THE ETRUSCAN WORLD

——— •◆• ———

The Etruscans can be shown to have made significant, and in some cases perhaps the first, technical advances in the central and northern Mediterranean. To the Etruscan people we can attribute such developments as the tie-beam truss in large wooden structures, surveying and engineering drainage and water tunnels, the development of the foresail for fast long-distance sailing vessels, fine techniques of metal production and other pyrotechnology, post-mortem C-sections in medicine, and more. In art, many technical and iconographic developments, although they certainly happened first in Greece or the Near East, are first seen in extant Etruscan works, preserved in the lavish tombs and goods of Etruscan aristocrats. These include early portraiture, the first full-length painted portrait, the first perspective view of a human figure in monumental art, specialized techniques of bronze-casting, and reduction-fired pottery (the *bucchero* phenomenon). Etruscan contacts, through trade, treaty and intermarriage, linked their culture with Sardinia, Corsica and Sicily, with the Italic tribes of the peninsula, and with the Near Eastern kingdoms, Greece and the Greek colonial world, Iberia, Gaul and the Punic network of North Africa, and influenced the cultures of northern Europe.

In the past fifteen years striking advances have been made in scholarship and research techniques for Etruscan Studies. Archaeological and scientific discoveries have changed our picture of the Etruscans and furnished us with new, specialized information. Thanks to the work of dozens of international scholars, it is now possible to discuss topics of interest that could never before be researched, such as Etruscan mining and metallurgy, textile production, foods and agriculture. In this volume, over 60 experts provide insights into all these aspects of Etruscan culture, and more, with many contributions available in English for the first time to allow the reader access to research that may not otherwise be available to them. Lavishly illustrated, *The Etruscan World* brings to life the culture and material past of the Etruscans and highlights key points of development in research, making it essential reading for researchers, academics and students of this fascinating civilization.

Jean MacIntosh Turfa is a Research Associate and occasional Lecturer in the Mediterranean Section of the University of Pennsylvania Museum and an adjunct professor in Classics at St. Joseph's University, Philadelphia. She has taught at the University of Liverpool, University of Illinois, Chicago, and Loyola University of Chicago, Drexel University, Dickinson and Bryn Mawr Colleges, St. Joseph's University and the University of Pennsylvania. She is a Member of the Istituto di Studi Etruschi e Italici.

THE ROUTLEDGE WORLDS

THE REFORMATION WORLD
Edited by Andrew Pettegree

THE MEDIEVAL WORLD
Edited by Peter Linehan, Janet L. Nelson

THE BYZANTINE WORLD
Edited by Paul Stephenson

THE VIKING WORLD
Edited by Stefan Brink in collaboration with Neil Price

THE BABYLONIAN WORLD
Edited by Gwendolyn Leick

THE EGYPTIAN WORLD
Edited by Toby Wilkinson

THE ISLAMIC WORLD
Edited by Andrew Rippin

THE WORLD OF POMPEI
Edited by Pedar W. Foss and John J. Dobbins

THE RENAISSANCE WORLD
Edited by John Jeffries Martin

THE EARLY CHRISTIAN WORLD
Edited by Philip F. Esler

THE GREEK WORLD
Edited by Anton Powell

THE ROMAN WORLD
Edited by John Wacher

THE HINDU WORLD
Edited by Sushil Mittal and Gene Thursby

THE WORLD OF THE AMERICAN WEST
Edited by Gordon Morris Bakken

THE ELIZABETHAN WORLD
Edited by Susan Doran and Norman Jones

THE OTTOMAN WORLD
Edited by Christine Woodhead

THE VICTORIAN WORLD
Edited by Marin Hewitt

THE ORTHODOX CHRISTIAN WORLD
Edited by Augustine Casiday

THE SUMERIAN WORLD
Edited by Harriet Crawford

Forthcoming:

THE FIN DE SIÈCLE WORLD
Edited by Michael Saler

THE ETRUSCAN WORLD

Edited by

Jean MacIntosh Turfa

Routledge
Taylor & Francis Group

LONDON AND NEW YORK

First published in paperback 2018

First published 2013
by Routledge
2 Park Square, Milton Park, Abingdon, Oxon OX14 4RN

and by Routledge
711 Third Avenue, New York, NY 10017

Routledge is an imprint of the Taylor & Francis Group, an informa business

British Library Cataloguing-in-Publication Data
A catalogue record for this book is available from the British Library

Library of Congress Cataloging-in-Publication Data
The Etruscan world / edited by Jean MacIntosh Turfa.
pages cm. -- (The Routledge worlds)
Includes bibliographical references and index.
ISBN 978-0-415-67308-2 (hardback : alk. paper) -- ISBN 978-0-203-52696-5
(ebook) 1. Etruscans. 2. Etruria--Civilization. 3. Etruria--Antiquities. 4. Material
culture--Italy--Etruria--History. I. Turfa, Jean MacIntosh, 1947-
DG223.3.E883 2013
937'.501--dc23
2012047206

ISBN: 978-0-415-67308-2 (hbk)
ISBN: 978-1-138-06035-7 (pbk)
ISBN: 978-0-203-52696-5 (ebk)

Typeset in Garamond 3
by Saxon Graphics Ltd, Derby

CONTENTS

———•◆•———

List of illustrations   x

List of contributors   xxix

Preface   xlv
Jean MacIntosh Turfa

Maps   xlvi

Introduction: time to give the Etruscans their due   1
Jean MacIntosh Turfa

PART I: ENVIRONMENT, BACKGROUND AND THE STUDY OF ETRUSCAN CULTURE

1 Etruscan environments   11
   Ingele M. B. Wiman

2 Massimo Pallottino's "Origins" in perspective   29
   Giovanna Bagnasco Gianni

3 Etruscan origins and the ancient authors   36
   Dominique Briquel

4 Fleshing out the demography of Etruria   56
   Geof Kron

PART II: THE HISTORICAL DEVELOPMENT OF ETRURIA

5   The Villanovan culture: at the beginning of Etruscan history   79
Gilda Bartoloni

6   Orientalizing Etruria   99
Maurizio Sannibale

7   Urbanization in southern Etruria from the tenth to the sixth century BC: the origins and growth of major centers   134
Robert Leighton

8   A long twilight: "Romanization" of Etruria   151
Vincent Jolivet

9   The last Etruscans: family tombs in northern Etruria   180
Marjatta Nielsen

PART III: ETRUSCANS AND THEIR NEIGHBORS

10   The western Mediterranean before the Etruscans   197
Fulvia Lo Schiavo

11   The Nuragic heritage in Etruria   216
Fulvia Lo Schiavo and Matteo Milletti

12   Phoenician and Punic Sardinia and the Etruscans   231
Rubens D'Oriano and Antonio Sanciu

13   Etruria and Corsica   244
Matteo Milletti

14   The Faliscans and the Etruscans   259
Maria Anna De Lucia Brolli and Jacopo Tabolli

15   Etruria on the Po and the Adriatic   281
Giuseppe Sassatelli and Elisabetta Govi

16   Etruscans in Campania   301
Mariassunta Cuozzo

17   Etruria Marittima, Carthage and Iberia, Massalia, Gaul   319
Jean Gran-Aymerich

PART IV: ETRUSCAN SOCIETY AND ECONOMY

18   Political systems and law   351
Hilary Wills Becker

19   Economy and commerce through material evidence: Etruscan goods in the Mediterranean world and beyond   373
Jean Gran-Aymerich with Jean MacIntosh Turfa

20   Mothers and children   426
Larissa Bonfante

21 Slavery and manumission   447
    Enrico Benelli

22 The Etruscan language   457
    Luciano Agostiniani

23 Numbers and reckoning: A whole civilization founded upon divisions   478
    Daniele Maras

PART V: RELIGION IN ETRURIA

24 Greek myth in Etruscan culture   495
    Erika Simon

25 Gods and demons in the Etruscan pantheon   513
    Ingrid Krauskopf

26 Haruspicy and Augury: Sources and procedures   539
    Nancy T. de Grummond

27 Religion: the gods and the places   557
    Ingrid Edlund-Berry

28 Archaeological evidence for Etruscan religious rituals   566
    Simona Rafanelli

29 Tarquinia, sacred areas and sanctuaries on the Civita plateau and on the coast: 594
    "monumental complex," Ara della Regina, Gravisca
    Giovanna Bagnasco Gianni

30 The sanctuary of Pyrgi   613
    Maria Paola Baglione

31 Orvieto, Campo della Fiera – *Fanum Voltumnae*   632
    Simonetta Stopponi

32 Worshiping with the dead: new approaches to Etruscan necropoleis   655
    Stephan Steingräber

33 The imagery of tomb objects (foreign and imported) and its funerary relevance   672
    Tom B. Rasmussen

PART VI: SPECIAL ASPECTS OF ETRUSCAN CULTURE

34 The science of the Etruscans   683
    Armando Cherici

35 The architectural heritage of Etruria   695
    Ingrid Edlund-Berry

36 Etruscan Town Planning and Related Structures   708
    Claudio Bizzarri

37 Villanovan and Etruscan Mining and Metallurgy   721
    Claudio Giardino

38 Technology, ideology, warfare and the Etruscans before the Roman conquest   738
    David George

39 The art of the Etruscan armourer   747
    Ross H. Cowan

40 Seafaring: shipbuilding, harbors, the issue of piracy   759
    Stefano Bruni

41 Princely chariots and carts   778
    Adriana Emiliozzi

42 The world of Etruscan textiles   798
    Margarita Gleba

43 Food and drink in the Etruscan world   812
    Lisa C. Pieraccini

44 The banquet through Etruscan history   823
    Annette Rathje

45 Etruscan spectacles: Theater and sport   831
    Jean-Paul Thuillier

46 Music and musical instruments in Etruria   841
    Fredrik Tobin

47 Health and medicine in Etruria   855
    Jean MacIntosh Turfa, with Marshall J. Becker

PART VII: ETRUSCAN SPECIALTIES IN ART

48 Foreign artists in Etruria   885
    Giovannangelo Camporeale

49 The phenomenon of terracotta: architectural terracottas   903
    Nancy Winter

50 Jewelry   914
    Françoise Gaultier

51 Engraved Gems   928
    Ulf R. Hansson

52 The Etruscan painted pottery   943
    Laura Ambrosini

53 The meanings of Bucchero   974
    Richard Daniel De Puma

54 Etruscan terracotta figurines   993
    Helen Nagy

55 Portraiture   1007
    Alexandra Carpino

56 Landscape and illusionism: qualities of Etruscan wall paintings   1017
    Helen Nagy

57 The bronze votive tradition in Etruria   1026
    Margherita Gilda Scarpellini

58 Mirrors in art and society   1041
    Richard Daniel De Puma

59 Science as art: Etruscan anatomical votives   1068
    Matthias Recke

60 Animals in the Etruscan household and environment   1086
    Adrian P. Harrison

PART VIII· POST-ANTIQUE RECEPTION OF ETRUSCAN CULTURE

61 Annius of Viterbo   1117
    Ingrid Rowland

62 The reception of Etruscan culture: Dempster and Buonarotti   1130
    Francesco De Angelis

63 Modern approaches to Etruscan culture   1136
    Marie-Laurence Haack

    Index   1147

ILLUSTRATIONS

— • ◆ • —

1.1	A bull of the Maremman *Bos Taurus*.	14
1.2	Mirror: the Vipinas brothers ambushing Cacu and the boy Artile.	23
2.1	Cover page of Pallottino's book on the origins of the Etruscans.	31
2.2	Pallottino's genealogical scheme of the provenance of the Etruscans according to literary sources.	32
2.3	Pallottino's sequence of the ancient cultures of the Italian Peninsula.	33
5.1	Schematic reconstruction of the birth of a proto-urban center.	82
5.2	Diffusion of the Villanovan culture.	82
5.3	Tomb of an adult man, Veii, Piazza d'Armi.	84
5.4	Finds from tombs at Veii, Quattro Fontanili.	85
5.5	Hut urn from Veii, Quattro Fontanili.	85
5.6	Grave group from Tarquinia.	86
5.7	Chamber tomb at Populonia: tomb of *rasoio lunato*.	87
5.8	Grave group from Tarquinia.	87
5.9	Etruscan material imported into Sardinia and Sardinian goods found in Etruria.	89
5.10	Enotrian juglet from Vulci.	90
5.11	Diffusion of Greek geometric cups in Italy.	92
5.12	Tomb AAI of the Veian necropolis of Quattro Fontani.	93
5.13	Tomb 1036 of the Veian necropolis of Casal del Fosso.	94
5.14	Tomb 871 of the Veian necropolis of Casal del Fosso: crested helmet.	94
5.15	Hut at Populonia.	95
5.16	Reconstruction of the banquet hall in the regia identified on the northern slope of the Palatine.	96
6.1	Bottle-vase (so-called inkwell) in bucchero with syllabary incised on body and model alphabet on ring-base.	101
6.2	Cauldron in bronze decorated in repoussé and with lion protomes.	101
6.3	Ribbed bowl in bronze. Cerveteri, Regolini-Galassi Tomb. 675–650 BC.	101
6.4	Grater in bronze. Provenance unknown. Seventh century BC.	102
6.5	Tripod-bowl, ceramic. Ceremonial vase of Phoenician type after Assyrian prototypes. From Vulci, formerly Raccolta Giacinto Guglielmi. 625–600 BC.	102

6.6	Fan in bronze. From Populonia, Tomba dei Flabelli. 675–625 BC.	103
6.7	Phoenician bowl. Processions of warriors and sacred nursing scene (cow and calf).	103
6.8	Hemispherical, double-walled cup of Phoenician manufacture.	103
6.9	Tarquinia. Fibula in gold decorated in granulation and filigree.	108
6.10	Gold appliqué plaque: rosette. Cerveteri, Regolini-Galassi Tomb.	109
6.11	Pectoral in beaten gold. Cerveteri, Regolini-Galassi Tomb.	109
6.12	Situla in silver ajourée, originally over a wooden body. Cerveteri, Regolini-Galassi Tomb.	110
6.13	Fibula in gold, with looped double spiral pendant on cross-piece. Vulci, Ponte Sodo. 675–650 BC.	111
6.14	Pendants from tomb 45 at Aššur, end fourteenth–thirteenth century BC, with motif of "cup-spirals."	111
6.15	Gold appliqué plaque: Hathor-head between "cup-spirals."	112
6.16	Bracelet in gold decorated in repoussé and granulation.	112
6.17	Cult-trolley in bronze. Cerveteri, Regolini-Galassi Tomb.	113
6.18	Egyptian amulet with zigzag motif in linear granulation. 1900–1800 BC.	114
6.19	Ornamental fibula in gold. Cerveteri, Regolini-Galassi Tomb.	114
6.20	Seated female figure in ceramic from the Tomb of the Five Chairs, Cerveteri. 650–600 BC.	116
6.21	Seated figures of ancestors in basalt from the Royal Tomb of Qatna, during excavation and after restoration.	117
6.22	Monumental access stair to the altar-platform of the Melone del Sodo II at Cortona.	118
6.23	Statuette of nude woman in ivory. Marsiliana d'Albegna, Circolo della Fibula, tomb XLI. 675–650 BC.	119
6.24	Tarquinia, Tumulo della Regina: view of external ceremonial area with staircase; on the walls painted plaster.	119
6.25	"Main tombs at Tarquinia necropolis."	120
6.26	Cinerary urn in form of a house. Cerveteri, Monte Abatone necropolis, tomb 426. 650 BC.	121
6.27	*Tomba a casa* with portico. Tuscania, Pian di Mola. 575–550 BC.	122
6.28	Krater of the "Bicenzo Group" decorated with geometric motifs and metopes with stylized birds.	122
6.29	Veio, Tomba dei Leoni Ruggenti. Circa 690 BC.	123
6.30	Cerveteri, Tomba dei Leoni Dipinti. 670–650 BC.	123
6.31	"Weeping" statuette in bucchero. Cerveteri, Regolini-Galassi Tomb.	124
6.32	Calabresi Vase: charioteer driving a pair of horses. Bucchero. Cerveteri, Tomba Calabresi. C. 660–650 BC.	124
6.33	Set of vases in silver. Cerveteri, Regolini-Galassi Tomb.	125
6.34	Fibula *a drago* in gold with dedicatory inscription in granulation.	125
6.35	Situla of *Plikaśna*. Gilded silver. From Chiusi. Circa 650 BC.	126
6.36	Olpe in bucchero, decorated with relief of Jasion, Medea, the Argonauts and Daedalus. From Cerveteri, Tumulus of San Paolo, tomb 2, 630 BC.	126
6.37	Veii, Monte Michele, Tomba Campana. Watercolor. The grave goods on the floor do not belong to this tomb. C. 600 BC.	127
6.38	Bronze figurine of draped female votary with *kyathos*. Provenance unknown. 625–600 BC.	127
7.1	Southern Etruria, topography with major and minor Early Iron Age sites.	135

7.2	Tarquinia, topography and archaeological features (with survey data from Mandolesi 1999).	137
7.3	Veii, topography and archaeological features (with survey data from Patterson 2004).	139
8.1	Found in the votive deposit of the Campetti sanctuary at Veii, this terracotta represents Aeneas carrying Anchises, which shows, in the fourth century BC, that the ideological association between the conquest of the city and that of Troy were still familiar to the residents of the area.	152
8.2	The recent excavations of Cerveteri have revealed the presence of a public, subterranean complex that was decorated with paintings and dated by the mention of the Roman praetor of Caere, C. Genucius Clepsina, consul in 276 and 270.	152
8.3	Plate made at Falerii, datable around the middle of the fourth century BC.	153
8.4	The stronghold of Musarna.	154
8.5	The inscriptions found in the vicinity of the forum of Tarquinia.	155
8.6	The François Tomb of Vulci.	155
8.7	The bath building constructed at Musarna around the end of the second century BC.	158
8.8	Bilingual inscription found at Pesaro and dated to the second half of the first century BC.	158
8.9	Kalyx krater in *ceramica argentata* ("silvered ceramic") from Bolsena, first half of the third century BC.	159
8.10	The hypogeum of the Velimna, probably of the last third of the third century BC.	159
8.11	Figure of a *haruspex* depicted on a *terra sigillata* vase.	160
8.12	The Perugia cippus and the Cortona Tablet.	161
8.13	Tomba Bruschi, dated from the end of the fourth century or the beginning of the next century.	161
8.14	Construction of the great *villae* on land confiscated from conquered cities.	162
8.15	The extraordinary Dionysiac throne in terracotta of the beginning of the second century BC.	163
8.16	Etruscan sarcophagi accompanied by the authority of a long written text relating the *cursus honorum* of the deceased.	164
8.17	Anatomical ex-votos in terracotta offered to different gods by members of the popular classes, both Etruscan and Roman.	165
8.18	Inscribed cippi.	165
8.19	The travertino urns of Strozzacaponi.	166
8.20	Ex-votos in bronze produced at Volterra in second half of the third century BC, known by the name of *"Ombra della serra"* ("Shadow of the Night").	167
8.21	Vulcian mirror of the last quarter of the fourth century BC.	167
8.22	Wedding basket found at Palestrina.	168
8.23	Statue of the Orator found near Perugia, dated to the end of the second century BC or the beginning of the next century.	168
8.24	The "Corsini throne".	169
8.25	Base discovered near the theatre of Caere.	170
9.1	The Tomb of the Velimna/Volumnius family, Perugia. Late third century BC.	182
9.2	The Inghirami Tomb, from Volterra.	184

9.3	The Inghirami Tomb: a male figure reworked into a female one.	185
9.4	The Inghirami Tomb: a female lid figure.	186
9.5	The Inghirami Tomb: a male lid figure.	187
9.6	The Inghirami Tomb: a fragmentary chest.	187
9.7	A couple being transported in a *carpentum*.	189
9.8	Female lid figure with the neck-tail coiffure of the Tiberian-Claudian period.	190
9.9	Livia's portrait head, from the Roman theatre at Vallebuona, Volterra.	190
10.1	Distribution map of the sites that are mentioned in this paper.	197
10.2	Chronological table of the Bronze Age and beginning of the Iron Age.	199
10.3	The *nuraghe* Arrubiu, Orroli (Nuoro).	200
10.4	Mycenaean materials found in Sardinia.	200
10.5	Bronze figurine from *nuraghe* Cabu Abbas, Olbia (Sassari) and Nuragic necked jar.	202
10.6	Distribution map of the oxhide ingots in the Mediterranean.	203
10.7	Funtana Coberta of Ballao (Cagliari) hoard: the container and the oxhide ingots.	204
10.8	Evidence of close contacts between Cyprus and Sardinia in the Late Bronze Age.	205
10.9	The biggest (38 cm) Nuragic bronze figurine of a warrior in Pigorini Museum, Rome.	206
10.10	Western "*Pistilliform*" sword and bronze figurine of the "Head of the Tribe" from Monti Arcosu, Uta (Cagliari) holding a sword of a similar shape on the shoulder.	208
10.11	Distribution map of the Iberian-type objects found in Sardinia.	208
10.12	Su Monte, Sorradile (Oristano) hoard.	210
10.13	Nuragic bronze boat from Pipizu, Orroli (Nuoro).	211
11.1	Map of Sardinia with the principal sites cited in the text.	217
11.2	Località Camposanto-Olmedo, bronzes (Lo Schiavo forthcoming 2).	219
11.3	Nuraghe Flumenelongu-Alghero, hoard (Lo Schiavo 1976).	219
11.4	Principal categories of Nuragic bronzes.	220
11.5	Nuragic daggers with short tangs from Sardinia.	223
11.6	Nuragic pendants in the shape of a "pilgrim flask" and quiver.	224
11.7	Nuragic buttons.	225
11.8	Vetulonia, grave goods from tomb 85/1897 of Poggio alla Guardia: Sardinian askoid jug, razor and armlet.	225
11.9	Vulci, "Tomb of the Sardinian Bronzes" from the Cavalupo necropolis: Nuragic bronzes (Bartoloni, Pitzalis 2011).	226
11.10	Populonia, hoard of Falda della Guardiola (photo Archivio SBAT).	227
12.1	The sea routes between Sardinia and Central Italy and the main Phoenician settlements on the Island.	231
12.2	The *nuraghe* Santu Antine of Torralba.	232
12.3	Mycenaean vase for perfume (alabaster) from *nuraghe* Arrubiu of Orroli (mid-fourteenth century BC).	233
12.4	Cypriot copper ox-hide ingot from Ozieri (thirteenth–eleventh century BC).	234
12.5	Bronze sword imported from Etruria from the nuraghe Attentu of Ploaghe (eleventh century BC).	234
12.6	Nuragic amphora imitating Phoenician amphorae from Nuragic village of Sant'Imbenia at Alghero (end of ninth century BC).	234

12.7	Area of Phoenician settlements in the Western Mediterranean in the mid-eighth century BC.	234
12.8	Etruscan jug (olpe) for wine, probably from Tharros (early sixth century BC).	236
12.9	Greek amphora with erotic scene imported into Tharros from Etruria (560–550 BC).	236
12.10	Etruscan cup (kantharos) for drinking wine, from Tharros (early sixth century BC).	237
12.11	Etruscan container for scented ointments (aryballos), probably from Tharros (first half of sixth century BC).	237
12.12	Olbia between the spheres of Phoenician, Greek and Etruscan settlement around 630 BC.	238
12.13	Greek cup (kotyle) for drinking wine, from Greek Olbia (about 600 BC).	238
12.14	Small bronze lion from the Nuragic sanctuary of Nurdòle – Orani (end of the sixth century BC).	239
12.15	Etruscan wine amphora from the sea on the east coast of Sardinia (mid-fifth to mid-third century BC).	240
12.16	Genucilia plate from Olbia (end of fourth–beginning of third century BC).	242
12.17	Vase for oil (askos) from Olbia (end of fourth–beginning of third century BC).	242
13.1	Map of Corsica with principal sites discussed in this chapter.	245
13.2	Molds for bronze casting.	247
13.3	Fibulae *ad arco serpeggiante* ("with serpentine-bow").	248
13.4	Peninsular axes: 1. Castifao-Corte; 2. *Maison Perragi* (Giardino 1995).	248
13.5	Cagnano, pendant of *"plume"* type (Museo Archeologico, Florence).	252
13.6	Fibulae of *Corsican* type.	253
13.7	Cagnano, fibula of Certosa type with tweezers.	253
13.8	Grotta Alessandro, beads of spirally twisted wire.	254
14.1	The area of the *Ager Faliscus*.	259
14.2	Map and aerial photo of *Falerii* (modern Civita Castellana).	260
14.3	Narce hill (from the south-east).	261
14.4	Bowl from Tomb 2 (XLVI), third necropolis of Pizzo Piede.	261
14.5	Map of *Falerii* drawn by Adolfo Cozza in 1889.	262
14.6	Map of Narce drawn by Adolfo Cozza in 1889.	263
14.7	Example of architectural terracottas from Falerii (via Gramsci).	264
14.8	Raniero Mengarelli's excavations at Pizzo Piede, Narce, 1933.	265
14.9	Pre-Roman quarry at *Falerii*.	265
14.10	Sanctuary of Juno Curitis at Celle, *Falerii*	266
14.11	"Krater of the Aurora," *Falerii*.	266
14.12	Apollo from the Scasato temple site, *Falerii*.	267
14.13	Falerii novi.	268
14.14	La Petrina and I Tufi necropoleis of Narce.	269
14.15	Reconstruction of Faliscan female and male dress based on tombs A36 (XXVI) and A38 (XXIX) La Petrina necropolis.	270
14.16	Types of tombs peculiar to Narce (eighth century BC).	271
14.17	Location of late cremation burials in Narce.	271
14.18	Cremation in open tomb, Grotta Gramiccia necropolis, Veii (in Drago 1997).	271
14.19	Examples of architectural terracottas from Narce, Pizzo Piede.	273

14.20	Sanctuary of Monte Li Santi-Le Rote, Narce.	273
14.21	Votive head from the sanctuary of Monte Li Santi-Le Rote, Narce.	274
14.22	View of Corchiano (from the east).	275
14.23	Types of tombs characteristic of Corchiano.	276
15.1	Map of *Etruria Padana* from ninth to eighth century BC.	282
15.2	Map of *Etruria Padana* from sixth to fourth century BC.	283
15.3	Map of Etruscan Bologna.	284
15.4	Bronze vessels from Benacci Caprara Tomb 39 of Bologna.	285
15.5	Biconical vase with stamped decoration from Bologna.	286
15.6	Malvasia Tortorelli Stele from Bologna.	286
15.7	*Cippi* from Rubiera (Reggio Emilia).	287
15.8	Herakles and Apollo from the acropolis of Villa Cassarini in Bologna.	288
15.9	Goods from the "Tomb of the Folding Stool" of Bologna.	288
15.10	Stele 168 from Bologna.	289
15.11	Stele from S. Michele in Bosco of Bologna.	289
15.12	Objects made of amber from the tombs of Verucchio.	290
15.13	Wooden throne from Verucchio.	290
15.14	Aerial view of the city of Marzabotto.	291
15.15	General plan of the city of Marzabotto.	292
15.16	Layout of the foundation ritual of the city of Marzabotto.	292
15.17	Reconstruction of House 1 of Regio IV-insula 2 of Marzabotto.	293
15.18	Photo and plan of the city temple of Marzabotto.	293
15.19	Acropolis of Marzabotto, altar D.	294
15.20	Palisade/embankment of Spina.	295
15.21	River pebble with inscription "*mi tular*" from Spina.	296
15.22	Attic vases from the funerary offerings at Spina.	296
15.23	Tomb at Monterenzio.	298
16.1	Campania from Iron Age to Archaic period: population distribution.	301
16.2	Pontecagnano. Princely Tombs.	303
16.3	Pontecagnano.	305
16.4	Pontecagnano.	306
16.5	Pontecagnano: necropolis and old settlement.	307
16.6	Capua.	313
16.7	The "Campanian system".	313
16.8	Pontecagnano: Kantharos in bucchero.	314
17.1	Mediterranean, Europe and remote Etruscan finds.	321
17.2	Marseille, site of *Îlot rue Cathédrale*, fragments of cooking stand and foot of basin-brazier, complete profile of cookware vase (*olletta d'impasto*).	322
17.3	Marseille, site of *Îlot la Madeleine, braciere ceretano*: red-slipped basin decorated with cylinder-stamped design.	323
17.4	Marseille, site of Collège Vieux Port, Etruscan inscription incised in large letters on the shoulder of a Greek wine amphora.	323
17.5	Coastal *oppidum* of Saint-Blaise, Etruscan inscription of commercial character incised on an Etruscan amphora, sixth century.	324
17.6	Coastal *oppidum* of Pech-Maho (Sigean, Aude), Etruscan inscription mentioning *Matalia* (*Massalia*, Marseille).	325
17.7	Greek colony of Empúries (Ampurias, *Emporion*), sector of the sanctuary of Aesculapius, feline paw from a bronze tripod, with inscription made at time of casting.	325
17.8	Votive deposit of one Etruscan amphora and one Phoenician amphora.	326

17.9	Shipwreck of Grand Ribaud F (East of Marseille), cargo of Etruscan amphorae.	326
17.10	Cargo of kitchen pottery from the wreck of Grand Ribaud F.	327
17.11	Carthage, old excavations of necropoleis.	329
17.12	Carthage, zone of Dar-Seniat, statuette of young woman offering.	331
17.13	Necropolis of Los Villares, province of Albacete (Castilla-La Mancha), plaques from a small box with representations of banquet, satyrs and birds. Carved ivory, end of the sixth century.	332
17.14	Site of Turuñuelo, Mérida, province of Badajoz (Estremadura), plaque from a box with centaur. Carved ivory, end of the sixth century.	333
17.15	Cancho Roano, Zalamea, province of Badajoz. Banquet tools, *simpula*. Bronze, end of the sixth century.	333
17.16	Plan of architectural complex of Cancho Roano.	334
17.17	Malaga, old excavations at the foot of the Alcazaba, handle in bronze with a young hero controlling human-headed bulls and a siren.	335
17.18	Empúries/Ampurias, fragment of *infundibulum* with figurine of a frog serving as hinge.	337
17.19	Empúries/Ampurias, terminal appliqué in form of a lion-head, bronze.	337
17.20	Etruscan mirror, from Empúries/Ampurias, old excavations in the necropolis. Bronze, engraved with the Judgment of Paris.	338
17.21	Ullastret, excavations of the *oppidum* of Puig Sant Andreu, attachment of moveable handle for stamnoid situla. Cast bronze.	338
18.1	The Etruscan city-states with suggested territorial boundaries.	353
18.2	Bronze weight with a lead center from Caere (Sant'Antonio).	357
18.3	A miniature model of the *fasces*, in iron, from the *Tomba del Littore*, Vetulonia.	357
18.4	Funerary cippus from Chiusi, now in Palermo, depicting magistrates judging contests.	358
18.5	A road cutting in the tufo near Pitigliano.	358
18.6	Etruscan roads radiating from Veii and Faliscan centers during the seventh to sixth centuries BCE.	359
18.7	Boundary stone from Poggio di Firenze reading *tular sp{ural}*.	361
19.1	Antenna-hilt sword in bronze of Villanovan type probably discovered in Egypt.	374
19.2	Crested helmets in bronze, of Villanovan type, discovered in the panhellenic sanctuary of Olympia.	375
19.3	Bronze, *bracciale di scudo* (armband of a shield), with figural decoration, from Olympia.	376
19.4	Belt in bronze of Late Villanovan type, discovered in Euboea.	377
19.5	Etruscan fibulae from various locations in Greece.	378
19.6	Tripod brought up from the sea off Cape Agde, Languedoc.	379
19.7	Reconstruction of original profile of kantharos from Camirus, Rhodes.	380
19.8	Beaked oinochoe, *Schnabelkanne*, from the tomb of Schwarzenbach.	380
19.9	Bronze Etruscan vases from tombs at Bourges-*Avaricum* and environs.	381
19.10	Three oinochoai with long spouts, *Schnabelkannen*, from the tombs of Bourges-*Avaricum* and environs.	381
19.11	Kantharos (reconstruction) from the *oppidum* of Camp-de-Chassey, Bourgogne.	384
19.12	Token in bronze, a sort of *tessera hospitalis*.	388

19.13	Handle attachment with palmette from large bronze basin, from the sanctuary of Fâ, Barzan, Charente-Maritime.	391
19.14	Figurine-attachment in bronze, representing a winged lion (or sphinx ?), *oppidum* of Mont Lassois, Bourgogne.	394
19.15	Villanovan razor and Etruscan fibulae from Bourges and environs.	399
20.1	Tomb of the Painted Vases, Tarquinia, rear wall.	428
20.2	Canopus from Dolciano, Chiusi. Enthroned image of male ancestor.	429
20.3	Limestone relief from Chiusi. Wedding procession.	431
20.4	Tomb of the Monkey at Chiusi. Deceased woman watching funeral games in her honor.	432
20.5	Bronze mirror, Praenestine.	432
20.6	Bronze mirror from Castelgiorgio.	433
20.7	Carved amber bow of a fibula, from Ancona	433
20.8	Black-figure vase. Satyr carrying off a friendly maenad.	434
20.9	Urn from Tragliatella (Cerveteri).	435
20.10	Bronze ring found on the body of a deceased woman in grave 153 of the necropolis of Castel di Decima, near Rome.	436
20.11	Life-size stone ash urn from Chiusi.	438
22.1	Stele from Kaminia (Lemnos).	458
22.2	*Liber Linteus*, from northern Etruria.	461
22.3	Detail of the Tablet of Capua.	461
22.4	Detail of the *Tabula Cortonensis*.	462
22.5	*Cippus* of Perugia.	462
22.6	Lead plaque from Magliano.	463
22.7	Sarcophagus of Laris Pulenas, from Tarquinia, 250–200 BC.	463
22.8	Gold plaque from Pyrgi.	464
22.9	Black-gloss kylix, from Capua.	466
22.10	Fragment of a "Spurinas"-plate, from Pyrgi.	466
22.11	Inscription on chamber tomb (Volsinii, necropolis of Crocifisso del Tufo, tomb 29).	466
22.12	Oinochoe, from Caere, 675–650 BC.	466
22.13	Bucchero vase in the shape of a rooster, from Corneto (Tarquinia).	466
22.14	Attic red-figure Kylix, from Tarquinia.	467
22.15	Black-gloss Kylix, from Suessula.	467
22.16	Tarquinia, dipinto on wall, Tomba dell'Orco I (350–325 BC).	468
22.17	Tarquinia, dipinto on wall, Tomb of the Spitus.	468
22.18	*Cippus* in the Tomb of the Reliefs at Caere.	468
23.1	Dice from Vulci.	479
23.2	List of the Etruscan numbers.	481
23.3	Mirror with the goddess Athrpa.	482
23.4	Reconstruction of a *groma*.	484
23.5	The Liver of Piacenza.	485
23.6	Division of sky.	485
23.7	The Etruscan numeral marking system compared to Latin.	488
24.1	Bucchero olpe found in Caere. Taitale (Daidalos).	496
24.2	Etruscan amphora, perhaps made in Caere.	496
24.3	Greek krater found in Caere with signature of Aristonothos.	497
24.4	"Caeretan" hydria, circa 525 BCE.	497
24.5	Attic volute krater (Kleitias krater) found in Chiusi.	498
24.6	Handle side of Fig. 24.5.	499
24.7	Chariot from Monteleone di Spoleto.	499

24.8	Side panel of the Monteleone chariot.	499
24.9	Wall painting in Tomba dei Tori, Tarquinii.	500
24.10	Etruscan (during the nineteenth century called "Pontic") amphora.	
and	Shoulder friezes on both sides: judgment of Paris. Munich,	
24.11	Antikensammlungen (n.31).	501
24.12	Bronze mirror from Praeneste.	502
24.13	Carnelian scarab.	503
24.14	Carnelian scarab. "Seven against Thebes."	503
24.15	Bronze mirror from Vulci.	504
24.16	Etruscan black figure amphora, shoulder frieze.	504
24.17	Terracotta votive from Veii.	505
24.18	Bronze mirror. Apollo (Aplu) and Dionysios (Fufluns).	505
24.19	Bronze mirror from Perugia.	506
24.20	Clay *acroterium* from Caere.	507
24.21	Clay *acroterium* from Astrone valley.	507
24.22	Clay *antepagmentum* from Pyrgi.	508
24.23	Alabaster urn from Volterra.	509
24.24	Terracotta urn from Perugia.	509
25.1	Mirror, Bologna.	514
25.2	Mirror, St. Petersburg B (or V) 505.	514
25.3	Schema of the regions of the sky.	515
25.4	Mirror, Florence.	518
25.5	Mirror, Vaticano.	518
25.6	Bronze statuette of Tinia.	520
25.8	Stamnos, red figure, Vaticano.	521
25.9	Tarquinia, Tomba dei Caronti: *Charun chunchulis* and *Charun huths*.	522
25.10	Sarcophagus of Hasti Afunei, Palermo.	523
25.11	Terracotta antefixes, Rome, Villa Giulia.	523
25.12	Plate, Pontic.	525
25.13	Tarquinia; Tomba dell'Orco II.	525
25.14	Bronze statuette, Florence.	526
25.15	Bronze coin, (incuse) = *LIMC* VII Poseidon/Nethuns 17. After plaster cast.	526
25.16	Red-figure oinochoe, vulture demon.	527
25.17	Wolf at night, "photo trap" near Daubnitz in the Lausitz.	527
26.1	Mirror with Pava Tarchies from Tuscania.	540
26.2	Gold ring bezel with Lasa Vecuvia, from Todi.	541
26.3	Painting of Vel Saties, from the François Tomb, Vulci.	541
26.4	Diagram of the Piacenza Liver.	542
26.5	Clay model of a sheep's liver from Mesopotamia.	543
26.6	Drawing of terracotta model of a liver from Falerii Veteres.	547
26.7	Mirror with Chalchas as haruspex.	549
26.8	Bronze handle of a pitcher (*Schnabelkanne*).	551
27.1	Monte Amiata.	558
27.2	Lago di Chiusi.	558
27.3	Tiber river.	559
27.4	Orvieto, Belvedere temple. Photo: Ingrid Edlund-Berry.	560
27.5	Mount Soracte.	561
28.1	Painted clay plaque.	567
28.2	Mirror in bronze. From *Praeneste*.	568
28.3	Funerary cippus in peperino.	570
28.4	Etrusco-Corinthian krater of the "Gobbi."	572

28.5	Black figure hydria.	573
28.6	Black-figure amphora.	574
28.7a–c	Etruscan *oinochoe* in overpainted red figure.	577
28.8	Mirror in bronze.	578
28.9	Black-figure krater.	579
28.10	Cinerary urn in tufo.	580
29.1	Tarquinia, "monumental complex," the natural cavity.	595
29.2	Tarquinia, "monumental complex," the two pits in front of the "altar temple" and the discovery of the bronzes.	596
29.3	Tarquinia, "monumental complex," *area* γ overlapping the Villanovan structures.	596
29.4	Tarquinia, "monumental complex," the location of the altars focusing the natural cavity in the centre.	597
29.5	Tarquinia, "monumental complex," "impasto" shard with a cross inscribed in a circle.	597
29.6	Tarquinia, "monumental complex," the well, surmounted by the arch.	598
29.7	Tarquinia, "monumental complex," the terracotta plaque found inside the well.	599
29.8	Tarquinia, "monumental complex," the "impasto" shard with the inscription χiiati.	599
29.9	Tarquinia, Ara della Regina sanctuary, aerial view (LiDAR).	600
29.10	Tarquinia, Ara della Regina sanctuary, from the West.	600
29.11	Tarquinia, Ara della Regina sanctuary, the south-east corner of the terrace with the Archaic structures.	601
29.12	Tarquinia, Ara della Regina sanctuary, the stone chest from the east.	601
29.13	Tarquinia, Ara della Regina sanctuary, the stone chest from the north-east.	602
29.14	Tarquinia, Ara della Regina sanctuary, *altar* α from the west.	602
29.15	The Winged Horses Group after restoration.	603
29.16	Pelike of the Kadmos.	603
29.17	Krater of the Painter of Lycurgus.	604
29.18	Reconstruction of the subject represented on the pediment of the third phase of the Temple of the Ara della Regina sanctuary at Tarquinia (Temple III).	604
29.19	Gravisca, sanctuary, general plan.	605
29.20	Gravisca, sanctuary, Aphrodite *promachos* from the southern area.	606
29.21	Gravisca, sanctuary, the *cippus* of Sostratos with the dedication in Greek to Apollo of Aegina from the southern area.	607
29.22	Gravisca, sanctuary, spearheads, miniature weapons and a warrior from the northern area.	608
29.23	Gravisca, sanctuary, the sixth phase (300–281 BC).	609
30.1	Aerial view of the territory of Pyrgi.	614
30.2	General plan of archaeological area.	614
30.3	Walls of the Roman colony in polygonal masonry.	615
30.4	Monumental sanctuary: phase-plans of Temple B and Temple A.	617
30.5	Reconstruction model of Temple B and of Sacred Area C (to left).	617
30.6	Reconstruction model of Temple A.	619
30.7	Architectural terracotta, replacement head from gable of Temple A.	620
30.8	Attic red-figure mesomphalic *phiale* from the southern sanctuary.	624
31.1	Campo della Fiera: aerial view of excavations.	633
31.2	Plan of central area of excavations.	634

31.3	Temple A.	635
31.4	Pavement of the *cella* of Temple A.	635
31.5	*Donario*, altar, trenches and quadrangular structure.	636
31.6	Base of statuette of figure seated on a throne.	636
31.7	Base with Archaic dedicatory inscription.	637
31.8	Black-gloss cup.	637
31.9	Bronze figurine of boy with ball.	638
31.10	Quadrangular structure emptied of fill.	638
31.11	Terracotta female head.	639
31.12	Bronze female head.	639
31.13	Terracotta female head on base.	640
31.14	Terracotta male head (front and back views).	640
31.15	Terracotta female head.	641
31.16	Terracotta female head during excavation.	641
31.17	Terracotta feet of female statue.	642
31.18	Attic vase in form of a Maenad's head.	643
31.19	Cavity in foundation course of the first *temenos* wall.	643
31.20	Threshold of the second *temenos* wall.	644
31.21	Via Sacra.	644
31.22	South Area: fountain and Temple B.	645
31.23	Spout of fountain in shape of leonine head.	645
31.24	Temple C.	646
31.25	Precinct of Temple C.	646
31.26	*Kylix* by Douris.	647
31.27	Etruscan red-figure cup.	647
31.28	Bucchero cup and detail of inscription *"atial."*	647
31.29	Plan of Temple C.	648
31.30	A *cassone* tomb in blocks of tuff.	649
31.31	Inhumation in the *a cassone* tomb and cremation in *olla*.	649
31.32	A *cassetta* tomb in a single block of tuff.	649
31.33	Feeding-vase.	650
31.34	Deposit on the floor-level outside Temple C.	650
31.35	Deposit with bucchero cup and objects in metal.	651
31.36	Plaques from the chariot.	651
31.37	Baths.	652
31.38	Fibula with twins suckled by the she-wolf.	652
32.1	Cerveteri, Banditaccia Necropolis, tumulus with profiled base of Orientalizing period.	657
32.2	Tarquinia, Doganaccia, Tumulo della Regina: antechamber with remains of wall plaster of Middle Orientalizing period.	657
32.3	Vetulonia, model of the Diavolino Tomb 2 of Orientalizing period.	658
32.4	Populonia, San Cerbone Necropolis, Tomb of the Funeral Beds.	659
32.5	San Giuliano, Tomb of Valle Cappellana 1.	659
32.6	Sarteano, Pianacce Necropolis: tomb dromoi with cippus.	660
32.7	Blera, Casetta Necropolis: half cube rock tomb of Archaic period.	660
32.8	San Giuliano, Caiolo Necropolis: Tomb of the Stag.	661
32.9	Populonia, San Cerbone Necropolis: aedicula tomb.	661
32.10	Cerveteri, Via degli Inferi: Tomb of the Doric Columns.	661
32.11	Sovana, Tomb of the Siren.	662
32.12	Sovana, model of the Ildebranda Tomb.	663
32.13	Manziana, stepped Etruscan rock altar.	664

32.14	Bomarzo, rock cube monument of Roman period.	664
32.15	Bomarzo, "Pyramide," rock monument of Roman period.	664
32.16	Barbarano Romano, monumental cippus in obelisk form from San Giuliano.	667
33.1	Attic black-gloss cup.	673
33.2	Tomba degli Auguri.	675
33.3	Etruscan black-figure (Ivy Group) one-handle kantharos.	676
33.4	Mirror with Hercle and Uni.	677
34.1	Division of the sky according to the *Etrusca disciplina*.	689
34.2	Plan of the Tuscan temple (*templum tuscanicum*).	691
34.3	The four prevailing positions of *Ursa Major*.	692
35.1	The Capitoline temple in Rome.	696
35.2	The Tuscan temple.	697
35.3	View towards the Capitoline hill.	698
35.4	Rusellae, House of the Impluvium.	700
35.5	Temple podia.	701
35.6	Rome, temple of Castor.	702
35.7	Sora, temple with Etruscan round moldings.	703
35.8a–b	Castiglion Fiorentino, Medieval wall and Etruscan gate.	704
36.1	Crocefisso del Tufo, plan of necropolis.	712
36.2	Plan and section of the Scala Mobile *cuniculus*.	713
36.3a–e	Vases found in excavation of the Scala Mobile *cuniculus*.	714
36.4	Etruscan private houses with cisterns: the "Tuscan atrium."	714
36.5	Cistern of the Archaic period connected with the main trunk of a *cuniculus*.	715
36.6	Plan of the area of the ancient monumental entrance to Orvieto to the West.	715
36.7	The west side of the tufa plateau of Orvieto.	716
37.1	Pair of bronze statuettes (*kore* and *kouros*).	722
37.2	Engraving: Etruscan mirror known as the "*Patera Cospiana*".	722
37.3	Pair of Etruscan earrings in gold produced by repoussé.	723
37.4	Fibula in gold decorated in granulation "*a pulviscolo*".	723
37.5	Orientalizing belt clasp in bronze with iron inlay.	723
37.6	Principal metal-bearing regions of Etruria.	724
37.7	Remains of ancient mines at Campo alle Buche.	725
37.8	Materials from the hoard of San Francesco.	726
37.9	Crucible from the Villanovan village of Bologna – Via Indipendenza.	726
37.10	Stone mold from the Villanovan village of Gran Carro.	727
37.11	Unseparated elements of a chain cast in tin from the Villanovan village of Gran Carro.	727
37.12	Fragment of a bloom from the Etruscan site of La Castellina del Marangone.	729
37.13	Remains of a furnace from Populonia.	730
37.14	Large tapped slag for iron smelting from Populonia.	730
37.15	Hammerscales from San Giovenale (Blera, Viterbo).	732
37.16	Lead ingots containing iron slag.	732
39.1	Poncho cuirass from Narce, Tomb 43.	747
39.2	Panoply of the Warrior of Lanuvium.	748
39.3	Panoply from the Tomb of the Warrior, Settecamini necropolis, Orvieto.	748
39.4	Etruscan cuirass with stylized musculature in Karlsruhe.	749
39.5	Italiote cuirass from Ruvo with naturalistic musculature.	749

39.6	Vetulonia-type pot helmet from the Tomb of the Duke, Vetulonia.	750
39.7	Montegiorgio Piceno helmet from Ancona.	750
39.8	Montelparo helmet from Cannae.	751
39.9	Picene helmet demonstrating transition from the Montelparo-type to the Belmonte-type Negau.	751
39.10	Volterra-type Negau helmet.	752
39.11	Vetulonia-type Negau helmet captured by the Syracusans off Cumae in 474.	752
39.12	Cast Montefortino helmet.	753
39.13	Votive statuette of a warrior wearing a fabric corselet reinforced with metal plates (420–400).	753
39.14	Votive statuette of a warrior in a scale or lamellar corselet.	754
39.15	Belly guard from Perugia.	754
39.16	Fully-armoured Achle on the Torre San Severo sarcophagus.	755
39.17	*Kopis* and *aspis* equipped warrior on an Etruscan oinochoe, 520–510.	755
39.18	From top, the exceptionally long *pilum* from Vulci (1.2 m), and Gallic-style (in scabbard) and late *kopis*-type swords from Perugia.	756
39.19	Statuette of Maris or Laran, 475–450.	756
40.1	Helmet from Olympia.	765
40.2	Wreck of Grand Ribaud F in the course of excavation.	767
40.3	*Olla* (jar) from Bisenzio, Olmo Bello necropolis, tomb 24.	769
40.4	Ship model in impasto from Tarquinia.	770
40.5	Oinochoe by the Pittore delle Palme, from Tarquinia (?).	770
40.6	Crater of Aristonothos, from Cerveteri.	771
40.7	Hydria by the Micali Painter, from Vulci.	771
40.8	Etruscan ship, reconstruction by Marco Bonino.	772
40.9	Etruscan cargo ship, reconstruction by Marco Bonino.	773
41.1–3	Etruscan amphora of the Heptachord Painter.	779
41.4	The reconstruction of the fast chariot from Populonia, Tumulo dei Carri.	780
41.5	Fragment from the original wooden chassis of the fast chariot from Vulci.	781
41.6	The fast chariot from Populonia, Tumulo dei Carri, 1:1 model.	782
41.7	The fast chariot from Populonia, Tumulo dei Carri.	782
41.8	The fast chariot from Vulci, Tomba del Carro di Bronzo, 1:1 model.	783
41.9	The fast chariot from Vulci, Tomba del Carro di Bronzo.	783
41.10	The reconstruction of the parade Chariot I from Castel San Mariano.	784
41.11	The parade chariot I from Castel San Mariano.	784
41.12	Chariot procession depicted on terracotta friezes of Veii-Rome-Velletri type, dating 530–520 BC.	785
41.13	The shock-absorbing system between the chassis and the axle in the parade chariot from Monteleone di Spoleto.	785
41.14	The parade chariot from Castro (near Vulci).	786
41.15	The wheels of the cart from Populonia, Tumulo dei Carri.	787
41.16	Virtual 3D reconstruction of the cart from Eretum.	788
41.17	The substructure of the same cart as Fig. 41.16.	788
41.18	The wedding procession on a terracotta plaque from Murlo, Poggio Civitate.	788
41.19	Attic black figure lekythos by the Gela Painter.	789
41.20	The bronze decoration of the cart from Castel San Mariano.	789

41.21	Diagram of the function of the iron brackets from Casale Marittimo,	
	Casa Nocera necropolis, tomb A.	790
41.22	Graphic reconstruction of the cart from Pontecagnano, Tomb 928.	785
41.23	The cart from Trevignano Romano, Tomba dei Flabelli.	791
41.24	The tomb of the Picene Princess of Sirolo (near Ancona).	792
41.25	The cart of Sirolo reconstructed as a model 1:4.	792
41.26	Chariot-racing depicted on terracotta friezes of Veii-Rome-Velletri type.	793
41.27	Old drawings of the scene with preparations for a chariot race,	
a–b	painted in the Tomb of the Triclinium of Tarquinia.	793
41.28	Chariot-racing depicted on a funerary stone relief of Chiusi.	794
41.29	Chariot-racing painted on a black-figure amphora by the Micali Painter.	794
42.1	Wooden throne from Tomba del Trono, Verucchio.	800
42.2	Bronze *tintinnabulum* from Tomba degli Ori, Arsenale Militare.	800
42.3	Spindle from Gran Carro.	801
42.4	Ceramic spindle whorls, Poggio Civitate di Murlo.	801
42.5	Warp-weighted loom and its position with: a) natural shed;	
	b) artificial shed.	802
42.6	Ceramic loom weights, Poggio Civitate di Murlo.	802
42.7	Tablet weaving.	803
42.8	Ceramic spools, Poggio Civitate di Murlo.	804
42.9	Textile fragment from Cogion-Coste di Manone.	805
42.10	Mineralized textile remains from the Tomba della Montagnola at	
	Sesto Fiorentino.	806
43.1	Tomb of Hunting and Fishing, Tarquinia.	813
43.2	Drawing of the principle characteristics of Italic cooking stands.	814
43.3	Caeretan brazier, circa 575 BC, Cerveteri, Monte Abatone Tomb 120.	815
43.4	Bucchero *focolare* (brazier set with bowls, lids and trays).	815
43.5	Caeretan brazier, circa 575 BC, Cerveteri, Banditaccia Tomb	
	Maroi III.	816
43.6	Bronze cheese grater, Cerveteri (?).	818
43.7	Composite fibula (bronze and amber) with pendant.	818
44.1	Lid of funerary urn from a tomb at Tolle (Tomb 23).	824
44.2	Lid of funerary urn from Montescudaio, territory of Volterra.	824
44.3	Frieze plaque, terracotta, from the Upper Building at Poggio	
	Civitate (Murlo).	825
44.4	Golini I tomb, Orvieto.	828
44.5	Tomb of the Shields, Tarquinia.	828
45.1	Amphora by the Micali Painter.	833
45.2	Tomba degli Olimpiadi.	835
45.3	Tomba degli Auguri.	836
45.4	Tomba degli Olimpiadi.	837
46.1	Terracotta plaque type C from Acquarossa.	841
46.2	The *cornu* at Museo Nazionale Etrusco di Villa Giulia.	843
46.3	The Tarquinia *lituus*.	843
46.4	Drawing of an *aulos* player in *Tomba dei Leopardi*, Tarquinia.	844
46.5	The Chianciano *aulos*.	844
46.6	Drawing of a *chelys lyra* in *Tomba dei Leopardi*, Tarquinia.	845
46.7	Drawing of a *barbiton* in *Tomba del Triclinio*, Tarquinia.	846
46.8	Mirror of a youth holding a concert *kithara*.	846
46.9	Rattling cup from Veii.	847
46.10	Sarcophagus and lid with portraits of husband and wife.	848

46.11	Amphora decorated by the Micali-painter.	849
46.12	Mirror of an athlete and an *aulos* player.	849
46.13	Terracotta plaque with banqueting scene, Poggio Civitate (Murlo).	850
47.1	Anatomical votive: model foot with bunion.	858
47.2	Poggio Colla Excavations, fragment of bucchero vase.	862
47.3	Elongated bronze votive figurine of a haruspex.	865
47.4	Liverpool uterus model.	866
47.5	Liverpool uterus model.	867
47.6	Manchester uterus model.	867
47.7	The "Decouflé bust" purchased by the Louvre, 2011.	868
47.8	Etruscan dental appliance.	871
47.9	Etruscan dental appliance.	871
48.1	*Antenne* sword from Fontivegge.	886
48.2	Krater by the Pescia Romana/Cesnola Painter.	888
48.3	Black Figure hydria by a painter of Micali Group.	892
48.4	The "Cannicella Venus," limestone statue, Orvieto, Cannicella necropolis.	893
48.5	Inscribed vase (fragmentary oinochoe).	894
48.6	Hellenistic urn of Volterran type.	895
48.7	Silver kotyle from Tomba del Duce, Vetulonia.	897
49.1	Poggio Civitate (Murlo): reconstruction of a pediment with sphinx acroterion.	906
49.2	Velletri, temple at Le Stimmate: reconstruction of the eaves.	908
49.3	Veii, Portonaccio sanctuary: reconstruction of a pediment with painted floral decoration.	910
50.1	Diadem, electrum. From the peripheral tomb II of the Pietrera at Vetulonia.	916
50.2	Pin. From the Tomb of the Lictor, Vetulonia.	917
50.3	Fibula *a sanguisuga*, gold, with stamped decoration.	918
50.4	Fibula *a sanguisuga*, gold, with granulated decoration *a pulviscolo*.	918
50.5	*A bauletto* earrings, gold, with granulation and other decoration.	920
50.6	Disc-earrings, gold.	920
50.7	Bracelet from Vulci.	921
50.8	Bulla: contest between Thetis and Peleus (?) between two female figures.	922
50.9	*A grappolo*-style earrings.	923
50.10	*A grappolo*/horseshoe earring, gold sheet.	924
51.1	Banded agate scarab depicting two Roman *salii*, inscr. *appius alce*.	930
51.2	Agate Scarab. Satyr. Greek.	931
51.3–5	Cornelian scarab. Warrior (Achilles/Achle).	932
51.6	Cornelian scarab. Hermes/Turms.	933
51.7	Cornelian scarab. Herakles/Hercle sailing on an amphora raft.	935
51.8	Cornelian scarab. Herakles/Hercle and Antaios, inscr. *hercle*.	936
51.9	Cornelian scarab. Herakles/Hercle and the Erymanthian Boar.	936
51.10	Banded agate. Odysseus/Uthuze, inscr. *uthuze*.	936
51.11	Cornelian scarab. Centaur. A *globolo* technique.	938
51.12	Sardonyx ringstone based on a scarab. Herakles/Hercle, inscr. *hercle*.	939
52.1	Etrusco-geometric *olla*, Narce tomb 23M.	944
52.2	Etrusco-Geometric skyphos, Vulci tomb 42F.	944
52.3	Etrusco-Geometric tripod pyxis, Narce tomb 1.	945
52.4	Red-on-White oinochoe, Narce tomb 1.	946

52.5	Red-on-White plate, Narce tomb 1.	946
52.6	Red-on-White biconical urn, Narce tomb 1.	947
52.7	White on Red conical stand and bowl, Narce tomb 7F.	949
52.8	Red on White "krater," Vulci tomb 66.	950
52.9	Etrusco-Corinthian oinochoe by the Bearded Sphinx Painter, Vulci/Pitigliano tomb 26.	951
52.10	Etrusco-Corinthian chalice by Painter of the Large Rosettes.	952
52.11	Black-figure amphora, from Orvieto.	955
52.12	Black-figure amphora and lid from Orvieto (Gruppo di Orvieto).	956
52.13	Faliscan beaked jug, Red (Gruppo di Barbarano).	959
52.14	Etruscan red-figure jug.	960
52.15	Genucilia plate from Ardea, *tomba a fossa*.	960
52.16	Genucilia star plate from Narce	960
52.17	*Ceramica Argentata* (silvered ceramic) amphora with sea-monster handles.	961
53.1a–c	Three *bucchero sottile kotylai* from Cerveteri, Banditaccia Necropolis, Tumulo 1, tomb 2, right chamber.	975
53.2	*Bucchero sottile* spiral amphora from Tarquinia, Monterozzi Necropolis, Cultrera tomb 25.	976
53.3	*Bucchero pesante* Nikosthenic amphora from Cerveteri, Bufolareccia tomb 999.	977
53.4	*Bucchero kantharos*, provenance unknown.	978
53.5	*Bucchero sottile* caryatid chalice, said to be from Chiusi or Volterra.	978
53.6	*Bucchero sottile* Cypro-Phoenician *oinochoe*.	979
53.7	*Bucchero pesante oinochoe*, provenance unknown.	981
53.8a–b	*Bucchero pesante* column krater, provenance unknown.	982
53.9a–b	*Bucchero pesante kantharos*, provenance unknown.	982
53.10	*Bucchero pesante* chalice from Orvieto.	983
53.11	*Bucchero pesante* jug, provenance unknown, probably Chiusi.	983
53.12	Incised inscription on a *bucchero sottile* cockerel, said to be from Viterbo.	985
54.1	Striding female figure, "Tanagra type."	994
54.2	"Apollo from Veii."	994
54.3a–b	Standing woman, rear and front views.	995
54.4a–b	Figure of woman by pilaster. Front and rear views.	995
54.5	Female head.	995
54.6	Female heads, one generation apart with adjustments as to adornments.	996
54.7a–e	Five seated figures from the Campetti Sanctuary at Veii.	996
54.8	Six seated figures from the Vignaccia Sanctuary at Cerveteri.	997
54.9a–b	Two male warriors from the Campetti Sanctuary at Veii.	998
54.10	Striding warrior figure from the Campetti Sanctuary at Veii.	998
54.11	Two male warrior figures from the Vignaccia Sanctuary at Cerveteri.	999
54.12	Figurine of Athena/Menerva from the Vignaccia Sanctuary at Cerveteri.	999
54.13	Seated figure of Athena/Menerva from the Vignaccia Sanctuary at Cerveteri.	1000
54.14	Athena/Menerva seated on a *kline*. From the Vignaccia Sanctuary at Cerveteri.	1000
54.15	Standing woman holding pig in right hand. From the Vignaccia Sanctuary at Cerveteri.	1001
54.16	Lyre bearing musician from the Campetti Sanctuary at Veii.	1001

54.17	Male figure holding lyre to left shoulder.	1002
54.18	Flute player and lyre bearer.	1002
54.19	Male and female pair holding lyre and bird perched between their heads.	1002
54.20	Terracotta relief from the Vignaccia Sanctuary at Cerveteri with Artumes sacrificing.	1003
54.21	Two women in *naiskos* flanked by musicians.	1003
54.22	Enthroned female holding patera (?Artumes).	1003
54.23	Double enthroned females holding patera.	1004
55.1	Male "Canopic" cinerary urn from Dolciano.	1008
55.2	Head of a woman, once part of a "Canopic" cinerary urn from Castelluccio di Pienza.	1009
55.3	*Pietra fetida* cippus in the form of a female half-figure from Chiusi.	1010
55.4	Bronze bust of a female from the so-called "Isis" Tomb in Vulci.	1011
55.5	Stone sarcophagus lid of an anonymous elite Etruscan man.	1011
55.6	Painted terracotta sarcophagus of Seianti Hanunia Tlesnasa from Poggio Cantarello, near Chiusi.	1011
55.7	Detail of the heads of the lid figures (a married couple) on a terracotta cinerary urn from Volterra.	1012
55.8	Bust of a woman from the Vignale deposit, Cerveteri.	1013
55.9	Over-life-sized bronze statue of Aule Meteli, found near Lake Trasimene.	1014
56.1	Rear wall of the "Tomb of the Roaring Lions," Veii.	1018
56.2	Tarquinia. Tomb of the Lionesses, rear wall.	1019
56.3	Tarquinia, Tomb of the Bulls: detail of rear wall.	1019
56.4	Tarquinia, Tomb of Hunting and Fishing.	1020
56.5	Tarquinia, Tomb of the Mouse.	1021
56.6	Tarquinia, Tomb of the Triclinium.	1021
56.7	Tarquinia, Tomb of the Ship.	1022
56.8	Tarquinia, Tomb of Orcus II.	1022
56.9	Tarquinia, Tomb of Orcus II.	1023
57.1a–b	Armed worshipper.	1027
57.2	Worshippers of the Hellenistic period.	1028
57.3a–c	Archaic statuette of bovine.	1029
57.4a–b	Statuette of *Tinia* from Arezzo.	1029
57.5	Minerva from Arezzo after the recent restoration.	1030
57.6a–b	Female worshipper.	1031
57.7a–c	Warrior from Brolio (550 BC).	1032
57.8	Putto from Montecchio.	1034
57.9a–b	*Kouros* from Arezzo: Fonte Veneziana (530–510 BC).	1034
57.10	Left leg of male statuette (400 BC).	1035
57.11	*Kouros* from Arezzo: Monte Lignano (500–480 BC).	1035
57.12	Athlete from Arezzo: Quarata (460–440 BC).	1035
57.13 a–c	*Kouros* from Lago degli Idoli (480–460 BC).	1036
58.1	Typical mirror sections.	1042
58.2	Undecorated tang mirror from Tarquinia.	1044
58.3a–c	Typical bronze tang mirrors and independent carved bone, ivory or cast bronze handles.	1044
58.4	"*Atunis* (Adonis) and *Lasa Achununa*," tang mirror.	1045
58.5a–c	Typical elliptical ("solar") and circular mirrors.	1045

58.6   Typical handle mirrors: Etruscan (left) and Praenestine (right).   1046
58.7   "*Uni* (Hera) nursing *Hercle* (Herakles)," mirror from tomb 65,
         Tarquinia, Fondo Scataglini.   1047
58.8   Spiky-garland mirror, provenance unknown.   1050
58.9   Dioskouroi mirror, provenance unknown.   1051
58.10   Lasa mirror, provenance unknown.   1051
58.11   Handle mirror with male Lasa, from the Tomb of Fastia Velsi, Chiusi.   1052
58.12   Tang mirror with male and female Lasae forming border,
         provenance unknown.   1053
58.13   Lasa mirror, provenance unknown.   1053
58.14   Lasa mirror, from the Tomb of Fastia Velsi, Chiusi.   1054
58.15   Lasa mirror, from Orvieto.   1054
58.16   "Toilette of Malavisch," provenance unknown.   1055
58.17   "Oracular Head of *Urphe*," so-called Casuccini Mirror, from Chiusi.   1057
58.18   "Oracular Head of *Urphe*," provenance unknown.   1057
58.19   Praenestine mirror with young couple playing a board game.   1059
58.20   "Paniscos and Marsyas," Praenestine mirror.   1059
58.21   Female skeleton with Lasa mirror, from Tomb A, Cannicella
         necropolis, Orvieto.   1061
59.1   Male votive head, from Veii.   1069
59.2   Female votive head (half-head), from Veii.   1069
59.3   Right Eye.   1070
59.4   Female breast, from Veii.   1070
59.5   Uterus, heart, bladder and three fragments of polyvisceral plaques,
         from Veii.   1070
59.6   Swaddled infant, from Veii.   1070
59.7   Fragment of a female votive statue with open abdominal cavity,
         from Veii.   1072
59.8   Female half-head, with hole for hanging, from Veii.   1072
59.9   Uterus from Veii.   1075
59.10   Penis.   1075
59.11   Votive ears, from Veii.   1076
59.12   Outstretched votive hand, from Veii.   1076
59.13   Votive torso with internal organs.   1077
59.14   Right foot.   1078
59.15   View of male torso.   1079
59.16   Male torso with open abdominal cavity.   1079
60.1   The classification system adopted for this chapter in terms of
         Etruscan animal motifs (see Table 60.1 for more details).   1087
60.2a–v Examples of Etruscan animal motifs on an array of different
         artifacts and diverse materials (see text for more details).   1090
60.3   Examples of Etruscan bird motifs on an array of different artifacts
         and diverse materials (see text and Table 60.2 for more details).   1095
60.4   Villanovan period. A graphic presentation of some 20 items
         spanning the years 900–780 BC depicting or representing animal
         motifs classified as per Fig. 60.1.   1103
60.5   Orientalizing period. A graphic presentation of some 86 items
         spanning the years 780–600 BC depicting or representing animal
         motifs classified as per Fig. 60.1.   1103

60.6	Archaic period. A graphic presentation of some 85 items spanning the years 600–480 BC depicting or representing animal motifs classified as per Fig. 60.1.	1104
60.7	Classical period. A graphic presentation of some 32 items spanning the years 480–323 BC depicting or representing animal motifs classified as per Fig. 60.1.	1105
60.8	Hellenistic period. A graphic presentation of some 35 items spanning the years 323–100 BC depicting or representing animal motifs classified as per Fig. 60.1.	1106
60.9	Etruscan animal categories collated according to find site.	1107
60.10	A possible role of animal motifs in the after-life beliefs of the Etruscans.	1110
60.11	The front panel relief of a Hellenistic Volterran alabaster urn.	1111
61.1	Anonymous seventeenth-century painter, *Annius of Viterbo*.	1118
61.2	View of Viterbo.	1119
61.3	Etruscan tombs along a street in Viterbo.	1119
61.4	Master Pasquale of Rome, *Sphinx*.	1122
61.5	Etruscan sarcophagi in the courtyard of Palazzo Civico, Viterbo.	1124
61.6	"Desiderius decree," supposedly 776.	1127
61.7	"Egyptian" stele, pastiche.	1127

CONTRIBUTORS

———•◆•———

Luciano Agostiniani was born in Pistoia in 1939, and received an MA degree at the University of Florence in 1972. From 1987 to 2009 he was Professor of General Linguistics and Comparative Philology in the University of Perugia, Faculty of Arts. He is a member of the Società Italiana di Glottologia, Società Internazionale di Linguistica e Filologia Italiana, Società di Linguistica Italiana, a member of the board of directors of the Istituto Nazionale di Studi Etruschi e Italici, and a correspondent member of the Accademia della Crusca. His main areas of research are: languages of ancient Italy, dialectology and sociolinguistics (in particular spoken Italian), semantics (also in connection with formulaicity and idiomaticity), linguistic historiography. On the ancient linguistics side, he is interested mainly in Etruscan and ancient Italic languages (his publications include books, *Iscrizioni anelleniche di Sicilia, I: Le iscrizioni elime*, Florence 1977; *Le "iscrizioni parlanti" dell'Italia antica*, Florence 1982; *Tabula Cortonensis*, Rome 2000; and various congress communications and articles in periodicals and miscellanies). One of his specific fields of interest is the structure and typological classification of Etruscan.

Laura Ambrosini is a researcher at the Institute for the Study of Italic and Ancient Mediterranean Civilizations of the National Research Council and Professor of Etruscology and Italic Antiquities at the University of Foggia. She obtained a postgraduate diploma with honors in Classical Archaeology as well as her PhD in Archaeology (Etruscology) with honors from the Department of Etruscology and Italic Antiquities of the University of Rome "La Sapienza," under the supervision of Professor Giovanni Colonna. She has participated in the excavation of the Etruscan city of Veii and the sanctuary of Pyrgi and in the reinstallations of the National Museums of Villa Giulia and Cerveteri. Her book on Veii won the prize "Promotion Research 2004" and in 2005 she won a National Research Council Prize in the area of Sciences of Antiquity. Her research has focused primarily on ancient sites of Etruria (Veii, Norchia), on the *Ager Faliscus* (Corchiano, Falerii Veteres, Narce), on craft (pottery, mirrors, *thymiateria*, gems), the Etruscan language and Archaeometric studies on pottery and metals. For these studies she has developed many partnerships with foreign museums and institutions (École Française de Rome; CNRS, France; the British Museum, London; Metropolitan Museum of Art, New York, Musée d'Aléria Corsica, among others). She is the author of five scientific books and over 90 scientific articles and book chapters.

Maria Paola Baglione, a student of Massimo Pallottino, graduated in 1971 from the University of Rome "La Sapienza," where, since 2000, she has been an associate professor. Her interests include

Etruria on the Tiber (*Il territorio di Bomarzo*, Rome, 1976) and the adjacent Faliscan territory, with special regard for the cultural character and chronological definition of the oldest phases (eighth–seventh centuries BC) of that culture. In collaboration with M. A. De Lucia Brolli (q.v.) she continues the reconstruction of nineteenth-century excavations in the region of Narce (showcased in the exhibition "Scavo nello Scavo," Viterbo, 2004, curated by A. M. Sgubini Moretti). She recently took over direction of the Pyrgi excavations on the retirement of Giovanni Colonna, and continues the excavation and publication of the new southern sanctuary; the excavations and the new Museo Archeologico Nazionale in Castello di S. Severa at Pyrgi offer a unique opportunity for students and scholars. Her own research at Pyrgi includes the analysis of offerings and rituals found in the southern shrine, and the Attic vases excavated there. In 2001 she curated the exhibition of a group of terracotta votive statues from the Veii Portonaccio sanctuary for the exhibition "Veio, Cerveteri, Vulci. Città a confronto" sponsored by the Soprintendenza Archeologica per l'Etruria Meridionale; and she also coordinated the study and display of materials acquired by the Antiquarium of the Villa Giulia from the Museo Kircheriano. She has presented her research at various international conferences (Convegni di Studi Etruschi, Regensburg, Copenhagen, Philadelphia) and continues (with Professor F. Gilotta) the study of Praenestine mirrors from the Barberini Collection in the Villa Giulia.

Giovanna Bagnasco Gianni is a Classics graduate and has a PhD in Archaeology; she is Associate Professor of Etruscan Studies at the Università degli Studi di Milano (since 2005), and director of the archaeological excavations at Tarquinia conducted by the Università degli Studi di Milano. Her research spans from the archaeological reports regarding Tarquinia to the conditions of cultural transmission among cultures in the ancient world, in particular between Etruscans and Greeks, through to the analysis and interpretation of the archaeological and epigraphic data. A member of the Istituto di Studi Etruschi ed Italici, she is co-director (with Maria Bonghi Jovino) of the series *Tarchna*, (with Federica Cordano) of *Aristonothos. Scritti per il Mediterraneo antico*, and (with Nancy de Grummond, q.v.) of the *International Etruscan Sigla Project*. She has published extensively on Etruscan archaeology and epigraphy, the site and art of Tarquinia and related issues, and participated in international conferences. She edited and contributed to *Bridging Archaeological and Information Technology Culture for community accessibility* (Milan, July 10–11, 2007; Rome 2008), and with Maria Bonghi Jovino has published a book on the Ara della Regina (Tarquinia) temples. She has assisted with several major exhibitions, including *Gli Etruschi di Tarquinia* (Milan 1986); *Acque profonde* (Tarquinia 1998); *Oltre le Colonne d'Ercole* (Milano 1999); *Tarquinia. Una nuova storia* (Tarquinia 2001).

Gilda Bartoloni graduated in 1967 in Etruscology, having studied with Massimo Pallottino at Rome. Since 1976 she has been Professor of Etruscology at the Universities of Lecce, Siena and Paris IV Sorbonne, and a visiting professor at the Universities of Copenhagen and Vienna. In 2001 she became full professor at the University of Rome "La Sapienza." Her scientific interests regard especially Etruscan and Latial Protohistory, and she has published handbooks on the Villanovan and Etruscan cultures and mortuary archaeology, as well as over 100 works on the relations between the Italic peoples and other Mediterranean cultures. She curated the exhibition on *Etruscan Princes Between Mediterranean and Europe*, held at Bologna in 2000. She has participated in and directed many archaeological excavations in Etruria and Latium, most recently, the Veii project of the University of Rome "La Sapienza" (the settlement of Piazza d'Armi) and the Villanovan necropolis of Poggio delle Granate at Populonia; in 2003 she began research at Poggio del Telegrafo (Populonia). In collaboration with the Soprintendenza of Toscana she is responsible for the excavation of the Campassini site (Monteriggioni), of the handicraft area of Quartaia (Colle Val d'Elsa) and of the Pugiano sanctuary (San Gimignano). She is an ordinary member and auditor of the Istituto di Studi Etruschi ed Italici, and has been director of the newly reinstalled Etruscan and Italic Antiquities Museum of the University of Rome "La Sapienza."

Hilary Becker is an assistant professor of Classics at the University of Mississippi. She earned her BA at Bryn Mawr College and her MA and PhD at the University of North Carolina. Her publications include articles dealing with Etruscan property, archives, *castella* and settlement patterns and she co-edited, with Margarita Gleba, the volume *Votives, Places and Rituals in Etruscan Religion* (Brill 2009). She is currently researching a Roman imperial pigment shop in the Area Sacra di S. Omobono in Rome as part of the ongoing excavations there.

Marshall Joseph Becker, Professor Emeritus in Anthropology at West Chester University, was trained at The University of Pennsylvania in all four fields of anthropology. He now applies multiple anthropological approaches to gather information about the people of ancient Etruria and elsewhere in the Mediterranean. His studies of skeletal populations from archaeological sites in Italy, Greece, Turkey, the Czech Republic and elsewhere in the European Union have appeared in dozens of articles and in a book co-authored with J. Turfa. Dr. Becker has published over 200 articles on the Lenape and other Native Americans as well as a number of book chapters and monographs on the peoples of the lowland Maya region. His research has been supported by grants from the National Science Foundation, the National Endowment for the Humanities, The American Philosophical Society, the National Geographic Society and the Social Science Research Council.

Enrico Benelli is a specialist in Etruscology and the archaeology of pre-Roman Italy. He worked in the Soprintendenza ai beni archeologici delle Marche from 1999 to 2001, becoming a researcher in the CNR (National Research Council), where he is currently responsible for research in Etruscan epigraphy and editor of the *Thesaurus linguae Etruscae* and the *Corpus Inscriptionum Etruscarum*. He developed a new chronological framework for the archaic cultures of inner central Italy, and conducted excavations in the Sabine necropolis of Colle del Forno (Eretum) from 2003 to 2009. His research includes Etruscan epigraphy, history and society, especially the later period; a series of studies of late Etruscan inscriptions from the area of Chiusi, combining epigraphical, archaeological and antiquarian topics, has led to innovative results, especially concerning the social history of Chiusi and the whole of Etruria. He has taught Etruscology in the University of Udine since 2005.

Claudio Bizzarri has a long record of achievements as director and collaborator on numerous Etruscan and Roman archaeological excavations; he was the American Institute of Archaeology Kress Foundation Lecturer in 2001–2002, and is now a corresponding member of the AIA. He received his doctorate from the University of Perugia and is currently the Director of the PAAO (Archaeological and Environmental Park of the Orvieto Area), a member of the board of the Fondazione per il Museo C. Faina, and Resident Professor for "Arizona in Italy," the Study Abroad Program in Italy of the University of Arizona in Tucson. He has published extensively on the archaeology and topography of the Orvieto region, and on Etruscan material culture, and has taught archaeology courses at the universities of Macerata, Camerino, and Foggia.

Larissa Bonfante received her BA at Barnard College, her MA at the University of Cincinnati, and her PhD at Columbia University, where she studied with Otto J. Brendel, Margarete Bieber and Meyer Schapiro. She is Professor Emerita of Classics at New York University and has published on Etruscan and Roman dress and Etruscan language and culture, particularly iconography. She recently edited *The Barbarians of Ancient Europe* (2011), in which she also deals with Etruscan influence in Europe, and is presently working on an edited book, *Nudity as a Costume in the Ancient Mediterranean*. For the last ten years, with Jane Whitehead, she has been co-editor of *Etruscan News*, the Bulletin of the US Section of the Istituto di Studi Etruschi. In 2007 she was awarded the Gold Medal of the Archaeological Institute of America. She is a member of the Archaeological Institute of America, the Istituto di Studi Etruschi ed Italici, the German Archaeological Institute, the

Société des Etudes Latines, and the American Philosophical Society. Her books *Etruscan Life and Afterlife* (ed.), *The Etruscan Language: An Introduction* (with Giuliano Bonfante), and *Etruscan Dress* have seen multiple editions in the US and abroad.

Dominique Briquel, born in Nancy (France) in 1946, studied classical philology at the École Normale Supérieure and at the Sorbonne University (Paris), where he attended the lessons of Jacques Heurgon, Raymond Bloch and Michel Lejeune, before spending three years (1971–1974) at the French School of Rome, Palazzo Farnese. He taught Latin at the École Normale Supérieure in Paris, before becoming a professor at the University of Dijon. Since 1997, he has been Professor in Classical Philology at the Sorbonne, and at the École Pratique des Hautes Etudes, Paris, where he teaches a seminar in Etruscology. His own research deals especially with the testimonies of ancient authors, Greek and Latin, on the Etruscans (and their ideas about Etruscan origins), Etruscan inscriptions (with the publication of Etruscan documents in French collections) and Etruscan religion (especially in its use by the "last pagans: against the rise of Christian religion). His recent books include *L'origine lydienne des Étrusques, histoire du thème dans la littérature antique* (1991), *Les Tyrrhènes, peuple des tours, l'autochtonie des Étrusques chez Denys d'Halicarnasse* (1993), *La civilisation étrusque* (1999), *Chrétiens et haruspices: la religion étrusque, dernier rempart du paganisme romain*, (1997), and *La prise de Rome par les Gaulois* (2008).

Stefano Bruni was born in Florence in 1960. After receiving a Bachelor of Arts degree at the Università degli Studi of Florence, was awarded the Dr. M. Aylwin Cotton Foundation grant; subsequently he became an archaeologist in the Ministero per i Beni Culturali e Ambientali, serving in the Soprintendenza ai Beni Archeologici della Toscana. After earning the degree of Dottore di ricerca in archeology (Greek, Roman and medieval: settlements, economy and culture), since 2000 he has been Professor of Etruscology and Italic Antiquities in the Faculty of Arts and Philosophy of the Università degli Studi di Ferrara. He has participated in numerous excavation campaigns in Etruria, in the center of Pisa and the territory of the lower Valdarno, as well as the Valdera district and the Colline Pisane Inferiori. He is responsible for more than 200 publications, including monographs, articles and reviews, which have been published in major Italian and international journals. His scientific research is concerned with problems of the Etruscan and pre-Roman Italic world, and ranges over a wide area of interests: pottery and numismatics, historical topography, bronze-working, terracotta sculpture and religion, iconography and problems of trade and commerce, funerary ideology and sculpture. An important area of his scientific activity is devoted to historiography and antiquarian studies, from a primarily historical viewpoint.

Giovannangelo Camporeale graduated from the University of Florence in 1956. He has held numerous academic posts, beginning as a professor in Etruscology and Italic Archaeology at the University of Florence in 1962. He has been a visiting professor at the British Academy (London), the École Normale Supérieure (Paris), and the Deutsches Archäologisches Institut (Berlin), and since 1995 he has been the Course Coordinator in Etruscology and Italic Antiquities of the Università Italiana per Stranieri of Perugia. He has also been President of the Istituto di Studi Etruschi ed Italici since 1995, and Lucumo of the Accademia Etrusca of Cortona since 2008. He was President of the *Lexicon Iconographicum Mythologiae Classicae (LIMC)*, and coordinator of several international exhibitions, including "Prima Italia," "Etruria Mineraria" and "The Etruscans and Europe." He directed the archaeological excavations of Massa Marittima (and thus Lago dell'Accesa) for many years, and is a member of numerous Italian and international professional groups, including the Scientific Council of the Istituto per l'Archeologia Etrusco-Italica of the Consiglio Nazionale della Ricerca (CNR) and the Foundation for the Museum "C. Faina" of Orvieto. Among his books are *La caccia in Etruria* (*The Hunt in Etruria*, 1984), *La tomba del Duce* (1967), *I commerci di Vetulonia in età orientalizzante* (1969), and works on the Alla Querce and C. A. Collections, on Orvietan bucchero and craftsmanship, and on the site of Lago dell'Accesa. His most recent work, *Gli Etruschi. Storia* *e civiltà* (2000) has gone into a third edition, and has appeared in German translation; *Gli Etruschi fuori dell'Etruria* (2001). It has also been issued in an English-language edition, *The Etruscans Outside Etruria* (2004).

Alexandra A. Carpino is Professor of Art History and Chair of the Department of Comparative Cultural Studies at Northern Arizona University. She is the author of *Discs of Splendor: The Relief Mirrors of the Etruscans* (2003) and has written articles on the historical, social and cultural meanings of the narratives found on engraved bronze mirrors. She is also the co-editor of the (forthcoming) *Companion to the Etruscans* (Wiley-Blackwell 2014), and the editor-in-chief of *Etruscan Studies: Journal of the Etruscan Foundation.*

Armando Cherici graduated from the Facoltà di Lettere of Florence University with a thesis in Etruscology, and earned the title of Dottore di Ricerca in Archeologia Italica at the University of Rome "La Sapienza." He holds a post-doctoral position at the University of Florence, where he teaches courses in Etruscology for the Centro di Cultura per Stranieri. He has held conferences and seminars in Italic Archaeology at the Sorbonne and University of Nantes, at the Scuola di Specializzazione in Archeologia of Florence University as well as the École Normale Supérieure of France. He has been a member of the scientific staff of the CNRS/University of Tübingen Franco-German excavations at Castellina del Marangone (Rome), and collaborated in publication of the *Lexicon der Antike "Neue Pauly," Lexicon Iconographicum Mythologiae Classicae (LIMC)*, and the *Thesaurus Cultus et Rituum Antiquorum (ThesCRA)*, and his numerous articles have appeared in archaeological and scientific journals. He is a member of the Deutsches Archäologisches Institut, the Istituto Nazionale di Studi Etruschi e Italici, and the Academia Etrusca of Cortona.

Ross Cowan is an independent scholar. He studied Classics at the University of Glasgow (MA 1997, PhD 2003), and is the author of six books and numerous articles on all aspects of Roman warfare. He has a particular interest in the military organizations and arms and armour of the peoples of pre-Roman Italy. Publications relevant to this project include "An important Italic helmet rediscovered" (in *Archäologisches Korrespondenzblatt* 37, 2007) and *Roman Conquests: Italy* (Barnsley, 2009).

Mariassunta Cuozzo is Associate Professor in Etruscology and Italic Archaeology at the University of Molise and at the University of Naples "Orientale." Her most relevant book for Etruscan studies is: *Reinventando la tradizione. Immaginario sociale, ideologie e rappresentazione nelle necropoli orientalizzanti di Pontecagnano*, Paestum (Salerno) 2003. She has published widely on Campanian, Greek, Etruscan and Italic Archaeology and on theoretical issues in European Archaeology. She is currently director of excavations in the Etruscan-Campanian settlement of Pontecagnano.

Francesco de Angelis holds a PhD in Classical Art and Archaeology from the Scuola Normale Superiore in Pisa, and is currently Associate Professor in the Department of Art History and Archaeology at Columbia University in New York. Among his interests are mythological images and their contexts; the role of monuments in the transmission of cultural memory and identity; the reception of the classical past in modern scholarship. He is the author of a monograph on the funerary urns of Chiusi, *Miti greci in tombe etrusche. Le urne cinerarie di Chiusi* (Rome: Accademia dei Lincei, 2012), and of numerous articles about Greek, Etruscan, and Roman art. He also has edited several books, the most recent of which is *Spaces of Justice in the Roman World* (Leiden-New York: Brill, 2010).

Nancy Thomson de Grummond is M. Lynette Thompson Professor of Classics at the Florida State University and specializes in Etruscan, Roman and Hellenistic art and archaeology, with special interests in Etruscan art, myth and religion. She directs the FSU excavations at the Etruscan site of Cetamura del Chianti. Among her books are *A Guide to Etruscan Mirrors* (1982, which included an international exhibition at FSU) and *Etruscan Myth, Sacred History and Legend* (2006). With Erika Simon, she chaired the Langford Conference "The Religion of the Etruscans," and has edited the book of the same title (2006, with Erika Simon). She is directing the *International Etruscan Sigla Project* with Giovanna Bagnasco Gianni (q.v.).

Maria Anna De Lucia Brolli, a student of Massimo Pallottino, graduated in 1975 with honors in Etruscology and Italic Antiquities from the University of Rome "La Sapienza" with a thesis on the manufacture of Archaic architectural terracottas. She joined the Ministero per i Beni e le Attività Culturali, serving with the Naples Museo Archeologico Nazionale and the Soprintendenza per i Beni Archeologici del Lazio. Since 1983 she has been an official with the Soprintendenza per i Beni Archeologici dell'Etruria meridionale, responsible for the protection of antiquities in the Faliscan territory (Narce, *Falerii*, Corchiano, Vignanello). She is Director of the Museo Archeologico dell'Agro Falisco in the Forte Sangallo of Civita Castellana, and has also been responsible for the reinstallation of the Faliscan galleries in the Villa Giulia Museum and for many other exhibitions. She has directed numerous excavations, including the definitive studies (and protection) of sanctuaries at Narce (Monte Li Santi-Le Rote), *Falerii* (Scasato II and via Gramsci sites) and the Underworld shrine at Grotta Porciosa. Her publications include *L'Agro Falisco* (Rome, 1991) and *Civita Castellana: Il Museo Archeologico dell'Agro Falisco* (Rome, 1991), and articles such as, with M. P. Baglione, "Le deposizioni infantili nell'agro falisco tra vecchi e nuovi scavi," *Scienze dell'Antichità* 14 (2007–2008) 869–893.

Richard Daniel De Puma is the F. Wendell Miller Distinguished Professor *Emeritus* of Classical Art and Archaeology, University of Iowa, where he taught for more than 35 years. He earned his BA at Swarthmore College, and holds both an MA and PhD in Classical and Near Eastern Archaeology from Bryn Mawr. He is an elected member of the Istituto Nazionale di Studi Etruschi ed Italici in Florence, a member of the Deutsches Archäologisches Institut in Berlin, and Research Associate at the Field Museum of Natural History in Chicago. He has organized exhibitions on Etruscan pottery and Roman portraits, and was Senior Curatorial Consultant for the exhibition "Art in Roman Life: Villa to Grave" at the Cedar Rapids Museum of Art. Most recently he collaborated on the major permanent reinstallation of the Etruscan Gallery at the Metropolitan Museum of Art in New York and contributed to the guidebook, *Art of the Classical World in the Metropolitan Museum of Art*, in 2007. His catalogue, *Etruscan Art in the Metropolitan Museum of Art*, will appear in 2013. For many years Professor De Puma was on the Advisory Board of the *American Journal of Archaeology* and continues to serve on the Advisory Board of *Etruscan Studies*. He has been a long-time lecturer for the Archaeological Institute of America, and conducted archaeological fieldwork in Italy, Turkey and India, and most recently co-directed excavations at Latin Crustumerium. He is the author of ten books (three on Etruscan mirrors) and more than 70 articles on various aspects of Etruscan and Roman art and archaeology. His book on *Art in Roman Life* was published in 2009.

Rubens D'Oriano, born at La Maddalena (province of Sassari, Sardinia), graduated from the University of Pisa in 1978 and joined the Soprintendenza per i Beni Archeologici delle province di Sassari e Nuoro (Sardinia) as an archaeologist, conducting excavations and research and publishing studies on Sardinia in the eighth century BC to the fifth century AD, especially on commercial and cultural contacts of the island with the rest of the Mediterranean.

Ingrid Edlund-Berry is Professor Emerita in the Department of Classics, The University of Texas at Austin. She received her fil. lic. degree at the University of Lund and PhD at Bryn Mawr College and has taught at the University of Georgia, University of Minnesota, the Intercollegiate Center in Rome, and the University of Texas at Austin. Her excavation experience includes Poggio Civitate (Murlo), S. Angelo Vecchio (Metaponto), and Morgantina. Her publications include books: *The*

Iron Age and Etruscan Vases in the Olcott Collection at Columbia University (Philadelphia 1980), *The Gods and the Place: Location and Function of Sanctuaries in the Countryside of Etruria and Magna Graecia (700–400 B.C.)* (Stockholm 1987), *The Seated and Standing Statue Akroteria from Poggio Civitate (Murlo)* (Rome 1992), with Lucy Shoe Meritt, *Etruscan and Republican Roman Mouldings,* (New York and Rome 2000); edited papers and books: "Architectural Theory and Practice: Readings of Vitruvius," *Memoirs of the American Academy* 50 (2005) 1–86, with Giovanna Greco and John Kenfield, *Deliciae Fictiles III: Architectural Terracottas in Ancient Italy: New Discoveries and Interpretations* (Oxford 2006), with Nancy T. de Grummond, *The Archaeology of sanctuaries and ritual in Etruria* (Portsmouth RI, 2011), articles, biographical essays, and book reviews.

Adriana Emiliozzi, a student of the famous Etruscologist Massimo Pallottino, graduated in 1971, and has made her career at the National Research Council (Rome). Today she is senior researcher at the Institute for the Study of Italic and Ancient Mediterranean Civilizations (ISCIMA). She took part in the publication of the corpus of bronze *Praenestine Cistae* and in the organization of the international *Corpus of Etruscan Mirrors (CSE)*. She reorganized and published the archaeological collections of the Civic Museum of Viterbo, renewing its galleries in 1994. With the exhibition *Carri da Guerra e prìncipi etruschi* she has opened new horizons for the study of the "culture of princes" in ancient Italy, and made fresh analyses of famous monuments, including the Chariot of Monteleone di Spoleto (Metropolitan Museum, New York), newly reconstructed in 2007 and published in 2011. She has made contributions to epigraphy and prosopography, Etruscan and Roman, as well as archaeology in general.

Françoise Gaultier is Deputy Director of the Department of Greek, Etruscan and Roman Antiquities of the Musée du Louvre. She holds a doctorate from the University of Paris X-Nanterre and was formerly a member of the École Française de Rome. Since 1981 she has been a curator for the Etruscan collections and has also taught at the École du Louvre. She has written a number of books and articles on Etruscan antiquities and the history of the Louvre Etruscan collections and has organized the following exhibitions: "Les Etrusques et l'Europe" (Paris, Grand Palais, September 1992–January 1993; Berlin, Altes Museum, February–May 1993) in conjunction with M. Pallottino and G. Camporeale; "Trésors Antiques, les bijoux de la collection Campana" (Paris, Musée du Louvre, October 2005–January 2006; Rome, Musei Capitolini, March–July 2006) with C. Metzger; and "Gli Etruschi dall'Arno al Tevere, le collezioni del Louvre a Cortona" (Cortona, MAEC, March–July 2011) with L. Haumesser.

David B. George holds degrees in Art History/Archaeology from the University of Missouri-Columbia, and received his MA and PhD in Classical Studies at the Ohio State University. Since 1995 he has been Professor of Classics and Chair of the Classics Department at St. Anselm College (Manchester, New Hampshire), and Director of its Institute for Mediterranean Archaeology. He is (with Claudio Bizzarri, q.v.) Co-Director of the Excavations at Coriglia, Castel Viscardo, in the territory of Orvieto, where he is studying an Etruscan settlement. He teaches Latin, Greek, Hebrew, ancient history and archaeology, and has published extensively on various problems in ancient history and Classics, and on scientific applications (such as XRF technology) for archaeological excavations, for which he has been awarded numerous grants. He has appeared in interviews on the television *History Channel* and advised on scripts for topics including the lives of Hannibal, Moses, Caesar, and for the television series "Battles BC" and "Clash of the Gods."

Claudio Giardino (PhD) is a researcher at the University of Salento, Lecce, and a member of several archaeological missions, in Italy and abroad. His interest focuses on archaeometallurgy and on the interaction between metals and society in antiquity. His publications include the books *Il Mediterraneo occidentale fra il XVI e l'VIII sec. a.C. Cerchie minerarie e metallurgiche – West*

Mediterranean between 14th and 8th Century BC: *Mining and metallurgical spheres* (Oxford 1995) and, *I metalli nel mondo antico. Introduzione all'archeometallurgia* (new edition) (Rome-Bari 2010).

Margarita Gleba obtained her PhD from the Department of Classical and Near Eastern Archaeology at Bryn Mawr College (USA). Her principal fields of research are pre-Roman Italy and textile archaeology. She has excavated at Poggio Civitate di Murlo (Siena, Tuscany), Campo della Fiera (Orvieto, Umbria), Cavallino (Lecce, Puglia), Poggio delle Civitelle (San Venanzo, Umbria), as well as in Turkey and Ukraine. She was research project manager at the Centre for Textile Research, University of Copenhagen, Denmark and has recently completed a Marie Curie Intra-European Research Fellowship at the Institute of Archaeology, University College London, UK. She is the author of *Textile Production in pre-Roman Italy* (Oxbow 2008) and co-editor of *Dressing the Past* (Oxbow 2008), *Places and Rituals in Etruscan Religion. Studies in Honour of Jean MacIntosh Turfa* (Brill 2009), *Communicating Identity in Italic Iron Age Communities* (Oxbow 2011) and *Textiles and Textile Production in Europe from Prehistory to AD 400* (Oxbow 2012). She is now the recipient of a European Research Council Starting Grant for the study of ancient textiles.

Elisabetta Govi is Associate Professor in Etruscology and Italic Archaeology at the Università degli Studi di Bologna, where she teaches Etruscan archaeology and epigraphy and Italic archaeology. Since 1988 she has been responsible for archaeological excavations in the Etruscan city of Marzabotto, and is currently excavating the recently discovered urban temple. Her research interests include the urbanism and Etruscan architecture of the Po Region, and domestic and sacred architectonics, in the broader context of the development of Tyrrhenian Etruria and its commercial and cultural contacts with Etruria Padana. In 2010, together with G. Sassatelli, she prepared the final report on the excavation of House 1, *Regio* IV-*insula* 2 of Marzabotto. Another research interest is the stone sculpture of fifth-century Bologna analyzed from the viewpoint of funerary ideology. She also studies funerary ritual of the sixth–fifth centuries at Bologna (especially in the Certosa necropolis) and Spina. She studies the diffusion of Etruscan writing in the Po region, and has published a book on Attic imports in Bologna: *La ceramica attica a vernice nera di Bologna* (Bologna 1994). She is a member of the Istituto di Studi Etruschi e Italici, and has collaborated with museums and cultural heritage agencies in the region.

Jean Gran-Aymerich was born in Barcelona. He holds the *Doctorat d'état* from the Sorbonne, and is Director of Research at the Centre National de la Recherche Scientifique (CNRS) in Paris. He is a member of the Istituto Nazionale di Studi Etruschi ed Italichi, and participated in the Franco-German excavations of the Etruscan site of La Castellina del Marangone in the territory of Caere (south of Civitavecchia). His research ranges from bucchero pottery to Etruscan trade and exchange in the Mediterranean, and his current research includes Carthage. He participates frequently in international conferences, and recently spoke on management of cultural heritage sites at Alésia in France and La Castellina (Italy) at the conference "Patrimoine et bonne gouvernance en Tunisie" (Tunis, July 2012). His publications include: *Corpus Vasorum Antiquorum, Louvre 20* (1982) and *Louvre 23* (1992); *Malaga phénicienne et punique. Recherches franco espagnoles 1981–1988*, 1991 (received the Prix R. Dusseigneur 1986 of the Académie des Inscriptions et Belles-Lettres); *La Castellina a sud di Civitavecchia: origini ed eredità. Origines protohistoriques et évolution d'un habitat étrusque* (2011); "Gli Etruschi fuori d'Etruria occidentale et dans l'Ouest de l'Europe," in *Votives, Places and Rituals in Etruscan Religion. Studies in Honour of Jean MacIntosh Turfa*, (M. Gleba, H. Becker eds, Leiden-Boston 2009) 15–41; "La presencia etrusca en Cartago y el circulo del Estrecho su relacion con las navegaciones en el Mediterraneo occidental durante los siglos VII–V, y el *Libyae lustrare extrema*. Realidad y literatura en la visi grecoromana de Africa," *Estudios en honor del profesor Jehan Desanges* (J. M. Candau Moron, F. J. Gonzalez Ponce, A. L. Chavez Reino eds, Séville 2009) 1–32.

Marie Laurence Haack is Professor of Ancient History at the Université de Picardie and member of the Institut Universitaire de France (IUF). She is the author of *Les haruspices dans le monde romain* (Bordeaux 2003) and *Prosopographie des haruspices romains* (Pisa-Rome 2006); and editor of Écritures, cultures, societies dans les nécropoles d'Italie ancienne (Table-ronde proceedings), and *Mouvements et trajectoires dans les nécropoles d'Italie d'époque orientalisante, archaïque et hellénistique* (Bordeaux 2009). She is currently working on a book dealing with the historiography of Etruscology in the twentieth century.

Ulf Hansson has a PhD in classical archaeology and ancient history from the University of Gothenburg, Sweden (2005); his dissertation was on late Etrusco-Italic engraved gems (the so-called "*a globolo*" style). He is currently a research fellow in the Department of Classics at the University of Texas at Austin and at the Swedish Institute in Rome. His research interests include Etruscan and Italic art and archaeology, ancient and neoclassical engraved gems, the history of archaeology, history of collecting, and reception of antiquity. He is currently working on a book about the German archaeologist Adolf Furtwängler (1853–1907), and a revised and expanded version of his dissertation.

Adrian Harrison, D.Phil (*Cantab*), Associate Professor of Animal Production Physiology at the Faculty of Health Sciences, Copenhagen University – has a background in animal production, research and teaching duties in physiology, and additional qualifications in animal nutrition and biochemistry. His private interest in ancient civilizations and the Etruscans has led to a few publications: "A Modern Appraisal of Ancient Etruscan Herbal Practices: Were natural forms of treatment for Fasciola hepatica available to the Etruscans?" (*International Journal of Medical Sciences* 7[5] 2010: 282–291); and "Metallurgy, environmental pollution and the decline of Etruscan civilization" (*Environmental Science and Pollution Research International* 17 [2010]: 165–180). Additionally, he has written articles on "*Fuscum Olympionico Inscriptum* – Olympic Victor's Dark Ointment," an ancient transdermal means of pain relief believed to have been used by Olympic athletes and listed under the *collyria* by Galen, work that has been undertaken in collaboration with the British Museum: *An Ancient Greek Pain Remedy for Athletes*, and *Transdermal Opioid Patches for Pain Treatment in Ancient Greece*. He is currently participating in a study of ancient Etruscan DNA and related materials.

Vincent Jolivet is *Chargé de recherche* at the CNRS, Paris (Centre National de la Recherche Scientifique), specializing in the archaeology of Etruria and pre-Roman Italy. His early excavation work included the sites of Saint-Blaise, Ruscino, Agde and other sites in the Languedoc, and the site of Claros, where he assisted with publication. A long-term affiliate of the École française de Rome, he participated in the excavation of Etruscan Marzabotto, and has directed excavations at the Hellenistic site of Musarna (1983–2003), and published extensively on topics including the Romanization of Etruria, Etruscan painted ceramics and black gloss and plain-ware ceramics (including the *CVA* Louvre 22) as well as art and artisans of the Hellenistic period. He has participated in the publication project for the finds from the French excavations of the city site of Bolsena, and the virtual museum project for the Etruscan collections in the Phoebe Hearst Museum, Berkeley (USA). He also studies Roman topography and Renaissance cartography, with publications on the Pincian excavations (1981–2005) and the topography of the northern Campus Martius. His recent research appears in *Musarna* volumes 4 and 5, and *Pincio* 2.

Ingrid Krauskopf wrote a dissertation on the "Theban legend-cycle and other Greek legends in Etruscan art" for her PhD from the University of Heidelberg (with Roland Hampe). She completed her *habilitation* with a thesis on S-handle oinochoai, "Bronzeschnabel-Kannen mit Bauchknick. Eine etruskische Form in Italien und Griechenland" (1982, University of Mannheim, with Wolfgang Schiering). In 1994 she became a professor of Classical Archaeology at the University of Mannheim, and in 2002 she continued this role in Heidelberg (she retired in 2010). She worked for the *LIMC (Lexicon Iconographicum Mythologiae Classicae)* and *ThesCRA (Thesaurus Cultus et Rituum Antiquorum)* projects at the Heidelberger Akademie der Wissenschaften (Heidelberg Academy of Sciences and Humanities). She has been a *Membro straniero* of the Istituto Nazionale di Studi Etruschi ed Italici since 1983 and has published numerous articles and books on Etruscan mythology and religion, including the basic reference on Etruscan demonology, *Todesdämonen und Totengötter im vorhellenistischen Etrurien* (Florence 1987) and numerous articles on Etruscan gods and heroes in the *LIMC*.

Geoffrey Kron, educated at the University of Toronto, teaches Greek history at the University of Victoria. His research focuses on Greco-Roman social and economic history, including: the ancient economy and the Bücher-Meyer controversy; Greek democracy and the influence of political and social democracy on the distribution of wealth and income and on economic development, both ancient and modern; nutrition, social equality and public health in the ancient world, and their consequences for life expectancy; and Greek and Roman agriculture, particularly animal husbandry, aquaculture, and game farming.

Robert Leighton is Senior Lecturer in Archaeology at the University of Edinburgh. His research interests are primarily in the later prehistory of the central-western Mediterranean, from about 2000–500 BC, with a particular focus on Italy and Sicily. He has edited *Early Societies in Sicily* (Accordia Research Centre, 1996) and is the author of *Sicily before History* (Cornell, 1999), *Tarquinia, an Etruscan City* (Duckworth, 2004), *Prehistoric Houses at Morgantina* (Accordia Research Centre, 2012) and a monograph on the site of *Pantalica* (in preparation).

Fulvia Lo Schiavo is an archaeologist, associated researcher and former Research Director at the Institute for Aegean and Near Eastern Studies (ICEVO) in the National Council of Research (CNR, Rome) 1999–2005. She was Archaeological Superintendent in Tuscany (Florence) from 2006–2010, and in Sardinia (Sassari and Nuoro) from 1987–1999. She specializes in the study of the Mediterranean Bronze Age, with special interest on Sardinian archaeology, and is engaged in projects to set up a local museum for the Sardinian site of *Sa Domu 'e Su Nuraxi Arrubiu*; and in a project to catalogue the Cypriot collections of the Florence Museo Archeologico. Her research and publications range from ancient metallurgy and the archaeology of Sardinia to Etruscan archaeology and metallurgy, including: *Oxhide ingots in the central Mediterranean* (F. Lo Schiavo, J. Muhly, R. Maddin, A. Giumlia-Mair, eds, Biblioteca di Antichità Cipriote 8, ICEVO-CNR, Roma 2009); *Le Fibule dell'Italia meridionale e della Sicilia, dall'età del bronzo recente al VI secolo a.C.* (Prähistorische Bronzefunde, Abteilung XIV, Band 14, Stuttgart 2010); *I complessi archeologici di Trestina e di Fabbrecce nel Museo Archeologico di Firenze* (A. Romualdi and F. Lo Schiavo, eds) *Monumenti Antichi dei Lincei, Serie Miscellanea vol. XII* (LXVI Serie Generale, Rome 2009); *Archeometallurgy in Sardinia from the origins to the beginning of the Early Iron Age* (F. Lo Schiavo, A. Giumlia-Mair, U. Sanna, R. Valera, eds) *Monographie Instrumentum* (30, Montagnac 2005, ed. Monique Mergoil).

Daniele Federico Maras completed his studies at the University of Rome "La Sapienza," receiving a PhD in Archaeology (Etruscan Studies) in 2002, where he taught Etruscan and Italic Epigraphy from 2006 to 2010. Since 2010 he has been a member of the Board of Teachers for the PhD in Linguistic History of the Ancient Mediterranean at the Libera Università di Lingue e Comunicazione IULM of Milan, and since 2012 he has been a member of the *Società Italiana di Storia delle Religioni*. As well as writing articles and contributing to journals and edited volumes, he is also author of *Il dono votivo. Gli dei e il sacro nelle iscrizioni etrusche di culto* (2009), and, with G. Colonna, he wrote of the *Corpus Inscriptionum Etruscarum*, II.1.5, dedicated to Veii and the Faliscan area (2006).

Matteo Milletti, a researcher in Etruscology, has collaborated for many years with the Cattedra di Etruscologia dell'Università di Roma "La Sapienza," in the archaeological excavations of the site of Populonia-Poggio del Telegrafo (Livorno) and is also part of the Italian team excavating in Corsica at Cuciurpula-Serra di Scopamena/Sorbollano and at Puzzonu-Quenza (*Corse-du-Sud*). He is currently participating in several research projects, including analysis of finds from the site of Veii-Piazza d'Armi (University of Rome "La Sapienza"), and on results of excavations by the Soprintendenza Archeologica della Toscana in the necropolis of Populonia-S. Cerbone. Since 2011 he has held a position as teaching assistant at the Università degli Studi of Siena. He has published numerous articles and edited proceedings of congresses, study seminars and exhibitions. In recent years he has devoted special attention to the analysis of the relations of Etruscan civilization with that of the great islands of the Tyrrhenian Sea during the Iron Age.

Helen (Ili) Nagy is Professor Emerita of Art History at the University of Puget Sound. She is an expert on Etruscan votive terracottas and has been involved for many years with the study of Etruscan mirrors. Her publications include a book, *Votive terracottas from the 'Vignaccia', Cerveteri, in the Lowie Museum of Anthropology* (Rome 1988) and articles on Greek sculpture, Etruscan terracottas and mirrors. She is currently finishing a co-edited (with Larissa Bonfante, q.v.) volume of the collection of antiquities at the American Academy in Rome.

Marjatta Nielsen earned her PhD from the University of Helsinki with a thesis on the late Etruscan funerary sculpture of Volterra, and has given lectures on Etruscan culture and ancient art at universities in Denmark, Sweden and Finland. Her research interests cover various aspects of the Etruscan civilization, with special emphasis on late Etruscan funerary art, women and family tombs, as well as the reception of classical art in later times. She has been co-editor of *Acta Hyperborea. Danish Studies in Classical Archaeology*, and co-organizer of exhibitions on the Etruscans at Volterra (1985 and 2007) and Helsinki (2003).

Lisa C. Pieraccini received her PhD at the University of California Santa Barbara under the guidance of Mario A. Del Chiaro. Pieraccini lived in Rome for many years where she taught and conducted research at the Etruscan site of Cerveteri. Upon her return to the US in 2006 she taught for Stanford University and since 2007 has been teaching at the University of California Berkeley. Active at the southern Etruscan site known today as Cerveteri, her research interests and publications include Etruscan archaic pottery, burial customs, wall painting and the reception of the Etruscans in the eighteenth and nineteenth centuries. She is a member of the Istituto di Studi Etruschi ed Italici. Her book, *Around the Hearth: Caeretan Cylinder-Stamped Braziers* (2003) is the first comprehensive study of a unique class of over 350 Etruscan braziers. She is currently working on a book dedicated to ancient Caere.

Simona Rafanelli, Etruscologist, has been, since 2002, Director of the Museo Civico Archeologico "Isidoro Falchi" of Vetulonia. In 2009 she re-opened the excavations of the Etruscan-Roman city of Vetulonia, exposing a new, exceptionally well-preserved *domus* (aristocratic house). In the Vetulonia Museum she has curated exhibitions on a variety of topics: Etruscan gold and amber jewelry, the Tomb of the Trident and the Tomba del Duce of Vetulonia, "Vetulonia at the center of the Mediterranean," "Ships of bronze, from the Nuragic sanctuaries to the Etruscan tumuli of Vetulonia," and (2012) "The inimitable model. Paths between Etruscan civilization, Oenotrians and Dauniams." Her latest book, co-authored by Paola Spaziani, is *Etruschi. Il privilegio della bellezza* ("Etruscans: The privilege of beauty," Aboca Edizioni, 2011). She has published numerous articles on Etruscan archaeology, Vetulonia, and Etruscan religious rituals and art, including "Cippi in pietra configurati a testa umana dall'agro volsiniese," in E. Pellegrini and S. Rafanelli "Vecchie scoperte e recenti indagini a Bolsena," *Archaeologiae. Research by Foreign Missions in Italy*, VI, 1–2, 2008, G. M. Della Fina (ed.), Pisa-Rome 2011; "Un nucleo di altorilievi frontonali dall'Arce

Minore di Vetulonia," in *Deliciae Fictiles IV. Atti del Convegno Internazionale sul tema "Terrecotte architettoniche dell'Italia antica. Immagini di dei, mostri ed eroi* (Roma-Siracusa, 21–25 October 2009), P. S. Lulof and C. Rescigno (eds), Oxford 2010, 236–241; "Terrecotte architettoniche a Roselle con fregi figurati: gli epigoni dei sistemi decorativi di I fase ?" ("Architectural Terracottas with Relief Friezes from Roselle: The Epigones of the "First Phase" Decorative Systems?"), in *Tetti di terracotta. la decorazione architettonica fittile tra Etruria e lazio in età arcaica. Atti delle Giornate di Studio* (Sapienza, Università di Roma, 25 March and 25 October 2010), Officina Etuscologia, semestrale d'archeologia, Rome 2011.

Tom B. Rasmussen recently retired as Senior Lecturer and Head of Art History and Visual Studies at the University of Manchester. He took a PhD in Classical Archaeology at Cambridge under the direction of Robert Cook, with a dissertation published as *Bucchero Pottery from Southern Etruria* (1979, reissued by Cambridge University Press in 2006). With Nigel Spivey and in honor of Robert Cook, he co-edited the book *Looking at Greek Vases* (CUP 1991, Greek translation 1997). Before coming to Manchester, he was a fellow of the Institute of Archaeology in Ankara, traveling in the Phrygian, Hittite and Urartian highlands and the Levant. A fellow of the Society of Antiquaries, he has taught Greek, Roman, Etruscan and Near Eastern art and archaeology, and participated in excavations in Italy, France and England, including the projects of the British School at Rome, especially the Tuscania survey project. His numerous publications include *Archaeological Reports* (1985, 1995), *The Macmillan Dictionary of Art* (now *Grove Dictionary*), as editor, and co-authored fascicules of the *CSE*, the corpus of Etruscan mirrors. With Graeme Barker he published the well known *The Etruscans* (Blackwell, 1998). Recent works include: "Etruscan urbanization," in *Mediterranean Urbanization 800–600 BC* (R. Osborne and B. Cunliffe (eds), Oxford 2005: 71–90) and "Herakles' apotheosis in Etruria and Greece," *Antike Kunst* 48 (2005) 30–39.

Annette Rathje, Associate professor of Classical Archaeology at the Saxo Institute and of Archaeology, Ethnology, Greek and Latin and History of the University of Copenhagen, Denmark, she has participated in several excavations in Central Italy and has written numerous articles about Etruscan and Italic culture in Pre-Roman Italy, including major works on Near Eastern imports in Etruria, and on the tradition of the banquet. She is particularly interested in the interconnection, interaction and communication amongst the peoples of the Mediterranean in the ninth to sixth centuries BC.

Matthias Recke is a classical archaeologist and Curator of the Antikensammlung of the Justus-Liebig-Universität in Giessen, Germany. He has published a book on the attitude of the Greeks to the phenomenon of war, and various articles on archaic sculpture and ancient pottery. Other research interests include acculturation phenomena in the Late Bronze and Iron Ages in the eastern Mediterranean (Pamphylia and Cyprus). Since 2011 he has been Field Director of the archaeological excavations of Hala Sultan Tekke in Cyprus. In the course of his museum duties, he has produced numerous publications on the history of research and on reception of antiquity in modern art. In 2008 he organized an exhibition on the Etruscan anatomical votive terracottas in the Deutsches Medizinhistorisches Museum in Ingolstadt (published, with Waltrud Wamser-Krasznai, as *Kultische Anatomie* [Ingolstadt, 2008]).

Ingrid D. Rowland is a professor at the University of Notre Dame School of Architecture and a frequent contributor to The New York Review of Books. She graduated from Pomona College and earned Master's and PhD degrees in Greek literature and Classical Archaeology at Bryn Mawr College. She is the author of the books *Giordano Bruno: Philosopher/Heretic* (Farrar, Straus, and Giroux, 2008); *The Place of the Antique in Early Modern Europe*; *The Culture of the High Renaissance: Ancients and Moderns in Sixteenth Century Rome*; *The Roman Garden of Agostino Chigi*, Horst Gerson Memorial Lecture (University of Groningen, 2005); *The Scarith of Scornello: a Tale of Renaissance*

Forgery (University of Chicago Press, 2004). Her essays in *The New York Review of Books* were collected in *From Heaven to Arcadia: The Sacred and the Profane in the Renaissance* (New York Review Books, 2005). She is a member of the Accademia dei Sepolti (Volterra), the Academia Bibliotecae Alexandrinae (Egypt), and the American Academy of Arts and Sciences, and has been a fellow of the Getty Research Institute and John Simon Guggenheim Foundation.

Antonio Sanciu was born at Buddusò (province of Sassari-Sardinia). A graduate of the University of Trieste, since 1979 he has worked as an archaeologist in the Soprintendenza per i Beni Archeologici of the provinces of Sassari and Nuoro. He has directed numerous campaigns of archaeological excavation and edited and published various studies on Punic and Roman Sardinia.

Maurizio Sannibale, born in 1961, completed his studies at the Università degli Studi di Roma "La Sapienza," where he took a degree in Arts, and then a diploma in the Scuola di Perfezionamento in Archeologia. He is a corresponding member of the Istituto Nazionale di Studi Etruschi (2010). Since 1996 he has been Director of the Museo Gregoriano Etrusco of the Musei Vaticani. In more than 80 published books and articles, he has treated various aspects of artistic and artisanal production, with particular regard for goldsmithing, bronze-working, sculpture and figured ceramics. His studies have also dealt with conservation and the evidence of ancient techniques of production. He has recently dedicated several works to iconography, Etruscan religion, and to the relations between cultures in the area of the ancient Mediterranean.

Giuseppe Sassatelli, Professor of Etruscology and Italic Archaeology at the University of Bologna, has held and still holds many academic and institutional charges, including at national level. He is a regular member of the Istituto di Studi Etruschi e Italici, and a corresponding member of the German Archaeological Institute. Since 1988 he has directed the Bologna University excavations of the Etruscan city of Marzabotto, and has collaborated with many museums and agencies in presenting temporary and permanent exhibitions. His research output has been devoted to: the reconstruction of the historic dynamics of the Etruscan presence in the Po region, with innovative studies of the population; urban development of the main cities of the territory; artistic, especially sculptural production; commercial and cultural exchange; individual mobility between *Etruria padana* and neighboring territories; relations among neighboring cultures of northern Italy; the Etruscan character of the frontiers; the role of the Etruscans in relations between the Mediterranean and Europe, with particular regard to the Celts. A great part of his scientific activity is dedicated to the theme of the diffusion of writing in the Po region, especially in its initial phases, to the implications of this phenomenon on the historical, social and cultural plane, to its transmission by means of the Etruscans to the other populations of northern Italy. Another interest is the historiography of Etruscan studies and its relation to the "political" history of Italy.

Dr. Margherita Gilda Scarpellini, Mayor of Monte San Savino (prov. Arezzo, 2012) and former Director of the Museo Civico Archeologico in Castiglion Fiorentino, specializes in the archaeology of Arezzo and Castiglion Fiorentino. She is a member of the Accademia Petrarca di Lettere Arte e Scienze di Arezzo, and is associated with the Soprintendenza per i Beni Archeologici della Toscana. In addition to research and lectures she has organized a number of exhibits, including "The wild boar in antiquity" in Castiglion Fiorentino and *"Sacra Mirabilia"* in Rome. Her publications include articles on the history of collections, excavations and museum exhibits, and museum catalogues, for example, "Il sacello tardo etrusco di villa Fatucchi ed appunti sui santuari di Arezzo etrusca," in *Atti e Memorie Accademia Petrarca Arezzo* 59–60 (1997–98 [2000] 29–55; "L'acqua degli Etruschi. Appunti per alcuni culti idrici della Valdichiana aretina," in *I sentieri dell'acqua: culto, ruolo e regime delle acque nel Castiglionese* (Castiglion Fiorentino 2008) 21–41; *Castiglion Fiorentino Tesori Ritrovati*, exhibition catalogue (Montepulciano 2002); *Il cinghiale nell' antichità, archeologia e* *mito*, exhibition catalogue (Cortona 2009); *Sacra Mirabilia Tesori da Castiglion Fiorentino*, exhibition catalogue (Florence 2010).

Erika Simon is Professor Emerita of Würzburg University, where she held the chair in Classical Archaeology and served as director of the antiquities section of the Martin-von-Wegner Museum. She is the author or editor of numerous articles in many fields of art history, Classics and ancient history, and ancient myth and religion, as well as many books on Greek, Roman, and Etruscan art, myth, religion and society, including *Ara Pacis Augustae* (1968), *Festivals of Attica: an Archaeological Commentary* (1983), *Schriften zur etruskischen und italischen Kunst und Religion* (1996), and *The Religion of the Etruscans* (2006, co-editor with Nancy Thomson de Grummond, q.v.). She has been the recipient of numerous honors, including the Festschrift *Kotinos* (1992, Mainz: von Zabern).

Stephan Steingräber is from Munich and has studied Classical Archaeology, Etruscology, Ancient History and Prehistory in Germany and Italy. He worked at the German Archaeological Institute in Rome and has taught mainly at the universities of Munich, Mainz, Tokyo, Rome, Padova and Foggia. He was visiting professor in Denmark, Italy and the United States, and lecturer for the Getty Foundation and the Archaeological Institute of America. He is currently Professor of Etruscology at the University of Roma Tre. His numerous publications deal mainly with the historical topography, urbanism, architecture and tomb painting of Etruria and Southern Italy. He is a member of the Istituto di Studi Etruschi (Florence), the Accademia Etrusca (Cortona) and the German Archaeological Institut (Berlin) and lives in the small Etruscan town of Barbarano Romano north of Rome, where he is Director of the Archaeological Museum. Among his prize-winning books and articles are: *Etruskische Möbel* (1979); *Etruria: Städte, Heiligtümer, Nekropolen* (1981); *Città e necropoli dell'Etruria* (1983); *Etruscan Painting: Catalogue raisonné of Etruscan wall paintings* (1986); *Volterra* (2002); and *Abundance of Life: Etruscan Wall Painting* (2006).

Simonetta Stopponi is Professor of Etruscology and Italic Antiquities at the University of Perugia, and has also taught at the University of Macerata. She is the author of numerous monographs and articles in specialized journals, covering various aspects of the discipline, and coordinating exhibitions of Etruscan material (from *Case e Palazzi d'Etruria* [1985] and the *Tomba della Scrofa nera* [1983] to the bucchero collection of the Museo C. Faina of Orvieto [with F. Capponi and S. Ortenzi, 2006] and *Museo comunale di Bettona. Raccolta archeologica* [2011]). She is particularly interested in the archaeology and antiquities of Perugia, Orvieto and the Picene territory. She has directed territorial surveys and excavations at Orvieto, and since 2000 she has directed excavation of the site of Campo della Fiera of Orvieto for the University of Perugia in collaboration with the University of Macerata. The results of the survey are of great importance: according to the latest evidence, the site of the federal sanctuary of the Etruscans, sought since the fifteenth century, has been found.

Jacopo Tabolli, born in Rome, has lived in both Italy and Egypt. He earned his BA and MA in Archaeology at the University of Rome "La Sapienza" and is the youngest PhD candidate in Etruscan Studies to have graduated there (2012). His PhD dissertation in Archaeology (Etruscology), *Along the borders of Veii and Ager Faliscus. The inhabited area and the necropoleis (Tufi and Petrina) of Narce, between the first Iron Age and the Orientalizing period*, combined the study of more than 170 tomb-groups with research in various archives, recovering unpublished documents of the nineteenth-century excavations and enabling the re-identification of famous tomb groups now in Italy, Philadelphia, and elsewhere. He has published articles on the chronology and archaeology of the *Ager Faliscus* and Internal Etruria in the First Iron Age and Orientalizing period. He has participated in excavations in Italy, Tunisia and Cyprus, including field projects of the Institute of Etruscology (Populonia and Veii) and of the Department of Sciences of Antiquities (Palatine Hill), since 2005. He supervised one sector within the excavation site of Veii Piazza d'Armi under the direction of Professor Gilda Bartoloni. He is currently a research fellow at Sapienza University of Rome and involved in several research projects: publications of Veii-Piazza d'Armi excavation campaigns 2000–2012, Veii Grotta Gramiccia necropolis, in collaboration with ISCIMA – National Council of Research, and the Cori-ancient polygonal walls project.

Jean-Paul Thuillier was an Etruscologist at the École française de Rome and is now Professor of Classics at the École normale supérieure, Paris. In addition to numerous articles, he is the author of *Les jeux athlétiques dans la civilisation étrusque* (Rome, École française de Rome, BEFAR, 1985), *Sport im antiken Rom* (Darmstadt, Wissenschaftliche Buchgesellschaft, 1999), *Les Etrusques. La fin d'un mystère?* (Paris, Gallimard-Découvertes, 1992), *Les Etrusques. Histoire d'un peuple* (Paris, Armand Colin, 2003), and with W. Decker *Le sport dans l'Antiquité. Egypte, Grèce, Rome* (Paris, Editions Picard, 2004) and *Les Etrusques* (Paris, Editions du Chêne, Grandes civilisations, 2006).

Fredrik Tobin is a PhD candidate in Classical Archaeology and Ancient History at Uppsala University in Sweden, where he is writing a dissertation on the tombs of San Giovenale. He holds a Master's degree in Classical archaeology and ancient history as well as an undergraduate degree in Church music from the University of Gothenburg and a Master's degree in Organ performance and literature from the Eastman School of Music, Rochester NY.

Jean MacIntosh Turfa received her PhD in Classical and Near Eastern Archaeology and Latin from Bryn Mawr College, and has participated in excavations in the US and abroad, including the Corinth excavations of the American School of Classical Studies and the Bryn Mawr Etruscan excavations at Poggio Civitate (Murlo). She has taught in the US and abroad (Universities of Liverpool, Illinois, and Pennsylvania, Loyola University, Dickinson University, Bryn Mawr College, and St. Joseph's University). She was a consultant for the permanent reinstallation of the Kyle M. Phillips Etruscan Gallery of the University of Pennsylvania Museum, where she is currently a Rodney Young Research Fellow. She has published extensively on various topics of Etruscan culture, including architecture and shipbuilding, trade and the Etruscan-Punic alliance, anatomical votives and health in Etruria, votive offerings and divination in Etruscan and Italic religion, and has appeared on television programs for the *History* and *Discovery* channels. Her books include *A Catalogue of the Etruscan Gallery of the University of Pennsylvania Museum* (2005) and *Divining the Etruscan World: The Brontoscopic Calendar and Religious Practice* (Cambridge, 2012), which formed the topic of the British Museum's Eva Lorant Memorial Lecture, which she delivered in 2011. She is a member of the Archaeological Institute of America and American Philological Association, and a foreign member of the Istituto di Studi Etruschi ed Italici.

Ingela M. B. Wiman is currently an Associate Professor at the Swedish Institute in Rome. Her commission is to conduct research and create a thematic course on the Etruscans and their civilization for a two-year period. She is affiliated with the department of Historical Studies at the University of Gothenburg and a member of the scientific committee of the *Corpus Speculorum Etruscorum* (CSE) where she aims to publish the Etruscan mirrors stored in Sweden and Norway. She has written many works on Etruscan mirrors and natural resource management, both Etruscan and worldwide.

Nancy A. Winter received her PhD in Classical Archaeology from Bryn Mawr College and was a librarian of the Blegen Library at the American School of Classical Studies at Athens, Greece. While in Athens, she organized and edited the proceedings of two conferences on Greek architectural terracottas, and published *Greek Architectural Terracottas from the Prehistoric to the End of the Archaic Period* (Oxford Monographs on Classical Archaeology, Oxford 1993). She later published *Symbols of Wealth and Power: Architectural Terracotta Decoration in Etruria and Central Italy, 640–510 B.C.* (Supplement to the *Memoirs of the American Academy in Rome* 9, Ann Arbor 2009). Some of her recent articles include: "New light on the production of decorated roofs of the 6th c. B.C. at sites in and around Rome," *JRA* 22 (2009) 6–28 (co-authored with I. Iliopoulos and A. J. Ammerman); "Sistemi decorativi di tetti ceretani fino al 510 a.C.," in *Studi in memoria di Mauro Cristofani* in *Mediterranea* 5, 2008 (2009) 187–196; "The Caprifico Roof in its Wider Context," in D. Palombi (ed.), *Il tempio arcaico di Caprifico di Torrecchia (Cisterna di Latina): I materiali e il contesto*, Cori 2010, 113–122; "Solving the Riddle of the Sphinx on the Roof," in *Etruscan by Definition. Papers in Honour of Sybille Haynes*, J. Swaddling and P. Perkins (eds), (British Museum Research Publication 173, London 2009, 69–72); and *Etruria I. Architectural terracottas and painted wall plaques. pinakes c. 625–200 BC* (Catalogue, Ny Carlsberg Glyptotek [co-authored with J. Christiansen], Copenhagen 2010). Her database of Etruscan architectural terracottas is available on the Beazley Archive website at the University of Oxford.

PREFACE

——·◆·——

Jean MacIntosh Turfa

We walk in the footsteps of giants, the many scholars who have preceded us in the study of ancient Etruria and Italy, and whose works you will find frequently cited in this volume.

We honor several of our colleagues who have recently been lost but will be remembered wherever Etruscan civilization is studied:

Claudia Giontella, Francesca Romana Serra Ridgway and David Ridgway, Antonella Romualdi, Brian Shefton, Paola Zamarchi Grassi.

This volume would not have been possible without the assistance of many colleagues and friends, especially Amy Davis-Poynter, Ingrid Edlund-Berry and Stephanie Budin, Nancy Thomson de Grummond, Larissa Bonfante, Rex Wallace, Greg Warden, Margarita Gleba and Cynthia Reed; and the advice and encouragement of all the authors, especially Gilda Bartoloni, Giovannangelo Camporeale, Richard De Puma, Fulvia Lo Schiavo, Erika Simon, Stephan Steingräber, Jacopo Tabolli, and the late David Ridgway; and the many individuals, institutions, and museums that have assisted with information, images, etc. A number of scholars who were not able to share in the writing of this book have assisted and encouraged in other ways: Anna Maria Bietti Sestieri, Fiona Campbell, Sybille Haynes, Ellen Macnamara, Georgina Muskett, John Prag, Judith Swaddling.

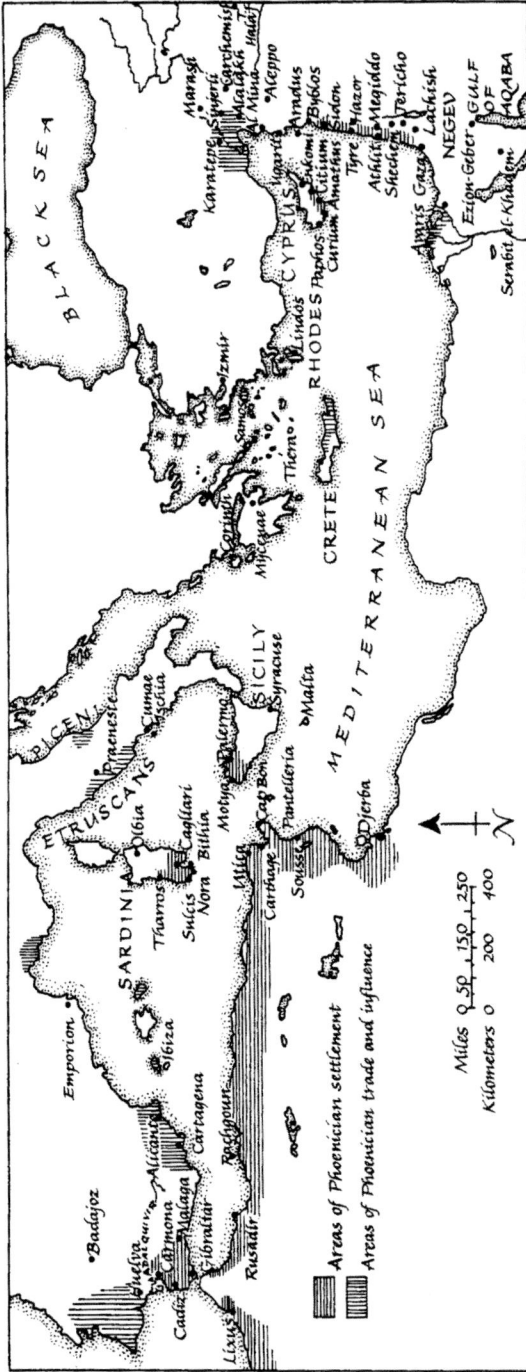

Map 1   The Mediterranean World in the first millennium bc: Etruria in the central Mediterranean, between the Greek and Punic Worlds and Europe. From W. Culican, *The First Merchant Venturers* (New York, 1966), Fig. 1. © Thames & Hudson.

RAETI CARNI

VENETI

Golasecca

GALLI

Verona Padua
Este
Adria

PO

HISTRI IAPODES

LIGURES

Spina

Nesactium LIBURNI

Monaco

Bologna
Marzabotto

ADRIATIC SEA

Luni Rimini
(Ariminum)
Fiesole Novilara
(Faesolae)
Pisa ARNO
Volterra Arezzo Ancona
Cortona Gubbio

Populonia UMBRI
Chiusi Perugia Belmonte

ELBA Vethlonia PICENTES
Orvieto Todi Ascoli (Asculum)
Vulci Piceno
Campovalano

CORSI Tarquinia Falerii SABINI VESTINI
Aleria SANNITES PAELIGNI
(Alalia) Cerveteri Palestrina Corfinium
Rome MARSI
Lavinium LATINI VOLSCI Sipontum
Satricum AURUNCI Lucera Arpi Canosa (Canusium)
DAUNI

Capua Melfi PEUCETI
Cumae MESSAPII
Olbia Naples (Neapolis) Brindisi
Ischia Pompeii (Brindisium)
(Pithekoussai) LUCANI Tarentum CALABRI

SARDI TYRRHENIAN Paestum OENOTRI Metapontum
SEA Velia Siris
Tharros Pyxos (Heraclea)
BRUTTII CHONES
Sybaris

Cagliari
Croton (Kroton)
Sulcis Nora

AEOLIAN ISLANDS MORGETES

Lipari Medma Caulonia
Palermo Messina ITALI Locri
(Zancle) Reggio (Rhegion)
Motya ELYMI Naxos
Selinus SICANI Catania
Agrigento SICULI
(Akragas) Leontini Megara Hyblaea
Gela Syracuse
Carthage Akrai
(Qart-hadasti)

Greek and
Phoenician colonies

Principal
native centers

Celts

Map 2   The Italian archipelago: cultural regions.
From M. Pallottino, *Genti e Culture dell'Italia Preromana* (Rome, 1981), Fig. 1

Map 3   Etruria: principal cities and sites.
From L. Banti, *The Etruscan Cities and Their Culture* (Berkeley and Los Angeles, 1973), p. 3.

INTRODUCTION

TIME TO GIVE THE ETRUSCANS THEIR DUE

———•◆•———

Jean MacIntosh Turfa

The world of the Etruscans has expanded greatly in recent years: in depth, due to new scientific areas of research such as archaeological biochemistry, DNA analysis, and materials science that can tell us more than we could fathom about the physical composition of their goods and their very bodies (on the DNA issue, see Chapters 3 and 4). We have also seen expanded the scope of Etruscan interaction in the Mediterranean and beyond, a field significantly broadened by analysis of archaeological finds of imports, exports, and details of interaction (travel, diplomacy, marriage, colonization) found in settlements, tombs, and underwater shipwrecks of the Mediterranean, North Africa, and Europe. Fresh scholarship enabled by the publication of corpora of Etruscan art (the *CSE, CVA, LIMC, ThesCRA*,[1] and catalogues of exhibitions, museums, and collections) is enhancing our perspective on works in many media; access to the panorama of Etruscan inscriptions and documents[2] is supporting new research into the personalities, lives, and society of the Etruscan-speakers of the first millennium BC (of all walks of life: see, for instance, Chapter 21).

Still there are historians, Classicists and art historians who have yet to enter the world of the Etruscans: it has not always been as accessible as it is today, in the wake of a number of general books in various languages, including several for Anglophone readers.[3] Many scholars in tangential fields have not felt comfortable with Etruscan culture or their ignorance thereof, and such feelings can often lead to denial – and to seeing the Etruscans merely as poor imitators of Greece or thoughtless enemies of Rome.

Why the shocking ignorance? We cannot expect others to read the Etruscan language – and we lack the Etruscan literature to compare to the works of Greek and Latin authors – but many scholars may feel unsteady in reading Italian publications, and all too many scholars may have been influenced by the Victorian schoolboy phenomenon: trained in the Classical heritage, perhaps even in Latin and Greek, they *know*, from the Classical historians like Herodotus and Livy, that Etruscans were the Others, the enemies, the implacable foes and despots like the Tarquins (whose heritage, *we* know, was after all, half Greek). In short, many thoughtful scholars have absorbed the Greek and Roman biases against an opponent who is now poorly known.

There is an unconscious element prompting denial in all of us: if history could fail to preserve even basic information on such a major culture, once dominant in a large sector of the Mediterranean, and the source of so much technology and cultural achievements, what does that say for our posterity? The fact is that the Etruscan language was lost, and in the absence of some unforeseen discovery, we may never have the literature that they produced and it didn't take a deliberate campaign by Rome to ensure its disappearance, all it took was a reliance on flimsy recording media (linen books, papyrus etc.) and the acquiescence of the descendants of native speakers (but do see Chapters 22 and 23 for how much has actually been rediscovered and restored).

It seems as if there is something about the Etruscans that makes everyone want to take sides. Romans and Greeks acted shocked that the Etruscans raised all the offspring of noble families (having implied that the paternity of said children was in question. In fact, we know what the Romans would have done to their illegitimate offspring, see Chapter 20). There are hints of human sacrifice, yet the Romans, who sacrificed a pair of Gauls and a pair of Greeks during the Hannibalic War, did not press this issue, either (Livy 22.57.6). The Etruscans could serve as symbols for all sorts of beliefs. D.H. Lawrence saw them as vibrant foils to the gray juggernaut of Roman fascism, and Annius of Viterbo claimed them as descendents of Noah – and his own ancestors (see Chapter 61). Today, familiarity with Etruscan culture sets a select group of archaeologists and historians apart from the general audience who know only the "mysterious Etruscans." The "mystery" is in our own minds, and the information offered in this volume will show that the reality of Etruscan culture is even stranger – and also more familiar, since much of it can be discerned in our own heritage.

Until now, for very many topics, key publications have only been available in Italian or otherwise less readily accessible to general audiences. For instance, the excavated finds of Etruscan and Italic chariots were never before compiled until Adriana Emiliozzi coordinated an exhibition "*Carri da Guerra dei Principi Etruschi*," ("War chariots of the Etruscan princes") in 1997 (catalogue published in Italian). Her latest findings appear here in Chapter 41. Likewise, many recent excavations and research discoveries have been presented here in English for the first time.

This book is not intended to replace the major recent works in English on Etruscan culture (see note 3), but rather to supplement and augment them with in-depth studies of special fields, and to present the very latest discoveries and analyses. It is plotted into major areas of inquiry where its authors have been able to make new contributions to our knowledge or to restore to the Etruscans developments that may have been credited elsewhere (Etruscan metallurgy, engineering, and surveying were admired by even their most severe enemies, and their monumental construction programs and safe, comfortable housing exceeded most standards of their day, yet there is no mention of the Etruscans in a major handbook of ancient (Classical) technology, published in 2008.) Some studies presented here are by the experts who actually discovered and/or excavated them; others synthesize the current picture of life in ancient Etruria from artistic, archaeological, and epigraphic evidence.

Certain topics were simply too big and complex to treat in the scope of one short article among many, and the state of the art is such that, already, complete volumes could be written to cover the relations of the Etruscans with their Italic neighbors, especially the Latins (including the Romans), with whom they had a variegated relationship over at least a full millennium. (A beginning for this study would be the works of Anna Maria

Bietti Sestieri, on the Italic peoples of central Italy, especially the Latins).[4] The later years of Etruscan relations with Italic peoples, especially Latins and/or Romans, are treated for the era of Romanization of Italy, in Chapter 8.

Another major topic would be the relations of the Greeks with Etruria: the tragic death of David Ridgway prevented publication of his planned chapter on first contact of Etruscans with the Euboeans (and others) who founded the colony of Pithekoussai.[5] (See here the relations of Etruscans in Campania, and comments of Cuozzo on the Hellenization phenomenon in Chapter 16.) The impact of this phenomenon cannot be overestimated, and its repercussions still resonate in Italy and Europe. The subsequent interactions and exchanges between Etruscans and Greeks are historically complex, and may be noted especially in the chapters here dealing with art and myth (see Chapters 6 and 48 on the Orientalizing and on-going phenomenon of foreign artisans settling in Etruria, and Chapters 24 and 25 on the impact of Greek myth and religion; see also the Chapters on art in Part VII; Chapters 45 and 46 indicate the reaction of Etruria to Greek athletics, spectacles, and music.)

This volume begins essentially with the dawn of the Etruscan identity in the Iron Age, around the beginning of the first millennium BC, the era of proto-history when the places that were to become cities, and where the distinctive technology (metallurgy) and material culture (pottery, agriculture, housekeeping etc.) were developed. For prehistory and Bronze Age associations, see Chapter 5 (Protovillanovan and Villanovan culture), and Chapter 10 (the western Mediterranean), and Chapters 11 to 13 on the wide-ranging pre- and proto-historic links to cultures from Mesopotamia to the Atlantic. The subsequent periods of Etruscan history, through the Hellenistic period/end of the first millennium BC, are covered (Chapters 8 and 9), as well as the later rediscovery/reception of Etruscan civilization (Chapters 61–63). The centuries between, the heydays of Etruscan culture, are developed through specialist studies of different aspects of government, society, religion, economy and trade, and the development of material culture. Etruscans, too, had their own era of colonization, although it progressed differently from the famous Phoenician and Greek waves of commercial migration. Etruscan colonization impacted upon the development of Europe and thus of modern Europe, ultimately bequeathing to us ways of life, transport, and technology – and especially literacy. Those "Roman numerals" that we use are, like our "Latin alphabet," an Etruscan invention. Etruscan art may have delved deeply into Greek conventions and themes, but in turn it was the inspiration for the long-lived Celtic art of Europe (as noted in Chapter 17).

With introductory background on the study of the Etruscans and their environment and the physical factors of their lives, and a final section on the post-antique reception of Etruscan culture and history, this volume covers major topics and fields of material culture. Part I begins with the physical environment of Etruria, indicating how this volcanic, storm-prone, agriculturally rich land fostered the unique culture of the Etruscans; Chapter 2 considers the old "origins" question in modern perspective as developed by Massimo Pallottino before DNA became an issue; that approach still offers useful means of appraising the new announcements of non-Etruscologists about their recent projects. This question of origins is old, at least as old as Herodotus and the Greeks who saw Etruscans as Others to be disdained or as foils for the burgeoning power of Rome: a full discussion and explanation of the ancient attitudes and their modern legacy is provided in Chapter 3. Chapter 4 fleshes out the population of Etruria with some thoughts on what their life was actually like, based on skeletal studies and the other tools of the demographer.

In Part II, the historical development of Etruria begins with the Villanovan culture (Chapter 5), and proceeds through the Orientalizing phenomenon and the infusion of foreign elements that stimulated special aspects of Etruscan culture (Chapter 6). Chapter 7 delves into the urbanization phenomenon that shaped the cities, central Italy, and ultimately Europe, down through the sixth century BC: the subsequent eras of great art, technology, and political developments of the Archaic through Hellenistic periods are covered in Parts IV through VII, broken down into key features of culture, religion or art, while Part II concludes with the waning of Etruria: the long twilight of the Roman takeover of the land (Chapter 8), and a personal view from the tombs of the great and the upstart families of northern Etruria who watched, but not meekly, as their homeland changed (Chapter 9).

Treating Etruria's relations with neighboring cultures, Part III traverses the Late Bronze Age through the Iron Age and Archaic period, beginning with the scene in the western Mediterranean at the dawn of the first millennium (Chapter 10), and describing the major indigenous cultures of the Italian archipelago and their relations with Etruscans: Nuragic Sardinia (Chapter 11), Phoenician and Punic Sardinia (Chapter 12), Corsica (Chapter 13), the Faliscans, the Italic people closest to Etruria in culture and society (Chapter 14), and Etruscan expansion and relations with the regions of the Po Valley/Adriatic (Chapter 15) and Campania on and beyond the Bay of Naples (Chapter 16). Part III ends with the maximum dispersion of Etruscans and their materials, from Etruria Marittima to Carthage, Iberia, Massalia, and Gaul (Chapter 17).

The basics of Etruscan society and daily life are analyzed in Part IV, beginning with the political and legal systems that so impressed Aristotle and supported a period of Etruscan hegemony that was never forgotten by the historians (Chapter 18). The economy and commercial relations of Etruria could form an entire volume (and has done so in the past): in this volume the latest discoveries attesting Etruscan activity far from home and Etruria's famous products, are presented in Chapter 19. The life of Etruscans at home is discussed under the topic of mothers and children (Chapter 20), and slavery and manumission, a topic often overlooked or misrepresented, although epigraphy and onomastic studies enable us to scrutinize it now (Chapter 21). The most pervasive, and distinctive, feature of Etruscan life, the language, is treated in Chapter 22, and in Chapter 23, where Etruscan numbers and reckoning – and their considerable legacy – are surveyed.

Part V comprises religion in Etruscan culture, beginning with the Etruscans' avid adoption or adaptation of Greek myth (Chapter 24) and the variegated identities of the Etruscan pantheon, where many native gods have been little understood (Chapter 25). The most famous of Etruscan religious practices, the fields of haruspicy and augury, respected even by the Romans, are discussed in Chapter 26. The gods and the places of Etruscan religion set the scene for studies of Etruscan sanctuary sites and temples (Chapter 27), and the archaeological correlates of Etruscan rituals, especially sacrifices, are explored in Chapter 28. The great (and still famous) shrines of Etruscan worship are surveyed in the next chapters: Tarquinia's urban and extra-mural shrines including the Civita plateau complex, the Ara della Regina and the seaside shrines of Graviscae (Chapter 29). The Caeretan international port sanctuary at Pyrgi, with its famous shrine marked with gold plaques and politically inspired artwork, is covered in Chapter 30. The great meeting point of all Etruria, the *Fanum Voltumnae* ("shrine of the god Voltumna/ Veltune"), only recently identified by the excavations of Campo della Fiera at Orvieto, is presented in Chapter 31. One final aspect of Etruscan worship is funerary cult, with the great necropoleis described in Chapter 32, followed by a brief consideration of the imagery and relevance of offerings placed in tombs (Chapter 33). The sanctuaries of Veii, the other major south Etruscan center, have not been discussed separately, but the Portonaccio sanctuary and its terracotta acroterial sculptures (such as the Apollo of Veii) have been studied and familiar for almost a century; with other Veian sanctuaries it has yielded massive votive deposits from the Iron Age through Late Republican periods. Many finds are discussed in various chapters throughout the book.[6]

Special aspects of Etruscan culture appear in Part VI: Etruscan science and inquiry (Chapter 34), Architecture (Chapter 35) and town planning (Chapter 36). We can never know exactly how much of modern science and technology we owe to Etruscan "trendsetters," passed on through Rome. We may be sure that, beneath its Greek ornamentation, Roman architecture (and thus our own) owes its structural core to Etruscan engineering and materials science. The hydraulic engineering and surveying in town planning, including implementation of gridded plans, are also Etruscan feats. Other major fields of Etruscan expertise, even fame, in antiquity include mining and metallurgy (Chapter 37), warfare and implementation of arms and armor (Chapters 38 and 39), including the chariots developed for war and display (Chapter 41), and seafaring: whether they were pirates or honest merchants, Etruscan seafarers were unequalled for centuries in the central and western Mediterranean (Chapter 40). On the home front, essentials of Etruscan life that are often overlooked today (but not in antiquity) include textiles and their production (Chapter 42), cuisine (Chapter 43) and its presentation in the banquet ceremony (Chapter 44), and entertainment, often a means of worship, honoring the ancestors, or maintaining political control with spectacle (Chapter 45) and with music (Chapter 46). Etruscan health and the unique character of medicine in central Italy are treated in Chapter 47.

The highly distinctive character of Etruscan art, in many media, follows in Part VII, beginning with Etruria's debt to immigrant foreign artists (Chapter 48), including the sudden creation and subsequent development of architectural terracotta in Etruria (Chapter 49). Chapters 50 through 58 survey a wide array of artistic media in which Etruscan artisans excelled: goldsmithing and jewelry; engraved gems, painted pottery (over several centuries), bucchero pottery, the black ware today (and in antiquity) emblematic of Etruscans, terracotta figurines, the art of portraiture, fresco painting, noted for its landscape motifs and illusionism, bronze votive figurines and statues, and Etruscan engraved mirrors. All these categories of art had profound impacts on society and economy in antiquity, and continue to do so today (as in Josiah Wedgwood's naming the location of his pottery "Etruria"). Sculpture in bronze and terracotta can also tell us much about religion, in its votive dedications, while luxury goods and monumental art reveal the interests of ruling classes, and pottery, manufactured at many levels of simplicity or extravagance, illuminates the daily lives and public occasions of all classes of society. The terracotta production of anatomical votive models combined religion and artistic representation, and has much to tell us of intellectual history and medicine in Late Republican Italy (Chapter 59). Animals, so pervasive in art of every period, are analyzed in a novel way through their artistic representations, indicative of animals' position in Etruscan life and thought (Chapter 60).

Processes of exchange and cultural interaction were undoubtedly much more dynamic than we often envisage from behind our desk or computer: exactly how did the alphabet come to be transferred from Etruria to the Scandinavian cultures? Was that rare object actually brought home from a pirate raid? As in Homer's epics, hosts would have regaled visitors with the colorful narrative of how a particular piece came into their possession. The objects that we view today as isolated works of art were originally made and used as the centerpieces of serious ceremonies such as banquets, sacrifices, divination rituals; and the belongings found in tombs, such as mirrors and armor, were once gifts displayed in betrothal, wedding, coming of age, and military rituals and processions. They held much greater significance in their original settings than we often grant them. As Sannibale writes in Chapter 6, the adoption or adaptation of artistic motifs and iconography never occurs without forethought and reference to belief: there are good reasons to think that the Etruscan princes (and princesses) and their court artists knew very well the meanings of Egyptian, Near Eastern, and Greek motifs and selected them quite deliberately. Likewise, without the intermarriage of Punic Sardinian craftsmen, the trade of Atlantic Iberia, the mediation of the peoples of Corsica and Campania, and the camaraderie of the Faliscans, Etruria could not have become what it was.

Part VIII concludes with the post-antique reception of Etruscan culture and history, from its early, and sometimes exceptionally imaginative, beginnings with "Annius of Viterbo" (Chapter 61), and early scholarly discoveries by Thomas Dempster, brought to a curious readership by Filippo Buonarotti (Chapter 62). Chapter 63 examines modern reception of the Etruscans and their art, with some curious proponents in Italy and abroad.

There are many instances of innovation, invention, and implementation of technology, statecraft, and social development to be found in these pages. For instance, the earliest stone architecture in Italy has been identified in the seventh century BC cult buildings at Tarquinia La Civita (Chapter 29); Etruscans, although not necessarily doctors, performed post-mortem C-sections and probably other surgery (Chapters 47, 59); the future of wheeled vehicles, from automobiles to railways, was determined when the Iron Age Etruscans began to make chariots, given the later development and spread of Rome and Roman roads (Chapter 41); the intricate creatures of Celtic art and manuscripts owe their birth to unnamed Archaic Etruscan artisans (Chapter 19). Etruscan cities led the way in metallurgy, agriculture, surveying and planning, in literacy and the uses of writing, in religious practice, especially divination, the techniques of urbanization and the dissemination of Greek iconography and myth through the European world. Roman portraiture and monumental painting, bronze-working and goldsmithing, glass-making and gem-cutting, would have taken a very different track without the Etruscans. The modern position of women in Western culture, the comforts of wooden architecture and home décor, the wines of France and games propelled by cubical dice, owe much of their character to Etruscan developments of the early first millennium BC. Today, the Etruscans still have much to offer and much for us to discover: welcome to their world – and ours.

NOTES

1   *Corpus Speculorum Etruscorum, Corpus Vasorum Antiquorum, Lexicon Iconographicum Mythologiae Classicae, Thesaurus Cultuum et Rituorum Antiquorum.*

2   *Corpus Inscriptionum Etruscarum, Testimonia Linguae Etruscae, Etruskische Texte, Rasenna* (online journal).

3   Sybille Haynes, *Etruscan Civilization. A Cultural History*, Los Angeles: Getty Press, 2000.
    M. Torelli, ed., *Gli Etruschi/The Etruscans*, (exhibition, Palazzo Grassi, Venice 2000) Milan: Bompiani, 2000.
    G. Barker and T. B. Rasmussen, *The Etruscans*, Oxford: Blackwell, 1998.

L. Bonfante, ed., *Etruscan Life and Afterlife*, Detroit: Wayne State, 1986.

G. Bonfante and L. Bonfante, *The Etruscan Language. An Introduction* (revised edition), Manchester University Press/Palgrave, 2002.

O. J. Brendel, *Etruscan Art*, New Haven: Yale, and others, 1978, 1995.

N. T. de Grummond and E. Simon, eds., *Religion of the Etruscans*, Austin: University of Texas, 2006.

N.T. de Grummond, *Etruscan Myth, Sacred History, and Legend*, Philadelphia: University Museum Press, 2006.

4   See, for instance, by A. M. Bietti Sestieri, *L'Italia nell'età del bronzo e del ferro. Dalle palafitte a Romolo (2200–700 A.C.)* (Rome: Carocci, 2010). See also *The Iron Age Community of Osteria dell'Osa: A Study of Socio-political Development in Central Tyrrhenian Italy*, (Cambridge University Press, 1992, 2009); and, with Anna De Santis, "Relative and Absolute Chronology of Latium Vetus from the Late Bronze Age to the Transition to the Orientalizing Period" in D. Brandherm and M. Trachsel, eds., *A New Dawn for the Dark Age? Shifting Paradigms in Mediterranean Iron Age Culture*, (Oxford: Archaeopress, 2008: 119–133).

5   Readers are recommended to consult his recently published scholarship on this and related topics, including: "Italy from the Bronze Age to the Iron Age," in *Cambridge Ancient History*, vol. 4, ch. 12 (2nd edn, 1988); "The Etruscans," in *Cambridge Ancient History*, vol. 4, ch. 13 (2nd edn, 1988); *The First Western Greeks*, (Cambridge University Press, Cambridge 1992); "Nestor's cup and the Etruscans," *Oxford Journal of Archaeology*, 16:3 (1997) 325–344, in which the mystery of the cheese grater is explained; "The first Western Greeks revisited," in *Ancient Italy in its Mediterranean Setting. Studies in honor of Ellen Macnamara*, (Accordia Research Institute, University of London, London 2000) 179–191; "An inscribed bucchero aryballos," *Journal of Roman Archaeology* 21 (2008) 248–254.

6   Again, Veii could easily fill more than one book. For basic background bibliography see S. A. Collins-Elliott and I. Edlund-Berry, "A bibliography of sanctuaries and ritual in Etruria," in [143–165] 162–163. Recently released: G. Bartoloni, ed., 2011. *Il culto degli Antenati a Veio. Nuove testimonianze da scavi e ricerche recenti*. Rome: Officina edizioni; and G. Bartoloni and M. G. Benedettini, 2011. *Veio. Il deposito votivo di Comunità Votive (Scavi 1889–2005)*. Rome: G. Bretschneider.

PART I

ENVIRONMENT, BACKGROUND AND THE STUDY OF ETRUSCAN CULTURE

———•◆•———

CHAPTER ONE

ETRUSCAN ENVIRONMENTS

———— •◆• ————

Ingela M. B. Wiman

THE TERRA FIRMA

The continents are in a state of flux, in a manner usually invisible to the naked eye but horribly obvious when the earth quakes or the tsunami swells. The Etruscan landscape was shaped by such disastrous events thousands of years ago. Today the African plate is still pushing over the Eurasian one in a north-easterly direction slowly pressing down the western land, resulting in a rise in sea level on the coastal plains of Italy since the time the Etruscans ruled.

Etruria proper was situated below the western Apennines and between the rivers: the Arno to the north and the Tiber to the south and east. Large parts of Latium were once controlled by the Etruscans as was the city of Rome in the sixth century BC. Etruscan-speaking people moved north-east and traversed the Po valley. Eventually they also founded trading cities on the Adriatic coast, Spina and Adria. The Tyrrhenian Sea now hides some of their ancient territory. Great rivers, however, especially the Arno, Ombrone and Tiber transgressed the lands in westerly, winding courses transporting silt and mud along their way, the so-called alluvium that created swamps and silted coastlines on the Tyrrhenian Sea. This is especially evident around the mouth of the Arno at Pisa. The large river system joining it there has considerably broadened the coastline from Livorno to Viareggio. Pisa was closer to the sea in ancient times,[1] unlike the San Cerbone cemetery and port of Populonia that in Antiquity reached a further 80 meters out from today's seashore. The port of Caere, Pyrgi, has seen its ancient shorelines hidden by the sea, whereas Rome had to deal with silted coasts at Ostia and Portus.

Rivers that cut through the porous volcanic tuffs, the Bruno, Mignone, Fiore, Marta and Vesca caused the deep gorges and plateaus that are so typical of the south Etruscan landscape, the beauty of which is often beyond words. The Apennines, the core of which is limestone that was once the bottom of the ocean, are continuously rising and folding due to the continental clash pressure, as are the smaller hills west of their high peaks, the sub-Apennines. As humans started to burn down the forests on the hills to make the land arable,[2] snow and rains from the mountains and hills have carried soils down their slopes to the valleys below forming the typical Mediterranean landscape of barren or *macchia* highlands covered in scrubland vegetation, and cultivated valley bottoms with olives or vines on the sloping hills. The precise time these occurrences started to reform the face of the Etruscan earth will be discussed in this chapter. Huge volcanic eruptions beginning in the Pleistocene shaped the band of lakes running in a north-south direction in the anti-Apennines, the heartland of Etruria: Lakes Bolsena, Monterosi, Bracciano and Vico. Each of their eruptions shed large amounts of pumice, large stones and hot lava into the surrounding environment. The youngest formations are the caldera-containing Lake Nemi and Lake Albano from a final eruption around 5000 years ago.[3] The Pleistocene is the geological period in which the four latest glaciations occurred. It is now considered to have lasted from 2.5 million years ago to the end of the last great ice age, the Würm, around 12,000 years ago. The period following it has been called the Holocene and persists today.[4] Since the welding process of lava occurs when the deposit is still hot, the various eruptions have formed lava of slightly varying compositions.[5] When solidified it became the porous reddish brown rock called tuff. The composition of the tuff and the various particles hidden in it can inform us of its origin when used in tombs or walls or other Etruscan edifices.[6] Predominating in the south around lake Vico is red or black tuff with black incrustations/ *tufo rosso (nere) di scorie nere, TR(N)SNV*. Earlier eruptions from the Paleobolsena crater in the area of Vulci shaped grey tuff of higher density (Nenfro Paleobolsena *NPB*) favored by the early Vulsinian sculptors for tomb art.[7] The magnitude of these volcanic explosions is unimaginable. One link in this volcanic chain is the bay of Naples with Vesuvius. The disaster of its eruption in the summer of 79 AD was witnessed by its contemporaries and has also been assessed through finds made during excavations. Pliny the Elder died there from asphyxiation of volcanic gases. A certain type of eruption is named after him, *Plinian*. It is characterized by a cloud rising from the volcano up to the stratosphere, toxic gases and an explosion forming a caldera. An *ultra-Plinian* occurs when the ash plume reaches 25 km and the volume of the eruptive material covers 10 square kilometers.[8] The row of lakes in the anti-Apennines today represents pleasant memories of a series of such devastating *ultra-Plinians* of the past.

The northern parts of Etruria have a lithosphere of conglomerates, sandstones and limestone, representing heritage from the Tethys Ocean that covered southern Europe in the Mesozoic era during the Triassic period 200 million years ago and separated the two large continents, Gondwana and Laurasia, from each other. Tectonic activity has also shaped these northern landscapes of Etruria forming hills with peaks up to 1000 meters above sea level. Looking at the map of the area comprising Elba and the inland bay we can see what appears to be a huge crater. Elba was connected to the Populonian peninsula during the Pleistocene, forming the largest of the islands of the archipelago where cities like Chiusi and Siena were once mere islets. The resulting layers of fine limestone can still be admired as the material of the famous Chiusine *cippi*. The hills around this are called the Colline Metallifere in Italy, the metal-bearing hills (see Chapter 37 for further research on mining). Elba is famous for the rich iron mines worked there in Etruscan times. The iron ores are of two general types, hematite, iron bound to oxygen, Fe_2O_3 and pyrite, iron bound to sulphur, FeS_2 (iron disulphide). The former, rich in iron and easily reducible, was the mineral the Etruscans worked. The beautiful, black, shining mineral has been favored for inlays in jewelry, especially during the nineteenth century AD. Sulphuric iron is more difficult to extract and was not mastered by the ancients. Copper also was present in ores on Elba but was mainly extracted in the inland hills. Copper in the area was bound to sulphur and had to be roasted in open-air blast furnaces in order to replace the sulphur with oxygen. The beautiful bronze objects for which the Etruscans are famous required copper and tin to form the gold-like bronze alloy. Tin was rare in Antiquity, but there are tin ores present in Campiglia, both in the form of microscopic grains and as lenses embedded in hematite ores. The cassiterite (tin bound to oxygen, Sn_2O) from Campiglia is unusually rich and contains 72 percent tin. George Dennis described the "Cento Camerelle" with traces of ancient extraction of tin. Certainly the metal-cunning Etruscans made use of this valuable raw material.[9] These areas have a documented mining history until 1975 when the last mines of Massa Marittima were closed.[10] The mineral deposits were among the wealthiest in the whole of the Mediterranean.

Unlike most cities of Etruria the largest northern city, Populonia, was situated close to the coast, a result of its importance as a port receiving the rich iron ores from Elba. Vetulonia and Roselle, also important metal trading cities in Etruscan times, were situated near the shore of the *Lacus Prilius*, which in the modern period is a dried out lake.[11] One lake of special interest in the northern area is Lago dell'Accesa, a karst lake 37–39 meters deep. In the seventh century BC a small mining community was built on its eastern shore. Several mines were used in Etruscan times in the vicinity, some only a few hundred meters from the settlement. It was abandoned at the end of the sixth century BC and it has been suggested that this abandonment was due to heavy metal (arsenic, As) poisoning as a result of combined climatic conditions and mineral working habits.[12] Production was resumed in the first century AD. The lake's importance derives from a series of pollen cores extracted there which give us a good deal of knowledge about the covering of trees and utility plants during Etruscan times and will be further discussed below.

The thermic dynamics below the Earth's crust in Italy cause hot spring waters to well from various localities. Sometimes these are mixed with sulphur. Native or free sulphur occurs chiefly in volcanic or sedimentary deposits such as those described above; in Etruria they are found in the band of volcano lakes from south to north. In Antiquity these sulphuric wells were considered most curative both for men and animals. Baths cured or improved skin diseases in animals, sheep-scab, foot rot in hoofed animals and were used to clean sheep before wool shearing. They were a very valuable asset.[13]

The Maremma, made famous by D. H. Lawrence's book *Etruscan Places*, published in 1932, is the vast south-western coastal area of Etruria stretching from Tarquinia in the south to the Colline Metallifere in the north. Today a thriving agricultural district, in Etruscan times it was a partially swampy area. The land was suitable only for grazing but was poor grazing land at that. Small Etruscan cities were placed on hilltops in the highlands above the Maremma proper and George Dennis describes how inaccessible parts of the area were during his visits in the 1840s. Roadless land, thorny bushes, swampy holes, sheep flocks and rabid dogs met him when he tried to reach Populonia.[14] His appreciation of the Maremma, however, is clear from his praise of it as "full of the picturesque and beautiful."[15] It had many shallow, lacustrine waters in Etruscan times, especially the so-called Maremma Livornese and Maremma Grossetana, most of which have perished due to land rise and the thorough drainage projects of Mussolini which finally put an end to the fearful fevers of the swamps. The malaria parasite is much favored by the agricultural practices of humans. It probably spread as a result of agriculture and sedentary life some 10,000 years ago. The Etruscan waters were surely full of gnats in ancient times but the malaria parasite seems not to have appeared in Italy before 500 BC,[16] even somewhat later in Etruria, possibly transferring from Africa during the Punic wars. A special culture has developed in the Maremma with *buttari* on horses herding cattle of a hearty stock that can survive on poor grazing conditions. Primitive lines of this breed, the Maremmana, resemble the aurochs, *Bos primigenus*, the wild ancestor of domestic cattle (extinct since

Figure 1.1   A bull of the Maremman *Bos taurus*. I. Wiman.

1627) in a number of features like the big protruding horns and dark furred bulls and lighter females. Aurochs were once common throughout the whole Eurasian continent.

To conclude, the Etruscan lithosphere and soils are a *mixtum compositum* of igneous and sedimentary geological processes characterized by deep ravines in the south and by a hilly, metalliferous landscape in the north. The petrified volcanic ash has made the soils very fertile and their porosity allows rain to permeate the soil and form sources of excellent drinking water. Metals and other raw materials were abundant. This was a land favored by the gods "...*primis Italiae fertilis*" (Livy 12.3). It is no wonder that it has attracted animals and humans from time immemorial.

CLIMATE AND VEGETATION HISTORY

The Mediterranean region is clearly vulnerable to the combined effects of climate and human activities. George Perkins March was perhaps first to realize the extent to which human beings have changed the face of the Earth. He travelled in the Mediterranean in the middle of the nineteenth century and became the first American ambassador to the new united Italian Kingdom. He noticed and remarked upon the careless deforestation that led to erosion, flooding and drought and lamented the ruined hills of the Mediterranean. In his famous book, *Man and Nature or, Physical Geography as Modified by Human Action* (1864), he clearly understood the influence of forests on vegetation, soil and water and, hence, their importance for local climatic conditions. He was the first to develop the thesis that man was himself a geological agent.[17] Since his time it has been debated whether the disappearance of the formerly large Mediterranean woods was a result of human activities, due to climate change, or possibly that the large Mediterranean forests of Antiquity were a mere myth.[18] These questions have stimulated scientists to systematically investigate the nature of the ancient environment to trace previous incidents of climate change or heavy anthropogenic impact in order to get a better understanding of past and present processes. Paleoecology is currently very important in the study of the history of climate change.

A number of probing cores have been taken from the maar lakes and coastal areas discussed above to acquire the tools to investigate this matter. One of the most famous investigations, published in 1970, was an account of the history and development of the Lago di Monterosi (hereafter cited as LdM). This small lake is almost invisible on the map but, according to Prof. G. Evelyn Hutchinson you will find it "on the north-eastern side of the Sabatinian volcanic complex, the centre of which is occupied by Lago di Bracciano."[19] Hutchinson invented ecology as a scientific discipline. His overall scientific contribution by the probing of LdM was the detection of the drastic system-wide change taking place in the waters of the lake as witnessed by the sediment archives. Since its creation around 26,000 years BP (Before Present) it had been in an oligotrophic state, i.e. poor in nutrition and biotic life. This changed almost overnight when the Romans built the via Cassia, linking Rome with central Etruria, near the southern shores of the lake. In fact, Roman road engineering was a process of civilization not confined to the road construction proper. It involved massive tree felling and clearance to achieve arable land. Before the arrival of the Romans, this area was primeval forestland, part of the *Silva Ciminia*, the fearful barrier to Sutri, "...the key and gateway to Etruria" (Livy 6.9.4). The via Cassia was a construction of strategic importance conducted by Lucius Cassius Longinus, consul in 171 BC, in order to gain easier access to the Roman colonies established on the territory of the conquered Veii (396 BC).[20] The debris from the cleared lands found their way into the lake along with nutritious sediments that rapidly converted the lake's ecological system to a eutrophic state, rich in biotic organisms and metabolism. This road, in fact, and its simultaneous clearance made possible the gradual subjugation of the central Etruscan cities by the Roman forces.

HERBS

What was learned by the innovative study of the LdM was that humans affect nature in various ways and can do so very rapidly. For periods when sediments were rich in the pollen of nettles, the scientists drew the conclusion that the area was heavily populated, since nettles thrive on the phosphoric soils caused by human garbage. Nettle, *urtica dioica*, is thus an indicator of human presence. Pollen from other species, for example, vine or cultivated olive,[21] which are not endogenic in Italy, indicate agricultural activity as does pollen from *triticum*, or wheat, a grass originating on the Anatolian high plateaus. Times of increased grazing can be traced by a cumulative amount of pollen from plantain, *Plantago major* or, especially, *Plantago lanceolata*, ribwort plantain. These species are perennial and hardy and thrive in trampled soils. Their growth is especially favored when the animals eat their concurrent grasses and other edible flowers of the meadows. Obviously plantain does not overly please the bovine or ovine palate. Other species, such as *Artemisia* (sagebrush and wormwood) or heathers (*ericaceae*) are indicative of the climate of the region in question. Sagebrush is characteristic of cold steppes and heathers of moorland. Rising frequencies of *poaceae*, wild grasses of various kinds and *rumex*, sorrels, indicate an increase in the distribution of open areas and human impact in the form of meadows and grasslands. Sorrels were appreciated for their sour taste and wormwood was a treasured ingredient in many liquids and medicinal remedies, therefore, people encouraged their growth. Man is always able to interfere in natural processes thus masking events of concern to, for instance, climatologists.

TREES

We have already touched upon the presumptive tree felling in Neolithic times. It has not always been easy to judge what caused a cessation in a diagram of pollen from a specific tree. Parasites or fungi of various kinds may cause its absence in a pollen sequence, as we witness today with the elms that are dying because of the *Ophiostoma* type fungi spread by a small black beetle whose larvae feed on the tree. Generally, however, declines of trees are caused either by climatic variations or human activity. In the period after the last glaciations, cold steppe vegetation predominated in Italy but from the mid Holocene c. 7000 years ago, large fir forests dressed hills and coastland in northern and western Italy.[22] At this time a major shift in the vegetation cover is detected from pollen samples taken in the area around the mouth of the Arno near Pisa. Large floods of the river, as well as sea level fluctuations, indicate climate change.[23] This caused the disappearance of conifer woods, especially the *Abies Alba*, common silver fir. Nowadays the fir appears in mountainous terrains, in some small populations in the Pyrenees, in the Alps and easterly to the Balkans. Today it occurs up to 1100 m above sea level (*asl*). Temperature falls by one degree Celsius per 100 meters *asl*. With a climate shift of minus one degree the fir tree line would subsequently fall 100 meters downhill and vice-versa as a result of climatic fluctuations. In reality, however, pollen-aerosol dynamics is a complex issue. Pollen from fir, for example, is very susceptible to winds and precipitation and thus the light pollen may travel long distances and the catchment area can be difficult to estimate. By observing small particles of charcoal in the sediments, scientists suggest that these were emitted through the fires caused by Neolithic man and thus are indicative of human deforestation.[24] Generally, sudden shifts may indicate human agency (especially when combined with charcoal) whereas changes of a *longue durée* often indicate climate change.[25] Eventually broadleaved trees like oaks and beech succeeded the fir. The former became dominant in the northern Alps around 3000 years ago.[26] These are trees that like warmer climate and were favored by rising temperatures. Further to the south in the Massetano, similar changes have been observed in the pollen sequences. The area around Lago dell'Accesa, as touched upon above, harbored large evergreen forests of *Quercus ilex* at the mid-Holocene. *Quercus ilex*, holm oak, has leathery dark-green leaves and a black bark. It reaches about 25 meters and the leaves are a bit spiky on the edges, especially in younger trees, to protect them from being eaten by hoofed animals. It is commonly believed that this was the species predominant in the later Mediterranean Holocene before the changes induced by humans were detectable. Taking good note of the difficulties combined with pollen spread discussed above, we have a series of investigations from a small lake in the Colline Metallifere that, combined with results from other lake samples from Toscana and Lazio, in various ways may shed new light on the issues problematical above.

DATA FROM LAGO DELL'ACCESA, MASSETANO, ITALY

Several probing campaigns have been made in Lago dell'Accesa situated close to Massa Marittima (42°59′N, 10°53′E). The objective of most of the soundings is to investigate climate versus man induced impact on the environment. The first of the series to be discussed here had a somewhat different agenda and was undertaken by the present author and the geologist Sten Ekman. Its specific objective was to investigate whether the Etruscans made use of coppice woods, or *silvia cauduae*, in their processing of the mineral ores melted here. Cato the Elder talks about the profitability of various forms of such coppice woods (Cato, *Agr. Orig.* 1.7). Pliny writes at length about the plantation and cultivation of trees including the use of coppice woods. He values chestnut as the most useful tree in this process, since it is easily worked and its rotation period is only six years (Pliny *HN* 17.35.147-159). The postulated question was how the Etruscans provided raw material and fuel to the metal industry on Elba and in Populonia. Estimations of the annual extent of the production differ widely from 10 million tons (which is unrealistic) to the lowest figure estimation of about 4–5000 tons of ore extraction. Calculations of the amount of charcoal needed for Etruscan type furnaces with two bellows estimate that 170 kilos of charcoal was needed to produce one kilo of wrought iron. In the furnace the carbon dioxide produced by the fuel reduced the iron from the ore. The product, the *blomma* ("bloom"), had to be reheated and hammered several times to remove slags and coal. Of course this process demanded huge amounts of wood. In his investigation of fuel used near the mines, John Nilén, in an unfortunately unpublished manuscript, identified two main types of wood used, oak and sweet chestnut.[27] He does not specify the type of oak species, but P. G. Warden has suggested that *Quercus cerris*, the Bush- or Turkish oak, was used for metal production at Poggio Civitate.[28] *Castanea sativa*, the sweet chestnut, originated in Asia and was first planted by the Greeks (hence its name *Sardis glans*, the nut from Sardis). Both the extraction and the processing of the ores were believed to have taken place near the sources on Elba. It has been shown by recent excavations in the ancient port area that from the mid-fifth century BC large-scale production was transferred to or concentrated in Populonia.[29] Most scholars believe that this shift took place after the island had become totally deforested. Elba today is still heavily marked by erosion and barren hills. In Populonia and the Massetano, however, production seems not to have caused irreducible deforestation and extraction in the Massetano continued into medieval times.[30] Therefore we intended to take a pollen sample in the year 1997 in order to investigate the possible use of coppice woods in Etruscan times. The results are given in short below and include only times of vegetational transitions and their interpretation.

Lago dell'Accesa: Results of pollen-core studies

6000–4000 BC – rising water levels, large forests of deciduous oak.
Analysis: relatively cold and wet climate, no clear evidence of human presence.

3700 BC – drier climate, appearance of pollen of wheat types, deciduous forests notably diminished.
Analysis: human reclamation of arable land for cultivation.

1450 BC – (beginning of Apennine Bronze Age) more humid climatic conditions, emergence of plants typical of grazed soil, tree, heather and oaks declined.
Analysis: arrival of herdsmen, pastoralism the chief economic strategy.

c. 900 BC – (beginning of Villanovan period) rising amounts of pollen from cultivated plants; olives, fruit trees, herbs of groves and meadows, chestnut and oak are increasing, decreasing amounts of plantain.
Analysis: open human shaped landscape with groves and meadows and olive cultivation, pastureland seemingly diminished.

300 BC – forest decreasing in favor of evergreen vegetation, especially the olive family, increased erosion processes, rising amount of wheat and olives, rising amounts of wild grasses and plantain.
Analysis: a greater degree of mining activities, increased cultivation of olives and crops, greater degree of pasture.

Around birth of Christ – drastic change, shoreline regressing, magnetic matter in abundance, increased amounts of *Castanea sativa*.
Analysis: increased erosion and mining activities in Roman times, pollen indicates very near-shore conditions, therefore, the presence of chestnut may indicate cultivation of this plant in coppice woods (although with a thorough and yearly cutting, trees do not bloom and thus do not produce pollen).

Conclusions drawn by this investigation combined with a survey of the Populonian beach area indicate that there was a good supply of trees, wild or cultivated and that extensive erosion processes did not occur until Roman times when both types of oaks as well as Beech/*Fagus* and Elm/*Ulmus* were markedly declining. The rising amount of *Castanea sativa* may not only be a result of agro-forestry and mining, however, since the large nut was used for food both in Antiquity and modern times. It was common to grind the nuts to make flour for baking "poor man's bread," as the product was called in the eighteenth and nineteenth centuries AD. The absence of grape pollen is a curious fact and may indicate that vines were not cultivated in this district. Charcoal found in furnaces located on the beach in Populonia indicates that at least twigs from coppice woods were used in Etrusco-Roman times.[31] At the time we conducted our survey we had no funding for examining what types of trees were used, but our samples are awaiting analysis.

How do these research data compare to results from later, more methodologically sophisticated analyses? At least three well-documented investigations have been carried out in the area. Two of the investigations were concerned mainly with earlier periods and with the question of climate change at Lago dell'Accesa and are not overly useful for evaluating the later Etruscan vegetation history.[32] The third investigation, however, discusses the vegetation cover and the climate from 15,000 years ago in the area.[33] The data are fully compatible with ours. Datings differ somewhat, possibly due to various sampling techniques for the C14 analyses. We analyzed the pollen cores themselves while the other investigation sampled wood and peat. Past lake-level changes are useful when trying to differentiate human versus climate impact and the lowest lake levels in Italy appeared around 1800 BC during an "aridity crisis."[34] Pollen from vines is almost negligible and indicates that the Colline Metallifere were not used for cultivating grapes on a larger scale. Both papers, however, stress the important fact that larger deforestation processes, combined with erosion processes, start around 300 BC with a marked rise around the first century AD. Contrary to Nilén, Mariotti Lippi *et al.* claim that the *Erica arborea*, tree heather, is the most important wood species for metal reduction.[35] This is a bush typical of wet or dry scrublands, extremely hard and heat-resistant. This might explain the small twigs we found in the slag heaps on the beach of Populonia.

To conclude, these combined data support the idea that large-scale, systematic deforestation activities were not part of Etruscan economic strategies. After the dry spell of the eighteenth century BC, the climate became more humid around 1400 BC and Etruscan times were a benign period as regards the climate, similar to today's, with rainy autumns and winters and dry and hot summers. In Roman times the climate became gradually warmer and dryer until about 400 AD.[36] The favorable climate of the Etruscan period allowed the inhabitants to live in cities and smaller villages supported by farmers and farmsteads in the countryside harvesting products from their land. Apart from tomatoes, maize and potatoes they could cultivate most of the products typical of contemporary Tuscany.

THE LAND OF THE FLOCKS

Etruscans hunted the woods for boars and deer. The importance of hunting for economy was probably small (approximately 5 percent of all meat consumed) and the images of hunting merely reflect an aristocratic concept of a life free from hard manual labor. Sheepherders and cattle breeders provided most meat.[37] The domesticated species now common in the Maremma, *Bos taurus*, have been the uncanny target of the heated debate on Etruscan origins. Scientists from the Catholic University of the Sacred Heart in Piacenza have extracted mitochondrial DNA (inherited in a maternal line) from cattle of Tuscan breed and found these grouping with cattle of the Near East, whereas other Italian species resemble cattle of northern Europe. Their conclusion was that this breed came to Italy in ships during the late Bronze Age.[38] Be that as it may, scholars no longer believe in permanent, local constancy. Professor Bonghi Jovino of the Milan University believes that small groups of immigrants may have caused the cultural discontinuity seen at the beginning of late Bronze Age/early Iron Age or proto-Villanovan times.[39] Long-distance trade and movements of people seem to have been the rule in prehistory as well as in modern times. A moving testament to this fact is the frozen body of "Ötzi," the "Iceman," who died as he travelled over the Alps 5,300 years ago. He can now be seen at the Archaeological Museum in Bolzano.

However impressive the Maremma breed is today, in Etruscan times oxen were mainly used for dragging the plough and the carriages used in agriculture to bring in harvests and to spread manure over the lands.[40] Most bones from oxen are of old animals that had been eaten when their working days were over. Bones from most excavations in Etruscan settlements demonstrate that sheep and pigs were the most common animals used for meat production and for fertilizing the fields.[41] Grassland and water are essential to a pastoral and farming economy. The hilly landscapes of Etruria provided grasslands all year round. In summer, when the coastal plains or valleys became dry and the grass withered, the herders took their sheep up to higher lands where grass was good and fresh. The animals grazing in coastal lands in Etruria in winter were herded to hilly parts of Umbria and Marche during summer. In order to preserve the products, cheeses were made in cottages and *tavernae* during this stay and were carried back or traded along the major transhumance roads.[42] The Etruscans had an early custom of placing a "*grattatoio*," a cheese-grater, among the symposium paraphernalia in their early tombs (see Chapter 43, also Chapter 6, Fig. 6.4) because apparently they liked to grate cheese into wine. A rich social life evolved along the roads and shepherds met and exchanged cheese recipes, stories and religious ideas. Heracles was worshiped in shrines along the various *calles* leading from valleys and up into the mountains of the peninsula, some nodes eventually growing into large commercial centers (for instance Hercules Victor at Tivoli).[43] These old pack-trails went through innumerable deep river valleys in the southern landscape. The *dogana*, for example, in function from Etruscan to modern times led from the coastal plains between Cerveteri and Tarquinia, passed San Giovenale on its way and herders and sheep had to cross the Vesca in order to proceed. Sometimes roads were cut into the cliffs to facilitate the movements of flocks and people or to gain access to the necropoleis and they can be traced near the ancient Etruscan cities, where they are often harmoniously adapted to the landscape. Old surviving Etruscan roads and *calles* are often mixed together following natural features of the landscape.[44]

In the above investigations of vegetation and animals of ancient Etruria it can be concluded that the land was organized as a *cultura promiscua*. In the hilltops sweet chestnuts, hazel and oaks grew, sometimes as coppice woods used for fodder and fuel. Further down the hills the soil had to be kept in place by dry-stone walls making a net of terraces on which olive groves and vineyards were planted. These had to be irrigated and the Etruscans are famous for their rock cut *cuniculi* leading water to fields as well as diverting water from roads.[45] In the lower lands were the fields with arable crops and vegetables, peas and beans, and in the barns were pigs. Sheep and goats grazed on meadows and plains of poorer or waterlogged soils. The impression is a land of small-scale agriculture well adapted to the environment. As stressed before, no large-scale deforestation or erosion processes is evident until Roman times.

THE SKY – LIGHT AND NOISE

The heavens were much studied by the Etruscans in order to decode the will of gods. It was important to scrutinize the flight of birds through the different heavenly sectors, likewise the course of lightning and the occurrence of thunder.[46] At night the Etruscans used oil lamps and torches during the night to guide them, to light up tombs or to gather around during evening conversations. Of course there was no pollution from electric lights. The heaven's stars shone like brilliant jewels in the night sky and the Milky Way could be seen as a shimmering band across the sky. The full moon lit roads and farms and its shifting trajectories and phases were familiar to the Etruscans and used to estimate the time. The morning star announced *Thesan*/Aurora, her rosy fingers painting the Earth. Likewise, the air surely would have been pierced by noises from the ports and towns. Hammering from the smith's anvil, smoke from his fires, shouted commands, roaring laughter, the crack and clatter of wagons' wooden wheels over pavements, horses whinnying and so on, but without the ceaseless, growling, murmur of traffic, motors and machines, the air would have been fresh and sound. Recently, at sunset at San Giovenale, the only perceptible sound was the tinkle of a distant bell tied to the neck of a female *Bos taurus*. For their view of the stars and extraordinary silence only, you could envy the Etruscans.

THE SEA

Another great asset was the wide Tyrrhenian Sea. When compared to the poisoned and over-fished sea we know today it provided animal protein to an extent impossible to perceive. Salt was valuable in Antiquity to make food spicier but it was also used as a preservative. *Salaria* were constructed with the aid of shallow pools where the water evaporated and left the salt as a crust on the bottom. Salt was also a valuable trading product to the sea-less interior and control of these trading roads was a great source of ancient conflict.[47]

Like all seafarers of the Mediterranean, the Etruscans, the Phoenicians and Greeks accused each other of piracy. There was a fine line between acquiring goods by trade or by capture. This line was often transgressed and the crew of a ship could easily fall victim to the slave market or kidnapping. In classical Greek accounts, the singer Arion won many valuable treasures when he sang in Sicily. On his way back home to Corinth the ship's crew decided to steal Arion's prize gold. He was allowed to sing one final song before he was hauled overboard. But the dolphins that heard him sing took him on their backs safely back to Corinth where the tyrant Periander eventually punished the sailors. Even gods could be assaulted at sea. Famous is the magnificent vase by Exekias, found in a tomb in Vulci. On this vase we see Dionysus sitting in his ship, with vines and grapes rising from the sail. Pirates, transformed to dolphins, surround the ship. In a sublimely humorous way the man-dolphin transformation is depicted on an Etruscan amphora of the late ninth century stored in the Toledo Museum (see Fig. 8,1 and Chapter 24). Evidence of the hard work onboard Mediterranean ships is a man believed to have been a sailor and killed or sacrificed and buried in the gorge sanctuary at the Pian di Civita Area Sacra, Tarquinia (see Chapter 29). His skeleton is marked with wounds and the wear of a hard-working life spent running on slippery decks and rowing in stormy weather.[48]

Although there was conflict at sea, the Greeks and Phoenicians worked and traded peacefully on Etruscan soil. The great emporia to the southern cities are famous, including Tarquinia's Graviscae, Caere's Pyrgi and Vulci's Regae. Greek influences, both religious and social, are particularly noticeable in Graviscae. Forty years of excavations at the site have unearthed various sanctuaries, among them one is devoted to Aphrodite situated in close connection to metallurgical activities in the area with large finds of slag from iron, copper and lead production together with smelting furnaces.[49] The connection between Aphrodite and metalwork is an ancient one in the eastern Mediterranean, especially at Cyprus where she is at times connected to Astarte. In Pyrgi the Phoenician element is more marked with the famous temples A and B and the adjacent L-shaped edifice with a row of small rooms for commerce and/or temple-prostitution, presenting everything for a visiting sailor's convenience (see Chapter 30).[50] These were among the ports exporting Etruscan surpluses of metals, olive oil and perhaps wine around the Mediterranean. Etruscan amphorae have been found in such remote places as Monte Polizzo, an inland mountain centre in the Elymian heart of Sicily.[51]

Also buccheroware – the black, shining, metal-imitating Etruscan pottery – was exported from these harbors, with or without contents. It was obviously highly esteemed in foreign countries, evidence perhaps of the cultural impact of the Etruscans in Archaic times. Just as Greek vases were imported to Etruria as prestige goods from a distant and sophisticated civilization and eventually placed in the proprietor's grave, Etruscan vases seemingly also had the same exotic value to places in the western Mediterranean and the cities to the north in France and Germany (see Chapters 17 and 19).[52] Another cultural achievement that was transmitted from such ports was the Greek alphabet from Euboea. Via the Etruscan script, these letterforms were adopted by the Romans and the Gallic people in France and travelled, with the aid of trading centers along the French and German rivers, up to the distant Nordic countries, where they would be developed in the form of runes.[53] The hitherto earliest inscription found in Italy is a small vase found in the tomb of a lady in Gabii (Osteria dell'Osa) from around 775 BC. Praising the woman's skill, the Greek word "*Eulin*," which means "good in linen," remains on her vase.[54] Pollen from linen is detected in most pollen analysis and cloth from linen and wool was highly valued in Etruria. Depictions of the splendid textiles now lost can be admired on tomb walls as paintings, for instance the detailed *toga picta* of Vel Saties in the François tomb, or the dress of the dancing lady from the tomb of the Lionesses.[55] The delicate transparent fabric of the dresses of the two attendants to *Malavish*, depicted on a famous mirror in the British Museum (inv. no. BM 626), demonstrates that the Etruscans were master weavers (see Chapter 42 for a survey of textile manufacture). We can speculate that the dye for coloring was traded from the Milesian Greeks, famous for their linen fabrics and purple dye. In return the Greeks may have bought manufactured bronzes, lamps, mirrors, or incense burners, *thymiateria*, for which the Etruscans were famous across the Mediterranean.[56]

A GLIMPSE OF IMAGES AND MYTHS CONNECTED TO THE ETRUSCAN LANDSCAPE

How can we estimate the interplay between man and nature in Etruria when no written material on this issue has survived? To understand a cultural system it is important to consider the ideological explanation that culture is the glue that maintains societal order. Did the Etruscans know they were Etruscans and to what degree did they feel united as a people? Did people living in the rich southern cities feel primarily like Etruscans or as Tarquinians, Caeretans, or Vulcians, were they rivals in power and goods? Did the tufo plateaus of southern Etruria instill in them the idea of limit, *tular*, so that the habitat of the living had to be separated from those of the dead? (See also Chapter 18.) To what extent did such ideas permeate the whole of the land of the *Rasenna/Rasna*?

Small fragments of original narrations appear in Etruscan imagery, such as those about the *Vipinas* or Vibenna brothers. Sometimes these images are older than the accounts by Roman writers but most of these pictorial narrations, however, are from later periods, beginning in the late fourth century, possibly as a result of dealings with a specific "other" who had conquering intents.[57] On a mirror we see the Vipinas brothers in a landscape consisting of rocks and two trees (Fig. 1.2). A human-like creature, using his left hand to heave himself up onto the highest cliff, gazes out of the scene towards the spectator. His right hand is almost hidden by the branches of a tree. He is crowned with a diadem from which two hornlike spikes protrude. It seems a fair guess that he is a satyr, a faun, a borderline figure that is part-nature part-culture. Surrounding the scene is a vine-garland with ripe grapes and a small boy with a vine-cutting tool is depicted on the extension. Thus, the scene reflects a nature that is composed of elements of humans, wilderness, cultivated grapes, and a harvester. The main scene shows a narrative of the *Vipinas* brethren who seem to have arrived to capture or kill the torque-wearing *Cacu*. The lyre player *Cacu* is a prophet or a seer in late Etruscan images.[58] In the Roman myths he is a bandit who dwells in a cave close to the Palatine in Rome to which he brings the cattle he stole from Hercules/*Hercle* in Erythiea, the red island of the setting sun.[59] Almost all later histories of Hercules are tied to Italy and the cattle he overcame by slaying Geryon on the island of the setting sun. From very early on, Heracles was established as a figure of central importance in all of "Italy" – a name Varro said was derived from its cattle (Varro, *RR* 2.5.3). In the Etrusco-Italic cultural sphere, *Hercle* seems to have enjoyed a special status, more elevated than the one he had in Greece, a hero-god approaching divine status. The Etruscan *Hercle* thus seems to have differed in significant respects from the Greek Heracles. He appears as one of few recognizable divinities on sixth-century terracotta slabs from central Etruscan settlements, as mastering the bull or the lion,[60] and also together with Geryon on the so-called Gobbi crater from Cerveteri, dated to c. 590/580 BC (or 560, according to some).[61] Italy was a land of pastoralists and Heracles

Figure 1.2   The Vipinas brothers ambushing Cacu and the boy Artile.
Note the Pan/Satyr overlooking the scene from above a cliff. Courtesy the Trustees
of the British Museum.

was, of course, the Master of Animals, the protector of flocks and herds, of shepherds and herdsmen.[62] Interestingly, Bagnasco Gianni proposes a reading of the name *Umaele*, as equivalent to Eumalos, a member of the Bacchiads from Corinth. His name means "rich in herds" and he appears on the famous mirror where *Tarchon* acts as haruspex (Chapter 26, Fig. 26.1).[63] The tools of these diviners were the livers from sacrificed animals, a tradition the Etruscans shared with Mesopotamian and Anatolian people. Heracles, himself liminal, is also seen as the defender of a goddess against creatures on the other side of the human *limes* (border), such as sirens and giants.[64] *Hercle*, as discussed above, became associated with water, especially running water.[65] A symbol of running water in Graeco-Roman and Etruscan iconography was often an amphora held either to the spout of a nymphaeum or simply the amphora was depicted lying on the ground with the mouth facing the onlooker, as seen on many mirrors depicting *Hercle*. Water for your flocks and to quench your own thirst was vital when travelling on long transhumance passages.

Nature or natural scenery often appears in tomb painting. It is sparse and, as in the Roman paintings of Pompeii, showing landscapes dominated by human beings and their enterprises. A wall in the Tomb of the Bulls at Tarquinia shows Achilles ambushing the young Troilos when he comes to water his horse (Chapter 24, Fig. 24.10). The outdoor landscape of nature is indicated by a row of trees embellished with ribbons and exotic flowers on tall stems. It does not get any wilder than this except for the untamed animals, hunting or being hunted, in long friezes, for instance in the François Tomb of Vulci. Birds are painted in flight or as targets for shooting and fish are to be hooked. "Nature" is an invention of the eighteenth century and the Etruscans seem to have taken it for granted. To them, nature was an arena in which people performed. The Underworld couple is surrounded by black cloud-like formations in later tombs, as are other creatures of the beyond. The Underworld seems to be a good place, where you meet your loved ones and join in a heavenly feast that never ceases, but the voyage to this final destination seems to be a very threatening and dangerous one. However, there are a few light and helpful creatures on that path, such as the *Vanth* who accompanies the dead and lights their way with torches (see Chapter 25).

Myths and images thus tell everyday life in Etruria and nature's role in it. They tell of the importance of cattle and sheep, of herders' troubles, fears and need for protection. Bad omens or early warnings are sent by natural phenomena and averted by the actions of the haruspex, who could exorcise evil. For these people, nature is spirited and inhabited by borderline beings. Nights were dreaded, to judge from the rejoicing exultation greeting the sunrise in the terracotta antefixes from Pyrgi, showing *Thesan*/Aurora with daybreak stars, *Usil*/Sol, with flaming rays and the cocky morning dew.[66] Dawn has broken![67]

NOTES

1 Mariotti Lippi *et al.* 2007, 279–295.
2 Colombarli *et al.* 2008, 679–692.
3 See excellent images of these volcanoes on NASA Space Station image ISS006-E-36701, 2003. Available at: <http://eol.jsc.nasa.gov/>.
4 Recently down-dated in 2009 by the International Union of Geological Sciences (IUGS) (Riccardi 2009).
5 Ciccioli *et al.* 2010, 9328–9343.
6 Ciccolo, Cattuto *et al.* 2010, 229–251.
7 Ciccolo, Cattuto *et al.* 2010, 229–251.
8 Winchester 2004, 12.
9 For a thorough discussion see Wiman 1990, 31–32.
10 Bianciardi and Cassola 1995.
11 Wiman and Ekman 2000–2001, 109–124.
12 Harrison *et al.* 2010, 165–180.
13 Santillo Frizell 2010, 26–51.
14 Dennis 1883, 213.
15 Dennis 1883, 194.
16 Packard 2007, 46.
17 Curtis and Lieberman 1982.
18 Meiggs 1982, cap. 13, 'Deforestation'; van Andel *et al.* 1986, 103–128.
19 Hutchinson 1970, 5.
20 Ward-Perkins in Hutchinson 1970, 10–12.
21 Foxhall 2007, Chapters 5 to 7.
22 Watson 1996, 805.
23 Bellini *et al.* 2009, 1169.
24 Columbarli *et al.* 2008, 679–692.
25 I am most grateful to Professor Bo Wiman who informed me of the *Abies Alba* dates and their relation to climate conditions.
26 Watson 1996, 805.
27 Nilén 1960.
28 Warden *et al.* 1982, 26–35.
29 Cristofani and Formigli 1981, 175–194; Miletti and Pitzalis, personal correspondence.
30 Francovich 1985, 313–340.
31 Wiman and Ekman 2000–2001, 122.
32 Finsinger *et al.* 2010, 1239–1247; Colombaroli *et al.* 2008, 679–692.

33   Drescher-Schneider *et al.* 2007, 279–299.
34   Mariotti Lippi *et al.* 2000, 295.
35   Mariotti Lippi *et al.* 2000, 279–295.
36   Lamb 1995, 157.
37   De Grossi Mazzurin 1985, 131–171.
38   Pellecchia *et al.* 2007, 1175–1179.
39   (As cited by New York Times, 'DNA Boosts Herodotus' Account of Etruscans as Migrants to Italy', Nicholas Wade April 3, 2007, www.nytimes.com/2007/04/03/science/03etruscan).
40   Cf. the Bronze sculpture of a ploughman from Arezzo, Edlund-Berry 2006, 117.
41   De Grossi Mazzorin 1985, 131–171.
42   Santillo Frisell 2009, 26–51.
43   Santillo Frisell and Wootin 2009, 219–230
44   Potter 1979, 80.
45   Potter 1979, 85.
46   MacIntosh Turfa 2006, 173–190; Thomson de Grummond 2006, 27–44.
47   Kurlansky 2002, *passim.*
48   Bonghi Jovini 2010, 161–180.
49   Fiorini and Torelli 2010, 29–45.
50   Colonna 1989, 171–183.
51   Mühlenbock 2008, Sandström (forthcoming).
52   Rasmussen 1979, 143–157.
53   Bonfante and Bonfante 1983, *passim.*
54   Cf. the discussion in Bartoloni and Delpino 2005, 478–483 and 493–494.
55   Pallotino 1952, 43–48; 115–124.
56   MacIntosh Turfa 1986, 66–91.
57   Wiman and Backe-Forsberg 2007, 109–124.
58   Small 1982, 3–67.
59   Wiman and Hansson, forthcoming.
60   Acquarossa, Velletri, Tuscania, see Strandberg Olofsson 2006, 517–530.
61   Rome, Villa Giulia. *LIMC* IV 1988, 188 Geryoneus no. 19.
62   Burkert 1979, 78–98; Bradley 2005.
63   Bagnasco Gianni 2009, 82–90; Thomson de Grummand 2006, 27–44.
64   Valenza Mele 1979.
65   *Roscher* 1:2, col 2237, s.v. Heracles (A. Furtwängler).
66   For an image see Haynes 2000, Fig 153.
67   I am grateful to PhD student Fredrik Tobin who informed me on volcanoes; to Professor Bo Wiman who provided data of *Abies Alba*; to Barbro Santillo Frizell for valuable comments on the paper; to Jean MacIntosh Turfa for encouragement and to the staff of the Swedish Institute in Rome, always helpful!

BIBLIOGRAPHY

Andels, van T., Runnels, C. N. and Pope, K. O. (1986) "Five thousand years of land use and abuse in Southern Argolid, Greece," *Hesperia*, 55, 1: 103–128.
Bagnasco Gianni, G. (2009) "The importance of being Umaele" in P. Perkins and J. Swaddling (eds), *Etruscan by Definition. Study day in honour of Sybille Haynes' 80th birthday*, 8 December 2006, London, 82–90.
Barker, G. and Rasmussen, T. (1998) *The Etruscans*, Blackwell, Oxford, 10–42.
Bartoloni, G. and Delpino, F. (2005) *Oriente e Occidente: metodi e discipline a confronto. Riflessioni sulla cronologia dell'età del ferro in Italia. Atti dell'Incontro di studi. Roma. 30–31 ottobre 2003. Mediterranea, 1 (2004)*, Pisa: Istituti Editoriali e Poligrafici Internazionali.

Bellini, C., Mariotti-Lippi, M. and Montari, C. (2009) "The Holocene landscape history of the NW Italian coasts," *The Holocene*, 19, 8: 1161–1172.

Bianciardi, L. and Cassola, C. (1995) *I Minatori della Maremma*, Cernusco L, Massa Marittima.

Bonfante, G. and Bonfante, L. (1983) *The Etruscan Language. An Introduction*, New York and London: New York University Press.

Bonghi Jovino, M. (2010) "The Tarquinia Project: A summary of 25 years of excavation," *AJA* 114, 1: 161–180.

Ciccioli, P., Plescia, P. and Capitani, D. (2010) "H, 29Si, and 27Al MAS NMR as a tool to Characterize Volcanic Tuffs and Assess Their Suitability for Industrial Applications," *J. Phys. Chem. C*, 114, 9328–9343.

Ciccolo, P., Cattuto, C., Plescia, P., Valentini, V. and Negrotti, R. (2010) "Geochemical and engineering geological properties of the volcanic tuffs used in the Etruscan Tombs of Norchia (Northern Latium, Italy) and a study of the factors responsible for their rapid surface and structural decay," *Archaeometry*, 52, 2: 229–251.

Colombarli, D., Vannière, B., Emmanuel, C., Magny, M. and Tinner, W. (2008) "Fire-vegetation interactions during the Mesolithic-Neolithic transition at Lago dell'Accesa, Tuscany, Italy," *The Holocene*, 18,5: 679–692.

Colonna, G. (1989) "Il Tempio B" in *Pyrgi : Scavi del Santuario Etrusco* (1969–1971). Suppl. 2 to *NSc* 42–43, 280–290.

Cristofani, M. (ed.) (1981) *Gli Etruschi in Maremma. Popolamento e attività produttive*, Silvana Editoriale, Milano.

Curtis, J. and W. and Lieberman, F. (1982) *The World of George Perkins Marsh, America's First Environmentalist. An Illustrated Biography*, The Countryman Press, Woodstock, Vermont.

Dennis, G. (1883) *The Cities and Cemeteries of Etruria*, (3rd edn), John Murray, London.

De Grossi Mazzorin, J. (1985) "Reperti faunistici dall'acropoli di Populonia: testimonianze di allevamento e caccia nel III secolo a. C.," *Rassegna di Archeologia*, 5: 131–171.

De Grossi Mazzorin, J., and Riedel, A. (1997) "La fauna delle terramare" in M. Bernabò Brea, A. Cardarelli, M. Cremaschi (eds), *Le Terramare. La Più Antica Civiltà Padana*, Electa, Milan.

Drerschler-Schneider, R., De Beaulieu, J.-L., Magny, M., Walter-Simmonet, A.-V., Bosset, G., Millet, L., Brugiapaglia, E. and Drescher, A. (2007) "Vegetation history, climate and human impact over the last 15,000 years at Lago dell'Accesa (Tuscany, Central Italy)," *Veget. Hist. Archaeobot*, 16: 279–299.

Finsinger, W., Colombaroli, D., De Beaulieu, J.-L., Vannière, B. and Vescovi, E. (2010) "Early to mid-Holocene climate change at Lago dell'Accesa (central Italy): climate signal or anthropogenic bias?," *Journal of Quaternary Science*, 12, vol. 25, 8: 1239–1247.

Foxhall, L. (2007) *Olive Cultivation in Ancient Greece: Seeking the Ancient Economy*, Oxford: Oxford University Press.

Francovich, R. (1985) *Un villaggio di minatori e fonditori di metallo nella Toscana del Medievo: San Silvestro (Campiglia Marittima). Rapporto preliminare*, ser. XII, 313–401.

Harrison, A. P., Cattani, I. and Turfa, J. M. (2010) "Metallurgy, environmental pollution and the decline of Etruscan civilisation," *Environmental science and pollution research international*,17, 1: 165–180.

Hutchinson, G. E. (1970) "Ianula: an account of the history and development of the Lago di Monterosi, Latium, Italy," *Transactions of the American Philosophical Society*, New Series 60: 4.

Kurlansky M. (2002) *Salt: A World History*, Walker Publishing Company, Inc., USA.

Lamb, H. H. (1995) *Climate. History and the Modern World*, (2nd edn), Routledge, London and New York.

MacIntosh Turfa, J. (1986) "International Contacts: Commerce, Trade, and Foreign Affairs" in L. Bonfante (ed.) *Etruscan Life and Afterlife. A Handbook of Etruscan Studies*, Aris and Phillips, Warminster, 67–91.

——(2006) "The Etruscan Brontoscopic Calendar" in N. Thomson de Grummond and E. Simon (eds) *The Religion of the Etruscans*, Austin: University of Texas Press, 173–190.

Mariotti Lippi, M., Giachi, G., Paci, S. and Di Tommaso, P.-L. (2000) "Studi sulla vegetazione attuale e passata della Toscana meridionale (Follonica – Italia) e considerazioni sull'impatto ambiente dell'attività metallurgica etrusca nel VI–V secolo a.C.," *Webbia* 55: 279–295.

Mariotti Lippi, M., Bellini, C., Trinci, C., Benvenuti, M., Pallecchi, P. and Sagri, M. (2007) "Pollen analysis of the ship site at Pisa San Rossore, Tuscany, Italy: the implication for catastrophic hydrological events and climate change during the late Holocene," *Vegetation History and Archaeobotany*, 16, 6: 453–465.

Meer van der, L. B. (ed.) (2010) Material Aspects of Etruscan Religion. Proceedings of the International Colloquium, Leiden, May 29 and 30, 2008. *BABesch, Annual Papers on Mediterranean Archaeology*, suppl 16, Leuven: Peeters

Meiggs, R. (1982) *Trees and Timber in the Ancient Mediterranean World*, Oxford: Oxford University Press.

Miletti, M., Pitzalis, F. *et al.* (2011) "Populonia, sepolture in località Casone," *XXVIII Convegno di Studi Etruschi ed Italici, La Corsica e Populonia*, 28 ottobre 2011.

Mühlenbock, C. (2008) *Fragments from a mountain society. Tradition, innovation and interaction at Archaic Monte Polizzo, Sicily.* GOTARC serie B. Gothenburg Archaeological Thesis 50.

Nilén, J. (1960) "The prehistoric iron industries on Elba," unpublished article; photocopies are available from Tekniska Museet, Box 27842, Stockholm 115 93, Sweden.

Pallotino, M. (1952) *Les Grand Siècles de la Peinture. La Peinture Étrusque*, Albert Skira, Genève.

Packard, R. M. (2007) *The Making of a Tropical Disease: A Short History of Malaria*, Johns Hopkins University Press, Baltimore.

Pellecchia M. *et al.* (2007) "The mystery of Etruscan origins: novel clues from Bos taurus mitochndrial DNA," *Proc. R. Soc. B*, 1175–1179.

Potter, T. W. (1979) *The Changing Landscape of South Etruria*, London: Paul Elek.

Riccardi, A. C. (2009) "IUGS ratified ICS recommendation on redefining of Pleistocene and formal definition of base of Quaternary." Available at: <http.//www.stratigraphy.org/upload/IUGS%20Ratification_Q%20&20Pleistocene.fdf>.

Sandström, C. (forthcoming) "Traces of trade. Imported transport amphorae from house I Monte Polizzo, Western Sicily."

Santillo Frizell, B. (2004) "Curing the flock. The use of healing waters in Roman pastoral economy," in Santillo Frizell (ed.) *Pecus: Man and Animal in Antiquity*, Rome.

——(2010) *Lana, Carne, Latte, Paesaggi pastorali tra mito e realtà*, Mauro Pagliai Editore, Florence.

Small, J. P. (1982) *Cacus and Marsyas in Etrusco-Roman Legend*, Princeton: Princeton University Press.

Strandberg Olofsson, M. (2006) "Creatures Great and Small. Animals on Etrusco-Italic Architectural Terracotta Reliefs" in (eds) E. Herrin, I. Lemos, F. Lo Schiavo, L. Vagnetti, R. Whitehouse and J. Wilkins, *Across Frontiers. Etruscan, Greeks, Phoenicians & Cyprus. Studies in honour of David Ridgway and Francesca Romana Serra Ridgway, Accordia Specialist Studies on the Mediterranean* 16, Accordia Research Institute, London, 523–4, 517–530.

Thomson de Grummond, N. (2006) "Prophets and Priests" in N. Thomson de Grummond and E. Simon (eds) *The Religion of the Etruscans*, Austin: University of Texas Press: 27–44.

Valenza Mele, N. (1979) "Eracle euboico a Cuma. La gigantomachia e la via Heraclea" in *Recherches sur les cultes grecs et l'Occident*, (Cahiers du Centre Jean Bérard, 5), Naples, 90–51.

Vannière, B., Magny, M., Emmanuel, C., Tinner, W. and Colombaroli, D. (2008) "Fire-vegetation interactions during the Mesolithic-Neolithic transition at Lago dell'Accesa, Tuscany, Italy," *The Holocene*, 18, 5: 679–692.

Warden, P. G., Maddin, R., Stech, T. and Muhly J. D. (1982) "Copper and Iron Production at Poggio Civitate (Murlo). Analysis of Metalworking By-products from an Archaic Etruscan Site," *Expedition*, 25:1, 26–35.

Watson, C. S. (1996) "The vegetational history of the northern Apennines, Italy: information from three new sequences and a review of regional vegetational changes," *Journal of Biogeography*, 23: 805–841.

Wiman, I. M. B. (1990) *Malstria-Malena, Metals and Motifs in Etruscan Mirror Craft*, SIMA, Jonsered.

Wiman, I. M. B. and Ekman, S. (2000–2001) "Man and nature in Etruria. Natural resources management in the Massetano Area (Tuscany, Italy)," *OpRom*, 25–26: 109–124.

Wiman, I. M. B. (1990) *Malstria – Malena. Metals and Motifs in Etruscan Mirror Craft* (SIMA, 91), Göteborg: Åström.

Wiman, I. M. B. and Backe-Forsberg, Y. (2006–2007) "Surfacing deities in later Etruscan art and the sacellum at San Givenale," *OpRom*, 31–32: 17–27.

Wiman I. M. B. and Hansson, U. (forthcoming) "Betwixt dawn and dusk. *Hercle* sailing on the amphora raft."

Winchester, S. (2004) *Krakatoa. The Day the World Exploded*, Perennial, Harper Collins, New York.

CHAPTER TWO

MASSIMO PALLOTTINO'S "ORIGINS" IN PERSPECTIVE

—•✦•—

Giovanna Bagnasco Gianni

During the 1920s and 1930s of the last century, some decades after Italian unification took place (1861), scholars were challenged to shape a Prehistory for the newborn nation together with her history of art. However, such a need occurred after some anti-Roman feelings had been growing during the previous century. They appeared together with the appraisal of the multifaceted aspects of the populations of the ancient Peninsula, showing a richness in culture and freedom that would shortly thereafter be strongly limited by the power of Rome (Harari 2012: 14–16).

Such a philo-Italic and philo-Etruscan attitude was also in effect during the 1920s, at the beginnings of the Fascist period, when a number of scholars were alerted to take part in the creation of the "Italian past". Among them there was Alessandro Della Seta who was of Jewish faith and thus destined to be relieved of his important appointments later on (1939). His outstanding life and scientific production reflect a twofold attitude towards the appearance of the Etruscans in the historical scenario. On the one hand he expressed his opinion about the need for shifting from a perspective focused on the problem of "origin" to that of "formation" (Della Seta 1922: 189–193); on the other hand he was convinced that the Etruscans had a Near Eastern origin. Therefore, when he became Director of the *Regia Scuola archeologica di Atene* he started excavations on the island of Lemnos in 1926, in order to assess the cultural environment of the "Tyrrhenian" stele, discovered there at Kaminia, because it was inscribed with a language very close to Etruscan (see Chapter 22).

Such a deep concern for the Etruscan culture, however, would be neglected after the great exhibition "Mostra Augustea della Romanità" (1937), that definitely showed that the Fascist regime had chosen Augustan Rome as the model for its propaganda.

Before such a strong Augustan revival put an end to the recognition of the Etruscans as the hard core of the common Italian past, nearly at the same time as Della Seta's investigations to unravel the problem of Etruscan origins, something related to such issues – but independent from the Italian political environment – was going on. In late March and early April 1927, D.H. Lawrence visited Etruria and wrote his last travel book, *Etruscan Places*, published only in 1932 (Lawrence 2011). His quotations of the authors he read in order to become acquainted with the Etruscans – George Dennis, Theodor Mommsen, Fritz

Weege and Pericle Ducati – make it possible to figure out at least his indirect knowledge of the opinions on Etruscan origins expressed by authors such as Herodotus, Dionysius of Halicarnassus and Livy (Hostettler 1985: 241). Therefore it is worth quoting a few of Lawrence's considerations about the beginnings of the Etruscan civilization.

> The Etruscans sailed the seas. They are even said to have come by sea, from Lydia in Asia Minor, at some date far back in the dim mists before the eighth century BC. But that a whole people, even a whole host, sailed in the tiny ships of those days, all at once, to people a sparsely peopled central Italy, seems hard to imagine. Probably ships did come – even before Ulysses. Probably men landed on the strange flat coast and made camps, and then treated with the natives. Whether the newcomers were Lydians or Hittites with hair curled in roll behind, or men from Mycenae or Crete, who knows. Perhaps men of all these sorts came, in batches. For in Homeric days a restlessness seems to have possessed the Mediterranean basin, and ancient races began shaking ships like seeds over the sea. More people than Greeks, or Hellenes, or Indo-Germanic groups, were on the move.
>
> (Lawrence 2011: 40–41).

Moreover, comparing the situation of Volterra to that of Tarquinia, Lawrence claims a difference of "tribe": "This was surely another tribe, wilder, cruder and far less influenced by the old Aegean influences. In Caere and Tarquinia the aborigines were deeply overlaid by incoming influences from the East." (Lawrence 2011: 193.)

As we shall see, such insights might eventually become crucial for reviewing the well-established concepts of "cultural growth" and "formation" introduced since 1939 by Massimo Pallottino, when he was founding modern Etruscan studies. The current archaeological consensus keeps converging on such concepts in order to represent the Etruscan culture as the result of different waves of populations and of subsequent and persistent inputs of foreign contacts with the autochthones of the Italian peninsula. Actually, it is worth noting that Lawrence's interest in the origins of the Etruscans is issued from a deep intention to meet the core of the Etruscan culture according to his peculiar approach of "pure attention" that he considered very close to the attitude of the Etruscan augur towards divination. In such a way "every great discovery or decision" is made possible, "even prayer and reason and research itself" (Lawrence 2011: 97–98). Therefore an intellectual perspective, intermingled with his personal poetics, permeates D.H. Lawrence's meditations on the Etruscans. However, something similar seems also to concern Massimo Pallottino, judging from the titles of two articles that he published after the Second World War.

"Participation" and sense of Drama in the figurative world of the Etruscans (Pallottino 1946) appeared shortly before he published his monograph on the origins of the Etruscans (Pallottino 1947). *Science and poetry in quest of the Etruscans* (Pallottino 1957) appeared ten years later. This second one directly reports his personal feelings towards Etruscan studies: "There is an Etruria for scholars and an Etruria for writers whose traditions run on diverging tracks and, in some ways, designed to remain without communication: the tradition of objective research and that of poetic insights" (Pallottino 1957: 10). Such a background was evidently part of M. Pallottino's approach towards his studies, especially in the case of the problem of Etruscan origins that was going to be crucial to him all his life (Briquel 2007). His scientific attitude was first of all historical, because he took into great consideration the prominent role of archaeology in historical reconstructions and, as a consequence, the role of Etruscan studies too (Bonghi Jovino 2008, pp. 16–17).

Nevertheless, according to the sequence of the above-mentioned stances, it might be possible that Massimo Pallottino developed his new perspective on Etruscan origins without disregarding the approach that he shared in some way with the world of "poetic insights." Akin to this could be considered his frequent use of figures of thought for conveying his theories. For example, in the case of the beginnings of Etruscan history he repeatedly used the example of the French nation, among other modern populations in Europe, which are actually difficult to confine within the stiff limits of a straightforward and linear evolution. He considered the French population as a peculiar blend of successive and persistent inputs of foreign contacts, Ligurians, Gauls, Romans or Franks (Pallottino 1947: 5).

As a consequence, Massimo Pallottino's new perspective focused on at least two core concepts, which he had already figured out as early as his first studies on the Etruscans. At the end of the 1930s he had already pointed out the idea of different levels of "cultural growth" according to the evidence he grasped in the territories of Etruria (1939). Shortly after he focused on the idea of "formation" in the chapter entitled "The problem of Etruscan origins" of the first edition of his famous book *Etruscologia* (Hoepli 1942). The whole question is studied in his major book, which is also outstanding for its peculiar outline, quite rare in human sciences immediately after the Second World War (Bagnasco Gianni 2012). For this reason his book deserves great consideration (Figure 2.1) (Pallottino 1947). To support his theory, he discussed and took advantage of the clashing opinions of Greek and Latin authors on the Etruscan origins that he also summed up in a table (Figure 2.2) pointing out the difference between Herodotus' and Dionysius of Halicarnassus' positions, respectively from the Near East and autochthonous. (See Chapter 3.) The book also deals with other evidence, exploring ancient Italian cultures that are also listed in a table from the Eneolithic (before the second millennium BCE) onwards (Figure 2.3), discussing linguistic issues and questioning the possibility to identify references to the Etruscans in Egyptian epigraphic sources of the second millennium BCE.

MASSIMO PALLOTTINO

L'ORIGINE
DEGLI
ETRUSCHI

SOCIETÀ ANONIMA TUMMINELLI EDITRICE
"STUDIUM URBIS"
CITTÀ UNIVERSITARIA · ROMA

Figure 2.1 Cover page of Pallottino's book on the origins of the Etruscans (Pallottino 1947).

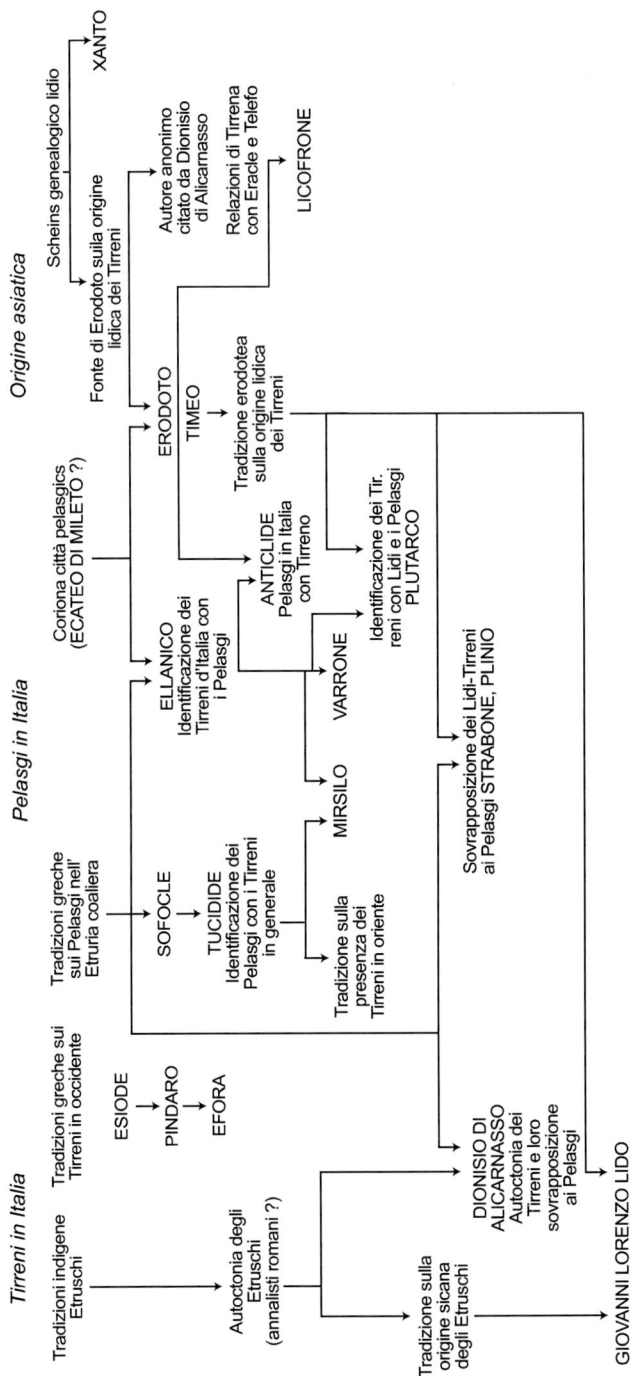

Figure 2.2 Genealogical scheme of the provenance of the Etruscans according to literary sources (Pallottino 1947, 50).

	Italia centro-meridionale	Regione etrusco-laziale	Italia settentrionale
	ENEOLITICO	ENEOLITICO	ENEOLITICO
Il millennio av.Cr.	APPENNINICO I (Conelle)	Rinaldone	Chiozza, Remedello ecc
	APPENNINICO II (Filottrano)	Parziale penetrazione dell'APPENNINICO in Etruria (Cetona)	APPENNINICO e TERREMARE in Emilia. Diffusione del rito della cremazione.
1000-700 circa	Diffusion sporadica della cremazione (Pianello, Timari ecc.). Inizio della CULTURE DEL FERRO MERIDIONALE e colonizzazione greca.	«VILLANOVIANO» in Etruria, manifestazioni dette «di transizione» e inizio della CULTURE DEL FERRO LAZIALE.	Bologna S. Vitale, Fontanella ecc. « VILLANOVIANO » in Emilia e inizio delle CULTURE DEL FERRO nell' Italia settentrionale
		«VILLANOVIANO» EVOLUTO in Etruria	«VILLANOVIANO» EVOLUTO in Emilia (Benacci II, Arnoaldi); CULTURE ATESTINA E DI GOLASECCA
700-575	Inizio delle CULTURE DEL FERROR nell' Italia centro-adriatica	ORIENTALIZZANTE CIVILTÀ ETRUSCA ARCAICA	
575-500			Penetrazione etrusca nella pianura padana (Certosa)

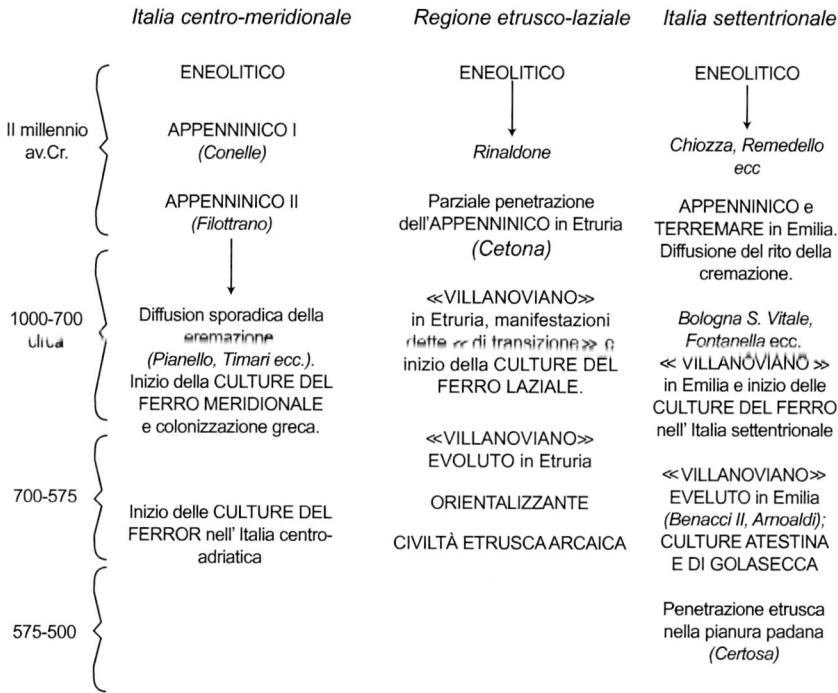

Figure 2.3 Sequence of the ancient cultures of the Italian Peninsula (Pallottino 1947, 96).

Summing up, as early as 1947 Massimo Pallottino considered the Etruscan nation to have appeared in the historical scenario in the first millennium BCE: "…the Etruscan nation and the Etruscan civilization have to be considered in no other way than a well defined result of ethnic, political, economic, cultural factors that came to converge and develop in central Italy at the beginning of the first millennium BCE." (Pallottino 1947: 5.)

Afterwards a number of contributions were dedicated to the same subject, spanning from chronological and historical issues to linguistics (Pallottino 1947–48; 1948–49; 1961; 1968; 1970; 1977; 1984; 1986), without ignoring the anthropological approach to the question raised by the Ciba Foundation Symposium held in London in 1958. His position was cautious, but nevertheless did not disregard the debate between historical anthropology and genetics (Pallottino 1961) and was in some ways ahead of the times (Bagnasco Gianni 2012). Nowadays we have the twofold opportunity to ignore indications based on genetic data generated from aDNA (ancient DNA), claiming closer relationships with Near Eastern than with modern Italian populations, or to meet the challenge and discuss the problem with different, but punctual and collaborative scientific approaches (Turfa 2006; Perkins 2009; Harari 2010).

In such a recent scenario it is worth noting that in 1985 Massimo Pallottino himself introduced another novel approach to the discussion. During the Second International Congress of Etruscan Studies he suggested that the Etruscan nation might have started its formation very early in Central Italy, during the Eneolithic culture of Rinaldone (from the third millennium to first half of the second millennium BCE) (Pallottino 1989: 61–62). With this he combined the movements of people from the East, the characters of the language shared with those of the island of Lemnos, already assessed since Della Seta's time, and the Herodotean account of Lydian origins for the Etruscan people. It is a matter of future research to carefully assess all the elements that are available to us and to arrive at results and theories that have been reflected upon and shared by a larger community of domain experts (Bagnasco Gianni 2012).

BIBLIOGRAPHY

Bagnasco Gianni, G. (2012) "Origine degli Etruschi" in Bartoloni, G. (ed.), *Introduzione all'Etruscologia*, Milan: Hoepli, 47–81.

Bonghi Jovino, M. (2008) "Crossing the bridge: the meeting of two cultures" in Bagnasco Gianni, G. (ed.), *Bridging Archaeological and Information Technology Culture for community accessibility (Milan, July, 10–11, 2007)*, Rome: L'Erma di Bretschneider, 13–19.

Briquel, D. (2007) "Massimo Pallottino e le origini etrusche" in Michetti, L. M. (ed.), *Massimo Pallottino, a dieci anni dalla scomparsa. Atti dell'Incontro di studio. Roma, 10 – 11 novembre 2005*, Roea: Edizioni Quasar, 29–41.

Della Seta, A. (1922) *Italia antica. Dalla caverna preistorica al palazzo imperiale*, Bergamo: Istituto Italiano d'Arti Grafiche.

Harari, M. (2010) "La questione delle origini etrusche: dati archeologici e linguistici a confronto coi risultati di una recentissima indagine genetica" in Negroni Catacchio, N. (ed.), *L'alba dell'Etruria. Fenomeni di continuità e trasformazione nei secoli XII–VIII. IX Incontro di Studi su Preistoria e Protostoria in Etruria (Valentano-Pitigliano, 12–14.09.08)*, Milan: Octavo, 37–48.

——(2012) "1. Storia degli Studi" in Bartoloni, G. (ed.), *Introduzione all'Etruscologia*, Milan: Hoepli, 19–46.

Hostettler, M. (1985) *D.H. Lawrence, travel books and fiction*, Berne and New York: Peter Lang.

Lawrence, D. H. (2011) *Etruscan Places. Travels through forgotten Italy*, London: Tauris Parke Paperbacks.

Pallottino, M. (1939) "Sulle facies culturali arcaiche dell'Etruria", *StEtr*, XIII, 85–129.

——(1942) *Etruscologia*, Milan: Hoepli.

——(1946) '"Partecipazione" e senso drammatico nel mondo figurato degli Etruschi', *Arti Figurative*, 3–5, 149–165.

——(1947) *L'origine degli Etruschi*, Rome: Tumminelli.

——(1947–48) "Note in margine al problema delle origini etrusche", *Antiquitas*, 2–3, 16–23.

——(1948–49) "Erodoto autoctonista?", *StEtr*, XX, 11–16.

——(1957) "Scienza e poesia alla scoperta degli Etruschi", *Quaderni dell'Associazione Culturale Italiana*, 24, 7–22.

——(1961) "Nuovi studi sul problema delle origini etrusche. Bilancio critico", *StEtr*, XXIX, 3–30.

——(1968) Review of Hencken, H. (1968) *Tarquinia. Villanovans and Early Etruscans I–II*, Cambridge (Mass.), *StEtr*, XXXVI, 493–501.

——(1970) "Etnogenesi uguale poleogenesi?" in *Studi sulla città antica. Atti del Convegno di studi sulla città etrusca e italica preromana*, Bologna 1966, Bologna: Isituto per la storia di Bologna, 75–76.

——(1977) "Il problema delle origini etrusche e la preminente incidenza del fatto linguistico nella sua discussione" in *Paleontologia Linguistica, Atti del VI Convegno Internazionale di Linguisti*, Milano 1974, Brescia: Paideia, 129–136.

——(1986) "Nota introduttiva. Immagini e realtà della civiltà etrusca" in Pugliese Carratelli, G. (ed.), *Rasenna. Storia e civiltà degli Etruschi*, Milan: Edizione Scheiwiller per il Credito Italiano, 3–12.

——(1989) "Prospettive attuali del problema delle origini etrusche" in Cristofani M. (ed.), *Atti del secondo congresso internazionale etrusco* (Firenze 26 maggio – 2 giugno 1985), Rome: G. Bretschneider, 55–62.

Perkins, P. (2009) "DNA and Etruscan identity" in Swaddling, J. and Perkins, P. (eds), *Etruscan by Definition: The Cultural, Regional and Personal Identity of the Etruscans*, London: The British Museum Press, 95–111.

Turfa, J. M. (2006) "Staring down Herodotus: mitochondrial DNA studies and claims about Etruscan origins", *Etruscan News*, 7, 4–5.

CHAPTER THREE

ETRUSCAN ORIGINS AND
THE ANCIENT AUTHORS

———•◆•———

Dominique Briquel

One aspect of the Etruscan mystery and the fascination that they evoke in the public, in addition to the persistent obscurity of their language, is the question of their origins. Massimo Pallottino designated this as "*l'annosa questione delle origini etrusche*"[1] ("the age-old question of Etruscan origins," see Chapter 2). This is in fact one of the classic issues that arise concerning the Etruscans: we do not know how this people was formed, or whence its formative elements and characteristic features were derived; its language, as Dionysius of Halicarnassus noted (1.30.2), was like no other known. Any treatise on Etruscology will include a section dealing with the question of origins: one can only note that the debate remains open and that contradictory theories have been proposed, none of which can claim to be convincing. Three main theses have been advanced in the history of Etruscan studies that may be considered to be based on scientifically admissible arguments. Two were inherited from Antiquity: that which maintains that the Etruscans came from the East and that which considers them an extension of the oldest established populations of the locales where we know them in historic times, that is to say by making them autochthonous, natives of Italy. A third was added in modern times, first by the Frenchman Nicolas Fréret, in his *Recherches sur l'origine et l'ancienne histoire des différents peuples de l'Italie* ("Researches on the origin and history of various ancient peoples of Italy") published in 1753. It was reprised by the big names of German learning of the nineteenth century, such as B. G. Niebuhr and T. Mommsen in their histories of Rome, published respectively in 1811 and 1856: this was the requirement that the ancestors of the Etruscans came over the Alps from the north, in the region where we know the Rhaetians. Their name had appeared to evoke the name *Rasenna* that, according to Dionysius of Halicarnassus, the Etruscans gave themselves in their own language (1.30.3); inscriptions show that the Rhaetians actually spoke a language related to Etruscan.

This is not the place to resume consideration of the issue or analyze the various theories advanced. This paper will consider how the "age-old question of Etruscan origins" had arisen for ancient authors. On this point, modern scholars have only resumed a debate that already existed in Antiquity: at the time when the Greeks, Etruscans and Romans rubbed shoulders, they could not but be struck by the singularity of their language, and had already posed the question, where did this people come from? But even then there was no unequivocal answer: the ancient authors were already advancing opposing views, of autochthony or of their coming by sea, the latter appearing in two distinct versions, one, by far the most widespread, expressed by Herodotus, that the first Etruscans were colonists from Lydia, yet also linking them to the Pelasgians, an extinct population at the time, but one that Greeks represented as having preceded themselves on the soil of Hellas. In a sense, the modern problem of Etruscan origins only prolongs a discussion that existed in ancient times, so it is useful to understand why this discussion took place and what the issues were. It is not irrelevant to note that the debate had not, despite appearances, a truly scientific character, but that the positions taken vis-à-vis the origin of the Etruscans expressed a perspective of rapport with this people – and thus had an ideological significance.

We have already twice invoked the testimony of Dionysius of Halicarnassus, the Greek rhetorician who settled in Rome at the time of Augustus, and wrote the *Roman Antiquities* to raise Greeks' awareness of the origins and early history of the city, which had then extended its empire across the Mediterranean world. This is a key source because, unlike Livy who adopts a narrowly Romanocentric view and tells us virtually nothing about other peoples with whom the Romans were in contact, Dionysius became interested in Etruscans – who, as we know, played a very important role in the early days of the existence of Rome, to the point where it was ruled in the sixth century BC by the Etruscan dynasty of the Tarquins. Concerning Etruscan origins, Dionysius has devoted five chapters of his first book (1.26–30), to a long excursus on the Etruscan issue.

There is nothing like it elsewhere in Greek and Latin literature and that is why Dionysius was often considered the first Etruscologist.[2] He had his own opinion on the origin of the Etruscans, who were to him natives of Italy. But that did not stop him considering the existence of other doctrines, the Lydian thesis and the thesis that recognized them as descended from the ancient Pelasgians. He exposes the whole range of theories, with a completeness and objectivity in presenting the views of his predecessors that we would recognize in a modern scientist. He often specifically quotes his predecessors, such as Xanthus of Lydia (1.28.2), Hellanicus of Lesbos (1.28.3) and Herodotus (1.29.3), and his testimony is all the more precious because, except for Herodotus for whom we have a text,[3] the authors he cites are no longer accessible except for a few fragments. For instance, if we did not have his quotation from the *Phoronis* of Hellanicus of Lesbos, we would be at a loss to know the Pelasgian doctrine as presented by this historian of the fifth century BC. Although Dionysius was a rhetorician, not a scholar, and probably did not conduct exhaustive research into the works of the authors he mentions, his view has merit: it is likely that he used information that had been collected by his slightly older contemporary, the great Roman scholar Varro, who recorded it in his great work of scholarship, *The Antiquities*. We no longer have the work of Varro and Dionysius has at least taken care, a rarity among ancient historians, to make a full statement on a controversial issue and not simply to state his own position.

Moreover, his approach was comparable to that found in modern presentations of the issue, since it is not confined to repeating the views of his predecessors with a bookish erudition. Today, an essential aspect of the problem of origins includes a review of the evidence of language and culture. Dionysius was already well aware of the importance in the debate of the linguistic data: the comparison he drew between Etruscans and Pelasgians or Lydians did involve the traits of language (for the Etruscans and Pelasgians (1.29.2), "their languages are different and preserve not the least resemblance to one another," for the Etruscans at 1.30.1, "they do not use the same languages")⁴ thus finding that the Etruscan language could not be reduced to either of these or even to any other known language. Dionysius reported in 1.30.2, "it is found to be a very ancient nation and to agree with none other in its language," indicating a correctness of observation that has been virtually proved by contradiction, in the failure of countless attempts at decipherment which have engaged generations of more or less enlightened spirits who sought to explain the Etruscan language by comparison to the most diverse languages. As for cultural data, again he took care not to neglect it, noting that the Etruscans "neither worship the same gods as the Lydians nor make use of similar laws or institutions, but in these very respects they differ more from the Lydians than from the Pelasgians" (1.30.1). The method of exposition therefore seems impeccable: we can say the same about how Dionysius conducts the discussion and advances its conclusion, leading to the selection of the autochthonist theory. One does not find in his work a peremptory statement of the doctrine, which he prefers, but an approach that reaches this conclusion only after a systematic discussion and criticism of the arguments submitted. It is through the subsequent rejection of other doctrines that the author demonstrates the validity of the theory of autochthony.

The excursus is too long to quote verbatim, but a summary in outline form clearly demonstrates the rigor of Dionysius' method:

- Introduction (1.26.2): presentation of two views of the origin of the Etruscans, as natives of Italy and one as immigrants ("some declare them to be natives of Italy, but others call them foreigners").

I) Statement of opposing arguments:
  - A) Short presentation of the thesis of autochthony (1.26.2), relative to authors who are not named ("those who make them a native race") and to which Dionysius is our only witness. This thesis advances a precise explanation of the name of the Etruscans in Greek, "Tyrrhenians," formerly "Tyrsenians," from the name of the towers, *turseis*, that this people had built and in which they lived.
  - B-1) Detailed presentation of the doctrine of the Etruscans as immigrants, in both forms, the first using the Lydians (1.27–28.1), concluding a discussion quoting Xanthus the Lydian (1.28.2); then one involving the Pelasgians (1.28.3–4). In detail, the statement of Dionysius is as follows:
    a) Presentation of a first version of the legend of Tyrrhenos, son of Atys king of Lydia, then called Maeonia, whose son Lydos inherited his father's kingdom and gave it the name of Lydia, while his brother Tyrrhenos left to colonize Etruria, which owes its Greek name, Tyrrhenia, to him (1.27.1–2).
    b) The form of the legend differs from that which is then reported (ascribed to Herodotus) in that there is no mention of a famine that would have forced a portion of the population to leave the country for Italy (1.27.3–4).⁵
    c) Brief presentation of two other variants of the theory of Lydian origins, amending the genealogy of Tyrrhenos and undoubtedly based on late re-workings of the legend (1.28.1). In the first, the hero is given as the son of Heracles and his Lydian mistress, Omphale. In the second, his father is Telephus; according to some texts actually he is the father of both Lydos and Tyrrhenos.⁶

d) Reference to Xanthos, the fifth-century BC Lydian author (1.28.2). In fact this passage is already used to criticize the Lydian thesis: Dionysius likes to point out that the Lydian historian "who was well acquainted with ancient history as any man and who may be regarded as an authority second to none on the history of his own country" was ignorant of the tradition of emigration to Italy by Lydians led by a son of Atys called Tyrrhenos.

- B-2) Presentation of the doctrine involving the Pelasgians (1.28.3–4).
  a) Thesis presented by a contemporary of Herodotus, Hellanicus of Lesbos, in his genealogical work, the *Phoronis*, devoted to the descendants of Phoroneus, in a passage quoted verbatim by Dionysius (1.28.3).
  b) Another tradition on the Pelasgians, not really about Etruscan origins, explains how Tyrrhenians (so the Etruscans by their Greek name) would have done the opposite course, travelling from Italy to Greece, and receiving because of their migration, the name Pelarges, that is to say "storks" in Greek, an ancient form retained in the name of the "Pelargic/Pelasgian Wall" of the Athenian Acropolis. This tradition of Athenian origin is attributed to an author of a *History of Attica*, Myrsilus, who lived in the third century BC (1.28.2).[7]

II) Discussion and rejection of doctrines that do not follow Dionysius, this time the order is reversed: first a critique of the Pelasgian thesis (1.29), followed by that of the Lydian theory (1.30.1).
- A) Discussion of the Pelasgian thesis.
  a) Potential for confusion between the Etruscans and Pelasgians because they were established near each other; examples of confusions that have occurred, notably in Italy where in the past Greeks indiscriminately designated as Tyrrhenians not only the Etruscans themselves but also the Latins and Umbrians, to the point of considering Rome an Etruscan city (*polis Tyrrhenis*, 1.29.1–2).
  b) A reference to a passage in Herodotus (1.57.3), quoted verbatim, on the language spoken by the Pelasgians of Placia and Sylace and the people of Cortona in Tuscany (according to the reading adopted in the *Roman Antiquities*). In this text, the language of the Pelasgians of Cortona is distinct from that of their neighbors who are Tyrrhenians, therefore Etruscans: it follows that Pelasgians and Etruscans do not speak the same language and are to be perceived as two distinct peoples (1.29.3–4).
- B) Discussion of the Lydian theory: this was already initiated by the citation of Xanthos (1.28.2), by whose authority Dionysius questioned the merits of tradition on Tyrrhenos, as well as the authority of Herodotus (1.57.3), allowing him to conclude that their language and ethnic character distinguished Pelasgians from Etruscans. As noted, Dionysius stresses the cultural and linguistic differences between Lydians and Etruscans, but without going into detail (1.30.1).
- Conclusion: accuracy of the autochthonist thesis (1.30.2). This conclusion is presented with the most explicit modesty: "those probably come nearest to the truth who declare that the nation migrated from nowhere else, but was native to the country." Dionysius does not extend the arguments which can be invoked in his favor (that is, the isolation of the Etruscans by language and cultural traits) and the justification of the doctrine of the Etruscans as an indigenous population of Italy is in its reasoning a rejection of the other two theses.

Dionysius' ultimately negative demonstration of the autochthony of the Etruscans is not satisfying. He may be accused of insufficiently developing positive aspects, including issues of language or civilization, which in the eyes of modern Etruscologists are obviously the most decisive. It must be said that his brief statement on the unique character of the Etruscans seems rather to beg the question, but let us not be overly critical. Dionysius is right on this point and, although he did not have available the means of modern linguistic analysis, we should at least give him credit for fully perceiving the peculiar nature of the Etruscan language and its heterogeneity in relation to Indo-European languages like Greek and Latin. In total, if one refers to the type of debate possible in his time, one cannot fail to admire how the rhetorician of Halicarnassus conducted his inquiry, which remains one of the finest examples of analysis and scientific discussion that Antiquity has bequeathed to us.

However, the seriousness and the (to our eyes) scientific approach of Dionysius, as in this passage, actually raise other questions. For if we take into account the personality of the orator of Halicarnassus, it seems paradoxical to regard him as a true scholar – as do the Etruscologists when they make him the first representative of their specialty. We know that his purpose in writing the *Roman Antiquities* was to defend a thesis which can hardly be regarded as scientifically founded: that the Romans were Greeks and had even become, over time, the best representatives of Hellenism. This paradoxical (if not absurd, to us) thesis he claimed to demonstrate in Book I: once the Siculi, indigenous barbarians who had at one time inhabited Latium, had disappeared, the soil of Rome had only received people of Hellenic descent. He serialized the traditions of the arrival in the region of first, the Aborigines, arbitrarily considered to be Arcadians (1.10–16), of the Pelasgians, defined as Greeks despite the express statement of Herodotus (1.57) that they were "barbarophones" and spoke a barbarian language (1.17–30), of the Arcadians of Evander (1.31–33), of the companions Heracles left behind upon his return from the expedition to capture the herds of Geryon (1.34–44), and then of the Trojans of Aeneas (1.45–69), with a genealogical demonstration to suggest that "the Trojans too were a nation as truly Greek as any," allowing us to move on to the embarrassing fact that the two nations clashed in the Trojan War. To this accumulation of various traditions, complacently reinterpreted as needed, he added the linguistic argument, actually supported by some ancient authors, that Latin was Greek (1.90), in its Aeolian variant (which corresponds to the fact that the Arcadians of Evander were regarded as speaking a dialect of this group).[8] And, throughout his history, he constantly compares Roman institutions to those of Greece, the notion that Rome was at its origin Hellenic.[9]

Obviously, the thesis of the Hellenism of the Romans, on which the historic vision of Dionysius was based, has no scientific validity: it responded to the desire, clearly stated at the beginning of his book, to reconcile his compatriots to the fact that they had been subjected to Roman rule, by showing them that they should not, in fact, consider the Romans to be barbarians, "one will find no nation that is more ancient or more Greek than these" (1.89.2). Now it is in the perspective of this totally artificial vision of Rome that we may understand why Dionysius had come to speak of the Etruscans – and adopt the autochthonist theory. The thesis of the Hellenism of Rome carried for him a corollary: the Romans (and those to whom they were related, such as the Latins) were the only ones in Italy who might benefit from such an origin, which lent them prestige among the Greeks; the other Italian peoples were barbarians – and that is why the historian systematically ignores the many traditions that proposed Greek heroes or peoples as the source of this or that people or city of the peninsula. But the Etruscans posed a particular problem: it was impossible not to mention them; given the role they played in the history of ancient Italy and especially of Rome. Dionysius was obliged to consider that the Etruscans had been the dominant group in Italy, north of the area directly affected by Hellenic colonization, and Greeks often saw Rome as an Etruscan city, in Greek *polis Turrhenis* (1.29.2), whereas it was for Dionysius a Greek city, *polis Hellenis* (1.89.1).[10] But traditions like making Etruscans former Pelasgians or Lydians (since they did not speak Greek they were, in the strict linguistic sense of the term, barbarians) had the disadvantage of reconciling them with the Greeks, integrating them into their own world – and so risked jeopardizing the privilege of the Romans to be the only representatives of Hellenism in Italy. To make Etruscans indigenous palliated this difficulty: being indigenous, the Etruscans were no more than the barbarians of Italy, without any relationship with the Greek world and its values.[11] It is in this sense, negative in terms of its implications for ethnic Greek mentality, that we must understand Dionysius' choice of the autochthonist thesis.[12]

Thus, far from responding to a disinterested approach, to a purely scientific concern the affirmation of the Etruscans' autochthony by Dionysius, although supported by arguments scientifically relevant to us, was in part ideologically oriented: it continued to depreciate the Etruscans vis-à-vis the Romans, who were themselves at the centre of his historical work. And it seems to have been there from the beginning, its aim to present the Etruscans as Italian barbarians and thus to devalue them in relation to the Greeks.

Dionysius is for us the only witness to this thesis. But the little he tells us is enough to show it was born in a Hellenic milieu (and does not reflect, as has sometimes been suggested, the vision that the Etruscans held of their own origins):[13] it included an explanation of the name of Tyrrhenians by *turseis*, "towers," which corresponds to the name of the people in Greek (presumably in opposition to the explanation of the eponymous hero Tyrrhenos associated with the thesis of Lydian origin). As for the environment in which this was created, one can think of Syracusan historians. That great Greek city of Sicily, which in the time of Hieron (474 BC) had already defeated the Etruscans in the waters off Cumae, had embarked, at the time of Dionysius I (431–367 BC) on a struggle against the Etruscans for control ("thalassocracy") of the seas bordering Italy.[14] The tyrant especially attacked the shrine of Pyrgi (which name also means "towers") and had justified the looting by the fact that in attacking this external harbor of Caere, he had taken a hideout for pirates, the reputation that attached to the Etruscans in the Greek world.[15] The conduct of the master of Syracuse had attracted the widespread condemnation of the Greeks, and it is likely in this context, seeking to justify his actions, that scholars of the entourage of Dionysius came up with this presentation of the origin of the Etruscans. Far from being descendants of the Lydians, according to the doctrine inherited from Herodotus, or of ancient Pelasgians, according to earlier views espoused by Hellanicus of Lesbos, the Etruscans were only Italian barbarians, clinging to their pirate lairs and living in the towers to which they owed their name. This presentation was clearly derogatory – and it is in this sense too, despite the appearance of a purely scientific treatise, that it has been used by Dionysius.[16]

The creation of the thesis of Etruscan autochthony presumably occurred not in answer to scientific concerns, nor from a desire to give a historically-based explanation as to how this people, undoubtedly one of the largest indigenous populations of Italy, was formed. One had tried to express a position with regard to the Etruscans themselves and in this case to present them unfavorably, by reducing them to mere barbarians, without anything to recommend them in the eyes of the Greek public for whom this discourse was intended. But if the autochthonist theory, as Dionysius presents it, appears to be an artificial development, responding to political ends, this is not necessarily true of other ideas about Etruscan origins that prevailed in Antiquity. We must now consider the other two doctrines, specifically those that contradict Dionysius of Halicarnassus, one using the Lydians and the other the Pelasgians.

We begin with the thesis of Lydian origin, for which the authority of the father of history, Herodotus, whose description in *Histories* (1.94) ensured a very wide dissemination in Antiquity. It appeared to be commonly accepted doctrine in Roman times – Dionysius, with his adoption of the autochthonist theory, is an isolated dissident figure.[17] Significantly, it was adopted by the Etruscans themselves: Tacitus tells us that, during the reign of Tiberius, the assembly (*concilium*) of the Etruscan people had issued a decree affirming their kinship with the people of Sardis in Lydia, which was home to the temple of the imperial cult whose construction had been decided (*Annals* 4.55). But we should see how this doctrine arose and consult the passage of Herodotus, which is its first presentation (1.94). We will analyze this text,[18] allowing us to see how it could be developed and the concerns – and again not purely scientific ones – to which it responded.

1.94 (2): According to what they themselves [the Lydians] say, the pastimes now in use among them and the Greeks were invented by the Lydians: these, they say, were invented at the time they colonized Tyrrhenia. This is their story: (3) In the reign of Atys son of Manes there was great scarcity of food in all Lydia. For a while the Lydians bore this with what patience they could; presently, when there was no abatement of the famine, they sought for remedies, and divers plans were devised by divers men. Then it was that they invented the games of dice and knuckle-bones and ball, and all other forms of pastime except only draughts, which the Lydians do not claim to have discovered. (4) Then, using their discovery to lighten the famine, they would play for the whole of every other day, that they might not have to seek for food, and the next day they ceased from their play and ate. This was their manner of life for eighteen years. (5) But the famine did not cease to plague them, and rather afflicted them yet more grievously. (6) At last their king divided the people into two portions, and made them draw lots, so that one part should remain and the other leave the country; he himself was to be the head of those who drew the lot to remain there, and his son, whose name was Tyrrhenus, of those who departed. Then one part of them, having drawn the lot, left the country and came down to Smyrna and built ships, whereon they set all their goods that could be carried on shipboard, and sailed away to seek a livelihood and a country; till at last, after sojourning with many nations in turn, they came to the Ombrici [Umbrians], where they founded cities and have dwelt ever since. (7) They no longer called themselves Lydians, but Tyrrhenians, after the name of the king's son who had led them thither.

This text is of course of paramount importance to the controversy over Etruscan origins, and the proponents of the theory of oriental origin, whether ancient or modern, have not failed to refer to it as evidence of a tradition of showing that those whom the Etruscans of the historical period recognized as their ancestors had come from beyond the seas, and specifically from Lydia. But, before drawing any conclusions whatsoever, it should be analyzed as it occurs. This is indeed a relatively long text, complex in composition and using a number of elements that need to be examined in detail. The idea of Lydian colonists sent to Italy and there founding Etruria would appear only after a long process, which involves many other considerations. One should be aware that this text does not appear in the context of a discussion of this particular problem. This is only mentioned in passing. Herodotus happened to speak about the migration of Lydian colonists to Etruria in covering another point: the question of the origin of the games, which the Lydians flattered themselves as having invented. The historian discusses the problem of Etruscan origins only because of the general circumstances surrounding the invention of the games, the sending of a Lydian colony to Italy. Added to that the narrative is presented as Lydian: at no time did Herodotus attribute it to the Etruscans nor did he say they themselves represented the birth of their nation in this way.

The question of the invention of the games is thus pivotal in this passage. But it is based on an idea that does not appear explicitly in the text, rather, as L. Pareti has shown, it only helped justify attributing to the Lydians the invention of games:[19] their ethnic name was near the linguistic base of the Latin word *ludus* ("game"), but which exists in other Indo-European languages (for example in the Greek verb *loidorein*, "play," "mock") and meaning "play." By their name, then, the Lydians appear to be those to whom the creation of games was attributed. We must realize that indeed, in the form of narrative that Herodotus gave, unlike the version that was released later under his name (which I have qualified as the "vulgate," and which Dionysius presents at 1.27.3–4), Tyrrhenos had no brother and there was no Lydos, whose name would explain the appearance of the ethnic name, Lydians: in this form of the tradition, the ancient Maeonians received their name from Lydos, son of Atys. In Herodotus, however, Lydos did not appear: but he did not have to appear, and the substitution of the name Lydians for Maeonians was explained in another way, by their invention of games.

In fact, this assertion of the invention of games by the Lydians, advanced by the Lydians themselves, was opposed to a Greek doctrine that maintained the games were the work of Palamedes,[20] one of the army of the Achaeans, who, during the Trojan War, was the first inventor, the *protos heuretes* of the games.[21] The history that Herodotus collected from his Lydian informants is indeed clear on this point, an imitation of the legend of Palamedes: it was also during a famine (depending on the version, either when the Greek fleet was blocked at Aulis, or during the siege of Troy itself) that the Greek hero imagined games with the same intention: to help his companions forget in the excitement of the game, that they had nothing to eat. The Lydians, considering their name as the "people of the games," had to grasp and insert it into their national traditions, placing the famine which justified the invention of games in the reign of King Atys, son of Manes, who, already in the local tradition reported by Xanthos (quoted by Dionysius 1.28.2), appeared to be the king to whom was related the transition from the old ethnic name of Maeonians into Lydians.[22]

Thus, the Herodotean story seems dependent on a complex development process that goes far beyond what would have been the mere recording of historical memory of the departure of Lydian colonists for Etruria. By this question of the invention of games, it bears the mark of a scholarly construction, making use of motifs drawn from the repertoire of Hellenic traditions taken up by the Lydians (since there is no reason to doubt the assertion of Herodotus that he reports a story of Lydian origin). One can make the same observation about other points of the story: for many reasons it appears to be a Lydian parallel to the narrative of Greek colonization (Tyrrhenos and his companions even embark at the Greek port of Smyrna). The Lydians were moved to send a colony abroad as a means to address the famine that had struck them (the games-solution, which had worked for eighteen years, proved insufficient!): famine was often advanced as justifying the Greek colonization enterprises, whether in a general history (situation of *stenochoria*, "lack of land") or as a reason for the creation of this particular colony (for example, the foundation of Chalcidian Rhegion or the founding of Cyrene from Thera). The Lydians leaving for Italy were designated by lot (and are thus not volunteers): the same method of selecting those who have to leave their homeland, combined, where appropriate, with the Delphic theme of a human tithe, was also cited for Rhegion and Cyrene, as well as Magnesia on the Maeander, close to Lydia. It seems that the Lydians had already developed a similar story about the Mysians, to whom they were related, explaining the origin as the result of sending settlers chosen in a time of crisis.[23] The story we read in Herodotus 1.94 is entirely a Greek story of colonization.

That the narrative form modeled on Hellenic parallels is not proof of non-historicity: the Lydians may very well have clothed their folk-memory of a migration, which in ancient times sent some of them to Italian shores, with Greek motifs of the foundation of colonies in such circumstances. But we may be facing a totally artificial reconstruction, without any reference to any historical reality. And that is where another type of account intervenes, one that has less to do with the historical background: a question which must remain open and that consideration of such a text cannot decide, than with the function it was to fulfill in the Lydian atmosphere in which it was elaborated.

The text of Herodotus is not limited to the passage of emigrants from Lydia to Italy where they would have laid the groundwork for the future Etruria. It takes account of the name of this people, by using the convenient method of the eponymous hero who gave his name to the nation. There is therefore a personalized aspect in this relationship between Lydians and Etruscans, and that at the highest level, since Tyrrhenos is presented as the son of the Lydian king. The linking of Lydians and Etruscans thus passes as ties of kinship. The eponymous hero to whom the new people in the West owe their ethnic name has a genealogical connection with Lydia. But this is a mode of expressing a relationship between two human groups that we meet very often. For example, the unity of the various components of the Greek world was expressed by the fact that the heroes who gave their names to each of its major subdivisions were all descendants of the eponymous Greek Hellen, son of Deucalion, to whom they were either the sons; like Doros and Aiolos, respectively eponymous for Dorians and Aeolians, or the grandsons (born to Xuthus, the third son of Hellen, the brother of Doros and Aiolos); like Athis and Ion, eponymous ancestors of the inhabitants of Attica and the Ionians. The Lydians in turn had developed this mode of expression, which perceived entire peoples as kinsmen. Xanthos, in the passage quoted by Dionysius of Halicarnassus (1.28.2), explained that the Lydians and the Torebians spoke closely related languages because they descended from two brothers, sons of King Atys, Lydos and Torebos.[24] Herodotus knew another tradition that presented Car, Lydos and Mysos, respectively eponymous of Carians, Lydians and Mysians, as brothers (1.171): thus he explained the fact that Lydians and Mysians were allowed to attend the temple of the great national god of the Carians, Zeus of Mylasa, who bore as an epithet the very name of their people.[25]

We are dealing with traditions of *syngeneia*, of "matching."[26] These were extremely common in Antiquity, both in the Greek world and elsewhere. It was usual for situations where a good relationship existed between two human groups, such as those that sanctioned a treaty of alliance, to be presented as based on a relationship that had united the ancestors of the two groups. This common distant origin justified the good understanding they demonstrated in the present. Greek epigraphy has furnished us with a series of such official claims of kinship: it was a mode of expression expected in diplomatic practice.[27] There is an example in the Bible that is almost a caricature, in the first *Book of Maccabees* (12.20–23), with the letter that Areios the king of Sparta sent in response to the request of alliance and friendship that Jonathan had made of him (there is no reason not to regard it as authentic): Areios supported his favorable response with the fact that "it has been found in writing concerning the Spartans and the Jews that they are brothers and they are the descendants of Abraham." It is doubtful that such a document existed or that the people of Sparta were actually considered as descendants of Abraham. But this very exaggeration shows how it was customary for the bonds of friendship to be presented as based on very ancient kinship.

With Herodotus' account of the birth of Etruria as a colony founded by the son of the Lydian king Atys, we are probably dealing with a development of this kind, with elements borrowed from the Greek world – stories of sending colonies, a tradition on the origin of games – to assert a relationship between Etruscans and Lydians. Construction as refined as this (going far beyond the simple assertion that Lydos and Torebos were brothers, as in the fragment of Xanthos quoted by Dionysius) is reminiscent of the atmosphere in the court of kings like the Mermnadai, such as Croesus, who had pursued an active diplomacy. It is probably in such a setting that such a story could be born, to reflect the good relations established between Lydia and the Tyrrhenian world. But we must admit that we can go no further in the analysis of this tradition, since it may refer not to the Etruscans of Italy but to the Tyrrhenians who were established in the islands of the Aegean. We must acknowledge our inability to determine more precisely how such a tradition of *syngeneia* could have been created: but that Herodotus' account falls into this category is not in doubt.

In any event, such a narrative, in itself, cannot be regarded as reflecting an ancient historical tradition based on memories of real events. The assertion of a relationship between Jews and Spartans shows that such statements could be completely artificial. But we cannot exclude it either: it is permissible to imagine that in building such a story, those who developed it would have remembered ancient population movements between the Aegean area and the Italian peninsula. However, the composition presented by Herodotus must be judged for what it is, a scholarly development of various elements around the idea of a kinship between Etruscans and Lydians. Whether or not it meets a historical reality cannot be inferred.

With the tradition of the Lydian origin, we are quite far from the Etruscan world itself. We are dealing with a Lydian story and can recognize what is explained in a Lydian context – what this text teaches us about the Etruscans themselves is reduced to very little: they are related to Umbrians, presented as their predecessors in the country they inhabit, and they developed an urban civilization, being organized in cities. But the last tradition we have to consider, that of the Pelasgian origin of the Etruscans, places us in a significantly different context: this time the place of the Etruscans in the shaping of the doctrine can be clearly defined, as well as the function of a story like the one in the fragment of Hellanicus preserved by Dionysius (1.28.3), cited from the *Phoronis*:

> Phrastor was the son of Pelasgus, their king, and Menippe, the daughter of Peneus; his son was Amyntor, Amyntor's son was Teutamides, and the later son was Nanas. In his reign the Pelasgians were driven out of their country by the Greeks, and after leaving their ships on the river Spines in the Ionian Gulf, they took Croton, an inland city; and proceeding from there, they colonized the country now called Tyrrhenia.

As in the legend of the Lydian Tyrrhenos, the origin of the Etruscans is linked to a hero who led the migration of the first representatives of the nation into Italy. But this time it is not an acronym, but a personage, Nanas, whose name, we shall see, refers to local data. Like the Tyrrhenos of Herodotus, it is he who causes the appearance of the name of the Etruscans and its substitution for the former ethnic group. In this tradition, this group consists of Pelasgians – and we find their eponymous source, because Nanas descends from Pelasgos in the fourth generation. He is a Pelasgian, it is to him that the formation of the Etruscan *ethnos* is attributed, he is the progeny of Pelasgos: we can still ascribe this tradition to the *syngeneia* legend, because it establishes a genealogical link between Pelasgos who represents the Pelasgians and Nanas who is responsible for the birth of the Etruscans.

This Pelasgos is linked to a Thessalian context. His father, Peneus, husband of Menippe, is a river god, personifying the Peneios that flows in this region. It is also in Thessaly that one must view the eviction of the Pelasgians and their replacement by the Greeks. Another presentation of the vicissitudes of the establishment of the first Greeks in Hellas in historical times, as related by Dionysius (1.17.3), states that after the arrival of Pelasgos in Thessaly, the Pelasgians had lived there for five generations (which corresponds to the computation of Hellanicus if one counts Pelasgos) before being driven out by Deucalion, who we know was considered the common ancestor of all the Greeks through his son the eponymous Hellen, and his grandsons Doros, Aiolos and Xuthus, the last having begotten Athis and Ion. But Pelasgos is not the only hero known by that name: and Dionysius, in the preceding passage (1.17.2), had spoken of a first Pelasgos, son of Zeus and Niobe daughter of Phoroneus, who had lived in Argos in the Peloponnese before his descendant in the sixth generation, another Pelasgos, this time given as the son of Poseidon and Larissa, who corresponds to the Pelasgos evoked by Hellanicus, and who made the decision to emigrate to Thessaly. These complex genealogical constructions (which Hellanicus published according to an ancient form of historiography built around genealogies of heroes, represented by writers like Acousilaos of Argos or Pherecydes of Athens)[28] were necessitated by the fact that the Pelasgian traditions were widespread in several regions of Greece – especially in Thessaly and the Argolid – and therefore several figures of an eponymous Pelasgos were created, between whom he had to imagine bonds of kinship.[29]

This tradition then made the ancient Pelasgians into the Etruscans. While preserving the fact that, linguistically, the Etruscans were barbarians it thus connected them with a people whom the Greeks represented as having been established on the soil of Hellas even before themselves and constituting the source of several Hellenic populations of later times (especially the Athenians, presented by Herodotus 1.56, as the finest example of a Greek people descended from the Pelasgians). Prior to the Greeks, Pelasgians could only be "barbarophones," as Herodotus concluded after a survey of Pelasgian populations extant in his time, including the inhabitants of Placia and Scylace on the Hellespont (1.57) – an investigation fortunately conducted not by him but by his predecessor Hecataeus of Miletus and followed up in his *Survey*.[30] He well understood an aspect that would be a positive in the eyes of the Greeks: being of Pelasgian origin, the Etruscans could be perceived, if not as Greeks in the strict sense (because they did not speak Greek), at least as related to a people with whom the Greeks were linked. In short, considered as ancient Pelasgians, the Etruscans were quasi-Hellenes.

This Pelasgian definition of Etruscans could only have positive consequences as regards the Greeks. Yet it is remarkable that, alone among barbarians, two Etruscan cities, Spina on the Adriatic and Caere on the Tyrrhenian Sea, were afforded the great privilege of building a treasury in the pan-Hellenic sanctuary of Delphi. It is thought that Spina and Caere had to take advantage of their Pelasgic origin: it is surely no coincidence that it is mainly around these two cities (and also Cortona) that traditions about the Pelasgians were developed.[31] It is no coincidence either that, around the time that Hellanicus developed the tradition of the Pelasgian origin of the Etruscans (fifth century BC), and probably already at the end of the previous century, with Hecataeus of Miletus who seems to have been the first to report this doctrine,[32] these two Etruscan cities were centers of active trade with the Greek world. They presented themselves as founded by the Pelasgians, highlighted their *syngeneia* with this nearly Hellenic people, and conferred on themselves a prestigious foundation for the bonds of exchange and commercial partnership which united the Spinetans, Caerites and Greeks.

It is probably the Pelasgian doctrine, as in the fragment of the *Phoronis* of Hellanicus, which best makes us feel the affirmation of a tradition of *syngeneia* about the Etruscans. In the text of Hellanicus the reference to Pelasgians – and specifically the Pelasgians of Thessaly – who were known to have occupied the soil of Greece before the Greeks themselves and who were therefore believed to have gone elsewhere, definitely serves to link people who do not speak Greek but are important to the Greeks as were the Pelasgians and the Etruscans, these barbarians with whom the Greeks of the sixth to fifth centuries BC had established successful trade relationships. This is not scientific inquiry about the identity of a people.

A detail of the text of Hellanicus also enables us to guess how the surviving narrative was developed by Dionysius of Halicarnassus.[33] The place where the Pelasgians disembarked was defined by the fifth-century historian as the Spinetic mouth of the Po. More explicitly, Dionysius, taking the legend, will present the city of Spina as a Pelasgian foundation (1.18.3–5). In other words, the Pelasgians were well placed, just as the ancestors of the Etruscans were – specifically related to historical Spina the Etruscan city on the Adriatic at the time that the Po valley was being developed between the late sixth century and the beginning of fourth century BC – to promote exchange between Etruscans and Greeks in the Adriatic Sea. It is suggested that the people of Spina were precisely the source of the tradition transmitted by Hellanicus.

Spina was a city inhabited by Greeks as well as Etruscans, although the authority was certainly exercised by the Etruscan element,[34] which clearly made its mark on the narrative of Hellanicus. The beginning of Hellanicus' text, with the genealogy of the Pelasgian rulers of Thessaly descended from Pelasgos, is purely Greek. Phrastor and Amyntor, whom we do not otherwise know, bear Greek names, formed with the suffix-of-agent nouns, *-tor* added to the verbs *amuno*, "I forbid," and *phrazo*, "I explain," meaning "defender" and "indicator." As for the name of Teutamides, it is a loan from Homer, describing in *Iliad* (2.840–843) the quota of Pelasgians who came to aid the Trojans, defined as "living in the fertile Larissa;" Homer described as "Teutamid" two leaders, Hippothous and Pylaios the son of Lethos. This is where we find a Teutamid, associated with Larissa in Thessaly, although it is absurd to make an individual name of what was a family name, a patronymic "son of Teutamos."[35] But the name that follows, Nanas, introduces us to a completely different context, this time Etruscan.

This Nanas, who led the migration of Pelasgians from Thessaly to Italy, is cited in relation to the town of Cortona, in north-eastern Tuscany which he reached by crossing the Apennines from Spina; he made it his base for conquering the whole of Tuscany.

This city appears to be the capital of Etruria, the center of the *dodecapolis*. Now, we know another tradition that plays a special role in relation to a character presented as established in Cortona and with a name very similar to that of Hellanicus' Pelasgian king, Nanos. This Nanos is mentioned in a passage of Lycophron's *Alexandra* (1242–1244), who said that Odysseus died among the Etruscans, at "Gortynaia," that is to say, in Cortona (805–806). These allusions by Lycophron are illuminated by his scholiasts, where we learn that Nanos was the name given by the Etruscans to Ulysses when, according to certain versions, he returned to Italy.[36] It is noted that this Ulysses-Nanos would have settled in the same town of Cortona as the Pelasgian-Nanas: it appears that we are dealing with two avatars of the same local legend, rotating about a local hero of Cortona bearing a name of the type Nana/Nanos.

Another tradition, more recent, specifies the background of these "Cortonan" legendary developments. In the Augustan age, Virgil in the *Aeneid* resumed a tradition of Etruscan origin implying that Dardanus, the ancestor of Aeneas, came to the Troad from a city of Corythus, which we recognize as Cortona: the journey of a Trojan hero to Italy appears to be the return to the home of his ancestors.[37] Commentators on Virgil suggest, however, that this Corythus was linked to a mountain, where his tomb would have been.[38] But for Ulysses-Nanos there is also a question of a tomb located on a mountain: Lycophron (805–806) recounted that "after his death, Perga, a mountain in the country of the Tyrrhenians, welcomed him, reduced to ash, to Gortynaia." So we assume the existence of a local hero, whose tomb, located on high ground near the Etruscan city, was in the course of history identified with different figures of Greek myth: Nanos the Pelasgian around the sixth/fifth century BC, the time of Hecataeus and Hellanicus, Ulysses, as the Etruscan Nanos in the fourth/third century BC, the time of Theopompus and Lycophron, and Corythus, the ancestor of Aeneas, in Virgil's time. There have thus been several interpretations of the same legendary local hero, the traditions associated with various ways of relating him to the Greek world. But it is basically the same local reality: the existence of a tomb of a character considered very important for the history of the city, which was probably the object of worship by its inhabitants. We have discovered a reality similar to that in the excavations of the heröon of Aeneas at Lavinium, described by Dionysius (1.64.5), which was originally the tomb of a Latin chief of the early seventh century BC before becoming a cult-place during the sixth century BC, probably for the mysterious figure of *Pater Indiges* even before it was identified with Aeneas.[39]

Why do we find this tradition of the Pelasgian Nanas, developed in the atmosphere of Greco-Etruscan Spina, attached to Cortona? We must consider that the Etruscans – who are behind the development of Etruria in the Po Valley in the late sixth century BC, transforming the old Villanovan culture maintained in Bologna and giving birth to new cities, colonial foundations of regular grid-plan, such as Marzabotto and Spina – came primarily from north-eastern Tuscany, the region of Chiusi, Perugia, Arezzo: a group of cities which formed a sort of triangle around the religious centre of Cortona. So they were traditions of this area where Cortona was viewed as the ancient metropolis of the whole of Tuscany, the city from which the other cities of the *dodecapolis* were founded – the same way that, for residents of the southern part of Etruria, Tarquinia, the city of Tarchon, played the role of metropolis, a city that gave birth to the eleven other members of the Etruscan federation. By inserting the Cortonan Nanos into the history of Pelasgian migration to Italy, the Spinetans, who had made theirs the port of arrival on Italian soil of the Pelasgian ancestors of the Etruscans, had integrated this relationship with a people linked to Greece with a truly Etruscan tradition, about the formation of the federation of the twelve cities, which they shared with the inhabitants of north-eastern Tuscany.

The text of Hellanicus that was handed down to us by Dionysius (who presumably reprised a presentation of the birth of Etruria already in Hecataeus) shows that the Etruscans, and specifically those of Spina, have used this form of tradition to clothe in a prestigious prehistory the intense commercial ties that bound them to their Hellenic partners. Again, this type of discourse on Etruscan origins was not neutral: it takes advantage of Pelasgian ancestry to give them an image entirely favorable in the eyes of the Greeks. Once again we are far from purely scientific concerns. The assertion that the Pelasgians were their ancestors had a propaganda value and made these barbarians – and the Etruscans indisputably were barbarians – appear Greek.

Indeed, the positive direction for the Greeks in the reference to Pelasgians, if clearly reflected in the shaping of the tradition we know from Hellanicus, does not explain the primary reason for the identification of Etruscans with Pelasgians. To understand its appeal, one must entertain other considerations. But one area where we admit the existence of Pelasgians in Antiquity was the Aegean, with its islands – especially those in the north, such as Samothrace – whose mysteries were attributed to this ancient population. But this region had also been the theatre of the Tyrrhenian pirates, whose depredations had left a lasting impression in the memories of Greeks and were illustrated by famous episodes, such as the metamorphosis into dolphins of pirates who had attacked the ship carrying Dionysus to Samos or the abduction of girls participating in the Athenian cult of Artemis at Brauron.[40] Those whom the Greeks called the Tyrrhenians had occupied some islands in the northern Aegean Sea, especially Lemnos, where the famous inscription found in Kaminia in 1887 revealed that they spoke a language very close to the Etruscan attested in Italy. Whichever way one explains the presence of these cousins of the Etruscans in the Aegean Sea, an issue that does not concern us directly here,[41] we may think that this establishing of Tyrrhenians in an area where the Pelasgians had once been known led to the identification of the two ethnic concepts.[42] And it is therefore in all probability, that the Greeks were able to identify the Tyrrhenians-Etruscans with the Pelasgians, before this relationship, rewarding for them, was taken over by the Etruscans themselves, especially the Etruscans of Spina, but probably also those of other regions, including Caere, a Pelasgian city where tradition has been particularly lively.[43]

Thus, initially, the identification of the Etruscans with Pelasgians would have resulted from an intellectual process noted in an article by E. Bickermann who has shown its importance for the ethnographic representations of the Greeks.[44] Faced with a non-Greek, and thus barbaric, population, they posed the question of identity in terms of origin and, to account for these *origines gentium* – to borrow from the title of Bickermann's article – they tended to use their own representations, attaching them to the vast repertoire of their own traditions involving heroes or Hellenic peoples. This is what must have happened in the case of the Pelasgians: the assimilation of the two ethnic concepts probably has not been the deed of the Etruscans. But they nonetheless played a part in awarding a certificate for virtual Hellenism that could only facilitate their profitable trade relations with the Greeks. Of course, it is difficult to assume that such constructions have had any historical foundation.

In fact this impression of a problem that does not meet scientific concerns really seems to characterize the set of doctrines that had been advanced in Antiquity on the question of Etruscan origins. Even when the authors seem to have approached this question with the detachment and objectivity of the scientist, as with Dionysius of Halicarnassus, it appears that they were responding to other purposes and sought above all to give a picture that could be either positive (with Lydian and Pelasgian theses) or unfavorable, at least from a Greek viewpoint (with the autochthonist thesis). One can probably not totally dismiss the idea that some proper historical memories may have survived through the texts of ancient authors who have discussed this issue (the followers of the Eastern origin of Etruscans believe that the passage of Herodotus in which the Lydians came to Italy could have retained the memory of an ancient population movement between the eastern basin of the Mediterranean and the Italian peninsula). But in any case where these possible historical memories have been fully taken up and integrated in reworked accounts, they are clearly artificial. Whether for the autochthonist thesis, or that identifying the Etruscans with the Pelasgians, or that they derived from Lydian colonists, their primary function was to account for the connections that existed at the time when these traditions were disseminated between the historical Etruscans and the Greeks. The meaning of a doctrine such as this, making the Etruscans natives of Italy, carried the corollary that they were mere Italian barbarians and were unrelated to Hellenism and its values: we recognize a development by hostile Greeks, probably the Syracusans at the time of their struggles against the Etruscans. The other two doctrines were rather favorable presentations: whether that of the Lydian origin, a typical assertion of *syngeneia* between the Lydians and Etruscans, responding to a kind of narrative power in Antiquity, to which it would be dangerous to assign any historical basis; or that of the Pelasgian origin, identifying the Etruscans as a barbarous people certainly, but one who played an important role in how the Greeks represented their own past. With all this we are far from scientific discourse.

But one cannot fail to be struck by the fact that when the debate was taken up by those who, in modern times, have addressed the issue of the formation of the Etruscan people, it was in the same terms that Massimo Pallottino clearly emphasized in his 1947 book *L'origine degli Etruschi*, that they continued to debate the origins of the Etruscans by contrasting different theories. We owe to this great Italian scholar the awareness that such a debate is insufficient: we cannot reduce a people to a single origin to account for all they have been in history. Every people has been the result of a melting pot, formed by the superposition and mixing of diverse elements. Any attempt to explain in terms of origin is historically simplistic and wrong. But if Etruscologists of modern times have so long strayed into a dead-end and reductionist debate, it is probably because it is the same debate that was conducted in Antiquity. It is important to understand that this ancient debate, which lasted to modern times, responded to issues other than those of pure science.

NOTES

1   The great Italian Etruscologist (1909–1995) dedicated a special work to the question, published in Rome in 1947: *L'origine degli Etruschi*. One may find in Pallottino's handbook, *Etruscologia*, a clear treatment of the problems, theories, and scholars who discussed them (1st ed., 1942, followed by new editions in 1947, 1953, 1957, 1963, 1968, 1984). See, in the final edition, Pallottino 1984: 81–117.

2   For a favorable appreciation of Dionysius as an Etruscologist, see, Pallottino 1947: 81–2, Altheim 1950: 68–9, Heurgon 1951, Hus 1980: 301.

3   There is nonetheless a problem concerning Dionysius' citation of Herodotus (1.57.3), that the language of the Pelasgians who inhabited Placia and Scylace, two towns on the Hellespont, was similar to that of the Crotoniates (and thus of the inhabitants of Cortona in north-west Tuscany); the manuscripts of Herodotus here do not name the Crotoniates, but the Crestoniates, of the city of Crestone in the Chalchidice. Scholars are divided on whether to follow the Herodotean manuscript tradition and view – that of Dionysius as incorrect – or to follow Dionysius and think that Herodotus wanted to establish a link between the people of the two little Hellespont towns and the Etruscan city. On this subject, see Briquel 1984:104–10 (and 101–68 for the place of Cortona in the tradition of a Pelasgian origin of the Etruscans).

4   Here and hereafter, quoting the *Loeb Classical Text* in the translation by E. Cary (1937–1950).

5   This version does not exactly conform to that in Herodotus 1.94. It concerns a pair of brothers: Lydos who remains at home and gives his name to the country until then called Maeonia, and Tyrrhenos, who departs to found Etruria. Herodotus only mentions that Tyrrhenos is son of Atys, and does not name any brother Lydos. It seems that in the Hellenistic period, the theory of the Lydian origin of the Etruscans was expanded in this version and referred to Herodotus, in somewhat modified form (which I have called the "Herodotean Vulgate," see Briquel 1991: 91–123).

6   On this version of the legend see Briquel 1991: 138–54.

7   On this tradition see Briquel 1984: 278–92, Gras 1985: 590–615.

8   On the thesis that Latin ought to be an Aeolian Greek dialect, Collart 1954: 215–18, see Gabba 1963, Briquel 1984: 444–53.

9   On the historical work of Dionysius and the meaning of his demonstration, refer to Gabba 1991.

10   On the issues of viewing Rome as either a Greek or an Etruscan city see Vanotti 1999.

11   This meaning of Etruscan autochthony in the work of Dionysius was masterfully treated by Musti 1970. It was disputed by Gabba 1991:104–105: such a negative ethnic perception of the Etruscans is incompatible with their role in the history of Italy, as shown by the fact the Dionysius had planned to write a book especially on the lofty deeds of this people (1.30.4: "In another book, I shall show what cities the Tyrrhenians founded, what forms of government they established, how great power they acquired, what memorable achievements they performed, and what fortunes attended them").

12   The attribution of Etruscan autochthony that made barbarians of them cannot be regarded in the same way as Athenian authochthony (on which see, in part, Montanari 1979–1981, Loraux 1981a, 1981b): for the inhabitants of Attica, literally born from the soil of Greece, an authochthonous origin is obviously positive.

13   This thesis, somewhat expanded, is presented by Micali 1832: 97–9, De Sanctis 1907: 128, Pareti 1926: 13, Pallottino 1947: 48, Torelli 1986: 18, Gabba 1991: 113, n. 42.

14   On this question, see in part Cristofani 1983, 1989, Giuffrida Ientile 1983, Gras 1985. For developments in the Adriatic, Braccesi 1971, 1977, 2004.

15   References in Briquel 1984: 196–201.

16   For a more detailed study of the question see Briquel 1993.

17   On the diffusion of the Lydian thesis at this time, Briquel 1991: 479–88. It appears, at least by allusion, in Cato, the Pseudo-Scymnos, Cicero, Catullus, Virgil, Ovid, Strabo, Verrius Flaccus, Valerius Maximus, Velleius Paterculus, Seneca, Silius Italicus, Pliny the Elder, Tacitus, Statius, Plutarch, Pollux, Appian, Tertullian, Justin, Festus, Hyginus the Fabelist, Solinus, Servius, Rutilius Namatianus, Isidore of Seville.

18   Quoted here in the translation of A. D. Godley, *Herodotus* vol. 1 : 123–24 (Loeb Classical Library, Cambridge, MA, 1920, revised 1926, 1966).

19   See Pareti 1926: 60. The idea was reprised in Pallottino 1947: 44, Sakellariou 1958: 71.

20   On this tradition, Briquel 1991: 47–9.

21 On the importance of the theme of the first inventor in Greece, Kleingünther 1933, Thraede 1962.
22 For references on Atys and Manes see Briquel 1991: 15–31.
23 References on these different traditions in Briquel 1991: 51–4 (Rhegion and Cyrene), 56–7 (Magnesia on the Meander), 54–65 (Mysians).
24 Xanthos, cited by Dionysius, 1.28.2: "He says that Lydus and Torebus were the sons of Atys; that they, having divided the kingdom they had inherited from their father, both remained in Asia, and from them the nations over which they reigned received their names. His words are these: 'From Lydus are sprung the Lydians, and from Torebus the Torebians. There is little difference in their language and even now each nation scoffs at many words used by the other, even as do the Ionians and Dorians.'" On the Torebians see Briquel 1991: 25–31.
25 Herodotus, 1.171: "There is an ancient temple of Carian Zeus at Mylasa, in which the Mysians and Lydians share as being brother races of the Carians, for they say that Lydos and Mysos were brothers of Car; these share in it, but those who being of another race have come to speak the same language as the Carians, these have no share in it."
26 On this notion, Musti 1963, Curty 1995.
27 The catalogue established by Curty (1995) lists 88 epigraphic documents citing decrees relating the ancestry of peoples or cities.
28 See Mazzarino 1966: 58–70 (Acousilaos), 75–9 (Hecataeus), von Fritz 1967: 65–71, Grant 1970: 15–9.
29 For an accessible analysis of the Pelasgian traditions see Lochner-Hüttenbach 1960.
30 On the Hecataean origin of this passage in Herodotus see Briquel 1984: 130–3.
31 See Briquel 1984: 3–30 (Spina), 169–224 (Caere).
32 Because the doctrine, in the form we know from Hellanicus and with a special role attributed to Cortona (and Spina) was already known to Hecataeus, see Briquel 1984: 125–6, 135–6, 144–5.
33 We are not necessarily dealing with the first version which links the Etruscans and Pelasgians, see below.
34 On Spina, see Berti, Guzzo 1994 and Rebecchi 1998.
35 See Briquel 1984: 145–9.
36 For more details, see Briquel 1984: 150–60.
37 On this legend and its Etruscan origin see Colonna 1983.
38 See Servius and his interpolator, commentary on Virgil, *Aeneid* 3.167, 170, 7.209, 10.719. Complete data and discussion in Briquel 1984: 161–5.
39 On the excavation at Lavinium, Castagnoli *et al.*, 1972, 1975; on the heröon of Aeneas, Sommella 1971–1972, Sommella, Giuliani 1977, Giuliani 1981.
   On the timing of the identification of the recipient of the monument with Aeneas, (and assuming a stage where it would have been considered Latinus, son of Ulysses and Circe), see Cogrossi 1982, Grandazzi 1988. On the important category of figures of legendary "fathers" attached to numerous Italian populations (known in a *Pater* for Pyrgi, Alba Fucens, Sabina, Reate, besides the Sardinian *Sardus Pater*), in which you must certainly place the Latin *Pater Indiges*, a synthesis is unfortunately lacking. For comparison of the evidence from Lavinium and the case of Nanas/Nanos/Corythus at Cortona, Briquel 1984: 166–7.
40 On the question of Tyrrhenians of the Aegean, in addition to the works cited in note 13, see Torelli 1974, Gras 1976, C. De Simone 1996.
41 Proponents of each of the ideas about the origins of the Etruscans were able to account for the presence of Tyrrhenians in the Aegean as part of their vision of the origins of this people. At the time of its discovery, Kaminia was used to support the thesis of Oriental origin, as evidence of a group related to the Etruscans who had remained behind when the Etruscans departed from Asia Minor for Italy. Other scholars, based on the autochthonist thesis, believed that there had to be the remnants of two related groups dating back to a pre-Indo-European

substrate who managed to stay on in two different areas of the Mediterranean (M. Pallottino), or, later, as the result of a movement of Etruscan pirates who settled in the Aegean in the early historic period (M. Gras, C. De Simone).

42   For a more detailed study see Briquel 2000.

43   Evidence in Briquel 1984: 169–224.

44   See Bickermann 1952.

BIBLIOGRAPHY

Altheim, F. (1950) *Der Ursprung der Etrusker*, Baden-Baden: Verlag für Kunst und Wissenschaft.

Berti, F. and Guzzo P. G. (eds) (1993) *Spina. Storia di una città tra Greci ed Etruschi. Catalogo della mostra, Ferrara, Castello Estense, 26 settembre 1993–15 maggio 1994*, Ferrara: Maurizio Tosi Editore.

Bickermann, E. J. (1952) "Origines gentium," *Classical Philology*, 47: 65–81; reprinted in *Religions and Politics in the Hellenistic and Roman Periods* (1985), Como: Edizioni New Press, 399–417.

Braccesi, L. (1971; 2nd edn 1977) *Grecità adriatica. Un capitolo della colonizzazione greca in Occidente*, Bologna: Pàtron.

Braccesi, L. (ed.) (2004) *La pirateria nell'Adriatico antico*, Hesperìa 19, Rome: "L'Erma" di Bretschneider.

Briquel, D. (1984) *Les Pélasges en Italie. Recherches sur l'histoire de la légende*, Bibliothèque des Écoles Françaises d'Athènes et de Rome 252, Rome: École Française de Rome.

——(1991) *L'origine lydienne des l'Étrusques. Histoire de la doctrine dans l'Antiquité*, Collection de l'École Française de Rome 139, Rome: École Française de Rome.

——(1993) *Les Tyrrhènes, peuple des tours, l'autochtonie des Étrusques chez Denys d'Halicarnasse*, Collection de l'École Française de Rome 178, Rome: École Française de Rome.

——(2000) "Pélasges et Tyrrhènes en zone égéenne" in F. Prayon and W. Röllig (eds) *Akten des Kolloquiums zum Thema Der Orient und Etrurien. Zum Phänomen des "Orientalisierens" im westlichen Mittelmeerraum (10.-6. Jh. V. Chr., Tübingen, 12.-13. Juni 1997*, Biblioteca di « Studi Etruschi » 35, Pisa-Rome: Istituti editoriali e poligrafici internazionali, 19–36.

Cary, E. (1937–1950) *Dionysius of Halicarnassus. Roman Antiquities* (vols. I–VII), Cambridge, MA: Harvard University Press (Loeb Classical Library).

Castagnoli, F. *et al.* (1972) *Lavinium, I. Topografia generale, fonti e storia delle ricerche*, Rome: De Luca.

——(1975) *Lavinium, II. Le tredici are*, Rome: De Luca.

Cogrossi, C. (1982) "Atena Iliaca e il culto degli eroi, l'heroon di Enea a Lavinio e Latino, figlio di Odisseo," *Contributi dell'Istituto di Storia Antica*, 18: 79–88.

Collart, J. (1954) *Varron, grammairien latin*, Paris: Les Belles Lettres.

Colonna, G. (1983) "Virgilio, Cortona e la leggenda etrusca di Dardano," *Archeologia Classica*, 32, 1980 (but 1983): 1–14; reprinted in *Italia ante Romanum Imperium. Scritti di antichità etrusche, italiche e romane (1958–1998)*, (2005), Pisa-Rome: Istituti editoriali e poligrafici internazionali, I, 189–200.

Cristofani, M. (1983; 2nd edn 1989) *Gli Etruschi del mare*, Milan: Longanesi.

Curty, O. (1995) *Les parentés légendaires entre cités grecques*, Hautes études du monde gréco-romain 20, Genève: Droz.

De Sanctis, G. (1907) *Storia dei Romani*, I, Turin: Fratelli Bocca.

De Simone, C. (1996) *I Tirreni a Lemnos. Evidenza linguistica e tradizioni storiche*, Biblioteca di « Studi Etruschi », Florence: Leo S. Olschki Editore.

Fraschetti, A. (1989) "Eraclide Pontico e Roma 'città greca'," in A. C. Cassio and D. Musti (eds) *Tra Sicilia e Magna Grecia. Aspetti di interazione culturale nel IV sec. a.C., Atti del Convegno, Napoli, 19–20 marzo 1987*, Annali dell'Istituto Universitario Orientale di Napoli, Dipartimento di Studi del Mondo Classico e del Mediterraneo Antico, Sezione filologico-letteraria 11, Rome: Edizioni dell'Ateneo, 81–95.

Fritz, K. von (1967) *Die griechische Geschichtschreibung*, Berlin: de Gruyter.

Gabba, E. (1963) "Il latino come dialetto Greco" in *Studi alessandrini in memoria di Augusto Rostagni*, Turin: Bottega d'Erasmo, 188–94.

——(1991) *Dionysius and the History of Archaic Rome*, Sather Classical Lectures 56, Berkeley – Los Angeles – Oxford: University of California Press.

Giuffrida Ientile, M. (1983) *La pirateria tirrenica, momenti e fortuna*, Supplementi a Kôkalos 6, Rome: Giorgio Bretschneider Editore.

Giuliani, C. F. (1981) "Santuario delle tredici are, heroon di Enea" in *Enea nel Lazio, archeologia e mito. Catalogo della mostra, Roma, 22 settembre–31 dicembre 1981, Campidoglio, Palazzo dei Conservatori*, Rom: Fratelli Palombi Editori, 169–77.

Grandazzi, A. (1988) "Le roi Latinus: analyse d'une figure légendaire," *Comptes Rendus de l'Académie des Inscriptions et Belles-Lettres*: 481–497.

Grant, M. (1970) *The Ancient Historians*, London: Weidenfeld and Nicolson.

Gras, M. (1976) "La piraterie tyrrhénienne en mer Égée, mythe ou réalité?" in *Mélanges offerts à Jacques Heurgon. L'Italie préromaine et la Rome républicaine*, Collection de l'École Française de Rome 27, Rome: École Française de Rome, 341–70.

——(1985) *Trafics tyrrhéniens archaïques*, Bibliothèque des Écoles Françaises d'Athènes et de Rome 258, Rome: École Française de Rome.

Heurgon, J. (1951) "Les pénestes étrusques chez Denys d'Halicarnasse (IX, 54)," *Latomus*, 18: 713–23; reprinted in *Scripta varia*, Collection Latomus 191 (1986), Bruxelles: éditions Latomus, 313–22.

Hus, A. (1980) *Les Étrusques et leur destin*, Paris: Picard.

Kleingünther, A. (1933) *Prôtos Heuretès, Untersuchungen zur Geschichte einer Fragestellung*, *Philologus* Suppl. 26, 1, Berlin: Akademie Verlag.

Lochner-Hüttenbach, F. (1960) *Die Pelasger*, Arbeiten aus dem Institut für vergleichende Sprachwissenschaft in Graz 6, Vienna: Gerold.

Loraux, N. (1981a) *L'invention d'Athènes: histoire de l'oraison funèbre dans la "cité classique,"* Paris: Mouton.

——(1981b) *Les enfants d'Athéna: idées athéniennes sur la citoyenneté et la division des sexes*, Paris: Maspero.

Mazzarino, S. (1966) *Il pensiero storico classico*, Rome-Bari, 1966: Laterza.

Micali, G. (1832) *Storia degli antichi popoli italiani*, Florence: Tipografia all'insegna di Dante.

Montanari, E. (1981) *Il mito dell'autoctonia: linee di una dinamica mitico-politica ateniese*, Rome: Agra, 2nd edn, Rome: Bulzoni.

Musti, D. (1963) "Sull'idea di *suggeneia* in iscrizion greche," *Annali della Scuola Normale Superiore di Pisa*, 32: 225–39.

Musti, D. (1970) *Tendenze nella storiografia romana e greca su Roma arcaica. Studi su Livio e Dionigi d'Alicarnasso*, Quaderni Urbinati di Cultura Classica 10, Rome: Edizioni dell'Ateneo.

Pallottino, M. (1947) *L'origine degli Etruschi*, Rome: Tumminelli.

——(1984), *Etruscologia*, 7th edn, Milan: Hoepli.

Pareti, L. (1926) *Le origini etrusche*, Florence, 1926: R. Bemporad e figlio.

Rebecchi, F. (ed.) (1998) *Spina e il delta padano, Atti del convegno "Spina : due civiltà a confront," Ferrara, Aula Magna dell'Università, 21 gennaio 1994*, Rome: "L'Erma" di Bretschneider.

Sakellariou, M. B. (1958) *La migration grecque en Ionie*, Collection de l'Institut Français d'Athènes 17, Athens: Institut Français d'Athènes.

Sommella, P. (1971–1972) "Heroon di Enea a Lavinium, recenti scavi a Pratica di Mare," *Rendiconti della Pontificia Accademia Romana di Archeologia*, 44: 47–74.

Sommella, P. and Giuliani, C. F. (1977) "Lavinium, compendio dei documenti archeologici," *Parola del Passato*, 32: 356–72.

Thraede, K. (1962) "Das Lob des Erfinders. Bemerkungen zur Analyse der Hereumata-Kataloge," *Rheinisches Museum*, 105: 158–86.

Torelli, M. (1974) "TYPPANOI," *Parola del Passato* 30: 417–33.

Torelli, M. (1986) "La storia" in *Rasenna, storia e civiltà degli Etruschi*, coll. Antica Madre, Milan: Libri Scheiwiller, Credito Italiano.

Vanotti, G. (1999) "Roma polis Hellenis, Roma polis Tyrrhenis," *Mélanges de l'École Française de Rome (Antiquité)*, 111: 217–55.

CHAPTER FOUR

FLESHING OUT THE
DEMOGRAPHY OF ETRURIA

———•◆•———

Geof Kron

The analysis of skeletal remains offers extremely important evidence for health, nutrition and changes in economic development and social equality, particularly for poorly documented civilizations, such as that of the Etruscans. Interpreting Etruscan physical anthropology is difficult, and we can only give a brief and tentative preliminary sketch at this stage of research, given the limited number of comprehensive anthropometric studies using the best methods; nevertheless, enough evidence exists to suggest that the Etruscans enjoyed an overall level of health and nutrition notably superior to that of the working classes of nineteenth-century Europe. This is true for most Greco-Roman populations from the late Archaic and Classical periods through the Roman republic and empire (Kron 2005), but the Etruscan diet, like that of many Classical and Hellenistic Greeks (Kron 2005: 72), seems, for the most part, to have been perceptibly better than that of the population of later Roman Italy.

Classical archaeologists have traditionally concentrated relatively little upon the techniques of the "New Archaeology," most importantly for our purposes, the exploitation of zooarchaeology, archaeobotany and physical anthropology when excavating in Italy (see MacKinnon 2007 for an overview). Etruscan archaeology, however, was a relatively early and significant exception to this general rule. The controversy, which dates from Classical times and the competing accounts of Herodotus and Dionysius of Halicarnassus, over the extent of Eastern Aegean or Near Eastern influence on the origins of Etruscan culture inspired Italian physical anthropologists, dating back at least as far as the 1880s (Coppa *et al.* 1997: 99 note 2; see Chapters 2 and 3 in this book), with an intense interest in determining the relationship between the "ethnicity" or "race" of this enigmatic people, and that of the other cultural groups in Iron Age, Roman, and modern Italy (see Ward-Perkins 1959, Perkins 2009 for two eminently sensible accounts). This obsession on the part of physical anthropologists with identifying ethnic groups, which owed much to the influence upon early anthropometric research of eugenics and social Darwinism, continues to channel much research away from the estimation of stature using long-bone measurement, for example, which would clarify the diet and living standards of these populations, towards studies designed to elucidate ethnic relationships, particularly statistical morphological studies of skulls or teeth (see, most recently, Pacciani *et al.* 1996; Coppa *et al.* 1997; Rubini *et al.* 1997, 2007; Claasen and Wree 2004), now supplemented by genetic studies comparing ancient, often Etruscan, and modern DNA (Vernesi *et al.* 2004a; Levy-Coffman 2005; Belle *et al.* 2006; Achilli *et al.* 2007). Although DNA has been used, for example, to identify the sex of poorly preserved skeletal remains (Vernesi *et al.* 1997; Vernesi 1999) or to show that bodies in a particular tomb group are genetically related and may represent a single family group (Cappellini *et al.* 2004), the most ambitious aim of ancient genetic studies has been the drive to clarify the geographic or ethnic origin of population groups. To this point, the results remain highly controversial, if not entirely unconvincing (Perkins 2009), and have arguably been deeply undermined by the failure to integrate archaeological, historical and ancient DNA evidence into the interpretation of the modern genetic material, which, while certainly more abundant, may not provide convincing evidence for population dynamics a few centuries ago in the Paleolithic or Neolithic, as is rather optimistically claimed (references in Simoni *et al.* 2000).

Some of the first large-scale studies of ancient DNA have focused upon the Etruscans, presumably inspired by the great appetite to clarify the origin of this mysterious people. They have revealed some dramatic discontinuities between Etruscan and modern Tuscan DNA profiles with some intriguing, if inconclusive, evidence of haplotypes rare in Europe, but not uncommon in modern Anatolia and the Middle East (Vernesi *et al.* 2004a; Belle *et al.* 2006; Achilli *et al.* 2007; Brisighelli *et al.* 2009). A number of scholars, most notably Hans-Jürgen Bandelt (Bandelt 2004; 2005; Gilbert *et al.* 2005), have charged that this Etruscan material, and much ancient DNA, present anomalies, which cast doubt on its authenticity, suggesting that it is likely to be contaminated or degraded by postmortem damage. On the other hand, the authors of this pilot Etruscan study claim that they used the most rigorous controls (Cooper and Poinar 2000), and, while there are a number of mutations which seem inconsistent with the results from much larger databases of modern genetic material, some of the incongruities are simple errors in reporting, and many of the nucleotides affected do seem to be prone to rapid mutation and need not invalidate the overall results (Vernesi *et al.* 2004b). Bayesian statistical tests of these Etruscan studies (Ligia and Rannala 2008) suggest that the anomalies are few and minor, and need not cast any doubt on the overall reliability of the results, and Vernesi and his co-authors are surely right to insist that we cannot assume that authentic ancient DNA studies may not yield results which seem surprising or inconsistent with what we know from contemporary material. Some extremely careful recent studies seem to give confidence that archaeological DNA samples can indeed yield reliable results. The analysis of Viking DNA from well-sealed contexts, for example, reveals haplotypes exceedingly rare in modern Scandinavian samples (Melchior *et al.* 2008), and significant discontinuities in ancient and modern genetic material can also be demonstrated for Iceland, Britain and the Netherlands (Guimares *et al.* 2009: 2164); whereas studies of ancient DNA from Iberians (Sampietro *et al.* 2005) and Sardinians (Ghirotto 2010), populations plausibly considered to have experienced limited immigration, reveal much greater consistency and continuity between ancient and modern genetic material. Until more studies of Italian material are completed, it will remain difficult to properly interpret these pioneering Etruscan studies, or to judge how typical they are of pre-Roman and Roman populations in Italy, but, as a recent study has shown (Guimares *et al.* 2009), the genetic material from samples in modern Tuscany seems entirely consistent with DNA from medieval sites. This suggests that the origin of the discontinuity lies sometime before 1000 AD, and most likely in the first millennium BC (see also Brisighelli *et al.* 2009 for a similar date). This is hardly surprising, for any number of reasons, most notably: 1) the dramatic expansion of Italian, and particularly Etruscan contacts with Greek, Phoenician and Carthaginian traders, artisans and colonists, in Italy and throughout the Mediterranean (Kracht 1991: 50–68, 80–5; Krinzinger 2000; Camporeale 2001: *passim*; Fletcher 2007; Bezecky 2008; Bourdin 2011); 2) the significant Etruscan import of chattel slaves from the Aegean and beyond, and the even more dramatic changes likely with the Roman conquest of Etruria and Italy; and 3) the expansion of the Roman hegemony (with its stimulus not only to the import of chattel slaves, but to the immigration of free *peregrini* from throughout the empire), continuing through the invasions of the Goths, Huns and Lombards (Heather 2009).

As Ward-Perkins, Perkins, Luraghi (2008) and also, more controversially, James (1999), emphasize, the late nineteenth and twentieth-century obsession with notions of race and ethnicity only confuses our reading of many ancient societies, given the relative willingness of the Greeks and Romans to accept people into their community based on shared political or cultural values, rather than ethnicity or direct descent (*pace* Isaac 2004), and their relative indifference to the notion of fixed ethnic groups based on kinship. One intriguing study (Coppa *et al.* 1998), for example, notes a great deal of homogeneity in morphological traits through much of Italy, including across the Apennines, and points out that the most important changes are in fact diachronic, presumably related to developments in lifestyle and culture. It is ultimately more helpful, therefore, particularly at this stage, to concentrate on social and cultural changes, and changes in diet, nutrition and health standards, if we want to exploit the evidence of physical anthropology in order to understand Etruscan society.

We face a number of challenges, however, in offering a full and up-to-date synthesis. Most of the important Etruscan necropoleis, such as those at Tarquinia, for example, have been thoroughly looted from Antiquity, leading to significant damage to the skeletal remains (Becker 2002: 691), moreover, since they have been relatively well-known and celebrated for centuries for their elaborate, well-appointed and often lavishly decorated tombs, many were poorly and unscientifically excavated decades or centuries ago, generally with limited attention to skeletal remains. Moreover, many anthropometric studies date from the beginnings of the science, and, at least until relatively recently, modern studies have, as we have already alluded, concentrated on morphological analyses of skulls and teeth, at times failing to consistently study or at least publish, and sometimes even to preserve, many long bones. A serious complication comes from the habit of many Italian physical anthropologists, through the 1970s and even the 1980s, and a few partisans of low-height estimates even today (Capasso 2001; for which cf. Becker 2003 and Lazer 2009: 182–3; Giannecchini and Moggi-Cecchi 2008: 290, Table 6) to favor using the less reliable and out of date Pearson and Manouvrier methods for estimating stature. Such methods may be adequate, perhaps, for some of the stunted populations of nineteenth century Western Europe, and for many very short Neolithic and early Bronze Age populations, but are likely to underestimate heights by 2–3 cm or more for taller Greco-Roman and Medieval populations, as has been confirmed by detailed studies using *in situ* measurements and the Fully-Pineau (1960) anatomical method (Bolsden 1984; Formicola 1993; Becker 1999b; Kron 2005: 79–81). Moreover, many not only use a range of methods to calculate stature, but also fail to publish the actual long bone lengths and other critical anthropometric data, which would allow stature and other data to be estimated by more reliable methods (Borgognini Tarli and Mazzotta 1986: 154). Finally, as is true of all but the most sophisticated of anthropological studies even today (e.g. Fox 2005), there is relatively little attention to standardization, quantification and careful contextualization, (or to the challenges of the "osteological paradox" (Wood *et al.* 1992), the potential of most anthropological samples, coming as they do from cemeteries, to misrepresent the health status of living populations), when analyzing possible indications of nutritional or health stress, such as linear enamel hypoplasia or LEH, Harris lines, cribra orbitalia or porotic hyperostosis, periostitis, caries, abscesses and ante-mortem tooth loss, arthritis and the like. Attempts are gradually being made to bring together and organize fairly large collections of Etruscan skeletal material (Coppa 1997: 21; cf. Becker *et al.* 2009), and a few significant synthetic articles, unfortunately now somewhat dated, cover certain important aspects of the data (Borgognini Tarli and Mazzotta 1986; Pacciani *et al.* 1996). Nevertheless, for the most part the Etruscan material is not nearly as well studied as the Roman, and this sketch must remain very broad and tentative, calling for significantly more up-to-date research, and more attention to skeletal remains in future excavations.

Although the stature evidence is arguably the most significant for our reading of Etruscan living standards, some of the data on other indicia of lifestyle, health and nutrition, while not yet studied in enough depth to allow clear conclusions to be drawn, do still deserve some brief discussion.

Archaeologists and physical anthropologists have collected and studied Etruscan teeth in some depth from a relatively early stage. Sophisticated gold and silver dental appliances have attracted considerable attention, and we have some good recent surveys of the evidence (Becker 1992a, 1995/1996; Bliquez 1996; Becker 1999, 2000). Roman literary sources, which suggested a medical use for such appliances, anchoring false teeth, rather than a cosmetic one, have been questioned (Becker 1999: 110–11) on the grounds that such appliances have yet to be found in Roman contexts (Becker 1999: 104), but this objection now seems to be contradicted by at least one recent find from Roman imperial times (Minozzi *et al.* 2007).

Most studies suggest relatively good levels of oral health and significantly fewer cases of caries than in most modern populations, the result of the absence of refined sugar and carious foods, and reasonably low levels of heavy tooth wear, LEH, abscesses, calculus and ante-mortem tooth loss. Still, dental hygiene is sometimes poor, and the Etruscans, like the Romans, although arguably to a significantly lesser extent (Capasso 1987), were more prone to cavities than pastoral or hunter-gatherer populations, as a result of less reliance on meat and fibrous foods, and greater access to processed cereals and carbohydrates (Fornacieri *et al.* 1984; Brasili Gualandi 1992; Brasili Gualandi *et al.* 1997; cf. Catalano *et al.* 2007). There is evidence for a very broad secular trend for human teeth to decline in size with the overall introduction of more soft cooked and processed foods, and the transition from a raw or poorly processed diet, with a great deal of grit, or the consumption of hard-to-eat foods that need to be gnawed or crushed, a trend beginning in the transition from the Paleolithic to the Neolithic and Bronze Ages, reaching a climax among the Etruscans and Romans, and, after a regression in the early Medieval period, resuming a broad secular decline to Greco-Roman levels among the moderns (Manzi *et al.* 1997; Manzi *et al.* 1999: 475 Fig. 1; Belcastro *et al.* 2007). Some of the more detailed, largely Roman era studies offer some helpful insights to interpreting the Etruscan evidence. For example, analyses of the caries rate, and its association with the consumption of processed carbohydrates, and perhaps also some honey and other luxury foods, can be documented by contrasting several suburban Roman necropoleis and the likely poorer rural settlement of Vallerano (Catalano *et al.* 2007). Likewise, two studies of the transition from the Roman era to the significantly harsher economic conditions of the early Medieval period (Manzi *et al.* 1999; Belcastro *et al.* 2007), in a number of different communities – ranging from the prosperous urban slaves, freedmen and middle classes of Portus, buried in Isola Sacra, to the rather poor rural mountain town of Lucus Feroniae, and several settlements in the Apennines – are significant. They demonstrate that the early Medieval population suffered much more severely from heavy tooth wear, abscesses, calculus, LEH and ante-mortem tooth loss than the Roman populations, particularly the urban middle class population of Portus, despite having slightly fewer caries and relatively good heights, indicative of reasonably good access to meat, as a result of their largely rural, and often pastoral, economy, although the contrast was muted for the economically marginalized community of Lucus Feroniae. One can also observe greater sexual dimorphism and overall internal variation in tooth size, arguably the result of class differences, among the rural population of Lucus Feroniae, than the more urbanized and prosperous people buried in Isola Sacra.

A few studies have also been made comparing Greco-Roman or Etruscan indicators of dental health and of general health stress, which are of some interest in putting the Etruscan and Greco-Roman experience in some perspective. One detailed comparison of Hellenistic and twentieth century Greek skeletal collections (Vanna 2007) revealed dramatically lower ancient levels of caries and ante-mortem tooth loss, significantly lower rates of periodontitis, and slightly lower levels of LEH for males, although not for females. Fractures are slightly less common in the ancient population, and dramatically so when ancient (0.08 percent) and modern (0.38 percent) females are compared – this result might suggest alarmingly high levels of spousal abuse in the modern period, as accidents or occupational injuries seem rather unlikely explanations. Modern levels of osteoarthritis are also higher, more so for women than for men.

The incidence of cribra orbitalia or porotic hyperostosis, a fine pitting particularly of the orbital vaults of the skull, found in skeletal samples from many ancient and modern cultures, is often taken as a likely indication of nutritional or health stress (e.g. Manzi *et al.* 2001). The aetiology is controversial, however. Theories of its origin include anemia brought on by an inadequate supply of iron in the diet, or the consumption of iron-depleting phytates in a largely cereal diet, or the result of the consumption of goat's milk rather than mother's milk by young children, as well as the possible nutritional stresses caused by parasitic infections or weanling diarrhea (Sandford *et al.* 1983; Stuart-Macadam 1987). Others explain it instead as evidence of an inherited thalassemia, like sickle cell anemia, a genetic response to chronic exposure to malaria on the part of previous, and perhaps contemporary generations (e.g. Angel 1966; Fornaciari *et al.* 1989). Unfortunately, many physical anthropologists simply note the presence of the syndrome, not noting the severity, for which there are few objective standards recognized, or the percentage of the population affected, or the extent to which the lesions are active or healed (Manzi *et al.* 2001 and Fox 2005 are notable models of good method). The relatively mild effects of most cases of cribra orbitalia typically encountered and duly noted in Etruscan and Greco-Roman skeletal samples, when compared to skeletal examinations of actual sufferers from thalassemia (Ascenzi and Balistreri 1977; Lagia *et al.* 2007), and the rarity of unhealed lesions in adults and their overwhelming preponderance in young children (at least before the successful challenge of senatorial power in the conflict of the orders, Salvadei *et al.* 2001: 714–5) suggest that sufferers from genetic anemias like thalassemia were relatively rare. More likely, we are primarily dealing with childhood iron deficiencies caused by nutritional iron deficits or by gastrointestinal complaints such as weanling diarrheal or parasitic infections. The severity and extent of this syndrome seems, even in relatively poor Roman communities like Lucus Feroniae, to have been significantly lower than in early Medieval populations (Salvadei *et al.* 2001), and cribra orbitalia do not seem particularly common or severe among the Etruscan population (see, e.g. Mallegni *et al.* 1979; Pacciani *et al.* 1996; Brasili Gualandi *et al.* 1997: 257; Robb *et al.* 2001: 219, table 4).

Linear enamel hypoplasia, or LEH, generally fine lines, or, in severe cases, visible grooves, on teeth, particularly canines, caused by short interruptions in the enamel forming process as a result of bouts of malnutrition or sickness in childhood, is also often seen as a helpful indication of poor health or nutrition (Goodman and Armegalos 1985). As with many cases of cribra orbitalia, however, LEH need not represent evidence of severe illness or acute malnutrition, and are relatively common, often in fairly mild forms and disproportionately affecting the poor or disadvantaged, in relatively healthy and tolerably well-fed populations, including many inhabitants of modern cities, and not just in the developing world. The syndrome is strongly associated with weaning stress, poor childhood nutrition, or periods of rapid dental development (Dobney and Goodman 1991; Goodman *et al.* 1992; Moggi-Cecchi *et al.* 1993). Such defects are therefore able to reveal, like cribra orbitalia, or studies of child growth and development, mild to moderate malnutrition or disease stresses. In a few instances, we can show individuals for whom a wide range of indicators of malnutrition, poverty and ill-health come together in severe form, as in the case of one, very short (150 cm), woman from Herculaneum (Erc 106), suffering from rickets and poor teeth, including several lost ante-mortem and others affected with very serious enamel hypoplasia, abscesses, or severe tooth wear (Bisel 1991: 16–18). The prevalence of LEH among the disadvantaged is also evident from an interesting study of the Sabine population of Corvaro di Borgorese, during the Republican period (Catalano 1996), which sees a notable increase in LEH, arguably connected with rapid urban growth and the associated health problems of the urban poor. The observation that the cases observed were excavated in a single restricted part of the burial ground (Catalano 1996: 435) suggests that among the ancient Italians, as in the contemporary studies cited above, socio-economic status is extremely important in predicting the likelihood of LEH. For a number of Roman populations, particularly those which were economically deprived, relatively large proportions were affected with LEH (e.g. Bonfiglioli *et al.* 2003; Cucina *et al.* 2006; see Lea 2010: 26–30), but in slightly more affluent communities, it seems that a significantly lower proportion, and often only a minority, are affected (Manzi *et al.* 1989; Lea 2010: 108). Certainly, our studies of Etruscan teeth, already cited, tend to suggest rather lower rates, although, admittedly, few studies are fully quantified or studied in the same depth as some of the more recently excavated Roman-era samples.

Many diseases fail to leave clear diagnostic evidence on bones, but studies of Etruscan skeletal remains have shown possible cases of leprosy (Mariotti 2005), acromegaly (Brasili Gualandi *et al.* 1997), brain injuries treated using trepanation (Fornaciari *et al.* 1990; Fornaciari 2004), and even, much more rarely, cardiovascular disease, such as aortic coarction (Ciranni and Fornaciari 2006). The most frequent ailments revealed in the skeleton are arthritic conditions, particularly common on the vertebral spine, which is generally vulnerable to damage, including cleft atlas, spina bifida of the sacrum and sacralization of the fifth lumbar spine, but also found in hip, elbow, shoulder and knee (Brasili Gualandi *et al.* 1997). Most of the pathological changes are related to aging or occupational causes, particularly the stress of relatively heavy work or repetitive movement, as have been very effectively explored in a detailed study by Alessandra Sperduti (1997). Studying the traces of over-development of the points of tendon attachment reveals not only injuries from overwork, but also can be helpful, along with analysis of the robusticity of bones (as, e.g. in Rubini 1996), in pinpointing muscular development. Such evidence could also potentially allow conjectures about likely body mass index, which is as significant as height as an indicator of likely health and life expectancy, but far more difficult to determine using physical anthropology. Evidence for physical training and a heavy musculature can be pointed out from one study of one well-built Roman soldier (Erc 26) killed in Herculaneum (Bisel and Bisel 2002: 468) and another athlete or body builder (Erc 86) from the same town (Laurence 2005: 88).

Osteoporosis, like arthritis, is an important health ailment, particularly for women, which can be documented using skeletal remains, and a very full recent study, again of a Roman rather than Etruscan site (Cho and Stuart 2011), reveals that the progress of the syndrome, at least for the tolerably well-off working and middle class population buried in Isola Sacra, is fairly typical of that normally found in modern studies (Cho & Stuart 2011: 12–13). Although the difficulty of accurately aging skeletal remains tends to make demographic conclusions from physical anthropology unreliable, this recent work on osteoporosis, along with an important observation identifying a large number of cases of a syndrome peculiar to post-menopausal women in skeletal remains from Pompeii (Lazer 2009: 153) suggests that life expectancy in Roman populations, and also presumably Etruscan and Greek populations, was likely to be significantly greater than is sometimes assumed from uncritical use of evidence of high infant mortality and poor life expectancy using nineteenth century comparative evidence (see Kron forthcoming c). Of course, our insight into ancient levels of infant mortality is severely limited by the custom of interring neo-nates and many children, and, in the case of the Etruscans, probably all who died at ages of less than around five and a half, in different locations from adults and older children (Becker 2007; 2012), and by our general failure, with the striking exception of the discovery of a massive children's cemetery at Astypalaia in Greece (Hillson 2009), to identify significant numbers of child burials.

The most significant and generally reliable evidence of overall levels of health and nutrition, however, come from anthropometric studies of mean final height, as has been extensively demonstrated in a massive modern anthropometric literature investigating the secular increase in height in Western Europe over the past two centuries, and in detailed studies of under-nutrition, ill-health, debility and reduced life expectancy worldwide (references in Kron 2005). Although some communities, such as the isolated mountain dwellers of Molise or the Apennines, already identified above with high levels of LEH and cribra orbitalia, clearly suffered significantly higher levels of under-nutrition, as did many chattel slaves and immigrants, and the poor, on the whole, Greco-Roman final heights suggest a significantly better level of nutrition and health than that experienced by the working classes of Western Europe prior to the mid-twentieth century for most countries (references in Kron 2005; Kron 2012b). Many nineteenth century European populations, most notably the Austrians and Spanish, were fed on a scant, overwhelmingly cereal-based diet, and urban dwellers suffered very heavy stress from gastro-intestinal diseases, as well as cholera and typhoid, caused by extremely poor sanitation and contaminated water supplies. As a result, in the eighteenth and nineteenth centuries, mean heights for many adult male populations range from as low as 158 cm to around 162 cm, whereas Roman era populations in Italy seem to have averaged mean male heights much closer to 168 cm, with Classical and Hellenistic Greeks typically reaching mean heights ranging from 170 to 172 cm. It must be acknowledged, however, that some Greek colonial populations, such as those at the cemetery of Pantanello in the *chora* of Metapontum (166.6 cm: Henneberg and Henneberg 1998: 520, Table 11.14), or Apollonia in the Tauric Chersonese (168 cm: calculated from data supplied by Anne Keenleyside, pers comm,) were somewhat shorter.

Two relatively full surveys comparing Roman and Etruscan skeletal remains show significantly higher values for the latter (Borgognini Tarli & Mazzotta 1986; Giannecchini and Moggi-Cecchi 2008: 289, Table 3; 291, Fig. 2; but note the under-estimate of the absolute height equivalence argued above), and suggest that the Etruscans were at least a good two centimeters or so taller on average. Both surveys do include, along with the Etruscans, a few results from rural Iron Age populations, in which, as in the early Medieval period, low population densities and the lack of urbanization allowed the population to keep their own domestic livestock, permitting a higher-protein diet and greater mean heights (cf. Kron 2005: 76–7; 78–9), perhaps thereby inflating the Etruscan average very slightly. Becker's chronological breakdown of Tarquinian heights shows that for this urbanized Etruscan population, living conditions seem to have improved as we move from the Orientalizing and Archaic period to the Classical, and held up well under the Roman hegemony (Becker 1997: Table 3: 167.24 cm (n=10) dated ca. 750–500 BC; 170.64 cm (n=19) dated 375–90 BC). The evidence from individual Etruscan sites corroborates the thrust of these broader surveys, showing mean male heights for populations in the core of the Etruscan region clustering around 169 cm or 170 cm or more, as, for example, at Tarquinia (Mallegni *et al.* 1979: 194, Table 2: 168.75 cm (n=31); Becker 1989: 169.2 cm (n=10); Becker 1990; Becker 1997: Table 3; Becker 2002), Camerano (Corrain 1977: 170.1 cm (n=23)), Selvaccia near Siena (Pardini 1981: 168.9 cm (n=9)), and Blera, near Viterbo (Becker 2004). Results from regions under heavy Etruscan influence, but still somewhat mixed in terms of their cultural background (e.g. Robb 2001: 214–5) and lifestyle, show a more complex picture, and sometimes, as in the very well studied large cemetery site of Pontecagnano (Pardini 1982; Lombardi Pardini *et al.* 1984; 1991; 1992; Sonego and Scarsini 1994; Scarsini and Bigazzi 1995; Robb 2001), seem decidedly poorer or more inegalitarian (Robb *et al.* 2001: 219, Table 4: 166.0–166.5 cm). The evidence is rather patchy, but does tend to reflect that regions under Etruscan influence were doing relatively well, and, in many cases, arguably better on the whole than they would under the Romans: Monte Bibele (Gruppioni 1980; Dall'Aglio *et al.* 1981; Brasili Gualandi 1989; Brasili Gualandi *et al.* 1997); Bologna (Sergi 1884: 166.7 cm (n=24); Facchini 1975: 168.1 cm (n=3)); Camerano (Corrain 1977: 170.1 cm (n=23)); Spina (Marcozzi 1969: 168.2 cm (n=5)); Civitanova (Corrain *et al.* 1982: 169 cm (n=67)); Capovalano, in Abruzzo (Coppa *et al.* 1987: 170.6 cm (n=7)); and Atesino, near Pavia (Corrain 1971).

Although the stunted heights often common among Neolithic and early Bronze Age farming populations (Auerbach 2011) are to some extent attributable to calorie under-nutrition, it is the lack of protein in the diet, typically derived from meat and other more expensive foods, that is the most significant limiting factor. Studies of trace minerals in bones, either zinc and strontium (an older and arguably less reliable method, given the tendency of these minerals to leach into or out of bones based on soil conditions) or stable isotopes of carbon and nitrogen in order to determine the importance of protein, whether herbivorous meat or marine sources, can be very informative in supplementing and explaining height data, and are adding a great deal to our understanding of the relatively rich Greco-Roman diet (Prowse *et al.* 2004; Fornaciari and Mallegni 1987; Kron 2012a), but few such studies have been carried out for Etruscan sites. One strontium/zinc analysis (Fornaciari and Mallegni 1987) suggests a fairly rich agricultural diet, slightly less rich than at Athens, but consistent with our height evidence, which likewise suggests nearly comparable levels of protein in the Etruscan diet. One of our few isotope studies (Scarabino *et al.* 2006) argues that their results suggest a largely vegetable or cereal diet, but their methodology is weak, failing to study the carbon and nitrogen isotope signatures in contemporaneous domestic animals, or to properly put the results into the context of other sites. Seen in this light, their results are, in fact, not inconsistent with a significant amount of meat in the diet, albeit mainly from herbivores rather than sea fish. Another isotope study (Calabrisotto *et al.* 2009) from Populonia, dating from the second century AD, based on radiocarbon dating and the find of a coin of Marcus Aurelius, and therefore unfortunately rather unhelpful to us, shows high meat and fish consumption. They estimate up to 30 percent of the protein in the diet may come from marine fish, and the rich grave goods, and relatively good height of 172 cm for the male, certainly make this credible.

One of the great advantages of anthropometric evidence over many crude measures of economic development, such as global estimates of GNP per capita, is its sensitivity to often subtle changes in mass living standards and changes in social inequality, which might otherwise be obscured by the prosperity of small elites. For example, the significant increase in social inequality in much of the United States over the latter half of the nineteenth century, concomitant with northern industrialization, urbanization and the backlash against southern reconstruction, is reflected in a very significant decline in American mean heights from well over 172 cm in Colonial times, to around 168 cm by circa 1900 (see Kron 2005: 70–1). While statistical evidence for increasing wealth inequality picks up this social transformation (Williamson & Lindert 1980), most economic historians would surely have argued that this remained a period of significant economic growth. Significantly, such anthropometric evidence, like that documenting poor English living standards during the industrial revolution, or the steep secular decline in Italian living standards over the late seventeenth and eighteenth centuries (see Kron forthcoming), is much more finely attuned to the actual effects of social changes as well as gross economic output.

Likewise, careful attention to differences in mean final height gives us some potential to identify and compare trends in social inequality, prosperity and poverty in Etruscan and Roman society. The data suggests, if we supplement it with housing data and other indications of likely wealth and income distribution and economic development, as I can only sketch briefly here, that Etruscan society may well have been closer to that of the Greeks, less conservative and inegalitarian than that of Republican and Imperial Rome, just as it was radically different from nineteenth-century Europe.

While many modern scholars suspect that Etruscan society was highly inegalitarian, some suspect it was even more so than Roman society after its conflict of the orders (Harris 1971: 114–29; Cornell 1995), their claims are far from conclusive. This theory is based heavily on the social conflicts between rich and poor allegedly exploited by the

Romans, who propped up the wealthy (see Harris 1971: 129–44), but a very different interpretation of the state of Etruscan society is equally plausible, since lower class agitation against Roman hegemony was even more marked among the clearly democratic Greeks.

Others base their hierarchical vision of Etruscan society on the lavish tombs and their elaborate grave goods, claiming that they suggest a society divided between wealthy chieftains and the poor, but, as Marshall Becker first posited in several original analyses of both skeletal remains and their archaeological context (Becker 1990; 1993; 2002), and as others have investigated in a similar fashion, for Pontecagnano (Robb *et al.* 2001) the reality is more complex, with a relatively broad and mobile elite and little clear evidence of radical inequality or long dynasties of princely power or wealth.

Given the evidence of broad prosperity and limited social inequality revealed by Etruscan skeletal remains, it is likely that Etruscan society was in fact a rather more egalitarian society than we have traditionally thought, with a significant middle class, in the sense of a broad middle income group, as in modern North American usage (see Mayer 2012; Kron forthcoming). While we cannot offer estimates of overall wealth inequality to show, the existence of a middle class as large as in some modern representative democracies and welfare states (Kron 2011), as at Classical Athens, or even to survey in full, large housing samples to provide a credible estimate of likely income inequality, as for Pompeii and Herculaneum (Kron forthcoming), we do have sufficient evidence to conclude that Etruscan society fits comfortably within a Greco-Roman and Carthaginian *koine* of broadly democratic and egalitarian middle class societies. Certainly, the Etruscans were widely recognized as one of the leading commercial civilizations of the Mediterranean, famed for their wealth and luxury (Potter 1979: 69–87; Liébert 2006), successful craft production and manufacturing (Barker and Rasmussen 1998: 201–10; Torelli 2001: 365–476; Camporeale 2001), highly prized metalwork (Barker and Rasmussen 1998: 206–9; Torelli 2001: 393–404) and bucchero pottery, widely exported into Italian and foreign markets (Barker and Rasumssen 1998: 214–5; Naso and Trojsi 2009).

Although a detailed discussion would be out of place here, it is worth noting that there is a great deal of corroborating archaeological evidence for the rise of a broad Etruscan middle class of prosperous traders, craftsmen and small farmers in the Archaic period. We can cite, for example, the precocious emergence of a broad mass market for craft manufactures, most notably bucchero ware (Potter 1979: 72), as well as a wide range of Greek and Phoenico-Carthaginian imports (Spivey 1991; Barker and Rasmussen 1998: 203–5; 214; Giudice 1999; Osborne 2001; Lewis 2003; Fletcher 2007: 100, Figs. 169–71; 121–4; Ambrosini 2009; Baldoni 2009), in the cities of Etruria. Survey archaeology (see Izzet 2007: 200, Table 6.1 and Potter 1979; Barker and Rasmussen 1988: 29–32; 38–9; Perkins 1999: 55–64; Enei 2001) documents an intensively cultivated landscape with many small farms, many of which were likely those of small tenant farmers or owner-occupiers, many of which are pretty substantial (Barker and Rasmussen 1998: 167–72), their numbers rising in the sixth century BC and filling the landscape by the fifth century BC (Rasmussen 1998; Izzet 2007: 193–207). A relatively sophisticated system of intensive mixed farming seems to have been practiced, with crop rotations and the integration of a full range of domestic livestock, and even a market for wild game (Barker and Rasmussen 1998: 182–200). A growing urban middle class begins to become clear archaeologically as Villanovan hut villages are transformed into populous Etruscan cities (Spivey and Stoddart 1990: 61; Cornell 1995: 204, Table 3; Barker and Rasmussen 1998: 153), with public squares, broad streets and well-planned *insulae* (Colonna 1986; Izzet 2007: 171–2 and Fig. 6.1; 174–81) divided into large multi-room houses (Brandt and Karlsson 2001). The excavated houses at Marzabotto are remarkably large, with a ground area ranging from 600 to 800 m² (Mansuelli 1963; Torelli 2001: 301–2), and while these are clearly the homes of an elite, it is a remarkably broad one. Although few excavations have investigated the domestic quarters as thoroughly as at Pompeii or Olynthus, the thatched wattle and daub huts which were typical in the Villanovan period (Boëthius 1962; Brandt and Karlsson 2001; Izzet 2007: 147–8; Izzet 2007: 148, Fig. 5.1. and cf. Liseno 2007) were now replaced by rectilinear mud-brick and stone buildings with tile roofs by the mid-seventh century BC (Izzet 2007: 148 citing Colonna 1986: 425; de Albentiis 1990: 29–30), and both elite and ordinary dwellings increased significantly in size. At San Giovenale and Aquarossa, over the seventh and sixth centuries BC, houses went from two rooms to an average of three to five "articulated spaces", with as many as 16 rooms in a number of fifth-century BC houses in Marzabotto (Izzet 2007: 158), and even the smallest houses now aspired to some degree of privacy and comfort (Izzet 2007: 149 Fig. 5.2 and see Stefani 1922: 379–85; Mansuelli 1963; Colonna 1986; Brandt and Karlsson 2001).

The evidence of physical anthropology, both of mean final heights, and of skeletal markers of chronic under-nutrition, disease, or stress, suggests that the Etruscans, like the Classical and Hellenistic Greeks, enjoyed reasonably good health and nutrition, marginally better on the whole than much of the population of Latium and Italy over the course of the Roman Republic and Empire, and certainly much better than that of the working classes of nineteenth century Western Europe. This good health is likely only partly as the result of greater overall prosperity, however. More likely, the key reason for the relatively good health of the Etruscans, lay in their success in significantly reducing the proportion of the population's suffering from extreme poverty, poor diet, over-work, and other health stresses which would be reflected in stunted heights or skeletal abnormalities. There is good reason to believe, based on both literary and archaeological evidence, that these indices of good health for the Etruscan population should be taken seriously as an indication of relative social equality, and that we ought to question the traditional view of Etruscan society as distinctly hierarchical, even more so than that of the Romans, according to some. Instead, I would suggest that we see the Etruscan political and social system as one of independent competing city-states, with substantial urban and rural middle classes, rather more akin socially and culturally to the Greeks, and arguably quicker to urbanize and democratize than their Roman and Latin rivals, and certainly quicker than most of the Italic tribes of the Iron Age and the Roman hegemony (Attema *et al.* 2010; Colivicchi 2011).

BIBLIOGRAPHY

Achilli, A., Olivieri, A., Pala, M., Metspalu, E., Fornarino, S., Battaglia, V., Accetturo, M., Kutuev, I., Khusnutdinova, E., Pennarun, E., Cerutti, N., Di Gaetano, C., Crobu, F., Palli, D., Matullo, G., Silvana Santachiara-Benerecetti, A., Cavalli-Sforza, L. L., Semino, O., Villems, R., Bandelt, H.-J., Piazza, A. and Torroni, A. (2007) "Mitochondrial DNA Variation of Modern Tuscans Supports the Near Eastern Origin of Etruscans," *American Journal of Human Genetics* 80: 759–768.

Ambrosini, L. (2009) "An Attic red-figured Kylik from Veii and the distribution of the Zalamea Group in Etruria" in Judith Swaddling and Philip Perkins (eds), *Etruscan by definition. The cultural, regional and personal identity of the Etruscans. Papers in honour of Sybille Haynes, MBE,* London: British Museum Press, 25–30.

Angel, J. L. (1966) "Porotic Hyperostosis, Anemias, Malarias and Marshes in the Prehistoric Eastern Mediterranean," *Science,* N. S. 153: 760–763.

Ascenzi, A. and Balistreri, P. (1977) "Porotic Hyperostosis and the Problem of Origin of Thalassemia in Italy," *Journal of Human Evolution* 6: 595–604.

Attema, P., Burgers, G. J. and van Leusen, M. (2010) *Regional Pathways to Complexity: Settlement and land-use dynamics in early Italy from the Bronze Age to the Republican period,* Amsterdam: Amsterdam University Press.

Auerbach, B. M. (2011) "Reaching Great Heights: Changes in Indigenous Stature, Body Size and Body Shape with Agricultural Intensification in North America" in *Human Bioarchaeology of the Transition to Agriculture,* R. Pinhasi and J. T. Stock (eds), Oxford: Wiley-Blackwel, 203–34.

Baldoni, V. (2009) *La ceramica attica dagli scavi ottocenteschi di Marzabotto,* Bologna: Antequem.

Bandelt, H.-J. (2004) "Etruscan artefacts," *American Journal of Human Genetics* 75: 919–20.

Bandelt, H.-J. (2005) "Mosaics of ancient mitochondrial DNA: positive indicators of nonaunthenticity," *European Journal of Human Genetics* 13: 1106–1112.

Barker, G. and Rasmussen, T. (1998) *The Etruscans,* Oxford: Blackwell Publishers.

Bartoli F., Mallegni F. and Vitiello A. (1991) "Indagini nutrizionali e odontostomatologiche per una definizione della dieta alimentare in un gruppo umano a cultura etrusca: Gli inumati della Necropoli dei Monterozzi di Tarquinia (VI–II sec a.C.)," *Studi Etruschi* LVI(III): 255–269.

Becker, M. J. (1990) "Etruscan Social Classes in the VI Century B.C.: Evidence from Recently Excavated Cremations and Inhumations in the Area of Tarquinia" in H. Heres and M. Kunze (eds) *Die Welt der Etrusker,* Akademie-Verlag: Berlin: 23–35.

——(1992) "An Etruscan gold dental appliance in the collections of the Danish National Museum: Evidence for the history of dentistry," *Tandlaegebladet* (Danish Dental Journal), 96: 695–700.

——(1993) "Human Skeletons from Tarquinia: A Preliminary Analysis of the 1989 Cimitero Site Excavations with Implications for the Evolution of Etruscan Social Classes," *Studi Etruschi* 58: 211–248.

——(1995/96) "Early dental appliances in the eastern Mediterranean," *Berytus* 42: 71–102.

——(1999a) "Etruscan Gold Dental Appliances: Three Newly 'Discovered' Examples," *American Journal of Archaeology* 103: 103–111.

——(1999b) "Calculating Stature from in situ Measurements of Skeletons and from Long Bone Lengths: an Historical Perspective Leading to a Test of Formicola's Hypothesis at 5th Century BCE Satricum, Lazio, Italy," *Rivista di Antropologia* 77: 225–47.

——(2000) "Re-constructing the Lives of South Etruscan Women from the Archaeological, Skeletal, and Literary Evidence" in A. E. Rautman (ed.) *Interpreting the Body: Insights from Anthropological and Classical Archaeology,* Philadelphia: University of Pennsylvania Press, 55–67.

——(2002) "Etruscan Tombs at Tarquinia: Heterarchy as Indicated by Human Skeletal Remains" in *Preistoria e protostoria in Etruria. Atti del Quinto Incontro di Studi* 2, ed. N. Negroni Catacchio, Milan: Onlus, 687–708.

——(2003) "Review of *I Fuggiaschi di Ercolano: Paleobiologia delle vittime dell'eruzione Vesuviana del 79 D.C.* by L. Capasso," *The Journal of Roman Studies* 93: 404–406.

——(2004) "Appendice II: Etruscan Skeletons of the Hellenistic Period from the Casacce Necropolis at Blera (Viterbo, Italy) Excavated in 1982," *Notizie delle Scavi* (2002–2003): 175–189.

——(2005) "Etruscan Women at Tarquinia: Skeletal Evidence for Tomb Use and Insights into Status Differences in South Etruria," *Analecta Romana* 31: 21–36.

——(2006a) "The Archaeology of Infancy and Childhood: Integrating and Expanding Research into the Past," *American Journal of Archaeology* 110: 655–658.

——(2006b) "Etruscan Women at Tarquinia: Skeletal Evidence for Tomb Use" in C. C. Mattusch, A. A. Donohue and A. Brauer (eds), *Common Ground: Archaeology, Art, Science, and Humanities. The Proceedings of the 16th International Congress,* Oxford: Oxbow Books, 292–294.

——(2007) "Childhood among the Etruscans: Mortuary Programs at Tarquinia as Indicators of the Transition to Adult Status" in *Constructions of Childhood in Ancient Greece and Italy*, Princeton: American School of Classical Studies at Athens, 281–292.

——(2012) "Coming of Age in Etruria: Etruscan Children's Cemeteries at Tarquinia, Italy," *International Journal of Anthropology* 27: 63–86.

Becker, M. J. and Salvadei, L. (1992) "Analysis of the Human Skeletal Remains from the cemetery of Osteria dell'Osa" in Anna Maria Bietti Sestieri (ed.), *La Necropoli Laziale di Osteria dell'Osa*, Rome: Quasar, 53–191.

Becker, M. J., Turfa, J. M. and Algee-Hewitt, B. (2009) *Human remains from Etruscan and Italic tomb groups in the University of Pennsylvania Museum*. Pisa: Fabrizio Serra Editore.

Belcastro, G., Rastelli, E., Mariotti, V., Consiglio, C., Facchini, F. and Bonfiglioli, B. (2007) "Continuity or Discontinuity of the Life-Style in Central Italy During the Roman Imperial Age-Early Middle Ages Transition: Diet, Health, and Behavior," *American Journal of Physical Anthropology* 132: 381–394.

Belle, E. M. S., Ramakrishnan, U., Mountain, J. L. and Barbujani, G. (2006) "Serial coalescent simulations suggest a weak genealogical relationship between Etruscans and modern Tuscans," *Proceedings of the National Academy of Sciences* 103: 8012–8017.

Bezeczky, T. (2008) "Amphorae from the West. Evidence of the long distance trade connection with Ephesus" in M. Hainzmann and R. Wedenig (eds), *Instrumenta inscripta Latina, 2. Akten des 2. Internationalen Kolloquiums Klagenfurt, 5.–8. Mai 2005*, Klagenfurt: Geschichtsvereines für Kärnten, 25–34.

Bisel, S. C. (1991) "The human skeletons of Herculaneum," *International Journal of Anthropology* 6: 1–20.

Bisel, S. C. and Bisel, J. F. (2002) "Health and Nutrition at Herculaneum: An Examination of Human Skeletal Remains" in W. M. F. Jashmeski and F. G. Mayer (eds), *The Natural History of Pompeii*, Cambridge: Cambridge University Press, 451–75.

Bliquez, L. (1996) "Prosthetics in Classical Antiquity: Greek, Etruscan, and Roman Prosthetics," *ANRW* 37:3: 2640–76.

Bolsden, J. (1984) "Statistical Evaluation of the Basis for Predicting Stature from Long Bone Lengths in European Populations," *American Journal of Physical Anthropology* 65: 305–11.

Bonfiglioli, B., Brasili, P. and Belcastro, M. G. (2003) "Dento-alveolar lesions and nutritional habits of a Roman Imperial age population (1st–4th c. AD): Quadrella (Molise, Italy)," *Homo* 54: 36–56.

Borgognini Tarli, S. M. and Mazzotta, F. (1986) "Physical anthropology of Italy from the Bronze Age to the Barbaric Age" in B. Kandler-Palsson (ed.) *Ethnogenese europäischen Völker*, Stuttgart: Fisher Verlag, 147–172.

Bouloumié, B. (1985) "Les vases de bronze étrusques et leur diffusion hors d'Italie" in, Mauro Cristofani (ed.), *Il commercio etrusco arcaico. Atti dell'Incontro di studio, 5–7 dicembre 1983*, Rome: Consiglio Nazionale delle Ricerche, 167–78.

Bourdin, S. (2006) "Fréquentation ou intégration: les présences allogènes dans les emporia étrusques et ligures (VIe-IVe s. av. J.-C.)" in F. Clément, J. Tolan, J. Wilgaux (eds), *Espaces d'échanges en Méditerranée. Antiquité et Moyen Age*, Rennes: Presses Universitaires de Rennes, 19–39.

Bradley, M. (2011) "Obesity, corpulence and emaciation in Roman art," *Papers of the British School at Rome* 79: 1–41.

Brandt, J. R. and Karlsson, L. (2001) *From Huts to Houses: Transformations of Ancient Societies. Proceedings of an International Seminar Organised by the Norwegian and Swedish Institutes at Rome, 21–24 September 1997*. Stockholm.

Brasili Gualandi, P. (1989) "I reperti scheletrici della necropoli di Monte Bibele (IV–II sec. a.C). Nota Preliminare" in V. Morrone (ed.), *Guida al Museo "L. Fantini" di Monterenzio e all'area archeologica di Monte Bibele*, Bologna: Provincia di Bologna, 52.

——(1992) "Food habits and dental disease in an Iron-Age population," *Anthropologischer Anzeiger*, Jahrg. 50: 67–82.

Brasili G., Patricia, F., Fiorenzo, S. P. and Mazzucato, L. (1997) "Reconstruction of the health status in a past human population: the Iron Age necropolis of Monte Bibele (Bologna, Italy)," *Anthropologischer Anzeiger*, Jahrg. 55: 247–264.

Brisighelli, F., Capelli, C., Álvarez-Iglesias, V., Onofri, V., Paoli, G., Tofanelli, S., Carracedo, A., Pascali, V. L. and Salas, A. (2009) "The Etruscan timeline: a recent Anatolian connection," *European Journal of Human Genetics* 17, 693–696.

Camporeale, G. (ed.) (2001) *The Etruscans Outside Etruria*. Los Angeles: The J. Paul Getty Museum.

Capasso, L. (1987) "Dental pathology of the Etruscan Population," *Studi Etruschi* 53: 177–91.

——(2001) *I fuggiaschi di Ercolano: paleobiologia delle vittime dell'eruzione vesuviana del 79 d.C.* Rome: "L'ERMA" di Bretschneider.

Cappellini, E., Chiarelli, B., Sineo, L., Casoli, A., Di Gioia, A., Vernesi, C., Biella, M. G. and Caramelli, D. (2004) "Biomolecular study of the human remains from tomb 5859 in the Etruscan necropolis of Monterozzi, Tarquinia (Viterbo, Italy)," *Journal of Archaeological Science* 31: 603–612.

Carandini, A. (2009) "I paesaggi del suburbio" in V. Jolivet, C., Pavolini, M. A., Tomei and R. Volpe (eds), *Suburbium II: Il suburbio di Roma dalla fine dell'età monarchica alla nascita del sistema delle ville (V–II secolo A.C)*, Paris: École Française de Rome, 295–310.

Carandini, A. and Carafa, P. (eds) (2000) *Palatium e sacra Via I. Prima delle mura, l'età delle mura e l'età delle case arcaiche*, Rome: Istituto Poligrafico e Zecca dello Stato.

Catalano, P. (1996) "La comunità di Corvaro (Rieti). Mutamenti delle condizioni di vita quotidiana in epoca arcaica e repubblicana. Ipotesi antropologiche" in *Identità e civiltà dei Sabini. Atti del XVIII Convegno di studi etruschi ed italici, Rieti - Magliano Sabina 30 May – 3 June 1993*, Florence: Olschki, 431–443.

Catalano, P., Caldarini, C., De Angelis, F., *et al.* (2007) "La carie dentaria a Roma. Indicazioni da alcuni sepolcreti suburbani d'epoca romana," *Medicina nei secoli, arte e scienza* 19: 745–61.

Cho, H. and Stout, S. D. (2011) "Age-associated bone loss and intraskeletal variability in the Imperial Romans," *Journal of Anthropological Sciences* 89: 000.

Cifani, G. (2004) "Recenti approcci e metodi per lo studio dell'edilizia antica: Il caso della Roma arcaica" in E. C. De Sena and H. Dessales (eds), *Archaeological Methods and Approaches: Industry and Commerce in Ancient Italy*, Oxford: BAR IS. 1262, 219–25.

Cipriani, M., Pontrandolfo, A. and Rouveret, A. (2003) "La céramique grecque d'importation à Poseidonia. Un exemple de réception et d'usage" in Pierre Roillard and Annie Verbanck-Piérard (eds) *Le vase grec et ses destins*, Munich: Biering & Brinkmann, 139–156.

Ciranni, R. and Fornaciari, G. (2006) "The aortic coarctation and the Etruscan man: morphohistologic diagnosis of an ancient cardiovascular disease," *Virchows Archiv* 449: 476–478.

Claassen, H. and Wree, A. (2004) "The Etruscan skulls of the Rostock anatomical collection – How do they compare with the skeletal findings of the first thousand years B.C.?" *Annals of Anatomy* 186: 157–163.

Colivicchi, F. (2011) "Local Cultures of South Italy and Sicily in the Late Republican Period: Between Hellenism and Rome," *Journal of Roman Archaeology*.

Colonna, G. (1986) "Urbanistica e architettura" in Giovanni Pugliesi-Caratelli (ed.), *Rasenna: Storia e civiltà degli Etruschi*, 371–530. Milan: Garzanti.

——(1990) "Città e territorio nell'Etruria meridionale del V secolo" in *Crise et transformation des sociétés archaïques de l'Italie antique au Ve siècle av. J.-C. Actes de la table ronde organisée par l'École Française de Rome et l'Unité de recherches étrusco-italiques associée au CNRS (UA 1132) Rome 19–21 November 1987*, 7–21. Rome: École Française de Rome.

Cooper, A. and Poinar, H. N. (2000) "Ancient DNA: do it right or not at all," *Science* 289: 1139.

Coppa, A. (1997) "Paleodata for different geographical areas," *Human Evolution* 12: 17–24.

Coppa, A., Cucina, A., Mancinelli, D., Vargiu, R. and Calcagno, J. M. (1998) "Dental Anthropology of Central-Southern, Iron Age Italy: The Evidence of Metric Versus Nonmetric Traits," *American Journal of Physical Anthropology* 107: 371–386.

Coppa, A., Mancinelli, D., Petrone, P. P. and Priori, R. (1987) "Gli inumati dell'Eta del Ferro di Campovalano (Abruzzo, area medio-adriatica)," *Rivista di Antropologia* 65: 105–138.

Coppa, A., Cucina, A., Mancinelli, D. and Vargiu, R. (1997) "Biological Relationships of Etruscan-Culture Communities," *Etruscan Studies*: Vol. 4, Article 9. Available at:<http://scholarworks. umass.edu/etruscan_studies/vol4/iss1/9>.

Cornell, T. J. (1995) *The Beginnings of Rome: Italy and Rome from the Bronze Age to the Punic Wars (c. 1000–164 BC)*, New York and London: Routledge.

Corrain, C. and Capitanio, M. (1971) "Dati osteometrici su resti umani antichi del Territorio Atesino (Padova)," *Oblatio – Raccolta di studi di Antichità ed arte in onore al Prof. Aristide Calderini*, 247–86. Como.

Corrain, C., Capitanio, M. and Erspamer, G. (1977) "I resti schelectrici della necropoli picena di Camerano nelle Marche (secoli VI–III a.C.)," *Archivio per l'antropologia e l'etnologia* 107: 81–153.

——(1982) "Alcune necropoli romane delle Marche," *Archivio per l'antropologia e l'etnologia* 112: 151–231.

Cristofani, M. (1989) *Gli Etruschi del mare*, Longanesi: Milan.

——(1990) *La Grande Roma dei Tarquini: Roma, Palazzo delle esposizioni, 12 giugno-30 settembre 1990*. Rome: "L'Erma" di Bretschneider.

Cucina, A., Vargu, R., Mancinelli, D., Ricci, R., Santandrea, E., Catalano, P. and Coppa, A. (2006) "The Necropolis of Vallerano (Rome, 2nd–3rd Century AD): An Anthropological Perspective on the Ancient Romans in the Suburbium," *International Journal of Osteoarchaeology* 16: 104–117.

Dall'Aglio, L., Giusberti, G., Gruppioni, G. and Vitali, D. (1981) "Monte Bibele: aspetti archeologici, antropologici e storici dell'insediamento preromano," *Mélanges de l'Ecole française de Rome. Antiquité* 93: 155–182.

De Albentiis, E. (1990) *La casa dei Romani*. Milan: Longanesi.

Dobney, K. and Goodman, A. H. (1991) "Epidemiological studies of dental enamel hypoplasias in Mexico and Bradford: Their relevance to archaeological skeletal studies" in H. Bush and M. Zvelebil (eds), *Health in Past Societies: Biocultural interpretations of human skeletal remains in archaeological contexts*, Oxford: Archaeopress, 81–100.

Enei, F. (2001) *Progetto Ager Caeretanus: Il literale di Alsium*. Rome.

Fletcher, R. N. (2007) *Patterns of Imports in Iron Age Italy*. Oxford: BAR.

Formicola, V. (1993) "Stature Reconstruction from Long Bones in Ancient Population Samples: An Approach to the Problem of its Reliability," *American Journal of Physical Anthropology* 90: 351–8.

Fornaciari, G. (2004) "La trapanazione del cranio in Età classica: Il caso di Pontecagnano, Salerno (IV secolo a.C.)," *Anthropos & Iatria* 8: 34–40.

Fornaciari, G., Brogi, M. and Balducci, E. (1984) "Patologia dentaria degli inumati di Pontecagnano (Salerno), VII–IV sec. a.C.," *Archivio per l'antropologia e la etnologia* 114: 73–93.

Fornaciari, G. and Mallegni, F. (1987) "Palaenutritional studies on skeletal remains of ancient populations from the Mediterranean area: An attempt to interpretation," *Anthropologischer Anzeiger*, Jahrg. 45: 361–370.

Fornaciari, G., Mezzetti, M. G. and Cuni, C. (1989) "Iperostosi porotica nella Campania costiera antica: malnutrizione o anemie emolitiche congenite? I risultati delle indagini paleonutrizionali a Pontecagnano, Salerno (VII–IV secolo a.C.)," *Rivista di Antropologia* 67: 149–160.

Fornaciari, G., Mezzetti, M. G. and Roselli, A. (1990) "Trapanazione cranica del IV secolo a.C. da Pontecagnano (Salerno)," *Studi Etruschi* 56: 285–286.

Formicola, V. (1993) "Stature reconstruction from long bones in ancient population samples: an approach to the problem of its reliability," *American Journal of Physical Anthropology* 90: 351–358.

Fox, S. C. (2005) "Health in Hellenistic and Roman Times: The Case Studies of Paphos, Cyprus, and Corinth, Greece" in Helen King (ed.), *Health in Antiquity*, London: Routledge, 59–82.

Fully, G. and Pineau, H. (1960) "Détermination de la stature au moyen du squelette," *Annales de Médecine Légale* 40: 145–153.

Ghirotto, S., Mona, S., Benazzo, A., Paparazzo, F., Caramelli, D. and Barjuni, G. (2010) "Inferring genealogical processes from patterns of Bronze-Age and modern DNA variation in Sardinia," *Molecular Biology and Evolution* 27: 875–86.

Giangreco, G., Lonoce, N. and Vetrugno, E. (2007) "Archeotanatologia e paleobiologia dei resti scheletrici umani rinvenuti nel 2006 a Bagnolo del Salento," *Archivio per l'antropologia e la etnologia* 137: 145–65.

Giannecchini, M. and Moggi-Cecchi, J. (2008) "Stature in Archeological Samples From Central Italy: Methodological Issues and Diachronic Changes," *American Journal of Physical Anthropology* 135: 284–292.

Gilbert, M., Thomas P., Bandelt, H.-J., Hofreiter, M. and Barnes, I. (2005) "Assessing ancient DNA studies," *TRENDS in Ecology and Evolution* 20: 541–4.

Giudice, F. (1999) "Il viaggio delle immagini dall Attica verse l'occidente," in F.-H. Massa-Pairault (ed.), *Le mythe grec dans l'Italic antique*, 267–327. Rome: Ecole Française de Rome.

Goodman, A. H. and Armelagos, G. J. (1985) "Factors affecting the distribution of enamel hypoplasias within the human permanent dentition," *American Journal of Physical Anthropology* 68: 479–493.

Goodman, A. H., Pelto, G. H., Allen, L. H. and Chavez, A. (1992) "Socioeconomic and Anthropometric Correlates of Linear Enamel Hypoplasia" in A. H. Goodman and L. L. Capasso (eds), "Children from Solis, Mexico" in *Recent contributions to the study of enamel developmental defects*, Teramo: Edigrafital, 373–80.

Gruppioni, G. (1980) "Prime osservazioni sui resti scheletrici del sepolcreto di Monte Bibele (Bologna) (IV–II sec a.C.)," *Atti della Società dei naturalisti e matematici di Modena* 111, 1–18.

Guimares, S., Ghirotto, S., Benazzo, A., Milani, L., Lari, M., Pilli, E., Pecchioli, E., Mallegni, F., Lippi, B., Bertoldi, F., Gelichi, S., Casoli, A., Belle, E. M., Caramelli, D. and Barbujani, G. (2009) "Genealogical discontinuities among Etruscan, Medieval, and contemporary Tuscans," *Molecular Biology and Evolution* 26: 2157–66.

Harris, W. V. (1971) *Rome in Etruria and Umbria*. Oxford: Clarendon Press.

Heather, P. (2009) *Empires and Barbarians: The Fall of Rome and the Birth of Europe*. New York: Oxford University Press.

Henneberg, M. and Henneberg, R. J. (1998) "Biological characteristics of the population based on skeletal remains" in J. C. Carter (ed.), *The Chora of Metaponto: The Necropoleis*. Austin: University of Texas Press, 503–556.

Hillson, S. (2009) "The world's largest infant cemetery and its potential for studying growth and development" in L. Schepartz, S. Fox and C. Bourbou (eds), *New Directions in the Skeletal Biology of Greece*, Princeton: American School of Classical Studies at Athens, 137–54.

Isaac, B. (2004) *The invention of racism in the Classical antiquity*. Princeton: Princeton University Press.

Izzet, V. (2007) *The Archaeology of Etruscan Society*. Cambridge: Cambridge University Press.

James, S. (1999) *The Atlantic Celts: ancient people or modern invention?* Madison: University of Wisconsin Press.

Kracht, P. (1991) *Studien zu den griechisch-etruskischen Handelsbeziehungen vom 7. bis 4. Jahrhundert v. Chr.* Bochum: Brockmeyer.

Krinzinger, F. (2000) *Die Ägäis und das westliche Mittelmeer. Beziehungen und Wechselwirkungen 8. bis 5. Jh. v.Chr. Akten des Symposions, Wien 24. bis 27. März 1999*. Vienna: Verlag der österreichischen Akademie der Wissenschaften.

Kron, G. (2002) "Archaeozoology and the Productivity of Roman Livestock Farming," *Münstersche Beiträge zur Antike Handelsgeschichte 21, 2*: 53–73.

———(2005) "Anthropometry, Physical Anthropology, and the Reconstruction of Ancient Health, Nutrition, and Living Standards" *Historia* 54: 68–83.

———(2008a) "Animal husbandry, Hunting, Fishing and Pisciculture" in John P. Oleson, *The Oxford Handbook of Engineering and Technology in the Classical World*, New York: Oxford University Press, 176–222.

———(2008b) "The Much Maligned Peasant. Comparative Perspectives on the Productivity of the Small Farmer in Classical Antiquity" in John Northwood and Luuk De Ligt (eds), *People, Land, and Politics: Demographic Developments and the Transformation of Roman Italy 300 BC–AD 14*, 71–119. Leiden: E. J. Brill.

———(2011) "The Distribution of Wealth at Athens in Comparative Perspective," *Zeitschrift für Papyrologie und Epigraphik* 179: 129–38.

———(2012a) "Food Production" in W. Scheidel (ed.), *The Cambridge Companion to the Roman Economy*, Cambridge: Cambridge University Press, 156–174.

———(2012b) "Nutrition, hygiene, and mortality. Setting parameters for Roman health and life expectancy consistent with our comparative evidence" in E. Lo Cascio (ed.), *L'impatto della "peste antonina,"* Bari: Edipuglia.

———(forthcoming) "Comparative evidence and the reconstruction of the ancient economy: Greco-Roman housing and the level and distribution of wealth and income" in François de Callataÿ and Andrew Wilson (eds), *Long-term quantification in ancient Mediterranean history*, Oxford: Clarendon Press.

Lagia, A., Eliopoulos, C. and Manolis, S. (2007) "Thalassemia: Macroscopic and Radiological Study of a Case," *International Journal of Osteoarchaeology* 58: 221–28.

Laurence, R. (2005) "Health and the Life Course at Herculaneum and Pompeii" in Helen King (ed.), *Health in Antiquity*, London: Routledge, 83–96.

Lazer, E. (2008) *Resurrecting Pompeii*. New York: Routledge.

Lea, C. (2010) "Prevalence and Timing of Enamel Hypoplasias in the Vagnari Skeletal Sample (1st–4th centuries AD)" *Theses*. Paper 351. Available at: <http://opensiuc.lib.siu.edu/theses/351>.

Levy-Coffman, E. (2005) "We Are Not Our Ancestors: Evidence for Discontinuity between Prehistoric and Modern Europeans," *Journal of Genetic Genealogy* 1: 40–50.

Lewis, S. (2003) "Representation and reception. Athenian pottery in its Italian context" in John B. Wilkins and Edward Herring (eds), *Inhabiting symbols. Symbol and image in ancient Mediterranean*, London: Accordia Research Institute, 175–92.

Liébert, Y. (2006) *Regards sur la truphè étrusque*. Limoges: Pulim.

Liseno, A. (2007) *Dalla capanna alla casa: dinamiche di trasformazione nell'Italia sud-orientale, VIII–V sec. a.C.* Bari: Progedit.

Lombardi, P. E, Polosa, D. and Pardini, E. (1984) "Gli inumati di Pontecagnano (Salerno), VII–VI sec.a.C.," *Archivio per l'antropologia e l'etnologia* 114: 3–62.

Lombardi, P. E., Fulciniti, G. and Pardini, E. (1991) "Somatologia, dimorfismo sessuale e struttura biologica di una popolazione campana del VII–IV secolo a.C.," *Archivio per l'antropologia e la etnologia* 121: 3–43.

Luraghi, N. (2008) *The ancient Messenians: constructions of ethnicity and memory*. Cambridge: Cambridge University Press.

MacKinnon, M. (2007) "State of the Discipline: Osteological Research in Classical Archaeology," *American Journal of Archaeology* 111: 473–504.

Mallegni, F., Fornaciari, G. and Tarabella, N. (1979) "Studio antropologico dei resti della necropoli di Monterozzi (Tarquinia)," *Atti della Società Toscana dei Scienze Naturali: Memorie*, Serie B, LXXXVI: 185–221.

Manzi G., Censi L., Sperduti A. and Passarello P. (1989) "Linee di Harris e ipoplasia dello smalto nei resti scheletrici delle popolazioni umane di Isola Sacra e Lucus Feroniae (Roma, I–III sec. d.C.)," *Rivista di Antropologia* 67: 129–148.

Manzi, G., Santandrea, E. and Passarello, P. (1997) "Dental Size and Shape in the Roman Imperial Age: Two Examples From the Area of Rome," *American Journal of Physical Anthropology* 102: 469–479.

Manzi G., Salvadei L., Vienna A. and Passarello P. (1999) "Discontinuity of life conditions at the transition from the Roman Imperial Age to Early Middle Ages: example from Central Italy evaluated by pathological dento-alveolar lesions," *American Journal of Human Biology* 11: 327–341.

Marcozzi, V. and Cesare, B. M. (1969) "Le osse lunghe della città di Spina (Osservazioni antropologiche)," *Archivio per l'antropologia e l'etnologia* 99: 1–24.

Mariotti, V., Dutour, O., Belcastro, M. G., Facchini, F. and Brasil, P. (2005) "Probable Early Presence of Leprosy in Europe in a Celtic Skeleton of the 4th–3rd Century BC (Casalecchio di Reno, Bologna, Italy)," *International Journal of Osteoarchaeology* 15: 311–325.

Matieu, L. M. and Rannala, B. H. (2008) "Bayesian inference of errors in ancient DNA caused by postmortem degradation," *Molecular Biology and Evolution* 23: 1503–11.

Mayer, E. (2012) *The Ancient Middle Classes*. Cambridge, MA: Harvard University Press.

Melchior, L., Kivisild, T., Lynnerup, N. and Dissing, J. (2008) "Evidence of Authentic DNA from Danish Viking Age Skeletons Untouched by Humans for 1,000 Years," *PLoS ONE* 3: e2214.

Messeri, P. (1963) "Scheletrici etruschi provenienti da Populonia," *Archivio per l'antropologia e l'etnologia* 93: 169–89.

Minozzi, S., Fornaciari, G., Musco, S. and Catalano, P. (2007) "A Gold Dental Prosthesis of Roman Imperial Age," *The American Journal of Medicine* 120: e1–e2.

Moggi-Cecchi, J., Crovella, S., Bari, A. and Gonella, P. (1993) "Enamel hypoplasias in a 19th century population from Northern Italy," *Anthropologischer Anzeiger* 51: 123–29.

Naso, A. and Trojsi, G. (2009) "Funde aus Milet: XXII. Etruscan Bucchero from Miletus: Preliminary Report," *Archäologischer Anzeiger*: 135–150.

Osborne, R. (2001) "Why Did Athenian Pots Appeal to the Etruscans?" *World Archaeology* 33: 277–295.

Pacciani, E. (1989) "Resti scheletrici umani da insediamenti etruschi: repertorio della collezione giacente presso la Soprintendenza Archeologica della Toscana," *Studi Etruschi* 55: 221–226.

Pacciani, E., Chiarelli, B., D'Amore, G. and Moggi-Cecchi, J. (1996) "Paleobiology of Etruscan populations," *Human Evolution* 11: 159–170.

Pardini, E. and Mannucci, P. (1980) "Studio antropologico degli scheletri etruschi (VI–V secolo a.C.) ritrovati nella tomba a tre celle scoperta a Selvaccia (Siena)," *Quaderni di Scienze Antropologiche* 5: 26–52.

——(1981) "Gli Etruschi di Selvaccia (Siena): studio antropologico," *Studi Etruschi* 49: 203–15.

Perkins, P. (2009) "DNA and Etruscan identity" in P. Perkins and J. Swaddling (eds), *Etruscan by Definition*, London: British Museum Press, 95–111.

Potter, T. W. (1979) *The Changing Landscape of South Etruria*. London: Paul Elek.

Prowse, T., Schwarcz, H., Saunders, S., Bondioli, L. and Macchiarelli, R. (2004) "Isotopic paleodiet studies of skeletons from the Imperial Roman cemetery of Isola Sacra, Rome, Italy," *Journal of Archaeological Science* 31: 259–272.

Robb, J., Bigazzi, J. R., Lazzarini, L., Caterina S. and Sonego, F. (2001) "Social 'Status' and Biological 'Status': A Comparison of Grave Goods and Skeletal Indicators From Pontecagnano," *American Journal of Physical Anthropology* 115: 213–222.

Rubini, M. (1996) "La necropoli arcaica di Casal Civitella (Riofreddo, Roma, Lazio)" in *Identità e civiltà dei Sabini. Atti del XVIII Convegno di studi etruschi ed italici, Rieti – Magliano Sabina 30 maggio – 3 giugno 1993*, 363–373. Florence: Olschki.

Rubini, M., Bonafede, E., Mogliazza, S. and Moreschini, L. (1997) "Etruscan Biology: The Tarquinian Population, Seventh to Second Century BC (Southern Etruria, Italy)," *International Journal of Osteoarchaeology* 7: 202–211.

Rubini, M., Mogliazza, S. and Corruccini, R. S. T. (2007) "Biological Divergence and Equality During the First Millennium BC in Human Populations of Central Italy," *American Journal of Human Biology* 19: 119–31.

Salvadei, L., Ricci, F. and Manzi, G. (2001) "Porotic hyperostosis as a marker of health and nutritional conditions during childhood: studies at the transition between Imperial Rome and the Early Middle Ages," *American Journal of Human Biology* 13: 709–717.

Sampietro, M. L., Caramelli, D., Lao, O., Calafell, F., Comas, D., Lari, M., Agustí, B., Bertranpetit, J. and Lalueza-Fox, C. (2005) "The Genetics of the pre-Roman Iberian Peninsula: A mtDNA Study of Ancient Iberians," *Annals of Human Genetics* 69: 535–48.

Sandford, M. K., Van Gerven, D. P. and Meglen, R. R. (1983) "Elemental Hair Analysis: New Evidence on the Etiology of Cribra Orbitalia in Sudanese Nubia," *Human Biology* 55: 831–44.

Scarabino, C., Lubritto, C., Proto, A., Rubino, M., Fiengo, G., Marzaioli, F., Passariello, I., Busiello, G., Fortunato, A., Alfano, D., Sabbarese, C., Rogalla, D., De Cesare, N., D'Onofrio, A. and Terrasi, F. (2006) "Paleodiet characterisation of an Etrurian population of Pontecagnano (Italy) by Isotope Ratio Mass Spectrometry (IRMS) and Atomic Absorption Spectrometry (AAS)," *Isotopes in Environmental and Health Studies* 42:2, 151–158.

Scarsini, C. and Bigazzi, R. (1995) "Studio antropologico dei resti umani" in A. Serritella (ed.), *Pontecagnano II.3. Le nuove aree di necropoli del IV e III sec. a.C*, Naples: Istituto Universitario Orientale, 135–146.

Simoni, L., Calafell, F., Pettener, D., Bertranpetit, J. and Barbujani, G. (2000) "Geographic patterns DNA diversity in Europe," *American Journal of Human Genetics* 66: 262–278.

Sonego, F. and Scarsini, C. (1994) "Indicatori scheletrici e dentari dello stato di salute e delle condizioni di vita a Pontecagnano (Salerno) nel VII–V sec. a.C.," *Bulletino* di *Paletnologia italiana* 85:1–25.

Sperduti, A. (1997) "Life Conditions of a Roman Imperial Age Population: Occupational Stress Markers and Working Activities in *Lucus Feroniae* (Rome, lst–2nd cent. AD)," *Human Evolution* 12: 253–267.

Spivey, N. (1991) "Greek vases in Etruria" in Tom Rasmussen and Nigel Spivey (eds), *Looking at Greek Vases*, Cambridge: Cambridge University Press, 131–50.

Spivey, N. and Stoddart, S. (1990) *Etruscan Italy: An Archaeological History*. London: Batsford.

Stuart-Macadam, P. (1987) "Porotic hyperostosis: New Evidence to Support the Anemia Theory," *American Journal of Physical Anthropology* 74: 521–6.

Swaddling, J. and Prag, J. (eds) (2002) *Seianti Hanunia Tlesana: The Story of an Etruscan Noblewoman*. London: British Museum Press.

Tang, B. (2005) *Delos, Carthage, Ampurias: The Housing of Three Mediterranean Trading Centres*. Rome: "L'ERMA" di Bretschneider.

Torelli, M. (1990) "La società etrusca della crisi: quali trasformazioni sociali?" in *Crise et transformation des sociétés archaïques de l'Italie antique au Ve siècle av. J.-C. Actes de la table ronde organisée par l'École Française de Rome et l'Unité de recherches étrusco-italiques associée au CNRS (UA 1132) Rome 19–21 November 1987*: 189–98. Rome: École Française de Rome.

——(1999) *Tota Italia. Essays in the cultural formation of Roman Italy*. Oxford: Clarendon Press.

——(ed.) (2001) *The Etruscans*. London: Thames and Hudson.

Treister, M. Y. (1996) *The Role of Metals in Ancient Greek History*. Leiden: E. J. Brill.

Trotter, M. and Gleser, G. C. (1952) "Estimation of stature from the bones of American whites and Negroes," *American Journal of Physical Anthropology* 10: 463–514.

——(1958) "A Re-evaluation of Estimation Based on Measurements of Stature taken During Life and of Long Bones after Death," *American Journal of Physical Anthropology* 16: 79–123.

Vanna, V. (2007) "Sex and Gender Related Health Status Differences in Ancient and Contemporary Skeletal Populations," *Papers from the Institute of Archaeology* 18: 114–147.

Vernesi, C. (1999) "Molecular sex determination of Etruscan bone samples (7th–3rd c. BC): a reliability study," *Homo* 50: 118–26.

Vernesi, C., Caramelli, D., Bramanti, B., Tilotta, G., Carbonell i Sala, S. and Chiarelli, B. (1997) "Analysis of Ancient DNA for Human Sex Determination," *Etruscan Studies* 4, Article 10. Available at: <http://scholarworks.umass.edu/etruscan_studies/vol4/iss1/10>.

Vernesi, C., Caramelli, D., Dupanloup, I., Bertorelle, G., Lari, M., Cappellini, E., Moggi-Cecchi, J., Chiarelli, B., Castri L., Casoli, A., Mallegni, F., Lalueza-Fox, C. and Barbujani, G. (2004a) "The Etruscans: A Population-Genetic Study," *American Journal of Human Genetics* 74: 694–704.

Vernesi, C., Barbujani, G., Caramelli, D., Castri L., Bertorelle, G. and Lalueza-Fox, C. (2004b) "Etruscan Artefacts Much Ado About Nothing," *American Journal of Human Genetics* 75: 923–27.

Ward-Perkins, J. B. (1959) "The Problem of Etruscan Origins Some Thoughts on Historical Method," *Harvard Studies in Classical Philology* 64: 1–26

Wiel-Marin, F. (2005) *La ceramica attica a figure rosse di Adria. La famiglia Bocchi e l'archeologia.* Padova: CLEUP.

Wood, J. W., Milner, G. R., Harpending, H. C., Weiss, K. M., Cohen, M. N., Eisenberg, L. E., Hutchinson, D. L., Jankauskas, R., Česnys, G., Katzenberg, M. A., Lukacs, J. R., McGrath, J. W., Roth, E., Abella, U., Douglas H. and Wilkinson, R. G. (1992) "The Osteological Paradox: Problems of Inferring Prehistoric Health from Skeletal Samples," *Current Anthropology* 33: 343–370.

Zanker, P. (ed.) (1976) *Hellenismus in Mittelitalien: Kolloquium in Göttingen vom 5. bis 9. Juni 1974,* 2 vols. Tübingen: Vandenhoek and Ruprecht.

PART II

THE HISTORICAL
DEVELOPMENT OF ETRURIA

———•◆•———

CHAPTER FIVE

THE VILLANOVAN CULTURE: AT THE BEGINNING OF ETRUSCAN HISTORY

——— •◆• ———

Gilda Bartoloni

The beginning of the cultural processes that would be concluded in the early Iron Age by the concentration of settlements at the sites of future Etruscan cities, in all likelihood is to be recognized in the Late Bronze Age, that is, in the second half of the second millennium BC. After a period of general cultural uniformity in ancient Italy, in the course of the tenth century BC there began to appear well-delineated areas equivalent to the large regions or territories that, in historic times, would correspond to well-defined *ethnè*: the Veneti, Etruscans, Latins, Sabines. The culture associated with the territory ultimately occupied by the Etruscans is defined as "Villanovan." Villanovan is understood as a system of customs, a typical expression of material civilization of the zone that would be historically Etruscan, namely that large area that diagonally crosses Italy, from the eastern basin of the Po to the central Tyrrhenian and finally to the Tiber, and which from there expanded into Campania.

The name comes from the accidental discovery made in 1853 by Giovanni Gozzadini at Villanova (approx. 8 km east of Bologna) of a series of cremation tombs: the ritual is characterized by the deposition of skeletal remains in vases of impasto (that is, of clay that is not purified, and is handmade and fired at a relatively low temperature). The urns are commonly defined as biconical because of their shape (similar to two juxtaposed truncated cones); for the most part they were covered by bowls also of black impasto. The cremation ritual is also represented by more or less valuable ornaments or other belongings of the deceased (especially fibulae, bracelets, necklaces, weapons, razors, etc.) and additional impasto ceramics (jugs, bowls, plates etc.). This definition of Villanovan was later extended to analogous funerary assemblages at Bologna, Tarquinia, Bisenzio, and other sites in Tyrrhenian Etruria, and then, as they were brought to light, to finds at the villages related to these necropoleis.

A continuity of life is well documented in the major Etruscan cities ever since the last phase of the Bronze Age ("Final Bronze Age"). Between the end of the Bronze Age and the beginning of the Iron Age, around the turn of the tenth century BC, the population almost completely abandons the sites of the previous period in order to settle in groups of a few hundred individuals in the territories of Veii, Tarquinia, Vulci etc., occupying distinct nuclei in the broad plains and adjacent hills. The Etruscans themselves traced the origin of the Etruscan nation to a date corresponding to the eleventh or tenth century BC: Varro (in Censorinus, *De die natali* 17.5–6 and Servius, Commentary on *Aeneid* 8.526) reports that the Etruscan *Libri rituales* ("Books of rituals") showed that the duration of the *nomen Etruscum* (literally "Etruscan name," meaning the Etruscan civilization) would not have exceeded ten "centuries;" Servius also notes (Commentary on *Eclogue* 9.46) that Augustus believed, on the basis of the teachings of the haruspices (divination priests), that during his reign the tenth *saeculum* (age, "century") would begin, the time of the end of the Etruscan people.

In the final phase of the Bronze Age (mid-twelfth to tenth century BC) the disposition of settlements appears to be better distributed, although they are no longer connected to the paths of the *tratturi* (drove roads for transhumance of flocks and herds) as they had been during the Middle Bronze Age. As evidence of the intensive exploitation of land and continuous population growth there are now known in Etruria at least 70 confirmed settlements, and several more sites with indications of at least temporary occupation. The typical town of this chronological phase generally occupies high ground or a *tufa* plateau of more than five hectares, isolated at the confluence of two watercourses. These small plateaus, naturally or artificially protected, are not completely built up: non-residential areas within the defenses were probably intended as collecting points for livestock or zones reserved for cultivation, land used only by certain groups, or areas designated for shelter in case of enemy attack.

For a number of years now the site of Castellaccio di Sorgenti della Nova (at the "Sources of the Nova" river) has hosted systematic research which shows a settlement articulated on the summit and on various terraces, naturally fortified and defended by steep walls and surrounded by two confluent ditches. The large terraced areas cut deeply into the flanks of the cliff. Its "urbanized" organization is quite complex: on the summit plateau are located houses of modest dimensions with sunken foundations and superstructure of perishable material, suitable to accommodate nuclear families; on the sides of the artificially terraced cliff, there open numerous artificial caves adapted for occupation, for places of worship, and for service facilities, while on the terraces in front, large houses intended for extended families were built along a small canal with foundations on an elliptical plan. Alongside the domestic structures are added rooms/structures of the same plan and construction technique but more or less reduced in size, probably used as storerooms and repositories; it has been thought that some of these small rooms were intended to house domestic animals. In the artificial caves at Sorgenti della Nova there were also exceptionally well-preserved ovens with domed walls of fired clay and braziers (*focolari*) for cooking food.

In other settlements (in Monte Rovello near Allumiere and at Luni on the Mignone River) structures of imposing dimensions (15–17 meters long and 8–9 meters wide) and rectangular plans have been identified, with the roof resting directly on a low bank of earth or stones. Probably these represent the homes of the heads of their respective communities, intended also for political and religious functions.

The funeral ritual can be documented systematically from the twelfth century BC, when the cremation of the dead begins to appear and then to prevail. This ritual, which corresponds to that of the Urnfields culture (*Urnenfelder*) of continental Europe, spread from the Alps to the north-eastern tip of Sicily in the Final phase of the Bronze Age, and is generally defined as "Protovillanovan," determined by its cultural affinity with the subsequent, Villanovan, culture which would be manifested at the beginning of the Iron Age only in certain parts of Italy.

Evidence of the passage from the custom of inhumation to cremation is found in the tumulus (mound-shaped) tombs in the necropolis of Crostoletto di Lamone on the left bank of the Fiora River, not far from the site of Castellaccio di Sorgenti della Nova, with burials, whether by inhumation or cremation, established since the Late Bronze Age. The urn used is almost always a biconical vessel, usually covered by an upended bowl. Sometimes the burials are double, that is, in the same well-shaped tomb (*tomba a pozzo*) or *custodia* (large container), two ossuaries are deposited at the same time.

Taken together, the data seem to indicate the presence of individuals or families at the head of different groups. And in the final phase of the Bronze Age, there must have begun the process that generated (at least two centuries later) a tribal society based on families and the increasingly widespread ownership of land.

In the ninth century BC the territory is divided instead into rather large districts, each belonging to a large village, divided internally into widely spaced groups of huts, and into a small number of isolated villages located in strategic positions, for which we can assume some form of dependence upon the larger settlements.

Compared to the preceding period, this type of aggregation is characterized by a higher concentration of the population. To the number of villages located mostly on inaccessible plateaus, with defensive priority assigned to the needs of agriculture, are added settlements over wide plains where the population was grouped into a single hilltop location. It is a sort of synoikistic process, so, for example, at Vulci people were gathered from the district of the Fiora and Albegna Rivers, while to Veii came the communities that inhabited the region from the Tiber River to Lake Bracciano, including the Faliscan and Capenate territories. The reference to Halesos, son of Saturn, the mythical founder of Falerii in the genealogy of Morrius the king of Veii (Servius, Commentary on *Aeneid* 8.285) may conceal this close relationship between Veii and the *Ager Faliscus* (the territory of the historical Faliscans).

The great movement of population that characterizes this period is unthinkable without political organizations that were able to impose their decisions on the individual village communities: the different groups, undoubtedly each consisting of nuclei linked by bonds of kinship, located within or outside the *tufa* plateaus that would be the future seats of the Etruscan city-states, have cultural links between them, also attested to by the analysis of craft production, such as to imply affiliation to the same political unit and enabling us to speak of such human concentrations as "proto-urban" (Fig. 5.1).

Strong indications of the change in relationship with the land are derived mainly from the radical change of the dislocation of the settlements and the tendency to concentrate the population sites on the plateau, surrounded by large areas of farmland. The development of large-scale cultivation of new land must have resulted in new business relationships. It seems hard to believe that the exploitation of resources over some hundreds of square kilometers could be implemented in a situation in which the land was still owned in common: it does not seem questionable to postulate for this period a subdivision of property.

The area in which Villanovan culture extends, from its first appearance, is not limited to the territory of Etruria proper (Fig. 5.2). In addition to the Tyrrhenian Villanovan culture, an Emilian Villanovan may be distinguished in the north, which includes the region south of the Po plain, with its capital at Bologna, and a Romagna-Villanovan

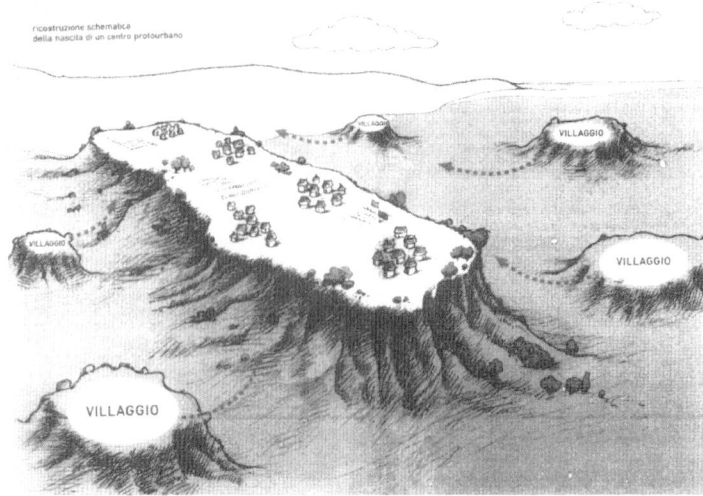

Figure 5.1   Schematic reconstruction of the birth of a proto-urban center (after P. Tamburini, *Il Museo territoriale del Lago di Bolsena. Vol 1. Dalle origini al periodo etrusco*, Bolsena 2007).

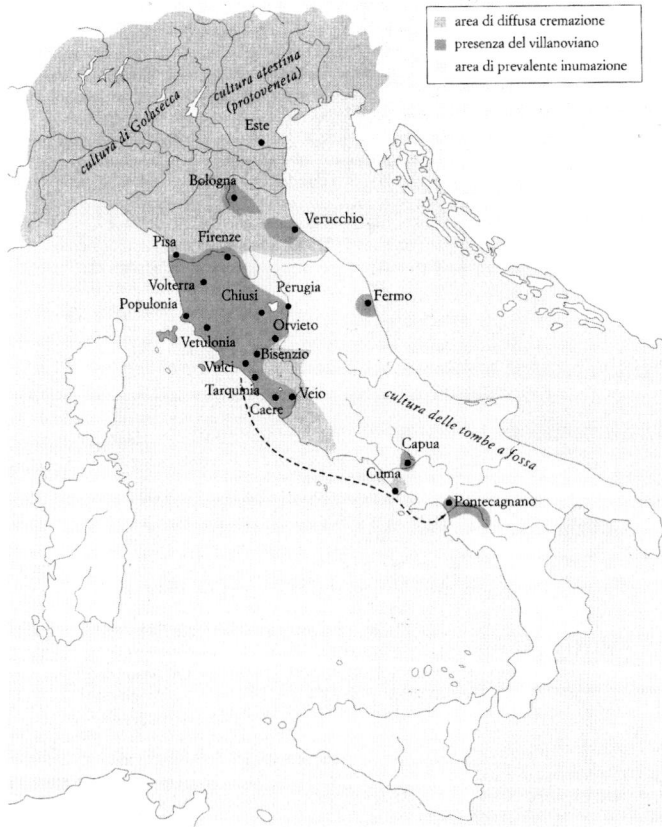

Figure 5.2   Diffusion of the Villanovan culture (after M. Torelli, ed., *Gli Etruschi*, Milan, 2000, p. 45).

attested especially in the Rimini area, at Verucchio. In the central peninsula, Fermo (Ascoli Piceno) was a completely isolated nucleus, while in the south, Villanovan characteristics can be recognized at Capua and in the Salerno region, with the necropoleis of Pontecagnano, Arenosola and Capodifiume near Paestum, probably a bridgehead to the other large southern Villanovan nucleus of Sala Consilina, located within the territory between Salerno and Lucania in the Valley of the Diano. Not only do we see similarities in the funerary customs but also other phenomena occur at the same time, in the typology of settlements and necropoleis, and as noted, the beginning of the process of formation of the Etruscan cities and even a colonial-type expansion. To give some plausibility to a possible "colonization," namely the presence of Etruscan people in these "Villanovan" settlements, there are the epigraphic and historical (literary) sources. On one hand are the comments of ancient authors such as Pliny (*Natural History* 3.70) that affirm that "the territory which stretches along three thousand paces from the Sorrento peninsula to the River Sele belonged to the Etruscans," but we do not know to what period to assign this report, or that of Verrius Flaccus (*Res etruscae* fr.1 P) who believed that Tarchon, eponymous hero of Tarquinia, and thus of the Tarquinian people, was responsible for the foundation of the twelve cities of Etruria in the Po Valley. On the other hand, of considerable interest is the evidence at Bologna of the use of Etruscan writing beginning at the end of the eighth century BC, a period that, especially in the district of Emilia, does not seem to break with the preceding phase, still to be defined as Villanovan. Such testimonies appear to be almost contemporary with the first evidence of inscriptions in Etruria proper.

The settlement pattern characteristic not only of Etruria proper (e.g. Tarquinia, Veii, Vetulonia) but also of peripheral centers (Pontecagnano, Fermo or Verucchio) is a town located on a large plateau (Veii, Cerveteri, Tarquinia, Vulci) or on a hill-plateau of average size (Orvieto-Volsinii, Vetulonia, Volterra) and of two groups of necropoleis (or two necropoleis) located generally to the north and south of the settlement, but also possibly to east and west. One of these appears to be the main necropolis, the other, smaller in number of tombs, shows characteristics of excellence.

The location of Populonia seems exceptional even for northern Etruria: unlike the other major Etruscan sites, which are in fact located on high ground and away from the sea or coastal lagoons, this is the only city located on the sea. The inhabited area (150/180 hectares) seems concentrated in the southern side of the promontory above the Gulf of Baratti. The *tufa* plateaus which will be the sites of future cities do not seem to be completely built up, but are divided into carefully spaced districts, with most of the plains used for agriculture or grazing. The internal organization is poorly understood because of the lack of systematic excavations of inhabited areas, but especially because of the type of facilities and urban structures, in large part constructed of perishable materials.

The momentum of the excavation of domestic sites in the last two decades has brought new information about settlement conditions, but it also has raised many questions: often among the remains of huts, inside or outside the structures, are more or less deliberate funerary depositions.

On the Civita plain of Tarquinia (Pian di Civita) was found a ninth-century BC enclosure with deposits of worked deer antlers, burials of newborns and of one child, an encephalopathic albino, which, according to the excavators, invokes the concept of *monstrum* (a prodigy in Roman religion, see Chapter 29). The further discovery in this area of burials of adults without accompanying grave goods is explained by M. Bonghi Jovino as part of religious practice; for one man, thought to be of Greek origin, they speak of a religious sacrifice. At Veii, at the center of the so-called Cittadella on Piazza d'Armi (the acropolis of the city), a structure with an oval plan, including a trench tomb (*tomba a fossa*) (Fig. 5.3), was interpreted as "a sort of mortuary chapel erected for the veneration of an exceptional death" (G. Colonna, unpublished conference paper), while on the great plateau near the north-west gate, at the center of a large oval hut of the ninth century BC, was found a burial within an earthen grave, with the skeleton of a 35-year-old woman with offerings of a few bronze objects.

We know the necropoleis better than the settlements: through their analysis it has become possible to see the bigger picture of cultural development. The examination of burial grounds as structured contexts allows the study of the economic, sociological, and intellectual aspects of ancient societies that are only partially illuminated by other evidence. The moment of death and the subsequent funeral ritual become important social occasions, although the funeral rites cannot be considered a simple statement of the values of a given community. The reflection of the society of the living in funeral customs can never be considered direct and immediate: it is mostly indirect, selective and mediated. During the ninth century, the exclusive rite of most Villanovan necropoleis was cremation, even though there are frequent examples of inhumation in trench graves as well: at Populonia, and at Cerveteri, for example, from the beginning of the use of the Sorbo necropolis the two rites co-existed. The tombs dug in virgin soil are usually *a pozzetto* (in "well-shaped," cylindrical pits) with the ossuary sometimes protected inside a *custodia* (container) made of *tufa* (at Veii, Bisenzio) or of *nenfro* (Tarquinia).

The funeral offerings, extremely limited in the earliest burials, seem mostly to consist of the ossuary (Fig. 5.4) inside which were the cremated bones, protected with a lid, and one or more fibulae of different styles depending upon the type of textile, hair-spirals (*fermatrecce*) and spindle whorls in female depositions, razors or pins in male

Figure 5.3   Tomb of an adult man, Veii, Piazza d'Armi (photo G. Bartoloni).

burials. In general accessory vessels are rare, and weapons are exceptional. The typical urn is represented by a biconical impasto vessel (Fig. 5.4) of elongated shape compared to its Protovillanovan predecessor, with one or two horizontal handles set at the point of maximum diameter. In the case of two-handled urns, however, one of the two handles is found deliberately broken. The rich incised decoration, obtained with a comb-like, multi-pointed instrument, occurs on the body and neck of the vessel, divided into more or less separate groups; more rare is ornamentation with applied metal inlays. The decorative technique, common in Italy, seems also to be common in the region of the French and Swiss platform-villages (*palafitte*) from the Late Bronze Age; because of this it was deduced that it had been disseminated from this region. The lid of the vase ossuary

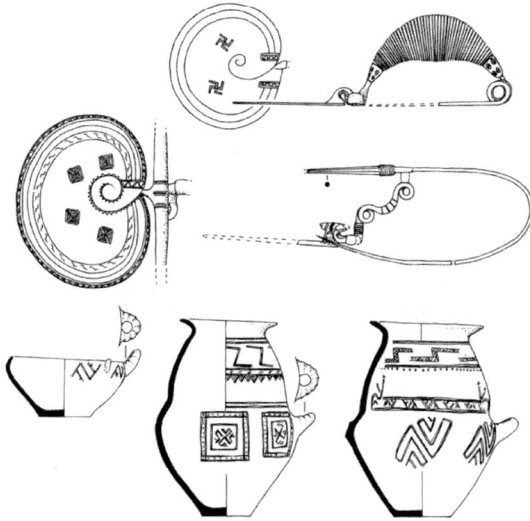

Figure 5.4   Finds from tombs at Veii, Quattro Fontanili (after *Annali dell'Istituto Orientale di Napoli. Archeologia e Storia Antica* VIII, 1986).

Figure 5.5   Hut urn from Veii, Quattro Fontanili (after Dalla *Capanna alla casa. I primi abitanti di Veio*, Formello 2003).

almost always consists of a bowl or dish with a conical body, incurving rim and ring handles set between two small pseudo-lugs. Already in the earliest phase, some ossuaries are closed not with bowls/plates but with conical helmets in clay (at Tarquinia, Veii, etc.) and later, with crested helmets reproducing bronze specimens.

Particularly prominent among the ossuaries are the previously noted model huts (Fig. 5.5); hut urns are attested mainly in coastal Etruria (at Vetulonia, Vulci, Tarquinia, Caere) and southern interior Etruria (Bisenzio and the territory of Veii): the percentage of these urns in the shape of houses is very low in contrast to the conventional biconical jars, amounting to one hut urn for every hundred biconical urns, thus indicative of their special character. In centers where there are models of housing functioning as ossuaries, the helmet-cover of biconical urns may have represented the gabled roof of the hut. In the biconical vase, the ideology of the armed warrior, expressed by the helmet, is augmented by that of the protector of the home: the two functions, of owner of the house and protector of the family inside, expressed through the symbols of the hut and the warrior, are associated with, and attributed to, a single personage.

In the earliest period of Villanovan culture, grave goods do not seem to reveal any difference in wealth or social status: they differ only in distinguishing women from men, and among these only a few are known as warriors, through the helmet or, rarely, weapons. Distinctive features such as hut urns are not solely the prerogatives of male or female: to a woman must be attributed a set of offerings (from Vulci?) in which are two miniature impasto spindles and a spindle whorl (see G. Bartoloni, *La cultura villanoviana. All'inizio della storia etruca*, Rome 2002: 188, Fig. 6.19). There is no difference in grave goods between depositions with hut urns and those in biconical urns.

Consequently, the documentation of the cemeteries seems to point to an entirely egalitarian system. Instead, it is more likely that, because of a constant funerary ideology, community members were considered equal in the rite of burial: one speaks of a combination of a common belief combined with the rigidity of cremation ritual.

About two or three generations after the advent of the so-called Villanovan revolution, funerary offerings, previously quite sober, are enriched with additional elements, signs

Figure 5.6   Grave group from Tarquinia (after M. Torelli, A. M. Sgubini Moretti, *Etruschi. Le antiche metropoli del Lazio*, Rome, 2008, photo Soprintendenza archeologica per la Toscana).

indicating an individual's prestige, showing frequent exchange of objects between different Etruscan communities and other communities of different cultures, especially those of Nuragic Sardinia (see Chapters 10 to 12). Alongside cremation burial, inhumation in earthen trenches appears and, in Populonia exceptionally, in chamber tombs with pseudo-vaults (Fig. 5.7). The deceased lies on his back fully clothed: more ornaments were placed with women, while men had weapons, and both sexes were accompanied by vases. The complement of ceramic vessels appears usual in all depositions whether cremation or inhumation. Weapons are now more often attested, but always in depositions that stand out with other elements (hut urns, scepters, etc.); more common among male burials are grave goods with helmet and razor, less common are those with helmet (mostly bronze), razor, sword and spear (Fig. 5.8). It is evidence, then, of a gradual transformation in funeral ritual, for which the previously sparse set of goods usually becomes more complex;

Figure 5.7   Chamber tomb at Populonia: tomb of *rasoio lunato* (after A. Minto, *Populonia*, Florence, 1943).

Figure 5.8   Grave group from Tarquinia (after F. Falchetti, *Etruschi*, Florence, 2000: photo Soprintendenza archeologica per la Toscana).

small groups of male and female burials that stand out either for the use of monumental tombs (chamber, trench, or pit-tombs with special covers) or for the presence of objects of particular prestige, such as weapons, pottery, ornaments in bronze and in precious materials.

These significant changes in funerary ideology, which indicate a process of social transformation taking place and exchange processes of a systematic and structural character, are mirrored by changes in regional planning. By examining the necropoleis we deduce a sharp increase in population in certain villages, despite the high infant mortality seen in paleoanthropological studies, and from an analysis of the grave offerings, emerges an impression of the uniformity of material culture and of the groups gravitating around the plateau.

From the end of the ninth century BC, there was in Italy a lively system of exchanges between communities both of the same culture and those far away. Relations with other Villanovan communities in the Po Valley and Salerno region are highlighted mainly by the distribution of bronze artifacts. Products of Bologna are popular in Etruria, both in coastal areas, especially Populonia and Vetulonia, and in the interior (Veii) by the end of the ninth century BC and then more often through the eighth century BC. It is generally razors and fibulae, bronze objects widely represented in Villanovan funerary offerings that are found in all areas. The presence of vessels and weapons among grave goods, usually defensive types (shields and later also helmets), indicates, from the end of the ninth century BC, a toreutic production whose models, styles and techniques seem to be closely linked to a larger, transalpine sphere, and especially to central and northern Europe.

The coastal communities of Etruria during this phase appear to take a major role in the Tyrrhenian Sea, engaging in trade with the Nuragic populations on one hand (Fig. 5.9) and the "Enotrian" communities of southern Italy on the other, via the Villanovan outposts in the Salerno region (see Chapter 16). If the mining centers of Etruria are more interested in relations with the islands of the Tyrrhenian (see Chapter 13), then those of southern coastal Etruria (Tarquinia and perhaps Vulci) seem to control the traffic along the Tyrrhenian coast.

As one gradually moves away from the first decades of the eighth century BC, the process of economic differentiation within society becomes more evident in the tombs that contain increasingly valuable material, and show us visible signs of a social gap. This delineates an elite in which a woman could be as privileged as a man and receive the same profusion of goods.

Generally, the birth of the middle-Tyrrhenian aristocracy is fixed within the eighth century BC. The funeral offerings of this period exhibit a progressive increase in quality and quantity; some burials stand out from the rest, throwing into relief movement within the body politic. In the first half of the century, we notice a contrast between some individuals recognized as persons of rank and the main group, which remains homogeneous.

In each community some male and female assemblages emerge (usually of warriors). The men are characterized as warriors/chariot-owners, and essential armaments are the circular shield of sheet-bronze decorated in repoussé and with an attached handle, crested helmet with horizontal tubes at the base, iron sword with bronze sheath, iron and bronze spears, and more rarely, axes. The materials relevant to these depositions show frequent contact between eminent persons: we find Enotrian material in Etruria (Fig. 5.10), and Villanovan material in Latium, from Campania to Calabria. Contact with the people

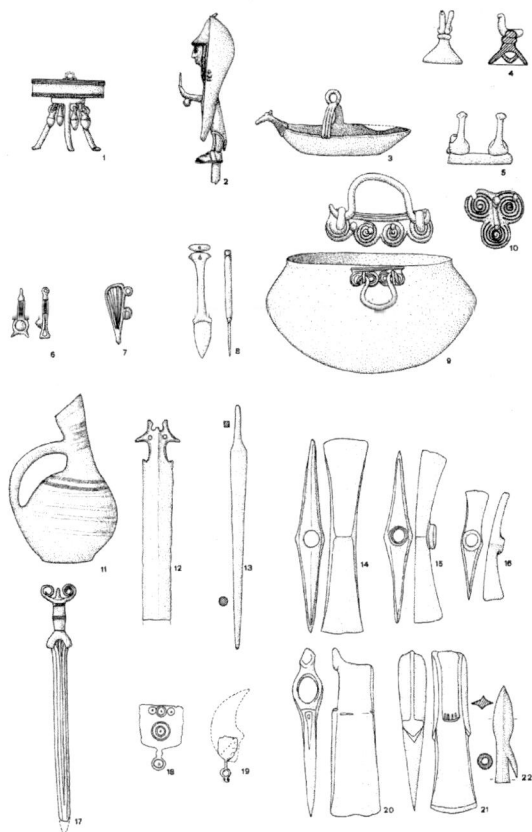

Figure 5.9   Etruscan material imported into Sardinia and Sardinian goods found in Etruria
(after *La Sardegna nel Mediterraneo tra il secondo e il primo millennio a.C.*, Cagliari, 1987).

of the eastern Mediterranean, which began early in the eighth century BC, continues to be widely attested in the middle decades of the century. In addition to the prestigious objects found in tombs of both sexes, male depositions are highlighted by weapons in various combinations, female burials are distinguished by ornaments belonging to rich headdresses and by impasto spindle whorls and *rocchetti* ("spools" or weaving weights) that were sometimes accompanied by spindles and distaffs in bronze.

The assemblages show significant enrichment with the presence of goods manufactured in the Near East and Greece: seals, scarabs, and pendants seem to be the materials of choice of the nascent local aristocracy, but there are also vases, as evidenced by the discovery in Tarquinia of a Phoenician-Cypriot jug type widespread in all the Phoenician settlements from Cyprus to Malaga, datable to the middle years of the eighth century BC, according to the stratigraphic sequence developed for Tyre (see Chapter 17).

In the necropoleis, tombs are arranged in small, no doubt family, groups: examination of the horizontal stratigraphy of burial at Veii, for example, shows a breakdown of the graves into more or less consistent groups, probably belonging to extended family groups, recognizable not only in their arrangement on the ground, but also for the combination of particular characteristics of the ritual and the grave goods.

Figure 5.10   Enotrian juglet from Vulci (after M. Torelli, A. M. Sgubini Moretti, *Etruschi. Le antiche metropoli del Lazio*, Rome, 2008, photo Soprintendenza archeologica per l'Etruria meridionale).

In the funeral ritual children are separated from the adult world because, as in life, they could not be considered active members of the community, with the exception of some depositions, almost always with rich offerings, where family ties have taken precedence over the rules. At Veii, in the Quattro Fontanili necropolis, some depositions identified as children's were accompanied by weapons and other items indicating that they undoubtedly belonged to a privileged line of descent in which lineage was more important than age, supporting the hypothesis that in death people often become what they were not in life.

Regarding the territorial layout, some rich tombs found in the countryside, outside the usual necropoleis, declare the desire to exhibit the acquisition of farmland by members of the aristocracy, and foreshadow the rise of many settlements scattered throughout the territory. This phenomenon that began in the eighth century BC asserts itself at the end of the century and especially during the early decades of the seventh century BC, probably following some sort of occupation of the land by large urban centers. Certainly it cannot be called a spontaneous phenomenon, but is rather an organized peopling of the landscape. The analysis of funerary ideology and of the typology of ceramic and metallic artifacts can indicate the different areas that correspond to the territories of the major cities.

The establishment of a hierarchy of stable and complex settlements from the mid/late eighth century BC represents a clear change in the history of the landscape. With the establishment of new settlements, we are seeing a turnaround in the terms of use of the territory compared to the situation that had arisen with the emergence of large proto-urban arrangements. The settlements reoccupy the territories that appear to have been abandoned in the early Iron Age, but it is now clear that a hierarchical relationship remained between the major and minor settlements. The impetus towards more systematic organization of the rural areas must be attributed to politically centralized institutions, which had to be the major Villanovan centers. This phenomenon has been linked to the emergence of a genuine agricultural nobility.

The ruling class shows that it consolidated its wealth, not only based on land ownership, but also on trade, understood in the broadest sense, including oppressive aspects such as the "economy of plunder" exercised through piracy or the exacting of tolls. The management of trade is the prerogative of some male figures, identifiable as warriors by the rich panoplies of their tombs, which were generally placed at the center of the burials of other members of the family clan.

If the goods and craftsmen show frequent movement, we must also imagine a dynamic of social mobility among the aristocracy, not only due to matrimony, but also to the pursuit of additional power and prestige. The use of gifts among prominent individuals, especially those of obvious prestige such as weapons or decorated vases, had to represent one of several forms of transfer of assets. The various modes of circulation, such as trade, marriage gifts, acquisition of spoils of war, gift exchange, relationships and related obligations of hospitality, the awarding of prizes for competitions, undoubtedly coexisted in the same environments.

The hundred years between the mid-eighth and mid-seventh centuries BC may therefore rightly be considered crucial for the relentless innovations that led to the passage from the great proto-urban centers to Greek-type *poleis* (cities), and from oral to written language, that is, from prehistory to history. A significant boost in the acceleration of the formation of urban communities in Tyrrhenian Italy has been attributed to contact with the Greek/Euboean communities located in the Bay of Naples from circa 770 BC. Indigenous communities established stable relations with the first Greek immigrants, who came first as prospectors on reconnaissance: the material evidence of exchanges between indigenous settlements and Greeks can be seen in the presence in funerary offerings at Tarquinia, Cerveteri and Veii of two-handled cups mainly of Euboean manufacture, painted on the zone between the handles with pendant semicircles (on the earliest examples) (Fig. 5.11), or with chevrons, or, on the later versions, with a metope enclosing a bird. These vases must be understood as a sign of relationships of hospitality, a custom acquired from abroad, and probably stimulated by occasional Greek presence.

Initially techniques and figural models were assimilated, and soon thereafter, more broadly cultural models were too (for example, with the introduction of writing, of a new method of banqueting, of a heroic funerary ideology, that is, a new mode of aristocratic living), such that the face of Etruscan society was profoundly changed. The principal cause for the escalation of these contacts must be attributed to the Greeks' interest in exploiting the Etruscans' metal resources. The communities with which the Greeks came into contact, then, seem to be well organized, used to contacting populations of similar or quite different cultures, fully interested in trade and ready to receive any sort of foreign stimulus. We witness, for example, the rapid adoption of new ceramic techniques and thus of foreign craftsmen.

For some scholars, the introduction of viticulture to Etruria and Latium is due to the Greeks: paleobotanical data, however, seem to place the diffusion of vines in Italy in a much earlier period. During the Villanovan period, whether in Etruria or Latium, we may detect a massive production of vessels connected with wine: kraters, jars (*olle*), and stands for both, two-handled cups (*kantharoi*), imitating more or less faithfully Greek models. Undoubtedly introduced by the Greeks was the ceremonial consumption of wine, which became a distinguishing element of aristocratic groups. Closely linked to contact with the Greek world is a new production of vases, first in purified clay, and then in thin-walled impasto turned on a fast potter's wheel and fired at high temperatures in kilns.

Moreover, among the grave goods classifiable in the eighth century BC, the increase in iron objects such as weapons, tools or ornaments, must be attributed to a development

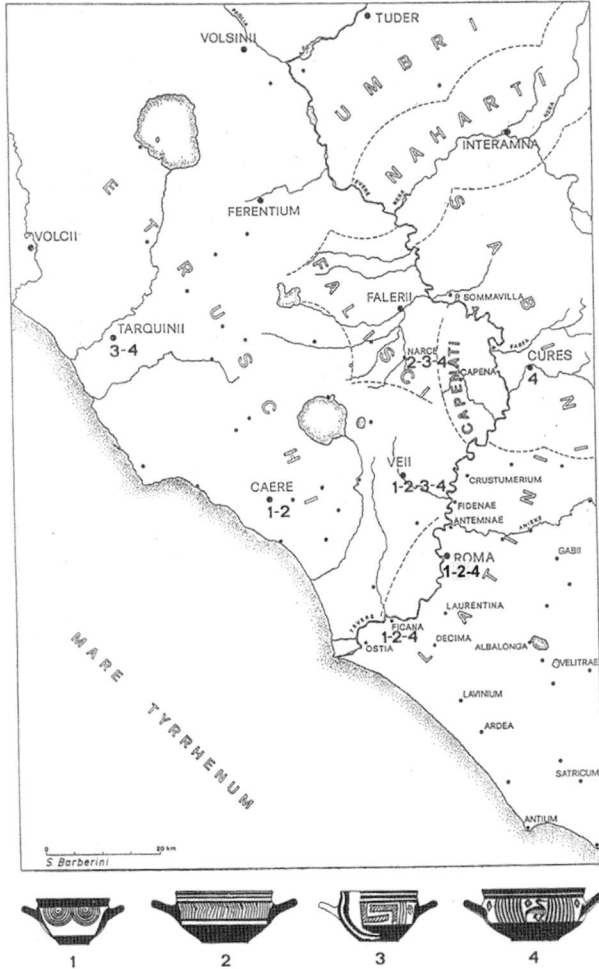

Figure 5.11 Diffusion of Greek geometric cups in Italy (*Magna Graecia. Archeologia di un sapere*, Milan, 2005, pp. 345–359).

or at least an increase, in the technology of working this metal, a technology intensively developed in the Aegean world; its transmission was presumably facilitated by contacts with Near Eastern populations. It is now the consensus, in fact, that the sophisticated techniques of working in many craft genres presuppose an apprenticeship spent with Greek or Near Eastern artisans, the keepers of a more advanced learning, whether sedentary or itinerant through various locations.

The Etruscan aristocrats tend, each one, to present himself as a *rex* ("king") within his own sphere, whether that is his family or the extended family, his *gens* (clan), *curia* ("tribe") or *populus* ("people", the entire community). (Note that we must use the Latin terms in the absence of Etruscan literature). At Veii, from the middle years of the eighth century through the entire seventh and into the first half of the sixth century BC, we may recognize the figures of the rulers (*capi*) who present notable parallels to the seven kings of Rome, to whom the oldest histories of Rome refer.

To one figure of a warrior were attributed all the powers of command, as he was buried with a special cremation ritual and with his ashes collected in a precious ossuary of bronze covered with a helmet and protected by a shield with anthropomorphic significance (Quattro Fontanili, tomb AA 1). His death must be dated to the decades after the middle of the eighth century BC (Fig. 5.12), recalling the death of a king well known for his merit in religious institutions, just as tradition refers to the second king of Rome, Numa Pompilius.

In tomb 1036 of the Veii necropolis of Casal del Fosso, excavated in 1915 but restored only in 2001, the deceased was covered by two bilobate shields; the rest of his armour consists of a crested helmet, a cuirass composed of two discs of sheet-bronze, two swords, a spear and a chariot symbolized by a pair of bronze horse-bits. The burial was completed by a scepter, a mace, and two bronze vases imported from the Danube region. (Fig. 5.13).

Armour composed of a cuirass, double shields, sword and spear appears commonly in Latial tombs of the tenth century BC, in a time when formal burials are the prerogative of the heads of villages with a more or less family character. The use of this type of

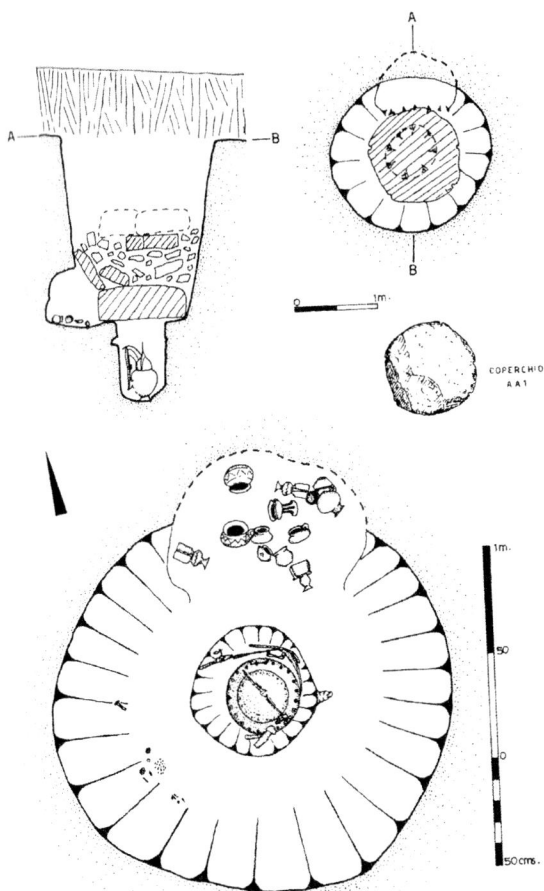

Figure 5.12 Tomb AAI of the Veian necropolis of Quattro Fontanili
(after *Notizie degli Scavi* 1970. pp. 292–308).

armament in a decidedly more recent context appears, then, undoubtedly symbolic and ritual in character. We must associate the personage buried in the Veii tomb with the priestly college of the Salii, founded by Numa, but attested in much later eras both in Latium and Etruria. Strictly associated with the cult of the Salii is also the mace used in rituals to strike the *ancilia*, the bilobate shields. There is a telling reference in this burial to the tomb of Morrius, king of the Veientines, whom Servius in the epitome to Virgil's *Aeneid* likens to Numa Pompilius in his explanation of the founding of the cult of the Salii.

At least twenty years later the same necropolis, tomb 871, also shows exceptional characteristics, with a very tall crested helmet (Fig. 5.14), a trapezoidal fan, a complete

Figure 5.13   Tomb 1036 of the Veian necropolis of Casal del Fosso (after *Etruschi, l'ideale eroico e il vino lucente*, Milano 2012).

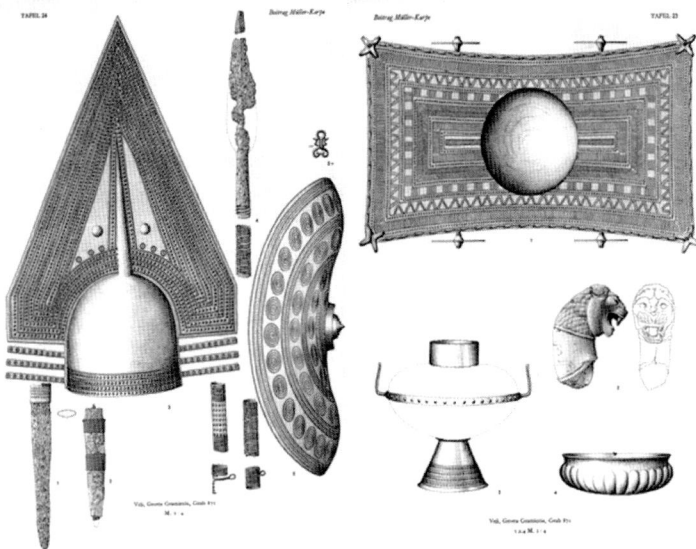

Figure 5.14   Tomb 871 of the Veian necropolis of Casal del Fosso: crested helmet
(after L. Drago Troccoli, in Dinamiche di sviluppo della città nell'Etruria Meridionale, Veio,
Caere e Vulci, Rome-Pisa 2005).

set of armour, a scepter and a footstool, no doubt symbolic of the throne, and a bronze rhyton perhaps of Assyrian origin). The visual reference is obviously to a monarch of Near Eastern type. Excavations in the settlements provide evidence of structures that begin to stand out from average huts: from the end of the eighth century BC, when the aristocratic class is already well defined, with emerging headmen/chiefs, some structures with rectangular plans, divided into two or three rooms, stand out from the common huts of oval outline, which are still the main type of habitation (Fig. 5.15). These great huts of wood, planned with multiple rooms and given porches and courtyards, may be considered royal residences. In the "houses of the king," true political centers and community institutions (Fig. 5.16) begin to develop community functions, with rituals especially linked to banquets.

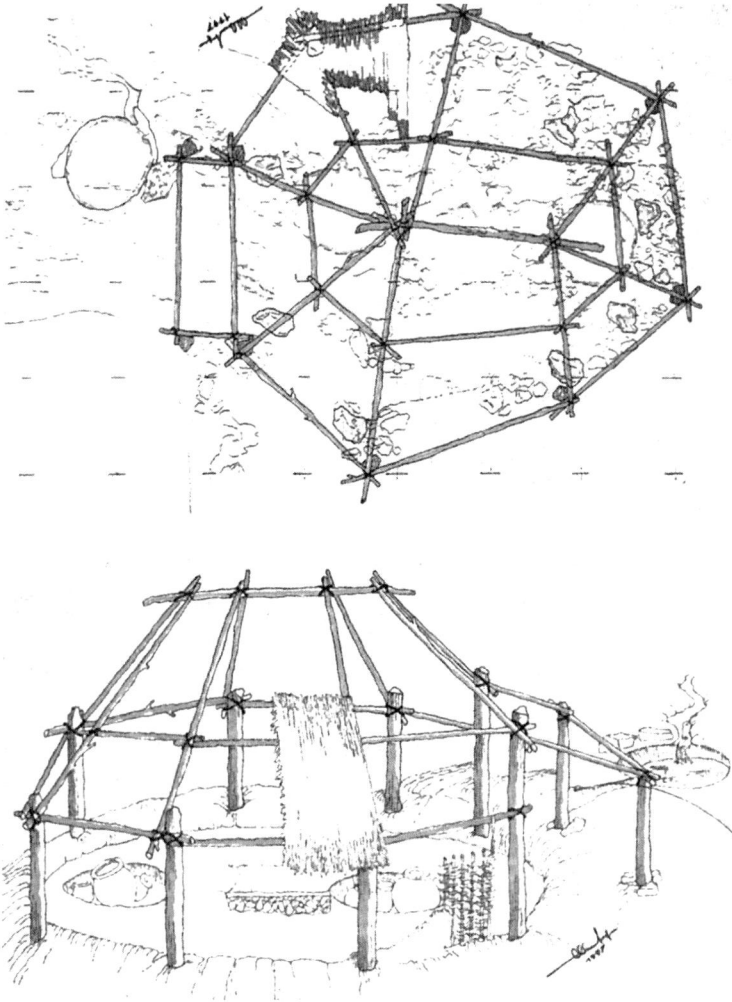

Figure 5.15   Hut at Populonia (Excavations G. Bartoloni, processing V. Acconcia, A. Di Napoli).

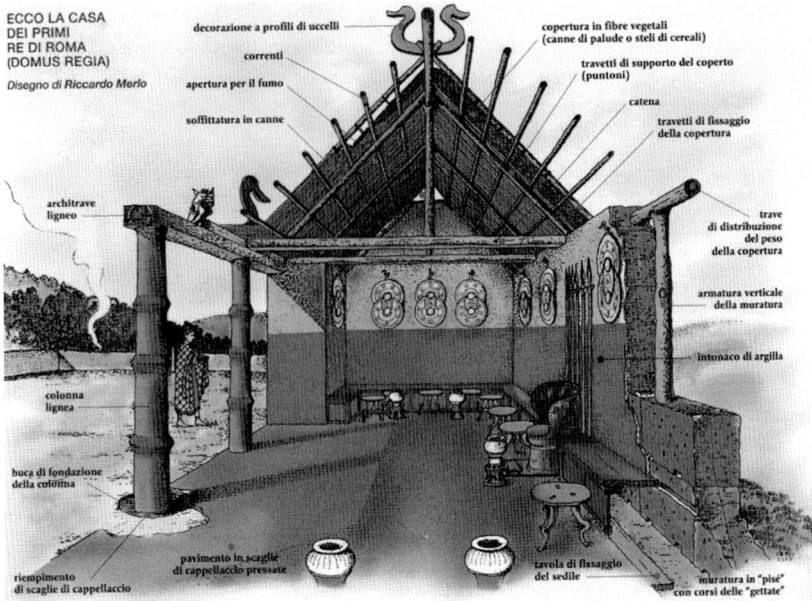

Figure 5.16   Reconstruction of the banquet hall in the regia identified on the northern slope of the
Palatine (excavations of A. Carandini, drawing R. Merlo).

BIBLIOGRAPHY

On the end of the Bronze Age:

Bietti Sestieri, A. M. (1996) *Protostoria. Teoria e pratica*, Rome: Carocci editore.

Negroni Catacchio, N. (ed.) (1998) *Preistoria e protostoria in Etruria. Terzo incontro di Studi. Protovillanoviani e/o Protoetruschi. Ricerche e scavi*, Milan: Centro studi di preistoria e archeologia.

Peroni, R. (1996) *L'Italia alle soglie della storia*, Bari: Laterza.

Zanini, A. (ed.) (1997) *Dal Bronzo al Ferro.Il II millennio a.C. nella Toscana Centro-Occidentale*, Livorno, pp. 27–31.

——(1998) "The final Bronze Age in Tuscany" in *Atti del XIII Congresso. Unione Internazionale delle Scienze preistoriche e protostoriche*, Forlì A.B.A.C.O, pp. 395–398.

On Villanovan culture in general:

Bartoloni, G. (2002) *La cultura villanoviana. All'inizio della storia etrusca*, Roma NIS 1989 (2nd edition Rome: Carocci editore).

Fugazzola Delpino, M. A. (1984) *La cultura villanoviana. Guida ai materiali della prima età del ferro nel Museo di Villa Giulia*, Rome: Edizioni dell'Ateneo.

On the process of urban formation:

Bartoloni, G. (2008) *La nascita delle metropoli dell'Etruria meridionale* in *Etruschi. Le antiche metropoli del Lazio*, Milan: Electa, 20, pp. 38–45.

D'Agostino, B. (2001) "La città" in *Dinamiche dello sviluppo delle città nell'Etruria meridionale: Veio, Caere, Tarquinia, Vulci, Atti del XXIII Convegno di Studi Etruschi e Italici (ottobre 2001)*, Pisa-Rome Istituti editoriali e poligrafici internazionali 2005, pp. 21–25.

On relations with Sardinia (see also Chapter 12):

Lo Schiavo, F., Falchi, P. and Milletti, M. (eds) (2008) *Gli Etruschi e la Sardegna tra la fine dell'età dell'età del bronzo e gli inizi dell'età del ferro*, catalogo della mostra, Florence: Contemporanea Progetti.

Paoletti, O. and Tamagno Perna L. (eds) (2002) *Etruria e Sardegna centro-settentrionale tra l'età del bronzo finale e l'arcaismo. Atti del XXI Convegno di studi etruschi ed italici*, Sassari – Alghero – Oristano – Torralba, 13–17 October 1998, Pisa-Rome: Istituti editoriali e poligrafici internazionali.

On relations with native centers of southern Italy:

Delpino, F. (1986) "Rapporti e scambi nell'Etruria meridionale villanoviana con particolare riferimento al Mezzogiorno" in *Archeologia nella Tuscia*, vol. II, "Quaderni di Archeologia etrusco-italica", 13, Rome: Consiglio nazionale delle ricerche, pp. 167–76.

On relations with central Europe:

Iaia, C. (2005) *Produzioni toreutiche della prima età del ferro in Italia centro-settentrionale. Stili decorativi, circolazione, significato*, Pisa-Rome: Istituto Editoriali e Poligrafici Internazionali.

On the beginnings of the aristocracies in Tyrrhenian Italy:

Bartoloni, G. (2003) *Le società dell'Italia primitiva. Lo studio delle necropoli e la nascita delle aristocrazie*, Rome: Carocci editore.

On the first relations with the Greek world:

Bartoloni, G. (2005) "Inizi della colonizzazione nel centro Italia" in *Magna Graecia. Archeologia di un sapere*, Milan: Electa, pp. 345–359.

On relations with the Near East:

Martelli, M. (1991) "I Fenici e la questione orientalizzante in Italia" in *Atti del secondo congresso internazionale di studi fenici e punici*, Rome: Consiglio Nazionale delle ricerche, pp. 1049–1070.

Sciacca, F. (2005) *Patere baccellate in bronzo.Oriente, Grecia, Italia in età orientalizzante*, Rome: "L'ERMA" di Bretscneider.

von Hase, F. W. (1995) "Ägäische, griechische und vorderorientalische Einflüsse auf das tyrrhenische Mittelitalien" in *Beiträge zur Urnenfelderzeit nördlich und südlich der Alpen*, Bonn: R. Habelt, pp. 239–286.

On women in Etruria (see also Chapter 20):

Sordi, M. (1981) "La donna etrusca" in AA.VV., *Misoginia e maschilismo in Grecia e in Roma*, Genova Istituto di filologia classica e medievale, Genoa: University of Genoa, pp. 49–67.

D'Agostino, B. (1993) "La donna in Etruria" in M. Bettini (a cura di). *Maschile femminile. Genere e ruoli nelle culture antiche*, Roma-Bari: Laterza, pp. 61–73.

von Eles, P. (ed.) (2005) *Le ore e i giorni delle donne* Verucchio: Pazzini editore.

Pitzalis, F. (2011) *Volontà meno apparente. Donne e società nell'Italia centrale tirrenica tra VIII e VII secolo a.C.*, Rome: "L'ERMA" di Bretschneider.

On Etruscan textiles (see also Chapter 42):

Gleba, M. (2008) *Textile Production in Pre-Roman Italy.* Ancient Textile Series, Oxford/Oakville, CT: Oxbow Books/David Brown, vol. 4 pp. 1–270;

Gleba, M., Herring, E. and Lomas, K. (eds) (2009) *Textile tools and specialisation in the Early Iron Age female burials. BAR International. Gender Identities in Italy in the First Millennium* BC., Oxford: Archaeopress, pp. 69–78.

Gleba, M. and Mannering, U. (2012) *Textiles & Textile Production in Europe From Prehistory to* AD 400, Oxford/Oakville, CT: Oxbow Books/David Brown.

CHAPTER SIX

ORIENTALIZING ETRURIA

———•◆•———

Maurizio Sannibale

GENERAL

The Orientalizing phase (circa 730–580 BC) is a vast cultural phenomenon involving the entire Mediterranean basin, with the movement of people and goods, technology exchanges, and contacts in Etruria which were to establish significant economic growth, a truly epochal "leap."[1] A crucial role in this phenomenon will be exercised by the renewed wave of Phoenician expansion, induced by Assyrian pressure on the Palestinian-Syrian coast between the reigns of Tiglath-pileser III (744–727 BC) and Esarhaddon (680–669 BC). This must have upset the liberty and economic structures of the Levantine states hitherto ruled by local dynasties,[2] and affected the colonial diaspora of Greeks to the west. It is in this cultural context in Greece that the compilation of the Homeric poems occurs, narrating much earlier events that are inevitably affected by the present conditions of those regions.

The Orientalizing is a crucial period, then, which sees Etruscan civilization at its grand beginnings, in a phase of rapid and significant changes that will leave their mark on all of Western culture: the rise of cities, large colonial settlements, the spread of writing. Men of different ethnicity who move and meet each other for trade and the search for raw materials will transfer knowledge and technology, and wealth will grow.

The Etruscan aristocracy, asserting itself in its leadership role and in consolidating riches, will look to the pomp of Eastern courts as a model. The practice of peer gift-exchange, around which revolve commercial and diplomatic relations, causes a wide spread of goods, creating bonds of reciprocity not only among men, but also between men and gods as occurred in the Greek world with offerings destined for sanctuaries. The objects found in tombs, made of bronze, but also in silver, gold, and exotic materials such as ivory and ostrich eggs, as well as amber, glass paste, wood, and iron, illustrate the powers and ceremony reserved for the sovereign in the course of life and in some way guaranteed them after death. The new goods,[3] imported or produced locally by immigrant craftsmen (see Chapter 48), are characterized by a virtuosity and eclecticism that tend to test the full potential of the materials. Along with the prestige goods are introduced themes, iconography and technologies from the eastern Mediterranean (Egypt, Syria, Cyprus, Rhodes, Greece) and the Near East (as far as Urartu and Mesopotamia).

Simultaneously, objects of Etruscan production, mainly bronzes and bucchero vases, will reach Greek sanctuaries and other sites in the Mediterranean.[4]

The Orientalizing phenomenon in Etruria is manifested mainly in southern cities not far from the coast and which are more open to contacts (Veii, Caere, Tarquinia, and next Vulci) while in contact with the mining district of the mountains of Tolfa. To the north, actually on the sea, we find Populonia, linked to mineral resources and the Colline Metallifere ("Metal-bearing Hills") and the island of Elba; the major cities of the interior include Chiusi, Vetulonia, and Volterra. In this period the process of urbanization comes to fruition and establishes a monumental and more permanent form for necropoleis as well, as in the notable case of Cerveteri, where there is a sudden burgeoning of the monumental tumulus, perhaps derived directly from the Near East; this will spread elsewhere.

Among the most important innovations incorporated in Etruria during the Orientalizing phase are surely the acquisition of the alphabet and writing technique that occurred by the late eighth century BC. The alphabet adopted by the Etruscans is basically the western Greek, Chalcidian script, which must have been acquired by the cities of southern Etruria as a result of their contact with Euboeans located in the Bay of Naples (Fig. 6.1). In the burials are ostentatious sample alphabets and syllabaries with the teaching sequence of the 26 letters of the Euboean alphabet, incised on objects that recall this recently introduced practice, such as the ivory tablet of Marsiliana d'Albenga and the so-called Regolini-Galassi inkwell. To formulae written during the practice of gift-exchange is thus added the memory of the event with the explicit mention of donor and recipient.

The contacts underway during colonization in the West led to the acquisition not only of goods but also of cultural models. Among these the custom of the banquet assumes the central place at court, following the Greek custom derived from the East,[5] to which may be traced the most precious objects and furnishings: bronze cauldrons with animal finials originating in eastern Anatolia and northern Syria (Fig. 6.2) and skewers used in the preparation of meat which was then divided according to specific codes of hierarchy among those admitted to the court.

Even the ritualized consumption of wine, an exotic and valuable drink, first imported and then manufactured in Etruria (archaeology increasingly reveals traces of early cultivation of the vine), will constitute a genuine prerogative of noble groups. Around the ritual of drinking among equals in a communal event will develop alliances and decisions, established relationships with foreigners: destined for this are pitchers, cups and chalices of precious or expensive material, such as glass and fine ceramics. In particular, there is the adoption of drinking vessels of solemn ceremonial function from the eastern courts, such as ribbed bowls (*patere baccellate*), which acquire a lofty symbolic value recognized as an attribute of rank, originally reserved for kings and their dignitaries at the Assyrian courts (Fig. 6.3).[6] At first imported and then widely produced in Italy, they did not remain confined to the aristocratic banquet of the living: their deposition among funerary offerings extends the theme of royalty to the feast of the dead and the ancestors. The same goes for the hemispherical cup, a banquet vessel of ancient Near Eastern tradition, introduced early in Italy (at Torre Galli in the ninth century, in bronze), of which there are adaptations in glass (Bernardini tomb, Palestrina) and imported versions in precious metal (see Fig. 6.8), or the local "scales cups" in silver, produced at Cerveteri (see Fig. 6.32).

The same consumption of wine in the ritualized conviviality of the banquet offers numerous opportunities for the simultaneous presence of accessories that bring together

Figure 6.1 Bottle-vase (so-called inkwell) in bucchero with syllabary incised on body and model alphabet on ring-base. From Cerveteri. Regolini-Galassi excavations. 650–600 BC Museo Gregoriano Etrusco 20349. Photo © Musei Vaticani.

Figure 6.2 Cauldron in bronze decorated in repoussé and with lion protomes. Cerveteri, Regolini-Galassi Tomb. 675–650 BC Museo Gregoriano Etrusco 20207. Photo © Musei Vaticani.

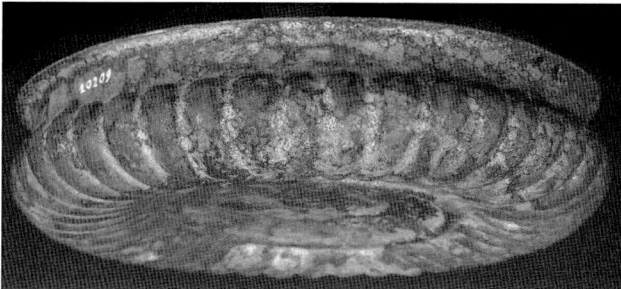

Figure 6.3 Ribbed bowl in bronze. Cerveteri, Regolini-Galassi Tomb. 675–650 BC Museo Gregoriano Etrusco 20209. Photo © Musei Vaticani.

the worlds of Greece and the Near East: the metal cheese graters, associated with pottery drinking cups, reminiscent of the ancient Greek custom of garnishing wine with cheese (Fig. 6.4), while some ceramic tripod-bowls, found in Etruria and Latium, were used as mortars for grinding aromatic substances intended to enhance the flavor of wine, and may be traced to northern Syria and the Phoenician colonies in the central Mediterranean (Fig. 6.5). In addition, fans, censers, plectra for stringed instruments, and spoons for cosmetics, precious ornaments for clothes, and jewelry eloquently evoke the splendor of palace life (Fig. 6.6). These objects also convey the image and the official ideology of the prince; always pictured as a warrior hero, whether on land or sea, as on the Aristonothos krater. On the Phoenician-Cypriot engraved *paterae* (bowls), objects worthy of a king, issues related to royalty stand out, such as hunting, war, the triumph of Pharaoh, divine nursing scenes, dynastic and eschatological symbols that summarize well the essence of the Orientalizing phenomenon: we are dealing with precious Phoenician craft creations, which draw upon an Egyptianizing iconographic repertoire with Near Eastern influences; they were received as prestige-gifts by Etruscan princes, but also by the lords of Palestrina and Pontecagnano (Figs. 6.7 and 6.8).

Figure 6.4   Grater in bronze. Provenance unknown. Seventh century BC. Museo Gregoriano Etrusco 11175. Photo © Musei Vaticani.

Figure 6.5   Tripod-bowl, ceramic. Ceremonial vase of Phoenician type after Assyrian prototypes. From Vulci, formerly Raccolta Giacinto Guglielmi. 625–600 BC Museo Gregoriano Etrusco 39704. Photo © Musei Vaticani.

Figure 6.6 Fan in bronze. From Populonia, Tomba dei Flabelli.
675–625 BC Firenze, Museo Archeologico Nazionale 89325.

Figure 6.7 Phoenician bowl. Processions of warriors and sacred nursing scene (cow and calf).
Gilded silver, decorated in repoussé and engraved. On the exterior is an Etruscan inscription
of possession: *larthia velthurus*. Cerveteri, Regolini-Galassi Tomb. 675–650 BC Museo
Gregoriano Etrusco 20364. Photo © Musei Vaticani.

Figure 6.8 Hemispherical, double-walled cup of Phoenician manufacture. Scenes of lion hunt, war
(processions of infantry, cavalry, chariots), sacred nursing (cow with calf in papyrus thicket), banquet.
Gilded silver, decorated in repoussé and engraved. Cerveteri, Regolini-Galassi Tomb. 675–650 BC Museo
Gregoriano Etrusco 20365. Photo © Musei Vaticani.

Despite the rarity of real weapons in the tombs where we often find enhanced, decorative examples and lighter, symbolic "parade" versions, even the shields hung on the walls, in sheet bronze or represented in relief, are already a symbol of power rather than a direct reference to warlike enterprise, as is the war chariot, a parade vehicle devoid of any real tactical use in the rugged terrain of the Middle Tyrrhenian (see Chapter 41). The same goes for the axe, more sacrificial tool than weapon, linked to the religious function of the sovereign and often echoed by the trident as a symbol of the beam of lightning and of divination.

The prince's wife, as a fundamental figure in the hereditary transmission of power, shared status and wealth with her husband, while retaining that prerogative in the house, so characteristic of the Homeric queens from Penelope to Helen: weaving, as is represented on the *tintinnabulum* ("ceremonial rattle") from the Tomba degli Ori of Bologna. Thus, together with jewels and precious vases, in the burials of women of rank we also find spindle-whorls for the processing of wool, reproduced, however, in precious materials.

The Etruscans are not mere collectors of imported models: in a central position, between the Mediterranean and Europe, they will play a role as a bridge between East and West. The pomp and ceremony of their courts will eventually seduce the Celtic princes of the transalpine region who will collect objects of Etruscan manufacture for their rituals and funerary offerings.

REFLECTIONS UPON ETRUSCAN ORIENTALIZING

When Helbig published in 1879 the Barberini Tomb of Palestrina, one of the most representative Orientalizing complexes of Middle-Tyrrhenian Italy, he could not help but draw on Homeric descriptions for interpreting funerary objects. In fact he unleashed a flood of Homeric archaeology (one that still flows today) in an approach that tends to interpret archaeological data from the Mycenaean to Archaic periods in light of the descriptions of Homer. Following Herodotus and the Bible, even in later studies, the German scholar did not fail to emphasize the presence of oriental objects and the role of the Phoenicians in the production and trade of luxury goods.[7]

Not very different was the approach of Italian palaeoethnologist Giovanni Pinza when in 1915 he studied the Regolini-Galassi Tomb of Caere, another cornerstone for the understanding of the Orientalizing phenomenon in Etruria. Although superseded in many points, Pinza's pan-Mediterranean study remains valid, and captures the interrelationships between Etruria, the Near East and the Aegean world, including Egyptian cultural influences.

Unfortunately, the decline of romantic nationalism and the moral and material devastation of two world wars, stimulated by a progressive anti-Semitic imprint, highly conditioned studies of the Orientalizing phase in Etruria. These did not fail to take chauvinistic tones and Etrusco-centric viewpoints. Even the monograph that historian Luigi Pareti devoted to the Regolini-Galassi Tomb in 1947 expresses an almost ideological rejection of the role of the Phoenicians (and thus Semitic culture) in the Mediterranean and the Tyrrhenian coast, when he says:

> There was a time when the Phoenicians and Phoenician thalassocracy were used to explain everything [...] But many archaeologists [...] have continued undeterred to

talk about those Phoenicians, masters of the seas, instructors of the Homeric bards and so on: and therefore to support the Sidonian or Syriac regions as the sources of Orientalizing Etruscan art [...] In any case the thesis of high-volume Phoenician import trade in Etruria [...] is completely unacceptable.[8]

It makes one reflect upon the coincidence of certain conclusions with some of the axiomatic statements that a few years earlier (1938) appeared in the "Manifesto of the Race," of sad and shameful memory, conceived by the fascist regime, of which I quote some passages:

> The population of Italy is currently, in the majority, of Aryan origin and Aryan civilization. This population of Aryan civilization has lived for several millennia in the peninsula, little has remained of the civilization of the pre-Aryan people [...] Of the Semites who over the centuries have landed on the sacred soil of our Country in general nothing is left.[9]

Throughout the second half of the twentieth century it would be necessary to overcome the ideological confrontation between East and West within paganizing classicism and recognize not only the presence of genuine goods and merchandise coming from the East, but also the circulation of people and ideas. Moreover, the same Homeric poems were recorded and perpetuated through the alphabet, the Semitic invention adopted by Greeks who themselves participated in Orientalizing culture.[10] To analyze Etruscan Orientalizing as a whole, yet seek to dissect the Greek from the Near Eastern in the logic of contrast, could therefore be a false problem.[11]

From the time when navigation was developed the Mediterranean joined rather than separated lands and peoples. These lines of union, which follow the seasonal routes of winds and currents, are not unidirectional. In addition to the mutual relationship between the departure and landing sites, infinite combinations were made possible by the intermediate stages, as indicated by the diverse array of cargoes of wrecks, from the Bronze Age onward.

The Orientalizing has been traditionally linked to the question of Etruscan origins, in particular the Eastern hypothesis (see Chapter 3) supported by the oldest literary tradition, in supposed agreement with the character of the archaeological record. In reality, the Etruscan *ethnos* appears already defined in the Late Bronze Age, in anticipation of the substantial identification of the early Iron Age Villanovans with the Etruscans who will be actors in the Orientalizing phenomenon. This phenomenon does not emerge out of nowhere; it connects with the dynamics of trade and contacts, related to the search for metals that had already transpired in the Bronze Age, and sailing to the west, the ends of the known world. The agents will be the Levant and the Aegean world and the large Mediterranean islands, including Crete, Cyprus, and Nuragic Sardinia, with which Etruria entertained strong and early relationships. Among the documents of these dynamics is the introduction into Italy of small anthropomorphic clay figurines begun in the Late Bronze Age; their magico-ritual aspects seem to evolve into forms of veneration in the Iron Age. In this case we should backdate the beginning of the process of anthropomorphizing the divine, re-attributing it to eastern influence.[12]

Iron Age material culture, especially in funerary offerings, already attests to the formation of elites who display weapons and horse trappings as well as pottery and bronze ornaments in their tombs. This connotation of the warrior classes was readily related to emerging new territorial organizations and the formation of large, populous proto-urban centers in locations that would become the Etruscan cities of the historical age, at the expense of abandoning older, smaller hilltop settlements scattered throughout the territory.

Already boat-shaped vases, which appear in Late Villanovan (*Villanoviano evoluto*) tombs, reveal the early Etruscans' special relationship with the sea, whether they symbolize the sea voyage to the Afterlife, or relate to actual navigation. Ancient sources attest to an actual Tyrrhenian mastery of the seas that delayed the Greek colonization of Sicily and prevented it moving north of the Bay of Naples, if not from landing on the French coast and there founding Massalia c. 600 BC.

The reading of the cultural dynamics that will lead Etruria in the age of metals to develop a complex urban civilization, able to interact with the most advanced peoples of the ancient Mediterranean, has sometimes suffered from a certain interpretative automatism. Basically, we have become accustomed to read and believe that given certain conditions, such as agricultural and agronomic development and availability of raw materials, the outcome could only be a spontaneous aggregation of villages, the foundation of cities, the emergence of a ruling class of "*principes*" that can establish and control a territory and its increased wealth. A consequence of this would have been a stimulus to exchange and trade, initially launched through the circuit of gift-exchange and import of precious objects of craftsmanship, some from distant lands. For many decades, the notion prevailed that Etruscan Orientalizing constituted only a tumultuous confluence of exotic goods, in exchange for raw materials and products from the new rich of the West, who were deemed to be only minimally involved with the culture that had produced those same goods.

The mere material aspects – even though they seem to be concrete – require an interpretive effort to determine what led to the intellectual and spiritual development of a culture: not all of these immaterial, intangible aspects leave archaeological traces. The circulation of precious objects and valuable material, of craftsmanship and sophisticated technology, constitutes, in purely economic perspective, an increase of value. This value tends to increase in passing from hand to hand through the circuit of gift-exchange and the consequent custom of hoarding. All this constitutes the intangible component of goods, linked as they are to the men and ideas with which they have circulated.

To reconstruct the story in the absence of history, that is, written sources, mechanistic approaches have sometimes been attempted, stating that, from a chaotic state of departure, a community of people eventually reaches a form of organization, in which there will emerge a certain percentage of individuals with the character of a leader, and finally, that given certain conditions, such as creating a surplus, the economy is necessarily destined to expand, increasing the level of trade with ever larger spheres of circulation. In our case it appears valid to propose a simple historical approach, based on events occurring in the ancient Near East between the ninth and seventh centuries BC, which led to a movement, a diaspora westward of heterogeneous cultural components.

Of course a reasonable doubt remains as to whether these artisans, scholars and traders moving westward were simple "orphans" of a palace and a city, or whether among them were also the bearers, some even the leading exponents, of a culture. Certainly in exporting and manufacturing of goods, gifts bringing highly symbolic and complex iconography, they consciously related to the Etruscan princes as counterparts and potential partners with much in common. In fact, we know what occurred during contact with the Greek world, but we cannot exclude the possibility that something similar may have occurred in the presence of Levantine individuals. The arrival of Demaratus in Etruria offers an interpretive parameter on the mobility and possibility for integration of a foreign individual into an already structured group, especially to introduce new knowledge. Demaratus, the father of the future king of Rome, Tarquinius Priscus, came from Corinth, exiled after the royal line of Bacchiads to which he belonged was outlawed in 657 BC by the new ruler, the tyrant Cypselus. Demaratus arrived in Tarquinia, tracing the routes westward which, as a wealthy merchant he had already traveled, along with others of his countrymen; their names are known for the close connection with arts and crafts: Eucheir ("skillful hand"), Diopos ("talented eye"), Eugrammos ("good at drawing"). Similar stories, or the possibility for a foreigner to be co-opted into the ranks in the Etruscan nobility, are implied in an Etruscan inscription on a vase discovered in the "Tumulus of the King" in the Doganaccia necropolis of Tarquinia, close to that of "The Queen" (see below), which quotes a certain Rutile Hipucrates, whose family name clearly expresses his Greek descent.

For decades the Etruscan *principes* seem to emulate the pomp and ceremony of Near Eastern courts. One wonders what their actual perception and cognition of such a distant world could have been. Was it sufficient to import and introduce new techniques and iconography to convey new cultural patterns and knowledge? Certainly image and symbol are able to replace the written word and the sign, but since their acquisition does not appear random here, the receptor must have been able to understand and perhaps to select them. A "dialogue" between cultures was necessary rather than a "silent barter" system.

It is believed that the Etruscan counterpart of this trade was in metals, agricultural, and livestock products, salt, perhaps even slaves. Of course our old image of the economy is strongly affected by our industrial civilization, with its abundance of goods and raw materials, ease of transport, and availability of large and immediate sources of energy. This should make us reflect on the real value of objects and materials in Antiquity. Think of the metals. Usually ships were not loaded with ore. In fact, there are ingots on the wrecks found and by the time an ingot appears, a whole process of transformation has already transpired. A metal ingot implies an intrinsic value, as a sort of non-perishable storage of energy and manpower, which have been spent for the research and curation of mineral deposits, the extraction and transportation, metallurgical processes, and access to energy sources, namely the burning of forests and the production of charcoal. On the one hand is the technological know-how, and on the other, specific and abundant manpower, supported by adequate food production. If the metal-smith can be thought of as a single, itinerant individual, the serial process of production that leads from the ore to the metal requires a territorial organization of resources that includes the control of the mines. It is perhaps no coincidence that coinage involves metallurgy.

Even textile art, with the production of clothing, represents a source of wealth, as well as a significant leap in the quality of life. Weaving was done in the home and carried on, almost as a prerogative, by women of rank. The clothes mostly remain in the negative, as archaeological documents, but there remains the presence of fibulae found in the graves, or even offered in Greek sanctuaries[13] (see Chapter 42). Iconographic documents such as the *tintinnabulum* from Bologna and the throne of Verucchio show the processing steps.[14] We should not forget that textiles may have carried decorative motifs and iconography. For all the crafts in the Orientalizing phenomenon we see that the specialization of roles, the urban experience, understood as an organization of public and private spaces within it, and land management, are both the preamble and the product.

BETWEEN TECHNOLOGY AND SYMBOL: THE TRANSFER OF THE GOLDSMITH'S ART AND OF ARTISANS

The technology transfer of the goldsmith's art to the West is a broad cultural phenomenon, the direct transmission of knowledge and empirical aspects, accompanying an intangible heritage linked to the formal aspects: iconography, symbol, message.[15] In investigating the contextual acquisition of typological and iconographic elements we cannot ignore the prevailing ritual character of production in the eastern areas that instilled a high degree of symbolism, which is where the symbol and analogy are the only direct form of conceptual communication, and we should not forget how this can be traced back to the realm of magic.

The technical principles of the Etruscan goldsmith, filigree and granulation, burst onto the Tyrrhenian Early Orientalizing scene without previous technological and formal predecessors, after only the briefest, minimal experimental phase (see Chapter 50). The link has now been identified in the construction of a "Villanovan" gold fibula, from a *tomba a pozzo* in Tarquinia, dated to the mid-eighth century BC (Fig. 6.9).[16] Its linear decoration and filled triangles evoke Eastern models distributed during the second millennium. But what now appear even more extraordinary are the technological elements that clearly distinguish the Tarquinia fibula from Etruscan jewelry: layout and grain size (0.4 mm), and the same welding technique with salts of silver instead of copper, making it in virtually all aspects identical to the goldwork of the East, including those extraordinary discoveries in the royal necropolis of Ebla. Similar Eastern techniques can be found in the jewelry of Cumae, which, however, appears toward the end of the eighth century BC, also as some of the first evidence in Italy of fine granulation technique with solder of copper salts, typical of Etruscan jewelry. It is likely that the area of the Phlegraean Fields was one of the "laboratories" in which the meeting of cultures fostered a decisive technological advance.[17]

It is no coincidence that new techniques are associated with the introduction of any new motifs that, in themselves, are more than mere decoration. Suffice it to consider the rising moon and sun motifs, the disc-shaped pendant-amulets common in Etruria, Latium, Campania, but also in Rhodes, during the eighth century. These are the delocalized and later descendents of far more ancient Near Eastern amulets, symbols of deities in aniconic phase,[18] in which we also find the reason for the star/rosette of Inanna/Ishtar,[19] as in the Tarquinia pendant.[20] Pendant-amulets, in the form of divine symbols, are worn by Ashurnasirpal II (883–859) and other Assyrian kings of the ninth and eighth centuries. It is reasonable to question whether the presence of these ancient symbols of astral divinity in the Orientalizing gold of Etruria is totally without meaning (Fig. 6.10).

Figure 6.9   Tarquinia. Fibula in gold decorated in granulation and filigree. Second half of eighth century BC. Photo Soprintendenza per i Beni Archeologici per l'Etruria Meridionale.

It is possible that the very adoption of gold, increasing more and more, was strongly determined by its original symbolic value in Eastern cultures, rather than its material value. Gold, absent from Italian indigenous deposits and material culture, is intimately bound in the ancient Near East and Egypt with the sphere of the divine and kingship, never separated entirely from magical-religious meanings. In Egyptian funerary ritual gold is associated with the concept of immortality of the body, represented as a palliative to Late Period mummification. Through the gold that covers it, the body of the deceased is regenerated by passing to the divine from the human state. Gold, associated with the sun and the stars, the prerogative of Ra and Hathor, is the incorruptible flesh of the gods. For example, in the "*Book of the Heavenly Cow*," the body of the sun god Ra is made up of precious metals: silver for the bones, gold for the flesh and lapis lazuli for the hair.[21]

In explicit connection with the matters set forth here is the singular golden "bib" (pectoral) from the Regolini-Galassi Tomb (Fig. 6.11), which in form and symbolism is directly linked to Egypt.[22] The large necklace (Egyptian "*usekhet*"), actually the pectoral,

Figure 6.10   Gold appliqué plaque: rosette. Cerveteri, Regolini-Galassi Tomb. Museo Gregoriano Etrusco. Photo © Musei Vaticani.

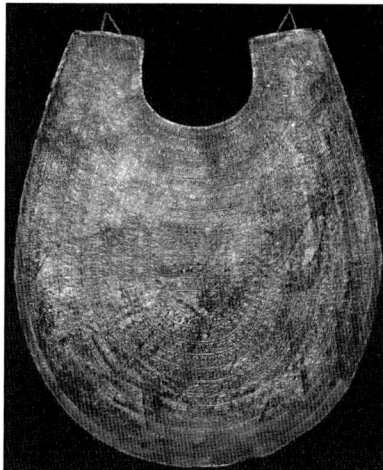

Figure 6.11   Pectoral in beaten gold. Cerveteri, Regolini-Galassi Tomb. Museo Gregoriano Etrusco 20553. Photo © Musei Vaticani.

is present in Egypt from the Early Dynastic to the Late Period. Linked to the concept of kingship, with the function of ensuring protection and incorruptibility to the bodies of the dead, it comes to be adopted in the Syro-Palestinian region and the Near East, in conjunction with the political and military expansion of the New Kingdom (Dynasties XVIII–XX, 1550–1070 BC). Considering the historical and decorative repertoire, it is likely that this reached Etruria through Levantine mediation.[23] The iconography associates motifs of different origins: from those more generically Near Eastern (winged woman with or without a lotus flower) to those from the Syro-Phoenician region (like the "Lord of Animals," griffin, Phoenician palmette), while the repertoire of fantastic animals (chimaera, pegasus) looks to Greece instead. Even the geometric pattern of hatched triangles, otherwise seen as a citation from the "indigenous" proto-historic repertoire, may portend a more ancient and widespread legacy, since it is repeated unchanged even on Egyptian funerary masks of Ptolemaic cartonnage.

The pectoral was relevant to the deceased woman who was placed in the main chamber of the tomb, where, through a window, ritually left open, we witness the epiphany of the deified dead, as befits a goddess or a queen, associated with the ancient oriental motif of the "Lady at the window" as an announcement of a sacred event. In the Regolini-Galassi Tomb, hanging on the side of the window was the *ajouré* silver and wood situla, which recalls symbolic ties with water in this container of ancient lineage (Fig. 6.12). The origin of the form goes back to the ancient Near East and Egypt, where it was used since the second millennium BC. It is precisely in Pharaonic Egypt that the situla appears closely connected with a particular ritual that also extended to funerary cult; it was used as a container for the holy water of the Nile but also for milk, from which follows a shape vaguely imitating a breast, thus significantly related to the concept of regeneration. In Assyrian reliefs the cylindrical situla is a constant attribute of the winged genii represented as touching the Tree of Life, in a propitiatory action. It therefore seems very significant that, in an atmosphere as educated and receptive as at Cerveteri, even in the sixth century urns that boast a row of breasts along the bottom edge are made.[24]

In the East, the techniques maintained a sort of ritual immutability, because they were bound to objects with sacred and symbolic purposes, where their very construction

Figure 6.12 Situla in silver ajouré, originally over a wooden body. Cerveteri, Regolini-Galassi Tomb. Museo Gregoriano Etrusco 20471. Photo © Musei Vaticani.

represented a ritual action, codified in gestures and in materials. Even the passage of knowledge from father to son, biological or metaphorical as fellow-members of the guilds, was cloaked in an aura of magic.[25] In this sense we might interpret the Semitic inscriptions on two Phoenician cups found in Italy, respectively, "Ešmunya'ad son of Ašto" at Palestrina and "Balašī son of the smith" at Pontecagnano. It is likely that at least a residual awareness of the scope of magical-religious symbols had survived among the artisans who prepared the funeral goods of the Middle Tyrrhenian *principes*.

In the golden fibula from Vulci-Ponte Sodo (Fig. 6.13) we observe looped double spiral pendants on the cross-piece, an ancient symbol of the Mesopotamian goddess Ninhursag, "lady of the mountain," the goddess of fertility, which we see reproduced in amulets in Ur, Tepe Hissar (Iran), and in cast-form at Nimrud and Aššur tomb 45 (fourteenth to thirteenth centuries). In the same tomb appears the prototype of the cup-spirals, the equivalent of the double spiral (Fig. 6.14), a pattern found in the plaques of gold and

Figure 6.13 Fibula in gold, with looped double spiral pendant on cross-piece. Vulci, Ponte Sodo. 675–650 BC. Munich, Antikensammlungen 2331. Photo Staatliche Antikensammlungen und Glyptothek München, photographer R. Kühling.

Figure 6.14 Pendant from tomb 45 at Aššur, end fourteenth-thirteenth century BC, with motif of "cup-spirals." Photo made at time of discovery. Formerly Staatliche Museen zu Berlin, Vorderasiatisches Museum. Photo Staatliche Museen zu Berlin.

electrum in the foundation deposit at Ephesus (seventh century BC), the Phoenician-Punic jewelry in Sardinia and Spain, as well as in the Orientalizing Etruscan jewels and artifacts, where one encounters a Hathor-head or a palmette (Fig. 6.15). With good evidence we could suppose that these are not simple decorative motifs, as the single palm tree is rather a compendium of the Sacred Tree or Tree of Life, as seen in the Assyrian reliefs of the north-west Palace of Nimrud and at Nineveh. The fusion of the palm branch with the lotus flower seems highly significant, especially when it is the attribute of a female character with Hathor-locks (Fig. 6.16).

In the cosmogony of ancient Egypt, the lotus flower is the first element to rise from the primordial waters, from which starts the creation of the world following the birth of the sun. It symbolizes the regenerative power of life with cosmic and universal value as regards the gods, kings and the whole living universe. The ceremonial act of offering

Figure 6.15 Gold appliqué plaque: Hathor-head between "cup-spirals." Cerveteri, Regolini-Galassi Tomb. Museo Gregoriano Etrusco. Photo © Musei Vaticani.

Figure 6.16 Bracelet in gold decorated in repoussé and granulation. Above: "Mistress of the Animals" and "Hero who kills a Lion." Below: Hathoric-figures with palm branch and lotus flower. Cerveteri, Regolini-Galassi Tomb. Museo Gregoriano Etrusco 20562. Photo © Musei Vaticani.

the lotus carried a powerful magical and symbolic charge. In Egyptian tombs true lotus petals have been found placed near the deceased.

In the Regolini-Galassi Tomb, twenty-eight bronze lotus flowers decorated the floor of the cultic trolley, a recurring offering in Etruscan Orientalizing princely graves (Fig. 6.17). The trolleys/miniature carts are a class of Eastern origin (Phoenician and Aegean) between the second and first millennium BC, found in Crete, Euboea, and recently also Israel. The *Book of Kings* speaks of ten bronze basins on wheels for Solomon's temple cast by Hiram of Tyre (do not confuse him with the king of Tyre in the same era), in his turn son of a Late Bronze Age craftsman.[26] Containers on wheels are also described by Homer as regal and divine attributes: a basket on silver wheels decorated with gold is given to Helen[27] and tripods on wheels of gold made by Hephaestus for the banquets of the gods are able to reach the assembly of gods and then return alone.[28] The cart is thus a link with the divine sphere by virtue of the attribute of wheels, whose magical properties of connection with the world of the immortals are implicit in the Homeric description of the tripods of Hephaestus.

In the Regolini-Galassi bracelets, the female figure with Hathor-locks, palm branch and lotus flower also appears between two rampant lions which quote the contemporary theme of the "Mistress of Animals" in conjunction with the masculine iconography of the "Hero who kills the lion with the sword." Both subjects show the inspiration of Near Eastern models and are linked by funerary connotations.

Among the most characteristic ornamentation of Orientalizing Etruscan gold stands the broken line or zigzag. This motif of ancient ancestry is made with the same technique as the second-millennium granulation on an Egyptian amulet (Fig. 6.18), also seen in goldwork from Syrian Alalakh (1460 BC). This is also not a simple decorative element but the symbolic representation of water. As such it is already found in Susa from the fourth millennium, combined with water birds and celestial phenomena. In the pectoral of Sheshonq I (XXII Dynasty, 945–924 BC), the solar boat floats on the expanse of water, rendered by the same broken lines as the corresponding hieroglyph. In Orientalizing, schematic representation of water with zigzags appears in Phoenician cups imported into Italy and in assorted Etruscan goldwork, including the cup from Palestrina in the Victoria and Albert Museum, its shape reflecting eastern prototypes. Prior to that it is already seen in the gold cup found at Nimrud in the tomb of Yabâ, Queen of Tiglath-Pileser III (745–727 BC).

In the great ornamental fibula of the Regolini-Galassi Tomb (Fig. 6.19), an unsurpassed masterpiece of goldsmithing anchored to Etruscan patronage, a symbolic apparatus seems to follow a certain thematic syntax. It starts at the lions surrounded by interlaced arches with palmettes on the disc, which evoke the theme of the sacred and the Lord/Lady of

Figure 6.17   Cult-trolley in bronze. Cerveteri, Regolini-Galassi Tomb. Museo Gregoriano Etrusco 20559. Photo © Musei Vaticani.

Figure 6.18 Egyptian amulet with zigzag motif in linear granulation. 1900–1800 BC.
London, British Museum. Photo © The Trustees of The British Museum.

Figure 6.19 Ornamental fibula in gold. Cerveteri, Regolini-Galassi Tomb.
Museo Gregoriano Etrusco 20552. Photo © Musei Vaticani.

the Animals, with a reference to the strength of the life cycle and the regenerative power of nature in this world. This sphere is physically and conceptually separated by water, symbolized by the zigzag patterns on the cross-piece that, if we accept the similarity of the Homeric plunge into the abyss of Hades, also carries inherent allusion to death.[29] This hiatus is reconstructed from the palmettes and lotus flowers hanging from the ends of the cross-piece. The palm alludes to the Tree of Life and combines with the lotus, a powerful reminder of regenerative power. The bow of the fibula rises from water, furrowed by water birds that bring into contact air, water and earth; this heavenly world is protected by legions of winged griffins, which guarantee inviolability, and reference the parallel sphere of the Underworld. Additionally, the motif of waterfowl, of Villanovan ancestry, in Etruscan Orientalizing, appears in connection with funerary themes and is regularly quoted in the apparatus of aristocratic tombs. The key to interpretation is given at the tip of the bow of the fibula by the head of Hathor, Egyptian goddess of the celestial sphere, a solar deity and mother accompanying the solar boat of Ra. In her primary essence as life-giver she is also the goddess of fertility and natural cycles of regeneration and in this sense may be understood her close relationship with the realm of the afterlife.

In the case of the Regolini-Galassi Tomb, where technique, style and iconography seem to follow a coherent program, one almost has the impression of facing the artisans of the "palace" who are certainly in possession of knowledge, but also in the suite of goods.[30] The disappearance of the palatial economy, and political and economic transformations during the first millennium BC, may have facilitated the movement of "free" artisans, according to a model more akin to what will be the situation of the Classical world. It remains an open question whether, in the eighth and seventh centuries BC, emancipated and autonomous Levantine specialized workers have come to Etruria, rather than submit to some form of hierarchy or subjugation, whereby they could still fall into the category of "goods," objects rather than agents in the dynamic of "gift" exchange.[31] According to the model of the Near East from the Bronze Age and mid-first millennium BC, artisans, as well as doctors, priests and magicians, were themselves prestige goods in the bureaucracy of the palace and could be the object of gift exchange and also of long distance diplomatic relations.[32]

At present, foreign immigrants of Levantine origin are frequently recognized in Etruria (see Chapter 48), in the case of architecture, sculpture, and various crafts, but it is even conceivable that one can add those artisans of the sacred that are wizards and priests. Forms and magical rituals are still closely tied to empirical aspects, such as the transmission of knowledge and technology. Certainly, divining practices as peculiar as hepatoscopy and brontoscopy should be traced back mainly to Mesopotamia rather than Latium and Tuscany.[33] Also associated with the Levantine world are rituals and foundation deposits in the construction of buildings, together with the practice of the banquet, also equally adopted by the Greeks.

THE CITY OF THE DEAD AND OF THE LIVING

The monumental evidence of tumuli in the city of the dead reflects the society of the living. The tumulus, a vastly more enduring monument than the royal houses, marks the territory in the image of the noble families who base their status on ownership and inheritance of land. This is well reflected by the onomastic inscriptions that soon take binomial shape, introducing the patronymic, clearly linked to the right of succession (see Chapter 22). At the same time smaller tumuli are arranged around the large ones, reflecting a social system based on *clientes*, with hierarchies and dependencies.

The carved bases of these tumuli, which can reach 50–60 meters in diameter, are characterized by a sequence of segments and moldings, similar to the architectural tradition of northern Syria and perhaps introduced by an architect of Eastern origin. They are the only discriminating elements of a monumentality that occurs suddenly and models a territory, according to Anatolian influences that are found only in Phrygia and in Lydia, where the necropolis of Bin Tepe in Sardis (Lydia), with dozens of huge tumuli (the Gyges Mound is 220 meters in diameter), is the closest parallel to the Etruscan necropoleis.[34]

From Tumulus MM ("Midas Mound") of Gordion – now dated to 740 BC and which thus precedes by at least a generation the mythical Phrygian king to whom it had been attributed[35] – comes a bronze situla with lion's head, a drinking vessel of Assyrian type that we see represented in the reliefs of the time of Sargon II (722–705 BC) at Nineveh and that we find actually exported to Veii in the second half of the eighth century BC.[36]

At the same time, the birth of a monumental sculptural tradition is attributed to Levantine masters who adopted Syro-Hittite models.[37] This is actually a model of ancient ancestry and looks very impressive in the form of enthroned ancestors in the Tomb of the Five Chairs at Cerveteri (Fig. 6.20) or in the Tomb of the Statues at Ceri (more directly related to Eastern models), keeping in mind corresponding figures of the two ancestors in the dynastic tomb of Qatna discovered in Syria in 2002 (Fig. 6.21). The two statues of basalt, placed on either side of the antechamber of the tomb located in the Royal Palace, are dated stylistically to the Middle Bronze Age II (1850/1800–1750/1700 BC) but the context is the Late Bronze Age (fifteenth to fourteenth centuries BC). The tomb documents archaeologically for the first time the *kispu* ritual, known from the literary sources of the Near East, namely the continued sustenance of the deceased with food, that here was ritually consumed in perfect communion between the living and the dead in the central chamber.[38] The similarities with the funeral rites of Etruria, several centuries later, are still impressive.

Some Caeretan tombs are also equipped with a stepped podium, which allowed access to the top of the artificial hill of earth, for the practice of funeral rites. The staircase of the Melone del Sodo II at Cortona is further enhanced by two carved antae with a warrior in the act of stabbing a sphinx that attacks him (Fig. 6.22). These monumental structures, built for reasons of worship, were probably not exclusive to Cerveteri and Cortona and it is possible that in future they will be discovered elsewhere.

Figure 6.20 Seated female figure in ceramic from the Tomb of the Five Chairs, Cerveteri. 650–600 BC. London, The British Museum D219.

Figure 6.21 Seated figures of ancestors in basalt from the Royal Tomb of Qatna, during excavation and after restoration. Manufactured eighteenth century BC, from a context of fifteenth-fourteenth century. Damascus, Musée Nationale. After Pfälzner 2008.

The funerary cult, earth-bound for libations and sacrifices, thus moved onto a terrace to simultaneously watch the sky. It is as if the ancestors, as will be shown in the acroteria of Murlo, and statues of deities on the roofs, were projected into the sky. The terrace is part of a cult in Near Eastern practice that has precedents in the Bronze Age, as in the case of the sacred area of Ishtar at Ebla, but that is reflected in the worship of Adonis in the West in the Classical and Hellenistic periods.[39] The contemporary appeal to ambivalent – chthonic and celestial female deities, both funerary and fertility – already present in Orientalizing iconography, seems at least conceivable by analogy. From the case of the goddess Hathor and sacred representations of nursing, one may trace the nude female figures that already occur in Italic proto-history, isolated or assembled on

Figure 6.22   Monumental access stair to the altar-platform of the Melone del Sodo II at Cortona.
Beginning of sixth century BC. Photo MAEC-Museo dell'Accademia Etrusca e della Città di Cortona.

ritual vessels, which converge in the essence of a goddess of fertility, generation and regeneration beyond death, according to the ancestral pattern of "Mother Goddess" and its subsequent sedimentation in the cults of Turan, Ishtar/Astarte, Aphrodite, Venus.[40] This understanding is also interpreted in the ivory statuette of a naked woman with her hand brought to the breast from Marsiliana d'Albegna, Circle of the Fibula, tomb XLI (675–650 BC) (Fig. 6.23).

An interesting feature appears in the Orientalizing tumuli of Tarquinia, which can provide a sort of small piazza in the external entry area, with monumental structures to accommodate seated spectators. To the well-known case of the Tomba Luzi in the Infernaccio necropolis, with a central staircase and three smaller ramps on the sides forming a sort of auditorium, is now added that of the "Tumulus of the Queen," the subject of recent excavations, still in progress, dated around the mid-seventh century BC (Fig. 6.24).[41] This is an impressive architectural construction about 40 meters in diameter, fitted with a monumental staircase, which creates an open-air enclosure for spectacles and ceremonies in honor of the noble dead. The "little square" was originally covered by a wooden canopy supported in front by three columns, the rock-cut foundations of which still remain. The roof also ensured the preservation of painted plaster. It does not take a great leap of imagination to picture in such a context, something like the funeral games for Patroclus recounted in the *Iliad* (Book XXIII). One may hypothesize that these monumental spaces were used by the presiding clan for noble assemblies of particular importance or solemnity, such as seeking the advice and divinatory protection of their ancestors. In particular, this should emphasize the affinity of the tumulus, even from an architectural point of view, with the royal tombs of Cyprus, such as those of Salamis. It is likely that even in the case of tumuli destined for the kings of Tarquinia, we may recognize the work of architects and craftsmen who arrived in the early seventh century BC from the eastern Mediterranean. Another element of these dynamics is provided by the discovery of remains of wall painting, intended to decorate the hall and two-sided chambers of the tomb of the royal personage buried in the "Tumulus of the Queen." In fact this pictorial document, dated c. 630 at the beginning of Late Orientalizing, deviates markedly, from the technological point of view, from all other known Etruscan painting, because the color support is composed of a thick layer of crushed-alabaster plaster, according to an

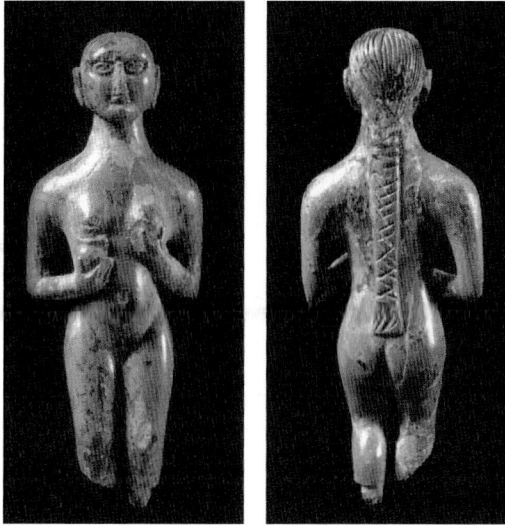

Figure 6.23   Statuette of nude woman in ivory. Marsiliana d'Albegna,
Circolo della Fibula, tomb XLI. 675–650 BC Firenze, Museo Archeologico Nazionale.

Figure 6.24   Tarquinia, Tumulo della Regina: view of external ceremonial area with staircase; on the
walls painted plaster. Photo Università degli Studi di Torino: courtesy of Alessandro Mandolesi.

established practice of the Near East (Egypt, Syria-Palestine, Cyprus). It is conceivable
that this ancient wall painting was created by hands of masters coming directly from the
eastern Mediterranean following a standard technique compatible with the climate of
the original areas, but totally unsuited to the environmental conditions of Etruria. For
this reason the plaster and colors appeared greatly deteriorated to the discoverers, to the
extent that they were almost illegible. It is possible that this rare survivor of the first
achievements in Tarquinia mural painting represents only a small sample of a broader and
unsuspected figurative heritage wrecked because of inherent technological limitations
that were incompatible with local conditions. A careful reading of the remains tends to
restore floral elements and perhaps human figures. In the "Tumulus of the Queen" the
painting is also associated with monumental statuary, as demonstrated by a fragmentary

statue of a lion or sphinx about two meters in height, which would thus bring the image of the tomb close to the fantasy reconstructions realized by Canina for the tumuli of the Sorbo necropolis at Cerveteri and at Tarquinia, that appear attractively decorated with statues (Fig. 6.25).

The Orientalizing also coincides with a systematic program of urban planning, which the most recent archaeological research has gradually unveiled, providing variety to our knowledge that would otherwise be dominated by funerary evidence. More careful excavations have also revealed the presence of foundation rituals, accompanied by bloody sacrifices, or the deposit of valuable and symbolic objects. They range from the biconical vase at Veii carefully deposited near the fortification walls of the late eighth century, to the foundation ritual attested in relation to the earliest fortifications at Populonia in the second half of the eighth century, the so-called hoard of Falda della Guardiola.

The case of Tarquinia is emblematic, in which urbanization revolves around the definition of a sacred-institutional complex on Pian di Civita (see Chapter 29). Here, at a place of worship already established in the tenth century BC in a natural cavity, there came into being ritual actions and structures with a highly symbolic meaning associated with royalty, the sphere of the sacred and foundation rites, which at the same time also powerfully evoke the Near East.[42] In the second half of the eighth century, to which are dated some stone walls, there took place the ritual burial of a man, perhaps a Euboean sailor, killed by a blow from an axe. Prototypes from the eastern Aegean and, in particular the Syro-Palestinian corridor, characterize the sacred building (Beta) fitted with a bench-like altar for animal sacrifice, built with the technique of pier-and-panel masonry; the foundation deposit would date it around the first quarter of the seventh century. The deposit consisted of a traditional axe of proto-historic type (tenth-ninth century), an early Orientalizing shield, and a trumpet-*lituus*, possibly manufactured in the Near East. These bronzes, termed "talking bronzes," which symbolize a role that is both political-military and priestly, recall the dawn of the city of Tarquinia and the image of a wise priest-king who paralleled Numa in the early history of Rome. Also in the first quarter of the seventh century, on the acropolis of Populonia (Poggio del Telegrapho) a house of rectilinear wooden structure composed of three rooms

Figure 6.25 "Main tombs at Tarquinia necropolis." After L. Canina, *L'antica Etruria marittima*, II, Roma 1849, pl. LXXXIX.

and a porch, and called "the king's house," was abandoned as a prelude to the rebuilding of a similar new structure. The event, perhaps a prelude to a change of leadership, was sealed by a solemn libation of 100 individuals, perhaps representing the various aristocratic families of Populonia. One hundred cups (*kyathoi*) and one *olla* (jar) were found in the pit formed by a post-hole of the structure that was demolished.[43] By the seventh century, we witness the building of fortified circuit walls on stone plinths with mud-brick superstructures as in the case of Roselle, a town in which was erected a sacred-institutional building with rectilinear plan and a circular room covered by a tholos-roof set in a large rectangular enclosure.

The "Palace," the privileged site of the splendor of the prince, plays a central role in relations between the great aristocratic families, both local and foreign. The interior of the tombs, especially those at Cerveteri, of course, is a valuable reflection of real architecture, which evolves from the representation of the oldest thatched roofing to reproduce the carved beams and coffers of a wooden roof covered with tiles. Above all, the vestibule, a large room sometimes with pillars with Aeolic or Doric capitals, presents a profusion of carved pieces of furniture such as beds, baskets, stools, thrones, and shields hung on the walls.

Roof-tiles are introduced around the mid-seventh century and the new structure of the house is also commemorated by the production of urns with gabled roof and architectonic decoration (Fig. 6.26). Towards the end of the century canonized in the tombs (and perhaps in real homes), rooms (usually three) side by side are preceded by a vestibule and porch. The rock-cut tomb at Tuscania, Pian della Mola, shaped like a house with gabled roof decorated with acroteria and a portico, is a striking, "petrified" example of a luxury residence (Fig. 6.27).

An Orientalizing urban center is exemplified in the Acquarossa houses, with side-by-side rooms whose tiled roofs are decorated with painted, cut-out, or plastic terracotta ornamentation. Peculiar is the case of the "Palace" of Murlo near Siena, a princely residence ritually destroyed about 530, whose Late Orientalizing phase is articulated within a colonnaded courtyard with decorative architectural terracottas, ambiguously suspended between sacred space and the celebration of the noble family. The scenes depicted on terracotta frieze-plaques are a succession of banquets, horse races, wedding

Figure 6.26   Cinerary urn in form of a house. Cerveteri, Monte Abatone necropolis, tomb 426. 650 BC. Cerveteri, Museo Nazionale Archeologico Cerite Claudia Ruspoli.

processions, and assemblies of gods, while on the roof above statues of seated ancestors and real and imaginary animals look down.

Also in Murlo, a multipurpose workshop, consisting of a roof on pillars, saw production processes presumably with exchanges of knowledge and workers: architectural tiles and terracottas, working of metal, bone, horn and ivory. The production model is certainly more akin to that of the Renaissance artist than the industrial revolution that would otherwise have resulted in the segregation (conceptual and spatial) and specialization of the various procedures.

THE ART

In Etruscan Orientalizing art there exists a certain duality of reference models: on one hand the geometric tradition, and on the other figurative style and animal subjects that bear the imprint of the East. The Euboean artisan-immigrants in Etruria in the eighth century had established a geometric tradition reflected in pottery decoration (Fig. 6.28)[44]

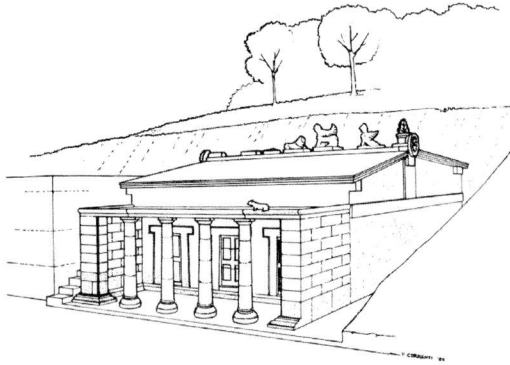

Figure 6.27 *Tomba a casa* with portico. Tuscania, Pian di Mola. 575–550 BC. After A. M. Sgubini Moretti, in *Atti II Congresso Internazionale Etrusco*, Roma 1989.

Figure 6.28 Krater of the "Bisenzio Group" decorated with geometric motifs and metopes with stylized birds. Second half of eighth century BC. Museo Gregoriano Etrusco 16321. Photo © Musei Vaticani.

as well as in bronzes (Bisenzio trolley and situla). In the seventh century, this tradition still exists in the ceramics and emerges in mural painting, as in the Tombs of the Roaring Lions (690 BC) and Ducks (680–670 BC) of Veii, sharing Etrusco-geometric style (Fig. 6.29). It is possible that wall painting, which we only know from tombs, was also used in the residences of the living.

The importation of refined and precious objects, such as the Phoenician-Cypriot cups discovered at Caere and Palestrina, ushers in a figurative and narrative repertoire that is also partially incorporated into painting.[45] At Cerveteri, c. 670–650 BC, a large group of tombs stands out for its exotic and fantastic animal themes, exemplified by the Tombs of the Painted Animals and the Painted Lions (Fig. 6.30). Into the latter fits the theme of "Lord of Animals," its female variant dominating the refined decoration of gold jewelry in the Regolini-Galassi Tomb (see Fig. 16). At the same time the Tomb of the Ship, unreadable in its details, must have retraced key narrative and celebration of the naval achievements of the "Prince" buried there. Narrative forays of evocative and magical flavor appear in the meal on the Montescudaio funerary urn, and in mourning statuettes that surrounded the bronze bed, and perhaps the ceramic urn, in the Regolini-Galassi Tomb (Fig. 6.31).

Figure 6.29   Veio, Tomba dei Leoni Ruggenti. Circa 690 BC Photo Soprintendenza per i Beni Archeologici dell'Etruria Meridionale.

Figure 6.30   Cerveteri, Tomba dei Leoni Dipinti. 670–650 BC. Watercolor by M. Barosso (1910–1913).

The transition from symbol to image also clearly involves the overcoming of aniconic forms in which images are hidden, or simply the embodiment of the dead. The cinerary urns gradually become individualized. At the same time, bronze sculpture, in the technique of *sphyrelaton*, passes from the symbolic volumes of the Marsiliana d'Albegna bust (with sphere for a head) or the more explicit "puppet" of the Tomb of the Chariot of Vulci (680–670 BC) to the more complete bust of the Egyptian goddess from which the Isis Tomb of Vulci (600–580 BC) is named.

The second quarter of the seventh century sees the emergence of bucchero, a typical Etruscan prestige product initially anchored to aristocratic patronage, as in the notable case of the Caeretan Tomba Calabresi (Fig. 6.32).[46] The technique of bucchero is interdisciplinary, also drawing on the knowledge of metallurgy and metal-working: reduction-firing to obtain the black color (even in section) is similar to the process for producing charcoal, while the technique of direct incision after firing is similar to the work of the engraver.[47] (See Chapter 34 on knowledge shared across disciplines.) The taste for mixed media, recurring in the Orientalizing period, is also expressed in the application of silver on the surface and of pigments in the engravings. Only later will more cursive and less expensive solutions be introduced, such as stamped and cylinder-seal decoration, the same as those found on pithoi and impasto braziers at Cerveteri.[48]

Figure 6.31   "Weeping" statuettes in bucchero. Cerveteri, Regolini-Galassi Tomb. Museo Gregoriano Etrusco. Photo © Musei Vaticani.

Figure 6.32   Calabresi Vase: charioteer driving a pair of horses. Bucchero. Cerveteri, Tomba Calabresi. C. 660–650 BC. Museo Gregoriano Etrusco 20235. Photo © Musei Vaticani.

Bucchero also includes eclectic typology, since it reproduces both the local forms of the oldest traditions and those of imported Phoenician, East Greek and Protocorinthian pottery, likewise emulating the thinness of the last.

A similar assortment of shapes and inspiration enters into replicas in precious metals (silver, sometimes with gilding) that, as in the case of the Regolini-Galassi Tomb, bear inscriptions in Etruscan engraved by the same craftsman, evidently for local patrons (Fig. 6.33). The exercise of the scribal art by artisans is even documented by virtuoso inscriptions in decorative granulation technique on the gold work (Fig. 6.34).[49] For the bronze cauldrons with animal-head attachments, well researched prestige objects, is indicated a dependence on generic models from the Near East, linked in general to the central Anatolian plateau where there arose the kingdom of Urartu, and to Assyria, and the Neo-Hittite kingdoms of northern Syria. The last are identified as a possible area of convergence of diverse currents of production, from which the cauldrons would then be exported to Greece and the West where they would then receive further processing. Monumental cauldrons, placed on tripods or supports, are present in the princely tombs of Etruria and other peripheral areas to the Greek world, as in Cyprus or in Lycia.

A different perspective of valuation is offered by the extraordinary discovery in Karmir-Blur, on the outskirts of Yerevan, Republic of Armenia, of a cauldron protome virtually identical to those of the Regolini-Galassi cauldron (see Fig. 6.2). The specimen is engraved with the name of the Armenian king of Urartu Sarduri II (764–730 BC) and thus provides not only a clear reference to the production area of the original model, but also a testimony to the prestige of such an object that, not surprisingly, was intended for the main chamber in a Cerveteri tomb. It is likely, also by virtue of meaning and value that, like other objects, the cauldron protomes could have arrived in Etruria after a long history.[50] By the second half of the seventh century, the Eastern influence is less and suggestions of the Greek world increase markedly. To the increasingly frequent imports of Protocorinthian vases, first present in the Caeretan Regolini-Galassi Tomb, and the

Figure 6.33 Set of vases in silver. Cerveteri, Regolini-Galassi Tomb. Museo Gregoriano Etrusco. Photo © Musei Vaticani.

Figure 6.34 Fibula *a drago* in gold with dedicatory inscription in granulation. From Castelluccio di Pienza, Chiusi. Paris, Musée du Louvre.

Tumulus of Montetosto, we may add the work of the immigrant vase-painter Aristonothos, who leaves his signature on the famous krater with the blinding of Polyphemus and a naval battle between Greeks and Etruscans.

The Plikaśna situla from Chiusi (650 BC), but attributed to Caeretan manufacture, combines the tradition of the Phoenician-Cypriot cups with Hellenic iconographic contamination, including funeral games and warriors with Corinthian-type hoplite armament (Fig. 6.35). Something similar happens with the ivory relief-carved pyxis from the Pania necropolis of Chiusi (620–580 BC), also produced in southern Etruria. In an exotic material and a craft-tradition of Levantine heritage are associated Greek mythological themes and heroes, where they seem to be identified with the Etruscan aristocracy (Figs 24.1 and 24.2). The bucchero olpe, with relief and incised decoration from Cerveteri, shows familiarity with the saga of the Argonauts (630 BC), a true incunabulum of the Greek myth with Etruscan transliteration for the characters of Medea (Metaia) and Daedalus (Taitale) (Fig. 6.36; see also Chapter 24). The incised stele

Figure 6.35 Situla of *Plikaśna*. Gilded silver. From Chiusi. Circa 650 BC. Florence, Museo Archeologico Nazionale. Photo Soprintendenza per i Beni Archeologici della Toscana (photographer: Fernando Guerrini).

Figure 6.36 Olpe in bucchero, decorated with relief of Jason, Medea, the Argonauts and Daedalus. From Cerveteri, Tumulus of San Paolo, tomb 2. 630 BC. Roma, Museo Nazionale Etrusco di Villa Giulia.

of Avele Feluske at Vetulonia at the end of the seventh century shows us an Etruscan warrior who displays a Corinthian helmet and a circular hoplite shield, without giving up his symbolic double axe.

It is in this context in Vulci that the workshops of the Painter of the Swallows, of East-Greek training, and the Bearded Sphinx Painter, founder of the Etrusco-Corinthian tradition, are implanted. The latter develops the Polychrome Group at Caere and Veii, which finds its counterpart in the Campana tomb at Veii (600 BC) (Fig. 6.37). The dense decoration of the painted wall makes one think, anachronistically, of a sort of "tapestry" in which the narrative theme of knights and the more symbolic register of real and imaginary animals are saturated with superabundant chains of floral ornaments.

The Late Orientalizing sees the founding of the first Etruscan temple at Veii – Piazza d'Armi (c. 600 BC) and the birth of the first votive bronze sculpture (Fig. 6.38). The aura of sacredness will tend to shift away from king's houses to sanctuaries on the wave

Figure 6.37   Veii, Monte Michele, Tomba Campana. Watercolor. The grave goods on the floor do not belong to this tomb. C. 600 BC. After Haynes 2000.

Figure 6.38   Bronze figurine of draped female votary with *kyathos*. Provenance unknown. 625–600 BC. Firenze, Museo Archeologico Nazionale 225.

of new social arrangements, a prelude to the gradual introduction of the human figure into the scale and representation of the divine according to rules more akin to the world of Archaic Greek art. If we really want to identify a boundary that history can later draw between East and West, this will be the transfer of the king into the world of mortals and the projection of man among the immortals.

NOTES

1 For general aspects of the Orientalizing phase, see: Bartoloni 2002; Bartoloni, Delpino 2005; Bonfante, Karageorghis 2001; Botto 2008; Burkert 1992; Camporeale 2004; Celuzza, Cianferoni 2010; Colonna 1994; D'Agostino B. 1999; *Dinamiche di sviluppo* 2005; Étienne 2010; *Etruria e Sardegna* 2002; *Etruschi* 2000; Della Fina 2006; Della Fina 2007; Haynes 2000; Magness 2001; Minetti 2004; Naso 2000; Naso 2011; Pacciarelli 2001; Prayon, Röllig 2000; *Principi etruschi* 2000; Rendeli 1993; Ridgway 2002; Riva, Vella 2006; Sciacca 2006–2007; Sciacca 2010; Stampolidis 2003; Strøm 1971; von Eles 2004; Turfa 2012.
2 Liverani 2000: 3–13.
3 Rathje 1979; Martelli 1991.
4 Naso 2001.
5 Rathje 1988; Rathje 1990.
6 Sciacca 2005.
7 Ampolo 2000.
8 Pareti 1947: 524 ff.
9 The document, consisting of ten paragraphs, signed by a group of Italian intellectuals and academics, was presented on July 26 1938 and published on the front page in *La difesa della razza*, ed. Telesio Interlandi, vol. I, no. 1, 5 August 1938.
10 Gras 2000. For oriental models in Greek Orientalizing art see Markoe 1996; Rocco 2006.
11 Burkert 1992; Liverani 2000.
12 Babbi 2008.
13 Naso 2001.
14 Bonfante 2005.
15 For a longer treatment of themes touched on in this paragraph, and for bibliographic references, see the articles Sannibale 2008a; Sannibale 2008b.
16 Hencken 1968: 184, Fig. 169c-d; Nestler – Formigli 1994: 30, Fig. 21.
17 Formigli, Scatozza Höricht 2010.
18 Maxwell-Hyslop 1974: 102–104, pl. 69. 141, pls. 108–109.
19 Maxwell-Hyslop 1974: 140–143, 151, pl. 108.
20 von Hase 1975: 118, pl. 23, lower left; Strøm 1971: 69, S 38.
21 For the cultural and magical significance of gold and minerals in ancient Egypt: Aufrère 1991: 308–392.
22 Especially emphasized, also for other aspects of the funerary ritual, by Bubenheimer-Erhart 2005: 154–162.
23 For Phoenician mediation in the propagation in Etruria of Egyptian motifs and goods from the mid-eighth to mid-seventh centuries BC, as well as the special role of Caere, see Camporeale 2006.
24 Jannot 2000: 90, Fig. 12.
25 Burkert 1992, 25 ff., 45 ff.
26 I *Kings* 7.27–39. For the significance of the passage of knowledge from father to son, see Burkert 1992: 25 ff., 45 ff.
27 Homer, *Odyssey* 4.131.
28 Homer, *Iliad* 18.373–377.
29 Homer, *Iliad* 16.742–750; cf. Cerchiai 2003: 34–36.
30 Camporeale 2006: 99 ssg.

31 Camporeale 2011.

32 Zaccagnini 1983.

33 For Mesopotamian influences in Etruscan religion, with particular evidence for the development of forms of divination such as hepatoscopy and brontoscopy, as well as the drafting of the correlate sacred texts, and the Etruscan relations – at the highest levels of their society – with Near Eastern cultures, see now Turfa 2012, in particular: 241–277.

34 Naso 1998.

35 Rose, Darbyshire 2011: 3, 16 fig. 1.2, 24 ff., 92 ff., 166. This research published recently by the Museum of Archaeology and Anthropology of the University of Pennsylvania, presents a revision of the chronology of the Iron Age at Gordion, combining archaeological data with the latest dendrochronological and radiocarbon dating. In particular the chronological sequence of a portion of the 150 known tumuli has been reassigned, changing their relation with the destruction level of the city, now raised to the end of the ninth century BC, approximately a century earlier than the traditional chronology. Many tumuli, as in the case of Tumulus MM, thus become contemporary with the reconstruction of the Middle Phrygian Citadel in the course of the eighth century BC, which shows a certain interconnection with the Levantine milieu in relation to the exchange of goods and commodities.

36 *Principi Etruschi* 2000: 128, no. 78 (M. Marchesi). For the example of Gordion, cf. ibid.: 96, 98 fig. without no. (F. Delpino).

37 Colonna, von Hase 1984.

38 Pfälzner 2008.

39 Di Filippo Balestrazzi 1999.

40 Delpino 2006: 51–54.

41 Cataldi, Mandolesi 2010; Mandolesi, De Angelis 2011.

42 Bonghi Jovino, Chiaramonte Treré 1997: 162–179, 217–220.

43 Bartoloni 2011: 102–110.

44 Boitani, Neri, Biagi 2010.

45 Naso 1996; Minetti 2003.

46 Sciacca, Di Blasi 2003.

47 Sannibale 2003.

48 Pieraccini 2003; Serra Ridgway 2010.

49 Fibula from Castelluccio di Pienza, Chiusi, 650–625 BC: H. Rix, *Etruskische Texte*, Tübingen 1991: Cl 2.3.

50 For the presence of Urartian and Assyrian bronze imports in Etruria, from the last 30 years of the eight to the beginning of the seventh century, with particular regard to the ribbed bowls, see Sciacca 2006.

BIBLIOGRAPHY

Ampolo, C. (2000) "Il mondo omerico e la cultura orientalizzante mediterranea" in *Principi etruschi* 2000, 27–35.

Aufrère, S. (1991) *L'univers minéral dans la pensée égyptienne* (= Bibliothèque d'Études 105.1–2), Cairo.

Babbi, A. (2008) *La piccola plastica fittile antropomorfa dell'Italia antica dal bronzo finale all'orientalizzante* (=*Mediterranea*, Supplemento, 1), Pisa-Rome 2008: Fabrizio Serra Editore.

Bartoloni, G. (2002) *La cultura villanoviana. All'inizio della storia etrusca*, Rome: Carocci.

——(2011) "Un rito di obliterazione a Populonia" in Maras, D. F. (ed.), *Corollari. Scritti di antichità etrusche e italiche in omaggio all'opera di Giovanni Colonna*, Pisa-Rome: Fabrizio Serra Editore, 102–110.

Bartoloni, G. and Delpino, F. (eds) (2005) *Oriente e Occidente: metodi e discipline a confronto. Riflessioni sulla cronologia dell'Età del ferro italiana*, Atti dell'Incontro di Studi (Roma 2003), (= Mediterranea 1 – 2004), Pisa-Rome: Istituti Editoriali e Poligrafici Internazionali.

Boitani, F., Neri, S. and Biagi, F. (2010) "Riflessi della ceramica geometrica nella più antica pittura funeraria veiente," *Papers of the XVII International Congress of Classical Archaeology (Roma 2008), Bollettino di Archeologia on-line*, I, F/F7/3, pp. 20–27. Available at: <www.archeologia. beniculturali.it /pages/pubblicazioni/html>.

Bonfante, L. (2005) "The Verucchio Throne and the Corsini Chair: Two Status Symbols of Ancient Italy" in *Terra Marique. Studies in Art History and Marine Archaeology in honor of Anne Marguerite McCann*, Oxford: Oxbow Books, 3–11.

Bonfante, L. and Karageorghis, V. (eds) (2001) *Italy and Cyprus in antiquity. 1500–450 BC. Proceedings of an international symposium held at the Italian Academy for Advanced Studies in America at Columbia University* (New York 2000), Nicosia: Severis Foundation.

Bonghi Jovino, M. and Chiaramonte Treré, C. (1997) *Tarquinia. Testimonianze archeologiche e ricostruzione storica. Scavi sistematici nell'abitato 1982–1988* (=Tarchna I), Roma, "L'ERMA" di Bretschneider.

Botto, M. (2008) "I primi contatti fra i Fenici e le popolazioni dell'Italia Peninsulare" in Celestino, S. and Rafel, N. (eds) *Contacto cultural entre el Mediterráneo y el Atlántico (siglos XII – VIII ane). La precolonización a debate*, Madrid: Consejo superior de investigaciones científicas, 123–148.

Bubenheimer-Erhart, F. (2005) "Einflüsse Ägyptens in Etrurien" in *Ägypten, Griechenland, Rom: Abwehr und Berührung*, Städelsches Kunstinstitut und Städtische Galerie. Ausstellung vom 26. November 2005 bis 26. Februar 2006, Tübingen: 154–162.

Burkert, W. (1992) *The orientalizing revolution. Near Eastern influence on Greek culture in the early archaic age*, London: Harvard University Press.

Camporeale, G. (2004) *Gli Etruschi. Storia e civiltà*, UTET: Torino.

——(2006) "Dall'Egitto all'Etruria. Tra villanoviano recente e orientalizzante medio" in *Gli Etruschi e il Mediterraneo. Commerci e politica* (Atti del XIII Convegno Internazionale di Studi sulla Storia e l'Archeologia dell'Etruria) in *Annali della fondazione per il Museo "Claudio Faina,"* 13: 93–116.

——(2011) "Maestri d'arte e mercanti d'arte ai primordi della storia etrusca" in Maras, D. F. (ed.), *Corollari. Scritti di antichità etrusche e italiche in omaggio all'opera di Giovanni Colonna*, Pisa-Rome: Istituti Editoriali e Poligrafici Internazionali, 19–23.

Cataldi, M. and Mandolesi, A. (2010) "Tarquinia. Ripresa delle indagini nell'area dei tumuli monumentali della Doganaccia," *Annali della Fondazione per il Museo "Claudio Faina,"* 17: 235–273.

Celuzza, M. and Cianferoni, G. C. (eds) (2010) *Signori di Maremma. Élites etrusche fra Populonia e Vulci*, Catalogo della mostra (Firenze 2010), Florence: Polistampa.

Cerchiai, L. (2003) "Il piatto della tomba 65 di Acqua Acetosa Laurentina e i pericoli del mare," *Ostraka* 11,1: 29–36.

Colonna, G. (1994) "Etrusca Arte" in *Enciclopedia dell'Arte Antica, Secondo Supplemento (1971–1994)*, II, 554–605 (= "Arte Etrusca" in *Italia ante Romanum Imperium*, Pisa-Rome: Istituti Editoriali e Poligrafici Internazionali 2005, 1419–1505).

Colonna, G. and von Hase, F.-W. (1984) "Alle origini della statuaria etrusca. La Tomba delle statue presso Ceri," *Studi Etruschi* 52: 13–59.

D'Agostino, B. (1999) "I principi dell'Italia centro-tirrenica in epoca orientalizzante" in Ruby, P. (ed.), *Les princes de la protohistoire et l'émergence de l'état*. Actes de la Table Ronde (Naples 1994), Naples-Rome: Centre Jean Bérard, Ecole francaise de Rome, 81–88.

Della Fina, G. M. (ed.) (2006) *Gli Etruschi e il Mediterraneo. Commerci e politica*. Atti del XIII Convegno Internazionale di Studi sulla Storia e l'Archeologia dell'Etruria (Orvieto 2005), *Annali della Fondazione per il Museo "Claudio Faina"*, 13.

——(ed.) (2007) *Etruschi, Greci, Fenici e Cartaginesi nel Mediterraneo Centrale*. Atti del XIV Convegno Internazionale di Studi sulla Storia e l'Archeologia dell'Etruria (Orvieto 2006), *Annali della Fondazione per il Museo "Claudio Faina"*, 14.

Delpino, F. (2006) "Una identità ambigua. Figurette femminili nude di area etrusco-italica: congiunte, antenate o divinità?," *Mediterranea* 3: 33–54.

Di Filippo Balestrazzi, E. (1999) "Adone, o quando la regalità è finzione. Dalla terrazza cultuale di Ebla al rito sul tetto nelle Adonie occidentali. Storia ed evoluzione di una festa" in *Ostraka* 8: 309–342.

Dinamiche di sviluppo 2005 = Dinamiche *di sviluppo delle città nell'Etruria meridionale.* (2005) *Veio, Caere, Tarquinia, Vulci.* Atti del XXIII Convegno di Studi Etruschi ed Italici (Roma-Veio-Pyrgi-Tarquinia-Tuscania-Vulci-Viterbo 2001), Pisa-Rome: Istituti Editoriali e Poligrafici Internazionali.

Étienne, R. (ed.) (2010) *La Méditerranée au VIIe siècle av. J.-C. (essais d'analyses archéologiques)*, Paris: De Boccard.

Etruria e Sardegna 2002 = Etruria e Sardegna centro-settentrionale tra l'Età del Bronzo Finale e l'arcaismo. Atti del XXI Convegno di Studi Etruschi e Italici (Sassari-Alghero-Oristano-Torralba 1998), Pisa-Rome: Istituti Editoriali e Poligrafici Internazionali.

Etruschi 2000 = Torelli M. (ed.) (2000) *Gli Etruschi*, catalogo della mostra (Venezia 2000), Cinisello Balsamo: Bompiani.

Formigli, E. and Scatozza Höricht, L. A. (eds) (2010) *Le prime lavorazioni dell'oro in area flegrea*, Siena: Nuova Immagine.

Gras M. (2000) "Il Mediterraneo in età Orientalizzante. Merci, approdi, circolazione" in *Principi etruschi* 2000, 15–26.

Haynes, S. (2000) *Etruscan Civilization. A Cultural History*, Los Angeles: Getty Press, 1–133.

Hencken, H. (1968) *Tarquinia, Villanovans and Early Etruscans*, Cambridge (Mass.): Peabody Museum.

Jannot, J.-R. (2000) "Etruscans and the afterworld," *Etruscan Studies. Journal of the Etruscan Foundation*, 7: 81–99.

Liverani, M. (2000) "Potere e regalità nei regni del Vicino Oriente" in *Principi etruschi* 2000, 3–13.

Magness, J. (2001) "A Near Eastern ethnic element among the Etruscan elite?" *Etruscan Studies. Journal of the Etruscan Foundation*, 8: 79–117.

Mandolesi, A. and De Angelis, D. (2011) "Il tumulo della Regina di Tarquinia fra tradizioni levantine e innovazioni etrusche," *Archeologica Classica* 62, 1: 7–39.

Markoe, G. (1996) "The emergence of Orientalizing in Greek art. Some observations on the interchange between Greeks and Phoenicians in the eighth and seventh centuries BC," *Bulletin of the American Schools of Oriental Research*, 301: 47–67.

Martelli, M. (1991) "I Fenici e la questione Orientalizzante in Italia," *Atti del II Congresso internazionale di studi fenici e punici* (Roma 1987), Rome: Consiglio Nazionale delle Ricerche, 1049–1072.

Maxwell-Hyslop, K. R. (1974) *Western Asiatic Jewellery c. 3000 – 612 BC*, London: Methuen & Co. Ltd., 1971.

Minetti, A. (ed.) (2003) *Pittura etrusca: problemi e prospettive*, Atti del Convegno (Sarteano-Chiusi 2001), Siena: Protagon Editori Toscani.

——(2004) *L'Orientalizzante a Chiusi e nel suo territorio*, Rome: "L'ERMA" di Bretschneider.

Naso, A. (1996) *Architetture dipinte. Decorazioni parietali non figurate nelle tombe a camera dell'Etruria meridionale. VII – V secolo a.C.*, Rome: "L'ERMA" di Bretschneider.

——(1998) "I tumuli monumentali in Etruria meridionale. Caratteri propri e possibili ascendenze orientali" in *Archäologische Untersuchungen zu den Beziehungen zwischen Altitalien und der Zone nordwarts der Alpen während der frühen Eisenzeit Alteuropas.* Ergebnisse eines Kolloquiums in Regensburg, 3. 5 November 1994, Regensburg: Universitätsverlag Regensburg GMBH, 117–157.

——(2000) "Le aristocrazie etrusche in periodo orientalizzante" in *Etruschi* 2000, 111–129.

——(2001) "La penisola italica e l'Anatolia, XII – V secolo a.C." in Muss, U. (ed.), *Der Kosmos der Artemis von Ephesos*, Österreichisches Archäologisches Institut, Sonderschriften Band 37, Wien, 169–181.

——(ed.) (2011) *Tumuli e sepolture monumentali nella protostoria e uropea*. Atti del convegno internazionale (Celano 2000), Mainz: Verlag des Römisch-Germanischen Zentralmuseums.

Nestler, G. and Formigli, E. (1994) *Granulazione etrusca. Un'antica arte orafa*, Siena: Nuova Immagine.

Pacciarelli, M. (2001) *Dal villaggio alla città. La svolta protourbana del 1000 a.C. nell'Italia tirrenica*, Florence: All'insegna del Giglio.

Pareti, L. (1947) *La Tomba Regolini – Galassi del Museo Gregoriano Etrusco e la civiltà dell'Italia centrale nel sec. VII a.C.*, Città del Vaticano.

Pfälzner, P. (2008) "The royal palace at Qatna: power and prestige in the late bronze age" in Aruz, J., Benzel, K. and Evans, J. M. (eds) *Beyond Babylon. Art, Trade and Diplomacy in the Second Millennium BC*, New York: The Metropolitan Museum of Art, 219–221.

Pieraccini, L. C. (2003) *Around the Hearth. Caeretan Cylinder-Stamped Braziers*, Roma: "L'ERMA" di Bretschneider.

Prayon, F. and Röllig, W. (eds) (2000) *Der Orient und Etrurien. Zum Phänomen des "Orientalisierens" im westlichen Mittelmeerraum* (10.-6. Jh. v.Chr.), Akten des Kolloquiums (Tübingen 1997), Pisa-Roma : Istituti Editoriali e Poligrafici Internazionali.

Principi etruschi 2000 = Bartoloni, G., Delpino, F., Morigi Govi, C. and Sassatelli, G. (eds) (2000) *Principi etruschi tra Mediterraneo ed Europa*, exhibition catalogue (Bologna 2000–2001), Venice: Marsilio.

Rathje, A. (1979) "Oriental imports in Etruria in the eighth and seventh centuries BC: Their origins and implications" in Ridgway, F. R. and D. (eds) *Italy before the Romans. The iron age, Orientalizing and Etruscan periods*, London-New York-San Francisco: Academic Press, 145–183.

——(1988) "Manners and customs in Central Italy in the Orientalizing period. Influence from the Near East," *Acta Hyperborea. Danish studies in Classical Archaeology*, 1: 81–90.

——(1990) "The adoption of the Homeric banquet in Central Italy in the Orientalizing period" in Murray, O. (ed.) *Sympotica. A symposium on the symposion. First Symposium on the Greek Symposion* (Oxford 1984), Oxford: Clarendon Press, 279–288.

Rendeli, M. (1993) *Città aperte: ambiente e paesaggio rurale organizzato nell'Etruria meridionale costiera durante l'eta orientalizzante e arcaica*, Roma: Gruppo Editoriale Internazionale.

Ridgway, D. (2002) *The world of the early Etruscans*, Göteborgs Universitet, The Félix Neubergh Lecture, 2000, Jonsered: Åström.

Riva, C. and Vella, N. C. (eds) (2006) *Debating Orientalization. Multidisciplinary Approaches to Change in the Ancient Mediterranean*, London: Equinox.

Rocco, G. (2006) "Modelli orientali e rielaborazioni greche: originali iconografie di creature fantastiche nell'orientalizzante" in *Varia iconographica ab Oriente ad Occidentem*, Roma: Universita degli studi di Roma "Tor Vergata," 29–48.

Rose, C. B. and Darbyshire, G. (eds) (2011) *The new Chronology of Iron Age Gordion*, Gordion Special Studies VI, Philadelphia: University of Pennsylvania Press.

Sannibale, M. (2003) "Nota sulle indagini scientifiche e sui restauri" in Sciacca, Di Blasi (2003) *La Tomba Calabresi e la Tomba del Tripode di Cerveteri*, 281–300.

——(2008a) "Gli ori della Tomba Regolini-Galassi: tra tecnologia e simbolo. Nuove proposte di lettura nel quadro del fenomeno Orientalizzante in Etruria," *Mélanges de l'École Française de Rome – Antiquité (MEFRA)* 120/2: 337–367.

——(2008b) "Iconografie e simboli orientali nelle corti dei principi etruschi," *Byrsa* 7, 1–2: 85–123.

Sciacca, F. (2005) *Patere baccellate in bronzo. Oriente, Grecia, Italia in età orientalizzante*, Rome: "L'ERMA" di Bretschneider.

——(2006) "Importazioni assire e urartee" in *Gli Etruschi e il Mediterraneo. Commerci e politica* (Atti del XIII Convegno Internazionale di Studi sulla Storia e l'Archeologia dell'Etruria), *Annali della fondazione per il Museo "Claudio Faina"* 13: 285–304.

—— (2006–2007) "La circolazione dei doni nell'aristocrazia tirrenica: esempi dall'archeologia," *Revista d'Arqueologia de Ponent* 16–17, 281–292.

——(2010) "Commerci fenici nel Tirreno orientale: uno sguardo dalle grandi necropoli," *Papers of the XVII International Congress of Classical Archaeology* (Roma 2008), *Bollettino di Archeologia on-line*, I, F/F2/5, 5–19. Available at: <www.archeologia.beniculturali.it/pages/pubblicazioni/html>.

Sciacca, F. and Di Blasi, L. (2003), *La Tomba Calabresi e la Tomba del Tripode di Cerveteri*, Museo Gregoriano Etrusco, Cataloghi 7, Città del Vaticano.

Serra, Ridgway F. R. (2010) *Pithoi stampigliati ceretani. Una classe originale di ceramica etrusca*, Roma: "L'ERMA" di Bretschneider.

Stampolidis, N. C. (ed.) (2003) *Sea Routes...From Sidon to Huelva. Interconnections in the Mediterranean 16th–6th centuries BC*, Catalogue of the exhibition (Athens 2003), Athens: Museum of Cycladic Art.

Strøm, I. (1971) *Problems Concerning the Origin and Early Development of the Etruscan Orientalizing Style*, Odense: Odense University Press.

Turfa, J. M. (2012) *Divining the Etruscan World. The Brontoscopic Calendar and Religious Practice*, Cambridge, New York: Cambridge University Press.

von Eles, P. (ed.) (2004) *La ritualità funeraria tra età del ferro e orientalizzante in Italia*. Atti del convegno (Verucchio 2002), Pisa-Rome: Istituti Editoriali e Poligrafici Internazionali.

von Hase, F.-W. (1975) "Zur Problematik der frühesten Goldfunden in Mittelitalien," *Hamburger Beiträge zur Archäologie* 5: 99–182.

Zaccagnini, C. (1983) "Patterns of Mobility among Ancient Near Eastern Craftsmen," *Journal of Near Eastern Studies* 42: 245–264.

CHAPTER SEVEN

URBANIZATION IN SOUTHERN ETRURIA FROM THE TENTH TO THE SIXTH CENTURY BC: THE ORIGINS AND GROWTH OF MAJOR CENTERS

———— •◆• ————

Robert Leighton

Urbanization is a recurrent theme in Mediterranean archaeology of the early first millennium BC and one that has been revisited frequently in recent years.[1] What is meant by urbanization (or, indeed, by a city) may vary according to time, place and scholarly or cultural tradition. As a process of development, urbanization overlaps state formation and questions of economic, socio-political and territorial organization. In Etruria, it most obviously concerns the origins and growth of the main centers, and their form, structure and function in a regional setting. The lives of many Etruscan cities extend for a millennium or more from the end of the Bronze Age, providing abundant material for multi-period narratives or site biographies, but they also raise difficult questions about the cause, pace and trajectory of change. The breadth and complexity of this topic permits only an introductory sketch, which considers the archaeological evidence for major cities during their first few centuries of life (circa 1000–500 BC). Priority is given here to settlement layout and the built environment, while territorial relationships, which tend to highlight economic and political questions and have been the subject of much important work, can only be touched on.

EARLY IRON AGE (VILLANOVAN) FOUNDATIONS, CIRCA 950–725 BC

As archaeological sites, most Etruscan cities can be ascribed Late Bronze or Early Iron Age (henceforth EIA) origins.[2] Tarquinia, Chiusi, Vulci, Vetulonia, Volterra and probably also Caere, were already occupied in the Final Bronze Age (Protovillanovan period, twelfth to eleventh centuries), or even earlier[3] (See Fig. 7.1). Initially they were part of a settled landscape of relatively numerous small or medium-sized settlements, but they seem to have grown considerably and achieved regional status in the EIA (Villanovan period, mid-tenth to eighth centuries). In southern Etruria, their rise to prominence coincided with the abandonment of neighboring settlements, which created an increasingly "monocentric" pattern characterized by a small number of relatively large strategically placed sites. How and why this occurred is hard to specify. Voluntary or coerced synoecism

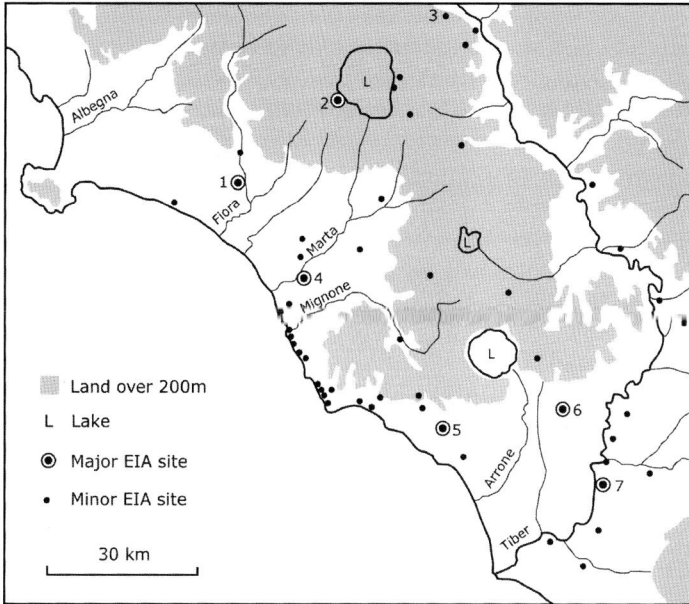

Figure 7.1 Southern Etruria, topography with major and minor Early Iron Age sites.
1.Vulci; 2. Bisenzio; 3. Orvieto (Volsinii); 4. Tarquinia; 5. Cerveteri (Caere); 6. Veii;
7. Rome (data mainly from Pacciarelli 2000).

(the aggregation of formerly separate communities in one place), perhaps for security in response to warfare or growing rivalry, is one possibility. Dominant central places also have greater potential for wealth accumulation and specialization, such as trade and craft production, which are increasingly important features of this period.[4]

The locations of the larger EIA sites, such as Veii, Caere, Tarquinia and Vulci are noteworthy: they occupy large promontories or a series of adjacent plateaus, covering from 120 to 200 hectares, with natural defenses and useful resources nearby, such as rivers and good arable and pastoral land. Evident vantage points on lines of communication along valleys or the coast, they were well placed to serve as the hubs of a wider settlement nexus, which is a key to their successful development. In fact, few major EIA sites failed to expand in subsequent periods; Bisenzio on Lake Bolsena is one such case. Likewise, few cities lack evidence of EIA foundations; Doganella and Roselle are examples,[5] but most Etruscan cities of historical times were already prominent places within an EIA regional context. Moreover, large EIA sites are not numerous or close to each other, which suggests that they did not tolerate the presence of competing centers nearby and that mutual distance may have been as important to their development as the particular configuration of the individual site locations or their proximity to resources. This also seems to anticipate their subsequent development as assertive independent city-states, whose fortunes were partly determined by their ability to control and exploit substantial surrounding territories.

Various coastal sites near Tarquinia and Vulci attest a growing use of maritime resources by communities most likely dependent on the major EIA centers.[6] Again, this echoes the more fully developed relationship between metropolis and emporium (such as Tarquinia-Gravisca) in later periods (below). Otherwise, surprisingly few sites are recorded within a 20-kilometer radius, none of which look like serious rivals.[7] This is a striking feature of EIA settlement patterns in southern Etruria, although the extent to which current distribution maps reflect past reality is questionable.[8] Small sites are undoubtedly under-represented. The nature of territorial control exerted by the main centers at this time is also hard to gauge. A sphere of influence dictated by political considerations rather than subsistence needs is more likely than a closely administered territory. The population of an EIA site (see below) must have been sustainable with just a few square kilometers of productive surrounding land, whereas the agricultural potential of a large territory would be hard to exploit effectively or intensively without a network of subsidiary affiliated sites, which are not well attested. On the other hand, looser territorial rights could be useful for transhumance, hunting, fishing, providing access to more distant pasture, woodlands, wetlands, the sea and, not least, the valuable resources of metal-bearing localities (such as the Tolfa hills in the case of Tarquinia and Caere, or the Colline Metallifere in the case of Populonia and Vetulonia).

Our knowledge of site layouts, however, is sketchy and biased towards cemeteries. Habitation zones are largely unexcavated or known only from scattered finds, often just potsherds from plough soil.[9] Dating is reliant on ceramic typologies rather than 14C dates and often approximate, particularly of houses, which are mostly badly preserved due to successive rebuilding and not necessarily long-lived or contemporary. Burials, however plentiful, provide limited compensation for such lacunae. Population estimates for EIA sites are problematic, ranging from several hundred to a few thousand people, although figures at the lower end of this scale may seem more plausible.[10] Nevertheless, the distribution and quantity of finds from the large sites has grown. They now come from all the main promontories of Tarquinia and are scattered over much of Veii, Caere and Vulci. This has cast doubt on the idea, first formulated in regard to Veii, that the large plateaus or hillocks of EIA sites typically hosted various independent villages. Rather than individually demarcated units, replicating each other in structure and function, many authors now consider them to be single communities sharing a large space, at least in the case of physically unitary sites.[11] This does not exclude a segmented and discontinuous distribution, however, that permitted some differential sub-group organization and identity.[12] The presence of distinct cemeteries around the fringes of promontories and residential areas, which they complement and help to define, is reconcilable with this idea.

In the Final Bronze Age, small communities at Tarquinia (Castellina, Corneto) and Veii (Isola Farnese) might have used the larger adjacent plateaus primarily for agriculture.[13] The large oval houses on the Monterozzi (Calvario) plateau (see Fig. 7.2), perhaps associated with the Arcatelle cemetery, probably date to the EIA (phase 1), while the smaller quadrangular buildings, with a more consistent orientation, could be residences of slightly later date (phase 2) and include one or two ancillary structures, perhaps for storage or animals.[14] EIA residential zones can be postulated on Civita and Cretoncini and it is possible that metal-working and cult activities (more visible in the next period) had already begun to concentrate in certain areas.[15] The dead were generally confined to cemeteries, but occasionally placed beside residential structures, evidently in connection with particular rituals or status considerations in certain cases.[16] Other kinds of cult places in open or enclosed spaces may also have been present.[17] In general, one might envisage rather sprawling settlements with funerary and corresponding residential zones of clustered free-standing houses (employing timber frameworks, wattle, daub

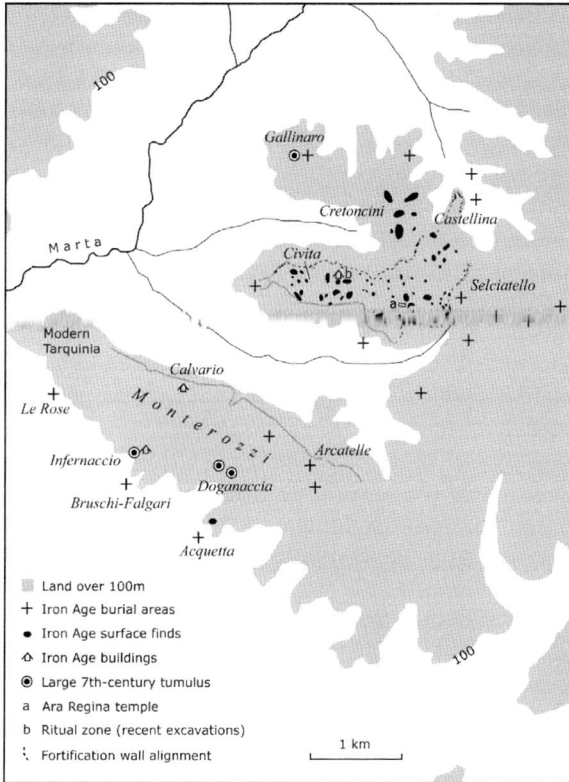

Figure 7.2 Tarquinia, topography and archaeological features
(with survey data from Mandolesi 1999).

and thatching), with nearby cultivation plots, animal pens, track ways and open spaces, allowing relatively unconstrained patterns of movement and interaction. By the early eighth century, however, there is evidence, notably from Veii, for substantial stone and earthen perimeter walls and ditches of a probably defensive and communal nature.[18]

Burial rites and artifacts to some extent connote the gender, rank and perhaps age and family ties of the deceased, while community traditions are suggested by differences between major sites and regions.[19] At Tarquinia, the main locus of power may have been in the Monterozzi-Arcatelle zone, where the tombs are slightly richer than elsewhere.[20] A generally limited degree of differentiation or complexity in the EIA, which may be essentially heterarchical and indicative of a layered, rather than pyramidal, social structure, becomes more marked and hierarchical in the eighth century, as suggested by elaborate weaponry in some graves, which are probably male, and by array of dress and other items in rich, probably female, graves. Vertical ranking is not easy to infer until the mid-late eighth century, and it is not until the seventh century that funerary rites involved architecturally prominent forms of long-lasting commemoration.

In sum, to call the large EIA sites "villages" downplays their size, articulation and regional status. Alternatives, like "township," are similarly burdened by variable modern connotations. While certain features evoke the chiefdoms or early state modules of archaeological theory in the late twentieth century, these labels have also lost traction through problems of definition and loose usage.[21] Proto-urban is the conventional term (in Italy), which justifiably stresses the EIA origins of most Etruscan cities, although "semi-urban" seems preferable to this author, since it avoids the overly evolutionistic or potentially teleological implications of "proto-urban" as an explanation of the causes and trajectory of subsequent growth. Likewise, while a more neutral or cautious view need not hesitate to describe the EIA as "foundational" for Etruscan state formation, the socio-political correlate of urbanization, the extent to which it is formative is more debatable and subject to re-evaluation as evidence grows. Nevertheless, one may at least credit it with an establishment or initial structuring of settlements, territorial relationships, patterns of land and resource exploitation and some cultural traditions along lines that sometimes anticipate, but do not predetermine, subsequent development and elaboration.

URBAN TRANSFORMATIONS, CIRCA 725–550 BC

Major changes occurred over the next 150 years, often called the "Orientalizing" period, although the evidence is still very uneven (see Chapter 6). Separation of the living from the dead seems stricter than before, while areas of "ritual" or ceremonial use become visible. At Tarquinia, the large Monterozzi plateau now served for burial, not housing as well, perhaps because it was easier to move the living elsewhere (onto the Civita-Regina plateau), as the dead steadily required more space. At Veii, a few tombs were added to older cemeteries, while new (seventh-century) burial grounds clustered near site entrances and exits; those to the north (at Riserva del Bagno for example) seem to be higher ranking than those to the south (Macchia della Comunità), perhaps associated with a *quartiere popolare* on the nearby promontory (see Fig. 7.3).[22]

Residential quarters, still little known, evidently coalesced on the central plateaus at the heart of most sites (Veii, Caere, Tarquinia, Vulci). Piazza d'Armi, an offshoot of the main promontory at Veii, was probably a higher status zone, but the houses of this period initially were no doubt still free-standing timber-framed buildings of variable shape (oval or quadrangular) with thatched roofs and open spaces in between. Even high-ranking individuals of the early seventh century, who constructed large burial mounds for the Afterlife (below), may well have lived in houses of traditional design, as represented by those at Veii, Satricum and the "hut tomb" at Caere.[23] Growing social divisions, however, were most likely reflected in private housing by the mid-seventh century and more emphatically thereafter, as suggested by increasingly elaborate funerary architecture at Caere and by multi-roomed buildings at secondary sites, such as Acquarossa and San Giovenale, or, most strikingly, at Murlo.[24]

This also involved greater use of stone, at least for wall foundations, as shown by excavated, but poorly preserved, structures from Veii and Caere, and the first use of roof tiles for domestic buildings in the late seventh century.[25] While it is easy to underestimate the potential monumentality of large timber buildings, quadrangular masonry houses with tiled roofs would have some advantages over traditional EIA houses in an urban setting, notably in terms of durability and diminished fire risk.[26] They also require less timber, possibly a diminishing resource in the vicinity of major settlements, which might help to explain the growing tendency to inhume rather than cremate at this time. A preference for stone and tile buildings, which were probably long-term investments intended to outlive their first occupants, might also relate to changing patterns of property ownership within the urban context, where descendents would perhaps inherit

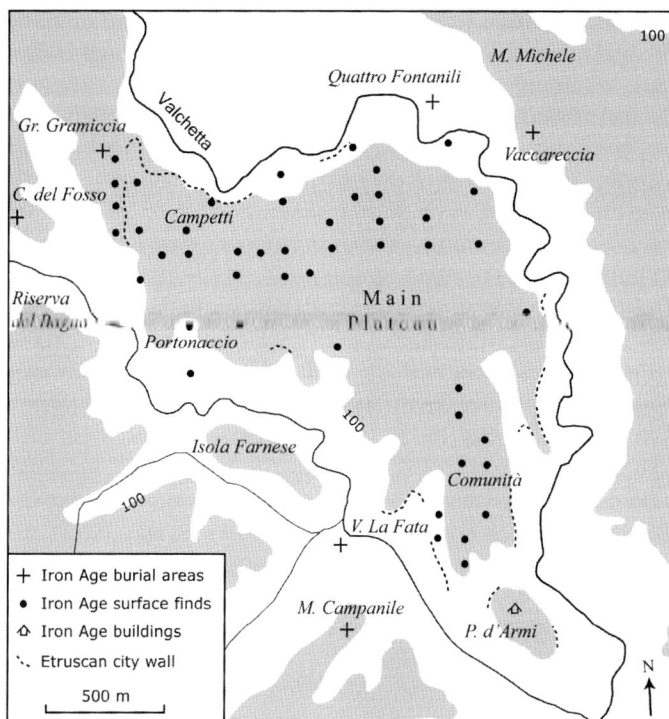

Figure 7.3   Veii, topography and archaeological features (with survey data from Patterson 2004).

houses or the plots on which they were built. A homologous phenomenon of the seventh century could be the multi-generational use of some burial mounds and chamber tombs (below), in contrast to the individual nature of EIA burials, and the signs of increasingly familial or dynastic claims to power, supported by personal wealth, invested in both urban and rural property (below).

An indication that growing social complexity in the eighth century was a precursor of urbanization comes from elite burials, albeit still in the EIA tradition, containing items of adornment, weaponry, horsemanship, wheeled vehicles and imported pottery, often connoting banqueting and drinking. They occur at several sites, including Veii and Tarquinia, as represented by the "warrior tomb" at Tarquinia, an inhumation associated with a hitherto unrivalled level of burial wealth.[27]

This heralds one of the most striking developments of the seventh century: the erection of large mounds, up to 60 m in diameter, over built or rock-cut burial chambers containing quantities of valuable grave goods, the products of both local and foreign craftsmanship, suggesting a more complex iconography of power than hitherto known.[28] Tumuli are an archetypal medium for expressing status, ideally suited to a burgeoning elite attempting to legitimate and consolidate authority by commemorating ancestral links, while showing their ability to command labor in the process. The skyward projection of the mound, surmountable by ramps or stairs and topped by an altar or shrine in some cases, probably referenced celestial powers. Such monuments also occur in parts of the eastern Mediterranean at this time and presumably were familiar to some foreign visitors as well.[29] At Tarquinia, the earliest are on the edges of burial areas, surrounding residential zones in a distant arc, as at Veii, where they would be most conspicuous on approaching or leaving the site. At Caere they dominate the Banditaccia cemetery. Others are on important thoroughfares or in the surrounding territory, where they probably affirmed family claims to the lands on which they were built.

Tumuli must have had considerable impact on urban and rural landscapes. By 550 BC, they had taken over large areas of the cemeteries at Caere and Tarquinia, where they imply a great investment in the creation of what must have resembled funerary theme parks, enhanced by large stone sculptures of humans and exotic or mythical animals. Even if primarily for individual or family aggrandizement, the mounds transformed their host sites in a very public, almost theatrical way, flanking roadways and creating labyrinthine pathways. They imply that urbanization was driven by an aspiring competitive class, comprising a growing number of families, and that the character and form of the early Etruscan city were shaped by markedly rhetorical statements, which were part of a new language of socio-political power, no doubt directed at rivals and lower orders. This does not conflict with the idea that they were also a locus of civic pride, reassurance and ritual temporalities (from recurrent funerals and ceremonies honoring and communicating with the dead), creating an aura of consecrated space around the emerging city.

The importance of ritual is also witnessed near the epicenter of Tarquinia (Civita), where cult activities are documented in an area already occupied in the EIA and which emerges in the eighth century, or even earlier, as a place of special significance.[30] This is indicated by unusual inhumation burials, probably ritual executions, and votive offerings. More substantial development in the early seventh century saw the construction of a two-roomed building (*beta*), possibly a shrine or even a priestly residence (*regia?*), including a pilaster masonry wall of Phoenician style, associated with pit depositions of iconic bronze artifacts (an axe, shield and trumpet), animal bones and pottery with feasting connotations.[31] The complex expanded during the seventh century with the addition of quadrangular courtyards, covering a substantial plot of ground. The emergence of elaborate buildings for ritual activities, not readily identifiable hitherto, anticipates one of the defining features of Etruscan cities, in which religious architecture figures prominently.[32]

By the seventh century, the audience for such conspicuous projects must have extended into the surrounding territory, which may have supplied part of the required labor or payment for them, presumably in some form of transferable surplus, such as goods, services, rents or tributes. Industrial activities were also intensifying, notably those involving pyrotechnology and kilns, located at the margins of some sites, but not others.[33] This also raises the question of how urbanization affected human health.[34] Increasing specialization is well exemplified by the expanding range, quality and volume of craft products in circulation, which include fine pottery, valuable metal and other items (glass and ivory), probably made in nucleated workshops.[35] One may also infer intensification and specialization in agricultural or subsistence activities geared to exchange, including a new emphasis on olives and viticulture. By this time, personal land ownership in the form of heritable estates, was probably well entrenched.

While the importance of ritual is manifest in Etruscan city formation, defensive walls and ditches, already noted at EIA Veii (above), are also attested by 750–700 BC at Vulci, along with a palisade at the west gate. By the later seventh century there were mud brick walls at Roselle, and rough stone walls around the acropolis of Castellina del Marangone and elsewhere.[36] The use of quadrangular stone blocks (*opus quadratum*) seems to follow in the sixth to fifth centuries at Veii, Tarquinia and other sites. Although these constructions resemble utilitarian public works, aside from defense, their purpose is not unlike that of elaborate cemeteries and cult buildings in that they also projected order, reassurance and prestige, while demarcating space in a way that is consonant with the development of a more formal, even juridical, notion or definition of a city.[37]

Another aspect of settlement evolution from 650–600 BC is the establishment at Veii (Piazza d'Armi) of a central track with side streets at right angles defined by cut grooves demarcating plots of ground, suggesting a re-organization of space along rectilinear, block-like principles in this zone. This may have respected older EIA alignments, although the area does not seem to have been heavily built up until the sixth century.[38] Open public spaces are implied at several sites.[39] At Tarquinia too, a by-product of the quadrangular cult precincts juxtaposed on Civita in the seventh century (above) must have been the creation of rectilinear passageways, even if a more elaborate street system with paved surfaces and underground conduits only appeared later, around the end of the sixth century.[40] Orthogonal planning is evident in the street-tombs at Caere (600–550 BC), at Orvieto (circa 550 BC) and, most strikingly, in the precisely gridded city blocks (*insulae*) at the northern town of Marzabotto (circa 540–500 BC), which incorporated workshops and even a temple (see Chapter 15).[41] In addition to various surprisingly modern features (wells, pavements, drains, wide streets, atrium houses) Marzabotto seems to have had smaller burial grounds relative to the residential zone and to the older southern Etruscan cities. Priorities had evidently changed. Perhaps there was also more awareness of the health risks in cramped and crowded urban settings.[42] Grid plans, which are better suited to certain sites – generally on level or virgin ground – were doubtless intended to regulate space and intra-community relations and activities, while mitigating tensions or rivalries, as required by the changing social configurations of the sixth century.[43] They were evidently adopted widely as one formal solution to the challenges of town planning at this time by authorities with considerable decision-making power in southern Italy, Sicily and the Etruscan world, further indicating the close cultural links between these areas.[44]

Distribution maps show an increasingly busy rural landscape in the late eighth and seventh centuries, with secondary centers emerging (which could be quite substantial, and include their own elites), as well as hamlets and small farms, probably reliant on good relations with the emerging regional metropolis, which was the catalyst for rural development and agricultural intensification.[45] Whatever the centralizing and exploitative tendencies of the city, with its enhanced political and decision-making powers, as well as size, it could provide some protection against outsiders or rivals, as well as a manufacturing center and regional market for the exchange of raw materials and finished goods. Recent research has stressed the evolution of increasingly hegemonic territorial relations in the sixth and fifth centuries, which included the use of frontier shrines and a more efficient road network.[46]

Of particular significance was the relationship between metropolis and local harbor or coastal emporium, most obvious in the juxtaposition of Caere and Pyrgi, Tarquinia and Gravisca, Vulci and Regisvilla. This association probably dates from the EIA in embryonic form (above). Castellina del Marangone, a coastal site equidistant from Caere and Tarquinia and already occupied in the Middle-Final Bronze Age, shows intensification of exchange and production activity in the eight to seventh centuries.[47] In the sixth century, however, these maritime sites were monumentalized with shrines and temples, evidently in response to a need for better support structures, formal trade agreements and bureaucratic regulation in which religious authorities played a central role. This development may also have characterized the situation at the main urban centers, where religious buildings would provide the physical backdrop and institutional oversight for all manner of civic activities, including meetings and markets, in adjacent spaces, which we might envisage as the forerunners of the later Roman forum.[48] At Tarquinia, for example, the massive 4th-century Ara della Regina temple was built at the highest elevation of the plateau on the site of earlier temples dating from the sixth century.[49] This might have been an important location before then, but its rise to prominence in the sixth century coincides suggestively with the end of the old Orientalizing cult place in area *beta* (Pian di Civita, above); this was probably a crucial period in the creation of a new urban focal point.

CONCLUSIONS

Urbanization has been discussed here mainly in terms of relationships within Etruria, according to the premise that – except in colonial contexts – it is an evolving process determined largely by local conditions, traditions and decisions, even if external forces can act as a stimulant. Comparable trajectories and pace of development between the major south Etruscan cities may be attributed to locational and socio-cultural similarities, proximity and interaction, including rivalry and emulation. While evolving in tandem, however, some sites seem more precocious or prosperous in certain periods. For example, Tarquinia appears to be ahead in the EIA, perhaps overtaken by Caere in the seventh century, although the general impression is of a rough equilibrium, unless disrupted by exceptional circumstances; an obvious case is the destruction of Veii by Rome in 396 BC. Comparable origins, histories and longevity doubtless also contributed to a similarly held sense of identity and status, perhaps encouraging self-definition and assertions of individuality, somewhat paradoxically, in order to maintain distinctions. Invented genealogies and foundation stories have a role to play here, such as those linked with Tarquinia, the city of Tarchon and Tages in literary tradition, which can only have enhanced its claims to religious authority.[50] This warns against extrapolating too much from smaller, often short-lived, rural sites. Ancient cities had more in common with each other than with the latter, regardless of whether they were in Etruria, Latium or southern Italy.

The urbanization of Etruria was also connected with that of neighboring regions and the wider Mediterranean, however, including those areas colonized by Phoenicians and Greeks, with whom the Etruscans were in close contact from at least 750 BC. How much weight should be given to external factors is debatable. Trade undoubtedly stimulated local production both in rural and urban settings, while privileged access to external sources of wealth helped local elites to differentiate themselves in the eyes of a potentially sceptical local audience, creating or magnifying class distinctions. The extravagant aggrandizing features of early Etruscan urbanism and much Orientalizing material culture arguably served essentially this purpose.

Similarly, the elaboration of religious ritual, for which the Etruscans were renowned, and which also hinges on restricted knowledge or access, would have been a useful tool in forging new identities and allegiances to particular people and places, especially in Etruria, which lacked any prior experience of urbanization and where the generally benign natural environment would be of limited help in the maintenance (or enforcement) of stable foci of aggregation and social control. In this connection, it is noteworthy that many older Etruscan cities were abandoned in late Antiquity and that few of the Renaissance cities in the region emerged on the same sites. Physical geography and resource proximity do not fully account for the spatial configuration of city-states in this area.

City formation was probably also fuelled by growing aspirations and ambitions peculiar to the late eighth and seventh centuries in which consumerism, fashion, cosmopolitanism and social networking played a part, albeit within the limits of a society dominated by strict social protocols, client-patron and clan-like relations.[51] At the same time, high-level treaties and strategic alliances with foreigners or foreign states, of a kind already mentioned by literary sources for the sixth century, were presumably more easily negotiated and maintained from within urban structures that were mutually recognizable, along with unmistakable symbols of status and authority, despite the linguistic or ethnic diversity of the parties involved.

Apart from forms of competition, symbolic entrainment and emulation, described under the heading of peer polity interaction,[52] more direct stimuli are conceivable in an age of increasingly good communications and movement of goods, ideas and people. Etruscan urban centers were undoubtedly able to expand autonomously and to absorb outsiders, as suggested by inscriptions or textual evidence. A corollary is their ability to colonize or found new sites, mostly within their own territories, but sometimes further afield.[53] Population estimates are notoriously difficult, but urban centers undoubtedly grew considerably after the EIA and contained several thousand people by the later sixth century (though perhaps no more than about 10,000 typically).[54]

For the seventh century, the story of Demaratus, a Corinthian merchant-nobleman, who moves to Tarquinia accompanied by craftsmen and fathers a future king of Rome by his Etruscan wife, seems as literally emblematic of cross-cultural fertilization as it is possible to imagine. Rather than a (Greek)-teacher/(Etruscan)-pupil model of interaction, which is how the story is sometimes read, it may signal a form of peer polity magnetism, in which the host city (Tarquinia) has already achieved a respectable size and internationally recognizable form of power and status in the eyes of a distant foreign metropolis (Corinth). From a diffusionist perspective, however, one might suggest that Etruscology has tended to underestimate the potential of contacts with Phoenicians who are under-represented in literary sources but who were the only people in the western Mediterranean in the eighth century with a long-prior knowledge and experience of life in urban city-states.

The origins and trajectory of Etruscan urbanization are also bound up with state formation, which takes us back to the EIA (or the Final Bronze Age), a period sometimes regarded as one of step-like rather than ramp-like change from an earlier (Middle-Late Bronze Age) stage. Archaeological work increasingly has revealed connections between the EIA and subsequent periods. Urbanization tends to be associated with the seventh and sixth centuries, when we can see a veritable building boom that did much to determine the layout, appearance and character of major Etruscan cities for centuries to come. However, if we reason that this must have been preceded locally by social and political change, then at least the second half of the eighth century seems no less crucial.

While the evidence is rather skewed towards ritual and monumentality, these were evidently powerful ingredients in Etruscan urbanization. Even the first use of writing, once regarded as a *sine qua non* for any respectable urban civilization, seems to be closely connected with ritual in Etruria.[55] It may be an exaggeration to call the sixth century a "new act" rather than just a "scene change" in Etruscan urbanism, but it raises the question of how the seventh-century city, with its ideologically charged manifestations of tumuli, cults and exotica, should be distinguished from its Archaic successor, and how monuments of earlier periods were reconciled with changing values and social realities in later times. Superficially at least, the later (sixth/fifth-century) cities may seem more bureaucratic, pragmatic and integrative, with their additional public works (better city walls, streets, water works and harbors) but the physical remains and symbols, if not also the memory and traditions, of their origins and early growth, must still have been apparent.

NOTES

1 For example, Osborne and Cunliffe 2005. I have prioritized recent works below.
2 The absolute chronology of the EIA is debated (Bartoloni and Delpino 2005). It can be subdivided between an earlier and later phase (Primo Ferro 1, roughly 950–825 BC; and Primo Ferro 2, roughly 825–725 BC). All centuries in my text are BC (or BCE) unless indicated otherwise.
3 di Gennaro and Guidi 2009; Pacciarelli 2009; 2010; Maggiani 2010. For Veii and Caere, see also Berardinetti *et al.* 1997: 317–8; di Gennaro *et al.* 2004; Cerasuolo 2008: 690–1.
4 For example, Bietti Sestieri 1997.
5 For Doganella, see Perkins 2010: 104–6, with references.
6 Pacciarelli 2000: 170; Barceló *et al.* 2002; Negroni Catacchio and Cardosa 2005.
7 San Giuliano, about 23 km east of Tarquinia, might represent a strategic outpost, safeguarding its hinterland (Pacciarelli 2010: 20). See also Bonghi Jovino 2005a: 45.
8 Barker and Rasmussen (1998: 61–3) note the limitations of dating survey pottery, which also makes it hard to chart the speed of change. For various debates with references, see Vanzetti (2004).
9 For example, Mandolesi 1999 (Tarquinia); Patterson 2004 (Veii).
10 For example, Rajala (2005: 710) suggests 500–1000 people for EIA Veii.
11 For example, Berardinetti *et al.* 1997: 319; di Gennaro *et al.* 2004. Chiusi is often regarded as a series of villages, although this is disputed by Pacciarelli (2000: 131–2). Villanovan Bologna, however, does not appear to have coalesced into a single physical unit until the eighth century (Ortalli 2008).
12 Pacciarelli (2010: 23) calls them corporate groups and suggests that the later institution of the Roman *curiae* (Smith 2005) may ultimately derive from this type of "horizontal" social organization.
13 di Gennaro and Guidi 2009: 434.
14 Pacciarelli 2000: 170, with references. A sequence from oval to rectangular buildings is indicated at Veii (Bartoloni 2009b: 65) and hinted at in the case of Caere (Maggiani and Rizzo 2005: 182).
15 Bonghi Jovino (2010: 163–5) stresses the ritual or cult dimension of EIA finds from Civita. However, cult and domestic functions could still be in close proximity in this period (Leighton 2004: 40); for ritual activities beside EIA dwellings at Caere, see Izzet 1999–2000: 136.
16 For example, Bartoloni 2007–8; Boitani *et al.* 2007–8 (Veii); Bonghi Jovino 2007–8 (Tarquinia).
17 For example, as at Sorgenti della Nova (Negroni Catacchio and Cardosa 2007: 56–9).
18 Boitani 2007–8: 836–8; Boitani 2008: 139–42. Defensive walls were probably widespread in Italy from the Late Bronze Age onward, and are also attested by impressive constructions at EIA Bologna (Ortalli 2008).

19 For example, Berardinetti *et al.* 1997; Toms 1998; Iaia 1999.

20 Iaia 1999: 69–71; Pacciarelli 2010: 27–8.

21 Bietti Sestieri (1997) describes the EIA polities of Etruria as early states.

22 Bartoloni 2009a: 9–11; Berardinetti *et al.* 1997: 332–4.

23 Boitani *et al.* 2007–8; Waarsenburg 2001.

24 For example, Prayon 2000; Donati 2000, for general surveys.

25 Boitani 2008: 139; Bartoloni *et al.* 2005; Bartoloni 2009a (Veii); Izzet 1999–2000: 138 (Caere).

26 For example, Damgaard Andersen 1997: 347.

27 Leighton 2004: 56–8, with references; Pacciarelli 2010: 32–3. For Veii, see De Santis 2005.

28 See Mandolesi 2008; Riva 2010, with references.

29 For Anatolian, North Syrian and Cypriot analogies, see Naso 1996; Mandolesi 2008: 14–15.

30 For summaries: Bonghi Jovino 2010; Leighton 2004: 40. On the burials: Bonghi Jovino 2007–8.

31 Bonghi Jovino 2005b; 2010: 168; Rathje 2006. For similarities between cult and aristocratic residences, see also Steingräber 2001: 25.

32 Prayon 2009 (for links between sacred and secular architecture).

33 Finds under the city wall at Tarquinia and Veii: Baratti *et al.* 2008: 161, 165; Boitani *et al.* 2007–8; Cascino and Di Sarcina 2005; but more integrated with housing at Doganella and Marzabotto (Perkins and Walker 1990: 70).

34 For example, Harrison *et al.* 2010, for discussion. And see note 42 below.

35 Nijboer 1997; 2004.

36 Moretti Sgubini 2008: 171 (Vulci); Cygielman and Poggesi (2008) suggest that the Roselle walls may be late seventh century and possibly for terracing; Prayon 2005 (Castellina del Marangone). See also Izzet 2007: 182–7; Fontaine 2008.

37 E.g. Briquel 2008.

38 Acconcia *et al.* 2005; Bartoloni 2007–8: 828.

39 Izzet 2007: 179–81, with references.

40 Chiaramonte Treré 2005, for roughly rectilinear parallel streets at Tarquinia.

41 Lippolis 2005, for Marzabotto; Perkins 2010: 106–7, with further examples.

42 A reduction in stature of central Italian populations during the first millennium BC might be due to increasingly unfavorable living conditions: Giannecchini and Moggi-Cecchi 2008.

43 For power and class relations, see, for example, Cerchiai 2000.

44 While the Greek colonies may have promoted such developments, forms of urban geometry recur at various times and places, for example, in the north Italian Middle Bronze Age "terramare" sites, and perhaps at Oderzo in the eighth century (Ruta Serafini and Balista 1999: 80–2).

45 For example, Bonghi Jovino 2005a (with bibliography); Zifferero (2005) suggests a more rapid development of Caere's hinterland not before the later seventh century; Perkins 2010, for sixth-century transformations in the Albegna valley.

46 Cifani 2010; Stoddart 2010; Zifferero 2005, with further references.

47 Prayon 2005.

48 For example, Nijboer 2004: 147–53.

49 Bonghi Jovino 2010.

50 For example, Leighton 2004: 75–8, with references.

51 For example, Foxhall 2005 for related discussion.

52 Renfrew and Cherry 1986.

53 For example, Camporeale 2005.

54 Perkins 2010: 109 for Albegna valley estimates (with further references).

55 For example, Wilkins 1996.

BIBLIOGRAPHY

Acconcia, V., Bartoloni, G. and ten Kortenaar, S. (2005) "The stratigraphical investigation at Piazza d'Armi (Veii; Rome): excavation campaigns of 1996–2002" in P. Attema, A. Nijboer and A. Zifferero (eds), *Papers in Italian Archaeology VI. Communities and Settlements from the Neolithic to the Early Medieval Period. Proceedings of the 6th Conference of Italian Archaeology, Groningen 2003, Vol.2*, Oxford: BAR International Series 1452 (II), 278–86.

Baratti, G., Cataldi, M. and Mordeglia, L. (2008) "La cinta fortificata di Tarquinia alla luce della nuova documentazione" in O. Paoletti and M. C. Bettini (eds), *La Città Murata in Etruria. Atti del XXV Convegno di Studi Etruschi ed Italici, Chianciano Terme-Sarteano-Chiusi, 30 marzo–3 aprile 2005*, Pisa-Rome: F. Serra editore, 155–69.

Barceló, J. A., Pelfer, G. and Mandolesi, A. (2002) "The origins of the city. From social theory to archaeological description," *Archeologia e Calcolatori*, 13: 41–64.

Barker, G. and Rasmussen, T. (1998) *The Etruscans*, London: Blackwell.

Bartoloni, G. (2007–8) "La sepoltura al centro del pianoro di Piazza d'Armi-Veio," *Scienze dell'Antichità* 14(2): 821–32.

Bartoloni, G. (ed.) (2009a) *L'abitato etrusco di Veio. Ricerche dell'Università di Roma 'La Sapienza'. I: Cisterne, pozzi e fosse*, Rome: Edizioni IUNO.

Bartoloni, G. (2009b) "Periodo protostorico, periodo etrusco: una sequenza ambigua" in S. Bruni (ed.) *Etruria e Italia Preromana. Studi in onore di Giovannangelo Camporeale*, Pisa-Rome: F. Serra Editore, 61–7.

Bartoloni, G., Acconcia, V. and ten Kortenaar, S. (2005) "Veio, Piazza d'Armi" in A. M. Sgubini Moretti (ed.), *Dinamiche di sviluppo delle città nell'Etruria meridionale. Veio, Caere, Tarquinia, Vulci. Atti del XXIII Convegno di Studi Etruschi ed Italici, Roma, Veio, Cerveteri/Pyrgi, Tarquinia, Tuscania, Vulci, Viterbo, 2001. Vol.1*, Pisa-Rome: Istituti editoriali e poligrafici internazionali, 73–85.

Bartoloni, G. and Delpino, F. (eds) (2005) *Oriente e occidente: metodi e discipline a confronto. Riflessioni sulla cronologia dell'età del ferro in Italia. Atti dell'incontro di studi, Roma 30–31 ottobre 2003 (Mediterranea I, 2004)*, Pisa-Rome: Istituti editoriali e poligrafici internazionali.

Berardinetti, A., De Santis, A. and Drago, L. (1997) "Burials as evidence for proto-urban development in southern Etruria: the case of Veii" in H. Damgaard Andersen, H. W. Horsnaes, S. Houby-Nielsen. and A. Rathje (eds), *Urbanization in the Mediterranean in the 9th to 6th Centuries BC. Acta Hyperborea*, 7, Copenhagen: Museum Tusculanum Press, 317–42.

Bietti Sestieri, A. M. (1997) "Italy in Europe in the Early Iron Age," *Proceedings of the Prehistoric Society*, 63: 371–402.

Boitani, F. (2008) "Nuove indagini sulle mura di Veio nei pressi di porta nord-ovest" in O. Paoletti and M. C. Bettini (eds), *La Città Murata in Etruria. Atti del XXV Convegno di Studi Etruschi ed Italici, Chianciano Terme-Sarteano-Chiusi, 30 marzo–3 aprile 2005*, Pisa-Rome: F. Serra editore, 135–43.

Boitani, F., Neri, S. and Biagi, F. (2007–8) "La donna delle fornaci di Veio-Campetti," *Scienze dell'Antichità* 14(2): 833–68.

Bonghi Jovino, M. (2005a) "Città e territorio. Veio, Caere, Tarquinia, Vulci: appunti e riconsiderazioni" in A. M. Sgubini Moretti (ed.), *Dinamiche di sviluppo delle città nell'Etruria meridionale. Veio, Caere, Tarquinia, Vulci. Atti del XXIII Convegno di Studi Etruschi ed Italici, Roma, Veio, Cerveteri/Pyrgi, Tarquinia, Tuscania, Vulci, Viterbo, 2001. Vol.1*, Pisa-Rome: Istituti editoriali e poligrafici internazionali, 27–58.

——(2005b) "Tarquinia. Monumenti urbani," in A. M. Sgubini Moretti, (ed.), *Dinamiche di sviluppo delle città nell'Etruria meridionale. Veio, Caere, Tarquinia, Vulci. Atti del XXIII Convegno di Studi Etruschi ed Italici, Roma, Veio, Cerveteri/Pyrgi, Tarquinia, Tuscania, Vulci, Viterbo, 2001. Vol.1*, Pisa-Rome: Istituti editoriali e poligrafici internazionali, 309–22.

——(2007–8) "L'ultima dimora. Sacrifici umani e rituali sacri in Etruria. Nuovi dati sulle sepolture nell'abitato di Tarquinia," *Scienze dell'Antichità*, 14.2: 771–93.

———(2010) "The Tarquinia Project: A Summary of 25 Years of Excavation," *American Journal of Archaeology*, 114: 161–80.

Briquel, D. (2008) "La città murata: aspetti religiosi" in O. Paoletti and M. C. Bettini (eds), *La Città Murata in Etruria. Atti del XXV Convegno di Studi Etruschi ed Italici, Chianciano Terme-Sarteano-Chiusi, 30 marzo–3 aprile 2005*, Pisa-Rome: F. Serra editore, 121–33.

Camporeale, G. (ed.) (2005) *The Etruscans Outside Etruria*, Los Angeles: J. Paul Getty Trust Publications.

Cascino, R. and Di Sarcina, M. T. (2005) "L'abitato di Veio tra età orientalizzante e conquista romana; l'interpretazione in base ai dati delle ricognizioni Ward-Perkins" in P. Attema, A. Nijboer and A. Zifferero (eds), *Papers in Italian Archaeology VI. Communities and Settlements from the Neolithic to the Early Medieval Period. Proceedings of the 6th Conference of Italian Archaeology, Groningen 2003. Vol.2*, Oxford: BAR International Series 1452 (II), 287–91.

Cerasuolo, A. (2008) "All'origine di Caere. Contributo alla conoscenza del processo formativo protourbano in un settore dell'Etruria meridionale" in N. Negroni Catacchio (ed.), *Preistoria e protostoria in Etruria, Atti dell'ottavo incontro di studi, Paesaggi reali e paesaggi mentali, Ricerche e scavi, vol.2*, Milano, 683–94.

Cerchiai, L. (2000) "The ideology of the Etruscan city" in M. Torelli (ed.) *The Etruscans*, Milan: Bompiani, 243–53.

Chiaramonte Treré, C. (2005) "Nuovi dati sull'urbanistica tardo-arcaica di Tarquinia" in A. M. Sgubini Moretti (ed.), *Dinamiche di sviluppo delle città nell'Etruria meridionale. Veio, Caere, Tarquinia, Vulci. Atti del XXIII Convegno di Studi Etruschi ed Italici, Roma, Veio, Cerveteri/Pyrgi, Tarquinia, Tuscania, Vulci, Viterbo, 2001. Vol.1*, Pisa-Rome: Istituti editoriali e poligrafici internazionali, 331–39.

Cifani, G. (2010) "State formation and ethnicities from the 8th to 5th century BC in the Tiberine valley (central Italy)," *Social Evolution and History*, 9(2): 53–69.

Cygielman, M. and Poggesi, G. (2008) "Cinta muraria di Roselle. Alcune considerazioni alla luce dei recenti lavori di restauro" in O. Paoletti and M. C. Bettini (eds), *La Città Murata in Etruria. Atti del XXV Convegno di Studi Etruschi ed Italici, Chianciano Terme-Sarteano-Chiusi, 30 marzo–3 aprile 2005*, Pisa-Rome: F. Serra editore, 244–61.

Damgaard Andersen, H. (1997) "The archaeological evidence for the origin and development of the Etruscan city in the 7th to 6th centuries BC" in H. Damgaard Andersen, H. W. Horsnaes, S. Houby-Nielsen and A. Rathje (eds) *Urbanization in the Mediterranean in the 9th to 6th Centuries BC. Acta Hyperborea*, 7, Copenhagen: Museum Tusculanum Press, 343–82.

De Santis, A. (2005) "Da capi guerrieri a principi: la strutturazione del potere politico nell'Etruria protourbana" in A. M. Sgubini Moretti (ed.), *Dinamiche di sviluppo delle città nell'Etruria meridionale. Veio, Caere, Tarquinia, Vulci. Atti del XXIII Convegno di Studi Etruschi ed Italici, Roma, Veio, Cerveteri/Pyrg, Tarquinia, Tuscania, Vulci, Viterbo, 2001, Vol.2*, Pisa-Rome: Istituti editoriali e poligrafici internazionali, 615–31.

di Gennaro, F., Schiapelli, A. and Amroroso, A. (2004) "Un confronto tra gli organismi protostatali delle due sponde del Tevere: le prime fasi di Veio e di Crustumerio" in H. Patterson (ed.), *Bridging the Tiber. Approaches to Regional Archaeology in the Middle Tiber Valley. Archaeological Monographs of the British School at Rome*, 13, Rome, 147–77.

di Gennaro, F. and Guidi, A. (2009) "Ragioni e regioni di un cambiamento culturale: modi e tempi della formazione dei centri protourbani nella valle del Tevere e nel Lazio meridionale," *Scienze dell'Antichità*, 15: 429–45.

Donati, L. (2000) "Civil, Religious, and Domestic Architecture" in M. Torelli (ed.), *The Etruscans*, Milan: Bompiani, 313–33.

Fontaine, P. (2008) "Mura, arte fortificatoria e città in Etruria. Riflessioni sui dati archeologici" in O. Paoletti and M. C. Bettini (eds), *La Città Murata in Etruria. Atti del XXV Convegno di Studi Etruschi ed Italici, Chianciano Terme-Sarteano-Chiusi, 30 marzo–3 aprile 2005*, Pisa-Rome: F. Serra editore, 203–20.

Foxhall, L. (2005) "Village to City: Staples and Luxuries? Exchange Networks and Urbanization" in R. Osborne and B. Cunliffe (eds), *Mediterranean Urbanization 800–600 BC*, Oxford: Oxford University Press, 233–48.

Giannecchini, M. and Moggi-Cecchi, J. (2008) "Stature in archaeological samples from central Italy: methodological issues and diachronic changes," *American Journal of Physical Anthropology*, 135: 284–92.

Harrison, A. P., Cattani, I. and Turfa, J. M. (2010) "Metallurgy, environmental pollution and the decline of Etruscan civilisation," *Environmental Science and Pollution Research*, 17: 165–80.

Iaia, C. (1999) *Simbolismo funerario e ideologia, alle origini di una civiltà urbana. Forme rituali nelle sepolture 'villanoviane' a Tarquinia e Vulci, e nel loro entroterra. (Grandi contesti e problemi della protostoria italiana, 3)*, Florence: All'Insegna del Giglio.

Izzet, V. (1999–2000) "Etruscan ritual and the recent excavation at Sant'Antonio, Cerveteri," *Accordia Research Papers*, 8: 134–48.

——(2007) *The Archaeology of Etruscan Society*, Cambridge: Cambridge University Press.

Leighton, R. (2004) *Tarquinia, an Etruscan City*, London: Duckworth.

Lippolis, E. (2005) "Nuovi dati sull'acropoli e sulla forma urbana di Marzabotto" in G. Sassatelli and E. Govi (eds), *Culti, forma urbana e artigianato a Marzabotto. Nuove prospettive di ricerca (Atti del Convegno di Studi, Bologna 2003)*, Bologna: Ante Quem, 139–65.

Maggiani, A. (2010) "Volterra. Formazione della città e del territorio" in P. Fontaine (ed.), *L'Étrurie et l'Ombrie avant Rome; cité et territoire. Actes du colloque internationale, Louvain-la-Neuve 2004*, Brussels: Belgisch Historisch Instituut te Rome, 35–61.

Maggiani, A. and Rizzo, M. A. (2005) "Cerveteri. Le campagne di scavo in loc. Vigna Parocchiale e S. Antonio" in A. M. Sgubini Moretti (ed.), *Dinamiche di sviluppo delle città nell'Etruria meridionale. Veio, Caere, Tarquinia, Vulci. Atti del XXIII Convegno di Studi Etruschi ed Italici, Roma, Veio, Cerveteri/Pyrgi, Tarquinia, Tuscania, Vulci, Viterbo, 2001.Vol.1*, Pisa-Rome: Istituti editoriali e poligrafici internazionali, 175–83.

Mandolesi, A. (1999) *La 'prima' Tarquinia. L'insediamento protostorico sulla Civita e nel territorio circostante. (Grandi contesti e problemi della protostoria italiana, 2)*, Florence, All'Insegna del Giglio.

——(2008) "Ricerca sui tumuli principeschi orientalizzanti a Tarquinia: prime indagini nell'area della Doganaccia," *Orizzonti. Rassegna di Archeologia*, 9: 11–25.

Moretti Sgubini, A. M. (2008) "Le mura di Vulci: un aggiornamento sullo stato della ricerca" in O. Paoletti and M. C. Bettini (eds), *La Città Murata in Etruria. Atti del XXV Convegno di Studi Etruschi ed Italici, Chianciano Terme-Sarteano-Chiusi, 30 marzo–3 aprile 2005*, Pisa-Rome: F. Serra editore, 171–9.

Naso, A. (1996) "Osservazioni sull'origine dei tumuli monumentali nell'Italia centrale," *Opuscola Romana*, 20: 69–85.

Negroni Catacchio, N. and Cardosa, M. (2005) "'Paesaggi d'acque'. Il progetto di ricognizione del Monte Argentario e dell'area lagunare costiera (Grosseto-Toscana)" in P. Attema, A. Nijboer and A. Zifferero (eds), *Papers in Italian Archaeology VI. Communities and Settlements from the Neolithic to the Early Medieval Period. Proceedings of the 6th Conference of Italian Archaeology, Groningen 2003, Vol.2*, Oxford: BAR International Series 1452 (II), 973–83.

Negroni Catacchio, N. and Cardosa, M. (eds) (2007) *Sorgenti della Nova. Un abitato tra Protostoria e Medioevo. Guida allo scavo.* Milan: Onlus.

Nijboer, A. J. (1997) "The role of craftsmen in the urbanization process of central Italy (8th to 6th centuries BC)" in H. Damgaard Andersen, H. W. Horsnaes, S. Houby-Nielsen and A. Rathje (eds) *Urbanization in the Mediterranean in the 9th to 6th Centuries BC. Acta Hyperborea, 7*, Copenhagen: Museum Tusculanum Press, 383–406.

——(2004) "Characteristics of Emerging Towns in Central Italy, 900/800 to 400 BC" in P. Attema (ed.), *Centralization, early urbanization and colonization in first millennium BC Italy and Greece. Part 1, Italy (Babesch, Supplement 9)*, Leuven: Peeters, 137–56.

Ortalli, J. (2008) "La prima *Felsina* e la sua cinta" in O. Paoletti and M. C. Bettini (eds), *La Città Murata in Etruria. Atti del XXV Convegno di Studi Etruschi ed Italici, Chianciano Terme-Sarteano-Chiusi, 30 marzo–3 aprile 2005*, Pisa-Rome: F. Serra editore, 493–506.

Osborne, R. and Cunliffe B. (eds) *Mediterranean Urbanization 800–600 BC, Proceedings of the British Academy 126*, Oxford: Oxford University Press.

Pacciarelli, M. (2000) *Dal villaggio alla città. La svolta protourbana del 1000 a.C. nell'Italia tirrenica (Grandi contesti e problemi della protostoria italiana, 4)*, Florence: All'Insegna del Giglio.

——(2009) "Verso i centri protourbani. Situazioni a confronto da Etruria meridionale, Campania e Calabria," *Scienze dell'antichità*, 15: 371–416.

——(2010) "Forme di complessità sociale nelle comunità protourbane" in P. Fontaine (ed.), *L'Étrurie et l'Ombrie avant Rome: cité et territoire. Actes du colloque internationale, Louvain-la-Neuve 2004*, Brussels: Belgisch Historisch Instituut te Rome, 17–33.

Patterson, H. (ed.) (2004) *Bridging the Tiber. Approaches to Regional Archaeology in the Middle Tiber Valley. Archaeological Monographs of the British School at Rome, 13*, Rome, 11–28.

Perkins, P. (2010) "The Cultural and Political Landscape of the *Ager Caletranus*, North-West of Vulci" in P. Fontaine (ed.), *L'Étrurie et l'Ombrie avant Rome: cité et territoire. Actes du colloque internationale, Louvain-la-Neuve 2004*, Brussels: Belgisch Historisch Instituut te Rome, 103–21.

Perkins, P. and Walker, L. (1990), "Survey of an Etruscan city at Doganella, in the Albegna valley," *Papers of the British School at Rome*, 58: 1–143.

Prayon, F. (2000) "Tomb Architecture," in M. Torelli (ed.) *The Etruscans*, Milan: Bompiani, 335–43.

Prayon, F. (2005) "Lo sviluppo urbanistico del sito etrusco di Castellina del Marangone (comune di Santa Marinella, prov. di Roma)" in A. M. Sgubini Moretti (ed.), *Dinamiche di sviluppo delle città nell'Etruria meridionale. Veio, Caere, Tarquinia, Vulci. Atti del XXIII Convegno di Studi Etruschi ed Italici, Roma, Veio, Cerveteri/Pyrgi, Tarquinia, Tuscania, Vulci, Viterbo, 2001, Vol.2*, Pisa-Rome: Istituti editoriali e poligrafici internazionali, 665–79.

——(2009) "The Atrium as Italo-Etruscan Architectural Concept and as Societal Form" in J. Swaddling and P. Perkins (eds), *Etruscan by Definition, Papers in Honour of Sybille Haynes, MBE*, London: British Museum Press, 60–3.

Rajala, U. (2005) "From a settlement to an early state? The role of Nepi in the local and regional settlement patterns of the Faliscan area and inner Etruria during the Iron Age" in P. Attema, A. Nijboer and A. Zifferero (eds), *Papers in Italian Archaeology VI. Communities and Settlements from the Neolithic to the Early Medieval Period. Proceedings of the 6th Conference of Italian Archaeology, Groningen 2003, Vol.2*, Oxford: BAR International Series 1452 (II), 706–12.

Rathje, A, (2006) "Il sacro e il politico. Il deposito votivo di Tarquinia" in M. Bonghi Jovino (ed.), *Tarquinia e le civiltà del Mediterraneo, Quaderni di Acme 77*, Milan, Cisalpino, 103–118.

Renfrew, C. and Cherry, J. F. (eds) (1986) *Peer polity interaction and socio-political change*, Cambridge: Cambridge University Press.

Riva, C. (2010) *The Urbanization of Etruria. Funerary Practices and Social Change, 700–600 BC*, Cambridge: Cambridge University Press.

Ruta Serafini, A. and Balista, C. (1999) "Oderzo: verso la formazione della città" in *Protostoria e storia del 'Venetorum Angulus', Atti del XX convegno di Studi Etruschi ed Italici, (Portogruaro, Quarto d'Altino, Este, Adria, 1996)*, Pisa, 73–91.

Smith, C. (2005) "The Beginnings of Urbanization in Rome" in R. Osborne and B. Cunliffe (eds), *Mediterranean Urbanization 800–600 BC (Proceedings of the British Academy 126)*, Oxford: Oxford University Press, 203–32.

Steingräber, S. (2001) "The process of urbanization of Etruscan settlements from the Late Villanovan to the Late Archaic period (end of the eighth to the beginning of the fifth century BC): presentation of a project and preliminary results," *Etruscan Studies* 8: 7–33.

Stoddart, S. K. F. (2010) "Boundaries of the state in space and time," *Social Evolution and History*, 9(2): 28–52.

Toms, J. (1998) "The construction of gender in Early Iron Age Etruria" in R. D. Whitehouse (ed.), *Gender and Italian archaeology. Challenging the stereotypes. Accordia Specialist Studies on Italy*, 7, London: Accordia Research Centre, 157–79.

Vanzetti, A. (2004) "Risultati e problemi di alcune attuali prospettive di studio della centralizzazione e urbanizzazione di fase protostorica" in P. Attema (ed.), *Centralization, early urbanization and colonization in first millennium BC Italy and Greece. Part 1, Italy (Babesch, Supplement 9)*, Leuven: Peeters, 1–28.

Waarsenburg, D. J. (2001) "Living like a prince: the habitation counterpart of *tombe principesche*, as represented at Satricum" in J. R. Brandt and L. Karlsson (eds), *From huts to houses: transformations of ancient societies. Proceedings of an international seminar organized by the Norwegian and Swedish Institutes in Rome, September 1997 (Skrifter Utgivna av Svenska Institutet i Rom 4, 56)*, Stockholm, 179–88.

Wilkins, J. B. (1996) "Urban Language Ritual" in J. B. Wilkins (ed,), *Approaches to the Study of Ritual, Italy and the Ancient Mediterranean*, London: Accordia Research Centre, 123–41.

Zifferero, A. (2005) "La formazione del tessuto rurale nell'agro cerite" in A. M. Sgubini Moretti (ed.), *Dinamiche di sviluppo delle città nell'Etruria meridionale. Veio, Caere, Tarquinia, Vulci. Atti del XXIII Convegno di Studi Etruschi ed Italici, Roma, Veio, Cerveteri/Pyrgi, Tarquinia, Tuscania, Vulci, Viterbo, 2001. Vol. 1*, Pisa-Rome: Istituti editoriali e poligrafici internazionali, 257–72.

CHAPTER EIGHT

A LONG TWILIGHT (396–90 BC): ROMANIZATION OF ETRURIA

———— ·•·——————

Vincent Jolivet

INTRODUCTION

The ambiguous term "Romanization," which indicates at once a work in progress and the end result of this process, can legitimately be applied to the slow phenomenon occurring in Etruria between the third and first centuries (all dates BC), which resulted in the almost complete disappearance, at the beginning of the Empire, of the Etruscan culture, institutions and language. Yet it is not a new or unique fact that Rome was founded in immediate contact with an Etruscan territory itself long permeable to Latin influences, and the "century of the Tarquins," the sixth century, resulted in a deep Etruscanization, against which transpired the birth of the Roman Republic. Latinization, and then Romanization of Etruria and Etruscanization of Rome formed a process that thus retained over more than seven centuries, a mixture of cultures that was more closely cemented by a solid mortar, that of the Greek culture which, in successive waves, touched, to varying degrees, all the peoples of the Italian peninsula. The Etruscan civilization was still alive at the beginning of the Roman conquest, which certainly did not put an abrupt end to its development, even though every one of the major city-states that formed Etruria – twelve, according to the tradition – presents very specific characteristics that deeply differentiate it from its neighbors. The idea of "decadence," dear to the scholars of the nineteenth century AD, still weighs heavily on the history of this period, and this is justified etymologically, since it opens with the loss of independence of Etruria. But these three centuries were also those of deep transformations in all areas, which led ultimately to a form of successful integration.

THE ROMAN CONQUEST

It did not take much more than a century for the early Roman Republic, after having driven out Tarquinius Superbus, to take the offensive and set out to destroy the nearest Etruscan city: Veii, one of the most powerful of the dodecapolis, fell in 396,[1] according to Livy after a siege of ten years, which ancient authors compared to that of ancient Troy (Fig. 8.1). The city was destroyed, its territory entirely forfeited to benefit the *ager publicus* of

Rome, and colonized; the survivors were enrolled in four new urban tribes, thus creating a tremendous economic boom for Rome. The treatment of Veii and the revelation of the danger represented by the Roman army led to a sudden realization on the part of other Etruscan cities, and resulted in a little over a century of new conflicts. The nearest neighbor of Rome, *Ceisra*-Caere, seized the opportunity offered by the Gaulish raid of 390 to move closer to Rome by hiding behind its walls Rome's Vestals and sacred objects. We find it, however, in 353, alongside Tarquinia in a war, after which Caere and Rome signed a truce (*indutiae*) of 100 years (Fig. 8.2). Soon after, the city entered the orbit of

Figure 8.1   Found in the votive deposit of the Campetti sanctuary at Veii, this terracotta represents Aeneas carrying Anchises, which shows, in the fourth century, that the ideological association between the conquest of the city and that of Troy were still familiar to the residents of the area (Rome, Villa Giulia; Camporeale 2004, Fig. 184).

Figure 8.2   The recent excavations of Cerveteri have revealed the presence of a public, subterranean complex that was decorated with paintings and dated by the mention of the Roman praetor of Caere, C. Genucius Clepsina, consul in 276 and 270 (Cristofani 1984, p. 58).

Rome, which granted it the status of *civitas sine suffragio*, not only was this a citizenship that does not include the right to vote, but Caere also saw the confiscation of half of its territory, including its coastline, whose strategic interest to the Romans was to prove decisive during the Punic Wars.

A little further north, the fall of Veii placed Roman territory in contact with two powerful cities, Falerii and Tarquinia, attacked jointly by Rome in 358. To the east, this largest city of the Faliscans, people with a Latin-like language but whose representatives, sitting on the annual Etruscan *concilium* at the *Fanum Voltumnae*, could take the measure of the threat from the first quarter of the fourth century, when the two Roman colonies of Nepi and Sutri were founded in its direct sphere of influence. The Romans neutralized the city with a 40-year truce, signed in 351 followed by a treaty (*foedus*) from 343, which opened the access corridor to the Etruscan territory formed by the middle valley of the Tiber (Fig. 8.3). However, after an attempted uprising in 298, the city was taken and completely destroyed in 241, on the pretext of a slave revolt, 6,000 of its inhabitants massacred, its gods displaced to Rome according to the rite of *evocatio*, and half of its territory confiscated; a new Falerii was then built on the plain, three miles west of the ruined city.

A few years after the capture of Veii, in 384–383, the Roman attacks were already concentrated on *Tarchna*-Tarquinia, which appears as the real bulwark of all Etruria because of the position of its territory, which extended from the Tyrrhenian Sea to the Tiber, the seniority and power of this city, and also of its political weight in the assemblies of the *Fanum Voltumnae*. A first major conflict begun in 353 ended in 351 with the signing of a truce that was upheld for 40 years, but in contrast to the contemporary situation with Falerii, this was not transformed into a treaty. So the war began again in 311 with the

Figure 8.3 Datable around the middle of the fourth century, this plate made at Falerii, where the model enjoyed a great success with the Etruscan workshop of Cerveteri and was exported all over the western Mediterranean, furnishes an inscription in Latin characters probably referring to the owner of the ceramic workshop, Poplia Genucilia (Rhode Island, Providence; Beazley 1947, Pl. 38).

support of other Etruscan cities, which besieged Sutri and fought the Roman army in 310, unsuccessfully, at Lake Vadimon. This conflict ended in 308 with a new 40-year truce between the two cities, which Tarquinia exploited to enhance the militarization of its territory (Fig. 8.4). But there is little doubt that the Tarquinians, among other Etruscans, were present at the battle of Sentinum, in 293, alongside the Gauls, Umbrians and Samnites, and at the second battle of Lake Vadimon in 283 alongside the Boii, that resulted in two decisive victories for the Romans. It is believed that the triumph celebrated in 281 by Q. Marcius Philippus *de Etrusceis* marks the end of the independence of Tarquinia, the leader of the coalition, and part of its territory was then confiscated by Rome (Fig. 8.5).

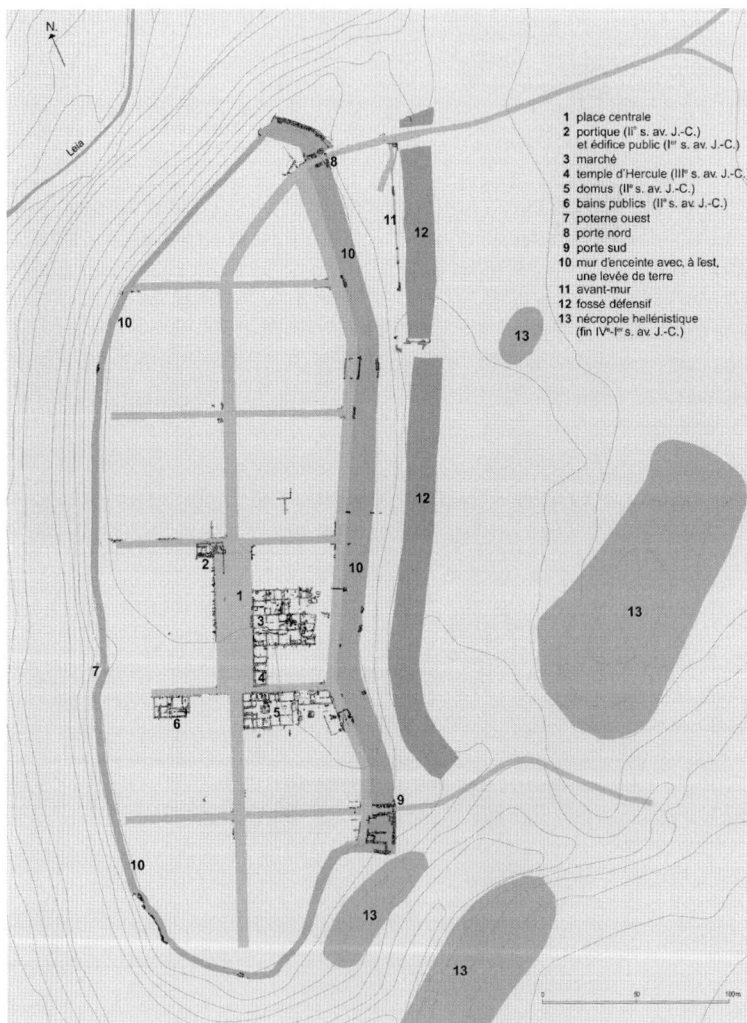

1 place centrale
2 portique (II° s. av. J.-C.)
  et édifice public (I° s. av. J.-C.)
3 marché
4 temple d'Hercule (III° s. av. J.-C.)
5 domus (II° s. av. J.-C.)
6 bains publics (II° s. av. J.-C.)
7 poterne ouest
8 porte nord
9 porte sud
10 mur d'enceinte avec, à l'est,
   une levée de terre
11 avant-mur
12 fossé défensif
13 nécropole hellénistique
   (fin IV°-I° s. av. J.-C.)

Figure 8.4 The stronghold of Musarna, created around the end of the fourth century in the center of the territory of Tarquinia presents in its five hectares all the characteristics of a city in miniature: orthogonal plan, division into lots of its 12 residential insulae, a central piazza, public monuments, capillary network of sewers, powerful fortifications and distinct areas of cemeteries.

Rome was therefore able to pursue its advance in Etruria either by diplomatic means or by war: the following year, in 280, a new triumph is celebrated by P. Tiberius Coruncanius *de Vulcentibus et Volsiniensibus*, the two cities of Vulci (Fig. 8.6) and Volsinii whose territory was to the north, in direct contact with that of Tarquinia. The other Etruscan cities, caught between the advance of Rome to the south and the threat of the Gauls and Ligurians to the north, appear to have preferred to deal with the Romans. The case of Arezzo is significant in this respect: the only Etruscan city, in 311, to refuse to

Figure 8.5   The inscriptions found in the vicinity of the forum of Tarquinia, known under the name of *elogia*, commemorate, at an unknown date between Tiberius and Trajan, some episodes of the glorious past of the great local family of the Spurinna: here, the expeditions led by Aulus Spurinna, four centuries earlier, to drive out of power Ogulnius the king of Caere, to put down a revolt of slaves at Arezzo and to conquer nine Latin strongholds (Tarquinia, Museo Archeologico Nazionale; *Rasenna* 1986, Fig. 6).

Figure 8.6   The François Tomb of Vulci, at the very beginning of the Hellenistic era, compares the deeds of the Trojan War with those of the local aristocracy in their fight against Rome: here, Marce Camitlnas kills Cnaeve Tarchunies Rumach, a Tarquin of Rome (Villa Albani; Torelli-Sgubini Moretti 2008, p. 191).

march against Rome, it does not sign in 308, together with Perugia and Cortona, a truce of 30 years with the city; in 302 the great family of the Cilnii sought the intervention of Rome to put down a slave revolt – a half-century earlier, under similar conditions, it was the Tarquinian General Aulus Spurinna who had intervened to restore order (see Fig. 8.5). In 284, when the city is threatened by the Gauls, it is likewise the Roman army that comes to the rescue.

From the late fourth century, the Roman army roamed freely in the territory of internal and northern Etruria, easily accessible thanks to past alliances with Faliscans and the Umbrians of Camerino and, from 299, with the founding of the colony of Narni: one finds it in operations around Roselle (302), Volterra and Volsinii (298), Chiusi and Perugia (295) and Volsinii and Roselle (294). This part of the conquest may be considered completed with the capture in 264 of *Velzna*-Volsinii, on whose territory was the great pan-Etruscan sanctuary, the *Fanum Voltumnae* (see Chapter 31): as at Arezzo, it was a slave revolt that led to Roman intervention at the request of at least a part of its ruling class. The destruction of the city, the plundering of its statues, the *evocatio* of its chief deity, Voltumna, and the deportation of the survivors to the shores of Lake Bolsena, about eight miles south-east, clearly showed the Roman determination to those Etruscan cities who wanted to retain or regain their independence. That year, the triumph of Fulvius Flaccus *de Vulsiniensibus* marks the end of all hope of independence of the Etruscan cities: in 259, the Roman capture of the Etruscan colony of Aleria, occupied by the Carthaginians since the beginning of the first Punic War, and the destruction of Falerii, in 241, are the latest episodes of this long history. All the Etruscan cities were now bound by a treaty with Rome, but it was only in 90 with the *lex Iulia*, followed in 89 by the *lex Plautia Papiria*, which put an end to the Social War, that their inhabitants became Roman citizens in their own right.

A NEW TERRITORIAL FRAMEWORK

The Roman colonization of large parts of Etruscan territory that then became *ager publicus* began just after the conquest of Tarquinia. During the first half of the third century, Rome founded a series of maritime colonies – small towns planned to accommodate some 300 peasant-soldiers and their families – along the Tyrrhenian coast, on land confiscated from the Etruscans, in the territory of Caere (*Castrum Novum*, Pyrgi, *Alsium* and *Fregenae*, between 286 and 245). In the territory of Vulci, at Cosa (273), was a colony under Roman law inhabited by at least 2,500 families. The second major phase of colonization is concentrated between 183 and 177, after the end of the second Punic War and the early Roman conquest of the East, this time it concerns the territories of Vulci, with Heba and Saturnia, Tarquinia with Gravisca, and Pisa, with Lucca and Luni. Several other colonies were founded thereafter, especially at the end of the Republic, by Sulla, Caesar or Octavian. The continued occupation of most sites, governed by a patchwork of different laws (Roman or Latin colonies, *municipia*, *praefecturae*, *fora* etc.), the presence of colonists on land sometimes depopulated by war against Rome, the Carthaginian and Gallic invasions, and conscription, and the mingling among settlers individually (*viritim*) or clustered in cities, have certainly been powerful factors in the Romanization of the Etruscan territory, especially in the areas closest to Rome. But only in a few cases (from Settefinestre to Heba and Saturnia; at Florence and Lucca) was it possible to demonstrate the presence of centuriation comparable to that attested in the rest of the peninsula.

Taking into account the threat posed by the Gauls (definitively vanquished at Talamone in 225 by the Romans, with the help of Etruscan auxiliaries) and by the Carthaginians (the first Punic War begins in 264, the same year as the fall of Volsinii and the founding of Pyrgi and Paestum), the efficiency of the Roman military could not be guaranteed solely by the capillary network of routes that linked the various Etruscan centers. Shortly after the mid-third century, the creation of the major north-south axes would therefore allow the conduct of rapid operations in an area recently conquered and still unstable, and would open to Rome direct access to areas occupied by warlike people, the Ligurians to the north-west and the Gauls in the north-east. The first of them, probably surveyed in 241, is the *Via Aurelia vetus*, which runs along the Tyrrhenian coast to Luni, thus linking five colonies of Rome, from *Fregenae* to Cosa. From 220, the *Via Flaminia* crosses a small part of the Etruscan territory, in the south-east, before reaching Umbria towards Rimini. The dating of the two pathways of the central part of the territory, which connect at the end of their journey with the *Via Flaminia*, is poorly known: the *Via Clodia*, perhaps in the late third century, connected Tuscania, Vulci and Cosa, the *Via Cassia*, probably created in the first half of the second century, linked Bolsena, Chiusi, Cortona, Arezzo, Florence and Pisa. Finally, breaking away from the *Cassia* at Nepi, the *Via Armerina* led directly to Perugia, crossing Umbrian territory. There is no doubt that the ancient Etruscan road network, carefully planned and drained, continued to be used. But with the founding of colonies and the distance that separated certain sites from the new routes favored by traffic and trade, the creation of these pathways contributed to unbalance the relationship that had long existed between the territory and its population centers, causing the depopulation or abandonment of some of them, now isolated, in favor of others better located.

Typical, also, of Roman culture – although Etruria already knew well-developed, but quite different, architectural forms – are the thermal baths (hygienic, therapeutic or beneficial, all factors of social ties) and the structures for spectacles (amphitheaters and theaters, powerful vehicles for disseminating language), perhaps erected through an act of benefaction by citizens of Roman ethnicity, as a symbol and vector of their social integration (Fig. 8.7). With temples dedicated to new gods, and soon to the imperial cult, these buildings were to diffuse in capillary fashion a lifestyle in every way similar to that of the inhabitants of Rome. Meanwhile, inscriptions – sometimes bilingual (Fig. 8.8) – help to define the progressive diffusion of Latin, slower in rural than in urban areas, and the appearance of new families in Etruria. In this respect, the differences from site to site are numerous: thus, in the late first century at Caere, where the transition from Etruscan to Latin had occurred a century earlier, half of the *gentilicia* (family/clan names) attested are of Latin origin, while at Tarquinia this figure is three times lower. It is certain that these differences betray significant differences in the degree of acculturation of the Etruscan cities.

RETENTION OF POWER AND THE CHANGING OF THE RULING CLASSES

Proud of its traditions and its history, the Etruscan aristocracy played a role of the first order throughout this period. Powerfully structured, it cemented together the various cities through marital ties and probably exerted a fascination on the Roman nobility, conscious of its debt to Etruria, whether in the domain of signs of power, of the architecture

Figure 8.7 The bath building constructed at Musarna around the end of the second century, public but reserved for the local aristocracy, introduces to this site various typically Roman innovations: *opus incertum*, the hypocaust floor, bath-technology, and above all, mosaics, the only example known of this type, which bear in Etruscan letters the name of the two magistrates responsible for its construction.

Figure 8.8 The bilingual inscriptions are reflections of an era when the Etruscan language, already marginalized, still tried to resist the progress of Latin; this one, found at Pesaro and dated to the second half of the first century, is from a certain L. Cafatius who practiced the profession of *haruspex* and of *fulguriator* (Pesaro, Museo Archeologico; Torelli 2000, p. 186).

of houses and temples or the military organization: in the late fourth century the Fabii, a family of the first rank, used to send their children to complete their education at Caere, just as the elite of Rome would later send their offspring to Athens. Although the Etruscan aristocracy certainly played a role, long after the conquest, as either supporters or opponents of Rome, Rome itself, far from imposing the principles of the Republic, extended its dominion over the power of this oligarchy: it was directly responsible for ensuring the social order and providing the city with tribute, goods or men, as circumstances required. The epigraphic corpus related to this class, consisting essentially of funerary inscriptions, is particularly rich, especially in the territories of Caere (on the walls of tombs) and Tarquinia (on sarcophagi); these inscriptions sometimes mention, particularly in Tarquinia, the *cursus honorum* of the deceased. The funerary furnishings, however, betray the difficulties of the aristocracy: the red-figure vases, once a status symbol par excellence, become a consumer product from the late fourth century, soon replaced by a very large production-series of vases decorated in superposed color and in black-gloss; throughout that century, the sets of large bronze vessels are replaced, notably at Falerii and Volsinii, by ceramic imitations (Fig. 8.9). Therefore, in the funerary realm,

Figure 8.9 From the beginning of the Hellenistic period, with the Roman conquest, the loss of economic power by the Etruscan aristocracies led them to substitute in their tombs high-quality ceramic replicas, not usable in daily life, for the vases in bronze of the sort that had been deposited in earlier times: kalyx krater in *ceramica argentata* ("silvered ceramic") from Bolsena, first half of the third century. (Florence, Museo archeologico 191.1; Torelli 2000, p. 153).

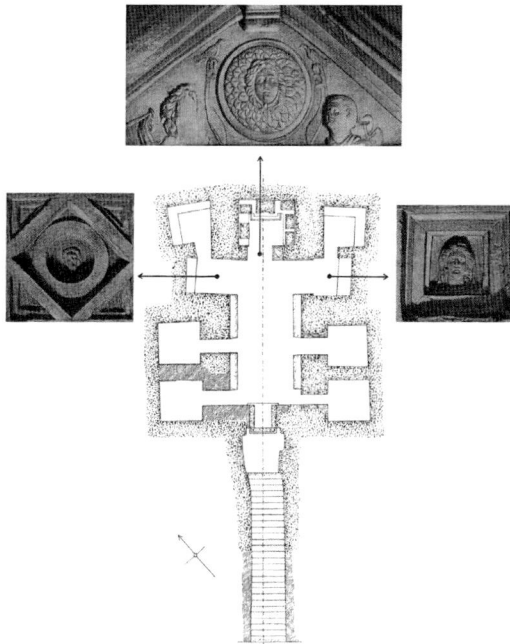

Figure 8.10 At Perugia, the hypogeum of the Velimna, probably of the last third of the third century, is the Etruscan tomb that most faithfully reproduces the canonical plan of the aristocratic house developed three centuries earlier, undoubtedly at Caere, and widely taken up later by the Romans. The lower portion has a central hall dedicated to the family and its heritage, while the two side rooms were probably reserved for women on the right, and for men on the left.

it is rather the architecture of the tombs, like that of the Velimna in Perugia (Fig. 8.10); their paintings, as in Tarquinia or the decoration of the sarcophagi or urns deposited there that most effectively depict the eminent status of the deceased, sometimes combining Etruscan iconography and Latin epigraphy.

The phase of Romanization is also reflected in the same class, by a significant evolution of the role of Etruscan women who appear to have enjoyed, at the beginning of the history of this people, a dignity comparable to that of their male counterparts, such that their liberty and license were considered scandalous by the Greeks and Romans. From the late fourth century, perhaps because the conflict with Rome had brought an exaltation of the typically male values of war, Etruscan women are most often represented in a subordinate position: reclining like men on their sarcophagi or urns, they very rarely hold the symbols of the banquet and sacrifice (patera, kantharos); in the paintings, they are no longer represented reclining, but sit at the foot of their husbands' couches; and finally, in funerary inscriptions, the custom of indicating the matronymic of the deceased, deeply rooted in Etruria from the Orientalizing period, almost disappears during the second century. The process in action, certainly a long-standing commitment, tends to install the Etruscan woman in a place conforming to the gender hierarchy that has long been in force in the Roman world.

Ultimately, it is religion, closely controlled by the Etruscan male ruling classes who provided the priests (Fig. 8.11), which appears to have curbed – most effectively to the benefit of Rome – the social and gender tensions that conquest could harshly release. Every gesture of public life, each new construction was regulated by a set of complex religious laws that comprised what is known as the Etruscan *disciplina*. The books which composed the *disciplina* contained detailed religious instructions that are still reflected, for instance, in the rituals inscribed on the linen bandages used later to wrap a mummy preserved today in Zagreb; and they undoubtedly also expressed respect for property and social hierarchies, as evidenced by a text of the early first century known as the "Prophecy

Figure 8.11   Along with various statuettes in bronze, this figure of a *haruspex* depicted on a *terra sigillata* vase produced in the Rasinius' workshop shows that this was a profession familiar to the clientele that purchased these vases in the Augustan period (Tübingen, Institut fur klassische Archäologie; 158; Torelli 2000, p. 276).

of Vegoia," by the Perugia cippus or by the recently discovered Cortona Tablet (Fig. 8.12). The great Etruscan families achieved, with Roman support, the ability to exert undivided power over their people for a long time (Fig. 8.13). After enactment of the *lex Iulia*, some of these dominant social groups chose to emigrate to Rome, where a dozen Etruscan families already had representatives in the Senate, some since the beginning of the Hellenistic period. But it was not true of all the Etruscan cities, some of which probably kept some of their old social structure and hierarchies even under the Empire.

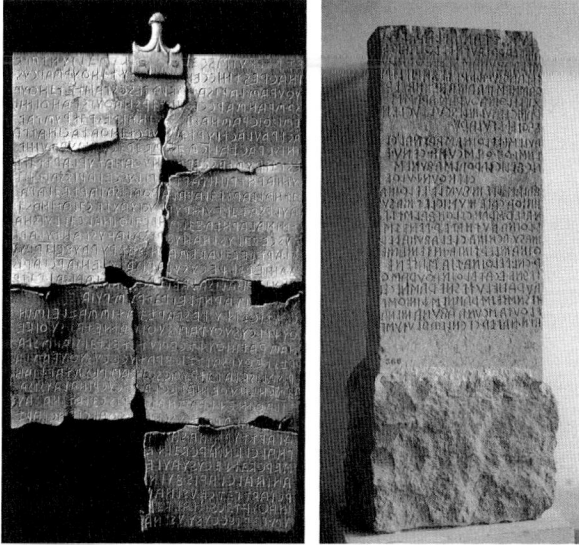

Figure 8.12   The Perugia cippus (left), one of the longest known Etruscan inscriptions, bears a text relating to the boundaries of the properties of the two great families of the city, the Velthina and the Afuna, during the second century (Perugia, Museo Archeologico; Cristofani 1984, p. 77). The Cortona Tablet (Tabula Cortonensis) (right), a copy of a mortgage agreement of the third or second century includes names of men and women of the Scevas and Cusu families (see also Fig 22.4). (Florence Museo Archeologico inv. 234.918).

Figure 8.13   In the course of the Hellenistic period, the images of the dance, the hunt, the banquet or the Underworld are replaced by processions of magistrates in togas, expressing the early influence of Roman decorum on the Etruscan aristocratic families: here, that of the Tomba Bruschi, dated from the end of the fourth century or the beginning of the next century (Camporeale 2004, Fig. 145).

PRESSURE FROM THE MIDDLE AND LOWER CLASSES

The other levels of Hellenistic Etruscan society are much less well known to us, whether by text or through archaeology, and it is reasonable to assume, again, significant disparities between the different cities, as well as between town and countryside. There was clearly a large middle class of small and medium landowners, traders, producers, as witnessed by the series of standardized urns of Volterra or Chiusi, and in which the gender balance appears to have been better observed than among the aristocrats.

At the lowest level of society, Etruria does not seem to have known a slave system directly comparable with those of Greece or Rome (see Chapter 21) – and the latter was introduced by force into the Etruscan territory with the creation, from the second century, of two types of slave domains: large villas, like Settefinestre (Fig. 8.14), built by the Sextii in the territory confiscated from Vulci, where wine was produced and exported in large quantities; and the small, "Catonian" sorts of farms where slaves were part of a small family. Our sources mention another particular category of dependents known in Etruscan as *lautni*, that the Greeks called *therapontes*, and the Latins *servi*. They appear in the texts with the revolts attested twice in Arezzo (the mid-fourth century and 302), and at Volsinii in 264 – having resulted in the complete destruction of the last city, by the massacre of its people and by the deportation of the survivors.

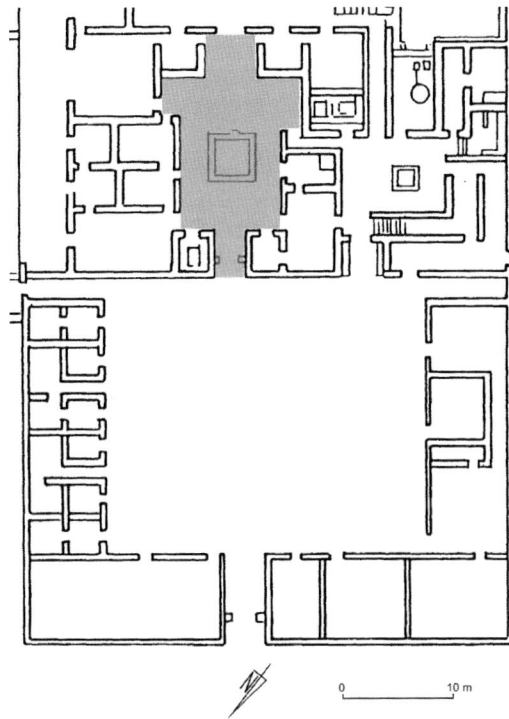

Figure 8.14   Profoundly foreign to the mentality of the Etruscan landowners, the construction of the great *villae* on land confiscated from conquered cities, as here that of Settefinestre constructed in the territory of Vulci around the middle of the first century by Lucius Sestius who was consul in 23 BC, will allow the diffusion of new models for exploitation of the land, but also of the ideology of chattel-slavery in an Etruria that until now only knew other forms of dependence.

It seems in any case that there existed in most of the Etruscan cities at the turn of the fourth century, increased pressure on the part of that class whose demands the Romans, for whom the *plebs* represented a fundamental element of the social and political order, had to consider while seeking to safeguard the interests of an Etruscan aristocracy increasingly well represented in the Senate. The Etruscan dependents probably formed the majority of the members of Bacchic *thiasoi* that were particularly numerous and organized in the southern part of Etruria, and whose disturbing success and seditious potential provoked, in 186, the intervention of the Roman senate who ordered the destruction of places of worship of Bacchus throughout Italy (Fig. 8.15).

AGRICULTURE AND METALLURGY, HANDICRAFT AND ART

It is to the activity of the middle or lower classes that the "obese Etruscan" (Fig. 8.16), associated with the idle aristocrat of the Hellenistic period, and a symbol of wealth in the region, owed his prosperity. An extraordinarily fertile land and rich in metals, Etruria offers, here too, a wide variety of situations because of the morphology of the sites, their geology and their position relative to major communication routes – main and secondary roads, the Tiber, the Tyrrhenian Sea. The only really concrete ancient evidence of this diversity is the inventory of contributions made – enthusiastically, according to Livy (28.45.13–21) – by Etruscan cities for the various military preparations of Scipio in 205. This text distinguishes two different types of production: metallurgy (Populonia, Arezzo) was apparently less developed than agriculture and forestry, with their products (Caere, Tarquinia, Perugia, Chiusi, Roselle, Volterra), comparable to the level of Etruscan expertise recognized in relation to drainage and land reclamation. Campaigns of archaeological survey have also revealed very different situations: in the region nearest

Figure 8.15   The extraordinary Dionysiac throne in terracotta of the beginning of the second century, found in the peristyle of a *domus* at Poggio Moscini in Bolsena demonstrates the success of Bacchic religion in southern Etruria, repressed as seditious by the Roman senate in 186 (Bolsena, Museo Archeologico; École française de Rome; picture M. Benedetti, Archivio SBAEM).

to Rome, just beyond its *suburbium*, the fields were entirely at the service of provisioning the city; they are found depopulated, however, to the advantage of the towns, in areas such as the Tyrrhenian coast, devastated by malaria, as described by Tiberius Gracchus in 125; and so they were still organized in capillary fashion, without fundamental changes seeming to have occurred in the size and distribution of rural sites, as at Volterra. The foundation of the colonies did not necessarily have a significant impact on the subdivision of land before the conquest: the 300 settlers of Gravisca each received only five *jugera* (1.26 hectares), less than 400 hectares for the entire population – but the 2,000 settlers of Saturnia received ten *jugera* each, or 2.5 ha, and those of Luni 51.5 *jugera*, about 13 ha each. Etruscan peasants and Roman colonists had to rub shoulders everywhere, in varying numbers, as evidenced perhaps in the votive healing-cults of the third-second centuries found in the rural sanctuaries they attended together: each culture seems to be represented according to its own customs (tunic and bareheaded for the Etruscans, toga, sacrificial veil, and children's *bullae* for Romans) (Fig. 8.17). The scarcity of large slave-villas in Etruria, except along the coastal strip and some main roads, seems, more generally, to testify the prudent policy of Rome in this region, as long as their management was left to the Etruscan aristocracy. Early in the first century there was probably a latent state of agrarian crisis, which caused the exile, all the way to Tunisia, of a group of inhabitants of Chiusi, as evidenced by the inscribed boundary *cippi* of Oued Miliane (Fig. 8.18).

Formerly highly developed in the mountain region of Tolfa, extraction and processing of metals are concentrated thereafter, until the depletion of deposits in the mid-first century on the exploitation of iron ore from Elba, controlled by the Romans after the conquest and elaborated in Populonia, situated opposite the island. Clay, stone and metal are the basis of the principal productions of this period, in terms of both art and craft, but in very different ways; for most object classes, local production is generally preferred to imports: only amphorae, imported in great quantities from across the Mediterranean as early as the third century, testify, with the export of wine and ceramics produced in central Italy, the existence of a maritime trade probably still managed partly by Etruscan ships.

Fig. 8.16   Over the course of the entire Hellenistic period, Etruscan sarcophagi, especially those of Tarquinia, offer an image of an aristocracy quite remote from Greek ideals, for whom opulence of forms is a sign of richness, of prestige and of power – above all when, as here, it is accompanied by the authority of a long written text relating the *cursus honorum* of the deceased: the decoration of the chest of the sarcophagus of Laris Pulena, dated to the middle of the third century, demonstrates a tragic vision of death (Tarquinia, Museo Archeologico Nazionale ; Torelli 2000, p. 481).

Figure 8.17 Until the end of the Hellenistic period, and for about two centuries, votive deposits in Etruria and Latium are characterized by a great number of anatomical ex-votos in terracotta offered to different gods by members of the popular classes, both Etruscan and Roman. These objects depict all the parts of the human body, as well as animals; in certain cases, such as at here in the territory of Vulci, one assumes that the dedicant was Roman because he is veiled, while the Etruscans had the custom of sacrificing with head bare (votive deposit of Tessennano; Costantini 1995, pl. 2b). See Chapter 59 for more examples.

Figure 8.18 To the agrarian crisis of the end of the second century and the beginning of the following century, that one attributes the migration of a group of Etruscan farmers to the north-east of Tunisia, in the Oued Miliane, where they marked the borders of their fields by placing in the ground a series of inscribed cippi, according to the custom of their homeland (Tunis, Musée du Bardo; *Rasenna*, Fig. 255).

The ceramic forms show a profound break with the previous period: from the third century, the black-gloss ceramic, long known, appears everywhere, and forms of "Campanian ware," adapt to a wider audience; for a long time produced in a multitude of small factories, they were dominated, from the early second century, by a group of workshops related to Campanian B, of which Etruria becomes a major production center. This strong trend undergoes a new acceleration with nearly industrial products that appear in Arezzo, imitating famous Eastern red vases, around the mid-first century (the *tyrrhena sigilla*, for Horace, *Epodes* 2.2.180); the workshop, with its different subsidiaries, supplied most of the fine table-ware of the classical world for nearly a century. All of these products available at low prices in a range of quite varied forms are widely disseminated and poorly differentiated in their decor. Clay and stone (and, just after the founding of Luni, marble from the Apuan Alps) were also involved: for funerary goods, and for the manufacture of sarcophagi or urns, which are mostly products of widely repetitive series. Yet, their different degrees of refinement and finish show that they were produced for different levels of the population, as their context of discovery can sometimes indicate: in Tarquinia (stone sarcophagi), Tuscania (terracotta sarcophagi), Volterra (urns of alabaster and tufa) or Chiusi (multicolored terracotta urns) (Fig. 8.19). These different classes of objects, deeply foreign to Roman art, as were the burial customs to which they bear witness, attest the vitality and originality of genuine Etruscan production (Fig. 8.20), although it often betrays a strong influence from Greece, with or without the mediation of Rome. Metal objects, especially bronzes, cease to appear in large numbers in tombs and instead of banquet dishes objects connected with the toilette appear: mirrors (Fig. 8.21) and strigils, still products of Etruria and of southern Etruria particularly, but whose workshops are increasingly challenged by those of Praeneste, which dominates the parallel production of *cistae* (Fig. 8.22). But the Etruscan cities retained a prestige production, as evidenced by different outright masterpieces of the Hellenistic period in Etruria such as the *Chimaera of Arezzo* or the *Oratore* (Fig. 8.23; see Chapter 57), and their artisans contributed, with Rome, to the development of portraiture (see Chapter 55).

Figure 8.19   The travertino urns of Strozzacaponi, found in recent excavations of a large Hellenistic cemetery, still offer a very rich polychromy which offsets reliefs that are very stereotyped but often relate to Greek myths: here, the Seven against Thebae (tomb of the Funerary Bed, urn 6; Cenciaioli 2010, p. 29).

Figure 8.20 Some products of Etruscan art and craftsmanship; the series of ex-votos in bronze produced at Volterra in the second half of the third century, known by the name of *"Ombra della sera"* ("Shadow of the Night") is without doubt the most original and the most modern. It has inspired the work of Alberto Giacometti (Volterra, Museo Guarnacci; Camporeale 2001, p. 11).

Figure 8.21 Etruscan mirrors present a rich repertoire of mythological scenes, sometimes difficult to understand; some relate to the history of relations between Etruria and Rome: on this Vulcian mirror of the last quarter of the fourth century, the brothers Aule and Caile Vibenna, *condottieri* originally from Vulci, surprise the prophet Cacu in order to learn the destiny of their people (London, British Museum; Barker-Rasmussen 1998, Fig. 39).

Figure 8.22 The remarkable mastery of bronze-working by Etruscan artisans fostered the birth and development, in the course of the Hellenistic period, of concurrent production in Latium, notably at Palestrina where the masterpiece is incontestably the Ficoroni cista of the second half of the fourth century. As the inscription it carries indicates, this sort of wedding basket found at Palestrina was made at Rome by an artisan with a Campanian name, Novios Plautios, for a certain Dindia Macolnia who made a gift of it to her daughter (Rome, Museo Etrusco di Villa Giulia; *Rasenna*, Fig. 592).

Figure 8.23 Among the other masterworks of the last Etruscan bronze-smiths, the statue of the Orator found near Perugia, dated to the end of the second century or the beginning of the next century, demonstrates at the same time the extraordinary expertise still present in the old Etruscan cities, and the purely Roman character of their production; the long votive dedication inscribed on the hem of his toga, written for one Aule Metellus, son of Vel and Vesi, is written entirely in Etruscan (Florence, Museo Archeologico Nazionale; Camporeale 2001, p. 72).

EPILOGUE

It is paradoxically the time when, around 6 BC, Augustus created the seventh region (Regio VII-Etruria), thus achieving the first true political and administrative unity of this region, that can be regarded as the complete integration of the Etruscan civilization with Roman culture; in the testimony of Pliny (*NH* 3.8–9), the region had 54 communities, including 27 colonies. But the memory of what the Etruscans had represented did not fade away until the end of the Empire (Fig. 8.24), thanks to the presence of their descendants in the Roman elite and the Senate. This included several characters of the first order, such as Maecenas, descendant of the Cilnii of Arezzo at the time of Augustus from Caere Urgulania the wife of the "Emperor-Etruscologist" Claudius (author of 20 books of *Tyrrhenika*), from Caere, or Otho, the ephemeral emperor born in Ferento, in the Romanized family of the Salvii; the Caecina of Volterra, for their part, in the fifth century AD still held an important place in Roman society. Each year, the games held at the *Fanum Voltumnae* recreated the atmosphere of the Etruscan League, restored in the form of the XII, later the XV populi (Fig. 8.25), and we find still a mention in the time of Constantine, who authorized their relocation to Hispellum. But it is significantly in the religious sphere, where their skill was universally acknowledged, that the Romans retained the longest living memory of the Etruscans, as evidenced by the restoration, from the first century, of the Ordo LX haruspicum: these divination priests who served the greatest personages of the State reappeared in different periods of the history of the Roman Empire, right up to the day of 410 AD when they would make their offer to Pope Innocent I to save Rome from its fall by unleashing the lightning on the army of Alaric (Zosimus 5.41.1–2). Finally, declining along with the Empire, Etruscan civilization had to wait ten more centuries to arouse the curiosity of the first antiquaries and contribute afresh in a significant way to two historical revivals in Italy (see Chapters 61–63), and thus to the Renaissance of Europe, with the splendor of the Tuscan Cosimo I and the slow construction of Italian unity during the Risorgimento.

Figure 8.24 The "Corsini throne" is an archaizing marble replica of the thrones of the Orientalizing era, of which many examples in bronze, terracotta or wood have been found in Etruscan tombs; created in the first century AD and based on models older by seven centuries it probably decorated the interior of the aristocratic *domus* of a rich Roman who was proud of his Etruscan origins (Rome, Palazzo Corsini; Pallottino 1992, fig. 106).

Figure 8.25 The base discovered near the theater of Caere was decorated with the personifications of the 12 principal cities of Etruria, of which only three have come down to us: from left to right, Vetulonia, Vulci and Tarquinia. Dated to the Julio-Claudian period, this monument illustrates well the phase of promotion of the Etruscan past in the era of the emperor Claudius (Rome, Musei Vaticani; Cristofani 1984, p. 138).

BIBLIOGRAPHY

Acconcia, V. (2012) Paesaggi etruschi in terra di Siena. L'agro tra Volterra e Chiusi dall'età del Ferro all'età romana, Oxford: Archaeopress, (*BAR* Int. Ser. 2422).

Agostiniani, L. and Nicosia, F. (2000) *Tabula Cortonensis*, Rome: "L'ERMA" di Bretschneider.

Amann, P. (2011) *Die antiken Umbrer zwischen Tiber und Apennin*, Vienna: Holzhausen.

Andreau, J., Broise, H., Catalli, F., Galeotti, L. and Jolivet, V. (2003) *Musarna 1. Les trésors monétaires*, Rome: École française de Rome (*CÉFR*, 304).

Bacci, M. (2006) "I confini del territorio di Populonia al tempo della romanizzazione. Nuovi dati per un'ipotesi di ricostruzione" in M. Aprosio and C. Mascione (eds), *Materiali per Populonia* 5, Pisa: ETS, pp. 445–451.

Barker, G. and Rasmussen, T. (1998) *The Etruscans*, Oxford.

Beazley, J. D. (1947) *Etruscan Vase-Painting*, Oxford.

Belfiore, V. (2010) *Il liber linteus di Zagabria : della testualità e del contenuto*, Pisa-Rome: F. Serra.

Benelli, E. (1994) *Le iscrizioni bilingue etrusco-latine*, Florence: Olschki.

——(1998) *Le iscrizioni funerarie chiusine di età ellenistica*, SE 64, pp. 225–263.

——(2001) "The Romanization of Italy through the Epigraphic Record" in S. Keay and N. Terrenato (eds), *Italy and the West. Comparative Issues in Romanization*, Oxford: Oxbow, pp. 7–16.

——(2001a) *Le iscrizioni funerarie chiusine di età ellenistica*, SE 64, 2001, pp. 225–263.

—— (ed.) (2009) *Thesaurus Linguae Etruscae, 1. Indice lessicale*, Pisa-Rome: F. Serra.

——(2009a) "Alla ricerca delle aristocrazie chiusine" in M. L. Haack (ed.), *Écritures, cultures, sociétés dans les nécropoles d'Italie ancienne*, Bordeaux: Ausonius, (*Ausonius, Études* 23), pp. 135–160.

Berrendonner, C. (2003) "L'Étrurie septentrionale entre la conquête et Auguste: des cités sans magistrats?" in M. Cébeillac-Gervasoni and L. Lamoine (eds), *Les élites et leurs facettes. Les élites locales dans le monde hellénistique et romain*, Rome-Clermont Ferrand: École française de Rome (*CÉFR* 309), pp. 149–169.

——(2005–2007) *La società di Chiusi ellenistica e la sua immagine : il contributo delle necropoli alla conoscenza delle strutture sociali, EtrNews* 10, pp. 67–78.

——(2006) *Les Tetnie a Vulci, MÉFRA* 118, pp. 21–34.

Berrendonner, C. and Munzi, M. (1998) *La gens Urinate, MÉFRA* 110, pp. 647–662.

Bianchi Bandinelli, R. and Giuliano, A. (2008) *Les Étrusques et l'Italie avant Rome*, Paris: Gallimard.

Biancifiori, E., Sarracino, D. and Taloni, M. (2010) "Lo scavo delle pendici sud-orientali di Poggio del Telegrafo (PdT). L'avvio della romanizzazione di Populonia" in G. Baratti and F. Fabiani (eds), *Materiali per Populonia*, 9, Pisa: ETS, pp. 27–60.

Borsi, F. (ed.) (1985) *Fortuna degli Etruschi*, exhib. cat., Milan: Electa.

Bradley, G. (2007) "Romanization. The End of the Peoples of Italy?" in G. Bradley, E. Isayev and C. Riva (eds), *Ancient Italy. Regions without Boundaries*, Exeter: University of Exeter Press, pp. 295–321.

Briquel, D. (1997) *Chrétiens et haruspices. La religion étrusque, dernier rempart du paganisme romain*, Paris: Presses de l'École normale supérieure.

Broise, H. and Jolivet, V. (1997) "Civita Musarna. La romanizzazione di un sito etrusco" in *Museo archeologico nazionale di Viterbo*, Milan: Electa, pp. 22–41.

——(eds) (2004) *Musarna 2. Les bains hellénistiques*, Rome: École française de Rome, (*CÉFR*, 344).

Brown, F. E. (1980) *Cosa. The Making of a Roman Town*, Ann Arbor: The University of Michigan Press.

Bruun, H. and Körte, G. (1870) *I rilievi delle urne etrusche*, Rome: coi tipi dei Salviucci, 1870–1916.

Bruun, P. (ed.) (1975) *Studies in the Romanization of Etruria*, Rome: Bardi (*Acta Instituti Romani Finlandiae* 5).

——(ed.) (1976) "On Exploring and Explaining the Disappearance of the Etruscans" in D. M. Pippidi (ed.), *Assimilation et résistance à la culture gréco-romaine dans le monde ancien*, Paris: Les Belles Lettres, pp. 131–137.

Bueno, M. Mosaici e pavimenti della Toscana. II sec. a. C.-V sec d.C., Rome, 2011 (Antenor Quaderni, 22).

Cambi, F. (2004) "Le campagne di Falerii e di Capena dopo la romanizzazione" in H. Patterson (ed.), *Bridging the Tiber. Approaches to Regional Archaeology in the Middle Tiber Valley*, Rome, pp. 75–101.

——(2005) *Cosa e Populonia. La fine dell'esperienza urbana in Etruria, WAC* 2, pp. 71–90.

——(2006) "Il territorio di Populonia e la romanizzazione. Geografica storica, ambiente, bacini di approvvigionamento" in *Materiali per Populonia*, 5, Pisa: ETS, pp. 437–444.

Camporeale, G. (1985) (ed.) *L'Etruria mineraria*, exhib. cat., Milan: Olschki.

——(ed.) (2001) *Gli Etruschi fuori d'Etruria*, Los Angeles.

——(2004) *Gli Etruschi. Storia e civiltà²*, Torino.

Camporeale, G. and Firpo, G. (eds) (2009) *Arezzo nell'antichità*, Rome: G. Bretschneider.

Carandini, A. (ed.) (1985) *La romanizzazione dell'Etruria : il territorio di Vulci*, Exhibition catalogue, Milan.

——(ed.) (1985a) *Settefinestre. Una villa schiavistica nell'Etruria romana, I. La villa nel suo insieme*, Modena: Panini.

Cardosa, M. (2005) "Paesaggi nel territorio di Vulci dalla tarda protostoria alla romanizzazione" in *Dinamiche di sviluppo delle città nell'Etruria meridionale. Veio, Caere, Tarquinia, Vulci, Atti del XXIII convegno di studi etruschi ed italici*, Pisa-Rome: Istituti editoriali e poligrafici internazionali, pp. 551–557.

Cenciaioli, L. (2010) (ed.) *I colori dell'addio. Il restauro delle urne di Strozzacaponi*, Perugia: Fabrizio Fabbri.

——(ed.) (2011) *L'ipogeo dei Volumnii. 170 anni dalla scoperta*, Città di Castello: Fabrizio Fabbri, pp. 167–182.

Chellini, R. (1997) "La romanizzazione nel Volterrano" in *Aspetti della cultura di Volterra etrusca*, *Atti del XIX convegno di strudi etruschi e italici*, Florence: Olschki, pp. 379–392

Chiesa, F. (2005) *Tarquinia. Archeologia e prosopografia tra ellenismo e romanizzazione*, Rome: "L'ERMA" di Bretschneider.

Ciampoltrini, G. (1981) *Note sulla colonizzazione augustea nell'Etruria settentrionale*, StClOr 31, pp. 41–55.

——(2004) *Insediamenti e strutture rurali nella piana di Lucca fra tarda Repubblica e piena età imperiale*, JAT 14, pp. 7–24.

——(ed.) (2007) *Ad limitem. Paesaggi d'età romana nello scavo degli orti del San Francesco in Lucca*, Lucca: Tip. Menegazzo.

——(ed.) (2008) *La Valdera romana fra Pisa e Volterra. L'area archeologica di Santa Mustiola (colle Mustarola) di Peccioli*, Peccioli: Pacini.

Cifani, G. (2003) *Storia di una frontiera. Dinamiche territoriali e gruppi etnici nella media Valle Tiberina dalla prima età del Ferro alla conquista romana*, Rome: Istituto poligrafico e zecca dello Stato.

Coarelli, F. (2011) *Le origini di Roma*, Milan: Jaca Book.

Colonna, G. (1999) *Epigrafi etrusche e latine a confronto. Atti del XI congresso internazionale di epigrafia greca e latina*, *1*, Rome: Quasar, pp. 435–450.

Corretti, A. and Firmati, N. (2011) "Metallurgia antica e medievale all'isola d'Elba : vecchi dati e nuove acquisizioni" in C. Giordano (ed.), *Archeometallurgia : dalla conoscenza alla funzione*, Bari: Edipuglia, (*BACT, Quaderno* 8).

Corsi, C. and Venditti, P. (2010) "The Role of Roman Towns in the Romanization Process in Corsica" in C. Corsi and F. Vermeulen (eds), *Changing Landscapes. The Impact of Roman Towns in the Westerne Mediterranean*, Bologna: Ante quem, pp. 69–84.

Costantini, S. (1995) Il deposito votivo del santuario campestre di Tessennano, Rome.

Cristofani, M. (1965) *La tomba delle Iscrizioni a Cerveteri*, Florence: Sansoni.

——(ed.) (1977) *Urne volterrane 2. Il Museo Guarnacci*, Florence: Centro Di.

——(1983) *La scoperta degli Etruschi : archeologia e antiquaria nel '700*, Rome: CNR.

——(ed.) (1984) *Gli Etruschi: una nuova immagine*, Florence.

Cristofani Martelli, M., Fiumi, E., Maggiani A. and Talocchini A. (eds) (1975) *Urne volterrane. 1. I complessi tombali*, Florence: CNR.

Cygielman, M. (2010) "Case a Vetulonia" in M. Bentz and C. Reusser (eds), *Etruskisch-italische und römisch-republikanische Häuser*, Wiesbaden: Reichert (*Studien zur antiken Stadt*, 9), pp. 173–181.

David, J.-M. (1997) *La romanisation de l'Italie*, Paris: Aubier.

de Ligt, L. and Northwood, S. J. (2008) *People, Land and Politics. Demographic Developments and the Transformation of Roman Italy, 300 BC–AD 14*, Leiden-Boston: Brill, (*Mnemosyne Supplements* 303).

de Cazanove, O. (2000) "Some Thoughts on the Religious Romanisation of Italy before the Social War" in *Religion in Archaic and Republican Rome and Italy. Evidence and Experience*, Edinburgh, 2000, pp. 71–76.

Della Fina, G. M. (ed.) (2011) *La fortuna degli Etruschi nella costruzione dell'Italia unita*, XVIII *convegno internazionale di Studi sulla storia e l'archeologia dell'Etruria*, AnnFaina 18.

——(ed.) (2012) *Il Fanum Voltumnae e i santuari comunitari dell'Italie antica, XIX convegno internazionale di Studi sulla storia e l'archeologia dell'Etruria*, AnnFaina 19.

Di Giuseppe, H. (2005) *Un confronto tra l'Etruria settentrionale e meridionale dal punto di vista della ceramica a vernice nera*, PBSR 73, pp. 31–84.

——(2012) *Black-Gloss Ware in Italy. Production Management and Local Histories*, Oxford: Archaeopress (*BAR Int. Series*, 2335).

Domenici, I. (2010) *Etruscae Fabulae : mito e rappresentazione*, Rome: G. Bretschneider.

Eckstein, A. M. (2006) *Mediterranean Anarchy, Interstate War and the Rise of Rome*, Berkeley-Los Angeles-London: University of California Press.

Emiliozzi, A. (1983) *Sull'epitaffio del 67 A. C. nel sepolcro dei Salvii a Ferento*, MÉFRA 95, pp. 707–717.

——(1993) *Per gli Alethna di Musarna*, QuadAEI 22, 1993, pp. 109–146.

Farney, G. D. (2010) *The Name-Changes of Legendary Romans and the Etruscan-Latin Bilingual Inscriptions. Strategies for Romanization*, EtSt 13, pp. 149–157.

Fentress, E. (2000) "Frank Brown, Cosa, and the Idea of a Roman City" in E. Fentress (ed.), *Romanization and the City. Creation, Transformations, and Failures*, Portsmouth: JRA, pp. 11–24.

——(ed.) (2003) *Cosa V : an Intermittent Town. Excavations 1991–1997*, Ann Arbor: The University of Michigan Press (*MAAR*, suppl. 2).

Firmati, M. (2009) "L'Arcipelago toscano e la romanizzazione : il contributo delle ultime ricerche" in F. Cambi, F. Cavari and C. Mascione (eds), *Materiali da costruzione e produzione del ferro. Studi sull'economia populoniese fra periodo etrusco e romanizzazione*, Bari: Edipuglia, pp. 187–193.

Fracchia, H. (1996) "Etruscan and Roman Cortona: New Evidence from the Southeastern Val di Chiana" in J. F. Hall (ed.), *Etruscan Italy. Etruscan Influences on the Civilization of Italy from Antiquity to the Modern Era*, Provo: Brigham Young University and Museum of Art, pp. 190–215.

Fraschetti, A. (1977) *A proposito dei "Clavtie" ceretani*, QuadUrbin 24, pp. 157–162.

——(1980) *I Ceriti e il "castello ceretano" in Diodoro*, AnnAStorAnt 2, pp. 147–155.

Gerhard, E. (ed.) (1843–1897) *Etruskische Spiegel*, Berlin: G. Reimer.

Gentili, M. D. (1994) *I sarcofagi etruschi in terracotta di età recente*, Rome: G. Bretschneider.

Giannattanasio, B. M. (ed.) (2006) *Aequora, pontos, jam, mare…Mare, uomini e merci nel Mediterraneo antico*, Borgo San Lorenzo: All'insegna del Giglio.

Giulierini, P. (2006–2007) *Famiglie e proprietà a Cortona tra tardo ellenismo e romanizzazione*, AnnAcEtr 32, pp. 183–214.

Glinister, F. (2006) "Reconsidering 'Religious Romanization'" in C. E. Schultz and P. B. Harvey, *Religion in Republican Italy*, Cambridge: Cambridge University Press, pp. 10–33.

Gran-Aymerich, J. and Domínguez-Arranz, A. (eds) (2011) *La Castellina a sud di Civitavecchia : origini ed eredità. Origines protohistoriques et évolution d'un habitat étrusque*, Rome: "L'ERMA" di Bretschneider (*Bibliotheca Archaeologica*, 47).

de Grummond, N. T. and Edlund Berry, I. (eds) (2011) *The Archaeology of Sanctuaries and Ritual in Etruria*, Portsmouth: JRA (*JRA* suppl. Series, 81).

Haack, M. L. (2003) *Les haruspices dans le monde romain*, Paris-Bordeaux: Ausonius (*Ausonius, Scripta Antiqua* 6).

——(2003a) "Le cas des haruspices des colonies et des municipes" in M. Cébeillac-Gervasoni and L. Lamoine (eds), *Les élites et leurs facettes. Les élites locales dans le monde hellénistique et romain*, Rome-Clermont Ferrand: Presses universitaires Blaise-Pascal (*CÉFR*, 309), pp. 451–463.

Hadas-Lebel, J. (2004) *Le bilinguisme étrusco-latin. Contribuiton à l'étude de la romanisation de l'Étrurie*, Louvain-Paris-Dudley: Peeters.

Harris, W. V. (1971) *Rome in Etruria and Umbria*, Oxford: Clarendon Press.

Herbig, R. (1952) *Die jüngeretruskischen Steinsarkophage*, Berlin: Mann.

Heurgon, J. (2002) *Daily Life of the Etruscans*, London: Phoenix.

Hohti, P. (1975) *Aulus Caecina the Volaterran. Romanization of an Etruscan*, AIRF 5, pp. 405–433.

Hus, A. (1971) *Vulci étrusque et étrusco-romaine*, Paris: Klincksieck.

Izzet, V. (2007) "Etruria and the Etruscans : Recent Approaches" in G. Bradley, E. Isayev and C. Riva (eds), *Ancient Italy. Regions without Boundaries*, Exeter: University of Exeter Press, pp. 114–130.

——(2009) "Women and the Romanization of Etruria" in E. Herring and K. Lomas, *Gender Identities in Italy in the First Millenium BC*, Oxford: Archaeopress (*BAR* Int Ser., 1983), pp. 127–134.

Jannot, J.-R. (1998) *Devins, dieux et démons*, Paris: Picard.

Jehasse, O. (1988) *Les suburbia d'Aleria et la romanisation de la Corse au second siècle de l'Empire*, Caesarodunum 32, pp. 247–258.

Jolivet, V. (1995) "Un foyer d'hellénisation et son rayonnement (IVᵉ–IIIᵉ s. av. J.-C.). Préneste et la diffusion des strigiles inscrits en grec" in *Hommages à André Nickels, Études Massaliètes* 4, Paris-Lattes: Errance, pp. 445–458.

——(2009) "Musarna et l'Ager Tarquiniensis à l'époque romaine" in É. Rebillard (ed.), *Musarna 3. La nécropole impériale*, Rome: École française de Rome (*CÉFR*, 415), pp. 7–29.

——(ed.) (2010) *L'Étrurie hellénistique et la Méditerranée, 330–90 av. J.-C.*, Bollettino di Archeologia On line, 2010, http://151.12.58.75/archeologia/.

——(2011) *Tristes portiques. Sur le plan canonique de la maison étrusque et romaine des origines au principat d'Auguste*, Rome: École française de Rome (*BÉFAR* 342).

——(forthcoming) *Nouvelles frontières, nouveaux horizons : les contours changeants du territoire de Tarquinia, Mélanges Dominique Briquel*, forthcoming.

Jolivet, V., Pavolini, C., Tomei, M. A. and Volpe, R. (eds) (2009a) *Suburbium 2. Il Suburbium di Roma dalla fine dell'età monarchica alla nascita del sistema delle ville (V–II secolo a.C.)*, Rome (*CÉFR*, 419).

Keay S. and Terrenato, N. (eds) (2001) *Italy and the West. Comparative Issues in Romanization*, Oxford: Oxbow.

Lambrechts, R. (1959) *Essai sur les magistratures étrusques*, Bruxelles-Rome: Academia Belgica.

Launaro, A. (2011) *Peasants and Slaves. The Rural Population of Roman Italy (200 BC to AD 100)*, Cambridge: Cambridge University Press.

Linderski, J. (2003) "*Regio VII in qua Etruria est*," *JRA* 16, pp. 495–499.

Liou, B. (1969) *Praetores Etruriae XV populorum*, Bruxelles: Latomus.

Liverani, P. (2005) "Il gruppo di ritratti imperiali da Caere : una messa a punto" in B. Adembri (ed.), *AEI MNESTOS. Miscellanea di Studi per Mauro Cristofani*, II, Florence: Centro Di, pp. 772–787.

——(2011) "La romanizzazione" in G. Bartoloni (ed.), *Introduzione all'Etruscologia*, Milan: U. Hoepli, pp. 227–252.

MacMullen, R. (2004) "Romanization in the time of Augustus" in *Roman Imperialism. Readings and Sources*, Malden Mass.: Blackwell, pp. 215–231.

Maffei, A. and Nastasi, F. (eds) (1990) *Caere e il suo territorio da Agylla a Centumcellae*, Rome: Istituto Poligrafico e Zecca dello Stato.

Maggiani, A. (2008) *Cilnium genus. La documentazione epigrafica etrusca*, SE 54, pp. 171–196.

——(2008) *Riflessi della pittura pergamena in Etruria. Il "Maestro del ratto di Proserpina,"* Rivista di archeologia 32–33, pp. 93–110.

Mansuelli, G. A. (1988) *L'ultima Etruria. Aspetti della romanizzazione del paese etrusco. Gli aspetti culturali e sacrali*, Bologna: Pàtron.

Marangio, C. and Laudenzi, G. (eds) (2009) *Palaia Philia. Studi di topografia antica in onore di Giovanni Uggeri*, Galatina: Mario Congedo.

Massa Pairault, F.-H. (1985) *Recherches sur l'art et l'artisanat étrusco-italiques à l'époque hellénistique*, Rome: École française de Rome (*BÉFAR*, 257).

——(1990) "Du mariage à la solidarité politique : quelques réflexions sur le cas de Clusium hellénistique" in J. Andreau and H. Bruhns (eds), *Parenté et stratégies familiales dans l'Antiquité romaine*, Rome: École française de Rome (*CÉFR*, 129), pp. 333–380.

——(1996) *La cité des Étrusques*, Paris: CNRS.

Michelucci, M. (1985) *Roselle. La Domus dei Mosaici*, Montepulciano: Editori del Grifo.

Mills, P. and Rajala, U. (2011) "Interpreting a Ceramiscene Landscape – the Roman Pottery from the Nepi Survey Project" in *TRAC 2010. Proceedings of the Twentieth Annual Theoretical Roman Archaeology Conference*, Oxford: Oxbow, pp. 1–17.

Morandi Tarabella, M. (2004) *Prosopographia etrusca I. Corpus. I. Etruria meridionale*, Rome: "L'ERMA" di Bretschneider.

Morel, J.-P. (1981) *Céramique campanienne : les formes*, Rome: École française de Rome.

——(2006) *Céramiques à vernis noir et histoire*, JRA 22, pp. 477–488.

Munzi, M. (2001) "Strategies and Forms of Political Romanization in Central-Southern Etruria. Third Century BC" in S. Keay and N. Terrenato (eds), *Italy and the West. Comparative Issues in Romanization*, Oxford: Oxbow, pp. 39–53.

Munzi, M. and Terrenato, N. (2000) *Volterra. Il teatro e le terme*, Florence: All'insegna del Giglio.

Nicosia, F. and Poggesi, G. (1998) *Roselle. Guida al parco archeologico*, Siena: Nuova Imagine.

Pailler, J.-M. (1988) *Bacchanalia. La répression de 186 av. J.-C. à Rome et en Italie*, Rome: École française de Rome.

Pailler, J.-M. *et al.* (1987) *Bolsena et la romanisation de l'Étrurie méridionale*, MÉFRA 99, pp. 529–659.

Pairault-Massa, F.-H. (2006) *Romanisation, hellénisme et société étrusque dans le contexte des deux premières guerres puniques*, Pallas 70, pp. 123–145.

Pallottino, M. (ed.) (1992) *Les Étrusques et l'Europe*, exhib. cat., Paris: Réunion des Musées Nationaux.

Paolucci, G. (1988) (ed.) *I romani di Chiusi*, Rome: Multigrafica.

Papi, E. (2000) *L'Etruria dei Romani. Opere pubbliche e donazioni private in età imperiale*, Rome: Quasar.

Paribeni, E. (2003) "Appunti sulla romanizzazione delle Apuane. Il territorio di Carrara" in G. Roncaglia, A. Donati and G. Pinto, *Appennino tra antichità e Medioevo*, Città di Castello: Petruzzi, pp. 197–204.

Patterson, H. (ed.) (2004) *Bridging the Tiber. Approaches to Regional Archaeology in the Middle Tiber Valley*, Rome: British School at Rome.

Patterson, H. and Coarelli, F. (eds) (2008) *Mercator placidissimus: The Tiber Valley in Antiquity*, Rome: Quasar.

Patterson, H., Di Giuseppe, H. and Witcher, R. (2004) *Three South Etrurian "Crises": First Results of the Tiber Valley Project*, PBSR 72, pp. 1–36.

Pellegrini, E. *et al.* (2011) *Bolsena e la sponda occidentale della Val di Lago: un aggiornamento*, MÉFRA 123, pp. 13–105.

Peyras, J. (2008) "Pouvoir romain et terre étrusque d'après des documents de l'Antiquité tardive" in T. Piel (ed.), *Figures et expressions du pouvoir dans l'Antiquité*, Rennes: Presses universitaires de Rennes, pp. 109–126.

Pfeilschifter, R. (2007) "The Allies in the Republican Army and the Romanisation of Italy" in *Roman by Integration. Dimensions of Group Identity in Material Culture and Text*, Portsmouth: JRA, pp. 27–42.

Piel, T. (2008) "Des contingents étrusques en Méditerranée occidentale : mercenaires ou forces d'intervention civique?" in T. Piel (ed.), *Figures et expressions du pouvoir dans l'Antiquité*, Rennes: Presses universitaires de Rennes, pp. 75–91.

Pucci, G. (ed.) (1992) *La fornace di Umbricio Cordo. L'officina di un ceramista romano e il territorio di Torrita di Siena nell'antichità*, Florence: All'insegna del Giglio.

Pucci, G. and Mascione, C. (1993) "Un' officina ceramica tardo-etrusca a Chiusi" in *La Civiltà di Chiusi e del suo territorio, Atti del XVII Convegno di Studi Etruschi ed Italici*, Florence: Olschki, pp. 375–383.

Radke, G. (1981) *Viae publicae romanae*, Bologna: Cappelli.

Rasenna (1986) Aut. Div, *Rasenna. Storia e civiltà degli Etruschi*, Milan.

Rebillard, É. (ed.) (2009) *Musarna 3. La nécropole impériale*, Rome: École française de Rome (CÉFR, 415).

Rendini, P. (2003) "Un caso di romanizzazione. Saturnia e il territorio della media valle dell'Albenga" in C. Mascione and A. Patera (eds), *Materiali per Populonia*, 2, Florence: All'insegna del Giglio, pp. 327–340.

Rix, H. (ed.) (1991) *Etruskische Texte*, Tübingen: G. Narr.

Roncalli, F. (1999) *Volsinii e il mondo italico al tempo della romanizzazione*, AnnFaina 6, pp. 31–39.

Roth, R. E. (2007) *Styling Romanisation. Pottery and Society in Central Italy*, Cambridge: Cambridge University Press.

——(2007a) "Ceramic Integration? Typologies and the Perception of Identities in Republican Italy" in *Roman by Integration. Dimensions of Group Identity in Material Culture and Text*, Portsmouth: JRA, pp. 59–70.

Santrot, M.-H. and J. (eds) (1995) *Bolsena, la citerne 5*, Rome: École française de Rome (*MAH*, suppl. 6).

Scapaticci, M. G. (2008) *Nuovi dati sul popolamento della pianura di Tarquinia durante la romanizzazione. Il caso della località "Il Giglio," OpAthRom* 1, pp. 123–135.

Scarano Ussani-Torelli, V., Torelli, M. (2003) *La Tabula Cortonensis: un documento giuridico, storico e sociale*, Naples: Loffredo.

Scullard, H. H. (1998) *The Etruscan Cities and Rome*,[2] Baltimore: Johns Hopkins University Press.

Sforzini, P. (1990) "Vasai 'aretini' in area falisca: l'officina di Vasanello" in *Atti del XV Convegno di Studi Etruschi ed Italici*, Florence: Olschki, pp. 251–274.

Shepherd, E. J., Capecchi, G. and de Marinis, G. (eds) (2008) *Le fornaci del Vingone a Scandicci : un impianto produttivo di età romana nella valle dell'Arno*, Florence: All'insegna del Giglio.

Söderlind, M. (2000) *Romanization and the Use of Votive Offerings in the Eastern Ager Vulcentis, OpRom* 25–26, pp. 89–102.

——(2002) *Late Etruscan Votive Heads from Tessennano*, Rome: "L'ERMA" di Bretschneider.

Steingräber, S. (ed.) (1986) *Etruscan Painting*, New York: Johnson Reprint Corp.

Talbert, R. J. A. (ed.) (2000) *Barrington Atlas of the Greek and Roman World*, Princeton and Oxford.

Tamburini, P. (1998) *Un Museo e il suo territorio. Il Museo territoriale del lago di Bolsena, 1. Dalle origini al periodo etrusco*, Bolsena: Città di Bolsena.

——(2001) (ed.) *Un Museo e il suo territorio. Il Museo territoriale del lago di Bolsena, 2. Dal periodo romano all'era moderna*, Bolsena: Città di Bolsena.

Terrenato, N. (1998) "The Romanization of Italy. Global Acculturation or Cultural Bricolage" in *TRAC 97. Proceedings of the Seventh Annual Theoretical Roman Archaeology Conference*, Oxford: Oxbow, pp. 20–27.

——(1998a) *Tam Firmum Municipium : the Romanization of Volaterrae and its Cultural Implications*, *JRS* 88, pp. 94–114.

——(ed.) (2001) *Italy and the West. Comparative Issues in Romanization*, Oxford: Oxbow, pp. 7–16.

——(2001) "A Tale of Three Cities. The Romanization of Northern Coastal Etruria" in S. Keay and N. Terrenato (eds), *Italy and the West. Comparative Issues in Romanization*, Oxford: Oxbow, pp. 54–67.

Torelli, M. (1969) *Senatori etruschi della tarda repubblica e dell'impero, DdA* 3, pp. 285–363.

——(1975) *Elogia tarquiniensia*, Florence: Sansoni.

——(1982) "Ascesa al senato e rapporti con i territori d'origine. Italia: Regio VII (Etruria)" in *Epigrafia e ordine senatorio*, II, Rome: Edizioni di storia e di letteratura (*Tituli*, 5), pp. 275–299.

——(1989) "Problemi di romanizzazione" in *Atti del secondo congresso internazionale etrusco*, I, Rome: G. Bretschneider, pp. 393–403.

——(1992) "Il quadro materiale e ideale della romanizzazione" in R. Cassano (ed.), *Principi imperatori vescovi. Duemila anni di storia a Canosa*, Venice: Marsilio, pp. 608–619.

——(1999) *Tota Italia. Essays in the Cultural Formation of Roman Italy*, Oxford: Clarendon Press.

——(ed.) (2000) *Gli Etruschi*, Exhib. Catalogue, Milan: Bompiani.

——(2006) "Tarquitius Priscus haruspex di Tiberio e il laudabilis puer Aurelius. Due nuovi personaggi della storia di Tarquinia" in M. Pandolfini Angeletti (ed.), *Archeologia in Etruria meridionale*, Rome: "L'ERMA" di Bretschneider, pp. 249–286.

Torelli, M. and Sgubini Moretti, A. M. (eds) (2008) *Etruschi. Le antiche metropoli del Lazio*, Exhibition catalogue, Milan.

Urso, G. (ed.) (2008) *Patria diversis gentibus una? Unità politica e identità etniche nell'Italia antica*, Pisa: ETS.

Vallat, J.-P. (2001) "The Romanization of Italy: Conclusions" in S. Keay and N. Terrenato (eds), *Italy and the West. Comparative Issues in Romanization*, Oxford: Oxbow, pp. 102–110.

Valvo, A. (1988) *La "profezia" di Vegoia." Proprietà fondiaria e aruspicina in Etruria nel I secolo a.C.*, Rome: Istituto italiano per la storia antica.

van der Meer, L. B. (2007) *Liber Linteus Zagrabiensis. The Linen Book of Zagreb. A Comment on the Longest Etruscan Text*, Louvain (*Monographs on Antiquity*, 4).

Vincenti, V. (2009) *La tomba Bruschi di Tarquinia*, Rome: G. Bretschneider (*Archeologica*, 150).

Will, E. L. (2005) "The Port of Cosa and Economic romanization in Gaul and the Danube Valley" in J. Pollini (ed.), *Terra Marique. Studies in Art History and Marine Archaeology in honor of Anna Marguerite McCann*, Oxford: Oxbow, pp. 255–262.

Witcher, R. W. (2006) *Settlement and Society in Early Imperial Etruria*, *JRS* 91, pp. 88–123.

Corpora and Reference Collections

CIE : *Corpus Inscriptionum Etruscarum.*
CSE : *Corpus Speculorum Etruscorum.*
CSVI : *Corpus delle stipi votive in Italia.*
CVA : *Corpus Vasorum Antiquorum.*
FI : *Forma Italiae.*
LIMC : *Lexicon Iconographicum Mythologiae Classicae.*
REE : *Rivista di epigrafia etrusca. Studi etruschi.*

BIBLIOGRAPHIC NOTE[1]

Prologue

Romanization of Italy: Torelli 1992; David 1997; Terrenato 1998; Torelli 1999; Keay-Terrenato 2001; Vallat 2001; Mac Mullen 2004; Eckstein 2006; Bradley 2007; Pfeilschifter 2007; de Ligt-Northwood 2008; Urso 2008; Marangio-Laudenzi 2009; Aman 2011 (Umbria); Launaro 2011.

The Roman conquest; A new territorial framework

Romanization of Etruria: Torelli 1969; Harris 1971; Bruun 1975; Ciampoltrini 1981 (Northern Etruria); Radke 1981 (Roman roads); Mansuelli 1988; Torelli 1989; Massa Pairault 1996; Scullard 1998; Papi 2000 (Southern Etruria); Torelli 2000; Munzi 2001 (Southern and Central Etruria); Terrenato 2001 (Northern Etruria); Heurgon 2002; Cifani 2003; Linderski 2003; Pairault-Massa 2006; Witcher 2006; Izzet 2007; Peyras 2008; Piel 2008; Jolivet *et al.* 2009a; Liverani 2011. See also the various volumes of *FI*.

Retention of power and the changing of the ruling classes; pressure from the middle and lower classes

Society: Lambrechts 1959 (magistrates); Torelli 1969 and 1982 (Roman Senate); Pailler 1988 (Bacchanal affair); Agostiniani-Nicosia 2000 and Scarano Ussani-Torelli 2003 (*Tabula Cortonensis*); Patterson 2004 (Tiber valley); Patterson-Coarelli 2008 (Tiber valley); Izzet 2009 (gender); Jolivet 2010 (trade) and 2011 (housing); Launaro 2011 (peasants and slaves).

Onomastic and epigraphy: Bruun 1975 and 1976; Benelli 1994; Berrendonner-Munzi 1998; Colonna 1999; Agostiniani-Nicosia 2000 and Scarano Ussani-Torelli 2003 (*Tabula Cortonensis*); Benelli 2001; Berrendonner 2003 (Northern Etruria); Hadas-Lebel 2004; Morandi Tarabella 2004 (Southern Etruria); Farney 2010. See also *CIE*, *REE*, Rix 1991 and Benelli 2009. See Chapters 21, 22, 23.

Religion: Valvo 1988; Briquel 1997; Jannot 1998; Cazanove 2000; Söderlind 2000 and 2002; Haack 2003 and 2003a; Glinister 2006; Meer 2007 and Belfiore 2010 (Zagreb mummy); Grummond-Edlund-Berry 2011. See also, for the various deities, *LIMC*. See Part V in this volume.

Agriculture and metallurgy, handicraft and art

Art and craftsmanship: Cristofani *et al.* 1975 and Cristofani 1977 (Volterran urns); Morel 1981 (black-gloss); Camporeale 1985 (metallurgy); Massa Pairault 1985 (art); Sforzini 1990 (*sigillata* ware); Pucci 1992 (ceramic production); Pucci-Mascione 1993 (ceramic production); Gentili 1994 (terracotta sarcophagi); Jolivet 1995 (strigils); Santrot 1995; Torelli 1999; Di Giuseppe 2005 (black-gloss); Roth 2007 and 2007a (black-gloss); Maggiani 2008 (urns); Shepherd-Capecchi-De Marinis 2008 (ceramic production); Bianchi Bandinelli-Giuliano 2008 (art); Morel 2009 (black-gloss); Vincenti 2009 (painting); Cenciaioli 2010 (urns); Domenici 2010 (urns and mirrors); Coarelli 2011 (art and coinage); Corretti-Firmati 2011 (metallurgy); Bueno 2011 (pavements); Di Giuseppe 2012 (black-gloss). See also Gerhard 1843 and *CSE* (mirrors), Bruun-Körte 1870 (urns), Herbig 1952 (sarcophagi), Steingräber 1986 (painting) and *CVA* (vases).

Epilogue

Liou 1969 (*XV populi*); Cristofani 1983 (XVIII c.); Borsi 1985; Pallottino 1992; Briquel 1997 (late Antiquity); Della Fina 2011 (Risorgimento).

The cities and their territory:

Aleria: Fraschetti 1977; Jehasse 1988; Corsi-Venditti 2010.

Arezzo: Maggiani 1986; Camporeale-Firpo 2009.

Caere: Cristofani 1965; Fraschetti 1977 and 1980; Maffei-Nastasi 1990; Liverani 2005; Gran Aymerich-Domínguez Arranz 2011.

Chiusi: Paolucci 1988; Massa Pairault 1990 ; Benelli 1998 and 2001a; Berrendonner 2004; Benelli 2009a; Acconcia 2012.

Cortona: Fracchia 1996; Agostiniani-Nicosia 2000; Scarano Ussani-Torelli 2003; Giulierini 2006.

Falerii: Sforzini 1990 (ceramica sigillata); Cambi 2004; Patterson-Di Giuseppe-Witcher 2004; Mills-Rajala 2011 (Nepi).

Florence: Ciampoltrini 2004 and 2007 (Lucca); Shepherd-Capecchi-De Marinis 2008 (ceramica).

Perugia: Cenciaioli 2011.

Pisa: Terrenato 2001; Paribeni 2003 (Carrara).

Populonia: Cambi 2005; Bacci 2006 and 2006; Giannattanasio 2006; Firmati 2009; Biancifiori-Sarracino-Taloni 2010; Corretti-Firmati 2011 (Elba).

Roselle: Michelucci 1985; Nicosia-Poggesi 1998; Liverani 2011.

Tarquinia: Torelli 1975; Emiliozzi 1983 (Ferento) and 1993 (Musarna); Gentili 1994 (Tuscania); Broise-Jolivet 1997 (Musarna); Andreau *et al.* 2003 (Musarna); Cifani 2003 (Tiber Valley); Broise-Jolivet 2004 (Musarna); Chiesa 2005; Torelli 2006; Scapaticci 2008; Rebillard 2009 (Musarna); Jolivet 2009 and forthcoming; Liverani 2011.

Veii: Patterson-Di Giuseppe-Witcher 2004; Liverani 2011.

Vetulonia: Cygielman 2010.

Volsinii/Bolsena: Pailler *et al.* 1987 (Bolsena); Santrot 1995 (Bolsena); Tamburini 1998 (Bolsena); Roncalli 1999 (Bolsena); Tamburini 2001 (Bolsena); Pellegrini 2011 (Bolsena); Della Fina 2012 (*Volsinii*).

Volterra and Siena: Hohti 1975; Chellini 1997; Terrenato 1998a and 2001; Ciampoltrini 2008; Liverani 2011; Acconcia 2012.

Vulci: Hus 1971; Brown 1980 (Cosa); Carandini 1985 and 1985a (Settefinestre); Söderlind 2000 and 2002 (Tessennano); Fentress 2000 and 2003 (Cosa); Vallat 2001 (Cosa); Rendini 2003 (Saturnia); Cambi 2005 (Cosa); Cardosa 2005; Will 2005 (Cosa); Berrendonner 2006.

Illustrations not included in main bibliography:

Barker, G. and Rasmussen, T. (1998) *The Etruscans*, Oxford: Blackwell.
Beazley, J. D. *Etruscan Vase-Painting*, Oxford: Clarendon Press.
Camporeale G. (ed.) (2001) *The Etruscans Outside of Etruria*, Los Angeles: J. Paul Getty Museum.
Camporeale, G. (2004) *Gli Etruschi. Storia e civiltà²*, Torino: UTET.
Cristofani, M. (ed.) (1984) *Gli Etruschi: una nuova immagine*, Florence.
Rasenna (1986) Aut. Div, *Rasenna. Storia e civiltà degli Etruschi*, Milan: Scheiwiller.
Torelli, M. and Sgubini Moretti, A. M. (eds) (2008) *Etruschi. Le antiche metropoli del Lazio*, exhibition catalogue, Milan: Electa.

NOTE

1   Most works on the Etruscans include a part on the period following the Roman conquest: we refer readers to these, without mention in the bibliography. Ultimately, readers are referred to G. Bartoloni (ed.), *Introduzione all'Etruscologia*, Milan, 2011, and a synthetic work is currently being prepared in Italy under the direction of Alessandro Naso. Information relating to this period is dispersed through the existing literature, particularly in the *Notizie degli Scavi*, the *Monumenti antichi della R. Accademia dei Lincei*, the *Studi Etruschi*, the *Atti* of the *Convegno di Studi Etruschi ed Italici,* and in museum or exhibition catalogs: it was obviously impossible to list them all. The main texts devoted to this period by M. Cristofani, G. Colonna and M. Torelli are today conveniently gathered in two works, M. Cristofani, *Scripta selecta*, I–III, Pisa-Rome 2001 and G. Colonna, *Italia ante Romanum imperium. Scritti di antichità etrusche, italiche e romane (1958–1998)*, I–IV, Pisa-Rome, 2005 and A. Sciarma (ed.), M. Torelli (2012) *SHMAINEN SIGNIFICARE. Scritti vari di ermeneutica archeologica*, Pisa-Rome; various recent Festschriften also contain a certain number of contributions on the Romanization of Etruria: B. Adembri (ed.), *AEI MNESTOS. Miscellanea di Studi per Mauro Cristofani*, Florence, 2005; D. Caiazza (ed.), *Italica ars: studi in onore di Giovanni Colonna per il premio I Sanniti*, Caserta, 2005; S. Bruni (ed.), *Etruria e l'Italia preromana: studi in onore di Giovannangelo Camporeale*, Pisa-Rome, 2009. Literature selected here brings together the most important, newer, publications, to complement that given in Liverani 2011, pp. 250–252. To facilitate research, we have gathered sources for the major themes of this chapter, and also for the main Etruscan cities. We indicate in bold some titles that are particularly important for the study of this period. One will find in Bianchi Bandinelli-Giuliano 2008 a chronology of this period put into perspective in relation to that of the Hellenistic world.

CHAPTER NINE

THE LAST ETRUSCANS: FAMILY TOMBS IN NORTHERN ETRURIA

———•◆•———

Marjatta Nielsen

From the last three centuries BC the Etruscans have left behind a huge amount of sarcophagi and ash chests (or cinerary urns), with or without name inscriptions or sculptural decoration. When decorated, the artistic level is highly varied, but the trend went decidedly from quality to quantity.[1] That is why only a few tomb complexes and a few fine examples of the late ash chests are illustrated in most books on the Etruscans. This contributes to a gloomy idea of "the period of decline," and the last generations of Etruscans who followed the old burial customs are rarely mentioned at all. Further, there is a tendency to consider everything Greek older than Etruscan, and everything Etruscan older than Roman, as if there were not considerable overlap.

Most of the Etruscan chests were placed in chamber tombs, many of which had space enough to remain in use for a considerable time, even for two or three centuries. When discovered, many tomb chambers were filled up to the brim. It seems that the late Etruscans preferred to be buried together in crowded tombs, rather than being buried alone or founding new tombs.

The material is, however, very unevenly distributed. It is understandable that the areas far from Rome, the north-Etruscan city-states and their territories, succeeded in maintaining Etruscan traditions for a longer period than the areas closer to Rome. Yet the Roman expansion not only in Italy, but also in the Eastern Mediterranean, has left traces in north-Etruscan funerary art, at least by the second century BC, when yet another wave of Hellenization reached Etruria. The traditions continued for most of the first century BC, either by following local traditions or by adopting artistic impulses from Rome. However, expert artists were no longer attracted to seek such commissions in Etruria, and the exciting novelties were created elsewhere or in other artistic fields.

In museums the "loose" late-Etruscan objects may be amusing or their number overwhelming, but entire tombs with their contents are much more revealing about the changing cultural and social circumstances in which they were created. There is much material particularly for the study of the social aspects. We seldom know anything about the persons and families in question, but we can study them through generations thanks to their name inscriptions. We know who were buried together, since the information about the relationships between the deceased gets increasingly detailed, including who married whom.[2] We can also follow the shift of language, from Etruscan to Latin and a number of inscriptions were given in both languages.[3]

With or without inscriptions, the sculptural decorations (banqueting lid figures and chests with reliefs) give a picture of the cultural horizons and ambitions of the families in question, and transform the – mostly roughly hewn – tomb chambers into banquet halls or scenes for funerary games and dramatic performances. In the following, I will give a rough idea of both these approaches.

THE RELATIONSHIPS BETWEEN THOSE BURIED TOGETHER

When analysing the genealogical ties between those buried in the same tombs, as documented by the inscriptions, different patterns take form: it is evident that there was no overall consensus about how far the obligation to bury family members reached.[4]

The prevailing custom was, however, the one which still appears most obvious: men – fathers and sons – in an agnatic lineage, as well as their wives/mothers, but no daughters (they were supposed to be buried with their husbands). Not seldom two or three brothers and their wives follow the parents and so forth, in parallel lineages, but there were limits as to how large a crowd the tomb was able to host.

A very restricted version of this norm is constituted by tombs where only men in an agnatic lineage were buried. The clearest case of such a tomb is that of the Cutus at Perugia: there are fifty men and no women.[5] This secured a place for a large crowd of male Cutus, who claimed descent from the same ancestor, an anonymous man buried in a sarcophagus in the back chamber of the tomb. Who the Cutus were married to can only be deduced from their mothers' names. On balance, some women married into such families solved their burial problem by founding separate tombs, with access only for women, in a more or less direct matrilineal line.[6]

An enlarged version of the normal pattern is represented by tombs with men and their wives, with the addition of one or more daughters, whose names do not mention any husband. They probably had died before getting married, but we cannot be sure.

The well-known Perusine Tomb of the Velimnas/Volumnii may be attributed to this category, in spite of its absolute male dominance (Fig. 9.1).[7] When it was discovered in 1840, only the back chamber contained chests, with five banqueting Velimna men. In the left back corner, however, was placed the sitting funerary statue of Veilia, daughter of Arnth Velimna. The dedicatory inscription tells that her father Arnth and uncle Larth built the tomb for their offspring (*husiur*): but, in fact, Velia is their only representative. Instead, the monuments belong to Arnth and Larth themselves, their brother Vel, as well as their father Aule and grandfather Thefri. All the magnificent monuments seem to have been executed at one moment.

The rest of the spacious tomb was found empty – perhaps the family had moved elsewhere. Yet the memory of the tomb was not forgotten, since one more chest, of marble and of Roman workmanship, was placed at the left front corner of the back chamber in the early Imperial period. Significantly, the name was given in both Etruscan and Latin: "*pup velimna au cahatial / P. Volumnius A.f. Violens Cafatia natus.*"[8] The chest must post-date the Perusine War of 42 BC, which resulted in a devastating (albeit accidental) fire in the city, and the "ritual" slaughtering of 300 Etruscan noblemen by Octavian. In the funerary

Figure 9.1 The Tomb of the Velimna/Volumnius family, Perugia. Late third century BC. S. J. Ainsley's drawing from 1843, The British Museum, Department of Prints and Drawings, cat. LB 62. [From Haynes 2000, 380.]

material, we can see a clear break after these disasters. The pompous reconstruction of *Augusta Perusia* would then attract newcomers, and perhaps even descendants of the old families, such as the Volumnii.

ACCEPTANCE OF COGNATIC KIN

The next step in widening the circle of persons admitted to Etruscan family tombs was that also married daughters were accepted, in spite of the fact that they ought to be buried in their husband's family tomb. Perhaps a daughter had returned to her own family as a widow or even a divorcee. There may also have been changes in the very notion of marriage: as in Rome more or less at the same time, the wife began to maintain close links with her family of origin (*matrimonium sine manu*).

Especially in the countryside in Northern Etruria we meet even wider acceptance of cognatic kin in otherwise agnatic tombs: not only a married daughter but also her sons, even husband or his nearest kin may have been buried in her family tomb. This may have been the result of almost systematic marriage alliances between certain families in the rural areas, so "his or her kin" were almost the same; further, the husband's family tomb may have been fully occupied.

THE DISINTEGRATION OF THE FAMILY TOMBS

In the Chiusine area the development went even further. When the back chamber of fine, old family tombs was filled up with magnificent chests or sarcophagi, smaller side chambers and several one-person niches, *loculi*, could be added along the long corridor leading down to the tomb. Such niches often contained small-sized terracotta chests, still decorated with reliefs and reclining lid figures, but these were not modeled individually, but cast in moulds, and they are counted in the thousands. An even cheaper alternative was a bell-shaped clay urn. Also small-sized, simple travertine chests were very numerous.

All these types of urns were less expensive and so anonymous that inscriptions were necessary for identification.[9]

The inscriptions are a goldmine of information. We can see that the range of names in this late period (from late second to late first century BC) was very mixed indeed. The common opinion attributes these kinds of tombs in small necropoleis to small farmers, former serfs, who were enfranchised through class struggles. However, the Chiusine aristocracy was still thriving (but less keen on spending money for burials), while the new, economic possibilities must have contributed to make the "lower classes" visible in the archaeological record. The "new" social strata were as keen to leave behind an epigraphic memory of themselves as the elite.[10]

The next step on the ladder of "breaking down the family-based burial customs" in the Chiusine countryside was corridor tombs with rows of one-person niches, *loculi*, along the walls, without any dominating family.[11] Related and seemingly unrelated persons were buried in the niches without regard to the family ties. Here we meet persons of high- and middle rank Etruscan ancestry, their ex-slaves of foreign origin, Romans married to Etruscan women: i.e. different social classes side by side, but in individual niches. Advanced Romanization and with that, increased mobility, may have scattered the families apart, and burials were probably laid in the hands of "egalitarian" burial associations.

VOLTERRA – AN ETRUSCAN STRONGHOLD

Such "mixed" tombs are not known from Volterra, which preserved the Etruscan traditions down to the Augustan period, and even beyond – and this in spite of the fact that the Volterrans had systematically sided with the loser in every possible Roman political struggle during the first century BC. At Volterra, the inscriptions are very unevenly divided, and therefore our knowledge of the social structure has great gaps. From the late fourth to the middle of the second century inscriptions are very rare, and continued to be so on the more modest tufa ash-chests. This does not prove a low rate of literacy: perhaps the name of the family was written outside the tomb, and the images helped posterity to remember who was who. Or, perhaps the place of the individual within the family community was not considered an important issue.

In the course of the second century BC, however, there was a big boom of producing decorated ash-chests and lids in large workshops, which furnished ready-made "portraits" with generic images, characterized only by gender and age. The tombs grew larger and the number of "monuments" increased considerably, which must have created the need for inscriptions to identify the deceased.

Many tombs had already been excavated by the eighteenth century when the scholars were keen on documenting the inscriptions. Since these were written on the lids, we know the provenance of many lid figures, while lids without inscriptions and all the chests are difficult to connect to any context.

This is also the case with the two large tombs of the family Ceicna/Caecina (already known from Roman literary sources), discovered in 1739 and 1785.[12] In the tomb discovered first, several inscriptions are written in Latin, in the second and therefore, older one, they are only in Etruscan. Nothing is known of the earliest phases of the tombs, not to mention the chests. Drawings of the situation at the discovery show that everything was thoroughly mixed up on the floor, whether due to robbers or natural damage.

THE INGHIRAMI TOMB AND THE ATIS

An exception to this disappointing situation is the so-called Inghirami tomb, discovered by the brothers Iacopo and Lodovico Inghirami in the Ulimeto necropolis just outside Volterra in 1861.[13] They took pride in keeping everything in its proper place to show to visitors. Now the relief scenes of the chests were at the centre of scholarly interest, and a list was written of their place in the tomb. Yet, the many fragments and arbitrary combinations of lids and chests make one suspect a more chaotic situation at the discovery.

In spite of the high artistic standards of the ash-chests, the inscriptions are few. These tell us, however, that the family in question was called Ati. As a family name it is only known from this tomb, but it is homonymous with the Etruscan word for "mother," *ati*. However, from the Volterran acropolis there are some dedicatory inscriptions to *Papa* (grandfather) and *Atia{l}* ("Mother's) – obviously ancestral deities who were venerated there.[14] It is tempting to guess that the Atis claimed a connection with the city's mother goddess.

From the Inghirami tomb there are no Latin inscriptions, although a number of lids are from the late period when Latin was written in Volterra. In Latin the name would have taken the form Atius/Attius. Persons with that name were known since the second century BC and onwards, especially in the Volscian area and at Rome, but not in Etruria. The most prominent members were Caesar's wife and Augustus' mother. We cannot be sure of any connection, since names of quite different origins may have resulted in the same form in Latin.

The original placing of the chests was maintained when the tomb was reconstructed in the garden of the Archaeological Museum in Florence in 1899–1902. There are some discrepancies as to the lids and fragments, but yet the tomb is still the one that gives the best impression of the whole (Fig. 9.2). The underground space is roughly hewn in the rock, but the reclining lid figures turn the room into a banquet hall for an eternal family feast. However, the space is not square, as a house, but rounded, with a large bench for the

Figure 9.2   The Inghirami Tomb, from Volterra, reconstructed in the garden of the Archaeological Museum in Florence. (Photo Scala).

chests along the walls. Apart from the central pillar, left to support the ceiling, the room rather looks like a theatre or an arena for games. The "cross-referencing" of the idea of a banquet hall and a scene for funerary games and theatrical performances is also reflected in the relief motifs on the ash-chests.

Only one lid figure in the Inghirami tomb belongs to the third century BC, but all the others are from the second century onwards. Perhaps the oldest chest ("generation 0") had been moved from an earlier tomb, which had proved inadequate. When filled up with some sixty chests, five or six generations had been hosted there. As to their genealogy, only fragments can be reconstructed – the definition of "generations" is rather based on the chronological sequence of the workshops that produced the monuments.

Not only did the workshops produce ready-made chests with a variety of motifs, but they also produced lid figures, which would give a general idea of the deceased – man, woman, young or middle-aged. The supply of male "portraits" was safe, but less so as to female figures (see Chapter 55). In the Inghirami tomb there is one case of a stock male figure being converted into a female one (Fig. 9.3).[15] There was no original "iconographical program" for the decoration of the tomb: generation after generation acquired chests with subjects typical of their time.[16] The motifs may be categorized in different ways – ornamental, funerary scenes such as farewell or journey to the Underworld, themes drawn

Figure 9.3 The Inghirami Tomb: a male figure reworked into a female one. The relief shows Pelops and Hippodameia departing for their horse race. Late second century BC. Florence, the Archaeological Museum, inv. 78495. Museum photo. (*UV* 1, 138; Nielsen 2007: 170).

from Greek mythology and especially dramatic literature, local stories (the latter ones are almost absent here) or biographical representations. Many of the Greek themes may contain learned, eschatological messages: divine will, commanding the death of a hero. But the philosophical level is not necessarily the only reason for the choice of subject.

Four times the motif of the "Recognition of Paris" was chosen for a chest, a popular motif because of its self-evident connection with funerary games (Fig. 9.4): Priam's son, the Trojan prince Paris had been exposed as a child in order to prevent the disasters predicted by his sister Cassandra. As a young shepherd he won the games arranged in the memory of the royal prince, believed to be dead. Angry with the "low-class" winner, the other princes, his brothers, tried to kill him. When Paris sought rescue at the altar with the victory palm in his hand, he was recognized as Priam's son and was rescued. What followed, is also represented on some of the relief.

Many other motifs have less evident explanations for their popularity. Some recurrent motifs were perhaps chosen in order to connect later generations with the founders of the tomb (like the Calydonian Boar Hunt, Fig. 9.5). Perhaps even the immediate visual impression of the scene has played an important role. Many scenes show banquets, as if to reproduce the image of the banqueting lid figures and banquets arranged at funerals. The priestesses pouring libations on the heads of Orestes and Pylades hold in their hands libation bowls similar to those in the male lid figures' hands, and probably those used for libations at funerals. Both the Calydonian Boar and some heroes are placed in a grotto, which might resemble the entrance of the tomb itself. Especially many reliefs in the first row show horse races (e.g. three moments of the Pelops cycle; cf. Fig. 9) – all galloping in the same direction, from left to right, as if to create an illusion of horse races arranged at funerals. The galloping horses also fit well with the circular form of the tomb, reproducing an illusion of a horse race arena. Furthermore, duel scenes also fit in the context of funerary games.

A particularly elaborate chest – regrettably fragmentary – was placed in front of the central pillar (Fig. 9.6).[17] The front shows Odysseus rescuing his companions at Circe's

Figure 9.4 The Inghirami Tomb: a female lid figure with a fan and rich jewelry, and a chest with the Recognition of Paris, circa 100 BC. Florence, The Archaeological Museum, inv. 78520. Museum photo (*UV* 1, 161).

Figure 9.5   The Inghirami Tomb: a male lid figure and a chest with the
Calydonian Boar Hunt, circa 150 BC. Florence, The Archaeological Museum, inv. 78484.
Museum photo (*UV* 1, 126; Nielsen 2007, 163).

Figure 9.6   The Inghirami Tomb: a fragmentary chest with Odysseus rescuing his
companions from Circe's banquet; at the corners, Centaurs abducting women; on the lower
frieze, a chariot race in circus. Late second century BC. Florence, The Archaeological
Museum, inv. 78522. (Drawing from H. Brunn 1870, pl. 89:3).

banquet: her magical potion is already transforming them into animals. At the corners, we see strong Centaurs abducting naked Lapith women. The rest of their equine bodies fill the short sides where we can see that they are mounted by young riders. Centaurs and Lapiths have nothing to do with the story of Odysseus and Circe, but the Centaurs, too, are "mixed creatures," as Odysseus' companions at the moment of their metamorphoses (see Chapter 25). At the same time, they may refer to the Centaurs framing the scene of the Calydonian Boar Hunt, the main monument in the place of honor at the centre of the back wall (though inconveniently invisible behind the central pillar, cf. Fig. 9.3).[18] The Centaurs do not belong to this scene either but represent the wild forces comparable to that of the boar (and of death itself).

Returning to the Odysseus and Circe relief, its lower front border has an unusual frieze, showing a horse race without mythical elements: symmetrically, from the left and from the right, three chariots pulled by two horses are heading in full gallop towards a central *meta*. On both sides, one of the horse pairs is stumbling and going to fall. This is perhaps the closest we come to a representation of "real" horse races (apart from Tarquinian wall-paintings). They probably formed a part of the expiatory rites in connection with funerals. Keeping Volterra's situation on the hilltop in mind, such chariot races must have been a very risky business, indeed.

The many theatrical motifs on the chests – by and large corresponding to Hellenistic adaptations of Euripides' tragedies and the developments of early Roman drama – strongly speak in favor of theatrical performances as making part of funerals and ritual festivals in Etruria, as "modernized" variants of the old-day expiatory games (see Chapter 45).

THE LAST ETRUSCANS – FOLLOWING ROMAN FASHIONS

In the Inghirami tomb, chests from the last phase of Volterran production are few. Perhaps the Atis were among those who abandoned the Etruscan customs – or the town. On the other hand, the tomb was filled up, and subsequent generations had to be buried elsewhere.[19] Some workshops began to produce quite different, more Roman-style chests without lid figures, parallel with the last Etruscan workshops. The Etruscan traditions were fading out, but not yet extinct.

Yet even this final period of Etruscan funerary art was not without novelties. A new version of the motif of the "Journey to the Underworld" had been introduced earlier in the century, namely the journey of the deceased in a *carpentum*, a covered wagon not unlike wagons of the American Wild-West. This motif became the most popular one in the workshop that was still producing at a relatively large scale. In several of these reliefs women and girls are represented wearing a hairstyle called "*nodus*" (cf. Tibullus 2.5.8), as do many female lid figures produced in the same workshop (Fig. 9.7). The name does not refer to the usual knot at the top of the head or at the neck, but to the bun at the centre of the forehead.[20] It had been introduced by Augustus' sister Octavia and his wife Livia, and worn by all the leading ladies of the Second Triumvirate and the Augustan age. With their images – coin portraits and statues – the "*nodus*" spread all over the Roman world.[21] Elsewhere in Etruria, it only appears on clearly Roman portrait sculpture and funerary reliefs (e.g. at Chiusi and Arezzo), but Volterra was the only place where the Etruscan style funerary sculpture was still vigorous and receptive enough to adopt it – as certainly did also the living women.[22]

One more fashionable female hairstyle found its way to Volterra, the so-called neck-tail, which dates to the reigns of Tiberius, Caligula and Claudius. Now the hair has again a central parting, but down the neck there is a plaited "tail." One female lid figure wears it (Fig. 9.8), but some of its features – the fish-like position on the stomach, rasp-marks, and other peculiarities – connect her with an analogous male figure, who is lying down clad in a large Roman toga.

A third lid figure to be connected with these two represents a boy, who holds in his hands writing tablets and a book-scroll, the customary attributes of the "Diptych Group" of the Augustan period, thus representing a link between the Augustan and the Tiberian periods.[23] With them, the Etruscan tradition dies out at Volterra. The Romanized and Latinized Etruscans were still living there, while others attended their careers at Rome.

With the donations of two ex-Volterrans, A. Caecina Severus and A. Caecina Largus, a Roman theatre was built on the slopes of the town, probably between the year 1 BC and AD 25. From the sculptural decoration of the theatre derive some Julio-Claudian portrait statues: a small-scale portrait of young Octavian, and bigger busts of Augustus and Tiberius. A head of Livia may serve as a significant link between this style icon and the Volterran ladies: originally, this portrait had a *nodus* bun on top of the forehead, but it was removed, leaving some rough chisel grooves on the spot. Probably stucco amendments turned it to a more up-to-date hairdo of the Tiberian era (Fig. 9.9).[24]

a

b

c

Figure 9.7 A couple being transported in a *carpentum* pulled by two mules to the Underworld. The woman in the wagon (b) and the girl at the left corner (c) wear *nodus*-coiffures. From Volterra. Circa 40–0 BC. London, the British Museum, D 67. Photos by the author.

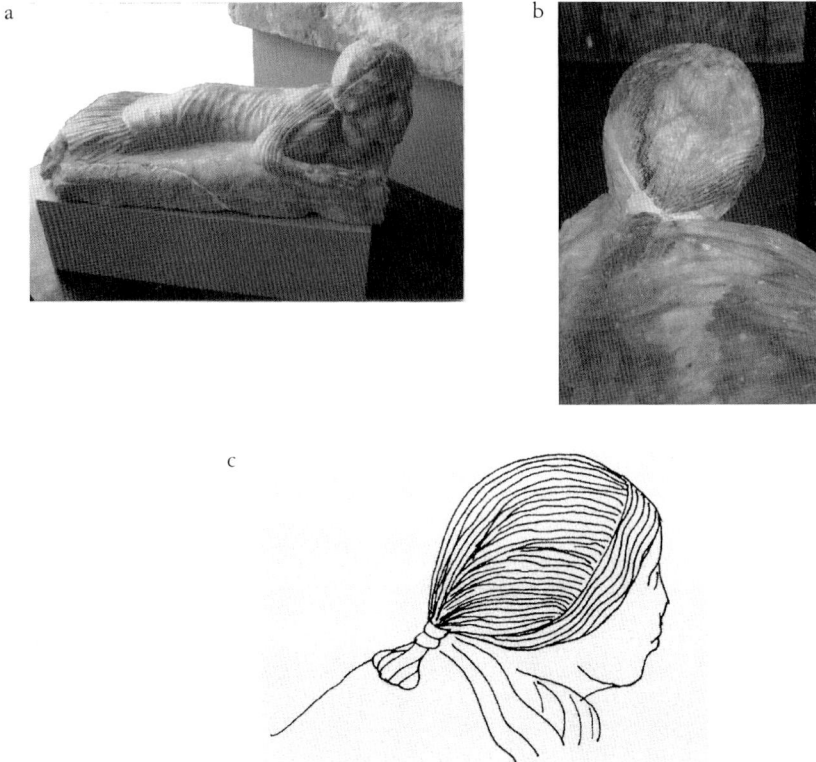

Figure 9.8   Female lid figure with the neck-tail coiffure of the Tiberian-Claudian period. Volterra, Museo Guarnacci, inv. 241. (Photos and drawing by the author).

Figure 9.9   Livia's portrait head, from the Roman theatre at Vallebuona, Volterra. Augustan period, but reworked by removing the *nodus* on the forehead, probably in the Tiberian period. Museo Guarnacci. (Photo by the author).

Keeping in mind the countless theatrical subjects on the chest reliefs, it is no wonder that the Caecinae chose to convince their fellow-citizens of the benefits of the new rule by giving them a monumental theatre built of stone. Under Roman rule, future fame would lie in such politically-motivated displays and not in the ostentation of the family tomb.

NOTES

1   Since this contribution is based on my own research through the years, the references do not give true credit to the vast scholarship on the field. I am happy to dedicate the study to my mother, Helvi Hokkanen-Pettersson, at her 103rd birthday.

2   For example, Nielsen 1989 and 2002, Amann 2006, Benelli 2009.

3   Kaimio 1975; Benelli 1994.

4   For the whole issue see Nielsen 1989 (esp. 82–89) and 2002.

5   Feruglio 2002.

6   Nielsen 1999.

7   Shortly on these aspects, Nielsen 2002: 100–101; latest, the many important contributions in Cenciaioli (ed.) 2011. "Pupli Velimna [son of] Avle and Cahatia/Publius Volumnius Violens son of Aulus born of Cafatia."

8   Benelli 1994, 18–20, no. 7.

9   For the Chiusine tombs and their contents, see for example, Haynes 2000: 333–342. For the different kinds of Chiusine sarcophagi, ash chests and urns, see various contributions in Barbagli and Iozzo (eds) 2007, 86–108 (alabaster and travertine urns: F. de Angelis and A. Rastrelli); 109–122 (terracotta urns: A. Rastrelli and M. Sclafani); 123–125 (bell-urns: E. Albani). For the terracotta urns, most recently, see Sclafani 2010; for the bell-urns, see also Bagnasco Gianni 2009.

10 Cf. Benelli 2009, esp. 157–158.

11 For example, Haynes 2000: 335. Such corridor tombs have recently been excavated by Monica Salvini at San Casciano dei Bagni (I owe this information to Giulio Paolucci).

12 *UV* 1:26–41 (Maggiani).

13 Maggiani 1975 and 1977; Nielsen 2007.

14 Bonamici 2007: 220–222.

15 *UV* 1, no. 138; for the phenomenon of recarving male figures into female ones see Nielsen 1986: 44–50.

16 Cf. Nielsen 1995: 322–323, tables with all Volterran motifs in chronological order.

17 Brunn 1870: pl. 89: 3; *UV* 1: no. 164; Nielsen 2007: 171 no. 17.

18 *UV* 1: no. 126; Nielsen 2007: 163.

19 In the tomb were also kept several undecorated and therefore "undatable" chests (now removed), which were not described in the nineteenth-century lists, where the focus was on decorated reliefs.

20 For the Volterran lid figures with *nodus*, see Nielsen 1976: 139. For the *carpentum* reliefs, see *UV* 2:1, nos. 188–214 (not one of the *nodus*-hairstyles have been mentioned; *ibid.*, no. 217 (a lid figure) describes the hairdo, without commenting on it.

21 Latest, Micheli 2011: 53–56, 61.

22 Other places, like Asciano, also present datable material from the Augustan period, but without sculptural decoration.

23 Nielsen 1985: 46–47 (all three); *UV* 2:2, no. 17 (the female figure; the neck-tail is not shown nor described). All the three lids are combined with older chests, whose pertinence is uncertain. For the neck-tail in general, most recently, Micheli 2011: 62–65.

24 For example, Cateni 2004: 81–82.

BIBLIOGRAPHY

Amann, P. (2006) "Verwandschaft, Familie und Heirat in Etrurien. Überlegungen zu Terminologie und Struktur" in P. Amann, M. Pedrazzi and H. Taeuber (eds), *Italo-Tusco-Romana. Festschrift für Luciana Aigner-Foresti*, Wien: Holzhausen, 1–12.

Bagnasco Gianni, G. (2009) "Un ossuario fittile a campana del Museo Archeologico di Milano," in S. Bruni (ed.), *Etruria e Italia preromana. Studi in onore di Giovannangelo Camporeale*, Pisa-Rome: Fabrizio Serra Editore, 45–55.

Barbagli, D. and Iozzo, M. (eds) (2007) *Etruschi. Chiusi Siena Palermo. La collezione Bonci Casuccini*, Siena: Protagon editori.

Benelli, E. (1994) *Le iscrizioni bilingui etrusco-latine* (Biblioteca di "Studi Etruschi" 27), Florence: Leo S. Olschki editore.

Benelli, E. (2009) "Alla ricerca delle aristocrazie chiusine" in M.-L. Haack (ed.) *Écritures, cultures, sociétés dans les nécropoles d'Italie ancienne (Table-ronde Paris 2007)*, (Ausonius éditions, Études 23), Paris-Bordeaux: De Boccard, 135–159.

Bonamici, M. (2007) "Culti e pratiche devozionali nel santuario dell'acropoli" in G. Cateni (ed.), 2007, 220–222.

Brunn, H. (1870) *I rilievi delle urne etrusche, vol. 1. Ciclo Troico*, Rome: Instituto di Corrispondenza Archeologica.

Cateni, G. (2004) *Volterra. Museo Guarnacci*, Pisa: Pacini editore.

Cateni, G. (ed.) (2007) *Etruschi di Volterra. Capolavori da grandi musei europei (Exhibition catalogue – Volterra)*, Milan: Federico Motta Editore.

Cenciaioli, L. (ed.) (2011) *L'Ipogeo dei Volumni 170 anni dalla scoperta (Atti del convegno di studi Perugia 2010)*, Perugia: Fabrizio Fabbri editore.

Feruglio, A. E. (2002) "La tomba dei *cai cutu* e le urne cinerarie perugine di età ellenistica" in G. M. Della Fina (ed.), *Perugia etrusca (Atti del IX Convegno Orvieto 2001)*, Annali Faina 9, Rome: Edizioni Quasar, 475–495.

Haynes, S. (2000) *Etruscan Civilization. A Cultural History*, London: British Museum Press.

Kaimio, J. (1975) "The Ousting of Etruscan by Latin in Etruria" in P. Bruun (ed.), *Studies in the Romanization of Etruria* (Acta Instituti Romani Finlandiae 5), Rome: Bardi editore, 85–245.

Maggiani, A. (1975) "Tomba XIX. Tomba Inghirami," in *UV* 1, 84–119.

——(1977) "Analisi di un contesto tombale: La tomba Inghirami di Volterra" in M. Martelli and M. Cristofani (eds), 124–136.

Martelli, M. and Cristofani, M. (eds) (1977) *Caratteri dell'ellenismo nelle urne etrusche (Atti dell'incontro di studi, Siena 1976)*, Florence: Centro Di.

Micheli, M. E. (2011) "Comae formatae" in M. E. Micheli and A. Santucci (eds), *Comae. Identità femminile nelle acconciature di età romana*, Pisa: Edizioni ETS, 49–78.

Nielsen, M. (1977) "I coperchi delle urne volterrane. Caratteristiche e datazione delle ultime botteghe" in M. Martelli and M. Cristofani (eds) 137–141.

——(1985) "Coperchio di urna cineraria, nos. 18–20" in A. Maggiani (ed.), *Artigianato artistico (Exh. cat. Volterra-Chiusi)*, Milan: Electa, 46–47.

——(1986) "Late Etruscan Cinerary Urns from Volterra at the J. Paul Getty Museum: A Lid Figure Altered from Male to Female, and an Ancestor to Satirist Persius," *The J. Paul Getty Museum Journal*, 14, 43–58.

——(1989) "Women and Family in a Changing Society: A Quantitative Approach to Late Etruscan Burials," *Analecta Romana Instituti Danici*, 17–18 (1988–1989), 53–98; a shorter version in Italian: "La donna e la famiglia nella tarda società etrusca" in A. Rallo (ed.), *Le donne in Etruria* (Studia Archaeologica, 52), Rome: L'Erma di Bretschneider (1989), 121–145.

——(1995) "Cultural Orientations in Etruria in the Hellenistic Period: Greek Myths and Local Motifs on Volterran Urn Reliefs" in P. Guldager Bilde, I. Nielsen and M. Nielsen (eds), *Aspects of Hellenism in Italy: Towards a Cultural Unity?* (Acta Hyperborea 5), Copenhagen: Museum Tusculanum Press, 319–357.

——(1999) "Common Tombs for Women in Etruria: Buried Matriarchies?" in P. Setälä and L. Savunen (eds), *Female Networks and the Public Sphere in Roman Society* (Acta Instituti Romani Finlandiae, 22), Rome, 65–139.

——(2002) "… stemmate quod Tusco ramum millesime ducis…" (Persius Sat. 3.28): Family Tombs and Genealogical Memory among the Etruscans" in J. Munk Højte (ed.), *Images of Ancestors* (Aarhus Studies in Mediterranean Antiquity, 5), Aarhus: Aarhus University Press, 89–126.

——(2007) "La tomba Inghirami" in G. Cateni (ed.) 2007, 156–171.

Sclafani, M. (2010) *Urne fittili chiusine e perugine di età medio e tardo ellenistica* (Archaeologica 160), Rome: Giorgio Bretschneider editore.

UV 1 (1975) M. Cristofani *et al.* (eds) *Urne volterrane. 1. I Complessi tombali* (*Corpus delle urne etrusche di età ellenistica, 1*), Florence: Centro Di

UV 2:1 (1977) M. Cristofani (ed.) *Urne volterrane. 2. Il Museo Guarnacci, 1* (*Corpus delle urne etrusche di età ellenistica, 2*), Florence: Centro Di.

UV 2:2 (1986) G. Cateni (ed.), *Urne volterrane 2, Il Museo Guarnacci, 2* (*Corpus delle urne etrusche di età ellenistica, 2*), Pisa: Pacini Editore.

PART III

ETRUSCANS AND THEIR NEIGHBORS

———•◆•———

CHAPTER TEN

THE WESTERN MEDITERRANEAN
BEFORE THE ETRUSCANS

———— •◆• ————

Fulvia Lo Schiavo

INTRODUCTION

In previous literature discussing the earliest phases of the Etruscans, the "Western Mediterranean" was more a geographical perspective than it was an historic one. Since west of the Tuscan and Latium coasts lies the island of Sardinia (Fig. 10.1), it seems only correct not to limit the analysis to the Tyrrhenian Sea but to consider also the connection and trade concerning Corsica, the Balearic Islands and the Iberian Peninsula, as far as

Figure 10.1   Distribution map of the sites that are mentioned in this paper (elab. Milletti 2012).

the Gibraltar strait and beyond. The "Far West" history (as it was called in a paper presented to the XXIX Taranto Conference in 1989) (Lo Schiavo, D'Oriano 1990) has greatly changed due to the publication of the recovery of the discarded pottery and ivory fragments and other items from Huelva (Gonzàles de Canales *et al.* 2004). The volume, dated to 2004, marked a revival of interest, still far from being exhausted, and the new, exciting discovery of Sardinian and Greek and more eastern findings on the Atlantic coasts, that will be mentioned below.

A second preliminary explanation concerns the expression "before the Etruscans," deliberately vague enough to include a large span of time, in order to allow us to evaluate synthetically what can have influenced "the sea of the Etruscans," therefore not only from the Late Bronze Age to the Early Iron Age, but beginning with references to the extraordinarily rich season of Mediterranean interconnections, and of expansion and flourishing of the archaeological local *facies* that occurred in the Recent Bronze Age (approximately thirteenth century BC).

In this framework, "the Etruscans" are extensively considered – far from any ethnic definition – the people of the Tyrrhenian coasts and inland of central Italy, that is present-day Tuscany, Umbria and north Latium, considering also the Picentino region that in the Iron Age became "Campanian Etruria," and other adjacent areas.

THE MYCENAEANS IN THE WESTERN MEDITERRANEAN

In the Recent Bronze Age (Fig. 10.2), the two main protagonists of the Mediterranean scene on the Western routes are the Mycenaeans and the Cypriots. Thanks to the pioneering studies of Lucia Vagnetti, here summarised, there is much to be added to our understanding of the way in which the Aegean sailors and merchants approached the people of Peninsular Italy and of the Islands (Vagnetti 1982a; 1982b; 1999a; 2000; 2011a; 2011b; Vagnetti, Jones 1988; Jones, Vagnetti 1991).

Three main phases of contacts can be traced, beginning with the first, dated Late Helladic I and II (Italian Middle Bronze Age, hereafter MBA, 1 and 2, middle of sixteenth century to the end of fifteenth century BC), the phase of the earliest approach to a few sites of Ionian and Tyrrhenian coasts, with a preference for small and rocky islands in front of open gulfs and river mouths, acquiring a naturally defended lookout in comparison with land routes that were wider and richer in resources but potentially dangerous. The best examples are well known sites such as Scoglio del Tonno and Porto Perone in the gulf of Taranto, Capo Piccolo and Torre Mordillo in the Sibaritide, Vivara in the Gulf of Naples, the Aeolian Islands north-east of Sicily and Monte Grande on the south coast of the island.

In the second phase, dated Late Helladic, hereafter LH, IIIA – IIIB early (Italian MBA 3 – beginning of Recent Bronze Age, end of fifteenth-beginning of fourteenth century BC), the archaeological evidence shows that the relationships between the Aegean and the Central Mediterranean were more and more regular and active. The most important sites are still Scoglio del Tonno, the Aeolian Islands, Thapsos, and other necropoleis in eastern Sicily.

The earliest Mycenaean materials found in Sardinia are dated to the LH III A2 (equivalent to the Italian MBA 3 phase), consisting in two very special finds, an almost complete *alabastron* from the foundation levels of Nuraghe Arrubiu-Orroli (Fig. 10.3;

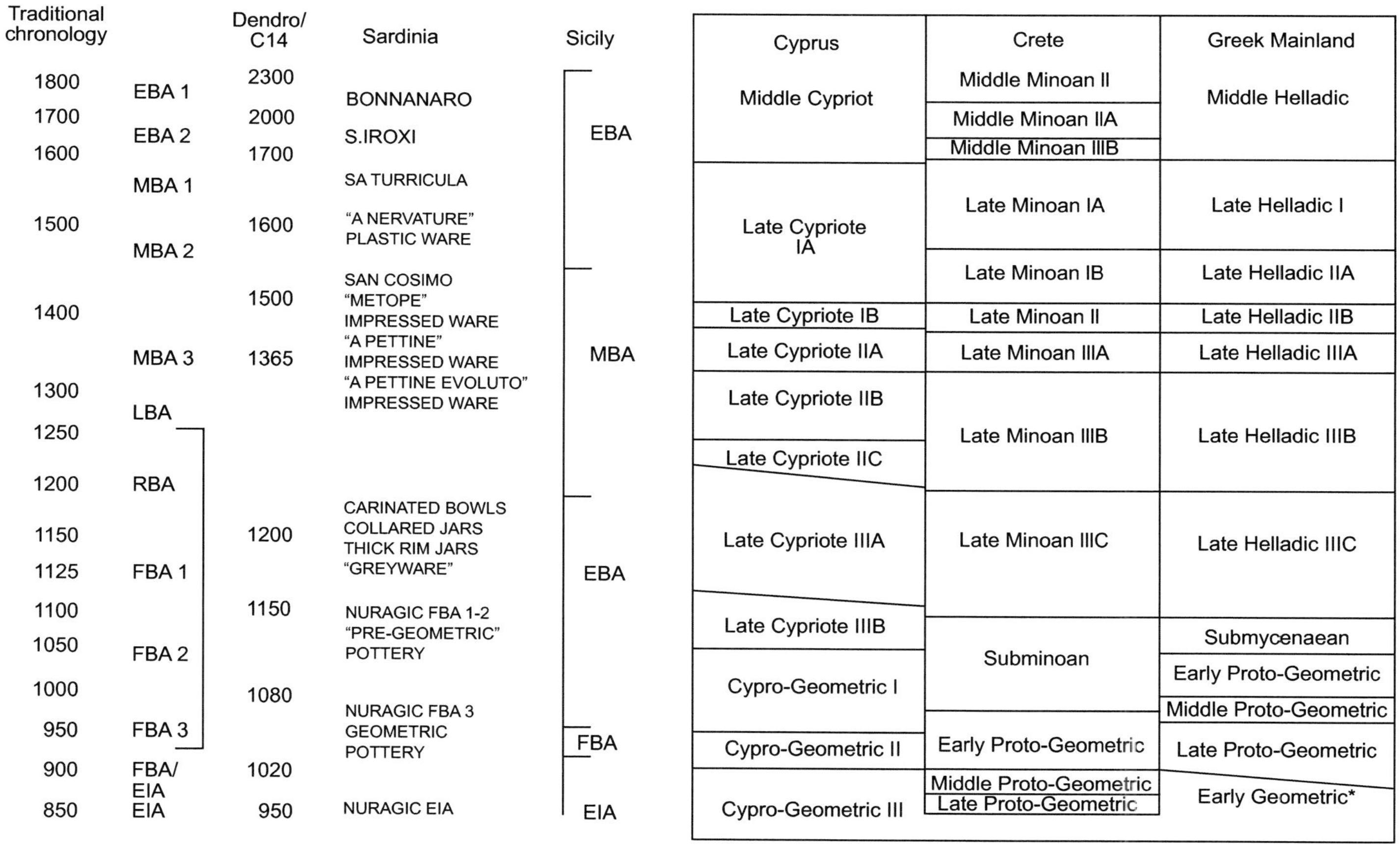

Traditional chronology		Dendro/C14	Sardinia	Sicily	Cyprus	Crete	Greek Mainland
1800	EBA 1				Middle Cypriot	Middle Minoan II	Middle Helladic
1700	EBA 2	2300	BONNANARO	EBA		Middle Minoan IIA	
1600	MBA 1	2000	S.IROXI			Middle Minoan IIIB	
		1700	SA TURRICULA		Late Cypriote IA	Late Minoan IA	Late Helladic I
1500	MBA 2	1600	"A NERVATURE" PLASTIC WARE	MBA		Late Minoan IB	Late Helladic IIA
1400		1500	SAN COSIMO "METOPE" IMPRESSED WARE / "A PETTINE" IMPRESSED WARE		Late Cypriote IB	Late Minoan II	Late Helladic IIB
	MBA 3	1365	"A PETTINE EVOLUTO" IMPRESSED WARE		Late Cypriote IIA	Late Minoan IIIA	Late Helladic IIIA
1300	LBA				Late Cypriote IIB		
1250					Late Cypriote IIC	Late Minoan IIIB	Late Helladic IIIB
1200	RBA	1200	CARINATED BOWLS, COLLARED JARS, THICK RIM JARS, "GREYWARE"	EBA	Late Cypriote IIIA	Late Minoan IIIC	Late Helladic IIIC
1150	FBA 1	1150	NURAGIC FBA 1-2 "PRE-GEOMETRIC" POTTERY		Late Cypriote IIIB		
1125							Submycenaean
1100	FBA 2				Cypro-Geometric I	Subminoan	Early Proto-Geometric
1050		1080	NURAGIC FBA 3 GEOMETRIC POTTERY				Middle Proto-Geometric
1000	FBA 3			FBA	Cypro-Geometric II	Early Proto-Geometric	Late Proto-Geometric
950	FBA/EIA	1020				Middle Proto-Geometric	
900	EIA	950	NURAGIC EIA	EIA	Cypro-Geometric III	Late Proto-Geometric	Early Geometric*
850	EIA						

Figure 10.2 Chronological table of the Bronze Age and beginning of the Iron Age (elab. Milletti 2012).

10.4, no. 2), and an ivory fragment representing a warrior head with a boar's-tusk helmet, which probably decorated a wooden casket, from Mitza Purdia-Decimoputzu (Fig. 10.4, no. 1). It is worth noting that the few sherds found in the Iberian Peninsula at Montoro-Cordoba in the upper Guadalquivir valley are chronologically placed in the same period (equivalent to the Iberian Las Cogotas 2 phase) (Martin de la Cruz 1988): what these three discoveries along the western routes have in common is the fact that they are still isolated, with no traces of other older preliminary contacts and, on the contrary, they are located quite inland, along the rivers such as Flumendosa in the case of Nuraghe Arrubiu and Guadalquivir in the case of Montoro, while the open site of Mitza Purdia lays at the foot of the Sulcis-Iglesiente mountain region, rich in metal deposits.

Figure 10.3   The *nuraghe* Arrubiu, Orroli (Nuoro). Photo M. Mereu.

Figure 10.4   Mycenaean materials found in Sardinia: 1. Ivory head with boar's-tusk helmet from Mitza Purdia, Decimoputzu (Cagliari); 2. Mycenaean *alabastron* from Arrubiu, Orroli (Nuoro); 3. Fragment of a Mycenaean imported *rhyton*; 4. Local imitation of Mycenaean crater and 5. Nuragic "slate-gray" *impasto* basin from *nuraghe* Antigori, Sarroch (Cagliari).

The third phase goes from late LH IIIB to advanced LH IIIC (Italian Recent Bronze Age [RBA] to Final Bronze Age [FBA] 1), when not only Mycenaean imports are still widely distributed, but there now begins, and takes hold, the frequent reproduction of Mycenaean pottery models: large containers for transport and storage (*dolia*), practical and everyday kitchen pottery, as well as elegant and refined ceramics. This local production imitating Aegean imported ware – demonstrated by archaeometric analyses (Vagnetti *et al.* in preparation) – in its turn originated a new and close contact network all over Peninsular Italy, where the best-known settlement is Broglio-Trebisacce in Calabria, and including south-central Sardinia, where the bulk of the discoveries took place in Nuraghe Antigori-Sarroch (Fig. 10.4, nos. 3–4), at the western extremity of Cagliari gulf (Vagnetti 2011b).

Later on in the LH IIIC and Submycenaean period (Italian FBA 1–2 and 3) the development both in the production of locally imitated Mycenaean pottery, as well as in participation in the metallurgical *koine*, show that the interconnections were deeply rooted and longstanding, for instance as in the two south Apulian sites of Rocavecchia and Santa Maria di Leuca, though the number of imports is decreasing (Bettelli 2002).

The evidence of Sardinia is particularly important for two reasons: first of all the highly fascinating and still open problem of reciprocal spheres of influences with the Cypriots, of which we will discuss below; secondly a phenomenon that began as sailing and trading contacts but that took root and expanded not only to many other sites in the more or less nearby areas, the last evidence of which being the sherds found at Sant'Antioco (ancient *Sulky*), but also to other fields of local activity, apparently influencing agricultural production and related pottery technique. Large containers in polished clay that were hard-fired so as to avoid porosity, as well as the beginning of the production of pitchers, can be linked to the growing frequency of the discoveries of olive pits and of grape seeds in Late Bronze Age deposits (Sa Osa-Oristano) (Usai A. 2010).

The "slate-gray" pottery, or "Nuragic-gray" pottery (Fig. 10.4, no 5), characterised not only by the colour of the clay due to a better hard burnishing but also by a whole set of very peculiar pottery shapes, is found mainly concentrated in south-central Sardinia and in association with Mycenaean imports and imitations. More and more this typical Nuragic production is found – and the number of sites where it is recognised is growing – bringing the evaluation of the trade routes in the Mediterranean from a unique East to West course to a two-way course. A southern route from south Sardinia goes to Cannatello in the Agrigento region of southern Sicily and then to the harbour site of Kommos in southern Crete, both in LH IIIA2-IIIB levels, reaching – as was very recently stated – Pyla-Kokkinokremos on the south-east coast of Cyprus, a short-lived site dated from Late Cypriot [LC] IIC and abandoned in 1200 (mid thirteenth-beginning of twelfth centuries BC) (Karageorghis 2011). A main point for the correct interpretation of historic pattern is the fact that all these RBA Nuragic clay sherds do not belong to prestige or votive elegant ceramics but to simple everyday pottery, common vessels used by travelers and sailors; moreover, the Nuragic jar with "inverted-elbow" handles found in Pyla-Kokkinokremos (Fig. 10.5) is broken and repaired with a large lead clamp, and the lead – analysed by lead isotope analysis – comes from the Sulcis-Iglesiente mining region, therefore it is certain that the jar traveled as an utilitarian container for food or other alimentary merchandise.

We are allowed to conclude that in order to explain the absence of finds of Mycenaean pottery in northern Tuscany where the richest metal deposits are located, though also depending from the chance of the discoveries, one must take into account Nuragic Sardinia and its Cypriot connection.

Figure 10.5   Bronze figurine from *nuraghe* Cabu Abbas, Olbia (Sassari) and Nuragic necked jar with "inverted-elbow" handles from Pyla-Kokkinokremos.

OXHIDE INGOTS IN THE MEDITERRANEAN

The copper trade originated in the eastern Mediterranean in the kingdom of *Alashjia* (generally identified with Cyprus); from there the oxhide ingots were distributed to Anatolia and Bulgarian regions along the Black Sea (Rotea 2004; Leshtakov 2007) to Egypt and to Greece and far west to Sicily and to Sardinia (Fig. 10.6). The northernmost discovery consists of the four fragments of at least two different oxhide ingots found in the hoard of Oberwilflingen (Baden-Württemberg), in association with bronze axes with broad edges of a transitional type of MBA/LBA date, no later than thirteenth century BC (Primas, Pernicka 1998; Primas 2005).

In Cyprus, mining and smelting processes have been thoroughly investigated and many achievements have been recognised, particularly on the characteristics and different locations of the various phases of the metallurgical process, on the smelting equipment, and on the earlier production preceding that of LC II. For the moment, no ingot fragments dating prior to the fourteenth century BC have been found on Cyprus, where the use of the oxhide ingot shape can be confirmed from the fourteenth down to the end of the twelfth century BC. Hopefully, future excavations will expand these chronological boundaries (Kassianidou 2009: 59).

The best document of the maritime copper trade are the two wrecks of Uluburun and Cape Gelidonya (Yalçin *et al.* 2005; Bass 1967), on the southern coast of Turkey, dated respectively to the end of the fourteenth and to the first half of the thirteenth centuries BC, giving us a different picture of the situation. The first wreck, which has been well-excavated and is still under in-depth study, is a merchant ship of selected goods that includes metal cargo, consisting of 354 copper oxhide ingots and about 100 tin ingots, intended for exchanges among dynasts; the second wreck carried copper (and

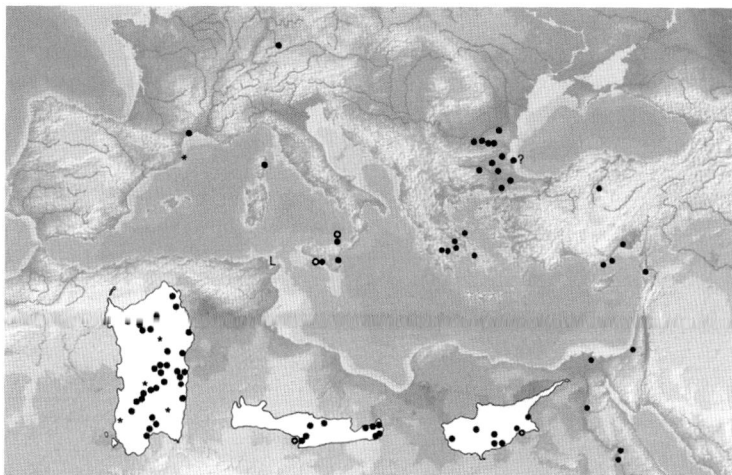

Figure 10.6 Distribution map of the oxhide ingots in the Mediterranean (elab. Milletti 2012).

probably also tin) ingots, together with a bronze craftsman with his tools, appointed to the retrieval and working of metal scraps, also carried on board, on the whole depicting a time of crisis (Vagnetti 2000: 66).

OXHIDE INGOTS IN THE WEST-CENTRAL MEDITERRANEAN

The situation of the discoveries of oxhide ingots in the west-central Mediterranean has been extensively studied recently (Lo Schiavo *et al.* eds. 2009) and the situation is not changed, as far as Sicily, Corsica and southern France are concerned. In Sicily, there is up to now only in Lipari a hoard with hundreds of fragments of oxhide and plano-convex ingots and scraps of weapons and tools; in the other two sites of Cannatello and Thapsos, one fragment each was found. Two whole oxhide ingots were discovered in north-east Corsica, at S. Anastasìa, south of Bastia and in the deep water of Sète, a coastal site of the Hérault.

Totally different is the situation in Sardinia, where not only is there actually the highest occurrence of finds outside of Cyprus, but also where new discoveries from the archaeological excavations are daily brought to light (Lo Schiavo 2011).

The first report of the discovery of oxhide ingots, at Serra Ilixi in central Sardinia in 1857, was by Giovanni Spano, Canon and Senator, which was followed by those discovered at Ayia Triada in Crete and published by Luigi Pigorini in 1904. Five ingots were found all together, side by side, during ploughing, at the base of a demolished *nuraghe* known as "Serra Ilixi"; one of the ingots was acquired by the Museo Archeologico Nazionale of Cagliari and two more by Spano, who later left them to the same museum, of which he was the founder and the Director and where they are on display.

The first well-dated closed association is the Arzachena-Albucciu hoard, of the Recent Bronze Age (LH IIIB, by comparison with the shape of the pottery found in dated levels at Kommos, Crete). Recently two important discoveries of the same period were added to the list: the Funtana Coberta-Ballao hoard (Manunza 2008) (Fig. 10.7) and Nuraghe Serucci-Gonnesa. It is possible that the appearance of Cypriot oxhide ingots happened earlier in Sardinia, as their burial in the foundation of a Nuragic tower (Bisarcio-Ozieri)

Figure 10.7   Funtana Coberta of Ballao (Cagliari) hoard: the container and the oxhide ingots.

suggests. As to the later pieces, there is no reason to believe that they were in use in the islands much later than the eleventh–tenth centuries BC when more plano-convex ingots are in circulation.

Complete or fragmentary oxhide ingots were found in more than 30 sites (31 listed and discussed in Lo Schiavo 2009; four more sites in Lo Schiavo 2011), but the number is destined to grow according to the archaeological research and analyses. At the moment, only four oxhide ingots in Sardinia are complete: three from Serra Ilixi-Nuragus (Nuoro) and one from S. Antioco of Bisarcio-Ozieri; all the others are fragmentary and found generally in hoards, mostly hidden in *nuraghi* and Nuragic villages, temples and sanctuaries.

THE CYPRIOTS IN THE WESTERN MEDITERRANEAN

While the presence/influence of the Mycenaeans in the West is mostly evidenced by a peculiar new pottery style and technique, the Cypriot presence/influence in the West is overwhelming in the domain of metallurgy, almost as a modern trade divided into clear-cut spheres of influence and "monopoly." A few years ago this assertion would have been censured for being overly modernistic. Nowadays, thorough study of the copper oxhide ingots and tin trade has built up a very different pattern from a simplistic *ex Oriente Lux* mode and added to the incredible – though preliminary – conclusion that even if the bulk of Cypriot copper was produced with a view to the western trade, it is not excluded that at least some of the contractors – specifically Nuragic people – covered the distance and came to the source, carrying the ingots aboard their own ships and perhaps acting as go-betweens for LBA emporia on the route in Crete (Kommos) and in Sicily (Cannatello, Lipari and possibly also Thapsos) (Lo Schiavo *et al.* 2009). A western-type Thapsos sword in the Uluburun wreck, though up to now an isolated item, can be considered a trace of the presence of traders/sailors of other western provenance.

Though extreme, this framework is feasible to explain both the overwhelming presence of oxhide ingots in Sardinia, and of smithing tools (sledge-hammers, raising-hammers, tongs, shovels), double-edged instruments (massive and simple double-axes, axe-adzes, picks), prestige objects (tripod-stands), bronze figurines and other items, strikingly similar to the Cypriote ones dated LC II/LC III (Italian LBA 1 and 2), frequently, if not always, associated (Lo Schiavo 1983; Lo Schiavo, Macnamara, Vagnetti 1985; Ferrarese Ceruti *et al.* 1987) (Fig. 10.8).

Even more impressive is the Cypriot influence in the field of metallurgical process, concerning the melting and casting in stone moulds of a wide range of instruments: axes of different shapes, chisels, drift punches and some personal items such as pins, weapons such as swords, daggers, *stilettos*, and an incredibly rich lost-wax technique manufacture of figurines of humans, animals, monuments, tools, weapons, containers, in some cases as big as statues (38 cm in the Great Warrior of the Pigorini Museum) (Fig. 10.9) and as small as pendants, amulets and buttons. Both techniques are applied to the production and ornamentation of bronze containers (jars, cauldrons and jugs).

The Nuragic metalworkers came to master the technique of production in moulds and the lost-wax process, and applied them to the local reproduction of the original Cypriot models, reaching, in their turn, a high level of mastery and originality. Since the presence of peculiar Nuragic pottery, dated RBA/FBA 1, had been established along the route of southern Sicily, southern Crete and southern Cyprus – openly following a route whose missing steps are expected to appear – there is nearly no doubt that we are not dealing with sporadic events or with the transmission of a few objects by single wandering travelers. It is rather a deeply-rooted network along precise sea routes: it has been suggested (Lo Schiavo 2001) that at least some metalworkers actually came and

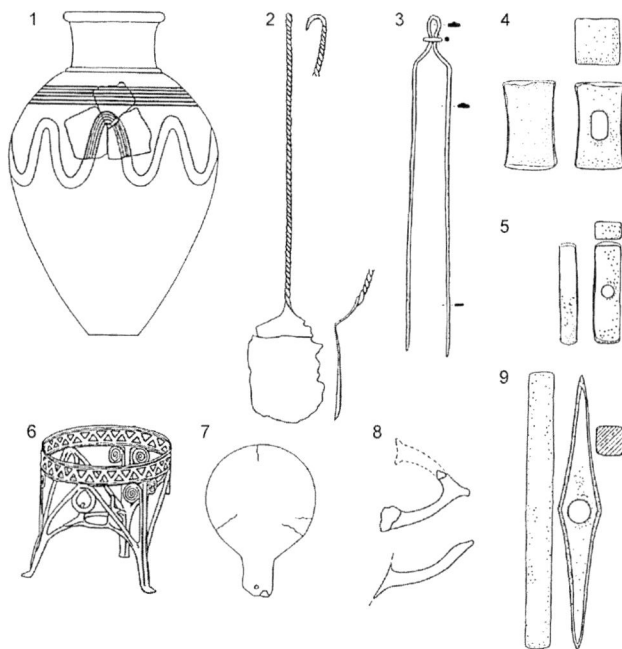

Figure 10.8   Evidence of close contacts between Cyprus and Sardinia in the Late Bronze Age: 1. and 8. Pithos and "wishbone" handle from *nuraghe* Antigori, Sarroch (Cagliari); 2. and 6. Bronze shovel and tripod-stand from a private collection, Oristano; 3. Fire tongs from Badde Ulumu, Sassari; 4. Sledgehammer from Nuchis, Sassari; 5. Raising hammer from Perfugas (Sassari); 7. Bronze mirror from Pirosu-Su Benatzu cave, Santadi (Cagliari); 9. Double axe from Ozieri (Sassari).

Figure 10.9   The biggest (38 cm) Nuragic bronze figurine of a warrior in Pigorini Museum, Rome.

settled in Sardinia, during the winter season, bringing with them their pure copper oxhide ingots, of whose quality they would have been sure, their technical prowess and such items as could serve as "models" both for the use and for the "significance" of the objects. The material presence at least of some Cypriot bronzeworkers in RBA Sardinia, even as itinerant seasonal coppersmiths as is documented by what was found on board the Cape Gelidonya ship, joined to parallel material presence of Nuragic sailors (traders) in LCII/LCIII Cyprus, as now seems to have been the case shown by the discovery of Nuragic pottery in Pyla-Kokkinokremos, could have been the base of the strong and long lasting Cypriot "imprinting" on Nuragic bronze production, in spite of the social structure and cultural differences between the two islands.

The Nuragic bronze items are mainly collected in hoards, deposited in temples and in sanctuaries, in such a quantity as to demonstrate the economic and political centralising "federal" power exerted by the Nuragic "Head-of-the-Tribe" conventions, till the end of the LBA.

THE LEGEND OF THE FOUNDATION OF CARTHAGE

Marcus Junianus Justinus (second century AD), in his epitome of *Historiarum Philippicarum* by *Pompeius Trogus*, reports the legend of Elissa, sister of the king of Tyre, fleeing to avoid persecution, to the bay of today Tunis, acquiring from the native people a piece of land as large as an ox skin. For this reason the queen invented the trick of cutting the skin into thin threads, tying them together in order to enclose a large piece of territory, on the *Byrsa* promontory. To the objections raised by W. Huss to this legendary interpretation, very much based on hellenizing etymology, a different interpretation, as a legendary transposition of a precise cultural situation, was suggested by S. Gsell and S. Moscati.

From the archaeological point of view, the circulation of oxhide ingots in the Mediterranean is so wide that it is difficult to accept the idea of the independent birth of a legend concerning a piece of land bought thanks to an ox skin – although through a trick – conceived as something having a great value. On the contrary, it seems plausible to think that the people of the region where Carthage was eventually to be founded had a direct knowledge of the oxhide ingots and experienced their metal value. In fact, nowadays it is known through chemical analyses that most if not all the copper oxhide ingots analysed had such a high degree of purity (the average is from 97% up to 99% Cu) as to allow their immediate use in any bronze workshop.

In a later period, fragments belonging to at least three different askoid jugs – a Nuragic FBA 3 production, see below – were found in Carthage in secondary context, but probably came originally from the earlier phase of settlement: this means that from the very beginning Carthage was tightly connected to the Mediterranean maritime routes (see also Chapter 17.)

ATLANTIC/MEDITERRANEAN INTERCONNECTIONS

The subject of the East/West interconnection was highlighted in two joint scientific major events: the International Conference held in Rethymno (Crete) in 2002, followed in 2003 by an outstanding exhibition displayed in the Cycladic Art Museum at Athens, of the same title: *Interconnections in the Mediterranean, ca. 1500–500 BC* and sharing the Greek word *ΠΛΟΕΣ* (*PLOES* = SHIP) as a logo, pointing out that the sea was the element that brought near distant lands and allowed and facilitated material and cultural long-distance transmission. In this framework, the network – focused on metallurgy – intertwining in Nuragic Sardinia is certainly impressive (Lo Schiavo 2003a; 2003b).

The Cyprus/Nuragic Sardinia and the Iberian peninsula/Nuragic Sardinia connections do not follow an equal pattern: from the chronological point of view, the oldest Cypriot models and materials are, as we said before, related to LCII and LCIII production (RBA and FBA 1 and 2, thirteenth-eleventh century BC), while the oldest western type *"Pistilliforme"* swords can be dated to the FBA 2 (eleventh century BC). Later on (FBA 3, about tenth century BC) the western prevails and outnumbers the eastern influence. In both cases Nuragic Sardinia most probably receives materials from an external region – ascertained by archaeometrical analyses only for the oxhide ingots – and modify the models according to local taste, fashion, necessity, thus creating the original and unique Nuragic bronze production, side by side with an outstanding architecture and with an incredible maritime and trading entrepreneurship. Thus, it is evident that trade is a part of the whole picture and not all of it.

Local Nuragic production of Cypriot models can be explained in the light of the considerable metallurgical experience acquired by Sardinian bronze craftsmen from those of the eastern Mediterranean, supported and based (as stated above) on the excellent quality and extreme pureness of the Cypriot copper; it obviously indicates a long-standing deep familiarity and cultural, even more than material, exchange. A parallel explanation must be sought for the reproduction – according to the results of the metallurgical analyses (Begemann *et al.* 2001) – and imitation of western bronze items by the Nuragic bronze craftsmen. If we should summarise this story using modern terminology it would be appropriate to say that the Nuragic economic import/export balance in the middle and late period of FBA inclined from East to West. There is still a lot to be said, but the reasons why the axis of the interconnections inclines from the East to the West are, at the moment, open to discussion and only some of them can be hypothesised (could it have been the search for western tin?)

A list of Iberian weapons, ornaments and tools found in Sardinia was discussed many years ago (Fig. 10.9): flanged hilted and "fenestrated" hilted swords, daggers, spear-heads and spear-butts, trunnion axes, flat single-loop and double-loop palstaves, flanged single-loop and double-loop palstaves, one-loop and double-loop socketed axes, flat and socketed sickles, razors, "elbow" fibulae, armlets, openwork handles (Lo Schiavo, D'Oriano 1990; Lo Schiavo 1991). Leaving aside much older (BA 2) examples, in the FBA 2 and 3, parallel to the Atlantic Bronze Age 2 and 3, *"Pistilliforme"* swords (Fig. 10.10) and flanged hilted, Huelva/Saint Philbert and Monte Sa Idda type swords, both imports and local reproductions are known in the island (Burgess, O'Connor 2008) (Fig. 10.11).

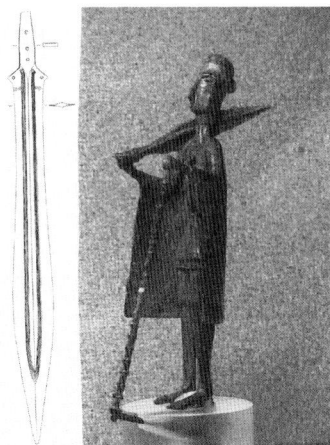

Figure 10.10   Western *"Pistilliform"* sword and bronze figurine of the "Head of the Tribe" from Monti Arcosu, Uta (Cagliari) holding a sword of a similar shape on the shoulder.

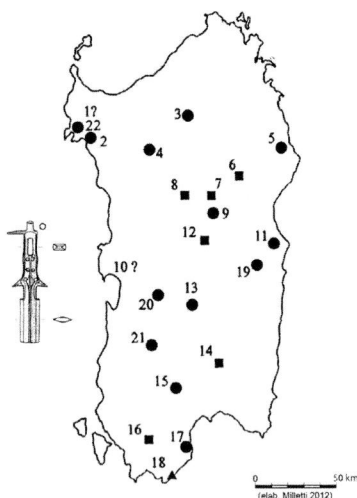

Figure 10.11   Distribution map of the Iberian-type objects found in Sardinia. (*Circle = hoard; Square = temple or sanctuary; Triangle = tomb; ? = unknown*). 1. Nurra region; 2. Flumenelongu, Alghero; 3. Tula; 4. Funtana Janna, Bonnanaro; 5. Oreo, Siniscola; 6. Su Tempiesu, Orune; 7. Nurdole, Orani; 8. Su Ederosu, Bolotana; 9. Sarule; 10. Oristano; 11. Ogliastra region; 12. Abini, Teti; 13. Forraxi Nioi, Nuragus; 14. S. Andrea Frius; 15. Monte Sa Idda, Decimoputzu; 16. Pirosu-Su Benatzu, Santadi; 17. Monte Arrubiu, Sarroch; 18. *Bithia*; 19. Villagrande Strisaili; 20. Brunku 'e S'Omu, Villaverde; 21. S. Maria de Urgu, S. Gavino Monreale; 22. S. Imbenia, Alghero. (elab. Milletti 2012).

Among this varied and peculiar collection of bronze items, one of the best documents of the west-east connections through the medium of Sardinia is the Atlantic-type revolving *obelos* – a technical device joining spit and firedogs – a fragment of which was found in the Monte Sa Idda hoard and a complete piece in Cyprus at Amathus, tomb 523, in the same tomb group as a bronze fire tongs and a shovel of characteristic LCII-III Cypriot types, frequently found and also locally produced in Nuragic Sardinia (Karageorghis, Lo Schiavo 1989).

Two points are by now acknowledged: the first, and already discussed above, is the Cypriot impact factor on Nuragic Sardinia, more than on any other western land, specifically connected to the metallurgy. The second is the intermediary active role of Nuragic Sardinia towards the contemporary regions of the western Mediterranean, where the central position of the island is undeniable. To begin with the two complete oxhide ingots found in Corsica and in southern France at the mouth of the Rhone river, to follow with Nuragic, Cypriot and Iberian materials, scattered from the FBA 3/EIA 1 hoards of Tyrrhenian Italy (modern Tuscany and Latium, but also as far inland as Umbria and through the Apennines to the San Francesco-Bologna hoard and S. Vitale-Bologna necropolis), the number of the discoveries is large and progressively increasing, and the variety of evidence is notable.

NURAGIC SARDINIA IN THE WESTERN MEDITERRANEAN BEFORE THE ETRUSCANS

Two items are more than any others characteristic of Nuragic Sardinia in the last phase of the Final Bronze Age (FBA 3): the askoid jugs and the miniature bronze boats.

The askoid jugs

Until not long ago, the peculiar Nuragic shape of a small pitcher, characterised by a round body and a thin strongly asymmetrical neck, connected to the belly by a ribbon handle and often decorated with geometrical incised and impressed patterns, was called "Vetulonian", on account of its diffusion in Early Iron Age (EIA) Vetulonia and other Villanovan necropoleis. At the same time the extent and variety of Nuragic production was almost unknown.

Today the prospects are totally changed: first came the discovery and publication of a similar jug from Khaniale Tekke in Crete (Vagnetti 1989; Ferrarese Ceruti 1991). Then a few sherds were found in Carthage. Subsequently, a fragment of a handle from Mozia (Marsala district, Trapani province) was found, recently followed by a second askoid jug from the same site, comparable to Nuragic FBA 3 type. Also from Dessueri, southern Sicily (Caltanissetta prov.) (Lo Schiavo 2005).

In the Iberian peninsula, the first to have been noted by Mariano Torres Ortiz was a fragment in the village of Carambolo, in association with impasto sherds but in a mixed level (Torres Ortiz 2004); next, an almost complete askoid jug was found in Cadiz, and many other fragments, together with other Nuragic pottery sherds, were published from Huelva. In Huelva, recent discoveries in archaeological excavations are bringing to light Nuragic askoid jugs in "pre-Phoenician" levels (Gomez Toscano, Fundoni 2010). A splendid example of askoid jug came to light in the excavation of one of the most striking Nuragic sanctuaries discovered recently, Su Monte (Sorradile district, Oristano province) (Fig. 10.12). On the basis of the associated finds, V. Santoni and G. Bacco dated the sanctuary to the RBA-FBA, consequently concluding that the jug should be dated within Nuragic FBA (Bacco, Santoni 2008).

The original Nuragic production of different shapes of askoid jugs is indisputable; they were precious and prestigious containers for a special liquid used in ritual ceremonies. Recent gas-chromatographic analyses indicate in Sardinia a content of (red) wine (Sanges 2008: 10); they have been found in Nuragic temples and sanctuaries. In Vetulonia, it is now demonstrated by way of pottery analyses that the majority of askoid jugs were local imitations, far more than the imports from the island, which are few and older (middle of ninth century BC), while the imitations continue in the eighth century to the beginning of the seventh (Cygielman, Pagnini 2002: 390–391 tab. III a–b); moreover, in Vetulonia the askoid jugs have a more mixed content, equally based in alcohol (flavoured wine?) Contrary to Sardinia, in Etruria the askoid jugs are mostly found in tombs; only recently have a few sherds been discovered in Populonia, in the settlement.

To sum up, Nuragic askoid jugs have been produced in Nuragic Sardinia within the FBA 2 and mostly FBA 3, which would explain such an early presence in Vetulonian tombs. Following on from this, we may suppose that from then onwards, because of the symbolic and material value both of the container and of the content, they were handled along Phoenician trade routes all over the Mediterranean. Indeed, the Phoenician *emporium* of Sant'Imbenia in northern Sardinia shows that a Near Eastern presence was established there from at least the ninth century BC onwards.

The miniature bronze boats

In Cyprus, right from the EBA, ships were reproduced both in clay and in bronze, and also in Minoan and Mycenaean frescos and vases (Basch 1987). In Sardinia, the earliest bronze boats are connected to the great season of the production of bronze figurines by the lost wax process, reproducing in miniature men and women, warriors and peasants, tools and weapons, pieces of furniture and monuments, containers, baskets and ritual objects, beginning in FBA 1 and 2.

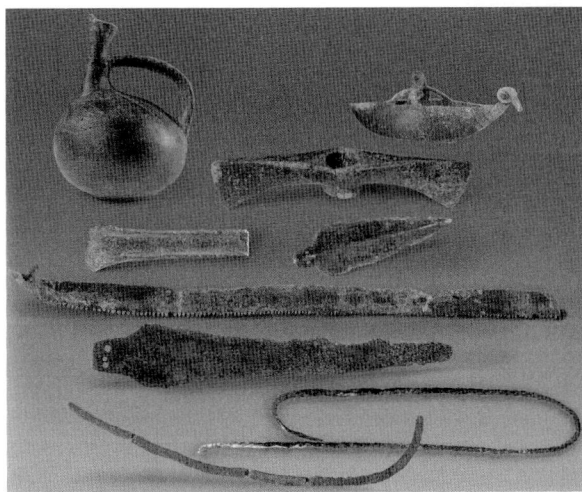

Figure 10.12   Su Monte, Sorradile (Oristano) hoard.

The Nuragic bronze boats (Fig. 10.13) were exactly what they seem, that is to say they are miniature reproductions of sailing craft, sufficiently faithful to the originals but not aimed – unlike the Cypriot examples – to represent the proportion and all the technical equipment necessary for sailing, including human figures sitting at the stern holding the helm or on the bench at the middle of the hull. In general, the shapes are the flat-bottomed craft or the *"sutiles naves"* of the most archaic forms, the round elongated boats or the "racing" ships suitable for rapid journeys, especially if equipped with a mast, namely a support system on which to haul up a sail, and the shorter, deeper round boats, perhaps with cabin and double deck, or the commercial cargo ships.

Up to now, in the Nuragic Bronze Age no clay boats are known: this shape appears in the EIA as a late reproduction of an old meaningful symbol (Lo Schiavo 2000; 2002). It is not surprising that the Nuragic peoples at the apogee of their civilization should portray the ship, for the very reason that it is the symbol of their familiarity with the sea, together with the ownership of land and agricultural resources, as it is shown by the yoked oxen, dogs, pigs/wild boars, birds and miniature Nuragic towers represented on board.

It seems possible to discern a systematic difference in the original destination of the boats in comparison to the other bronze figurines, which may have had an influence on the subsequent ancient destinations in the Italian Peninsula: they were probably votive offerings, but not to the gods of the waters or to chthonic divinities. If the boats appear more frequently in the hoards it is on account of their intrinsic meaningfulness, because they signified power and wealth, superiority and prestige. Perhaps the sea enterprise could have at least reinforced, if not substituted, the sign (iconography) of power, and perhaps the ownership of the boat was something similar to a royal attribute.

In this way, the deposition in Orientalizing tombs, even many centuries later, would find a rational explanation: not of a simply old valuable item such as can be bought, even if at high price, through eastern traders, but an extremely precious heritage of a by-then extinct mythical people, and the Tyrrhenian peoples were their direct heirs, as much as the Phoenicians who settled on the island and revitalised it. Considering the far greater intrinsic value of the boats, in addition to their symbolic and "historical" significance, it

Figure 10.13 Nuragic bronze boat from Pipizu, Orroli (Nuoro).

does not seem inconvenient to have preserved them for many centuries after the period of manufacture, which was perhaps followed by reproductions in clay.

The 100 or so small reproductions of bronze boats, of various forms and dimensions, but all ending with an animal head at the prow, mostly found in Sardinia and in small numbers in Etruria and Latium as well, constitute incontrovertible evidence of how the Nuragic peoples, in reality or by way of symbol, had knowledge of the sea and of navigation.

CONCLUSION

This is the scenario into which the Phoenicians arrive and in a short time take hold of the southern trade routes from the Levantine coasts to the Atlantic, evidently following preceding maritime enterprises and, as far as Sardinia is concerned, prospecting all the island including the east coast, establishing a joint-venture trade in Sant'Imbenia, probably attracted by the rich Calabona copper mines (Giardino, Lo Schiavo 2007), but soon discovering the better option of the wine trade, in amphoras produced on the spot, shaped according to their Levantine models, foreign to Nuragic Sardinia, and (finally) settling in south-west "Shardana" land; it appears clearly that they were following a path known to them or/and familiar to their next of kin.

The coming of the age of Iron, as was said many years ago, is not only a chronological boundary, but an epochal change, due to strictly interconnected metallurgical, technological, economical and social changes. Things are not the same at the end of the Final Bronze Age in Sardinia, but the Nuragic Heritage had a fundamental role to play in Tyrrhenian Peninsular Italy, throughout the Iron Age and all through the Phoenician material and cultural influence.

BIBLIOGRAPHY

Bacco, G. and Santoni, V. (2008) "Il Bronzo Recente e Finale di Su Monte – Sorradile (Oristano)" in *La Civiltà nuragica. Nuove acquisizioni*, Atti del Convegno, Senorbì, 14–16 dic. 2000, II. a cura di P. Bernardini and G. Bacco: 543–656.

Basch, L. (1987) *Le musée imaginaire de la marine antique*, Athénes 1987.

Bass, G. F. (1967) *Cape Gelidonya: a Bronze Age Shipwreck*, Trans.Am.Phil.Soc. 58, Philadelphia.

Begemann, F., Schmitt-Strecker, S., Pernicka, E. and Lo Schiavo, F. (2001) "Chemical composition and lead isotopy of copper and bronze from Nuragic Sardinia," *European Journal of Archaeology*, 4, 1: 43–85.

Bettelli, M. (2002) *Italia Meridionale e Mondo Miceneo. Ricerche su dinamiche di acculturazione e aspetti archeologici, con particolare riferimento ai versanti adriatico e ionico della penisola italiana*. Firenze.

Burgess, C. and O'Connor, B. (2008) "Iberia, the Atlantic Bronze Age and the Mediterranean" in *Contacto cultural entre el Mediterráneo y el Atlántico (siglos XII–VIII ane): la precolonización a debate*, S. Celestino, N. Rafel and X. L. Armada (eds), Madrid: 41–58.

Cygielman, M. and Pagnini, L. (2002) "Presenze sarde a Vetulonia: alcune considerazioni" in *Etruria e Sardegna centro- settentrionale tra l'età del Bronzo Finale e l'Arcaismo*, Atti del XXI Convegno di Studi Etruschi ed Italici, (Sassari–Alghero-Oristano-Torralba, 13–17 Ottobre 1998) Pisa-Roma: 387–418.

Ferrarese Ceruti, M. L. (1991) "Creta e Sardegna in età postmicenea: una nota" in *Il passaggio dal Miceneo all'alto Arcaismo. Dal palazzo alla città*, Convegno Internazionale, Roma, 14–19 marzo 1988, Roma: 587–591.

Ferrarese Ceruti M. L., Vagnetti, L. and Lo Schiavo, F. (1987) "Minoici, Micenei e Ciprioti in Sardegna nella seconda metà del II millennio a.C." in *Nuragic Sardinia and the Mycenaean World*, SSA.III. BAR Intern.Series 387, Oxford: 7–37.

Giardino, C. and Lo Schiavo, F. (eds), (2007) *I ripostigli sardi algheresi della tarda età nuragica. Nuove ricerche archeometallurgiche*, Roma.

Gómez, Toscano F. and Fundoni, G. (2011) "Relaciones del Suroeste con el Mediterráneo en el Bronce Final (siglos XI–X a.C.). Huelva y la isla de Cerdeña," *Anales de Arqueología Cordobesa* 21/22, 2010 – 2011: 17–56.

Gonzàles de Canales Cerisola, F., Serrano Pinchardo, L. and Llompart Gòmez, J. (2004) *El Emporio Fenicio precolonial de Huelva, (ca. 900–770 a.C.)* Biblioteca Nueva, Madrid.

Jones, R. and Vagnetti, L. (1991) "Traders and Craftsmen in the Central Mediterranean: Archaeological Evidence and Archaeometric Research" in N. H. Gale (ed.) *Bronze Age Trade in the Mediterranean. Studies in Mediterranean Archaeology* 90: 127–147.

Karageorghis, V. (2011) "Handmade Burnished Ware in Cyprus and elsewhere in the eastern Mediterranean' and Appendix I–IV," in *On cooking pots, drinking cups, loomweights and ethnicity in Bronze Age Cyprus and neighbouring regions*, An International Archaeological Symposium held in Nicosia, November 6th–7th, 2010, Vassos Karageorghis and Ourania Kouka (eds), Nicosia 2011: 87–112.

Karageorghis, V. and Lo Schiavo, F. (1989) "A West Mediterranean Obelos from Amathus", *Rivista di Studi Fenici* 17, 1: 15–28.

Kassianidou, V. (2009) "Oxhide ingots in Cyprus" in F. Lo Schiavo, J. Muhly, R. Maddin and A. Giumlia-Mair (eds) *Oxhide Ingots in the Central Mediterranean*, Biblioteca di Antichità Cipriote, ICEVO-CNR, Roma: 41–81.

Leshtakov, K. (2007) "The Eastern Balkans in the Aegean Economic System during the LBA. Ox-Hide and Bun Ingots in Bulgarian Lands," in *Between the Aegean and Baltic Seas: Prehistory across Borders*, Proceedings of the International Conference, *Bronze and Early Iron Age Interconnections and Contemporary Developments between the Aegean and the Regions of the Balkan Peninsula, Central and Northern Europe*, University of Zagreb, 11–14 April 2005, edited by I. Galanaki, H. Tomas, Y. Galanakis and R. Laffineur, *Aegaeum* 27: 447–458.

Lo Schiavo, F. (1983) "Le componenti egea e cipriota nella metallurgia della tarda età del Bronzo in Italia," in *Magna Grecia e Mondo Miceneo*, Atti del XXII Convegno di Studi sulla Magna Grecia, (Taranto, 7–11 ottobre 1982) Napoli: 285–320.

——(1991) "La Sardaigne et ses Relations avec le Bronze Finale Atlantique" in *Le Bronze Atlantique*, Ier Colloque de Beynac, 10–14 Sept. 1990, Beynac-et-Cazenac, pp.213–226.

——Lo Schiavo, F. (2000) "Sea and Sardinia: Nuragic bronze boats'" in *Ancient Italy in its Mediterranean Setting*, Studies in honour of Ellen Macnamara, D. Ridgway, F. R. Serra Ridgway, M. Pearce, E. Herring, R. D. Whitehouse and J. B. Wilkins (eds), Accordia 4, London: 141–158.

——Lo Schiavo, F. (2001) "Late Cypriot bronzework and bronzeworkers in Sardinia, Italy and elsewhere in the West" in *Italy and Cyprus in Antiquity*. New York, Italian Academy, Columbia University, November 16–18, 2000, L. Bonfante and V. Karageorghis (eds), Nicosia 2001: 131–152.

——Lo Schiavo, F. (2002) "Osservazioni sul problema dei rapporti fra Etruria e Sardegna in età nuragica – II" in *Etruria e Sardegna centro-settentrionale tra l'età del Bronzo Finale e l'Arcaismo*, Atti del XXI Convegno di Studi Etruschi ed Italici, Sassari – Alghero – Oristano – Torralba, 12–17 ottobre 1998, Pisa-Roma, a cura di O. Paoletti: 51–69.

——Lo Schiavo, F. (2003a) Sardinia between East and West: Interconnections in the Mediterranean, *PLOES. Sea Routes ... Interconnections in the Mediterranean, c.1600–600 BC.*, Proceedings of the International Symposium held in Rethymnon, Crete, Sept. 29 – Oct. 2, 2002, N. Ch. Stampolidis and V. Karageorghis (eds), Athens 2003: 15–34.

——Lo Schiavo, F. (2003b) "Sardinia between East and West: Interconnections in the Mediterranean," in *Sea Routes…From Sidon to Huelva. Interconnections in the Mediterranean, 1600–6th c. BC.*, N. Chr. Stampolidis (ed.), Museum of Cycladic Art, Athens 2003: 152–161.

——(2005) "Le brocchette askoidi nuragiche nel Mediterraneo all'alba della storia" in *Sicilia Archeologica* 103: 101–116.

——(2009) "The oxhide ingots in Nuragic Sardinia" in Lo Schiavo *et al.* (eds) (2009): 225–390.

——(2011) "Gli Altri: Nuragici e Ciprioti a confronto" in *I Nuragici, i Fenici e gli Altri: Sardegna e Mediterraneo tra Bronzo Finale e Prima Età del Ferro*, Atti del I Congresso Internazionale in occasione del venticinquennale del Museo "Genna Maria" di Villanovaforru, 14–15 dicembre 2007, a cura di Paolo Bernardini e Mauro Perra, Sassari: 15–53.

Lo Schiavo F., Albanese Procelli R. M. and Giumlia-Mair A. (2009) "Oxhide ingots in Sicily" in Lo Schiavo *et al.* (eds), 2009: 135–221.

Lo Schiavo, F., Macnamara, E. and Vagnetti, L. (1985) "Late Cypriot Imports to Italy and their influence on local Bronzework," *Papers of the British School Rome* 53: 1–71.

Lo Schiavo, F., Muhly J., Maddin, R. and Giumlia-Mair, A. (eds) (2009) *Oxhide Ingots in the Central Mediterranean*, Biblioteca di Antichità Cipriote 8, ICEVO-CNR, Roma 2009.

Lo Schiavo, F. and D'Oriano, R. (1990) "La Sardegna sulle rotte dell'Occidente" in *La Magna Grecia e il lontano Occidente*, Atti del XXIX Convegno di Studi sulla Magna Grecia (Taranto, 6–11 ottobre 1989), Napoli: 99–161.

Manunza, M. R. (2008) "Gli strati nuragici" in *Funtana Coberta. Tempio nuragico a Ballao nel Gerrei*, a cura di M. R. Manunza, Ballao.

Martin de La Cruz, J. (1988) "Mykenische Keramik aus Bronzezeitlichen Siedlungsschichten von Montoro am Guadalquivir", *Madrider Mitteilungen* 29: 77–92.

Primas, M. (2005) "Ochsenhautbarren in Europa" in Ü. Yalçın, C. Pulak and R. Slotta (eds), *Das Schiff von Uluburun/The Ship from Uluburun, Welthandel vor 3000 Jahren/Global Trade 3000 years ago*, Deutsches Bergbau-Museum Bochum, vom 15. Juli 2005 bis 16. Juli 2006, Bochum: 385–392.

Primas, M. and Pernicka, E. (1998) Der Depotfund von Oberwilflingen. Neue Ergebnisse zur Zirkulation von Metallbarren, *Germania* 76: 25–65.

Rotea, M. (2004) "Non-Ferrous Metallurgy in Transylvania of Bronze Age," *Acta Musei Napocensis* 39–40/1, 2002–2003: 7–17.

Sanges, M. (2008) *La vite e il vino in Sardegna dalla preistoria alla fine del mondo antico*, in *Sardinia Insula Vini*, a cura di M. Sanges, G. Lovicu, Nuoro, pp. 7–23. Available at: <www.sardegnaagricoltura.it/documenti/14_43_20080505182810.pdf>.

Usai, A. (2010) "L'insediamento prenuragico e nuragico di Sa Osa-Cabras (OR). Topografia e considerazioni generali," in *L'insediamento di Sa Osa-Cabras (OR) sul fiume Tirso*, A. Usai (ed.), *Tharros Felix* 4, a cura di A. Mastino, P. G. Spanu, A. Usai and R. Zucca, Università degli Studi di Sassari: 157–319.

Vagnetti, L. (1982a) "Quindici anni di studi e ricerche sulle relazioni tra il mondo egeo e l'Italia protostorica," *Magna Grecia e mondo miceneo. Nuovi documenti*, XX Convegno di Studi sulla Magna Grecia (Taranto 1982), Napoli: 4–40.

Vagnetti, L. (ed.) (1982b) *Magna Grecia e mondo miceneo. Nuovi Documenti*. XXII Convegno di Studi sulla Magna Grecia (Taranto 1982), Taranto, Istituto per la Storia e l'Archeologia della Magna Grecia.

Vagnetti, L. (1989) "A Sardinian askos from Krete," *Annals of the British School at Athens* 84: 355–360.

——(1999a) "Mycenaeans and Cypriots in the Central Mediterranean before and after 1200 BC" in *The Point Iria Wreck: Interconnections in the Mediterranean ca. 1200 BC*. Proceedings of the Intern. Conference, W. W. Phelps, Y. Lolos and Y. Vichos (eds), Island of Spetses 1998, Athens: 187–208.

——(2000) *I Micenei fra Mediterraneo orientale e occidentale dopo la fine dei palazzi*, in *Magna Grecia e Oriente mediterraneo prima dell'età ellenistica*, Atti XXXIX Conv. Studi Magna Grecia, Taranto 1999, Napoli: 63–89.

——(2011a) "Le ceramiche egeo-micenee ed italo-micenee" in *Il nuraghe Antigori di Sarroch. Scavi M.L. Ferrarese Ceruti 1979–1986, preprint*, Usai A. (ed.), Cagliari: 23–25.

——(2011b) "Western Mediterranean," in *Oxford Handbook*, Chapter 66, Oxford (Chicago) 2011: 891–905.

Vagnetti, L., Levi, S. T. and Bettelli, M. (in preparation). *The Mycenaeans and Italy: The Archaeological and Archaeometric Ceramic Evidence.*

Vagnetti, L. and Jones, R. E. (1988) "Towards the Identification of Local Mycenaean Pottery in Italy," in *Problems in Greek Prehistory*, E. B. French and K. B. Wardle (eds), Bristol Classical Press, Bristol: 335–348.

Yalçin, Ü., Pulak, C. and Slotta, R. (eds) (2005) *Das Schiff von Uluburun/The Ship from Uluburun, Welthandel vor 3000 Jahren/Global Trade 3000 years ago*, Deutsches BergbauMuseum Bochum, vom 15. Juli 2005 bis 16. Juli 2006, Bochum.

CHAPTER ELEVEN

THE NURAGIC HERITAGE IN ETRURIA

——•◆•——

F. Lo Schiavo and M. Milletti

THE NURAGIC HERITAGE (F. LO SCHIAVO)

Inheritance is the practice of passing on property, titles, debts and obligations upon the death of an individual. It has long played an important role in human societies. (Online Dictionary, author's emphasis)

To begin with Latin, all Romance or Neo-Latin languages agree that the meaning of the word "inheritance," both in real and in symbolic terms, concerns the transmission of a property from a dead to a living person (Lo Schiavo, Milletti, Toms forthcoming). For some years now this idea has dominated the studies of the last phases of Bronze Age Nuragic Sardinia, in relation to the beginning of the Villanovan and Etruscan cultures. Peninsular Italy and particularly the Tyrrhenian regions of Central Italy receive the heritage of Nuragic Sardinia that, after an extraordinary development in the Middle, Recent and Final Bronze Age, is now no more the same but has deeply changed from the social, economic and political point of view, that is, in customs, ideology, way of life, seafaring and external connections.

It is not a question of "death" but of "resurrection": in the Early Iron Age, Sardinia is not empty and not in a period of decline; on the contrary, it is an extraordinary period of renewal, experimentation and varied application of many different influences that reach the island from the East (the Levantine peoples, from the late ninth century BC onwards, mainly represented by the Phoenicians) and from the West, since the western routes, opened as early as the eleventh century BC, are now flourishing in both directions (see Chapter 10). Later on, the Phoenicians will play an important role in the distribution of Sardinian products from the West to the South and to the East, widening and stabilizing a trade network already opened in the Bronze Age by the Cypriot–Nuragic connection.

THE COMING OF THE AGE OF IRON
(WERTIME AND MUHLY 1980)

The close of the Bronze Age marked the end of an era in which the alloying of copper and tin dominated trade and technology. The Bronze Age was succeeded by the Age of Iron, already known in the West but not familiar universally. While iron artefacts from Elba and metals from Campigliese and Monte Amiata had not escaped the attention of Bronze Age Nuragic Sardinians, there are no definitive traces of the systematic use of iron before the Iron Age. With the introduction of this new material, the Nuragic civilization ended without internal and external traumas and, as far as archaeological evidence can show, without war or slaughter. On the contrary, the descendants of the Nuragic people in the Final Bronze Age (FBA 2 and 3) must have opened the way to the search for and actively participated in the utilization of new resources, markets and trade partnerships.

The people of northern, central and southern Sardinia (Fig. 11.1) were exceptionally skilled in the complex techniques of mineral exploitation and metallurgy, expert in the

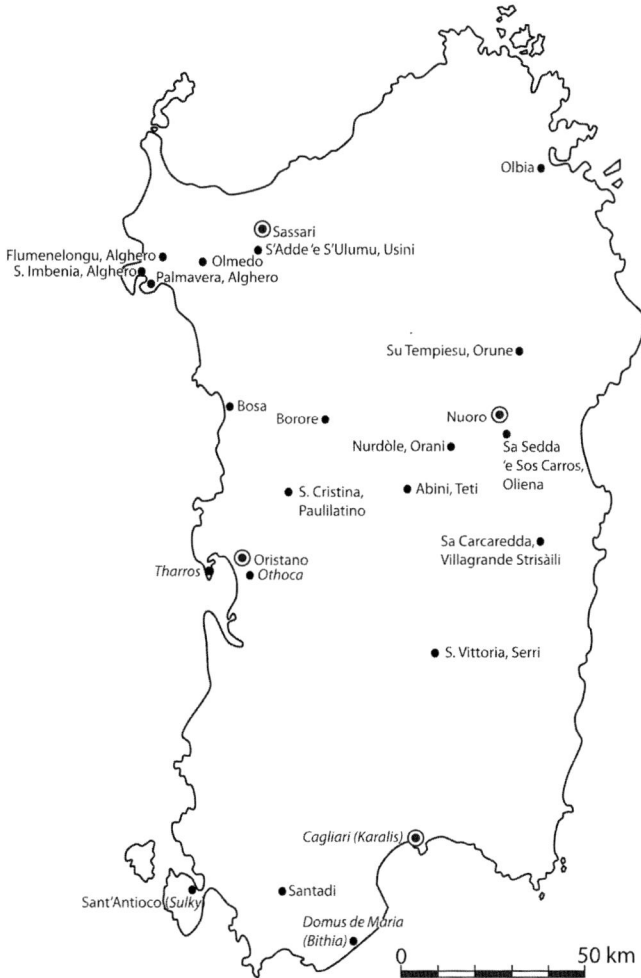

Figure 11.1   Map of Sardinia with the principal sites cited in the text.

Mediterranean sea routes, and experienced traders, with contacts in both the Near East and the Far West. In the very end of the Bronze Age and in the Early Iron Age, their life and destiny changed, stressing differences that could have been distinguished also in the previous period.

Northern Sardinians strengthened their relationship with the Tyrrhenian area, gravitating more and more towards the opposite shore and introducing ancient Sardinian customs to the local cultures of peninsular Italy. With this clear increase in contact between Sardinia and the mainland, the Tyrrhenian Sea became a stage for joint naval ventures. Trade and piracy were linked in written sources, evidenced by the interconnected genealogies, mythologies and common designations ("*Trsha*," "*Thyrsenoi*"?). Piracy and trade dominated the Tyrrhenian Sea until stronger land-based powers took the fore on both sides, and fought over the sea.

The Nuragic people living in the inland central Nuoro region ("*Barbaroi*," today "*Barbaricini*"), knew and participated in cultural developments throughout Sardinian prehistory and protohistory, such as changes in artefact form and rituals, and even acted as cultural intermediaries. Sanctuaries continued to be used for centuries, from the FBA 3/EIA 1 up to the Middle Ages, showing local reverence for early symbols and traditions (Sa Sedda'e Carros-Oliena, Nurdole-Orani, Sa Carcaredda-Villagrande Strisàili, S. Vittoria-Serri, etc.) This is confirmed by the letters of the pope Gregorius Magnus to the "Judge" ("*Giudice*") Ospito, in which he complains about the persistent adherence to the ancient cults.

At the end of the Bronze Age, the Nuragic peoples living in the south-west center of the island ("*Srdn*," "*Shardana*"?), having opened land and markets to the Levantines and later on Phoenicians, shifted materially and ideologically towards the newcomers settled on the coast. Later on, the foundation of the new cities: *Bosa*, *Tharros*, *Othoca*, *Sulki*, *Bithia* and *Karalis* brought a new way of life, with new ideology and rituals, developing to the adoption of Near-Eastern and Phoenician religion and deities. Past rituals were transformed, from the monumental collective Tomba dei Giganti ("Giant's tomb") and its later developments to individual pit and cist burials, often grouped in necropoleis, at first rarely and later more and more often enriched with personal grave goods. Pottery production for ritual purposes often imitates old Nuragic shapes, such as the elbow-handled jars, the askoid jugs, the carinated bowls, produced now in the new technique of wheel-thrown clay and sometimes covered with a new red lustrous paint, apparently influenced by the early Phoenician's pottery style. Traditional bronze weapons and ornaments, such as daggers and detachable-head bronze pins are now partially or entirely made in iron. The production of amulets, symbolically reproducing in miniature the Nuragic panoply (the so-called "little quivers," "*faretrine*" in Italian), long-handled traditional flanged axes, well-known pottery shapes such as "pilgrim's flasks" (the so-called "pendulum" pendants), and so on, increase.

In the Early Iron Age the Phoenicians followed the Mediterranean routes, where in the MBA 3/RBA Cypriot copper oxhide ingots circulated and, beyond, reached the far western regions of the Iberian peninsula, to the Atlantic coast. The Algherese area in the north-western region, among the most densely populated of Nuragic Sardinia, and with a multitude of bronze finds in the temples (Camposanto-Olmedo: Fig. 11.2) and the hoards (Flumenelongu-Alghero: Fig. 11.3; S. Imbenia 3-Alghero), shows evidence of this cultural integration. The focus shifted from the Nuragic villages such as Palmavera-Alghero

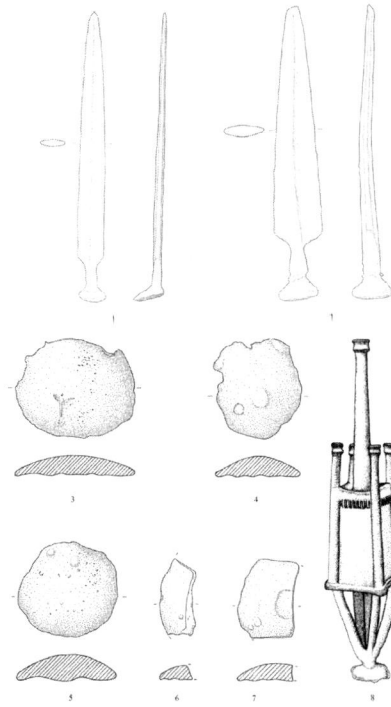

Figure 11.2   Località Camposanto-Olmedo, bronzes (Lo Schiavo forthcoming 2).

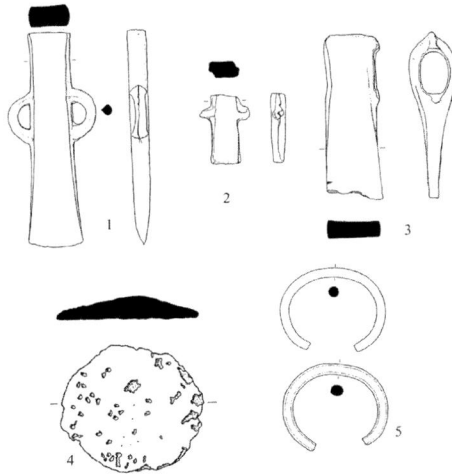

Figure 11.3   Nuraghe Flumenelongu-Alghero, hoard (Lo Schiavo 1976).

to the new Phoenician and "international" emporium in the formerly Nuragic village of S. Imbenia, a short distance away on the outskirts of Porto Conte bay. At S. Imbenia, two hoards of copper ingots were gathered up and buried in amphorae, one a local *"impasto"* reproduction, and the other a Phoenician manufacture. Metallurgical analysis showed that it came from the nearby deposits at Calabona (Giardino, Lo Schiavo eds 2007). The same shape of locally made S. Imbenia amphoras carrying wine have been traced from Sardinia to Tyrrhenian Italy and all over the Iberian peninsula to the Atlantic seaboard. The incentive for trade in the Bronze Age had been copper, but most evidently in the Iron Age trade was driven not so much by metal, but by wine (Lo Schiavo forthcoming).

THE NURAGIC HERITAGE

Focusing on materials produced in Nuragic Sardinia and found in Etruria, Umbria, *Latium Vetus*, "Villanovan Campania" and possibly elsewhere in southern Italy (Nuragic bronze boat from Capo Colonna in the Hera Lacinia sanctuary) and Sicily (askoid jugs from Dessueri and Motya), one must bear in mind three materially, culturally and chronologically distinct sequences of events (Fig. 11.4).

The first event is the original production in Sardinia of objects either for a precise destination or under a specific commission, which have a more or less long life.

The second is the "transport" of objects from Sardinia to the place of the discovery in peninsular Italy. This "movement" can imply a wide ranges of possibilities: either a family transmission by a wedding or by a father-to-son entrustment, or a second "commission" in a regular merchant trade, or a casual event such as sea piracy.

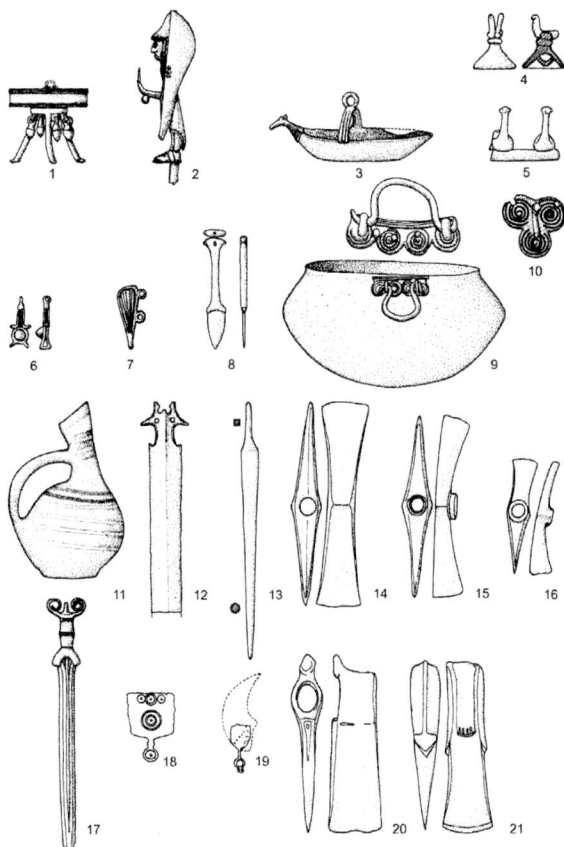

Figure 11.4 Principal categories of Nuragic bronzes imported into the peninsula (1–16) and of peninsular bronzes imported into Sardinia (17–21) (Lo Schiavo, Ridgway 1987).

The third and final event is the burial of objects, preceded by a more or less long "second" life, in some cases including breaking and restoration of the piece.

In this line of events, the problem is tracing down the actors and the dates that must be hypothesized from the beginning to the end, considering that often only the end can be dated (when the object is not derived from a private collection, lacking in data of provenance of any kind). That is why the discovery of Nuragic objects in Villanovan and Etruscan tombs led to the wrong conclusion of an indiscriminate EIA manufacture in the island, acquired at the moment by market trade as any other merchandise.

A totally different chain links up *the imitation* of Nuragic handiwork found in peninsular Italy, firstly, because its manufacture can have taken place either in Sardinia or in Etruria (as in the case of the Vetulonian askoid jugs) and secondly, because it is more difficult to determine the time needed from the making to the burial, when a new and highly debatable parameter is added, that is the time for the model to reach and penetrate a foreign environment, up to the point to determine a cultural rather than a material need (a material need can have been the craving for a new and renowned Sardinian wine, while the cultural need dictated the shape of the container and the placement in the grave).

It must never be forgotten that one of the strongest and most peculiar features of Nuragic Sardinia is the miniature reproduction of human beings, animals, monuments, weapons, tools, clay and wickerwork containers and other objects of ritual value. This means that reproducing and placing an object of a symbolic aspect not in a Nuragic sanctuary but in a tomb is far from a casual acquisition of an ornament in a marketplace, but implies a deep understanding of a common cultural basis, ascribing importance to images and subjects though in a deliberately smaller size (Lo Schiavo 2011).

The second sequence, as it is now demonstrated by new and exciting discoveries, not only happens between Sardinia and peninsular Italy, but also between Sardinia and the Iberian peninsula: see the fragments of a miniature bronze tripod-stand from La Clota-Teruel in Bajo Aragon, apparently made in the same region as the discovery (Rafel Fontanals 2002; Rafel *et al.* 2010), typologically identical to the miniature bronze tripod-stand from Pirosu-Su Benatzu cave in Santadi (Lilliu 1973; Usai, Lo Schiavo 1995); see also the "inverted-elbow" handle jar from *Sulki*-S. Antioco (Bartoloni 1989) and from La Rebanadilla-Malaga (Arancibia *et al.* 2011 Fig. 14), an EIA reproduction of a Nuragic FBA 2 shape (Campus, Leonelli 2006).

Evidently, from now onwards, the main target is to distinguish if the object is an *original* Nuragic Bronze Age product or if it is an *imitation*, and if it was made in Sardinia or elsewhere. The answer to this question opens a world of different cultural meaning. To this aim, the most thorough typological *and* analytical and technical studies are absolutely necessary and cannot at any cost be omitted, also taking under examination items that up to now were considered as secure.

THE NURAGIC HERITAGE IN ETRURIA (M. MILLETTI)

With few exceptions, such as the votive small bronze boat discovered in the sanctuary of Hera Lacinia at Crotone in Calabria (Spadea 1996), or the one found recently during the dredging of Lake Trasimene in Umbria (Marzatico *et al.* 2011), almost all of the Nuragic material found on the Italian peninsula comes from Etruscan territories, especially from the northern mining districts of Vetulonia and Populonia, in (modern) Tuscany (Bartoloni 1991, 2002; Lo Schiavo 1981, 2002; Milletti 2012), but with concentrations also reported in southern Etruria, at Tarquinia (Babbi 2002) and the Villanovan-Campanian site of Pontecagnano (Lo Schiavo 1994). There are both ornamental items (buttons, pins, Fig. 11.4, nos. 4, 13) or those with a strong symbolic value (pendants, small bronze boats, anthropomorphic figurines, Fig. 11.4, nos. 2, 3, 6, 7), and also weapons (daggers, swords, Fig. 11.4, nos. 8, 12), tools (axes, Fig. 11.4, nos. 14–16), ceramic vases (askoid jugs, Fig. 11.4, no. 11) and metal vessels (bowls, Fig. 11.4, nos. 9–10). A close partnership would thus seem to unite the people of Sardinia, and in particular, as mentioned above, those of the Alghero district with those of northern Etruria, and this special relationship surely must have been developed by sharing experiences and common interests in the exploitation of mineral resources, metallurgy and seafaring enterprises. The difficulties that the Greek and Levantine products meet during the Iron Age in their diffusion into northern Etruria (Botto 2007) may indicate an attempt by the Nuragic Sardinian people to maintain a non-exclusive but preferential channel of trade with this part of Etruria: the "conquest" of this market by Greek ceramics in fact coincides with the crisis in the system of Sardinian-northern Villanovan exchange, indicated by the gradual reduction in the number of materials that testify to the exchanges between the two areas since the second half of the eighth century BC. In contrast, in Sardinia there are reported, both in the north at Sant'Imbenia-Alghero, and in the south of the island at Sulky-Sant'Antioco (Rendeli 2005), some of the oldest ceramic Euboean imports known in the western Mediterranean (Ridgway 2006). These data confirm that the role of mediator was played by Nuragic Sardinians in limiting the spread of these products to the upper Tyrrhenian Sea, in an attempt to maintain direct control of the routes that connected the island with northern Etruria, passing along the coasts of Corsica, where, before the arrival of the Phoenicians at Aleria, one can detect the same lack of Greek and Levantine products (Milletti *et al*. forthcoming). Although the recent discoveries of Gallura in Olbia might suggest early attempts in the north of the island (D'Oriano 2010), the late-eighth century BC consolidation of the Phoenician settlement of Sardinia, with the deduction of the first "colonies" of the south, would then lead to the disruption of this system of relations. The acculturation of the Sardinian people occurred in a gradual manner and its timing varies from one area to another (Bernardini, Perra eds, 2011); it thus helps to open up to the Levantine peoples and Greeks the markets of northern Etruria, which still maintains a special relationship with the island, albeit through agents of different cultural backgrounds.

NURAGIC OR IMITATION NURAGIC MATERIALS IN ETRURIA: HISTORY AND DISTRIBUTION

Consolidation of relations between Sardinia and Etruria is already indicated at the end of the Bronze Age, but a significant increase in the exchange of materials would seem to indicate that the height of contact should be placed during the transition between Villanovan periods I and II. Most of the Nuragic products or those denoting distinctive style or that belong to the formal repertoire with a clear Sardinian imprint actually come from contexts dating from the late ninth and the first half of the eighth century BC, while the latest evidence are sporadic pieces limited almost exclusively to objects of the highest prestige, kept for their strong ideological value.

Among the earliest Nuragic bronze products to arrive on the peninsula are two double axes with converging edges found on the island of Elba and dated to the full Final Bronze Age (Carancini 1984). A similar history might apply to some large daggers with short tang or simple base, richly decorated with engraving (see Fig. 11.5, nos. 1–3) and reported mostly in Populonia and Vetulonia (Lo Schiavo 1981). The link of these weapons with the masculine world, as indicators related to gender and social prerogatives, is attested by their frequent offering in Nuragic temples and shrines/sanctuaries (?), where the daggers were deposited in large amounts, affixed in stone plaques specially prepared to hold dedicants' offerings or inserted between the stone blocks of the walls (Lo Schiavo 2003). We are dealing with objects of intense personal relevance and their arrival on the peninsula seems connected with the acceptance of individuals of Sardinian origin among the local population.

Prevalent, if not exclusively so, in northern Etruria are some of the most typical categories of small Nuragic bronzes such as pendants and "pilgrim flasks" (Fig. 11.6, nos. 1–3), a vase form of oriental style attested early in Sardinia (Lo Schiavo 2000), or the objects, on the other hand typically Sardinian, called "*faretrine*" ("small quivers," Fig. 11.6, nos. 4–7), not really reproductions of quivers for arrows, but rather representing an actual dagger sheath (Deriu 2009), preserving on one side a pocket where the weapon could be sheathed and on the opposite side usually one to three slots to accommodate the long, tough Nuragic pins probably used not only as ornaments, but also as daggers and throwing weapons (stilettos). A greater and more even distribution in Etruria seems instead to encompass other categories of bronzes, like the so-called "buttons," actually appliqués to be sewn onto clothing, often characterized by a finial that can be zoomorphic, with images of doves, oxen or mouflon (Fig. 11.7, nos. 1–6), and, more rarely, a stylized *nuraghe* or hunting scene (Fig. 11.7, nos. 7–10). Obvious stylistic differences are found between the *faretrine* and the buttons of peninsular origin and those discovered on the island, leading us to believe that some of the examples found in Etruria constitute local re-workings of more traditional, older Nuragic models (Milletti 2008), on the basis of

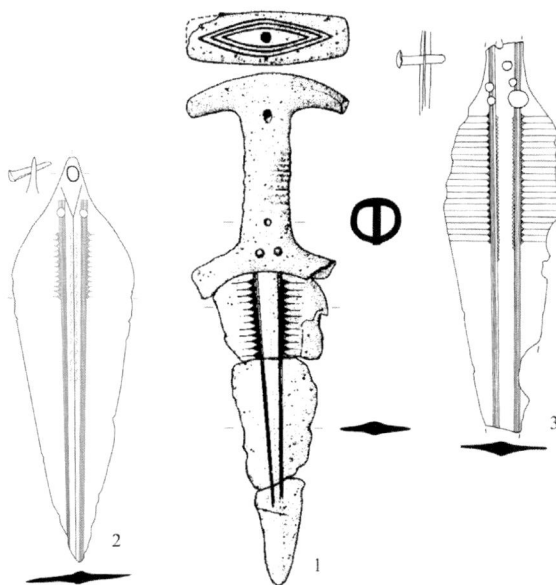

Figure 11.5   Nuragic daggers with short tangs from Sardinia: 1. Vetulonia, Colle Baroncio (Milletti 2012); 2. Duos Nuraghes, Borore (Lo Schiavo 1997); 3. Marcellano di Gualdo Cattaneo, Perugia (Bonomi Ponzi 1991).

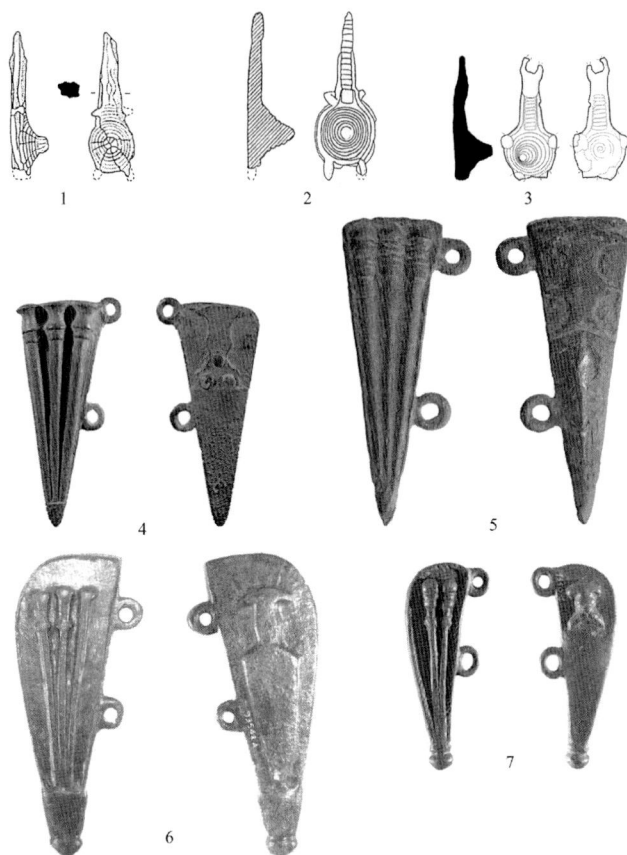

Figure 11.6 Nuragic pendants in the shape of a "pilgrim flask" and quiver: 1. Su Tempiesu-Orune (Fadda, Lo Schiavo 1992); 2. Vetulonia, Le Cortine (Lo Schiavo 2000); 3. Vetulonia (Milletti 2012); 4. Abini, Teti (Milletti 2012); 5. *Tharros* (Zucca 1987); 6. Località Caldana-Venturina, Populonia (Milletti 2012); 7. Etruria (Milletti 2012).

what has been found for the ceramic series of askoid jugs at Vetulonia, only few of which (Fig. 11.8), according to the mineralogical and petrographic analyses, were imports (Cygielman, Pagnini 2002); in Sardinia these vessels, starting from the full Final Bronze Age (Campus, Leonelli 2006), are widely used and it seems reasonable to assume that the Sardinian association is now the driving force for their diffusion in northern Etruria while askoid jugs are still rare in other Villanovan areas.

Some Nuragic bronzes are only sporadically attested in Etruria: the *tintinnabula* ("rattles") for example, in the form of a stool or anthropomorphic figurines, currently reported only in the famous tomb of the Cavalupo necropolis of Vulci (Fig. 11.9) and recently recognized as a multiple cremation (Arancio, Moretti Sgubini, Pellegrini 2010) called the "Tomb of the Sardinian Bronzes" because of the presence among the offerings of two of these objects and a miniature reproduction of a basket, also from the island. On the other hand, the hypothesis of intermarriage between the populations of Sardinia and the Italian peninsula seems corroborated by the presence of Nuragic objects in Etruscan burials, mostly female (Bartoloni 1997).

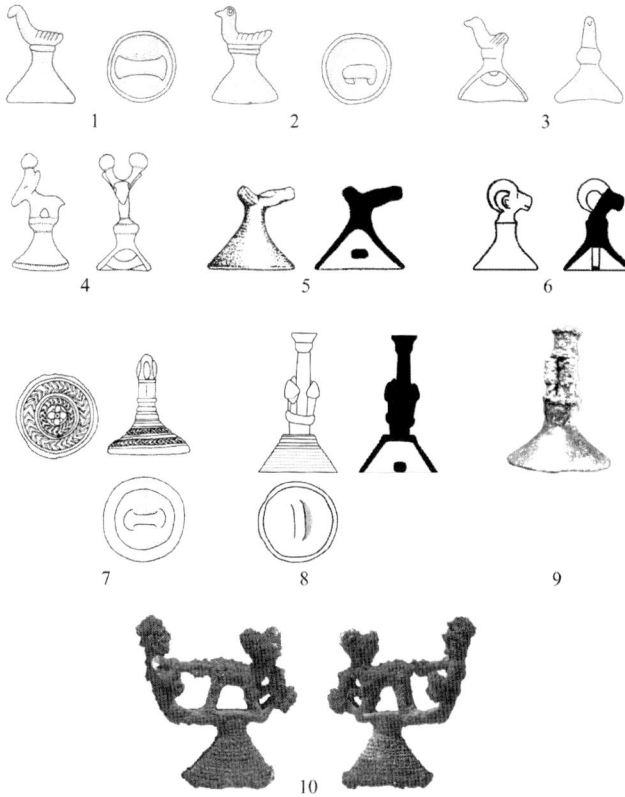

Figure 11.7   Nuragic buttons: 1. & 2. S. Vittoria di Serri (Lo Schiavo 1994); 3. Pontecagnano, tomb 2207 (Lo Schiavo 1994); 4. Pontecagnano, tomb 2198 (Lo Schiavo 1994); 5. Populonia, S. Cerbone, tomb 40 (Bartoloni 1991); 6. Populonia, Piano delle Granate, tomb 10/1915 (Bartoloni 1989); 7. Abini-Teti (Lo Schiavo 1994); 8. Vetulonia, Le Cortine (Milletti 2012); 9. Nuraghe Palmavera, Alghero (Moravetti 1992); 10. Nuraghe Cuccurada, Mogoro (Atzeni *et al.* 2005).

Figure 11.8   Vetulonia, grave goods from tomb 85/1897 of Poggio alla Guardia: Sardinian askoid jug, razor and armlet (photo Archivio SBAT).

A separate discussion is merited for some objects of prestige and strong ideological value, such as ship models and swords, found on the peninsula in tombs belonging to prominent individuals or offered in votive deposits. To the latter category belong the sword of Monte Sa Idda type and the small bronze boat from the hoard of Falda della Guardiola at Populonia (Lo Schiavo, Milletti 2011), in context deposited during the advanced third quarter of the eighth century BC, perhaps behind a city gate in the lower circuit of walls, variously attributed from the Archaic to Hellenistic period, but whose route may follow that of the oldest fortifications, as seen for example, at Veii (Boitani 2008). The hoard (Fig. 11.10), probably a foundation offering (Bartoloni 1991), also consists of five axes and a fibula now dispersed, but that probably fastened a fabric wrapped around the other objects. The offering of two Sardinian bronzes, kept for a long time before the deposition, part of this collective ritual, perhaps made by one or more prominent figures of the local community, indicates the high ideological value attributed to them in Etruria and, consequently, the strong interpenetration of the Villanovan and Sardinian cultures, with an implicit recognition of the importance of the latter in the formation process of the society of Populonia (Lo Schiavo, Milletti 2011). On the other hand, Nuragic ship models were found in the most important Vetulonian Orientalizing burials, up to three in the same tomb, as in the case of the Tomba delle Tre Navicelle ("Tomb of the Three Ship Models"). The case of the small bronze boat from the Tomba del Duce (Vetulonia) can be considered emblematic: the object, decorated with a rich and complex file of figurines on the sides, was selected and placed in the burial of one of the greatest personalities of the local environment of the seventh century BC. So even in the full Orientalizing period, very much alive in the memory of Etruria a lively season of contacts persisted with the Nuragic culture; reaffirming the ties with the latter would be an important factor in determining the status of a *princeps*.

Figure 11.9   Vulci, "Tomb of the Sardinian Bronzes" from the Cavalupo necropolis: Nuragic bronzes (Bartoloni, Pitzalis 2011).

Figure 11.10   Populonia, hoard of Falda della Guardiola (photo Archivio SBAT).

BIBLIOGRAPHY

Arancibia Román, A., Galindo San José, L., Juzgado Navarro, M., Dumas Peñuelas, M. and Sánchez Sánchez-Moreno, V. M. (2011) "Aportaciones de las últimas intervenciones a la arqueología fenicia de la Bahía de Málaga" in Manuel Álvarez Martí-Aguilar (ed.), *Fenicios en Tartesos: nuevas perspectivas*, BAR International Series 2245: 129–149.

Arancio, M. L., Moretti Sgubini, A. M. and Pellegrini, E. (2010) "Corredi funerari femminili di rango a Vulci nella prima età del Ferro: il caso della tomba dei Bronzetti sardi" in N. Negroni Catacchio (ed.), *L'alba dell'Etruria. Fenomeni di continuità e trasformazione nei secoli XII–VIII a.C. Ricerche e scavi*, Atti dell'IX Incontro di Studi di Preistoria e Protostoria in Etruria (Valentano-Pitigliano 2008), Milan: Onlus, 321–334.

Atzeni, E., Cicilloni, R., Ragucci, G. and Usai, E. (2005) "Un bronzetto con scena di caccia dal nuraghe Cuccurada-Mogoro (OR)" in P. Bernardini and R. Zucca (eds), *Il Mediterraneo di Herakles. Studi e ricerche*, Atti del Convegno di Studi (Oristano-Sassari, 26–28 March 2004), Pisa: Carocci, 223–231.

Babbi, A. (2002) "Appliques e pendenti nuragici della Raccolta Comunale di Tarquinia" in *Etruria e Sardegna centro- settentrionale tra l'età del bronzo Finale e l'arcaismo*, Atti del XXI Convegno di Studi Etruschi e Italici (Sassari, Alghero, Oristano, Torralba 1998), Pisa-Rome: Istituti Editoriali e Poligrafici Internazionali, 433–452.

Bartoloni, G. (1989) "Marriage, sale and gift. A proposito di alcuni corredi femminili delle necropoli populoniesi dell'Età del Ferro" in A. Rallo (ed.), *Le donne in Etruria*, Rome: "L'ERMA" di Bretschneider, 35–54.

——(1991) "Populonium Etruscorum quodam hoc tantum in litore," *Archeologia Classica*, XLIII: 1–37.

——(1997) "Bronzetti nuragici importati nell'Italia peninsulare" in A. Zanini (ed.), *Dal Bronzo al Ferro. Il II millennio a.C. nella Toscana centro occidentale*, catalogo della mostra (Livorno 1997), Pisa: Pacini editore, 27–31.

——(2002) "Strutture sociali e rituali funerari: il caso di Populonia" in *Etruria e Sardegna centro-settentrionale tra l'età del bronzo Finale e l'arcaismo*, Atti del XXI Convegno di Studi Etruschi e Italici (Sassari, Alghero, Oristano, Torralba 1998), Pisa-Rome: Istituti Editoriali e Poligrafici Internazionali, 343–362.

——(2003) *Le società dell'Italia primitiva. Lo studio delle necropoli e la nascita delle aristocrazie*, Rome: Carocci.

Bartoloni G. and Pitzalis F. (2011) "Mogli e madri nella nascente aristocrazia tirrenica" in V. Nizzo (ed.), *Dalla nascita alla morte: antropologia e archeologia a confronto*, Atti del I Congresso Internazionale di Studi Antropologia e Archeologia a confronto (Rome, 21 May 2010), Rome: ESS, 137–160.

Bartoloni, P. (1989) "Nuove testimonianze arcaiche da Sulcis," *Nuovo Bullettino Archeologico Sardo*, 2: 167–192.

Bernardini, P. and Perra, M. (eds) (2011) *I Nuragici, i Fenici e gli altri*, Atti del I Congresso Internazionale in occasione del venticinquennale del Museo "Genna Maria" di Villanovaforru (Villanovaforru 2007), Sassari: Carlo Delfino editore.

Boitani, F. (2008) "Nuove indagini sulle mura di Veio nei pressi della porta Nord-Ovest," with appendix of F. Biagi and S. Neri in *La città murata in Etruria*, Atti del XXV Convegno di Studi Etruschi e Italici, (Chianciano Terme, Sarteano, Chiusi 2005), Pisa-Rome: Istituti Editoriali e Poligrafici Internazionali, 135–143.

Bonomi, Ponzi L. (1991) "Materiali delle collezioni Bellucci e Guardabassi," in *Mevania. Da centro umbro a municipio romano*, catalogo della mostra (Bevagna 1991), Venice: Electa, 30–39.

Botto, M. (2007) "I rapporti fra la Sardegna e le coste medio-tirreniche nella Penisola italiana: la prima metà del I millennio a.C." in *Etruschi, Greci, Fenici e Cartaginesi nel Mediterraneo Centrale*, Atti del XIV Convegno Internazionale di Studi sulla Storia e l'Archeologia dell'Etruria, Rome: Quasar, 75–136.

Campus, F. and Leonelli, V. (2006) "La Sardegna nel mediterraneo fra l'età del Bronzo e l'età del Ferro. Proposta per una distinzione in fasi" in *Studi di Protostoria in onore di Renato Peroni*, Florence: All'Insegna del Giglio, 372–392.

Carancini, G. L. (1984), *Le asce nell'Italia continentale*, PBF IX.12, Munich: Beck'sche Verlagsbuchhandlung.

Cygielman, M. and Pagnini, L. (2002) "Presenze sarde a Vetulonia: alcune considerazioni" in *Etruria e Sardegna centro- settentrionale tra l'età del bronzo Finale e l'arcaismo*, Atti del XXI Convegno di Studi Etruschi e Italici (Sassari, Alghero, Oristano, Torralba 1998), Pisa-Rome: Istituti Editoriali e Poligrafici Internazionali, 387–410.

——(2006) *La tomba del Tridente a Vetulonia*, Pisa-Rome: Istituti Editoriali e Poligrafici Internazionali.

Deiru, L. (2009) "Le "faretrine" nuragiche. Contributo allo studio delle rotte fra Sardegna ed Etruria" in A. Mastino, P. G. Spanu and R. Zucca (eds), *Naves plenis velis euntes (Tharros Felix 3)*, Rome: Carocci, 136–177.

D'Oriano, R. (2010) "Fenici, Indigeni, Greci, Cartaginesi, Romani, Vandali. Stratificazione e interazione culturale ad Olbia (Sardegna) dall'VIII sec. a.C. al V d.C." Available at: <http: 151.12.58.75/archeologia/index.php?option=com_content&view=article&id=14&Itemid=14>.

Fadda, M. A. and Lo Schiavo, F. (1992) *Su Tempiesu di Orune. Fonte sacra nuragica*, (Quaderni della Soprintendenza ai Beni Archeologici per le province di Sassari e Nuoro 18), Ozieri: Il Torchietto.

Giardino, C. and Lo Schiavo, F. (eds) (2007) *I ripostigli sardi algheresi della tarda età nuragica. Nuove ricerche archeometallurgiche*, Rome: Bagatto.

Lilliu, G. (1973) "Tripode bronzeo di tradizione cipriota dalla grotta Pirosu-Su Benatzu di Santadi (Cagliari)" in *Estudios dedicados al Prof. Luis Pericot*, Barcelona: 283–307.

Lo Schiavo F. (1976), *Il ripostiglio del nuraghe Flumenelongu (Alghero-Sassari)*, (Quaderni della Soprintendenza ai Beni Archeologici per le Province di Sassari e Nuoro 2), Sassari: Il Torchietto.

——(1981) "Osservazioni sul problema dei rapporti fra Sardegna ed Etruria in età nuragica" in *L'Etruria mineraria*, Atti del XII Convegno di Studi Etruschi e Italici (Firenze, Piombino, Populonia 1979), Florence: Istituti Editoriali e Poligrafici Internazionali, 299–314.

——(1994) "Bronzi nuragici nelle tombe della prima età del Ferro di Pontecagnano" in *La presenza etrusca nella Campania meridionale*, Atti delle giornate di studio (Salerno, Pontecagnano 1990), Florence: Olshki, 61–82.

——(1997) "Borore (Nuoro). Località Duos Nuraghes. Bronzi nuragici. Notizia preliminare," *Bollettino d'Archeologia* 43–45: 240–242.

——(2000), "Forme di contenitori di bronzo e di ceramica: documenti ed ipotesi" in P. Bartoloni and L. Campanella (eds), *La ceramica fenicia in Sardegna. Dati, problematiche, confronti*, Atti del I Congresso Internazionale Sulcitano (Sant'Antioco 1997), Rome: Consiglio Nazionale delle Ricerche, 207–223.

——(2002) "Osservazione sul problema dei rapporti fra Sardegna ed Etruria-II" in *Etruria e Sardegna centro- settentrionale tra l'età del bronzo Finale e l'arcaismo*, Atti del XXI Convegno di Studi Etruschi e Italici (Sassari, Alghero, Oristano, Torralba 1998), Pisa-Rome: Istituti Editoriali e Poligrafici Internazionali, 51–70.

——(2003) "Uomini e Dei: ripostigli ed offerte nella Sardegna nuragica," *Rendiconti della Pontificia Accademia di Archeologia*, LXXV (2002–2003): 3–32.

——(2011) "Immagini e simboli di là dal mare" in S. Rafanelli, P. Spaziani and F. Colmayer (eds), *Navi di bronzo: dai Santuari nuragici ai Tumuli etruschi di Vetulonia*, Catalogo della Mostra (Vetulonia, 16 luglio–6 novembre 2001), Viterbo: 20–25.

——(forthcoming 1) "The Bronze Age in Sardinia" in Anthony Harding (ed.) *Oxford Handbook Oxford*. Oxford: Oxford University Press.

——(forthcoming 2) "Pezzi scelti e produzione destinata all'offerta nei ripostigli e nei santuari della Sardegna nuragica" in B. Toune (ed.), *Pezzi scelti. Distruzione e manipolazione di beni tra l'età del Bronzo e del Ferro: dal riciclo al sacrificio*, Atti del Convegno (Rome, 16–18 February 2012), Rome.

Lo Schiavo, F. and Milletti, M. (2011) "Una rilettura del ripostiglio di Falda della Guardiola (Populonia, LI)," *Archeologia Classica*, LXII: 309–355.

Lo Schiavo, F., Milletti, M. and Toms, J. (forthcoming) (2010) "Le tombe 33, 91, 99 e 202 della necropoli di Selciatello Sopra e l'eredità nuragica di Tarquinia" in M. D. Gentili (ed.), *Studi e ricerche a Tarquinia e in Etruria*, Simposio Internazionale in ricordo di Francesca Romana Serra Ridgway (Tarquinia 24–25 September 2010).

Lo Schiavo, F. and Ridgway, D. (1987) "La Sardegna e il Mediterraneo occidentale allo scorcio del II millennio" in *La Sardegna nel Mediterraneo tra secondo e primo millennio a.C.*, Atti del II Convegno di Studi *Un millennio di relazioni fra la Sardegna e i Paesi del Mediterraneo* (Selargius-Cagliari, 27–30 November 1986), Cagliari: Edizioni della Torre, 391–418.

Lo Schiavo, F. and Usai, L. (1995) "Testimonianze cultuali di età nuragica: La grotta Pirosu in località su Benatzu di Santadi" in *Carbonia e il Sulcis. Archeologia e territorio*, Carbonia: Editrice S'Alvure, 147–190.

Marzatico, F., Gebhart, R. and Gleischer, P. (eds) (2011) *Le grandi vie della Civiltà. Relazioni e scambi fra Mediteranneo e centro Europa dalla preistoria alla romanità*, catalogo della mostra (Trento, 2011), Trento: 411–412.

Milletti, M. (2008) "Riflessioni sul tema dei contatti tra la Sardegna e l'Etruria tra Bronzo Finale e prima età del Ferro" in F. Lo Schiavo, P. Falchi and M. Milletti (eds), *Gli Etruschi e la Sardegna. Tra la fine dell'età del Bronzo e gli inizi dell'età del Ferro*, catalogo della mostra (Sa Corona Arrubia 2008), Cagliari: Contemporanea Edizioni, 17–23.

——(2012) *Cimeli d'indentità. Tra Etruria e Sardegna durante la prima età del Ferro*, (*Officina Etruscologia* 6/2012), Rome: Officina Edizioni.

Milletti, M., Pêche Quilichini, K., Amici, S., Biancifiori, E., Mottolese, C., Palmieri, S., Palone, V., Sagripanti, L., Sartini, E. and Volpi, A. (forthcoming) "Cuciurpula, Serra-di-Scopamena/Sorbollano (Corse-du-Sud): nuovi dati su un insediamento protostorico corso (campagne 2008–2011)" in G. Facchin and M. Milletti (eds), *Materiali per Populonia 10*, Pisa: ETS.

Moravetti, A. (1992) *Il complesso nuragico di Palmavera*, Sassari: Carlo Delfino editore.

Rafel Fontanals, N. (2002) "Un tripode de tipo chipriota procedente de La Clota," (Calaceite, Teruel), *Complutum* 13: 77–83.

Rafel, N., Montero, I., Rovira, M. C. and Hunt, M. A. (2010) "Sobre el origen y la cronología del trípode de varillas de la Clota (Calaceite, Teruel): nuevos datos arqueométricos / On the origin and chronology of the rod tripod from la Clota (Calaceite, Teruel): new archaeometric data," *Archivo Español De Arqueología*, 83: 47–65.

Rendeli, M. (2005) "La Sardegna e gli Eubei" in P. Bernardini and R. Zucca (eds), *Il Mediterraneo di Herakles. Studi e ricerche*, Atti del Convegno di Studi, Pisa: 91–124.

Ridgway, D. (2006) "Early Greek Imports in Sardinia" in G. R. Tsetskhladze (ed.) (2006), *Greek colonisation. An account of Greek Colonies and Other Settlements Overseas*, Vol. 1, Leiden: Brill, 239–252.

Spadea, R. (1996a) "Il tesoro di Hera," *Bollettino d'Arte* 88 (1994): 1–34.

Wertime, T. A. and Muhly, J. D. (1980), *The Coming of the Age of Iron*, Yale: Yale University Press.

Zucca, R. (1987) "Bronzi nuragici da Tharros" in *La Sardegna nel Mediterraneo tra secondo e primo millennio a.C.*, Atti del II Convegno di Studi *Un millennio di relazioni fra la Sardegna e i Paesi del Mediterraneo* (Selargius-Cagliari, 27–30 November 1986), Cagliari: Edizioni della Torre: 117–132.

CHAPTER TWELVE

PHOENICIAN AND PUNIC SARDINIA
AND THE ETRUSCANS

—·◆·—

Rubens D'Oriano and Antonio Sanciu

PHOENICIAN SARDINIA AND THE ETRUSCANS
(RUBENS D'ORIANO)

The close relations that bound Sardinia and Etruria in Antiquity were motivated by important geographical and cultural factors that can be summarized as follows: the presence of important agro-pastoral and mineral resources in both areas; the vocation to maritime commerce of human groups who were the protagonists of these relationships; geographical proximity of the territories they inhabited, connected by short-distance maritime routes whether along coastal paths (from Sardinia to northern Etruria via the east coast of Corsica and the Tuscan Archipelago) or by deep sea (directly to the Etruscan coast of Italy opposite eastern Sardinia) (Fig. 12.1) known through archaeological and literary sources (speaking, for example, for an era that is indeterminable but certainly quite old, of the "pirates" operating between Sardinia and Pisa).

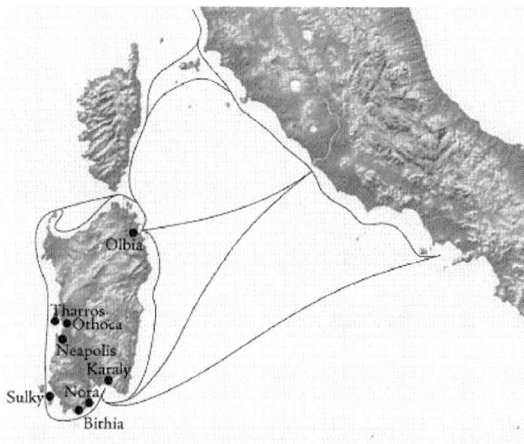

Figure 12.1   The sea routes between Sardinia and Central Italy and the main
Phoenician settlements on the island.

231

SARDINIA BEFORE THE PHOENICIANS

However, one cannot fully understand the reasons and dynamics of the relationship between the Phoenicians and the Etruscans of Sardinia without at least a brief description of the context of Mediterranean relations from which these relationships are derived, thus extending the boundaries of the chronological and geographical scene and presenting the appearance of additional representative actors, including especially the indigenous people of Sardinia.

Between the sixteenth and eleventh centuries BC the Nuragic civilization grows in the island and reaches its apogee, occupying the territory with at least 8,000 capillary *nuraghi* (megalithic towers from which the culture takes its name), including very large villages, often imposing shrines, large collective tombs, etc. in a sort of competition between communities which resulted in many cases in the erection of monuments that are unrivalled for grandeur in the contemporary western Euro-Mediterranean world (*nuraghi* with four or five towers and even up to 18 towers, some originally as high as 20 meters, Fig. 12.2) nor for refinement (sacred wells and sanctuaries in stone masonry cut with geometric precision). The development of metallurgy was extremely important, thanks to the significant local mineral resources and trade with other Mediterranean populations.

Towards the middle of the fourteenth century BC Nuragic Sardinia was itself the scene of an epochal cultural and historical change: the discovery of the island by the Mycenaean Greeks (Fig. 12.3) and thereafter the opening of the western half of the Mediterranean from Sicily to Iberia (known probably via Sardinia), with its lively world of various indigenous peoples already in contact with each other for the exchange of important resources, especially metals, which were the prime interest for the Mycenaeans. These were the first to acquire – and therefore to spread to both East and West – the notion of the complete development of the Mediterranean from its banks further east to the Atlantic. The Mycenaeans then put into communication, for the first time by direct and continuous communications, the two halves of the ancient world, while up until that time, exchanges had taken place only in brief sessions, and generally only between adjacent areas. From now on the relations between the peoples of the West will intensify, and begin the long process of direct communication between them and the shores of the Aegean as shown, for Sardinia, by Nuragic artifacts found in Crete and Cyprus.

Figure 12.2   The *nuraghe* Santu Antine of Torralba.

Figure 12.3   Mycenaean vase for perfume (alabaster) from *nuraghe* Arrubiu of Orroli (mid-fourteenth century BC).

THE PHOENICIANS IN SARDINIA AND IN THE WESTERN MEDITERRANEAN

After the collapse of the Mycenaean world, from the twelfth century BC the role of protagonists in the voyages from the East to the Western Mediterranean is inherited by the merchants settled between Cyprus (Fig. 12.4) and the opposite Syro-Palestinian coast, and by the mid-ninth century BC the Phoenicians begin to distinguish themselves and to prevail, especially the city of Tyre.

These eastern merchants, focusing on metallurgy, reach Nuragic Sardinia, which then is the main carrier on routes of commerce that connect the Iberian-Atlantic area and the Etruscan-Latial regions (Fig. 12.5). The island is such an important point-connection of these circuits with the traffic that reaches from the East. Its navy is first the precursor and then an important partner (perhaps initially functioning as a leader) of the Levantine merchants and then of the Phoenicians providing the knowledge and first access to the mineral resources of Iberia and of Etruria.

The success of this commerce induces the Phoenicians from the late ninth century BC to strengthen their presence in the West, whether through traditions of hospitality with indigenous communities, as in Huelva in Iberia and Sant'Imbenia at Alghero, Sardinia (Fig. 12.6), or with the establishment of their own autonomous settlements such as Carthage itself, to cite only the most famous case. This second mode of appropriation will soon become the most important and widespread, and throughout the eighth and seventh centuries BC, stable Phoenician settlements dot the shores of the Western Mediterranean from Sicily to the Atlantic via Sardinia, North Africa and Iberia (Fig. 12.7), weaving and consolidating over time a network, previously established (ninth-eighth century BC), of pan-Mediterranean enterprises, sometimes in partnership with the Greeks and the indigenous peoples of the West, including the Nuragic Sardinians, and then more and more independently. The main Phoenician centers are Tharros, Othoca (Santa Giusta), Neapolis, Sulky (Sant'Antioco), Nora, Bithia, Karaly (Cagliari), Olbia (Fig. 12.1).

Parallel to this was the projection of the Greeks to the west, perhaps initially with the Phoenicians thanks to the close relationship the two peoples entertained on the shores of the Aegean and Eastern Mediterranean. They then settled permanently from the third quarter of the eighth century BC in Southern Italy, therefore called Magna Graecia, and in central-eastern Sicily, weaving there too a global network of trade in ways similar to

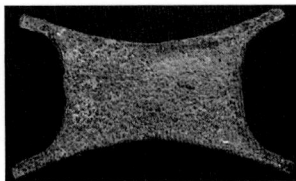

Figure 12.4   Cypriot copper ox-hide ingot from Ozieri (thirteenth-eleventh century BC).

Figure 12.5   Bronze sword imported from Etruria from the *nuraghe* Attentu of Ploaghe (eleventh century BC).

Figure 12.6   Nuragic amphora imitating Phoenician amphorae from Nuragic village of Sant'Imbenia at Alghero (end of ninth century BC).

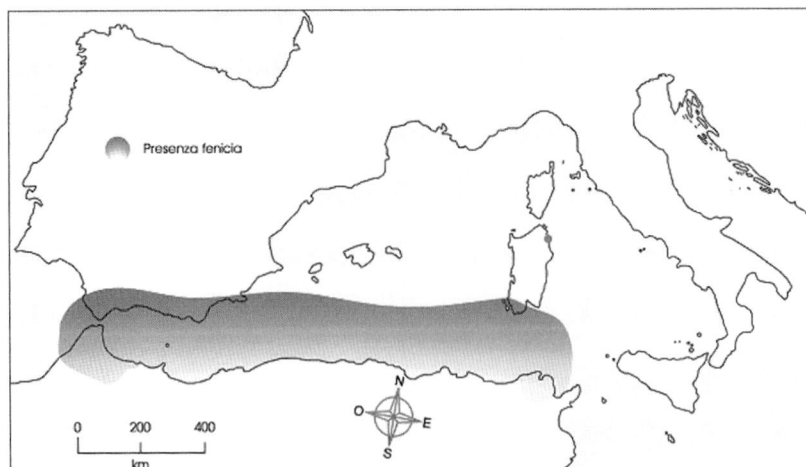

Figure 12.7   Area of Phoenician settlements in the Western Mediterranean in the mid-eighth century BC.

those adopted by the Phoenicians. It is certainly the case that simultaneously with the spread of these early models of urban life in the West, the same phenomenon begins in the Etruscan world, and in neighboring Latium with the birth of Rome itself. But not in Sardinia.

Between the eleventh and the eighth-seventh centuries BC, partially in parallel (eighth and seventh century BC) with the birth of the Phoenician centers on the coast of the island, Nuragic civilization undergoes one or more phases of massive change, on the nature of which – breakdown, change, reorganization, crisis and recovery, etc. as well as its history, methods, motives and outcomes – there is no consensus among scholars, especially because of the different dating, higher or lower, assigned to entire categories of objects essential to the chronologies of contexts, some of which (wine jugs and bronze figurines) are crucial for the study of relations with the Phoenician and Etruscan world. In any case at the end of this phase, between the eighth and seventh century BC, the Nuragic population, though of course far from disappearing, gradually abandoned the field of Mediterranean trade that for Sardinia is now firmly in the hands of the Phoenicians, albeit with the assistance of the Etruscans and Greeks especially in the seventh and sixth centuries BC.

THE PHOENICIANS OF SARDINIA AND THE ETRUSCANS

And so we come finally to the specific theme of this work, the relationship between the Phoenicians of Sardinia and the Etruscans. This is a very articulate argument for which the ever more abundant and sophisticated studies devoted to it have reached considerable depth, covering individual and highly detailed local issues to the overall very intricate Mediterranean scenario in which these relationships occur (a quasi-global world in the modern sense, in which roughly "anyone can sell anything, anywhere"). Because it is not feasible to give here an account of the full scope of this complexity, and the abundance and diversity of findings that describe it, we will proceed by summarizing the key issues especially about the ebb and flow of trade and its cultural implications.

From Phoenician Sardinia between the eighth and sixth centuries BC, products enter Etruria both from the island and from the Phoenician colonial world of the West and the East from the motherland. It is important to emphasize that among them there are also some objects of artistic production of the most refined workmanship, executed in materials of great value, such as ivory and precious metals, which have played a part in shaping not only the language of Etruscan art but also the ideological forms of display of the power of the *principes* ("princes") of Etruria. It should, however, be considered that goods from the Phoenician motherland and the western Phoenician colonial world could arrive in Etruria from circuits that do not involve Sardinia, i.e. directly from the production areas and /or other regions, that are not even Phoenician, but which are also intermediary.

Conversely, Etruscan products from Etruria reached Sardinia and even the indigenous world, mainly through the predominantly Phoenician ports (Fig. 12.8), but there were also Greek goods, which, as we shall see, the island received directly from maritime circuits (Fig. 12.9) that did not necessarily involve Etruria. It is very likely that Sardinia has in turn carried these goods to the Phoenician world of Iberia and Carthage, for they were quite popular in those regions, where they also came from different trade routes that did not touch on the island. In essence what we know of this trade through archaeological

Figure 12.8   Etruscan jug (olpe) for wine, probably from Tharros (early sixth century BC).

Figure 12.9   Greek amphora with erotic scene imported into Tharros from Etruria (560–550 BC).

finds of high profile goods, especially items related to the banquet, and particularly for the consumption of wine (amphorae containing wine, and pottery, also metal vessels for preparation and drinking: Fig. 12.10), objects for personal care and ornaments (jewelry and perfumes: Fig. 12.11), and to a lesser degree offerings and various objects that allow the display of rank (bronze figurines, etc.). We are dealing with objects moving in aristocratic circles generally as gifts functioning to initiate the exchange of other goods between the human ethnic-cultural peer groups at the origin and destination of the goods (this included the indigenous elites of Sardinia) and these goods are often valuable indicators of the sharing, whether partial or deep-seated, of similar social values, such as public expression of rank at the banquet, funeral rites, etc.

We can ascertain from archaeological finds, however, only the tip of the iceberg; the massive component of trade was probably represented by goods of widespread and popular consumption (such as agro-pastoral and marine products, minerals, etc., And we are missing other perishable and valuable assets like textiles, spices, slaves, and so on. We know only in part the intangible yet vital components such as the sharing of information (geographical, historical, etc.), technology (naval, metallurgical, ceramics, etc.), world views, diplomatic agreements, myths, legends, etc., in short, culture in the broadest and most proper sense.

As for carriers of these exchanges, it is possible that before the massive explosion of Etruscan maritime commerce in the late seventh century, there was a clear preponderance of Phoenician activity, and later we have to imagine a shared venture with Etruscans though perhaps more in the scope of a Phoenician leadership. An important clue to this partnership, beyond the usual archaeological material, is a fragment of an Etruscan

Figure 12.10   Etruscan cup (kantharos) for drinking wine, from Tharros (early sixth century BC).

Figure 12.11   Etruscan container for scented ointments (aryballos), probably from Tharros
(first half of sixth century BC)

inscription on stone, discovered in 1891 in the city of Oristano that was in ancient times in the hinterland of the Phoenician city of Othoca and Tharros, and may be related to an unknown sanctuary.

However, there is an exception, an important element of interference in the picture now: the appropriation around 630 BC of the city of Olbia by the Greeks of Phokaia ("Olbía" in Greek); this became the only center of Hellenic Sardinia (Fig. 12.12). Olbia was originally a Phoenician settlement of the mid-eighth century BC, certainly important for trade with Etruria, as the only independent Phoenician center in the Tyrrhenian Sea north of Sicily, (i.e. not an enclave shared by other nations as in Greek Pithekoussai or Nuragic Sant'Imbenia). It strategically overlooked the coast of Italy. This was an ideal position to attract the attention of Phokaians as the first base for their insertion into the Western Mediterranean, an ideal starting point for the subsequent discovery and settlement of the Celtic world (Massalia, Marseille, was founded around 600 BC) and of Corsica (Alalíe, Aleria, founded around 565 BC). The Greek Olbia therefore must be considered as a third actor, along with Phoenicians and Etruscans, in the scenario of traffic in the central Tyrrhenian Sea, especially as regards the conveyance of Greek pottery to the island (Fig. 12.13), in addition to its arrival in Etruria from the Aegean centers of production.

The situation thus far summarized undergoes a sudden change from the second half of the sixth century BC when Carthage, now the most powerful Phoenician colony in the Western Mediterranean, first takes military action to gain control of Sardinia at the expense of the Phoenician cities of the island, and then concludes a military alliance with the Etruscan city of Caere in order to counteract the increasingly aggressive expansionism of the Phocaeans. Both operations are successful. With the naval battle that the Greek literary sources name for "the Sardinian Sea" ("Sardónion" = Sardinia) around 540 BC, the Etruscans and Carthaginians forced the Phokaians to abandon Alalíe and Corsica, which fall under the power of the Etruscans, and in subsequent years, the North African city gains control of the whole of Sardinia, including Olbia which the Greeks therefore

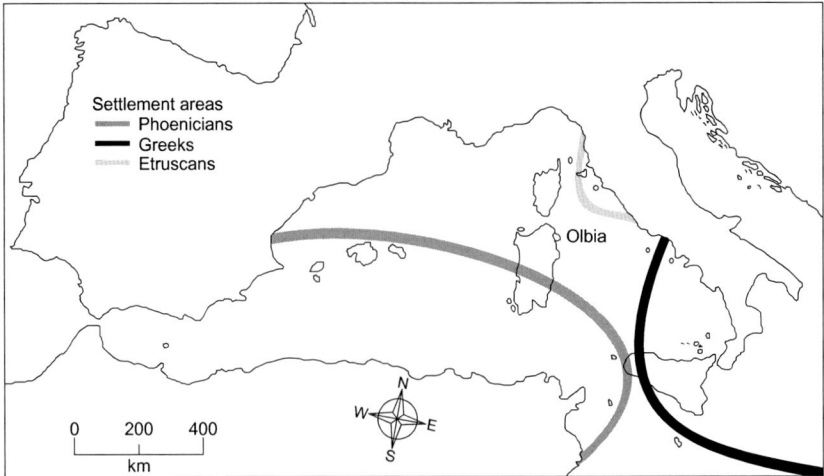

Figure 12.12   Olbia between the spheres of Phoenician, Greek and Etruscan settlement around 630 BC.

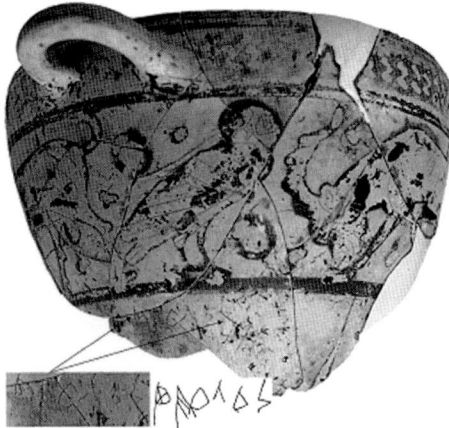

Figure 12.13   Greek cup (kotyle) for drinking wine, from Greek Olbia (about 600 BC).

abandon; Carthage does this as much to check the growing power of Rome, with a treaty signed in 509 BC permitting them to land freely on these shores. In this new definition of spheres of power, hitherto unknown in the Western Mediterranean for clarity and scope, the relationships between the Etruscans and Sardinia, which in time will become increasingly "Punic", will continue in ways and forms in part similar to the past and partly different, but certainly diminished in quantity.

PUNIC SARDINIA AND THE ETRUSCANS (ANTONIO SANCIU)

In the last decades of the sixth century BC Carthage took possession of Sardinia, occupying the Phoenician cities and, more generally, the coastal landing points. The conquest of the island, which corresponded to the entrance of Corsica into the sphere of influence of the Etruscans, completely changed the political and economic landscape in this part of the Mediterranean. In particular, Punic relationships with the opposite shore of the Tyrrhenian changed by immediately concluding a treaty with Rome dating from 509 BC, the text of which was handed down by Polybius (3.22). The date coincides with the fall of the monarchy and the birth of the republic in Rome and is just five years before the end of the domination of the Etruscans in Latium, with the defeat they suffered at Aricia at the hands of the Latins who were in alliance with the tyrant Aristodemus of Cumae. The treaty, signed with clauses giving conditions unfavorable to Rome, clearly stated in regard to Sardinia but also for Libya (i.e. North Africa), that the Romans were not allowed to carry on trade in the island except in the presence of officials in charge of Carthaginian commerce, in essence, customs officials tasked with charging a duty. Thus ended the autonomy of the Phoenician cities of the island which, previously, had managed their own trade with the Etruscan area and, generally, in the Mediterranean: thus, even in places that had not suffered destruction during the conquest by Carthage, because the Punic protectionist policy took effect during a crisis, in some cases even a severe one – with some exceptions like Tharros – it affected many of these settlements, at least for most of the fifth century BC. They gradually took back the urban dimension and prospered, precisely by means of Carthage, which brought into the network new centers for international trade activities, in particular, open to the markets of Athens, as in the case of Neapolis, in the Gulf of Oristano, which flourished perhaps to the detriment of the nearby town of Othoca. Despite the good business relations between Carthage and Etruria, especially with Caere, there was still, at this stage, a decrease in imports from the Etruscan world, whether into Africa, or to Sardinia.

Among the bronze artifacts introduced into the island from the Etruscan world, there are a few finds from the indigenous area, including the fragment of a handle with palmette-anchor ornament, from a wine pitcher (oinochoe of "*Schnabelkanne*" type), dated from the end of the sixth to the fifth century BC, found in the *nuraghe* of Adoni Villanova Tulo the small bronze lion (Fig. 12.14) of the end of the sixth century BC and the horizontal handle of a wine cup (kylix) dated between the mid-fifth and mid-fourth centuries BC, from the Nuragic sanctuary of Nurdòle in the countryside of Orani. From Tharros and Nora come, however, some plaques belonging to small caskets, made of ivory and bone and decorated with carvings depicting couchant rabbits and cattle, which are, in all likelihood, the productions of the region of Tarquinia; they must have reached the island by way of the African metropolis.

Figure 12.14   Small bronze lion from the Nuragic sanctuary of Nurdòle – Orani
(end of the sixth century BC).

With regard to ceramics, it is especially Nora that has furnished us with assorted evidence, also linked to the sphere of the symposium, among which are two wine-cups (kantharoi) in bucchero of the second half of the sixth century BC and, in gray bucchero, fragments of closed shapes, an oinochoe and a jug of the second half of the sixth century, and of a bowl of the end of the sixth century-first half of the fifth century BC. There is also evidence relating to trade and consumption of Etruscan wine on the island. The fragment of an amphora from Vulci of Py type 5, dated to the second half of the sixth century BC, was also found at Nora. Some Py 4 amphorae, dating from the mid-fifth to the mid-third century BC, were found in the waters of the east coast, particularly between the Ogliastra and Cagliari (Fig. 12.15): this is clearly a stretch of the route from Etruria, reaching Corsica and the re-born Etruscan center of Alalia (formerly the Greek "Alalíe") with the island of Elba as the bridge, then continuing along the Sardinian coast towards Carthage. Other finds of Etruscan amphorae of the same type are associated instead with the west coast and especially seem to concern the city of Neapolis.

The ancient sources are silent on Sardinia in the fifth century BC, while for the next century, Diodorus relates two incidents that could be linked. In 379 BC (or 387 BC) a revolt of Sardinians and Libyans broke out, and shortly after, in 378 or 377 BC (or 386 BC) (Diod. 15.27.4), the Romans attempted to establish their first colony outside the peninsula by sending 500 settlers to Sardinia. This information, which was previously questioned by some scholars, seems now to be accepted by most. A similar attempt would also have occurred, according to Theophrastus (*Historia Plantarum* 5.8. 2), in Corsica, but we do not have in this case a precise chronological reference-point for the event. The location of the Sardinian colony is unknown, but could reasonably be placed on the east coast, perhaps at Posada, where according to the coordinates provided by Ptolemy (*Geography* 3.3.4) there existed, in the second century AD, a center called *Pheronía polis*, which some experts correlate with the colony. The name brings to mind the *Lucus Feroniae* in

Figure 12.15 Etruscan wine amphora from the sea on the east coast of Sardinia (mid-fifth to mid-third century BC).

fact, the sanctuary, in the territory of Capena, of the goddess Feronia, associated with redemption from servitude and the right of asylum; it may imply the Sabellic origin and the servile status of the colonists; behind the initiative there had to be the pressure of the Roman *plebs* and its implementation was probably made possible by Caere, which may have supplied the Romans with the ships needed to implement the enterprise. Moreover, in this part of the east coast, there seems to be a strong Etruscan and Italic aspect, perhaps from the ethnic viewpoint, since, again according to the account of Ptolemy, it may have been established as the center of the population of Aesaronenses, whose name is certainly traceable to the Etruscan area, even if we do not actually know when they settled on the island. We are not aware of the duration of the foundation, or if the "Feronia" of Ptolemy is in fact related to it and not created after the Roman conquest of the island, but it is certain that Carthage had to quickly resume control of this part of the island. In fact, according to Polybius (3.24), in 348 BC Rome and Carthage concluded a new treaty under which the Romans were not allowed to carry on trade or to found any city in Libya and Sardinia, regions that are now all officially recognized. In these territories landing was only permitted in case of necessity and only for the time necessary to supply and repair and in any case, even in the event of storms, for not more than five days. Trade was, however, allowed in Sicily and in Carthage itself. From the moment that Libya is included, we do not know if the ban on founding cities in Sardinia can be related precisely to the previous Etruscan-Roman attempt at colonization; it is, however, certain that since the middle years of the fourth century BC, Carthage had proceeded to strengthen its control on the central north-east coast of Sardinia, undoubtedly as an anti-Roman maneuver, and in this light we should probably view the birth of the new city of Olbia. Similarly, the Punic presence should be considered also, attested since the second half of the fourth century BC, on the cliff of Posada, another focal point in the defense of a large tract of coastal land behind, perhaps not coincidentally, near, or perhaps the same place where the Romans had allegedly attempted the foundation of their first colony in Sardinia.

From this period, Sardinia, along with the rest of the Punic world, received massive imports of black gloss pottery from Attica with which, however, was associated black gloss pottery produced in Latium, among which vases from the *atelier des petites estampilles* were found especially in contexts dating from the second half of the fourth century BC. Attested, but to a lesser extent, are ceramics produced in southern Etruria which could be related to the trade in Etruscan wine which still persists in this phase. Among these products are included the Genucilia plates, made in Falerii and Caere; documented at Alalia in abundance, they were also found in various centers of Sardinia and, in particular, and perhaps not coincidentally, just down the east and southern coast at Olbia (Fig. 12.16), Sarcapos and Cagliari, where some of them have been identified to come from Caere. Tied to the same commercial circuit could also be a vessel for drinking wine (skyphos) at Olbia, of which is preserved a fragment of wall with decoration in superposed color, comparable with vases attributed to the "Group of Ferrara T 585," also well documented in Alalia, and a few other vessels, also dating from the late fourth and early third century BC, including a truncated biconical container for oil (askos) from the Funtana Noa necropolis of Olbia (Fig. 12.17), a cup of the Morel 2621 series from the necropolis of Tuvixeddu in Cagliari, and two oinochoai with bag-like mouth, one from Monte Sirai and the other from Tharros. With the Roman conquest of the island in 238 BC comes the definite end of any relationships, at least in Sardinia, between the Etruscan and Punic worlds.

Figure 12.16   Genucilia plate from Olbia (end of fourth-beginning of third century BC).

Figure 12.17   Vase for oil (askos) from Olbia (end of fourth-beginning of third century BC).

BIBLIOGRAPHY

Aubet, M. E. (1973–1974) "El origen de las placas en hueso de Nora" in *Studi Sardi*, 23: 125–130.

Bernardini, P. (2010) *Le torri, i metalli, il mare. Storie antiche di un'isola mediterranea*, Sassari: Carlo Delfino editore.

Bernardini, P., Spanu P. G. and Zucca, R. (eds) (2000) *La battaglia del Mare Sardonio. Studi e ricerche*, Cagliari-Oristano: La Memoria Storica-Mythos.

Bonamici, M. (2002) "Frammenti di ceramica etrusca dai nuovi scavi di Nora" in Paoletti, O. (ed.) *Etruria e Sardegna centro-settentrionale tra l'età del bronzo finale e l'arcaismo. Atti del XXI Convegno di Studi Etruschi ed Italici, Sassari, Alghero, Oristano, Torralba, 13–17 ottobre 1998*, Pisa-Rome: Istituti editoriali e poligrafici internazionali, 255–264.

Botto, M. (2007) "I rapporti tra la Sardegna e le coste medio-tirreniche della Penisola Italiana: la prima metà del I millennio a.C.," *Annali della Fondazione per il Museo Claudio Faina*, XIV: 75–136.

——(2011) "Interscambi e interazioni culturali fra Sardegna e Penisola Iberica durante i secoli iniziali del I millennio a.C." in Martí-Aguilar, M. A. (ed.), *Fenicios en Tartesos: nuevas perspectivas*, BAR International Series 2245, Oxford: Archeopress.

Celestino Perez, S., Rafale i Fontanals, N. and Armada Pita, X. L. (eds) (2008) *Contacto cultural entre el Mediterráneo y el Atlántico (siglos XII-VIII ANE). La precolonización a debate*, (Escuela Española de Historia y Arqueológia, Roma. Serie arqueológica, 11), Madrid: Consejo Superior de Investigaciones Científicas.

D'Oriano, R. (1985) "Contributo al problema di Feronìa polis" in *Nuovo Bullettino Archeologico Sardo*, II: 229–247.

D'Oriano, R. (2010) "Indigeni, Fenici e Greci a Olbia" in D'Oriano, R. (ed.) *Fenici, Indigeni, Greci, Cartaginesi, Romani, Vandali. Stratificazione e interazione culturale a Olbia (Sardegna) dall'VIII sec. a. C. al V d. C.: 12–25*, in Dalla Riva, M. and Di Giuseppe, H. (eds) *Meetings between Cultures in the Ancient Mediterranean. Proceedings of the 17th International Congress of Classical Archaeology, Rome 22 26 sept. 2008, Bollettino di Archeologia on line, I, Volume speciale A/ A4/3*. Available at: <http://151.12.58.75/archeologia/bao_document/articoli/3_D'Oriano_paperfinal.pdf>. (Last accessed 21 December 2011).

Garau, E. (2007) *Disegnare paesaggi della Sardegna*, Ortacesus: Nuove grafiche Puddu.

Madau, M. (1997) "Fenici e indigeni a Nurdole di Orani," in Bernardini, P., D'Oriano, R. and Spanu, P. G. (eds), *Phoinikes b Shrdn. I Fenici in Sardegna : nuove acquisizioni*, Cagliari: La Memoria Storica, 71–76.

Oggiano, I. (2002) "Nora: un'area sacra sul promontorio del Coltellazzo" in Paoletti, O. (ed.) *Etruria e Sardegna centro-settentrionale tra l'età del bronzo finale e l'arcaismo. Atti del XXI Convegno di Studi Etruschi ed Italici, Sassari, Alghero, Oristano, Torralba, 13–17 ottobre 1998*, Pisa-Rome: Istituti editoriali e poligrafici internazionali, 265–275.

Paoletti, O. (ed.) (2002) *Etruria e Sardegna centro-settentrionale tra l'Età del Bronzo Finale e l'Arcaismo. Atti del XXI Convegno di Studi Etruschi e Italici. Sassari-Alghero-Oristano-Torralba, 13–17 ottobre 1998*, Pisa-Rome: Istituti Editoriali e Poligrafici Internazionali.

Rendeli, M. (2009) "La ceramica greca ed etrusca" in Bonetto, J., Falezza, G. and Ghiotto, A. R. (eds), *Nora. Il foro romano, I Materiali preromani*, II, 1, Padova: Edizioni Quasar, 7–72.

Sanciu, A. (2000) "La ceramica a vernice nera," in Cavaliere, P., D'Oriano, R., Manconi, F. and Sanciu, A. – Wilkens B., *Olbia punica: intervento di scavo in via delle Terme, in Rivista di Studi Punici* I: 21–37.

——(2011) "Nuove testimonianze d'età punica da Posada e dalla Sardegna centro-orientale" in *Sardinia, Corsica et Baleares antiquae*, Pisa-Rome: Fabrizio Serra Editore, 9.

Sanges, M. (2002) "Materiali di provenienza tirrenica e nuragici di prima età del ferro dal Nuorese" in Paoletti, O. (ed.) *Etruria e Sardegna centro-settentrionale tra l'età del bronzo finale e l'arcaismo. Atti del XXI Convegno di Studi Etruschi ed Italici, Sassari, Alghero, Oristano, Torralba, 13–17 ottobre 1998*, Pisa-Rome: Istituti editoriali e poligrafici internazionali, 481–490.

Sanna, B. (2006) "Testimonianze fenicie, greche ed etrusche da Cornus" in Mastino, A., Spanu, P. G. and Zucca, R. (eds) *Tharros Felix* 2: 81–93.

Uberti, M. L. (1975) "Gli avori e gli ossi" in Acquaro, E., Moscati, S. and Uberti, M. L. (eds), *Anecdota Tharrhica*, Rome: C.N.R., 93–108.

Zucca R. (1984) "Tre piattelli di Genucilia dalla Sardegna" in *Annali della facoltà di Lettere e Filosofia dell'Università degli Studi di Perugia*, XXI, 7: 307–311.

Zucca R. and Ugas G. (1984) *Il commercio arcaico in Sardegna*, Cagliari: Angelo Viali Editore.

CHAPTER THIRTEEN

ETRURIA AND CORSICA

———•◆•———

Matteo Milletti

Corsica (Fig. 13.1), the fourth largest island in the Mediterranean after Sicily, neighboring Sardinia and Cyprus, is located a short distance from the coast of Etruria, so that it is directly visible from large parts of the northern Tyrrhenian coast. It is therefore natural that the island nations have had, since the early days, preferential relationships with the people of the territories of the future Etruria. However, the rough and mountainous center of Corsica has fostered a certain isolation of the interior from the south-western and eastern coastal regions, the latter, by contrast, fully integrated into the framework of Tyrrhenian trade routes, certainly to an extent greater than what can yet be perceived from the new study of island archaeology. This strong regionalism and the archaeological knowledge of the rather "disorganic" area are certainly at the basis of the significant uncertainties in the periodization of the Bronze and Iron Ages. In particular, the beginning of the latter is placed, depending on the area and the various opinions of scholars, between the late ninth and early seventh century BC; even the canonical subdivision of a First and Second Iron Age, to coincide with the arrival of Phocaean settlers at Aleria around the mid-sixth century BC, does not seem valid if extended to the rest of the island. This results in an objective difficulty in reconstructing a reliable picture of the Corsican civilization and of its contacts with other bordering areas, especially in the centuries between the second and first millennia BC; however, as we shall see, there is concrete evidence of the relationship and common interests which bound Corsica to the territories of the future Etruria, already in the full Bronze Age, and which serve as a prelude to the consolidation of contacts between the two areas that occurred in the following centuries. Corsica is also a meeting place between the main cultural *facies* of the peninsula and the Nuragic environment; on the other hand, some of the main routes linking Sardinia, a crucial junction of important seaborne Mediterranean trade routes, and the peninsula were to affect the coast of Corsica. The strait that separates the two islands could be crossed either at the *Fretum Gallicum* (today's Strait of Bonifacio), still considered dangerous, however, due to strong currents, or by drawing a route between a promontory of north-eastern Sardinia and south-east Corsica; it is logical to think that navigation would follow along the eastern coast of Corsica, with some provisioning stations located at the mouths

Figure 13.1   Map of Corsica with principal sites discussed in this Chapter.

of major rivers, which were to enable connection to the interior of the island, from that of Stabiacco in the Gulf of Porto-Vecchio, through the Solenzara, located slightly farther north, and the Tavignano, in communication with Aleria, up to the mouth of the Golo, the largest river of the island, just south of Bastia. The crossing of the Tyrrhenian should take advantage of the natural bridge formed from the archipelago of Tuscany, which is at least under the control of the emerging city of Populonia (Bartoloni 1991) since the late Bronze Age and the only Etruscan town built on the sea and overlooking the island of Elba, which is reached in a few hours by boat from Poggio del Telegrafo, along with the nearby site of Poggio del Castello, the location of the historic city.

THE CONTACTS OF CORSICA WITH THE PENINSULA AND WITH SARDINIA DURING THE BRONZE AGE

At the beginning of the Bronze Age, material culture, whether in the production of vases or bronze-working, already presents interesting analogies with that of the peninsular *facies* of *Lavagnone-Polada* and the Sardinian *Bonnanaro* (Camps 1979; Lanfranchi 1992; Lanfranchi Weiss 1997; Lanfranchi 2006; Melis 2007); however, it is in the following period that the relationship between island civilization and the surrounding areas seems to consolidate within a framework of shared cultural experiences.

During the Middle and Recent Bronze Age, ceramic development shows the existence of established relationships with the peninsula, and especially with some areas of the future northern Etruria. Local production, in fact, adopts some styles and vase forms and decorative motifs of *Protoappenninic* tradition, a cultural *facies* that characterizes, among others, some coastal areas of northern Tuscany and, to a lesser extent, was borrowed from the *facies* of peninsular *Grotta Nuova* (Camps 1979, 1988; Lanfranchi 1992; Atzeni, Depalmas 2006; Lorenzi 2007; Pêche-Quilichini 2012). The relations of southern Corsican ceramic production, and particularly of the *Apazzu-Castidetta-Cucuruzzu facies*, are yet to be deepened with that of northern Sardinia (Pêche-Quilichini 2010c). The affinity and contacts of the south of the island with neighboring Sardinia are indeed evident both in the articulation of social structures, and in similar architectural experiences, so as to suggest an original common cultural substratum. In this regard, the information handed down by Pliny (*NH* 3.7.85) is suggestive: he notes the presence in Gallura, during the Roman period, of the population of *Corsi* (Mastino, Spanu, Zucca 2005).

BETWEEN THE NINTH AND EIGHTH CENTURIES BC: THE STRENGTHENING OF CONTACTS WITH MIDDLE-TYRRHENIAN ETRURIA

On the threshold of the Iron Age (Lanfranchi, Weiss 1975; Lanfranchi, Weiss 1997; Cesari 2010), the view of the trade and relationships with the peninsula and in particular of Etruria's relations with Corsica, vital since the previous centuries, is well established in its essential features. By the end of the Bronze Age, Corsica had entered a period of profound economic and social restructuring, evidenced by a progressive failure of the settlement system of previous centuries, centered in the southern sector in the so-called *castelli* (Lanfranchi 2006), or fortified villages, often surrounded by Cyclopean walls. Located on hills and naturally protected granite *chaos* areas or on sites of low defensive potential but strategically positioned to exploit patterns of significant resources, these settlements are generally characterized by the presence, in a dominant position, of at least one tower (*torra*) and a monument, consisting of several buildings located close to the latter, while the rest of the village was spread over neighboring terraces, often extended or regularized by artificially imposing walls of the substructure, with housing units obtained by integrating the natural ledges of bedrock or by adapting caves and rock shelters for this purpose. To these settlements, some of which continue to be populated, it is appropriate to add new finds, such as Cuciurpula (Pêche-Quilichini 2010a, 2010b; Pêche-Quilichini *et al.* 2012; Milletti *et al.* 2011), Cozza Torta in the south (Milanini 2012), or E. Mizane in the north of the island (Antolini 2012), which are arranged along the main routes of transhumance and the routes linking the interior and the coast. The transition to a system of "scattered" settlements, with more widespread occupation of the territory, is paired with a definite openness to contacts with the future historical territories of Etruria. Contributing to the strengthening of ties between the two areas are common experiences related to metallurgy, in the context of a general movement of materials and ideas involving the large islands of Tyrrhenian and Middle-Tyrrhenian Etruria (Milletti 2012a). Although the Corsican bronze-working of the centuries around the turn of the first millennium BC is not comparable to that of the Nuragic culture or the territories of northern Etruria, whether in volume of production or for the originality of the models, nonetheless, the discovery of a number of molds for metal casting (Fig. 13.2) seems to

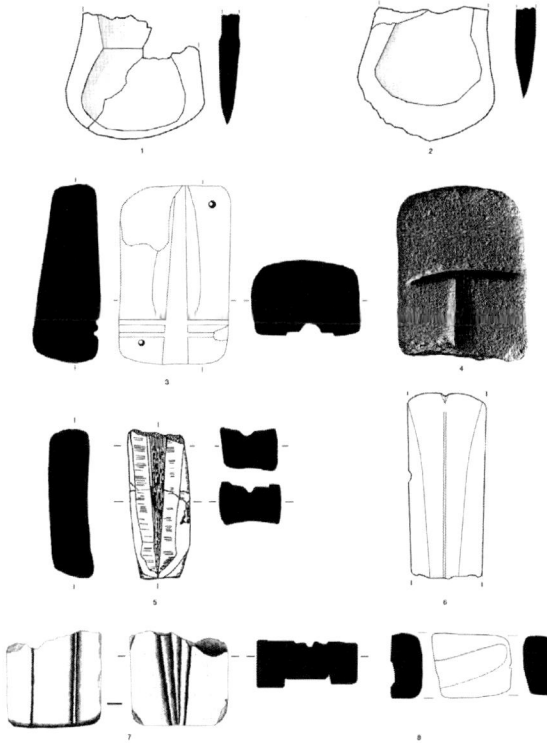

Figure 13.2 Molds for bronze casting: 1–2. Alò Bisucce (Lanfranchi 1992); 3. Mutola (Lanfranchi 1978); 4. Castidetta (Cesari, Nebbia 1996); 5. Castiglione (Cesari 1996); 6. Marze (Antolini 2008); 7. Punta Ficcaghjola (Pêche-Quilichini 2009); 8. Capula (Lanfranchi 1978).

indicate a certain vitality in local metallurgy (Pêche-Quilichini 2009; Milletti 2012b), with some island shapes that betray clear links with the mainland tradition, especially among the fibulae. Simply, the adoption of these into local costume shows the strength of the contacts with Middle-Tyrrhenian Etruria; in fact, these bronzes occur as the principal element in the offerings of Corsican burials of the First Iron Age, in contrast to what happens in nearby Sardinia, where fibulae, although attested since the Late Bronze Age, are not yet in evidence in the tombs and are only occasionally offered at sanctuaries. Among the various styles, in Corsica those "*ad arco serpeggiante*" ("with serpentine bow") predominate; certainly to be considered local productions are some large fibulae with multiple loops in the bow or with elbow bends (Lanfranchi, Weiss 1997; Milletti 2012b). The larger specimens can reach up to 20 cm in length and the section near the bow is decorated with a burin (Fig. 13.3 nos. 4–5). But there are also less frequent shapes with a bow of one or two loops (Fig. 13.3 nos. 1–3), characteristic of the northern sector of Etruria, imported and imitated not only in Corsica but also in Sardinia (Delpino, 1981, 1997). As for the other categories of bronze-work arriving on the island there are some peninsular axes, such as a winged example from Castifao, Corte (Fig. 13.4 no. 1), attributable to the Vetulonia type, and a socketed axe from *Maison Perragi*, Aleria-Corte (Fig. 13.4 no. 2), paralleled by the San Francesco type with broad shoulders (Carancini 1984). Both types are widely diffused in northern Etruria (Lo Schiavo, Milletti 2011).

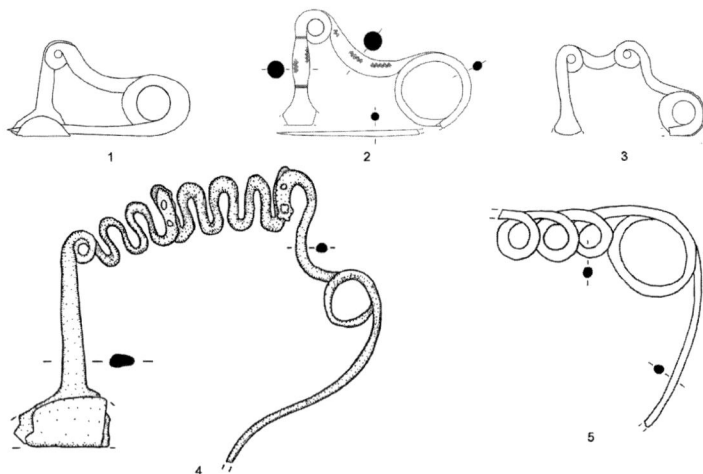

Figure 13.3 Fibulae *ad arco serpeggiante* ("with serpentine-bow"): 1–3. Corsica, provenance unknown (Delpino 1981); 4. "La Teppa" (Magdeleine, Milleliri, Ottaviani 2003); 5. "La Teppa" (Museo Archeologico, Florence).

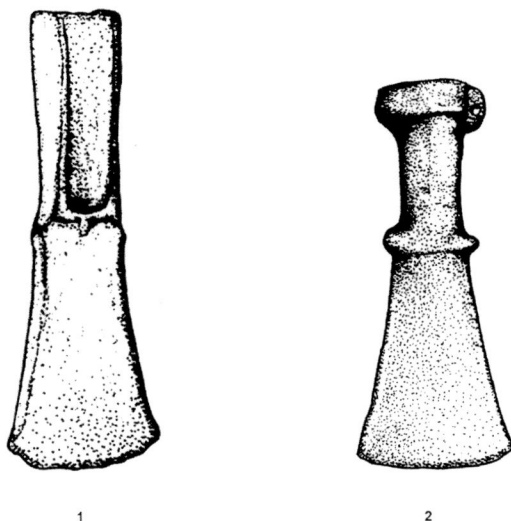

Figure 13.4 Peninsular axes: 1. Castifao-Corte; 2. *Maison Perragi* (Giardino 1995).

To date, there are no known imports of Corsican products of the ninth and eighth centuries BC in Etruria, but it is possible that archaeological research will soon fill this gap. More generally, there is a reflection of the contacts with the Nuragic and Corsican environment, in a framework of mutual influences that must have invested not only the handicrafts but also the sphere of customs and local behaviors. This has been hypothesized for some peculiarities of burial customs in the area of Populonia (Bartoloni 2002; Bartoloni 2003), such as the early appearance of the practice of inhumation, in some cases with collective ritual and burials deposited in natural cavities, as illustrated on the mainland in the shelter of Biserno, San Vincenzo-LI (Fedeli *et al.* 1989) and, more frequently, on the island of Elba (Zecchini 2001). In Corsica, in particular, the practice of inhumation with collective ritual is virtually exclusive until the height of the Archaic period and remains clearly predominant in the following centuries (Milanini 1996, 2006; David 2001; Milletti 2012a), with the sole exception, for historical reasons to which we will return later, of the area of Aleria. The Tuscan Archipelago therefore figures as one of the crucial hubs of the traffic between northern Etruria and the major islands of the Tyrrhenian Sea, and its early entry into the orbit of Populonia must have secured for this area the role of privileged intermediary, along with Vetulonia, in relations with Corsica and Sardinia, for the entire First Iron Age (Bartoloni 1991, Fedeli, Galiberti, Romualdi 1993; Bartoloni 2004; Acconcia, Milletti 2009; Acconcia, Milletti 2011; Bartoloni forthcoming).

CORSICA BETWEEN THE SEVENTH AND THE FIRST HALF OF THE SIXTH CENTURY BC: A PERIOD DIFFICULT TO READ

Serious gaps in the documentation prevent a reliable reading of the development of Corsican civilization in the centuries immediately preceding the arrival of Phocaean colonists in Aleria. What little information we have, however, allows us to hypothesize modalities of occupation of the land similar to those of previous centuries and to see clear evidence of continuity in relations with the mainland and especially with Etruria. Some collective tombs on the east coast of the island, such as those of Cagnano, Luri in Cap Corse (Chantre 1901; Romagnoli 1912), "La Teppa" of Lucciana, Vallecalle near present-day Bastia (Magdeleine, Milleliri, Ottaviani 2003), or dell'Ordinacciu, Solaro (Lanfranchi, Weiss 1975), just north of the river Solenzara, in fact, have produced, along with a mass of material dating from the mid-sixth century BC to at least the mid-third century BC, a fair number of the oldest imported bronzes, among which we note some fibulae (Jehasse 1987; Lechenault 2012) and other ornaments, which demonstrate that dialogue with Tyrrhenian Etruria never stopped and that, at the same time, there was a certain openness to contacts with central-European areas (Lechenault 2011). However, in large parts of the interior of the island, such as the Alta Rocca region in the southern portion of Corsica, we can detect the extreme scarcity of imported materials, and the apparent persistence of forms of settlement and land-use similar to those of previous centuries, which agree well with the local material culture, especially in the pottery, which is still tied to that of the Iron Age, with an apparently limited circulation of metals, and an especially flourishing lithic industry.

THE FOUNDATION OF ALERIA AND RELATIONS WITH ETRURIA FROM THE ARCHAIC PERIOD TO THE ROMAN CONQUEST (259 BC)

The situation changed substantially after the middle decades of the sixth century BC, when, according to literary sources (Jehasse 2003), colonists from Phocaea, founded in 565 BC following an oracular response, the city of Aleria/Alalia (Herodotus 1.165) on the east coast of Corsica (Κύρνος), perhaps on an existing native settlement (Jehasse, Jehasse 1973; Gran-Aymerich, Jehasse 2006). The city's name is of uncertain etymology, if derived from the war cry αλαλή (Gras 1997, 2000), a hypothesis that now seems to find greater consensus, ἅλς from the Greek word "salt" (Jehasse 1962) or from a local word (Jehasse,

Boucher 1959). It is possible that this first settlement was a mere trading post, operated by Greek prospectors in collaboration with the local population; its geographical position, a short distance from the coast of Etruria and along one of the main routes of Tyrrhenian traffic, must have made Aleria an important crossroads of trade immediately, while the same location on a not very large (about 30 ha) but very high plateau, at the mouth of the Tavignano, one of the major rivers of the island and overlooking a large coastal lagoon, allowed, in addition to a smooth landing-place from the sea, the exploitation of the considerable resources of the hinterland (Cristofani 1993). The subsequent arrival of a new contingent of colonists, more substantial than the first, and who had been driven from their homeland by the Persian army of Harpagos (Herodotus 1.164), provoked the reaction of the Etruscans and Carthaginians, concerned over the consolidation of the Greek presence in the Middle and Upper Tyrrhenian. According to Herodotus, in fact, the newcomers, unlike the first group, in addition to founding sanctuaries, perhaps *Artemisia*, turned to piracy, in all likelihood attacking the Etruscan cities and those of Punic Sardinia. The high tension culminated in 540 BC, in the famous battle of the Sardinian Sea, which saw a league composed of the major Tyrrhenian Etruscan cities, Caere at its head, and the Carthaginians (Bernardini 2001), opposing the Phocaeans of Aleria. The latter became aware of the intention of the allies to attack and plunder their city, preferring to confront the enemy forces, which totaled 60 Carthaginian ships and as many Etruscan, in a pitched battle, which gathered, according to various hypotheses, off Olbia (Colonna 2000) or near the Tuscan coast (Gras 1972) or in front of *Pyrgi*, one of Caere's harbours (Jehasse, Jehasse 1973). The Phocaeans won the victory, thus defined as "Cadmean" (Colonna 1989), at a high price, losing 40 of the 60 ships with which, despite obviously being outnumbered, they fought against the allies, while the remaining ships were rendered unsound for war by the loss of their *rostra* (rams). The position of Aleria now became untenable and, therefore, the victorious Phocaeans sailed to the city and picked up their wives, children and everything else possible, then abandoned it and sailed to Rhegion, where parties would later leave to found Velia (Υέλη) near Poseidonia in Campania (Herodotus 1.166–167).

The Etruscans benefitted more from the departure of the Phocaeans; the Caeretans especially were able to take advantage of the victory to strengthen their trade and that of the growing power of Rome, but also the Populonians established a fruitful dialogue with the Etruscan center (Νίκαια?) that replaced the Phocaean colony (Diodorus 5.13.3–4). More generally, the occupation of Aleria and the expulsion of the Greeks allowed the Etruscans to control the Tyrrhenian Sea for about a century, until the blockade of Cumae in 474 BC, which caused the victorious intervention of the Syracusans and, subsequently, the incursions of the latter who, in 453–452 BC, reached Elba for the first time, occupying it and Corsica (Colonna 1981). The central role of Cerveteri in the affair of the Sardinian Sea is confirmed by the event of the stoning to death by Caeretans of the Phocaean prisoners from the battle (Gras 1984, 1985): the place where this sort of collective human sacrifice happened, perhaps near a major extra-urban road (Colonna 1963, 2000), became contaminated and "since then all the living things of Agylla, be they sheep, pack animals or men, who were passing near the place where lay the Phocaeans who had been stoned, became crippled, maimed or were paralyzed" (Herodotus 1.167.1). The Caeretans sent to Delphi to ask for the means of atonement, and received from the Pythia the order to offer sacrifices to the dead and hold gymnastic and equestrian games.

Unfortunately, archaeological research has not yet provided confirming evidence for the original Greek foundation of Aleria; to the subsequent Etruscan occupation there are attributed the remains of a circuit wall with bastions, discovered near the south-eastern boundary of the plateau and partially obliterated by the Roman amphitheater, and a nearby residential quarter but above are the traces, highlighted by aerial photographs, of a system of division of land, centered on an axis along which are arranged some intersections, which seem to presuppose a colonial occupation, not unlike the kind practiced by the Etruscans in other peripheral areas (Cristofani 1993; Jehasse, Jehasse 1997, 2001; Donati 2001; Gilotta 2001, Jehasse 2004; Gran-Aymerich, Jehasse 2006). The pre-Roman Aleria, however, is known primarily for the discovery of the necropolis of Casabianda (Jehasse, Jehasse 1973, 2001), located south of the plateau of the city, with a portion of the tombs which appear aligned along the axes set by the division of land established by the Etruscan occupation. The oldest burials date only to the late sixth or early fifth century BC and the necropolis appears to remain in uninterrupted use, at least until the mid-third century BC. The burials of Casabianda, whether for the tomb types, among which the chamber tombs with dromos and internal benches stand out, or for the funerary rituals, with the appearance of individual cremations, mark a decisive break with the island traditions, anchored in the rest of the island to the practice of collective burials in caves and rock shelters; this indicates a clear influence from Etruscan culture. In particular, choosing to emphasize, in many male burials, the connotation of the deceased as a warrior, and also in tombs with complex funerary offerings of vessels that recall, at the same time, the practice of the "Greek-style" symposium, fits perfectly with the character of Aleria as a center of the frontier, constantly exposed to serious threats, in sharp contrast with what is found, for example, in fifth-century BC Populonia, which in other respects denotes strong ties with the Corsican city (Romualdi 2001). There is a close correspondence, for example, between the imports of Attic pottery found in the necropoleis of the two centers (Martelli 1981; Romualdi 2001), but belonging to production workshops that are only sparsely represented in southern Etruria (Gilotta 2001; Romualdi 2004). This confirms the common business interests of Populonia and Aleria, and the full inclusion of the latter, situated along the main sea connection that led from the south of the peninsula to the centers of southern Gaul and Liguria, into the economic and cultural *koine* of the Upper- and Middle-Tyrrhenian metal-bearing district. From the second quarter of the fifth century BC, moreover, the ceramic vessels and the main bronze products found in the Casabianda necropolis, which remain at a high level even after the Syracusan raids of 453 and 384 BC, demonstrate the broad spectrum of the commercial relationships of Aleria, with an increased volume of trade with some port-centers of Campania, Gaul, Spain and – supposedly through the mediation of Populonia – with the Adriatic emporium of Spina, through which much of the pottery from Greece arrived in the Corsican center (Romualdi 2004). From the middle decades of the fourth century BC, however, the volume of imported Attic pottery to Aleria sees a drastic reduction in a meaningful analogy with what was observed in Populonia but, especially from the end of the century, imports from workshops of Latium and southern Etruria gain in quantity. As regards, for example, the Etruscan red-figure vases, the Caeretan component has a decided priority compared to other products attested in the Corsican center, that come from the Faliscan, Chiusine-Volterran, Tarquinian and Vulcian territories (Ambrosini 2007; see Chapter 52). This new orientation of the commercial interests of Aleria seems connected with the growing power of Rome, which would eventually be a driving force for the economy of the main centers of Latium and especially Cerveteri, bound to the *Urbs* by privileged agreements. The mining district built on the combination of Elba-Populonia, with the latter perhaps linked to Rome by treaties of privileged partnership as early as the late fourth century BC (Miletti, Pitzalis forthcoming), is still an important pole of attraction up to the first half of the third century BC and Aleria represents one of the main "gateways" of access to it. If, for example, it is likely through Populonia that black-gloss pottery arrives in Corsica from the *atelier des petites estampilles* Group (Romualdi 1992), we assume the reverse path for at least a substantial part of the Punic and Iberian pottery that occurs in significant analogy in the necropoleis of both Casabianda and Populonia. To the end of the fourth century BC are dated the oldest finds on the peninsula of *peignée*-type ceramics, a production run of vases, with a unique morphology mainly restricted to jugs and jars, identified by the treatment of the raw surfaces with an instrument like a comb, as well as by the use of asbestos as a degreaser in the production of the island (Jehasse 1973; Rizzitelli *et al.* 2003; Paolini-Saez 2012; Acconcia, Milletti 2011). Its distribution on the peninsula is interesting, in the present state of our knowledge, the Tyrrhenian district of Populonia, where a significant concentration of imitations is attested (Pallecchi 2001), and all the way to Pisa. On the contrary, as regards Corsican bronze production, we note the limited movement in Etruria of the types of objects more peculiar to the island's production, such as the so-called *plume* pendants (Fig. 13.5), with a few examples of fibulae of Corsican type (Fig. 13.6), similar in style to the Certosa type (Fig. 13.7) and confirmed in Corsica from at least the second quarter of the fifth until the end of the third century BC (Acconcia, Milletti 2011 with references). The gradual decay of Aleria during the second half of the third century BC, indicated by the low standard of material deposited in the tombs, is perhaps connected with the events related to the Roman conquest (259 BC) and the crisis of its main intermediary in Etruria, Populonia, that, starting from the second half of the third century BC, is experiencing a period of recession, from which, however, it will recover by the end of the century (Romualdi 1996).

Figure 13.5 Cagnano, pendant of *"plume"* type (Museo Archeologico, Florence).

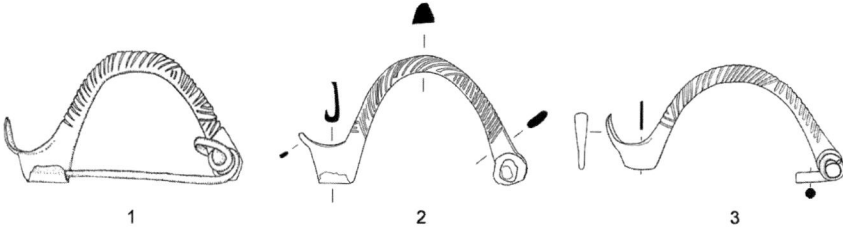

Figure 13.6   Fibulae of *Corsican* type: 1. Val di Cornia (Maggiani 1979); 2. Figa La Sarra, Olmeto (Cesari 2001); 3. Pinzu a Vergine, Barrettali (Museo Archeologico, Florence).

Figure 13.7   Cagnano, fibula of Certosa type with tweezers (Museo Archeologico, Florence).

In Corsica Aleria represents an exceptional rather than a paradigmatic case and it would be wrong to extend the considerations expressed above to the rest of the island. The impact of the Etruscan culture is evident only in the colony and neighboring areas, while elsewhere it is much less marked, although our limited knowledge of Archaic sites on the island (ceramic imports, transport amphorae and bucchero are reported for the village of Cozza Torta in the Gulf of Porto-Vecchio, Milanini 2012) do not allow us to make definitive judgments, but also in the region of Cap Corse, closer to the coast of Etruria, the offerings in collective burials show a clear preference, almost complete in the ceramic vases, less generalized in the sets of personal ornaments (Fig. 13.8), for objects of local tradition, though, since the mid-fifth century BC, there seems to be a gradual increase in the incidence of bronzes coming from Etruria and the Celtic areas of northern Italy. In contrast, in one of the main funerary contexts of the south of the island, the burial of Tappa 2, Porto-Vecchio, the pottery deposited is strictly local (Milanini *et al.* 2010) and the prevalence of island products among the Archaic and Classical materials is also found in other tombs of the southern sector, such as those of Nulachiu and San Ciprianu (Pasquet 1979). The local

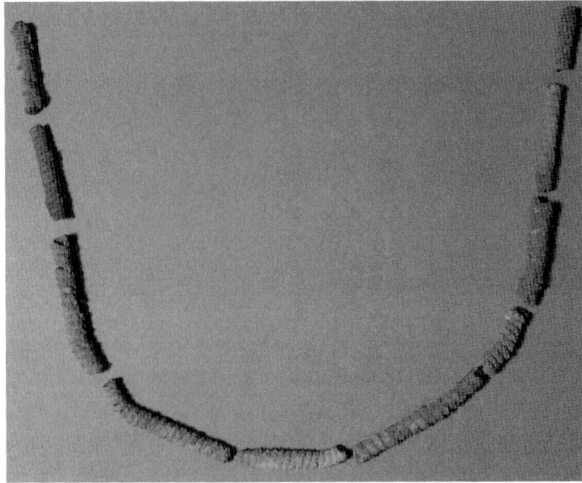

Figure 13.8 Grotta Alessandro, beads of spirally twisted wire (Museo Archeologico, Florence).

people, therefore, while remaining in continuous contact with the other bordering areas, remain strongly anchored in local traditions, even in the funeral ritual that, with certain exceptions, such as the individual cremation of San Simeone, Ajaccio (Doazan 1967), remains that of collective inhumation up to the period of full Hellenism. On the other hand, if Strabo, about two and a half centuries after the Roman conquest, defines the natives who inhabit the mountains as "wilder than the animals" (*Geography* 5.2.7), we hypothesize that the process of Romanization has concentrated primarily on the coastal ranges of the island, pivoting likewise on Aleria and, later, the colony of Mariana, located some tens of kilometers further north. In conclusion, the archaeological evidence in our possession, however flawed, permits us to perceive an uninterrupted common thread of contacts between Corsica and Etruria over the course of centuries, amassed by a dense network of common interests and by inclusion in the same policies of seaborne trade.

BIBLIOGRAPHY

Acconcia, V. and Milletti, M. (2009) "Pratiche metallurgiche e circolazione dei saperi all'origine di Populonia" in F. Cambi, F. Cavari and C. Mascione (eds), *Materiali da costruzione e produzione del ferro. Studi sull'economia populoniese fra periodo etrusco e romanizzazione*, Borgomanero, Edipuglia: 141–147.

Acconcia, V. and Milletti, M. (2011) "Populonia e la Corsica: alcune riflessioni" in G. Facchin and M. Milletti (eds), *Materiali per Populonia 10*, Pisa, ETS: 445–457.

Ambrosini, L. (2007) "La ceramica etrusca e falisca a figure rosse da Aléria" in *Etruschi, Greci, Fenici e Cartaginesi nel Mediterraneo centrale*, Annali per la Fondazione per il Museo Claudio Faina XIV, Roma, Quasar, 365–403.

Antolini, G. F. (2008) *Le Niolu préhistorique*, Ajaccio.

——(2012) "L'Âge du Fer dans le Niolu," in K. Pêche-Quilichini (ed.), *L'Âge du Fer en Corse: acquis et perspectives*, Actes de la table ronde de Serra-di-Scopamène (Serra-di-Scopamène 2009). Ajaccio, Associu Cuciurpula ed: 58–75.

Atzeni, E. and Depalmas, A. (2006) "I materiali appenninici di Filitosa" in *Materie prime e scambi nella preistoria italiana*, Atti della XXXIX Riunione Scientifica dell'Istituto Italiano di

Preistoria e Protostoria (Florence, 2004), Florence, Istituto Italiano di Preistoria e Protostoria: 1173–1184.

——(1991) "Populonium Etruscorum quodam hoc tantum in litore," *Archeologia Classica*, XLIII: 1–37.

——(2002) "Strutture sociali e rituali funerari: il caso di Populonia" in *Etruria e Sardegna centro-settentrionale tra l'età del bronzo Finale e l'arcaismo,* Atti del XXI Convegno di Studi Etruschi e Italici (Sassari-Alghero-Oristano-Torralba 1998), Pisa-Rome, Istituti Editoriali e Poligrafici Internazionali: 343–362.

——(2003) *Le società dell'Italia primitiva. Lo studio delle necropoli e la nascita delle aristocrazie,* Rome, Carocci.

——(2004) "Populonia: l'insediamento della prima età del Ferro," in M. L. Gualandi and C. Mascione (eds), *Materiali per Populonia 3*, Florence, All'Insegna del Giglio: 237–249.

——(forthcoming) "Populonia e le isole del Tirreno central tra VIII e VII secolo a.C." in *La Corse et Populonia/La Corsica e Populonia*, Atti del XXVIII Convegno di Studi Etruschi e Italici (Bastia-Aléria-Piombino-Populonia 2011), Pisa-Roma, Istituti Editoriali e Poligrafici Internazionali.

Bernardini, P. (2001) "La battaglia del Mare Sardo: una rilettura," *Rivista di Studi Fenici*, 29: 135–158.

Camps, G. (1979) "La préhistoire dans la région d'Aleria", *Archeologia Corsa*, 4: 5–21.

——(1988) *Préhistoire d'une île*, Paris, Editions Errance.

Carancini, G. L. (1984) *Le asce nell'Italia continentale*, (PBF IX.12), Munich, Beck'sche Verlagsbuchhandlung.

Cesari, J. (1996) "Castiglione, Grosseto-Prugna," *Gallia Informations*, 1996 (1994–1995): 16–17.

——(2001) "Le dolmen de Figa alla Sarra (Olmeto, *Corse-du-Sud*) dans son contexte archéologique" in *Architettura, arte e artigianato nel Mediterraneo dalla Preistoria all'Alto Medioevo*, Atti della tavola rotonda internazionale in memoria di Giovanni Tore (Cagliari 1999), Oristano, S'Alvure: 9–45.

Cesari, J. (ed.) (2010) *Corse Antique*, Paris, éditions du patrimoine.

Cesari, J. and Nebbia, P. (1996) "Castidetta-Pozzone," *Gallia Informations*, 1996 (1994–1995): 23–26.

Chantre, E. (1901) "La nécropole préhistorique de Cagnano, prés de Luri (Corse)" in Actes du Congrés de l'Association Française pour l'Avancement des Sciences, Ajaccio: 715–723.

Colonna, G. (1963) "Un nuovo santuario dell'agro ceretano," *Studi Etruschi*, XXXI: 135–147.

——(1981) "Presenza greca ed etrusco-meridionale nell'Etruria mineraria" in *L'Etruria mineraria*, Atti del XII Convegno di Studi Etruschi e Italici (Florence-Piombino-Populonia 1979), Florence, Leo Olschki Editore: 443–452.

——(1989) "Nuove prospettive sulla storia etrusca tra Alalia e Cuma" in Atti del Secondo Congresso Internazionale Etrusco (Florence 1985), Rome, Leo S. Olschki Editore: 361–374.

——(2000) "I *Tyrrhenói* e la battaglia del Mare Sardonio" in P. Bernardini, P. G. Spanu and R. Zucca (eds), Μαχη. *La battaglia del Mare Sardonio. Studi e ricerche,* Cinisello Balsamo, Edizioni La Memoria Storica-Mythos: 47–56.

Cristofani, M. (1993) "Il testo di Pech-Mao, Aleria e i traffici del V secolo a.C.," *Mélanges de l'Ecole française de Roma* 105: 833–845.

Cygielman, M., Lo Schiavo, F., Milletti, M. and Pagnini, L. (forthcoming), *Populonia e Vetulonia fra Corsica e Sardegna* in *La Corse et Populonia/La Corsica e Populonia*, Atti del XXVIII Convegno di Studi Etruschi e Italici (Bastia-Aléria-Piombino-Populonia 2011), Pisa-Rome, Istituti Editoriali e Poligrafici Internazionali.

David, H. (2001) *Paléoanthropologie et Pratiques Funéraires en Corse, du Mésolithique à l'âge du Fer*, (BAR IS 928), Oxford, Tempus Reparatum.

Delpino, F. (1981) "Aspetti e problemi della prima età del Ferro nell'Etruria settentrionale marittima" in *L'Etruria mineraria*, Atti del XII Convegno di Studi Etruschi e Italici (Florence-Piombino-Populonia 1979), Florence, Leo S. Olschki Editore: 265–298.

——(1997) "La metallurgia" in A. Zanini (ed.), *Dal Bronzo al Ferro. Il II millennio nella Toscana centro occidentale*, catalogo della mostra (Livorno 1998), Pisa, Pacini: 23–27.

Doazan, L. (1967) "Documents pré- et protohistoriques au portes d'Ajaccio", *Corse Historique*, 27–28: 5–30.

Donati, L. (2001) "Gli Etruschi in Corsica" in G. Camporeale (ed.), *Gli Etruschi fuori d'Etruria*, Verona, Arsenale Editrice: 274–279.

Di Fraia, T. and Grifoni Cremonesi R. (2007) "Rapporti fra Italia centrale, Corsica e Sardegna durante l'età dei metalli" in A. D'Anna, J. Cesari, L. Ogel and J. Vaquer (eds), *Corse et Sardaigne Préhistoriques. Relations et échanges dans le contexte méditerranéen*, Actes des congrés nationaux des sociétés historiques et scientifiques 128e (Bastia, 2003), Paris, CTHS: 265–274.

Fedeli, F., Galiberti, A., Pacciani, E. and Di Lernia, S. (1989) "Lo scavo del riparo Biserno (San Vincenzo, Livorno)," *Rassegna d'Archeologia*, VIII: 147–185.

Fedeli, F., Galiberti, A. and Romualdi, A. (1993) *Populonia e il suo territorio. Profilo storico- archeologico*, Florence, All'Insegna del Giglio.

Giardino, C. (1995) *Il Mediterraneo Occidentale fra il XIV ed VIII secolo a.C. Cerchie minerarie e metallurgiche*, (BAR IS 612), Oxford, Tempus Reparatum.

Gilotta, F. (2001) "Aleria" in A. Romualdi (ed.), *Le rotte nel Mar Tirreno: Populonia e l'emporio di Aleria in Corsica*, catalogo della mostra (Piombino 2001), Suvereto, Isografiche: 7–13.

Gran-Aymerich, J. and Jehasse, O. (2006) "Les îles du monde étrusque: le cas de la Corse et Alaliè", *Mediterranea*, 3: 141–171.

Gras, M. (1972) "À propos de la 'bataille d'Aléria'", *Latomus*, 32: 698–716.

——(1984) "Cité greque et lapidation" in *Du châtiment dans la cité. Supplices corporeis et peine de mort dans le monde antique*, Table ronde de Rome (Rome 1982), Rome, École française de Rome: 77–89.

——(1985) *Trafics tyrrhéniens archaïques*, (Bibliothèque des Ecoles françaises d'Athènes et de Rome 258), Rome, École française de Rome.

——(1997) "L'Occidente e i suoi conflitti" in S. Settis (ed.), *I Greci: storia, cultura, arte e società. 2. Una storia greca. II. Definizione*, Torino, Einaudi: 61–85.

——(2000) "La battaglia del Mare Sardonio" in P. Bernardini, P. G. Spanu, R. Zucca (eds), Μαχη. *La battaglia del Mare Sardonio. Studi e ricerche,* Cinisello Balsamo, Edizioni La Memoria Storica-Mythos: 37–46.

Jehasse, J. (1962) "La 'victoire à la cadméenne' d'Hérodote (I, 166) et la Corse dans les courants d'expansion grecque", *Revue des études anciennes*, 1962: 241–286.

——(1975) "La Céramique modelée d'Aleria Préromaine", *Etudes Corses*, XXX: 143–163.

Jehasse, J. and Boucher J. P. (1959) "La côte orientale corse et les relations commerciales en Méditerranée", *Revue des Etudes Corses*, 1959: 45–72.

Jehasse, J. and Jehasse, L. (1973) *La nécropole préromaine d'Aléria (1960–1968) avec une étude des graffites par Jacques Heurgon,* Gallia XXVe suppl., Paris.

——(1997) *Aleria rediviva. Aleria ressuscitée*, Ajaccio, La Marge édition.

——(2001) *Aléria. Nouvelles données de la nécropole*, Travaux de la Maison de l'Orient méditerranéen 34, Lyons, Maison de l'Orient méditerranéen.

——(2004) *Aleria métropole. Les remparts préromains et l'urbanisation romaine*, Ajaccio, Éd. du "Journal de la Corse."

Jehasse, O. (1987) "Nouveaux elements sur les fibules de Corse a propos d'une decouverte recente sur la commune d'Osani", *Archeologia Corsa*, 10–11 (1985–1986): 59–64.

——(2003), *Corsica Classica. La Corse dans le textes anciens. VIIᵉ siècle av. J.-C-an 1000*, Ajaccio, La Marge ed (ed. 1986¹, 1987²).

de Lanfranchi, F. (1978) *Capula. Quatre Millénaires de survivances et de traditions*, Bastia, Offset Imprimerie.

——(1992) "La Corse entre le XVI et le XIV siècle dans se rapports avec les faciès italiens", *Rassegna di Archeologia*, X (1991–1992): 581–591.

——(2006) *Le temps des tribus. Un autre approche de la protohistoire*, Bastia, Editions Anima Corsa.

de Lanfranchi, F. and Weiss, M. C. (1975) *La civilisation des Corses. Les peuplades de l'Age du Fer*, (*Numéro spécial du Bulletin de la Société des Sciences Historiques et Naturelles de la Corse*), Bastia.

de Lanfranchi, F. and Weiss, M. C (eds) (1997) *L'aventure humaine préhistorique en Corse*, Ajaccio, La Marge édition.

Lechenault, M. (2011) "L'età del Ferro in Corsica fra sviluppo endogeno e flussi mediterranei" in G. Facchin and M. Milletti (eds), *Materiali per Populonia 10*, Pisa, ETS: 367–376.

——(2012) "Les fibules de l'âge du Fer corse : aspects méthodologiques et état des recherches" in K. Pêche-Quilichini (ed.), *L'Âge du Fer en Corse: acquis et perspectives*, Actes de la table ronde de Serra-di-Scopamène (Serra-di-Scopamène 2009), Ajaccio, Associu Cuciurpula ed: 96–106.

Lorenzi, F. (2007) "La céramique apenninique en Corse," in A. D'Anna, J. Cesari, L. Ogel and J. Vaquer (eds), *Corse et Sardaigne Préhistoriques. Relations et échanges dans le contexte méditerranéen*, Actes des congrés nationaux des sociétés historiques et scientifiques 128e (Bastia, 2003), Paris, CTHS: 213–224.

Lo Schiavo, F. and Milletti, M. (2011) "Una rilettura del ripostiglio di Falda della Guardiola (Populonia, LI)," *Archeologia Classica*, LXII: 309–355.

Magdeleine, J., Milleliri, A. and Ottaviani, J. C. (2003) "La 'Teppa di Lucciana'. Nécropole protohistorique. Commune de Vallecalle (Haute-Corse)", *Bulletin de la Société des Sciences Historique et Naturelles de la Corse*, 702–703: 7–80.

Maggiani, A. (1979) "Urna cineraria con corredo dalla Val di Cornia. Contributo alla definizione del territorio volterrano in età ellenistica" in *Studi per Enrico Fiumi*, Florence, Pacini Editore: 99–108.

Mastino, A., Spanu, P. G. and Zucca, R. (2005) (eds) *Mare Sardum. Merci, mercati e scambi marittimi della Sardegna antica (Tharros Felix 1)*, Roma, Carocci.

Martelli, M. (1981) "Populonia: cultura locale e contatti con il mondo greco" in *L'Etruria mineraria*, Atti del XII Convegno di Studi Etruschi e Italici (Florence-Piombino-Populonia 1979), Florence, Leo Olschki Editore: 399–427.

Melis, P. (2007) "Una nuova sepoltura della cultura di Bonnanaro da Ittiri (prov. di Sassari, Sardegna) ed i rapporti fra la Sardegna settentrionale e la Corsica nell'antica età del Bronzo" in A. D'Anna, J. Cesari, L. Ogel, J. Vaquer (eds) (2003) *Corse et Sardaigne Préhistoriques. Relations et échanges dans le contexte méditerranéen*, Actes des congrés nationaux des sociétés historiques et scientifiques 128e (Bastia, 2003), Paris, CTHS: 275–286.

Milanini, J. (1998) "La sépulture à l'Age du Fer: acquis et problèmes" in *Bulletin de la Société des Sciences Historique et Naturelles de la Corse*, 682–683–684: 9–31.

——(2006) "Lieux et pratiques des cultes en Corse à l'âge du Fer", *Documents d'Archéologie Méridionale*, 27: 237–249.

Milanini, J. L. (2012) "Cozza Torta et la question du premier âge du Fer dans l'extrême sud de la Corse" in K. Pêche-Quilichini (ed.), *L'Âge du Fer en Corse: acquis et perspectives*, Actes de la table ronde de Serra-di-Scopamène (Serra-di-Scopamène 2009).

Milanini, J. L., David, H., Pasquet, A. and Tramoni, P. "La sépulture de l'âge du fer de Tappa, 2 (Porto-Vecchio, *Corse-du-Sud*)", *Documents d'Archéologie Méridionale*, 31: 131–151.

Milletti, M. (2012a) *Cimeli d'identità. Tra Etruria e Sardegna nella prima età del Ferro*, (*Officina Etruscologia 6/2012*), Roma, Officina Edizioni.

——(2012b) "Brevi note di metallurgia corsa", in K. Pêche-Quilichini (ed.), *L'Âge du Fer en Corse: acquis et perspectives*, Actes de la table ronde de Serra-di-Scopamène (Serra-di-Scopamène 2009), Ajaccio, Associu Cuciurpula ed: 87–95.

Milletti, M., Pêche-Quilichini, K., Amici, S., Biancifiori, E., Delvaux, S., Lachenal, T., Mottolese, C., Palmieri, S., Palone, V., Pretta, G., Py V., Sagripanti, L., Sartini, E. and Volpi, A. (2011) "Cuciurpula, Serra-di-Scopamena/Sorbollano (*Corse-du-Sud*): nuovi dati su un insediamento protostorico corso (campagne 2010–2011)" in G. Facchin and M. Milletti (eds), *Materiali per Populonia 10*, Pisa, ETS: 377–444.

Milletti, M. and Pitzalis, F. (forthcoming): "Populonia-Baratti (LI): sepolture alto-ellenistiche in località Casone" in *La Corse et Populonia/La Corsica e Populonia*, Atti del XXVIII Convegno di Studi Etruschi e Italici (Bastia-Aléria-Piombino-Populonia 2011), Pisa-Rome, Istituti Editoriali e Poligrafici Internazionali.

Pallecchi, P. (2001) "Indagini mineralogico-petrografiche sui boccali di tipologia corsa" in A. Romualdi (ed.), *Le rotte nel Mar Tirreno: Populonia e l'emporio di Aleria in Corsica*, catalogo della mostra (Piombino 2001), Suvereto, Isografiche: 22–23.

Paolini-Saez, H. (2012) "Les productions à pâtes amiantées à l'âge du Fer: origines et evolution," in K. Pêche-Quilichini (ed.), *L'Âge du Fer en Corse: acquis et perspectives*, Actes de la table ronde de Serra-di-Scopamène (Serra-di-Scopamène 2009), Ajaccio, Associu Cuciurpula ed: 76–86.

Pasquet, A. (1979) "Contribution a l'atlas préhistorique de la région de Porto Vecchio," *Archeologia Corsa*, 4:53–81.

Pêche-Quilichini, K. (2009) "Note sur un moule double découverte sur la Punta Ficcaghjola (Appietto/Alata, Corse-du-Sud)", *Bulletin Archéologique et d'Histoire de la Corse*, 3 (2005–2007): 31–41.

——(2010a) "Cuciurpula, un village de l'âge du Fer dans la montagne corse," *Archeologia*, 477: 16–27.

——(2010b) "Le vase de fondation zoomorphe du premier âge du Fer de Cuciurpula (Serra-di-Scopamène/Sorbollano, Corse-du-Sud)", *Bulletin de la Société Préhistorique Française*, 107: 371–381.

——(2010c) "La ceramica del Bronzo finale nel sud della Corsica (sec. XII–IX): la *facies* 'Apazzu-Castidetta-Cucuruzzu'" in N. Negroni Catacchio (ed.), *L'alba dell'Etruria. Fenomeni di trasformazione e di continuità nei secoli XII–VIII*, Atti del IX Incontro di studi del comitato "Preistoria e Protostoria dell'Etruria" (Valentano-Pitigliano, settembre 2008), Milan, Onlus: 573–592.

——(2012) "Révision chrono-culturelle des vaisselles de l'âge du Bronze de Filitosa-Turrichju (Sollacaro, Corse-du-Sud)", *Documents d'Archéologie Méridionale*, 32 (2009): 161–210.

Pêche-Quilichini, K., Bergerot, L., Lachenal, T., Martinetti, D., Py, V. and Regert, M. (2012) "Les fouilles de Cuciurpula: la structure 1" in K. Pêche-Quilichini (ed.), *L'Âge du Fer en Corse: acquis et perspectives*, Actes de la table ronde de Serra-di-Scopamène (Serra-di-Scopamène 2009), Ajaccio, Associu Cuciurpula ed: 35–57.

Rizzitelli, C., Costantini, A., Ghizzani, F. and Mileti, C. "La ceramica dei saggi I-II e IX" in C. Mascione and A. Patera (eds), *Materiali per Populonia 2*, Florence, All'Insegna del Giglio: 55–81.

Romagnoli, A. (1912) "Relation sur une découverte archéologique à Cagnano (Corse) de l'époque proto-historique (ver la fin de l'âge du Fer) en décembre 1900," *Bulletin de la Société des Sciences Historiques et Naturelles de la Corse*, 346–348: 323–328.

Romualdi, A. (1992) "La ceramica a vernice nera" in A. Romualdi (ed.), *Populonia in età ellenistica. I materiali dalle necropoli*, Atti del seminario (Florence 1986), Florence, Arti Grafiche "Il Torchio": 110–151.

——(1996) Voce "Populonia," *Enciclopedia dell'Arte Antica*, Roma, Treccani.

——(2001) "Populonia" in A. Romualdi (ed.), *Le rotte nel Mar Tirreno: Populonia e l'emporio di Aleria in Corsica*, catalogo della mostra (Piombino 2001) Suvereto, Isografiche: 14–17.

——(2004) "Riflessioni sul problema della presenza di Greci a Populonia" in *I Greci in Etruria*, Annali per la Fondazione per il Museo Claudio Faina XI, Roma, Quasar: 181–200.

Zecchini, M. (2001) *Isola d'Elba. Le origini*, Lucca, San Marco.

CHAPTER FOURTEEN

THE FALISCANS AND THE ETRUSCANS

———•◆•———

Maria Anna De Lucia Brolli and Jacopo Tabolli

FALISCAN CULTURE, EIGHTH CENTURY BC
TO ROMANIZATION

At the dawn of the unification of Italy, between the 1880s and 1890s, a large project for the Archaeological Map of Italy brought to the attention of scholars a particular region north of Rome, known from literary sources as the *Ager Faliscus* (Barnabei *et al.* 1894, Gamurrini *et al.* 1972; Cozza – Pasqui 1981) (Fig. 14.1). The Faliscans were a population of Italic origin, as evidenced by the language commonly spoken and documented by numerous inscriptions, the oldest of which date from the seventh century BC. The inscriptions may be traced back to a common Latin origin (Deecke 1888, Giacomelli 1963, Bakkum 2009).

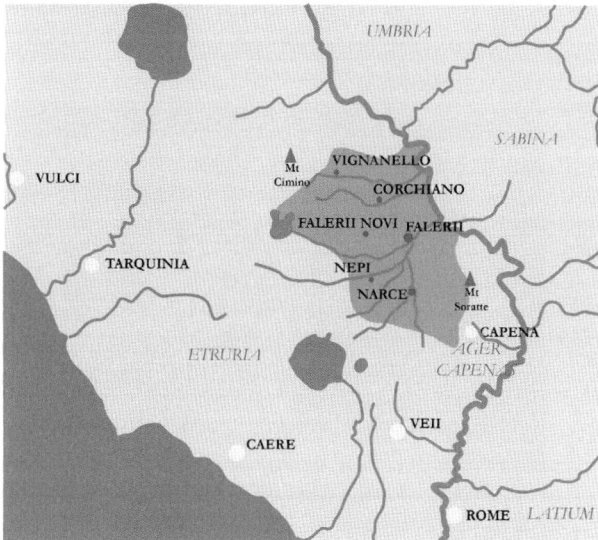

Figure 14.1   The area of the *Ager Faliscus*.

259

The geographic region of the *Ager Faliscus*, in the basin of the Treja River Valley, one of the greatest tributaries of the Tiber River, has a uniquely clear-cut boundary, represented precisely by the Tiber River that separates the area from the Sabine and Umbrian sectors. The other boundaries are more blurred on the geomorphological level: Mount Soracte on the south-east, to the south the slopes of the Sabatino volcano with Lake Bracciano, to the west the volcanic complex of Vico and the Ciminian Forest. Soracte, the mountain sacred not only for the Faliscans, but also for the Etruscans, the Sabines and Capenates, due to the presence of the cult of *Pater Soranus*, in ancient times was a meeting point and at the same time the border with neighboring populations, especially the Capenates (most recently, Colonna 2009) (see Fig 27.5, this volume). The name of the *Falisci* is formed on the same etymological root as *Falerii*, the only city to be specifically mentioned in Greek and Roman sources (apart from *Fescennium*, a site to which we will return). From the beginning of the seventh century BC, and until the Roman conquest in 241 BC, *Falerii* was configured as the primary urban reality of the region, its importance surviving over time despite the Roman destruction. Even today, Civita Castellana, founded on the ruins of the ancient Faliscan city, is the main center of the province after Viterbo (Fig. 14.2).

Falerii exercised its hegemony over a large territory which saw, further to the north, the presence of smaller centers, some of which are fully structured in an urban sense such as Corchiano and Vignanello; these settlements, which have developed at different times depending on the control of the territory, have followed the fortunes of the main site which rapidly declined after the Roman conquest (De Lucia Brolli 1991, Poleggi

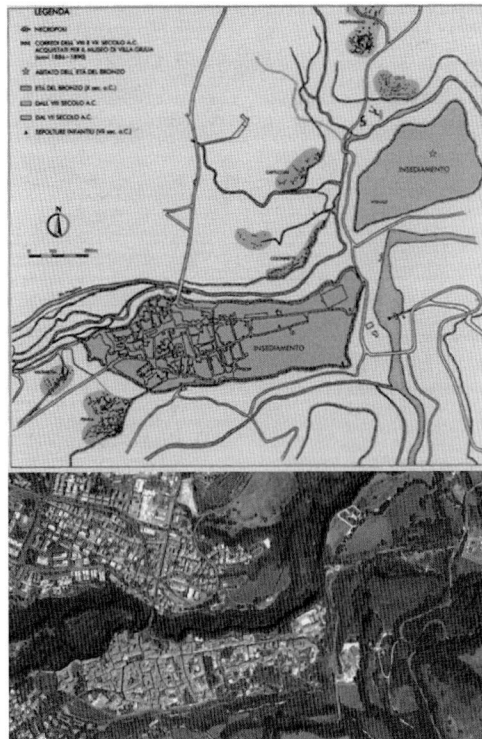

Figure 14.2   Map and aerial photo of *Falerii* (modern Civita Castellana).

1995). The other main center, located in the southern sector of the *Ager Faliscus*, is Narce between Mazzano Romano and Calcata (now a part of the necropolis lies also in the Municipality of Faleria). The old center, anonymous, is universally known by the name that identifies one of the major hills of the settlement and which preserves the memory of a site perched on high ground (Latin *in - arce*) (Fig. 14.3). It has been suggested that over time we should recognize in Narce the *Fescennium* cited by ancient sources, but of uncertain location (Barnabei *et al.* 1894, Potter 1976, Colonna 1990). The situation is not entirely convincing since there are no significant archaeological traces to substantiate it. Recently it has been suggested that Narce should be identified with the name *Tevnalthia*, a city (*spura*) name which occurs in the inscription on a hemispherical footed bowl from Tomb 2 (XLVI) of the third necropolis of Pizzo Piede (Maras 2012) and which recalls linguistically a site of probable Italic origin (Fig. 14.4).

A special position is also assumed by the center of Nepi that in the south-west of the Faliscan territory was already considered old by Livy (6.9.5); together with Sutri it was

Figure 14.3   Narce hill (from the south-east).

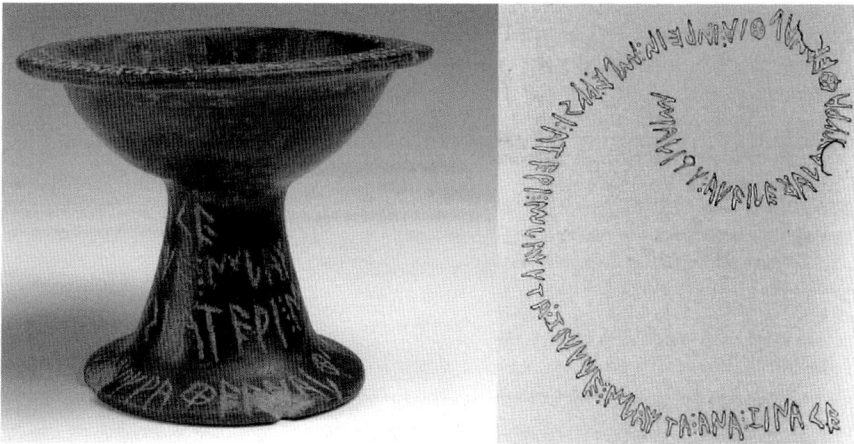

Figure 14.4   Bowl from Tomb 2 (XLVI), third necropolis of Pizzo Piede.

one of the gateways of Etruria. Recent excavations, still largely unpublished, highlight the cultural relevance of Nepi to the Faliscan territory, nor was it devoid of external influences, especially from Narce and Veii (Rizzo 1996). Several sites of the *Ager Faliscus* such as *Falerii*, Narce and Nepi have furnished evidence of a phase of uninterrupted occupation from the Middle Bronze Age until the end of the Final Bronze Age (Gennaro 1982, 1986, Barbaro 2011). Following the witness of the oldest villages of the Bronze Age there follows in the First Iron Age (ninth century BC according to traditional chronology) a period of depopulation of the area indicated by the complete absence of data (Gennaro 1986). The proto-urban revolution involving southern Etruria also sees the entire Faliscan territory participate in the synoecism of Veii. The repopulation of the *Ager Faliscus* is attested both at *Falerii* and Narce, and seems to be concentrated in the first half of the eighth century BC. To the thrust of Italic population, movements are added, especially at Narce, a minority participation by the same Etruscans from Veii in an analogy of the well-known rite of *ver sacrum* ("sacred Spring" – Colonna 1986, Baglione and De Lucia Brolli 1990, Tabolli 2012 forthcoming).

It is especially in the main centers of *Falerii* and Narce that the archaeological record allows us to follow the history and dynamics of development of settlements through the different phases (De Lucia Brolli and Baglione 1997). In the second half of the eighth century BC the formation of settlements leads to two different solutions. At *Falerii* we are witnessing a gradual occupation of the two nuclei that will form the village, the high point of Vignale and, from the last decade of the eighth century BC, the adjacent larger plateau. So the necropolis of Montarano, associated with the first settlement on Vignale, is succeeded by the establishment of the burial grounds of Penna and Valsiarosa to mark the western boundary of the town (Fig. 14.5). At Narce, instead, the settlement now involves the three main hills of Narce, Monte Li Santi and Pizzo Piede, which together

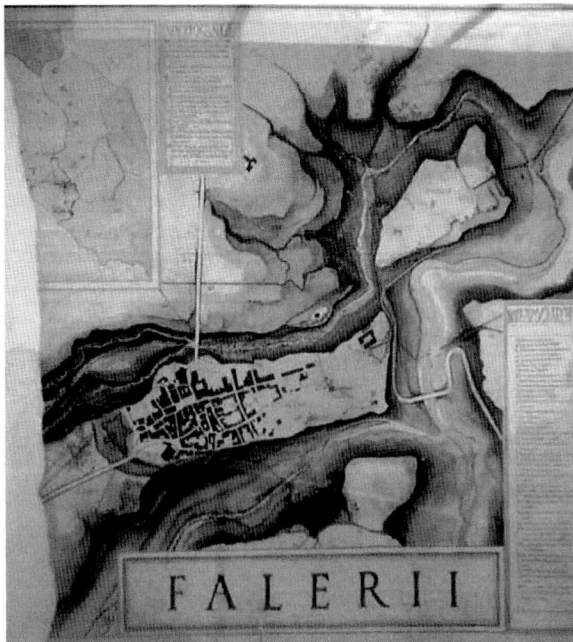

Figure 14.5 Map of *Falerii* drawn by Adolfo Cozza in 1889.

seem to constitute a unitary reality (Torelli 1982, Colonna 1990, De Lucia Brolli and Baglione 1997). The oldest necropoleis – I Tufi and La Petrina – are developed in the valley directly linked to the system Narce - Monte Li Santi, which, united by a natural saddle, in the Archaic period are also connected by a monumental structure: a viaduct in squared blocks of tufa, now partly obliterated by the passage of the provincial road from Mazzano to Calcata (Fig. 14.6).

In this phase in the territory the rites of cremation and inhumation burial coexist in general. The most common tombs are equally distributed *pozzo* and *fossa* types (well-pits and trenches) which are sometimes accompanied, by mid-century, by a niche for the deposition of grave goods, while it is only at the end of the eighth century BC that the type of trench with a special burial niche (*loculus*) of "Narce type" spread (di Gennaro 1988, Belelli Marchesini 2010). The subsequent development of the latter probably led, in the first quarter of the next century to a pseudo-chamber with access from a *caditoia* (shaft entrance). In the course of the seventh century BC, both sites appear to have completed the process of urban formation. The cemeteries now have a radial pattern around all the nuclei of the settlement. The monumental character of the burials, the presence of a monumental tumulus at Narce (in the necropolis of Petrina C, Tomb 2 [XLVII]) like the oldest chamber tombs in *Falerii* – characterized by long access *dromoi* that, in some cases, are oriented toward the emerging urban center (De Lucia Brolli 2012). In conjunction with the wealth of the funerary offerings, they now attest to the conclusion of the process of social differentiation and the emergence of a fully structured aristocratic class. At *Falerii* the presence of specialized artisans is also evident: the production of impasto vases, in fact, appears organized according to criteria of almost "industrial" character, with wide distribution both domestic and external (Biella 2007, 2010, 2011; 2011th). At

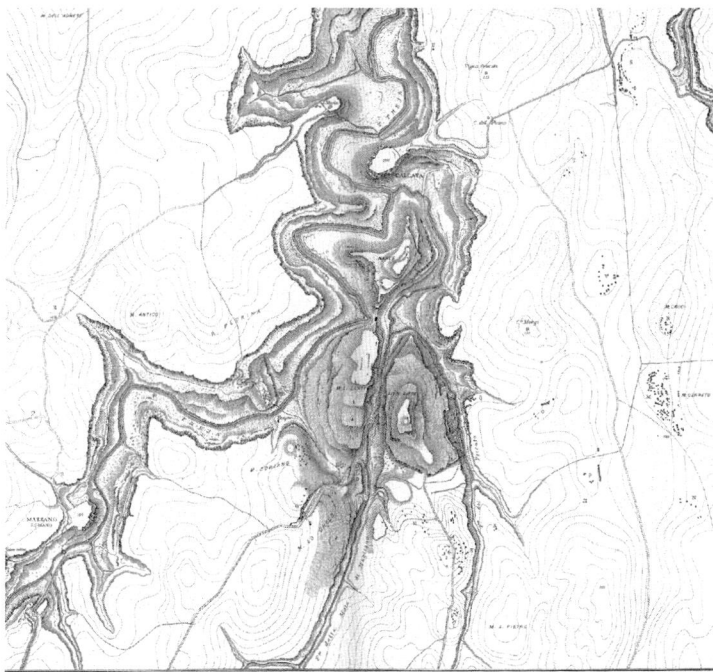

Figure 14.6   Map of Narce drawn by Adolfo Cozza in 1889.

Narce instead, local pottery production is characterized by a greater variety of types and expression, not so much of an organized artisanal system as of single artistic personalities active at Narce and not only the famous "Painter of Narce" (Canciani 1974, Martelli 1987, Micozzi 1994, Szilágy 2005, Boitani *et al.* 2010).

With the Archaic period between the sixth and fifth centuries BC it is particularly *Falerii* that progressively tends to assume a central role in the political and economic system of the region, consolidating its hegemony over the territory and satellite communities placed in control of the focal points. The city is endowed with a system of urban and suburban sanctuaries located along the access roads and near the city gates. Strategically positioned in front of the acropolis of Vignale, on the valley floor, from the first half of the sixth century BC the shrine of Juno Curitis becomes a landmark not only for the Faliscan community (Colonna 1985, p. 110–113; Benedettini, Carlucci, De Lucia Brolli 2005; Albers 2007) (Fig. 14.7). *Falerii* becomes at this stage one of the towns most receptive of Attic pottery of high quality, first black-figure and then red-figure pottery that, creating a substrate of familiarity, will form the basis for subsequent local figured products (Ambrosini 2005, 2009).

Our knowledge on the articulation of internal organization of settlement at Narce is more limited. The only extensive investigation, in 1933 by R. Mengarelli, was on the plain of Pizzo Piede (De Lucia Brolli and Baglione 1997; Baglione and De Lucia Brolli 2004). The urban excavations have revealed a small but significant group of architectural terracottas that reveal the presence of an urban sanctuary from at least the late sixth century BC (Fig. 14.8).

The existence of a belt of suburban sanctuaries is tied to the foot of Monte Li Santi, where, corresponding to two small areas along the alluvial plain of the Treja, were found the remains of a temple building abandoned early (1890–1891 and 1901 excavations) and a very sophisticated complex of buildings and open-air altars from the first half of the fifth century BC lasting until the end of the second century BC (Excavations 1985–2003) (De Lucia Brolli 1990, 1990a; Benedettini *et al.* 1999, De Lucia Brolli - Benedettini 2002). Given the limited information on actual areas of the settlement in this chronological horizon, the

Figure 14.7   Example of architectural terracottas from *Falerii* (via Gramsci).

extensive surveys in the necropoleis during the late-nineteenth century tell us that Narce had a decrease in the number of burials and necropoleis used (down to four out of 20) but their scope is marked by funerary offerings of special prestige and economic wealth. In contrast, at *Falerii* we witness an increase in the number of chamber tombs, which appear with an increasing number of *loculi* for funerary deposition, a sign of population growth.

At the beginning of the fourth century BC *Falerii*, building on its economic potential, faces a complex restructuring of the town, organizing the plateau according to a regular system (of which traces have been recognized in several excavations, partly unpublished) (for the excavation of Via Gramsci: De Lucia Brolli 2006). Recent investigations, still unpublished, have identified a monumental pre-Roman quarry of tufa blocks to the west of the settlement, from which comes, in all likelihood, the building material used in the city (Fig. 14.9).

It is at this stage that the reconstruction of most of the temple buildings is implemented, both in urban areas such as the temple of Scasato II, sacred to the triad Jupiter, Juno, Minerva, and also in the suburban area where the temple of Juno Curitis assumes an orientation parallel to the course of the Rio Maggiore, similar to that of the temple of Argive Hera at Greek Argos (Fig. 14.10). This is also the time when the vase-painters

Figure 14.8   Raniero Mengarelli's excavations at Pizzo Piede, Narce, 1933.

Figure 14.9   Pre-Roman quarry at *Falerii*.

develop in the wake of the arrival of the important masters of Attic figured pottery, producing masterpieces in both red-figure and superposed color, such as the *Dis Pater* Painter, the Krater of Aurora, the works of the Nazzano Painter and so on (Adembri 1987) (Fig. 14.11). The tradition of coroplastic production so expertly begun in the first

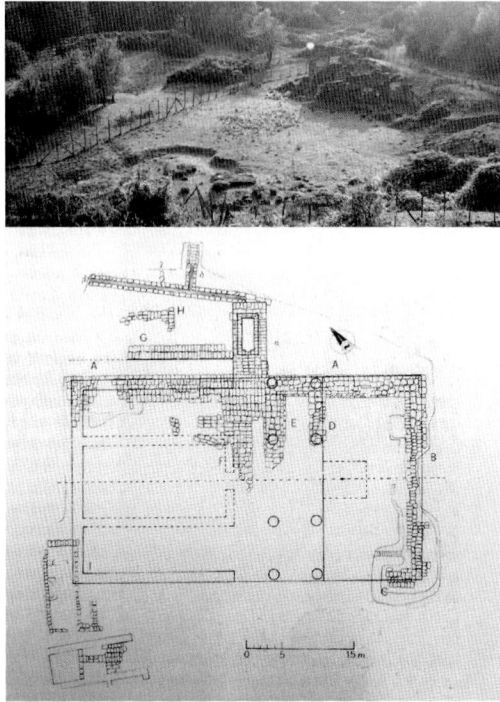

Figure 14.10 Sanctuary of Juno Curitis at Celle, *Falerii*.

Figure 14.11 "Krater of the Aurora," *Falerii*.

266

half of the fifth century BC is expressed in the fourth century BC in world-class works such as the Apollo of Scasato (Fig. 14.12) and the cycle of sculptures that adorned the temple in the sanctuary built in the second half of the century in a prominent position within the higher plateau (area of the Forum?). Simultaneously Narce was affected by the fall of Veii that in 396 BC was overwhelmed by Rome. It follows that in that year, according to Livy (5.24–27), the Roman army led by Furius Camillus conquers Capena in successive stages, devastating the countryside and reaching the walls of *Falerii*, which surrendered. There is no evidence to assert that Narce was struck by the Roman advance of that year, but the social and economic crisis of the city has emerged from the archaeological context known thus far (De Lucia Brolli and Baglione 1997). Once again, the grave goods in the necropoleis of this center suggest a form of survival of the communities located on the plateau of Monte Li Santi and Pizzo Piede albeit in a smaller number of families. The few funerary offerings, for the most part in reused tombs, denote a substantial economic decline. Again Livy (10.46) tells of a triumph in 293 BC over the Faliscans celebrated by the consul Spurius Carvilius Maximus, which surely brought about a harsher bending of the social structure of Narce that in less than a century would lead to its permanent abandonment, with the exception of the suburban sanctuary of Monte Li Santi-Le Rote. In 241 BC *Falerii* also permanently surrendered after a brave resistance. The sources tell of total destruction and forcible transfer of the population to a nearby lowland site where a settlement, *Falerii Novi*, was built over a pre-existing one (a collection of sources is in Di Stefano Manzella 1990). The Romanization of the territory, the watershed of which lies in the date of 241 BC, is actually a process of longer duration that has its origins in the increasingly close relations between some families of notables of *Falerii* and the Roman *gentes* ("clans"). Probably these relations created a policy of occupation of the countryside with the creation of large estates that preceded the formal founding of *Falerii* while at the same

Figure 14.12   Apollo from the Scasato temple site, *Falerii*.

time encouraging its birth (De Lucia Brolli 1995–96; De Lucia Brolli – Michetti 2005) (Fig. 14.13). The Roman conquest had an economic impact on the entire Faliscan sector, also determined by the interrupted flow of production of ceramics on an industrial scale, which were widely exported, and formed the basis of the economic fabric of the Faliscan metropolis. After 241 BC the necessity of territorial control by Rome led to the construction of two major roads, the Via Amerina (post 241 BC) and the Flaminia (220 BC); their paths excluded the original *Falerii*, while in the countryside, along new roads, there developed *villae rusticae* which are recognized in areas of tile fragments. Almost all the temples survived the Roman conquest, both in *Falerii* and its hinterland (Grotta Porciosa), and in Narce (Monte Li Santi – Le Rote), which seem to have been completely abandoned in a planned and programmed fashion around the end of the second-beginning of the first century BC (Benedettini, Carlucci, De Lucia Brolli 2005 and 2010).

ETRUSCANS AND FALISCANS: WHAT RELATIONSHIP?

The geographical position of the *Ager Faliscus*, nerve center of communications in the Middle Tiber Valley, creates a sub-region in close contact between the various peoples of central Italy, with whom relations were also facilitated by their common gravitation to the large artery of the River Tiber (Baglione 1986). Since the early Iron Age it had demonstrated this phenomenon of social mobility that certainly favored the interface between the different populations, resulting in similarities in the manifestations of material culture and funeral ideology. In particular, the contiguity of the Faliscan territory with that of the Capenates and the apparent similarities until a few years ago resulted in the scientific literature using the term "Faliscan-Capenate" for the expressions of Faliscan culture. It is only in recent decades that a clear ethnic-cultural demarcation has been delineated between Faliscans and Capenates (most recently, Biella 2007 and 2012), although not abandoned by all scholars (Camporeale 2005). Similarly, the Faliscans were often juxtaposed to the Etruscans, with whom, as the sources tell us, they sometimes shared their history repeatedly allying against Roman expansion. The political proximity with the Etruscans is particularly pushed into prominence by the presence of Faliscans, like that of the Capenates among the confederated peoples who annually gathered at the

Figure 14.13   *Falerii novi.*

shrine of the *Fanum Voltumnae* at Orvieto (see Chapter 31). The two main times when the anti-Roman alliances operated were in the conflict of Rome and Veii (402–395 BC) when the Faliscans and Capenates sided with Veii, and the Roman-Tarquinian War of 357–351 BC which saw *Falerii* ally with Tarquinia. In general the close relationship between Etruscans and *Falisci* is measured primarily in the trade in goods and materials, and in the circulation of ideas and cultural patterns, marked by relations of reciprocity. With respect to the universe of trade, we must consider what influence direct relations with the Etruscans would have had on some Faliscan sites.

In defining the Faliscan territory two regions that are both geographical and cultural may be recognized: the southern *Ager Faliscus*, which has its epicenter in Narce, and the central-northern *Ager Faliscus* that sees in *Falerii* the hegemonic center that exerts a wide control even on smaller sites like Corchiano and Vignanello. The two sub-regions interact in more or less direct proportion to the proximity of the neighboring Etruscans. In the earliest phase Narce is certainly the site to witness more direct contacts determined by its proximity to Veii, the nearest Etruscan center, only 25 km distant (Baglione and De Lucia Brolli 1990, 1997). Trade between the two centers is significant from the beginning of the eighth century BC, so as to have often caused confusion in the ethnic-cultural identification of Narce, thought by some scholars, albeit cautiously, to have been a colony of Veii (Cifani 2005); trade continued uninterrupted until the fall of Veii. One of the elements that, in the earliest phase (eighth century BC) are common and show strong affinities between the two sites is the field of funerary ideology (Baglione and De Lucia Brolli 1997). Among the oldest tombs of the necropoleis of I Tufi and La Petrina are recognized some contexts that apparently are directly associated with the funerary ideology and material culture of Veii (Baglione and De Lucia Brolli 1990) (Fig. 14.14).

But if one observes the burials in detail there is a wide range of differences: associations in grave goods include a set composition of personal ornaments and pottery strongly influenced by local decisions, and often in connection with Etruscan, rather than Latin and Sabine, funeral customs (Turfa 2005: pp. 13–21; Pitzalis 2011) (Fig. 14.15).

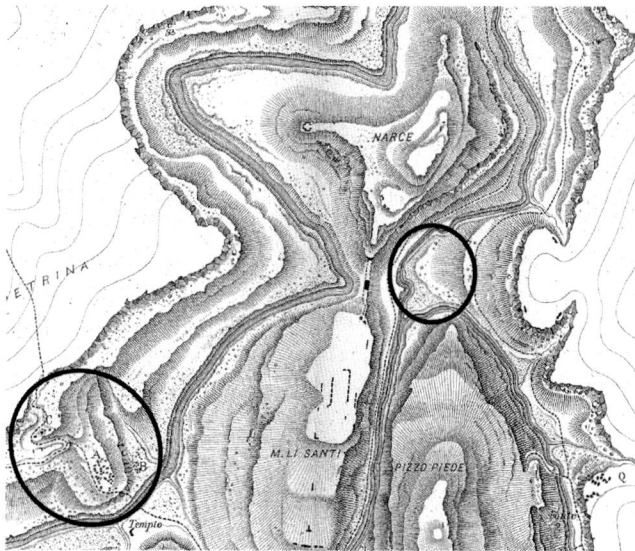

Figure 14.14   La Petrina and I Tufi necropoleis of Narce.

Figure 14.15   Reconstruction of Faliscan female and male dress based on tombs A36 (XXVI) and A38 (XXIX) La Petrina necropolis (by Jacopo Tabolli and Matteo Gennaro).

Compared to Veii, the evolution of funerary architecture of the oldest tombs furnishes different structures (for example, the *pozzo* type and well-shaped tomb built with a rectangular stone lining) or the adoption of the sarcophagus of tuff not only for infant burials, as at Veii, but for different age groups: at Narce the wooden coffin appears in a chronologically more recent horizon than the tuff sarcophagi, while at Veii the two types are used simultaneously (Fig. 14.16). Thus the simple *pozzi* (well-pits) and *fosse* (trench tombs) often simply denote later graves instead of being the starting point of an evolution towards more complex forms, as happens in the Etruscan site (for Veii see Bartoloni *et al.* 1997; for Narce, Tabolli forthcoming 2012). One of the characteristics of Narce is the long duration of the rite of cremation that goes beyond the chronological limits of the custom at Veii, and is attested in sectors of the necropoleis specifically intended for cremation: Petrina B, Monte Li Santi, the South Group of I Tufi (Baglione and De Lucia Brolli 1997) (Fig. 14.17). The similarities and differences that accumulated in the eighth century BC in the funerary ideology are reproduced between the end of the sixth and the beginning of the fifth century BC, when Narce looks towards Veii in adapting to local needs a particular type of tomb with burial area open to the sky and niches (*loculi*) to hold the cinerary urns (Fig. 14.18). While some of these tombs have a rich collection of goods that signals the higher social strata of the population (Petrina B 89), others are relatively bare or have a set of offerings that is reduced to essentials, illustrating in this a reflection of the sumptuary laws that in this period affected southern Etruria and *Latium Vetus* (De Lucia Brolli and Baglione 1997).

The small number of tombs in which this ideology is expressed is distributed within the necropoleis (Petrina B, Monte Soriano), which belonged to the communities established on the heights of Narce/Monte Li Santi. At the same time in the community of Pizzo Piede the close relationships with the Etruscan cities are crystallized: evidence

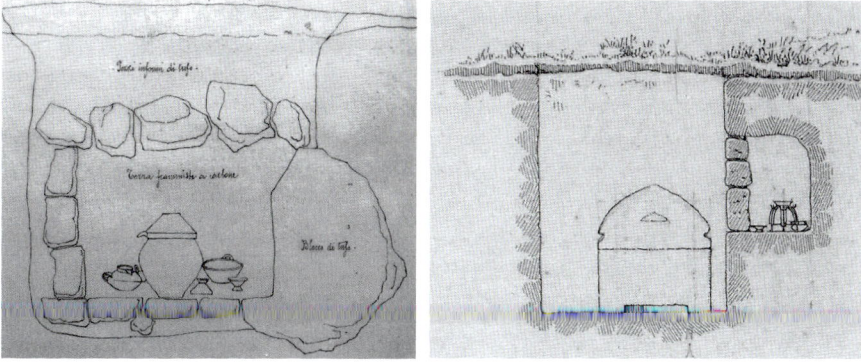

Figure 14.16   Types of tombs peculiar to Narce (eighth century BC).

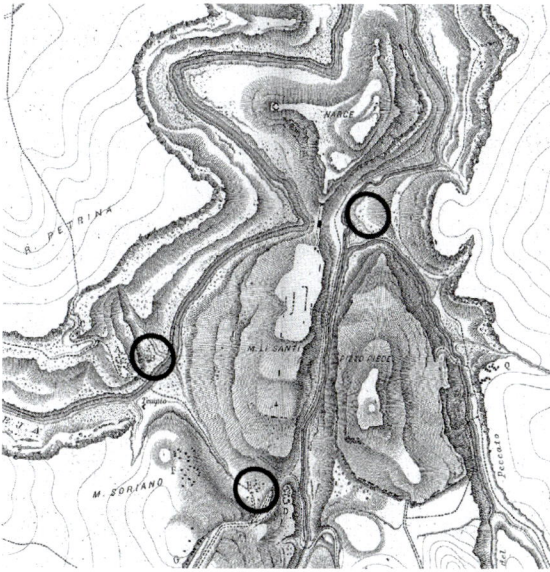

Figure 14.17   Location of late cremation burials in Narce.

Figure 14.18   Cremation in open tomb, Grotta Gramiccia necropolis, Veii (in Drago 1997).

from the archaeological excavations of Mengarelli in 1933 records a strong Veian component in the decoration of the city temple, where the architectural terracottas were derived from the same molds used for the decor of the sanctuary at Veii-Portonaccio around 510 BC (De Lucia Brolli and Baglione 1997, 2004). The marking on the back of the slabs in Etruscan, functional to their implementation, is a technical device, which is reflected in the complex at Veii. Moreover, the presence of the figure of Achelous, although extremely fragmentary, in the decorative system of the sanctuary of Pizzo Piede was interpreted as an allusion to the heroic cycle of Herakles, whose role in the sanctuary of Portonaccio is particularly relevant around the end of the sixth century BC (Fig. 14.19). The close relationship between the two shrines indicates a profound influence on the part of Veii, which could also be interpreted in political terms, at least for the community of Pizzo Piede. This relationship is not random, however, since the establishment of Pizzo Piede is naturally connected to Veii by a clearly identified road. On the other hand this is the sector which over time has produced the largest number of Etruscan inscriptions in funerary contexts, and from inside the area, the oldest and most numerous are dated in the seventh century BC (Gamurrini 1894, Cristofani 1988, Bagnasco Gianni 1996, Colonna and Maras 2006). It should be remembered that Narce is characterized precisely by the large number of Etruscan inscriptions in contrast to a very limited presence of Faliscan inscriptions, which, however, are late and come exclusively from the suburban sanctuary of Monte Li Santi-Le Rote (De Lucia Brolli 2012 in press). This too has been interpreted in favor of the Etruscan character of Narce (Cifani 2005) or the presence of an Etruscan-speaking community, permanently implanted in the Faliscan center (Cristofani 1988). In fact, if we look at the inscriptions that have been preserved, especially the oldest ones, as part of a more general reference to the writing system of Veii, we recognize peculiarities in the script that would attest, according to recent studies, an independent local writing tradition (Maras 2012). A striking example is the association of the three sibilants in the writing system, a feature absent in contemporary texts at Veii. On the other hand, the inscriptions – of gift, of possession, and of amatory content, very long and literary in character – are displayed on movable objects, which could be the result of trade and not related in a precise and unambiguous way to a stable presence of Etruscans within the social structure of Narce (for reading and analyzing texts, see Colonna and Maras 2006). A recent re-reading of the inscriptions has highlighted the contribution of Veii as a center of radiation for the dissemination of epigraphic models adopted by the Faliscan elites, and especially from nearby Narce, where the nascent aristocracy express their dominant role over the town's population through the use of Etruscan, but in a local reinterpretation. The same lemma *Tevnalthia*, which could be the oldest name of Narce, is written in Etruscan characters, but this reveals certainly not an Etruscan etymological origin, but probably it is Italic instead (Maras 2012). Even at *Falerii*, indeed, the oldest attestations of writing are in the Etruscan language: witness the *olla* from the tomb of the necropolis of Montarano 43, which, placed on a typical support of local production like the *olla* itself, bears, in Etruscan and not Faliscan (as in a previous reading), the very suggestive ritual prescription, "Do not put me down" (Colonna 2011).

However, it should be remembered that Faliscan inscriptions are also attested at Narce, albeit late and limited in number and coming exclusively from the suburban sanctuary of Monte Li Santi-Le Rote (De Lucia Brolli 2012 in press) (Fig. 14.20). It is precisely this shrine that offers additional insights into the close ties between Narce and Veii. Among the votives, the presence of heads from the first half of the fifth century BC

Figure 14.19 Examples of architectural terracottas from Narce, Pizzo Piede.

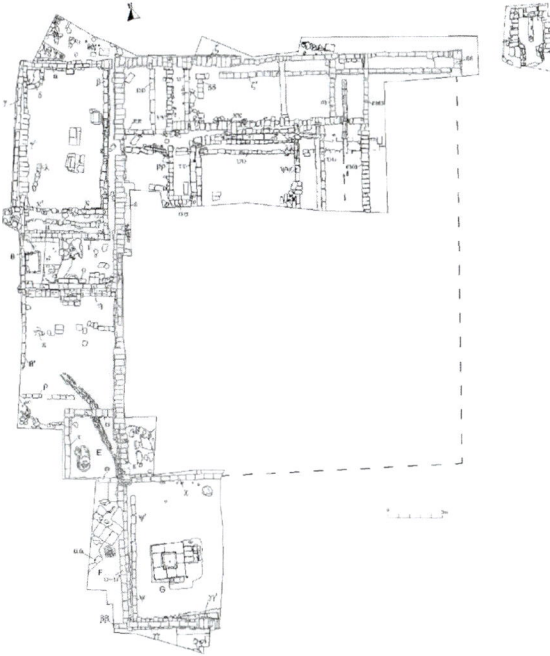

Figure 14.20 Sanctuary of Monte Li Santi-Le Rote, Narce.

is a highly distinctive cultural element, assimilating Narce with another great Faliscan center, *Falerii*, but especially with the nearby Veii and stressing once again that the tradition of votive heads originates in the Faliscan-Veian area (on this issue Comella 1997) (Fig. 14.21). At *Falerii* votive heads, mostly female, dating from the fifth century BC are present in the sanctuaries of Celle and Vignale (see Comella 1986) and in votive deposits connected to the sacred area of Ninfeo Rosa (Blanck 1990). At Veii, the votive deposit of Campetti has furnished many heads dated between the late sixth and fifth centuries BC (Vagnetti 1971; Comella – Stefani 1990) with an overwhelming preponderance of female types that are due to a religious cult of Demeter-Ceres practiced in the sanctuary (Comella 1981). Beyond that significant common thread, though, which qualifies the comparisons, a substantial autonomy on the part of Narce is revealed with respect to *Falerii*, showing, moreover, even in the early third century BC, a gravitation towards the region of Veii-Rome. One more signal that points in this direction is represented by the presence of both male and female heads almost exclusively veiled (*capite velato*), against a very small percentage of non-veiled heads, in contrast with what is documented in *Falerii* (Comella 1986). It was noted that the representation of the offrant with veiled head is prevalent in the territories politically dependent upon Rome, while the bare-headed types are most common in southern Etruria and Campania (Pensabene *et al.* 1980, pp. 47–48). At Veii, the gradual spread of veiled heads, attested to a lesser extent in the fourth century BC, becomes prominent in the second century BC; it may illustrate the overlap of the Roman religious tradition with that of the Etruscans (Comella 1982). At *Falerii*, on the other hand, the adoption and persistence of the Greek rite could find its ideological motivations in superb vindication of the epic origins of the city, which, according to a theory formed no later than the fifth century BC, and further consolidation in the imperial age, was supposedly founded by the Argive Halesus (Camporeale 1991). The different behavior of Narce versus *Falerii* seems to emphasize its affinities with the neighboring Veii, and with the Etruscan area in general, and this is also well attested in the cultural context of the funeral, and could be a further sign of the lower resistance of the old southern center of the *Ager Faliscus* in its contacts with the Roman conqueror.

Mobility phenomena concern also the broad Faliscan northern center, and in this context the relationship between Etruscans and Faliscans finds its fullest realization especially at Corchiano, which, under the control of *Falerii*, implements a policy of openness towards the Etruscan cities of the northern Tiber valley, Volsinii and Chiusi, with significant results in the field of urban, cultural and socio-economic development (on the issue most recently De Lucia Brolli - Michetti 2005) (Fig. 14.22). The site has furnished significant archaeological and epigraphic evidence that proves the presence of Etruscan-speakers as early as the late Archaic age (the *zuchu* of clear Chiusine origin, *CIE* 8384) and a strong penetration of elements of Etruscan origin in the Faliscan social structure, concentrated especially between the fourth and third centuries BC.

Figure 14.21   Votive head from the sanctuary of Monte Li Santi-Le Rote, Narce.

Figure 14.22   View of Corchiano (from the east).

The dynamics that have led this center to accommodate an increasing number of persons from outside are to be found in the elements of the formation of the site, which only becomes a city in the late sixth century BC, when *Falerii*, now fully organized as a hegemonic center of the *Ager Faliscus*, implements a policy of territorial control in ways that could be called "colonization." The result of a well-planned settlement is evident on an urbanistic level: the necropolis of Vallone shows right at the end of the sixth century BC a rational organization of space that is unparalleled in the rest of the territory and recalls analogous processes implemented in Etruria and in particular at Cerveteri and Orvieto. Direct influences from the area of Volsinii are also recognized in the use of basalt stones placed as markers on the tombs and in the evidence of the noble Faliscan cognomen *hescuna* linked to the Hescanas family (Colonna 1990, note 52, Fig. 4).

There has been much debate over time, precisely determined by the extent of this phenomenon, on the origin and the historical moment at which we place the arrival of Etruscan people at Corchiano. There are two main hypotheses: the first identifies the starting area in the territory of Chiusi (especially Peruzzi 1990, p. 289), attributing the transfer of individuals and groups to the diaspora that followed the destruction of Volsinii in 264 BC (Cristofani 1988, p. 21); the other believes it possible that an Etruscan colonization was instigated by Norchia and fully implemented by the fourth century BC, at the urging of Tarquinia, as an anti-Roman gesture (Colonna 1990, p. 118–123).

Whatever the reasons behind the phenomenon, the presence of Etruscans is in any event significant enough to interfere with the management of public affairs, as revealed by the monumental inscription *"larθ velarnies"* (CIE 8379) carved on the walls of the so-called rock-cut roadway of Cannara or San Egidio and probably attributable to the constructor of the road, which is one of the main routes that led into the town, connecting it with the territory to the south-west (see Moscati 1985, p. 93, fig. 62, section 2, Figs. 74–78). There is consistently a remarkable capacity for integration into local families, well marked by epitaphs furnished by the burial grounds closely related to the urban class, and through these it is possible to follow the full sequence of writing and the local language appropriate to Etruscan-speakers.

In the countryside surrounding the town we find a different situation: distant from the truly urban area are found tombs with rock-cut façades, some isolated, some arranged in pairs within the smaller nuclei of the necropolis, which recall the type of architectural models borrowed from Etruscan Norchia (Fig. 14.23). These impressive tombs, scattered over a wide range, indicate a complex occupation of the countryside by families of Etruscan origin – according to the hypothesis of Giovanni Colonna, probably coming from the territory of Tarquinia – more bound to their ethnic and cultural roots, and different from the Etruscans who were already integrated into urban communities. It is possible that once again we can recognize, in this territorial process of taking root, the long arm of *Falerii* that in the context of complex political-military alliances intertwined with Tarquinia around the mid-fourth century BC, with anti-Roman purpose, may have ceded large swathes of territory to the Etruscan alliance.

In conclusion, the picture painted highlights the complexity and long duration of the mutual relations between Faliscans and Etruscans. And although the small region of the *Ager Faliscus* clearly manifests deep influences from the wider and more structured world of the Etruscans, the Faliscans nevertheless retained their independence over time as well as their specific cultural identity, conversing as equals with their powerful neighbor. This inseparable relationship does not stop the advance of Romanization: it is significant that both territories would become part of the same *Regio VII Augustea*.

Figure 14.23   Types of tombs characteristic of Corchiano.

BIBLIOGRAPHY

Adembri, B. (1990) "La più antica produzione di ceramica falisca a figure rosse. Inquadramento stilistico e cronologico" in *La civiltà dei Falisci*, Atti del XV Convegno di Studi Etruschi e Italici (Civita Castellana, 28–31 maggio 1987), Florence: Leo S. Olschki, 233–244.

Albers, J. (2007) *Der Tempel von Celle in Civita Castellana: Untersuchungen zur etruskischen Architektur, zum Terrakottaschmuck und Sakralwesen am Beispiel eines faliskischen Heiligtums von 6. Bis 1. Jahrh. V. Chr.*, Berlin: Tenea.

Ambrosini, L. (2005) "Circolazione della ceramica attica nell'agro falisco e volsiniese: un confronto," in *Orvieto, l'Etruria meridionale interna e l'agro falisco*. Atti del XII Convegno Internazionale di

Studi sulla Storia e l'Archeologia dell'Etruria (Orvieto 2004), in *Annali Faina* XII, Rome: Quasar, 301–336.

——(2009) "Sulla ceramica attica a figure rosse del primo quarto del IV secolo a.C. da *Falerii Veteres*," in *Etruria e Italia Preromana. Studi in onore di Giovannangelo Camporeale*, 17–26, Pisa-Roma: Fabrizio Serra Editore.

Baglione, M. P. (1986) "Il Tevere e i Falisci," in *Il Tevere e le altre vie d'acqua del Lazio antico*, Atti del VII Incontro di Studio del Comitato per l'Archeologia Laziale (*Quaderni di Archeologia Etrusco Italica* 12): 124–142, Rome: Consiglio Nazionale delle Ricerche.

Baglione, M. P. and De Lucia Brolli, M. A. (1990) "Nuovi dati sulla necropoli de "I Tufi" di Narce" in *La civiltà dei Fallisci*, Atti del XV Convegno di Studi Etruschi e Italici (Civita Castellana, 28–31 maggio 1987), 61–102, Florence: Leo S. Olschki.

——(1997) "Veio e i Falisci" in G. Bartoloni (ed.), *Le necropoli arcaiche di Veio*, (1997), 145–171.

——(2004) "Il santuario urbano di Pizzo Piede a Narce" in A. M. Moretti Sgubini (ed.), *Scavo nello scavo. Gli Etruschi non visti*, catalogo della mostra (Viterbo, 5 marzo–30 giugno 2004), Rome: Ministero per i Beni e le attività culturali, Soprintendenza per i beni archeologici per l'Etruria meridionale.

Bartoloni, G. (1997) (ed.) *Le necropoli arcaiche di Veio*, Rome: La Sapienza.

Bakkum, G. C. L. M. (2009) *The Latin Dialect of the Ager Faliscus*. 150 Years of Scholarship, Amsterdam: Amsterdam University Press.

Barbaro, B. (2011) *Insediamenti, aree funerarie ed entità territoriali in Etruria meridionale nel bronzo finale*, Florence: All'insegna del Giglio.

Barnabei, F., Cozza, A. and Pasqui. A. (1894) *Degli scavi di antichità nel territorio falisco (Monumenti Antichi dei Lincei IV)*, Rome: Accademia dei Lincei.

Belelli Marchesini, B. (2010) "Necropoli di *Crustumerium*: bilancio delle acquisizioni e prospettive" in *AIAC* 2008.

De Lucia Brolli, M. A. and Benedettini M. G. (2002) "Narce: santuario suburbano di Monte Li Santi-Le Rote" in *Arte, Fede e Religioni. Trentacinquemila anni di storia*, (Catalogo mostra Roma 2002), 60, Rome: Tipograf sr.l.

Benedettini, M. G., Catalli, F. and De Lucia Brolli, M. A. (1999) "Rinvenimenti monetali nel territorio dell'antica Narce. Il santuario suburbano in località Monte Li Santi, Le Rote" in *Bullettino Numismatica Romana* 32–33: 47–102, Rome: Istituto Poligrafico dello Stato.

Benedettini, M. G., Carlucci, C. and De Lucia Brolli, M. A. (2005) "I depositi votivi dell'Agro falisco. Vecchie e nuove testimonianze a confronto" in A. Comella and S. Mele (eds) *Depositi votivi e culti dell'Italia antica dall'età arcaica a quella tardo-repubblicana*. Atti del Convegno di Studi, Perugia, 1–4 giugno 2000: 219–228, Bari: Edipuglia.

Biella, M. C. (2007) *Impasti orientalizzanti con decorazione ad incavo nell'Italia centrale tirrenica*, Rome: G. Bretschneider.

——(2010) "Le metamorfosi degli impasti in bucchero. Ovvero come gli artigiani falisci seppero adattarsi alla moda dei tempo" in *Tra centro e periferia. Nuovi dati sul bucchero nell'Italia centrale tirrenica. Officina Etruscologia* 3, Rome: Officina Edizioni.

——(2011) "Impasti orientalizzanti falisci e capenati con decorazione incisa: un primo bilancio" in XVII International Congresso f Classical Archaeology, *Bollettino d'Archeologia on-line*, 32–41.

——(2011a) *La collezione Feroldi Antonisi De Rosa. Tra indagini archeologiche e ricerche di un'identità culturale nella Civita Castellana postunitaria*, Rome: l'Erma di Bretschneider.

Blanck, H. (1990) "Ritrovamenti dal cosiddetto ninfeo Rosa di *Falerii* Veteres" in *La civiltà dei Falisci*. Atti del XV Convegno di studi etruschi ed italici, (Civita Castellana 28–31 maggio 1987): 223–230, Florence: Leo S. Olschki.

Boitani, F., Biagi, F. and Neri, S. (2010) "Riflessi della ceramica geometrica nella più antica pittura funeraria veiente" in *Bullettino di Archeologia on line*: 20–27, Rome.

Camporeale, G. (1991) *L'ethnos dei Falisci secondo gli scrittori antichi* in *Archeologia Classica* 43: 209–221, Rome: l'Erma di Bretschneider.

Canciani, F. (1974) *CVA. Tarquinia, Museo Nazionale* 3. Italia 55. Rome: Istituto Poligrafico dello Stato.

Carlucci, C., De Lucia Brolli, M. A. and Keay, S. (2007) "An archaeological survey of the Faliscan settlement at Vignale, *Falerii* Veteres (province of Viterbo)" in *Papers of the British School at Rome* 75: 39–121, London: British School at Rome.

Camporeale, G. (2005) "Dall'agro falisco e capenate all'agro volsiniese e all'alta valle del Fiora" in *Orvieto, l'Etruria meridionale interna e l'agro falisco.* Atti del XII Convegno Internazionale di Studi sulla Storia e l'Archeologia dell'Etruria (Orvieto 2004) in *Annali Faina* XII: 269–299, Rome: Quasar.

Cifani, G. (2005) "I confini settentrionali del territorio veiente" in G. Camporeale (ed.) *Dinamiche di sviluppo delle città nell'etruria meridionale. Veio, Caere, Tarquinia, Vulci. Atti del XXIII Convegno di Studi Etruschi ed Italici, Roma, Veio, Cerveteri/Pyrgi, Tarquinia, Tuscania, Vulci, Viterbo, 1–6 ottobre 2001.*, Volume 1 151–161: Pisa, Rome: Istituti editoriali e poligrafici internazionali.

Colonna, G. (1985) (ed.), *Santuari d'Etruria*, Catalogo della mostra: 110–113, Milano: Electa.

——(1986) "Il Tevere e gli Etruschi" in *Il Tevere e le altre vie d'acqua del Lazio antico,* Atti del VII Incontro di Studio del Comitato per l'Archeologia Laziale (*Quaderni di Archeologia Etrusco Italica* 12): 37–53, Rome: Consiglio Nazionale delle Ricerche.

——(1990) "Corchiano, Narce e il problema di Fescennium" in *La civiltà dei Fallisci,* Atti del XV Convegno di Studi Etruschi e Italici (Civita Castellana, 28–31 maggio 1987), 111–140, Florence: Leo S. Olschki.

——(2009) "L'Apollo di Pyrgi, Śur/Śuri (il "Nero") e l'Apollo *Sourio*" in *Studi Etruschi* 73: 101–134, Rome: l'Erma di Bretschneider.

——(2011) *REE* in *Studi Etruschi* LXXIV 2008: 399–401, Rome: G. Bretchneider editore.

Colonna, G. and Maras, D. F. (2006) *Corpus Inscriptionum Etruscarum,* fasc. II, 1, 5 et additamentum fasc. II, 2, 1, *Inscriptiones Veiis et in agro Veientano, Nepesino Sutrinoque repertae, additis illis in agro Capenate et Falisco inventis, quae in fasciculo CIE II, 2, 1 desunt, nec non illis perpaucis in finitimis Sabinis repertis,* Florence: Leo S. Olschki.

Comella, A. (1981) "Tipologia e diffusione dei complessi votivi in Italia in epoca medio- e tardo-repubblicana" in *Mélanges de l'Ecole française de Rome. Antiquité* 93, 7ss. Rome: L'Ecole française de Rome.

Comella, A. (1986) *I materiali votivi del Falerii* (CSV I, Regio VII, 1), Rome: l'Erma di Bretschneider.

——(1997) "Circolazione di matrici in area etrusco-laziale e campana" in *Le Moulage en terrecuite dans l'antiquité: création et production dérivée, fabrication et diffusion,* Actes du XVIIIe Colloque de Recherches Archéologiques, (Lille III, 7–8, décembre 1995), Villeneuve D'Ascq, 333–351.

Comella, A. and Stefani, G. (1990) *Materiali votivi del santuario di Campetti a Veio. Scavi 1947 e 1969,* Rome: G. Bretschneider.

Cozza, A. and Pasqui. A. (1981) *Carta Archeologica d'Italia (1881–1897). Materiali per l'Agro Falisco* (Forma Italiae s. II, doc. 2, Florence: Leo S. Olschki.

Cristofani, M. (1988) "Etruschi nell'agro falisco" in *Papers of the British School at Rome* LVI: 13–24, London: British School at Rome.

Deecke, W. (1888) *Die Falisker,* Strasbourg: Karl J. Trübner.

De Lucia Brolli, M. A. (1990) "Un nuovo santuario a Narce sulla sponda del Treja" in *La civiltà dei Falisci,* Atti del XV Convegno di Studi Etruschi e Italici (Civita Castellana, 28–31 maggio 1987), 173–195, Florence: Leo S. Olschki.

——(1990a) "Area del santuario suburbano. Il deposito votivo. Monte Li Santi-Le Rote, Narce (Viterbo)" in *Bollettino di Archeologia*, 3: 65–71, Rome: Istituto Poligrafico e Zecca dello Stato, Libreria dello Stato.

——(1991) *Civita Castellana. Il Museo Archeologico dell'Agro Falisco*, Rome: Quasar.

——(1991a) *L'Agro Falisco*, Rome: Quasar.

——(1995–96) *"Falerii* Novi: novità dall'area urbana e dalle necropoli" in Atti *della Pontificia Accademia Romana di Archeologia. Rendiconti* LXVIII: 21–68, Vatican City: Tipografia poliglotta vaticana.

——(2006) "Dalla tutela alla ricerca: recenti rinvenimenti dall'area urbana di *Falerii"* in M. Pandolfini (ed.), *Archeologia in Etruria Meridionale. Atti delle giornate di studio in ricordo di Mario Moretti* (Civita Castellana, 14–15 novembre 2003): 65–89, Rome: l'Erma di Bretschneider.

——(2010) "Un culto ctonio nell'"hinterland" di *Falerii"* in *I riti del costruire nelle acque violate.* Atti del convegno internazionale, Roma, Palazzo Massimo 12–14 giugno 2008; 343–357, Rome: Scienze e lettere.

——(2012) "Appunti sulla tomba 5 della necropoli di Valsiarosa" in G. Cifani (ed.) *Identità e cultura dei Falisci* (Atti del seminario della British School at Rome, Roma, 19 maggio 2011), Rome, Quasar.

De Lucia Brolli, M. A. (ed.) (forthcoming) *Il santuario di Monte Li Santi – Le Rote*, Pisa-Roma, Fabrizio Serra editore.

De Lucia Brolli, M. A. and Baglione, M. P. (1997) "I Falisci: il caso di Narce" in *Nomen Latinum*, Atti del Convegno Internazionale (Rome, 24–26 ottobre 1995) (*Eutopia* IV.2): 53–94, Rome: Quasar.

De Lucia Brolli, M. A. and Michetti, L. M. (2005) "Cultura e società tra IV e III sec a.C. *Falerii* e Orvieto a confronto" in *Orvieto, l'Etruria Meridionale e l'agro falisco. Annali Faina* (XII): 375–427, Rome: Quasar.

di Gennaro, F. (1982) "Organizzazione del territorio nell'Etruria meridionale protostorica" in *Dialoghi d'Archeologia*, 2: 102–137, Milan: Il Saggiatore.

——(1986) *Forme di insediamento tra Tevere e Fiora dal bronzo finale al principio dell'età del ferro*, Florence: Leo S. Olschki.

——(1988) "Primi risultati degli scavi nella necropoli di *Crustumerium*: tre complessi funerari della fase IV A" in *Archeologia Laziale* IX, 1988 (*Quaderni di Archeologia Etrusco Italica* 16), 113–123, Rome: Consiglio nazionale delle ricerche.

Di Stefano-Manzella, I. (1990) "Lo stato giuridico di *Falerii* Novi dalla fondazione al III sec. d.C." in *La civiltà dei Falisci*, Atti del XV Convegno di Studi Etruschi ed Italici (Civita Castellana 28–31 maggio 1987), Florence: Leo S. Olschki.

Gamurrini, G. F., Cozza, A., Pasqui, A. and Mengarelli, R. (1972) *Carta Archeologica d'Italia (1881–1897). Materiali per l'Etruria e la Sabina* (Formae Italiae s. II, doc.1), Florence: L.S. Olschki.

Giacomelli, G. (1963) *La lingua falisca*, Florence: L.S. Olschki.

Maras, D. F. (2012) "Questioni di identità: Etruschi e Falisci nell'agro falisco" in G. Cifani (ed.) *Identità e cultura dei Falisci* (Atti del seminario della British School at Rome, Roma, 19 maggio 2011), Florence: Leo S. Olschki.

Martelli, M. (1987) "La ceramica orientalizzante" in M. Martelli (ed.), *La ceramica degli Etruschi*, 16–22, Novara: Istituto geografico De Agostini.

Micozzi, M. (1994) «*White on red*». *Una produzione vascolare dell'orientalizzante etrusco*, Rome: GEI.

Moscati, P. (1985) "La viabilità di una regione: l'Agro Falisco" in Boitani F. *et al.*, *Strade degli Etruschi. Vie e mezzi di comunicazione nell'antica Etruria*, 89–97, Rome: Autostrade - Concessioni e Costruzioni Autostrade.

Pensabene, P. *et al.* (1980) *Terrecotte votive dal Tevere*, Rome: l'Erma di Bretschneider.

Peruzzi, E. (1990) "Gli Etruschi di Corchiano" in *La civiltà dei Falisci*, Atti del XV Convegno di Studi Etruschi e Italici (Civita Castellana, 28–31 maggio 1987), 277–289, Florence: Leo S. Olschki.

Pitzalis, F. (2011) *La volontà meno apparente. Donne e società nell'Italia centrale tirrenica durante l'Orientalizzante antico*, Rome: L'Erma di Bretschneider.

Poleggi, P. (1995) *Una città falisca di frontiera: Vignanello dall'VIII al III secolo avanti Cristo*, Viterbo: Stab. tip. Agnesotti.

Potter, T. W. (1976) *A Faliscan Town in South Etruria. Excavations at Narce 1966–71*, London: British School at Rome.

Rizzo, D. (1996) "Recenti scoperte dall'area di Nepi" in *Identità e civiltà dei Sabini*, Atti del XVIII convegno di Studi Etruschi ed Italici (Rieti – Magliano Sabina, 30 maggio – 3 giugno 1993): 477–494, Florence: Leo S. Olschki.

Szilàgyi, J. G. (2005) "Dall'Attica a Narce, via Pitecusa" in *Mediterranea*, II, Fabrizio Serra editore: 27–55.

Tabolli, J. (2012) "Narce nella prima età del Ferro" in G. Cifani (ed.) *Identità e cultura dei Falisci* (Atti del seminario della British School at Rome, Roma, 19 maggio 2011), Rome: Quasar.

——(2012) *L'abitato e le necropoli I Tufi e La Petrina di Narce tra la prima età del Ferro e l'Orientalizzante Antico. Al confine dell'Agro falisco con il territorio di Veio*, Rome *forthcoming*.

Torelli, M. (1982) "Veio, la città, l'*arx* e il culto di Giunone Regina" in H. Blanck, S. Steingräber (eds), *Miscellanea archeologica Tobias Dohrn*: 117–128, Rome: G. Bretschneider.

MacIntosh Turfa, J. (2005) *Catalogue of the Etruscan Gallery of the University of Pennsylvania Museum of Archaeology and Anthropology*, Philadelphia: University of Pennsylvania Museum of Archaeology and Anthropology.

Vagnetti, L. (1971) *Il deposito votivo di Campetti a Veio. Materiali degli scavi 1937–1938*, Florence: Sansoni.

CHAPTER FIFTEEN

ETRURIA ON THE PO AND
THE ADRIATIC SEA

———•◆•———

Giuseppe Sassatelli and Elisabetta Govi

INTRODUCTION (GIUSEPPE SASSATELLI)

The ancient historical traditions, both Greek and Latin, agree that the presence and domination of the Etruscans in the Italian peninsula extended well beyond what has normally been regarded as their homeland, that is, (modern) Tuscany and northern Lazio. In particular, Livy, who defines the Etruscans as the most important people, well known from the Alps to Sicily, states that after setting their roots in Etruria, they penetrated into Campania to the south and spread north, crossing the Apennines, until they occupied most of the Po Valley with a massive colonial movement whose outcome was the establishment of twelve cities, on analogy with Tyrrhenian Etruria (Livy 5.33.9–10). We are not in a position to recognize a true dodecapolis in the Po region, but the stabile presence of the Etruscans in the Po Valley and their efficient organization on a commercial as well as political and institutional framework, thus represents a consolidated historical fact that the ancient authors knew well. The conquest of the fertile lands watered by the River Po is attributed by the sources to two characters: Tarchon, the founder of Tarquinia and of the Etruscan "nation," and Ocnus, Etruscan king of Perugia, founder of Bologna and Mantua. This dual tradition probably reflects two distinct Etruscan occupations of the Po Valley, dating back to an earlier, Villanovan stage and a more recent settlement corresponding to the sixth century BC, when the entire area underwent a reorganization that led to the establishment of new cities and the creation of a powerful trading system.

Etruscan interest in this area since the ninth century BC can be traced in part to the exploitation of natural resources, but also to the enormous commercial potential of an area that is central and convenient to the main routes linking Etruria, northern Italy and Europe, between the Adriatic and the Tyrrhenian Sea. The Etruscan population in the earliest, Villanovan, phase is thus concentrated in the area of the plains around Bologna, which is the hub of manufacturing activities as well as an extensive network of long distance contacts, and in the hilly area of Verucchio (near Rimini) overlooking the Adriatic Sea (Fig. 15.1). While Bologna developed from the outset a widespread occupation of the surrounding area for agricultural purposes, Verucchio was itself set up as a frontier center for commercial purposes, open to contacts with neighboring peoples and the peoples of the opposite shore of the Adriatic. During the Orientalizing period the two centers are fully integrated into the commercial circuits associated with all of Tyrrhenian Etruria, and they have furnished extraordinary evidence of the culture of the *principes* ("princes"), among which stands out the monumental sculpture in stone and the acquisition of writing in Bologna, and the elaborate funerary rituals of Verucchio. The Etruscans of Bologna then transmit the art of writing to all other populations of northern Italy, west to the Celtic Golasecca culture and east to the Venetic culture of Este. In these areas, the Etruscans, again via Bologna and the Po Valley, also distribute manufactured goods as well as important cultural and productive impulses particularly if we but think of all the "art of the situlae" peculiar to the Venetic area, but originating from an influx of Tyrrhenian craftsmen, coming from Bologna.

The political and economic order of Etruria Padana (Etruria of the Po Valley) in the earliest phases (Villanovan and Orientalizing) hinged primarily on Bologna and Verucchio and a dense network of smaller towns, widely disseminated in the territory since the mid-sixth century BC, shows a radical transformation linked with the broader picture of the Tyrrhenian and Western Mediterranean. The conflicts between the Etruscans, Greeks and Carthaginians end in naval clashes in the upper Tyrrhenian Sea and begin the gradual erosion of the Etruscans' unchallenged dominion of the sea. The increasing risks along the routes in the northern Tyrrhenian Sea led to an inevitable decline of trade with Celtic Europe, until then channelled along the route to Marseilles and the Rhone Valley. It is at this time that the Po region assumes a new importance because of its access to the Adriatic Sea, a trade route known to the Greeks for a long time but only now fully valued on the basis of contacts with the Celts across the Alps. The entire Po Valley was reorganized and the founding *ex novo* of the cities of Marzabotto in the Bolognese Apennines, Spina on the Adriatic coast and Mantua just north of the Po and on the River Mincio, as well as the "refounding" of Bologna, the capital of this new system, which allows the creation of a formidable economic

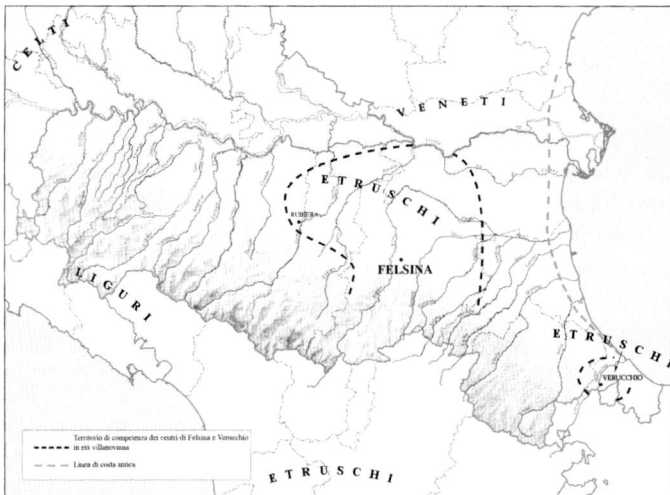

Figure 15.1   Map of *Etruria Padana* from ninth to eighth century BC (Dipartimento di Archeologia di Bologna).

structure, based on a dense network of exchanges between Tyrrhenian Etruria, Greece and transalpine Europe (Fig. 15.2). From Tyrrhenian Etruria there reached the Po Valley, in addition to manufactured products, also raw materials (copper and iron) to be transformed into products in special factories whose level of production was especially high. The close business relationship with the Greek world involves a deep acculturation of this Etruscan territorial sector, which was particularly receptive and open to cultural stimuli.

From this moment on the same lines of trade form the backbone of a new system of economic and political aggregation adopting essentially the urban form, in which an important role was also played by Adria, which is located further north on the Adriatic and near the territory of the Veneti. The newly founded cities are characterized by regular plans that required formal rituals of foundation, reconstructed mainly at Marzabotto. A dense network of villages of rural character or small towns, especially well documented in western Emilia, then joins the large urban centers. This radical reorganization of the Etruscan Po-territory ("Etruria Padana") has suggested a phenomenon of internal colonization from Etruria (Chiusi and Volterra). Etruscan epigraphy shows, however, that in the newly founded cities such as Marzabotto the names of local origin significantly outweigh others; therefore, the Etruscans of the Po region were above all the protagonists in this great process of development.

FELSINA/BOLOGNA

Bologna functioned at this point in an executive capacity, and may be considered the "capital" of Etruria Padana. Pliny the Elder reports that within the confederation of twelve cities of the Po Valley, Bologna, the ancient Felsina, was awarded a distinction of great importance: "*Bononia Felsina vocitata tum cum Etruriae esset princeps*" (Pliny, *Naturalis Historia* 15.112). The statement could have a meaning more chronological than political-institutional, so as to be understood as a synonym of metropolis, "mother-city" with a key role in the genesis and formation of the same Etruscan *ethnos*, on analogy with

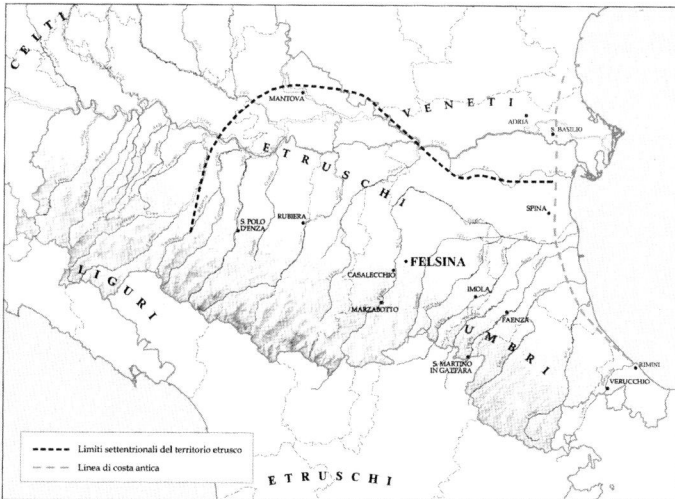

Figure 15.2   Map of *Etruria Padana* from sixth to fourth century BC (Dipartimento di Archeologia di Bologna).

Cortona and Pyrgi. Analogous with what happened in most of the Tyrrhenian centers, from the ninth century BC on, in Bologna also the population is concentrated in at least three villages, topographically distinct, already gathering around the area of the future historic city. During the first half of the eighth century BC one of these villages, the one closest to the hills, becomes the fulcrum of a single settlement that is already proto-urban in character, extending over 200 hectares, but still sparsely occupied. The inhabited area is bordered by two rivers and around it are placed the necropoleis according to a spatial organization, which already requires the ability for long-term planning (Fig. 15.3). The sparse population of the valley during the earlier Bronze Age makes one think that the rapid emergence of the great center of Bologna is due to the arrival of the Etruscans from the Tyrrhenian (the first colonization event). In fact, it is possible to recognize the economic and commercial conditions of the phenomenon in some sites of the Bronze Age, such as Frattesina (Fratta Polesine-Rovigo), which are already integrated into the great circuits designed for the supply of metals and basic materials sent out on one side to the Aegean and from the other towards Tyrrhenian Etruria. It is therefore likely that the formation of the proto-city of Bologna between the ninth and eighth centuries BC is due to local people, albeit with the participation of Etruscan elements that came from the Tyrrhenian. In the eighth century BC, after an initial period of adjustment the village began a process of gradual conquest of a vast surrounding area used for an extensive type of agriculture devoted mainly to crops like cereals. This expansion was not immune to conflict with other entities, as confirmed by Livy (5.34.9) who relates the story of the battle of the Ticino, fought by the Etruscans and Gauls in the time of Tarquinius Priscus, evidence of an ancient conflict between groups who resided near the Po. Useful testimony in this regard is the stone funerary *cippus* (late seventh century BC) found in Rubiera (in western Emilia), on which an inscription mentions the *zilath*, a "military leader" of a border community certainly controlled by Bologna.

We are poorly informed on the internal organization of the city of Bologna, especially in this earliest phase (eighth to seventh century BC), but we know that along the northern border an imposing *agger* (defensive earthwork) flanked by ditches was built. Inside, the settlement was laid out in part with large groups of huts, initially separated by wide open spaces intended primarily for agriculture. Already at this stage a consistent metallurgical activity is well documented, as demonstrated by the hoard of Piazza San Francesco, closed

Figure 15.3   Map of Etruscan Bologna (Dipartimento di Archeologia di Bologna).

in a large jar in the late eighth or early seventh century BC, with nearly 15,000 bronze objects carefully stored inside. Accumulated over time, these objects weighed about 1418 kg, and all were destined to be recast. This was certainly the reserve storage of one or more workshops, as evidenced by the presence of many tools related to metallurgy (saws, files, hammers, anvils and crucibles). There are also many ingots of pure copper, perhaps from the mines of Tyrrhenian Etruria. Other work tools (saws, drills, rasps, chisels and axes) can be traced back to woodworking or tool making, while large scythes, sickles and the pennate axes indicate different crops, and viticulture and arboriculture.

The cemeteries of Bologna have furnished more than 3,000 graves for the Villanovan phase (ninth to eighth century BC) and Orientalizing period (seventh to sixth century BC) and about 1,000 for the next phase conventionally called the "Felsina phase" (from the mid-sixth to beginning of the fourth century BC). They began to bury in the areas closest to the village and proceeded to spread out almost in haphazard fashion. After an initial phase characterized by a substantial uniformity in the grave goods, attested by a biconical urn and few other objects, from the mid-eighth century BC differences begin to appear in the funeral ritual, the consequence of radical structural changes that correspond to economic and social transformations. The population is now heading towards a rapid cultural and political development, which will lead at the end of the eighth century BC to the emergence of an aristocratic class, just as happens in the centers of Tyrrhenian Etruria. Symptomatic in this respect is the indication of possession of a horse through the deposition in the tomb of bits and other items of tack, alluding to a higher social level. More and more numerous in the tombs is the banquet service of fine vessels, often made of bronze (Fig. 15.4), and especially lavish is the system of personal ornaments such as fibulae, pins and belts made of bronze. The rare presence of weapons in graves evokes special functions of a military character, but the rite of burial in Bologna did not envisage the connotation of the deceased as a warrior, in contrast to the situation in the Tyrrhenian area. During the seventh century BC the high level of production and artistic attainment is evidenced by the appearance of painted pottery in imitation of Greek wares and the stamp-decorated ceramics that are a feature of Bologna (Fig. 15.5). But above all there is the emergence of funerary sculpture in stone, perhaps due to craftsmen from the East who came to Bologna, indicating a strong economic development and a high artistic culture, supported by the aristocracy. The Orientalizing stelae (so-called "proto-Felsina stelae") exhibit an iconographic repertoire that extends from the Near Eastern (sphinxes, tree of life, the lord in the chariot) and ends with the exhibition of the social and political values of the class in power (Fig. 15.6). Another event of great significance in cultural terms, forever linked to this group of *aristoi*, is the early acquisition of writing in the early seventh century BC. The inscription on an amphora from the Melenzani necropolis dating from the late seventh century BC, the longest in Bologna and one of the longest of all the Etruscan area, recalls a solemn gift

Figure 15.4   Bronze vessels from Benacci Caprara Tomb 39 of Bologna (Museo Civico Archeologico di Bologna).

between aristocrats finalized at the end of the text with the signature of the guarantor who wrote the inscription. The confirmation of a full and generalized acquisition of writing across the Po Valley area controlled by the Etruscans comes from the addition of two stone *cippi* from Rubiera in the Secchia valley, funerary monuments dating from the late seventh and early sixth century BC, inscribed and decorated in relief with Orientalizing motifs (Fig. 15.7).

Figure 15.5   Biconical vase with stamped decoration from Bologna
(Museo Civico Archeologico di Bologna).

Figure 15.6   Malvasia Tortorelli Stele from Bologna (Museo Civico Archeologico di Bologna).

Figure 15.7   *Cippi* from Rubiera (Reggio Emilia) (Soprintendenza per i Beni
Archeologici dell'Emilia Romagna).

During the sixth century, following the radical economic and commercial transformations affecting the whole territory of Etruria Padana, Bologna will capture the signs of a general restructuring that leads to full development in an urban sense. The city is now equipped with houses with stone foundations and roofs of clay tiles, and a genuine *arx*-type elevated Etruscan acropolis with a temple building and carved *cippi* of travertine and marble, also intended to hold offerings, among which stand out two bronze statuettes of Hercules with the apples of the Hesperides and of Apollo as lyre player, testimony of the cults that were practiced (Fig. 15.8). From the *arx* the eye could embrace the whole urban area, the necropolis and much of the *chora* (adjacent farmland); the *arx* is perfectly suited to the function of *auguraculum*, i.e. "ritual observatory," where the augur could conduct the rites of foundation in relation to a quadripartition oriented in space that transformed the city into a *templum*, according to the prescribed Etruscan discipline. As in the previous stage, we know very little about the structure and organization of the town, already destroyed by the Romans and buried beneath the medieval and modern city. The necropoleis, however, provide important evidence of the new urban organization and especially the economic, social and political characteristics of the civic community. The tombs are still arranged along the route of the access roads to the city. In the greater funeral sector, the Certosa site to the west, several important projects of monumental character have been documented, such as the construction of a large, 15-meter wide road, a very old track that is now paved with pebbles and side drains, creating a large public work commissioned by the whole city community. On either side of the street the richest and most important tombs were prepared, indicated by above ground monumental stone markers, which constitute the most distinctive peculiarities of Felsina of the fifth century BC.

The funeral offerings from the tombs include items of Etruscan production and Attic imports associated with the banquet and the symposium. Large vessels (kraters, amphorae and stamnoi), cups and utensils (strainers, ladles and jugs) allude to the preparation and consumption of wine. In a well-known tomb of the Giardini Margherita necropolis, sumptuous vessels of the funerary offerings were grouped around and over a folding stool of ivory, the *sella curulis* that belonged to a local magistrate (Fig. 15.9). The tomb offers a picture of an urban society in which political office, rather than wealth, indicates the social rank of the deceased, as shown by the stone tomb-markers produced in the mid-fifth century BC, the so-called "Felsina stelae," horseshoe-shaped and decorated in low relief. Indeed, they represent the various social categories (the hoplite, the knight, the priest, the mature man, young woman, etc.), but on the most monumental tombstones, decorated with multiple registers, there also appear scenes of processions with characters bearing emblems that pay homage to the deceased, or in particularly solemn ceremonies, including the conduct of games in honour of the deceased, which refer to the deceased as vested with an important role in the political and institutional realm (Fig. 15.10). In some exceptional cases we find an explicit reference through inscriptions citing the office of *zilath*, the supreme urban magistracy whose functions are similar to those of a Latin *praetor*. The imagery of the "Felsina stelae," a unique phenomenon in the panorama of Etruscan sculpture, also reveals the salient traits of funerary ideology that at this stage focuses on the concept of the journey to the Afterlife and the change in status that death causes. And in tune with the Greek ideological universe, mutated in the region of Etruria Padana through commercial contacts, pictures of demonic psychopompoi and Charon himself with an oar accompany the transit of the deceased to the Afterlife (Fig. 15.11).

Figure 15.8   Herakles and Apollo from the acropolis of Villa Cassarini in Bologna (Soprintendenza per i Beni Archeologici dell'Emilia Romagna).

Figure 15.9   Goods from the "Tomb of the Folding Stool" of Bologna
(Museo Civico Archeologico di Bologna).

Figure 15.10   Stele 168 from Bologna (Museo Civico Archeologico di Bologna).

Figure 15.11   Stele from S. Michele in Bosco of Bologna (Museo Civico Archeologico di Bologna).

VERUCCHIO

The Etruscan center of Verucchio, in Romagna, perched on an easily defended hill and just fifteen miles from the sea, like many cities of Tyrrhenian Etruria was born with a commercial vocation and developed through control of the Adriatic coast and the direct connection to the hinterland and with the centers of the Tiber and southern Etruria. It is very likely that Verucchio had its port near Rimini. The importance and precocity of the Etruscans in the Adriatic is also indirectly confirmed by the testimony of Livy on the Etruscan domination of both seas of the peninsula, namely the Tyrrhenian and Adriatic.

The hill chosen for the settlement consists of a plateau of about 50 hectares, 300 meters above sea level, reminiscent of landscapes typical of Tyrrhenian Etruria (think of the cliff-top city of Orvieto). At the foot of this hill and around it, were arranged the necropoleis. In the town were found the remains of huts as well as houses with stone foundations and roof tiles, and workshops are well documented. The tombs have yielded materials of extraordinary importance and quality: raw and carved amber from the Baltic (Fig. 15.12), for which Verucchio was a sorting and processing site; horse-bits; weapons, which constitute an element of strong differentiation in Bologna; textiles of rare refinement (see Chapter 42), and the extraordinary variety and richness of fibulae, necklaces and earrings in which there is a massive and sophisticated use of amber, the ossuaries and utilitarian pottery, richly stamp-decorated. These are just some of the outstanding features of this Etruscan town, but above all the wooden artifacts stand out, preserved in large quantities and now, after some recent discoveries in Bologna, as yet unpublished, they are less isolated as a feature of Etruria Padana. From a princely tomb comes an extraordinary wooden throne, similar to specimens in bronze from Tyrrhenian Etruria (Fig. 15.13); its back is decorated with carvings of very complex figurative scenes that refer to the ceremonial and aristocratic ideology of hegemonic groups. The extraordinary documentation of Verucchio's funerary rituals reflects the development and economic and commercial potential of the community and reveals a plurality of contacts with neighboring cultural areas that make this Etruscan border town unique.

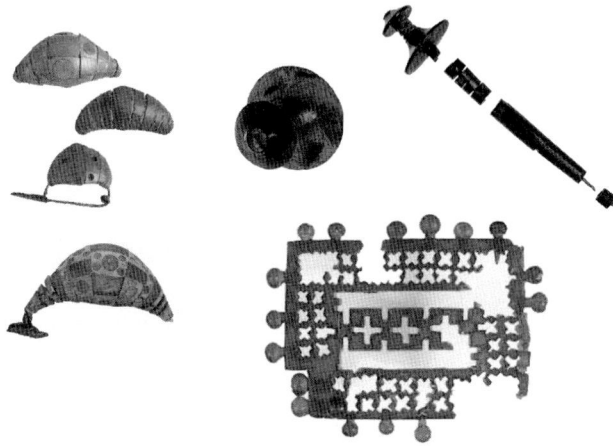

Figure 15.12   Objects made of amber from the tombs of Verucchio (Soprintendenza per i Beni Archeologici dell'Emilia Romagna).

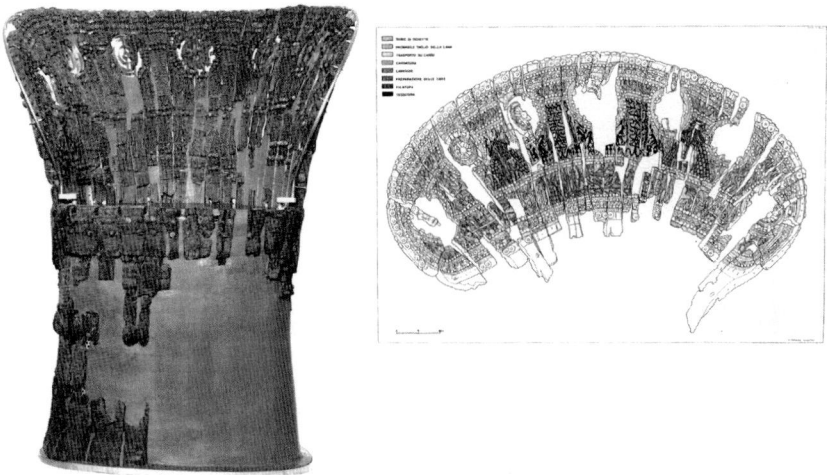

Figure 15.13   Wooden throne from Verucchio (Soprintendenza per i Beni Archeologici dell'Emilia Romagna).

MARZABOTTO (ELISABETTA GOVI)

Located in the Reno Valley, which ever since the Villanovan period has been the main route of communication between Tyrrhenian Etruria and Etruria Padana, the city of Marzabotto is known for its urban layout that has been perfectly preserved (Fig. 15.14); behind its regular and perfect astronomical orientation are the clearly identifiable traces and structures of a foundation ritual attributed by ancient sources precisely to the Etruscans. Established *ex novo* in the second half of the sixth century BC, the town assumed its permanent and regular layout around the beginning of the fifth century BC (Fig. 15.15). Of this development, in the urban sense, there is perhaps testimony in the ancient name of the city, which came to light recently in an inscription, *Kainua*, that may be traced to the Greek *kainon*, meaning "new [city]," just like Neapolis in Magna Graecia. Urban regularity on one side and a connection with the Etruscan ritual of a celestial *templum* projected on the earth on the other, have always captured the attention of scholars since the first excavations in the nineteenth century. Today we are able to reconstruct the foundation ritual that here finds an exact match in the famous passage of Festus, showing the time and methods for the *inauguratio*, for which they needed two "seats," ritually linked according to a sort of *stipulatio*. In the *auguraculum*, placed on the acropolis and thus in a dominant position, the augur, sitting on the *tescum* and facing east-south-east, embracing a view of the entire inhabited area, could perform the *spectio*, an operation that allowed the transposition of the axes of the celestial *templum* onto the earth. Below, at the center of the projected *templum* is where the two main urban axes crossed and where there was driven into the ground the stone with the *crux* (inscribed cross-hairs), in what is considered the *sedes inaugurationis*, the auspice-taker stood, tasked with implementing the instructions of the augur. The defining principle of the geometry of the city is the observation of the sun in its annual cycle, given that the urban form corresponds exactly to the figure that connects the endpoints of the sunrise and sunset at the summer and winter solstices (Fig. 15.16). The plan of the city was then based on the two diagonals, connecting these points that always crossed at the *crux* on the stone marker.

Figure 15.14   Aerial view of the city of Marzabotto (Soprintendenza per i Beni Archeologici dell'Emilia Romagna).

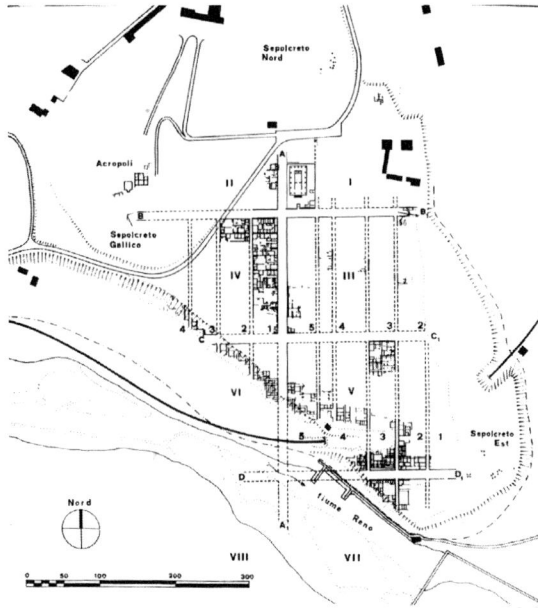

Figure 15.15   General plan of the city of Marzabotto (Dipartimento di Archeologia di Bologna).

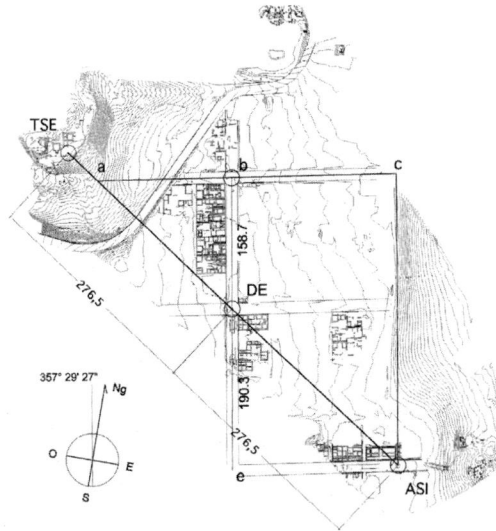

Figure 15.16   Layout of the foundation ritual of the city of Marzabotto
(Dipartimento di Archeologia di Bologna).

The genuinely Etruscan foundation ritual combines with inspiration and urbanistic experiences of the Greek colonial world, developed between the late sixth and early fifth century BC. The town of Marzabotto is thus built according to strict criteria of regularity and urban planning: a large, 15-meter-wide road (*plateia* A) runs through the town in a north-south direction and is crossed perpendicularly by three other roads also 15 meters wide (*plateiai* B, C and D), all with a central roadway of at least five meters for vehicular traffic and two sidewalks used for pedestrian traffic as well as for a resting place and shops. Roads less than five meters wide (*stenopoi*) were used to define the individual blocks that held the houses, factories and production facilities, but also the great city temple of Tinia that was recently discovered. The houses are characterized by a planimetric variety (Fig. 15.17), had strong foundations of large river pebbles, superstructures in unfired clay bricks dried in the sun or of "*graticcio*" ("lattice-system" construction), and roofs of pan and cover tiles. Along the main street, *plateia* A, are the houses with structures of a compluviate atrium, belonging to the upper class. The production workshops were used in particular for two craft activities: metallurgy and production of ceramics and tiles. The metallurgy was practiced not only in small domestic workshops but also in large and specialized ateliers. The production of ceramics and tiles is also evidenced by small kilns scattered everywhere in the urban area and in a very large facility of *Regio II-Insula 1*, in the service of the temple of the city-cult dedicated to Tinia, corresponding to Greek Zeus (Fig. 15.18). The temple, built in the early fifth century BC, is perfectly placed in the urban

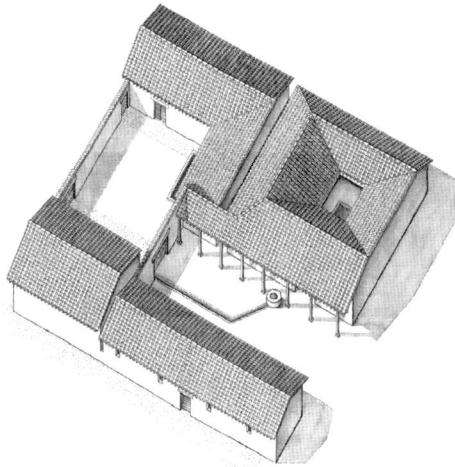

Figure 15.17   Reconstruction of House 1 of Regio IV-insula 2 of Marzabotto (Dipartimento di Archeologia di Bologna).

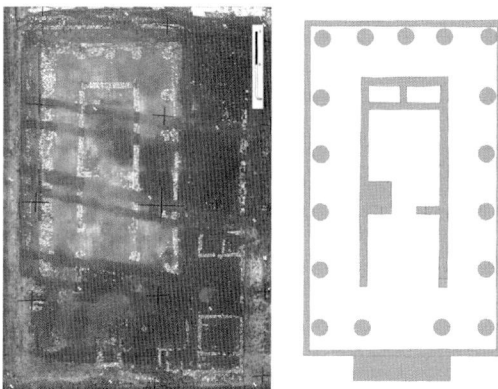

Figure 15.18   Photo and plan of the city temple of Marzabotto (Dipartimento di Archeologia di Bologna).

fabric, to the north of the monumentalized northern entrance of the road that came from Bologna. The temple, a large peripteral structure (35.50 x 21.75 m), which is connected to important developments in the Tyrrhenian area (Vulci and Pyrgi), was probably a combination of political and social center for the citizens, like the agora of Greek cities.

The town had important infrastructure that ensured a high quality of life for its citizens: wells present in all homes; channels to the sides of roads to ensure the smooth flow of rainwater, a water system structured as a *castellum aquae* for purified water from a natural spring with special settling basins that drained it clean into the city below. To the north and east of the urban area were located two necropoleis, on both sides of two major roads into the city, one that came from Bologna and the other from Tyrrhenian Etruria. To the north-east on the small plateau overlooking the city was placed the acropolis with a complex of religious buildings (temples and their altars). One of these in particular, a podium-altar with stairs and a central well, which was found filled with the remains of sacrifices; it corresponds to the *mundus* (offering pit) for worship of the infernal deities and sacred in particular to Dis-Pater, a deity to whom Tarchon had dedicated the newly founded cities in Etruria Padana (Fig. 15.19).

SPINA

The Etruscan town of Spina is the answer to the early Greek presence in the northern Adriatic, well documented in the first half of the sixth century BC at Adria. Founded around 540 BC, Spina is certainly an Etruscan town (the epigraphic evidence shows that the majority of its inhabitants spoke and wrote in Etruscan), despite the presence of many individuals of other ethnic groups, especially Greeks, and as such it seems to inherit the function of control over the Adriatic port, Verucchio, that in previous ages had exerted but now entered a phase of relative decline. With Spina a new chapter in relations with the Greek world, and especially Athens, opens to the Etruscans of the Po Valley.

Figure 15.19   Acropolis of Marzabotto, altar D (Soprintendenza per i Beni Archeologici dell'Emilia Romagna).

The site of Spina (near present-day Comacchio) was not far from the sea in ancient times. It stood in a hostile environment in terms of climate, made difficult due to constant tidal flooding. The enormous efforts to control the waters and counter the gradual silting of the harbour make clear the importance of the *emporium* of Spina in relation to the network of trade affecting the whole of Etruria Padana. Of the city and its internal organization we know little, but we are familiar with wooden structures and pilings used both to strengthen the ground and to raise the living floors above the water level (Fig. 15.20). So far the only area of the town that has been discovered has an area of 5–6 hectares and corresponds to a naturally elevated expanse, like an island emerging from the surrounding lagoon. There must surely have been other islands of this kind forming the city of Spina, which has a very large number of tombs (over 4,000) and which in Antiquity must have played a major role, if it was permitted to erect a *"thesauròs"* (treasury) in the sanctuary at Delphi. The houses discovered to date have a regular structure made of wood, including the superstructure (the use of tiles for the roofs seems to arrive here very late). The urban plan shows characteristics of regularity like the larger cities of the Etruscan Po region, from Marzabotto to Bologna, and even the origin of Spina probably involved a foundation ritual, witnessed by a stone marker with the *crux* and inscribed *"mi tular"* ("I [am] the border"), such as is documented precisely at Marzabotto (Fig. 15.21). The town, probably with regular houses and canals, was also equipped with a large artificial canal built by the Etruscans to enable connection to the sea, cutting through all the coastal dunes and ensuring the arrival of Greek goods at the docks of Spina then to be redistributed to the rest of Etruria Padana.

The archaeological evidence of Spina, so limited as regards the town, is rather extraordinary for the burial grounds discovered in the last century; the sites of Valle Trebba and Valle Pega, where thousands of graves and associated funerary objects are the most lively and most vital signs of trade and of the relations that this Etruscan city had with Athens in particular. One of the most common types of goods was, in fact, the Attic pottery conveyed to Etruscan Spina, and not only the practice of the symposium now assimilated by the Etruscans, but also mythological themes and epics, and more generally the image of the society and culture of Athens of the fifth century BC (Fig. 15.22). The epithet of "Greek city" (*polis hellenìs*) that is given to Spina by Strabo and by the Pseudo Scylax, however, should not be understood in the ethnic sense but refers to its full commercial accessibility for the Greeks who in this *emporion* could be welcomed and speak their own language.

Figure 15.20   Palisade/embankment of Spina (Soprintendenza per i Beni Archeologici dell'Emilia Romagna)

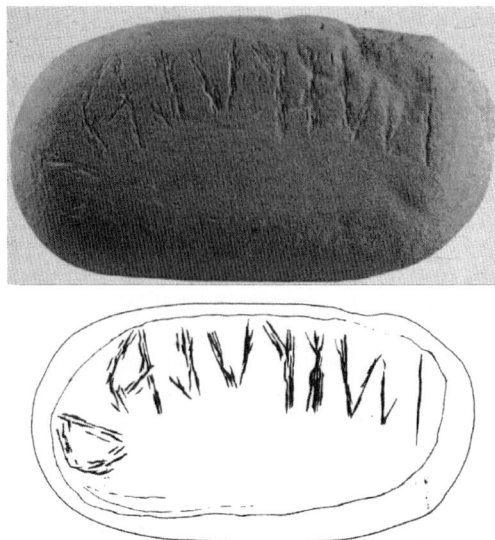

Figure 15.21   River pebble with inscription *"mi tular"* from Spina (Soprintendenza per i Beni Archeologici dell'Emilia Romagna).

Figure 15.22   Attic vases from the funerary offerings at Spina (Soprintendenza per i Beni Archeologici dell'Emilia Romagna).

At Spina also were landed many amphorae for transport of Greek olive oil and wine. These products were distributed by the Etruscans to the other populations of northern Italy, in addition to the transalpine world, as evidenced by the Corinthian, Chiote, Samian, Attic, Mendesian and perhaps also Thasian transport amphorae present at Spina, Marzabotto and Forcello near Mantua. Also, bronze vessels of Etruscan production, linked to the banquet, are present in northern Italy and beyond the Alps where they arrived in large quantities along with the precious figured and black gloss Attic pottery, introducing to the Celtic princes the Mediterranean tradition of the symposium and the consumption of wine.

The unique trading system created by the Etruscans of the Po region was based on availability, as return goods of agricultural products, particularly wheat (which, like all great cities, Athens needed) and also of other products related to food supply such as livestock, are mentioned in the literary sources and documented archaeologically. Pig-raising was definitely a very common type of farming, as well as the rearing of smaller animals, reminding us of the "chickens of the Adriatic," already known to Hecataeus. It is likely then that metal, too, carried weight in this kind of exchange, and it would have come from Tyrrhenian Etruria.

MANTUA

Mantua, which is located north of the Po, was the northernmost of the Etruscan cities of the Po Valley. It was the base for the routes from this area aimed primarily toward the Italic populations (Veneti, Raeti and Celts of Golasecca) and later to transalpine Europe. Its Etruscan origin is widely attested in the sources, but we know the city very much from archaeological evidence. While a little further south, at the confluence of the Po and the Mincio, in the town of Forcello di Bagnolo San Vito, on a hillock of artificial origin, there was brought to light a town of about 12 hectares whose relationship with Mantua is still under discussion. This town is characterized by a regular grid of street-blocks, located along roads or canals that intersect at right angles, by houses built with perishable materials (wood and clay), and by intensive activities of production and trade. The exploration also found in several locations the presence of a solid artificial terrace fitted with a palisade, an *agger terreus* (earthen embankment), which in addition to playing a defensive role was also to protect the town from the frequent and intense flooding of the Mincio. Here, as in Spina, in a far from favorable environment, the Etruscans decided to found a settlement on the basis of connections, especially by river; on the one hand to the Adriatic and the port of Spina, and on the other to the interior, with a strategic role in the system of exchanges between the Mediterranean and Europe that the Etruscans themselves had created and tightly controlled. The town has a regular plan, like other newly founded cities in Etruria Padana, and was crossed by canals, which are also navigable. One excavated area produced the traces of a house made of wood and occupied by individuals dedicated to the most sophisticated practices of the symposium, as evidenced by the Attic vases and wine amphorae found there.

THE END OF ETRURIA PADANA

At the beginning of the fourth century BC, Gauls from Europe and the Transpadane region fell heavily on the territory of the Etruscans and the Umbrians and then pushed on to Rome, which was besieged and taken. The invasion of the Gauls had strong, disruptive effects, at least in its early stage, on the entire system of cities created by the Etruscans in the Po Valley. This started with Marzabotto, which lost its urban identity, becoming a sort of outpost to control the valley of the Reno. In Bologna, events were probably less traumatic, at least in appearance. The city seems to maintain a prominent position within the territory controlled by the Gauls, but in its urban structure significant changes occurred, including a clear general impoverishment. The Gauls undermined at its base the urban model created by the Etruscans in the Po Valley with the consequent fragmentation of the territory within, which both the routes and the characteristics and distribution of settlements changed rapidly. According to Livy (33.37.3–4) Bologna, which he continues to call Felsina, in addition to being qualified as an *urbs* ("city") in homage to its fully urban Etruscan past, is sometimes also referred to as *oppidum* ("fortified town"), surely a result of the dismantling by the Gauls. The organization of the territory is no longer "by city," as in the previous Etruscan phase, but by "*vici*," i.e. lowland settlements related to agricultural production, or by "*castella*," settlements on high ground with distinct functions, including military, of supervision and control of the land and of the new routes of communication. With this radical transformation, the Gauls themselves intended to become the main intermediary between the Mediterranean and continental Europe, taking over from the Etruscans. For this purpose, new trade routes were activated, more to the east and more aimed at the Romagna region, emptying the Etruscan cities of Bologna and Marzabotto of their historical role and depriving them of their economic function, instead lending great strength and importance to new settlements like the Celtic town of Monte Bibele (Monterenzio) (Fig. 15.23).

Only Mantua and Spina survived this upheaval, the first because of its strategic position, the second because it was decentralized and surrounded by marshes and dunes. Spina became a collection point for many Etruscans of the Po region who fled after the Gallic onslaught, and who devoted themselves to trade and piracy on the Adriatic Sea. The continuity of Etruscan presence on the sea is not just at Spina, but covers a wide coastal strip running from Adria to Ravenna, where there is massive importation of Etruscan ceramics (from Volterra, but also from other centers of northern and interior Etruria) and, to a lesser extent, of goods from Magna Graecia and Sicily, if we think of the "Greco-Italic" amphorae. Here there is also a significant local production of pottery and ceramics both figured and undecorated, most notably those of "Upper-Adriatic" type, a typical production of the Etruscans of the northern Adriatic, perhaps also aided by the arrival of artists from interior Etruria and from the *Ager Faliscus* ("Faliscan territory," see Chapter 14).

The economic vitality of this Adriatic coast and especially of Spina at this late stage is also evidenced by epigraphic documentation at Spina, where Veneti, Italic groups, Faliscans, Messapians and also Gauls resided. The piracy of the Etruscans of the Po region is perhaps the reason for the famous Athenian decree of 325–324 BC, relating to a

Figure 15.23 Tomb at Monterenzio (Soprintendenza per i Beni Archeologici dell'Emilia Romagna).

colonization scheme to protect Greek traffic in the northern Adriatic. This late Adriatic-Etruscan culture survives long into the third century BC and is welded chronologically to the first episodes of the Romanization of the Po Valley, which begins right from Rimini, an ancient Etruscan town that has now become a true "Adriatic port" for the entire Po region.

BIBLIOGRAPHY

On Etruria Padana in general:

Harari, M. (2000) *Gli Etruschi del Po*, Edizioni Libreria Cardano, Pavia.
Govi, E. (forthcoming) *Etruscans in Po Valley Etruria: urbanism and domestic architecture* in *Housing and habitat in the Mediterranean World: responses to different environments* (International Archaeology Conference, Monash Prato Centre, 2011).
Malnati, L. and Manfredi, V. (1991) *Gli Etruschi in Val Padana*, Il Saggiatore, Milan.
Sassatelli, G. (2000) *L'espansione etrusca nella Valle Padana* in *Gli Etruschi* (Catalog of Exhibition, Venice), Bompiani, Cinisello Balsamo, pp. 169–179.
——(2001) *Gli Etruschi nella pianura padana* in G. Camporeale (ed.), *Gli Etruschi fuori d'Etruria*, Arsenale Editrice, Verona, pp. 168–191.
——(2008) "Gli Etruschi nella Valle del Po. Riflessioni, problemi e prospettive di ricerca" in *AnnFaina*, 15, pp. 71–114.

On Bologna:

Macellari, R. (2002) *Il sepolcreto etrusco nel terreno Arnoaldi di Bologna, 550–350 a.C.*, Marsilio, Venice.
Principi etruschi tra Mediterraneo ed Europa (Catalog of Exhibition, Bologna) (2000) Marsilio, Venice.
Sassatelli, G. and Donati, A. (eds) (2005) *Storia di Bologna, 1. Bologna nell'antichità*, Bononia University Press, Bologna, pp. 75–385.
Sassatelli, G. and Govi, E. (2007) [2009] "Ideologia funeraria e celebrazione del defunto nelle stele etrusche di Bologna" in *StEtr*, 73, pp. 67–92.

On Verucchio:

Gentili, G. V. (2003) *Verucchio villanoviana. Il sepolcreto in località Le Pegge e la necropoli al piede della Rocca Malatestiana*, G. Bretschneider, Rome.
Sassatelli, G. (2001) "Verucchio, centro etrusco di 'frontiera'" in *Ocnus*, 4, 1996, pp. 247–268.
von Eles, P. *et al.* (2002) *Guerriero e sacerdote. Autorità e comunità nell'età del ferro a Verucchio. La Tomba del Trono*, All'insegna del Giglio, Borgo S. Lorenzo.

On Marzabotto:

Baldoni, V. (2009) *La ceramica attica dagli scavi ottoceneschi di Marzabotto*, Antequem, Bologna.
Govi, E. (ed.) (2007) *Marzabotto, an Etruscan town*, Antequem, Bologna.
Govi, E. (2008) "Reconstructing History from Material Culture. The Case of Etruscan Marzabotto" in *ARCHAIA: Case Studies on Research Planning, Characterisation, Conservation and Management of Archaeological Sites*, BAR, Oxford, pp. 137–146.
——(forthcoming) *Etruscan urbanism in Po Valley Etruria* in J. A. Becker – E. C. Robinson (eds), *Studies in Italian Urbanism: the First Millennium BCE* in JRA Supplementary Series.
Govi, E. and Sassatelli, G. (2003) *Marzabotto. La casa 1 della Regio IV – insula 2* (Studi e Scavi 26), Antequem, Bologna.

Gottarelli, A. (2010) "Templum solare e culti di fondazione. Marzabotto, Roma, Este: appunti per una aritmo-geometria del rito (IV)" in *Ocnus*, 18, pp. 53–74.

Sassatelli, G. (ed.) (1994) *Iscrizioni e graffiti della città etrusca di Marzabotto*, University Press Bologna, Bologna.

Sassatelli, G. and Govi, E. (ed.) (2005) *Culti, forma urbana e artigianato a Marzabotto. Nuove prospettive di ricerca* (Atti del Convegno di Studi, Bologna 2003), Antequem, Bologna.

Sassatelli, G. and Govi, E. (2010) *Cults and Foundation Rites in the Etruscan City of Marzabotto* in L. B. van der Meer (ed.) *Material aspects of Etruscan religion* (Proceedings of the International Colloquium, Leiden 2008), "BaBesch" Supplementa 16, Leuven, pp. 17–27.

Vitali, D., Brizzolara, A. M. and Lippolis, E. (2001) *L'acropoli della città etrusca di Marzabotto*, University Press Bologna, Imola.

On Spina:

Berti, F. and Guzzo P. G. (eds) (1993) *Spina. Storia di una città tra Greci ed Etruschi* (Catalogo della Mostra, Ferrara), Ferrara Arte, Ferrara.

Berti, F. and Harari, M. (eds) (2004) *Storia di Ferrara II. Spina tra archeologia e storia*, Ferrara.

Govi, E. (2006) "'L'ultima' Spina. Riflessioni sulla tarda etruscità adriatica," in *Rimini e l'Adriatico nell'età delle guerre puniche* (Atti del Convegno Internazionale di Studi, Rimini 2004), Antequem, Bologna, pp. 111–135.

Rebecchi, F. (ed.) (2004) *Spina e il delta padano. Riflessioni sul catalogo e sulla mostra ferrarese* (Atti del Convegno, Ferrara 1994), L'Erma di Bretschneider, Roma 1998.

Sassatelli, G. "Gli Etruschi di Spina" in *Hesperìa: Studi sulla grecità d'Occidente*, 19, pp. 21–30.

On Mantova:

de Marinis, R. C. (ed.) (1986–1987) *Gli Etruschi a Nord del Po* (Catalog of exhibition, Mantova), Mantova.

de Marinis, R. C. and Rapi, M. (eds) (2005) *L'abitato etrusco del Forcello di Bagnolo S. Vito (Mantova): le fasi arcaiche*, Tipografia operaia, Mantova.

CHAPTER SIXTEEN

ETRUSCANS IN CAMPANIA

———— •◆• ————

Mariassunta Cuozzo

The ancient perception of the Etruscan character of some districts of Campania is attested in the ancient literary sources. According to Pliny the Elder (*NH* 3.70), at one time the Picentine region belonged to Etruscans, extending for thirty miles from Sorrento to the River Sele (D'Agostino 1988; Cuozzo 2003, Cerchiai 2010). For Livy (7.3.1) and Strabo (5.4.3), Capua is an *urbs maxima* at the head of an Etruscan do Dodecapolis in Campania. (Fig. 16.1).

Nevertheless, the archaeological picture of the region presents noteworthy elements of complexity and the significance of the occurrence of cultural traits of "Villanovan" type in Campania has been the subject of heated debate. Today, the composite cultural panorama, rather than being interpreted in terms of ethnic contrasts, seems to take shape from the very beginning as a dynamic and dialectic situation of population, which in

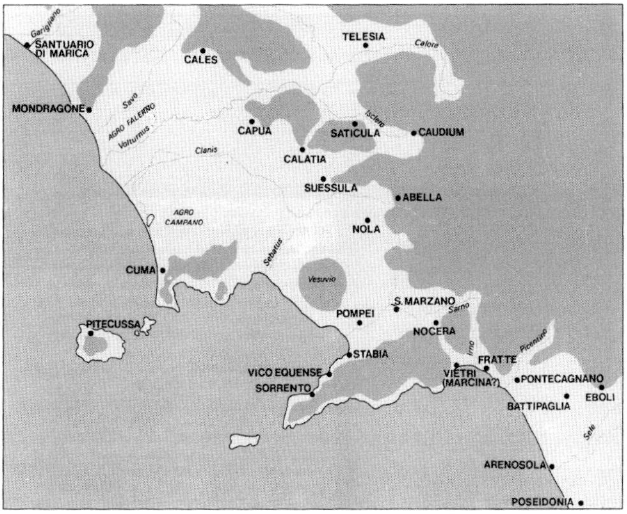

Figure 16.1   Campania from Iron Age to Archaic period: population distribution.

the current state of its variegated aspects is difficult to define: for the longest part of their history, many communities of ancient Campania appear to be "open societies," cultural composites so as to evoke in recent years the anthropological definitions of "*cultures metisses*" or hybridization (Amselle 1990; 2010; D'Agostino-Cerchiai 2004; Van Dommelen 1997; 2006; Cuozzo 2012) or the theory of the "Middle Ground" (Malkin 2002).

The Etruscan presence in Campania in the First Iron Age – traditionally labeled as the so-called first "Etruscanization" (*etruschizzazione*) – rather than indicating a huge displacement of peoples and the enslaving or forced acculturation of the local populations, should instead probably be considered a form of cultural hegemony brought about by groups of southern Etruscans who enjoyed an advanced socio-economic and cultural level. This enabled them to stimulate, through a widespread integration of indigenous people, a process of territorial re-organization and a concentration of settlement in a proto-urban pattern (Cerchiai 2010).

The population of Campania during the Iron Age is usually subdivided into several principal cultural districts. Traditionally indigenous groups, characterized by their funerary ritual of inhumation, occupy the northern coastal area and internal southern Campania: the horizon of the *fossa*-tombs comprises pre-Hellenic Cumae and similar sites on the island of Ischia, the communities of the Valley of the Sarno, the southern Hirpini region corresponding to the cultural assemblage termed *Oliveto-Cairano* (Valleys of the Sele and Ofanto). People of the "*Villanovan*" horizon, traceable to the principal centers of southern and central Etruria, have been recognized as the rulers of coastal southern Campania, up to the boundary of the Gulf of Salerno, corresponding to the modern-day small town of Pontecagnano with the neighboring *ager picentinus* and in the northern interior sector of the region, in the fertile plain of the Volturno around the ancient Capua (Santa Maria Capua Vetere). One last Villanovan nucleus has been identified at Sala Consilina in the Valley of the Diano, thus beyond the confines of the ancient regions, and so it will not be considered in this chapter. In the second half of the eighth century BC Campania became the site of the oldest Greek foundations in the West. As both the literary sources and material culture testify, these are people from Euboea who settle at Pithekoussai on the island of Ischia, and at Cumae on the mainland opposite, and they profoundly change the order of the Tyrrhenian region.

As regards the debate on the Campanian "*Villanovan*" cultural horizon (Cuozzo 2012 with previous bibliography), according to one early hypothesis (Pallottino; D'Agostino) the so-called "first Etruscanization" is a phenomenon of "colonization," paralleling the Villanovan expansion into the region of Etruria Padana, connected with the displacement from the central area of the peninsula of people associated with an agricultural population but also aimed at acquiring control of the strategic maritime- and river-junctions of the region. Such an identity appears diachronically attested, beyond the description of the literary sources, by the long-term bonds between Pontecagnano, Capua and Etruria, according to the epigraphic and cultural evidence. Conversely, a second reading of the evidence, led by Renato Peroni and his "school," does not attribute an ethnic value to Villanovan cultural traits but suggests a similar process of socio-economic development at the time of creation in both Etruria and Campania of cohesive, politically structured communities, already organized in a proto-urban fashion.

The discoveries of recent years make it difficult today to maintain the absence of Etruscan components not only in the case of Pontecagnano, where all the material evidence and settlement organization are tied to the antiquity of the extraordinary epigraphical documentation from the middle of the seventh century BC (Fig. 16.4.3), but also in the case of Capua, in the light of the results of recent excavations in the necropoleis (necropolis of the Nuovo Mattatoio, Fig. 16.6). At the same time, very recent discoveries have furnished indications of a broad sphere of interaction between the diverse components of the Campanian population as early as the beginning of the First Iron Age (Cuozzo 2012 with bibliography).

The stabile presence of Greeks in Campania enriched and complicated the situation described. The settlement of Pithekoussai, which was established by Chalkis and Eretria according to the ancient sources, points to the conclusion of a phase when the coasts of the Tyrrhenian Sea were frequented by seafarers coming above all from Eubeoa and from the Cyclades, following the routes of the Phoenicians. These first contacts, at a time when the West was still unknown territory, are attested by the mythical locations of the *Odyssey*. The community of Pithekoussai does not seem to follow the rigid norms of a Greek *polis* but constitutes an emblematic example of integration and cohabitation among ethnically

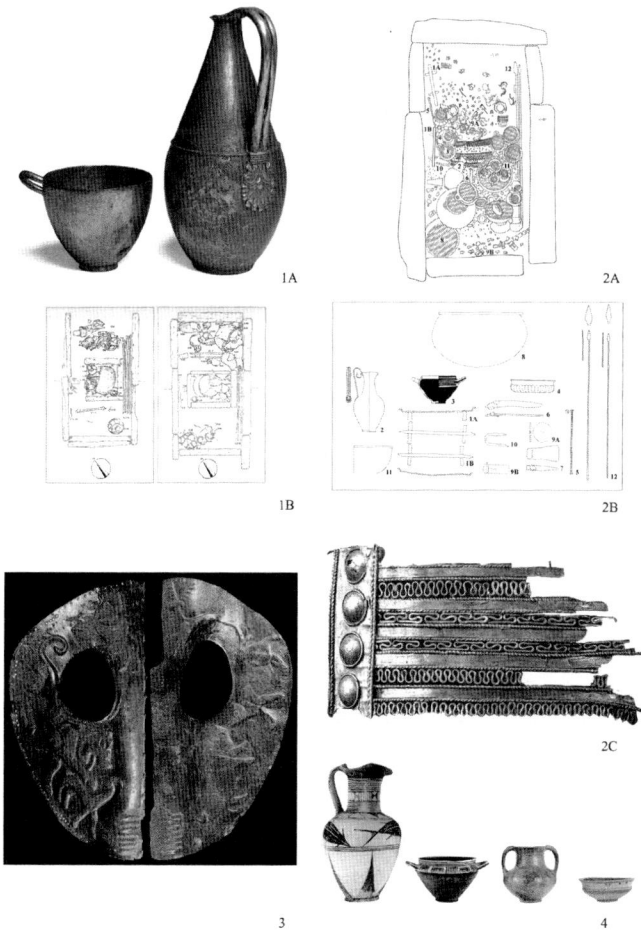

Figure 16.2   Pontecagnano. Princely Tombs. 1. Tombs 926–928; 2. Female princely Tomb 2465 with a selection of the grave goods; 3. Horse armor (mask) from Tomb 4461; 4. The "basic set" of Orientalizing grave goods.

and culturally diverse components; Greeks, Phoenicians, indigenous peoples (Ridgway, 2000). The island shows a distinctive artisanal and commercial physiognomy: in the second half of the eighth century BC Pithekoussai establishes a broad network of relations of interaction whether with Etruria and the Etruscan cities of Campania or with the native sphere, which implies in the first place the mobility of artisans above and beyond the circulation of raw materials and/or goods and the diffusion in Etruria, as in Campania and in other regions, of products of "Greek type" reworked to suit the taste and needs of the local elites (Gras 2000; D'Agostino 2011a; Cerchiai 2010). The foundation of Cumae, traditionally dated to 725 BC, but according to new discoveries probably even older, implies significant changes in the Tyrrhenian and Campanian equilibria.

The development of the relations between Greeks and local populations has turned out to be quite diverse: if with the Etruscan sphere and the Etruscan components of Campania, especially with neighboring Capua, there prevails an agreement based on respect and reciprocal exchange that can be traced over a long period through alternating phases, in contrast, in the case of the indigenous sphere, after the violent conquest of the Phlegraean littoral, attested by the ancient sources (Phlegon of Tralles in *FGH* II 257), the local populations will be in part reduced to a servile condition, in part pushed towards the hinterland and the Apennine zones to the borders of the Samnite territory. The period between the Early and Middle Orientalizing (last quarter of eighth to mid/third quarter of seventh century BC), represents for Campania a moment of extraordinary flowering (Fig. 16.2). The history of the Etruscan components of the region is known above all through the rich documentation of Pontecagnano and the *ager picentinus* that in recent years has been enriched by the results of new excavations at the site of Monte Vetrano (Cerchiai *et al.* 2009; Campanelli 2011).

The physiognomy of the composite material culture for Pontecagnano between the end of the First Iron Age and the Orientalizing period configures a role of the first order in the scope of the Tyrrhenian and the Mediterranean: the Picentine center (*ager picentinus*) appears to be a true and proper crossroads of peoples and cultures, bound by tight bonds as much to the Etruscan and Latial (Latin) world as to the Greeks of Pithekoussai and Cumae; intensive relations are attested with Greece and with Phoenician and/or Near Eastern components; complex relationships that also imply phenomena of mobility are documented with the surrounding Campanian and Italic communities, first with the groups of *Hirpini* of the so-called *Oliveto Citra-Cairano* horizon, the communities of the valley of the Sarno, Capua, and the Enotrian sphere (Fig.16.3).

The affirmation of powerful aristocracies of a hereditary character is attested in the funerary sphere by the well-known phenomenon of the "princely tombs," a sign of recognition and of the comprehensive solidarity of the Tyrrhenian elites whether of Greek, Etruscan, or indigenous origin, which transcends ethnic differences in favor of the expression of an above-normal status (see *Debating Orientalisation*): from Tomb 104 of the Fondo Artiaco at Cumae, to the "princely" tombs of Etruria and Latium, via tombs 926–928, 4461 and now also 2465, a woman's tomb (Fig. 16.2, 16.4) of Pontecagnano (Cuozzo 2012). Although the "princely" customs were foreshadowed by the exceptional assemblage of Fornaci tomb 922, still datable to the end of the First Iron Age (D'Agostino 2011), the princely tombs that constitute a distinctive sign of the aristocracy in the Tyrrhenian region seem until now absent at Capua in the full Orientalizing period. It is possible, however, that this absence is to be attributed to the current state of research and to the vast backlog of evidence that remains unpublished (Bellelli 2005; Johannowsky 1996).

Traditionally, a second period of "Etruscanization" of Campania appears to coincide with the final phase of the Orientalizing and the Archaic period (sixth century BC). In this case also, today one tends to consider this phenomenon a form of cultural influence rather than a process of colonization (D'Agostino-Cerchiai 2004; Cerchiai 2010). The Etruscan cultural contribution occurs in four main aspects that affect the entire region, beyond the limits traditionally assigned to the Etruscan component of Campania:

- an extensive process of urbanization and settlement aggregation;
- the beginning of local production of bucchero and expansion on a regional scale;
- the elaboration of a "Campanian system" in the ornamentation of public buildings (Fig. 16.7), based on a standardized complex of revetments in polychrome terracotta designed for temple structures of Tuscan type with superstructure in perishable material, the result of the amalgamation of Etruscan, Greek, and indigenous craft experience (see Chapter 49);
- the spread of Etruscan writing, even in areas of indigenous tradition, documented by many inscriptions incised on vessels found in funerary offerings. Next to the Etruscan names and in the presence of Greek names, in fact, there appears an extensive documentation of indigenous onomastic formulas often completed by the noble family name (*gentilizio*), to indicate the success of those aristocracies of local origin that will play a crucial role in the later history of Campania (Fig.16.4).

A document of exceptional character is the so-called *Tabula Capuana,* one of the longest public texts surviving in the Etruscan language, datable in its original form between the end of the sixth and the beginning of the fifth century BC, but recopied in the course of the fifth century (Fig. 16.8 no. 4; see Chapter 22).

Current historical-archaeological reflection, however, also tends to privilege in this phase the profound integration of the elites, attested by the archaeological and epigraphic evidence, that seems to transcend, in this phase, the ethnic differences, and appears to mark a fundamental stage in the process of formation of an identity for the Campanian

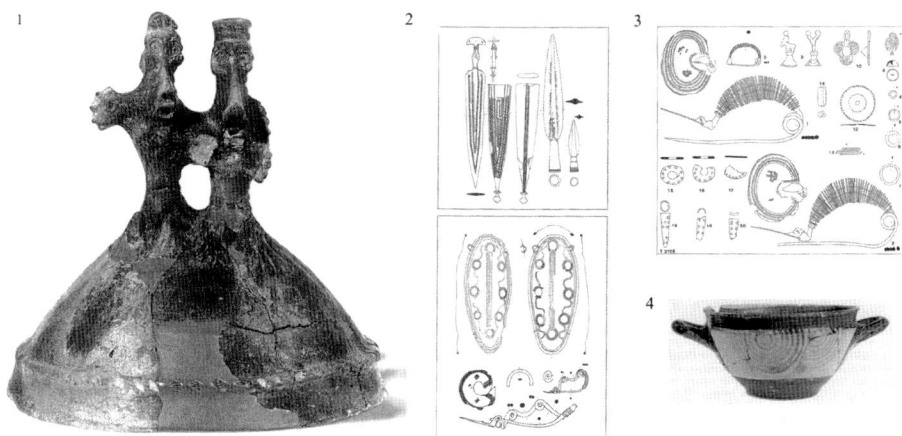

Figure 16.3   Pontecagnano. 1. Helmet-lid with anthropomorphic figures; 2. Tomb 180: the panoply; 3. Tomb 2198: selection of grave goods with Nuragic bronze figurine; 4. Cup with pendant semicircles from Tomb 7129.

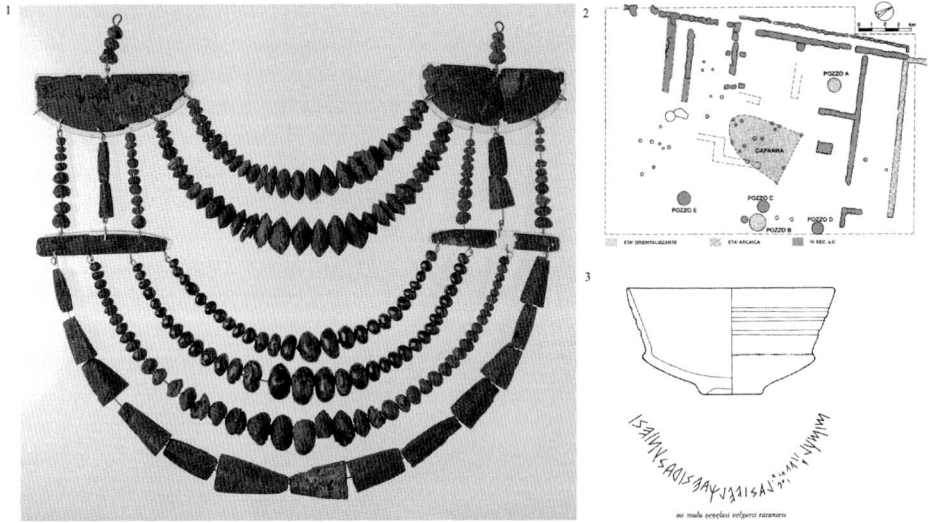

Figure 16.4 Pontecagnano: 1.The necklace-pectoral from Tomb 2465; 2. Orientalizing apsidal
building in southern sector of the settlement; the oldest Etruscan inscription in Campania
(Tomb 3509, mid-seventh century BC).

world that will be fully realized in the course of the fifth century BC. One of the aspects
investigated with more attention in recent years is the capillary process of urbanization
that invests Campania, paralleling the other regions of ancient Italy, in the course of the
Archaic period. Urban planning is implemented in a rigorous functional articulation of
spaces that will remain unchanged up until the Roman conquest and in a progressive
monumentalization of public areas, first of all the sanctuaries. The urban plan is usually
based on a regular grid of streets that subdivide blocks designated for residences and
separates the residential quarters from the areas designated public and from the zones to
be used for artisanal activities.

The process of urbanization and the renewed Etruscan interest in Campania are
manifested not only in those centers that represent a continuity of Etruscan components
in Campania – Capua and Pontecagnano – but above all they determine the formation of
a new network of settlements in areas that were not previously urbanized: the Sorrento
peninsula (Sorrento, Vico Equense, Stabiae); the territory of Nola (Nola); the Valley
of the Sarno (Nocera and Pompei). The Etruscan *Marcina* has been identified with
the settlement of Fratte di Salerno, founded at the mouth of the Irno, and destined to
supplant Pontecagnano, over the course of the sixth century BC, in the control of shipping
and interior routes. In northern Campania, apart from Capua – for the entire Archaic
period the principal Etruscan city of Campania – the urbanization extended to the nearby
Suessula and *Calatia*. In southern Campania two main spheres of influence seem to be
interwoven, the Etruscan and the Greek, the latter represented by new foundations
(*Poseidonia* and *Velia*). But it is the privileged axis Capua-Cumae that plays a dominant
role in the history and culture of archaic Campania.

Capua, as has been said, according to the sources capital of an Etruscan dodecapolis,
and Cumae, in the last part of the sixth century BC governed by the tyrant Aristodemos
(504–484 BC), experienced an extraordinary flowering as testified by the expansion and

urban restructuring with the realization of great public works projects (walls, hydraulic construction, sanctuaries) and of a fertile season of artisanal creativity. A preferred archaeological indicator of the cultural synergy between the two cities is the "Campanian system" characterized as early as the first half of the sixth century BC by female-head antefixes, by the last quarter of the sixth century BC arising from a lotus bud. The "Campanian system" would be met with noteworthy popularity even outside the region (Rome, Pyrgi, Volterra and southward even as far as Sicily; D'Agostino-Cerchiai 2004).

From these homogenizing characters the main Etrusco-Campanian centers present peculiarities and specific developments that should be considered individually.

PONTECAGNANO

The Etrusco-Campanian center of Pontecagnano rose near the River Picentino, 10 km to the south of Salerno (Fig. 16.5), on a plain bounded by mountains of the same name; it is actually known above all for the vast necropoleis (Cuozzo 2003; D'Agostino 2006) that have furnished up to today more than 10,000 tombs mainly datable between the ninth and fourth centuries BC, although still little is known about the settlement, in spite of important finds in recent years (Cerchiai 2010; Pellegrino-Rossi 2011; Scavi Autostrada 2012). The principal necropoleis of Pontecagnano are located to the west and east of the town, in the locality of S. Antonio a Picenza: a plateau extending 80 hectares, defined by surveys and by recent archaeological campaigns (Fig. 16.5). The settlement occupied a strip of land today almost entirely bounded on the north by the route of the Salerno-Reggio Calabria autostrada, to the south by the Strada Statale 18; to the west and south the ancient boundary followed natural ravines, in the first case corresponding to the river bed of the Picentino. The name of the ancient city of Etruscan origin is still unknown, while today we may consider as sure the identification of the Roman phase with the *oppidum* of *Picentia* (268 BC).

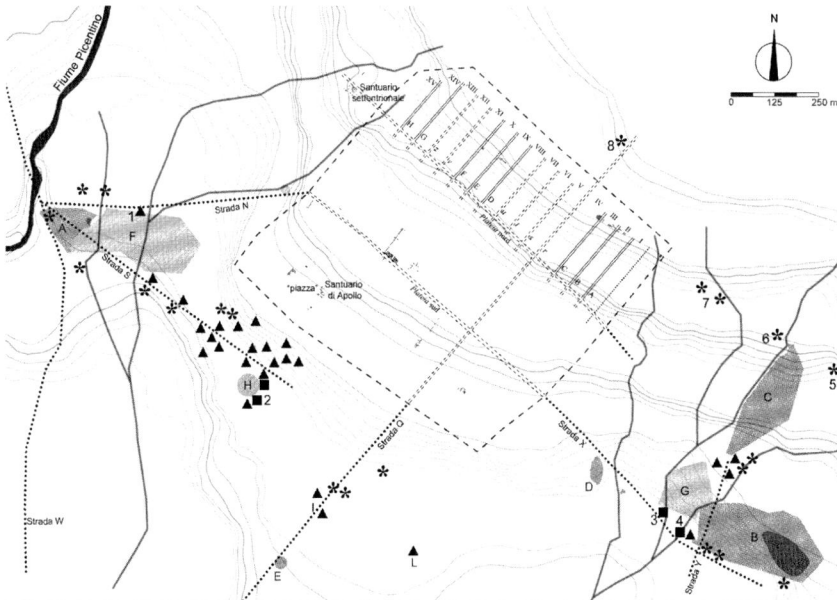

Figure 16.5   Pontecagnano: necropoleis and old settlement.

The history that emerges from the archaeological research at Pontecagnano provides an excellent outline, from its beginnings, of cultural openness and interaction among the various people who lived in or frequented Campania. As has been stated, between the First Iron Age and the Orientalizing period, the Picentine center acquires a first-rate role in the Tyrrhenian region, demonstrating a strong network of relationships with Etruria, Greek components, Phoenicians, Near Easterners, and Italic peoples.

Orientalizing Pontecagnano has been known until now mostly for the "princely" tombs 926–928 and 4461, all of them male and located in the western necropolis (Figs 16.2, 16.5). The partial publication of the tomb of the "princess" 2465 (Figs 16.2, 16.4) and the systematic survey of the necropoleis have revealed the multidimensional character of the community, enhancing previous readings and proposing questions on the diversity of its identities, differences and shared characteristics that appear to characterize the Campanian center.

THE FIRST IRON AGE

The widely prevalent funerary ritual is cremation with deposition in a biconical impasto ossuary placed usually directly in *a pozzetto* tombs (well-shaped pits) (Pontecagnano II.1; *Dinamiche di sviluppo* 2005). For the First Iron Age, apart from two principal necropoleis to the north-west and south-east of the settlement, one further burial ground is known, located two kilometers to the south (loc. Pagliarone) that seems associated with a minor settlement, perhaps a lagoon harbor.

The ceramic imitation of a bronze helmet constitutes in many cases the cover for male biconical urns; the others are usually covered with an overturned bowl. As in Etruria, in the first half of the ninth century BC an egalitarian ideology seems to prevail, a sort of "isonomic" ideal that is manifested in the absence of a marked differentiation between grave goods and in a prohibition against depositing real weapons in the burials. Some elements of the funeral offerings seem generally connected to the gender of the deceased, probably also in relation to the deceased's status, such as the typology of the fibulae which distinguishes between male and female types, the textile equipment that denotes a certain number of female burials from the first half of the ninth century BC on, and on the male side, the razor, and from the end of the ninth/beginning of the eighth century BC, offensive arms (spear and sword; Tomb 180, Fig. 16.3).

The material culture of Pontecagnano is characterized, from the beginning, by the emergence of a plurality of influences: apart from the obvious integration into a Campanian milieu in the ceramic repertoire, the privileged relations with coastal southern Etruria (Tarquinia, Veii) are evident. Among the most meaningful indicators one notes, alongside the biconical vases already mentioned, the presence of a hut-urn (Bietti Sestieri 1992), vases in bronze sheet, the repertoire of the arms and razors. Early contacts are documented with the Phoenician and Nuragic world (Sardinian bronzes, Tomb 563); and with Torre Galli, in modern-day Calabria (greaves, Tomb 180). The complexity of the ideologies, of the rituals and of the religious forms is attested by the famous cover of an ossuary depicting as its final hand-modeled figurines of a couple. Some scholars (D'Agostino 1988; Cerchiai 2010) interpret the female figure as a goddess who welcomes a hero to his destination in the Underworld (or perhaps it is part of a scene of *hieros gamos,* "sacred marriage" with a divinity: Torelli 1997); in a further hypothesis to be projected in a supernatural dimension, it may be the conjugal couple that in this phase is also emphasized in the structuring of the burials.

Between the second and third quarters of the eighth century BC, the advanced restructuring of endogenous social dynamics and the process of concentration of resources in the hands of a few groups are enhanced by the opening of new contacts with the Greek world. Early ceremonial exchanges are attested with the Euboean-Cycladic navigators of the "pre-colonial" phases: from the beginning, Pontecagnano plays a privileged role as attested by the concentration there of Greek ceramics; first the cups with pendant semicircles are present in the Picentine center in quantities unknown anywhere else, then the chevron cups and bird-bowls and the other ceramic types of this period (D'Agostino 2006; 2011a; Cerchiai 2010). With the settlement of Pithekoussai, between the middle and third quarter of the eighth century BC, and especially with the foundation of Cumae in the last quarter of the century, the relations between Greeks and the Tyrrhenian centers change profoundly. It remains now to assess the complex implications of its character and the significance of the results of the most recent excavations in the *ager picentinus* territory, in particular of the settlement of Monte Vetrano at the mouth of the River Picentino. This outpost, separated from the main center and controlling a port, has furnished for the moment of transition from First Iron Age to the Orientalizing phase some tombs of exceptional wealth and especially characterized by an extraordinary concentration of imports, signs of intense relations with Greek and Near Eastern components as well as with Etruria and Pithekoussai in whose sphere are indicated a Near Eastern bronze cup of the type "of the bulls" ("*dei tori*"), a Nuragic boat model and a scarab of the Lyre Player Group (Cerchiai-Nava 2009; Campanelli 2011). The site disappears in the sweeping territorial transformations that signal the transition to the Orientalizing period.

THE ORIENTALIZING PERIOD

The passage to the Orientalizing period is configured in the necropoleis of Pontecagnano by the funerary representation of a true and proper "reinvention of tradition" (Cuozzo 2003), implying profound transformations of the symbolic and ideological heritage: the protagonists are the hereditary aristocracies, comparable to the powerful *gentes* ("clans") of which the literary sources speak for Latium and Etruria, associated with the assertion of a pyramidal social structure at the apex of which are found the "princes" who centralize in their own persons the political, military and religious power and the guarantee of the system of relationships within the group and the control of the ritual field (D'Agostino 1977; 1999). Integral parts of this social structure are the new forms of funerary ideology based on an accentuated and intentional discontinuity with the First Iron Age, with the abandonment of the oldest burial grounds – following a behavior attested in the main southern Etruscan centers – and the construction of an apparatus of new symbols and new behaviors. The full representation and visibility of the burials of children in the necropoleis, a category under-represented or marginalized in other cultural areas of the peninsula, demonstrates the affirmation of a renewed perception of the central importance of kinship and of the continuity of the clan groups that appears to open up new fields of symbolism. Such ideological dynamics seem connected to a decisive stage in the long process of urban formation. Of special importance, there now appear the first testimonies found of the settlement in the zone where, in the Archaic-Classical period, there would arise the sanctuary of Apollo; and the traces of a territorial reorganization with extensive reclamation of farmland (Fig. 16.4.2; Cerchiai 2010).

In both the principal necropoleis of Pontecagnano (Fig. 16.2), inhumation is now the dominant ritual, the tombs are usually *a fossa* (trench-shaped) or *a cassa* (cist-shaped) made of travertine slabs; cremation, or an allusion to this, only returns in the case of the "princely" tombs 928–926, 4461 (Cuozzo 2004–2005; Bonaudo *et al.* 2009). The renovation of the funerary landscape is based for the most part in cases of a centripetal structuring of the cemetery plan centered on the presence of clan tombs within the area of privileged burials and reserved also with regards to the presence of elements of enclosure and the creation of cult places for funerary cult still active into the fifth century BC (Fig. 16.2). As the variegated material culture testifies, Pontecagnano appears to be an "open" community that tends to integrate and rework various contributions and components that are at the same time in competition. The enhanced dialectic within the social body through the norms of the community, strategies of groups or of individuals and the complex dynamics of interaction with diverse cultural spheres are at the core of radical changes in the rituals and in the composition of the funerary offerings.

The establishment of rules and prohibitions of collective type occurs primarily in the selection of a "basic set" of grave goods which focuses on the association of a small impasto amphora, preferred indicator of the material culture of Pontecagnano, with a "wine service" of Greek type, totally innovative compared to the First Iron Age: it is an essential level of ritual, adopted by the community towards the end of the eighth century BC, for all components of gender and age group, men, women, children, and kept unchanged at least until the second half of the seventh century BC. Privileged bonds with the Etruscan world are manifested through the preferential use of writing and the gentilicial name (*gentilizio*): as has been noted, from Pontecagnano comes the oldest Etruscan inscription in Campania, the first in the region to document the adoption of the two-part name formula with the indication of a noble (gentilicial) name of unequivocal Etruscan origin ("*mi mulu venelasi velchaesi rasuniesi*") (Cerchiai 2010). The most recent results of research show that in Pontecagnano, as in contemporary contexts of Etruria and Latium, the heads of clans may be both male and female (Cuozzo 2003).

A marked dialectic in which identities are intertwined with status and gender seems to preside over the forms of re-elaboration of "princely" rituals in the context of a clear ideological confrontation between the East and West necropoleis. On the one hand, in the western necropolis, the "prince-hero" is affirmed, an Etruscan-Tyrrhenian ideological construct, partly evocative of Homeric places, the exclusive preserve of a few personages of male gender, like the individuals buried in the well-known tombs 926–928, 4461, and on the other hand, in the eastern necropolis, there appears the figure of the princely female of Tomb 2465, probably covered by a tumulus and the center-point for the surrounding funerary space. In Tombs 926–928, the ritual selected is cremation with the deposition of the bones, wrapped in fine cloth, in one or more containers of bronze sometimes also draped with textiles. The architecture of tombs 926–928 provides for the setting up of two distinct symbolic spaces (Fig. 16.2). Particular attention is paid in Tomb 928 to the wine service, the oinochoe and kotyle decorated, under the rim, with an inscription in false hieroglyphs, the product of Phoenician craftsmen working on the coast of Syria (Fig. 16.2 no. 1A). Symbols of luxury and of the princely lifestyle, these exotic objects, imported from the Orient and characterized by the quality of materials and technical refinement, appear in the main aristocratic tombs of Etruria and Latium. Offerings related to the status of the deceased, to the guarantee of the community and to the relationship with the gods, include precious and exotic imports, weapons and, most importantly, a set of multipurpose tools alluding to the function of the sacrifice, the banquet with meat and the display of the hearth (hatchets, axes, *machaira* [dagger/knife], knives, andirons, fire tongs) and, therefore, symbols of assurance of the continuity of the group or community, and at the same time signs of power. The possession of one or more horses is attested for tombs 926–928; in Tomb 4461 a royal type of horse armor appears, unique for its kind, consisting of a pair of equine masks in bronze with repoussé decoration of hunting scenes (Fig. 16.2, no. 1C).

A quite different scenario is outlined in the eastern necropolis. In this case, the lady of Tomb 2465 (Fig. 16.2) is the sole "princely" figure, and not merely the wife of the prince: in the funerary representation she seems to be the sole guarantor of the system of signs associated with the legitimization of the family line, the guarantee of the continuation of the group, a form of authority and power. For the woman, there is configured in the eastern necropolis of Pontecagnano a centrality of conception of the family line that could imply the existence of bilinear systems of descent (Cuozzo 2003). To female figures, the sole custodians of the prerogative of the chariot/cart, of royal symbols like the fan, sacrificial instruments and the hearth (axe, knife, fire-dogs, spits), major roles seem to be assigned, particularly in the sacred sphere. As various ancient sources recount, the deep bonds between divinities and those administering their cults at times could comprise a genuine personification of the gods through the splendor of the costumes and the presence of specific attributes, as has been hypothesized for the lady buried in the Regolini-Galassi Tomb of Caere (Colonna-diPaolo 1998; Cuozzo 2003), so the garments of the princess of Pontecagnano Tomb 2465, enriched with rare jewelry with repoussé and filigree decoration of Etruscan and/or Greco-Campanian manufacture (Fig. 16.4), are stiff in their lower half, entirely covered by a tight network of ornaments in metal plate. It has also been noted that the valorization of the female line of descent, together with typologies of uxorilocal matrimony with a foreigner, are attested in the ancient world precisely in relation to royal or princely conditions. However, in the case of Tomb 2465, as in that of the Regolini-Galassi Tomb of Caere, the construction of a funerary landscape of feminine type leads one to consider the possibility of a transitory female pre-eminence in the creation of the group and/or of power, perhaps in conjunction with one of those crucial periods of transition that, at times, seemed connected, in the ancient sources, with momentary changes in power relations (Rathje 2000; Bartoloni 2003).

CAPUA

The settlement was displaced to a strategic position that allowed it to control both the river routes to the Tiber region and interior Etruria through the valleys of the Sacco and Liri, and by the access routes to the Apennines through the Samnite territory (Cerchiai 2010). With respect to its foundation, the literary sources are not uniform, even if they all agree on the Etruscan character of the city. A well-known passage of Velleius Paterculus (1.7), that constitutes the principal testimony for this issue, proposed two different traditions: one, espoused by the author, places the foundation around 800 BC, the other, attributed to Cato, instead dates the event 260 years before the Roman conquest. In the light of the most recent archaeological discoveries, both dates seem to reveal a correspondence with crucial moments in the history of Capua: the "high" date must refer to the first foundation of the city which today is amply confirmed in the necropoleis of "Villanovan" type of the First Iron Age; the "low" chronology, instead, would indicate a phase of urban "re-foundation" experienced in the first quarter of the fifth century BC (D'Agostino 2011c). As in the majority of the examples described, the archaeological history of the site during the oldest phases is entrusted almost exclusively to the necropoleis: the beginning of occupation is set around the end of the tenth and beginning of the ninth century BC at the transition from Final Bronze Age to First Iron Age.

Until recent years, the Etruscan characteristics at Capua during the earliest phases seemed rather attenuated with respect to the Picentine region, first because of the absence of the biconical urn and helmet-lid, usually replaced with a jar (*olla*) covered with a bowl, and for the subsequent periods, by the more recent appearance of the epigraphic documentation (second half of the sixth century BC) compared to Pontecagnano. Profound changes to this interpretation are today prompted by the results of recent excavations in the locality of the "Nuovo Mattatoio." The necropolis, located to the north toward Monte Tifata, has furnished ample evidence (approximately 400 tombs), for the most part unpublished, representing especially the earliest phase of the First Iron Age until now lacking in the Capuan necropoleis. The new evidence attests the presence at Capua of the biconical ossuary and of the helmet-lid, the appearance of Villanovan types in the repertoire of swords and fibulae and, above all, a comprehensive adherence to forms of funerary ideology comparable with Tyrrhenian Etruria and Pontecagnano (Fig. 16.6; Johannowsky 1996; Melandri 2011).

With respect to settlement typology, it is especially the layout of the urban necropoleis (necropolis of Fornaci; Cappuccini; etc.; Fig. 16.6.1), that from the second half of the ninth century BC delimits a vast area of about 200 hectares, later occupied by the city of the historical period, which demonstrates a criterion of proto-urban organization, according to a practice characteristic of the contemporary centers of Etruria proper. A picture of the opening-up and cultural interaction in the Tyrrhenian region and the Mediterranean not dissimilar to that described for Pontecagnano is restored, until late in the ninth century BC, by the composite and diverse material culture with Greek and Near Eastern components as well as those of Etrusco-Italic type. The emergence of hereditary aristocracies in the last part of the First Iron Age finds confirmation in the funerary associations. The repertoire of ornaments is enriched by an exceptional local production of fibulae in bronze, and especially in large scale, characterized by zoomorphic and/or anthropomorphic appliqués.

In the final moment of the First Iron Age (phase II C), still in the third quarter of the eighth century BC, is dated Tomb 722 of the Fornaci necropolis (D'Agostino 2011c), a female deposition of an extraordinary level for the quantity and quality of the offerings and the ornamental apparatus, dated by a cup of Aetos 666 type of Pithekoussan manufacture. It is doubtful that also belonging to this tomb group is a valuable silver urn with a scale-pattern around the rim, a type until now known only much later, in the grave goods of some of the main princely burials of Cumae, Praeneste, Caere. This set of offerings appears even more surprising in contrast with the evidence of the full-blown Orientalizing period when these vessels seem to be until now absent from the princely tombs at Capua.

It is only much later, actually within the Archaic period, with the beginning of the sixth century BC, that the Capuan aristocracies choose to recover Etruscan paradigms for the display of Orientalizing gentilicial (clan) power in a similar way to what happens in other areas of interior Etruria (for example, the Chiusine region). Even today, this phase is only known thanks to two nineteenth-century finds: these are the Tomba Dutuit, distinguished by the find of an extraordinary cart of Etruscan provenance, with sides decorated in repoussé, and by a sumptuous banquet service consisting of imported Laconian bronze vessels (Bellelli 2005).

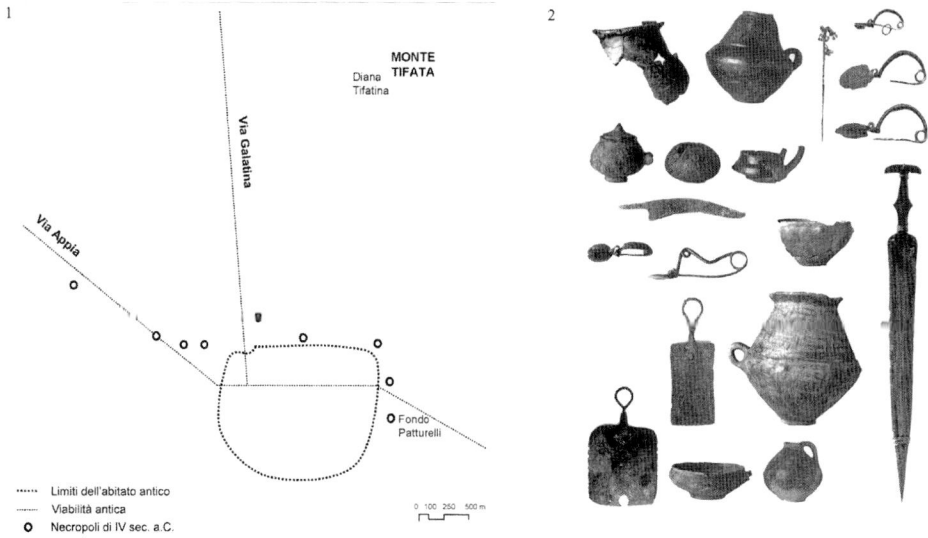

Figure 16.6   Capua. 1. Necropolis and settlement; 2. Necropolis of the Nuovo Mattatoio: selection of grave goods of the First Iron Age.

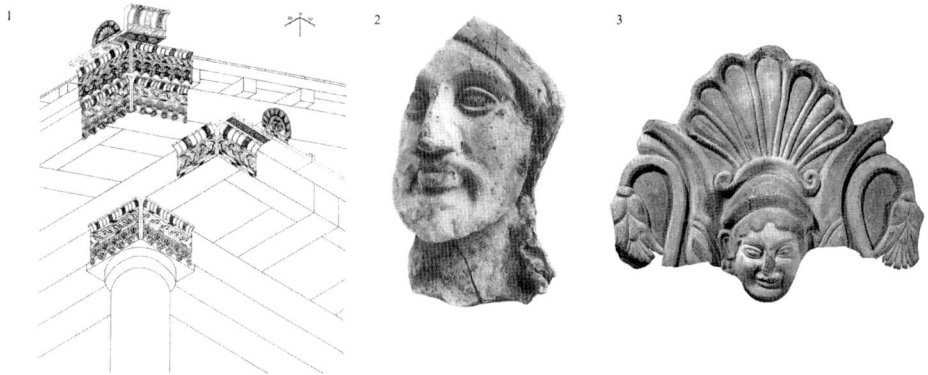

Figure 16.7   1. The "Campanian system." 1. Pompeii: decorative system of Archaic Temple of Apollo; 2. Capua: antefix with female head; 3. Fratte: Male head in terracotta from a cult statue (Zeus?).

The Archaic period is a time of the maximum flowering of Capua celebrated in the ancient sources as the axis of Campania together with Cumae, with which it shows inseparable bonds in this phase, documented above all by the development and the diffusion of the "Campanian system" in public building programs (Fig. 16.7).

The exploration of a residential area, which was recently brought to light at the eastern edge of the settlement (loc. "Siepone"; Cerchiai 2010), centered on a non-orthogonal system of axial streets with dwellings made of tufa foundations and elevations in mudbricks, with hearths and drainage channels, has furnished fundamental information for the understanding of the pre-Roman settlement that was otherwise particularly lacking. The urban and territorial planning of the Archaic period is accompanied by the monumentalization of the public spaces, first of all the sanctuaries. A decisive contribution to the understanding of the system of the cults in the Etrusco-northern territory of the city is furnished by the *Tabula Capuana*, (Fig. 16.8 n.4; Cechiai 2010), a text of liturgical character, incised in boustrophedon style (lines alternating direction) before firing on a terracotta plaque and written in the alphabet prevalent in the Capuan area and traceable to the southern Etruscan region (Veii). The sacred calendar bears the inscription of rites dedicated to several deities of the Etruscan celestial and chthonian pantheon associated with basic references to specific cult places: the sanctuary of Uni corresponds probably to the sanctuary at Fondo Patturelli; compare also the mention of another sanctuary in the region of *Hamae*.

The first monumental phases of the suburban sanctuary of Fondo Patturelli, situated at the eastern edge of the Capuan settlement, are dated to the Early Archaic period. We are dealing with a context severely damaged by ancient destruction and clandestine excavations: the occupational phases and the character of the cult are mainly reconstructed through the architectural or votive terracottas and the epigraphic documentation. The patron deity is female, associated with the protection of fertility and procreation. The information derived from the *Tabula Capuana* has suggested an affinity with Uni (Hera, Juno) or with Italic divinities such as Fortuna or Mater Matuta. The sanctuary today is known above all for the vast production of votive terracottas of the "Campanian mother" type (see Chapter 20), with the goddess enthroned and nursing one or more swaddled babies. This is a cult that persists to the end of the second century BC (Fig. 16.8, no. 3).

The first "Battle of Cumae" is dated to 524 BC, and sets the people of Cumae against a coalition formed by the Etruscans of the Adriatic shore, Umbrians and Daunians, and signals the ascent of Aristodemos as a *condottiero* and politician. Aristodemos will become "tyrant" of the city only later, in the sphere of events connected with the expulsion of

Figure 16.8   1. Pontecagnano: Kantharos in bucchero with dedication to Apollo in Greek letters, from the southern sanctuary; 2. Capua: The Barone *lebes* (London, British Museum); 3. Sanctuary of the "Fondo Patturelli": votive statue of the Campanian "Mother" type; 4. The *Tabula Capuana*; 5. Coinage in silver of the *Campani* (end of the fifth century BC).

Tarquinius Superbus (509 BC), the last Etruscan king of Rome, and the establishment of the Republic following a war conducted against the city of Porsenna, king of Chiusi; in the Battle of Ariccia of 504 BC, the Cumaean *condottiero* defeats Arruns, son of Porsenna, and upon his return to Cumae succeeds in seizing power. The age of Aristodemus signals both at Cumae and at Capua a period of development, grandiose public works and expansion of production in the atmosphere of an inseparable relationship with Cumae, attested by the adoption by the elites of the same ideologies and of similar categories of luxury. Special importance is expressed in the production of bronze dinoi (cauldrons) with lids surmounted by figural scenes made of bronze figures in the round. The best-known but challenging example of this class is the so-called "Barone *lebes*," dated to the end of the sixth century BC (Fig. 16.8, no. 2). The conclusion of this phase of artisanal expansion and the contemporaneous waning of the Campanian architectonic system corresponds to a comprehensive crisis in the history of the city and of Campania (Cerchiai 2010 with bibliography).

FROM THE SECOND BATTLE OF CUMAE (474 BC) TO THE ETHNOGENESIS OF THE CAMPANIANS

The historic events that signal definitively the end of an epoch and the opening of a different phase in the history of the region are the assassination of Aristodemus (484 BC) and the second "Battle of Cumae" (474 BC). The Etruscan defeat ends the privileged relationship between Etruria and Campania and the naval power of Syracuse is affirmed along with the role of the new foundation of Neapolis. The crisis that follows is reflected in the scope of a much larger process that affects the Tyrrhenian portion of Etruria, Latium, and Campania, and signals the end of Etruscan thalassocracy in the Tyrrhenian and the progressive assertion of other realities in the Italic world (Cerchiai 2010 with bibliography). As a consequence of these events at Cumae and Capua, there occurs a phenomenon of contraction and of oligarchic closing of ranks.

The expression of dynamics of conservatism and of social strife acquires an ethnic flavor and seems to be documented on the archaeological level by radical actions of urban restructuring, with the appearance of true and proper areas (formal cities or colonies) that were refounded, and by the concomitant building up or reconstructing of fortifications. A phenomenon of accentuated discontinuity seems signaled in the case of Capua by the literary tradition and by archaeological evidence that indicates a significant cessation in occupation within the settlement (the depletion of the "Siepone" quarter) and the erection of fortifications. We are probably dealing with a true and proper act of refounding on the part of a restricted oligarchy of Etruscan origin that might be paralleled in the new designation of *Volturnum* recorded by Livy and in the Etruscan name Velthur documented in the *Tabula Capuana*, associated with the erudite tradition of *vultur*, the vulture that is linked to auspices in the rite of inauguration. A similar sequence of alterations of the urban plan with the building of fortifications and of a new residential quarter is documented both at Pontecagnano and at Fratte. The dominance of conservative forces from the old aristocracies of Etruscan and Greek origin results in the escalation of ethnic-social tensions within urban structures that acquire the appearance of claims of "ethnic self-consciousness." The historical-archaeological panorama of Campania from the fifth century BC on seems dominated by the conflict between the two principal ethnic groups that emerged from the reorganization of the Italic populations of the region and the neighboring areas, the Campanians and the Samnites. The ethnogenesis of the "people of the Campanians" is dated to 438 BC with the successive conquest of Capua (423 BC) and Cumae (421 BC). The literary sources suggest that control of the Campanian plain and of the region of the Bay of Naples accrued to the Campanians, while the influence of the Samnites extended from the Caudine and Hirpine region out to southern Campania, from the Sele to the Sorrento peninsula (Cerchiai 1995; Cuozzo 2012).

BIBLIOGRAPHY

Amselle, J. L. (1990) *Logiques metisses. Antropologie de l'identite en Afrique et ailleurs*, Paris: Editions Payot.

Bartoloni, G. (ed.) (1997) *Le necropoli arcaiche di Veio. Giornata di studio in memoria di Massimo Pallottino*, Rome: Università degli Studi di Roma "La Sapienza".

Bellelli, V. (2005) *La tomba in localita Quattordici Ponti*, Rome, "L'ERMA" di Bretschneider.

Bietti Sestieri, A. M. (ed.) (1992) *La necropoli laziale di Osteria dell'Osa*, Rome: Quasar.

Bonaudo, R., Cuozzo, M., Mugione, E., Pellegrino, C. and Serritella, A. (2009) "Le necropoli di Pontecagnano: studi recenti" in R. Bonaudo, L. Cerchiai and C. Pellegrino (eds), *Tra Etruria, Lazio e Magna Greci: indagini sulle necropoli*, Paestum: Pandemos.

Buchner, G. and Ridgway D. (1993) *Pithekoussai I, MonAL. n.s. IV*i, Rome: G. Bretschneider.

Campanelli (ed.) (2012) *Dopo lo Tsunami – Catalogo della Mostra Salerno 18 November – 28 February 2012*.

Cerchiai L. (1995) *I Campani*, Milan: Longanesi.

——(2010) *Gli antichi popoli della Campania – Archeologia e storia*, Rome: Carocci.

Cerchiai, L. and Nava M. L. (2008–2009) "Uno scarabeo del lyre-plyer group da Monte Vetrano (Salerno)," *AionArchStAnt*, n.s. 15–16, pp. 97–104.

Colonna, G. and Di Paolo, E. (1998) "Il letto vuoto, la distribuzione del corredo e la finestra della tomba Regolini-Galassi" in G. Nardi, M. Pandolfini, L. Drago and A. Berardinetti (eds), *Etrusca e Italica. Scritti in onore di M. Pallottino I*, Pisa and Rome: Istituti editoriali e poligrafici internazionali.

Cuozzo, M. (2003) *Reinventando la tradizione. Immaginario sociale, ideologie e rappresentazione nelle necropoli Orientalizzanti di Pontecagnano*, Paestum-Salerno: Pandemos.

——(2012) "Gli Etruschi in Campania" in G. Bartoloni (ed.), *Introduzione all'Etruscologia*, Milan: Hoepli.

——(2004–2005) "Ripetere, moltiplicare, selezionare, distinguere nelle necropoli di Pontecagnano. Il caso della T. 4461" in *Pontecagnano: la città, il paesaggio*, pp. 145–154.

D'Agostino, B. (1977) "Grecs et 'indigènes' sur la côte tyrrhénienne au VIIe siècle: la transmission des idéologies entre élites sociales," *Annales. ESC*, 1, 1977, pp. 3–20.

——(1988) "Le genti della Campania antica" in G. Pugliese Carratelli (ed.), *Italia omnium terrarum alumna*. Milan: Scheiwiller, pp. 531–589.

——(1996) "Pontecagnano," *BTCGI*, 1996, pp. 187–199.

——(2006) "The first Greeks in Italy" in *Greek Colonisation. An account of Greek colonies and other settlements overseas*, Leiden-Boston: Brill, pp. 201–237.

——(2011a) "Pithecusa e Cuma nel quadro della Campania di età arcaica," *RM* 117, pp. 35–53.

——(2011b) "La tomba 722 di Capua loc. Le Fornaci e le premesse dell'Orientalizzante in Campania" in D. Maras (ed.), *Corollari. Scritti di antichità etrusche e italiche in omaggio all'opera di G.Colonna*, Pisa-Rome: Fabrizio Serra, pp. 33–45.

——(2011c) "Gli Etruschi e gli altri in Campania settentrionale" in *Gli etruschi e la Campania settentrionale, Atti del Convegno di Studi Etruschi* (2007), Pisa-Rome: Fabrizio Serra, pp. 69 ff.

D'Agostino, B. and Cerchiai, L. (2004) "I Greci nell'Etruria Campana" *Annali Faina* 11, pp. 271–288.

Dinamiche di sviluppo delle città nell'Etruria Meridionale – Veio, Caere, Tarquinia, Vulci – Atti del XXIII Convegno di Studi Etruschi (2005).

Gras, M. (2000) "Il Mediterraneo in età Orientalizzante: merci, approdi, circolazione" in AA.VV. *Principi Etruschi tra Mediterraneo ed Europa*, Bologna/Venice: Milan: Marsilio, pp. 15–26.

Hodder, I. (1999) *The Archaeological Process. An Introduction.* Oxford: Blackwell.

Johannowsky, W. (1996) "Aggiornamenti sull prima fase di Capua" *AION ArchStAnt* n.s.

Kourou, N. (1999) Rec. a *Prima di Pitecusa*, AION ArchStAnt, pp. 219–222.

Melandri (2011) *L'eta del ferro a Capua. Aspetti distintivi del contesto culturale e suo inquadramento nelle dinamiche di sviluppo dell'Italia protostorica* (= BAR S2265), Oxford: Archaeopress.

Moretti Sgubini (2000) *Veio, Cerveteri, Vulci Città d'Etruria a confronto – Catalogo della Mostra Rome 1° October – 30 December 2001*, edited by A. M. Moretti Sgubini, Rome: "L'ERMA" di Bretschneider.

Parker Pearson, M. (1999) *The Archaeology of Death and Burial*, Phoenix Mill: Texas A & M University.

Pellegrino C. and Rossi, A. (2011) *Pontecagnano I.1. Città e campagna nell'Agro Picentino (Gli scavi dell'autostrada 2001–2006)*, Fisciano: Pandemos.

Pontecagnano II. La necropoli del Picentino 1.Le tombe della Prima Età del Ferro (=AIONArchStAnt Quad.5), (1988), Naples: "L'ERMA" di Bretschneider.

Rathje, A. (2000) "'Princesses' in Etruria and Latium Vetus?" in D. Ridgway, F. R. Serra Ridgway, M. Pearce, E. Herring, R. D. Whitehouse and J. B. Wilkins (eds), *Ancient Italy in its Mediterranean Setting. Studies in Honour of Ellen Macnamara*, London: Accordia Research Institute, pp. 295–300.

Ridgway, D. (2000) "The First Western Greeks Revisited" in D. Ridgway, F. R. Serra Ridgway, M. Pearce, E. Herring, R. D. Whitehouse and J. B. Wilkins (eds), *Ancient Italy in its Mediterranean Setting. Studies in Honour of Ellen Macnamara*, London: Accordia Research Institute, pp. 179–191.

Riva, C. and Vella, N. C. (eds) *Debating Orientalization – Multidisciplinary approaches to change in the Ancient Mediterranean*, London: McGill-Queen's University Press.

Torelli, M. (1997) *Il rango, il rito, l'immagine. Alle origini della rappresentazione storica romana*, Milan: Electa.

van Dommelen, P. (1997) *On Colonial Ground*, Leiden: Brill.

——(2006) "The orientalising phenomenon: Hybridity and material culture in the western Mediterranean" in C. Riva and N. Vella (eds), *Debating orientalisation. Multidisciplinary approaches to change in the ancient Mediterranean*, London: McGill-Queen's University Press, pp. 134–152.

NOTE ON BIBLIOGRAPHY

On issues of theory and methodology:

The definition of *cultura meticcia* ("*mestizo* culture") is treated by:

Amselle, J. L. (1990) *Logiques metisses. Antropologie de l' identite en Afrique et ailleurs*, Paris : Editions Payot.

——(2009) *Il distacco dall'occidente*, Rome: Meltemi.

Bourdieu, P. and Wacquant, L. J. D. (1992) *Réponses. Pour une anthropologie réflexive*, Paris: Seuil.

Fabietti, U. (1999) *Antropologia culturale. L'esperienza e l'interpretazione*, Rome: Laterza.

van Dommelen, P. (1998) *On colonial grounds*, Leiden: Brill.

For the interpretation of necropoleis:

Compare with the following titles in particular:

Cuozzo, M. (2003) *Reinventando la tradizione. Immaginario sociale, ideologie e rappresentazione nelle necropoli Orientalizzanti di Pontecagnano*, Paestum-Salerno: Pandemos.

D'Agostino, B. (1985) "Società dei vivi, comunità dei morti: un rapporto difficile," *Dialoghi di Archeologia*, 3s. (3): pp. 47–58.

D'Agostino, B. and Schnapp, A. (1982) "Les morts entre l'object et l'image" in G. I. Hodder (1992) *Theory and Practice in Archaeology*, London: Routledge.

Hodder, I. (ed.) (1999) *The Archaeological Process. An Introduction*, Oxford: Blackwell.

Morris, I. (1987) *Burial and Ancient Society*, Cambridge: Cambridge University Press.

Parker Pearson, M. (1999) *The Archaeology of Death and Burial*, Phoenix Mill: Texas A & M University.

Vernant, J. P. and Gnoli, G. (eds) (1990) *La mort, le morts dans les sociétés anciennes*, 14–25, Cambridge and Paris: Éditions de la Maison des sciences de l'homme.

On the issue of the position of women in Etruscan and Italic culture:

Bartoloni, G. (ed.) (2012) *Introduzione all'Etruscologia*, Milan: Hoepli (with earlier bibliography).

D'Agostino, B. (1999) "I principi dell'Italia centro-tirrenica epoca Orientalizzante" in P. Ruby (ed.) *Les princes de la protohistoire et l'émergence de l'état*, Naples and Rome: Centre Jean Bérard, pp. 81–88.

Sordi, M. (1981) "La donna etrusca" in C. Grottanelli (ed.), *Misoginia e maschilismo Grecia e Roma*, Genova: Università di Genova, Istituto di filologia classica e medievale, pp. 49–67.

CHAPTER SEVENTEEN

ETRURIA MARITTIMA: MASSALIA AND GAUL, CARTHAGE AND IBERIA

———•◆•———

Jean Gran-Aymerich

INTRODUCTION

The diffusion of Etruscan products in the Mediterranean is amply documented in the seventh and sixth centuries (all dates BC), during the "Belle Époque" of Etruscan civilization. The archaeological discoveries relating to maritime trade confirm the attestation of the historian Livy concerning the Etruscans who "had long extended their dominion over land and sea."[1] Often we envisage the emergence of this Etruscan Golden Age in an overly schematic manner. Thus, one might think that the Etruria of the Orientalizing period marks a phase of opening-up, after a long period of "Proto-Etruscan" gestation when the Villanovan villages would have lived in isolation from each other and cut off from the wider world. In the eighth century it was the Greek colonies in southern Italy, and Phoenicians from Carthage to Sardinia and even up to south-eastern Iberia, who induced a complete transformation of Etruscan civilization. Etruscan art, and as well the entire culture and fringe technology, were quite simply transformed based on Greek and oriental models (see Chapter 6). And so it was only around 670 that the Etruscans embarked on their sea voyages, which the Greeks, their primary maritime rivals, denounced as acts of piracy.

This vision of the first Etruscans on the sea and of piracy as a first resort and source of wealth is simplistic and a *reductio ad absurdum*. In truth, the opening of Etruscan settlements at the end of the Iron Age has proto-historic precedents. Exchanges in the Tyrrhenian Sea and relations with transalpine regions had been frequent since the final phases of the Bronze Age. Furthermore, at the dawn of the Iron Age, Etruria was far less isolated than one might imagine. Villanovan-style objects appear in transalpine regions and very far to the east – as far as Greek sanctuaries and perhaps even in Egypt – but as well to the west (Villanovan ceramics at Huelva), whereas continental (amber), oriental (faience, bronze), and Greek (subgeometric vases) objects arrived in Etruria. We have only a small percentage of the evidence for this trade, including primary materials (copper, tin, gold, silver, ivory, amber, colorants), consumer products (food, wine, oils, unguents, perfumes) and perishables (cloth, skins, fur, wood); likewise, the real impact of personal and cultural exchange escapes us. The distribution of Etruscan objects far from Etruria is not the result of a sudden and unexpected apparition, but rather of an evolution that accelerated in the seventh century and attained its apogee in the first half of the sixth century in the Mediterranean and in the latter half of the sixth century and the beginning of the fifth in the Celtic hinterland. This general paradigm has been accepted since the end of the nineteenth century AD, since the discovery of Etruscan bronzes in temperate Europe, notably *Schnabelkannen*-type oinochoai, and the first discoveries of bucchero vases in Marseille, Sicily, and Carthage. In the middle of the twentieth century AD the panorama was considerably enriched, especially by the identification of Etruscan transport amphorae on several shipwrecks and amongst the settlements of southern France (*le Midi*) and Catalonia. If today the three most trustworthy indicators of the long-range diffusion of Etruscan objects remain the *Schnabelkannen*, bucchero kantharoi and transport amphorae, then the history of exchange is in reality very rich, dense and complex (see Chapter 19) (Fig. 17.1).

THE NORTH-WESTERN MEDITERRANEAN: MARSEILLE AND GAUL

The sailing routes of the central Mediterranean that reach the littoral of the Gaulish isthmus, between Provence and Catalonia, extend into the mainland via the Rhône and through Aquitaine, before rounding the gulf of Lyon and heading for the Iberian littoral. This is the region outside of Italy that has furnished the largest number and the greatest range of Etruscan objects. The discoveries include over one hundred deposits, primarily from habitations, but also from tombs, ritual areas and shipwrecks.

The phenomenon which we have dubbed the "French exception" refers to the fact that certain mercantile goods distributed via the maritime network in the south of France were introduced to the interior via the Rhône-Saône, where these goods were joined, at certain sites in the hinterland, by other exports which followed the land routes crossing the Alps.[3] The study of Etruscan and Italic imports, both in the Mediterranean world and the European hinterland, is as indispensable for research into the protohistory of the local populations of the river regions and the interior as it is regarding Etruscan and Italic history.[4]

Marseille-Massalia-Matalia

Marseille is without a doubt the critical point in envisioning the "Etruscans as seen by the Gauls."[5] One must recall that it is the first site in the north-western Mediterranean where, in the twentieth century AD, bucchero vases were identified.[6] In spite of the many excavations carried out, it is still difficult to evaluate the respective place of Greeks, Etruscans, and local populations in Marseille since the city's earliest history in the late seventh-early sixth centuries. Such a situation is shared amongst other emerging port sites in the western Mediterranean, where multiple maritime operators crossed paths.[7] The recent reports – archaeological and historical – have reinforced not only the interpretation of the Greek colony at Marseille, but also her many regional contacts, especially concerning the region of the Rhône.[8] The statistical study of imports and of the earliest local ceramics produced in Marseille has been especially fruitful.[9] Despite the precocious identification of bucchero vases at Marseille, the extensive excavations at the habitation site of Saint-Blaise revealed far more numerous Etruscan goods.[10] However, the recent excavations conducted at Marseille have considerably augmented the Etruscan

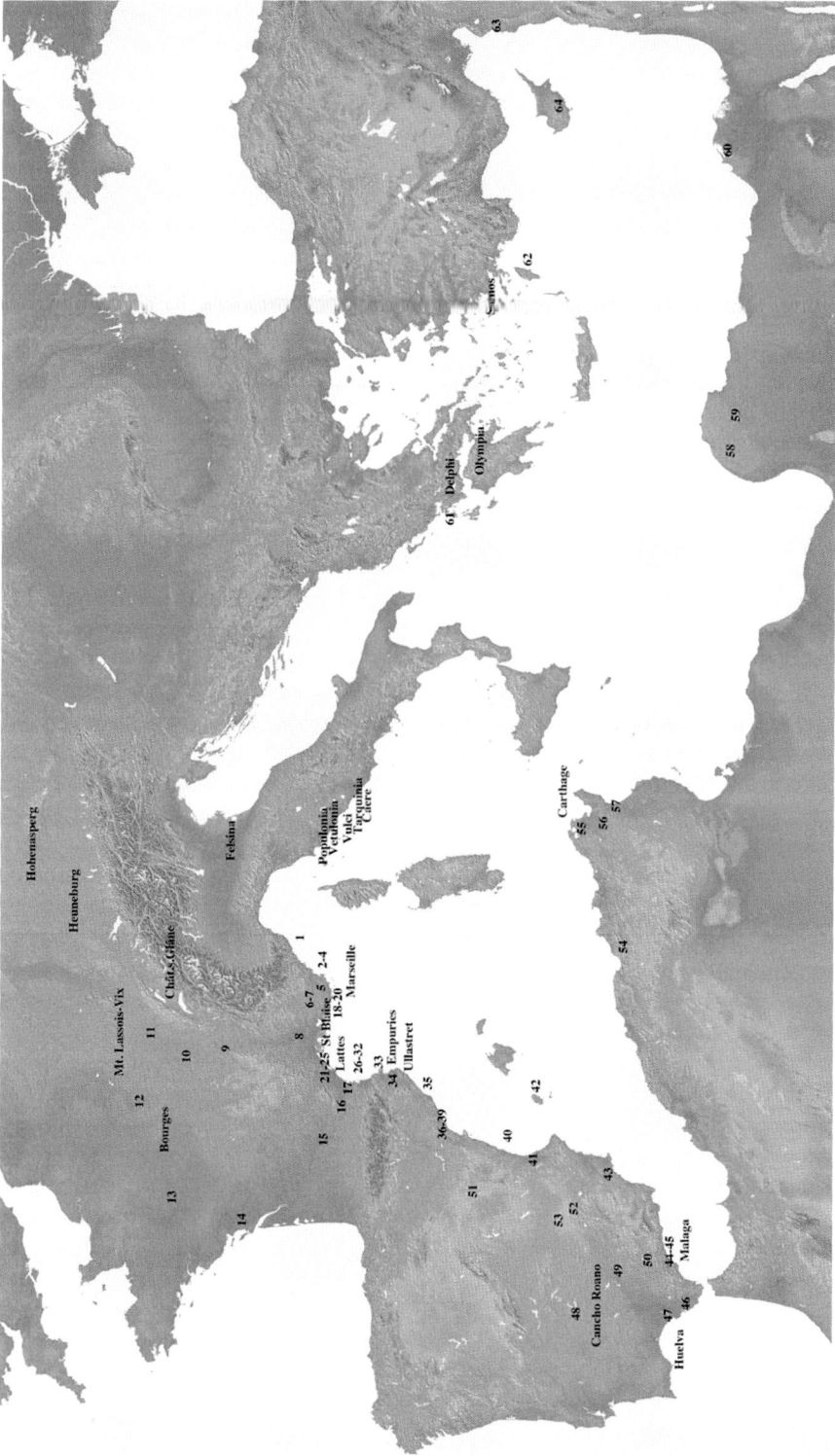

Figure 17.1   Mediterranean, Europe and remote Etruscan finds © Gran-Aymerich.[2]

complement, both quantitatively and qualitatively. Certain Etruscan discoveries at Marseille are truly exceptional, completely unprecedented outside of Italy, and they open new perspectives on the presence of the Etruscans.

The most numerous and remarkable Etruscan discoveries have emerged in the constructions situated in the oldest part of the port conglomerate at Marseille and in proximity to the piers. The first levels of occupation on the site *Îlot rue Cathédrale* (or *Îlot* 55) date to the beginning of the sixth century and have revealed quadrangular constructions of sub-basements in stone and a notable concentration of Etruscan ceramics.[11] Other than the well-known repertoire of bucchero vases, Etrusco-Corinthian vases, and transport amphorae, there are also common ceramics pertaining to everyday life. Amongst the cooking ceramics are vases of *impasto* with a coarse, sandy coating, and objects of common usage, such as basins/mortars, cooking-ware and small storage vessels, *ollae*, and lid-bowls (*ciotola-coperchio*). More remarkable are the fragments of cook-stands with tenons (*fornello*) of a type well known in Etruria and possibly having served for on-board cooking before reaching its final, land-based destination (Fig. 17.2).[12] Of greatest interest is the discovery, for the first time outside of the Italian peninsula, of a red-slipped Caeretan *focolare* (brazier) at the Marseille site of *Îlot la Madeleine* (Fig. 17.3). It is decorated on the flat rim with an animal register in relief in the Orientalizing tradition, an exact parallel to the stamp-decorated basins of Caere dating to the second quarter of the sixth century. It is a unique example of a flaw in fabrication of the roller-stamped decoration,[13] which indicates that it must have been used as a domestic utensil, rather than for a ritual or votive purpose. Amongst the most salient Etruscan discoveries at Marseille are two bucchero vases of a type unknown outside of Etruria. The one is a cup of the type *a maschera umana* (with relief of a human face), of which the closest parallel

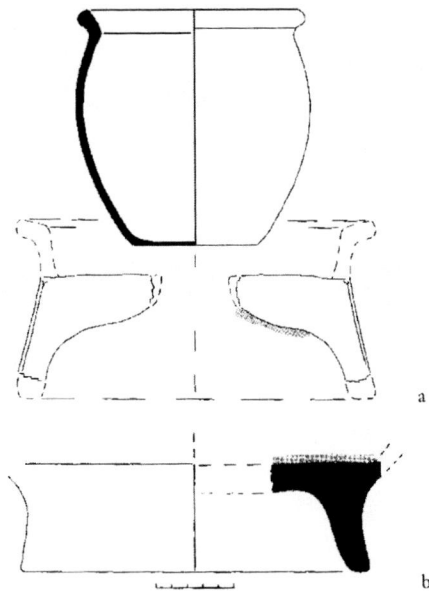

Figure 17.2   Marseille, site of *Îlot rue Cathédrale*, fragments of cooking stand and foot of basin-brazier, complete profile of cookware vase (*olletta d'impasto*) from Saint-Blaise (Gran-Aymerich 2006a, drawing G.-A.).

outside of Etruria is an Etrusco-Corinthian painted example from Ullastret in Catalonia. The other is a sturdy oinochoe, with lion masks decorating the handle attachments that surround the spout. This vase and its decoration are well known amongst the products of Caere of the second quarter of the sixth century.[14] Additionally, we note that the proto-historic habitation closest to Marseille, the *oppidum* of Saint-Marcel, today in the area of the modern city, has yielded a local version of this bucchero oinochoe in a local grey-black fabric; the adaptation of the lion masks presents a common characteristic of the earliest Celtic art.[15]

The recent works at Marseille contribute equally to the realm of epigraphy. The first Etruscan signs and letters from Marseille were revealed in the port quarter where the important Etruscan ceramic deposit was discovered. These graffiti appear on monochrome ceramics, bucchero, and *impasto* of the first half of the sixth century, mostly from Caere, to judge from the mineral content.[16] These are isolated letters and signs, carved on the external base or upon the everted rims of the *ollette*. The marks carved before firing on the common food-preparation vessels (*ollae*, lid-bowls), may be associated with the fabrication and export of the ceramics, whereas the graffiti incised after firing may have commercial reasons, as for certain amphorae but may in other cases pertain to an ostentatious display of ownership (Fig. 17.4). Other examples of Etruscan vases marked with letters or symbols were found in the excavations of the eastern sector of the old port, at the sites of Jules Verne and Bargemon.[17]

Figure 17.3 Marseille, site of *Îlot la Madeleine, braciere ceretano*: red-slipped basin decorated with cylinder-stamped design (drawing G.-A.).

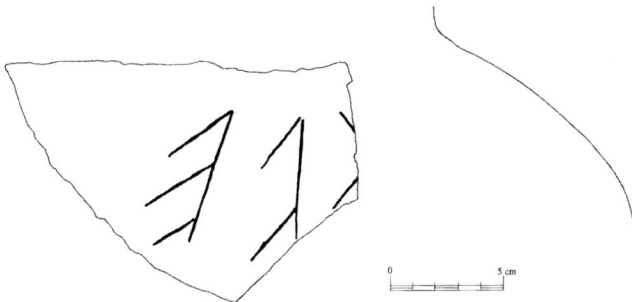

Figure 17.4 Marseille, site of Collège Vieux Port, Etruscan inscription incised in large letters on the shoulder of a Greek wine amphora made in Marseille (Gran-Aymerich 2006c).

Two very remarkable inscriptions were discovered in the western quarters of the old city, at the site of Collège Vieux Port. The shorter inscription was deeply engraved on the external base of an *impasto* lid-bowl, dated to the second half of the sixth century; it is two signs that read with no difficulty "*va*," probably an abbreviation of the name of the owner.[18] The mineral inclusions in the clay permit the identification of the origin of this bowl as Caere. The second inscription was doubtless incised after firing at Marseille itself. In truth, this text was engraved upon the upper, and thus most visible, portion of a wine amphora made in Marseille (the ware and inclusions are perfectly identifiable) at the end of the sixth century or the beginning of the fifth century. The truncated inscription is written right to left, of which three letters are visible, ...*ve*, preceded by a letter of which all that remains are two oblique strokes (Fig. 17.4). The object was discovered in the context of a singular edifice, identified by the excavator as a "dining room". This important document gives evidence for the presence of a lettered Etruscan and was in all probability offered as a diplomatic gift at a ceremonial banquet or meeting in a high level architectural complex.[19]

The littoral of Provence, Languedoc, and Catalonia

Before the recent discoveries in Marseille, this north-western littoral fringe of the Mediterranean had already revealed the first Etruscan epigraphic documents in southern France, of which many are of singular importance. At the *oppidum* of Saint-Blaise, for example, certain amphorae bear inscriptions and marks of a commercial character (Fig. 17.5).[20] A graffito inscribed on the base of an Attic cup of the fifth century, long considered to be illegible, is now understood by Giovanni Colonna to be a dedication in Greek letters but Etruscan language to the Etruscan divinity Uni.[21] The harbor of Lattes has furnished inscribed, everyday pottery, of which the bowls in bucchero and *impasto* have provided graffiti corresponding to feminine names.[22] The *oppidum* of Ensérune is well known for its Iberian inscriptions, of which one was reinterpreted as a Celtic name written with Etruscan letters.[23] The *oppidum* of Pech-Maho (Sigean) brought forth a truly first-rate document, a veritable text, apparently a letter of commercial character, inscribed upon a sheet of lead, of which the verso is an even older Greek text.[24] This document, dating from the beginning of the fifth century, furnishes the oldest epigraphic reference to Marseille-*Massalia*, *Matalia* in Etruscan. Given the presence of the word *zik* (letter, writing, book) and of the word *eitva*, comparable to the Oscan *eituva* (money,

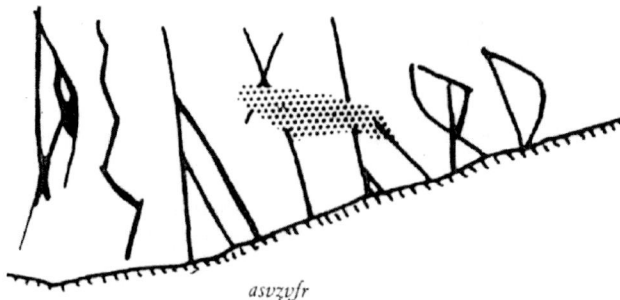

asvzvfr

Figure 17.5   Coastal *oppidum* of Saint-Blaise, Etruscan inscription of commercial character incised on an Etruscan amphora, sixth century. (Gran-Aymerich 2006c).

coinage), this text on lead could correspond to a sort of bill of exchange (Fr. *lettre de change*; Eng. bill of lading or promissory note, bill of exchange), (Fig. 17.6).[25] Finally, the Greek foundation of Empúries-Ampurias in Catalonia (Girona) has revealed a document unique outside of Etruria: a feline paw in bronze – probably part of a tripod – bearing the inscription *CAR*. This inscription was clearly written in the mould when the object was first made, revealing the original votive character of the object (Fig. 17.7).[26]

The regions of the north-western Mediterranean that provide the largest number and variation of Etruscan imports are: Marseille and Saint-Blaise in Provence, Lattes in Languedoc, Ampurias and Ullastret in Catalonia. The Etruscan transport amphorae are numerous at these sites, and are even in the majority during the first half of the sixth century, whereas, during the second half, the Greek amphorae of Marseille appear and multiply rapidly. Concerning Phoenician amphorae, they appear in quite minor but non-negligible quantities up to the river port of Arles, and we note here the quite remarkable association of an Etruscan amphora and a Phoenician amphora deposited in the grotto sanctuary of Le Bouffens near Caunes-Minervois (Aude), at the entrance of the Aquitaine corridor (Fig 17.8). This path of penetration into Aquitaine is marked by Etruscan vases reported as far as Toulouse and by borrowed Etruscan ceramic forms rendered in the local black ceramics, for example, the oinochoe of Carsac, to the south of Carcassonne.[27]

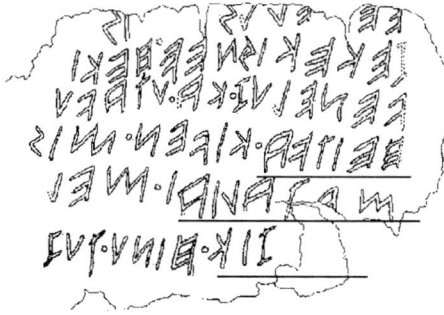

Figure 17.6 Coastal *oppidum* of Pech-Maho (Sigean, Aude), Etruscan inscription mentioning *Matalia* (*Massalia*, Marseille), on lead sheet, with Greek inscription on reverse, fifth century. Each is a letter of correspondence of commercial or diplomatic character, differing in content (Gran-Aymerich 2006b).

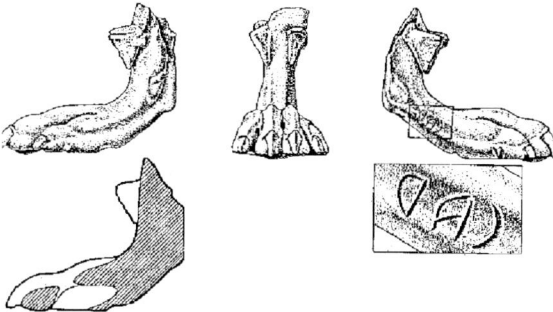

Figure 17.7 Greek colony of Empúries (Ampurias, *Emporion*), sector of the sanctuary of Aesculapius, feline paw from a bronze tripod, with inscription made at time of casting, end sixth to beginning fifth century. (Gran-Aymerich 2006a).

Thus, in their considerable majority, the Etruscan exports to the south of France were discovered in settlements, but we note also their presence in contexts both funerary and votive. Certain aristocratic tombs of the local populations contain Etruscan ceramics with associated metalwork, such as the tumulus of Agnel at Pertuis, the necropolis of Saint-Julien at Pézenas, or again at Cayla de Mailhac. The tombs of Etruscans *per se* are not attested, but certain tombs near Lattes do suggest them: thus the tomb containing a strigil and a bossed-rim basin.[28] Several finds correspond to Etruscan offerings (the inscription of Saint-Blaise, the Etruscan amphora of the grotto of Caunes-Minervois, probably the inscribed bronze from Ampurias) or diplomatic gifts (the inscription on the Greek amphora from Marseille).

Alternatively, the shipwrecks with cargoes of Etruscan amphorae and vases discovered in southern France reveal the magnitude of Etruscan mercantile enterprises, even if one equivocates still on the identification of the ships and their crews, whether Etruscans or Greeks.[29] Nevertheless, the existence of Etruscan entrepreneurs appears quite likely, as it pertains to homogeneous cargoes of Etruscan provenance, as is the case of the shipwrecks of Antibes, of Écueil du Miet 3, and of Grand Ribaud F. The Grand Ribaud F (Fig. 17.9) dating to the end of the sixth century, is of particular interest, not only for the possibilities offered by the wreck's state of preservation, lying at 90 meters deep, but also

Figure 17.8   Votive deposit of one Etruscan amphora and one Phoenician amphora, of the type "Area del Estrecho" (Gibraltar area), from the cave-sanctuary of Caunes-Minervois, Aude. First half of the sixth century. (photo G.-A.).

Figure 17.9   Shipwreck of Grand Ribaud F (East of Marseille), cargo of Etruscan amphorae (photo G.-A.).

for the information furnished by the earliest soundings. It is the largest complement of Etruscan amphorae known to date, estimated at several hundred containers, and amongst the complement are stacked groups of small, bronze dishes and inscribed vases (Fig. 17.10).[30] These discoveries and their display at expositions in Marseille and Hauterive in Switzerland presented opportunities to re-examine the entire situation of archaic shipwrecks in the western Mediterranean.[31]

We have considerable information about the numerous habitations in the region of Marseille, of which the most important is Saint-Blaise. The apparent decline of Saint-Blaise in the fifth century could have been associated with the decreased contacts with Etruria and Marseille's monopoly over regional exchanges, which translated into the development of the site of the island of Martigues, before the renaissance of Saint-Blaise in the Hellenistic period.[32] The dynamism of the local populations and the rise of Mediterranean Gaul, from the final Bronze Age to the second Iron Age, have been profoundly re-evaluated.[33] The relations amongst the local populations and the Mediterranean navigators over the long haul were complex and multiform, as is revealed by recent studies on the presence of Gaulish objects from southern France in Italy, Sicily, and Greece.[34]

The change of mentalities in the proto-historic West occurred via the introduction of figural representation. A precise example of the adaptation of iconography since the sixth century is provided in Marseille by the bucchero oinochoe decorated with lion masks at the handle-attachments; likewise by a parallel example in grey-black ware from the *oppidum* of Saint-Marcel.[35] Lattes attests to the early introduction of stone statuary in southern France with the statue of a kneeling archer discovered in fill, *spolia*, and which formed part of a commemorative monument most certainly of the fifth century.[36] At Saint-Blaise, the presence of a sanctuary is suggested by the presence of sculpted architectural elements, and by the Etruscan inscription, in Greek characters, interpreted as a dedication to Uni.[37] All in all, it is a concatenation of serious transfers both material and cultural amongst local and foreign populations.[38]

The Rhône and the Celtic hinterland

The path of distribution of Etruscan (and Greek) goods by the Rhône corridor, and thus the Saône, is studded with Etruscan finds in the lower Rhône Valley, in Saint-Rémy-de-Provence, in Arles, and farther north in Vienne, in the region of Lyon and up to Burgundy in Chassey (Chassey-le-Camp en Saône-et-Loire) and in Bragny-sur-Saône. For the

Figure 17.10 Cargo of kitchen pottery from the wreck of Grand Ribaud F (photo G.-A.).

distribution of Etruscan goods in the hinterland see Chapter 19. However, we note here the connection between the Etruscan bucchero forms in the black wares and proto-historic grey wares of southern France in the Rhône-Saône corridor, and found through Burgundy and beyond. We know, especially through the works of Charlette Arcelin-Pradelle, of the phenomenon of adaptation of bucchero forms through a small percentage of local grey or black ware, called *"grise du Midi,"* or *"de Provence"* and we have identified some of these at Marseille itself.[39] Returning to the Rhône axis, imitations of Etruscan kantharoi have been confirmed up to the region of Lyon and at Chassey in Burgundy.[40] The *oppidum* at Bourges, in the Centre region, has furnished examples of open forms, which might be connected to these wares of Provence.[41] The latest works at the *oppidum* of Mont-Lassois at Vix and the excavation of the large apsidal building (the "Princess Palace") have furnished amphorae from Marseille, Attic ceramics of high quality, and proto-historic black wares and oinochoai which partake of Etruscan forms.[42] Other examples of the influence of Etruscan forms amongst the Celtic ceramics of the hinterland were known, including the *Schnabelkannen*-type oinochoai,[43] while, for the cups, this influence was proposed for certain carinated cups and in particular those decorated with notches on the carination.[44]

THE SOUTH-WESTERN MEDITERRANEAN: FROM CARTHAGE TO THE IBERIAN PENINSULA

The exchanges between Carthage and the Etruscan cities such as Caere, Tarquinia or Vetulonia from the end of the eighth century were critical for the introduction and adoption in the Etruscan world of products, fringe technologies, and new iconographic models. The most important cultural and human exchanges pertained to craft: specialized handcrafts, artisans, and artists from the Near East plied their trades in the Etruscan cities.[45] In return, we note the first introduction of Etruscan products, and more copiously those of the central Tyrrhenian area, at Carthage and in the Phoenician colonial world up to Huelva.[46] The discovery of Sardinian ceramics of a late Villanovan style at Malaga (Churriana, near the international airport), Cadiz and Huelva opened new avenues of study.[47] Etrusco-Phoenician economic and diplomatic relations experienced an especially intense phase during the second half of the seventh century and throughout the sixth, as evidenced by the Etruscan and Phoenician inscriptions upon the gold plaques from Pyrgi – the principle port of Caere – which cast light on the first Romano-Carthaginian treaty.[48]

Carthage, Karthazie

For a site so far from Etruria Carthage has revealed an exceptional concentration of Etruscan goods. The collection is unique as much for the quantity of finds – which exist in the hundreds in both habitations and necropoleis – as for the extensive chronology of the discoveries (from the seventh through to the fourth centuries); some of these finds are of inestimable value in the study of Etrusco-Carthaginian relations. The contrast is striking with the paucity of Etruscan finds identified in the rest of North Africa: bucchero kantharoi were found at Naukratis, and perhaps at Tocra; Cyrene furnished a plate of the Genucilia type, and Cyrenaica has provided a belt-buckle; the presence of bucchero at Karnak has yet to be confirmed.[49] The finds in Greece and in the eastern Mediterranean constitute a specialized dossier and have been the objects of multiple studies.[50] The case of Malta is peculiar because of insularity and its proximity to the Tyrrhenian Sea.[51]

Farther west, the materials from Utica and Tipasa have yet to be verified.[52] It is once again necessary to mention the two Etruscan inscriptions dating to the Republican period: one is upon a bronze disc, a kind of *tessera hospitalis*, from Gouraya (Gunugu) some 150 kilometers west of Algiers.[53] The other appears upon a set of three boundary stones that repeat a legal proclamation, collected in the valley of Miliane, to the south-west of Carthage.[54] Thus, the rich concentration of Etruscan discoveries at Carthage confirms that the Punic capital was a privileged port in regards to Etruscan relations with North Africa and maritime trade in the southern Mediterranean, constituting the major east-west axis of the so-called "Phoenician corridor."[55]

The archaeological dossier of Etrusco-Punic relations emerged in the nineteenth century AD upon the first discovery at Carthage of Etruscan objects, associated with objects identical in style to the Orientalizing works found at Carthage and in wealthy Etruscan tombs, such as faience flasks for unguents and perfumes.[56] Today, Etruscan banquet ware, in ceramics as well as bronze, and perfume vessels (Fig. 17.11) are well known through over 100 examples associated with some 30 different types. These discoveries primarily derive from tombs close to the summit of the hill of Byrsa (Saint-Louis) and out to the sectors of Sainte Monique and Bordj-Djedid, although without further particulars concerning the exact distribution.[57]

The bronze vessels from the funerary goods in Carthage consist of several oinochoai of types either common or very close to Etruscan styles. Certain groups appear to be local productions, while others show close affinities with Campanian products, or those of Magna Graecia; some are clearly Etruscan. We recognize four primary categories: the Rhodian type, decorated with Orientalizing and Egyptianizing motifs (palmettes, uraeus, Hathor masks); the type with anthropomorphic handles; the type with handles raised and decorated or not with a mask at the lower attachment; and finally the most famous Etruscan form, an oinochoe with cylindrical body and long spout – the *Schnabelkanne* – the most common form of export. Amongst the examples of the Rhodian type, other than the famous gilded bronze from the Byrsa, we know of two from Ard el-Mourali and two others from Ard el-Kheraïb, which appear to be of Carthaginian manufacture and which date to somewhere between the end of the seventh century and the beginning of the sixth.[58] The oinochoai with figured handles and those with simple raised handles would be

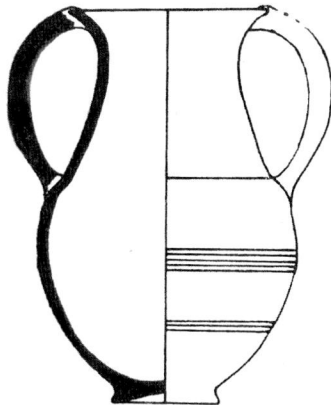

Figure 17.11 Carthage, old excavations of necropoleis, small amphora of bucchero *sottile* with registers of incised horizontal lines, Musée du Louvre. End of the seventh century (drawing G.-A.).

Etruscan, dating to the Archaic and late Archaic periods, while those with the decorated handle-bases come from Etruria proper, from Campania or Magna Graecia, and date to the end of the sixth century through to the beginning of the fifth.[59] The *Schnabelkannen* are represented at Carthage by at least seven examples, from the end of the sixth century to the middle of the fifth.[60] Even while waiting for a complete study of these materials, it is evident that, outside of Italy and Aleria in Corsica, it is Carthage that offers the densest concentration of Etruscan metallic pieces.[61]

The most remarkable Etruscan discovery in Carthage comes from a tomb in the necropolis of Sainte Monique. It is a mid-sixth century ivory plaque in the form of either a boar or perhaps a feline, of which the reverse bears an Etruscan inscription. This *tessera hospitalis* would have belonged to a *Puinel Karthazies*, a Carthaginian who would have benefited from this document that guaranteed him sea travel and a welcome in Etruria.[62] Also quite exceptional is a funerary *cippus* in the form of a column, clearly identifiable at Caere as an indicator of male burials.[63] It may be dated to the fourth or early third century and is contemporaneous with painted Genucilia-type plates from Caere, localized in the necropolis of Sainte Monique.[64] This *cippus*, with its missing socle, must have been part of a small monument, and it served to mark the tomb of an Etruscan from Caere.[65] We know of no other examples outside of Italy except for those amongst the tombs of Aleria.[66] Another dossier, considered many times, consists of the sarcophagi with reclining effigies from the necropolis of the Rabs at Sainte Monique, which raises the question of cultural and artistic exchanges between Carthage and Tarquinia (where an identical sarcophagus was found) during the Hellenistic age.[67]

Concerning domestic contexts, the excavations undertaken in the archaic levels of Carthage have considerably revised both the chronology and typology of Etruscan ceramics there, which extend from the seventh century, or even the end of the eighth, to the Hellenistic period. This consists not only of drinking vessels and perfume containers, as was the case for the tombs, but also common wares and transport amphorae.[68] The recent excavations in the archaic levels of the lower city, near the shore, have permitted an identification of handmade Sardinian and Etrusco-Italic ceramics from the eighth century, *impasto non tornito*, and Etrusco-Italic or proto-Etruscan transport amphorae dating to the dawn of the seventh century, the so-called ZITA-Amphoren, type-5.[69] The most widespread Etruscan amphorae to emerge from sixth-century contexts, and the Etruscan ceramics of the sixth to fourth centuries, were the monochrome wares (*impasto tornito, bucchero*, cream wares) and painted vases (Etrusco- or Italo-Geometric, Etrusco-Corinthian, and red-figure ware of the Genucilia type).[70] This diversity of ceramic finds in the quarters close to the shore, although their numbers are relatively humble in comparison to the large quantity of Punic wares, does not appear to support the hypothesis of imports destined for a Carthaginian clientele. The Etruscans, be they transient or permanent residents, and the presence of Etruscan women at Carthage – in a context of exchanges and mixed marriages – might explain this presence of perfume containers, cooking wares, and common wares in the Punic metropoleis.[71] Apart from the various possible hypotheses, these Etruscan discoveries confirm the permanence of the close ties between Etruria and Carthage.

Other, less common finds from Carthage attest to the distinctive relations held between the Punic metropolis and Etruria. Such is the case of three *bullae* of fired clay from the Mago quarter, which reveal the presence of Etruscan documents amongst the vestiges of the archives discovered in this excavation.[72] Finally, amongst the discoveries made at

Carthage at the beginning of the twentieth century AD, there is the statuette salvaged amidst the contents of the cisterns of Dar-Seniat, to the south of Sidi Bou-Saïd, which we have recently re-evaluated.[73] Here, a young woman in frontal pose wears a tight chiton, which she holds to the side in her left hand; she holds forward her right hand, palm down (Fig. 17.12). It is a fine product of Etruria, dating to the end of the sixth or the beginning of the fifth century, which might be associated with a workshop in southern Etruria, Caere or Veii, or possibly northern Etruria, perhaps Volterra. The votive character of this statuette is evident, and the most likely hypothesis is that it comes from a sanctuary from which the discards served as fill in the Roman cisterns. Other such debris from *favissae* have emerged from the edge of Bordj-Djedid and the necropolis of Sainte Monique.[74] The statuette from Dar-Seniat depicts the female donor, and is associated with the cult of a feminine deity, such as Uni-Turan, Venus-Aphrodite, or Astarte, whom we might connect with a fountain-sanctuary identified near where the statuette was discovered.[75] The presence at Carthage of this offering, clearly that of an Etruscan lady, corresponds to a moment of heightened diplomatic relations between Caere and Carthage at the end of the sixth century and at the dawn of the fifth. Aristotle's citation (*Politics* 3.5.10–11) of a formal treaty maintained between Carthage and "the Etruscans" (we do not know which cities) attests the high level of economic importance in these relationships; the objects identified hint at the individuals who must have administered the treaties' provisions.

The Southern Iberian Peninsula

The relations, real or supposed, between Etruria and the Iberian Peninsula have sparked numerous works following different disciplines (philological, stylistic, archaeological), for which we have elsewhere established a historiographic chronology.[76] Certain propositions, such as the hypothetical influence on the iconography and architecture of Iberia, have been abandoned (as for the ramparts of Tarragona) or have not received formal confirmation.[77] The Etruscan discoveries from the Iberian Peninsula rather often incite perplexity and hypercritical attitudes, inspired by ignorance of the general context of the hinterland and the littorals, of the Atlantic coast, and of the Mediterranean, both in southern

Figure 17.12 Carthage, zone of Dar-Seniat, statuette of young woman offering. Beginning of the fifth century. (Gran-Aymerich 2008a).

France and on the peninsula. Furthermore, the quantitative approach adopted often excludes typological associations and restricts a global interpretation. A clear example of this reductive phenomenon is illustrated by the under-evaluation of the interest in sets of dining paraphernalia formed from the Etruscan oinochoai and the Orientalizing bronze basins (*braserillos*), located in the rich tombs at Huelva and at Cigarralejo, which have not received sufficient recognition as elements in prestige banquets. Additionally, the fragmentary state of the ceramics discovered in the settlements rendered their identification difficult, as much for the bucchero vases as for the transport amphorae, and as well the common wares or even the painted pottery (Huelva, Ullastret).[78] The graffiti themselves are often first confused with Iberian inscriptions (Lattes, Ensérune).[79] The associations at certain sites, such as Huelva, Malaga, Ullastret and Ampurias of bucchero vases, transport amphorae and Etruscan bronzes recommend perspectives other than the merely quantitative.

The list, hardly exhaustive, of Etruscan discoveries on the Iberian Peninsula renders a minimum of 45 confirmed sites: 13 for Catalonia, 16 for the Levante and Baleares, 16 for the southern half of Spain. This ensemble includes 29 sites on the littoral, 12 in the hinterland, and four underwater locations that suggest shipwrecks.[80] The main concentrations of Etruscan discoveries correspond to differentiated sites: the foundations of colonies Greek (Ampurias) or Phoenician (Malaga, Cerro del Villar, Toscanos), as well as indigenous sites with maritime access (Ullastret, Huelva). There is the example of a votive deposit in a littoral sanctuary (La Algaida on the mouth of the Guadalquivir) and others most likely deriving from urban sanctuaries (Ampurias, Malaga). Etruscan high-value objects – bronzes and ivories – were found in princely tombs of the littoral (Huelva) and the hinterland (Pozo Moro and Los Villares for complete contexts) (Fig. 17.13) and

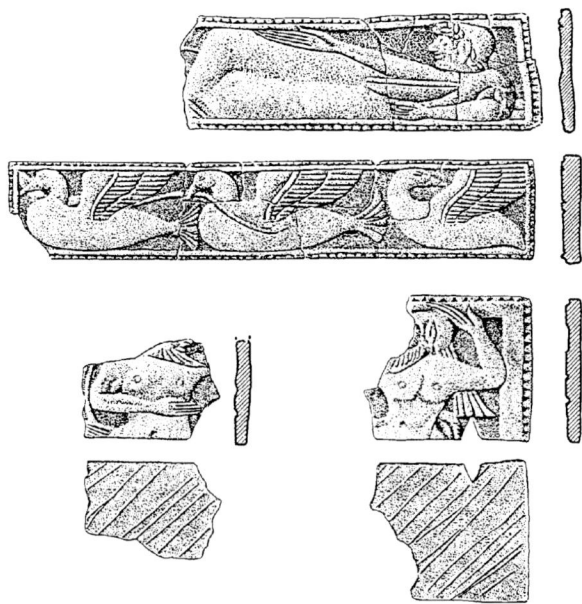

Figure 17.13 Necropolis of Los Villares, province of Albacete (Castilla-La Mancha), plaques from a small box with representations of banquet, satyrs and birds. Carved ivory, end of the sixth century. (Gran-Aymerich 2006c).

amid residential contexts (Cancho Roano, El Turuñuelo) (Fig. 17.14–15). This grouping of contexts diverse yet complementary, linking commercial enterprises, the centers of economic power, and local indigenes, forces a re-evaluation of the dossier of trade goods and Etruscan enterprises on the Iberian Peninsula. While the dossiers from Ampurias and the Catalan littoral are closely linked to Marseille and the diffusion of Etruscan objects in the north-western Mediterranean, southern Iberia is primarily linked to Carthage and the network of western Phoenician colonies.

The Etruscan goods documented the farthest from Etruria derive from the Atlantic coast, at the port site of Huelva, and in the Tartessian hinterland by the palace-sanctuary of Cancho Roano, to the south of Mérida in Estremadura (Figs 17.15, 17.16a).[81] The site of Huelva, sheltered at the base of its harbor, is the most important indigenous habitation

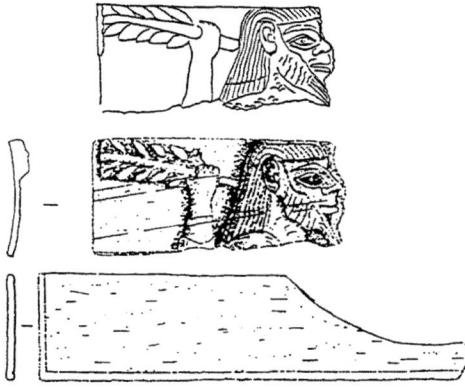

Figure 17.14   Site of Turuñuelo, Mérida, province of Badajoz (Estremadura), plaque from a box with centaur. Carved ivory, end of the sixth century. (Gran-Aymerich 2006c, top drawing G.-A.).

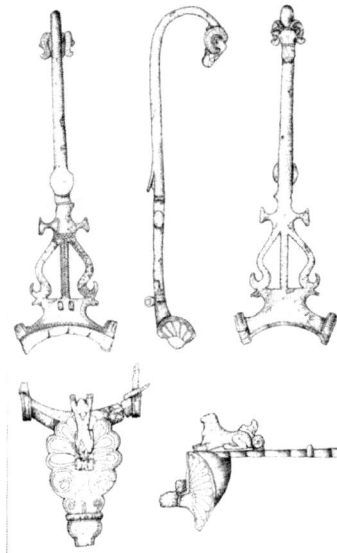

Figure 17.15   Cancho Roano, Zalamea, province of Badajoz. Banquet tools, *simpula*. Bronze, end of the sixth century. (Gran-Aymerich 2006c).

of the Tartessian littoral and is at the heart of a very rich mining belt, with resources in copper and silver alongside the tin lode of the Atlantic coast. The princely tombs close to the town have revealed two Rhodian-style bronze oinochoai,[82] while the port quarter has revealed a remarkable series of ceramics: bucchero kantharoi, transport amphorae and Etrusco-Corinthian pottery.[83] Within a context of proto-historic local ceramics with Phoenician, Cypriot, and Greek imports dated to the eighth century, Sardinian vases have recently been identified as well as two fragments of *impasto* of Villanovan type, from either southern Etruria or Campania.[84]

The Mediterranean port farthest from Etruria to have furnished pottery, transport amphorae and a bronze vase of high quality is Malaga. The colonial foundations around *Malaka* and its harbor appear very early at the heart of Phoenician enterprises on the Mediterranean coast close to the Straits of Gibraltar. The Malaga bay was no stranger to Archaic Greek commerce and corresponds to the location of the mythical colony of *Mainake* (Toscanos?).[85] This littoral also provides a notable concentration of sites with Etruscan goods, mainly bucchero vases and transport amphorae: the habitations of the city of Malaga (mouth of the Guadalmedina), Cerro del Villar (mouth of the Guadalhorce),

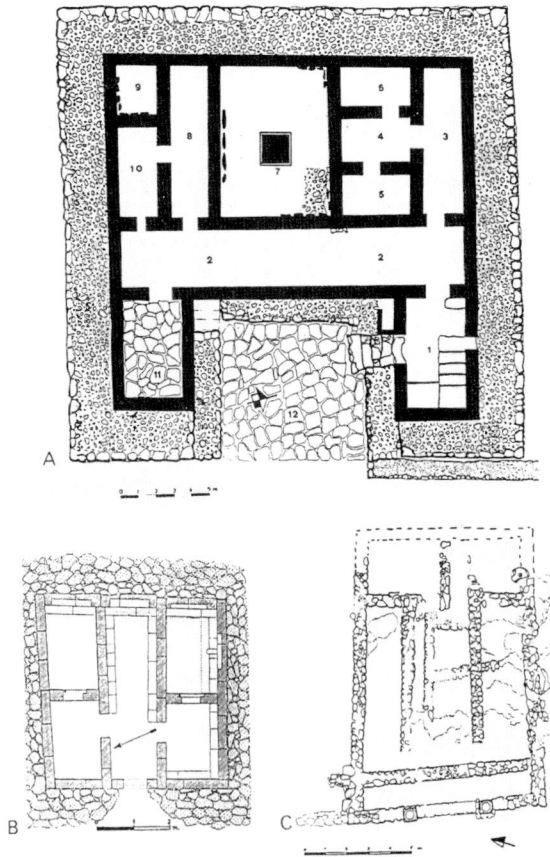

Figure 17.16a–c   Plan of architectural complex of Cancho Roano (a) and plans of structures with possible Etruscan influence in southern Iberia: great tomb of Toya, Jaén (b) and building with portico *in antis* at la Illeta, Els Banyets, Alacant-Alicante (c) (Llobregat 1991).

and Toscanos (mouth of the Vélez). The extensive excavations at Toscanos have revealed the presence of Etruscan ceramics, and although a detailed study has yet to be made of these goods, an appreciable number of bucchero kantharoi has already been identified. For the record, we shall recall the recent attribution to this littoral region of an Etruscan mirror, of Hellenistic date, an unconfirmed and suspect discovery.[86] The exemplary excavations at the insular port of Cerro del Villar have revealed several types of bucchero vases, of which some are unique on the Iberian Peninsula: the extremely characteristic small Caeretan amphorae decorated with incision like those at Carthage, and possible imitations of kantharoi and grey-black ware, as at Marseille.[87] The central city of Malaga has furnished bucchero vases, Etruscan amphorae and Etrusco-Corinthian ceramics, while the slopes of the citadel of Malaga, the Alcazaba, revealed two exceptional objects, one Punic, one Etruscan, both attributable to a sanctuary erected on the summit in the sixth century. The Punic object is an ivory plaque, whose relief carving and Egyptianizing decoration find their closest parallels in Carthage.[88] The second object is a handle in bronze in the shape of a *despotes therōn* mastering two man-headed bulls and a siren.[89] This bronze, of exceptional quality, is certainly a product of Etruria, dating to the end of the sixth century (Fig. 17.17) and it has close parallels at Carthage and at Schwarzenbach in the Celtic hinterland (see Fig. 19.8).[90] The Malaga bronze, like the Etruscan bronzes of the sanctuary at La Algaida (mouth of the Guadalquivir) would have been a votive offering.[91]

CONCLUSIONS

Etruscan maritime enterprises in the Mediterranean beyond the Tyrrhenian Sea differed from those of the Phoenicians and Greeks, as they did not rely on a network of colonial foundations. However, their maritime accomplishments were as extensive as their expeditions upon land, and in fact their power was both considerable and significant

Figure 17.17   Malaga, old excavations at the foot of the Alcazaba, handle in bronze with a young hero controlling human-headed bulls and a siren. End of the sixth century (Gran-Aymerich 1991 *et al.*, photos G.-A.).

in both arenas, as Livy recalled. Based on the data furnished by Carthage and Marseille, and the study of Etruscan relations with these two major colonial foundations, the one Phoenician, the other Greek, which played a significant role in the maritime history of the western Mediterranean, I have formulated the hypothesis of the Etruscan *"fonduk"* (Arabic *funduq*, a sort of inn or manor house, see below).

THE HYPOTHESIS OF THE ARCHAIC ETRUSCAN FONDUK

The word *fonduk* (*fondaco, fondouk, fonde*), borrowed from the Arabic language, appeared in the twelfth century AD to designate the warehouse or storage unit in a Mediterranean commercial city open to foreign powers referred to as *pandokeion* in Greek.[92] Specifically, it is where ships are authorized to drop off merchandise, as well as a place for lodgings, meetings, and diplomatic accommodations. The traits that seem to define an archaic *fonduk* are:

1. The presence of a coherent and homogeneous ensemble of imported objects and merchandise in a structure.
2. This ensemble of imports is *relatively* small and remarkable in its find context.
3. The imports come from maritime transport.
4. The discovery site has a quay.
5. This quay connects with a habitation and forms a continuous entity with either a city or a neighboring major habitation.
6. The imports are concentrated in a peripheral position of the habitation and in close proximity to the port region.
7. In best-case scenarios a construction is identified as a warehouse, residence or meeting house.
8. The historic context may support the hypothesis of a *fonduk*: that is to say, an architectural complex with warehouse, place of lodging and meeting, used for transactions, accords or ceremonies tied to on-going commercial ventures.

Profiles of different possible Etruscan fonduks

An establishment of this type for Etruscan merchants and sailors could have been located in an emporium or a colony of a powerful naval ally or even in a native port context. According to our present documentation, the hypothesis of an Etruscan *fonduk* is likely in three separate instances: in the Greek colonial context (Marseille, Ampurias), in the indigenous context (Saint-Blaise, Lattes, Ullastret, Huelva) and in the Punic colonial context (Carthage, Malaga).

The Greek colonial context: at Marseille, the first building complex on *Îlot rue Cathédrale*, located right next to the anchorage of the western habitation, has furnished the most remarkable batch of Etruscan ceramics in ancient *Massalia*, all from an early sixth-century stratigraphy. The most ancient building, dated to between 600 and 580, was designated by Lucien François Gantès during the excavation as the "Etruscan House" because of the number and variety of Etruscan vases in bucchero, Etruscan common wares in *impasto*, Etrusco-Corinthian wares, and transport amphorae. At the building site of Collège Vieux Port, also near the anchorage, the architectural complex interpreted as a

Greek banquet hall revealed an Etruscan inscription upon an amphora from Marseille dated to the end of the sixth century (Fig. 17.4).[93] The Etruscan finds from Ampurias (Palaiopolis, Neapolis and the necropoleis) merit a full study of recent finds and a deep scrutiny of the old ones so as to bring to light a panorama no doubt vastly richer than what is currently understood.[94] Based on identification from the old finds and amongst the Etruscan banquet wares are a *simpulum* ("ladle," *infundibulum* or "strainer") with frog figurine[95] (Fig. 17.18) and the two figurines and feline paw with inscription,[96] the last three identified as offerings.[97] The head of a lion decorating a chariot or piece of furniture (end of the sixth century, Fig. 17.19)[98] and especially the Etruscan mirror (end of the fourth century, Fig. 17.20) might be understood as markers of an Etruscan presence at this Greek colony.[99]

The indigenous context: the *oppidum* of Saint-Blaise (Bouches-du-Rhône, Provence) dominates a large marshy sector that formerly communicated directly with the sea. The complement of Etruscan goods, numerous and varied, was noted in the excavations of the upper city and the lower town by the ramparts. Bernard Bouloumié revealed the presence of a remarkable concentration of fragments of Etruscan amphorae at the foot

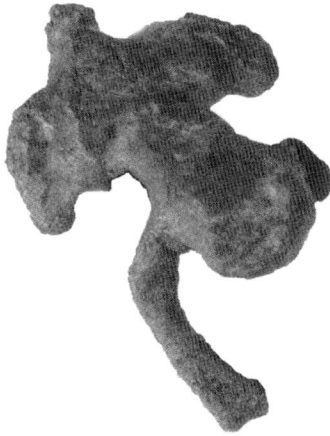

Figure 17.18   Empúries/Ampurias, fragment of *infundibulum* with figurine of a frog serving as hinge. (Catalogue Empúries 2007).

Figure 17.19   Empúries/Ampurias, terminal appliqué in form of a lion-head, bronze. (Catalogue Empúries 2007).

of the hill, in the area used for disembarkation at the edge of the Lavalduc salt-water pond.[100] The small port-site of Lattes (Hérault, Languedoc) is dominated by the modern city of Montpellier and the location of the *oppidum* of *Substantion* which brought to light excellent Attic ceramics of the fifth century and vestiges of an important proto-historic site. To the extreme south of Lattes, the constructions that furnished the most important concentration of Etruscan ceramics as well as the bowls bearing the inscriptions pertaining to women's names were identified by Michel Py as "Etruscan structures."[101] The *oppidum* of Ullastret (Girona-Gerona, Catalonia) furnished a rich ensemble of Etruscan ceramics and bronzes (Fig. 17.21) the study of which continues to supply unexpected data.[102] Antonio Arribas Palau published in the 1960s the amazing "*hallazgo cerrado*" (closed deposit) of Ullastret, which includes a complete Etruscan drinking set, possibly used for a ceremonial gathering.[103] At the foot of the *oppidum* Illa d'en Reixac corresponds to a quay that has brought to light some partially explored structures and which contained Etruscan goods. Huelva (Atlantic façade of the Andalusian littoral) provides continual, uninterrupted new evidence for its proto-historic origins, which attest to an active maritime commerce, both varied and of long duration. The Etrusco-Italian imports have been noted in several princely tombs around the area, as well as in the region close to the quays in a context of quadrangular architectural constructions.[104]

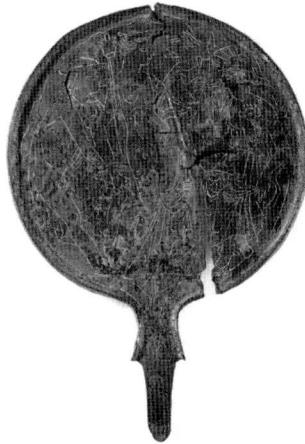

Figure 17.20   Etruscan mirror, from Empúries/Ampurias, old excavations in the necropolis. Bronze, engraved with the Judgment of Paris, end of the fourth century (Gran-Aymerich 2006c).

Figure 17.21   Ullastret, excavations of the *oppidum* of Puig Sant Andreu, attachment of moveable handle for stamnoid situla. Cast bronze (Gran-Aymerich 2006c).

The Punic-Phoenician Colonial Context: Malaga and Carthage. Etruscan imports in the bay of Malaga appeared in significant quantity in the Phoenician foundations of Toscanos (mouth of the Vélez), Cerro del Villar (mouth of the Guadalhorce) and in the heart of the ancient *Malaka* (mouth of the Guadalmedina). These port sites are tied to the old, indigenous habitations of Veléz-Malaga for the Velez valley, Cartama and Churriana for the Guadalhorce valley.[105] During the long-standing excavations begun in AD 1964 at Toscanos, Hans Georg Niemeyer and Hermanfried Schubart underlined the importance of this littoral zone for the foundations of the Phoenician colonies for Greek commerce linked to the port which the texts call *Mainake*, and they confirmed the presence of Etruscan goods.[106] The excavations at Toscanos have brought about many controversies, both for the chronology of the large ditch and its ramparts in large, carved stone blocks and also over the identification of Structure C, which the excavators took for a large warehouse or storage room, and others have identified as a building for aristocratic residential or even ceremonial use.[107] Our work in the center of the city of Malaga has allowed us to identify the first Etruscan ceramics of Punic *Malaka* and to link several exceptional discoveries to a sanctuary at the peak of the citadel.[108] Near to Malaga, the insular port of Cerro del Villar has also revealed Etruscan ceramics in a context, which Maria Eugenia Aubet Semmler has identified as a market, consisting of a street flanked by "*casas de mercado.*"[109]

Concerning Carthage, other than the numerous and various Etruscan discoveries, we know of at least one certain tomb of an Etruscan – more precisely that of a voyager from Caere, as attested by the columnar *cippus* which the person in charge of the funeral took care to order. The bronze statuette from Dar-Seniat is utterly exceptional as it demonstrates the votive actions of an Etruscan woman (Fig. 17.12). The feminine world is equally represented by Etrusco-Corinthian alabastra and the *anforette* in bucchero used as perfume containers. The quarter close to the shore at Carthage has been the site of deep excavations that have revealed Etruscan vases in bucchero, *impasto* and cream wares. The surprising concentration of Etruscan objects at Carthage calls for an intense study, so as to explain the presence of Etruscan women at Carthage and the possibility of mixed marriages. The hypothesis of an Etruscan *fonduk*, as a scale of the maritime commerce also merits examination. One might already affirm, to judge from the Etruscan goods at Carthage, that this Etruscan presence at Carthage would have been quite active during the sixth century and continued up until the Hellenistic period.

Commercial and diplomatic relations: arguments in favor of the Etruscan fonduk hypothesis

The historiographic sources and epigraphic documents provide precious evidence for interpreting Etruscan enterprises outside of Etruria, especially for establishing diplomatic alliances. The most explicit texts are those pertaining to relations with Carthage – especially the Caere-Carthage coalition during the Battle of Aleria and matters pertaining to the Tyrrhenian Sea[110] – as well as the first Roman-Carthaginian treaty, for which Caere played a premier role.[111] Amongst the inscriptions found in Etruria, the gold Pyrgi Plaques have shed new light on the relations (social, religious, diplomatic and economic) between Caere and Carthage for the crucial period that extends from the end of the sixth century to the first decades of the fifth.[112]

THE ETRUSCAN INSCRIPTIONS FROM THE MEDITERRANEAN REGION: EVIDENCE FOR LONG-RANGE TRAVEL AND CULTURAL TRANSFERS

The most exceptional of the known Etruscan texts was discovered very far from Etruria. This is the *liber linteus*, used to wrap an Egyptian mummy now in Zagreb (see Chapter 22). We do not know all the circumstances leading to the relocation of this object to Egypt, but it is reasonable to believe that this text accompanied an Etruscan, most likely a priest, in his long peregrinations to the land of the Pharaohs. Amongst the texts traced to Etruria we might also count the ivory plaque from Carthage, which, without doubt, provided safe conduct or some manner of *tessera hospitalis*. Another, similar document of more recent chronology is the inscribed bronze disc discovered in Gouraya, Algeria. The short inscription from Ampurias that appears upon a bronze feline paw would have been inscribed during the casting process in Etruria and is a very particular piece outside of Etruria. The Etruscan pottery exported might present marks and inscriptions related to commercial uses or manufacture, and certain pieces might have been inscribed in Etruria before export, as is proven by the presence of inscribed vases in the Grand Ribaud F shipwreck or by certain common wares found at Marseille whose inscriptions were rendered before firing.

Amidst all this, one must admit that the majority of Etruscan table wares and common wares with graffiti would have been inscribed at the sites where the fragments themselves were discovered, even though it is not possible to determine this with any certainty. Such documents have been identified in Greece and in southern Gaul.

Greece has furnished a widely dispersed and varied array of Etruscan objects with inscriptions. In the pan-Hellenic sanctuaries, where Etruscan objects and Villanova-style bronzes are frequent, we are quite familiar with the Greek inscriptions on Etruscan helmets dedicated by the Syracusans after the Battle of Cumae.[113] The Athenian agora has brought to light two Etruscan inscriptions upon bucchero vases,[114] while the majority of inscribed documents, and Etruscan vases, have been found in port sanctuaries or mercantile cities. At Corinth, bucchero kantharoi were found in the Potters' Quarter and other bucchero vases formed part of the discarded merchandise in the courtyard of a Trader's House on the Lechaion Road.[115] The bucchero kantharos from the sanctuary of Aphaia on Aegina, which bears the mutilated name of an Etruscan, has furnished the clearest epigraphic evidence of such a presence in a sanctuary outside of Etruria.[116] Concerning the sanctuary at Perachora, the engraved sealstone of a ring now in New York, which depicts the death of Ajax and bears the name of a "*mercante etrusco*" (Naniva) has been authenticated and recognized as Etruscan.[117] From the same sanctuary comes the inscription of a Corinthian – Nearchos – who incised his name upon a bucchero kantharos.[118]

For the north-western Mediterranean, the Etruscan inscriptions from Marseille, Saint-Blaise, Lattes, Ensérune, Pech-Maho and Ampurias open a fruitful avenue of research. This ensemble is rich and complex, and provides new perspectives through attentive readings of the graffiti coming from the habitation excavations.[119] Nevertheless, the most exceptional of the texts coming from southern France remains the lead sheet discovered at Pech-Maho in Languedoc, which bears an engraved letter, presumably commercial; epigraphic and philological analysis confirm its redaction in a "colonial" context.[120] The inscription engraved upon an amphora from Marseille, found in a sort of banquet hall according to L. F. Gantès, director of the excavations of the building complex at Collège

Vieux Port, confirms the presence at the end of the sixth century of a literate Etruscan and suggests the celebration of diplomatic ceremonies at which he participated. The majority of the graffiti on the bucchero and *impasto* vases from Marseille, Saint-Blaise and Lattes are understood as marks of ownership and the particularly exalted status conferred upon those using the script. The bowls from Lattes marked with women's names are of exceptional interest and appear to confirm the presence of Etruscan or Etruscanized women and the practice of mixed marriages. An analogous conclusion emerges from certain non-epigraphic documents from Carthage, specifically the perfume vessels in bucchero or Etrusco-Corinthian wares and the votive statuette from Dar-Seniat.

Southern Gaul has also furnished certain inscriptions that suggest a heretofore unsuspected cultural transfer of Etruscan origin. One is the graffito from Saint-Blaise upon the base of an Attic cup, in Greek characters but in Etruscan language and with a dedication to the goddess Uni: this reading was proposed by G. Colonna and suggests the cultural miscegenation of a presumably local person of high status.[121] The other inscription, which also appears to reveal an analogous result, is the graffito of Ensérune: J. de Hoz proposes to read the name of an indigene, of Celtic extraction, transcribed into Etruscan characters.[122]

FUNERARY STRUCTURES AND CONSTRUCTIONS WHICH CAN BE TRACED BACK TO AN ETRUSCAN PRESENCE

Until now the tombs and architectural remains the farthest from Etruria yet still tied to an Etruscan presence were those of Aleria on Corsica. Carthage has certainly furnished proof positive of the tomb of the Etruscan from Caere, marked by the aforementioned *cippus*, although unfortunately disassociated with its original locus. Near Lattes we noted a tomb with Etruscan goods and the oldest strigil found in Gaul, suggesting a deceased foreigner, possibly Etruscan. In one of the tombs of Ampurias, the exceptional discovery of an Etruscan mirror appears to indicate the high status of an Etruscan lady, or at least an Etruscanized one. A distant parallel might be the burial (in tomb 25) at Ras el Bassit (Syria) of an infant with a bucchero kantharos.[123] Other than in a few remarkable cases, imported objects present in distant necropoleis are difficult to interpret vis-à-vis matters of ethnicity or community. Effectively, tomb goods are in no way sufficient for determining with certainty the identity of the deceased. However, this restriction does not impede scientifically grounded avenues of research or the formation of new hypotheses. At Carthage, for example, one might suggest the attribution of certain tombs to "assimilated foreigners."[124] The dossier is complicated but merits further examination.

Concerning structures built in the settlements, the data are sparse and difficult to interpret, given the lack of extensive excavation contemporary with the levels of the Etruscan imports. For the north-western Mediterranean, in spite of such designations as "Etruscan house" for a construction at the building site of *Îlot rue Cathédrale* at Marseille, and for several rooms in a quarter at Lattes, no complete architectural ensemble is identifiable with certainty as an Etruscan residence or storeroom. However, the earliest levels of Lattes do appear to attest to a new style of architecture introduced into the local, indigenous context; likewise the apparition in southern France of stone statuary, manifest in the sculpture of a kneeling archer which was part of a commemorative monument of the fifth century, later reused in fill.[125]

The south-western Mediterranean and the Straits of Gibraltar have furnished very rich elements of colonial architecture, exclusively deriving from oriental sources, Phoenician and Punic. For example, the site of Toscanos has revealed a singular construction in use in the sixth century and designated "storeroom C," a sort of warehouse with three aisles which some have taken as a prestige structure.[126] The port site of El Campello (Illeta dels Banyets, Alicante) contains two buildings – A and B – interpreted as two cultic structures, which may have had a hypothetical Etruscan influence (Fig. 17.16c).[127] At Cerro del Villar (Malaga), Etruscan goods are concentrated in several constructions of the so-called "*casas y calle del mercado*,"[128] and at Huelva most of the Etruscan ceramics have been located in the buildings of the Calle del Puerto and its environs.[129] At none of these sites was there a strong, direct correlation between Etruscan imports and any specific building.

However, the localization and the excavation of a coherent architectural ensemble with its contents may permit the identification of a *fonduk*, as is the case for the exclusively Phoenician site of Abul at the mouth of the Sado River, to the south of the Tagus and Lisbon, whose city center has otherwise recently furnished the vestiges of a Phoenician habitation and presence since the seventh century.[130] The site of Abul itself goes back to this early period and constitutes the sole complete example of an isolated warehouse, composed of aisles and rooms around a central court. The residential character of this complex and its attested ritual function augment its storage functions and unite the ensemble of characteristics, which might correspond to a Phoenician *fonduk* established on the Atlantic coast.

To conclude: the Etruscans, in the context of long-range expeditions and, as with many aspects of their civilization, are, by their uniqueness, a subject of permanent paradox for researchers. Etruscan naval activities beyond the Tyrrhenian Sea appear to function without colonial foundations or their own ports. The Etruscans had developed their long-range enterprises on a "non-colonial" thalassocracy. Rather than transporting Etruscan freight on Greek or Phoenician ships, the entrepreneurs and shippers of the most prosperous Etruscan maritime cities appear to have made use of ports open to their ships and their products, thanks to prearranged treaties. The very clear increase in Etruscan goods in the western Mediterranean, notable from the end of the seventh and throughout the sixth century, would have resulted from the emergence of several base networks or ports-of-call for the merchandise, the sailors and Etruscan voyagers.[131] These harbor access points, guaranteed by treaty, manifest elements characteristic of establishments close to the *fonduks* spread throughout the Mediterranean throughout the ages.[132]

The Bibliography for this chapter can be found at the end of Chapter 19.

NOTES

1 *Ab Urbe Condita* 5.33.
2 Main Etruscan cities involved in long-distance trade: Caere, Tarquinia, Vulci, Vetulonia, Populonia, Felsina.
   Etruscan major ports of trade, *emporia* or *fonduk* in the western connection: Carthage, Málaga, Huelva, Marseille-*Massalia*, Saint-Blaise (Bouches-du-Rhône), Lattes-*Lattara* (Montpellier), Empúries (Ampurias, *Emporion*), Ullastret (Puig Sant Andreu and Illa d'en Reixac). Aristocratic residences in the European and Iberian hinterland: Hohenasperg, Heuneburg, Châtillon-sur-Glâne, Mont Lassois-Vix, Bourges, Cancho Roano (Zalamea).
   Main concentrations in Greek sanctuaries: Olympia, Delphi, Samos.

Principal locations cited in chapters 17 and 19: 1. Antibes, shipwreck La Love; 2. Cassis, shipwreck Cassidaigne; 3. East of Marseille, shipwreck of Estéou dou Miet; 4. id. shipwreck Grand Ribaud F; 5. Saint-Marcel, Marseille; 6. Vauvenargues, Bouches-du-Rhône; 7. Pertuis, Vaucluse; 8. Arles; 9. Lyon-Vaise; 10. Chassey, Bourgogne; 11. Bragny, Saône valley; 12. Auxerre; 13. Saint-Gemmes, Loire valley; 14. Fâ, Barzan, Gironde; 15. Toulouse; 16. Carcassonne, Carsac and La Cité; 17. Roc de Buffens and Le Cros, Caunes-Minervois, Languedoc; 18. Tamaris, Bouches-du-Rhône; 19. L'Arquet, id; 20. Saint-Pierre-les-Martigues, id; 21. Agde, *Agathé*, Languedoc; 22. shipwrecks of Rochelongue and others, id; 23. La Liquière, Calvisson, Gard; 24. Saint Julien, Pézenas; 25. Ensérune; 26. Béziers; 27. Montlaurès, Narbonne; 28. Cayla de Mailhac; 29. Pech-Maho, Sigean; 30. Collioure, Roussillon; 31. Elne, *Illiberris*; 32. Perpignan, *Ruscino*; 33. shipwreck Cap Creus, Girona; 34. La Fonollera, Girona; 35. shipwreck Cava, Barcelona; 36. Penya del Moro, Barcelona; 37. Moleta del Remei, Tarragona; 38. La Gessera, id; 39. Tarragona; 40. shipwreck near Valencia; 41. Xabia-Javea, Alacant; 42. Ibiza and Balaeric area; 43. Villaricos, Almeria; 44. Toscanos, Vélez-Málaga; 45. Cerro del Villar, Guadalhorce; 46. Cádiz; 47. La Algaida, Guadalquivir; 48. Turuñuelo, Mérida; 49. Alcurrucén, Córdoba; 50. Mirador de Rolando, Granada; 51. Segóbriga, Cuenca; 52. Los Villares, Albacete; 53. Pozo Moro, id; 54. Gouraya, Algeria; 55. Utica, Tunisia; 56. Miliane valley, Tunisia; 57. Ksour es Saaf, Tunisia; 58. Tocra, Libya; 59. Cyrene, Libya; 60. Naukratis, Egypt; 61. Corfu, Greece; 62. Rhodes; 63. Ras-el-Bassit, Syria; 64. Cyprus (Amathus and Kition).

3   Among the sites where the two paths of distribution most certainly meet, via the south of France and via the Golasecca region and the Alps, we count Lyon and Bragny-sur-Saône on one side, and the Heuneburg on the other. Several principle settlements of the Celtic hinterland have been identified in this regard, such as Bourges, Mont Lassois, Châtillon-sur-Glâne and the Heuneburg. See Gran-Aymerich 2006c, 2008c, 2012. For the debate concerning the southern French route versus that of the Alps, see Kimmig 1975, 1983, 2000; Shefton 1995, 2000; Rolley ed. 2003; Rolley 2006.

4   Pioneers in this field are the works of Joseph Déchelette (1862–1914), Pere Bosch-Gimpera (1891–1974), Wolfgang Kimmig (1910–2001). See in particular: Bernard, Roure 2010.

5   Gras 2004, 213–235.

6   These discoveries were contemporaneous with scientific research conducted on the north bank of the Old Port by Gaston Vasseur (1855–1915), and then by Michel Clerc (1857–1931) with the support of Edmond Pottier (1855–1934) for the study of Greek and Etruscan ceramics. Sourisseau 2002.

7   Niemeyer 1990, 1995, 2005.

8   Rothe, Tréziny 2005; Actes Marseille 1999; Delestre dir. 2006; Hermary, Hesnard, Tréziny 2006; Sourisseau 2002 and 2004; Gantès, Sourisseau, Verger 2003.

9   Gantès 1992 and 1999.

10 Bouloumié 1982; Gantes, Sourisseau, Verger 2003.

11 Gantès 2002.

12 Gantès 2005, 695, 705, 729; Gran-Aymerich 2006b.

13 Gran-Aymerich 2010, 218–221, no 2, forthcoming b; Catalogue Marseille 2013, 132, Fig. no 5.

14 Gran-Aymerich 1992: 86, pl. 38.2–9, 39 and 2006a.

15 Gran-Aymerich 1998, 2004.

16 Velde *et al.* 2002; Velde 2006.

17 Marchand 2006, 281–304, Fig. 3. BN07; Gran-Aymerich 2006a, 219, pl. I.c.

18 Briquel, Gantès, Gran-Aymerich, Mellinand 2006, 42–43; Briquel, Gran-Aymerich 2006, 69; Gantès 2006, 105, Fig. 72, no 204; Gran-Aymerich 2006b, 280, Fig. 23; id. 2009a, Fig. 4; Catalogue Marseille 2013, 174, Fig. no 52.

19 Briquel, Gantès, Gran-Aymerich, Mellinand 2006, p. 42; Briquel, Gran-Aymerich 2006, p. 69; Gantès 2006, 105, Fig. 72, no 32; Gran-Aymerich 2006b, 280, Fig. 24; id. 2009a, Fig. 4; Catalogue Marseille 2013, 174, Fig. no 51, for the restitution of the architectural complex Fig. 20, 37.

20 Colonna 1980, 2006b, 664, Fig. 2.

21 Colonna 2006b, 667, pl. Ic, Fig. 6. For the presence of an *intra muros* sanctuary to which we might attach this find: Gran-Aymerich 2009a, 28–29.

22 Colonna 1980, 2006b, 665, Fig. 3; Py 2009.

23 De Hoz 2008.

24 Cristofani 1983, 1993, 1995; Colonna 1980, 1988, 2006b; Belfiore forthcoming.

25 I thank Jean Hadas-Lebel for the exchange of information in this regard, while releasing him from any responsibility for this interpretation.

26 Sanmartí 1993, photo in the opposite direction; Gran-Aymerich 2006c, 2009a, 253, Fig. 4.

27 Catalogue Carcassonne 1989, Fig. coul. 121, "oenochoe de terre cuite de type étrusque de la nécropole de Las Peyros à Couffoulens (il s'agit, probablement, d'une copie languedocienne)".

28 According to C. Landes concerning the tombs with exclusively Etruscan furnishings recently discovered in the excavations outside Lattes, see Catalogue Lattes 2002.

29 Catalogue Marseille 2002; Catalogue Hauterive-Laténium 2005; Pomey 2006.

30 Long, Gantès, Drap 2002, Fig. 1–2: Etruscan amphora of the type "Bon Porté," with signs inscribed on the rim, a small, globular *olpe* (Etruscan?) with signs inscribed on the base, an amphora from Magna Graecia with an incised inscription on the neck.

31 Catalogue Marseille 2002; Catalogue Hauterive-Laténium 2005.

32 Chausserie-Laprée 2005a and 2005b, 5–9; Gantès 2003, 65–69, notices 1.1–23, 1.31–52.

33 Garcia 2004 and 2006; Garcia, Vital 2006; Ugolini 2010; Arcelin 2004; Py 1993 and 2003.

34 Verger 2003, Fig. 11. For a recent study of the protohistoric bronzes of southern France: Campolo, Garcia 2004.

35 Gran-Aymerich 2006a, Fig. 10, mouth of a bucchero oinochoe from the area of the Bourse at Marseille; Fig. 11, mouth of a pitcher in grey monochrome ware from Saint-Marcel.

36 Catalogue Lattes 2002, 129–139; Py, Dietler 2003; Py, Lebeaupin, Sejalon, Roure 2006, pl. V.

37 For the inscription, Colonna 2006b, 667, Fig. 6. For the identification of an *intra muros* sanctuary at Saint-Blaise: Gran-Aymerich 2009a, 28–29, "Un sanctuaire intra-muros à Saint-Blaise, Bouches-du-Rhône et une probable dédicace à Uni".

38 For a historiographic approach on the various points of view on the evolution and/or acculturation of southern French Gaul: Bernard, Roure 2010.

39 Gran-Aymerich 2006a, 214, Fig. 6 and 2006b, Fig. 11.

40 Gran-Aymerich 2006a, 214, Fig 8.

41 Gran-Aymerich 1995a, 1997, 2002a.

42 Mötsch 2008; Balzer 2009; Maffre, Chazalon forthcoming.

43 Abels 1992; Vorlauf 1997.

44 Kimmig 1991, 1999; Sankot 2006, Fig. p. 19, with examples of carinated cups with perpendicular incisions from Tuchomerice, Bohemia, dating to the Late-Hallstat period.

45 Thus for the ivory workshops at Caere, the first cut-stone walls at Tarquinia, the first stone sculptures at Ceri in the region of Caere, or in Casale Marittimo in the region of Vetulonia.

46 Botto, Vives Ferrándiz 2006, Fig. 4, importazioni "villanoviane"; Gran-Aymerich 2006b, 255.

47 Botto 2011.

48 Pallottino 1963; Heurgon 1965b and 1993; Scardigli 1991; Colonna 2007.

49 For the Cyrenaica finds: Jolivet 1980; Cristofani 1983; Hase 1992 (1989), 327–328, n. 2, Fig. 27; Naso 2006c and 2011; Camporeale *et al.* 2001; Camporeale 2004, 231. For the hypothetical presence of bucchero at Karnak: Naso 2011, 80, no 34.

50 Hase 1979 and 1997; Gras 1985, 651–680; Bellelli, Cultraro 2006; Naso 2000a–c, 2006a–b and 2009a–b.

51 Bonanno 1993.

52 The presence of bucchero at Utica (MacIntosh Turfa 1977, 370, n. 94; Naso 2011, 79, no 18) and Tipasa (Hase 1992 (1989) 27, n. 2, via information furnished by M. Torelli; Naso 2011, 79, no 2) has not yet been confirmed, and the Etrusco-Corinthian ceramics of Leptis Magna have been refuted: Frère 2006, 253, carte Fig. 3; Naso 2011, 79.

53 On the bronze disc from Gouraya, *tessera hospitalis* of the 3rd cent. BC: Briquel 2006; Naso 2011, 79, no 1.

54 Heurgon 1969a (= Heurgon 1986, 433–447) and 1969b; Carruba 1976; Colonna 1983; Briquel 2006, 59.

55 Niemeyer 1990, 1999 and 2005.

56 As with the "Divine Nile" (*Hapy*) flasks, the "New Year" flasks, and the cylindrical faience vessels (with green glaze coating) from Carthage, Motya, and Tarquinia, representing Egyptianizing scenes with the name of the Pharaoh Bocchoris (720–715). Bissing 1933 and 1941; Vercoutter 1945; Aubet Semmler 1980b, Cintas 1976, pl. LXXV; Catalogue Venise 1988, no 425, 655; Redissi 1997.

57 The Etruscan vases from Carthage are now stored in the museums of Carthage and Bardo, but others have been dispersed. I have found two examples at the Louvre (Département des Antiquités grecques, étrusques et romaines): Gran-Aymerich 1982, pl. 15.3–4, inv. AO 3208, 55–56; Gran-Aymerich 1983, Fig. 1c–d, 78–79. Concerning Carthaginian tombs with Etruscan vases: Boucher 1953; Colozier 1953; Cintas 1976, Fig. 45a, has reassembled the Punic and Etruscan materials from a tomb at Douïmés; MacIntosh 1974; Turfa 1977; Morel 1981; Gras 1985; Thuillier 1985; Hase 1992 (1989), 231, Fig. 2, 1996 and 2004, 73–77. For the whole study of the necropoleis of Carthage: Benichou-Safar 1982.

58 Picard 1959; Cintas 1976, 319, Fig. 48, pl. LXXXI; Jiménez Ávila 2002, figs. 30, 59.15 for the example from Byrsa, pl. 81.1. For the Rhodian-style oinochoes: Shefton 1979; Rolley 1987; Jiménez Ávila 2002, figs. 29, 53–55. The votive razor from Kerkouane, in the Bardo Museum, is a high-quality piece ornamented with a sphinx or siren, probably a Carthaginian piece showing the influence of Etruscan bronze vases: Catalogue Venise 1988, no 304, 635, photo p. 432; Catalogue Paris 1995, photo p. 46.

59 Catalogue Venise 1988, nos 293–294, 635, photo p. 432; Catalogue Paris 1982, 77, no 99, for an example with two nudes decorating the handle; Picard 1959. The Rabs sector of the necropolis of Sainte Monique provides a dense concentration of bronze oinochoai of the fifth–fourth centuries with figures decorating the lower handle attachments: Cintas 1976, 373, n. 952, pl. 81.6–8: "R. P. Delattre notes that in three months he discovered 15 oinochoai (*aiguières*)."

60 Jacobsthal-Langsdorff 1929; Reinecke 1933; Bouloumié 1973, 169–170, 231, 287, 301; Cintas 1976, 340–341, Fig. 55, pl. 81.2; Hase 1992 (1989), 378, Fig. 32, pl. 33, and 2004, 78, figs. 25–28b; Vorlauf 1997. Also: Morel 1994.

61 For an introduction to the bronze metallurgy of Carthage: Tekki 2009. The necropolis of Aléria in Corsica has furnished several hundred Etruscan bronzes, but the site is itself unique as a possible Etruscan maritime colony, which nevertheless is located in the Tyrrhenian Sea: Gran-Aymerich, Jehasse 2007, with bibliography. In the Celtic hinterland we know of a large dispersion of Etruscan bronzes, several hundred objects, which might be contrasted with a few isolated Greek pieces of very high quality and often exceptionally large, such as the Vix Krater or the Hochdorf Cauldron: Bouloumié 1987; Shefton 1995; Rolley *et al.* 2003; Haffner 2003; Rolley 2005 and 2006; Gran-Aymerich 2013a.

62 See in particular: Moscati, Pallottino 1966, 12, pl. I,1; Catalogue Venise 1988, 632, no 289, color photo p. 536. Finally, with bibliography, Maggiani 2006, 319–321, Fig. 1.1, 2.1, and 2007 with a new reading.

63   Missing the upper portion. The preserved fragment measures 50 cm, the diameter at the base is 32.5 cm; Pallottino 1964, 114 (= Pallottino 1979, I, 393, pl. VIII, 1); MacIntosh 1974; Turfa 1977, 369, n. 2; Blumhofer 1993, 190–194, type I; Hase 1996, 189, and 2004, 76, 79.

64   For the Etruscan *cippus* and the plates of Genucilia type: Morel 1980, 29, 38, 65, 71, and 1981; Jolivet 1980; Hase 1996, 188–189, figs. 1–3. On the presence of funerary stelai in the Carthage necropoleis (mostly from the Rabs sector of Sainte-Monique), and distinctions among the stelai of the sanctuary: Cintas 1976, 359–360; Bénichou-Safar 1982.

65   Hase 1996, 194, n. 26.

66   Concerning the 29 *cippi* of Aléria, themselves without engraved inscriptions (but possibly originally painted) as is the case for Carthage: Gran-Aymerich, Jehasse 2007; Hase 1996, 193, notes the marble example from Tomb 87, from the beginning of the fourth century. The Etruscan *cippi* of this type were discovered at Spina and Marzabotto: Hase *ibid*. 191, n. 14, with bibliography.

67   Bissing 1933, 119–129; Colozier 1953; Cintas 1976, 377–381, pl. LXIIILXV, LXVII, 2–3; Haumesser 2007.

68   Boucher 1953; Ferron 1966; MacIntosh 1974; Turfa 1977 and 1986; Morel 1981; Thuillier 1985; Hase 1992 (1989); Niemeyer–Docter *et al.* 1993; Mackensen 1999; Lancel ed. 1982; Lancel 1995; Docter *et al.* 1997; Vegas 1997; Docter 1998, 2000 and 2007; Mansel 2011.

69   Docter 1998, 2000 and 2007.

70   See in particular: Hase 1992 (1989), Fig. 2: "Arealen A1, A3, A7"; Vegas 1997; Trias 1999; Docter 2007. For the early diffusion of Sardinian ceramics in the western Mediterranean and at Carthage: Botto 2011.

71   We have observed on many occasions the remarkable presence at Carthage of Etruscan flasks and small containers for perfumed oil (aryballoi, alabastra, small bucchero and *impasto* amphorae): Morel 1981; Gran-Aymerich, Bonnet, Domínguez-Arranz 2010. The majority of these vessels pertain to the women's world (with the probable exclusion of some aryballoi believed to belong to the world of men): Szilágyi 1998; Naso 2011, 79, no 8. One might deduce from the use of these vessels of perfumed oil the presence of Etruscan women at Carthage. The figurine from Dar-Seniat (see below) seems to constitute an additional proof in this regard: Gran-Aymerich 2008a and 2009a.

72   Berges 1993, 253, 255, pl. 67, 4–6 and 1997; Hase 2004, 78, notes the exceptional character of these three impressions, probably made with Etruscan seals, amongst the 1437 discovered examples. On the first discoveries of clay bullae with sealings found in the quarter next to the Carthage littoral: Cintas 1970, 304, n. 213; Sznycer 1969, figs p. 141–142.

73   Gran-Aymerich 2008a and 2009a.

74   Delattre 1923.

75   Chelbi 2006.

76   Gran-Aymerich 1991 and 2006b; Gran-Aymerich and Gran-Aymerich 2006.

77   Llobregat 1982, 1991 and 1998; Colonna 2006a, Fig. 19.

78   Arribas, Trias de Arribas 1961; Donati 1991; Gran-Aymerich 2006b; Botto, Vives Ferrándiz 2006; Colonna 2006a; Bruni 2007.

79   Colonna 1980, 2006a and 2006b; de Hoz 2008; Py 2009.

80   Actes Barcelone 1990; Fernández, Gómez Bellard, Ribera 1993; Catalogue Marseille 2002, 21; Bardelli, Graells 2012; Graells forthcoming.

81   Celestino Pérez 2001; Gran-Aymerich 1995d, 2006 and 2008a; Gran-Aymerich, du Puytison, Lagarce 1995.

82   Shefton 1979; Jiménez Ávila 2002; Botto, Vives-Ferrándiz 2006, Figs 9 (Huelva) and 10 (from "Granada," perhaps Malaga).

83   One of the Etrusco-Corinthian vases is part of the Senza Graffito Group from Tarquinia: Gran-Aymerich 2006b; Colonna 2006a, Fig. 1; Botto, Vives-Ferrándiz 2006, Fig. 8.

84 González de Canales, Serrano Pichardo, Llompart Gomez 2004: for the *impasto* of Villanovan type, Fig. p. 98–99, pl. LIX.10–11; for the ceramics of Sardinia, Fig. pp. 100–105; Botto, Vives-Ferrándiz 2006, Fig. 4.

85 Niemeyer 1995; for the interpretation of Mainake in a historic period, favorable to Greek Commercial enterprises, see Gran-Aymerich 1990; Gran-Aymerich *et al.* 1991, 136–139.

86 Mansel 1998.

87 For the Etruscan finds at Malaga and those of Cerro del Villar: Gran-Aymerich *et al.* 1991, 128–134; Gran-Aymerich 1994, with bibliography; Aubet Semmler 2007. For the kantharoi in bucchero and grey monochrome ware from Marseille: Gran-Aymerich 1998, 2006b, 2004, 2006a, pl. Id-e.

88 Gran-Aymerich *et al.* 1991, pl. IV, Fig. 97; Gran-Aymerich 2008a, Fig. 6.

89 Gran-Aymerich *et al.* 1991, pl. III, Gran-Aymerich 2006b, Fig. 8; 2008a, Fig. 5; Colonna 2006a, Fig. 5.

90 Haffner 1976, 147–148, pl. 9.2.

91 Colonna 2006a, Fig. 2; Botto, Vives Ferrándiz 2006, Fig. 11; Gran-Aymerich 2008a, Fig. 4, and 2009a, Fig. 2; Bardelli, Graells 2012, 25, Fig. 1–3.

92 On the earliest *fondachi* of Venice, the etymology of the term, and the origins of such a commercial "stop-over" location protected according to the oriental model of the mercantile storage unit (the *pandokeion* of Greeks in the East): Concina 1997, 9–20. On the Phoenician model of the *enoikismoi* (Italian "'*fondachi*'"): Niemeyer 1990, 1995, 1999, 158 and 2005. Also Gras *et al.* 1989, 105–115; Aubet Semmler 1994, 87–94.

93 Gantès 2006, 195, Fig. 72, no 32; Briquel, Gantès, Gran-Aymerich, Mellinand 2006; Gran-Aymerich 2009a; Catalogue Marseille 2013, 174, Fig. no 51.

94 Aquilué, Castanyer, Santos, Tremoleda 2006.

95 Castanyer, Santos 2007, Fig. p. 57, "petita granota de bronze … trobat a Sant Marti d'Empuries"; Bardelli, Graells 2012, p. 32, Fig. 15.

96 Gran-Aymerich 2008a, Figs 8–9, and 2009a, Figs 5–6

97 Sanmartí 1993; Gran-Aymerich 2008a, Fig. 7, and 2009a, Fig. 7.

98 Castanyer, Santos 2007, Fig. p. 57, "procedeix de l'anomenada Tomba Cazurro".

99 Catalogue Paris 1992a, 259, no 300, col. pl. p. 177; Almagro-Gorbea 1992; Gran-Aymerich 2006b, Fig. 14.

100 Bouloumié 1982; Gran-Aymerich 2009a, 28–29.

101 Py 2009; Py, Garcia 1993; Py, Lebeaupin, Sejalon, Roure 2006.

102 For the amazing deposit of Etruscan vases: Arribas Palau, Trías de Arribas 1961. For the presence of a bronze attachment of an Etruscan stamnos-situla: Gran-Aymerich 2006c, Fig. 13; Botto, Vives-Ferrándiz 2006, Fig. 59; Bardelli, Graells 2012, 33, Fig. 16. For the presence of vases inspired by Etruscan forms: Donati 1991. For the presence of a vase by the Micali Painter: Bruni 2007.

103 Arribas Palau, Trías de Arribas 1961. On this subject see: Catalogue Paris 1992a, Fig. p. 176, 259–260, no 301–303; Gran-Aymerich 2009a, 21.

104 Fernández Jurado, García Sanz 2001, Fig. 7.

105 Gran-Aymerich *et al.* 1991, map Fig. 2–3.

106 Niemeyer *et al.* 1988, 169, Fig. 9.g, 134, Fig. 6.e; Gran-Aymerich, Andérica 2000.

107 Niemeyer 1995; for an interpretation as a prestige residence with similar function to Cancho Roano: Almagro-Gorbea *et al.* 1990. See also: Celestino Pérez 2001; Dies Cusi 2001. For the oriental origins: Kochavi 1998.

108 Gran-Aymerich *et al.* 2001, Figs 4–5; Gran-Aymerich 2008a, 91–94 and 2009a, 29–30.

109 Aubet Semmler *et al.* 1999.

110 Pallottino 1963; Heurgon 1993; Gras 2000; Fantar 2000; and more in MAXH 2000.

111 Pallottino 1963; Heurgon 1965b; Scardigli 1991; Colonna 2007.

112 Wikander 2008.

113 Cristofani 1983, Fig. 59; Gras 1985, 681–694, pl. VIII.

114 Colonna 2009, notes 16 and 43.

115 MacIntosh 1974; Williams 1974.

116 Cristofani 1983 and 1994.

117 Colonna 2009.

118 Hase 1997, 317, Fig. 24.1; Naso 2006b, 364; Colonna 2009, 219.

119 See in particular: Cristofani 1993 and 1995; Colonna 1980, 1988 and 2006b; de Hoz 2008; Briquel *et al*. About the very "special" pottery tablet with Greek inscription about "Etruscan ware," perhaps from Ampurias: Dunst 1969; Mangas, Plácido 1998, 344–345.

120 Cristofani 1993.

121 Colonna 2006b, 667, Fig. 6.

122 De Hoz 2008.

123 Courbin 1993, 31–32, 68, 175, Fig. 17.8, pl. 19.3–4. A few tombs in Phoenician Cyprus also held Etruscan vases (bucchero, Etrusco-Corinthian wares): Turfa 2001, 276–278.

124 Gras, Rouillard, Teixidor, 226.

125 Catalogue Lattes 2002, 129–139; Py 2009.

126 Almagro-Gorbea *et al*. 1990: Niemeyer 1995; Dies Cusi 2001.

127 Llobregat 1982, 1991 and 1998.

128 Aubet Semmler *et al*. 1999.

129 Fernández Jurado , García Sanz 2001; Fernández Jurado 2005.

130 Mayet, Tavares da Silva 2001. See also: Martín Bravo 1998.

131 For these investigations: Gran-Aymerich 2008a, 2009a, 2013b, forthcoming a, b, d, and h.

132 See Chapter 19 for bibliography to this chapter.

PART IV

ETRUSCAN SOCIETY AND ECONOMY

CHAPTER EIGHTEEN

POLITICAL SYSTEMS AND LAW

———•◆•———

Hilary Becker

Greek and Roman authors inform us that the administration of Etruscan cities began with kings and, in fits and starts, transitioned to elected magistrates at the end of the Archaic period, contemporary to similar developments in Athens and Rome. While the ancient authors are not overly interested in the mechanics of the Etruscan political system, this study will examine Etruscan evidence, along with evidence from Greek and Roman authors, in order to flesh out a diachronic impression of political life in Etruria, aiming to demonstrate in particular how the different city-states were governed across their territories, and to what extent there was any federal activity in Etruria. Such a study also provides an idea of what Etruscan citizens might have expected from their magistrates and their city-state overall, in terms of administration, public works and law.

A DIACHRONIC OVERVIEW OF ETRUSCAN MAGISTRACIES:

The monarchical period

By the middle of the eighth century BCE elite leaders (*principes*) at the head of Etruscan *gentes* (clans), according to Roman authors, shared their power to form the Etruscan city-state. As with the contemporary Romans and Greeks, the preferred political form for these nascent city-states was monarchical. The Etruscan word for king was *zilath*, denoting "head ruler" or "commander".[1] This political term remains in use throughout Etruscan political history, although its precise constitutional meaning changes over time. The use of the term *zilath* during the monarchical period can be found on a cippus from Rubiera (near Modena) dating to the end of the seventh century BCE.[2] This inscription specifically states that this magistrate, whose name is no longer legible, was a *zilath* at Misala or Sala.

Etruscan kings are familiar in Greek and Roman authors, and even the *Aeneid* associates early Etruria with kingship, in the form of Mezentius of Caere.[3] An Etruscan king Arimnestos was the first non-Greek to make a dedication (a throne) at Olympia,[4] and other notable kings include Porsenna, as well as the kings of Etruscan descent at Rome. Mastarna is one of the more notable kings from Etruscan and Roman history, mostly as a man of Etruscan origin who would come to be king of Rome. Exploring his origin story allows us to understand early magisterial titles even further.

Etruscan legend (preserved by the Etruscophile emperor Claudius) presents Mastarna as a local hero from Vulci, who was a *condottierro*-like figure who fought in league with the Vibennae brothers. These exploits are depicted in the frescoes of the François Tomb in Vulci, undoubtedly the best-extant reflection of an Etruscan historical past. In these scenes the trio fights against a range of people from central Italic cities including a figure labeled as a Gnaeus Tarquinius of Rome, who is otherwise unknown to us. A speech given by Claudius relates that Mastarna immigrated to Rome with the remnants of a private army (that of his comrade, Caelius Vibenna) and changed his name to Servius Tullius.[5] And while the Roman historical tradition preserves alternate origin stories for their sixth king,[6] his value for an understanding of Etruscan magistracies is significant. This is because the name "Macstrna," as he is labeled in the François tomb, also contributes to the general understanding of Etruscan political nomenclature. Once the suffix *–na*, which is often used to denote Etruscan family names, is removed, the name is similar to the Latin noun *magister*.[7] As Jacques Heurgon demonstrated, the Latin term *magister* originally referred to magistrates such as the *magister equitum* and is the term from which *magistratus* ultimately derives. There is also an Etruscan magistracy (of debated function) known as *macstrev* (*-c*).[8] The Romans also had a word that they thought was the Etruscan word for kings, *lucumones*,[9] which also was the first name of their first "Etruscan" king, Tarquinius Priscus, who was born as *Lucumo* in Tarquinia.[10] This word was probably a Latin translation of the popular Etruscan first name *Lauchume*.

Two ancient sources may shed light on the social relationship that the king enjoyed with the people of his city-state. The first is a passage from Macrobius that relates a tradition wherein the Etruscan people would pay their respects to the king (*regem suum salutabant*) every ninth day, presumably at a gathering when the town and country spheres would come together and the power of the supreme leader would be reinforced.[11] A second, very different picture reveals a fear of the monarchy but its date is problematic. The Brontoscopic Calendar of Nigidius Figulus was a sixth century CE Greek translation of a Latin version of Ciceronian date, which in turn was drawn from an Etruscan original of a presumed eighth century to early seventh century BCE date.[12] If it thunders, it could portend danger to the king on one particular day, on another oppression by the king, and on yet another the king might be overthrown, but even so, thunder on December twenty-seventh could bring help from the king to many.[13] It is entirely possible that such references to the king in the calendar reflect a time of transition from the monarchy, as in Rome, when people may have been wary of kings (see Veii below).

Transition to republican government

Thefarie Velianas, ruler of Caere (*C[a]isra*), dedicated the golden, inscribed Pyrgi plaques around 500 BCE (see Chapter 30).[14] Thefarie Velianas, like Arimnestos, was also active in the international sphere, as he evidently worked with Phoenician/Punic persons and received the help of their goddess, Astarte (equated with Uni in this Etruscan text), to whom he dedicates a temple and a statue. In the Etruscan version of the inscription, Thefarie Velianas is described as a *zilath*, and the translation of "king" seems appropriate because the term used to describe his status in the Phoenician text is *mlk*, a Semitic term indicating dynasty.[15] In spite of the Phoenician text, there is some debate as to what kind of official Thefarie was, and this debate stems partly from the fact that the same term *zilath* will be used to describe the highest-ranking republican magistrates that follow the monarchy.[16] His precise status draws attention because his title was given a descriptive adjective, so that he is a *zilac seleitala*, a title that may not describe a king any longer but instead could be something comparable to the Roman *praetor maximus* who would have been one magistrate among colleagues. Thefarie Velianas, if this is correct, could be at the precipice of a new oligarchic system, which is republican in its nature.

Towards the end of the Archaic period cities began the transition from kings to elected magistrates, and Thefarie Velianas could be a part of this revolution. Indeed, during the Archaic and Classical periods there is a great deal of experimentation and transition in the political sphere, so that some cities might have monarchies while others had republics; in this respect we see how the different city-states behaved independently from one another and were autonomous (Fig. 18.1). This situation is best represented in the city of Veii as

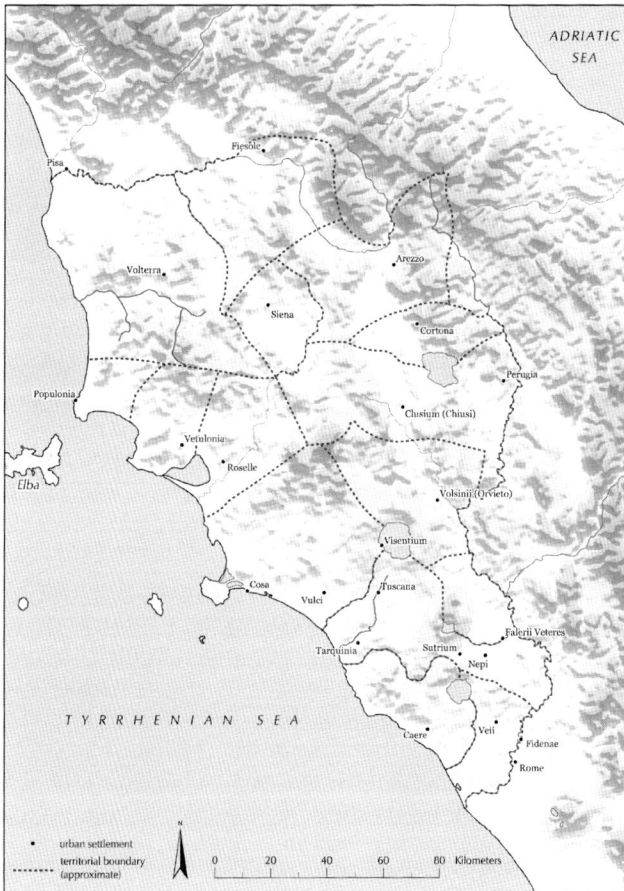

Figure 18.1   The Etruscan city-states with suggested territorial boundaries. Map by H. Becker and T. Elliott, Ancient World Mapping Center, www.unc.edu/awmc. Territorial boundaries after L. Bonfante, ed. 1986 with modifications. Reconstruction of ancient coastline following W. V. Harris (Maps 41 and 42) and N. Purcell (Map 44) in Talbert, R. J. A. ed. 2000 *Barrington Atlas of the Greek and Roman world*. Princeton, N.J: Princeton University Press.

it re-introduces the kingship repeatedly even though its peer city-states have abandoned monarchy. In 437 BCE there is a King Tolumnius of Veii whose defeat provided *spolia opima* for Rome.[17] The Veientines switched to elected office at some point afterwards but evidently grew tired of it (*taedio annuae ambitionis*) and elected a king again in 403 BCE. The other Etruscan city-states apparently had oligarchic governments and disapproved of this decision so much so that they did not help Veii in its ultimate battle against Rome.[18]

Another set of texts that are helpful in understanding this important period of transition are the *Elogia Tarquiniensia*, Latin inscriptions set up in the Julio-Claudian era to honor the storied ancestors of T. Vestricius Spurinna. All three Spurinnae are listed as *praetors*, and at least two of them were leading armies. For this reason, the sphere of experience of a republican *zilath* seems to be roughly equivalent to that of a *praetor*. These definitions become even more interesting through the account of the life of Aulus Spurinna, who was three times elected as a *praetor*. He drove out a king Orgolnius of Caere (*Caeritum regem*), showing that there were still occasional monarchical flare-ups.[19] The date of Aulus Spurinna's activities has been debated, but may fall anywhere from later in the fifth century to the mid fourth century BCE.[20]

The city-state and republican administration

Many different titles for magistracies occurred as the different Etruscan city-states transitioned from monarchy to oligarchy. As we have seen, the *zilath* is the chief official of a city, who as with the other magistracies, is drawn from the patrician class. A person could be a *zilath* more than once, such as a Larth from Tarquinia, who, "the son of Arnth Plecu and of Ramtha Apatrui, having been *zilath* twice, died at the age of forty-nine years".[21] The second century BCE Vulcian Larth Tute out-served him by serving as a *zilath* (lit. *zilchnu* "having performed the *zilath*-ship") eight times.[22] One could evidently hold this position at a young age because Sethre Tutes was a *zilath* at Vulci three times before he died at the age of 25.[23] One of the most basic functions of the *zilath*-ship is that it was eponymous and used to date the year, such that in Tarquinia the *Tomba degli Scudi* was built during the magistracy (*zil*) of Vel Hulchnie[24] and the *Tomba dell'Orco* I during the magistracies of Larth Hulchnies and Marce Caliathe, allowing us to see that there can be one or two *zilaths* in a given year.[25]

Many different attributes could be added to the title *zilath* (such as *marunuchva, parchis*, or *eterau*), and as with Thefarie Velianas, these attributes are important in so far as they may add to or delimit the jurisdiction and responsibilities of an office. The *zilath eterau*, for example, may have been a magistrate of the youths.[26] These magisterial titles are not all understood but are recognizable because a word typically follows *zilath* in the genitive, such as a magistrate from Chiusi who was labeled as *zilath scuntnues*; the meaning of this second term is not known but may be related to the root "*scun*," a role that may be connected to building.[27] Jacques Heurgon likens these multiple magistracies in each city-state to Athens, where there was an *archon eponymous*, a king *archon*, an *archon polemarch*, and the six junior archons, the *thesmothetae*.[28]

In addition to *zilaths* in charge of the central city of a city-state, this role is also attested in secondary centers. Information supporting this can be found from magisterial inscriptions in Norchia, Musarna and Tuscania that seem to distinguish between the magistracies held in these locations and those held in the capital city of Tarquinia.[29] For example, a group of inscriptions from the Tarquinian town of Musarna provide information on the prominent *gens Alethna*, seven of whose members held offices during the second half of the third century and second century BCE.[30] Most of these magistracies were probably carried out in Musarna itself. One member of the family, Arnth Alethna, was an urban *zilath* (*zilach{nce} spurethi*) and it seems that the *spura* (i.e. Etruscan for urban center) in question could reasonably be Musarna.[31] Another member of the Alethna *gens* had an even more specific title, clearly indicating that he was not a local *zilath*, because his inscriptions states that he was a *zilath tarchnalthi*, a "*zilath* at Tarquinia".[32]

Of all the different magisterial titles that contain the term *zilath*, the *zilath mechl rasnal* is perhaps the best known and, of late, most debated. The key to understanding this phrase lies with the term *rasna*, which the Greek author Dionysius of Halicarnassus defined as the term that the Etruscans used to describe themselves, different from "*Tyrsenoi*" or "*Tyrrhenoi*" as the Greeks called them or "*Tusci*" as the Romans did.[33] So if Dionysius is correct that *rasna* is the word used to describe all of Etruria, then this word may take on a federal character. That said, the term *zilath mechl rasnal* has been translated as a *zilath* "of the Etruscan people" (i.e. *mechl*, an unknown word, being read as "people"). Thus defined, the *zilath mechl rasnal*, must be, in that case, a federal magistracy and thus, the person who presided over the Etruscan League (discussed below). But the head of the Etruscan League was, according to Livy, a *sacerdos*.[34] This position came to be known as an *aedilis* during the Julio-Claudian period and a *praetor (Etruriae) XV populorum* by the Hadrianic era.[35] In the *Elogia Tarquiniensia* above, the term *praetor* was equated to the role of a *zilath*. But according to Rix's interpretation, the term *zilath mechl rasnal* is not equivalent to the *praetor (Etruriae) XV populorum* because in the Julio-Claudian period, when we know that a *zilath* is thought to be a *praetor*, the leader of the League is only an *aedilis*. Further problems arise when we consider an inscription from Orvieto from the *Tomba Golini I*, one of only three commemorating individuals who achieved this rank (the other two are from Tarquinia proper).[36] Among other magistracies, Vel Leinies was a *mechlum rasneas clevsinsl zilachnve*. But what does the modifying term *clevsinsl* add to our understanding of this magistracy? *Clevsinsl* is the genitive adjective for the city of Chiusi; if this is added to the phrase as it is traditionally understood, it is clear that "a federal magistrate (i.e. of all the Etruscan people) of Chiusi" does not make much sense. This prompted Helmut Rix (and then Adriano Maggiani) to attempt to redefine *rasna* and they suggest that the word may not have the federal sense of "Etruscan" but simply "people" (*populus*).[37] Viewing the Etruscans as "peoples" finds resonance as Livy does not refer to the 12 city-states of Etruria, but to the 12 peoples,[38] and this preference is retained in the aforementioned title of the imperial magistrate of the Etruscan League. A relief from Julio-Claudian Caere includes pictorial personifications of the cities of Tarquinia, Vulci, and Volsinii, but these personifications are labeled as the groups that comprise these cities, that is, rather than "Tarquinii", the city known today as Tarquinia, it is labeled as *Tarquinienses*, the "people of Tarquinia" (Fig. 8.25).[39]

Under this hypothesis, if *rasna* is to be read as *populus*, *mechl* might be equivalent to the Latin *res*, thus rendering *mechl rasnal* as *res publica*, the Latin term for state. If this is true, then Vel Leinies was a *zilath* of the Clusine state. With this redefinition in mind, a scenario emerges such that there could be *zilaths* in the capital cities but also in some minor centers, like Musarna. Perhaps it was then that the *zilath mechl rasnal* had authority over all the other *zilaths*, people and land within the area of the city-state. This idea is strengthened by the *Tabula Cortonensis* (discussed below), wherein there is a *zilath mechl rasnal*, as well as eponymous *zilaths*, who are not the same individuals.

Other Republican magistracies

Other positions are also attested beyond the varied degrees of *zilath*.[40] The *marunuch* is a magistracy first attested in the monarchical period, in an inscription on the Tragliatella cippus dated to the mid-sixth century BCE and it remains in use amongst other republican offices.[41] Like the zilathship (*zilach*), inscriptions commemorating a *maru* may add the attributive description of *spural* or *spurana*, such as the magistrates Arnth Churcles of Norchia and Larth Curunas from Tarquinia who both held the position of urban *marunuch*.[42] The duties of a *maru* are not perfectly understood, but inscriptions over time suggest that this position may have been collegial and may have involved both religious and civic duties, and it is a position that Maggiani suggests may have had some of the duties of a Roman *aedilis* and *quaestor*.[43] There is also a magistrate known as the *purth* (or *purthne*), which seems to have been a high-ranking office or charge that could be held concurrently with that of *zilath*.[44] The aforementioned Larth Tute was not only a *zilath* eight times, but he also was a *purth*.[45] There are various hypotheses as to what the *purth* was responsible for, with one scholar likening the position to a "first minister" (thus relying on a possibly etymological connection to the Greek executive officers, the *prutaneis*) while another suggests it could be a special appointment outside of the traditional *cursus*, akin to the Roman *censor*.[46]

Magisterial duties and the activities of the city-state

We have seen that there were different types of *zilaths*, of different rank and charge as well as lower-ranking magistracies. The delimiting adjectives that further defined the magistracy (e.g. *eterau*) surely served to distinguish and separate the *zilath* from lower ranking magistrates and, in turn, would have served to prescribe their duties. We already have seen that the *zilaths* of the major cities gave their names, eponymously, to the year. And while this practice could be simply used for dating, as in the funereal examples listed above, in other contexts a listing of the eponymous magistrate(s) might serve to add authority to the object under consideration. In this case, one thinks of a bronze weight from Caere that was dedicated to *Turms* (Mercury) during the zilathship (*zilc*) of La(r)th Nulathe (Fig. 18.2).[47] On the sixth line of the inscription there are numerals (*IIC* = 286.5 grams) that indicate the object's weight. This weight finds comparison with a similar practice in the Roman world where the name of an *aedilis* (or later, that of the *praefectus urbi*) upon an inscribed donative weight served to indicate that the weight had been checked against an official group of weights. There is also a bronze tablet from Tarquinia, and while it is only partially legible, the preamble begins with the eponymous date provided by two magistrates, before a discussion of some matter (a will?) relating to a member of the Clevsina family.[48] This tablet had nail holes so that it could be affixed to a wall or post. In the case of this inscription, we do not know how directly the magistrates were involved, but the Pyrgi plaques certainly show that an Etruscan magistrate could post official documents (in that case, of a predominately religious nature).

The actions of Thefarie Velianas certainly prompt us to think at what point different, ostensibly political magistracies may have had religious duties as a part of their regular *munus*. It is clear that the *zilaths* as well as other magistrates would have taken part in ceremonial processions, using instruments such as the *sella curulis* and the *fasces* (Fig. 18.3). Other high-profile activities, such as administering or even judging games might

Figure 18.2   Bronze weight with a lead center from Caere (Sant'Antonio). Dated from the fourth century to first part of the third century BCE. Villa Giulia Museum. After Maggiani 2001c, Fig. 35.

Figure 18.3   A miniature model of the *fasces*, in iron, from the *Tomba del Littore*, Vetulonia. End of the seventh century BCE. Photo: H. Becker. Museo Archeologico di Firenze.

also have been a part of a particular magistrate's purview. In this relief from Chiusi, two magistrates (recognizable because of their curved staffs) sit on a dais to judge contests; they are flanked by a *lictor* who holds rods and guards the wineskins used as prizes (Fig. 18.4).[49] Whether these games, as depicted, are civic in nature or were held for a funeral (consider the many games decorating Etruscan tomb paintings of the Archaic and early Classical periods) is open to speculation, but what is interesting here is that the officials were accompanied not only by a *lictor* but also by a scribe who recorded the winners. Other magisterial duties might have included minting coins, managing markets, and even a task with combined religious-political import such as managing the calendar.

Local magistrates may also have administered the Etruscan road network. The roads of cities such as Volsinii Veteres, Veii or Falerii Veteres are some of the most easily detected Etruscan roads because they were carved out of the *tufo* bedrock (Fig. 18.5). The roads

Figure 18.4 Funerary cippus from Chiusi, now in Palermo, depicting magistrates judging contests. Second quarter of the fifth century BCE. Jannot 1984, Fig. 171.

Figure 18.5 A road cutting in the *tufo* near Pitigliano. Photo credit: Parco Archeologico Città del Tufo.

radiated out of these cities, serving the needs of all of the citizens of their territories, whether for trade, war, or basic communication needs (Fig. 18.6). The territories of Veii, Caere and Falerii Veteres also had extensive networks of *cuniculi*, or manmade tunnels, carved into the *tufo* and used to channel and divert water. The use of *cuniculi* would have supported the agricultural needs of each city's territory and helped to maintain the roads, thus *cuniculi* represented very good investments for a city.

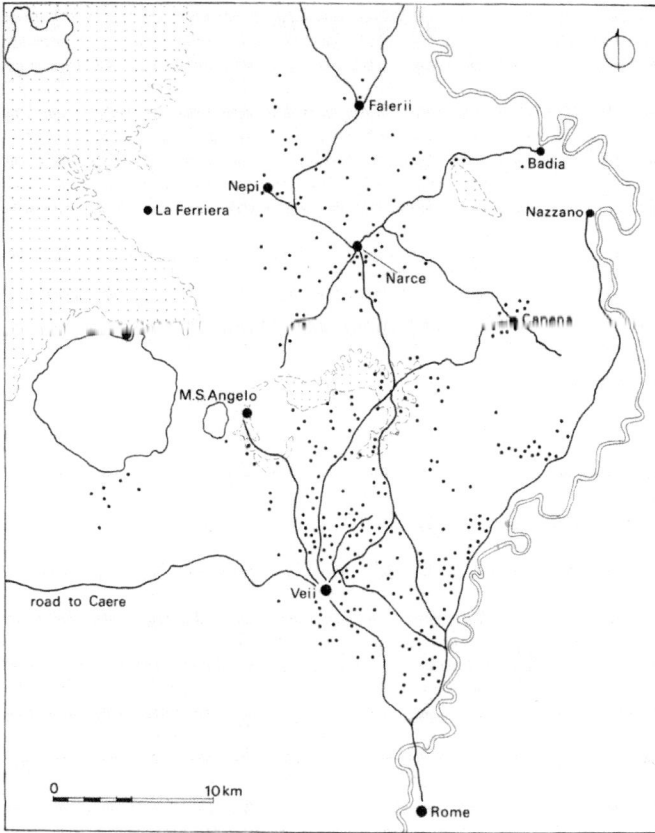

Figure 18.6 Etruscan roads radiating from Veii and Faliscan centers during the seventh to sixth centuries BCE. Potter 1979, Fig. 21.

The territory of Veii had a network of more than 25 km of *cuniculi*, a comprehensive scheme that is indicative of centrally organized construction.[50] Over time, roads and *cuniculi* would require maintenance, thus a central organizing office could have best assigned individual tasks over such a large area. Only one inscription gives a hint of the administration that might have existed and it was found on a small road branching off from Via degli Inferi in Caere's Banditaccia necropolis. The inscription, cut into the side of the road, announces that it was carried out under the marunship of Larth Lapicanes.[51] Here, we see the magistracy of *marunuch* operating in the orbit of public works. Maggiani likens this position to the similarly titled Umbrian magistrates known as *marones* "who often oversee the execution of buildings and public monuments".[52]

Another aspect that these magistrates share is the fact that we know about them in the first place. There are 72 extant magisterial inscriptions (with 47 of those coming from Tarquinia and its larger territory alone).[53] In addition there are tomb paintings and many sarcophagi that depict the magistrates who may be identified by means of their costume, attendants and symbols of office. For example the sarcophagus of Ramtha Višnai was intended for her and only mentions her husband, Arnth Tetnies, in the course of her identification (*arntheal tetn{i}es puia*).[54] And while it makes sense that Arnth Tetnies' *cursus honorum* was not listed, we can still tell that he was a magistrate because he is depicted on the sarcophagus relief being followed by attendants bearing a *sella curulis*, a *lituus*, a ceremonial trumpet, and a double flute (see Fig. 46.10). The many epigraphical and figural attestations reveal that it was an honor to hold these magistracies and one that would serve to define them for the rest of their lives as well as in the Afterlife.

ETRUSCAN PROPERTY AND STATE PROPERTY

We can also glean information about the city-state by considering the property that it owned. We know little about whether there were public buildings for Etruscan magistrates to use,[55] but we can say at least that Etruscan city-states owned property. The ability to own property underscores the public recognizability of the state as an entity while at the same time revealing that the state had some wherewithal with which to acquire property. Objects owned by a city-state are marked with various permutations of the word *spura,* or its genitive *spural* (of the city), whether it is the abbreviation *sp* or *spu* or even the adjective *spurana*.[56] These inscriptions, dating from the Archaic and Hellenistic periods, are wide-ranging, including Campania in the south to Populonia and Fiesole in the north. From these inscriptions it is clear that the state could own a range of items from vases (one of which was even bronze), a helmet, tiles, and a bronze weight. A few of these objects merit particular consideration. First, how were the tiles used? Were these tiles used for community owned buildings, about which we know little or nothing? Other interesting objects in this category include a small bronze object, thought to have been a weight (or a piece of *aes rude*), that was inscribed with the letters *sp*, as well as a *dolium* from Chiusi inscribed *mi spural*, or "I am community (or city-state) property".[57] Certainly the *dolium*, and perhaps the bronze object, finds resonance with the official weights and measures from the Athenian agora that read *demosion*.[58]

BOUNDARIES AND THE DELINEATION OF POLITICAL TERRITORIES

The Etruscans had a keen interest in boundaries, whether those boundaries were temporal or sacral, and these boundaries also contribute to an understanding of their political realities. Ritually defined spaces, such as the cities founded according to Etruscan ritual (*Etrusco ritu*),[59] were an important facet of Etruscan religion so much so that boundaries, whether celestial, terrestrial, or temporal were a part of the *etrusca disciplina* (see Chapter 27).[60] Instances of this can be seen in the fact that the orientation of the sky was important for augury and temporal orientation, and that even sacrificial livers were carefully sectioned off and assigned to the relevant divine forces.[61] The Etruscans also had calendars and believed that they even could determine the length of time allotted to their own civilization.[62]

Etruscans were also very interested in territorial boundaries and had words to differentiate between various parts of their territory. The ritual text known as the *Liber Linteus* refers to the *sacnicleri cilthl spureri methlumeric enas*, which may mean, "for the sacred fraternity/priesthood (*sacnica*) of the citadel (*cilth*), for the city-state (*spura*) and for the city (*methlum*) of *ena* (of whomsoever)".[63] This ritual calendar was written at some point between the middle of the third century and the early first century BCE and was written with observations specific to one place (perhaps Perugia).[64] This calendar is city-state specific much as the Brontoscopic calendar of Nigidius Figulus was said to be written specifically for Rome.[65] If priests were recording observances discretely in each city, it would be important to know just where the city and all of its boundaries, such as those referred to in the *Liber Linteus*, begin and end. Knowing where the boundaries are located for a city's *pomerium*, immediate *ager*, and the boundaries of its city-state would also have important political implications in terms of day-to-day administration, war, boundary disputes, and the like. The political importance of boundaries can be seen in the time of Tarquinius Priscus when the town of Collatia submitted to the Romans, because not only did Collatia surrender their citizens, their city, fields, shrines, and water to Rome, but even their boundaries (*terminos*).[66]

ETRUSCAN BOUNDARY MARKERS

Of particular interest in this context is understanding the markers that Etruscans used, predominantly in North Etruria, to demarcate their territory. These markers bear the word *tular*, meaning "boundaries" or "confines" and mark boundaries or *pomeria*, more precisely "the public boundaries emanating from the authority of the state" (Fig. 18.7).[67] The find spots of markers labeled *tular spural* have been plotted in an attempt to determine what civic boundaries they once marked. Giovanni Colonna believes that extant markers are found along both what might be termed the limits of the *urbs* and also the *ager* of a city.[68] Following Colonna's reading, the boundaries of the *spura* include all that might be in the *civitas*. A different picture is presented by a boundary marker installation at Bolsena (*Volsinii Novi*) that was found before one of the main entrances leading into the city.[69] The inscription reads *thval methlum*, and while the meaning of the first word remains unknown, the second word *methlum* describes the *urbs*. Thus this stone marked the entrance to the *pomerium* of Bolsena, the boundary inside which an augur could take his readings (see Chapter 26).[70]

Figure 18.7   Boundary stone from Poggio di Firenze reading *tular sp{ural}*.
Second century BCE. Lambrechts 1984, 326 Fig. I.

Magistrate names are also found on all five boundary stones marking the *tular spural*, providing an eponymous date as well as signifying under whose authority these stones were erected.[71] Added to this picture is the much earlier (seventh century BCE) Tragliatella cippus, which was found on the street that connected Caere to Veii.[72] Only part of the inscription is legible but it mentions a *maru*, an official who, if this stone was indeed a boundary marker, was also certifying a boundary.[73] These boundary markers certainly had religious import, in that they were marking *pomeria* but the inscribed names underscore the legal and political importance of these boundaries and inform us as to the activities of these officials.

Finally, a *tular rasnal* inscription found about 1.5 kilometers from the city of Cortona probably once marked the road leading into Perugia.[74] This marker has been traditionally translated as, "boundaries of the Etruscan people," and thought to represent an ethnic boundary separating Etruria from Umbria. However, many scholars have of late balked at the idea that the boundaries of not even just the city-state, but Etruria itself would lie nearly at the "gates" of Cortona.[75] We return again to the term *rasna*, this time without the accompanying term *mechl*. If *rasna* means "people", what then are the boundaries of the people?

Colonna has recently suggested that *tular rasnal* does not mark the boundaries of Etruria, or even the urban *pomerium* of Cortona, but the city's immediate *ager*. This limit is comparable to the *ager Romanus antiquus*, the boundary that was three to six miles outside Rome, providing an additional layer of defense; it remained largely fixed over time.[76] The reason that the term *rasna* applies to this boundary may be then because this area is larger than city alone, and contains the resources that are necessary for basic sustenance and defense; this is the area of the *populus*, specifically those "people" who are capable of defending the city.[77]

As with the magisterial title *zilath mechl rasnal*, the meaning of the term *rasna* in these cases has great political import for understanding how the city-state was conceived and governed. The jurisdiction of the *Liber Linteus* was described above in concentric rings, using a political institutional vocabulary of the city and its larger territory, with the *cilth* (the citadel or arx), the *methlum* (city), and the *spura* (city-state); the *Liber Linteus* does not refer to *rasna* as a part of these jurisdictional rings, but if this interpretation of the boundary stone from Cortona is correct, we might add in an additional territorial division. Maggiani best explained the significance of these boundaries to Etruscan vocabulary, when he wrote that, "it is highly probable that each of these political-territorial institutional situations matched a well-defined network of administrative offices, which for the most part eludes us, especially as regards diachrony".[78]

Etruscan boundaries were so important that they were even a part of the Etruscan mythological canon, wherein there is the nymph Vegoia and her prophecy, which deals with the boundaries that separate private property. This prophecy was said to be transmitted from the nymph, and was presumably transmitted through Etruscan culture and came to be recorded among the Latin *agrimensores*.[79] This text sets the penalties for moving property boundary markers (*termini*) and reveals a real anxiety surrounding the boundaries between people's property. In the prophecy, Jupiter had helped to survey and set the limits of fields, marking the borders with boundary stones as a check against human avarice and people who move the boundary markers for their own benefit. To discourage such behavior, penalties are detailed for the slave (*servus*) (and potentially his master [*dominus*]) who commits such an offense.[80]

PROPERTY AND THE LEGAL SPHERE

Boundary markers like those referred to in the prophecy were indeed used to mark private property such as the two *cippi* from Bettona that mark the boundaries of the Larnas family within a necropolis.[81] Another cippus found in Castiglione del Lago, reads *tular alfil*;[82] the familial name *Alfial* is attested in the territory of Chiusi and Perugia.[83] All of these markers date from the fourth and third centuries BCE.

Another boundary marker, the Cippus of Perugia, itself a functional boundary stone, provides rare insight into boundaries, property, and Etruscan law. The Cippus of Perugia records an adjudicated agreement concerning the use of private land. The contract was struck between the families of Larth Afuna and Aule Velthina and allows Larth Afuna to draw water from the property of Velthina (a legal servitude analogous to the Roman *aquae haustus*).[84] The inscription also deals with the apportionment to Larth Afuna of land within the necropolis that was owned by Aule Velthina. The *Tabula Cortonensis* also provides valuable information about land ownership and legal provisions, as well as the opportunity to speculate about the political world behind these contracts.[85] This bronze tablet has a handle that would have allowed it to be posted and serves as a contract between Petru Scevas and Arntlei, his wife, and the Cusu family. The fact that a woman plays a part in a legal matter, and potentially owned property herself, is itself worthy of note. In this contract the Cusu family owns agricultural property and may be receiving it back from Petru Scevas, who may have rented it.

These documents have some aspects in common, and thus give insight into the workings of Etruscan legal processes. The first is that they both provide precise measurements for the land under discussion. The second is that both contracts are officially witnessed, as in the case of the Perugia Cippus where the witness ([*t*]*eurat*) was Larth Rezus. The *Tabula Cortonensis* not only has many as two groups of witnesses that certify the arrangement, but also names Larth Cucrina Lausisa, *zilath mechl rasnal* who served as a witness.[86] The text is even dated on the reverse side with the inclusion of the names of the local *zilaths*, Larth Cusus and Laris Salini. The convergence of both the eponymous *zilaths* and the *zilath mechl rasnal* supports the idea of the distinction between a *zilath* who is in charge of a city or town and one who presides over the entire territory, in this case, Cortona. This inscription also gives us a rare view into Etruscan political life and magisterial activities because we can see that the *zilath mechl rasnal* was involved in this legal proceeding and may have had some juridical authority.

In the case of the Cippus of Perugia, on the basis of a close study of the inscription, Francesco Roncalli has concluded that the surviving inscription does not represent the initial iteration of the text, but is rather a copy, a conclusion reached on the basis of the awkward spacing of text.[87] This observation of Roncalli lends credence to an argument that inscriptions of this type were not singular, in that copies were made of them, thus underscoring the official nature of these records. Even stronger evidence for this can be found within the inscription of the *Tabula Cortonensis* that specifically mentions that other copies of the agreement should be stored in the home of the Cusu family, as well as the homes of four men (all of whom have elite names and are presumably to be counted among the local *principes*).[88] It is possible, then, that a copy of the text preserved on the Cippus of Perugia was also written on a less durable medium and stored for reference. What is interesting about this storage is that, at least in the case of the *Tabula*, it is clear that an agreement important enough to have official involvement is not stored in a public building. We know from Cicero that in Late Republican Rome public records (*tabulae publicae*) were not stored in the senate house, but were kept in private homes.[89] That private buildings could take on a public function certainly underscores, again, the role of the *principes* within their community. And while this circumstance does not solve the problem of puzzling out whether there were public buildings in Etruria, it informs us that, at least on this one point, a public building such as an archive might not have been needed. These two inscriptions, along with their *tular* marker peers, also give insight into property law, and permit us to consider the nature of Etruscan property law and when it developed. Important to this consideration is the knowledge that one aspect of the *etrusca disciplina* was a *liber iuris Terrae Etruriae*, literally a "book of the law of the land of Etruria".[90] Nothing is known about this book, or whether there were any other books addressing different legal concerns. This question naturally can extend beyond the *etrusca disciplina* and be applied to the political world of the Etruscans. Did the magistrates pass laws, similar to law codes like the Twelve Tables from contemporary Rome? Ancient authors do refer to Etruscan laws in passing but there is much still that we would like to know about the coverage of Etruscan law.[91] Were there provisions for debt bondage and slaves, citizenship, and inheritance?

There may have been laws or regulations regarding commerce (consider the aforementioned weight from Caere) and an important inscription sheds light on this. The Pech Maho contract, found beyond Etruria (in Languedoc), reflects two contracts – one written in Etruscan, and the other, written on the reverse side, in Greek.[92] The contracts are similar in that they both list the individuals conveying goods and a location involved (Massalia and Emporion, respectively). Both documents are written so that the goods and corresponding payment for which can be tracked, such that both mention a down payment.[93] The Greek contract, which is better preserved, has two lists of Iberian witnesses present for two transactions. It is not clear whether the Etruscan version had that same degree of juridical formality.[94] But like the Cippus of Perugia and the *Tabula Cortonensis*, this contract deals with property, property that is important enough to be written down (*zik* which compares with similar formulae on the other contracts).[95] It is hoped that future finds of inscriptions may shed even more light on what matters were worthy of making contracts and further, what magistrates and citizens were involved in the law. One final question remains, since we have considered the territorial application of magistracies, and that is, what was the territorial application of laws and contracts – e.g. did the *liber iuris Terrae Etruriae* apply to all of Etruria, or did it vary from city-state to city-state?

ETRUSCAN LEAGUE

As much as we have been interested in defining the boundaries of Etruria, it is worthwhile to explore, finally, the one regular occasion when the boundaries were less important. The *Fanum Voltumnae*, or shrine of Voltumna, was a pan-Etruscan shrine where an annual religious festival was held.[96] Leading men from all over Etruria (*principes ex omnibus populis*) would meet at the *Fanum Voltumnae*.[97] The festival consisted of sacral activities, games, and an opportunity for members of various city-states to talk. It is very likely that marketing also occurred in this pan-Etruscan meeting place, much like at *Lucus Feroniae*.[98] When Livy mentions that the Romans learned of a particular meeting of the *Fanum Voltumnae* and its potential implications, the Romans learn of this event from the *mercatores* who were there.[99]

The ancient historians did not record where the *Fanum Voltumnae* was located but an important clue can potentially be found in a rescript from the Constantinian period from Spello that refers to the festival occurring *"aput Vulsinios"* (near Volsinii) according to ancient custom (*consuetudo prisca*).[100] The poet Propertius is helpful here, as well, as he describes the god Vertumnus abandoning his Volsiniian fires in favor of Rome.[101] A likely candidate has emerged at Campo della Fiera, to the west of modern Orvieto (see Chapter 31).[102] Campo della Fiera is a natural crossroads at the foot of Volsinii where the roads connecting the Tiber River valley, the Tyrrhenian Sea, Chiusi and Arezzo converge. The name of the site itself, Italian for the "fairgrounds field," is also revealing, and we know that the site was used as a fairground into the Middle Ages. In addition, recent excavations have revealed a sacred site of long duration, with continuous activity occurring from the sixth century BCE into the sixteenth century.

The attendees of the *Fanum Voltumnae* were the residents of the 12 city-states of Etruria (*duodecim populi Etruriae*), although sometimes they are referred to as the 15 peoples. The number of 12 principal cities is canonical, and is matched by other reputed sets of 12 affiliated Etruscan cities, located to the north of Etruria in the Po Valley and to the south in Campania. The number 12 also matches that of the member city-states of the Ionian League.[103] Most importantly, while many of the long-standing members of the *Fanum Voltumnae* can be guessed (Tarquinia, Caere, Chiusi, etc.), no ancient author specifically lists them *in toto*; additionally, the member city-states probably changed over time. To this end, Servius mentioned specifically that Populonia was founded too late to be a member of the league.[104] Similarly the Faliscans and Capenates were almost certainly not a part of this league, but they were still received in an audience of 397 BCE when they asked for help for Veii (because of their position in relation to Rome) and ultimately for themselves.[105] Twelve representatives presided over the ceremonies and they elected a priest among themselves.[106] In 403 BCE, before Veii's final king fell into disfavor with the other Etruscans for preserving the monarchy, he first withdrew the actors he had sponsored for the communal games, once he had lost the nomination for this very priesthood.[107]

One of the most lingering questions about the Etruscan League is whether it could have had a federal, military and political character. Dionysius of Halicarnassus believed that it could, and described a Tyrrhenian custom wherein each of the 12 cities would contribute a *fasces*, all of which would be handed over to the leader of a joint Etruscan military expedition.[108] He discusses this custom in the context of a series of protracted campaigns between the Latins and Etruscans against Tarquinius Priscus. At first, a confederation of only the northern cities (Chiusi, Arezzo, Volterra, Roselle, and Vetulonia) fought against Rome, but soon after, any city that does not join the war is threatened with exclusion from the league.[109]

At the end of the sixth century BCE, even the status of one of Etruria's most famous kings is muddled in the sources. Livy, Dionysius and Plutarch call Porsenna the king of Chiusi,[110] but (if it is the same personage) he is called the king of *Volsinii* by Pliny the Elder at one point,[111] and the king of Etruria elsewhere by Pliny the Elder and Florus.[112] It may be that in the course of Porsenna's military campaigns, he had authority over more than just the people of Chiusi. Even so, these episodes may just represent *ad hoc* alliances in the case of a perceived regional threat. We know so little from the Etruscans themselves about their military history, but even from the *Elogia Tarquiniensia*, where Tarquinia is involved against Caere and later Arezzo, we see that the Etruscan cities were probably more often fighting against each other than working together on a regular basis.

CONCLUSIONS

This chapter has been concerned with understanding the political system of Etruria, in so far as it is known. Part of the toolkit for understanding this system is being aware of the internal partitions within Etruria. We have considered the boundaries within the city-state such as the *cilth, methlum,* and *spura* – these are boundaries that any priest would have needed to know to perform augury but they clearly had great implications for the political jurisdiction of magistrates. Awareness of the boundaries has, in turn, brought out in relief the autonomy of the city-states and how they operated distinctly from one another. In addition, we have also considered those times when broader Etruscan alliances might have developed across the city-states.

NOTES

1 Cristofani 1984, 131–132.
2 Haynes 2000, 71; Torelli 2000, 201. *ET Pa* 1.2.
3 Verg. *Aen.* VII. 647; VIII. 482; X. 786–907 also Liv. 1.2. A kylix of *impasto grigio* dated between 680–640 BCE was inscribed with the name of Laucie Mezentie (lit. the cup reads *mi Laucies Mezenties*). This cup probably came from Caere and confirms that the gentilician name, otherwise only known from a mythic Caeretan character in Roman mytho-history, was one used in Caere (C. de Simone. 1991. "Etrusco Laucie Mezentie," *Arch Class* 43: 559–73.
4 Paus. 5.12.5.
5 *CIL* XIII, 1668.
6 *CIL* XIII, 1668; Liv. 39.4–6; Dion. Hal. *Ant. Rom.* 4.1–2.
7 Heurgon 1964, 48.
8 Maggiani 2001a, 237; d'Aversa 1994, 33.
9 Ser. *Aen.* 2.278.
10 Liv. 1.34.
11 Macrob. *Sat.* 1.15.13.
12 Turfa 2006 and 2012.
13 Turfa 2006. For these events, see the prophecies for October 19th, November 16th, December 7th and 30th and January 16th and 21st; winter was apparently rough on monarchies.
14 *TLE* 873–874; *ET Cr* 4.4.
15 Migliorati 2003, 42.
16 Maggiani 1996, 102–5.
17 Liv. 4.17; Dion. Hal. *Ant Rom.* 12.5; Flor 1.2.9; Cic. *Phil.* 9.4; Plut. *Rom.* 16.
18 Liv. 5.1.
19 Torelli 1975, 56–92.
20 Torelli 1975, 82–92; Migliorati 2003, 42; Maggiani 2005, 63.
21 Heurgon 1964, 18; *TLE* 136.
22 *TLE* 324; Heurgon 1957, 83; Bonfante and Bonfante 2002, 97.
23 *ET Vc* 1.94; *TLE* 1.94; Cristofani 1984, 131–132; Maggiani 2001a, 237.
24 Morandi Tarabella 2004, 243; *TLE* 90 and 91.
25 Morandi Tarabella 2004, 243 and 319; *TLE* 84. This inscription (and the magistracy) dates c. 380–370 BCE.
26 Maggiani 2001a, 233–234.
27 Maggiani 2001a, 237. The inscription, an epitaph, is damaged at the crucial term: see Turfa 2005: 263–265 no. 295.
28 Heurgon 1964, 50.

29 Colonna 1988, 24.
30 Heurgon 1957, 97; Emiliozzi 1993.
31 *ET AT 108.*
32 Maggiani 1996, 106; van der Meer 2004, 24; *AT 100.*
33 Dion. Hal. *Ant. Rom.* 1.30.
34 Liv 5.1.5.
35 Rix 1984, 461.
36 Rix 1984, *TLE* 233.
37 Rix 1984 and Maggiani 2001a, 237–238.
38 Liv. 1.8.3.
39 Cristofani 1984, 124.
40 It should be noted that this review concentrates only on the most visible, political magistracies and is not by any means exhaustive; for this reason, non-political positions, such as *cepen* (or priest) are not included.
41 Maggiani 2001a, 229; Maggiani 2001b, 40.
42 *ET AT* 121; *TA* 1.196; van der Meer 2004, 24–25; Maggiani 2006, 109–113.
43 Maggiani 2001a, 235–237.
44 Maggiani 1996, 114–116; Maggiani 2001a, 237.
45 *TLE* 324.
46 For the first suggestion, see Heurgon 1964, 51, for the latter see Maggiani 1996, 116 and Maggiani 2001a, 237.
47 Maggiani 1996, 101 and 136, n. 69; Maggiani 2001c, 72–73; Maggiani 2002, 167–168.
48 Facchetti 89–94, *ET Ta* 8.1.
49 Colonna 1976; Jannot 1984, 48–49, figs. 171–73; Palerme 8385. This cippus dates to the second quarter of the fifth century BCE.
50 Potter 1979, 85.
51 SE LV 1989, 325–326, n. 95, tav: XLV; Maggiani 2001a, 236; Morandi Tarabella 2004, 270.
52 Maggiani 2001a, 236. On such projects at Volsinii, see the new discoveries, Chapter 36.
53 Maggiani 1996.
54 Haynes 2000, 287. *CIE* 5312; *TLE* 320. The sarcophagus is dated to the mid-fourth century BCE.
55 See Becker (forthcoming).
56 For a full list of these inscriptions, see Watmough 1997, 47–51; Becker 2010. It is also possible that a black glaze bowl inscribed *maru*, the name of the type of magistracy itself (but without the specific name of the magistrate), might belong to this category. If this bowl was intended for a city *maru*, it should be considered whether this bowl was also city property and if so, for what was it to be used (*SE* 2007 73: 289–90)?
57 The small bronze piece was found at Suana/Sovana, in the territory of Populonia and has three tick marks on the reverse side (*SE* 1972 v. 40, 408–409 no. 13). For the Clusine *dolium*, see *ET Cl* 2.27 and *SE* 1978 v. 46, 370–71 no. 123; *TLE* 487. Both objects are now housed in the Museo Archeologico di Firenze.
58 See for example, G. R. Davidson and D. B. Thompson. 1943. *Small Objects from the Pnyx*, v. 1. (*Hesperia*; supplement 7), 28 no. 3, 30 no. 26. Athens: American School of Classical Studies and J. C. Donati. 2010. "Marks of state ownership and the Greek agora at Corinth." *AJA* 114.1: 3–26.
59 Varro. *L.L.* 5.143. For more on the nature of Etruscan boundaries, see Edlund-Berry's (2006) authoritative survey.
60 Front. *de limitibus* F22, 10–11.
61 See respectively, N. L. C. Stevens. 2009. "A new reconstruction of the Etruscan heaven." *AJA* 113.2: 153–64 and L. B. van der Meer. 1987. *The bronze liver of Piacenza.* Amsterdam: J.C. Gieben.

62 Cens. *DN* 14.6 and 15.

63 van deer Meer 2009, 217–18.

64 Having personalized resources such as these compiled and amended by local priests for each city reveals that the city was a centralized authority in its area for religious matters.

65 Turfa 2006.

66 Liv. 1.38.2.

67 Colonna 1988, 19.

68 Colonna 1988, 17–21.

69 Colonna 1988, 21.

70 Cristofani 1984, 121–22.

71 Lambrechts 1970, 26–50; Lambrechts 1984.

72 Alternatively, it could be possible that this inscription marks not a boundary but work done by the *maru* on the road.

73 Cristofani 1984, 127; Maggiani 1996, 109, 133 n. 5; Maggiani 2005, 62. Alternatively, this stone could be simply commemorating public works, as seems to be the case with the *maru* Larth Lapicanes.

74 *TLE* 632. This cippus dates to the third century BCE.

75 Quotation from Rix 1984, 467; see also Cristofani 1984, 122; Colonna 1988, 25–28.

76 Colonna 1988, 26–8; Gargola 1995, 84. See also A. Alföldi 1962. "*Ager Romanus Antiquus.*" *Hermes* 90.2: 187–213.

77 Colonna 1988, 28.

78 Maggiani 2001a, 231–2.

79 Heurgon 1959; Harris 1971, 31–40. See also K. Lachmann, ed. 1848. *Die Schriften der Römischen Feldmesser.* Berlin: G. Reimer, 350–51.

80 "*Si servi faciant, dominio mutabuntur in deterius. Sed si conscientia dominica fiet, caelerius dominus extirpabitur, gensque eius omnis interiet.*" (de Grummond 2006, 191 no. II.1).

81 *TLE* 692. See also S. Stopponi, ed. 2006. *Museo comunale di Bettona,* 315 n. 263–4. Milan, Electa. These date to the late third century BCE.

82 Lambrechts 1970, 22 no. 2, 61; *TLE* 530. The inscription is now lost.

83 *CIE* 719–721, 1344, 1671–1674, 3378, 3410–3412, 3509–3510, 3745, 3769–3772, 4021, 4172, 4331, 4573, 4586. See also H. Rix. 1963. *Das etruskische Cognomen: Untersuchungen zu System, Morphologie und Verwendung der Personennamen auf den jüngeren Inschriften Nordetruriens.* Wiesbaden: O. Harrassowitz, 246.

84 Maggiani 2001d, 98; Facchetti 2000, 19–21; Wylin 2003; Becker 2010.

85 Becker 2010; The *Tabula Cortonensis* is dated to the late third to early second century BCE.

86 Maggiani 2001d, 107; Wallace 2008, 206, 210, and 212–3.

87 Roncalli. 1985 [1987], 167.

88 Maggiani 2001d, 107; Facchetti 2005, 62; Wallace 2008, 212–3. Note that one of the four individuals is also of the Cusu family, i.e. Velche Cusu, son of Aule.

89 Culham 1984, 19: Cic. *Sull.* 15.42.

90 Serv. *ad Aen.* 1.2. Rand's commentary rejects the alternate reading of *ruris* (in place of *iuris*) and finds support in Cicero *De Div.* 2.50 (Rand 1946, 10). See also: Scarano Ussani and Torelli 2003, 42; Facchetti 2000, 46–8.

91 Dion. Hal. *Ant. Rom.* 3.60; Val. Max. 9.1.ext.2.

92 Cristofani 1993; Facchetti 2000, 95–9. See also J. Chadwick. 1990. "The Pech Maho Lead. *ZPE* 82: 161–66 and H. Rodríguez Somolinos. 1996. "The Commercial Transaction of the Pech Maho Lead: A New Interpretation." *ZPE* 111: 74–8.

93 Cristofani 1993, 833.

94 Cristofani 1993, 835.

95 Bonfante and Bonfante 2002, 115; Becker 2010.

96 Liv. 4.23.5; 4.25.7–8; 4.61.2; 5.1;6.2.2.

97 Liv. 6.2.2.

98 Liv. 1.30.5; Dion. Hal. *Ant. Rom.* 3.32.1.

99 Liv. 6.2.2.

100 The rescript refers to a festival that alternated between *Volsinii* and the Umbrian city of Hispellum, in which the rescript was found (CIL XI.5265). See also Bradley, G. J. 2000. *Ancient Umbria: State, culture, and identity in central Italy from the Iron Age to the Augustan era.* Oxford: Oxford University Press and K. Tabata, 1995. "The Date and Setting of the Constantinian Inscription of Hispellum," in *Studi Classici e Orientali* 45, 369–405.

101 Prop. 4.2.2–4. Additionally, the comment of Valerius Maximus, where he says that *Volsinii "Etruriae caput habebatur,"* may also be a clue (Val. Max. 9.1.ext.2).

102 Stopponi, 2007; Harris 2007, Stopponi 2011.

103 Haynes 2000, 135.

104 Servius *ad Aen.* 10.172. However, Populonia could have taken the place of Veii once it was destroyed (Heurgon 1957, 86).

105 Briquel 1994, 358; Liv. 5.17.7.

106 Servius Aen. 8.475; Liv. 5.1.5; Dion Hal. *Ant. Rom.* 3.61.2.

107 Liv. 5.1.5.

108 Dion. Hal. *Ant. Rom.* 3.61.2. Strabo 5.2.2 describes an Etruria that at one time was united under one authority and carried out successful military ventures.

109 Dion. Hal. *Ant. Rom.* 3.51.4, 3.57.1; see also 3.57.5 and 3.59.3–4.

110 Livy 2.9; Dion. Hal. *Ant. Rom.* 21; Plut. *Public.* 16.

111 Plin. *HN* 2.54.140.

112 Plin. *HN* 36.19.91 and Flor. 1.4.1. For a discussion of this status, see Di Fazio 2000, 396; Capdeville 1993, 68; Jannot 1984, 403–406; Pallottino 1993, 20.

BIBLIOGRAPHY

Agostiniani, L. (1997) "Considerazioni linguistiche su alcuni aspetti della terminologia magistratuale etrusca" in R. Ambrosini (ed.), *Scríbthair a ainm n-ogaim: scritti in memoria di Enrico Campanile*, Pisa: Pacini Editore, 1–16.

Aigner Foresti, L. (1994) "La Lega etrusca" in *Federazioni e federalismo nell'Europa antica. Alle radici della casa comune europea. I. Bergamo, 21–25 September 1992.* Milan: Vita e pensiero. 327–350.

——(2001) "Momenti di aggregazione e momenti di disgregazione nei sistemi politici degli Etruschi" in *Identità e valori. Fattori di aggregazione e fattori di crisi nell'esperienza politica antica. Atti del Convegno Bergamo 1998,* 97–128.

Becker, H. (2010) "The Written Word and Proprietary Inscriptions in Etruria," *Etruscan Studies* 13: 131–48.

Becker, J. A. (forthcoming) "Italic architecture of the earlier first millennium BCE" in R. B. Ulrich and C. Quenemoen (eds), *Blackwell Companion to Roman Architecture,* London: Wiley-Blackwell.

Bellini, V. (1960) "Sulla genesi e la struttura delle leghe nell'Italia arcaica. I-II. La dodecapoli etrusca," *Revue internationale des droits de l'antiquité* 7: 273–305.

Bonfante, G. and Bonfante, L. (2002) *The Etruscan Language. An Introduction.* Manchester: Manchester University Press.

Briquel, D. (1994) "I passi liviani sulle riunioni della lega etrusca" in L. Aigner Foresti (ed.), *Federazioni e federalismo nell'Europa antica. Alle radici della casa comune europea. I. Bergamo, 21–25 September 1992,* 351–72. Milan: Vita e Pensiero.

——(2003) "Le *Fanum Voltumnae*: remarques sur le culte fédéral des cités étrusques" in A. Motte et al. (ed.), *Dieux, fêtes, sacré dans la Grèce et la Rome antiques : actes du colloque tenu à Luxembourg du 24 au 26 October 1999,* 133–59. Turnhout, Belgium: Brepols.

Capdeville, G. (1993) "Porsenna, re del Labirinto" in G. Maetzke and L. Tamagno Perna (eds), *La civiltà di Chiusi e del suo territorio. Atti del XVII Convegno di Studi Etruschi e Italici. Chianciano Terme 28 May–1 June 1988*, 53–71. Florence: L.S. Olschki.

Cerchiai, L. (2001) "The Ideology of the Etruscan City" in M. Torelli (ed.), *The Etruscans*, New York: Rizzoli, 243–253.

Colonna, G. (1976) "'Scriba cum rege sedens'," *L'Italie préromaine et la Rome républicaine. Mélanges offerts à Jacques Heurgon*. Paris: Ecole française de Rome, 187–95.

——(1988) "Il lessico istituzionale etrusco e la formazione della città, specialmente in Emilia Romagna," *La Formazione della città preromana in Emilia Romagna: atti del convego di studi, Bologna-Marzabotto, 7–8 dicembre 1985*, Bologna: Centre Studi sulla Città Antica, 15–36.

Cristofani, M. (1967) "Un *cursus honorum* di Cerveteri," *SE* 35: 609–18.

——(1984) "Diritto e amministrazione dello Stato" in M. Cristofani (ed.), *Gli Etruschi: Una nuova immagine*, 120–34.

——(1993) "Il testo de Pech-Maho, Aleria e I traffici del V secolo A.C.," *MEFRA* 105: 833–45.

——(1995) "Novità sul commercio etrusco arcaico: dal relitto del Giglio al contratto di Pech Maho" in J. Swaddling, S. Walker and P. Roberts (eds), *Italy in Europe: Economic Relations 700BC–AD 50*, London, British Museum, 131–37.

Culham, P. (1989) "Archives and Alternatives in Republican Rome," *CP* 84.2: 100–15.

d'Aversa, A. (1994) *Dizionario della lingua etrusca*. Brescia: Paideia.

de Grummond, N. T. (2006) *Etruscan Myth, Sacred History, and Legend*. Philadelphia: University of Pennsylvania Museum of Archaeology and Anthropology.

Di Fazio, M. (2000) "Porsenna e la società di Chiusi," *Athenaeum* 88.2: 393–412.

Edlund Berry, I. (2006) "Ritual Space and Boundaries in Etruscan Religion" in N. T. de Grummond and E. Simon (eds), *The Religion of the Etruscans*, Austin: University of Texas Press, 116–31.

Emiliozzi, A. (1993) "Per gli Alethna di Musarna," *Miscellanea etrusco-italica, I, QuadAEI* 22: 133–41.

Facchetti, G. M. (2000) *Frammenti di diritto private etrusco*. Florence: L.S. Olschki.

——(2005) "Some new remarks on the Tabula Cortonensis," *Lingua Posnaniensis* 47: 59–63.

Gargola, D. J. (1995) *Lands, laws & gods: Magistrates & ceremony in the regulation of public lands in Republican Rome*. Chapel Hill: University of North Carolina Press.

Harmon, D. P. (1985) "Religion in the Latin Elegists" in *Aufstieg und Niedergang der Römischen Welt*, II.16.3, 1909–1973. New York: De Gruyter.

Harris, J. (2007) "*Fanum Voltumnae*: Is the Mystery Resolved?" *Current Archaeology* 26: 23–6.

Harris, W. V. (1971) *Rome in Etruria and Umbria*. Oxford: Clarendon Press.

Haynes, S. (2000) *Etruscan civilization: A cultural history*. Los Angeles: J. Paul Getty Museum.

Heurgon, J. (1957) "L'état étrusque," *Historia* 6: 63–97.

——(1959) "The Date of *Vegoia's Prophecy*," *JRS* 49: 41–5.

——(1964) *Daily life of the Etruscans*. London: Weisenfeld and Nicolson.

——(1967) "Magistratures republicans et magistratures étrusques" in E. Gjerstad *Les Origines de la République romaine*, 99–132. Vandœuvres-Genève: Fondation Hardt pour l'étude de l'Antiquité classique.

Jannot, J.-R. (1984) *Les reliefs archaïques de Chiusi*. Roma: Ecole française de Rome.

Lambrechts, R. (1959) *Essai sur les magistratures des républiques étrusques*. Brussels: Palais des académies.

——(1970) *Les inscriptions avec le mot tular et le bornage étrusques*. Florence: L. S. Olschki.

——(1984) "S/s'pur- = populus ou une nouvelle borne du territoire fiesolan" in G. Maetzke, M. G. M. Costagli and L. T. Perna (eds), in *Studi di antichità in onore di Guglielmo Maetzke*, II, Rome: Giorgio Bretschneider Editore, 325–28.

Maggiani, A. (1996) "Appunti sulle magistrature etrusche," *SE* 62: 95–138.

——(2001a) "Republican Political Forms" in M. Torelli (ed.), *The Etruscans*, New York: Rizzoli, 227–241.

——(2001b) "Magistrature cittadine, magistrature federali" in *La lega etrusca dalla Dodecapoli ai Quindecim Populi. Atti della giornata di studi, Chiusi 9 October 1999*, 37–48. Pisa: Istituti Editoriali e Poligrafici Internazionali.

——(2001c) "Pesi e balance in Etruria" in C. Corti and N. Giordani (eds), *Pondera. Pesi e misure nell'antichità*, Campogalliano: Museo della bilancia, 67–74.

——(2001d) "Dagli archivi dei Cusu. Considerazioni sulla tavola bronzea di Cortona," *Rivista di Archeologia* 25: 94–114.

——(2002) "La libbra etrusca. Sistemi ponderali e monetazione," *SE* 65–68: 163–199.

——(2005) "Da Veio a Vulci. Le istituzioni politiche" in O. Paoletti (ed.), *Dinamiche di sviluppo delle città dell'Etruria meridionale. Veio Caere Tarquinia Vulci (Atti di Congresso)*, 61–9. Pisa: Istituti editoriali e poligrafici internazionali.

Menichetti, M. (2001) "Political Forms in the Archaic Period" in M. Torelli (ed.), *The Etruscans*, New York: Rizzoli, 205–25.

Migliorati, G. (2003) "Forme politiche e tipi di governo nella Roma etrusca del VI sec. A.C.," *Historia* 52.1: 39–66.

Morandi Tarabella, M. (2004) *Prosopographia etrusca*. Volume 1. Rome: "L'ERMA" di Bretschneider.

Pallottino, M. (1993) "La funzione storica di Chiusi nel mondo etrusco" in G. Maetzke and L. Tamagno Perna (eds), *La Civiltà di Chiusi e del suo territorio. Atti del XVII Convegno di Studi Etruschi e Italici. Chianciano Terme 28 May–1 June 1988*, 19–21. Florence: L.S. Olschki.

Potter, T. W. (1979) *Changing Landscape of South Etruria*. New York: St. Martin's Press.

Rand, E. (1946) *Servianorum in Vergilii carmina commentariorum editoinis Harvardianae volumen*. Lancaster, PA: Societatis Philologicae Americanae cura et impensis.

Rix, H. (1984) "Etr. *mec rasnal* = lat. *res publica*" in G. Maetzke, M. G. M. Costagli and L. T. Perna (eds), *Studi di antichità in onore di G. Maetzke* II, Rome: Giorgio Bretschneider Editore, 455–68.

Roncalli, F. (1985 [1987]) "Sul Testo del 'Cippo di Perugia," *SE* 53: 161–70.

Scarano Ussani, V. and Torelli, M. (2003) *La Tabula Cortonensis. Un documento giuridico, storico e sociale*. Naples: Loffredo.

Scullard, H. H. (1967) *The Etruscan cities and Rome*. Ithaca, New York: Cornell University Press.

Stoddart, S. K. F. (1990) "The political landscape of Etruria," *The Journal of the Accordia Research Centre* 1: 39–51.

Stopponi, S. (2007) "Notizie preliminari dello scavo di Campo della Fiera" in G. Della Fina (ed.), *Etruschi, greci, fenici e carthaginesi nel Mediterraneo centrali. Atti del XIV Convegno internazionale di studi sulla storia e l'archeologia dell'Etruria*, 495–530. Rome: Quasar.

——(2011) "Campo della Fiera at Orvieto: new discoveries" in N. T. de Grummond and I. Edlund Berry (eds), *The Archaeology of Sanctuaries and Ritual in Etruria*, *JRS* 81, 16–44.

Torelli, M. (1975) *Elogia tarquiniensia*. Florence: Sansoni.

——(1984) "Classi e trasformazioni sociali" in M. Cristofani (ed.), *Gli Etruschi: Una nuova imagine*, Florence: Giunti Martello, pp. 101–119.

——(2000) "The Etruscan city-state" in M. H. Hansen (ed.), *A comparative study of thirty city-state cultures: an investigation*, Copenhagen: Kongelige Danske Videnskabernes Selskab, 189–208.

——(2001) "Un cippo confinario etrusco da Cortona" in C. Masseria (ed.), *10 anni di archeologia a Cortona*. Rome: Giorgio Bretschneider, 129–40.

Turfa, J. M. (2005) *Catalogue of the Etruscan Gallery of the University of Pennsylvania Museum of Archaeology and Anthropology*. Philadelphia: University Museum.

——(2006) "Appendix A: The Etruscan Brontoscopic Calendar" in N. T. de Grummond and E. Simon (eds), *The Religion of the Etruscans*, Austin: University of Texas Press, 173–190.

——(2012) *Divining the Etruscan World. The Brontoscopic Calendar and Religious Practice*. Cambridge: Cambridge University Press.

van der Meer, L. B. (2004) *Myths and more on Etruscan stone sarcophagi*. Louvain (Belgium): Peeters.

——(2009) "On the enigmatic deity Lur in the *Liber linteus zagrabiensis* (LL)" in M. Gleba and H. Becker (eds), *Votives, Places and Rituals in Etruscan Religion*, Leiden: Brill, 217–227.

Wallace, R. (2008) *Zikh Rasna: A manual of the Etruscan language and inscriptions*. Ann Arbor: Beech Stave Press.

Watmough, M. M. T. (1997) *Studies in the Etruscan loanwords in Latin*. Florence: L.S. Olschki.

Wylin, K. (2003) "Review of *Frammenti di diritto privato etrusco*, by G. M. Facchetti," *Etruscan News* 3. Winter 2003: 11–2.

CHAPTER NINETEEN

ETRUSCAN GOODS IN THE MEDITERRANEAN WORLD AND BEYOND

———·◆·———

Jean Gran-Aymerich with Jean MacIntosh Turfa

INTRODUCTION

A good estimate of Etruria's wealth and economy, and its impact upon neighboring – and subsequent – cultures may be predicated upon a survey of its imports and exports and the range of foreign influences it embraced and adapted. The meeting of different cultures is discussed in Part III of this book, and the interaction and immigration of foreign craftsmen (and others) is treated in Chapters 6 and 48. The character of the evidence, both objects and contexts, differs from east to west across the Mediterranean, with – thanks to quite recent excavations – a rapidly growing body of material to be analyzed for the western Mediterranean, both Europe and North Africa.

Etruria and the central Italian Peninsula occupy a favorable position vis-à-vis Mediterranean and European exchange (Fig.17.1). This region, at the heart of the Tyrrhenian Sea, is roughly the same distance from Marseille, from the foothills of the Alps, and from Carthage, and, at a larger scale, just as far from Gibraltar as from Cyprus. At the end of the proto-historic period, the tenth through eighth centuries (all dates BC), Etruscan objects appear all along these long circuits of distribution, in both the Mediterranean and temperate Europe. During the seventh century this diffusion took place by both land and sea. The apogee of maritime exports occurred in the sixth century, lasting into the fifth century for exports into the Celtic hinterland. These first exports from the Italic Peninsula did not cease in later eras, but marked the beginning of a long period of exchanges, both cultural and human, which continued into the Roman Republican period. At the core of our enquiry is the period of the greatest diffusion of Etruscan objects, from the seventh to the fifth centuries. The clearest evidence of these far-flung Etruscan enterprises are bucchero kantharoi, transport amphorae and bronze vessels. However, the reality is far richer and more complex than these simple categories might suggest, especially for the regions of the western Mediterranean where Etruscan objects are the most numerous and varied.[1]

THE DISCOVERIES

The identification of Etruscan objects far from Etruria dates back to the nineteenth century AD. The dossier is composed of a large number of works and publications continually augmented by new discoveries and restudy of past finds. The following survey offers the most up-to-date introduction possible of this material, by category.

Armaments and equestrian harnesses

Etruscan warrior gear appears in Europe in the tenth through eighth centuries (see Chapter 39). These Villanovan-type objects, either originals or imitations, are those singular items which bestow a sense of prestige upon the local aristocrats and what might be termed the "knightly class": antenna swords, crested helmets and horse bits. These pieces come from the cities of maritime and southern Etruria, such as Tarquinia, Veii and Vetulonia. At the end of the eighth century, as was the case at Verruchio, horse bits of Vetulonian type (or imitations based on styles typical of the Etruscan world) appeared north of the Alps, at Alpenquai near Zurich, Vadena-Pfatten, Zolyom in Slovakia, Cluj-Napoce in Romania, and at Olympia. These accoutrements of the mounted warrior may also be attested in the seventh century at Stična in Slovenia amongst a funerary deposit containing two vessels, one in bronze and the other in Etrusco-Corinthian-style ceramic.[2]

Antenna swords appear in the tenth through to the eighth centuries in Adige in Este, in Brandenburg in Austria, at Steyr, along the Rhine in the Swiss cantons, and along the Rhône-Saône corridor up to Chandon by Amboise on the Loire.[3] These swords seem to have Mediterranean-wide distribution, based on finds (unconfirmed and thus requiring caution) from the Iberian Peninsula, from Bétera by Saguntum and from Egypt, (Fig. 19.1).[4] The dossier of these Mediterranean discoveries, unique in their extreme age, is now supported indirectly by the presence of contemporary objects from the Tyrrhenian littoral in Carthage and south-eastern Iberia, such as askoid pitchers and Sardinian bronzes.[5] To the north of the Alps, the axe from Étrembières in Haute-Savoie has a thickening of the flanged "wings" of a type found on Villanovan examples from Bologna and Vetulonia, and an "Etruscan" letter or symbol engraved on the shaft.[6] For the late Archaic period and later, one might envision an Etruscan influence based on the diffusion of *machaira*-type swords in Iberia. This hypothesis is reinforced by the Etrusco-Italic armaments from the Etruscan tombs of Aléria in Corsica (see Chapter 13) and the evidence from Languedoc and the north-eastern Iberian Peninsula.[7]

Villanovan-type crested helmets (Fig. 19.2, examples from Olympia) appear in western Ukraine, in Austria at Hallstatt, and in France at Armancourt in Oise;[8] while Etrusco-Italic skull-cap helmets appear to have served as prototypes in Slovenia.[9] Certain helmets of local production are decorated in Etruscan style, as with the row of semicircles and palmettes on the helmet from Novo Mesto.[10] Archaic-period Etruscan helmets are known

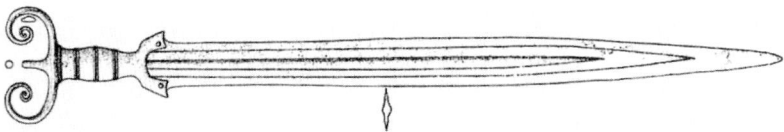

Figure 19.1   Antenna-hilt sword in bronze of Villanovan type probably discovered in Egypt.
Ninth–eighth century. (Bianco Peroni 1970).

amongst the panoplies from the tombs of Aléria, from the remnants of the shipwrecks at Sète, Agde and Gava in the Llobregat delta south of Barcelona, and other examples identified in the settlements of the Catalan-Languedoc littoral.[11]

Deposits of Etruscan shields of Villanovan type are attested in several Panhellenic sanctuaries, especially Olympia and the Samian Heraion, Dodona and (probably) Delphi.[12] Other than the examples from the tombs of Aléria, shields decorated with bosses in Catalonia have been interpreted as evidence of Etruscan influence.[13] The introduction into the western Mediterranean of disc-cuirasses and greaves amongst high-status warriors is partially attributable to the Etruscans. So much is the case for the prehistoric populations of the Catalan littoral, at the sites of Mas de Mussol and La Oriola – close to the mouth of the Ebro River and north up to Cayla de Mailhac and the necropolis of Corno-Lauzo in Languedoc.[14] The statue of a warrior from Lattes has decorated discs taken from prototypes in the Etrusco-Italic world and which have parallels in Iberia.[15] From Olympia is known a wonderful figured flat bronze strip (possibly the handle of a shield) (Fig. 19.3) and in North Africa the amazing bronze triple-disc cuirass from Ksour es Saaf (Tunisia), of the Hellenistic period.[16] Finally, the recent restoration of the parade panoplies from Aléria has revealed high quality incised mythological scenes upon a pair of Etruscan greaves.[17]

Thrones and chariot paraphernalia

The numerous fragments of repoussé bronze sheet from Olympia have been shown to belong not only to shields but also to Etruscan thrones.[18] In the Celtic hinterland, the bench or triple throne of Hochdorf reflects models known in Etruria.[19] In the palatial context of the Tartessos hinterland in the southern Iberian Peninsula, several pieces of cast bronze would have belonged to seats or benches similar to Etruscan productions.[20] Other Etruscan-style bronzes have been attributed to chariots at Gornja Radgon in Slovenia, in Bavaria and in the Rhineland.[21] The Greek colony of Empúries (Ampúrias, *Emporion*) in Catalonia has revealed a terminal piece in the form of a lion's head, which was originally part of a piece of furniture or the shaft of a chariot or sledge (see Fig. 17.19).[22]

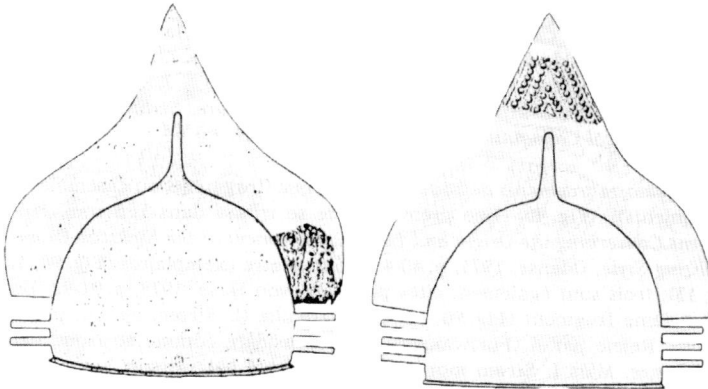

Figure 19.2   Crested helmets in bronze, of Villanovan type, discovered in the panhellenic sanctuary of Olympia. Ninth-eighth century. (Kilian 1977).

Objects of personal adornment and toilette, caskets and pyxides

Etruscan gold and silver jewelry has not been clearly identified far from Etruria, with the exception of the rich tombs of Aléria. In the far West, we have the very uncertain matter of the small gold fibula of *sanguisuga* type from Saint-Aignan, not far from the mouth of the Loire.[23] The recent excavations at Bourges have furnished, in the area of a razed funerary tumulus, a large pin decorated with the granulated head of a ram, of clear Mediterranean manufacture and probably to be attributed to Etruria. This piece of jewelry may be compared with personal ornaments in granulated gold from Ins-Anet and Jegenstord (Switzerland). This technique of granulation also appears on other gold items: the bracelet from Ensisheim, the earrings from Gurgy (Auxerre) and farther south at Lanouille (Dordogne), as well as the headband from the grotto sanctuary of Roc du Buffens at Caunes-Minervois (Aude). Etruscan influence is suggested for all these pieces of jewelry.[24] Jewelry of gold filigree, also clearly tied to Etruscan influence, has been noted in Kleinklein in Styria and recently in the *"Keltenblock"* tomb of the Lady of Heuneburg.[25] We have suggested the possible Etruscan technical and stylistic influences for the protohistoric goldworking of the Iberian Peninsula, with the clearest example being the stamped gold leaf from Peña Negra (Alacant-Alicante).[26]

The Etrusco-Italic bronze fibulae of the eighth–seventh centuries are well represented in the Celtic world, and more discretely in the Mediterranean region, especially by the finds discovered in Corsica and Sicily. The fibulae in bronze *a navicella* and *a sanguisuga* are common from Slovenia to Gaul, with a strong concentration in the Alpine region; in France they cluster along the corridors of the Seine and the Rhône, and in Provence in the region of Avignon.[27] Certain fibulae were found in funerary contexts, such as the

Figure 19.3 Bronze, *bracciale di scudo* (armband of a shield), with figural decoration, from Olympia. Sixth century. (Camporeale 2001).

serpentine fibulae with disc-shaped terminal from Besançon and from Bourges (see Fig. 19.15c) or likewise the fibula *a navicella* from tumulus I at Colmar-Riedewir in the Haut-Rhin department.[28] As with figurines, fibulae are preserved in the basements of museums amongst the various objects deemed to be local finds but not certifiably so.[29] The fibulae from past dredging of the Saône at Lyon and from the Seine at Paris have achieved a new credibility through the discovery in 1991 of a fibula *a sanguisuga* and of a tin bar in the deep excavations at Bercy at the edge of the river in Paris, which also revealed the famous proto-historic, wooden dugout (*monoxile*) canoes.[30] The Villanovan-style belts with a large bronze, lozenge-shaped plaque are known through the example from Châtel-Gérard, between the Yonne and the Seine, and that from Nantes, although whether this latter example was in fact a real local discovery remains controversial. A fine Villanovan belt in Paris (Cabinet des Medailles) (Fig. 19.4) is believed to have come from Euboea, indicating that dealings among aristocrats also proceeded in the Greek homeland.[31] Such female accessories as Villanovan belts and feminine fibulae types (Fig. 19.5) imply intermarriage or even deliberate visits (as pilgrims? members of diplomatic entourages?) – the belts are really for ceremonial wear, as they would impede any sort of normal work or leisure, and the fibulae were surely offered attached to complete garments, either robes of state, the suppliant's favorite belonging pledged to the gods in a sanctuary, or samples of the Etruscan lady's own weaving expertise.[32] Semi-lunate razors appear throughout northern Italy, where they inspired several imitations. They appear in Austria and in Dalmatia,[33] while in France they have come to light in the Alpine regions of Pralognan-la-Vanoise and possibly from the lake at Bourget, as well as in Mulhouse Forest, also in Bourges (see Fig. 19.15a).[34]

Etruscan mirrors brought to light outside of the Italian Peninsula are extremely rare. Outside of Aléria, the strongest example is that of a tomb in the Greek foundation of Empúries in Catalonia, decorated with a scene of the Judgment of Paris (Fig. 17.20). Another Etruscan mirror is alleged to come from Torre del Mar in Malaga.[35] For the record, let us note the mirror with the Dioskouroi, discovered in an Imperial Roman tomb in Paris at the Boulevard of Port-Royal.[36]

Other than the cylindrical, bronze-clad pyxis dating to the seventh century from Appenwihr in Alsace, Etruscan quadrangular pyxides are known in the Mediterranean from the last quarter of the sixth century. These small coffers or caskets, covered in ivory or bone with figural decoration, were found in the eastern Mediterranean at Athens, Delos, Rhodes, Cyprus, Kavala and in the heart of the Balkans at Atenica.[37] They also appear in the western Mediterranean at Malta, Ibiza, and in the hinterland of southern Iberia at Los Villares (Albacete), and at Turuñuelo, near Merida (Figs 17.13 and 17.14).

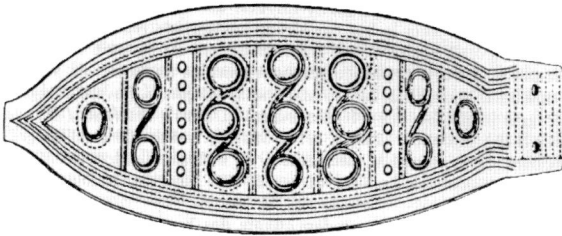

Figure 19.4   Belt in bronze of Late Villanovan type, discovered in Euboea.
Eighth–seventh century. (Cristofani 1983).

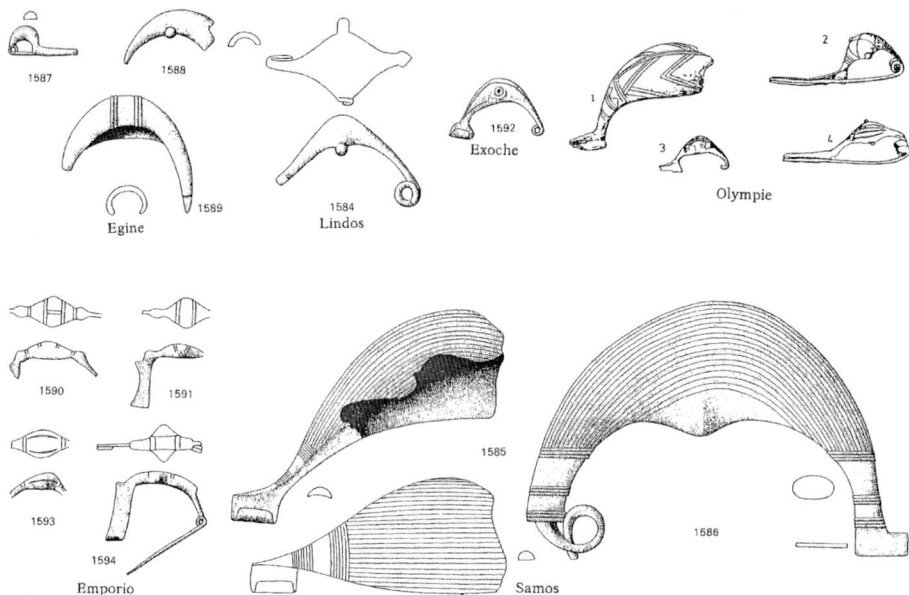

Figure 19.5   Etruscan fibulae from various locations in Greece: Olympia, Aegina, Samos, Exoche, Lindos, Emporio. Eighth–seventh century. (Gras 1985).

Statuettes, figurine attachments and figured vase handles

The introduction of anthropomorphic representations in central Europe manifests a new way of thinking, and in this regard Etruscan products are accorded a role in the transmission of the new iconography and ideas. So much is true for the figurines on the seventh-century cultic bronze chariot from Strettweg, and the figurines from Frög in Austria.[38] A rich repertoire of Etruscan statuettes found in Gaul has been catalogued, but much information on context is missing – some may derive from the Italian antiquities market, while others may be of an archaizing style but date to the Gallo-Roman period. Only a small number of statuettes definitively belong to the Etruscan dossier. The most remarkable examples are those from Thorigné-en-Charnie (Mayenne), from Châtillon-sur-Seiche (Île-et-Vilaine), from Montalin (Seine-et-Marne), and the figurine from the sanctuary at Fontaines-Salées or Vézelay, south of Auxerre in Burgundy.

The attached figurines and protomes decorate tripods, cauldrons and other vessels (oenochoae, amphorae, basins). The best-known example is the tripod and cauldron set from La Garenne at Sainte-Colombe, a site connected to the princely center of Mont-Lassois. On the littoral, the most intact piece is the tripod recovered off the coast of Agde (Fig. 19.6). Far more numerous are the handles adorned with figural or vegetal decoration, which are found as frequently in the Celtic regions as in the western Mediterranean and in the interior of Iberia. Figures in repoussé are well known in the regions north of the Adriatic, and even more of the *Arte delle Situle*, and north-west of the Alps where feline iconography adorns a pyxis from Appenwihr in Alsace. The influence of the figural decoration of Etruscan bronze vases is recognizable in the earliest Celtic art (masks, man-eating monsters, bestiaries), especially in the iconographic repertoire on the handles of Etruscan *Schnabelkanne*-type oinochoai, whose form inspired local production.[39]

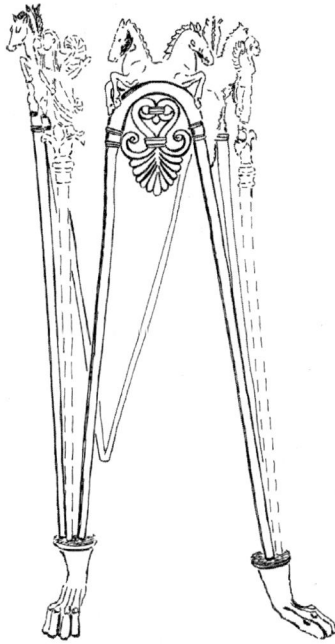

Figure 19.6 Tripod brought up from the sea off Cape Agde, Languedoc. Cast bronze, a letter incised on the back of one of the appliqué figures, beginning of the fifth century. (drawing G.-A.).

Metallic vases

Etruscan bronze vessels are well represented in the western Mediterranean and in the European hinterland, even though vases in precious metals have not been clearly identified. The cup of Kameiros (Rhodes), in heavy silver with gold plating and now in the Louvre, shows a characteristic carinated profile and two neatly raised handles which identify the object as a luxurious version of an Etruscan kantharos (Fig. 19.7). However, this cup was probably made in a workshop on Rhodes.[40] The gilded silver mesomphalic phiale from the tomb at Vix may be either an Etruscan creation, or the result of Etruscan influence, and likewise a similar piece in gold from Apremont (Gray) in Haute-Saône.[41]

Pouring vessels are the primary Etruscan bronze exports, distributed as much by sea as by land. Late seventh- and early sixth-century Rhodian-style oinochoai discovered in western Europe appear likely to be of Etruscan manufacture.[42] These oinochoai appear in the Celtic hinterland at Kappel and Vilsingen (Inzigkofen, Sigmaringen, Baden-Württemberg), and in the Rhône corridor in the region of Vienne and in the tomb of Pertuis (Vaucluse). In the western Mediterranean, Rhodian-style oinochoai of apparent Etruscan manufacture have been found in Carthage and in the southern Iberian Peninsula (Grenada-Malaga and Huelva), while other oinochoai of a more clearly Orientalizing style correspond to local productions, both Phoenico-Punic and Tartessian.[43] *Schnabelkannen*, oinochoai with long spouts, from the second half of the sixth and fifth centuries, are the most numerous Etruscan bronzes among the exports: there are some one hundred examples north of the Alps, with a primary concentration in the Rhine region of the Hunsrück-Eiffel Culture.[44] In the distribution of *Schnabelkannen* in the Mediterranean, the concentrations in Aléria and Carthage truly stand out, complemented by some isolated discoveries in Cayla de Mailhac (Languedoc) and Le Cigarralejo in Mula (Murcia). *Schnabelkannen* are classified according to their handles and handle-attachments (anchor, palmette, serpent). The oinochoai with handle in the form of a youth are illustrated by localized examples in the Celtic hinterland at Schwarzenbach (Fig. 19.8); by several examples from Carthage, of which some appear to be Etrusco-Campanian; and in Spain by the handles from Malaga, from Pozo Moro (Albacete), and from Cuenca (Castilla-La Mancha).[45] Squat oinochoai of the *Plumpekanne*-type appear in the Celtic hinterland at Hatten (Bas-Rhin), and in the Mediterranean, with variants at Aléria (where rounded oinochoai of Beazley type IX are better known), and possibly also at Cayla de Mailhac and at Carthage.

Small olpai with raised handles, well represented at Aléria, are equally well known on the littoral and in the Iberian backlands: El Oral (San Fulgencio, Alacant-Alicante), Alcurrucén (Pedro Abad, Cordoba), Escuera and Mirador de Rolando (Granada), Cabecio del Tesoro (Murcia), Segóbriga (Cuenca). Concerning the two examples from the former

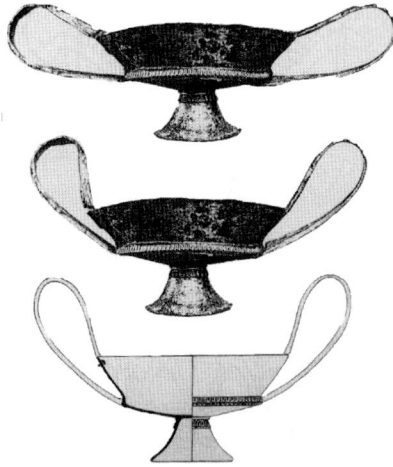

Figure 19.7   Reconstruction of original profile of kantharos from Kameiros, Rhodes. Silver and gold leaf, Musée du Louvre, sixth century. (Gran-Aymerich 1995b, drawing G.-A.).

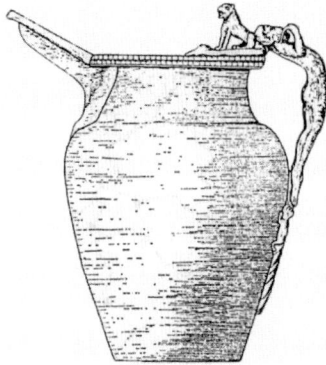

Figure 19.8   Beaked oinochoe, *Schnabelkanne*, from the tomb of Schwarzenbach. Cast bronze and repoussé, fifth century. (Gran-Aymerich 1995b).

Saavedra collection at the National Archaeological Museum in Madrid, these are probably of Andalusian origin.[46] These small olpai have appeared in western France from older excavations; some of these have received recent confirmation.[47] The Etruscan bronze amphorae, less common amongst the exports, are known from the Celtic hinterland, at Schwarzenbach (Palatinate) and through almost identical examples from Conliège and from Bourges. (Fig. 19.9a). The handle from Clermont-Ferrand is still contested.[48] Amongst deep-bodied bronzes of Etruscan origins or influence in central and eastern Europe are biconical vases from the end of the Villanovan period, although these are somewhat controversial save for some precise examples such as an urn from Gevelinghausen (Meschede).[49] Situlae illustrate well the bilateral, north-south currents of distribution. In that region between the Rhine and Burgundy we recognize examples from Vetulonia, dated to the first half of the seventh century; but, in the eighth through seventh centuries we also note a current running north to south, manifested by the situlae of Kurd type with cruciform attachments, or those decorated with registers of stamped dots and circles, which appear from Vetulonia down to Praeneste.[50] In the sixth and fifth centuries, corded bronze situlae, so widespread in the Celtic milieu, serve as examples

Figure 19.9   Bronze Etruscan vases from tombs at Bourges-*Avaricum* and environs. Cast bronze and repoussé. Fifth century. (Gran-Aymerich 1995a, 1995c).

Figure 19.10   Three oinochoai with long spouts, *Schnabelkannen*, from the tombs of Bourges-*Avaricum* and environs. Cast bronze and repoussé. Fifth century. (Gran-Aymerich 1996).

of imports in the region south of the Alps, or may be local replications. The Etruscan stamnos followed the same path as the situla, and they are occasionally found together in the necropoleis of Bourges or La Picardie (Gurgy, Auxerre).[51] The site of Ullastret (Girona) has revealed a stamnos handle attachment (Fig. 17.21).[52]

Amongst the vessels destined to be placed upon tripods are large basins and cauldrons. Concerning these, there is a complete ensemble from La Garenne (Saint-Colombe), the protome from Angers, the cauldron from Hassle (Sweden), likewise the heads of an example from Olympia, which would appear to be Etruscan.[53]

The bronze basins of Etruscan origin and their copies are abundantly represented to the north of the Italian Peninsula and in the Celtic hinterland.[54] The series of bossed-rim basins appear in significant numbers in southern France, and the Grand Ribaud F shipwreck has revealed a stack of smaller pieces within a cargo that contained several wine amphorae (Figs 17.9 and 17.10). On the coast of Agde was discovered, not far from the tripod, a basin-cauldron with plain rim identical to the deep-bodied basins and of Etruscan and Etrusco-Campanian great dimensions.[55] Basins with attached solid handles belong to those categories of grave goods distinctive of high-status tombs, such as the one in Vix dating to the second half of the sixth century. The most recent examples, fifth–fourth centuries, have elaborately decorated handles and appear at Verna (Saint Romain de Jalionas, Isère), at Saint-Gemmes-sur-Loire (Angers) and up to the Atlantic coast in Gironde, at Barzan, in the deepest levels of the Fâ sanctuary (Fig. 19.13).[56] Bourges is known for its remarkable concentration of Etrusco-Italic bronzes (nearly twenty) coming from tombs and from peripheral deposits, while the domestic area later revealed an Etruscan basin handle of the "omega" type.[57] Concerning the littoral of the Iberian Peninsula, several basins originally identified as Etruscan have been reclassified, but we might still look to the one example from Peña Negra (Alacant-Alicante) as Etruscan.[58]

Etruscan bronze cups of long-range distribution are known from the seventh century in the ribbed *phialai – Rippenschalen* – known from Frankfurt, Poiseul-la-Ville, from the environs of Lyons, and from Appenwihr Colmar, (where the *phiale* accompanied a bronze *pyxis*).[59] These two objects, the *phiale* and *pyxis*, would most likely have been products of Vetulonia, but the possibility of an artisan from this region working in northern Italy or on the northern slope of the Alps should also be considered.[60] Etruscan *paterae* (shallow bowls) of "Cook" type have been identified on the north-east of the Iberian Peninsula, in the tomb of Ferrers at Calaceite and in the region of Empúries.[61]

Other metallic objects appropriate to the banquet

Etruscan tripods are known in the European context from early examples of the type *ad occhiello nelle zampe* – a characteristic product of Vetulonia in the mid-seventh century – an example of which comes from Novo Mesto in Slovenia.[62] Amongst the rod-tripods and lion-footed tripods is one that held the cauldron of La Garenne at Sainte-Colombe, as well as the tripod from Auxerre which was (definitively?) removed from the list of local finds.[63] The example from the Grafenbüll tomb may be Etruscan.[64] In the Mediterranean, other than those from Aléria (tall candelabras on iron tripods), we know the complete example from Agde, an inscribed example from Empúries, and the appliqué from La Algaida from near the mouth of the Guadalquivir, although the interpretation of this last one as a tripod is controversial.[65]

Etruscan *infundibula* (strainers) appear in very far-flung regions: in the eastern Mediterranean at Argos (Heraion), Olympia (Sanctuary of Zeus), Lindos (Rhodes) and up to the coast of the Black Sea (Pantikapaion, Kertch). To the south, they appear in the Maghreb, at Cyrene (Sanctuary of Demeter and Persephone). North of the Alps, they have come from the deposit in Arbedo (Switzerland). To the extreme west, several examples are known from the Iberian littoral: Empúries, Ullastret, Poble Nou (Vila Joiosa-Villajoyosa, Alacant-Alicante), and from underwater finds at Xabia-Jávea (Alacant-Alicante) and from the shipwreck of Cala S. Vicenç (Balearics). The interior of the Iberian Peninsula has also revealed several of these objects, at Mirador de Rolando and Izanalloz (Granada), Alcurrucén (Cordoba), with two examples coming from Cancho Roano (Badajoz) (Fig. 17.15).[66]

The small cheese-grater, *gratuccia*, used to flavor wine, is a characteristic utensil among Etruscan banquet utensils (see also Chapter 6, Fig. 6.5; Chapter 43, Fig. 43.6). Such objects have come to light in southern France (*oppidum* of La Cloche, Les Pennes-Mirabeau) and at Empúries.[67] South of the Ebro, in the little *oppidum* of Oral (San Fulgencio, Alacant-Alicante), a *gratuccia* and a small olpe in bronze were also found.[68]

Concerning those banquet items associated with cooking, to the north of the Alps, iron andirons and spits have been found; the custom of depositing them in tombs seems to derive from Etruscan influence.[69] In the Celtic world, the monumentalization of princely tombs in the sixth century goes hand in hand with a profusion of bronze goods placed in the funerary chambers, goods which – as with the Etruscans and probably under their influence – create the atmosphere of a banquet hall.[70] North of the Alps, a so-called *harpago* (once equated with a meat-hook, now identified as a torch-holder) has been identified at Gornja Radgona/Radkersburg, probably as further evidence of banqueting or other night-time ceremonies.[71]

Ceramic fine wares

Etruscan ceramic wares are practically absent from the continental hinterland, as well as the interior of the Iberian Peninsula. Several possible examples are uncertain or remain unverifiable.[72] The presence of cups and oinochoai of the Etruscan-Corinthian type seems to be confirmed at Stična in Slovenia, while an Etrusco-Corinthian olpe from Haguenau retains the benefit of the doubt.[73] Bucchero kantharoi would have been introduced to the region of Toulouse by way of the isthmus of Aquitaine, and via the Rhône corridor up to the region of Lyons. Adaptations of Etruscan kantharoi into the local grey and black wares have been identified at Marseille itself, at many sites in Provence, and towards the interior up to the region of Lyons, at Saint-Paul-Trois-Châteaux, and in Burgundy at Camp-de-Chassey (see Fig. 19.11).[74] Finally, adaptations in local black ware of Etruscan oinochoai have come to light in the region of Carcassonne and in Burgundy in the latest excavations of the large apsidal building *in antis* (the "Princess palace") at Mont Lassois.[75] Further east bucchero vases with Chiusine-style reliefs have been discovered, although these are still in need of confirmation. These derive from finds from *Lauriacum* in Enns (near Lorch by the Upper Danube), and from Alte Gleisberg (near Jena in Thuringia).[76]

On the Mediterranean rim, in contrast to the interior, Etruscan ceramics are amply distributed. The primary object dispersed in this maritime diffusion is the bucchero kantharos, found in Anatolia and Syria, Greece and Egypt, all the way to the Atlantic façade of Iberia in Huelva.[77] In truth, we do not know of a single site bearing archaic

Etruscan ceramics that has not brought to light an example of a bucchero kantharos, while there are some sites that have revealed these vessels exclusively. This extraordinary dispersion is very irregular, and a large number of discoveries correspond to unique or rare pieces at isolated sites, or sites otherwise very remote from other Etruscan finds. So much is the case in the eastern Mediterranean and in North Africa, with the exceptions of Carthage and the Corinthian Trader's establishment, which was clearly an importer/exporter of a wide range of Greek and other luxury pottery (see below).

On the borders of the western Mediterranean farthest from Etruria we have found three important concentrations of Etruscan ceramics. In spite of some similarities, we note extreme distinctions among these three regions.

In the first region, the north-western Mediterranean, there are large deposits around some two hundred sites of various types and the discoveries are numerous and varied. This is also the case for the primary settlements, such as Marseille, Saint-Blaise, Lattes, Béziers, Empúries, and Ullastret. Finds also derive from smaller settlements (Tamaris, La Liquière, Marduel, Montlaurès, Mailhac, Pech-Maho, Turo de la Font de la Canya, Penya del Moro, Moleta del Remei and others). Etruscan ceramics are likewise present in a large number of funerary contexts and as votive offerings. In addition, there are several underwater finds, and shipwrecks whose main commodities were basically amphorae but which also contained Etruscan ceramic wares.

For the second region, the south-western Mediterranean, Carthage contains an extraordinary ensemble of Etruscan ceramics and finds, and offers a contrast with the rest of the Maghreb where such finds are sporadic and isolated.

The third region, the littoral of the Iberian Peninsula south of the Ebro, offers a singular situation. Etruscan ceramics, associated with bronzes, appear intermittently there, remarkably on both the Mediterranean and Atlantic façades of the Straits of Gibraltar: to the east at Malaga and in the west at Huelva.

Within this well distributed repertoire of Etruscan ceramics (bucchero, impasto, Etrusco-Corinthian, cream ware), those with figural decoration are extremely rare. For that which concerns the hinterland, we know of only two isolated and unconfirmed

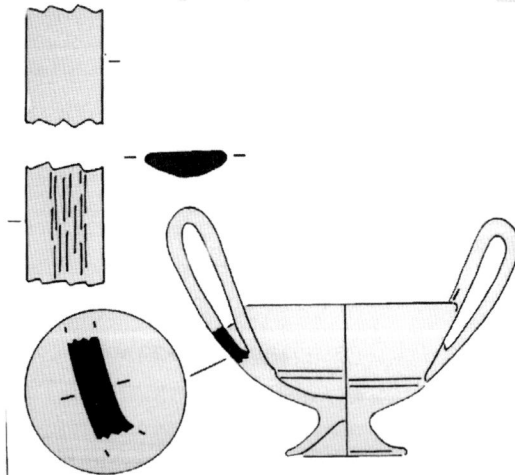

Figure 19.11 Kantharos (reconstruction) from the *oppidum* of Camp-de-Chassey, Bourgogne. Local version in grey-black fabric of the Midi. Sixth century. (Gran-Aymerich 2006a).

examples of bucchero with such figures, at Enns and Jena. In the Mediterranean, Etrusco-Corinthian vases decorated with animals (such as an alabastron of the *Pittore delle Code Annodate*) appear at Carthage, and later so do Genucilia plates. Etrusco-Corinthian ceramics with animal decoration also appear at Huelva (a plate by the *Pittore senza Graffito*). The north-western Mediterranean offers a more consistent range of figural ceramics. The site of Ullastret has revealed Etrusco-Corinthian ceramics, as well as local imitations, of such items as a face-cup (*a maschera umana*) and an exceptional Black Figure vase by the *Micali Painter*.[78] Saint-Blaise has provided a good repertoire of Etrusco-Corinthian wares, including a piece by the *Pittore senza Graffito*. Marseille offers, in addition to Etrusco-Corinthian wares with animal décor, several exceptional pieces: in bucchero there is a *face-cup* and an oinochoe with two stamped lion-masks around the handle-base. In red-slipped impasto is a Caeretan brazier decorated with a figural impression made by cylinder seal (Fig. 17.3).[79] The small number of these Etruscan ceramics with figural decoration amongst the exports corresponds especially to the contemporary styles produced and well known in southern Etruria, Caere and Tarquinia.

Food and fire wares

The presence of Etruscan common wares, evidence of everyday living, far from Etruria has received very little attention for far too long. The examples from Carthage and Marseille are important and significant, as it is only in recent excavations in the deepest levels that it has been possible to identify sherds of common wares, designated sandy, dull black and unpainted fine clay. The sites with the best examples of Etruscan ceramics tied to everyday life are Marseille, Saint-Blaise, Lattes and Empúries. In these areas, we note especially the mortarium-type basins, and small jars of the type *olletta* used for food preparation and preservation. Additionally, Marseille has revealed several exceptional fire accessories, up until now unique outside of Etruria. These consist of portable stoves of the type *fornello* (Fig. 17.2) and the Caeretan brazier with rolled stamped decoration (Fig. 17.3).

Amphorae and other storage vessels

Etruscan amphorae, although discovered very early on,[80] were definitively identified thanks to local examples found in underwater rescue excavations at sites along the southern coast of France. Cargoes of Etruscan amphorae, known from a half-dozen shipwrecks of the sixth century, offer evidence of the trade in Etruscan wine and constitute the principal evidence of an active commercial trade in Maritime Etruria. The discrete presence of amphorae in the intermediary settlements of southern France is tied to the local consumption of wine, whereas the larger quantities discovered at the principal sites (Marseille, Saint-Blaise, Lattes) would indicate not only localized consumption but also a regional redistribution and long-distance trade routes by land. Transportation via the Rhône is confirmed by the discovery of Etruscan amphorae at Lyons and Bragny-sur-Saône in Burgundy, where the evidence is definitive if slight. The role of Etruscan amphorae on the littoral of Provence and in Catalonia is, conversely, very important at the end of the seventh century and through the mid-sixth, and continues until the beginning of the fifth, when a decline is noticeable. Statistical studies of the earliest levels of occupation at Marseille reveal that up until the middle of the sixth century Etruscan amphorae outnumber those imported from Greece, while local Greek (from Marseille) amphorae were produced from the middle of the century.[81] The prestige associated with the Etruscan transport amphorae and their contents is also manifest by their presence in southern France in funerary assemblages and in the grotto sanctuary of Roc de Buffens at Caunes-Minervois, Aude (Fig. 17.8).

The little jars – *ollette d'impasto* – were not only used in food preparation but also in the transport and conservation of foodstuffs.[82] These vessels appear at the principle port sites of Marseille, Saint-Blaise, Lattes, Empúries and in the cargo of the shipwreck at Antibes.

Flasks and other small vessels pertaining to the conservation of perfumed oils and unguents appear amongst the exported Etruscan vases. The region of the littoral from Provence to Catalonia revealed a certain number of Etrusco-Corinthian alabastra and aryballoi, contrasting with the absence of certain pottery forms in bucchero, notably the small amphorae with flat handles which are so common in Carthage. The Iberian littoral attests to the isolated presence of Etrusco-Corinthian aryballoi at Ibiza (Puig dels Molins), Tortosa (Mas de Mussols), La Fonteta (Alacant-Alicante), Villaricos (Almeria), Malaga (Palacio de Buenavista) and possibly Huelva.[83] Carthage presents an exceptional concentration of perfume vases in its necropoleis, consisting of Etrusco-Corinthian vases (alabastra, aryballoi) but also bucchero vases (small amphorae with flat handles, possibly certain aryballoi). This plethora of Etruscan perfume vessels also appears in the Punic colonies of Sardinia and is echoed at Malaga (small amphora with flat handles in bucchero from Cerro del Villar, at the mouth of the Guadalhorce).[84]

Foodstuffs and perishable products

We recognize the Etruscan contribution to the diffusion of new products by maritime and terrestrial routes in southern France and in the Celtic hinterland. Transport amphorae confirm the overwhelmingly important role of the wine trade, tied to wine-drinking ceremonies, banquets and the diffusion of drinking vessels, especially oinochoai and kantharoi. One might contest the *importance* of the volume of wine distributed during the Archaic period, but not the phenomenon itself. Among other products introduced into temperate Europe from the Mediterranean are coral, ivory, faience, perfume and incense.[85] Woven fabrics, and possibly certain colorants and mordants, probably played a role in the exchanges between the Mediterranean and the Celtic world (see Chapter 42).[86] Woven fabrics from long-distance trade were recognized at the port site of Lattes and in the tomb at Hochdorf, which preserved traces of the red luxury textile of Mediterranean (Etruscan?) origin wrapped around its king or prince.[87] It is also possible that a link exists between the Etrusco-Italic fibulae and the imported fine fabrics, which would have been worn by foreigners or natives who adopted the new fashions.[88]

If we consider the importance of the diffusion of entire cargoes of Etruscan amphorae in the north-western Mediterranean, the main product of Etruscan commerce in the sixth century would certainly appear to have been a trade in wine, in spite of the presence revealed by the shipwrecks of some amphorae – larger and with flat bases – which appear to have been used to transport oils, olives and other commodities (e.g. resin). If the consumption of Etruscan wine is not in any way in doubt for the littoral regions where the amphora are plentiful, we might contrast this with the Celtic hinterland, where Etruscan amphorae are very rarely attested and Greek amphorae are also few in number. Recent excavations of the princely residences of Heuneburg, Mont Lassois and Bourges confirm the minimal presence of amphorae from Marseille and, up until now, an absence of Etruscan amphorae. In truth, Etruscan amphorae have been found in small numbers and accompanying Greek amphorae along river piers, at Lyons and at Bragny-sur-Saône. An analysis of the final contents of the handled cauldron from Hochdorf showed a strong concentration of honey, which would suggest, according to certain hypotheses, a local beverage and perhaps offers an explanation for the minimal consumption of wine at the princely sites. However, there is also the possibility that this mixture, rather than being a beverage, was a ceremonial fluid used to embalm the deceased.[89] Even if the numbers are small, the definitive presence of Greek, and likewise Etruscan, amphorae in the Celtic hinterland suffices to prove the introduction of wine into the heart of the Continent in the sixth century.[90] Otherwise, the transport of wine along extensive land routes may have occurred, after the initial export, in containers of wood or in skins which were better adapted for land travel, as described in the *Odyssey*.[91]

The diffusion of perishable products transported in small quantities (oils, perfumes, incense) might be deduced from the presence of appropriate vessels and through laboratory analysis.[92] In the Celtic hinterland, the so-called *pyxis* from Appenwihr has provided an exceptional piece of evidence: formerly considered to be some kind of container, and not an incense-burner, its association with a ribbed *phiale* indicated a ceremonial usage, which may have implicated an Etruscan, according to G. Camporeale.[93] The small Etruscan coffers, quadrangular and covered with ivory or sculpted bone revetments, found in southern Iberia and in the Punic colonial circuit, may have served as containers for incense or other aromatics. We have already referred to the Etruscan perfume vessels, both in bucchero and in Etruscan-Corinthian ware: to use these flasks requires refilling, and thus suggests a trade in perfumed oils and unguents in containers of larger size.

The possibility of architectural evidence

No vestiges of Etruscan architecture have as yet been clearly identified in regions far from Etruria, and for a long time the chimeric interpretations of A. Schulten concerning the Cyclopean ramparts of Tarragona and Etruscan primitive origins have received other explanations.[94] Until now, the clearest evidence of Mediterranean – and possibly Etruscan – architecture, suggesting the movement of the architects themselves, has been the ramparts with quadrangular towers and mud-bricks at Heuneburg. At this same princely site, the plans of the aristocratic houses suggest a distant influence from Etruscan houses.[95] Otherwise, the interpretation of two apsidal buildings recently brought to light at Mont Lassois, of which the larger has a façade *in antis,* is caught between the two equally compelling hypotheses, of Mediterranean influence or the evolution of the local architecture.[96] In the Celtic hinterland once again, one might note the possibility of an Etruscan influence for the sanctuary of Zavist, built on a monumental platform, in the region of Prague.[97] In the funerary domain, the large Celtic tombs of the sixth century have been considered in relation to Etruscan architecture, both in terms of the accent on their monumentality and the use of funerary chambers designed to resemble banquet halls.[98]

Concerning southern France, let us focus on two constructions. Marseille, on the *Îlot Cathédrale (Îlot 55),* has brought to light the "House of the Etruscans" a partially excavated, quadrangular architectural unit with stone foundations. At Lattes, the "Etruscan Houses" pull together several continuous structures. In these two cases, we are dealing with quadrangular constructions with stone foundations located in proximity to the ancient harbors. Additionally, for both, the "Etruscan" designation applied by the archaeologists derives from the remarkable concentration of Etruscan vases at both sites.[99]

In the south of the Iberian Peninsula, chamber tombs constructed in ashlar masonry, as at Toya (Jaén), have suggested to some a relationship with fine Etruscan funerary architecture (Fig. 17.16b).[100] On the littoral, buildings of a certain scale, such as buildings A and B at Illeta dels Banyets (El Campello, Alacant-Alicante), and taken to be temples or warehouses, may show a very hypothetical Etruscan influence (Fig. 17.16c).[101]

Concerning vestiges or *spolia* of monuments, the site of Lattes has revealed (re-used and mutilated) a Late Archaic sculpture of a kneeling warrior (archer?), of Etrusco-Italic influence, for which parallels exist in the Iberian world. This statue would have been part of a commemorative monument of unknown location.[102] The funerary *cippus* in fine calcite in a distinctly Caeretan columned style, discovered and preserved at Carthage, would have no doubt crowned the tomb of an Etruscan from Caere.[103] It is the only certain example of an Etruscan's tomb, and of Etruscan influence of a monumental nature, outside of Aléria in Corsica. The historical sources (Strabo 5.220 or 5.2.3) mention the construction of two Etruscan chapels at Delphi (attributed to Caere-Agylla, and Spina). However, the suggestion that the anonymous structure located next to the *thesaurus* ("treasury") of the Massaliots is to be attributed to Caere has not received unanimous support.[104]

Written documents and inscribed objects

Etruscan inscriptions identified in archaeological contexts far from Etruria constitute the most meaningful evidence for this culture. Putting aside the very specialized case of the Stele of Lemnos, which does not pertain to our topic (see Chapter 22, Fig. 22.1), it is necessary to mention the *liber linteus* from Egypt now in Zagreb. This unique document, the longest text preserved in Etruscan, would have been written in south-central Etruria and gives evidence for an Etruscan priest travelling to Africa, probably during the late Republican period. An analogous case is presented by three cimarking territory in the Oued Miliane Valley (Bir Mcherga), to the south of Carthage, although in this instance the inscriptions were done on site, in the Late Roman Republican period, after the destruction of Carthage and the forced immigration of Etruscans probably at the orders of Sulla.[105] Amongst the later Etruscan inscriptions, we should also recall the bronze token from Gouraya-Gunugu, Algeria (see also Chapter 17) (Fig. 19.12).[106]

Figure 19.12 Token in bronze, a sort of *tessera hospitalis*, discovered at Gounougou, Gouraya, Algeria. Second century. (Briquel 2006).

The eastern Mediterranean provides inscriptions from the Archaic period which show the movements of Etruscans. In the panhellenic sanctuaries, in which there are numerous Etruscan bronzes, the inscriptions left by the Etruscans are written in Greek, as at Delphi on the base for a tripod dating to the beginning of the fifth century.[107] From the same site, an effaced inscription, a sort of palimpsest, is no longer deemed to be Etruscan.[108] In the harbor sanctuaries, where offerings of bucchero vases are well attested, Etruscan inscriptions also appear.[109] In the eastern Mediterranean, bucchero kantharoi deposited in sanctuaries in the city of Corinth might have been marked with an 'A' as a commercial sign, or it may have been an acronym for *aisar*, "the gods." At the seamen's shrine of Hera on the promontory of Perachora opposite Corinth, the inscription on a bucchero kantharos states in Greek that "*Nearchos anetheke*" ("Nearchos has dedicated"), and a bucchero sherd deposited at the Athenaion at Ialysos (Rhodes) is also a dedication in Greek, showing some close connection between Greeks and Etruscans.[110]

In the Maghreb, Carthage brought to light an exceptional document, a *tessera hospitalis*, inscribed on an ivory plaque, which commemorated the burial of a Punic man at Carthage who probably made diplomatic excursions to Etruria over the course of the second half of the sixth century.[111]

The north-western Mediterranean has furnished the richest collection of inscriptions, marks and Etruscan signs gathered outside of Etruria, once again excluding Aléria, which is located on the shores of the Tyrrhenian Sea on the route to Gaul (see Chapter 13). We count in southern France a small number of inscriptions definitely transported from Etruria, copious evidence for inscriptions probably written *in situ*, and several Etruscan wares containing graffiti which certainly could have been incised *in situ*.

The first category – inscriptions done in Etruria – pertains to inscribed amphorae that were discovered in shipwrecks and settlements such as Saint-Blaise, inscriptions which were commercial in nature. In this category we might also include vases that were marked prior to firing – primarily small jars, *ollette* – inscribed with a letter or sign on the internal rim of the pouring spout: in Etruria this is generally understood to mark mass-produced vases. An exceptional item in this category is the griffin from a bronze tripod from Empúries, which was inscribed with the letters *CAR* before casting, as is the case with other votive bronzes from Etruria (Fig. 17.7).

The category of inscriptions certainly rendered outside of Etruria contains two remarkable documents. The older is a fragment of a Massaliot amphora shoulder (end of the sixth century) discovered at Marseille in the Collège Vieux Port construction site. In truth, this container bears a truncated Etruscan inscription, of which several large and well-incised characters remain (Fig. 17.4). The second document is the lead sheet from Pech Maho (Sigean, Aude), which bears an Etruscan inscription upon one side, incised at the beginning of the fifth century, mentioning Matalia (*Massalia*, Marseille) (Fig. 17.6). On the other side of the sheet an older commercial letter had been written in Greek. The Etruscan inscription presents lexical variants deemed appropriate for a "commercial" or "colonial" style.[112]

The final category contains numerous inscriptions, letters and signs identified on Etruscan vases. These are graffiti incised after firing, although we cannot tell if they were executed after transport. However, a number of interlocking and likely factors strongly suggest that these inscriptions were rendered at their site of discovery. They appear exclusively on mass-produced vases deemed disposable after use, and we do not know of a single example of an Etruscan inscribed vase from the funerary or votive assemblages.

The most interesting case is that of the bucchero and impasto bowls from Lattes, bearing feminine forenames, which G. Colonna considered to be of possible indigenous origin. These vases would have been inscribed in Etruria and transported by their owners, or possibly could have been inscribed *in situ*. But, in any case, the inscriptions function as status markers for women of a certain social rank: Etruscan women relocated to Lattes, or Etruscanized indigenous women.[113] The largest number of engraved signs on Etruscan vases discovered in Marseille, Saint-Blaise and Lattes appears to have been done by individual Etruscans anxious to establish their status.

Several examples show peculiar characteristics. Thus the foot of an Attic cup from Saint-Blaise (second half of the fifth century) bears an inscription interpreted as Etruscan language in Greek letters and consisting of a dedication to the Etruscan goddess Uni.[114] The settlement of Ensérune has furnished several graffiti considered to be Iberian, one of which was reinterpreted as the name of a Celt incised in Etruscan characters.[115] Finally, for the Celtic hinterland, the graffito of Montmorot (Jura) used Etruscan characters for an inscription of north Italic origin which was associated with a cultural group at Golasecca.[116]

A PRELIMINARY CLASSIFICATION OF CONTEXT TYPES AND FINAL USES OF ETRUSCAN GOODS

An inquiry into the role and significance of long-range Etruscan objects, which would examine each example in its context of discovery, still needs to be accomplished and would resolve numerous difficulties. The list that follows constitutes a preliminary classification, which takes into consideration the primary categories.

Offerings: war booty, votive deposits, diplomatic gifts

Certain Etruscan bronzes discovered in the panhellenic sanctuaries are clearly war booty dedicated by the Greeks. Such is the case of the well-known helmets consecrated by the Syracusans at the temple of Zeus at Olympia after the Battle of Cumae (474 BC, Fig. 39.11).[117] However, the majority of these Etruscan objects (Villanovan crested helmets, fibulae, shields, thrones, horse-bits, cauldrons) are uninscribed, and thus it is not possible to identify the donors with any certainty – they could have been Greeks just as easily as Etruscans.[118] In many Greek harbor sanctuaries we find Etruscan objects, some bearing Etruscan inscriptions and thus evidence of Etruscan involvement. So much is so for a bucchero kantharos and a sealstone from a ring, said to be from Perachora.[119] Likewise, from the sanctuary at Aegina we know of an example of a Greek having incised his inscription upon a bucchero kantharos, an act we might interpret as an offering relating to the relations between the Greeks and Etruscans.[120] Most such offerings are Iron Age to Archaic in date, but again, these goods are more distinctive and thus more readily recognized in Greek deposits. Other types of offerings have perished (organic materials) or lost recognizable form (metal melted down). Rare survivors include the cast, figured decoration of a late sixth-century Vulcian tripod dedicated on the Athenian Acropolis[121] and a fifth-century tripod/incense burner with kneeling youths astride feline paws deposited at Olympia sometime after 450.[122]

For a long time the distribution pattern of these deposits offered a clean contrast between the eastern Mediterranean, where Etruscan objects were mainly found in sanctuaries, and the western Mediterranean, where such goods, utterly lacking votive characteristics, were found in domiciles, necropoleis and shipwrecks. The dossier of Etruscan votive objects in the west has benefitted recently from an inquiry which has permitted us to re-evaluate these ancient finds, such as at Carthage for the statuette of Dar Seniat, and at the sanctuary of La Algaida at the mouth of the Guadalquivir River, for the figurine forming part of a tripod or other bronze furniture, and likewise the Etruscan amphora in the grotto deposit near Caunes-Minervois. Several exceptional Etruscan bronzes are also now considered to have been offerings, such as the griffin from the inscribed tripod at Empúries (temple sector of Aesculapius), the *despotes therōn* handle from Malaga (at the foot of the Alcazaba), or the palmette handle from the deepest levels of the sanctuary of Fâ at Barzan in Gironde (Fig. 19.13). In the interior of Gaul we have the figurine from the sanctuary at Fontaines-Salées (or possibly nearer to Vézelay according to some indicators) in Burgundy, which has been included in the tentative dossier of Etruscan statuettes without context from Gaul.[123] Two exceptional inscriptions pertain to this dossier of offerings: one is a dedication in the Etruscan language but written in Greek characters inscribed upon the foot of an Attic cup from Saint-Blaise, which, according to G. Colonna, is addressed to the goddess Uni.[124] The other inscription, this time in Etruscan characters, appears upon a Massaliot amphora discovered at Marseille, at the Collège Vieux Port site, and is considered to be a diplomatic gift for a group of notables.[125]

Finally, on the Languedoc littoral, there is the utterly extraordinary deposit of an Etruscan amphora and a Phoenician amphora (Fig. 17.8) in a rich context of metal offerings (including a headband of a gold-silver alloy decorated with granulation), at the grotto sanctuary of Roc de Buffens near Caunes-Minervois (Aude), at the entry to the Aquitaine corridor (Fig. 17.1).[126]

Funerary ensembles

In temperate Europe and in the western Mediterranean, the presence of Etruscan objects amongst high status tombs is attested for a long duration, from the seventh through to the fourth centuries. For such a space and for such an extent of time, it is evident that the content and distribution of the various assemblages will vary according to place and time.

Figure 19.13   Handle attachment with palmette from large bronze basin, from the sanctuary of Fâ, Barzan, Charente-Maritime. End of the fifth to the beginning of the fourth century. (Gran-Aymerich 2009).

In the Celtic hinterland, from the very first excavations (as at Klein Aspergle), the princely tombs dating to the late Hallstatt and the beginning of the La Tène periods attest the frequent presence of an Etruscan bronze vase, more rarely two or three (as at Vix). They are high quality pieces, well made even if mass-produced, which the Celtic world has brought to light in considerable numbers – some 200 examples (oinochoai, stamnoi, situlae, basins). Likewise, Archaic Greek bronze vases are known though only a very small number of masterpieces, remarkable for the quality of the work and, for some, for their large dimensions (the hydria from Grächwill, the Vix krater, the cauldron from Hochdorf). The primary distribution of these tombs with Etruscan metal vases, at the end of the sixth century and the beginning of the fifth, is the upper Danube valley and the Rhine, with a strong concentration in the Hunsrück-Eiffel area. This distribution extends to the western regions traversed by the upper Seine (for Vix) and the elbow of the middle Loire (for Bourges). No tomb in the Celtic hinterland has yet revealed Etruscan ceramics, although Attic cups are attested and, quite exceptionally, a small Greek transport amphora in the tumulus of Mercey-sur-Saône.[127]

For the Iberian hinterland, we observe the same absence of Etruscan ceramics and the same presence of Greek cups, even though several tombs contained a bronze vase or an expensive item such as an ivory casket. Thus the *Schnabelkanne* from tomb 57 in Cigarralejo (Mula, Murcie), the vase with the *ephebe*-style handle from the monumental tomb at Pozo Moro (Albacete), the ivory casket from the necropolis of sculpted monuments at Los Villares (Albacete) (Fig. 17.13). One might also add the Etruscan bronzes from the interior of the peninsula whose funerary origins appear assured, such as the examples from Segobriga and Cuenca (Castille-La Mancha), from Alcurrucén (Cordoba) and from Cabecico del Tesoro (Murcia). Huelva, located at the mouth of the river open to the Atlantic, is remarkable in this respect: two bronze vases (Rhodian style oinochoai) are attested in the rich assemblages of two tombs from which Etruscan ceramics are absent, even though at the port sector close to the necropolis bucchero and Etrusco-Corinthian ware are well attested, and even Etruscan transport amphorae. The recent discovery in the settlement of Huelva of late Villanovan style *impasto* vases (eighth century) must also be noted here.[128]

The Mediterranean littoral presents a more structured and complex panorama. Outside of the Tyrrhenian Sea, we note the presence of funerary assemblages with Etruscan objects in three regions: the north-western Mediterranean, the Balearics and southern Iberia and the site of Carthage. Bronzes and ceramics are represented to different degrees, but their combined presence in the same funerary context, as at Pertuis in Provence, the Cayla de Mailhac in Languedoc or Empúries/Ampurias in Catalonia, is utterly rare.[129]

The north-western Mediterranean littoral, from Provence to Catalonia, reveals tombs with Etruscan goods, some being located in proximity to important port sites such as Lattes (tomb with a strigil, tombs with Etruscan vases) and Empúries (tomb of the mirror, tombs with ceramics). In Agde, the necropolis of Peyrou has brought to light two apparently Etrusco-Geometric cups from the second half of the seventh century.[130] The majority of tombs in the south of France containing Etruscan objects are located near the seaside. In western and central Languedoc, the tombs with Etruscan amphorae are known in the larger necropoleis, such as Saint-Julien de Pézenas and the Grand-Bassin at Mailhac, as well as isolated examples.[131] Amongst the most remarkable assemblages from the Midi are the tumuli of Pertuis in Provence (Vaucluse), containing a Rhodian style oinochoe and an Etrusco-Geometric cup from the end of the seventh century. Le Cayla de Mailhac, in Languedoc (Aude) has revealed Etruscan goods from the sixth and fifth centuries, including a *cista a cordoni* and several fragments of bronze oinochoe handles, assigned to necropoleis (Corno-Lauzo and Grand-Bassin II), but also from the settlement, as with a *Schnabelkanne*.[132]

In the Iberian littoral, the specific case of the Ampurda area (Empúries and Ullastret) and the funerary depositions as far as the Ebro valley, have been the subjects of recent studies.[133] We note on one hand the presence of Etruscan goods, which appear in the Massaliot orbit, and on the other hand their influence on local productions, even at the level of ceramics and bronzes.[134]

South of the Ebro, the Mediterranean littoral has hardly revealed a trace of Etruscan objects in the funerary assemblages. The excavations of the past few years in the necropolis of Poble Nou at Vila Joiosa-Villajoyosa (Alacant-Alicante) have brought to light a *simpulum* (ladle) thought to be Etruscan, but its typology and the late chronology of the tomb (second half of the fifth through to the fourth centuries) call for prudence in interpretation.[135] In the maritime context under Punic influence, the funerary depositions from Ibiza (Puig dels Molins) stand out, containing a kantharos, an Etrusco-Corinthian aryballos, and the bone plaque from a casket with zoomorphic decoration.[136]

Etruscan funerary goods from Carthage are exceptional for their richness, but otherwise they are comparable with those from other sites in the Phoenicio-Punic colonial orbit, such as Sardinia, for example. Etruscan objects at Carthage are characterized by their variety and long duration. We have several dozen such objects from tombs, the oldest in the region dating to the mid- or later seventh century (tombs with vases in *impasto* and fine bucchero), with more dating to the end of the seventh and the sixth centuries (small amphorae, kantharoi and oinochoai in bucchero, Etrusco-Corinthian vases), with the latest dating to the fourth century (Genucilia plates). What is exceptional is the number of bronze vases, represented by a large quantity of only one shape: the oinochoe. Amongst the oinochoai in bronze are about ten of the most distinctive Etruscan type of beaked jug (*Schnabelkannen*); the others would be Etrusco-Campanian and from Magna Graecia, or of local production, such as the Rhodian-style oinochoai with clearly Orientalizing features.[137] A large proportion of the past finds from the Carthaginian necropoleis are without context, but it appears that no tomb had both Etruscan ceramic *and* bronze vases. This fact might correspond to two different deposition profiles: bronze vases for high status Carthaginians, Etruscan ceramics to designate Etruscans or other people who maintained a relationship with the Etruscans.

The tombs of Etruscans that are far from their native cities were clearly identified at Aléria on Corsica. Carthage furnished irrefutable proof of such a presence – the cippus of a style fashionable in Caere (also known at Aléria) found in one of the necropoleis of the African metropolis.[138]

The hypothesis of an Etruscan owner of the assemblage and tomb at Appenwihr in Alsace is suggestive, but still remains somewhat problematic.[139] Near Lattes there were recently discovered tombs with distinctive assemblages that suggest the presence of foreigners, possibly Etruscans, such as the tomb with the Etruscan amphora, dagger, small boss-rimmed bowl in bronze, and the oldest bronze strigil yet identified in Gaul.[140] In a tomb from Empúries, the mirror depicting the Judgment of Paris might constitute a mark of social status for a lady, either Etruscan or particularly associated with the Etruscan world.

In the eastern Mediterranean, burials with bucchero are rare, and may mark the routes of seafarers, diplomats or others with strong Etruscan associations, as at Kameiros, Rhodes (noted above), Amathus Cyprus, or the infant buried in the Syrian necropolis at Ras el Bassit (a city probably later known under the Greek name of Poseideion).[141] All of the firm evidence is of the Archaic period, although some Etruscan goods, such as Genucilia plates, have been recognized in other contexts of the fifth–third centuries.

Etruscan objects in residential contexts or singular structures

In the regal residences of the Celtic world, Etruscan imports are known, indirectly, by the placement of bronze banquet vases in the tombs, as at Hohenasperg, Vix or Bourges. The simultaneous presence of Attic cups, both in the tombs and in the residences, supports the idea that imports connected with drinking were used in banquets before having been placed in the funerary assemblages the same as in Etruria. The residences themselves give evidence for these wares in bronze. From Heuneburg comes a clay mould of a masked, bearded man, a satyr, identical to representations that appear as appliqués on Etruscan bronzes.[142] Mont Lassois has brought to light a small, bronze attachment of a winged lion or a sphinx, of Etruscan production or influence (Fig. 19.14). In this citadel, the excavation of the large apsidal structure with a façade *in antis* – interpreted as a residential palace ("*le palais de la Princesse de Vix*") has revealed most recently two ceramic, handmade oinochoai inspired by Etruscan models.[143] The latest investigation at the settlement of Bourges has furnished a bronze basin-handle of Etruscan type.[144]

The Iberian Peninsula has brought to light, in the hinterland of Tartessos, the most admirably conserved example of a palace-sanctuary from the early Iron Age, with clearly oriental architectural characteristics. Indeed, the palace at Cancho Roano, south of Mérida, has revealed the westernmost Etruscan bronzes found so far: two *infundibula* in an exceptionally wealthy context with hundreds of banquet vases, most of them Attic cups,[145] of a clearly ceremonial nature (Fig. 17.15).

Marseille offers a very different case. The excavation of Collège Vieux Port has allowed us to identify a notable building, exceptional for the dimensions of the main room, for the small, juxtaposed rooms or "chapels" (the remains of which are coated with paint) and for the rich assemblage of Greek ceramics dating to the end of the sixth century. This

Figure 19.14   Figurine-attachment in bronze, representing a winged lion (or sphinx ?), *oppidum* of Mont Lassois, Bourgogne. End of the sixth century. (Gran-Aymerich 2013a).

building has been interpreted by L.-F. Gantès, director of the excavations, as a ceremonial banquet hall, a dining room.[146] From this single context comes the fragment of a Greek Massaliot amphora bearing a truncated inscription in large Etruscan letters permitting identification as a gift of a diplomatic character (Fig. 17.4).[147]

Extraordinary concentrations of Etruscan objects in domestic contexts

In the western Mediterranean, Etruscan ceramics found far from Etruria appear primarily in domestic contexts and are of an apparently dispersed nature. It is true that no houses with Etruscan goods have been the subject of extensive excavations, save for the partial exception of Saint-Blaise, Lattes and Empúries; none of the sixth-century levels was sufficiently documented so as to allow for a room-by-room comparative analysis. However, we might note two important facts. The first is the recurrent association of certain categories of objects: bucchero vases, Etrusco-Corinthian vases and transport amphorae appear near the port settlements in the northern maritime sector (Marseille, Saint-Blaise, Lattes, Empúries, Ullastret) and also in the southern maritime sector (Carthage, Malaga, Huelva). Many of these sites have revealed Etruscan bronzes, either in the settlements themselves (Lattes?, Empúries-Ampurias, Ullastret, Malaga, Carthage) or in the necropoleis (Lattes?, Empúries, Huelva, Carthage). The second fact concerns some of these settlements where we observe Etruscan ceramics gathered in buildings located in proximity to the ancient harbors: Marseille (the earliest habitation on *Îlot Cathédrale*), Saint-Blaise (rim of the Lavalduc pond), Lattes (zone 27), Ullastret (Illa d'en Reixac), Malaga (Cerro del Villar), Huelva (Calle del Puerto). This concatenation of interlocking data suffices to open an inquiry into the hypothesis of the Archaic Etruscan *"fonduk"* as suggested in Chapter 17.[148]

Shipwrecks, underwater and river finds

The discovery of Etruscan objects sunk in transport is of capital importance when evaluating the commercialization of goods coming from Etruria. A string of shipwrecks dating to the sixth century and transporting Etruscan cargoes (amphorae, dining wares, bronzes) was recognized on the route reaching between southern Etruria and southern Gaul: Isola del Giglio, Antibes, Bon Porté, Dattier, Pointe Lequin, Grand Ribaud F, and the area of Cap d'Agde. In the waters of the Isle of Giglio were identified no fewer than three shipwrecks containing Etruscan amphorae, the most important of which is Campese, dating to the beginning of the sixth century. It is the oldest underwater deposit of Etruscan vases, while the ship itself is in general considered to be Greek.[149] The Giglio shipwreck, although heavily looted, has furnished a parade helmet, musical instruments, writing implements, ingots of copper and lead, as well as Etruscan and Greek ceramics and amphorae for the transport of wine, oil, and olives. The shipwreck from Cap d'Antibes, dating to the mid-sixth century, contained a cargo of Etruscan amphorae (approximately 180 examples), several Greek amphorae, and bucchero vases (40 kantharoi and 25 oinochoai approximately), Etrusco-Corinthian vases (seven cups and three plates), basins, *ollette* and bowls in *impasto*, as well as a Punic lamp with two spouts.[150] The other shipwrecks have mainly furnished amphorae, while the excavated portion of Grand Ribaud F (end of the sixth century) has revealed a cargo containing amphorae – some inscribed – ceramics and piles of small dishes in bronze.

The Mediterranean waters of the Iberian Peninsula have been scoured for Etruscan amphorae and bronzes: in the province of Gerona in Catalonia, along Castellon de la Plana, and at Cabanyal-Malvarrosa, along Valencia. Likewise are the bronzes further to the south, along Xabia-Javea (Alacant-Alicante) and in the Balearics in the shipwreck of Cala S. Vicenç.[151]

These underwater discoveries offer us a picture of interrupted commerce, and are potentially very rich in data. Although none of these shipwrecks has furnished a complete cargo, they all reveal a remarkable diversity of merchandise, objects and origins. For the Antibes shipwreck, the discovery of a Punic lamp has been suggested as evidence of a Punic man on board, either as a sailor or traveler. For the Giglio shipwreck (Campese), the ceremonial armor – including the finely decorated Corinthian style helmet – associated with the writing tablets and musical instruments (flutes) suggest the presence on board of a *naukleros*, a ship-owner or merchant, either Greek or Etruscan.[152] The presence of a Punic water jar apparently used by the crew of the Giglio merchantman, raises issues of "registry" in the ethnicity of the seafarers.

This ensemble of shipwrecks carrying Etruscan goods is evidence of out-going commercial enterprises originating from Etruscan ports, regardless of the origins of the ships themselves. By contrast, we know of no shipwrecks along the return journey. Only the underwater deposit of Rochelongue (Agde) suggests this hypothesis: hundreds of salvaged bronzes dating to different proto-historic periods, the copper ingots and the packets of tin beads would constitute the remains of a shipwreck from the seventh century, sailed in the direction of Marseille and Etruria.[153] It is good to remember here a shipwreck and the traces of a second on the route from the Straits of Gibraltar heading towards the central Mediterranean, even if, in appearance at least, it would not appear to have anything to do with Etruscan seafaring: the shipwrecks of Bajo de la Campana (Almería littoral) and of Mazarrón (Murcia, Carthaginian littoral). These two deposits have furnished whole elephant tusks, some of which were inscribed in Punic.[154] This is the only evidence of the trade in ivory for the Orientalizing and Archaic periods, and we know that the most active ivory centers in the West in these periods were in the southern Iberian Peninsula, whence came these two ships heading to Carthage and to Etruria (principally Caere and Vulci).

The interior of Gaul has furnished Etruscan objects amongst the river finds. In truth, fibulae and other Etruscan bronzes have appeared during previous excavations of the Seine at Paris and the confluence of the Rhône-Saône at Lyons, and as well in the Auron at Bourges and in the Loire by Amboise and close to Tours. These discoveries have often inspired skepticism, but the recent discoveries of Etruscan imports in the ports on the large rivers seem to support the existence of such distribution by fluvial routes. Indicative of this are the Etruscan amphorae discovered at Bragny sur Saône and at Lyons on the Rhône, and likewise the Etruscan fibula *a sanguisuga*, associated with a small tin ingot brought to light in Bercy (Paris) on the banks of the Seine.[155]

In the eastern Mediterranean, however, the picture is different, in large part due to the state of excavation of the old Greek and Near Eastern cities and to the difficulties of identifying goods other than distinctive bucchero or Vulcian bronzes. It is likely that most Etruscan exports are no longer recognizable in the archaeological record, as they would have been metal ingots, or even ore, shipped through the Italian archipelago, as attested in the discovery of Elban hematite (iron ore) in the industrial quarter of the eighth-century colony of Pithekoussai.[156] Likewise, timber, agricultural products, leather and textiles or *materia medica* would be difficult to recognize in the archaeological record. This may also explain why today we see so few Etruscan goods in Greece and the eastern Mediterranean; while in the practice of cabotage, sailing along the coast making frequent stops, a ship would have seen many ports of call between leaving Etruria and reaching the Greek islands, Cyprus or Anatolia and the Levant. "Identity items" (isolated objects) such as bucchero kantharoi are scattered throughout the region, and into the Black Sea ports (Olbia), but the bulk cargoes, such as ingots or timber loaded in Populonia, for example, may have been dispersed before the ships reached Cyprus, Tarsus or Sidon. Etruscan art of the seventh and sixth centuries depicts deep-hulled fast-sailing merchant vessels probably modeled on Cypro-Phoenician long-distance freighters, but apart from paintings and models, no actual ships of this scale have yet been found.[157]

But the picture was undoubtedly more complicated still: if bucchero kantharoi were given away to participants in banquet toasts and ceremonies of friendship, they were also part of marketplace commerce. At Corinth, a prosperous importer's home/shop in a prime location on the Lechaion Road that connected the sprawling center of the city with the great port, held piles of imported ceramics that had been discarded and dumped in its courtyard. The catalogue of fabrics found there mirrors the composition of Archaic cargoes in shipwrecks, including Laconian and Chiote painted vases, East Greek and Corinthian wares, and Etruscan bucchero in the form of kantharoi but also larger vessels. Bucchero kantharoi in the Potters' Quarter were associated with the homes/workshops of the Corinthian potters, but may have been kept as curiosities or dedicated in household shrines.[158]

Unique finds

Certain far-flung Etruscan discoveries are quite surprising and often remain inexplicable. Without a doubt the most troubling piece is the tablet of fired clay with a Greek inscription, which supposedly comes from Empúries-Ampurias in Catalonia. The text makes reference to the firing of black, Etruscan vases. The authenticity of this document (now dispersed in private hands) has not been confirmed and indeed it may be a counterfeit.[159] The Etruscan mirror without precise context, believed to come from the sector Torre del Mar (Morro de Mezquitilla) at Malaga, is extraordinary because of its supposed origin. Let us recall the unexplained but real discovery of an Etruscan mirror during the excavation of the Roman necropolis on the Boulevard of Port-Royal in Paris.[160] The mirror from Empúries-Ampurias, although unique, appears to come from one of the tombs from this Greek colony. These discoveries, real or counterfeit, remind us of others, such as the Villanovan swords from Egypt and from Bétera in Spain, which raise doubts.[161] But, after all, other Etruscan finds no less extravagant have been perfectly authenticated, such as the *liber linteus* from the Zagreb mummy, which remains in Egypt. It is possible in the long run that such extraordinary objects found so far from Etruria belonged – in the case of the authenticated examples – to Etruscan travelers or expatriates.

Among the unusual finds it is good to remember the numismatic data. The presence of far-flung Etruscan coins is shown in the didrachma of Populonia depicting a gorgon of Aléria on its obverse. Southern France has brought to light silver obols thought to be Etruscan or of regional production from the lower Rhône, at Sainte-Maxime de Gignac-la-Narthe and at Arles.[162] Further south, a cut-up didrachma from Populonia with a gorgon on the obverse would have come from the region close to Ebro at El Penedès (Tarragona).[163]

Other uncommon objects of Etruscan origin would have belonged to aristocrats coming from Etruria. In this category belong, in Carthage, the statuette of Dar Seniat, the funerary cippus of Caeretan style and the ivory *tessera hospitalis*. This last object, discovered in the tomb of a Carthaginian is evidence of his diplomatic relations with Etruria and recalls the presence of a Punic lamp on the shipwreck at the Cap d'Antibes. One might once again evoke the underwater discoveries of parade armor (Giglio, Agde, Gavà at the mouth of the Llobregat south of Barcelona), which give evidence of travelers or sailors of high status. The best complete panoplies of Etruscan parade armor located far from Etruria were found in the tombs of Aléria: one pair of greaves in the process of restoration revealed high quality decoration with mythological themes.[164]

CONCLUSION

This survey of Etruscan objects discovered very far from Etruria reveals numerous scenarios depending on chronology and geography. A universal interpretation is unlikely as the evidence is multifaceted and dispersed, corresponding to different realities and with similar objects meaning different things in different situations. The need for minute examination and interdisciplinary expertise for each case does not, nevertheless, make it impossible to draw broad conclusions from the evidence.

Amongst the recurrent questions surrounding this matter of widespread Etruscan objects are those pertaining to commercial enterprises, be they real or supposed, and especially concerning the real authors of these maritime distributions, the Etruscans themselves, or perhaps the Greeks or even the Phoenicians. The land-based distributions raise the problem of knowing if the dispersions are "random," or if rather they were part of long distribution circuits by caravan and river, controlled by the local aristocrats. Finally, we might question whether objects as curious as bucchero kantharoi, often appearing in very small numbers in far-away lands, were really understood as merchandise. In truth, these exceptionally singular vases by their very peculiar form could have served other functions, especially in the wine-drinking ceremony.[165]

To deal with these questions, we turn our attention here to explicitly mercantile products (*saleable goods*), to personal possessions that would indicate an Etruscan presence (*personal effects*) and to singular vases (kantharoi) which dot the Etruscan outward venture (*accompanying products*).

Saleable goods

The shipwrecks with Etruscan cargoes give the best proof of commercial traffic in the region of Etruria: that of wine amphorae. In the western Mediterranean, Etruscan amphorae are well represented in the sixth century, while Phoenician amphorae – and in their wake those of the Greeks and the *Zentralitalischenamphoren* – knew a much earlier diffusion. These amphorae were accompanied by a representative range of banquet wares in ceramic and bronze. These Etruscan bronzes, used in the consumption of wine, would have been the object of a very active trade on specific circuits of distribution: in the direction of the princely sites of the Celtic hinterland, which controlled the continental exchange routes; and in the direction of the maritime cities and trade centers of the western Mediterranean, such as Marseille and Carthage, masters of large portions of the sea.

The great majority of Etruscan bronzes are mass-produced vases, widely distributed and sometimes taken as prototype models by distant workshops. These three criteria – mass-production, diffusion of a number of relatively standardized pieces, and the adoption of forms or decoration – provide serious arguments for including these banquet paraphernalia amongst the goods in the commercial circuits. Moreover, a portion of the cargo from Grand Ribaud shipwreck F is comprised of stacks of Etruscan bronzes, small dishes, destined for southern France.

Thus far, complete commercial cargoes of Etruscan goods have not been identified in the wrecks of the eastern Mediterranean, but for the sixth century, the Corinthian Trader's House attests intensive Greek involvement in the distribution of Etruscan and Italic wares.

Personal effects

For the oldest periods, throughout the eighth and seventh centuries, isolated pieces (a fibula, a razor) of which there are a few examples far from Etruria, appear to be objects for personal use, whose far-flung presence may have resulted from personal travel or transmission by persons abroad (Fig. 19.15). Certain object combinations, such as the *patera* and *pyxis* from Appenwihr, raise the hypothesis that a person (Etruscan?) could, in the midst of the Celtic realm, have practiced ceremonies with the aid of these objects and specific products (incense?).[166]

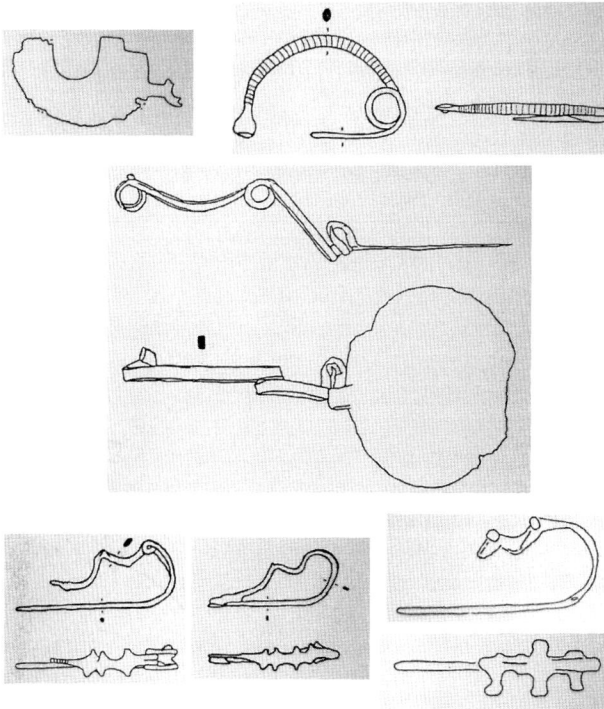

Figure 19.15   Villanovan razor and Etruscan fibulae from Bourges and environs.
Eighth–sixth century. (Gran-Aymerich 1995a).

At the dawn of the Archaic period, non-commercial Etruscan objects become more numerous and clearly identifiable. Carthage in particular has revealed several of those mentioned above: the small ivory plaque with Etruscan inscription, the statuette from Dar Seniat and the funerary cippus of Caeretan style. These objects correspond to very isolated and specific functions: the first corresponds to the *tessera hospitalis* of a Punic person who maintained relations with the Etruscans; the second would have been the offering of an Etruscan woman at Carthage; the third is proof of an Etruscan from Caere buried in the Punic metropolis.

Marseille has brought to light exceptional documents which are not commercial objects and which appear to have pertained to traveling Etruscans: such is the case for the Etruscan inscription traced upon a Massaliot amphora, which would appear to be a diplomatic gift tied to an official meeting or banquet. Concerning the Caeretan stamp-decorated brazier (Fig. 17. 3; see Figs 43.3 and 43.5), this does not appear to belong to the network of sales products so characteristic of Caere, but belonged to an Etruscan, who could have used it as a ritual object or more probably as a functional instrument, as is suggested by the wear on the stamped decoration and the amazing fact that this is a unique, failed cylinder impression. Moreover, the buildings in the port sector of ancient Marseille have furnished portable stoves, *fornelli*, as well as common dining wares, which show similar usage.

Unique vases which dot the long-range routes

The commercial status of the bucchero vases dispersed in the Mediterranean, and especially the kantharos – the most original and widely-dispersed form – has regularly been cast into doubt and deemed dissimilar to the commerce in Greek cups. If one might consider – reasonably – that some of the most far-flung discoveries of bucchero could not have been a response to consumer demand, it becomes clear that the wide dispersion of these vases responded to a variety of circumstances. Thus, the votive placement of kantharoi, with or without inscriptions, in the Greek sanctuaries is not a commercial act, even if it reveals close relations between the Greeks and the Etruscans. The presence of very modest quantities of bucchero kantharoi at port sites as far away as Naucratis and Huelva, Malaga and Miletos suggests that these vases, in certain circumstances, were objects of ritual use, destined for a votive dedication, with libation, or for ceremonies involving the consumption of wine. This hypothesis on the ritual role of bucchero vases finds support if we consider that these objects are found in isolation, not having been distributed in large numbers, and were scarcely objects of imitation.

Certainly, contact with the East had a strong influence on the character of Etruscan culture. The earliest monumental stone sculpture (and possibly architecture; see Chapters 6 and 48), gold-smithing techniques and designs (Chapters 6 and 50), chariotry and breeding of draught horses (Chapter 41), shipbuilding (probably), elements of religious discipline such as Greek mythology and iconography (Chapters 24 and 25) and Eastern haruspicy and brontoscopy (Chapter 26) came to Etruria from Greece and the Levant (also channeling Mesopotamia). The concerted and long-term commercial arrangements, reflected in part by the treaties of Etruscan cities with Carthage (see Chapter 17), and by the story of Demaratus (see Chapter 49), are only tokens for a much broader process of interaction, travel and trade between many different people that must have deeply affected all those involved.

By contrast, the situation in the north-western Mediterranean is completely different. In truth, for the first half of the sixth century especially, one finds in this zone the most important concentrations of bucchero kantharoi and vases outside of Etruria, not only at the principle sites but also along a ring of intermediary sites. We know of cases of provincial regions adopting the forms and decorations of bucchero vases in local productions: we have identified as much at Marseille even for kantharoi in grey ware, and likewise in the *oppidum* of Saint-Marcel for an oinochoe decorated with relief masks. Far into the interior, we know of reproductions of kantharoi in the region of Lyons and all the way to Burgundy. We can affirm that, on the littoral of Provence, Languedoc, and Catalonia, bucchero vases were commercialized with other trade goods, and that this region of the Mediterranean is the furthest from Etruria where this phenomenon is clearly attested. Moreover, certain shipwrecks carrying Etruscan amphorae contained a cargo of kantharoi and other vases in bucchero. For example, the shipwreck at the Cap d'Antibes was transporting a shipment of several dozen kantharoi and oinochoai.

To conclude, the Etruscans "as powerful on land as on sea," according to Livy, benefited on land from their location on the Po plain by promoting exchanges with the intermediary populations in the direction of the Celtic world; indeed, colonies like Marzabotto were founded, still within peninsular Italy of course, to facilitate manufacture, processing of goods and their trade with burgeoning markets across the Alps (see Chapter 15). The period when the distribution of Etruscan bronzes north of the Alps is at its strongest – at the end of the sixth and during the fifth centuries – coincides with the apogee of the Etruscan cities in the plains of the Po River. Etruscan commercial enterprises very much made use of the Alpine trade circuits and benefited from their role as active intermediaries between the populations of the northern Adriatic and the Alpine valleys.

By sea, Etruscan enterprises conducted beyond the Tyrrhenian did not take the form of proper colonial settlements. Rather, and this is beyond doubt, the Etruscans were the first people of western Europe to set up maritime cities from which to distribute and market their products throughout the whole of the Mediterranean. The north-western Mediterranean was the principal target of the Etruscan merchants, as is attested by the considerable number of objects and commodities found in this region. Although we can affirm for southern Gaul – the region most concerned with the sale of wine and drinking paraphernalia – that "there was no 'Etruscan commerce' itself creating an economic network,"[167] we might envision another interpretation of the phenomenon: Etruscan long-range ventures appear to have been based on a "non-colonial model" that adapted to the demands and profited from the possibilities of the Greek and Phoenician colonial networks. Enquiry is still ongoing on this matter, supporting the hypothesis of archaic Etruscan "*fonduks*" (see Chapter 17), because these Etruscans who took so much from the Orient and offered so much to the Occident have never ceased to amaze us.

NOTES

1   See to this effect Chapter 17 on relations between Etruria Marittima, Carthage, Iberia and Gaul.
2   von Hase 1969, 9, Fig. 1.8; *id.* 1981; Herrmann 1984; Catalogue Paris 1992a, 158.
3   Catalogue Paris 1992a, 158, 193, Fig. 254.
4   For Spain: Brandherm 2007, 1, n. 4. For Egypt: Bianco Peroni 1970, 113, n. 35, pl. 45; Naso 2011, Fig. 1.
5   Botto 2011; Naso 2011, 75.

6   Catalogue Paris 1992a, 180.

7   Catalogue Barcelona 1990; Gran-Aymerich, Jehasse 2007; Graells 2008, 2010a, 2011, forthcoming.

8   Catalogue Paris 1992a, 158.

9   Catalogue Paris 1992a, 159.

10 Catalogue Paris 1992a, 162.

11 Izquierdo, Solias 1990, 601, pl. I–II; Graells 2008a, 2010a and 2011.

12 Geiger 1994; von Hase 1997, 298, 310–313.

13 Actes Barcelone 1990, 158, Fig. 4, Mianes shield; Graells 2011.

14 Actes Barcelone 1990, 107–154, Figs 1–3; Catalogue Collioure-Bellesta 2011; Graells 2011.

15 Py, Dietler 2003; Py *et al.* 2006; Py 2009.

16 For Ksour-es-Saaf: Ben Younès 2001. For Olympia: Camporeale *et al* 2001: 95, figure.

17 Verger 2013 and forthcoming; Gran-Aymerich forthcoming b.

18 Strøm 2000.

19 Verger 2006.

20 Actes Barcelone 1990, 457–463, pl. I–XVI; Jiménez Ávila 2002.

21 Catalogue Paris 1992a, 159.

22 Catalogue Empúries 2007, 57, figure.

23 Jannot 1990 and 1995b.

24 Eluere 1989, 48–55, and in Catalogue Paris 1987, 41. For the pin of Bourges: Gran-Aymerich 2013a, Fig. 5.

25 Catalogue Paris 1992a: 159; see the websites for the Heunebourg *"Keltenblock"* tomb.

26 Perea 1986, 307; Jiménez Ávila 2004; Botto, Vives-Ferrándiz 2006, 143.

27 Adam 1992; Garcia 2012.

28 Bonnet, Plouin, Lambach 1991.

29 Adam *et al.*, 1987–1992; Jannot 1995b; Milcent 2006b; Gran-Aymerich 1992c, 1995a, 1996, 1997, 2002a, 2013a; Santrot 2001 and forthcoming.

30 Catalogue Paris 1992b, 12, Fig. no 12, decorated fibula *a sanguisuga*; Fleury, Marquis 2000, 33–39.

31 Von Hase 1997, 302–303, Fig. 7.

32 The *Palatine Anthology* (Book 6) offers Greek examples of woman donating clothing and ornaments, and the sanctuary of Artemis at Brauron received clothing of women who died in childbirth; on votives, see Turfa 2006.

33 Catalogue Paris 1992a, 158.

34 Catalogue Paris 1992a, 180; Gran-Aymerich 1992c, 1995a, 1995c, 2002a, 2013a.

35 Empúries: Catalogue Paris 1992a, 177, color Fig. cat. 300; Malaga: Mansel 1998.

36 Adam *et al.*, 1989, vol. II, 31.

37 Martelli 1985; Bellelli, Cultraro 2006, on Fig. 22, p. 248 "map of the distribution of Etruscan *cofanetti* (boxes) in ivory and bone" the point at Carthage corresponds in reality to the small ivory plaque of the *tessera hospitalis*.

38 Catalogue Paris 1992a, 162–163, Fig. cat. 242.

39 Kimmig, von Vacano 1973; Abels 1992; Gran-Aymerich 1998, 2004, 2006c; Kruta 1992; Jud 1996; Hase 2000; Jung 2008; Mötsch 2008; Balzer 2009; Bardel 2009; Bardel, Kasprzyz 2011.

40 Kameiros kantharos (in Louvre Museum: Catalogue Paris 1979, 147, no 83) with a restoration of its original profile: Gran-Aymerich 1995b, pl. 10, 72. For a bronze kantharos from the sanctuary at Taxiarchis at Didie (Turkey): Naso 2006b, 379.

41 Kimmig 1991, 1999; Eluère 1989; Eluère, Drillon, Duval 2003; Krausse 2003.

42 Shefton 1979. The argument suggesting that the oinochoai from the tombs at Huelva are Greek (the general absence of Etruscan finds) has been overturned by the discovery of Etruscan ceramics in the habitations of Huelva. See now Shefton 2009 in which he reassesses the identification of so-called Rhodian oinochoai, finding certain types (Types A and B) to

be definitely Etruscan in manufacture. Shefton furnishes an updated list (2009: 128–138) of "Rhodian" oinochoai, thus altering the picture of Archaic Mediterranean trade, since some reached Sicily (Ragusa), Spain (Huelva), the Danube region, and even Rhodes, where an Etruscan oinochoe was buried in Kameiros tomb A22.

43 Jiménez Avila 2002; Tekki 2009.

44 Mainly Jacobsthal, Langsdorff 1929; Reineke 1933; Bouloumié 1973; Haffner 1976, 1993; Abels 1992; Vorlauf 1997.

45 Almago-Gorbea 1983; Gran-Aymerich 1994; Graells 2008b; Bardelli, Graells 2012, 34–35.

46 Bardelli, Graells 2012, 34–35; Graells forthcoming.

47 Santrot and Santrot forthcoming.

48 Bouloumié 1986; Shefton 1995; Milcent 2006b.

49 Catalogue Paris 1992a, 193.

50 Catalogue Paris 1992a, 166, Figs 264–265.

51 Delor, Rolley 1995.

52 Gran-Aymerich 2006c, 278, Fig. 13; Botto, Vives-Ferrándiz 2006, 196, Fig. 59; Bardelli, Graells 2012, 33, Fig. 16.

53 Rolley 2005; Jantzen 1955, "groupe de Cumes."

54 Bouloumié 1986, 1987; Catalogue Lattes 1992.

55 Bérard-Azzouz, Feugère 1997; basin no 1141, from La Petite Roche; Gran-Aymerich 2006b, 210, Fig. 5.

56 Robin, Soyer 2003; Adam 2003; Gran-Aymerich 2008a, map Fig. 1, 2009a, 252, Fig. 3.

57 Milcent 2007, Fig. 17; Catalogue Saint-Germain 2009, Fig. III.11, 159.

58 Actes Barcelone 1990, 337, 364, Fig. 2; Botto, Vives-Ferrándiz 2006; 143, Fig. 52; Bardelli, Graells 2012, 34–35.

59 Hase 1992; Adam 2003, 2006.

60 De Marinis 2000b; most recently Camporeale 2009.

61 Graells 2010a, 2011; Graells, Sarda, forthcoming.

62 Catalogue Paris 1992a, 159, Fig. 267; Camporeale 2009, 13.

63 Amourette, Nadalini, Rolley 1993. The necropolis of La Picardie (Gurgy), at the foot of Auxerre, has revealed several Etruscan bronze vases (*stamnoi*: Delor, Rolley 1995) and earrings decorated with filigree of a possibly Etruscan influence: Eluère 1989.

64 Following the opinion of C. Rolley, vid. Verger 2006, 42.

65 Catalogue Barcelona 1990, 399, pl. VI; Torelli 1986; Gran-Aymerich 2008a, 90, Fig. 4, 2009a, 252, Fig. 2; Bardelli, Graells 2012, p. 25, Fig. 1–3.

66 Cancho Roano: Gran-Aymerich 2006b, Figs 3–4; Botto-Ferrándiz 2006, Fig. 23; Cyrene: Naso 2011, 78, Fig. 5. For Spain: Bardelli, Graells 2012.

67 Vigie 2011, Fig. 32. All our thanks to Marta Santos in Empúries and François Gantès in Marseille for their personal communications on this topic.

68 Botto, Vives-Ferrándiz 2006, Figs 51.1, 51.3; Gran-Aymerich 2006b, Figs 10.1–3 with also a bronze spit. For the role of the small wine jug with rounded mouth in the Etruscan symposium and its diffusion outside of Etruria, see most recently Donati, forthcoming.

69 Catalogue Paris 1992a, 164.

70 Verger 2006, 36–37.

71 Catalogue Paris 1992a, 159. See Jurgeit 1999, 515–516 no. 865.

72 Such as the bucchero kantharos of Koscielec, Cujavia in Poland (Fogel, Makiewicz 1989) or the "*frammento di bucchero relativo alla parete di una forma chiusa*" from Karnak in Egypt (Naso 2011, 80, no 34).

73 Bouloumié 1976, 23; Catalogue Paris 1992a, 159, Fig. cat. 269.

74 Bellon, Perrin 1992; Perrin, Bellon 1992; Bellon *et al.*, 1992; 1995a, 2006a, 2012b. Gran-Aymerich 1998, Fig. 5.

75 Catalogue Carcassonne 1989, 121; Mötsch 2008; Chaume, Mordant 2011.

76 Rupprechtsberger 1982; Simon 1999, 63–64, Figs 3–4, 83, Fig. 19; Gran-Aymerich 2006c, 2008c, 2009c, forthcoming c.

77 For the first distribution maps of bucchero ware in the Mediterranean basin: Gran-Aymerich 1973, 297, Fig. 32 and 1992a, 631–632, Figs 1–2; Hase 1992 (1989), Fig. 1; Catalogue Paris 1992, 64–65.

78 Catalogue Paris 1992, 176, no 303; Donati 1991; Bruni 2007.

79 For the bucchero oinochoe with relief masks from Marseille (Bourse) and an imitation in grey ware from the *oppidum* of Saint-Marcel: Gran-Aymerich 1995a, 73, pl. 11.1–2, *id.* 1998, 219, Fig. 2a–2b, Fig, 9; *id.* 2004, Figs 12–13; *id.* 2006a, Fig. 4, 6; *id.* 2006b; *id.* 2008c; *id.* 2009c. For the *tazza a maschera umana* in bucchero from Marseille (*rue Cathedrale*): *id.* 2006a, Fig. 5. For the brazier decorated by cylinder seal from Marseille (îlot de la Madeleine): Catalogue Marseille 2013, p. 132, Fig. 5; Gran-Aymerich forthcoming b in Actes Bastia-Piombino 2011.

80 Gsell 1891, typological table of pl. suppl. A–B, no 40.

81 Gantès 1992, 1999; Sourisseau 2002.

82 Gran-Aymerich, Domínguez-Arranz 2011, chaps. 3–4, 20, 40.

83 This is in contrast to the finds from Almaraz in Portugal (Frère 2006) and Medellín in Estremadura, Spain (Almagro-Gorbea dir. 2008, 578, Fig. 676).

84 Catalogue Barcelone 1991, 383–398; Gran-Aymerich 1994, 245, Figs 2.1–4; Aubet Semmler 2007.

85 Champion 1976; Mohen in Actes Paris 1987; Perrin 2000; Rondi, Costanzo 1997; Raposso, Ruggiereo 1995; Rondi, Costanzo, Ugolini 2000; Mederos Martín, Ruiz Cabrero 2004; Ugolini, Olive 2006; Catalogue Trento 2011, 30–35. For the cargo of the Late Bronze Age Uluburun Ship and its origins: Pulak 2001.

86 For colorants and for salt: Fernández Uriel 1995, 2000. For the role of alum as a mordant, and Etruscan access to this material from the *allume* of the Tolfa mountains, hinterland of Civitavecchia: F. Curri, intervento, p. 25, in Actes Florence-Populonia-Piombino 1979; Toti 1996; Actes Naples 2003.

87 For Hochdorf: Banck-Burgess 1999; Verger 2006. For the material from Lattes, which may derive from the plateau of central Asia: Catalogue Lattes 2002, 137.

88 Dunning 1991; Adam, R. 1992; Adam, A.-M. 1992.

89 Verger 2006.

90 Wells 1980; Kimmig 1983; Bouloumié 1986, 1987; Perrin 2004; Brun 1987, 2008; Marchetti Lungarotti, Torelli 2006.

91 "We had not yet gone through the red wine we had on board, as each one had his fill in the amphorae" (9.144–180, 212–215). Goatskins are attested by their Etruscan name – *naplan* – of Phoenician origin. Heurgon 1965a, and Gilotta 1987, 234–235, Figs 94–95, and by their depiction on the Sarcophage des Époux, ("Sarcophagus of the Married Couple") conserved at the Louvre, according to the hypothesis of M. Martelli (in *Prospettiva* 22, 1980: 101).

92 Catalogue Mariemont 2008; Actes Rome 2009; Gran-Aymerich, Bonnet, Domínguez-Arranz 2010; Frère, Gran-Aymerich 2010; Gran-Aymerich 2012.

93 Camporeale 2009, 6.

94 See, with bibliography, Gran-Aymerich, J. and E. 2006.

95 Verger 2007, 2010.

96 Chaume, Mordant 2011.

97 Bouzek 1985, 1992.

98 Verger 2006.

99 For Marseilles: Gantès 2002; Catalogue Marseille 1990, 1999. For Lattes: Py, Garcia 1993; Py *et al* 2006; Py 2009; Gran-Aymerich forthcoming d, Fig. 8–9.

100 Llobregat 1991; Colonna 2006a.

101 For sacred function and Etruscan influence: Llobregat 1982, 1991, 1998. For aristocratic residence and warehouse function: Almagro Gorbea 1983.

102 Py, Dietler 2003.

103 Pallottino, Moscati 1966, 12, pl. I.2; Pallottino 1979, 393, pl. VIII.1; von Hase 1996; Gran-Aymerich 2008a, 2009a, 2013b, forthcoming d and h; Naso 2011, 79, no 15. Since such stone monuments are rare outside of Etruria proper, one wonders if this person had been a shipper, who, like the fourth-century Tarquinian Partunu family, had access to means of transporting by sea heavy cargoes such as sculptural stone.

104 Cristofani 1983, 77; Gras 1985, 686; Catalogue Marseille 2013.

105 Bir Mcherga, Miliana valley inscribed *ci* of Etruscan settlers: *ET* Af 8.1–8.8; Bonfante and Bonfante 2002, 183–185 no. 60, Heurgon 1969a b, 1986, 446; Curruba 1976; Colonna 1983; Gran-Aymerich 2009a, 26; Naso 2011, 79, n° 17.

106 Briquel 2006.

107 Delphi tripod base: Cristofani 1983, Fig. 58, *"cippo reggitripode da Delfi con iscrizione dedicatoria di Etruschi; inizi del V secolo a.C."*

108 Cristofani 1983; Gras 1985; Colonna 1993; Briquel 1998.

109 Cristofani 1994; Colonna 2009.

110 MacIntosh 1974; Martelli 1988; von Hase 1997, 317 fig. 24, with references.

111 Catalogue Venise 1988, 632 no. 289, color photo p. 536; Maggiani 2006, 319–321, Fig. 1.1, 2.1, with bibliography, and 2007 with a new reading of the inscription.

112 Cristofani 1993, 1995.

113 Colonna 1980, 2006b; Catalogue Lattes 2002, 136–137; Py 2009.

114 Colonna 2006b.

115 De Hoz 2008 .

116 Catalogue Saint-Germain 2009, 106, Fig. II.27.

117 Catalogue Paris 1992a, 124, Fig. no 75–76.

118 Von Hase 1981, 15, Fig. 3; Herrmann 1984, 290, Figs 20–21; Camporeale 2009, 10–11.

119 Von Hase 1997; Naso 2000a–b, 2006a; Colonna 2009.

120 Cristofani 1983; Colonna 2009.

121 References in Turfa 1986, 73 note 80.

122 Haynes 1985, 288–289 no. 118.

123 For the statuette of the Vezelay area: Gran-Aymerich 2009a, 256, fig. 9. For the whole inquiry: Adam 1987–1992; Milcent 2006a–b.

124 Colonna 2006b.

125 Briquel, Gantès, Gran-Aymerich, Mellinand 2006; Gran-Aymerich 2006c, 2009a, Fig. 4; Gantès 2008; Catalogue Marseille 2013, 174, Fig. 51.

126 Catalogues Lattes 2002, 20–21; Herubel, Gailledrat 2006; Gran-Aymerich 2013b, Fig. 3, and forthcoming d, Fig. 5.

127 Catalogue Paris 1987, 73.

128 Gónzalez de Canales Cerisola, Serrano Pichardo, Llompart Gomez 2004; Botto, Vives-Ferrándiz 2006; Gran-Aymerich 2006.

129 Bouloumié 1990; Taffanel 1970; Actes Barcelone 1990, Castanyer, Santos 2007, 57 for the "Cazurro tomb" with the Etruscan lion bronze head Fig. 17.19.

130 Janin 2006; Catalogue Lattes 2002, 19.

131 Landes 2002, Catalogue Lattes 2002, 132.

132 Taffanel 1970; Bouloumié 1973, 1986.

133 Aquilué, Castanyer, Santos, Tremoleda 2006; Marzoli 2005; Graells 2010a, 2011.

134 Donati 1991; Bruni 2007; Graells 2011, forthcoming.

135 Botto, Vivez-Ferrándiz 2006, 144.

136 Botto, Vives-Ferrándiz 2006; Gran-Aymerich 2006c, 2008a, 2009a.

137 Jiménez Avila 2002; Torres Ortiz 2002; Gran-Aymerich 2008a, 2009a; Tekki 2009.

138 Pallottino, Moscati 1966; Pallottino 1979, I, 393, pl. VIII, 1; Turfa 1974, 1977, 369, n. 2; Blumhofer 1993, 190–194, type IIb; von Hase 1996, 189, 2004, 76–79; Gran-Aymerich 2008a, 2009a, and forthcoming d.

139 Camporeale 2009, 6.

140 Catalogue Lattes 2002, 132–133, and personal communication from Ch. Landes about a tomb with exclusively Etruscan ceramics.

141 References in Turfa 2001.

142 Kimmig, von Vacano 1973; Kimmig 1975; Jud 1996; von Hase 2000.

143 Mötsch 2008; Balzer 2009; Chaume 2011; Chaume, Mordant 2011.

144 Catalogue Saint-Germain 2009; Milcent 2009.

145 F. Gracia Alonso in S. Celestino ed. 2003.

146 Gantès 2006; Catalogue Marseille 2013, 37, Fig. 20.

147 Briquel, Gantès, Gran-Aymerich, Mellinand 2006; Gran-Aymerich 2008b; Catalogue Marseille 2013, 174, Fig. 51.

148 Gran-Aymerich 2013b and forthcoming a, d, h.

149 Campese shipwreck, Isle of Giglio, near by the Isle of Elba; objects conserved at the Archaeological Museum of Florence. Lead ingots of a flat, oval shape, one side convex, the other flat, 47 cm, two letters engraved on the bottom; copper ingot circular in shape, 41/43 cm.: McKee 1984, 1985; Bound 1985, 1987, 1991; Rendini 1993; Catalogue Paris 1992a, no 4–5: 110. There is not, however, consensus on the ship's "registry": its sewn construction (with ligatures of cordage holding planking together) also has parallels in the Tyrrhenian and Adriatic: see Turfa, Steinmayer 1999, 2001.

150 Pruvot 1971; Cristofani 1983; Catalogue Marseille 1990; Catalogue Marseille 2002; Catalogue Hauterive-Laténium 2005.

151 Fernández, Gómez Bellard, Ribera 1993; Alvar 1993; Botto, Vives Ferrándiz 2006; Vives Ferrándiz 2007; Graells 2008, forthcoming.

152 Bound 1991; Cristofani 1995; Colonna 2006b.

153 Bérard-Azzouz, Feugère 1997; Feugère, Rouquette, Tourrette 2001; Catalogue Lattes 2002; Catalogue Marseille 2002; Catalogue Hauterive-Laténium 2005, 41.

154 Mederos Martín, Ruiz Cabrero 2004; Negueruela *et al.* 2000.

155 Catalogue Paris 1992b; Fleury, Marquis 2000.

156 Ridgway 1992, 91–96.

157 Turfa 2001, 280–284; further on Etruscan cargo ships, see Turfa, Steinmayer 1999, 2001.

158 MacIntosh 1974.

159 Dunst 1969; Mangas, Placido 1998, 344–345.

160 For the Malaga mirror: Mansel 1998. For the mirror from Paris: Adam 1987–1992, vol. II, 1989, 31.

161 But Bronze Age precedents do exist: the Uluburun wreck, a small vessel with a "royal cargo" of luxury goods and enough tin and copper ingots to arm a city militia, sank late in the fifteenth century with an Italian bronze sword in its hold (also a stone Bulgarian mace head): did the sword belong to an Italian guard or diplomat? See Pulak 2001, 45–46, Fig. 5.

162 These remain to be verified. See Cristofani 1983, Actes Marseille Lattes 2002, *passim*.

163 Asensi 1990; Asensi Estruch 2011; Domínguez-Arranz, Gran-Aymerich 2011; Graells 2011, 120, Fig. 44, "*tesoro del Penedès 1930.*"

164 S. Verger and J. Gran-Aymerich, to appear in Actes Bastia-Piombino 2011; Verger 2013.

165 The two-handled cup is for sharing and toasting, so that one drinker may pass it easily to the next. Kantharoi in far-away places, like the sailors' shrine at Perachora, would have been recognized as symbols of hospitality and foreign-born guests or hosts. We thank doctoranda Jenny Muslin for sharing her MA thesis (2009, University of Buffalo) on the iconography of the kantharos.

166 In the opinion of Camporeale 2009, 6.

167 Catalogue Lattes 2002, 33.

BIBLIOGRAPHY TO CHAPTERS 17 AND 19

Abbreviations for volumes of proceedings (ACTES plus place and date of conference) and exhibitions (CATALOGUE plus place and date of exhibition)

Actes Barcelone 1990: J. Remesal, O. Musso (eds) *La presencia de material etrusco en la Península Ibérica*, Barcelona, 1991.

Actes Bastia-Piombino 2011: *La Corsica e Populonia. XXVIII Convegno di Studi Etruschi ed Italici. Bastia, Aléria, Piombino, Populonia* (2011), forthcoming.

Actes Clermont-Ferrand 1999: D. Frère (ed.) *De la Méditerranée vers l'Atlantique. Aspects des relations entre la Méditerranée et la Gaule centrale et occidentale (VIIIe-IIe siècle av. J.-C)*, Rennes.

Actes Florence 1985: *2° Congresso Internazionale Etrusco*, Florence, 1989.

Actes Florence-Populonia-Piombino 1979: *L'Etruria mineraria. XII Convegno di Studi etruschi e italici*, Florence, 1981.

Actes Londres 1992: J. Swaddling, S. Walker and P. Roberts (eds) *Italy in Europe. Economic Relations 700 BC–AD 50*, (British Museum 1992), London, 1995.

Actes Marseille 1999: H. Bouiron, M. Tréziny, (eds) *Trames et paysages urbains de Gyptis au Roi René. Colloque international Marseille, 1999*, Aix-Marseille, 2001.

Actes Marseille-Lattes 2002: *Gli Etruschi da Genova ad Ampurias. XXIV Conv. Studi Etruschi Italici Marseille-Lattes 2002*, Pise-Rome, 2006.

Actes Milan 1990: M. Bonghi Jovino (ed.) *Produzione artigianale ed esportazione nel mondo antico. Il bucchero etrusco*, Milan, 1993.

Actes Naples 2003: P. Borgard, J.-P. Brun, M. Picon (eds) *L'alun de Méditerranée, colloque international*, Naples-Aix, 2005.

Actes Orvieto 2005: *Gli Etruschi e il Mediterraneo. Commerci e politica. XIII Conv. Internazionale Studi, Orvieto 2005 (Annali Fondazione Museo "C. Faina" XIII)*, Rome, 2006.

Actes Paris 1987: *Les princes celtes et la Méditerranée. Rencontres École du Louvre* (1987), Paris, 1988.

Actes Ravello 1987: T. Hackens (ed.) *Navies and Commerce of the Greeks, the Carthaginian and the Etruscans in the Tyrrhenian Sea. PACT 20, 1988. European Symposium Ravello 1987*, Strasbourg, 1993.

——(1996) J.-P. Morel, C. Rondi-Costanzo, D. Ugolini (eds) *Corallo di ieri. Corallo di oggi. Symposium Ravello 1996*, Bari, 2000.

Actes Ratisbonne 1994: *Archäologische Untersuchungen zu den Beziehungen zwischen Altitalien und der Zone nordwärts der Alpen. Kolloquium Regensburg*, Ratisbonne, 1998.

Actes Rome 1983: *Il commercio etrusco arcaico*, M. Cristofani, P. Pelagatti (eds), (*Quaderni Centro studio Archeologia etrusco-italica* 9), Rome, 1985.

——(2009) D. Frère, L. Hugot (eds) *Les huiles parfumées en Méditerranée occidentale et en Gaule VIIIᵉ s. av.-VIIIᵉ s. ap. J.-C., Colloque Universités Bretagne Sud et La Rochelle, École française de Rome*, Rennes 2012.

Actes Sassari 1998: *Etruria e Sardegna centro-settentrionale tra l'età del bronzo finale e l'arcaismo, XXI Conv. Studi Etruschi Italici, Sassari, Alghero, Oristano, Torralba 1998*, Pise-Rome 2002.

Actes Vienne 1989: *Etruskische Präsenz in Norditalien und nördlich der Alpen*, Vienne, 1992.

Catalogue Bologna 2000: *Principi etruschi tra Mediterraneo ed Europa*, Venise.

Catalogue Carcassonne 1989: *Carsac et les origines de Carcassonne, Musée des Beaux-Arts*, Carcassonne.

Catalogue Collioure-Belesta 2011: *Des vases pour l'éternité. La nécropole de Negabous et la Protohistoire du Roussillon*, Perpignan, 2010.

Catalogue Empúries 2007: *Animals d'Empúries. Cataleg*, Ampurias.

Catalogue Florence 1985: *Civiltà degli etruschi. Catalogo Museo archeologico*, Milan.

Catalogue Francfort 2010: *Fürsten. Feste. Rituale. Bilderwelten zwischen Kelten und Etruskern*, Francfort-sur-le-Main.

Catalogue Hauterive-Laténium 2005: *Amphore à la mer! Epaves grecques et étrusques. Laténium, Hauterive*, Neuchâtel.

Catalogue Lattes 2002: *Les Étrusques en France. Archéologie et collections. Catalogue exposition Lattes 2002*, Lattes, 2003.

Catalogue Mariemont 2008: *Parfums de l'Antiquité. La rose et l'encens en Méditerranée*, Musée Royal de Mariemont.

Catalogue Marseille 1990: *Voyage en Massalie. 100 ans d'archéologie en Gaule du Sud*, Marseille.

——(1999) *Parcours de villes. Marseille: 10 ans d'archéologie, 2600 ans d'histoire*, Marseille.

——(2002) *Les Étrusques en mer. Épaves d'Antibes à Marseille*, Aix-en-Provence.

——(2013) *Le Trésor des Marseillais. 500 av. J.-C., l'éclat de Marseille à Delphes*, Paris-Marseille 2012.

Catalogue Martigues 2000: *Le temps des Gaulois en Provence*, Martigues.

Catalogue Paris 1979: *Mer Egée Grèce des Iles. Musée du Louvre*, Paris.

——(1982) *De Carthage à Kairouan. 2000 ans d'art et d'histoire en Tunisie. Musée du Petit Palais*, Paris.

——(1987) *Trésors des princes celtes. Galeries nationales du Grand Palais*, Paris.

——(1992a) *Les Etrusques et l'Europe. Galeries Nationales du Grand Palais*, Paris.

——(1992b) *Les pirogues néolithiques de Bercy. Exposition à la Mairie du XIIe arr.*, Paris.

——(1995) *Carthage, l'histoire, sa trace et son écho, Musée du Petit Palais*, Paris.

Catalogue Saint-Germain 2009: *Golasecca, du commerce et des hommes à l'âge du Fer (VIIIe-Ve siècle av. J.-C.), Musée National de Saint-Germain-en-Laye*, Paris.

Catalogue Trente 2011: *Le grandi vie delle civiltà. Relazioni e scambi fra Mediterraneo e il Centro Europa dalla Pristoria alla Romanità*, Trente. (= *Im Licht des Südens. Begegnungen antiker Kulturen zwischen Mittelmeer und Zentraleuropa*, Munich, 2012).

Catalogue Venise 1988: *I Fenici, Palazzo Grassi Venezia*, Milan.

——(2000) *Gli Etruschi, Palazzo Grassi Venezia*, Milan.

Catalogue Wurtzbourg 1995: *Luxusgeschirr keltischer Fürsten. Griechische Keramik nördlich der Alpen*, Wurtzbourg.

Note that abbreviations for periodicals are from *Archäologische Bibliographie*

Abels, B.-U. (1992) "Eine Tonschnabelkanne von der Ehrenburg in Oberfranken", *AKorrBl* 22, 79–82.

Adam, A.-M. (1992) "Signification et fonction des fibules dans le cadre des relations transalpines du VIIIe au Ve siècle avant notre ère," *Actes Vienne 1989*, 117–120.

——(1993) "Importation et imitation de bronzes méditerranéens en milieu celtique: quelques problèmes de méthode," *Archaeologia Mosellana 2. XIe colloque AFEAF, Sarreguemines 1987*, Luxembourg, 361–374.

——(2003) "De l'imagerie hallstattienne aux décors laténiens: quelles filiations?," *Décors, images et signes de l'âge du Fer européen, XXVIe colloque AFEAF, Paris 2002*, Tours, 27–36.

——(2006) "L'Europe tempérée dans ses contacts avec le monde méditerranéen (Ve-IIe s. av. J.-C.)," *Les Civilisés et les Barbares du Ve au IIe siècle avant J.-C.: Celtes et Gaulois. Table ronde Budapest 2005*, Glux-en-Glenne, 193–203.

Adam, R. (1992) "L'apport d'objets italiques dans le Jura: voie unique ou voies alternatives?," *L'Âge du Fer dans le Jura, XVe colloque AFEAF, Pontarlier 1991*, Lausanne, 181–187.

Adam, R., Briquel, D. and Gran-Aymerich, J. (1992) "Les relations transalpines," *Catalogue Paris 1992a*, 180–187.

Adam, R. *et al.* (1987–1992) *Répertoire des importations étrusques et italiques en Gaule*, vol. I (1987), II (1989), III (1990), IV (1992), Tours.

Almagro-Gorbea, M. (1983) "Pozo Moro," *MM* 24, 177–193.

——(1989) "L'Etruria e la Penisola Iberica. Stato attuale della questione sui ritrovamenti di ceramiche," *Actes Florence 1985*, 1149–1160.

——(1992) "Les Étrusques et la péninsule Ibérique," *Catalogue Paris 1992*, 174–179.

Almagro-Gorbea, M., Domínguez de la Concha, A. and López-Ambite, F. (1990) "Cancho Roano. Un palacio orientalizante en la Península Ibérica," *MM* 31, 251–308.

Almagro-Gorbea, M., Lórrio, A. J., Mederos, A. and Torres, M. (2008) *La necrópolis de Medellín. II. Estudio de los hallazgos*, Madrid.

Alvar, J. (1993) "El tráfico comercial etrusco hacia el Extremo Occidente," *Actes Ravello 1987*, 373–391.

Amourette, P., Nadalini, G. and Rolley, C. (1993) "Une importation à supprimer: le trépied d'Auxerre," *RAE* 44, 191–192.

Aquilué, X., Castanyer, P., Santos, M. and Tremoleda, J. (2006) "El comercio etrusco en Emporion: evidencias sobre la presencia de materiales etruscos en la Palaia Polis de Empúries," *Actes Marseille-Lattes* 2002, 175–192.

Arcelin, P. (2004) "Les prémices du phénomène urbain à l'âge du Fer en Gaule méridionale les agglomérations de la basse vallée du Rhône," *Gallia* 61, 223–270.

Arribas Palau, A. and Trías de Arribas, G. (1961) "Un interesante 'hallazgo cerrado' en el yacimiento de Ullastret" *AEspA* 34, 18–40.

Asensi, R. M. (1990) "Una moneda etrusca a la provincia de Tarragona," *Faventia* 12–13, 175–179.

——(2011) *Inventari dels materials etruscs procedents de colleccions dels museus catalans*, Barcelone.

Aubet Semmler, M. E. (1980) "Nuevos objetos orientales hallados en Vulci," *CuadRom* 14, 53–73.

——(1994) *Tiro y las colonias fenicias de Occidente*, Barcelone, (1st ed. 1987; *The Phoenicians and the West*, Cambridge, 1993).

——(2007) "East Greek and Etruscan Pottery in a Phoenician Context" in S. White Crawford (ed.), *Up to the Gates of Ekron. Essays Archaeology and History of Eastern Mediterranean in Honor of Seymour Gitin*, Jérusalem, 447–460.

Aubet Semmler, M. E. *et al.* (1999) *Cerro del Villar. I. El asentamiento fenicio en la desembocadura del río Guadalhorce y su interacción con el hinterland*, Séville.

Augier, L., Buchsenschutz, O. and Ralston, I. B. M. (eds) (2007) *Un complexe princier de l'âge du Fer. L'habitat du promontoire de Bourges (VIe-Ve s. av. J.-C.)*, Bourges.

Bakhuizen, S. C. (1993) "The Tyrrhenian Pirates: Prolegomena to the Study of the Tyrrhenian Sea," *Actes Ravello 1987*, 25–32.

Balzer, I. (2009) "Die Drehscheibenkeramik aus den Altgrabungen des Mont-Lassois, ein Zwischenbericht" in B. Chaume (ed.) *La céramique hallstattienne : approches typologique et chrono-culturelle, colloque Dijon 2006*, 51–68.

Banck-Burgess, J. (1999) *Die Textilfunde aus dem späthallstattzeitlichen Fürstengrab von Eberdingen-Hochdorf*, Stuttgart, 1999.

Bardel, D. (2009) "Les artisans potiers à l'époque de la civilisation hallstattienne," *Artisans et savoir-faire des Gaulois, Dossiers d'Archéologie* 335, 30–37.

Bardel, D. and Kasprzyk, M. (2011) "La céramique protohistorique et antique du grand bâtiment," *Chaume, Mordant* 2011, 547–635.

Bardelli, G. (forthcoming) "Cavalli senza cavalieri. Il tripode di Cap d'Agde e i tripodi etruschi tardo-arcaici con protomi equine," *Contacts et acculturations en Méditerranée Occidentale. Colloque Hommages à M. Bats, 15–18 sept. à Hyères-les-Palmiers*, Lattes.

Bardelli, G. and Graells i Fabregat, R. (2012) "*Wein, Weiss und Gesang*. A propósito de tres apliques de bronce arcaicos entre la Península Ibérica y Baleares," *AEspA* 85, 23–42.

Belfiore, V. (forthcoming) "Il testo etrusco di Pech Maho e i testi su lamine di età arcaica," *Contacts et acculturations en Méditerranée Occidentale. Colloque Hommages à M. Bats, 15–18 sept. à Hyères-les-Palmiers*, Lattes.

Bellelli, V. and Cultraro, M. (2006) "Etruria, penisola balcanica ed Egeo settentrionale," *Actes Orvieto 2005*, 197–252.

Bellon, C. and Perrin, F. (1992) "Nouvelles découvertes de l'Age du Fer à Lyon-Vaise (Rhône)," *RAE* 43.2, 269–292.

Bellon, C., Courtial, J.-C., Durand, E., Perrin, F. and Sergent, F. (2006) "A propos des importations étrusques de la moyenne vallée du Rhône aux marches de l'Auvergne," *Actes Clermont-Ferrand 1999*, 19–56.

Ben Younès, H. (2001) "La cuirasse de Ksour es Saaf au Sahel Tunisien. Problème de chronologie," *Pallas* 56, 67–70.

Bénichou-Safar, H. (1982) *Les tombes puniques de Carthage. Topographie, structures, inscriptions et rites funéraires*, Paris.

Bérard-Azzouz, O. and Feugère, M. (1997) *Les bronzes antiques du musée de l'Ephèbe. Collections sous-marines*, Agde.

Berges, D. (1993) "Die Tonsiegel aus dem karthagischen Tempelarchiv," *RM* 100, 250–256.

——(1997) "Die Tonsiegel aus dem karthagischen Tempelarchiv," *Karthago II. Die deutschen Ausgrabungen in Karthago*, F. Rakob (dir.), Mayence, 10–244.

Bernard, L. and Roure, R. (2010) "Naissance de la protohistoire méridionale" in S. A. de Beaune (ed.), *Écrire le passé. La fabrique de la préhistoire et de l'histoire à travers les siècles*, Paris, 351–361.

Bernardini, P. (2001) "La battaglia del Mare Sardo: una rilettura," *RStFen* 39.2, 135–158.

——(2009) "Tra il Mediterraneo e l'Atlantico. I viaggi fisici, i viaggi mentali," *AnnSassari* 1, 185–224.

Bianco Peroni, V. (1970) *Le spade nell'Italia continentale (PBF IV.1)*, Munich.

Bigeard, H. and Feugère, M. (2011) "Les bronzes figurés antiques du musée de Mâcon (Saône-et-Loire)," *Instrumentum* 33, June 2011, 18–23.

Bissing, F. von (1933) "Karthago und seine griechischen und italischen Beziehungen, *StEtr* 7, 83–134.

——(1941) *Zeit und Herkunft der in Cerveteri gefundenen Gefässe aus ägyptischer Fayence und glasiertem Ton (Sitzungsberichte der Bayerischen Akademie der Wissenschaften II.7)*, Munich.

Blumhofer, M. (1993) *Etruskische Cippi. Untersuchungen am Beispiel von Cerveteri (Diss.)*.

Bonanno, A. (1993) "Evidence of Greek, Carthaginian and Etruscan Commerce South of the Tyrrhenian: the Maltese Case," *Actes Ravello 1987*, 417–428.

Bondi, S. F. (1999) "Carthage, Italy and the 'Vth century problem'," *Phoenicians and Carthaginians in the Western Mediterranean*, G. Pisano (ed.), Rome, 39–48.

Bonfante, L. (1981) *Out of Etruria. Etruscan Influence North and South*, BAR IS 103, Oxford.

——(ed.) (2011) "The Etruscans: Mediators between Northern Barbarians and Classical Civilization," *The Barbarians of Ancient Europe*, Cambridge, 233–281.

Bonfante, L. and Bonfante, G. (2002) *The Etruscan Language. An Introduction.* (2nd ed.), Manchester-New York.

Bonet, Ch., Plouin, S. and Lambach, F. (1991) "Le tumulus I de Colmar-Riedewihr (Haut-Rhin)," *Gallia* 48, 2–57.

Botto, M. (2011) "Interscambi e interazioni culturali fra Sardegna e Penisola Iberica durante i secoli iniziali del I milenio" in M. Alvarez Marti-Aguilar (ed.), *Fenicios en Tartesos. Nuevas perspectivas*, (BAR Int. Sers. 2245), Oxford, 33–67.

Botto, M. and Vives-Ferrrándiz, J. (2006) "Importazione etrusche tra le Baleari e la Penisola Iberica (VIII-prima meta del V sec. a.C.)," *Actes Orvieto 2005*, 117–196.

Boucher, E. (see also Colozier) (1953) "Céramique archaïque d'importation au Musée Lavigerie de Carthage," *CahByrsa* III, 11–86.

Bouloumié, B. (1973) *Les oenochoés en bronze du type "Schnabelkanne" en Italie*, Paris-Rome.

——(1976) "Un vase étrusco-corinthien (?) trouvé en Alsace (?)," *Mélanges Jacques Heurgon. L'Italie préromaine et la Rome républicaine*, Paris-Rome, 49–58.

——(1982) "Saint-Blaise et Marseille au VIe s. avant J.-C. L'hypothèse étrusque," *Latomus* 41, 74–91.

——(1986) "Vases de bronze étrusques du service du vin," *Actes Londres 1982*, 63–79.

——(1987) "Le rôle des Etrusques dans la diffusion des produits étrusques et grecs en milieu préceltique et celtique," *Hallstatt-Studien. Tübinger Kolloquium 1980*, Weinheim, 20–43.

———(1990) "Les tumuli de Pertuis. Les tumuli de Vauvenargues," *Voyage en Massalie. 100 ans d'archéologie en Gaule du sud. Catalogue, Musées de Marseille*, 131–137.

Bound, M. (1985) "Una nave mercantile di età arcaica all'isola del Giglio," *Actes Rome 1983*, 65–69.

———(1987) "The Etruscan Metal Trade and the Evidence from the Pre-Classical Wreck at Campese Bay, Giglio Island," *Seaborne Trade in Metals and Ingots*, Oxford, 33–47.

———(1991) "The pre-classical wreck at Campese Bay, island of Giglio. Second interim report. 1983 season," *SteMat* 6, Florence, 199–244.

Bouzek, J. (1985) "Die Bauten auf der Akropolis von Zavist und die mediterrane Welt," *LF* 108, 68–69.

———(1992) "Die Etrusker und Dölmen," *Actes Vienne 1989*, 361–370.

Brandherm, D. (2007) *Las espadas del Bronce Final en la Península Ibérica y Baleares*, PBF IV.16, Stuttgart.

Briquel, D. (1998) "Le città etrusche e Delfi. Dati d'archeologia delfica," *Etrusca disciplina. I culti stranieri in Etruria. IV Convegno internazionale* (*Annali "C. Faina"* 5), 143–169.

———(2006) "Rapporti tra Etruschi e Africa del Nord: uno sconosciuto documento epigrafico," *Actes Orvieto 2005*, 59–92.

Briquel, D., Gantès, L.-F., Gran-Aymerich, J. and Mellinand, P. (2006) "Marseille, nouvelles découvertes grecques et étrusques," *Archéologia* 432, 36–43.

Briquel, D. and Gran-Aymerich, J. (2006) "Les inscriptions étrusques," in Gantès, Mellinand (eds) 2006, 69.

Brun, P. (1987) *Princes et princesses de la Celtique. Le premier âge du Fer en Europe, 850–450 av. J.-C.*, Paris.

Brun, P. and Ruby, P. (2008) *L'âge du Fer en France. Premières villes, premiers États celtiques*, Paris.

Bruni, S. (2007) "Ullastret e il Pittore di Micali. Appunti sulla produzione di kylikes nell'Etruria arcaica," *StEtr* 72 (2006), 97–116.

Buchsenschutz, O. and Ralston, I. B. M. (eds) (2001) *L'occupation de l'âge du Fer dans la vallée de l'Auron à Bourges* (*Bituriga, Monographie 2001–2*), Bourges.

Campolo, J. and Garcia, D. (2004) *Bronzes protohistoriques du Musée Calvet d'Avignon*, Avignon.

Camporeale, G. (2004) *Gli Etruschi. Storia e civiltà*, Turin, 2004 (first ed. 2000, last ed. 2008, trad. *Die Etrusker. Geschichte und Kultur*, Zürich-Dusseldorf, 2003).

———(2006) "Gli Etruschi in Provenza e in Linguadoca," *Actes Marseille-Lattes 2002*, 13–20.

———(2009) "Da Vetulonia verso la Renania e la Costa d'Oro nel VII secolo A.C.," *StEtr* 73–2007, 3–16.

———(2011) "Maestri d'arte e mercanti d'arte ai primordi della storia etrusca," *Corollari. Scritti omaggio Giovanni Colonna*, Pise-Rome, 19–23.

Camporeale, G. *et al.* (2001) *Gli Etruschi fuori d'Etruria*, Vérone (*The Etruscans outside Etruria*, Los Angeles, 2005).

Carruba, O. (1976) "Nuova lettura dell'iscrizione etrusca dei cidi Tunisia," *Athenaeum* 54, 163–173.

Castanyer, P. and Santos, M. (2007) "La representació d'animals en la torèutica, glíptica i joieria d'Empúries," *Cataleg Empúries 2007. Animals d'Empúries*, Empúries, 56–58.

Celestino Pérez, S. (2001) "Los santuarios de Cancho Roano. Del indigenismo al orientalismo arquitectónico" in D. Ruiz Mata, S. Celestino Pérez (eds), *Arquitectura oriental y orientalizante en la Península Ibérica*, Madrid, 17–56.

Celestino Pérez, S., Gracia Alonso, F., Jiménez Avila, J. and Kurtz, G. (2003) *Cancho Roano VIII. Los materiales arqueológicos I*, Mérida.

Champion, S. (1976) "Coral in Europe: Commerce and Celtic Ornament" in P.-M. Duval, C. Hawkes (eds), *Celtic Art in Ancient Europe, Congress Oxford 1972*, London, 29–40.

Chaume, B. (2002) *Vix et son territoire à l'âge du Fer. Fouilles du mont Lassois et environnement du site princier*, Montagnac.

——(2011) *Archéologie en Bourgogne. Vix (Côte-d'Or), une résidence princière au temps de la splendeur d'Athènes*, Dijon.

Chaume, B. and Mordant, C. (eds) (2011) *Le complexe aristocratique de Vix. Nouvelles recherches sur l'habitat, le système de fortification et l'environnement du mont Lassois*, Dijon.

Chausserie-Laprée, J. (2005a) *Martigues, terre gauloise. Entre Celtique et Méditerranée*, Paris.

——(2005b) "Villages gaulois de l'ouest de l'étang de Berre," *L'Archéologue. Archéologie nouvelle, Dossier: Provence gauloise. Celtes de Méditerranée*, 5–9.

Cintas, P. (1970–1976). *Manuel d'archéologie punique*, vol. I–1970, vol. II–1976, Paris.

Colonna, G. (1980) "Graffiti etruschi in Linguadoca," *StEtr* 48, 181–185.

——(1983) "Virgilio, Cortona e la leggenda etrusca di Dardano," *ArchCl* 73–1980, 1–15.

——(1988) "L'iscrizione etrusca del piombo di Linguadoca," *ScAnt* 2, 547–555.

——(1993) "Doni di Etruschi e di altri barbari occidentali nei santuari panellenici" in A. Mastrocinque (ed.), *I grandi santuari della Grecia e l'Occidente, convegno Trento 1991*, Trente, 43–67.

——(2006a) "Il commercio etrusco arcaico vent'anni dopo (e la sua estensione fino a Tartesso)," *Actes Orvieto 2005*, 9–28.

——(2006b) "A proposito della presenza etrusca nella Gallia meridionale," *Actes Marseille-Lattes 2002*, 657–678.

——(2007) "Novità su Thefarie Velianas," *Etruschi, Greci, Fenici e Cartaginesi nel Mediterraneo centrale (Annali "C. Faina"* 14), Rome, 9–24.

——(2009) "Un etrusco a Perachora. A proposito della gemma già Evans col suicidio di Aiace," *StEtr* 73–2007, 215–222.

Colozier, E. (see also Boucher) (1953) "Les Étrusques et Carthage," *MEFRA* 65, 63–98.

Concina, E. (1997) *Fondaci. Architettura, arte e mercatura tra Levante, Venezia e Alemagna*, Venise.

Courbin, P. (1993) *Fouilles de Bassit. Tombes du Fer*, Paris.

Cristofani, M. (1983) *Gli Etruschi del mare*, Milan.

——(1985) "Pirateria e commercio," *Catalogue Florence 1985*, 225–241.

——(1993) "Il testo di Pech-Maho, Aleria e i traffici del V secolo A.C.," *MEFRA* 105, 833–845.

——(1994) "Un etrusco a Egina," *StEtr* 59–1993, 159–162.

——(1995) "Novità sul commercio etrusco arcaico: dal relitto del Giglio al contratto di Pech Maho," *Actes Londres 1992*, 131–137.

——(1996) *Etruschi e altre genti nell'Italia preromana. Mobilità in età arcaica*, Rome.

Daveau, I. and Py, M. (forthcoming) "Grecs et Étrusques à Lattes : nouvelles données à partir des fouilles de la Cougourlude," *Contacts et acculturations en Méditerranée Occidentale. Colloque "Hommages à M. Bats", 15–18 September, Hyères-les-Palmiers*, Lattes.

De Hoz, J. (2008) "A Celtic Personal Name on an Etruscan Inscription from Ensérune, Previously Considered Iberian (*MLH* B.1.2b)" in J. L. García Alonso (ed.), *Celtic and other languages in ancient Europe*, Salamanca, 17–27.

Delattre, A.-L. (1923) "Une cachette de figurines de Déméter et de brûle-parfums votifs à carthage," *CRAI*, 354–365.

Delestre, X. (ed.) (2006) *Marseille 27000 ans d'histoire, Dossier spécial Archéologia* 435.

De Marinis, C. (2000a) "Il corallo nella cultura di Golasecca," *Actes Ravello 1996*, 159–175.

——(2000b) "I principi celti," *Catalogue Bologne 2000*, 379–389.

Delor, J.-P. and Rolley, C. (1995) "Gurgy (Yonne), La Picardie," *Fastes des Celtes anciens, Catalogue de l'exposition des musées de Troyes et de Nogent-sur-Seine*, 86–91.

Dies Cusi, E. (2001) "La influencia de la arquitectura fenicia en las arquitecturas indígenas de la Península Ibérica (s. VIII–VII)," in D. Ruiz Mata, S. Celestino Pérez (eds), *Arquitectura oriental y orientalizante en la Península ibérica*, Madrid, 69–122.

Docter, R. F. (1998) "Die sogenannten ZitA-Amphoren: nuraghisch und zentralitalisch," *Festschrift H. G. Niemeyer (Veröff. Joachim Jungius-Ges. Wiss. Hamburg* 87), Hamburg, 359–373.

———(2000) "Carthage and the Tyrrhenian in the 8th and 7th Centuries B.C. central Italian transport amphorae and fine wares found under the Decumanus Maximus," *IV Congreso Internacional Estudios fenicios y púnicos, Cádiz 1995*, Cadix, 329–338.

———(2006) "Etruscan pottery: some case studies in chronology and context," *Actes Marseille-Lattes 2002*, 233–240.

———(2007) "Die importierte griechische und zentralmediterrane Feinkeramik archaischer Zeit," "Archaische Transportamphoren," Carthage. *Die Ergebnisse der Hamburger Grabung unter dem Decumanus Maximus II (Hamburger Forsch. Arch.* 2), Mayence, 453–491, 616–661.

Domínguez-Arranz, A. and Gran-Aymerich, J. (2011) "Protomoneda y tesaurización en la fachada tirrénica de Italia central (s. XI–VI a.C.)," *Barter, money and coinage in the ancient Mediterranean (10th–1st centuries BC), IV encuentro peninsular de numismática antigua, Madrid, 2010*, Madrid, 85–96.

Domínguez Monedero, A. J. (1991) "El enfrentamiento etrusco-foceo en Alalia y su repercusión en el comercio con la Península Ibérica," *Actes Barcelone 1990*, 239–273.

Donati, L. (1991) "Considerazioni su un'oinochoe da Ullastret," *Actes Barcelone 1990*, 577–585.

———(forthcoming) "Il simposio 'all etrusca' ad Aleria," *Actes Bastia-Piombino 2011.*

Dunning, C. (1991) "Parures italiques sur le Plateau suisse" in A. Duval (ed.), *Les Alpes à l'Age du Fer (RAN suppl.* 22), 375–380.

Dunst, G. (1969) "Ein griechisches Tontäfelchen von der Küste bei Ampurias," *MM* 10, 146–154.

Eluère, C. (1989) "A 'Gold Connection' between the Etruscans and early Celts?," *Gold Bulletin (World Gold Council, Geneva)* 22.2, 48–55.

Eluère, C., Drillon, F. and Duval, A.-R. (2003) "Le torque. L'or et l'argent de la tombe de Vix," Rolley (ed.) 2003, 171–175.

Ettel, P. (1995) "Verbreitung und Rezeption italischer Fibelmoden nördlich der Alpen," *Catalogue Wurtzbourg 1995*, 48–51.

Fantar, M. H. (2000) "Carthage au temps de la bataille de la Mer Sardonienne," MAXH 2000, 73–84.

Fernández, A., Gómez Bellard, C. and Ribera, A. (1993) "Las ánforas griegas, etruscas y fenico-púnicas en las costas del Pais Valenciano," *Actes Ravello 1987*, 317–333.

Fernández Jurado, J. (2005) "Y por fín llegaron los Fenicios a Huelva," in S. Celestino Pérez, J. Jimenez Avila (eds), *El Período orientalizante en la Península Ibérica. III Simposio Internacional Arqueología de Mérida. Protohistoria del Mediterraneo Occidental, (Anejos AEspA* 35), Madrid, 731–742.

Fernández Jurado, J. and García Sanz, C. (2001) "Arquitectura orientalizante en Huelva" in D. Ruiz Mata and S. Celestino Pérez (eds), *Arquitectura oriental y orientalizante en la Península Ibérica*, Madrid, 159–172.

Fernández-Uriel, P. (1995) "Algunas consideraciones sobre la púrpura: su expansión por el lejano Occidente," *IIIe Congrès International Études phéniciennes et puniques, Tunis 1991*, Tunis, 39–53.

———(2000) "La industria de la sal," *IV Congreso Internacional Estudios fenicios y púnicos, Cádiz 1995*, Cadix, 345–349.

Ferron, J. (1966) "Les relations de Carthage avec l'Étrurie," *Latomus*, 689–709.

Feugère, M. (1992) "Une phiale étrusque du Musée de la civilisation gallo-romaine, à Lyon," *Gallia* 49, 1–7.

———(2011) "Bassins en bronze du IVe s. av. notre ère," *Instrumentum* 34, December, 25–30.

Feugère, M. and Freises, A. (1996) "Un casque étrusque du Ve s. av. notre ère trouvé en mer près d'Agde (Hérault)," *RANarb* 27–28/1994–1995, 1–7.

Feugère, M., Rouquette, D. and Tourrette, C. (2001) "Agde (F., Hérault): nouveaux bronzes antiques du secteur de Rochelongue," *Instrumentum* 14, 11–12.

Fleury, M. and Marquis, P. (2000) "Un patrimoine redécouvert," *Archéologia*, 372, 33–39.

Fogel, J. and Makiewicz, T. (1989) "La sconosciuta importazione etrusca in Cujavia (Polonia centrale) e la questione della presenza degli Etruschi sul Baltico," *StEtr* 45, 123–130.

Frère, D. (2006) "La céramique étrusco-corinthienne en Gaule," *Actes Marseille-Lattes 2002*, 249–280.

Frère, D. and Gran-Aymerich, J. (eds) (2010) *Parfums dans l'Antiquité, Dossiers d'Archéologie 337*.

Gantès, L.-F. (1992) "La topographie de Marseille grecque. Bilan des recherches (1829–1991). L'apport des fouilles récentes à l'étude quantitative de l'économie massaliète," *Marseille grecque et la Gaule. Actes Marseille 1990 (Collection Études Massaliètes 3)*, Marseille, 71–88, 171–178.

——(1999) "La physionomie de la vaisselle tournée importée à Marseille au VIe siècle av. J.-C.," *Céramique et peinture grecques. Modes d'emploi. Colloque École du Louvre*, Paris, 365–381.

——(2002) "Les fouilles de l'îlot de la Cathédrale ou îlot 55," *Catalogue Marseille 2002*, 104–105.

——(2003) "Catalogue des objets céramiques du site de Saint-Blaise," *Catalogue Lattes 2002*, 65–69.

——(2005) "Les céramiques archaïques et classiques de l'Espace Bargemon" in P. Mellinand (ed.), *Espace Bargemon à Marseille. Rapport final d'opération. INRAP, no 2002/168*, Nîmes, 695–729.

——(ed.) (2010) *Rapport final d'opération de la fouille archéologique des places de la Madeleine et du Refuge à Marseille*, Marseille.

Gantès, L.-F. and Mellinand, P. (eds) (2006) *Rapport final d'opération de la fouille archéologique du collège Vieux-Port à Marseille*, Nîmes.

Gantès, L.-F., Sourisseau, J. C. and Verger, S. (2003) "Saint-Blaise," *Catalogue Lattes 2002*, 61–80.

Garcia, D. (2004) *La Celtique méditerranéenne*, Paris.

——(2006) "Les Celtes de Gaule méditerranéenne. Définition et caractérisation," *Les Civilisés et les Barbares du Ve au IIe siècle avant J.-C.: Celtes et Gaulois. Table ronde Budapest 2005*, Glux-en-Glenne, 63–76.

——(2012) "Provence. La Protohistoire," *Archéologia 496*, 27–30.

Garcia, D. and Vital, J. (2006) "Dynamiques culturelles de l'âge du Bronze et de l'âge du Fer dans le sud-est de la Gaule," *La préhistoire des Celtes, Celtes et Gaulois. Table ronde Bologne 2005*, Glux-en-Glenne, 64–80.

Geiger, A. (1994) *Treibverzierte Bronzerundschilde der italischen Eisenzeit aus Italien und Griechenland*, Stuttgart.

Gilotta, F. (1987) "La tomba François di Vulci," *La tomba François. Catalogo Vaticano 1987*, 234–235.

González de Canales Cerisola, F. (forthcoming) "Tarsis-Tarteso desde los hallazgos de Huelva" in C. Gómez Wagner, P. Moret and M. Torres Ortiz (eds), *Tarsis-Tartessos. Mito, historia, arqueología. V Coloquio Centro Estudios fenicios y púnicos, Madrid, 2007*, Madrid.

González de Canales, F., Serrano Pichardo, L. and Llompart Gomez, J. (2004) *El emporio fenicio precolonial de Huelva (ca. 900–770 a.C.)*, Madrid.

——(2006) "Las evidencias mas antiguas de la presencia fenicia en el Sur de la Península," in M. Corrales Aguilar, M. Gontan Morales, E. Martín Cordoba, B. Mora Serrano and A. Recio Ruiz (eds), *Tiempos de púrpura. Málaga antigua, antigüedades hispanas I, (Mainake 28)*, Malaga, 105–128.

Graells i Fabregat, R. (2008a) "Un aplique de casco etrusco de la Antigua colección Vives," *Herakleion 1, 2008*, 69–84.

——(2008b) "Vasos de bronce con asas 'a kouroi' en el occidente arcaico: a la luz de un nuevo ejemplar procedente de Cuenca", *AEspA 81*, 201–212.

——(2010a) *Las tumbas con importaciones y la recepción del Mediterraneo en el nordeste de la Península Ibérica (VII–VI a.C.)*, Lleida.

——(2010b) "'Palais' et 'lieux de culte' archaïques dans le nord-est de la péninsule Ibérique," *Palais en Méditerranée de Mycènes aux Tarquins. Dossiers d'Archéologie 339*, 74–79.

——(2011) "*Mistophoroi* ilergetes en el siglo IV AC: el ejemplo de las tumbas de caballo de la necrópolis de La Pedrera (Vallfagona de Balaguer-Térmens, Catalunya, España)," *JbRGZM 55–2008*, 81–158.

————(forthcoming) "The Etruscans in the Iberian peninsula" in A. Naso (ed.), *Etruscology*, New York.

Graells i Fabregat, R. and Sarda Seuma, S. (forthcoming) "Respuestas materiales a estímulos ideológicos: instrumental Mediterráneo de banquete en el noroeste de la Península Ibérica (s. VII–VI a.C.)," *Meetings between Cultures in the Ancient Mediterranean. XVII International Congress of Classical Archaeology. Incontri tra culture nel mondo Mediterraneo antico*, *Roma 2008*, forthcoming.

Gran-Aymerich, J. (1973) "Un conjunto de vasos en bucchero inciso. Ensayo de formalización," *TrabPrehist* 30, 217–307.

————(1974) "Observaciones sobre la presencia etrusca en el Mediterráneo occidental," *Simposio de colonizaciones, Barcelona-Ampurias, 1971*, Barcelone, 47–52.

————(1982) *Corpus Vasorum Antiquorum. France 31. Louvre 20*, Paris.

————(1983) "Les céramiques phénico-puniques et le bucchero étrusque. Cas concrets et considérations générales," *I Congresso Internazionale Studi Fenici e Punici, Roma 1979*, Rome, 77–87.

————(1989) "Oenochoés et amphores dans l'Étrurie archaïque," *Actes Florence 1985*, 1483–1493.

————(1990) "Mainaké et les récentes découvertes en Andalousie," *XXIX Convegno di Studi sulla Magna Grecia, La Magna Grecia e il lontano Occidente, Taranto 1989*, Naples, 91–93.

————(1991) "Etruscos y materiales etruscos en la Península Ibérica: historia de un tema controvertido y sus perspectivas actuales," *Actes Barcelone 1990*, 625–632.

————(1992a) "Malaga dans le détroit de Gibraltar. Les données géo-stratégiques de l'expansion phénicienne," *Lixus. Actes du colloque de Larache 1989*, Rome, 59–69.

————(1992b) "Les témoignages des textes et la céramique étrusque dans la Rome des rois," *La Rome des premiers siècles. Table Ronde en l'honneur de M. Pallottino*, Paris, 99–109.

————(1992c) "Les matériaux étrusques hors d'Etrurie: le cas de la France et les travaux en cours à Bourges-Avaricum," *Actes Vienne 1989*, 329–359.

————(1992d) *Corpus Vasorum Antiquorum. France 34. Louvre 23*, Paris.

————(1993) "Observations générales sur l'évolution et la diffusion du bucchero," *Actes Milan 1990*, 19–41.

————(1994) "Los Etruscos y la Península Ibérica: los hallazgos de Málaga y su significación," *Homenaje J.-M. Blázquez*, Madrid, t. II, 237–248.

————(1995a) "Les importations étrusques au cœur de la Gaule. Le site princier de Bourges et les nouvelles découvertes à Lyon et Bragny-sur-Saône," *Actes Londres 1992*, 45–74.

————(1995b) "Le bucchero et les vases métalliques," *Vaisselle métallique, vaisselle céramique. Productions, usages et valeurs en Étrurie*. Colloque Nantes 1994 (*REA* 97.1–2), 1995, 45–76.

————(1995c) "Griechische Vasen und etruskische Bronzen aus Bourges in ihrem archäologischen und historischen Kontext," "Griechische Keramik aus Bourges im Loirebecken," *Catalogue Wurtzbourg 1995*, 71–74, 131–135.

————(1995d) "La Méditerranée et les sites princiers de l'Europe occidentale. Recherches en cours dans le cercle du détroit de Gibraltar et dans l'isthme gaulois," *IIIe Congr. Int. Etudes Phéniciennes et Puniques, Tunis 1991*, Tunis, vol. II, 97–109.

————(1996) "Bronzes étrusques et vases grecs à Bourges," *Bourges. Hors série Archéologia*, Dijon, 8.

————(1997) "Les premières importations méditerranéennes de Bourges," *Vix et les éphémères principautés celtiques. Les VIe-Ve s. av. J.-C. en Europe centre-occidentale, Colloque Châtillon-sur-Seine 1993*, Paris, 201–212.

————(1998) "Les premiers vases étrusques et le décor figuré dans le Midi de la Gaule et la Celtique," *Actes Ratisbonne 1994*, 217–248.

————(2000a) "La problématique des échanges à l'époque orientalisante: matières premières et produits élaborés, *Der Orient und Etrurien, Tübinguen, 1997*, Pise-Rome, 89–103.

————(2000b) "La tombe de Vix," *Les fabuleuses découvertes du XXe siècle. Dossiers d'archéologie 259*, 106–111.

——(2002a) "Les importations grecques et étrusco-italiques à Bourges," *Les âges du Fer en Nivernais, Bourbonnais et Berry oriental, XVIIe colloque AFEAF, Nevers 1993*, Glux-en-Glenne, 97–106.

——(2002b) "L'Étrurie méridionale, la Sardaigne et les navigations en Méditerranée occidentale à la fin du VIIe siècle," *Actes Sassari 1998*, 135–141.

——(2004) "Le fauve carnassier dans l'art étrusque et son influence sur le premier art celtique," *La Tarasque de Noves. Réflexions sur un motif iconographique et sa postérité. Colloque Avignon 2001*, Avignon, 15–27.

——(2006a) "La diffusion des vases étrusques en Méditerranée nord-occidentale: l'exception gauloise," *Actes Marseille-Lattes 2002*, 205–219.

——(2006b) "Les Étrusques et l'extrême Occident (VIIe-Ve siècles av. J.-C.): regards sur l'Isthme gaulois et la péninsule Ibérique," *Actes Orvieto 2005*, 253–283.

——(2006c) "Les sources méditerranéennes de l'art celtique occidental, VIe-Ve s. av. J.-C.," *Actes Clermont-Ferrand 1999*, 19–56.

——(2008a) "La presencia etrusca en Cartago y su relación con las navegaciones en el Mediterráneo occidental y el círculo del Estrecho durante los siglos VII–V" in J. M. Candau Morón, F. J. González Ponce and A. L. Chávez Reino (eds), *Libyae lustrare extrema. Estudios en honor de Jehan Desanges*, Séville, 1–32.

——(2008b) "New Light on Etruscans outside Etruria. Etruscan Inscriptions and Offerings in the Western Mediterranean," *Etruscan News* 9, 13–16.

——(2008c) "Bourges et la celtique: les échanges avec Marseille et l'Étrurie," *Les Phocéens et leur commerce vus de Lyon et d'ailleurs. Colloque Lyon, Maison l'Orient Méditerranéen, 1996, (BAParis)*, Paris, 23–50.

——(2009a) "*Gli Etruschi fuori d'Etruria*: dons et offrandes étrusques en Méditerranée occidentale et dans l'Ouest de l'Europe" in M. Gleba and H. Becker (eds), *Votives, Places and Rituals in Etruscan Religion. Studies in Honor of J. MacIntosh Turfa*, Leiden-Boston, 15–42.

——(2009b) "L'Étrurie orientalisante. À la périphérie du Proche-Orient et au centre de la Méditerranée," *Centre et périphérie. Approches nouvelles des Orientalistes. Actes 2006, Société asiatique, Collège de France*, Paris, 127–159.

——(2009c) "Le bucchero: réflexions sur la diffusion regionale et les exportations" in S. Bruni (ed.), *Etruria e Italia preromana. Studi Giovannangelo Camporeale*, Pise, 465–470.

——(2010) "Le bassin étrusque décoré de l'îlot Madeleine à Marseille" in Gantès, 218–221.

——(2012) "Aux origines de la vogue des vases à parfum et onguents étrusques: réception et transmission (Xe-VIIe s. av.J.-C.)," *Actes Rome 2009*, 93–100.

——(2013a) "Entre Méditerranée et Atlantique: les bronzes étrusques dans les relations commerciales," *Hommages Olivier Buchsenschutz (ed. Ausonius)*, Bordeaux, 429–445.

——(2013b) "Etruscans at Marseilles and Carthage: the *fondouk* evidence", *Etruscan News* 15, 5–9.

——(forthcoming a) "Les relations entre Caeré et Carthage et la diffusion d'objets étrusques jusqu'à l'Atlantique (VIIe-Ve siècles av. J.-C.," *VIIe Congrès International Études Phéniciennes et Puniques, Hammamet 2009*, Tunisia.

——(forthcoming b) "L'Étrurie méridionale, Aléria, Marseille et la Gaule," *Actes Bastia-Piombino 2011*, Florence-Pisa.

——(forthcoming c) "Le bucchero de Chiusi, une étonnante richesse et une forte spécificité," *Hommages Luigi Donati*.

——(forthcoming d) "Maisons-entrepôts d'époque archaïque en Méditerranée occidentale et les vestiges lointains d'une présence étrusque," *Urbanisme et architecture en Méditerranée antique et médiévale à travers les sources archéologiques et littéraires. Colloque Tunis, 2011*.

——(forthcoming e) "Le bucchero étrusque, entre tradition et innovation," *Hommages Maria Bonghi Jovino*.

——(forthcoming f) "Le bucchero: céramique de prestige et céramique commune, en Étrurie et en Méditerranée occidentale," *Hommages Mario A. Del Chiaro*.

————(forthcoming h) "'L'Ami étrusque' et ses traces en Méditerranée occidentale: l'hypothèse d'un fondouk archaïque à Carthage," *Hommages Dominique Briquel.*

Gran-Aymerich, J. *et al.* (1991) *Malaga, phénicienne et punique. Recherches franco-espagnoles 1981– 1988*, Paris.

Gran-Aymerich, J. and du Puytison-Lagarce, E. (1995) "Recherches sur la période orientalisante en Étrurie et dans le Midi Ibérique," *CRAI*, 569–604.

Gran-Aymerich, J. and Andérica, J.-R. (2000) "Populations autochtones et allogènes sur le littoral méditerranéen andalou: de Málaga à Vélez-Málaga et Frigiliana (VIII–VIe s. av. J.-C.)," IV Congreso Internacional Estudios fenicios y púnicos, *Cádiz 1995*, Cadix, 1811–1814.

Gran-Aymerich, J. and Gran-Aymerich, E. (2006) "Les Étrusques en Gaule et en Ibérie: du mythe à la réalité des dernières découvertes," *The Etruscans Now British Museum XXVI Classical colloquium, London, 2002 (EtrSt 9, 2002)*, Fremont, Michigan, 207–226.

Gran-Aymerich, J. and Jehasse, O. (2007) "Les îles du monde étrusque: le cas de la Corse et Alaliè," *Mediterranea 3–2006*, 141–172.

Gran-Aymerich, J. and Domínguez-Arranz, A. (eds) (2011) *La Castellina a sud di Civitavecchia, origini ed eredità. Origines protohistoriques et évolution d'un habitat étrusque*, Rome.

Gran-Aymerich, J., Bonnet, C. and Domínguez-Arranz, A. (2010) "La diffusion des parfums de Carthage à la péninsule Ibérique," *Parfums dans l'Antiquité. Dossiers d'Archéologie 337*, 52–57.

Gras, M. (1985) *Trafics tyrrhéniens archaïques*, Rome.

————(2000) "La battaglia del mare sardonio. Appunti e ricordi," *MAXH 2000*, 37–46.

————(2004) "Les Étrusques vus de la Gaule. Échanges maritimes et implantations," *DocAMerid* 27, 213–235.

Gras, M., Rouillard, P. and Teixidor, J. (1989) *L'univers phénicien*, Paris (*L'universo fenicio*, Turin, 2000).

Gsell, S. (1891) *Fouilles dans la nécropole du Vulci*, Paris.

Haffner, A. (1976) *Die westliche Hunsrück-Eifel Kultur*, Berlin.

————(1993) "Die keltischen Schnabelkannen von Basse-Yutz in Lothringen." *XIe Colloque AFEAF, Sarreguemines 1987 (AMosel 2)*, Luxembourg, 337–360.

————(2003) "Le torque. Type et fonction," Rolley (ed.) 2003, 176–188.

Hase, F.-W. von (1969) *Die Trensen der Früheisenzeit in Italien (PBF XVI.1)*, Munich.

————(1979) "Zur Interpretation villanovazeitlicher und frühetruskischer Funde in Griechenland und der Ägäis. Überlegungen zum gegenwärtigen Forschungsstand," *Kleinen Schriften aus dem Vorgeschichtlichen Seminar Marburg* V, 1979.

————(1992/1989) "Der etruskische Bucchero aus Karthago. Ein Beitrag zu den frühen Handelsbeziehungen im westlichen Mittelmeergebiet (7.-6. Jahrhundert v. Chr.)," *JRGZM* 36–1989 1992, 327–410; (in Italian, "Il bucchero etrusco a Cartagine," *Actes Milan 1990*, 187–194).

————(1992) "Etrurien und Mitteleuropa -zur Bedeutung der ersten italisch-etruskischen Funde der späten Urnenfelder- und frühen Hallstattzeit in Zentraleuropa," *Actes Vienne 1989*, 187– 196, 235–266.

————(1997) "Présences étrusques et italiques dans les sanctuaires grecs (VIIIe–VIIe siècle av. J.-C.)," *Les Étrusques, les plus religieux des hommes. Colloque École du Louvre 1992*, Paris, 293–323.

————(1998) "Einige Überlegungen zum Fernhandel und Kulturtransfer in der jüngeren Hallstattzeit," *Actes Ratisbonne 1994*, 285–319.

————(2000) "Zur Giessform der figürlichen Henkelattasche von der Heuneburg," *Importe und mediterranee Einflüsse auf der Heuneburg (Heuneburgstudien XI)*, Mayence, 177–195.

————(2004) "Karthager und Etrusker in archaischer Zeit," *Hannibal ad portas. Macht und Reichtum Karthagos. Austellung Karlsruhe 2004–2005*, Stuttgart, 70–80.

Haumesser, L. (2007) "Étrusques, Puniques et Grecs: la circulation des sarcophages en marbre peints," *Etruschi, Greci, Fenici e Cartaginesi nel Mediterraneo centrale (Annali "C. Faina" 14)*, Rome, 271–291.

Haynes, S. (1985) *Etruscan Bronzes*, London.

Hermary, A., Hesnard, A. and Tréziny, H. (eds) (1999) *Marseille Grecque. La cité phocéenne (600–49 av. J.-C.)*, Paris.

Herrmann, H.-V. (1984) "Altitalisches und Etruskisches in Olimpia," *AnnScArchAtene* 61 (1983), 271–279.

Herubel, F. and Gailledrat, E. (2006) "Répartition et chronologie du mobilier étrusque en Languedoc occidental et en Rousillon (VIe-IVe s. av. J.-C.)," *Actes Marseille-Lattes 2002*, 159–174.

Heurgon, J. (1965a) "La coupe d'Aulus Vibenna," *Mélanges J. Carcopino*, Paris, 515–522.

——(1965b) "Les inscriptions de Pyrgi et l'alliance étrusco-punique autour de 500 av. J.-C.," *CRAI*, 89–105.

——(1969a) "Inscriptions étrusques de Tunisie," *CRAI*, 526–551.

——(1969b) "Les Dardaniens en Afrique," *REL* 47, 284–293.

——(1986) *Scripta varia*, Bruxelles.

——(1993) *Rome et la Méditerranée occidentale jusqu'aux guerres puniques*, Paris, (first ed. 1969).

Isler, H. P. (1967) "Etruskischer Bucchero aus dem Heraion von Samos," *MdI* 82, 77–88.

Izquierdo, P. and Solias, J. M. (1991) "Dos cascos de bronce de tipología etrusca procedents d'un derelicte romà trobat a l'ancoratge de Les Sorres (Gavà, Baix Llobregat)," *Actes Barcelone 1990*, 601–614.

Jacobsthal, P. and Langsdorff, A. (1929) *Die Bronzeschnabelkannen. Ein Beitrag zur Geschichte des vorrömischen Imports nördlich der Alpen*, Berlin.

Janin, T. (2006) "Systèmes chronologiques et groupes culturels dans le Midi de la France de la fin de l'âge du Bronze à la fondation de Marseille: communautés indigènes et premieres importations," *Actes Marseille-Lattes 2002*, 93–102.

Jannot, J. R. (1977) "La production d'étain de la Péninsule armoricaine à l'époque antique," *Les Pays de l'Ouest. 97 Congrès National Sociétés savantes Nantes 1972*, vol. 1, 19–22.

——(1990) "A propos d'une fibule étrusque. La fibule d'or de Saint-Aignan (Loire-Atlantique)," Adam, R. *et al.*, 1990, 85–87.

——(1995a) "Les navires étrusques, instruments d'une thalassocratie?," *CRAI*, 743–778.

——(1995b) "Peut-on parler de commerce étrusque en Gaule du nord-ouest?," *Actes Londres 1992*, 75–91.

——(2006) "L'axe ligérien, voie de contacts entre Méditerranée et Gaule de l'Ouest?," *Actes Clermont-Ferrand 1999*, 77–83.

Jantzen, U. (1955) *Griechische Greifenkessel*, Berlin.

Jiménez Ávila, J. (2002) *La toréutica orientalizante en la Península Ibérica*, Madrid.

——(2004) "Orfebrería y toréutica orientalizante en la Península Ibérica. Comportamientos diferenciales" in A. Perea, I. Montero and O. García-Vuelta (eds), *Tecnología del oro antiguo*. Madrid, 209–215.

Jolivet, V. (1980) "Exportations étrusques tardives (IVe-IIIe siècles) en Méditerranée occidentale," *MEFRA* 92, 681–724.

Jud, P. (1996) "Eine etruskische Satyr-Attasche aus Pratteln," *Trésors Celtes et Gaulois. Le Rhin supérieur entre 800 et 50 av. J.-C. Catalogue d'exposition*, Colmar, 173–177.

Jung, M. (2008) "Palmettengesichter auf Attaschen etruskischer Kannen als mögliche Vorbilder latènezeitlicher Gesichtsdarstellungen?," *AKorrBl* 38.2, 33–39.

Jurgeit, F. (1999) *Die etruskischen und italischen Bronzen sowie Gegenstände aus Eisen, Blei und Leder im Badischen Landesmuseum Karlsruhe*, Pise-Rome.

Kilian, K. (1973) "Zum italischen und griechischen Fibelhandwerk des 8. und 7. Jahrhunderts," *HambBeitrA* III.1, 1973, 1–39.

——(1977) "Zwei italische Kamenhelme aus Griechenland," *BCH, Suppl. VI, Etudes delphiques*, 429–442.

Kimmig, W. (1975) "Die Heuneburg an der oberen Donau," *Ausgrabungen in Deutschland 1950–1975. Monographien des Römisch-Germanischen Zentralmuseums* 1, 192–211.

——(1983) "Die griechische Kolonisation im westlichen Mittelmeergebiet und ihre Wirkung auf die Landschaften des westlichen Mitteleuropa," *JbRGZM* 30, 5–79.

——(1984) "Zu einem getriebenen Bronzeblech aus dem Musée Dobrée in Nantes (Frankreich)," *AKorrBlat* 14, 293–298.

——(1988) *Kleinaspergle. Studien zu einem Fürstengrabhügel der frühen Latènezeit bei Stuttgart*, Stuttgart.

——(1990) "Zu einem etruskischen Beckengriff aus Borsdorf in Oberhessen," *AKorrBlat* 20, 75–85.

——(1991) "Edelmetallschalen der späten Hallstatt- und frühen Latènezeit," *AKorrBlat* 21, 241–253.

——(1999) "Coupes en métal précieux du Hallstatt final et du début de La Tène," *Archéologie des Celtes. Hommages R. Joffroy*, Montagnac, 195–206.

——(ed.) (2000) *Importe und mediterrane Einflüsse auf der Heuneburg* (Heuneburg Studien XI), Mayence.

Kimmig, W. and Vacano, O. W. von (1973) "Zu einem Gussform-Fragment einer etruskischen Bronzekanne von der Heuneburg a.d. oberen Donau," *Germania* 51, 72–85.

Kochavi, M. (1998) "The Eleventh Century BC Tripartite Pillar Building at Tel Hadar" in S. Gitin, A. Mazar and E. Stern (eds), *Mediterranean Peoples in Transition. Studies T. Dothan*, Jérusalem, 468–478.

Køllund, M. (1998) "Sardinian Pottery from Carthage" in M. S. Balmuth and R. Tykot (eds), *Sardinian Stratigraphy and Mediterranean Chronology*, Oxford, 355–358.

Krausse, D. (2003) "La phiale," Rolley (ed.) 2003, 217–230.

Krings, V. (1998) *Carthage et les Grecs (c. 580–480 av. J.-C.)*, Leyde.

——(2000) "Quelques considérations sur l'empire de Carthage". A propos de Malchus," *IV Congreso Internacional Estudios fenicios y púnicos, Cádiz 1995*, Cadix, 161–172.

Kruta, V. (1992) "Art étrusque et art celtique," *Catalogue Paris 1992a*, 206–213.

Lancel, S. (ed.) (1982) *Byrsa II. Mission archéologique francaise à Carthage. Rapports préliminaires des fouilles 1977–1978 (niveaux et vestiges puniques)*, Paris-Rome.

——(1995) "Carthage et les échanges culturels en Méditerranée," *Catalogue Paris 1995*, 24–48.

Lebeaupin, D. (2010) "Lattes et les Étrusques," *Lattes, une cité antique du sud de la Gaule. L'Archéo-Thema* 11, 20–25.

Lepore, E. (1993) "L'emporion: alcuni problemi storiografici e metodologici," *Actes Ravello 1987*, 47–55.

Long, L., Gantès, L.-F. and Drap, P. (2002) "Premiers résultats archéologiques sur l'épave Grand Ribaud F (Giens, Var)," *CahASubaqu* 104, 17–52.

Llobregat, E. (1982) "Iberia y Etruria: notas para una revisión de las relaciones," *Lucentum* 1, 71–91.

——(1991) "Vias paralelas: templos y tumbas en Etruria y en Iberia," *Actes Barcelone 1990*, 309–336.

——(1998) "La Illeta dels Banyets (El Campello, Camp d'Alacant Fou un Emporion?," *Homenatge Miquel Tarradell*, Barcelone, 3–127.

Lüscher, G. (1998) "Die Importkeramik" in B. Dietrich-Weibel, G. Lüscher and T. Kilka (eds), *Posieux/Châtillon-sur-Glâne. Keramik/Céramiques (6.-5. Jh.v.Ch./VIe-Ve siècles av.J.-C.)*, Fribourg, 119–210.

MacIntosh, J. (see also Turfa) (1974) "Etruscan Bucchero Pottery Imports in Corinth," *Hesperia* 43: 34–44.

Mackensen, M. A. (1999) "Vorrömische Funde" in F. Rakob (ed.), *Karthago III. Die deutschen Ausgrabungen in Karthago*, Mayence, 530–544.

Maffre, J.-J. and Chazalon, L. (forthcoming) "Trouvailles anciennes et trouvailles récentes de céramique attique en Bourgogne : Vix et le Mont Lassois," *BantFr* 2012.

Maggiani, A. (2006) "Dinamiche del commercio arcaico: le *tesserae hospitales*," *Actes Orvieto 2005*, 317–350.

——(2007) *REE, StEtr* 71 (2005), 82.

Marchand, F. (2006) "La céramique étrusque des chantiers Jules-Verne et Villeneuve-Bargemon de Marseille," *Actes Marseille-Lattes 2002*, 281–304.

McKee, A. (1984) "Rescue records-Giglio and Giannutri," *IntJNautA* 13, 83–84.

——(1985) *Tarquin's ship*, London.

MAXH (2000) *MAXH. La battaglia del Mare Sardonio. Atti Oristano 1998*, P. Bernardini, P. G. Spanu and R. Zucca (eds), Cagliari-Oristano.

Mangas, J. and Plácido, D. (eds) (1998) *La Península Ibérica en los autores griegos: de Homero a Platón, T.H.A. IIA*, Madrid (344–345 pottery tablet from Ampurias).

Mansel, K. (1998) "Ein hellenistisch-etruskischer Spiegel vom Morro de Mezquitilla (Algarrobo, Malaga)," *MM* 39, 143–150.

——(2007) "Die Metallfunde" in H. G. Niemeyer, R. F. Docter and K. Schmidt (eds), *Karthago. Die Ergebnisse der Hamburger Grabung unter dem Decumanus Maximus. II*, Mayence, 796–813.

——(2011) "Cartago y la Península Ibérica en los siglos VIII–VI a.C." in M. Alvarez Martí-Aguilar (ed.), *Fenicios en Tartesos. Nuevas perspectivas*, (BAR Int. Ser. 2245), Oxford, 69–85.

Mansuelli, G. A. (1993) "Fonti greche e latine sulla navigazione etrusca," *Actes Ravello 1987*, 11–24.

Marchetti Lungarotti, M. G. and Torelli, M. (eds) (2006) *Vino. Tra mito e cultura*, Milan.

Martelli, M. (1985a) "I luoghi e i prodotti dello scambio," "Tessera hospitalis," *Catalogue Florence 1985*, 175–224, 229–233.

——(1985b) "Gli avori etruschi tardo arcaici: botteghe e aree di diffusione," *Actes Rome 1983*, 207–248.

——(1988) "La stipe votiva dell'Athenaion di Jalysos: un primo bilancio" in S. Dietz and I. Papachristodoulou (ed.), *Archaeology in the Dodecanese*, Copenhagen.

Martín Bravo, A. M. (1998) "Evidencias del comercio tartésico junto a puertos y vados de la cuenca del Tajo," *AEspA* 71, 37–52.

Marzoli, D. (2005) *Die Besiedlungs- und Landschaftsgeschichte im Empordà von der Endbronzezeit bis zum Beginn der Romanisierung*, Mayence.

Mayet, F. and Tavares da Silva, C. (2001) "Abul e a arquitectura Orientalizante na costa portuguesa," in D. Ruiz Mata and S. Celestino Pérez (eds), *Arquitectura oriental y orientalizante en la Peninsula ibérica*, Madrid, 249–260.

Mederos Martín, A. and Ruíz Cabrero, L. A. (2004) "El pecio fenicio del Bajo de la Campana (Murcia, España) y el comercio del marfil norteafricano," *Zephyrus* 57, 263–281.

Mele, A. (1993) "Il Tirreno tra commercio eroico ed emporia classica," *Actes Ravello 1987*, 57–68.

Milcent, P.-Y. (2006a) "Les importations italiques au nord-ouest du Midi gaulois (milieu du Xe-debut du IVe s. av. J.-C.): inventaire et perspectives d'interprétation," *Actes Marseille-Lattes 2002*, 319–356.

——(2006b) "Examen critique des importations méditerranéennes en Gaule centrale et occidentale: les attributions douteuses, erronées ou falsifiées," *Actes Clermont-Ferrand 1999*, 117–133.

——(2009) "A l'extrémité occidentale du réseau d'échanges: Avaricum," *Catalogue Saint-Germain 2009*, 138–142.

Morel, J.-P. (1980) "Les vases à vernis noir et à figures rouges d'Afrique avant la deuxième guerre punique et le problème des exportations de Grande Grèce," *AntAfr* 15, 29–71

——(1981) "Le commerce étrusque en France, en Espagne et en Afrique," *L'Etruria Mineraria. XII Convegno Studi etruschi e italici. Firenze-Populonia-Piombino 1979*, Florence, 463–508.

——(1990a) "Nouvelles donneés sur le commerce de Carthage punique entre le VIIe et le IIe siècle avant J.C.," *Carthage et son territoire dans l'antiquité. IV Colloque international (Strasbourg, 1988)*, Paris, 67–100.

——(1990b) "Les amphores massaliètes en Afrique du Nord et particulièrement à Carthage" in M. Bats (ed.), *Les amphores de Marseille grecque. Chronologie et diffusion (VIe-Ier s. av. J.-C.). Table-ronde Lattes 1989*, Lattes, Aix-en-Provence, 269–272.

——(1994) "Une oenochoé en bronze à inscription grecque de Carthage," *Eukrata. Mélanges C. Vatin*, M.-Cl. Amouretti and P. Villard (eds), Aix-en-Provence, 179–188.

——(2006) "Les Étrusques en Méditerranée nord-occidentalae: résultats et tendances des recherches récentes," *Actes Marseille-Lattes 2002*, 23–46.

Mötsch, A. (2008) "Keramische Adaptionen mediterraner Bronzekannen auf dem mont Lassois," *AKorrBl* 38.2, 201–210.

Naso, A. (2000a) "Etruscan and Italic Artefacts from the Agean" in D. Ridgway, F. R. Serra Ridgway, M. Pearce, E. Herring, R. D. Whitehouse and J. B. Wilkins (eds), *Ancient Italy in its Mediterranean Setting. Studies Ellen Macnamara*, London, 193–208.

——(2000b) "Etruskische und italische Weihungen in der Ägais: Altbekannte und die neue Funde" in P. Krinzinger (ed.), *Die Ägais und das westliche Mittelmeer. Beziehungen und Wechselwirkungen 8 bis 5. Jh. v.Chr. Symposions Wien 1999*, Vienne, 157–163.

——(2000c) "Materiali etruschi e italici nell'Oriente mediterraneo," *Magna Grecia e Oriente mediterraneo prima dell'età ellenistica. XXXIX Convegno Taranto 1999*, Naples, 185–205.

——(2006a) "Etruschi (e Italici) nei santuari greci," *Stranieri e non cittadini nei santuari greci, convegno Udine 2003*, Florence, 325–358.

——(2006b) "Anathemata etruschi nel Mediterraneo orientale," *Actes Orvieto 2005*, 351–416. Rome.

——(2006c) "Etruscan and Italic Finds in North Africa, 7th–2nd century BC" in A. Villing and U. Schlotzhauer (eds), *Naukratis. Greek Diversity in Egypt. Studies on East Greek Pottery and Exchange in the Eastern Mediterranean*, Londres, 187–198.

——(2009a) "Un thymiaterion etrusco a Didima?" in S. Bruni (ed.), *Etruria e Italia preromana. Studi Giovannangelo Camporeale*, Pise-Rome, 639–646.

——(2009b) "Funde aus Milet XXII. Preliminary Report. Etruscan bucchero from Miletos," *AA*, 135–150.

——(2011) "Manufatti etruschi e italici nell'Africa settentrionale (IX–II SEC. A.C.)," *Corollari. Scritti in omaggio all'opera di Giovanni Colonna*, Pise-Rome, 75–83.

Negueruela, I., Pinedo, J., Gomez, M. *et al.* (2000) "Descubrimiento de dos barcos fenicios en Mazarrón (Murcia)," *IV Congreso Internacional Estudios fenicios y punicos. Cádiz 1995*, Cadix, 1671–1684.

Niemeyer, H. G. (1990) "The Phoenicians in the Mediterranean. A Non-Greek Model for Expansion and Settlement in Antiquity" in J. Descoeudres (ed.), *First Australian Congress Class. Archaeology held in honour A.D. Trendall, Sydney 1989*, Oxford, 469–489.

——(1993) "Trade Before the Flag? On the Principles of Phoenician Expansion in the Mediterranean," *Biblical Archaeology Today. Second International Congress Biblical Archaeology. Jerusalem 1990*, Jérusalem.

——(1995) "Phoenician Toscanos as a Settlement Model? Its Urbanistic Character in the Context of Phoenician Expansion and Iberian Acculturation," *Social Complexity and the Development of Towns in Iberia (Proceedings British Academy 86)*, 67–88.

——(1999) "Die frühe phönizische Expansion im Mittelmeer. Neue Beiträge zu ihrer Beschreibungen und ihren Ursachen," *Saeculum* 50, II, 153–175.

——(2005) "Phoenicians vs. Greeks. Achievements and polemics in archaeological research since the discovery of Al Mina" in A. Spano Giammellaro (ed.), *V Congresso Int. Studi fenici punici Marsala-Palermo 2000*, Palermo, vol. I, 11–17.

Niemeyer, H. G., Briese, C. and Bahnemann, R. (1988) "Die Untersuchungen auf dem Cerro del Peñon," *Forschungen zur Archäologie und Geologie im Raum von Torre del Mar 1983/84*, Mayence.

Niemeyer, H. G., Docter, R. *et al.* (1993) "Die Grabung unter dem Decumanus Maximus von Karthago. Vorbericht über die Kampagnen 1986–1991," *RM* 100, 201–244.

Pallottino, M. (1963) "Les relations entre les Étrusques et Carthage du VIIe au IIIe siècle avant J.-C.," *CahTun* XI, 1963, 23–29 (Pallotino 1979, vol. I, 371–376).

——(1979) *Saggi di antichità*, vol. I–III, Rome.

Pallottino, M. and Moscati, S. (1966) "Rapporti tra Greci, Fenici, Etruschi ed altre popolazione italiche alla luce delle nuove scoperte," *Problemi attuali di scienza e di cultura. Accad. Naz. dei Lincei Quaderni* no 87), Rome, 1966, p.11–16 (Pallottino 1979, vol. I, 391–397).

Perea, A. (1986) "La orfebreria púnica de Cádiz," *Los Fenicios en la Península Ibérica*, Barcelona, 295–322.

Perrin, F. (2000) "L'origine de la mode du corail méditerranéen (*Corallium rubrum L.*) chez les peuples celtes: essai d'interprétation," *Actes Ravello 1996*, 193–203.

——(2004) "Le vin et le fromage," "La découverte du vin par les Celtes," *Le vin nectar des Dieux. Génie des Hommes. Exposition Lyon*, 102–103, 126–135.

Perrin, F. and Bellon, C. (1992) "Mobilier d'origine et de filiation méditerranéennes dans la moyenne vallée du Rhône, entre Alpes et Massif Central," *Marseille grecque et la Gaule, Ve Congrès archéologique de Gaule méridionale. Marseille 1990*, Lattes-Aix, 419–430.

——(1997) "L'occupation du premier âge du Fer des bords de Saône à Lyon (Rhône)" in P. Brun and B. Chaume (ed.), *Vix et les éphémères principautés celtiques, Actes Châtillon-sur-Seine 1993*, Paris, 157–164.

Picard, C. (1959) "Les oenochoés en bronze de Carthage," *RA*, 35–164.

Pittau, M. (1996) "Gli Etruschi e Cartagine: i documenti epigrafici," *Africa Romana* XI, 1657–1674.

Pomey, P. (2006) "Les navires étrusques: mythe ou réalité?," *Actes Marseille-Lattes 2002*, 423–434.

Provost, M. (1983) "Une anse de chaudron étrusque à Saint-Gemmes-sur-Loire (Maine-et-Loire)," *Gallia*, 209–215 (and in "Les découvertes du confluent Maine-Loire," Adam, R. *et al.* vol. III, 1990, 93–94).

Pruvot, G. (1971) *Epave antique étrusco-punique (ou celto-ligure?) au cap d'Antibes, VIe s. av. J.-C.*, Antibes.

Pulak, C. (2001) "The Cargo of the Uluburun Ship and Evidence for Trade with the Aegean and Beyond" in L. Bonfante and V. Karageorghis (eds), *Italy and Cyprus in Antiquity: 1500–450 BC*, Nicosia, 13–60.

Py, M. (1993) *Les Gaulois du Midi. De la fin de l'Age du Bronze à la conquête romaine*, Paris.

——(2003) *Les Celtes du Midi*, Paris.

——(2009) *Lattara (Lattes, Hérault), comptoir gaulois méditerranéen entre Étrusques, Grecs et Romains*, Paris.

Py, M. and Garcia, D. (1993) "Bilan des recherches archéologiques sur la ville portuaire de Lattara (Lattes, Hérault)," *Gallia*, 1–93.

Py M. and Dietler, M. (2003) "Une statue de guerrier découverte à Lattes (Hérault)," *DocAMérid* 26, 235–249.

Py, M., Lebeaupin, D., Sejalon, P. and Roure, R. (2006) "Les Étrusques et Lattara: nouvelles données," *Actes Marseille-Lattes 2002*, 583–608.

Raposso, B. and Ruggierro, M. G. (1995) "Ambra, osso e pasta vitrea nell'Etruria protovillanoviana," *Preistoria e protoistoria in Etruria. Secondo Incontro di Studi, Farnese 1993*, Milan, 247–251.

Redissi, T. (1997) "Les objets de toilette égyptiens et égyptisants du mobilier funéraire de Carthage," *RM* 104, 359–369.

Reinecke, P. (1933) "Zu den Bronzeschnabelkannen aux Carthago," *Germania* 17, 52–73.

Rendini, P. (1993) "Isola del Giglio: acquisizioni sul commercio etrusco," *Actes Ravello 1987*, 191–201.

Ribera Lacomba, A. and Fernández Izquierdo, F. (1989) "Ánforas etruscas en el Pais Valenciano," *Actes Florence 1985*, vol . II, 1115–1124.

Ridgway, D. (1992) *The First Western Greeks*, Cambridge.

Riva, C. (2010) "Trading settlements and the materiality of wine consumption in the North Tyrrhenian Sea region" in P. van Dommelen and A. Bernard Knapp (eds), *Material Connections in the Ancient Mediterranean. Mobility, Materiality and Mediterranean Identities*, London, 210–232.

Robin, K. and Soyer, C. (2003) "Fragment d'une anse de bassin étrusque découvert à Barzan (Charente-Maritime)," *Aquitania* 19, 285–290.

Rolley, C. (1962) "Trouvailles méditerranéennes en Basse-Bourgogne," *BCH* 86, 476–493.

——(1987) "Les bronzes grecs: recherches récentes," *RA*, 335–360.

——(ed.) (2003) *La tombe princière de Vix*, Paris.

——(2005) "Les bronzes grecs et romains: recherches récentes," *RA*, 2005/2, 333–358.

——(2006) "Les routes de l'étain en Méditerranée et ailleurs," *Les Civilisés et les Barbares du Ve au IIe siècle avant J.-C.: Celtes et Gaulois. Table ronde Budapest 2005*, Glux-en-Glenne, 185–192.

Rondi-Costanzo, C. (1997) "Corail de Béziers, du Midi de la Gaule et de Méditerranée entre le VIIe et le IIIe s. av. J.-C." in D. Ugolini (ed.), *Languedoc occidental protohistorique. Fouilles récentes, VIe-IVe s. av. J. C., Aix en Provence*, 197–239.

Rondi-Costanzo, C. and Ugolini, D. (2000) "Le corail dans le bassin nord-occidental de la Méditerranée entre le VIe et le IIe s. av. J.-C.," *Actes Ravello 1996*, 177–191.

Rothé, M.-P. and Tréziny, H. (eds) (2005) *Carte archéologique de la Gaule 13/3 – Marseille et ses alentours*, Paris.

Rupprechtsberger, E. M. (1982) "Ein etruskisches buccherofragment aus Lauriacum," *Jahrbuch des Oberösterreichischen Musealvereines* 127, 25–28.

Sankot, P. (2006) "Les tombes à épée du Ve siècle avant J.-C. en Bohême," "Nouvelles données sur la production artisanale des ateliers du début de la période laténienne," *Les celtes en Bohême, en Moravie et dans le nord de la Gaule. Les Dossiers de l'Archéologie* 313, 10–15, 16–21.

Sanmartí, E. (1993) "Ampurias," *Historia 16. Cuadernos del Arte Español* 93, 3–31.

Santrot, J. (2001) "La dame de Nivillac ou le voyage d'un bronze archaïque méditerranéen jusqu'aux rivages de la Vilaine," *Hommages J. L'Helgouac'h et J. Briard*, Rennes, 295–306.

Santrot, J. and Santrot, M.-H. (forthcoming) "Une olpè étrusque en bronze trouvée près de Redon (Ille-et-Vilaine)?," *Hommages J.-R. Jannot*.

Sassatelli, G. (2011) "I rapporti tra Mediterraneo ed Europa e il ruolo degli Etruschi," *Catalogue Trente 2011*, 255–267.

Scardigli, B. (1991) *I trattati romano-cartaginesi*, Pisa.

Schönfelder, M. (2001) "Die etruskischen Bronzebecken aus dem Samsbacher Forts, Lkr. Schwandorf," *RGZM* 48–1, 309–335.

Schweitzer, J. (1996) "L'olpé étrusque de Kappelen," *Trésors Celtes et Gaulois. Le Rhin supérieur entre 800 et 50 avant J.-C., catalogue d'exposition*, Colmar, 167–171.

Shefton, B. B. (1979) *Die "Rhodischen" Bronzekannen. Marburger Studien zur vor-und Frühgeschichte* 2, Mayence.

——(1995) "Leaven in the dough: Greek and Etruscan imports north of the Alps-The Classical period," *Actes Londres 1992*, 9–44.

——(2000) "The material in its northern setting" in Kimmig (ed.) 2000, 27–41.

——(2009) "Oinochoai and other Etruscan, Italic and Greek Vessels in Bronze from Trestina" in F. Lo Schiavo and A. Romualdi (eds), *I Complessi Archeologici di Trestina e di Fabbrecce nel Museo Archeologico di Firenze*, Rome, 107–141.

Simon, K. (1999) "Ein buccero-Fragment vom Alten Gleisberg bei Bürgel (Thüringen)," *ArbFBerSächs* 41, 61–96.

Sourisseau, J. C. (2002) "Les importations étrusques à Marseille: de Gaston Vasseur aux grandes interventions d'archéologie préventive : une découverte progressive, des problématiques renouvelées," *Catalogue Marseille 2002*, 88–95.

——(2004) "Les amphores ibériques et phénico-puniques en Provence et dans la basse vallée du Rhône (VIe-Ve s. av. J.-C.)," *DocAMerid* 27, 319–346.

Strøm, I. (2012) "A Fragment of an Early Etruscan Bronze Throne in Olympia?" *PoDIA* 3: 67–95.

Szilágyi, J. G. (1998) *Ceramica etrusco-corinzia figurata. Parte II. 590/580–550 a.C.*, Florence.

Sznycer, M. (1969) "La littérature punique," *Carthage. Sa naissance, sa grandeur (Archéologie vivante* I.2, déc. 1968–févr. 1969), Paris, 141–148.

Taffanel, J. and Taffanel, O. (1970) "Trois bronzes de type étrusque à Mailhac (Aude)," *RANarb* III, 21–31.

Tekki, A. (2009) *Recherches sur la métallurgie punique, notamment les objets en alliages à base de cuivre à Carthage*, Doctoral thesis, University Aix-Marseille.

Thuillier, J.-P. (1985) "Nouvelles découvertes de bucchero à Carthage," *Actes Rome 1983*, 155–163.

Torelli, M. (1981) "Colonizzazioni etrusche e latine di epoca arcaica," *Gli Etruschi e Roma, Atti incontro di studio in onore di M.Pallottino, Roma 1979*, Rome.

———(1986) "Dialogue sur le trépied étrusque," *DialHistAnc* 12, 120–121.

———(1997) "Ibérie et Étrurie, étude comparative de deux régions périphériques du monde classique," *Les Ibères. Dossiers d'Archéologie* 228, 28–31.

———(2004) "La bataille pour les routes maritimes: de 1000 à 300 av. J.-C." in David Abulafia (ed.), *Méditerranée, berceau de l'histoire (Mediterranean in History, London, 2003)*, Paris, 99–126.

Torres-Ortiz, M. (2002) *Tartessos*, Madrid.

———(forthcoming) "El Período Orientalizante: una perspectiva postcolonial" in C. Gómez Wagner, P. Moret, M. Torres Ortiz (eds), *Tarsis-Tartessos. Mito, historia, arqueología. V Coloquio Centro Estudios Fenicios y Púnicos, Madrid 2007*, Madrid.

Toti, O. (1996) "L'allume nel processo economico dei Monti della Tolfa nel periodo delle testimonianze micenee," *Secondo congresso internazionale Micenologia, Roma-Napoli 1991*, Rome, 911–921.

Trias, G. (1999) "Etrusco-corinthian Ware," F. Rakob (ed.), *Karthago III. Die deutschen Ausgrabungen in Karthago*, Mayence, 264–266.

Turfa, J. (vid. MacIntosh) (1974) *Etruscan-Punic Relations*. (Diss. Bryn Mawr College), Michigan: University Microfilms.

———(1977) "Evidence for Etruscan-Punic Relations," *AJA* 81, 368–374.

———(1986) "International Contacts: Commerce, Trade and Foreign Affairs" in L. Bonfante (ed.), *Etruscan Life and Afterlife. A Handbook of Etruscan Studies*, Detroit, 66–91.

———(2001) "The Etruscans and the Phoenicians of Cyprus: 8th–6th centuries B.C.," in L. Bonfante and V. Karageorghis (eds), *Italy and Cyprus in Antiquity: 1500–450 BC*, Nicosia, 271–290.

———(2006) "Votive Offerings in Etruscan Religion" in N. T. de Grummond and E. Simon (eds), *The Religion of the Etruscans, Proceedings of Sixth Langford Conference, Florida State University 1999*, Austin, 90–115.

Turfa, J. M. and Steinmayer, A. G. Jr. (1999) "The Earliest Foresail, on Another Etruscan Vase," *IJNA* 28.3, 292–296.

———(2001) "Sewn Hulls and Self-Defense," *IJNA* 30.1, 122–127.

Ugolini, D. (2010) "Présences étrangères méditerranéennes sur la côte du Languedoc-Roussillon durant l'âge du Fer: de la fréquentation commerciale aux implantations durables," *Pallas* 84, 83–110.

Ugolini, D. and Olive, C. (2006) "De l'arrivée à la consommation: l'impact des trafics et des produits étrusques en Languedoc occidental," *Actes Marseille-Lattes 2002*, 555–582.

———(2012) *Carte archéologique de la Gaule 34/4, Béziers Paris*, 2012.

Vegas, M. (1997) "Der Keramikimport in Karthago während der archaischen Zeit," *RM* 104, 351–358.

Velde, B. (2006) "Les inclusions minérales des céramiques étrusques d'époque archaïque. Une étude comparative dans le Midi (Marseille, Saint-Blaise) et en Étrurie méridionale (Caere-Pyrgi, Tarquinia, La Castellina près Civitavecchia)," *Actes Marseille-Lattes 2002*, 241–248.

Velde, B., Trojsi, D., Guidi, G.F., Gran-Aymerich, J., Delpino, F. and Bellelli, V. (2002) "Ceramiche antique. L'analisi delle argile e le ricerche CNRS-CNR," *Actes Marseille-Lattes 2002*, Poster.

Vercoutter, J. (1945) *Les objets égyptiens et égyptisants du mobilier funéraire carthaginois*, Paris.

Verger, S. (2003) "Des objets gaulois dans les sanctuaires archaïques de Grèce, de Sicile et d'Italie," *CRAI*, 525–573.

———(2006) "La grande tombe de Hochdorf, mise en scène funéraire d'un *cursus honorum* tribal hors pair," *Siris* 7, 5–44.

———(2007) "Les Etrusques, l'Italie du Nord et l'Europe transalpine (XIe-Ve s. av. J.-C.)," *Les Etrusques dernières découvertes 1992/2007, Dossiers d'Archéologie* 322, 94–101.

———(2010) "Résidences aristocratiques et espaces publics en Italie du Nord et en Allemagne du Sud," *Palais en Méditerranée de Mycènes aux Tarquins. Dossiers d'Archéologie* 339, 66–73.

———(2013) "Some observations regarding Greaves in Tomb 90 of the Casabianda Necropoleis at Aléria (Corsica)", *Etruscan News* 15, 20.

———(forthcoming) "Une paire de cnémides archaïques de la nécropole d'Aléria," *Actes Bastia-Piombino 2011*.

Vigie, D. (2011) "La Provence celto-ligure. Les collections du musée d'Archéologie méditerranéenne," *Archéologia* 484, 26–37.

Vives-Ferrandiz Sánchez, J. (2006) "Negociando encuentros. Situaciones coloniales e intercambios en la costa oriental de la península Ibérica (ss. VIII–VI a.C.)," *Cuad Arqueol Mediterranea* 12–2005, Barcelona, 33–52.

———(2007a) "A propósito de un *infundibulum* etrusco hallado en aguas de la bahía de Xabia (Alacant)," *MM* 48, 33–43.

———(2007b. "La vida social de la vajilla etrusca en el este de la *Península* Ibérica. Notas para un debate", *El valor social i comercial de la vaixella metàl-lica en el Mediterrani centre-occidental durant la protohistoria*, R. Graells (ed.), *Revista d'Arqueologia de Ponent* 16–17, 2006–2007, 318–324.

Vorlauf, D. (1997) *Die etruskischen Bronzeschnabelkannen. Eine Untersuchung anhand der technologisch-typologischen Methode (Internazionale Archäologie* 11), Espelkamp.

Wagner, C. G. (2011) "Fenicios en Tartessos: ¿Interacción o colonialismo?" in M. Alvarez Martí-Aguilar (ed.) *Fenicios en Tartesos. Nuevas perspectivas, (BAR Int. Sers.* 2245), Oxford, 119–128.

Wells, P. (1980) *Culture Contact and Culture Change. Early Iron Age Central Europe and the Mediterranean World*, Cambridge.

Wikander, O. (2008) "The religio-social message of the gold tablets from Pyrgi," *Opuscula Athens and Rome* 1, 79–84.

Williams, C. K. (1974) "Excavation at Corinth, 1973," *Hesperia* 43, 14–24.

CHAPTER TWENTY

MOTHERS AND CHILDREN

————— •◆• —————

Larissa Bonfante

INTRODUCTION

Some of the most powerful human images and symbols are those related to male and female, sex and marriage, and the nursing mother. It is in just these areas that Etruscan life and ideals differed most radically from those of the Greeks and Romans.

In contrast to the sources available for the history and habits of Greece and Rome, whose rich tradition of historical and literary texts can tell us what these classical people said and thought about the subjects of gender, families, women and children, the evidence available for Etruscan customs is archaeological and visual. Unfortunately, no literary texts by the Etruscans have come down to us – no epic, drama or lyric poetry. We only have half a dozen religious inscriptions – dedications, contracts, liturgies, religious calendars – and some 9,000 very brief epitaphs (see Chapter 22). There is, however, a great deal of art and material culture from which we can learn about Etruscan daily life, as Jacques Heurgon showed in his 1964 book.[1] This chapter will focus on what we know of the situation of women and children in the world of the Etruscans and how it differs from the reality and the ideals of the classical Greek world with which we are so much more familiar.

Their art and material culture illustrate Etruscan customs, beliefs and ideals, but these must be translated – just as Greek and Latin texts must be translated – in order for us to properly understand them. Just as the Etruscans used the Greek alphabet to write in their peculiar language, Etruscan artists and craftsmen used the vocabulary of Classical Greek art to express their particular rituals, customs and beliefs, and to represent the world around them – a world in which the status of women was very different from other classical societies.

ETRUSCAN WOMEN

There is not much about the Etruscans in Greek and Latin literature. The longest single literary passage, however, an account by the fourth-century historian Theopompus, quoted in Athenaeus' later scandal-mongering compilation, *Deipnosophistae, Sophists at Dinner,* deals with Etruscan sexual customs, and emphasizes the role of women in Etruscan social life. The Greek author has much to say about the shocking behavior of the Etruscans.

They share women in common and display a total lack of shame or modesty, showing themselves naked and speaking openly about sexual intercourse. Etruscan women are beautiful, powerful and promiscuous, mingle freely with men, recline with them on the same couch, and even offer toasts at the banquets and drinking parties that were for the Greeks traditionally all-male events. These banquets, because of their sexual license and lack of restraint, were orgies rather than normal social occasions. Here is the passage:

> Among the Etruscans, who were extraordinarily pleasure-loving, Timaeus says... that the slave girls wait on the men naked. Theopompus, in the forty-third book of his Histories, also says that it is normal for the Etruscans to share their women in common. These women take great care of their bodies and exercise bare, exposing their bodies even before men, and among themselves: for it is not shameful for them to appear almost naked. He also says they dine not with their husbands, but with any man who happens to be present; and they toast anyone they want to.
>
> And the Etruscans raise all the children that are born, not knowing who the father is of each one.
>
> It is no shame for the Etruscans to be seen having sexual experiences...for this too is normal: it is the local custom there. And so far are they from considering it shameful that they even say, when the master of the house is making love, and someone asks for him, that he is "involved in such and such," shamelessly calling out the thing by name. When they come together in parties with their relations, this is what they do: first, when they stop drinking and are ready to go to bed, the servants bring in to them – with the lights left on! – either hetairai, party girls, or very beautiful boys, or even their wives.
>
> When they have enjoyed these, they then bring in young boys in bloom, who in turn consort with themselves. And they make love sometimes within sight of each other, but mostly with screens set up around the beds; these screens are made of woven reeds, and they throw blankets over them. And indeed they like to keep company with women: but they enjoy the company of boys and young men even more.
>
> And their own appearance is also very good-looking, because they live luxuriously and smooth their bodies; for all the barbarians in the West shave their bodies smooth... They have many barber shops.

Athenaeus also quotes the remark of Aristotle, that "Etruscans eat with their wives, reclining at table with them under the same blanket, and that Etruscan slaves are very beautiful and dress better than is the custom of slaves."[2]

There are all the standard charges and clichés of Greek *truphe* or Roman *luxuria* – the love of ease and pleasure of an exotic people, the lust and luxury characteristic of the barbarian way of life, the fancy barbers and emphasis on physical beauty, the promiscuity, the wild parties and lack of modesty – Etruscans allegedly are not even ashamed to have intercourse with the lights on.

Yet a comparison of this description with the picture derived from archaeological discoveries and Etruscan art allows us to distinguish some of the reality behind the scandal-mongering gossip. Sixth-century BC archaic tomb paintings of Tarquinia illustrate the ideals, realities and conspicuous consumption of aristocratic ceremonies, and the life of the members of the noble families who set up these tombs as monuments to their wealth and prestige. The banquet scenes painted on their walls offer striking parallels to those described by the Greek author. Their animated, colorful atmosphere pictures the *joie de vivre* of the banqueters, husbands and wives reclining together on elegant couches covered in bright textiles, while youthful slaves bustle around them serving wine from huge containers, or sit nearby preparing fresh garlands (Fig. 20.1).[3] It was the sight of Etruscan men and women reclining on the same couch that most shocked Theopompus. Respectable Greek women did not attend dinners or drinking parties; only party girls reclined together with the men.[4] The authors making charges of Etruscan sexual license interpreted the social situation and the behavior of the women in the light of the far different Greek customs of the classical period, and in particular from the point of view of the stricter Greek moral attitude of the fourth century BC.[5]

There is more that can be said about two specific passages. The author's remarks on the great care the women take of their bodies, and their custom of exercising naked, "exposing their bodies even before men, and among themselves, for it is not shameful for them to appear almost naked," may refer to Sparta, where the women exercised like the men, and thus joined them in an exclusively male context. To an Athenian, the custom appeared strange and even perverse. Plato advocated adopting it – but only in theory.[6]

The statement that women can raise any children they have, on the other hand, may well be based on a real difference between Greek and Etruscan attitudes to the exposure of children at birth. Jews and Egyptians were said to rear every child that was born to them. The Germans did not limit the number of children, and considered it shameful to expose them to die.[7] Etruscan wealth and resources would also have allowed them to indulge a love of children and avoid resorting to exposure of newborn babies, as was the custom for ancient Greeks during most of their history.

The passage might also refer to the legal situation of Etruscan women, who could perhaps bring up their own children no matter what the status of the father, a situation Greek laws did not permit. In Greece and Rome, the father decided whether a child should be brought up or exposed. An Etruscan upper class woman, in contrast, could pass on her status, and perhaps her property, to her children.[8] This would agree with the use of the matronymics that appeared in Etruscan epitaphs, though far less frequently than patronymics. Etruscan women also had their own names – Tanaquil, Ramtha, Thana – in contrast to their neighbors the Romans, where daughters simply took their father's name, Cornelia, Lucretia, Julia.[9]

Figure 20.1 Tomb of the Painted Vases, Tarquinia, rear wall. Married couple attending a banquet reclining on the same couch. To the right, a naked cupbearer, on the left, seated, their children. C. 500 BC. (*MonInst* 1869–73, pl. 13).

THE ETRUSCAN ARISTOCRACY

The basic element of society in classical Greece was the male citizen and soldier. In Rome it was the *pater familias*. In Etruscan society, which retained its aristocratic nature throughout its history, it was the married couple that represented one generation in the continuous chain of generations of a great family in which the wife's noble birth was as important as that of the husband.[10] This Etruscan aristocracy arose at a certain point in the history of the cities between the Arno and the Tiber, when it marked the juncture between prehistory and history. Archaeology can trace its development from the necropoleis, the cities of the dead, whose rich graves provided these great families with an opportunity to exhibit their wealth, connections and prestige.

In the more or less egalitarian burials of the prehistoric Iron Age, the Villanovan period, men and women were distinguished by their grave goods; the men's armor that identified their role as warriors, and the textile tools and jewels with which women were provided in the afterlife.[11] The canopic urns that held their ashes were made to seem lifelike, and indeed anthropomorphic, by a process of animism that was felt to magically restore some life to the deceased ancestor. The urns were buried fully dressed, or had their garments and jewelry painted on.[12] Though the cloth garments have mostly disappeared, the bronze fibulas or safety pins that held them in place have survived, and we can see that their forms differed – those of the women were leech-shaped, while the men's had a twisted, serpentine form. The gender of the deceased whose ashes were placed in the canopic urns was also identified by their lids: those of the men were either actual helmets or clay substitutes, while the women's urns were covered by shallow bowls used for funerary libations or liquid sacrifices. Many were topped by schematic figures, pairs of males and females standing together or holding each other in a final embrace.[13] At Chiusi urns were placed on a throne, males and females distinguished by their hairstyles, beards and jewelry. (Fig. 20.2). In the Tomb of the Five Chairs at Cerveteri, five ancestors – three males and two females – were placed on seats of honor before a table, as at a banquet.[14]

Figure 20.2   Canopus from Dolciano, Chiusi. Enthroned image of male ancestor. Chiusi, Museo Archeologico Nazionale. Villanovan, 650–600 BC. (Photo Courtesy Soprintendenza per I Beni Archeologici della Toscana).

The contents of the richly furnished Villanovan tombs excavated at Verucchio, near modern Rimini, on the amber route along the Adriatic, are unusual because of their early date (c. 680 BC), as well as for the organic material preserved by the favorable conditions of the soil in which they were buried. Here were toga-like mantles for the lord and grave goods identifying him as a warrior and priest. Women's tombs held quantities of amber and glass paste jewelry and delicate amber spindles, symbolic of their owner's status rather than useful tools. From a man's grave came a richly carved wooden throne showing scenes of men and women involved in wool work, the women working at the loom and other phases of the craft, as well as a somewhat mysterious ritual being carried out by two women protected by armed guards (see Fig. 15.13).[15]

With the Orientalizing period of the eighth and seventh centuries BC, Etruscan wealth, international contacts and prestige were at their highest. We now see the rise of the monumental, multi-chambered family tombs of the aristocracy, which were distinguished by the richness of their grave goods, in contrast to the earlier, more egalitarian Iron Age burials, and where the women's graves had equal and often greater riches than those of the men. The graves of these aristocratic, wealthy princesses included two chariots, a light woman's *calesse* (cart) and a parade *biga* (two-horse chariot).[16] From graves at Tarquinia, Cerveteri and Praeneste and farther north at Chiusi come treasures of gold and silver and amber jewelry, bronze chariots and thrones, tableware for great banquets, imported faience, decorated ostrich eggs, and the fine glossy bucchero that became an Etruscan specialty, modeled on their bronze symposium ware. Writing now appears for the first time, as abecedaria on writing implements, or used to write the owner's name on an object: *mi larthia telicles lechtumuza*, states a tiny perfume vase, speaking in the first person, "I am the little lekythos of Larthia Telikles."[17] And so we learn that these people are the Etruscans, who use the Greco-Phoenician alphabet to write their language, which is unlike any other known to us.[18]

MARRIAGE

Couples are ubiquitous in Etruscan art from early times, and marriage is often represented or alluded to. Countless images of upper class married couples populate the lively banquets painted on the walls of the tombs at Tarquinia, or are shown in effigy reclining on their funeral couches. An actual wedding ceremony appears on an archaic relief from Chiusi: though it is unfortunately fragmentary, enough remains to show the bride, groom and priest under a *huppah*-like canopy that covers them like a wedding blanket (Fig. 20.3).[19] Here and elsewhere, the blanket or veil that covers husband and wife is a favorite symbol of marriage. On the archaic sarcophagus of the Bride and Groom – actually of the Married Couple, "degli Sposi" – the husband's mantle covers the legs of his wife like a blanket. On the fourth-century BC sarcophagus from Vulci in Boston, it is the man's rounded, toga-like *tebenna* that covers them both like a blanket: idealized in death, the handsome couple lie in each other's arms in their marriage bed, naked, their parallel nudity and their embrace representing the consummation of their marriage beyond the grave.[20] Husbands and wives in Etruscan art often display an affection not usually seen in classical art. Some couples on the covers of Iron Age Villanovan cinerary urns are tenderly embracing. A gesture signifying marital affection, the chin-chuck, is shown on a seventh-century BC vase from Cerveteri as well as in a banquet scene from Tarquinia (Fig. 20.1). Another gesture, that of the husband placing his hand on his wife's breast, comes from the Greek repertoire, where it is found in images of Zeus and Hera, for example.[21]

Figure 20.3 Limestone relief from Chiusi. Wedding procession, with priest, musician, and attendants preceding the wedding party – bride, priest, and bridegroom – standing under a fringed cover. Chiusi, Museo Archeologico Nazionale. (Soprintendenza alle Antichità d'Etruria).

In the necropoleis, gender differences are emphasized by the shapes of the beds, by the grave markers placed outside the tomb, even by the women's breasts modeled along the lower edge of the house-shaped ash urns. In all these cases, women's burials are associated with the house shape.[22] Women's domain was the family, its prestige and continuity, but women were by no means confined to the house, or to private religious ceremonies. Their prominence in a public role may be shown by a group of inscriptions from a tomb at Vulci that identify women with the title of *hatrencu*. A recent study convincingly suggests that this is a civic rather than a religious, priestly title, perhaps even an official magistracy, assumed by Etruscan women in particular historical circumstances.[23] The way the women dressed, with shorter skirts and more outerwear, shows that they did in fact live a more public life than Greek women.[24]

We have seen that funerary art, which is the principal form of evidence we have for Etruscan customs and beliefs, regularly shows husband and wife reclining together at the banquet and symposium. Roman women, unlike Greek women, also accompanied their husbands to parties and banquets – an orator asks, "What Roman would be ashamed to take his wife to a dinner party?"[25] But unlike Etruscan women, Roman wives sat primly beside their husbands' couches, they did not lie down beside them.

In the grave and beyond, women were accorded wealth and honors (Fig. 20.4). In real life, they enjoyed considerable freedom and autonomy both within and outside the marriage. The importance of the married couple, the fact that an Etruscan woman had her own name, the use of the matronymic implying her importance and that of her family and the possibility that she could provide status and perhaps even citizenship all point to the important role women played in Etruscan society. But there was no matriarchy – the husband was the head of the family, which is why we know the word for "wife," *puia*, but not the word for "husband."[26]

In Etruscan iconography, mythological scenes emphasize the marriage and family bonds of divinities and heroes,[27] often choosing obscure alternate forms of the Greek myth represented or transforming the story radically. Such scenes were incised on the backs of the engraved bronze mirrors that brides received on their wedding day, and that they took to their graves with them when they died.[28] One mirror shows Admetus and

Alcestis as a loving couple on their wedding day, flanked by the symbolic images of their marriage and their death. A Praenestine mirror represents the reconciliation and perhaps the marriage of Juno and Heracles, crudely expressed by male and female sexual organs (Fig. 20.5). Prophecy, frequently represented or alluded to in scenes of preparation for the marriage, was evidently part of the wedding ritual. We see it on a beautiful mirror in which Thetis is bathing and adorning herself. As she looks into the mirror, Peleus, who has just come upon the scene, recoils in horror at the vision he sees there – the tragic result of their union, the birth of Achilles and the Trojan War (Fig. 20.6).[29]

Some of these images might have functioned like modern wedding portraits on the mantel, recording the formation of the family. The inscriptions that identify the figures are often detached from them, their principal function being apparently to move the scene to a mythological level, as in an *epithalamium,* equating the married couple to divine or heroic lovers. One scene shows Turan, goddess of love, bringing together the adulterous lovers, Paris and Helen,[30] who are here presented as an ideal couple and an example for the married pair.

Figure 20.4   Tomb of the Monkey at Chiusi. Deceased woman watching funeral games in her honor. (*MonInst* 5, 1849–53, pl. 14–16).

Figure 20.5   Bronze mirror, Praenestine. Juno (Iuno) and Heracles (Hercele) approach from either side Jupiter, who is seated on an altar (Iovei). Juno is flanked by a female herm, Heracles by a phallus. New York, Metropolitan Museum. Late fourth or early third century BC. (Bonfante, 1997, *CSE* USA 3.7).

Turan herself, the love goddess, is a frequent example for mortal lovers. She is shown together with her lover, Adonis (Atunis). Along with her swan, Tusna, she appears with Atunis on a beautiful amber group in the Metropolitan Museum, holding an alabastron from which she will apply a fragrant perfume or unguent to ratify their union (Fig. 20.7).[31] On another mirror, Turan and an older, taller, adult Atunis appear in a conjugal embrace in front of the marriage bed: the *anasyrma* gesture of Turan announces the forthcoming consummation of their marriage.[32]

Figure 20.6   Bronze mirror from Castelgiorgio. Peleus, rushing in from the left, sees Thetis at her toilette, looking into her mirror. New York, Metropolitan Museum. (Bonfante, 1997, *CSE* USA 3.14).

Figure 20.7   Carved amber bow of a fibula, from Ancona. Aphrodite (Turan) reclining on a couch with her lover Adonis (Atunis); her swan curls up behind her back. New York, Metropolitan Museum. C. 500 BC.

In Greek mythology and Greek art, Dionysos and Ariadne are almost the only divine happily married pair. Etruscan art is populated by such affectionate couples as Zeus and Hera (Tinia and Uni);³³ Dionysos and Ariadne (Fufluns and Areatha); Leda and Tyndareus (Latva and Tuntle); and Hades and Persephone (Aita and Phersipnai), rulers of the Underworld. Satyrs and maenads, frequently shown dancing together (Fig. 20.8), are on friendlier terms than in Greek art, where lustful satyrs pursue frightened maenads and nymphs.³⁴ Vanth and Charu work together as partners.³⁵ The pairs are not always married couples or lovers: they can be brother and sister, as in the case of Apollo and Artemis, or mother and son, like Fufluns, shown in a tender embrace with his mother, Semla, or Thetis and Achilles on the early sixth-century BC Monteleone Chariot (Figs 24.7 and 24.8). Often pairs of divinities are made up of a younger male and an older – and larger – female figure: Turan with Atunis, the youthful Fufluns with his mother.³⁶ And instead of the Greek representations of pairs of warriors or male wrestlers, Praenestine bronze cista handles of the fourth century BC show men and women together, wrestling – recalling the contest of Peleus and Atalanta – or carrying the body of a dead warrior.³⁷

Before we leave this mythological world we might mention a peculiar aspect of some Etruscan divinities. Thalna, Lasa, and a few other deities seem to have no fixed gender, but appear as either male or female at various times.³⁸ Does a representation of the seer Teiresias, shown with feminine dress and demeanor along with the attributes of a man, express a special interest in such shifting gender, or is it a picturesque rendering of the story that he had been turned into a woman and was familiar with both the male and female sex?³⁹

Aside from the married couple, we see pairs of women sitting together on some of the votive terracottas, where they perhaps represent some kind of ceremonial society, or group of women involved in family rites. The two women riding in a carriage on one of the plaques from the decoration of the early archaic aristocratic residence at Murlo (Poggio Civitate) have been interpreted as the bridal party approaching the bride's future home.⁴⁰

CHILDREN, BIRTHS AND BABIES

Greek myth had transferred the childbearing function to Zeus. Etruscan mythology restored it to the mother, and often illustrated family values. Tinia, unlike Zeus, is usually a faithful husband, often shown with his wife, Uni.⁴¹ On one mirror, a family group includes Tyndareus and Leda looking fondly at the egg from which the baby Helen

Figure 20.8 Black-figure vase. Satyr carrying off a friendly maenad. New York, Metropolitan Museum. Sixth century BC. (Metropolitan Museum of Art, Inv. 22.139.83).

will hatch.[42] Paris [Elachsantre] is seated like a good father at the bedside of Elina, who is in bed nursing the baby Ermania, while Turan, goddess of love, visits the happy family (see Chapter 24, Fig. 24.13).[43]

Birth scenes in general are much more popular in Etruscan than in Greek art.[44] While the divine conceptions and births in Greek myth are uniformly unnatural, Etruscan renderings often bring out their more practical, normal aspects. Tinia is shown on a mirror giving birth to a large, fully armed Menerva with two beautifully dressed midwives at his side, comforting him and bandaging his aching head.[45] Elsewhere we see the baby Dionysos, wearing protective amulets, emerging from Tinia's thigh, where he has been incubated; a female attendant nurse, Mean, holds an unguent jar and dipstick: is it to assuage the birth pangs of Tinia, the new father, or to anoint the new-born baby?[46] An Etruscan scene shows the conception of a god as an actual sexual union, as Semla lifts up her skirt in an *anasyrma* gesture to have intercourse with the great god: a satyr shows that the conception of the god Fufluns/Dionysos will be the result.[47]

Scenes of the nuclear family, father, mother and child together, appear in Etruscan art, but it is not always easy to distinguish the children, the Roman *liberi*, from the *servi*. On the seventh-century BC Tragliatella urn, a man and a woman stand facing each other with a small figure between them. The inspiration for the group could be Theseus and Ariadne with Ariadne's nurse. But the figures are given Etruscan names, so that the smaller figure represents a real child (Fig. 20.9).[48] Young boys and girls shown serving at banquets on tomb paintings seem to be servants, but a unique scene on the wall of the Tomba del Barone, may represent a formal family portrait of father and mother with their son. In the fourth-century BC François Tomb, Arnza, "little Arnth," stands next to Vel Saties and releases the birds from which the seer reads the omens; is Arnza his attendant or his son?[49]

Images of many stages of the lives of children, from birth to adolescence, appear in Etruscan art and material culture. Most prominent are the babies, perhaps related to the fact that the Etruscans were among a number of non-Greek cultures that did not practice child infanticide, or abandonment – *expositio* in Latin. They, like the Egyptians, the Jews, the Germans, but unlike the Greeks of classical and Hellenistic times, valued all their children and raised them.[50]

Figure 20.9   Urn from Tragliatella (Cerveteri). Nuclear family, military parade, erotic symplegma and other scenes. C. 600 BC. Rome Capitoline Museum. (Giglioli 1929, pl. 26).

Two surprising references to birth have recently been added to the repertoire. The remarkable image of a baby actually emerging from the mother's body is a birth scene of a type previously unknown.[51] It occurs on two tiny seals from a seventh-century BC bucchero fragment excavated at the Etruscan site of Poggio Colla, in the Mugello (see Fig. 47.2). The crouching mother giving birth is portrayed with her face in profile, her hair in the long back braid typical of the seventh century BC, her knees and one arm raised. Although images of a crouching woman are known from Etruscan art of this period, none shows the baby being born.[52]

Also recent is an intriguing interpretation of a heretofore-mysterious object, a large bronze circle or flat ring, sometimes decorated with a geometric pattern, found on or near the body of a deceased woman in numerous graves of the seventh century BC. According to Gilda Bartoloni, the object signified that the woman has given birth, and as a symbol of childbirth further attesting to the importance of child bearing and children in the world of early Italy (Fig. 20.10).[53]

KOUROTROPHOS

Once the child is born, the natural first act of the mother is to nurse it at her breast. This image is known by the Greek term *kourotrophos*, originally referring to anyone rearing or taking care of a child, but used today for a female figure holding or nursing a child. The image of the woman and child is so familiar to us in Western art from representations of the Virgin Mary with the Christ child that we tend to take for granted its interpretation

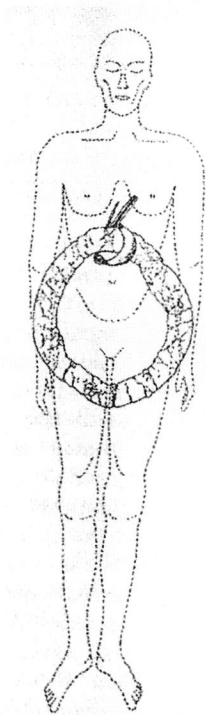

Figure 20.10 Bronze ring found on the body of a deceased woman in grave 153 of the necropolis of Castel di Decima, near Rome. (Bartoloni 2008, Fig. 2).

as a universal symbol of maternity and of the close physical and emotional bond between mother and child.[54] The motif of the *kourotrophos* was not universal, however. It was relatively rare in comparison to other images of women in most of the ancient world, and served a number of different symbolic functions, ranging from honoring the king of Egypt, to adding strength to magical spells, to depicting scenes of daily life.[55]

The importance in Italy in the art of all periods of the figure of the female *kourotrophos* contrasts with its absence in the official religion of the Greeks – though not in cult, where ancient practices survive into much later times[56] – and its occurrence in Italy constitutes the most visible and remarkable difference between this imagery and that of mainland Greece. Groups of the "holy family," with father, mother, and child, are almost unknown as a motif in Greek art. After the little Mycenaean "divine nurses" of the thirteenth century BC, images of mothers and children are also rarely found in Greek art before the Hellenistic period. Greek myth, as well as art, shows divine babies handed over to foster mothers or tutors, to be nursed by nymphs or animals. The chances of mythological babies being nursed by their own mothers are slim.

What accounts for this reluctance on the part of the Greeks to show this act, so natural in real life? Much of it stems from religious reasons. As we have seen, the male gods were in charge. In addition, male-dominated Greek society looked upon nursing and the baring of the breasts with revulsion and dread. Two strong taboos were involved, nudity and milk. Mother's milk was a powerful magic and strong medicine, used by Egyptians, Greeks and Romans – and no doubt by Etruscans, though we have no information on that account. A recent study finds that human milk, a heavily symbolic and highly-effective substance, was used in different ways in Greek and Roman pharmacopias, and varied according to the patient's gender. It was connected with therapies involving animal excrements and with the Greek idea of women's pollution and cathartic treatment: early Greek sources recommend human milk, sometimes specifically from "a woman who has borne a male child," almost exclusively in treating women. Human milk therapies in the Roman context, on the other hand, are not gender specific, since, owing perhaps to Etruscan influence, Roman society was less polarized sexually than Greek, and more accepting of the female body. Noting the remarkable difference between Greek and Roman ideas, the author of the study concludes that different conceptions of gender are involved – the Romans not associating women with pollution in the same degree as the Greeks.[57]

The second taboo was the universal rule against showing the naked female body and the related requirement that the sexual organs and women's breasts be covered in public at all times. This taboo, too, involved a powerful magic. In Greek art the sight of a nursing mother had far different connotations from those we associate with the maternal, protective aspects of the Virgin Mary. It signified vulnerability and impending danger for both mother and child: a red-figure hydria shows Amphiaraos going off to war and death, as his wife, soon to be a widow, nurses their infant son; and a Pompeian fresco, taken from a Greek image, shows Danae nursing Perseus at her breast, at her side the open chest in which the child will be sent off to die.[58] The bared breast that Clytemnestra offers to the matricidal Orestes, often shown in art, belongs in this same context of impending danger. The breast need not be maternal; the Niobids also bare their breasts in their headlong flight.[59]

Images of *kourotrophoi* and nursing mothers are frequent in Italy from the eighth century BC on and continue well into Roman times; they are by no means limited to the

Etruscan world – examples are found in Latium, in Campania, and throughout the former Greek colonies of southern Italy and Sicily.[60] The earliest image appears on a bronze horse trapping from an eighth-century BC woman's tomb at Decima, in Latium, near the border of Etruria, where it had been deposited along with the chariot that indicated her high status. It represents two naked human figures, a woman nursing a child and a man with two birds pecking out his eyes: as often, it is hard to tell whether they are meant to represent a divine, mythological or a human couple. Two archaic statues, the *kourotrophos* representing Leto with the baby Apollo in her arms from the roof of the temple at Veii, and the so-called Mater Matuta from Chiusi, a seated funerary figure of an enthroned goddess with a baby (Fig. 20.11), were probably influenced by Greek models, for they hold the babies, but do not nurse them.[61] Such unusual figures as the life-size, sixth-century BC funerary limestone statue of a woman nursing two babies found at Megara Hyblaea, in Sicily, or the life-size, standing statue of a woman with a baby from Volterra, the so-called Maffei statue, based on a Greek fourth-century BC model to which the Etruscan artist has added the baby,[62] all demonstrate the lack of stabile Greek models for this motif. For Etruscan religion and ideals, on the other hand, the need for such images was important enough to cause artists and craftsmen to invent new models and modify old ones, breaking through the prohibition against representing nursing or viewing the naked female breast.

The fourth to second centuries BC saw a proliferation of these nursing mothers, in a variety of forms, functions, sizes, styles, iconography and context that reflect the local importance of the motif and the impelling need for such an image for the devout. The many later nursing *matres* from Capua, and the hundreds of terracotta figurines of *kourotrophoi* from sanctuaries all date from this period (see Chapter 54).

Figure 20.11   Life-size stone ash urn from Chiusi. Enthroned woman or goddess, so-called Mater Matuta, holding swaddled baby on her lap. Florence, Museo Archeologico. 450–425 BC. (Soprintendenza alle Antichità d'Etruria.)

The scene of Herakles nursing at the breast of Hera was known in Greek literature in the myth of the origin of the Milky Way, created by the milk spurting out of the breast of an angry Hera when she realized that Zeus had tricked her into nursing Herakles, hoping thereby to have her adopt him. It is not, however, known in Greek mainland art. In fact it occurs only on four Etruscan mirrors and a south Italian vase of the fourth century BC. The scene of Hera nursing the hero reflects an earlier belief in an amicable relationship of Hera and Herakles, which would account for his theophoric name of "Glory of Hera." The adoption scene is carried out according to an Eastern ritual whereby the goddess grants divinity or royalty to her favorite by nursing him at her breast (see Fig. 20.11).[63]

LITERACY AND EDUCATION

An intriguing aspect of the status of aristocratic Etruscan women from early times is their literacy. Furthermore, from the time when writing was first adopted in Italy, a series of discoveries testifies to a close connection between writing and women.[64] Writing is found in the earliest wealthy tombs, most of which belong to women. Scholars have noted the close relationship of texts to textiles, which were traditionally the province of women.[65] The letters or *sigla* appearing on loom weights and other wool-working implements used by women are the objects of current study.[66] Also belonging to this context is an interpretation of what seems to be the earliest Greek inscription, on an eighth-century BC vase from Osteria dell'Osa; the word is read as EULIN, perhaps meaning "good spinner," and the object is seen as a container used to hold wool for spinning.[67]

Much has been written about a later source for our knowledge of women's literacy: the bronze mirrors given to brides on their wedding day. Made in several Etruscan cities and Etruscanized Praeneste from the fifth to the third centuries BC, they are often decorated with images from myths, or more rarely daily life, and are often inscribed with the names of the characters. The images testify to women's literacy and to the Etruscans' interest in and knowledge of Greek mythology and drama.[68]

We know something about the education of the upper classes, but as usual we know little about that of the lower classes.[69] The Etruscans' technical ability in many fields, from road building to chariot making, music and working terracotta and bronze, is clear from what remains of their monuments, cities, sanctuaries and necropoleis. Their neighbors, the Romans, knew and respected their knowledge of divination and communication between the divine and human spheres. In the fourth century BC, Roman aristocrats sent their sons to Caere to learn divination, as they later sent them to Athens to study literature.[70] Laris Pulenas had himself represented on his sarcophagus holding the scroll with his genealogy and titles: one of his ancestors was Creice, "the Greek", and he wrote a book on divination.[71] This would have been a path followed by many sons of the Etruscan aristocracy, who would study the various books of rituals and divination, and eventually become haruspices, highly skilled and respected at home and abroad.

CONCLUSION

This chapter has attempted to make use of the available evidence to put together a plausible picture of the situation of women and children in the world of the Etruscans. The loss of Etruscan literature, the hostility of historical accounts, and generally the absence of the textual evidence that allows us to feel more familiar with the reality and the ideals of women in the classical Greek and Roman worlds, all this is more than balanced by the abundance of Etruscan archaeological, epigraphic, artistic and iconographical evidence. Etruscan women were more visible alongside the men, as wives and mothers, priestesses and seers. The families and clients of aristocratic women celebrated their weddings and their funerals, and furnished their graves with expensive and luxurious objects, unhindered by the sumptuary laws of the Greeks and Romans, often specifically aimed at controlling the wealth, power and prestige of women. But there was no matriarchy like that envisioned by Bachofen, who exaggerated the different roles of women in these classical societies as meaning that the roles of men and women were reversed.

NOTES

1. Heurgon 1964.
2. Theopompus, *Histories,* in Athenaeus 517d–518a. English translation, Gulick 1927, 41, 12. 517–518. Lefkowitz and Fant 2005, 88–89, No. 100, with a different translation.
3. Tomb of the Painted Vases, Steingräber 1986, 353–355, No. 123: "the rear wall has an intimate air, with a married couple and the children seated alongside them." The small figure on the right is a cupbearer. For the garlands, see also the pediment of the Tomb of Hunting and Fishing, Steingräber 1986, No. 50, Fig. 46. Steingräber 2006, many examples.
4. Pomeroy 1995, 143.
5. Dover 1974.
6. Pomeroy 2002, 25–27. Plato, *Republic* 457 a–b.
7. Tacitus, *Germania* 19: *Numerum liberorum finire aut quemquam ex adgnatis necare flagitium habetur.* "To restrict the number of children, or to kill any of those born after the heir, is considered wicked." Translation, Mattingly-Handford 1970, 117–118. Judaism prohibits infanticide. Josephus, *Against Apion* II 5: God "forbids women to cause abortion of what is begotten, or to destroy it afterward."
8. Torelli 1997a, 52–86, especially 77. See Pomeroy 2002, 48, 90–91 for possible Spartan examples.
9. Bonfante 1994, 249, with refs. Women had less of a public presence than men, and were expected to keep their names, like their persons, private. According to Anglo-Saxon etiquette in the not-so-distant past, a married woman should use her husband's full name in public; a name taboo required her to hide her given name and reserve the intimacy of knowing it to close relatives and family friends.
10. Bonfante 1981, 157–187.
11. For grave goods according to gender, see Cougle 2009, 58.
12. Bonfante 2003, Figs. 3–9, 14–16.
13. For fibulas, see Torelli 2000, 547–548. For stylized images of men and women, see De Puma 1996, with Turfa review, 1998. For the final embrace, see Säflund 37–38, Figs. 23–25.
14. For enthroned canopi, see Torelli 2000, 549. Tomb of the Five Chairs, Haynes 2000, 92–95.
15. Torelli Von Eles 2002, 2006, 2007.
16. In the seventh and sixth centuries BC, women were buried with rich grave goods and two chariots – a biga or *currus* and a ladies' *calesse* – in Etruria, Latium, and the neighboring Picene area, as well as across the Alps, in Gaul. Emiliozzi 1997. Bartoloni, Grottanelli 1989, 59–61. Landolfi 1997, 236.
17. Telikles: TLE 761, Rix OA 2.2. Bonfante and Fowlkes 2006, 111, 113, No. 33: seventh century. The lekythos is now on loan at the Metropoltan Museum of Art. For women, textiles and writing, see below, note 83.
18. See chapter on language, in this volume.
19. Wedding on Chiusi relief: Bonfante 1994, 252, Fig. 8.6. Haynes 2000, 248, and cf. 240–241. Couples: Säflund 1993, 36–123. Haynes 2000, 361.

20 Sarcophagus of the Married Couple: Haynes 2000, 214–215. Sarcophagus from Vulci: Bonfante 1994, 250–251, Fig. 287. On Etruscan "parallel nudity" of men and women, see Bonfante 1993, 27–55. For a mantle covering seated husband and wife, see Haynes 2000, 361, Fig. 283.

21 Iron Age urns: Säflund 1993, 37–38, Figs. 23–25. Chin-chuck: Tomb of the Painted Vases, Bonfante 1994, 244; Säflund 119, Fig. 87. On the vase from Monte Abetone, Cerveteri (Haynes 54–55, Fig. 35, in color), the gesture has been interpreted as the affectionate caress of an anonymous couple, or as a pleading gesture, in a mythological scene showing Helen and Menelaos at the end of the Trojan War. For later meanings of the chin-chuck, see Steinberg 1996, 110–118. For the double chin-chuck on a thirteenth-century emblem of marriage, see Lavin and Lavin 2001, 18, 25, Fig. 23. The authors also cite the motif of the overlapping position of the legs to allude to the sexual aspect of the marriage. For the hand of the husband on his wife's breast, see Bonfante, *CSE* USA 3, 6 (Admetus and Alcestis), Haynes 2000, 255, Fig. 213 (Tinia and Uni?), and de Grummond, 2006, 59. The last image is cited as an example for medieval images of the marriage of Christ and Mary, Lavin and Lavin 2001, 11 and 18, fig. 22.

22 Haynes 2000, 90–91.

23 *Hatrencu*: Lundeen 2006, 34–61. From the Tomba delle Iscrizioni, Vulci; it is a distinctly local phenomenon. Morandi Tarabella 2004, 384–387. Nielsen 1989b, 143, 384–387. Haynes 2000, 285–286. Lundeen notes that the women are buried in the tomb because of their *hatrencu* status, rather than their family relationship. We may compare the Vestal Virgins, who are unmarried and cut off from their families during their term of office, or the "widows" or deaconesses of the early Christian church: Miller 2005, 49: these are, however, religious, not civic offices.

24 Bonfante 2003, 88–89.

25 Cornelius Nepos, *Lives*, *praef*. 6.L (Lefkowitz, Fant 2005, 164–165, No. 209), comments on the prudery of the Greeks: "They consider that many of the customs we think are appropriate are in bad taste. No Roman would hesitate to take his wife to a dinner party, or to allow the mother of his family to occupy the first rooms in his house and to walk about in public..."

26 Bachofen's (1861) claim that there was an Etruscan matriarchy has had a long-lasting influence. *Puia*: Bonfante and Bonfante 2002, 111.

27 On the importance of family ties, see de Angelis 2012, 218, 242.

28 For mirrors in general see de Grummond 1982; 239–243; Van der Meer 1995; Haynes 2000, 239–243. Many mirrors in de Grummond 2006.

29 Bonfante, *CSE* USA 3.6 (Admetus and Alcestis); 3.7 (Jupiter, Juno and Herakles); 3.14 (Peleus and Thetis). On the prophecy before the marriage, see van der Meer 1995, 91; de Grummond 2006, 33–35, 160.

30 Bonfante, *CSE* USA 3.9.

31 Amber group: Picón *et al*. 2007, 284–285, 471, No. 326. For Tusna and Zipna, see de Grummond 2006, 94, 98, Fig. V.28.

32 De Grummond 2006, 153, fig. VII.8.

33 Haynes 2000, 255, 259, Fig. 213.

34 Satyr and maenad: Metropolitan Museum Inv. 22.139.83. Bonfante and Swaddling 2006, 41, 15, 50.

35 Vanth and Charu: Haynes 2000, 274–275. De Grummond 2006, 213–225.

36 For the Monteleone Chariot see now Emiliozzi 2011, 8–132. For couples on mirrors see Van der Meer 1995, 182–200; 228–235 (Spiky Garland Group); 187, No. 89, and 197, No. 95; 228–235 (larger female figures).

37 Coppola 2000, 76–84. The muscles of the women have led one scholar to claim that they are androgynous: Sandhoff 2011, 71–96.

38 Haynes 2000, 274. De Grummond 2006, 21. Bonfante and Swaddling 2006, 50.

39 Bonfante and Swaddling 2006, 32–33.

40 Murlo plaque: Haynes 2000, 121–123, Fig. 103. Bruni 2004, 24–25, No. 15 (*pompa nuptialis*), thinks the veiled woman (the bride?), is accompanied by a second figure, whose gender is unspecified (a servant?), holding the parasol.

41 E.g. Haynes 2000, 42; de Grummond 2006, 58–59, Fig. IV.8.

42 Bonfante and Swaddling 2006, 15, Fig. 3.

43 Rome, Villa Giulia. The sphinx swooping down from above represents an epiphany of the goddess: Erika Simon, Hampe-Simon 1964, 43, Fig. 9. I am grateful to Adriano Maggiani for this reference.

44 On the prevalence of birth scenes and babies, see Bonfante 1989, 85–106; van der Meer 1995, 119–134; Haynes 2000, 361–363, on babies and small children; and de Grummond 2006, 59–63.

45 The attendants' dress includes the shoulder tassel, a sign of status and prestige: Bonfante 2003, 189. Practical Etruscan artists represented bandaging scenes in surprising circumstances, perhaps tongue in cheek, as when Asclepius (Esplace) bandages Prometheus (Prumathe) on a mirror in the Metropolitan Museum (*CSE* USA 3.11).

46 De Grummond (2006, fig. IV.11) compares this ritual anointing to a christening, perhaps giving immortality.

47 De Grummond 2006, 59. Supra, note 25.

48 Tragliatella urn: Giglioli 1929. Haynes 2000, 97–99. The Latin term *liberi*, used of the *familia's* legitimate children in contrast to the slaves, implies that this was also true in real life. The Latin term *puer*, used of a slave, corresponds to calling a slave "boy" in the Old South, implying his inferior status. For children and servants, see the Tomb of the Painted Vases, above, note 3.

49 Tomb of the Baron, rear wall: Steingräber 1986, 285, No. 44, with different interpretations of the scene. Haynes 2000, 224, Fig. 183. François Tomb: Steingräber 1986, 377–378, No. 178, Fig. 185, sees Arnza as the servant of Vel Saties. Haynes 280–281, Fig 227.

50 Still basic is the article on Athenian infanticide by Glotz, who however calls it a universal custom: Ernout-Meillet, s.v. *expositio*. Jews (Josephus, *Apion* 2.202; Diodorus Siculus, 40.3.8), Egyptians (Diodorus Siculus 1.80.3; Strabo, *Geography* 17.2.5).

51 Nutt 2011, 17. Lorenzi 2011, 17.

52 De Grummond 2006, 111–112, Fig.V.43.

53 Bartoloni 2006, 16–18; 2008, 30–34, Figs. 2–12.

54 For a detailed discussion of the topic, see Bonfante 1997, 174–196.

55 Budin 2011. Images of the child being bathed are connected with childbirth and illustrated in the art of Rome, for example Kleiner and Matheson 2000, 57.

56 For their presence in cult, see Burkert 1985, 41, 184. Nursing mothers are conspicuous by their absence from Greek art; Hadzisteliou Price 1978 includes images of men and animals as child-care providers in her study of the Greek *kourotrophos*.

57 Laskaris 2005, 174–189; 2008, 459–464. Review by Horster 2006. The Greek medicinal use of mother's milk was adapted from an Egyptian ritual calling for the "milk of one who has borne a male child," to be poured from an anthropomorphic vase in the form of a mother nursing an infant. The Egyptian application was not gender specific.

58 Amphiaraos: Bonfante 1989, pl. XLVIII.2. Danae: fresco from Casa dell'Orso, *LIMC*, s.v. Perseus, 86.

59 Cohen 1997, 66–92.

60 Bonfante 1989, 85–106.

61 Bonfante 1997, 177–178. Mater Matuta: Haynes 2000, 296–298.

62 Megara Hyblaia: Bonfante 1989, pl. XXXV. Kourotrophos Maffei: Haynes 2000, 357, Fig. 279. Ranuccio Bianchi Bandinelli's *bon mot* about this statue, whose head was missing (it was later found), was that it showed "a woman who lost her head and found herself with a baby in her arms."

63 Bonfante 1997, 180–183. For the Greek myth, see Gantz 1993, 378, and Rasmussen 2005, 30–39. On the Isis examples, see Tran Tam Tinh 1973. The subject became a favorite among Baroque painters; Caravaggio's painting in Naples, *La carità romana* (1606), includes it, and by the time of Rubens it was not unusual.

64 Bagnasco Gianni 1999, 85–106.

65 For *sigla* see Bagnasco Gianni 1999, 86–92, and Bagnasco Gianni and de Grummond, forthcoming.

66 Bagnasco Gianni 1999, 93–98, with bibliography. Scheid and Svembro 1994, 134–135. In *Texts and Textiles* 2004, Edmunds, Jones and Nagy show how the Greeks and Romans conceived of poetic composition and writing in terms of weaving.

67 Its interpretation is still controversial, Bagnasco Gianni 1999, 101–103; Huxlos 1998, 204; Gras 2000, 21–21–22. Ridgway (1996, 87–97), sees the hole as serving the practical purpose of letting the wool out of the vase gradually without having it become matted.

68 De Grummond 1982.

69 For Rome, see Horsfall 2003.

70 Livy 9.36.3. Bonfante and Bonfante 2002, 57.

71 Bonfante and Bonfante 2002, 149–151, Source No. 31.

BIBLIOGRAPHY

Bachofen, J. J. (1967) *Myth, religion, and mother right; selected writings of J. J. Bachofen.* (*Mutterrecht* originally published 1861). Princeton, NJ.

Bagnasco Gianni, G. (1999) "L'acquisizione della scrittura in Etruria: materiali a confronti per la ricostruzione del quadro storico e culturale" in Bagnasco Gianni, Cordano 1999, 85–106.

Bagnasco Gianni, G. and F. Cordano (eds) (1999) *Scritture Mediterranee tra il IX e il VII secolo a.C.* Atti del Seminario. Università degli Studi di Milano, Milan.

Bagnasco Gianni, G. and N. T. de Grummond. (forthcoming) "Introducing the International Etruscan Sigla Project" in *Etruscan Literacy in its Social Context*, Kathryn Lomas and John B. Wilkins (eds), Accordia Research Centre. London.

Bartoloni, G. (2006) "Madri di Principi" in Petra Amann (ed.) *Studi in onore di Luciana Aigner Foresti.* Vienna, 13–22.

——(2008) "Le donne dei principi nel Lazio protostorico," *Aristonothos* 3: 23–45.

Bartoloni, G. and C. Grottanelli (1989) "Il carro a due ruote nelle tombe femminili del Lazio e dell'Etruria" in Rallo 1989, 55–73.

Becker, Marshall J. (2007) "Childhood Among the Etruscans" in Ada Cohen, Jeremy B. Rutter, (eds) *Construction of Childhood in Ancient Greece and Italy.* Princeton, NJ, 286.

Beer, C. (1987) "Comparative votive religion: the evidence of children in Cyprus, Greece and Etruria," *Boreas*, 15, 21–29.

——(1994) *Temple-boys. A study of Cypriote votive sculpture. Part 1. Catalogue.* Jonsered.

Bettini, M. (1998) *Nascere. Storie di donne, donnole, madri ed eroi.* Turin.

Bettini, M. and A. Borghini (1979) *Il bambino e l'eletto. Storia di una peripezia culturale*, Mat. disc. an. test. Class. 3: 121–153.

Bettini, M. and G. Guidorizzi (2004) *Il mito di Edipo. Immagini e racconti dalla Grecia a oggi*, Turin.

Bietti Sestieri, A. M. (ed.) (1992) *La necropoli laziale di Osteria dell'Osa.* Rome.

Bonfante, L. (1981) "Etruscan Couples and their Aristocratic Society," *Women in Antiquity. Women's Studies* 8 (1981) 157–187.

——(1984) "Dedicated mothers," *Visible Religion. Annual for Religious Iconography* 3: 1–17.

——(1986) *Etruscan Life and Afterlife.* Detroit.

——(1986) "Votive terracotta figures of mothers and children" in J. Swaddling (ed.) *Italian Iron Age Artefacts in the British Museum. Papers of the Sixth British Museum Classical Colloquium.* London, 195–201.

——(1989) "Iconografia delle madri: Etruria e Italia antica" in Rallo 1989, 85–106.

——(1993) "Etruscan Nudity" in L. Bonfante (ed.) *Essays on Nudity in Antiquity in Memory of Otto Brendel. Source. Notes in the History of Art*, 12 (1993) 47–55.

——(1994) "Excursus: Etruscan Women" in E. Fantham *et al.* 1994, 243–259.

——(1997) "Nursing mothers in Classical Art" in Koloski Ostrow, Lyons, 1997, 174–196.

——(1997) *Etruscan Mirrors. CSE USA* 3. *New York, Metropolitan Museum of Art*. Rome.

——(2003) *Etruscan Dress*. Updated edition. Originally published 1975. Baltimore.

Bonfante, L. and B. Fowlkes (2006) *Classical Antiquities at New York University*. Rome.

Bruni, S. (2004) "Pompa Nuptialis," *ThesCRA* 1, 23–25, No. 15.

Buchholz, H. G. (1987) "Das Symbol des gemeinsamen Mantels," *JdI* 102 (1987) 1–55.

Budin, S. L. (2011) *Images of Woman and Child from the Bronze Age: Reconsidering Fertility, Maternity, and Gender in the Ancient World*. Cambridge.

Burkert, W. (1985) *Greek Religion*. Harvard, Cambridge, MA.

Burn, L. 2000. "Three terracotta *kourotrophoi*" in G. R. Tsetskhladze, A. M. Snodgrass, A. J. N. W. Prag (eds) *PERIPLOUS. To Sir John Boardman from his Pupils and Friends*. London - New York, 41–49.

Cameron, A. (1932) "The Exposure of Children and Greek Ethics," *CR* 46 1932, 105–14.

Cameron, A. and A. Kuhrt (1983) *Images of Women in Antiquity*. Detroit.

Celuzza, M. (2011) "La cura dei bambini nella società etrusca," Rafanelli and Spaziani 2011, 34–47.

Cohen, B. (1997) "Divesting the Female Breast of Clothes in Classical Sculpture" in Koloski Ostrow, Lyons, 1997, 66–92.

Comella, A. (2004) "*Kourotrophoi*," "Fanciulli," "Bambini in fasce," *ThesCRA* 1, 335.

Coppola, F. (2000) *Le Ciste prenestine. I. Corpus. 3. Manici isolati*, Rome.

Cougle, L. (2009) "Latial Iron Age mortuary contexts: the case of Osteria dell'Osa" in Edward Herring, Kathryn Lomas (eds) *Gender Identities in Italy in the First Millennium BC*. BAR. Oxford.

Crawford-Brown, S. (2010) "Votive Children in Cyprus and Italy," *Etruscan News* 12 (2010) 5, 31.

Dasen, V. (ed.) (2001) *Naissance et petite enfance dans l'Antiquité*. Actes du colloque de Fribourg, 28 novembre – 1er décembre 2001. Paris.

Dasen, V. and T. Späth (eds) (2010) *Children, Memory, and Family Identity in Roman Culture*. Oxford, New York.

De Angelis, F. (2012) *Miti greci in tombe etrusche: le urne cinerarie di Chiusi*. Rome.

de Grummond, N. T. (ed.) (1982) *A Guide to Etruscan Mirrors*. Tallahassee, FL.

——(2006) *Etruscan Myths, Sacred History, and Legend*. Philadelphia, University Museum Press.

De Puma, R. (1996) *CVA USA* 31. The J. Paul Getty Museum. Malibu, fasc. 6. Malibu, CA.

Dixon, S. (1988) *The Roman Mother*. Norman, OK and London.

Dolansky, F. (2008) "*Togam virilem sumere*: Coming of Age in the Roman World" in J. Edmondson and A. Keith (eds) *Roman Dress and the Fabrics of Roman Culture*. Toronto, 47–70.

Dover, K. J. (1974) *Greek Popular Morality in the Time of Plato and Aristotle*. Oxford, Blackwell.

Emiliozzi, A. (ed.) (1997) *Carri da guerra e principi etruschi*. Rome.

——(2011) "The Etruscan Chariot from Monteleone di Spoleto," *MMJournal* 46: 8–132.

Fantham, E., H. P. Foley, N. B. Kampen, S. B. Pomeroy and H. A. Shapiro (1994) *Women in the Classical World*. Oxford.

Giglioli, G. Q. (1929) "L'oinochoe di Tragliatella," *Studi Etruschi* 3: 111–159.

Gantz, T. (1993) *Early Greek Myth*. Baltimore, MD.

Gras, M. (2000) "Il Mediterraneo in età orientalizzante: merci, approdi, circolazione" in *Principi Etruschi* 2000, "Donne, commercio, scrittura," 21–22.

Gulick, C. B. (1927–41) *Athenaeus: Deipnosophistae*. Loeb Classical Library. Revised 1955. Cambridge, MA. 6 vols.

Hadzisteliou Price, T. (1978) *Kourotrophos. Cults and Representations of the Greek Nursing Deities*. Leiden.

Harlow, M. and R. Laurence (eds) (2010) *A Cultural History of Childhood and Family in Antiquity.* New York, Oxford.

Haynes, S. (2000) *Etruscan Civilization. A Cultural History.* Los Angeles, CA. 2000. On the role of women in Etruscan art and life.

Herring, E. and K. Lomas (eds) (2009) *Gender Identities in Italy in the First Millennium* BC. BAR International Series 1983. Oxford.

Heurgon, J. (1964) *The Daily Life of the Etruscans.* New York. English translation of *La vie quotidienne chez les Étrusques.* Paris 1961.

Hodos, T. (1998) "The Asp's Poison: Women and Literacy in Iron Age Italy" in R. D. Whitehouse 1998, *Gender & Italian Archaeology.* Accordia Specialist Studies on Italy 7. London, 197–208.

Horsfall, N. (2003) *The Culture of the Roman Plebs,* London, Duckworth.

Horster, M. (2006) Review of Laskaris 2005. *BMCR* 2006.07.14.

Kleiner, D. E. E. (2000) "Family Ties. Mothers and sons in Elite and Non-Elite Roman Art" in Kleiner and Matheson 2000, 43–60.

Kleiner, D. E. E. and S. B. Matheson (eds) (2000) *I Claudia* II. *Women in Roman Art and Society. Yale University Art Gallery.* Austin, TX.

Koloski Ostrow, A. O. and C. L. Lyons (eds) (1997) *Naked Truths. Women, Sexuality, and Gender in Classical Art and Archaeology.* London and New York.

Laes, C. (2011) *Children in the Roman Empire: Outsiders Within.* Cambridge.

Landolfi, M. (1997) "I simboli di rango di una principessa picena" in Emiliozzi 1997, 229–236.

Laskaris, J. (2005) "Error, loss, and change in the generation of therapies" in Philip J. van der Eijk (ed.) *Hippocrates in Context.* Papers read at the XIth International Hippocrates Colloquium. University of Newcastle upon Tyne, 27–31 August 2002. Studies in Ancient Medicine 31. Leiden, Brill, 174–189.

——(2008) "Nursing Mothers in Greek and Roman Medicine," *AJA* 112 (2008) 459–464.

Lavin, M. A. and I. Lavin (2001) *The Liturgy of Love: Images from the Song of Songs in the Art of Cimabue, Michelangelo, and Rembrandt.* The Franklin D. Murphy lectures XIV. The Spencer Museum of Art, The University of Kansas.

Lefkowitz, M. R. and M. B. Fant (2005) *Women's Life in Greece and Rome. A Source Book in Translation.* Third edition. Baltimore.

Lewis, S. (2002) *The Athenian Woman. An Iconographic Handbook.* New York, London, Routledge.

Lorenzi, R. (2011) "Ancient Images of a Mother Giving Birth Found," *Discovery,* accessed Oct 19, 2011. Reprinted, *Etruscan News* 14, 2011, 17.

Lundeen, L. (2006) "In Search of the Etruscan Priestess" in *Religion in Republican Italy,* edited by C. Schultz and P. Harvey. Cambridge.

Martelli, M. "Opulence" in Torelli 2000, 566–567.

Miller, P. C. (ed.) (2005) *Women in Early Christianity.* Washington, DC.

Morandi Tarabella, M. (2004) *Prosopografia etrusca.* I. *Corpus. L'Etruria meridionale.* Rome.

Morgi Govi, C. (ed.) (2001) *Principi Etruschi tra Mediterraneo ed Europa.* Bologna, Marsilio.

Neils, J. (2011) *Women in the Ancient World.* London and Los Angeles, CA, 58–78.

Nielsen, M. (1989a) "Women and Family in a Changing Society: A Quantitative Approach to Late Etruscan Burials," *AnalRom* 17–18 (1989) 53–98.

——(1989b) "La donna e la famiglia nella tarda società etrusca" in Rallo 1989, 121–145.

——(1992) "Portrait of a Marriage. The Old Etruscan Couple from Volterra" in *Acta Hyperborea* 4, 1992, 89–141.

Nutt, W. (2011) "Digging it Up," *Etruscan News* 14, 2011, 17.

Pesarino, A. (2000) "Contributo allo studio del tipo della 'Virgo lactans': il papiro PSI XV 1574 dell'Istituto Papirologico G. Vitelli di Firenze," *Latomus* 59 (3) 640–646. Representation of the Madonna suckling the Christ-child on a 5th-early 6th century Coptic papyrus found at Antinoe, Egypt in 1936–1937 and now in Florence. This representation is considerably earlier than previously attested examples of the theme of the 'Virgo Lactans' in Egypt; the origin and development of this theme is surveyed.

Picón, C. A., J. R. Mertens, E. J. Milleker, C. S. Lightfoot and S. Hemingway (2007) *Art of the Classical World in the Metropolitan Museum of Art*. New York.

Pomeroy, S. B. (1983) "Infanticide in Hellenistic Greece" in Cameron and Kuhrt 1983, 207–219.

——(1995) *Goddesses, Whores, Wives and Slaves. Women in Classical Antiquity*. Originally published in 1975. New York.

——(2002) *Spartan Women*. Oxford 2002.

Rafanelli, S. and P. Spaziani (2011) *Etruschi. Il privilegio della bellezza*. Aboca, Florence.

Rallo, A. (ed.) (1989) *Le donne in Etruria*. Rome.

Ramussen, T. (2005) "Herakles' apotheosis in Etruria and Greece," *Antike Kunst* 48: 30–39.

Rawson, B. (ed.) (2011) *A Companion to Families in the Greek and Roman Worlds*. Malden, MA.

Ridgway, D. (1996) "Greek Letters at Osteria dell'Osa," *Opuscula Romana* 20: 87–97.

Säflund, G. (1993) *Etruscan Imagery. Symbol and Meaning*. Jonsered, Paul Åströms Verlag.

Sandhoff, B. (2011) "Sexual Ambiguity? Androgynous imagery in Etruria," *Etruscan Studies* 14 (2011) 71–96.

Scheid, J. and J. Svenbro (1996) *The Craft of Zeus: Myths of Weaving and Fabric*. Cambridge, MA.

Smith, C. J. (2000) "Worshipping Mater Matuta: Ritual and Context" in E. Bispham and C. J. Smith (eds) *Religion in Archaic and Republican Rome and Italy*. Edinburgh, 136–155.

Steinberg, L. (1996) *The Sexuality of Christ in Renaissance Art and in Modern Oblivion*. Chicago.

Steingräber, S. (1986) *Etruscan Painting*. New York, Johnson Reprints. Still the most complete repertoire, with information on each tomb.

——(2006) *Abundance of Life. Etruscan Wall Painting*. Los Angeles, CA. J. Paul Getty Museum. Includes the latest finds.

Text & Textile: An Introduction to Wool-Working for Readers of Greek and Latin (2004) (Video). S. Edmunds, P. Jones and G. Nagy. Department of Classics, Rutgers University, New Brunswick, NJ. Order from *http://classics.rutgers.edu*.

Tite, P. L. (2009) "Nurslings, Milk and Moral Development in the Greco-Roman Context: A Reappraisal of the Paraenetic Utilization of Metaphor in 1 Peter 2.1–3," *JSNT 3ÌA*, 371–400.

Torelli, M. (1997a) "Domiseda, lanifica, univira. Il trono di Verucchio e il ruolo e l'immagine della donna tra arcaismo e repubblica" in Torelli 1997b, 52–86.

——(1997b) *Il rango, il rito e l'immagine. Alle origini della rappresentazione storica romana*. Milan.

——(2000) *The Etruscans*. London.

Tran Tam Tinh, V. (1973) *Isis Lactans. Corpus des monuments gréco-romains d'Isis allaitant Harpocrate*. Leiden, Brill.

Turfa, J. M. (1998) Review of De Puma 1996. *BMCR* 1998.08.10.

——(2004) "Anatomical votives," *ThesCRA* 1, 359–368.

van der Meer, L. B. (1991) "Etruscan *Rites de Passage*," *Stips Votiva, Papers Presented to C.M. Stibbe*, (ed.) M. Gnade. Amsterdam, 119–126.

van der Meer, L. B. (1995) *Interpretatio Etrusca. Greek Myths on Etruscan Mirrors*. Amsterdam.

von Eles, P. (ed.) (2002) *Guerriero e Sacerdote. Autorità e comunità a Verucchio nell'età del ferro. La tomba del Trono*. Quaderni di Archeologia dell'Emilia Romagna 6.

——(ed.) (2006) *La ritualità funeraria tra età del ferro e orientalizzante in Italia*. Atti del Convegno, Verucchio, 26–27 June 2002. Biblioteca di "Studi Etruschi" 41. Istituti Editoriali e Poligrafici Internazionali. Pisa, Rome.

——(ed.) (2007) *Le ore e i giorni delle donne. Dalla quotidianità alla sacralità tra VIII e VII secolo*. Verucchio.

von Staden, H. (1992) "Women and Dirt," *Helios* 19: 7–30.

CHAPTER TWENTY ONE

SLAVERY AND MANUMISSION

———•◆•———

Enrico Benelli

HISTORICAL EVIDENCE

The existence of the institution of slavery in Etruria has never been doubted. Ancient historians and, more frequently, antiquarian sources refer repeatedly to Etruscan slaves; their somehow abnormal behavior (as seen from Greek standards) is a major component in the build-up of the image of Etruscan *tryphè*.[1] It is precisely these sources that inspired a reconstruction of Etruscan slavery as something completely different from similar Greek and Roman institutions; historians, at least before the last decades of the twentieth century, attempted to demonstrate that the Etruscan civilization, usually conceived as genuinely anti-classical before the diffusion of the historical approach first introduced by Pallottino's methods in the new discipline of Etruscology, never knew the inhumane custom of chattel slavery before its incorporation in the Roman world (and forced adoption of Roman laws and behaviors). This is the outcome of a long debate about the existence in Antiquity of more "humane" and morally acceptable forms of slavery, based on long-established family bonds, in which the relationship between master and slave assumed the paternalistic overtones that usually served to justify the various forms of serfdom widely diffused in modern Europe until at least the beginnings of the nineteenth century (but in some places even later); examples were found mostly in the Greek world, first of all in the Spartan institution of helotage. The widespread repugnance for chattel slavery favored an equally diffused appreciation of these forms of dependence, thought of as milder, morally justifiable, and somehow "humane" and "natural" (an idea about which the Helots themselves would have presumably dissented).[2]

It is probably no accident that the first assemblage of sources aimed at reconstructing some kind of helotry in the Etruscan world appears in Karl Ottfried Müller's handbook:[3] the same author was best known for his monumental work *die Dorier* ("that perniciously influential 1000-page fantasia...in which the helots and the dependent labour in other so-called Dorian states were together squeezed into twenty pages of blatant apologetics," in M. I. Finley's words).[4] Müller's ideas received widespread support and were later (supposedly) backed by linguistic arguments especially developed by Karl Pauli and Wilhelm Deecke (the latter arranged for a second edition of the handbook, with a substantial updating dealing especially with language and epigraphy).[5] This reconstruction, further implemented by S. P. Cortsen,[6] found its final triumph in the furiously anticlassical mood of the years immediately following World War II,[7] and it has required some pain to dismantle the collection of heterogeneous sources that supposedly backed it (while linguistic arguments had already evaporated thanks especially to Emil Vetter, Helmut Rix and Karl Olzscha).[8] The modern approach to these sources has completely changed.[9]

The idea of a slavery of the helotic kind as something completely different from a "real" slavery (usually identified with chattel slavery) appears in Greek political theories after the success of the Messenian revolt in 370/69 BC.[10] Aristotle, discussing the various forms of slavery, concluded that helotry was more dangerous for masters than chattel slavery, because the connection of Helots with the territory where they lived could provide a common ground on which to build up revolts (as it effectively happened), whilst slaves deprived of any common identity were less likely to pose such problems (he could of course not anticipate the slave revolts of the Roman late-republican period).[11] Modern historians accepting this categorization, starting from Müller himself, completely upturned this assumption, stating that it was chattel slavery that represented a "danger" for societies (a danger of a moral kind, of course). The definition of a supposedly widespread category of slavery of the helotic kind was reconstructed following lists of such "half-slaves" concocted by late-antique lexicographers, that included groups which were outright slaves and others who were on the contrary undoubtedly free people (only deprived of full political rights, as often happened in strongly oligarchic societies); these sources are now considered of limited or no use in reconstructing the real status of the various human groups mentioned in them.[12]

The equation between Etruscan lower classes and the Thessalian *Penestai* (a category frequently mentioned in relation with Helots and other supposedly similar population groups), often assumed through the evidence of Dionysius of Halicarnassus, can be ruled out by the non-technical use the author made of this word;[13] in any case, when the term πενέσται was used in a more technical sense, it always implied a conquest and enslaving of local populations by invading groups,[14] a process Dionysius could hardly have imagined for Etruria, as he was the almost sole supporter of a tradition of a totally autochthonous origin of the Etruscans.[15] On the other hand, other sources often cited to concoct the reconstruction of Etruscan "helotry" have completely different meanings: the description attributed to Posidonius, for example, must be interpreted in the framework of a somehow conventional view of Etruscan *tryphè*,[16] while the property right supposedly enjoyed by Etruscan slaves sometimes reconstructed on the basis of the "Prophecy of Vegoia," as well as on the evidence of the *peculium* of the Vergilian character Tityrus (implying a highly unlikely survival of Etruscan law in Augustan-age Mantua), is absolutely inconsistent, the instances cited completely understandable in the context of Roman custom.[17]

SLAVE REVOLTS

Slave revolts in Etruria are attested at least twice in our sources, in addition to the famous case of Volsinii in 265 BC, which requires special attention. The events of 196 BC were hardly a problem confined to Etruria itself, as they are only a part of a series of outbreaks of slave revolts in various areas of Italy.[18] It is possible that these events originated from the massive flow of slaves towards Italian markets following the Second Punic War (as explicitly stated in the case of the troubles at Setia in 198 BC), which resulted in large groups of enslaved persons of homogeneous ethnic origin finding themselves at work in the same places (exactly the circumstances Aristotle considered most dangerous). The mention of a *servile bellum* in Arretium in the *elogium* of Aulus Spurinna is somehow more puzzling; the first editor, Mario Torelli,[19] thought that the period of activity of this prominent Tarquinian magistrate should be set around the middle-fourth century BC; his intervention should therefore be considered in a framework of outright Tarquinian hegemony in the whole of Etruria. Archaeological evidence suggests that at some time before this period Tarquinii had conquered stretches of territory originally belonging to the neighboring cities of Caere and Volsinii; the prominence of Tarquinii in the wars against Rome is explicitly stated in historical sources, at least until the last decade of the fourth century BC, when it was for the first time heavily defeated, never to recover its previous standing. Moreover, a brief entry in Livy (10.3.2) recording internal disturbances in Arretium leading to a Roman intervention in 302 BC, could suggest the existence of mounting social tensions around those years. Mauro Cristofani, relying on the mention of a king of Caere in the same inscription, suggested that the actions of Aulus Spurinna should be pushed back at least a couple of centuries; epigraphic evidence, discovered only after Torelli's edition of the *elogia,* shows that monarchy had already disappeared in Caere by the middle-fourth century BC.[20] If this high dating of Aulus Spurinna is accepted, the "slave war" should therefore be considered something similar to what happened in high republican Rome, when slaves were employed more than once in the context of attempted coups, which some abridged narratives hastily defined as outright *bella servilia.*[21]

The great revolt which broke out in Volsinii in 265 BC was something completely different. The sources about this momentous event sketch it as a coup by elements labeled by most of the Latin authors as "freedpersons", "slaves" in other narratives, first of all the Greek one of Zonaras (eventually achieving their freedom by themselves, once they had attained full control of the government); in both traditions, the coup was fostered by the fact that the ruling classes of Volsinii had previously committed significant positions in state administration, and even in army command, to persons enjoying a subordinate status. The intervention by the Roman state, following a request by the dispossessed aristocrats, required a major siege by a consular army, resulting in pillage and destruction of the city, massacre of all rebels, and resettlement of the survivors in the new Volsinii on the shores of the Bolsena lake.[22] The Romans were obviously preoccupied with maintaining peace in central Italy while preparing the gigantic effort of the war against Carthage, and could not tolerate a radical change in policy of an allied state. What kind of people are to be understood under the definition of "slaves" or "freedpersons" is not entirely clear. It has often been thought that the narrative could fit well into the framework of Etruscan helotry reconstructed by nineteenth-century scholars, disregarding the fact that in societies exploiting slave institutions of this kind a mass enfranchisement was never remotely contemplated,[23] let alone commitment of governmental or military responsibilities. A high danger of ferocious uprisings was always present, as clearly stated by Aristotle. Present-day scholars prefer to interpret these "slaves" as plebeians living in a condition of legal marginality, whose real status was crucially misunderstood by Greek and Roman historians;[24] this would justify the apparent extent of the uprising. On the other hand, it should not be forgotten that the new Volsinii was a large and prosperous city, and its inscriptions reveal a significant continuity in family names with the old one. It is clear that enough of the inhabitants survived the massacre following the siege of 265/264 BC to people a new city of no lesser dimensions than the old one; a mass slaughter of the entire plebeian class seems highly unlikely.

EPIGRAPHIC EVIDENCE: FREEDPEOPLE

Not surprisingly, epigraphic evidence for freedpersons is more extensive than that available for slaves. The Etruscan word for freedman, *lautni/lavtni* (fem. *lautniθa/lavtniθa*, "freedwoman"), has traditionally been connected with *lautn,* "family," *lautni* meaning something like "man of the family."[25] The archaic feminine form *lauteniθa*, documented by a recently published inscription from Orvieto (see below), raises some doubts about this reconstruction. The archaic form of the word for "family," *lavtun*,[26] is also attested as stem of an onomastic series, which is not related with an indication of social condition; it starts with the archaic name *Lavtunie* from Marzabotto (*TLE* 706 = ET Fe 1.13[27]), whose (typically gentilicial) suffix *-ie* suggests it is to be interpreted as a family name (although an individual name cannot be entirely ruled out). The recent-age form of family name *Lautne/Lavtne* (fem. *Lautnei/Lavtnei*) is attested throughout Etruria (from Caere to Perusia, Arretium, Cortona, Volaterrae: *ThLE* I,² *s. vv.*). The female Clusine *cognomen Latuni* (whose male form is as yet unknown) belongs probably to this same series, while *Latni* is, at least once, only a syncopated form of the well-known family name *Latini* (and, in some instances, a simplified form for *lautni*: see *ThLE* I,² *s. vv.*, for references).

The most ancient freedperson known to us is *Kanuta*, freedwoman of a *Larecena* (and wife of an *Aranθ Pinie*) who was the author of a dedication of an altar in the Volsinian sanctuary of Campo della Fiera (*REE* 74, 140; see Chapter 31). The inscription belongs probably to the late Archaic period, as is shown by some characteristic epigraphic features, like the use of <f>, but especially the breaking of the text into separate lines, introduced in Etruscan writing not earlier than 510/500 BC. This individual was probably a freedwoman of a somehow privileged status, as is shown not only from her very appearance as a dedicator of an inscribed stone altar, but also from her marriage with a freeborn person (whose family name is already unknown in Orvieto: he belonged presumably to a lesser family than the *Larecena* themselves). Roman law began to intervene into matters regarding slaves and freedpersons at least by the time of the Twelve Tables (mid-fifth century BC), revealing that the sphere of action of such persons had begun to cross the borders of the gentilicial clans and to involve the whole society.[28] This required intervention by the State, especially concerning relations between slaves (and freedpersons) and freeborn people outside the *gens* to which they belonged; traditional customs centered on the authority of the *pater familias* were probably considered no longer sufficient to regulate such matters (although it is possible that such traditions continued to work inside the *gentes* themselves). As a result, at least from the mid-fifth century BC onwards, the status of slaves and freedpersons in the civic community as a whole was defined by public law. It is possible that Etruscan cities underwent similar developments, especially in the framework of the increased definition of the political sphere that characterized the late Archaic phase. It is probably no accident that epigraphic evidence for freedpeople and slaves begins exactly in the late Archaic period.[29]

After that one late Archaic testimony, inscriptions referring to freedpersons appear again in the third century BC, their number increasing dramatically between the second and the early first centuries BC, as a consequence of the enormous diffusion of chattel slavery in Italy after the Second Punic War. Most of the freedpersons in this period bore

Graecanic names, which betray their origin from Eastern Mediterranean slave markets. The evidence is heavily imbalanced between southern and northern Etruria; in the south of the region, only three freedmen are known, all of them from votive inscriptions,[30] while southern Etruscan funerary epigraphy remained impervious to lower social classes. In the northern cities, on the contrary, a couple of hundred funerary inscriptions of freedpersons are known, the greatest part of them from Clusium and Perusia and their territories. Their incidence in epigraphy is comprised between 3% in Volaterrae and 4% in Clusium: a remarkable success for former chattel slaves, most of them of foreign origin, only attainable in the exceptional conditions of robust economic growth of second- and first-century BC northern Etruria.

Etruscan slaves, when enfranchised, retained their individual name, transforming it into a family name, and adding to it a citizen *praenomen*; the former master's name is almost always mentioned, as is the indication of status (*lautni/lavtni* or *lautniθa/ lavtniθa*, sometimes abbreviated, syncopated or otherwise truncated); this last element is important especially when (as often happens) the *praenomen* is not explicitly written in the funerary inscriptions,[31] and the name could otherwise appear as a slave's name. As far as our evidence goes, freedpersons were hardly ever buried in their former master's family grave (as often happened in the Roman world),[32] but usually chose (or were obliged) to do otherwise; this was facilitated by the fact that in some northern Etruscan cities (Clusium, especially, but also Perusia) it was possible to buy individual spaces in common tombs, and even families or individuals who could not afford the construction of a private tomb of their own were allowed access to formal burial (and, consequently, to archaeological and epigraphic visibility). Freedpersons are found buried in tombs together with freeborn people belonging to other families, in some cases even of high standing, since common tombs were in no way reserved to individuals of lesser social level only. Typical of the later period (first century BC) are marriages between immigrant freedmen and freeborn women of local origin, probably belonging to minor families, as their family names usually appear for the first time in epigraphy in these occasions: it is reasonable to assume that the social gap had been crossed thanks to a (relative) wealth possessed by these immigrants; such marriages proved advantageous for both parties concerned (providing social recognition for immigrant freedpersons, and economic improvement for the local families).[33] We do not know what kind of legal ties bound the freedperson to his/her former master, and whether Etruscan law or custom contemplated something like the duties Roman *patroni* could ask their freedpeople to perform.[34]

Some Etruscan funerary inscriptions of freedpersons from Clusium and Perusia show a name formula of the Roman kind, with the family name reproducing the former master's one; they must refer to enfranchisements following the *lex Iulia* of 90 BC, and the consequent adoption of Roman law by Etruscan cities.[35] It is interesting that the only freedman attested from Caere, to be dated probably into the third century BC, had a genuinely Roman name formula; the city of Caere had received Roman citizenship at some point between 390 and 273 BC, and even names of freeborn people, from the third century BC onwards, followed Roman customs.[36]

EPIGRAPHIC EVIDENCE: SLAVES

The Etruscan word for "slave" is not known to us,[37] despite some proposals by nineteenth-century scholars, that have astonishingly survived their dismissal by linguistic research at least from the mid-twentieth century. The Etruscan slave had an individual name followed by his/her master's name in the genitive case. In the Archaic period a name formula of that kind could be easily confused with the one currently used by freeborn people (often displaying the "afunctional genitive" -*s* ending): this is why an enclytic pronoun -*sa* (not to be confused with the determinate article -*śa*) was added to the master's name. We know, for instance, of a *Kape Mukaθesa*, Kape (slave) of a Mukaθe (CIE 11147 = ET Vc 6.1), and of an *Aranθ Heracanasa*, Aranθ (slave) of a Heracana (REE 30, p. 284, 1 = ET Ta 7.12[38]). In the later period, when only a handful of *praenomina* were deemed acceptable for freeborn people, and the "afunctional genitive" was gradually dropped, it had become impossible to make such mistakes; the enclytic -*sa* consequently disappeared. Epigraphic documents mentioning slaves are very uncommon: a *Murila Hercnas* making a luxurious dedication in a sanctuary of Tarquinii (CIE 10007 = ET Ta 3.6)[39], a *Tasma Śatnas* buried near Bagnoregio, in the territory of Volsinii (REE 35, p. 546 = ET Vs 1.257), and an *Antipater Cicuś* buried in the territory of Clusium (CIE 2004 = ET Cl 1.1502) are the only individuals clearly recognizable as slaves from a body of evidence comprising several thousands of inscriptions. Two of their names belong to the Graecanic type, the third (*Tasma*) is an Etruscan transcription of a Messapian name,[40] suggesting the existence of different sources for slaves in Hellenistic age Etruria. A number of slave names are known also from captions in the famous scene of food preparation for their masters' (Underworld) banquet painted on the walls of the Tomb Golini I at Porano (near Orvieto).[41] In addition to these instances, it must be taken into account that at least some of the many isolated names commonly found in proprietary inscriptions could have belonged to slaves (or freedpersons), but it is impossible to achieve a reasonable degree of certainty in the absence of a clear indication of a master's name.

NOTES

1   See especially Liébert 2006, with references.
2   Finley 1998, pp. 79–134.
3   Müller 1828, pp. 376–380.
4   Finley 1998, p. 89.
5   See especially Deecke 1884, pp. 35–36.
6   Cortsen 1925, pp. 77–89.
7   See for example Heurgon 1957; Mazzarino 1957; Frankfort 1959.
8   See especially Vetter 1948, c. 66; Rix 1963, p. 371 n. 165; Olzscha 1968. See also Benelli 2003 for a comprehensive history of studies.
9   The best account on this topic is Harris 1971, pp. 114–124.
10 See especially Cartledge 2003, p. 16; Cartledge 2011, with literature.
11 *Politics* 1330 a 25–8; the idea of helotage as potentially dangerous was already present in Plato's *Laws*: see Garnsey 1996, pp. 53–56.
12 See especially van Wees 2003; Cartledge 2011, pp. 78–82, with references.
13 9.5.4; for a brief review of literary evidence see Benelli 1996.
14 About Thessalian *Penestai*, after the classical study by Ducat 1994, see especially van Wees 2003, pp. 53–63, and Welwei 2008.
15 See especially Briquel 1993.
16 Diodorus 5.40.3 (to be read in comparison with the famous description by Theopompus, in Athenaeus 12.14.517d–518b, about scandalous and immoral Etruscan customs); see Liébert 2006, pp. 51–176, with references. The idea that inappropriate behavior by slaves (including exhibition of wealth and excessive freedom) is a sign of a "degeneration" of slavery, leading

ultimately to subversion of rules and destruction of social order, is not uncommon in Greek political thought; it reappears, for instance, in the charges against Athenian democracy in Ps.-Xen. Ath. Pol. 1.10–12 (Cataldi 2000).

17 Use of *peculium* in the form of land-plots and other goods as an incentive for agricultural slaves: see especially Cha 1988, p. 434; Roth 2005, p. 291; Aubert 2009, pp. 179–183, with references.

18 Bradley 2011, pp. 246–247; sources on slave uprisings before the outbreak of the first great revolt in Sicily in 141 BC: Capozza 1966 (the ideological bias of this unquestionably precious work can be hardly overestimated).

19 Torelli 1975, pp. 80–82.

20 Cristofani 1995, pp. 29–30. The odd municipal government of Imperial-age Caere (comprising a *dictator*, an *aedilis iure dicundo*, an *aedilis annonae* and a *censor perpetuus*: see CIL XI, 3593, 3614, 3616–3617) probably reproduced Etruscan age magistracies, culminating with a single eponymous *zilath*, and had nothing to do with a kingship that had presumably long since disappeared. Some lines of the inscription of the *aequipondium* from Caere with *zilath*-dating are poorly preserved, and various readings have been proposed; the most reliable is probably Maggiani's one: Moretti Sgubini 2001, p. 153.

21 Sources in Capozza 1966, pp. 17–72; see also Storchi Marino 1997, p. 196.

22 The best account of the evidence is Harris 1971, pp. 115–118. The narrative of events in Volsinii is probably not unrelated to widespread ideas about Etruscan *tryphè*: the behavior of the supposed "slaves" and their masters fits suspiciously into such a framework: see especially Liébert 2006, pp. 242–255. The inevitable connection between all narratives of the Volsinian uprising and the theme of *tryphè/luxuria* is correctly stressed also by Capozza 1997, a thorough examination of the literary sources about the event, with fundamental references to the significance the ancient authors themselves could have attributed to this episode (a circumstance helping to explain the differences between the sources).

23 Even the exceptional and innovative policy adopted by Nabis to attempt a renewal of Spartan fortunes was not intended to free all helots, but only a part of them – maybe even a minority: see Cartledge & Spawforth 1989, pp. 69–70.

24 See for instance Colonna 2003, p. 145.

25 Rix 1994, pp. 96–116. In some inscriptions, the word *lautni* is used as an adjective meaning "belonging to the family" (*e.g.* CIE 5470 > ET Ta 1.182, *śuθi lavtni*, "family tomb").

26 This archaic form appears only in the *Tabula Capuana*: see Cristofani 1995a, pp. 52, 101–105, but also Rix 1994, p. 115.

27 The inscription, despite its classification in ET, is not funerary at all; it is incised on a stone weight, and is generally recognized either as proprietary, or as a mention of the person whose authority guaranteed the weight itself.

28 See especially López Barja de Quiroga 2007, pp. 108–113; Bradley 2011, pp. 243–244 and Gardner 2011, with references.

29 About slavery in Etruria and Rome in the Archaic period, and the possible sources of slaves before the establishment of large slave markets in the middle- to late-republican age, see (especially) Welwei 2000, Auliard 2002 and Nash Briggs 2002–2003 (maybe over-simplistic).

30 CIE 11155 (Volcii); Colonna 1989–90, p. 895, of unknown provenance (but safely attributable to Caere thanks to palaeographical elements); *ibid.* p. 891, of unknown provenance (generically from southern Etruria).

31 Funerary inscriptions from Clusium and Perusia often did not reproduce the complete official name of the deceased; fundamental components of the name formula could be omitted, while other elements could be added. This probably reflected the circumstance that inscriptions were usually on objects put inside the tomb, and not on public display; the inscribed name identified the deceased in a form that suited the needs of the group that had access to the tomb. This is true for freeborn people as well as for freedpersons, whose names appear

frequently in abridged forms; the personal name (*praenomen*) introduced after manumission is often omitted. I suspect that in name forms like, for instance, *Haśti Preśnteś lavtnita* (REE 71, 66) it is the freedperson's family name (= his/her former individual name as slave) that is lacking: anyway, in most similar cases (like the present one) archaeological dating shows that the burial belongs to a very late period, and it is highly likely that their manumission took place under Roman law (after 90 BC); if this is the case, the freedperson's family name will be identical with their former master's one (see below).

32   The exceptions are very few, and for the best part are referred to the first century BC, and to freedpeople originating from immigrant, non-native families.

33   see Benelli 2012.

34   Waldstein 1986 provides the most comprehensive review about this topic. The evidence from burial customs seems to suggest that the Etruscan *lautni* were more independent from their former masters' families than the Roman *liberti*: but this same evidence could be read otherwise (for instance, it is possible that freeborn families, especially of higher status, simply could not accept sharing their tombs with their former slaves).

35   These occurrences are not recognized in the lists by Rix 1994, pp. 100–106: see Benelli 2009, pp. 309–310, nn. 21–22.

36   Kaimio 1975, p. 195; the inscription is cited above, n. 30.

37   Rix 1994, pp. 66–67, with references.

38   The reading of this inscription in ET is untenable.

39   Ambrosini 2002, pp. 233 n. 119; 428–430.

40   Cf. the *praenomina Dazimas*, MLM 6 Cae. (masculine); *Dazomas*, MLM 4 Cae., 21 Gn., 27 Gn., 23 Ro. (masculine); *Dazoma*, MLM 3 Ro. (feminine); and other related forms.

41   See Feruglio 1995, pp. 29–52, with references.

BIBLIOGRAPHY

Ambrosini, L. (2002) *Thymiateria etruschi in bronzo di età tardo classica, alto e medioellenistica*, Rome: "L'ERMA" di Bretschneider.

Aubert, J.-J. (2009) "Productive investments in agriculture: *instrumentum fundi* and *peculium* in the later Roman republic," in J. Carlsen and E. Lo Cascio (eds), *Agricoltura e scambi nell'Italia tardo-repubblicana*, Bari: Edipuglia, pp. 167–185.

Auliard, C. (2002) "Les esclaves dans les butins républicains des premiers siècles de la conquête" in M. Garrido-Hory (ed.), *Routes et marchés d'esclaves. 26ᵉ colloque du GIREA* (Besançon 2001), Paris: Presses universitaires Franc-comtoises, pp. 51–64.

Benelli, E. (1996) "Sui cosiddetti penesti etruschi," *La Parola del Passato* 51, pp. 335–344.

——(2003) "Una misconosciuta nota di Gustav Herbig e l'etrusco *etera*" in *Miscellanea etrusco-italica* III, Rome: C.N.R, pp. 209–221.

——(2009) "La società chiusina fra la guerra annibalica e l'età di Augusto. Osservazioni archeologiche ed epigrafiche," *Ostraka* 18, pp. 303–322.

——(2012) "Matrimoni misti e identità in cambiamento: Chiusi da città etrusca a municipio romano" in S. Marchesini (ed.), *Matrimoni misti: una via per l'integrazione tra i popoli. Atti del convegno* (Verona-Trento 2011), Trento, pp. 103–109. Trento: Provincia Autonoma di Trento.

Bradley, K. (2011) "Slavery in the Roman Republic" in Bradley and Cartledge, pp. 241–264.

Bradley, K. and P. Cartledge (eds) (2011) *The Cambridge world history of slavery, 1, The ancient Mediterranean world*, Cambridge: Cambridge University Press.

Briquel, D. (1993) *Les Tyrrhènes peuple des tours. Denys d'Halicarnasse et l'autochtonie des Étrusques*, Rome (Collection de l'École Française de Rome, 178).

Capozza, M. (1966) *Movimenti servili nel mondo romano in età repubblicana, I. Dal 501 al 184 a. Cr.*, Rome: "L'ERMA" di Bretschneider.

——(1997) La tradizione sui conflitti sociali a Volsini nel III secolo a.C.: dai servi agli *oiketai* attraverso i *liberti* in *Atene e Roma* 42, pp. 28–41.

Cartledge, P. (2003) "Raising hell? The Helot Mirage – a personal review" in Luraghi and Alcock, pp. 12–30.

——(2011) The Helots: a contemporary review, in Bradley and Cartledge, pp. 74–90

Cartledge, P. and A. Spawforth (1989) *Hellenistic and Roman Sparta. A tale of two cities*, London-New York: Routledge.

Cataldi, S. (2000) "Ἀκολασία e ἰσηγορία di meteci e schiavi nell'Atene dello Pseudo-Senofonte: una riflessione socio-economica" in M. Sordi (ed.), *L'opposizione nel mondo antico*, Milan: Vita e pensiero, pp. 75–101.

Cha, Y.-G. (1988) The function of peculium in Roman slavery during the first two centuries A.D. in T. Yuge and M. Doi (eds), *Forms of control and subordination in antiquity (Proceedings of the International Symposium for Studies in Ancient Worlds*, Tokyo 1986), Leiden: Brill, pp. 433–436.

CIE – *Corpus Inscriptionum Etruscarum*.

CIL – *Corpus Inscriptionum Latinarum*.

Colonna, G. (1989–1990) "Le iscrizioni votive etrusche," *Scienze dell'Antichità* 3–4, pp. 875–903.

——(2003) "Le vicende storiche di Orvieto etrusca" in G. M. Della Fina (ed.), *Storia di Orvieto, 1. Antichità*, Perugia: QuattroEmme, pp. 125–146.

Cortsen, S. P. (1925) *Die etruskischen Standes- und Beamtentitel durch die Inschriften beleuchtet*, Copenhagen: Høst & Son.

Cristofani, M. (1995) "Le città etrusche e Roma," *Eutopia* 4,2 (= Atti del convegno internazionale "*nomen Latinum*) Rome: Leo S. Olschki , pp. 21–31.

——(1995) *Tabula Capuana. Un calendario festivo di età arcaica*, Florence.

Deecke, W. (1884) *Etruskische Forschungen und Studien, VI. Die etruskischen Beamten- und Priester-Titel*, Stuttgart: Heitz.

Ducat, J. (1994) *Les Pénestes de Thessalie*, Paris: Les belles lettres.

ET – H. Rix (1991) *Etruskische Texte*, Tübingen: Narr Verlag.

Feruglio, A. E. (1995) *Porano. Gli Etruschi*, Perugia: QuattroEmme.

Finley, M. I. (1998) *Ancient slavery and modern ideology*. Expanded edition edited by B. D. Shaw, Princeton: Wiener Publishers.

Frankfort, T. (1959) Les classes serviles en Étrurie, *Latomus* 18, pp. 3–22.

Gardner, J. F. (2011) "Slavery and Roman law" in Bradley and Cartledge, pp. 414–437.

Garnsey, P. (1996) *Ideas of Slavery from Aristotle to Augustine*, Cambridge: Cambridge University Press.

Harris, W. V. (1971) *Rome in Etruria and Umbria*, Oxford: Clarendon Press.

Heurgon, J. (1957) "L'État étrusque," *Historia* 6, pp. 63–97.

Kaimio, J. (1975) "The ousting of Etruscan by Latin in Etruria" in *Studies in the romanization of Etruria, Acta Instituti Romani Finlandiae*, 5, pp. 85–245.

Liébert, Y. (2006) *Regards sur la truphè étrusque*, Limoges: Presses universitaires de Limoges.

López Barja de Quiroga, P. (2007) *Historia de la manumisión en Roma. De los orígenes a los Severos*, Madrid: Universidad Complutense de Madrid, (Gerión Anejos, IX).

Luraghi, N. and S. E. Alcock (eds) (2003) *Helots and their masters in Laconia and Messenia. Histories, ideologies, structures* (Papers from a workshop, Harvard 2001), Washington: Center for Hellenic Studies.

Mazzarino, S. (1957) "Sociologia del mondo etrusco e problemi della tarda etruscità," *Historia* 6, pp. 98–122.

MLM – C. de Simone and S. Marchesini (eds) (2002) *Monumenta linguae Messapicae*, Wiesbaden: Reichert.

Moretti Sgubini, A. M. (ed.) (2001) *Veio, Cerveteri, Vulci. Città d'Etruria a confronto* (Catalogo della mostra, Rome 2001), Rome: "L'ERMA" di Bretschneider .

Müller, K. O. (1828) *Die Etrusker*, Breslau: J. Max & Comp.

Nash Briggs, D. (2002–2003) "Servants at a rich man's feast. Early Etruscan household slaves and their procurement," *Etruscan Studies* 9, pp. 153–176.

Olzscha, K. (1968) "Etruskisch *lautn* und *etera*," *Glotta* 46, pp. 212–227.

REE – *Rivista di epigrafia etrusca* in *Studi Etruschi*.

Rix, H. (1963) *Das etruskische Cognomen*, Wiesbaden: Harassowitz.

Rix, H. (1994) *Die Termini der Unfreiheit in den Sprachen alt-Italiens*, Stuttgart: Steiner Verlag.

Roth, U. (2005) Food, Status and the *Peculium* of Agricultural Slaves, *Journal of Roman Archaeology* 18, pp. 278–292.

Storchi Marino, A. (1997) "Schiavitù e forme di dipendenza in Roma arcaica. Alcune considerazioni" in M. Moggi and G. Cordiano (eds), *Schiavi e dipendenti nell'ambito dell'"oikos" e della "familia."* *Atti del XXII Colloquio GIREA* (Pontignano 1995), Pisa: ETS, pp. 183–212.

ThLE, I² – *Thesaurus linguae Etruscae*, I, Indice lessicale, Pisa-Roma: Fabrizio Serra Editore 2009.

TLE – *Testimonia linguae Etruscae*

Torelli, M. (1975) *Elogia Tarquiniensia*, Florence: Sansoni.

van Wees, H. (2003) Conquerors and serfs: wars of conquest and forced labour in archaic Greece in Luraghi and Alcock, pp. 33–80.

Vetter, E. (1948) "Die etruskischen Personennamen *leθe, leθi, leθia* und die Namen unfreier oder halbfreier Personen bei den Etruskern," *Jahreshefte des Österreichischen archäologischen Instituts* 37, Beiblatt, cc. 57–112.

Waldstein, W. (1986) *Operae libertorum. Untersuchungen zur Dienstpflicht freigelassener Sklaven*, Stuttgart: Steiner Verlag.

Welwei, K.-W. (2000) *Sub corona vendere. Quellenkritische Studien zu Kriegsgefangenschaft und Sklaverei in Rom bis zum Ende des Hannibalkrieges*, Stuttgart: Steiner Verlag.

Welwei, K.-W. (2008) Neuere Forschungen zur Rechtstellung der Penesten, in P. Mauritsch, W. Petermandel and R. Rollinger *et al.* (eds), *Antike Lebenswelten. Konstanz – Wandel – Wirkungsmacht. Festschrift für Ingomar Weiler zum 70. Geburtstag*, Wiesbaden: Harassowitz, pp. 393–411.

CHAPTER TWENTY TWO

THE ETRUSCAN LANGUAGE

—— ·◆· ——

Luciano Agostiniani

THE DOCUMENTATION

Etruscan[1] is a dead language, the knowledge of which – in contrast to other dead languages like Latin or Greek – has been completely lost, and therefore it is accessible for us only through the surviving evidence: the written documents and the so-called "Etruscan glosses." The latter contribution to our knowledge of the language is minimal. We are dealing, as is known, with about sixty words – the greater part of them reported by the *Lexicon* of Hesychius and by the *Liber Glossarum*, and the rest by authors such as Varro, Verrius Flaccus, Dioscorides, Strabo and others – that the ancients have passed down to us as Etruscan, providing a Greek or Latin translation. Their number, in itself modest, decreases further when one considers that some of them, such as κάπρα or δέα reported by Hesychius, are obviously not Etruscan words but rather Latin-Italic. Moreover, the words often appear in Graecized or Latinized form (as exemplified by the case of αισ-οῖ, "gods," also in Hesychius, with an inflectional ending -οῖ, which is a Greek nominative plural): this makes them very unreliable evidence for the sounds or forms of Etruscan.

Therefore, our knowledge of the Etruscan language rests essentially on written documents, which – except in one case, as we shall see – consist of inscriptions. Now, if by "inscription" is meant, in a very general sense, every manifestation of writing that is in itself complete (although possibly lacking one or more parts, due to accidents occurring in the transmission of the text), including also alphabetic *sigla*, abbreviations and the like, we can say that Etruscan is attested by about 11,000 inscriptions, and this testifies to a highly developed use of writing. Their upper chronological limit falls at the very beginning of the seventh century BC (the earliest Etruscan inscription seems to be the graffito from Tarquinia, Ta 3.1), while the lower limit is the first century AD, with the bilingual inscription on a funerary urn from Arezzo, Ar 1.8 (in agreement with the testimony of Dionysius of Halicarnassus 1.30, who says that Etruscan was still spoken in the time of Augustus).

GEOGRAPHICAL AND
CHRONOLOGICAL DISTRIBUTION

Geographically, the inscriptions are distributed in an area that includes Etruria proper and the areas of Etruscan expansion: Campania (Capua, Suessula, Nola), Emilia-Romagna (Piacenza, Bologna, Ravenna, Adria, Spina), Lombardy, Corsica (Aleria). Other inscriptions are regionally eccentric, and should probably be considered the result of a sporadic and occasional presence of Etruscans: thus the funerary stele of the late sixth century BC found at Busca in Piedmont, Li 1.1, and the *"tessera hospitalis"* ("visiting card"), also of the sixth century BC, found at Carthage (Af 3.1).

Harder to explain is the presence of a certain number of inscriptions, all of the second half of the sixth century BC, found on the island of Lemnos in the Northern Aegean: fifteen graffiti on vases, a votive offering-base of stone inscribed with a dedication, and the funerary stele of Kaminia (Fig. 22.1), dedicated to a warrior, Holaie Phokiaš, which mentions his age and some events in his life. The language is nothing but a variety of Etruscan – and not a generally "Etruscoid" language as stated in the past – characterized, it seems, by linguistic features that are more archaic than those predictable according to the dating of the text. On the historical significance of the presence of an Etruscan inscription on Lemnos debate remains open (Agostiniani 2012): are we dealing with Etruscans who came from Italy, perhaps in connection with trading activities or even piracy? Or rather – as those claim who accept the hypothesis of an origin of the Etruscans from Asia Minor, in the tradition of Herodotus – a settlement linked to a "migration" from East to West? Undoubtedly, playing against the first hypothesis is the fact, reported by archaeologists, that on Lemnos there is no other trace of Etruscan material culture; and it cannot be proven – as has been maintained – that the text of the stele references institutions and usages typical of the Etruscans of Italy (such as eponymy, the use of the metronymic or a formula with indication of the age of the deceased).

Figure 22.1   Stele from Kaminia (Lemnos), late sixth century BC
(Athens, National Archaeological Museum).

ASPECTS OF VARIABILITY

As a whole, the Etruscan inscriptions all appear to reflect the same language: and this implies the existence of a standardized variety, at least in written language. But within the written standard uniformity is not absolute: just as one would expect, given that the inscriptions are distributed over a wide geographic area and over a period of at least seven centuries.[2] Accordingly, it has long been established that there are two historical varieties, one called "Archaic Etruscan," which includes the inscriptions of the seventh through fifth centuries BC, the other named "Late Etruscan," or "Neo-Etruscan," which includes the inscriptions of the fourth to first centuries BC. Compared to Archaic Etruscan, Late Etruscan is characterized by the presence of phenomena of weakening and disappearance of vowels, so *turuce* "dedicated" > *turce, RamuΘa* (woman's name) > *RamΘa*, and so on; by the monophthongization of the archaic diphthong *ai* to *e*, for which the name of Ajax, *Aivas* > *Evas*; and finally, by the lowering of some original *i*s to *e*, as in *ica* "this" > *eca* (to all these phenomena we shall return later, when describing the sounds). As regards the existence of geographical diversity, there is the recent discovery that at least one trait seems to characterize linguistically the two varieties of Etruscan, the "northern" and "southern", which are already differentiated by letter forms: namely, the presence, in the northern inscriptions, of the palatal *s* / š / in the same contexts in which the southern inscriptions have a dental *s* / s / (we will also return to this when describing the sounds).

Analogous aspects of variability are found in the writing of the texts.[3] It has been established that the alphabet used was originally a Greek alphabet, namely the Euboean (Chalcidian) version brought by Greek settlers to Campania and passed on to the Etruscans through cultural contacts. But, obviously, the form of some letters has changed over time and there are distinguished – to simplify greatly – archaic alphabetic varieties (where, for example, *my* and *ny* are the type 𐌌 and 𐌍) from recent varieties (in which the two signs are, respectively, of the type 𐌟 and 𐌦). On the other hand, adaptation of the alphabet to the needs of the Etruscan language entailed a number of problems: first, how to bridge two gaps in the model alphabet (the absence of signs to represent / š / and / f /, sounds alien to Greek); and second, how to choose between graphic alternatives (the model alphabet had two signs for / s /, *sigma* 𐊖 and *sade* 𐌌, and two signs for / k /, *kappa* 𐌊 and *koppa* 𐊥).

This has led to the formation of two different geographic varieties, the northern and southern. The northern area shows the use, from the earliest manifestations of writing, of a system with a high degree of functionality and is therefore quite stable: / k / is represented by a single sign, 𐌊 (compared to the three that, as we shall see, characterize the early southern scripts); and the functional contrast between / s / and / š / is made through the use of two different signs, respectively 𐌌 and 𐊖.

Compared to this writing system, one that remains substantially unchanged over time, in the southern area the situation is far more complex. For the representation of / k / Etruscan at first used not only 𐌊 and 𐊥 as in the Greek model, but added 𐌂, therefore: 𐌊A 𐊥V 𐌂𐌙 𐌂I (the selection of the letter depends on the vowel that follows). This system, objectively complex, is simplified at an early stage (in the most recent southern varieties / k / is always written with 𐌂), and constitutes the basis of the Latin alphabet (later passed on to modern languages). As regards the representation of / s / and / š /, initially the same sign, 𐊖, is used for both, but soon different centers in southern Etruria sought to remedy the situation of "graphic under-differentiation," and in different ways: at Tarquinia, 𐊖 for

/ s / is joined by M for / š /, while at Caere the sign for / š / is ⋜ ("four-stroke sigma"); and finally, at Veii (but also at Caere) / s / is represented by a cross mark X (also ╀), while ʃ represents / š /.

In diagram:

	/s/	/š/
Tarquinia	ʃ	M
Caere	ʃ	⋜
Veii (and Caere)	X	ʃ

For the rendering of / f / there is evidence in the southern area, at first, of the use of a digamma, �ᚺᛘ or ᛗᚺ, which is replaced (but only in the late sixth century BC) by a unique sign, 8, taken from one of the Italic alphabets. For the northern area archaic evidence is lacking, and the only sign that we find in use is 8.

TEXT TYPES

If we consider what kind of texts comprise the Etruscan epigraphic corpus,[4] it is easy to see that all those that were lost, predictably, were the documents of "normal" use in writing in the Etruscan world: papyri, parchments, waxed tablets, all the linen books with a single exception, and most of the lead plaques. Their loss is largely due to the perishable nature of the supports, or because of their reuse, in the case of metals such as bronze or lead. Hence the almost total absence from the corpus of texts representative of certain kinds of writing, such as literary texts, archival documents – legal texts, annals and other historical texts, letters, dictionaries, grammars.

In fact, the so-called "long texts" of the Etruscan corpus, i.e. that select handful of fewer than ten texts that exceed 30/40 words, on which rests much of what we know about the language, belong to one of these categories, especially that of archival documents. If they have come down to us, it is due to fortuitous and exceptional circumstances: for example, the occasional use of non-perishable material, such as clay in the case of the "Tablet of Capua"; or the fact that the document was transcribed on non-perishable medium (stone in the case of the "*Cippus* of Perugia," bronze in the case of the "*Tabula Cortonensis*"); or a "recycling" such as that to which we owe the preservation of the manuscript of the "*Liber linteus*" (see below); or pure chance, for texts using materials that are typically reused, such as lead or gold (so the "Magliano Lead Plaque," the "S. Marinella Plaque," the "Pyrgi Plaques").

The longest extant Etruscan text is the "Manuscript of Zagreb,"[5] the only non-epigraphic document in the Etruscan corpus. This is a "*liber linteus*," i.e. a manuscript written with a brush on a linen cloth, dating to the third-second century BC. It ended up, it is not known how, in Egypt, where it was re-cut horizontally into long strips used as bandages to wrap a mummy. It was originally divided into twelve rectangular panels, each with 34 lines of writing. The cloth was folded "accordion-fashion" along the lines of the vertical panels: these functioned like the pages of a book. Only some of the strips

are preserved, so that the manuscript has large gaps. The text consists of approximately
1,350 words and about 400 different lexical units (some of the lexical units appearing
more than once). It is a ritual calendar, describing the ceremonies that should be made
on established days for the benefit of various divinities. Example (LL VIII.3) (Fig. 22.2):

(1)	*celi*	*huθiś*	*zaθrumiś*	*flerχva*	*neθunsl*	*śucri* ...
	On September	six	twenty	offerings	to Neptune	are to be dedicated (?)

["On September twenty six offerings are to be dedicated (?) to Neptune"]

Second in text length is the so-called "Capua Tablet" (Fig. 22.3), incised on a slab of
terracotta found at S. Maria Capua Vetere in Campania.[6] It is divided into ten sections by
horizontal lines, and is currently made up of 62 lines, some with lacunae, and of about
390 words, not all completely preserved. The lexical units present are about 200. The
script is the one used in Campania around the mid-fifth century BC. It is, as in the case of
the "Zagreb mummy," a "ritual calendar": it prescribes the ceremonies to be performed
at certain dates (and in some places) in favor of some deities.

An example from Section I, lines 2–3:

(2)	... *leθamsul*	*ci*	*tartiria*	*ci-m*	*cleva*	*acasri* ...
	to Lethams	three	*tartiria*	and three	*cleva*	are to be offered (?)

The "*Tabula Cortonensis*,"[7] recently retrieved, is a bronze tablet with a text of 32 rows on
one side, eight rows on the other – for a total of 206 words, which puts it in third place
among the "longer texts" in the Etruscan corpus. This is a legal document, dating from

Figure 22.2 *Liber Linteus*, from northern Etruria, second century BC (Zagreb, Archaeological Museum).

Figure 22.3   Detail of the Tablet of Capua, fifth century BC, first half (Berlin, Staatliche Museen).

the late third–early second century BC, which registers a transaction that relates to land (presumably, the subdivision of a *latifundium*, for which historical and archaeological parallels are not lacking in this period). Almost half of the words are personal names. The lexical units are 60, some appearing more than once; the total occurrences of lexical units are 90. Let's cite the beginning of the text (Fig. 22.4):

(3) *et* *pêtruś scêvês* *êliun-tś* *vina-c* *restm-c* *cenu*
thus by Petru Scevas the *eliun* the vineyard and the *restm* (were) Xed,

["thus, the vineyard and the *restm* (were) Xed by Petru Scevas, the *eliun*"]

Another legal document is the so-called "*Cippus* of Perugia," (Fig. 22.5) a rectangular travertine stone *cippus* (block-like marker), found near Perugia. The inscription, dated between the third and second century BC, runs in 24 lines on the front and continues on

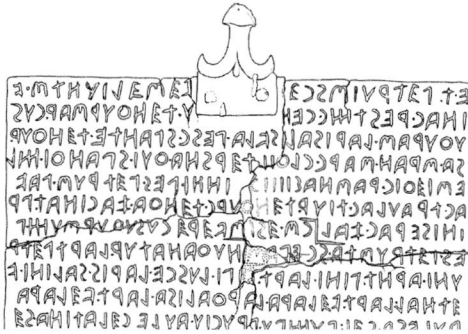

Figure 22.4   Detail of the *Tabula Cortonensis*, late third-second century BC
(Cortona, Museo dell'Accademia Etrusca e della Città di Cortona).

Figure 22.5   *Cippus* of Perugia, early second century BC
(Perugia, Museo Archeologico Nazionale dell'Umbria).

one of the short-sides with 22 rows, for a total of 128 words. It is the transcript on stone of a judgment concerning property issues between the Velthina and Afuna families of Perugia.

The other "long texts" are even shorter: four inscriptions, which are here listed and briefly described. The "Santa Marinella Plaque" (Cr 4.10) is a sheet of lead, found in the sanctuary of Punta della Vipera.[8] It is preserved in two non-joining fragments. The text, for a total of about 80 words (of which only 40 are legible) is incised on both sides. It dates from the late sixth or early fifth century BC, and is believed to be an oracular response. The "Lead Plaque of Magliano" (AV 4.1) is also a lead plaque, roughly circular in shape.[9] The inscription runs in a spiral on both sides (Fig. 22.6), and dates back to the mid-fifth century BC. It consists of about 70 words and is thought to be a description of rituals. The "Inscription of Laris Pulenas" (Ta 1.17) (Fig. 22.7) is carved on the *volumen* (scroll) held in the hand of a figure of the deceased, carved on a sarcophagus lid found in Tarquinia. The text, dating back to the first half of the second century BC, consists of 59 words and deals with the genealogy and the events of the life of the

Figure 22.6 Lead plaque from Magliano, late fifth century BC
(Florence, Museo Archeologico Nazionale).

Figure 22.7 Sarcophagus of Laris Pulenas, from Tarquinia, 250–200 BC
(Tarquinia, Museo Archeologico Nazionale).

deceased. There are, finally, the two gold foil plaques from Pyrgi (Cr 4.4–4.5) (Fig. 22.8), which carry texts, respectively, of 36 and 15 words. Found in the sanctuary along with a third sheet of gold, inscribed in Phoenician, they record, like the Phoenician text, the dedication to Uni/Astarte of a temple by a local Etruscan ruler around 500 BC.

In general, the longer texts are written language productions in which the creative aspect is prevalent. However, they do not lack repeated turns of phrase and various stereotypes. So, for example, the descriptions of the various rituals of the "*Liber linteus*" repeat several times the expression *cisum pute tul θans hatec repinec*, which we find on pages III (lines 22–23), IV (lines 3–4 and 16), IX (lines 4–5, 11–12 and 20). The same applies to the "Tablet of Capua": for example, *isvei tule ilucve apirase* appears in section II, line 8 and again in section III, line 17. Quite different is the case of the vast majority of shorter inscriptions. Some are totally devoid of an articulated structure, as in the case of *sigla* and abbreviations – presumably of proper names or words of some sort – or by the proper names inscribed on an object to indicate (without formulating it linguistically) a relationship between the object and the person designated by name. We may find either simple names, or onomastic formulas that are more or less complex. This is the most common type of inscription in the case of tomb markers, urns and sarcophagi. The following serve as examples:

(4) Cm 2.44 (Capua, graffito on vase, fifth century BC, first half): *cupe veliesa* "Cupe, (son) of Velie" (Fig. 22.9)
(5) Cl 1.393 (Chiusi, lid of cinerary urn, second century BC): *peθna larces remznal* "Pethna, (son) of Larce and of Remznei"

Figure 22.8 Gold plaque from Pyrgi, early fifth century BC (Rome, Museo di Villa Giulia).

Other short inscriptions, albeit linguistically structured, are marked by a distinctly formulaic character. The text is composed starting from a pre-existing form (a "formulaic schema"), which indicates linguistically the ownership of an object by a certain person, or the dedication of the object (by a certain person) (to a certain person), occurring in statements such as "of X," "this object is of X," "I am of X," "X has given me (to Y)." The object may be the tomb and the owner or dedicatee may be a deity, according to the form of votive dedications (Maras 2009).

Examples:

(6)   Vs 2.8 (Orvieto, vessel, fifth century BC): *uχus* "of Uchu"
(7)   Cr 4.8 (Pyrgi, dipinto on vase, late sixth-early fifth century BC): *unial* "of Uni" (Fig. 22.10)
(8)   Cr 2.51 (Caere, vase, 575–550 BC): *uχus θafna* "cup of Uchu"
(9)   Cr 2.13 (Caere, vase of silver, 650–600 BC): *mi larθia* "I (am) of Larth"
(10) Vs 1.4 (Volsinii, lintel of chamber tomb, 550–500 BC): *mi mamarces velθienas* "I (am) of Mamarce Velthienas" (Fig. 22.11)
(11) Cr 2.20 (Caere, graffito on vase, 675–650 BC): *mi qutum karkanas* "I (am) the pitcher of Karkana" (Fig. 22.12)
(12) Cr 2.33 (Caere, vase, 650–625 BC): *mi squrias θina mlaχ mlakas* "I (am) the pitcher of Squria, a beautiful thing for a beautiful woman"
(13) Ve 3.6 (Veii, graffito on vase, c. 600 BC): *mini mulvanice karcuna tulumnes* "Karcuna Tulumnes has given me"
(14) AT 3.1 (Corneto, graffito on vase, seventh century BC, second half): *mi mulu kaviiesi* "I (was) given to Kavie" (Fig. 22.13)
(15) Ta 3.2. (Tarquinia, graffito on vase, late sixth century BC): *itun turuce venel atelinas tinas cliniiaras* "Venel Atelinas has dedicated this (kylix) to the sons of Tinia' (the Dioscuri) (Fig. 22.14)
(16) Cm 2.13 (Suessula, graffito on vase, late fifth century BC, first half): *mi χuliχna qupes alθrnas ei minipi capi* "I (am) the cup of Cupe Althrna, do not take me" (Fig. 22.15)

It is remarkable that, especially in the Archaic period, these inscriptions of possession or gift/dedication are made in the form of so-called "speaking inscriptions" based on a stylistic pretense that it is the object on which the inscription is found which declares its ownership or its destination for a certain personage. It is also remarkable that the form of "speaking inscriptions," like others such as "prohibition against theft" or the stylistic feature of the "beautiful object of/for a nice person," used to supplement the formula for possession or a gift/dedication, goes beyond the scope of the Etruscan language, and is found in Greek, Latin and other languages of ancient Italy. So to the aforementioned *mi larθia* "I (am) of Larth" correspond formulas such as Latin *Marci sum* "(I) am of Marcus," Oscan *Kanuties sim* "(I) am of Kanutie" and Greek Σοταίρō εἰμί, "(I) am of Sotairos"; to the formula cited above, *mi Squrias θina mlaχ mlakas* "I (am) the pitcher of Squria, a beautiful thing for a beautiful woman," corresponds non-urban Latin (Faliscan) *eco quton...Titias duenom duenas* "I (am) the *koton*...of Titia, a beautiful thing for a beautiful woman" and Greek Αριστοκλείας εμί τας καλάς καλά "(I) am the beautiful (kylix) of beautiful Aristokleia." To *ei minipi capi* cited above, finally, correspond Latin expressions like *ne atigas me* "don't touch me," *noli me tangere* "don't touch me," *noli me tollere* "don't take me away," and the like, and in Greek inscriptions, μέ θίγες "do not touch (me)," μή με άνοιγε "do not take me away," and the like.

Figure 22.9   Black-gloss kylix, from Capua, fifth century BC, first half
(once Staatliche Museen, Berlin, today lost).

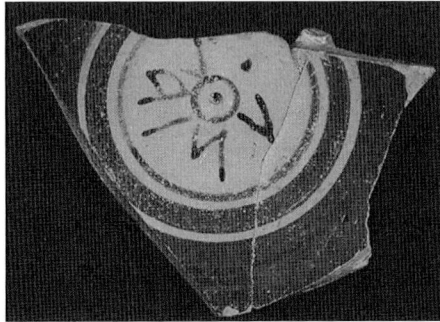

Figure 22.10   Fragment of a "Spurinas"-plate, from Pyrgi, late sixth-early fifth century BC
(Rome, Museo di Villa Giulia).

Figure 22.11   Inscription on chamber tomb (Volsinii, necropolis of Crocifisso del Tufo, tomb 29).

Figure 22.12   Oinochoe, from Caere, 675–650 BC (Paris, Musée du Louvre).

Figure 22.13   Bucchero vase in the shape of a rooster, from Corneto (Tarquinia), seventh century BC,
second half (Boston, Museum of Fine Arts).

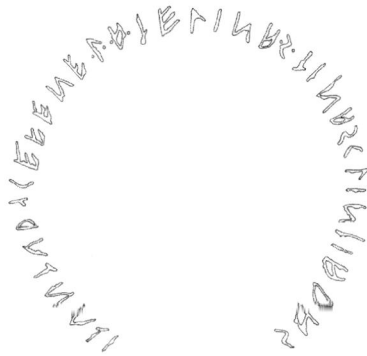

Figure 22.14 Attic red-figure Kylix, late sixth century BC, from Tarquinia
(Tarquinia, Museo Archeologico Nazionale).

Figure 22.15 Black-gloss Kylix, from Suessula, fifth century BC, first half
(Naples, Museo Archeologico Nazionale).

Formulas also appear repeatedly in more complex inscriptions, especially to complement the markers on tombs, urns, etc. Here, the mention of the person is followed by statements that provide information about his personality, his deeds, possible offices held, the age at death, and more. For example:

(17) Ta 7:59: (Tarquinia, painted on the wall of a tomb, 350–325 BC): (Fig. 22.16)

... *spur}inas*	*an*	*zilaθ*	*amce*	*meχl*	*rasnal*
Spurinas	who	zilath	was	rei	publicae

("...Spurinas who *zilath* was of the commonwealth")

(18) Ta 1.167 (Tarquinia, dipinto on wall, Tomb of the Spitus family third century BC, first half): (Fig. 22.17)

metli	*arnθi*	*puia*	*amce*	*spitus larθal*	*svalce*	*avil LXIIII*	*ci clenar*	*acnanas arce*
Metli	Arnthi	wife	was	of Larth Spitu;	she lived	years 64	to three sons	gave birth

("Metli Arnthi was wife of Larth Spitu; she lived 64 years, (and) she gave birth to three sons")

(19) Cr 5.3 (Caere, stone *cippus*, fourth century BC, second half): (Fig. 22.18)
vel matunas larisalisa an cn śuθi ceriχunce "Vel Matunas, (son) of Laris, who this tomb built"

Figure 22.16 Tarquinia, dipinto on wall, Tomba dell'Orco I (350–325 BC).

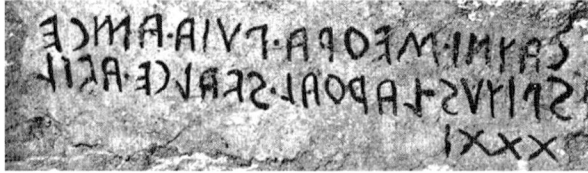

Figure 22.17 Tarquinia, dipinto on wall, Tomb of the Spitus family, third century BC, first half.

Figure 22.18 *Cippus* in the Tomb of the Reliefs at Caere, fourth century BC, second half.

Finally, we consider a special case, the captions that appear in relation to images: mostly painted on walls of tombs or incised on the backs of mirrors. In the vast majority of cases, the caption proclaims the name of the person depicted. So, for example, in the Tomb of Orcus in Tarquinia, dated 325–300 BC (Ta 7.64, 7.66, 7.72, 7.74), we find mentioned φersipnei "Persephone," *eivas* "Ajax," *θese* "Theseus," *uθuste* "Odysseus" and on the back of a mirror, also from Tarquinia, of the fourth century BC (Ta S.3) we read *apulu* "Apollo," *menrva* "Minerva" and *hercle* "Hercules." In very few cases, the caption does not relate to the single character, but to the entire scene, and therefore assumes the structure of a sentence. Thus in the scene of Herakles nursed by Hera that appears on a mirror of the fourth-third century BC from Volterra (Vt S.2), the sentence is recorded, *eca sren tva iχnac hercle unial clan θrasce*: "this image shows [or similar] how Heracles became (?) the son of Uni." And a similar structure seems to be recognized in the sentence *eca ersce nac aχrum flerθrce,* commenting on the farewell scene between Admetus and Alcestis painted on a vase of the late fourth century BC from Vulci (Vc 7.38).

THE STRUCTURE OF THE LANGUAGE

In the absence of a continuity of transmission and of knowledge of the Etruscan language, all that we know about it today – the sounds, forms, lexical meanings, syntactic structures – results from a reconstruction process achieved through the interpretation of written texts.[10] Among the approaches to the meaning of the texts we cannot reasonably count what is traditionally known as the "etymological method": i.e. the comparative procedure which, assuming a genealogical bond of Etruscan with another known language, claims to derive the meanings of the unknown Etruscan words from the words of the known language that are similar in form. The method is correct in itself, but wrong in its application to Etruscan, for the obvious reason that Etruscan is a language genealogically isolated, and that any supposed kinship with this or that language – Hebrew, Basque, Armenian, Finno-Ugric, Ural-Altaic languages, Caucasian languages, Berber languages, Tuareg, Micro-Asiatic languages, Sanskrit, Latin and Italic languages, Greek – are quite clearly totally illusory.

The case is different with what is traditionally defined as the "combinatory method," which originally was based exclusively – contrary to what is claimed by proponents of the "etymological method" – on the identification, comparison and classification of words and forms in the texts. Obviously, such a procedure is still indispensable and preliminary to the analysis of a text in an unknown language, or to the reconstruction of the characteristics of the language. But it must be said that such a type of analysis, which works exclusively with the forms, would not by itself be able to provide information on the overall meaning of a text, the meaning of words, or the value of forms of grammar. To tap into this type of data, one must integrate the formal analysis of information in different ways, by reviewing, for example, the contexts of the inscriptions, the type of the object on which the inscription appears, the reference to proper names, etc.

The third of the traditionally recognized methods, the so-called "bilingual method" (also "parallel texts method") quite naturally integrates with the formal analysis, providing clues to the meaning and structure of the texts. It is based on the idea that the well-known cultural community existing between the different peoples of ancient Italy must have resulted in, among other things, the use of similar text elements. Thus the structure and meaning of a text in a known language, say Umbrian, will give us indications about the meaning and structure of an Etruscan text. In fact, even our partial knowledge of the contents of the rituals of the *Liber linteus* and the Capua Tablet rests largely on the parallelism of the text with that of the other great ritual text of ancient Italy, the "Iguvine Tables." And we may recall, in confirmation, the proofs of convergence that we have seen before with the "speaking inscriptions," the "prohibition of appropriation" or the form of "beautiful object of/for a nice person."

To the three methods traditionally recognized, one can add a fourth[11] that could be called the "typological method." This refers to aspects of the typology of languages, especially – but not solely – the fact that some of the traits of a language are influenced by the existence of other traits. For example, if a language puts the direct object before the verb, it will also generally put the genitive before the head noun, and will generally use postpositions rather than prepositions (see below, the description of Etruscan morphosyntax). From a typological perspective it is possible to discover in Etruscan the presence of certain traits, and also to verify the real presence of others proposed on the basis of different methods, for example the combinatory method.

Phonology

Our current knowledge of Etruscan is anything but meager, when one considers the substantial poverty of written documentation on which the reconstruction of the language has ultimately been based. Almost paradoxically, since it is a dead language, its best known aspect is phonology. It is possible to reconstruct the series of functional sounds (phonemes) of Etruscan, the natural classes both of vowels and of the consonants, through a series of indications provided mainly by the values of the Greek alphabetic signs in the model alphabet upon which Etruscan script was based, and also by the phonetic treatment of lexical loans in Etruscan, the evolution of the script, the general criteria of phonological typology, and a few explicit testimonies of ancient authors.[12]

The vowel system of Etruscan, at least for the Archaic period, is a system of four vowels, marked by *iota, alpha, epsilon* and *ypsilon*: thus it is formed by the three basic vowels / i a u / plus / e /. Such systems are widely attested in the languages of the world. We believe[13] that for the Archaic period, the / a / was a back vowel (as in French *pâte*), and that in the recent phase of the language it became centralized (the / a / is a central vowel in Italian, Spanish and many other languages). This is shown by the different treatment, in both the Archaic and Late phases of the language, of the diphthong / ou / in the Italic loanwords in Etruscan, by which the Italic personal name *Loucios* is rendered in archaic Etruscan as *Laucie* or *Lavcie*, in Late Etruscan as *Luvcie*; or even by the different output of the genitive of stems in a dental consonant, like the personal names *Larθ* and *Laris*, that in Archaic Etruscan are not *Larθial* and *Larisal* (as will instead occur in the Late period, and as required by the "pertinentive" form – see more below), but *Larθia* and *Larisal* with the absorption of the final / l / (which was velarized in Etruscan) into the back (velar) / a /: a form of absorption which is no longer possible in Late Etruscan, when the / a / will have lost its velar character. The Archaic Etruscan vowel system has therefore a quadrangular symmetry and in the Late period, a triangular asymmetry. In outline:

Archaic Etruscan		Late Etruscan	
i	u	i	u
		e	
e	a		a

The discovery of the *Tabula Cortonensis* has shown, however, that things are even more complex – certainly owing to the variety of language of Cortona, and perhaps also to other varieties, if not all.[14] In the Cortona text there are two different / e /, one marked with an *epsilon* that follows the direction of the writing (from right to left), the other with the same sign but retrograde (the opposite direction). The regularity of their distribution shows that we must be dealing with different sounds, distinguished phonetically by the different length and/or by different height. Under these conditions, the vowel system of Late Etruscan increases its asymmetry: no longer two, but three palatal vowels in contrast to one velar vowel.

Before analyzing the consonant system, we must note two developments that distinguished the vowel system of Late Etruscan from that of the Archaic period. The first is the presence of / e / as a substitute for / i / in a stressed syllable: to Archaic *itan*, "this," corresponds *etan*; and *cipen*, "priest" (or more likely "all"),[15] in the Tabula Capuana corresponds to *cepen* in the *Liber Linteus*, and so on. This lowering of / i / into / e / appears to be blocked by the presence, in the next syllable, of one high vowel: by which *vipina* does not turn into **vepina* and *cicu* does not become **cecu*. From this diachronic change the variation (free?) between / e / and / i / within Archaic Etruscan, whether in a stressed or unstressed syllable, must be distinguished.[16] This is the case, for example, of the personal name *Pisna* vs. *Pesna*, both of the end of the seventh century BC; or of *Hirmina* vs. *Hermena*; of *Piθe* vs. *Peθe*; of *muluvanice*, "he donated," vs. *muluvanece*. In *Numesie* vs. *Numisie*, the expression with *e* actually precedes that with *i* by more than a century.

The second characteristic feature of Late Etruscan is the monophthongization of the diphthong / ai / to / e / : by which the Etruscan name of Ajax is *Aivas* in the oldest inscriptions, *Evas* in later ones. If in the female gentilicial (family) names – and occasionally elsewhere, for example in *Eivas* the name of Ajax – we find *ei* and not *e* as the evolution of *ai* (for example, in *velimnei* and not **velimne* compared to the Archaic *velimnai* and the masculine *velimna*), this is due to a restructuring for functional requirements:[17] the *-i* being the mark of female gender (as we shall see below), a form like *velimnai* is immediately identifiable as a woman's name, as opposed to the masculine *velimna*; but once that / ai / is reduced to a monophthong, / e /, the mark is no longer "visible" and must be reintroduced.

For the class of consonantal sounds, there are no major differences between the archaic and the most recent phase of the language, except, as we shall see, in the case of the sibilants. We can reconstruct a system that has a double set of stops, aspirated and not aspirated: / p t k pʰ tʰ kʰ /; an affricate, / ts /; two liquids, / l r /, and two nasals, / m n /; four fricatives, / f s š h /; two semivowels, / j w /. This is a system that from a typological point of view appears highly plausible.[18] All the phonemes that are included, in fact, belong to the 20 most common consonants in the languages of the world and, moreover, the system generally complies with the implications relationship established by typology: in the sense that, for example, the presence, for the series of fricatives, of / f s š h / respects the typological principle by which if there is only one fricative, it is / s /, if two, then / f s /; if three, then / f s š /; if four, then / f s h š /. The absence of voiced stops / b d g / is indicated by the non-use of *beta* and *delta* and by the use of *gamma* for the voiceless velar. This is also confirmed by the testimony of Varro, who gives *itus* as the Etruscan word for "the Ides,"[19] and by the treatment of Greek loan-words: see the series *paχa, tiφile, creice* for *Βάκχος, Δίφιλος, Γραῖκος*, where Greek / b d g / are replaced by the phonetically close series / p t k /.

As for the subsystem of the sibilants, the written evidence already mentioned shows that Etruscan provided two, one apical / s /, the other palatal / š / (the arguments put forward in the past to claim that the distinction was based on a feature of length/intensity, where / s *vs.* ss /, are to be rejected). The frequency of / š / is much higher in the inscriptions of northern Etruria, 59.78 per cent against 16.19 per cent of southern Etruria:[20] the northern variety shows palatalization of the sibilant when it is found in front of a consonant, or in contact with an / i / or a / j /. So one of the words for "city" is [š]*pur-* in northern varieties, while it appears as [s]*pur-* in the south; Pesna the personal name appears as *pe*[š]*na* in the north, *pe*[s]*na* in the south; the personal name Laris is *lari*[š] in the north, *lari*[s] to the south; the family name Keisi- is *kei*[š]*i-* in the North, *kei*[s]*i-* in the-South, and so on.

Other aspects of the consonant system are more marginal. One recalls the de-aspiration of / th / in the final position in a word, typical of Late Etruscan in the North, with the formation of morphophonemic alternations (in the *Tabula Cortonensis*, regularly *lart* vs. *larθ-ial*). It is worth briefly discussing the syllabic structure and accent.[21] In Archaic

Etruscan the basic syllable structure is the open syllable, or at most closed by / m n r l /. As for the accent, it had to be predominantly melodic and non-dynamic, as evidenced by the fact that this syllabic structure was maintained for a very long period, from the seventh to fifth centuries BC. In the first half of the fifth century BC, Neo-Etruscan developed a strong accent on the first syllable of the word. This eventually led to the loss of unstressed vowels, especially those that followed the accented syllable, thus reducing the number of syllables of the word and the appearance of more or less complex closed syllables. For example, the Archaic trisyllabic *turuce* ("dedicated") corresponds to the Late Etruscan bisyllabic *turce*; to *avile*, a male personal name, corresponds *avle*; to *ramuθa*, a female personal name, corresponds *ramθa*; to *venel*, a male personal name, corresponds *vel* (from **venl*); to *clutumusta*, a local version of the name of Clytemnestra, corresponds *clutmsta*. The loss of vowels was preceded by a phase of weakening, resulting in oscillating written results: see the series *aχile – aχele – aχale* (then *aχle*), a personal name, or *avile – avele – avale* (then *avle*), another personal name.

Morphosyntax

On the morphosyntax of Etruscan our information is far less comprehensive. It has been established that it is an agglutinating language (but see below), in which each grammatical category is expressed by a morphemic segment placed after the lexical base[22] (a radical, followed or not by derivative suffixes).[23] The sequence of the constituent elements of the words is as expected: "radical (+ derivative morphology) + number + case." The noun has an uninflected form, the absolute case, and then a series of marked cases. Taking the word for "son" as an example, and comparing the structural homology with Turkish, another agglutinative language, in contrast with the Latin (a fusional language), we have:

clan	*clen-ar*	*clen-si*	*clen-ar(a)-si*
oğul	*oğul-lar*	*oğul-a*	*oğul-lar-a*
fili-us	*fili-i*	*fili-ō*	*fili-is*
"child"	"children"	"to the child"	"to the children"

Apart from the absolute case, the cases marked for Etruscan are the genitive, ablative, locative and pertinentive. Formally, the pertinentive[24] is close to the genitive: see for example the declension of proper names such as *Larθ* (gen. *Larθ-ia Larθ-ial*, pert. *Larθ-ial-e*), *Venel* (gen. *Venel-us*, pert. *Venel-us-i*), *Marce* (gen. *Marce-s*, pert. *Marce-s-i*). But the genitive case, in spite of what has been said in the past, is functionally distinct: the genitive expresses belonging, the pertinentive[25] the destination. *Turuce*, "he dedicated," is constructed with the genitive, *muluvanice*, "he donated" with pertinentive, and so on. Even the ablative[26] is formally close to the genitive, as shown, again, in the declension of proper names such as *Larθ* (gen. *Larθ-al*, abl. *Larθ-al-s*), *Tute* (gen. *Tute-s*, abl. *Tute-i-s*), *Vel* (gen. *Vel-u-s*, abl. *Vel-u-i-s*), *Tarna* (gen. *Tarna-s*, abl. *Tarn-e-s* from **Tarna-i-s*). The case is well attested, especially in Late Etruscan, in its function either as prototypical expression of origin:

(20) TCo II.1:

cên zic	ziχuχe	sparzêstiś	śazleiś in	θuχti CusuΘuraś	suΘiu
this writing	was written	from the table	śazle that	in the house of the Cusu	(is) lying

or of agent:

(21) Vc 1.64:

Larθ Tutes	anc	farθnaχe	Veluis Tuteis	Θanχviluis-c Turials-c
Larth Tutes	who	was generated	by Vel Tutes	and by Thanchvil Turi

It is apparent that both the pertinentive and the ablative are complex cases, derived from the genitive through the addition of phonetic segments. Despite the presence of a case system, the direct object is not marked morphologically, and for this the absolute case is used: except for the category of pronouns, which in the objective function have a marker / n /, which expresses the definiteness (*mi* "I": *mi-ni*, *in* "that thing which" [inanimate]: *in-ni, ika, ita* "this": *ika-n, ita-n*).

The fact that there is a variety of endings in the case inflexion and in the formation of the plural does not agree[27] with the agglutinative character of the language, and would seem to indicate – as do other features of the language – that Etruscan is an originally agglutinating language that is evolving toward a different type. The allomorphy may be explained by natural evolutionary facts, such as the loss of morphological categories – for example, the category of the collective next to the plural, or the syncretism between the genitive and another case, perhaps a sort of partitive.[28]

Among pronouns[29] and personal pronouns, demonstratives and relatives are attested. We have already given some examples: *mi* "I," *ica, ita* "this," *an, in* "which," "what thing." The demonstratives are also found – in Late Etruscan in phonetically reduced form – in the enclitic position, for example, in the *Tabula Cortonensis*, II: *pes pêtrus-ta scevaś* "the house, that of Petru Scevas." The segment / -ša / accompanying forms of the genitive, in the type *Velu{š}a* < *Vel-us+/ša/*, is to be considered a mark of the possessive rather than an enclitic pronoun.[30] Our knowledge of the morphology of Etruscan verbs[31] is even more fragmentary than that of the morphology of nouns and pronouns. We mention some of the most obvious and well-established features. An opposition between active and passive is documented by two forms of the preterite, / -ke / vs. / kʰe /:[32] see above, *zilaθ amce* "he was *zilath*" (17), *itun turuce* "he dedicated this" (15), *avil svalce LXIIII* "lived 64 years;" but *cên zic ziχuχe*, "this writing was written" (20),…*anc farθnaχe*…"who was generated/born." Participial forms[33] are to be identified in the type of *acnanas* (18), and in the forms ending in -*u* of the type *mulu* "given" (14), *cenu* "?" (3), *lupu* "dead," and so on. For mood, apart from the predictable use of the verb stem for the imperative (as in *suθ* "place" or *trin* "talk" in the *Liber Linteus*), we detect the existence of a necessitative form: for example, *śucri* "must be offered," or *acasri* "must be sacrificed."[34] Beyond that, not much can be said, except for the negative fact of the absence of the copula: it is no accident that the "speaking inscriptions" use the pronoun *mi* in contrast to the Greek model εἰμί ("I am"). And if *amce* is to be read as "was" in phrases like *zilaθ amce*, "was *zilath*," the situation is comparable to that attested in a language like Russian: the verb only has the function to mark the past tense.

In terms of the syntax we note three important points. The first concerns the reciprocal position, within a construction, of the element that determines and the element that is determined:[35] as we see already from the structure of compounds such as *Θana-cvil* (proper name of a woman) or *tins-cvil* ("votive offering," from a previous value of * "gift of Tins"), in Etruscan the determinant is placed to the left of the determined (unlike, for example, romance languages like French or Italian). So the direct object precedes the verb, as in formulae of the type of *ci clenar…arce* "three children…generated" or *cn ziχ…acasce* "this writing…he made," (respectively in Ta 1.167 and Ta 1.17); the genitive precedes the name (see the formulas *LarΘal clan* "son of Larth"); morphemes, whether inflectional or derivative, are composed exclusively of suffixes; there are no prepositions, only postpositions[36] (see expressions such as *aritimi-pi* and *turan-pi,* "for Aritimi," "for Turan" of Ve 3.34, or the formula *clen ceχa* "for the benefit of the son"). On the other hand, the adjective seems to follow the noun, as in phrases of the type **caper zamΘic,* "vase of gold" (LL VIII.10), or *ziχ neΘsrac* "writing on/about haruspicy" (AT 1.105). We know, however, that in many languages the adjective behaves in this matter in unexpected ways.

The second point to note is that Etruscan does not have a grammatical distinction of gender[37] like Latin, which opposes a masculine *mons* ("mountain") to a feminine *vallis* ("valley") and a neuter *flumen* ("river"), and that we recognize only from the concordance of *magnus mons,* distinguished from *magna vallis* and *magnum flumen.* Concord phenomena of this kind are entirely absent in Etruscan. Nouns belong to two semantically motivated classes,[38] animate and inanimate. Only animate nouns show the marking of the plural when accompanied by a numeral, when there is more than one: so we see *clen-ar ci* "three children" (*clan* "son"), but *ci avil* "three years" (*avil* "year"). Furthermore, the marking of the plural takes place through the use of two different morphemes for animate and inanimate nouns: *ais-er* "gods," *clen-ar* "sons," *hus-ur* "boys" on the one hand, and *avil-χva* "years," *cilΘ-cva* "fortresses," *culs-cva* "doors" on the other. The first of the two phenomena is normal in language typology. The marking of the plural numerals in the presence of more than one is favored for animate nouns, for example in languages such as Amharic or Pashto. Much less likely – but examples do exist – is a marking of the plural in both classes of nouns.

Lexicon

We must now address the vocabulary.[39] We have already noted the absence, in the written documentation of Etruscan, of the most obvious manifestations of writing, from literature to correspondence. One of the most unfortunate consequences of this situation is that the few hundred words in our texts, surely only a fraction of the actual vocabulary of a cultured language such as Etruscan, are only those required by the type of texts that we have found. The result is that we are quite well informed about certain very specific and technical areas of the Etruscan vocabulary, for example, the names of vases, such as *qutum,* "pitcher," *aska,* "askos," *leχtum,* "lekythos," *culiχna,* "cup," *pruχum,* "pitcher," *spanti,* "plate," *θina,* "jar," and others. But we miss very broad areas of basic vocabulary. We know that "to be" is represented by *am-* (*amce* "was," *ame* "is," etc.), "gold" by *zam(a)θi,* that *mlaχ* is "beautiful," *cel* is "earth," *avil* is "year," *tiur* is "moon/month," and, after the recovery of the *Tabula Cortonensis,* that *mal-* means "watch" (or "see") and "plain" is *span;* but we are entirely ignorant of obvious concepts such as "stay," "go," "come" and "eyes," "hand," "head," "change," "seek," "open," "easy," "full," "slow," and so on.

In fact, the areas of the basic Etruscan lexicon that we know best are the kinship terms, and the names of numbers. For the first, we can list *apa* "father"; *ati* "mother";

clan "son"; *sec* "daughter"; *husur* "boys"; *papals* and *tetals* "grandson"; *nefts* "nephew"; and *prumts* "great grandchild" (by indirect descent?); *apa nacna* and *ati nacna* "grandfather" and "grandmother." As for the names of numbers,[40] for the first ten we are certain of the values from one to six – in the order: *θu (n), zal, ci, sa, maχ, huθ* - and "ten", which is *sar*. The terms for "seven," "eight" and "nine" are definitely **cezp, *nurφ* and **semφ*, though it is not possible to determine which term corresponds to which value. For the tens there is *zaθrum* "20," of unknown etymology, and the series formed with a suffix *-alχ*, a multiplier: *cialχ* "30," *sealχ* "40," *muvalχ* "50" (?) **huθalχ* "60," *cezpalχ, semφalχ, *nurφalχ* "70–80–90." Neither the word for "100" nor that for "1000" is attested. The rest of the numbers are formed through processes of addition and subtraction. Addition is used for the first six numbers in the tens: for example, *ci sar* "13," *huθzar* "16," *ci zaθrum* "23," **sa- zaθrum* "24," and so on. For the last three numbers we revert to a subtractive process. So "19" is *θun-em zaθrum* "one-without //twenty" (i.e. "twenty without one"), as Latin *undeviginti*; "18" is *esl-em zaθrum*, like Latin *duodeviginti*. Etruscan use of the subtractive system is more extensive than the Latin, for "17" is *ci-em zaθrum* against the form of Latin *septemdecim*; it is not impossible that, as the Roman system of graphic notation of numerals is of Etruscan origin, they also show a subtractive process, which in fact was not reflected in the Indo-European matrix of Latin.

As a general conclusion, we can say that all the vocabulary examples above confirm what already seems clear from the facts of morphosyntactic structure: the Etruscan language is genealogically isolated. This does not imply that Etruscan is lacking in individual lexical items that can be traced to Greek or Latin-Italic languages. Many of the names of the vessels mentioned above, as *culiχna, aska, pruχum*, are lexical borrowings from the Greek (respectively, κύλιξ ἀσκός πρόχουν), evidently because of the prestige attached to the Greek mode of wine consumption (the Etruscan word for "wine," *vinum*, is likewise a loan word, from Ϝοῖνος). Also reflecting Greek is *elaiva-* "olive" from ἐλαίϜα. Words like *nefts* "nephew," or *prumts* "great grandchild," were borrowed from an Italic language (presumably Umbrian), while to Latin are attributed *cela*, "cell," or *macstr-* (at the root of Mastarna) from *magister*. But the absence of any systematic correspondences in basic vocabulary for the names of relatives, or for the numerals, shows that similarities, such as those recognizable in names, are due to long-standing contacts between Etruscans and the other peoples of ancient Italy.

NOTES

1   Abbreviations identifying inscriptions refer to the *Etruskische Texte* (Rix ed. 1991). Other abbreviations are common ones. In the transliterated texts the values of signs are generally intuitive, while it is to be noted that φ represents /pʰ/, θ /tʰ/ and χ /kʰ/; among the sibilant consonants *ś* represents Μ (sade), while *s* transcribes + (or ✕); lastly, *ê* represents the "backward" *epsilon* in the *Tabula Cortonensis*.
     I would like to thank Jean MacIntosh Turfa for translating, in a very satisfactory way, the original Italian text; I am especially grateful to Elizabeth Jane Shepherd for checking, improving and correcting my changes in the English translation, sometimes all other than linguistically faultless.
2   Agostiniani 2006; Van Heems 2011.
3   Cristofani 1991, pp. 11–31; Agostiniani 2006, pp. 181–187.
4   Benelli 2007; Wallace 2008, pp. 135–195.
5   Belfiore 2010.

6   Cristofani 1995.
7   Agostiniani-Nicosia 2000.
8   Massarelli in press.
9   Massarelli in press.
10 De Simone 1996; Agostiniani 1992, pp. 59–66.
11 Agostiniani 1993.
12 Rix 1984, pp. 214–222.
13 Agostiniani 1992, p. 48.
14 Agostiniani-Nicosia 2000, pp. 47–52.
15 So Adiego 2006.
16 Agostiniani 2006, pp. 177–178.
17 Agostiniani 1995b, pp. 16–17.
18 Agostiniani 1993, pp. 29–30.
19 De Simone 1968; 1970a.
20 Agostiniani 2006, p. 180.
21 Agostiniani 1992, pp. 52–53.
22 Agostiniani 1992, p. 53.
23 Pfiffig 1969, pp. 163–173; Steinbauer 1999, pp. 107–143.
24 Colonna 1975; Rix 1984, pp. 227–228.
25 Agostiniani 2011.
26 Cristofani 1971; Rix 1984, pp. 226–227.
27 Agostiniani 1992, pp. 53–54.
28 Agostiniani 2011, pp. 18–19.
29 Rix 1984, pp. 229–231.
30 Pfiffig 1969, pp. 119–120.
31 Wylin 2000.
32 De Simone 1970b.
33 Rix 1984, pp. 234–235.
34 See preceding two notes.
35 Pfiffig 1969, pp. 207–211; Agostiniani 1993, pp. 232–33.
36 Facchetti 2002, pp. 75–82.
37 Fiesel 1922.
38 Agostiniani 1993, pp. 33–38.
39 Wallace 2008, pp. 123–134.
40 Agostiniani 1995a.

BIBLIOGRAPHY

Adiego, I.-X. (2006) "Etrusco marunuχva cepen," *Studi Etruschi* 72, pp. 199–214.

Agostiniani, L. (1985) "La sequenza tinascliniiaras e la categoria del numero in etrusco" in AA.VV., *Studi linguistici e filologici per Carlo Alberto Mastrelli*, Pisa: Pacini, pp. 13–19.

——(1986) "Sull'etrusco della Stele di Lemno e su alcuni aspetti del consonantismo etrusco," *Archivio Glottologico Italiano* 71, pp. 15–46.

——(1992) "Contribution à l'étude de l'épigraphie et de la linguistique étrusque," *Lalies* 11, pp. 37–74.

——(1993) "La considerazione tipologica nello studio dell'etrusco," *Incontri Linguistici* 16, pp. 23–44.

——(1995) "Sui numerali etruschi e la loro rappresentazione grafica," *AIΩN* 17, pp. 21–65.

——(1995b) "Genere grammaticale, genere naturale e il trattamento di alcuni prestiti lessicali in etrusco" in AA.VV., *Studi linguistici per i 50 anni del Circolo Linguistico Fiorentino*, Florence: Olschki, pp. 9–23.

——(2006) "Varietà (diacroniche e geografiche) della lingua etrusca," *Studi Etruschi* 70, pp. 173–187.

——(2011) "Pertinentivo" in G. Rocca (ed.), *Atti del Convegno Internazionale "Le lingue dell'Italia antica: iscrizioni, testi, grammatica. In memoriam Helmut Rix (Milano 7–8 marzo 2011)*, Milan (= *Alessandria* 5), pp. 17–44.

——(2012) "Sulla grafia e la lingua delle iscrizioni anelleniche di Lemnos" in V. Bellelli (ed.), *Le origini degli Etruschi. Storia, archeologia, antropologia*, Rome: "L'ERMA" di Bretschneider, pp. 169–194.

Agostiniani, L. and Nicosia, F. (2000) *Tabula Cortonensis*, Rome: "L'ERMA" di Bretschneider.

Belfiore, V. (2010) *Il Liber Linteus di Zagabria. Testualità e contenuto*, Pisa-Rome: Fabrizio Serra.

Benelli, E. (2007) *Iscrizioni etrusche: leggerle e capirle*, Ancona: Saci.

Bonfante, G. and Bonfante, L. (2002) *The Etruscan Language. An Introduction*, Manchester.

Caffarello, N. (1975) "Avviamento allo studio della lingua etrusca" in AA.VV., *Archaeologica. Scritti in onore di A. Neppi Modona*, Florence: Olschki, pp. 41–148.

Colonna, G. (1975) "A proposito del morfema etrusco -si," in AA. VV., *Archaeologica. Scritti in onore di Aldo Neppi Modona*, Florence: Olschki, pp. 165–171.

Cristofani, M. (1971) "Sul morfema etrusco -als," *Archivio Glottologico Italiano* 56, pp. 38–42.

——(1991) *Introduzione allo studio dell'etrusco*, Florence: Olschki.

——(1995) *Tabula Capuana. Un calendario di festività di età arcaica*, Florence: Olschki.

De Simone, C. (1968) *Die griechischen Entlehnungen im Etruskischen, I*, Wiesbaden.

——(1970a) *Die griechischen Entlehnungen im Etruskischen, II: Untersuchung*, Wiesbaden.

——(1970b) "I morfemi etruschi -ce (-ke) e -χe," *Studi Etruschi* 38, pp. 115–139.

——(1989) "L'ermeneutica etrusca oggi" in AA.VV., *Atti del secondo congresso internazionale etrusco*, Rome: Giorgio Bretschneider, pp. 1305–1320.

Facchetti , G. (2002) *Appunti di morfologia etrusca*, Florence: Olschki.

Fiesel, E. (1922) *Das grammatische Geschlecht im Etruskischen*, Göttingen: Vandenhoeck & Ruprecht.

Maras, D. F. (2009) *Il dono votivo. Gli dei e il sacro nelle iscrizioni etrusche di culto*, Pisa-Rome: Fabrizio Serra.

Massarelli, R. (forthcoming) *I testi etruschi su piombo*, Pisa-Rome: Fabrizio Serra.

Pallottino, M. (1989) *La langue étrusque. Problèmes et perspectives*, Paris: Belle Lettres.

Pfiffig, A. J. (1969) *Die etruskische Sprache*, Graz: Akademische Druck.

Rix H. (1963) *Das etruskische Cognomen*, Wiesbaden.

——(1984) "La scrittura e la lingua" in AA.VV., *Gli Etruschi. Una nuova immagine*, Florence: Giunti, pp. 210–238.

——(1987–88) "Zur Morphostruktur des etruskischen s-Genetivs," *Studi Etruschi* 55, pp. 169–193.

——(1989) "Per una grammatica storica dell'etrusco" in AA.VV., *Atti del II Congresso Internazionale Etrusco*, Rome: Giorgio Bretschneider, pp. 1293–1306.

——(ed.) (1991) *Etruskische Texte. Editio minor. I: Einleitung. Konkordanz. Indices, II: Texte*, Tübingen (= *ET*).

Steinbauer, D. (1999) *Neues Handbuch des Etruskischen*, St. Katharinen: Scripta Mercaturae Verlag.

Van Heems, G. (2011) "Essai de dialectologie étrusque. Problèmes théoriques et applications pratiques" in G. Van Heems (ed.), *La variation linguistique dans le langues de l'Italie préromaine*, Lyon: Publications de la Maison de l'Orient et de la Méditerranée, pp. 69–90.

Wallace, R. (2008) *Zikh Rasna. A Manual of the Etruscan Language and Inscriptions*, Ann Arbor, Michigan: Beech Stave Press.

Wylin, K. (2000) *Il verbo etrusco. Ricerca morfosintattica delle forme usate in funzione verbale*, Rome: "L'ERMA" di Bretschneider.

CHAPTER TWENTY THREE

NUMBERS AND RECKONING: A WHOLE CIVILIZATION FOUNDED UPON DIVISIONS

——— •◆• ———

Daniele F. Maras

According to the literary sources, the Etruscans paid special attention to division of land as well as to partitions of time, regions of the sky and generally to an orderly distribution of every natural and human phenomenon within precise boundaries.

Boundaries: this seems to be the key to understanding the core of the Etruscan meaning of life.[1] Certainly it is not by chance that the only surviving fragments of Etruscan literature, in translations by Latin (and Greek) authors, are passages of the so-called *Gromatici veteres*, the ancient land surveyors (among them the famous Prophecy of Vegoia),[2] and Nigidius Figulus' brontoscopic calendar, handed down in a Greek version by John Lydus.[3]

Classical authors indeed suggest that the Etruscans were obsessed with the correct disposition of space and time, measuring and observation of which could result in the interpretation of the true will of the gods.

In such a civilization, which cared so much for measuring and divisions and is even said to have invented the astronomically oriented division of land (Hyg. Grom., *Const. lim.*, 166 Lach.),[4] it is not surprising to find a good amount of information about numbers and their application both in ordinary life and in sacred as well as public contexts.

In the following pages I will outline the archaeological, linguistic and historical evidence on this critical concept in Etruscan culture.

NUMBERS

As the first step in our journey through Etruscan reckoning systems, we need to show what evidence we have about the lexical and grammatical forms of the numbers,[5] which have been dealt with as an independent aspect of Etruscan studies for more than a century.

The key to the knowledge of the names of the first six numbers has been the finding of two dice in Vulci (not at Tuscania, as is often stated[6]), which do not show the usual numbers in the form of a series of dots or lines, but the corresponding Etruscan words inscribed on each face (Fig. 23.1). On opposite faces, whose sum should be 7 if the Etruscans used the same system as other classical peoples (s. *Anth.Pal.* XIV, 8),[7] are

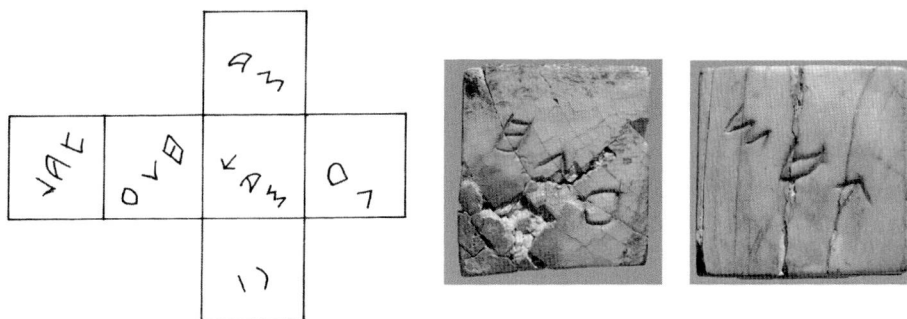

Figure 23.1 Dice from Vulci: the Etruscan names of the first six numbers are incised on each face. Paris, Bibliothéque Nationale. (Photo © Bibliothéque Nationale de France; drawing from M. Cristofani, *Introduzione allo studio dell'etrusco*, Florence, Olschki, 1991).

written the following pairs: *θu~huθ*; *zal~maχ*; *ci~śa*. Some generations of scholars have battled over the correct attribution of values to these names of numbers, either respecting or disregarding the "rule of seven."[8]

A further key to the problem is provided by the major gold tablet of Pyrgi, whose Punic translation provides the number *śls*, "three," in place of Etruscan *ci*, so giving one secure starting point to the series of the dice.[9]

Furthermore, the occurrence of the numbers *zal* and *ci* within epitaphs and inscriptions, recording the number of children a mother had had or how many times somebody had held an office or magistracy in his life, confirm they were among the lowest numbers: probably "two" and "three." And another argument for this identification comes from the subtractive system for numbers preceding tens (see below), which also provides the meaning "one" for number *θu*.

According to the "rule of seven" the meaning of *śa* should be "four," but another piece of evidence seems to point in a different direction. Scholars have long noticed that some non-Indoeuropean words of Greek language, coming from a substrate, share form and meaning with Etruscan words (for example, Gr. ὀπυίω, "to marry," vs. Etr. *puia*, "wife"); so, the observation that, according to the late grammarian Herodian, the previous name of the town Tetrapolis in Attica (literally the "city of four") was *Hyttenía*, seemed to provide a translation for the Etruscan number *huθ*.

More recently, perceptive studies by Adriana Emiliozzi and Luciano Agostiniani of some funerary inscriptions from Tuscania and Musarna have argued that the verbal forms *zelarvenas* and *śarvenas*, containing respectively the roots of the numbers *zal* and *śa*, should be interpreted as "having duplicated" and "having quadruplicated" the space of the tomb (*tamera*), as analysis of the funerary chambers shows that that was what had happened.[10] Furthermore, lately a complete research on type and features of dice in Etruria from the eighth to the third century BCE shows that the "rule of seven" was regularly respected from the fifth century BCE onwards.[11]

So, against the evidence of the comparison with the pre-Greek name of the town, we are forced to agree with the former interpretation of the number *śa* meaning "four" and *huθ* meaning "six," leaving as a consequence the value "five" for *maχ*.[12]

To reconstruct the sequence of the numbers from "seven" upwards, we have further evidence in the indication of the age of the deceased in funerary inscriptions, whenever it is given in words and not by means of numeral marks, and in some calendar dates as expressed in the *Liber Linteus* from Zagreb or on the *Tabula* from Capua. From these sources we can list the following numeral words (listed in the probable order from 7 to 10):

semφ, cezp, nurφ, sar

Obviously it is even more difficult to establish the correct sequence of these numbers, though we can be almost certain that *sar* has the meaning "ten."

Possible help comes from late literary information about the name of the month of October, which in Etruscan sounded *Xosfer*, probably to be read **Chosfer* and compared with number *cezp*, whose meaning can be inferred as "eight."

Finally, a hypothesis has recently been proposed by Giulio Giannecchini for the number "twelve," which is probably represented by the Etruscan word *snuiaφ/snuiuφ*, occurring in some passages of the *Liber Linteus* and in the final sentence of the minor golden tablet of Pyrgi:[13] *vacal tmial avilχval amuce pulumχva snuiaφ*, to be translated approximately as "the (number of) ritual(s) (*vacal*) of the years of the temple was (testified by) twelve *bullae*."[14]

The names of tens are expressed by the suffix *-alχ* added to the names of units with some phonetic adaptation: *cealχ*, "thirty," from *ci*; *śealχ*, "forty," from *śa*; *muvalχ*, "fifty," from *maχ*[15]. An exception is the name for "twenty," *zaθrum* (perhaps relating in some way to *zal*), which differs from the others just as Latin *viginti* from *triginta*, or Greek εικοσι to τριακοντα).

Much remains to be said about the numbers above ten, which use an additive and subtractive system similar to that in Latin: so *ci sar* is "thirteen" and *huθ sar* is "sixteen," but to say "seventeen," "eighteen" and "nineteen" respectively the subtractive forms *ci-em-zaθrumis*, *esl-em-zaθrumis* and *θun-em-zaθrumis* were used (literally like Latin *tres-*, *duo-* and *unum-de-viginti*).[16] About the higher numbers there can only be hypotheses, founded upon the presence of certain words where we expect numerals: for example in the sequence *masu naper* on the Cippus from Perugia (where *naper* is an unit of length, see below) the word *masu* is perhaps a number,[17] and since it seems to appear again in the sequence *masuvem maniχiur* on a long and obscure Archaic inscription from Caere, it could be a possible candidate for "one hundred" (and the latter sequence could be *centum-de-mille*, thus "900"?)[18] (Fig. 23.2).

DIVISIONS

Once we have described the Etruscan numeral system and the available evidence for the value of every known number, we can go further in exploring what kinds of divisions are attested in Etruscan culture by the sources at our disposal.

Divisions of time

In his work *De die natali* ("*On the day of birth*"), Censorinus provides some information about the contents of the Etruscan *Libri Rituales*, which also dealt with the fixed length of the life of men, towns and peoples (17.5–6).

Censorinus tells us that, according to Etruscan theory, the length of each *saeculum* (approximately one century) was determined by the oldest person alive at the time of the end of the preceding *saeculum*, to start with the foundation of a town or a people:[19]

1	*θu*
2	*zal*
3	*ci*
4	*śa*
5	*maχ*
6	*huθ*
7	*semφ* (?)
8	*cezp* (?)
9	*nurφ* (?)
10	*sar*
...	
13	*ci sar*
...	
17	*ciemzaθr(u)m(i)s*
18	*eslemzaθrumis*
19	*θunemzaθrum(i)s*
20	*zaθrum*
...	
30	*cealχ*
40	*śealχ*
50	*muvalχ*
...	
100	*maśu* (??)
...	
1000	*maniχiur* (???)

Figure 23.2 List of the Etruscan numbers.

obviously the length was variable and Censorinus himself states that the first four *saecula* of Etruscan civilization lasted 100 years, while the following three lasted respectively 123, 119 and 119 years.[20]

As we can see, Etruscan *saecula* are something quite different from our conception of centuries as well as from the ancient reckoning by generations: their function was strictly related to the doctrine of the *haruspices*, and was the basis of the science of interpretation of prodigies, which took place at every change of *saeculum* (see Chapter 26).

The *Libri Fatales* (part of the wider *Rituales*) described the correct length of a human life, fixed in twelve *hebdomadai*, that is to say periods of seven years; everybody could attend religious practices until they were 70, eventually gaining a further 14 years; at 84, everybody "lost their minds" and could no longer receive prodigies (Cens., *De die natali* 14.6).

Thus, people living more than 84 years were an exception[21] and their death could mean the end of a *saeculum*, which was of crucial importance to the Etruscans, whose civilization had been prophesied to be going to last just ten *saecula*.[22] When a comet appeared in the sky at the death of Caesar and Octavian stated that it was the mark of his adoptive father becoming a god, the haruspex Vulcanius stood up against this statement and said that the comet meant the end of the ninth *saeculum* and that, having revealed a secret against the gods' wishes he would die immediately (Serv., *in Buc.*, 9, 46).[23]

We can thus infer that Etruscan attitudes on time were deeply intertwined with religion; and further evidence comes from references to the calendar in sacred texts such as the *Liber Linteus* of Zagreb or the *tabula* from Capua, both providing prescriptions of ceremonies and rituals to be held in certain parts of the year.[24] Even Latin terminology is a debtor to Etruscan for such an important calendar-word as *idus* (the half-way point of a month), which according to Macrobius came from an Etruscan verb *iduare*, "to divide."[25]

At this regard it is interesting to compare the two Etruscan gold tablets of Pyrgi: the major one gives to us two dates, referring to a month (*ilacve tulerase*) and to a day (*teśiameitale ilacve alśase*), translated into Phoenician respectively as "in the month of the sacrifice to the sun" and "in the month of KRR in the day of the god's burial";[26] both dates (especially the latter) seem actually to refer conceptually to Punic rituals and religion, though they have been transferred into the Etruscan calendar system.

The minor tablet refers to a month (*masan*, occurring in the *Liber Linteus* too), which is said to have become *tiur unias*, probably "month of Uni's festivity";[27] the decision took place twelve years (*snuiaφ*, see above) after the dedication of the temple, what was confirmed by the number of *bullae*, golden-headed nails, driven into its door (see above).

The last remark refers to the so-called ritual of *clavifixio*, the insertion of a nail at a fixed time of every year, which took place in Volsinii in the sanctuary of Nortia as well as in Rome in the *cella* of Minerva in the Capitoline temple.[28] Once again religion is linked with the flow of time and its regulation (Fig. 23.3).

Figure 23.3   Mirror with the goddess Athrpa, corresponding to the Greek Athropos, driving the nail of Fate in the head of a boar between two unhappy pairs of the myth whose end was decided during a hunt (from A. J. Pfiffig, *Religio Etrusca*, Graz, Akademische Druck und Verlagsanstalt, 1975).

Divisions of land

From a passage of Festus (358 L.) we gain another piece of information about the *Libri Rituales* that told Etruscans which rite (Latin *ritus*) was to be used to consecrate towns, altars and temples; which inviolability (*sanctitas*) to consecrate walls; which law (*ius*) to consecrate gates and how to divide tribes, *curiae*, *centuriae*, armies and any other things relating to war or peace.[29]

Clearly these books were a true collection of religious and ritual conduct on different matters, in different situations and for different purposes. From our point of view it is interesting to see that the so-called Etruscan *disciplina* also concerned itself with the foundation of towns and the definition of their main parts, which is confirmed by other authors (Serv., *in Aen.*, I, 422; Vitr., I, 7, 1), but as a consequence, it was also concerned with the division of land, which was determined by means of cardinal points, regarded as eternal and heavenly (Hyg. Grom., *Const. lim.*, 166 Lach.):[30] unchangeable for human purposes.

In fact, this is the core of the Prophecy of Vegoia: the longest and most interesting fragment of Etruscan literature still surviving in a Latin translation within the writings of the land surveyors (*Gromatici Veteres*).[31] Boundaries and landmarks were first established by Jupiter himself (Etruscan *Tinia*) and disturbing or simply moving them would cause terrible punishments and plagues.[32]

The literary sources focus special attention on the Etruscan rite for the foundation of towns, which was also used outside of Etruria above all in Latium and in Rome in particular.

The *disciplina* of the Etruscan *haruspices* required that an imaginary line be drawn in the sky from north to south and then a second one from east to west:[33] the result was what was called in Latin the *templum caeleste*: the sky divided into four quadrants, whose projection onto the ground became the *templum in terris*, to be used for divinatory and consecratory purposes (see below).[34]

Excavations in towns of new foundation – or better re-founded in the historical age, such as Marzabotto near Bologna – show how such astronomical partition was the basis for the organization and orientation of parts of town and of buildings. Studies on these practices give evidence for the importance of further ideal lines drawn from south-east to north-west and from south-west to north-east, relating to solsticial dusk and dawn points, whose outcome was a division of the sky into eight sectors.[35]

Consequently there were many possible orientations of altars, streets, sacred and public buildings, according to their function.[36]

A fair number of *cippi*, often marked with a cross – a symbol of the division of the sky – have been found in Etruscan towns, to mark junctions of main streets or outer boundaries, as a trace of the land surveyors' work.

Their doctrine was so famous and highly esteemed in ancient Italy, especially by the Romans, that it was regarded as the origin of Roman land-measuring techniques:[37] the Latin name of the measuring instrument itself, the *groma*, was of Etruscan origin, coming from **cruma*, an adaptation from Greek *gnomon*, literally "ruler" (Fig. 23.4).[38]

Divisions of the skies

The Latin poet Martianus Capella (Mart. Cap., *nupt. Merc. et Phil.*, I, 45 ff.) has handed down to us in poetical form an all but complete list of gods inhabiting the sixteen partitions of the sky, moving clockwise from north to east, south, west and back to north.[39]

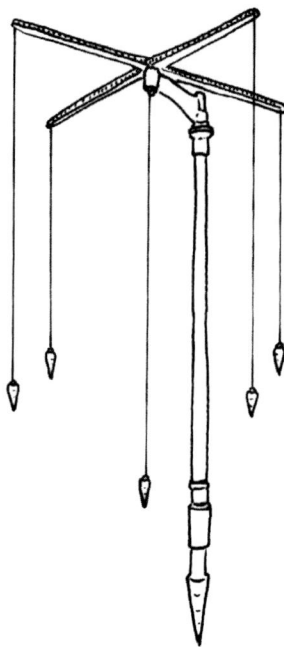

Figure 23.4 Reconstruction of a *groma*, the principal tool of the Roman land surveyors, whose name derived from Greek *gnomon* borrowed through the Etruscan language (**cruma*).

From other sources we know that Etruscan divination was based upon the classification of signs happening in the sky – from lightning to flying birds – to be interpreted by seers on the basis of their place and direction within a fixed scheme, determined by the oriented observation point of the *templum in terris*.

The same procedure was used by the *haruspices* in orienting, partitioning and interpreting the liver of sacrificed victims, such as sheep, as shown by the most famous bronze model, dating from the first century BCE, called the Liver of Piacenza (Fig. 23.5).

The shape of the model is modified to host an external flat border that is divided into sixteen regions, each inscribed with the name of a god, showing a strong resemblance to Martianus' series:[40] obviously the correspondence is not perfect owing to the several centuries of distance between the sources and to different divination schools perhaps existing even among the *haruspices*.

But it is possible to recognize a further clustering of the regions into four wider partitions corresponding respectively to most favorable and favorable gods (from north to east and from east to south) and to terrible and most terrible gods (from south to west and from west to north), whose meaning is further highlighted by the simple division into two parts, occurring on the back of the Liver, dedicated to sun (*usil*) and moon (*tiur*) (Fig. 23.6).[41]

And we happen to know the Etruscan word defining the "regions" of the sky, *luθ* (or *lut*, pl. *luθcva*), occurring on a stone tile marking the "house of Tinia" (*tinś lut*) in an *auguraculum* found in the sanctuary of Castelsecco near Arezzo.[42] Such a discovery perhaps allows us to translate a passage of the *Liber Linteus* relating to something to be offered "to Tinia in the tenth region" (*tinś in śarle luθti*).[43]

Figure 23.5 The Liver of Piacenza (from M. Cristofani [ed.], *Gli Etruschi. Una nuova immagine*, Florence, Giunti, 2000).

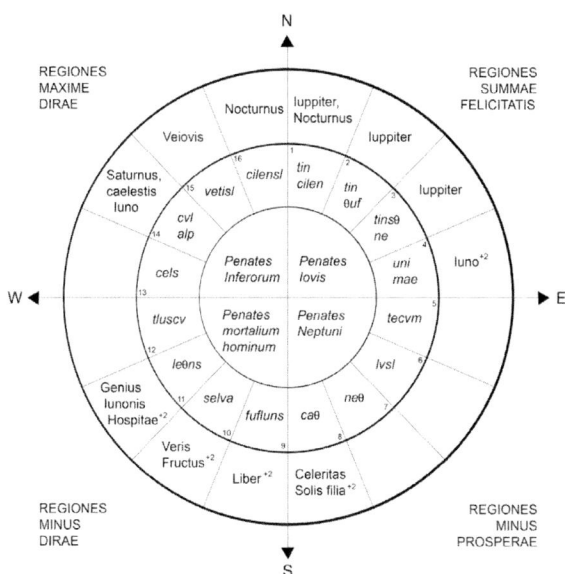

Figure 23.6 Division of sky, with sixteen regions corresponding to as many divinities, according to the outer ribbon of the Liver of Piacenza (middle circle), compared with a passage of Nigidius Figulus (inner circle) and the list of gods provided by Martianus Capella (outer circle: some correspondences, following the mark "+2," have been moved two regions forward).

The development of the doctrine of the sky from four to eight and from eight to sixteen partitions seems to have been a specific Etruscan peculiarity, depending on the acknowledged skill of the *haruspices* in most specialities of divination.

In fact, evidence of such a doctrine is given by the position of the first tombs dug within the Orientalizing *tumuli* in Caere and elsewhere in Etruria, constantly occurring within the north-west quadrant,[44] and probably also by the peculiar symbolic program of the famous "*lampadario di Cortona*" (the "Cortona Lamp") consecrated in a funerary context, which has sixteen lights set among mythological figures.[45]

An attempt to reconcile the Etruscan system of sixteen with the near-eastern astrological system of twelve (linked to the zodiac and the months) can be perhaps recognized in the inner partitions of the Liver of Piacenza, which seem to be partially clustered in the six boxes of the "wheel" on the left and in a rectangular six-box group on the right, repeating most of the gods' names occurring in the outer 16-box border.[46]

MEASURES

Length and area

Despite the special care devoted by the Etruscans to the subject of boundaries, testified by a fair number of *cippi*, often inscribed, we are unable to form a complete picture of the Etruscan measuring system and its units. The only name we can confidently attribute to a unit of length is *naper*, which occurs four times on the famous *"Cippus of Perugia,"* one of the longest Etruscan inscriptions, and twice on two similar *cippi* with shorter inscriptions.

The word has been compared with Latin *napurae*, occurring in a passage of Festus and meaning a kind of "rope"; thus possibly the Etruscan unit corresponded to the fixed measure of a rope: presumably a medium unit of length.[47]

From the archaeological evidence we can infer that a shorter unit of measurement was used in architecture and in everyday life, and by analogy with the Greek and Roman lexicon it was called "foot."

There seems to be evidence of a shorter "Italic foot" of about 27 cm versus a longer "Attic-Roman foot" of 29.6 cm, both of which used in different buildings and contexts in the Archaic age, for example in Rome[48] and in Latium,[49] while in Marzabotto only the latter was used, which spread across Italy during the Republican age.[50]

The attention paid by the Etruscans to measures in architecture is strongly emphasized by Vitruvius in describing the so-called *Tuscanicae dispositiones*, which had been used to achieve absolutely perfect proportions in the Temple of Jupiter Capitolinus in Rome (incidentally in this sacred building the Attic-Roman foot was used exclusively.)[51]

The mathematical nature of such proportions is evident from their relationship with the golden rectangle, which would have been first theorized and described later in Greek literature by Euclid, at the beginning of the third century BCE.[52]

Weight and coinage

Adriano Maggiani has dedicated two recent studies to Etruscan weight systems, on the basis of recent finds of metal and stone weights, which provide the data to be considered, together with the evidence of coinage.[53]

Maggiani identifies a heavy *libra* of 358.125 grams and a light *libra* of 286.5 grams (the latter having a variant of 315.15 grams in Vetulonia, perhaps for trade purposes).

For both units two whole systems were created whose fractions are attested by weights and multiples with, for example, ratios of 1/25, 1/10, 1/2, 2/1, etc. Both systems seem to have functioned at least from the fifth to the third century BCE.

Clearly, the identification of Etruscan weight systems has the potential to affect our understanding of the spread of coinage in Etruria and its chronology; but in practice there are few links between the systems identified by Maggiani and the coinage.[54]

The credit for a first intervention in monetary matters is attributed by Pliny to king Servius Tullius,[55] who is also said to have instituted weights and measures in general, as well as the classes and *centuriae* of the Servian "constitution" (*de vir. ill.* VII, 8).

The chronology traditionally assigned to his reign is compatible with that of the cast bronze ingots marked with a branch-like decoration ("*a ramo secco*"), found all over Italy, as well as Sicily, but concentrated in Etruria.[56] Actually these ingots seem to follow no detectable weight pattern, and are usually found in fragments; moreover, they hardly correspond to the expression *signavit aes* that Pliny refers to Servius Tullius, probably meaning to say (quite mistakenly) that he struck coinage.[57] There are small, isolated and episodic issues of gold and silver coinage, probably from the fifth century BCE and later;[58] but the only substantial issue is the massive gold and silver coinage of Populonia in the first half of the third century BCE; in the same period, Populonia as well as Vetulonia produced large bronze coinages. These, as well as the cast bronze coinage of Volaterrae and the massive cast and struck bronze issues from inner Etruria, were based in principle on a unit weighing roughly half a Roman pound; but the archaeological evidence shows that they are all much earlier than the use of the unit at Rome in the last quarter of the third century BCE. There were also substantial struck bronze issues, similar, for example, to those of Neapolis.

Some issues have legends referred to names of towns or, rarely, to names of private people; but they are generally rather problematic.[59]

A silver unit of 8.72 grams is presumably borrowed from the so-called Euboic-Attic system,[60] a silver unit of 5.73 grams has been taken as "Asiatic";[61] but we do not have enough evidence to interpret these choices, and the subject would require much more attention than what can be discussed in this short contribution[62].

It is at least clear than weight reductions within a particular coinage were common, as at Rome and in Magna Graecia.[63] Two series, probably from Vulci, with the legend *θezi vel sim.*, show a ratio of 2 : 1 in weight (10.84 grams vs. 5.28 grams), but it is not clear whether they are contemporary or sequential.[64]

EPILOGUE

As expected, numbers were an important part of the daily life of the Etruscans, widespread in religious practices and theory, but also used in architecture and law.

There is still some important evidence to be considered, coming from *graffiti* with numerals, present in epigraphy at least from the Orientalizing period. In this regard it is interesting to see how one of the main uses of the alphabet since its introduction in Etruria was for reckoning purposes: at the beginning of the seventh century BCE the bronze deposit of S. Francesco at Bologna contained several objects marked with single letters or with numeral marks in order to be checked and counted by the craftsman who owed them.[65]

Similarly the series of decorated terracotta revetments of the temple of Portonaccio in Veii were marked with syllabic groups of two or three letters (*ca-ce-ci*...on the right of the roof and *cra-cre-cri*...on the left), whose function was simply numeral, as testified by the comparison with more recent revetment systems in Veii and elsewhere, which show common numeral marks.

The numeral marking system in Etruria, developed during the Archaic age, originally had single vertical lines for units and "X"'s for tens; then, by cutting the cross in half they generated a mark for five (an upside-down V), while the mark for 100 was obtained by driving a vertical line through the middle of the cross; the bottom half of it became the mark for 50 (identical to an upside down trident-shaped *chi*).[66]

It is not surprising that the Roman system was derived from the Etruscan, since we know that for a long time children from the most important Roman families were sent to Etruria in order to study *litterae*, thus ensuring long-term contact and cultural exchange with Rome (Fig. 23.7).[67]

The use of numbers in religious practice and divinatory science was carried on by Etruscan *haruspices* even after the complete Romanization of Etruria, as shown by late authors such as Martianus Capella (see above), but by then they were integrated into Latin culture. When lightning hit the base of a statue of Augustus causing the letter "C" of "CAESAR" to fall down, the event was interpreted by seers: in one hundred days (marked with "C" in the Roman system) the emperor would be accepted among the gods, since "AESAR" is "god" in Etruscan (Suet., *Aug.*, 97).[68]

A final remark is proper on a technical loanword in Latin, *mantis(s)a*, which means "addition of weight," according to Festus (Paul. Fest. 119, 9), "but worsening (or decreasing) it, because un-useful": it has been interpreted as something conceptually similar to "tare," an indispensable reckoning instrument for trade purposes, which had been presumably theorized and named by Etruscans.[69] But the obscurity of the passage does not allow us to be sure.[70]

Value	Etruscan	Latin
1	I	I
5	Λ	V
10	X	X
50	↑	L
100	✳	C
1000	☉	M

Figure 23.7 The Etruscan numeral marking system compared to Latin.

NOTES

1 Bonfante 2005: 153 ff.; Edlund-Berry 2006: 116 ff.
2 De Grummond 2006: 41 f.
3 Turfa 2004 and 2010.
4 Campbell 2000: 134.
5 A complete survey of actual knowledge about Etruscan numerals has been provided by Agostiniani 1995.
6 Colonna 1978: 116.
7 Artioli, Nociti, Angelini 2011: 1031 ff.; but see also Agostiniani 1995: 23 ff.
8 Agostiniani 1995: 22.
9 Agostiniani 1995: 26.
10 Emiliozzi 1993 and Agostiniani 1997.
11 While before that date a different correspondence was applied (1~2, 3~4, 5~6); Artioli, Nociti, Angelini 2011.
12 Agostiniani 1995: 30; Wallace 2008: 54 ff.
13 Giannecchini 1997.
14 Maras 2009: 364.
15 Agostiniani 1995: 31 ff.
16 Van Heems 2009.

17 See also Facchetti 2000: 22 (quoting A. J. Pfiffig), with different opinions.
18 About the use of high cyphres in religious context, see also number MMMCCC, "3,300," on the lead plaque of S. Marinella, probably inscribed with an oracular response (Maras 2009: 282).
19 Edlund-Berry 2006: 120.
20 De Grummond 2006: 42 ff.; Mora 2008: 173 ff.
21 A complete survey of ages of deceased people as recorded by epitaphs has been given in Turfa forthcoming, with further statistical and medical considerations.
22 Bonfante 2005: 159 f.
23 Mora 2008.
24 See respectively Belfiore 2010: 55 ff., with further bibliography, and Cristofani 1995.
25 Macr., *sat.*, I, 15; see also Varro, *l.L.*, VI, 28.
26 Maras 2009: 352 ff.
27 Maras 2009: 363.
28 Torelli 1986: 215 f.; Van der Meer 2011: 117 ff.
29 Van der Meer 2011: 86
30 Campbell 2000: 134 and 384; Van der Meer 2011: 86 f.
31 Campbell 2000: 256 ff.; Bonfante 2005: 155.
32 De Grummond 2006: 41 f.
33 Dilke 1971: 32 f.
34 Edlund-Berry 2006: 118 f.; Van der Meer 2011: 91.
35 Van der Meer 2011: 88 ff.
36 Colonna 2006: 132 ff.
37 Campbell 2000: xlv.
38 Dilke 1971: 33; Van der Meer 2011: 88.
39 De Grummond 2006: 44 ff.
40 van der Meer 1987: 9 ff. and 22 ff.
41 van der Meer 1987: 147 ff.
42 Maras 2009: 226 f., with further bibliography; Van der Meer 2011: 91.
43 Belfiore 2010: 138, with some different opinions.
44 Van der Meer 2011: 95.
45 Van der Meer 1987: 28 f.; Fiorini 2005: 291 and 298 f., with further bibliography.
46 Maggiani 1982: 77 f. On astrological and near-eastern influences in the cosmos of the liver, see also with different opinions Torelli 1986: 196; Van der Meer 1987: 153 ff.
47 Facchetti 2000: 14.
48 Cifani 2008: 239 f.
49 L. Quilici, in Emiliozzi (ed.) 1999: 75.
50 A forthcoming work on building systems in Archaic Etruria has been discussed as a PhD thesis in Rome by B. Belelli Marchesini in 1994 (title: *L'edilizia in Etruria meridionale dal VII al IV secolo a.C.: tecniche e accorgimenti costruttivi*). See also Belelli Marchesini, forthcoming.
51 Ridley 2005: 102; Cifani 2008: 239; Mura Sommella 2009: 338.
52 Cherici 2006: 19 ff., who points out a possible relationship with observation of the sky and divination, and Cherici 2007. On close relationships between architectural proportions and mathematics in Etruria, see Cavalieri 2008.
53 Maggiani 2002 and 2007. See also recently Pare 1999.
54 For further bibliography, see N. K. Rutter, A. M. Burnett, M. H. Crawford, *et al.*, *Historia numorum. Italy*, London, British Museum Press, 2001, 23–42; and lastly the contributions of A. Burnett, I. Vecchi and specially of N. Vismara in a thematic section on numismatics of *Etruscan Studies*, 10, 2004: 81–116.
55 Plin., *nat. hist.*, XVIII, 12.
56 Pallottino 1993: 260 f.

57 See M. H. Crawford, "From *aes signare* to *aes signatum*," *Schweizerische Numismatische Rundschau*, 88, 2009: 195–197.

58 At times with marks of value, providing matter for metrologic and analytic studies; Maggiani 2002: 193 f.

59 Catalli 2000: 92 ff.

60 Catalli 2000: 89.

61 That is to say 1/50 of the Etruscan light *libra* (according to Maggiani 2002, p. 172), which allows an easy ratio of 2 : 3 with the Euboean-Attic foot.

62 See Maggiani 2002 and 2007, with further bibliography.

63 About numeral marks "X" and "XX" on two sequential series from Populonia, see Catalli 2000, 91; Maggiani 2002: 181 ff. and 195 f.

64 Maras 2003: 408 ff. (sequential); but see Maggiani 2002: 192 ff., who infers a ratio of 2 : 1 between contemporary denominations.

65 Colonna 1988: 12 ff.

66 Agostiniani 1995: 54 f. and 58; Keyser 1988.

67 Agostiniani 1995: 51 f.

68 Actually "AESAR" is likely to Etruscan plural word *aiser*, "gods," and the sign for 100 was different in the Etruscan system: so this tale shows an interesting syncretism of Etruscan and Latin elements.

69 Cherici 2006, p. 27.

70 I would like to thank Prof. Michael H. Crawford for his invaluable help: of course, only the author can be held responsible for the views expressed as well as for any remaining errors.

BIBLIOGRAPHY

Agostiniani, L. (1995) "I numerali etruschi e la loro rappresentazione grafica," *AION*, ling., 17: 21–65.

——(1997) "Sul valore semantico delle formule etrusche *tamera zelarvenas* e *tamera* šarvenas" in A. Catagnoti *et al.* (eds), *Studi linguistici offerti a Gabriella Giacomelli*, Padova: Quaderni del Dip. di Linguistica. Florence, 4. 1–18.

Artioli, G., Nociti, V. and Angelini, I. (2011) "Gambling with Etruscan dice: a tale of numbers and letters," *Archaeometry*, 53.5: 1031–1043.

Belelli Marchesini, B. (forthcoming) *Considerazioni sui sistemi di misurazione e sui criteri metrologici impiegati in campo edilizio in ambito etrusco-laziale* in G. van Heems (ed.), *Regler l'usage: norme et standard dans l'Étrurie hellenistique*, Actes de la rencontre (Rome, 2009).

Belfiore, V. (2010) *Il liber linteus di Zagabria. Testualità e contenuto*, Pisa-Roma: F. Serra.

Bonfante, L. (2005) "Etruscan Boundaries and Prophecy" in T. Atkin and J. Rykwert (eds), *Structure and Meaning in Human Settlements*, Philadelphia: University Museum of Archaeology and Anthropology, 153–163.

Campbell, B. (2000) *The Writings of the Roman Land Surveyors. Introduction, Text, Translation and commentary*, London: *JRS*, Monographs, no. 9.

Capogrossi, L. (2009) "Il diritto delle XII tavole e l'inizio della *centuriatio*," *Agri Centuriati* 6: 241–251.

Cavalieri, M. (2008) "*Genus numeri*, relations mathématiques sous-jacentes à l'architecture étrusque. Le cas du temple de l'*Ara della Regina* à Tarquinia," *Res Antiquae*, 5: 3–14.

Cherici, A. (2006) "Per una scienza etrusca," *Science and Technology for Cultural Heritage*, 15: 9–28.

——(2007) "Per una scienza etrusca 2. *Templum*, templi e rettangolo aureo," *Science and Techology for Cultural Heritage*, 16: 9–29.

Cifani, G. (2008) *Architettura romana arcaica. Edilizia e società tra Monarchia e Repubblica*, Rome: "L'ERMA" di Bretschneider.

Colonna, G. (1978) "Archeologia dell'età romantica in Etruria: i Campanari di Toscanella e latomba dei Vipinana," *Studi Etruschi*, 46: 81–117.

——(1988) "L'écriture dans l'Italie centrale à l'époque archaïque," *Revue de la Société des élèves, anciens élèves et amis de la section des sciences religieuses de l'É.P.H.É.*: 12–31.

——(2006) "Sacred Architecture and the Religion of the Etruscans" in N. T. de Grummond and E. Simon (eds), *The Religion of the Etruscans*, Austin: University of Texas, 132–168.

Cristofani, M. (1995) *Tabula Capuana. Un calendario festivo di età arcaica*, Florence: Olschki.

De Grummond, N. T. (2006) *Etruscan Myth, Sacred History, and Legend*, Philadelphia, PA: University of Pennsylvania Museum of Archaeology and Anthropology.

Dilke, O. A. W. (1971) *The Roman Land Surveyors. Introduction to the Agrimensores*, Newton Abbot: David & Charles.

Edlund-Berry, I. E. M. (2006) "Ritual Space and Boundaries" in N. T. de Grummond and E. Simon (eds), *The Religion of the Etruscans*, Austin: University of Texas, 116–131.

Emiliozzi, A. (1993) "Per gli Alethna di Musarna," in *Miscellanea etrusco-italica I*, Roma: *Quaderni dell'Istituto di Archeologia Etrusco-Italica*, 22, 1993: 109–146.

——(ed.) (1999) *Carri da guerra e principi etruschi*, Catalogue of the exhibition (Viterbo-Rome, 1998–1999), Rome: "L'ERMA" di Bretschneider.

Facchetti, G. M. (2000) *Frammenti di diritto privato etrusco*, Florence: Olschki.

Fiorini, L. (2005) "I santuari del territorio" in S. Fortunelli (ed.), *Il Museo della città etrusca e romana di Cortona. Catalogo delle collezioni*, Florence: Polistampa, 291–299.

Giannecchini, G. (1997) "Un'ipotesi sul numerale etrusco per 'dodici,'" *La Parola del Passato*, 52: 190–206.

Keyser, P. (1988) "The Origin of the Latin Numerals 1 to 1000," *American Journal of Archaeology*, 92.4: 529–546.

Maggiani, A. (1982) "Qualche osservazione sul fegato di Piacenza," *Studi Etruschi*, 50: 53–88.

——(2002) "La libbra etrusca. Sistemi ponderali e monetazione," *Studi Etruschi*, 65–68: 163–199.

——(2007) "La libbra etrusca. Addenda," *Studi Etruschi*, 73: 135–147.

Maras, D. F. (2003) "Numismatica ed epigrafia. Nuove osservazioni sulle serie a legenda θezi e leθez, *Scienze dell'Antichità*, 11: 403–416.

——(2009) *Il dono votivo. Gli dei e il sacro nelle iscrizioni etrusche di culto*, Pisa-Rome: F. Serra.

Mora, F. (2008) "I *saecula* etruschi," *Res Antiquae*, 5: 173–180.

Mura Sommella, A. (2009) "Il tempio di Giove Capitolino: una nuova proposta di lettura," *Annali della Fondazione per il Museo C. Faina di Orvieto*, 16: 333–372.

Pallottino, M. (1993) *Origini e storia primitiva di Roma*, Milan: Rusconi.

Pare, C. F. E. (1999) "Weights and weighing in Bronze age central Europe." *Eliten in der Bronzezeit. Ergebnisse zweier Kolloquien in Mainz und Athen*, Römisch-Germanisches Zentralmuseum, Monographien, 43. Mainz: von Zabern, 421–514.

Ridley R. T. (1995) "Unbridgeable Gaps: the Capitoline Temple at Rome," *Bullettino della Commissione Archeologica Comunale*, 106: 83–104.

Torelli, M. (1986) "La religione," *Rasenna. Storia e civiltà degli Etruschi*, Milan: Scheiwiller, 157–237.

Turfa, J. M. (2004) "The Etruscan brontoscopic calendar and modern archaeological discoveries," *Etruscan Studies*, 10: 163–173.

——(2010) "The Etruscan Brontoscopic Calendar" in N. T. de Grummond and E. Simon (eds), *The Religion of the Etruscans*, Austin: University of Texas, 173–190.

——(forthcoming) "The *Obesus Etruscus*: any basis in fact?," *International Journal of Medical Science*, 9.

Van der Meer, L. B. (2011) *Etrusco ritu. Case Studies in Etruscan Ritual Behaviour*, Leuven: Peeters.

Van Heems, G. (2009) "Nombre, chiffre, lettre: formes et réformes des notations chiffrées de l'étrusque," *Révue Philologique*, 83.1: 103–130.

Wallace, R. E. (2008) *Zikh Rasna. A Manual of the Etruscan Language and Inscriptions*, Ann Arbor, New York: Beech Stave Press.

PART V

RELIGION IN ETRURIA

CHAPTER TWENTY FOUR

GREEK MYTH IN ETRUSCAN CULTURE

———— •◆• ————

Erika Simon

G reek myth is present in all phases of Etruscan figural art. As far as we know, the first medium for mythical scenes were vessels of clay, and the earliest depictions represented adventures of the Argonauts and of Odysseus – no wonder in a country of seafaring people.[1] According to Homer's *Odyssey* (12.70), Argo, the ship of the Argonauts, was "in all men's minds" at that time.

In 1988 a bucchero jug from an Etruscan grave in Cerveteri (ancient Caere), an olpe (Fig. 24.1) came to light. It is dated by context and style towards 630 BCE.[2] The decoration – in flat relief and engraved – shows (among unnamed figures) two persons with inscribed mythical names: Metaia, Taitale (Fig. 24.1), in Greek Medea, Daidalos. They do not belong to the same myth, therefore they are not represented in the same scene. Medea, a princess from Kolchis (north-east of the Black Sea), used her magic power to help Jason, the leader of the Argonauts, to get the golden fleece.[3] He took her to Greece as his wife. On the bucchero jug she is shown at a magic kettle rejuvenating a man, perhaps her husband Jason. Daidalos was of Athenian origin and a famous artist, architect and inventor.[4] He built the labyrinth for Minos, the king of Knossos, and flew from Crete to Sicily with self-made wings. He also came to the island Sardinia,[5] not far from the Etruscans. The bucchero jug shows him winged and running with lifted arms (Fig. 24.1). In archaic style this is flying – a dream of mankind.

About two generations earlier, the Etruscans had learned letters from Greek colonists at the bay of Naples. However, name inscriptions on Etruscan clay vessels remained rare. Many more mythical names are found on bronze mirrors (see Figs. 24.12, 24.15, 24.18, 24.19). It is interesting that those names in Etruscan art often seem to be derived from Dorian dialect.[6] This was not the language of Homer but of the Greek chorus song, even on the theater stage of classical Athens. Therefore, we should consider that the Etruscans not only knew about Greek myths from epic poetry but also from lyric song.[7] According to ancient historians the noble Corinthian Demaratos emigrated from his (Dorian speaking) home town to Tarquinii with a group of people[8] and among them were artists.[9]

There are other mythical scenes on early clay vases, but without names. An amphora of about 670 BCE (Fig. 24.2)[10] shows a figural frieze: a man holding a seven-stringed lyre and a *plektron* stands between five acrobatic dancers. They wear breastplates and some of

Figure 24.1   Bucchero olpe found in Caere. Taitale (Daidalos). Rome, Villa Giulia (n. 2).

Figure 24.2   Etruscan amphora, perhaps made in Caere. Orpheus and *pyrrhiche* of young Argonauts.
Wuerzburg, M. v. Wagner Mus. (n. 10).

them have weapons. With them they perform an armed dance (*pyrrhiche*), which is known from early cult and myth in Anatolia, Greece and Italy.[11] Young Argonauts danced the *pyrrhiche* to the music of Orpheus on mount Dindymon in honor of the divine mother Rhea.[12] Her cult personnel consisted of young armed dancers called *kouretes*. The goddess enjoyed the *pyrrhiche*, created on waterless Dindymon, "Jason's Spring" as it was called (Ap. Rhod. 1.1148). With their dance, the Argonauts also wished to appease the soul of a hero (Kyzikos), whom they had killed inadvertently. I think that dance was mentioned in the early epic about the Argo (lost to us) and is represented on the amphora. Therefore, the musician is Orpheus and the frontal lion head above him is the gargoyle of "Jason's Spring" (Fig. 24.2). The purpose of that *pyrrhiche* – appeasement of a soul – fits well with an amphora in a tomb. We shall see that depictions of Greek myth in Etruria were often made for the dead (see Figs. 24.7–8, 24.23–24 and others).

According to Martelli the amphora (Fig. 24.2) was produced in Caere, where vases of the same workshop were found.[13] They are a generation older than the bucchero jug (Fig. 24.2). Caere, after all, was much interested in Greek mythology. This town, also called

Agylla, was said to have been founded by Pelasgians from Thessaly.[14] It is possible that Greeks lived there, or in Caere's harbor Pyrgi, in the first half of the seventh century BCE, and among them was one called Aristonothos. He signed the famous krater found in Caere (Fig. 24.3). It shows the blinding of Polyphemus by Odysseus and his comrades.[15] In this case, inscriptions of mythical names are not needed – the unique adventure from the ninth book of the *Odyssey* (402 ff.) speaks for itself. A century later, in the second half of the sixth century BCE, the "Caeretan hydriae" turn up.[16] They were made in Etruria, probably in Caere, by immigrants from East Greece. About half of them show mythical scenes, but not the Argonauts. A frequent figure on them is Herakles.[17] His adventure with the hell dog, Kerberos – a typical theme for a grave – was represented by the two main artists of Caeretan hydriae, the Eagle Painter and the Busiris Painter.[18] To the first one is ascribed a hydria in the Getty Museum (Fig. 24.4).[19] It shows Herakles

Figure 24.3 Greek krater found in Caere with signature of Aristonothos. Blinding of Polyphemus. Rome, Musei Capitolini.

Figure 24.4 "Caeretan" hydria, circa 525 BCE, ascribed to the Eagle Painter, an East Greek artist who perhaps worked in Caere. Herakles and Iolaos fight against the Lernaean Hydra. Photo © The J. Paul Getty Museum, Villa Collection, Malibu, California (n. 19).

and his brother Iolaos, both armed, in their fight against the Lernaean Hydra, a multi-headed serpent monster. To the right, at the heel of Herakles, a large crab appears and between Iolaos' legs a fire burns. The flames were explained as a weapon against the Hydra, but Iolaos uses a *harpe.* According to astral mythology, Hera sent the Cancer of the zodiac against Herakles when he fought with the Hydra. That sign appears together with the Dog Star (Sirius) in high summer.[20] At this time of the year – according to archaic poets – men were flabby and exhausted.[21] Crab and fire on the Caeretan hydria, after all, symbolize the summer heat, sent by Hera against her stepson.

Many vases were imported from Greece, at first from Eastern Ionian regions and from Corinth and then later (after 580/70 BCE) more and more often from Athens. The style of the different ceramic origins was imitated in Etruria. In the "Corinthianizing" period (630–540 BCE) mythical scenes are rare,[22] whereas in the Etruscan "Black Figure" pottery (550–480 BCE) various myths appear.[23] One of the most famous Athenian vases, the Kleitias krater in Florence (565/60 BCE, also known as the "François Vase"), was found in a tomb of Chiusi (Figs. 24.5–6).[24] It is decorated with nine mythical scenes. The main frieze, which runs around the krater, shows Olympian gods visiting the newly married couple Peleus and Thetis, the future parents of Achilles. Achilles appears in the two framing friezes on the main side (Fig. 24.5), his dead body is transported by Aiax (Fig. 24.6) on both handle sides.[25] After all, more than half of the Kleitias krater is connected with the myth of Achilles.

The chariot from Monteleone di Spoleto in New York (540 BCE) was made in an Etruscan workshop (Figs. 24.7 and 24.8)[26] and is adorned with Achilles' heroic life. At an exhibition in Viterbo and Rome that was held towards the end of the last century, spectators were surprised at the high number of tombs with chariots from ancient Italy, many belonging to noble Etruscans.[27] The Monteleone chariot is the best preserved. Its wood, of course, is entirely new (see Chapter 41). The metalwork, beaten and engraved bronze, consists of three panels. Two *kouroi* connect the big central panel with the sides. The big central panel of the chariot (Fig. 24.7) illustrates the beginning of book 19 of the *Iliad*: Thetis brings new weapons for her son Achilles. A frieze beneath one of the side panels (Fig. 24.8) shows a centaur, a winged figure and a youth, who wrestles

Figure 24.5   Attic volute krater (Kleitias krater) found in Chiusi. Front side, main frieze: Olympian gods visit the wedding of Peleus and Thetis. Above: Achilles organizes the chariot race at the funeral for his friend Patroklos (*Iliad* book 23). Below: Achilles pursues Troilos who is on horseback (see Fig. 10). Florence, Mus. Arch. (n. 24).

Figure 24.6   Handle side of Fig. 24.5: Aiax with the dead body of Achilles (repeated on the other side).

Figure 24.7   Chariot from Monteleone di Spoleto. Drawing of the three panels: Achilles kills Memnon; Thetis brings new weapons to her son; Achilles on a chariot with winged horses (n. 26–27).

Figure 24.8   Side panel of the Monteleone chariot: Memnon, the son of Eos (see Fig. 24.21) killed by Achilles. Beneath: Cheiron, Iris and the boy Achilles wrestling with a panther. New York, Metr. Mus.

with a panther. He is Achilles with his teacher Cheiron and the divine messenger Iris between them. One of the side panels has a scene from the lost epic *Aithiopis:* Achilles (on the right) fights against Memnon, a son of the goddess of the dawn (Eos, Etruscan Thesan) and the Trojan prince Tithonos (see note 54). Memnon came with Aethiopians to help Troy. On the panel (Fig. 24.8) his breast is hit by Achilles' lance, whereas his lance fails on Achilles' helmet. Beneath them lies a dead Aethiopian. The other side panel shows Achilles after his death, driving his chariot with two winged horses.

The lost epic *Kypria,* the first of the Trojan cycle, was especially important for visual art. It contained events around Troy before the *Iliad,* such as the judgment of Paris or the death of Troilos. The latter was, like Paris, a son of Priam. According to an oracle, the Achaeans could not take Troy if Priam's youngest son became an adult. Therefore Troilos died early by the hand of Achilles. This myth is painted in the Tomba dei Tori in Tarquinii of 530 BCE (Fig. 24.9).[28] Troilos rides to Apollo's sanctuary to water his horses. Behind the fountain, Achilles appears with a knife. He will kill Troilos in the sacred grove. Later, Apollo took revenge for this crime by killing Achilles. The god's grove is indicated by the palm tree that is near the basin, by laurel and by other plants. It continues in the frieze below, where the laurel trees are adorned with ritual ribbons. Mythical scenes are rare in Etruscan tomb painting, whereas Apollo's laurel grove frequently occurs.[29] This is why the myth of Troilos is depicted here. The spiky object beneath his horse is not a plant but a demon of death rising from the earth.

As mentioned above, on the main frieze of the Kleitias krater the Olympians come to celebrate the wedding of Peleus and Thetis (Fig. 24.5). On this occasion, a quarrel about beauty arose among the goddesses Hera, Athena and Aphrodite. Zeus ordered his messenger Hermes to take them to Paris (Alexandros), Priam's son, who then was a herdsman on Mount Ida. He had to judge which of the three goddesses was the most beautiful. The earliest preserved picture of that judgment in ancient art (640/630 BCE) is preserved on an olpe from Corinth, the Chigi vase, found near Veii.[30] The most famous judgment of Paris in Etruscan art is on a black-figured amphora from Vulci (540 BCE). It is attributed to the "Paris Painter" who is named after this vase.[31] Both shoulder friezes

Figure 24.9 Wall painting in Tomba dei Tori, Tarquinii. Achilles waylays Troilos in the grove of Apollo (n. 28–29).

belong together. On the left side (Fig. 24.10), cattle are guarded by a dog. The noble cowherd Paris does not look towards his animals, but turns to the other side, where five persons approach (Fig. 24.11).

Two men, one white-haired and one young, each with a herald's staff (*kerykeion*), lead the three goddesses. Amusingly, they show stage fright. Hera seizes her veil with a great gesture and whispers with Hermes. The helmet of Athena is worn like a hat, and Aphrodite pulls up her garment to show her elegant shoes and legs. The genial painter did not copy Greek models. The cattle and the raven behind Paris as well as the old herald in front of him are original creations. The white-haired herald and Hermes appear

Figure 24.10

Figures 24.10 and 24.11   Etruscan (during the nineteenth century called "Pontic") amphora. Shoulder friezes on both sides: judgment of Paris. Munich, Antikensammlungen (n.31).

on another amphora by the same painter,[32] together with the centaur Cheiron, the future
teacher of Achilles (see Fig. 24.8). They are about to lead the three goddesses from the
wedding festival on Mount Pelion in Thessaly to Mount Ida in the Troad. The old man
is Aiakos (Aeacus), father of the bridegroom Peleus.[33] He was said to be the fairest of all
humans. He will have influence on the judgment of Paris, as well as Apollo's oracular
bird, the raven, sitting behind him (Fig. 24.10).

Aphrodite had promised to Paris the most beautiful woman on earth. On a bronze
mirror from Praeneste (470/60 BCE), which has Etruscan name inscriptions, the goddess
fulfils her promise (Fig. 24.12).[34] Paris, as young as on the amphora (Fig. 24.10), is seated
at the bed where Helen has given birth to her daughter. He looks up to the majestic
Aphrodite (Turan), who will help him to abduct the mother without the baby. Three
sphinxes appear as fate symbols, one above Helen, whose abduction caused the Trojan
War. The scene has a special flair, typical for Etruscan mirrors (see Chapter 58). They were
privately used. The same may be said about gems. Men and women wore them, mostly on
rings. The Etruscans learned to cut gems from East Greek and oriental artists (see Chapter
51). The "Master of the Boston Dionysos" (last quarter of sixth century BCE) belonged to
the first generation of Etruscan gem artists.[35] Like his colleagues he preferred to represent
single figures: a hero, a god, a demon.[36] Mythical scenes with three and more persons
are rare. One of his carnelian scarabs is such an exception (Fig. 24.13).[37] In the center
Herakles grasps at the wrist of a small old man. Some scholars call him Nereus, the grey
god of the sea; others prefer Geras, the personification of Old Age. I think the latter fits
well in the private sphere of a gem. The goddess behind Herakles is Athena, the female
figure on the other side is not convincingly named. I think she is Herakles' Olympian
bride Hebe, the personification of Youth.[38] She congratulates him with a flower in her
raised hand. He defeats Old Age and will live with her. A carnelian scarab, made famous
by Winckelmann, shows a scene of the "Seven against Thebes" (Fig. 24.14, early fifth

Figure 24.12   Bronze mirror from Praeneste. Helen in childbirth, Paris and Aphrodite (Turan).
Rome, Villa Giulia (n. 34).

century BCE).[39] This piece in Berlin, with name inscriptions, is the best among several gems which illustrate the same situation. The seer Amphiaraos, who is seated between some of the Seven, announces a dark future for them. The heroes are depressed. I think those ring stones warned their owners against quarreling in their own family: Oedipus' sons, the brothers Eteokles and Polyneikes, fought against each other and died (Fig. 24.23).

The Theban cycle was in Etruria as popular as the Trojan. People were fascinated by seers like Amphiaraos and Teiresias, because prophecy was an important part of their religion.[40] Teiresias also turns up in the *Nekyia* of the *Odyssey* (11.90 f. translation R. Lattimore): "Now came the soul of Teiresias the Theban, holding a staff of gold". In a long speech (38 verses) Teiresias tells how Odysseus can make peace with Poseidon. This scene appears on a mirror from Vulci with name inscriptions (Fig. 24.15, second quarter fourth century BCE).[41] Odysseus (Uthuze) is seated and holds the knife with which he has ritually slaughtered a ram (not represented). The animal's blood brings to life the shadow of Teiresias (*hinthial Teriasas*). He has a female head, because for a part of his life he had been a woman.[42] The figure at his side is Hermes *Psychagogos*, escort of souls, in the inscription *Turms Aitas* = Hermes of Hades. He does not appear in Homer's *Nekyia* but in the Aeschylean drama based on it, the *Psychagogoi*.

Figure 24.13   Carnelian scarab. Herakles and Geras (Old Age), flanked by Athena (Menerva) and Hebe, the goddess of Youth. Boston, MFA (n. 37).

Figure 24.14   Carnelian scarab. "Seven against Thebes." Berlin, Staatl. Mus. (n. 39).

During the fifth century BCE Greek myths came to be known by a new type of poetry: drama. Elsewhere I have shown that Etruscan art was influenced by the Athenian theater.[43] Many famous tragedies about Theban myths exist, for example, "The Seven against Thebes" of Aeschylus or the Oedipus tragedies of Sophocles.

Finally, the Theban and Trojan cycle and other myths were highly regarded, because they dealt with genealogy and ancestors. One of the most famous was Aeneas, a member of the Trojan royal house who fled Troy with his father, son and comrades to central Italy.[44] This myth was already circulating in Etruria in the sixth century BCE – half a millennium before Vergil wrote his epic. Many black-figure Athenian vases decorated with the flight of Aeneas were found in Etruscan graves.[45] An *Iliad* scene with Aeneas (5.511–518) is shown on the shoulder of a late black figure Etruscan amphora (Fig. 24.16).[46] His mother Aphrodite (Turan) rescues him from the battlefield. She makes Aeneas invisible to Diomedes by throwing her mantle upon him. Turan is winged as often in earlier Etruscan art. The Aeneas myth even became a cult. Excavations in Veii brought to light votive statuettes of terracotta (Fig. 24.17).[47] They represent Aeneas, who carries his father Anchises on his shoulder.

Figure 24.15   Bronze mirror from Vulci. Odysseus (Uthuze), the shadow (*hinthial*) of Teiresias and Hermes (Turms). Berlin, Staatl. Mus. (n. 41).

Figure 24.16   Etruscan black figure amphora, shoulder frieze: Aphrodite (Turan) throws her mantle on Aeneas. Wuerzburg, M. v. Wagner Mus. (n. 46).

Vessels like kraters and cups were used for festive drinking. This is the reason why vases often show the world of Dionysos (Fufluns). An Etruscan black-figure hydria (earlier in Toledo/Ohio) is decorated with a scene from the Homeric hymn to Dionysos (500 BCE, Fig. 8.1).[48] In this poem the god's ship is attacked by Tyrrhenian – i.e. Etruscan – pirates. The god transforms them into dolphins. The hydria shows six figures upside down above waves. Most of them still have human legs and heads of dolphins, but a human bust with a dolphin's tail appears to the left side, together with ivy, the holy plant of Dionysos.

There are special Dionysian scenes in the private world of Etruscan mirrors. An inscribed one from the second quarter of the fourth century BCE in Berlin (Fig. 24.18)[49] shows Apollo (Aplu) with a laurel staff and Dionysos (Fufluns) who is embraced by his

Figure 24.17   Terracotta votive from Veii. Statuette of Aeneas carrying his father Anchises. Rome, Villa Giulia (n. 47).

Figure 24.18   Bronze mirror. Apollo (Aplu) and Dionysios (Fufluns) who is embraced by his mother. Berlin, Staatl. Mus. (n. 49).

mother Semele (Semla). A satyr boy plays a double pipe at Apollo's side. This god and Dionysos had near relations in Delphi and Delos, where they owned the same temple.[50] At the Delphic festival *Herois* Semele's resurrection from Hades was celebrated. It is represented on the mirror in a frame of Dionysian ivy. A similar mirror, showing the same types of figures, was excavated near Orvieto.[51] However, apart from Apollo, the names are different. Aphrodite (Turan) and Adonis (Atunis) embrace, and instead of the satyr the boy Eros (Turnu) sits at the left side. He plays with an *iynx*, a little wheel with magical power. Love is the subject of many mirrors. One of the grandest, in early Hellenistic style, currently housed in Berlin, was found in Perugia (Fig. 24.19).[52] The names of the five figures are taken from Greek myth, but the main person, Athrpa (Atropos, one of the three *Moirai,* Fates) behaves in a purely Etruscan fashion. She is about to fasten a nail with her hammer, an action of irreversible fate. Both loving couples on the sides of the goddess – Aphrodite and Adonis, Meleager and Atalante – were separated by an early death. Adonis was killed by a boar. Atalante and Meleager met at the Calydonian boar hunt. For this sake Athrpa fastens the head of a boar with her nail.

We now move from these private works of art to architectural sculpture. In Etruria this consists mainly of terracotta. One of the earliest preserved pieces (last quarter of the sixth century BCE) is a central *acroterium* in Berlin (Fig. 24.20).[53] It was found at a temple in Cerveteri. The winged goddess, also with wings at her shoes, originally appeared above a pediment. This is Eos (Thesan), the goddess of the dawn, and she has a boy in her arms. Some scholars state he is Kephalos, but he is surely the Trojan prince Tithonos, the future father of Memnon, the hero who would come to Troy with the Aethiopians and would be killed by Achilles (see Fig. 24.8). On Etruscan mirrors Thesan instead carries Memnon, her fallen son.[54]

We turn from an early sculpture to a late one, which is Thesan as well (Fig. 24.21).[55] The lifesize clay figure was excavated in 1986 in the Astrone valley, south-west of Chianciano Terme. The winged goddess originally appeared flying above the right side of a Hellenistic pediment. With the gesture of *aposkopein* she looks back to the central

Figure 24.19 Bronze mirror from Perugia. The fate goddess Atropos (Athrpa) fastens a nail between two loving couples (Aphrodite and Adonis, Meleager and Atalante). They were separated by early death. Berlin, Staatl. Mus. (n. 52).

acroterium, which I think depicts the sun god (Usil) with his horses. The goddess of the dawn held a vessel in her left hand for spilling the morning dew.

The most famous architectonic sculptures, excavated near Veii,[56] date from the late sixth century BCE. They belong to different groups that had been placed on the highest beam of a building in the sacred precinct.[57] One particular group showed Apollo and Herakles debating over the deer of Artemis.

Apollo is better preserved than the others, while only Hermes' beautiful head exists. We may call him "Turms of Tin," because Zeus sent him to make peace between Apollo and Herakles. Etruscan gods lived in harmony.

Whereas Greek pediments could be filled with figural scenes already in the sixth century BCE, the Etruscans adorned the ends of the main beams with square reliefs (see Chapter 49). An *antepagmentum* of this type was found in Caere's harbor Pyrgi (Fig. 24.22),[58] from a

Figure 24.20   Clay *acroterium* from Caere. Eos (Thesan) with Tithonos in her arms.
Berlin, Staatl. Mus., inv. TC 6681.1 (n. 53).

Figure 24.21   Clay *acroterium* from Astrone valley. The dawn goddess Thesan.
Chianciano Terme, Mus. (n. 55).

temple of the second quarter of the fifth century BCE. The terrible scene belongs to the Seven against Thebes. Zeus (Tin) in the center throws his lightning bolt at Kapaneus who cries. Athena (Menerva) at the side of Zeus has a vessel in her right hand. She wanted to bring the drink of immortality to the mortally wounded Tydeus,[59] but she is horrified by his behavior and departs. He is biting into the head of the fallen Melanippos in order to drink his brain.

Figures of pedimental compositions are known from Hellenistic Etruria. They were excavated, for example, together with the Thesan *acroterium* (Fig. 24.21),[60] but the interpretation is not clear. A terracotta pediment from Talamone (second quarter of second century BCE) in Florence[61] shows the fate of the Seven against Thebes. Oedipus kneels in the center between his dying sons Eteokles and Polyneikes. Behind him is the wall of Thebes with Kapaneus on a ladder. On the right side Amphiaraos sinks with his chariot into the earth, on the left Adrastos leads his horses in the other direction. He was the only one of the Seven who survived.

The central scene of the Talamone pediment recurs on Northern Etruscan ash urns (– second-first century). On the lids of these urns the persons whose remains are buried in them are at the eternal symposium. An alabaster urn in Volterra (Fig. 24.23)[62] shows a man with scroll and drinking horn. His name is inscribed on the *kline.* The relief beneath is framed by two nearly naked female statues, and the one on the left holds a torch. They are fate goddesses like the Greek *Moirai* (see Fig. 24.19) and the Etruscan Vanth (see Fig. 24.24). Oedipus laments kneeling in the center, supported by a warrior. At each of his sides his sons Eteokles and Polyneikes die in the arms of comrades. Behind them Kreon, king of Thebes, speaks with a long-haired woman. I think she is Antigone who will bury her brother Polyneikes in spite of Kreon's ban. The fate goddesses as well as themes of mourning and burying are appropriate to ash urns. This is one of the reasons why Theban mythology often appears on them. Perhaps there were also genealogical reasons. We know for example, from Vergil's *Aeneid* (10.198–200) that his home town Mantua was named after Manto, the daughter of Teiresias. The poet certainly did not invent this. The tale must have been popular in Northern Etruria at the time of the urns.

Many of them also were made of terracotta, for example an urn at Perugia with a couple on its lid.[63] Fig. 24.24 shows a drawing after the terracotta relief. The myth, I think, is situated in Corinth, a town connected with Etruria even more closely than

Figure 24.22 Clay *antepagmentum* from Pyrgi. Zeus (Tin) killing Kapaneus, one of the Seven, with his lightning. Athena (Menerva) leaves with her drink of immortality, denying it to Tydeus, who bites into the head of Melanippos. Rome, Villa Giulia (n. 58).

Figure 24.23 Alabaster urn from Volterra. Oedipus between his dying sons; behind him Kreon and Antigone. Volterra, Mus. Guarnacci (n. 63).

Figure 24.24 Terracotta urn from Perugia. Sisyphos offering at his own grave, and Death in the shape of a wolf demon. Perugia, Mus. (n. 63).

Thebes. The bearded man with *pileus* (conical cap) is the Corinthian king Sisyphos. Hades had allowed him to return to life to perform tomb rites at his own grave. But Sisyphos fettered Thanatos (Death) with the consequence that nobody could die. In the relief Sisyphos pours a libation, while chained Death (with wolf paws) rises up and seizes one of the king's companions. Behind him the Etruscan fate goddess Vanth appears. Death will be freed and Sisyphos will have his eternal punishment: pushing a rock up a hill.

In this article metalwork, apart from mirrors, is rarely discussed. The Etruscans were masters of metalwork, but during hard times bronze statues were chopped up and sold as raw material. The same was the case for Greek and Roman bronzes. In 1553 the famous Chimaera was found outside Arezzo, buried at a depth of 5 meters.[64] The monster with a lion's body and three heads (of lion, goat and serpent) was cast by an Etruscan artist in the early fourth century BCE. The goat's head is wounded and Chimaera is represented with her mythical adversary, Bellerophon, riding on Pegasus. The inscription on her right foreleg tells us that the group was a votive in the sanctuary of Tin, the highest Etruscan god.

Apart from mythical scenes there are single figures from Greek myth in Etruscan art. We find them on gems especially and some of them have inscriptions.[65] In earlier archaeological literature these figures and scenes were thought to be copies after Greek originals. Many Etruscan artists, however, created original works (Figs. 24.10–13 and others). They mixed their symbols and figures with Greek ones (Figs. 24.19, 23–24). A part of them surely was bilingual. Etruscans were the first to be fascinated by Greek mythology outside Greece.

NOTES

1   Krauskopf (2011) 133–137; below n.14.
2   Rome, Villa Giulia. M. A. Rizzo, M. Martelli, "Un incunabolo del mito Greco in Etruria." *ASAtene* 66/67, 1988/89, 7–56; A. M. Moretti Sgubini, *Il Museo Nazionale Etrusco di Villa Giulia. Guida breve* (Rome 1999) 35 fig. 27; Krauskopf (2011) 134, n. 11 (literature).
3   *LIMC* V (1990) 629–638 "Iason" (J. Neils).
4   *LIMC* Suppl. 2009, 165–159 "Daidalos et Ikaros" (J. E. Nyenhuis).
5   Diodorus 4, 30; Pausanias 10, 17,4.
6   C. de Simone, *Die griechischen Entlehnungen im Etruskischen* (Wiesbden 1970); H. Rix, "Das Eindringen griechischer Mythen in Etrurien nach Aussage mythologischer Namen." *Schriften des DArV* 5 (Mannheim 1981) 96–106.
7   See below n. 43.
8   Strabo 5.2.2 p. 220 C; commentary: St. Radt, *Strabons Geographika* 6 (Goettingen 2007) 29–31.
9   Pliny, *NH* 35,152; Steingräber (2006) 41 f; von Hase (2008) 223.
10 Wuerzburg, M. v. Wagner Mus. ZA 66 (Nereus foundation). Martelli (1987) 18. 262 f. no. 38 pl. 92; *eadem* AA 1988, 285–296; Simon (1996) 99–104; Krauskopf (2011) 133 f.
11 *DNP* 10 (2001) 642–644 "Pyrrhiche" (R.Harmon). In Rome armed dances were performed by the priesthood of the Salii: *RE* I A 2 (1920) 1873–1894 "Salii 1" (F. Geiger).
12 Ap. Rhod. 1, 1134 ff: "By command of Orpheus the young men in full armour moved round in a high-stepping dance, beating their shields with their swords" (translation E. V. Rieu). *Kouretes* in the cult of Rhea (Cybele): *LIMC* VIII (1997) 736–741 "Kouretes/Korybantes" (R. Lindner).
13 Martelli (1987) 18.
14 Strabo 5, 2, 3 p. 220 C; above n. 8. The Argo sailed from Thessaly to the Black Sea. Etruscans interested in Thessalian myths: *LIMC* VIII (1997) 154 "Tyro" (E. Simon).
15 Aristonothos krater from Caere. Blinding of Polyphemus. Rome, Mus. Cap. Inv. Castellani 172. Martelli (1987) 263 f. no. 40 pl. 93; v. Hase (2008) 225 Fig. 3.
16 *DNP* 2 (1997/99) 907 f. "Caeretaner Hydrien" (M. Steinhart).
17 Hemelrijk (1984) 141 f.
18 Hemelrijk (1984) 14 no. 4 pl. 32 f. and 23 f. no. 11 pl. 54.
19 Malibu, Getty Mus. 83. AE 346. Hemelrijk (1984) 41 no. 23 pl. 88. 89 a; *LIMC* V (1990) 37 "Herakles" no. 2016 pl. 56.
20 Simon (2009) 53 f.
21 Hesiod, *Works and Days* 585–587; E. Lobel and D. Page, *Poetarum Lesbiorum Fragmenta* (Oxford 1955) 270 frg. 347 (Alcaeus).
22 Martelli (1987) 23–30.
23 Martelli (1987) 31–42 (M. A Rizzo).

24 von Hase (2008) 223 Figs. 1 a. b; T. Hirayama, *Kleitias and Attic Black-Figure-Vases in the Sixth Century B.C.* (Tokyo 2010).

25 Simon (2009) 109 Fig. 2.

26 Hampe, Simon (1964) 53–67 pls. 22–25s. 16–17; Gisler-Huwiler (1986) 244 no. 82 pl. 195; Simon 2001, 157 f.; von Hase (2008) 229 f.

27 A. Emiliozzi, (ed.) *Carri da Guerra e Principi Etruschi* (Rome 1999) 179–190 Figs. 1–6 pls. XII–XVII (M. Bonamici, A Emiliozzi). A. Emiliozzi, *Metro. Mus. Journal* (New York) 46, 2011, 8–132.

28 Steingraeber (2006) 91; von Hase (2008) 228 Fig. 8.

29 Simon (1996) 60–70.

30 Rome, Villa Giulia 22679. Kossatz-Deissmann (1994) 179 no. 26.

31 Munich, Antikensammlungen VAS 837 "Pontic amphora." Hampe, Simon (1964) 36–39 pls. 16–17; Kossatz-Deissmann (1994) 180 no. 42.

32 New York Metr. Mus. 55. 11. 1. Hampe, Simon (1964) 35–44 pls. 12–15; Gisler-Huwiler (1986) 240 no. 43.

33 Simon (2012) 58–62.

34 Rome, Villa Giulia 1691. Hampe, Simon (1964) 35 n. 4; 43 f. Fig. 9; Simon (2001) 154. 159 Fig. 161.

35 Spier (2000) 330–335.

36 For mythical figures on Etruscan scarabs: Krauskopf (1995); see also Chapter 51.

37 Boston, MFA 21.197. H. Heres, M. Kunze (eds) *Die Welt der Etrusker* (Berlin 1988) 289 pl. 56, 1–2 (P. Zazoff); Schwarz (1990) 229 no. 305; Spier (2000) 333 Fig. 4.

38 *LIMC* IV (1988) 458–464 "Hebe"(A-F. Laurens).

39 Krauskopf (1974) 85.108 Sie 1 pl. 20, 1; Kunze (2009)15. 45. 95–97 Fig. 110; other gems with the same subject: Krauskopf (1974) 108 Sie 1 a -Sie 4; Krauskopf (1994) 715f.

40 de Grummond, Simon (2006) 27–44 (N. T. de Grummond).

41 Vatican, Mus. Greg. Etr. 12687. Harari (1997) 106 no. 103; Simon (2000) 517–519 Fig. 7.

42 R. Merkelbach, R. M. West, *Fragmenta Hesiodea* (Oxford 1967) 134–136 frg. 275.

43 Simon (2000) 511–521.

44 *Enciclopedia Virgiliana* II (Rome 1985) 221–234 "Enea" (N. Horsfall, P. Grimal, F. Canciani); *LIMC* Suppl 2009, 34–38 "Aineias" (E. Simon).

45 K. Schauenburg, *Gymnasium* 67, 1960, 176–191 and *Gymnasium* 76, 1969, 42–53.

46 Wuerzburg, M. v. Wagner Mus. L 799. CVA Wuerzburg 3 (1983) 64–66 pls. 47,1 and 49,1; Simon (2001) 155, 159 Fig. 162.

47 Rome, Villa Giulia 40272. *LIMC* I (1981) 388 "Aineias" no. 96 pl. 303 (F. Canciani).

48 Martelli (1987) 311 no. 130 pl. 176; *LIMC* VIII (1997) 155 "Tyrsenoi" no. 1 pl. 115 (M. Harari).

49 Krauskopf (1984) 342 no. 36 pl. 289; Simon (1996) 64–66 fig. 8.

50 E. Simon, "Apollon und Dionysos," *In memoria di Enrico Paribeni* II (Rome 1998) 451–460.

51 de Grummond, Simon (2006) 50 f. Fig. IV.6.

52 de Grummond, Simon (2006) 22 Fig. II.19 (L. Bonfante); Simon (1996) pl. 7.

53 Bloch (1986) 795 no. 29; Simon (2007) 52 pl. XXI c.

54 Bloch (1986) 795 f; Simon (1996) 181–193.

55 Simon (2007) 47–54 pl. XIX.

56 Rome, Villa Giulia. Krauskopf (1984) 339 no. 12 pl. 287 (Aplu); Schwarz (1990) 222 no. 222 (Hercle); Harari (1997) 104 no. 76 pl. 78 (Turms).

57 For the problems of their position: Simon (1996) 71–78.

58 Rome, Villa Giulia. Krauskopf (1994) 741 no. 47 pl. 545.

59 In Etruscan *Tute*. He often appears on gems: Krauskopf (1995) 60; *LIMC* VIII (1997) 142–145 "Tydeus" no. 1–6; Kunze (2009) 45. 97 fig. 111; *LIMC* Suppl. 2009, 489 f. "Tydeus" (S. Lorenz).

60 Above n. 55.

61 B. von Freytag gen. Loeringhoff, Das Giebelrelief von Telamon und seine Stellung innerhalb der Ikonographie der "Sieben gegen Theben." *RM Erg.H.* 27 (1986); Krauskopf (1994) 741 no. 48.
62 Volterra, Mus. Guarnacci 374. *LIMC* IV (1988) 31 "Eteokles" no. 28 pI. 17 (I. Krauskopf).
63 M. Sprenger, G. Bartoloni, *Die Etrusker* (Hirmer, Munich 1977) 160 no. 265; Simon (1996) 90–95 fig. 12.
64 *LIMC* III (1986) 261 "Chimaira in Etruria" no. 11 pI. 210 (G. Cianferoni, M. Iozzo, E. Setari (eds) *Myth, Allegory, Emblem: The Many Lives of the Chimaera of Arezzo. Proceedings of the International Colloquium, Malibu 4 December* 2009, The J. Paul Getty Museum, Rome: Aracne.
65 Krauskopf (1995); see above n. 39. 59.

BIBLIOGRAPHY

Bloch, R. (1986) "Eos/Thesan," *LIMC* III, 789–797.
Cianferoni, G., Iozzo, M. and Setari, E. (eds) (2012) *Myth, Allegory, Emblem: The Many Lives of the Chimaera of Arezzo. Proceedings of the International Colloquium, Malibu 4 December* 2009, The J. Paul Getty Museum, Rome: Aracne.
Gisler-Huwiler, M. (1986) "Cheiron," *LIMC* III, 237–248.
de Grummond, N. T. and Simon, E. (eds) (2006) *The Religion of the Etruscans*, University of Texas, Austin.
Hampe, R. and Simon, E. (1964) *Griechische Sagen in der frühen etruskischen Kunst*, Zabern, Mainz.
Harari, M. (1997) "Turms," *LIMC* VIII, 98–111.
von Hase, F.-W. (2008) "Zur Rezeption Homerischer Dichtung in der frühen etruskischen Bildkunst" in J. Latacz and others (eds) Exh. cat. *Homer. Der Mythos von Troia in Dichtung und Kunst* 221–231, Hirmer, Munich.
Hemelrijk, J. M. (1984) *Caeretan Hydriae. Kerameus* 5, Zabern, Mainz.
Kossatz-Deissmann, A. (1994) "Paridis iudicium," *LIMC* VII, 176–188.
Krauskopf, I. (1974) *Der thebanische Sagenkreis und andere griechische Sagen in der etruskischen Kunst*, Zabern, Mainz.
——(1984) "Apollon/ Aplu," *LIMC* II, 335–363.
——(1994) "Septem," *LIMC* VII, 730–748.
——(1995) *Heroen, Götter und Dämonen auf etruskischen Skarabäen. Peleus, Beiheft 1 zu Thetis*, Mannheim.
——(2011) "Seefahrergeschichten…Zur Faszination des griechischen Mythos in der etruskischen Kultur," in D. F. Maras (ed.) *Corollari. Scritti…in omaggio all' opera di Giovanni Colonna* 133–137, Pisa/Rome.
Kunze, M. (ed.) (2009) *Die Etrusker. Die Entdeckung ihrer Kunst seit Winckelmann* Cat. exh. Winckelmann Mus. Stendal. Rutzen, Ruhpolding/Mainz.
Martelli, M. (ed.) (1987) *La Ceramica degli Etruschi*, Novara.
Schwarz, Sh. J. (1990) "Herakles/Hercle," *LIMC* V, 196–253.
Simon, E. (1996) *Schriften zur etruskischen und italischen Kunst und Religion*, Steiner, Stuttgart.
——(2000) "Teatro attico e arte etrusca del V e IV secolo A.C" in *Scienze dell'Antichità* 10, 511–521. Rome.
——(2001) "Rom und Troia." In M. Korfmann and others (ed.) Exh. cat. *Troia. Traum und Wirklichkeit* 154–173. Stuttgart. (2007) "Thesan-Aurora" in *Studi Etruschi* 71, 2005 (Rome 2007) 47–54.
——(2009) *Ausgewählte Schriften* III, Rutzen, Ruhpolding/Mainz.
——(2012) *Ausgewählte Schriften* IV, Rutzen, Ruhpolding/Mainz.
Spier, J. (2000) "From East Greece to Etruria: a Late Sixth-Century BC Gem Workshop" in G. R. Tsetskhladze and others (ed.) *Periplous. Papers…presented to Sir John Boardman,* 330–335, Thames & Hudson, London.
Steingräber, St. (2006) *Etruskische Wandmalerei*, Schirmer/Mosel, Munich.

CHAPTER TWENTY FIVE

GODS AND DEMONS IN THE ETRUSCAN PANTHEON

. ♦ .   —

Ingrid Krauskopf[*]

SOURCES

We owe what we know about Etruscan gods and demons to three groups of sources:

Representations in art: These are by far the largest group, but they give a somewhat one-sided impression. The gods are often shown in Greek mythological scenes; they are identifiable through the mythological context, attributes, and/or inscriptions, which can, above all, be found on engraved bronze mirrors from the fifth century BC on. In such cases, those gods who have a Greek counterpart are preferentially depicted, but there are also exceptions. At the Birth of Athena, for example, not only are Tinia/Zeus, Menrva/Athena, and Sethlanś/Hephaistos named by inscriptions, but so too are two female figures who correspond to Greek depictions of Eileithyai. However, in contrast to the Eileithyia they have names that have also been handed down in other contexts: Thalna, Thanr, and Ethauśva[1] (Fig. 25.1). Inscriptions are numerous also on mirrors that show no mythological scenes, but that do show groups of gods and demons, especially from Turan's/Aphrodite's entourage; here the inscriptions characterize a number of purely Etruscan demons and gods at least approximately: they fit the circle of Turan/Aphrodite[2] (Fig. 25.2).

Roman and Greek literature: Etruscan gods are named in Roman and Greek literature primarily in connection with divination techniques, in which the Etruscans specialized, and which also interested the Romans. And so we learn that, besides Jupiter (Tinia), eight other gods could hurl thunderbolts: those named are Juno (Uni), Minerva (Menrva), Volcanus (Sethlanś), Mars (Laran), Saturnus (Satre?), probably also Hercules (Hercle), and Summanus. Jupiter can throw three different types of thunderbolts; in the case of the two more dangerous types of thunderbolt, councils of gods have to give their consent, the *dii consentes* or *complices*, respectively, the *dii superiores et involuti*.[3] In connection with lightning-interpretation, the division of the sky into 16 regions is mentioned, a reminiscence of which is preserved in the Late Antique pantheon constructed by the author Martianus Capella (see below and, above all, Chapter 26). Arnobius (*Adv. nat.* 3, 40, following

* The author would like to thank Robert Avila for his help with the English translation of this text.

Figure 25.1 Mirror Bologna, Museo Civico Archeologico It. 1073: Birth of Athena.
After Gerhard, *ES* pl. 66.

Figure 25.2 Mirror St. Petersburg B (or V) 505. Turan and Atunis, with trabants in the outer circle.
After Gerhard, *ES* pl. 322.

Nigidius Figulus) hands down a subdivision of the sky in which the Penates of Jupiter (N–E), Neptune (E–S?), the Underworld (*inferorum*, W–N) and the mortals (*mortalium omnium*, S–W?), are assigned to the four sections.[4] In another schema (Pliny *NH* 2.143–144), the regions of the sky are ordered according to their effects: in the north-western quarter there are the *regiones maxime dirae*, in the north-east, the *regiones summae felicitatis*, in the south-east, the *minus prosperae*, and in the south-west, the *minus dirae* (Fig. 25.3).

Occasionally, the chief divinities of sanctuaries which were of interest to the Greeks or Romans are named: Leukothea (or Eileithyia) or Mater Matuta, as well as Apollo in Pyrgi (see below); in Veii Juno, who (as a statue), after the Roman conquest of Veii, had been brought to Rome in the rite of *evocatio*, and was dedicated a temple on the Aventine as

Juno Regina (Livy 5. 21.1; 23.7; 31.3); as well as Voltumna, in whose sanctuary (*fanum*) near Volsinii the Etruscan "League" convened (Livy 4.23.5; 25.7; 61.2; 5.17.6; 6.2.2, cf. also 5.1), and who is elsewhere known as the *deus Etruriae princeps* (Varro, *L.L.* 5.46).[5]

Etruscan literary sources:[6] These are undoubtedly the most authentic source, but are very limited in number. The few longer Etruscan texts, such as the mummy-wrappings from Zagreb, hand down several gods' names. However, these are not very helpful as far as the characterization of the gods named is concerned. The most important source are the inscriptions on the model of a sheep's liver found in 1877 near Piacenza, and which has 16 compartments along its edges with – in some cases, abbreviated – gods' names, and there are others inside (see Chapter 26).[7] The compartments along its edges show some striking parallels to Martianus Capella's pantheon, so that a combination of the Roman sources with the liver provides substantial information for a number of gods. But many of the divinities known from pictorial art can't be found there, for example, Aplu, Menrva, Sethlans, and Turan. In other words, some of the gods who, according to Roman tradition, could also hurl thunderbolts. Surprisingly, Hercle (Herakles) is represented on the liver. Tinia has three compartments on the outer edge, and two more in an inner field between the edge and the gall bladder, and is, in this manner, associated with another deity: Cilens thvf(ltha), thne, neth(uns); other gods are also named in another god's compartment, which points out a peculiarity of Etruscan religion (see below). In the past decades, inscriptions on votive offerings have increasingly been consulted – those already known to us, as well as numerous new finds – which have strongly promoted understanding of the Etruscan pantheon.[8]

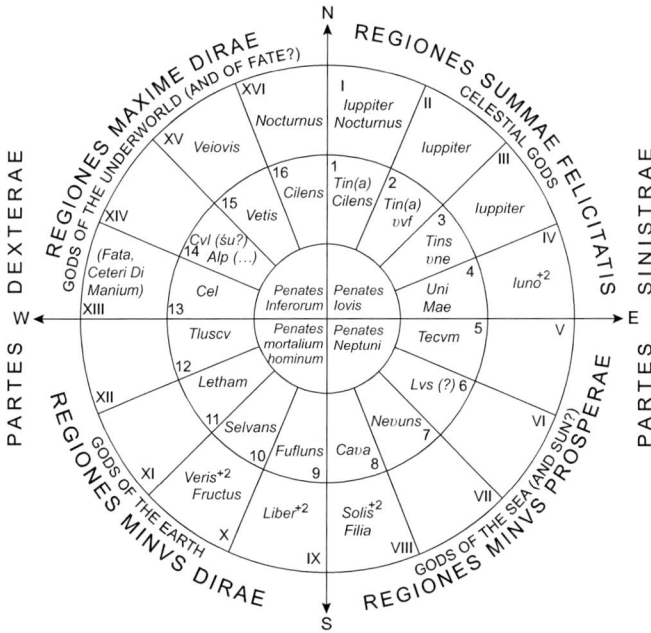

Figure 25.3 Schema of the regions of the sky, following Nigidius Figulus (inside), the liver of Piacenza (middle), Martianus Capella (outer circle) and Pliny and others (margin). The fields marked with +2 in the circle of Martianus Capella are shifted by two fields compared with the liver of Piacenza. After A. Maggiani in M. Cristofani (ed.) *Gli Etruschi. Una nuova immagine* (1984) Fig. on p. 139.

A LOOK AT THE HISTORY OF RESEARCH: CULT DEITIES VS. MYTHOLOGICAL FIGURES AND THE LOOSENING OF THE RIGID SCHEMA

While the amalgamation of Etruscan and Greek conceptions in the Etruscan realm of the gods had long been accepted, the discrepancy between the gods depicted in art and those on the liver from Piacenza eventually resulted in some scholars wanting to separate the Etruscan cult divinities radically from those of Greek mythology. The suggestion that depictions of Greek gods had a religious background in Etruria was disputed and they were compared to the representations of Greek gods and myths in the Renaissance:

> Simply using a subject which belongs to a foreign religion or belief does not necessarily mean that the religion is accepted[9]...In Etruria, one finds Apollo only in mythological scenes. It is not only the case that there is no votive inscription with his name, but the god is not named on the liver from Piacenza, which is an indication that he had no cult in Etruria.[10]

At this point, it should really have been asked how the ancient reports could then be judged, according to which Caere, after the stoning of the prisoners from the battle of Alalia, had sent a delegation to Delphi to ask how this killing could be expiated (Herodotus 1.167); that Caere and Spina had treasuries in Delphi (Strabo 5.214.220); and that there was a sanctuary of Apollo in Pyrgi, Caere's harbor (Ael. var. 1.20).

When these lines were being written, the excavations which were to call this rigid schema into question had already begun. In the harbor sanctuary in Pyrgi, known from Greek literature (see Chapter 30), the northern sanctuary was excavated first. Its chief god, as it turned out, was Uni, who, on bilingual golden tablets, is equated with the Phoenician Astarte. However, in Etruscan art Uni is, without exception, identified with Hera in all of the representations of Greek myths. Conversely, it was obviously impossible for the Greeks to recognize their Hera in the goddess of Pyrgi. Rather they saw in her their Leukothea or Eileithyia – the Romans saw Mater Matuta.[11] In the subsequently excavated southern sanctuary, Śuri and Cavtha were chiefly worshipped; in Śuri, one could – by way of the god of the mountain Soracte (Soranus – Apollo – Dispater) – recognize the Apollo mentioned by Aelian.[12] In the excavations that began just a little later (1969) at Gravisca[13], Tarquinia's harbor, there were at first votives dedicated (in Greek) – presumably by Greek seafarers – to Aphrodite, Hera, and Demeter, as well as to Apollo. When frequentation of the sanctuary by Greeks diminished, the Greek names disappeared: the recipients of the votives were now Turan, Uni, and Vei. Obviously, the Greeks as well as the Etruscans always took pains to recognize their own gods in the foreign ones. Thus, the question of the relationship of the original Etruscan religion to Greek mythology had to be posed anew. In this endeavor, it was primarily important to study the former more precisely. Progress was made through further excavations and through the intensive analysis of the votive inscriptions.[14]

THE PRESENT STATE OF RESEARCH:
THE ANTHROPOMORPHIZATION OF THE
ETRUSCAN PANTHEON UNDER GREEK INFLUENCE

At present, there is a broad consensus that the Etruscan deities were not originally conceived in human form, but rather as forces which manifested themselves through their effects. In modern terminology, the term *numen* was often used, which, however, does not quite correspond to the ancient meaning of the word, and is very controversial;[15] for that reason, the term coined by A. Prosdocimi, *divinità-atto* (divinities defined by their actions), is preferred.[16] A certain parallel to Roman religion could be recognized in this, in which this concept is sometimes unduly exaggerated. For example, Aius Locutius was worshipped there, who had been perceived only once as a voice that spoke in the Grove of Vesta and warned against the approaching Gauls (Liv. 5, 32, 6; 50, 5). The Romans did not question from which god this voice could have come, but immediately named it (Aius Locutius). This principle led to a large number of divinities in Rome, but did not exclude the existence of chief gods with a great plenitude of power. There were such chief gods in Etruria as well, and, in fact, there was also a multitude of gods' names; but on this basis it is not possible to know with certainty to what extent the Roman system can be taken as a model for Etruscan religion.

It is quite probable that the gods had originally not been envisioned in human form. Some observations speak in favor of this assumption, as, for example, the lack of clarity regarding their sex. Some figures are represented mostly as female, but in individual cases, however, they are also represented as male. This happens once each for Thalna, Alpan/Alpnu, Achviser, Evan, and Artumes.[17] The name-endings are also not sex-specific, the best-known examples being Turan (Aphrodite/Venus) and Laran (Ares/Mars). But it is not only the endings in -a(n) but also those in -i (Vei/ Demeter, Śuri/Apollo), -u (Culsu/a female death-demon, Ap(u)lu/Apollo), -na (Tin(i)a/Zeus, Thalna), and -ns (Culsans/Janus, Sethlans/Hephaistos, Cilens/a goddess without a direct Graeco-Roman equivalent) that make the sex of the spiritual being named impossible to recognize. It is also quite probable that it was Greek, and, to a lesser extent, also Oriental influences that led to the Etruscans beginning to think of the gods in human form.[18] Whenever a comparable Greek deity could be found for an Etruscan one, the latter is shown in the former's appearance; and not only the appearance was adopted, but so too were the myths associated with the god. The Greek *divinità-mito* were therefore amalgamated with the Etruscan *divinità-atto*. Gods for whom a Greek counterpart couldn't so easily be found probably remained in essence without any myth.[19] Whenever only pictorial representations were lacking, the Etruscans themselves became active designers, for example, drawing upon oriental models. For instance, this happened in the depictions of the sun-god,[20] and even when the Greek depictions of Helios with his four-horse chariot predominated, a mirror (Fig. 25.4) shows, in its completely unique pictorial creation, even more influences: we see the sun-god on his quadriga, driving to the right, and, above that, he is shown a second time, in a boat, together with two companions, moving to the left. A waterspout, out of which a thick stream flows, separates both of these scenes. It is Okeanos, on which Helios in the sun-barque returns to the sunrise during the night. Neither the waterspout nor Helios' companions are elements of Greek iconography. The sun-barque recalls depictions of the Egyptian sun-god's nightly voyage through the Underworld.[21]

In spite of the superimposition of the original Etruscan conceptions of gods by foreign, above all, Greek archetypes and myths, the nature of Etruscan beliefs remained essentially the same. A good example for this is the representation on a mirror[22] (Fig. 25.5), on which Thetis and Eos/Thesan, the immortal mothers of Achilles and Memnon, implore Zeus/Tinia that he allot life and victory to their respective sons. In the Greek myth, Zeus uses a scale[23] for the decision. Tinia, on the other hand, holds two different thunderbolts in his hands. Memnon will die, which means that the thunderbolt directed toward Thesan is the Destroyer – it has the typical Etruscan form with a point, whereas

Figure 25.4 Mirror Florence, Mus. Arch. 73798: the sun-god on his quadriga, and, above, returning in the sun-barque, together with two companions. After Gerhard, *ES* V pl. 159.

Figure 25.5 Mirror Vaticano, Mus. Greg. Etr. 12257; Thetis and Eos/Thesan, the immortal mothers of Achilles and Memnon, implore Zeus/Tinia for the lives of her sons, Achilles and Memnon. Tinia with two types of thunderbolts. After Gerhard, *ES* pl. 396.

the milder one, by Thetis, consists of symmetrical wavy lines. Usually, Tinia is shown with a single thunderbolt, the one with the point, his most dangerous one (Fig. 25.6).[24]

The equation of Etruscan and Greek gods was not always as unproblematical in all cases as in that of Zeus and Tinia. It was obviously especially difficult for Apollo. Due to a lack of name inscriptions, we do not know how this god was named in the Archaic Etruscan illustrations of Greek myths. The Caeretans worshipped Śuri in Pyrgi, the god that Greek historians later equated with Apollo, and they had made this identification presumably as early as the sixth century BC; it is appropriate to Śuri's sinister nature that Apollo, in Archaic Etruscan depictions, mostly appears with the bow as a death-sending, crime-punishing god (Fig. 25.7).[25] In the Portonaccio sanctuary in Veii, where the well-known Apollo from Veii was found, Menrva is, in fact, the chief divinity, but there are also terracotta votive gifts, which depict Aplu. Giovanni Colonna[26] has identified this Aplu with the god Rath, who is named in a votive inscription in the Portonaccio sanctuary, and is named as the owner of the sanctuary (Rathlth: in the sanctuary of Rath) on the mirror on which the liver inspection of Pavatarchies takes place (see Fig. 26.1).[27] Rath would then, above all, be a prophetic god. Finally, Ap(u)lu is added, at first only in inscriptions on mirrors, but then also in a votive inscription.[28] His name is obviously derived from the Latin Apollo, because the final "n" is missing, which is otherwise always retained when Greek names are adopted (Agamemnon-Achmemrun, Iason-(H) eiasun). Possibly, the introduction of the Apollo-cult in Rome, and the dedication of the temple of *Apollo medicus* in the year 431 BC after an epidemic, contributed to making the Roman form of the name known in Etruria.[29] The three Etruscan names of the Greek Apollo cannot be brought into full agreement with the three functions of avenging wrong, prophecy, and warding off plagues and diseases, but it is conceivable that, among the three gods, one of these aspects respectively stood out. On the liver from Piacenza, none of the three is mentioned. The functions named were, therefore, presumably still associated with other gods.

Figure 25.6   Bronze statuette of Tinia, Heidelberg, Antikenmuseum der Universität F. 148.

Figure 25.7 a–b   Pontic amphora Paris, Bibl. Nat. 171: a) Aplu killing Tityos who tried to abduct Aplu's mother, Letun. b) Two demons dragging the unfaithful Koronis and her lover Ischys to Aplu and Artumes. After MonInst. II (1835) pl. 18 (= Hampe/Simon 6–7).

Etruscan divinities and their Greek counterparts do not fully correspond to one another in other cases either. Even in the case of the Dioscuri, which had been borrowed without direct Etruscan parallels from Greek religion under the translated name of *tinas cliniar* ("Sons of Zeus"), new functions were added which, in fact, fit well with their myth, but are not known from Greece for them. In Etruria, they belong to the divinities who protected the dead on their way to the Underworld (see Chapter 28).[30] The Greek Hermes was divided into two gods: Turms,[31] who was associated with Tinia, and Turms Aitas, associated with Aita/Hades, and who corresponds to the Greek Hermes Psychopompos (Fig. 25.8). Even more examples could be given, but that would far exceed the bounds of this article.

A PECULIARITY OF ETRUSCAN RELIGION: CIRCLES AND COUNCILS OF GODS

With Turms Aitas, we have reached an area that could belong to the core of Etruscan religion: the attribution of a god to the circle of another, or the combination of two divinities, as in some of the compartments on the liver from Piacenza (s. above). F. D. Maras[32] has drawn attention to circles of gods which form themselves around a divinity: in an inscription, for example, Turan(?) and Selvans are designated as *thanral* ("belonging to Thanr"); there is a group centered on the underworld-god Calus, to which Tinia and

Figure 25.8   Stamnos, red figure, Vaticano, Mus. Greg. Etr. Z. 38: Turms discusses with his
underworld counterpart Turms Aitas. Photo Mus. IV.34.17.

Pethan belong; and there are apparently such groupings around Fufluns and Thufltha. One naturally recalls, under this aspect, the god-councils mentioned in Latin literature, the *dii consentes* and the *dii superiores et involuti*, as well as the groups in the division of the sky (and those known as Penates) handed down by Arnobius. The cooperation of several *divinità-atto* was obviously necessary, or at least beneficial, if a certain effect was to be brought about. Further, it is characteristically Etruscan that gods and groups of gods have a fixed seat in the sky,[33] and that this division makes certain techniques of divination in earthly matters at all possible, as, for instance, the sheep's liver reflects. While god-groups have a certain parallel in Umbrian religion,[34] the *deorum sedes* are apparently specifically Etruscan.

DEMONS AND THE ETRUSCAN PANTHEON

The numerous demon-figures are also an Etruscan peculiarity, for which Greek parallels can scarcely be found. In this regard, the Etruscans were, so to speak, compelled to become inventive image-designers, and they did it with great success. Depictions of death-demons,[35] above all, are numerous, which is probably due to the fact that in Etruria the cemeteries were better preserved, and for a long time they were more intensively excavated than cities and sanctuaries. There were probably demons in all of the manifestations of Etruscan religion.

What are demons, and how can they be distinguished from gods? The modern use of the term with regard to ancient demons corresponds roughly to the use that Plato gives in the *Symposion*; there, the priestess Diotima characterizes Eros. Walter Burkert has given a summary:[36]

> Eros would be a being that is neither god nor mortal, but mid-way, a *daimon*; because of such kind are the *daimones*: they stand in the middle between gods and men, they are interpreters and ferrymen, who transmit the messages and gifts of men to the gods, and from gods to men, prayers and sacrifices from the one group, orders and rewards from the other side.[37]

Accordingly, demons stand in closer contact with humans than gods, but they can always only be recognized by the fact that they affect something. They are inconceivable as pure existence without any relationship to human beings. The question is, how this can be reconciled with the hypothesis of the Etruscan *divinità-atto*, who could be perceived only through the effects of their actions. A thesis imposes itself which is not in the least provable, and has probably been developed out of the question posed: it could be that there were originally many beings that were each responsible for a certain process, approximately corresponding to the Roman "special gods" (*Sondergötter, indigitamenta*),[38] and whose necessary cooperation one later ascribed to direction by higher gods.

If we take a closer look at the few sources on Etruscan demons with this thesis in mind, then the result is as follows:

1) Demons are presumably those spirits which appear in plural, or at least, in close relationship to many other beings of similar, or of the same sort. The best examples for this concept are the male and female death-demons[39] which, in general, are summarized under the names of Charun and Vanth. While, however, Vanth is named in inscriptions only in the singular, several Charun-depictions are found together with various epithets (Fig. 25.9). In addition, there is also a demon, Tuchulcha, which is obviously different in appearance from Charun. For the female death-demons of the Late Classical and Hellenistic epochs, which closely resemble each other, besides Vanth, there is another name attested that brings its bearer unambiguously in connection with a passage or a gateway: Culsu (Fig. 25.10). She therefore exercised the function of a gate-keeper or door-opener. One should then consider dividing the large throng of death-demons into a multitude of spirits, each respectively responsible for a single aspect, but this theory finds no support, either in iconography, or in the – not all too common – name inscriptions. And the god that they all do the groundwork for is, in the hellenized version, Aita/Hades,

Figure 25.9   Tarquinia, Tomba dei Caronti: *Charun chunchulis* and *Charun huths*.
After DAI Rom neg. 81.4359.

not simply the supreme organizer, but rather the ruler over the kingdom of the dead, something fundamentally different. Here, the hypothesis cited above obviously does not quite work out.

2) Turan is just as little a summarization of all of the figures that are assembled on mirrors in her realm. Some of them have names that originally seem to have been plural forms: Achvizr and Ethausva.[40] They were, therefore, originally a group. It is possible, as Mauro Cristofani has assumed,[41] that some of the figures of her circle correspond to the personifications that are found on Attic vases since the later fifth century BC. Because they too stand for certain characteristics or effects they could fit unproblematically into the circle of the original Etruscan demons.

3) Maris,[42] who is always portrayed as youthful, and even twice in plural as a small child, has various epithets, some of which are derived from other gods' names (Turan, Hercle). He also appears alone, and is represented three times on the liver from Piacenza, in two of them without any epithet. The conception of demons defined above does not seem to be quite appropriate for him, but he can nonetheless appear in plural.

4) When we consider the area of the divinities of the weather and of the heavenly bodies,[43] we find plural beings, winged female figures who pour water out of a vessel, perhaps personifications of clouds (Fig. 25.11). And in the series of antefixes from the

Figure 25.10   Sarcophagus of Hasti Afunei, Palermo, Mus. Arch. Reg. Coll. Casuccini: Culsu and other female demons. After Herbig, Steinsarkophage pl. 57a (photograph in the possession of the Arch. Inst. Heidelberg).

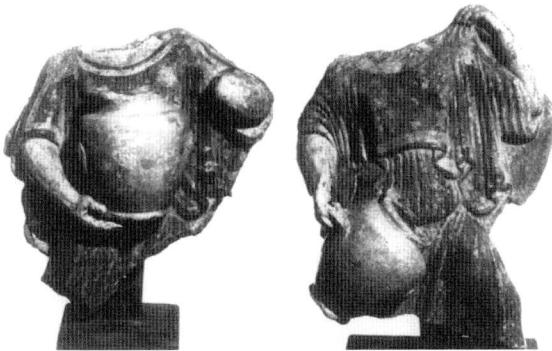

Figure 25.11   Terracotta antefixes, Rome, Villa Giulia. From Veio, Macchia Grande: Female demons with water jars, representing clouds (?). Photo Mus. 26919 and 35499.

building with the many rooms in Pyrgi (see Chapter 30), we find a being with the head of a rooster, which, as the harbinger of the day, hurries ahead of the sun-god. One would like to designate such apparitions as demons, although they do not come into contact with human beings.

All of these difficulties may probably be explained by three circumstances: 1) In Etruria, there was no fundamental difference, between gods and demons – it was a gradual difference. Both of them had the same origin. 2) The Etruscan pantheon was not a closed, dogmatic system, but – to express it casually for once – it was an open society, into which foreigners were integrated and in which the old-established could change their appearance, partly according to foreign models, or even extend their competence under foreign influence, or remain what they had always been. Some of them had probably had different names in different places of worship. Some of them became dominant (gods), others were more concerned with the concrete execution of divine plans (demons); this second group must have been more numerous than the first one. 3) We are acquainted with this society only in its latest phases, which permits only some few conclusions on its original state. Typically, Etruscan gods had a pronounced inclination to cooperation and to group formation, as well as fixed "domiciles" in the sky.

SUPPLEMENT: ON THE THERIOMORPHISM OF ETRUSCAN GODS AND DEMONS: THE ART OF SHAPING THE DEMONIC

In Etruscan art, theriomorphic components are seldom combined with the human form in the case of the "great" gods, but this occurs more frequently among demons. This led to the assumption that gods – in a primitive stage of religion, and precisely also in Etruria – were first imagined in the form of animals, and later – perhaps under Greek influence – in human form.[44] Even if this "prehistoric theriomorphism"[45] is scarcely discussed in the meantime, it is nevertheless not to be overlooked that, at least in the case of death-demons and underworld-gods, something of the sort can be perceived: demons by which human traits are combined with wolf- or vulture-traits occur from the sixth century BC into the Hellenistic period. During the Orientalizing period, hybrids of lions and wolves stand for the realm of death.[46] At that time, the Etruscans had probably begun to furnish the lion, the dangerous predator unfamiliar to them, and which they had borrowed from Greek and oriental art, with the features of the most-feared animal of the native fauna. The fact that wolves and vultures, likewise native animals, could be emissaries of a nearing death must have been common knowledge then. Wolf-demons are depicted in the subsequent centuries in the most varied combinations of human and animal characteristics (Fig. 25.12), until the basic concept found its perfect expression in the representation of Aita in the Tomba dell'Orco II in Tarquinia (Fig. 25.13) and in the Tomba Golini I near Orvieto. The wolf's head appears above the god's human head. The formal model was probably Herakles with the lion's skin, but this isn't the skin of a dead animal, but a living wolf with a huge, staring eye. Behind Aita's human body, the wolf's body is visible. One could hardly better illustrate the conception that the God of Death can appear in more than one form. But he is neither a human being nor a wolf, he is the God of Death.

Figure 25.12 Plate, Pontic. Rome, Villa Giulia 84444: wolf demon.
Photo Mus. detail, tondo: wolf demon.

Figure 25.13 Tarquinia; Tomba dell'Orco II, head of Aita. After DAI Rom neg. 82.635.

Aita is an exception inasmuch as animal parts are more frequently seen on "lesser" gods and on demons. But in their realm, the hybrid form became accepted: there are youths above whom a swan appears[47] (Fig. 25.14); they probably personify the stimulating, refreshing coolness, which radiates from bodies of water during the summer heat. Gods or demons of the sea wear a cap in the form of a Ketos-head (reptilian sea-monster, Fig. 25.15), or of an entire dolphin; on some coins,[48] the animal reproduced (boar?) cannot be exactly identified.

On the basis of all of these depictions, however, one should not conclude that the Etruscans thought of the gods in an earlier phase as animals and then later as human beings. It is much rather a question of two possibilities for giving an abstract concept,

Figure 25.14   Bronze statuette, Florence, Mus. Arch. 547, so-called Jason.

Figure 25.15   Bronze coin, (incuse) = *LIMC* VII Poseidon/Nethuns 17. After plaster cast.

for example, death, a concrete form. In one case, this could have been the animal form, in another, the human form, or both forms could have been developed in parallel. The Etruscans' image-shaping imagination, which otherwise receded behind the overwhelming influence of Greek art, also expressed itself in details. Many death-demons have huge, staring eyes, as in a vulture-demon on a red figure vase (Fig. 25.16);[49] in the Tomba della Quadriga infernale,[50] this eye is emphasized by being shown *en face*, while all of the eyes of humans there are shown, as is usual in the stylistic convention of the time, in profile. Every animal, and human beings as well, finds it an unpleasant experience when someone stares at them; one involuntarily has the feeling that it cannot mean anything good. It must have been much more eerie when two eyes suddenly become visible in the dark (Fig. 25.17); they constituted a very real, lethal menace.

Figure 25.16 Red-figure oinochoe, vulture demon. Vatican Mus. Greg. Etr. 18200. (See *LIMC Supplementum* 2009 Daemones anonymi 5). Photo Mus.

Figure 25.17 Wolf at night, "photo trap" near Daubnitz in the Lausitz. By permission of Wildbiologisches Büro LUPUS. Dorfstrasse 16 02979 Spreewitz (Sachsen).

NOTES

This table shows a selection of the gods about whom we know more than just their names.

* Denotes numbers after Maggiani 1982 and de Grummond/Simon 2006, Fig. II.2; ( ) = second in the field of another god, e.g. tin/cilen; field 41 and 42 are on the other, convex side of the liver denoting day and night. Divinities mentioned only in one field and otherwise unknown. For reasons of space it was not possible to include the names mentioned in the mummy-wrapping of Zagreb (e.g. Letham, Nethuns, Thesan, Tinia, Uni) and the tile from Capua (Tabula Capuana), where Letham(s) seems to dominate. For both texts, see Chapters 22–28.

****bold** = a probable main deity of a sanctuary.

Etruscan (and similar Etr. deities)	Equivalent Greek	Equivalent Roman	Equiva-lent Other Rel.	Possible attributes (and some remarks)	Field in the Liver from Piacenza*	Evidence for cult places**: I = inscriptions (after Maras 2009), S = votive statues or statuettes (more than five expl.)
Aita, Eita (Calu)	Hades	Pluto, Dispater		Wolf's cap, sceptre		
Ap(u)lu (Śuri, Rath)	Apollon	Apollo		Bow, lyre or kithara, laurel branch		Arezzo, presso Santa Croce (I, sors); Cerveteri, Vignaccia (S); Narce, Monte Li Santi (?, I: apalus); Veii, Campetti (S); Veii, Portonaccio (S), for I s. Rath. Campania: Pontecagnano, north sanctuary
Artumes, Aritimi	Artemis	Diana		Bow, as huntress short chiton and boots		Cerveteri, Vignaccia (S); Gravisca (I); Roselle (I); Tarquinia, Ara della Regina (I, sors); Veii, Portonaccio (I)
Calu (god of the Underworld, s. also Aita)					8.23	Roncoferraro (Mantova) (I); Cortona (I). Calusnal or Kalusnal (=Circle of C.): Orvieto, Belvedere (I: tinia calusna), Vulci, town (I) Corciano (Pethns calusnal)
Catha (sun god or =cavtha?, s. Maras 2009, 303)						

Etruscan name	Greek	Roman	Other	Attributes/description	No.	Findspots
Cav(a)tha, Kav(u)tha Sech [= daughter, Kore]	Persephone, Kore (Colonna 1991/92), Artemis, Hekate (Maggiani 1997)					Pyrgi, South Sanctuary (I), Populonia, San Cerbone (I), Orvieto (I), San Feliciano (east of Lago Trasimeno) (I)
Cel	Ge, Gaia	Tellus, Terra Mater			13	Castiglione del Lago (West of Lago Trasimeno (I); Volterra, Casabianca (I?). Campania: Nola (I)
Cilen(s)		Nocturnus (?)		Female in a terracotta relief from Bolsena (see note 19)	16. 36. (1)	
Culsans		Ianus		Head with two faces	14? (= cvlalp)	Cortona, Piazza del Mercato presso Porta Ghibellina (I, S), cvl: Bagnoregio (Orvieto) (I Culsans or Culsu?)
Esplace	Asklepios	Aesculapius				
Fufluns, Fufluns Pachies, Pacha	Dionysos	Bacchus, Liber		Thyrsos, ivy, kantharos	9.24	Pyrgi, south sanctuary (I: circle of E); Todi (I); Vulci, Pian dell' Abbadia (I).
Her(e)c(e)le	Herakles	Hercules	Phoen.-Punic Melqart	Lion's skin, bow, club	29	Caere? (I); Caere, San Antonio (I); Pyrgi, south sanctuary (I); Veii; Portonaccio (S);
Laran	Ares	Mars		Cuirass, helmet, lance, shield		Bettona (Perugia) (I); Cerveteri, Vignaccia (S?); Orvieto, Belvedere (I: circle of?) Veii, Campetti (S); Vulci (I?)
Lasa				Wings, often represented in the circle of Turan	19	
Letham(s), Lethan					11.18.32.37. 27? (= leta)	
Lurs, Lurmi				With sword together with Tinia on a mirror		Bolsena, Il Poggetto (I , Corchiano, necropoli di San Antonio tomb 20 (I); Gravisca (I); Perugia (I); Vulci, Poggio Olivastro (I)

Table continued overleaf

Table continued

Etruscan (and similar Etr. deities)	Equivalent Greek	Equivalent Roman	Equivalent Other Rel.	Possible attributes (and some remarks)	Field in the Liver from Piacenza*	Evidence for cult places**: I = inscriptions (after Maras 2009). S = votive statues or statuettes (more than five expl.)
Lvsa					6.34	
Maris		Genius (de Grummond)		Young male (Baby or youth, frequently plural with different bynames)	26.30.39	Chiusi (I)
Men(e)rva	Athena	Minerva		Helmet, aegis, lance, shield		**Veii, Portonaccio** (I. S); **S. Marinella, Punta della Vipera (I,** S; Cerveteri, Vignaccia (S); Perugia, Palazzone, tomba degli Acsi (I); Pyrgi, south sanctuary (I); Tarquinia, Monterozzi (I)
Nethuns	Poseidon	Neptunus		Trident	7.28. (22)	Caere, Banditaccia(?) (I); Pyrgi, north sanctuary (I.?: net[...])
Phersipnai, Phersipnei	Persephone	Proserpina		Snakes in the hair		
Rath (Aplu)	Apollon?	Apollo?		Laurel branch		Bolsena, Fosso di Arlena (I); Caere, San Antonio (I);Chiusi (I); Pyrgi, south sanctuary (?, I); San Polo d'Enza (I); Veii, Portonaccio (I);
Satre		Saturnus?			35	
Selvans		Silvanus			10.31	Bolsena, Pozzarello (I); Cortona, Piazza del Mercato presso Porta Ghibellina (I on S); probably Sarteano (I); Tarquinia, town (I) see also Maras 2009, 391sg. (Umbria)
Sethlanś	Hephaistos	Vulcanus		Hammer, tongs		

Etruscan name	Greek	Latin / other	Attributes	No.	Attestations
Šuri (Aplu)	Apollon	Soranus (Apollo, Dispater, Pater Pyrgensi?)			**Pyrgi, South Sanctuary** (I); Arezzo, presso Santa Croce (I, sors); Bettona (Perugia) necropoli (I); Orvieto, Belvedere (I); Tarquinia, town (I); Viterbo, Cipollara (I, sors); Vulci, Pian di Maggio(?) (I); Vulci, town (I)
Tecum, Tec sans			Together with Cel and Cavtha (*kanthas*) part of a *templum* formed by the lake (s. above note 14)	5	Tuoro (north of Lago Trasimeno) (I)
Thanr					Perugia (?; I), probably Sarteano (I: circle of Thanr), cf. also Maras 2009, 313 (*originis incertae*); Spina, Valle Mezzana (town) (I)
Thesan	Eos	Aurora	Quadriga, wings		Pyrgi, north sanctuary I); Spina, Valle Pega, tomb 102C (I)
Thupltha, Thuftha				21 (2. 20)	Chiusi region (I); Montalcino, loc. Castello di S. Angelo in Colle (I); Montecchio (Cortona) (I); Mucigliano (Siena) (I): Tarquinia, town, edificio d (I); Vulci, Pian di Maggio (?) (I, circle of Th.?)
Tin(i)a	Zeus	Iupiter	Lightning bolt	1.2.3. 20.22	**Bolsena, Il Pogetto (I : Marzabotto, temple in regio I** (I); Adria, town (I); Bolsena, town (I); Feltre (Belluno) (I); Pyrgi, north sanctuary (I?); Roselle, town; Tarquinia (I); Tinia calusna: Orvieto, Belvedere (I). For *tinscvil* see Maras 2009, 91 s.
Tinas cliniar	Dioskouroi	Castores	With Horses, stars, amphorae, dokana		Tarquinia, Monterozzi, in a tomb (I)

Table continued overleaf

Table continued

Etruscan (and similar Etr. deities)	Equivalent Greek	Equivalent Roman	Equivalent Other Rel.	Possible attributes (and some remarks)	Field in the Liver from Piacenza*	Evidence for cult places**: I = inscriptions (after Maras 2009), S = votive statues or statuettes (more than five expl.)
Tiv, Tiur	Selene	Luna		Crescent of the moon	41	Chianciano, loc. Acquasanta(?) (I); Veii, Campetti (I)
Tluscv					12.33.40	
Turan	Aphrodite	Venus				**Gravisca** (I); Probably Sarteano (I); Veii, Portonaccio (I); Narce, Monte in Mezzo ai Prati, tomb 5 (I, circle of T.)
Turms	Hermes, as Turms Aitas = Hermes Psychopompos	Mercurius		Kerykeion, hat with wings		Caere, San Antonio (I)
Uni	Hera, Uni of Pyrgi in Greek interpretation: Leukothea, Eileithyia	Iuno, Uni of Pyrgi in Roman interpretation: Mater Matuta	Phoenic. Astarte	Iuno Sospita type: goat's skin	4	**Pyrgi, north sanctuary** (I); Cortona (I); Gravisca (I); Vulci, Fontanile di Legnisina (I)
Usil (Catha?)	Helios	Sol		Quadriga, sun disk	42	
Vanth				As a female death demon: wings, boots, torch, snakes, scroll		Marsiliana d'Albegna, loc. Perazzeta, in a tomb (I); Spina, Valle Pega tomb 707C

Etruscan name	Greek	Latin	Notes	No.	Attestations
Vatimi			Proposed as god of Vetulonia (Vatl.) by Banti (*StEtr* 5, 1931, 185–201), in that case with a dolphin or ketos on the head: coins *LIMC* VII Po-Poseidon/Nethuns 16-19, but inscriptions from inner Etr.		Corchiano, necropoli ci San Antonio tomb 20 (I) cf. two other I of uncertain origin (Maras 2009, 304-305.315)
Vei	Demeter	Ceres			Caere, Vigna Parocchiale (I); **Gravisca** (LS); Orvieto, Canicella (I); Pian delle Vigne presso Norchia (I); Pyrgi, north sanctuary (I); Regae, loc. Le Murelle (I); Roselle, town (I); San Polo d'Enza (I); Vulci, Fontanile di Lenigsina (I)
Veltune, Voltumna, Vortumnus (Latin) (=Tinia?)		Vertumnus (?)	*Deus princeps Etruriae, Fanum Voltumnae,* see above (note 5)	15	
Vetis, Veive		Veiovis?			Pyrgi, south sanctuary (I)

BIBLIOGRAPHIC NOTES

Lists and short characterizations of the most important divinities in: Jannot 1998, 153 –174; de Grummond 2006, 53–172; Simon 2006, 152–167; see also Bentz 1992; Maras 2009, 101–153; for the gods of the Piacenza liver, van der Meer 1987, 30–140.

In the *Lexicon Iconographicum Mythologiae Classicae* I–VIII (1984–1997, Zurich Munich Duesseldorf: Artemis Verlag), there are articles on gods and demons who are identifiable in pictorial art (in individual cases, when false interpretations have to be refuted, figures without an own iconography are also included). In the case of figures which are attested only once in inscriptions, it is sometimes uncertain whether this is a case of demons or heroes of an unknown myth. In this case, the name is italicized.

I 214–216 Achvizr; 573–576 Alpan; 665 Aminth. II 169–176 (Aphrodite)/Turan; 335–363 (Apollon)/Aplu; 498–505 (Ares)/Laran; 774–792 (Artemis)/Artumes; 1050–1074 (Athena)/Menerva. III 1–2 Athrpa; 184 Catha; 185 Celsclan (Sohn der Cel, Erde = Giant); 225–236 (Charon I)/Charun; 294–295 Cilens; 306–308 Culsans; 308–309 Culsu; 531–540 (Dionysos)/Fufluns; 597–608 (Dioskouroi)/Tinas Cliniar; 789–797 (Eos)/Thesan; 810–812 Epiur; 1070–1077 (Ariadne)/Ariatha. IV 1–12 Eros (in Etruria) with Svutaf und Purthisph, on the last, see Snenath; 24–25 Esplace (= Asklepios); 38 Ethausva; 126–128 Evan; 128–129 Evrphia; 330–345 Gorgones (in Etruria); 394–399 (Hades)/Aita, Calu; 654–659 (Hephaistos)/Sethlanś; V 196–253 (Herakles)/Hercle; 1038–1047 (Helios)/Usil. VI 217–225 Lasa; 249–250 Leinth; 256 Letham; 264–267 (Leto)/Letun; 296 Lur; 346–349 Malavisch; 358–360 Maris; 383–385 Mean; 627 Mlacuch; 681–685 Mousa, Mousai (in Etruria); 688–689 Munthuch; 711–712 Nathum; 934–935 Nortia. VII 329–332 Phersipnai (= Persephone); 479–483 (Poseidon)/Nethuns; 506 *Preale;* 622 Reschualc; 623 Rescial; 648 *Rutapis;* 718 Selvans; 795 *Sleparis;* 823–824 Suri; 900–902 Thalna; 908 Thanr. VIII 19 Thupltha; 52 Tretu; 85–90 Tritones (in Etruria); 97–98 Tuchulcha; 98–111 Turms (= Hermes); 114 *Tvami;* 159–171 Uni (= Hera); 173–183 Vanth; 183–184 Vegoia; 185 *Veltune;* 236 Vesuna; 281–282 Voltumna; 400–421 (Zeus)/Tinia; 488–489 Zinthrepus; 489–490 Zipna.

LIMC Supplementum 2009: 19–20 Achvizr; 73–78 (Aphrodite)/Turan; 79–82 (Apollon)/Aplu; 86 (Ariadne)/Ariatha; 143–156 Daemones anonymi (in Etruria); 180–183 (Dionysos)/Fufluns; 205–206 (Eos)/Thesan; 212–213 Eros (in Etruria); 232–233 Gorgo, Gorgones (in Etruria); 244–264 (Herakles)/Hercle; 279–281 (Hermes)/Turms; 457–458 Snenath; 472 Thalna; 473 Thanr; 483–484 *Thuluter;* 484 Thupltha.

NOTES

1. *LIMC* VIII Zeus/Tinia **40. 41*. 43***; *CSE* Italia 1 Bologna, Museo Civico 1 (Roma: "L'ERMA" di Bretschneider, 1987) 32–35 no. 13 fig. 13a.b; de Grummond 2006, 64s. fig. IV.12.13; 81 fig. V.10.

2. Ill.: St. Petersburg, Hermitage B 505: LIMC I Achvizr **5*** = VI Lasa **15** = VIII Zipna **3**; de Grummond 2006: 98 Fig. V.28; de Grummond/Simon 2006 52 fig. IV.7. Besides those named, there also appear together with Turan: Alpan, Aminth, Evan, Lasa, Malavisch, Mean, Munthuch, Reschualc, Snenath, Thalna and Thanr, mainly the two latter and Lasa are not at all confined to that circle. For the satellites of Turan see M. Cristofani, "Faone, la testa di Orfeo e l'immaginario femminile," *Prospettiva* 42 (1985) 2–12 = *idem, Scripta Selecta* (Pisa-Roma, Istituti Editoriali e Poligrafici Internazionali, 2001) II, 587–597.

3. The sources are listed by Pfiffig 130f. and de Grummond/Simon 2006, 213–217. Who the eighth thunderbolt-casting god was, hasn't been handed down. The most important source for thunderbolt-hurling: Pliny *NH* 2.138–144.

4   S. de Grummond/Simon 2006, 217 Source IX.3. For the problem of the *deorum sedes* see, most recently, A. Maggiani, *"Deorum sedes.* Divinazione etrusca o dottrina augurale romana?" *AnnFaina* 16 (2009) 221–237.

5   On Voltumna: Cristofani. M., "Voltumna: Vertumnus," *AnnFaina* 2 (1985) 75–88; Capdeville, G., "Voltumna ed altri culti del territorio volsiniese," *AnnFaina* 6 (1999) 109–135.

6   See Chapter 22 and Bonfante. L., "Etruscan Inscriptions and Etruscan Religion" in de Grummond/Simon 2006, 9–26.

7   van der Meer 1987; Colonna, G., "A proposito degli dei del Fegato di Piacenza," *StEtr* 59 (1993) 123–136. L. Bonfante in de Grummond/Simon 2006, 10–11. Details in Chapter 26. The study by Maggiani (1982) took a decisive step forward.

8   Bentz 1992, 185–218; Maras 2009, 101–158.

9   Banti, L. (1973) *Etruscan Cities and Their Culture*, London, B. T. Boteford, 186 (*eadem, Il mondo degli Etruschi* (1969) Roma: Biblioteca di Storia Patria, 246.

10 Translated from Banti, L., (1960) *Die Welt der Etrusker* (Stuttgart: Cotta'sche Buchhandlung Nachfolger) 116.

11 Literary source, attempts at an explanation, and more: *Die Göttin von Pyrgi. Akten des Kolloquiums Tübingen 16.–17.1.1979* (Biblioteca di Studi Etruschi 12, Firenze 1981: Olschki)

12 G. Colonna, "Novità sui culti di Pyrgi," *Rendiconti della Pontificia Accademia Romana di Archeologia* ser. 3, 57 (1984–1985) 57–88.

13 Fiorini, L./Torelli, M., "Quarant'anni di ricerche a Gravisca" in *Material Aspects of Etruscan Religion. Proceedings of the International Colloquium Leiden, May 29–30, 2008* (ed. L. Bouke van der Meer). *BaBesch* Suppl. 16 (2010) Louven – Paris – Walpole: Peeters, 29–49, see also Chapter 29.

14 Some examples: Colonna, G., "La dea etrusca Cel e i santuari del Trasimeno," *Scritti in memoria di Gianfranco Tibiletti* (=*Rivista Storica dell'Antichità* 6–7, 1976/77) 45–62; Rendeli, M., "Selvans tularia," *StEtr* 59 (1993) 163–166; Maras, D. F., "La dea Thanr e le cerchie divine in Etruria: nuove acquisizioni,"*StEtr* 64, 1998 (2001) 173–197; Maras, D. F. (2000) "Le iscrizioni sacre etrusche sul vasellame in età tardo-arcaica e recente," *Scienze dell'Antichità* 10 (2000) 121–137; a summary now by Maras 2009.

15 See on this point concisely Scheid, J. (2003) *An Introduction to Roman Religion*, Edinburgh: Edinburgh University Press, 153.

16 Prosdocimi, A. L., "Le religioni degli Italici" in: *Italia omnium terrarum parens* (ed. G. Pugliese Carratelli, 1989, Milano: Libri Scheiwiler) esp. 484–448. The opposite are the *divinità-mito*.

17 On this aspect and on the following: M. Cristofani, "Sul processo di antropomorfizzazione nel pantheon etrusco" in: *Miscellanea etrusco-italica 1* (= *QuadAEI* 22) (1993) 9–21; idem., "Masculin/Féminin dans la théonymie étrusque" in: *Les Étrusques, les plus religieux des hommes. État de la recherche sur la religion étrusque. Actes du colloque international Grand Palais 17.–19.11.1992* (eds F. Gaultier and D. Briquel, Paris: La Documentation Francaise, 1997) 209–219; in summary: Krauskopf, I., "Männlich / weiblich in der etruskischen Welt" in *ThesCRA* VIII.5.a (p. 263f) 2012. Los Angeles: The J. Paul Getty Museum. Polarités de la vie religieuse a. Abschnitt 3 [in print, appears at the end of 2011].

18 Some deliberations on this point: Krauskopf, I., "Seefahrergeschichten – Göttergeschichten oder der Hunger nach Bildern. Zur Faszination des griechischen Mythos in der etruskischen Kultur" in *Corollari. Scritti di antichità etrusche e italiche in omaggio all'opera di Giovanni Colonna* (a cura di D. F. Maras, Pisa-Roma: Fabrizio Serra editore, 2011, 133–137).

19 They can, however, at least in the late period, be present in mythological scenes, as for example, Letham at the Birth of Athena (*LIMC* VI Letham 1 = VIII Zeus/Tinia **45**; van der Meer 1987 68 fig. 31) and Cilens, who is depicted as a woman, together with Menrva in an unidentifiable scene (*LIMC* II Athena/Menerva **140*** = III Cilens 1; de Grummond 2006 color pl. II on CD Rom).

20 Krauskopf, I., "EX ORIENTE SOL. Zu den orientalischen Wurzeln der etruskischen Sonnenikonographie," *Archeologia Classica* 43 (1991) = *Miscellanea etrusca e italica in onore di Massimo Pallottino,* 1261–1283; *LIMC* V addenda *s. v.* Helios/ Usil. Another "oriental" demon: Maggiani, A., "Vita effimera di un mostro etrusco," *RdA* 30 (2006) 47–56.

21 Mirror Firenze, Mus. Arch. 73798: *LIMC* VI Helios/Usil **30*** with bibl.; Pfiffig 1975 243f., fig. 106; M. Tirelli, "La rappresentazione del sole nell' arte etrusca," *StEtr* 49 (1981) pl. 16d;. The inscription *"Cathesan"* can be interpreted in various ways, s. *loc. cit.* 1046; *LIMC* III *s. v.* Catha.

22 Vatican, Mus. Greg. Etr. 12257: *LIMC* II Athena/Menerva **168°** = III Eos/Thesan **33** = VIII Zeus/Tinia **65***; de Grummond 2006 54 fig. IV.1; de Grummond/Simon 40 Fig. III.16. We owe the discovery of this *interpretatio etrusca* to J. Heurgon: "De la balance aux foudres (à propos du miroir étrusque, Gerhard, E.S. IV 396)" in *Melanges de litterature et d'épigraphie latines, d'histoire ancienne et d'archéologie. Hommage à la memoire de Pierre Wuilleumier* (1980, Paris: Soc. d'edition les belles lettres) 165–196.

23 *LIMC* III Eos/Thesan 293–298.

24 Bronze statuette Heidelberg, the University's Museum of Antiquities F 148: *LIMC* VIII Zeus/Tinia **105***. De Grummond/Simon 2006, 46 fig. IV.1

25 S. *LIMC* II 338–341. 352–355 s. v.Apollon/Aplu. Here fig. 6 :Pontic amphora, Paris, Bibl. Nat. 171 (*LIMC* Apollon/Aplu 3*. 7*)

26 Colonna 1987, 431–435.

27 *LIMC* VII Pavatarchies 1; Colonna 1987, 436 Abb. 21; de Grummond/Simon 2006, 30 Fig. III.4.30.

28 M. Bentz./D. Steinbauer, "Neues zum Aplu-Kult in Etrurien," AA (2001) 69–77.

29 Livy 3.63.7, see, for example, E. Simon, Die Götter der Römer (Munich: Hirmer, 1990) 28. On M.-L. Haack's thesis ("Apollon médicin en Ètrurie," *Ancient Society* 37 (2007) 167–190, who recognizes an *Apollo medicus* in the god of the Portonaccio sanctuary on the basis of the votive terracottas, see Krauskopf, I., *LIMC Supplementum* 2009, 82 s.v. Aplu.

30 G. Colonna, "Il *dokanon*, il culto dei Dioscuri e gli aspetti ellenizzanti della religione dei morti nell' Etruria tardo-arcaica" in: *Scritti di antichità in memoria di Sandro Stucchi* II (= *StMisc* 29, 1996) 165–184.

31 Besides the articles in *LIMC* VIII and *LIMC Supplementum* 2009 see also M. Harari, "Turms: il nome e la funzione" in *Image et religion dans l'antiquité gréco-romaine. Actes du Colloque de Rome 11.–13. décembre 2003* (Napoli : Centre Jean Bérard, 2008, 345–354. Sannibale, M., „Gli Etruschi e l'Aldilà," in: *Aldilà. L'ultimo mistero. Cat. exhibition* Illeggio 2011 (ed. Castri, S.- Geretti, A.) pp. 222f. no. 33.

32 Maras 1998/2001; Maras 2009, 153–157.

33 It is controversial to which extent these *deorum sedes* are reflected in the orientation of temples. S. F. Prayon, "Deorum sedes. Sull'orientamento dei templi etrusco-italici,"*ArchCl* 43 (1991) 1285–1295 with earlier literature. One also has to consider that, e. g., the sunrise-point oscillates through the seasons, and that we can't be certain that the Etruscans didn't find this point to be more important than the fixed point of the sun's zenith in the south, see on this N.L.C. Stevens, "A new reconstruction of the Etruscan heaven," *AJA* 113 (2009) 153–164.

34 Literature by Maras 1998/2001, 196f. n. 78.

35 See note 38.

36 W. Burkert, *Griechische Religion der archaischen und klassischen Epoche*, Stuttgart Berlin Köln Mainz: Verlag W. Kohlhammer, 1977, pp. 487f. There and pp. 278–282 on the complex ancient terms, *daimon* and *daimonion*.

37 Original quote from W. Burkert: "Eros sei ein Wesen, das weder Gott noch sterblich ist, sondern ein mittleres, ein *daimon*; denn solcher Art seien die *daimones*: sie stehen in der Mitte zwischen Göttern und Menschen, sie sind Dolmetscher und Fährleute, die Botschaften und

Gaben von den Menschen zu den Göttern und von den Göttern zu den Menschen übermitteln, Gebete und Opfer von der einen, Aufträge und Belohnungen von der anderen Seite."

38 D. Elm, "Die Kontroverse über die Sondergötter," *Archiv für Religionsgeschichte* 5.1 (2003) 67–79; M. Perfigli, Indigitamenta: divinità funzionali e funzionalità divina nella religione romana. *Anthropoi* 2. Pisa: Edizioni ETS, 2004.

39 See the respective articles in *LIMC*, further Krauskopf 1987, J.- R. Jannot, "Charun, Tuchulcha et les autres," *RM* 100, 1993, 59–81; *idem*, "Charu(n) et Vanth, divinités plurielles?." In *Les Étrusques, les plus religieux des hommes. État de la recherche sur la religion étrusque. Actes du colloque international Grand Palais 17.–19.11.1992* (eds F. Gaultier and D. Briquel, Paris 1997) 139–166.

40 See Maras 1998/2001, p. 193, see also n. 2.

41 See n. 2.

42 *LIMC* VI *s. v.* Maris; de Grummond 2006, 140–144.

43 *LIMC Supplementum 2009, s. v.* Daemones anonymi (in Etruria) 151–153 with bibl.

44 So, for example, A. Stenico, "Di alcune divinità italiche," *Athenaeum* 25 (1947) pp. 55ff. esp. 58.

45 F. Dirlmeier, *Die Vogelgestalt homerischer Götter* (Sitzungsberichte der Heidelberger Akademie der Wissenschaften. Philosophisch-Historische Klasse, 1967, 2. Heidelberg: Carl Winter Universitätsverlag) p. 35.

46 I. Krauskopf, "Sul teriomorfismo di dèi etruschi e italici" in *Forms and Structures of Religion in Ancient Central Italy. III Convegno Internazionale dell'Istituto di Ricerche e documentazione sugli antichi Umbri (IRDAU)* Perugia-Gubbio, 21.–25. settembre 2011. For Aita s. also the *LIMC*-article and Krauskopf 1987.

47 LIMC *Supplementum* 2009, 153–155; I. Grau, "Der sogenannte Jason im Archäologischen Museum von Florenz," *Hefte des Archäologischen Seminars Bern (HASB)* 18, 2002, 23–44.

48 *Loc. cit.* 151; *LIMC* VII Poseidon/Nethuns 16–19 = VIII Tyrsenos 2–5

49 For example, the wolf-demon on the Pontic plate Rome, Villa Giulia (*LIMC Supplementum* 2009 Daemones anonyma 1 = Monstra anonyma in Etruria 22*; de Grummond/Simon 2006 75 fig. V.14) and the wolf's "cap" of Aita in the Tomba dell'Orco (*LIMC* IV Hades/Aita 6*; de Grummond/Simon 2006, 71 Fig. V.7–8), the vulture-demon on an oinochoe in the Vatican (*LIMC Supplementum* 2009 Daemones anonymi 5*) or the Charun in the Tomba degli Aninas (*LIMC* III Charon/Charun 60*).

50 *LIMC Supplementum* 2009 Daemones anonymi 26*; S. Steingräber, *Abundance of Life. Etruscan Wall Paintings*, Los Angeles, The J. Paul Getty Museum, 2006, pl. 230; Minetti, A., *La tomba della Quadriga Infernale nella necropoli delle Pianacce di Sarteano* (Roma, L'ERMA di Bretschneider 2006).

BIBLIOGRAPHY

Bentz, M. (1992) *Etruskische Votivbronzen des Hellenismus*, Florence: Biblioteca di Studi Etruschi 25, Florence: Leo Olschki.

Colonna, G. (1987) "Note preliminari sui culti del santuario di Portonaccio a Veio," *Scienze dell'Antichità* 1, 419–446.

——(1991/92) "Altari e sacelli. L'area sud di Pyrgi dopo otto anni di ricerch," *RendPontAcc* 64, 63–115.

——(1997) "Divinités peu connues du panthéon étrusque" in F. Gaultier and D. Briquel (eds) *Les Étrusques, les plus religieux des hommes. État de la recherche sur la religion étrusque. Actes du colloque international Grand Palais 17.–19.11.1992*, Paris: La Documentation Francaise, 167–184.

——(2012) "Il pantheon degli Etruschi – 'i più religiosi degli uomini' – alla luce delle scoperte di Pyrgi," *Atti della Accademia Nazionale dei Lincei, anno CDIX -2012 classe di scienze morali, storiche e filologiche. Memorie ser. IX vol. XXIX fasc. 3557–595.*

de Grummond, N. T. (2006), *Etruscan Myth, Sacred History and Legend*, Philadelphia, University of Pennsylvania Museum of Archaeology and Anthropology.

de Grummond, N. T. and Simon, E. (2006) (eds) *The Religion of the Etruscans*, Austin: University of Texas Press, with English translations of the important literary sources to Etruscan religion, 191–218.

Herbig, R. and Simon, E. (1965) *Götter und Dämonen der Etrusker*, edited and revised by Erika Simon, Mainz: Philipp von Zabern.

Jannot, J. -R. (1998) *Devins, dieux et démons. Regards sur la religion de l'Étrurie antique*, Paris: Picard.

Krauskopf, I. (1987) *Todesdämonen und Totengötter im vorhellenistischen Etrurien. Kontinuität und Wandel*, Biblioteca di Studi Etruschi 16, Florence: Leo Olschki.

Maggiani, A. (1982) "Qualche osservazione sul fegato di Piacenza," *StEtr* 50, 53–88.

——(1997) "Vasi attici figurati con dediche a divinità etrusche." Suppl. 18 alla *RdA*, Rome: Giorgio Bretschneider.

——(2002) "I culti di Perugia e del suo territorio," *AnnFaina* 9 (Roma: Edizioni Quasar) 267–299.

——(2004) "L'homme et le sacré dans les rituels et dans la religion étrusque" in J. Ries (ed.) *Les civilisations méditerranéennes et le sacré*. Turnhaut: Brepols. 183–203, (translated from original Italian edition J. Ries (ed.) (1991) *Le civiltà del Mediterraneo e il sacro*, Jaca Book: Milano).

Maras, D. F. (1998/2001) "La dea Thanr e le cerchie divine in Etruria: nuove acquisizioni," *StEtr* 64, 1998 (2001) 173–197.

——(2009) *Il dono votivo. Gli dei e il sacro nelle iscrizioni etrusche di culto*, Pisa Rome: Fabrizio Serra.

Pfiffig, A. (1975) *Religio Etrusca*, Graz: Akademische Druck- u. Verlagsanstalt.

Simon, E. (2006) "Gods in Harmony: The Etruscan Pantheon" in N. T. de Grummond and E. Simon (eds) *The Religion of the Etruscans*, Austin: University of Texas Press, 45–65.

ThesCRA = *Thesaurus Cultus et Rituum Antiquorum* I–VIII Los Angeles, The J. Paul Getty Museum 2004–2012.

van der Meer, L. B. (1987) *The Bronze Liver of Piacenza. Analysis of a Polytheistic Structure*, Amsterdam: Gieben.

CHAPTER TWENTY SIX

HARUSPICY AND AUGURY: SOURCES AND PROCEDURES

———•━•———

Nancy T. de Grummond

INTRODUCTION

Haruspicy and augury are forms of divination practiced assiduously by the Etruscans.[1] At its most basic, haruspicy may be defined as the art of divining the will of the gods, especially by examining the entrails of animals (Lat. *extispicium*). In Rome, the practitioner was called a *haruspex* (pl. *haruspices*), a word that was explained in Antiquity as one who inspects the entrails of a *hariuga* (sacrificed animal).[2] In a bilingual Latin/Etruscan inscription from Pesaro (*ET* Um 1.7; CIL XI 6363; 1st century BCE), the Etruscan word *netśvis* is found as a translation of *haruspex*. The *–vis* may also refer to "one who inspects" and thus *netś* may have the same meaning as *hariuga*. As will be noted below, the haruspices also interpreted a wide variety of other types of signs, but the emphasis in this article will be on extispicy, especially in regard to the liver.

Augury or *augurium* referred – at least in Rome – to watching the activities of birds and deciding whether they showed favorable or unfavorable omens from the gods. The Etruscan word for such a religious practice is uncertain. It is safe to conclude that the Etruscans did practice augury, but we cannot be sure that their responses were similarly limited, or whether there were more nuanced answers depending on the species, number, color or activity of the birds. Augurs occasionally dealt with other prodigies as well.[3]

SOURCES

Truly primary sources on Etruscan divination are exiguous and only modestly informative. Of Etruscan inscriptions the aforementioned Pesaro bilingual is among the most illuminating: *{L. CA}FATIUS.L.F.STE.HARUSPE{X} FULGURIATOR cafates. lr.lr.netśvis.trutnvt. frontac.* It tells us, besides the Etruscan word for *haruspex*, that such an individual of the first century BCE in Pesaro on the Adriatic coast could also be skilled in the reading of lightning. The Etruscan phrase *trutnvt.frontac*, using two words in place of *fulguriator* (=*frontac*?) may refer to additional competency.[4] The title of *netśvis*, with a slight variation in spelling was given to a certain Nae Cicu, son of Pethnei, buried at Poggio al Moro, Chiusi.[5] One of the longest Etruscan inscriptions known, still meager at 59 words, gives an epitaph of a priest from Tarquinii, L(a)ris Pulenas (circa 250–200 BCE).[6] It reveals that he wrote a book on haruspication (*ziχ neθśrac*) and served as a priest of Catha and Pacha (counterpart to Bacchus). The inscription lists his genealogy more fully than usual in Etruscan epitaphs, perhaps to indicate that he came from a family of seers.

A good many representations of Etruscan divination and priests have survived, along with *realia* in the form of excavated artifacts pertaining to ritual, that give glimpses of the appearance and practices of haruspication and augury.[7] Fundamental is the engraving on a bronze Etruscan mirror from Tuscania that shows a young haruspex labeled Pava Tarchies (Fig. 26.1), standing with a liver in his left hand, propped on his upraised left leg, in turn braced on a tall rock. He wears the hat with apex typical of the Etruscan priest. A group of deities and mortals crowd around him, including a certain Avl Tarchunus, who rests his chin upon his hand in an intent attitude of contemplation. He, too, has the apical hat, though it is not placed on his head; hanging behind him, it suggests that he may be preparing to become a haruspex and then will officially wear the hat. It is worth noting that Pava Tarchies is a youth, and seems to be instructing the older man.[8] They may be legendary or mythological figures. A goddess labeled Lasa Vecuvia, also seen on a gold ring bezel from Todi, where she is naked (Fig. 26.2), and on a bronze mirror, where she is called Lasa Vecu and dressed and winged, seems to have been an important Etruscan divine prophetic figure, called Nymph Vegoia by Roman writers, who recorded her as the source of books on lightning.[9] There are many other scenes on mirrors and gems that allude to divination, including an Etruscan mythical or legendary prophetic figure named Umaele, who reads a liver on one mirror and tends an oracular head on others.[10] He is thus far unknown in the ancient literary record; there is no evidence that he was the author of any books.[11] Another prominent prophet is Cacu, seen on a mirror and in

Figure 26.1   Mirror with Pava Tarchies from Tuscania. Early third century BCE Florence, Museo Archeologico Nazionale (after Torelli, 1988, Fig. 1).

reliefs on ash urns, with the attribute of the lyre to aid in his prophesying and a youthful assistant, Artile, by his side.[12] He is attacked by the Vipinas brothers, Avle and Caile, who are thought to be real historical individuals, active at Rome, Vulci and Veii.[13] But Cacu himself, like Umaele and unlike Tages and Vecuvia, does not seem to have emerged in the sacred history of the Etruscans as an author of written prophecy. Vel Saties (Fig. 26.3) the head of an Etruscan noble family of Vulci, is certainly an historical figure,

Figure 26.2   Gold ring bezel with Lasa Vecuvia, from Todi. Early third century BCE Rome, Museo Etrusco di Villa Giulia (Photo: Courtesy of the Soprintendenza per i Beni Archeologici dell'Etruria Meridionale).

Figure 26.3   Painting of Vel Saties, from the François Tomb, Vulci. Watercolor copy by C. Ruspi, Vatican Museums (after Buranelli, 1992, 85).

depicted in his tomb performing an act of augury as his small assistant Arnza prepares to release a bird. Gazing upward and wearing a wreath of vegetation, Vel is dressed in an honorific robe decorated with a scene of nude male warriors, the whole suggesting that he had a dual role as priest and magistrate or general.[14]

As for *realia*, without doubt the single most important piece of evidence on Etruscan divination is the Piacenza Liver (Fig. 26.4),[15] a truly astonishing object that has created a focal point for understanding disparate bits of evidence from literary sources, archaeological sites and other artifacts. Discovered casually in 1877 by a farmer, the bronze model of a sheep's liver (maximum length 12.6 cm) was probably created in the second or first century BCE and is inscribed in a script used locally around Cortona. The upper surface features incisions that create 40 cells of varying shapes and sizes, each with one or more names of gods. Another model liver, made of terracotta, comes from Falerii Veteres (circa 300 BCE; Fig. 26.5),[16] a city in which Faliscan and Etruscan culture were blended.

The Romans were acquainted with various sacred books written in Etruscan, which gave instructions for communicating with the gods. Collectively referred to as the *Etrusca disciplina*,[17] these books pertained not only to entrails and the flight of birds, but also to divination through thunder and lightning and through prodigies.[18] Of the references to books that have come down to us, it is not always easy to tell what the contents were or whether different names may have been used for one particular book. There are general references to the *Etrusci libri*,[19] *Etruscorum libri*,[20] *Etrusca scripta*,[21] *chartae etruscae*,[22] *Tuscorum litterae*,[23] *Etruscae disciplinae volumina*,[24] *Tusci libelli*,[25] *Tyrrhena carmina*,[26] as well as to the *libri Vegoici*, "books of Vegoia," and the *libri Tagetici*,[27] "books of Tages," attributed to the two best known prophets of the Etruscans.

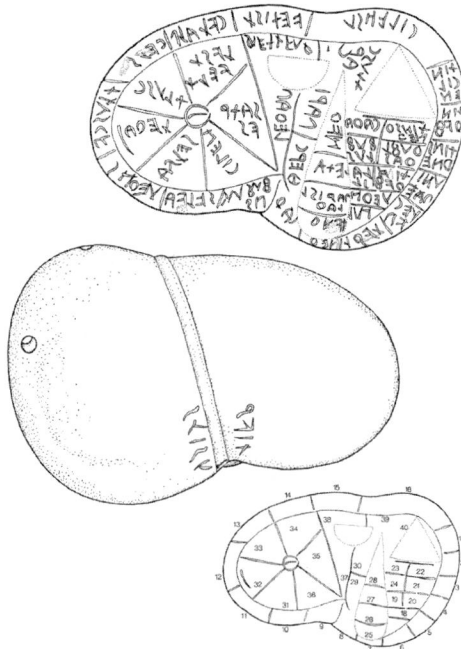

Figure 26.4   Diagram of the Piacenza Liver. Second–first century BCE (after Torelli 1986, 211).

Figure 26.5   Clay model of a sheep's liver from Mesopotamia, eighteenth century BCE. Inv. BM Bu
89–4–26, 238. London, British Museum.

Then there are numerous references to books with particular categories of information. Vegoia (=Etruscan Vecuvia or Lasa Vecuvia) was said to have written about lightning, and thus the books referred to as *fulgurales...libri* and *Etrusci libri de fulguratura* may have been contained in the *libri Vegoici*.[28] Tages, the wizened child who emerged from a ploughed furrow at Tarquinii and revealed the basic tenets of divination to the city founder, Tarchon, is especially associated with haruspication; he is said to have first demonstrated *extispicium*, the examination of *exta* (i.e. entrails).[29] Thus *aruspicinae libri* or simply *haruspicini* may refer to a part of the *libri Tagetici*.[30] Tages is also said to have treated *sacra Acheruntia*, rites that have to do with fate and the Afterlife, and rituals related to founding cities and delimiting boundaries.[31] The former may have been contained in the *libri fatales*; the latter were certainly in the *libri rituales*.[32] *Libri exercituales* may have been for the use of *haruspices* in the army.[33] Etruscan books on auspicious birds were so detailed that there were even illustrations to identify each bird that was being observed.[34]

Cicero relates that at Rome prodigies were to be delegated to Etruscan haruspices,[35] thereby indicating that *haruspicina* actually embraced a good bit more than the reading of entrails. In fact there are several passages in Cicero's *De divinatione* (2. 42; 49–50) in which the word *haruspicina* seems to apply to divination in general and thus to be loosely equivalent to the *Etrusca disciplina*. Cicero's well-known text of 56 BCE on the response of the haruspices (*De haruspicum responsis*) notes that the haruspices are charged with interpreting a *strepitus cum fremitu* ("a clamor, with roaring") in the *ager Latiniensis*. Other prodigies referred to the haruspices by the Romans are numerous and remarkable: lightning, monstrous births, androgynies, a rain of stones, a rain of blood, talking cows, oxen climbing stairs, a statue that is blown over, a statue weeping, flames from the earth, a trumpet blast from the sky, a speaking infant, a rain of iron, bees on the Capitol.[36] All of these belong to the period of the Republic, and stand a reasonable chance of indicating matters of concern to the Etruscans themselves within their own political bodies and society.

The names of various Roman antiquarians and scholars are associated with the study and preservation of Etruscan books and teachings, falling roughly into two time periods – the Late Republic/Early Empire and Late Antiquity. From the earlier period,[37] the illustrious polymath Varro (116–27 BCE) is a leading figure in antiquarian study of religious traditions. His *Antiquitates rerum divinarum*, unfortunately known mainly from fragments quoted or passages alluded to by other authors, passed on information about the Etruscan art of interpreting lightning, priesthoods in early Rome, and the use of divination in relation to the four elements of air, fire, earth and water. In other works he recorded information about the rituals of laying out a city, as well as information about omens provided by fish, in his *libri navales*.[38] An elusive figure whose name seems to have been C. Fonteius Capito,[39] evidently a contemporary of Varro and close friend of Antony, was recorded to have written a thunder calendar and to have disseminated the story of Tages and Tarchon.

No individual is more important for problems of Etruscan divination than Publius Nigidius Figulus (circa 98–45 BCE), also a contemporary of Varro as well as a friend of Cicero, an enormously prolific writer whose works have mostly disappeared.[40] Nigidius probably came from Etruscan Perugia to Rome, where he enjoyed a respectable political career and moved in intellectual circles in which religious and philosophical systems of explaining the universe were much studied and discussed. His posture on philosophy and Roman government in the first century BCE – Pythagorean, *magus*, astrologer and supporter of Pompey – sometimes put him at a disadvantage, and he found himself exiled after Caesar came to power. Nigidius is viewed as someone interested in the occult and magic, a serious scholar of religion who wrote a treatise *De augurio privato* and another *De extis*, directly concerned with extispicy. Most significant for this discussion is his Latin translation of an Etruscan brontoscopic calendar attributed to Tages himself, which has survived in a Byzantine Greek translation by Johannes Lydus, made in the sixth century CE.[41]

Tarquitius Priscus,[42] from a distinguished family of the first century BCE and friend of Varro, was known for having made a Latin translation of the *libri Vegoici*. The one surviving fragment of an Etruscan prophecy, recorded in the *Gromatici Veteres* and said to have been delivered by Vegoia to a certain Arruns, is thought to derive from the scholarship of Tarquitius.[43] He also produced an *Ostentarium Tuscum*, as well as a work on prophesying from trees, and *Libri Tarquitiani* were still available in the fourth century CE. For *ostenta* from the period of the Late Republic, the obscure Julius Obsequens is important. Details of his life are quite unknown, except that he compiled a *Liber prodigiorum*; it contains entries from 190 to 11 BCE and bears a close relationship to the various prodigy lists in Livy's history.[44]

Yet another significant figure of the period of the later Roman Republic was Aulus Caecina, who studied Etruscan texts and attempted to transmit tenets of the Etruscan discipline.[45] Like Nigidius, he came to Rome from an Etruscan city (Volaterrae), and was in the circle of Cicero, participating in philosophical and religious inquiries. Cicero defended him in regard to a claim on property at Tarquinii (69 BCE), but his position as an opponent of Caesar hindered him until he recanted and was helped by Cicero to be pardoned. He had intimate knowledge of Etruscan teachings, having learned from his father in the traditional Etruscan manner, and he passed on his knowledge in a Latin treatise, *De etrusca disciplina*, which has been described as a "major event" in the intellectual life of the Late Republic.[46] The loss of this document is felt keenly by those trying to understand Etruscan religion. He was especially important as a source on Etruscan interpretation of lightning.[47]

The case of Cicero is difficult for other reasons. Himself an augur of the Roman state (from 53 BCE), he nevertheless had an ambivalent position on the nature and efficacy of divination. His many references to the *Etrusca disciplina* and to haruspices must be seen in the context of the debates he staged in his treatises *De natura deorum* and *De divinatione* (45–44 BCE). Having studied thoroughly the tenets of the various schools of philosophy of the Hellenistic period in his youth and again in his later years, he described himself as an academic who, with open mind, also gave his full attention to other schools; for divination this meant in particular the Stoics and Epicureans. Thus in the *De divinatione*, in Book I the remarks of his brother Quintus representing the Stoic view stress the successes of divination (with the Etruscans mentioned side by side with other peoples devoted to the art), while in Book II his own remarks as Marcus are aimed at refuting the claims of divinatory practice. Perhaps the most cited statement is his snide quote from Cato, who had wondered why one haruspex did not laugh aloud when he met another haruspex (*De div.* 2.52). And while we may be grateful to Cicero for preserving a tidy version of the story of the prophecies of Tages, usually no one cites his own personal reaction to the story:

> Who in the world is stupid enough to believe that anybody ever ploughed up – which shall I say – a god or man?…Could not this so-called god have delivered this art to mankind from a more exalted station? But if this fellow Tages was a man, pray, how could he have lived covered with earth? Finally, where had he himself learned the things he taught others?[48]

It has been argued that Cicero's knowledge of Etruscan divination was superficial,[49] but certain parts of the *De divinatione* give us precious information. Quintus relates the story, for example, of Attus Navius, augur for Tarquinius Priscus, searching for the best grape cluster to offer to Jupiter, delimiting his vineyard by standing in the middle, facing south, and dividing it first into quarters, then eliminating three of the quarters through augury, and finally subdividing the final quarter to achieve success (*De div.* 1.31). The description has a ring of authority and authenticity, and gives reason to believe that such Etruscan divination may have already been practiced in Rome in the time of Tarquinius Priscus (a legendary figure, but traditionally assigned to the late seventh-early sixth century BCE). Still, it leaves further details to be revealed by the Augustan-era Greek historian and antiquarian, Dionysius of Halicarnassus (d. after 7 BCE), who relates how birds helped the augur as a boy to select the appropriate quadrant for the best grape cluster (*Roman Antiquities*, 3.73.3).[50]

Certainly, Livy is an important source for the activities of Etruscan priests and details of Etruscan ritual embedded in his historical accounts. His description of the expansion of the city of Rome under Servius Tullius, for example, sheds light on the meaning of the *pomerium* and the ceremonial inauguration of spaces (1.44.3). Attention has been given appropriately to his various reports of prodigies, seemingly drawn from pontifical archives.[51] Other distinguished literary figures of the Augustan period who were formed in the intellectual climate described above were able to relate easily to information about ancient Etruscan religious practice in their poetry. Propertius (4.2) has left the memorable description of the statue of Vertumnus, "chief god of Etruria" (Varro, *De lingua latina* 5.46), while Vergil in the *Aeneid* and Ovid in his *Fasti* and *Metamorphoses* related imaginative stories and customs that provide hints about Etruscan traditions.[52]

From the early Empire, Pliny's *Natural History* (circa 77 CE) provides numerous miscellaneous observations on various practices of divination. Of particular usefulness are his reports on the interpretation of the activities of birds,[53] and his section on lightning bolts is regarded as "most valuable of all" the sources of information about the practices of lightning divination (*NH* 2.138–144).[54] Pliny's identity is that of the encyclopedic who researches all topics that have to do with *Natural History*. Seneca (d. 65 CE), on the other hand, writes as a philosopher, devoting space in his *Quaestiones Naturales* to a searching review of Etruscan beliefs about lightning as a scientific subject. Both authors had consulted the writings of Caecina, but they show some points of disagreement.[55]

A resurgence of interest in the religion and antiquities of the Etruscans occurred in Late Antiquity, in the third, and especially fourth and fifth centuries CE. Many of the works known during the Republic were still consulted, within an ambient of theological and philosophical inquiry in the critical years of the decline of the pagan system. Though now remote from the actual practice of the *Etrusca disciplina*, scholars often used works that have since been lost, and transmitted antiquarian information worth sifting through. The grammarian Censorinus, using Varro, described the Etruscan doctrine of the cycles of time and how to calculate the periods of time allotted to cities and to the Etruscan *nomen* (Etruscan civilization) itself (*De die natali*, 238 CE).[56] Arnobius, a rhetorician and apologist for Christianity from North Africa, while attacking and refuting pagan religion, preserved curious details regarding Etruscan beliefs in his *Adversus Nationes* (circa 297–303 CE).[57] He, too, consulted Varro, as well as Cicero. Very reliable and diverse are the notes of Servius, the pagan grammarian regarded as one of the most learned men of his generation, in his commentary on works of Vergil, written around 400 CE.[58] A priceless document is the text of Martianus Capella called by modern scholars *De nuptiis Philologiae et Mercurii*, created in the 420s CE, wherein Mercury marries Philology in a charming fantasy. Invitations are sent out to all the gods who are described in a most unusual way to dwell in a sky divided into 16 regions.[59] This information resonates on the one hand with a comment by Cicero that the Etruscans uniquely divided the heavens into 16 parts so that they might identify the region from which a bolt of lightning came[60] and on the other hand with the 16 cells running around the top side of the Piacenza liver, each designated as the place of presence of one or more gods. Last to be mentioned of the late antique savants is Johannes Lydus, the Byzantine scholar of the sixth century CE who assembled a bonanza of divinatory material in his *De ostentis*, including the *Tonitruale* and myth of Tages culled from Fonteius, and the most important of all surviving Etruscan religious documents, the brontoscopic calendar of Nigidius Figulus,[61] said to derive from Tages.

PROCEDURES AND COMPARISONS

There can be no doubt that there was a connection between divinatory practices in the ancient Near East and those in Greece and Italy. There are many valid comparisons and cross-references among the types of divination practiced – *extispicium*, augury, brontoscopy, the reading of prodigies – and the procedures followed. Somehow practices in Mesopotamia from as early as circa 2000 BCE were transmitted to the Etruscans, first becoming visible in the archaeological record in Italy by around 500 BCE,[62] but probably beginning earlier than that date. The date and route of diffusion of these procedures cannot be proven, but it is certain that the arts that developed in early Babylon remained continuously in use in the Near East down into Seleucid times, and had particular vitality at the courts of the Neo-Assyrian kings in the eighth and seventh centuries BCE.[63] This is the time of the "Orientalizing" phenomenon when a vast array of cultural material was transmitted westward, absorbed and transformed, in Greece, Italy, North Africa, Spain and France. The trade lanes to Italy have been identified, and they run from the area dominated by the Neo-Assyrian kings, Esarhaddon (680–669 BCE) and Ashurbanipal (668–627 BCE), great users of state divination,[64] to Cyprus, the Greek islands and Euboea, and on to the Euboean colony of Pithekoussai on the Bay of Naples and from there to Etruria. Along with the dazzling objects imported into Italy[65] came other cultural cargo. Burkert argued that the scenario implies traveling charismatic figures who may have come to visit local princes and thereby introduced well-developed divination practices.[66] (The tale of Megales, the Phrygian seer who taught augury to the Sabines,[67] though related at a considerably later date, provides an example of the paradigm). Turfa hypothesizes exchange among individuals of the upper classes who shared economic and political concerns (ship owners, diplomats, aristocrats, princes) that would have facilitated transmission of such a fundamentally useful art as divination.[68] In addition, it is highly probable that fresh infusions into divinatory practice in Italy came about in later centuries, especially in the Hellenistic period, when the international ferment of ideas about divination and its relation to philosophical and scientific views of the universe swept through intellectual circles in Rome. Cicero's *De divinatione* provides detailed references.

The similarities between the Babylonian and Etruscan traditions are well known and often cited.[69] Both practiced the sacrifice of sheep in particular, both made models of livers with significant markings on them, both used a system of orientation to determine which parts of the liver were favorable and which unfavorable.[70] Equally well known are the differences. The Babylonian liver models seem to be records of readings, as may be seen in an unusually detailed example in the British Museum (Fig. 26.5),[71] featuring a grid in which blemishes from past readings were indicated, whereas the Piacenza liver, the most revealing of the Etruscan liver models, seems to be a guide to the presence of gods on the liver under consultation.

It is true that Babylonian liver reading also called for a determination of the presence of the god; if the god was not present, the consultation was terminated. The terracotta liver from Falerii (Fig. 26.6) presents some very precise details that show the direct connection between the two traditions, but also reveal how a new and different system was developed. A line running down the middle of the left lobe on the Falerii liver

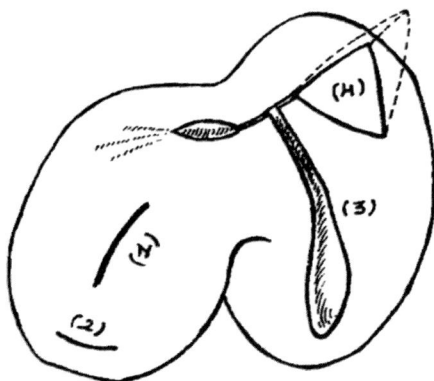

Figure 26.6 Drawing of terracotta model of a liver from Falerii Veteres, area of the temple of Lo Scasato. Circa 300 BCE. Rome, Museo Nazionale di Villa Giulia. Drawing after Nougayrol, 1955, p. 513).

is apparently identical with one called the *Manzāzu*, "Presence," in Babylonian lore.[72] Another line on the lower left seems to be the same as the Babylonian *Padānu* ("Path"). These same two marks may be identified on the left lobe of the Piacenza liver (in the circle in the middle is the "Presence" and in cell 32, belonging to *Letha*, on the far left is the "Path").[73] But the Etruscan system of identifying the gods seems to have become extremely elaborate, involving as it did a multitude of deities, whereas Near Eastern extispicy was directed mainly at Shamash, the sun god, and Adad, the storm god.[74]

Another way in which the Etruscan and Near Eastern systems were alike was in the use of formulas with protasis ("If...") and apodosis ("then....").[75] The clearest Etruscan examples occur in the brontoscopic calendar of Nigidius Figulus, which claimed the authority of Tages. Here are several examples from the month of October:

Oct. 1.   If it thunders, it threatens a corrupt tyrant over the affairs of state.
Oct. 3.   If it thunders, it signifies hurricanes and disturbances by which the trees will be overturned; there will be a great disruption in the affairs of common people.
Oct. 4.   If it thunders, the lower classes will have the upper hand over their betters, and the mildness of the air will be healthy.
Oct. 5.   If it thunders, there will be a surplus of all the necessities excepting grain.
Oct. 6.   If it thunders, appearance of future abundance, yet harvest will be less plentiful and autumn practically empty of fruit.
Oct. 8.   If it thunders, an earthquake with roaring is to be expected.
Oct. 10. If it thunders, it signifies the downfall of a praiseworthy man.[76]

The predictions are specific and vary greatly in their concerns. Obviously many details relate especially to certain individuals in political power, while others may affect a whole populace. Matters of weather, health and agriculture occur repeatedly.[77] If we look at the records of liver divination noted by Roman writers as coming from Etruscan haruspices, there are many further *comparanda*, basically reflecting a formula of "if ....then..." The "head" of the liver, the *caput iecoris* (in modern scientific terminology, the *processus caudatus*) was always a conspicuous and significant element, and there are several reports on its nature that demonstrate clearly how a liver might be interpreted with protasis and apodosis. If the head was absent this was a negative sign, but if the head was enlarged this was a positive indication.[78] If the head was doubled this could be again a sign of strength according to one interpretation.[79] But another priest at another time might take it as a negative sign, because it could signal civil conflict between two competing generals.[80] Other parts of the liver might have a narrower context for a conditional interpretation: the gall bladder had a particular connection with the god Neptune and with water (the Etruscan name Nethuns is written on the gall bladder of the Piacenza liver). Augustus found a double gall bladder in the victim on the day of his naval victory at Actium.[81]

The 16 divisions around the edges of the liver corresponded with the 16 divisions of the heavens, and these in turn were keyed to compass points. The mapping of the heavens was essential for interpreting lightning, which began with determining which of the gods who hurled lightning (there were nine in all) may have sent a particular bolt. Here, as on the liver, the Etruscans manifested the approach to different kinds of omens in the way in which they carefully demarcated the areas where they sought the omen. The laying out of a zone in the air, on the ground, or underground, known as a *templum* in Latin,[82] probably originated within the Etruscan belief system, characterized by a virtual obsession with orientation. The Etruscan curved ritual wand known in Latin as the *lituus* was used by the priest to mark out a *templum*.[83] The *templum* was further articulated into categories of "in front" (*pars antica*), "behind" (*pars posterior*), "on the left," (*in sinistrum*) and "on the right" (*in dextrum*). Obviously ritual stance was important, as may be seen not only in the scene of Pava Tarchies (Fig. 26.1), but also in a much earlier depiction of hepatoscopy, the mirror in the Vatican showing Chalchas as a winged diviner (Fig. 26.7). Like Pava Tarchies, he stands with his left leg raised and braced on a rock, his left hand outstretched to hold the liver so that he may observe it closely. On the table/altar next to him are placed other parts of the victim (windpipe? lungs?), indicating that at this time, the liver was not the only item for *antispicium*. It is not incidental that the left side is so emphasized in such a scene. Etruscan doctrine taught that the left side was normally the auspicious side, because it indicated the east: Tinia, the chief Etruscan god, took up his post in the north, looking south; his left side and hand thus were turned toward the east, the happy, light-filled zone where the day originates. In contrast, the Greek Zeus was thought to be facing north and for the Greeks the right side then became the auspicious one.

There are, of course, many and valuable comparisons for the procedures of divination from Greece and Italy, the latter continuing down into the period of the later Roman Empire. The stream of tradition becomes murky, however, especially in relation to the haruspices at Rome. They are popularly referred to as Etruscan, but most of the ones who were truly ethnic Etruscans belong to the period of the first century BCE or early first century CE; the list of names of haruspices from the early Empire on suggests that, in general, the priests were not Etruscan by birth, language or training.[84] Some haruspices of Rome were named as members of the prestigious *Ordo LX haruspicum*, supposed to be recruited from Etruria; others served an emperor or governor and thus also clearly had Roman-style state jobs. Still others will have served individuals in a public or private capacity. In these circumstances the *Etrusca disciplina* may have undergone important changes; to be cautious it is perhaps best to refer to the situation as the Roman phase of the Etruscan discipline and the haruspices.

Figure 26.7   Mirror with Chalchas as haruspex. Circa 400 BCE. Vatican Museums. (After *ES* 2.223).

Thus in describing the procedures of Etruscan haruspication it is always necessary to filter the evidence. It seems likely that one difference between the early Etruscan approach to *exta* and that of the haruspices in the Roman phase was that the Etruscans removed the *exta* from the animal, while the later ritual sometimes (perhaps normally?) left them attached to the animal.[85] Further, the Piacenza liver, with all of its inscriptions, tells us that the reading of a liver was a far more complex procedure for the Etruscans than it was for either the Greeks or the Romans, who normally sought a simple answer in the response, either favorable or unfavorable.[86] The Etruscan system must have been much more than binary, since the priest would have to determine first of all which god or gods were present on the liver being consulted. Then, with a subtle interpretation based on protasis and apodosis, a nuanced answer could be produced.

Many of the characteristics of divination by liver, lightning and thunder that noted above apply to the surviving evidence about augury obtained by studying the activities of birds.[87] But here, perhaps more than elsewhere in ancient divination, it is difficult to separate out the beliefs of the Etruscans, because prophesying from birds was widespread and long-lasting in Greece and Italy, and again there is a rich background of Near Eastern practices.[88] The *Iliad* and the *Odyssey* both contain references to augury, and the Greek perception that the skill was developed early was confirmed in the story of Prometheus, who gave mankind many gifts, including prophecy from birds.[89] For the Romans no story was more basic than the foundation legend detailing the conflict between Romulus and Remus, the resolution of which was based on messenger birds from the gods.[90] As for the priesthoods, just as the haruspices represented Etruscan tradition, the augurs were solidly Roman, formed into a college with a well-developed tradition of law and employed to consult sacred chickens on whether or not to go to battle.[91]

Certainly, augury was well developed among the Etruscans, and it is no surprise that among the few glosses surviving on Etruscan vocabulary are the words for falcon, *capys*; eagle, *antar*; crane, *gnis*; and hawk, *arak*.[92] Pliny refers to birds that were *depicta in Etrusca disciplina*, (*N.H.* 10.37) implying that Etruscan augurs had sacred books to help them to identify birds. The number, color, conspicuous size and variety of action of the birds painted in Etruscan tombs strongly suggest that the artists attempted to show birds of omen, whether good or bad.[93] Among artistic representations, an evocative image of a semi-nude, bearded man gazing towards the heavens (Fig. 26.8), with his head resting on his hand in a pose of meditation (cf. Avl Tarchunus, Fig. 26.1), may show a legendary or divine augur taking the auspices.[94]

At the end of this inquiry, we return to what was observed at the beginning. The primary sources for studying Etruscan divination are meager and difficult to interpret. If we had even a few more of the various treatises in the corpus of *Etrusci libri*, it would revolutionize our understanding of how the Etruscans practiced divination. The reclaiming by Turfa of the brontoscopic calendar of Nigidius Figulus opens windows in many directions for the study of the origins, history and praxis of the *Etrusca disciplina* and shows how advances can be made. Intensified research into ancient libraries or the (highly unlikely) discovery of new documents could likewise advance comprehension in a dramatic way. An encouraging development, not central to this essay on haruspicy and augury, is the examination of Etruscan images and artifacts that may tell about other forms of divination known to have been practiced in the ancient world, which have not been studied in relation to the Etruscans because there is little or no textual evidence for them. The evidence to prove, for example, that the Etruscans practiced sortition (casting

Figure 26.8   Bronze handle of a pitcher (*Schnabelkanne*) with relief of a priest gazing upward, fifth century BCE. Arezzo, Museu Archeologico Mecenate. (Photo: Soprintendenza per i Beni Archeologici della Toscana-Firenze).

of lots) is mounting.[95] Careful review of religious iconography makes it all but certain that the Etruscans utilized *lekanomanteia* (divination by gazing into a bowl of liquid), another practice known from the Near East,[96] and *catoptromanteia* (divination with mirrors), a ritual missing in the Near Eastern corpus, but known in many places in the world at many different times and shared by the Etruscans, Greeks and Romans.[97] For some other types of divination (dreams, smoke, dice),[98] we may never identify any specific evidence, but given the demonstrable devotion of the Etruscans to haruspicy, brontoscopy and augury, as well as the attention to prodigies, it would not be surprising to find that some of these other divinatory techniques were included in the *disciplina etrusca*.

NOTES

1   Fundamental bibliography: Thulin 1968; Pfiffig 1975, 115–155; Torelli 1985, 210–216, 236–237; van der Meer 1987; Briquel 1997; Capdeville 1997; Maggiani 2005; de Grummond 2006b.

2   Thulin II, 3. Maggiani, 2005, 54, with alternate spellings for *hariuga*. Cf. also Haack 2006, 13, for the many variant spellings of *haruspex* in Latin inscriptions. The spelling *harispex* prevails in inscriptions relating to individuals with a strong Etruscan connection.

3   Maggiani 2005, 65–66.

4   TLE 697. ET Um 1.7. An inscribed grave cippus from Tarquinia also tells that Arnth Apries was a *trutnuθ*, but gives no further illumination on the meaning of the word. ET Ta 1.174.

5   TLE 524. ET Cl 1.1036.

6   TLE 131. ET Ta 1.17. Bonfante 2006, 13.

7   Maggiani 1989; de Grummond, 2006b; Roncalli 2010. For a thorough listing of such depictions see Turfa 2006b. The emphasis in the present essay is upon Etruscan figures, both

real and mythological, that may provide information about Etruscan religious practice. Greek prophetic figures were represented in Etruria as well, such as Chalchas, reading a liver (Fig. 7), and Urphe (Orpheus), whose severed head seems to prophesy; de Grummond 2006a, 37–40.

8 De Grummond 2006a, 27 and 2006b, 27–30. Some have argued that Pava Tarchies is equivalent to Tages, the leading Etruscan prophet, discussed below.

9 On the bezel she may be divining by means of a mirror, as a second naked nymph stands nearby. De Grummond 2006a, 29–31; de Grummond 2006b, 30–31.

10 de Grummond 2011, 325–328.

11 Note, however, that on two mirrors that seem to show Umaele as intermediary for a prophecy, a scribe seems to be writing down the prophecy delivered in the scene. De Grummond 2006a, 33–34.

12 Small 1982; de Grummond, 2006a, 27–29.

13 de Grummond, 2006a, 175–180.

14 The scene is saturated with Etruscan political and social content and Arnza should not be construed as a child playing with a bird, as recently argued (cited in Maggiani 2005, 65).

15 Van der Meer, 1987; Maggiani 1982.

16 Nougayrol 1955; Rasmussen 2003.

17 Basic is Thulin 1968. For the various names of books see especially 1–12. See also de Grummond 2006a. In spite of Thulin's masterly account, there is still no systematic critical treatment of the individual sources for our knowledge of the *Etrusca disciplina*. Phillips, 2006, 13–17, while reviewing ancient scholarship on Roman religion, mentions and evaluates a number of the authors who were writing on Etruscan religious matters.

18 What is perhaps in the end surprising is that there is little indication that the Etruscans practiced astrology in their systems of divination. Weinstock (1951) argued for such, but so far the evidence is indirect.

19 Cic. *de har. resp.* 37; Censor. *d.d. nat* 17; Serv. D. *Aen* 3.537 and 8.398.

20 Macrob. *Sat.* 3.7.2.

21 Cic. *de har. resp.* 25.

22 Cic. *de div.* 1.20.

23 Pliny *N.H.* 2.138.

24 Pliny *N.H.* 2.199.

25 Juven. 5.13.62.

26 Lucret. 6.381.

27 Amm. Marc. 17.10.2.

28 Thulin I, 3–4.

29 Mart. Cap. II. 157. Cf. Fulgentius *Serm.* 48; Isid. *Orig.* 8.9.34; Festus 359; Cic. *de div.* 2.50.

30 Serv. *Aen.* 8.398; Cic. *de div.* 1.72.

31 Serv. *Aen.* 8. 398; Macrob. *Sat.* 5.19.13.

32 Censor. 14.6 (*fatales*); Festus 285 (*rituales*).

33 Amm. Marc. 23.5.10.

34 Pliny, *NH* 10.37

35 *Leg.* 2.21.

36 Listed in MacBain 1982, 82–104, *passim.*

37 Rawson 1985, 303–315 is the best general coverage of divination in Rome during this period.

38 Rawson 1985, esp. 312–316; de Grummond, 2006, 3. On the *libri navales,* Thulin I, 11–12, quoting Vegetius, *Epit. rei militaris* 4.41.

39 Weinstock 1950 reviews the scraps of evidence and creates a coherent picture.

40 Turfa 2012 is basic. Rawson 1985, *passim* but esp. 309–312. Turfa, 2006a, 174–175.

41 Turfa, 2006a; Turfa 2012.

42 Thulin, III, 76–78. Rawson 1985, 28, 94; Heurgon, 228–229, 233. de Grummond, 2006a, 2.

43 De Grummond, 2006a, 30–31 and de Grummond and Simon, Appendix B, 191–192.

44 Rosenberg 2011, 293 gives a date for Julius Obsequens in the fourth century CE. MacBain 1982. Peter L. Schmidt, s.v. "Obsequens, Julius." *Brill's New Pauly.*

45 Hohti 1975, esp. 427–429. Rawson 1985, 304–305.

46 Schofield 1986, 49 (quoting Rawson).

47 Weinstock 1951, esp. 124–125.

48 *De div.*, tr.

49 Wardle 2006, 282 (quoting Briquel).

50 For other passages in Dionysius that are relevant, see Thulin I, 7. and Vaahtera 2001, 113, 117–122. The other Greek historian noted for recording relevant information on Etruscan divination is Plutarch (ca. 46–120 CE), who as a priest at Delphi had a natural interest in religious practice. Thulin 1909, 7, 21, 67. For evaluation of the usefulness of Greek historical writing as source material for Etruscan religion, see Vaahtera 2001.

51 McBain 1982.

52 Of course, they must always be read as creative reconstructions of Etruscan culture. For some key examples, see de Grummond, 2006a, 3, 197–198, 208–211.

53 *NH* 10.28, 30, 33, 35–49; de Grummond, 2006a, 41–42.

54 Weinstock 1951, 123.

55 *QN* 2.32, 39, 41, 45, 47, etc; de Grummond and Simon, 2006, Appendix B, 214–215. Weinstock 1951.

56 K. Sallmann, s.v. "Censorinus," *Brill's New Pauly*, vol. 3, col. 105; Pfiffig, 1975, 159–160.

57 F. Mora, s.v. "Arnobius," *Brill's New Pauly*, 2, cols 17–18.

58 W. Suerbaum, s.v. "Servius," *Brill's New Pauly* 13, cols 333–335.

59 *De nuptiis* 1.45–61. See de Grummond 2006a, 44–46.

60 *De div.* 2.18.42. See also van der Meer 1987, 27–29.

61 Definitively published and discussed in Turfa 2012.

62 The earliest evidence for augury known to me appears in a bronze statuette of a priestly figure looking up toward the heavens, probably in an act of augury: Cristofani 1985, 267 (no. 39; ca. 500–480 BCE); de Grummond 2005, 307. Roncalli 2010, 124–125, contextualizes a gold ring bezel (likely dating to the 6th century BCE) as having a divinatory significance, perhaps showing the practice of *lekanomanteia*, another technique shared between Mesopotamia and Etruria.

63 Rochberg 2004, 3–4, notes the relevance of the phrase of A. L. Oppenheim, "stream of tradition," in regard to Mesopotamian transmission of omen texts from Sumerian and Akkadian times down to the Neo-Assyrian and Neo-Babylonian phases.

64 Starr 1983, 1, 5, 108–109, referring to the great library of Ashurbanipal at Nineveh, where the divinatory texts are proportionately the largest body of material.

65 Rathje 1979.

66 Burkert 1992, 41–42.

67 Related in the second century BCE by Gellius. Small 1982, 45–46.

68 Turfa 2012, Chapter 10.

69 Burkert 1992, 46–48; Rasmussen 2003, 135 and notes 196–197; Annus 2010, 11. For examples of Babylonian model livers, see Nougayrol 1955.

70 Maggiani 2005, 57; Starr 1983, 15.

71 Burkert 1992, 46, 181; Flower 2008, 33–34; Rasmussen 2003, 137.

72 Koch-Westenhoff, 51–52. The term *Manzāzu*, is sometimes translated as "Station," but is better understood to mean "the Presence."

73 Nougayrol 1955; Maggiani 1982, 85.

74 Oppenheim 1977, 196; Starr 1983, 44–45; Rasmussen 2003, 138.

75 Rochberg 2010.

76 Turfa 2012, part II.

77 Turfa 2012, Chapter 10, brings up numerous comparanda for the concerns of the omens from the Near East but, as she notes, there is no Eastern brontoscopic calendar that matches

closely the calendar of Nigidius Figulus. The vitality of the tradition evolving outside of Mesopotamia is clear.

78 Maggiani 2005, 57–58; Liv. 27.26.13–14; Pliny *N.H.* 11.189.

79 Pliny *N.H.* 11.189.

80 Thus the historical Etruscan augur Arruns in Lucan 1.626, obviously alluding to Caesar and Pompey.

81 Maggiani 2005, 58; Pliny *N.H.* 11.195.

82 Torelli 2005.

83 Once again the Near Eastern parallels are not lacking. It has been shown convincingly that the *lituus* has striking parallels in Mesopotamia, Syria and Anatolia: Ambos and Krauskopf 2010. Near Eastern usage of the curved wand in orientation, however, does not seem to have been demonstrated.

84 Haack 2006. Cf review by Turfa, 2006b.

85 Note the famous Trajanic relief in which the sacrificed bull lies on its back as the officiants examine the protruding entrails. Beard, North and Price 1998, II, 178–179.

86 See Collins 2008, especially 319 and 324. He notes, however, that there were nuances in the interpretation depending on color, texture and presence or absence of features such as the caudate lobe.

87 In general see Thulin, III, 106–115; Pfiffig 1975, 150–152; Schilling 1992, 94–97; Maggiani 2005, 65–66; Capdeville, forthcoming.

88 West 1997, 46–47; Flower 2008, 25, 51, 78–79, 90–91.

89 *Iliad* 1.69; *Odyssey* 15.525–34; Aesch. *Prometheus* 484–99.

90 *De div.* 1.107–108. The dispute is not so easily resolved in Livy 1.6.4.

91 Linderski 1986; Schilling 1992, 94–96.

92 *TLE*, 807, 810, 821, 835.

93 Steingräber 1984, 289, Tomba degli Auguri (Augurs); 299–300, Tomb della Caccia e Pesca (Hunting and Fishing); and especially 315–316, Tomba dei Giocolieri (Jugglers), which depicts a pair of black birds flying toward an unusual plant and a scene of a man defecating, all most likely referencing an omen.

94 Roncalli 2010, 123.

95 Maggiani 2005, 66–69.

96 Roncalli 2010, 122–124.

97 de Grummond 2002.

98 Oppenheim 1977, 207–209.

BIBLIOGRAPHY

Ambos, C. and Krauskopf, I. (2010) "The Curved Staff in the Ancient Near East as a Predecessor of the Etruscan *lituus*" in L. B. van der Meer (ed.), *Material Aspects of Etruscan Religion, BABesch, Annual Papers on Mediterranean Archaeology*, Suppl. 16. Leuven: Peeters, 127–153.

Annus, A. (2010) "On the Beginnings and Continuities of Omen Sciences in the Ancient World" in A. Annus (ed.), *Divination and Interpretation of Signs in the Ancient World.* Chicago: University of Chicago, 1–18.

Beard, M., North, J. and Price, S. (1998) *Religions of Rome.* Cambridge: Cambridge University Press.

Bonfante, Larissa (2006) "Etruscan Inscriptions and Etruscan Religion" in N. T. de Grummond and E. Simon (eds), *The Religion of the Etruscans*, Austin: University of Texas Press, 9–26.

Burkert, W. (1992) *The Orientalizing Revolution: Near Eastern Influence on Greek Culture in the Early Archaic Age.* Cambridge, Mass.: Harvard University Press.

Buranelli, F. (1992) *The Etruscans, Legacy of a Lost Civilization,* N. T. de Grummond (ed. and tr.). Memphis: Wonders.

Capdeville, G. (forthcoming) "L'uccello nella divinazione in Italia centrale" in A. Ancillotti (ed.), *Forme e strutture della religione nell'Italia mediana antica, Atti del III Convegno Internazionale dell'Istituto di Ricerche e Documentazione sugli Antichi Umbri*.

Collins, D. (2008) "Mapping the Entrails," *AJP* 129 : 319–345.

de Grummond, N. T. (2002) "Mirrors, Marriage and Mysteries," *JRA, Supplement* 47, 63–85.

——(2005) "Roman Favor and Etruscan Thuflthas: A Note on Propertius 4.2.34," *Ancient West and East* 4.2, 296–317.

——(2006a) *Etruscan Myth, Sacred History and Legend*. Philadelphia: University Museum of Anthropology and Archaeology.

——(2006b) "Prophets and Priests" in N. T. de Grummond and E. Simon (eds), *The Religion of the Etruscans*. Austin: University of Texas Press, 27–44.

——(2011) "A Barbarian Myth? The Case of the Talking Head" in L. Bonfante (ed.), *The Barbarians of Ancient Europe: Realities and Interactions*. Cambridge: Cambridge UP, 313–345.

ET (1991) H. Rix *et al.*, *Etruskische Texte. Editio minor. I: Einleitung, Konkordanz, Indices; II: Texte*. Tübingen.

Flower, M. A. (2008). *The Seer in Ancient Greece*. Berkeley: University of California Press.

Haack, M. L. (2006) *Prosopographie des haruspices romains. Biblioteca di Studi Etruschi* 42. Pisa and Rome: Istituto Nazionale di Studi Etruschi ed Italici, Istituti Editoriali e Poligrafici Internazionali.

Hohti, P. (1975) "Aulus Caecina, the Volaterran, Romanization of an Etruscan" in *Studies in the Romanization of Etruria. Acta Instituti Finlandiae*, 5. Rome: Bardi: 409–433.

Koch-Westenhoff, U. (2000) *Babylonian Liver Omens: The Chapters Manzāzu, Padānu and Pān tākalti of the Babylonian Extispicy Series Mainly from Aššurbanipal's Library*. Copenhagen: Museum Tusculanum Press.

Linderski, J. (1986) "The Augural Law," *ANRW* II.16.3, 2147–2312.

MacBain, B. (1982) *Prodigy and Expiation: A Study in Religion and Politics in Republican Rome*. Brussels: Collection Latomus, 177.

Maggiani, A. (1989) "Immagini di aruspici" in *Atti del Secondo Congresso Internazionale Etrusco, Florence 26 May–2 June 1985*, vol. *III* (Supplemento di *Studi Etruschi*) 1557–1563.

——(2005) "La divinazione in Etruria" in *ThesCRA*, III. Los Angeles: The J. Paul Getty Museum: 52–78.

Nougayrol, J. (1955) "Les rapportes des haruspicines étrusque et assyro-babylonienne et le foie d'argile Falerii Veteres (Villa Giulia 3786)." *CRAI*: 509–20.

Oppenheim, A. L. (1977) *Ancient Mesopotamia, Portrait of a Dead Civilization*. Chicago: University of Chicago Press.

Pfiffig, A. (1975) *Religio etrusca*. Graz: Akademische Druck-u. Verlagsanstalt.

Phillips, C. R., III. (2007) "Approaching Roman Religion: the Case for *Wissenschaftsgeschichte*" in J. Rupke (ed.), *A Companion to Roman Religion*. Blackwell.

Rathje, A. (1979) "Oriental Imports in Etruria in the Eight and Seventh centuries B.C.: Their Origins and Implications" in D. and F. R. Ridgway (eds), *Italy before the Romans, The Iron Age, Orientalizing and Etruscan Periods*, London, 145–183.

Rasmussen, S. W. (2003) *Public Portents in Republican Rome*. Rome: L'Erma di Bretschneider.

Rawson, Elizabeth (1985) *Intellectual Life in the Late Roman Republic*. London: Duckworth.

Rochberg, F. (2004) *The Heavenly Writing, Divination, Horoscopy, and Astronomy in Mesopotamian Culture*. Cambridge: Cambridge University Press.

——(2010) "'If P, then Q': Form and Reasoning in Babylonian Divination" in A. Annus (ed.), *Divination and Interpretation of Signs in the Ancient World*. Chicago: University of Chicago. 19–27.

Roncalli, F. (2010) "Between Divination and Magic: Role, Gesture and Instruments of the Etruscan Haruspex" in L. B. van der Meer (ed.), *Material Aspects of Etruscan Religion, BABesch, Annual Papers on Mediterranean Archaeology*, Suppl. 16. Leuven: Peeters, 117–126.

Rosenberg, V. (2011) "Republican Nobiles: Controlling the Res Publica" in J. Rüpke (ed.), *A Companion to Roman Religion*. N.p.: Wiley-Blackwell, 292–303.

Schofield, M. (1986) "Cicero for and against Divination." *JRS* 76, 47–65.

Small, J. P. (1982) *Cacus and Marsyas in Etrusco-Roman Legend*. Princeton: Princeton University Press.

Starr, I. (1983) *The Rituals of the Diviner. Bibliotheca Mesopotamica*. 12. Malibu: Undena Publications.

Steingräber, S. (1984) *Catalogo ragionato della pittura etrusca*. Milan: Editoriale Jaca Book.

Swoboda, A. (1964) *P. Nigidii Figuli Operum Reliquiae*. Amsterdam: A.M. Hakkert.

TLE (1968) *Testimonia Linguae Etruscae*, M. Pallottino (ed.) Editio Altera. Florence: "La Nuova Italia" Editrice.

Torelli, M. (1986) "La religione" in M. Pallottino *et al.* (eds), *Rasenna, Storia e civiltà degli etruschi*, Milan: Scheiwiller, 159–237.

——(2005) "Templum" in *ThesCRA*, IV. Los Angeles: The J. Paul Getty Museum, 340–347.

Turfa, J. M. (2006a). "The Etruscan Brontoscopic Calendar," Appendix A in N. T. de Grummond and E. Simon (eds) *The Religion of the Etruscans*. Austin: University of Texas Press, 173–190.

——(2006b) Review of M-L. Haack, *Prosopographie des haruspices romains*. *BMCR*, 12.34. Available at: <http://bmcr.brynmawr.edu/2006/2006-12-34.html>.

——(2012) *Divining the Etruscan World, The Brontoscopic Calendar and Religious Practice*. Cambridge: Cambridge University Press.

Thulin, C. O. (1968) *Die Etruskische Disciplin*. Repr. of I. *Die Blitzlehre* (1905); II. *Die Haruspicin* (1906); III. *Die Ritualbücher und zur Geschichte und Organisation der Haruspices* (1909). Darmstadt: Wissenschaftliche Buchgesellschaft.

Vaahtera, J. (2001) *Roman Augural Lore in Greek Historiography, A Study of the Theory and Terminology*. Historia Einzelschriften 156. Stuttgart.

van der Meer, L. B. (1987) *The Bronze Liver of Piacenza, A Polytheistic Structure*. Amsterdam: J. C. Gieben.

Wardle, D. (2006) *Cicero on Divination*. Oxford: Clarendon Press.

Weinstock, S. (1946) "Martianus Capella and the Cosmic System of the Etruscans," *Journal of Roman Studies* 36, 101–129.

——(1950) "C. Fonteius Capito and the 'Libri Tagetici'," *PBSR* 18, 44–49.

——(1951) "Libri fulgurales," *PBSR* 19, 122–153.

West, M. L. (1997) *The East Face of Helicon*. Oxford: Clarendon Press.

CHAPTER TWENTY SEVEN

RELIGION: THE GODS AND THE PLACES

———·◆·———

Ingrid Edlund-Berry

There is no spring that is not sacred (*Nullus enim fons non sacer*, Servius *Aen.* 7.84).

Springs are an important part of the Etruscan landscape, as are rivers, hills and mountains, valleys and plains, forests and groves, and, as far as we can tell, each could serve as a place of worship under divine protection.[1] The deities were known by name, and their sphere of power was carefully defined in the sky and on earth, as shown on the Piacenza liver and in the text of Martianus Capella.[2]

To the Romans this all-encompassing practice of defining sacred space was known as *Etrusca disciplina*, and as puzzled as they were by all the rituals observed by their neighbors and rivals, many such traditions were absorbed into Roman religion, including the desire to negotiate with the deities about the future through observations of signs in the sky and through sacrifices. In the process, many names of Greek, Etruscan, Latin, and Italic deities became assimilated, while in each culture the gods and goddesses maintained their own identity and their specific places of worship.[3]

In examining the sacred places within the geographic area dominated by Etruscan culture from the Iron Age into the Roman Republic, it is clear that the Etruscans, identified primarily through their non-Indo-European language and certain cultural characteristics in terms of habitations, art, and trade, shared much with their neighbors in other parts of Italy. While certain practices may be common to all or most of ancient Italy, there are also significant differences between individual Etruscan sanctuaries, and any general statement of what the Etruscans did or believed usually needs to be qualified with specific examples.[4]

Although Etruscan speakers lived as far north as the Po valley and as far south as Campania, the area considered the homeland of Etruscan culture ranges from the river Arno in the north to the Tiber in the east and south.[5] Bordering areas such as Umbria and Latium display many Etruscan cultural features, and Rome in particular shows a cultural affinity with Etruria, documented by the reign of Etruscan kings in the seventh and sixth centuries BC, but questioned by many who prefer to see Rome as mainly part of Latium.[6]

Within Etruria proper, the mountain ranges of the Apennines mark the spine of the peninsula, and accentuate the valleys crossing from west to east. In addition to long stretches of mountainous areas, isolated mountaintops such as Monte Falterona, Monte Giovi, and Mount Soracte provide a visual link between the earth and the skies, and, as can be expected, provide evidence of ancient places of worship. Others, such as the majestic Monte Amiata, of volcanic origin, create a focal point between north and south Etruria, and may have served as central gathering places (Fig. 27.1).[7]

With the exception of the Trasimene Lake, the lakes of Etruria (Lago di Bolsena, Lago di Vico, Lago di Chiusi, Lago di Bracciano) are formed from volcanic craters that stand out in the landscape (Fig. 27.2). Evidence of sanctuaries and votive offerings (statuettes) suggest that the borders of the lakes were considered sacred, and that the transition between land and water had to be protected.[8]

The main rivers of Etruria, which also defined its boundaries, are the Arno and the Tiber. Smaller rivers (Ombrone, Marta, etc.) provided access to the Tyrrhenian sea, and

Figure 27.1   Monte Amiata. Photo: Ingrid Edlund-Berry.

Figure 27.2   Lago di Chiusi. Photo: Ingrid Edlund-Berry.

could also be perceived as boundaries between city territories (Fig. 27.3). Although river gods were prominent in both Greek and Roman religion, Etruscan cult places were most likely connected with the crossing of rivers rather than with the river itself.[9]

Roads fulfill an important function by providing connections between settlements, but they also provide transitions from within communities to the outside, including burial grounds. It is therefore to be expected that sacred places and offerings be placed at the point of entry or exit to a town or village, at the entry to burial grounds, or at the crossing of roads.[10]

Transhumance represents a form of travel peculiar to Etruria as well as other areas of ancient Italy. Here, the herds of animals dictated the rules of passage, and places of rituals therefore could include stops along the way at holy cleansing waters, at sulphur springs, or at other points of healing.[11]

The Etruscans were feared at sea, but on land the sanctuaries that faced the sea were also very much part of the inland communities (for example, Pyrgi, the harbor town of Caere/Cerveteri). Most settlements were located away from the sea, with the exception of harbors and smaller outposts. As points of entry for foreign traders, such outposts (for example, Gravisca) provided an influx of non-Etruscan cults that co-existed with the local cults.[12]

Regardless of location, the sacred places chosen by the Etruscans were planned in accordance with the demands on the location in relation to nature and to the habitations. Often difficult to document, but vital for our understanding of Etruscan sacred places and sanctuaries, is the relation between approach and access especially within larger sanctuaries with many different cult areas (for example, Pyrgi, Campo della Fiera, Tarquinia).[13] While studies have suggested that the orientation of temples was chosen because of the deities worshipped there, it seems that other factors played a role as well.[14] If one assumes that the front of a temple is the visual goal of a visitor, the Belvedere temple at Orvieto is turned towards someone coming from the city (Fig. 27.4), whereas both temples at Pyrgi are facing the sea and not the city (Caere/Cerveteri), which they represented.

Before the time of written documentation in the form of dedicatory inscriptions and other texts, we are completely dependent on the archaeological remains to identify the practices of the people who worshipped at sacred places in Etruria. Rituals such as

Figure 27.3   Tiber river. Photo: Ingrid Edlund-Berry.

Figure 27.4   Orvieto, Belvedere temple. Photo: Ingrid Edlund-Berry.

depositions of pottery and small objects, evidence for sacrifice, and even production of pottery or metals may suggest actions that continued for a long time in areas visited or inhabited from the Bronze Age into historic times. Even though it may be presumptuous to call these early inhabitants "Etruscans," their practices, and, in particular, the location of their practices, often coincide with later documented Etruscan sanctuaries, as seen, for example, at Pian di Civita in the ancient city of Tarquinia.[15]

Sacred places in nature did not depend on any particular group of people, language, or culture, and seem to have existed from the time of the first human presence in ancient Italy. While caves and springs provide essential shelter and water for both people and animals, they were also used as the sites for deposits of modest offerings of pottery or metals. Landmarks such as mountains and hilltops give travelers direction, but are also connecting points between the land and the heavens, and become centers of worship (for example, Mount Soracte, Fig. 27.5).

As the Etruscans (and their Iron Age predecessors) settled throughout Etruria, the places chosen were for the most part on isolated hilltops or on clusters of hills. Some of these may already have been considered sacred, but as settlements they became equipped with places of worship within the urban community. While we traditionally think of Etruscan sanctuaries as dominated by temples (see below), an urban sacred place (sanctuary) could be identified by the presence of votive offerings or an altar, perhaps as a remnant of a sacred place in nature.[16]

Because of the location of Etruscan settlements, the natural formation of a hilltop provided an obvious boundary or defense against that which is outside and not belonging to the community. Where the natural boundary did not exist or needed to be further accentuated, manmade walls with gates provided a visual (as well as strategic) point of transition, and as such came under the divine protection of extramural sanctuaries.[17] Such sanctuaries were placed in close proximity to the city boundaries, and could range in form from a temple complex (Portonaccio temple at Veii) to places for votive offerings.

As defined by the landscape or by smaller settlements, major Etruscan cities included a surrounding territory with extra-urban sanctuaries that were politically and culturally dependent on the city. These included the roadside sanctuaries that served various

Figure 27.5 Mount Soracte. Photo: Ingrid Edlund-Berry.

different functions, whether to protect travelers and trade or to provide a ritual passage from the community of the living to the burial ground outside the city. Within the burial ground, rituals could be performed around the tomb, but also at funerary shrines for the cult of a deity (Cannicella sanctuary at Orvieto).[18]

To the extent that the ties between a city and an extra-urban sanctuary can be defined, the territory of any given Etruscan city also contained rural sanctuaries. While for practical purposes, any sanctuary located outside the city (for example, along the roads), could be considered "rural," a rural sanctuary proper would be one where the cult practices pertain to agriculture or animal husbandry (including transhumance).[19]

Depending on the location and function of the extra-urban and rural sanctuaries, they could serve to define and secure the boundaries for any given city. As such, they would guarantee safe travels along the roads, safe crossings of rivers and mountains, and perhaps control trade from one region to another.

But, in addition to the need for establishing and maintaining boundaries, the Etruscan cities also recognized that collaboration between groups of cities could require distinct gathering places for political purposes but obviously under divine protection. Such "political sanctuaries" included the Fanum Voltumnae, probably to be identified with the sanctuary at Campo della Fiera, just south of modern Orvieto. Since in principle all sanctuaries could serve as centers for gatherings as part of the cult rituals, there are no absolute criteria for how a sanctuary would rank as "political," whether the location or layout, and considering the overall assumption that in Etruria all aspects of human activity must be under divine protection, it is possible that places such as Lucus Feroniae or the monumental building at Poggio Civitate were used for assemblies of a political (as well as religious) nature.[20]

In spite of the fact that our knowledge of Etruscan sanctuaries is limited by the preservation of material remains, it is noteworthy that no two sanctuaries are alike. Whether due to preservation or original plan, the appearance of sanctuaries varied from isolated votive deposits, altars, and modest small buildings of different functions, to a network of sacred spaces within or outside a community (as documented at, for example, Vulci, Arezzo, or Civita Castellana) or major complexes, usually extramural or extra-urban, with one or more temples, other buildings, a number of altars, areas for votive offerings (as documented at, for example, Pyrgi, the Portonaccio temple at Veii, and Campo della Fiera at Orvieto). In some cases, there were a number of sacred spaces other than temples (for example, at Gravisca), but usually the sanctuary was identified by its main architectural feature, the temple.[21]

Our appreciation of Etruscan temples is usually determined by Vitruvius's description of the ideal features of a Tuscan temple. Only when we realize that what Vitruvius describes is an abstract image of what he saw in his own time (during the reign of Augustus) and what might have existed some five hundred years earlier, hence the use of *Tuscanicus*, which refers to something "Tuscan-like," not actually Tuscan or Etruscan.[22]

Regarded as houses for the deities, temples were a common but not required part of an Etruscan sanctuary. Like other markers of sacred activity such as altars or votive deposits they were located within the setting of nature or in relation to a habitation (urban, extramural, extra-urban etc.), but are unfortunately often studied out of context.

As described by Vitruvius, the Tuscan temple was a squarish building (with the proportions 6:5 in length and width, *de arch.* 4.7) with one or more rooms (*cellae*) for the cult statues of the deities in the back, and a colonnade towards the front. The rooms could consist of a central wider *cella*, with a narrower room or open wing (*ala*) on either side. The number of columns varied, both at the front and along the sides, and sometimes also the back. The temple was placed on a podium resting on the below ground foundations, and was accessed by steps at the front.

Although it seems to be every archaeologist's dream to unearth a temple that fits all the criteria proposed by Vitruvius, the truth is that Vitruvius himself provides a caveat to his ideal plan by stating that temples be designed according to the rituals of each deity (*de arch.* 4.8.6). Furthermore, as can be expected, even during the peak of Etruscan culture in the seventh-early fifth centuries BC no two buildings are identical, and even by the time Etruscan and Roman architectural traditions had merged in the third century BC and later, local variations were the norm.

A brief overview of reasonably well-preserved temples from Etruria proper shows much variety in plan and execution. The late Archaic Portonaccio temple at Veii, famous for its terracotta roof statues of Apollo and other deities, has a square floor plan and is usually reconstructed with three *cellae*, whereas the slightly earlier temple B at Pyrgi (510 BC) is peripteral and with only one main *cella*. The main urban temple at Vulci (early fifth century BC) also has one *cella*, whereas the later temple A at Pyrgi (470–460 BC) is tripartite, like the temple at Fontanile di Legnisina (fifth-fourth century BC) and the Belvedere temple at Orvieto (fifth century BC). Some temples were remodeled, such as the monumental Ara della Regina temple at Tarquinia, which was expanded and the floor plan changed during the many phases of its history (sixth-third centuries BC) with rooms added to the original interior. Others such as the temple at Fiesole (fourth-third century BC) maintained their original plan with one *cella* and flanking *alae*. Although Vitruvius described podia, many Etruscan temples were placed fairly close to the ground, with some notable exceptions such as the Ara della Regina temple at Tarquinia.[23]

When viewed in an urban context or as part of large extramural or extra-urban sanctuaries rather than as isolated buildings, Etruscan temples play an integral role in the rituals connected with the deity or deities worshipped. As Vitruvius points out, the temples should be oriented in such as way that worshippers be able to view the cult statue with the eastern sky as a backdrop (*de arch.* 4.5), and the columns spaced in such a way that there be enough space for the matrons (*matres familiarum, de arch.* 3.3.2) to be able to walk up towards the *cella* with the cult statue.

The temples thus served as the space connecting the deities with their worshippers who also participated in the rituals at the altar (not always oriented in the same direction as the temple and often in a different location in the sanctuary such as at the Portonaccio temple at Veii) and witnessed the observation of the signs performed by the especially assigned priests in their designated inaugurated space (*templum*). All of these activities were further coordinated with the deposition of votive offerings, and probably processions with music that entered the sanctuary space winding their way towards the perceived center, whether the main temple, altar, or other important area.

For Vitruvius, there was a distinction between the Etruscan/Tuscan land and "Tuscan-like" architecture. For us today, modern Tuscany is very different from ancient Etruria, yet the spirit of the Etruscan gods and their places is very much present. Even where hotels, factories and highways dot the landscape, the distinctions in nature between mountain tops and valleys, the transitions between farmland and city, and the roads connecting as well as separating communities remind us of the close interaction between human activity and topography. While we may no longer attribute our actions to the wishes of the ancient deities, we owe the continuity of settlements and appreciation of the land to the Etruscans and their *Etrusca disciplina*.

NOTES

1   Etruscan deities tend to seem abstract and aloof. The Etruscan landscape, on the other hand, is real and demands our close attention and appreciation (Edlund 1987). The images included here serve as cues for readers abroad, but nothing can substitute the actual experience of the Tuscan land. I thank Jean Turfa for suggesting the topic, and Beth Chichester (Department of Classics, The University of Texas at Austin) for her expert help in preparing the images for publication.

2   De Grummond and Simon 2006.

3   See Chapters 24 and 25.

4   In the following discussion, the term "sacred place" refers to any location where there is evidence of an ancient (Etruscan) cult, whether an isolated offering, an altar or a building. "Sanctuaries" refer to locations that preserve more elaborate features such as precincts, temples or other buildings, or altars. If we focus on the relation between the place and its function for religious rituals, a "sacred place" tends to emphasize the overall setting in nature, whereas a "sanctuary" focuses on the manmade features. It is noteworthy that most textbooks on ancient architecture present the building (temple etc.) totally void of its context, including the approach and access.

5   Barker and Rasmussen 1998.

6   The degree to which Rome historically and culturally was part of Etruria continues to be a topic of intense debate (Cornell 1995). In particular, examples of early architecture in Rome (Capitoline temple, S. Omobono temples and architectural terracottas) may suggest that already in the Archaic period Rome had ambitions grander than those of her Etruscan neighbors (Hopkins 2010). I tend to believe that at least in the Archaic period, the architectural practices were quite similar, with local variations, in the area of Etruria and Latium, including Rome. For the sake of simplicity, I have included only examples from Etruria proper concerning the gods and the places.

7   Edlund 1987; Edlund-Berry 2006.

8   Giontella 2006 and 2012. The important contributions by Claudia Giontella will always be remembered as we mourn her death.

9   Edlund 1987; Edlund-Berry 2006.. For rivers serving as demarcation of boundaries, see also Campbell, 2012.

10 See Chapter 7 and Chapter 36.

11 See Frizell 2010.

12 See Chapters 29 and 30.

13 Meyers 2003. See Chapters 29–31.

14 Prayon 1997.

15 See Chapter 29.

16 Since the publication of Colonna 1985 and Edlund 1987, our knowledge of the Etruscan countryside and its sanctuaries has increased drastically. Thanks to surveys and excavations, it is now possible to evaluate the presence of sanctuaries at different locations in relation to the cities, see, for example, Zifferero 2005 for Caere/Cerveteri. Because of the complexity of the material, it seems still too early to evaluate all of rural Etruria, especially in consideration of the sacred places in nature.

17 For the walled cities of Etruria, see Camporeale 2008. The question of how the gates related to the visual and real approach and access from the countryside is still in need of continued study, see Edlund-Berry 2010 and also Chapter 35.

18 See Chapter 31.

19 See above, n. 17.

20 The issue of what constitutes a "sanctuary" rather than a civic or private building complex is very complicated, and the terminology varies greatly depending on the writer's perspective. I maintain that it is important to avoid imposing modern perspectives on ancient Etruscan religious and political systems for which we have such limited knowledge, see Edlund-Berry 2011, 8–10.

21 Colonna 2006.

22 See Chapter 35.

23 Colonna 2006.

BIBLIOGRAPHY

Barker, G. and Rasmussen, T. (1998) *The Etruscans*, Oxford: Blackwell.

Campbell, B. (2012) *Rivers and the Power of ancient Rome*, Chapel Hill, NC: The University of North Carolina Press.

Camporeale, G. (ed.) (2008) *La città murata in Etruria. Atti del XXV convegno di Studi Etruschi ed Italici*, Pisa and Rome: Fabrizio Serra editore.

Colonna, G. (ed.) (1985) *Santuari d'Etruria*, Milan: Electa.

Colonna, G. (2006) "Sacred Architecture and the Religion of the Etruscans" in N. T. de Grummond and E. Simon (eds) *The Religion of the Etruscans*, Austin, TX: University of Texas Press, 132–168.

Cornell, T. J. (1995) *The Beginnings of Rome*, London and New York: Routledge.

de Grummond, N. T. and Simon, E. (eds) (2006) *The Religion of the Etruscans*, Austin, TX: University of Texas Press.

Edlund, I. E. M. (1987) *The Gods and the Place. Location and Function of Sanctuaries in the Countryside of Etruria and Magna Graecia (700–400 B.C.)*, Stockholm: Paul Åströms förlag.

Edlund-Berry, I. (2010) "Öppen eller stängd? Den etruskiska stadsporten som kontaktpunkt och gränsmarkör för stad och landsbygd" in F. Faegersten, J. Wallensten and I. Östenberg (eds) *Tankemönster. En festskrift till Eva Rystedt*, Lund: Faegersten, 45–52.

——(2011) "Introduction" in N. T. de Grummond and I. Edlund-Berry (eds), *The Archaeology of Sanctuaries and Ritual in Etruria*, Portsmouth RI: Journal of Roman Archaeology, 7–15.

Edlund-Berry, I. E. M. (2006) "Ritual Space and Boundaries in Etruscan Religion" in N. T. de Grummond and E. Simon (eds) *The Religion of the Etruscans*, Austin, TX: University of Texas Press, 116–131.

Frizell, B. S. (2010) *Lana, carne, latte. Paesaggi pastorali tra mito e realtà*, Florence: Mauro Pagliai.

Giontella, C. (2006) *I luoghi dell'acqua "divina." Complessi santuariali e forme devozionali in Etruria e Umbria fra epoca arcaica ed età romana*, Rome: Aracne.

Giontella, C. (2012) *"…nullus enim fons non sacer…": culti idrici di epoca preromana e romana (Regiones VI–VII)*, Pisa and Rome: Fabrizio Serra editore.

Hopkins, J. N. (2010) "The Topographical Transformation of Archaic Rome: A New Interpretation of Architecture and Geography in the Early City" unpublished PhD dissertation, The University of Texas at Austin.

Meyers, G. E. (2003) "Etrusco-Italic Monumental Architectural Space from the Iron Age to the Archaic Period: An Examination of Approach and Access" unpublished PhD dissertation, The University of Texas at Austin.

Prayon, F. (1997) "Sur l'orientation des édifices cultuels" in F. Gaultier and D. Briquel (eds) *Les Étrusques, les plus religieux des hommes. État de la recherche sur la religion étrusque*, Paris: La Documentation française, 357–371.

Zifferero, A. (2005) "La formazione del tessuto rurale nell'agro cerite: una proposta di lettura" in O. Paoletti and G. Camporeale (eds) *Dinamiche di sviluppo delle città nell'Etruria meridionale: Veio, Caere, Tarquinia, Vulci. Atti del XXIII convegno di Studi Etruschi ed Italici*, Pisa and Rome: Istituti editoriali e poligrafici internazionali, 257–272.

CHAPTER TWENTY EIGHT

ETRUSCAN RELIGIOUS RITUALS: THE ARCHAEOLOGICAL EVIDENCE

———— •◆• ————

Simona Rafanelli

As I begin this short route through the customs and ritual religious practices adopted and implemented by the Etruscans, I would like to echo the words with which Gregory Warden opened his contribution on "Remains of the Ritual at the Sanctuary of Poggio Colla," asserting that "Ritual is a physical manifestation of belief, but a ritual is also an action,"[1] and more specifically, as he emphasized in 2011, it is a type of action by its nature "performative, repetitive and reproducible,"[2] and for this reason permeated by physicality and temporality, although its broader meaning, i.e. the intersection between action and belief, cuts the bonds of time and space, managing to put the human element in connection with the divine. What remains of this action, the material outcome of the ritual, is indeed that "*sacro detrito*," the "sacred debris," on which the attention of scholars has been more and more frequently focused, aroused by the growing accumulation of data derived from surveys of excavations conducted in sacred spaces of the sanctuaries and necropoleis of the Etruscans.[3]

THE SACRED STRUCTURES: THE ALTARS

Located within funerary areas or sanctuary sites, the altar represents the center of the sacrificial action, for it is in the killing, in the bloody violence, synthesized in the image of the altar stained with blood[4] where, at the peak of religious exaltation and of the sacredness of the ritual, the contact of man with divinity is resolved.

In accordance with what N. T. de Grummond has very recently observed, it is sufficient to cast a glance at the rapid succession of typological classifications of Etruscan sacred structures developed in recent years,[5] to understand how the study of the documentation fails to proceed in parallel with the fast-paced series of new discoveries.[6]

The exploration of the large Etruscan cultic complexes and sanctuaries of Tarquinia (Ara della Regina and La Civita: see Chapter 29) and of Pyrgi (monumental sanctuary and southern area: see Chapter 30), alongside that of the sacred areas of smaller places, identified among the so-called "rural sanctuaries" or "boundary sanctuaries" like those of Cetamura del Chianti and of Poggio Colla, has shown and continued to provide outstanding results for the progress of our knowledge about the ritual practices of the Etruscans. Yet it is the documentary category of altars that is unquestionably the main archaeological evidence of ritual activity.[7] It has received the greatest increase thanks to the identification of a discrete number of "precarious" sacred structures which have led us to further define the character of those ancient structures dating back to an era pre-dating that of Numa, known from the literary sources as the *"temporaria de caespite altaria."*[8]

"Primitive" altars, raised at first with sods of earth, and gradually replaced with piles of stones, their appearance would have reflected that provided by the image of such a mound reproduced on the side of the sarcophagus of Torre San Severo (Orvieto) with the sacrifice of Polyxena at the hands of Achilles.[9] It takes on tangible form, apart from the "provisional" altar of cobblestones identified in the sanctuary of Gravisca,[10] in the altars of sub-circular/elliptical/rectangular plan recognized in structures "ζ" (Zeta), "ι" (Iota) and "ν" (Nu) of the southern area at Pyrgi,[11] which, under the aspect of ideology and cult, refer to the so-called "lenses of clay" of the "monumental complex" of La Civita at Tarquinia,[12] and in the Hellenistic altar No. 2 of Cetamura del Chianti, which can be compared not only to the Pyrgi altars, but also to those found in the sanctuary of Piana del Lago (Montefiascone) on Lake Bolsena.[13]

On the other hand, like the "precarious" cult structures, from the category of permanent altars that could be called "canonical" due to types already known with rectangular plan/ with *antae* and superstructure of rectilinear profile, sometimes with crowning moldings, or with an entirely molded profile[14] (Fig. 28.1), an articulation with moldings that seems to respond to an entirely Etruscan tradition,[15] the picture has been progressively enriched with new acquisitions furnished by the excavation of Campo della Fiera near Orvieto[16] (see Chapter 31), which scholars now almost unanimously tend to recognize as the *Fanum Voltumnae* celebrated by the Latin sources. In particular, the structure "with double

Figure 28.1   Painted clay plaque. Paris, Louvre, Campana Collection S 4034. From Cerveteri, Necropoli della Banditaccia. 530 BC (after Roncalli 1965, tav. 3).

opposed echinus and abacus" reconstructed through the recovery of an inverted ashlar block to form a "monumental molded altar," variously interpreted as a cult structure or an offering table to hold bronze votives, by virtue of the presence of holes in the flat upper surface of the top element, expands the "hourglass" type of altar widely documented in iconographic representations (Fig. 28.2).[17]

In the extremely varied typological framework of Etruscan altars documented between the Archaic and Late Hellenistic periods,[18] the variety of altar is determined mainly by the different combinations of a traditionally circular/rectangular plan, either a Greek "T-shaped" or a Greek *"in antis"* plan, with rectilinear superstructure or articulated in the peculiar shape of a pair of chiastically recurved moldings of Etruscan inspiration. A special mention, for the ritual implications inherent in the structure, is due to the type of altar in the version with *antae*, with a U-shaped abacus on the top, recognized in the altar described in the ritual text of the *Tabulae Iguvinae*, where the term *ereçlo* designates the protected space prepared to receive the sacrificial fire for the cooking of the meats butchered on the surface of the abacus.[19] The actual examples of this type, admirably represented by the altars of the Sanctuary of the Thirteen Altars of *Lavinium* and by the two altars of the Sacred Area of S. Omobono at Rome,[20] seem to be recognized, in the Etruscan sphere, in the foundations of the altars with *antae* of the sanctuaries of Veii-Portonaccio and S. Marinella-Punta della Vipera, and perhaps in the small rural sanctuary of Grasceta dei Cavallari in the Monti della Tolfa and, in a funerary context, in the vicinity of the Tumulus of the Cuccumella at Vulci.[21]

In the sanctuary of Campo della Fiera, an altar for sacrifices has been identified with a monolithic altar with square base, inverted echinus, and fascia with cavetto and abacus[22] comparable to type c2 of the crowning molding of the cube-tombs (*tombe a dado*) of Sovana[23] and, among representational examples, with the low altar toward which a

Figure 28.2   Mirror in bronze. Florence, Museo Archeologico Nazionale, inv. n. 646. From *Praeneste*. End of sixth century BC (after Rafanelli 2004, 153, no. 127)

personage is leaning in the process of sacrificing a bird on a sardonyx gem preserved in Vienna.[24] To this may be added, in the same Orvietan sanctuary, two other altars with inverted echinus profile, one of which[25] is comparable for shape and dimensions, to an example from the necropolis sanctuary of the Cannicella, with lower recesses,[26] already defined as a sort of altar chopping-block very likely reserved for operations in the killing and butchering of the body of the animal victim.[27]

In the framework of the classification of altars proposed by Colonna (2006), a form of monumental structure, provided with elements associated with a catachthonic cult, such as channels, pits, holes, pipes and conduits is identifiable now with a single construction, as in the case of the altar in the sanctuary of Punta della Vipera (S. Marinella) in the Caeretan countryside, now with a complex cultic apparatus formed by the association of a "pierced" altar, and an altar constructed above ground, wells, bases for offerings, which are attested in Etruria within sanctuary precincts, as shown by the examples from Area C of Pyrgi or by the sacred area with the "precinct" of the Veian sanctuary of Portonaccio.[28] These would actually constitute a kind of open-air worship, passed down in literary sources in the dual formulation of the *"loca sine tecto diis sacrata"*[29] or of the *"locus parvus deo sacratus cum ara."*[30] In the extreme variety of typological variations thereon, such cultic reality would come to include monumental "podia" with T-shaped plan and rectilinear/molded profile, like the structures "B" and "D" of the sanctuary on the Acropolis of Marzabotto, already fortunately defined, also by Colonna, as a "self-sufficient unit of worship,"[31] capable of combining planimetric elements drawn from the Greek world (T-shaped plan, etc.) with Etruscan structural elements and cultic valences. With a certain degree of probability, we may assign them respectively to a cult devoted to the celestial gods (altar "D") and to Underworld/chthonic gods (altar "B"); the two "podia" seem to lend reason to that ambivalence of destination, *"urania/infera"* ("heavenly/underworld"), already emphasized,[32] that seems to characterize, from the Archaic period on, the above-ground Etruscan cultic structures corresponding to the Greek *bomos* (raised altar),[33] also located in sanctuary and funerary contexts and assignable to divinities and cults labeled either celestial or subterranean.

As regards sanctuary spaces, structures related to chthonic/underworld cults[34] are recognizable, in addition to the structures mentioned above, in the nenfro block of truncated conical shape, with a small cavity, situated within the sacred area of Pian di Civita at Tarquinia, near the entrance to area "γ" (Gamma), and compared by Bagnasco Gianni[35] with the two stone blocks, also provided with cavities and a gutter, placed in the *sacellum* ("chapel") "γ" (Gamma) of Pyrgi, interpreted as altars[36] and ritually connected to *bothros* "ε" (Epsilon). In the sanctuary of Cetamura,[37] Altar 1, identified in an irregular, tetragonal platform of large, rough stones and presumably related to the NW channel prepared to convey offerings of a liquid nature into the natural cavity opening into the rocky bank (cf. the cultic structural complex constructed at the Civita site at Tarquinia in connection with the natural cavity there[38]), exhibits, on its flattened upper surface, a circular depression perhaps used for the same sort of cultic procedures.

A similar variety of shapes and sizes, accompanied by an equal semantic-functional complexity, recurs, always in the presence of elements such as conduits, channels, etc. in the structures used for the cult of the dead and for the catachthonic gods, in those contexts where the actual use of the monument within burial areas, or the contiguous relationship of the structure with the tomb construction, openly declares their funerary connotation.

Operationally assimilated to the "podia" of Marzabotto, altar "λ" (Lambda) of the sanctuary in the southern area of Pyrgi seems to furnish a valid parallel to the so-called "great" altar found at Populonia, in the area of the necropolis discovered very recently on the Gulf of Baratti, below sea-level, along with other buildings dating from the final decades of the seventh century and the beginning of the sixth century BC, interpreted as structures associated with cults honoring chthonic deities in whose sphere the dedication of arms plays an important part.[39]

If today the imposing altar/base for display of cippi erected in the cult space/stepped theatral area of the Grotta Porcina,[40] near the monumental tumulus of the necropolis, continues to represent a *unicum* in the context of Etruscan Archaic funerary architecture, it is, on the other hand, possible to recognize within the funerary context, a sort of thread of continuity in the implementation of a particular type of cult structure that, in conforming to the same formal and conceptual principal, leads from the so-called terrace-altars with stepped access in the Orientalizing and Archaic eras, related to the tumuli of the Caeretan, Florentine, Cortona complexes, passing through the cultic platforms of the Viterbo hinterland (Tuscania, Pian di Mola; San Giuliano, Tumulo Cima) and the crowning structures of the cube-tombs of *Etruria rupestre* (the cliff-regions of southern Etruria, Norchia, Castel d'Asso, Blera, Sovana),[41] up to that peculiar class of monuments concentrated in the same areas as the rock-cut tombs, and variously defined as "pyramidal stepped monuments,"[42] (Fig. 28.3) capable of combining in the same structural unit the double value of funerary monument and structure for worship,[43] which can be deduced from the considerable figural documentation, enriched in recent times by the latest evidence.[44]

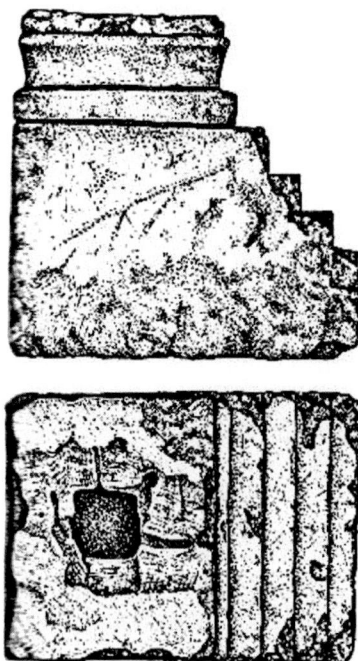

Figure 28.3   Funerary cippus in peperino. Graphic relief (plan and profile to scale 1:5), made by architect Marica Rafanelli. Vulci, Castello dell'Abbadia, *Antiquarium*.
First decades of third century BC (rilievo arch. Marica Rafanelli).

THE BLOODY OFFERING: THE ANIMAL VICTIMS, THE GODS, THE PURPOSES OF SACRIFICE

The detailed analysis of necropolis contexts, among which those of Pontecagnano and of Verucchio,[45] have in recent times permitted us to deepen the meaning and content of a second major category of archaeological evidence, represented by abundant finds of bones furnished by cult areas which, in the reconstruction of ceremonial behavior, serve to accompany and support the evidence of the altars, and more generally, of the structures designed for the performance of ritual activities. Passing over the vast field of evidence furnished by the innumerable, mold-made offerings that are distinctly north-Etruscan or Etruscan-Latin-Campanian that comprise the deposits of ex-votos, predominantly of bronze in the first group, and of terracotta in the latter, which have become the subjects of thematic studies[46] and of individual in-depth contributions like that of Jean Turfa,[47] I wish to concentrate on that which Ingrid Edlund-Berry has defined as one of "the two most important ritual activities,"[48] represented by a particular meaning of offering to the gods, conceived as the offering of the flesh and organs of the animal victim, inseparably associated with the libation of the blood of the sacrificed animal and of non-bloody liquids derived from the vegetable and animal world (wine, cereals, milk, etc.)

The contribution of new data acquired from the analysis of offerings derived from the vegetable and animal kingdoms has formed the subject of an important study-meeting held in Tarquinia in 2003,[49] specifically of accurate observation of the bone remains and the remains of non-bloody offerings found in the sanctuary areas of Pyrgi,[50] Tarquinia,[51] Poggio Colla,[52] Cetamura del Chianti,[53] Campo della Fiera[54] and from funerary contexts at Pontecagnano[55] and Verucchio.[56] These studies complement the extensive and increasing masses of data collected by Luigi Donati under the heading of "Sacrifice in the Etruscan World,"[57] which already included in preliminary notice, some of the data provided by excavations carried out in the Sanctuaries of the Acropolis of Volterra[58] and of Ortaglia, in Volterran territory.[59]

Among the most important results of these analyses, there is the apparent confirmation of the presence, in the context of bloody sacrificial offerings, of some peculiar species, such as tortoises, edible and non-edible fish, molluscs, birds, foxes, badgers, etc…alongside categories of domestic and wild animals that are well represented, such as cattle, pigs, sheep/goats, deer, dogs, horses.

It appears difficult to understand the identity of the deities worshipped in a specific sacred area (sanctuary or funerary), beginning with an analysis of the osteological finds recovered there, both for the still elusive contours of the various divine personages of the Etrusco-Italic pantheon and for the hybrid nature of these, sometimes agglutinating and taking on the attributes, appearance or spheres of action of multiple divinities that seem more traditionally distinct within the better known Greek pantheon, or on the contrary replicated in an unknown number of different cultic hypostases.[60] Nevertheless, the repeated occurrence of the same species of animal victim in similar ritual contexts, or the evident repetition of the same ritualized modalities of killing the animal, or any correlation with specific types of cult structures[61] permit us to make some inferences primarily on the nature of the cult practice in the sacred area, whether celestial or underworld/chthonic.

The largest portion of an ox, sacrificed and deposited in a single act, as distinct from that of deposition in jars filled with remains of plants and animals of other species, in the so-called "repeated deposit" of the Civita site at Tarquinia,[62] ultimately underscores the value of "*hostia sacrificalis princeps*" ("foremost sacrificial victim") covered by a domestic species that, because of its market value and above all the importance derived from its role as a man's "companion in work," expressed in the agricultural activity of the "ox-as-ploughman," represented in every respect a type of offering of great value in the context of the sanctuary. The same value was to be bestowed in funerary spaces, as shown by the analysis of ritual contexts furnished in the necropolis of Verucchio,[63] where whole animals, cattle, horses and sheep/goats, were placed to mark the outer limits of the necropolis, or to divide individual groups of burials; they come to assume the significance of offerings of consecration of the area. The same objective of consecration probably explains the eighteen heads of cattle, of which the skulls and jaws are preserved, found along the so-called "alignment" that marked the northern limit of the sanctuary in the southern area of Pyrgi.[64]

The rare figural representations of sacrifice, with some plausibility related to the funerary sphere[65] (Fig. 28.4), seem in fact to show a predilection for this victim *par excellence*, in which we might recognize one of the "*certae hostiae*" ("certain victims") that were offered in sacrifice to "*certis diis*" ("certain gods") that allowed the souls of the dead to achieve immortality (Arnobius 2.62)[66] and to transform them into the *Dii animales* ("Spirit gods") identified by Servius with the Penates and the Viales (they are the Lares Viales, the gods who protected the country-streets) of the Romans (Servius *Ad Aen.* 3.168)[67]. On the other hand, when confronted with the abundant bone remains of domestic species such as cattle, sheep/goats, pigs, furnished by sanctuary areas, it is more difficult to recognize representations of this type of location (sanctuary areas) in the sphere of figural images, where any desire to set a sacrificial scene within a sanctuary is entrusted simply to a few iconic and highly suggestive signs, such as columns or pilasters surmounted by large vases (Fig. 28.5).[68]

The prevalence of one domestic species over another, within a ritual context, would seem in fact to direct attention toward a different divine recipient of the offering of the animal victim; on the basis of comparison with the Greek paradigm, it would seem permissible to recognize this divine recipient, in the case of the so-called "monumental complex" at Pian di Civita of Tarquinia, wherein the offering of sheep/goats prevails, in a goddess of chthonic valence, called by the epithet of *Uni* in the Orientalizing period,[69] capable of assuming eastern values in the guise of *Uni-Astarte* (the Phoenician *Ishtar*),[70] also venerated in the northern sanctuary of Pyrgi,[71] to whom the offering of a tortoise is well suited, the remains of which were also found in the sanctuary of Ortaglia, in the Volterran countryside, and in that of the Acropolis of Volterra.[72]

Figure 28.4   Etrusco-Corinthian krater of the "Gobbi." Painter of the "Knotted Tails." Cerveteri, Museo Archeologico, inv. no. 19539. From Caere. 590–570 BC (after Martelli 1987: 291)

On the other hand, the sacrifice of sheep is also well suited for sacrificial rituals in honor of gods such as Dis Pater, to whom it is perhaps permissible to ascribe the ceremonies practiced in the sanctuaries of the Acropoleis of Marzabotto and of Volterra, respectively, in the monumental podium structure "B," also interpreted as a *mundus*, and in the sacred area that seems to qualify as the primitive cultic nucleus of the city. Sheep are also appropriate to a Tinia imbued with underworld-chthonic connotations like the one worshiped in Area C of Pyrgi, or in the Orvietan Belvedere sanctuary, where the dedication incised on a *poculum* (drinking cup), repeats the *epiclesis* (invocation) of the god Calusna.

Widely documented in ritual, sanctuary and funerary contexts,[77] the offering of *ovis vel capra* ("sheep or goat" – whose bones cannot be differentiated in most archaeological contexts) must also represent in the Etruscan world the most common and recurring type of animal sacrifice, where the title of "*hostia sacrificalis princeps*," already postulated for the ox in terms of the honor and value of the victim and thus of the greater rarity and quality of the offering, could be attributed to this domestic species based on its exact opposite in the domestic economy, because of the relative cheapness and widespread availability of the animal, used primarily for human food and a wide range of ritual destinations. If in fact the species of sheep/goat, in combination with cattle and pigs, formed the core of the principal sacrificial procedures known in official Roman ceremonies like that of the *suovetaurilia*, the data obtained from the analysis of osteological finds in the context of sanctuary and burial complexes seem to deliver, with the prevalence of these species over others domestic or wild, a direct confirmation of the appearance of the famous "triptych" in Etruscan ritual as well. This predominance of sheep/goats seems to be reflected in the figural documentation, in which the representation of *ovis vel capra* occurs on a conspicuous number of monuments[78] and in different contexts, sometimes ascribable to the private and/or funerary sphere, as perhaps seems to occur in the scene of sacrifice of a sheep near a *naiskos* at the end of a sacred(?) *pompe* (procession), on the front panel of an urn in London (British Museum D69).[79] Other times, it is linked, by virtue of the presence of a person sacrificing in the costume of a priest, to the sphere of public ceremonies very probably occurring in a sanctuary.[80]

A propitiatory/celebratory intent, tinged with shades of initiation, would seem to be found in the sacrificial scene reproduced on the front of the black-figure amphora in the Museum of Dresden (Fig. 28.6),[81] that displays a male figure engaged in an armed dance within the framework of a religious festival[82] in honor of a god with Dionysian traits, in which the purpose of the celebration is in keeping with the presumed initiation value of

Figure 28.5   Black figure hydria. Eagle Painter. Copenhagen, Nat. Mus. 13567. From Caere. 530–520 BC (after Hemelrijk, J. M. (1984) Caeretan Hydriae: 29–30 n. 15 tavv. 67–69.

Figure 28.6   Black-figure amphora. Gruppo Vaticano 265/Gruppo Monaco 883.
Dresden, Skulpturenslg. ZV 1653. First quarter of the fifth century BC. (After Martelli 1992:
342–346, pls. 73, 3–4; 74).

the Pyrrhic dance,[83] a kind of sacrifice intended to honor a deity who is positioned to assist the "passage" of a male individual from the state of adolescent athlete/ephebe into the essential condition of a mature man, integrated into society. Precise correspondences with the model offered by the Greek *thusia*, generally characterized by the double intention of propitiation and mantic (prophetic) rite,[84] are revealed in the sacrificial ritual depicted on the shoulder of the "Ricci *Hydria*,"[85] where the floral framing of the *temenos* with ivy and grapevines, the same species of victims, especially the goat, together with the altar-*bomos* surmounted by burning flames,[86] in the presence of the priest and in the staging of the sequence of operations required to fulfill the sacrificial ritual of bloody and bloodless offerings, seem to betray the official character of the ceremony, set in the space of a sacred area *"en plein air"* and the destination of the rite, for a divine person with Dionysian traits.

The frequent use of the sheep as an expiatory victim, along with pigs and dogs, is partly substantiated by the documentation relating to the Latin rites of expiation of lightning, carried out by the Etruscan haruspex through the offering of a sheep with just two infant teeth, called *bidens*, from which the name was given to the place struck by lightning, called *bidental*.[87] The diffusion of this ritual custom, going back to Etruria and marked, according to Livy, by the execution of *"quaedam occulta solemnia sacrificia"* (Livy 1.31), only partly takes into account the prominent position likely held in Etruria by the expiatory sacrifices. This hypothesis would seem to be supported by the same analogy, often found within the "neighboring" Italic-Iguvine and Roman ritual setting, where every manifestation of abnormal phenomenon (*portentum*) and every mistake made during the course of the ritual demanded a prompt expiation and reparation.

Not too dissimilar from the sacrifices of expiation of lightning were those for the placing of a so-called border-marker and the so-called "foundation" sacrifices, both involved in equal measure, with elements of offering and consecration. If the indirect Latin sources preserve, in the legend of the *sulcus primigenius* ("first-born furrow") ploughed by Romulus during the foundation of Rome, the memory of Etruscan ritual sacrifice, ending with the propitiatory sacrifice of the bovine team yoked to the plough, then the bones of pigs/sheep found in a jar in *edificio* "α" (Alpha) of Gravisca, along with the remains of plants and a roasting spit,[88] testify to the fact that the rituals involving blood sacrifice of the victim were associated with vegetable offerings. The ritual use of the jars, also intended for the cooking of the *exta* (internal organs) of the sacrificed animals (*exta aulicocta*)[89] is widely documented in the sacred area of the Civita at Tarquinia, where the only "repeated deposit"[90] has furnished numerous examples of cooked vegetable and animal offerings, to which are added the two impasto jars found in the so-called "area α,"[91] under the Archaic wall; they contained the remains of a foundation deposit,[92] including burnt fish bones and bones of a piglet.

Consistent with the primary role that in Etruria must have imbued the sacrifices with an expiatory character, and rituals of foundation marked by the same value, there are numerous small animal victims alongside the sheep in these contexts, represented mainly by dogs, foxes and suckling piglets.

The excavations conducted in the last decade in the sanctuary areas of Pian di Civita in Tarquinia, in the so-called "monumental complex,"[93] and at Ortaglia[94] have furthered the documentation of the use of foxes as sacrificial victims, designated, as with the wolf/dog[95] and the piglet, with a specific value justifying their use in expiatory ritual. This is proven in the field of art by the reproduction of these animals designated for the infernal deities, as in the case of the Cortona bronze figurine depicting a canid,[96] with an inscription containing the name of the god.[97] To the skeletal remains already noted of a dog and piglet found "whole" in the main shrine at Pyrgi, in the wells placed respectively in front of Temple A and in Sacred Area C,[98] and perhaps related – like the structures – to the divine figure of *Uni-Eileithyia* and to a chthonic *Tinia*, and to [the bones] of foxes found in the same Caeretan sanctuary,[99] we may add the remains of canids found in the well in the sanctuary of Ortaglia and in the "monumental complex" of Tarquinia – La Civita,[100] and the remains of complete skeletons of foxes recovered from the well of the sanctuary at Ortaglia and in the same Tarquinian "monumental complex,"[101] as well as the remains of pigs and piglets from the same contexts.[102]

The pig was widely used in foundation sacrifices, as evidenced by the finds in the Sanctuary of the Acropolis of Volterra,[103] and especially those recovered inside Area "α" (Alpha) of Tarquinia – La Civita,[104] where, in the votive deposits, there is recorded the distinct predominance of the remains of pigs over those of sheep/goats. A suckling pig, in particular, seems to constitute the offering more likely to fulfill that custom very deeply rooted in the Etruscan religious system,[105] represented by the ritualized construction of boundary-walls, the precepts of which, useful to separate from profane space entire or partial buildings and to regulate "the foundation and consecration of cities, altars, temples" (Festus 285 L. "*quo ritu condantur urbes, arae, aedes sacrentur*"), had to be preserved at the heart of the *Libri Rituales* ("Books of Rituals") of the *Etrusca Disciplina*.[106]

The concept of the sacredness of the structure, together with that of the sacredness of the individual, both achieved through the same religious ritual of consecration, deeply interrelated, dominates, in Warden's opinion,[107] ancient religious ideology during the entire first millennium BC, inserting the man and the structure into the same circular path that leads inexorably from construction to destruction and to burial in the context of a process marked by stages shared by the two identities, human and structural.

In the Sanctuary of Poggio Colla, near a cylindrical stone element, variously understood as a column or altar, there came to light in 2006 a bronze bowl filled with pig bones and resting on more bones of the same species, in relation to which one would like to recognize a sacrifice of purification, in terms of a parallelism that may be established between funerary practice, where the body of the individual is returned to the earth through rituals that purify, placate and sanction the end of the life cycle, and the so-called "deposit of inscription" that associates the sacrifice of the piglet, characterized by the same ritual finality, with the burial of the bases of statues and of altars. Accumulation of purificatory, expiatory, propitiatory valences, and the species of swine, notably in the form of a suckling piglet, present its candidature as an appropriate animal victim recurring in sacrificial rituals marked by such purposes and intended for a divine personage also characterized by chthonic and cata-chthonic/infernal connotations.

To the divine catachthonic couple, *Dis Pater – Ceres* we may assign respectively the offerings of sheep/goats and swine, to which may be added those of rooster and tortoise for the female deity with strong Demetriac values, widely attested in the sanctuary of the Acropolis of Volterra,[108] assimilated by virtue of the presence of *oikoi*, courtyards, *bothroi*, vases turned upside down and buried, vessels for the pressing of vegetal offerings (wine?), but above all of pierced clay pipes for conveying liquid offerings, bloody and bloodless, into the depths of the earth, at the Orvietan sanctuary of the Cannicella, also sacred to Demeter/Vei, at the Veian Campetti sanctuary, attributed to the same goddess, and, in Siceliote territory, to the Demeter sanctuary of the *Malophoros* at Selinus (Sicily).

The link to a cult of Demeter-Ceres seems apparent also in the rural sanctuary of Cetamura del Chianti, where the occurrence of newborn piglets and puppies[109] in two open refuse pits in the naturally rocky hillside, in full consonance with the ritual evidence that characterizes the sacred area of Pian di Civita at Tarquinia, since the end of the Bronze Age centered on the centrality of worship at the so-called natural cavity, reveals the sacrality of the same rocky plain, beyond the scope of the expiatory and purificatory character of the ritual actions.[110]

IMAGES AND RITUALS

"A sacrificial ritual is defined exclusively, differentiated from the others, in relation to the combination of gestures that make up its internal structure, implemented according to an order and precise arrangements, primarily involving differential treatment of the object sacrificed."[111]

Formulated by Jean Rudhardt about the Greek world, these observations show in even greater extent their validity when applied to the Etruscan sacrificial sphere, where the overall assessment of real and pictorial documentation has highlighted the difficulty of identifying the various sacrificial types on the basis of victim, equipment and altar used in the sacred action. If in fact the possible correlation of a raised altar, surmounted by flames, with an infernal-chthonic deity prevents establishing a fixed relationship between the altar-*bomos* and the celestial divinity, the indiscriminate use of the same instruments of death for the different animal species sacrificed, or the presence of crowns and flutes in all types of context (funerary or not), also precludes the establishment of a clear correspondence between a particular sacrificial rite and the categories of "objects" both animate and inanimate involved in ritual action. Ignoring the nature of the latter, the specific appearance assumed by a rite will depend therefore on the modes and forms of their combination and interaction within the ritual, which vary depending on the purpose pursued by the action of sacrifice. Apart from defining the types of sacrifice, the attempt to grasp the various purposes proposed for the fulfillment of the sacrificial rite becomes fundamental, determining the intrinsic configuration of the ritual act.

The uncertainty of the data provided by the residues of plant and animal offerings is well suited to the words of J. P. Vernant: "If the remains of the ritual are silent...we may ask what the images and the myth are telling us."[112] It is precisely the analysis of the figural representations that, in the Etruscan world, generates the attempt to reconstruct the sacrificial ritual in the different stages that, within a rigid and previously established order, ought to lead, from the selection of the animal to be allocated for sacrifice, to its ritual killing, preceded and followed by the series of operations associated with the bloodless offering.[113] Then comes the yet more complex objective, to seek to locate the main purposes, thus, the typologies of the sacrifice.

The analysis of some figured documents, probably linked to the sphere of cult and more specifically of funerary ritual practices, allows us to explore this ritual "path," tentatively proposing a "reconstruction" and trying to shed light on the nature and on the values of some divine figures chiefly related to the infernal-funerary sphere.[114] An example for illustration is a red-figure *oinochoe* in the Museo Nazionale Etrusco di Villa Giulia (Fig. 28.7a-c).[115]

The scene depicted on the body of this Vulcian *oinochoe* reproduces, in a kind of synoptic and synthetic representation, the sequence of the bloody rite to be performed at the end of the *pompè* (procession), by which the offerings have been performed near the place of sacrifice, at the moment of suspension (*epochè*) that precedes the killing of the victim in proximity to the altar and the libation of the bloodless offerings before and after the shedding of the victim's blood and the cooking of its flesh.[116]

Essential to the formulation of an exegetical hypothesis for the sacrificial rite represented, would seem to be the small bloodless offerings deposited on the top of the *trapeza* (table) to the side of the altar: the triangular outline of these items[117] suggests, in fact, an immediate comparison to those small pyramid-shaped flour-concoctions known in Greek sacrificial ritual.

The protagonist of the bloody act, identified primarily because of his knife, although it is devoid of a specific priestly connotation,[118] would take on the double role of sacrificer (*sacrificante*), understood as one who directs the sacrificial ceremony, and that of the one killing (*sacrificatore*), the *magheiros*, who materially carries out the killing of the victim.[119]

Figure 28.7a-c   Etruscan *oinochoe* in overpainted red figure. Rome, Museo Nazionale Etrusco di Villa Giulia, inv. no. 63649. From Vulci, Osteria necropolis, tomb no. 52 (Scavi Mengarelli 1925–34). Middle of the fourth century BC. (After Rafanelli 2009, figs. 1–4).

"Presentation" of the victim[120] to the divinity in front of the altar, bloodless libations that precede and follow the immolation of the animal and the offering of its flesh, constitute a ritual sequence that seems to be supported by the recent interpretation furnished by H. Rix of the "parallel rituals" of the *Liber Linteus* of Zagreb ("Linen Book," see Chapter 22),[121] where the "presentation" of the victim to the god precedes in fact the prescription for the bloodless offering of *vinum* (wine) and of *fase* (*polta?* "cakes"?) and the killing of the animal victim, in similar fashion to that illustrated in the *Tabulae Iguvinae* (the bronze *Tablets of Gubbio*)[122] and to what we learn from the reading of the descriptions of sacrificial ceremonies in contemporary Greece.[123]

Also concerning the instruments of death, in parallel with what happens in the contemporary Greek and Roman spheres, the knife or the short sword represent the weapons generally used for victims of small and medium size,[124] cut down while standing or atop the altar, once freed from the constraints of the rope with which the animal is bound and led in the ritual procession up to the place of sacrifice.

The animal victim, ultimately destined for sacrifice, identifiable as a deer, could well form part of a funerary ritual devoted to a god of the Underworld, consistent with the provenance of the *oinochoe* from a tomb. If the association of the animal with Hermes in other Etruscan figural documents[125] fits the scope of a funerary sacrifice on the basis of the god's psychopompic abilities (able to lead souls to the Afterlife), on the other hand the association of the deer with other gods with chthonic aspects, such as the infernal Apollo, assimilated precociously to *Šuri* in the Etruscan world, or a funerary *Dionysos*, may be validated by the appearance of other "secondary" elements in the figured representation.[126]

The funerary provenance of the vase could therefore endorse the eschatological meaning of the representation of the sacrificial rite, correlated to the initiational dimension of a *Dionysos Baccheios* attested at Vulci[127] by vase inscriptions since 460 BC and understood as the god who liberates one from the chains of death through initiation into his Mysteries.

The species of the victim, a piglet, the *katharmos par excellence* in Greek civilization,[128] (Fig. 28.8) as in Roman-Italic culture, and the sacrificial animal most closely connected

Figure 28.8 Mirror in bronze. Philadelphia, University of Pennsylvania Museum inv. No. MS 5444. Second half of the fourth century BC. (Courtesy of the University of Pennsylvania Museum; drawing by permission of the artist, R.D. De Puma, *CSE* U.S.A. 4: no. 34).

to the divine personages of *Dionysos-Bacchus* and *Demeter-Ceres-Vei*, depicted on the side of a kalyx-krater (inv. 4112) in the Florence Museo Archeologico (Fig. 28.9),[129] directs the vector of research toward the particularly cathartic sphere of the mystery cult. The origin of the krater in the territory of Vulci, a venue in the Late Classical era for Dionysiac mysteries, is corroborated further by iconographic subjects found in other vases of this pictorial group. The Maenads with *thyrsus* and *Charun* with his hammer lead us to the Dionysian hopes for an afterlife and the Bacchic procession; *Charun* is the ultimate protagonist of the *anodos* of the deceased, who will be "awakened" in the Underworld and initiated into a "new" life." The entire figured decoration of a bell-krater from the necropolis of Aleria[130] would also fit within a horizon filled with the same mysterious "spirit"; it juxtaposes to the winged female personage making a sacrifice, and provided with deerskin, candelabrum and instruments for libation, the reverse scene, interpreted mythologically as the liberation of *Peirithöos* from Hades and from tortures inflicted by infernal monsters. The evidence of the appeal to the Dionysiac eschatological message, comes in the feminine figure of a *Vanth,* wearing the *nebris* (fawn-skin) of the Maenads, who reconciled the fear of death with the belief in the "eternal" life of the soul.

To the cult, likewise imbued with mystical elements, of an infernal-chthonic goddess with traits of Demeter, or to that, equally catachthonic, addressed to the *Manes* (in Rome, chthonic gods, equated with departed souls) of the deceased, one could easily relate the sacrificial representation displayed on the front of Volterran urn no. 212 of the Museo Guarnacci (Fig. 28.10).[131] "*Naiskos*" with blazing fire, piglet, bloodless offerings of grains, liquids and incense, alluded to by the jug and *cistae* introduced into the scene by participants in the ritual, appear to be correlated equally with funerary or Demeter-ritual, where the blood of the victim, besides placating the spirit of the dead, would purify the members of the family, washing away every impurity derived from contact with the pestilential *miasma* of death. On the other hand, to a Demeter both chthonic and funerary, probably recipient of the sacrifice depicted on the Etruscan urn, the Romans used to sacrifice, a "*porca praesentanea*," "*familiae purgandae causa*" (a "sow for the purpose of purifying the family") near the tomb of the deceased.

Figure 28.9 Black-figure krater. Berlin Funnel Group Painter. Florence, Museo Archeologico Nazionale, inv. no 4112. Second half of the fourth century BC. (After Del Chiaro 1974, no 4, tav. 5).

Figure 28.10 Cinerary urn in tufo. Volterra, Museo Etrusco Guarnacci, inv. no. 212. Second half of the second century BC (after *CUE* II 1, 176 n. 240).

Funeral sacrifices addressed to the souls of the dead and to an infernal-chthonic *Dionysos*, are probably recognizable in the sacrificial friezes reproduced on the *Plikasna* situla, on the funerary *cippus* from Perugia and on the panels of the Chiusine sarcophagus in the Louvre,[132] regarding, in the last two cases in particular, monuments strictly connected with the funerary sphere. Characterized by a purpose distinct from the merely purificatory-expiatory or simply propitiatory, the sacrificial rituals presented in these monuments were thus aimed specifically at satisfying the catachthonic gods and at "restoring" the dead to life through the conjoined action of sacrifice, music and dance. Perfectly interrelated within the ritual, in equal measure, were blood sacrifice, orchestral choruses, the sound of the flute, ritual armed combat, each in the specificity of their expressive language, in "recalling" to life. This is the guiding principle of the whole funeral ceremony, which finds its main references in the divine persons of a *Ceres*, understood as a pan-Italic divinity, and of a *Dionysos* clad in the infernal-chthonic valences connected to the implications of rebirth and salvation.

Masterfully analyzed by I. Krauskopf,[133] the Etruscan dimension of the Afterlife, which formed the subject of the *Libri Acheruntici*, on whose contents only the passages of Arnobius and Servius mentioned above can throw any light, was marked ever since as the oldest conception of Etruscan funerary ideology by elements symbolic of passage identifiable in the doors depicted on wall frescoes in the tombs of Tarquinia, or symbolic of boundary, detected, for example, in the Tomb of the Blue Demons, in the representation of the boat and the cliffs placed so as to close at its two ends the journey made by the deceased, in that sort of interim space between the World of the Living and the Kingdom of the Dead, identified by Krauskopf (2006: 773–76) with a sort of Antechamber of Hades (*vestibulum Orci*). Within what we might almost interpret as a space of "return," the deceased could, assimilated *post mortem* to the divine figures of the twin sons of Zeus, guardians and guides of the dead in their passage between the two "worlds," through the implementation of certain sacrificial rituals cross back over the threshold of Hades in the direction of that "anteroom," sometimes located inside the burial chamber itself, in order to assist his family members and to receive the honors bestowed on him through certain ceremonies. The existence, proven by the passages in ancient authors, of particular sacrificial rites capable of ensuring the attainment of immortality, even deification, by departed souls may substantiate the possible occurrence of different rituals, alongside those of expiatory-purificatory and propitiatory character, intended to appease the "wrath" of the dead, and aimed at infusing new strength and life-blood[134] into the souls of the departed, enabling them to reach the goal of the eternal banquet arranged in the Underworld, having survived a journey fraught with dangers and populated by monstrous demons.

Well-versed, with the aid of special structures or cultic equipment, in honor of the infernal-catachthonian gods or of the dead themselves, for the benefit of their souls, the offerings of blood more than any others had to have the power to "feed" and "reinvigorate" the spirits of those who had passed over, endowing them with the same principle of life. And it is in just this "unified revitalizing program," implemented by separate sacrificial rites, that it connects in itself the multiplicity of forms and designs of Etruscan funerary cult, with connotations of the initiatory and mystery valences in the Dionysiac tradition,[135] carried out mainly through the blood-offering, intended to placate with blood the eternal and inextinguishable "thirst" of the souls of the dead.

RITUAL AND SIGNIFICANCE

Building on that sort of "mystical finality"[136] that seems to spring from the analysis of the well-known passage of Seneca (*Quaest.Nat.* 2.32.2),[137] coming to permeate all aspects of the earthly and otherworldly life of the Etruscan people, we could therefore claim in this regard that the ritual, understood as religious practice that underlies every action – and which is itself a performative action – punctuated each stage of the life journey of man, whether conceived as an individual or as a social community.[138] Warden's metaphor of the temple, identified as a "living thing,"[139] is extended to all elements, animate and inanimate, that make up the social, religious, ideological and political universe of the Etruscans, united by the fundamental moments of birth and death (of the end and the beginning), placed under the guardianship of one or more gods.[140]

The same principle of life understood, in line with the main Heracleitan philosophical principles, as a stream in motion of an eternal becoming, then as a continuous cycle of transformation, is inexorably marked by the stages in which this becoming is articulated, and each of these phases is accompanied by a ritual. Here van Gennep's rites of passage,[141] set free and at the same time validated by the two stages of birth and inevitable death, ratify and regulate all forms of passage, and surging to the parameters with which the whole life process of becoming is unified. The offering itself, in the dual and often complementary form of bloodless and bloody offering, is accomplished according to a precise and unalterable sequence of steps and operations to which its progress and its outcome are shackled. The "closed" and chained mechanism of the ritual procedure, the ordering principle of the rite itself, becomes at the same time, the director and guarantor before the deities, reflecting in the sacred action that same (divine) order that informs the cosmos.

Man and gods participate equally in the formation of that cosmos, where the sacred action elevates a key reading of the order based on the dialogue between man and god, of which the ritual, within which the offering is fulfilled, becomes the ineffable instrument of decoding. And it is "essentially in the scrupulous fidelity to the ritual and to the religious tradition" that comes to reveal itself, that "centrality of the sacred"[142] emerges solidly "in the Roman vision of the Etruscan culture" and that forms the principal characteristic of a people who, echoing the very famous words of Livy (5.1.6), "excelled in the art of cultivating religious practices."

NOTES

1   Warden 2009a: 107.
2   Warden 2011: 55.

3   See Collins-Elliot and Edlund-Berry 2011, for an updated view of the bibliography relative to the state of studies and discoveries concerning the Sanctuaries and, more broadly, the Etruscan sacred cultic areas.

4   Burkert 1983: 22–23.

5   Colonna 2006; Menichelli 2009.

6   See de Grummond, N. T. 2011b: 139, which emphasizes how the documentation of the typology of altars is being continually expanded.

7   See Edlund-Berry 2011: 11, where the scholar stresses that the altars and votive offerings constitute the two principal indications of ritual activity.

8   Tertulliano, *Apology* 24.

9   Colonna 2006: 136, Fig. VIII.9.

10 Rafanelli 2004, III.G.2.294: end of the sixth century BC.

11 Colonna 1994: 63 ss.; Colonna 2000: 251 ss.; Colonna 2006: 132 ss.; Colonna 2012: 213, Fig. 17.

12 Bonghi Jovino 2005: 74, with previous bibliography.

13 De Grummond 2011: 80–81; Colonna 2012: 213, Fig. 20.

14 See the peculiar outline of the altar depicted on the Campana plaque 4034 preserved in the Musée du Louvre: Roncalli 1965: 18–19, n. 3, pl. 3; Rafanelli 2004, III.E.2.a.221, with previous bibliography.

15 Cf. Edlund-Berry 2008; about the characteristic "Etruscan round," corresponding to a full half-round or to a quarter-round or oval, as seen in Stopponi 2011: 21, note 17; see Shoe Meritt and Edlund-Berry 2000.

16 Stopponi 2009: 425 ff.; Stopponi 2011: 16 ff. During the writing of the present book, *AnnFaina XIX* published "Il Fanum Voltumnae e I Santuari comunitari dell'Italia antica" (Orvieto 2012), to which I refer in a few notes here, that was entirely dedicated to the Orvietan sanctuary of Campo della Fiera and included important contributions on this topic by many scholars amongst whom are: S. Stopponi, G. Colonna, A. Frascarelli, B. Belelli Marchesini, C. Carlucci, M. D. Gentili, L. M. Michetti, *et al.*

17 Cf. among the *"realien,"* the altars of Pieve a Socana (fifth century BC) and of Fiesole (beginning of the third century BC), for which see Comella 2005: 166–168, IV.A. 4, 8, and, among figural representations, the altar reproduced on the mirror in Berlin and those represented on the amphora in Dresden, on the mirror in Florence, and on the stamnos in Boston, for which see Donati 2004, III.B.7, 127, 128, 133; see also Pieraccini 2011: 129–131, Figs 5–6. Speaking of the monumental structure of Campo della Fiera, see now Frascarelli 2012: 131–160, fig. 1–40.

18 On the altars, most recently, Comella 2005: 166–171; Colonna 2006; Menichelli 2009; cf. also Studnizka 1903: 123 ff.; Steingräber 1982: 103–119; Euwe-Beaufort 1985: 101 ff.; Roncalli 1987: 47–60; *idem* 1990: 229–243; Pianu 1991: 193–199, pls 55–56; Thuillier 1991: 243–247; Prayon 1997, 357–373; Steingräber 1997: 97–116.

19 Castagnoli 1959–1960: 153, note 23; *contra* Roncalli 1990: 108–109. TI (*Tabulae Iguvinae*) IV, 19; IV, 17: offerings *super ereçle* and *supu ereçle*.

20 See Castagnoli 1959–1960: 145 ff.; Coarelli 1984: 22–23; Cristofani 1990: 11 ff.; in particular, for the bibliography of the sacred area of Sant'Omobono, see Terrenato 19 *et al.* 2012.

21 For the altar of Veio-Portonaccio sanctuary, see Comella 2005: 166–169, IV.A.3; for the altar of S. Marinella-Punta della Vipera, see S. Stopponi in Colonna 1985: 149–154; for Grasceta dei Cavallari, see G. Gazzetti in Colonna 1985: 155–157; Colonna 2006: 148, VIII.26; for the altar near the Vulcian tumulus of the Cuccumella, see Chiesa 2005: 107.

22 Menichelli 2009: 110; Stopponi 2011: 28, Fig. 28.

23 For which cf. Maggiani 1978: 17, 20 ff., Fig. 15; Rafanelli 1997, 34, Figs 1–4.

24 Donati 2004, III.B.11, 177; Martini, *Ringsteinglyptik* 134 n. 29 tav. 8, 4.

25 Stopponi 2011: 21, Fig. 13.

26 Roncalli 1994, pl. VII, pp. 103–108.

27 Rafanelli 2004, III.G.2.297.

28 Colonna 1986: 102, 129. Sometimes built elevated or excavated entirely in the earth, the "perforated" (*forati*) altars could be associated with the altar-*bomos* completing complementary cults – burnt sacrifice and libation – as proven by the case of the emporium-sanctuary of Pyrgi, area "C" (Rafanelli 2004, III.G.2.298; Comella 2005: 166–169, IV.B.13), dedicated to a chthonic Tinia (Thuillier 1991, op.cit. *supra* note 18), and of the Veian sanctuary of the Portonaccio, with a sacred area dedicated to Menerva (Rafanelli 2004, III.G.2.299; Comella 2005: 166–169, IV.B.12). Cf. also the Caeretan sanctuary of Santa Marinella – Punta della Vipera. Comella 2005: 166–169, IV.B.17.

29 Festo, 318 L.

30 Gellio, 7, 12, 5.

31 Colonna 1985: 23.

32 Rafanelli 2004, III.D.2.a; III.G.2.295.

33 See Yavis, G., *Greek Altars* [1949] 43) for the Greek world. In the Etruscan world, the terms remain unknown that designated the various types of altars equivalent to the Greek terms of *bomos* (constructed altar), *eschara* (sacrificial trench), *bothros* (sacrificial well). The only exegetical hypothesis in this sense has been formulated for the term *spanti* ("plate": cf. LL: *spanza*, "small *spanti*"), interpreted by extension as the floor-area of the altar, based on comparison with the Umbrian ritual texts of the *Tabulae Iguvinae* (Castagnoli 1959–1960, *op. cit. supra* note 19; Colonna 1973–74: 132 ff.). The terms *spanthi/spante*, recurring in the *Tabula Cortonensis* (Agostiniani/Nicosia 2000) where they are translated as "in the floor/plain," have permitted us to hypothesize the existence of a term **span*, plain, from which *spanti* ("plate") would have been derived. The great antiquity of the term in Etruria and its deep roots in the structures of the Etruscan language would seem to exclude the hypothesis of an origin in the Umbrian language.

34 One seems to detect in the Hellenistic period a greater occurrence of canals/conduits in the sanctuary areas in contrast to funerary spaces: cf. the terracotta pipes in the sanctuary on the Volterran acropolis (for which see Bonamici 2005, 4–5).

35 Bagnasco Gianni 2005: 91, 95 ff.

36 Colonna 2006: 140, where the scholar defines the altars of the sacellum "γ" (cf. Comella 2005: 166–169, IV.B.15) as the simplified version of the *mensae* for libations and bloodless offerings intended for the domestic and funerary cult of the ancestors and offers in comparison, among other examples, the funerary altars found in the Caeretan tombs Campana 1 and Tomb of the Five Chairs and some stone blocks from the region of Orvieto. Found inside the tomb structures, the altars, so-called "*a cuppelle*" ("with hollowed cups") and "*a trono*" ("throne-type"), distributed through the valley of the Fiora and the region of Volsinii, represent a particular type of altar reserved for the funerary cult (Bloch 1955: 64–70), used near or within the burial place. These altars, of Archaic date, are found in the form of a simple slab, furnished with cup-like cavities and with little channels in the top surface, or in the form of a block hollowed across the front and top (Rafanelli 2004, III.G.2.301), associated with a second block placed vertically which gives it the shape of a throne. On the other hand, the Hellenistic so-called "pierced" ("*forati*") altars of the Volsinian territory (two at Bolsena of which one is lost: cf. Rafanelli 2004, III.G.2.300; two at Orvieto; one at Bagnoregio; see also Comella 2005: 166–169, IV.B.18–20) constitute in this context a peculiar class: they are small monuments in tufo, nenfro or peperino, a truncated-conical or truncated-pyramidal block crossed vertically by a channel, originally placed in the open in modest sacred areas. The presence of a dedicatory inscription (TLE 205) allows them to be connected with a catachthonic cult directed especially to Tinia, in his underworld-funerary aspect, but also to *Culsu*.

37 De Grummond 2011: 77 ss., 85–86.
38 Recently, Bonghi Jovino 2005: 73 ff.; see also Bonghi Jovino 1987: 59 ff.; *Tarchna* I.
39 Milletti *et al.* 2011 forthcoming.
40 Rafanelli 2004, III.D.2.b; III.G.2.296; Comella 2005: 166–168, 170, IV.C.29; Colonna 1993: 321–347; Steingräber 1997: 104 Fig. 3.
41 v. Steingräber 1982; Steingräber 2009: 123 ff.; Colonna 1986: 371–530; Colonna, G./ Colonna-Di Paolo, E. 1978 (Norchia); Maggiani 1978: 15 ff. (Sovana); Prayon 1975; Prayon 1985: 441 ff.; Zamarchi Grassi 1998: 19 ff. (Cortona).
42 Rafanelli 1997, 33–35; Rafanelli 2010 forthcoming; Steingräber and Prayon: 91–95; cf. the so-called *"ad ara"* monuments of Roman date: Colonna-Di Paolo 1984: 523–526.
43 Cf. Prayon 1985: 447–449. Some details allow us to clarify the nature of these extremely unusual monuments, which may be resolved in the function of the tomb and the funerary altar: we are dealing with steps, terraces, and built-in features on the top, presumably intended to house urns and funerary vases and for the sacrificial practice of libation (Colonna Di Paolo, E. 1984: 513–526). As well, the lack of remains of bones on the surface also seems to confirm a cultic practice directed toward employing the blood of the victim. Such an interpretation can be supported by the scene on the Gobbi krater (Donati 2004, II.16), where the patera (bowl) held by the female figure in the principal frieze alludes to the bloodless libation, while the sprinkling of blood is implied in the presence of the animal victim in the minor frieze who is being led in the direction of the stepped altar.
44 See Winter 2009: 451–452, 6.D.1.c., Ill. 6.14; Rafanelli 2010 forthcoming.
45 Bailo Modesti *et al.* 2005: 37 ff.; Von Eles 2005: 29 ff.
46 Comella-Mele 2005, Rendini, 2009.
47 Turfa 2006, with previous bibliography; Nagy 2011, with previous bibliography.
48 Edlund-Berry 2011, v. *supra* note 7.
49 Bonghi Jovino, Chiesa 2005.
50 Most recently, see Sorrentino 2005; cf. also Cardini, L. (1970) 616 ff.; Caloi, L./Palombo, M. R. (1988–1989), 131 ff.
51 Bonghi Jovino 2005, Chiesa 2005, Bagnasco Gianni 2005.
52 Warden 2009, 2011.
53 De Grummond 2011.
54 Stopponi 2009; 2011.
55 Bailo Modesti *et al.* 2005.
56 Von Eles 2005.
57 Donati 2004, III.B.
58 Bonamici 2005.
59 Bruni 2005.
60 Bonghi Jovino 2005: 82–83.
61 In the extreme difficulty of attributing a precise typology of altar to a specific divinity, it is possible to note a repeated association of the altar "with *antae*" with the goddess *Menerva*, as seems to be shown in the examples offered in the Etrusco-Latial region, by the sanctuaries of S. Marinella-Punta della Vipera, Veio-Portonaccio, *Lavinium*-Thirteen Altars, and Roma-S. Omobono.
62 Bagnasco Gianni 2005: 92 ff.
63 Von Eles 2005: 33 ff.
64 Sorrentino 2005: 129–130.
65 See the Etrusco-Corinthian krater by the Painter of the Knotted Tails, the Certosa situla, the Chiusine sarcophagus in the Louvre, and the Volterran urn Museo Guarnacci 493 (Donati 2004, II.16; III.B.1, 50, 52, 55). See also the Caeretan architectural plaque in Winter 2009: 451–452, 6.D.1.c., Ill. 6.14; Rafanelli 2010 forthcoming. Among the oldest representations of the sacrifice of an ox, cf. the reproduction of the man with the animals in the plastic

decoration of the shoulder of the bronze *olla* from tomb 22 of the Olmo Bello necropolis of Bisenzio (Maggiani 1997: 439; Donati 2004, II.15).

66 Rafanelli 2004, III.A.2.28.

67 Rafanelli 2004, III.A.2.32.

68 Cf., for example, the Caeretan *hydria* in Copenhagen in Donati 2004, III.B.1, 51.

69 Bonghi Jovino 2005: in particular, 80 ff.

70 The cult of the goddess, with strongly oriental traits of the Phoenician *Ishtar*, must also have included ritual processions with music and circle dances (Johnstone 1956), perhaps recalled in the representation of the choros of women that winds around the body of the Caeretan *alabastron* in Donati 2004, III.B.1.176, where the offering to the deity is represented as a goose.

71 Cf. Colonna 2000, 251 ff.

72 Donati 2004, III.B.1.10; Bruni 2005: 23; Bonamici 2005: 7 ff.

73 The offering of sheep/goats is associated in Greece with divinities like *Hermes* and Apollo, guardians of the flocks and herds (Donati 2004, III.B.7). In the sphere of Etruscan figural representations, on votive terracottas from the Vignaccia deposit at Caere, a goat is associated with the figure of *Artumes* (Nagy 1994; in relation to the gods venerated in the sacred area, see also Millemaci 1998: 11–61), while, on the bronze plaques designed to cover one or more funerary couches at Bomarzo, the recipient of an offering of a goat conducted by a procession of satyrs seems to be Herakles, distinguished by the characteristic attribute of the club (Donati 2004, III.B.7.129–131). (For terracotta figurines, see Chapter 54).

74 Colonna 1985: 88 ff., 4.10; Sassatelli 1992: 605–606; Rafanelli 2004, III.G.2.295; Colonna 2006: 140–141; Colonna 2012: 210, Fig. 11.

75 Perhaps this was also the site of a *mundus* reserved for the cult of *Dis Pater*, to whom the epithet of *papa* ("grandfather") may refer, intended as the original divinity of the sacred area (Bonamici 2005, 7–9).

76 For the Sanctuary of the Belvedere at Orvieto, see S. Stopponi in Colonna 1986, 80–83; Colonna 2006: 160, VIII.43; *LIMC* VIII Zeus/Tinia 400. Cf. also, in Volsinian territory, the "pierced" altars evoking the form of a subterranean cult, with dedications to *Tinia Tinscvil*, for which see Comella 2005: 166–169, IV.B.18 (TLE² 205 = CIE 5168): see *supra* note 36.

77 Cf. Donati 2004, III.B.7.105–129 bis.

78 Cf. Donati 2004, III.B.7.123–138.

79 Donati 2004, III.B.7.138.

80 Cf. The representations on the amphora in Dresden, on the Praenestine mirror in the Museo Archeologico Nazionale of Firenze, on the mirror in Berlin with the depiction of one of the mythological episodes belonging to the cycle of the Labors of Herakles (Donati III.B.7.128, 127, 134).

81 Donati 2004, III.B.7.128, with previous bibliography: in particular, see Colonna 1997: 195 ff.; see also Paolucci and Colonna 2005: 332 ff.; Paolucci 2007: 13, Fig. 2; Pieraccini 2011: 129, Fig. 3.

82 Martelli 1992: 342–346, pls 73, 3–4; 74. See also, especially for the figure of the Satyr, occurring in the context of a probable representation of an "Etruscan Festival," Paleothodoros 2007, 191–193.

83 Scarpi 1979: 78 ff.; Camporeale 1987: 41–42.

84 The double intent, both propitiatory and mantic, very probably also found a place in Etruria, similar to that of the Greek *thusia*, among the autonomous sacrificial rites or those able to join in themselves a number of valences. The exegesis of the figural Etruscan representations could in effect orient the inquiry toward a correlation of the mantic intent with the propitiatory, in a function in which it would acquire a sense also of the practice of haruspicy.

85 Donati 2004, III.B.7.126; Pieraccini 2011: 135, Fig. 14a–c.

86 As regards the altar-*bomos*, heart and "iconic synthesis of the sacrificial device" and of the "sacrificial fire," see Durand 1991, 45 ff.

87 Donati 2004, III.B.7.

88 Rafanelli 2004, III.G.2a.191 = 109a.

89 Livius, 41, 15, 1a. On the offering of the *exta*, generally understood as the portion reserved, in the course of the sacrificial rite, for the priest, see Le Guen-Pollet 1991, 13 ff.

90 Bagnasco Gianni 2005: 92 ff.

91 Chiesa 2005: 104 ff.

92 Corresponding to Group II in the classification of M. Bonghi Jovino in Bonghi Jovino 2005b: 35–36.

93 Bonghi Jovino 2005a: 73 ff., in particular, see table 6.

94 Bruni 2005: 22.

95 Bruni 2005: 22–23. For the linking of the wolf, in the Etruscan sphere, with the underworld god *Suri*, a sort of catachthonic Apollo, see Bruni 2002: 22, note 78, where the author takes into consideration the representation depicted on a black-figured vase, Donati 2004, III.B.2a.67, in which he identifies the probably Etruscan version of a ritual ceremony absorbed into that celebrated on Mount Soracte by the *Hirpi Sorani*. For the Etruscan cult of Apollo, the contribution of E. Simon (1973) remains fundamental.

96 Donati 2004, III.B.2.333.

97 In questo caso l'infero *Calus*, contenuto nell'iscrizione *Calustla* (*TLE* 642).

98 Donati 2004, III.B.2a.60; 9, 150. Per il lupo, cf. Bruni 2005: 23, notes 50–51.

99 Donati 2004, III.B.2c.69–70.

100 Donati 2004, III.B.2a.59bis e 63.

101 Donati 2004, III.B. 2c.67bis, 71.

102 Donati 2004, III.B.9.147bis, 151, 155.

103 Bonamici 2005: 6, in particular.

104 Chiesa 2005: 104 ff.

105 Chiesa 2005: 106.

106 According to the rite of *consecratio*, the altar takes on a perennial sacrality and inviolability. Particularly evident in the case of the Archaic cultic structure near the temple of the Ara della Regina of Tarquinia (cf. most recently Bagnasco Gianni 2011: 45 ff., with previous bibliography, among which: Colonna 1985, 70–78; Colonna 2006: 161–163) or of the two Hellenistic examples of Fiesole, incorporated into the later structures (for which, see G. Maetzke in Colonna: 1985, 93–95 and Colonna 2006: 163–164).

107 Warden 2011: 61 ff.

108 Bonamici 2005: 5 ff. Among the vegetable offerings is noted the fig (p. 6), a fruit rich in seeds and especially adapted (like the pomegranate) to symbolize the sphere of fecundity and of reproduction.

109 De Grummond 2011: 72–73.

110 Perhaps also the sacrifice of the fallow deer, whose remains were found beneath the south-east wall of area G, room 1 (de Grummond 2011: 72, note 9: twelfth ritual context?), attests to the presence of a foundation ritual marked by an expiatory-purificatory character, joining this species of animal with those already connoted by this valence, such as the piglet, dog, wolf and fox.

111 Rudhardt 1958.

112 Cf. Warden 2009b: 301.

113 Rafanelli 2004, III.H.2. Cf., in particular, for the iconography understood as an instrument to introduce the understanding of ritual, Durand 1991: 45 ff.

114 See, in this regard the still important contribution of I. Krauskopf (1987).

115 Donati 2004, III.B.3.76; Rafanelli 2010: 1–10, Figs 1–4.

116 Rafanelli 2004, III.F.174.

117 Differently on the plaques from Bomarzo (Donati 2004, III.B.7.153, nos. 129–131; Cristofani 1995, 114, n.3, pl. 20a; Baglione 1976, 105–107, Gruppo A, nos. 1, 1b, 2, pls 62–64, Fig.

2), the triangular elements on the upper surface of the low altar may be interpreted as stylized flames. Cf., also Rafanelli 2004, H 2.B.179.

118 Maggiani 1989: 1557 ff. pls 1–3; Roncalli 1991: 124 ff.; de Grummond 2006: 33–39.
119 Rafanelli 2004, III.E.2.164–165.
120 *ET LL* VIII, 17–18. Rafanelli 2004, III.A.1.140, n. 21; III.H.2.a.178–179.
121 Rix 1997: 391–398.
122 Prosdocimi 1984.
123 See for example that of the ritual calendar of the Island of Kos (Herzog 1928, in *Abh. Akad. Berlin*, 6).
124 Rafanelli 2004, III.H.1.177.
125 Cf., for example, the carnelian scarab Furtwangler n. 33 (*LIMC* VIII Turms, n. 8); see also Donati 2004, III.B.3.147–148.
126 The mixture of elements of Apollo and Dionysiac cults, in this case, on one side recognizable in the presence of the laurel crown on the altar, and, perhaps, in the armlet with *bullae* on the arm of the person sacrificing, and on the other, in the possible association of the animal victim with the *nebris* (fawnskin), characteristic attribute of Maenads, is on the other hand not uncommon in Etruscan ritual representations. (Rafanelli 2010: 5).
127 The provenance of the vase from Vulci, a city permeated, ever since the fifth century BC, with mystery beliefs in which, in a sense, Dionysiac beliefs prevailed, could indicate that the recipient of the offering was to be *Fufluns Pachie*, to whom the frieze of ivy leaves would be appropriate that adorns the shoulder of the little vase, framing and acclimatizing the figured scene, as does the headband, held in the left hand of the person standing to the right of the altar, an attribute that marks the initiates of the mystery cult of Dionysos (see Colonna 1991: 124).
128 Cf., among others, the mythological representations of the purification of Orestes by means of the blood of a piglet whose throat is slit, like that shown on the back of the Etruscan mirror. Donati 2004, III.B.9.161, where Apollo himself (*Aplu*) sacrifices the piglet over the head of *Urste* in the presence of *Metua* and *Vanth*; for the scene on the same mirror see also Ambrosini: 230, 14.
129 Donati 2004, III.B.9.160.
130 Del Chiaro 1974a, n. 36, p. 45, Fig. 34; Del Chiaro 1974b.
131 Donati 2004, III.B.9.162.
132 Donati 2004, III.B.7.123; Rafanelli 2004, III.E.2a, 220; Donati 2004, III.B.1.52.
133 Krauskopf 2006: 66 ff.
134 Cf. Warden 2009b: 301 ff., where the scholar stresses the concept of the blood sacrifice as a means of communication and osmosis between human and animal, from which necessarily follows the extreme importance attributed by the Etruscans to the cult of the deceased ancestors, celebrated and divinized by means of particular bloody sacrificial rites (see *supra*, note 66).
135 Cf. Colonna 1991: 117 ff.
136 Cf. Maggiani 2012: 408, where the scholar stops to examine the passage of Seneca in which the Roman philosopher emphasized the difference between the Etruscans and the Greeks and Latins, reiterating the assumption that the Etruscans attributed to the gods themselves the will to determine phenomena with the intention of communicating to men, through them, their intentions, while the Greeks and Latins maintained that the phenomena happened because the conditions had been created that made them occur.
137 Cf. N. T. de Grummond "Selected Latin and Greek Literary Sources" in de Grummond and Simon 2006, Appendix B, no. VIII.1.
138 Cf. Censorinus, *De Die natali*, 14.15, which surveys the life cycle of man in twelve periods of seven years (*hebdomades*), and in ten *saecula* the existence of the Etruscan *nomen* (cf. Maggiani 1984: 150).

139 See *supra* nota 107.
140 Maggiani 1992: 194–195.
141 Van Gennep 1909.
142 Maggiani 1992: 191.

BIBLIOGRAPHY

Agostiniani, L. and Nicosia, F. (2000) *Tabula Cortonensis*, Roma: "L'ERMA" di Bretschneider.

Ambrosini, L. (2006) "Le raffigurazioni di operatori del culto sugli specchi etruschi" in *Gli operatori cultuali* (= SEL 23). Verona, 197–233.

Anathema (1992) *Regime delle offerte ed economia dei santuari nel Mediterraneo antico. 1989–1990*, Atti del Convegno Internazionale, Rome, June 1989. *Scienze dell'Antichità*. Storia Archeologia Antropologia 3–4, 1989–1990.

Baglione, M. P. (1976) "Il territorio di Bomarzo" in *Ricognizioni archeologiche in Etruria*, Rome, CNR.

Bagnasco Gianni, G. (2005) "Tarquinia, il Deposito reiterato: una preliminare analisi dei comparanda" in M. Bonghi Jovino and F. Chiesa (eds), 91–102.

——(2011) "Tarquinia: excavations by the University of Milan at the Ara della Regina Sanctuary" in N. T. de Grummond and I. Edlund-Berry (eds), 45–54.

Bartoloni, G. (2009) "The earliest Etruscan toast. Considerations on the earliest phases of Populonia" in M. Gleba and H. Becker (eds), 159–170.

Beazley, J. D. (1947) *Etruscan Vase Painting*, Oxford: Clarendon Press.

Belelli Marchesini, B., Carlucci, C., Gentili M. D. and Michetti, L. M. (2012) "Riflessioni sul regime delle offerte nel santuario di Pyrgi" in *AnnFaina* XIX, 227–263.

Bloch, R. (1955) "Découverte d'un habitat étrusque archaïque" in *MEFRA* 67, 64–70.

Bonamici, M. (2005) "Appunti sulle pratiche cultuali del Santuario dell'Acropoli di Volterra" in M. Bonghi Jovino and F. Chiesa (eds), 1–14.

Bonghi Jovino, M. (1987) "Gli scavi nell'abitato di Tarquinia e la scoperta dei "bronzi" in un preliminare inquadramento," in M. Bonghi Jovino and C. Chiaramonte Treré (eds), *Tarquinia: ricerche, scavi e prospettive*, Milano, 59–78.

——(2005a) "Offerte, uomini e dei nel "complesso monumentale" di Tarquinia. Dallo scavo all'interpretazione" in M. Bonghi Jovino and F. Chiesa (eds), 73–90.

——(2005b) "*Mini muluvanice-mini* turuce. Depositi votivi e sacralità: dall'analisi del rituale alla lettura interpretativa delle forme di religiosità" in A. Comella and S. Mele (eds), 31–46.

Bonghi Jovino, M. and Chiesa, F. (eds) (2005) *Offerte dal regno vegetale e dal regno animale nelle manifestazioni del sacro* (Atti dell'incontro di studio Milano 26–27 June 2003) *Tarchna*, Supplemento I.

Briquel, D. (1999) *La religion étrusque* in Y. Lehmann (ed.), *Religions de l'Antiquité*, Paris, 7–75.

Bruni, S. (2002) *Nugae de Etruscorum fabulis* in "L'immagine in Etruria," Seminario, Roma, Istituto Archeologico Germanico, 21–22 gennaio 2000 [*Ostraka* X, 1]: 7–28.

——(2005) "Il Santuario di Ortaglia nel territorio volterrano: appunti sulle pratiche cultuali" in M. Bonghi Jovino and F. Chiesa (eds), 15–28.

Brunn, H. and Körte, G. (1870–1916) *I rilievi delle urne etrusche*, I–III.

Burkert, W. (1983) *Homo necans*, Berkeley.

Caloi, L. and Palombo, M. R. (1988–1989) "La fauna" in *NotSc* Suppl., 131–138.

Camporeale, G. (1987) "La danza armata in Etruria" in *MEFRA* 99, 41–42.

——(2004) La religione in *Gli Etruschi. Storia e civiltà*, 131–152.

Cardini, L. (1970) "Materiale osteologico" in *NotSc* Suppl., 616–625.

Castagnoli, F. (1962) "Sulla tipologia degli altari di Lavinio" in *Bullettino della Commissione Archeologica Comunale di Roma* 77 (1959–1960), 145–72.

Chiesa, F. (2005) "Un rituale di fondazione nell'area α di Tarquinia" in M. Bonghi Jovino and F. Chiesa (eds), pp. 103–112.

Coarelli, F. (1981) "Sull'area sacra di S. Omobono" in *La Parola del Passato* 36, 35–38.

——(1984) *Roma Sepolta*, Biblioteca di Archeologia, Roma: Curcio ed.

Collins-Elliot, S. A. and Edlund-Berry, I. E. M. (2011) "A bibliography of sanctuaries and ritual in Etruria" in N. T. de Grummond and I. Edlund-Berry (eds), 143–165.

Colonna, G. (1973–74) "Nomi etruschi di vasi," 132ss. in *Arch. Cl.* XXV–XXVI, 147 ss.

——(ed.) (1985) *Santuari d'Etruria* (Catalogo della Mostra, Arezzo) Milano.

——(1986) "Urbanistica e architettura" in Pugliese Carratelli, G. (ed.) *Rasenna*, 369–530.

——(1986a) "Novità sui culti di Pyrgi" in *RendPontAcc* 57, 57–79.

——(1987) "Note preliminari sui culti del Santuario di Portonaccio a Veio" in *Scienze dell'Antichità* I, 419–446.

——(1991) "Riflessioni sul dionisismo in Etruria" in F. Berti (ed.), *Dionysos. Mito e mistero* (Atti Convegno Internazionale Comacchio 1989), 117–155.

——(1991–92) "Altari e sacelli. L'area sud di Pyrgi dopo otto anni di ricerche" in *RendPontAcc* 64 (1994) 63–115.

——(1993) "Strutture teatriformi in Etruria" in *Spectacles sportifs et scéniques dans le monde étrusco-italique*, Actes de la Table Ronde, 321–347.

——(1997) "L'anfora etrusca di Dresda col sacrificio di *Larth Vipe*" in *Amico Amici*, Gad Rausing den 19 Maj 1997, Kristianstad, 195–216.

——(2000) "Il santuario di Pyrgi dalle origini mitistoriche agli altorilievi frontonali dei Sette e di Leucotea" in *Scienze dell'Antichità* 10, 251–336.

——(2001) "Portonaccio" in A. M. Moretti Sgubini (ed.), *Veio, Cerveteri, Vulci, Città d'Etruria a confronto*, catalogo della mostra, 37–44.

——(2006) "Sacred Architecture and the Religion of the Etruscans" in N. T. de Grummond and E. Simon (eds), 132–168.

——(2012) "I Santuari comunitari e il culto delle divinità catactonie in Etruria" in *AnnFaina* XIX, 203–226.

Colonna, G. and Colonna Di Paolo, E. (1978) *Norchia* I, Roma.

Colonna Di Paolo, E. (1978) *Necropoli rupestri del viterbese*, Novara.

——(1984) "Su una classe di monumenti funerari romani dell'Etruria meridionale" in *Studi in onore di G. Maetzke* II, 513–526.

Comella, A. and Mele, S. (eds) (2005) *Depositi votivi e culti nell'Italia antica dall'età arcaica a quella tardo-repubblicana*, Convegno di Studi Perugia (1–4 giugno 2000).

Comella, A. (200) "Altari" in ThesCRA, IV, 166–171.

Cristofani, M. (ed.) (1984) *Gli Etruschi. Una nuova Immagine*, Firenze.

——(ed.) (1990) *La grande Roma dei Tarquini*, 111–130, Roma.

——(1995) *Tabula Capuana. Un calendario festivo di età arcaica.* Istituto nazionale di Studi Etruschi e Italici. Biblioteca di «Studi Etruschi», 29, Firenze.

de Grummond, N. T. (2006) "Prophets and Priests" in N. T. de Grummond and E. Simon (eds), 132–168.

——(2011a) "Ritual practices at the Sanctuary of the Etruscan artisans at Cetamura del Chianti" in N. T. de Grummond and I. Edlund-Berry (eds), 68–88.

——(2011b) "Conclusion" in N. T. de Grummond and I. Edlund-Berry (eds), 139–141.

de Grummond and Edlund-Berry (eds) (2011) *The Archaeology of Sanctuaries and Ritual in Etruria*, Portsmouth, Rhode Island.

de Grummond, N. T. and Simon, E. (eds) (2006) *The Religion of the Etruscans*, Austin: University of Texas Press.

Del Chiaro, M. A. (1974a) *The Etruscan Funnel Group*, Florence: Sansoni Ed.

——(1974b) "Etruscan red-figured pottery at ancient Alalia" in *Riv. Corse Historique*.

Donati, L. (2004) "Il sacrificio nel mondo etrusco" in *ThesCRA* I, Processions. Sacrifices. Libations. Fumigations. Dedications, 2.a. Sacrifices/Sacrifices/Opfer/sacrifici, Etr., 136–182.

Durand, J. L. (1991) "Images pour un autel," in R. Étienne et M.-T. Le Dinahet (eds), *L'Espace sacrificiel dans les civilisations méditerranéennes de l'Antiquité.* Actes du Colloque de Lyon (1988), 45–51, Figs 1–14.

Edlund-Berry, I. E. M. (2008) "The language of Etrusco-Italic architecture: new perspectives on Tuscan temples" in *AJA* 112, 441–447.

——(2011) "Introduction. Rituals at Etruscan Sanctuaries" in N. T. de Grummond and I. Edlund-Berry (eds), 10–13.

Euwe-Beaufort, J. (1985) "Altari Etruschi" in *BABesh* 60, 101 ss.

Frascarelli, A. (2012) "Un donario monumentale a campo della Fiera" in *AnnFaina* XIX, 131–160.

Gaultier, F. and Briquel, D. (eds) (1997) *Les plus religieux des hommes. État de la recherche sur la religion étrusque*, Atti Colloquio Internazionale (Parigi, 17–19 novembre 1992).

Gleba, M. and Becker, H. (eds) (2009) *Votives. Places and Rituals in Etruscan Religion. Studies in honor of Jean MacIntosh Turfa* in *Religions in the Graeco-Roman World*, vol. 166, Brill, Leiden – Boston.

Jannot, J. R. (1988) *Devins, dieux et demons*, Paris.

Johnstone, M. A. (1956) *The dance in Etruria*, Firenze.

Krauskopf, I. (1987) *Todesdämonen und Totengötter in vorhellenistischem Etrurien*, Florence.

——(1997) "Influences grecques et orientales sur les représentations de dieux étrusques" in F. Gaultier and D. Briquel (eds), 25–36.

——(2006) "The Grave and Beyond in Etruscan Religion" in N. T. de Grummond and E. Simon (eds), 66–89.

Le Guen-Pollet, B. (1991) "Espace sacrificiel et corps des betes immolées. Remarques sur le vocabulaire designant la part du pretre dans la Grece antique, de l'epoque classique a l'epoque imperiale" in R. Étienne et M.-Th. Le Dinahet (eds), *L'Espace sacrificiel dans les civilisations méditerranéennes de l'Antiquité.* Actes du Colloque de Lyon (1988), 13–23.

Maggiani, A. (1978) "Le tombe a dado di Sovana" in *Prospettiva* 14, 15–30.

——(1989) "Immagini di aruspici" in *Atti del II Congresso Internazionale Etrusco* (Firenze 1985), 1557–1563, tav. I–III.

——(1992) "L'uomo e il sacro nei rituali e nella religione etrusca" in J. Ries (ed.), *Le civiltà del Mediterraneo e il sacro. Trattato di antropologia del sacro*, 3, 191–212.

——(1997) "Réflexions sur la religion étrusque primitive: de l'époque villanovienne à l'époque archaïque" in F. Gaultier and D. Briquel (eds), 431–447.

——(1999) "Culti delle acque e culti in grotta in Etruria" in *Ocnus*, 7, 187–203.

——(2003) "Un santuario vetuloniese di età ellenistica" in *Miscellanea Etrusco-Italica* III, *Quaderni di Archeologia Etrusco-Italica*, 137–154.

——(2012) "La religione" in G. Bartoloni (ed.) *Introduzione all'Etruscologia*, 395–418, Milano: Editore Ulrico Hoepli.

Maggiani, A. and Simon E. (1984) "Il pensiero scientifico e religioso" in M. Cristofani (ed.), 136–167.

Martelli, M. (ed.) (1987) *La ceramica degli Etruschi*, Novara.

——(1992) "Festa etrusca" in *Kotinos*. Festschrift für Erika Simon, Mainz.

Menichelli, S. (2009) "Etruscan Altars from the 7th to the 4th Centuries B.C.: Typology, function, Cult" in *Etruscan Studies* 12, 99–125.

Milani, L. A. (1912) *Il Regio Museo Archeologico di Firenze*, Firenze.

Millemaci, G. (1998) "Il deposito votivo della Vignaccia a Caere. Le divinità di culto" in *Atti e Memorie dell'Accademia toscana di Scienze e Lettere La Colombaria*, vol. LXII, n.s. XLVIII, Anno 1997, 11–61.

Milletti, M. *et al.* cds. in *XXVIII Convegno di Studi Etruschi e Italici* "La Corsica e Populonia," Bastia, Aléria, Piombino, Populonia, 25–29 ottobre 2011.

Modesti, B., Frezza, G. A., Lupia, A. and Mancusi, M. (2005) "Le acque intorno agli dei: rituali e offerte votive nel Santuario Settentrionale di Pontecagnano" in M. Bonghi Jovino and F. Chiesa (eds), 37–64.

Nagy, H. (1994) "Divinities in the Context of Sacrifice and Cult on Caeretan Votive Terracottas" in R. D. De Puma and J. P. Small (eds), *Murlo and the Etruscans. Art and Society in ancient Etruria.* Madison Wisc., 211–223.

——(1992) *The Vignaccia Deposit of Cerveteri* in *Anathema*, 733–736, Figs 4–6.

——(2011) Etruscan votive terracottas and their archaeological contexts: preliminary comments on Veii and Cerveteri, in Grummond and Edlund-Berry 2011, pp. 113–125.

Paleothodoros, D. (2007) "Dionysiac Imagery in Archaic Etruria" in *Etruscan Studies. Journal of the Etruscan Foundation* (Etruscans Now; Proceedings of the symposium held at the British Museum, 2002, part II), vol 10, 2004–2007, 187–201.

Paolucci, G. (2007) "La Collezione Grossi di Camporsevoli nel Museo Civico Archeologico di Chianciano Terme" in QC6, Quaderni del Museo Civico Archeologico di Chianciano Terme, Rome.

Paolucci, G. and Colonna, G. (2005) "*Ager Clusinum*: Camporsevoli" in REE StEtr LXX, 2004 (2005), 332–34, no. 53.

Pianu, G. (1991) "Gli altari di Gravisca" in R. Étienne et M.-Th. Le Dinahet (eds), *L'Espace sacrificiel dans les civilisations méditerranéennes de l'Antiquité.* Actes du Colloque de Lyon (1988), 193–199, tavv. 55–56.

Pieraccini, L. C. (2011) "The wonders of wine in Etruria" in N. T. de Grummond and I. Edlund-Berry (eds), 127–137.

Prayon, F. (1975) "Frühetruskische Grab- und Hausarchitektur" in *RM* Erg.- H. 22.

——(1979) "Felsthrone im Mittelitalien" in *RM* 86, 87–101.

——(1985) "L'architettura funeraria etrusca. La situazione attuale della ricerca e problemi aperti" in Atti del II Congresso Internazionale Etrusco, Florence, 441–449.

——(1997) "Sur l'orientation des édifices cultuels" in F. Gaultier and D. Briquel (eds), 357–373.

Prosdocimi, A. L. (1984) "Rites et sacrifice dans les Tables d'Iguvium" in *Sodalitas. Scritti in onore di A. Guarino*, 7, 3317–3340.

Rafanelli, S. (1997) "Altare su podio a gradini. Nota su un cippo funerario dell'Antiquarium di Vulci," in *RdA* XXI, 1997, 33–37, Figs 1–4.

Rafanelli, S. (2004) "Il sacrificio nel mondo etrusco" in *ThesCRA* I, Processions. Sacrifices. Libations. Fumigations. Dédications, 2.a. Sacrifices/Sacrifices/Opfer/sacrifici, Etr., 136–182.

——(2010) "La religione etrusca in età ellenistica. Rituale e iconografia fra tradizione e contaminazioni" in *Bollettino di Archeologia on line*, Direzione generale per le antichità, volume speciale, Roma 2008 – International Congress of Classical Archaeology, Meetings between Cultures in the ancient Mediterranean, in collaborazione con AIAC (Associazione Internazionale di Archeologia Classica).

——(2012) cds (Atti del V Convegno Internazionale sulle Mura Poligonali, Alatri ottobre 2010).

Rendini, P. (ed.) (2009) *Le vie del sacro. Culti e depositi votivi nella valle dell'Albegna*, Badesse, Monteriggioni (SI): Industria Grafica Pistolesi.

Rix, H. (1986) "Etruskisch Culs – 'Tor' und der Abschnitt VIII, 1–2 des Zagreber Liber Linteus" in *VjesAMuzZagreb*, 19, 17–40.

——(1997) "Les Prières du Liber Linteus de Zagreb" in F. Gaultier and D. Briquel (eds), 391–398.

Roncalli, F. (1965) *Le lastre dipinte da Cerveteri*, Florence.

——(1981) "Die Tracht des Haruspex..." in *Die Aufnahme fremder Kultureinfluesse in Etruria...*, Mannheim, 124–132.

——(1987) "Le strutture del santuario e le tecniche edilizie" in *AnnFaina* 3, 47–60.

——(1990) "La definizione pittorica dello spazio tombale nell'età della crisi" in *Crise et transformation des sociétés archaïques de l'Italie antique au Ve s. av. J.-C.* Actes Table Ronde Ec. Franç. Rome, 229–243.

——(1994) "Cultura religiosa, strumenti e pratiche cultuali nel santuario di Cannicella a Orvieto" in *"Tyrrhenoi Philotechnoi,"* Atti della Giornata di studio (Viterbo, 13 Ottobre 1990), Roma, 99–119.

Rudhardt, J. (1958) *Notions fondamentales de la pensée religieuse et actes constitutifs du culte dans la Grèce ancienne*, Genève, Droz (réédité chez Picard à Paris en 1992).

Sassatelli, S. (1992) "Culti e riti in Etruria Padana: qualche considerazione" in *Anathema*, 599–617.

Sassatelli, G. and Govi, E. (2005) "Il tempio di Tinia in area urbana" in *Culti, forma urbana e artigianato a Marzabotto. Nuove prospettive di ricerca* (Atti del Convegno, Bologna 2003), 9–62.

Scarpi, P. (1979) "Pyrrhìche o le armi della persuasione" in *DdA* n.s. I 1, 78 ss.

Shoe Meritt, L. T. and Edlund-Berry, I. E. M. (2000) "Etruscan and Republican Roman mouldings. A reissue of the Memoirs of the America Academy in Rome," 28 (1965) (Univ. of Pennsylvania Mus. Monog. 107).

Simon, E. (1973) "Die Tomba dei Tori und dert etruskische Apollon-kult" in *JdI 88*, 27–42

Sorrentino, C. (2005) "Analisi paleozoologiche a Pyrgi" in M. Bonghi Jovino and F. Chiesa (eds), 127–134.

Steingräber, S. (1982) "Überlegungen zu etruskischen Altären" in *Miscellanea Tobias Dohrn dedicata*, 103–119.

——(1997) "Le culte des morts et les monuments de pierre des nécropoles étrusques" in F. Gaultier and D. Briquel (eds), 97–116.

——(2009) "The Cima Tumulus at San Giuliano: an aristocratic tomb and monument for the cult of the ancestors of the late Orientalizing period" in M. Gleba and H. Becker (eds), 123–133.

Steingräber, S. and Prayon, F. (2011) *Monumenti rupestri etrusco-romani tra I monti Cimini e la valle del Tevere* Associazione Canino Info Onlus, Grotte di Castro (VT).

Stopponi, S. (2007) "Notizie preliminari dallo scavo di Campo della Fiera" in *AnnFaina* XIV, 493–530.

——(2009) "Campo della Fiera di Orvieto: nuove acquisizioni" in *AnnFaina* XVI, 425–478.

——(2011) "Campo della Fiera: new discoveries" in N. T. de Grummond and I. Edlund-Berry (eds), 16–44.

Studnizka, F. (1903) "Altare mit Gruben Kammem" in *Oest. Jahr.* 6, 123 ss.

Tarchna I. (1997) M. Bonghi Jovino and C. Chiaramonte Treré, *Tarquinia. Testimonianze archeologiche e ricostruzione storica. Scavi sistematici nell'abitato. Campagne 1982–1988*, Roma.

Terrenato, N., Brocato, P., Caruso, G., Ramieri, A. M., Becker, H. W., Cangemi, I., Mantiloni, G. and Regoli, C. (eds) (2012) "The S. Omobono Sanctuary in Rome: Assessing eighty years of fieldwork and exploring perspectives for the future", Internet Archaeology 31 (Internet bibliography) available at http://dx.doi.org/10.11141/ia.31.3

ThesCRA Thesaurus Cultus et Rituum Antiquorum.

Thuillier, J. P. (1991) "Autels d'Etrurie" in R. Etienne and M. T. Le Dinahet (eds) *L'espace sacrificiel dans les Civilisations Méditerranéennes de l'Antiquité* (Actes du Colloque tenu à la Maison de l'Orient, Lyon, 4–7 juin 1988) Paris, 243–247.

Torelli, M. (1986) "La religione," in G. Pugliese-Carratelli (ed.), *Rasenna*, 159–237.

——(1997a) "Secespita, praefericulum. Archeologia di due strumenti sacrificali romani" in *Etrusca et Italica. Scritti in ricordo di Massimo Pallottino*, Pisa, 575–598.

——(1997b) *Il rango, il rito, l'immagine. Alle origini della rappresentazione storica romana*, Milano.

——(2000) "La religione etrusca" in M. Torelli (ed.), *Gli Etruschi*, Cinisello Balsamo, 272–289.

Turfa, J. (2006) "Votive Offerings in Etruscan Religion" in N. T. de Grummond and E. Simon (eds), 90–115.

Van Gennep, A. (1909) *Les rites de passage*, Paris.

Von Eles, P. (2005) "Verucchio. Dalla terra e dal mare: la proiezione dell'ambiente nell'ambito funerario" in M. Bonghi Jovino, F. Chiesa, 29–36.

Warden, P. G. (2009a) "Remains of the Ritual at the Sanctuary of Poggio Colla" in M. Gleba and H. Becker (eds), 107–121.

——(2009b) "The blood of animals: predation and transformation in Etruscan funerary representation" in S. Bell and H. Nagy (eds), *New perspectives in Etruria and Rome: papers in honor of Richard De Puma*, Madison WI, 301–329.

——(2011) "The temple is a living thing: fragmentation, enchainment and reversal of ritual at the acropolis Sanctuary of Poggio Colla" in N. T. de Grummond and I. Edlund-Berry (eds), 55–67.

Winter, N. A. (2010) *Symbols of Wealth and Power, Architectural Terracotta Decoration in Etruria & Central Italy, 640–510 BC*, Memoirs of American Academy in Rome, Supplementary Vol. IX, Ann Arbor, Michigan: The University of Michigan Press.

Zamarchi Grassi, P. (1988) "Un edificio per il culto funerario. Nuovi dati sul tumulo II del Sodo a Cortona" in *RdA* 22, 19–26

CHAPTER TWENTY NINE

TARQUINIA, SACRED AREAS AND SANCTUARIES ON THE CIVITA PLATEAU AND ON THE COAST: "MONUMENTAL COMPLEX," ARA DELLA REGINA, GRAVISCA

——— •◆• ———

Giovanna Bagnasco Gianni

The Civita plateau, where the Etruscan city of Tarquinia was situated, is hidden from the seashore and the ancient ports by the hill that hosts the necropolis of Monterozzi, where the medieval town of Corneto was erected in the eighth century AD. On the coast, where the salt plants are still visible, halfway between the sea and the Etruscan settlement of Gravisca, there was a sanctuary open to Etruscans and foreigners.

THE CIVITA PLATEAU

Two Etruscan sacred areas were built on the Civita plateau of Tarquinia both related to local religious tradition, but differently conceived: the "monumental complex" with its peculiar architecture is meant to preserve the natural features of an ancestral sacred space whereas the huge Ara della Regina sanctuary could be seen from far away.[1]

The "monumental complex"

Maria Bonghi Jovino has recently summarized the main chronological phases of the "monumental complex" and the results of the excavations held since 1982, which can be found in the three volumes of the *Tarchna* series and in other major contributions.[2] Thanks to her outstanding work, what is already well known is the antiquity of the sacred area (since the Villanovan era) in a pre-civic dimension that has been very well described: "Here we have a unique occasion to witness the very creation of cultic practices, and to follow the development of religious and institutional activities, and their transformations through cultural contacts, and deliberate choice between continuity and change."[3]

In the past ten years the excavations have brought to light confirmations of the previous interpretations and opened up new spaces of thought regarding the continuity of religious and ceremonial practices of this peculiar religious landscape, where supernatural manifestations took place and the local community gathered for sacred and public purposes.[4] After the basic characteristics were settled in its first crucial phases of foundation, the "monumental complex" was permanently structured in the Archaic

594

period. Its limits and setting coincide with the very beginning of the story of the site and confirm its continuity and memory through centuries, showing persistent relationships between objects and sacred spaces, built or open air, to carry out the same cult practices, until the era of Romanization.[5]

More peculiar aspects are the marking of relevant areas of the bedrock of the "monumental complex" with stabile and perishable structures and human burials. The deposition of the child affected by the *morbus sacer* (epilepsy) near the natural cavity, which is the focus of the whole "monumental complex," belongs to the very core of the reasons of its foundation (Fig. 29.1). Among human burials there are a number of sacrificed individuals: for example the so-called seaman, who was probably a Greek man according to the fragmentary vase found in connection with him, shows an articulated situation of Mediterranean contacts and foreign presences. These are also unraveled by the technical features of the subsequent Orientalizing phase inspired by eastern Mediterranean masonry (pilaster-wall linked by sections of smaller stones). In this period its sacred and political destination is demonstrated by the deposition of the three famous bronzes in front of building β, the "altar temple" dedicated by a *rex* ("king") at the beginning of the seventh century BC to the main Etruscan goddess Uni (Fig. 29.2). Her presence has recently been proven as will be described below.

In the Archaic period architectural devices, such as stone blocks and altars of raw stones and earth, were positioned to keep ever present the memory of previous Villanovan cultic spots. This happens for example in *area* γ where the Villanovan evidences are

Figure 29.1   Tarquinia, "monumental complex," the natural cavity. Courtesy of Università degli Studi di Milano, "Progetto Tarquinia" archive.

preserved inside an elevation of the floor, marked by walls and votive deposits (Fig. 29.3).[6] Therefore these archaeological evidences are tightly connected to the concepts of memory, authority and recognizability that are crucial for the survival of traditions and place attachment for the majority of ancient communities.[7]

The central axis, oriented south-north, which definitively overlies the natural cavity in the Archaic period, is evidently the result of the very early design of the precincts of the west and east areas of the Orientalizing period. Two recently discovered cultic arrangements, located west and east of the natural cavity and dating back to the first phases of the area, open the way to the thesis of the crossing of two main axes over the natural cavity (Fig. 29.4). The result is the partition of the whole area into four quadrants, which

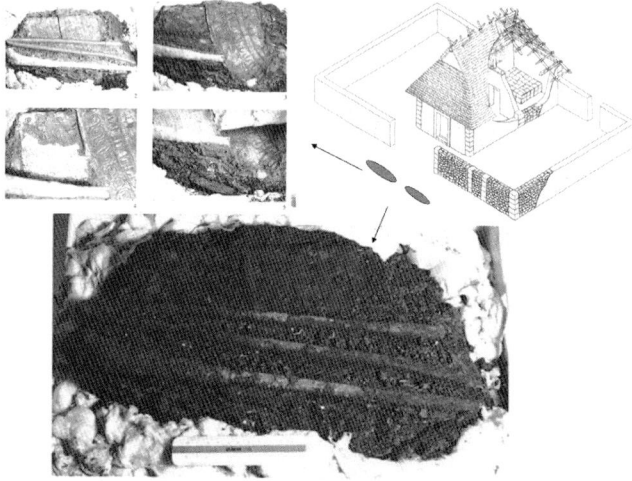

Figure 29.2   Tarquinia, "monumental complex," the two pits in front of the "altar temple" and the discovery of the bronzes. Courtesy of Università degli Studi di Milano, "Progetto Tarquinia" archive.

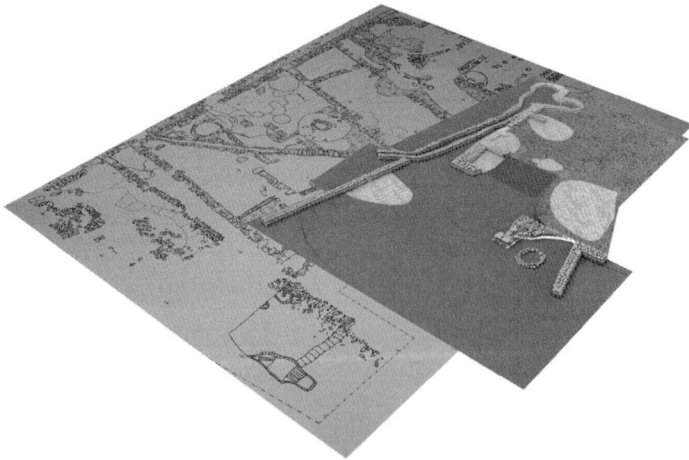

Figure 29.3   Tarquinia, "monumental complex," *area* γ overlapping the Villanovan structures. (Graphic reconstruction by Matilde Marzullo). Courtesy of Università degli Studi di Milano, "Progetto Tarquinia" archive.

seems to be very close to the treatment of the sacred space according to the principles of the *Etrusca Disciplina* (division, delimitation and orientation) that also emerge from the epigraphic documentation of the Italian peninsula. A cross that is inscribed in a circle seems to evoke the above-mentioned fundamental concepts of the Etruscan sacred space thanks to its relation to the object on which it is inscribed.[8] Such signs, probably used for their immediate visual eloquence, are called *sigla* and bear meanings that can be compared, in terms of communication, to those produced by proper writing[9] (Fig. 29.5). Also in the "monumental complex," from the transition between the Villanovan and Orientalizing periods up to the Hellenistic, pottery is often marked with such *sigla*.

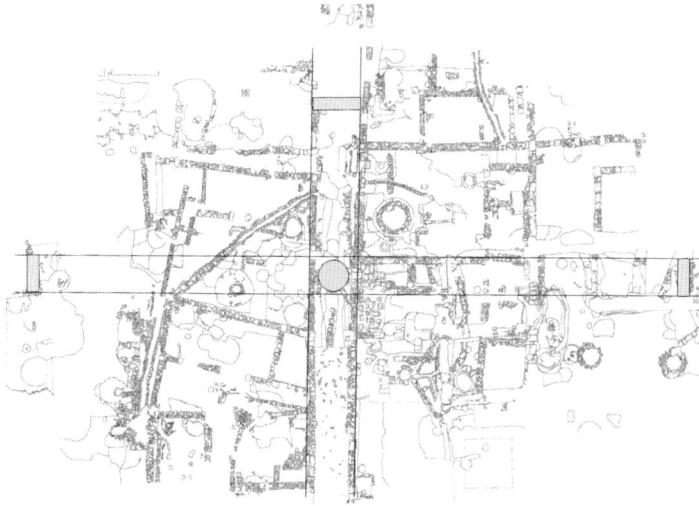

Figure 29.4   Tarquinia, "monumental complex," the location of the altars focusing on the natural cavity in the center. Courtesy of Università degli Studi di Milano, "Progetto Tarquinia" archive.

Figure 29.5   Tarquinia, "monumental complex," "impasto" shard with a cross inscribed in a circle. Courtesy of Università degli Studi di Milano, "Progetto Tarquinia," archive.

According to a similar background, the structures unearthed so far in the different spots and quadrants within the design of the "monumental complex" seem to assume different meanings. For example, in the north-east sector, which is the most favorable according to the Etruscan religion, near the north-east cornerstone of the "monumental complex," an outstanding monument was discovered: a well surmounted by an arch, inserted into a wall (Fig. 29.6).

The well has been dug directly in the bedrock and shows an articulated section. It is bell-shaped in the upper part, with a diameter at its base of 1.90 m and a height of 2.20 m, whereas it goes straight down in its bottom part with a diameter of 1.2 m. The depth reached so far is 21.50 m, due to the presence of water, which could be reached thanks to holes carved at a regular distance in the walls of the well.

The arch on top of the well could be seen only from the north because the wall in which it is inserted is part of the terrace built to retain the huge amount of clay forming the pavement in front of the east entrance to the "monumental complex." This terrace was built in the second half of the seventh century BC and, if our researches prove the same chronology for the arch and the wall, the arch is probably going to be the most ancient found in Etruria so far. On the whole, the architectural setting has no other comparisons, except for the literary description of the *cloaca maxima* in the Rome of Tarquinius Priscus, which nevertheless had another purpose.

The presence of water together with a thick filling in the upper part of the well – formed by large fragments of black glaze, thin-walled and "impasto" pottery often inscribed with texts and *sigla*, fragments of a terracotta plaque and stones – show a violent and deliberate action performed when the well was still in use, in order to obliterate it. The chronology of the pottery sealing the well indicates that the destruction took place in a short period of time during the second century BC, to be placed after the chronology suggested by the stylistic dating of the outstanding terracotta high-relief plaque with a warrior in battle. The plaque was probably part of a small pediment to be dated between the second half of the third and the first decade of the second century BC[10] (Fig. 29.7). Pediment and pottery were probably moved from somewhere else in the "monumental complex," but always related to cultic practices held in the immediate surroundings.

Figure 29.6   Tarquinia, "monumental complex." The well, surmounted by the arch. Courtesy of Università degli Studi di Milano, "Progetto Tarquinia," archive.

Besides *sigla* with the cross inscribed in the circle, a number of shards are inscribed with a name that can hardly be referred to a common person because it is written either complete or in abbreviation, in Etruscan and Greek, and by different hands. These inscriptions, now under study, come along with the latest epigraphic documentation so far found on the site, recalling the above-mentioned main Etruscan goddess Uni worshipped since its foundation.[11] The ultimate evidence of her presence is proven by the inscription χiiati, which means "related to χia," inscribed on an "impasto" pottery shard found in these same premises (Fig. 29.8). In fact the inscription refers to χia, which defines the chthonic nature of the goddess Uni, whose features are already well known thanks to the documentation of Cerveteri and Pyrgi (see Chapter 30).[12]

Figure 29.7 Tarquinia, "monumental complex," the terracotta plaque found inside the well. Courtesy of Università degli Studi di Milano, "Progetto Tarquinia," archive.

Figure 29.8 Tarquinia, "monumental complex," the "impasto" shard with the inscription χiiati. Courtesy of Università degli Studi di Milano, "Progetto Tarquinia" archive.

Ara della Regina sanctuary

The Ara della Regina sanctuary was built in monumental features from its very architectural beginning to become one of the largest in Etruria. The detailed publication of the Archaic phases (from the beginning of the sixth to the end of the fifth century BC) is now available.[13] The sanctuary had, on the whole, approximately four main phases built one on top of the other, taking advantage of the foundations and of the previous elevations of the Temples, according to a practice well known in Magna Graecia and Sicily (Fig. 29.9).

The first two phases had a similar layout with a high base of regular leveling courses of stone blocks (34 x 55 m) built to enlarge the hill and create a flat ground level on top of which a podium was built to host Temple I (around 570 BC) and, shortly after, Temple II (around 530 BC). Temple I had an elongated *cella* with *pronaos* (12 x 27 m) that became the core of Temple II when it was equipped with two *alae*. It was much larger than Temple I (25 x 40 m) and decorated with terracotta plaques. The area in front of the east entrance to both temples was delimited by a polychrome wall (*wall* γ), which can be followed for 40 meters, and had the function to both control the thrust of the earth from the hill behind and adjust the ground level around a stone chest located in front of the south-east corner of the Temple (Figs. 29.10–11). The stone chest had a different

Figure 29.9   Tarquinia, Ara della Regina sanctuary, aerial view (LiDAR). Courtesy of Università degli Studi di Milano, "Progetto Tarquinia," archive.

Figure 29.10   Tarquinia, Ara della Regina sanctuary, from the West. Courtesy of Università degli Studi di Milano, "Progetto Tarquinia," archive.

orientation (340°) from that of the temples (east-west) and its features are hard to assess because it was sealed under *altar* α of the subsequent third phase of the sanctuary, which is the most evident (Figs 29.11–12). Observing its layout and ignoring the presence of the stone chest, the previous literature review supported the idea that *altar* α, with the adjacent *precinct* β, was Archaic and celebrated the ancestral spot where Tages sprang from a clod in the ground. According to literary sources Tages was the child who appeared looking like an old man who taught Tarchon, the founder of Tarquinia, the secrets of the *Etrusca disciplina*. Nevertheless, the results of excavations held since 1983 show that both *altar* α and *precinct* β belong to the third phase of the sanctuary and that their orientation depends on that of the cultic arrangement focused on the Archaic stone chest and *wall* γ.

The third phase of the sanctuary, set at the beginning of the fourth century BC, represents the most consistent refurbishing of the whole sanctuary with the construction of a huge terrace in front of the base of the Temples. The terrace incorporated *wall* γ, which was partially destroyed, and the location of the stone chest, which was sealed under *altar* α. At the same time a hero cult presumably was conducted only once on top of the

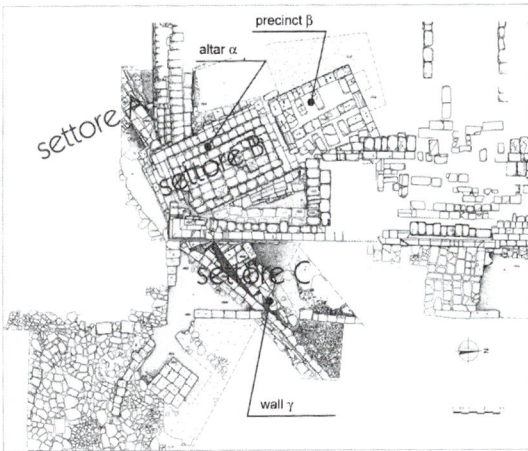

Figure 29.11   Tarquinia, Ara della Regina sanctuary, the south-east corner of the terrace with the Archaic structures. Courtesy of Università degli Studi di Milano, "Progetto Tarquinia," archive.

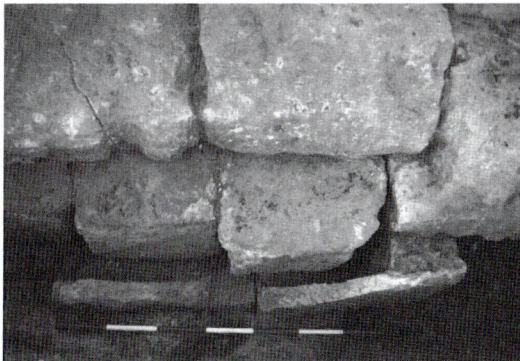

Figure 29.12   Tarquinia, Ara della Regina sanctuary, the stone chest from the east. Courtesy of Università degli Studi di Milano, "Progetto Tarquinia" archive.

altar: the stone chest was cut and left partially protruding under the east side of *altar* α in order to receive liquid offerings. The altar is evidently symbolic, because it is now impossible to reach it from its regular entrance from the south-east (Fig. 29.14). Connecting the evidence of the stone chest, which has the dimensions of a sarcophagus, with a Latin inscription quoting the hero-founder Tarchon, found by P. Romanelli on the same side of the Temple terrace, M. Bonghi Jovino[14] thinks that the sanctuary maintains across time the memory of the cenotaph where Tarchon the hero-founder of Tarquinia was worshipped.

Figure 29.13 Tarquinia, Ara della Regina sanctuary, the stone chest from the north-east. Courtesy of Università degli Studi di Milano, "Progetto Tarquinia" archive.

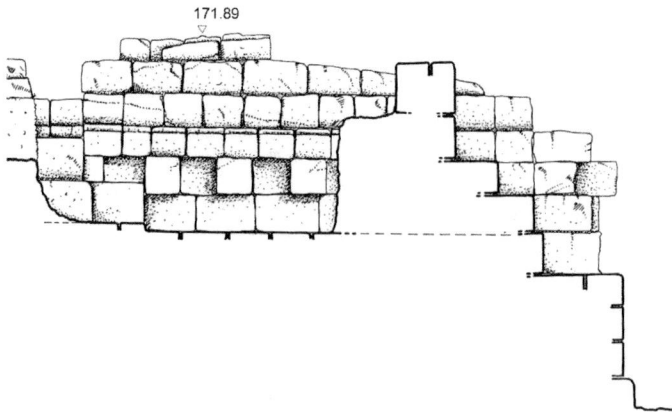

Figure 29.14 Tarquinia, Ara della Regina sanctuary, *altar* α from the west. Courtesy of Università degli Studi di Milano, "Progetto Tarquinia," archive.

Temple III was equipped with the famous terracotta plaque of the Winged Horses Group (Fig. 29.15); its chronology accords well with this phase from a formal, stylistic and iconographic point of view. The recent reconstruction of the Group is based on two more terracotta fragments that share the style, technique and ceramic composition of the Winged Horses: the bottom part of a female figure, whose dress is decorated with star motifs, and a vessel of closed form. From an iconographic point of view, considering all three surviving elements of the pediment, only the story of Herakles' apotheosis, after his burning on the pyre, seems to include them all. The best come from the repertoire of earlier Attic red-figure pottery, for example the red-figure pelike attributed to the Painter of Kadmos (450–400 BC) (Fig. 29.16), and on more or less contemporary Apulian figured ware, for example the krater of the Painter of Lycurgus (370–350 BC) (Fig. 29.17), that combine all these elements.

In these examples the main scene is distributed over several levels and this is one of the reasons why we confirm M. Pallottino's solution of a "closed" pediment for the Temple of the Winged Horses:[15] other important issues come along with the 22° slope of the top of the plaque, the width of the base of the pediment (25.5 m) and the metrological analysis

Figure 29.15 The Winged Horses Group after restoration. Tarquinia, Museo Nazionale Tarquiniense. Thanks to Soprintendenza per i Beni Archeologici per l'Etruria Meridionale.

Figure 29.16 Pelike of the Kadmos Painter (Beazley). Munich, Antikensammlungen, inv. 2360. Bagnasco Giannni 2009: 125, Fig. 19.

to determine the size of the chariot behind the horses and the number of its possible occupants.[16] As a consequence the *biga* with the walking Winged Horses could have been placed in the upper register of the pediment, with the head of the *auriga* in the middle and Hercle mounting the chariot for his apotheosis, symmetrically positioned behind the horses. In the bottom register, female figures, holding closed vessels, could be positioned around the remains of a possible pyre, according to the dimensions of the other two surviving elements associated with the pediment as a whole[17] (Fig. 29.18).

After all Hercle is not a new entry at the Ara della Regina sanctuary, since his deeds were recalled by Archaic terracotta fragments there (the plaque with the cattle of Geryon and the pedimental high relief with the Hydra). His meaningful presence is also implied by the genealogy of Tarchon from Herakles developed in the local tradition.[18] Temple IV represents the last refurbishment that was most recently assessed, it is late Hellenistic and can be perceived in the ultimate setting of the two arms flanking the stairway to the terrace and in the courses of black stone (*nenfro*) framing its crucial spots such as *altar* α protruding from the south side of the terrace.

Figure 29.17   Krater of the Painter of Lycurgus, Milano, Collezione Banca Intesa.
Bagnasco Gianni 2010: 224, Fig. 4.

Figure 29.18   Reconstruction of the subject represented on the pediment of the third phase of the Temple of the Ara della Regina sanctuary at Tarquinia (Temple III) (Drawing by Massimo Legni). Courtesy of Università degli Studi di Milano, "Progetto Tarquinia" archive.

GRAVISCA

The sanctuary of Gravisca on the coast is organized as a considerable middle ground for the meeting of Etruscans and foreigners. The shrines of its southern part show multifaceted cultic practices to honor different Greek gods in a modest architectural setting, whereas the northern sanctuary is focused on two imposing chthonic altars probably dedicated to two Etruscan gods, Śuri and Cavatha (Apollo and Persephone according to the Greek *interpretatio*) (Fig. 29.19).

The results of the forty-year excavations in these two main areas of the sanctuary of Gravisca in their detailed chronological phases and relationships have been recently presented, therefore an up-to-date overview of the whole sanctuary is now possible.[19]

The beginning of the sanctuary is unraveled in its southern area thus far. At the end of the seventh century BC, Greek visitors from Phocaea were hosted in the favorable natural shelter of the lagoon of Gravisca, which is rich in good fresh water. This probably happened coincidentally with the foundation of the Etruscan settlement of Gravisca further north[20] that has always been part of the territory of Tarquinia. This is clearly stated by Livy when he reports the deduction of the colony of Gravisca in 181 BC: "Colonia Grauiscae eo anno deducta est in agrum Etruscum, de Tarquiniensibus quondam captum." ("The colony of Graviscae was founded in Etruscan territory, formerly occupied by the Tarquinians," Livy, *Ab Urbe condita* 40.29).[21]

Such very early cult practices developed in an open-air setting (*sub divo*), but shortly thereafter a shrine devoted to Aphrodite was built. The area around it was enlarged and articulated through almost three architectonic phases carried out by east Greek builders under the control of local authorities that also guaranteed international exchanges.[22] The

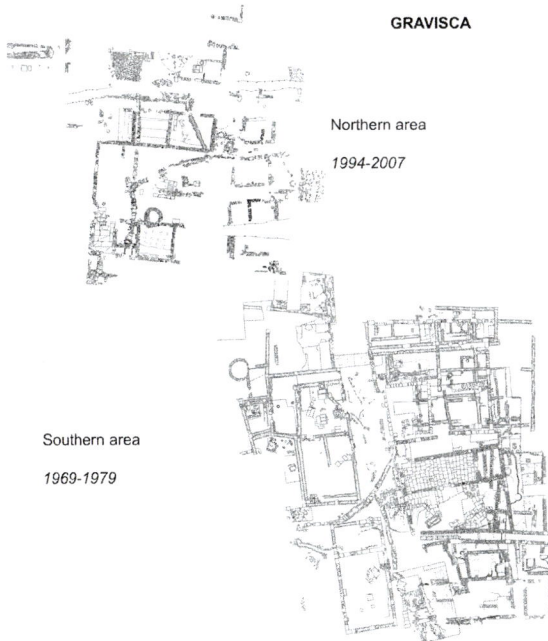

GRAVISCA

Northern area

1994-2007

Southern area

1969-1979

Figure 29.19   Gravisca, sanctuary, general plan. Thanks to Lucio Fiorini,
Università degli Studi di Perugia.

religious landscape of these early phases of the southern area of the sanctuary, open to the south, is characterized by the presence of arrangements for the production of copper and iron around the *naiskos* (small temple) of Aphrodite. Such activities recall both her union with Hephaestus[23] and probably the presence of the Etruscan counterpart famous for its metallurgical skills.[24] Therefore the social structure seems to be modest, formed by subaltern intermediaries, enrolled by outstanding groups (tribal/familial groups) from Ionia and Aegina, who probably worked together with small groups of local artisans, as a few Etruscan votive inscriptions declare.[25]

The first phase (580–550 BC)

The southern area of the sanctuary recalls a Phocaean presence. A *sacellum* devoted to Aphrodite, with *adyton* and entrance open to the west, was built; among the votive offerings, an impressive bronze statuette of Aphrodite *promachos* (Fig. 29.20) confirms her cult in connection with the inscriptions bearing her name that were found in the upper levels.

The second phase (550–530 BC)

A consistent number of Samian worshipers probably introduced the cult of Hera in the east side of the shrine and addressed to her a number of votive inscriptions. The previous *sacellum* was transformed into a *megaron* flanked by a *temenos*, a well and a porch whose north/west corner was marked by the offering of an Attic *lebes* (cauldron) containing coral. Since coral is such a material part of the cult practices of Adonis, well documented in the later phases of the sanctuary, it is possible to argue that he was worshiped also in this earlier phase.[26] Recent excavations north-west of the previous southern shrines exposed a swampy zone, that was later built up and supplied with canals. The earliest chronology reached so far is the second half of the sixth century BC, when two cultic spots, formed by strata of cinders mixed with animal bones (*escharai*), were deposited.[27]

Figure 29.20   Gravisca, sanctuary, Aphrodite *promachos* from the southern area.
Fiorini and Torelli 2010: 31, Fig. 4.

The third phase (530–480 BC)

After the southern area was destroyed by fire, thick layers of earth were leveled to build two joint *sacella* of Aphrodite and Hera focused on a south-north axis with a unique *pronaos* open to the south. The ultimate construction of the Heraion near the Aphrodision possibly implies the presence of Greeks from Aegina, which could be also supported by finds, in second deposition, belonging to this same chronological phase, such as the famous *cippus* of Sostratos dedicated in Greek to Apollo of Aegina (Fig. 29.21).[28] In the meantime the *escharai* of the north-west area were monumentalized with two altars (δ and ε) that find parallels in Magna Graecia and Sicily.[29] They are near the spot where a votive deposit was sealed in secondary deposition, after the destruction of the sanctuary carried out by the Romans in 281 BC. The composition of the votive deposit, belonging to the most consistent period of worship of this northern part of the sanctuary, is very important to assess its religious destination.[30] Such offerings find impressive comparisons with the chthonic cult practices held in honor of Śuri and Cavatha in the southern sanctuary of Pyrgi. At Gravisca, Śuri's cult is attested by the presence of spearheads, miniature weapons and a warrior figurine (Fig. 29.22) together with shining stones recalling thunderbolts and the *baityloi* offered to the god,[31] whereas Cavatha's cult emerges from the recurrence of *skyphoi* and *olpai* with a standard capacity.[32] On the whole, such offerings together with the shape of the altars, are considered by the excavators to be expressions of a massive influence from the Sicilian tyrants; this was particularly strong in such historical circumstances when Rome was also looking for involvement with the strong economic power of Sicily.[33]

The fourth phase (480–400 BC)

Probably as a consequence of the loss of power in the Tyrrhenian Sea suffered by all Etruscans after the defeats inflicted by the Greeks in 480 BC (battle of Himera and victory of Syracuse against the Carthaginians, the Etruscans' allies), and in 474 BC (battle of

Figure 29.21   Gravisca, sanctuary, the *cippus* of Sostratos with the dedication in Greek to Apollo of Aegina from the southern area. Thanks to Lucio Fiorini, Università degli Studi di Perugia.

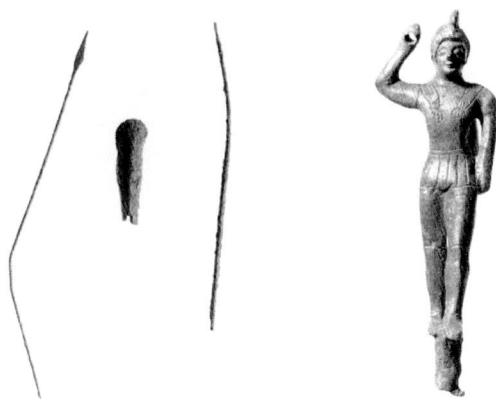

Figure 29.22 Gravisca, sanctuary, spearheads, miniature weapons and a warrior from the northern area. Fiorini and Fortunelli 2011: 45, Figs 4–5.

Cumae and victory of Syracuse under Hieron I), the plan of the southern area of the sanctuary and its destination radically changed. The metallurgical activity stopped together with the *emporion*, and commercial enterprises were entirely transferred to Etruscan control.[34] The influence of Tarquinia became stronger and a new porch that faced north was built on the north side, probably to underline such changes in the political relationships with foreign subjects. The Aphrodision and the Heraion were equipped with separate entrances differently oriented and with courtyards built over the previous metallurgical zones. The *temenos* of Aphrodite was enlarged westwards to include a road running north-south; in the south-west corner of the *temenos* the cult of Adonis was expressed by the presence of his stone chest. The finding of the above-mentioned *cippus* of Sostratos, together with another inscription addressed to the same god in the premises located to the west of the *temenos* of Aphrodite, make it possible to identify nearby a new sacred space dedicated to Apollo.[35] The altars of the north-west sanctuary remained in use,[36] but in the decade between 430 and 420 BC they were dismantled.

The fifth phase (400–300 BC)

A new design of urban spaces was defined and the north-south road was crossed by *stenopoi* (narrow alleys). On the west sector the largest *stenopos* divided the southern area of the sanctuary from the northern. The southern *sacella* were articulated in different blocks and definitely focused on cults peculiar to a single god, with selected types of offerings and vessels for cult practices: Aphrodite (building γ), Adonis (building δ), Apollo (building α), Demeter (building β, courtyard F and zone X); building ε had probably a service purpose.[37] In the northern area, after a series of expiatory sacrifices, a new *sacellum* was built on the southern side of a large courtyard closed by a porch in its northern side. Around the mid-fourth century BC an imposing drainage channel was set to organize the leveling terrace of a new architectonic phase (60 x 40 feet), still respecting the previous *sacellum* of the southern side, now endowed with a well rich in water. The previous porch of the northern side was divided into three rooms probably for cult reasons, and where altar ε previously stood, a new smaller altar α was built and oriented according to the rest of the sanctuary.[38]

The sixth phase (300–281 BC)

The southern *sacella* remained basically unchanged, with a general tendency to strengthen their walls. Nevertheless, some premises were modified (Fig. 29.23). The Heraion in building γ was dismantled and the cult of Hera was transferred to the nearby Aphrodision, which was therefore divided into two areas with different concentrations of offerings according to the two goddesses: Aphrodite-Turan in area L and Hera-Uni in area M.[39] The *naiskos* devoted to Apollo in building α became one single room and zone X between buildings α and β was monumentalized with pilaster-walls and a round altar, probably in connection with a Sicilian influence.[40]

In the northern area no consistent changes were accomplished, except for the refurbishing of the *sacellum* and the integration of the well within its premises. One more altar β was built in the west side of the sacred space, which was paved with slabs of local stone probably used for sacrificial purposes and supplied with a small chthonic well.[41] In 281 BC Gravisca was annexed to Roman territories. Nevertheless, the southern *sacella* were attended again by the local population mostly in the Aphrodision and in the Adonion where a votive inscription was dedicated (*Adon* on an Arretine cup).[42] In the northern area of the sanctuary the dispersed sacred objects were collected after the Roman destruction and sheltered in the above-mentioned votive deposit of its northern side.[43]

Figure 29.23 Gravisca, sanctuary, the sixth phase (300–281 BC).
Thanks to Lucio Fiorini, Università degli Studi di Perugia.

NOTES

1   In 1982 the excavations of the Università degli Studi di Milano were started by Maria Bonghi Jovino within the "Tarquinia Project" gathering many different interdisciplinary approaches: Bonghi Jovino 2010. The research is now directed by Giovanna Bagnasco Gianni (since 2004). The author warmly thanks Prof. Maria Bonghi Jovino for involving her in the stratigraphic excavations at Tarquinia since the beginning, Prof. Susanna Bortolotto and Prof.

Stefano Valtolina who collaborate to the enterprise of this inter-disciplinary work. The other members of the project Andrea Garzulino, Enrico Giovanelli, Matilde Marzullo, Claudia Piazzi are also warmly acknowledged. Lucio Fiorini's advice and support has been essential in dealing with the results of the excavations of Gravisca.

2 Bonghi Jovino 2010: 2–15, referring to previous literature. For more recent contributions see the bibliography listed in Bagnasco Gianni 2008a.

3 Damgaard Andersen 2001: 28.

4 Bonghi Jovino 2009a.

5 Bagnasco Gianni 2008a.

6 Bagnasco Gianni 2005a; Chiesa 2005.

7 Bagnasco Gianni 2005b.

8 Bagnasco Gianni 2008b; Bagnasco Gianni, Gobbi, Scoccimarro, forthcoming.

9 Bagnasco Gianni and de Grummond, forthcoming.

10 Chiesa, forthcoming.

11 The literature review recently summarized (Maras 2009: 391) shows scepticism about the interpretation of the inscription *mi uni* as a quotation of the name of the goddess Uni. Nevertheless, even before the discovery of the inscription *χiiati* confirming her presence, the small *corpus* of Etruscan texts found in the "monumental complex" show the recurrence of abbreviations of her name (Bagnasco Gianni 2005a: 96).

12 Colonna 2002: 300.

13 Bonghi Jovino and Bagnasco Gianni, 2012. For previous references: Bonghi Jovino 1997; Bonghi Jovino 2010: 16–19; Bagnasco Gianni 2011b.

14 Bonghi Jovino 2009b: 21–22.

15 Bagnasco Gianni 2009, 106–108.

16 Emiliozzi 2009.

17 Bagnasco Gianni 2010a.

18 Bagnasco Gianni, forthcoming.

19 For a recent literature review: L. Fiorini, in Fiorini and Fortunelli 2011: 39. The author is grateful to Prof. Lucio Fiorini for his essential support in dealing with the results of the excavations of Gravisca.

20 L. Fiorini, in Fiorini and Torelli 2010: 29.

21 Torelli 1990.

22 Bonghi Jovino 2006; M. Torelli, in Fiorini and Torelli 2010: 43.

23 L. Fiorini, in Fiorini and Torelli 2010: 31.

24 M. Torelli, in Fiorini and Torelli 2010: 44.

25 M. Torelli, in Fiorini and Torelli 2010: 44–45.

26 L. Fiorini, in Fiorini and Torelli 2010: 32.

27 L. Fiorini, in Fiorini and Torelli 2010: 39; L. Fiorini, in Fiorini and Fortunelli 2011: 40–41.

28 M. Torelli, in Fiorini and Torelli 2010: 43.

29 L. Fiorini, in Fiorini and Torelli 2010: 39–40.

30 S. Fortunelli, in Fiorini and Fortunelli 2011: 42–46.

31 L. Fiorini, in Fiorini and Fortunelli 2011: 46–47.

32 L. Fiorini, in Fiorini and Torelli 2010: 41; S. Fortunelli, in Fiorini and Fortunelli 2011: 42–46.

33 M. Torelli, in Fiorini and Torelli 2010: 44.

34 M. Torelli, in Fiorini and Torelli 2010: 43.

35 L. Fiorini, in Fiorini and Torelli 2010: 33.

36 L. Fiorini, in Fiorini and Torelli 2010: 41.

37 L. Fiorini, in Fiorini and Torelli 2010: 33–35; L. Fiorini, in Fiorini and Fortunelli 2011: 39.

38 L. Fiorini, in Fiorini and Torelli 2010: 41.

39 L. Fiorini, in Fiorini and Torelli 2010: 36

40 L. Fiorini, in Fiorini and Torelli 2010: 35–36.
41 L. Fiorini, in Fiorini and Torelli 2010: 41–42.
42 L. Fiorini, in Fiorini and Torelli 2010: 36–37.
43 L. Fiorini, in Fiorini and Torelli 2010: 38–39.

BIBLIOGRAPHY

Bagnasco Gianni, G. (2005a) "Tarquinia. Il deposito votivo reiterato: una preliminare analisi dei *comparanda*" in *Tarchna. Suppl. 1*, 91–102.
——(2005b) "Sui 'contenitori' arcaici di ex-voto nei santuari etruschi" in A. M. Comella and, S. Mele (eds), *Depositi votivi e culti dell'Italia Antica dall'età arcaica a quella tardo-repubblicana* Atti del Convegno (Perugia 1–4 giugno 2000), Bari: Edipuglia, 351–358.
——(ed.) (2008a) *Tra importazione e produzione locale: lineamenti teoretici e applicazioni pratiche per l'individuazione di modelli culturali. Il caso di Tarquinia* in M. Dalla Riva (ed.), *Meetings between Cultures in the Ancient Mediterranean. Proceedings of the 17th International Congress of Classical Archaeology*, Rome 22–26 sept., Rome: MIBAC. Online. Available at: <http://151.12.58.75/archeologia/index.php?option=com_content&view=article&id=59&Itemid=59>. (Accessed 21 December 2011).
——(2008b) "Rappresentazioni dello spazio 'sacro' nella documentazione epigrafica etrusca di epoca orientalizzante" in X. Dupré Raventós. S. Ribichini and S. Verger, (eds), Saturnia Tellus. *Definizioni dello spazio consacrato in ambiente etrusco, italico, fenicio-punico, iberico e celtico.* Atti del Convegno Internazionale svoltosi a Roma dal 10 al 12 November 2004, Rome: CNR, 267–281.
——(2009) "I Cavalli Alati di Tarquinia. Una proposta di lettura" in M. Bonghi Jovino and F. Chiesa (eds), 93–139.
——(2011a) "The Winged Horses on the Ara della Regina temple at Tarquinia" in P. Lulof and C. Rescigno (eds), *Deliciae Fictiles IV. Architectural Terracottas in Ancient Italy Images of Gods. Monsters and Heroes. Proceedings of the International Conference held in Rome (Museo Nazionale Etrusco di Villa Giulia, Royal Netherlands Institute) and Syracuse (Museo Archeologico Regionale 'Paolo Orsi'),* October 21–25, 2009, Oxford and Oakville: Oxbow Books, 222–225.
——(2011b) "Tarquinia: Excavations by the University of Milano at the Ara della Regina Sanctuary" in I. E. M. Edlund-Berry and N. T. de Grummond (eds), *The Archaeology of Sanctuaries and Ritual in Etruria, JRA*, Supplement 81, 45–54.
——(forthcoming) "Lo specchio della tomba 65 del fondo Scataglini e la questione dell'apoteosi di Hercle a Tarquinia" in *Studi e ricerche a Tarquinia e in Etruria. Simposio internazionale in ricordo di Francesca Romana Serra Ridgway*, Tarquinia 24–25 settembre 2010, Pisa-Rome: Fabrizio Serra Editore.
Bagnasco Gianni, G. Gobbi, A. and Scoccimarro, N. (forthcoming) "Segni eloquenti in necropoli e abitato" in M. L. Haack (ed.), *L'écriture et l'espace de la mort*, Rencontres internationales (Roma, 5–7 mars 2009), Rome: Ecole Française de Rome.
Bagnasco Gianni, G. and de Grummond, N. T. (forthcoming) "Introducing the International Etruscan *Sigla* Project," *Etruscan Literacy in its Social Context,* Institute of Classical Studies University of London, 22–23 September 2010, London: Accordia.
Bonghi Jovino, M. (1997) "La phase archaïque de l'Ara della Regina à la lumière des recherches récentes" in F. Gaultier and D. Briquel (eds) *Les Étrusques. Les plus religieux des hommes*, Paris: La documentation Francaise, 69–95.
——(2006) "Contesti, modelli e scambi di manufatti. Spunti per un'analisi culturale e socio-economica. La testimonianza Tarquinia-Gravisca" in *Gli Etruschi da Genova ad Ampurias*, Atti del XXIV Convegno di Studi Etruschi ed Italici, Marseille-Lattes 2002, Pisa – Rome: Fabrizio Serra Editore, 679–689.
——(2009a) "L'ultima dimora. Sacrifici umani e rituali sacri in Etruria. Nuovi dati sulle sepolture nell'abitato di Tarquinia," in G. Bartoloni and M. G. Benedettini (eds), *Sepolti tra i vivi. Evidenza*

ed interpretazione di contesti funerari in abitato (Roma, 26–29 aprile 2006), *Scienze dell'Antichità*, 14 (2007–2008), 771–794.

——(2009b) "Il santuario dell'Ara della Regina: preliminare proposta di ricostruzione dei templi arcaici e indicazioni sul luogo di culto" in M. Bonghi Jovino and F. Chiesa (eds), 7–45.

——(2010) "The Tarquinia Project: A Summary of 25 Years of Excavation," *AJA*, 114: 161–180.

Bonghi Jovino, M. and Bagnasco Gianni, G. (eds) (2012) *Tarquinia. Il santuario dell'Ara della Regina. I templi arcaici*, Rome: "L'ERMA" di Bretschneider.

Bonghi Jovino, M. and Chiesa, F. (eds) (2009) *L'Ara della Regina di Tarquinia, aree sacre, santuari mediterranei*. Atti della Giornata di studio, Milano 2007, Milan: Cisalpino.

Chiesa, F. (2005) "Un rituale di fondazione nell'*area alpha* di Tarquinia" in *Tarchna, Suppl. 1*, 103–109.

——(forthcoming) "Scene di una battaglia eroica. Lastra fittile con guerriero combattente dal 'complesso monumentale; di Tarquinia" in *Studi e ricerche a Tarquinia e in Etruria. Simposio internazionale in ricordo di Francesca Romana Serra Ridgway*, Tarquinia 24–25 September, 2010, Pisa-Rome: Fabrizio Serra Editore.

Colonna, G. (2002) "Il santuario di Pyrgi dalle origini mitistoriche agli altorilievi frontonali dei Sette e di Leucotea," *Scienze dell'Antichità* 10: 251–336.

Damgaard Andersen, H. (2001) Review of *Tarchna I 1997* in *Acta Hyperborea* 8: 280–285.

Emiliozzi, A. (2009) "La biga con i cavalli alati di Tarquinia" in M. Bonghi Jovino and F. Chiesa (eds), 141–152.

Fiorini, L. and Torelli, M. (2010) "Quarant'anni di ricerche a Gravisca" in L. B. van der Meer (ed.), *Material Aspects of Etruscan Religion*, Proceedings of the International Colloquium (Leiden, May 29 and 30 2008), *BABesch* Annual Papers on Mediterranean Archaeology, Supplement 16, 29–49.

Fiorini, L. and Fortunelli, S. (2011) "Si depongano le armi. Offerte rituali di armi dal santuario settentrionale di Gravisca" in C. Masseria and D. Loscalzo (eds), *Miti di guerra. Riti di pace. La guerra e la pace: un confronto interdisciplinare*, Bari: Edipuglia, 39–50.

Maras, D. F. (2009) *Il dono votivo. Gli dei e il sacro nelle iscrizioni etrusche di culto* (Biblioteca di Studi Etruschi 46), Pisa-Rome: Fabrizio Serra Editore.

Tarchna, Suppl. 1 (2005). Bonghi Jovino, M and Chiesa, F. (eds) *Offerte dal regno vegetale e dal regno animale nelle manifestazioni del sacro, Atti dell'Incontro di Studio, Milano 26–27 giugno 2003*, Rome: "L'ERMA" di Bretschneider.

Torelli, M. (1990) "Gravisca" in Bibliografia Topografica della colonizzazione greca in Italia e nelle isole tirreniche 8, Pisa-Rome: Pacini Editore, 172–176.

CHAPTER THIRTY

THE SANCTUARY OF PYRGI

———•◆•———

Maria Paola Baglione

The port and Etruscan sanctuary of Pyrgi were situated along the shore of the Tyrrhenian Sea to the north of Rome, about 52 kilometers along the modern Via Aurelia, which roughly traces the route of the Roman consular road. In the Etruscan period the coast extended at least 70 meters beyond the modern coastline because of the greater depth of sea level today, and the entire landscape was more articulated, rich in coastal lagoons and watercourses that descended from the hills nearby inland, covered with forests where several species of tall trees were growing, such as white firs, oaks, cypress, beech, remains of which have been found in the excavations.

Located in one of the most beautiful spots on the coast north of Rome and still relatively untouched, the district of Pyrgi is a large area in which are gathered diverse archaeological sites. To the north there is an exceptional overlapping of settlement phases that covers more than a millennium: on a small promontory stands the medieval castle of Santa Severa, the earliest phase of which dates back to the tenth century AD. The castle and its village overlies the Roman *colonia maritima,* founded around 268 BC to fortify the coasts in anticipation of the first Punic War. The massive "Pelasgian Walls," large polygonal blocks of limestone from the quarries of the neighboring Monti della Tolfa, bordered the perimeter of the colony and even today are a formidable witness of Roman building techniques of the Middle Republican era (Figure 30.2). In turn, the Roman colony is superimposed on the Etruscan village, which occupied the headland behind the Etruscan port. As seems clear from the erosion escarpment visible along the beach, the Etruscan settlement was established around the second half/end of the seventh century BC and, thanks to the stratigraphy preserved, it was possible to identify at least five distinct levels of occupation up to the Roman Republican period.

The excavations that led to the discovery of the monumental sanctuary began in 1957, to the south of the castle. Under the direction of Massimo Pallottino, following the discovery of architectural terracottas in a field during agricultural work, this important discovery allowed the great Etruscan expert to precisely define the site where the shrine of Eileithyia-Leucothea stood, the only Etruscan sanctuary that has been located precisely from the Greek and Latin sources because it is linked to the main harbor of the Etruscan city of Caere, the most important port facility in Tyrrhenian Etruria.

Figure 30.1 Aerial view of the territory of Pyrgi; to north, the castle and area of the Roman colony; to the south, the two sanctuaries on the seashore. (Googlemap).

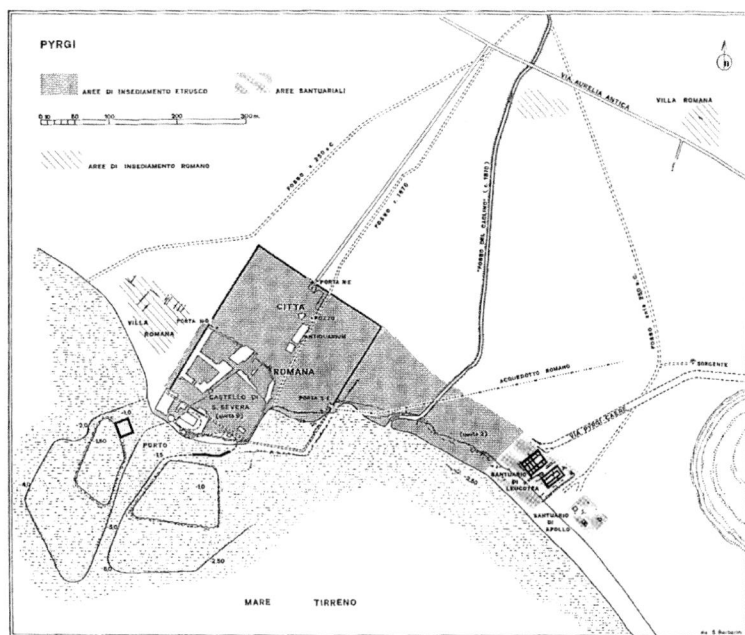

Figure 30.2 General plan of archaeological area.

In the first half of the nineteenth century, Luigi Canina, the Roman architect to whom we owe considerable studies on the territory of Caere, speculated that the sanctuary arose in the area enclosed by the "Pelasgian" wall circuit belonging to the Roman *colonia maritima*; only the excavations have made possible the evaluation of the whole archaeological area of Pyrgi, stretching for more than 800 meters from the Castle to the sanctuaries, along a north-south axis. (Figure 30.3).

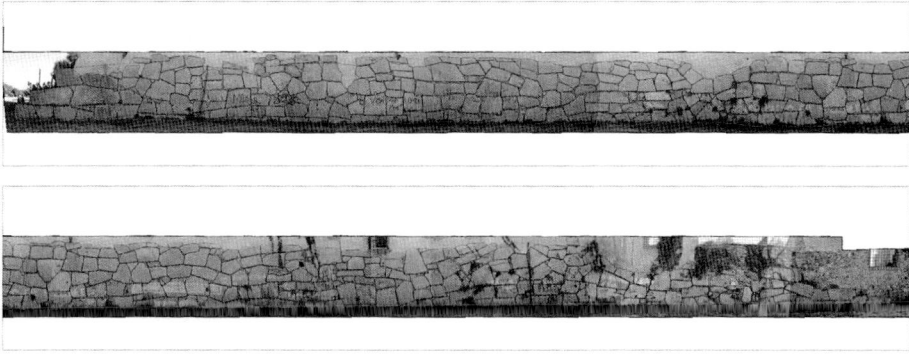

Figure 30.3   Walls of the Roman colony in polygonal masonry. (Prepared by B. Belelli Marchesini).

This systematic excavation has allowed us to investigate stratigraphically the largest sanctuary of Etruria and to reconstruct the stages of its life, from its foundation to the dismantling after the installation of the Roman colony around 270/268 BC, and the consequent obliteration of the Etruscan sanctuary-center. Gradually, the team from the University of Rome "La Sapienza," under the guidance of Massimo Pallottino first and then Giovanni Colonna, have brought to light and restored to the heritage of our culture an area crucial for the history of ancient Italy. Both the harbor and the sanctuary were well known and frequented by ancient peoples who scoured the routes of the Mediterranean. Greeks and Phoenicians were the first, and certainly, beginning at the end of the sixth century BC, the evidence gathered in the excavations allows us to affirm that the great emporium-sanctuary of Caere played the role of international sanctuary at the center of the Mediterranean.

According to G. Colonna, the port of Pyrgi combined commercial functions with those of a military arsenal; it is very likely that the fleet that engaged in battle against the Phocaeans of Alalia in the Sardinian Sea, that occurred circa 540 BC, was armed and launched from Pyrgi itself, where the coastal lagoons could accommodate haulage basins. The fortune of the port of Pyrgi was guaranteed by its special geological situation and by the abundant supply of fresh water provided by a copious spring that flows from the nearby hinterland, also used by the Roman colonists and active at least until the end of the eighteenth century of our era.

The mother-city, Caere, located inland 13 kilometers to the east, attached particular importance to its connections with its main port: to this end it arranged to construct a broad roadway, 10.4 meters wide, completely paved, which in an almost straight course linked the port to the city, replicating the proven system used in Athens-Piraeus. This exceptional piece of engineering followed a path already defined during the second half of the seventh century BC; exiting Caere the road passed between the great Orientalizing tumulus of Monte Tosto and the temple built in the sixth century to atone for the killing of the Phocaean prisoners after the battle of the Sardinian Sea already mentioned, and, after crossing the Caeretan plain, reached the back of the monumental sanctuary. From here it turned at a sharp angle to the north and, proceeding straight, parallel to the coast for about 800 meters, arrived in the northern district of the town located behind the harbor. Another quarter of the Etruscan town also extended to the south, almost as far as the sanctuary; thanks to the latest excavations (2009–2011), it is now possible to reconstruct more clearly the regular grid of the city blocks facing the sea, and intended either for residential use or for the warehousing/storage of foodstuffs. The Caere-Pyrgi road clearly marked the eastern boundary of this portion of the town that was subdivided by the parallel paths of regular city streets that joined the great thoroughfare to the sea.

The focus of the interest of Caere concentrates on the band to the south of the settlement at the end of the sixth century BC, when a radical intervention has a profound effect on the morphological character and on the organization of the territory through the use of a monumental sacred area intended to become a major attraction in the coastal landscape. In fact, since at least the middle of the century, in this sector is indicated the presence of unidentified sacred buildings to which belong fragments of architectural terracottas of the first phase that have been found in the course of excavations; but the fifty years between 510 and 470/460 BC is the period in which the attention of the political power of Caere is concentrated in the basic restructuring of the two sanctuaries that rose side by side along the coast, the famous monumental sanctuary and the southern sanctuary, identified in 1983, which is not more than 4000 square meters. In their maximum stage of development, the two sanctuaries will extend over a frontage of more than 180 meters, covering an area of about 14,000 square meters; the extension of the entire sacred area and its position in direct contact with the sea are an absolute exception in Etruria and find parallels only in the great sanctuary complexes of Greece and Magna Graecia. The Greek and Latin sources, for whom port and sanctuary were an indivisible system, ennobled the origins of this important place of worship, making them go back to the mythical population of the Pelasgians, and highlighting its great riches, the object of a sudden and disastrous raid conducted by Dionysius the Elder of Syracuse in 384 BC, who robbed the sanctuary of the fabulous sum of 1,500 talents of silver.

By the end of the sixth century BC, steps are taken in the great work of the parallel restructuring of the two sanctuaries. The most challenging interventions are reserved for the monumental sanctuary, which from now on will become a sort of manifesto of Caeretan political propaganda directed to the outside world (Figure 30.4). The works begin with the creation of a huge earthwork of clay to improve and raise the area, situated at a lower level than the settlement; on the embankment Temple B will be raised by digging a network of foundation trenches and employing blocks of red tuff extracted from the quarries of Caere, which are transported to the building site, in the construction. The construction of a monumental sacred building of the scope of Temple B requires a high level of technical and organizational expertise; the building techniques adopted in Etruria in the Late Archaic period involve not only walls of plastered tuff blocks but also roofing with wooden structures and, above all, the installation of a complex system of terracotta architectonic revetments to which was entrusted the dual responsibility of protecting the structures and conveying the message chosen for the decorative program.

The plan adopted for Temple B was inspired by a Greek model, perhaps mediated directly by familiarity with Campania: the temple, with façade facing the sea, has a peripteral plan (18.64 x 28.41 m) with two rows of columns on the façade and a narrow cella placed almost against the rear porch (Figure 30.5). The terracotta decoration of the building represented an innovative creation of the Caeretan artisans who conceived of a new homogeneous system comprising revetment plaques for the architraves and for the slopes of the roofs surmounted by simas, and, on the flanks, antefixes with the head of a

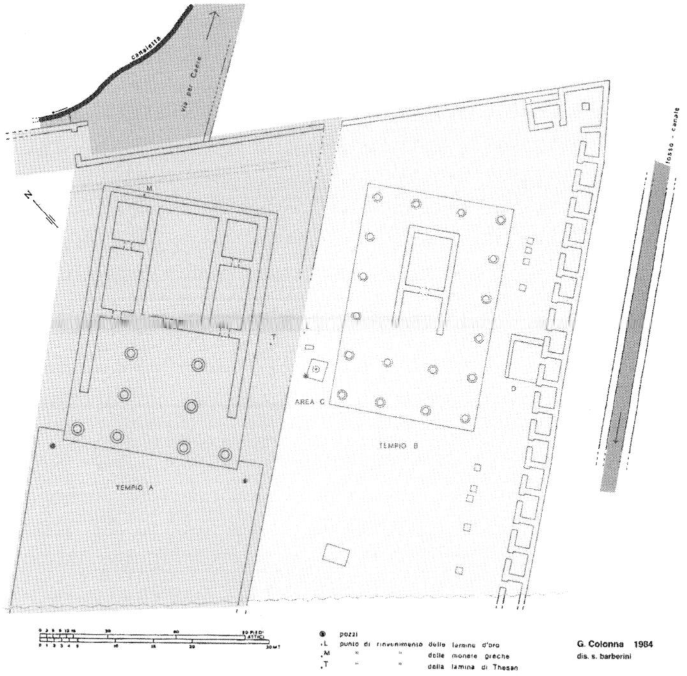

Figure 30.4   Monumental sanctuary: phase-plans of Temple B and Temple A
(Prepared by B. Belelli Marchesini).

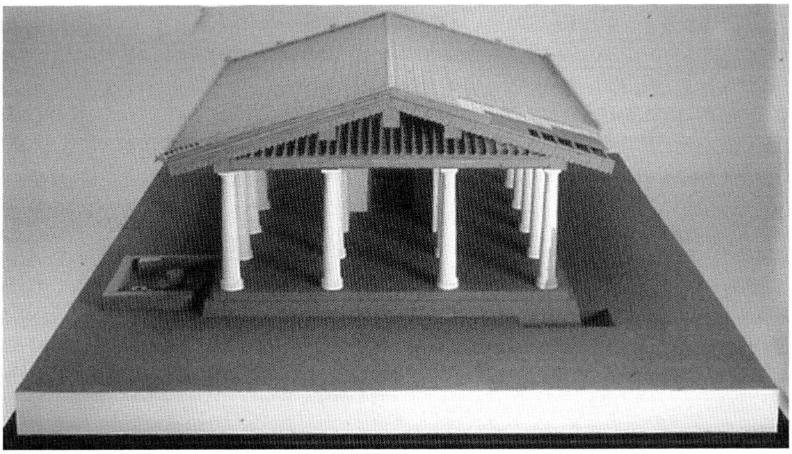

Figure 30.5   Reconstruction model of Temple B and of Sacred Area C (to left); Rome, Museo delle
Antichità Etrusche e Italiche, Università La Sapienza.

maenad, a silen or a negro inserted within a perforated nimbus. The figured decoration
was concentrated in large high-relief plaques designed to cover the ends of the main roof
beams with episodes from the myth of Heracles; the prominent position on the gable
end of the roof was reserved for the pair of acroterial statues depicting the hero with the
titular goddess of the temple, Uni (Hera/Juno).

From the outset, Temple B was placed inside a rectangular area defined by the north wall of the temenos including an impressive entrance portico open in the southeast corner and to the south of the long "hall" defined as the "building of the twenty cells." Covered by a roof with a single slope, it was decorated by an original system of antefixes with complete figures, symbolizing the different phases of the day. G. Colonna has proposed that the cells harbored the priestesses who practiced sacred prostitution, according to a cult practice imported from the Phoenician area, perhaps from the sanctuary of Aphrodite on Mount Eryx (Sicily), controlled in the sixth century BC by the Phoenicians.

The close connection with the Phoenician world that characterized the political program of Caere towards the end of the sixth century BC is revealed by the most important Etruscan epigraphic discovery of the second half of the twentieth century, the three gold plaques found in 1964 (see Figure 22.8), together with a fourth plaque in bronze, in Area C, a small quadrangular space set against the northern wall of Temple B and intended for open-air cult celebrations, with a courtyard paved with blocks of tuff. In the quadrangle were placed a cylindrical altar in gray tuff, with a large central hole that reached an underground cavity, intended for chthonic cults, a second, trapezoidal, altar in peperino, and a well that provided water essential to the rituals. When the temple was dismantled in the early third century BC, Area C was considered a sort of "area of respect" and to the east of the well was built a small enclosure with materials taken from the temple, in which were laid, carefully folded back on themselves, the three gold plaques and the bronze plaque. From the parallel texts of two gold plaques, one in Etruscan and one in Phoenician language, there opens a window into the history of archaic Caere: the temple with its outbuildings was built and dedicated to the Etruscan goddess Uni, assimilated to the Phoenician Astarte, by *Thefarie Velianas* the king-tyrant of Caere, which places the sanctuary of Pyrgi at the center of philo-Punic politics. The choice of the decorative program linked to the cycle of Heracles agrees well with the special attention that the *tyrannoi*, in Greece as in Italy, reserved for the figure of the hero. The change in the balance of the Tyrrhenian Sea has weighty impacts at Caere as well: the defeat of the Carthaginians at Himera in 480 BC, mainly engineered by the Syracusans, marks the beginning of difficulties in the southern Tyrrhenian Sea for the Etruscans; further serious defeat suffered by the Etruscans in the waters off Cumae in 474 BC, again at the hands of Syracuse, further reduces the importance of the maritime cities of Etruria in the Tyrrhenian, instead strengthening the role of Syracuse as champion of Hellenism. In this profoundly altered political climate very probably the tyranny's regime was toppled at Caere, as had happened at Cumae; continuing to regard the sanctuary of Pyrgi as the point intended to open access to the mother city for foreigners who sailed in the Tyrrhenian, the new regime vowed the construction of a new and more imposing temple, Temple A, which will be constructed a little over 20 meters to the north of its predecessor and perfectly parallel to it, around 470/460 BC. The sacred area was more than doubled to the north with a second extremely massive clay earthwork; also the road between Caere and Pyrgi, at the rear of Temple A, will be remodelled in order to create a courtyard intended for processions, which preceded a monumental entrance placed behind the temple.

For temple A the native plan of "Tuscanic" type was adopted, with three flanking cellae in the back and a deep, shady porch with three rows of columns between projecting *antae* (Figure 30.6). More impressive and spectacular than Temple B, Temple A presented itself to those who arrived from the sea, raised on a wide podium on a terrace at the corners of which were dug two wells to collect the dripwater from the roof. For the system of terracotta revetments the same types already in use at Caere and at *Falerii veteres* were adopted; all the care and attention were concentrated in the decorative program of the plaques designed to cover the ends of the ridge beams of the roof. The temple was most likely dedicated to the Etruscan goddess Thesan, as witnessed by a votive dedication of a worshiper, Tanchvil Catharnai (*ET* Cr 4.2). Assimilated to Latin Mater Matuta and to the Greek Leucothea, this powerful female deity forms part of the panorama attested in the Greek and Magna Graecian maritime sanctuaries in which the titulary gods hold powers as protectors of sea voyages, of passages between two places, and of all the events considered "passages": the birth of the day and the birth of human beings. To the Theban Leucothea, protector of sailors, who was received on the Italic coast by Heracles after having thrown herself into the sea to escape the jealousy of Hera, is attributed the head with wind-swept hair found in one of the wells beside Temple A (Figure 30.7). The choice of a myth rooted in the cultural heritage of Greek sailors for the decorative program, intended for the front gable, had been dictated by the desire to evoke the function of welcome and shelter developed for the nearby port.

On the rear, to the end of the ridge beam, was affixed the high-relief terracotta plaque, which measures a little over 1.50 m, in which are concentrated the most dramatic events of the saga of the Seven Against Thebes, with an amazing, free and innovative "unity of time and space" (see Figure 24.24). The unknown Etruscan master reveals a very clear personality and a confident and accomplished technique in exploiting the full potential of malleable clay. Characterized by a strong polychromy, the image was clearly visible to those approaching the temple from Caere and proceeding along what had come to assume the character of a "sacred way": in the background, Capaneus shouts his challenge to Zeus who, in front of him, raises his arm ready to hurl the thunderbolt that will blast him. In the foreground, below, Tydeus and Melanippus, wounded, are locked in mortal combat; in a last act of impiety, Tydeus bites his opponent in the head, to devour his brain. On the

Figure 30.6 Reconstruction model of Temple A; Rome, Museo delle Antichità Etrusche e Italiche, Università La Sapienza.

Figure 30.7   Architectural terracotta, replacement head from gable of Temple A, fourth century BC.

left, Athena, raising the vial of immortality intended for Tydeus, withdraws in disgust at the sight of such an act of cannibalism. The condemnation of impiety and arrogant challenge to the will of the gods and the universal, unwritten laws of human society and order were a warning to those who arrived from the mother city: the choice of such a theme, inserted in the climate of ethical tension that permeates contemporary Greek tragedy, expresses a clear condemnation of the previous tyrannical regime of Thefarie and reveals, in the entire scope of work performed in the sanctuary, the clear desire of the mother city to enshrine before foreign visitors the complete change that had occurred in the government of the city.

In full archaism, Caere has now definitely entered fully into its urban development and in this historical phase there is also definitively consolidated the role of the sanctuaries as promoters of cultural exchange and of artistic innovation and production; in the same way, it should be noted that the sanctuaries guaranteed safety and welcome to foreigners and also controlled commerce, guaranteed by their titulary gods.

The sanctuary continued to be frequented until about 273 BC, a date which marks the shift in Roman-Caeretan relations, resulting in the foundation of the *colonia maritima* of Pyrgi on the site of the former Etruscan settlement. Following the founding of the colony it was arranged to dismantle the sacred buildings and to deposit in the earth the complex architectural decorations, thus marking the end of worship.

The southern sanctuary, identified in 1983, was brought to light almost in its entirety; its surface area is very modest compared to the northern sanctuary (measuring approximately 2000 square meters). The bed of a channel, now dried up, at that time fed from a spring behind the sacred area, divides the two shrines, marking a limit and a ritual passage. The soil, which at this point formed a slight depression, was not profoundly altered by agricultural activities and has preserved, in an optimal situation, traces of ritual actions related to the life of the sanctuary, which excavation has allowed us to "read," furnishing information of great importance from a historical-religious viewpoint (Figure 30.2). The traits of the southern sanctuary, the rituals reconstructed, the typology of the offerings and the dedicatory inscriptions have recently led to the conclusion that in this area has been implanted perhaps the oldest cult place of the Demeter cult in Etruria, a cult most likely directly imported by the Greek sailors who landed on the Caeretan coast. This is not at odds with the passage of Aelian, author of the third century AD, who recounts how Syracuse, perhaps in the course of the raid of 384 BC, had carried off "the riches of Apollo and of Leucothea," also taking possession of the silver *trapeza* ("table") consecrated to the god; this leads to the conclusion that the second sanctuary can be ascribed to the god Apollo. The rich corpus of dedicatory inscriptions mentions mainly a pair of titulary divinities: in the first place the goddess Cavatha, assimilated to the Greek Kore, daughter of Demeter, and the *paredros* ("companion") Śuri, equated by G. Colonna originally to Faliscan Apollo Soranus, a deity with double aspect, both oracular and chthonic, and then assimilated to the god Hades, the husband of Kore.

In this sanctuary we do not find the interest in monumental organization that was evident in the northern sanctuary; the entire area is characterized by simple buildings, by modest equipment, and by altars made with different techniques, some with simple stone mounds, scattered at random. At first sight, it seems that altars and shrines have been made without any connection to a prearranged plan, but rather to meet the needs of worship dictated by temporary circumstances and details. This small shrine was in operation at the same time as the great official sanctuary, probably welcoming non-Etruscan visitors coming to the port to the north. The different stages of its life played out roughly parallel to those of the monumental sanctuary.

After an initial phase, indicated by the discovery of archaic antefixes with female heads, datable around 540 BC, at the close of the sixth century BC the cult appears concentrated in the center of the area, where there are gathered three basic elements from the point of view of ritual: the sacellum β, the altar ν, and the deposit ρ. The shrine was probably dedicated to two titulary divinities (as a foundation offering, beneath the left cella were found a pair of gold earrings, referring to the goddess Cavatha); an exceptional pair of busts of rampant Acheloos, placed on the corners of the roof as lateral acroteria, portray the mythical river-god symbolizing the strength of river waters conquered by Heracles in the course of his Labors, evocative of the work of controlling the watercourses next to the sanctuary. Covered at the top by a stone slab, altar ν was located inland, facing the entrance room of the shrine, a couple of meters from the deposit ρ, which perhaps constituted the foundation deposit. The latter, found intact, is one of the complexes of interest in the southern area, not only in terms of the interpretation of worship but also for the quality and the number of the offerings – made up of 46 vessels all complete when reconstructed, all deposited according to a precise ritual, inside a cylindrical cavity about 80 cm in diameter and about one meter deep. It is clear that the vases were placed in a circular pattern surrounding an Attic black-figured amphora, containing a number of valuable female ornaments (including a pendant in sheet silver in the form of a tortoise), arranged in three layers. In the two lower layers, the forms chosen are drinking vessels (*kylikes*), vases for pouring wine (*olpai*) and vases containing perfumed oils (*lekythoi*). With particular attention, they had tried to preserve the association of vases for drinking with vases for pouring, safeguarding in this way a precise memory of the various actions of libations with liquids (wine?) first poured from the *olpe* into the *kylix*, and from this onto the earth. In the top layer were deposited vases of larger dimensions, especially amphorae, which we may assume contained the liquids used in the performance of the ceremony. Almost all the vessels used in the performance of the ritual consist of Attic pottery, thanks to which it is possible to determine a good approximation of the date of the formation of the deposit, dating at least to the beginning of the fifth century BC. The creation of a small enclosure (*temenos* τ), incorporating these three "points of interest" further emphasizes the importance of separating them from the rest of the sacred area.

About the same time as the expansion of the monumental sanctuary occurred, the minor sanctuary was also expanded to the south. In the southeast sector the tholos-type altar λ was erected, which was accessed by a short ramp, the only feature with a character of monumentality, with which was probably associated the structured deposit κ, functioning as a votive deposit (see plan). Within the circumference of stones that delimited altar λ the exceptional offering of a group of lead ingots was buried (see Figure 37.16), while the contiguous deposit κ was made in three different nuclei deposited in succession. The act of consecration began in sector A, where the ground was prepared first by pouring the liquid from three different containers of perfumed substances (one *lekythos*, one *alabastron* and one *aryballos*) placed next to a "package" of leaves in iron and bronze sheet and covered with a rough row of stones on which was overturned a bronze basin. Inside the basin were also found three perfume vases, more valuable than those preceding (a pair of *alabastra* in alabaster and a small *oinochoe* in glass paste). The objects are clearly related to a female divinity, to whom the "package" of metal leaves also alludes, reminiscent of a ritual reserved for Demeter, the *phyllobolia* ("offering of leaves"). Further to the south, a cluster of vessels all of open forms, deposited without order, marks the second act and an ideological change in the rite. In the group, an Attic kantharos, datable to 470 BC, seems relatively isolated; attributed to the workshop of the Painter of the Syriskos, it is formed of masks of a silen and a maenad joined together. Since the *kantharos* is *par excellence* the vessel of Dionysos for drinking, and maenads and silens form part of the god's cortege, it is obvious that an attempt was made to characterize this deposit as "Dionysiac." This character is then reprised by the pair of column-craters, these too Attic, deposited closer to altar λ; one of the craters is decorated with Heracles in repose, who extends a large *kantharos* toward a silen who is ready to pour the wine from a goatskin; under Heracles' foot is the Etruscan inscription *mi fuflunusra*. This is a "speaking inscription" in which the vase announces that it belongs to Fufluns, the Etruscan version of Dionysos, with a precise match betweeen the language of the inscribed text, the image and the function of the vase, which was considered the symposium vase *par excellence*.

Other offerings, placed at the side of the two craters, emphasize a particular connection between the spheres of Demeter and Dionysos. A pair of female protome-busts, which in Etruria find their closest parallels in those from the newly discovered deposit of the sanctuary of the *emporium* of Gravisca, may be considered offerings linked to the cult of the pair of Demeter, tied to the cycles of nature and rebirth, and her daughter Kore. To the rituals of chthonic character reserved for the two goddesses may be assigned as well a large *olla* in impasto, placed in a hollow beside the busts, and containing heavy fragments of *aes rude*. The *olla* had certainly been used for an offering of chthonic character, because its base had been drilled and subsequently closed, allowing liquid to filter over the bronze. In this complex deposit the two deities, in charge of agricultural activities essential in the Greek and Etruscan worlds (the vine and wheat), probably were associated in a perspective within which the same relevance to the mystery religions is considered an integral part of the complex of beliefs and rituals associated with the cycles of rebirth of the forces of nature and of man himself.

In the corner towards the sea was built a second shrine, designated γ, about a decade later; with an elongated plan, it had been built so as not to allow a view from the threshold of the inner cella, isolated on all four sides, as if it had been conceived to define an obligatory path around its perimeter, according to rituals appropriate to the processions of Demeter cult. This particular value of the cults practiced in the sanctuary received a clear confirmation from the discovery of two documents, both of which carry a clearly interpretable message. First it is necessary to recall the lower part of a votive statue, of two-thirds life-size, assigned to the late Classical period, depicting a personage carrying a piglet held by the hind legs. This important votive fits into the scheme of the canonical ex-votos of the Demeter sanctuaries, where the "offrant with piglet" evokes a fundamental step in the rituals followed there. The second document, likewise unequivocal, consists of an inscription dedicated to Demeter, one of the few Greek inscriptions recovered from the southern area; it was found in the open space along the sea, in front of the shrine designated β and called the "west piazza." This is the second of two squares defined within the sacred space, the larger one, the "north piazzale," stretched over nearly a quarter of the area of the sanctuary, in the northeast sector. The realization of these spaces, framed by the various altars and shrines of which traces remain, has been traced to a massive renovation that was begun after the serious act of impiety linked to the looting by Dionysius. The violation of the consecrated area and of what was contained in it made it necessary to reconsecrate the sanctuary, obliterating existing structures and gathering up what had been consecrated to the gods as offerings or as instruments of worship. The southern area was obliterated and the two squares, north and west, were made using a massive "fill" in which votive offerings were mixed, the remains of animal sacrifices, and instruments used for the cult which, as such, could not be removed from the sacred area. In this way, a collection was formed that even now constitutes an assemblage for research that is privileged in the variety of materials present, and above all, by the exceptional quality and quantity of the Attic ceramics, all reduced to minute fragments and dispersed over many different spots. Despite the poor state of conservation, the recovered fragments have made it possible to reconstruct a single framework for the sanctuaries of Etruria, thanks to the presence of very special pieces, whose interest has increased significantly because it belongs to a find-context which confers on the complex, and on each individual piece, a value quite different from that inherent in grave goods (to date our most common source for such vases).

It should be noted, firstly, that in the fills in the squares, it appears clear that a deliberate selection was made in the choice of Attic pottery, privileging some very peculiar forms, that have been associated with vases present in various sanctuaries of the Greek world dedicated to female divinities presiding over the rites of passage from childhood to the age of fertility (as in the sanctuary of Artemis at Brauron), or, to the sphere of fecundity, as is the case in Demeter sanctuaries and in others related to them such as the sanctuary of the Malophoros at Selinus. In the deposits in the squares at Pyrgi there recur thus series of the little *oinochoai* in the form of a female head, certainly to be assigned to rituals linked to female deities, and an even more numerous series of *lekythoi*, of varying capacity and quality, from the most common types produced in large numbers from the end of the sixth century BC, to the more rare pair of red-figured *lekythoi* by the Berlin Painter. A substantial number of plates, almost exclusively black-figured, is another find outside the usual situation for Etruscan sanctuaries; also extraordinary is the presence of the precious Attic white-ground pottery, a product that, by its very delicacy, was not intended for common use, but recurs as an offering in the sanctuary of Eleusis, and is represented in Pyrgi by a kylix and two plates. In the sanctuaries of goddesses, especially Brauron and Eleusis, there are known the pair of black-figured *epìnetra,* objects culturally related to the Greek world, where they were used to facilitate the work of spinning and, as an engagement gift, symbolized the change in status of girls. The strong socio-religious valence of such objects, which accompanied the offerings associated with rites of passage, falls outside the Etruscan mentality and is a strong indication of the presence of visitors accustomed to express important religious acts, such as the consecration of objects that symbolize the passage of status, according to methods and means that are purely Greek.

Among the materials recovered from the great southern sanctuary is a *phiale mesomphalos*, which patient conservation has enabled us to partially reconstruct from numerous fragments scattered throughout the fill of the northern square; it represents the most significant offering consecrated in the southern sanctuary, for its dimensions, its quality and for its decorative subjects (Figure 30.8). The *phialai* were ritual vases intended for libations; in this case, the exceptional size (41.7 cm in diameter) does not make it suitable for this use, but places it in a category of objects produced solely for the

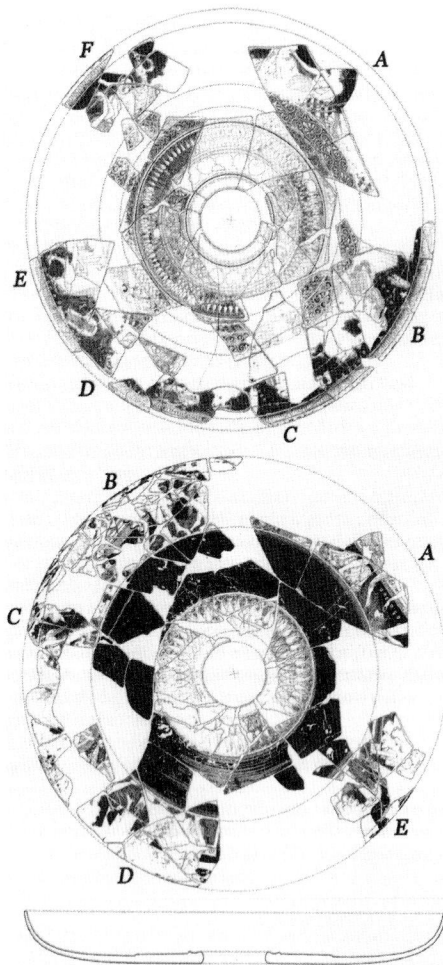

Figure 30.8 Attic red-figure mesomphalic *phiale* from the southern sanctuary: Odysseus and the Suitors.

purpose of offering, analogous to what has been attested in the case of the great *kylix* attributed to Onesimos and dedicated to Heracles in the sanctuary of Porta S. Antonio in the mother city, Caere. This large vessel, in size and in the profile of its very thin walls, testifies above all to the great skill of the potter, certainly presented technical difficulties in the process of its throwing and firing. The break restored in antiquity with small bronze clamps may have been produced or manifested just after firing.

The subject chosen for the decoration of the exterior, as in the case of the high relief in the gable of Temple A, is a sign of a precise ethico-political ideology that entrusts to the figural message a stern warning on the observance of the laws of hospitality and social life. On the exterior, in a figural register slightly over 13 cm in height, runs a continuous frieze of a complex composition that depicts with great excitement the dramatic conclusion of the banquet of the wicked Suitors, executed by Odysseus after his return. The decapitation of the diviner Leiodes, the final victim of Odysseus, is clearly identifiable in the severed head that has fallen beneath a couch. From the *kline* ("couch") hang, now inert, the arms of the slain suitors and all the drama of the event appears in the overlap of lifeless bodies and fallen, overturned couches, in the meticulous depiction of the tremendous upheaval that struck the banquet hall, where nothing more (pottery, tripods, tables) is intact or in place. Significantly, the interior frieze contrasts with the tragic outcome of the wicked banquet, carried out in defiance of the laws of hospitality and society. The work of a vase painter of great skill in drawing and composition, which was put to the test in this, the oldest representation remaining to us of the massacre of the Suitors, the *phiale* can be attributed to the mature phase of the unknown master known as the "Brygos Painter," around 470 BC.

The organization of the decoration is knowingly calibrated: while on the interior a series of elaborate decorative friezes frame the figured field and the hole where the *omphalos*, now lost, was placed, on the exterior the figured field is spread over a wide black band using the full height of the visible part of the wall, with a desired effect of contrast. On both exterior and interior the decorative theme is the symposium, with contrasting results: while on the interior frieze the banqueters, leaning on cushions, are enjoying everything that a banquet among free men can offer (wine, music and song, the company of *hetairai*), in the exterior frieze the banquet hall, sumptuously furnished, is the scene of the massacre of the guests. The different atmosphere that prevails in the two scenes has a profound impact on the composition: on the interior the space is marked by the calm figures of the diners, joined in groups formed of wreathed youths facing young girls, in two cases portrayed with long flowing hair, a genuine "bravura piece" of the potter. The figurative repertoire is that adopted by the Athenian vase painters of the years around 490/480 BC; the melody of the double flute played by a standing youth induces an ecstatic atmosphere to which a banqueter on a couch has abandoned himself in a rare frontal view.

On the exterior, the continuous overlapping of bodies on different levels, the bold views of overturned and destroyed furniture, illustrate the drama of the event. On the exterior is one of the rare representations of the massacre of the Suitors that has come down to us, perhaps the oldest yet known. In this case the final phase of the massacre is represented, where the hero Odysseus rather ruthlessly restores order to his house and punishes those who have violated the sacred rules of hospitality and banquet. The subject therefore represented a stern warning to comply with the norms governing the coexistence of citizens with full rights and such a reminder of the rules of coexistence "among equals" could be linked to a particular political situation in the mother city of Caere. The decorative scheme chosen for the gable of the monumental Temple A reveals the same ethico-political tension that conforms to the ideals espoused by Athens in the decade of the Persian Wars. The sources recall that in the stoa of Athena Areia at Plataea, rebuilt by the Athenians after the war, the same themes present at Pyrgi recurred in two frescoes: Polygnotus portrayed Odysseus near the end of the slaughter of the Suitors, and Onasias depicted the expedition of Adrastus and of the Seven against Thebes (Pausanias 9.4.2).

At Caere as at Pyrgi, the sanctuaries appear to be the recipients of the products of great effort, the implementation of which certainly constituted an example of the technological and stylistic innovations of the most successful ceramic workshops of Athens. The period around the Persian Wars is one of the most innovative and fruitful, and we cannot exclude the possibility that such demanding products were executed by famous masters upon commission. Two hypotheses have been advanced on defining the personality of the master who decorated the *phiale*: Onesimos (Williams 1993), to whom we owe the great kylix from Caere (exhibited in the Caere Museum, *sala* Castellani), or the Brygos Painter (Baglione 2000), certainly related to the first period of his career, in that period of major activity in the years around 480/470 BC.

Details of the Mesomphalic Phiale: interior

The banqueters are depicted in the pose of the "Banquet on the ground" leaning on cushions but without couches; from above, moving to the right are identified: A – first couple, with female figure with long, light-colored hair; B – isolated female figure to left, with hair gathered in a *sakkos*; C –male couple, with diner on right striking the strings of a *barbiton* (lyre); D – second couple (probably man and woman) of whom only intertwined arms are visible; E – flute-player in transparent chiton who with melody of a double flute induces a state of euphoria in the guest, depicted collapsed on the pillows, his face frontal; F – finally, a youth who extends his right hand to stroke the chin of a girl in front of him, followed by the body of another guest, isolated. Between the banqueters other instruments are hung by cords (one lyre and one *cithara*).

Mesomphalic Phiale: exterior

The pivotal point of the representation is the detail of the decapitated male head that has fallen to the ground (A) framed between the bloodied arms of two slain banqueters dangling over the edge of the *kline* and the right foot of a fleeing personage; on the left, facing the scene, an armed man (lower part of his cuirass visible); at the extreme left corner, alongside the leg of a second *kline*, one can see the head of another fallen man, his face to the ground (B). The fragment which remains most clearly legible illustrates one of the final events of *Odyssey* Book 22, dedicated to the slaughter of the suitors: Odysseus, despite the pleas of the *haruspex* Leiodes, cuts off his head with a sword he has snatched from the ground: "and the head, still speaking, finished in the dust" (*Odyssey* 22.329). In the following groups of fragments it is possible to identify other elements that emphasize the ruthlessness of the massacre: Group B (left): two men fallen back onto a *kline* (the arm of one can be seen), the second, wreathed, has his head on the ground; C – on a third, broken, *kline* lies a victim (the color of the fragment is due to exposure of the vase to fire), while in front runs a man armed with greaves; before a fourth *kline* – D – from which hangs the hand of another victim, a personage wrapped in a large, draped cloak is in flight; beneath the kline a *trapeza* (serving-table) is still standing, holding food and furnishings. After a gap, a *trapeza* and perhaps a *kottabos* (gaming-stand) overturned in front of the last kline – E. It is not possible to discern additional characters from those mentioned in the *Odyssey*. The richness of the furnishings (the covers all have long fringes, the *klinai* have finely carved feet, and bronze vessels and a tripod are identifiable) evokes an atmosphere of high social rank that is well suited to the home of Odysseus.

BIBLIOGRAPHY

General works on the history of inhabited territory:

Annovazzi, V. (1853) *Storia di Civitavecchia dalla sua origine fino all'anno 1848*, Rome.

Belelli Marchesini, B. (2001) 'L'abitato costiero di Pyrgi: osservazioni sull'impianto urbanistico e sugli aspetti edilizi' in J. Rasmus Brandt and K. Larsson (eds), *From huts to houses. Transformation of ancient societies*, Proceedings of an International Seminar organized by the Norwegian and Swedish Institutes (Rome, 21–24 September 1997), Stockholm, pp. 395–405.

Canina, L. (1840) 'Pyrgi degli Agillei o dei Ceriti,' *AnnInst* 12, pp. 34–44, pls. E–F.

Castagnoli, F., Cozza, L. (1957) 'Appunti sulla topografia di Pyrgi,' *PBSR* 25, pp. 16–21.

Colonna, G. (1963) 'Prima ricognizione dell'entroterra pyrgense,' *StEtr* 31, pp. 149–167.

——(1968) 'La via Caere-Pyrgi' in *La via Aurelia da Roma a Forum Aureli, QuadIstTopRoma* 4, pp. 75–87.

——(1996) *Pyrgi, EAA*, II suppl., IV, pp. 678–684.

——(1997a) 'Divinités peu connues du pantheon étrusque' in F. Gaultier and D. Briquel (eds), *Les étrusques plus religieux des hommes. État de la recherche sur la religion étrusque,* Actes du Colloque International (Paris 17–19 November 1992), Paris, pp. 167–184.

——(2001) 'Divinazione e culto di Rath/Apollo a Caere (a proposito del santuario in località S. Antonio),' *ArchCl* 52, 2001, pp. 151–173.

Steingräber, S. (1981) *Städte, Heiligtümern, Nekropolen*, Munich, pp. 455–462.

Torelli, M. (1980) *Etruria* (Guide archeologiche Laterza, 3), Bari, pp. 96–105.

Excavation reports:

Complete reports on the excavation campaigns in the monumental sanctuary are published in:

Pallottino, M. and Colonna, G. (eds) (1959) *Pyrgi*.

Aa.Vv. (1970) *Santa Severa (Rome). Scavi e ricerche nel sito dell'antica* Pyrgi, 1957–1958, NSchttp://www.db.dyabola.de/dya/dya_srv2.dll?07&dir=X6KB60AQ&RecNo=482518, pp. 143–263.

Aa.Vv. (1970) *Pyrgi. Scavi del Santuario etrusco (1959–1967). NSc* XXIV, II suppl., Rome.

Aa.Vv. (1992) *Pyrgi. Scavi del santuario etrusco (1969–1971)*, NSc, 1988–89, XLII–XLIII, II suppl., Rome.

The sanctuaries:

Baglione, M. P. (ed.) (2011c) *Massimo Pallottino. Tre momenti nella vita di uno studioso: Veio, Pyrgi, Milano '55* Exhibition catalogue (Polo Museale dell'Università La Sapienza, Rome 15 May 2010), Rome.

Baglione, M. P., Belelli Marchesini, B., Carlucci, C., Gentili, M. D. and Michetti, L. M. (forthcoming) 'Pyrgi, un santuario al centro del Mediterraneo' in *Sanctuaries and the power of consumption. Networking and the formation of elites in the archaic western Mediterranean world*, Proceedings of the International Conference (Innsbruck, 20–23 March 2012).

Belelli Marchesini, B., Carlucci, C., Gentili, M. D. and Michetti, L. M. (forthcoming) 'Considerazioni sul regime delle offerte nel santuario di Pyrgi' in *Il fanum Voltumnae e i santuari comunitari dell'Italia antica*, Atti del XIX Convegno Internazionale di studi sulla storia e l'archeologia dell'Etruria (Orvieto, 16–18 December 2011).

Colonna, G. (1998a) 'Il santuario etrusco di *Pyrgi*' in L. Drago Troccoli (ed.), *Scavi e ricerche archeologiche dell'Università di Roma "La Sapienza,"* Rome: L'Erma di Bretschneider, pp. 125–132.

——(2000) 'Il santuario di Pyrgi dalle origini mitistoriche agli altorilievi frontonali dei Sette e di Leucotea,' *ScAnt* 10, pp. 251–336.

The monumental sanctuary:

Carlucci, C. (2006) 'Osservazioni sulle associazioni e sulla distribuzione delle antefisse di II fase appartenenti ai sistemi decorativi etrusco-laziali' in I. Edlund-Berry, J. Kenfield and G. Greco (eds), *Deliciae Fictiles III. Architectural Terracottas in Ancient Italy: New Discoveries and Interpretations*, Proceedings of the International Conference (Rome, 7–8 November 2002), Oxford, pp. 2–21.

Colonna, G. (1965b) 'Il santuario di Pyrgi alla luce delle recenti scoperte,' *StEtr* 33, pp. 191–219.

——(1966) 'Nuovi elementi per la storia del santuario di Pyrgi,' *ArchCl* XVIII, pp. 85–102.

——(ed.) (1985) *Santuari d'Etruria*. Exhibition catalogue (Arezzo, 19 May–20 October 1985), Milan, pp. 127–141.

——(ed.) (1996) *L'altorilievo di Pyrgi. Dei ed eroi greci in Etruria*, Rome.

The southern sanctuary:

Baglione, M. P. (1989) 'Quelques données sur les plus recentes fouilles de Pyrgi' in *Ancient Greek and related pottery*, Proceedings of the 3rd Symposium on ancient Greek and related pottery (Copenhagen 1988), Copenhagen, pp. 17–24.

——(1989–90) 'Considerazioni sui santuari di Pyrgi e di Veio-Portonaccio,' *Anathema*, pp. 651–667.

——(1997a) 'Cratere a colonnette a figure rosse con Herakles simposiasta' in A. Maggiani (ed.), *Vasi attici figurati con dediche a divinità etrusche*, Rome: G. Bretschneider, pp. 85–93.

——(1997b) 'Ritrovamenti dall'area sud di Pyrgi: due askoi frammentari del *Seven Lobster-Claws Group*' in *Etrusca et Italica. Scritti in ricordo di Massimo Pallottino*, Pisa-Rome 1997, 1–24.

——(2000) 'Rinvenimenti di ceramica attica dal santuario dell'area sud' in *Dei ed eroi greci in Etruria*, Atti del Colloquio Internazionale (Rome 1997), *ScAnt* 10, pp. 337–382.

——(2004) 'Il santuario sud di Pyrgi' in M. Bentz and C. Reusser (eds), *Attische Vasen in etruskischem Kontext. Funde aus Häusern und Heiligtümern*, Beihefte CVA Deutschland, II, Munich 2004, pp. 85–106.

——(2008a) 'Esame del santuario meridionale di Pyrgi,' *Atti Roma*, pp. 301–318.

——(2009) 'Culti e culture dal santuario dell'Area Sud di Pyrgi' in S. Fortunelli and C. Masseria (eds), *Ceramica attica da santuari della Grecia, della Ionia e dell'Italia*, Atti del Convegno Internazionale (Perugia 14–17 March 2007), Venosa, pp. 217–232.

Colonna, G. (1991–92) 'Altari e sacelli. L'area Sud di *Pyrgi* dopo otto anni di ricerche,' *RendPontAc* 64, pp. 63–115.

——(1994) 'L'Apollo di Pyrgi' in *Magna Grecia Etruschi Fenici*, Atti XXXIII, Convegno di Studi sulla Magna Grecia (Taranto, 8–13 October 1993), Taranto, pp. 345–375.

——(1995) 'Scavi e Scoperte. Pyrgi (Com. di S. Marinella, Rome),' *StEtr* 61, pp. 440–446.

New excavations:

Baglione, M. P. (ed.) (2011b), *Fili e tele. Dee, donne e case. Un deposito rituale dallo scavo di Pyrgi. Settembre 2010*, Exhibition catalogue (Rome 2011), Rome, pp. 32–33.

Baglione, M. P., Belelli Marchesini, B., Carlucci, C. and Michetti L. M. (2010) 'Recenti indagini nel comprensorio archeologico di Pyrgi (2009–2010),' *ScAnt* 16, pp. 541–560.

The epigraphic heritage:

Colonna, G. (1965) 'La donazione pyrgense di Thefarie Velianas,' *ArchCl* 17, pp. 286–292.

——(1970) *Le lamine di Pyrgi* Quaderni Accademia nazionale dei Lincei 147, Rome.

——(1997) 'L'iscrizione del cratere di Pyrgi con Eracle bevitore' in A. Maggiani (ed.), *Vasi attici figurati con dediche a divinità etrusche*, Rome: G. Bretschneider, pp. 94–98.

Pallottino, M., Colonna, G., Vlad Borrelli, L. and Garbini, G. (1964) 'Scavi nel santuario etrusco di Pyrgi. Relazione preliminare della settima campagna di scavo 1964 e scoperta di tre lamine d'oro inscritte in etrusco e in punico,' *ArchCl* 16, pp. 49–117.

The Roman colony:

Baglione, M. P. (1988–89) 'Le monete' in *Pyrgi* 1988–89, pp. 126–131, 322–324.

——(forthcoming) 'Osservazioni sull'organizzazione territoriale del comprensorio di Pyrgi' in *Caere e Pyrgi: il territorio, la viabilità e le fortificazioni*, Atti della Giornata di Studio (Rome, 1 March 2012), *Caere* 6.

——(2011a) 'Il deposito Rho' in Baglione 2011, pp. 42–45.

——(2011b) 'Pyrgi, santuario meridionale – deposito rho' in Baglione 2011b, pp. 43–45.

——(forthcoming) 'Analisi delle fortificazioni della colonia romana e rapporti con l'abitato etrusco' in *Caere e Pyrgi: il territorio, la viabilità e le fortificazioni*, Atti della Giornata di Studio (Rome 1 March 2012), *Caere* 6.

——(forthcoming) 'Le mura della colonia marittima di Pyrgi' in *Mura di legno, mura di terra, mura di pietra: fortificazioni nel Mediterraneo antico* Atti del Convegno (Rome, 7–9 May 2012), *ScAnt* 19.

Bartoloni, G., Colonna, G. and Grottanelli C. (eds) (1989–90) *Anathema. Regime delle offerte e vita dei santuari nel Mediterraneo antico* (Atti del Convegno Internazionale, Rome, 15–18 June 1989), *ScAnt* 3–4, pp. 13–927.

Belelli Marchesini, B. (1988–89) *L'abitato etrusco di Pyrgi* (Tesi di Laurea, Università degli Studi di Roma La Sapienza).

——(2012) 'Il circuito e le porte delle mura "pelasgiche" di Pyrgi' in L. Attenni and D. Baldassarre (eds), *Atti del Quarto Seminario Internazionale di Studi sulle mura poligonali* (Alatri, 7–10 October 2009), Rome, pp. 303–311.

Cavallini, M., Drago, L., Felli, F. and Saviano G. (2003) 'Metallurgy in Etruria: data analyses on lead, copper, bronze and iron objects from Veii and Pyrgi' in *International Conference Archaeometallurgy in Europe* (Milan 24–26 September 2003), Milan, vol. 2, pp. 475–482.

Cluverius, P. (1624) *Italia antiqua*, Lugduni Batavorum.

Coccolini, G. and Follieri M. (1980) 'I legni dei pozzi del tempio A nel santuario etrusco di Pyrgi,' *StEtr* 48, pp. 277–291.

Colonna, G. (1959) 'Osservazioni sull'area urbana etrusca e romana' in *Pyrgi* 1959, pp. 253–258.

——(1960) 'Fistula iscritta da Pyrgi' in *NSc*.

——(1965a) 'Fortificazioni romane di Pyrgi,' *BdA* 50, p. 126.

——(1970) 'Il Tempio B. Le strutture' in *Pyrgi* 1970, pp. 275–289.

——(1981a) 'La dea di Pyrgi. Bilancio aggiornato dei dati archeologici (1978)' in *Die Göttin von Pyrgi,* Atti dell'Incontro (Tübingen 16–17 gennaio 1979) (Biblioteca di Studi Etruschi, 12), Florence, pp. 13–34.

——(1984) 'Apollon, les Étrusques et Lipara,' *MEFRA* 96, pp. 557–578.

——(1984–85) 'Novità sui culti di Pyrgi,' *RendPontAc* 62, pp. 57–88.

——(1985) 'Anfore da trasporto arcaiche il contributo di Pyrgi' in *Il commercio etrusco arcaico.* Atti dell'incontro di studio (5–7 December 1983), *QuadAEI* 9, pp. 5–18.

——(1988–89) 'Il Tempio B. Le strutture' in *Pyrgi* 1970, pp. 171–183.

——(1989–90a) 'Pyrgi,' *StEtr* LVI, (*REE*), pp. 313–324, nn. 21–41.

——(1989–90b) 'Tempio e santuario nel lessico delle lamine di Pyrgi,' *Anathema*, pp. 197–216.

——(1996a) 'L'Apollo di Pyrgi' in Magna Grecia, Etruschi, Fenici, Atti del XXXIII Convegno di Studi sulla Magna Grecia, Taranto 1993 (Napoli 1996), pp. 345–375.

——(1996b) 'Pyrgi' in *Enciclopedia dell'arte antica*, II suppl., pp. 678–684.

——(1998b) 'Pelagosa, Diomede e le rotte dell'Adriatico,' *ArchCl*, 50, pp. 363–378.

——(2003) *REE* 2003 (*StEtr* 69,), pp. 319–322, n. 29.

——(2004a) 'I Greci di Caere' in *Atti Orvieto* 2007, pp. 69–94.

——(2004b) 'La "disciplina" etrusca e la dottrina della città fondata,' *StRom* 52, 2004, pp. 303–311.

——(2005a) 'Caere' in *StEtr* 71, pp. 168–188, nn. 26–37.

——(2005b) *Italia ante Romanum Imperium. Scritti di antichità etrusche, italiche e romane*, 4, Pisa-Rome.

——(2006a) 'Cerveteri. La Tomba delle Iscrizioni Graffite' in *Atti Civita Castellana* 2006, pp. 419–451.

——(2006b) 'Sacred architecture and the religion of the Etruscans' in N. Thomson de Grummond and E. simon (eds), *The Religion of the Etruscans*, Austin 2006, pp. 132–168.

——(2007a) 'L'Apollo di Pyrgi, Šur/Šuri (il "Nero") e l'Apollo *Sourios*,' *StEtr* 73, pp. 101–134.

——(2007b) 'Novità su Thefarie Velianas' in *Atti Orvieto* 2007 pp. 9–24.

——(2010a) 'A proposito del primo trattato romano-cartaginese (e della donazione pyrgense ad Astarte)' in *Atti Orvieto* 2010, pp. 275–304.

——(2010b) 'The "Seven Against Thebes" Relief (Tydeus and Capaneus at the Siege of Thebes), Unknown Etruscan artist' in C. Dell (ed.), *What Makes a Masterpiece? Encounters with Great Works of Art*, London 2010, pp. 34–37.

——(forthcoming) 'Ancora su Šur/Šuri. 1. L'epiteto *Eista ("il dio"). 2. L'attributo del fulmine,' *StEtr* 75.

——(forthcoming) 'Il pantheon degli Etruschi – "i più religiosi degli uomini" – alla luce delle scoperte di Pyrgi,' *RendLinc*.

Colonna, G. and Maras, D. F. (2003) 'Pyrgi,' *StEtr* 69, (*REE*), pp. 307–337, nn. 19–54.

Colonna, G., Maras, D. F. and Morandi, M. (1998) 'Pyrgi,' *StEtr* 64, (*REE*), pp. 369–422, nn. 33–96.

Coppi, A. (1838) 'Dei castelli di Pirgi, S. Severa, S. Marinella, Loterno, Castel Giuliano e Sasso,' *DissPontAcc* 8, pp. 77–91.

Cristofani, M. (1986) 'Nuovi dati per la storia urbana di Caere,' *BdA* 35–36, pp. 1–24.

De Rossi, G. M., Di Domenico, P. G. and Quilici, L. (1968) 'La via Aurelia da Roma a Civitavecchia, *QuadIstTopRoma*' 4, pp. 13–73.

Della Fina, G. M. (ed.) (2003) *Tra Orvieto e Vulci*, Atti del X Convegno internazionale di Studi sulla Storia e Archeologia dell'Etruria (Orvieto 2002), *AnnFaina* 10, Rome.

——(ed.) (2004) *I Greci in Etruria*, Atti XI Convegno Internazionale di Studi sulla storia e l'archeologia dell'Etruria (Orvieto 2003), *AnnFaina* 11, Rome.

——(ed.) (2007) *Etruschi, Greci, Fenici e Cartaginesi nel Mediterraneo centrale*, Atti XIV Convegno internazionale di Studi sulla storia e l'archeologia dell'Etruria (Orvieto 2006), *AnnFaina* XIV, Rome.

——(ed.) (2009) *Gli Etruschi e Roma. Fasi monarchica e alto-repubblicana*, Atti XVI Convegno internazionale di Studi sulla storia e l'archeologia dell'Etruria (Orvieto 2008), *AnnFaina* 16, Rome.

——(ed.) (2010) *La grande Roma dei Tarquini*, Atti XVII Convegno Internazionale di Studi sulla Storia e l'Archeologia dell'Etruria (Orvieto 2009), *AnnFaina* 17, Rome.

Drago Troccoli, L. (2012) 'Ancore litiche, ancore in piombo ed altri "oggetti del sacro" in metallo dal santuario meridionale di Pyrgi' in V. Nizzo and L. La Rocca (eds), *Antropologia e acheologia a confronto: rappresentazioni e pratiche del sacro* (Atti del 2° Congresso Internazionale di Studi (Rome 20–21 May 2011), Rome 2012, pp. 827–840.

——(forthcoming) '*Aes rude* e lingotti. Tra esperienze premonetali e offerte votive' in *Il metallo come misura della ricchezza*, Atti del IV Convegno Internazionale di Archeologia Sperimentale (Civitella Cesi, 13–15 April 2012).

Dupré Raventós, X., Ribichini, S. and Verger S. (eds) (2008) Saturnia tellus. *Definizioni dello spazio consacrato in ambiente etrusco, italico, fenicio-punico, iberico e celtico*, Atti del Convegno Internazionale (Rome 2004), Rome.

Enei, F. (1994) 'Pyrgi: recupero del circuito murario romano. Relazione di attività 1992–1993,' *Archeologia Uomo-Territorio, Rivista scientifica dei G.A. d'Italia*, 13, pp. 244–250.

——(2001) *Progetto* Ager Caeretanus. *Il litorale di* Alsium, Santa Marinella.

——(2004) *Pyrgi sommersa. Ricognizioni archeologiche subacquee nel porto dell'antica Caere, Pyrgi*, Santa Marinella.

——(2008) *Pyrgi sommersa. Ricognizioni archeologiche subacquee nel porto dell'antica Caere*, Santa Marinella.

——(2011) 'Alle origini del porto etrusco di Pyrgi: i presupposti preistorici,' *Archaeologia maritima mediterranea* 8, pp. 13–28.

——(2012) 'Pyrgi e le sue mura poligonali: recenti scoperte nel castrum e nell'area portuale' in L. Attenni and D. Baldassarre (eds), *Atti del Quarto Seminario Internazionale di Studi sulle mura poligonali* (Alatri, 7–10 October 2009), Rome 2012, pp. 313–324.

Fortunelli, S. and Masseria, C. (eds) (2009) *Ceramica attica da santuari della Grecia, della Ionia e dell'Italia*, Atti Convegno Internazionale Perugia 2007, Venosa.

Frau, B. (1990) 'I porti ceretani di Pyrgi e Castrum Novum," in A. Maffei and F. Nastasi (eds), *Caere e il suo territorio. Da Agylla a Centumcellae*, Rome 1990, pp. 319–327.

Giuliani, C. F. and Quilici, L. (1964) 'La via Caere-Pyrgi,' *QuadIstTopRoma* 1, pp. 5–15.

Linington, R. E. (1963) *Esplorazione geofisica a Pyrgi. Giugno-luglio 1962*, *ArchCl* 15, pp. 256–261.

——(1969) 'Prospezione geofisica a Pyrgi. II campagna,' *ArchCl* 21, 2, pp. 297–298.

——(1970) 'La prospezione geofisica' in *Pyrgi* 1970, pp. 744–755.

Maggiani, A. (1997) *Vasi attici figurati con dediche a divinità etrusche, RdA* Suppl. 18, Rome.

Maras, D. F. (2000) 'Le iscrizioni sacre etrusche sul vasellame in età tardo-arcaica e recente,' *ScAnt* 10, pp. 121–137.

——(2007) 'Divinità etrusche e iconografia greca: la connotazione sessuale delle divinità solari ed astrali,' *Polifemo* 7, 2007, pp. 101–126.

——(2008) 'Pyrgi,' *StEtr* 74, 2008 (REE), pp. 317–324, nn. 70–78.

——(2009a) *Il dono votivo. Gli dei e il sacro nelle iscrizioni etrusche di culto* (Biblioteca di Studi Etruschi 46), Rome.

Melis, F. (1970) 'Tempio A. Le terrecotte eseguite a stampo' in *Pyrgi* 1970, pp. 83–188.

——(1985) 'Modello di ricostruzione del Tempio B,' *Santuari d'Etruria* 1985, p. 130.

Odysseus (1999) B. Andreae (ed.), *Odysseus. Mythos und Erinnerung*, Exhibition catalogue, (Munich 1999), Mainz.

Pallottino, M. (1957) 'Scavi nel santuario etrusco di Pyrgi: relazione preliminare della prima campagna, 1957,' *ArchCl* 9, pp. 206–222.

——(1965) 'Nuova luce sulla storia di Roma arcaica dalle lamine d'oro di Pyrgi,' *StRom* 13, pp. 1–13.

Rallo, A. (1970) 'Le terrecotte non figurate' in *Pyrgi* 1970, pp. 203–234.

Rovere, A., Antonioli, F., Enei, F. and Giorgi, S. (2011) 'Relative sea level change at the archaeological site of Pyrgi (Santa Severa, Rome) during the last seven millennia,' *Quaternary* n. 232, 1, pp. 82–91.

Saviano, G., Felli, F. and Drago, L. (2007) 'Etruria meridionale e Lazio: analisi su reperti metallici e fittili provenienti da Veio, dal santuario di Pyrgi e dall'area dell'Artemisio' in M. Cavallini, G. Gigante (eds) *De Re Metallica. Dalla produzione antica alla copia moderna*, Rome 2007, pp. 73–102.

Scarpignato, M. (1985) *Oreficerie etrusche arcaiche*, Rome.

Serra, F. R. (1970) 'Le ceramiche grezze' in *Pyrgi* 1970, pp. 509–552.

Sorrentino, C. (2005) 'Analisi paleozoologiche a Pyrgi,' *Atti Milano* 2005.

CHAPTER THIRTY ONE

ORVIETO, CAMPO DELLA FIERA –
FANUM VOLTUMNAE

———— •◆• ————

Simonetta Stopponi

The Etruscan *Velzna* (Latin Volsinii), the current Orvieto, was an important *polis* exalted by the ancient writers for its wealth and power.[1] Valerius Maximus (9.1, ext. 2), for example, defines it as *"opulenta, moribus et legibus ordinata, Etruriae caput."* The latest modern criticism believes that near the city was located the *Fanum Voltumnae*, the federal sanctuary of the Etruscans of which Livy writes on several occasions (4.23.5, 4.25.7, 4.61.2, 5.17.6, 6.2.2), but without ever stating the name of the center, which was the seat of the sanctuary. From the historian we know that representatives of the league of the twelve peoples met regularly at the *Fanum* to make decisions together, including decisions on foreign policy as happened during the clash between Rome and Veii. The god worshiped in the sanctuary was Voltumna-Vertumnus, defined by Varro (*Lingua Latina* 5.46) as the *"deus Etruriae princeps"* and assimilated to Tinia. During the meetings there were held, as well as religious ceremonies, fairs, markets, theatrical spectacles and solemn games that it was forbidden to interrupt. The location of the sanctuary in Orvieto is suggested by the so-called *Rescript of Spello* (*CIL* XI.5265), written between 333 and 337 AD, by which the emperor Constantine granted the right to celebrate the annual religious ceremonies and *ludi*, imposed as an ancient custom, to the inhabitants of Spello in their city without having to go through difficult paths to Volsinii. The poet Propertius also attests to the Volsinian origin of Vertumnus (4.2.1–4), summoned to Rome in 264 BC when the consul Fulvius Flaccus conquered Volsinii (*CIL* I.2, 46). Festus (s.v. *toga picta*, 228 L) reports that in the Aventine temple of the god the consul was depicted as a *triumphator*. According to an account by Pliny (*NH* 34.16.34) the Romans plundered the town of 2,000 bronze statues: the number, perhaps exaggerated, is surely indication of the existence of a rich sanctuary.

To the west of the cliff on which Orvieto stands is a vast flat area that was for centuries designated for the conduct of markets and fairs, as evidenced by its name: Campo della Fiera. In 1876 excavations in this locality brought to light walls and architectural terracottas belonging to a cult-place. These are now preserved in Berlin. The brief notes left on the surveys did not indicate the exact location, the sacred character of the cult, or the identity of the patron divinities, making it appropriate to resume investigation at the site. Since 2000, excavations have been conducted by the University of Perugia, in collaboration with the University of Macerata, directed by myself and funded by the Foundation of the Cassa di Risparmio of Orvieto, and with the participation of students from universities in Italy, Europe and the US. Several reports have already been published which are summarized here to make room for recent discoveries. It should be noted that this is work in progress: the study of the finds must still be completed and the excavation of some structures must be finished. The materials found so far are large and numerous, especially the architectural terracottas, one of which matches an antefix in Berlin, suggesting that the site investigated is indeed that of the nineteenth-century excavations.

The surface area explored to date is more than three hectares (Fig. 31.1). A massive structure of walls, 2.5 meters thick and standing on one side in polygonal masonry, was brought to light in one of the areas at higher levels. Downhill from this wall was exposed a kind of "plateau" (leveled) area, dating to between the second and first century BC, which covered a dump of different architectural elements of diverse chronology. Nearby, the area is crossed by a paved road built in the mid-third century BC. The track, exposed for more than 50 meters, was five meters wide and furrowed by the passage of wagons, connecting Orvieto with Bolsena. The road narrows, probably to decrease traffic flow in the central part of the area, where the cult has persisted for a long time, from the sixth century BC into the Roman Imperial age. This area is defined by a boundary wall, which was rebuilt several times over the centuries: here there are superimposed remodeling phases of the Republican and Imperial periods.

Within the sacred enclosure, characterized by the presence of two wells (Fig. 31.2 nos. 1, 9), are three small adjoining rooms (Fig. 31.2 no. 2), leveled in the Roman period, which already existed in the second half of the fifth century BC as proven by the deposit in a large clay container placed near one of the walls. The remains could be read as a primitive building, whose religious function is supported by the fact that it is oriented to the east, like the nearby temple called A (Fig. 31.2 no. 3). We do not know with certainty the period of construction of this temple, but the building shows multiple reconstructions (Fig. 31.3). It certainly existed in the fourth century BC, followed by a

Figure 31.1   Campo della Fiera: aerial view of excavations.

Figure 31.2 Plan of central area of excavations (drawing S. Moretti Giani): 1. Well; 2. Primitive building; 3. Temple A; 4. Quadrangular structure; 5. Donario; 6. Trenches; 7. Thesaurus; 8. Altar; 9. Well; 10. First *temenos*; 11. Second *temenos*; 12. Third *temenos* in opus reticolatum; 13. Fourth *temenos*; 14. Via Sacra; 15. Baths.

restructuring of the entire sector to which are assigned the slabs of trachyte that at the northeast corner of the podium replace blocks of tuff. On the front are large slabs of tuff that probably constituted the foundations of the projecting walls on either side of the stairs. Further intervention, between 50 and 25 BC, sees the resurfacing of the floor decorated with inlays of stone fragments and bicolor-motifs (Fig. 31.4). Along the south wall of the temple, flanked by a paved pathway, were found numerous bronze nails. Some, in perfect condition, do not seem to have been used. The most likely interpretation of the nails is for architectural terracottas, but the presence of such a large number of specimens raises the appeal to the Volsinian tradition of the *clavus annalis*, which was affixed to the temple of the goddess Nortia (Cincius *apud* Livy 7.3.7), recognized by some in the Orvietan Belvedere temple.

Figure 31.3   Temple A.

Figure 31.4   Pavement of the *cella* of Temple A.

Aligned with the temple stands a great *donario* (offering table) of trachyte with moldings that are reminiscent of the Lavinium altars, but especially of the altars that Fulvius Flaccus erected at Rome in front of the temples of Sant'Omobono after the conquest of Orvieto (Fig. 31.2 no. 5 and Fig. 31.5, right). On the upper side holes remain for the housing of bronze statuettes. Beside the *donario* is a monolithic altar in tuff, which was almost completely covered with layers of burnt remains of apparent sacrifices. Here was found the graffito *apas* ("of the father"), written on the interior of a bucchero cup. Between the altar and the *donario* was placed a *thesaurus* (treasure repository), found intact (Fig. 31.2 no. 7), which has furnished more than two hundred bronze and silver coins, the most recent of which is dated to 7 BC.

In this same sector of the sanctuary is a square structure defined by ashlar blocks of tuff (Fig. 31.2 no. 4 and Fig. 31.5). Inside were found important materials datable within a wide time span. Among the most indicative to be noted are an Ionicizing statuette of a seated god, an Attic oinochoe in the shape of the head of Dionysus, ram-head rhyta in Attic pottery and black-gloss, many feminine objects, bases from which bronze statuettes had been violently removed (but one still retains three bronzes), including a parallelepiped support in trachyte with holes and grooves for the attachment of a small figure sitting on a throne (Fig. 31.6) and the large base with Archaic dedicatory inscription

Figure 31.5 *Donario*, altar, trenches and quadrangular structure.

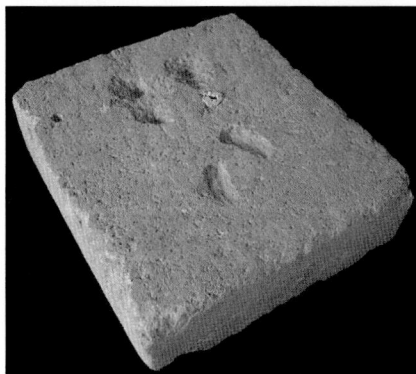

Figure 31.6 Base of statuette of figure seated on a throne.

that commemorates the gift of Kanuta (Fig. 31.7), a woman of Oscan origin, freedwoman of the Larecenas family and wife of Aranth Pinies, to the *Tluschva* deities worshiped in the "heavenly place." Under the large base was a black-gloss cup dating from the late fourth to early third century BC (Fig. 31.8), which contained a large number of objects intentionally placed inside: a leaf of gold and one of bronze, an image of a child who offers a ball (Fig. 31.9), three small *bullae*, six rings and a pair of tweezers, beads of amber and glass paste, sixteen fibulae, thirteen pieces of *aes rude* and fragments of Attic pottery. When the filling was removed a huge boulder was revealed that had been intentionally trimmed to nearly oval shape and fit perfectly in the building, although not in a central position (Fig. 31.10). We do not know if the square enclosure had been created for the purpose of a sacred ritual deposition or whether it originally remained empty, as a *chasma* open to the Underworld, affording a view of the big rock that resembles an *omphalos*, the

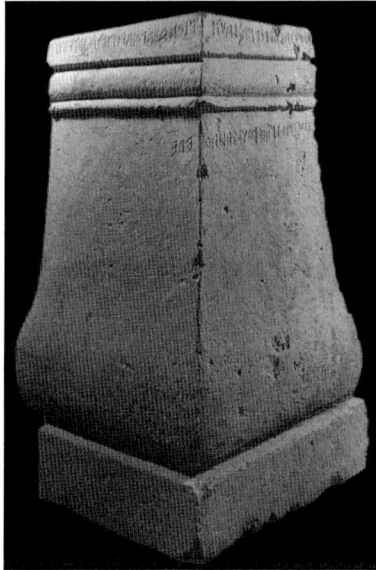

Figure 31.7 Base with Archaic dedicatory inscription.

Figure 31.8 Black-gloss cup.

Figure 31.9 Bronze figurine of boy with ball.

Figure 31.10 Quadrangular structure emptied of fill.

presence of which has undoubtedly played a key role in emphasizing the area and the structure itself. Some of the finds show that the cavity was filled in the Proto-Augustan age with objects that had suffered the depredations of the army of Fulvius Flaccus, as evidenced by the empty bases of statues that recall the Plinian account of the looting of 2,000 bronzes.

Between the *temenos* wall, *donario*, altar and quadrangular structure have been found two large trenches lined with large and irregular blocks of different sizes (Fig. 31.2 no. 6 and Fig. 31.5). They were covered by layers of burning that obscured altar and *thesaurus*, and had been filled in a single procedure. Fragments of thin-walled vases, *terra sigillata*, glass vases and an *as* minted after 211 BC show that the filling is coeval with that of the quadrangular structure. The materials recovered are many: the most striking evidence is furnished by votive heads and statues. The oldest is a terracotta female head with *tutulus* and a diadem with rosettes superimposed on her wavy hair (Fig. 31.11). At the top there is the hole for a *meniscus* that indicates an outdoor location. The stylistic features point to the last decade of the sixth century BC. It is broken at the neck and one cannot determine whether it was an isolated head or belonged to a statue. A prestigious bronze gift was deposited, a small bronze female head (Fig. 31.12), a true masterpiece of Etruscan metalwork, dated circa 490–480 BC, which probably belonged to a stone base which retains the lead in the top where the head was affixed. To the Late Archaic period belong

Figure 31.11   Terracotta female head.

Figure 31.12   Bronze female head.

two terracotta heads with faces derived from the same mold as antefixes of Orvietan type. Another woman's head, similar to the previous in iconographic and stylistic characters, but slightly larger, is applied to a stand (Fig. 31.13). Between the head and the upper edge of the base remains a small gap, perhaps functioning to receive liquid offerings.

The same mold for the larger female heads was also used for a male head, as shown by the red color of the skin (Fig. 31.14). The hair on the forehead was shaved, perhaps for the application of a crown or the front of a helmet. On the back it looks like a helmet or a hat attached to the skull. At the top is a hole, larger than usual, for the *meniscus* or for an attribute similar to the *apex* (pointed hat) of a *flamen*. The male head, derived from female prototypes, evocatively recalls the elegy of Propertius, the passage in which Vertumnus says that if he wears garments of Cos he becomes a "gentle maiden." The

Figure 31.13   Terracotta female head on base.

Figure 31.14   Terracotta male head (front and back views).

head is broken at the neck and may have been part of a statue as suggested by fragments in similar clay, which reconstruct the lower portion of a standing male figure, from the groin to the legs. The comparison is with a statue from Orvieto obtained by the Ny Carlsberg Glyptothek in Copenhagen in 1924. On that date, or shortly before, finds are not recorded in Orvieto, but the materials were also sold long after their discovery, as may have happened for architectural terracottas purchased for the University of Pennsylvania Museum of Philadelphia, which – upon autopsy – are shown to be identical to some found at Campo della Fiera.

Dated to the mid-fifth century BC is a female head on a square base (Fig. 31.15). It is typical of the acceptance in the Tiber region of Etruria of models from classical Greece and Magna Graecia, like two other beautiful female heads, one almost intact, the other fragmentary (Fig. 31.16), whose stylistic characteristics find parallels in the head in the round from Vigna Grande at Orvieto.

Figure 31.15   Terracotta female head.

Figure 31.16   Terracotta female head during excavation.

Exceptional is a larger than life-size arm in stone, to which belongs a hand holding a pomegranate painted in red. A rectangular recess under the elbow shows that it was supported and connected to the armrest of a seat. The image of deities sitting on thrones is similar to that reconstructed for the parallelepiped support found in the quadrangular structure (Fig. 31.6). The iconography conjures up images of Hera enthroned with pomegranate from the first half of the fifth century BC from Poseidonia or those of Persephone from the sanctuary of Demeter at Selinunte and at Tegea. Then the complex base of a terracotta statue of a woman was found, of which the feet remain, clad in sandals with elongated toes (Fig. 31.17), dated to the first half of the fourth century BC.

Other objects found in the two trenches are finger-rings of bronze and silver with signets of gold, and rock crystals also, one of them in the shape of an eye, fragments of small vases of alabaster, glass paste beads and ointment jars, amber, a gold pendant, many fibulae, a large amount of *aes rude* and inscribed bases. Among the ceramics was a small Attic Maenad-head vase (Fig. 31.18). The trenches have produced female elements especially, such as those in the quadrangular deposit pit. This suggests that the worship of the sanctuary prevalent in this area had the character of Demeter- and chthonic-cults, practiced by women and addressed to female deities, whether they were recognized as *Vei*, according to a rereading proposed by Giovanni Colonna for an inscription on a loom weight from this same area, or as *Cavatha*, partner of *Apollo Sourios* that – according to the same scholar – would be present at Campo della Fiera. However, one name emerges clearly from the documents: the deities *Tluschva*, which are also found at Sant'Antonio at Cerveteri and have been read by Adriano Maggiani as a divine feminine group linked to nature and vegetation. With regard to Campo della Fiera, it is to be noted that the base of Kanuta was found with materials associated with Dionysus, and we should not forget that in the liver of Piacenza the theonym *Tluschva* appears in the same sectors as Fufluns.

The latest research has indicated the progression of different enclosure walls. It would be premature to establish an absolute chronology, but it is possible to propose some dating. The oldest wall (Fig. 31.2 no. 10) may be assigned to a period between the fifth and fourth century BC, and is aligned with the eastern side of the quadrangular structure, which is becoming more and more essential and fundamental for the sacred area.

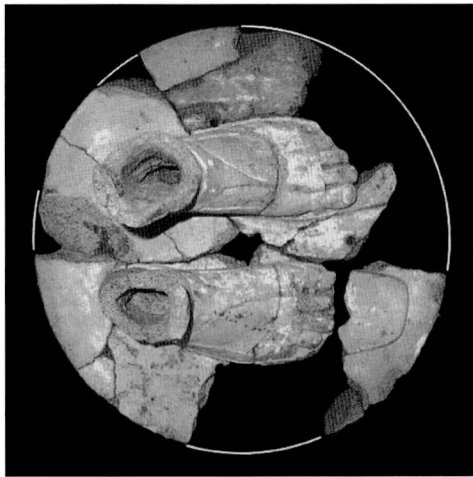

Figure 31.17 Terracotta feet of female statue.

Ceramic fragments found in a small hole dug in the first surviving row (Fig. 31.19) can be attributed to a rite of re-foundation of the boundary during the construction of the second *temenos* wall. This partially overlaps the first one and then diverges to the east (Fig. 31.2 no. 11). It is provided with a threshold of blocks of trachyte with stop and hinge holes for a door that opens from the inside of the enclosure (Fig. 31.20). The material used for the threshold is the same as all other architectural elements that belong to a significant structural change subsequent to the events of 264 BC.

A third wall built in *opus reticulatum* narrows the space (Fig. 31.2 no. 12) and closes an area that includes the monuments evidently considered the most significant (Temple A, altar, *thesaurus*, *donario*, and quadrangular structure). One wall in *opus reticulatum* begins from Temple A and ends at the northern limit of the threshold of trachyte, where the door is re-constructed with housings of the cornerstones with *cubilia*. The walls in *opus reticulatum* are to be connected to the resurfacing of the floor of Temple A. At the same time, remains of votive offerings were placed in the three deposits.

Figure 31.18   Attic vase in form of a Maenad's head.

Figure 31.19   Cavity in foundation course of the first *temenos* wall.

Later, in imperial times, further remodeling closes the door with a rough stone structure that rests on layers containing African pottery (Fig. 31.2 no. 13). Structures and materials thus show the long Roman use of this area. This statement should also be considered with regard to the cult practiced, although changes may have occurred in the ritual forms of worship including a possible transformation of the cults.

The central area of the excavation is crossed by an imposing paved road to be identified with the "Sacred Way" (Via Sacra) of the sanctuary, flanked by bases for altars and statues (Fig. 31.21). It saw three phases of construction, one above the other, the dates of which are provided by fragments of Etruscan ceramics in bucchero and superposed color: the first phase is dated after the middle of the sixth century BC, the second phase in the fifth century BC and the last phase around the middle of the fourth century BC. About 70 meters of the road has been brought to light and shows a progressively increasing slope to the south, toward the slope of the hill overlooking Campo della Fiera. The middle of the roadway is marked by a row of paving stones. The eastern part has ruts set 1.2 meters

Figure 31.20   Threshold of the second *temenos* wall.

Figure 31.21   Via Sacra.

apart corresponding to the distance between the wheels of a chariot (*biga*) like the *currus* from the Tomb of the Chariots of Populonia. The shallow depth of the ruts, ending where the slope is steeper, indicates that the passage of vehicles was not frequent, contrary to what happened in the road from Orvieto to Bolsena. The Via Sacra was thus somewhat passable by wagons and partly pedestrian, finally becoming exclusively pedestrian toward the south. It is a kind of ritual and triumphal path. The road ran behind a modern villa, which unfortunately occupies the path towards the highest portion, where powerful structures have been brought to light (South Area).

The South Area is characterized by the presence of a large structure before which a wall encloses a monumental fountain (Fig. 31.22). From the fountain comes a leonine waterspout (Fig. 31.23) and a black-gloss plate with graffito *ve* (abbreviation of the name *Veltune*?). The basement is probably related to a sacred building (named B). From the temple one can see the area below: the location makes it a dominant feature and underlines its importance. From the typology of building techniques and materials it can be inferred that it was an Archaic building in use until the Republican era. Although the investigation had to be suspended for economic reasons, it seems possible to speak of the intentional abandonment of the site.

Figure 31.22   South Area: fountain and Temple B.

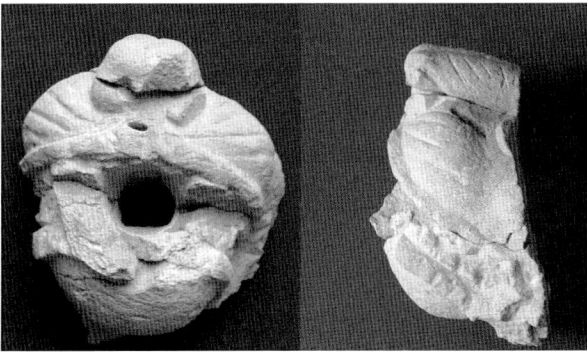

Figure 31.23   Spout of fountain in shape of leonine head.

Important news comes from the southern sector of the Via Sacra, where it extends for more than nine meters along the lateral walkways and where the wagon-ruts terminate. And here there emerged the third temple (called C), of which the first course of blocks of tuff remains (Fig. 31.24 and Fig. 31.1 no. 1). Unfortunately the center was devastated by digging for a modern sewage line that has interrupted the continuity of the building by removing the material that covered the structures. The monument is about 13 meters long and 8.6 meters wide. In the south wall remains the underpinning of a column that indicates that the temple is facing southwest. Pronaos and *cella* are separated by a partition wall. Parallel to the north side of the building runs a wall, which forms a boundary of the precinct of the temple (Fig. 31.25 and Fig. 31.29 nos. 2). The pavement outside the building is at the same level as the Archaic phase of the Via Sacra. Over the structures was found a large quantity of fragments, in particular Attic black-figure and

Figure 31.24   Temple C.

Figure 31.25   Precinct of Temple C.

red-figure ceramics. Some are recomposed as a cup by Douris of 490–480 BC, with a bearded male figure holding up a hare and the acclamation *Hippodamas kalos*, and under the foot, the Etruscan graffito *la* (Fig. 31.26). Also found were an Etruscan *kylix* of the third quarter of the fourth century BC depicting Etruscan Fufluns (Fig. 31.27) and a cup in grey bucchero incised on the rim with the word *atial* ("of the mother," Fig. 31.28), the explicit female counterpart of the *apas* ("of the father") found in the precinct of Temple A. On the vessel interior are incised two syllables, one of which is repeated on the exterior

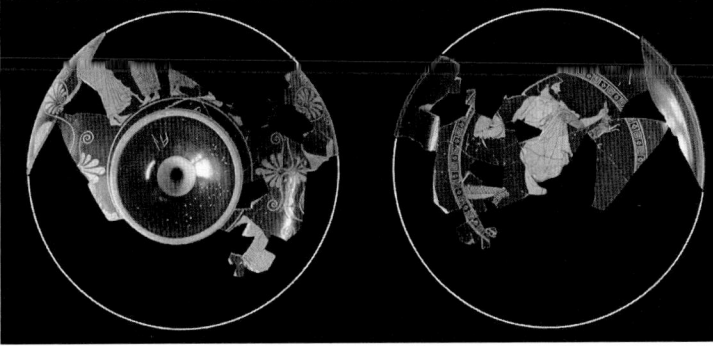

Figure 31.26   *Kylix* by Douris.

Figure 31.27   Etruscan red-figure cup.

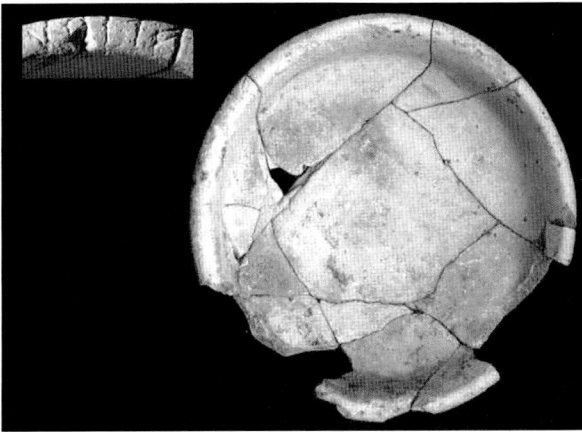

Figure 31.28   Bucchero cup and detail of inscription "*atial*."

base. Gold jewels and fine threads of gold once part of fine textiles were also found, as were Etruscan ceramics including black-gloss, but no fragments of the Roman period were found. The latest materials seem to be anchored at the end of the fourth-the first half of the third century BC.

Near the long walls of the temple were two pits (Fig. 31.29 no. 3): one filled with bones from one or more large animals whose species is as yet unidentified, the other with a large amount of fragments of plain pottery, a few bones which radiocarbon analysis assigns to the late fourth century BC, and the mold for the frame (nimbus) of a head-antefix. The two trenches are the result of a single act perhaps related to the ritual deconsecration of the temple.

Along the perimeter of the building are located three tombs (Fig. 31.29 nos. 4–6). A chest of slabs of tuff, its cover provided with holes for liquid offerings (Fig. 31.30), contained an infant lying in a wooden chest (Fig. 31.31). Osteological analysis indicated the deceased was a male, who died between three and five years of age. The grave goods are a miniature bowl in a grey fabric found near the head, and the base of a black-gloss cup cut off around the stamp-decorated tondo and resting on the feet, dating from the late fourth or early third century BC. Adjacent to the southern wall of the tomb was a small *olla* in plainware, covered by a black-gloss cup, which contained the burnt bones of an infant between 18 months and two years of age, perhaps of the same family as the preceding child, given the close proximity of the burials. Next to the southern wall of the temple and intercepted by a Roman channel in *cocciopesto* (Fig. 31.29 no. 6), another burial consisted of a block of tuff into which were dug four slots for the feet of a chest. The contents were disturbed, but not enough to prevent the partial reconstruction of the grave goods (Fig. 31.32): the bottom of a black-gloss skyphos, two spindle whorls, a mirror, a stamped strigil and a feeding bottle in black-gloss dated 350 ± 50 BC (Fig. 31.33). The analyses show this individual's age is about a year and perhaps show female

Figure 31.29 Plan of Temple C (drawing S. Moretti Giani): 1. Temple C; 2. Precinct wall; 3. Trenches; 4. A *cassone* tomb; 5. Cremation burial in *olla*; 6. A *cassetta* tomb.

Figure 31.30   A *cassone* tomb in blocks of tuff.

Figure 31.31   Inhumation in the *a cassone* tomb and cremation in *olla*.

Figure 31.32   A *cassetta* tomb in a single block of tuff.

gender. The most recent dating of the fragments found so far on the ruins of the temple is thus supported by the date of the depositions. A link between the presence of graves and the abandoned building can hypothetically be explained by a relationship between children's graves, and veneration of a matronly deity, as implied by the inscription *atial*.

The ground level outside the temple contained many fragments of an à la brosse amphora dating from 510 BC, which had been ritually broken. After the destruction of the temple, a deposit of objects plausibly belonging to the sacred building was left on the ground level (Fig. 31.34 and 35): a bucchero cup, above which lay a bronze chariot element, a kyathos comparable to Tarquinian specimens, a *bulla*, a cista foot configured as an anguiped satyr and other small decorative bronze fragments. Sheets from the side of a chariot decorated with a palmette and a figure of Nereus were carefully folded (Fig. 31.36). To the chariot belonged a plaque representing a Gorgon, without iconographic parallels, with earrings and necklace, long eyelashes, eyebrows with each hair drawn separately, and tongue marked by thick dots. Chariot, cup and kyathos can be dated to the Late Archaic period.

Figure 31.33   Feeding-vase.

Figure 31.34   Deposit on the floor-level outside Temple C.

For the end of the history of the destruction of Temple C, the material evidence thus far indicates a period prior to 264 BC. The historical events to which it refers are in the period between the late fourth and early decades of the third century BC: in 308, Decius Mus took the *castella* (hill-forts) of Volsinii and caused such terror that the *nomen etruscum*, probably meeting at the *Fanum*, concluded a *foedus* (Livy 9.41.6). In 294 BC, Postumius comes not far from the city walls after having devastated the countryside and killed 2,800 Etruscans (Livy 10.37.1–2), but it is Atilius Regulus who celebrates the triumph *de Volsonibus* (*CIL* XI².45). In 285 BC, a new conflict began (Livy, *perioch.* 11). In 280 BC, the *Fasti* record the triumph of *Coruncanius de Vulsiniensibus* (*CIL* XI².46). The clashes with Rome cannot have left the sanctuary unscathed: what seems certain at the moment is that neither in Temple B nor Temple C did the cult continue to function into Roman times, but worship was reserved for Temple A, where the *temenos* wall was restored several times.

The floor of the northern section of the Via Sacra was raised in the Roman period with a rich layer of iron slag and a bath complex was built with rooms decorated with floor mosaics (Fig. 31.37). From the baths comes a fibula with an image of the twins

Figure 31.35 Deposit with bucchero cup and objects in metal.

Figure 31.36 Plaques from the chariot.

suckled by the wolf (Fig. 31.38). The building may have originally housed the marble portrait that had been carefully placed in a pit near Temple A. Although the identity is unknown, manner and place of burial indicate a personage of great importance, perhaps a *Praetor Etruriae*. Above the destruction level of the baths was a habitation phase of the fifth century AD, a *domus* laid out inside the rooms that were no longer in use. The most important space occupies the original *tepidarium*. The large amount of pottery found undamaged in the original position of use and faunal remains lead to the interpretation of the area as the kitchen. With the exception of a *catillus* (small bowl) for grinding and a North African amphora, the ceramics are mostly for cooking, table service and pantry storage. The chronology of this occupation is confirmed by the discovery of a silver coin of the end of the fifth century BC, attributed to Theodoric.

Figure 31.37   Baths.

Figure 31.38   Fibula with twins suckled by the she-wolf.

To Late Antiquity is also assigned the mosaic of the brick building erected atop Roman structures in *opus reticulatum*, which were in turn built on Etruscan structures (perhaps related to Temple D of Campo della Fiera). With the sixth-seventh centuries, the site is occupied by a necropolis with graves dug in the earth. Next the tombs change in typology and those of the eighth-ninth centuries are in chests made of slabs of tuff. At the end of the occupation the church of San Pietro in Vetere, known in medieval documents, will be built over the former buildings. The last act is marked by the mass burials of those who died in the Black Death of 1348.

SUMMARY

At Campo della Fiera, after initial sporadic finds of Villanovan pottery, the materials become more numerous in the mid-sixth century BC. The oldest documents are represented by architectural terracottas of the first phase and by Attic pottery, the presence of which becomes especially conspicuous in the age of Porsenna. Umbrian bronzes and coins from Greek and Sicilian-Punic mints indicate the presence of devotees who were not exclusively Etruscan. More modest offerings are represented by loom weights, sometimes inscribed and others of miniature type, or by small bronze figurines, while the empty bases that once supported statues recall the looting during the Roman conquest of the city. The Etruscan period is followed by occupations in the Roman era: those of the Augustan period correspond to the propaganda scheme of revitalization of ancient and important sacred sites. Next, Christianity replaced the pagan sanctuary with a cemetery and then a church.

From the sixth century BC the life of the site continues uninterrupted until the fourteenth century AD, for almost 2,000 years. From this framework it appears clearly that the research at Campo della Fiera is bringing to light the structures of the *Fanum Voltumnae*, sought in vain since the fifteenth century.

NOTE

1   All photos courtesy of Campo della Fiera Excavations (Dipartimento di Scienze Storiche dell'Antichità dell'Università di Perugia).

BIBLIOGRAPHY

Bizzarri, C. (2012) "Gli inizi del santuario di Campo della Fiera: la ceramica greca," *Annali Faina* 19: 77–114.

Colonna, G. (2007 [2009]) "L'Apollo di Pyrgi, *Sur/Suris* (il "Nero") e l'Apollo *Sourios*," *Studi Etruschi* 74:101–134.

——(2008 [2010]) "*Volsinii*. Santuario in località Campo della Fiera," *REE* (*Studi Etruschi* 73): 382–383, n. 137bis, 388–389, n. 141.

——(2012) "I santuari comunitari e il culto delle divinità ctonie in Etruria," *Annali Faina* 19: 203–226.

Cruciani, M. (2012) "Campo della Fiera di Orvieto: la Via Sacra," *Annali Faina* 19: 161–182.

Frascarelli, A. (2012) "Un donario monumentale a Campo della Fiera," *Annali Faina* 19: 131–160.

Gilotta, F. (2010) "Clusium e il Clusium Group. Un nuovo documento dagli scavi di Orvieto," *Opuscula* 3: 179–184.

Giontella, C. (2009) "Pavimenti in "signino" (cementizio) a Campo della Fiera, Orvieto," *Atti del XIV Convegno AISCOM*, Tivoli: scripta manent Edizioni: 111–118.

——(2011) "Lo scavo archeologico di campo della Fiera ad Orvieto," *Il Capitale culturale. Studies on the Value of Cultural Heritage* 2, EUM: edizioni università di Macerata, 285–298.

——(2012) "Una prestigiosa offerta da Campo della Fiera: donna o dea?," *Annali Faina* 19: 115–130.

Leone, D., Simonetti, S. (2012) "Campo della Fiera, Orvieto: dal santuario etrusco all'insediamento tardo antico" in A. Bravi (ed.), *Aurea Umbria. Una regione dell'Impero nell'era di Costantino (III–IV sec. d.C.)*, *Bollettino per i Beni Culturali dell'Umbria* n.s., Catalogo della Mostra, 224–226.

Maggiani, A. (2011) "*Tluschva*, divinità ctonie" in D. F. Maras (ed.) *Corollari. Scritti di antichità etrusche e italiche in omaggio all'opera di Giovanni Colonna*, Studia erudita 14, Pisa-Roma: Fabrizio Serra editore, 138–149.

Ranucci S. (2011) "A stone *thesaurus* with a votive coin deposit found in the sanctuary of Campo della Fiera, Orvieto (*Volsinii*)," *Proceedings of the XIV International Numismatic Congress, Glasgow 2009*: 954–959.

——(2009) "Il *thesaurus* di Campo della Fiera, Orvieto (*Volsinii*)," *Annali Istituto Italiano Numismatica* 55: 103–139.

Satolli, F. (2007) *Un caso suburbano di continuità insediativa (IV–XV secolo)*, in G. M. Della Fina, C. Fratini (eds), *Storia di Orvieto II. Medioevo*, Perugia: Quattroemme, 233–253.

——(2009) *Pavimentazioni antiche nel contado orvietano: lo scavo della chiesa di Campo della Fiera*, *Atti del XIV Convegno AISCOM*, Tivoli: scripta manent Edizioni, 119–127.

Simonetti S. (forthcoming) "Le pavimentazioni dell'impianto termale di Campo della Fiera di Orvieto," *Atti del XVIII Colloquio AISCOM*.

Stopponi S. *et al.* (2002) "GIS e Geo-Archeologia in loc. Campo della Fiera presso Orvieto (TR), poster," 6a Conferenza Nazionale ASITA (Perugia, 5–8 November, 2002).

——(2003) "I templi e l'architettura templare" in G. M. Della Fina (ed.) *Storia di Orvieto I. Antichità*, Perugia, 235–273.

——(2002–03 [2006]), "Recenti indagini archeologiche in loc. Campo della Fiera di Orvieto (TR)," *Etruscan Studies* 9: 109–121.

——(2006) "*Volsiniensia disiecta membra*" in I. Edlund-Berry, G. Greco, J. Kenfield (eds), *Deliciae fictiles* 3, *Proceedings of the International Conference held at American Academy in Rome* (November 7–8. 2002), Oxford: Oxbow Books, 210–221.

——(2007) "Les fouilles de Campo della Fiera à Orvieto," *Les Dossiers d'Archéologie*, juillet–août: 68–73.

——(2007) "Notizie preliminari dallo scavo di Campo della Fiera," *Annali Faina* 14: 493–530.

——(2007) "Etruria e Roma. Il tempio ritrovato fra archeologia e storia," Prolusione tenuta in occasione dell'inaugurazione dell'Anno Accademico 2006/2007 dell'Università degli Studi di Macerata, Macerata, 26–37.

——(2010) "Orvietaner Heiligtümer, Tempel und Architekturterrakotten" in S. Steingraeber, G. M. Della Fina, *Orvieto*, Mainz, 33–52.

——(2010) "Orvieto" in S. Bruni (ed.) *Gli Etruschi delle città*, Cinisello Balsamo, 138–147.

——(2009) "Campo della Fiera: nuove acquisizioni," *Annali Faina* 16: 425–478.

——(2011) "Campo della Fiera at Orvieto: new discoveries" in N. Thomson De Grummond and I. Edlund-Berry (eds), *The Archaeology of Sanctuaries and Ritual in Etruria*, *JRA*, Suppl. Ser., 81: 16–43.

——(2008 [2010]) "*Volsinii*. Orvieto, Campo della Fiera," *REE* (*Studi Etruschi* 73): 292–294, nn. 52–53, 379–388, nn. 134–140.

——(2011) "Frammenti di "Prima Fase" da Orvieto," *Tetti di terracotta. La decorazione architettonica fittile tra Etruria e Lazio in età arcaica*, Atti delle Giornate di studio (Sapienza – Università di Roma, 25 marzo e 25 ottobre 2010), Officina Etruscologia 5: 65–72.

——(2012) *Il Fanum Voltumnae: dalle divinità* Tluschva *a San Pietro*, *Annali Faina* 19.

CHAPTER THIRTY TWO

WORSHIPING WITH THE DEAD: NEW APPROACHES TO THE ETRUSCAN NECROPOLIS

———•◆•———

Stephan Steingräber

INTRODUCTION[1]

In spite of many excavations, discoveries and research into Etruscan urban areas and sanctuaries in recent decades, the thousands of necropoleis and tombs in Etruria still remain our main sources of information about Etruscan culture, art, life and religion and, of course, particularly burial customs, funeral rites and specific aspects of the Etruscan Afterlife. They often reflect historical, economic and social changes too. Without any doubt the Etruscans – more than any other population or culture – invested a great deal of financial resources and architectural, technical and artistic know-how in their cemeteries and tombs, which means, in some way, an investment in the Afterlife. Unfortunately we are still missing a complete "handbook" on Etruscan tombs and tomb architecture, and many Etruscan necropoleis and tombs – specifically those of Cerveteri – are not really thoroughly published. Of course, there are different kinds of approaches to this extremely complex and interesting topic – more technical-architectural, more art historical, more religious, more social, etc. In this modest contribution I can touch only briefly on the most important aspects and, via a quite rich and extended bibliography, hope to stimulate further interest and research on Etruscan necropoleis and tombs.

HISTORY OF DISCOVERIES AND RESEARCH

The first discoveries of important Etruscan tombs and tomb monuments and resulting research go back to the Renaissance. In 1507, the huge Tumulo of Montecalvario near Castellina in Chianti with its four chamber tombs of the late Orientalizing period was discovered and functioned perhaps as a model for the design of a tomb monument by Leonardo da Vinci. Particularly rich in discoveries were the second halves of the eighteenth and nineteenth centuries. But even now every year new tombs come to light in many parts of Etruria both through regular excavations and by the activities of tomb robbers and casual finds. The general and overview publications we owe mostly to non-Italian archaeologists such as F. Prayon (1975) and J. P. Oleson (1982), but neither of these works can be considered as a general "handbook" including all areas and sites of Etruria and all-important aspects of Etruscan necropoleis, tombs and tomb architecture.

NECROPOLEIS

We can distinguish between single tombs (sometimes in isolated and dominating positions), small groups of tombs and real necropoleis. Some of the Etruscan necropoleis are among the most extensive of the ancient world. In the Villanovan period the necropoleis were still isolated from each other but during the Orientalizing and Archaic periods they were extended until they entirely surrounded the inhabited area of a city and even outstripped it in area. The large necropoleis in particular – real "cities of the dead" – around the main Etruscan metropoleis offer good possibilities for the study of their ground plans, organization, extension, development and changes. The different geological and geographical conditions in Southern and Northern Etruria often resulted in different forms of cemeteries and tombs. In Cerveteri the Necropoli della Banditaccia – the most impressive and best preserved necropolis of Etruria – and in Orvieto the Necropoli del Crocefisso del Tufo are outstanding examples and extremely instructive reflecting in part the layout of the cities. During the sixth century BC, with the rise of a new middle class, hundreds of *tumuletti* and later hundreds of cube-tombs were planned and erected according to the direction of the necropolis streets and accessible directly from them. After the middle of the sixth century BC parts of the necropoleis are characterized by a kind of Hippodamean system with an orthogonal network of roads and rectangular squares and mostly uniform cube tombs, which is not only a sign of better use of space but also a clear reflection of new tendencies in the urban system (such as in Marzabotto after 500 BC). At the same time they also reflect social changes and probably new laws and norms intended to limit the opulence of burials.

TOMBS AND TOMB MONUMENTS

We should always clearly distinguish between tombs and tomb monuments and their respective typology, chronology, topographic distribution, architectural elements and decorations. In Etruscan we know two words, "*suthi*" and "*cana*" which mean "monument" and "tomb" respectively, (cf. Greek "*sema*," Latin "*cippus*"). Among the main tomb types we find *pozzo/pozzetto* = well/pit tombs (for cremation burials), *fossa* tombs, *loculus* tombs, niche tombs, chamber tombs, *cassone* tombs (Vulci), sarcophagus and stone cist tombs. Among the tomb monuments we can distinguish between stone circles (interrupted and continuous, especially in Vetulonia and Marsiliana d'Albegna), tumuli and *tumuletti*, cubes, half cubes and false cubes, houses, *porticus*, temples, *aediculae* and *tholoi*. According to the different regions, sites, geological conditions, local traditions and social status there is a great variety of types and variants. A very important change in burial custom took place in the early seventh century BC with the transformation of larger *fossa* tombs into chamber tombs destined for the burial of family groups. We can observe this change from single to collective burial particularly well in the extended necropoleis of Cerveteri. This change was connected with the construction of large tumuli (up to 80m in diameter) both in Southern and in Northern Etruria (but not in *Etruria padana*, the Po region) replacing the small "archaic tumuli" and with the definitive confirmation of a new leading aristocratic class. The general tendency of monumentalization is well documented in Southern Etruria not only in Cerveteri and its territory (Blera, San Giuliano, San Giovenale) but in Vulci, Tarquinia and Veii too (Figs 32.1, 32.2). In Northern Etruria the chamber tombs and the tumuli are mostly built in limestone or sandstone blocks and slabs (Populonia, Vetulonia, Artimino, Quinto Fiorentino, Castellina in Chianti, Cortona), whereas in Southern Etruria structures hollowed out in the soft volcanic tufa stone are clearly prevailing. Characteristic for the north (especially between the areas of Volterra and Florence) in the middle and late Orientalizing period are round burial chambers with false cupola and sometimes a central pillar = the so-called *tholos* tombs which remind one of the much older Mycenean *tholoi*

Figure 32.1   Cerveteri, Banditaccia Necropolis, tumulus with profiled base of Orientalizing period.

Figure 32.2   Tarquinia, Doganaccia, Tumulo della Regina: antechamber with remains of wall plaster of Middle Orientalizing period.

but reveal probable architectural connections with the Sardinian nuraghe (Fig. 32.3). An early predecessor we find only in Populonia toward the end of the ninth and beginning of the eighth century BC in a much smaller size but already characterized by a circle of slabs and a small tumulus, a single entrance, a circular chamber and a false cupola. During the Orientalizing period in Vetulonia and Populonia the circular false cupola rests on a square chamber. The tombs of Cortona, Castellina in Chianti and Artimino are characterized mainly by the arrangement of rectangular chambers with corbelled vaults on a longitudinal axis. The development of tomb architecture during the seventh and sixth centuries BC in Southern Etruria and particularly in Cerveteri is extremely varied and interesting and was divided by F. Prayon (1975) into six main types (A – F) according to their ground plans, type of dromos, door and window shapes, types of roofs, ceilings and "furniture" such as tomb beds, sarcophagus beds, benches, thrones, chairs, baskets and altars, columns, pillars, capitals and profile bases, and the type of tomb monument and exterior architecture. The large tumuli of the Orientalizing period – characterized normally by a profiled base – often contain more chamber tombs, in a few cases up to six or seven. These tombs often go back to different periods/generations and thus have a different typology. Each tumulus belonged to a particular family/*gens* (clan) and served for several generations (Figs 32.4, 32.5). The oldest tomb in a tumulus is always oriented toward north-west, which means it is toward the section of the underworld gods on the Etruscan celestial scale. The Regolini Galassi Tomb and the Tomb of the Hut (or "Thatched Roof") belong to the oldest chamber tombs in Cerveteri with a long open dromos and the chambers in longitudinal axis. Whereas the corbelled vault of the Regolini Galassi Tomb is built in tufa slabs, the two chambers of the

Figure 32.3   Vetulonia, model of the Diavolino Tomb 2 of Orientalizing period
(Vetulonia, Museo Archeologico).

Figure 32.4   Populonia, San Cerbone Necropolis, Tomb of the Funeral Beds: chamber with remains of
the stone beds of Orientalizing period.

Figure 32.5   San Giuliano, Tomb of Valle Cappellana 1: two chambers with tuscan columns and stone
beds of Late Orientalizing period.

other tomb are completely hollowed out and – concerning the vaults – clearly influenced
by contemporary hut architecture. A very characteristic tomb type (type D according
to Prayon) clearly influenced by house architecture (Veii, Acquarossa) was common in
Cerveteri and its territory during the late seventh and the first half of the sixth century BC.
It is characterized by a large antechamber and three burial chambers behind it and often
by a rich "furnishing" (as in the Tomb of the Shields and Chairs in Cerveteri). We find the
same ground plan after the middle of the sixth century BC in the temple architecture too
("*templum tuscanicum*" according to Vitruvius). After the middle of the sixth century BC the
cube tombs with their square appearance prevailed particularly in Cerveteri, in the rock

tomb area (Blera, San Giuliano) and in Orvieto (Figs 32.8, 32.9, 32.10). In Populonia
the tumuli were replaced by *aedicula* tombs with characteristic gabled roofs (Figs 32.6,
32.7). A strong change happened toward the end of the sixth century BC when the tombs
– especially in the Cerveteri area – no longer imitated real houses and consisted normally
only of one square chamber with simple benches along the walls. This quite simple
and monotonous one-room tomb type remained typical during the following centuries.
Only after the middle of the fourth century BC some tombs of new aristocratic families,
especially in Cerveteri, Tarquinia and Vulci, became once again more richly decorated
with architectural (pilasters, wall niches, beds) and painted or stuccoed elements (like
in the Tomb of the Reliefs in Cerveteri belonging to the Matuna family) imitating in
an abstract way the central part of contemporary dwellings = atrium houses, while the
smaller rooms = *cubicula* of those houses are reduced in the tombs to simple *loculi* used for
burials. The burial of the tomb's founder couple was particularly emphasized normally in
a big alcove/niche in the middle of the back wall according to the idea of heroization of

Figure 32.6   Sarteano, Pianacce Necropolis: tomb dromoi with cippus of fourth century BC.

Figure 32.7   Blera, Casetta Necropolis: half cube rock tomb of Archaic period.

Figure 32.8   San Giuliano, Caiolo Necropolis:
Tomb of the Stag – cube rock tomb of Hellenistic period.

Figure 32.9   Populonia, San Cerbone Necropolis: aedicula tomb with gabled roof of
Late Archaic period.

Figure 32.10   Cerveteri, Via degli Inferi: Tomb of the Doric Columns of Late Archaic period.

the deceased (Tombs of Reliefs and Alcova and Torlonia in Cerveteri, Mercareccia Tomb in Tarquinia). The huge number of burials of several generations underlines the continuity of the gentilicial group. Also, the external façades of monuments were often remodeled with architectural and sculptural decorations. Quite different is the tomb type with barrel vaulting built in stone blocks which is documented first in the Early Hellenistic period in Cerveteri (Tomb of the Demons in Loc. Greppe Sant'Angelo) and Orvieto and later mainly in the territories of Chiusi, Cortona and Perugia partly covered by *tumuletti*.

ROCK TOMB ARCHITECTURE

This phenomenon was characteristic for the inner parts of Southern Etruria (and the Faliscan area) and unique in Italy from the first half of the sixth century BC until the end of the third/beginning of the second century BC. The main sites are San Giuliano, Blera and Tuscania for the Archaic period and Norchia, Castel d'Asso and Sovana for the Hellenistic period (Fig. 32.11). Great attention and care were paid to the external appearance of the monument often characterized by profiles and painted decorations. Especially in the later period the monument and exterior façade became more monumental and elaborated whereas the tomb chambers situated under the façade became simpler and appeared sometimes like rough-hewn caves. Concerning the typology we find cube, house, *aedicula*, temple, *porticus* and *tholos* tombs. The most common type was the cube or half-cube tomb probably inspired by the cube tombs of Cerveteri. A variation is the so-called cube tomb with *sottofacciata*/under-façade, a space furnished with benches and a false door. The most noble rock tombs such as the temple and *porticus* tombs in Norchia and Sovana reveal influences from temple and palace architecture and are richly decorated with reliefs and sculptures. The Ildebranda tomb in Sovana shows the ground plan of a *"peripteros sine postico"* and has to be connected with the concept of heroization of the deceased (Fig. 32.12). It was obviously the owner's intention to attract attention to the splendor of his tomb and to keep himself and his family alive in the memory of his descendants.

Figure 32.11   Sovana, Tomb of the Siren: rock aedicula tomb of Hellenistic period.

Figure 32.12   Sovana, model of the Ildebranda Tomb – temple rock tomb of Hellenistic period
(Sovana, Museo Archeologico).

Many of these splendid rock tombs had a permanent visual contact with the city of the living. Most of them did not serve only for burials but were conceived as cult places and monumental altars too (Fig. 32.13). The upper platform of the cube tombs could be reached indeed by lateral stairs.

ROCK MONUMENTS OF THE LATE ETRUSCAN AND ROMAN PERIOD

The Etruscan tradition of rock monuments mostly of funerary character continues even in Roman times – especially in the first century BC and the first century AD. A conspicuous number of monuments called "Piramidi," "Predicatori," "Massi" etc. are concentrated between the Monti Cimini and the Tiber Valley in the triangle between Bomarzo, Soriano nel Cimino and Vitorchiano (Prov. of Viterbo) and partly characterized by Latin inscriptions indicating the names of the deceased, the donators and some gods such as the Bona Dea (Figs 32.14, 32.15).

INFLUENCES FROM HOUSE, PALACE AND TEMPLE ARCHITECTURE

Often one can read that Etruscan tomb architecture is an imitation of house architecture. This assertion is only partly true – we have to distinguish between the different periods, tomb types and architectural elements. But without any doubt tomb architecture is a partial and precious substitute for the mostly destroyed and lost Etruscan house and palace architecture and this is especially valid for Cerveteri where the tombs of the second half of the seventh century BC and of the greater part of the sixth century BC are reproducing many details of the interior shape of the houses. This concept of the tomb or tomb monument as the hut or house of the dead is reflected already by the cinerary hut urns of the Villanovan period imitating the structures of the dwelling huts of the deceased, leaving them within their usual environments and furnishing them with everything they liked and which could be useful for their Afterlife. Different kinds of furniture, implements

Figure 32.13   Manziana, stepped Etruscan rock altar.

Figure 32.14   Bomarzo, rock cube monument of Roman period, probably with altar function.

Figure 32.15   Bomarzo, "Pyramide" – rock monument of Roman period, probably with altar function.

and weapons, as well as perishable items such as food were left for the dead. Real house and palace architecture is reflected particularly in the Cerveteri tomb type D (especially in the Tomb of the Tablinum) and later for example in the Tomba François in Vulci and the Volumnii Tomb in Perugia with their symmetrical layout of several chambers grouped around a T-shaped nucleus resembling the patrician *atrium-tablinum* house type, which is obviously of Etrusco-Italic origin and goes back to the Archaic period. The thrones in the antechamber of tomb type D may symbolize the *potestas* and social position of the *pater* and *mater familias*, and their position in the vestibule corresponded probably to the position of the so-called *solium* in a contemporary patrician house. Influences of palace architecture manifest themselves particularly in the façade of the house tomb with *porticus* at Pian di Mola near Tuscania of the Early Archaic period, influences of temple architecture in the façades of the temple rock tombs in Norchia (Tombe doriche) and Sovana (Tombe Ildebranda and Pola) of the Early Hellenistic period. We find other elements of house and palace architecture such as coffered ceilings in tombs at Chiusi, Vulci and Sovana.

LOCAL ELEMENTS AND FOREIGN INFLUENCES

In Etruscan tomb architecture, both local elements and foreign influences, models and parallels are manifesting themselves though such influences are not always easy to prove. According to the different periods and areas in Etruria we can notice influences from Asia Minor (Phrygia, Lydia), Cyprus (Salamis), Syria (Ugarit), Macedonia, Apulia and Campania. The huge (mainly South) Etruscan tumuli of the Early and Middle Orientalizing period reveal similarities and possible influences particularly from Phrygia, Lydia, Syria and Cyprus.

The so-called Macedonian tomb type was introduced via Northern Apulia (Daunia) and Campania first in Southern Etruria (Cerveteri, Orvieto) and later in North Etruria (Chiusi, Cortona, Perugia). The Hellenistic temple and *porticus* tombs in the South Etruscan rock tomb area (Norchia, Sovana) are influenced both in architectural and ideological sense by the monumental Mausolea and Heroa in Asia Minor, connected with the idea of heroization of the deceased. Their decorations reveal influences mostly from Magna Graecia and Apulia. The general custom of rock tomb architecture was particularly common in several areas of Asia Minor – especially in the south-west in Lycia and Caria.

ELEMENTS OF THE ANCESTOR CULT

Etruscan tombs and tomb monuments did not only serve as burial places but also were sites for funeral rites and for the worship of the dead. Discoveries and researches especially during the last decades have revealed that particular – mostly architectural – elements of the tombs and tomb monuments were destined exclusively for the cult and rites in honor of the deceased and ancestors. Some of these elements are of monumental character and size. In Cerveteri, Vulci and San Giuliano we find tomb chambers with remains of altars, thrones and chairs, tables and chests but without any burials, which functioned as cult rooms for sacrifices and rites in honor of the ancestors and deceased. A unique example is the left lateral room of the Tomb of the Five Chairs in Cerveteri. Among the different furnishings, which are on a smaller scale than normal, on the five chairs were seated small terracotta figures representing the ancestors in the act of pouring libations and eating together with the tomb-founder couple buried in the back chamber. Many tumuli have ramps (especially in Cerveteri) or added platforms (as in Artimino) or terraces and many cubes have lateral stairs that allow entrants (priests and relatives of the dead) to climb up to the top of the monument obviously for ritual purposes. The upper platforms of the cube tombs had the size and function of monumental altars. The *sottofacciata* areas with their benches probably served funeral banquets. Also the *dromos* or an open space in front of the burial chamber could be used to deposit offerings or to make libations. A really impressive example is the so-called *terrazza-altare* of the Tumulo del Sodo II in Cortona-Camucia, decorated with palmettes of Ionic type and two sculptural groups and dating from the Late Orientalizing period. From this monumental terrace-altar one could climb up to a *naiskos/aedicula* on the top of the tumulus. Both structures were clearly intended for funeral rites and ceremonies. We know of open squares and "ritual theatres" also in Grotta Porcina (in combination with a round altar), Vulci (in front of the main tomb of the Cuccumella) and Tarquinia (in front of the tomb in the Luzi Tumulo). Unique in Etruria is the rectangular base originally with two rows of monumental obelisk-like *cippi* beside the Tumulo Cima in San Giuliano. This *"area cultuale all'aperto"* (G. Colonna, 1985) was probably an uniconic monument in memory of the ancestors of the aristocratic owner family of the tumulus.

TOMB INSCRIPTIONS

Tomb inscriptions were rather rare in the early periods apart from the Orvieto tombs but later documented on *cippi* and façades such as in Norchia and Castel d'Asso. In the case of Orvieto the inscriptions give us information about the different provenance of the tomb owners (from Umbria and even from the Celtic area). Frequent carved or painted inscriptions in the gentilicial (extended family) tombs of the Hellenistic period enable us to partially reconstruct the genealogy of the owner family.

CIPPI AND TOMB SCULPTURES

Cippi = tomb signs in stone could be erected in front of the tomb entrance, upon the tomb monument or sometimes even in the tomb and indicated specific burials. Their size, material and typology are different according to local customs and different periods in Etruria (Fig. 32.16).

Sculptures of wild animals and monsters, standing as "guardians" in front of the tomb monument or tomb entrance, were probably of apotropaic character and mainly common in the Archaic period but later too. In Vulci and its territory this custom was particularly popular.

BURIAL GIFTS

The composition, materials, number and richness of the burial gifts – in most cases unfortunately no longer intact – give us a lot of information about age, sex, social status, taste etc. of the deceased and of course, about the chronology and duration of the use of a tomb. Additionally, the composition of the burial gifts, including often both local and foreign objects, informs us about the economic and cultural relations between the respective Etruscan town and other Etruscan towns and foreign areas. In the Orientalizing

Figure 32.16   Barbarano Romano, Museo Archeologico: monumental cippus in obelisk form from San Giuliano.

period especially the burial gifts of the aristocratic tombs = *"tombe principesche"* were particularly rich including partly imported objects from the Near East and the Greek world (for illustrations, see Chapters 6 and 33).

RECENT DISCOVERIES, EXCAVATIONS AND RESTORATIONS

Among the most important discoveries of the last three decades we should emphasize the Tomb of the Demons in Loc. Ripe Sant'Angelo of Cerveteri, the new excavations around the Tomb of the Five Chairs at Cerveteri and the Tumulo del Sodo II at Cortona-Camucia, the Doganaccia Tumuli at Tarquinia (see Fig. 32.2), the Cutu Tomb at Perugia, the painted tombs at Tarquinia (Tomb of the Blue Demons), Sarteano (Tomb of the Infernal Quadriga) and Veii (Tomb of the Roaring Lions) and the restoration of the Cuccumella Tumulus at Vulci. It is impossible to mention here many other more or less important discoveries (see, for instance, Chapters 55 and 56).

VARIA

During the last decades paleoanthropological, paleozoological and paleobotanical finds and researches also became more important telling us a lot about daily life and burial customs in Etruria.

CONCLUSION

Some of the main Etruscan necropoleis such as the Banditaccia necropolis of Cerveteri are not yet completely or sufficiently published. We should make every possible effort to close these painful gaps. The main desiderata that should be considered in the future are increased international cooperation, the creation of valid and helpful databases, even more paleoanthropological, paleozoological and paleobotanical research for the reconstruction of general living conditions in Etruria, and the preparation and publication of a well elaborated handbook on Etruscan necropoleis, tombs, and tomb architecture including the most recent excavations, discoveries and research.

NOTE

1   All photos by the author.

BIBLIOGRAPHY

A.A.V.V. (1988) *Etrusker in der Toskana. Etruskische Gräber der Frühzeit.* Ausstellungskatalog, (ed. M. Cygielman) Frankfurt (and Florence). Frankfurt: Museum für Vor-und Frühgeschichte.

Akerström, A. (1934) *Studien über die etruskischen*, Gräber, Uppsala: C.W.K. Gleerup.

Barbieri, G. (ed.) (2010) *La Tomba dei Demoni alati di Sovana. Un capolavoro dell'architettura rupestre in Etruria*, Siena: Nuova Imagine Editrice.

Bartoloni, G. (1972) *Le tombe da Poggio Buco nel Museo Archeologico di Firenze*, Florence: Leo S. Olschki.

——(2000) "La tomba" in *Principi etruschi tra Mediterraneo ed Europa*. Comune di Bologna, Museo Civico Archeologico, Venezia: Marsilio, pp. 163–190.

——(2003) *Le società dell'Italia primitiva. Lo studio delle necropoli e la nascita delle aristocrazie*, Rome: Carocci Editore, pp. 70–72.

——(ed.) (2012) *L'architettura, in Introduzione all'Etruscologia*, Milan, pp. 253–308

Becker, M. J., MacIntosh Turfa, J. and Algee-Hewitt, B. (2009) *Human remains from Etruscan and Italic Tomb Groups in the University of Pennsylvania Museum*, Pisa and Rome: F. Serra Editore.

Bianchi Bandinelli, R. (1925) "Chiusi" in *Monumenti Antichi* 30, pp. 210–551.

——(1929) "Sovana," Florence: Rinascimento del libro.

Blanck, H. and Proietti, G. (1986) *La Tomba dei Rilievi di Cerveteri*, Rome: De Luca.

Boethius, A. (1978) *Etruscan and Early Roman Architecture*, Harmondsworth: Penguin Books.

Boethius, A. *et al.* (1962) *Etruscan Culture – Land and People*, New York/Malmö: Columbia University Press.

Boethius, A. and Ward Perkins, J. B. (1970) *Etruscan and Roman Architecture*, Harmondsworth: Penguin Books.

Bonamici, M., Stopponi, S. and Tamburini, P. (1994) *Orvieto. La necropoli di Cannicella*, Rome: "L'Erma" di Bretschneider.

Bosio, B. and Pugnetti, A. (1986) *Gli Etruschi di Cerveteri. La necropoli di Monte Abatone*, Modena: Panini.

Bulgarelli, F., Maestri, D. and Petrizzi, C. V. (1977) *Tolfa etrusca e la necropoli di Pian Conserva*, Rome: Quaderni del G.A.R. 6.

Camporeale, G. (1968) *La tomba del Duce*, Florence: Leo S. Olschki.

Canina, L. (1846–1851) *L'antica Etruria Marittima I–II*, Rome 1846–1851. Rev. Camera apostolica.

Chiostri, F. and Mannini, F. (1969) *Le tombe a tholos di Quinto Fiorentino*, Sesto Fiorentino: Associazione turistica Pro Sesto.

Coen, A. (1991) *Complessi tombali di Cerveteri con urne cinerarie tardo-orientalizzanti*, Pisa – Rome: Leo S. Olschki.

Colonna, G. (1967) "L'Etruria meridionale interna dal villanoviano alle tombe rupestri" in *Studi Etruschi* 35, pp. 3–30.

——(1986) "Urbanistica e architettura" in G. Pugliese Carratelli (ed.) *Rasenna. Storia e civiltà degli Etruschi*, Milan: Libri Scheiwiller, pp. 369–530.

——(1994) "Etrusca Arte: Urbanistica e Architettura" in *EAA II* Suppl. II, Rome, pp. 554–565.

Colonna, G. and von Hase, F.-W. (1984) "Alle origini della statuaria etrusca: la Tomba delle Statue presso Ceri" in *Studi Etruschi* LII, pp. 13–59.

Colonna di Paolo, E. (1978) *Necropoli rupestri del Viterbese*, Novara: De Agostini.

Colonna di Paolo, E and Colonna, G. (1970) *Castel d'Asso I–II*, Florence: CNR.
(1970) *Norchia I*, Florence: CNR.

Cristofani, M. (1965) *La Tomba delle Iscrizioni a Cerveteri*, Florence: Sansoni.

——(1969) *Le tombe da Monte Michele al Museo Archeologico di Firenze*, Florence: Leo S. Olschki.

D'Agostino, B. (1977) "Tombe 'principesche' dell'orientalizzante antico da Pontecagnano" in *Monumenti Antichi Misc. II*: 1.

Demus-Quatember, M. (1958) *Etruskische Grabarchitektur*, Baden-Baden: B. Grimm Verlag.

Dennis, G. (1848) *The Cities and Cemeteries of Etruria*, London: John Murray.

Donati, L. (1989) *Le tombe da Saturnia nel Museo Archeologico di Firenze*, Florence: Leo S. Olschki.

Drago Troccoli, L. (2006) *Cerveteri*, Rome: Istituto Poligrafico e Zecca dello Stato.

Falchi, I. (1891) *Vetulonia e la sua necropoli antichissima*, Florence: Successori Le Monnier.

Fedak, J. (1990) *Monumental Tombs of the Hellenistic Age: A Study of Selected Tombs from the Pre-Classical to the Early Imperial Era*, Toronto: University of Toronto Press.

Gargana, A. (1990) "La necropoli rupestre di San Giuliano" in *Monumenti Antichi* 33, pp. 297–468.

Gaugler, W. M. (2002) *The Tomb of Lars Porsenna at Clusium and its religious and political implications*, Bangor-Maine: Laureate Press.

Haynes, S. (2000) *Etruscan Civilization. A Cultural History*, London: British Museum Press.

Hencken, H. (1968) *Tarquinia, Villanovans and Early Etruscans*, Cambridge, Massachusetts: Peabody Museum.

Izzet, V. (1996) "Exploring space and surface in Etruscan funerary architecture" in J. B. Wilkins (ed.) *Approaches to the Study of Ritual. Italy and the Ancient Mediterranean*, London: Accordia Research Centre, University of London, pp. 55–72.

——(2007) *The Archaeology of Etruscan society*, Cambridge: Cambridge University Press.

Koch, H. von Mercklin, E. and Weickert, C. (1915) "Bieda" in *Römische Mitteilungen* 30, pp. 161–310.

Maggiani, A. (1990, 1994) "Tombe con prospetto architettonico nelle necropoli rupestri d'Etruria" in M. Martelli (ed.) *Tyrrhenoi Philotechnoi. Atti della giornata di studio*, Viterbo and Rome, pp. 119–159.

Mandolesi, A. (2008) "Ricerca sui tumuli principeschi orientalizzanti di Tarquinia. Prime indagini nell'area della Doganaccia" in *Orizzonti*, 9, pp. 11–25.

Martinelli, M. and Paolucci, G. (2006) *Luoghi Etruschi*, Florence: Scala.

Messerschmidt, F and von Gerkan, A. (1930) *Nekropolen von Vulci*, Berlin.

Minto, A. (1922) *Populonia. La necropoli arcaica*, Florence: R. Bemporad & Figlio, Editori.

Moretti, M. (1974) *Tarquinia*, Novara: De Agostini.

——(1977) *Cerveteri*, Novara: De Agostini.

Morselli, C. (1980) *Sutrium*, Florence: Leo S. Olschki.

Moscatelli, G. and Mazzuoli, G. (2008) *Le necropoli rupestri della Tuscia*, Grotte di Castro: Canino Onlus.

Nardi, G. (1999) "Tomba" in M. Cristofani (ed.), *Dizionario della civiltà etrusca*, Florence: Giunti, pp. 298–303.

Naso, A. (1991) *La Tomba dei Denti di Lupo a Cerveteri*, Pisa and Rome: Leo S. Olschki.

———(1995) "Alle origini della pittura etrusca: decorazione parietale e architettura funeraria" in *Etruria meridionale nel VII secolo a.C.* in *JRGZM* 37, 1990 (1995) pp. 439–499.

———(1996a) *Architetture dipinte: Decorazioni parietali non figurate nelle tombe a camera dell'Etruria meridionale* (VII – V secolo a.C.), Rome: "L'Erma" di Bretschneider.

———(1996b) "Osservazioni sull'origine dei tumuli monumentali nell'Italia centrale" in *Opuscula Romana* 20, pp. 69–85.

———(1998) "Tumuli monumentali in Etruria meridionale: caratteri propri e possibili ascendenze orientali" in *Archäologische Untersuchungen zu den Beziehungen zwischen Altitalien und der Zone nordwärts der Alpen während der frühen Eisenzeit Alteuropas*. Akten des Kolloquiums Regensburg 1994, Regensburg 1997, pp. 117–157.

———(2001) "Dalla capanna alla casa: riflessi nell'architettura funeraria etrusca" in J. Rasmus Brandt and L. Karlsson (eds), *From Huts to Houses. Transformations of Ancient Societies. Proceedings of an International Seminar organized by the Norwegian and Swedish Institutes in Rome*, September 1997, Stockholm 2001, pp. 29–39.

———(2007) "Etruscan style of dying. Funerary architecture, tomb groups and social range at Caere and its hinterland during the seventh-sixth centuries B.C." in N. Laneri (ed.), *Performing death. Social analyses of funerary traditions in the ancient Near East and Mediterranean*, Chicago 2007, pp. 141–162.

Nati, D. (2008) *Le necropoli di Perugia*, Città di Castello: Edimond.

Nicosia, F. (1966) *Il Tumulo di Montefortini e la Tomba dei Boschetti a Comeana*, Florence: Tipografia Giuntina.

Oleson, J. P. (1982) *The Sources of Innovation in Later Etruscan Tomb Design (ca. 350–100 B.C.)*, Rome: G. Bretschneider.

Origo Crea, B. (ed.) (1984) *Etruria svelata. I disegni di Samuel James Ainsley nel British Museum*, Rome: Edizioni dell'Elefante.

Orioli, F. (1826) *Dei sepolcrali edifizi dell'Etruria media e in generale dell'architettura tuscanica*, Ficsole: Poligrafia fiesolana.

Pallottino, M. (1937) "Tarquinia" in *Monumenti Antichi* 36.

———(1971) *La Necropoli di Cerveteri*, Rome: Istituto Poligrafico dello Stato.

Pellegrini, E. (1989) *La Necropoli di Poggio Buco. Nuovi dati per lo studio di un centro dell'Etruria interna nei periodi orientalizzante e arcaico*, Florence: Leo S. Olschki.

Pareti, L. (1947) *La Tomba Regolini Galassi*, Vatican: Tipografia poliglotta vaticana.

Pohl, I. (1972) *The Iron Age Necropolis of Sorbo at Cerveteri*, Stockholm, Acta Instituti Romani Regni Sueciae 4° XXXII.

Prayon, F. (1975) *Frühetruskische Grab- und Hausarchitektur*, Heidelberg: F.H. Kerle Verlag.

———(1979) "Felsthrone in Mittelitalien" in *Römische Mitteilungen* 86, pp. 87–101.

———(1989) "L'architettura funeraria etrusca. La situazione attuale delle ricerche e problemi aperti," *Atti del II Congresso Internaz. Etrusco* (Florence 1985), Rome, pp. 441–450.

———(1995) "Ostmediterrane Einflüsse auf den Beginn der Monumentalarchitektur in Etrurien" in *JRGZM* 37, 1990, pp. 501–519.

———(2000) "Tomb Architecture," in M. Torelli (ed.), *The Etruscans*, Milan: Bompiani, pp. 334–343.

———(2006) *Die Etrusker. Jenseitsvorstellungen und Ahnenkult*, Mainz: Philipp von Zabern.

Prayon, F. and Bonfante, L. (eds) (1986) "Architecture" in *Etruscan Life and Afterlife*, Warminster: Aris & Phillips, pp. 174–202.

Quilici Gigli, S. (1970) *Tuscana*, Rome: Forma Italiae.

———(1976) *Blera*, Mainz: Philipp von Zabern.

Ricci, G. *et al.* (1955) "Caere" in *Monumenti Antichi* 42.

Riva, C. (2010) *Urbanization of Etruria – Funerary Practices and Social Change, 700–600 BC,* Cambridge: Cambridge University Press.

Romanelli, R. (1986) *Necropoli dell'Etruria rupestre*. Architettura, Viterbo: Edizioni Cultura.

Romualdi, A. (ed.) (1992) *Populonia in età ellenistica. I materiali dalle necropoli. Atti del Seminario,* Florence 1986, Florence 1992: Il Torchio.

Romualdi, A. and Settesoldi, R. (eds) 2009 *Populonia. La Necropoli delle Grotte. Lo scavo nell'area della cava,* Pisa: Edizioni ETS.

Rosi, G. (1925) "Sepulchral architecture as illustrated by the rock façades of Central Etruria. Part 1" in *Journal of Roman Studies* 15, pp. 1–59.

——(1927) "Sepulchral architecture as illustrated by the rock façades of Central Etruria. Part 2" in *Journal of Roman Studies* 17, pp. 59–96.

Steiner, D. (2004) *Jenseitsreise und Unterwelt bei den Etruskern. Untersuchungen zur Ikonographie und Bedeutung,* Munich: Hubert Utz Verlag.

Steingräber, S. (1981) *Etrurien. Städte, Heiligtümer, Nekropolen,* Munich: Hirmer.

——(1985) "Felsgrabarchitektur in Etrurien" in *Antike Welt* 16, 2, pp. 19–40.

——(1991) "Etruskische Monumentalcippi" in *Archeologia Classica* 43, pp. 1079–1102.

——(1993) "L'architettura funeraria chiusina" in *La civiltà di Chiusi e del suo territorio. Atti del XVII Convegno di Studi Etruschi e Italici. Chianciano Terme 1989,* Florence, pp. 171–182.

——(1996) "New Discoveries and Research in Southern Etruscan Rock Tombs" in *Etruscan Studies* 3, pp. 75–104.

——(1997) "Le culte des morts et les monuments de pierre des nécropoles étrusques" in F. Gaultier and D. Briquel (eds), *Les Etrusques: les plus religieux des hommes. Etat de la recherche sur la religion étrusque. Actes du colloque international,* Paris 1992, Paris 1997, pp. 97–116.

——(ed.) (2000) "Investing in the Afterlife – royal and aristocratic Tombs in ancient Etruria, Southern Italy, Macedonia and Thrace," Exhibition Catalogue, The University of Tokyo Museum, Tokyo: University of Tokyo Press.

——(2002) "Ahnenkult und bildliche Darstellungen von Ahnen in etruskischen und unteritalischen Grabgemälden aus vorrömischer Zeit" in J. Munk Hojte (ed.), *Images of Ancestors,* Aarhus, pp. 127ss.

——(2009a) "Etruscan rock-cut chamber tombs: origins, characteristics, local and foreign elements" in J. Swaddling and P. Perkins (eds), *Etruscan by Definition. Papers in Honour of Sybille Haynes,* London: British Museum, pp. 64–68.

——(2009b) *La necropoli etrusca di San Giuliano e il Museo delle necropoli rupestri di Barbarano Romano,* Canino: Canino Onlus.

——(2010) "Il monumento funerario etrusco dal VII al III secolo a.C.: genesi, sviluppo, significato" in *Monumento e Memoria. Dall'Antichità al Contemporaneo. Atti del Convegno, Bologna,* 11–13 October 2006 (ed. by S. De Maria – V. Fortunati), Bologna, pp. 7–15.

Steingräber, S. and Prayon, F. (2011) *Monumenti rupestri etrusco-romani fra la Valle del Tevere e i Monti Cimini,* Canino: Canino Onlus.

Torelli, M. (1980) *Etruria,* Rome: Laterza.

——(1982) *Necropoli dell'Italia antica,* Milan: TCI.

van Eles, P. (ed.) (2006) *La ritualità funeraria tra età del Ferro e orientalizzante in Italia. Atti del Convegno, Verucchio,* June 2002, Pisa – Rome: Istituti Editoriali e Poligrafici Internazionali.

von Duhn, F. (1924–1939) *Italische Gräberkunde I–II,* Heidelberg: Carl Winter's Universitätsbuchhandlung.

von Stryk, F. (1910) *Studien über die etruskischen Kammergräber,* Dorpat: Laakmanns.

Zamarchi Grassi, P. (1993) *La Cortona dei Principes. Catalogo della Mostra,* Cortona: Calosci.

Zifferero, A. (1991) "Forme di possesso della terra e tumuli orientalizzanti nell'Italia centrale tirrenica" in E. Herring, R. Whitehouse and J. Wilkins (eds), *Papers of the Fourth Conference in Italian Archaeology. The Archaeology of Power,* Part 1, London, pp. 107–134.

——(ed.) (2000) *L'architettura funeraria a Populonia tra IX e VI secolo a.C. Atti del Convegno* (Populonia, 30–31 ottobre 1997), Florence: All'Insegna del Giglio.

CHAPTER THIRTY THREE

THE IMAGERY OF TOMB OBJECTS (LOCAL AND IMPORTED) AND ITS FUNERARY RELEVANCE

———•◆•———

Tom B. Rasmussen

The Monte Abatone necropolis is one of Cerveteri's largest. In 1961 a rich tomb was excavated here, and numbered 610. There was no metalware or jewelry, but it contained a large variety of pottery dating to the late sixth and early fifth century BC, ranging from local bucchero to some striking Athenian black-figure ware together with a fine red-figure cup by Oltos with Herakles wrestling a sea-god (Moretti 1966; Beazley 1963: 1623, 66bis). In many ways MA 610 is not untypical of Etruscan tomb assemblages of this period, as often they consist of a mix of objects from different regions (metalware has usually been removed by earlier tomb-robbing), and in the late Archaic period the most important external source was Greece, especially Athens.

But were the objects placed in tombs chosen at random or is there some logic to their choice? If the latter, are there specific funerary interpretations that can be placed on the imagery they display? A further question is whether there is a tie-up between the iconography of tomb objects and tomb paintings, the funerary purpose of which is more assured?

Most imported Greek pottery is of shapes that are suited to the banquet or drinking party (Osborne 2001: 291), and these would, of course, have been useful for any banquets that took place at Etruscan funerals. A quick answer as to why certain objects are found in tombs could be that whatever equipment was used at the funerary banquet was simply collected up afterwards and interred with the tomb occupants, as suggested by Werner (2005: 75) for Etruscan black-figure pottery. But even if this were the case, it still leaves questions about the imagery featured on tomb goods.

Where Etruscan painted pottery is concerned, it is worth noting that it is first and foremost an urban, and primarily a funerary, phenomenon. In fact, 99 percent of Etruscan black-figure pottery of known provenance has been found in tombs (Paleothodoros 2011: 45). It is clear from a number of field surveys that, apart from very frugal amounts of the Etrusco-Corinthian fabric, out in the farming communities of the countryside (for example in the Albegna valley: Perkins 1999) there was minimal circulation of painted pottery. In the case of imported pottery, Attic is plentiful at town sites, at Roselle for example (Donati 1994: 100), and even at minor urban centers (Reusser 2002: 204). The finest pottery, especially in the case of Etruscan and Attic figured wares, seems to have been used (ultimately, at any rate) for dedication at sanctuaries and for placing in tombs.

An important issue is whether painted pots and the other contents of tombs were possessions of the deceased when alive or whether they were bought or manufactured expressly for burial. One thinks of the gold jewelry that is such a striking feature of the great "princely" tombs of the seventh century BC. Many of these items are suitable for actually wearing, but others, such as the 30-centimeter-long Regolini-Galassi granulated brooch (see Chapter 6, Fig. 6.20; Sprenger and Bartoloni: 1977: pl. 18), are unlikely to have been worn. Was this made specially as a solace for the dead person in the grave? Not necessarily: the fabulously wealthy had to store their gold in some form, and having huge ornaments made out of it was perhaps as convenient a form for the storeroom as any other. There are also indications that some tomb goods, pottery especially, were in use before burial. For example, a couple of bucchero chalices had had their feet carefully repaired before being placed in a tomb at Orvieto (Bizzarri 1962: 127, Fig. 41), some bucchero jugs show decoration that is worn from repeated placement of the thumb on the handle while pouring (Regter 2003: nos 17, 78), while among the pots of Monte Abatone 610 were three Athenian black-glazed cups, the largest of which has repair holes drilled for the handle and foot (Fig. 33.1).

If such care could be given to vessels of modest appearance it is no surprise that ancient repairs to Athenian figured pottery are also known (Elston 1990), and the fine condition of some of these items suggests they also come from tombs, most probably from Etruria. How the Etruscans acquired their Greek pots is not irrelevant here. Most Athenian painted pots were for the symposium, and the theory that many of them were used once at Athens and then shipped off to Etruria to be traded second-hand found little favor when first proposed (Webster 1972) but it has more recently enjoyed increasing acceptance

Figure 33.1 Attic black-gloss cup, detail of repair holes (after Moretti 1966). Excavated at Cerveteri, Monte Abatone tomb 610; Museo Etrusco di Villa Giulia.

(Johnston 1991: 216–18; Rasmussen 2008). Second-hand trade is still difficult to prove, but is the best explanation for many of the prize Panathenaic amphoras found in Etruscan tombs (Rystedt 2006: 503). As equally important as how they were traded is whether any thought was given to their appropriateness for burial use. What, for example, were two Attic cups with erotic scenes doing in a Tarquinian tomb? Both are by the same artist (attributed to the Triptolemos painter) and must have been collected as a pair (Boardman and La Rocca 1978: 114; Beazley 1963: 367, nos. 93, 94). Moreover, there are many hundreds of such scenes, both homoerotic and heterosexual, on similar imported red-figure vessels, and the great bulk of those with known provenances come from Etruscan tombs (Kilmer 1993: 205). Although they are rare on Etruscan pots and other objects, it so happens that it is at Tarquinia that tomb painting sometimes features erotic groups (Tombs of: the Bulls, the Whipping, the Chariots), which are usually explained in a symbolic way – protecting the tomb occupants, or energizing them for renewed life. So, rather than being placed in the tomb as erotica for its own sake, the Greek vases may have been chosen to perform this "secondary" symbolic function.

A more common subject for the painted walls of Etruscan tombs is sports and games, which are usually thought to signify the games staged at funerals. A number of Athenian pots with similar decoration are also found in the tombs, and this is perhaps where the mythological wrestling of the Oltos cup fits in. Some of them belong to the black-figure Perizoma Group, which gets its name from the very un-Greek loincloth which athletes are shown wearing. These pots actually copy vessel shapes that originated in Etruria, as well showing, in addition, scenes of banqueting – itself perhaps the most popular of all the themes of Etruscan tomb decoration. Moreover, there are two aspects of these scenes that follow local Etruscan customs: the banqueting is directly on the ground, rather than on couches, and is in Etruscan mixed-gender fashion where males and females are portrayed as of equal status. It seems that this particular Athenian workshop was in some way aware of the specific iconographic needs of Etruscan funerary practice (Spivey 1991: 144; Shapiro 2000).

Some sports shown on Athenian pots seem to involve a bloody outcome: in London there is a black-figure amphora painted with a scene of boxers where blood pours from their noses; it was produced in the Nikosthenes workshop (Tosto 1999: no. 135), which was very fond of showing boxers and which exported almost its entire output to Etruria, but this pot seems to have been diverted to Sicily (Agrigento). Sports depicted on Etruscan tomb walls could also result in maiming or even perhaps death, as is apparent from the spills depicted in chariot racing scenes (Tomb of the Olympic Games), and in the "Phersu game" of the Tomb of the Augurs where the "sport" consists of a hooded man trying to beat off a vicious dog (Steingräber 1986: pl. 20; see Fig. 45.3). One detail of this tomb was already badly damaged when it was discovered and is best seen in a published drawing (Becatti and Magi 1955: Fig. 9; Fig. 33.2). It shows, on the entrance wall either side of the door, a tug-of-war, but this is hardly a comic scene or one of light relief as suggested by Thuiller (1985: 592): if the restored drawing is correct, the rope passes around the waist of one contestant and around the neck of the other – who would be in danger of losing his life. It has also been suggested that the vicious dog in the Phersu sequence may in fact be a wolf-like creature from the Underworld (Elliot 1995) which may also be recognized in monstrous figures emerging from wells carved on late ash-urns and in the chained beast on a well known seventh century BC bronze urn from a tomb at Bisenzio (De Grummond 2006: 13–15; see also Chapter 25). If that should be the case,

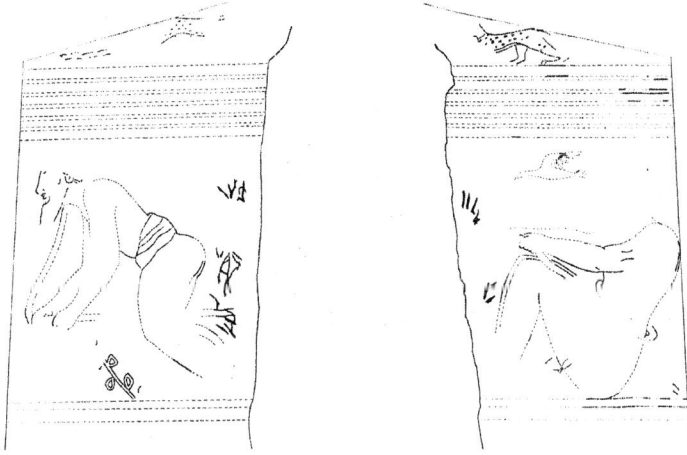

Figure 33.2   Tomba degli Auguri, detail (after Becatti and Magi Fig. 9).

then we have an interesting tie-up between tomb decoration and objects placed in tombs, as well as early indications in Archaic tomb painting of Underworld references.

One of the glories of the Louvre collections is the red-figure Antaios krater by the Athenian vase-painter Euphronios, found in a Cerveteri tomb (Beazley 1963: 14, 2). There are many Greek scenes of Herakles grappling and wrestling with opponents but this is one of the few that shows the moment of death (the pupil of the giant's eye rolls upwards, and his mouth is open in a final gasp). Was the pot, therefore, chosen because wrestling at funeral games sometimes ended in unconsciousness or death? Did Etruscan burial rites on occasion include human sacrifice? Or, as seems more likely for most occasions, was the deceased's need for sustenance from human blood satisfied by its depiction alone?

Another way of providing for the deceased, in addition to putting objects in the tomb or painting the tomb walls, was to represent such objects by means of relief sculpture. Best seen in the Tomb of the Reliefs at Cerveteri (Blanck and Proietti 1986) this is especially illuminating for us because for the tomb designer it was a time-consuming process and needed to be carefully planned in advance. On the walls and pillars of this tomb is represented a variety of status objects: a fan (*flabellum*) and staff (*lituus*), also a probable writing tablet; homely objects: ladles, knives, pickaxes, crockery (metalware and pottery). Most importantly, almost all these items can be found in other tombs – not just in relief or painting but also in the form of real objects. Whoever designed this tomb knew he was not simply replicating some sort of house or a room in a house, but a tomb of the dead. Hence there is a three-headed Cerberus on the far wall together with a snaky-legged "Scylla," both creatures associated with the Underworld. One could even draw the conclusion that the iconography of this tomb suggests a space that is at one and the same time the house, the tomb, and the Underworld.

But the point worth stressing here is that the pots from tombs are identical to those found in domestic situations, even though it is sometimes said that in real life wealthy Etruscans used only metalware and that the pottery found in tombs was a cheap substitute purchased for honoring the dead (Vickers 1985–6). In actuality metal services do exist from tomb contexts, and a good example is the silverware found with the sarcophagus of Seianti Hanunia Tlesnasa from near Chiusi and now in the British Museum – even though the objects have since been lost (Ginge 2002: 11, pl. 11); however, most metal items tend to have fallen foul of tomb-robbers from Roman times onwards.

When we come to pictures on pots, it might be possible to separate out those pots made specifically for the tomb and those that were not. However, for Attic products imported into Etruria there seems to be no discernible difference between the images (banquets, Herakles scenes, and so on) on vessels found in houses, sanctuaries or tombs (Reusser 2002). The situation for Etruscan painted pottery is rather different. It is far less plentiful than Attic, and a recent study of tomb contexts that contain both Etruscan and Attic concludes that the former was able to supply images that were less generic and of greater local significance (Paleothodoros 2009: 58). In Etruscan black-figure pottery a striking example is a one-handled kantharos with a scene of *prothesis* or lying-in-state (Werner no. 2.2, pl. 3; Fig. 33.3) – which, interestingly, is matched by no less than three Attic one-handlers of the above-mentioned Perizoma Group, showing the *ekphora* or funeral cortège, all made for the Etruscan market. Also of local significance are those pots that display images of Underworld demons such as Charun and Vanth. One example is an Etruscan red-figure krater in Paris showing the sacrifice of a Trojan prisoner with "Charu" swinging his mallet. On the other side of the pot we are in the Underworld itself: a Charun faces two Amazons, one is labeled as a *hinthial* (shade) and the other named as Pentasila (Greek Penthesilea), both are bandaged to indicate their violent deaths, and both have their heads covered with their draperies to underline further that they are no longer alive (Martelli 1987: no. 174, Beazley 1947: pl. 31). Also in Paris is the equally well-known krater with Alcestis and Admetus (Etruscan Alcsti and Atmite), framed by Charun and a snake-brandishing demon (Beazley 1947: 133, pls 30.1–2). What is important here is not just the presence of demons but also the stories illustrated: the deaths of the Trojan and Amazons, and the impending sacrificial death of Alcsti, from which she was in the end spared. Both these pots come from the necropolis at Vulci. A good many others in Etruscan-red figure showing death-demons are briefly surveyed by Beazley (1947: 8–9).

Also placed in tombs were mirrors, as is clear from the excellent state of preservation of many of them, as well as the legend *suthina* – "for the tomb" – written on several (De Grummond 2009). A silver mirror was found in the Seianti tomb (see above), and a decorated bronze mirror in New York (Bonfante 1997: no. 6) again shows Alcsti (here Alcestei) and Atmite, with enigmatic flanking figures that are not obviously demons. A

Figure 33.3   Etruscan black-figure (Ivy Group) one-handle kantharos, British Museum 99.7–21.1.
Courtesy of Trustees of the British Museum.

mirror in Florence (Fig. 33.4), which has often been discussed (most recently: Rasmussen 2005, Feruglio 2006), shows Hercle (Herakles) nursing at Uni/Hera's breast. The subject is Hercle's apotheosis (which seems to be explained in the "caption" held by Tinia/Zeus on the right), but so far little consideration has been given to the female figure behind Uni who demands our attention in being not only the central figure but also the only one who engages the viewer with her eyes. The distinctive hem of her garment also enfolds the Uni/Hercle group, linking her strongly to it, and the likeliest identification for her is Hebe, daughter of Uni and Tinia. Her drapery is pulled over her head in the bridal pose as she awaits her bridegroom, Hercle.

Hebe, goddess of eternal youth and Hercle's reward for his life of toil and heroism, is in many ways the pivotal figure of this mirror, and one can imagine it originally being a marriage gift for a young woman and later thought suitable – with its connotations of immortality – for inclusion in her burial. One can imagine a similar history, involving actual use before burial, for the New York mirror with Atmite and Alcestei. However, a red-figure skyphos in Boston with the same subject but with a winged demon standing behind the pair (Brendel 1995: Fig. 271; Beazley 1947: pl. 37) would seem to have been made especially for the tomb. This must have been the case too with the red-figure pots displaying demons discussed above, and it may be worth pointing out that, on one of them, the figure of the Trojan being sacrificed is very reminiscent of a similar scene painted in the François Tomb at Vulci (Buranelli 1987: 94, Fig. 7). The pot was also painted at Vulci at very much the same time, in the second half of the fourth century BC.

Sarcophagi and ash-urns need also to be considered, however briefly, as they are a necessary part of tomb furniture especially in the later periods. One would expect the relief scenes shown on their sides to display a funerary flavor, and of course many do. For example, the rocky divide between this world and the Underworld is shown on a number of sarcophagi, including the one belonging to Laris Pulenas at Tarquinia which

Figure 33.4 Mirror with Hercle and Uni, Florence Museo Archeologico
(after E. Gerhard, *Etruskische Spiegel* V, 60).

features the deceased at the center, flanked by two Charuns, as he approaches the rock and, just beyond, the Greek hero Sisyphus who is threatened by a Vanth as he crouches by the boulder that he is doomed continually to roll uphill (Roncalli 1996). But other scenes, such as battles between Greeks and Amazons, are harder to interpret in a funerary light. So too with the subjects on ash-urns: some, such as the journey to the Underworld on a mule-driven cart, are clearly linked to the purpose of the urn; others, such as scenes with local heroes we know as the Vibenna brothers, are more difficult to connect. But it is likely that as the scenes on burial containers are studied in more detail, so further Underworld connections will be made.

In summary, the burial containers apart, it seems that a minority of items found in Etruscan tombs were made specifically for them, or ordered for them in the case of imported objects, others were not. In the case of pots, Etruscans put Etruscan pottery in their tombs, but preferred – if they could get it – Greek, because they must have appreciated its superior quality. It should, however, be borne in mind that Etruscan red-figure ware continued through the fourth century BC when Athenian figured ware was much less readily available. Apart from exceptional products such as the Perizoma Group, most of the Athenian imagery is neither tomb- nor Etruria-specific. For the most part, what was utilized, whether Etruscan or Greek, was simply what came to hand; often this was perhaps from among the deceased's possessions, and then it was a matter of choosing what was iconographically most appropriate, if the range of material allowed it. The idea of an Etruscan hanging around the port of Tarquinia for the latest shipment of pornographic pots from Athens, because these images harmonized with his views of death, seems an unlikely scenario. On the other hand, pots with erotic pictures were in circulation in Etruria, and from their number suitable items could be chosen for inclusion in burial. Similarly, pots with other kinds of scene might be selected from a household's possessions that offered a particular funerary spin.

More generally, Etruscan taste in Greek pots seems to have coincided very much with our own today. Few, if any, Etruscans would have heard of the name of the Athenian vase-painter Oltos, even though he was among the very best of his contemporaries, yet many almost unerringly sought out the pots of highest quality. Etruscan purchasers might have been canny operators in the salesrooms of today, though they would have been staggered at current prices. For it is clear from all the evidence available that the Etruscan who originally purchased the Oltos cup, later to be put in a tomb, would have given for it no more than he might have paid a craftsman for a day or two's work.

Why the pot was placed in a tomb is the big question, and why indeed often scores of pots, together with other objects, were placed in single tombs. Perhaps one should not expect a simple logical answer to be available. To quote E. R. Dodds (1951: 137): "There is no domain where clear thinking encounters stronger unconscious resistance than when we try to think about death" – a remark that has relevance far beyond the Greek context for which it was made.

BIBLIOGRAPHY

Beazley, J. D. (1947) *Etruscan Vase Painting*. Oxford: Clarendon Press.
——(1963) *Attic Red-figure Vase-painters*, 2nd ed. Oxford: Oxford University Press.
Becatti, G. and Magi, F. (1955) *Monumenti della pittura antica scoperti in Italia. Sezione prima: la pittura etrusca. Tarquinii fasc. III–IV: Le pitture delle Tombe delle Auguri e del Pulcinella*. Rome: Libreria dello Stato.

Bizzarri, M. (1962) "La necropoli del Crocefisso del Tufo in Orvieto." *Studi Etruschi* 30: 1–135.

Blanck, H. and Proietti, G. (1986) *La Tomba dei Rilievi di Cerveteri*. Rome: De Luca.

Boardman, J. and La Rocca, E. (1978) *Eros in Greece*. London: John Murray.

Bonfante, L. (1997) *CSE USA 3: New York, The Metropolitan Museum of Art*. Rome: "L'ERMA" di Bretschneider.

Brendel, O. (1995) *Etruscan Art*. 2nd ed. New Haven and London: Yale University Press.

Buranelli, F. (ed.) (1987) *La Tomba François di Vulci*. Rome: Edizioni Quasar.

de Grummond, N. T. (2006) *Etruscan Myth, Sacred History, and Legend*. Philadelphia: University Museum of Archaeology and Anthropology.

——(2009) "On mutilated mirrors" in M. Gleba and H. Becker (eds) *Votives, Places and Rituals in Etruscan Religion. Studies in honor of J. MacIntosh Turfa*: 171–182. Leiden: Brill.

Dodds, E. R. (1951) *The Greeks and the Irrational*. Los Angeles: University of California Press.

Donati, L. (1994) *La Casa dell'Impluvium. Architettura etrusca a Roselle*. Rome: G. Bretschneider.

Elliot, J. (1995) "The Etruscan wolfman in myth and ritual." *Etruscan Studies* 2: 17–33.

Elston, M. (1990) "Ancient repairs of Greek vases in the J. Paul Getty Museum." *J. Paul Getty Museum Journal* 18: 53–68.

Feruglio, A. E. (2006) "Hercle e Uni a Orvieto" in B. Adembri (ed.), *Aeimnestos: miscellanea di studi per Mauro Cristofani*: 558–565. Florence: Centro Di.

Ginge, B. (2002) "The sarcophagus, the tomb and the Seianti family in their archaeological context" in J. Swaddling and J. Prag (eds) *Seianti Hanunia Tlesnasa. The Story of an Etruscan Noblewoman*: 11–15. London: Trustees of the British Museum.

Johnston, A. (1991) "Greek vases in the marketplace" in T. Rasmussen and N. Spivey (eds), *Looking at Greek Vases*: 203–231. Cambridge: Cambridge University Press.

Kilmer, M. (1993) *Greek Erotica on Attic Red-figure Vases*. London: Duckworth.

Martelli, M. (1987) *La ceramica degli etruschi. La pittura vascolare*. Novara: Istituto Geografico De Agostini.

Moretti, M. (1966) *Tomba Martini Marescotti. Quaderni della Villa Giulia 1*. Milan: Lerici Editori.

Osborne, R. (2001) "Why did Athenian pots appeal to the Etruscans?" *World Archaeology* 33: 277–295.

Paleothodoros, D. (2009) "Archaeological contexts and iconographic analysis. Case studies from Greece and Etruria" in V. Nørskov, L. Hannestad, C. Isler-Kerényi, and S. Lewis (eds), *The World of Greek Vases*: 45–62. Rome: Edizioni Quasar.

——(2011) "A complex approach to Etruscan black figure vase painting." *Mediterranea* 8: 33–82.

Perkins, P. (1999) *Etruscan Settlement, Society and Material Culture in Central Coastal Etruria*. Oxford, British Archaeological Reports.

Rasmussen, B. B. (2008) "Special vases in Etruria: first- or secondhand?" in K. Lapatin (ed.), *Papers on Special Techniques in Athenian Vases*: 215–224. Los Angeles: J. Paul Getty Museum.

Rasmussen, T. (2005) "Herakles' apotheosis in Etruria and Greece." *Antike Kunst* 48: 30–39.

Regter, W. (2003) *Imitation and Creation. Development of Early Bucchero Design at Cerveteri in the Seventh Century BC*. Amsterdam: Allard Pierson Museum.

Reusser, C. (2002) *Vasen für Etrurien. Verbreitung und Funktionen Attischer Keramik in Etrurien des 6 und 5 Jahrhunderts vor Christus*. Zurich: Akanthus.

Roncalli, F. (1996) "Laris Pulenas and Sisyphus: mortals, heroes and demons in the Etruscan underworld." *Etruscan Studies* 3: 45–64.

Rystedt, E. (2006) "Athens in Etruria. A note on Panathenaic amphorae and Attic ceramic imagery in Etruria" in E. Herring, I. Lemos, F. Lo Schiavo, L. Vagnetti, R. Whitehouse and J. Wilkins (eds), *Across Frontiers: Etruscans, Greeks, Phoenicians and Cypriots. Studies in honour of David Ridgway and Francesca Romana Serra Ridgway*: 497–506. London: Accordia Research Institute.

Shapiro, H. A. (2000) "Modest athletes and liberated women: Etruscans on Attic black-figure vases" in B. Cohen (ed.) *Not the Classical Ideal: Athens and the Construction of the Other in Greek Art*: 313–337. Brill: Leiden.

Spivey, N. (1991) "Greek vases in Etruria" in T. Rasmussen and N. Spivey (eds), *Looking at Greek Vases*: 131–150. Cambridge: Cambridge University Press.

Sprenger, M. and Bartoloni, G. (1977) *The Etruscans. Their History, Art, and Architecture.* New York: Harry N. Abrams.

Steingräber, S. (ed.) (1986) *Etruscan Painting: Catalogue Raisonné of Etruscan Wall Painting.* New York: Harcourt Brace Jovanovich.

Thuiller, J-P. (1985) *Les Jeux athlétiques dans la civilization* étrusque. Rome: École Française de Rome.

Tosto, V. (1999) *The Black-figure Pottery Signed* ΝΙΚΟΣΘΕΝΕΣΕΠΟΙΕΣΕΝ. Amsterdam: Allard Pierson Museum.

Vickers, M. (1985–6) "Imaginary Etruscans: changing perceptions of Etruria since the fifteenth century." *Hephaistos* 7–8: 153–68.

Webster, T. B. L. (1972) *Potter and Patron in Classical Athens.* London: Methuen.

Werner, I. (2005) *Dionysus in Etruria. The Ivy-leaf Group.* Stockholm: Paul Åströms Forlag.

PART VI

SPECIAL ASPECTS OF ETRUSCAN CULTURE

———•◆•———

CHAPTER THIRTY FOUR

THE SCIENCE OF THE ETRUSCANS

———•◆•———

Armando Cherici

Tyrrhenia is the country, and Tyrrhenians are the so-called Etruscans. A sage wrote their history, and said that the demiurge, the creator god of all things, granted 12,000 years to his creatures, and distributed them into twelve seats (Gk. *oikoi*, "houses"). In the first millennium he created the heavens and the earth. In the second he created the visible firmament, calling it heaven. In the third the sea and all waters of the earth. In the fourth all the great lights: the Sun, Moon, stars. In the fifth all living things: birds, reptiles, quadrupeds in the air, on the earth, in the water. In the sixth he created man; to man remain 6,000 years.

This looks like a passage from the first book of the Bible, but it is actually the entry "Turrenia" in the *Suda* (Fr. 7.706 J), an encyclopedia of the ancient world compiled in Byzantium between the tenth and eleventh centuries of our era. Accordingly, the Etruscan cosmogony must have been closely related to that attested in priestly circles in Jerusalem around the sixth century BC (*Genesis* 1, 1–2, 4), including the equation that one divine day = 1,000 human years (*Psalms* 90.4; 2 *Peter* 3.8). The topic is of considerable interest: for the seventh century BC, imports from the Phoenician and Cypriot regions are well documented, and through cultural contact this borrowing may be plausible,[1] but – if the entry in the *Suda* is credible and we are clearly dealing with external influence – Etruria would have accepted a cosmogonic system of thought quite different from that of the other two "classic" cultures of the ancient Mediterranean, the Greek and Roman, cultures adjacent to the Etruscans, and with which it substantially shared its pantheon. The questions remain open and require directed study; here, I would simply like to indicate that what is reported in the *Suda* is not entirely foreign to the Etruscan culture, having indeed certain elements that are unique to it, as well as other elements most likely from other sources: the doctrine of a definite time, granted to the life of the individual man, or to a civilization as a whole (Censorinus, *De natali die* 14.6), and the 12 "houses" (*oikoi*), reminiscent of the 16 *sedes* ("seats") into which the Etruscan *templum* is divided (Pliny, *Nat.Hist.* 2.60.142; Martianus Capella 1.45–46).[2]

Let us now proceed to the topic of our chapter. What is a cosmogony? It is man's first attempt to explain the origin and nature of himself, as well as the universe and the world in which he lives, an attempt which, for the first time in the history of thought, takes an organized form. In an era so ancient, the answer can only be religious, yet the different cosmogonies can give us clues to a crucial aspect of "pre-scientific" thought on how a culture has observed the world around them. And the Etruscan cosmogony handed down to us by the *Suda* confirms a mindset and a mode of observation – and cataloging – that are paralleled in other manifestations of this culture.

The Universe and Earth are not perceived and interpreted from a spiritual point of view, there do not appear the primal forces of the Greek theogony, there is a creator, as in Plato, but not his world of ideas: the primary attention is focused on the physical world. Of the creative act – presented as religious certainty – it evaluates and ranks what is physically perceptible, identifying coherent sets: the terrestrial fire is correlated to the celestial "great fires" (*similia similibus*, "like to like"), animals are classified with an internal logic that works up to modern science: those that fly, those who walk or crawl (quadrupeds and reptiles), those that swim. The waters of the sea are distinguished from those of the land (thus, salt- and fresh-waters).

We rely on a sample of only a few lines that have survived the overall disappearance of a great written culture. Although they have perhaps been interpolated, with all due prudence we can assume that these necessarily meaningful words, dictated by a "wise man," confirm some features of Etruscan culture, features that we find in other sources and that can definitely be classified as pre-scientific basics: direct observation of nature, the classification of its phenomena, the development of a series, the final compilation of corpora, handbooks that interpret from a religious perspective every phenomenon visible in the world, from the shape and direction of lightning to the flight of birds to the appearance of the entrails of sacrificed animals. Certainly the results are far from a scientific conclusion, and natural phenomena are seen as divine signs, caused or created by the gods, but the intent in studying them is not simply religious, but rather a magico-religious approach to achieving human advantage through interpretation and subsequent action. Of religion we have the evidence of rituals that refer to their collective needs and fears and contingencies, but we do not find devotion; of magic – and of science – we have first interpretation, then manipulative intent: a god is not induced to kindness with piety, or prayer, but one may determine the position that will serve to remove an obstacle, or create a condition that can be fulfilled, forcing the fulfillment of an act indicated by data from the phenomena observed and classified in a specific corpus.[3] Observation, cataloging, recording, the ability to use data from any person who has access to them, interpretation, channeling forces or events to human benefit: these are essential components of science itself, even if accrued and managed with complex incentives and magico-religious intent. And in fact, in the same Latin sources, not least the passage of Seneca (*Quaest. nat.* 2.32.2) usually taken as a symbol of the religious obsession of this people, we witness that the Etruscans have unwittingly formed their observations into a complete scientific procedure.

However, let us begin with a passage in which the scientific value of a typically Etruscan discipline, haruspicy, is told to us explicitly, by a "technical" author, Vitruvius. The Roman architect records the method for choosing the site for a new human settlement:

> For the ancestors, having sacrificed sheep which were grazing in those places where towns or permanent camps were being established, used to examine the livers, and if they were pale and infected the first time, they would sacrifice another group,

wondering whether they were injured because of disease or because of spoiled fodder. When they had tested many animals and demonstrated the whole and solid nature of the livers [that resulted from good] water and fodder, there they established their fortifications; if however they found [the livers] tainted they thus confirmed the judgment that a future pestilence would grow in the bodies of humans in these places even though there was ample food and water, and so they would move elsewhere and change area, seeking good health in all particulars. (*De architectura* 1.4.9).[4]

The expertise gained by the ancestors in observation of entrails, especially the liver, led to the observation of anomalies or what we now define as a "biological indicator," and relating them to the relationship between the environment and the health of animals is an appropriate course of science, just as it is proper for science to affect the outcome of such a course for the benefit of man. Some may object that we are faced with an interpretation gained from Vitruvius on a practice that the Etruscans followed without their having understood its "scientific" value; but this is possible, just as it is possible that the technical-empirical Vitruvius actually passed on a genuine Etruscan document, without the filter of philosophy by which his contemporary Seneca opposes the Etruscan religion to Greek and Roman rationalism, a filter that perhaps also continues to influence the way we see that civilization.

Let us revisit the famous passage of Seneca:

This is the difference between us and the Etruscans, with whom resides the utmost learning for interpreting lightning: we believe that lightning is caused by clouds colliding, whereas they believe that clouds collide in order to create lightning. Since they attribute everything to the divine, they are led to believe not that events have a meaning because they have happened, but that they happen in order to express a meaning.[5]

I note that here there have also surfaced the stages of a scientific process: the Etruscans see a god as the cause of the movement of the clouds – and this is a religious matter – but they have nevertheless established a relationship of cause and effect between clouds that collide and the generating of lightning. This is a scientific acquisition, caused by a series of observations of a specific natural phenomenon, which is cataloged in its different manifestations, in a corpus (the *Libri Fulgurales, Books of Lightning Divination*) that will enable all specialists to recognize elements – form, direction etc. – that are identified as significant, unique responses from which to draw. Roman thought is generally considered to be more rational, but Seneca speaks in the first century AD, when the Latin culture has been secularized, while the Etruscan wisdom-tradition to which he refers is centuries old: it is now fixed by the time of written texts, but its first formation precedes the advent of writing, given that even in the fully historical period, its transmission was entrusted to the ancestral mnemonic technique of verse.[6] The image of Etruria as haunted by religion is – at least in part – due to a stereotypical judgment that, during the Roman Empire, was attributed to a culture of centuries earlier, a culture that was particularly based on those observations that gradually led to the concept of "natural philosophy" formulated by Newton, and from there to modern science.

These observations never really matured into a true science, even if they have consolidated an empirical approach and awareness of a whole series of relations of cause and effect. Why the next steps toward actual scientific progress did not occur is difficult to say. Perhaps because of the gradual marginalization of Etruria compared to that world of contacts and exchanges that will give life to Ionian philosophy, and then to Hellenistic science. Perhaps because an important scientific tool precociously and systematically used by the Etruscans, the hoarding of wisdom literature in the pages of written texts, has not permitted the subsequent development of a doctrine or of an observation, but rather its crystallization. Its ultimate codification with the written word, once data is written down, excludes the need to continue the direct observation of natural phenomena that had served as the *raison d'etre* of the book itself. A book that, as a further element of "crystallization," was attributed to semi-divine sages – Tages, the nymph Vegoia, the "sage" of the passage in the *Suda*, perhaps even Pythagoras[7] – who were believed to be infallible, like their writings. This "fossilization" of the written data recurs often in the history of science, e.g. the contrasting positions of Galileo's experimentalism and the Aristotelians who, having drawn their positions on the texts and the weight of one particular author, denied the need for further direct observation of nature. But, in the case of the Etruscans, there definitely was observation of nature, and it was translated into a magico-empirical culture that is not quite science because, as far as we know, it did not result in the formulation of laws that explain phenomena, but it was the antechamber to science, and it has sometimes caused science-like outcomes, especially in practical matters.

The scientific orderliness of successive empirical observations has provided us with one of the symbols of the Etruscan civilization: bucchero pottery. A production that mimics – and sometimes goes beyond – the prestige of metal ware: in form, in thickness, delicacy, color, surface, even in sound. It took modern science a long time to understand the degree of absolute specialization of this ceramic, made in special kilns that consumed (reduced) the oxygen content of the clay:[8] the Etruscans surely did not come to determine the chemical and physical mechanisms that produce this result, but with observation, with an endless series of tests, with the ability to record the results, they had finally identified components and constructed the kilns in order to obtain a product of the utmost specialization. This is empirical science, or scientific empiricism.

A similar procedure was evident in gold-working, by developing unsurpassed techniques such as granulation, *a polviscolo* granulation (use of components the size of dust) and filigree. Even here there is no detailed elucidation of the physical-chemical mechanisms that allowed the goldsmith to manufacture and solder in a pattern tiny gold spheres or filaments, without melting them all. The technique (colloidal soldering) that the artisans of the Orientalizing period are proven to have demonstrated, however, is undoubtedly the result of long experimentation made possible by a rich and stable society, able to accommodate, train, and retain craftsmen who were not only working in material of great intrinsic value, but also needed time, protection and security, which would enable them to develop and impart their knowledge. The disappearance of *bucchero sottile* ("delicate bucchero") during the Archaic period, along with the finest gold-working techniques, is probably due to the waning of favorable economic conditions that had supported the progress of this research and the transmission of acquired skills.

For ceramics and jewelry the archaeological evidence can attest, for other areas in which Etruscan empirical science has achieved lasting results, at least in part transmitted to other cultures, we must return to the scant traces of literary sources. More than one author mentions the Etruscan Pharmacopoeia (Aeschylus, *El. Fragm.* 2, Bergk. 2.571; Theophrastus, *Hist. plant.* 9.15.1; Martianus Capella chap. 6.637), and Dioscorides recalls thirteen plant species for which the Etruscans recognized medicinal value still accepted today:[9] their identification lies well within the scientific capacity of observation, classification and recording of data that we have proposed to identify as characteristic of Etruscan culture, and here we may trace the transmission of the results of experiments conducted on the use of a specific plant essence, which was identified over time and distinguished with its own name: an accomplished scientific process.

The hydraulic engineering expertise of the Etruscans, known from ancient sources and archaeological evidence that is not easy to date,[10] pertains especially to the organizational-technical realm and that of practical management: an impressive work force must have been employed, and considerable care must then have been devoted to the maintenance of complex works, above ground or underground, such as the drainage systems of the Po delta, the Formello *cuniculus* (tunnel) at Veii (more than half a kilometer long) or the Cloaca Maxima in Rome (with a course estimated at slightly under a kilometer). But if familiarity with the site and the ready availability of slave labor can explain works of such extension, still, some of their characteristics imply a scientific-empirical process: through digging underground tunnels that could not be supervised from the surface we can imagine that they had developed specific geodetic techniques based on the ability to survey, to lay out alignments, to measure angles, capabilities that were assumed theoretically in the doctrines of the *limites*, of the founding of cities, of the consecration of temples and altars, and contained in the procedures of the *Libri rituales* (Festus 358L).

Even here we are at a severe disadvantage in having, from this wisdom-heritage, only tiny fragments that we continue to place – perhaps distorted by historical perspective – in the world of Etruscan religious obsession. It is again Festus (351L), who helps us to understand how a religious ceremony, the augural ritual, would in fact make the building a geodesic landmark, that is, a point of reference for reading the landscape (and sky): "*stellam significare ait Ateius Capito [...] auctoritatem secutus P. Servilii auguris, stellam quae ex lamella aerea adsimilis stellae locis inauguratis infigatur.*" In the altars and temples consecrated according to augural rites was fixed a bronze "star,"[11] that is a reference to the two cross-pieces of the *groma*,[12] the surveying instrument that will allow the Romans to plan the use of land in all its forms, from laying out the path of the roads, to the slope of the aqueducts, and the centuriation (precise land division) of the fields. That there already existed in the Etruscan period a cadastral awareness linked to the concept of *terminatio*, the design of artificial boundaries, is demonstrated by the finds of inscribed *cippi* and recorded in a document of the knowledge handed down from semi-divine figures: the prophecy of Vegoia. It is perhaps also possible to go beyond an exclusively religious interpretation here: the *termini* surely belong in the scope of the sacred, but this is also true for Rome, where they are protected by Terminus and are celebrated in the Terminalia festival. If from Roman culture there remained only this last piece of information, we would have considered the Roman concept of *termini* only from a religious point of view (as we tend to do for the Etruscans), whereas we know that they were the concrete foundation of an agrimensorial science (that of measuring the land), which was based on a remarkable ability for geometric abstraction and application, in teaching skills that in Etruscan doctrine are vested in a priest, in his designating a *templum* in which to observe and recognize the phenomena of nature.

Posidonius of Apamea, who lived between the second and first centuries BC, while direct information on the Etruscan culture was still available, informs us how letters, natural science, theology were maintained (in Diodorus 5.40.2): it is certainly possible that these areas interpenetrated – even if our sources differentiate them – and that certain topics were handed down in dogmatic form, as also in the Pythagorean school; moreover, as in any ancient culture, it is possible to imagine that religious knowledge and scientific knowledge would mingle and converge in the same person: the priest or the king (who was originally also a priest, as witnessed in Rome in the survival of the institution of the *rex sacrorum*). The soothsayer of Veii who interpreted the flooding of Lake Albano (Livy 5.15.12), thus demonstrates that technology and religion are mingled. Pliny in his *Naturalis Historia* (2.140) recalls how Porsenna dispatched – by evoking a lightning-bolt – the monster Olta, who threatened the city of Volsinii after having ravaged the countryside: the passage is complicated, in part because Porsenna is known as king, not at Orvieto, but at Chiusi. The myth that Pliny seems to speak of involves one of the many "monsters" that were devouring the fields, with which the ancient world associated malaria and the uncertainty of life around the marshes, and this is possible, given that between Chiusi and Orvieto is located the southern edge of the marshes of the Chiana, synonymous in the Middle Ages with a hostile and unhealthy environment:[13] a land destined to be swampy, if regimentation of water works would not allow water to flow into the Tiber, and Pliny (3.53) places here a river – the Clanis – that was regulated by dams. It is not impossible to see behind the myth the outcome of a lengthy procedure of hydraulic works, the memory of which came to be attributed to a prominent figure such as Porsenna, in the role of a powerful priest-king:[14] religion, technical skills, history and myth, may be conjoined in ancient times, but modern research can perhaps isolate individual elements, with great caution and the awareness that we are operating in a "marshy" land.

Some aspects of the Etruscan world – as in the ancient world in general – still elude us because of an imperfect synergy between "humanistic" and "scientific" disciplines, disciplines which struggle to communicate. In modern archaeological publications, the orientation of temples, altars and tombs is always referenced to magnetic north, and entrusted to a graphic symbol that is too small, making it impossible to assess the exact degrees of a structure's orientation: it offers a notion of orientation, but is not sufficient to interpret it. Our cardinal points are not the same as those prevailing in the mental geography of Antiquity, and, at least in the Roman world, any map would have placed our East at the top, as indicated by the *Tabula Peutingeriana* and as evidenced by the names of the Adriatic Sea (*Mare Superum*, the "Upper Sea") and the Tyrrhenian Sea (*Mare Inferum*, "Lower Sea"). Since the Etruscan *templum* (a sacred enclosure for augury/divination) was based on points determined by the rising and setting of the sun (*aequinoctialem exortum, aequinoctialem occasum*: Pliny, *Hist. nat.* 2.143), in order to document and interpret the orientation of a structure properly, we need to detect the point on the structure itself where the rising and setting of the sun is perceived on certain dates, such as the solstices. These points should be on the visible horizon, in fact, and not astronomical reference points: if we are to the east and there are mountains nearby, then the sun will appear late over the horizon, and then will move southward in winter, north in summer; the opposite happens if the temple is on top of a hill.

Also, in the latitudes of Etruria, in the six months between the two equinoxes the point where the sun rises every day moves southward or northward: between the two solstices the points of dawn and sunset (Fig. 34.1) describe an arc of about 66 degrees!

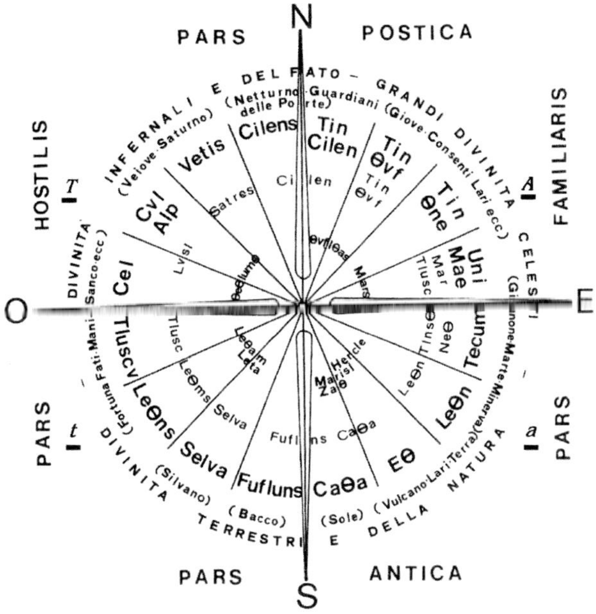

Figure 34.1 Division of the sky according to the *Etrusca disciplina*, diagram by M. Pallottino. Added: A and a = position of the sun at dawn (Ital. *Alba*) on the summer and winter solstices; T and t = position of the sun at sunset (Ital. *Tramonto*) on the same dates.

This means that the lateral sighting lines of an Etruscan temple cannot be indicated by only a small sign for north on the plan. In Temple C and altar A of Marzabotto, oriented N/S, whoever stood on the ground and ran his eye along the outer edge of the wall, could identify the exact date of the two solstices, days when the sun rose and set exactly on the projection of the wall to the left or right of the observer, but if Temple C (as is possible) had its columns arranged as in the Tuscan temple described by Vitruvius, the observer could see, behind the columns to his left and right, the sunrise and sunset of the winter solstice. In the Temple of the Belvedere in Orvieto, and perhaps in the Temple of Jupiter Capitolinus in Rome, the left-hand projection would seem to correspond to sunrise of the summer solstice, and the right-hand projection corresponds to the sunset of the winter solstice, the opposite for the temple of Punta della Vipera at Santa Marinella and the temple beneath the Chiesa delle Stimmate of Velletri: the optical line of sight on the left would correspond to the dawn of the winter solstice, that on the right would correspond to sunset on the summer solstice, thus providing two precise dates for dividing the year. The two temples of Pyrgi instead seem to have the facade oriented toward the winter solstice sunset. In the funerary context, the long *dromos* of the Montagnola Tomb at Artimino seems oriented toward the dawn of the winter solstice: it may be a coincidence, but this particular dawn corresponds to the time when the days begin to lengthen, on which the sun is "born again," as still remembered today in the ritual of our Christmas. At Cerveteri the very long *dromos* of the oldest tomb in the Tumulus of the Colonel is instead oriented towards the sunset of the summer solstice, i.e. the time when the sun begins to "die." The monumental stairway of the Tumulus of Sodo in Cortona would seem, rather, to be facing the sunrise in the winter equinox: the slight declination from the east could be due to the delayed appearance of the sun from behind the mountain that overlooks the site. Such evidence – if it is not random – should not surprise us: centuries before, sacred Sardinian buildings such as the well of Santa Cristina in Paulilatino (Oristano) allowed the rays of the sun to penetrate the structure on the equinoxes, many centuries before the oculus of the dome of the Pantheon would project them on the threshold at noon on the summer solstice, and in the eleventh century AD, a hole in the dome of the Baptistery of Florence followed the annual motion of the sun, as was observed even two centuries later by Giovanni Villani (1.61).

I would like to emphasize that the foregoing has outlined only the merits of a proposition: the documentation available for the Etruscan monuments does not allow a reliable assessment of orientation with respect to the apparent motion of the sun visible on the horizon. And as I emphasize, especially in this field, a complete study would require collaboration between several scientific disciplines. The great religious buildings have long been, in human history, places of celestial observation for reasons many and complex: their size ensured more accurate readings, their arrangement in the environment enabled them to escape the demands of everyday life that impose conditions on civic buildings, only the priests had the available time – and knowledge – to make a complete series of observations, only the priests were able to transmit and consolidate the results of such research, and with the ability to chart the year, essential in an agricultural economy, the priests solidified their power: the calendar in Rome was regulated by the Pontifex Maximus, and it is precisely in 46 BC, when Julius Caesar holds this position, that we have his first reform, the Julian calendar that remained valid until 1582, when again a pontifex, Pope Gregory XIII, reformed it.

From analyzing the literary sources, however, it seems highly probable that the Etruscans had developed their own research and techniques for tracking and scanning the calendar year. John the Lydian (*De magistratibus* 1.1 W) informs us that he wrote at length about this in his book *De mensibus*: part is unfortunately lost, but the space devoted to this subject shows that the Etruscan culture had addressed the issue with elements that were original and substantial enough to provide a wealth of material even in the Byzantium of the fifth-sixth centuries AD. And in fact, we know from Servius that the new day began, in Etruria, with the dawn (*ad Aen.* 5.738, 6.535); from Varro and Macrobius that the Roman Ides – a movable date that divided the month – were designed by Etruscans (*Lingua latina* 6.28; *Saturnalia* 1.15); and the jurist Antistius Labeo stated that it would have been their idea to reduce the days of February (in Lydus, *De mensibus* 3.10). If we add to the latter two pieces of information, the ritual of the *clavus annalis* ("year-nail") that was celebrated in Volsinii (Livy 7.3; Festus s.v.), we may reasonably suspect that the Etruscans had devoted much attention to the problems of the exact measurement of the calendar year. The rite of the nail provides a chronological fixed point before and after the movable date of the Ides, and especially the shortening of February, which allowed them to adapt the division of the months of the year, perhaps to coordinate with the luni-solar calendar, which began in February with the first full moon of spring: this most ancient, pastoral calendar, was easier to follow but not sufficiently accurate for the strict needs of a complex agriculture. Choosing to assign a variable, shorter length to February, which is thus configured as the last month, it also meant that there would be less intrusion on any organized activity: in February farm-fields, trade and war are still closed down,[15] which is a socio-economic valuation because the need to link the length of the months and of the year to the course of the sun is an expression of socio-economic order, and of its value. And here, once again, empiricism, science, economics and religion are mingled, given that Etruscan mastery in projecting a ray of fixed boundaries into a given territory, which is devoid of markers – the horizon and the dome of the sky – is represented by the *templum*, based on the equinoctial points (Fig. 34.1).

The *templum* could use the reference points offered by the bronze star that we encountered above, but also the very structure of the Tuscan temple could possibly fulfill this function. Vitruvius, describing the plan in a well-known passage (4.7), adopts, only for this purpose, a very particular frame of reference, based on proportional measurements easily made on site with a system of ropes and stakes. Such empirical procedure allows one to realize, without resorting to algebraic calculations, a building with two geometrical characteristics, which I believe are of interest to this study. 1) The *pars antica* and *pars postica* both have the dimensions of the golden rectangle, a relationship that seems present in many Etruscan monuments, which should be a topic-specific interdisciplinary study.[16] 2) Whoever places himself with his back to the central cella could see the *pars antica* of the *templum*, divided into eight segments from its plot of six visible columns, because the sight of the two corner columns is covered by the two inner columns (Fig. 34.2).[17] This evidence is easily plotted; I do not consider this to be random, but it is very difficult to pursue the idea further. On the one hand we must resign ourselves to the absolute paucity of written sources; on the other, there should be more accurate documentation and interdisciplinary analysis that would locate the temple in the daytime landscape, as in that of the night: archaeology has largely neglected the world of the constellations into which was projected much of ancient mythology, that is – as we said earlier – the pre-scientific way of explaining the nature of things, *de rerum natura*. The swastika, an element that appears through the millennia in the development of any agricultural culture, from China to Etruria, might arise from the seasonal positions of *Ursa Major* (Fig. 34.3), which the Greeks called *helix*, "spiral," as the swastika is a spiral.[18]

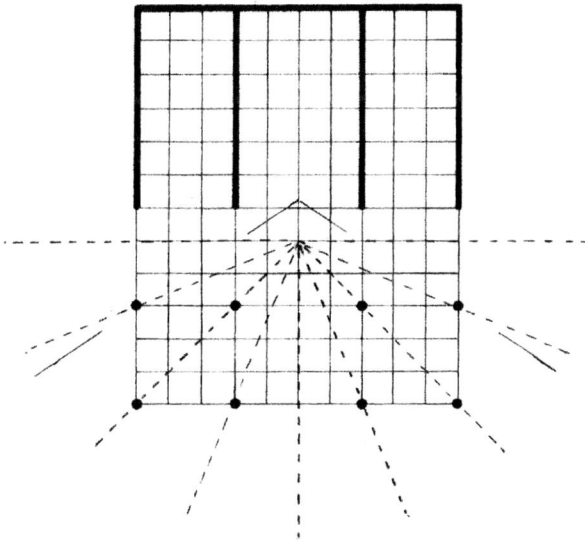

Figure 34.2   Plan of the Tuscan temple (*templum tuscanicum*) according to Vitruvius (Knell), with indication of the golden rectangle in the *pars postica* and of the lines of sight of the eight sectors of the *pars antica* of the *templum*.

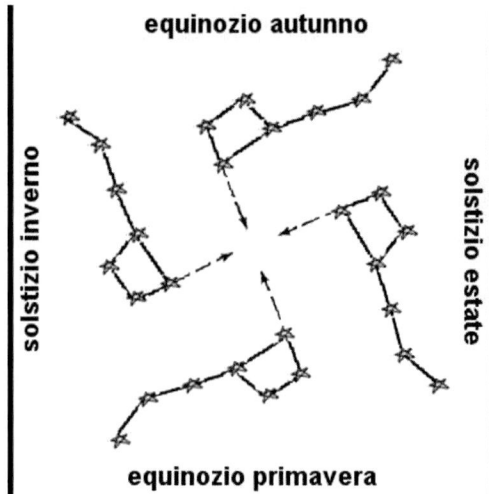

Figure 34.3 The four prevailing positions of *Ursa Major* form a swastika pattern in the sky.

These are fascinating areas of possible further inquiry, which one could explore only with an interdisciplinary approach,[19] or at least one that is not exclusively art-historical. Thus we discover that fluid dynamics were known not only for what concerned the great hydraulic works mentioned above, but also in the behavior of water moving under pressure through pipes: a series of vessels with internal baffles or vent holes were arranged to distribute liquid selectively, or to prevent the formation of bubbles; bucchero cups with internal tubes allowed one to suck the liquid by creating a vacuum with the mouth,[20] or to mix fluids by the principle of communicating vessels that allowed water to pour into isolated above-ground monumental fountains.[21] Late Etruscan anatomical votives document a remarkable knowledge of the internal organs, accessible only with surgical techniques.[22] We are on the threshold of science, in the empirical and cognitive phase, but the Etruscan culture always shows a marked ability to abstract and render these observations concrete, and useful: in the practice of trade in Etruria there was created the economic concept of "tare" (Festus 129; *TLE* 844), today still an essential concept in mercantile science.

NOTES

1   See now also results of Near Eastern borrowing in the Etruscan Brontoscopic Calendar (Turfa 2012, chapter 8).
2   On which: Van Der Meer 1979; Stevens 2009.
3   The episode of the victim's entrails stolen at Veii (Livy 5.21.8) is significant: it is not devotion that influences the outcome of the sacrifice, but he who physically completes a specific act; cf. also the story of the *Caput Oli* (Servius, *ad Aen.* 8.345).
4   Vitruvius' original text: "*Maiores enim pecoribus immolatis, quae pascebantur in îs locis, quibus aut oppida aut castra stativa constituebantur, inspiciebant iocinera, et si erant livida et vitiosa primo, alia immolabant dubitantes, utrum morbo an pabuli vitio laesa essent. Cum pluribus experti erant et probaverant integram et solidam naturam iocinerum ex aqua et pabulo, ibi constituebant munitiones; si autem vitiosa inveniebant, iudicio transferebant item humanis corporibus pestilentem futuram nascentem in his locis aquae cibique copiam, et ita transmigrabant et mutabant regiones quaerentes omnibus rebus salubritatem.*" (*De architectura* 1.4.9).

5   Seneca's original text: *"Hoc inter nos et Tuscos {...} interest: nos putamus, quia nubes collisae sunt, fulmina emitti, ipsi existimant nubes collidi, ut fulmina emittantur, nam, cum omnia ad deum referant, in ea opinione sunt, tamquam non, quia facta sunt, significent, sed quia significatura sunt, fiant."*

6   Livy 5.15.4; Lucretius *De rerum natura* 6.381; Censorinus, *De die natali* 4.13.

7   Cherici 2006, p. 11 ff.

8   Cuomo Di Caprio 2007, p. 438 ff.

9   Cherici 2006, p. 10 f.; Johnson 2006; Scarborough 2006; Harrison, Bartels 2006; Harrison, Turfa 2010.

10 Bergamini 1991. See Chapter 36.

11 Cherici 2006, p. 22 ff. A star is traced on the platform of the rock-cut tomb at Bomarzo, the "Sasso del Predicatore" ("Stone of the Preacher") (Steingräber-Prayon 2011, p. 35 ff.).

12 Daremberg-Saglio, S.V. Stella.

13 Dante, *Inferno* 29.46 f.; Fazio Degli Uberti, *Dittamondo* 3.10.22 ff.; L. Pulci, *Morgante* 23.41.

14 Cherici 1994.

15 Cherici 2006, p. 16 ff.

16 Cherici 2007; Idem 2012.

17 Cherici 2007, Figs. 1, 2.

18 Cherici 2006, p. 24.

19 Cherici 2006, p. 24.

20 Cristofani 1985, No. 5.2; Cf. Peruzzi 1998, p. 43.

21 Maggiani 2011.

22 Baggieri, Rinaldi Veloccia 1996.

BIBLIOGRAPHY

Baggieri, G. and Rinaldi Veloccia M. L. (eds) (1996) *Speranza e sofferenza nei votivi anatomici dell'antichità*, Rome: MelAMi.

Bergamini, M. (ed.) (1991) *Gli Etruschi maestri d'idraulica*, Perugia: Electa.

Cherici, A. (1994) "Porsenna e Olta, riflessioni su un mito etrusco" in *Mélanges de l'Ecole française de Rome* 106, p. 353–402.

——(2006) "Per una scienza etrusca" in *Science and Technology for cultural Heritage* 15, p. 9–28.

——(2007) "Per una scienza etrusca. 2. Templum, templi e rettangolo aureo" in *Science and Technology for cultural Heritage* 16, p. 9–29.

——(forthcoming) "Il rettangolo aureo nell'Etruria Rupestre" in S. Steingräber (ed.), *L'Etruria Rupestre dalla protostoria al medioevo*.

Cristofani, M. (ed.) (1985) *Civiltà degli Etruschi*, Milan: Electa.

Cuomo di Caprio, N. (2007) *La ceramica in archeologia, 2: antiche tecniche di lavorazione e moderni metodi d'indagine*, Rome: "L'ERMA" di Bretschneider.

Fabbri, F. (2005) "Votivi anatomici fittili e culti delle acque nell'Etruria di età medio- e tardorepubblicana" in *Rassegna di Archeologia*, 21B, p. 103–152.

Harrison, A. P. and Bartels, E. M. (2006) "A Modern appraisal of ancient Etruscan herbal practices" in *American Journal of Pharmacology and Toxicology*, p. 21–24.

Harrison, A. P. and Turfa, J. M. (2010) "Were natural forms of treatment for fasciola hepatica available to the Etruscans?" in *International Journal of Medical Sciences* 7, p. 282–291.

Herz-Fischler, R. (1987) *A mathematical History of Division in extreme and mean Ratio*, Waterloo, Canada: Wilfrid Laurier University Press.

Johnson, K. P. (2006) "An Etruscan Herbal?" in *Etruscan News*, 5, pp. 1, 8.

Maggiani, A. (forthcoming) "Le fontane monumentali nei santuari etruschi" in *Annali Faina* XIX, [in press].

Nestler, G. and Formigli, E. (2004) *Granulazione etrusca. Un'antica arte orafa*, Siena: nuova immagine.

Peruzzi, E. (1998) *Civiltà greca nel Lazio preromano*, Florence: L.S. Olschki.

Scarborough, J. (2006) "More on Dioscurides' Etruscan Herbal" in *Etruscan News* 6, pp. 1, 9.

Steingräber, S. and Prayon, F. (2011) *Monumenti rupestri etrusco-romani tra i Monti Cimini e la Valle del Tevere*, Grotte di Castro: Annulli Editori.

Stevens, N. L. C. (2009) "A new Reconstruction of the Etruscan Heaven" in *American Journal of Archaeology* 113, p. 153–164.

Turfa, J. M. (2007) "The Etruscan Brontoscopic Calendar and Modern Archaeological Discoveries" in *Etruscan Studies* 10, p. 163–173.

——(2012) *Divining the Etruscan World. The Brontoscopic Calendar and Religious Practice*, Cambridge: Cambridge University Press.

van der Meer, L. B. (1979) "*Iecur Placentinum* and the Orientation of the Etruscan Haruspex" in *BABesch* LIV, p. 49–64.

CHAPTER THIRTY FIVE

THE ARCHITECTURAL HERITAGE
OF ETRURIA

——— ·◆· ———

Ingrid Edlund-Berry

VITRUVIUS AND THE TUSCAN TEMPLE

Etruscan architecture is an acquired taste for those expecting well-preserved ancient buildings such as the Greek temples or the Roman bath complexes. Instead of gleaming marble and indestructible brick walls, it is the bare remains of a foundation course, a threshold, a column base, a tile fragment, or a cutting for a post hole that provide evidence for reconstructing an Etruscan temple or other building. Yet, thanks to references in the ancient texts as well as an increasing body of archaeological remains, it is recognized, sometimes somewhat reluctantly, that Etruscan architecture is important, and that its heritage deserves to be acknowledged.

Although Etruscan buildings and monuments are mentioned in a variety of ancient texts, it is thanks to the Roman architect Vitruvius that the architectural heritage of Etruria was known and appreciated long before the discovery of actual Etruscan temples and other buildings excavated in the nineteenth century and later. Vitruvius lived in Rome at the time of Augustus, and his work, *de architectura*, reflects his interests in both architectural theory and building practices.[1] Before the advent of archaeology he represented the most esteemed source for ancient architecture, and his work was studied in great detail throughout the Renaissance and later.[2] At the same time, it was also recognized that Vitruvius could not be counted on to describe and analyze only what he saw with his own eyes, but rather that he was a theorist providing models and suggesting solutions, some of which were purely theoretical and philosophical, others based on architectural practice.

As a result, when Vitruvius describes Etruscan architecture we need to be aware of the context of his narrative and of his terminology. Thus, in referring to Etruria as a region of Italy (for example, 2.6.4 or 2.10.1) or the location of temples as prescribed by Etruscan priests (1.7.1), he uses words such as "*Etruria*" and "*Etruscus*" to indicate that which pertained to the Etruscans, their land, and culture. On the other hand, in discussing architectural styles, he prefers the adjective "*tuscanicus*," derived from the Latin noun "*Tuscus*," a variant of "*Etruscus*," in contexts which indicate that he is analyzing a form that resembles Etruscan models, but which because of its age and tradition should be perceived of as "Etruscan-inspired" rather than historically or culturally "Etruscan."[3]

In his survey of different types of temples, Vitruvius describes those that are built of wood rather than stone as "straddling, top-heavy, low, and broad" (3.3.5) and as having the gables decorated with statues of terracotta or gilt bronze in the Etruscan-inspired fashion ("*tuscanico more*"). As examples of such temples in Rome, he includes the temple of Ceres at Circus Maximus, Pompey's temple of Hercules, and the Capitoline temple (Figure 35.1), all of which one assumes he would have examined firsthand. Of the temples mentioned, only the temple of Hercules was recent, whereas the construction of the other two dates back to the monarchy and early Roman Republic, and Vitruvius may here imply that the temples he saw looked old-fashioned, although in the original form the sculptures would have been placed on the roof rather than in the pediment.[4]

Vitruvius further uses the same adjective, "*tuscanicus*," in describing the plan and proportions of a temple style which follows his analysis of the familiar Doric, Ionic, and Corinthian types (4.6.6–4.7.5). According to the "Etruscan-inspired design" (4.6.6 *de tuscanicis dispositionibus*), such a temple should have set proportions with six parts in length and five parts in width; the length of the temple building should be divided into a front porch with columns, and a rear part with three rooms, of which the center one was wider than the other two (Figure 35.2). The columns should be aligned with the temple walls, and have a fixed ratio of height and diameter in proportion to the base, the shaft, and the capital. The arrangement of columns in the "Etruscan-inspired type" (4.8.5 "*tuscanicum genus*") of architecture could appear by itself or be combined with Greek types, whether Corinthian or Ionic.[5]

Understandably, Vitruvius' authoritative analysis of architectural styles became regarded as the norm for architectural principles, and editions of his text as well as separate treatises were published with drawings and reconstructions by famous artists and architects who interpreted his text and applied his principles to Renaissance and

Figure 35.1 The Capitoline temple in Rome (Rome, Musei Capitolini. Archivio Fotografico dei Musei Capitolini).

later buildings.[6] Thus, what became known as the "Tuscan Order" in architecture was studied and copied long before there was any archaeological evidence to confirm or modify Vitruvius' analysis.

With the early nineteenth-century excavations not only reported in scholarly publications, but also by travelers such as George Dennis, the world of the Etruscans was brought to light, including the discovery of their architecture, first the tombs and later their temples and houses.[7] Well acquainted with the text of Vitruvius, archaeologists and architects eagerly anticipated the discovery of more Etruscan buildings, temples in particular, but it soon became apparent that the Etruscan architectural heritage known to Vitruvius did not correspond with the archaeological reality.[8] In particular, the proportions and plans of excavated Etruscan temples did not correspond with Vitruvius' definition, and architectural historians were at a loss as to how to define either "Etruscan" or "Etruscan-inspired" forms of architecture.

The effect of this difficulty in reconciling Vitruvius' text and the archaeological remains is perhaps most apparent in the discussion of the Capitoline temple in Rome, dedicated to Jupiter Optimus Maximus, Juno, and Minerva.[9] It is listed by Vitruvius among the temples that were decorated with roof sculptures in the Etruscan-inspired style ("*tuscanico more*" 3.3.5), and based on the excavated remains, the temple has been reconstructed to include three rooms and a front porch with columns. Since the ancient texts (Livy, Pliny, and others) include the construction of this major temple among the achievements of the Etruscan rulers in Rome, the Tarquin dynasty, it has generally been considered the epitome of all Etruscan temples, only to be dedicated in the first year of the Roman Republic, in 509 BC.

But, in spite of its presumed Etruscan origin and style, the Capitoline temple is in many ways an anomaly, in particular because of the size of the foundation, and the estimated size of the temple itself, assuming that it filled the whole surface of the foundation. It has therefore been suggested that we should consider this temple a Roman creation, inspired in form and detail from traditions in Etruria as well as in Latium and in the Greek world, but brought together in a new and unsurpassed monumentality in Rome.[10] If so, Vitruvius' choice of words in describing the pedimental sculptures is very appropriate in that they represented a tradition known in Etruria, but one that had been disseminated to other areas, including Rome.

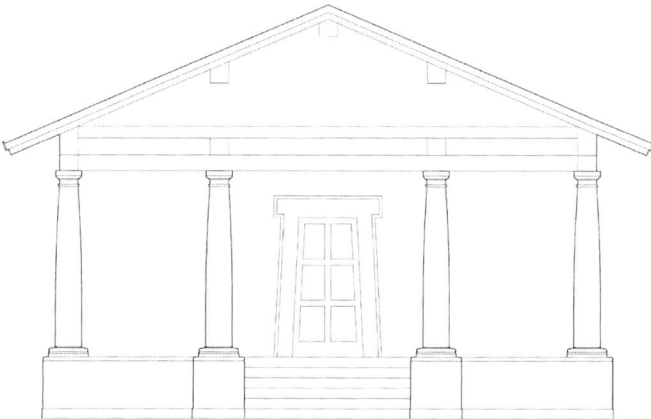

Figure 35.2 The Tuscan temple (courtesy P. Gregory Warden and Jess Galloway).

Yet, regardless of how "Etruscan" the Capitoline temple may be in its execution, the concept of its location on the Capitoline hill and its role as a religious landmark in Rome ties in with the location of temples in Etruria proper (Figure 35.3; see Chapter 27). Viewed as a symbol of what Rome stood for, this Roman monument (in Etruscan clothing) was adopted by city planners in areas of Italy where Roman or Latin colonies were founded and a major temple was erected as part of a new or modified city plan, and the tradition was further spread in the Roman cities throughout the Mediterranean. Ultimately, the Capitolium temple of the Roman Republic belongs in the tradition of the Etruscan temples, but with a superimposed set of features which may or may not ever have been used together in an original Etruscan form. The Capitolia, as we see them in Roman Imperial cities – usually at the end of a forum – tend to be raised high above the ground, resting on a podium, usually with mouldings, to be approached through the steps at the front of the building, with the columns placed in front and usually on the long sides of the temple proper, which contains the main room (*cella*) as one room, or with rooms on either side.

In spite of the fact that Etruscan temples do not always fall into the category of Vitruvius' Tuscan temple, his work continues to inspire our study of Etruscan architecture. It is thanks to him that we can trace the Etruscan-inspired architectural heritage ("*tuscanico more*") from his time to the Renaisssance and later. For the centuries before Vitruvius, we will need to rely on the archaeological evidence to provide the Etruscan background for the development of a Roman architectural tradition that was founded on a mixture of local traditions and contacts with the world around it.[11]

VITRUVIUS AND THE TUSCAN ATRIUM

Unlike George Dennis and early travelers to Tuscany who were limited to seeing recent discoveries of tombs and city walls, we can today view remains of Etruscan houses at a number of sites, and discover that they, like so many other things Etruscan, represent a

Figure 35.3 View towards the Capitoline hill. Photo: Ingrid Edlund-Berry.

variety of traditions.[12] As living quarters for Etruscans, houses were built within cities and in the countryside. Like other buildings, they were constructed from local stone, wood, and clay, and for the most part only the foundation courses remain. Evidence of walls, and, in particular, the well-developed system of terracotta roof tiles and architectural revetments allow for a reasonably accurate reconstruction of the houses, large and small.

The interest in the Etruscan house as a phenomenon derives from two separate sources, one modern and one ancient. The modern one, expressed by scholars such as Einar Gjerstad and Axel Boëthius, is the relationship between the Oriental *"liwan"* house with three rooms and the Etruscan domestic dwelling, also related to the temple plan, as the house of the deities, with three rooms.[13] This emphasis on three rooms has influenced much of Etruscan architecture, and has led to interpretations that highlight clusters of three rooms that are either isolated or form part of courtyard buildings such as the Archaic monumental building at Poggio Civitate (Murlo).[14]

Linked to the modern discussion of the three-room concept is Vitruvius' presentation of the types of the Roman atrium house, of which the "Etruscan-inspired" one is described as having a roof opening (*compluvium*) with four sides sloping down to allow rain water to collect in basin in the floor of the interior courtyard (6.3).[15] Following the definition of the different types of interiors depending on the slope of the roof, and the use of columns, if any, is a description of the ideal proportions of the atrium, including the presence of *"alae"* or wings, and of the *tablinum* and other rooms.

This passage and the brief reference that Greek houses lack atria (6.7.1) have created much confusion as to the origin of the traditional Roman atrium house. If, as Vitruvius suggests, the Etruscan-inspired house has an Etruscan origin, parallels may be found in the Etruscan tombs that display, carved in the tufo rock, ceilings with fake openings similar to the *compluvia* and courtyards of the atrium type.[16]

Of course, the problem of tracing the heritage of the presumed Etruscan-inspired house in domestic Etruscan architecture lies in the fact that we have no actual house preserved to the full height of the walls and roof, other than those suggested by the models of houses. A missing link may, however, exist in the House of the Impluvium from the Etruscan site of Rusellae (Figure 35.4).[17] There we find a sequence of dwellings, of which the one from the Archaic period includes an atrium with *impluvium*, comparable to what Vitruvius describes except for the fact that the reconstruction includes three posts for supporting the roof.[18] Examples of atrium-style houses have also been uncovered at Marzabotto, the northern Etruscan outpost near Bologna,[19] whereas Rome may provide evidence of both courtyard buildings (for example, the Auditorium)[20] and atrium houses (along the Velia; used as regal residences).[21]

As our evidence for Etruscan domestic architecture increases it should be possible to define more clearly which features are distinctly Etruscan and which tend to be common to the architectural traditions in central Italy.[22] The question of three-room structures, whether for sacred or secular use, remains open-ended, and the relation between so-called atrium houses and courtyard buildings needs to be documented more clearly. That both are anchored in Etruscan architecture seems, however, certain, and the traditions continue both in Rome and in other parts of Italy. Does this mean that the Etruscans were pioneers in creating domestic architecture? Perhaps not, but they certainly experimented with a variety of forms, and those that were successful were used extensively, even long after the Etruscan political power had disappeared.

Figure 35.4   Rusellae, House of the Impluvium. Photo: Ingrid Edlund-Berry.

ARCHITECTURAL TRADITIONS IN CENTRAL ITALY

Because of the similarities in building materials, construction, form, and decoration between buildings created in Etruria proper and in neighboring areas such as Rome and Latium, it is difficult to attribute innovation to one culture rather than another. Since the written evidence for events in Rome is so much greater than for any other area of central Italy, it is tempting to credit Rome and her citizens as the innovating force in both political and cultural spheres. But, as indicated by the archaeological evidence, all communities were in contact with each other through trade and as people and ideas traveled in all directions technical skills were shared in production of goods and construction of buildings.[23] At least for the Archaic period, before 500 BC, it would seem that Etruria and Latium, including the Faliscan territory, shared many of the same achievements, and it was not until Rome had confirmed her status as the leading city that we can witness a separation of traditions between Etruscans, Latins, and, ultimately, Romans. But, at the same time, the architectural heritage of Etruria was transferred from the Etruscan cities into Rome, once ruled by Etruscan kings, where it was combined with the traditions of Latium. Thus Roman culture, including architecture, absorbed a heritage that it was destined to transmit to the peoples of the Mediterranean and Europe.

ETRUSCAN TEMPLES AND MOULDINGS

The Etruscans were known for their practice of religion, and their sanctuaries contained temples and other buildings as well as altars and places for worship. Because local stone, clay, and wood were the primary building materials, Etruscan buildings were not meant to last, and had to be constantly rebuilt to withstand the vicissitudes of weather and time.[24] By the time of Vitruvius, the most revered building in Rome, the Capitoline temple, was still standing, but only because of continuous maintenance. It is therefore likely that what Romans and others knew about early Etruscan architecture was based less on autopsy than on hearsay, perhaps with the exception of stone temple foundations that were reused or incorporated into other buildings. Models of buildings, used as votive offerings, would give some indication of building traditions,[25] and the continued use of terracotta decoration, including large-scale statues, on Etruscan as well as Roman temples must have impressed each generation of builders and craftsmen.[26] These traditions of construction and decoration of buildings were, of course, not limited to the immediate area around Rome. Many temples that reflected local traditions as well as those inspired by contact with Etruria and Rome were built in Umbria and in the Samnite communities.[27]

With a keen architect's eye, Vitruvius outlines the construction of a temple from the ground up (3.4), with solid foundations providing the support for the cella and surrounding columns. Although the proportions of the elements could vary, he carefully defines the details of the steps in front and the podium on the remaining three sides (in buildings where there were no steps around all four sides). The elements of the podium are described, from the bottom up, as a plinth (*quadra*), base moulding (*spira*), dado (*truncus*), cornice (*corona*), and '*lysis*' (? cavetto moulding). As is often the case with Vitruvius' descriptions of architectural details, there are many variables to the basic sequence of elements, that is, the crowning and base mouldings, separated by a vertical dado of varying height (Figure 35.5).[28]

Although the use of mouldings is shared by Greek, Roman, and Etruscan architectural traditions, the Etruscan varieties are distinctly different from others, both in their form, proportions, and use.[29] The most common type is a round, similar to a Greek ovolo, but used as a base moulding, usually very large. This round, often referred to as the Etruscan round, occurs in a variety of monuments, including temples in Etruria proper but also in neighboring areas, including Latium and Rome, and it can be argued that it may have been part of different architectural traditions, both Latin and Etruscan, if indeed the two can be separated.[30]

To Vitruvius, and to the Roman world around him, a podium was an essential part of a temple, and such temples could be found in many towns within Italy and in parts of the Mediterranean dominated by Rome. While many of the early temples in Rome, including the Capitoline temple, the temples of Saturn and of Castor in the Roman forum (Figure 35.6), and the Archaic temple at S. Omobono, were built on podia of varying

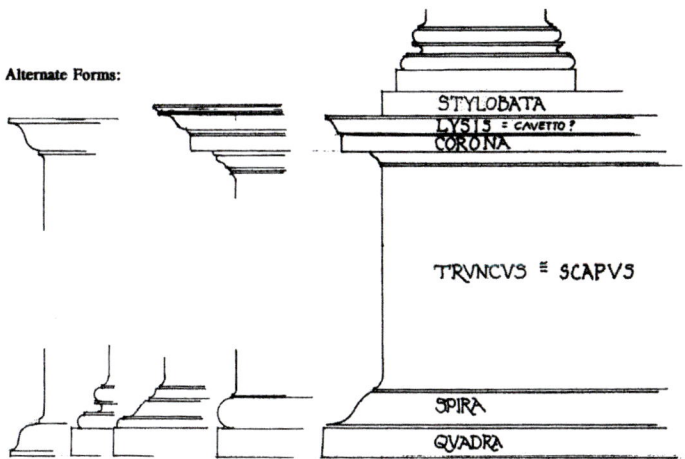

Figure 35.5 Temple podia (courtesy T. N. Howe, from Rowland and Howe 1999, Figure 45).

heights,[31] evidence for Etruscan round mouldings is lacking for the Capitoline temple and the temple of Saturn. The first Archaic temple at S. Omobono has a small Etruscan round above the dado, but no base moulding, and it is not known how the moulding fragment from the temple of Castor was originally placed.[32]

Good examples of temple podia with Etruscan round crowning and base mouldings have been found at Ardea in Latium.[33] In addition to the Casalinaccio temple in the ancient city, recent discoveries at Fosso dell'Incastro on the coast include a sanctuary with well-preserved temple podia,[34] whereas fragments of mouldings at Satricum and Pyrgi may belong to similar temple podia with crowning and base mouldings.[35]

Podia with double Etruscan rounds, of the same or different sizes, but without the separating dado, appear in the second Archaic temple at S. Omobono,[36] and later in the Ara della Regina temple at Tarquinia from the fourth century BC.[37] This design, known also from monumental altars in Etruria and Latium,[38] is further used in temples built in communities that had become part of the Roman political sphere, either in general terms (as for example, the temple at Villa S. Silvestro) or specifically as colonies such as Isernia and Sora (Figure 35.7).[39]

The presence of podia became the hallmark of Roman temples built within Italy and throughout the Roman Empire, often regarded as Capitolia, representing the religious and political traditions of the mother city.[40] The Etruscan round moulding continues as a variant form for temple podia even in the second century BC at Cosa in Etruria, both as a crowning and base moulding, and at Samnite Pietrabbondante (Temple A) as a base moulding, and even other mouldings (cyma reversa or cyma recta) often show rounded elements derived from the Etruscan round.[41]

With time, the Etruscan round was replaced in Imperial Roman architecture by a very complex set of mouldings, but the use of a single horizontal round can be noted throughout

Figure 35.6 Rome, temple of Castor. Photo: Ingrid Edlund-Berry.

Figure 35.7   Sora, temple with Etruscan round mouldings. Photo: Ingrid Edlund-Berry.

European architecture, whether in churches or monumental public buildings.[42] Whether its Etruscan heritage was acknowledged is debatable, but the form can be found also in very modern buildings where the moulding is applied as a separate strip onto a brick or cement wall, thus creating a horizontal transition between floors.[43]

ETRUSCAN WALLS

One can speculate over what a visitor to Etruria during the latter centuries of the Roman Republic would actually have been able to see of Etruscan buildings, including the monumental temples. What would have been in full view, however, were the very impressive city walls that served to protect the Etruscan cities from invaders, including the Romans.[44] Even in cities where the steep hills on which they were built served as natural fortifications, the circuit of walls and heavily defended gates sent any potential intruder a message not only of the inhabitants' intent on defense but also of their highly developed technical engineering skill in creating the walls. Of course, as we know from the ancient texts, the Etruscan cities ultimately fell to Rome, but the walls and the gates were preserved as a visual reminder to generations to come of who the original builders were. In the handbooks on Etruscan cities, the city walls are often referred to as of Etrusco-Roman date, and as a further indication of continuity, many walls were later incorporated into Medieval and later fortification systems, as seen for example at Castiglion Fiorentino (Figure 35.8a–b).[45]

ETRUSCAN MONUMENTAL TOMBS

In intentional contrast to the Etruscan cities perched on top of steep hills were the cemeteries, placed along the roads leading out of the cities or on the slopes of hills. These

Figure 35.8a–b Castiglion Fiorentino, Medieval wall and Etruscan gate. Photos: Ingrid Edlund-Berry.

were the cities of the dead, and while the tomb chambers often resembled the houses of the living with doorways and windows carved in the volcanic rock, the monumental tumulus mounds that covered the tombs at Caere/Cerveteri and other sites created a vision of earth reaching the sky, perhaps as a link between the deities of the Underworld and those of the heavens. Although the burial grounds varied from city to city, it is noteworthy that the Romans developed monumental tombs for their rulers and members of important families, perhaps inspired by tomb monuments familiar to them from their Etruscan neighbors.[46]

THE ARCHITECTURAL HERITAGE OF ETRURIA

As suggested by the examples above, the architectural heritage of Etruria is reflected in many different ways, whether in the overall plan or in minute details. Overall, however, what is important is the connection between the location of buildings and the setting in the landscape. Whether viewed from afar or close up, a building is appreciated in terms of how its approach and access relate to the surrounding area. As Etruscan buildings and building details were viewed by neighbors and travelers, and even by their enemies, ideas were transmitted, first to Rome, where they were incorporated into already existing traditions, and later examined by Vitruvius as examples of systems comparable to those of the Greek architectural world. With the Renaissance architects as our intermediaries we can thus view with our own eyes the traditions of the Tuscan architectural form, at the same time as the archaeological evidence provides a wealth, confusing at times, of examples of Etruscan innovations in city planning, temple designs, houses and gathering places, fortification systems, and funerary architecture. What the Romans and other peoples in Italy perceived as Etruscan-inspired traditions became incorporated into the architectural practices of Italy, many of which have disappeared with time, while others such as the Etruscan round mouldings, have survived, surprisingly, in the architectural world of today.

NOTES

1 See Rowland and Howe 1999.
2 See, for example, Morolli 1992.
3 Edlund-Berry 1997; Rowland and Howe 1999, 229.
4 For the placement of statues, see Winter 2009.
5 For the translation of Latin *genus* as "type" rather than order, see Rowland and Howe 1999, xiii.
6 Rowland and Howe 1999: xiii–xiv.
7 Dennis 1848.
8 Lake 1935; Boëthius 1978.
9 The literature on the Capitoline temple is vast. See, for example, Albertoni 2008 and Hopkins 2012.
10 Davies 2006.
11 According to Boëthius 1978, 136–137, Vitruvius uses the term *"consuetudo italica"* for the blend of traditions that created Roman architecture, both native Italian and Greek. Much of what looks Greek in Roman buildings is the use of decorative elements, whereas the structural core reflects traditional Etrusco-Italic features.
12 For an overview, see Morandini 2011.
13 See Boëthius 1978, 90. Also Torelli 1985, 29.
14 See Phillips 1993, 9.
15 Prayon 2009.
16 See examples in Boëthius 1978.
17 Donati 1994; Winter 2009, 19.
18 Donati 1994: Fig. 37.
19 Bentz and Reusser 2008, 80–89 (See Chapter 15).
20 The history of the Auditorium villa in Rome is complex because of its possible connection with the nearby sanctuary of Anna Perenna (see for example, Morandini 2011). Both courtyard buildings (Winter 2009, 567–568) and atrium houses share the open space surrounded by sets of rooms used for gathering, sharing of meals and rituals, and as living quarters. It would seem that the roof construction and sequence of three rooms are secondary to the overall purpose of these structures, and that they should be studied together as examples of the approach and access to indoor and outdoor spaces (Meyers 2012).
21 Cifani 2008.
22 The terminology of Etruscan, Etrusco-Italic, Roman, and Latial reflects the varying approaches, depending on the researcher's interests. Part of the tension expressed with these regional and cultural terms derives from the issue of whether Rome is to be considered part of the Etruscan culture, at least during the rule of the Tarquins, or from early on its own master (see, for example, Cornell 1995).
23 It is difficult to grasp the full impact of trade. Not only were precious objects such as ivories or decorated pottery transported to and within Italy, but a close analysis of both the material and the themes depicted has allowed Patricia Lulof to suggest that terracotta roofs from Campania were shipped to Satricum in Latium (Lulof 2006).
24 Boëthius 1978.
25 Boëthius 1978.
26 Winter 2009.
27 See, for example, Bradley 2000: Appendix I; Stopponi 2006: 231–249; Strazzulla 2006.
28 See Rowland and Howe 1999: Fig. 45.
29 Shoe Meritt and Edlund-Berry 2000.
30 Edlund-Berry 2008; Potts 2011.
31 Shoe Meritt and Edlund-Berry 2000.
32 Shoe Meritt and Edlund-Berry 2000.

33 Di Mario 2007.
34 Di Mario 2009.
35 Edlund-Berry 2008.
36 Edlund-Berry 2008.
37 Shoe Meritt and Edlund-Berry 2000.
38 Menichelli 2009; Stopponi 2011.
39 Edlund-Berry 2008.
40 Boëthius 1978.
41 Shoe Meritt and Edlund-Berry 2000; Edlund-Berry 2008.
42 Edlund-Berry 2006.
43 http://en.wikipedia.org/wiki/Molding_%28decorative%29 (accessed 29 December 2011).
44 Camporeale 2008.
45 Zamarchi Grassi 2006.
46 Boëthius 1978: 94–102; 213–214 and n. 96 (On tombs, see Chapter 32).

BIBLIOGRAPHY

Albertoni, M. (ed.) (2008) *Il tempio di Giove e le origini del Colle Capitolino*, Milan: Electa.
Bentz, M. and Reusser, C. (2008) *Marzabotto. Planstadt der Etrusker*, Mainz: Philipp von Zabern.
Boëthius, A. (1978) *Etruscan and Early Roman Architecture*, New Haven and London: Yale University Press.
Bradley, G. (2000) *Ancient Umbria*, Oxford: Oxford University Press.
Camporeale, G. (ed.) (2008) *La città murata in Etruria. Atti del XXV convegno di Studi Etruschi ed Italici*, Pisa and Rome: Fabrizio Serra.
Cifani, G. (2008) *Architettura romana arcaica*, Rome: "L'ERMA" di Bretschneider.
Cornell, T. J. (1995) *The Beginnings of Rome*, London and New York: Routledge.
Davies, P. J. E. (2006) "Exploring the International Arena: The Tarquins' Aspirations for the Temple of Jupiter Optimus Maximus" in C. C. Mattusch, A. A. Donohue and A. Brauer (eds), *Proceedings of the XVIth International Congress of Classical Archaeology. Boston August 23–26, 2003. Common Ground: Archeology, Art, Science, and Humanities*, Oxford: Oxbow Books, 186–189.
Dennis, G. (1848) *The Cities and Cemeteries of Etruria*, London: J. Murray [and later editions].
Di Mario, F. (2007) *Ardea, la terra dei Rutuli, tra mito e archeologia: alle radici della romanità. Nuovi dati dai recenti scavi archeologici*. Rome: Soprintendenza per i Beni Archeologici del Lazio.
——(2009) "Ardea, l'area archeologica in località Le Salzare-Fosso dell'Incastro," *Lazio e Sabina* 5: 331–346.
Donati, L. (1994) *La casa dell'Impluvium. Architettura etrusca a Roselle*, Rome: Giorgio Bretschneider.
Edlund-Berry, I. E. M. (1997) "'Etruscheria' in Vitruvius and Strabo" in B. Magnusson *et al.* (eds), *Ultra Terminum Vagari. Scritti in onore di Carl Nylander*, Rome: Quasar, 77–79.
——(2006) "The Etruscan Heritage in Postmodern Architecture" in C. C. Mattusch, A. A. Donohue, and A. Brauer (eds), *Proceedings of the XVIth International Congress of Classical Archaeology. Boston August 23–26, 2003. Common Ground: Archeology, Art, Science, and Humanities*, Oxford: Oxbow Books, 147–150.
——(2008) "The language of Etrusco-Italic architecture: new perspectives on Tuscan temples," *American Journal of Archaeology* 112: 441–447.
Hopkins, J. N. (2012) "The Capitoline Temple of and the Effects of Monumentality on Roman Temple Design" in M. L. Thomas and G. E. Meyers (eds), *Monumentality in Etruscan and Early Roman Architecture: Ideology and Innovation*, Austin, TX: University of Texas Press, 111–138.
Lake, A. K. (1935) "The Archaeological Evidence for the 'Tuscan Temple'," *Memoirs of the American Academy* 12: 89–149.

Lulof, P. (2006) "'Roofs from the South': Campanian Architectural Terracottas in Satricum" in I. Edlund-Berry, G. Greco, and J. Kenfield (eds), *Deliciae Fictiles III. Architectural Terracottas in Ancient Italy: New Discoveries and Interpretations*, Oxford: Oxbow, 235–242.

Menichelli, S. (2009) "Etruscan Altars from the 7th to the 4th Centuries B.C.: Typology, Function, and Cult," *Etruscan Studies* 12: 99–129.

Meyers, G. E. (2012) "Introduction: The Experience of Monumentality in Etruscan and Early Roman Architecture" in M. L. Thomas and G. E. Meyers (eds), *Monumentality in Etruscan and Early Roman Architecture: Ideology and Innovation*, Austin, TX: University of Texas Press, 1–20.

Morandini, F. (2011) "Le fattorie arcaiche di Pian d'Alma (Scarlino – GR) e Marsiliana d'Albegna (Manciano – GR): modello "urbano" esportato in campagna o modello "extra-urbano" radicato nella tradizione?" in A. Ellero *et al.* (eds), *La città. Realtà e valori simbolici*, Padova: S.A.R.G.O.N., 79–100.

Morolli, G. (1992) "L'ordine tuscanico nella concezione rinascimentale e postrinascimentale" in M. Pallottino (ed.), *Gli Etruschi e l'Europa*, Paris and Milan: Fabbri, 292–297.

Phillips, K. M., Jr. (1993) *In the Hills of Tuscany*, Philadelphia: The University Museum.

Potts, C. R. (2011) "The Development and Architectural Significance of Early Etrusco-Italic Podia," *BABESCH* 86: 41–52.

Prayon, F. (2009) "The Atrium as Italo-Etruscan Architectural Concept and as Societal Form" in J. Swaddling and P. Perkins (eds), *Etruscan by Definition. Papers in Honour of Sybille Haynes, MBE*, London: The British Museum, 60–63.

Rowland, I. D. and Howe, T. N. (1999) *Vitruvius Ten Books on Architecture*, Cambridge: Cambridge University Press.

Shoe Meritt, L. and Edlund-Berry, I. E. M. (2000) *Etruscan and Republican Roman Mouldings*, Philadelphia: University Museum and American Academy in Rome.

Stopponi, S. (2006) *Museo Comunale di Bettona*, Perugia: Mondadori Electa.

——(2011) "Campo della Fiera at Orvieto: New Discoveries" in N. T. de Grummond and I. Edlund-Berry, *The Archaeology of Sanctuaries and Ritual in Etruria*, Portsmouth, R. I.: Journal of Roman Archaeology, 16–44.

Strazzulla, M. J. (2006) "Le terrecotte architettoniche nei territori italici" in I. Edlund-Berry, G. Greco, and J. Kenfield (eds) *Deliciae Fictiles III. Architectural Terracottas in Ancient Italy: New Discoveries and Interpretations*, Oxford: Oxbow, 25–41.

Torelli, M. (1985) "Introduzione" in S. Stopponi (ed.), *Case e palazzi d'Etruria*, Milan: Electa, 21–32.

Winter, N. A. (2009) *Symbols of Wealth and Power*, Ann Arbor, Michigan: University of Michigan Press.

Zamarchi Grassi, P. (2006) "Le terrecotte architettoniche dal tempio etrusco del Piazzale del Cassero (Castiglion Fiorentino)" in I. Edlund-Berry, G. Greco, and J. Kenfield (eds), *Deliciae Fictiles III. Architectural Terracottas in Ancient Italy: New Discoveries and Interpretations*, Oxford: Oxbow, 135–150.

CHAPTER THIRTY SIX

ETRUSCAN TOWN PLANNING AND RELATED STRUCTURES

—— ·◆· ——

Claudio Bizzarri

What the Etruscan city – once it could be called a city[1] – looked like depends in great part on the structures of an immaterial nature, those social structures functional in the urban fabric for which they were created, as well as the purely material aspects. One of the most notable cases often dealt with is the forum of Rome,[2] the political center of the Urbs, which entailed reclamation work beginning with one of its kings of Etruscan origins.[3]

The strong bond between Rome and the territories that stretched northwards from the "*litus etruscum*"[4] also determined the introduction of techniques and knowledge borrowed in turn from the Etruscans in the Mediterranean area, thus highlighting the vast and fertile cultural exchange already present in the Archaic period and which also touched on the territories south of Rome.[5]

In the panorama of Etruria proper, with the passage of time, studies regarding the major cities and smaller centers have gradually focused on the planning of spaces. It may be relevant to mention a few before going on to provide a swift overview of the development of private architecture, characterized by the extreme perishability of the materials used, and then turning to a symbolic case: the settlement of Orvieto.

Even recently the existence, or at least the political importance, of the Etruscan dodecapolis[6] has been questioned. While on the one hand it does not invalidate the current analysis, it is a factor that nonetheless introduces an element of breakdown that helps us to understand, as previously in the funerary field, the extent and type of autonomy adopted by each individual community in the field of town planning. It should not be forgotten that the structural layout precedent to a sort of monumentalization of the settlement and the aspects connected to the geo-pedological nature are determining factors in some of the choices made. The long history of archaeological studies in Etruria must, of course, be kept in mind, where initially attention was centered on an exploration of the rich necropoleis rather than the inhabited centers that often, but not always, were located underneath the medieval and modern settlements.[7]

In a recent article Stephan Steingräber[8] listed a series of elements on which he based his study of Etruscan town planning. On the whole his opinions can be validated, but there are a few exceptions. As is often the case in a systematic type of approach – necessarily simplified and simplifying – there is always "a maverick," something hard to fit in since it is extraneous to the schemes worked out. In the case of Steingräber's study the division between the "public" area and the "religious" space is probably not as distinct as proposed, for what was public had a strong sacred connotation, and vice versa. It was therefore at times difficult to establish the boundaries – a term that in this place is more than appropriate – and a private sphere that had both sacred and public overtones at one and the same time is a valid possibility. The most obvious example is the valence given to the boundary, as a spatial caesura, where the *terminus* is of such importance that beginning with Numa,[9] the person who moved the position of the boundary stone was considered *sacrum* or *accursed: Numa Pompilius statuit eum qui terminus exarasset et ipsum et boves sacros esse* (Numa Pompilius decreed that who moved – uprooted – a boundary *cippus* (marker) would he himself and the oxen become *sacer*). *Sacer*, that is, given over to the gods, no longer belonging to the human sphere:[10] *quidquid quod deorum habetur.*[11] The connotation of *sacer* is in any case negative and prerogatives held by the other members of the community[12] are lost. The late prophesy of the nymph Vegoia is just as clear and is proof of how attention to the boundary markers, the ownership of the land and the relative questions were still very topical even centuries later.[13]

At this point the way in which Colonna organized the lexical elements *cilth, spura, methlum, rasna* and *tuthina* can help us understand the solutions adopted by the Etruscans in defining different areas (fields), all with a precise physical and public-sacred connotation,[14] probably marked by *cippi*. The correlation between *spura* and *tota* in the Gubbio tablets[15] has already been identified, where *spura* is to be taken in its meaning of "civic," within which the *cilth* assumes a restricted and sacred connotation, perhaps comparable to the area of the *arx*. *Methlum* has been identified as the probable indication of the *urbs*, different from the *spura* but more complex than the *arx*. The term was found on a *cippus* from Bolsena located at one of the entrance roads. There would then be a *spura* with subdivisions in *methlum* and *cilth*: relative territory – county – city limits and downtown, with less important satellite centers, *pagi*, gravitating as a whole around a specific *polis*, which, if the term is acceptable, could have been the *tuthina*.

An inscription from Bolsena concerning a gift to Selvans the god of boundaries (*tularias*) by Aule Havranas also includes as a parathetic player a *tuthina apana*, interpreted by Wylin, I believe correctly, as a paternal *pagus*.[16] So here we have a triad that oscillates between the private (Aule Havranas), the divinity (Selvans of the boundary *cippi*) and a *pagus*, a settlement known to be of a public nature. Another interesting element is provided by the travertine *cippus* from Perugia,[17] found in 1822 on the hill of San Marco. The inscription is in the alphabet used in northern inland Etruria and dates to the Hellenistic period. The text regards a legal deed between two families: the Velthina, probably Perugian, and the Afuna, from the Chiusi area. They divide the property or the use of the property in which the family tomb of the aristocrats of Perugian origin is located. What interests us here is that in line 8 there is explicit mention of *tularu*, the boundary markers, obviously indispensable elements in a legal act that provides for the respect and functional presence.

The foundation rites, as taken from the literary sources,[18] are scrupulously organized in a precise series of consecutive acts: the *precatio* was the formal addressing of the deity or deities in a ritual. The word is related by etymology to "prayer," and Pliny says that the slaughter of a sacrificial victim is ineffectual without *precatio*, the recitation of the prayer formula.[19] The *liberatio* (from the verb *liberare*, "to free") was the "liberating" of a place (*locus*) from "all unwanted or hostile spirits and of all human influences," as part of the ceremony inaugurating the *templum* (sacred space). It was followed by the *effatio*, the creation of boundaries (*fines*). The verb *effari* means "to create boundaries (*fines*) by means of fixed verbal formulas."[20]

One of the most regular urban layouts is the one that can be seen in Marzabotto, where several structures, located in the area west of the town, on a slightly raised portion of land, are altars and the *auguraculum* from which the priest would have performed the operations previously described. The orientation of the structures is the same as the one followed in the regular layout of the streets of the Etruscan settlement, named Misa or Kainua (see Chapter 15).[21] Located near Pian di Misano,[22] this city has most frequently been taken as an example of perfect town planning – a settlement that corresponds to the Hippodamean layout but dates to the fifth century BC, with a plan that Aristotle would have considered unsuitable in guaranteeing proper defense in case of attack.[23] Its distinctive feature of regular organization allows for a rapid and unimpeded movement of men, and potential invaders would have no problem in entering a city with an urban grid plan. The main street, up to 15 meters in width, runs from north to south and is intersected by at least three streets of the same size that constitute the east-west layout of the grid. Parallel to the *plateia* that recalls the Roman *cardo*, are narrower lanes, the *stenopoi*, creating a regular grid on which the blocks of dwellings and public areas are located.

The technical instruments that could have been used at the time were very rational even if simple from a technological point of view. One of the most effective ones is the *groma*, a vertical rod with four horizontal cross pieces mounted at right angles. A plumb line with lead weights hangs down vertically at the end of each arm. They were used in correctly leveling and guaranteeing the quality of the readings. Sighting along the arms of the cross (orthogonal arms) intersecting straight lines forming 90° angles could be established.[24] The center of the *groma* was their point of origin. Using graduated yards (*stadiae*) and a water level, straight lines, always pointing in the same direction, could be traced even on slopes. Surveying tools of this kind underlie the organization of the infrastructural network required by a settlement with determined characteristics. There are two examples in areas that are not urban which help us better understand some of the chronological and technical aspects: the tunnels of the lakes of Latium and those of the Roman aqueduct called Buso della Casara, near Valnogaredo at Padua.

With regards to the former, Filippo Coarelli has identified the general historical sphere in which the subterranean system of sub-horizontal conduits, the *cuniculi* or tunnels,[25] were adopted. With regards to the great works connected to the overflow (*scolmatori*) channels[26] of the lakes of Nemi and Albano, these works fall into the area of a hydraulic culture in archaic Latium, in which the chronology of the two effluents is an important element. Since that of Albano is older, there is less information available. Then comes that of Nemi, also dating to the sixth century BC, and therefore much earlier than the taking of Veii (396 BC), an event to which reference is traditionally made in view of the stories told by Livy and Plutarch[27] concerning Veii and the lake of Albano, two things only apparently unconnected.[28] An explanation for the flooding of the waters of the lake in the fourth century BC might be the result of the improper functioning of a pre-existing conduit (cause: technical obstruction), or the fact that the religious procedural systems were not respected (cause: divine punishment). Coarelli solved the problem when he identified various procedural irregularities both in the election of the military tribunes in Rome and in the carrying out of the Latin *ferie* (festivals) and the sacrifice on Monte Albano. The unrest of the plebs in the Urbs was not isolated but also included other peoples in the Latin league. It was actually the hegemony of Rome, subsequently to be clearly affirmed, that "caused" the *portentum*, a sign of danger for the existence of the Latin league itself, soon to be dismantled (338 BC). From a technical point of view,[29] therefore, how was the problem to be solved? The overflow was collected in underground conduits, thus regulating the water level in the volcanic basins, and was discharged at lower altitudes in the countryside surrounding the craters. The tunnels are impressive in their length: over 1600 meters for Nemi and 1200 for Albano. The correct direction, since there are no vertical shafts (*lumina*), could only be obtained by using a *groma* and a water level.

Although the Buso della Casara is much later, it helps us understand the technical approach adopted in the creation of these underground conduits. As his point of departure the author[30] notes that in the aqueduct he studied there were recurrent modules connected to the stretches that could be dug before calculating anew the direction to follow. The direction was calculated on the basis of measurements taken in the gallery, an important element in simplifying (speeding up) the excavation procedures. In short, the working program might have called for the excavation of a certain number of modules – each generally 20 feet or approximately 5.9 meters long. A length of this sort allows us to imagine the use of a rod or a rope marked with the correct distance, at the end of which the direction was calculated anew. An analysis of the angles measured in the aqueduct studied by Pesaro tells us that it was always a multiple of 18, as if the measurer had used an instrument that made it possible for him to effect calculations of this kind, a sort of alidade divided into 18-degree sections. Examination of the various options has demonstrated that this is easier to use in a tunnel and is the most trustworthy. The use of relatively simple equipment coupled with technical-scientific knowledge can therefore be hypothesized. The instrument that comes closest seems to be the dioptra of Hero of Alexandria,[31] a scientist who probably lived around the middle of the first century AD.

With a *groma* the *scolmatori* could be planned on the ground with a simple operation that allowed the excavation to start from both sides at once and the direction could be followed, also in underground spaces, with the *dioptra*.[32] The above-named aspects, both of a specifically religious-cultic and of a technical-operative nature, find their ideal application in the city of Orvieto, the ancient *Velzna*.

THE CASE OF ORVIETO

Concerning Smyrna, Strabo said: "the regular division of the streets of Smyrna is noteworthy; the streets are as straight as possible and paved...There is one error, not a small one, in the work of the engineers, that when they paved the streets they did not give them underground drainage."[33] This is not the case with the city of Orvieto where the subterranean structures bear witness to the *a priori* planning of the city layout, involving a whole series of implications of a socio-political nature of considerable importance, confirmed by the careful arrangement of the funerary buildings in the city's ring necropolis.[34] A glance at the layout of the urban necropoleis (Fig. 36.1), of which only the stretches of Crocefisso del Tufo and, in part of Cannicella, respectively on the northern and southern slopes of the city, are visible today, are indications of how the social body that held power in archaic Orvieto was capable of regulating the private sphere, including the funerary sphere.[35]

The layout of the cube-shaped monuments, practically identical and laid out in regular blocks, might refer to that of the houses and structures like the dwellings seen, for example, in the ancient city of Marzabotto. In Orvieto the percentage of variability is very low, due in part to the lay of the land at the base of the cliff and the terraced structure of the necropolis that develops on a slope, in a probably centrifugal arrangement. While little evidence of the urban structure of the ancient city remains on the top of the plateau, what is present can help us understand how the city of the living was organized and what type of functional plan had been used as early as the sixth century BC. The author of this paper[36] has drawn up a typology of the underground works connected to the water supply for the Etruscan settlement. Consolidation works carried out in the past thirty years or so[37] have provided further information regarding some of the *cuniculi*. Here we wish to focus on a portion of a *cuniculus* studied in the course of work for an important segment of the city's alternative mobility system aimed at limiting traffic in the historical center. The *cuniculus* in question (Fig. 36.2) was intersected in the course of the excavation for the escalators connecting the parking lot of the Foro Boario (erroneously known as ex-Campo della Fiera) with Piazza Ranieri. The system of *cuniculi* consisting of a main branch with smaller *cuniculi* branching off at right angles encountered in the upper portion of the passageway was spared. The ogival cross section of the conduit is similar to other works of a hydraulic nature dating to the Etruscan period. The scientific dig carried out in the *cuniculus* fill brought to light archaeological material dating to the Hellenistic period, although there was some that went back to the Archaic period, reflecting the development of the settlement on the cliff. This system falls under the classification of tunnels or *cuniculi* with orthogonal ramifications.

According to Adolfo Cozza[38] the tunnels in Orvieto were dug beneath the streets of the city and today we can add that they received the overflow of rainwater from the cisterns in the *atria*. One example of the tunnel/street system has been identified near the area of the Temple of Belvedere,[39] at the eastern end of the plateau, in correspondence

Figure 36.1   Crocefisso del Tufo, plan of necropolis.

with a portion of a paved street uncovered in the excavations for the foundations of the barracks' infirmary in the first half of the twentieth century. The escalator *cuniculus* is however the first subterranean conduit whose organization reveals that it was dug scientifically.[40] The plan shows a regular course with side branches that intersect the main tunnel, leaving, where necessary, a containment wall for the water. The height was probably carefully calculated on the basis of that of the cisterns at its origins. There is also an interesting cistern defined as belonging to the first type[41] near the conduit. It is perfectly preserved in the underground premises of a restaurant. The cistern with walls in isodomic masonry and covered by projecting radial brackets was discovered around the 1920s by the local historian Pericle Perali who drew it without, however, seeing it as part of the larger system regarding the preservation of water and tunnels hypothesized in this paper. Unfortunately the tunnel was not completely excavated but the detritus is still there and further investigation will hopefully continue in the future. The dig, however, did provide finds of unquestionable value such as fragmentary kylikes in bucchero, plates, *olle*, lekythoi (Fig. 36.3).

Our current knowledge regarding the underground structures of Orvieto supplies a basis for the identification of a complex infrastructural organization. Created together with the dwelling units, it consisted of cisterns located beneath the impluvium in the atrium, which Vitruvius not by chance called Tuscan atrium,[42] where rainwater was collected (Fig. 36.4). When the water in the cistern reached a certain level, the excess was channeled into the *cuniculi* that emptied into the main trunk (Fig. 36.5). This in turn disgorged the water outside the cliff. It is important to highlight the fact that in this system the pairing of cisterns/*cuniculi* was exclusively used for the processing of clear water, while the tunnels/paved streets added a less noble component, regimenting the water from the street.

On the basis of these implications it is particularly interesting to analyze other proposals for the urban plan of the Etruscan city of Velzna. In a book that deals with work carried out in the sphere of the previously mentioned law, and which also included archaeological assets, Anna Eugenia Feruglio touches on the importance of the wall in Via della Cava,

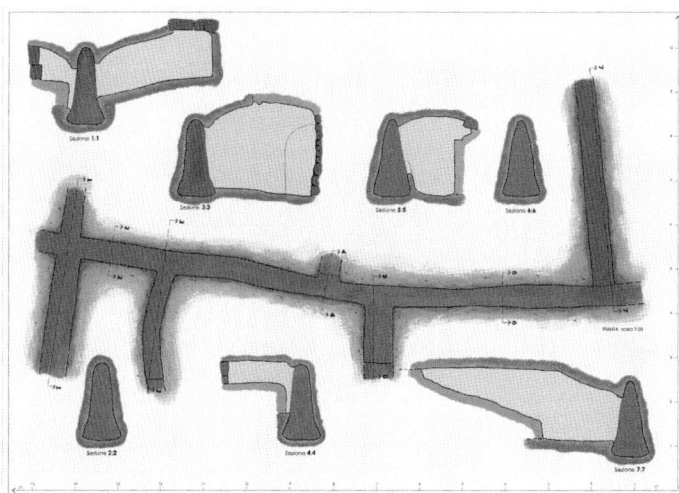

Figure 36.2   Plan and section of the Scala Mobile *cuniculus*. (Drawing by Simone Moretti Giani).

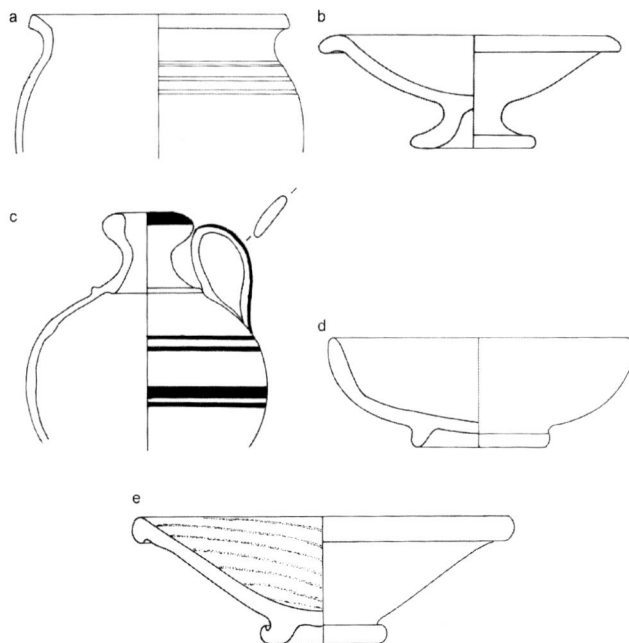

Figure 36.3a–e   Vases found in excavation of the Scala Mobile *cuniculus*: a) *olla*: common ware ovoid large container, this kind of vase is documented in Etruria since the mid-sixth century BC while in Orvieto, in funerary contexts, it appears from the second half of the century; b) *Piattello*: grey bucchero stemmed-foot small plate, this shape in Orvieto appears around the end of the sixth century BC and follows into the first half of the following century; c) *Lekythos*: globular vase used for scented oil, the body is decorated with painted lines; production of this vase seems to be peculiar to Orvieto in the Archaic period; d) Cup: grey bucchero cup with a ring base, a very common shape in Southern Etruria, is attested in Orvieto since the third quarter of the sixth century BC; e) *Piattello spirale a stralucido*: common ware plate decorated with a "burnished spiral line" on the interior surface called "*spirale a stralucido,*" peculiar of the productions of Orvieto from the end of the sixth century BC to the third century BC.

Figure 36.4   Etruscan private houses with cisterns: the "Tuscan atrium."
(Drawing by Simone Moretti Giani).

714

a terrace structure indispensable in the organization of the Etruscan settlement located near the main gate of the city.[43] She plots a series of lines on the plan of the modern city that refer to some of the basic *directrices* of the ancient urban plan (Fig. 36.6). A rapid examination of the Etruscan remains visible beneath the church of Saints Andrea and

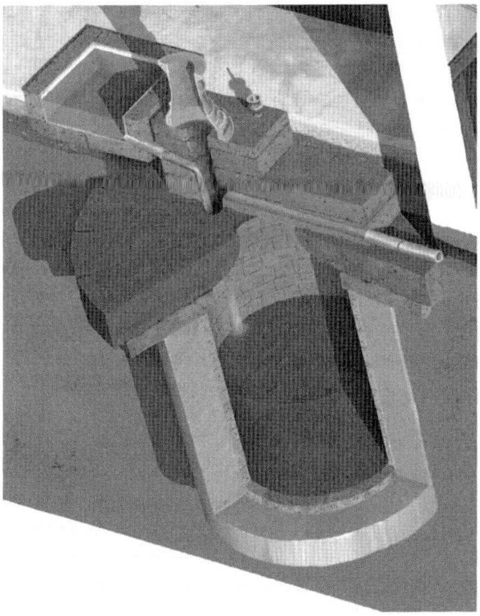

Figure 36.5   Cistern of the Archaic period connected with the main trunk of a *cuniculus*.

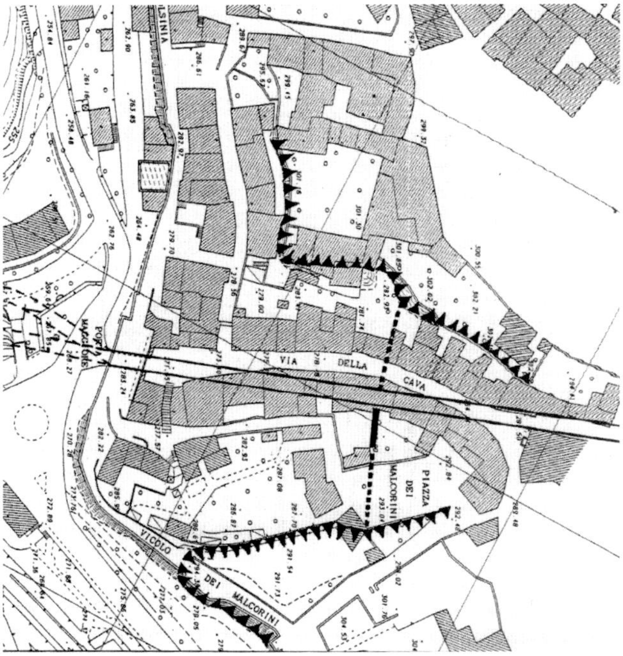

Figure 36.6   Plan of the area of the ancient monumental entrance to Orvieto to the West; the dotted line corresponds to the so-called Muro di Via della Cava (elaborated from Feruglio 1998).

715

Bartolomeo in Piazza della Repubblica reveals another highly important element to be considered in understanding the prospective urban grid of the ancient city. The remains of the Early Christian church clearly ignore those of the precedent Etruscan settlement,[44] consisting of tufa platforms set next to cisterns and shafts for water, remains of dry-stone masonry and stone paving. All these structures do not follow the lines of the present fabric, connected to the medieval city, and are organized according to an axis a few degrees off of the magnetic north. The same orientation appears in some of the remains excavated in the courtyard of Palazzo Monaldeschi and also in some remains belonging to an Etruscan house.[45] Davanzo attempted a reconstruction of the urban grid of Etruscan Orvieto on the basis of an analysis of the layout of some of the extant *directrices* and orientation of some monuments, and the result is quite interesting.[46] This is particularly the case for the medieval quarter (Fig. 36.7), keeping in mind that the Etruscan city probably stopped all correspondence with the area now known as Fontanasecca/Piazza dei Montemarte, as Gamurrini[47] has previously indicated. A second complex of *cuniculi* in the area corresponding to Piazza Ranieri (escalator *cuniculi*) supplies another important element pertinent to a general evaluation. Located beneath Palazzo Gaddi, they also consist of a main conduit and orthogonal branches. The fact that it lies not far from the previously mentioned complex of Piazza Ranieri and that its orientation does not correspond completely, indicates that the individual city blocks could develop according

Figure 36.7 The west side of the tufa plateau of Orvieto, Davanzo outlined some interesting elements of the urban grid, in particular the dotted line in the left area located in the medieval quarter (from Davanzo 2007).

to autonomous *directrices* forming an auto-sufficient system (tunnel – road – cisterns – drains). This may also be in relation to the planimetric and altimetric configuration of the various areas of the plateau. The picture obtained is therefore compatible with the general subdivision proposed by Davanzo, but this still needs to be submitted to verification concerning the presence of infrastructures, of systems whose function was connected with the inhabited center. Since these infrastructures are underground, they have in part been preserved.

From this perspective, the study of the man-made cavities in the cliff of Orvieto, suggested by Perali[48] years ago, could be extremely useful in providing us with a picture of what the Etruscan city that stood on this volcanic butte might have been like.

NOTES

1   Bruno D'Agostino has warned about problems inherent in a generalized approach concerning Etruscan town planning: "...how dangerous it is to draw up a "unified" history of the city in Etruria, overlooking the profound differences that characterize the different territorial areas" (D'Agostino 1998, p. 125 ff).

2   Moccheggiani Carpano 1984 pp. 164–178.

3   Livy 1.38.6, Livy 1.56.2.

4   Hor. *Carm.* I.2.14; Lydia ripa, *Stat. Silv.* IV.4.4.

5   De la Blanchere 1882; Coarelli 1990, pp. 141–148; *contra* Quilici Gigli 1996, p. 196; here she proposes a later chronology to the Republican period.

6   See the forthcoming 2011 Faina Foundation 19th meeting papers; the title was "Il Fanum Voltumnae e i santuari comunitari dell'Italia Antica."

7   For Tarquinia the words of Lawrence are always useful: "Therefore, if the ancient city of Tarquinia lay on this hill, it can have occupied no more space, hardly, than the present little town of a few thousand people. Which seems impossible. Far more probably, the city itself lay on that opposite hill there, which lies splendid and unsullied, running parallel to us." (Lawrence 1932 p. 65).

8   Steingräber 2001. Available at: http://scholarworks.umass.edu/etruscan_studies/vol8/iss1/1

9   Festus, Ep. (p. 505 L. = p. 368 M.).

10 Morani 1981, p. 40.

11 Macrobius (*Sat.,* II 3,2).

12 See the examples in Fugier 1963, p. 69 ff.

13 For the prophecy see Valvo 1988; for Vegoia see de Grummond 2006, p. 30; for boundaries and boundary stones see Oniga, 1990 p. 102 ff and Edlund-Berry 2006, p. 116 ff.

14 Colonna 2005, 1871–1890; see Morandini 2011, p. 80.

15 Prosdocimi 1978, pp. 587–607; Prosdomici 1984; Ancillotti Cerri 1996.

16 REE 55.128; Wylin 2000; *contra* Morandi 1985, p. 16, where *tuthina apana* becomes "(as) a fatherly gift," in connection with the verb *turuche*. See also Bonfante 2002, p. 167.

17 TLE 570; Facchetti 2000, p. 9.

18 For Rome see Carandini 2000, p. 122.

19 Pliny, *Nat. Hist.* 28.11.

20 Festus, 146 (Lindsay).

21 Colonna 1974, n. 44; Sassatelli 2005, pp. 47–55; Staccioli 2005, p. 186; Govi 2007, p. 65.

22 Mansuelli-Brizzolara-de Maria-Sassatelli-Vitali 1982; Malnati 1987, pp. 125–137; Sassatelli 1992; Sassatelli 1994; Vitali-Brizzolara-Lippolis 2001.

23 Aristotle, *Politics* 2.5.1 (1267b); he says that Hippodamus from Miletus, son of Euripus, was the one who invented the regular grid for urban plans; for the reference to motives of security see 7,10,4 (1330b); see Humphrey, Oleson, Sherwood 1998, p. 435ff.

24 A good reproduction can be seen in Adam 1984, p. 11.

25 Coarelli 1991, p. 35 ff.

26 The term *"scolmatore"* refers to a canal, in this case subterranean, that deviates the water from a basin when it reaches the high water mark, discharging it elsewhere.

27 Traditionally it is said that the waters of the lake flooded even though it had not rained – a prodigious event – and that then the drainage canal (*scolmatore*) was created on indication of an augur from Veio captured by the Romans and on indications received from the Delphic oracle, since the water of the lake must not be mixed with that of the sea, that is flow off normally, or Veio would not be taken or even Rome would fall; Cic. *De div.* I 44, 100; II 32, 69: *si lacus Albanus redundasset isque in mare fluxisset Romam perituram; si repressus esset Veios* (see Ferri 2009, p. 222).

28 See in this regard what Coarelli wrote in Coarelli 1991, p. 36 ff.; an excellent example of how integration concerned with the antique sources and archaeological evidence can contribute to the correct interpretation of historical events.

29 Castellani-Dragoni 1991, p.43 ff.

30 Pesaro 2005, pp. 106–111.

31 Paoletti 1984, p. 119 ff.; for a reconstruction of the dioptra see Adam 1984, p. 9.

32 Adam 1984, p. 16.

33 Strabo, *Geog.*, 14.1.37; see note 22.

34 For an updated bibliography on Crocefisso del Tufo see Feruglio 2007, pp. 275–328.

35 This brings us back to the original hypothesis, where mention was made of various socio-cultural levels.

36 Bizzarri 2007, pp. 317–350.

37 The first "special" law for Orvieto and Todi was n.545, voted during 1987.

38 Adolfo Cozza would study some *cuniculi* at the end of the nineteenth century but his work would be published only in 1972 (Cozza – Pasqui 1972).

39 Minto 1934, p. 89 ff.

40 The excavation was carried out by the company Archeostudio s.n.c., whose members I would like to thank for letting me present for the first time some data.

41 Perali 1928, p. 79, n. 66, pl. V, n. 37.

42 Vitruvius 6.3.

43 The wall was discovered by Mario Bizzarri in the 1960s and its importance was immediately clear since it partially solved one of the problems connected with the identification of *Volsinii* with the city of Orvieto, in line with the description by Procopius of Caesarea in his *Bellum Gothorum*, where he describes an imposing wall as an element that characterized Etruscan *Volsinii* (Bizzarri 1966; Feruglio 1998a, pp. 107 ff.).

44 Feruglio 1998b, p. 94 ff. and plans p. 90.

45 Bizzarri 1998.

46 Davanzo 2007.

47 Gamurrini 1881.

48 Perali 1928, where he also attempts an archaeological map of the city.

BIBLIOGRAPHY

Adam, J.-P. (1984) *L'arte di costruire presso i Romani. Materiali e tecniche*, Longanesi. (English edition: *Roman Building. Materials and Techniques*, trans. A. Mathews, London: Batsford).

Ancillotti, A. and Cerri, R. (1996) *Le tavole di Gubbio e La Civiltà degli Umbri*, Perugia: Jama.

Bizzarri, M. (1963–1964) "Una importante scoperta per l'antica topografia di Orvieto" in *Bollettino dell'Istituto Storico Artistico Orvietano*, XIX–XX, pp. 118–125.

Bizzarri, C. (1998) "Area archeologica di palazzo Monaldeschi" in Bruschetti, Feruglio, pp. 99–106.

———(2007) "Strutture ipogee di Orvieto etrusca: proposta di inquadramento tipologico" in *Atti I Congresso Nazionale di Archeologia del Sottosuolo: Bolsena 8–11 December 2005. Archeologia del Sottosuolo: Metodologie a Confronto*. Volume 1. *{Hypogean Archaeology – BAR International Series 1611}*, pp. 317–350.

Bonfante, G. and Bonfante, L. (2002) *The Etruscan Language: An Introduction*, Manchester: Manchester University Press.

Bruschetti, P. and Feruglio, A. E. (eds) (1998) *Todi – Orvieto, Interventi per il consolidamento e il restauro delle strutture di interesse archeologico*, Perugia.

Castellani, V. and Dragoni, W. (1991) "Opere arcaiche per il controllo del territorio: gli emissari sotterranei artificiali dei laghi albani" in *Gli Etruschi maestri di idraulica*, Perugia: Mondadori Electa, pp. 43–60

Coarelli, F. (1990) "Roma, i Volsci ed il Lazio antico" in *Crise et transformation des Sociétés archaïques de l'Italie antique au V siecle av. J. C.*, in Coll. Ec. Fr. Rome, p. 137.

———(1991) "Gli emissari dei laghi laziali: tra mito e storia" in *Gli Etruschi maestri di idraulica*, Perugia: Mondadori Electa, pp. 35–42.

Colonna, G. (2005) "Il lessico istituzionale etrusco e la formazione della città (specialmente in Emilia Romagna)" in C. Ampolo and G. Sassatelli (eds), *Italia ante romanum imperium. Scritti di antichità etrusche, italiche e romane (1958–1998)*, Pisa-Rome, pp. 1871–1890.

———(1974) in *REE*.

Cozza, A. and Pasqui, A. (1972) "Carta archeologica dell'Etruria. Opere di completamento al rettangolo Orvieto-Bolsena" in *Forma Italiae*, serie II, I, Florence.

D'Agostino, B. (1998) "La non polis degli etruschi" in L. Canfora (ed.), *Venticinque secoli dopo l'invenzione della democrazia*, Rome: Donzelli ed.

Davanzo, R. (2007) "Il disegno e i disegni della città medievale" in G. M. della Fina and C. Fratini (eds), *Storia di Orvieto*, II, *Il Medioevo*, pp. 345–405.

de Grummond, N. T. (2006) "Prophets and priests" in de Grummond, Simon 2006, pp. 27–44.

de Grummond, N. T. and Simon, E. (eds) (2006) *The Religion of the Etruscans*, Austin: University of Texas Press.

de la Blanchere, M. R. (1882) "La malaria de Rome et le drainage antique" in *MEFRA* 2, pp. 94–106.

Edlund-Berry, I. E. (2006) "Ritual space and boundaries in Etruscan religion," in de Grummond, Simon, pp. 116–131.

Facchetti, G. M. (2000) *Frammenti di diritto privato etrusco*, Florence: Olschki.

Ferri, G. (2009) "Il significato e la concezione della divinità tutelare cittadina nella religione romana, *tesi dottorato* Università degli Studi di Roma 'Tor Vergata,' XXI ciclo."

Feruglio, A. E. (1998) "Il muro di via della Cava" in Bruschetti, Feruglio, pp. 107–114.

———(1998b) "I resti sotto la chiesa di S. Andrea" in Bruschetti, Feruglio, pp. 91–98.

———(2007) "Le necropoli etrusche" in G. M. della Fina (ed.), *Storia di Orvieto*, I, *Antichità*, pp. 275–328.

Fugier, H. (1963) *Recherches sur l'expression du sacré dans la langue latine, les Belles lettres* (Saint-Amand, impr. C.-A. Bédu), Paris.

Gamurrini, G. F. (1881) "Volsinii etrusca in Orvieto" in *AnnIst*, pp. 28–59.

Govi, E. (ed.) (2007) *Marzabotto una città etrusca*, Bologna: Ante Quem.

Humphrey, J. W., Oleson, J. P. and Sherwood A. N. (1998) *Greek and Roman Technology: A Sourcebook. Annotated Translations of Greek and Latin Texts and Documents*, New York: Routledge.

Lawrence, D. H. (1932) *Etruscan Places*.

Malnati, L. (1987) "Marzabotto. La fase arcaica" in *La formazione della città in Emilia Romagna* (Exhibition catalogue), Bologna, pp. 125–137

Mansuelli, G. A., Brizzolara, A. M., De Maria, S., Sassatelli, G. and Vitali, D. (1982) *Guida alla città etrusca e al museo di Marzabotto*, Bologna: Edizioni Alfa.

Minto, A. (1934) "Trovamenti archeologici durante gli sterri a Vigna Grande per la costruzione della Caserma avieri" in *Notizie degli Scavi*, pp. 89 ff.

Moccheggiani Carpano, C. (1984) "Le cloache dell'antica Roma" in R. Luciani (ed.), *Roma Sotterranea*, Rome: Quasar di Severino Togno, pp. 164–178.

Morandi, A. (1985) AI, II, p. 18; III, p.16.

Morandini, F. (2011) "Le fattorie arcaiche di Pian D'Alma (Scarlino – GR) e Marsiliana d'Albegna (Manciano – GR): modello "urbano" esportato in campagna o modello "extra-urbano" radicato nella tradizione?" in A. Ellero, F. Luciani and A. Zaccaria Ruggiu (eds), *La Città. Realtà e valori simbolici. 7 – Quaderni del Dipartimento di Scienze dell'Antichità e del Vicino Oriente*, Venice: Università Ca' Foscari Venezia, pp. 79–100.

Morani, M. (1981) "Lat. *'sacer'* e il rapporto uomo-dio nel lessico religioso latino" in *Aevum*, LV, pp. 30–46.

Oniga, R. (1990) *Il confine conteso: lettura antropologica di un capitolo sallustiano, Bellum Iugurthinum 79*, Bari: Edipuglia.

Paoletti, M. L. (1984) "16, Gli strumenti: Vitruvio ed Erone" in AA.VV *Misurare la terra: centuriazione e coloni nel mondo romano*, Modena: Franco Cosimo Panini, pp. 119–121.

Perali, P. (1928) *Orvieto Etrusca*, Rome: Tipografia del Sonato.

Pesaro, A. (2005) "Evidenze di regolarità strutturali nel tracciamento di opere in cunicolo. Il caso del 'Buso della Casara' in *In Binos Actus Lumina. Rivista di studi e ricerche sull'idraulica storica e la storia della tecnica*, II, Atti convegno Narni October 2001, pp. 106–111.

Prosdocimi, A. L. (1978) "L'Umbro," in *Lingue e dialetti dell'Italia antica*, Rome: Biblioteca di Storia Patria, pp. 587–607.

——(1984) *Le Tavole Iguvine*, I, Florence: Olschki.

Sassatelli, G. (1992) *La città etrusca di Marzabotto*, Bologna: Grafis.

——(ed.) (1994) *Iscrizioni e graffiti della città etrusca di Marzabotto*, Bologna: University Press Bologna.

——(2005) "Un altro documento epigrafico e il nome etrusco della città" in *Culti, forma urbana e artigianato a Marzabotto. Nuove prospettive di ricerca*, Bologna: Ante Quem, pp. 47–55.

Staccioli, R. A. (2005) *Gli etruschi. Un popolo tra mito e realtà*, Rome: Newton Compton Editori.

Quilici Gigli, S. (1996) *Uomo, acqua e paesaggio: atti dell'incontro di studio sul tema Irreggimentazione delle acque e trasformazione del paesaggio antico*, S. Maria Capua Vetere, 22–23 November, Rome: L'Erma di Bretschneider.

Steingräber, S. (2001) "The Process of Urbanization of Etruscan Settlements from the Late Villanovan to the Late Archaic Period (End of the Eighth to the Beginning of the Fifth Century B.C.): Presentation of a Project and Preliminary Results," *Etruscan Studies*: Vol. 8, Article 1, pp. 7–34.

Valvo, A. (1988) *"La Profezia di Vegoia,"* Rome: Istituto Italiano per la Storia Antica.

Vitali, D., Brizzolara, A. M. and Lippolis, E. (2001) *L'acropoli della città etrusca di Marzabotto*, Bologna: University Press Bologna.

Wylin, K. (2000) "Il verbo etrusco. Ricerca morfosintattica delle forme usate in funzione verbale," *Studia Philologica* 20, Rome.

CHAPTER THIRTY SEVEN

VILLANOVAN AND ETRUSCAN MINING AND METALLURGY

——— •◆• ———

Claudio Giardino

Etruria is rightly considered one of the main metallurgical centers of the ancient world. Its fame is due both to the rich metal ore deposits throughout the Tyrrhenian region and to the abundance of metallic objects that were recovered from burial grounds, from hoards and from settlements, from the end of the Bronze Age onward. This prosperity is particularly evident in the tombs of Caere, Tarquinia, Vulci, Populonia and Vetulonia and was linked to the control exercised by these centers on the mining areas and on trade in raw materials to Europe and the Mediterranean (Banti 1969: 46–47, 64, 184–185; Pallottino 1973: 129–131; Camporeale 1985: 29–33). Etruscan craftsmanship enjoyed a high reputation in antiquity: in the mid-fifth century BC candelabra and other bronze objects of Etruscan manufacture constituted sought-after furnishings for the finest Greek houses (Pherekrates and Kritias, quoted by Athenaeus, *Deipnosophistai* 15. 60.700 c, 1.50.286). Despite this, research on aspects of production, such as the exploitation of mines, ore smelting and manufacturing of metal items was largely neglected until recently by concerted archaeological research.

THE TECHNIQUES

Since the Final Bronze Age, metal technology had reached very high levels, as is evident from the refined repoussé decoration that appears on cups, pendants and fibulae in the hoard of Coste del Marano (Tolfa). Whether in the Villanovan or Orientalizing period, the centers of Etruria produced sophisticated metal artifacts in bronze, silver and gold.

The Etruscan technical experts were able to master metallurgical techniques, producing works of high artistic value. Skill in the use of lost-wax casting is attested by many bronzes, including figurines (Fig. 37.1) and the few statues that have come down to us, such as the Chimaera of Arezzo or the Mars of Todi. But we know that these works had once been very numerous: according to Pliny, the sack of Volsinii alone, in 264 BC, yielded to the Romans 2,000 bronze statues (*Nat. Hist.* 34.16.34).

Excellent examples of chiseling are provided by the mirrors on the surface of which were often engraved complex mythological scenes (Fig. 37.2). The art of toreutics has also left significant evidence, as exhibited in the parade chariots from Castel San Mariano (Perugia) and Monteleone di Spoleto where the decoration is made in repoussé, embossed with the pattern beaten from the back of the sheet metal and finished on the front with the chisel (see Chapter 41). Many objects, including fibulae, were then finished by stamping, by means of punches that imprinted the ornamental motif on the sheet metal (Fig. 37.3).

The Etruscans certainly excelled in filigree; they were especially expert in the granulation technique, obtained by soldering tiny gold spheres onto a metal substrate: it is considered that on the surface of a leech-fibula from Tuscania were soldered about 25,000 beads of 0.12 mm diameter (Nestler, Formigli 1994: 15) (Fig. 37.4). To further

Figure 37.1 Pair of bronze statuettes (*kore* and *kouros*) made by lost-wax casting technique; from Monte Acuto Ragazza (Bologna) (courtesy of the Museo Civico Archeologico, Bologna).

Figure 37.2 Engraving: Etruscan mirror known as the "*Patera Cospiana*"; from Arezzo (courtesy of the Museo Civico Archeologico, Bologna).

improve the strength and appearance of iron weapons, Etruscan blacksmiths applied the technique of pattern welding by alternating different layers of iron during forging, as is observed in a spear head of the fourth-third century BC from Montefiascone (Panseri, Leoni 1967: 223). Iron was sometimes used to inlay bronze objects and thus obtain decorative color effects: examples are some large Orientalizing belt clasps from the territory of Siena (Camporeale 1985: 29) (Fig. 37.5).

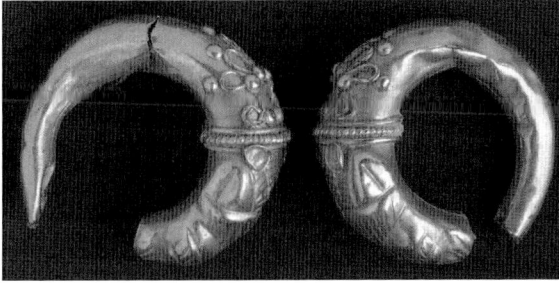

Figure 37.3   Pair of Etruscan earrings in gold produced by repoussé (courtesy of the Museo Civico Archeologico, Bologna).

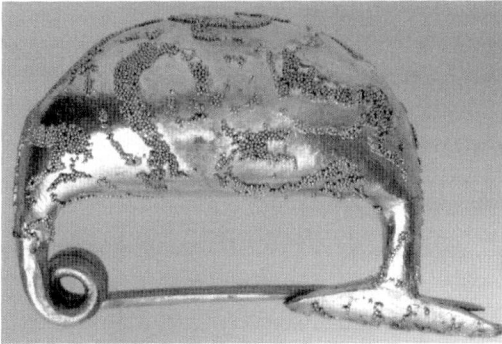

Figure 37.4   Fibula in gold decorated in granulation "*a pulviscolo*"; from Bologna, Arsenale Militare, tomb 5 (courtesy of the Museo Civico Archeologico, Bologna).

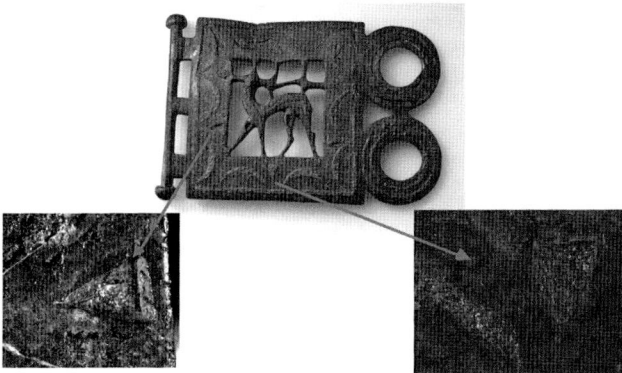

Figure 37.5   Orientalizing belt clasp in bronze with iron inlay; from Murlo (Siena). Magnification: ×6.5 (courtesy of Museo Preistorico-etnografico "L. Pigorini," Rome).

MINERAL RESOURCES AND MINES OF ETRURIA

The ore deposits

Tyrrhenian Etruria is the richest region of subalpine Italy for metal deposits. In its many ore bodies are present, also in considerably rich mineralizations, copper, iron, lead, silver, antimony, zinc, arsenic and tin. This consists of two main distinct geographical units, with different metallogenic characteristics. The first area is located south of the Arno, in Tuscany, and includes the important mining districts of the Colline Metallifere (the "Metal-bearing Hills") and the island of Elba, and the second is in southern Etruria, with the ore deposits of the Tolfa Mountains and the Maremma. There are also several other minor outcrops in the Rognosi Mountains, in the region of Siena, in the Val di Cecina, in the Apuan Alps, and near Florence at Impruneta (Lotti 1908: 179–182; Del Caldo *et al.* 1973: 160–167; Riccobono 1992; Giardino 2008: 73–74) (Fig. 37.6). This difference is reflected – in the common cultural matrix – even in the aspects and regional characteristics of the Villanovan period: while Tuscany appears connected to the northern regions – as it had been in the Late Bronze Age – and particularly to the Bologna area, southern Etruria plays an autonomous role with the development of large proto-urban centers, which will become the major cities of the historical age (Bietti Sestieri 2010: 252–253).

The mines

In Etruria, mining began in prehistoric times, as attested by the miners' stone-hammers found at Poggio Malinverno in the Tolfa Mountains (northern Lazio) (Giardino, Steiniger 2011). Traces of "prehistoric" exploitations have occasionally been observed also in Tuscany, in the mines of Campiglia Marittima, Monte Rombolo, Boccheggiano and

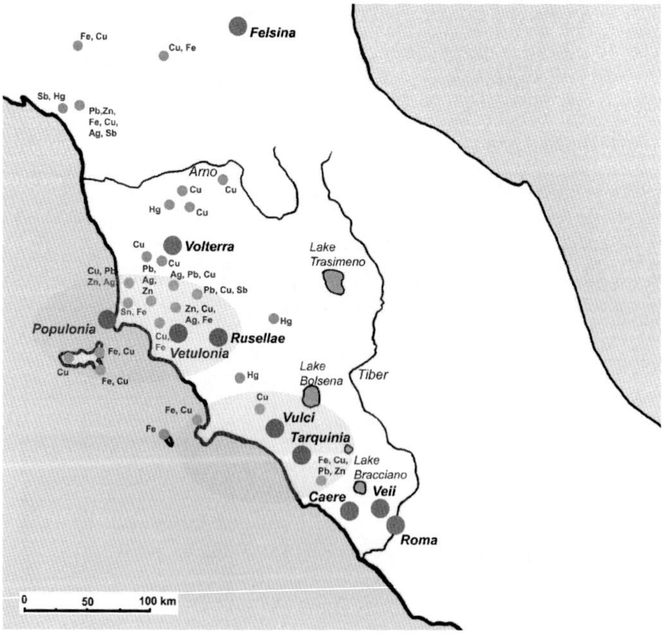

Figure 37.6 Principal metal-bearing regions of Etruria.

Montieri (Andrée 1922). Even for the ancient Etruscan period our knowledge of mines is scarce: in the nineteenth century, as a result of new extraction on an industrial scale, in many places the remains of ancient workings were observed, such as the island of Elba, in the area of Populonia, in the Campiglia region, in Massa Marittima, Montecatini, the Apuan Alps, and Tolfa Mountains. Some of them were probably linked to medieval activities, others to the Etruscan or proto-historical periods (Simonin 1858; Badii, 1931; Tanelli 1985: 37) (Fig. 37.7).

The better-known and better-investigated workings are those of Campiglia, although the paucity of actual archaeological excavations makes it difficult to distinguish between the activity of medieval times (tenth-fourteenth century AD) and that of the Etruscan period (seventh-first century BC), also taking into account the similarity in mining techniques and the reuse of the oldest pits in later periods (Cascone, Casini 1998). The Etruscan mines often appear to be pits that follow the mineralized veins; the mouth gives direct access to vertical shafts. The excavations sometimes reached a depth of more than 120 meters from the opening. The pits were connected by short horizontal galleries, between 80 cm and two meters high. Occasionally the pits opened into large rooms that also exploited natural underground cavities. Traces of tools were detected on the rock; they were produced mainly by iron picks. On the walls, small niches held the oil-lamps. The miners had to live in villages near the mining areas, such as the one excavated near the lake of Lago dell'Accesa in the territory of Vetulonia, a settlement that has furnished, in addition to the remains of several buildings, some groups of tombs (Camporeale *et al.* 1985: 128–130).

THE CENTERS OF METALLURGY

The Villanovan period

The importance of metallurgy in Etruria is evident from the Late Bronze Age, as shown by the hoards of metal objects found in the region. In the Iron Age, the large quantity and variety of metal artifacts are reflected, in addition to the hoards, in the tomb offerings. Among the hoards, the San Francesco hoard in Bologna stands out; it was deposited in

Figure 37.7   Remains of ancient mines at Campo alle Buche (Campiglia Marittima, Livorno).

a large jar of impasto in the first decades of the seventh century BC and contained about 14,800 pieces, weighing over 1,400 kg in total (Zannoni 1888) (Fig. 37.8). The analyses of the ingots contained within it indicate that these were normally made up of copper nearly free of impurities (Antonacci Sanpaolo *et al.* 1992: 164–166; Bietti Sestieri *et al.* 2002: 679), intended for alloying with tin or to be added during the recasting of bronze scraps.

For the Villanovan period, certainly the clearest evidence of metallurgical activities is offered from Bologna where in the Iron Age settlement there were areas with installations for the metal working. A *tuyere*, crucibles and slag come from these areas (Taglioni 1999: 51–52, 100, 182); these pieces of evidence are in addition to the San Francesco hoard, that contained ingots, waste and casting residues. The analyses carried out by X-ray fluorescence (ED-XRF) on copper residues still adhering to the inside of the crucible found in Via Indipendenza demonstrate how it was used in casting operations (Fig. 37.9): in fact, the metal was an alloy of copper and tin, with the presence of lead. Other workshops were also located near Bologna, such as Castenaso (Forte 1994: 195, 198) and Casalecchio (Peyre 1968: 376–377). Apart from the Bolognese region, traces of Villanovan metallurgical activities have also been reported from other centers of Etruria, such as Verucchio (Gentili 1986), Monfestino (Modena), and Monte Pezzola (Reggio Emilia) (Vitali 1983: 163; Moretto 1995: 68–69).

Figure 37.8   Materials from the hoard of San Francesco, Bologna
(courtesy of the Museo Civico Archeologico, Bologna).

Figure 37.9   Crucible from the Villanovan village of Bologna – Via Indipendenza
(courtesy of the Museo Civico Archeologico, Bologna).

Tyrrhenian Etruria appears to be relatively poor in evidence, although the distribution of several Early Iron Age discoveries near the mining areas is an indirect indication of the exploitation of the ore deposits (Giardino 1995: 109–133, Figs 53, 56, 58, 127). In southern Etruria evidence of metallurgical activities comes from Tarquinia and Bolsena. At Tarquinia, on the terrace of Pian di Civita, shapeless pieces of molten copper (*aes rude*), a piece of slag, and some fragments of hematite were found during surveys along with fragments of impasto, probably to be dated to the Iron Age (Zifferero 1992: 82–83). The Villanovan settlement of Gran Carro on Lake Bolsena – an area centrally situated with respect to the territories of Vulci, Tarquinia and Volsinii-Orvieto – provided several pieces of evidence related to the metallurgy of copper alloys, consisting of ingots, casting residues, semi-worked pieces, an unrefined lead ingot and a stone mold for the manufacture of three different artifacts (Tamburini 1995: 308, 315–316) (Fig. 37.10). At Gran Carro, tin artifacts were also recovered: small chain rings of almost pure tin, not yet separated after casting (Fig. 37.11), and a tiny strip of the same metal, most probably to inlay the pottery with tin foils (Giardino, Gigante 1995), a decoration that occurred with relative frequency in the grave goods of Etruria (Stjernquist 1960; Bartoloni, Delpino 1985). The archaeometric analyses carried out by X-ray fluorescence on the finds from Gran Carro detected in some of the bars the presence of tin, an indication that they were obtained from metal recycling.

Figure 37.10   Stone mold from the Villanovan village of Gran Carro (Bolsena, Viterbo).

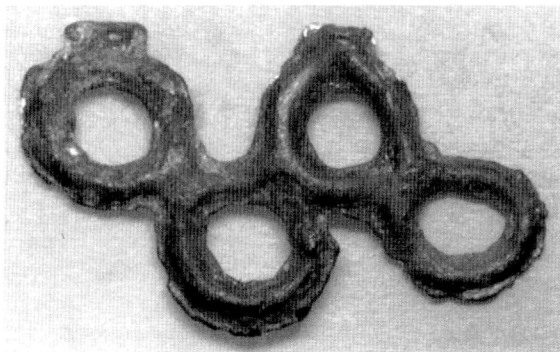

Figure 37.11   Unseparated elements of a chain cast in tin from the Villanovan village of Gran Carro (Bolsena, Viterbo).

They also showed significant contents of antimony and arsenic, probably related to the use of copper ores containing these elements, like the copper minerals from northern Lazio and southern Tuscany.

In Tuscany, relatively little metallurgical evidence can be clearly ascribed to the Iron Age. Metalworking is attested on the island of Elba, which also has copper- and lead-ore deposits as well as those of iron: the pseudo-Aristotle (*De mir. Ausc.* 93) stated that on Elba, copper was mined first and it was only later that iron was mined. In the site of Colle Reciso (or perhaps at Santa Lucia) a fragmentary sandstone mold for casting axes was discovered in the nineteenth century, associated with molten copper and slag (Cocchi, 1865: 10, pl. I: 11–12; Foresi, 1867: 18–19; Delpino 1981: 275, note 27). At Colle Reciso – where there are iron and copper outcrops – a bronze hoard was also discovered (two other hoards were found at Chiessi-Valle Gneccarina and in an unknown place on the island) (Giardino 1995: 119–122).

Evidence of Iron Age metallurgical activities is also present in the Populonia region: at the Villanovan site of Poggio del Molino, on the Gulf of Baratti, a stone mold for multiple castings was found (Fedeli 1982–83: 157–164); additionally, the first installation of the furnaces at Val Fucinaia should be attributed to the Villanovan and Orientalizing periods (Minto 1954: 302–303). The late Villanovan lead axes from the Volterra region are a local production, and therefore they testify a casting activity that is almost exclusive to the Val di Cecina area: examples were discovered at Bibbona, Lustignano and Volterra, in the Guerruccia necropolis; only a single piece comes from Sarteano, which is in the territory of Siena. These axes are probably related to the exploitation of lead ore deposits from the Colline Metallifere (Giardino 1995: 129, Fig. B 62).

With regard to iron, its use develops in Etruria during the Early Iron Age, first in the centers of southern Etruria (Tarquinia and Veii) and then in those of Tuscany. At Vetulonia only a small number of iron artifacts date from the eighth century BC; the widespread diffusion occurs especially from the Orientalizing period onward (Gualtieri 1977: 221–222; Delpino 1988: 63–65; Giardino 2005: 498–499).

The Etruscan period

Ancient sources on mining activities in Etruria are quite scarce. Strabo records the existence of already abandoned old mines in the environs of Populonia (Strabo 5. 2.6). Information on the smelting activities is also rare in literature. The presence of iron smelting furnaces is mentioned on island of Elba, which owes its Greek name (Aithalia) to the pollution of smoke (*aithalos*) that surrounds it. In the first century BC, Diodorus Siculus outlined the iron and steel processes that took place there:

> ...For the island possesses a great amount of iron-rock, which they quarry in order to melt and cast and thus to secure the iron, and they possess a great abundance of this ore. For those who are engaged in the working of this ore crush the rock and burn the lumps which have thus been broken in certain ingenious furnaces; and in these they smelt the lumps by means of a great fire and form them into pieces of moderate size which are in their appearance like large sponges. These are purchased by merchants in exchange either for money or for goods and are then taken to Dicaearchia (modern Pozzuoli, Naples) or the other trading-stations, where there are men who purchase such cargoes and who, with the aid of a multitude of artisans in metal whom they have

collected, work it further and manufacture iron objects of every description. (Diodorus 5.13.1–2; translation by Loeb Classical Library edition, 1939).

This passage shows, *inter alia*, that at least some iron was exported still unrefined, as bloom, to be refined elsewhere: this was confirmed by the archaeometallurgical analysis of some bloom fragments found in the Etruscan settlement of La Castellina del Marangone, near Civitavecchia (Giardino 2011: 991) (Fig. 37.12). The iron ore was exported from Elba into the Tyrrhenian area starting from the sixth-fifth century BC; it probably reached, as well as Populonia, Follonica, Pisa and Genoa (Corretti, Benvenuti 2001: 142).

Elban industry remained very prosperous as late as the third century BC, since the Elban military contingent, who participated on the Roman side at the battle of Cannae in 216 BC, was very proud of using weapons made from iron extracted from their own mines (Silius Italicus, *Punica* 8.615–616). Even Arezzo, like Populonia, must have had a flourishing metallurgical industry. In 205 BC, during the Second Punic War, the two cities were the only ones among the Etruscans supplying metal objects to the Roman army: Arezzo provided Rome with 50,000 weapons including shields, spears, helmets, spurred spears, as well as tools such as axes, hoes and sickles; Populonia supplied Rome with a large amount of iron (Livy 28.45).

Few details are known about the settlements associated with mining. As well as the above-mentioned village near Lago dell'Accesa – which is just over a kilometer from the rich deposits of mixed sulphides at Capanne – settlements that are also likely to be related to mining activities include the hill settlements of Castello di Procchio and Castiglione di San Martino where the floors rest on a base set up made with iron slag, dating from the fifth-fourth centuries to the first century BC (Camporeale 1985: 24).

Iron smelting slags have been found in Tuscany, along the coast of Follonica (Cucini Tizzoni, Tizzoni 1992: 47–51); and at Follonica, in the Via Massetana, 21 furnaces have been found, arranged in battery (Aranguren *et al.* 1998). However, the main evidence of the Etruscan iron industry comes from Populonia, on the Gulf of Baratti, where even into the early twentieth century the slag covered an area of 200,000 square meters, reaching a depth of ten meters (D'Achiardi 1929: 397). The archaeological excavations of the industrial district, from the 1970s to the present day, show that in this area iron metallurgy had developed since the mid-sixth century BC (Martelli 1981; Buonamici 2006). Investigations have identified furnaces, with a similar shape to those of Follonica.

Figure 37.12   Fragment of a bloom from the Etruscan site of La Castellina del Marangone (Santa Marinella, Rome).

They were cylindrical shaft furnaces that tapered upwards, with the base partially sunk into the ground; they appear to be approximately half a meter high with an internal diameter of about 30 cm (Fig. 37.13). The walls, about 15 cm thick, were made of hewn stones and slag held together by clay; inside, the air intake was through nozzles (*tuyeres*) positioned toward the bottom of the furnace (Voss 1988: 92–96; Giardino 1996: 271–272). The furnaces allowed the escape of the slag during the smelting process: the slags of Populonia are indeed flattened and have the characteristic traces of sliding tracks associated with their run-off from the furnace in a semi-fluid state ("tapped slag") (Fig. 37.14). The analyses carried out on slags have shown that the furnaces operated at temperatures of around 1200 – 1300°C, allowing easy transformation into metallic iron of the ore that consisted of iron oxides: hematite and magnetite. From this was obtained a spongy mass, the bloom, consisting of a porous mass of iron, charcoal and slag. Therefore a subsequent forging process was necessary, to obtain the iron by means of hot hammering (Giardino 2010: 205–206).

Figure 37.13   Remains of a furnace from Populonia.

Figure 37.14   Large tapped slag for iron smelting from Populonia.

The ore that supplied the iron industry in Populonia came from the neighboring island of Elba, and also from iron-bearing deposits in the district of Campiglia Marittima. This area also provided, presumably, the copper ore that was smelted in the furnaces of the city. The lowest levels of the deposits on the Baratti beach, in fact, contain numerous slags from the copper smelting, an indication that at Populonia a relevant production of this metal too occurred around the sixth-fifth century BC (Benvenuti *et al.* 2000: 74).

Evidence of copper metallurgy, dating from the seventh and sixth centuries BC, was found in Poggio Civitate (Murlo), a site near the Colline Metallifere, a strategic point between the Etruscan inland and coastal centers. Here, at Pian del Tesoro, in different areas of the plateau, there came to light distinct areas associated with both copper smelting and working and the remains of smelting furnaces (Nielsen 1993). From Poggio Civitate comes evidence of iron working, too: a scorified bar of iron, in particular, seems to have been produced during an experimental attempt to obtain metallic iron from wüstite existing in the copper slag, through an ingenious process of re-smelting (Warden 1993: 44–45).

Evidence of metallurgical activity, not related to the ore smelting, but rather to copper casting and to iron forging, is attested in some of the centers of southern Etruria. At Vulci, the only indication of such an activity is constituted by a clay mold drawn from a metal object, most likely used to produce multiple bronze objects (Kent Hill 1981). Nevertheless, the presence of a large number of metal artifacts in the tombs ever since the Villanovan period led to the hypothesis that an important craft center flourished here, specialized in the production of metal ornaments, weapons, tableware, etc. Unfortunately, especially in the past, the archaeological excavations have been concentrated on cemeteries, neglecting the settlement until relatively recent times (see Arancio *et al.* 2006: 61–66).

The settlement of La Castellina del Marangone, near Civitavecchia (Rome), yielded abundant evidence of metallurgy, indicating that the site had to be a base for intense activity of artisans who not only worked bronze, but also worked iron; remains of crucibles, nozzles, semi-finished artifacts and smithing slag were found together with finished objects (Giardino 2011). Of particular interest are a couple of crucibles: their analyses have shown that on the site copper, lead and tin were alloyed, mixing together these metals; tin was used in the form of its mineral (cassiterite), or else as a pure metal (Rovira 2011: 977–980).

Evidence of craft activities also comes from the Etruscan settlement of San Giovenale (seventh-fifth century BC), in the territory of Blera (Viterbo), where slags from hammering were found in many areas of the "Borgo" and in the Acropolis, clear evidence of forging of iron (Fig. 37.15); a small bar of bronze, evidently a semi-finished product, indicates also the manufacture of copper alloys (Guidi *et al.* 2005). Substantial waste from production processes was found in Cerveteri. One smithing slag was found from an Orientalizing context in the urban area of Caere (Sant'Antonio) (Guidi, Trojsi 2001). There are numerous metallurgical indicators from excavations in the area of Vigna Parrocchiale too, where the dump of a foundry came to light that was specialized in the casting of bronzes using the lost wax technique (Guidi, Trojsi 2003; Bellelli 2005). Large conical crucibles (some over 50 cm in diameter), *tuyeres* (bellows' nozzles) and residues of the refractory external mantles used in the manufacture of the articles have been found there. The analysis of the slag shows that iron objects were forged at the site, in addition to copper casting. It should be noted that in the early fifth century BC the complex was close to a sacred area, which suggested that it was used for the construction yard of the temple.

A similar situation, where the metallurgical activity served the construction of a temple, is also likely to be present in Rome of the Tarquins: evidence of iron forging has been found in the area where the Temple of Jupiter Capitolinus was erected (Giardino, Lugli 2001). Even at Pyrgi the presence of metallurgical activity is attested, connected again with the sanctuary. Some lead ingots from inside the sacred area actually contained fragments of hematite and iron slag, the latter linked to smithing activity (Fig. 37.16). The ingots, dating to the early decades of the fifth century BC, were apparently produced by deliberately putting in them waste material that was stored in the vicinity; this insertion may perhaps have been for ritual purposes. The ingots were produced most probably at the site: a lead melting activity is testified by the recovering of lead clasps and casting drops (Saviano et al. 2006: 78–79).

From the sanctuary of Gravisca comes evidence for the processing of iron, copper and lead attributable to the sixth-fifth century BC: clay fragments of furnaces were observed – of which the bases are preserved – together with slag, casting residues, and blacksmith's tongs (Fiorini 2001: 136–137; Franceschi, Luciano 2005).

A copper ingot fragment with low impurities was found near the village of Piano di Stigliano (Canale Monterano, Rome), near the Tolfa Mountains: the association with pottery allows it to be dated to the sixth century BC (Zifferero 1992: 84–85).

Figure 37.15   Hammerscales from San Giovenale (Blera, Viterbo).

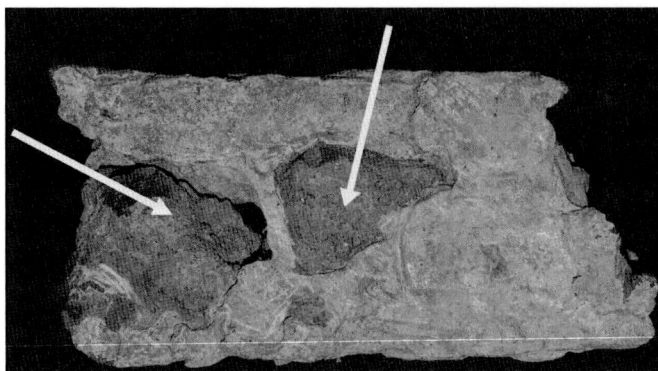

Figure 37.16   Lead ingots containing iron slag (see arrows), from Pyrgi (Santa Severa, Rome).

There are many indications of metal-working on Etruscan sites in Etruria Padana (the Po Region), probably because the raw metal from Tuscany arrived here to be marketed in the Po Valley and beyond the Alps. In fact, some of the main metallurgical centers appear along the lines of communication between Tuscany and Emilia, for instance, Marzabotto (province of Bologna) on the River Reno or San Polo on the River Enza (province of Reggio Emilia) (Moretto 1995). Marzabotto certainly represents an important metallurgical center, where the working of both bronze and iron took place: here, the production facilities were located in the center of town, near the main road that crossed the city from north to south. The workshops, found both in *Regio V* (*insulae* 3 and 5) (Massa-Pairault 1997; Locatelli 2005), and in *Regio IV* (*insulae* 1 and 2) (Sassatelli 1989: 53–58, 62; Taglioni 1990), were particularly dedicated to the production of bronze, although there also happen to be some iron works. Excavations have unearthed the remains of furnaces, casting pits, numerous fragments of crucibles and molds in refractory clay, slags and casting residues, as well as pieces of pumice stone. The pumice implies that in the same workshops where the casting operations took place there also occurred the finishing of the products, which were cleaned and polished with the use of abrasive materials. The discovery of metal fragments and ingots suggests that here too, as in Villanovan Bologna, the bronze-smith's workshop made use of recycled bronze mixed, if necessary, with pure copper. The productive plant of *insula* 5, except for the room where the metal was cast, had a floor of fired clay on which occurred the final processing, such as the finishing of the products and any processes of hammering, soldering and annealing; a further cobbled area was set aside for the accumulation of semi-finished pieces and waste for recasting.

Additional evidence of metalworking is documented in other centers of Etruria Padana, both within large urban centers such as Bologna-Felsina (Taglioni 1999: 67) or Spina (Uggeri Patitucci, Uggeri 1973), and in small villages, as at Case Nuove di Siccomonte (Parma), Servirola (Reggio Emilia), Casale Rivalta (Reggio Emilia), Voghiera (Ferrara), Monte Bibele di Monterenzio (Bologna), and Pianella di Monte Savino (Bologna) (Moretto 1995, 68–71).

CONCLUSION

This brief summary shows that both the ancient sources and the archaeological data agree in stressing how metallurgy constituted one of the main economical and cultural engines of the Etruscan centers ever since the proto-historic period. In recent decades, the intensification of research and greater attention to aspects of production has greatly enriched our knowledge, shedding new light on the complex network of trade and cultural relations that linked the different parts of Etruria. An increasingly extended use of analytical techniques on archaeological materials is a prerequisite for the development of archaeometallurgy, a discipline whose contribution is essential to understand the economic and socio-cultural dynamics of a people so deeply bound to the exploitation and processing of metals, as the Etruscans certainly were.[1]

NOTE

1   I would like to thank the Museo Civico Archeologico of Bologna, which has kindly authorized the publication of the finds in its collections; the illustrations were furnished by the Archivio Fotografico of the Museum itself. I would also like to thank the Museo Preistorico-etnografico "L. Pigorini" of Rome, which has given permission to reproduce the inlaid clasp from Murlo.

BIBLIOGRAPHY

Andrée, J. (1922) *Bergbau in der Vorzeit*, Leipzig: Kabisch.

Antonacci Sanpaolo, E., Follo, L. and Canziani Ricci, C. (1992) "Il deposito di S. Francesco (Bologna) ed il contributo delle indagini archeometallurgiche" in E. Antonacci Sanpaolo (ed.), *Archeometallurgia Ricerche e prospettive. Atti del Colloquio Internazionale di Archeometallurgia (Bologna, Dozza Imolese 1989)*, Bologna: Clueb, pp. 159–206.

Arancio, M. L., Brotzu, A., Cavallini, M., Moretti, A. M. and Pellegrini, E. (2006) "Approccio metodologico preliminare alle problematiche della produzione metallurgica vulcente nella prima età del Ferro" in M. Cavallini, G. E. Gigante (eds), *De Re Metallica, dalla produzione antica alla copia moderna*, Rome: "L'ERMA" di Bretschneider, pp. 61–72.

Aranguren, B., Giachi, G. and Pallecchi, P. (1998) "La struttura dei forni" in *Follonica Etrusca, i segni di una civiltà*, scheda 11, Follonica.

Badii, G. (1931) "Le antiche miniere del Massetano (Massa Metallorum)" in *Studi Etruschi* V, pp. 455–473.

Banti, L. (1969) *Il mondo degli Etruschi*, Ente per la diffusione e l'educazione storica, Rome.

Bartoloni, G. and Delpino, F. (1985) "Un tipo di orciolo a lamelle metalliche" in *Studi Etruschi* XLIII, pp. 3–45.

Bellelli, V. (2005) "Αγυλλιος χαλκος" in *Dinamiche di sviluppo delle città nell'Etruria meridionale: Veio, Caere, Tarquinia, Vulci. Atti del XXIII Convegno di studi etruschi ed italici, Roma, Veio, Cerveteri, Pyrgi, Tarquinia, Tuscania, Vulci, Viterbo (2001)*, I, Istituti editoriali e poligrafici internazionali, Pisa-Rome, pp. 227–236.

Benvenuti, M., Mascaro, I., Costagliola, P., Tanelli, G. and Romualdi, A. (2000) "Iron, copper and tin at Baratti, Populonia: smelting processes and metal provenances" in *Historical Metallurgy* 34, 2, pp. 67–76.

Bietti Sestieri, A. M. (2010) *L'Italia nell'età del bronzo e del ferro: dalle palafitte a Romolo (2200–700 a.C.)*, Carocci, Roma.

Bietti Sestieri, A. M., Giardino, C., Gigante, G. E., Guida, G. and Ridolfi, S. (2002) "Primi risultati delle indagini non invasive mediante EDXRF sul ripostiglio di S. Francesco di Bologna" in C. D'Amico (ed.), (2002) *Atti del Secondo Congresso Nazionale di Archeometria (Bologna)*, Bologna: Pàtron, pp. 669–682.

Buonamici, M. (2006) "Nuove ricerche nell'area degli edifici industriali di Populonia," in *ΑΓΩΓΗ. Atti della Scuola di Specializzazione in Archeologia dell'Università di Pisa* III, Edizioni Plus, Pisa: Pisa University Press, pp. 255–268.

Camporeale, G. (1985) "Introduzione" in G. Camporeale (ed.), *L'Etruria mineraria*, Milan: Electa, pp. 21–36.

Camporeale, G., Canocchi, D. and Donati, L. (1985) "Massa Marittima, Lago dell'Accesa" in G. Camporeale (ed.), *L'Etruria mineraria*, Milan: Electa, pp. 125–177.

Cascone, G. and Casini, A. (1998) "Pre-industrial mining techniques in the mountains of Campiglia Marittima (Livorno)" in S. Milliken and M. Vidale (eds) *Craft Specializaion: Operational Sequences and Beyond. Papers from the EAA Third Annual Meeting at Ravenna 1997*, IV, BAR int. Series 720, Oxford: Hadrian Books, pp. 149–151.

Cocchi, I. (1865) "Di alcuni resti umani e degli oggetti di umana industria dei tempi preistorici raccolti in Toscana" in *Memorie della Società Italiana di Scienze Naturali*, I, pp. 1–32.

Corretti, A. and Benvenuti, M. (2001) "The Beginning of Iron Metallurgy in Tuscany, with Special Reference to *Etruria Mineraria*" in J.-P. Descoeudres, E. Huysecom, V. Serneels and J.-L. Zimmermann (eds), *Aux origines de la metallurgie du fer. Actes de la 1ère Table ronde internationale d'archéologie. L'Afrique et le basin méditerranéen (Genève 1999), Mediterranean Archaeology* 14, pp. 127–145.

Cucini Tizzoni, C. and Tizzoni, M. (1992) *Le antiche scorie del Golfo di Follonica (Toscana). Una proposta di tipologia. Notizie dal Chiostro del Monastero maggiore. Rassegna di studi del Civico museo archeologico e del Civico gabinetto numismatico di Milano*, suppl. IX, Milan.

D'Achiardi, G. (1929) "L'industria metallurgica a Populonia" in *Studi Etruschi* III, pp. 397–404.

Del Caldo, A., Moro, C., Gramaccioli, C. M. and Boscardin, M. (1973) *Guida ai Minerali*, Milan: Fratelli Fabbri.

Delpino, F. (1981) "Aspetti e problemi della prima età del ferro nell'Etruria settentrionale marittima" in *L'Etruria mineraria. Atti del XII Convegno di Studi Etruschi e Italici (Florence, Populonia, Piombino 1979)*, Florence: Olschki, pp. 265–298.

——(1988) "Prime testimonianze dell'uso del ferro in Italia" in G. Sperl (ed.), *The First Iron in the Mediterranean, PACT* 21, Strasbourg: Council of Europe, pp. 47–68.

Fedeli, F. (1982–83) "Forma per fusione da Populonia (Piombino, Livorno)" in *Rassegna di Archeologia* 3, pp. 157–165.

Foresi, R. (1867) *Sopra una collezione composta di oggetti antistorici trovati nelle isole dell'Arcipelago Toscano e inviata alla Mostra Universale di Parigi. Lettera inviata al prof. L. Simonin*, Florence.

Forte, M. (1994) "Lo scavo dell'insediamento di Castenaso-Via Gramsci: le strutture (1981)" in M. Forte and P. von Eles (eds), *La pianura bolognese nel villanoviano. Insediamenti della prima età del Ferro*, Catalogo della mostra archeologica di Villanova di Castenaso (1994–1995), Florence, pp. 193–199.

Franceschi, E. and Luciano, G. (2005) "I metalli" in L. Fiorini, *Topografia generale e storia del santuario : analisi dei contesti e delle stratigrafie*, Edipuglia, Bari, pp. 499–506.

Gentili, V. G. (1986) "L'età del ferro a Verucchio: cronologia degli scavi e scoperte ed evoluzione della letteratura archeologica" in *Studi e Documenti di Archeologia* II, pp. 1–41.

Giardino, C. (1995) *Il Mediterraneo occidentale fra il XVI e l'VIII sec. a.C. Cerchie minerarie e metallurgiche – West Mediterranean between 14th and 8th century B.C. Mining and metallurgical spheres, BAR Int. Series 612*, Oxford: Tempus Reparatum.

——(2005) "Metallurgy in Italy between the Late Bronze Age and the Early Iron Age: the Coming of Iron" in P. Attema, A. Nijboer and A. Zifferero (eds), *Papers in Italian Archaeology VI, Communities and Settlements from the Neolithic to the Early Medieval Period. Proceedings of the 6th Conference of Italian Archaeology (Groningen 2003), BAR Int. Series 1452 (II)*, Oxford: Archaeopress, pp. 491–505.

——(2006) "L'estrazione del ferro a Populonia. Nuove evidenze" in *ΑΓΩΓΗ. Atti della Scuola di Specializzazione in Archeologia dell'Università di Pisa* III, Edizioni Plus, Pisa: Pisa University Press, pp. 269–284.

——(2008) "Paesaggi minerari dell'Etruria pre-protostorica" in *Atti VIII Incontro di Studi Preistoria e Protostoria in Etruria (Valentano (Vt) – Pitigliano (Gr) 2006)*, Milan: Centro Studi di Preistoria e Archeologia, pp. 73–89.

——(2010) *I metalli nel mondo antico. Introduzione all'archeometallurgia* (new edition), Rome-Bari: Laterza.

——(2011) "Indagini archeometallurgiche sui reperti" in J. Gran-Aymerich and A. Domínguez-Arranz (eds), *La Castellina a sud di Civitavecchia : origini ed eredità. Origines protohistoriques et évolution d'un habitat étrusque*, Rome: "L'ERMA" di Bretschneider, pp. 981–998.

Giardino, C. and Gigante, G. E. (1995) "Ricerche archeometriche sui materiali metallici del "Gran Carro" (Bolsena – VT): alcuni risultati preliminari mediante ED–XRF" in P. Tamburini, *Un abitato villanoviano perilacustre. Il "Gran Carro" sul Lago di Bolsena (1959–1985)*, Rome: G. Bretschneider Editore, pp. 316–232.

Giardino, C. and Lugli, F. (2001) "L'attività siderurgica nel Giardino Romano" in *Bullettino della Commissione Archeologica Comunale di Roma* CII, pp. 327–328.

Giardino, C. and Steiniger, D. (2011) "Evidenze di miniere preistoriche nell'Etruria Meridionale" in C. Giardino (ed.), *Archeometallurgia: dalla conoscenza alla fruizione Atti del Workshop, 22–25 maggio 2006 (Cavallino (LE), Convento dei Dominicani), Beni archeologici – conoscenza e tecnologie, Quaderno 8*, Bari: Edipuglia, pp. 289–292.

Gualtieri, M. (1977) *Iron in Calabria in the Ninth and Eighth Centuries B.C.*, Dissertation in Classical Archaeology – University of Pennsylvania, Ann Arbor, Michigan: Xerox Microfilms.

Guidi, G. F. and Trojsi, G. (2001) "II.A.3.2. Spugna di ferro" in A. M. Moretti Sgubini (ed.), *Veio, Cerveteri, Vulci: città d'Etruria a confronto, catalogo della mostra (Roma, Museo Nazionale Etrusco di Villa Giulia 2001)*, Rome: "L'ERMA" di Bretschneider, Ingegneria per la cultura, p. 130.

——(2003) "Appendice: i residui delle attività produttive" in M. Cristofani (ed.), *Caere. 4, Vigna Parrocchiale: scavi 1983–1989 : il santuario, la "residenza" e l'edificio ellittico*, Pisa-Rome: Istituti Editoriali e Poligrafici Internazionali, pp. 259–265.

Guidi, G. F., Giardino, C. and Trojsi, G. (2005) "L'insediamento etrusco di San Giovenale (Blera, Viterbo). Caratterizzazione chimico-fisica dei residui delle attività produttive" in *Opuscula Romana* 30, pp. 73–84.

Kent Hill, D. (1981) "From an Etruscan Door" in *Studi di antichità in onore di Guglielmo Maetzke*, II, Rome: G. Bretschneider, pp. 321–324.

Locatelli, D. (2005) "La 'fonderia' della Regio V, insula 5: elementi per una definizione dell'attività produttiva" in G. Sassatelli and E. Govi (eds), *Culti, forma urbana e artigianato a Marzabotto. Nuove prospettive di ricerca, Atti del Convegno di Studi (Bologna 2003)*, Bologna: Ante Quem, pp. 213–237.

Lotti, B. (1908) "Cenni sulla geologia della Toscana" in *Bollettino del R. Comitato Geologico d'Italia* IX, 3°, pp. 165–190.

Martelli, M. (1981) "Lo scavo di edifici nella zona "industriale" di Populonia" in *L'Etruria mineraria. Atti del XII Convegno di Studi Etruschi e Italici (Firenze, Populonia, Piombino 1979)*, Florence, pp. 161–172.

Massa-Pairault, F.-H. (1997) "Témoignages sur le bronze et le travail du bronze" in F.-H. Massa-Pairault (ed.), *Marzabotto. Recherches sur l'insula V, 3*, Rome: École Française de Rome.

Minto, A. (1954) "L'antica industria mineraria in Etruria ed il porto di Populonia" in *Studi Etruschi* XXIII, pp. 291–319.

Moretto, T. (1995) "Dati e considerazioni sulla metallurgia in Etruria padana" in L. Quilici and S. Gigli Quilici (eds), *Atlante tematico di topografia antica. I Supplemento. Agricoltura e commerci nell'Italia antica*, Rome: "L'ERMA" di Bretschneider, pp. 65–71.

Nestler, G. and Formigli, E. (1994) *Granulazione Etrusca. Un'antica tecnica orafa*, Siena: Nuova Immagine.

Nielsen, E. (1993) "Further Evidence of Metal Working at Poggio Civitate" in E. Formigli (ed.), *Antiche officine del bronzo, materiali, strumenti, tecniche, Atti del seminario di studi ed esperimenti (Murlo 1991)*, Siena: Nuova Immagine, pp. 29–40.

Pallottino, M. (1973) *Etruscologia* (VI ed.), Milan: Hoepli.

Panseri, C. and Leoni, M. (1967) "Research on an Iron Spearhead from the Etruscan Sanctuary of Fanum Voltumnae, fourth to third centuries B.C." in M. Levy (ed.), *Archaeological Chemistry. A Symposium*, Philadelphia, pp. 205–229.

Patitucci Uggeri, S. and Uggeri, G. (1973) "Spina" in *Studi Etruschi* XLVII, pp. 402–406.

Peyre, C. (1968) [Rapport des fouilles de l'École française] "À Casalecchio di Reno" in *Chronique. Mélanges d'archéologie et d'histoire – École française de Rome*, 80, pp. 376–389.

Riccobono, F. (1992) "I giacimenti minerari" in F. Giusti (ed.), *La Storia Naturale della Toscana Meridionale*, Milan: Amilcare Pizzi Editore, pp. 107–139.

Rovira, S. (2011) "Estudios analítico de materiales pirometalúrgicos" in J. Gran-Aymerich and A. Domínguez-Arranz (eds), *La Castellina a sud di Civitavecchia: origini ed eredità. Origines protohistoriques et évolution d'un habitat étrusque*, Rome: "L'ERMA" di Bretschneider, pp. 971–981.

Sassatelli, G. (1989) *La città etrusca di Marzabotto*, Casalecchio di Reno: Grafis.

Saviano, G., Felli, F. and Drago, L. (2006) "Etruria meridionale e Lazio: analisi su reperti metallici e fittili provenienti da Veio, dal santuario di Pyrgi e dall'area del santuario dell'Artemisio" in M. Cavallini and G. E. Gigante (eds), *De Re Metallica, dalla produzione antica alla copia moderna*, Rome: "L'ERMA" di Bretschneider: pp. 73–101.

Simonin, L.-L. (1858) "De l'exploitation des mines et de la métallurgie en Toscane pendant l'Antiquité et le Moyen Age" in *Annales des Mines* V, XIV, pp. 557–615.

Stjernquist, B. (1960) "La decorazione metallica delle ceramiche villanoviane" in *Civiltà del ferro. Studi pubblicati in occasione della ricorrenza centenaria di Villanova*, Bologna: Arnaldo Forni, pp. 429–442.

Taglioni, C. (1990) "Le attività metallurgiche" in G. Sassatelli and A. M. Brizzolara (eds), I Nuovi scavi dell'Università di Bologna nella città etrusca di Marzabotto : mostra fotografica (Bologna 1990), Bologna: Clueb, p. 29.

Taglioni, C. (1999) *L'abitato etrusco di Bologna*, Bologna: Bologna University Press.

Tamburini, P. (1995) Un abitato villanoviano perilacustre. Il "Gran Carro" sul Lago di Bolsena (1959–1985), Rome: G, Bretschneider Editore.

Tanelli, G. (1985) "I giacimenti minerari dell'Etruria e le attività estrattive degli Etruschi" in G. Camporeale (ed.), *L'Etruria mineraria*, Milan: Electa, pp. 37–38.

Vitali, D. (1983) "L'Età del Ferro nell'Emilia occidentale: dati, considerazioni e proposte" in *Studi sulla città antica: l'Emilia-Romagna*, Rome: "L'ERMA" di Bretschneider, pp. 129–172.

Voss, O. (1988) "The Iron Production in Populonia" in G. Sperl (ed.), *The First Iron in the Mediterranean, PACT* 21, Strasbourg: Council of Europe, pp. 91–100.

Warden, P. G. (1993) "Copper, Iron and Smelting Technologies in Iron Age Etruria: New Evidence from Poggio Civitate (Murlo)" in E. Formigli (ed.), *Antiche officine del bronzo, materiali, strumenti, tecniche, Atti del seminario di studi ed esperimenti (Murlo 1991)*, Siena: Nuova immagine, pp. 41–49.

Zannoni, A. (1888) *La fonderia di Bologna scoperta e descritta*, Bologna: Azzoguidi.

Zifferero, A. (1992) "Giacimenti minerari e insediamenti nel Lazio settentrionale: recenti acquisizioni e prospettive di ricerca" in E. Antonacci Sanpaolo (ed.), *Archeometallurgia. Ricerche e prospettive. Atti del Colloquio Internazionale di Archeometallurgia (Bologna-Dozza Imolese 1988)*, Bologna: Clueb, pp. 81–103.

CHAPTER THIRTY EIGHT

TECHNOLOGY, IDEOLOGY, WARFARE AND THE ETRUSCANS BEFORE THE ROMAN CONQUEST

———— •◆• ————

David B. George

War as it is practiced and armies as institutions are expressions of the complex of behaviors that make up a culture. Certainly, the physical realities of biology, physics – as well as the nature of the adversary – shape and refine the particular practice of war, but more than anything else it is the value system of culture that gives definition to the craft of war on the field of battle. Technology plays a role, yet technology does not configure the battlefield; rather, culturally valued selections determine the art and exercise of war.

In this chapter, I shall examine several aspects of how differences in civic ideology within the Etruscan cities might have shaped their appropriating of military technology. The aim is to tease out of the material culture, particularly from the hoplite-type armor and the traditions that survive in the literary record about martial ideologies, suggestions of evidence for this relationship.

Indeed, one must recognize here the same problem that one finds when discussing the Greek *poleis* at war – because of the focus on technology, diversity of civic ideology is sometimes glossed over in the treatment of military matters. And one must state at the outset that when considering the Etruscans the problem is even more complicated than when examining the Greek *poleis*. We know much more about the Greek world than we do the Etruscans'. We possess their notions, in their own voices, about Greeks waging war whereas for the Etruscans we have only Romanized Greeks and Romanized Etruscans, Romans themselves, and the odd pre-Romanized Greek voice to give us some indication about Etruscan culture and ideology. Moreover, the quantity of material culture that relates to warfare is not exceedingly large and is mostly from funerary contexts. Yet even this material, such as it is, from funerary contexts reflects some profound differences between Northern and Southern Etruria especially in the seventh to the fifth centuries BCE, as well as some deep differences between the Etruscan cities that make up the two broad regions.

In war, as in all other aspects of Etruscan society, the very deep stratifications of society color everything. When the Etruscans took to the field they brought that stratification with them. Indeed almost to the end of their identity as a people, the aristocracy was still characterizing its right to lead based upon martial skill and leadership in most of the cities. In many cities the ability, on one's own authority and from one's own resources, to field and presumably arm troops was a mark of aristocratic greatness.

Consider for example Dionysius' (9.5.4) account of a battle near Veii around 480 BCE. As the Roman consuls advance on Veii, Dionysius describes them as unnerved by what they see. Spread out in front of the city, in good order, is arrayed the might of the enemy (ἡ τῶν πολεμίων δύναμις ἐξεστρατευμένη πρὸ τῆς πόλεως πολλή τε καὶ ἀγαθή). It was considerable in both number and quality. But here Dionysius gives an important piece of information. The city army of Veii has been augmented by the chief men of rank, (οἱ δυνατώτατοι – *hoi dynatotatoi*) from other cities throughout Etruria (ἐξ ἁπάσης Τυρρηνίας) with their own clients and dependents (τοὺς ἑαυτῶν πενέοτας ἐπαγόμενοι). The word πενέστης (*penestes*) likely refers to that class of people who were not quite in servile status but not quite free and tied to a specific δυνατώτατος (*dynatotatos*), clan or family with obligations to work the land as well as supply military service.[1] (On social classes, see Chapter 21.) It is likely that the δυνατώτατος (*dynatotatos*) was under some sort of a personal or familial obligation to whoever was requesting help for the city. There was no citywide political structure to approve, deter, or compel aristocratic participation in a particular conflict. Also, it is quite likely that the δυνατώτατος (*dynatotatos*) himself was responsible for equipping his dependents. His personal glory and honor would be reflected in both the number of troops and how finely they were equipped. This is likely the origin of the 125 Negau type helmets that were found in 1905 at Vetulonia deposited near the walls of the *arx* and inscribed with the gentilicial name *haspnas*.[2] These helmets would have been owned by the *haspnas gens* (clan) and distributed to the *penestes* and perhaps other dependent classes when needed.

This rather archaic social structure for levying troops would have been reflected on the battlefield in a number of ways. As noted, in this case, the consuls were taken aback by both the size of the army (πλῆθος) and the quality of its weapons (τὴν λαμπρότητα τῶν ὅπλων).[3] This implies that there was no means for anticipating, by friend or foe alike, the number or quality of troops who would turn out for any particular battle. The other implication of this is that the various elements of the army are not likely to have trained together or been armed in the same way. It would have been composed of two distinct groups, the aristocratic class and the πενέστης (*penestes*), each with very narrowly defined functions.

The πενέσται (*penestai*), if fully armed, would have been equipped with a round Etruscan style helmet, a sword or ax and perhaps a shield. But it is likely that at times they would have had, other than a helmet, only an offensive weapon.[4] Their weapons would not have required much training and would not have been very different from agricultural implements. Indeed the use of a scythe on a farm would be good practice for use of the curved sword (*kopis*). These weapons would have necessitated fighting in loose formations and so battle would tend to be individual against individual.

For the aristocratic warrior ideology, we have a good deal of evidence from material culture. One interesting piece is a *bucchero pesante* oinochoe from Ischia di Castro now in the Villa Giulia. It presents the aristocratic elements of the Etruscan army in the field. Dating to the last quarter of the seventh century BCE,[5] the vase has four components, each depicting different figures: two of the figures are wearing crested Corinthian helmets, who carry round shields and appear to wear cuirasses. They are engaging each other with thrusting spears. Next to them is an archer, presumably dead, with a crested Corinthian helmet, wearing a cuirass, reclined on his back with drawn bow. Advancing on the scene is a figure wearing a bell-shaped helmet (like that from Todi now in Perugia: for illustration and discussion of actual arms and armor, see Chapter 39). He wears a cuirass and a skirt in a two-wheeled chariot followed by a rider wearing a Corinthian helmet without crest. Rounding off the scene are two equine creatures. The oinochoe presents a coherent image of the aristocratic elements of the Etruscan battlefield. There are heavily armed men engaged in single combat, archers, cavalry and warriors who ride out in the Homeric way on a chariot. The helmets are diverse and could represent rank or more likely reflect the hodgepodge of armor that Etruscan aristocrats bring to the field. Here, the aristocratic ideal is evinced not only by signs of wealth (horses or armor) but also of skill, practice and some training (handling horses, chariots, close-quarter spears, or the bow). The aristocratic use of the bow is in direct opposition to the Greek hoplite ideal in that it does not depend upon the corps but upon the individual.[6]

The aristocratic fighters would have been on the field of battle then as archers, or cavalry or have been very splendidly armored and have ridden to the battlefield in a chariot in a Homeric manner. The aristocratic fighters who rode out on horse would have served as the scouts, and in battle would have engaged other cavalry.[7] If they rode out in a chariot they would have served as the command and control of their contingent. While there would have been some variance in his equipment, it is likely that the heavily armored δυνατώτατος (*dynatotatos*) would have had a breastplate, a shield, sword and spear(s) and perhaps greaves. His right to lead would rest upon his ability to fight, to lead and to direct his men, as well as his capacity to supply his dependents with the equipment they needed to fight. Presumably, he would have been responsible for feeding his contingent as well. Given this arrangement there would have been a strong likelihood for class to fight class. More specifically, there would have also been a tendency for the δυνατώτατοι (*dynatotatoi*) on such a battlefield to engage in *monomachia* (single combat) with other δυνατώτατοι. Evidence from the visual depiction of individual combat on sarcophagi and wall paintings reinforces this notion.

One may add as an example the tradition that survives about the deaths of Arruns, son of Tarquin, and Lucius Iunius Brutus at the battle of Silva Arsia; it provides interesting material to contemplate. I do not argue for the historicity of the battle, Arruns or Brutus, though I see no reason why the tradition should be entirely baseless. In comparing the recasting of the tradition by Livy and Dionysius of Halicarnassus several important features emerge as instructive.

Livy's version of the story is that as Tarquin makes his rounds of the cities of Etruria to seek help his primary focus is on the Veii and the Tarquinii. His general pleas are personal and presume gentilicial connections (*ne ex se, eiusdem sanguinis, extorrem…*2.6). He presents himself as the reason for Roman expansion and success (*se regem, augentem bello Romanum Imperium*) and so implies that the Etruscan cities have nothing to fear by joining him; they will be able to avenge their losses (*suas quoque veteres iniurias ultum irent…*). In a perhaps intentionally proleptic response, the Veians are moved by the latter (*amissa repetenda*) but the Tarquinii by the former (*pulchrum uidebatur suos Romae regnare*). Thus Tarquinia and Veii send armies. Here, according to Livy's account the consuls do not move against the Etruscan armies until they have crossed into Roman territory (*postquam in agrum Romanum uentum est, obuiam hosti consules eunt*) at which point they move to obstruct the Etruscan armies' movement. Livy's implication of course is that Rome, without Tarquin, is not interested in expansion against the Etruscan cities; they are just defending themselves, a common Livian *topos*. When the advance scouts under the command of Arruns and Brutus happen upon each other, Livy plays down Brutus' temper and focuses on Arruns' (*inflammatus ira*) in their charge to mutual death. As Brutus perceives Arruns' assault, Livy has him turn to meet the young prince with gusto (*avide*) but gives the consul cover for what might be seen as an imprudent act by declaring that at that time it was proper and fitting for generals to engage with one another in battle (*decorum erat tum ipsis capessere pugnam ducibus*). On the whole a very pro-Roman, pro-Brutus story.

Dionysius' account (5.14–15) differs in important ways. It has long been argued that he is likely to have had solid Etruscan sources and is thus a better source than Livy for Etruscan affairs. And indeed his narrative seems richer in details that appear to be genuinely Etruscan. For example, when he discusses the aid that the Etruscan cities are giving to the family of Tarquin he is much more subtle in his characterization of it. His account describes Tarquinia and Veii openly helping (ἐκ τοῦ φανεροῦ) as entire cities but other cities send help piecemeal, presumably drawn by individual leading men from their own personal resources in men and arms or simply hiring mercenaries to fulfill whatever obligations they had (ἐκ δὲ τῶν ἄλλων ἐθελοντάς τινας, οὓς μὲν ὑπὸ φίλων παρασκευασθέντας, οὓς δὲ μισθοφόρους). I take the first phrase to refer to the Etruscan practice of having an aristocrat individually promise to levy troops that he would draw from his own dependants. The fact that clans within a city could send troops to fight on behalf of the clan and not the city does tend to diminish the authority of city institutions but elevate that of the individual aristocrat and his clan.

Thus in Dionysius' account two Etruscan cities, Tarquinia and Veii, are openly engaged in hostilities as city entities because it is likely their social structures required corporate action (e.g. they are functioning more like poleis). While it is possible that all their leading families may have come to some sort of consensus, it seems more likely that their collective behavior reflects a difference in social structure from those cities that are still functioning in the more archaic gentilicial structures and so have leading men marching out with their own troops on their own authority (ἐθελοντάς) to acquire personal glory by helping in person. Thus we have in this tradition a reflection of a divergence between Etruscan cities of the north and south with southern cities developing a more city centered authority. Again, I am not arguing for historicity of the story but rather for a better reflection of Etruscan traditions and institutions in the material he had to work with.

Dionysius also describes the Romans as being more aggressive. Unlike Livy's narrative, Dionysius describes them as not waiting to suffer the first incursion but preemptively crossing to meet the Etruscan host before it can arrive in Roman territory (καὶ πρὶν ἐκείνους διαβῆναι τὸν ποταμὸν αὐτοὶ τὰς δυνάμεις διαβιβάσαντες ἐχώρουν πρόσω). But his account of the deaths of Arruns and Brutus evinces the most significant contrasts to Livy. For example, he does not present the event as a chance meeting of scouting parties but rather the two armies are already drawn up in battle formations in preparation to close with the enemy (μελλόντων δ' αὐτῶν εἰς χεῖρας ἰέναι). Arruns rides between the lines, close enough to be seen as an individual by the enemy and close enough to heap insult directly upon Brutus (λόγους ὑβριστὰς εἰς τὸν ἡγεμόνα τῶν Ῥωμαίων Βροῦτον ἀπερρίπτει). Besides one very personal charge, that Brutus killed his own son (θηρίον ἄγριον ἀποκαλῶν καὶ τέκνων αἵματι μιαρόν), the other abuses have a general (Homeric) feel – the want of manhood (ἀνανδρία) and cowardice (δειλία) as does the final calling out to settle the point by single combat (εἰς τὸν ὑπὲρ ἁπάντων ἀγῶνα προὐκαλεῖτο μόνον αὐτῷ συνοισόμενον). The taunts, in Dionysius, had their effect. Brutus' honor was pricked (οὐκ ἀξιῶν τοὺς ὀνειδισμοὺς ὑπομένειν) and contrary to the advice of his friends he rode out between the lines to take up Arruns' challenge and meet his fated death (ἤλαυνε τὸν ἵππον ἐκ τῆς τάξεως, ὑπεριδὼν καὶ τῶν ἀποτρεπόντων φίλων ἐπὶ τὸν κατεψηφισμένον ὑπὸ τῆς μοίρας θάνατον ἐπειγόμενος). Aside from the Homeric color that Dionysius gives the story there is also the general impression that this is an ekphrasis.

His prose is worth quoting at length verbatim for its force.

> Both carried along with like courage, making no calculation for what would happen, other than what they wanted to do, spurring on their horses – from opposite sides explosively crashing into each other, both inflicting on each other with their sarissas inescapable death blows through their shields and corslets, each drenching his spear in the opposite side of the other's ribcage. Their horses entangled, breast to breast, are thrown back on their hind legs by the force of the charge and rearing up having thrown their riders. The fallen riders lay stretched out bleeding out great quantities of blood from their wounds as they die...[8]

There is much here that points to an ekphrasis of a painting or mosaic beyond simple rhetorical flourish. The careful description of the position of the wounds, the careful placement of the horses raised in a triangle with the fallen heroes laying prone to bring the lines out but having a counter thrust of the lines with the spears reinforcing the triangle, all point to a Hellenistic painting. But be that as it may, both Livy and Dionysius preserve in the Brutus-Arruns story a tradition of *monomachia*. Livy states outright that in days of old such single combat between generals was "acceptable" (*decorum*).

With Book 3 of the *Iliad* in mind, scholars have tended to dismiss any notion of *monomachia* either in plastic or literary arts as a device or convention. In plastic art it is a result of the difficulties of showing many men engaged in battle; in literature it is the desire to increase the pathos by focusing on the individual for the whole – a *synecdoche*. But that neglects the fact that such single combats do in fact occur not only in Etruria but also throughout the Greek and Roman worlds. They can be the result of ritualized behavior, *ad hoc* loss of temper (people do get mad and do silly things in war), or a calculus to reduce the damage of a conflict.[9] And importantly, they are at times commemorated in works of art as paradigms for aristocratic emulation, as for example, the hero Echemos at Tegea (Herodotus 9.26.4; Pausanias 8.53.10).[10]

It is likely that the frequency of depictions of single combat on Etruscan sarcophagi is meant to reinforce the aristocratic ideal of *monomachia*. In a Roman context *monomachia* is tied to the honor of the *spolia opima*. This continues quite late. In terms of the Etruscan aristocratic context there is perhaps another reason for *monomachia*. The aristocracy was still functioning in many places as if their right to rule rested on their prowess at arms. But here there are some subtle differences between northern and southern cities that one needs to reflect on.

The spread of hoplite armor from the Greek world to the Etruscan (and Roman) has long been studied both in terms of the armor and the transference of tactics.[11] The broad consensus seems to be that given the fact that in funerary contexts the armor seems to be found rarely in complete panoplies and that the offensive weapons frequently include typical Etruscan weapons, like the axe, which are incompatible with a hoplite formation, and the bow, which is incompatible with hoplite ideology, that the hoplite types of armor were adopted without the tactics. Thus the hoplite armor recovered from elite tombs would have been analogous to other Hellenic or Hellenizing objects found in funerary contexts (cf. Chapter 33). It was intended to represent individual status of wealth and participation in an aristocratic sympotic culture. Indeed in many cases the panoply could have been a gift intended to be worn in parade, or for ritual use, or for a public display of one's participation in the Hellenic ideal rather than actual use on the battlefield.[12] Some of the body armor is meant to be worn but others would clearly have considerably restricted mobility in the field, which reinforces questions about its purpose.[13] In any case when it did appear in the field it was piecemeal and in accord with the general cultural structure of the Etruscan army. It would have generally been restricted to the elites while the *penestes* would have continued to fight as they always did.

An interesting contrast in the application of this technology to the warfare is seen at Vulci and Velzna (Volsinii/Orvieto). The two towns were closely tied commercially and many of the Greek vases recovered from Velzna passed through Vulci. Yet the two cities' aristocracies seem to have been functioning differently. In Vulci, there appears to be an elite society based on martial skills whereas at Velzna the aristocracy seems to have allowed the development of a class of proto-hoplites, men who were not aristocratic or particularly wealthy but who defined themselves by their ability to participate in the defense of the city. A good view into this contrasting ideology can be gleaned from the Tomb of the Warrior at Vulci and the many *cippi* from the Orvieto area that depict hoplites.

The Tomb of the Warrior has a single burial of an individual with a full panoply of hoplite armor, a pair of greaves, four spearheads, an iron sword, and a helmet of strikingly Etruscan type. Even in its Hellenism the panoply still has markers to indicate that it is Etruscan. The grave also contains a number of Attic-figured vases tied to sympotic culture as well as a Panathenaic amphora depicting a boxing match. When one considers the Tomb of the Warrior, it is clear that the traditional markers of Etruscan gentilicial affiliation are lacking and this is likely to reflect the funerary ideology of an emerging timocratic elite.[14] Taken in the context of other burials with hoplite armor, the image of the deceased is that of a member of the elite who displays his status through connection to the Greek sympotic ideal. The armor is a status symbol reflecting Hellenized ideals, not a reflection of the deceased's status as a hoplite.

The situation is somewhat different at Velzna. Here there is, at least in a funerary context, a somewhat equalitarian ideology reflected in the treatment of family tombs. All are of equal size and similar configuration. This implies that, whatever wealth or gentilicial differences existed in reality with regard to position within the civic ideology, there was a type of family-based equality. Such an ideology seems to be reflected in the region's treatment of the image of the hoplite. There are a large number of *cippi* with figures armored as hoplites. The very quantity of these images would tend to indicate that they were not meant to mark elite burials but rather belonged to the graves of a broader class. It would be interesting to know whether these *cippi* were associated with graves that contained armor or if the armor belonged to the family or city and was not placed with the deceased. But since most of these *cippi* have survived disassociated from their graves we shall likely never know. Given, however, the typical treatment of tombs that have been systematically excavated around Orvieto, it would seem that such graves that do have armor placed within them belonged to elites, and others associated with the *cippi* would not contain armor or contain a helmet only. The depiction of the hoplite on the *cippus* would then be intended to indicate the status of the grave's occupant as part of a class that participates in the defense of the city. It is likely, however, that there never was a true hoplite class even at Velzna, but rather that the iconography of the hoplite had become fixed to a Hellenic ideal and the image simply indicates "warrior."

This is bolstered by the tradition, though a much later one, that the Etruscan elites of Velzna lost control of the city to their freed men and slaves because they had turned, among other things, the control of their army over to them. Dio Cassius' (Book 10 p.141 = Zonaras 8.7) narration of the sad story of the end of Etruscan Velzna indicates a number of conditions still prevailing in the aristocracy and how they related to military matters. As part of the general meme of Etruscan luxury and decadence (ἁβρότης), he notes that the once mighty elites of Velzna "turned the administration (διοίκησις) of their city over to their household slaves (οἰκέτης) and even quite frequently (ὡς τὸ πολύ) conducted military expeditions (στρατεία) through them." While there is much that is problematic with this passage, not the least of which its date and location, it is clear that Dio still envisioned the now-decadent elite to be, at times, required to go out with the army themselves. However, they would send their οἰκέται out in their place as often as they could. Again this implies that there were times when they were obliged to sally forth with the army. Moreover, the most natural way of understanding οἰκέτης is that it refers to freedmen rather than the class of semi-free *penestes* who were likely to still be working the land even as late as the third century BCE. Thus this does not reflect the natural transformation of a class into citizen-soldiers but rather the simple usurpation of control of the city by those who were handed the management of the city organs and control of the weapons. But, moving back to the sixth and fifth centuries BCE, another factor that would mitigate against a true hoplite class is the nature of the Etruscan battlefield; it was simply not suited to hoplite strategy or formations. It is more likely, should any of the hoplite panoply have been present on the battlefield, that like the *haspnas* clan's helmets it was owned by the family (or clan or city) and supplied piecemeal to the fighters.

There was a persistent class division that shaped Etruscans on the battlefield. The division resulted in two classes of fighters, aristocrats who were well armed and had some practice in the craft of warfare and another class made up of the poor and dependent and in some cases semi-servile folks who were armed by their patrons with simple offensive weapons that required no or very little training. But even within this situation there were different practices that reflected local variants of ideology that helped determine how and by whom new military equipment would be used.

NOTES

1   On this class in general see: Heurgon, 1970; Torelli, 1981, 79–83, as well as 1987, 87–95.

2   Egg, 247–50; Maggiani, 48–49; Massa-Pairault, F. 261–264.

3   D'Agostino 80 (1990) holds, on the basis of ὁμονοοῦσαν at 9.5.5, that Dionysius envisages these troops arrayed as hoplite. I think he misses the point. The contrast is between the factional strife that riddles the Roman army and unison of the Etruscan elites (στασιαζούσῃ δυνάμει τῇ σφετέρᾳ πρὸς ὁμονοοῦσαν τὴν τῶν πολεμίων); that is the reason for the consuls' fear. Such unison results in numbers and quality.

4   Martinelli 2004 gives a solid review of armor and its uses.

5   (Inv. 64578) Falconi Amorelli, 171–172 # 10 tav XXVIII a–f; cf. Stary 1981 pl. 7; D'Agostino (1990), 70, Fig. 4.

6   The fact that the bowman is armored, as well as the skill required, moves him into the aristocratic side of things. This is one more bit of evidence for the lack of a hoplite ideology among the Etruscans when one considers the treatment of bowmen in the Greek hoplite context. Cf. George 145–8.

7   Martinelli (1998) and Jannot (1986) have good discussions of the uses of the cavalry in its full range of usages.

8   Dionysius in the original: "ὁμοίῳ δ' ἀμφότεροι θυμῷ φερόμενοι καὶ λογισμὸν οὐχ ὧν πείσονται λαβόντες, ἀλλ' ὧν ἐβούλοντο δρᾶσαι, συρράττουσι τοὺς ἵππους ἐξ ἐναντίας ἐλαύνοντες καὶ φέρουσι ταῖς σαρίσαις ἀφύκτους κατ' ἀλλήλων πληγὰς ἀμφότεροι δι'ἀσπίδων τε καὶ θωράκων, ὁ μὲν εἰς τὰ πλευρὰ βάψας τὴν αἰχμήν, ὁ δ' εἰς τὰς λαγόνας· καὶ οἱ ἵπποι αὐτῶν ἐμπλέξαντες τὰ στήθη τῇ ῥύμῃ τῆς φορᾶς ἐπὶ τοῖς ὀπισθίοις ἀνίστανται ποσι και τοὺς ἐπιβάτας ἀναχαιτίσαντες ἀποσείονται. οὗτω μὲν δὴ κεῖόντες ἔκειτο πολὺ διὰ τῶν τραυμάτων ἐκβάλλοντες αἷμα καὶ ψυχορραγοῦντες."

9   Pritchett (p. 15) after noting "as to the many duels in the *Iliad*, it is often overlooked that *monomachia* appears to have been an ancient military practice common to all the peoples around the Mediterranean basin" reviews the principle examples (17–20) from the Greek world. Harris, 39, note 1 gives a number of Roman examples. One account of Scipio Aemilianus' *monomachia* is historical (Polybius 35.5.1), the other fictitious (Appian, *Lib.* 45) but may date from second century BCE Scipionic self-promotion.

10 The theme was apparently repeated, Daux 811 reports, with a photo (Fig. 5) of a Hellenistic stele with the image of Echemos fighting.

11 Snodgrass is, of course, the starting point and essentially argues for a transfer of tactics with technology. But Cherici (2009) and Jannot (1991) as well as Spivey and Stoddart give good reasons to question the transfer of tactics. For armor in general Stary is still the standard.

12 Turnure has an interesting discussion on possible ritual uses of Etruscan armor.

13 Turfa, 111 argues that the Narce cuirass was so restrictive that its use might have been for a warrior who was engaged in command and control functions and didn't need mobility. I suspect that its function was ritual and not intended for the battlefield.

14 D'Agostino, 78 has a good discussion of the tomb with relevant bibliography as well as the *cippi* found around Orvieto.

BIBLIOGRAPHY

Cerchiai, L. (2001) "The Ideology of the Etruscan City" in M. Torelli (ed.), *The Etruscans*, New York: Rizzoli, 243–253.

Cherici, A. (2009) "Etruria-Roma: Per una storia del rapporto tra impegno militare e capienza politica nelle comunità antiche," *Annali della Fondazione per il Museo "Claudio Faina"* 16, 155–173.

D'Agostino, Bruno (1990) "Military Organization and Social Structure in Archaic Etruria" in O. Murray and S. Price, *The Greek City from Homer to Alexander*, Oxford: Clarendon Press, 59–82.

Daux, George (1968) "Chronique des foulles de découvertes archéologiques en Grèce en 1967," *Bulletin de correspondance hellénique* (92) 711–1135.

Falconi Amorelli, M. T. (1968) "Materiali di Ischia di Castro conservati nel Museo di Villa Giulia," *Studi Etruschi* 36, 169–177.

Egg, M. (1988) "Italische Helme mit Krempe," *Antike Helme*, Mainz, 222–270.

George, D. B. (1994) "Euripides; Herakles 140–235: Staging and the stage iconography of Herakles' bow", *Greek, Roman, and Byzantine Studies* 35, 145–157.

Harris, W. V. (1979) *War and Imperialism in Republican Rome*, Oxford: Oxford University Press.

Heurgon, J. (1970) "Classes et ordres chez les Étrusques" in *Recherches sur les structures sociales dans l'Antiquité classique*, Paris: Editions du Centre National De La Recherche Scinetifique, pp. 29–41.

Jannot, J.-R. (1986) "Les cavaliers étrusques. Armement, mode de combat, fonction. VIIème au IVème siècle." *Mitteilungen des Deutschen Archaeologischen Instituts, Römische Abeilung* 93, 109–133.

——(1989) "Armement, tactique et societé. Réflexions sur l'example de l'Etrurie archaïque" in B. S. Frizell, *Arte Militare et architettura nuragica: Nuragic architecture in its military, territorial and socio-economic context : proceedings of the First International Colloquium on Nuragic Architecture at the Swedish Institute in Rome, 7–9 December, 1989*, Stockholm: P. Åströms, 73–81.

Martinelli, M. (1997) "Guerra e controllo del territorio in Etruria tra età del bronzo ed età del ferro" in M. Pearce, M. Tosi (eds), *Papers from the EAA Third Annual meeting at Ravenna 1997. Pre-and Protohistory v 1 (British Archaeological Reports International S.)* 51–45.

——(2004). *La lancia, la spada, il cavallo: Il fenomeno Guerra nell'Etruria e nell'Italia centrale tra età del bronzo ed età del ferro*, Florence: Regione toscana.

Maggiani, A. (1990) "La situazione archeologica dell'Etrurie settentrionale nel V sec. a.C." in *Crise et Transformation des sociétés archaïques de l"Italie antique au Ve siècle av. J.C.*, Rome, 23–49.

Massa-Pairault, F. (2001) "The social structure and the serf question" in M. Torelli (ed.), *The Etruscans*, New York: Rizzoli, 255–271.

Pritchett, W. Kendrick (1985) *The Greek State at War (Part IV)*, Berkeley: University of California Press.

Snodgrass, A. M. (1965) "The Hoplite Reform and History," *JHS* 85, 110–122.

Spivey, N. and Stoddart, S. (1990) *Etruscan Italy: An archaeological history*, London: Batsford, 127–139.

Stary, P. F. (1981) *Zur eisenzeitlichen Bewaffnung und Kampfesweise in Mittelitalien. (Marburger Studien zur Vor- und Frühgeschichte, 3.)* Mainz: Philipp von Zabern.

Torelli, M. (1981) *Storia degli Etruschi*, Rome-Bari: Editori Laterza.

——(1987) *La società etrusca. L'età arcaica, l'età classica*, Rome: Nuova Italia Scientifica.

Turfa MacIntosh, J. (2005) *Catalogue of the Etruscan Gallery of the University of Pennsylvania Museum of Archaeology and Anthropology*, Philadelphia: University of Pennsylvania Museum.

Turnure, J. (1965) "Etruscan ritual armor," *AJA* 69, 39–48.

CHAPTER THIRTY NINE

THE ART OF THE ETRUSCAN ARMOURER

———•◆•———

Ross H. Cowan

The legend of Mamurius Veturius, who crafted perfect replicas of the *ancile* for Numa
Pompilius (Ov. *Fast.* 3.379–392), reflects the skills of the armourers of Etruria and
Central Italy, and the expectations of their patrons in the eighth and seventh centuries.
Take, for example, the unique "poncho" cuirass crafted for a chief of Narce (Fig. 39.1) in
the final quarter of the eighth century (all dates BC). Tailored to fit an individual with
very broad shoulders and a heavily muscled chest, the cuirass, formed from a single sheet
of bronze and extensively decorated in repoussé, is a fine example of form and function.
This combination would continue to characterize Etruscan and Faliscan arms and armour
for another 450 years.[1]

If we leap forward in time to about 475, an armourer of Vulci fashioned an exceptional
cuirass for a nobleman from Lanuvium in Latium. It is by far the earliest surviving

Figure 39.1   Poncho cuirass from Narce, Tomb 43 © University of Pennsylvania Museum of
Archaeology and Anthropology, image no. 152663.

example of the muscle cuirass. Despite its early date, the Lanuvium cuirass is remarkably advanced; the muscle cuirass was probably developed by Italiote Greeks, but the form was rapidly adopted and adapted by the armourers of Etruria (Fig. 39.2).[2]

The musculature of the Lanuvium cuirass is exaggerated and stylized, features which continued to distinguish Etruscan cuirasses from the more naturalistic Italiote examples into the fourth and early third centuries. The musculature of another Vulcian cuirass, but dating to the second half of the fourth century, is remarkably similar to the Lanuvium cuirass. Other later fourth to early third century Etruscan cuirasses have markedly stylized musculature: two examples from Bomarzo, including one that was ritually destroyed; the cuirass from the Tomb of the Warrior, Settecamini necropolis, Orvieto (Fig. 39.3); and an example of uncertain provenance in Karlsruhe. The inscribed cavalry cuirass from Falerii

Figure 39.2 Panoply of the Warrior of Lanuvium. National Museum of Rome
© Ursus/Wikimedia Commons.

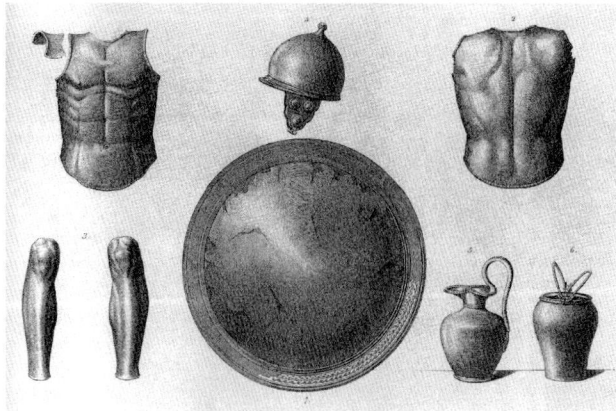

Figure 39.3 Panoply from the Tomb of the Warrior, Settecamini necropolis, Orvieto.
Note the Montefortino helmet with triple-disc cheek guards, after G. C. Conestabile (1865)
Pitture murale a fresco, Florence: tav. 12.

(made especially wide at the hips to facilitate riding) is more naturalistic and assumed to be of Italiote manufacture. However, the treatment of the pectoral muscles, and the strong line running from the neck to the belly button, is reminiscent of the style of Etruscan cuirasses (Fig 39.4). Such armour had to be made to measure (cf. Xen. *Mem.* 3.10.9), and one wonders if the cuirass was the work of an Etruscan or Faliscan armourer. Like the Warrior of Lanuvium, did a wealthy Faliscan *eques* commission his fitted armour from a Central Italian artisan?[3]

It is often assumed that muscle cuirasses were hammered from bronze sheet, but the breastplate of an Italiote example appears to have been roughly cast and then hammered into its final shape (Fig 39.5). A triple-disc cuirass, of a type cast in matrices by Italiote armourers for Oscan warriors, was apparently discovered at Vulci. It is possible that a Vulcian armourer copied the casting technique, but it seems more likely that it arrived there by trade or as booty.[4]

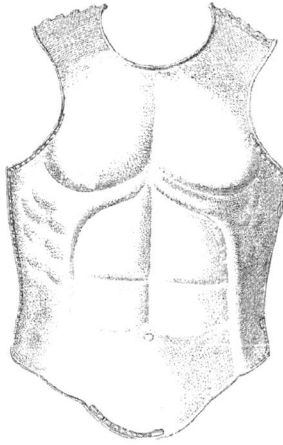

Figure 39.4   Etruscan cuirass with stylized musculature in Karlsruhe, after A. Baumeister (1888) *Denkmäler des klassischen Altertums*, Leipzig: abb. 2246.

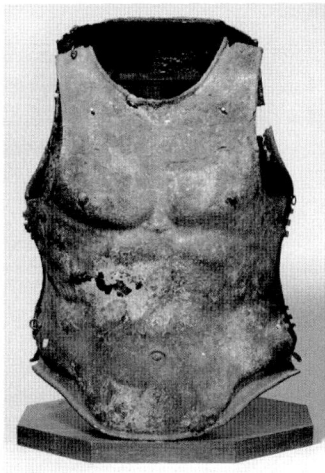

Figure 39.5   Italiote cuirass from Ruvo with naturalistic musculature © Trustees of the British Museum.

The Warrior of Lanuvium was armed with an axe, a spear, two javelins (perhaps actually a short proto-*pilum* and a *sauroter*), and a massive *kopis*, 81.7 cm in length. This curved sword was perhaps an Etruscan innovation. Already in the seventh century a swordsmith succeeded in making a *kopis* with a pattern-welded blade for a warrior of Vetulonia. A spear head from Montefiascone (fourth century) and a sword blade from Chiusi (third century), forged from alternating layers of hard and soft iron, also demonstrate advanced production techniques, but such high standards cannot be assumed for all Etruscan weaponry.[5]

A fine Vulcian helmet of cast bronze, with decorative eyes of silver, gold and glass paste, protected the head of the Warrior of Lanuvium. It was a variant of the Negau-type, which was ultimately derived from the "pot" helmet (Fig. 39.6). In the first half of the seventh century, a Vetulonian armourer produced a helmet with a one-piece, rather than a composite, bowl. It was the proto-type of the Central Italian pot helmet.

By the later seventh century, the Vetulonia helmet had crossed the Apennines and Picene smiths produced their own adaptations, the first being the Montegiorgio Piceno-type, which, in the first half of the sixth century, developed into the Montelparo-type with embossed decoration of animal horns and ears (Fig. 39.7), and a waist between bowl and

Figure 39.6 Vetulonia-type pot helmet from the Tomb of the Duke, Vetulonia.
After *Notizie degli scavi*, 1887, tav. 14.

Figure 39.7 Montegiorgio Piceno helmet from Ancona © Trustees of the British Museum.

turned brim. This, in turn, evolved into the mid-sixth century Belmonte-type, with a medial ridge running along the bowl and splitting into volutes above the brow. This was the earliest form of the famed Negau helmet (named after the find-spot of a late variant in Slovenia). Vetulonia, Montegiorgio, Montelparo (Fig. 39.8) and some Belmonte helmets feature bosses: small and located near the crown (Vetulonia, early Montegiorgio), or large, hemispherical and filled with lead, and placed on the sides of the bowl (later Montegiorgio, Montelparo and Belmonte). Their purpose was probably defensive rather than decorative, because Central Italian warriors fought at close quarters with swords, maces and axes, concentrating on blows to the head. A high proportion of male skeletons from the early Samnite necropolis at Aufidena exhibit serious cranial trauma.[6]

The Etruscans adopted the new Negau helmet and made it their own (Fig. 39.9). The earliest Etruscan variant, the Volterra-type (Fig. 39.10), dates to the third quarter of the sixth century. It dispensed with the volutes of the Belmonte, but some examples are highly decorative. The best-known type of Negau, which predominated from the end of the sixth century, is also named after Vetulonia. Simple but elegant in style, it remained popular into the fourth century. Vulci was probably a production centre for Negau helmets. Pegasus and Bellerophon crest holders, and prancing horse protomes seem to be "trademarks" of Vulcian workshops.[7]

Figure 39.8   Montelparo helmet from Cannae © Trustees of the British Museum.

Figure 39.9   Picene helmet demonstrating transition from the Montelparo-type to the Belmonte-type Negau © Culture and Sport Glasgow (Museums).

Vetulonia-type Negau helmets seem to have been cast as blanks and then worked into shape by hammering (Fig. 39.11). An extravagantly decorated *prunkhelm* of Etruscan (Vulcian?) manufacture, but discovered in a tomb in Lombardy, was completely cast. Early Etruscan versions of Corinthian helmets (some composed of two halves) were hammered from sheet bronze, but later examples of much thicker metal (including the Chalcidian variant), may have been cast as blanks and then hammered. In the fourth century, Etruscan armourers perfected their adaptation of the Gallic helmet, best known as the Montefortino-type (Fig. 39.12). These were cast by the lost wax method: an example now in Philadelphia retains a partial fingerprint from the original wax model. Arretium was a major producer of this helmet (and of *pila*) in the third century (Liv. 28.45.15).[8] Other Etruscan and Faliscan armour included simple pectoral breastplates (Fig. 39.13), linen and scale (or lamellar) corselets (Fig. 39.14) (as worn by the Mars of Todi), greaves,

Figure 39.10   Volterra-type Negau helmet. Note the horse protome © University of Pennsylvania Museum of Archaeology and Anthropology, image no. 151540.

Figure 39.11   Vetulonia-type Negau helmet captured by the Syracusans off Cumae in 474 © Trustees of the British Museum.

Figure 39.12   Cast Montefortino helmet © University of Pennsylvania Museum of Archaeology and
Anthropology, image no. 151537.

Figure 39.13   Votive statuette of a warrior wearing a fabric corselet reinforced with metal plates
(420–400) © Trustees of the British Museum.

and supplementary armour like belly, thigh and arm guards. Although most examples
are of early date, pectorals are still depicted in the art of the fourth century; a bronze
belly guard from Perugia (Fig. 39.15) was perhaps intended for use with a pectoral.
Thigh guards are worn by warriors depicted on a temple acroterium from Falerii (early

Figure 39.14 Votive statuette of a warrior in a scale or lamellar corselet. Burrell Collection (Glasgow Museums) © Ross H. Cowan.

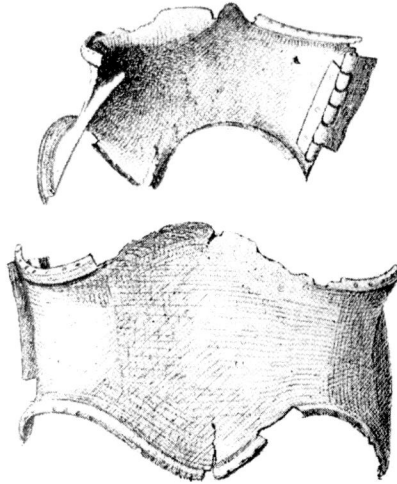

Figure 39.15 Belly guard from Perugia, after Messerschmidt 1932, tav. 25.

fifth century). Similar short thigh guards are worn by the figure of Achle on the Torre San Severo (Orvieto) sarcophagus (circa 300) (Fig. 39.16). He also wears upper and lower guards on both arms; combined with his greaves and muscle cuirass, he is protected by a full "suit" of plate armour. A pair of upper and lower wraparound arm guards, strikingly similar to those depicted on the sarcophagus but sixth or fifth century in date, were amongst the armour excavated from a tomb at Aufidena. A fragment of bronze plate from the Tomb of the Warrior, Settecamini (Orvieto) may belong to an arm guard.[9]

From the mid-seventh century, the Etruscan warrior fought with the bronze-faced *aspis* (Fig. 39.17). Complete facings exist from the Tombs of the Warriors at Vulci (circa 520) and Settecamini (Orvieto), but the most important example is the fifth or fourth century shield from Bomarzo. It retains substantial parts of its wooden core and fragments of leather lining.[10]

Despite a Roman assertion to the contrary (*Ineditum Vaticanum* 3), use of the Greek shield did not turn Etruscan warriors into hoplites, for it was used in combination with javelin, axe and *kopis*. The axe is more prominent in the seventh and sixth centuries; the late seventh century stele from Vetulonia of Auvele Feluskes is the classic image of the combination of battle-axe and *aspis*. The *kopis* remained popular throughout our period. Early examples, such as from Bomarzo, were cutting weapons. The blade of the later *kopis* had a curved edge on one side, a straight back on the other, and a point for thrusting (Fig. 39.18). Other cut-and-thrust swords were in use, mostly adapted from Greek models, but in the fourth century Etruscan warriors were experimenting with straight-edged blades inspired by the swords of the Senones and Boii.[11] A Roman tradition attributed the invention of the *pilum* to legendary Tyrrhenus (Plin. *HN* 7.201), and an Etruscan example of

Figure 39.16 Fully-armoured Achle on the Torre San Severo sarcophagus. Museo Faina, Orvieto © J. D. Lasica.

Figure 39.17 *Kopis* and *aspis* equipped warrior on an Etruscan oinochoe, 520–510 © Trustees of the British Museum.

the javelin, with a notably long shank, comes from Vulci (possibly fourth century). The arms frieze in the Giglioli Tomb at Tarquinia (circa 300) depicts a trio of *pila* between a pair of *aspides*, demonstrating that they were used together, just like the classic Roman combination of *pilum* and *scutum*. Perhaps as an indication of their importance in Etruscan warfare, the *pila* were painted above the main sarcophagus in the tomb.[12] The arms and armour of the Etruscans give us clues to their fighting style. The javelin is a weapon of fluid open order combat. The *kopis* and axe, being weapons of individual combat, were not appropriate to the close-order phalanx of the Greek hoplite. Equally, the large Etruscan *aspis*, up to 95 cm in diameter, is quite appropriate for use in open-order combat. That Etruscan warriors required armourers to produce limb protectors, and smiths to forge *pila* and battle-axes, indicates their method of fighting was the opposite of that practiced by hoplite spearmen, who fought shoulder to shoulder and enjoyed the supplementary protection of their comrades' shields (Thuc. 5.71.1). Livy's picture of late fourth century Etruscans, organized in maniples and fighting with javelins and swords (9.39.5–11), is probably accurate (Fig. 39.19).

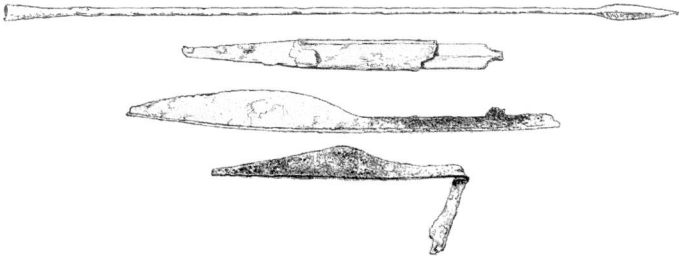

Figure 39.18 From top, the exceptionally long *pilum* from Vulci (1.2 m), and Gallic-style (in scabbard) and late *kopis*-type swords from Perugia. After Reinach 1907, Fig. 5 and Messerschmidt 1932, tav. 25, 28.

Figure 39.19 Statuette of Maris or Laran, 475–450. The modelling of the right hand shows that it originally held a javelin with a throwing thong. The *porpax* (armband) of an *aspis* remains attached to the left arm © Trustees of the British Museum.

NOTES

1 Turfa 2005, 111.
2 Lanuvium: Zevi 1993, 434–437. Development: Jarva 1995, 30–32.
3 Vulci: Cahn 1989, 84–86. Bomarzo: Buranelli 1992, 96; Buranelli and Sannibale 1998, 229–233. Orvieto: Adembri 1982, 77–78; Karlsruhe: Hagemann 1919, 47. Falerii: Zimmermann 1986.
4 Italiote: Peltz 2004. Vulci: Connolly 1986, 118; Treister 2001, 209–210.
5 Lanuvium: Zevi 1993, 417–419. Innovation: Connolly 2006, 99; Stary 1979, 196 is less sure. Vetulonia, Chiusi swords: Mapelli 2006. Montefiascone: Pansieri and Leoni 1966.
6 Lanuvium: Zevi 1993, 431–434. Such highly decorative helmets have been labeled *prunkhelme* (Egg 1988, 250–254), a better description than "parade helmet," which assumes flamboyant armour was reserved for ceremonial purposes. Development from Vetulonia- to Belmonte-type: Egg 1986, 6–17; 44–48; Cowan 2007. Cranial trauma: Paine 2007.
7 Etruscan Negau-types: Egg 1986, 41–64; Egg 1988, 243–250. Vulci "trademarks": Ferraguti 1937, 118; Neugebauer 1943.
8 Negau: Feugère and Freises 1994. Corinthian: Weiss 1977; Manti and Watkinson 2008. *Prunkhelm*: Egg 1988, 250. Montefortino: Born 1991; Turfa 2005, 146–147.
9 Fabric, scale/lamellar, pectorals: Connolly 2006, 97–100. Pectoral in art: Blázquez 1960; cf. Polyb. 6.23.14 for Roman use of pectorals in the third century. Belly guards: Jarva 1995, 59–60; Hill 1982 (Capena, seventh century); Messerschmidt 1932, 512 (Perugia, fourth century). Limb guards: Beazley 1947: 91, 136–137; Jarva 1995, 74–75, 82–83 (Falerii). Torre San Severo: Galli 1916. Aufidena: Mariani 1901, 579. Orvieto: Adembri 1982, 84–85.
10 Vulci: Ferraguti 1937, 116. Orvieto: Adembri 1982, 79. Bomarzo: Blyth 1982.
11 Axe: Stary 1979, 188 and 192. For an axe from a later fourth to early third century warrior tomb at Castellonchio (Orvieto), see D. Diffendale (2007) "Central Italian Panoplies – 4ᵗʰ c. BC Umbria," online: http://www.sas.upenn.edu/~dpd/italica/armor/c-panoplies.html (accessed 25 October 2011). Auvele Feluskes: Maggiani 2007. Bomarzo *kopis*: Buranelli 1992, 101. Late *kopis*, Gallic sword: Messerschmidt 1932, 512, 518 (Perugia). Other swords: Connolly 2006, 98–99.
12 Vulci: Reinach 1907 (II), 129–130. Giglioli: Cristofani 1967; Connolly 2006, 100.

BIBLIOGRAPHY

Adembri, B. (1982) "La Tomba del Guerriero" in *Pittura etrusca a Orvieto*, Rome: Kappa, 75–85.
Beazley, J. D. (1947) *Etruscan Vase-Painting*, Oxford: Clarendon Press.
Blázquez, J. M. (1960) "Espejos etruscos figurados del Museo Arqueológico Nacional de Madrid," *Archivo Español de Arqueología*, 33: 145–155.
Blyth, P. H. (1982) "The Structure of the Hoplite Shield in the Museo Gregoriano Etrusco," *Bollettino Monumenti, Musei e Galerie Pontificie*, 3: 5–21.
Born, H. (1991) "Zur Herstellung der etruskischen Bronzehelme mit Scheitelknauf," *Archäologisches Korrespondenzblatt*, 21: 73–78.
Buranelli, F. (1992) *The Etruscans: Legacy of a Lost Civilization*, Memphis: Lithograph.
Buranelli, F. and Sannibale, M. (1998) "Reparto Antichità Etrusco-Italiche (1984–1996)," *Bollettino Monumenti Musei e Gallerie Pontificie*, 18: 139–441.
Cahn, D. (1989) *Waffen und Zaumzeug*, Basel: Antikenmuseum Basel und Sammlung Ludwig.
Connolly, P. (1986) "Notes on the Development of Breastplates in Southern Italy" in J. Swaddling (ed.), *Italian Iron Age Artefacts in the British Museum*, London: British Museum Publications, 117–125.
——(rev. edn 2006) *Greece and Rome at War*, London: Greenhill.

Cowan, R. H. (2007) "An Important Italic Helmet Rediscovered," *Archäologisches Korrespondenzblatt*, 37: 379–387.

Cristofani, M. (1967) "Il fregio d'armi della Tomba Giglioli di Tarquinia," *Dialoghi di Archeologia*, 1: 288–303.

Egg, M. (1986) *Italische Helme: Studien zu den ältereisenzeitlichen Helmen Italiens und der Alpen*, Mainz: Verlag des Römisch-Germanischen Zentralmuseums.

——(1988) "Italische Helme mit Krempe" in A. Bottini, *et al.* (eds), *Antike Helme*, Mainz: Verlag des Römisch-Germanischen Zentralmuseums.

Ferraguti, U. (1937) "I bronzi di Vulci," *Studi Etruschi*, 11: 107–120.

Feugère, M. and Freises, A. (1994) "Un casque étrusque du Ve siècle av. notre ère trouvé en mer près d'Agde (Hérault)," *Revue archéologique de Narbonnaise*, 27–28: 1–7.

Galli, E. (1916) "Il Sarcofago etrusco di Torre San Severo," *Monumenti Antichi*, 24: 5–114.

Hagemann, A. (1919) *Griechische Panzerung*, Leipzig: B. G. Teubner.

Hill, D. K. (1982) "Early Italic Armor at Vassar College," *American Journal of Archaeology*, 86: 589–591.

Jarva, E. (1995) *Archaiologia on Archaic Greek Body Armour*, Rovaniemi: Pohjois-Suomen Historiallinen Yhdistys.

Maggiani, A. (2007) "Auvele Feluskes: della Stele di Vetulonia e di altre dell' Etruria settentrionale," *Rivista di Archeologia*, 31: 67–75.

Manti, P. and Watkinson, D. (2008) "From Homer to Hoplite: Scientific Investigations of Greek Copper Alloy Helmets" in S. A. Piapetis (ed.), *Science and Technology in Homeric Epics*, Dordrecht: Springer, 167–179.

Mapelli, C., Nicodemi, W., Venturini, R. and Riva, R. (2006) "Risultati derivanti da nuovi esami realizzati su manufatti bellici del VII a.C. e III a.C. rinvenuti in Etruria," *Metallurgia Italiana*, 98: 15–24.

Mariani, L. (1901) "Aufidena," *Monumenti Antichi*, 10: 225–638.

Messerschmidt, F. (1932) "Inedita Etruria," *Studi Etruschi*, 6: 509–524.

Neugebauer, K. A. (1943) "Archaische Vulcenter Bronzen," *Jahrbuch des Deutschen Archaologischen Instituts*, 58: 206–278.

Paine, R. R., Macinelli, D., Ruggieri, M. and Coppia, A. (2007) "Cranial Trauma in Iron Age Samnite Agriculturalists, Alfedena, Italy," *American Journal of Physical Anthropology*, 132: 48–58.

Panseri, C. and Leoni, M. (1966) "Sulla tecnica di fabbricazione delle armi in ferro presso gli Etruschi: Esame di una cuspide di lancia del IV Sec. a.C. da Montefiascone," *Metallurgia Italiana*, 10: 381–389.

Peltz, U. (2004) "Ein apulischer Brustpanzer – seine Restaurierung und Überlegungen zur Herstellung," *Beiträge zur Erhaltung von Kunst-und Kulturgut*, 1: 81–88.

Reinach, A. (1907) "L'origine du *pilum*," *Revue Archéologique*, I: 243–252 and 425–425; II: 125–136 and 226–244.

Stary, P. (1979) "Foreign Elements in Etruscan Arms and Armour: 8th to 3rd Centuries BC," *Proceedings of the Prehistoric Society*, 45: 179–206.

Treister, M. Y. (2001) *Hammering Techniques in Greek and Roman Jewellery and Toreutics*, Leiden: Brill.

Turfa, J. M. (2005) *Catalogue of the Etruscan Gallery of the University of Pennsylvania Museum of Archaeology and Anthropology*, Philadelphia: University of Pennsylvania Press.

Weiss, C. (1977) "An Unusual Corinthian Helmet," *California Studies in Classical Antiquity*, 10: 195–207.

Zevi, F. (1993) "La tomba del Guerriero di Lanuvio" in *Spectacles sportifs et sceniques dans le monde etrusco-italique*, Rome: École française de Rome, 409–442.

Zimmerman, J.-L. (1986) "La fin de Falerii Veteres: Un témoignage archéologique," *Getty Museum Journal*, 14: 37–42.

CHAPTER FORTY

SEAFARING: SHIP BUILDING, HARBORS, THE ISSUE OF PIRACY

——— •◆• ———

Stefano Bruni

The historical importance of the relationship between the Etruscan world and the sea was cultivated by the ancients themselves, and became one of the recurrent themes in the discussions of Greco-Roman ethnography concerning the Etruscans. From Poseidonius, quoted by Diodorus (5.40.2), Late Hellenistic historiography has repeatedly emphasized the intimate connection of the Etruscans with the sea, noting that the district of the Mediterranean, which according to its geographical orientation the Greeks called θάλασσα νότια and the Romans *mare inferum* (cf. Pliny *NH* 3.75) more commonly took on the name of τυρρηνικόν πέλαγος/*mare tuscum* not because it washed the coast of Etruria, but because the Etruscans had exercised a lasting dominion over that sea, such that a late tradition also attributed the name of the hero Tyrrhenos to the Ionian Sea (Isid., *Etym.* 13.16, derived from Serv. *Ad Aeneid.* 3.211) and the island of Malta would itself be εν τῷ τυρρηνικῷ πελάγαι (Schol.Clem.Alex. 337.26). Equally, the sea from the other side of the Peninsula, the *mare superum*, has assumed for its northern mirror, namely that area facing the Gulf of Trieste and the area of the Po delta, the name Adriatic from Adria, *Tuscorum colonia*, as Livy noted also in a famous passage which summarizes the earlier traditions (5.33.7–8). If, in regard to this last district, a passage in Hecataeus (fr. 99 Nenci) dates the use of this name back at least to the end of the sixth century BC, and in the advanced fourth century BC, it will extend to the entire middle Adriatic coast, all the way to the Gargano, then the name of the Tyrrhenian Sea seems to boast a tradition just as old, as indicated by a famous fragment of the *Triptolemos* of Sophocles quoted by Dionysius of Halicarnassus (1.12.2), which records the τυρσενικός κόλπος, the "gulf," or better the sea, (cf. Thuc. 6.62) "of the Tyrrhenians."

Inasmuch as the name of the Etruscans does not appear in the list of thalassocracies handed down by Eusebius (*Chronikon* 1.225) and recorded by Diodorus (7.11), who had perhaps derived it from an historian of the fifth century BC, the ancient literature recalls several times how the Etruscans had exercised dominion over the sea for a long time (Diod. 5.40.2; 11.51; Dion. Hal. 1.11; Strabo 5.2.5 C 222; Livy 5.33.7).

However, it remains difficult to determine the coordinates of the complex map of this thalassocracy, also an echo of the Etruscans as *thalassokrátores*, "rulers of the seas," that remain in the memory of numerous ventures throughout the Mediterranean basin. In addition to the episode of the epic confrontation in the waters of the Sardinian Sea shortly after the middle of the sixth century BC (Herodotus 1.163–167; Justin 18.7.11 and 43.5.2; and also Strabo 6.1.1 C 252; Paus. 10.8.6–7 and 18.7), or that of the battle off the promontory of Cumae in 474 BC (Diod. 11.51), or again the participation, on the side of the Athenians, in the summer of 414/413 BC in the siege of Syracuse by sending three pentekonters (Thuc. 6.103.2), the sources recall the presence of Etruscans who were driven to Lipari (Callimac. Frg. 93 Pfeiffer; Strabo 6.2.10 C 275) and were in the waters of the Strait of Sicily, where in the first decades of the fifth century BC, the tyrant of Rhegion, Anaxilaos, fortified the Isthmus of Skyllation in order to protect the zone against the Tyrrhenians (Strabo 6.1.5 C 257). Etruscans were also in Sardinia (Strabo 5.2.7 C 225), in Corsica (Diod. 5.13), in the Balaeric Islands and the Iberian Peninsula (Steph. s.v. *Banaurides*; Auson. *Epist.* 27.88–89), all the way to the far west, beyond the Pillars of Heracles, where they had tried to settle on an Atlantic island in the region of Cadiz (Diod. 5.20), to which the recent news of an exceptional discovery of a large deposit of Etruscan material of the First Iron Age at Huelva, the main port of Tartessos, provides an important historical perspective. The fame of the seapower of the Etruscans had to have been very great, however, if in the fourth century BC (if not a century earlier), there were attributed to the Tyrrhenoi some ventures such as the kidnapping of the statue of Hera from Samos (Menodot. *FGrHist* 541 F 1 = Athen. 15.671e – 674a), or the raids on Attica with which was associated the establishment of the cult of Aphrodite Koltas (Suid., s.v. Κώλτας), or even the abduction of young girls from Brauron (Philoc. *FGrHist* 328 F 100, and also *FGrHist* 328 F 101 [= schol. Hom. *Il.* 1.594]; Plut. *Mul.virt.* 8 and *Aetia gr.* 21), which the oldest tradition unanimously referred to the Pelasgians, as evidenced, in this last case, by the lost tragedies, the *Hypsipyle* of Aeschylus and the *Lemniai* of Sophocles, as well as Herodotus (6.138.1 and also 4.145.2). The phenomenon is undoubtedly complex and seems to be related to piracy, the activities practiced by the descendants of the Pelasgians who inhabited the Chalcidice region and Lemnos. The presence of the Etruscans in the eastern basin of the Mediterranean, however, need not have been episodic or limited to the network of trade routes. This is confirmed by an inscription of 299 BC, which mentions that the inhabitants of Delos were forced to borrow five thousand drachmas from the temple treasury to prepare defenses against the *"Tyrrhenoi"* (*IG* 11, 2, 148, 73 – 74).

In the Greek and Latin sources, the Etruscan world seems to be a blurred reality, in any case, inasmuch as it is complex, and it is not always easy to recognize the various components in their actual historical dimension; Etruria was a limited geographical reality, yet full of particular connotations where, as is natural, the various voices that refer to the entire area give glimpses of distinct and different events, and also the phenomenon of thalassocracy will be measured on the scale of these individual entities at the cost of compromised understanding – or at least of a merely generic view of its history.

The participants in this adventure are, of course, the *poleis* ("city-states") of the Tyrrhenian *paralia* ("shore"), and, on the Adriatic coast, the centers of Adria and Spina, to which will be added, at the end of the fourth century BC, Ravenna. However, the case of Vel Kaikna, who was buried in *Felsina* (Bologna) but who was in all likelihood a *navarch* (commander of a warship) at Spina, in a complex and highly-organized territorial political system that sees that center as a civil and military port at the mouth of the Po serving the entire sector of *Etruria padana* ("Etruria of the Po region": Sassatelli 2009; see Chapter 15), gives a glimpse of a situation that is much more complicated.

If one excludes Populonia, the only *polis* of Etruria located on the sea and which had its own port adjacent to the city with a landing and two docks at the foot of the promontory on which stood the settlement (see Strabo 5.2.6 C 223), all the other cities were located at some distance from the coast and their ports were completely separate, standing along the coast, according to the strategies of the population that were evaluated so positively in a famous passage of Aristotle's *Politics* (7.4).

The loss of the *periplus* (a written account of a sailing circuit) of Etruria in the *portolan* attributed to Scylax of Caryanda (cf. § 17) has deprived us of an important source for understanding the panorama that Etruria offered during the course of the Late Archaic period. Only the *periplus* of Etruria by Pomponius Mela (*Chorographia* 2.65) records for the Etruscan coasts the ports of *Pyrgi, Minio, Castrum Novum, Gravisae, Cosa, Telamon, Populonia, Caecina, Pisa*; but if the presence of *Telamon* (modern Talamone) along the coast, on a promontory at the northern shore of the estuary of the Osa, which disappeared during the civil war between the Sullans and Marians in the years between 82 and 80 BC, provides a secure *terminus ante quem* for the chronology of this situation, the landscape described by Mela is one that was created by the Romanization of the region and is, in substance, comparable to the text of Strabo and to the maritime geography of the ports of Etruria in the Augustan period offered by Virgil's listing of the maritime allies of Aeneas.

Yet the evidence of the finds permits us to recognize many harbors along the coast of Etruria and ports of some importance, sometimes located near the mouths of rivers and streams. For each *polis* was linked to an *epineion* ("seaport"), sometimes flanked by landings and/or minor ports in a complex system of infrastructures that mark the relationship of the various cities with the sea.

This is the case of Cerveteri, which from the first Archaic phase maintained its principal port at Pyrgi, 13 kilometers distant from the city and connected to it by a monumental roadway, built in the first half of the sixth century BC, and which was complemented by the ports of Alsium to the south, near modern Palo, and of Punicum in the north, corresponding to the town of Santa Marinella. Similarly, at the opposite end, just before the Ligurian Sea, in the case of Pisa, at one time distant from the shore by 20 stadia (Strabo 5.2.5 C 222), or less than four kilometers, within a structured landscape hemmed by lagoons – very different from today – and marked by the courses of the Arno and the Auser, there existed a complex system of ports and minor landings directly linked to the city and to some extent controlled by it, distributed along the coast of the Tyrrhenian Sea from the mouth of the Fine in the south to the area in the north where, in around 177 BC, Luni was founded. Alongside some minor landings, ground surveys have made it possible to glimpse from the Archaic period on a port district in the area of the early medieval basilica of San Piero a Grado near the mouth of the northern branch of the Arno, a site that seems, albeit with changes, and in its surroundings still partly obscure, to have preserved the character of the first ports of call of the Tyrrhenian routes related to Pisa in Roman times. In fact, a tradition that dates back to the Carolingian period fixed in this location the first landing of the Apostle Peter on his voyage to Rome in 42 or 61 AD. A second *epineion*, known in modern antiquarian literature as "Porto delle Conche," must have been situated to the north, at the mouth of the Auser, to which must be related the harbor located in the north-west of the settlement that was brought to light by the excavations begun in 1998 and still in progress, in the area of the railway station of "Pisa – San Rossore." Beginning with the end of the fourth–beginning of the third century BC, a third port comes to mark the extension of Pisa over the sea, nine miles south of the *epineion* of San Piero a Grado, in the inlet between the present-day mouth of the Calambrone, Santo Stefano ai Lupi; and the promontory of Livorno develops what Roman tradition will remember by the name of *Portus Pisanus*, an infrastructure that, since the third century BC, has played a leading role in the field of trade that was directed toward Rome, whether in relation to commercial developments and especially in the realm of political policy surrounding the confrontations with Sardinia, Gaul and the Iberian region (see Polybius 2.27.1; 28.1; Livy 21.39; Polybius 3.56.5; and also 3.96.9), this being the only port to the north of Populonia before the foundation of Luni in 177 BC (even though a landing certainly existed here by the end of the third century BC).

The Tyrrhenian coast was thus marked by a complex series of ports and docks. If a passage of Dionysius (3.44.1) observes that the mouth of the Tiber did not present port inlets, a port of call should rather be found at the mouth of the river, as suggested by the tradition that attributed to Ancus Martius (fourth king of Rome, seventh century BC) the foundation of Ostia and the organization of the salt pans on the left bank. From there the course of the river went up, marked by a thorough and widespread series of docks and vital river harbors ever since the first Archaic phase. Further north it was the port at the mouth of the Arrone, near modern Fregene, in connection with the city of Veii. Then, after the landings in the territory of Cerveteri, the ports of Tarquinia were developing, *Graviscae* and further north, *Martanum* on the right bank of the Marta, near the mouth of the ditch of Bandita di Pian di Spille, where a dock has been identified that is certainly related to an artisanal workshop of the Late Hellenistic period. In connection with Vulci there was the port of *Regae/Regisvilla*, identified in the area of Le Murelle on the coast of Montalto di Castro, while further north, after the port of *Telamon* and various smaller landings were found the ports of call of the Argentario, whose function corresponds to the actual route to the Island of Giglio, then the port of Umbro at the mouth of the Ombrone associated with Roselle, while for Vetulonia there must have been a dock on Lake Prile. After Populonia and the system of ports and landings on Elba, in the area to the right of the mouth of the Cecina was found the port of Vada Volaterrana and then, after the course of the Fina, the series of ports of the Pisan territory, from Quercianella to the mouth of the Rogiolo, to which are added, at the beginning of the Hellenistic period, Castiglioncello and some minor landings in the various coves along the coast of Livorno, to the settlement at the tip of Livorno, and up to the coast of Versilia, studded by a dense and varied series of coastal settlements ever since the full Archaic period.

In the absence of concrete remains of the various docks and infrastructure of the ports of call very little is known of the port facilities. The issue of archaeology of the ports of the Etruscans remains, in essence, an irritating problem, to repeat the expression used over fifty years ago by Le Gall referring to navigation on the Tiber, and only recently has it seen a revival of research on the subject; still, the little that is known offers a glimpse of a very complex and articulated situation, even on a purely architectural level. While the uncertainty of their history remains, there is the realization of impressive architectural works, perhaps dating to the Late Archaic period in the docking basin of Gravisca, and reported in the zone of Porto Clementino at Tarquinia, while investigations in the urban cove area of Pisa showed that already at the turn of the fifth century BC, probably in relation to the changing techniques of naval engineering, the functional structures for dry-docking ships come to be remodeled, when the wooden ramps made in the manner of the moorings of the Archaic period, which functioned to draw boats out of the water for dry-docking, are replaced with quays made of stone and wood, which were to moor the various boats and with which all the operations could take place that normally were performed inside the port basin.

It is a widely held opinion that the main source of the Etruscan thalassocracy should be identified in Caere, which would be joined by Vulci and Tarquinia, to varying degrees and in different timeframes, after the setback marked by the battle of Cumae in 474 BC, first, and by the incursions of Syracuse in 453 BC in the Upper Tyrrhenian, and then, at the end of the fifth century BC, Tarquinia seems to assume some sort of leadership on the sea, leading the expedition, alongside the Athenians, against Syracuse, if we are to believe a Latin inscription that commemorates the venture of a noble Tarquinian, Velthur Spurinna, the first Etruscan leader to have crossed the sea with an army, reaching Sicily, and that gives us, perhaps not without uncertainties, the name of the commander of the Etruscan contingent that participated in the siege of Syracuse in 413 BC. However, even the centers of the northern district must have exercised an extensive command of the sea. Among these certainly Pisa, whose projection into the Tyrrhenian Sea, overshadowed by the characteristics of the material culture of the center ever since the earliest origins of the settlement, is confirmed by the ideology underlying the "royalty" of the *princeps* for whom, at the turn of the eighth century BC, or shortly after, the monumental tumulus of via San Jacopo was erected, or by the spread of artistic products of the city over a wide area of the north-western sector of the Mediterranean starting from the end of the seventh century BC. Another center that participates in this reality is Vetulonia: if in the Orientalizing period it reveals an aristocracy strongly marked by a relationship with the sea, as seems to be shown in the paradigm of the signs of power revealed by the grave goods of the so-called *Circolo del Tridente* ("Circle of the Trident"), then in the course of the Hellenistic era it is ideologically identified with the personage who has the skin of a *ketos* (reptilian sea-monster) displayed on the obverse of the city's coinage, and with the figure holding an oar over his shoulder with his right hand, the eponymous hero or tutelary deity that is identified with the *populus* of the *Vetulonienses* on the relief of the so-called "Throne of Claudius" discovered during the excavations of the theater of the Julio-Claudian era at Cerveteri.

Similar to what may be found for the Greek world, in this age of the oldest dominion over the sea, there were also achievements in the form of piracy, activities closely related to the modalities of the *prexis* of the age of the dominant aristocracies; and not without reason. In a random passage of Ephorus, transmitted by Strabo (6.2.2 C 267), he recounts how the Greeks, in the years before the first *apoikiai* ("colonies"), refrained from sailing for commercial purposes in the waters off Sicily because of the issue of actions by Etruscan pirates.

The ληστήρια of the Tyrrhenians is one of the *topoi* related to the Etruscan world in Greek and Roman tradition, a *topos* that has had a very specific historical situation and sees, among other things, during the fifth century BC the projection by the Greeks into the dimension of myth the disturbing Etruscan presence in the region of the Straits (of Messina). Related to the situation to which Dionysios of Phocaea was opposed at the beginning of the century, and to the Etruscan occupation of Lipari in the years between 485 and 475 BC we should probably also refer the epithet of τυρσηνίς attributed by Euripides (*Medea,* 1342 and 1359) to Scylla, the monster with whom the rocky cliffs above the Strait of Messina were identified, the daughter of Tyrrhenos, according to a tradition noted by one scholiast of the *Republic* of Plato (588 c) and, perhaps, from an uncertain passage of the epitome of Apollodorus (*Ep.* 7.20), who, in contrast to the more common version, already attested in Hecataeus, said Scylla was the daughter of Phorcys.

To the phenomenon of Etruscan piracy of the Archaic period should also be referred the myth of the abduction of Dionysus by the Tyrrhenian pirates and their subsequent punishment by transformation into dolphins, a story most probably developed in Corinth at the close of the seventh century BC, in the more general context of the thriving Corinthian Dionysiac cult, in relation to the dangers that the Etruscan ληισταί presented to the Corinthian *naukleroi* and *emporoi* (shipmasters and merchants) in their navigation to the West. The myth has had a wide circulation and, even if we must expunge the testimony offered by a famous Samian cup of the mid-sixth century BC, because it most likely portrays a file of Dionysian chorus members costumed as dolphins, the animal lovers of dance and song, still the theme is well known in Etruria from the end of the sixth century BC at least up to the early Hellenistic period, as attested on the one hand by a black-figure hydria by the Painter of Vatican 238 (see Fig. 24.19), that came from a tomb in southern coastal Etruria and ended, through the meshes of the antiquities market, at the Museum of Arts of Toledo, and on the other hand, a plate of the Genucilia series found during the excavations of the Curia in the Forum Romanum.

It is, however, within the framework of the anti-Etruscan Athenian propaganda of the late Classical period that the myth played a role of some importance. Apart from recalling that mentioned in the prologue of the *Cyclops* of Euripides (verses 11–17), an important testimony to this saga is the seventh of the hymns attributed to the name of Homer, which, although uncertain and difficult to date, seems to date, at least in the version handed down, not before the end of the fifth century BC, if not in the fourth century BC, given the many reminiscences of formulae and forms rarely attested and taken from Euripides, and in particular, from his *Bacchae*. There is, for example, the same term used to indicate "pirates," the rare Ionic-Attic form ληϊστής, -οῦ in place of ληιστήρ, -ήρος attested in the epic (Hom., *Od.* 3.73; 9.254; 13.427; etc.) and in the Homeric Hymns (*Hym.Cer.* 125; *Hym. Apol.* 454; *Hym. Herm.* 14), but it is present, in addition to Herodotus' (4.17) reference to Dionysius of Phocaea, significantly, in Euripides (fr. 112,1 and fr. 151b,13). To confirm what is probably the fourth century BC date is the use in the hymn at verse 13 of the rare technical verb κατατανύω used to indicate the action of tightening the ropes, which is found only in the treatise *De fracturis* attributed to the *Hippocratic corpus* of Aristotelian date, if not later (cf. 13.53; 19.22; 44.4). In the face of this evidence is the monument erected in Athens in 334 BC by Lysicrates near the Theater of Dionysus, which a long tradition of studies has linked with the venture against the pirates successfully accomplished by Diotimos in 335 BC (cf. *IG* 2, 2, 1263; and also ps.Plut., *Mor.* 844a).

Piracy is a diffuse activity: it was the people of Lipari who in 392 BC captured the tithe of the spoils of Veii that the Roman ambassadors were taking to Delphi (Livy 5.28; Val.Max 1.4; Diod. 14.93); Aeginetans were the ones who on behalf of Sparta made raids against Athenian shipping in 347 BC; Greeks – perhaps Syracusans – were the pirates who in 345 BC infested the sea from Antium to the Tiber (Livy 7.25–26). In the literature of the late Classical period, however, the phenomenon has an especially Etruscan tinge, and it is especially in the full Classical age and the fourth century BC when Etruscan piracy assumed dimensions that had to worry the Greek world, whether Athens, which already in the third quarter of the fifth century BC had contracted *philia* (a compact of friendship) with a Messapian dynast, perhaps the same Artas of the *symmachia* (state military alliance) made on the occasion of the Sicilian expedition of 414–412 BC, to ensure smooth sailing in the area of the *Ionios kolpos* (*IG* 1², 53) and who in 325 BC decreed the establishment of a colony, never realized, in the middle or upper Adriatic, to ensure the φυλακῆς ἐπί τυρρηνοῖς ("guard-post against the Tyrrhenians": *IG* 2, 2, 1629), or instead Syracuse, which in 384 BC promoted a strong expedition of 60 triremes and 40 transport ships, personally led by the same Dionysius, into the north-central Tyrrhenian Sea against Etruscan pirates, during which he attacked and looted the port of Pyrgi and its sanctuary (ps.Aristot. *Oec.* 2, p. 1349 b; Diod. 15.14.3; Strabo 5.2.8 C 226; Aelian. 1.20; Polyaen. 5.2.21; see Chapter 30).

The phenomenon of Etruscan piracy during the second half of the century had reached a significant size and was not limited to the Adriatic district, if indeed it was the Tyrrhenian where the Campanian region was with the base of Postumius who overran the sea with at least 12 ships and in 339 BC appeared in the harbor of Syracuse to offer his services to Timoleon (Diod. 16.82). Equally, the Etruscans of the Tyrrhenian region of southern Etruria, or the group from Campania, must be those pirates who, along with the Antiati (men from Antium/Anzio), were raiding in Magna Graecia and against whom the first Alexander, in 334 BC, and then, near the end of the fourth century BC, Demetrius Poliorcetes, invited Rome to take action (Memnon, *FGrHist* 434 F 18; Strabo 5.3.5 C 232).

If the famous Etruscan helmet dedicated by Hieron at Olympia for the victory in the waters off Cumae (474 BC), now in the British Museum (see Fig. 39.11), together with the other helmet of the Archaeological Museum at Olympia (Fig. 40.1), is an exceptional testimony on the level of monumental evidence, of an episode of Etruscan history on the sea, to which may be added the case of the two helmets from the years around the middle of the fifth century BC, one found at Populonia in the waters of the Gulf of Baratti, the other in the area in front of the necropolis of Buche delle Fate, which then may be suggestive when connected with the events caused by the two Tyrrhenian expeditions of Syracuse in 453 BC, led by Phayllos and Apelles, although a helmet of the same type was recovered from the seabed to the east of the center of Agde, in the Gulf of Lyons, also witnessing a maritime circulation of this type of military equipment, still, archaeological evidence for piracy remains scarce. Inasmuch as the interpretative possibilities are necessarily ambiguous, mute testimony of pirate action seems to be the wreck of the ship found in the waters off the island of Spargi in the archipelago of La Maddalena, in north-western Sardinian waters, the remains of which show traces of a

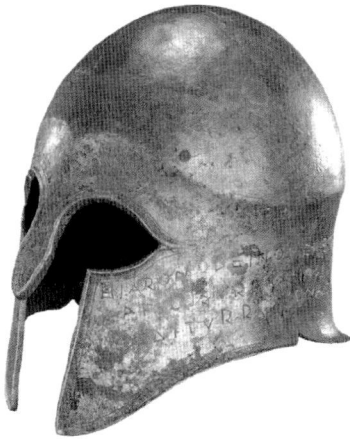

Figure 40.1   Helmet from Olympia. Olympia, Archaeological Museum, inv. M9.

violent impact suffered by the ship, that cannot be attributed to the physical conditions of the seabed or other natural obstacles. A confirmation of the sinking of this cargo vessel (Latin: *navis oneraria*) following a pirate action is also the recovery among the materials of the cargo, which fix the date of the sinking in the last decades of the second century BC, of a fragment of the calotte of a human skull still wearing a bronze helmet, probably belonging to one of the sailors, which is more likely than one of the pirates who had attacked the vessel. Much more ambiguous is the possibility of reading the spearhead found among the materials of the *Bon Porté 1* wreck of the full Archaic period, and equally open to quite a few options of interpretation, is the case of the extraordinary cache of arms (helmets of the class "*a bottone*," Coarelli type C, in bronze and iron, bronze muscle cuirasses, swords, iron spear-points and ends of spears and javelins) found on the beach of the Gulf of Baratti, an area in ancient times certainly set well back from the shoreline in comparison to what it is today, but otherwise associated with the *epineion* of Populonia.

Similarly, there is nothing to identify people who practiced piracy in the finds of the various Etruscan necropoleis, even in a center like Spina, which especially after the Celtization of the inland Po valley in the fourth century BC, had to be at the center of Etruscan piracy in the Adriatic. Since it cannot be ruled out that the headquarters of Adriatic piracy can be recognized in Ravenna, this situation does not seem to depend on the inability of us moderns to read the signs, but rather should be explained by the funerary ideology of this community, which seems oriented according to parameters which exclude from the composition of grave goods expressions of military *areté* ("honor/excellence") and of *polemos* ("war").

As in the case of port facilities, our knowledge of Etruscan naval engineering is also limited. The wrecks definitely known to date are, in substance, many, but in practice limited to a few cases from the southern French coast between Antibes and Agde, to which has recently been added the case of the wreck from Calafuria, found on the seabed immediately south of Livorno, which, with its load of Etruscan amphorae (Py type 4A), and by virtue of the characteristics of other materials stowed on it, including a Massaliote amphora of Bertucchi type 2B and a Phoenico-Punic amphora (of the group of Torres T-1,4 between 2 and 5), seems to be dated to the second half of the fifth–beginning of the fourth century BC. However, if in the case of the wreck of La Love at Cap d'Antibes, and in that of Écueil du Miet 3 in the little archipelago of Marseilleveyre in the Bay of Marseille, of Cassidaigne in the bay of Cassis, or that of Point du Dattier, or in those of Pointe Lequin 1B in front of the north coast of the island of Porquerolles, only materials from the cargoes and on-board equipment are known; the only data available on characteristics of the hulls are for the wrecks of Bon Porté 1 of the second half of the sixth century BC, found off the island of San-Tropez, between Cape Camarat and Cape Taillat, and that excavated only partially in the waters off the south-east of the small peninsula of Giens to the west of the islet of Grand Ribaud (wreck F), dated between the end of the sixth and the first decades of the fifth century BC (Fig. 40.2).

In the case of the wreck of Bon Porté 1 there are more than a few doubts about the origin of the vessel and its *naukleros*. The cargo included about 20 amphorae of Py type 5 of Vulcian production, fewer than 10 amphorae of Massaliote Bertucchi type 1, two specimens of the so-called Corinthian B type from Magna Graecia, and two or three Clazomenian amphorae seem to place the activity of this ship as part of a circuit of a Massaliot *emporos* ("merchant") redistributing goods of various origins. The characteristics of the engineering of the hull would seem to agree with this perspective, a boat a dozen

Figure 40.2 Wreck of Grand Ribaud F in the course of excavation.

meters in length, with a rounded hull and slender at the ends, built according to the archaic technique of assembling the various parts of the hull with ligatures. These features are common techniques in the Mediterranean, but the comparison with one of the wrecks of the Archaic period brought to light in Jules-Verne square in Marseille (wreck 9), which certainly came out of the local shipyards and was made according to the same artisanal tradition, together with the character of the boat, which is lighter and faster, but a small vessel intended for coastal navigation (cabotage), or for fishing, seem to indicate with some likelihood a Massaliote origin for the vessel.

Likewise the hull of the Grand Ribaud F wreck, a vessel at least 20 feet long, if not larger, and with a capacity of between 30 and 38 tons, finds meaningful similarities of engineering with the archaic Greek wreck Jules-Verne 7, so that it is not possible to establish with certainty its shipyard of origin (whether Greek or Etruscan). In addition to Greek and Etruscan ceramics, as well as a series of bronze basins, the cargo comprised 1,000 amphorae found still stacked in at least five superimposed and firmly linked layers, consisting mostly of specimens of Etruscan type Py 4 from a workshop in southern Etruria, to which were joined some "Ionic-Massaliote" examples sometimes attributed to the Chalcidian zone of the Strait and to Ionian Sicily, and sometimes to the Locrian region. The inscriptions present on some objects, and in particular those on an Ionian-Massaliote amphora, now considered part of the on-board equipment and not part of the cargo proper, and that on the base of a plain, black gloss cup, also belonging to the on-board equipment of the ship, refer to the Latin world, to which "Manios" belonged who most probably commanded the vessel and who had "Etruscanized" his name to *Maniie*, with which he marked his personal possession of that amphora of Magna-Graecian wine. The characteristic letterforms may be traced to the region of Tarquinia, according to Giovanni Colonna, and that is where the merchant belonged who had marked an amphora in the cargo with his own *trademark*.

If the proposed reconstruction has any chance of acceptance, it follows that the ship of the Grand Ribaud F wreck is in all likelihood Etruscan and that, at least in the Archaic period, the Etruscan engineering aspects must have been very similar to those known for the shipyards of the Phocaean Greeks of the western Mediterranean if not more generally of the Greek navy.

Ancient antiquarian tradition, however, attributed to Etruscan shipbuilding its own inventive autonomy, projecting onto the mythical figure of the hero Pisaeus, the son of Tyrrhenus (Pliny *NH* 7.56.207) the innovation of adding a rostrum to the bow of a vessel for a more effective offensive role, perhaps evoking the famed arsenals of Pisa with the name of this *protos euretés* ("first discoverer"). A bronze example of this prow-fitting, now in the Fitzwilliam Museum in Cambridge, England, dated to the Hellenistic period, was found off the coast of North Africa: it is a tripartite *rostrum* (ram) with its base open in a V-shape and crossed vertically at an angle by a sort of curved bar that seems to fit well on the convex curve of a prow, the appearance of which seems to fully justify the image incised on a small impasto jug from tomb I of the excavations of 1928 in the necropolis of Veii-Macchia della Comunità (beginning of the seventh century BC), which depicts a ship provided with a rostrum fitted horizontally to interrupt the profile of the symmetrically curved keel, typical of a round ship (thus a cargo vessel). In the case of purely representational evidence, it would not seem feasible to distinguish the presence of a rostrum, or even of a simple cutwater, since prow-overhangs seem to continue in the majority of Etruscan ships of the Orientalizing and early Archaic periods (oinochoai of the Pittore delle Palme, the Pania pyxis, bronze plaques now in Copenhagen, Etrusco-Corinthian plate by the Kithara Painter, etc.): the keel curves, flexing in profile, in a different fashion from what is observed for the Greek world. The case seems different for longships of marked military (naval) use, for instance the one that is attacking a *navis oneraria* on the famous crater of Aristonothos, or the penteconters on a Vulcian hydria by the Micali Painter now in the British Museum, and the stele of Vel Kaikna of Bologna, where the *rostrum* continues the straight line of the keel following an engineering system also common to Greek and Carthaginian shipbuilding. Other information can be inferred from the corpus of images of ships, in design and pattern, which marked the Etruscan iconographic repertoire from the early Iron Age until the full waning of Etruria in the Roman world, and shows that quite a few ship types were in use in Etruria since the early Iron Age, differentiated both diachronically and in their mode of use and functions. A wide range of ritual vases that replicate, in clay, the structure of ships and boats found in the necropoleis of many centers of southern and interior Etruria allow a glimpse inside the framework of types of Etruscan naval architecture of the earliest era, showing a diverse typology and a very fine level of engineering already in those years. Craft designed for river navigation or as small coasting vessels (cabotage) are in all likelihood portrayed on some vases from Veii (Tomb of Monte Oliviero), Capena (necropolis of S. Martino, tomb 16) and Orvieto, which replicate in impasto the form of monoxile (dugout) canoes like that actual one, exceptionally well known, of the mid-eighth century BC from the necropolis of Caolino near Sasso di Furbara in the territory between Pyrgi and Cerveteri, or instead ships constructed by assembling the various parts of the hull seams with ligatures ("sewn ships"). Also likely to have been designed for lake sailing are the reproductions found in the necropoleis of Bisenzio: these are flat-bottomed boats, whether small craft or with symmetrical, round hulls with keels and curved ends, with stempost and sternpost and skin made of planking sewn with ligatures; a gaudy ornament in the form of an animal protome was on the stempost of both types, jutting upwards, while, apparently only in the round-hulled ship above the stempost was found a circular element protruding out beyond the hull, which formed the seat for the helmsman who steered the ship, as confirmed by the boat propelled by two oarsmen painted on a nearly contemporary *olla* (jar) from tomb 24 of the necropolis of Olmo Bello (Bisenzio; Fig. 40.3).

Figure 40.3   *Olla* (jar) from Bisenzio, Olmo Bello necropolis, tomb 24. Rome, Museo di Villa Giulia, inv. 57069/4.

The little model boat of tomb 10 of the burial ground of Porto Madonna has a short cutwater on the bow, in a continuation of the line of the keel. Boats of the same type are also documented in Tarquinia (Fig. 40.4) and San Giuliano, where they are part of important contexts, which are characterized by the presence of helmets as covers for the ossuaries and by miniature chariots. If the hypothesis that these grave goods can refer to ranking individuals who exercised a hegemony on land (the chariot) and by sea (the ship) is contrasted with the same evidence from some contexts relevant to female figures (e.g. tomb 8 of Tarquinia-Poggio Selciatello), it leads us to prefer interpretative perspectives that are more closely linked to funeral ideology, the series of Tarquinian vessels furnishes many important reasons that are pertinent here. Although this is not so much the case for the study of the engineering aspects, since we may notice some deformation in the reproduction of boats, especially as regards the proportions of length and width, however it can well be appreciated that both in general, and for the profiles and details of the stempost and sternpost. Among other things, two ship models deserve special attention, obviously restoring the image of ships of a certain size that are clearly intended for navigation on the high seas. In both cases they are round-hulled vessels with the nearly vertical stempost topped with a great bird-shaped protome similar to that of the stern at the extremity of which was the place for the helmsman at the steering-oar, and propelled by a series of oars on both sides, seven pairs in the ship model from Arcatelle, and perhaps six pairs in the fragmentary model from Poggio dell'Impiccato, according to the number of holes that pierce the sides just below the gunwale. The latter also included a mast for the sail, which had to be inserted into a cavity present in the central frame and also affixed by stays running fore and aft (one or two – the right-hand side is incomplete), the fastenings of which are rendered plastically. Some details show that the ship had a shell of "sewn" planks, reinforced by an internal framework of five frames held together at the top by the gunwale. At the end of the keel at both bow and stern, there is a spur, probably a cutwater. Compared to the model ship from Arcatelle, with the slender profile and propelled only by oars, the vessel from Poggio dell'Impiccato has a decided enlargement in the middle, giving the ship a "mixed" character, as well as the mixed propulsion system, driven both by oars and sail: intended essentially for transport, the ship was still agile and ready, as needed, to defend or attack according to the dialectic between *prexis* and *lesteia* that characterizes sea traffic in this age.

The many depictions of ships and boats that characterize the Etruscan artistic repertoire confirm that since the first decades of the seventh century BC, there are in circulation in the Mediterranean Etruscan vessels of different types, as evidenced by the two oinochoai of the so-called Pittore delle Palme, active at Tarquinia in the years between 700 and 675 BC (Fig. 40.5), and which are echoed in mid-century by the famous Caeretan crater signed by Aristonothos (Fig. 40.6): to a roundship, heavy, with high sides and driven by sail, intended for commercial use (cf. the στρογγύλη ναῦς, "roundship," in Herodotus 1.163.2), is contrasted a leaner and quicker vessel, with curved keel that is nearly straight, driven by a set of oars; the character of the ship is associated with warlike and predatory activity which is reiterated by its exaggerated cutwater sheathed

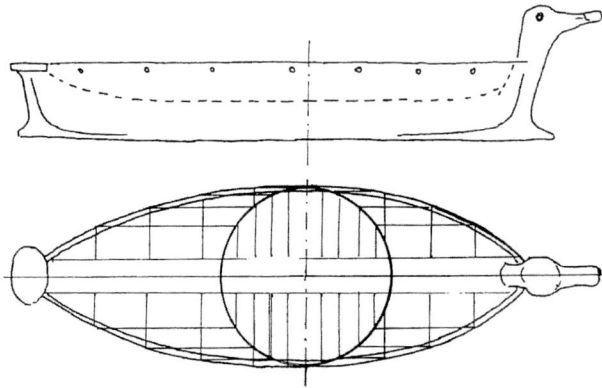

Figure 40.4   Ship model in impasto from Tarquinia. Tarquinia, Museo Archeologico Nazionale, s.inv. Plan and reconstruction by Marco Bonino.

Figure 40.5   Oinochoe by the Pittore delle Palme, from Tarquinia (?). Columbia, University of Missouri, Museum of Art and Archaeology, inv. 71.114.

with a ram. The graffiti on an impasto olla from the nineteenth-century excavations of Monterozzi at Tarquinia, and the scene painted on a plate from tomb 65 of the necropolis of Acqua Acetosa Laurentina (Cerveteri), however, show that during the seventh century BC there were in use ships of "light" construction with mixed propulsion, characterized by an angular, sharply cut *akrostolion* on the prow and by an *aphlaston* that curved back and over the stern.

Although only documented at the turn of the sixth century BC, the image on a hydria from Vulci by the Micali Painter, now in the British Museum (Fig. 40.7), perhaps as early as the seventh century BC, the Etruscans, like the Greeks, must have adopted for their seafaring the ship of dual propulsion, whose invention, although not grasped historically, is generally attributed to the Phoenician world. Greek tradition attributed the construction of the first bireme to Eretria, as evidence by a passage of Damon referring back to the era of the Euboean navy and *emporia*. To the same type, for which the Greek navy used the name of *pentecontera diera* ("double-oar pentekonters") also belongs the ship carved on the Bologna stele of Vel Kaikna, attesting to how the *akrostolion* of the bow,

Figure 40.6   Crater of Aristonothos, from Cerveteri. Rome, Musei Capitolini, formerly Coll. Castellani, inv. 172.

Figure 40.7   Hydria by the Micali Painter, from Vulci. London, British Museum, inv. B 60.

which in Archaic times was straight, in the last decades of the fifth century BC develops a sinuous profile and begins to acquire the monumentality that characterizes the naval architecture of the Hellenistic and Roman periods (see Fig. 40.8). Vessels of the type on the Bologna stele are the three ships that transfer the Etruscan contingent to Sicily in the summer of 413 BC (Thuc. 6.103.2).

The appearance of an Etruscan cargo ship offshore, corresponding to the Greek *holkades* and the Phoenician *gauloi*, is offered in the same years by the extraordinary seascape of the so-called Tomb of the Ship of Tarquinia (Fig. 56.7), where among the many boats depicted is a great merchant ship. The vessel is in line with Mediterranean shipbuilding of the era (Fig. 40.9), as is documented by the iconographic repertoire of the Greek world. If, as is likely, it remains only hypothetical that already at that time there have been introduced, in place of the archaic practice of *sutiles naves* ("sewn ships") the constructive methods of fastening the shell with *harmoniai* and *gòmphoi*, that is "wedges" and "dowels" (mortise and tenon) the hull, large and roomy, seems to be equipped with a cutwater at the bow, which makes it suitable for sailing close to the wind and making way. There are two masts, one mainmast in the center, and one forward, smaller, to carry the foresail with which it could perform an intricate set of maneuvers.

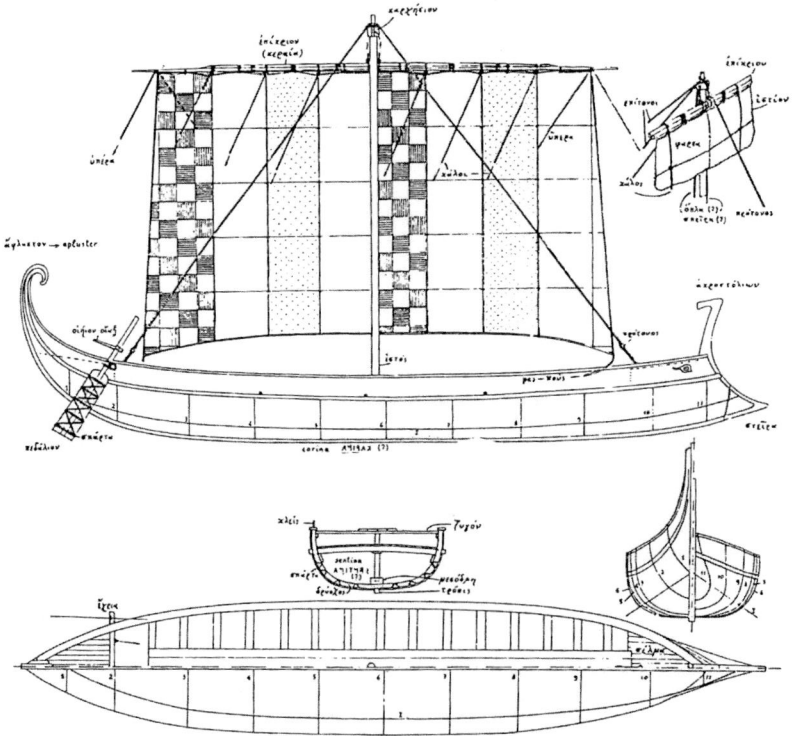

Figure 40.8   Etruscan ship, reconstruction by Marco Bonino.

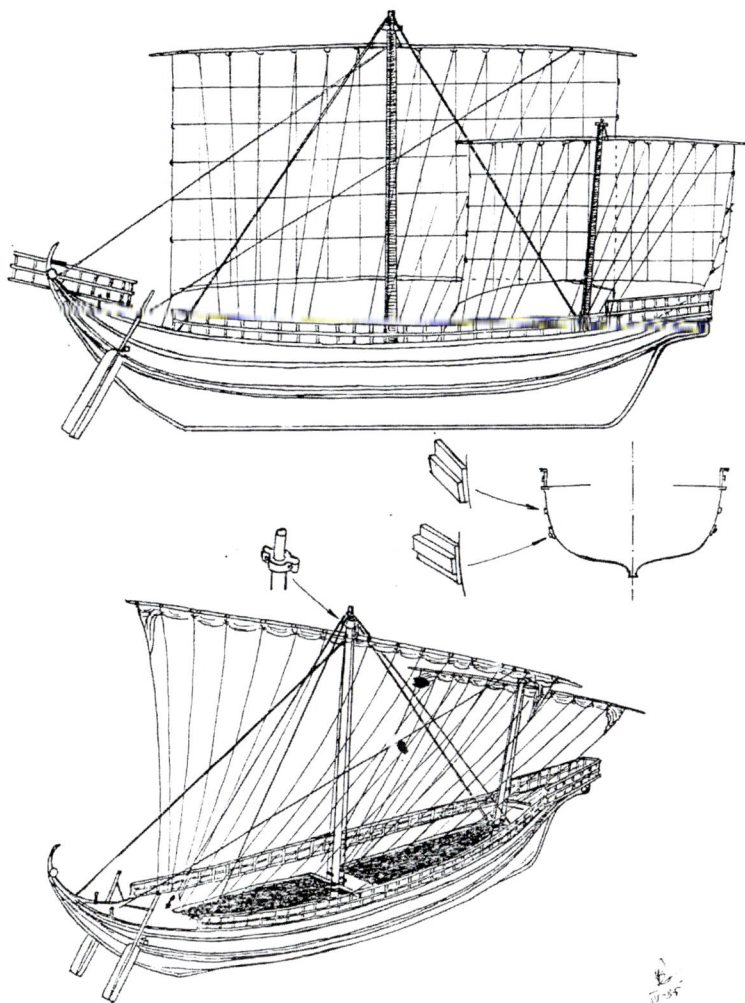

Figure 40.9 Etruscan cargo ship, reconstruction by Marco Bonino.

BIBLIOGRAPHIC NOTES

In general: Cristofani 1983; Idem 1984, 2–20; Gras 1985a; Gras 1985b, 149–159; Cristofani 1987, 51–76; Jannot 1995, 743–778; Pettena 2002; Cherici 2006, 439–482; Atti Piombino – Orbetello 2010. For the name of the Tyrrhenian Sea: Cordano 2006, 305–316; for that of the Adriatic: Colonna 2003, 160–161.

For the ports in general: Oleson – Hohlfelder 2011, 809–833; for the situation in the first imperial age: Ciampoltrini 1991, 79–98; for southern Etruria: Gianfrotta 1988, 11–16; for the Caeretan territory, also: Enei 2001 e 2008; for the port of Gravisca: Frau 1981; for Regae: Morselli – Tortorici 1985, 27–40, Fig. 1; for Pisa: Bruni 2006, 513–534.

For the routes of the Upper Tyrrhenian: Maggiani 2006, 435–454. On the concept of thalassocracy: Momigliano 1944, 1–7; Idem 1987, 127–138.

On the theme of piracy, also: Gras 1976, 341–369; Giuffrida 1978, 175–200; Mele 1979; Giuffrida Ientile 1983; Bakhuizen 1988, 25–3; Atti Venezia 2004. On the Homeric Hymn to Dionysos, see now: Nobili 2009, 3–35, and Capso 2003, 79–98; and also Spivey – Rasmussen 1986, 2–8; Harari 1988, 33–46. For the Athenian monument of Lysikrates: Ehrhardt 1993. On the Spargi wreck and underwater finds associated with pirate activity: Gianfrotta 1981, 227–242; for the helmets from Populonia: *Venezia* 2000, 562 n. 68 (A. Romualdi). For the deposit of arms on the beach of Populonia: Romualdi 2009, 373–380.

For Etruscan wrecks: *Marseille* 2002, with earlier bibliography, and also Pomey – Long 1992, 189–198; Krotscheck 2008. For the wreck *Grand Ribaud F:* Long – Gantes – Drap 2002, 5–40; Long – Gantes – Rival 2006, 454–496; Colonna 2006, 657–678. For the wreck of Calafuria: Papo – Citi – Marini 2005. For the dugout canoe from Sasso di Furbara: Brusadin Laplace 1977–1982, 355–379.

On Etruscan ships: Paglieri 1960, 210–231; Biers – Humphrey 1977, 219–228; Pomey 1981, 225–251; Hagy 1986, 221–250; Corretti 1988, 241–258; Bonino 1989, 1517–1536; Bonino 1995, 83–98; Pekary 1999, 156 n. I-C 8, 160–162 nn. I-F 10–19, 204 n. I-P 6, 302 nn. I-T 1–5, 308–312 nn. I-V 15–43, 322 n. NL-1; Höckmann 2000, 77–87; Höckmann 2001, 227–308; Pomey 2002, 109–112; Idem 2006, 423–434; Carlson 2011, 379–405; Pomey 2011, 2–8.

For Etruscan ship models of the First Iron Age, in addition to the collection of Götlicher 1978, see Quilici Gigli 1986, 85–89; Iaia 1999, 26–27; Iaia 2002, 729–730; Mandolesi – Castello 2009, 9–28; cf. also Johnston 1985.

For the wrecks of Marseille: Pomey 1995, 459–484; Idem 1998, 147–154.

For ancient techniques of navigation, in general: Medas 2004.

On the Etruscan artistic repertoire of the sea: Pizzirani 2005, 251–270, as well as for fisheries: Lubtchansky 1998, 111–146.

BIBLIOGRAPHY

Atti Marseille – Lattes (2006) *Gli Etruschi da Genova ad Ampurias*, Atti del XV convegno di Studi Etruschi ed Italici, Marseille – Lattes, 26 settembre – 1 ottobre 2002, Pisa-Rome.

Atti Piombino – Orbetello (2010) *Il mare degli Etruschi*, Atti del convegno Piombino – Orbetello, 17–20 settembre 2009, Florence.

Bakhuizen, S. C. (1988) "The Tyrrhenian Pirates: Prolegomena to the Study of the Thyrrhenian Sea" in (ed.) T. Hackens, *Flotte e commercio greco, cartaginese e etrusco nel Mar Tirreno, PACT 20*, pp. 25–32.

Biers, J. C. and Humphrey, S. (1977) "Eleven Ships from Etruria" in *The International Journal of Nautical Archeology and Underwater Exploration* 5, pp. 219–228.

Bonino, M. (1989) "Imbarcazioni arcaiche in Italia: il problema delle navi usate dagli Etruschi," in *Atti del Secondo Congresso internazionale Etrusco, Firenze 1985*, Rome pp. 1517–1536.

Bonino, M. (1995) "Sardinian, Villanovan and Etruscan crafts between the IX and the VIII cent. B.C. From bronze and clay models," in *Tropis* III, Athens, pp. 83–98.

Bruni, S. (2006) "Pisa e i suoi porti nei traffici dell'alto Tirreno: materiali e problemi" in Atti Marseille – Lattes, pp. 513–534.

Brusadin Laplace, D. (1977–1982) "L'imbarcazione monossile dalla necropoli del Caolino al Sasso di Furbara" in *Origini. Preistoria e protostoria delle Civiltà Antiche* 11, pp. 355–379.

Capso, E. (2003) "The Dolphins of Dionysos," in (ed.) M. C. Miller, *Poetry, Theory, Praxis. The Social Life of Myth: Word and Imagine in Ancient Greece. Essays in Honour of William J. Slater*, Oxford, pp. 79–98.

Carlson, D. N. (2011) "The Seafarers and Shipwrecks of Ancient Greece and Rome" in Catsambis – Ford – Hamilton, pp. 379–405.

Catsambis, A., Ford, B. and Hamilton, D. L. (2011) (eds) *The Oxford Handbook of Maritime Archaeology*, Oxford.

Cherici, A. (2006) "Talassocrazia: aspetti tecnici, economici, politici con un brevissimo cenno a Novilara, Nesanzio e ai Feaci" in *Gli Etruschi e il Mediterraneo. Commerci e politica*, Atti del XIII convegno internazionale di studi sulla storia e l'archeologia dell'Etruria, Orvieto, 16–18 dicembre 2005, [*Annali della Fondazione per il Museo "Claudio Faina,"* XIII], Rome, pp. 439–482.

Ciampoltrini, G. (1991) "Porti dell'Etruria augustea" in *Athenaeum* 79, pp. 255–259

Colonna, G. (2006) "A proposito della presenza etrusca nella Gallia meridionale" in Atti Marseille – Lattes, pp. 657–678.

Cordano, F. (2006) "I confini del Mar Tirreno" in *Gli Etruschi e il Mediterraneo. Commerci e politica*, Atti del XIII convegno internazionale di studi sulla storia e l'archeologia dell'Etruria, Orvieto, 16–18 dicembre 2005, [*Annali della Fondazione per il Museo "Claudio Faina,"* XIII], Roma, pp. 305–316.

Corretti, A. (1988) "Contributo alla discussione sulle strutture del commercio arcaico: le navi" in *PACT* 20, pp. 241–258.

Cristofani, M. (1983) *Gli Etruschi del mare*, Milan.

Cristofani, M. (1984) "Nuovi spunti sul tema della talassocrazia" in *Xenia* 8, pp. 3–20.

Cristofani, M. (1987) *Saggi di storia etrusca arcaica*, Rome.

Ehrhardt, W. (1993) "Der Fries des Lysikratesmonument" in *Antike Plastik* 22, pp. 7–67.

Enei, F. (2001) *Progetto Ager Caeretanus. Il litorale di Alsium, ricognizioni archeologiche nel territorio dei Comuni di Ladispoli, Cerveteri e fumicino (Alsium – Caere – Ad Turres – Ceri)* Santa Marinella.

Enei, F. (2008) *Pyrgi sommersa. Ricognizioni archeologiche subacquee nel porto dell'antica Caere*, Pyrgi – Santa Severa.

Frau, B. (1981) *Graviscae. Il porto antico di Tarquinia e le sue fortificazioni*, Rome.

Gianfrotta, P. A. (1981) "Commerci e pirateria: prime testimonianze archeologiche sottomarine" in *Mélanges de l'Ecole Française de Rome. Antiquité* 93, 1, pp. 227–242.

——(1988) "Le coste, i porti, la pesca, in Etruria meridionale. Conoscenza, conservazione, fruizione," *Atti del convegno, Roma, 29 novembre–1 dicembre 1985*, Rome, pp.11–16.

Giuffrida, M. (1978) "La 'pirateria etrusca' fino alla battaglia di Cuma" in *Kokalos* 24, pp. 175–200.

Giuffrida Ientile, M. (1983) *La pirateria tirrenica. Momenti e fortuna*, Rome.

Götlicher, A. (1978) *Materialen für ein Corpus der Schiffesmodelle im Altertum*, Mainz.

Gras, M. (1976) "La piraterie tyrrhenienne en mer Egée: mythe ou réalité?" in *Italie preromaine et laRome républicaine. Mélanges offerts à Jacques Heurgon*, Roma, pp. 341–369.

——(1985a) *Trafics tyrrhéniens archaiques*, Rome.

——(1985b) *Aspects de l'économie maritime étrusque*, in *Ktema* 10, pp. 149–159.

Hagy, J. W. (1986) "800 Years of Etruscan Ships" in *The international Journal of Nautical Archeology and Underwater Exploration* 15, 3, pp. 221–250.

Harari, M. (1988) "Dioniso, i pirati, i delfini," in (ed.) T. Hackens, *Flotte e commercio greco, cartaginese e etrusco nel Mar Tirreno. PACT* 20, pp. 33–46.

Höckmann, O. (2000) "Schiffahrt der Etrusker" in *Der Orient und Etrurien. Zum Phänomen des "Orientalisierens" im westlichen Mittelmeerraum (10. – 6. Jh. v. Chr.)*, Akten des Kolloqiums, Tübingen, 12–13 giugno 1997, Pisa – Rome, pp. 77–87.

——(2001) "Etruskische Schiffahrt," in *Jahrbuch des Römisch-Germanischen Zentralmuseums Mainz* 48, pp. 227–308.

Iaia, C. (1999) *Simbolismo funerario e ideologia alle origini di unacività urbana. Forme rituali nelle sepolture "villanoviane" a Tarquinia e a Vulci. e nel loro retroterra*, Florence.

Iaia, C. (2002) "Oggetti di uso rituale nelle sepolture "villanoviane" di Tarquinia" in Atti del V incontro di studi sulla preistoria e protostoria dell'Etruria, Sorano – Farnese 2000, Milan, pp. 729–738.

Jannot, J.-R. (1995) "Les navires étrusques, instruments d'une thalassocratie?" in *Comptes rendus des séances de l'Académie des Inscriptions et Belles Lettres*, pp. 743–778.

Johnston, P. F. (1985) *Ship and Boat Models in Ancient Greece,* Annapolis.

Krotscheck, U. (2008) *Scale, Structure, and organization of Archaic Maritime Trade in the Western Mediterranean: the "Pointe Lequin 1A,"* Diss. University of Stanford, Ann Arbor.

Long, L., Gantes, L.-F. and Drap, P. (2002) "Premiers résultats archéologiques sur l'épave Gran Ribaud F (Giens, Var). "Quelques éléments nouveaux sur le commerce étrusque en gaule, vers 500 avant J.-C." in *Cahiers d'Archéologie Subacquatique* 14, pp. 5–40.

Long, L., Gantes, L.-F. and Rival, M. (2006) "L'épave Grand Ribaud F. Un chargement de produits étrusques du debut du Ve siècle avant J.-C." in Atti Marseille – Lattes, pp. 454–496.

Lubtchansky, N. (1998) "Le pêcheur et la mètis. Pêche et statut social en italie centrale à l'époque archaique" in *Mélanges de lEcole Française de rome. Antiquité* 110, 1, pp. 111–146.

Maggiani, A. (2006) *Rotte e tappe nel Tirreno settentrionale,* in Atti Marseille – Lattes, pp. 435–454.

Mandolesi, A. and Castello, C. (2009) "Modellini di navi tirrenico-villanoviane da Tarquinia" in *Mediterranea* 6, pp. 9–28.

Marseille (2002) Long, L., Pomey, P. and Sourisseau, J. C. (eds), *Les étrusques en mer. Épaves d'Antibes à Marseille,* catalogo della mostra Marseille.

Medas, S. (2004) *De rebus nauticis. L'arte della navigazione nel mondo antico,* Rome.

Mele, A. (1979) *Il commercio greco arcaico. Prexis ed emporie,* Napoli.

Momigliano, A. (1944) *Sea Power in Greek Thought,* in *CR* 58, pp. 1–7.

——(1987) *Storia e storiografia antica,* Bologna.

Morselli, C. and Tortorici, E. (1985) "La situazione di Regisvilla" in *Il commercio etrusco arcaico,* Atti dell'incontro di studio, Rome, 5–7 December 1983, Rome, pp. 27–40.

Nobili, C. (2009) "L'inno omerico a Dioniso (*Hymn. Hom.* VII) e Corinto" in *Acme* 62, 3, pp. 3–35.

Oleson, J. P. and Hohlfelder, R. L. (2011) "Ancient Harbours in the Mediterranean" in Catsambis – Ford – Hamilton, pp. 809–833.

Paglieri, S. (1960) "Origine e diffusione delle navi etrusco italiche" in *Studi Etruschi* 28, pp. 210–231.

Papo, A., Citi, G. and Marini, L. (2005) *Un relitto etrusco tra i rinvenimenti di Calafuria. Note preliminari e parziali,* Livorno.

Pekàry, I. (1999) *Repertorium der hellenistischen und römischen Schiffsdarstellungen,* Münster.

Pettena, G. (2002) *Gli Etruschi e il mare,* Torino.

Pizzirani, C. (2005) "Da Odisseo alle Nereidi. Riflessioni sull'iconografia etrusca del mare attraverso i secoli" in *Ocnus* 11, pp. 251–270.

Pomey, P. (1981) "L'epave du Bon Porté e les bateaux cousus de Mediterranée" in *The Mariner's Mirror* 67, 3, pp. 225–251.

——(1995) *Les épaves grecques et romaines de la place Jules-Verne à Marseille,* in *Comptes-rendus des séances de l'Académie des Inscriptions et Belles Lettres*, pp. 459–484.

——(1998) "Les épaves grecques du VIe siècle av. J.-C. de la place Jules-Verne à Marseille" in *Archaeonautica* 14, pp. 147–154.

——(2002) "Navires ètrusques, navires misterieux ?" in *Marseille*, pp. 109–112.

——(2006) "Les navires étrusques: mythe ou réalité ?" in Atti Marseille – Lattes, pp. 423–434.

——(2011) *Defining a Ship: Architecture, Function, and Human Space,* in Catsambis – Ford – Hamilton, pp. 25–46.

Pomey, P. and Long, L. (1992) "Les premiers échanges maritime du Midi de la Gaule du VIe au IIIe siècle av. J.-C. à travers les épaves" in *Marseille grecque et la Gaule,* Actes du colloque international, Marseille, 18–23 November 1990, Lattes – Aix-en-Provence, pp. 189–198.

Quilici Gigli, S. (1986) "Scali e traghetti sul Tevere in età arcaica" in *Il Tevere e le altre vie d'acqua del Lazio antico,* Atti del settimo incontro distudio del Comitato perl'archeologia laziale, Roma, pp. 71–89.

Romualdi, A. (2009) "Un deposito di armi da Populonia" in *Mélanges de l'Ecole Française de Rome. Antiquité* 121, 2, pp. 373–380.

Sassatelli, G. (2009) "Riflessioni sulla 'stele della nave' di Bologna" in *Etruria e Italia preromana. Studi in onore di Giovannangelo Camporeale,* Pisa-Rome, pp. 833–840.

Spivey, N. J. and Rasmussen, T. (1986) "Dioniso e i pirati nel Toledo Museum of Art" in *Prospettiva* 44, pp. 2–8.

CHAPTER FORTY ONE

PRINCELY CHARIOTS AND CARTS

———— ·◆· ————

Adriana Emiliozzi

When the Assyrian artists decorated the royal palaces of Kalhu (Nimrud), of Khorsabad or of Nineveh with the scenes of the conquests, ceremonies or hunts of their sovereigns (from Tiglathpileser III to Ashurbanipal, between 745 and 627 BC), the figurative arts of the Etruscans included only the timid beginnings of narrative episodes of mythological character, denying us the possibility of observing the regal lifestyle of the leaders of these people even through their artistic representations. Thus, while we are in a position to be able to observe the form and to understand the use of Middle Eastern chariots between the eighth and seventh centuries BC, although we do not have the original (vehicles) we do have the odd representation to insert directly into the ancient reality of the remains of the numerous vehicles found in the Etruscan tombs of the same period. A good example of the oldest is a vase by the Caeretan Painter of the Heptachord (circa 670 BC), on which the arrival of a warrior on the field of battle echoes that of a mythical hero: armed with a sword, he descends from the *biga* (two-horse chariot) driven by a charioteer, as an attendant rushes up behind the chariot to bring him the rest of the arms he needs to fight on foot, that is, the spear and the round shield (Figs 41.1–41.3).[1] Other scenes with personages in chariots appear during the seventh century BC, but it will be necessary to wait for the development of the arts in the next century in order to see more complex scenes of military processions, of parades and of chariot races, carved, modeled, painted, beaten or incised on monuments of various types.

An accurate list of Etruscan and Italic wheeled vehicles coming from excavations and known from representations up to 1903 was furnished by Nachod 1909 (43–71). In 1978, Woytowitsch published a systematic collection of the remains of actual vehicles from the Italian peninsula, of representations and of small scale models, while Stary in 1980 and 1981, and other authors (also in the 1980s) have discussed the function of the chariot in Etruria.[2] The exhibition *Carri da guerra e principi etruschi* (Emiliozzi 1997) inaugurated the era of modern studies for the reconstruction – graphic and material – of the princely Etruscan and Italic vehicles datable between the last decades of the eighth and the sixth century BC.[3] A new book by Joost Crouwel is dedicated to all the vehicles of pre-Roman Italy, known through representations and models, as well as those buried in

Figures 41.1–3   Etruscan amphorae of the Heptachord Painter. Princeton University Museum of Art (loan from private collection). Photographs D. Niccolini, New York.

tombs, and extends the study to what is known about the roads, about the draft animals and about the manner of harnessing and driving them, as well as the uses for which such teams were intended (Crouwel 2012).

As in Cyprus, the Celtic world and among the non-Greek peoples of the Italian peninsula, in Etruria it was the custom to deposit in the tombs of members of the elite the vehicles that in life had marked their social status. The chariots found in Etruria and datable from 775–750 to 475 BC are all two-wheeled, whether we are dealing with chariots (Latin *currus*) and with carts (Latin *carpentum* and *cisium*), or whether we are dealing with utilitarian carts. A deceased person, man or woman, could be accompanied by a chariot alone, by a chariot and a cart, and in exceptional cases, also by a utility cart, ultimately used for the funeral ceremony.[4] In some cremation tombs there are found the metal remains of vehicles with obvious traces of fire, a sign that they had been burned on the pyre of the dead person. When they are not burnt, as happens in all the inhumation burials, the vehicles sometimes come to be buried complete, sometimes disassembled and stacked or otherwise deprived of their functionality (for example, with the draft pole broken), according to the ritual practices in use in a given place and time, but perhaps also dependent upon the amount of space available in the tomb.

From the end of the eighteenth century right up to today, in Italy the remains of more than 300 vehicles have been found, half of them in princely tombs in Etruscan territory. Such remains generally consist of the tire rims of iron and of other accessories belonging to the wheels, because the body of the chariot was composed of organic materials – wood, leather and rawhide – connected by joints and ligatures of rawhide, without the aid of nails. Sometimes a vehicle was enriched by decorations in bronze, sometimes inlaid in iron or encrusted with ivory.

CHARIOTS

From their first appearance in the tombs of the elite (775–750 BC) until the end of the Orientalizing period (circa 575 BC) chariots to be driven from a standing position were designed for speed and served for transporting the warrior prince to and from the battlefield, for the hunt and for ceremonial processions (Fig. 41.4).

By using seasoned wood the axle was made robust and rectilinear, intended to keep the wheels steady, to support the chariot body and to fasten the draft pole. The result of the joining of these parts was a compact and rigid structure, in which only the wheels

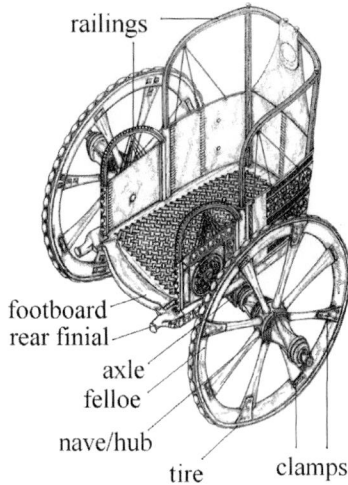

Figure 41.4   The reconstruction of the fast chariot from Populonia, Tumulo dei Carri
(project by A. Emiliozzi, drawing by G. Corsi).

turned freely in the axle arms, obtained by thinning the two ends of the axle. The length
of the axle arms matched the size of the hubs, with a surplus useful for inserting the
linchpin that kept the wheels in place. The length of the hub was important, so as to
guarantee the stability of the vehicle. This was carved from a tree trunk, trimmed so as
to obtain the greatest diameter in the central portion, to which were joined six, eight
or more spokes. These spokes, suitably filed to create less resistance to the movement
of rotation were mortized into the hub and the felloe (the wooden circle that forms the
circumference of a wheel). In Etruria the most common method of constructing a felloe
consisted of two concentric layers of wood, which were joined together. The outside layer
was formed of segments that were arcs of a circle cut from planks (usually four segments,
but they could also be in three) and the inside layer was a branch shaped under steam.
In less frequent cases the felloe was composed of single segments or of two concentric
branches. The junctions between the parts were affixed with nailed clamps, usually of
metal, but also of untanned hides, possibly decorated with a sheathing of a thin sheet
of bronze nailed on the outer side. The tire (the part that touches the road) was always
constructed of two semi-circles of iron bands, nailed to the felloe through holes prepared
prior to assembly.

On the central stretch of the axle was attached the floor frame, on which was constructed
the box of the vehicle. The floor frame was made by either steam-bending a tree branch,
which was then closed behind with a crossbar or by joining together four separately
constructed elements: in the first case (steam-bending) the chassis assumed the shape of a
"U" with the arms of the "U" flared slightly to the sides; and in the second case, a nearly-
rectangular shape that is less rounded across the front. The floor was made of woven
tongues or strips, also seen in vehicles in Egypt and the Near East. The material used
in Etruria seems to have been untanned hide, which was secured to the frame while still
damp through holes along the perimeter (Fig 41.5); as it dried, the woven leather became
so stiff that it could support the weight of the crew and so elastic that it could absorb the
effects of shaking that could otherwise have torn the rigid substructure.

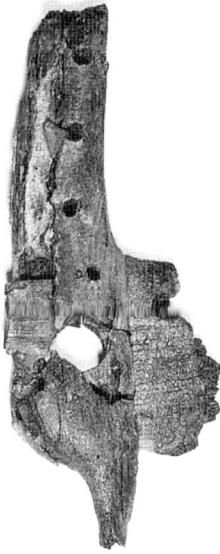

Figure 41.5   Fragment from the original wooden chassis of the fast chariot from Vulci (see Fig. 41.8). There are holes for the woven tongs of the floor and remains of leather fastened with nails of bronze. From Emiliozzi 1997, pl. V,1. Photograph E. Bianchi.

The sides of the vehicle were formed mainly from light wooden railings, located in front and along the sides, obtained by bending young branches of appropriate timber species, that functioned as parapets and constituted a firm grip for movements of entry or dismounting and for balance while maneuvering in the chariot. Around the middle and lower parts of the railings was stretched a covering of leather, that closed the cockpit of the vehicle on three sides. The box was always balanced on the axle and in it two persons could stand one behind the other, one person at the front and the other behind the line of the axle. This method of riding the vehicle depended on the type of harnessing of the two draft horses, to whom was always attached a neck yoke, in contrast to mainland Greece where a dorsal yoke was used.[5]

Almost all the Etruscan and Italic fast chariots were designed for a team of three (*trigae*) or four (*quadrigae*). The functional devices for the addition of a third and fourth horse protruded from the upper ends of the front rail and are found in the form of metal rings or pegs to suspend loops of rawhide, through which would pass the traces of the outrigger horses,[6] who are thus linked to the body of the chariot.[7]

In the most luxurious fast chariots a metallic decoration was applied over the covering of leather, which was designed to resist the jolting without being damaged. The finest of these examples of the Orientalizing period is the chariot of the Tumulo dei Carri (Tumulus of the Chariots) at Populonia (Fig. 41.6, 675–650 BC), which is also the only one where arrowheads were found with it, a sign that it was used also for hunting. The individual plaques of bronze inlaid with iron that formed the decoration on the box were affixed to the rawhide beneath with metal pins and by "seams" to obtain a sort of mosaic, ready to twist and flex at the slightest jolt without risk of damage. The result is a decorative syntax in superimposed registers (Fig. 41.7). In the upper register appear files of animals including men armed with long spears, presumably hunters; but in the lower register only animals are present. The iconography and the style of such ornaments accord well with the Orientalizing decorative taste of the first half of the seventh century BC, documented in the decoration of the shields and gold jewelry produced in the workshops of southern Etruria (cf. Chapters 6 and 50).

The same criterion of application of decoration was employed for the celebrated "biga" of the Regolini-Galassi Tomb (560–550 BC), recently subjected to a new reconstruction. Here we are dealing with bronze plates decorated in repoussé, with compositions of animals and ornamental elements in superimposed registers, worked in separate pieces and applied to the leather in a pattern to create the desired sequence. The decoration of the chariot from the Tomb of the Bronze Chariot at Vulci (700–675 BC) was also produced using similar devices, although they are less obvious. The bronze sheet that covers the front panel, decorated in repoussé with the use of punches, is worked in two halves and applied to the leather beneath, which in turn is affixed to the wood of the frame and the railings (Figs 41.8 and 41.9).

From the second quarter of the sixth century BC on, with the decline of the aristocracies of the Etruscan cities, the custom of burying in the tombs the vehicles used in life as a

Figure 41.6   The fast chariot from Populonia, Tumulo dei Carri, 1:1 model
(project by A. Emiliozzi, drawing by G. Corsi, model by C. Usai).

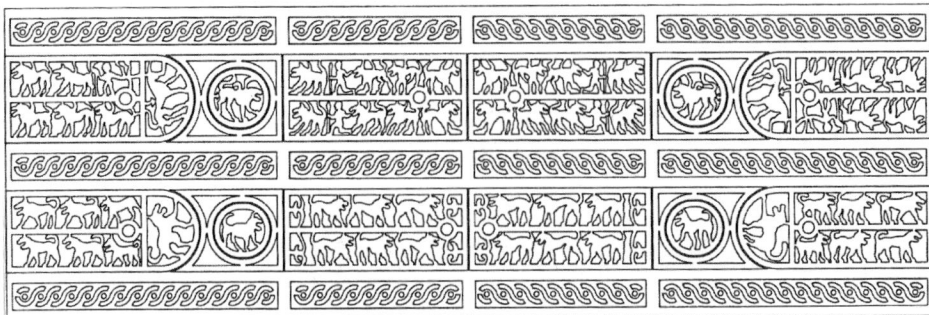

Figure 41.7   The fast chariot from Populonia, Tumulo dei Carri. Reconstruction drawing of the metal decoration of the front panel (project by A. Emiliozzi, drawing by G. Corsi).

Figure 41.8   The fast chariot from Vulci, Tomba del Carro di Bronzo, 1:1 model
(project by A. Emiliozzi, drawing by G. Corsi, model by C. Usai).

Figure 41.9   The fast chariot from Vulci, Tomba del Carro di Bronzo. Bronze sheeting of the front
panel. Photograph E. Bianchi.

symbol of power ceased. However, in the peripheral centers, which had remained alien
to the phenomenon of urbanization and of the process of the isonomic transformation
of society, some aristocratic groups in fact acquired just that custom, and they have left
us the most beautiful chariots ever built in the Italic peninsula. The characteristic that
they share is their projected use, exclusively ceremonial, given that in their construction
they were not designed for rapid travel. Functional innovations were introduced in the
construction of their wooden structure, which in some cases could be completely covered
in sheet bronze, from the chariot body to the wheels and from the draft pole to the yoke,
as shown in the parade chariots from Castel San Mariano near Perugia[8] (Figs 41.10 and
41.11), and in the splendid chariot preserved in the Metropolitan Museum of Art in New
York, which came from Monteleone di Spoleto but was built in Etruria (Emiliozzi 2011).

Figure 41.10   The reconstruction of the parade Chariot I from Castel San Mariano
(project by A. Emiliozzi, drawing by G. Corsi).

Figure 41.11   The parade chariot I from Castel San Mariano. A segment of the bronze sheeting of the
neck yoke. From Emiliozzi 1997, p. 222, fig. 13. Photograph E. Bianchi.

In the construction of the fast chariots the tops of the railings are never covered in leather
so that the top could function as hand-holds. In the parade chariots, however, as they are
intended to be used at walking speed only, the railings do not need to function as hand-
holds: for the charioteer, the reins are sufficient to help him balance, he can lean his body
against the front panel and the second occupant can balance himself without need of solid
hand-grips because he can lean his hand on the side panel or on the charioteer's shoulder,
as shown in the images of processions of chariots (Fig. 41.12).[9]

The front rail, whether covered only by leather or enriched with attached ornaments,
takes the form of an inverted "U" and rises above the front curve of the U-shaped floor
frame for a consistent fit (around 80–82 cm). In the arrangement of the side rails one
notes instead a showy innovation: they contract toward the front rail and are proportioned
at two-thirds of their height. At the place they originally occupied behind the axle,
there is sometimes introduced a small rectangular panel, as if to compensate for the
open space; we are actually dealing with a non-functional appendage, which in the more
luxurious chariots is covered in bronze sheathing.[10] This modification seems also to affect
the dimensions of the wheels, which in the reconstructed examples given thus far seem to
be smaller, and the length of the chassis is re-proportioned to their diameter. We cannot
determine if we are dealing with a general reorganization designed for the function of
parade chariots, given that in the sixth century BC the same characteristics appear in

Etruscan and Latin representations of racing chariots. This might be due to the fact that at the beginning of the sixth century BC, around 580, the technology employed by the wheelwrights of the preceding generations is updated to meet the needs of a new elite, for whom the ideological bond between the possession of a chariot and its military function, of Near Eastern origin, has now been weakened. A suggestion proposed for the reconstruction of the Dutuit Chariot of Capua (Emiliozzi 2006a; see Chapter 16), dated around 580 BC, illustrates the advanced phase of the "gestation" of the sixth-century BC parade chariot type with U-shaped sides, for which the construction of the Monteleone Chariot seems to have established the canon.

In the fast chariots the floor frame is always affixed directly to the axle and to the draft pole. The union of the three parts forms a rigid line meaning the vehicle can be ridden only by applying a woven tongue flooring, which is meant to absorb the effects of bouncing during the march, as noted above. In the parade chariots a complex system of joining between the floor frame and the axle is reconstructed instead, acting as shock absorber (Figs. 41.13, 41.14). Such a system must be employed in cases where the floor it not made of woven strips, but is a rigid surface, which could be made of wooden slats.

Figure 41.12   Chariot procession depicted on terracotta friezes of Veii-Rome-Velletri type, dating 530–520 BC. From Fortunati 1993.

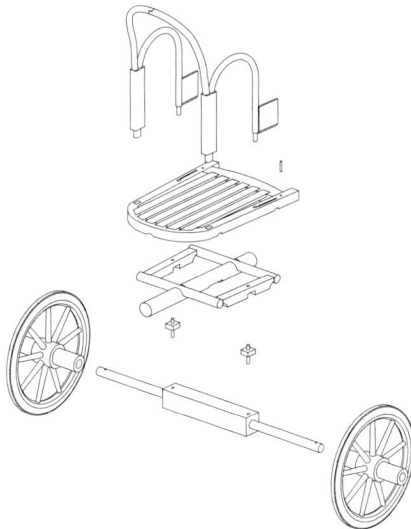

Figure 41.13   The shock-absorbing system between the chassis and the axle in the parade chariot from Monteleone di Spoleto (project by A. Emiliozzi, drawing by D. Lamura).

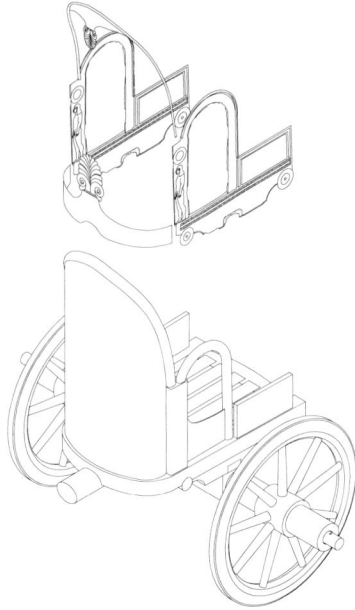

Figure 41.14 The parade chariot from Castro (near Vulci) with the same system to absorb the shock (project by A. Emiliozzi, drawing by D. Lamura).

The vehicle could thus process but not run, as shown by the fact that there are chariots provided with a shock-absorbing system that have wheels partially or entirely covered in bronze sheathing.[11]

In contrast to the fast chariots, none of the parade chariots recovered by excavations and studied to date seem to have been furnished with loops for the traces of the outriggers. Among the representations of *trigae* and *quadrigae* of the sixth century BC there is only one type of chariot provided with holes in the body, through which the traces could pass: this is on the frieze of an architectural terracotta from Caere,[12] but the vehicle is a fast chariot of a type not known to date from any actual chariots of ancient Italy. It is possible that the slow gait of the parade chariot, with the horses walking flanked by a footman, as shown in numerous representations, did not require the anchoring of outriggers to the chassis of the chariot.

CARTS

In 1921 the most elaborate and monumental wheels that a cart could have had in the ancient Mediterranean were discovered (Fig. 41.15), coming from the already-named Tumulus of the Chariots of Populonia and placed in a chamber separate from that containing the remains of the chariot. The large diameter (114 cm) meant the wheelwright had to construct them of two concentric felloes separated by two series of spokes, four on the inner and eight on the outer circumference. The entire surface of these wheels – hub, felloes and spokes – was thus covered in bronze sheet, cropped into long cusps along the outer edge adjacent to the rim of iron.

At a superficial glance it might seem that similar wheels could only belong to a ceremonial vehicle, for the same reasons that we have explained for parade chariots. In reality, only recently has it been understood that these did not belong to a chariot at all, but to a cart that was driven from a seated position, pulled not by horses but by donkeys or mules and that had to be used at a forcibly slowed gait because the axle belonged to the type that revolved together with the wheels. This mechanism has been amply studied for Greek carts and wagons (Crouwel 1992), but only in the last 20 years has the study been deepened to include the vehicles of Etruria and the other Italic regions.[13] Unfortunately, the cart of Populonia was found in a secondary deposition (Romualdi 1997), such that we cannot know whether or not its box was originally covered with metallic decoration over the leather like the sumptuous cart that came from the necropolis of Sabine Eretum, later in date by more than half a century,[14] or if its sides were open or covered only with leather. What can be suggested is that its wooden structure did not differ much from that example (Figs. 41.16, 41.17) or from the bridal cart on the Etruscan terracotta frieze plaques of Murlo (Fig 41.18), nor indeed from those Attic black-figured lekythoi of the Amasis Painter and Gela Painter (Fig. 41.19),[15] dated to the third quarter and end of the sixth century BC respectively. In favor of a carriage of the type depicted by the Gela Painter militates the presence – among the remains in iron found together with the wheels – of a series of 12 eyelets for suspension from wooden elements, that indicate the presence of two footrests (see below), one in front and one behind, on which the passengers seated in the vehicle could rest their feet. In this case we can attribute to the Populonia carriage another four bindings made in iron, in matching pairs, made to fit the heads of the long arms of the rectangular frame, from which hung the footrests.[16]

Unlike the Sabine region of the Tiber, where around the end of the seventh century BC there appeared, in the city of Eretum, the cart of the Ny Carlsberg Glyptothek in Copenhagen, splendidly covered in bronze sheets (see Fig. 41.16), in Etruria we must wait at least one more generation to see a similar and equally sumptuous cart, which is that of Castel San Mariano near Perugia (Fig. 41.20).[17] Unfortunately the conditions of its discovery in 1812, and of the recovery of its metal fragments and their subsequent dispersal into various collections and museums across Europe, has made the several attempts at a restoration of its wooden structure difficult. The only thing certain is that its box was closed on three sides, that is, also across the back. This fact, together with the application of an elaborate decoration hammered into low relief on three large sheets of bronze (apart from the minor friezes), makes it certain that it was designed for a ceremonial function as in the parade chariots, excluding any sort of utilitarian usage. It is further likely that it had two spoked wheels of Etruscan type and not the two

Figure 41.15   The wheels of the cart from Populonia, Tumulo dei Carri. From Emiliozzi 1997, pl. X. (Photograph courtesy of Soprintendenza per i Beni Archeologici della Toscana, Florence).

Figure 41.16 Virtual 3D reconstruction of the cart from Eretum. From the website principisabini.it. Project by A. Emiliozzi, 3D elaboration by R. Cavalli).

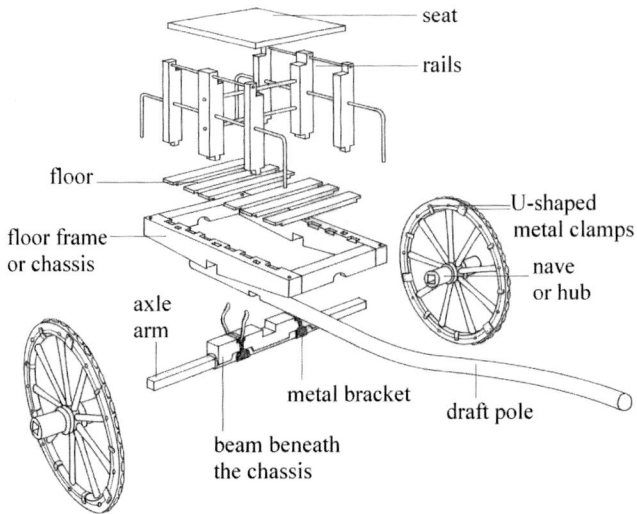

Figure 41.17 The substructure of the same cart as Fig. 41.16 (project by A. Emiliozzi, drawing by M. T. Francisi).

Figure 41.18 The wedding procession on a terracotta plaque from Murlo, Poggio Civitate. From Emiliozzi 1997, p. 65, s. 10.

Figure 41.19   Attic black figure lekythos by the Gela Painter. From Emiliozzi 1997, p. 61, s. 3.

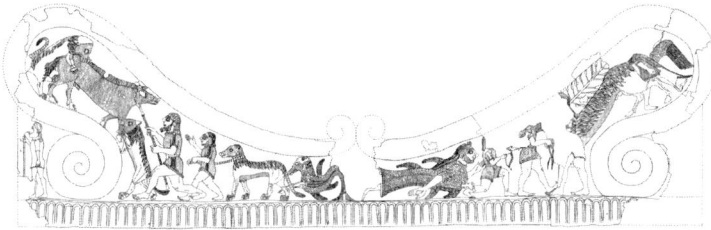

Figure 41.20a–c   The bronze decoration of the cart from Castel San Mariano: a) proper right side; b) rear side; c) minor frieze. Drawings from Höckmann 1982.

or four cross-bar wheels of Greek type, as has been suggested in various attempts at reconstruction, both graphic and three-dimensional.[18] Because of the dispersal noted for the excavated material and the loss of any elements in iron – which did not excite the interest of the excavators nor of the antiquarians of the era – we do not know whether such wheels were made with a revolving axle and fixed hubs or with hubs revolving in a fixed axle. In the first case the cart was intended for a slow pace in its design, and among the lost materials in iron we might be able to find the two brackets intended to hold the axle while it revolved beneath the beam crossing beneath the chassis. This consisted of broad bands in the form of a more or less open U, provided with slots to pass the rawhide thongs that bound it to the beam beneath the chassis; between these and the axle was placed the fat rind of a pig with the function of lubricating (Fig. 41.21, see also Fig. 41.17).

As can be understood from these observations, the recovery of all the metal fragments during the excavation of a vehicle – even those that seem insignificant – is essential if we are to know whether the disintegrated structure made only of wood, leather and rawhide belonged to a cart or to a chariot. To the present day we have distinguished seven metal elements that securely identify the deposition of a cart in a tomb: 1) bushings for the hubs provided with a quadrangular opening;[19] 2) axle caps in the form of a parallelepiped;[20] 3) U-shaped brackets;[21] 4) trident-shaped finial of the Y-pole;[22] 5) cylindrical clamps for the Y-pole;[23] 6) eyelets for the footrest;[24] 7) two or more perforated plates for keeping the seat in place.[25] Obviously it is not necessary to find all these elements associated with each other, but a single one of them is sufficient to classify a two-wheeled vehicle as a cart and not a chariot. On the other hand, even if the entire group of these is found together, but no longer joined, it is not possible to reconstruct the vehicle in a quite accurate manner, as could be done in the case of the cart of Sirolo.

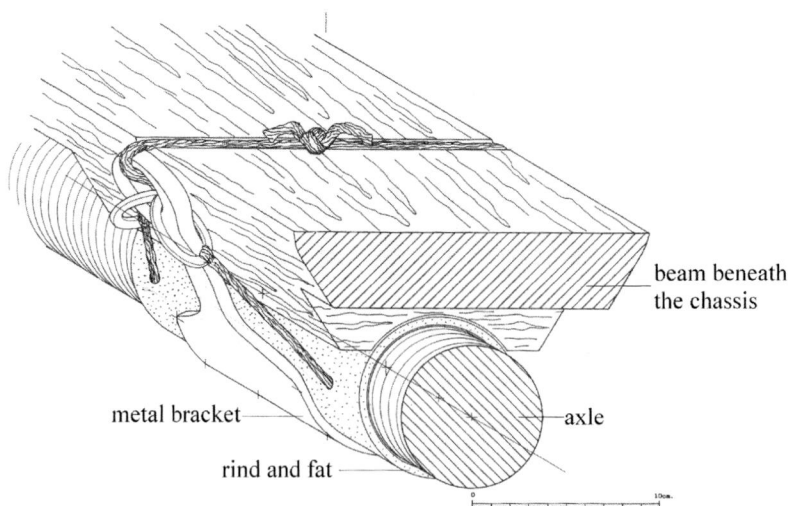

Figure 41.21   Diagram of the function of the iron brackets from Casale Marittimo, Casa Nocera necropolis, tomb A (project by A. Emiliozzi, drawing by M. Risaliti).

***

A second type of cart may be observed in the sketched reconstruction of that of Tomb 928 of Pontecagnano (Fig. 41.22, 675–650 BC) in Campanian Etruria or that of the Tomba dei Flabelli (Tomb of the Fans) of Trevignano Romano (Fig. 41.23, 675–625 BC) in southern Etruria, made possible by the study of some structural elements that may be compared with the remains of a later example found in 1989 in the Tomb of the Princess of Sirolo, in the Picene territory: buried after being dismantled and stacked (Fig. 41.24), this preserves all the metal parts in the original position, giving us the possibility of reconstructing a model of the vehicle (Fig. 41.25).

The principal distinguishing characteristic of this type is the Y-pole, formed by the extension of the side rods that contribute to construct a floor, appropriately heat bent in the direction of the yoke, to be affixed to the pair of draft animals, generally mules or donkeys. The Y-pole required a tip suitable not only to connect the two ends of the Y, but

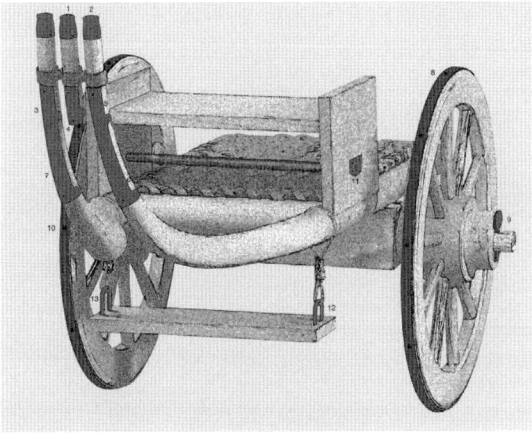

Figure 41.22   Graphic reconstruction of the cart from Pontecagnano, Tomb 928. The numbering indicates the remains of metal parts (project by A. Emiliozzi, drawing by L. Schiavoni).

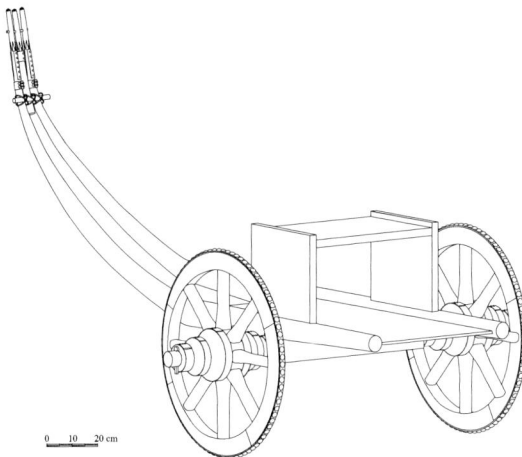

Figure 41.23   The cart from Trevignano Romano, Tomba dei Flabelli. The proposal of the reconstruction (project by A. Emiliozzi, drawing by D. Lamura).

also to a third element, which could be a short bar placed between them and useful to affix the yoke. To form the end, capsules of rawhide obtained from the deboned limbs of an animal, preferably swine (boar), were connected by through-pins and/or strips of rawhide. Between this more economic version and that luxurious one realized completely in metal – iron, cast bronze and bronze sheet (see Fig. 41.25) – there existed an intermediate variety of cases in which the presence of metal was always more consistent and not always made in a single piece (see Figs 41.22, 41.23).[26] There exist cases in which the trident-shaped metal finial is provided with more than three and up to five tines.[27] From these one must deduce that the shaft was not properly in the shape of a "Y," but had other intermediate rods issuing from the frame, for a better strengthening of the drive system. Probably in these cases a more flexible type of woodwork was used, such as wicker.

In the scope of the finds of metal elements belonging to carts, it would seem that on the trident-shaped finial for the Y-pole there are not associated the metal accessories used for a revolving axle. If this circumstance does not depend on chance (or on the sparse documentation of old excavations), we must conclude that this type of cart was relatively fast. It could thus serve the lord to travel across his vast land holdings and possibly to carry a cargo or luggage on the floor. Furthermore, with this type there has not yet been found a valuable decoration, which would have made the structure too fragile. It would

Figure 41.24   The tomb of the Picene Princess of Sirolo (near Ancona) during the excavation: the cart was dismantled and stacked. From Emiliozzi 1997, pl. XXV, 1 (photograph courtesy of the Soprintendenza per i Beni Archeologici delle Marche, Ancona).

Figure 41.25   The cart of Sirolo reconstructed as a model 1:4, now preserved in Antiquarium of Sirolo. From Emiliozzi 1997, pl. XXV, 2.

be nice to think that in these carriages the seat always would have been attached to the anterior part of the floor (see Figs 41.22, 41.25), to allow the loading of luggage and household goods in the middle and rear part. In the same fashion, the metal accessories for the revolving axle are sometimes associated with showy bronze coverings (see Figs 41.15–17), which confirms that this type of cart was designed exclusively for ceremonies that took place in the town, in the sanctuary or the necropolis.

The possession and display of a chariot as a status symbol among the Etruscan aristocracy, and sometimes as a medium for figurative projects of self-representation in the same way as proper and permanent monuments dissuades us from seeking – among the remains found in tombs – the traces of chariots that were actually used in sporting competitions. From the rich grave goods in all the tombs with chariots we may deduce that the patrons led an aristocratic lifestyle, while we know that the racing jockeys were of servile origin and did not receive a burial like those of the lords who organized the races of *bigae* and *trigae* on the occasion of civil or religious holidays or for funerals.

The form of such chariots is known from figural monuments beginning in the third quarter of the sixth century BC (Bronson 1965, Jannot 1984, Decker 1991; see Chapter 45), in the friezes in terracotta of noble residences and temples (Fig. 41.26), in funerary sculpture and painting (Figs. 41.27, 41.28), but also in vase painting (Fig. 41.29). Such representations do not fall within the theme of this chapter, but are useful to illustrate the basic construction of a fast chariot in wood, leather and rawhide alone, and are useful for understanding why we find only the iron rims of the wheels in the majority of the remains of vehicles from the princely tombs of preceding centuries.

Figure 41.26   Chariot-racing depicted on terracotta friezes of Veii-Rome-Velletri type, dating 530–520 BC. From Fortunati 1993.

Figure 41.27a–b   Old drawings of the scene with preparations for a chariot race, painted in the Tomb of the Triclinium of Tarquinia. From Steingräber 1984, pp. 296–297.

Figure 41.28 Chariot-racing depicted on a funerary stone relief of Chiusi. From Thuillier 1993, Fig. 7.

Figure 41.29 Chariot-racing painted on a black-figure amphora by the Micali Painter. Copenhagen, Ny Carlsberg Glyptothek. From Rome 1988, pl. 4.

NOTES

1   Emiliozzi 1997,pl. I, 1–2; Martelli 2001, pp. 2–7, Figs. 2–3. Until recently I knew only the side of the vase with the chariot, from which seemed to be the familiar iconography of the warrior who rides on the wagon to go to the place of battle. The view of the opposite side (Fig. 41.1) now shows that it is rather the arrival at the battlefield, where the warrior will fight on foot after completing its panoply.

2   Bartoloni and Grottanelli 1984; Galeotti 1986–88.

3   See Emiliozzi 1996, 1999; Cygielman and Pagnini 2005; Emiliozzi 2006a, 2006bA; A. Emiliozzi, in Emiliozzi, Moscati and Santoro 2007, pp. 150–154; De Marinis and Palermo 2008; Emiliozzi 2010, 2011.

4   During the recent works and studies for a new reconstruction of the vehicles from the Regolini-Galassi Tomb at Cerveteri (Pareti 1947), I came to understand that the four-wheeled wagon does not really exist: it must be rebuilt as a two-wheeled vehicle, with the long rectangular platform balanced on the axle and encased between removable side walls, decorated with bronze sheets. Normally, it could be used without sides as a wagon for the transport of luggage and household goods, not of people. During its last funeral ceremony it was used, complete with side walls, for the transport of the dead. A similar situation should occur for the princely carriage from the tomb of Monte Michele at Veii (published by Boitani 1983), which should be launched to a new and accurate study.

5 Among the remains of vehicles found in the tombs, however, there are indications of sporadic adoption of the dorsal yoke, evidently under the influence of the exclusive use that was made in mainland Greece (see Emiliozzi 2010, p. 12f, cat. no. 11, Fig. 21).

6 References are in Emiliozzi 2011, note 33 to section II.

7 References are in Emiliozzi 2011, note 34 to section II.

8 Höckmann 1982, pp. 11–118; Emiliozzi 1997, pp. 21 off.; Feruglio 1997; Bruni 2002, p. 26 f., with a complete bibliography on the burial complex from which the chariots come (pp. 21–23, note 1).

9 See Winter 2009, nos. 2.D.2.a,c, 5.D.3.a,c.

10 A detailed examination of this part of the structure is provided by Emiliozzi 2011, section II, B.

11 See the examples from Monteleone di Spoleto (Emiliozzi 2011) and from Via Appia Antica near Rome (Emiliozzi 1997, pp. 191–202).

12 Colonna 1997, p. 17, Fig. 2.

13 See Emiliozzi 1997, pp. 102–103, 280f, 294–297, 349–353, and *passim* among references listed in note iii.

14 Emiliozzi 1997, pp. 291–297; A. Emiliozzi, in Emiliozzi, Moscati and Santoro 2007, pp. 150–154; website principisabini.it, Il calesse in 3D.

15 For the lekythos of the Amasis Painter (ca. 550–530 BC) see Crouwel 1992, pp. 79, 81, 89f, 93, Fig. 2, pls 38–39; Emiliozzi 1997, pl. 24. For that of the Gela Painter (ca. 500 BC) see Crouwel 1992, notes 377, 389, 467, 500; N. Eschbach, in Emiliozzi 1997, p. 61f, s. 3.

16 Emiliozzi 1997, pp. 176–177.

17 Höckmann (1982, pp. 40–42), followed by a majority of scholars, dates it to 560 BC; Bruni (2002, pp. 36–39) dates it to 580–575 BC. Maggiani (2007) thinks it should be dated after 580–570 BC, that is, after the Paolozzi Sheets.

18 Attempts have been made by Höckmann 1982 (pp. 26–31, Fig. 12), Bruni 2002 (pp. 27ff, Figs. 8–9, 11–14) and most recently by the National Archaeological Museum in Perugia, where parts of the bronze revetments of the vehicle are preserved.

19 See a picture in Emiliozzi 1997, pl. X (Populonia).

20 For example, Emiliozzi 1997, p. 264, Fig. 1d (Vetulonia).

21 Some examples are in Emiliozzi 1997, p. 103, Fig. 8 (Veii), p. 297, Fig. 26 (Eretum).

22 Examples in Emiliozzi 1997, pp. 102–103, 249–253, pl. XXVI (Sirolo); 280, no.12, Fig. 12 (Barbarano Romano).

23 For example, Emiliozzi 1997, p. 282f, nos. 13–14, Figs 13–14, pl. XIX, 3 (Barbarano Romano).

24 Examples in Emiliozzi 1997, pp. 282f, no. 15, Fig. 15 (Barbarano Romano); moreover p. 235, Fig. 10 (tomb of the Princess of Sirolo, were they were found in the original arrangement at depth of -211 and -217); also Fig. 22 on p. 253 for their placement in the vehicle.

25 Emiliozzi 2006b, Figs 1 (no. 7), 3–4.

26 See Emiliozzi 2010 in respect of the cart from Trevignano Romano.

27 Camerin and Emiliozzi 1997, nos. 165 (Veii-Vaccareccia tomb 5), 167 (Veii-Vaccareccia tomb 7), with bibliography.

BIBLIOGRAPHY

Bartoloni, G. and Grottanelli, C. (1984) "I carri a due ruote nelle tombe femminili del Lazio e dell'Etruria," *Opus* 3, 383–404.

Boitani, F. (1983) "Veio. La tomba principesca della necropoli di Monte Michele," *Studi Etruschi* 51, 535–556.

Bronson, R. C. (1965) "Chariot Racing in Etruria," *Studi in onore di Luisa Banti*, Rome: "L'ERMA" di Bretschneider, pp. 89–106.

Bruni, S., (2002) "I carri perugini: Nuove proposte di ricostruzione" in G. M. Della Fina (ed.), *Perugia Etrusca: Atti del IX Convegno Internazionale di Studi sulla Storia e l'Archeologia dell'Etruria, Orvieto*. (Annali della Fondazione per il Museo Claudio Faina 9), Rome: Edizioni Quasar, pp. 21–47.

Camerin, N. and Emiliozzi, A. (1997) "Repertorio dei carri provenienti dalla Penisola Italiana," in Emiliozzi 1997, pp. 305–39.

Crouwel, J. H. (1992) *Chariots and Other Wheeled Vehicles in Iron Age Greece*. Amsterdam: Allard Pierson.

Cygielman, M. and Pagninim, L. (2005) *La tomba del Tridente a Vetulonia*, Pisa-Rome: Istituti Editoriali e Poligrafici Internazionali.

De Marinis, G. and Palermo, L. (2008) "Il currus e il calesse" in M. Silvestrini and T. Sabbatini (eds), *Potere e splendore. Gli antichi Piceni a Matelica*, Exhibition catalogue, Palazzo Ottoni, Matelica, pp. 234–244. Rome.

Emiliozzi, A. (1996) "Il carro [Castel di Decima, Tomba 15]" in M. Bedello Tata (ed.), *Memorie dal sottosuolo: Una pagina di scavo dalla necropoli di Castel di Decima*, Exhibition catalogue, Museo dell'Alto Medioevo, Rome.

——(ed.) (1997) *Carri da Guerra e principi etruschi*, Exhibition catalogue, Palazzo dei Papi, Viterbo; Museo del Risorgimento, Rome; Mole Vanvitelliana, Ancona. Rome. Revised ed. 1999; reprinted 2000.

——(1999) " La sepoltura del carro nell'Italia antica. I carri dalla Tomba A di Casale Marittimo" in A. M. Esposito (ed.), *Principi Guerrieri* (Exhibition catalogue), Milan: Electa, pp. 43–47.

——(2006a) "Ipotesi di ricostruzione del Carro Dutuit" in V. Bellelli, *La tomba "principesca" dei Quattordici Ponti nel contesto di Capua arcaica*, Rome: "L'ERMA" di Bretschneider, pp. 131–48.

——(2006b) "Nuovi spunti per una lettura del calesse dalla tomba 928 di Pontecagnano," *AION*, n.s., sezione tematica, 11–12, 2004–2005 (2006), pp. 139–144.

——(2010) *I veicoli della tomba dei Flabelli di Trevignano Romano. Museo civico e area archeologica. Supplemento*, Trevignano Romano: Museo Civico.

——(2011) "The Etruscan Chariot from Monteleone di Spoleto," *MMAJ* 46, 2011, pp. 9–132.

Emiliozzi, A., Moscati, P. and Santoro, P. (2007) "The Princely Cart from Eretum" in *Virtual Museums and Archaeology (Archeologia e calcolatori*, suppl. 1), Borgo San Lorenzo, Florence: All'insegna del Giglio, pp. 143–62.

Feruglio, A. E. (1997) "Le applicazioni e gli accessori metallici" in Emiliozzi 1997, pp. 213–25.

Fortunati, F. R. (1993) "Il tempio delle Stimmate di Velletri: Il rivestimento arcaico e considerazioni sul sistema decorativo" in Eva Rystedt, Charlotte Wikander, and Örjan Wikander (eds), *Deliciae fictiles: Proceedings of the First International Conference on Central Italic Architectural Terracottas at the Swedish Institute in Rome, 10–12 December 1990*, Stockholm, pp. 255–65.

Jannot, J.-R. (1984) *Les reliefs archaïques de Chiusi*. Rome: Collection de l'École Française de Rome 71.

Galeotti, L. (1986–88) "Considerazioni sul carro a due ruote nell'Etruria e nel Latium Vetus," *Archeologia Classica* 38–40: pp. 94–104.

Höckmann, U. (1982) *Die Bronzen aus dem Fürstengrab von Castel San Mariano bei Perugia*, Munich: Beck.

Littauer, M. A. and Crouwel, J. H. (1979) *Wheeled Vehicles and Ridden Animals in the Ancient Near East*, Leiden: Brill.

——(1997) "Antefatti nell'Oriente Mediterraneo: Vicino Oriente, Egitto e Cipro" in Emiliozzi 1997, pp. 5–10.

Nachod, H. (1909) *Der Rennwagen bei den Italikern und ihren Nachbarn*, Leipzig: Radelli & Hille.

Pareti, L. (1947) *La tomba Regolini-Galassi del Museo Gregoriano Etrusco e la civiltà dell'Italia centrale nel sec. VII a.C.*, Città del Vaticano: Tipografia poliglotta vaticana.

Roma (1988) *Un artista etrusco e il suo mondo il Pittore di Micali*. Exhibition catalogue, Rome.

Romualdi, A. (1997) "Il complesso monumentale" in Emiliozzi 1997, pp. 155–157.

Stary, P. F. (1980) "Zur Bedeutung und Funktion zweirädrige Wagen während der Eisenzeit in Mittelitalien," *HBA* 7, pp. 7–21.

——(1981) *Zur eisenzeitlichen Bewaffnung und Kampfesweise in Mittelitalien (ca. 9. bis 6. Jh. v. Chr.).* 2 vols. Marburger Studien zur Vor- und Frühgeschichte 3, Mainz.

Steingräber, S. (1984) *Catalogo ragionato della pittura etrusca*, Milan: Jaca Book.

Thuillier, J.-P. (1993) "Les représentations sportives dans l'oevre du Peintre de Micali" in *Spectacles sportifs et scéniques dans le monde étrusco-italique* (Actes de la table ronde de Rome 1991), Rome: École Française, pp. 21–44.

Winter, N. A. (2009) *Symbols of Wealth and Power: Architectural Terracotta Decoration in Etruria and Central Italy, 640–510 B.C. MAAR*, Supplementary volume 9, Ann Arbor: University of Michigan Press.

Woytowitsch, E. (1978) *Die Wagen der Bronze- und frühen Eisenzeit in Italien.* Prähistorische Bronzefunde 17, vol. 1, Munich: Beck'sche Verlagsbuchhandlung.

CHAPTER FORTY TWO

THE WORLD OF ETRUSCAN TEXTILES

———— •◆• ————

Margarita Gleba

INTRODUCTION

A ubiquitous commodity in Etruscan life, one that required not only substantial material but also human resources, was cloth.[1] As an item of consumption, textiles range between luxury and necessity and are ideal for the creation of specialized products, the manufacture of which may be narrowly localized. Such localization creates demand and necessitates redistribution, resulting in textile trade. Hence, two developmental directions can be observed.[2] The first is towards production of luxury items needed for status display and (long-distance) gift exchange between the elites, which leads to the development of highly specialized/skilled craftsmanship and a network of exchange and resource and object circulation, which can be archaeologically traced through the distribution of objects. The second is directed towards the quick production of necessity goods, which are in demand by the developing urban communities. This in turn leads to a development of more organized modes of production and trade in these necessity products. Unlike many other specialized crafts that appeared in Etruria already during the Iron Age (e.g. glass or certain metal and pottery types), textile production was not a new craft. Instead, part of the production shifted from making subsistence products to the manufacture of non-essential or luxury goods. Thus, in addition to the adoption of new weaving techniques, technological changes were also induced by an organizational shift in production, i.e. a change in purpose, intensity and scale of organization of textile production. As such, textiles present a special case in the production system of Etruria.

Despite the poor preservation of textiles on the Apennine Peninsula, we can get a glimpse of the rich world of Etruscan textiles and their economic, social and religious significance through archaeological, iconographic and written evidence. Textiles were used for a variety of purposes by the Etruscans. Colorful garments are depicted on Etruscan figurines, statues, vases and tomb paintings and reflect not only changes in fashion through time but also the meaning of textiles as conveyors of individual and group identity.[3] Textile fibers were also used for a particular kind of linen armour, used during the fourth century BCE and illustrated in Etruscan tomb art.[4] In addition to garments, objects such as colorful bed covers, cushions, tablecloths, wall hangings and other utilitarian textiles are frequently represented in Etruscan tomb paintings.[5] A rather unique use of textiles in Etruria was for books, the *libri lintei*, which were made of linen and used for recording religious rituals. Fragments of one such book, the so-called "Zagreb mummy wrappings," were preserved in Egypt.[6] Another important utilitarian use of textile fibers was for sails and ship rigging. Etruscans were well known throughout the Mediterranean as sailors and – according to their enemies – notorious as pirates. Their ship-building technology was among the most sophisticated of their era, including the use of the earliest foresail.[7] The production of this multitude of textiles used on a daily basis by the Etruscans required considerable skills, resources, organization and planning.

TEXTILE FIBERS

The creation of a textile involves raw material acquisition and preparation, spinning, weaving, dyeing and finishing. Since resources for making textiles include plant and animal products used for fibers and dyes, textile production is closely linked to agriculture (e.g. flax cultivation), animal husbandry (e.g. sheep farming) and exploitation of environmental resources (e.g. fibers from nettle and tree bast, wild dye plants such as woad and madder and minerals for mordants used in dyeing such as alum).

Fiber is a basic unit of raw material having suitable length, pliability and strength for conversion into yarns and fabrics. In Etruria, two basic fiber groups, divided on the basis of their origin into plant and animal, were used in textile manufacture. Plant fibers were derived from the bast of linen, hemp, nettle, esparto and from trees such as linden, oak and willow. Cotton arrived in Europe only during the Roman period. The major animal fiber of antiquity was sheep's wool, with occasional use of goat hair. The other important animal fiber, silk, did not come into use in Italy until Roman times. Asbestos, an unusual mineral textile fiber derived from a mineral amphibole was used for special fabrics such as funeral shrouds due to its unique quality of withstanding extremely high temperatures.[8] The most sumptuous textiles incorporated gold thread.[9]

The most common fibers, flax and wool, were obtained from cultivated plants and domesticated animals, cultivation and husbandry of which in itself required expenditure of significant resources: land, labor and time. Additional time and effort went into the preparation of fibers for textile production. Wool had to be removed from sheep, sorted into various qualities and combed to prepare it for spinning. Flax had to be harvested, retted in standing water or dew, and then processed to remove the unwanted parts of the plant.

Once procured and prepared, the fiber mass could be spun into yarn, which in turn was woven into cloth. Several Etruscan iconographic documents illustrate these production stages of textile manufacture, underlining the economic and social importance of the craft for the Etruscan society. Spinning and weaving women are carved on the wooden throne found in Tomb 89 at Verucchio, dated circa 700 BCE (Fig. 42.1).[10] A bronze rattle or *tintinnabulum* found in Tomb 5 of Bologna's Arsenale Militare necropolis, dated circa 600 BCE (Fig. 42.2) illustrates the processes of dressing the distaffs, spinning, preparation of the warp and, finally, weaving on an unusual two-storied warp-weighted loom.[11] Both of these iconographic documents indicate that various textile production stages are associated with particular tools. Unlike the textiles themselves, many textile implements are ubiquitous on Etruscan archaeological sites. This great number of implements associated with textile manufacture can be used to study the craft and its technological and economic aspects.

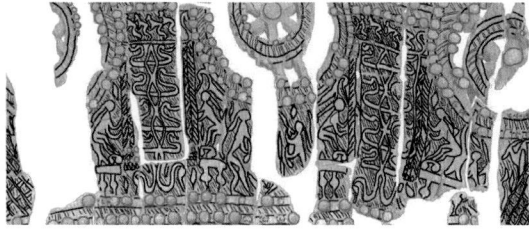

Figure 42.1 Wooden throne from Tomba del Trono, Verucchio, circa 700 BCE: two central scenes in the top register depict women at their looms (after von Eles 2002, Fig. 127).

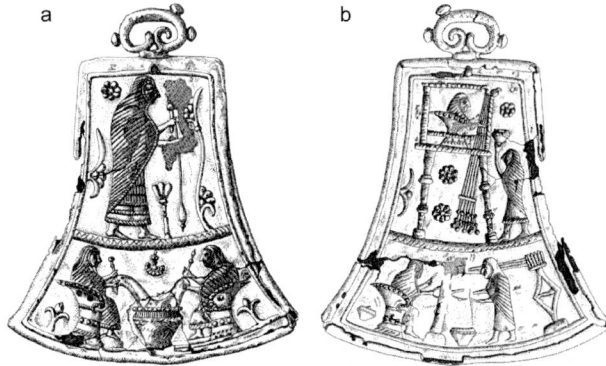

Figure 42.2 Bronze *tintinnabulum* from Tomba degli Ori, Arsenale Militare, Bologna, late seventh century BCE: a) side A, with scenes of spinning (top) and dressing the distaffs (bottom); (b) side B, with scenes of weaving (top) and warping (bottom). © Bologna Museo Civico Archeologico, reproduced with permission.

SPINNING

After the fiber mass has been prepared, it can be converted into a yarn by twisting and drawing out, or drafting, the fibers – the process known as spinning. Spinning was accomplished in Etruria on a suspended or drop spindle. A drop spindle is a simple rod with a hook or dent on top to attach the thread and a clay or stone whorl to sustain rotary movement. The type of spindle used in ancient Italy, and north of the Mediterranean in general, was a low-whorl spindle, in which the whorl was attached to the lower end of the spindle rod. An actual example of such a spindle has been found in the submerged village of Gran Carro in Lake Bolsena, dated to the early ninth century BCE (Fig. 42.3).[12] However, since most spindle shafts used in Antiquity were made of wood, often the only evidence for their use consists of the less perishable spindle whorls. The vast majority of spindle whorls in Italy are made of fired clay (Fig. 42.4), although examples made of luxury materials such as glass and amber have also been found in Etruscan burial contexts. Spindle whorls, often in large numbers, have been found on practically every settlement site in Etruria. A variety of whorl shapes and sizes are known and may reflect a relationship between the shape of the whorl, the speed of spinning and the tightness of the twist. A smaller diameter will cause the whorl to rotate faster and, therefore, to produce a tighter twist than could be accomplished with a wider whorl of the same weight. Hence, different whorls were required for different types of yarn.

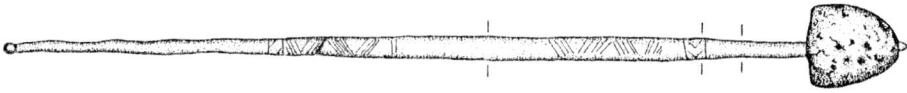

Figure 42.3 Spindle from Gran Carro, ninth century BCE (after Tamburini 1995, Fig. 51 no. 2081).

Figure 42.4 Ceramic spindle whorls, Poggio Civitate di Murlo, seventh-sixth century BCE.
Courtesy of Anthony Tuck.

As seen on the *tintinnabulum* depiction of a spinning lady, in addition to the spindle, spinning involved the use of another tool, a distaff, which is used to hold the prepared fiber. Short hand-held distaffs were used for spinning short-stapled fibers, while longer ones, held under the arm or in the belt, were used for longer fibers, such as flax. Distaffs were usually made of wood; even a simple forked stick would have been sufficient for the task. Considerably less frequent were items made of metals, including bronze, iron, silver and precious materials like glass and amber. Yet, while wooden distaffs have not survived in archaeological contexts, numerous examples of objects identified as distaffs made of luxury materials have been found in tombs of notable wealth.[13]

Spindles and distaffs were so closely associated with women in Etruria that women's contribution to the community as textile workers was symbolized by the deposition of spinning implements in their burials.[14] Textile tools, particularly spindle whorls, are common burial goods in Etruscan female graves. Examples such as a set of a bronze spindle and a bronze distaff from the eighth-century BCE Benacci-Caprara Tomb 56 in Bologna suggest that women were accompanied to their graves by a set of spinning tools.[15] Their symbolism continued well into the Roman period, when brides carried a spindle and a distaff during wedding processions.[16]

WEAVING

Once the required quantity of yarn has been spun, weaving can begin. Weaving is accomplished on a loom, a special frame that keeps the warp system in place, while allowing the weft to be passed in between warp threads. North of the Mediterranean in general, and in Etruria in particular, a warp-weighted loom was used (Fig. 42.5).[17] The loom was made up of two upright wooden beams that stood at a slight angle to the vertical plane, and a single horizontal or cloth beam, to which warp was attached. In a warp-weighted loom, as suggested by its name, the warp is kept taut by the weights attached at the bottom to groups of threads. Since these weights were made of stone or clay, they survive well in the archaeological contexts and allow us to trace the presence and sometimes even location of a warp-weighted loom on sites. The trapezoidal or truncated pyramidal shape of loom weights seems to have been prevalent in Etruria (Fig. 42.6), although ring-shaped loom weights were common north of the Arno River.[18] Occasionally loom weights are found *in situ* having fallen to the ground when the warp to which they were originally attached was destroyed or deliberately cut, as for example, at Poggio Baccherina near Chianciano.[19] A set of loom weights is typically composed of six to thirty implements, although it could reach as many as eighty.[20] Fewer loom weights would be needed if they are heavy and/or wide and more if they are light and/or narrow.[21]

The weaving on a warp-weighted loom started at the top, hence the weft had to be packed upwards. In the simplest tabby weave the warp is divided by pulling every second thread and inserting a rod or shed bar between the two groups in such a way that one of the groups is in front of it. Such a position creates an open or natural shed through which the weft could be passed all at once. The artificial or counter shed is then achieved by providing the back set of warp threads with heddles, or individual holders, usually made out of string for each individual warp end thread, which are attached to a heddle bar. When the heddle bar is lifted, it separates the threads in the direction opposite to the original shed. In more complex twill weaves, the warp is divided into more groups, attached to several heddle bars which are lifted in a specific sequence to achieve a particular pattern.

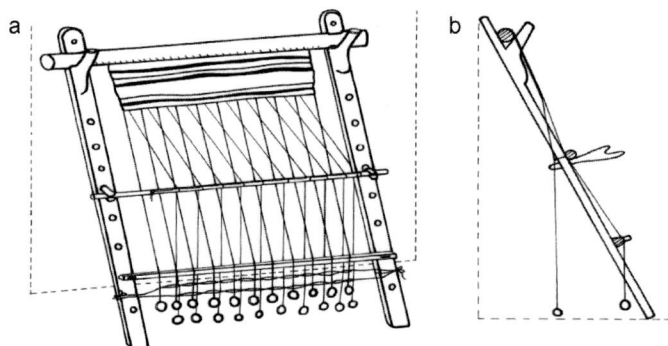

Figure 42.5 Warp-weighted loom and its position with: a) natural shed; b) artificial shed.
Courtesy of Eva Andersson Strand.

Figure 42.6 Ceramic loom weights, Poggio Civitate di Murlo, seventh-sixth century BCE.
Courtesy of Anthony Tuck.

Before weaving could begin, however, the warp had to be prepared separately from the loom and then attached to the cloth beam. This was accomplished by making a starting border or heading band, the weft of which becomes the warp of the loom. This band could be made on a special band loom in order to measure out and organize the warp threads. The only likely representation of such a device is seen on the Bologna *tintinnabulum* (Fig. 42.2). Another method was tablet weaving.

Tablet weaving involves passing threads through holes in the corners of (usually) square tablets (sometimes called cards), which, when rotated forward or back, force the threads to form different sheds (Fig. 42.7). By rotating cards in different combinations, it is possible to achieve numerous patterns. This method is suitable for weaving narrow bands, such as belts, heading bands for the warp of a warp-weighted loom, or decorative borders for the base textile. Tablet weaving in Etruria is attested not only by the presence of such borders on textiles but also by the finds of tablets, metal clasps, bone spacers with pegs and, particularly, by terracotta spools (*rocchetti*) (Fig. 42.8).[22] The latter were probably used as weights in tablet weaving.

FINISHING

After the textile had been taken off the loom, it had to be finished. Linen cloth could be subjected to various rough treatments to make it softer or it could be rubbed with a special stone or glass piece to give it extra luster. Linen could also be bleached in the sun. Wool cloth could be subjected to fulling, a treatment with water and, sometimes, soap that produces a very tight fabric. The surface of a wool fabric could also be raised to produce a nap. Another finishing process for both linen and wool textiles was pleating, as demonstrated by representations of Etruscan garments in art, which depict regular and often elaborate pleating of certain garments, particularly mantles, as for example in the case of the Apollo of Veii. Some of the textiles found at Verucchio provide the first hard evidence of such practice.[23]

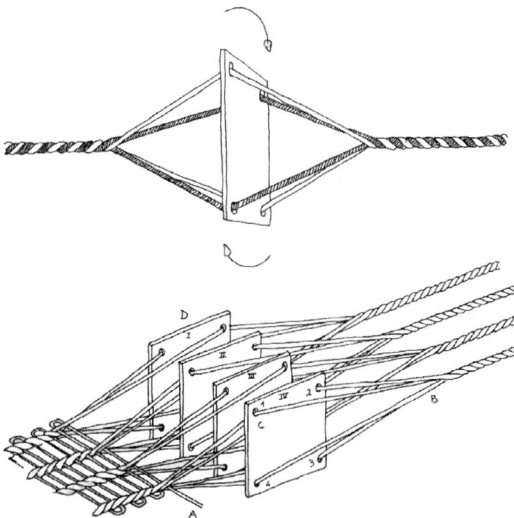

Figure 42.7 Tablet weaving. Courtesy of Lise Ræder Knudsen.

Figure 42.8 Ceramic spools, Poggio Civitate di Murlo, seventh-sixth century BCE.
Courtesy of Anthony Tuck.

Although ancient Italy is commonly regarded as the area of the "woven to shape" or "off-the-loom" textiles,[24] archaeological finds indicate that the needle was in use for both structural and decorative purposes. For example, some of the finds from Verucchio have seams and hems,[25] while stitches are visible on the garments of the Augurs depicted in the Tomb of the Augurs at Tarquinia.[26] Applied decoration was used in Etruscan textiles and could consist of seeds, glass beads, amber or metal attachments. The evidence of sewing activities also comes to us in the shape of numerous finds of bronze and bone needles.[27]

DYEING

While plant fibers resulted in uniformly colored shades of grey-white, wool came in a variety of natural shades, which could be used for decorative purposes, and white wool could be dyed many bright colors. Tomb paintings illustrate Etruscan garments and utilitarian textiles resplendent in reds, blues, greens, yellows and purples. A variety of plants and animals could have been used for the purpose.[28] Dye analyses of surviving textiles from Verucchio and Sasso di Furbara demonstrate the popularity of reds, blues and purples. Blue color could be obtained from woad (*Isatis tinctoria* L.). Reds and oranges were some of the most sought after and expensive colors. The root of dyer's madder (*Rubia tinctorum* L. and other similar species like *Rubia peregrina* L.), native to south Europe and cultivated by Roman times, was probably the most commonly used red dye source. According to later sources, Etruscans called it *lappa minor*.[29] Yellows could be obtained more easily and from a larger variety of plants, such as weld or dyer's weed (*Reseda luteola* L.), dyer's greenweed (*Genista tinctoria* L.) and many others. In addition to the bright colors, often requiring expensive and rare dyes, a variety of shades could be obtained from plants common throughout the Italian Peninsula. Many trees produce tannin-bearing dyes, which are also used for the curing of hides. Thus, oak and sumac can be used to dye textiles yellow, brown, or black, while pine produces brown and yellow dyes. Galls and nuts were commonly used for brown. The berries of *Sambucus nigra* L. produce green or black color while blueberries create a violet, pink, or blue-grey effect. River cane can be used to dye fiber green or yellow and nettle yellow-green or grey-green. Lichens produce brown, yellow and purple shades. The most expensive dye of antiquity, royal or shellfish purple has recently been identified in textiles from three Hellenistic period burials at Strozzacapponi, Perugia.[30] This is the first direct evidence for the use of purple in Etruria as seen in stripes and decorations on dresses such as those depicted on the images of the women of the Seianti family from second-century BCE Chiusi.[31]

ETRUSCAN TEXTILES

The resulting textiles and items made out of them are illustrated not only by the rich Etruscan iconographic sources but also by the archaeological remains. The vast majority of Etruscan textiles have been recovered from burials in Italy. One important exception is represented by the fragments of an Etruscan linen book, which was taken to Egypt sometime during the Hellenistic period and survived in the dry Egyptian climate because it was torn into strips and used as mummy wrappings.[32]

Etruscan textiles survive in either original organic, charred or, most frequently, mineralized state. The largest groups of textile remains still in their organic shape have been excavated at Verucchio[33] and at Sasso di Furbara.[34] Other finds come from Casale Marittimo and Cogion-Coste di Manone (Fig. 42.9).[35] Mineralized textiles are formations in which either metal corrosion products or calcium salts form casts around fibers retaining their external morphology and size almost unaltered (Fig. 42.10).[36] Even minute traces can provide a considerable amount of information about ancient textiles. Textiles preserved in association with metal objects are known from Bologna, Chiusi, Chianciano, Veii, Vulci, Tarquinia, Casale Marittimo, Murlo and numerous other sites.[37]

The surviving textiles demonstrate that Etruscans were familiar with diverse fibers, dyes and sophisticated weaving techniques. A variety of techniques were used to create textiles, including loom weaving, tablet weaving, soumak and some type of twining. The basic weaves include a variety of tabbies and twills.[38] Although regarded as an Iron Age feature of textile technology, twill developed during the Bronze Age and by the Early Iron Age complex twills are ubiquitous throughout Europe. The sophistication of twills from Verucchio and Sasso di Furbara points to a well-established and settled technology.

Figure 42.9   Textile fragment from Cogion-Coste di Manone, fourth century BCE © University of Pennsylvania Museum, reproduced with permission.

Figure 42.10   Mineralized textile remains from the Tomba della Montagnola at Sesto Fiorentino, seventh century BCE: a-b) tabby from bronze armour; c) twill from funerary bed.
Courtesy of Larissa Bonfante.

Furthermore, yarns of opposite twists were frequently combined to create spin-patterned twills, as in the cases of Verucchio and Sasso di Furbara. The reason for this tendency may be aesthetic, but it also reflects the knowledge of technique and appreciation of the subtlety of spin pattern. By the Hellenistic period, there is evidence of tapestry weaving, as illustrated by the elaborate representation of figures dancing a war dance on the triumphal mantle of Vel Saties in the fourth century BCE François Tomb, at Vulci.

The mantles and tunic-shaped garments found at Verucchio have been demonstrated to be ceremonial garments[39] and their tablet-woven borders appear to be status markers not only by their presence but also by their width bearing significance. The specifics of the presence of spools in Early Iron Age burials of Italy and the ubiquitous presence of borders in Etruscan garment representations further argue that these borders were not purely decorative but communicated a very clear and important message of status not only to the Etruscans but also among other European Early Iron Age cultures. Tablet-woven borders are also found on textiles from the princely burials in Central and Western Europe (e.g. Hallstatt, Austria; Hochdorf and Hohmichele, Germany; El Cigarralejo, Spain).[40] Moreover, the toga, the Roman descendant of the Verucchio mantles, retained the border as the status symbol, in this case dyed purple.

TEXTILE PRODUCTION AND ITS DEVELOPMENT
THROUGH TIME

The textile finds from Sasso di Furbara and Verucchio show many similarities, including the use of thread with varied twist direction to create a pattern, and the tablet-woven borders technique, as well as complex dyeing procedures. They demonstrate that by the seventh century BCE a sophisticated technology with the capacity to produce highly complex and labor-consuming luxury textiles existed in Etruria. The production of these textiles not only required highly specialized materials and skills, available only to the members of the elite classes of society, but was also in itself an exclusive, elite female occupation marked at death by the funeral deposition of associated tools. Thus, the *tintinnabulum* of Bologna and the Verucchio throne, both depicting textile production scenes, are prestige objects in their own right, indicating not only that textiles constituted a source of wealth and/ or status for their owners, but also that specialized textile production, specifically the manufacture of ceremonial garments, was the prerogative of the elite women represented.

Despite the high degree of specialization that characterizes this type of textile production in the Early Iron Age, it remained confined to the household level, as indicated by the regular finds of small quantities of textile instruments on settlement sites. By the seventh century BCE, however, a new production mode seems to come into play, appearing at certain sites, such as Murlo and Acquarossa, where large quantities of tools were found concentrated in small areas or in specific structures.[41] The size, shape, material and, often, decoration, of the tools themselves show increasing standardization, and they were most likely produced by specialists. Frequently, textile implements are concentrated in areas where other kinds of production, such as ceramic or metal, have been documented, suggesting a household or even workshop mode of manufacture and the existence of at least part-time specialist craftspeople. This change coincides with the specialization and professionalization of other crafts, most notably metallurgy and ceramic production.[42]

These changes also coincide with the emergence of urban centers in Etruria. Socio-political power became more and more concentrated in the hands of wealthy families who controlled both trade and production. Changes in economic demands led to "a gradual shift from production of luxury goods to subsistence goods and intensification of local specialized production" during the seventh and sixth centuries BCE.[43] The picture that emerges from the funerary context is one of textile production that is no longer controlled by the elites in the same way as it was in the Early Iron Age. The bronze distaffs that were common during the Villanovan period disappear by the sixth century BCE, as do the spools, which are found mainly in tombs dated from the tenth through to the sixth centuries BCE, with a few exceptional cases dated between the fifth-fourth centuries BCE. The weaving of ceremonial textiles is no longer the prerogative of elite ladies but is now handled by specialists or even slaves on a more "industrialized" level.

Robes such as the Verucchio mantles were made for specific ceremonial purposes and would probably have circulated through gift exchange. During the Orientalizing and Archaic periods there is a significant increase in the scale of textile production, indicated by the large number and standardization of tools. Cloth was likely produced for commercial purposes and textile trade in Etruria has been tied to salt, amber, slaves and other commodities.[44] Textile trade seems to be indicated indirectly by the spread of Etruscan fashion to central Europe as attested in the Situla Art.[45] While there is no evidence that textile production in Etruria ever reached an industrial scale of organization before the Roman period, there is strong indication of a manufacture mode, which greatly exceeded in quantity the simple subsistence production.

CONCLUSION

The abundance of textile tools on settlements and in burials from the Villanovan period onwards demonstrates that various stages of textile production were among the main economic activities and sources of wealth in Etruria. As one of the most important and labor-intensive crafts of the ancient world, textile production had great social significance in Etruria. This was expressed in funerary ritual through the inclusion of textile implements among the burial goods, as well as in religious activities through the deposition of textile tools in votive and foundation deposits.[46] Textile production was also an integral part of local and regional economies and local, regional and international trade.

The sophistication of Etruscan textiles – from the Villanovan Verucchio mantles to the Hellenistic triumphal mantle of Vel Saties depicted in the François Tomb at Vulci – demonstrates the high level of technical and artistic skills of the local textile makers, which did not diminish with changing political and economic fortunes of the Etruscans. As the power of the military aristocracy declined, social and political power was transferred to the more mercantile element of society, and large urban centers developed that were able to afford to have specialists to produce not only luxury but also subsistence goods (see Chapter 7). Textile production thus became an enterprise on a much larger scale, moving from individual specialists of the early Iron Age to a specialized workshop-based manufacture during the Archaic and later periods. It should come as no surprise that many aspects of the Etruscan world were mirrored in its textiles and their production.

NOTES

1   On textiles in antiquity, see Barber 1991 and Gleba and Mannering 2012.
2   Schneider and Weiner 1989.
3   On Etruscan dress, see Bonfante 2003.
4   Gleba 2012.
5   See Steingräber 1985 and 2006 *passim*.
6   van der Meer 2007. Cf. Chapter 22 in this volume.
7   Turfa and Steinmayer 1999. Cf. Chapter 40 in this volume.
8   Pionati Shams 1987: 3–11. Pliny the Elder (36.19–21) calls it live or incombustible linen and praises its usefulness for making funeral shrouds, napkins, lamp wicks, and fishing nets. The British Museum has an example of presumably Etruscan asbestos; see Gleba 2008: 63–64.
9   Pliny the Elder (*HN* 7.196) quotes Verrius Flaccus who said that the Etruscan king of Rome Tarquinius Priscus (traditional dates 616–578 BCE) celebrated a triumph wearing a golden tunic. On gold thread in ancient Italy, see Gleba 2008: 81–82.
10 Torelli 1997: 68–69; von Eles 2002.
11 Morigi Govi 1971.
12 Tamburini 1995: 169 no. 2081, Fig. 51.
13 Gleba 2008: 109–122.
14 Gleba 2009a.
15 Forte and von Eles 1994: 55 no. 32

16 Pliny *HN* 8.194; see Torelli 1984: 131, 133; Cottica 2007.
17 Hoffmann 1964.
18 On loom weight typology in Etruria and pre-Roman Italy in general, see Gleba 2008: 127–138.
19 Paolucci 1997: 56–57.
20 Barber 1991, 104.
21 Functional aspects of loom weights are discussed by Mårtensson *et al.* 2010.
22 On tablet weaving and tools involved, see Gleba 2008: 138–152; Raeder Knudsen 2012.
23 Stauffer 2012: 250.
24 Granger-Taylor 1982.
25 Stauffer 2012: 249.
26 Steingräber 1986: Pls 14–15.
27 Gleba 2008: 156–158.
28 On ancient and historic dyes and their sources, see Cardon 2007.
29 Bonfante 2002: 190 gloss 842.
30 Gleba and Vanden Berghe in press.
31 Swaddling and Prag 2002.
32 For the history of the find and a complete bibliography, see van der Meer 2007.
33 Traces of actual textiles have been found in numerous burials dating from 700 to 650 BCE and are undergoing analysis. Detailed studies of textiles from the male burials can be found in Stauffer 2002; 2003; 2004; 2012.
34 A large number of wool textile fragments were retrieved in 1953 at the Caolino necropolis at Sasso di Furbara in central-west Italy, found by construction workers in a wooden monoxile (dugout) boat, interpreted as a cenotaph; for analysis see Masurel 1982; Mamez and Masurel 1992. The boat was ^{14}C dated (radiocarbon dated) to the eighth century BCE, which is consistent with the stylistic dating of the materials found in the surrounding necropolis; Brusadin Laplace and Patrizi Montoro, 1982.
35 Esposito 1999; Gleba 2008: 50–51.
36 On textile mineralization in the presence of metal, see Chen *et al.* 1998.
37 See catalogue in Gleba 2008: 50–56.
38 On different weaves, see Barber 1991.
39 Stauffer 2002; 2012.
40 Raeder Knudsen 2012: 262.
41 For Acquarossa, see Östenberg 1975: 11–12; for Murlo, see Gleba 2000.
42 Nijboer 1998.
43 Nijboer 1997: 400.
44 Wells 1980: 43–44; Nash Briggs 2003: 253.
45 Bonfante 2003: 4–5, 132.
46 Gleba 2009b.

BIBLIOGRAPHY

Barber, E. J. W. (1991) *Prehistoric Textiles. The Development of Cloth in the Neolithic and Bronze Ages*, Princeton: Princeton University Press.

Bonfante, L. (2003) *Etruscan Dress*, 2nd ed., Baltimore: Johns Hopkins.

Bonfante, G. and Bonfante L. (2002) *The Etruscan Language: An Introduction*, Revised Edition, Manchester and New York: Manchester University Press.

Brusadin Laplace, D. and Patrizi-Montoro, G. and S. (1992) "Le necropoli protostoriche del Sasso di Furbara III: Il Caolino ed altri sepolcreti Villanoviani." *Origini* 16, 221–94.

Buranelli, F. (1983) *La necropoli villanoviana "Le Rose" di Tarquinia*, Roma: Consiglio Nazionale delle Ricerche.

Cardon, D. (2007) *Natural Dyes – Sources, Tradition, Technology, Science*, London: Archetype.

Chen, H. L., Jakes, K. A. and Foreman, D. W. (1998) "Preservation of Archaeological Textiles Through Fibre Mineralization," *Journal of Archaeological Science* 25: 1015–1021.

Cottica, D. (2007) "Spinning in the Roman World: from Everyday Craft to Metaphor of Destiny" in C. Gillis and M.-L. B. Nosch (eds), *Ancient Textiles – Production, Crafts and Society*, Oxford: Oxbow Books, 220–228.

Esposito, A. M. (1999) *I principi guerrieri. La necropoli etrusca di Casale Marittimo*, Milan: Electa.

Forte, M. and von Eles, P. (eds) (1994) *La pianura bolognese nel Villanoviano. Insediamenti della prima età del Ferro*, Florence: All'Insegna del Giglio.

Gleba, M. (2000) "Textile Production at Poggio Civitate (Murlo) in the 7th c. BC," in D. Cardon and M. Feugère (eds), *Archéologie des textiles des origines au Ve siecle. Actes du colloque de Lattes, oct. 1999*, Monographies Instrumentum 14, Montagnac: Éditions Monique Mergoul, 75–80.

——(2008) *Textile Production in Pre-Roman Italy*, Oxford: Oxbow Books.

——(2009a) "Textile tools and specialisation in the Early Iron Age female burials" in E. Herring and K. Lomas (eds), *Gender Identities in Italy in the First Millennium BC*, BAR Int. Ser. 1983, Oxford: Archaeopress, 69–78.

——(2009b) "Textile Tools in Ancient Italian Votive Contexts: Evidence of Dedication or Production?" in M. Gleba and H. W. Becker (eds), *Votives, Places and Rituals in Etruscan Religion. Studies in Honour of Jean MacIntosh Turfa*, Leiden, Brill, 69–84.

——(2012) "Linen-clad Etruscan warriors" in M.-L. Nosch (ed.), *Wearing the Cloak: Dressing the Soldier in Roman Times*, Oxford: Oxbow Books, 45–55.

Gleba, M. and Mannering, U. (eds) (2012) *Textiles and Textile Production in Europe from Prehistory to AD 400*, Oxford and Oakville: Oxbow Books.

Gleba, M. and Vanden Berghe, I. (forthcoming) "Textiles from Strozzacapponi (Perugia/Corciano), Italy – new evidence of purple production in pre-Roman Italy" in C. Alfaro (ed.), *Purpureae Vestes IV*, València.

Granger-Taylor, H. (1982) "Weaving Clothes to Shape in the Ancient World: The Tunic and Toga of the *Arringatore*," *Textile History* 13(1): 3–25.

Hoffmann, M. (1964) *The Warp-Weighted Loom. Studies in the History and Technology of an Ancient Implement*, Studia Norvegica 14, Oslo: Universitetsforlaget.

Mårtensson, L., Nosch, M.-L. and Andersson Strand, E. B. (2009) "Shape of Things: understanding a Loom Weight," *Oxford Journal of Archaeology* 28(4): 373–398.

Mamez, L. and Masurel, H. (1992) "Étude complémentaire des vestiges textiles trouvés dans l'embarcation de la nécropole du Caolino à Sasso di Furbara," *Origini* 16: 295–310.

Masurel, H. (1982) "Les vestiges textiles retrouvés dans l'embarcation," *Origini* 11: 381–414.

Morigi Govi, C. (1971) "Il tintinnabulo della 'Tomba degli Ori' dell'Arsenale Militare di Bologna," *Archeologia Classica* 23: 211–235.

Nash Briggs, D. (2003) "Metals, salt and slaves: economic links between Gaul and Italy and France from the eighth to the late sixth centuries BC," *Oxford Journal of Archaeology* 22(3): 243–259.

Nijboer. A. J. (1997) "The Role of Craftsmen in the Urbanization Process of Central Italy (8th to 6th Centuries BC)," *Acta Hyperborea* 7: 383–406.

——(1998) *From Household Production to Workshops*, Groningen: Groningen Institute of Archaeology.

Östenberg, C. E. (1975) *Case etrusche di Acquarossa*. Rome: Multigrafica Editrice.

Paolucci, G. (1997) *Museo Civico Archeologico delle Acque di Chianciano Terme*, Siena: Protagon Editori Toscani.

Pionati Shams, G. (1987) *Some Minor Textiles in Antiquity*, Gothenburg: Paul Åströms Förlag.

Raeder Knudsen, L. (2012) "The tablet-woven borders of Verucchio" in M. Gleba and U. Mannering (eds), *Textiles and Textile Production in Europe from Prehistory to AD 400*, Oxford and Oakville: Oxbow Books, 254–265.

Schneider, J. and Weiner, A. B. (1989) "Introduction" in A. B. Weiner and J. Schneider (eds), *Cloth and Human Experience*, Washington and London: Smithsonian, 1–29.

Stauffer, A. (2002) "I tessuti" in P. von Eles (ed.), *Guerriero e sacerdote. Autorità e comunità nell'età del ferro a Verucchio. La Tomba del Trono*, Florence: All'Insegna del Giglio, 192–219.

——(2003) "Ein Gewebe mit Schnurapplikation aus der 'Tomba del Trono' in Verucchio (700 v. Chr.)" in L. Bender Jørgensen, J. Banck-Burgess and A. Rast-Eicher (eds), *Textilien aus Archäologie und Geschichte. Festschrift für Klaus Tidow*, Neumünster: Wachholtz Verlag, 205–208.

——(2004) "Early Etruscan Garments from Verucchio," *Bulletin du CIETA* 81: 14–20.

——(2012) "Case Study: The Textiles from Verucchio, Italy" in M. Gleba and U. Mannering (eds), *Textiles and Textile Production in Europe from Prehistory to AD 400*, Oxford: Oxbow Books, 242–253.

Steingräber, S. (1986) *Etruscan Painting. Catalogue Raisonné of Etruscan Wall Paintings*, New York: Harcourt Brace Jovanovich.

——(2006) *Abundance of Life: Etruscan Wall Painting*, Los Angeles: The J. Paul Getty Museum.

Swaddling, J. and Prag, J. (eds) (2002) *Seianti Hanunia Tlesnasa. The Story of an Etruscan Noblewoman*, The British Museum Occasional Paper Number 100, London: British Museum.

Tamburini, P. (1995) *Un abitato villanoviano perilacustre. Il "Gran Carro" sul lago di Bolsena (1959–1985)*, Rome: Giorgio Bretschneider Editore.

Torelli, M. (1984) *Lavinio e Roma*, Rome: Edizioni Quasar.

——(1997) "'Domiseda, lanifica, univira.' Il trono di Verucchio e il ruolo e l'imagine della donna tra arcaismo e repubblica" in M. Torelli, *Il rango, il rito e l'immagine. Alle origini della rapresentazione storica romana*, Milan: Mondadori Electa, 52–85.

Turfa, J. M. and Steinmayer, A. G. Jr. (1999) "The Earliest Foresail, on Another Etruscan Vase," *International Journal of Nautical Archaeology* 28(3): 292–296.

van der Meer, B. (2007) *The Liber linteus zagrabiensis. The Linen Book of Zagreb. A Comment on the Longest Etruscan Text*, Leiden: Peeters.

von Eles, P. (ed.) (2002) *Guerriero e sacerdote. Autorità e comunità nell'età del Ferro a Verucchio. La Tomba del Trono*, Florence: All'Insegna del Giglio.

Wells, P. S. (1980) *Culture Contact and Culture Change: Early Iron Age Central Europe and the Mediterranean world*, Cambridge: Cambridge University Press.

CHAPTER FORTY THREE

FOOD AND DRINK IN THE ETRUSCAN WORLD

———·◆·———

Lisa C. Pieraccini

The topic of food and drink in the Etruscan world usually conjures up images of the so-called "banquet." But outside of the banquet, which we must remember was limited to an elite few, where else do we see evidence of food and drink in Etruria? The habitation sites thus far excavated reveal the use of hearths, cooking stands and other utensils for cooking food; an essential part of daily life in ancient Italy from the Bronze Age onward.[1] But do we find evidence of the preparation of food outside of the home? Did food and drink play a role at civic and religious feasts and rituals – and what were the Etruscans eating and drinking on these occasions? Tomb paintings depict banquets, but did loved ones leave food in the tomb as part of the funerary ritual? Deciphering the archaeological record for such an inquiry is challenging to say the least, not only due to the lack of Etruscan literature but also for the food substances that have simply not survived. But new advances in the way in which we interpret material culture coupled with recent studies of food utensils and cooking equipment reveal a broader picture of Etruscan customs surrounding food and drink. This study will not include an analysis of the banquet *per se*, (which is already covered in this book, see Chapter 44) but rather will focus on the evidence of food and drink outside of the banquet. Of particular interest is how food and drink were incorporated into civic and funerary rituals and how food and their utensils may have communicated status and wealth. Such a study uncovers another dimension to the overall picture of drinking and eating and its significant place in Etruscan life and Afterlife.

THE FERTILE LANDS OF ETRURIA: GRAIN, GRAPES, AND OLIVES

Archaeological evidence suggests that the basis for the rapid social and economic surge in Italy during the ninth-seventh centuries BC stems from agriculture and metallurgy, both important components of the Etruscan economy.[2] Although the Etruscans have not left us with their agricultural treatises, cookbooks and general thoughts on food, the Romans had much to say about Etruscan agriculture. In fact, multiple accounts show

how Romans repeatedly described Etruria's lush lands and abundant grains, especially *farro* (spelt) as a rich resource (Diod. V, 40; Varro *Rust.* I, 44).[3] *Farro* (*puls*), which was a staple in the Roman diet, certainly had its roots in Etruria.[4]

The Romans documented the plentiful Etruscan crops as early as the fifth century BC when Etruria provided grain to Rome during several famines (Dio. Hal. *Ant.* VII, 1, 2–5; Livy II, 34–3, IV, 52; XXII, 3, 1–7).[5] Romans also mention Etruscan sites for their splendid vineyards, olives, and figs (Dion Hal. *Ant.* I, 37, 1–4; Livy, V, 33; Plut, *Cam.* XV, 1–6). The quantity of grain was so abundant in Etruria that we hear of Cerveteri, Roselle, Volterra, Chiusi, Perugia and Arezzo giving large amounts of grain to the Roman general Scipio during the Punic Wars (Livy XXVIII, 45).[6]

Fruit too played a significant role in the ancient Etruscan diet, the vineyards, olive groves and wild fig trees supplied drink, oil, and food and formed a staple component of the ancient Mediterranean diet. Fava beans, peas and chestnuts were widely abundant and we know that chickpeas were cultivated as well.[7] The various meats available to the Etruscans consisted of wild boar, pig, sheep, bovine and goat, not to mention chickens, ducks and various other fowl, which also provided eggs.[8] The lakes and rivers, as well as the Tyrrhenian Sea, certainly supplied a variety of fish for local fishermen.[9] One of the most important testimonies of this is the celebrated Tomb of Hunting and Fishing at Tarquinia dating to circa 530 BC.[10] The back wall of the second chamber offers a snapshot of life on the coast with fishermen pulling up their nets, a hunter using a sling to capture colorful birds who swoop above the fishermen, while dolphins dive in and out of the sea (Fig. 43.1). Although this tomb features an aristocratic banquet in the upper pediment of the same wall, the actions below belong to the world of fishermen and hunters. Likewise, the Golini Tomb I in Orvieto offers an image of slaves preparing food for the banquet, a unique scene indeed.[11] Although we cannot assume that the slaves were consuming the same food items as the aristocracy, at least we know what was available in Etruria at this time; from this we can postulate that some of the population outside of the aristocracy, farmers, hunters and fishermen for example, were consuming high-protein foods whenever possible.

Figure 43.1   Tomb of Hunting and Fishing, Tarquinia, circa 530 BC. The back wall depicts fishermen pulling up nets while dolphins dive in and out of the water (Soprintendenza per i Beni Archeologici dell'Etruria Meridionale).

KITCHENS, COOKING AND COOKING UTENSILS

The Swedish excavation of Acquarossa reveals a number of Etruscan Iron Age huts and archaic houses along with a large quantity of cooking stands and fixed hearths.[12] Likewise, the huts and houses on the acropolis at San Giovenale provide rich evidence of fixed hearths, cooking stands and braziers used in a domestic setting.[13] However humble ancient cooking stands and braziers may appear to the modern viewer, they were an essential part of civilized life offering heat, warmth and light, not to mention their ability to prepare meals.[14] The most comprehensive assessment to date of ancient Italic cooking stands is C. Scheffer's work conducted at Acquarosssa (1981–82).[15] The cooking stand supports a container for cooking (Fig. 43.2), while the brazier is a pan, dish or "stand" used for holding coals.[16] Long neglected before Scheffer's important study, cooking stands and braziers prove to be remarkable artifacts in their own right. If anything, they offer one of the finest examples of continuity in form within the realm of ancient Mediterranean pottery.[17]

One of the most plentiful classes of Etruscan decorated braziers was produced at ancient Caere (Cerveteri) from the end of the seventh to the end of the sixth century BC (Fig. 43.3).[18] The braziers were made in the same workshop as the large *pithoi* and were adorned by rolling a cylinder stamp around the rim of the vessel, leaving a decorative relief. Although both vessels have routinely appeared in Caeretan tombs dating from the Archaic period, the braziers fulfilled a role well beyond that of the tomb;[19] used as portable hearths serving numerous functions in the domestic, civic and funerary worlds.[20] It appears that the *pithoi* were destined for the tomb to accompany the deceased

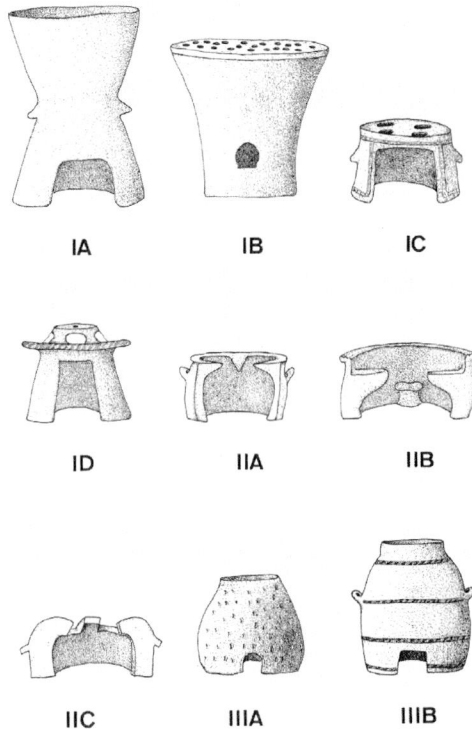

IA   IB   IC

ID   IIA   IIB

IIC   IIIA   IIIB

Figure 43.2 Drawing of the principle characteristics of Italic cooking stands (after Scheffer 1981, Fig. 2).

in the Afterlife (perhaps symbolically representing a plentiful surplus of food).[21] Chiusi produced handsome *bucchero pesante* "dining sets" dated to the sixth century BC, which often included bowls with lids, cups, plates, and serving utensils, placed in a so-called *focolare* tray and may have been for the deceased to use in the Afterlife. (Fig. 43.4).[22] The Etruscans have left us a plethora of cooking utensils at domestic sites (cooking stands, hearths, etc.), at sanctuaries (vases, dishes, pouring utensils, etc.) and in tombs (braziers, roasting spits, etc.). Depictions of cooking ware and cooking utensils are not hard to find featured in Etruscan art. Take for example, the Tomb of the Reliefs at ancient Caere, where skewers for meat, cooking pots, a butchering knife, and a pestle are just some of the items portrayed in painted relief in the tomb.[23]

FOOD AND THE ARCHAEOLOGICAL RECORD: RITUAL MEALS

Examples of meals prepared and offered or eaten for ritual use at the temple and tomb have survived.[24] The most obvious being the sacrificial remains of animals left at temples and sanctuaries throughout Etruria (which tells us much about the type of animals butchered and eaten). The bones from pig, goat, sheep and bovine are the most commonly found remains at such sites (see Chapter 1). Exactly who was eating the meat and how these portions were divided up is lost upon us today, although most scholars would agree that priests and "religious officials" were privy to such meals.[25]

Figure 43.3   Caeretan brazier, circa 575 BC, Cerveteri, Monte Abatone Tomb 120. The Monte Abatone Sphinx cylinder relief decorates the rim (after Pieraccini 2003, Fig. 16).

Figure 43.4   Bucchero *focolare* (brazier set with bowls, lids and trays), second half of the sixth century BC, Chiusi (after Turfa 2005, no. 124–135), University of Pennsylvania Museum, image no. 5096.

Fortunately, the latter part of the twentieth century saw many excavations aimed at civic centers and sanctuaries allowing for further study of the material culture present at such sites.[26] The Vigna Parrocchiale sanctuary at Cerveteri is a good place to assess such material. Evidence shows that food offered to the gods or prepared by priests for the gods, was done so in utilitarian ware.[27] In this case, undecorated vessels were destined for the gods; often they feature inscriptions with names of various deities. A recent find at the sanctuary of the Vigna Parrocchiale features an impasto *olla* (jar) with the inscription *VEI*, a chthonic goddess who may be connected to the Greek goddess Demeter, and therefore with agriculture and the harvest.[28] Such *ollae* are commonly found at numerous Etruscan habitation sites.[29] It is important to note that the *olla* at the Vigna Parrocchiale is described not as a votive, but rather as part of the equipment of the priests for serving/offering food to the resident deity.[30] Likewise the so-called *sacellum* at San Giovenale offers a fascinating view of how food was incorporated in ritual at a unique shrine (*sacellum*) connected to a bridge. Evidence of a brazier, charcoal and a fixed hearth suggests that eating took place there.[31] In addition, inscriptions referring to the deities *Vesuna* and *Laran* appear as well, implying that offerings (meals?) were prepared in their honor.[32]

Chickpeas (*cicer arietinum*) were recently discovered in a votive deposit at Cetamura del Chianti. The legumes were prepared in a terracotta vase and cooked so that the hulls separated from the seeds (perhaps to make a soup). The vase was cut in such a way that only the lower portion of the base was deposited, a symbolic act before leaving the "soup" as an offering. Chickpeas, which do not grow in the wild, had to be cultivated. They offered an important source of protein to the ancient Etruscan diet. With further archaeobotanical studies from Etruria, we will learn more about the role of such legumes.

Although it is extremely difficult to find remains of a meal prepared over 2,000 years ago, there are a few scant leftovers. One artifact, not associated with banquet equipment, offers a remarkable example of vessels used for the funerary meal in the tomb, namely, the Caeretan brazier best exemplified from the Maroi Tomb III at Cerveteri, which contained coals, small vases, a bronze poker and eggs (the residuals of a funerary meal, no doubt) (Fig. 43.5).[33] Eggs arguably played a much greater role in the Etruscan funerary feast than previously thought.[34] Not just a portable food item packed with protein, eggs may

Figure 43.5   Caeretan brazier, circa 575 BC, Cerveteri, Banditaccia Tomb Maroi III. The brazier was found with coals, vases, a bronze poker and eggs inside (after Pieraccini 2003, Fig. 10).

have carried powerful messages of status and fertility, life and rebirth.[35] Eggs or eggshells have survived in other Etruscan tombs, for example at Tarquinia, and were just recently found in a tomb outside Grosseto.[36] For the Etruscans, eggs may have made up an important component of the funerary feast in the tomb, marked by their inclusion on the walls of painted tombs from the Archaic to the Hellenistic periods. Perhaps they held symbolic meaning for the elite who are seen holding and passing them on the painted walls of Tarquinian tombs. We may be able to understand these eggs as part of a small funerary meal, as well as a symbolic offering for the deceased to take to the afterlife. In fact, the visual rhetoric of food can now be understood as communicating power and status.

MEAT, CHEESE AND WINE

Bronze roasting spits, and irons and skewers survived in many of the wealthy Orientalizing tombs and demonstrate the importance of "meat eating" to the wealthy Etruscans. These roasting spits appear to have declined in popularity by the Classical period, but their presence in early tombs speaks clearly of their association with a "meat eating" aristocracy. But many of the *ollae* found throughout the Etruscan period and used on cooking stands to cook vegetables, grains and legumes must have served for stews with meat as well.[37]

The production of cheese in ancient Italy predates the Etruscan period. Pottery vessels with perforations attest to cheese making in the Bronze Age.[38] Pictorial evidence can be helpful, as seen in the Tomb of the Reliefs at ancient Caere where an item featured on the wall just may be a wicker ricotta basket.[39] Cheese graters too, add to our knowledge of the production of cheese by the Etruscans (Fig. 43.6; see also Fig. 6.5). Close to 20 cheese graters have survived from the Tyrrhenian shores, a good many of them from Orientalizing tombs in Etruria. D. Ridgway's recent examination of bronze cheese graters reveals that many survive in wealthy male or "princely tombs" of the seventh century BC and are directly related to the cross pollination of goods, culture and ideas coming from abroad.[40] In effect, these graters can be traced to the Euboean Greeks at Lefkandi two centuries earlier where three have surfaced in warrior graves.[41] The Euboeans were charting the Tyrrhenian shores in the eighth century BC, best exemplified by one of the most celebrated Greek artifacts yet to surface in the Mediterranean, namely an imported drinking vessel found at Pithekoussai (Ischia) and bearing a metrical Greek inscription referring to Nestor's cup.[42] Actually, bronze cheese graters appear to be intimately connected to the material cache that reflected Homeric cultural identity.[43] Here we are reminded of the graters used in the preparation of *kykeon* (a mixture of wine and cheese) perhaps prepared in Nestor's cup, used, as Homer tells us, to revive a wounded hero (Hom. *Iliad* 11. 628–643).[44] One of the earliest graters found in Italy comes from the eighth century BC Tomb of the Warrior in the Polledrara cemetery at Vulci and was discovered with an Egyptian scarab mounted in silver.[45] In Etruria, cheese graters are commonly found with fine bronze vessels for the pouring and drinking of wine.[46] Their placement in male or "princely tombs" may symbolize heroic status as practical utensils associated with the consumption of "aristocratic food" namely, cheese.[47] That these graters symbolized "status" is hard to deny, as a miniature bronze cheese grater in the form of a pendant, which hung from a bronze fibula, has survived from Tomb 23M at Narce (Fig. 43.7).[48] An important discovery of two bronze graters from Cetamura del Chianti, a humble, inland Hellenistic site, reveals much about the continued use and perhaps "symbolic" aspects of these graters. The first specimen survives in five small fragments found in a votive pit –

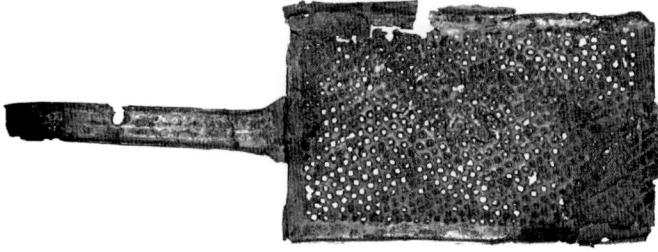

Figure 43.6   Bronze cheese grater, Cerveteri (?), Villa Giulia Museum, Rome.

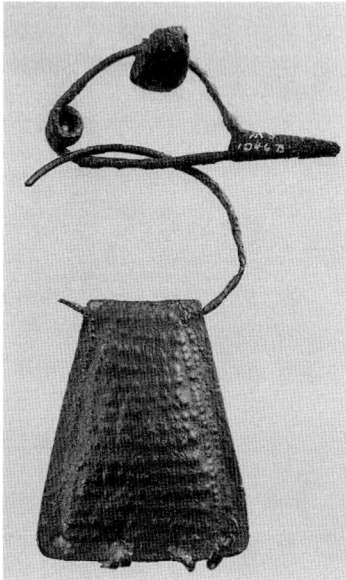

Figure 43.7   Composite fibula (bronze and amber) with pendant, early seventh century BC, Narce, Tomb 23M (after Turfa 2005, no. 34), University of Pennsylvania Museum, image no. 3918.

evidently the grater had been ritually destroyed.[49] The significance of ritual destruction is difficult to decipher here. The other bronze grater, found intact, was located in a refuse pit with Roman debris. These two specimens provide important data regarding graters found outside the tomb, dating to the Hellenistic period, as well as coming from a small inland site, like Cetamura.

One of the most abundant sources for understanding food and drink in Etruria are their containers. The thousands of drinking and pouring vessels produced by the Etruscans and imported from Greece make them the most common ceramic artifact in Etruria. Wine held a sacred place in Etruscan life, as we find wine vessels painted on the walls of tombs, left as offerings at sanctuaries, and packed in tombs for the deceased to use in the Afterlife.[50] It is hard to deny the importance of this liquid. It most certainly was the drink of choice and was a fundamental contributor to Etruscan economics and agriculture. Images of wine in Etruscan art are too numerous to count. Simply put, no other food or beverage held such an important place in Etruscan culture.

CONCLUSIONS

The ongoing excavations of Etruscan habitation sites will certainly amplify our understanding of fixed hearths, portable braziers and cooking stands – pottery shapes that changed precious little over time. Because of the combined archaeological work and scientific analysis of vessels, we are now beginning to learn more about the foods consumed by the Etruscans. This field promises to expand our knowledge of the Etruscan diet and enhance our understanding of the social implications of food. Likewise, careful analysis of sanctuaries and tombs can better supply us with evidence for ritual – remembering that the ritual use of food is often linked to transformation.[51] In the same way, the humbler inland sites, like Cetamura, have left us with remains of food in addition to food utensils from the Hellenistic period, providing evidence of cooking practices, votive offerings and the use of special utensils (graters). As studies regarding food increase, we may begin to see how food and drink played a notable role in conveying rank and that certain food items such as cheese, meat and eggs and beverages like wine, communicated a wide range of status and symbolic meaning.[52]

NOTES

1 *L'alimentazione* 1987 offers a wide variety of articles on agriculture, meat, fish, grain and grapes. For cooking stands see Scheffer 1981: 97; 1987: 102–103. It must be remembered that much of the cooking was done outside of the home.

2 Barker and Rasmussen 1998: 179–215; Bonamici 2000: 73.

3 Barker and Rasmussen 1998: 179–215, Fig. 67 depicts carbonized grains of barley. Giulierini 2005: 66.

4 Zifferero 2004. This paper explores methodological problems concerning pre-Roman coarse-ware and the transformation in ceramic forms due to a change from spelt to wheat.

5 Giulierini 2005: 66.

6 Ibid.

7 *L'alimentazione* (1987); Barker and Rasmussen 1998, 183ff. For chickpeas see de Grummond 2009: 189–190.

8 Barker and Rasmussen 1998: 185ff; Barbieri 1987.

9 Gianfrotta 1987; Barker and Rasmussen 1998: 199ff; Giulierini 2005: 70–77.

10 Steingräber 1986: no. 50.

11 Steingräber 1986: no. 32. We may not know what slaves were eating, but can infer that those who served and cooked for such events were introduced to the concept of the "banquet" and therefore had knowledge of "aristocratic" food items.

12 Scheffer 1981; 1982; Östenberg 1975: for "*focolari, camini, comignoli, e forni*" see p. 40. For hearths see p. 72, Zone B and p. 70, Zone E. For a fixed oven or hearth, see p. 106.

13 Karlsson 2006: 42. House III shows traces of more than one fixed hearth. For House II, see 73ff., Figs. 102–103. Even Caeretan cylinder-stamped braziers and *pithoi* were found in this house (77, no. 83, pl. 15). For a general assessment of the kitchen-ware and cooking stands see pp. 132–133.

14 Scheffer 1981: 9.

15 Scheffer 1981; 1982.

16 Scheffer 1981; Pieraccini 2003: 168f.

17 Scheffer 1981: 28–63.

18 Pieraccini 2003.

19 For braziers see Pieraccini 2003; for *pithoi* see Ridgway 2010.

20 For braziers found in tombs, see Pieraccini 2003: 32. For braziers found in an urban context, see Pieraccini 2006.

21 Serra Ridgway 2010.

22 Turfa 2005: no. 124–135.

23 Blanck 1987: esp. 115–116.

24 Pieraccini 2003; Bellelli, forthcoming.

25 Few, if any, images survive of Etruscans actually eating.

26 For sanctuaries see Colonna 1985; de Grummond and Edlund-Berry eds. 2011 offers an up to date bibliography of sanctuaries and ritual in Etruria.

27 Bellelli forthcoming.

28 Bellelli forthcoming. For the goddess *VEI*, see N. T. de Grummond 2006: 112.

29 Scheffer 1982: 67 n. 289.

30 Bellelli forthcoming.

31 Wiman and Backe-Forsberg 2008: 19–20.

32 Ibid 19. In addition, fascinating evidence from the hut pits discovered at Satricum contributes to our knowledge of ritual meals in early Latin domestic cults. See Maaskant-Kleibrink 1995.

33 Pieraccini 2003: 173; Pieraccini forthcoming.

34 Pieraccini forthcoming.

35 Pieraccini forthcoming.

36 Carpino 2008: Tombs 5859, 5862 were found with egg-shell. *Corriere della Sera* reported eggs found in an Etruscan tomb near Grosseto, "Uova travate in una tomba etrusca,"novembre 2, 2011.

37 Scheffer 1987: 97–103.

38 Barker and Rasmussen 1998: 192.

39 Barker and Rasmussen 1998: 193. Blanck (1987, 115) refers to this not as a basket but as a cushion.

40 Ridgway 1997: 325.

41 Ridgway 1997; 2008; 2009; forthcoming.

42 Ridgway 2009: 699–791.

43 Riva 1999: 332. Riva discusses the aristocratic lifestyles of Mediterranean elites and their deep connection to Homeric epics. See also Ridgway 1997; 2009; forthcoming.

44 Ridgway 1997: 326. See also the comedies of Aristophanes (*Wasps, Birds, Lysistrata*) for references to cheese graters.

45 Ridgway 2009: 790.

46 Ridgway 2008: 1; 1997, 331ff; forthcoming.

47 Ridgway 2008; forthcoming.

48 Turfa 2005: no. 34.

49 de Grummond 2009: 57, no. 18, fig. 18.

50 Ciacci and Zifferero 2005; Crisofani 1987; Pieraccini 2011.

51 For the ritual use of food see Lindsay 1998: esp. 70. With regard to food found in tombs, namely eggs, see Pieraccini 2003: 171–173 and Pieraccini (forthcoming).

52 This may force us to rethink the way in which we interpret banquet imagery, funerary feasts and ritual meals.

BIBLIOGRAPHY

L'alimentazione nel mondo antic: gli etruschi (1987) Rome: Istituto Poligrafico e Zecca dello Stato.

Barbieri, G. (1987) "L'alimentazione carnea degli Etruschi" in *L'alimentazione nel mondo antico: gli etruschi*, Rome: Istituto Poligrafico, 49–53.

Barker, G. and Rasmussen, T. (1998) *The Etruscans*. Oxford: Blackwell.

Bellelli, V. (forthcoming) "Il pasto ritual in Etruria: qualche osservazione sugli indicatori archeologici" in *Cibo per gli uomini cibo per gli dei*. Catania: Bonanno.

Blanck, H. (1987) "Utensili della cucina etrusca" in *L'alimentazione nel mondo antico: gli etruschi*, Rome: Istituto Poligrafico, 107–113.

Bonamici, M. (2000) "Economic structure" in M. Torelli (ed.), *The Etruscans*, New York: Rizzoli, 73–87.

Carpino, A. (2008) "Reflections from the Tomb: Mirrors as Grave Goods in Late Classical and Hellenistic Tarquinia" in *Etruscan Studies* 11: 1–33.

Ciacci, A. and Zifferero, A. (eds) (2005) *Vinum*, Siena: Ci Vin.

Colonna, G. (1985) *Santuari d' Etruria*, Milan: Electa.

Cristofani, M. (1987) "*Duo sunt liquores*" in *L'alimentazione nel mondo antico: Gli Etruschi*, Rome: Istituto poligrafico e Zecca dello Stato, 37–40.

de Grummond, N. T. (2006) *Etruscan Myth, Sacred History, and Legend*, Philadelphia: University of Philadelphia Musuem.

——(ed.) (2009) *The Sanctuary of the Etruscan Artisans at Cetamura del Chianti: The Legacy of Alvaro Tracchi*, Florence: Edifi.

Gianfrotta, P. A. (1987) "I prodotti del mare" in *L'alimentazione nel mondo antico: gli etruschi*, Rome. Istituto Poligrafico, 55–58.

Giulierini, P. (2005) "Cibo e alimentazione in Etruria: produzione e consumi" in G. C. Cianferoni (ed.), *Cibi e sapori nel mondo antico*, Livorno: Sillabe, 66–77.

Karlsson, L. (2006) *San Giovenale: Area F East: Huts and Houses on the Acropolis, Vol. IV, Fasc. 1*, Lund: Gleerup.

Lindsay, H. (1998) "Eating with the Dead: The Roman Funerary Banquet" in I. Nielsen and H. S. Nielson (eds), *Meals in a Social Context*, Oxford: Aarhus University Press, 67–80.

Maaskant-Kleibrink, M. (1995) "Evidence of households or of ritual meals? Early Latin cult practices: a comparison of the finds at Lavinium, Campoverde and Borgo Le Ferriere (Satricum)" in N. Christie (ed.), *Settlement and Economy in Italy 1500 BC – 1500 AD Papers of the Fifth Conference of Italian Archaeology*, Oxford: Oxbow Monograph 41: 123–33.

Östenberg, C. (1975) *Case etrusche di Acquarossa*, Rome: Monografie della Tuscia.

Pieraccini, L. (2003) *Around the Hearth – Caeretan Cylinder-Stamped Braziers*, Rome: L'Erma di Bretschneider.

——(2006) "Home is Where the Hearth Is: The Function of the Caeretan Brazier," *Ancient West and East* 5: 80–89.

——(2011) "The Wonders of Wine in Etruria" in N. T. de Grummond and I. Edlund-Berry (eds), *The Archaeology of Sanctuaries and Ritual in Etruria*, JRA suppl.: 127–136.

——(forthcoming) "L'inafferabile uovo etrusco" in M. D. Gentili (ed.), *Studi e ricerche a Tarquinia e in Etruria: Atti del simposio internazionale in ricordo di F. R. Serra Ridgway*, Rome.

Ridgway, D. (1997) "Nestor's cup and the Etruscans," *Oxford Journal of Archaeology* 16 (3): 325–344.

——(2009) "La coppa di Nestore e una grattugia da Vulci" in S. Bruni (ed.), *Etruria e Italia Preromana. Studi in onore di Giovannangelo Camporeale*. Rome: Fabrizio Serra Editore, 789–791.

——(forthcoming) "The Bronze Cheese-Graters" in I. S. Lemos (ed.), *Lefkandi III: Toumba Cemetery, Annual of the British School at Athens, Suppl.* 29.

Ridgway, F. R. S. (2011) *Pithoi stampigliati Ceretani: una classe originale di ceramica etrusca*, Rome: L'Erma di Bretschneider.

Riva, C. (1999) "Funerary Ritual, Cultural Identity and Memory in Orientalizing South Etruria" in R. F. Docter and E. M. Moormann (eds), *Proceedings of the XVth International Congress of Classical Archaeology*, Amsterdam: Allard Pierson Museum, 331–335.

Scheffer, C. (1981) *Acquarossa, II.1: Cooking and Cooking Stands in Italy 1400–400 BC* (ActaRom-4° 38:2): Stockholm.

——(1982) *Acquarossa, II.I: The Cooking Stands* (ActaRom-4° 38:2.1): Stockholm.

Steingräber, S. (1986) (ed.) *Etruscan Painting: catalogue raisonné of Etruscan wall painting*, New York: Harcourt Brace Jovanovich.

Turfa, J. (2005) *Catalogue of the Etruscan Gallery of the University of Pennsylvania Museum of Archaeology and Anthropology*, Philadelphia: University of Pennsylvania Museum of Archaeology and Anthropology.

Wiman, I. M. B. and Backe-Forsberg, Y. (2008) "Surfacing Deities in Later Etruscan Art and the *Sacellum* at San Giovenale," *Opuscula Romana* 31–32: 17–25.

Zifferero, A. (2004) "Ceramica pre-romana e sistemi alimentari: elementi per una ricerca" in H. Patterson (ed.), *Bridging the Tiber – Approaches to the Regional Archaeology in the Middle Tiber Valley*, Archaeological Monographs of The British School at Rome, 255–266.

CHAPTER FORTY FOUR

THE BANQUET THROUGH ETRUSCAN HISTORY

——— ·◆· ———

Annette Rathje

What is banqueting? Banqueting means eating and drinking together at formal parties, rituals and ceremonies. Eating as well as drinking is associated with initiations, burial rites and hospitality, indeed many aspects of human life. How can we understand the banquets of the Etruscans? They did not leave us with written descriptions about their manners and customs. The Greek and Latin literary sources are late and often marked by hidden agendas. We have to turn to archaeological sources and in this case we can analyze actual remains of food and drink,[1] places where it was prepared and places where it was consumed as well as banquet equipment. Representations of food and depictions of eating behavior can add to our knowledge and fortunately, the imagery of the Etruscans is abundant. The Etruscans have left us with a spectacular world of images from which we must carefully examine the evidence.

THE EARLY BANQUETS

Banquets are evidenced from the earliest Etruscans. The incinerated dead were put into urns that are sometimes anthropomorphic and, especially at Chiusi, placed on throne-like chairs before tables with food and drink. This custom must be seen in connection to the cult of the forefathers that distinguished this people from the Iron Age on.[2] The burials from Tolle in the Chiusine area are good examples, and from the same location we have the earliest representation of a reclining banquet (Fig. 44.1) on top of a lid belonging to an urn.[3] One of the earliest representations of a meal is seen on the lid of another terracotta urn from Montescudaio (territory of Volterra) (Fig. 44.2) from circa 650 BC.[4] The small fragmentary figures are made in the round and the motif is quite clear. A man is seated at a table laden with food (bread, *focacce?*) and a female servant (?) is fanning him. The scene suggests that he is a person of a certain rank and has adopted a Near Eastern custom. He raises his right arm in a gesture, likely he is performing a toast. A large vessel for mixing wine and water is next to the table and traces of a round base might refer either to a round chair for another person or to another vessel.[5]

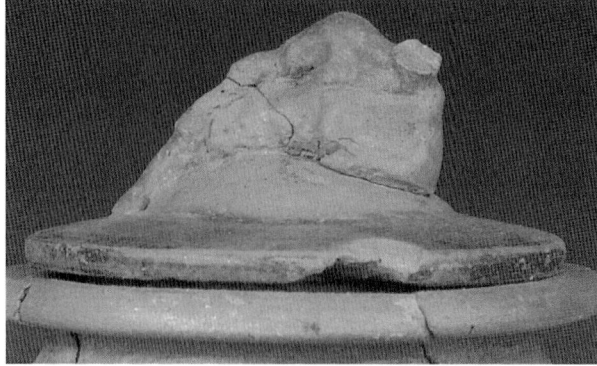

Figure 44.1   Lid of funerary urn from a tomb at Tolle (Tomb 23), circa 630–620 BC. Museo Civico
Archeologico di Chianciano Terme, courtesy of Giulio Paolucci.

Figure 44.2   Lid of funerary urn from Montescudaio, territory of Volterra, seated banquet circa 650 BC.
Florence, Museo Archeologico Nazionale, courtesy of A. M. Esposito.

AN UPPER CLASS PHENOMENON

Banquet equipment has been found from the elite tombs of the Orientalizing period
(roughly from the second half of the eighth century BC to the end of the sixth century
BC) and is interpreted as a reflection of the adoption of foreign manners and customs. The
period in question represents a process of selection of Greek, Near Eastern and occasionally
Egyptian goods. Material objects and perishable goods as well as foreign customs and new
ideas circulated among the Etruscans, as they were part of the Mediterranean cultural
trade networks. It is, however, important to understand that the Etruscans selected and
adapted foreign cultural elements to their own traditions.[6] They adopted the Greek way
of drinking and combined it with Near Eastern splendor. The way of feasting seems to
have changed, as feasts became a display of conspicuous consumption. The echelons of

society would be sitting or reclining on couches at their tables, made of ivory, wood or metal. The equipment would excel by quality and quantity; local items are made by the finest craftsmanship and many items are imports from abroad and thus very valuable. Items of gold, silver and bronze are often seen together with objects made of more exotic materials like glass, ostrich egg, shells or faience. We are talking about vessels for mixing (wine and water), pouring and drinking; cauldrons for mixing liquids as well as cooking meat, fire-dogs and spits for roasting and last but not least plates, dishes and bowls for serving the food. These items together with the actual food and drink were status bearing; they separated the persons of status, the "*aristoi*" from the rest of society. The banquet served as a paramount status marker both to the host and to the participants. The food was the best and boiled, stewed or roasted dishes of meat were accompanied with local as well as imported wines.[7] When many items are involved we might even be able to distinguish internal hierarchies, some persons were treated to the best piece of meat or were given the best wine. Sometimes we can even distinguish a division of drinking habits between men and women.

The feast based on meat and wine, where guests were either seated or reclining, connects the elites of the cultures around the Mediterranean and further east. The Etruscans have not left any written descriptions, we have no literary records from their hand, but we know of the phenomenon from the Homeric epic, the Old Testament, Assyrian records and elsewhere.[8]

BANQUETING AT MURLO

A fabulous party has been immortalized at Poggio Civitate, Murlo near Siena. A large palace-like building (60 x 60 m approx.) consisting of four wings around a courtyard was decorated with terracotta friezes with four different motives of which one is representing a banquet (Fig. 44.3).[9] Banquet equipment like that represented on the frieze has been found associated with the structure and it can thus be concluded that the representations symbolize real banquets that actually took place in the building. In fact, the northern wing probably functioned as a banquet hall. The great building had an earlier predecessor from around 630 BC. This older construction was destroyed by fire but has left us with a deposit of banquet equipment that was actually large enough to accommodate a large

Figure 44.3   Frieze plaque, terracotta, from the Upper Building at Poggio Civitate (Murlo), scene of reclining banquet, circa 575 BC. Illustration by Thora Fisker.

group of people.[10] So, the new building represents continuity in this respect. The persons depicted in the friezes of the great building at Murlo represent religious, political, juridical and military power. The banquet on the architectural terracotta decoration shows a large-scale consumption event in a courtly setting. The participants recline on finely cut beds covered with blankets and cushions, three-legged tables are placed in front of them laden with dishes and plates, some of which are filled with what look like eggs, fruits or cakes. A big metal cauldron is seen in the center on top of its elaborate stand. Two couples recline on the couches, to the left a man and a woman, to the right a man and cithara player who is possibly a woman. The men are drinking from hemispherical metal bowls while the women use ceramic cups with handles. Cupbearers, another servant and a flute player attend these people. It is very difficult to determine whether the banquets held in these surroundings represent the public or private sphere. The private and the public spheres are, however, very much entangled in this moment of history and the exact function of the great building is still under discussion.[11] The palatial complex must surely have been multifunctional including residential, political and ritual activities. The banquet scene shows a social ceremony dedicated to the exhibition of power, wealth and status. Other houses for feasting have been found at Roselle, Acqua Rossa (zone F) and San Giovenale.[12]

IMAGES ARE NOT ALWAYS WHAT THEY SEEM

Feasting and drinking practices are fundamental in securing social ties and alliances and also to ceremonies and rituals, as can be evinced from the finds of sanctuaries and tombs. Certainly the tombs have rendered the fullest picture of Etruscan feasting that can be gathered from the aforementioned finds and from tomb paintings from the Archaic period onwards. More than 50 tombs, mostly from Tarquinia but also from Cerveteri, Chiusi and Orvieto, are painted with banquet scenes, it *is* the most important representation. Actually a tradition was constructed when depicting the banquet in the Etruscan tombs, the "language of the images" was Greek. Therefore the banquet scenes are often called *symposia*. However, it must be stressed that the Greek *symposion* is quite another institution. It is a drinking event combined with literary and other performances and the participants were males; if women were ever present they were certainly not wives and daughters but courtesans, the so-called *hetaerae*.[13] On the contrary, Etruscan women were agents of their life and enjoyed an elevated position in the family, as we understand from images and epigraphic evidence. In fact, the presence of women stresses the significance and power of family. It is very interesting that women are not represented as mothers at these occasions.

Many of the tomb paintings only allude to real banquets. The men and women are set up reclining and sitting without being active participants. A discussion is ongoing about the whereabouts of these banquets. Do they depict real life? Or are they funerary banquets held to honor the deceased who leaves this life? Or do they represent a fantasy about the "eternal party" in another world? Perhaps, they are a welcome party by the forefathers for the newly dead? Thus the banquet can be intended as a religious symbol of the Otherworld where the living shared a meal with their dead relatives. In other words, the paintings also reflect a belief in continuity between life and death.[14] When studying ancient societies we must bear in mind that their images contained a contextual meaning as well as a meaning in the minds of the viewers. To understand images you must understand the mentality of the chosen period to be able to decode consciously chosen metaphors and meaning. Certainly, much of the evidence is ambiguous and provides an opportunity for different interpretations.

A POPULAR MOTIF

Banqueting is a very common motif in the Etruscan image-repertoire and apart from painted and sculptured funerary banquets and terracotta architectural decoration this theme is shown on numerous objects like painted vases, tableware, braziers with cylinder-stamped decoration, bronze items like tripod stands, basins and mirrors, ivory boxes, votive figurines etc. Their find contexts mark whether they were domestic or public, mundane or sacred. Certainly, objects can function as a "language" as subtle as a spoken language. Unfortunately, the practice of tomb robbing has destroyed, often completely, the message that these objects were meant to give when first placed in the tomb. The objects found in the tombs could refer to both the living and the dead. From the Archaic time on, Etruscan tombs were filled with the finest vases from Athens in combination with their own splendid bronze equipment and these items were even depicted in some of the tombs as, for instance, the Tomb of the Painted Vases.[15] Many of the vases from Athens depict sympotic scenes and some of them include women, and therefore the question has been raised if these motifs were made on Etruscan demand.[16]

WOMEN AND LUXURY

The matron of the house and her husband were often seen banqueting together as, for instance, on the back wall of the Tomb of the Leopards (see the cover of this book) thus confirming what it was that distressed the ancient authors from the fourth century BC, like Theopompos (Athenaeus, *Deipnosophistai* 12. 517d–518b), because to them it represented an immoral life. The Etruscans were indeed considered luxurious, frivolous and depraved (Timaeus in Ath. *Deip.* 4.153 d; Diodorus Siculus 5.3). A few authors mention the sumptuous tables that were prepared twice a day, the richly colorful rugs covering the beds of the reclining banqueters and the gorgeous equipment used.

LARGE FAMILY DINNERS

While the evidence from the period just mentioned gives witness to a larger diffusion of banqueting, the last centuries of Etruscan civilization have left us with the large family tombs of various cities. The paintings from Tomba Golini I at Orvieto give a full description of a rich banquet. Although the paintings were rather damaged already by the time they were drawn in 1865, we can still get an impression (Fig. 44.4).[17] A partition wall divided the tomb chamber. In the left part of the tomb the actual food preparation is documented, near the entrance an ox, various birds, a hare and a deer are hanging, so that we get the impression of a larder by this ostentatious display. This scene is followed on the side wall by a male servant chopping meat next to other servants, both females and males, engaged with the setting of four (movable) tables laden with grapes, pomegranates, *foccace* and eggs to the sound of a flute player, and another person who is bent over his work: kneading or pounding something in a *mortarium*. Then we see two men working with saucepans near a big, lighted oven and following this scene three more servants appear around a table with prepared food in numerous smaller vessels. In the right side of the tomb are four beds with reclining persons who are all participants to the banquet, which also includes Aita and Phersipnai, the gods of the Netherworld, sitting on a very ornate throne next to a splendid collection of metal vessels, framed by burning candles on two big candelabra and a burning censer. In front of the gods of the Netherworld a couple, man and woman, recline, while the other banqueters are all men. This tomb has depicted a candle light dinner for five generations of the Leinie family as can be learned from the inscriptions. So, here we are witnesses to collective consciousness about the past.

We meet the Velcha family from Tarquinia in the paintings of the Tomb of the Shields (Fig. 44.5).[18] Here the family banquet of two generations is seen in the central room,

Figure 44.4 Golini I tomb, Orvieto, mid-fourth century BC, family banquet and its preparation. Illustration by Thora Fisker.

Figure 44.5 Tomb of the Shields, Tarquinia, banquet of the Velcha family, mid-fourth century BC. Illustration by Thora Fisker.

the so-called *vestibulum,* to the right of the entrance to the main chamber. The founder of the tomb, Larth Velcha, was probably still alive when this tomb was inaugurated to the memory of his parents.[19] The images possibly show the living at banquet with the dead. The men are reclining while their wives are sitting at their side on beautiful, richly ornamented couches behind tables with food, where at least grapes and bread are distinguishable.

Although the custom is known already from the Archaic period on, it is especially from the third to the first centuries BC that the Etruscans from high and middle classes chose to be represented on their sarcophagi in the south and cinerary urns in the north. Reclining on pillows, they attend the eternal banquet both on the lids as well as on the front of the containers. Both women and men are seen holding a fan or a *patera,* however, in many cases they do not hold anything; in this moment of auto-celebration and coming together, they are "miming" a banquet. No food or drink is necessary, the inner space of the tomb has been transformed into a banqueting hall for the expanded family as seen in the Inghirami tomb for instance (see Fig. 9.2), no longer a material space but a symbolic space.

NOTES

1   See Chapter 43.
2   Tuck 1994; Kistler 2001.
3   Maggiani & Paolucci 2005: 5–8, 12–14. The tomb is dated 630–620 BC.
4   Maggiani & Paolucci 2005: 4.
5   Magi 1967.
6   Ridgway 2010: 51–54.
7   Rathje 2005; Rathje 2010: 25.
8   See Barjamovic 2011 for a very recent presentation of the Assyrian banqueting praxis, and Nijboer forthcoming.
9   Rathje 1994; Winter 2009: 157, 159, 187–189; cf. also Rathje 2011: 60–61.
10   Berkin 2003: 120–125.
11   De Grummond 1997.
12   Rathje 2004: 63.
13   Wecowski 2011; Murray 2000.
14   Krauskopf 2006, 75.
15   Steingräber 1986, no. 123: 353–354; Weber Lehmann 2001. For a recent bibliography of Attic vases in Etruria cf. Hatzivassilou 2010: 106–107.
16   Lewis, 2003: 189–190.
17   Steingräber 1986, no. 32: 278–279.
18   Steingräber 1986, no. 109: 341–343.
19   Maggiani 2005, 125.

BIBLIOGRAPHY

Barjamovic, G. J. (2011) "Pride, Pomp and Circumstance: Palace, Court and Household in Assyria 879 – 612 B.C." in J. Duindam and M. Kunt (eds) *Royal courts in dynastic states and empires: A global perspective,* Leiden: Koninklijke Brill, 27–61.
Berkin, J. (2003) *The Orientalizing Bucchero from the Lower Building at Poggio Civitate (Murlo),* Archaeological Institute of America. Monographs New Series, 6, University of Pennsylvania Museum of Archaeology and Anthropology: Philadelphia PA.
De Grummond, N. T. (1997) "Poggio Civitate, a Turning Point," *EtrSt* 4: 23–39.

Hatzivassiliou, E. (2010) *Athenian Black Figure Iconography between 510 and 475 BC*, Rahden/Westf.: Leidorf.

Kistler, E. (2001) "Thronende vor üppig beladener Tafel – orientalisierenden 'Fürsten' in Chiusi" in S. Bussi *et al.* (eds), *Zona Archeologica. Festschrift für Hans Peter Isler zum 60. Geburtstag.* Bonn: Dr. Rudolf Habelt, 219–37.

Krauskopf, I. (2006) "The Grave and Beyond" in N. T. de Grummond and E. Simon (eds), *The Religion of the Etruscans*, Austin: University of Texas Press, 66–89.

Lewis, S. (2003) "Representation and reception of Athenian pottery in its Italian context" in J. B. Wilkins and E. Herring (eds), *Inhabiting Symbols. Symbol and Image in the ancient Mediterranean*, Accordia Specialist Studies on the Mediterranean 5, London: 175–192.

Maggiani, A (2005) "Simmetrie architettoniche, dissemetrie rappresentative. Osservando le pitture della Tomba degli Scudi di Tarquinia" in F. Gilotta (ed.), *Pittura parietale, pittura vascolare: richerche in corso tra Etruria e Campania* ATTI Napoli 2003, Neaples: Arte Tipografica, 115–132.

Maggiani, A. and Paolucci G. (2005) "Due vasi cinerari dall'Etruria settentrionale. Alle origini del motivo del 'recumbente' nell'iconografia funeraria," *Prospettiva* 117–118: 2–20.

Magi, F. (1969) "L'ossuario di Montescudaio" in *Atti del primo simposio internazionale di protostoria italiana*, Roma: "L'Erma" di Bretschneider, 119–135.

Murray, O. (2000) "La convivialitè dans les cultures de l'Antiquité: la Méditerranée et la Chine," *Actes des Colloques 1996–1998 CGITA* 13: 7–22.

Nijboer, A. J. (forthcoming) "Banquet, Marzeah, Symposion and Symposium during the Iron Age: disparity and mimicry" in F. de Angelis (ed.), *Regionalism and Globalism in Antiquity: Exploring their limits, Colloquia Antiqua* 7, Peeters, Leuven.

Rathje, A. (1994) "Banquet and Ideology. Some New Considerations About Banqueting at Poggio Civitate" in R. D. de Puma and J. P. Small (eds), *Murlo and the Etruscans. Art and Society in Ancient Etruria*, Madison: University of Wisconsin Press, 95–99.

——(2004) "Life in central Italy in the Archaic period" *Accordia Research Papers* 9 2001–2003: 57– 67.

——(2005) "Fabulous Feasts" in V. Karageorghis, H. Matthäus and S. Rogge (eds), *Cyprus: Religion and Society from the Late Bronze Age to the End of the Archaic Period*, Möhnnesee-Wamel: Bibliopolis, 215–223.

——(2007) "Murlo, Images and Archaeology," *Etruscan Studies* 10 2004–2007: 175–184.

——(2010) "Tracking down the orientalising," *Bolletino di Archeologia on Line* I 2010 Volume Speciale F/ F2/2. Available at: <www.archeologia.beniculturali.it/pages/pubblicazioni.html>.

——(2011) "Il Caso di Murlo" in *Tetti di Terracotta. La decorazione architettonica fittile tra Etruria e Lazio in età arcaica*. Atti delle giornate di studio Sapienza Università di Roma, 25 March and 25 October 2010, *Officina Etruscologia* 5: 57–64.

Ridgway, D. (2010) "Greece, Etruria and Rome: Relationships and Receptions," *Ancient West and East* 9: 43–61.

Steingräber, S. (1986) *Catalogue raisonné of Etruscan Wall Paintings*, New York: Harcourt Brace Jovanovich Publishers.

Tuck, A. (1994) "The Etruscan Seated Banquet: Villanovan Ritual and Etruscan Iconography," *American Journal of Archaeology* 98: 617–628.

Weber-Lehmann, C. (2001) "Zur Ausstattung etruskischer Klinengelage: Ergebnisse historischer und moderner Dokumentation der Grabmalerei Tarquinias" in A. Barbet (ed.), *La Peinture Funéraire Antique. Actes du VIIe Colloque de l'association Internationale pour la Peinture Murale Antique*, Vienne Errance Paris 1998, 29–37.

Węcowski, M. (2011), *Sympozjon.czyli wspólne picie. Początki greckiej biesiady arystokratycznej (IX–VII wiek p.n.e.)*, Summary: Symposion, or drinking together. The rise of the Greek aristocratic Banquet (9th to 7th century B.C.) 351–359 Warszawa: Wydawnictwo Sub Lupa.

Winter, N. A. (2009) *Symbols of Wealth and Power. Architectural terracotta decoration in Etruria and Central Italy*, 640–510, MemAmAc, Suppl. IX, Ann Arbor MI.

CHAPTER FORTY FIVE

ETRUSCAN SPECTACLES: THEATER AND SPORT

———•◆•———

Jean-Paul Thuillier

INTRODUCTION: THE SITES OF SPECTACLES

Those who are interested in the various spectacles offered by Roman civilization will soon turn their attention to the many buildings of the Empire that have hosted them: circuses, theaters, odeons, and of course amphitheaters. Is not the Colosseum often presented as the symbol of Roman civilization? The same approach applied to Etruria would prove *a priori* very disappointing since we know of virtually no permanent Etruscan performance structures, with the exception of the theater of Castelsecco in Arezzo, but by then we are in the Hellenistic period, with "Romanization" in full swing, and the elliptical building at Cerveteri, the purpose of which is at best ambiguous (Camporeale 2004: 165, 337). Does this mean that Etruria was not a society of the spectacle, in contrast to Roman civilization? Obviously not: the chronological question is the key here, indeed prior to the first century BCE in Rome itself one could not cite many stone theatral structures: by contrast, places of entertainment constructed in perishable materials, wood especially, were numerous, in Etruria as well as in Rome.

In the absence of actual public buildings, it can be noted that from the seventh century BCE, several tombs of Orientalizing Tarquinia (the tumuli of Doganaccia, Poggio del Forno, Poggio Gallinaro, the Infernaccio) have a structure that has been described as "theatriform" (theater-shaped): a wide *dromos*, similar to a small courtyard or piazza, is often bordered on several sides by steps designed to accommodate spectators, and especially members of the nobility, who could watch not only stage dances but also boxing or wrestling matches, as part of funeral games. Other religious ceremonies such as sacrifices could obviously be celebrated there. Later, in the sixth century BCE, the tomb of the famous Cuccumella at Vulci, or the rock-cut cliff complex of Grotta Porcina near Blera, with an altar or a base for *cippi*, still retain similar structures (Colonna 1993).

The frescoes in the Tomb of the *Bigae* ("Tomb of the Chariots") of Tarquinia, dated circa 500 BCE, offer a remarkable picture of facilities for spectators. One can see the wooden grandstands protected by *vela* (awnings), that seem to illustrate the description of the Circus Maximus at the time of the Etruscan king Tarquin the Elder, as told by Livy or Dionysius of Halicarnassus (Thuillier 1985: 622–634). While young servants, stretched out under the stands, amused themselves with more or less innocent games, "noble" spectators were seated on benches, men and women mixed, and this public socializing is a highly significant trait, since, in at least one case, it is a woman who seems to occupy the foreground, if not the place of honor, on the grandstand. This image would not be seen in the Greek stadia, like that of Olympia, where no female spectators were allowed – although an exception was made for the priestess of Demeter Chamynē – and this image brings us closer to Rome where the Circus Maximus, according to Ovid (*Amores* 3.2; *Ars amatoria* 1.135–162), was a privileged place for attempted seduction.

LUDI CIRCENSES ET SCAENICI: THE CONTRIBUTION OF TEXTS

The importance and antiquity of stage shows and sports in Etruria proper are, instead, fully attested by literary sources that reveal unambiguously that the Romans borrowed heavily from their Tuscan neighbors in this field. Thus according to Livy (7.2) the *ludi scaenici*, the Roman theater productions, sprang up in 364 BCE after an epidemic (*pestis*), which traditional religious means failed to end, ravaged Rome: in the event of such a failure of properly Roman techniques then a "foreign rite" (*res peregrina*) must be involved and it is the Etruscans who are then called upon to help appease the gods (in the passage, this rite of proxy, the institution of games, *ludi*, to stop the divine wrath and the epidemic sent by the gods, appears as a typically Italic, Etruscan and Roman rite, and quite alien to the world of Hellenic religion). The fact remains that "without words in verse, without mime imitating the action of a poem, performers called from Etruria were dancing to the sound of the flute and, in the Etruscan manner, were striking graceful poses." These are modest beginnings, no doubt, that will include the intervention of the Roman youth and then the contribution of authors such as Livius Andronicus who arrived from Tarentum or Naples with a Greek repertoire. But the local actors (*vernaculi artifices*) will now be called "*histriones*" because "*ister*" is the Etruscan word to denote a professional performer: thus our theatrical lexicon also retains the Etruscan imprint.

As Livy shows again in the same chapter (7.2.3), before the fourth century BCE the Romans knew nothing more than the "*spectaculum circi*": and clearly these circus games are equally associated with Etruria. At the end of the seventh century BCE, Tarquin the Elder organized the most sophisticated games yet in Rome to celebrate his victory over the Latins – which shows how the Romans had already experienced sports-entertainments – the program (*ludicrum*) includes *equi*, horses, (mounted or driven?) and *pugiles*, boxers, who had been brought especially from Etruria (1.35.5–7). Thus we see that the Etruscans, for example, Veientines, who live so close to the *Urbs* (legend held that Ratumenna was a Veientine charioteer who gave his name to one of the gates of Rome) did not have to wait for the Greeks in order to see both equestrian and athletic sporting events. This theory of a Hellenic origin to sports in Italy, which is part of a powerful Grecocentrism in Etruscology and the history of sport in Antiquity, relies primarily on a passage in Herodotus (1.166–167) concerning the Battle of Alalia in the years 540–535 BCE. Following prodigies and yet another epidemic, the Etruscans of Caere appealed to the Pythia to avert it and the oracle at Delphi had advised them to set up gymnastic and equestrian games. Besides the fact that the Greek historian deliberately concealed the techniques of Etruscan expiation of prodigies to enhance the role of the sanctuary at Delphi and to distract from the defeat suffered by the Phocaeans, we see from the narrative of Livy that the *ludi circenses* had already been organized in some Etruscan cities at least a century earlier.

THEATER IN ETRURIA

If we are to believe Varro (*Lingua Latina*, 5, 55), the Etruscans wrote plays of classical type: a man called Volnius who has a Latinized name but who is of Etruscan origin wrote tragedies in Etruscan (*Volnius, qui tragoedias Tuscas scripsit*). All indications are that this author lived in the Hellenistic period, the time of the Gracchi, and one can imagine that his plays would have been staged in a theater like that of Arezzo, to which we have already referred, that dates precisely to the second half of the second century BCE (Heurgon 1961: 298–304). In earlier times, it is the iconography that furnishes testimonies of scenic games, private or public; this certainly comes closer to Livy's text since one sees there a number of *ludiones/histriones* (acrobats/actors). Likewise, a fragment of an Etruscan black-figured amphora in the Louvre dated to the years around 480 BCE shows us two characters disguised as satyrs, but wearing entirely local clothing (pointed cap, tunic with embroidered flowers) and dancing to music in an embryonic form of dramatic art (Szilagyi 1981).

Other documents, funerary paintings and especially Archaic reliefs from Chiusi, even testify that the Etruscans, from the sixth or fifth century BCE, were not satisfied with such simple dances as those described by Livy: there were performers, masked or not, and armed dancers, thus presenting a warlike theme. But the Etruscans also knew choreographed dances such as the dances of Silens and Maenads that illustrate the abduction of a woman, and ballets that are based on a mythological or non-mythical premise. J.-R. Jannot was able to identify, on a Chiusine relief preserved in Copenhagen, a ballet about Phineus, which was danced by professional actors playing the Boreads and the Harpies. On another Chiusine base in Florence, is depicted a boxing-dance – a choreographic theme reprised in our time – where three boxers dance rhythmically under the direction of a flute-player (Jannot 1984: 21–22, 28, 329–330; Jannot 1985). Black-figure pottery is revealing, as we have seen above, and we cannot forget to mention the amphora BM 64 of the British Museum (Fig. 45.1), the work of the Micali Painter, in the late sixth century BCE, on which we see a chorus of satyrs accompanying a Pyrrhic dancer (Beazley 1947: 2–3, pl. 2–2a, Jolivet 1993: 353–364; van der Meer 1986: 439–445).

In the Hellenistic period, small terracotta masks found in tombs of Tarquinia and Vulci of the end of the fourth century BCE may have been deposited among the grave goods as symbols of dramatic spectacles that the families of the deceased could not afford to organize at the time of the funeral. But slightly later, it is mainly the urns of Volterra, Chiusi and Perugia that are introduced into the debate in support of the existence of stage shows in Etruria. The reliefs represented on the chest of these urns often illustrate mythological themes of the Trojan or Theban cycles that are part of the Greek tragic repertoire,

Figure 45.1   Amphora by the Micali Painter, British Museum BM 64, various forms of entertainment and competition, circa 500 BCE, courtesy Trustees of the British Museum.

and also of Archaic Latin tragedy. And above all, one may find on these urns, which in Volterra are often produced in alabaster, elements of a theatrical setting (palace gates, caves, harbors, towers, temples), and of stage-setting accessories (altars): all this could have been directly inspired by representations of tragedies (Etruscan?) played in Etruria itself, and here we reach the Varronian allusion to Volnius (Camporeale 2004 :163–167).

SPORT IN ETRURIA

The quote from Livy concerning *ludi* held in Rome by Tarquin the Elder places the existence of such games in Etruria itself during the seventh century BCE. Etruscan iconography confirms this assertion, in particular for combat sports. An *olla* of incised bucchero, found at Veii and now lost, dating to the last third of the seventh century BCE, permits us to observe a beautiful scene of a fight, two boxers are squaring off, their arms are raised in high guard and they are dressed in short tunics (Thuillier 1985: 57–65). At Caere, on a painted urn, also from the seventh century BCE, a boxing match is represented (Martelli 1987: 260). We visit the same period and same city (the tomb of San Paolo) on an olpe of bucchero decorated with mythological scenes with Daedalus and Medea, and Jason (if indeed it is him) who is boxing. (Rizzo 2001: 170–171; see Chapter 24, Figs 24.1–2). Finally, and from the seventh century BCE again, a painted *olla* attributed to the Painter of Civitavecchia allows us to attend a boxing match that is accompanied by a musician, a flute-player for the first time: this practice will now be a constant among the Etruscans (Bruni 2000: 556). Boxing is not the only competition at this early period in Etruria, since a small bronze group found in Murlo, south of Siena, and dating from the late seventh century BCE, also shows two wrestlers in action watched by a referee armed with a long staff.

Athletic competitions: combat sports

But it is boxing that remains the favorite sport of the Etruscans, although as indicated in the passage from Livy, chariot races are very popular too. We see quite a number of representations of boxing in the sixth and fifth century BCE, especially in the frescoes of Tarquinia, where the boxers are sometimes the only athletes represented, and where they often occupy a prominent place, such as framing the doorway like two guards ready to threaten any undesirable visitors (Cardarelli Tomb) (Steingräber 1985: no. 53). This popularity of boxing can also be found on the tombstones of Felsina (Bologna) where it is essentially the only athletic sport – sometimes represented beside the chariot race: moreover, this sport also has a privileged place in the decoration of tombs, for example on the stele No. 169 (according to the catalog of P. Ducati), the boxing scene is spread over an entire register with five characters (the two athletes, the second with the sponge, the musician and the referee: see also the Amphora BM 64 by the Micali Painter) (Sassatelli 1993: 45–67). A *tibicen*, a flute-player, is almost always present alongside Etruscan boxers (Thuillier 1985: 231–254). Several Greek authors have noted this custom, wanting to see it as a sign of weakness, an indication of the dissolute life with which the Etruscans often were reproached in Antiquity. This grievance concerning *"truphē"* ("excessive luxury") as regards the musical accompaniment of Etruscan boxing was totally inappropriate. As seen today in traditional Thai boxing, which is certainly not "soft," it was the task of the musicians to pace the moves of both opponents and even wake up their fighting spirit as well, if it were ever waning.

The importance of boxing in the sporting customs of the Etruscans is also seen on the Archaic Chiusine relief already cited, which illustrates a ballet of boxing, with three athletes boxing and dancing rhythmically under the direction, even more necessary here, of a flautist (Jannot 1984: 329 ff.; Jannot 1985). Such choreography is not ignored today, either. But in Chiusi, a relief with a classic boxing scene was recently discovered and it shows great enthusiasm for wrestling (Thuillier 1997: 243–260): on both the reliefs and the frescoes of Chiusi, a wrestling hold is taken to a spectacular level and one can see that one of the adversaries actually seems to hover in the air over another competitor. This particular move would end one round of the game – if the Etruscans did take on the Greek rule of three "falls" – in any case, it appears as a signature of the artists of Chiusi.

Other athletic events

We can see on one of the two main walls of the Tomba degli Olimpiadi ("Tomb of the Olympic Games") of Tarquinia a set of three events: runners on foot, a long jumper and a discus thrower (Fig. 45.2). This wall also offers the typically Etruscan Phersu-game: we see a hooded man armed with a club who is being attacked by a vicious dog, spurred on by a masked executioner. The last is called *Phersu*, that is to say, the "Mask" (a word that corresponds to the Latin *persona*). (See Fig. 45.3, Phersu in the Tomba degli Auguri.) Some would wrongly see in this the prefiguring of the Roman gladiatorial combats that seem to find their source not in Etruria but actually in Campania/Lucania, as shown in many tomb paintings of Paestum (Pontrandolfo-Rouveret 1992). The combination of the three athletic events mentioned above might suggest that the Etruscans were also familiar with the Greek pentathlon, which included wrestling and javelin throwing. At the same time, on some Panathenaic amphorae are depicted a set of games (also including wrestling and javelin throwing) that indicate an athlete's victory in the pentathlon. And this is confirmed by other documents such as the British Museum amphora (BM 64) by the Micali Painter, where one can see a discus thrower and a javelin thrower side by side, and on an Archaic Chiusine relief preserved in Palermo, on which the same athlete holds both a discus and a javelin at the time of the awards. However, uncertainty remains on this point, because of the lack of literary texts or inscriptions.

Figure 45.2 Tomba degli Olimpiadi, right wall, Greek athletic games, Tarquinia, circa 510 BCE. Photo courtesy of Stephan Steingräber.

Figure 45.3 Tomba degli Auguri, right wall, scene with *Phersu*, man and dog, Tarquinia, circa 520 BCE. Photo courtesy of Stephan Steingräber.

Other questions remain: the runners of the Tomb of the Olympic Games are going to sprint, but will they run a *stade*-race? Are they at the end of a long distance race? What was the distance of this *dolichos* (usually just under 5000 m), and was there also in Etruria a *diaulos*-competition (a double *stade*)? The images certainly allow us to see that the Etruscan long jumper usually used jumping weights to improve his performance; the javelin thrower propelled his instrument with a strap called the *amentum* in Latin (and we see a beautiful representation of it in the frescoes in the Tomb of the Monkey at Chiusi). To see the awkwardness with which Etruscan artists often portray the gesture of the discus thrower, one can assume that the latter exercise was not very popular in Etruria. But it is also true that from around the mid-fifth century BCE, especially in Etruria Padana (the Po Valley), many bronzes or finials for votive candelabra for example, represent a pentathlon athlete. A small bronze from Bologna seems to depict a shot putter but the competition was rarely attested in Antiquity, so did it actually exist in Etruria?

Greek influences were important, but the Etruscan athletic games are not a simple copy of the Hellenic *agones*. On this point as on others, Etruscan originality is not to be underestimated, as we have seen with the musical environment of Tuscan boxing. Beyond the technical details, other significant differences should be highlighted. The issue of nudity might be at first an essential criterion, because the Greeks themselves claimed athletic nudity as a trait that radically distinguished them from the Barbarians. In fact, on this point there is not a problem regarding Etruscan society, since Etruscan wrestlers appear entirely nude, as in the Tomb of the Augurs at Tarquinia (Thuillier 1988). The realism of Etruscan art, at least in the late sixth and early fifth centuries BCE, allows increased understanding of certain practices that the idealization of the athlete in contemporary Attic art has almost completely hidden. Thus do we see, for example, that some Etruscan athletes are provided with an "athletic support": genitals are held in by a small cord itself attached to a belt. The frescoes in the Tomb of the Monkey at Chiusi offer particularly clear examples of this practice. Indeed, the Greeks cannot have done otherwise: in fact, some very rare vase-paintings, among them a beautiful krater by Euphronios, actually confirm this. The Etruscans were not "true barbarians": we have thus evidence that Etruscan artists were not content to merely reproduce Greek images, as is too often assumed, but they actually portrayed quite unmistakably the local realities (Thuillier 1985: 369–404).

Horse racing

The originality of Etruria is even more striking in relation to the horse races that were, as they would be later in Rome, and as with boxing, the sport par excellence of this people. In addition to the *equi* brought from Etruria to Rome for the games of Tarquin the Elder (circa 610–600 BCE), terracotta plaques uncovered in an aristocratic residence at Murlo show us that just shortly after 600 BCE a bareback horse race is held, where the jockeys compete for the prize of victory: a cauldron placed on a column, a true Etruscan Palio, especially as Murlo is near Siena (Root 1973). But the tomb frescoes of Tarquinia and Chiusi are remarkable and incredibly informative. This is particularly true of the Tomb of the Olympic Games already cited for its athletes. On the left wall of this small tomb, next to the boxers, we see four chariots rush to a vertical pole located on the track, indicating the finish line: the lead charioteer turns to see where his opponents are (Fig. 45.4), and we see that the fourth charioteer is the victim of a "wreck," a spectacular fall. The dress of these drivers is significant: with their mid-thigh length tunics, leather helmets and whips, they are very different from Greek charioteers, who, like the Charioteer of Delphi, wear a long robe, are bareheaded and have a goad (the *kentron*). Their driving technique is also remarkable: in Etruria, so they do not fall from the chariot, the reins are tied around the waist with a huge knot; in contrast, Greek charioteers simply take the reins in their hands – a wad of reins falling inside the box of the chariot allows better control (Bronson 1965). However, as can be seen on many documents – mosaics, reliefs, terracotta, glass, intaglios – from the equipment to the driving technique the Romans learned everything from the Etruscans and not from the Greeks.

The type of chariot used in these equestrian competitions is also significant. In the frescoes of Tarquinia mentioned above, these are *bigae*, chariots drawn by two horses. Etruscan iconography also never shows races of *quadrigae* (four-horse chariots) in contrast

Figure 45.4   Tomba degli Olimpiadi, left wall, chariot race, Tarquinia, circa 510 BCE.
Photo courtesy of Stephan Steingräber.

to what happens in Greece, where victory in the *quadriga* is reserved for a social and political elite: it is well known that the Charioteer of Delphi ran on behalf of a Sicilian tyrant. But the Etruscans had a predilection for the *triga*, the chariot drawn by three horses, with two draft horses and a horse harnessed on the outside in traces and, on Archaic reliefs of Chiusi, almost half of the chariot races are with *trigae* (Jannot 1984: 350–355; Bronson 1965). But the Greeks never held such races, while the Romans will take this contest into their circuses, as shown by Dionysius of Halicarnassus and several inscriptions presenting the victories of star charioteers. There was at Rome, in the Campus Martius along the Tiber, an equestrian training site called the *Trigarium* because of the *triga* races that were held there. This *Trigarium* dated from the Etruscan presence in the *Urbs* under the Tarquins (Coarelli 1977). Regarding races on horseback, we must emphasize the interest of the Etruscans and Romans for horse races and acrobats (in Latin, the *desultores*), who "jumped down" from their mount at a particular moment of the race, or who jumped from one horse to another, while neither the Etruscans nor the Romans almost ever depicted classic races with jockeys (after the evidence of Murlo, we no longer find such representations in Etruria) (Thuillier 1989). The Romans certainly later adopted *quadriga* races, but on the whole issue of horse games we can only note the proximity between Etruria and Rome, and the differences between Etruria and Greece.

CONCLUSION: RELIGIOUS ASPECT, SOCIAL ASPECTS

While symbolist interpretations have sometimes been proposed, it is clear that the frescoes of Tarquinia and Chiusi and the Archaic reliefs of the latter city (to confine ourselves to these two types of documents) evoke the funeral games in the ceremonies held at the funeral of the founder of the tomb. The Etruscans clearly were familiar with a ritual like the one described by Homer for the funeral of Patroclus in Book 23 of the *Iliad*, with various equestrian competitions – the *biga*-race is the most important – and athletic contests, among the latter, especially boxing and wrestling. This is one phase of a rite of passage that also includes other events: in addition to the viewing of the dead (*prothesis*) and transporting the remains, which some pictures (on the reliefs of Chiusi) or analysis of the furnishings of certain great tombs permit us to restore, we can quote at least the banquet, dance and "scenic" (theatrical) performances associated with sports in several frescoes. But, in the absence of texts describing the funeral ceremonies, it is difficult to establish with certainty the order of the rites, even if it can be assumed that the games come last (Jannot 1998: 66).

These rites are intended for the dead but also for the living: the family group, and even beyond, neighbors and some of the inhabitants of the city are at times tested and devastated by this loss that endangers society and that it is therefore necessary to overcome. Competitions, dances, the banquet (see Chapter 44), allow the group to overcome this psychological trial, to refresh themselves in every sense of the term and regain strength for the future of their community (D'Agostino 1989: 1–10). If the funeral games can be called initially private, since they are organized by a family (clan) group, and these games and their images endeavor to illustrate the status, power and wealth of the family in question – they exceed this framework to become almost public on certain occasions. The case of the Tomb of the Bigae and the grandstands depicted there is a good example, and you may even wonder whether or not the deceased was a *zilath* (magistrate/*praetor*) of Tarquinia. The Etruscans also knew of public and sacred games organized by cities or by the Etruscan League, as is evident when the inhabitants of Caere are encouraged to celebrate gymnastic and equestrian games each year after the Battle of Alalia, to atone for the sacrilege committed by their city after the naval victory.

As for the deceased himself, he may find solace in the paintings that extend in some way the effectiveness of ritual games, and he can rejoice in this vision, if one believes that he will see a more leisurely life in the Afterlife. The violent and dangerous nature of some Etruscan sports that readily shed blood is evident for example, in the boxing scenes (Tomb of the Olympics, Tomb of the Funeral Bed) where one of the boxers loses abundant blood, perhaps this is meant to revitalize the deceased, to give him a supplement of life (Jannot 1998: 67). Note however, that the bloody violence of fist fights or chariot crashes, possibly fatal to the driver, are not the sole preserve of Etruria: these motifs also exist in Greece (and Rome) and it is likely that it is these episodes, sports details, in a way quite realistic, that animate and give spice to the spectacle and its representation.

Livy again concludes by offering us essential information on the religious and social aspects of Etruscan shows. In book 5.1, the Latin historian returns to the siege of Veii in the early fourth century BCE that resulted in the sack of the city by the Romans who took advantage of the disunity of the cities of the Dodecapolis (a league of "Twelve Cities"). The Veientines sparked the ire of their Etruscan neighbors not only because they had restored the monarchical system at home, but especially because of the personality of the king:

> Earlier, he had become unbearable to the nation for his pride, that of a wealthy man, in committing the impiety of ruining games by a sudden interruption: that day, in fact, a setback had irritated him, a vote of the Twelve Peoples who had elevated to the priesthood another than him, and as the artists were almost all his slaves, in the middle of the performance he had suddenly withdrawn them.

Although Livy does not feel the need to clarify, this sacrilege, rightly known as "the most religious of all," which had struck the Etruscans, must have occurred during the *ludi* at the *Fanum Voltumnae*, that is to say during Pan-Etruscan games organized annually by the League of XII Nations in honor of Voltumna, an *epiklēsis* (additional name) of the god Tin(ia), celebrated here as the patron deity of the Etruscan confederation (Thuillier 1985: 480–482; see Chapter 31). These shows must have comprised, with the sacrifices, various religious ceremonies and a market fair, the main link between cities that never had a shared political system or defense policy. Thus the Etruscans held federated games that were evocative of those of Delphi and Olympia for the Greeks. If these are the same games that we find mentioned in the Rescript of Spello (*CIL* XI, 5265), probably in 337 AD during the reign of Constantine, centuries after the end of Etruscan independence, we find that the program always included *ludi scaenici* alongside gladiatorial combats that were probably introduced later (Gascou 1967).

But unlike the participants in Greek contests, Etruscan *artifices* (professional performers) were slaves: these "artists" are actually all professional performers of the *ludicrum*, the spectacle, and the term must also denote the athletes, riders, charioteers involved in spectator sport, as well as the actors, dancers, acrobats of all kinds involved in the stage show. Let us pass over the term *servi* used by Livy, since that does not prove that the Etruscans knew a classic system of slavery: Livy indicates that there are "dependents" attached to a lord, and although we cannot identify exactly their status, they clearly did not enjoy full legal freedom. The epigraphic analysis leads to similar conclusions since we find that Etruscan athletes have only a single, individual name where citizens would have been labeled with a double name of *praenomen* and clan/family (gentilicial) name (Thuillier 2009). We are therefore far from the Hellenic *agones* (competitions) where, at that time, only citizens were allowed to compete, but at the same time we are close to the Roman *ludi*: Roman citizens and the social elite are in the stands as spectators, and they would blush to think of participating in a show before an audience. This is one of the dividing lines between Greece and Rome as Cornelius Nepos has well demonstrated, and one may also wonder in this respect whether the Etruscan model was not the decisive one.

BIBLIOGRAPHY

Beazley, J. D. (1947) *Etruscan Vase-painting*, Oxford: Clarendon Press.

Bronson, R. C. (1965) "Chariot racing in Etruria" in *Studi in onore di L. Banti*, Rome: "L'ERMA" di Bretschneider, pp. 89–106.

Bruni, S. (2000) [Exhibition catalogue] in M. Torelli (ed.), *Gli Etruschi*, Venice: Bompiani.

Camporeale, G. (2004.) *Gli Etruschi. Storia e civiltà*, Turin: UTET Libreria.

Coarelli, F. (1977) "Il Campo Marzio occidentale. Storia e topografia," *MEFRA*, 89, pp. 807–846.

Colonna, G. (1993) "Strutture teatriformi in Etruria" in J.-P. Thuillier (ed.), *Spectacles sportifs et scéniques dans le monde étrusco-italique*, Rome: Ecole française de Rome, pp. 321–347.

D'Agostino, B. (1989) "Image and society in Archaic Etruria," *JRS*, 79, pp. 1–10.

Gascou, J. (1967) "Le rescrit d'Hispellum," *MEFRA*, 79, pp. 609–659.

Heurgon, J. (1961) *La vie quotidienne chez les Etrusques*, Paris: Hachette.

Jannot, J.-R. (1984) *Les reliefs archaïques de Chiusi*, Rome: Ecole française de Rome.

——(1985) "De l'agôn au geste rituel," *Ant. Class.*, 54, pp. 66–75.

——(1998) *Devins, dieux et démons. Regards sur la religion de l'Etrurie antique*, Paris: Editions Picard.

Jolivet, V. (1993) "Les jeux scéniques en Etrurie. Premiers témoignages (VIe-IVe siècle av. J.-C.)" in J.-P. Thuillier, *Spectacles sportifs et scéniques dans le monde étrusco-italique*, Rome: Ecole francaise de Rome, pp. 349–377.

Martelli, M. (1987) *La ceramica degli Etruschi. La pittura vascolare*, Novara: De Agostini.

Pontrandolfo, A., Rouveret, A. (1992) *Le tombe dipinte di Paestum*, Modena: Panini.

Rizzo, M. A. (2001) [Exhibition catalogue] in A. M. Moretti Sgubini (ed.) *Veio, Cerveteri, Vulci. Città d'Etruria a confronto*, Rome: "L'ERMA" di Bretschneider.

Root, M. C. (1973) "An Etruscan horse race from Poggio Civitate," *AJA* 77, pp. 121–137.

Sassatelli, G. (1993) "Giochi atletici in monumenti funerari di area padana" in J.-P. Thuillier (ed.), *Spectacles sportifs et scéniques dans le monde étrusco-italique*, Rome: Ecole francaise de Rome, pp. 45–67.

Steingräber, S. (1985) *Etruskische Wandmalerei*, Zürich-Stuttgart: Belser.

Szilàgyi, J. G. (1981) "*Impletae modis saturae*," *Prospettiva*, 24, pp. 2–23.

Thuillier, J.-P. (1985) *Les jeux athlétiques dans la civilisation étrusque*, Rome: Ecole française de Rome.

——(1988) "La Nudite Athlétique (Grèce, Etrurie, Rome)," *Nikephoros*, 1, pp. 29–48.

——(1989) "Les desultores de l'Italie antique," *CRAI*, pp. 33–53.

——(ed.) (1993) *Spectacles sportifs et scéniques dans le monde étrusco-italique*, Rome: Ecole française de Rome.

——(1997) "Un relief archaïque inédit de Chiusi," *RA*, 1997, pp. 243–260.

——(2009) "Un pugiliste serviteur de deux maîtres. Inscriptions 'sportives' d'Etrurie" in *Etruria e Italia Preromana* (Studi in onore di G. Camporeale), Pisa-Rome: Fabrizio Serra, pp. 877–880.

van der Meer, L. B. (1986) "Greek and local elements in a sporting scene by the Micali Painter" in J. Swaddling (ed.) *Italian Iron Age Artefacts in the British Museum*, London, British Museum, pp. 439–445.

CHAPTER FORTY SIX

MUSIC AND MUSICAL INSTRUMENTS
IN ETRURIA

———•◆•———

Fredrik Tobin

INTRODUCTION

Figure 46.1   Terracotta plaque type C from Acquarossa, second quarter of sixth century BCE. Courtesy of the Swedish Institute in Rome.

Even though we have no evidence of Etruscan musical notation and will never know the details of how Etruscan music sounded, quite a lot can be said about the way in which music and instruments figured in Etruscan society. And, while a definitive study of music and instruments in Etruria has yet to be published, there has recently been a lot of scholarly writing on the subject.[1] Just as in many other aspects of Etruscan culture, the evidence is fragmentary but enticing. Our knowledge of Etruscan music and instruments draws on a variety of sources that can be divided into three broad categories; images, archaeological evidence and texts.

The importance of images for our understanding of Etruscan culture has long been recognized and the rich and often multifaceted Etruscan imagery presents interpretative opportunities as well as challenges. The basic problem is that ancient images do not need to have a "one-to-one" relationship to ancient reality. The instruments that are most commonly seen in paintings are not necessarily the ones that were most common in real life nor do the instruments in images need to look exactly like they did in real life.[2] This should not keep us from using images as source material for scholarly discussions, but it should affect the types of questions we pose and encourage us to combine the use of images with archaeological findings and literary evidence.

Several musical instruments have appeared in excavations in Etruria. The fact that most of them have been uncovered in tombs is a reflection both of earlier archaeological practice (which for a long time focused on tombs) and also of the superior conditions for preservation that tombs provide. Unfortunately, the majority of the archaeological evidence does not come from controlled excavations but either from poorly documented excavations, as is the case of many of the finds made before the middle of the twentieth century, or from the collectors' market where objects often appear as the result of illegal operations.

When it comes to the literary evidence there is no ancient treatise devoted specifically to the subject of Etruscan instruments or music in Etruria. Instead we have to deal with fragmentary information and discussions in the works of a variety of Greek and Latin writers.[3] Often, these sources are very late and say more about other cultures' views of the Etruscans than about the Etruscans themselves.

THE INSTRUMENTS OF THE ETRUSCANS

The musical instruments for which we have evidence in Etruria, as archeological finds or in locally produced images, to a high degree correspond to the instruments found in other places around the Mediterranean in Antiquity. They can be categorized in a number of ways, and will here be dealt with in three groups: wind instruments, string instruments and percussion instruments. Since we do not know what the instruments were called in the language of the Etruscans, they will be referred to using Latin or Greek terms. In a few cases (such as the *lituus* and the *tuba*), the names of ancient instruments also correspond to a medieval or modern instrument; it should be noted that in those cases the ancient instruments have little or nothing in common with their later namesakes. It is also worth remembering that the ancient use of a Latin or Greek word is not always as consistent as the modern reader would like it to be. In many cases we cannot be certain exactly what an ancient writer meant when they used a certain term. There is for example, uncertainty regarding the distinction between the *lituus* and the *bucina* among some Latin writers,[4] and regarding precisely which instrument Greek writers were referring to when they wrote about the *tyrsenike salpinx*.[5] That being said, there are established modern conventions of what to call the ancient instruments and those names are the ones that will be used here.

Wind instruments

The wind instruments known to the Etruscans can be divided into lip-reed instruments (or brass instruments as they are commonly called today), air-reed instruments and reed instruments. The lip-reed instruments are musical instruments where air is set vibrating through the use of the player's lips. Air-reed instruments produce sound by directing air against a fixed edge, while reed instruments use a vibrating reed.

Broadly speaking, the lip-reed instruments in Etruria take three general shapes: the *cornu*, which is curved (Fig. 46.2); the *lituus*, which is straight but ends with a short curve (Fig. 46.3); and finally the *tuba* (Greek *salpinx*), which is straight. The fact that the shape of the *lituus* closely resembles that of the augural staff is probably the reason they bear the same name in Latin. To distinguish the two, the musical instrument is sometimes called trumpet-*lituus* in the scholarly literature.

The archaeological evidence for *cornua* consists of three relatively complete instruments and a number of smaller fragments.[6] Two of the complete instruments are in the British Museum in London and one is in the Museo Nazionale Etrusco di Villa Giulia in Rome (Fig. 46.2). The two *cornua* in London were found in the tomb of the Vipinana family in Tuscania where they were deposited probably sometime between the end of the fourth century BCE and the mid-second century BCE, while the *cornu* in the Museo Nazionale Etrusco di Villa Giulia does not have a known "findspot." It has recently been suggested that both the instruments in London and the one in Rome might consist of loose pieces assembled after having been excavated.[8]

Three complete *litui* from Etruria survive. One is in the collections of the Vatican Museo Gregoriano Etrusco, a second has surfaced in the antiquities market and a third, the only one with a secure find context, was excavated in Tarquinia in the 1980s (Fig. 46.3).[9] The Tarquinia *lituus* was found in the middle of the ancient settlement in a deposition dating to the early seventh century BCE. The instrument had been folded up before being deposited together with other bronzes in a pit in front of a building of sacred character.[10]

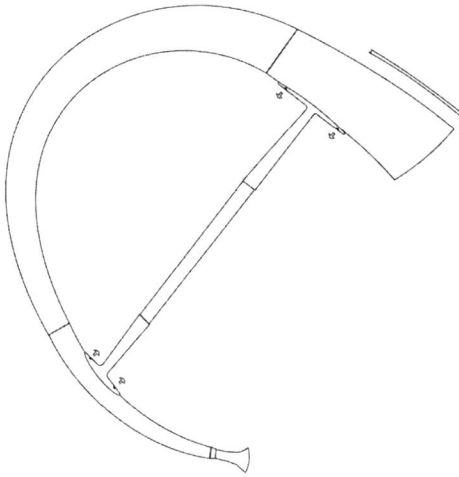

Figure 46.2   The *cornu* at Museo Nazionale Etrusco di Villa Giulia. Drawing by Peter Holmes.

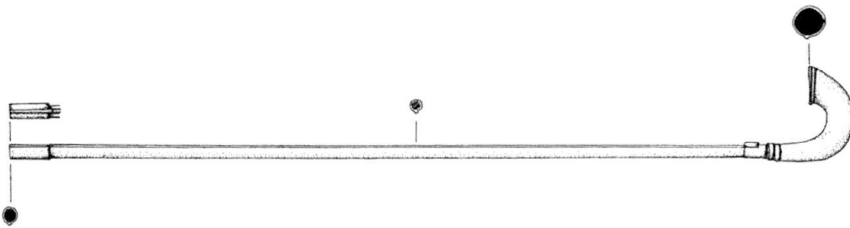

Figure 46.3   The Tarquinia *lituus*, first quarter of the seventh century BCE.
Courtesy of the Tarquinia excavations.

In Etruria, the *tuba* is found only in a handful of images.[11] It is not clear if it was a lip-reed or reed instrument, though the find of a Roman lip-reed *tuba* from Pompeii might indicate that also earlier *tubae* were lip-reed instruments. The possibility of the existence of a *tuba* with a reed can of course not be completely dismissed on such little evidence.[12]

From its appearance on Etruscan pottery in the middle of the seventh century BCE and down to Roman times, the *aulos* (Fig. 46.4) is one of the most ubiquitous instruments in Etruscan imagery.[13] Even though the Greek term *aulos*, just like the Latin equivalent *tibia*, is sometimes misleadingly translated into English as "flute" or "double flute" it is in fact a reed instrument. Since the *auloi* were usually made primarily of wood or bone they are very rarely found in excavations. One fragment of a bone pipe has been found in Chianciano (Fig. 46.5) and a few pipes of wood and bone have been recovered from the Giglio shipwreck.[14] A few details distinguish Etruscan images of *auloi* from Greek ones.[15] The most obvious difference is that *auloi* in Etruscan images often end with a flare,

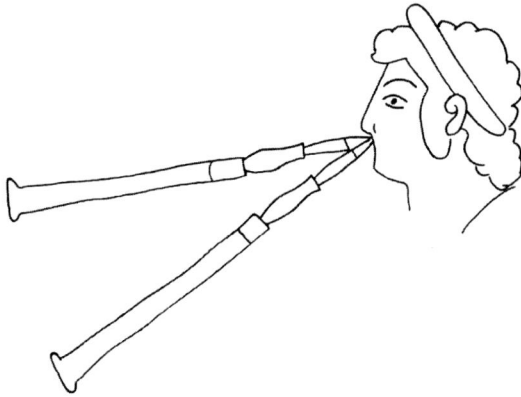

Figure 46.4 Drawing of an *aulos* player in *Tomba dei Leopardi*, Tarquinia.

Figure 46.5 The Chianciano *aulos*. Courtesy of the Museo Etrusco di Chianciano Terme.

something that is very unusual in Greek ones. Additionally Etruscan images often show instruments conical in shape. This has caused a debate whether the Etruscans had *auloi* with conical bores in addition to the ones with cylindrical bores, or if the conical shapes are just freer depictions of instruments with flared ends.[16]

Air-reed instruments rarely appear in Etruria and only in images.[17] The earliest known depiction of a *syrinx*, or panpipe, from Etruria proper is found in the *Tomba dei Giocolieri* in Tarquinia the paintings of which are dated to the end of the sixth century BCE.[18] The instrument also appears on *situlae* from north Italy dated to approximately the same time.[19] An air-reed instrument that is even rarer and occurs exclusively in the Late Etruscan period is the traversal flute. It can be seen most clearly on a cinerary urn from *Tomba dei Volumni* in Perugia but also possibly occurs on three urns from Volterra.[20]

String instruments

The only string instruments that were widely depicted in Etruria were members of the lyre-family; we lack evidence for harps or lutes.[21] Physical remains of lyres have been found in Greece and Magna Graecia but not in Etruria.[22] One of the earliest depictions of a lyre in Etruria can be found on an amphora painted by the Heptachord painter in the first half of the seventh century BCE[23] and lyres appear continuously in Etruscan art all the way to the Roman period. They come in a variety of forms and there exist differing opinions among modern scholars on how to divide them into sub-types. The problem is especially pronounced when dealing with Archaic depiction of lyres, where the amount of realism in the images can be questioned. Four relatively distinct types of lyres will be mentioned here: the cylinder *kithara*, the *chelys lyra*, the *barbiton* and the concert *kithara*.[24]

The cylinder *kithara* is a round bottom *kithara*[25] with peculiar cylindrical or quasi-cylindrical features placed where the arms meet the body of the instrument.[26] The instrument also appears in Greece and Anatolia but was not as long-lived there as it was in Etruria.[27] The *chelys lyra*'s (Fig. 46.6) most defining characteristic is its soundboard,

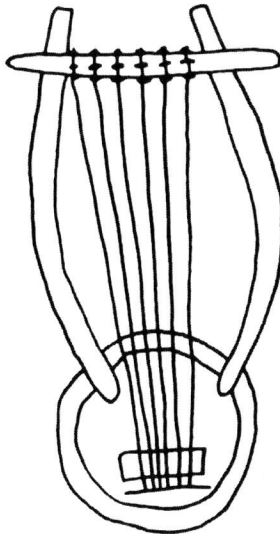

Figure 46.6 Drawing of a *chelys lyra* in *Tomba dei Leopardi*, Tarquinia.

which was made from tortoise shell or a wooden imitation of such a shell. The *barbiton* (Fig. 46.7) looks very similar to the *chelys lyra* but has longer arms (and consequently longer strings) that diverge as they extend from the body and curve in sharply at the top. The concert *kithara* (Fig. 46.8) is a flat bottom lyre with very elaborately constructed arms. Neither the *barbiton*[28] nor the concert *kithara*[29] are common in Etruscan images. Oddities in some of the depictions of concert *kitharas* have even led to the suggestion that the Etruscan painters didn't actually see the instrument themselves but worked only from Greek images.[30]

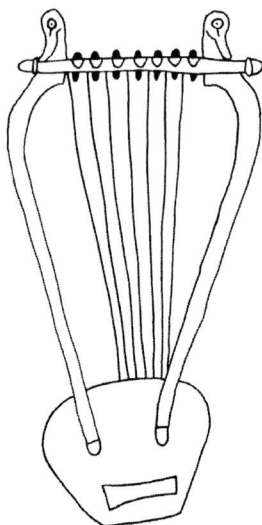

Figure 46.7   Drawing of a *barbiton* in *Tomba del Triclinio*, Tarquinia.

Figure 46.8   Mirror, now at the Museum of Fine Arts, Boston, of a youth holding a concert *kithara*, 400–350 BCE. Drawing by Richard de Puma.

Percussion instruments

Percussion instruments are less visible than string or wind instruments in Etruscan images, but they do occur and they are also present in the archaeological record.[31] One of the earliest attested instruments in Etruria overall is the rattle which occurs between the middle of the ninth century BCE and the end of the seventh century BCE.[32] The examples that survive are mostly made of clay, but bronze examples do exist. Interestingly, rattles are found almost exclusively in female burials.[33] Another percussion instrument that occurs is the *crotalum*, an instrument similar to modern castanets that consists of two pieces of metal, bone or wood.[34] Together with the *tympanum*, or hand drum, they are the instruments most associated with dancers.

There seem to have been no *sistra* in Etruria. The only possible exception is an ivory example in the British Museum, which for a long time was thought to have come from Orvieto and date to the Orientalizing period. A recent investigation however suggests that it is in reality a second–first century BCE instrument from Campania.[35]

A peculiar form of sound-creating device is the so-called rattling cup (Fig. 46.9). There are only two known examples from Etruria, found at Veii and (probably) Chiusi, dating to the late seventh–early sixth century BCE and the late sixth or fifth century BCE respectively.[36] Both are drinking vessels that were made with a void containing clay pellets so that they would rattle if shaken. It has been suggested that they were used as rhythm instruments by dancers cleaning off the table following a banquet, but perhaps it is just as likely that they were made simply for the surprise and amusement of the drinker. There is also a unique example of a bronze bracelet in the Museo Archeologico di Chiusi, which is hollow and contains bronze fragments that create a rattling sound when shaken.[37]

MUSIC AND INSTRUMENTS IN ETRUSCAN CULTURE

The well-known impact of Greek culture on Etruria also affected the field of music. But while it seems clear that new instruments entered Etruria through contact with the Greek world it is impossible to say what kind of music the Etruscans played on the newly acquired instruments. Some scholars have gone so far as to suggest that the music of Greece and Etruria were practically identical in terms of rhythms, scales and melodic structures.[38] It cannot be emphasized enough that this view is not built on any direct evidence but only on the assumption that the adoption of new instruments also means the

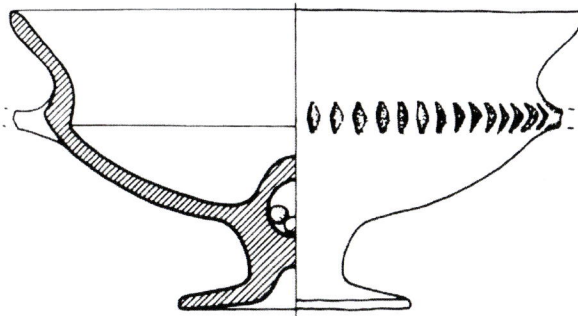

Figure 46.9   Rattling cup from Veii, late seventh–early sixth century BCE. Drawing by G. Calandra.

adaption of a related new repertoire of music. And while it is entirely possible that some Greek musical practices, and perhaps even practicing musicians, came to Etruria with the introduction of the new instruments, that is not reason enough to assume that the music of Greece and Etruria were identical (Fig. 46.10).

Although some instruments, like the *aulos*, were used by the Etruscans on all kinds of occasions, other instruments seem to have had more specifically defined uses. Brass instruments, for example, do not appear in banquet scenes but seem instead to be connected to civic and military matters. There is a widespread ancient tradition of ascribing the invention of different brass instruments to the Etruscans[39] and several ancient authors (the earliest including Aeschylos, Sophokles and Euripides) talk about the *tyrsenike salpinx*, or Etruscan trumpet.[40] Although the exact meaning of *tyrsenike salpinx* is elusive[41] and even though the attribution of the invention of the trumpet to the Etruscans is factually suspect, it is clear that the Greeks associated the Etruscans closely with brass instruments. In light of the way the instruments appear in Etruscan images of public processions[42] and the nature of the Tarquinia *lituus* deposition mentioned above, it does seem that brass instruments played an important role in Etruscan society. Considering the strong Etruscan tradition in metalworking this is not surprising.

Several ancient writers comment on the Etruscan use of musical instruments in very diverse contexts, specifically while baking, practicing boxing and flogging slaves.[43] We do not have any supporting evidence for the claim that the Etruscans played music while flogging their slaves, and when it comes to baking to the accompaniment of music the pictorial evidence is sparse and hard to interpret. A painting in the *Tomba Golini* I in Orvieto does show a meal being prepared in the presence of an *aulos* player,[44] as does the Campana *dinos* in Boston. In the latter case it should be noted that the scene can hardly be interpreted as an everyday cooking scene, but probably displays some sort of Dionysian event.[45] When it comes to the connection between music and boxing in Etruria there are several images to support the claim, for example a black-figure amphora decorated by the Micali-painter, now in London (Fig. 46.11).[46] Other kinds of athletes also appear together with musicians. A bronze mirror from Chiusi, dating to around 500 BCE, shows a long jumper mid-jump; to the left of him is a servant holding a strigil and to the right, an *aulos* player (Fig. 46.12).[47] String instruments do not appear with athletes, only the *aulos*, the *lituus* and the *crotalum* do.[48]

Figure 46.10   Sarcophagus and lid with portraits of husband and wife (1975.799).
Late fourth-early third century BCE, Vulci. Photo © Museum of Fine Arts, Boston.

Figure 46.11   Amphora decorated by the Micali-painter, detail © Trustees of the British Museum.

Figure 46.12   Mirror, now at the Museum of Fine Arts, Boston, of an athlete and an *aulos* player, circa 500 BCE. Drawing by Richard de Puma.

Musical instruments sometimes appear in Etruscan images of sacrifices or altars.[49] The most common instrument in such instances is the *aulos*, followed by the lyre and the *tympanon*.[50] However, a recent study found the relative occurrence of *auloi* in Etruscan sacrificial images to be as low as less than five percent.[51] We can therefore not claim that Etruscan sacrifices were usually conducted to the sound of musical instruments, only that some probably were.

Images of musical instruments often occur, as isolated objects or in the hands of a person, in tombs or on other kinds of funerary monuments. No instrument seems to have been considered unsuitable for this purpose. In some cases the instruments are placed quite conspicuously, as in the *Tomba dei Rilievi*, Cerveteri or the *Tomba Giglioli*, Tarquinia where brass instruments frame the entrance of the tomb.[52] Players of the *kithara* and the *aulos* can also be seen in more generic funerary images, often appearing as flanking elements around a central element like a door,[53] or as in the case of the *Tomba della Pulcella* in Tarquinia, a *loculus* in the back wall.[54] *Aulos* players are also present in *prothesis* scenes.[55]

Figure 46.13 Terracotta plaque with banqueting scene, Poggio Civitate (Murlo).
Courtesy of the Poggio Civitate excavations.

There is a strong correlation in Etruscan imagery between banqueting and music. Musicians often appear in pairs to play the *aulos* and the lyre for the reclining participants[56] (Fig. 46.1) and in several cases the banqueters themselves play instruments (Fig. 46.13), often they play lyres but in a few cases *auloi* are also played.[57] The *chelys lyra* is never used by the attending musicians, only by the banqueters, indicating perhaps that the instrument had aristocratic connotations.[58]

The second–third century CE writer Aelian recalls a story about how Etruscan hunters used sweet and soft music to lure animals into their traps.[59] A much earlier, seventh century BCE, metal vessel from Chiusi commonly known as the Plikaśna situla (see Chapter 6) has a frieze with an *aulos* player followed by a dog and a row of wild boars, seemingly portraying a similar story.[60] The Etruscans probably did use instruments to drive game during hunts[61] and to gather their herds.[62]

Etruscan music-making had a strong impact on Roman culture, perhaps seen most clearly in the Roman adoption of the *cornu* and *lituus*.[63] Strabo writes in the early first century CE that trumpets [*salpinges*] and all music used publicly by the Romans, as well as many other things including *fasces*, sacrificial rites and divination, had come from Tarquinia.[64] Livy similarly claims that scenic performances outside of the circus were introduced by instrumentalists and dancers imported from Etruria.[65] The authors may be exaggerating, but there is no reason to doubt that the influence on Roman music coming from their South Etruscan neighbors was vast. In Latin, only three instruments have names that do not derive from Greek and they are all wind-instruments: *tibia*, *lituus* and *tuba*.[66] Even if this fact doesn't speak to the question of who "invented" these instruments it does support the idea that there was a strong local wind instrument tradition in Central Italy.

NOTES

1   The most important recent work is Carrese, Li Castro and Martinelli 2010. The last synthesis in English is brief and outdated (Fleischhauer 1980), although there have been more recent ones in other languages (Jannot 1988, Fleischhauer 1995, Jannot 2004, Morandini 2011, Paolucci and Sarti 2012).

2   For a recent discussion of this issue (albeit in a Roman context) see Lawson 2008.

3   For an overview see Grandolini 2010; for a thorough investigation of Etruscan brass instruments in the textual sources see Berlinzani 2007 and Berlinzani 2010.

4   Meucci 1989.
5   Petretto 1996: 39–45; Berlinzani 2007: 16–21; Alexandrescu 2010: 34–35, 45–46.
6   See Alexandrescu 2010: 362–364 and Holmes 2010 for discussions of the archaeological evidence for *cornua* in Etruria and Alexandrescu 2008: 165–167 for a discussion of the instruments in the British Museum.
7   Alexandrescu 2008: 167.
8   Alexandrescu 2010: 363.
9   Alexandrescu 2010: 366–367.
10 Bonghi Jovino 2007.
11 Holmes 2008. To his list of sources can be added an early sixth century BCE krater from Cerveteri (Martelli 1987: 289–291, no. 85) and the hunting scene in *Tomba Querciola* 1 (Steingräber 2006: 156).
12   Holmes 2008: 245.
13 Jannot 1974 gives a full treatment of the subject.
14 Martinelli & Melini 2010 and Martinelli 2007: 29–35.
15 Sutkowska 2010.
16 Sutkowska 2010: 82–83. A similar issue can be observed in depictions of *salpinges* (Holmes 2008: 249).
17 Jannot 2010.
18 Jannot 2010: 183, Fig. 5.
19 For a discussion of musical instruments on *situlae* see Bermond Montanari 1999.
20 Fleischhauer 1964: 36, 44, nos 12, 20; Martinelli 2007: 22–23.
21 Jannot 1979: 471. See Sarti 2010 for a recent overview of string instruments in Etruria.
22 Lawergren 2007: 120–121.
23 Martelli 1987: 262–263, no. 38.
24 Lawergren 2007.
25 The instrument is sometimes called cradle kithara in English (the equivalent of the German term *Wiegenkithara*, French term *cithare en berceau* and Italian *cetra a culla*), but, following the argument put forward by Lawergren (1984: 156; 1993: 58–59), the more specific term cylinder kithara will be used here to avoid it being confused with other round bottom lyres (for examples of other such lyres see Lawergren 1984: Figs 10–14).
26 Lawergren 1984: 171.
27 Lawergren 1993: 59.
28 Jannot 1979: 473, 478; Del Papa 2010: 217, Fig. 2, nos 7–10.
29 Jannot (1979: 489–492) gives four examples. Lawergren (1993: 58, n. 20) has expressed doubts about them and in his most recent article only discusses *Tomba della Pulcella* and *Tomba della Fustigazione* (Lawergren 2007: 124, Fig. 5) the latter of which Jannot did not have in his list. See Sarti 2010: 187–188 for further examples.
30 Lawergren 2007: 122, 127; Sarti 2010: 188.
31 See Carrese 2010: 265–268 for a survey of the available evidence.
32 Carrese 2010: 231.
33 Brocato and Buda 1996: 86–87; Carrese 2010: 268, tab. 3.
34 See Brocato and Buda 1996: 87, n. 74 for a list of occurences of *crotala* in the tombs of Tarquinia.
35 Swaddling 2009.
36 Rasmussen 1995.
37 Iozzo 2009.
38 Pallottino 1975: 155; Fleischhauer 1980: 288; For an example of an opposing view see Lawergren 2007: 133, n. 2.
39 Ath. 4.184a; Diod. Sic. 5.40; Isid. *Etym.* 3.21.3; Poll. *Onom.* 4.85; Serv. 8.526; Alexandrescu 2010: 34.

40 Aesch. *Eum.* 567–568; Eur. *Heracl.* 830–831, *Phoen.* 1377–1378, *Rhes.* 988–989; Soph. *Aj.* 17.
41 See note 5.
42 Jannot 2004: 394–395.
43 Ath. 12.518b; Plut. *Mor.* 460; Poll. *Onom.* 4.56.
44 Steingräber 2006: 213.
45 Warden 2008: 127–128.
46 Fleischhauer 1964: 30, no. 7.
47 De Puma 1993: 26–27, no. 5.
48 Jannot 1979: 500, n. 51.
49 Hugot 2008: 62–63.
50 Hugot 2008; Verg. *G.* 2.192.
51 Hugot 2008: 72.
52 Alexandrescu 2008: 166, Figs 10–11.
53 See for example Jannot 1988: Fig. 6 or Steingräber 2006: 159.
54 Steingräber 2006: 158.
55 Jannot 1974: 124; Jannot 1988: 324, Fig. 5; Jannot 1990: 46–47.
56 A practice that seem also to have been present in early Rome (Quint. *Inst.* 1.10.20).
57 Jannot 1974: 125–126; Jannot 1990: 45.
58 Jannot 1979: 500.
59 Aelian *NA* 12.46.
60 Haynes 2000: 109–110; Martinelli 2007: 121.
61 See for example the hunting scene in *Tomba Querciola* 1 (Steingräber 2006: 156).
62 Polybius 12.4.
63 For an overview of the Etruscan influence on Roman music see Powley 1996.
64 Strabo 5.2.2.
65 Livy 7.2.4.
66 Berlinzani 2007: 15.

BIBLIOGRAPHY

Alexandrescu, C.-G. (2008) "Archaeological Finds of 'Brass' Instruments in Funerary Contexts" in A. A. Both, R. Eichmann, E. Hickmann and L.-C. Koch (eds), *Studien zur Musikarchäologie VI: Herausforderungen und Ziele der Musikarchäologie: Vorträge des 5. Symposiums der Internationalen Studiengruppe Musikarchäologie im Ethnologischen Museum der Staatlichen Museen zu Berlin, 19.–23. September 2006*, Rahden: Verlag Marie Leidorf, 163–178.
——(2010) *Blasmusiker und Standartenträger im römischen Heer: Untersuchungen zur Benennung, Funktion und Ikonographie*, Cluj-Napoca: Mega.
Berlinzani, F. (2007) "Strumenti musicali e fonti letterarie," *Aristonothos*, 1:11–88. Available at: <http://riviste.unimi.it/index.php/aristonothos/issue/view/54> (accessed January 1 2012).
——(2010) "Trombe etrusche nella prospettiva letteraria greco latina" in M. Carrese, E. Li Castro and M. Martinelli (eds), *La musica in Etruria: Atti del convegno internazionale: Tarquinia 18/20 settembre 2009*, Tarquinia: Comune di Tarquinia, 281–290.
Bermond Montanari, G. (1999) "Gli strumenti musicali nell'arte delle situle" in O. Paoletti (ed.), *Protostoria e storia del 'venetorum angulus': Atti del XX convegno di studi etruschi ed italici: Portogruaro – Quarto d'Altino – Este – Adria: 16–19 ottobre 1996*, Pisa: Istituti Editoriali Poligrafici Internazionali, 487–500.
Bonghi Jovino, M. (2007) "La tromba-lituo di Tarquinia nel suo contesto di rinvenimento," *Aristonothos*, 1:1–10. Available at: <http://riviste.unimi.it/index.php/aristonothos/issue/view/54> (accessed January 1 2012).

Brocato, P. and Buda, C. Z. (1996) "Phormiskos o platagè? Crepundia? Sulla funzione di un oggetto fittile in ambito greco, etrusco e latino," *Annali dell'Istituto Universitario Orientale di Napoli, sezione di archaeologia e storia antica*, 3: 73–90.

Carrese, M. (2010) "La documentazione degli strumenti e oggetti sonori in Etruria alla luce della classificazione organologica" in M. Carrese, E. Li Castro and M. Martinelli (eds), *La musica in Etruria: Atti del convegno internazionale: Tarquinia 18/20 settembre 2009*, Tarquinia: Comune di Tarquinia, 229–268.

Carrese, M., Li Castro, E. and Martinelli, M. (2010) *La musica in Etruria: Atti del convegno internazionale: Tarquinia 18/20 September 2009*, Tarquinia: Comune di Tarquinia.

De Puma, R. D. (1993) *Corpus Speculorum Etruscorum: U.S.A. 2: Boston and Cambridge: Boston – Museum of Fine Arts: Cambridge – Harvard University Museums*, Ames: Iowa State University Press.

Del Papa, B. (2010) "Suoni del mondo etrusco (metodo di ricerca)" in M. Carrese, E. Li Castro and M. Martinelli (eds), *La musica in Etruria: Atti del convegno internazionale: Tarquinia 18/20 settembre 2009*, Tarquinia: Comune di Tarquinia, 205–228.

Fleischhauer, G. (1964) *Etrurien und Rom* (Musikgeschichte in Bildern, Band 2: Musik des Altertums, Lieferung 5), Leipzig: Deutscher Verlag für Musik Leipzig.

——(1980) "Etruria" in S. Sadie (ed.), *The New Grove Dictionary of Music and Musicians*, 6, London: Macmillan Publishers, 287–291.

——(1995) "Etrurien" in L. Finscher (ed.), *Die Musik in Geschichte und Gegenwart: Allgemeine Enzyklopädie der Musik begründet von Friedrich Blume*, Sachteil 3, Kassel/Stuttgart: Bärenreiter/ Metzler, 188–199.

Grandolini, S. (2010) "La musica etrusca nelle fonti letterarie" in M. Carrese, E. Li Castro and M. Martinelli (eds), *La musica in Etruria: Atti del convegno internazionale: Tarquinia 18/20 settembre 2009*, Tarquinia: Comune di Tarquinia, 281–290.

Haynes, S. (2000) *Etruscan Civilization: A Cultural History*, London: The British Museum Press.

Hugot, L. (2008) "A propos des gras Tyrrhéniens qui devant l'autel soufflaient dans l'ivoire: Les représentations de musiciens autour des autels en Étrurie" in V. Mehl and P. Brulé (eds), *Le sacrifice antique: Vestiges, procédures et stratégies*, Rennes: Presses universitaires de Rennes, 61–80.

Holmes, P. (2008) "The Greek and Etruscan Salpinx" in A. A. Both, R. Eichmann, E. Hickmann and L.-C. Koch (eds), *Studien zur Musikarchäologie VI: Herausforderungen und Ziele der Musikarchäologie: Vorträge des 5. Symposiums der Internationalen Studiengruppe Musikarchäologie im Ethnologischen Museum der Staatlichen Museen zu Berlin, 19.–23. September 2006*, Rahden: Verlag Marie Leidorf, 241–260.

——(2010) "The Lazio Toscana U-Shaped *Cornua* in the British Museum" in M. Carrese, E. Li Castro and M. Martinelli (eds), *La musica in Etruria: Atti del convegno internazionale: Tarquinia 18/20 settembre 2009*, Tarquinia: Comune di Tarquinia, 125–154.

Iozzo, M. (2009) "Un nuovo strumento musicale nel Museo Archeologico di Chiusi" in S. Bruni (ed.), *Etruria e Italia preromana: studi in onore di Giovannangelo Camporeale*, Pisa: Fabrizio Serra, 481–486.

Jannot, J.-R. (1974) "L'aulòs étrusque," *Antiquité Classique*, 43: 118–142.

——(1979) "La lyre e la cithare: Les instruments à cordes de la musique étrusque," *Antiquité Classique*, 48: 469–507.

——(1988) "Musique et musiciens étrusques" in *Comptes-rendus des séances de l'Académie des inscriptions et belles-lettres*, 132/2: 311–334.

——(1990) "Musique et rang social dans l'Etrurie antique" in H. Heres and M. Kunze (eds), *Die Welt der Etrusker: Internationales Kolloquium 24.–26. October 1988 in Berlin*, Berlin: Akademie-Verlag Berlin, 43–51.

——(2004) "Musique et religion en Etrurie" in *Thesaurus Cultus et Rituum Antiquorum*, II. Los Angeles: The J. Paul Getty Museum, 391–396.

——(2010) "Les trois syringes étrusques: Des instruments propres à certains rites?" in M. Carrese, E. Li Castro and M. Martinelli (eds), *La musica in Etruria: Atti del convegno internazionale: Tarquinia 18/20 settembre 2009*, Tarquinia: Comune di Tarquinia, 177–184.

Lawergren, B. (1984) "The Cylinder Kithara in Etruria, Greece and Anatolia" in *Imago Musicae*, I: 147–174.

——(1993) "Lyres in the West (Italy, Greece) and East (Egypt, the Near East), ca. 2000–400 BC," *Opuscula Romana*, 19: 55–76.

——(2007) "Etruscan musical instruments and their wider context in Greece and Italy," *Etruscan Studies*, 10/1: 119–138.

Lawson, G. (2008) "Representation and Reality in the Late Roman World: Some Conflicts between Excavated Finds and Popular Images of Panpipes, Lyres and Lutes" in A. A. Both, R. Eichmann, E. Hickmann and L.-C. Koch (eds), *Studien zur Musikarchäologie VI: Herausforderungen und Ziele der Musikarchäologie: Vorträge des 5. Symposiums der Internationalen Studiengruppe Musikarchäologie im Ethnologischen Museum der Staatlichen Museen zu Berlin, 19.–23. September 2006*, Rahden: Marie Leidorf, 179–196.

Martelli, M. (1987) *La ceramica degli etruschi: La pittura vascolare*, Novara: Istituto Geografico de Agostini.

Martinelli, M. (2007) *Spettacolo e sport in Etruria: Musica, danza, agonismo e rappresentazioni tra Italia e Mediterraneo*, Florence: Regione Toscana.

Martinelli, M. and Melini, R. (2010) "L'aulòs etrusco di Chianciano: indagini attraverso la comparazione archeologica ed iconografica" in M. Carrese, E. Li Castro and M. Martinelli (eds), *La musica in Etruria: Atti del convegno internazionale: Tarquinia 18/20 settembre 2009*, Tarquinia: Commune di Tarquinia, 93–120.

Meucci, R. (1989) "Roman Military Instruments and the Lituus," *The Galpin Society Journal*, 42: 85–97.

Morandini, F. (2011) "All'origine della comunicazione musicale in Etruria" in C. Antonetti, G. Masaro and L. Toniolo (eds), *Comunicazione e linguaggi, Università Cà Foscari di Venezia. Contributi della scuola di Dottorato in Scienze Umanistiche*, Padova: Sargon, 135–158.

Pallottino, M. (1975) *The Etruscans*, revised and enlarged edition, trans. J. Cremona, London: Allen Lane.

Paolucci, G. and Sarti, S. (eds) (2012) *Musica e archeologia: Reperti, immagini e suoni dal mondo antico*, Rome: Quasar.

Petretto, M. A. (1996) "Musica e guerra: note sulla salpinx," *Sandalion*, 18: 35–53.

Powley, H. (1996) "The Musical Legacy of the Etruscans" in J. F. Hall (ed.), *Etruscan Italy: Etruscan Influences on the Civilizations of Italy from Antiquity to the Modern Era*, Provo: Brigham Young University and Museum of Art, 287–303.

Rasmussen, T. (1995) "Rattling among the Etruscans and Greeks" in J. Swaddling, S. Walker and P. Roberts (eds), *Italy in Europe: Economic Relations 700BC–AD50*, London: Department of Greek and Roman Antiquities, 195–203.

Sarti, S. (2010) "Gli strumenti a corda degli Etruschi: uso e iconografia" in M. Carrese, E. Li Castro and M. Martinelli (eds), *La musica in Etruria: Atti del convegno internazionale: Tarquinia 18/20 settembre 2009*, Tarquinia: Commune di Tarquinia, 185–204.

Sutkowska, O. (2010) "Etruscan and Greek Double Pipes: An Iconographical Comparison of their Organology" in M. Carrese, E. Li Castro and M. Martinelli (eds), *La musica in Etruria: Atti del convegno internazionale: Tarquinia 18/20 settembre 2009*, Tarquinia: Commune di Tarquinia, 79–92.

Steingräber, S. (2006) *Abundance of Life: Etruscan Wall Painting*, Los Angeles: J. Paul Getty Museum.

Swaddling, J. (2009) "Shake, Rattle and Rôle: Sistra in Etruria" in J. Swaddling and P. Perkins (eds), *Etruscan by Definition: The Cultural, Regional and Personal Identity of the Etruscans*, London: The British Museum Press, 31–47.

Warden, G. (2008) "Ritual and Representation on a Campana Dinos in Boston," *Etruscan Studies*, 11/1: 121–133.

CHAPTER FORTY SEVEN

HEALTH AND MEDICINE IN ETRURIA

——— •◆• ———

Jean MacIntosh Turfa with Marshall J. Becker

ETRUSCAN HEALTH

Health and conditions of nutrition and safety were a constant concern for the ancient world. Diodorus Siculus (5.40.2) says that the Etruscans "perfected writing and the study of nature (φυσιολογία) and theology," but if Etruria had an equivalent of Hippokrates (and there is no evidence for this), his or her works have not survived. Much of our information derives from religious sources such as votive cult or divination. Varro (*De re rustica* 1.2.27) recorded a charm for foot pain that he attributed to Etruscan wisdom, perhaps to one "Tarquenna," a form of incantation to be delivered while spitting on the ground: *ego tui memini, medere meis pedibus, terra pestem teneto, salus hic maneto in meis pedibus* ("I am mindful of you, cure my feet, let earth hold the affliction, let health stay here in my feet"). Many excavations and museum finds, textual analyses and medical studies have appeared since Mario Tabanelli published *La Medicina nel mondo degli Etruschi* in 1963, but we have not yet acquired sufficient data to comprehensively assess the state of medical practice or the average health of the Etruscans. Life in Etruria can be rated according to environmental conditions of food supply, climate, pollution and occupational hazards, but evidence for actual treatment, training in or understanding of health conditions remains scarce.

Environment: general health, nutrition and environmental safety

Ancient authors knew that Etruria was well-off in terms of climate, agriculture and the use of natural resources, from timber and fish to metals (Diodorus 5.40; see Chapter 1): what has become apparent through archaeological evidence is that many Etruscans paid for affluence in compromised health from environmental causes, or from an affliction of plenty, such as dental troubles due to the presence of complex-carbohydrate foods in their diet. Any estimate of health in Etruria must take all this into account.

Food and famine

Nutrition is a key aspect of human health and welfare, and Greek and Latin literature furnishes us with examples of people's concerns over assuring an adequate food supply. Not

855

as evident as famine, imperfect nutrition can be a crucial factor to survival if a community is otherwise assaulted, as in wartime, seasons of bad weather or volcanic eruption, or epidemics of infectious disease. Bronze Age eruptions of Vesuvius and other finds have preserved evidence for populations on the Bay of Naples (Sant'Abbondio, San Paolo Belsito) that may be extrapolated for most of Italy, including Etruria. Tafuri (2005) noted an increase in cases of iron deficiency (anemia) in the Neolithic Italian population, especially among women of childbearing age: perhaps caused by reliance on cereals to supply most calories, a problem that would be exacerbated by frequent childbirth or lactation.

In general, the people of Etruria would have eaten well, and studies of bones confirm the Mediterranean diet described by authors such as Cato, Varro and Pliny, based on cereals (barley, wheat, often consumed as porridge rather than bread), with a high vegetable content and relatively little meat or milk products (see Bartoli *et al.* 1997; Brocato 2000; Chapter 43). Cities near the sea would also have had seafood, and everywhere nuts and berries were gathered. Studies of burials at Sant'Abbondio show that, in contrast to many cultures, girls and women enjoyed the same diet as men and boys and were not deprived of calories or protein. Still, the condition of *cribra orbitalia*, a growth of the bone of the skull and eye-sockets that betrays anemia, has been identified in many skeletons of all periods in central Italy including Etruria. Harris lines on bones and hypoplasia of dental enamel attest that children's early years saw a series of periods of poor nutrition and/or fevers and illness that affected their absorption of iron and other nutrients. This could have resulted from famine, infectious disease, or parasitic infections.

Parasites must have abounded: the "Iceman" from the Italian Alpine Similaun glacier was infected with whipworms (Aspöck *et al.* 1996; Dickson *et al.* 2000), and other Italian and European populations, from the Neolithic on, have harbored roundworm (*Ascaris*), tapeworm (*Taenia*) (Aufderheide and Rodríguez-Martín 1998: 222–246) and liver fluke (*Fasciola hepatica*: Turfa and Gettys 2009). The huge middens of the Bronze Age Terramare culture in northern Italy must have harbored all sorts of pathogens (cf. Cocchi Gennick 1998: *passim*), although sanitation and fresh water supply in Iron Age Etruscan settlements must have supported much better living conditions (consider the Archaic Etruscan engineering feats of the Roman Cloaca Maxima, the *cuniculi* of Veii or the waterworks at Orvieto: Chapter 36).

Environment

Etruscan wealth and power derived in great part from Etruria's natural resources, and especially its mines and metallurgy (see Chapters 1 and 37). But environmental and occupational hazards accompanied the procedures by which thousands of families were supported: the ancient mining and smelting processes liberated large amounts of heavy metals and sulphur compounds into air, land and water, and some regions, such as that around Scarlino, Lago dell'Accesa and Massa Marittima, have had to undergo remediation today (Mascaro *et al.* 2001; Drescher-Schneider *et al.* 2007; Camporeale and Giuntoli 2000; Harrison *et al.* 2010). In the cool, rainy climatic period circa 800–500 BC, the heyday of Etruscan iron mining and bronze production, rainwater swept toxic compounds into the miners' food stores and houses (some of which had foundations of iron slag), and at Accesa and elsewhere settlements had to be relocated. Etruscan practices of divination could have contributed to the abandonment of toxic sites, as well as avoidance of pastures infected with parasites like sheep liver fluke (Turfa and Gettys 2009; Harrison *et al.*

2010). Vitruvius (*De architectura* 1.4.9) might have been speaking of Iron Age Etruria when he described such divination:

> For the ancestors, having sacrificed sheep which were grazing in those places where towns or permanent camps were being established, used to examine the livers, and if they were pale and infected the first time, they would sacrifice another group, wondering whether they were injured because of disease or because of spoiled fodder. When they had tested many animals and demonstrated the whole and solid nature of the livers [that resulted from good] water and fodder, there they established their fortifications; if however they found [the livers] tainted they thus confirmed the judgment that a future pestilence would grow in the bodies of humans in these places even though there was ample food and water, and so they would move elsewhere and change area, seeking good health in all particulars.

Congenital conditions

The social customs of early Etruria, such as the intermarriage of the ruling families of major cities (Tarquinia, Caere, Orvieto, Vulci etc.) well documented in epitaphs, might have led to genetically related problems. In the Bronze Age village of Nola-Croce del Papa, destroyed by a Vesuvian eruption circa 1780 BC, footprints of *livestock* show toe-like hooves on some cattle, a trait of inbreeding (Mastrolorenzo *et al.* 2006; Albore Livadie 2002). Huts preserved by ash show that pregnant goats and other livestock were kept in close proximity to human homes, under conditions conducive to the spread of zoonoses (Turfa 2012: 156–158, 197–198).

Some congenital conditions are potentially markers of lineage and are thus of interest to those who follow the pseudo-controversy of Etruscan origins. One such condition is bifurcate tooth roots, a harmless situation that merits further study: it has been found in modern Italians, and in Etruscan and Italic skeletons, but also appears in European populations. A number of women buried in the eighth-century BC colony of Pithekoussai had front teeth with bifurcate roots, which might identify them as Etruscan and Italic natives who had married Greek or Levantine colonists (Becker 1995; Becker and Donadio 1992).

A more curious possible situation is thus far only known from artistic representations: the condition of a didelphic or bicorporate, bicornate uterus, as depicted in highly stylized form in terracotta anatomical votive models found in large numbers in many Etruscan and Italic deposits (Turfa 1994: 227, Fig. 20.2, E-H). Anomalies of the reproductive organs are often passed on to descendents, and this might be a marker of ancestry, although there is no way of determining its incidence in the Etruscan population. (See below on anatomical models, and also Chapter 59).

HIGH INFANT-MORTALITY?

The past published record of Etruscan burials may have been inadvertently skewed by the fact that some communities buried under-age children apart from their elders; past excavations may also have neglected the rather ephemeral evidence of small depositions (Becker 2012). Careful analyses now show predictable infant/childhood mortality rates for Etruria. Of 168 skeletons of the seventh century BC studied at Adriatic Etruscan Verucchio, 40 were of children up to seven years old, and another eight were between seven and 14 years at death (Onisto 2002). Marshall Becker (2012) has found that in the affluent necropoleis of Tarquinia, approximately 10 per cent of the population died between 5.5 and 16.5 years, which he found consistent with mortality rates across Etruria, and in modern, pre-industrial societies in general. (Again, such tombs represent the upper classes of Etruria, not peasants or even urban commoners).

Other environmental or "occupational" issues

Of the rare literary references to Etruscan life, one, a gloss of a supposed Etruscan word, may preserve a hint of occupational orthopedic problems. Servius, in his commentary on *Aeneid* (10.145) says that the Etruscans used the term *capyas*, "falcon," as a nickname for men who have "their big toes curved under like the birds, falcons." In fact, this is a known deformity today called "claw foot" in which the toes resemble the talons of a bird of prey. It is normally only found in populations that wear shoes, and is caused by ill-fitting footwear. Curiously, some Etruscan anatomical votive models of feet do seem to show bunions (Fig. 47.1), which are also caused by bad shoes, and one wonders whether the Etruscan term *capys/capyas* was a response to frequent foot problems, or if the Etruscan reputation for luxury and showy costume, with men wearing boots and shoes, led ancient authors to associate foot troubles with them (Turfa forthcoming a). Surely the *"tyrrhenika"* sandals with high wooden platform soles and hinges on the instep (Turfa 2005: 32, 163–165 no. 143), found in numerous tombs, which were copied by Greek women and worn by Athena on the gold and ivory statue in the Parthenon, offered orthopedic hazards to Etruscan women of the sixth century BC and later.

SOURCES OF INFORMATION

In the material culture that survives, we see the religious approach rather than scientific investigation in the depiction or expiation of threatening health conditions, perhaps because "normal" books and documents do not survive, but religious texts do, to a slight extent (see Chapter 22).

Figure 47.1   Anatomical votive: model foot with bunion, University of Pennsylvania Museum L-64-478. See Turfa 2005: 247 no. 275.

Bodies/bones

New techniques of DNA analysis are proving useful in determining sex and consanguinity in family tombs; intriguing studies to identify the DNA of pathogens in bodies are now underway (e.g. A. Harrison and colleagues at University of Copenhagen) and could substantially change our views of disease in Antiquity. Archaeological context might at some time offer evidence of disease conditions, for instance, where multiple burials of persons of different ages were made in a short period of time: these might be the result of infectious disease entering a community. The burial of mother, father, son and daughter in a third-century BC tomb in the Tarquinian Calvario necropolis might one day be explained if the DNA of pathogens is identified (e.g. Cappellini *et al.* 2004). Another curious case is the Iron Age Latial burial at Osteria dell'Osa (Gabii) of a 30-year-old man re-opened before his bones became disarticulated for deposition of an elderly woman's cremated remains (Bietti Sestieri 1992: 121–125; Becker and Salvadei 1992: 177–178). Likewise, burials of older children, past the dangerous age of weaning, might be interpreted as resulting from infectious disease. Certainly, the recent results of studies on tissue from the Chalcolithic "Iceman" have changed our views, since they show that he was lactose intolerant and infected with Lyme disease (Keller *et al.* 2012).

Discoveries in the 1980s at the Tarquinia Pian di Civita site exposed some cases of human sacrifice (a child and an eighth-century BC swordsman who was dispatched by a blow perhaps from a winged axe), and also a special burial of a ninth-century BC boy who apparently died of a congenital condition (aneurism) after a short life of seeing and hearing things (from pressure on the brain) that no-one else could. (His affliction, seen in marks inside the skull, has suggested to some scholars that he was the prototype for the supernatural prophet Tages, said to have dictated the Etruscan scriptures (*disciplina etrusca*) before disappearing into the plowed earth whence he had come. (See Chapter 29; Fornaciari and Mallegni 1997).

Many diseases and causes of death, from plague to heart attack to murder, leave no telltale signs in the bones, but occasionally, conditions affecting bone such as anemia or cancer have been identified. A case of Pott's disease (a type of tuberculosis, known in Italy since the Neolithic period) was identified in a skeleton discovered in a tomb at Pozzuolo near Perugia (affecting the sacrum and lumbar spine (Capasso and Di Tota 1997: 553–554). At Bozzolo near Mantua, a child of eight–nine years and three middle-aged men were said to have symptoms of rheumatoid arthritis (Cattaneo and Mazzucchi 2005).[1]

In the rock-cut necropolis of Norchia, a tomb of the third century BC held the *"donna con i sandali"* and her newborn infant: she wore a pair of fashionable *tyrrhenika* sandals and a second pair was placed beside her (Barbieri and Becker 1996–97). Another case of death related to childbirth was a Faliscan woman of the seventh century BC whose urn held the bones of her newborn mingled with her own; gifts within included special miniature objects (De Lucia Brolli 2004).

Trauma

Chance finds of individuals who show evidence of trauma show a dangerous world, whether through war or accidents. For instance, at Tarquinia, Calvario Tomb 6100 (third century BC) held a man who died aged 45; the fibula of one leg had a healed fracture (Cavagnaro Vanoni 1996: 349). At Chiusi, possibly as early as 600 BC, a swordsman's combat or practice resulted in a broken nose – which healed well, although he probably carried a rakish scar for the rest of his 40 years of life. Even this affluent man showed mild signs of anemia (*cribra orbitalia*), and had poor dental hygiene (back teeth lost long before death in lower jaw and bad dental calculus: Becker *et al.* 2009: 78–79).

In an outlying necropolis of fifth-century BC Marzabotto, one man's cause of death appears to have been high-energy trauma, perhaps a fall from a horse or a height, which caused a pelvic ring fracture. Hemorrhage in such cases produced a high mortality rate in the past and still claims some modern victims; this find is said to be the oldest known example of this particular trauma (Pascarella *et al.* 2009).

In a fourth-century BC rock-cut tomb at Populonia, the skeleton of a man aged 45–50 years was identified to have metastatic cancer, its osteolytic lesions affecting skull, ribs, humerus and femur. The man had robust muscular development and worn upper incisors, presumably from occupational activities; while the doctors analyzing the bones felt this was a common worker, perhaps employed in Populonia's famous metals industry (Ciranni and Tempestini 2008), his burial in a rock-cut tomb would seem to indicate a more affluent status. Still, his affliction with cancer raises issues of industrial pollution, although the likeliest cause of his lesions is said to be either myeloma, lymphoma, renal cell or thyroid cancer, not lung cancer. At Tarquinia, a tumor on the femur of an otherwise unidentified skeleton was described by Virchow in 1884 (Brown 1960).

A number of men show broken and healed bones of legs, arms, feet, or the effects of warfare; but women too sustained serious injuries, provoking the question, if an affluent woman can be grievously injured, what is her environment like? Or is she in fact, just a reckless chariot-driver? The second-century BC terracotta sarcophagus of Seianti Hanunia Tlesnasa in the British Museum still contained her skeleton, of which a thorough study was made (Swaddling and Prag 2002), suggesting that her effigy on the lid was indeed a deliberate likeness. But Seianti's skeleton had some anomalies not portrayed in her sculpture: as a teenager, she had sustained some trauma of the soft tissues (not fractures) of her right pelvis and lower lumbar spine that caused changes in the bones due to crushing, necrosis and hematoma and causing later arthritis and pain. Seianti also suffered from a temporomandibular joint injury that occurred around the same time and left her with poor dental health and other discomfort. R. W. Stoddart (2002) suggested the injuries resulted from a fall while riding horseback; Seianti lived into old age with good nutrition, which probably included specially prepared soft foods.

Aging

Many skeletons of both men and women show the long-term effects of daily physical labor (microtrauma) in the deterioration of joints and arthritic conditions, sometimes leading to infections such as osteochondritis, seen for instance, in remains found in burials at Castenaso, Budrio, and Pontecagnano (Mainardi and Pacciani 1994; Losi 1994; Giusberti 1994; Fornaciari 1997).

Some Hellenistic sarcophagi show the signs of aging for men whose lined faces, set jaws and heavy chins are sometimes accompanied by fat bellies, made more prominent by Etruscan formal dinner dress (the Greek himation exposing chest and abdomen). The issue of the *obesus etruscus* (raised because of Catullus' comment, *Carmen* 39.11) could imply poor health due to overindulgence by Etruscans, but apart from a few Hellenistic sarcophagi and urns, there is no real evidence of obesity or related problems among

Etruscans. There is as yet no indication in skeletal collections of cases of morbid obesity manifested in such conditions as DISH (diffuse idiopathic skeletal hypertrophy, in which the vertebrae show a strange pattern of overgrowth of bone). This condition has, however, been identified in some Flavian-era victims of Vesuvius at Pompeii and Herculaneum (Turfa forthcoming a; Bradley 2011: 25–26).

Longevity

Over 4,400 Etruscan epitaphs are known, mainly from the fourth century BC and Hellenistic period; of these, over 250 inscriptions, most from Tarquinia and Volterra, recorded age at death. Children age two and older are represented (infrequently), and some men reached high ages, such as Lars Felsnas, who died aged 106, and had campaigned with Hannibal. Although none record people in their nineties, one woman died at 90, one man at 100 years of age (see Turfa forthcoming a). Men in their twenties saw the highest *recorded* death rate – this might not be an index to the general population, but might mean they were commemorated as casualties of war or because their lives were cut short. The death rate for women who received Etruscan epitaphs is nearly steady between the ages of 20 and 60, with some decrease in the forties – again, the quantities may be the result of family and social issues rather than actual death rates.[2]

Rare representational evidence

There are a few representations of events such as childbirth or of unusual conditions. The tomb of the Satie family, the fourth-century BC François Tomb of Vulci, preserves a carefully rendered portrait of a rachitic dwarf, Arnza ("Little Arnie") assisting the tomb's founder, Vel Saties, releasing a bird in a ritual of divination; clearly he is a valued member of the family, his shape, posture, reddish hair and wrinkled face are carefully depicted (Andreae 2004: 56 Fig. 42). The alabaster lid of a Hellenistic Volterran urn bears an effigy of an emaciated youth with wan but plucky face that must portray a wasting illness, of which he presumably died, for the epitaph (in Latin) of A. Caecina Selcia gives his age as 12 years (Cristofani *et al.* 1975: 28–29, no. 9).

Another representation is an Orientalizing stamped relief from a fragmentary bucchero vase found at Poggio Colla near Florence (Lorenzi 2011). It depicts a scene of childbirth with a crouching woman with long back braid and a baby just emerging beneath her (Fig. 47.2). The pose of seated or crouching childbirth must be true to life, and is even repeated in scenes of the birth of Dionysos or Menrva in engraved mirrors (see Fig. 25.1; van der Meer 1995: 119–124, Figs 52–56), where Zeus is seated and held by midwife goddesses like Thalna and Thanr, although, of course, Menrva will emerge from his head (which they then bandage)! Terracotta anatomical votives from dozens of shrines across central Italy show that infants were swaddled at least part of the time (and boys wore amuletic *bullae*) (Pautasso 1994: 33–44, pls 12–25).

Images painted in color in the Tomba dei Caronti at Tarquinia (third century BC) attest that some Etruscans were well aware of the consequences of snakebite: the Underworld demons Tuchulcha and Charu(n) are depicted with black-mottled blue or green skin which approximates the condition of flesh bitten by an adder or viper (Hostetler 2007).

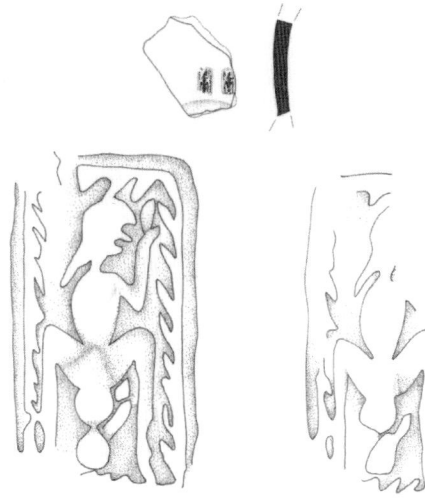

Figure 47.2   Poggio Colla Excavations, fragment of bucchero vase with stamped relief of childbirth scene. By kind permission of the Mugello Valley Archaeological Project. Drawing by Morgan Burgess.

Anatomical votive models

A tradition that had begun with small metal votives in the Archaic period came into its own with the social changes of the late fourth century BC. From about 300 BC into the Augustan period, more than 200 sacred sites in Etruria and elsewhere in the peninsula created deposits of a unique type of votive offering, model human bodies, heads, limbs or organs in terracotta, given as thank-offerings for fulfillment of vows requesting healing. Most are hands or feet, the parts most likely to need healing; almost none depict any sort of pathology, presumably because healing had already begun. Some models depict a plaque-like arrangement of multiple internal organs in reasonably correct placement; others in large numbers depict genitalia, internal and external, and a number of hearts, all highly stylized. Only four inscribed models have been found, one donated by a freedman, two uteri naming Vei, and a heart given by a Latin woman to Menrva. Thousands of models have been found, but they fail to enlighten us much on Etruscan knowledge of anatomy or physiology, since all are highly stylized; laboring uterus models may furnish some circumstantial evidence (below).

In the votive deposit of a presumed healing cult at Vignale-Tempio Maggiore, Falerii, some of the anatomical models of female external genitals clearly depict the physiology of the elderly, a sign of women's status in Etruria and the *Ager Faliscus* (Comella 1986: 78, pl. 42a–b). This contrasts with the much more common worry over non-maturation: many Etruscan and Italic votive deposits include juvenile/infantile male genitalia, probably offerings made in cases of delayed onset of puberty (see Turfa 2004: 361).

Diseases

Detecting infectious diseases that leave no marks on the skeleton is obviously difficult, but some tangential or circumstantial evidence is available, in addition to comments in the classical Greek and Latin authors. It seems reasonable to extrapolate from the

Hippokratic corpus and other literary sources, and also from archaeological sites of the Bronze Age cultures of the peninsula, and the finds from Pompeii and Herculaneum. Although the Etruscans and their neighbors suffered from a number of diseases, we may eliminate many others as not having reached the Mediterranean yet (yellow fever, bubonic plague, cholera; on leprosy, see possibly Mariotti *et al.* 2005), or as being density-dependent. When a severe disease first strikes a community, it may kill a large number of individuals, but usually survivors will develop some immunity, and such infections will die out without a constant supply of unexposed individuals. A community producing a steady stream of babies and children, if the population is large enough, can support such things as the childhood diseases of the twentieth century like measles or chickenpox. But such a high birth rate occurs only in large groups, and the towns and even cities of Etruria seldom if ever reached such a size (the populations of Volsinii, Caere, Vulci, or Tarquinia in the sixth century BC probably did not exceed 25,000–40,000 souls: Cornell 1995: 204–208; Heurgon 1964: 145–148; Rasmussen 2005: 86–88; Perkins 1999).

The density dependence of many diseases, for instance the rhinoviruses that cause today's colds, means they would not have been endemic in the Etruscan population, although a single event could have infected and harmed many people. Since we know many parasites were present in the Mediterranean and Italian environment, scholars have assumed that many gastrointestinal infections, such as salmonella, shigella and *E. coli*, which have long evolutionary histories, would have affected ancient Etruscan populations (Nataro *et al.* 2003). Any serious disease striking a naïve group will be terrifying, and Roman history records such "plague" events, from the time of Romulus and the *morbus pestifer* in the reign of Numa Pompilius, through the Republic and beyond, as recorded by Livy and epitomized by Julius Obsequens (Schlesinger 1959: *passim*).

Some other afflictions such as treponema infection have at times been proposed for ancient Italian populations, for instance, Classical-era skeletons from the countryside of the Greek colony of Metaponto, but this diagnosis of endemic syphilis (Henneberg and Henneberg 1998: 527–537) remains controversial. The presumed lesions found in many individuals, even young children, may be due to erosion in burial, or to porotic hyperostosis and anemia produced by different conditions (cf. Aufderheide and Rodríguez-Martín 1998: 154–171); no syphilis antigen was detected (Jeske-Janicka and Janicki 1998).

Divination: The *Brontoscopic Calendar*

Another source on health and disease in Etruria is the *Brontoscopic Calendar* (Turfa 2012), a Byzantine Greek translation of a Late-Republican Latin version of an Etruscan divination text, which cites many different diseases or afflictions that could occur in the aftermath of thunder, including cough, diarrhea, skin lesions of various sorts, "spotted diseases" (which may be cutaneous anthrax, common among sheep-herding groups, cf. Brachman and Kaufmann 1998; Wilkinson 1993). "Wasting away" is perhaps tuberculosis: on analogy to modern populations, for every one person with skeletal damage, like the Neolithic persons buried in the Arene Candide caves (Formicola *et al.* 1987), or the Etruscan woman at Pozzuolo (Capasso and Di Tota 1997: 553–554), 100 to 300 people may have suffered the respiratory effects of tuberculosis. Many times a disease prediction accompanies other adverse conditions such as famine or war, as might be expected. Such effects would have been painfully familiar to ancient observers.

Other Brontoscopic predictions warn of "plague but not life-threatening." Since this cannot be the bubonic plague (which first appeared in the late Empire), it may be Brucellosis, Malta- or undulate-fever, acquired from unpasteurized goat's (or other) milk (Aufderheide and Rodríguez-Martín 1998: 192–193; Young and Hall 1998; T-W-Fiennes 1978: 95–96). This is known to have infected Napoleon, and would have been present in settlements keeping livestock: survivors have compromised health, gastrointestinal problems and frequent bouts of fever. In the absence of soft tissue it is hard to diagnose in ancient populations, but Capasso (1999) describes what he believes to be a case in one of the victims of Herculaneum. Brucellosis is a zoonosis, a disease passed between humans and animals, often (like today's swine and bird influenzas) because of filthy conditions where humans and livestock live together (for more on possible diseases, see Turfa 2012, Chapter 6). A major symptom of Brucellosis in livestock is spontaneous abortion: the origins of the Roman Lupercalia festival might have some association, for the women in Romulus' town were miscarrying (Ovid *Fasti* 2.425–453; Wiseman 1995: 84, 127). His remedy, naked youths thwacking the women with raw goatskins, seems destined to spread the disease but it might illustrate the perceived association with goats.

Poliomyelitis and typhoid are also known to have been present in the Mediterranean world; polio, an immunizing gastrointestinal infection prior to modern sanitation techniques, was documented in sixth-century BC Italy (Wyatt 1993). Typhoid was described in the Hippokratic *Epidemics* I and IV: infection peaks in cold winters and kills up to 25 percent of patients, but usually spares children (Grmek 1991: 89, 346–350; Levine 1998; Longrigg 2000).

Malaria may well have been one of the foremost diseases in *Roman* Italy, with fresh infections arriving on cargoes of foreign slaves, debilitating many and killing persons already weakened by other poor conditions. DNA of malaria has been identified in the Imperial Roman population (see Weiland 2011; Sallares 2002; Scheidel 1996 on Roman death rates). Malaria has also been suggested as one of the causes of the tragically high infant mortality rates detected in the colonial Pithekoussan necropolis: many adults would have developed a tolerance to the strains of their homeland, but the strains of *Plasmodium* in the Bay of Naples were completely new (Becker 1995; Becker and Donadio 1992). Many scholars have pointed to cases of anemia as indication of a long-term, evolutionary response of the population to the threat of malaria, as anemic red blood cells are not conducive to the infection. Gaspare Baggieri (2005: 707) recognized thalassemia in a skeleton in the necropolis of Etruscan San Giovenale, and a child buried in the seventh century BC at Oscan/Etruscan Pontecagnano was diagnosed with the disease due to a spinal deformity (Fornaciari 1997: 470). If this is correct, it may represent a genetic response to endemic malaria, implying that Etruscan ancestors had acclimated to the Italian environment over a period of millennia.

"Healthful leanness?"

The *Brontoscopic Calendar* offers an odd prediction at December 29: "If it thunders, it signifies the most healthful leanness for bodies." While modern readers are familiar with the benefits of being thin, we expect that ancient audiences valued corpulence, if only as the sign of well-being and freedom from want. A few votive models and figurines, however, do seem to portray slimness – exaggerated for artistic effect – and not as a condition of ill health (Fig. 47.3). Fine bronze figures of gods (Diana) and priests (haruspices) are

Figure 47.3 Elongated bronze votive figurine of a haruspex, third century BC, Museo Etrusco di Villa Giulia, Rome 24478 (formerly Collezione Kircheriana). Sketch after Pfiffig 1975: 119, Fig. 50.

shown thin and attenuated but with healthy faces (Terrosi Zanco 1961; Cristofani 1985: *passim*; *Santuari d'Etruria* 1985: 92–94, 113–115; Turfa 2012: 182), and a number of terracotta statues or partial figures are rather thin and elongated, for instance, torsos from the Caeretan Manganello sanctuary (Nagy 2011: 123, Fig. 19); and Veii Comunità deposit (Bartoloni and Benedettini 2011: pl. 79).

MEDICINE: CAN WE DETECT ANY EVIDENCE OF DELIBERATE MEDICAL INTERVENTION FOR DISEASE OR INJURY?

We know of some religious aspects of healing cults because of votive religion (see Chapter 59), yet the so-called healing sanctuaries do not offer evidence of hospitals or other medical aspects except for the imported cult of Aesculapius at Rome, Fregellae and perhaps Antium.

Once the Aesculapius cult was installed in Rome (293–291 BC) it received the same, rather inaccurate anatomical votive models as all the other shrines, yet it established a hospital and must have been strongly influenced by Hippokratic institutions (Turfa 2006).

Diagnosis

In diagnosis, although there was always a religious cast to the statements, it appears that divination provided some links between environmental conditions and health or disease. The text of the Etruscan *Brontoscopic Calendar* predicts, following the phenomenon of thunder, the occurrence of various diseases or related issues such as famine (see Turfa

2012). Predictions keyed to days of the calendar year often warn of multiple events such as storms, wind or rain, famine or compromised food supply, and disease; likewise, war and hunger seem to be linked to disease. This might be the result of long folk traditions and orally transmitted wisdom. For example:

> AUGUST 13 If in any way it should thunder, there will be plague upon the bodies of both humans and dumb animals.

> MARCH 18 If it thunders, it signifies a period of severe rain, and disease, and the birth of locusts, barrenness [of crops] near at hand.

Treatment

The most famous aspect of Etruscan divination, haruspicy, involved the excision of a victim's liver and scrutiny thereof by a specially trained priest. As has been noted in relation to Egyptian mummification practices, this sort of dissection in extispicy does not seem to have transferred anatomical or physiological learning to any sort of medical practice (although lack of anaesthetics and antibiotics would have made surgery impractical).

Trepanation, known in many cultures and eras, has been practiced in Italy since the Neolithic period and is found in Etruria occasionally, apparently as treatment for skull fracture or other trauma, for instance near Mantua in fifth-century BC Bozzolo: the bone is unhealed, implying the patient did not survive (Mazzucchi *et al.* 2009; Cattaneo and Mazzucchi 2005; see Chapter 4 for additional cases in Classical Italy).

The scores of votive models of swaddled infants testify to the happy outcome of many births, and other models imply some level of obstetrical/gynecological care or intervention: highly stylized uteri, often depicting the wave-like ridges of third-stage labor contractions, are perhaps the best circumstantial evidence for knowledge of human reproduction (Figs 47.4–5). The simplified form can only represent a primate's uterus,

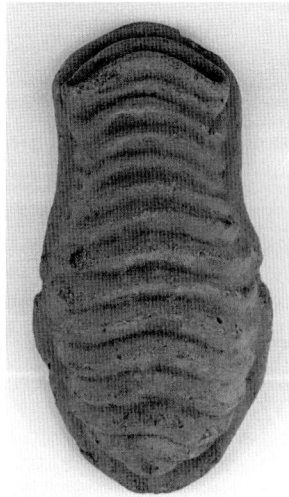

Figure 47.4   Liverpool uterus model, inv. 10.4.84.48, collected in nineteenth century by Joseph Mayer. Courtesy of National Museums Liverpool (World Museum).

and some examples show (highly rationalized) details such as malformations (a second, vestigial but functional uterus attached), or fibroid tumors, or a sectioned cervix that shows scars of previous births. (Analysis of pelvic bones to determine prior births is not widely accepted). Allegrezza and Baggieri (1999: 68–69, Figs 68–70) present X-ray studies of terracotta uterus models from Fontanile di Legnisina (Vulci) showing the incorporation inside the hollow organs, of one or two carefully fashioned clay pellets: undoubtedly a complex ritual accompanied the manufacture of these votives, presumably coded with requests for fertility or fecundity.

One mold-made example in the Manchester Museum had hand-modeled portions of the urinary tract added to it, presumably to indicate tissues that had been damaged in childbirth and healed (Fig. 47.6). (I have suggested that such details also indicate some familiarity with post-mortem C-section, a procedure cited in early Roman law and probably preceded by Etruscan traditions, Turfa 1994: 227–232). Some uterus models are flat, like the two inscribed "to Vei" (Demeter) at Vulci-Fontanile di Legnisina (Ricciardi 1988–89: 189, Fig. 48) and might represent a recently-emptied organ, the result of a post-mortem attempt at fetal salvage, although this cannot be proven. Live C-sections

Figure 47.5   Liverpool uterus model, inv. 10.4.84.49, collected in nineteenth century by Joseph Mayer; possible congenital anomaly (?). Courtesy of National Museums Liverpool (World Museum).

Figure 47.6   Manchester uterus model, with added details of urinary tract, Manchester Museum inv. 35152, ex Sharp Ogden Collection. Courtesy of the Manchester Museum.

were not performed in Italy in Antiquity, although there is some indication of successful operations in India where silk thread could be used.

Uterus models in several styles, along with a number of seemingly pregnant lower bodies (as at Tessennano, wearing modesty skirts but with navels exposed: Unge Sörling 1994: 48–49, Figs 1–2) were offered at many Etruscan and Italic sanctuaries, indicative of the position of women and the status accorded to their petitions in a wide variety of cults including the major goddesses. Models of draped and undraped men, women and children with an array of internal organs in relief on the torso (Fig. 47.7) are mirrored in large plaques or partial reliefs depicting schematically rendered internal organs. Tabanelli (1962) was able to show that there is no human anatomy lesson here – the best of the models can be sorted into beef/pork/or chicken, much as one might see in a butcher's shop, but clearly they are intended to remind the gods of healed afflictions. The recently published deposit at the site of Veii Comunità has several nude and draped, male and female torsos, many with exposed organs: the torsos have truncated necks, arms, legs reminiscent of modern medical illustrations, but the organs themselves are completely fanciful (Bartoloni and Benedettini 2011: 567–575, pls 73–78).

Recke (see Chapter 59) has presented the material evidence, from statues to limbless torsos, for knowledge or practice of surgery in Hellenistic Etruria and Latium, fewer than 40 sculptures depicting viscera against an otherwise lively human body. Of these, only a few pieces deliberately depict anything like a surgical incision – the most compelling example is the nude male torso, headless and limbless, in the Ingolstadt Collection (Figs 59.17–19), which appears to show marks representing surgical sutures along the edges of the "wound." A few other fragmentary torsos seem to show sawed-off ribs in the incision

Figure 47.7 The "Decouflé bust" purchased by the Louvre, 2011, from the estate of medical scholar Pierre Decouflé and probably found at Canino (Vulci). Third/second century BC, inv. no. MNE1341, photo © RMN-Grand Palais (musée du Louvre)/Stéphane Maréchalle. (See J. M. Turfa, "Exceptional Etruscan man joins the Louvre," *Etruscan News* 14 (Winter 2012) 23.

site surrounding the viscera. As Recke notes, such surgery is not easily survivable, yet it might have been occasionally attempted, or information gained from such attempts used to help those suffering from internal problems. Such depictions certainly attest to a new attitude in which expressing knowledge of the body and making very pointed, direct requests for specific kinds of healing was countenanced by society and the gods. Society had moved away from the atmosphere of archaic aristocracies.

Pharmacopeia

From Theophrastus at the end of the fourth century BC to Martianus Capella (fifth century AD), ancient authors respected the Etruscans expertise in herbalism and pharmacology. Theophrastus (*Historia plantarum* 10.15) said that Aeschylus in his elegies had spoken of the Etruscan race as a people skilled in compounding drugs (φαρμακοποιόν ἔθνος); Martianus Capella (*De nuptiis Mercurii et Philologiae* 6.37) called Etruria *remediorum origine celebrata.* We have the Etruscan names (preserved as glosses) for several plant species that were used as drugs in Antiquity (and many are still found today, in Italy and elsewhere, some even in the modern pharmacopeia (Harrison and Bartels 2006; Harrison and Turfa 2010; Leonti *et al.* 2009; Scarborough 2006). There are problems with some of these names, for they are actually Latin or Greek rather than Etruscan words (see Briquel 2006; Torelli 1976; Bertoldi 1936).

Many of the species cited in the glosses were used as vermifuges, toxic substances that can eliminate intestinal worms, and were still used in folk medicine in Campania as late as the twentieth century, when Jashemski and her colleagues (2002) catalogued the plants depicted or preserved in the cities destroyed by Vesuvius in 79 AD. While this is not strictly Etruscan culture, the finds do show the availability of these substances in Italy in Antiquity, and one may suspect that much of the Roman pharmacopeia was based on previous Etruscan folk medicine. The plants with antihelminthic properties included chamomile (*apiana: TLE* 808) and wormwood/absinthe, which were also thought to have anti-inflammatory properties and were used to treat gastrointestinal problems. Although not listed in the literary sources as specifically Etruscan, pomegranates have been used in modern times for their ability to eliminate worms and are depicted frequently in Etruscan art from the Archaic period on (Jannot 2009; Guarrera 1999; Jashemski *et al.* 2002; Harrison and Turfa 2010.) Jannot (2009) illustrates Etruscan familiarity with the lotus and poppy, which, as in other regions, were probably also valued for medicinal purposes as well as religious and funerary symbolism.

Among the plants with preserved "Etruscan" names are many still used in folk medicine or recently (re-) studied for potential healing properties: feverfew (Etr. *kautam* – sedative, pain control, reduce inflammation), gentian (Etr. *cicenda* – digestive treatments), henbane (Etr. *fabulonia* – sedative, painkiller, treatment of spasms, asthma), immortelle (Etr. *garuleum* – digestive issues, anti-inflammatory, analgesic), cuckoo-pint (Etr. *gigarum* – anti-bacterial, anti-fungal), pimpernel (Etr. *masuripos, tantum* – diuretic, expectorant, treatment of rashes), thyme (Etr. *mutuka* – expectorant, treatment of coughs, bronchitis), rough bindweed (Etr. *radia* – laxative, treatment of skin conditions), tuberous thistle (*spina alba* – actually Latin -emetic, emmenagogue), valerian (Etr. *sucinum* – treatment of digestive disorders, eczema, insomnia).

Some other plants were linked to Etruscan medicine by authors such as Pliny, but their Etruscan names have not survived, for instance, *millefolium* (water-milfoil), which

Pliny said grew in Etruria and was used to treat toothache and wounds, when mixed with lard was used to treat oxen accidentally cut by the plow (*NH* 24.152). The lily-like plant with aromatic flowers known in Antiquity as *Ephemeros* (L. *cicuta*) has been variously identified by scholars but was associated by ancient authors with Etruscan drug production. Theophrastus (*Historia plantarum* 9.16.6; Pliny *NH* 24.16) said that the Tyrrhenians (Etruscans) of the town of Heraclea (now unknown) were the special producers of a drug from this toxic species (see Bonacelli 1936: 484, note 1).

Seemingly trivial materials may have been recognized for health or safety benefits (as today, for instance, kohl eyeliner protects against fly-borne diseases of the eyes, and the specific gravity of ingredients in cosmetics or perfumes makes them effective antibacterial compounds). An alabaster unguent vase buried in the second century BC at Chiusi still contained traces of its original contents, possibly a skin- or face-cream with a base of mastic and pine resins, and moringa oil (probably) imported from Egypt/Africa (Colombini *et al.* 2009). The moringa oil may have protected the skin from infection, or even from the side effects of cosmetics such as face powder containing heavy metals (cf. Fahey 2005). See Becker 2009 for comments on the containers for drugs and unguents.

On analogy to the survival of ancient herbalism in modern Italian folk medicine, some modern and Roman-era spas with mineral waters or hot springs might have Etruscan origins (cf. Tabanelli 1963: 109–115). Many sanctuaries included features of springs, pools or running water (e.g. the Cannicella shrine in the Orvietan necropolis, the "Fountain shrine" at Marzabotto, the monumental pool at the Portonaccio sanctuary of Veii). The water features of Mezzomiglio, near the modern spa of Chianciano Terme, included a temple-like shrine and large immersion pool employing thermal springs high in sulfates, carbonates and calcium; according to excavator David Soren, "the spa certainly functioned from at least late Etruscan times," the third century BC, although its height came in the Trajanic period (Soren 2010: 13).

DENTAL HEALTH AND DENTISTRY IN ETRURIA (MARSHALL JOSEPH BECKER WITH JEAN MACINTOSH TURFA)

The origins of dental extraction and related surgeries almost certainly predate the period during which the recognizable Etruscan cities emerged. We may be certain that one of the early health-related occupations in Etruria involved the extraction of teeth and perhaps the related pharmaceutical skills (Becker 2009). Analgesic use and the delicate techniques needed for the successful removal of a problematical tooth are cited in the Hippocratic corpus and certainly were known to the Etruscans. The absence of direct evidence for these activities in Etruria has more to do with the absence of extensive written reports. The one aspect of Etruscan medicine for which intervention is most clearly attested relates to a very different aspect of dentistry. The striking evidence for the use of dental pontics among the Etruscans, however, is strongly linked to the medical procedures involving dental bridges. The earliest Etruscan examples of gold pontics were designed as ornaments that were related to a cultural activity involving tooth evulsion (the deliberate removal of one or more anterior teeth as a cosmetic activity for specific members of some cultures, often associated with coming-of-age rituals). How this was determined involves the study of dental health among the Etruscan and Italic peoples. Twenty burials have been found within ancient Etruria with skeletons still wearing gold dental appliances that held replacements for one or both missing front teeth, or central incisors (Bliquez 1996; Becker 1992, 1994A, 1994B, 1999A, 1999B). Nearly all of the examples of Etruscan dental appliances were found prior to the advent of modern archaeological methods, and we cannot be sure that the jaws in which the appliances were displayed or sold were really those of the original "owners" – some most definitely were not!

The earliest known prosthesis that can be assigned a date is one of a very few that can be placed in time. This piece, found in a tomb at Satricum (Borgo Le Ferriere, Tumulus C, tomb XVIII) and dated circa 630 BCE, was fashioned from a very narrow band of sheet-gold into which a single replacement tooth made of gold had been cold-welded (cf. Becker 2003). This is the only known example of the use of a gold replacement tooth. That this was also an early example suggests that it may have been a prototype for the concept.[3] The rapid development of wider and more stable gold bands and the use of cut-down human teeth or other materials to fashion the replacement tooth suggests an evolution in the technology. Those few examples clearly made from re-cut human teeth (Fig. 47.8), and some others that were cut to resemble human teeth, were attached to the band using tiny golden rivets. The band itself was anchored by loops extending from either end that were placed around adjacent living teeth (Fig. 47.9). Two examples in the Liverpool Museum illustrate replacements and the once-living teeth that served as anchors.[4] These appliances would have been made – and installed – by a goldsmith (Turfa forthcoming b; Becker and Turfa forthcoming).

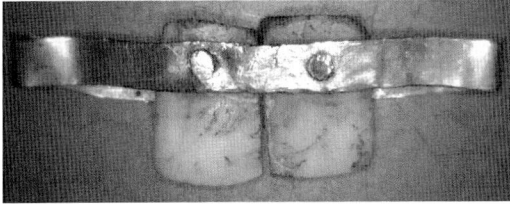

Figure 47.8 Etruscan dental appliance, gold with human teeth carved as replacements for missing teeth (empty spaces fit over original teeth). Liverpool Museum inv. M 10334, Mayer Collection. Photo by Margarita Gleba (2011). Courtesy of National Museums Liverpool (World Museum).

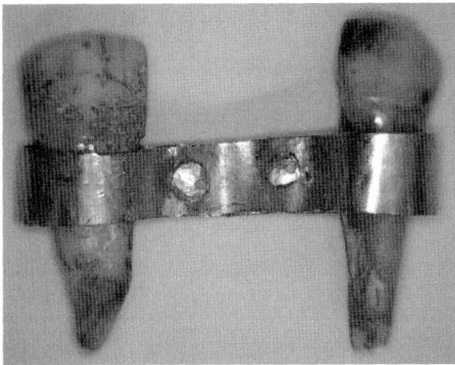

Figure 47.9 Liverpool, Etruscan dental appliance, gold with human anchor-teeth remaining, the replacement teeth missing. Liverpool Museum, inv. M 10335, Mayer Collection. Photo by Margarita Gleba (2011). Courtesy of National Museums Liverpool (World Museum).

The use of these Etruscan pontics for aesthetic purposes can be inferred through two distinct lines of evidence, both relating to the study of the dental health of the population. The review below summarizes the evidence for the pattern of dental loss that was common in ancient Etruria. Dental health was relatively good until later middle age. By age 50 the loss of first molars to extensive decay was not uncommon, with the second and third molars, and often second premolars, commonly following. Despite this progressive decay and loss in advanced age, and correlated periodontal disease, the loss of the anterior teeth was rare other than in individuals who lived to ages beyond 70 or 75. Even arthritic "little old ladies" (in Faliscan Narce) usually retained their own teeth past age 65 (cf. Becker 1993A). Thus it seems likely that the gold pontics that attract our interest were intended for use by people who did not lose one or both central incisors through natural, disease induced loss. We may infer that deliberate and culturally normative tooth evulsion, so widely practiced in cultures around the world, was responsible for the loss (Becker 1995B, 1995C, 2002A).

A second factor in understanding the full process through which healthy, living teeth were deliberately removed and replaced by false teeth was revealed through the study of Etruscan skeletal biology (Becker 1999C). The metric data from studies of ancient dentition indicate that tooth size, and body size in general, is strongly correlated with the biology of sex (Becker 2005). Many of the known Etruscan dental appliances now have spurious teeth with them, or have been placed in unrelated skulls where they mislead the unwary evaluator. By measuring the few surviving teeth definitely associated with these appliances and by measuring the sizes of the sockets in the appliances themselves, we find that all the dimensions of the original teeth fall well within the range of small tooth sizes expected for Etruscan *women*. The ornamental replacement of the teeth of these women, teeth that had been ritually removed,[5] enabled the elite Etruscans to continue a cultural tradition for upper-class women as well as to display their wealth (Becker 1998B, 2002C).

Several of the gold dental appliances appear to have had true medical functions. These functional prostheses seem to date from a later period in the era of gold pontics, perhaps reflecting Roman pragmatism in adopting this concept for specific medical uses. Roman variations on Etruscan pontics are mentioned by a number of classical authors. In addition, the use of these pontics in mortuary contexts was governed by Roman law.[6] These functional examples are of two distinct types. One variety consists of a series of gold rings that have been cold-welded together in the Etruscan fashion and used both to hold replacement (artificial) teeth and to stabilize natural teeth that had become loose (Becker 1996). A second variety of functional appliance consists of a simple, elongate oval band used only to stabilize loose teeth. These long bands also may have served as ornamentation.

A completely separate and somewhat later tradition in dental prostheses has been identified from the eastern shores of the Mediterranean. "Phoenician" dental appliances were fashioned from gold or silver (Becker 1997), and perhaps should be called Levantine or Near Eastern in type. The later date (Roman era) and purely functional aspects of these wire prostheses indicate a completely independent tradition. This tradition of wiring loose teeth to stabilize them continued to be used in dental medicine well into the twentieth century.

Dental problems, abscesses and gum disease contributed significantly to the ill health, and even the death of many ancient sufferers in various parts of the world. This has been suggested by several studies of Egyptian mummies and related populations. While claims have been made for serious dental lesions affecting the Etruscans (see Lilley 2002), the statistical incidence is extremely low (see Becker 2002B, 1993B). Dental health was fairly good among Iron Age Italic populations, to judge from surviving skeletal finds. Many people had very worn teeth, reflecting the consumption of whole grains that have tough silicate covers. Stone-ground cereals are more abrasive for their natural aspects than for any minerals that might be added in the milling process, as suggested by Cattaneo and Mazzucchi (2005). (Milling stones in every society are selected for qualities including hardness). With improvements in food supply and urbanization, it would seem that many more Etruscans began to eat "junk food" (refined carbohydrates such as white bread instead of barley porridge). This is suggested by the many skeletons of the Archaic through Hellenistic periods that reveal extensive dental calculus and lost teeth. Some of these factors may be related to social class. These observations correspond only somewhat with the dental example from Etruscan individuals now in the collections of the University of Pennsylvania Museum, excavated at Narce, Vulci, Chiusi, and Montebello (see Becker *et al.* 2009: 41–61 *passim*, 71–76, 78–79, 98, 132–138). However, this is an extremely limited sample. A greater sample from each of these many sites would be needed to confirm any hypothesis. A number of individuals in this group, and from other necropolis populations, also have premolars with distinctive bifurcate tooth roots. The statistical significance of this trait remains to be explored. The Iron Age skeletal population was generally quite short in stature. This is particularly evident among the women, who were often under five feet in height and had delicate skulls and jaws (Becker 2005). Many of them did not have third molars ("wisdom teeth"). Statistical surveys of specific dental aspects of the skeletal population of ancient Italy, factored for specific periods of time, would be useful.

Under the general concept of Etruscan dental medicine, note should be made regarding various claims of finds of various materials used as dental implants. These claims have been reviewed elsewhere (Becker 1994C, 1998A), and in some detail (Becker 1999D). As with many other claims, these are based entirely on misidentification of artifacts found in or around the oral cavities of individuals. The recent developments in dental techniques have, with the enormous progress of the past few decades in metallurgy as well as medicine, achieved extremely high rates of success in implantology. To believe that any group in Antiquity had achieved any degree of success in this field is to give credit to the Etruscans far beyond any that is due.

HEALTH AND WELL-BEING IN ETRURIA

Life was undoubtedly a challenge throughout Etruscan history. A year or two of poor harvests would have threatened lives, health and political regimes, and even the epitaphs of the nobility show death stalking young and old alike. Those suffering illness or trauma had recourse to religious vows, and, during the third-second centuries BC, thousands of votive models attest the healing of many individuals, commoners and freedmen as well as nobility, although there is scant evidence of any medical intervention, apart perhaps from post-mortem attempts at fetal salvage. The votive use of anatomical models of internal organs and sculptural plaques or statues with exposed viscera attests a certain level of recognition of anatomy and physiology by the general public, even if the models are schematic and highly stylized. In healing cults as in nutrition and society in general, women's concerns were on a par with men's. The population as a whole certainly enjoyed improved food and water supply, comfort, and sanitation because of Etruscan agricultural and engineering advances – and it may have suffered due to industrial pollution and the movement of foreign immigrants, ultimately brought in by Rome's conquests. Rome probably benefitted from Etruscan medicine as it certainly did from agriculture and engineering, but the authors of the Late Republic and Augustan periods might not have realized this and in any case were beguiled by the literature of Hellenistic Greek culture, and so we do not see acknowledgment of this. As in other fields, it remains for archaeological and scientific research to fill in the lacunae.

NOTES

1   This is only a sampling of published data; see Chapter 4 for more on evidence of disease and trauma; for review of paleopathological research in Etruria, see Mallegni and Vitiello 1997, and articles in *Journal of Archaeological Science*, and medical and anthropological literature.

2   Social considerations may skew our data: in funeral cippi inscribed with Latin epitaphs at Tarquinia (first century BC), in addition to octogenarian men, two Etruscan women (Spurinnia and Netia) reached 94 and 95 years, so we are not safe in making determinations from small samples. See Kaimio 2010: nos 91 and 227.

3   The provenance of one other example, said to be from Bisenzio, could possibly be Iron Age/late seventh century BC, since this settlement appears to have been abandoned around the end of the Archaic period; at the moment the piece is considered lost, however. The 19 finds from peninsular Italy range from Satricum and Bisenzio over all of Etruria (Bolsena and Bracciano lake regions, Orvieto, Tarquinia [possibly four examples], perhaps Cerveteri and Vulci, and the territory of Chiusi) and into the *Ager Faliscus* (Valsiarosa = Falerii-Celle), Latium (actually Satricum, also Palestrina/Praeneste) and Campania (Teano, one of the latest, dated circa 300 BC).

4   The Liverpool objects were collected by goldsmith and antiquarian Joseph Mayer, but lack provenance information; much of his collection was purchased in the second quarter of the nineteenth century, and came from the excavations of the Vulci necropoleis, and it seems possible that the pontics also came from Vulci.

5   The likelihood of an accidental or medical loss of a front tooth in such populations is extremely low; these are the last teeth to be lost in an aging individual, and front teeth can usually be detected in the ancient skeletal populations of central Italy.

6   The Roman *Law of the Twelve Tables*, recorded by the early fifth century BC, and with likely older antecedents, states *"ne aurum addito"*: "No gold may be added" to a body that is about to be buried, but for decorum allows gold prostheses to be left in place, a serendipitous confirmation of their use in archaic Italy.

BIBLIOGRAPHY

For thorough background on diseases etc. in antiquity, see Aufderheide and Rodríguez-Martín 1998 and Kiple 1993; for zoonoses see T-W-Fiennes 1978 and Turfa 2012, chapter 6.

Albore Livadie, C. (2002) "A First Pompeii: the Early Bronze Age village of Nola-Croce del Papa (Palma Campania phase)," *Antiquity* 76: 941–942.

Allegrezza, L. and Baggieri G. (1999) "Come leggere i votivi anatomici" in G. Baggieri and M. L. Rinaldi Veloccia (eds), *L'antica anatomia nell'arte dei donaria (Ancient Anatomy in the Art of Votive Offerings)*, Rome: MelAMi, 34–76.

Andreae, B. (2004) "La Tomba François ricostruita" in A. M. Moretti Sgubini (ed.), *Eroi Etruschi e Miti Greci. Gli affreschi della Tomba François tornano a Vulci*, Calenzano (FI): Edizioni Cooperativa Archeologia, 41–57.

Aspöck, H., Auer, H. and Picher, O. (1996) "*Trichuris trichiura* Eggs in the Neolithic Glacier Mummy from the Alps," *Parasitology Today* 12: 255–256.

Aufderheide, A. C. and Rodríguez-Martín, C. (1998) *The Cambridge Encyclopedia of Human Paleopathology*. Cambridge, UK: Cambridge University Press, 240–241.

Baggieri, G. (2005) "Paleopatologia scheletrica degli individui della necropoli di Monterozzi e di San Giovenale" in O. Paoletti and G. Camporeale (eds), *Dinamiche di Sviluppo delle Città nell'Etruria Meridionale. Veio, Caere, Tarquinia, Vulci. Atti del XXIII Convegno di Studi Etruschi ed Italici, Roma, Veio, Cerveteri/Pyrgi, Tarquinia, Tuscania, Vulci, Viterbo, 1–6 ottobre 2001*. Pisa and Rome: Istituti Editoriali e Poligrafici Internazionali, vol. II: 703–713.

Barbieri, G. and Becker, M. J. (1996–1997) "Tomba della donna con i sandali," *NS* 1996–1997: 343–355.

Bartoli, F., Mallegni, F. and Fornaciari, G. (1997) "Le risorse alimentari nel mondo etrusco: aspetti della paleodieta in due gruppi umani a cultura etrusca" in *Aspetti della cultura di Volterra etrusca fra l'età del ferro e l'età ellenistica. Atti del XIX Convegno di Studi Etruschi ed Italici (Volterra 1995)*. Florence: Istituto di Studi Etruschi, 477–488.

Bartoloni, G. and Benedettini, M. G. (2011) *Veio. Il Deposito votive di Comunità (Scavi 1889–2005)*. Rome: G. Bretschneider.

Becker, M. J. (1992) "An Etruscan gold dental appliance in the collections of the Danish National Museum: Evidence for the history of dentistry," *Tandlaegebladet (Danish Dental Journal)* 96 (Nr. 15): Cover, 695–700.

——(1993a) "Seianti Hanunia Tlesnasa: An Analysis of Her Skeleton in the Sarcophagus at the British Museum" in G. Maetzke (ed.), *La Civiltà di Chiusi e del Suo Territorio (Atti del XVII Convegno di Studi Etruschi ed Italici, Chianciano Terme, 1989)*, Florence: Leo S. Olschki, 397–410.

——(1993b) "Human Skeletons from Tarquinia: A Preliminary Analysis of the 1989 Cimitero Site Excavations with Implications for the Evolution of Etruscan Social Classes," *Studi Etruschi* 58 (for 1992): 211–248.

——(1994a) "Etruscan Gold Dental Appliances: origins and functions as indicated by an example from Valsiarosa, Italy," *Journal of Paleopathology* 6 (2): 69–92.

——(1994b) "Etruscan Gold Dental Appliances: Origins and Functions as Indicated by an Example from Orvieto, Italy, in the Danish National Museum," *Dental Anthropology Newsletter* 8 (3): 2–8.

——(1994c) "Spurious 'Examples' of Ancient Dental Implants or Appliances," *Dental Anthropology Newsletter* 9 (1): 5–10.

——(1995) "Human Skeletal Remains from the Pre-Colonial Greek Emporium of Pithekoussai on Ischia (NA): Culture Contact in Italy from the Early VIII to the II Century BC" in N. Christie (ed.), *Settlement and Economy in Italy 1500 BC to AD 1500. Papers of the Fifth Conference of Italian Archaeology* (Oxbow Monograph 41). Oxford: Oxbow Books, 273–281.

——(1995b) "Female Vanity Among the Etruscans: The Copenhagen Gold Dental Appliance," *Actas del I Congreso Internacional de Estudios sobre Momias, 1992* (ed.), Arthur C. Aufderheide. Santa Cruz de Tenerife: Museo Arqueológico y Etnológico de Tenerife. Volume II: 651–658.

——(1995c) "Tooth Evulsion Among the Ancient Etruscans: Recycling in Antiquity," *Dental Anthropology Newsletter* 9 (3): 8–9.

——(1996) "An Unusual Etruscan Gold Dental Appliance From Poggio Gaiella, Italy. Fourth in a Series," *Dental Anthropology Newsletter* 10 (3): 10–16.

——(1997) "Early Dental Appliances in the Eastern Mediterranean," *Berytus* 42 (1995/6): 71–102.

——(1998a) "A Roman 'implant' reconsidered," *Nature* 394 (No. 6693): 534.

——(1998b) "Etruscan Gold Dental Appliances: Evidence for Cultural Processes" in *Treating Illnesses: Historical Routes, 1st Internatl. Conf. Of Anthropology and History of Health and Disease*, Vol. 2 (ed.), Antonio Guerci. Genoa: Erga edizioni, 10–21. Also issued by Erga multimedia as, "*Guarire ieri e oggi. Domani?/Healing, Yesterday and Today. Tomorrow?*"

——(1999a) "Etruscan Gold Dental Appliances: Three Newly 'Discovered' Examples in America," *American Journal of Archaeology* 103: 103–111.

——(1999b) "The Valsiarosa Gold Dental Appliance: Etruscan Origins for Dental Prostheses," *Etruscan Studies* 6: 43–73.

——(1999c) "Calculating stature from *in situ* measurements of skeletons and from long bone lengths: an historical perspective leading to a test of Formicola's hypothesis at 5th century BCE Satricum, Lazio, Italy," *Rivista di Antropologia* (Rome) 77: 225–247.

——(1999d) "Ancient 'Dental Implants:' A Recently Proposed Example from France Evaluated with other Claims," *International Journal of Oral & Maxillofacial Implants* 14: 19–29.

——(2002a) "Etruscan female tooth evulsion: gold dental appliances as ornaments" in G. Carr and P. Baker (eds), *Practices, Practitioners and Patients: New approaches to medical archaeology and anthropology*. Oxford: Oxbow Books, 236–257.

——(2002b) "Seianti Hanunia Tlesnasa: A Re-Evaluation of her Skeleton in the British Museum" in *Seianti Hanunia Tlesnasa: The Story of an Etruscan Noblewoman*, J. Swaddling and J. Prag (eds), The British Museum Occasional Paper Number 100. London: The Trustees of the British Museum, 17–69.

——(2002c) "Etruscan Tombs at Tarquinia: Heterarchy as Indicated by Human Skeletal Remains" in *Paesaggi d'Acque – Ricerche a Scavi. Preistoria e Protostoria in Etruria: Atti del Quinto Encontro di Studi (12–14 May 2000)*, Vol. II (ed.), N. Negroni Catacchio. Milano: Onlus, for the Centro Studi di Preistoria e Archeologia, 687–708.

——(2003) "Etruscan Gold Dental Appliances: Evidence for Early 'Parting' of Gold in Italy through the Study of Ancient Pontics" in G. Tsoucaris and J. Lipkowski (eds), *Molecular and Structural Archaeology: Cosmetic and Therapeutic Chemicals*, Dordrecht: Kluwer Academic (NATO Science Series, 117), 11–27.

——(2005) "Etruscan Women at Tarquinia: Skeletal Evidence for Tomb Use," *Analecta Romana Instituti Danici* 31: 21–36.

——(2009) "Etruscan Origins of Pharmaceutical Vessel Shapes: Four Apothecary Jars From Early Chiusi, Toscana, Italy" in S. Bruni (ed.), *Etruria e Italia Preromana: Studi in onore di Giovannangelo Camporeale*, Volume I. Pisa: Accademia Editoriale, 69–72.

——(2012) "Coming of Age in Etruria: Etruscan Children's Cemeteries at Tarquinia, Italy," *International Journal of Anthropology* 27(1–2): 63–86.

Becker, M. J. and Donadio, A. (1992) "A summary of the analysis of cremated human skeletal remains from the Greek colony of Pithekoussai at Lacco Ameno, Ischia, Italy," *Old World Archaeology Newsletter* 16(1): 15–23.

Becker, M. J. and Salvadei, L. (1992) "Analysis of the Human Skeletal Remains from the Cemetery of Osteria dell'Osa" in A. M. Bietti Sestieri (ed.), *La Necropoli Laziale di Osteria dell'Osa*. Rome: Quasar, 53–191.

Becker, M. J. and Turfa, J. M. (forthcoming) *Etruscan Dental Appliances* (monograph).

Becker, M. J., Turfa, J. M. and Algee-Hewitt, B. (2009) *Human Remains from Etruscan and Italic Tomb Groups in the University of Pennsylvania Museum* (Biblioteca di Studi Etruschi 48), Pisa/Rome: Fabrizio Serra.

Bertoldi, V. (1936) "*Nomina tusca* in Dioscoride," *Studi Etruschi* 10: 295–320.

Bietti Sestieri, A. M. (1992) *The Iron Age Community of Osteria dell'Osa. A study of socio-political development in central Tyrrhenian Italy*. Cambridge: Cambridge University Press.

Bliquez, L. (1996) "Prosthetics in Classical Antiquity: Greek, Etruscan, and Roman Prosthetics" in W. Haase (ed.), *Aufstieg und Niedergang der römischen Welt, Teil II: Principat*, Vol. 37.3: [2640–2676] 2650–2651 on Etruscan.

Bonacelli, B. (1928) "La natura e gli Etruschi," *Studi Etruschi* 2: 427–569.

Brachman, P. S. and Kaufmann, A. R. (1998) "Anthrax" in A. S. Evans and P. S. Brachman (eds), *Bacterial Infections of Humans. Epidemiology and Control* (3rd edn). New York: Plenum, 95–108.

Bradley, M. (2011) "Obesity, Corpulence and Emaciation in Roman Art," *Papers of the British School at Rome* 79: 1–41.

Briquel, D. (2006) "Les glosses étrusques," *Res Antiquae* 3: 301–318.

Brocato, P. (2000) *La necropoli etrusca della Riserva del Ferrone. Analisi di una communità arcaica dei Monti della Tolfa.* Rome: Edizioni Quasar.

Brown, A. J. (1960) "Cancer in antiquity: natural history," *Notes on the History of Cancer. Victorian Cancer News* 2: 8.

Camporeale, G. and Giuntoli, S. (2000) *The Accesa Archaeological Park at Massa Marittima*, trans. J. Denton. Follonica, Editrice Leopoldo II.

Capasso, L. and di Tota, G. (1997) "Le malattie infettive degli Etruschi" in G. Maetzke and L. Tamagno Perna (eds), *Aspetti della cultura di Volterra Etrusca fra l'età del ferro e l'età ellenistica e contributi della Ricerca Antropologica alla conoscenza del popolo etrusco (Atti del XIX Convegno di Studi Etruschi ed Italici. Volterra 15–19 ottobre 1995).* Florence: Olschki, 551–557.

Cappellini, E., Chiarelli, B., Sineo, L., Casoli, A., Di Gioia, A., Vernesi, C., Biella M. C., and Caramelli, D. (2004) "Biomolecular study of the human remains from tomb 5859 in the Etruscan necropolis of Monterozzi, Tarquinia (Viterbo, Italy)," *Journal of Archaeological Science* 31: 603–612.

Cattaneo, C. and Mazzucchi, A. (2005) "L'alimentazione degli etruschi di Bozzolo (V secolo a.C.), and Necropoli di Bozzolo, corte Alta Cerese" in E. M. Menotti (ed.), *Cibo: vita e cultura nelle collezioni del Museo Archeologico Nazionale di Mantova.* Mantova: Tre Lune, 89–92, 216–217 (English).

Cavagnaro Vanoni, L. (1996) *Tombe tarquiniesi di età ellenistica: Catalogo di ventisei tombe a camera scoperte dalla Fondazione Lerici in località Calvario.* Rome: "L'ERMA" di Bretschneider.

Ciranni, R. and Tempestini, R. (2008) "Speculations About Osteolytic Lesions in an Etruscan Skeleton," *American Journal of Medicine* 121(8): 738–739.

Cocchi Genick, D. (1998) *L'antica età del bronzo nell'Italia centrale: profilo di un'epoca e di un'appropriata strategia metodologica.* Florence: Octavo.

Colombini, M. P., Giachi, G., Iozzo, M. and Ribechini, E. (2009) "An Etruscan ointment from Chiusi (Tuscany, Italy): its chemical characterization," *Journal of Archaeological Science* 30: 1–8 (doi: 10.1016/j.jas.2009.02.011).

G. Colonna (ed.) (1985) *Santuari d'Etruria.* Exhibition, Arezzo, Museo archeologico C. Cilnio Mencenate, 19 May – 20 October 1985. Milan: Electa.

Comella, A. (1986) *I materiali votive di Falerii.* Rome: G. Bretschneider.

Cornell, T. J. (1995) *The Beginnings of Rome.* London: Routledge.

Cristofani, M. (1985) *I Bronzi degli Etruschi.* Novara: Istituto Geografico De Agostini.

Cristofani M., Cristofani Martelli, M., Fiumi, E., Maggiani, A. and Talocchini, A. *Urne volterrane. 1. I Complessi tombali. (Corpus delle urne etrusche di età ellenistica.)* Florence: Centro Di; 1975.

De Lucia Brolli, M. A. (2004) "Una tomba a cremazione entro custodia litica dall'Agro falisco" in A. M. Moretti Sgubini (ed.), *Scavo nello scavo: gli Etruschi non viste: ricerche e 'riscoperte' nei depositi dei musei archeologici dell'Etruria meridionale: 5 marzo 2004–30 giugno 2004. Viterbo, Fortezza Giulioli.* Rome: Soprintendenza per I Beni Archeologici per l'Etruria Meridionale/ Union Printing Edizioni, 109–11, (112–117 catalogue).

Dickson, J. H., Oeggl, K., Holden, T. G., Handley, L. L., O'Connell, T. C. and Preston, T. (2000) "The Omnivorous Tyrolean Iceman: Colon Contents (Meat, Cereals, Pollen, Moss and Whipworm) and Stable Isotope Analyses," *Philosophical Transactions of the Royal Society London. (Biol Sci)* 355: 1843–1849.

Drescher-Schneider, R., de Beaulieu, J.-L., Magny, M., Walter-Simonnet, A.-V., Bossnet, G., Millet, L., Brugiapaglia, E. and Drescher, A. (2007) "Vegetation history, climate and human impact over the last 15,000 years at Lago dell'Accesa (Tuscany, Central Italy)," *Vegetation History and Archaeobotany* 16: 279–299.

Fahey, J. W. (2005) "Moringa oleifera: a review of the medical evidence for its nutritional, therapeutic, and prophylactic properties. Part 1," *Trees for Life Journal* 1(5). Available at: <http://www.tfljournal.org/article.php/20051201124931586>.

Formicola, V. Q., Milanesi, C. and Scarsini, C. (1987) "Evidence of spinal tuberculosis at the beginning of the fourth millennium BC from Arena Candida Cave (Liguria, Italy)," *American Journal of Physical Anthropology* 72: 1–7.

Fornaciari, G. (1997) "Paleopatologia di gruppi umani a cultura etrusca: il caso di Pontecagnano, Salerno (VII-IV sec. a.C.)" in *Aspetti della cultura di Volterra etrusca fra l'eta del ferro e l'età ellenistica. Atti del XIX Convegno di Studi Etruschi ed Italici (Volterra 1995)* Florence: Istituto di Studi Etruschi, 467–475.

Fornaciari, G. and Mallegni, F. (1997) "I resti paleoantropologici" in M. Bonghi Jovino and C. Chiaramonte Treré (eds), *Tarquinia. Testimonianze archeologiche e ricostruzione storica*, Rome: "L'ERMA" di Bretschneider, 100–102.

Giusberti, G. (1994) "Nota antropologica relativa ad uno schel etro di epoca villanoviana rinvenuto nel territorio di Quarto Inferiore (metà VI sec. A.C.)" in M. Forte and P. von Eles (eds), *La Pianura Bolognese nel Villanoviano. Insediamenti della prima età del Ferro.* Ministero Beni Culturali e Ambientali, and Soprintendenza Archeologica dell'Emilia Romagna. Studi e documenti di archeologia, *Quaderni* 5, 306–309.

Grmek, M. D. (1991) *Diseases in the Ancient Greek World* trans. M. Muellner and L. Muellner, French edition, 1983. Baltimore: Johns Hopkins.

Guarrera, P. M. (1999) "Traditional antihelmintic, antiparasitic and repellent uses of plants in Central Italy," *Journal of Ethnopharmacology* 68: 183–192.

Harrison, A. P. and Bartels, E. M. (2006) "A modern appraisal of ancient Etruscan herbal practices," *American Journal of Pharmacology and Toxicology* 1(1): 21–24.

Harrison, A. P. and Turfa, J. M. (2010) "Were natural forms of treatment for Fasciola hepatica available to the Etruscans?" *International Journal of Medical Sciences* 7(5): 282–291.

Harrison, A. P., Cattani, I. and Turfa, J. M. (2010) "Metallurgy, environmental pollution and the decline of Etruscan civilization," *Environmental Science and Pollution Research International* 17: 165–180; Available at: <http://www.ncbi.nlm.nih.gov/pubmed/19333636>.

Henneberg, M. and Henneberg, R. J. (1998) "Biological characteristics of the population based on analysis of skeletal remains" in J. C. Carter (ed.), *The Chora of Metaponto. The Necropoleis* II. Austin, TX: University of Texas, 503–556.

Heurgon, J. (1964) *Daily Life of the Etruscans*, trans. J. Kirkup. New York: Macmillan.

Hostetler, K. L. (2007) "Serpent Iconography," *Etruscan Studies* 10: 203–209.

Jannot, J.-R. (2009) "The Lotus, Poppy and other Plants in Etruscan Funerary Contexts" in J. Swaddling and P. Perkins (eds), *Etruscan by Definition. Papers in Honour of Sybille Haynes, MBE.* British Museum Research Publication Number 173: 81–86.

Jashemski, W. F., Meyer, F. G. and Ricciardi, M. (2002) "Plants: Evidence from Wall Paintings, Mosaics, Sculpture, Plant Remains, Graffiti, Inscriptions, and Ancient Authors" in W. F. Jashemski and F. G. Meyer (eds), *The Natural History of Pompeii.* Cambridge: Cambridge University Press, 80–180.

Jeske-Janicka, M. and Janicki, P. K. (1998) "Appendix 11A.5. Detection of Treponema Pallidum Antigens" in J. C. Carter (ed.), *The Chora of Metaponto. The Necropoleis* II. Austin, TX: University of Texas, 557–559.

Kaimio, J. (2010) *The Cippus Inscriptions of Museo Nazionale di Tarquinia.* Rome: Giorgio Bretschneider Editore.

Keller, A., Graefen, A. *et al.* (2012) "New insights into the Tyrolean Iceman's origin and phenotype as inferred by whole-genome sequencing," *Nature Communications* 3, Article 698; doi: 10.1038/ncomms1701 (28 February 2012).

Kiple, K. F. (ed.) (1993) *Cambridge World History of Human Disease*. Cambridge, UK: Cambridge University Press, 603–604 and 703.

Leonti, M., Casu, L., Sanna, F. and Bonsignore, L. (2009) "A comparison of medicinal plant use in Sardinia and Sicily – De Materia Medica revisited?" *Journal of Ethnopharmacology*, 121: 255–267.

Levine, M. M. (1998) "Typhoid Fever" in A. S. Evans and P. S. Brachman (eds), *Bacterial Infections of Humans. Epidemiology and Control* (3rd edn). New York: Plenum, 839–858.

Lilley, J. D. (2002) "5. Seianti Hanunia Tlesnasa: Some Observations on the Dental Features" in J. Swaddling and J. Prag (eds), *Seianti Hanunia Tlesnasa. The Story of an Etruscan Noblewoman*. London: British Museum Occasional Paper Number 100, 23–26.

Longrigg, J. (2000) "Death and Epidemic Disease in Classical Athens" in V. M. Hope and E. Marshall (eds), *Death and Disease in the Ancient City* London: Routledge, 55–64.

Lorenzi, L. (2011) "Ancient images of a mother giving birth found," *Discovery News* October 19, 2011. Available at: <http://news.discovery.com/etruscan-mother-birth-art111019.html>. Reprinted in *Etruscan News* 14 (Winter 2012): 17.

Losi, A. (1994) "La sepoltura di Quarto Inferiore" in M. Forte and P. von Eles (eds), *La pianura bolognese nel villanoviano. Insediamenti della prima età del Ferro*. Ministero Beni Culturali e Ambientali, and Soprintendenza Archeologica dell'Emilia Romagna. Studi e documenti di archeologia, *Quaderni* 5: 301–305.

Mainardi, S. and Pacciani, E. (1994) "Nota antropologica sullo scheletro umano rinvenuto a Castenaso- Via Gramsci nella struttura η" in M. Forte and P. von Eles (eds), *La pianura bolognese nel villanoviano. Insediamenti della prima età del Ferro*. Ministero Beni Culturali e Ambientali, and Soprintendenza Archeologica dell'Emilia Romagna. Studi e documenti di archeologia, *Quaderni* 5: 213–217.

Mallegni, F. and Vitiello, A. (1997) "Le ricerche antropologiche sui gruppi umani a cultura etrusca" in *Aspetti della cultura di Volterra etrusca fra l'età del ferro e l'età ellenistica. Atti del XIX Convegno di Studi Etruschi ed Italici (Volterra 1995)* Florence: Istituto di Studi Etruschi, 17–32.

Mariotti, V., Dutour, O., Belcastro, M. G., Facchini, F. and Brasil, P. (2005) "Probable Early Presence of Leprosy in Europe in a Celtic Skeleton of the 4th-3rd Century BC (Casalecchio di Reno, Bologna, Italy)," *International Journal of Osteoarchaeology* 15: 311–325.

Mascaro, I., Benvenuti, M., Corsini, F., Costagliola, P., Lattanti, P., Parrini, P. and Tanelli G. (2001) "Mine wastes at the polymetallic deposit of Fenice Capanne (Southern Tuscany, Italy). Mineralogy, geochemistry and environmental impact," *Environmental Geology* 41: 417–429

Mastrolorenzo, G., Petrone, P., Pappalardo L. and Sheridan, M. F. (2006) "The Avellino 3780-yr-B.P. catastrophe as a worst-case scenario for a future eruption of Vesuvius," *Proceedings of the National Academy of Sciences* 103.12 (March 21, 2006): 4366–4370.

Mazzucchi, A., Gaudio, D., Galassi A. and Cattaneo, C. "The study of cranial trauma in ancient populations: trepanation to therapy in four cases from northern Italy. *XXI Congress of the International Academy of Legal Medicine (IALM)*, Poster Session P.D$_2$ (Session D, May 29) Lisbon 2009. Available at: <http:.handle.net/2434/166917>.

Nagy, H. (2011) "Etruscan votive terracottas and their archaeological contexts: preliminary comments on Veii and Cerveteri" in N. T. de Grummond and I. Edlund-Berry (eds), *The Archaeology of Sanctuaries and Ritual in Etruria*. Portsmouth, RI: *Journal of Roman Archaeology* Suppl. 81, 113–125.

Nataro, J. P., Stine, O. C., Kaper, J. B. and Levine, M. M. (2003) "The archaeology of enteric infection: *Salmonella, Shigella, Vibrio*, and diarrheagenic *Escherichia coli*" in C. L. Greenblatt and M. Spigelman (eds), *Emerging Pathogens. The Archaeology, Ecology, and Evolution of Infectious Disease*. Oxford: Oxford University Press, 167–174.

Onisto, N. (2002) "7.1.Analisi morfologica e metrica dei resti ossei umani" in P. von Eles (ed.), *Guerriero e sacerdote. Autorità e comunità nell'età del ferro a Verucchio. La Tomba del Trono* (Quaderni di Archeologia dell'Emilia Romagna 6). Florence: all'Insegna del Giglio, 277–289.

Pallottino, M. (1968) *Testimonia Linguae Etruscae*, (= TLE) 2nd edn Florence: La Nuova Italia Editrice.

Pascarella, R., Marchesini Reggiani, L. and Boriani, S. (2009) "Pelvic ring fracture – Dislocation in a 2400-year-old Etruscan man," *Injury* 40: 223–225.

Pautasso, A. (1994) *Il deposito votive presso la Porta Nord a Vulci*, Rome: G. Bretschneider.

Perkins, P. (1999) *Etruscan settlement, society and material culture in central coastal Etruria*. Oxford: John and Erica Hedges.

Pfiffig, A. (1975) *Religio Etrusca*. Graz: Akademische Druck- und Verlagsanstalt.

Rasmussen, T. B. (2005) "Urbanization in Etruria" in R. Osborne and B. Cunliffe (eds), *Mediterranean Urbanization 800–600 BC*. Oxford: Oxford University Press, 71–90.

Ricciardi, L. (1988–89) "L'altare monumentale e il deposito votivo" in B. Massabò, "CANINO (Viterbo). – Il santuario etrusco di Fontanile di Legnisina a Vulci: Relazione delle campagne di scavo 1985 e 1986: il tempio," *Notizie degli Scavi* 42–43: 137–209.

Sallares, R. (2002) *Malaria and Rome*. Oxford: Oxford University Press.

Scarborough, J. (2006) "More on Dioscorides' Etruscan Herbs," *Etruscan News* (Summer 2006) 6: 1, 9.

Scheidel, W. (1996) *Measuring Sex, Age and Death in the Roman Empire* (= *JRA* Suppl. Ser. 21). Portsmouth, RI: *JRA*.

Schlesinger, A. C. (1959) *Livy with an English translation. XIV. Summaries, Fragments, and Obsequens*. Cambridge, MA: Harvard University Press (Loeb Classical Library).

Soren, D. (2010) "Introduction to Volume 2" in D. Soren and P. Mecchia (eds), *An Ancient Roman Spa at Mezzomiglio, Chianciano Terme, Tuscany*, Volume 2, with Dr. Paola Mecchia (BAR I.S. 2171, Oxford: Archeopress) 13–17.

Stoddart, R. W. (2002) "Remains from the Sarcophagus of Seianti Hanunia Tlesnasa: Pathological Evidence and its Implications" in J. Swaddling and J. Prag (eds), *Seianti Hanunia Tlesnasa. The Story of an Etruscan Noblewoman*. London: British Museum Occasional Paper Number 100, 29–38.

Swaddling, J. and Prag, J. (eds) (2002) *Seianti Hanunia Tlesnasa. The Story of an Etruscan Noblewoman*. London: British Museum Occasional Paper Number 100.

Tabanelli, M. (1962) *Gli ex voto poliviserali etruschi e romani. Storia, ritrovamenti, interpretazione*, Florence: Olschki.

——(1963) *La medicina nel mondo degli Etruschi*. Florence: Leo S Olschki.

Tafuri, M. A. (2005) *Tracing Mobility and Identity. Bioarchaeology and bone chemistry of the Bronze Age Sant'Abbondio cemetery (Pompeii, Italy)*. (BAR Int.Ser. 1359.) Oxford: Archaeopress.

Terrosi Zanco, O. (1961) "Ex-voto allungati dell'Italia centrale," *Studi Etruschi* 29: 423–59.

Torelli, M. (1976) "Glosse etrusche: qualche problema di trasmissione" in *Mélanges offerts à Jacques Heurgon: L'Italie préromaine et la Rome républicaine*. Rome: École française de Rome, 1001–1008.

Turfa, J. M. (1994) "Anatomical Votives and Italian Medical Tradition" in R. D. de Puma and J. P. Small (eds), *Murlo and the Etruscans*. Madison, WI: University of Wisconsin Press, 224–240.

——(2004) "[Weigeschenke: Altitalien und Imperium Romanum. 1. Italien.] B. Anatomical votives" in *Thesaurus Cultus et Rituum Antiquorum (ThesCRA) I. Processions – Sacrifices – Libations – Fumigations – Dedications*, Los Angeles, 359–368.

——(2005) *Catalogue of the Etruscan Gallery of The University Museum*, Philadelphia: University Museum Press.

——(2006) "Was There Room for Healing in the Healing Sanctuaries?" *Archiv für Religonsgeschichte* 8: 63–80.

——(2012) *Divining the Etruscan World: The Brontoscopic Calendar and Religious Practice*. Cambridge: Cambridge University Press.

——(forthcoming a) "The *Obesus Etruscus*: any basis in fact?" in A. P. Harrison (ed.), *International Journal of Medical Sciences*, special issue, (May 2012).

——(forthcoming b) *Catalogue of the Etruscan and Italic Antiquities in the Liverpool Museum*, G. Muskett (ed.).

Turfa, J. M. and Gettys, S. (2009) "The Skill of the Etruscan Haruspex: A Biological Basis for Successful Divination?" *Bulletin Antieke Beschaving* 84: 41–52.

T-W-Fiennes, R. N. (1978) *Zoonoses and the Origins and Ecology of Human Disease*. London/New York: Academic Press.

Unge Sörling, S. (1994) "A Collection of Votive Terracottas from Tessennano (Vulci)," *Medelhavsmuseet Bulletin* 29: 47–54.

van der Meer, L. B. (1995) Interpretatio Etrusca. *Greek Myths on Etruscan Mirrors*, Amsterdam: Gieben.

Viegi, L., Pieroni, A., Guarrera, P. M. and Vangelisti, R. (2003) "A review of plants used in folk veterinary medicine in Italy as a basis for a databank," *Journal of Ethnopharmacology* 89: 221–244.

Weiland, J. (2011) "Malaria in Etruria," *Etruscan Studies* 14: 97–105.

Wilkinson, L. (1993) "Anthrax" in K. F. Kiple (ed.), *Cambridge World History of Human Disease*. Cambridge: Cambridge University Press, 582–583.

Wiseman, T. P. (1995) *Remus. A Roman Myth*. Cambridge: Cambridge University Press.

Wyatt, H. V. (1993) "Poliomyelitis" in K. F. Kiple (ed.), *Cambridge World History of Human Disease*. Cambridge: Cambridge University Press, 942–950.

Young, E. J. and Hall, W. H. (1998) "Brucellosis" in A. S. Evans and P. S. Brachman (eds), *Bacterial Infections of Humans. Epidemiology and Control* (3rd ed.). New York: Plenum, 155–168.

PART VII

ETRUSCAN SPECIALTIES IN ART

——·◆·——

CHAPTER FORTY EIGHT

FOREIGN ARTISTS IN ETRURIA

———·◆·———

Giovannangelo Camporeale

The natural materials and mineral resources of the region inhabited by the Etruscans – agriculture, the forest, animal husbandry, fishing, salt-pans, metal-bearing ores, quarries of valuable stone (see Chapter 1) – furnished products in substantial quantities that not only satisfied local demands, but also were extensively exported. The area affected by this development extends from the Mediterranean basin into transalpine Europe: in general, raw materials were shipped from Etruria and manufactured goods of refined artistic value arrived in return. In the same movement, merchants themselves also arrived, as well as commercial agents and, sometimes, master artists. In regard to the latter, the indications offered until now in the archaeological literature are either general comments or refer only to individual cases (Szilágyi 1972, pp. 70–71; Cristofani 1976; Torelli 1976; Colonna 1980–1981 (1982); Canciani 1981; Martelli 1981; Maggiani, in Bocci – Maggiani 1985, pp. 51–54; Colonna, in Colonna – v. Hase 1986; Torelli 2000; Bellelli 2004; Iaia 2005, pp. 234–236; Lulof 2005; Ridgway 2010, p. 52; Maggiani 2011). In this chapter I will seek to briefly outline an overall picture, tracing the phenomenon from the earliest to the latest manifestations of Etruscan civilization. The starting point is not clear-cut: in Etruria, signatures of native artists are rare (on these, see Colonna 1975; Pfiffig 1976; Cristofani 1988; Martelli 1989; Colonna 1993; Bruni 2005), and those of foreign artists working in Etruria are especially rare. Obviously, the signatures of artists on goods made abroad and imported into Etruria will not be taken into account here, though they are not infrequent (Phoenico-Cypriot bowls of the seventh century BC, Greek black- and red-figure vases). The theory has occasionally been advanced that Greek potters and painters could have produced in Etruria some of the vases found there and attributed to them, but this has often not been based on concrete evidence. The many suggestions offered in its wake, by a variety of scholars, are occasionally certain, at other times merely likely or simply hypothetical.

From a tomb of the late ninth century BC at Tarquinia (Villanovan *facies*, phase IA–B) comes a bronze mirror originating in the Aegean-Cypriot region (Hencken 1968, p. 47, fig. 35 *b*; Delpino 1998–1999; Delpino 2000); from a contemporary tomb at Vulci come three Sardinian bronzes: a statuette of a warrior-priest, a rattle in the form of a footstool, and a miniature basket (see Fig. 11.9 and Chapter 11; Falconi Amorelli 1966; Bernardini 2002). Both tombs held female depositions. We may entertain the notion that such gifts were frequently incorporated into a "matrimonial policy" in the sense that one foreign woman (or man) had married an Etruscan spouse and had brought with her/him objects characteristic of their homeland, but with the qualification that in the ninth century BC a marriage between individuals of geographically (and culturally) distant countries implied that the commercial activities (and/or military enterprises) in which they were engaged involved their whole social framework, or rather, the families of both spouses.

Beginning at the end of the ninth, and for the entire eighth century BC (the Villanovan *facies*), some Etruscan grave goods are distinguished by the presence of finely crafted bronze arms, in particular, helmets and swords: signs of elevated social rank. Several types of helmet are known, including the crested and bell-helmets, which have many local ceramic imitations. Both types are disseminated through Central Europe and the Italian peninsula (see von Merhart 1941; Hencken 1959, pp. 34–35; Hencken 1971, pp. 78–96; Stary 1981, pp. 22–24; von Hase 1988). The crested helmets found in peninsular Italy, although greater in quantity, are distinguished from the others by the curved extension of the sides of the crest and by the presence of repoussé decoration and bosses set in horizontal bands near the base of the calotte (cf. Fig. 5.8). The general type may be considered central-European, while the variant is to be assigned to the Etruscan sphere and in all likelihood to central-European bronzesmiths who have come to Etruria; some examples of this variant were exported: to Sala Consilina, Asti, Hallstatt, and Zavadintsy in Ukraine (Hencken 1971, pp. 78–96; Stary 1981, pp. 22–23; 421–422, Beil 1, 1, Karte 17; L. Aigner Foresti, in AA.VV. 1992, p. 158). The bell-helmets found in Etruria also are differentiated from those found in central-northern Europe, in having decoration in beaten relief and bosses near the base of the calotte, just like the Etruscan-made crested helmets (Hencken 1971, pp. 43–55; Stary 1981, pp. 23–24; 422, Beil. 1, 2, Karte 2). In this case also, the general type is central-European, and the Etruscan variant may be associated with central-European bronzesmiths active in Etruria. Among the swords, the *antenne*-sword is another type common in central-northern Europe and Etruria (Fig. 48.1): those found in Etruria are numerous and characterized by *"antenne"* that are relatively short, with a single curve (Hencken 1959, p. 36; Bianco Peroni 1970, pp. 112–119; Stary 1981, pp. 36–37; 438–440, Beil. 1, 10–11, Karte 17). Once again, it is likely that these were made by central-European masters who had moved to Etruria, (on this problem lately, with previous bibliography, see Camporeale 2012; Iaia 2012) where they developed some new details for this type (for more on armor, see Chapter 39).

Likewise, small jugs of impasto, of Sardinian origin, usually less than a half-liter in capacity, are found in funerary offerings of the end of the ninth through the eighth century BC

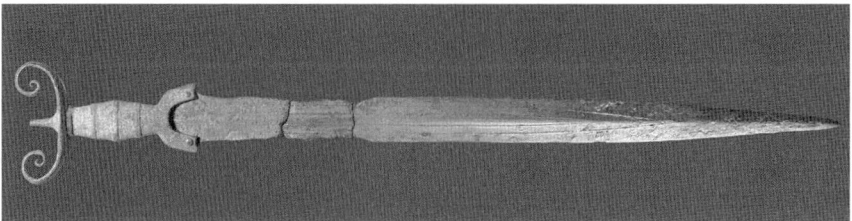

Figure 48.1   *Antenne* sword from Fontivegge. Perugia, Museo Archeologico Nazionale inv. 508.
By permission of the Soprintendenza per i Beni Archeologici dell'Umbria.

(see Fig. 5.9 no. 11). Characterized by a bulging belly and elongated, asymmetrical straight neck, they must have held some valued beverage meant to be poured sparingly in special ceremonies. Their distribution in Etruria is distinctive, evident by the fact that one to five examples are found in different centers: Caere, Tarquinia, Vulci, Bisenzio, Populonia, Volterra, whereas more than 40 are found in Vetulonia and its territory. These last, according to typological and chemical-physical examination, may be divided into two groups, those originals made in Sardinia, and local imitations (Cygielman – Pagnini 2002; Delpino 2002). The high number may be explained by the arrival in Vetulonia of groups of Sardinians, engaged in procedures of mining and metallurgy, activities which had been underway in Sardinia for a few centuries, and which were then being developed at Vetulonia (Camporeale 1998, pp. 42–43). The Sardinians continued to practice familiar customs in their new place of residence. We may ask whether among them there was not perhaps a potter commencing production at Vetulonia (see Chapter 5).

In the Etruscan decorative repertoire of the eighth century BC (Villanovan *facies*, evolved phase) the motif of Sun-ship becomes popular: a horizontal element with upright ends that terminate in bird-protomes, the hull curved with room for the sun-disc; this is worked on sheet-bronze in repoussé technique with punched dots and bosses. In this typology and technique, the motif may be traced back to the final phase of the Urnfields culture of the Carpathian-Danube region, where it must have had symbolic meaning: the cult of the sun, allusion to the voyage of the star with alternation of day and night (Camporeale 2012, with previous bibliography). A closely-dated example from Etruria is found in a bronze biconical vase from tomb AA1 of the Quattro Fontanili necropolis of Veii, a tomb with a rich set of offerings dated to Veii phase IIB 1 (Franco – Mallet – Wacher 1970, especially p. 300, n. 17, Figs 72–73). In such cases the most obvious interpretation is that a transalpine master has moved into Etruria (Camporeale 2012). It is not out of the question that the motif here retains the same symbolic meaning that it had in its homeland. In Etruria, the same motif, also sometimes a bit degenerate, had a continued life: it reappears on other vases on sheet-bronze, in the lids/roofs of hut-urns, the cheek-pieces of horse-bits, the handles of razors and censers, shield-pendants, sheet-bronze coverings of wooden *cistae*, and handles of cups (Camporeale 2012). And so it is clear that foreign masters are not only active in Etruria, but they are training other artisans.

Among Etruscan grave goods of the eighth century BC, objects made of amber are relatively common, usually in the form of human or animal figures or (necklaces of) beads of various types, especially in certain centers: Veii, Falerii, Vetulonia, Verucchio (cf. Fig. 15.12) (Massaro 1943; Negroni Catacchio 1989, pp. 661–680; Forte 1994). The subsequent history of these products is linked to the exotic and precious character of the material and – perhaps at that time – to the belief in their apotropaic and therapeutic value (Pliny, *Nat. Hist.* 37.11.44; 37.12.51). The raw amber originated in Baltic northern Europe, but the large number of pieces found in Etruria and the choice of ornament of the typically native objects (for example beads covering the bows of fibulae) indicate that they were made locally. In all likelihood the first workshops in the various Etruscan centers would have been founded and operated by north-European masters, experts in the treatment of amber who had arrived along with the raw material and tools necessary for working it. The tradition could have been continued by local apprentices. The amber certainly arrived in Etruria in the rough, but even in this state its magical- and market-values were recognized, given that we see unworked pieces in some funerary offerings, for instance at Vetulonia in the trench tomb of Castelvecchio that may be dated to the years bridging the eighth and seventh centuries BC (Camporeale 1966, p. 33, n. 39).

The same pattern developed for other materials of foreign origin such as ivory and gold, used extensively in artistic craftsmanship in Etruria. Evidence for these materials in the eighth century BC is sporadic, but they become common – naturally at higher levels of society – from the beginning of the next century. The first ivory carvings found in Etruria are either imports or are made locally by foreign masters who came from the source-region of the material (the Near East), and adapted their art to local ideologies: the master of animals, fights between fierce animals or monsters, processions of animals. Also the first products of goldsmiths, from the seventh century BC, may be attributed to masters from these areas because of the use of techniques, like granulation and filigree, common in the Aegean and Near East (see Chapter 50). They would have arrived in Etruria with their tools and would have begun the tradition of working these materials. In short, amber, ivory and gold have intrinsic market value, and their finished products are the prerogative of the rich class, the class that could adequately compensate the foreign masters who were introducing new and innovative arts.

Beginning in the middle years and for the rest of the eighth century BC, ceramic cups and kraters of Euboean manufacture, brought by Euboean seafarers, are found among Etruscan grave goods (Fig. 48.2). These are a novelty, in contrast to the local pottery of coarse impasto, while they stand out for their fine clay, wheel-made technique, decorative friezes painted in panels, and for their decorative repertoire of geometric elements like the chevron, broken meander, waterbird motif (*anatrella*), blossoming flower, checkerboard, and wavy line (*linea a tremolo*). They are vases used for wine-service, and their arrival in Etruria marks the arrival of wine, of the ceremony of the symposium, and of the associated aristocratic ideology (Ridgway 1984 [1992], pp. 143–169; Camporeale 1991). In the last decades of the eighth century and first decades of the seventh century BC, many vases for

Figure 48.2   Krater by the Pescia Romana/Cesnola Painter, of Euboean background, circa 730–710 BC, from Pescia Romana. Grosseto, Museo di Archeologia e d'Arte della Maremma, inv. 1426. With thanks to Dott.ssa Mariagrazia Celuzza.

wine service are found in Etruria (kraters, large jars, jugs, cups), all made with the potter's wheel and decorated with the same geometric ornaments but in local clay (Coldstream 1968; La Rocca 1973–1974; La Rocca 1982; Isler 1983; Rizzo 1989). It is very likely that they are the work of Euboean potters and/or painters, practicing their profession in Etruria to accede to the demands of a (rich) local clientele that has now been introduced to the symposium. Along with the Euboean masters others probably also arrived from Argos, because some vases for symposium service are painted with motifs from the Argive geometric repertoire, for example, the angular panels decorated with zig-zag or birds, and leaf-like fish (*pesce-foglia*) (Colonna 1980; Isler 1983, pp. 26–28).

In the first half of the seventh century BC, Greek potters were active at Caere (cf. Chapter 52). We are certain of some of foreign origin: the case of the artist Aristonothos (Euboean? Attic? Cycladic?) who has a Greek name and signed his work in Greek (language and alphabet), and Greek formula (*Aristonothos epoiesen*) on a krater circa 670–660 BC that depicts the blinding of Polyphemos on the front and a battle between two ships on the reverse. Other vase painters active in southern Etruria (Caere) in the first half of the seventh century BC – the Painters of the Cranes, of the Fishes (of Civitavecchia, of Stockholm, and of Amsterdam), of the Heptachord – show in their repertoire that they have assimilated the developments of Proto-Attic and Cycladic painting (Martelli 1984; 1987a; 1987b; 1988; 2001): very likely under the tutelage of Greek masters (present in Etruria?). They are the transmitters of an event of great cultural importance: the introduction of Greek myth into Etruria, a happy result that will become widely diffused in the following years (see Chapter 24).

The Regolini-Galassi Tomb of Caere and the Barberini and Bernardini Tombs of Praeneste are dated to the second quarter of the seventh century BC. They are usually called "princely tombs" for the richness of their contents and the precious materials of many of the finds (see Chapter 6). Notable among these are the bowls of gold, gilded silver, and silver, produced by the workshops of Phoenicia and/or Cyprus (cf. Figs 6.8 and 6.9). The decoration, in repoussé and incision, is distributed in shallow concentric friezes and consists of processions of animals or narrative scenes such as the royal hunt, hunting of monsters, armed combats, the parade of warriors on foot, on horseback or in chariots, which are all scenes located in a carefully observed, naturalistic setting. The same motifs were used in the decoration of vases in precious metal, in forms not Phoenician or Cypriot in origin but rather Corinthian (*kotylai*): that is to say, the master is a Phoenician, who knew the technique and decorative repertoire for working in precious metal, but functioned in an environment in which the vases available to him as models were Corinthian forms (cf. Fig. 6.35). Etruria, and Caere in Etruria, seems the most likely place for these accomplishments (Martelli 1973; Camporeale 2006, pp. 100–103), since there surely arrived, from diverse regions of the Mediterranean, both the imports found locally (at Caere) and used as models, and those redistributed into the interior, for instance, at Praeneste (Camporeale 1998, pp. 42–43; Camporeale 2003a, pp. 14–18).

Also dated to the first half of the seventh century BC are two enthroned statues that face each other in the front chamber of the Tomb of the Statues at Ceri: carved in stone, each, with throne, measures 1.23 m in height; they are the oldest examples of Etruscan monumental sculpture (Colonna – v. Hase 1986). The fact that there are no precedents in Etruria, their near-life-size scale, the stone-carving, the iconography of the majestically seated figure, are traits that recall Syrian tradition, and imply the work of a Syrian master (Colonna [– v. Hase] 1986, pp. 52–54). Among other things, contemporary Syrian masters have been proposed at Bologna for the rectangular stelai surmounted by a disc, with related decorative schemes: tree of life, heraldic rampant animals (Colonna [– v. Hase] 1986, pp. 52–54).

For the years around the mid-seventh century BC there is the information, reported by Strabo (5.2.2 C219), by Cornelius Nepos (*ap.* Pliny, *Nat. Hist.* 35.5.16) and Pliny (35.43.152), relating to the arrival in Tarquinia from Corinth of various artists in the retinue of the merchant Demaratus: the painter Ekphantos and the coroplasts Eucheir, Eugrammos and Diopos, the latter responsible for introducing the art of modeling into Etruria (see Chapter 49). Theirs are clearly professional, "speaking" names. There is little to add to the declaration of the ancient authors on the professions of Ekphantos (painter) and Eucheir (expert in use of the hands), but Eugrammos (expert in drawing) and Diopos (expert in surveying) could refer respectively to the graphic arts and to architecture or city-planning. The field, then, would comprise various artistic pursuits and would be broader in scope than Pliny implied. Of these masters cited, we know no works, although hypotheses have been offered. In all probability, these traditions were elaborated much later than the mid-seventh century BC, but they prompt the conviction that, at least in the art criticism of the last years of the Republic, a Corinthian component was perceived in the Etruscan art of the seventh century BC, including the direct involvement of Corinthian masters in this field.

Also belonging to the middle decades of the seventh century BC are some bronze cauldrons (*lebetes*) with handles ornamented with a blooming lotus flower between two rampant lions or two protomes of a lion or bull. The iconography of animals and flowers together, their application to the handles of bronze vessels, and the comma-shaped handle attachment, are found in other vases of the workshops of Vetulonia. One example, preserved in the Berlin Antikenmuseum, has a finely incised geometric ornament resembling "music paper" around its mouth, a peculiar type found in bronzes of the Carpathian-Danube region of the Hallstatt culture. This example is unique both in Vetulonia and in Etruria. It appears that the head of the workshop had worked at Vetulonia, but he must have been trained in an area of Hallstatt culture. (Camporeale 1986 [1988]). From the same region other bronzes reached Vetulonia: situlae (Secondo Circolo delle Pellicce, Circolo delle Sfingi) and cups (*capeduncole*), which were also copied in local ceramic imitations (Camporeale 1969, pp. 28–34). Nor can one exclude the possibility that the situlae of Kurd type from Vetulonia and other Etruscan centers are the works of masters from the Hallstatt region, where the type is widely disseminated (von Merhart 1952, pp. 29–33; 69–70 [= von Merhart 1969, pp. 321–327; 376–377]).

For the entire seventh century in Etruria one finds the massive arrival of Corinthian or East Greek vases, associated with the service of wine (amphorae, kraters, olpai, oinochoai, skyphoi, kotylai, cups) and of others for the toilette and obviously acquired for their contents (aryballoi, alabastra, pyxides, plastic vases). With these innovations developed fashions of body-care, practiced by women, by athletes, and by families to anoint their dead. At this time the Etruscan market was controlled by Corinthian and East Greek partners who replaced the Euboeans. With these vases, too, came masters (see Chapter 52). Those acknowledged today are two vase-painters who operated at Vulci during the last 30 years of the seventh century BC, the Bearded Sphinx and Swallows Painters, who originated one in Corinth (Szilágyi 1992, pp. 96–128, with previous bibliography) and the other in East Greece (Giuliano 1963; Giuliano 1967; Giuliano 1975). They initially adhered to the rules of their respective home schools, but gradually, living in the same environment and time, influenced each other: thus the Bearded Sphinx Painter came to use the typically East Greek outline technique (see Fig. 52.9), and the Swallows Painter came to paint aryballoi and olpai, Corinthian forms, with typically Corinthian dot-rosettes as fill ornaments. The Bearded Sphinx Painter was very prolific and founded a school, beginning the Etrusco-Corinthian tradition that would survive into the middle decades of the sixth century BC. The Swallows Painter had no followers.

From the beginning of the sixth century BC, Attic vases began to arrive in Etruria in large quantity and/or high quality, and, along with the East Greek wares, edged out Corinthian products. They were destined always for the symposium or as part of a person's toilette. Their movement is now in the hands of East Greek merchants and, near the end of the century, of Aeginetans: one recalls the comments of Herodotus (1.163.1–4) on the Phokeians who had discovered – for commercial benefit – the Adriatic, as well as Etruria, Iberia and Tartessos, or of Herodotus' remarks (4.152.3) on the Aeginetan Sostratos, the merchant with whom no one could compete. This mixture of products appears in the great emporium sanctuaries, the most famous of which are in the ports of Pyrgi and Gravisca. Greek iconography, myth, and the style of Archaic Greek art are increasingly present in the figural art of Etruria. The presence of Greek masters may be assigned to the second half of the century, especially after the Persian conquest of Asia Minor (546 BC), when a large portion of the Greek residents of this region evaded the Persian yoke and abandoned their homeland: suffice it to recall the flood of Phocians who arrived at Alalia in Corsica (Herodotus 1.165), where about 20 years earlier a sub-colony of Phocian Marseille had been founded.

Artists also took part in this influx of migrants, and settled in Etruria. Many hypotheses have been put forward for this. These artists from various countries of the Aegean coast of Asia Minor introduced diverse stylistic traditions and to the same artists are attributed the paintings of several tombs at Tarquinia of the last decades of the sixth century BC, for instance the Tombs of the Augurs, Acrobats, Olympic Games, Inscriptions, Bacchants, Baron (Cristofani 1976): the style is East Greek, the decorative repertoire is adapted to local commissions. The so-called Pontic vases are also probably by East Greek painters, active at Vulci in the third quarter of the sixth century BC, like the Paris or Amphiaraos Painters (Hannestad 1974; Hannestad 1976). Surely the East Greek artists are the painters of the Campana *dinoi* (see Martelli 1978, pp. 192–193, with bibliography) and of the Caeretan hydriae, who worked in Caere in the second half of the century. These hydriai have a metallic profile that distinguishes them from other versions of this shape. The style and the insistence on Greek myth, with some figures, seen on an example in the Louvre, labeled with Greek names (*Odios, Aias, Nestōr*), alphabet and language (Hemelrijk 1984, pp. 46–47, tavv. 107–108), indicate a workshop founded and run by Greek masters. To the second half of the sixth century BC are dated some architectural terracottas still from Caere – acroteria with Herakles and Athena, antefixes, raking simas and terminal tiles – which in the type and decoration (broken meander, birds, flowers, tongues) are paralleled in the East Greek repertoire: the current notion is that they are the work of local workshops, formed by immigrant Greek masters (Andrén, 1939–1940, pp. CXLVII–CXLIX; Bellelli 2004; Lulof 2005; Winter 2009, pp. 395–493; see Chapter 49). Also on a black-figured hydria of the Micali Group (Fig. 48.3; Spivey 1987; Rizzo 1988), dated to the end of the sixth-early fifth century BC, with a representation of a worker in bronze, are found Greek formulaic inscriptions (*epoios kalos, kalos* [...]), written in the same black paint as the vase, possibly to be attributed, because of the name, to a master with East Greek training (Bocci – Maggiani 1985). The painting is not of high

Figure 48.3   Black Figure hydria by a painter of Micali Group, bronze sculptor in his workshop (Greek inscription above his head). Florence, Museo Archeologico Nazionale, inv. 96780. Courtesy of Soprintendenza per i Beni Archeologici della Toscana.

quality, but it gives evidence that not only great foreign masters but also those of mediocre quality reached Etruria. An amphora in Würzburg close to the Micali Painter is signed by an artist, *Kape Mukathesa*, interpreted "Kape (slave) of Mukathe", in the same formula as *Aranth* (slave) of *Heracana*, who signed the painting in the Tomb of the Acrobats at Tarquinia (last decades of sixth century BC): in each case, the signatures are of Etruscan painters, who lack a *gentilicium*, but indicate only their link to a *patronus* (Colonna 1975; see Chapter 21).

A special situation may be proposed for the so-called Cannicella Venus (Fig. 48.4): a statue in Naxian marble, found in a sanctuary within the Cannicella necropolis of Orvieto, and dated to the middle decades of the second half of the sixth century BC. Current opinion holds that it may be an East Greek import that was restored in antiquity, for instance, in the replacement of the breasts (also in Greek island marble, but different in source from the statue itself) (Andrén 1967a, pp. 10–24; Andrén 1967b, pp. 50–51; Cristofani 1987). If one accepts the (quite likely) hypothesis about the restorations, it is necessary to acknowledge the presence in Orvieto of the raw material (Naxian marble) used in the restoration by a sculptor expert in working marble. Moreover, following research conducted in the storeroom of the Orvieto museum and in the old excavation notes, other fragments of Naxian marble statues had been found there (Andrén 1967a, pp. 24–25; Andrén 1967b, pp. 51–52, nos. 2–3; Maggiani 1999). Therefore, the number of examples increases and they are concentrated in Orvieto. In such a situation, the probable hypothesis is that a sculptor arrived in Orvieto from East Greece along with tools for carving statues. The only statue (fragmentary) also in Naxian marble, found in Etruria outside Orvieto comes from Chiusi (Cappuccini 2004); we cannot eliminate the possibility that this last statue was imported from Orvieto because an intensive network of interchange in sculptural production existed between the two centers in the Archaic period (Hus 1961, pp. 298–308; Camporeale 2003b, pp. 157). To a Greek sculptor – by birth or by training – has been attributed a head (of a statue), made in marble from the Apuan Alps and found in the stores of the Bargagli Collection in Casole d'Elsa Museum (Cianferoni 2012).

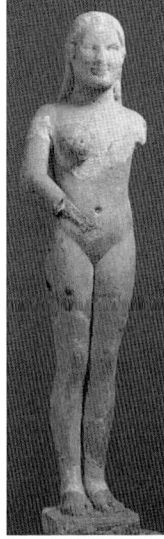

Figure 48.4   The "Cannicella Venus," limestone statue, Orvieto, Cannicella necropolis. Museo Faina, Orvieto © 2012. Photo Scala, Florence.

To the first years of the fifth century BC is attributed a reference of Varro (*ap.* Pliny, *Nat. Hist.* 35.45.154), in which he states that in Rome the ornamentation of temples was Etruscan (*tuscanica*) prior to the arrival of Damophilos and Gorgasos, masters coming from a region of Greek culture – Greece or more likely Magna Graecia or Sicily – who would have worked on the pictorial and coroplastic decoration of the Temple of Ceres, Liber and Libera, inaugurated in 493 BC (Colonna 1980–1981 [1982], pp. 170–172). It is true that this is the case for Rome, but *Latium Vetus* and Etruria during the Archaic period shared the same cultural and visual-artistic trend (Ridgway 2010, pp. 48–49). The reference confirms deductions made from archaeological evidence on the presence of East Greek coroplasts at Caere in the preceding decades. In other words, the migration of artists and the trade of artifacts toward Italy continues.

Between the second half of the sixth and the first decades of the fifth century BC, Attic vase workshops were producing in large part for the Etruscan market: the masterpieces of Attic pottery in Black and Red Figure are arriving there. Production included vases destined for the symposium (kraters, amphorae, oinochoai, jugs, cups, stamnoi), many especially produced by the Attic workshop of Nikosthenes (third to fourth quarter of the sixth century BC), which combine shapes of Etruscan origin with painted Greek decoration: amphorae, semi-cylindrical stands, kantharoi, skyphoi, stamnoi (the issue has been raised by various scholars: Martelli 1985, p. 180; for amphorae: Hirschland Ramage 1970, p. 22; Verzár 1973, pp. 51–52; Rasmussen 1979, pp. 74–75, type 1g; Gran Aymerich 1982, p. 39; Rasmussen 1985, pp. 34–35; for semi-cylindrical stands: von Bothmer 1972; Paribeni 1974, p. 132; for kantharoi, kyathoi, stamnoi: Isler Kerényi 1976; Rasmussen 1985; Brijder 1988; Ortenzi 2006; Giuman, Pilo 2012). Certainly, at least one master also arrived, originally perhaps from Sicily or Rhegion and active at Vulci in the second quarter of the fifth century BC, he signed an amphora (now in the Cabinet des Médailles, Paris) painted with scenes from the life of Achilles, in a technique of Red figure but in superposed color; this is the Praxias-Group, if the two inscribed names, on the rim (Praxias) and on the handle (Arnthe), refer to the same person (Beazley 1947, pp. 195–200; recently, with previous bibliography, Wachter 2001, pp. 194–196; Poccetti 2009). It is difficult to say whether he is a potter or painter, because the verb that would specify this is omitted. His Greek origin is confirmed by the fact that the picture labels are written in Greek letters, and this is repeated in other vases of the Group. He has been integrated into Etruscan society, taking a typical Etruscan *praenomen* and transforming his original Greek name into the *gentilicium*: an analogous phenomenon had occurred in the seventh century BC with *Rutile Hipucrates* (Fig. 48.5), attested in an inscription at Tarquinia (*TLE* 155), in which the *praenomen* is a local, or perhaps Latin, personal name and the *gentilicium* is an Etruscan version of his Greek name (Hippokratēs). Likewise, Larth Telicle, attested in an inscription from southern Etruria (*TLE* 761), has taken a characteristically Etruscan *praenomen* and has used for *gentilicium* a Greek name (Teliklēs).

After the naval defeats inflicted on the Etruscans by the Syracusans at Cumae in 474 BC and Elba in 453 BC, the ports of the southern Etruscan metropoleis, Caere, Tarquinia and Vulci, were barred from commerce in Attic goods; the only port remaining open to this commerce is Populonia in the mining region of northern Etruria. Numerous Attic vases of high quality of this period are found in Populonian tombs. Around the years 450–440 BC an artist's signature appears pertinent to our enquiry: *Metru menece*, on an Attic red-figured cup close to the style of the Penthesilea Painter, found at Populonia but perhaps made in Vulci (indicated by the ending of the verb in perfect tense, -*ce*, with the palatalized guttural). *Metru* is the Etruscan adaptation of the Greek name *Mētrōn* (De Simone 1968, p. 94; De Simone 1970, pp. 231–232) and *menece* is the Etruscan verb designating the action of the master (potter or painter?). He is a Greek who works for an Etruscan clientele and writes in Etruscan, but he lacks an Etruscan *gentilicium* and thus is a metic, not fully integrated into Etruscan society (Colonna 1975, pp. 190–191; Colonna 1980–1981 [1982], pp. 171–172). His position and civic status in Etruscan society is different from that noted for Arnth Praxias, also active in Vulci.

From the mid-fifth century BC, Greek influence in Etruria continues, but it is no longer focused on the cities of the Tyrrhenian coast, but rather toward the hinterland, traveling along the valleys of the Tiber, Chiana and Arno (to Veii, Falerii, Orvieto, Chiusi, Arezzo). Many sculptures in terracotta or stone in these cities, belonging to the decoration of temples or to cinerary statues hollowed to receive human remains, show that the

Figure 48.5 Inscribed vase (fragmentary oinochoe), dedication of Rutile Hipucrates, from Monterozzi, Doganella, Tumulo del Re (Tarquinia), seventh century BC. Drawing, after Hencken, *Tarquinia, Villanovans and early Etruscans* (1967), vol. I, p. 381 fig. 371, g, following L. Cultrera, "Tarquinia – Scoperte nella necropoli," *Notizie degli Scavi* 1932, 100–116.

stylistic accomplishments of Greek art of the Classical period, like those of the great artists Polykleitos or Pheidias, have been assimilated, although we cannot exclude the possibility that at least some sculpture could be the work of Greek masters who emigrated to Etruria. One immediate effect of the defeats at Cumae and Elba and the subsequent blocking of commerce in the southern Etruscan ports was the crisis in Attic vase production, which no longer had access to the metropolitan ports just mentioned. The reception of Attic vases at Populonia in northern Etruria and at Numana and Spina in the middle and upper Adriatic is not comparable quantitatively to what had occurred at Caere, Tarquinia and Vulci in the sixth century and in the first decades of the fifth century BC. This is undoubtedly the result of the political strategy of Syracuse, which succeeded in punishing its rival Athens in the industrial and commercial sector. The Attic potters and vase-painters had trouble surviving in their own country and emigrated to various sites in the Mediterranean, where they founded workshops: at Kertsch in the Black Sea, in Sicily, Apulia, Lucania, Campania and also Etruria. The city with the advantage in Etruscan territory is Falerii, the first city approached as one ascends the Tiber Valley (Veii having been occupied and destroyed by the Romans in 396 BC), where in the first half of the fourth century BC several Athenian-trained vase-painters were working, for instance the *Diespater*, Nazzano, Aurora, and *Foied* Painters, who for the most part produced large vases for the symposium (kraters, stamnoi) decorated with Dionysiac themes; moreover, they were responsible for the transmission into Etruria of Greek myths and cults (Beazley 1947, pp. 70–112). They were integrated into Faliscan society, insomuch as they used the local language for the labels of personages represented. Their pupils would have worked during the entire second half of the century in other Etruscan cities: Caere, Tarquinia, Vulci, Orvieto, Chiusi, Volterra. To the first half of the fourth century BC is dated the activity of other painters of Etruscan red-figured vases, who arrived in other centers of the region and brought with them the experience of Attic or Magna Graecian masters. In this context the Arnò Painter, originally from Lucania, began his career as a vase-painter at Tarentum and continued in Etruria, where he is recognized as the Perugia Painter (Gilotta 2003, pp. 211–213).

Two trends, Pergamene and Attic, are manifested in Hellenistic Etruria, in production of architectural terracottas and of cinerary urns in the northern cities (Volterra, Chiusi, Perugia: see Fig. 48.6); they show the assimilation of contemporary Greek art (see several papers in Martelli-Cristofani 1977; Maetzke 1992). It cannot be rules out that the

Figure 48.6   Hellenistic urn of Volterran type, death of Myrtilos, alabaster. Museo Archeologico Nazionale di Firenze. Courtesy of Soprintendenza per i Beni Archeologici della Toscana.

masters who initiated the new formal language in Etruria were foreigners come from the regions in which their styles were popular; it is probable that they passed through Rome and from there arrived in Etruria. However, in the same years, vases from Rome (*pocula deorum*) reached Etruria, as well as coins (series with device of ship's prow) but it was the masters especially who came and who worked on building the Roman (military) colonies that were being founded, not to mention the coincidental appearance of subjects from the Trojan and Theban mythological cycles in both archaic Latin tragedy and the decoration of the aforementioned Etruscan urns.

In conclusion, it is possible to recall a few general points.

1. This survey, far from being exhaustive, has only the scope of indicating some issues relative to the opening up of Etruria to foreign figurative and cultural influences, and to the mobility of foreign artists active in this region and to their integration into local society.

2. Their activity, as proven, or reasonably well hypothesized, translates into prestigious works, distinct from the products of local artisans and as a rule associated with rich contexts: on the other hand, only the rich were able to adequately compensate hired persons whose services would have cost more than those of natives. Therefore, a closer tie was forged between (figurative) culture and the aristocratic class.

3. The role of foreign artists in Etruscan society is not easily defined. The scarcity of signatures with complete name-formulae (*praenomen, gentilicium*, patronymic, verb indicating exact professional activity) precludes definitive identifications. Thus, their role was probably not much different from that of native artists. Certainly, it is necessary to consider possible changes in status over time (Etruscan civilization coincided with the entire first millennium BC), in their environment, and in the type of commission (public or private, monumental or smaller works). The masters in the entourage of the rich merchant Demaratus in the seventh century BC retained their original Greek names and thus were not fully integrated into Etruscan society as was Demaratus. The master who instead has an Etruscan or Etruscanized *praenomen* and a *gentilicium* – such as Arnth Praxias in the early fifth century BC – is in effect an Etruscan citizen, treated the same as the Faliscan Cavios Frenaios, active in the fourth century BC. Exactly when such a changeover happened is hard to pinpoint. Certainly it must have varied from case to case, considering how, in Vulci, approximately 50 years after Arnth Praxias, Metru met with quite a different treatment – a case similar to that of the Etruscan Pheziu Paves who signed a red-figured cup in the environs of Siena in the years 380–350 BC, if the text is to be interpreted, as proposed (Cristofani 1988, p. 329, n. 178, 1, with bibliography), "Pheziu of Pave."

4. The homelands of the foreign artists in Etruria are for the most part those which were sources for the valuable materials and manufactured goods they purveyed. The initial contact was probably made by merchants, with artists arriving in a second wave, after it was decided that Etruria could accommodate them. The tradition of Demaratus can serve as an example of this.

5. The works of foreign masters, once their artistic superiority over natives was acknowledged, primarily appealed to the taste of their targeted consumers and then to other residents in the areas where they settled.

6. These works also impacted on the native culture. It is significant that they made vases designed for specific ceremonies, part of a precise ideology (one thinks of the symposium

and its social, aristocratic implications), or that represent scenes of myth which usually have a symbolic value and recall particular political and/or social situations: these vases are analogues to the Greek patterns for the shape, function, and decoration.

7. The impact on an aesthetic and cultural level exercised by active foreign masters in Etruria is more pronounced than that simply exerted by objects coming from the same region as the artists. The presence of people implies the direct and immediate transmission of techniques, customs, ideas. The process of acculturation is broader and deeper, flowing from contact between the two worlds, and generates a whole series of positive results, when there are real persons as protagonists. The comparison between Etruria and Magna Graecia or Sicily is instructive: here, through the Greek colonial movement, there is a sort of peripheral Hellenism, where customs and *mores* of the motherland are preserved, while in Etruria acculturation develops on a local base that still is never obliterated and always emerges in a clear manner.

8. Etruria is the destination for – in addition to master-artists – merchants (one thinks of Demaratos or Sostratos), for commercial agents, especially in the port-sanctuaries, for artisans and slaves, all of whom contributed – in different ways – to the acculturation of Etruria. It is natural, as already noted, that the master artist, as a highly trained man, would have an impact on those who interacted with him. A different situation was produced by the artists who worked in the homeland, manufacturing objects for export to a foreign country – and for consumers from a different culture than their own. Also different is the case of the master who works on commission in his own country for foreign customers, usually through the intermediary of a commercial broker.

9. Ultimately, there surfaces the question of whether the foreign masters operating in Etruria produced works that belonged to the art of their homeland, or to the corpus of Etruscan art. Certainly, as we have had occasion to note above, the style, iconography, and techniques of their products belong to the homeland, but the master, while he worked in Etruria, inevitably adapted to the local context, to the taste and requirements of his clientele, for whom an iconography might be altered to give it a new meaning. Eloquent examples are found in the works of the middle decades of the seventh century BC Phoenician master mentioned above, active at Caere. From his workshop came the gilded silver kotyle from the Tomba del Duce of Vetulonia (Fig. 48.7): the shape of the vase is of Corinthian origin; the technique of incision on precious sheet-metal, the distribution of the decoration in parallel, low friezes that cover the entire surface of the vase, and the figural repertoire of animals and hybrid creatures are all Phoenician in origin.

Figure 48.7 Silver kotyle from Tomba del Duce, Vetulonia. Florence Museo Archeologico inv. 73582, after drawing from I. Falchi, *Vetulonia e la sua necropoli antichissima* (Florence, 1891), reproduced in G. Camporeale, *La Tomba del Duce* (Florence: Olschki, 1967) p. 99 no. 68, pl. B no. 3.

Some iconographic details, like the flame-patterned dorsal mane of felines, have parallels in Protocorinthian and Etruscan vase-painting (Brown 1960, pp. 28–30; Camporeale 1967, pp. 99–107; Camporeale 2006, p. 102). From the same workshop comes the *Plikaśna* situla of Chiusi (see Fig. 6.35): the form is peculiar, lacking parallels in contemporary Etruscan or related production; the technique of incising precious metal and the organization in low, parallel friezes, are linked to Phoenician bowls; the helmets with nose-guard worn by the warriors of the upper register recall the world of Corinth; the themes of swine-herd or files of warriors and athletes are of local origin, perhaps executed on commission as a sort of self-representation and exaltation of the recipient (Martelli 1973; Camporeale 2006, pp. 102–103). The master lived and worked in an environment – probably Caere – in which existed the background inspiration for his works. In this environment the master, of Phoenician origin, combined diverse components in a single product. This process occurred in Etruria, in an Etruscan cultural context, and at the behest of Etruscan consumers. I would say that to study a work of art, we must recognize that it is not static, composed of elements that can simply be identified and listed: the master's combining of various elements is only the beginning of a new and integrated work, instilled with the flavor of his own personality as well. Thus, the works in question may logically be attributed to Etruscan art. The debate, obviously, has a general character and may apply to all the works passed in review.

BIBLIOGRAPHY

AA.VV. (1992) *Gli Etruschi e l'Europa*, Milan: Fabbri Editore.

Andrén, A. (1939–1940) *Architectural Terracottas from Etrusco-Italic Temples*, Lund-Leipzig: Gleerup-Harrassowitz.

——(1967a) "Il santuario della necropoli di Cannicella ad Orvieto" in *Studi Etruschi* XXXV, pp. 41–85.

——(1967b) "Marmora Etruriae" in *Antike Plastik* VII, Berlin: Gebr. Mann, pp. 7–42.

Beazley, J. D. (1947) *Etruscan Vase-Painting*, Oxford Clarendon Press.

Bellelli, V. (2004) "Maestranze greche a Caere: il caso delle terrecotte architettoniche" in *Annali della Fondazione per il Museo 'Claudio Faina'* XI, pp. 95–118.

Bernardini, P. (2002) "I bronzi sardi di Cavalupo di Vulci e i rapporti tra la Sardegna e l'area tirrenica nei secoli IX–VI a.C. Una rilettura" in O. Paoletti (ed.), *Etruria e Sardegna centro-settentrionale tra l'età del Bronzo Finale e l'Arcaismo (Atti del XXI convegno di studi etruschi ed italici)*, Pisa-Rome: Istituti Editoriali e Poligrafici Internazionali, pp. 421–431.

Bianco Peroni, V. (1970) *Le spade nell'Italia continentale*, Munich: Beck.

Bocci, P. and Maggiani, A. (1985) "Una particolare hydria a figure nere del Museo Archeologico di Firenze" in *Bollettino d'Arte* LXX, pp. 49–54.

Brijder, H. A. G. (1988) "The shapes of Etruscan bronze Kantharoi from the seventh century B.C. and the earliest Attic black-figure Kantharoi" in *BABesch* LXIII, pp. 103–114.

Brown, W. L. (1960) *The Etruscan Lion*, Oxford: Clarendon Press.

Bruni, S. (2005) "Cavios Frenaios ceramista a Falerii" in *Annali della Fondazione per il Museo 'Claudio Faina'* XII, pp. 365–374.

Camporeale, G. (1967) *La tomba del Duce*, Florence: Olschki.

——(1969) *I commerci di Vetulonia in età orientalizzante*, Florence: Sansoni.

——(1986) (1988) "Presenze hallstattiane nell'Orientalizzante vetuloniese" in *Studi Etruschi* LIV, pp. 3–14.

——(1988) "Dall'Europa transalpina all'Etruria. Facies villanoviana" in *Archäologische Untersuchungen zu den Beziehungen zwischen Altitalien und der Zone nordwärts der Alpen während der frühen Eisenzeit Alteuropas*, Bonn: Universitätsverlag Regensburg, pp. 37–47.

——(1991) "Considerazioni sul commercio etrusco in età arcaica" in J. Remesal, O. Musso (eds), *La presencia de material etrusco en la península Ibérica*, Barcelona: University of Barcelona, pp. 61–68.

——(2003a) "Sulla decorazione a ventaglietti nel bucchero etrusco" in *Studi Etruschi* LXIX, pp. 13–23.

——(2003b) "L'artigianato artistico" in G. M. Della Fina, (ed.), *Storia di Orvieto I. Antichità*, Perugia: Quattroemme, pp. 147–216.

——(2006) "Dall'Egitto all'Etruria. Tra Villanoviano recente e Orientalizzante medio" in *Annali della Fondazione per il Museo 'Claudio Faina'* XIII, pp. 93–116.

——(2012) "La barca solare nella cultura villanoviana: evoluzioni iconografiche e semantiche" in P. Amann (ed.), *Kulte – Rite – religiöse Vorstellungen bei den Etruskern und ihr Verhältnis zu Politik und Gesellschaft*, Wien: Österreichische Akademie der Wissenschaften, pp. 235–249.

Camporeale, G., Banti, L. and Uggeri, G. (1966) "Vetulonia. Esplorazione di una tomba a tumulo e di una fossa in località Castelvecchio" in *Notizie degli Scavi*, pp. 28–51.

Canciani, F. (1981) "Griechische und orientalische Handwerker in Mittelitalien" in F. Hiller (ed.), *Die Aufnahme fremder Kultureinflüsse in Etrurien und das Problem des Retardierens in der etruskischen Kunst*, Mannheim: Vorstand des Deutschen Archäologen-Verbandes und Archäologisches Seminar der Universität Mannheim, pp. 53–59.

Capponi, F. and Ortenzi, S. (2006) *Museo Claudio Faina di Orvieto. Buccheri*, Perugia" Electa.

Cappuccini L. (2004) "Un frammento in marmo greco da Chiusi" in *Annali della Fondazione per il Museo 'Claudio Faina'* XI, pp. 207–219.

Cianferoni C. G. (2012) "Testa femminile di statua" in G. Baldini, M. Bezzini and S. Ragazzini (eds), *La Collezione Bargagli nel Museo Civico Archeologico di Casole d'Elsa*, Colle Val d'Elsa: Salvietti & Barabuffi, pp. 86–87.

Coldstream, J. N. (1968) "A figured Geometric Oinochoe from Italy" in *Bulletin of the Institute of Classical Studies* XV, pp. 86–96.

Colonna, G. (1975) "Firme arcaiche di artefici nell'Italia centrale" in *Römische Mitteilungen* LXXXII, pp. 181–192 (= *Italia ante Romanum Imperium*, Pisa-Rome: Istituti Editoriali e Poligrafici Internazionali, 2005, pp. 1795–1806).

——(1980) "Parergon. A proposito del frammento geometrico dal Foro" in *MEFRA* XCII, pp. 591–605 (= *Italia ante Romanum Imperium*, Pisa-Rome: Istituti Editoriali e Poligrafici Internazionali, 2005, pp. 877–885).

——(1980–1981 [1982]) "La Sicilia e il Tirreno nel V e IV secolo" (Atti del V congresso internazionale di studi sulla Sicilia antica), in *Kokalos* XXVI–XXVII, pp. 157–183 (= *Italia ante Romanum Imperium*, Pisa-Rome: Istituti Editoriali e Poligrafici Internazionali, 2005, pp. 161–180).

——(1993) "Ceramisti e donne padrone di bottega nell'Etruria arcaica" in AA.VV., *Indogermanica et italica. Festscrift für Helmut Rix zum 65. Geburtstag*, Innsbruck: Insitut für Sprachwissenschaft, Univeristät Innsbruck, pp. 61–68 (= *Italia ante Romanum Imperium*, Pisa-Rome: Istituti Editoriali e Poligrafici Internazionali, 2005, pp. 1899–1905).

Colonna, G. and von Hase, F.-W. (1986) "Alle origini della statuaria etrusca: la tomba delle Statue presso Ceri" in *Studi Etruschi* LII, pp. 13–59 (= *Italia ante Romanum Imperium*, Pisa-Rome: Istituti Editoriali e Poligrafici Internazionali, 2005, pp. 901–940).

Cristofani M. (1976) "Storia dell'arte e acculturazione: le pitture tombali arcaiche di Tarquinia" in *Prospettiva* 7, pp. 2–10 (= *Scripta selecta*, Pisa-Rome: Istituti Editoriali e Poligrafici Internazionali, 2001, pp. 467–483).

——(1987) "La 'Venere' della Cannicella" in *Annali della Fondazione per il Museo 'Claudio Faina'* III, pp. 27–39 (= *Scripta selecta*, Pisa-Rome: Istituti Editoriali e Poligrafici Internazionali, 2001, pp. 681–695).

——(1998) "La ceramica ellenistica" in M. Martelli (ed.), *La ceramica degli Etruschi*, Novara: Istituto Geografico De Agostini, pp. 313–331.

Cygielman, M. and Pagnini, L. (2002) "Presenze sarde a Vetulonia: alcune considerazioni" in O. Paoletti (ed.), *Etruria e Sardegna centro-settentrionale tra l'età del Bronzo Finale e l'Arcaismo* (Atti del XXI convegno di studi etruschi ed italici), Pisa-Rome Istituti Editoriali e Poligrafici Internazionali, pp. 387–410.

Delpino, F. (1998–1999) "Uno specchio miceneo da Tarquinia" in *Rendiconti della Pontificia Accademia Romana di Archeologia* LXXI, pp. 29–51.

——(2000) "Ancora sulla tomba Poggio Selciatello 77 di Tarquinia" in N. Negroni Catacchio (ed.), *Preistoria e Protostoria in Etruria* (Atti del IV incontro di studi, Montalto di Castro – Valentano 1997), Milan: Centro Studi Preistoria e Archeologia, University of Milan, pp. 215–219.

——(2002) "Brocchette a collo obliquo dall'area etrusca" in O. Paoletti (ed.), *Etruria e Sardegna centro-settentrionale tra l'età del Bronzo Finale e l'Arcaismo* (Atti del XXI convegno di studi etruschi ed italici), Pisa-Roma: Istituti Editoriali e Poligrafici Internazionali, pp. 363–385.

De Simone, C. (1968) *Die griechischen Entlehnungen im Etruskischen* I, Wiesbaden: Harrassowitz.

——(1970) *Die griechischen Entlehnungen im Etruskischen* II, Wiesbaden: Harrassowitz.

Falconi Amorelli, M. T. (1966) "Tomba villanoviana con bronzetto nuragico" in *Archeologia Classica* XVIII, pp. 1–15.

Forte, M. (ed.) (1994) *Il dono delle Eliadi. Ambre e oreficerie dei principi etruschi di Verucchio*, Rimini: Soprintendenza Archeologica dell'Emilia Romagna.

Franco, M. C., Mallet, P. and Wacher, A. (1970) "Veio (Isola Farnese). Continuazione degli scavi nella necropoli villanoviana in località 'Quattro Fontanili.' Nona campagna di scavo (Giugno, 1966)" in *Notizie degli Scavi*, pp. 296–308.

Gilotta, F. (2003) "Aspetti delle produzioni ceramiche a Orvieto e Vulci tra V e IV sec. a.C." in *Annali della Fondazione per il Museo 'Claudio Faina'* X, pp. 205–240.

Giuliano, A. (1963) "Un pittore a Vulci nella II metà del VII sec. a.C." in *Jahrbuch des Deutschen Archäologischen Instituts* LXXVIII, pp. 183–199.

——(1967) "Un pittore a Vulci nella II metà del VII sec. a.C. (addenda)" in *Archäologischer Anzeiger*, pp. 7–11.

——(1975) "Il 'Pittore delle Rondini" in *Prospettiva* 3, pp. 4–8.

Giuman, M. and Pilo, C. (2012) "Il *kyathos* attico. Un vaso etrusco nel Ceramico di Atene" in S. Angiolillo, M. Giuman and C. Pilo (eds), *Meixis. Dinamiche di stratificazione culturale nella periferia greca e romana*, Rome: Giorgio Bretschneider, pp. 19–36.

Gran Aymerich, J. M. J. (1982) *CVA, France* 31, *Louvre* 20, Paris: De Boccard.

Hannestad, L. (1974) *The Paris Painter. An Etruscan Vase-Painter*, Copenhagen: Munksgaard.

——(1976) *The Followers of the Paris Painter*, Copenhagen: Munksgaard.

Hemelrijk, J. M. (1984) *Caeretan Hydriae*, Mainz/Rhein: Philipp von Zabern.

Hencken, H. (1959) "Archaeological Evidence for the Origin of the Etruscans" in *A Ciba Foundation Symposium on medical Biology and Etruscan Origins*, London: J. & A. Churchill, pp. 29–47.

——(1968) *Tarquinia, Villanovans and early Etruscans*, Cambridge, MA: Peabody Museum.

——(1971) *The earliest European Helmets*, Cambridge, MA: Peabody Museum.

Hirschland Ramage, N. (1970) "Studies in Early Etruscan Bucchero" in *Papers of the British School at Rome* XXXVIII, pp. 12–61.

Hus, A. (1961) *Recherches sur la statuaire en pierre étrusque archaïque*, Paris: De Boccard.

Iaia, C. (2005) *Produzioni toreutiche della prima età del Ferro in Italia centro-settentrionale. Stili decorativi, circolazione, significato*, Pisa-Rome: Istituti Editoriali e Poligrafici Internazionali.

——(2012) "Metalwork, rituals and the making of elite identity in central Italy at the Bronze Age-Iron Age transition" in M. E. Alberti and S. Sabatini (eds), *Exchange Networks and Local Transformations. Interaction and local change in Europe and the Mediterranean from the Bronze Age to the Iron Age*, Oxford and Oakville: Oxbow Books, pp. 106–116.

Isler, H. P. (1983) "Ceramisti greci in Etruria in epoca tardo-geometrica" in *Numismatica e Antichità Classiche* XII, pp. 9–48.

Isler, H. P. and Kerényi, C. (1976) "Stamnoi e stamnoidi" in *Numismatica e Antichità Classiche* V, pp. 33–52.

La Rocca, E. (1973–1974) "Due tombe dell'Esquilino. Alcune notizie sul commercio euboico in Italia centrale nell'VIII secolo a.C." in *Dialoghi di Archeologia* VIII, pp. 86–103.

—— (1982) "Ceramica d'importazione greca dell'VIII secolo a.C. a Sant'Omobono. Un aspetto delle origini di Roma" in AA.VV., *La céramique grecque ou de tradition grecque au 8e siècle en Italie centrale et méridionale*, Naples: Centre Jean Bérard, pp. 45–53.

Lulof, P. S. (2005) "Una bottega-tettoia ionica a Caere" in O. Paoletti (ed.), *Dinamiche di sviluppo delle città dell'Etruria meridionale: Veio, Caere, Tarquinia, Vulci* (Atti del XXIII convegno di studi etruschi ed italici), Pisa-Rome: Istituti Editoriali e Poligrafici Internazionali, pp. 209–213.

Maetzke, G. (ed.) (1992) *La coroplastica templare etrusca fra il IV e il II secolo a.C.* (Atti del XVI convegno di studi etruschi e italici), Florence: Olschki.

Maggiani, A. (1999) "Un frammento di kore marmorea da Orvieto" in *Annali della Fondazione per il Museo 'Claudio Faina'* VI, pp. 235–251.

——(2011) "Rapporti tra l'arte etrusca e greca" in F. Marzatico, R. Gebhard and P. Gleirscher (eds), *Le grandi vie della civiltà*, Trento: Povincia Autonoma di Trento, pp. 213–219.

Martelli, M. (1973) "Documenti di arte orientalizzante da Chiusi" in *Studi Etruschi* XLI, pp. 97–120.

——(1978) "La ceramica greco-orientale in Etruria" in AA.VV., *Les céramiques de la Grèce de l'Est et leur diffusion en Occident*, Paris-Naples: CNRS-Centre Jean Bérard, pp. 150–212.

——(1981) "Un askos del Museo di Tarquinia e il problema delle presenze nord-ioniche in Etruria" in *Prospettiva* 27, pp. 2–14.

——(1984) "Prima di Aristonothos" in *Prospettiva* 38, pp. 2–15.

——(1985) "I luoghi e i prodotti dello scambio" in M. Cristofani (ed.), *Civiltà degli Etruschi*, Florence-Milan: Regione Toscana-Electa, pp. 175–181.

——(1987a) "Per il Pittore delle Gru" in *Prospettiva* 48, pp. 2–11.

——(1987b) "Del Pittore di Amsterdam e di un episodio del nostos odissiaco. Ricerche di ceramografia etrusca orientalizzante" in *Prospettiva* 50, pp. 4–14.

——(1988) "Un'anfora orientalizzante ceretana a Würzburg ovvero il Pittore dell'Eptacordo" in *Archäologischer Anzeiger*, pp. 285–296.

——(1989) "Una "firma d'artista" dell'Orientalizzante ceretano" in M. Cristofani (ed.), *Miscellanea ceretana* I, Rome: CNR, pp. 45–49.

——(2001) "Nuove proposte per i pittori dell'Eptacordo e delle Gru," *Prospettiva* 101, pp. 2–18.

Martelli, M. and Cristofani, M. (eds) (1977), *Caratteri dell'Ellenismo nelle urne etrusche* (Atti dell'incontro di studi, Università di Siena, 28–30 aprile 1976), Florence: Centro D.

Massaro D. (1943) "Le ambre di Vetulonia" in *Studi Etruschi* XVII, pp. 31–46.

Negroni Catacchio, N. (1989) "L'ambra: produzione e commerci nell'Italia preromana" in G. Pugliese Carratelli (ed.), *Italia omnium terrarum parens*, Milan: Scheiwiller, pp. 659–696.

Paribeni, E. (1974) "Intervento" in AA.VV., *Aspetti e problemi dell'Etruria interna* (Atti dell'VIII convegno nazionale di studi etruschi ed italici), Florence: Olschki, pp. 131–133.

Pfiffig, A. J. (1976) "Etruskische Signaturen" in *Österreichische Akademie der Wissenschaften. Hist.-Phil. Klasse. Sitzungsberichte. Band 304, 2. Abhandlung*, Wien.

Poccetti, P. (2009) "Un greco etruschizzato o un etrusco grecizzato? Nota sulle iscrizioni del vaso vulcente di Praxias" in C. Braidotti, E. Dettori and E. Lanzillotta (eds), *Ou pan ephemeron. Scritti in memoria di Roberto Pretagostini*, Rome: Università degli Studi di Roma "Tor Vergata", pp. 403–416.

Rasmussen, T. B. (1979) *Bucchero Pottery from Southern Etruria*, Cambridge: Cambridge University Press.

——(1985) "Etruscan Shapes in Attic Pottery" in *Antike Kunst* XXVIII, pp. 33–39.

Ridgway, D. (1984) (1992) *L'alba della Magna Grecia²*, Milan: Longanesi, (revised English edition: *The First Western Greeks*, Cambridge: Cambridge University Press, 1992.)

——(2010) "Greece, Etruria and Rome: Relationships and Receptions" in *Ancient West & East* IX, pp. 43–61.

Rizzo, M. A. (ed.) (1988) *Un artista etrusco e il suo mondo: il Pittore di Micali*, Rome: De Luca.

——(1989) "Ceramica etrusco-geometrica da Caere" in M. Cristofani (ed.), *Miscellanea ceretana* I, Rome: CNR, pp. 9–39

Spivey, J. (1987) *The Micali Painter and his Followers*, Oxford: Clarendon Press.

Stary, P. F. (1981) *Zur eisenzeitlichen Bewaffnung und Kampfesweise in Mittelitalien (ca. 9. bis 6. Jh. v. Chr.)*, Mainz/Rhein: Pilipp von Zabern.

Szilágyi J. G. (1972) "Le fabbriche di ceramica etrusco-corinzia a Tarquinia," *Studi Etruschi* XL, pp. 19–73.

——(1992) *Ceramica etrusco-corinzia figurata. Parte I, 630–580 a.C.*, Florence: Olschki.

Torelli, M. (1976) "Greek Artisans and Etruria. A Problem concerning the relationship between two cultures" in *Archaeological News* V, pp. 134–138.

——(2000) "L'ellenizzazione della società e della cultura etrusche" in M. Torelli (ed.), *Gli Etruschi*, Milan: Bompiani, pp. 141–155.

Verzár, M. (1973) "Eine Gruppe etruskischer Bandhenkelamphoren: Die Entwicklung von der Spiralenamphora zur nikosthenischen Form" in *Antike Kunst* XVI, pp. 45–56.

von Bothmer, D. (1972) "A unique Pair of Attic Vases," *Revue Archéologique*, pp. 83–92.

von Hase, F.-W. (1988) "Früheisenzeitliche Kammhelme aus Italien" in M. Egg (ed.), *Antike Helme*, Mainz: Verlag des Römisch-Germanischen Zentralmuseums, pp. 195–211

von Merhart, G. (1941) "Zu den ersten Metallhelmen Europas" in *Bericht der Römisch-Germanischen Kommission* XXX, pp. 4–42 (= *Hallstatt und Italien*, Bonn: Habelt, 1969, pp. 111–148).

——(1952) "Studien über einige Gattungen von Bronzegefässen" in AA.VV., *Festschrift des Römisch-germanischen Zentralmuseum in Mainz* II, pp. 1–71 (= *Hallstatt und Italien*, Bonn: Habelt, 1969, pp. 280–379).

Wachter, R. (2001) *Non-Attic Greek Vase Inscriptions*, Oxford: Oxford University Press.

Winter, N. A. (2009) *Symbols of Wealth and Power. Architectural Terracotta Decoration in Etruria and Central Italy, 640–510 B.C.*, Ann Arbor: University of Michigan Press.

CHAPTER FORTY NINE

THE PHENOMENON OF TERRACOTTA: ARCHITECTURAL TERRACOTTAS

———·◆·———

Nancy A. Winter

INTRODUCTION

The Etruscan decorative spirit found one of its most impressive expressions in the roofs of baked clay that adorned houses and public buildings beginning in the third quarter of the seventh century BC. Thanks largely to the important excavations at Acquarossa near Viterbo and Poggio Civitate (Murlo) near Siena, an astounding assortment of terracotta roofs have been documented spanning the Late Orientalizing to Archaic periods (640/630–510/500 BC). Although early Rome, even under Etruscan kings, appears to have limited the use of decorated roofs to civic and religious buildings, while providing even the houses of important personages with undecorated tiled roofs, more and more sites in Etruria are providing evidence for the early Etruscan practice of decorating even private buildings with elaborate terracotta roofs.

The evolution and types of decorative systems are now becoming clearer. An early predilection for painted decoration in the white-on-red technique can be linked to local pottery production but the use of molds for human and feline heads, apparent already by 630 BC, may be an imported technique; especially notable are the cut-out floral and figural plaques placed on the ridges of Late Orientalizing roofs (640/630–600 BC). Moldmade decoration in relief, with painted details in red, white and black, becomes one of the hallmarks of Etruscan roofs of the sixth century BC, especially for antefixes and figured friezes on raking simas and on revetment plaques that protected the rafters of the pedimental slopes, architrave, wall plates and rafter-ends along the eaves; these roofs form part of what Della Seta defined as the "First Phase" of Etruscan terracotta roofs.[1] Handmade statues in the round, some nearly life-size, are the successors of the cut-out ridge acroteria of the Late Orientalizing period, maintaining the strong emphasis on the ridge of certain buildings. After 560 BC, no private houses with decorated roofs have been documented, but the roofs of temples, civic and funerary structures are outstanding examples of Etruscan coroplastic art. By the late sixth century BC, large plaques with handmade sculpture in high relief are applied to the ends of the ridge beam (*columen*) and smaller side beams (*mutuli*) in the open pediment of temples, with a secondary roof on the pediment floor. Most frequently they accompany terracotta roofs designated by Della Seta as the "Second Phase,"[2] characterized by floral decoration instead of figural decoration on the revetment plaques, a style that adapted well to the larger temples they adorn from the fifth century BC on.

TERRACOTTA ROOFS OF THE LATE ORIENTALIZING PERIOD, 640/630–600 BC

The earliest terracotta roofs in Etruria, datable in the third quarter of the seventh century BC, all share the same basic use of a flat pan tile to carry rainwater off the slope, a convex cover tile to protect the space between pan tiles, and a convex ridge tile to cover the ridge of the double-sloped roof. In addition, other roof elements were invented to protect the rafters of the slopes on the short ends of the building and the rafter-ends along the eaves of the roof on the long sides of the building: flat terracotta revetment plaques that could be nailed to the wooden elements they protected. Closures for the lowest cover tile at the eaves formed antefixes, which prevented winds from dislodging the tiles. These roof elements provided protection from rain for the wooden roof frame and mud-brick walls, and were fireproof, unlike thatch. The roof elements along the ridge and the roof edges also provided a blank field for embellishment, and embellish they did.

At Poggio Civitate (Murlo), three buildings of the Late Orientalizing period carried ridge tiles to which flat upright plaques were attached, oriented along the axis of the ridge. These acroteria took the form of double volutes (more rarely animals) with cut-out edges that follow the contour of the design and painted decoration in the white-on-red technique.[3]

The hand painting on revetment plaques at Acquarossa provided the widest scope for the creative spirit of the local artisans, with a wide medley of designs from figural to geometric: horses, birds, snakes, fish, stags, a lion, a seated human; semicircles, scale patterns, circles, cross-hatched triangles, lozenges, hourglasses, hooked ray patterns, and herringbone patterns.[4] Their arrangement is paratactic and no attempt at narrative is apparent. The white-on-red technique and many of the patterns betray their origin in contemporary south Etruscan and Faliscan pottery.

Evidence for molds comes from Poggio Civitate (Murlo) where an actual mold for an antefix with canopic-style head was excavated in a workshop that made terracotta roofs, destroyed in 590–580 BC.[5] Other moldmade roof elements from the site include antefixes with female head[6] and feline-head waterspouts from a lateral sima that decorated the eaves of the roof of the same workshop.[7] Moldmade feline heads have been excavated at Acquarossa as well.[8]

THE TRANSITION FROM LATE ORIENTALIZING TO EARLY ARCHAIC TERRACOTTA ROOFS, 600–580 BC

A change was in the air already around 600 BC when outside influences from western Greece become apparent in the decoration of the terracotta roofs of Etruria. The painted guilloche appears on flat revetment plaques at Acquarossa around this time,[9] in the same white-on-red technique as before when more local motifs were favored. Accompanying them are flat, semicircular antefixes with a painted half-rosette or floral design.[10]

The use of a raking sima along the sloped edges of the roof is a late introduction into terracotta roofs in Etruria, probably only appearing around 600 BC. The morphology and decoration (a vertical plaque with cavetto profile, painted tongue pattern and painted anthemion),[11] as well as those of the revetment plaques with painted guilloche, suggest the possible influence of western Greek roofs of Sicily.

In the early sixth century BC, some cut-out acroteria at Poggio Civitate (Murlo) evolve from the flat plaque with painted interior details into a plaque with incisions on one side to define interior details of the double volute or, in one case, a rider.[12] The ridge acroteria of this period from houses at Acquarossa decorated the front end of the final ridge tile at the edge of the roof and sat perpendicular to the axis of the ridge. Some are formed of large plaques, pelta-shaped and with interior grooves for definition, made separately from the ridge tile and with a curved opening to fit over the tile.[13] The same mounting technique and orientation is found on a bow-volute acroterion with relief-modeled figural decoration at Poggio Civitate (Murlo)[14] that forms a technological transition to acroteria of statues in the round that will soon follow.

TERRACOTTA ROOFS OF THE SO-CALLED FIRST PHASE, 580–550/540 BC

The first major shift in the decoration of Etruscan roofs occurs around 580 BC with the introduction of moldmade figural reliefs for the decoration of revetment plaques and some raking simas. Scenes seem to draw inspiration especially from Corinthian vase painting. The appearance of figured friezes in Etruria comes shortly after their use in Rome on various roofs of public buildings on the Capitoline hill and in the Roman Forum.[15] In Rome, the relief revetment plaques are decorated primarily with processions of felines recalling animal friezes on Corinthian painted pottery, but at least one horse rider is documented, part of a larger scene of unknown type.[16] At Veii, the nearest Etruscan site to Rome, some similar plaques appear to imitate these earlier Rome revetments, with a few animal friezes[17] and several military scenes that include horse riders accompanying a departing warrior mounting his chariot.[18] Further north at Poggio Buco revetment plaques with animal processions and horse riders[19] have a cavetto profile decorated with squat convex strigils close in proportion to those of the Rome revetment plaques. A wider array of scenes is found on the revetment plaques of the courtyard building at Poggio Civitate (Murlo): a horse race, a cart procession, a seated assembly and a banquet, each scene allocated to a different part of the building.[20] Some of these scenes have been compared to Early Corinthian vase painting, a probable source also for the scene of hounds chasing hares on the raking sima from the same building.[21]

The courtyard building at Poggio Civitate (Murlo) (Fig. 49.1) provides an exceptional wealth of information on the full complement of terracotta roof decoration around 580–575 BC in Etruria. In addition to its figural raking sima and revetment plaques on the edges of the roof, the ridge was richly decorated with handmade terracotta statues mounted on large convex ridge tiles: at least ten seated male figures with beards and wide-brimmed hats and nine or more female seated statues of smaller scale, both types mounted perpendicular to the axis of the ridge;[22] at least four standing or walking human statues oriented along the axis and at least six human statues wearing helmets or the hats of *flamines*;[23] mythical creatures (a running figure, probably a Gorgon, a possible centaur, sphinxes, a griffin, a hippocamp),[24] and animal statues of ten different types and two different sizes (felines, horses, a boar, a ram, bulls),[25] all oriented along the axis of the ridge. Findspots of fragments of these statues suggest that the seated statues were primarily on the northern flank ridge together with standing or striding figures wearing helmets. Sphinxes appear to have decorated the four corners of the building, while other animals were distributed on the east, west, and south flanks; the smaller-size animals probably decorated the south ridge, which may have been set at a lower level than the ridges of the east and west flanks. The interior of the courtyard carried a roof with a lateral sima decorated with handmade feline-head waterspouts and moldmade female heads covering the opening between individual sima blocks.[26] Antefixes with Gorgoneia[27] were found in a row with revetment plaques with banquet scene along the line of the collapsed northern wall, at a distance that suggests the north flank had two stories. A large handmade Gorgoneion with nail holes probably served as protection for the end of a ridge beam.[28] A final curiosity of this roof is a series of feline heads[29] that appear to have covered the spaces between blocks of raking simas.

Similar roofs, none quite so elaborate, existed at other sites in Etruria but are less well preserved. In addition to the roof from Poggio Buco mentioned above, other roof elements that form part of this same decorative system have been excavated at Vulci (antefixes with Gorgoneion and a probable *columen* plaque with Gorgoneion)[30] and Rusellae (antefix with feline head, revetment plaque with horses).[31]

While the early figured friezes of Poggio Buco and Poggio Civitate (Murlo) seem to depict convivial scenes, other sites follow Veii in a preference for terracotta roofs with military scenes that include horse riders accompanying a departing warrior mounting his chariot. Included in this group of roofs are a series of buildings at Acquarossa and nearby Tuscania, the latter excavated in the cemeteries at Ara del Tufo and Guadocinto and belonging to funerary structures, while the former appear to have a more civic nature; a temple of Aplu/Apollo or Artumes/Artemis at Tarquinia; a possible funerary structure at Il Sodo near Cortona; a probable temple from Vigna Marini-Vitalini at Caere and an identical roof at nearby Pyrgi.[32] Characteristic of this decorative system, in addition to the raking simas and revetment plaques with figured friezes depicting military scenes

Figure 49.1 Poggio Civitate (Murlo): reconstruction of a pediment with sphinx acroterion.
Drawing by Renate Sponer Za.

(particularly the departing warrior scene, chariot processions with armed warriors and groups of armed riders),[33] are antefixes with female heads with simple panels of hair alongside the face[34] and eaves tiles with painted floral patterns on the underside,[35] which are visible from below the deeply projecting eaves of the roof. Individual pieces that belong to this decorative system, even if an entire roof cannot be reassembled from the fragments, come from Otricoli, Castellina del Marangone, Tarquinia, Rusellae, Poggio Buco, Vulci, Caere, and Vignanello.[36] Some of the military scenes have been excavated with revetment plaques depicting banquets and dancing[37] or bulls and a possible rape scene.[38] Roofs of funerary naiskoi using this decorative system apparently had acroteria, some archaizing in style; cut-out acroteria at Ara del Tufo and Guadocino near Turcania, and at Il Sodo near Cortona; a seated statue and a probable rider perhaps from Ara del Tufo.[39] Some technical advances evident in this group of roofs include the use of piece molds (separate molds for figured frieze and for crowning moldings on the revetment plaques) and use of the mold for female-head antefixes for the face of the otherwise handmade acroteria.

TERRACOTTA ROOFS OF THE SO-CALLED FIRST PHASE, 540/530–510/500 BC

An influx of artisans from Asia Minor is apparent in the introduction of two new decorative systems circa 540/530 BC, one of which is characterized by its wealth of figured friezes in relief and the other by its polychrome painted decoration that expands the palette from the previous red, white and black to include shades of brown, blue and green.

The former decorative system, known as the Veii-Rome-Velletri decorative system (Fig. 49.2) because of the sites at which examples have been discovered, first appears around 530 BC.[40] Although it includes many characteristics of preceding roofing systems, such as figured friezes in relief on its raking simas and revetment plaques (now including scenes of a chariot race in addition to armed riders, chariot processions, a seated assembly and a banquet), use of a lateral sima combined with antefixes with female head, and statues in the round as acroteria (including a central group of Herakles and Athena, flanked by volute acroteria, and sphinxes at the corners of the roof), new hallmarks of East Greek influence are the insertion of a relief meander enclosing a bird and a star-flower in boxes between the figured frieze and crowning molding of revetment plaques, and scenes of chariot races, both documented earlier on roofs of Asia Minor;[41] in addition, the sculptural style of the acroteria is Ionicizing. Technical innovations include mounting the acroterial statues on a plinth that is inserted into a separately made base, some of which are elaborately decorated with moldings and painted details.[42] At least six roofs sharing the same molds for the figured friezes are known, one from the Portonaccio sanctuary at Veii (but with other fragments excavated also on the Piazza d'Armi), at least four at Rome (on the Capitoline hill, the second-phase temple of Mater Matuta at S. Omobono in the Forum Boarium, the fourth-phase building on the site of the later Regia in the Roman Forum, and on the Palatine hill), and one at Velletri. Another set of related roofs with the same general morphologies for the different roof elements but that differ mainly in the military aspect of the figured friezes, the restricted number of scenes (lacking are the seated assembly and banquet), and the somewhat later style, are found in Rome (possible repairs to the roof of the second-phase temple of Mater Matuta at S. Omobono, and a probable replacement roof for the temple on the Palatine hill) and at Caprifico near Cisterna, south of Rome.[43]

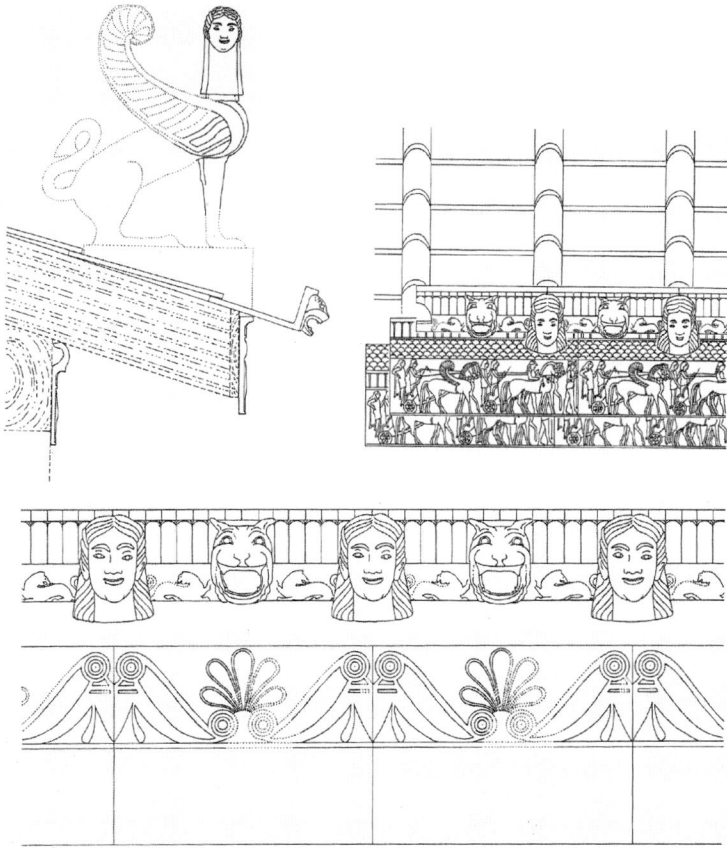

Figure 49.2   Velletri, temple at Le Stimmate: reconstruction of the eaves.
Drawing by Renate Sponer Za.

Their slightly later date and close connection with temples in Rome that had roofs of the Veii-Rome-Velletri decorative system suggest that these are later products of the same workshop, a hypothesis that is supported by petrographic analyses showing that the same formula for the mixing of clays and inclusions was used in all of these roofs.[44] More roofs that can be considered products of this same workshop continue to appear, most recently at Fosso dell'Incastro at Ardea.[45] One or more local workshops in Etruria at Tarquinia, Rusellae and Vetulonia produced a very similar set of roofs.[46]

The second decorative system with clear East Greek overtones originated in a workshop at Caere that has close ties with artisans producing Caeretan hydriae.[47] Typical are a series of raking simas decorated in paint only, with no relief, with cavetto profile or L-shaped;[48] most commonly the main motif on the vertical plaque is a painted meander enclosing alternating boxes with a bird and a star-flower, but floral patterns with star-flowers are also popular. Figural scenes are rare. Some of these raking simas have S-volute finials at the ends of the slopes, or even finials in the form of riding Amazons and warriors mounted along the top.[49] Below the raking sima on the pedimental slopes were revetment plaques, which, at least initially, carried figured scenes in relief, including chariot races and armed riders;[50] one group, however, had figured friezes that were painted only. Some of these painted revetment plaques depict typical scenes of armed riders or chariots, but another series carries running dogs, centaurs, or fighting animals, scenes closely linked iconographically with cylinder-produced reliefs on Caeretan braziers.[51] Along the eaves are antefixes with female heads, of which some 19 different molds can be counted, resting on eaves tiles with a painted underside, usually a floral band, with at least ten different patterns.[52] Some of the roofs carried central acroteria at the end of the ridge (Herakles and Athena, flanked by volutes; a hippocamp rider; a standing warrior) and at the corners of the roof (sphinxes); bases for the lateral acroteria were attached to the back of the raking sima and were decorated on three sides and the underside.[53] Finally, Caere may be one of the earliest workshops to introduce handmade high-relief sculpture on *columen* and *mutulus* plaques in the open pediment, with scenes of battle.[54] All of these roof elements share a distinctive emphasis on the painted decoration, which includes several polychrome examples. One of the earliest roofs of this decorative system is found at Satricum in southern Latium, where the entire roof appears to have been imported by sea from Caere, as indicated by petrographic analyses in addition to the style of the roof.[55] Other products of this Caeretan workshop are found nearby at Punta della Vipera, Castellina del Marangone, Pyrgi, and Sasso di Furbara.[56]

FORERUNNERS OF THE SO-CALLED SECOND PHASE, 550/540–520/510 BC

The arrival in Etruria of artisans from Asia Minor brought with it another style of roof less tied to the Etruscan tradition of figural decoration: floral decoration in relief or paint. From Tarquinia comes an antefix with a palmette above a double volute, a revetment plaque with a double anthemion in relief, and eaves tiles with painted star-flowers on the underside.[57] A lateral sima with a painted anthemion comes from the nearby sanctuary at Gravisca.[58]

East Greek influence appears in a roof from the Portonaccio sanctuary (Fig. 49.3), possibly belonging to the *sacellum* of Menerva/Athena, with raking sima and revetment plaques decorated with a relief meander above a painted anthemion; a slightly later version in relief, and an eaves tile with a similar painted anthemion on the underside, may represent a replacement roof.[59] Some painted revetment plaques from the workshop at Caere employing Asia Minor artisans, discussed above, are characterized by purely floral motifs, these with blues and greens that are especially unusual.[60]

TERRACOTTA ROOFS OF THE SO-CALLED SECOND PHASE, AFTER 510 BC

The second major shift in terracotta roof decoration in Etruria occurs at the end of the sixth century BC when floral friezes in relief replace the figural scenes of the "First Phase." Roofs of this so-called Second Phase generally decorate temple buildings of larger scale than before, often of the Vitruvian Tuscan order with a high podium carrying the triple cellae preceded by two rows of columns and accessible by stairs only at the front. This new decorative system, which remains in use over several centuries in Etruria and Central Italy, includes the following roof elements: a tall raking sima with cavetto profile, tall strigils, central painted fascia with a half-round molding above, and a large half-round base molding that ends at the corners of the roof in a ram's head or animal protome;

handmade figures of snakes or riders superimposed on the front of some simas; an open-work cresting, separately made, inserted into a channel in the top of the raking sima; revetment plaques with palmettes and lotus flowers in relief, often with circumscribing bands and cut-out bottom edge following the contour of the floral design, on the rafters of the pedimental slopes, architrave, rafter-ends on the eaves, and wall plates; eaves tiles with a painted underside (generally zigzags or meanders) and antefixes decorated with heads of women (probably maenads) and silens, surrounded by a nimbus of concave tongues or a floral pattern in relief; handmade, figural high reliefs on the larger ridge beam (*columen*) and smaller side beams (*mutuli*) in the open pediments; antefixes, sometimes full-figure creatures such as Typhon or Sirens, other times smaller antefixes with female and silen heads surrounded by a nimbus of tongues, on the floor of the open pediment.[61] One of the earliest and most complete roofs in Etruria with all of these elements decorated the temple of Apollo in the Portonaccio sanctuary at Veii, dated 510–500 BC, where life-size statues of deities walked along the ridge.[62] Some early fifth century BC roofs have instead figural central acroteria framed by inward-curving volutes, with relief on the front and painted decoration on the flat back.[63] Some of the finest examples of Classical and Hellenistic Etruscan terracotta sculpture decorated pediments at Falerii and Orvieto.[64]

By the third century BC smaller temples with a single cella, prostyle columns at the front and back, and no decoration in the pediments retain the tall raking simas and floral revetment plaques typical of the Second Phase, but have full-figure antefixes often depicting *potnia theron* along the eaves; a floral central acroterion crowns the end of the ridge.[65] Closed pediments with figural decoration of the first half of the second century BC have elaborate compositions of handmade terracotta sculptures mounted on flat backgrounds designed as a whole, then cut into segments for firing, and recomposed and nailed to wooden backers.[66] These complex scenes demonstrate the persistence of Etruscan technical skill and love of decoration down to the end of their existence, long after most of Etruria had succumbed to Roman domination.

Figure 49.3   Veii, Portonaccio sanctuary: reconstruction of a pediment with painted floral decoration. Drawing by Renate Sponer Za.

NOTES

1   Della Seta 1918, 128–132.
2   Della Seta 1918, 132–144.
3   Winter 2009, 101–106.
4   Winter 2009, 88–92.
5   Winter 2009, 88 (87–88: antefixes from the mold).
6   Winter 2009, 85–87.
7   Winter 2009, 78–80.
8   Winter 2009, 77–78.
9   Winter 2009, 93–95.
10 Winter 2009, 82–84.
11 Winter 2009, 72–74.
12 Winter 2009, 104–108.
13 Winter 2009, 109–112.
14 Winter 2009, 114–116.
15 Winter 2009, 144–148 (590–580 BC).
16 Winter 2009, 178.
17 Winter 2009, 259–260.
18 Winter 2009, 251–259.
19 Winter 2009, 181–183.
20 Winter 2009, 183–189.
21 Winter 2009, 162–165.
22 Winter 2009, 196–198; Edlund-Berry in Lulof and Rescigno 2011, 19–20.
23 Winter 2009, 198–200.
24 Winter 2009, 201–206.
25 Winter 2009, 206–208.
26 Winter 2009, 166–169. Mold for the female head: Winter 2009, 167. Similar lateral sima from Poggio Buco: Winter 2009, 165.
27 Winter 2009, 172–173.
28 Winter 2009, 192.
29 Winter 2009, 193–194.
30 Winter 2009, 159, 173–174 (antefixes), 192–193 (*columen* plaque).
31 Winter 2009, 159, 174 (antefix), 186 (revetment plaque).
32 Winter 2009, 229–231, 235 (Acquarossa); 229, 231–233 (Ara del Tufo); 234–235 (Tarquinia); 236 (Il Sodo); 236–239 (Caere); 239 (Pyrgi). Moretti Sgubini and Ricciardi in Lulof and Rescigno 2011, 155–163 (Guadocinto).
33 Winter 2009, 241–245 (raking simas) and 251–259, 260–278, 282–285 (revetment plaques).
34 Winter 2009, 245–250.
35 Winter 2009, 303–305.
36 Winter 2009, 261–262 (Otricoli); 263–264 and 267–268 (Castellina del Marangone); 264–265, 275–277, 277–278, 284–285 (Tarquinia); 264, 269 (Rusellae); 272 and 274 (Poggio Buco); 272 (Vulci); 248, 282, 288–293 (Caere); 282–283 (Vignanello).
37 Winter 2009, 278–280, 287–288 (banquets), 280–281 (dancing); Moretti Sgubini and Ricciardi in Lulof and Rescigno 2011, 158, Fig. 8.
38 Bulls: Winter 2009, 260 (unknown provenience), 285–287 (Tarquinia, Castellina del Marangone). Rape scene: Winter 2009, 274 (Poggio Buco).
39 Winter 2009, 106 (Ara del Tufo cut-out acroterion), 296–298 (Louvre statues, Il Sodo). Moretti Sgubini and Ricciardi in Lulof and Rescigno 2011, 156, Fig. 4 (Guadocinto).
40 Winter 2009, 311–393.

41 Star-flowers and relief meanders on revetment plaques from Sardis in Asia Minor: Åkerström 1966, pls. 44–45; Winter 1993, 237 (dated 550–540 BC). Herodotus I.166–167 might indicate the introduction of chariot racing in Etruria followed the battle of Alalia in 540 BC; earlier raking simas with chariot races from Asia Minor: Åkerström 1966, pls. 19 and 21 (Larisa), fig. 65.1 and 3 (Phokaia), pls. 39 and 41 (Sardis); Winter 1993, 237–238 (550 BC).

42 Winter 2009, 386–387.

43 Palombi 2010.

44 Winter *et al.* 2009, 19–20.

45 Ceccarelli in Lulof and Rescigno 2011, 194.

46 Winter 2009, 324–328.

47 Winter 2008, 190–194.

48 Winter 2009, 406–424.w

49 Lulof 2008; Winter 2009, 479–480 (S-volutes), 480–481 (riding Amazons); Lulof in Christiansen and Wintwer 2010, 154–157.

50 Winter 2009, 445–452.

51 Winter 2009, 453–461. Connections with Caeretan braziers: Winter, forthcoming.

52 Winter 2009, 425–443 (antefixes), 482–491 (eaves tiles).

53 Winter 2009, 466–468 (Herakles and Athena), 473 (volute); Rizzo in Lulof and Rescigno 2011, 140, figs. 4–8 (volutes). Hippocamp rider: Winter 2009, 470–471; Christiansen in Christiansen and Winter 2010, 148–149 (Provenience uncertain but the clay resembles that of Caere). Standing warrior: Winter 2009, 472–473; Lulof in Christiansen and Winter 2010, 158–159. Sphinxes: Winter 2009, 474–477. See also Christiansen in Christiansen and Winter 2010, 145–147 (Provenience uncertain but the clay resembles that of Caere). For lateral acroterion bases, see, e.g., Winter 2009, 478–479.

54 Lulof 2008, 200–206; Winter 2009, 463–466; Lulof in Christiansen and Winter 2010, 160–166.

55 Winter 2009, 398–400.

56 Winter 2009, 403–405.

57 Winter 2009, 498–500, 502–503. For the antefix, cf. examples from the Rhoikos temple at Samos (575–550 BC) and Assos (540 BC): Åkerström 1966, pls. 5.1 (Assos), 52.1–2 (Samos).

58 Winter 2009, 497–498.

59 Winter 2009, 495–497. Cf. the relief anthemion on lateral simas from Sardis: Åkerström 1966, pls. 46–47; Winter 1993, 243 (560 BC). Eaves tile: Winter 2009, 503–504.

60 Winter 2009, 461–463 (520–510 BC). Cf. revetment plaques with similar floral pattern in relief from Larisa am Hermos: Åkerström 1966, pl. 32.4; Winter 1993, 246 (550–540 BC).

61 Cf. the temple roof model with open pediment of a Second Phase roof from the sanctuary of Diana at Nemi, dated fourth/third century BC. Staccioli 1968, 39–40, pls. XXXIV–XXXVII. Examples of decorated *columen* plaques: Colonna 2006, 156–160, Fig. VIII.42 (Temple A at Pyrgi, 470–460 BC); Bagnasco Gianni in Lulof and Rescigno 2011, 222–225 (Ara della Regina temple at Tarquinia, early fourth century BC).

62 See, most recently, Michetti, Maras and Carlucci in Lulof and Rescigno 2011, 96–127.

63 For example, Opgenhaffen in Lulof and Rescigno 2011, 54–59 (Sirens); Bellelli in Lulof and Rescigno 2011, 134, Fig. 17 (Caere); Menichelli in Lulof and Rescigno 2011, 148–154 (Falerii); Stopponi in Lulof and Rescigno 2011, 164–176 (Cannicella sanctuary in Orvieto).

64 Falerii: Comella 1993. Orvieto: Strazzulla 1989; Stopponi 2003, 240–243, Figs. 4–5.

65 See, for example, the full-scale replica of the temple of Alatri, reconstructed in the garden of the Museo Nazionale Etrusco di Villa Giulia in Rome: Cozza in Colonna 1985, 63–65, no. 3.2.

66 For example, Freytag-Löringhoff 1986 (Talamone); Vilucchi 2001 (Catona); Rossi in Lulof and Rescigno 2011, 287–294 (Fosso dell'Incastro, Ardea).

BIBLIOGRAPHY

Åkerström, Å. (1966) *Die architektonischen Terrakotten Kleinasiens*, Lund: CWK Gleerup.

Christiansen, J. and Winter, N. A. (2010) *Etruria I: Architectural Terracottas and Painted Wall Plaques, Pinakes, c. 625–200 B.C.* (Catalogue Ny Carlsberg Glyptotek), Copenhagen: Ny Carlsberg Glyptotek.

Colonna, G. (1985) *Santuari d'Etruria*, Milan: Electa.

——(2006) "Sacred Architecture and the Religion of the Etruscans" in N. T. de Grummond and E. Simon (eds), *The Religion of the Etruscans,* Austin: University of Texas Press, 132–168.

Comella, A. M. (1993) *Le terrecotte architettoniche del santuario dello Scasato a Falerii: Scavi 1886– 1887*, Naples: Edizioni scientifiche italiane.

Della Seta, A. (1918) *Museo di Villa Giulia*, Rome: Danesi Editore.

Freytag-Löringhoff, B. von (1986) *Das Giebelrelief von Telamon und seine Stellung innerhalb der Ikonographie der "Sieben gegen Theben,"* Mainz: P. von Zabern.

Lulof, P. S. (2008) "Le amazzoni e i guerrieri di Vigna Marini-Vitalini: La ricostruzione di un frontone 'straordinario'" in *Munera Ceretana: Studi in memoria di M.Cristofani (Mediterranea 5)*, Pisa/Rome: Fabrizio Serra Editore, 197–214.

Lulof, P. and Rescigno, C. (eds.) (2011) *Deliciae Fictiles IV: Architectural Terracottas in Ancient Italy. Images of Gods, Monsters and Heroes. Proceedings of the International Conference Held in Rome (Museo Nazionale Etrusco di Villa Giulia, Royal Netherlands Institute) and Syracuse (Museo Archeologico Regionale 'Paolo Orsi'), October 21–25, 2009*, Oxford/Oakville: Oxbow Books.

Palombi, D. (ed.). (2010) *Il tempio arcaico di Caprifico di Torrecchia (Cisterna di Latina): I materiali e il contesto*, Rome: Edizioni Quasar.

Staccioli, R. A. (1968) *Modelli di edifici etrusco-italici: I modelli votivi*, Florence: Sansoni Editore.

Stopponi, S. (2003) "I templi e l'architettura templare" in G. M. Della Fina (ed.), *Storia di Orvieto I: Antichità,* Perugia: Quattroemme, 235–273.

Strazzulla, M. J. (1989) "La decorazione frontonale del tempio del Belvedere di Orvieto" in *Atti del secondo congresso internazionale etrusco, Firenze, 26 maggio–2 giugno 1985*, Rome: Giorgio Bretschneider, 971–982.

Vilucchi, S. (2001) "Il tempio dell'area santuariale della Catona" in *Etruschi nel tempo: I ritrovamenti di Arezzo dwal '500 ad oggi*, Florence: Nuova Grafica Fiorentina, 249–286.

Winter, N. A. (1993) *Greek Architectural Terracottas from the Prehistoric to the End of the Archaic Period* (Oxford Monographs on Classical Archaeology), Oxford: Clarendon Press.

——(2008) "Sistemi decorativi di tetti ceretani fino al 510 a.C." in *Munera Ceretana: Studi in memoria di M.Cristofani (Mediterranea 5)*, Pisa/Rome: Fabrizio Serra Editore, 187–196.

——(2009) *Symbols of Wealth and Power: Architectural Terracotta Decoration in Etruria and Central Italy, 640–510 B.C.* (Supplement to the *Memoirs of the American Academy in Rome* 9), Ann Arbor: University of Michigan Press.

——(forthcoming) "Confronti fra scene su bracieri ceretani e terrecotte architettoniche" in *Studi e ricerche a Tarquinia e in Etruria. Simposio internazionale in ricordo di Francesca Romana Serra Ridgway, Tarquinia, 24–25 settembre 2010.*

Winter, N. A., Iliopoulos, I. and Ammerman, A. J. (2009) "New Light on the Production of Decorated Roofs of the 6th c. B.C. at Sites in and around Rome," *Journal of Roman Archaeology* 22, 6–28.

CHAPTER FIFTY

ETRUSCAN JEWELRY

———•◆•———

Françoise Gaultier

The Greek literary sources readily describe the Etruscans as a people with a refined and lavish lifestyle: according to Diodorus Siculus (8.18.1) the inhabitants of Sybaris, known for their own wealth and taste for luxury, preferred them for this reason "to any other people among the Barbarians" and appreciated them as "the equal of the Ionians among the Greeks." The Etruscans were thus particularly distinguished by their work in gold, in the creation and manufacture of jewelry, the beauty, splendor, and technical qualities of which have until now defied goldsmiths.[1]

The extraction of copper and iron ores, and the early working of metal placed Etruria within a network of trade routes and exchange favorable to technological and cultural transmission and contributed significantly to its growth (see Chapter 37). The first jewelry enriched with precious metals or made of gold, silver or electrum, goes back to the Villanovan period (ninth–eighth centuries BC). Attested sporadically in the first half of the ninth century, it is more common in the second half of the century and especially in the eighth century BC. Found in the necropoleis like almost all the Etruscan jewelry that has come down to us, it characterizes a few rare grave assemblages when these are generally still modest: their appearance may be related to the beginning of the process of economic growth and social differentiation.

These jewels in which the precious metal is often associated with bronze or amber, even with bone or ivory, are mostly the same forms as the ornaments of bronze. These are hair-fasteners ("hair-spirals") made of spiral gold wire,[2] circular pendants of gold or of bronze covered with gold leaf, decorated with stamped geometric patterns,[3] but especially fibulae used to fasten clothing, tunics, cloaks, veils and other headgear.[4] Their forms and sizes are varied (the bow can be simple, swollen, or *a sanguisuga* ["leech-shaped"], or serpentine, the catch-plate can be extended into a disc). These forms may be indicative of the gender and age of the deceased: the serpentine fibulae usually belong to men's clothing, the fibulae with *sanguisuga*-type bow to women's clothing, and miniature ornaments to children's dress. The decoration is also very diverse, the bows of fibulae, in gold or silver, can be smooth, decorated with engraved patterns (herringbone most often),[5] or more rarely twisted (*cordelé*);[6] the bows of bronze fibulae can be covered with a spirally coiled gold wire and their pin adorned with amber and silver rings. The bow of *sanguisuga* type in certain fibulae in bronze can also be composed of segments of amber, bone and/or wood alternately covered or not with gold foil decorated with stamped geometric motifs. Some very fine examples come from the necropoleis of Veii or Bisenzio.[7] The bracts, strips of gold or bronze plates covered with gold leaf cut in the shape of a swastika, meander, triangles etc. and decorated with stamped geometric patterns, constitute another class of ornaments relatively abundant in the Villanovan period: pierced with holes at the corners or along the edge, they were sewn onto fabrics.[8]

In the second half of the eighth century BC the populations of the Near East, deprived of their resources and their traditional markets by Assyrian expansion, turn to the West in search of new markets and new sources of foodstuffs and minerals. The Phoenicians are increasing their presence on the coasts of North Africa and Spain, in western Sicily, and in Sardinia. The Greeks, faced with the narrowness of their lands, attracted by the iron and copper of Etruria and the fertile lands of southern Italy, settled on the southern coasts of the peninsula, from Apulia to Campania, and in the eastern part of Sicily. Into Etruria flowed objects and precious materials from Greece and the Near East (Asia Minor, Phoenicia, Syria and Assyria, Cyprus and Egypt). In the grave goods gold jewelry proliferated from the beginning of the Orientalizing period (720–580 BC – see Chapter 6) and shows the rapid enrichment of the Etruscan aristocracy, who take advantage of increased Mediterranean traffic, of the trade in iron and metal objects, products of agriculture, including wine, and accumulate, as signs of power and status symbols, precious metals and prestige objects imported from various regions of the Near East: gold, silver, electrum, ivory, faïence, glass vases, ostrich eggs or tridacna shells, jewelry, vessels or textiles. Etruscan artisans are inspired by the new repertoire of forms and images offered to them, and by blending these create a composite language characteristic of local products; they become familiar through the immigrant populations with the symbolism of oriental iconography[9] and learn from artisans, probably for the most part Phoenicians, the techniques specific to the working of precious metals, such as filigree and granulation (see Chapter 48). Expert from an already long experience with metallurgy, the Etruscans took these techniques to an extreme degree of sophistication, involving drawing motifs on the smooth surface of the background with a thin gold wire or spheres of gold of one to two millimeters in diameter soldered with the aid of copper salts which lower the melting temperature of the gold ("colloidal soldering").[10]

The two main centers of jewelry production in the Orientalizing period have been identified as Cerveteri and Vetulonia. One usually attributes to the workshops of Cerveteri, which was the hub and clearinghouse for articles imported from the Near East, a large portion not only of the jewelry found in the great Orientalizing princely tombs of southern Etruria, but also those in Latium and Campania. A characteristic of the production of the workshops of Vetulonia, founded probably by craftsmen from southern Etruria, is a decoration produced with the aid of extremely fine granulation, also called *pulviscolo* or "gold-dust," which also lends itself well to the portrayal of narrative scenes[11] and decorative friezes, like the file of fantastic animals that adorn the pin from the Tomb of the Lictor.[12] The gold granules create silhouettes and not merely a contour line. This technique is also demonstrated at Bologna where its appearance is attributed to the arrival of craftsmen coming from Vetulonia (Fig. 37.4).[13]

Certain types of jewels of eastern origin, already attested at the end of the Villanovan period, become more frequent during the last decades of the eighth century BC. This is the case for the circular pendants made of a copper alloy covered with gold or silver, well attested in Etruscan territory (at Bisenzio, Tarquinia, Veii, Vulci, Vetulonia – as far as Bologna) as well as in Campania (at Sala Consilina, Pontecagnano, or Cumae) and in Latium (at Acqua Acetosa, Castel di Decima, Praeneste, or Tivoli): the geometric and stamped decoration that characterizes these pendants during the Villanovan period is now enriched with plant and animal motifs, as well as astral motifs (crescent moon and solar disc) sometimes produced in granulation.[14] Provided with a bail for suspension, these discs become components of the necklaces worn by women and children, along with beads of glass, amber, faïence or gold, the pendants in the form of a lotus flower, or a palmette surmounted by a female bust with Hathor-locks.[15]

Other ornaments are becoming more sophisticated, such as the hair-spirals that take various forms, from a simple gold or silver wire wound in a spiral,[16] to complex models made of a spiral tube decorated with filigree and granulation, the ends terminating in the head of a snake or a lion, and on to the type made of a band obtained by the juxtaposition and alternation of smooth and spirally twisted wires terminating in a geometric or floral motif or in granulation, or even with a small plaque embossed with a head.[17]

Some new types are emerging, such as diadems, pins, and brooches. The diadems are very few in number,[18] but one recalls two sets of jewels recovered from female burials, the ribbon-shaped diadem from the Isis Tomb (Vulci, Polledrara necropolis), today in the British Museum, cut from a gold sheet and decorated with stamped motifs in several registers: walking lions and chimaeras, intertwined arches supporting palmettes,[19] or that from the peripheral Pietrera Tomb II at Vetulonia in electrum, also decorated with stamped motifs, an exceptional piece which reproduces part of a hairstyle arranged in bangs and side-braids (Fig. 50.1).[20]

The pins are of various shapes and designs: one can recall, in addition to the pin from the Tomb of the Lictor (Fig. 50.2) cited above, decorated with a frieze of walking animals in silhouette achieved *a pulviscolo*, that of the Barberini Tomb of Praeneste on which the head of the pin is worked in the shape of a flower.[21]

The great brooches, characteristic of men's clothing, belong to two types: the bar-type, of which the Barberini and Bernardini Tombs of Praeneste, with their examples decorated with small three-dimensional figures of animals and fantastic animals, detailed in granulation, offer the most sumptuous illustrations, and the type in the form of a comb, with stamped decoration and sometimes also enhanced with granulation, illustrated by a statuette from the Tomb of the Five Chairs of Cerveteri and by examples from the Circolo di Perazzetta of Marsiliana[22] and by the Bernardini Tomb of Praeneste.[23]

Figure 50.1   Diadem, electrum. From the peripheral tomb II of the Pietrera at Vetulonia. Mid-seventh century BC. Florence, Museo Archeologico Nazionale, inv. 74841.

Figure 50.2   Pin. From the Tomb of the Lictor, Vetulonia. Circa 630 BC. Florence, Museo Archeologico Nazionale, inv. 77260.

The most common models of brooches are inspired by Near Eastern models, most likely Phoenician, and consist of small stamped plaques detailed in granulation and decorated with a figure of the *potnia therôn* ("Mistress of Animals") in a very stylized design, reduced to a female head between floral volutes surmounted with a feline head. Furnished with a series of eyelets around the edges, these plaques were also used as a simple ornament for clothing: they are usually attributed to the workshops of Caere.[24]

One of the forms of bracelet most widely distributed in the Orientalizing period consists of three superimposed bands made of alternating smooth and decorated openwork filigree in serpentine pattern strips. Relatively old and probably created in southern Etruria, this type of bracelet is attested at Marsiliana d'Albegna, Cerveteri, Tarquinia, Populonia and Vetulonia.[25] Some examples are decorated on the central strip with a dimple and a crescent, presumably referring to the moon and sun, astral motifs attested very early in Mesopotamia and related to the worship of Astarte, mistress of life and death.[26] These motifs and that of the female head with Hathor-hairstyle can also be stamped on the plaques that link the different strips in some examples.[27] Also relatively common are bracelets consisting of a broad band of gold decorated with stamped designs, detailed or not with granulation, and characteristic of the Orientalizing repertoire: Phoenician palmettes, fantastic animals, in file or confronted on either side of a tree-of-life, female figures wearing Hathor-locks and holding a fan, sometimes framed by geometric motifs as in the examples from the Regolini Galassi Tomb (Fig. 6.17).[28] One notes also three bracelets, one in the Louvre composed of three parts attached to each other by means of hinges, and two, incomplete, in the Dallas Museum, are made of parallel strips created by the juxtaposition of round and twisted wires, held by transverse elements of the same type and terminated at their ends by motifs stamped in the round.[29]

The jewels best represented in the Orientalizing grave goods remain fibulae. The fibulae with serpentine bow and their numerous variants are frequently made in gold or silver without additional ornamentation, but they may also present a more complex decoration. The finest are decorated like the fibula from the Tomb of the Warrior of Tarquinia in the Berlin Museum, an openwork filigree motif,[30] or like the fibula from Vulci in the British Museum or the Corsini fibula from Marsiliana d'Albegna in the Florence Museo Archeologico, with small three-dimensional figures made in two halves and detailed in granulation, distributed over the entire length of the bow and the catch-plate, which are decorated with geometric motifs in granulation.[31]

The fibulae with bow *a sanguisuga* also furnish varied decoration. The oldest are ornamented with geometric motifs, no longer engraved but drawn using granulation,[32] the latest can be decorated with motifs of oriental origin (sphinx, walking griffins), stamped[33] or drawn in granulation: both types are well illustrated in the Tomb of the Lictor of Vetulonia (Figs 50.3, 50.4). Some have recourse to particularly sophisticated techniques: on a few examples the bow and the upper surface of the catch-plate can be constructed by a juxtaposition of short and thin gold ribbons bent at the ends to form bows to add plastic effects to the graphic decoration of the catch-plate.[34]

The workmanship of Orientalizing jewelry, in agreement with an art that is deliberately ostentatious, is not concerned with either excess or overload: the decoration of the great pectoral from the Regolini Galassi Tomb (Vatican Museo Gregoriano Etrusco) (Fig. 6.12), which is decorated with multiple stamped rows of motifs of Eastern type, and the large ornamental plaques from the Barberini and Bernardini Tombs of Praeneste (Villa Giulia Museum), which is decorated with a multitude of real and fantastic animal figures, play upon their repetition and emphasize rather the overall effect of the details, yet are

Figure 50.3   Fibula *a sanguisuga,* gold, with stamped decoration. From the Tomb of the Lictor, Vetulonia. Circa 630 BC. Florence, Museo Archeologico Nazionale, inv. 72258.

Figure 50.4   Fibula *a sanguisuga,* gold, with granulated decoration *a pulviscolo*. From the Tomb of the Lictor, Vetulonia, circa 630 BC. Florence, Museo Archeologico Nazionale, inv. 77261.

carefully drawn by means of granulation. Sometimes too fragile to have actually been worn, these jewels must have had an essentially ceremonial and/or funerary function. One may recall in this context the famous disc-fibula of the Regolini Galassi Tomb, which repeats a form common in the Villanovan era, but its size – it measures more than 30 cm in length – renders it practically unfit for use (Fig. 6.20). We can also recall the fibula from a tomb in the necropolis of Tolle near Castelluccio di Pienza in the region of Chiusi, today in the Louvre (Fig. 6.34). Exceptional, it bears an inscription, doubly meaningful because writing is the preserve of the aristocracy and its mastery itself a sign of prestige. This inscription: "I am the fibula of Arath Velavesna, Mamurke Tursikina gave me" refers to a practice well attested in archaic societies, the exchange of gifts between people of high rank, used to seal a marriage alliance or to conclude a contract, a practice illustrated, for example, in Book 23 of the *Iliad*, where a silver krater made by the Sidonians, given to Thoas by the Phoenicians, then by the son of Jason to Patroklos to ransom Lycaon the son of Priam, passes thus from hand to hand.

The accumulation of jewelry and the abundance of banquet vessels in gold and silver that characterize female sets of jewels and the furnishings of the great "princely" tombs of Etruria and Latium are not the expression of a simple taste for refinement and pomp, they must be understood as a symbolic representation and as an exhibition of the opulence and power of the great families.

In the Archaic period the cities assert their authority: more widely distributed, wealth is no longer hoarded (treasured), but invested in the activities and the structures of the city, in the building of temples and the decoration of sanctuaries. Often still a great refinement, jewelry is now more discrete, but around the middle of the sixth century BC, the rise of a new aristocratic class and the installation of Ionian populations fleeing the Persian menace then being exerted on the Greek cities of Asia Minor, gives rise to a revival of jewelry. Often reproduced on the walls of the painted tombs of Tarquinia, or in antefixes or funerary monuments in terracotta, jewelry is also relatively common in female burials of the second half of the sixth century BC. New types of jewelry are emerging, some are local creations, many may be attributed to the artisans newly arrived from Ionia: it is to their workshops established in southern Etruria that one attributes, around 530 BC, the first engraved gems in Etruria (see Chapter 51),[35] often mounted in rings[36] and sometimes in pendants, and the introduction of disc-earrings and cartouche-type finger-rings, or even the use of glass and hard stones.

Earrings are among the most common jewelry of the Archaic period. The barrel-shaped earrings (in Italian *a bauletto*, "carpet-bag-shaped") (Fig. 50.5) are widely diffused between the mid-sixth century[37] and the early fifth century BC through all of Etruria as well as the Faliscan territory, and attested as far as Spain[38] and one can imagine several production centers for this original creation of the Etruscan workshops. The earrings of this type, consisting of a rectangular gold leaf folded on itself in a half-circle, overlapped the earlobe, to which they were attached by a transverse gold wire. The front part of these loops, which are decorated in granulation, filigree and stamping, can be decorated with geometric and floral motifs, but also with figures of animals and more rarely with female heads.[39] Their backs, less visible, are decorated simply with geometric patterns such as parallel lines or a star. In the latest and most complex examples, a semicircular element or a palmette masks the fastening system, and the sides are completely or partially closed.

The disc-shaped earrings (Fig. 50.6),[40] of East-Greek origin, are decorated with a central motif and concentric friezes composed of geometric and floral motifs, bosses and

Figure 50.5   A *bauletto* earrings, gold, with granulation and other decoration. Second half of the sixth century BC. Philadelphia, University of Pennsylvania Museum nos. MS 3345A, B, C, image no. 234212.

Figure 50.6   Disc-earrings, gold. Second half of the sixth century BC. Paris, Musée du Louvre, Bj 45–46 © RMN (Musée du Louvre) Gérard Blot/Christian Jean.

granules. A small rod, attached to the rear of the disc, passed through the ear lobe to keep the earring in place.

Most necklaces preserved in museums are the result of more or less fanciful modern remounting and some are outright pastiches. This is the case for the famous necklace with scarabs from the Campana Collection (now in the Louvre), which served as a prototype for numerous scarab necklaces that were made during the 1860s in Rome by the Castellani goldsmith shop for a clientele that was spread across Europe and all the way to the United States.[41] The few necklaces unearthed in recent excavations and reconstructed based on the dimensions of the different components are all the more precious. This is particularly true of the necklaces from Tomb II of Sodo Tumulus II near Cortona that furnish a good example of the jewelry of the late Archaic period (480–460 BC). There are necklaces some of which are composed of beads decorated in granulation and in filigree and smooth beads separated from each other by separator rings, and others of openwork beads constructed of two hemispheres originally enclosing a bead of colored glass, and others with pendants cut from rock crystal, or the tooth of an animal the upper part of which was inserted in a sort of gold case decorated with filigree and/or granulation, alternating with bars as separating strips. Tomb II of Sodo Tumulus II offers us the rare example of amber pendants in the shape of a scarab, supported by cylindrical bars decorated with granulation, and still other types, more common, were in the form of a pinecone, acorn, grape-cluster, or a ram's head.[42] Also known are a number of pendants in the shape of the head of a lion or Acheloos, the river god endowed with apotropaic virtues. The Louvre preserves a beautiful example of the latter in which the fine granulation and filigree are used with extreme dexterity to make the beard and curls of the hair, constructed with a smooth spirally twisted wire and punctuated by a granule of gold.[43]

Archaic fibulae are abundant but less varied than before. We are dealing essentially with fibulae with a bow *a sanguisuga* and an elongated catch-plate adorned with granulation, filigree and vegetal patterns, sometimes with a covering of flowers in gold foil, to which can be added at the end of the catch a figure in the round of an animal (lion, bird, hare) or fantastical animal (winged lion, sphinx) in part at least attributed to the workshops of Vulci;[44] also there are fibulae with swollen bow or of the Certosa type.[45]

The oval signet or "cartouche" rings with incised, carved or repoussé decoration, divided into registers according to Phoenician fashion or forming a single scene in Greek fashion,[46] are decorated with figures of animals real and imaginary or with actual narrative scenes influenced by Greek myths in a style close to that of the vases of the Pontic Group or the Group of La Tolfa, themselves of East Greek descent.

The bracelets are mostly simple rings of gold, open or closed. The closed bracelets can be adorned with rings carrying a decoration in granulation or filigree.[47] The open bracelets are usually adorned at their ends by lion protomes.[48] Some rare examples were made in glass, such as a blue glass bracelet found at Vulci in a set of funerary offerings datable to the end of the sixth or beginning of the fifth century BC (Fig. 50.7).[49]

The crisis following the naval defeat of the Etruscans off Cumae in 474 BC and primarily affecting the centers of southern Etruria, causes the impoverishment of the funeral offerings of this region, but quickly enriches the inland centers and the Tiber Valley, which benefit from the referral of commercial traffic to the Adriatic route, and

Figure 50.7   Bracelet from Vulci. End of the sixth–beginning of the fifth century BC. Rome, Museo di Villa Giulia, inv. 59791 © Soprintendenza per i Beni Archeologici dell' Etruria Meridionale.

grave goods there continue to furnish fine pieces. Recovery is, however, quite clear in southern Etruria from the fourth century BC. Everywhere the old aristocracies make a new display of wealth and foster the creation of new types, whether original or influenced in the last decades of the century by Macedonian and Tarentine fashions.

Symbols of victory as in Greece, the Etruscan wreaths/crowns,[50] stamped in the form of bay leaves, olive, ivy, oak, vine or myrtle, usually arranged in groups attached to a support, have a specific typology. Their extreme fragility surely reserves them for a ceremonial or funerary usage. Mixed with arms or jewelry, with banquet vessels in male or female burials, they evoke both the social status of the deceased during his earthly life and his victory over death. Associated with arms, the crown evokes both the military triumphs of the dead warrior and his status as a hero and his identification with divinity in the Afterlife. Associated with the image of the banquet it also refers to Dionysian cult, which unites the themes of symposium and triumph, or some mystery religion such as Orphism, which reflects his vision of bliss in the hereafter through the image of an eternal banquet and ordained to adorn the body of the deceased with a crown for his participation in the banquet of the blessed.[51] The manufacture of these crowns is attributed in large part to the workshops of Vulci, and for the rest of them, to Chiusi, Populonia and Volterra, and in a more hypothetical fashion to the factories of Perugia and Spina.[52] It is usually assumed that these are the same workshops that produced the diadems, mainly those of Vulci, from which come examples of very high quality, or *bullae*, two-piece discoidal amulets with stamped decoration from Greek mythology (Fig. 50.8), that appear in the first half of the fourth century BC alongside plain *bullae*, undecorated or with decoration limited to the zone of the suspension bail.

The most common type of earrings in the fourth century BC are the *a grappolo* earrings.[53] This female attire is often reproduced in antefixes, votive terracottas and tomb paintings. The simplest type, also regarded as the oldest (Fig. 50.9), is composed of an upper horseshoe-shaped element, decorated with simple lines of stamped ("dapped") dimples,

Figure 50.8   Bulla: contest between Thetis and Peleus (?) between two female figures. First half of the fourth century BC. Paris, Musée du Louvre, Bj 745 © RMN (Musée du Louvre) Gérard Blot/Christian Jean.

which fits on the thickest part of the ring which is itself, and in front view, a large oblong to the lower part of which are affixed hollow spheres arranged in a cluster, with intervening smaller spheres and granules.[54] During the course of the fourth century BC the upper plate tends to take an oval shape and its decoration will go so far as to accommodate human protomes and figures of marine animals. This type of earring is sometimes presented in a simplified form, reduced to a simple stamped plaque: it is a cheaper alternative exclusively for funerary use. Another well attested type is in the form of a simple curved tube. In the second half of the fourth century BC, this tube can be enriched on its front surface with a convex plate decorated with stamped designs and a ring to carry in turn a pendant vase, globular or amphora-shaped.

A series of signet rings with almond-shaped bezel, decorated with a mythological or erotic scene surrounded by rows of tongues are collected under the name of Fortnum Group (Fig. 50.10)[55] from the name of a collector; it testifies to the same taste for stamped and popular decoration, quite distant from contemporary Greek jewelry, which is more sober and refined, the models of which will be widely disseminated and reproduced in Etruria after Alexander's conquests at the turn of the fourth to third century BC. The jewelry found in Etruscan tomb furnishings then reconnects with the refined techniques of filigree and granulation, and mingles various other materials with the gold: amber, garnet, glass or enamel, illustrating the research into polychromy of the Hellenistic period. However, it becomes difficult in the third–second centuries BC, even in the most abundant series such as earrings in the form of a disc or *pelta* (shield), with chains and pendants in the shape of an amphora, bird or inverted pyramid (disc-and-pendant class), or in the earrings in the shape of an open-ring decorated with a head of an animal or a Negro, to distinguish between the productions of southern Italy, where Tarentum is an important center of production, and those of the workshops of Etruria.[56]

Figure 50.9   A *grappolo*-style earrings. Fourth century BC. Paris, Musée du Louvre, Bj 322–323
© RMN (Musée du Louvre) Gérard Blot/Christian Jean.

Figure 50.10 *A grappolo*/horseshoe earring, gold sheet. Perhaps from Orvieto. Mid-fourth century BC. Philadelphia, University of Pennsylvania Museum MS 310, image no. 234213.

NOTES

1 On the place of Etruscan jewelry in the fashion of archaeological-style jewelry, cf. Weber Soros, Walker 2004; Pirzio Biroli Stefanelli 2005.

2 These spirals can be terminated in wavy loops at each extremity: cf. for example, Cristofani, Martelli 1983, p. 29, Fig. 2.4 and p. 33, note 39 (M. Martelli).

3 On the type of these disc-pendants, their origin, diffusion, decoration: Cristofani, Martelli 1983, p. 30, 36, no. 4, 5, 7, 90, 91; Botto 1996 (bibl.); Sannibale 2004, p. 74–75 (bibl.); Cygielman 2007, p. 35 (bibl.).

4 A fibula with swollen bow in gold was found beneath the skull of the deceased woman of tomb AA 12 A in the Quattro Fontanili necropolis at Veii and has kept clearly under the neck the head-covering in perishable material, of which only the tiny bronze buttons are preserved on the forehead: cf. Cristofani, Martelli 1983, p. 28 (M. Martelli).

5 Cf. Martelli, Cristofani 1983, p. 26, 32, note 2 for some examples from the Quattro Fontanili necropolis at Veii.

6 Cf. for example Cristofani, Martelli 1983, no. 1 p. 250.

7 Cf. for example Cristofani, Martelli 1983, p. 29 Fig. 3.3 (M. Martelli), p. 251 nos. 6–7 (M. A. Rizzo).

8 Cf. for example Cristofani, Martelli 1983, p. 27 Fig. 2.5, p. 30–31, p. 34 note 56 (M. Martelli); Cygielman 2007, p. 34 and Fig. 4.

9 Sannibale 2008.

10 On the beginnings of filigree and granulation and the role of immigrant artisans: cf. Cristofani, Martelli 1983, p. 36; on the role of Near Eastern artisans in the introduction of these techniques, see most recently: Sannibale 2008, p. 346.

11 Like the hunt-scene that decorates a pendant-seal of Near Eastern inspiration discovered at Vulci and preserved in the museum of Munich, its very fine granulation is considered to be a southern predecessor of the *pulviscolo* of Vetulonia: cf. Cristofani, Martelli 1983, p. 279 n° 94 (M. Martelli).

12 Cf. Martelli, Cristofani 1983, p. 270 no. 58 (M. Martelli).

13 Cf. Martelli, Cristofani 1983, p. 283 no. 109 (M. Martelli).

14 See the bibliography in note 3.

15 One may see for example Cristofani, Martelli 1983, p. 277 ff., nos. 87–91 (M. Cristofani).

16 For example Cristofani, Martelli 1983, no. 30 (M. Cristofani), no. 48 (M. Martelli). Cygielman 2007, p. 35 Fig. 2.

17 M. Martelli in Cristofani, Martelli 1983, p. 36 ; Gaultier 2005, p. 56–57.

18 Coen 1999, pp. 155–156.

19 Cristofani, Martelli 1983, p. 275 no. 77, (M. Martelli); Coen 1999, p. 155 note 2 [bibl.].

20 Cygielman 2007, pp. 34–47: p. 41, Fig. 14–15. One might also cite the diadem from the Tomba Avvolta of Tarquinia, today lost (C. Avvolta, *Annali dell'Instituto*, 1829, pp. 95–98; Coen 1999, p. 156 note 4 [bibl.]).

21 Cristofani, Martelli 1983, p. 258 no. 20 (M. A. Rizzo).

22 Martelli, Cristofani 1983, p.112 no. 57 (M. Martelli); Cygielman 2007, p. 37 Fig. 11.

23 Martelli, Cristofani 1983, p. 254 no. 10 (M. A. Rizzo).

24 Cf. Gaultier 2005, p. 58 (bibl.).

25 On this type of bracelet one may see *Trésors des Etrusques* 1989, nos. 1–2 p. 15 (bibl.); Sannibale 2004, pp. 102–103 no. 130.

26 This is the case for the Louvre examples Bj 985–986: Gaultier 2005, p. 57.

27 *Trésors des Etrusques* 1989, pp. 24 f. nos. 35–36.

28 Cf. Cristofani, Martelli 1983, p. 263 no. 36 (M. Cristofani), pp. 279–280 nos. 95–96 (Marina Martelli).

29 Deppert Lippitz 1996, p. 129 no. 29; Gaultier 2005, p. 57.

30 On this type of fibulae: cf. M. Martelli in Cristofani, Martelli 1983, p. 36, 269; example from Tarquinia, Tomb of the Warrior: Bartoloni 2002, pp. 112–113, from Veii, Grotta Gramicia, tomb 446 and from Casale del Fosso, tombs 1011 and 1031: Bartoloni 1997, p. 56, Fig. 24 and pl. VIb, p. 64 and pl. VIIa (bibl.), from Cerveteri (collection Castellani): *L'or magique* 1996, p. 109 no. 10 (bibl.).

31 Cristofani, Martelli 1983, p. 281 no. 101 (M. Cristofani) and pp. 266–267 no. 50 (M. Martelli).

32 Cristofani, Martelli 1983, p. 98 nos. 33–34 (M. Cristofani).

33 Martelli, Cristofani 1983, p. 271 sq. no. 62–66 (M. Martelli).

34 Gaultier 2005, p. 58 Fig. 5.8–5.9 (bibl.).

35 See, for example, on this topic: Boardman 1970, pp. 152 f.; Spier 2000.

36 Cf. Cristofani, Martelli 1983, p. 57 and p. 300 nos. 188 ff.

37 They belong to prototypes of the first half of the sixth century BC and perhaps derive from examples of the Orientalizing period: cf. Cristofani, Martelli 1983, p. 53; Trümpler 1990, pp. 291–293. For the examples illustrated in Fig. 50.5, see J. M. Turfa, *Catalogue of the Etruscan Gallery of the University of Pennsylvania Museum*, Philadelphia, 2005: 175, 215–216, nos. 164 and 226.

38 Blàzquez 1963, pl. 4–12; Trümpler 1988, p. 107.

39 The heads that decorate certain *a bauletto* earrings find the closest parallels in a series of small rectangular plaques intended to be sewn onto clothing, and decorated with a *kore* figure and attributable to the workshops of Cerveteri.

40 On this form of earrings, see: M. Martelli in Cristofani, Martelli 1983, p. 54; Scarpignato 1985, pp. 12 f. (bibl.).

41 Gaultier 2005, pp. 42 f.

42 For a catalog of the jewelry of Tomb II of the Sodo: Fortunelli 2005, pp. 176–180.

43 Cf. Gaultier 2005, pp. 39–40, Fig. 4.2, pp. 60–61, Fig. 5.18.

44 Cristofani, Martelli 1983, pp. 55, 58 (M. Martelli), p. 297 no. 172 (M. Cristofani).

45 Cristofani, Martelli 1983, no. 132 (M. Cristofani); Cygielman 2007, p. 43.

46 On this type of ring, see Boardman 1967; M. Martelli in Cristofani, Martelli 1983, pp. 56–57.
47 Gaultier, Metzger 2005, p. 60; p. 128, no. II.31.
48 For example, Marshall 1911, nos. 1368–1369.
49 Cristofani 1985, p. 174 no. 4 (M. A. Rizzo); for a similar exemplar in Dallas Museum: Deppert-Lippitz 1996, p. 129 no. 30.
50 Concerning this issue, see: Coen 1997; Coen 1999; Buranelli, Sannibale 2003, p. 129.
51 M. Cristofani in Cristofani, Martelli 1983, p. 66; Coen 1997, p. 103.
52 Coen 1999, pp. 158 ff.; Buranelli, Sannibale 2003, p. 129.
53 M. Cristofani in Cristofani, Martelli 1983, p. 63; Castor 2010 (bibl.).
54 Some have thought that these hollow spheres pierced in the back could have been used to contain perfumed products: see most recently Minetti, Rastrelli 2001, p. 113, no. 32 B. 32. Others prefer to think that the hole pierced in them corresponds to a technical requirement: Buranelli, Sannibale 2003, p. 129.
55 On this type of ring see Boardman 1966, pp. 10 ff.; Cristofani, Martelli 1983, p. 66.
56 On the subject and on attribution to Etruscan workshops of earrings with a Negro head in amber cf. Metzger 2005, p. 68.

BIBLIOGRAPHY

Bartoloni, G. (2002) *La cultura villanoviana*, 2nd edn, Rome: Carocci.
Boardman, J. (1967) "Archaic Finger Rings," *Antike Kunst* 10, pp. 3–28.
——(1970) *Greek Gems and Finger Rings. Early Bronze Age to Late Classical*, London: Thames and Hudson.
Botto, M. (1996) "I pendenti discoidali: considerazioni su una tipologia di monili di origine orientale presente nel *Latium Vetus*" in *Alle soglie soglie della Classicità. Il Mediterraneo tra tradizione e innovazione, Studi in onore di S. Moscati*, Pisa-Rome, pp. 559–568.
Buranelli, F. and Sannibale, M. (2003) *Vaticano, Museo Gregoriano Etrusco*, Rome: F.M. Ricci.
——(eds) (2004) *Etruscan Treasures from the Cini-Alliata Collection*, exhibition catalog Shawnee, Mabee-Gerner Museum of Art, Rome: Crisalide.
Castor, A. Q. (2010) "Horseshoe Earrings: a native Jewelry," *RM*, 116, pp. 159–204.
Coen, A. (1999) *Corona etrusca*, Daidalos 1, Viterbo: Università della Tuscia.
Cristofani, M. (ed.) (1985) *Civiltà degli Etruschi*, Exhibition catalogue, Florence: Electa.
Cygielman, M. (2007) "Gli ornamenti" in *Moda, costume, bellezza nel mondo antico, ornamenti nel museo archeologico di Firenze dall'Egitto all'Etruria*, exhibition catalogue Palermo, Museo Archeologico Regionale "Antonino Salinas," Livorno: Sillabe, pp. 34–47.
Deppert-Lippitz, B. (1996) *Ancient gold Jewelry at the Dallas Museum of Art*, Dallas: Dallas Museum of Art in association with the University of Washington Press.
Trésors des Etrusques (1989) Exhibition catalogue, Nantes, Rennes: Grand-Huit.
Gaultier, F. and Metzger, C. (eds) (2005), *Trésors antiques. Bijoux de la collection Campana*, Exhibition Catalogue, Paris, musée du Louvre, Milan-Paris: Cinq Continents-musée du Louvre.
Fortunelli, S. (2005) *Il Museo della Città etrusca e romana di Cortona*, Florence: Polistampa.
Gaultier, F. (2005) "Les bijoux étrusques," in Gaultier, Metzger 2005, 56–63.
von Hase, F.-W. (1975) "Zur Problematik der frühesten Goldfunden in Mittelitalien," *Hamburger Beiträge zur Archäologie* 5, pp. 99–181.
L'or magique (1996) *Trésors des Etrusques et des Romains*, Exhibition Catalogue, Brussels, Musées Royaux d'Art et d'Histoire, 1996 Arezzo – Brussels: Centro Affari e Convegni, Fondation pour les arts.
Marshall, F. (1911) *Catalogue of the Jewellery Greek, Etruscan and Roman in the Department of Antiquities*, British Museum, London: The British Museum.
Martelli, M. and Cristofani, M. (eds) (1983) *L'Oro degli Etruschi*, Novara: De Agostini.

Metzger, C. (2005) "Les bijoux grecs," in Gaultier, Metzger 2005, 64–69.

Pirzio Biroli Stefanelli, L. (2005) "La collection Campana et le bijou de style archéologique" in Gaultier, Metzger 2005, 85–101.

Sannibale, M. (2004) "Catalogo" in Buranelli, Sannibale 2004.

——(2008) "Gli ori della Tomba Regolini-Galassi: tra tecnologia e simbolo," *MEFRA* 120/2: pp. 357–367.

Scarpignato, M. (1985) *Monumenti, Musei e Gallerie pontificie, Museo Gregoriano etrusco, Oreficerie etrusche arcaiche*, Rome: L'Erma di Bretschneider.

Spier, J. (2000) "From East Greece to Etruria: a late Sixth-Century BC Gem Workshop," in G. R. Tsetskhladze, A. J. N. Prag and A. M. Snodgrass (eds), *Periplous. Papers on Classical Art and Archeology presented to Sir John Boardman*, London: Thames & Hudson, pp. 330–335.

Trümpler, C. (1988) "Goldschmuck" in C. Reusser, *Antikenmuseum Basel und Sammlung Ludwig, Etruskische Kunst*, Basel: Antikenmuseum Basel und Sammlung Ludwig, pp. 103–110.

——(1990) "Die etruskischen Körbchenohrringe" in H. Heeres and M. Kunze (eds), *Die Welt der Etrusker, actes du colloque Berlin 1988*, Berlin: Akademie-Verlag, pp. 291–298.

Weber Soros, S. and Walker, S. (eds) (2004) *Castellani and Italian Archeological Jewelry*, exhibition catalog New York, Bard Center, New Haven-London: Yale University Press.

CHAPTER FIFTY ONE

ENGRAVED GEMS

——— •◆• ———

Ulf R. Hansson

The technique of engraving harder stones with the aid of a bow-driven drill and cutting-wheel was introduced in Etruria sometime in the third quarter of the sixth century BCE.[1] The technically highly accomplished early works indicate that local craftsmen did not acquire the technique gradually from studying imported gems only, but that they learnt the craft from immigrant gem-engravers who had studied and mastered it elsewhere, most likely somewhere in the East Greek world, before settling in Etruria.

Etruscan gem-engravers used predominantly semi-precious stones of the chalcedony family, which have a hardness of 6.5–7 on the Mohs scale. Most popular throughout production was the red cornelian, which in Etruscan works is remarkably consistent in color, possibly indicating that the stones came from a single source or that they were subjected to color manipulation through some form of heat treatment or immersion, either by the Etruscans themselves or by their stone suppliers.[2] The sources whence the Etruscans obtained their stones have not been identified, but would most likely have been found somewhere in the East. In addition to cornelian, Etruscan engravers also used agates and striped sardonyx, and to a lesser extent jasper of various colors, onyx, and milky white chalcedony. Softer stones like green serpentine and non-lithic materials such as amber and bone were sporadically used,[3] and in the later phase colored glass paste was occasionally used for so-called *a globolo* scarabs (see below).

The shapes include: (1) the scarab gem, where the engraving of the curved back of the stone more or less faithfully imitates the anatomical parts of the scarab beetle; (2) the scaraboid, which retains the overall shape of the scarab gem but with little or no engraving on the curved backside; and (3) the pseudo-scarab, which has an image carved in relief on its curved backside instead of a beetle. All three types have a flat, oval underside which carries an engraved miniature image (device) within a decorated border which is usually hatched, but can also be, for example, dotted, cable, zigzag, or just a simple line, as on the late so-called *a globolo* scarabs. The device is invariably engraved in *intaglio* (from the Italian *intagliare*, to carve), i.e. the design is carved into the flat surface of the stone so that a raised or positive imprint is produced when the surface is pressed into a softer material such as wax or clay. The cameo technique, where the actual image is carved in relief, was not used by Etruscan engravers except for some images on the backs of pseudo-scarabs. A limited number of scarab gems with no intaglio device on the flat underside have survived, which suggests that at least some of these stones were delivered with ready-made beetle sides and that an engraved miniature image was added later. This seems especially plausible in the late period of production, when the beetle typologies became gradually more standardized.

All three gem types were invariably pierced lengthways so that they could be mounted on swivel hoops, for example, and worn either as pendants or as finger-rings. The gems were most likely worn with the intaglio device facing inwards, although some scarab gems were set in ring designs with a fixed device facing outwards. In the later phase of production, a fourth shape was introduced: the flat or very slightly convex ringstone, intended to be set, immobile, in metal finger-rings.

Gem-cutting requires no built structures, the basic equipment of the gem-engraver being more or less limited to a cutting wheel, drill-heads of various shapes and sizes, and a bow for rotating the drill.[4] A "workshop" would therefore have consisted of little more than the craftsman himself and his set of tools. This means that the person practicing this craft could be itinerant, carrying with him his light equipment, or at least his artistic output, from city to city in search of new clients. Apart from the gems, no other archaeological evidence for this craft has survived, and it is extremely difficult to link the glyptic production to a specific city or region, unless there is a concentration of similar works in a single find location. But very few of the approximately 2,600 surviving gems have been found during controlled excavation,[5] and the vast majority of them lack information on find location. Where the earliest archaic production is concerned, stylistic affinities have been noted with vase-painting and metalwork produced in the larger artistic centers of southern Etruria such as Tarquinia, Caere (Cerveteri) and Vulci, but also with stone reliefs produced in Volterra in the north.[6] Tarquinia is relatively rich in finds throughout the period of production, and in the late period inland Chiusi may be added to this list. But, as mentioned, both gems and engravers travel easily.

The fact that the gems were engraved by local craftsmen and not imported means that they more or less directly reflect the actual tastes and needs of the local customer groups catered for. In the beginning, gems may have been made on commission for members of the Etruscan elite, but in the late period the engravers would rather have anticipated the general tastes of a much expanded and socially diverse group of potential customers by producing series of gems carrying popular subject-matter, and the prospective client would probably have had a selection of gems to choose from. Scholars disagree on the question of whether the Etruscans ever used their engraved gems for sealing purposes or chiefly as personal adornment. It is true that some of the more elaborate gold settings that have been preserved seem impractical for sealing purposes. But clay imprints of Etruscan gems have been found in contemporary temple archives at Carthage,[7] and most metal mounts nevertheless seem to allow the gems to be fully functional as sealstones. Either way, there is no reason to doubt that the strong symbolic connotations of the sealstone would have been fully understood by the Etruscans. In this context should be mentioned an unprovenanced pendant bone seal in the form of a hare and bearing the inscription *mi larthia chulnas*, "I [am the seal of] Larth Chulna," tentatively attributed to mid-sixth-century BCE Chiusi.[8] Even if later inscriptions referring to a specific owner are exceptional,[9] like the late fourth- or early third-century BCE scarab gem in Florence with the inscribed name *appius alce* (Fig. 51.1), a device image was probably most carefully chosen, as it would be expected to represent or reflect its owner in some way or other. The same would be true of gems with devices chosen mainly for their protective or "amuletic" properties. The link between the engraved gem and its owner would in both cases have been a strong and personal one.

Figure 51.1 Banded agate scarab depicting two Roman *salii*, inscr. *appius alce*. Late fourth or early third century BCE. Florence, Museo Archeologico Nazionale, inv. 14400 © Soprintendenza per i Beni Archeologici della Toscana.

EARLY IMPORTED WORKS AND IMMIGRANT ENGRAVERS

Prior to the introduction of new techniques for engraving harder stones in the second half of the sixth century BCE, there are few examples of indigenous stone seal production.[10] Three gems in softer serpentine (hardness 2.5–5 on the Mohs scale) deserve to be mentioned. The earliest one is a scaraboid fragment found in the so-called *edificio beta* in the *Pian di Civita* complex at Tarquinia and datable to the late eighth or early seventh century BCE;[11] the other two are a scaraboid and a pendant seal found in the destruction layers of the earliest palace at Poggio Civitate, Murlo, and datable to the late seventh century BCE.[12] These and numerous finds of imported scarabs and scaraboids in the larger Etruscan and Faliscan centers show that such types of objects were circulated in the area at least from the early eighth century BCE onwards, when they begin to appear in burial contexts.[13] Imported material includes late ninth- and eighth-century BCE scarabs and scaraboids in various materials of Egyptian, Syro-Phoenician and/or Island manufacture, and late eighth-century BCE red and green serpentine scaraboids and scarabs belonging to the so-called Lyre-Player Group, which were carved by North-Syrian or Cilician engravers, possibly also by gem-carvers active on the island of Rhodes.[14]

In the late third and fourth quarters of the sixth century BCE, scarabs in hard, semi-precious stones attributed to East Greek workshops also begin to surface in Etruria. Where these early works are concerned, it is virtually impossible to distinguish imported stones from those that may actually have been engraved by immigrant Greek craftsmen active in Etruria, or for that matter by local gem-carvers trained by immigrants. Several of the gems in John Boardman's *Greek Robust Style* have allegedly been found in Etruria, and there is good reason to assume that at least some of these gems were actually carved by engravers active there. This has been suggested to be the case with the so-called "Master of the London Satyr" (Fig. 51.2).[15] These early gems from the last three decades of the sixth century BCE present affinities with works in other media made by Ionian artists who arrived in Etruria following the Persian invasion of their East Greek homelands. But Greek and Etruscan glyptic soon developed along different lines, making identification somewhat easier. The beetle sides of Etruscan scarabs are generally more detailed, carefully cut and

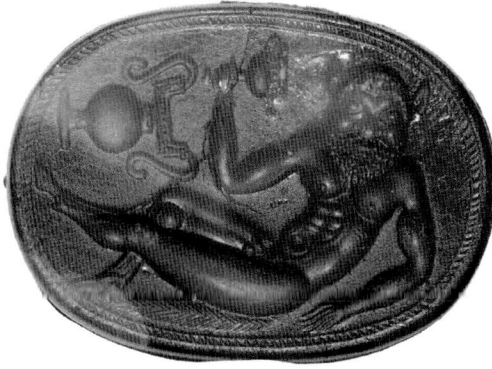

Figure 51.2 Agate Scarab. Satyr. Greek, Master of the London Satyr, circa 530–520 BCE. London, British Museum, inv. GR-1876.12–7.106 © Trustees of the British Museum.

highly polished than is the case with Greek works, and they normally lack the raised spine or carination that Greek scarabs often have. From the late Archaic period onwards, Etruscan scarabs usually also have a characteristic decoration on the plinth beneath the beetle, which further distinguishes them from Greek works. Most common is a neatly hatched band (*orlo etrusco*), which is sometimes double or triple, but there are many other kinds of decoration, like the kymation, zigzag, hatched triangles, and fishbone. While the scarab gem soon went out of fashion in the Greek world where it was replaced with the scaraboid and other shapes, it remained the preferred shape in Etruria well into the third century BCE.

LATE SIXTH- AND EARLY FIFTH-CENTURY WORKSHOPS

The preserved material from the Archaic period, circa 530/520–480 BCE, is very limited. The first engraver who may be called "Etruscan" has been named the "Master of the Boston Dionysos" after one of his more ambitious works, now in Boston: a pseudo-scarab which has an exceptional four-figure intaglio device showing Herakles/Hercle fighting Nereus (or possibly Geras), and an image of Dionysos carved in relief on its backside (see Fig. 24.14). Eight or nine works have been plausibly attributed to this master-engraver,[16] who was active sometime in the last decades of the sixth century BCE, although there are no known datable find contexts for any of his works. These gems share a number of defining features. They are of exceptionally high technical quality and very small in size – the gem in Florence depicting Achilles/Achle, illustrated here, measures only 9 mm across (Figs. 51.3–5). The beetles are meticulously carved and polished, but lack the plinth decoration that later on becomes characteristic of Etruscan works. A string of tiny drill-holes surrounds the intaglio devices, and an even finer round drill-head has been used for some details such as Achilles' shield and sword on the gem in Florence. The figures are stocky, depicted in the archaic manner with frontal upper torso and the rest of the body and head in profile. Their heads are somewhat over-proportioned and angular, the back of the skulls usually hollowed-out and highly polished, and the longish hair neatly held in place by a hair band or diadem. Facial features are carefully outlined. The armour of Achilles in the work illustrated here is very detailed, and the long garments

Figure 51.3–5 Cornelian scarab. Warrior (Achilles/Achle). Master of the Boston Dionysos, circa 520 BCE. Florence, Museo Archeologico Nazionale, inv. 15260. Photo Fernando Guerrini © Soprintendenza per i Beni Archeologici della Toscana.

of the figures on other gems in the group exhibit a mannered, linear drapery. Apart from the group's name piece and two compositions with two and three figures depicting the arming of Achilles by Thetis and Hephaistos/Sethlans, these early archaic gem devices show single figures: Hermes/Turms, Achilles, unidentified youths and a female figure.[17] The works attributed to the Boston Master exhibit close stylistic affinities with three scarab gems found at Uşak in modern Turkey, suggesting links with workshops active in this part of the ancient world.[18] Even if he seems to have had no close followers, this master-engraver can be said to mark the beginning of the Etruscan production.

Another characteristic group of Archaic gems consists of representations of the armed Athena/Menrva and the occasional Zeus/Tinia in a similar compositional schema. These works were probably produced slightly later than those of the Boston Master, one of them was found in a tomb at Populonia with black-figured vases dated circa 500 BCE.[19] Gods (Fig. 51.6), warriors and hero-figures from Greek myth were favored by the engravers and their patrons, who adapted them to suit their own specific needs for self-representation, protection etc. Female figures, mostly goddesses like Athena, Thetis, and Artemis/Artumes, constitute a relatively large group in the Archaic period, after which they virtually disappear from the glyptic material. Animals and monsters are conspicuously absent from the early glyptic repertory, as are satyrs and maenads. The gem-engravers of the Archaic period were influenced by the work of other artists active in Etruria and by imported Greek black- and early red-figure vase-painting.[20] The scarabs are all small in size, with meticulously carved beetles and intaglio devices. The beetles usually have small, decorated winglets in the upper exterior corners of the wings, and whiskered legs carved in relief. Some late archaic scarabs have decorated plinths.

Figure 51.6 Cornelian scarab. Hermes/Turms, circa 500 BCE. Copenhagen, National Museum of Denmark, Collection of Near Eastern and Classical Antiquities, inv. 2267. Photo Ulf R. Hansson, courtesy of the National Museum of Denmark.

FIFTH-CENTURY WORKSHOPS

From the early fifth century BCE onwards fewer Greek gems seem to have been circulated in Etruria, while there was a continuous influx of Attic vases. This is reflected in the repertory of the Etruscan gem-engravers, who continued to skillfully borrow and adapt single figures from more complex multi-figure compositions now found especially in red-figure vase-painting. Other influences include toreutics, sculpture, and perhaps even monumental painting, probably via transmitting minor arts. But the various mechanisms of this dynamic creative process, especially the inherent difficulties involved in introducing new subject-matter from other media and adapting it to the micro-format, which to some extent would explain the conservative nature of this craft, remain insufficiently studied.

During the Early Classical period, circa 480–430 BCE, Etruscan gem-engravers developed their craft along lines that had begun in the preceding period, retaining some characteristic traits such as the preference for rendering upper torsos frontally and the rest of the human figures in profile, and the careful detailing of coiffures and faces. Works from this period, which are sometimes labeled "Severe style," are characterized by greater formal and iconographic diversity due to an increased number of active engravers, and by a growing interest in the careful rendering of the nude male body, often with highly-skilled foreshortenings. There is a continued preference for single figures such as warriors, heroes, athletes, hunters, and youths, who are depicted standing, stooping, seated, collapsing, walking, running or kneeling. Achilles and Herakles remain popular, and there is a growing interest in the Theban heroes Kapaneus/Capne and Tydeus/Tute, who seem to have enjoyed greater popularity in Etruria than in Greece. The Early Classical repertory also includes the old eastern motif of fighting animals, one or two winged figures carrying a dead or wounded hero, warriors in council, as well as many two-figure compositions, for example, Herakles and Kyknos/Kukne, Ajax/Aifas and Kassandra, Ajax and Achilles, Aeneas and Anchises and others, which all show that Etruscan engravers did not shy away from ambitious multi-figure scenes; such compositions are actually more common on Etruscan gems than on Greek ones. The most famous of these more complex miniature compositions, the so-called "Gemma Stosch," which is now in Berlin, shows no less than five named heroes from the Seven Against Thebes story (see Fig. 24.15). An interesting scarab from Corchiano, now in Copenhagen, has an intaglio device depicting the reclining Herakles, with club and bow, sailing on a raft supported by six amphorae (Fig. 51.7). This subject matter, which seems to have been confined to engraved gems and bronze mirrors, becomes very frequent on later gems in the so-called *a globolo* technique (below).

It is sometimes still possible to attribute two or more works to the same "hand." Devices with little or no compositional variation occasionally make an appearance, sometimes with mirrored images. Once a compositional theme was successfully mastered and proved popular with patrons, it was generally retained. Some figure-types thus became standardized early on and sometimes used for more than one mythological figure, the precise identity of which could be indicated by the addition of a characteristic attribute or an inscribed name. These inscriptions, which amount to about 160 and mostly belong in the fifth and fourth centuries BCE, almost always name the figure(s) depicted, not the engraver or owner of the gem. They are mostly Etruscan variants of the names of Greek heroes.[21] Scholars often assume that the Etruscan engravers arbitrarily applied these

Figure 51.7 Cornelian scarab. Herakles/Hercle sailing on an amphora raft. From Corchiano. Early to mid-fifth century BCE. Copenhagen, National Museum of Denmark, Collection of Near Eastern and Classical Antiquities, inv. 3711. Photo Ulf R. Hansson, courtesy of the National Museum of Denmark.

Greek heroic names to various stock figures, but in most cases the names seem wholly appropriate for the figures represented in terms of action and/or attributes.[22] In some cases, names seem to have been added to assure correct identification of a depicted figure when his or her identity was not immediately clear from either attributes or action.[23] Sometimes names have been added to figures already identifiable through attributes or action, a form of "supercharging" that would instead have been aimed at maximizing the effectiveness or potency of the image.

The beetle sides continue to be meticulously carved and polished throughout the fifth century BCE, revealing a continued interest in the realistic rendering of the scarab beetle, but also a decorative inventiveness in details such as winglets and plinth decoration.

LATE FIFTH- AND FOURTH-CENTURY WORKSHOPS

The Late Classical period, circa 430–320 BCE, is characterized by continued formal and iconographic diversity. The label "Free style" is often applied to these works. Attic vase painting continues to be a major influence, together with coins, sculpture and painting, as well as indigenous Etruscan works such as bronze mirrors and *cistae*. The prevalent single- or two-figured compositions usually fill the whole space inside the oval decorated border, which is still mostly hatched but occasionally more elaborate, like the dotted line of the early scarab illustrated here, depicting Herakles wrestling with Antaios (Fig. 51.8), and found in a tomb in Populonia together with pottery dated to the mid-fifth century BCE.[24] A higher degree of realism and plasticity is introduced in the rendering of human bodies, which are muscular but successively more slender and at times statuary-like (Fig. 51.9). The figures, which tend to have large, sometimes squarish heads and coiffures with finely engraved strands of hair, are often clad in a characteristic short mantle or *chlamys* and frequently stand with their legs slightly apart or crossed, occasionally bent over an object or an animal (Fig. 51.10). Engravers excel in various foreshortenings of backs, arms and legs, and some figures are depicted performing an action such as speaking (with the characteristic raised-hand gesture), sacrificing, or practicing various crafts. Some scholars have interpreted such scenes as taken from everyday life, but the majority

Figure 51.8 Cornelian scarab. Herakles/Hercle and Antaios, inscr. *hercle*. From Populonia. Mid-fifth century BCE. Florence, Museo Archeologico Nazionale, no inv. © Soprintendenza per i Beni Archeologici della Toscana.

Fig. 51.9 Cornelian scarab. Herakles/Hercle and the Erymanthian Boar. From Chiusi. Fourth century BCE. London, British Museum, inv. GR 72.6-4.1140 © Trustees of the British Museum.

Figure 51.10 Banded agate. Odysseus/Uthuze, inscr. *uthuze*. From Orvieto. Fourth century BCE. Copenhagen, National Museum of Denmark, Collection of Near Eastern and Classical Antiquities, inv. 3097. Photo Ulf R Hansson, courtesy of the National Museum of Denmark.

of them are more likely linked to mythological figures;[25] defining actions such as these probably served to make depicted figures more easily identifiable. Figures from Greek myth remain popular, especially Herakles who is depicted alone or together with various figures and creatures such as Athena, Hermes, Acheloos, Kerberos, the Nemean Lion, and the Hydra. Other recognizable figures include Hermes, Achilles, Ajax, Peleus/Pele, Perseus/Pherse, Odysseus/Uthuze, Theseus/These, Kastor/Castur, Kadmos, Kapaneus, and Tydeus, but there are also many numerous nameless warriors, archers, athletes, hunters, youths, lyre-players etc. Animals and various hybrid creatures begin to surface, as do satyrs. The beetle-sides continue to be detailed and finely carved, with a variety of plinth decorations.

LATE FOURTH TO SECOND CENTURIES BCE

For a long time scholars doubted that purely Etruscan workshops continued to be active after the fourth century BCE. But authors like Peter Zazoff and Wolfram Martini have shown that Etruscan craftsmen continued to engrave gems well into the second century BCE, turning out works in different, parallel styles and techniques, and even introducing a new shape into their repertory, the fixed ringstone. But this important period is still highly problematic in a number of ways, and in need of further study. What can be safely said is that, towards the end of the fourth century BCE, Etruscan workshops offered an artistic output that was not only much more varied than previously, but it may also already have been partly aimed at customer groups outside Etruria. This is most likely the case with the two major new classes of gems, the so-called *a globolo* scarabs and the ringstones. But scarabs engraved in the various extensions of the Late Classical or "Free" style continued to be produced for a long time, with subject matter drawn from all previous periods of production. Engravers now leave more space around the increasingly elongated and statue-like figures, which are reminiscent of Hellenistic sculpture. Some stones tend to be somewhat flatter and wider, resulting in distorted beetle anatomies. The backsides are generally more summarily carved than before.

A globolo scarabs

Round drill-heads of various sizes were used throughout production not only for details, but also for producing larger cavities in the stone surface in preparation for additional engraving with finer tools. This technique is evidenced already in the earliest Etruscan works. But on some gems from the fifth and fourth centuries BCE such blob-like forms, mostly confined to heads of human figures and later also to animals and various objects, have been left more or less as they are and appear side by side with more detailed engraving achieved with finer tools. Such hybrid works prepare the way for a new important class of gems, the *a globolo* scarabs, which dominated the glyptic production of the late fourth and early third centuries BCE, and in which most or all engraving was done with a limited number of round drill-heads (Fig. 51.11).[26] There are many more datable find contexts for these gems, which had a very wide geographical distribution even outside Etruria and the Italian peninsula.[27] The *a globolo* gems constitute more than two thirds of the preserved corpus of Etruscan scarabs and were mostly serially-produced. This interesting development towards formal abstraction resulted in simplified, at times strikingly bold and effective images, which allowed for greater variety in interpretation. This engraving

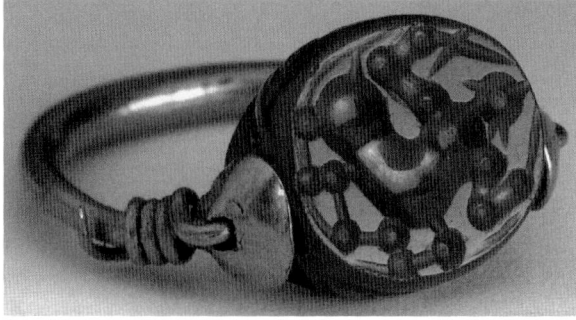

Figure 51.11 Cornelian scarab. Centaur. *A globolo* technique. Third century BCE. London, British Museum, inv. GR 1862.6-4.15 © Trustees of the British Museum.

technique and and resulting formal vagueness were probably deliberate ways of adapting to an ever-expanding market, whose specific demands and tastes had to be anticipated. The final decision on the specific identity of a figure depicted could be left to the future owner of the gem. Some scholars want to place the production of these works in non-Etruscan, Italic workshops, and it is very likely that engravers working in this style were active in or catered to customers in other regions of Italy as well. But the fact remains that there is considerable thematic continuity between the Etruscan scarab production of the fifth and fourth centuries BCE and the *a globolo* scarabs, where this established repertory is expanded to include images of chariots and equestrians, man-and-animal scenes, and various winged figures which are all less frequent on earlier gems. A variety of animals and monsters such as horses, deer, hares, dogs, birds, dolphins, Geryon, Pegasus, Kerberos, Chimaera, Scylla, giants, tritons, centaurs, griffins, harpies, sirens, sphinxes, and hippocamps are also new additions more or less confined to this class of gems. Of the identifiable figures, Herakles remains the most popular by far. He is depicted sailing on an amphora raft, collecting water from a spring or fountain, mastering animals or monsters like the Lion, the Hind, or Kerberos, or just standing or resting. At times he is replaced by a satyr performing the same characteristic actions. Other recognizable figures include Hyakinthos riding on a swan or driving a swan *biga*, the collapsing Kapaneus with the thunderbolt of Zeus, the brooding Achilles, Ajax committing suicide, Phaeton on the sun *biga*, Hermes *psychopompos*, Poseidon/Nethuns with his trident, Phalanthos/Taras riding on the dolphin, and Theseus with his father's sword. But these figures are no longer named, as *a globolo* gems with inscriptions are extremely rare – most of them are probably modern additions.

The beetles of the *a globolo* scarabs are highly standardized, winglets are now mostly hinted at by one to three diagonal grooves; in the late phase of production, the legs become reduced to a few incised lines, the plinth decoration disappears, and the common hatched border surrounding the intaglio device is replaced with a simple line or is omitted altogether. But the stones remain highly polished, the bold design of the device creating an attractive play of light.

Ringstones

The new important class of gems constituted by ringstones intended to be set, immobile, in metal finger-rings has much in common with the scarabs of the Early and Late Classical periods in terms of style and iconography.[28] And some scarab gems actually had their backs sawed-off in order to be reused as ringstones, like a sardonyx in London with an intaglio device showing the weary Herakles, illustrated here (Fig. 51.12). The ringstones, which vary in shape from circular and oval to more angular, have remained a problematic group of gems, both in terms of dating and workshop attribution, since virtually none of them have been found during controlled excavation, and provenance information is scarce.[29] Single, statuary-like figures from Greek myth are popular even here: Achilles, Herakles, Hermes, Odysseus, Kapaneus, Tydeus, and Kadmos, but so too are figures that are less common or absent on Etruscan scarabs, such as Prometheus, Orpheus, Philoktetes, and Oidipus with the Sphinx. There are also many anonymous warriors and youths, but very few female figures. The relative popularity of devices with what appears to be *Maschialismos* scenes or severed heads should be noted. There are very few inscriptions, most of them are written in Latin letters and seem to refer to the owner of the gem.[30] Some scholars have attributed this whole production to non-Etruscan workshops, and it is true that there are some differences in subject matter, but these probably say more about customer tastes than about the engravers. It is reasonable to assume that Etruscan workshops were responsible for initializing this production sometime in the second half of the fourth century BCE. They may have continued to produce ringstones well into the second century BCE, but, given the lack of datable contexts, chronology remains a controversial issue.[31] In the third and second centuries BCE they would have had competition from engravers active in other parts of central and southern Italy.

THE END OF ETRUSCAN PRODUCTION

The scarcity of datable find contexts makes the end of Etruscan glyptic production difficult to pinpoint. As mentioned, engravers probably began to adapt their artistic output to suit more socially and culturally heterogeneous customer groups, including non-Etruscan components, already towards the end of the fourth century BCE, by

Figure 51.12 Sardonyx ringstone based on a scarab. Herakles/Hercle, inscr. *hercle*.
From Arna (Perugia?) Fourth century BCE. London, British Museum inv. GR 1814.7-4.1299
© Trustees of the British Museum.

introducing new subject matter, techniques, and shapes. Both the *a globolo* scarabs and the ringstones are firmly rooted in the Etruscan glyptic tradition but could be seen as successful attempts to attract new customer groups, whether still Etruscan, Italic, Roman or Romanized. These classes of gems became popular outside Etruria, production soon included engravers active in other parts of central and southern Italy, and the enduring influence of Etruscan gem-engraving on the artistic output of later Italic and Roman-Republican workshops can be studied for a considerable period of time.[32] In the third and second centuries BCE, the fixed ringstone replaced the scarab gem as the most popular shape, and workshops were rapidly being established in various parts of Italy, notably in Campania and Latium, and later at Aquileia in the north, founded in 181 BCE. The earliest gems found at Aquileia are in fact *a globolo* scarabs.[33] But very few, if any, purely Etruscan workshops would still have been active after the mid-second century BCE.[34]

NOTES

1 For example, Zazoff 1983: 215–217 and refs; Spier 2000. For Etruscan gems in general, see Zazoff 1968, 1983: 214–259; Richter 1968: 173–213; Martini 1971; Boardman 1975: 37–45; Krauskopf 1995; Martelli and Gilotta 2000; Hansson 2005; Zwierlein-Diehl 2007: 81–97; Ambrosini 2011.
2 Boardman 1991.
3 Martelli 1981; Devoto 1990; Fábry 2009; Giovanelli 2012.
4 For engraving techniques, see for example, Boardman 1970: 379–382; Devoto and Molayem 1990: esp. 192–206.
5 Most gems with a known archaeological find context come from tombs, both male and female burials. The figure 2,600 gems is based on an inventory of known collections. The actual number of surviving gems may of course be much higher.
6 For example, Zazoff 1968: 20.
7 Berges 1997: nos. 461, 490, 573, 574, 592, 641, 642, 657, 658, 770.
8 Martelli 1981.
9 Ambrosini 2011: 74–77 EDP 1–10.
10 For an overview of earlier scaraboids and sealstones in amber and serpentine, see Giovanelli 2012.
11 Chiesa 2009.
12 Phillips 1978.
13 For example, Hölbl 1979, II, nos. 36, 39, 126f., 226 and *passim*; Bartoloni *et al.* 2000: 137–140 nos 92–108.
14 Martelli and Gilotta 2001: 455.
15 Boardman 1968: 173; 1970: 145, 152f.
16 We owe this attribution to Peter Zazoff (for example, 1968: 17–24, 1983: 215–217).
17 For the most recent list see Spier 2000: 333f.
18 Spier 2000.
19 Podere San Cerbone, tomb 13. *Notizie degli scavi,* 1908, 202.
20 Zazoff 1968: 30.
21 Ambrosini 2011.
22 For example, Krauskopf 1995: 5–19; 1996: 413; Ambrosini 2011.
23 For example, Krauskopf 1995: 11; 1996.
24 Pod. San Cerbone, Tomba del Bronzetto di un Offerente, *Notizie degli scavi*, 15, 1961: 63–67.
25 For example, Krauskopf 1995: 5–19; 1996.
26 Zazoff 1968: 118–141; 1983: 241–247; Hansson 2005; Zwierlein-Diehl 2007: 93–95.

27 Hansson 2005: 43–68. Southern Italy is especially rich in finds, but *a globolo* gems have been found all over the Mediterranean region and as far away as the coastal areas around Kertsch in Crimea.

28 Martini 1971.

29 Martini 1971: 21–23, 164: Aquileia, Chiusi, Dalmatia, Rome.

30 Martini 1971: 119–122, 164.

31 Martini 1971: 116–126. See also Zazoff 1983: 250–259; Zwierlein-Diehl 2007: 95–97.

32 For example, Sena Chiesa 1966; Zazoff 1983: 260–305; Zwierlein-Diehl 2007: 98–107.

33 Sena Chiesa 1966: nos. 567, 874, 1051, 1052.

34 Zazoff dates the end of scarab production circa 100 BCE (1983: 237–247).

BIBLIOGRAPHY

Ambrosini, L. (2011) *Gemme etrusche con iscrizioni*, (Mediterranea, Suppl. 6) Rome: Fabrizio Serra.

Bartoloni, G. *et al.* (2000) *Principi etruschi: tra Mediterraneo e Europa*, Venice: Marsilio.

Berges, D. (1997) *Die Tonsiegel aus dem karthagischem Tempelarchiv*, Mainz: von Zabern.

Boardman, J. (1968) *Archaic Greek Gems: Schools and artists in the sixth and early fifth ceturies BC*, Evanston: Indiana University Press.

——(1970) *Greek Engraved Gems: Archaic to early Classical*, London: Thames & Hudson.

——(1975) *Intaglios and rings, Greek, Etruscan and Eastern, from a private collection*, London and New York: Thames & Hudson.

——(1991) "Colour questions," *Jewellery Studies*, 5: 29–31.

Chiesa, F. (2009) "Uno scaraboide figurato dal 'complesso monumentale' a Tarquinia" in S. Bruni (ed.), *Etruria e Italia preromana: studi in onore di Giovannangelo Camporeale*, Rome and Pisa: Fabrizio Serra, pp. 227–232.

Devoto, G. (1990) "Scarabei etrusco-italici in serpentina," *Acta geoarcheologica urbica* 2: 34–36.

Devoto, G. and Molayem, A. (1990) *Archeogemmologia: pietre antiche, glittica, magia e litoterapia*, Rome: La Meridiana.

Fábry, N. B. (2009) "Lo scarabeo della Tomba 7 di Monterenzio Vecchio e le parures d'ambra delle necropoli etrusco-celtiche della Valle dell'Idice," *Ocnus* 17: 23–28.

Giovanelli, E. (2012) "Le prime testimonianze di glittica etrusca: scaraboidi e sigilli tra VIII e VII a.C." in *Preistoria e protostoria in Etruria: Atti del decimo incontro di studi. L'Etruria dal Paleolitico al Primo Ferro: lo stato delle ricerche*, Milan: Centro di Studi di Preistoria e Archeologia, II: 783–796.

Hansson, U. R. (2005) "*A globolo* gems: late Etrusco-Italic scarab intaglios," Unpublished PhD Diss., Gothenburg University. Forthcoming publication.

Hölbl, G. (1979) *Beziehungen der ägyptischen Kultur zu Altitalien*, Leiden: Brill.

Krauskopf, I. (1995) *Heroen, Götter und Dämonen auf etruskischen Skarabäen: Listen zur Bestimmung*, (Peleus, Beiheft zu Thetis, 1) Mannheim: University of Mannheim.

——(1996) "Interesse privato nel mito: il caso degli scarabei etruschi" in F.-H. Massa-Pairault (ed.), *Le mythe grec en Italie antique: fonction et image*, (CEFR, 253), Rome: École Française de Rome, pp. 405–421.

Martelli, M. (1981) "Un sigillo etrusco," *Quaderni Urbinati di Cultura Classica*, 9: 169–172.

Martelli, M. and Gilotta, F. (2000) "Sphragistics and glyptics" in M. Torelli (ed.), *The Etruscans*, New York: Rizzoli, pp. 455–462.

Martini, W. (1971) *Etruskische Ringsteinglyptik*, Heidelberg: F.H. Kerle.

Phillips, K. M. (1978) "Orientalizing gem stones from Poggio Civitate (Murlo)," *Parola del Passato*, 33: 355–369.

Richter, G. M. A. (1968) *The Engraved gems of the Greeks, Etruscans and Romans*, 1, London: Phaidon.

Spier, J. (2000) "From East Greece to Etruria: a late sixth-century BCE gem workshop" in G. R. Tsetskhladze, A. J. N. W. Prag and A. Snodgrass (eds), *Periplous: papers on classical art and archaeology presented to Sir John Boardman*, London: Thames & Hudson, pp. 330–335.

Torelli, M. (1997) "*Appius Alce*: la gemma fiorentina con rito saliare e la presenza dei Claudii in Etruria," *Studi Etruschi* 63: 227–255.

——(2002) "Autorappresentarsi: immagini di sé, ideologia e mito greco attraverso gli scarabei etruschi," *Ostraka*, 9: 101–155.

Zazoff, P. (1968) *Etruskische Skarabäen*, Mainz: Philipp von Zabern.

——(1983) *Die antiken Gemmen*, (Handbuch der Archäologie), München: C.H. Beck.

Zwierlein-Diehl, E. (2007) *Antike Gemmen und ihr Nachleben*, Berlin and New York: De Gruyter.

CHAPTER FIFTY TWO

THE ETRUSCAN PAINTED POTTERY

———— ·◆· ————

Laura Ambrosini

In this study the most important topics relating to Etruscan painted pottery have been selected and necessarily synthesized.[1] An attempt was made to focus not only on the artistic aspects of the pottery, but also on the technical aspects and on the organization of pottery workshops. This choice was made because in Antiquity the organization of work, different from today, stimulated many cultural exchanges, the fruits of which are evident for us even in the objects that have survived. As is known, while we have a large amount of iconographic and archaeological evidence for the organization of pottery workshops in Greece, for the Etruscans we are less fortunate. However, it is the oldest period that, almost surprisingly, gives us a greater number of documents.

ETRUSCO-GEOMETRIC POTTERY[2]

For the oldest productions we are all grateful to Marina Martelli who has carried out many studies on Etrusco-Geometric pottery, Orientalizing and Etrusco-Corinthian pottery, making our work of synthesis easier. Her study emphasizes the important role played by the islands (especially the Cyclades),[3] but also by Attica (Fig. 52.1), so far underestimated in favor of Euboea and Pithekoussai,[4] in the birth and development of Etrusco-Geometric ceramics. She stresses the main role of Caere, a city that since the beginning of the seventh century BC becomes the center of excellence in pottery decoration. As we all know the Greek (Euboean) craftsmen and traders who had set up a base on Pithekoussai (Ischia) circa 770 BC, moved to the mainland and established the colony of Cumae (750 BC). A large quantity of Greek pottery imports reached southern Etruria. After a period of production in the last decades of the eighth century BC imitating Greek drinking cups with geometric decoration (almost Euboic), i.e. running chevrons and concentric design known as the "pendant semicircle," Greek potters went to Etruria from the new colonies: from Euboean mother cities and Cycladic islands, they introduced in Campania and southern Etruria new technologies and new ideas. These new technologies were the use of purified clay, the fast potter's wheel, and the firing at high temperature in closed kilns. The new ideas were the decoration in Late Geometric style, with figures of birds, quadrupeds, fish, and occasional human beings (such the *Despotes hippōn* ["Master of horses"], ritual acts like the *choros* or dance, military acts like horsemen in parade, acts of worship like libation or adoration).

In the phase between 720–700 BC the production is rather limited and concentrated in Tarquinia and Vulci (Fig. 52.2), while between 700–675 BC the axis moves significantly to Tarquinia. Around the second quarter of the seventh century BC Veii and Caere innovated the production by introducing a very large number of new shapes of vases and then, circa 650 BC, monopolized the production of fine painted ceramics, while the production of Vulci and Tarquinia underwent a dramatic collapse. The peak of production seems to be reached between 700 and 675 BC; it was almost certainly linked to the practices of the symposium, the status symbol of the Hellenized aristocracy, followed by some setbacks in 675–650 BC and in 650–625 BC and the exhaustion of the class in the late seventh century BC, in connection with the emergence of new classes of pottery such as Etrusco-Corinthian. Etrusco-Geometric vases are widespread in southern Etruria and the surrounding countryside (*Ager Faliscus* and *Capenate*) (Fig. 52.3) and *Latium Vetus*.

The first examples of painted Etrusco-Geometric vases come from Veii, the city that receives the early Greek pottery. These vases produced in Veii at the third quarter of the eighth century BC (750–725 BC) are so similar to those found in Greece that, without

Figure 52.1   Etrusco-geometric *olla*, Narce tomb 23M, early seventh century BC. University of Pennsylvania Museum MS 1032, image no. 151475. Turfa 2005: no. 177.

Figure 52.2   Etrusco-Geometric skyphos, Vulci tomb 42F, early seventh century BC. University of Pennsylvania Museum MS 680, image no. 151423. Turfa 2005: no. 33.

Figure 52.3 Etrusco-Geometric tripod pyxis, Narce tomb 1, early seventh century BC. University of
Pennsylvania Museum MS 2732A–B, image no. 152699. Turfa 2005: no. 142.

a clay analysis (mostly Mössbauer spectroscopy), it is almost impossible to distinguish
the Etruscan from the Greek examples.[5] Also, in Tarquinia and Vulci Geometric Greek
vases or vases of the second quarter of the eighth century BC in Geometric Greek style
have been found.[6] They are decorated with concentric circles and ovals connected by
S-lines, lozenges with checkered pattern etc. The production of Veii and Caere shows
contacts with *Ager Faliscus* and *Capenate*. Other workshops were located in Vulci and
Tarquinia, Bisenzio and Poggio Buco. From the late eighth or early seventh century BC
the production is standardized. At Vulci, thanks to the Cesnola Painter who comes from
Naxos (according to Kourou) and not from Euboea, from 730 BC workshops of Kraters
were born (the workshop of the First Kraters, the Vulci Biconic workshop, and circa
720 BC, the workshop of the Ticinese Krater). The Krater is an important shape for the
symposium. The vases of the Cesnola Painter are the nucleus of the Late Geometric style
of Naxos, full of Attic influences. There are also Argive influences with contaminations
from Attica or from Naxos (Argive Painter). At Bisenzio the Euboean tradition prevails,
but the workshops also test less common shapes (i.e. bird-shaped askoi). At Tarquinia
are produced mainly oinochoai of Cypro-Phoenician type and Protocorinthian type,
mediated by Cumae. From the beginning of the seventh century BC there begin to appear
in Tarquinia the oldest mythical and epic events of the Hellenic heritage (690–680 BC)
with Theseus, Ariadne and the companions of the hero who perform the dance of the
geranos (the Elongated Horses Painter). The Elongated Horses Painter is a master of
probable Euboean-colonial origin, with Protoattic and Protocorinthian influences. At
the beginning of the seventh century BC the Bocchoris Painter is active and, in the first
quarter of the seventh century BC, also the Painter of the Palms, both with Protocorinthian
influences.

SUBGEOMETRIC POTTERY[7]

In the Early and Middle Orientalizing period the Subgeometric pottery with heron
patterns was routinely produced at Caere and Veii. It was also found in the *Ager Faliscus*

(Fig. 52.4) and Latium. Its presence in Campania and Sicily into the seventh century BC seems to be regarded as "coming back" merchandise that testifies the liveliness of the Greek frequenting of the middle Tyrrhenian Sea. The herons seem to be the Villanovan waterbird with contamination from Greek models. The vessel shapes are plates (Fig. 52.5), stamnoid ollae, oinochoai, large cups with high foot and ring askoi. In the Subgeometric production there still live elements of Euboean and Protocorinthian ancestry. The Subgeometric pottery with herons is absolutely the first Caeretan production with characteristics of uniformity and standardization that allow us to reconstruct a high level of organization of craft production already in the early seventh century BC.

Figure 52.4 Red-on-White oinochoe, Narce tomb 1, first half of the seventh century BC. University of Pennsylvania Museum 36–15–1, image no. 151671. Turfa 2005: no. 180.

Figure 52.5 Red-on-White plate, Narce tomb 1, early seventh century BC. University of Pennsylvania Museum MS 3071, image no. 151636. Turfa 2005: no. 179.

The ceramics decorated with herons are the same shapes as those with simple linear decoration: this shows that they were probably produced in the same workshops. The strong similarities between the current and the previous series point out that there were possibilities for exchanges and contacts, perhaps between workshops responsible for the production of both series. There is a dichotomy between the district of Caere-Veii and Tarquinia-Vulci. Tarquinia acts as a hinge between the two spheres of production. In the map of southern Etruria, the dividing line of distribution between *Metopengattung* and Subgeometric pottery runs at Tarquinia. Between 720 and 650 BC starts the *Metopengattung* production, repeating Euboean-Cycladic and Late Geometric motifs. The decoration consists of metopes and checkerboard with diamond; the shapes are jars, dippers and oinochoai. The *Metopengattung* production is widespread in Vulci and Tarquinia in the first half of the seventh century BC. The *Metopengattung* decoration comes from the additional decoration present on the vases of the Vulci Biconic workshop and of the Argive Painter. The Narce Painter (680–675 BC) (Fig. 52.6) is an Attic painter with Cycladic influences who produces in Veii vases decorated with feeding horses and herons. Some scholars think that he is also a decorator of tombs, such as the Roaring Lions Tomb; Marina Martelli thinks that the artisan active in the workshop of the Narce painter has painted the Tomb of the Ducks and the Roaring Lions Tomb (dated between 680 and 675 BC), while S. Neri considers the Tomb of the Roaring Lions to be by a different artist, active around 700 BC. Recent discoveries in Veii of vases by the Narce Painter, with independent features, which mark much of the subsequent production of the workshop, have induced F. Boitani to think that he moved from Caere to Veii, as already suggested by Dik. During the period of transition between the eighth and seventh centuries BC in Tarquinia the Painter of the Palms is active; he has assimilated the shapes and the decorative motifs of the Eastern tradition.

Figure 52.6   Red-on-White biconical urn, Narce tomb 1, early seventh century BC. University of Pennsylvania Museum MS 2730, image no. 151624. Turfa 2005: no. 16.

THE ORIENTALIZING POTTERY[8]

The decoration was first branded Subgeometric (fish and herons), then, in the middle of the seventh century BC a change of style takes place, bringing big heraldic animals and decorative motifs (with the Painter of the Calabresi Urn[9] and the Painter of the Birth of Menerva). At the beginning of the Late Orientalizing the mythological themes spread on these and other Caeretan productions. In the first generation we have the Workshop of the Civitavecchia Fishes, the Workshop of the Stockholm Fishes and the Cranes Painter. In Caere, in the first quarter of the seventh century BC is located the Workshop of the Civitavecchia Fishes Painter and later the Workshop of the Stockholm Fishes with fishes of Protocorinthian-Cumaean origin; the Cranes Painter, active in Caere, has Hellenic character with Cycladic influence and uses a monumental and figurative style. In the first half of the seventh century BC the Cranes Painter is the pioneer of the Orientalizing pottery decoration of Caere in impasto and in fine pottery; he is also the author of the first models in "white on red"-figured decoration. Recent discoveries in Veii suggested to F. Boitani that the Painter of the Cranes had moved from Caere to Veii. He is limited in the choice of subjects and is mainly bound to the zoomorphic repertoire and to Subgeometric texture. He extends the decorative repertoire, however, also working in the "white on red" technique, and paints not only fishes and birds, but also other animals and even humans (warrior) and demi-humans (Centaur).

The human figure becomes the protagonist of monumental pottery decoration: the innovation is due to the Caeretan Heptachord Painter (680–660 BC),[10] who prefers narrative scenes of mythic content. He is an experimentalist who belongs to a mythological and epic tradition of Greek origin. We can see the change in customers' taste: on the Heptachord Painter's vases we have the narrative scenes, zoomorphic figures, but also the knowledge of Greek sagas (probably Helen and Menelaus). He is an innovator with creative abilities; his anthropomorphic figures, drawn with the silhouette technique, do not have the serial nature of the Subgeometric repertoire. In the eponymous vase he depicts a *cithera*-player in a poetic performance while five armed men perform a dance (for a party or a ceremony of worship). The local *aristoi* want to buy vases that will reflect their ethics and behavior through comparison with characters of Greek myth and epic cycles.

Narrative scenes that denote the knowledge of Hellenic legends are introduced (see Chapter 24). Aristonothos[11] is a Greek itinerant artisan who worked in Caere and who signed his vases. His monumental style is inspired by the Cycladic Orientalizing and by Early and Middle (Early) Protoattic (perhaps he is Cycladic). The figures are taken from episodes of the Trojan cycle, and probably from the Theban cycle. The work of Aristonothos is not isolated, but, with courtly monumental tones, fits into the local tradition in which are Late Geometric influences together with the first results of Greek Orientalizing. Between the middle and the end of the seventh century BC, other adventures of Odysseus, set in the Tyrrhenian Sea, the blinding of Polyphemus and the escape from his cave, the collision with Scylla, are incorporated in Etruria. This highlights the symbolic importance of the Tyrrhenian *nostos* of Odysseus for the Etruscan aristocracy, as a symbol of the dangerous experiences of sea journeys. In the Middle Orientalizing stands the Amsterdam Painter, who uses a shape of amphora derived from SOS amphorae or from the Chiot amphorae. In the eponymous vase with Medea and the dragon of Colchis (660–640 BC), he uses an Orientalizing decorative dossier and expressions of Hellenic imprint. The theme of Medea, by the extrapolation of the Golden Fleece and the myth of the Argonauts, was, perhaps, a theme linked to the transmarine travels.

WHITE ON RED[12] AND RED ON WHITE POTTERY

The White on Red pottery (Fig. 52.7) is an impasto pottery with decorations in white over a red slip. The most ancient vases sporadically appeared in Tarquinia (780–760 BC), later in the interior of Etruria (Bisenzio and *Ager Faliscus*), and before that on the Tyrrhenian coast (middle-late IIB phase). This technique is developed in the moment of transition between the Late Villanovan phase and the beginning of Early Orientalizing. In the Orientalizing culture there is a general renewal even in the traditional indigenous arts: in the first half of the seventh century BC the impasto pottery painted in white on red ("White on Red") appears at Caere, Veii and in the *Ager Faliscus*. This fabric has been studied extensively by Marina Micozzi (1994, see note 9). The class includes plates, bowls, *holmoi, dolia*, amphoras, urns and cylindrical pyxides. The production starts in the first quarter of the seventh century BC at Caere with a repertoire of Subgeometric types with extremely stylized natural elements taken from the zoomorphic repertoire, such as herons and fishes. In the second half of the seventh century BC is a great turning point with animals (heraldic and in procession) and ornate decorations such as chains of palmettes.

The best representative of the Calabresi Urn Workshop is the Painter of the Birth of Menerva (perhaps to be identified with the Painter of Bufolareccia 86),[13] whose personality was approached in the art of the Tomb of the Painted Animals and the Tomb of the Painted Lions. His style is Phoenicianizing (linear Geometric patterns, chains of lozenges, Phoenician palmettes). The Etruscan inscription *kvsnailise*,[14] as repainted (see Gaultier-Geppert 2000) seems to be the name of the Painter of the Birth of Menerva, active in the third quarter of the seventh century BC. The production of Caere is characterized by complex formal and stylistic elements, but in the third quarter of the seventh century BC incorporates Geometric linear syntax enriched with typically Corinthian ornate effect, connected to the Demaratean phase. In the *Ager Faliscus* the production is characterized

Figure 52.7   White on Red conical stand and bowl, Narce tomb 7F, first half of the seventh century BC. University of Pennsylvania Museum MS 1221, image no. 152688. Turfa 2005: no. 27.

by a decoration of Subgeometric type with repetitive elements. Some new discoveries seem to prove that the Latin site of Crustumerium has been a center of production of this pottery type.[15]

A recent study of the production around Lake Bolsena and along the upper valley of the Fiora has avoided the excessively broad definition of "Bolsena Group," referring to the "White on Red of middle-interior Etruria."[16] The "Red on White" (Fig. 52.8) shares with the "White on Red" the decorative syntax, the adoption of decoration such as the target- and metope-patterns. Already in the second half of the eighth century BC, the "Red on White" technique is used for the decoration of Subgeometric vases in such internal sites as Bisenzio. In the *Ager Faliscus* the technique proceeds side by side with that of "White on Red," and often the two techniques are used with the specific desire to play with two-tone (for example, even in Poggio Buco in the first half of the seventh century BC). The decorative syntax is simple and standardized, with linear and metopal decorations. The class is present at Bisenzio until the Middle Orientalizing.

ETRUSCO-CORINTHIAN POTTERY[17]

For Etrusco-Corinthian pottery we have the monumental work of Szilágyi.[18] The Etrusco-Corinthian pottery seems to develop directly from the Etrusco-Geometric tradition in the late seventh century BC, encouraged by the emergence of new social classes. Etrusco-Corinthian figured pottery from the beginning was characterized by specialization in the decoration of certain shapes of vases. Around 630 BC a strong Hellenic acceleration occurs in Caere and Vulci: Etrusco-Corinthian production starts. The Etrusco-Corinthian pottery production is divided into three generations (first generation 630–600 BC, second-generation 600–580 BC, the third generation 580–550 BC). The input to production of the Etrusco-Corinthian vases is given by Corinthian imports (for example, the famous Chigi Olpe by the Macmillan Painter, a masterpiece of the Middle Proto-Corinthian 650–630 BC, from Veii, Chigi Tumulus).

Figure 52.8   Red on White *olla*, Vulci tomb 66, end of eighth–early seventh century BC. University of Pennsylvania Museum MS 566, image no. 151416. Turfa 2005: no. 25.

First generation: 630–600 BC

The most valuable artistic productions seem to be created in the first phase: the amphora was inspired by Corinthian models, initially of the Transitional period and then properly Corinthian, whose influx into Etruria lasted until the mid-sixth century BC. At the end of the third quarter of the seventh century BC, thanks to the influence of massive importing of Corinthian pottery, in Vulci and Caere, Etrusco-Corinthian black-figure pottery was born. In the early period the production of Caere includes the Polychrome Group (the Mount Abatone Cycle) and the miniature black-figure style of the Scale Group of large amphorae (630–580 BC). At Veii we have the Castellani Painter (630–620 BC), who produces aryballoi of Late Proto-Corinthian type, decorated in miniature style. At Vulci the Bearded Sphinx Painter was active (630–600 BC) (Fig. 52.9), the first great figure of Etrusco-Corinthian vase-painting, who, according to Szilágyi, would move from Vulci to Caere. At Vulci the Swallows Painter[19] was also active (620–610 BC), a follower of the Eastern Greek "Wild Goat Style."

Second generation: 600–580 BC

At this time the best synthesis between the Etruscan and the Corinthian spirit was reached; among the shapes of vases, the accessories of the banquet predominate. At Vulci the masters of the second generation are mainly the Feoli Painter, the leader of the school, the Pescia Romana Painter, the Painter of Boehlau, the Volunteer Painter, the St. Louis Painter. In Tarquinia another center of production is formed, more provincial and dedicated to mass production (Vitelleschi Painter, attributed by Szilágyi to the third generation).

Third generation: 580–550 BC

The decorative motifs are repetitive and the production, which is low-quality from an artistic point of view, becomes routine (containers for perfumes are also produced). The predilection for certain shapes shows the change of the social classes interested in these vessels. The Painter of Hercle, the Painter of Large Rosettes (Fig. 52.10), the Painter

Figure 52.9   Etrusco-Corinthian oinochoe by the Bearded Sphinx Painter, Pitigliano tomb 26, last quarter of the seventh century BC. University of Pennsylvania Museum MS 642, image no.152662. Turfa 2005: no. 189.

Figure 52.10   Etrusco-Corinthian chalice by Painter of the Large Rosettes, circa 590/580–560 BC.
University of Pennsylvania Museum MS 4837, image no. 151658. Turfa 2005: no. 211.

of the Knotted Tails and the Casuccini Painter produced patterned vases frozen in pre-established formulas; mass production was the main goal. The production is split into three groups: The Human Mask Group, which decorated kylikes especially with birds (the artistic level is very low), the Cycle of the Birds, which produced perfume containers decorated with birds, both particularly popular in Latium, the Confronted Cocks Cycle, numerically higher, which produced perfume containers, found mostly in Campania. A sudden increase occurs in plastic vases in all three groups. In Latium and in Campania[20] local production of Etrusco-Corinthian pottery existed. The Etrusco-Corinthian pottery was also exported overseas as an integral part of the large Etruscan trade. In southern Gaul were found vases of Vulci third generation (for example, the Painter of Large Rosettes, the Painter of the Knotted Tails) and Tarquinia (Wolf's Heads Painter and Painter without Graffito) and Human Mask Group (not in Carthage). In Etrusco-Corinthian production, from 580 BC, two huge production cycles dominate, the Olpai and Rosettes Cycles. After 560 BC the workshops are still active for a decade or two, but without any artistic pretensions (Human Mask Group, a Caeretan production, and others).

In conclusion, according to Szilágyi, in the first generation the Etrusco-Corinthian vases were destined for the wealthy, in the second for the refined ruling class that had a Hellenic style, and in the third generation for the less demanding middle-class. In the first phase, gravitating to the areas of Caere and Veii, we can see the preference given to the polychrome technique, while at Vulci the black-figure technique begins; the transition from one class to another is very gradual, as evidenced by the coexistence of different series in tombs of 630–600 BC. Initially, the predominant role is played by Caere, and by Vulci in the second generation. The primacy of Vulci lasts substantially even with the advent of third generation.

On an *omphalos phiale* dedicated in the Portonaccio sanctuary at Veii by Laris Lethaies, the signature has been identified as *mi(ni) zinace Vel{thur A}ncinies*, in the handwriting of Veii; the phiale was assigned by G. Colonna to the craftsman Velthur Ancinies, a young colleague of the Rosettes Painter, from whom he had departed stylistically, once he moved to Veii.[21] In Etrusco-Corinthian pottery the percentage of vases with depictions of the human figure is very low (about 1 percent); the number of images that refer to Greek mythology is surely irrelevant (in one case Achilles and Troilus, in one case Herakles and Geryon).

THE CAERETAN HYDRIAI,[22] THE CAMPANA GROUP (DINOI AND HYDRIAI),[23] THE NORTHAMPTON GROUP,[24] THE RICCI HYDRIA[25]

The Caeretan *Hydriai*

Some painters immigrated to Etruria from North Ionia and painted vases of large luxury shapes (*dinoi, hydriai* and *amphorae*) for the symposium, aimed at a prestigious clientele, often with symposiac themes and more often with mythological themes (in the Caeretan *Hydriai*). The East Greek component will have a strong influence in Etruscan culture also in the painting of tombs. The Caeretan *hydriai*, about 40 at this time, show both mythological and human genre themes. The style is wholly Ionian, and of remarkable quality. We can distinguish at least two painters: the Eagle Painter and the Busiris Painter. The first painter has a more calligraphic drawing style, the second is hastier. A context with fragments of a Caeretan hydria by the Eagle Painter has been recently dated to the last two decades of the sixth century BC.[26]

The Campana group

This group consists of an amphora, *hydriai* and *dinoi*, produced between 530–520/510 BC. In the Campana *dinoi* can be recognized, according to Hemelrijk, three painters (the Painter of Louvre E 737–E 739 or Ribbon Painter, the Painter of Louvre E 736 or Eight Painter, the Hoof Painter) who worked in the same workshop, active in Vulci around 530–520 BC. They specialized in a shape of vessel for the drinking of wine, decorated with Dionysian motifs. The style is Eastern Greek and the clay is apparently similar to that of Klazomenai. Hemelrijk believes that the Campana *dinoi* were even produced in East Greece, and imported into Etruria, but new evidence and clay analysis is needed to conclusively decide this matter.

The Campana *hydriai* with animal friezes, which have a touch of the Euboean, seem to have been made in Etruria. A. Waiblinger is inclined to attribute the *hydriai* to an Etruscan workshop that produces in the style of the Tyrrhenian amphorae. To the Louvre E 739 Painter or Ribbon Painter (Louvre E 737 to 739 of Hemelrijk) is attributed the famous Ricci *hydria*. While showing an undeniably East Greek style, near to the Enmann Group (ascribed to Phocaea by M. Martelli), the vase, according to Martelli, would be characterized by Etruscan accents and barbarization of the Ionian style. It must be stressed that a recent archaeometric analysis conducted on the clay of the Ricci *hydria* does not seem to show affinities with a group made up of two Campana *dinoi*, one Caeretan *hydria* and Etruscan black-figure pottery. The clay of this group contains very similar quantities of chromium and nickel.[27] Archaeometric analysis should be extended to all vases assigned to these classes.

The Northampton group

The belly amphora of the Northampton Group (circa 540–530 BC) from Vulci, with excellent quality of clay and paint (related to the clay of the Caeretan *Hydriai*), although based on Attic models, shows an extreme elegance and exuberance in the vegetal decoration. One could think that it was the work of an East Greek potter who, after working in North Ionia (his environment of origin and training), moved to work in

Etruria (Martelli), or even an Ionic product imported into Etruria (Hemelrijk). Martelli includes the belly amphora in her Chanenko Group.[28] This group comprises also small neck amphorae.

THE BLACK-FIGURE POTTERY[29]

Despite the formidable competition of imported figured ceramics, a production of Etruscan black-figured pottery is emerging. Among the masters, in the first place, is the Ionizing Paris Painter who founded in Vulci the so-called Pontic workshop around 550 BC or shortly after.

The Pontic Group operates in Vulci between 550/540 and about 520 BC. The Pontic vases were initiated by a Greek immigrant from Ionia, since their style is pure Ionian. Most of the vases are amphorae with myth and animal friezes, following the model of the Attic "Tyrrhenian" amphorae, vases for the élites of the major Etruscan cities of the Tyrrhenian coast (Caere and Vulci). We can distinguish different groups: Pontic Ceramic[30] (Paris Painter,[31] Amphiaraos Painter,[32] Tityos Painter,[33] Silenus Painter[34] and the Bibliothèque Nationale 178 Painter), La Tolfa Group,[35] Ivy Leaf Group,[36] Micali Painter and his school.[37]

One of the themes most frequently represented by the Paris Painter is a horseback race. In the first phase of his activities the Corinthian influence is stronger and the themes are generic files of human figures or animalistic ornaments, while later episodes related to the world of myth and heraldic groups of animals in secondary positions appear. The Amphiaraos Painter and the Tityos Painter are more eclectic and closer to Etruscan taste. In works by the Amphiaraos Painter (530–520/515 BC) the figures are disproportionate and often overflowing, mythological scenes are very rare, the animal repertoire is varied. The Tityos Painter uses dynamic pattern, with quick drawing of figures, almost sketches. He is particularly inclined to decorate vases with mythological scenes, especially with the myths of Heracles. The Painter of Bibliothèque 178 (530–510 BC) in the first part of the last quarter of the sixth century BC painted vases with narrative scenes in which he inserts decorative animals. The Painter of Silenus (530–515/510 BC), a student of the Paris Painter, favors Dionisiac themes, although the ambush of Troilus by Achilles appears on only two vases, as also the sacrifice of Polyxena.

The Ivy Leaf Group (540–520 BC), localized at Vulci, takes its name from the large leaves of ivy held in the hands of leading figures. According to a recent hypothesis of L. Bonfante they would reproduce leaves of cloth, wood or other materials carried in procession during ceremonies.[38] This group shows a strong Attic influence (Amasis Painter and Nikosthenes) and includes about fifty vases, almost all amphorae (all of type B), characterized by extreme rigidity of the figures, and an overabundance of phytomorphic decoration. Often there are animals and imaginary creatures. A local echo of the North-Ionian narrative vein occurs in the Tolfa Group.

The Tolfa Group (530–510 BC) (Fig. 52.11) consists of neck-amphorae (typical shape of Caere), decorated with large metopes on the shoulder and body. The themes are simple: human (or riders on seahorses or horses, newts, winged figures) or zoomorphic (panthers, horses, deer, Chimeras, Sphinxes, griffins, Sirens), and the only mythological episode is Achilles' ambush of Troilus. In this group, during the third quarter of the sixth century BC, there are two Painters: (Painter A or the Fat Painter or the Lotus Painter; and Painter B or the Thin Painter or the Painter of Group B). The workshops appear to be localized

Figure 52.11   Black-figure amphora, from Orvieto, sixth century BC. University of Pennsylvania
Museum MS 2491, image no. 4689 & 4690. Turfa 2005: no. 176.

at Caere (22 of 77 vases definitely attributable to the group were found in Caere), and
connected to the production of Caeretan *hydriai* (under the direct influence of Caeretan
hydriai, according to Hemelrijk). The shape of the vase, the table amphora for wine, is
linked to the wine production of Caere.

Between 520 and 490 BC Etruscan pottery production is dominated by the Micali
Painter and his school, with Ionian influence, but a more decorative style (cf. Fig. 48.3).
More than 200 vases are ascribed directly to his hand. Hundreds of vases of the Micali
Painter were for the most part ultimately intended for deposition in tombs. The early
works of the Painter (Early I) are influenced by the late works of Pontic pottery (Tityos
Painter with whom he worked); the scenes contain fantastic animals, the draftsmanship
is quick. In the second phase (Early II) the friezes are separated by bands of birds in
static poses. In the mature phase (Middle I and II) are included many vases, with more
diversified shapes and scenes with a study of proportions and anatomy of the human
figure. In the late phase (Late) (520–510 BC), under the influence of Attic pottery, the
figures are the most dynamic in pose and the phytomorphic friezes increase.

The Micali Painter vases present to us a world of jaunty centaurs, sirens, sphinxes,
winged horses and satyrs. His workshop seems to have been particularly prolific (Painter
of Vatican 238, Kyknos Painter, Group of *Kape Mukathesa*, Group of Florence 80675,
Orbetello Group and Bisenzio Group). *Kape* (slave) of *Mukathe* is working in the workshop
of the Micali painter. *Kape* signed a little amphora from Vulci preserved in Würzburg (see
Chapter 21).

In Orvieto, during the late sixth and the first quarter of the fifth century BC, the Group
of Monaco 892, Monaco 883, and Vatican 265 produces large vases with silhouette scenes
often featuring two figures (athletes, youths, battle scenes) made without internal details
(sometimes overpainted in white). The Orvieto Group (Fig. 52.12), with its flaws and

955

Figure 52.12 Black-figure amphora and lid, Orvieto, circa 500–480 BC. University of Pennsylvania Museum MS 2490A–B, image no. 4687. Turfa 2005: no. 213.

imperfections of firing techniques, shows some engagement with the Micali Painter and the desire to imitate the perspective of Attic pottery. In the early decades of the fifth century BC the same themes also interest the Dancing Satyrs Painter[39] (Lotus Flowers Workshop) who works in Caere almost to the middle of the fifth century BC. The scenes of his vases have themes of Attic imitation, with new functions in an Etruscan key, and subjects related to military values.

THE ANCIENT OVERPAINTED POTTERY: THE PRAXIAS GROUP[40] AND THE VAGNONVILLE GROUP[41]

Around 480 BC, to mimic the red-figure pottery, the use of overpainted pottery is introduced in Etruria. The technique, called "Six's technique" in its simplest form involves laying on figures in pink or orange on an all-black surface and incising details (so that the black shows through). This technique was used on Athenian black figure vases from the first half of the sixth century BC. The drawback is that the pale paints used are fugitive.

One of the initiators of the overpainting technique in Etruria is Arnthe Praxias, active around 480 BC. His signature, in the Greek Chalcidian alphabet, is painted before firing on the rim and on the handle of an amphora kept in Paris. He is a *metic* who uses his Greek name as a *gentilicium* to demonstrate his incorporation into civic society and takes an Etruscan personal name (see Chapter 48). However, it is possible that he is actually the Etruscan son of a Greek immigrant. In his workshop the hands of several painters can be distinguished: the style is subarchaic, in some ways still linked to the Micali Painter. The Jahn Painter in the early decades of the fifth century BC shows an Atticizing line of pioneering experiences with contacts traced by Prag to the Attic Painter of Copenhagen. The Vagnonville Group, a sort of subsidiary of the Vulcian Praxias workshop, can be placed in the third quarter of the fifth century BC. The founder of the workshop, the Bonci Casuccini Painter, prefers mythological representations. The provenence of the vases has suggested a localization of the workshop in Chiusi.

THE RED-FIGURE POTTERY[42]

The real red-figure technique seems to have been born at Vulci, apart from some strongly Atticizing large vases, made in inner Etruria (Orvieto and Chiusi) even in the fifth century BC, which are still connected with the black-figure (Orvieto Group) and with the Praxias Group. The Rodin[43] cup, made in Vulci, seems to date from around 400 BC The external decoration copies faithfully an Attic kylix of the Oedipus Painter found at Vulci and that of an amphora by the Painter of Achilles. In the internal tondo, in addition to the two satyrs, is the overpainted inscription *Avles V(i)pnas naplan* which mentions Aulus Vibenna who would come with Caelius to Rome with the fellow Mastarna, who would seize power and take the name of Servius Tullius. The groups gathered around the Stamnos of Bologna 824[44] and the kylikes, that mimic the Attic red-figure[45] kylikes, with Atticizing style and Lucanian characters highlighted by Cristofani and Harari. Both the Perugia Painter and the Sommavilla Painter[46] still have an Atticizing style but use only the relief line technique. Around the end of the fifth century BC the production called "earlier red-figure,"[47] of Attic influence, starts. The style is a little barbaric and simplified. In this production the Painter of Stamnos Casuccini, the Argonauts Painter, the Perugia Painter and the Sommavilla Painter are included. Recently, M. Denoyelle[48] proposed identifying the Perugia Painter (end of the first decades of the fifth-fourth century BC) with the Lucanian Arnò Painter, who may have moved to Etruria. Gilotta stressed these contacts with the Lucanian pottery involving, in general, the Creusa-Dolon Group, the Intermediate Group and the Primacy Group.[49] In the vases of the Argonauts Painter there are links with the Proto-Lucanian Amykos Painter (last quarter of the fifth century BC). Probably the transfer of Magna-Graecian craftsmen into Etruria may be connected with the foundation of Thurii (444/3 BC). The production of Faliscan red-figured pottery was born in *Falerii Veteres* (now Civita Castellana, near Viterbo) around 380–370 BC by the transfer of Attic artisans into the *Ager Faliscus* (for example, Del Chiaro Painter). This phenomenon has been linked to the economic crisis resulting from the Peloponnesian War, the conflict between Sparta and Athens for hegemony over Greece, lasted almost thirty years (from 431 BC to 404 BC). Additionally, the arrival of Attic red-figure vases at *Falerii Veteres* in the first decades of the fourth century BC, for example, the vase of the Talos Painter, the Painter of London F 64 and the Workshop of the Meleager Painter,[50] certainly brought new life to the local pottery production in the iconography (themes and representations), in the schemes for the composition of scenes, and in the style and more appropriately in the technique (for example, the wise use of white overpainting). Around 380 BC at *Falerii Veteres* some Greek craftsmen started the production of red-figure pottery.

The Del Chiaro Painter, founder of Workshop A (identified by B. Adembri) was probably Greek (Attic painter of the Jena Painter circle), and the next generation of painters were already of local origin. The workshop continues to produce in the following decades with the Nepi Painter and the *Diespater* Group, accepting stimuli both Attic and Italiote and adapting to a very local taste. Two other workshops are active (B and C), headed by the Painter of Vienna 4008 (370 BC) and the Villa Giulia Painter 8361 (360 BC) respectively.

Connected to the Faliscan is the workshop where the Painter of London F 484 and Painter of the Vatican Biga workshop, whose products circulate mainly in Vulci. These vases, together with others, refer to Lucanian products. The Campanizzante Group[51] in the second quarter of the fourth century BC produced vases in southern Etruria and Falerii with a Campanizing/Paestanizing language. The Settecamini Painter worked in internal Etruria (Chiusi or Orvieto) inspired by Faliscan painters. The Vanth Painter,[52] with Faliscan training, in his workshop in Orvieto produced monumental vases for the tombs. Clusium Volaterrae Group:[53] in the third quarter of the fourth century BC, the Clusium Group, made up of the Sarteano and Montediano Painters, spreads to Chiusi and the Val di Chiana producing *kylikes*, plastic vases and small *skyphoi*; while later, around 320 BC, a couple of workshop teachers moved to Volterra and specialized in the production of large column-kraters (*kelebai*) (Fig. L-29-57 Turfa 321), which were intended primarily for funeral use, and *stamnoi*. The tondi of *kylikes* are decorated with scenes related to the Dionysian or erotic themes. This production does not seem derived, as was supposed, from a branch of the mid-fourth century BC Faliscan *kylikes*. The leading figure of the Group is the Montediano Painter. The production of northern Etruria has three phases: "early" (320–300 BC) with the plain style of the Group of Transition, the "ornate" style with the Painter of Hesione and his circle, a fully-developed phase (300–275 BC) with the Painter of the Pigmy Trumpeter (or Monteriggioni Painter), the Painter of the Tuscan Column and the Nun Painter. The scenes with a meaning, often funereal, seem to depict rites of initiation and/or passage of persons related to the sphere of Dionysus.[54]

In the area of Vulci it is possible to locate the Group of Alcestis, whose most famous vase, by the Painter of Alcestis, with the embrace of Admetus and Alcestis, and bearing the inscribed names of characters, dates from around 330 BC. Still in Vulci, the Turmuca Group depicts in a kalyx-krater the shade of Andromache (*hinthi Aturmucas*) (330–300 BC) accompanied by Pentasila, both veiled and cloaked, in front of Charun and a girl. It is a *Nekyia* scene where the three girls are waiting on the shore of the Acheron to be ferried by Charon. The production of Vulci enriched the red-figured pottery with iconographic and symbolic-religious meanings that are evident in the Funnel Group.[55] The Funnel Group, considered Vulcian (possibly with a Tarquinian branch), was brought back recently by Gilotta to craftsmen with Faliscan training. To the Hague Painter, active around 300 BC, leader of the Frontal Workshop of the Funnel Group, are assigned two twin *stamnoi*, the Fould *stamnoi*,[56] one with Dionysiac scenes and the other with stories of Achilles and a kalyx-krater. He is a skilled designer, attentive to spatial effects, *chiaroscuro* and anatomy.

The Faliscan workshops at the mid-fourth century BC begin to produce for the middle class more standardized vases, especially *kylikes*, first with the relief line (class α – Würzburg 818), and then without the relief line (class β – Wurzburg 820), with themes mainly Dionysian. In class α is the Foied Group, a group of at least four *kylikes* (around 350 BC) with a painted inscription "*foied vino pafo cra carefo*" ("now I drink wine, tomorrow I run out of it"), which bears a representation of the embrace between Fufluns (Dionysus) and Semla (Semele). Among the later *kylikes* the Satyr and Dolphin Group[57] stand out, showing an interesting selective use of cartoons along with the *paterae* of the Forum Group,[58] named by the discovery of a fragment in the Roman Forum in Rome, in the Cloaca Maxima.

This is a production of *paterae* with red figures of the last quarter of the fourth century BC by two workshops, one Faliscan (perhaps in *Falerii Veteres*) and one in Tarquinia. The

Faliscan workshops in the second half of the fourth century BC made a standardized production of ordinary quality, with erotic or Dionisiac themes (Faliscan Figured Group, 340–280 BC), the Full Sakkos Group,[59] so-called by the distinctive headgear worn by the women on the vessels, and the Barbarano Group (Fig. 52.13), consisting of *oinochoai* decorated with a female head in profile.

The Fluid Group is late Faliscan, named for the appearance of diluted paint on most vases. The style is smooth, rounded, easy and fluid. The maeander has the "soft" form, with no relief line. The vases are *stamnoi*, amphorae, kalyx kraters, *oinochoai, skyphoi* etc. The themes are Nikai, Dionysos, Maenads and Satyrs. It is possible to detect a Caeretan figured production (340–300/280 BC?) dependent on the Faliscan. In the Caeretan Figured Group,[60] the oldest painter and one of the most prolific, the Villa Giulia Caeretan Painter,[61] is probably still active at Falerii (Falisco-Caeretan style), and later the production moved to Caere (Caeretan early style, medium and recent). The Torcop Group[62] of the second half of the fourth-early third century BC is named after vases in the museums of Toronto and Copenhagen. The vases are *oinochoai* decorated with female profiles (two confronted on the body and one on the neck); concerning the location of production Del Chiaro formulated the hypothesis of Caere. The production period is placed between the second half of the fourth and early third century BC. The area of diffusion of the Torcop Group, much larger than that of Caeretan figured vases (Fig. 52.14), includes coastal Etruria and the Faliscan and Latin areas.

The Genucilia plates:[63] still fundamental here is the study of Del Chiaro.[64] The eponymous plate in Providence (US), perhaps purchased at *Falerii veteres*, shows the name *Poplia Genucilia* pictured below the foot. The first name is typical of the Faliscan area, not Latin, and the *gentilicium* is attested in the nearby countryside of the *Ager Capenate* at Lucus Feroniae. Production begins at *Falerii veteres* (350–325 BC) and then continues in Caere. The plates are decorated with a female head (Fig. 52.15) (in the Faliscan and in the Caeretan productions) or with a star (in the Caeretan production) (Fig. 52.16).

Figure 52.13   Faliscan beaked jug, Red Figure, late fourth-early third century BC. University of Pennsylvania Museum L-64-218, image no. 151404. Turfa 2005: no. 322.

Figure 52.14   Etruscan red-figure jug, fourth century BC. University of Pennsylvania Museum MS 2517, image no. 151609 & 151608. Turfa 2005: no. 319.

Figure 52.15   Genucilia plate, Ardea, *tomba a fossa*, first half of the fourth century BC. University of Pennsylvania Museum MS 2841, image no. 46893. Turfa 2005: no. 136.

Figure 52.16   Genucilia star plate, Narce, mid- to late-fourth century BC. University of Pennsylvania Museum MS 3193, image no. 151637. Turfa 2005: no. 236.

But there are also local products. As is known, the Genucilia plates were popular for funerary offerings, in the votive deposits, in buildings related to worship and in the sanctuaries of Latium and Etruria. To a Genucilia plate, with the inscription *HRA* in black paint on the rim, found in the urban area of Caere (Vigna Parrocchiale), Del Chiaro has attributed a votive function. A number of other Genucilia plates from Caere, painted with the same inscription, allowed M. Cristofani to analyze the issue more thoroughly and to interpret the inscription as an abbreviation of the Greek theonym "HRAKLES," a deity who, at Caere, had a specific cult connected with the water. The inscription would be contrary to Hera, according to G. Colonna, followed by M. D. Gentili. The use of the Greek language would be due to Greek-speaking officials working in the cult of the goddess.

THE SILVERED POTTERY[65]

The silvered pottery, the yellow slip pottery, the polychrome pottery (Fig. 52.17) and the unglazed relief pottery were created to mimic metal prototypes. Volsinian, Faliscan and Volterran productions have been identified. Noteworthy are their contacts with Apulia and Macedonia: for example, the oinochoe shape VI is borrowed from Macedonian specimens (from Stauropolis, Derveni, Arzos and Vergina). In the repertoire there are many scenes of Amazons, derived from the decoration of the Mausoleum of Halicarnassus, revised and distributed through sketches in the Etruscan and Italiote areas. There are also the labors of Herakles, as in Greece and in Magna Graecia on mirrors and helmets.[66]

THE BLACK GLAZE WARE WITH OVERPAINTED DECORATION[67]

The second half of the fourth century BC sees the spread of the black glaze ware with over-painted decoration, that initially mimics the Attic red-figured ware. During the fourth century BC, the presence of Greek metics (probably Greeks, also Campanians) is attested by the

Figure 52.17 *Ceramica Argentata* (silvered ceramic) amphora, Orvieto, fourth century BC. University of Pennsylvania Museum MS 2511, image no. 151607. Turfa 2005: no. 317.

signature *Sokra(tes)* on a overpainted vase of the mid-fourth century BC from *Falerii Veteres*, head of a large production for the middle classes (Sokra Group[68]). The Phantom Group[69] was started by a Faliscan artist who emigrated to Caere (Jolivet) or to Tarquinia (Pianu) at the time of the war of 358–351 BC, in which Tarquinia and *Falerii Veteres* were allied against Rome.[70] Bruni has also suggested a greater articulation of production (one workshop was probably in Latium).[71] The latter hypothesis, pending confirmation, however, would make likely, I think, the wide distribution of this group through southern Latium and Rome itself. With this group is associated the Ferrara T 585 Southern Group or the Palmetta Southern Group[72] (late fourth or early third century BC), that includes *skyphoi* with white triangular palmette within a metope; the Northern one,[73] 330–300 BC, includes the Ferrara T 585 Group (small Volterran *skyphoi* with palmettes), the Ferrara T 156 Group (small Volterran *skyphoi* with swan and palmettes) and the Ferrara T 408 Group (or the Volterran Swan) with swan on side A and B. The technical characteristics of the Saint Valentin Group[74] vases and of the Imitation of Gnathia Style[75] vases seem to refer back to southern Etruria, especially to Tarquinia. Many features are a symptom of the transmission of technical know-how that took place through a direct contact between craftsmen, perhaps by transfer of Apulian artisans to Etruria.[76]

For that period, the problem has been discussed especially in relation to the *Pocola deorum* production.[77] The *Pocola deorum*, dated between the late fourth and early decades of the third century BC, are a small number of vases with an overpainted inscription and almost always overpainted decoration, influenced by Apulian vase painting, connected to a part of the *Atelier des Petites estampilles* production. The vases are dominated by figures of Eros, enriched with inscriptions in Latin of all deities, which include some cults introduced in Rome between 303 and 291 BC such as Salus, Bellona, Venus and Aesculapius. Cristofani thought that the production of *Pocola deorum* was related to the transfer to Rome of Vulcian artisans after the Roman conquest of Vulci in 280 BC. The Hesse Group (300–280 BC) is connected by technique and overpainted decoration but the style is more properly Etruscan. The group is tentatively attributed to Vulci. The cup from Vulci, currently in London, that depicts a hunter sitting in a gesture of meditation shows a genre of painting that some scholars have identified with that of Protogenes of Ialysos, a painter of the age of Alexander the Great. There are close contacts with Gnathia pottery of Taranto, even if the quality is much higher in this case. The Etruscan figurative pottery leaves the field to the black gloss ware, which henceforth will be destined to dominate not only in Etruria, but in the entire Mediterranean basin.

NOTES

1   I would like to thank Jean MacIntosh Turfa for inviting me to write this important chapter. I am also grateful to Jean for giving me the opportunity to illustrate some vases in the University of Pennsylvania Museum of Archaeology and Anthropology of Philadelphia (US) and for the revision of my English translation of the text. The vases illustrated are also in MacIntosh Turfa (2005). For a good overall view of the subject please refer to Martelli (1987b). In this book you will also find beautiful color photographs of the masterpieces of the Etruscan vase-painting mentioned in this chapter. See also Ambrosini, Jolivet (2013). Since the bibliography of each production and each individual artist is large, here it has necessarily been selected and will be mentioned especially in the most recent publications. The abbreviations used for the periodicals are those of the *Archäologische Bibliographie*.

2 For a new critical point of view on Etrusco-geometric pottery: Martelli (2008). Among the recent publications: Szilágyi (2005a); Neri (2008); Michetti (2009); Paoletti (2009); Williams (2009); Hussein (2009); Boitani, Neri, Biagi (2010); Neri (2010); Boitani (2010).

3 See, for example, Rizzo, M. A. (2000).

4 See, for exemple, Szilágyi (2005a).

5 Boitani (2001); Boitani (2005); Rizzo (2005).

6 Rizzo (2005a), 333.

7 Leach (1986); Leach (1987).

8 Martelli (1987a); Martelli (1987c); Martelli (1988); Simon (1995); Modenese (1997).

9 Buranelli (1985); Micozzi (1994).

10 Menichetti (1998); Martelli (2001); Camporeale (2007).

11 Dougherty (2003); Izzet (2004); Bagnasco Gianni (2007); Bonaudo (2008–09).

12 Coen (1992); Micozzi (1994); Geppert (2000); Geppert, Gaultier (2000); Strandberg Olofsson (2004); Micozzi (2005); Vistoli (2008); Medori (2010).

13 Micozzi (2005).

14 Martelli (1989).

15 De Puma (2010).

16 Botto (2006); Medori (2010).

17 Among the most recent publications on Etrusco-Corinthian vases, are noted: Johansson (1993); Szilágyi (1993a); Szilágyi (1993b); Martinez-Pinna (1994); Szilágyi, Fless (1999); Sidorova (2004); Strøm (2004–05); Voegtle (2005); Frère (2008); Bruni (2009); Bellelli (2009); Gabrielli (2010).

18 Szilágyi (1992); Szilágyi (1998).

19 Giuliano (2000).

20 Cerchiai (1990).

21 Colonna (2006).

22 Hemelrijk (1956); Kallipolitis (1956); Friis Johansen (1962); Schauenburg (1969); Hemelrijk - Lubsen-Admiraal (1977–78); Isler (1983); Hemelrijk (1984); Cahn (1986); Hemelrijk (1989); Rizzo (1989); Gaultier (1995); Hemelrijk (2000); Pedroni (2000–01); Pedroni (2002); Bonaudo (2003); Bonaudo (2004); Rizzo (2005b); Hemelrijk (2008); Hemelrijk (2009); Rizzo (2010–11).

23 For the Campana *dinoi* see Hemelrijk (2007) and Ambrosini (2008), 339, with all the references at note 50; for the Campana *hydriai*: Waiblinger (1974), with references.

24 Cook, Dupont (1998), 108.

25 See Martelli (1981), 9–10; Cerchiai (1995), with references (and the unfavorable remark in Hemelrijk (2007), 380–381, 389, note 127; Rizzo (2010–11).

26 Rizzo (2005b).

27 Ambrosini (2008).

28 Martelli (1981).

29 For recent synthesis: Gaultier (1995); Gaultier (2000); Gaultier (2003); Gaultier (2005); Rizzo (2007).

30 Hannestad (1976); Tiverios (1976); Stibbe (1977); Buccellato - Gatti (1978); Drukker (1979); Rizzo (1981); Raeder (1983); Rizzo (1983); Ginge (1988); Lund - Rathje (1988); Wehgartner (1988); Schianchi (1990); Williams (2005); Prata (2006–07); Rizzo (2009).

31 von Bothmer (1956); Hannestad (1974); Hannestad (1976).

32 Hannestad (1976); Rizzo (1981); Rizzo (1983).

33 Raeder (1983).

34 Drukker (1979).

35 Lombardo (1961); Zilverberg (1977); Zilverberg (1986); Gaultier (1987); Rizzo (1994); Rallo (2009).

36 Schauenburg (1963); Scheffer (1977); Drukker (1986); Werner (2005).

37 Among the most recent publications: Ambrosini (1998a), with references; Olivier (2000–01); Palmieri (2005); Szilágyi (2005b); Bruni (2006); Bonaudo (2006–07); Bentz (2009); Bonfante (2009); Bruni (2010).

38 Bonfante (2009).

39 Szilágyi (2004); Martelli (2004).

40 Szilágyi (1973). Two articles by M. Scarrone and S. Bruni are now in press.

41 Waiblinger (1980); Bruni (1988); Bruni (1993); Bonamici (2005a); Bonamici (2005b).

42 See: Beazley (1947); Del Chiaro (1974a); Pianu (1980); Jolivet (1982); Jolivet (1984); Cavagnaro Vanoni, Serra Ridgway (1989); Cristofani (1992); Harari (2000).

43 Heurgon (1966); Shefton (1967).

44 Gilotta (1986); Gilotta (1998).

45 Bocci Pacini (1979a).

46 Bocci Pacini (1982); Melli (2009).

47 Gilotta (1981); Gilotta (1984a); Gilotta (1984b); Gilotta (1985); Adembri (1985); Adembri (1988); Gilotta (1988); Bertoletti Zanchi (1989); Adembri (1990); Gilotta (1990); Adembri (1991); Gilotta (1991); Gilotta (2003); Gilotta (2005).

48 Denoyelle (1993).

49 Gilotta (2003).

50 Ambrosini (2009a).

51 Bocci Pacini (1979b).

52 Adembri (1981); Arias (1985); Colonna (1985); Dragoni (2006).

53 Stenico (1965); Harari (1980); Harari (1985); Del Chiaro (1986a); Harari (1988a); Harari (1988b); Del Chiaro (1989); Harari (1990a); Mangani (1992); Canocchi (1998); Muggia (2000); Rastrelli (2009); Gilotta (2010).

54 Cristofani (1995).

55 Del Chiaro (1974b); Harari (1990b).

56 Villard, Gaultier (1985).

57 Ambrosini (1999–2000); Ambrosini (2001).

58 Ambrosini (1998b); Ambrosini (2004); Ambrosini (2007).

59 Del Chiaro (1964).

60 Del Chiaro (1966); Del Chiaro (1974a); Jolivet (1982).

61 Ambrosini (2009), 49–50, with references.

62 Ambrosini (2009b) 52–53, with references.

63 Ambrosini (2009b), 53–56, with references.

64 Del Chiaro (1957).

65 Most recently, Guzzi (2002); Barbieri (2003); Michetti (2003); Michetti (2005); Jolivet (2006); Ambrosini (2010a).

66 Ambrosini (2010b).

67 See: Pianu (1978); Jolivet (1980); Pianu (1982); Pianu (1988); Bruni (1992).

68 Rupp (1972); Pianu (1978); Jolivet (1980); Del Chiaro (1986); Gorini (1986–87); Michetti (1993).

69 Pianu (1978); Knops (1987); Bruni (1992); Berti (1997); Ambrosini (2009b), 59–60, with references.

70 Pianu (1978), 184.

71 Bruni (1992), 62.

72 Ambrosini (2009b), 91–92, with bibliographic references.

73 Vismara (1985); Riccioni (1987).

74 Bruni (1992).

75 Bruni (1992); Ambrosini (2009b), 64–66, with bibliographic references.

76 Ambrosini (2010b).

77 Cifarelli, Ambrosini, Nonnis (2002–2003).

BIBLIOGRAPHY

Adembri, B. (1981) "Due nuovi Gruppi di vasi orvietani a figure rosse," *Prospettiva* 27, 14–26.

——(1985) "Ceramica falisca ed etrusca a figure rosse. Qualche precisazione" in *Contributi alla ceramica etrusca tardo-classica*, 17–20.

——(1988) "The earliest Faliscan red-figured workshops and their relationship with Attic and South Italian vase-painting" in Christiansen, Melander (1988) 7–16.

——(1990) "La più antica produzione di ceramica falisca a figure rosse. Inquadramento stilistico e cronologico" in *La civiltà dei Falisci. Atti del XV Convegno di studi etruschi ed italici, Civita Castellana 28–31 maggio 1987*, Florence: Olschki, 233–244.

——(1991) "Il Pittore di Berlino F 2948 nell'ambito dei pittori di kylikes falisci," *Prospettiva* 63, 40 47.

——(ed.) (2005) Αειμνηστος. *Miscellanea di studi per Mauro Cristofani*, Florence: Centro Di.

Ambrosini, L. (1998a) "Il Pittore di Micali. Nota iconografica sulla raffigurazione di due teste isolate," *ArchCl* 50, 343–361.

——(1998b) "Il Gruppo del Foro (The Foro Group) nel quadro della ceramica falisca a figure rosse. Un esempio di uso selettivo di cartoni," *StEtr* 64, 149–172.

——(1999–2000) "Ceramica falisca a figure rosse: the Satyr and Dolphin Group (Pittore di Würzburg 820) e lo schema del Dolphin-Rider," *ArchCl* 51, 245–276.

——(2001) "The Satyr and Dolphin Group. Un addendum," *ArchCl* 52, 223–227.

——(2004) "Novità sul Gruppo del Foro," *ArchCl* 55, 295–304.

——(2007) "Ceramica etrusca e falisca a figure rosse ad Aleria," *AnnFaina* 14, 365–404.

——(2008) "Su un dinos a figure nere da Falerii Veteres," *ArchCl* 59, 323–356.

——(2009a) "Sulla ceramica attica a figure rosse del primo quarto del IV secolo a.C. da *Falerii Veteres*" in Bruni (ed.), 17–26.

——(2009b) *La cisterna arcaica con l'incluso deposito di età ellenistica. (Scavi Santangelo 1945–1946 e Università di Roma "La Sapienza" 1996 e 2006). Il santuario di Portonaccio a Veio.* III, Monumenti Antichi dei Lincei, Serie Miscellanea Vol. XIII, Rome: Giorgio Bretschneider.

——(2010a) "Sui vasi plastici configurati a prua di nave (trireme) in ceramica argentata e a figure rosse," *MEFRA* 122, 73–115.

——(2010b) "Produzioni artistiche e artigianali" in Dalla Riva, Di Giuseppe (2010) F / F8 / 6. Available at: http://151.12.58.75/archeologia/bao_document/articoli/6_AMBROSINI.pdf, 54–80.

Ambrosini, L. and Jolivet, V. (eds) (2013) *Les potiers d'Étrurie et leur monde: contacts, échanges, transferts. Hommages à Mario A. Del Chiaro*, Paris: Éditions Armand Colin, in press.

Amyx, D. A. (1962) "A Pontic oinochoe in Seattle" in M. Renard (ed.), *Hommages à Albert Grenier*, Collection Latomus Vol. LVIII, Bruxelles: Berchem, 121–134.

Arias, P. E. (1985) "Sulla ceramica orvietana di tarda età classica ed ellenistica," *AnnFaina* 2, 133–141.

Bagnasco Gianni, G. (2007) "Aristonothos. Il vaso," *Aristonothos. Scritti per il Mediterraneo antico* 1, V–XV.

Barbieri, G. (2003) "Ceramica argentata da Viterbo," *MEFRA* 115, 207–229.

Bartoloni, G. and Delpino, F. (eds) (2005) *Oriente e Occidente: metodi e discipline a confronto. Riflessioni sulla cronologia dell'età del ferro in Italia*, Atti dell'Incontro di studi, Rome, 30–31 October 2003, numero monografico di "Mediterranea," I, 2004, Pisa-Rome: Istituti editoriali e poligrafici internazionali.

Beazley, J. D. (1947) *Etruscan Vase Painting*, Oxford: Clarendon Press.

Bellelli, V. (2009) "Etrusco-Corinthian notes. A class of pottery and its socio-economic context in two centuries of scholarship" in V. Nørskov, L. Hannestad, C. Isler-Kerényi *et al.* (eds), *The world of Greek vases*, Analecta Romana Instituti Danici. Supplementa, 41, Rome: Quasar, 77–87.

Bentz, M. (2009) "Der Micali-Maler in Bonn" in Bruni (ed.) (2009), 83–89.

Berti, F. (1997) "Una oinochoe del Phantom-Group a Spina" in *Studi in onore di Nereo Alfieri*, Ferrara: Lito-tipografia artigiana, 43–51.

Bertoletti Zanchi, D. (1989) "Uno stamnos protofalisco della Collezione Torno di Milano," *NotMilano* 43–44, 1–15.

Bocci Pacini, P. (1979a) "Alcune coppe etrusche di imitazione attica" in *Studi per Enrico Fiumi*, Pisa: Pacini Editore, 61–72.

——(1979b) "Nota su alcuni vasi etruschi a figure rosse del Gruppo Campanizzante," *AnnAcEtr* 11, 73–83.

——(1982) "Il Pittore di Sommavilla Sabina ed il problema della nascita delle figure rosse in Etruria," *StEtr* 50, 23–39.

Boitani, F. (2001) "La ceramica greca e di tipo greco a Veio nell'VIII secolo a.C." in A. M. Moretti Sgubini (ed.), *Veio, Cerveteri, Vulci. Città d'Etruria a confronto*, Exhibition catalogue, Rome: "L'ERMA" di Bretschneider, 106.

——(2005) "Le più antiche ceramiche greche e di tipo greco a Veio" in Bartoloni, Delpino (eds), 319–332.

——(2010) "Veio. La Tomba dei Leoni Ruggenti: dati preliminari" in P. A. Gianfrotta, A. M. Moretti (eds), *Archeologia nella Tuscia. Atti Incontro di Studio Viterbo 2007. Daidalos* 10, Rome: "L'ERMA" di Bretschneider, 23–47.

Boitani, F.- Neri, S. and Biagi, F. (2010) "Riflessi della ceramica geometrica nella più antica pittura funeraria veiente" in Dalla Riva, Di Giuseppe (eds), F / F7 / 3. Available at: http://151.12.58.75/ archeologia/bao_document/articoli/3_BOITANI.pdf, 20–27>.

Bonamici, M. (2005a) "Scene di viaggio all'aldilà nella ceramografia chiusina" in Gilotta (ed.), 33–44.

——(2005b) "Dalla vita alla morte tra Vanth e Turms Aitas" in Adembri (ed.), 522–538.

Bonaudo, R. (2003) "L'ascesa di Efesto all'Olimpo. Il caso delle hydriae ceretane" in I. Colpo, I. Favaretto and F. Ghedini (eds), *Iconografia 2001. Studi sull'immagine. Atti convegno Padova 2001*, Rome: Quasar, 101–109.

——(2004) *La culla di Hermes. Iconografia e immaginario delle hydriai ceretane*, Monografie della rivista "Archeologia classica," 1, Rome: "L'ERMA" di Bretschneider.

——(2006–07) "Dalla ceramica a figure nere alla Tomba del Triclinio. Un immaginario visuale delle rappresentazioni degli uccelli su alcuni monumenti figurati etruschi," *AnnAStorAnt* 13–14, 157–172.

——(2008–09) "In rotta per l'Etruria. Aristonothos, l'artigiano e la metis di Ulisse," *AnnAStorAnt* 15–16, 143–149.

Bonfante, L. (2009) "Manici di specchi dionisaci" in Bruni (ed.) (2009), 151–155.

Brijder, H. A. G., Drukker, A. A. and Neeft, C. W. (eds) (1986) *Enthousiasmos. Essays on Greek and Related pottery presented to J.M. Hemelrijk*, Amsterdam: Oxbow Books.

Bruni, S. (1988) "Autour d'un groupe de vases étrusques surpeints" in Christiansen Melander, (eds), 88–98.

——(1992) "Le ceramiche con decorazione sovradipinta" in A. Romualdi (ed.), *Populonia in età ellenistica. I materiali dalle necropoli. Atti del seminario, Florence 30 June 1986*, Florence: Il Torchio, 58–109.

——(1993) "Ceramiche sovradipinte del V secolo a.C. dal territorio chiusino. Il Gruppo Vagnonville. Una proposta di definizione" in *La civiltà di Chiusi e del suo territorio. Atti del XVII Convegno di studi etruschi ed italici, Chianciano Terme 28 May–1 June 1989*, Florence: Olschki, 271–295.

——(2006) "Ullastret e il Pittore di Micali. Appunti sulla produzione di kylikes nell'Etruria arcaica," *StEtr* 72, 97–116.

——(ed.) (2009) *Etruria e Italia preromana. Studi in onore di Giovannangelo Camporeale*, Pisa-Rome: Fabrizio Serra Editore.

——(2009) *Le ceramiche corinzie ed etrusco-corinzie. Gravisca*, 2, Bari: Edipuglia.

——(2010) "Note micaliane. Contributi per il catalogo del Pittore di Micali," *Mediterranea* 7, 17–47.

Buccellato, A. and Gatti, S. (1978) "Gruppo dei vasi pontici. Alcune osservazioni sul problema dei rapporti con la coeva pittura tombale tarquinese," *ArchCl* 30, 193–200.

Buranelli, F. (1985) *L'urna Calabresi di Cerveteri*, Studia archaeologica, 41, Rome: "L'ERMA" di Bretschneider.

Cahn, H. A. (1986) "Addendum caeretanum" in Brijder, Drukker and Neeft (eds), 35–38.

Camporeale, G. (2007) "Ancora sull'anfora di Würzburg del Pittore dell'Eptacordo," *PP* 62, 441–450.

Canocchi, D. (1998) "Due kylikes del Gruppo Clusium. Nuove proposte" in *In memoria di Enrico Paribeni*, Rome: Giorgio Bretschneider, 103–106.

Cavagnaro Vanoni, L. and Serra Ridgway, F. R. (1989) *Vasi etruschi a figure rosse. Dagli scavi della Fondazione Lerici nella necropoli dei Montarozzi a Tarquinia*, Studia archaeologica, 51, Rome: "L'ERMA" di Bretschneider.

Cerchiai, L. (1990) *Le officine etrusco-corinzie di Pontecagnano,* AIONArch. Quaderni, 6, Naples: Istituto Universitario Orientale.

——(1995) "Il programma figurativo dell'hydria Ricci," *AntK* 38, 81–91.

Christiansen, J. and Melander, T. (eds) (1988) *Proceedings of the 3rd Symposium of Ancient Greek and Related Pottery, Copenhagen August 31–September 4, 1987*, København: Nationalmuseet - Ny Carlsberg Glyptotek, Thorvaldsens Museum.

Cifarelli, F. M., Ambrosini, L. and Nonnis, D. (2002–2003) "Nuovi dati su Segni medio-repubblicana a proposito di un nuovo pocolom dall'acropoli," *RendPontAcc* 75, 245–325.

Coen, A. (1992) "Un gruppo vulcente di vasi in White-on-Red," *Prospettiva* 68, 45–53.

Colonna, G. (1985) "Società e cultura a Volsinii," *AnnFaina* 2, 101–131.

——(2006) "Un pittore veiente del Ciclo dei Rosoni: Velthur Ancinies" in M. Bonghi Jovino (ed.), *Tarquinia e le civilità del Mediterraneo (Atti Convegno internazionale Milano 2004) Quaderni di Acme* 77, Milan: Cisalpino Istituto Universitario, 163–185.

Contributi alla ceramica etrusca tardo-classica. Atti del Seminario, Rome 11 May 1984, Rome: CNR.

Cook, R. M. and Dupont, P. (1998) *East Greek Pottery*, London-New York: Routledge.

Cristofani, M. (1992) "La ceramografia etrusca fra età tardo-classica ed ellenismo," *StEtr* 58, 89–114.

——(1995) "'Mystai kai bakchoi.' Riti di passaggio nei crateri volterrani," *Prospettiva* 80, 2–14.

Dalla Riva, M. and Di Giuseppe, H. (eds) (2010) *Meetings between Cultures in the Ancient Mediterranean. Proceedings of the 17th International Congress of Classical Archaeology*, Rome 22–26 September 2008. *BA* on line I 2010/ Volume speciale I.

Del Chiaro, M. A. (1957) *The Genucilia Group. A Class of Etruscan Red-Figured Plates. University of California publications in classical archaeology*, 3, 4, Berkeley-Los Angeles: University of California Press.

——(1964) "The Full-Sakkos Group. Faliscan red-figured skyphoi and bell-kraters," *StEtr* 32, 73–87.

——(1966) "The Caeretan figured Group," *AJA* 70, 31–36.

——(1974a) *Etruscan red-figured vase-painting at Caere*, Berkeley-Los Angeles: University of California Press.

——(1974b) *The Etruscan Funnel Group. A Tarquinian red-figured Fabric*, Florence: Sansoni Editore.

——(1986a) "A Clusium Group duck-askos in Malibu" in *Greek vases in the J. Paul Getty Museum*, 3, 139–142.

——(1986b) "An Etruscan Sokra Group kylix in Texas," *NumAntCl* 15, 125–127.

——(1989) "Two Etruscan vases in Japan. A Clusium-Group duck-askos and a Volterran kelebe," *RM* 96, 293–303.

Denoyelle, M. (1993) "Sur la personnalité du Peintre d'Arnò. Un point de jonction entre Grande-Grèce et Etrurie," *RA*, 53–70.

De Puma, R. D. (2010) "Crustumerium and Etruria" in Dalla Riva and Di Giuseppe (eds), /F / F6 / 8. Available at: http://151.12.58.75/archeologia/bao_document/articoli/8_DEPUMA.pdf, 96–101.

Dougherty, C. (2003) "The Aristonothos krater. Competing stories of conflict and collaboration" in C. Dougherty and L. Kourke (eds), *The cultures within ancient Greek culture. Contact, conflict, collaboration*, Cambridge: Cambridge University Press, 35–56.

Dragoni, C. (2006) "I vasi del gruppo di Vanth del Museo Claudio Faina in Orvieto. Alcune precisazioni" in *Italia antiqua*, 189–213.

Drukker, A. (1973) "Een pontische oinochoe in het Allard Pierson Museum," *VerAmstMeded* 7, 4–5.

——(1979) "An Amphora without Silens by the Silen Painter," *BABesch* 54, 65–71.

——(1986) "The Ivy Painter in Friesland" in Brijder and Drukker (eds), 39–48.

Fleming, S. J. (1970) "Thermoluminescent authenticity testing of a Pontic amphora," *Archaeometry* 12, 129–131.

Frère, D. (2008) "Deux vases inédites du Peintre de Castellani," *BAntFr* (2002) [2008], 189–200.

Freyer-Schauenburg, B. (1975) "Die Geranomachie in der archaischen Vasenmalerei. Zu einem pontischen Kelch in Kiel" in *Wandlungen. Studien zur antiken und neueren Kunst Ernst Homann-Wedeking gewidmet*, Waldsassen: Stiftland-Verlag, 76–83.

Friis Johansen, K. (1962) "Eine neue Caeretaner Hydria," *OpRom* 4, 61–81.

Gabrielli, R. (2010) *Materiali del Museo archeologico nazionale di Tarquinia, 19. Ceramica etrusco-corinzia del Museo archeologico di Tarquinia*, Archaeologica 155, Rome: Giorgio Bretschneider.

Gatto, M. (2006) "Una classe vascolare falisca d'età orientalizzante. I biconici fittili" in *Italia antiqua*, 239–278.

Gaultier, F. (1987) "Dal Gruppo della Tolfa alla Tomba dei Tori. Tra ceramica e pittura parietale" in M. Bonghi Jovino (ed.), *Tarquinia. Ricerche, scavi e prospettive. Atti del convegno internazionale di studi "La Lombardia per gli Etruschi," Milan 24 – 25 June 1986*, Milan: Edizioni ET, 209–218.

——(1995) *Corpus vasorum antiquorum. France, 35. Musée du Louvre, 24*, Paris: Boccard.

——(2000) "Le ceramiche dipinte di età arcaica" in Torelli (ed.), 420–437.

——(2003) *Corpus vasorum antiquorum. France, 39. Musée du Louvre, 26*, Paris: Boccard.

——(2005) "Céramiques à figures noires de Cerveteri. La production du début du Ve siècle avant J.-C." in *Dinamiche di sviluppo delle città nell'Etruria meridionale. Veio, Caere, Tarquinia, Vulci. Atti del XXIII Convegno di studi etruschi ed italici. Roma, Veio, Cerveteri-Pyrgi, Tarquinia, Tuscania, Vulci, Viterbo. 1 – 6 October 2001*, Pisa-Rome: Istituti editoriali e poligrafici internazionali, 639–644.

Geppert, K. (2000) "Vrais vases, faux décor. Nouvelles considérations sur le décor de deux vases étrusques du Louvre," *RLouvre* 50, Nr. 1, 33–38.

Geppert, K. and Gaultier, F. (2000) "Zwei Pasticci und ihre Folgen. Die Bildmotive der Caeretaner Pyxiden D 150 und D 151 im Louvre" in F. Prayon and W. Röllig (eds), *Der Orient und Etrurien. Zum Phänomen des Orientalisierens im westlichen Mittelmeerraum, 10.–6. Jh. v.Chr. Akten des Kolloquiums, Tübingen 1997*, Pisa : Istituti editoriali e poligrafici internazionali, 211–218.

Gilotta, F. (1981) "Cratere etrusco a figure rosse da Populonia," *Prospettiva* 25, 30–36.

——(1984a) "Contributo alla ceramografia vulcente tardo classica," *BdA* 69, Nr.24, 41–52.

——(1984b) "A proposito della oinochoe di Castle Ashby," *Prospettiva* 37, 46–51.

——(1985) "Il problema 'earlier Red Figure'" in *Contributi alla ceramica etrusca tardo-classica*, 25–33.

——(1986) "Appunti sulla più antica ceramica etrusca a figure rosse," *Prospettiva* 45, 2–18.

——(1988) "Notes on some early Etruscan Red-Figure workshops" in Christiansen, Melander (ed.), 195–200.

——(1990) "Il cratere F 2959 nei Musei di Berlino" in H. Here and M. Kunze (eds), *Die Welt der Etrusker. Internationales Kolloquium 24.–26. Oktober 1988 in Berlin*, Berlin: Akademie-Verlag, 259–263.

——(1991) "Da Cerveteri," *ArchCl* 43, 955–959.

——(1998) "Addenda alla più antica ceramica etrusca a figure rosse," *StEtr* 64, 135–148.

——(2003) "Aspetti delle produzioni ceramiche a Orvieto e Vulci tra V e IV secolo a.C.," *AnnFaina* 10, 205–240.

——(2005) "L'Aiace di Palermo tra teatro e ideologia funeraria" in Gilotta (ed.), 73–77.

——(ed.) (2005) *Pittura parietale, pittura vascolare. Ricerche in corso tra Etruria e Campania. Atti della giornata di studio Santa Maria Capua Vetere 28 May 2003*, Naples: Arte tipografica.

——(2010) "Chiusi e il Clusium Group. Un nuovo documento dagli scavi di Orvieto," *OpAthRom* 3, 179–184.

Ginge, B. (1988) "A new evaluation of the origins of Tyrrhenian pottery. Etruscan precursors of Pontic ceramics" in Christiansen, Melander (eds), 201–210.

Giullano, A. (2000) "Ancora sul Pittore delle Rondini" in *Damarato. Studi di antichità classica offerti a Paola Pelagatti*, Milan: Mondadori Electa, 126–129.

Gorini, P. (1986–87) "Una kylix lacunosa del gruppo Sokra da Populonia (Livorno)," *RassAPiomb* 6, 265–271.

Guzzi, O. (2002) "Note su alcune composizioni narrative nella ceramica volsiniese," *Prospettiva* 106–107, 118–125.

Hannestad, L. (1974) *The Paris Painter. An Etruscan vase-painter*, København: Munksgaard.

——(1976) *The followers of the Paris Painter*, Det kongelige danske videnskabernes selskab. Historisk-filosofiske meddelelser, 47, 4, København: Munksgaard.

Harari, M. (1980) *Il Gruppo Clusium della ceramografia etrusca*, Bibliotheca archaeologica, 1, Rome: "L'ERMA" di Bretschneider.

——(1985) "Nuove considerazioni sui Gruppi Clusium e Volaterrae" in *Contributi alla ceramica etrusca tardo-classica*, 35–54.

——(1988a) "Les gardiens du paradis. Iconographie funéraire et allégorie mythologique dans la céramique étrusque à figures rouges tardive," *NumAntCl* 17, 169–193.

——(1988b) "Iconographie funéraire et allégorie mythologique dans la céramique étrusque à figures rouges tardive" in Christiansen, Melander (ed.), 231–241.

——(1990a) "Ceramiche volterrane a Spina. Per un'interpretazione storica" in A. Cambitoglou and J.-P. Descoudres (eds), Εὐμουσία. *Ceramic and iconographic studies in honour of Alexander Cambitoglou, Mediterranean Archaeology Supplement*, Sydney: Meditarch, 247–252.

——(1990b) "Il Pittore dell'Aja a Leida e il problema del Gruppo Funnel," *OudhMeded* 70, 33–45.

——(2000) "Le ceramiche dipinte di età classica ed ellenistica" in M. Torelli (ed.), 439–453.

Hemelrijk, J. M. (1956) *De Caeretaanse hydriae*, Rotterdam: Wegeling's Drukkerijen.

——(1984) *Caeretan hydriae, voll. I–II*, Forschungen zur antiken Keramik. 2. Reihe. Kerameus, 5, Mainz: Philip von Zabern Verlag.

——(1989) "An alabastron produced by the workshop of the Caeretan hydriae" in *Atti Secondo Congresso Internazionale Etrusco*, Florence 1985, Rome: Giorgio Bretschneider, 729–732.

——(2000) "Three Caeretan hydriai in Malibu and New York" in *Greek vases in the J. Paul Getty Museum*, 6, 87–158.

——(2007) "Four New Campana Dinoi, a New Painter, Old Questions," *BABesch* 82, 365–421.

——(2008) "A fake or not a fake…An ancient practical joke?," *BABesch* 83, 47–60.

——(2009) *More about Caeretan hydria. Addenda et clarificanda*, Allard Pierson series, 17, Amsterdam: Allard Pierson Museum.

Hemelrijk, J. M. and Lubsen-Admiraal, S. M. (1977–78) "Notes on some Caeretan hydriae," *BABesch* 52–53, 1–15.

Heurgon, J. (1966) "La coupe d'Aulus Vibenna" in *Mélanges d'archéologie, d'épigraphie et d'histoire offerts à Jérôme Carcopino*, Paris: Hachette, 515–528.

Hussein, A. M. (2009) "Imports, imitations, and immigrants. A note on Pithekoussai" in *Koine. Mediterranean studies in honor of R. Ross Holloway*, Oxford: Oxbow Books, 75–77.

Isler, H. P. (1983) "Drei neue Gefässe aus der Werkstatt der Caeretaner Hydrien," *JdI* 98, 15–56.

Italia antiqua. Storia dell'Etruscologia tra archeologia e storia della cultura. Atti del II corso di perfezionamento (Anno accademico 2003–2004). L'arte e la produzione artigianale in Etruria. Atti del III corso di perfezionamento (Anno accademico 2004–2005) Rome: Quasar.

Izzet, V. (2004) "Purloined letters. The Aristonothos inscription and krater" in K. Lomas (ed.), *Greek identity in the western Mediterranean. Papers in honour of Brian Shefton*, Leiden: Brill, 191–210.

Johansson, C. (1993) "Un olpe del Pittore della Sfinge Barbuta," *MedelhavsMusB* 28, 82–90.

Jolivet, V. (1980) "Exportations étrusques tardives, 4e–3e siècles, en Méditerranée occidentale," *MEFRA* 92, 681–717.

——(1982) *Recherches sur la céramique étrusque à figures rouges tardive du Musée du Louvre*, Paris: Éditions de la Réunion des musées nationaux.

——(1984) *Corpus vasorum antiquorum. France, 33. Musée du Louvre, 22*, Paris: Boccard.

——(2006) "Vases étrusques de céramique argentée provenant de Volsinies, Faléries et Volterra," review of "Le ceramiche argentate e a rilievo in Etruria nella prima età ellenistica," *JRA* 19, 396–400.

Kallipolitis, V. (1956) "Une nouvelle hydrie de Caere," *MonPiot* 48, Nr. 2, 55–62.

Knops, G. F. H. M. (1987) "Fünf Vasen der Phantomgruppe aus niederländischem Besitz," *MededRom* 47, 51–78.

Leach, S. (1986) "Subgeometric Heron pottery. Caere and Campania" in J. Swaddling (ed.), *Italian Iron Age Artefacts in the British Museum. Papers of the Sixth British Museum Classical Colloquium. London 1982*, London: Trustees of the British Museum by The British Museum Press, 305–307.

——(1987) *Subgeometric pottery from Southern Etruria*, Studies in Mediterranean archaeology and literature. Pocket-books, 54, Göteborg: Åström.

Lombardo, A. M. (1961) "Vaso etrusco a figure nere del gruppo di La Tolfa nel Museo Archeologico di Firenze," *StEtr* 29, 311–316.

Lund, J. and Rathje, A. (1988) "Italic gods and deities on Pontic vases" in Christiansen, Melander (ed.), 352–368.

MacIntosh Turfa, J. (2005) *Catalogue of the Etruscan Gallery of the University of Pennsylvania Museum of Archaeology and Anthropology*, Philadelphia: University of Pennsylvania, Museum of Archaeology and Anthropology.

Mangani, E. (1992) "Le fabbriche a figure rosse di Chiusi e Volterra," *StEtr* 58, 115–143.

Martelli, M. (1981) "Un askos del Museo di Tarquinia e il problema delle presenza nord-ioniche in Etruria," *Prospettiva* 27, 9–10.

——(1984) "Prima di Aristonothos," *Prospettiva* 38, 2–15.

——(1987a) "Per il Pittore delle Gru," *Prospettiva* 48, 2–11.

——(ed.) (1987b) *La ceramica degli Etruschi. La pittura vascolare*, Novara: De Agostini.

——(1987c) "Del Pittore di Amsterdam e di un episodio del nostos odissaico. Ricerche di ceramografia etrusca orientalizzante," *Prospettiva* 50, 4–14.

——(1988) "Un'anfora orientalizzante ceretana a Würzburg ovvero il Pittore dell'Eptacordo," *AA*, 285–296.

——(1989) "Una firma d'artista dell'Orientalizzante ceretano" in *Miscellanea ceretana*, 1, Rome: CNR, 45–49.

——(2001) "Nuove proposte per i Pittori dell'Eptacordo e delle Gru," *Prospettiva* 101, 2–18.

——(2004) "Un'anfora capitolina del Pittore dei Satiri Danzanti," *BMusRom* 18, 7–26.

——(2008) "Variazioni sul tema etrusco-geometrico," *Prospettiva*, 132, 2–30.

Martinez-Pinna, J. (1994) "L'oenochoé de Tragliatella. Considérations sur la société étrusque archaïque," *StEtr* 60, 79–92.

Medori, M. L. (2010) *La ceramica "White-on-Red" della media Etruria interna*. Sistema museale del lago di Bolsena. Quaderni, 11, Bolsena: Città di Bolsena Editrice.

Melli, P. (2009) "Un nuovo vaso del Pittore di Sommavilla e le importazioni di ceramica etrusca a figure rosse a Genova" in Bruni (ed.), 591–598.

Menichetti, M. (1998) "La pyrriche degli eroi. A proposito di un'anfora del Pittore dell'Eptacordo," *Ostraka* 7, 71–84.

Michetti, L. M. (1993) "Vasi sovradipinti della prima metà del IV secolo a.C. da Corchiano," *ArchCl* 45, Nr.1, 145–183.

——(2003) *Le ceramiche argentate e a rilievo in Etruria nella prima età ellenistica.* Accademia nazionale dei Lincei. Monumenti antichi. Serie miscellanea, 8, Rome: Giorgio Bretschneider.

——(2005) "La ceramica argentata volsiniese. Temi iconografici e scelte stilistiche," *MEFRA* 117, 99–136.

——(2009) "Note su un'anfora orientalizzante dal Tumulo di Monte Aguzzo a Veio" in Bruni (ed.), 607–615.

Micozzi, M. (1994) *White-on-red. Una produzione vascolare dell'Orientalizzante etrusco,* Terra Italia, 2, Pisa-Rome: Gruppo editoriale internazionale.

——(2005) "'White on Red': miti greci nell'Orientalizzante antico" in Adembri (ed.), 256–266.

Mingazzini, P. (1973) "Über die Echtheit dreier pontischer Amphoren," *BJb* 173, 112–116.

Modenese, C. (1997) "Uno skyphos ceretano del Pittore delle Gru?," *NotMilano* 59–60, 7–14.

Muggia, A. (2000) "La sfera infantile e il simbolismo iconografico. Alcuni casi dalla necropoli di Valle Trebba a Spina," *Ostraka* 9, 87–94.

Neri, S. (2008) "Una nuova fiasca del pellegrino. Integrazioni al repertorio vascolare veiente dell'Orientalizzante," *Aristonothos. Scritti per il Mediterraneo antico* 3, 87–109.

——(2010) *Il tornio e il pennello. Ceramica depurata di tradizione geometrica di epoca orientalizzante in Etruria meridionale (Veio, Caere, Tarquinia, Vulci)* Rome: Officina edizioni.

Olivier, Y. (2000–01) "Zwei Fragment des Micali-Malers in der Antikensammlung der Friedrich-Alexander-Universität Erlangen-Nürnberg," *Boreas* 23–24, 53–62.

Palmieri, A. (2005) "L'anfora del Pittore di Micali RC 1042 del Museo di Tarquinia. Un caso di 'special commission'?," *Mediterranea* 2, 107–132.

Paoletti, O. (2009) "Ceramica figurata etrusco-geometrica. Qualche osservazione" in Bruni (ed.), 653–660.

Pedroni, L. (2000–01) "Mito e storia su alcune idrie caeretane," *Boreas* 23–24, 63–72.

——(2002) "La battaglia del Mar Sardo su un'idria caeretana" in *Etruria e Sardegna centro-settentrionale tra l'età del bronzo finale e l'arcaismo. Atti XXI Convegno di studi etruschi ed italici, Sassari – Alghero – Oristano – Torralba 1998,* Pisa-Rome: Istituti editoriali e poligrafici internazionali, 143–148.

Pianu, G. (1978) "Due fabbriche etrusche di vasi sovradipinti. Il Gruppo Sokra ed il Gruppo del Fantasma," *MEFRA* 90, 161–187.

——(1980) *Materiali del Museo Archeologico Nazionale di Tarquinia. 1. Ceramiche etrusche a figure rosse,* Rome: Giorgio Bretschneider.

——(1982) *Materiali del Museo Archeologico Nazionale di Tarquinia. 3. Ceramiche etrusche sovra dipinte,* Archaeologica, 21, Rome: Giorgio Bretschneider.

——(1988) "Ceramiche etrusche sovradipinte di Tarquinia. Un addendum" in M. Torelli and F. H. Massa Pairault (eds), *Studia Tarquiniensia, Archaeologica,* Rome: Giorgio Bretschneider, 101–107.

Prata, E. (2006–07) "Dionysos Sphaleotas, Telephos e l'immaginario visuale. Alcune osservazioni su in'oinochoe pontica," *AnnAStorAnt* 13–14, 145–156.

Raeder, J. (1983) "Fussteller des Tityos-Malers im Antikenmuseum," *JbPreussKul* 20, 169–177.

Rallo, A. (2009) "Addenda al gruppo La Tolfa" in Bruni (ed.), 749–766.

Rastrelli, A. (2009) "Una kylix del Gruppo Clusium-Volaterrae dal territorio di Empoli" in Bruni (ed.), 767–771.

Riccioni, G. (1987) "Dalle necropoli di Spina. Valle Trebba. Gli skyphoi etruschi a palmette suddipinte della tomba 585 e revisione critica dell'eponimo Gruppo di Ferrara T. 585 del Beazley" in D. Vitali (ed.), *Celti ed Etruschi nell'Italia centro-settentrionale dal V secolo a.C. alla romanizzazione. Atti del Colloquio internazionale, Bologna 12–14 April 1985*, Bologna: University Press, 149–166.

Rizzo, M. A. (1981) "Corredi con vasi pontici da Vulci," *Xenia* 2, 13–48.

——(1983) "Contributo al repertorio iconografico della ceramica pontica," *Prospettiva* 32, 48–59.

——(1989) "Una nuova hydria ceretana ed altri prodotti della ceramografia arcaica d'Etruria," *BdA* 74, Nr. 56–57, 1–16.

——(1994) "Percorsi ceramografici tardo-arcaici ceretani," *Prospettiva* 73–74, 2–20.

——(2000) "Un'anfora dell'Orientalizzante cicladico da Cerveteri" in *Studi in onore di Paola Pelagatti*, Milan: Electa, 199–207.

——(2005a) "Ceramica geometrica greca e di tipo greco da Cerveteri" in Bartoloni and Delpino (eds), 333–378.

——(2005b) "Nuovi frammenti di un'hydria ceretana del Pittore dell'Aquila" in Adembri (ed.), 388–394.

——(2007) "La ceramica etrusca a figure nere" in D. Barbagli and M. Iozzo (eds), *Etruschi. Chiusi, Siena, Palermo. La Collezione Bonci Casuccini*, Siena: Protagon Editori Toscani, 182–197.

——(2009) "Una nuova anfora pontica del Pittore di Paride" in Bruni (ed.), 793–797.

——(2010–11) "I corredi delle hydriai ceretane e dell'hydria Ricci," *AION*, n.s. 17–18, in press.

Rupp, D. W. (1972) "The Sienese workshop of the Sokra Group," *ArchCl* 24, 13–22.

Schauenburg, K. (1963) "Eine neue Amphora des Efeumalers," *AA*, 404–430.

——(1969) "Eine caeretaner Hydria," *AntK* 12, 98–101.

Scheffer, C. (1977) "An Etruscan black-figured amphora of the Ivy-Leaf Group," *MedelhavsMusB* 12, 53–61.

Schianchi, L. (1990) "Note su due vasi Pontici inediti," *RassAPiomb* 9, 365–371.

Shefton, B. B. (1967) "Attisches Meisterwerk und etruskische Kopie," *WissZRostock* 16, 529–537.

Sidorova, N. (2004) *Corpus vasorum antiquorum. Russia, 7. Pushkin State Museum of Fine Arts, Moscow. Corinthian and Etrusco-Corinthian vases*, Rome: "L'ERMA" di Bretschneider.

Simon, E. (1995) "Argonauten beim Waffentanz, in Telemanniana et alia musicologica" in *Festschrift für Günter Fleischhauer zum 65. Geburtstag*, Oschersleben: Ziethen, 28–33.

Stenico, A. (1965) "Nuove pitture vascolari del Gruppo 'Clusium'" in *Studi in onore di Luisa Banti*, Rome: "L'ERMA" di Bretschneider, 293–307.

Stibbe, C. M. (1977) "Pontic vases at Oxford," *MededRom* 39, 7–12.

Strandberg Olofsson, M. (2004) "White-on-Red from Acquarossa. Some large decorated vessels and their chronological implications," *OpRom* 29, 73–89.

Strøm, I. (2004–05) "Il Pittore di Pozzuolo," *ScAnt* 12, 739–752.

Szilágyi, J. G. (1973) "Zur Praxias-Gruppe," *APol* 14, 95–114.

——(1981) "Impletae modis saturae," *Prospettiva* 24, 2–23.

——(1992) *Ceramica etrusco-corinzia figurata, 1. 630 – 580 a.C.*, Monumenti etruschi, 7, Florence: Olschki.

——(1993a) "Quelques remarques à propos de l'histoire de l'Atelier 'Senza Graffito' de Tarquinia," *BMusHongr* 78, 21–37.

——(1993b) "'Da buon Etrusco.' Il Pittore di Civitavecchia," *BMusBrux* 64, 39–59.

——(1998) *Ceramica etrusco-corinzia figurata, 2. 590/580–550 a.C.*, Monumenti etruschi, 8, Florence: Olschki.

——(2005a) "Dall'Attica a Narce, via Pitecusa," *Mediterranea* 2, 27–55.

——(2005b) "Due kyathoi" in Adembri (ed.), 361–377.

Szilágyi, J. G. and Fless, F. (1999) "Neuerwerbungen aus der Sammlung des Archäologischen Instituts der Universität zu Köln," *KölnJb* 32, 903–908.

Tiverios, M. A. (1976) "Οι "τυρρηνικοί" (αττικοί) αμφορείς. Η σχέση τους με τους "ποντιακούς" (ετρουσκικούς) και τον Νικοσθένη," *AEphem*, 44–57.

Torelli, M. (ed.) (2000) *Gli Etruschi*, Exhibition catalogue, Venice, Milan: Hoepli.

Villard, F. and Gaultier, F. (1985) "Les stamnoi Fould. Un dernier éclat de la peinture sur vases en Etrurie," *MonPiot* 67, 1–30.

Vismara, N. (1985) "Ceramiche ellenistiche sovradipinte. Il Gruppo Ferrara T 585," *StClOr* 35, 239–281.

Vistoli, F. (2008) "Una nuova acquisizione di ceramica 'White-on-Red' dall'ager Veientanus," *OpAthRom* 1, 63–77.

Voegtle, S. (2005) "Vier etrusko-korinthische Gefässe des Hercle-Malers in der Archäologischen Sammlung," *ASammlUnZürch* 31, 9–18.

von Bothmer, D. (1956) "Two Etruscan vases by the Paris Painter," *BMetrMus* 14, 127–132.

Waiblinger, A. (1974) *Corpus vasorum antiquorum. France, 26. Musée du Louvre, 17*, Paris: Boccard.

——(1980) "Deux vases étrusques à couleur superposée du Musée du Louvre," *CRAI*, 140–156.

Wehgartner, I. (1988) "Eine neue Pontische Oinochoe und Überlegungen zur Genese ihrer Form," *AA*, 303–325.

Werner, I. (2005) *Dionysos in Etruria. The Ivy Leaf Group.* Skrifter utgivna av Svenska institutet i Rom. 40, 58, Stockholm: Åström.

Williams, D. (2005) "The beginnings of the so-called Pontic Group and other Italian black-figure fabrics" in Adembri (ed.), 352–360.

——(2009) "The Hamilton Gray Vase" in J. Swaddling and P. Perkins (eds), *Etruscan by Definition. The Cultural, Regional and Personal Identity of the Etruscans. Papers in honour of Sybille Haynes, MBE*, London: Oxbow Books, 10–20.

Zilverberg, M. (1977) "Een La Tolfa amfoor in het Allard Pierson Museum," *VerAmstMeded* 13, 9–11.

——(1986) "The Tolfa Painter" in Brijder, Drukker and Neeft (eds), 49–60.

CHAPTER FIFTY THREE

THE MEANINGS OF BUCCHERO

———•◆•———

Richard Daniel De Puma

WHAT IS BUCCHERO?

Bucchero is the name we apply to a specific type of black pottery produced extensively by the Etruscans. It is sometimes called a "national" pottery or, unfairly, their "only independent invention."[1] The name comes from the Spanish *búcaro* first applied to South American pottery made from pungent black clay and later imitated by Portuguese potters who called it *pocaro*.[2] Discoveries of black Etruscan pottery reminded early excavators of this New World *búcaro* and so an Italian variant of the name, *bucchero*, stuck. The name has remained popular despite its having no direct connection whatsoever to the Etruscans. We have no idea what they called this kind of pottery. The modern study of bucchero is complex and cannot be examined closely here.[3]

Many scholars believe that the earliest bucchero evolved slowly from a type of impasto pottery made by the latest potters of the Villanovan culture, in other words by the people who became the Etruscans. Other experts have noted the strong similarities between certain metallic (and ivory) shapes that may have influenced the development of early bucchero. A kind of proto-bucchero is called *buccheroid impasto* by archaeologists. In *buccheroid impasto*, vessels are fired in a partial reduction atmosphere creating a black or blackish-brown surface but a lighter core. These vessels are mostly hand-built of poorly levigated clay. The earliest true bucchero appears to have been developed at ancient workshops in and around Caere (modern Cerveteri) in Southern Etruria, about 25 miles north-west of Rome. This material dates to circa 675 BC, is thrown on the wheel and is quite refined.[4] Shapes have thin walls, elegant profiles and often finely impressed, incised or modeled decoration. Some of these earliest examples are clearly derived from Greek shapes and may have been intended to imitate metallic originals. For example, very fine *kotylai* are precisely the shape of Protocorinthian *kotylai* and even have similar decorative ray motifs incised (rather than painted) around the base (Fig. 53.1, a–c). Some pieces, it is reported, were found with a silver coating still adhering to their outer surfaces to enhance the imitation of expensive metal originals (Fig. 53.1, b).[5] The high metallic sheen, so prevalent in the earliest bucchero, is probably a combination of burnishing and the application of a thin organic wash before firing.[6] The distinctive radiating patterns of burnishing, which may be achieved with a smooth pebble or the thumbnail, are often visible upon close examination. Recent studies have demonstrated that the impressed or incised decoration on many bucchero vessels was enhanced by the application of a chalky ochre or cinnabar.[7] This would have made the designs much more legible. Very rarely bucchero was painted. Traces of color, especially white and red, are visible on a few examples where they either enhance incised figures on *bucchero sottile* shapes or, more often, emphasize the relief designs of *bucchero pesante*, a later category of bucchero production.[8]

Examples of Tombs in Southern Etruria with the Earliest *Bucchero Sottile:*

Cerveteri.	Banditaccia Necropolis, Tumulo delle Nave, tomb 2, right chamber.[9]
	Banditaccia Necropolis, Tumulo I, tomb 2, right chamber.[10]
	Sorbo Necropolis, Tomba Calabresi.[11]
	Tumulo di Montetosto, tomb 2.[12]
	San Paolo, tombs 1–2.[13]
Ceri:	Casaletti, tomb 2.[14]
Veii:	Monte Michele, tomb 5, lower chamber.[15]
Tarquinia:	Tumulo di Poggio Gallinaro.[16]

Experiments conducted by a number of chemists and archaeologists have tried to duplicate this black pottery. It is important to realize that the clay is black throughout, not only on the exterior surfaces. It was long ago realized that the distinctive black sheen of bucchero was not a glaze or slip but rather the result of a reduction firing process that turned the clay black. In a reduction firing, the fire is stoked and deprived of oxygen so that a chemical change occurs in the clay. The clay's ferric oxide is reduced to ferrous oxide turning it from a reddish-brown color to black. The more complete the reduction, the blacker the core clay becomes. However, at some sites (notably the Volsinii-Orvieto area) a less than complete reduction was purposely used to produce a gray variety of bucchero. (Gray bucchero, a type of undecorated, utilitarian ware, will not be treated in this essay.)

Early archaeologists and connoisseurs noted that there were two basic types of bucchero: *bucchero sottile* ("light" bucchero) and *bucchero pesante* ("heavy" bucchero). In *sottile* the shapes are often refined, have thin walls and relatively simple decoration usually consisting of stamped or incised motifs. In *pesante* the shapes are larger, heavier (i.e. have thicker walls) and have modeled decoration. Incision is normally used to outline relief ornaments. In general, *bucchero sottile* appears in the earliest phases of production and is typical of Caeretan workshops in Southern Etruria. *Bucchero pesante* is a later product especially common in workshops at Vulci, Tarquinia, Chiusi and Orvieto. If we place the

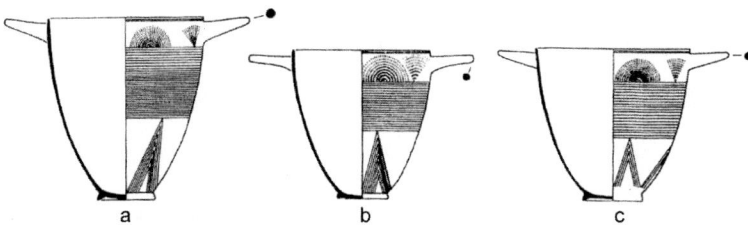

Figure 53.1a–c   Three *bucchero sottile kotylai* from Cerveteri, Banditaccia Necropolis, Tumulo 1, tomb 2, right chamber, circa 675–650 BC. Drawings from Rasmussen 1979, p. 187, Figs 116–118.

beginnings of true *bucchero sottile* at circa 675 BC, the earliest *bucchero pesante* appears about a century later, circa 575 BC, but continues to be produced into the early fifth century BC. Some scholars have seen an intermediate form of bucchero evolving from *sottile* to *pesante* in the late seventh century BC. This *bucchero transizionale* is less prestigious and more utilitarian. In the Etruscan Hellenistic period bucchero is largely replaced by a fine black-gloss pottery called Malacena Ware.

INDIGENOUS SHAPES OF *BUCCHERO SOTTILE*

Several pottery shapes that are popular in bucchero are indigenous to Italy. Perhaps the most important is the spiral amphora (Fig. 53.2), so-called because many are decorated with an incised spiral design on each side of the belly. This distinctive shape has a small, low foot, a bulbous belly, often with incised ornament, and wide ribbon-like handles that spring from the shoulder and join the rim of the flaring mouth. This shape appears very metallic and, in fact, a fine silver version with gold handles was found in the Regolini-Galassi Tomb at Caere, circa 675–650 BC.[17] This range of dates also applies to the earliest appearances of the spiral amphora in bucchero. The latest examples come from the end of the seventh century BC.

Three types of decoration appear frequently on spiral amphoras: incision (often in the form of double spirals, placed horizontally on the belly and usually framed by W-shaped designs below the handles); rouletting[18] (usually impressed "fan" motifs set vertically on the neck); ribbing (parallel striations set vertically on the belly). On some examples a small bird, fish or horse is incised above the spiral design but, in general, it is rare to find figural ornament on this shape. Several examples show incised or roulette decoration on the outer surfaces of the wide ribbon handles.

This important shape had its beginnings in hand-built impasto versions that eventually led to more refined examples that were thrown on the potter's wheel. (Some buccheroid examples as well as almost all bucchero spiral amphoras are wheel-made.) As time progresses, the shape generally becomes less squat, the foot becomes taller and more

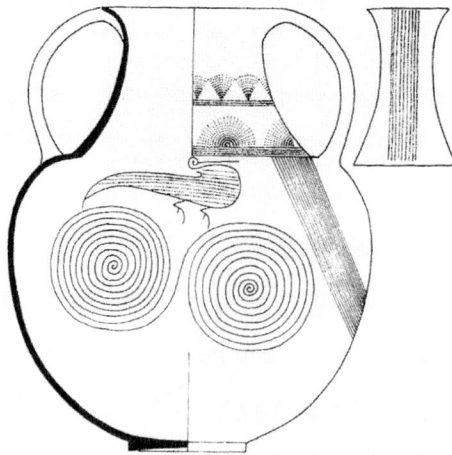

Figure 53.2 *Bucchero sottile* spiral amphora from Tarquinia, Monterozzi Necropolis, Cultrera tomb 25, circa 625–600 BC. Drawing from Rasmussen 1979, p. 163, Fig. 2.

trumpet-shaped, and the neck and handles taller. In fact, because these later examples are distinctive and represent an evolution in the shape, they have been given a different name by archaeologists: Nikosthenic amphoras (Fig. 53.3). The shape was first recognized in the work of the black-figure Athenian potter, Nikosthenes, who often signed his name *Nikosthenes epoiesen*. We now realize that Nikosthenes and his workshop of potters (active circa 530–500 BC) were imitating an indigenous Italic shape – specifically, one that was popular at Caere – but decorating it in Greek techniques (black figure, red figure or Six's technique), designed to appeal to the Etruscan market. In fact, almost all of these Greek Nikosthenic amphoras were found in and around Caere.[19] In bucchero, this shape becomes quite elegant. The proportions are attenuated and the decoration is refined. The wide ribbon handles are fully exploited as an area for both relief and, more frequently, cut-out (*ajour*) decoration, often enhanced with incision.[20] On a few exceptional pieces, there are an extra pair of handles. In addition, the wide belly friezes on Nikosthenic amphoras are sometimes incised with animal processions and other narratives. The spiral amphora and its gradual evolution into the Nikosthenic form represent a fascinating example of the steady progress of improved technical and decorative features of bucchero.

A second indigenous Italic shape is the *kantharos* (Fig. 53.4). This too, like the spiral amphora, has several metallic features and occurs in bronze examples. The standard form has a deep bowl, often with strongly-notched carination, on a tall trumpet-shaped foot. There are two high ribbon handles with struts. Decoration is often incised, and roulette fans, open or closed, frequently ornament the bowl whose carination is usually notched. In the later *pesante* examples, especially at Chiusi, the handles and bowls have relief decoration. Simple *kantharoi* with minimal incised ornament are the most common shape in bucchero.

Variants of the *kantharos* shape include a single-handled form, the *kyathos*, as well as a variant with no handles, the chalice. In both of these, we see the same variations on the theme: low feet gradually becoming taller and more flaring. An especially elaborate

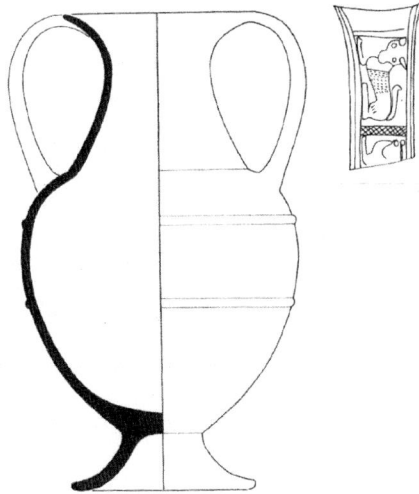

Figure 53.3 *Bucchero pesante* Nikosthenic amphora from Cerveteri, Bufolareccia tomb 999, circa 575–550 BC. From Rasmussen 1979, p. 168, Fig. 23.

form of the chalice is the so-called caryatid chalice (Fig. 53.5) with carinated bowl (often with an omphalos) and a flat ring base with four figural or perforated supports. Two ivory examples, from the Barberini Tomb at Praeneste, suggest that the ultimate inspiration for the type may be the ancient Near East. However, the distinctive carinated bowl of this and the other versions of this shape (*kantharos, kyathos*, chalice) appears in much earlier impasto examples and is thought to be Italic in origin.

BUCCHERO SOTTILE SHAPES INSPIRED BY NEAR EASTERN OR GREEK PROTOTYPES

As just mentioned, the distinctive figural supports on caryatid chalices may have been derived from Near Eastern prototypes, but the carinated bowls of the chalice shape seem to be Italic. A good example of a shape that is entirely derived from one in the Near East is the so-called Cypro-Phoenician *oinochoe* (Fig. 53.6). This jug's most characteristic feature is a tall, conical neck terminating in a small mouth. Examples appear in impasto and a number of metal examples have been found. Silver *oinochoai*, some with added gold ornaments, come from the Regolini-Galassi Tomb at Cerveteri, from Pontecagnano, and

Figure 53.4   *Bucchero kantharos*, provenance unknown, early sixth century BC. University of Iowa Museum of Art, Iowa City, inv. 1971.248. Photograph by B. Yarborough.

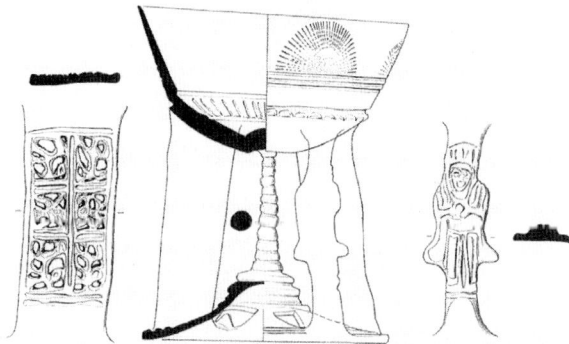

Figure 53.5   *Bucchero sottile* caryatid chalice, said to be from Chiusi or Volterra, circa 620–580 BC. From Perkins 2007, p. 98, Fig. 70a.

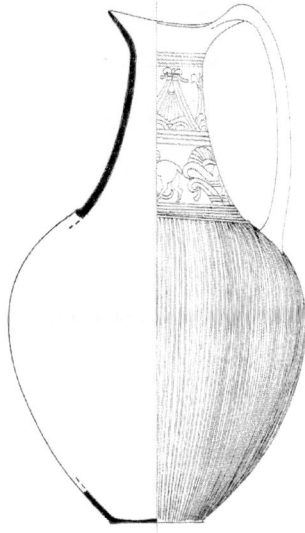

Figure 53.6 *Bucchero sottile* Cypro-Phoenician *oinochoe*, said to be from the Calabresi Tomb, Cerveteri, circa 650 BC. (Vatican, Museo Gregoriano Etrusco, inv. 20252.) Drawing adapted from Sciacca and Di Blasi 2003, p. 53, no. 14.

a number of other sites as far north as Vetulonia.[21] All date between circa 700 and 650 BC. These are almost certainly imports from the Near East, but some bronze examples (e.g. from Caere, Populonia, Narce and other sites) may represent a local response to the more precious silver and gold examples. The early bucchero examples (e.g. Tomba Calabresi, Caere[22]) are clearly inspired by these metal prototypes and are likely imitations of them. However, unlike the continuity seen in the spiral amphora form, the Cypro-Phoenician *oinochoe* evolves into a far less elegant, albeit related form in later bucchero. Instead, the original shape disappears from the Etruscan bucchero repertoire circa 625–600 BC.

Greek pottery had a strong influence on both the shapes and decorative schemes of Etruscan bucchero. An early example of this influence is the *bucchero sottile kotyle* (sometimes called a *skyphos*) from the Regolini-Galassi Tomb, Cerveteri (Fig. 53.1, b). The shape, a tall cup without lip and two horizontal handles placed near or at the rim, is a precise copy of the Protocorinthian *kotyle* and is popular in bucchero from circa 675–650 BC with variations as late as circa 600 BC. Even the decoration follows the Greek model although in bucchero incision replaced paint. Here too there are Etruscan examples in gold, silver and bronze: the famous gold *kotyle* with granulated sphinxes from the Bernardini Tomb at Praeneste;[23] important silver examples from Pontecagnano, Marsiliana d'Albegna and the Bernardini Tomb,[24] the last of which also has bronze versions. The *bucchero sottile* examples are among the finest productions of this type of pottery. Many have incredibly refined and thin walls, some less than one millimeter thick, and they are meticulously decorated with delicately impressed fans and incised lines. Exceptional pieces have modeled relief decoration.

It is interesting that the *kotyle* does not continue into later *bucchero pesante*. Rather, it is replaced by shapes imitating other types of Greek cups like the *kylix*. "The classification of bucchero cups presents some special problems. Greek influence is obvious, but not always easy to pin down with precision."[25] One important feature is that several characteristics (for example, deep or shallow bowls, lipless, or more or less pronounced lips and carinations) can occur on examples from the same context. There appears to be no simple evolution of forms. Late Protocorinthian and Ionic cups appear to be the major influences on the shapes of bucchero cups. Attic shapes, especially the Lip-cup popular in Greece circa 565–535 BC, appear to be confined to bucchero workshops in Central Etruria. Generally, decoration is simple: incised horizontal lines, rows of closed fans, the occasional ray pattern. Rarely do we find figural friezes that are incised or in relief.[26]

To summarize this first portion of the chapter, it is instructive to consider an excellent *bucchero sottile* jug (circa 650–630 BC) that was discovered in 1988 in tomb 2, San Paolo at Cerveteri (see Fig. 6.37). The shape, although the upper portion is missing, is clearly an *olpe*, a type of jug invented at Corinth that was imported in large numbers by the Etruscans and ultimately was imitated by them. In fact, there are hundreds of examples of Etrusco-Corinthian *olpai* and it is probably the most common shape for that painting style. In this specific case, the shape of the San Paolo *olpe* most closely resembles the famous Chigi vase, an *olpe* produced in Corinth circa 650 BC and exported to Etruria.[27] The tomb chamber in which the San Paolo *olpe* was found also contained locally made impasto vessels, some additional bucchero, a Protocorinthian *oinochoe*, three Protocorinthian *olpai* and one Etrusco-Corinthian *olpe*. Thus, it represents a typical collection of local and imported wares, with an especially strong concentration on Corinthian products.

The San Paolo *bucchero sottile olpe* has two wide friezes in relief with added incisions to enhance details. The technique is clearly reminiscent of metalwork. At the top, in the handle zone, the frieze depicts three felines. Two of them are devouring humans. In each case, a single leg hanging from the animal's mouth is the only part of the human that remains visible. This motif, which appears frequently on early bucchero pottery, is of uncertain significance.[28] The lower frieze (see Fig. 6.37) shows eleven human figures in three groups, plus one independent figure. Incised inscriptions identify two of these characters as well as an object (see also Chapter 24). Occupying the central position is a woman shown in profile facing left and inscribed *metaia* (Medea) (see Fig 6.37). In front of her a youth, unlabelled, emerges from a cauldron and almost certainly represents the figure of Jason, rejuvenated by Medea's magic. Six young men, carrying a long object, stride toward Medea. The object is inscribed *kanna*, perhaps "gift" or "prize," and may represent a lengthy piece of cloth (it has zigzag fringes and hems), the Golden Fleece, or a ship's folded sail.[29] To the left of the Jason figure, and separated from him by an incised six-pointed star, is a pair of youthful male athletes who appear to be boxing. In front of the boxers and facing the six youths carrying the *kanna* is the most fantastic of the figures, a running man with voluminous wings. He is inscribed *taitale* (Daidalos) (see Fig 24.1). How this figure of the legendary artisan and inventor precisely fits into the story of Jason, Medea, the Argonauts and the boxers has taxed the interpretative skills of several archaeologists. One point of consensus is that the *olpe* appears to document the increasing commercial contacts (represented by the Argonauts) and consequent exchange of technical knowledge (Daidalos) between Greece and Etruria during the seventh century BC.

BUCCHERO PESANTE: UNUSUAL SHAPES AND ELABORATE ORNAMENT

Approximately one century after the earliest appearance of *bucchero sottile* pottery in Etruscan tombs, a new variant, which we call *bucchero pesante* ("heavy bucchero"), became popular. The name is accurate because this new style is indeed much heavier due to its thick walls, larger scale, and more elaborate ornament. Simple, delicate motifs like the open and closed fans, so common on *bucchero sottile*, are replaced with stamped or modeled figures and designs in relief. In general, incision is used sparingly and often only to accentuate or articulate a relief. The combination of wheel-made portions of a vase and the hand-worked application of molded reliefs is typical. Scale is an important feature: some vases in this technique are among the largest the Etruscans ever produced. They rival the tallest Caeretan Red Ware pithoi.[30] These large vases are not utilitarian because they are poorly fired, quite friable and often intentionally perforated before firing. Many seem to have been made expressly for funerary purposes, much like *ceramica argentata*, a type of pottery associated with Volterra in the Etruscan Hellenistic period. *Bucchero pesante* was primarily made at Vulci, Chiusi and Orvieto, centers of the most active new ceramic workshops. Perhaps because it is considered less refined, repetitious and more likely "mass-produced" than elegant *bucchero sottile*, *bucchero pesante* has not received the attention it deserves in modern scholarship. It is an acquired taste.

There are many oddities about this kind of pottery. I would like to examine a few representative *bucchero pesante* shapes. First, let us consider shapes that derive from familiar prototypes. A large *oinochoe* in the Antikenmuseum Basel (Fig. 53.7) illustrates many features of *bucchero pesante*. The shape (a variant of Rasmussen's type 3e) is ultimately derived from Protocorinthian *oinochoai*. Several elements retain the appearance of metal: the wide, flat handle; the clamp-like handle attachment decorated with four modeled human heads; the thick horizontal bands at the base and foot; the repeated mold-made figures in relief that ornament the belly. Above the larger frieze, which perhaps depicts Theseus fighting the Minotaur, is a shoulder frieze composed of tear-drop-shaped gadroons, one of the most common decorative motifs of *bucchero pesante*. The lower figural frieze shows a pair of young men, perhaps boxers, confronting each other. This pair is repeated twelve times to form the frieze but, of course, each pair derives from the same mold. Vases of this type are often associated with workshops in Tarquinia.[31] The Basel *oinochoe* dates to circa 560–540 BC.

Figure 53.7   *Bucchero pesante oinochoe*, provenance unknown, circa 560–540 BC. (Antikenmuseum Basel, inv. Zü 146 A–B.) Photograph: Courtesy of Antikenmuseum Basel.

A *bucchero pesante* column krater (Fig. 53.8a–b) illustrates another shape derived from Corinthian prototypes but elaborated with a plethora of new Etruscan ornaments.[32] The basic Greek shape is retained but, in addition to the usual columnar handles, two struts modeled in the form of human masks are added between the shoulder and the rim (Fig. 53.8b). Ornamenting the shoulder and belly is a series of palmettes and small female heads in relief. When the large scale is added to the elaborate decorative scheme, the overall effect is one of great richness and complexity. In these impressive productions, achieving those qualities was surely the goal of many potters. Metal vessels are an obvious source of inspiration and some of these *bucchero pesante* vases even have clay "rivets" holding the handles in place. This column krater, as well as the related parallels and similarly decorated *hydriai*, *stamnoi*, amphoras and other shapes, are all associated with workshops in Vulci.[33]

Etruscan *kantharoi*, the popularity of which continues throughout the sixth century BC, undergo a similar *pesante* embellishment. An example in Iowa City (Fig. 53.9a–b) will illustrate the changes.[34] The basic *kantharos* shape with its distinctive tall ribbon handles

Figure 53.8a–b *Bucchero pesante* column krater, provenance unknown, circa 600–550 BC. University of Iowa Museum of Art, Iowa City, inv. 1970.57. Photographs by B. Yarborough.

Figure 53.9a–b *Bucchero pesante kantharos*, provenance unknown, sixth century BC. University of Iowa Museum of Art, Iowa City, inv. 1971.249. Photographs by B. Yarborough.

is maintained. However, the handles are now wider and support molded relief figures of the "Mistress of Animals" (Fig. 53.9b) whose head is buttressed by wide, vertical flanges that curve down the outside of each handle.[35] The bowl's rim now flares and undulates in a decidedly baroque manner. Below the deep carination on each side is a frieze of three molded protomes depicting a sphinx or siren. Vases of this sort are especially associated with workshops in Chiusi and probably date to the second half of the sixth century BC. A very similar decorative format, but often with crouching lions rather than sphinx protomes or other variations, is employed on contemporaneous *bucchero pesante kyathoi*, chalices (Fig. 53.10), goblets and *oinochoai*.

A highly-unusual jug in the shape of a siren (Fig. 53.11) illustrates the fanciful and imaginative virtuosity of many *bucchero pesante* artisans.[36] Conventional elements include the trefoil spout and strap handle with strut. Everything else is atypical: the large smiling

Figure 53.10 *Bucchero pesante* chalice from Orvieto, circa 550–500 BC. (Antiquities Collection, American Academy in Rome, inv. 285.) Drawing by R. De Puma.

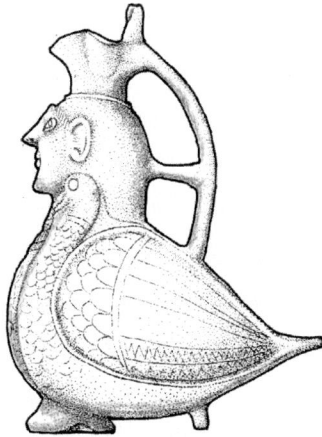

Figure 53.11 *Bucchero pesante* jug, provenance unknown, probably Chiusi, circa 550–500 BC. (Metropolitan Museum of Art, New York, inv. 18.145.25.) Drawing adapted from E. Camerini, *Il bucchero etrusco* (Rome: Gruppo Archeologico Romano, 1985), pl. XXXIX, 2.

face of the siren has almond-shaped eyes, prominent incised eyebrows, pointed nose and large abstract ears. Sirens are hybrid combinations of human females and birds, so we would expect to see their wings, but here they are subsumed by the wings of swans depicted in relief on each side of the siren's body. Usually, sirens have clawed bird's feet, but this one has fat human feet and apparently wears slippers. Incision is used abundantly to articulate feathers, facial features and to provide irrelevant but decorative ornaments like the elaborate palmette design on the siren's breast. This fine jug was probably made at Chiusi and dates circa 550–500 BC.

One final Chiusine product in *bucchero pesante* is typical of that inland city and its surrounding villages. Archaeologists call this footed tray a *foculum*.[37] These objects are either rectangular and footed, like an example in the Metropolitan Museum, New York (inv. 96.9.145), or circular and without feet. They usually have two horizontal handles and almost always have an opening cut out at the front. They were used as offering trays and deposited in tombs with other items dedicated to the cremated deceased. Several of these trays contain a variety of small bucchero dishes, containers, spoons, spatulas and palettes that may have been used to prepare (perhaps symbolically for the deceased) cosmetics or edibles. The New York *foculum* is displayed with several of these small items, but – as in almost every case – we cannot be certain that they were found with it.

Ornament on this *foculum* is typical of other *bucchero pesante* products: a combination of many modeled reliefs and few incisions. In this case, three large palmettes mark the midpoints of the tray's back and side walls. Four recumbent lions, modeled in the round, are stationed at each corner, and the front wall is flanked by hooded female heads that look at each other across the opening. Incised reliefs depicting a sphinx and a siren flank the opening and appear again on the back wall. These trays were popular at Chiusi throughout the sixth century BC. The example in New York is most likely a product of circa 550–500 BC.

SUMMARY OF BUCCHERO DECORATIVE TECHNIQUES

Open or closed "fans," made with a small notched tool of wood, and long lines of notched patterns, probably made with a roulette, are hallmarks of *bucchero sottile*. On many vases, especially *kantharoi* and *kyathoi*, the carination is often cut with notches. This, as well as parallel vertical ribbing, are other simple but effective devices that articulate the contours of the vase. We have seen that shallow relief designs, whether figural, vegetal or geometric, decorate bucchero vessels from the earliest period of production. These reliefs were often mold-made and affixed to the vase with a slip of diluted clay while still leather-hard. In *bucchero pesante* the reliefs are often not only more numerous and varied than in earlier *bucchero sottile* but also higher (i.e. made from deeper molds). Sometimes ornament includes small sculptures in the round. Reliefs may be cut out to form open (*ajour*) designs, a technique popular for the handles of Nikosthenic amphoras and the struts of caryatid chalices.[38]

Incision is the other universal technique and appears throughout bucchero production. Sometimes the incisions are parallel horizontal lines running around the rim of a *kantharos*, adding a simple but effective accent. At other times they may create a complex picture with multiple figures[39] or simply outline or articulate figures added in relief. Another popular decorative technique with a long history involves the use of small stamps or cylinder seals (*cilindretti*) to impress a design onto a leather-hard vase. Often these small cylinder seals are carved with processions of stylized figures or animals. When rolled on the vase they produce a continuous frieze whose complexity and small scale add considerably to the decorative quality of the vase. Scholars have meticulously studied and categorized these seals.[40] Thus, we have a key indicator of where certain seals were used and can employ the designs to determine regional or workshop differences and preferences.

INSCRIPTIONS ON BUCCHERO

From the first appearances in the early seventh century BC until its gradual disappearance during the fourth century BC, bucchero pottery was often inscribed. These inscriptions may be as short as a single letter, perhaps to indicate a particular potter or workshop (i.e. a kind of trademark), or they may be as long as a dedication mentioning donor and divinity to whom the offering was made. A number of inscriptions address the reader directly to state the name of the owner. These *iscrizioni parlanti* are important documents recording not only names of specific Etruscan individuals but also sometimes the Etruscan word for the particular vase shape on which it is inscribed.[41]

Among the early inscriptions on bucchero are two important alphabets. These two objects are roughly contemporary and date circa 630–620 BC. The first appears on the body of a stylized bucchero cockerel.[42] This shows an incised alphabet with 26 letters (one letter, an "*S*," appears twice) moving from left to right (Fig. 53.12). This small object has a lid that can be affixed with a cord to the body and probably served as an inkwell. Another bucchero container of conical shape was discovered in 1836 near the Regolini-Galassi Tomb at Cerveteri.[43] It too is probably an inkwell. All of the inscriptions move from left to right. In this case, the alphabet is incised around the base while above, on the body, is a syllabary. The syllabary, consisting of five lines, combines thirteen consonants with the four vowels used by the Etruscans (*i, a, u, e*). Thus, this little inkwell provides a handy reference for someone learning how to write.

We have already noted above the one-word inscriptions identifying specific mythical characters like *metaia* (Medea) and *taitale* (Daidalos) on the San Paolo *olpe* (see Figs 6.37 and 24.1). Another type of inscription, frequent on bucchero and other types of pottery, is one showing ownership or dedication. A good example is a bucchero object, perhaps the foot and stem of a large chalice or part of an incense burner. This was excavated at the Portonaccio Temple, Veii, and dates to circa 550 BC.[44] There are two inscriptions. The one at the base is simply a series of repeated "*r*" letters, for which we have no explanation. The upper inscription, moving from right to left, reads:

mine muluv{an}ece avile vipiiennas = I have been given/dedicated by Avile Vipiiennas

Figure 53.12   Incised inscription on a *bucchero sottile* cockerel, said to be from Viterbo, circa 630–620 BC. (Metropolitan Museum of Art, New York, inv. 24.97.21a, b.) Drawing from *Etruscans: Italy's Lovers of Life* (Alexandria, VA: Time-Life Books, 1995) p. 23.

Most formulaic inscriptions record the names of unfamiliar Etruscans. However, this one mentions *avile vipiiennas*, an archaic Etruscan form of a name equivalent in Latin to Aulus Vibenna. This seems to prove that the legendary brothers, Aulus and Caelius Vibenna of Vulci, did exist and that the tradition connecting them with Servius Tullius (also known as Mastarna or in Etruscan *macstrna*), one of Rome's early kings, has some basis in historical reality.[45] Furthermore, the date of the bucchero inscription and the date assigned by later Roman historians to the events surrounding the Vibenna brothers are consistent, both belonging to the middle of the sixth century BC.

BUCCHERO AND ETRUSCAN COMMERCE

The abundant natural resources and geographical centrality of Etruscan Italy assured its success as a major commercial center. Of the many trade items – raw ores like iron and copper, agricultural products like grain, wine, olives, olive oil, perfumed oils, unguents, and bronzes – bucchero was perhaps the most common type of Etruscan pottery to find its way to foreign emporia. This is an especially dynamic area of Etruscan studies and new research is continually refining our understanding of it.[46] It can be treated only superficially here.

Trade in Antiquity was never a simple operation but often involved a long series of contacts and exchanges. One foundation may well have been "gift-exchange." This process could be used by elite members of Etruscan society, the landowners who controlled a natural or manufactured resource, who wished to establish a profitable relationship with other local or foreign elites. Etruscan communities might exchange goods with neighbors and those living near a river route could eventually ship their products to the coast. From there they might begin another long series of exchanges along a changeable route of emporia that eventually led to a distant foreign territory. As time went on, these exchanges might have evolved from simple "silent commerce" as described by Herodotus (4.197) in connection with the Carthaginians and people living in parts of North Africa beyond the Straits of Gibraltar, to more formal trade contracts and partnerships.

If one plots a map of sites where bucchero has been found outside Etruria, one sees that it appears at locations throughout Italy, especially in Campania, Sicily and Sardinia, and the Mediterranean basin. Areas that have especially numerous finds include southern Gaul (essentially from Antibes west to Ampurias) and portions of southern Spain. More remote locations include Tarsus in southern Asia Minor, Naukratis in the Nile Delta, Tocra in Libya and Kościelec in northern Poland. Often the bucchero found at these sites is fragmentary, although most can be identified as *kantharoi*, and is associated with Etruscan transport amphoras used to ship wine or olive oil.

There has been a steady, concerted effort on the part of many Etruscologists in recent decades to demonstrate the importance of bucchero as a significant indicator of Etruscan cultural influence, trade, technical skill and taste. Numerous public and private collections of bucchero have been carefully studied or reassessed, a great deal of technical data has been collected and interpreted, and it is fair to claim that we are today in a much better position to appreciate the relevance of bucchero in the greater context of Etruscan civilization.

NOTES

1 For example, Ridgway 2005, 612.

2 Camporeale 2000: 405–406. F. Cortier-Angeli (in Jucker 1991: 294, n. 1) quotes a recipe from Artusi's famous nineteenth-century cookbook, *La scienza in cucina e l'arte di mangiar bene* (recipe no. 659). "...as the 17th century was ending and at the beginning of the 18th, in imitation of [Spanish] taste, perfumes and odorous essences came into great fashion. Among the odours, none was so exciting as bucchero, the use of which became so widespread that even druggists and confectioners would stick some into pastilles and victuals. Whence was this famous odour extracted and what was it like? Hark and wonder how extravagant may tastes and men be: it was the dust of crockery fragments and its perfume resembled that exhaled by sun-beaten earth under summer rain; the smell of earth, in short, produced by certain vases called buccheri, thin and fragile, unvarnished [unglazed], the name of which was perhaps given to dark-red color; but the most appreciated were of shiny black. These vases had been brought to Europe from South America first by the Portuguese and were used for drinking and for boiling perfumes and odorous waters, their rubble being then utilized in the above-said manner."

3 Readers who wish to explore this aspect of Etruscology should consult summaries in Perkins 2007, Camporeale 2000 and Martelli 1994. These sources also provide excellent bibliographies on what has become a vibrant but unwieldy and voluminous topic.

4 Colonna 1968: 268, no. 5; 269, fig. 3. Recent studies (e.g. Palmieri 2001) show that Veii and Tarquinia may not have been far behind Caere in this early production.

5 Ramage 1970: 17–18; Gran Aymerich 1982: 42, nos 11–12. Remains of gilding appear on two chalice caryatids circa 620–600 BC from Vulci, now in the Antikensammlungen, Munich (inv. 2364–2365), Cristofani and Martelli 1983: 286, no. 117; Gran Aymerich 1995: 65, pl. 3. For an unsubstantiated mention of gold leaf on a bucchero vessel, see *Notizie degli Scavi* 1894: 351–354.

6 Dohan 1942, 3–4.

7 Gran Aymerich 1995; Santamaria and Artizzu 2003.

8 Painted *bucchero sottile kantharos*: Jucker 1991: 203, no. 268. Painted *bucchero pesante* Nikosthenic amphoras: Gran Aymerich 1982: 81–83, pl. 39, 1–6. Martelli 1994, 763 mentions an unpublished painted bucchero vase from the Grand Tumulus at Monte dell'Oro, Cerveteri. See also, New York, Metropolitan Museum acc. no. 74.4.26, a painted *bucchero pesante* chalice: De Puma, forthcoming, 2013 Fig. 4.65. During the late nineteenth century some authentic bucchero vases were painted and varnished, one assumes to enhance their appeal and market value.
I realize that the use of terms like *bucchero sottile* and *pesante* is controversial because it suggests a simple division of what is certainly a far more complex and fluid situation. However, I have decided to use them in a general way to suggest an evolution in bucchero production that, I think, bears some validity. Only when one attempts to apply very specific chronological divisions to this material does one tread on thin ice. For more on this problem, see Berkin 2003: 5.

9 Rasmussen 1979: 9, where this tomb is dated circa 700–675 BC.

10 Rasmussen 1979: 10–11, where this tomb is dated ca. 700–650 BC.

11 Sciacca and Di Blasi 2003. Sciacca dates the tomb to ca. 660–650 BC. See also, Riva 2010: 166–171.

12 Rasmussen 1979: 12–14, probably circa 650 BC.

13 Maria Antonietta Rizzo, "Le tombe orientalizzanti di San Paolo" in Moretti Sgubini (ed.) (2001), *Veio, Cerveteri, Vulci. Città d'Etruria a confronto*, Rome: "L'ERMA" di Bretschneider, 163–176.

14 Colonna 1968: 268–271.

15 Boitani 1983. See also, Maria Helena Marchetti, "La produzione del bucchero a Veio: alcune considerazioni" in Naso (ed.) 2004: 17–27.

16 Petrizzi 1986: 211–214, nos. 576–595. Most of the vases are not "true" bucchero, but a very close approximation called *buccheri a superficie bruno-marrone*. Petrizzi dated this tomb circa 675–650 BC. See also, Daniela Locatelli, "Tarquinia" in Naso (ed.) 2004: 50–56, pl. 1.

17 Cristofani and Martelli 1983: 265, no. 45. Note that the decorative motifs are exactly like those found on most bucchero examples.

18 The word implies a notched wheel-like device (*roulette*) that could be rolled into the leather-hard clay to produce dotted lines before firing. Regter (2003: 24) has shown that "fans" were more likely made with a simpler notched blade, probably of wood. However, I suspect that impressed decoration consisting of longer lines and other (non-fan) motifs could have been made (more easily) with a roulette, as well as (very carefully) with a notched blade (see Regter 2003, fig. 6, b.5).

19 Martelli 1994, 763.

20 The relief designs on the wide handles of Nikosthenic amphoras were produced with matrices that have not survived. These are probably the same kind of matrices, perhaps made of wood, used to impress the friezes on contemporaneous Caeretan red impasto pithoi and braziers. For more on these, see Pieraccini 2003: 182–188; Serra Ridgway 2010: 129–134.

21 Cristofani and Martelli 1983: 43–44, fig. 6; 264–265, no. 42.

22 Sciacca and Di Blasi 2003: 52–61, nos 14 and 15 (fragmentary) with comparisons.

23 Rome, Museo di Villa Giulia inv. 61544: Canciani and von Hase 1979, no. 9; Cristofani and Martelli 1983, no. 19.

24 Canciani and von Hase 1979, no. 28, pl. 19, 2. This silver *kotyle* shows the distinctive dotted fan patterns so common on *bucchero sottile* vessels. See also, the fragmentary example no. 29, pl. 18, 4–5.

25 Rasmussen 1979: 117.

26 De Puma 2009: 306, Table I, nos 10–12; Sciacca and Di Blasi 2003: 79–80, Fig. 13.

27 The Chigi vase was found in 1881 at Monte Aguzzo, near Veii, and is now in the Villa Giulia, Rome, inv. 22679.

28 For a recent interpretation, see Warden 2009.

29 For these interpretations, see Rizzo 2001; Belelli 2002–2003; Bonfante and Bonfante 2002: 134–136; Riva 2010: 63–71. My own preference is that it represents a folded cloth thanks to the fringes and hems, details not likely to appear on a ship's sail or the Golden Fleece.

30 Serra Ridgway 2010.

31 For related vases, see Bruni 1989; Camporeale 1991: 93–95, no. 83; Perkins 2007: 16, no. 16. For bucchero associated with Tarquinia, see Daniela Locatelli, "Tarquinia" in Naso (ed.) 2004: 49–89.

32 University of Iowa Museum of Art, Iowa City inv. 1970.57: De Puma 1974.

33 See, most recently, Barbara Belelli Marchesini, "Appunti sul bucchero vulcente" in Naso (ed.) 2004: 91–147. A number of closely related parallels may be added now to the list I published in 1974: see Pellegrini 1989, 81–83, nos 261–264, pls LIV–LV and Belelli Marchesini in Naso (ed.) 2004, 97–101, pl. 4, 1–3 and pl. 6, 1–4.

34 University of Iowa Museum of Art inv. 1971.249, unpublished. For a closely related example, see University of Pennsylvania Museum of Archaeology and Anthropology inv. L–64–539, on loan from the Philadelphia Museum of Art (original inv. no. 14–335): Turfa 2005: 39, Fig. 25; 198–199, no. 201.

35 Sometimes these handles can become very ornate with multiple sculptural elements. See, for example, Berkin 2003: nos 22–23, 29–36, figs. 13–17, pls 6–11. For the Mistress of Animals motif, see Valentini 1969.

36 Metropolitan Museum of Art, New York (inv. 18.145.25): Camporeale 1973–74, 117, pl. XXX, 1–2; De Puma in Picón *et al.*, 2007, no. 321, 277, 469–470; De Puma, forthcoming, 2013, Fig. 4.85.

37 Metropolitan Museum of Art, New York (inv. 96.9.145a–i): De Puma in Picón *et al.*, 2007, no. 322, 277, 470; De Puma, forthcoming, 2013, Fig. 4.79a.

38 Verzár 1973; Capecchi and Gunella 1975; Salskov Roberts 1988.

39 Gran Aymerich 1973.

40 See, for example, Scalia 1968; Camporeale 1972. For a typical example associated with Chiusi, see De Puma 1986: 67–69, no. CA 14.

41 Agostiniani 1982.

42 Metropolitan Museum of Art, New York (inv. 24.97.21a, b), said to be from Viterbo: Pandolfini and Prosdocimi 1990: 22, no. 1, 3; De Puma in Picón *et al.*, 2007, no. 318, pp. 275, 469; De Puma, forthcoming, 2013, Fig. 2.1.

43 Museo Gregoriano Etrusco, Vatican (inv. 20349): Pareti 1947: 322–324, no. 327, pl. XLVI; Pandolfini and Prosdocimi 1990: 26–29, no. I, 6; F. Buranelli in Morigi Govi (ed.) 2000: 318–320, no. 431.

44 See M. Pallottino, "Il fregio dei Vibenna e le sue implicazioni storiche" in Buranelli (ed.) 1987: 225–234, and no. 93 (by F. Boitani). For a very similar inscription on the handle of a monumental bucchero oinochoe from Veii, see Moretti Sgubini (ed.) (2001), *Veio, Cerveteri, Vulci. Città d'Etruria a confronto*, Rome: "L'ERMA" di Bretschneider. = 45–46, no. I.F.I.1 (Villa Giulia depositi; exc. inv. VTP 222).

45 All three characters, with identifying Etruscan inscriptions, appear in the painted François Tomb. See Buranelli (ed.) 1987: 96–97, Fig. 8. For more on Etruscan writing, including additional examples of inscribed bucchero and writing implements, see G. Camporeale, "L'écriture et la civilization des livres" in *Les Etrusques et l'Europe* 1992: 86–91, 147–150; G. Sassatelli, "Il principe e la pratica della scrittura" in Morigi Govi (ed.) 2000: 309–326; De Puma (forthcoming, 2013), chapter II.

46 Bonghi Jovino 1993; Michel Gras, "Trade" in Torelli (ed.) 2000: 97–109; Bernard Bouloumié, "Le commerce maritime dans le Sud de la France" in *Les Etrusques et l'Europe* 1992: 168–175, 254–258; Mauro Menichetti, "Piracy and Trade" in Torelli (ed.) 2000: 549–551; Gran Aymerich 2006.

BIBLIOGRAPHY

Agostiniani, A. (1982) *Le 'iscrizioni parlanti' dell'Italia antica*, Florence: Leo S. Olschki Editore.

Bagnasco Gianni, G. (1996) *Oggetti iscritti di epoca orientalizzante in Etruria*, Florence: Leo S. Olschki Editore.

Batignani, G. (1965) "Le Oinochoai di bucchero pesante di tipo 'chiusino,'" *Studi Etruschi* 33: 295–316.

Belelli, V. (2002–2003) "Gli Argonauti all'imbarco," *Annali dell'Istituto Orientale di Napoli. Archeologica e Storia Antica*, n.s. 9–10: 79–94.

Berkin, J. (2003) *The Orientalizing Bucchero from the Lower Building at Poggio Civitate (Murlo)*, *Archaeological Institute of America Monographs*, n.s. 6, Philadelphia: The University of Pennsylvania Museum of Archaeology and Anthropology.

Boitani, F. (1983) "Veio: La tomba 'principesca' della necropolis di Monte Michele," *Studi Etruschi* 51: 536–556.

Bonamici, M. (1972) "Contributi alla classificazione del piú antico bucchero decorato a rilievo. I buccheri di produzione ceretana," *Studi Etruschi* 40: 95–114.

——(1974) *I buccheri con figurazioni graffite*, *Biblioteca di 'Studi Etruschi'* 8, Florence: Leo S. Olschki Editore.

Bonfante, G. and Bonfante, L. (2002) *The Etruscan Language: An Introduction*, Manchester and New York: Manchester University Press.

Bonghi Jovino, M. (1993) *Produzione artigianale ed esportazione nel mondo antico: il bucchero etrusco. Atti del colloquio internazionale, Milan 10–11 May 1990*. Milan: Edizioni ET.

Bouloumié, B. (1982) "Le bucchero nero d'Etrurie," *Latomus* 41: 773–784.

Bruni, S. (1989) "Note su un gruppo di oinochoai di bucchero con decorazione a stampo di produzione tarquiniese," *Annali dell'Istituto Orientale di Napoli. Archeologica e Storia Antica* 11: 121–153.

——(ed.) (forthcoming, 2013) *"Lautus erat tuscis Porsena fictilibus": Studi e ricerche sul bucchero dell'area chiusina per Luigi Donati*. Pisa: Edizioni ETS.

Buranelli, F. (ed.) (1987) *La tomba François di Vulci* (Exhibition catalogue, Vatican City, Braccio di Carlo Magno). Rome: Edizioni Quasar.

Camporeale, G. (1972) *Buccheri a cilindretto di fabbrica orvietana*, Studi dell' Accademia Toscana di Scienza e Lettere 'La Colombaria' 21. Florence: Leo S. Olschki Editore.

——(1973–1974) "Vasi plastici di bucchero pesante," *Archeologia Classica* 25–26: 103–122.

——(1991) *La Collezione C.A.: Impasto e Buccheri* I, Rome: Giorgio Bretschneider.

——(2000) "Archaic Pottery: Impasto and Bucchero Wares" in M. Torelli (ed.), *The Etruscans*, Milan: Bompiani, 405–419.

Canciani, F. and von Hase, F.-W. (1979) *La Tomba Bernardini di Palestrina* = *Latium Vetus* II, Rome: Consiglio Nazionale delle Ricerche.

Capecchi, G. and Gunella, A. (1975) "Calici di bucchero a sostegni figurati," *Atti e Memorie dell'Accademia Toscana di Scienza e Lettere 'La Colombaria'* 40: 35–116.

Colonna, G. (1968) s.v. 'Caere' in "Rivista di Epigrafia Etrusca," *Studi Etruschi* 36: 268–271.

Cristofani, M. and Martelli, M. (eds) (1983) *L'Oro degli Etruschi*, Novaro: Istituto Geografico de Agostini.

De Puma, R. D. (1974) "A Bucchero Pesante Column Krater in Iowa," *Studi Etruschi* 42: 25–36.

——(1986) *Etruscan Tomb-Groups: Ancient Pottery and Bronzes in Chicago's Field Museum of Natural History*, Mainz: Verlag Philipp von Zabern.

——(1988) "Nude Dancers: A Group of Bucchero Pesante Oinochoai from Tarquinia" in J. Christiansen *et al.* (eds), *Proceedings of the Third International Symposium on Greek and Related Pottery*, Copenhagen: National Museum, 130–143.

——(1996) *Etruscan Bucchero and Impasto—Corpus Vasorum Antiquorum U.S.A.* 31, J. Paul Getty Museum 6, Malibu: J. Paul Getty Museum.

——(2009) "An Inscribed Bucchero Kantharos in New York" in S. Bruni (ed.), *Etruria e Italia preromana: Studi in onore di Giovannangelo Camporeale*, Pisa and Rome: Accademia Editoriale, I, 303–308.

——(forthcoming, 2013) *Etruscan Art in the Metropolitan Museum of Art*, New York and New Haven: The Metropolitan Museum of Art and Yale University Press.

Dohan, E. H. (1942) *Italic Tomb-Groups in the University Museum*, Philadelphia: University of Pennsylvania Press.

Les Etrusques et l'Europe (1992) (Exhibition catalogue Galeries Nationales du Grand Palais, Paris, 15 September–14 December 1992. Altes Museum, Berlin, 25 February–31 May 1993). Paris: Reunion des Musées Nationaux.

Gran Aymerich, J. M. J. (1972) "Situles orientalizantes du VII siècle en Etruria," *MEFRA*, 84, 7–59.

——(1973) "Un conjunto de vasos de bucchero inciso: Ensayo de formalizacion," *Trabajos de Prehistoria* 30: 217–300.

——(1982) *Corpus Vasorum Antiquorum France* 31, *Musée du Louvre* 20, Paris: Diffusion de Boccard.

——(1995) "Le bucchero et les vases métalliques," *Revue des Études Anciennes* 97: 45–75.

——(2006) "La diffusion des vases etrusques en Mediterranée nord-occidentale: l'exception gauloise" in S. Gori and M. C. Bettini (eds), *Gli Etruschi da Genova ad Ampurias. Atti del XXIV*

Convegno di Studi Etruschi ed Italici, Marseille-Lattes 26 settembre–1 ottobre 2002, 205–218. Pisa: Istituto editoriali e poligrafici internazionali.

Jucker, I. (ed.) (1991) *Italy of the Etruscans*, Mainz: Verlag Philipp von Zabern.

Lollini, L. (1959) "Bucchero" in *Enciclopedia dell'arte antica, classica e orientale* 2: 203–210. Rome: Istituto della Enciclopedia Italiana.

Martelli, M. (1994) "Bucchero" in *Enciclopedia dell'arte antica, classica e orientale, Secondo Supplemento (1971–1994)* I, 761–767, Rome: Istituto della Enciclopedia Italiana.

Morigi Govi, C. (ed.) (2000) *Principi etruschi tra Mediterraneo ed Europa* (Exhibition catalogue, Museo Civico Archeologico, Bologna). Venice: Marsilio Editori.

Naso, A. (ed.) (2004) *Appunti sul bucchero. Atti delle giornate di studio*. Florence: All'Insegna del Giglio.

Palmieri, A. (2001) "Alle origini del bucchero. Contributo al riconoscimento di una fase sperimentale della produzione tarquiniese," *Archeologia Classica* 52: 175–189.

Pandolfini, M. and Prosdocimi, A. (1990) *Alfabetari e insegnamento della scrittura in Etruria e nell'Italia antica = Biblioteca di Studi Etruschi* 20, Florence: Leo S. Olschki Editore.

Pareti, L. (1947) *La tomba Regolini-Galassi del Museo Gregoriano Etrusco e la civiltà dell'Italia centrale nel VII sec. a. C.*, Vatican City: Tipografia Poliglotta Vaticana.

Pellegrini, E. (1989) *La necropoli di Poggio Buco. Nuovo dati per lo studi di un centro dell'Etruria interna nei periodi orientalizzante ed arcaico*, Florence: Leo S. Olschki Editore.

Perkins, P. (2007) *Etruscan Bucchero in the British Museum*, London: The British Museum.

Petrizzi, C. (1986) "Il tumulo monumentale di Poggio Gallinaro" in M. Bonghi Jovino (ed.), *Gli Etruschi di Tarquinia* (exhib. cat.), Milan and Modena: Edizioni Panini, 206–215.

Picón, Carlos, *et al.* (2007) *Art of the Classical World in the Metropolitan Museum of Art: Greece, Cyprus, Etruria, Rome*, New York and New Haven: The Metropolitan Museum of Art and Yale University Press.

Pieraccini, L. (2003) *Around the Hearth: Caeretan Cylinder-Stamped Braziers*, Rome: "L'ERMA" di Bretschneider.

Ramage, N. H. (1970) "Studies in Early Etruscan Bucchero," *Papers, British School at Rome* 38: 1–61.

Rasmussen, T. (1979) *Bucchero Pottery from Southern Etruria*, Cambridge: Cambridge University Press.

——(1985) "Etruscan Shapes in Attic Pottery," *Antike Kunst* 28: 33–39.

Regter, W. (2003) *Imitation and Creation: Development of Early Bucchero Design at Cerveteri in the Seventh Century B.C. Allard Pierson Series* 15. Amsterdam: Allard Pierson Museum.

Ridgway, D. (2005) "Etruria and Surroundings" reviews of five books including Naso (2004), *Classical Review* 55: 610–614.

Riva, Corinna (2010) *The Urbanisation of Etruria: Funerary Practices and Social Change. 700–600 BC*, Cambridge: Cambridge University Press.

Salskov Roberts, H. (1988) "Some Observations on Etruscan Bowls with Supports in the Shape of Caryatids or Adorned by Reliefs" in T. Fischer-Hansen (ed.), *East and West: Cultural Relations in the Ancient World = Acta Hyperborea* 1 (Copenhagen: Museum Tusculanum Press), 69–80.

Santamaria, U. and Artizzu, G. (2003) "Indagini scientifiche" in Sciacca and Di Blasi 2003: 271–279.

Scalia, F. (1968) "I cilindretti di tipo chiusino con figure umane," *Studi Etruschi* 36: 357–401.

Sciacca, F. and Di Blasi, L. (2003) *La Tomba Calabresi e la Tomba del Tripode di Cerveteri*, Vatican City: Direzione dei Musei dello Stato della Città del Vaticano.

Serra Ridgway, F. R. (2010) *Pithoi stampigliati ceretani: Una classe originale di ceramica etrusca*, edited by Lisa Pieraccini. Rome: "L'ERMA" di Bretschneider.

Torelli, M. (ed.) (2000) *The Etruscans* (Exhibition catalogue Palazzo Grassi, Venice, 26 November 2000–1 July 2001). Milan: Bompiani.

Turfa, J. MacIntosh (2005) *Catalogue of the Etruscan Gallery of the University of Pennsylvania Museum of Archaeology and Anthropology*, Philadelphia: University Museum Publications.

Valentini, G. (1969) "Il motivo della potnia theron sui vase di bucchero," *Studi Etruschi* 37: 413–442.

Verzár, M. (1973) "Eine Gruppe etruskischer Bandhenkelamphora: Die Entwicklung von der Spiralamphora zur Nikosthenischen Form," *Antike Kunst* 16: 45–56.

Warden, P. Gregory (2009) "The Blood of Animals: Predation and Transformation in Etruscan Funerary Representation" in S. Bell and H. Nagy (eds), *New Perspectives on Etruria and Early Rome in Honor of Richard Daniel De Puma* (Madison: University of Wisconsin Press), 198–219.

CHAPTER FIFTY FOUR

ETRUSCAN TERRACOTTA FIGURINES

———•◆•———

Helen Nagy

Ancient religious practice throughout the Near East and the Mediterranean relied heavily on the offering of gifts to the gods.[1] In Etruria thousands of dedicatory objects of various sizes, materials and types fill the storerooms of museums and excavations. Terracotta figurines comprise the largest votive category with a long chronological span and a great variety of subjects from simple animal forms to elaborately detailed representations. Many types, especially the "Tanagras," display strong Greek influence (Fig. 54.1), others reflect Cypriot and Near Eastern styles.[2] Since clay is easily manipulated and reproduced, this medium lends itself to mass production[3] alterations. Etruscan terracotta figurines exhibit a particular tendency to "customize" or alter existing molds by changing attributes, duplicating figures and creating new groupings. A closer look at a selection of categories of figurines from Cerveteri and Veii reveals the rich variety that could result in this medium with very little effort.

HISTORY AND TECHNIQUE

Pliny the Elder tells us (*HN* 35, etc.) that the art of modeling in clay was brought to Italy around the middle of the seventh century BC by Demaratus of Corinth who fled to Italy and settled in Tarquinia. According to sources (Pliny, *HN* 35.43.152; Livy 1.33) he was accompanied by artists who helped spread the technique of clay working (pottery and sculpture). By the early sixth century BC, "…this art had already been brought to perfection by Italy and especially by Etruria…" says Pliny (*HN* 35.45,157) referring to Varro's account of the contract received by Vulca of Veii for the statue of Jupiter Capitolinus. A short time elapsed between learning and perfecting the technique. One has only to look at the statues of the Portonaccio Temple in Veii (Fig. 54.2; see also Chapter 30) to appreciate the validity of Varro's assessment.[4] These impressive and powerful large statues attest to a superb mastery of the terracotta technique on a large scale.

The preferred technique for producing terracotta figurines involves the use of a matrix (or mold) taken from a hand modeled prototype or an existing figurine.[5] Usually a matrix is used only for the front, and the back of the figurine is a slab with a vent-hole to ensure successful firing (Fig. 54.3a–b). Some figurines will have both front and back molded

Figure 54.1 Striding female figure, "Tanagra type." Inv. No. 8–2512. Photo: author. Courtesy of the Phoebe A. Hearst Museum of Anthropology, University of California, Berkeley.

Figure 54.2 "Apollo from Veii." Museo Nazionale di Villa Giulia. Photograph courtesy of the Soprintendenza per i Beni Archeologici dell'Etruria Meridionale.

in a matrix; these tend to be of high quality (Fig. 54.4a–b). Heads are often produced separately and attached after firing (Fig. 54.5).[6] Larger figurines with outstretched arms will have these limbs separately molded. They may be fired together with the body, or attached after firing.[7] It is common to have matrices made from an existing figurine with a resulting reduction of 20 per cent in size. Fig. 54.6 features two heads one generation apart. The head ornament on the smaller head has been altered and the earrings omitted to produce variety. The earrings on the larger head may have been taken from a mold made for casting gold earrings.[8] Some figurines from Veii exist in as many as four generations.[9]

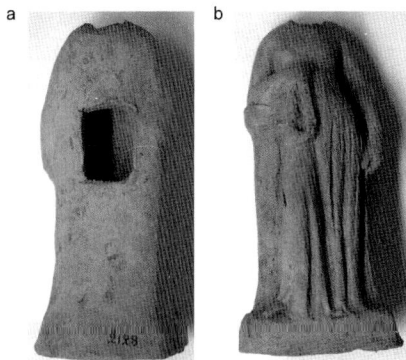

Figure 54.3a–b Standing woman, rear and front views. Inv. No. 2128.
Photo: author. Collection of the American Academy in Rome.

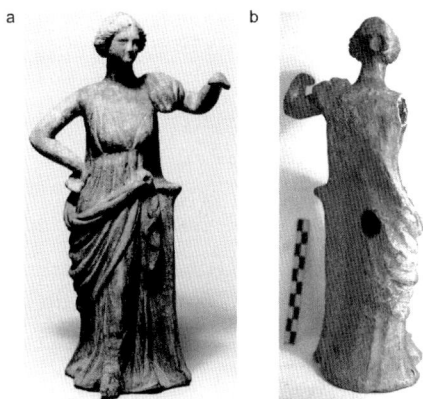

Figure 54.4a–b Figure of woman by pilaster. Front and rear views. Inv. No. 82. Photo: B. Bini.
Collection of the American Academy in Rome.

Figure 54.5 Female head. Inv. No. 1724. Photo: D. Wright.
Collection of the American Academy in Rome.

ETRUSCAN APPROACHES TO TERRACOTTA FIGURINE PRODUCTION

The variety and number of Etruscan figurine types is enormous.[10] Many derive directly from imported prototypes, and each local workshop seems to have developed its own prototypes. This brief section focuses on a selection of types and their derivatives to demonstrate some of the resulting varieties.

The kourotroph: variations on a type

The maternal type has a primary place among Etruscan votive figurines. Fertility and the safety and care of infants were of primary concern at all sanctuaries, regardless of the identity of the presiding divinity.[11] A few examples from Veii and Cerveteri suffice to demonstrate some of the varieties of this type. Fig. 54.7 represents five figurines depicting enthroned women, three with infants, from the Campetti sanctuary of Veii.[12]

Figure 54.6 Female heads, one generation apart with adjustments as to adornments. Inv. Nos. 8–2824 (L.) and 8–2826 (R). Photo: author. Courtesy of the Phoebe A. Hearst Museum of Anthropology, University of California, Berkeley.

a   b   c   d   e

Figure 54.7a–e Five seated figures from the Campetti Sanctuary at Veii. After Vagnetti 1971, Nos. G21, G20a, G28a, G20b, G27a. Museo Nazionale di Villa Giulia. Courtesy of the Soprintendenza per i Beni Archeologici dell'Etruria Meridionale.

These provide only a small sample of the many varieties of this type: enthroned women with or without child. Vagnetti's category G21 (See Fig. 54.7a) is typologically related to G20a (Fig. 54.7b), an enthroned figure without child, and to G20b (Fig. 54.7d), an enthroned woman holding both hands of a child on her lap, facing front. Throne type, garments, especially the parallel diagonal folds over the legs, and features such as the large head with emphasized bulging eyes, point to a common prototype. G28a (Fig. 54.7c) harks back to a different prototype, more closely related to Greek, Ionian types. Her proportions are more slender, the head is smaller, features less exaggerated. G27a (Fig. 54.7e) is related to G28a in proportions, but her mantle covers most of her chest including a small child whose tiny head projects above the mother's lap. A type close to G27a is also found in the Vignaccia deposit at Cerveteri (Fig. 54.8a).[15] Again, the ultimate prototype may have been a common type of Ionian Greek votive, reworked at the least possible effort into a mother. The variations from Cerveteri illustrated in Fig. 54.8 represent two main iconographic types: the nursing, or cradling mother (Fig. 54.8, a, c, d and f) and the mother displaying the infant (Fig. 54.8b and e), in the manner of the Byzantine *"Theotokos"* ("God bearing") Virgin.[14] The distinction between the two must have been significant for the Etruscans, as it was for the Byzantine Christians.

Figure 54.8 Six seated figures from the Vignaccia Sanctuary at Cerveteri. Inv. Nos. a) 8–2425; b) 8–2426; c) 8–2427; d) 8–2543; e) 8–2433; f) 8–2548. Photo: author. Courtesy of the Phoebe A. Hearst Museum of Anthropology, University of California, Berkeley.

The Warrior and Athena /Menerva: variations from site to site

Two iconographic types, the warrior and Athena/Menerva, illustrate typological differences between sites. Both occur at Cerveteri as well as Veii in some variations, but the typologies are different. In one type at Veii, a young warrior, nude except for a helmet, holds a round shield by his left thigh, right arm close to his body (Fig. 54.9a). The body proportions and stance, left leg slightly out and bent, recall Classical Greek works. Another type (Fig. 54.9b), related in stance and proportions to the nude warrior, wears armour over his upper body, a Greek type of helmet, and holds his round shield out to the side on his left lower arm. A third type of warrior is seen in a conventional profile pose, head and lower body in full profile, upper body almost full front. He is striding toward his left, shield on left arm with a short sword held upright in the same hand. His right hand is on his hip, arm akimbo. He wears an enormous crested helmet and a short tunic (Fig. 54.10). All three types occur both at the Campetti and at the Portonaccio sanctuaries at Veii.[15] The warrior type at Cerveteri differs significantly from its

a   b

Figure 54.9a–b Two male warriors from the Campetti Sanctuary at Veii. Photograph courtesy of the Museo Nazionale di Villa Giulia, Soprintendenza per i Beni Archeologici dell'Etruria Meridionale.

Figure 54.10 Striding warrior figure from the Campetti Sanctuary at Veii. Museo Nazionale di Villa Giulia. Photograph courtesy of the Soprintendenza per i Beni Archeologici dell'Etruria Meridionale.

Veii counterparts (Fig. 54.11). The frontal figure wears a modeled cuirass over a short-sleeved tunic and a double crested helmet. He leans to his left on a large oval shield. In all examples, a flange surrounds the head and the shoulders of the figure creating a relief-like effect. On the back the crest of the helmet is rendered in a cursory fashion, an illogical detail given the flange that surrounds the head. The awkward stance, heavily outlined, exaggerated features and the odd treatment of the helmet suggest that this type is a local creation,[16] perhaps to serve as a "companion" to the stylistically similar Menerva types[17] (Fig. 54.12). Several examples show her enthroned, with a Gorgon head decorating her aegis and a couple of owls perched on the back of the throne to either side of the rather startled face of the goddess (Fig. 54.13). An unusual version shows Menerva seated on a *kline.* (Fig. 54.14).[18]

Figure 54.11   Two male warrior figures from the Vignaccia Sanctuary at Cerveteri. Photo: author. Inv. Nos. 8–2461 and 8–2581. Courtesy of the Phoebe A. Hearst Museum of Anthropology, University of California, Berkeley.

Figure 54.12   Figurine of Athena/Menerva from the Vignaccia Sanctuary at Cerveteri. Inv. No. 2464. Photo: author. Courtesy of the Phoebe A. Hearst Museum of Anthropology, University of California, Berkeley.

Figure 54.13   Seated figure of Athena/Menerva from the Vignaccia Sanctuary at Cerveteri. Inv. No. 82431. Photo: author. Courtesy of the Phoebe A. Hearst Museum of Anthropology, University of California, Berkeley.

Figure 54.14   Athena/Menerva seated on a *kline*. From the Vignaccia Sanctuary at Cerveteri. Inv. No. 8–2561. Photo: author. Courtesy of the Phoebe A. Hearst Museum of Anthropology, University of California, Berkeley.

The variations on this type at Cerveteri suggest that Menerva had a special role here, accompanied by the warrior and a third type, a woman of similar aspect to the Menerva and warrior who holds a small pig in her right hand, associating her with the chthonic realm[19] (Fig. 54.15). Athena/Menerva also occurs at Veii, but in a more conventional, classical style. She holds a figure-8 shield by her left leg and her right arm is raised probably to hold a spear.[20] The local stylistic and typological distinctions of the warrior and Menerva figures indicate that while many types (such as the Tanagras) were favored at most sites, some were created specifically for the patrons of a particular sanctuary, or city.

Musicians; paired and duplicated figures

Music was an important part of ancient cult (see Chapter 46). The lyre and double flutes accompanied religious ceremonies and served as the "voice" of the divine.[21] In a number of examples from Veii, a nude male figure in a Classical pose, left leg bent, carries a lyre in his left hand (Fig. 54.16).[22]

The musicians from the Vignaccia at Cerveteri vary in type from a Classically inspired figure,[23] to one closer in style to the Warrior – Minerva figures, recalling Near Eastern/Cypriot prototypes[24] (Fig. 54.17). Occasionally these types are paired (Fig. 54.18) with each other, or the lyre-bearing figure may be paired with a woman (Fig. 54.19) in which case, the group could be interpreted as Apollo and Artemis (Aplu and Artumes).[25] In some instances, the two musicians flank a group enclosed in an architectural frame, or *naiskos*, similar to the arrangement of the goddess flanked by flute and lyre player at Boğazköy in Phrygia.[26] An example of such a group is the plaque from Cerveteri representing a scene of sacrifice (perhaps performed by Artemis) where a single flute player assists at the altar (Fig. 54.20).[27] In another instance, a duplicated seated female type is enclosed in an architectural frame flanked by the musicians (Fig. 54.21). A sacrificing Artemis/Artumes type, depicted seated on an altar (?) occurs both in a single and a duplicated version (Figs 54.22 and 54.23). Do we understand the latter as two separate identities or as an actual duplication of the same divinity, perhaps to underscore two of her aspects?[28] In all three examples, the same mold seems to have been employed to create new combinations.

Figure 54.15   Standing woman holding pig in right hand. From the Vignaccia Sanctuary at Cerveteri. Inv. No. 8–2481. Photo: author. Courtesy of the Phoebe A. Hearst Museum of Anthropology, University of California, Berkeley.

Figure 54.16   Lyre bearing musician from the Campetti Sanctuary at Veii. Museo Nazionale di Villa Giulia. Courtesy of the Soprintendenza per i Beni Archeologici dell'Etruria Meridionale.

Figure 54.17 Male figure holding lyre to left shoulder. Inv. No. 8–2576. Photo: author. Courtesy of the Phoebe A. Hearst Museum of Anthropology, University of California, Berkeley.

Figure 54.18 Flute player and lyre bearer. Inv. No. 86. Photo: B. Bini. Collection of the American Academy in Rome.

Figure 54.19 Male and female pair holding lyre and bird perched between their heads. From the Vignaccia Sanctuary at Cerveteri. Inv. No. 8–2580. Photo: author. Courtesy of the Phoebe A. Hearst Museum of Anthropology, University of California, Berkeley.

Figure 54.20   Terracotta relief from the Vignaccia Sanctuary at Cerveteri with Artumes sacrificing. Boston Museum of Fine Arts, Everett Fund, 88.364 © Boston Museum of Fine Arts.

Figure 54.21   Two women in *naiskos* flanked by musicians. Probably from the Vignaccia Sanctuary, Cerveteri. Inv. No. 37850. Siena Museo Archeologico. Courtesy of the Soprintendenza alle Antichità d'Etruria, Florence.

Figure 54.22   Enthroned female holding patera (?Artumes). From the Vignaccia Sanctuary at Cerveteri. Inv. No. 8–2436. Photo: author. Courtesy of the Phoebe A. Hearst Museum of Anthropology, University of California, Berkeley.

Figure 54.23 Double enthroned females holding patera. From the Vignaccia Sanctuary at Cerveteri. Inv. No. 8–2552. Photo: author. Courtesy of the Phoebe A. Hearst Museum of Anthropology, University of California, Berkeley.

CONCLUSION

The aim of this brief chapter has been to highlight some practices of Etruscan terracotta production in order to demonstrate the possibilities of creating variety within existing types. To do this, I have selected two sites out of the many and a few types out of the hundreds or more at each site. The number of terracotta figures from Etruria is staggering, as are the problems faced by the scholar attempting to organize and interpret them.

NOTES

1 The group of statuettes from Tell Asmar in the collection of the Oriental Institute at the University of Chicago is many students' first encounter with this phenomenon. (Janson 2007: 26, fig. 2.6.). A good source on votive religion in the Mediterranean is Van Straten 1981.

2 Nagy 1994: 213–214, 220–221, notes 22, 23.

3 Cabinet 32 of the Veii Storeroom at the Villa Giulia in Rome displays series of figurines from the Campetti sanctuary. Numerous examples are from a single mold. For instance: male warriors and musicians, Vagnetti 1971: types J2, J3, J5, J7, J8.

4 Haynes 2000: 205–211, fig. 170.

5 Muller 2010: 100–103, on technique, specifically of Tanagras, but applies to most terracotta production. Vagnetti 1971: 157–165. Hand modeled figurines are far less frequent and usually not reproduced.

6 Often the head is on a "stem" as in Fig. 54.6, but some have only a stub. The join between the body and the neck was usually masked by a thin layer of clay. Nagy 1988: 7.

7 The arm was removed from Fig. 54.5a for conservation. The join was masked by the drapery and a thin layer of clay.

8 For example, Fig. 54.7a, Hearst Museum 8–2824. Andrén 1955–56: 213–217; Briguet 1974: 247–252.

9 Veii: the standing musician type Vagnetti 1971: Iiv series. My notes from 1985 indicate at least 70 examples of this type in cabinet 32 of the Orologio storeroom at the Villa Giulia Museum in Rome.

10 Vagnetti 1971: 18. At least 3,000 terracotta pieces of at least 150 distinct types from the 1935–38 excavations at the Campetti sanctuary. Vignaccia, Cerveteri: Rosati 1890: 169–171, refers to ca. 6,000 terracottas. At least 800 of these are now in the Hearst Museum.

11 For the type in general, see: Price 1978. Etruscan and Italic mother types: Bonfante 1984: 1–17, and Bonfante 1986: 195–203.

12 Vagnetti 1971: Types (from left to right): G21, G20a, G28a, G 20b and G27a. All of these types exist in numerous examples and in more than one generation. My notes from 1986 indicate that on shelf 1, Cabinet 31 of the Orologio Storeroom at the Villa Giulia Museum, there were 27 examples of the type representing three generations with slight modifications. Shelves 2, 3 and 4 held another 99 examples of the type.

13 Nagy 1988: 36–37. Inventory no. 8–2425: 206, IID2.

14 *Theotokos*: for example, the famous sixth century encaustic icon of the Virgin and Child with Saints from the monastery of St. Catherine at Sinai: Rodley 1994: 43, Fig. 78. Both iconographic types occur in significant numbers at Veii as well as at Cerveteri and numerous other sites, and in more variations than those shown here. Satricum, a Latin site with strong Etruscan connections, has produced a tremendous variety of mother figures in great numbers. I have consulted the material stored in the Satricum Deposito of the Villa Giulia Museum and found 24 variations on the Kourotroph type. These can be divided into two major iconographic categories: nursing/cradling and frontal display of the child. For updates and further bibliography consult the journal: *Satricum: Reports and Studies of the Satricum Project*. Leiden: 1987.

15 Campetti: Vagnetti 1971: 180. Frontal nude type: J7, J8 numerous examples; with armor: J 2, J3; profile, striding: J5. Comella and Stefani 1990: type nos. E1 through E4, include types not discussed here. Portonaccio: Colonna 2002: No. 674, pl. 56, no. 681, pl. 59.

16 Maule and Smith 1959: 1–59 provide an exceedingly involved discussion of the warrior type, (Gaul or Maris) at the Vignaccia. 109–115: warrior type as Maris. Nagy 1988: 41–42, brief discussion of the type, suggesting that the type represents Laran, the Etruscan Mars.

17 Nagy 1988: 28–29, discussion of the type. Note that the crest of the helmet continues in the back as with the warrior type.

18 Nagy 1988: 196–197, Type IIIB16c. For the *Kline*: Breitenstein 1941: pl. 87, No. 784, but with a seated veiled woman.

19 Nagy 1988: 34–35, discussion of the type and parallels.

20 For example, at the Portonaccio: Colonna 1987: 423–424, fig. 2.

21 Strabo 5.220; Bittel 1963: 20; Nagy 1994: 213–214.

22 Vagnetti 1971: 180, identifies the type as representing Aplu. At least 400 examples of I 4 at the Villa Giulia.

23 Nagy 1988: 40–41 on musicians in general; 213–214, nos. IIE2 and IIE3, Figs 197–198.

24 Karageorghis 2000: 132–133, nos 197–199; Bittel 1963: fig. 5; Blinkenberg 1931: part 1, cols 425–427, part 2, pls 69–70, nos 1701–1710.

25 Nagy 1988: 31, 41, 245, No. IIG21, Fig. 258.

26 Bittel 1963: 7–21.

27 Boston, Museum of Fine Arts, Everett Fund, 88.364. Nagy 1994: 211–214; Nagy 2011: 120–121.

28 Maule and Smith 1959: 95, n. 104 identify the figure as a "kourotrophic Artemis." Nagy 1994: 214–215; Nagy 2011: 121. For double figures see: Hadzisteliou-Price 1971: especially 52–54.

BIBLIOGRAPHY

Andrén, A. (1955–56) "Una matrice fittile etrusca," *Studi Etruschi* 24: 207–219.
Bittel, K. (1963) "Phrygisches Kultbild aus Boğazköy," *Antike Plastik*, 2:7–21, 1–8.

Blinkenberg, C. (1931) *Lindos* II *Les petits objets*, Berlin: W. De Gruyter.

Bonfante, L. (1984) "Dedicated Mothers," in *Visible Religion* III *Popular Cults*, Leiden: Brill, 1–17.

——(1986) "Votive terracotta figures of mothers and children" in J. Swaddling (ed.), *Iron Age Artefacts in the British Museum*. Papers of the Sixth British Museum Classical Colloquium, London: British Museum Publications, 195–203.

Breitenstein, N. and Calvert, W. E. (1941) *Danish National Museum. Catalogue of Terracottas*, Copenhagen: E. Munksgaard.

Briguet, M.-F. (1974) "Petite tête feminine étrusque," *Revue du Louvre*, 247–252.

Colonna, G. (1987) "Note preliminare sui culti del santuario di Portonaccio a Veio," *Scienze dell'Antichità* 1: 419–445.

——(2002) *Il santuario di Portonaccio a Veio 1. Gli scavi di Massimo Pallottino nella zona dell'altare (1939–1940). Monumenti Antichi*, Serie miscellanea VI.3, Rome: Giorgio Bretschneider.

Comella, A., Stefani, G. (1990) *Materiali votive del santuario di Campetti a Veio: scavi 1947 e 1969*, Rome: Giorgio Bretschneider.

Hadzisteliou-Price, T. (1971) "Double and multiple representations in Greek art and religious thought," *Journal of Hellenic Studies* 91: 48–69.

Haynes, S. (2000) *Etruscan Civilization. A Cultural History*, Los Angeles: The J. Paul Getty Museum.

Janson, H. W. and Davies, P. J. E. *et al.* (2007) *Janson's History of Art: the Western Tradition*, 7th Edition, Upper Saddle River, N. J.: Pearson Prentice Hall.

Karageorghis, V. (2000) *Ancient Art from Cyprus. The Cesnola Collection in the Metropolitan Museum of Art*, New York: The Metropolitan Museum of Art.

Linders, T. and Nordquist, G. (eds) (1987) *Gifts to the Gods. Proceedings of the Uppsala Symposium. Acta Universitatis Upsaliensis* 15, Uppsala: Academia Ubsaliensis.

Maule, Q. and Smith, H. R. W. (1959) *Votive Religion at Caere: Prolegomena*, Berkeley and Los Angeles: University of California Press.

Muller, A. (2010) "The technique of Tanagra coroplasts. From local craft to 'global industry'" in V. Jeammet (ed.), *Tanagras. Figurines for Life and Eternity*, Valencia: Fundación Bancaja.

Nagy, H. (1988) *Votive Terracottas from the "Vignaccia," Cerveteri, in the Lowie Museum of Anthropology. Archaeologica* 75, Rome: Giorgio Bretschneider.

——(1994) "Divinities in the context of sacrifice and cult on Caeretan votive terracottas" in R. D. De Puma and J. P. Small (eds), *Murlo and the Etruscans. Art and Society in Ancient Etruria*, Madison, WI: University of Wisconsin Press, 207–219.

——(2011) "Etruscan votive terracottas and their archaeological contexts" in N. T. de Grummond and I. Edlund-Berry (eds), *The Archaeology of Sanctuaries and Ritual in Etruria. Journal of Roman Archaeology*. Supplementary series 81: 113–125.

Price, T. H. (1987) *Kourotrophos. Cults and Representations of the Greek Nursing Deities. Studies of the Dutch Archaeological and Historical Society*, vol. 8, Leiden: E. J. Brill.

Rodley, L. (1994) *Byzantine Art and Architecture. An Introduction*, Cambridge: Cambridge University Press.

Rosati, F. (1890) *Cere e suoi monumenti*, Foligno: F. Salvati.

Vagnetti, L. (1971) *Il deposito votivo di Campetti a Veio. (Materiali degli scavi 1937–1938)*, Florence: Sansoni.

Van Straten, F. F. (1981) "Gifts for the Gods" in H. S. Versnel (ed.), *Faith Hope and Worship. Aspects of religious Mentality in the Ancient World*, Leiden: E. J. Brill, 65–151.

CHAPTER FIFTY FIVE

PORTRAITURE

———•◆•———

Alexandra A. Carpino

INTRODUCTION

Like their contemporaries in ancient Greece, Etruscan artists focused a great deal of attention on renderings of the human body, bodies which portrayed, in the majority, actual men and women rather than deities or figures of heroic origin. Beginning in the seventh century BCE, representations of anonymous and named Etruscans were crafted in a variety of materials (terracotta, bronze, stone) and styles (abstract, stylized, idealized, realistic), and placed in either funerary or religious contexts.[1] The circumstances surrounding the creation of these images – commissions to portray either the deceased or the donor – stimulated Etruscan artists to move, at a very early date, in the direction of portraiture, albeit within the context of contemporary artistic conventions and traditions. In his comprehensive treatment of Etruscan art, Otto Brendel argued that the Etruscans were not only the first to make "the transition from generic to specific representations"[2] but also that their "sculptors of the seventh century BCE produced the first portraits of western art, ... [motivated by] the demand for memorial images."[3] He also proposed that "a turn from 'typical' to 'real' portraits...happened in Etruria about or shortly after 350 BCE."[4]

Although we can never know the extent to which recognizable representations of specific individuals were captured by the Etruscans' artists,[5] an interest in physiognomy and personality "expressed in terms of irregularity and uniqueness"[6] is readily apparent in their surviving imagery. This interest, moreover, led to a distinctive approach to the human figure: rather than focusing on the body as a whole, Etruscan artists concentrated on the heads and chests of their subjects, emphasizing their physical differences as well as aspects of their age, state of health and "social persona."[7] Thus, their likenesses became highly personalized, and a genre of art not previously articulated in the Classical world was born, spearheaded by local customs and traditions.

PORTRAITS IN FUNERARY CONTEXTS

The Etruscans' cult of the ancestors, with its emphasis on what Brendel calls "memorial portraits,"[8] provided the impetus for the production of images of the deceased which were placed in a variety of funerary contexts, both within and outside the tomb, as early as the seventh century BCE. Evidence suggests that this tradition originated in the Villanovan period (circa 750 BCE), when the Proto-Etruscans' distinctive funerary ossuaries – the biconical urns – were anthropomorphized through coverings – either a helmet or a bowl – which many scholars believe "symbolize[d] the head of the deceased."[9] Jocelyn Penny Small, for example, recently described the design that appears on the bronze hemispherical helmet from Tarquinia's so-called "Tomb of the Priest" as both "an abstraction and as a face...[there are] precisely formed circles for the 'eyes' and the center of the 'mouth' [is] placed between a more roughly produced brow and nose line."[10] The survival of this stylized face not only suggests that there was "a conceptual link between the deceased and the burial urn already in existence in the Villanovan period,"[11] but its presence in a tomb surrounded by grave goods that identify the deceased as a warrior also demonstrates the close connection between personal and social identity at this time.[12]

During the seventh century BCE, the ideas manifested by these Villanovan receptacles appear to have generated what many scholars agree is the Etruscans' earliest portrait tradition,[13] visible in the terracotta and/or bronze cinerary urns from the Chiusi region in central Tuscany, which take the form of vessels covered with lids in the form of human heads (Figures 55.1 and 55.2). These funerary vessels effectively convey both the character and physical traits of the deceased, along with elements demonstrating their social identity. Small, for example, hails the sense of "personality" that exudes from a three-dimensional viewing of these artifacts, noting that "the Etruscan combination of the abstract with the real"[14] resulted in works that appear "at first glance to be unrealistic and cartoon-like" but which "capture...recognizable likenesses."[15] Moreover, as Brendel has observed, "individual variety indeed became a theme of [this] art" and for the first time, "Etruscan art...achieved the transition from generic to specific representations."[16] A close study of the heads found on the Chiusine urns, moreover, reveals that none is exactly like any other – thus, their artists worked consciously to portray different individuals, each with their own physiognomy, thereby giving us, in the words of Brendel:

Figure 55.1   Male "Canopic" cinerary urn from Dolciano, late seventh-early sixth century BCE. Museo Archeologico Nazionale, Chiusi. (Photo: author).

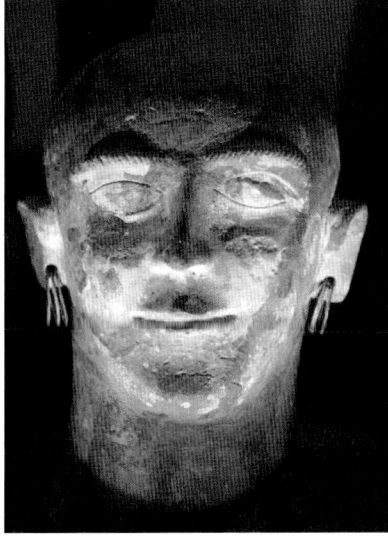

Figure 55.2   Head of a woman, once part of a "Canopic" cinerary urn from Castelluccio di Pienza, late
seventh-early sixth century BCE. Museo Archeologico, Siena (Photo: author).

...evidence of a remarkable new concept of art; namely, the inclusion within its
range of a concept of personality. This concept, aiming at the specific elements which
constitute humans as persons – not merely as types – at the same time represents an
endeavour very proper to art; for a portrait can never be achieved by verbal description
alone: it has to be shown.[17]

Nevertheless, Brendel shies away from describing the Chiusine heads as "portraits in the
modern sense;" instead, he calls them "proto-portraits" since they "incorporate a true
concept of personality" and "individual traits [do] prevail over the typical."[18] John Prag
concurs with this assessment, noting that they "mark a very important psychological and
artistic step away from the general,"[19] especially at a time when no other contemporary
culture was exploring this same concept.[20]

In other regions of Etruria during the seventh and sixth centuries BCE, patrons
commissioned statues in terracotta, stone and bronze, which were placed both inside and
outside the tomb. These include the men and women found inside the Pietrera Tomb
in Vetulonia, which have been variously interpreted as mourners, substitute bodies or
as the ancestors of the family buried within the tomb.[21] While their faces cannot be
characterized as portraits in the true sense of the word, Brendel observes that, "their
richness of realistic detail – hair style, necklaces, and personal ornament – furthers [the]
illusion [of]...a personal note... . They *are* the dead. Also, they are people of wealth and
refinement, an aristocratic lot."[22] Likewise, the figures that recline on the well-known
terracotta sarcophagi from Cerveteri, now in the Villa Giulia and the Louvre, represent
a married couple but do not depict individual physiognomies. Rather, as Haynes notes
in her discussion of the Louvre example, "the couple's smooth oval faces have identical
features...[and represent] a type of face that was adopted by Etruscan artists in the
second half of the sixth century."[23] Brendel notes a similar treatment in the faces found
on the contemporary cinerary statues from Chiusi: "we cannot doubt that, as with the

contemporary Canopic urns, the intention was to give material form to the likeness of a person once alive. But the features do not show it. They are strictly typical and not at all personalized."[24] The same goes for the cippi in the form of female half-figures (Figure 55.3), which have also been found in the Chiusi region: their physiognomic and structural uniformity suggests that they do not represent specific individuals but rather guardian figures.[25] In contrast, Brendel characterizes the hammered bronze bust of a female (Figure 55.4) from the so-called "Isis" Tomb in Vulci as a "possible portrait" since

> the forms of her face…do not quite fall in line with [known] types…but seem rather more individual. This deviation from the norm would not in itself guarantee a true representation of individuality, that is, the portrayal of a definite person, but it may indicate an awareness of the fact that irregularities of form – deviations from the type – are essential characteristics of a human individuality. In this sense the bust evidently does represent 'a person,' though it does not necessarily give a true portrait.[26]

Sybille Haynes, however, interprets this bust as "one of the oldest surviving cult images of a goddess" since, despite being discovered within a tomb, it was not "part of an ash urn."[27] Likewise, it is not clear if the seventh century BCE busts from Marsiliana d'Albegna functioned as "symbolically generalized image[s] of the deceased,"[28] or if they portray images of divinities, though consensus favors the former hypothesis.

The statues of the men (Figure 55.5), women (Figure 55.6) and couples (Figure 55.7) which appear on the covers of Etruscan sarcophagi and cinerary urns from the Classical and Hellenistic periods further attest to the long-standing nature and persistence of memorial portraiture in Etruria. While some of these, despite the presence of names, correspond more to types and might better be termed quasi-portraits "with features and traits that fall within a coded social vocabulary,"[29] and others depict similarities that may result from familial resemblances,[30] enough of the extant heads display a "remarkable diversity of visages…[which] support the claim that a genuine concept of portraiture,

Figure 55.3 *Pietra fetida* cippus in the form of a female half-figure from Chiusi, first half of the sixth century BCE. Museo Archeologico Nazionale, Chiusi. (Photograph: author).

Figure 55.4 Bronze bust of a female from the so-called "Isis" Tomb in Vulci, early sixth century BCE. The British Museum, London, Inv. 434 (Photograph: Courtesy of the British Museum).

Figure 55.5 Stone sarcophagus lid of an anonymous elite Etruscan man, early third century BCE. Museo Archeologico Nazionale, Florence (Photograph: Courtesy of Michele Myra Archila).

Figure 55.6 Painted terracotta sarcophagus of Seianti Hanunia Tlesnasa from Poggio Cantarello, near Chiusi, second century BCE. The British Museum, London, Inv. GR 1887.6–8.9 (Photograph: Courtesy of the British Museum).

Figure 55.7   Detail of the heads of the lid figures (a married couple) on a terracotta cinerary urn from Volterra, late second-early first century BCE. Museo Etrusco Guarnacci, Volterra, Inv. 613. (Photograph: author).

equal to the modern, materialized in Etruscan art for the first time in history."[31] Moreover, when the survival of a skeleton – such as the one found in the sarcophagus of Seianti Hanunia Tlesnasa – provided scholars with the opportunity to test the veracity of the Etruscans' portraiture, they discovered that the artist who crafted her face modeled her features to reflect her facial proportions and some aspects of her physical appearance and her age.[32] Thus, it is difficult not to see the individualized faces of many of the named and anonymous Etruscans from this period as being true to life.

PORTRAITS IN SANCTUARY CONTEXTS

The Etruscans never went before "the gods empty-handed,"[33] and one of the most common types of offerings in their shrines from the early fifth-first centuries BCE were either hand-sculpted or mold-made terracotta votive heads and busts.[34] The earliest examples appear to have been produced in Veii,[35] and as with their funerary counterparts, they "offer a rare confirmation of identity in votive images."[36] While many of these heads "were inexpensive and easily duplicated items…deposited by a cross section of society"[37] who could not afford a customized gift, Ingrid Edlund-Berry recently observed that "the variety of facial features, even on mold-made heads where the details were added individually, suggests an effort made by the artist to make each head unique, perhaps even as a portrait of the dedicant."[38] For this reason, in spite of the manner of their production,[39] Brendel considered these heads as "portrait[s] of a kind," especially since the attributes of physiognomy, age and personality incorporated into the customized versions must have been intended to represent "satisfactory likenesses."[40] Frequently cited in this respect are some of the terracotta heads from the Manganello deposit at Cerveteri[41] where the same mold was used to portray youths, young women and old men"[42] and contrasting likenesses were created through incised retouching. As noted by Helen Nagy, these heads represent "individualized portraits that depict specific aspects of the donor's appearance. These need not have been modeled directly on an individual's physiognomy, but they were probably 'customized', in some cases at least, to emphasize the salient recognizable features."[43] Other terracotta votive heads, however, "clearly show that realistic portraiture in terracotta was not inconceivable at this time."[44] Examples include the bust of a woman from Cerveteri (Figure 55.8),[45] the Malavolta head from Veii, which Brendel describes as "a near-portrait" since the artist gave the young man "an emphatically non-conformist, personal face,"[46] and male heads from Tessennano,[47] the Manganello deposit (this one may represent "a stroke victim")[48] and the Ara della Regina sanctuary at Tarquinia.[49] Thus, the customized terracotta votives were primarily male,[50] with artists focusing both on age and individual facial characteristics, as well as, at times, the state of the donors' health.

Votive heads in bronze, either alone or as part of a full-length statue, were also produced in the Late Classical and Hellenistic periods, and these are more easily characterized as portraits even though, like their terracotta counterparts, they share some standardized features that most likely represent the styles of workshops that produced them. Striking examples include the heads of a boy now in Florence and a young man from Fiesole,[51] as well as those found on the bust of the so-called "Brutus,"[52] and the statue of Aule Meteli (Figure 55.9), known as an outstanding example of Etruscan craftsmanship since its discovery in 1566.[53]

CONCLUSION

The interest in physiognomic individualization in Etruscan art, which began in the seventh century BCE and remained strong through the Hellenistic period, generated the creation of realistic likenesses and "can hardly be explained as anything other than an attempt at portraiture."[54] This genre, therefore, in all of its possible manifestations – typical, real, proto and quasi – was not only one of the most distinctive features of Etruscan art, but it also demonstrates that the beginnings of modern portraiture can be traced to their customs and achievements.

Figure 55.8   Bust of a woman from the Vignale deposit, Cerveteri, third century BCE. Vatican Museums, Inv. 14107. (Photo: Courtesy of Museo Gregoriano Etrusco, Vatican).

Figure 55.9 Over-life-sized bronze statue of Aule Meteli, found near Lake Trasimene, second–first century BCE. Museo Archeologico, Florence (Photo: Courtesy of Jessica Gardin).

NOTES

1   As Warden (2011: 1) has observed, the "display, at least as it has been preserved, [of Etruscan sculpture] was closely connected to religious observance, to funerary ritual, and to votive religion and thus has been found almost exclusively in either mortuary or sanctuary contexts."

2   Brendel 1995: 103.

3   Ibid: 87.

4   Ibid: 396.

5   Small 2008: 57. See also Brendel (ibid.: 104) who writes: "...in the absence of written documentation not only does any definition of an early Etruscan work as a portrait rest on assumption, but also the degree of physiognomical similitude and the concept itself, of what exactly was expected of a portrait, remain hypothetical factors." He also notes that that "even the most photographic portrait cannot give a complete record of a person" (ibid.). Finally, as Small (2003: 129) has pointed out, a similar problem exists for Roman portraits: "Roman portraits from the late Roman Republican period and after seem to capture physical likeness remarkably well. The portraits look like real people, but in the absence of any knowledge of what those people looked like, we cannot tell how accurate the portraits are."

6   Brendel 1995: 105.

7   Stewart 2003: 53. What Prag (2002: 62) calls "total portraits, where all the parts of the body have been rendered to depict one particular individual," did not exist in either Etruria or even later in Roman art. Stewart (ibid: 47) observes: "The enormous range of Roman portrait heads in stone was also tailored to a relatively small range of body-types. There is usually nothing about the body or pose that specifies the identity of the portrait subject in anything other than generic terms: it is the head which is, so to speak, tailor-made..."

8   Brendel 1995: 109: "the need for memorial portraits...was rooted in the Etruscan way of life...It was put to [their] artists to account for the differences between persons, in visible forms, as something essential to the human experience."

9 Tuck 1994: 624.
10 Small: 40, 43 and 202: no. 18.
11 Tuck 1994: 624 and Figures 9–10.
12 Brendel 1995: 106: "In their own way, the Villanovan ossuaries covered with a helmet already expressed the same thought [e.g. 'they were the last and lasting bodies of the dead'], for a helmet was the personal attribute and prerogative of a warrior, and therefore a badge of social distinction as well." Also see Warden 2008: 96–97.
13 Brendel: 1995: 106; Prag 2002: 60; Small 2008: 56.
14 Small 2008: 49.
15 Ibid: 48.
16 Ibid: 109.
17 Ibid.
18 Ibid: 130–131.
19 Prag 2002: 60.
20 See also Small 2008: 48–49, who notes that "Greek art doesn't achieve recognizable likenesses until the fifth century BCE at the earliest, and not consistently until the Hellenistic period."
21 Brendel 1995: 92 and Figures 62–63; Haynes 2000: 83.
22 Brendel 1995: 93.
23 Haynes 2000: 216.
24 Brendel 1995: 133.
25 Haynes 2000: 170.
26 Brendel 1995: 104–105.
27 Haynes 2000: 155.
28 Warden 2008: 98.
29 Prag 2002: 62; Söderlind 2002: 208–239.
30 Small 2008: 57–58.
31 Brendel 1995: 392–93; Prag 2002: 62.
32 Ginge 2002: 12; Prag 2002.
33 Barker and Rasmussen 1998: 224.
34 Turfa 2006; Edlund-Berry 2008: 88.
35 Turfa 2005: 244.
36 Turfa 2006, 102; see also Brendel (1995: 393) who writes that these heads "most probably stood for the devotees who dedicated them; possibly, they served as a symbolic substitute for the whole person – a *pars pro toto*."
37 Nagy 2011: 124.
38 Edlund-Berry 2008: 89.
39 Prag (2002: 61) wonders "whether this 'personalising' approach of a 'typical' product... represents the true Etruscan attitude to individual portraiture, or [if it] was merely the result of technical convenience.
40 Brendel 1995: 394.
41 Nagy 2011: 123 and Figure 20.
42 Prag 2002: 61.
43 Nagy 2011: 123–124, with further bibliography, and Fig. 20.
44 Söderlind 2002: 232.
45 Vatican Museums, Inv. 14107.
46 Brendel 1995: 320 and Figure 241; Torelli 2001: 631 (no. 302).
47 Söderlind 2002: 227–232 and Figure 139.
48 See Turfa 2006: 102, and Figure VI.14; Torelli 2001: 631 (no. 304).
49 Söderlind 2002: 232; Turfa 2006: Figure VI.6a; Torelli 2001: 631 (no. 305).
50 See Nagy (2011) and Steiner (2008: 143) for a discussion of the less individualized female votives.

51 Brendel 1995: 398 and Figures 305–306.
52 Ibid. 399 and Figure 308.
53 Colonna 1991; Torelli 2001: 631 (no. 306).
54 Brendel 1995: 106.

BIBLIOGRAPHY

Barker, G. and Rasmussen, T. (1998) *The Etruscans*, Oxford: Blackwell Publishers.

Brendel, O. (1995) *Etruscan Art*, 2nd edition, New Haven: Yale University Press.

Colonna, G. (1991) "Il posto dell'Arringatore nell'arte etrusca di età ellenistica," *Studi Etruschi* 56, 99–119.

Edlund-Berry, I. (2008) "Temples and the Etruscan Way of Religion" in P. G. Warden (ed.) *From the Temple and the Tomb: Etruscan Treasures from Tuscany*, Dallas: Meadows Museum, SMU, 66–93.

Ginge, B. (2002) "The Sarcophagus, the Tomb and the Seiante Family in their Archaeological Context" in J. Swaddling and J. Prag (eds) *Seianti Hanunia Tlesnasa: The Story of an Etruscan Noblewoman*, London: The British Museum Press, 11–15.

Haynes, S. (2000) *Etruscan Civilization: A Cultural History*, Los Angeles: The J. Paul Getty Museum.

Nagy, H. (2011) "Etruscan votive terracottas and their archaeological contexts: preliminary comments on Veii and Cerveteri" in N. T. de Grummond *et al.* (eds), *The Archaeology of Sanctuaries and Ritual in Etruria*, Portsmouth, RI: Journal of Roman Archaeology, 113–125.

Prag, A. J. N. W. (2002) "Seianti and Etruscan Portraiture" in J. Swaddling and J. Prag (eds), *Seianti Hanunia Tlesnasa: The story of an Etruscan Noblewoman*, London: The British Museum Press, 59–66.

Small, J. P. (2003) *The Parallel Worlds of Classical Art and Text*, Cambridge: Cambridge University Press.

——(2008) "Looking at Etruscan Art in the Meadows Museum" in P. G. Warden (ed.), *From the Temple and the Tomb: Etruscan Treasures from Tuscany*, Dallas: Meadows Museum, SMU, 40–65.

Söderlind, M. (2002) *Late Etruscan Votive Heads from Tessennano. Production, Distribution, Sociohistorical Context*, Rome: "L'ERMA" di Bretschneider.

Steiner, A. (2008) "The Etruscans and the Greeks" in P. G. Warden (ed.), *From the Temple and the Tomb: Etruscan Treasures from Tuscany*, Dallas: Meadows Museum, SMU, 142–163.

Stewart, P. (2003) *Statues in Roman Society. Representation and Response*, Oxford: Oxford University Press.

Torelli, M. (ed.) (2001) *The Etruscans*, New York: Rizzoli.

Tuck, A. (1994) "The Etruscan Seated Banquet: Villanovan Ritual and Etruscan Iconography," *American Journal of Archaeology* 98.4, 617–628.

Turfa, J. M. (2005) *Catalogue of the Etruscan Gallery of the University of Pennsylvania Museum of Archaeology and Anthropology*, Philadelphia: University of Pennsylvania Museum of Archaeology and Anthropology.

——(2006) "Votive Offerings in Etruscan Religion" in N. T. de Grummond and E. Simon (eds), *The Religion of the Etruscans*, Austin: University of Texas Press, 90–115.

Warden, P. G. (2008) "The Tomb: The Etruscan Way of Death" in P. G. Warden (ed.), *From the Temple and the Tomb: Etruscan Treasures from Tuscany*, Dallas: Meadows Museum, SMU, 94–113.

——(2011) "Etruscan Sculpture" in *Oxford Bibliographies Online: Classics*, New York: Oxford University Press. Available at: <www.oxfordbibliographiesonline.com>.

CHAPTER FIFTY SIX

LANDSCAPE AND ILLUSIONISM: QUALITIES OF ETRUSCAN FUNERARY WALL PAINTING

———•◆•———

Helen Nagy

The influence of Greek art on Etruscan painting is undeniable.[1] At the same time large-scale Etruscan painting has a distinct quality of its own, as Otto Brendel pointed out, "…there is a great deal both about their style and their themes which strikes us as properly Etruscan and, to that measure, not Greek."[2] The aim of this essay is to highlight landscape as one particularly Etruscan aspect of the frescoes by analyzing, in chronological order, a few examples of tomb paintings, mainly from Tarquinia.

LOCATION AND TECHNIQUES

Etruscan fresco paintings are mainly preserved on the walls of tombs, while a small number of large plaques painted in this technique come from non-funerary contexts as well.[3] Both types were produced in the fresco technique on a gesso surface, but the working conditions of the artists were significantly different. The plaques were probably painted in workshops with plenty of available light and fresh air; the artist working in the subterranean tomb chamber had little of either.[4] The tomb painter had to make do with lamps, tapers or a torch for lighting that was uneven and probably flickering. The humid atmosphere of the tomb made for technical difficulties, as did the less than ideal quality of the various wall surfaces.[5] A brief comparison between a plaque and a contemporary wall painting shows that the artist of the former could apply greater precision of intricate detail on a smooth even surface. This is a generalization based on only a few extant examples of plaques, but it raises the question of what we might be missing in terms of quality.[6] The tombs were private commissions, to be viewed by few; the non-funerary plaques were intended for a larger public and it seems reasonable to assume that in the hierarchy of a workshop, the more experienced artist would receive the more public commission.[7]

SPACE, LANDSCAPE AND ILLUSIONISM

The intense feline creatures and their avian companions floating in disarray on the walls of the Tomb of the Roaring Lions (Tomba dei Leoni Ruggenti) at Veii (Fig. 56.1), circa

700–590 BC,[8] have a certain abstract appeal. They hover over black and yellow stripes that separate the back wall into "ground" and "space." Rudimentary aquatic birds disposed in two uneven rows, occupy the wall above the lions. The birds, therefore, must be understood as "in the sky," and the lions, "on the ground." There is no narrative; the creatures represent living aspects of nature in an environment of death. They are perhaps meant to be apotropaic, or just symbolic of life. The forms of these animals can be traced to vase painting from Euboea via Pithecusae,[9] but their enlarged shapes, awkward disposition, and location are definitely Etruscan.

The connection between vase painting (Greek Corinthian and Etrusco-Corinthian) and wall painting is conspicuous in the early sixth century BC Campana Tomb,[10] also at Veii, but now the artist is experimenting with creating orderly decorative and "narrative" fields. The rear wall of the first chamber is decorated with two superimposed and tightly arranged compositions on either side of an opening to the rear chamber. The carefully rendered scenes are clearly based on the repertoire of Corinthian vase-painting.[11] Lions, panthers, fantastic animals and a few human figures overlap one another and are intertwined with decorative elements, mainly palmettes, creating a sense of *horror vacui,* a familiar quality of much of the vase painting of this period. The upper register on the right omits the fantastic beasts and depicts a horse and rider with companions, a reference to hunting or to a mythological event (Fig. 6.38).[12] The abstract plants now serve as landscape elements. There is ground, background (overlapping) and landscape (albeit symbolic) on a large scale. While the general style, individual forms and composition point to an origin in Greek vase-painting, the size, location and disposition of the paintings are not those of a vase-painter. The precision of line, graceful proportions and creative polychromy suggest an artist comfortable with the larger scale. Although the artist may not have been Greek, given the traffic in Greek vases and the presence of Greek artisans in Etruria, he would have been aware of the Greek visual vocabulary.[13]

Beginning in the period that coincides with the height of the Greek Archaic (circa 575–480 BC), the tomb painters of Tarquinia developed a standard decorative treatment of the chamber walls.[14] The resulting effect is that of a house or a tent with a tympanum zone at either end of the chamber set apart from the main frieze by a polychrome decorative

Figure 56.1   Rear wall of the "Tomb of the Roaring Lions," Veii. Image courtesy of the Soprintendenza per i Beni Archeologici dell'Etruria Meridionale.

strip. Below the frieze, a dado, variously decorated or consisting of a monochrome field, separates the ground from the main action. In the Tomb of the Lionesses (circa 520 BC, Fig. 56.2) the lowest (dado) zone represents the wavy sea with leaping dolphins and blue birds above. A straight thin red line of the cord impression, used in planning the composition, runs along the top of the waves.[15]

The Greek story of the Ambush of Troilus by Achilles decorates the back wall of the main chamber of the Tomb of the Bulls (circa 530 BC) at Tarquinia. The scene is familiar in black figure Greek vase paintings.[16] (Fig. 56.3) The Etruscan artist provides a fresh and lively rendering of the event. The scene adheres to the basic elements of the story as depicted on Greek vases, but Troilus' sister, Polyxena, has been omitted. The necessary prop, the large fountain with recumbent lion spouts dominates the center of the composition. On the left lurks Achilles, knife raised in his left hand, ready to strike. On the right, water flows from the lion spout into a basin as Troilus approaches on the back of a large reddish-beige horse. The artist obviously started with the horse, had a bit of

Figure 56.2   Tarquinia. Tomb of the Lionesses, rear wall. Image courtesy of the Soprintendenza per i Beni Archeologici dell'Etruria Meridionale.

Figure 56.3   Tarquinia, Tomb of the Bulls: detail of rear wall: Achilles and Troilus. Image courtesy of the Soprintendenza per i Beni Archeologici dell'Etruria Meridionale.

trouble and corrected its head and legs, and then squeezed Troilus on top, so that his head is far too small and projects into the striped border. The naked young prince sports fancy pointed soft leather shoes (*calcei repandi*), indicating his high status. A large fig tree in the center and various other plants as well as the frieze of trees hung with swags below the main panel, set the action in a grove. The artist is not yet comfortable with converting vase painting into a large-scale figural scene, but the attempt indicates that he has gone beyond the essentially decorative confines of pottery and the result is not an attempted copy but a new rendering on a large flat surface of a great dramatic event. The emphasis on landscape elements of trees and plants, especially the wonderful fig tree in the center, are the hallmark of this Etruscan hand.

The Tomb of Hunting and Fishing (circa 510–500 BC, Fig. 56.4) is one of the most remarkable creations of the Archaic period in Etruria.[17] It is almost as if the artist had decided to convert the formulaic waves, dolphins and birds of the dado zone of the Tomb of the Lionesses (Fig. 56.2) into a panorama of life on the sea on all four walls of the small back chamber. The water is a narrow dado zone teeming with life. Birds, dolphins and men are engaged in a variety of activities: net and spear fishing from colorful boats, diving off a striped rock sprouting plants, and hunting birds with a slingshot from another colorful rock.[18] Garlands hang into this happy atmosphere from the upper zone and a lively banquet is in progress in the tympanum of the rear wall. The overall composition is astonishing in its spontaneity, yet it is surprisingly well balanced. The blank background reads not as solid surface; this landscape could easily exist as a lovely seascape without the human figures.[19]

At this period of Etruscan painting overlapping is the only technique used to create spatial relationships. Small and large figures and objects share the same space, perhaps to be read according to hierarchic relationships as in the tympana of the Tomb of Hunting and Fishing (Fig. 56.4) and the Tomb of the Lionesses (Fig. 56.2). Landscape elements such as trees, plants, waves, rocks and interspersed animals provide a sense of life within these dark burial chambers. One of the most touching examples of this is the little mouse, precariously perched on the tip of a leaf in the Tomb of the Mouse (Fig. 56.5).[20]

The figural conventions of Etruscan wall paintings continue to follow the stylistic developments in Greek vase painting: increasingly complex poses, overlapping and a trend toward naturalism in the depiction of the human figure. The varied and contorted

Figure 56.4 Tarquinia, Tomb of Hunting and Fishing: Rear wall of inner chamber. Image courtesy of the Soprintendenza per i Beni Archeologici dell'Etruria Meridionale.

poses of the dancers in the Tomb of the Triclinium, Tarquinia, (circa 470 BC, Fig. 56.6) recall the work of the nearly contemporary red-figure Athenian Brygos Painter.[21] The high quality of the paintings has led scholars to suggest a Greek artist or an Etruscan one trained by a Greek. If so, the painter could not have been specialized in vase painting. The contorted poses of the Etruscan dancers surpass their small-scale Greek contemporaries in creating the sense of arrested motion and the expressive gestures of their exaggeratedly enlarged hands are genuinely Etruscan. The large colorful figures perform in a grove inhabited by a variety of birds and at least one feline on each wall. The trees, on a disproportionately small scale compared with the figures, display a rich variety of foliage, now mostly faded, but accessible through the precise *lucidi* executed in the nineteenth century by Carlo Ruspi.[22] Figures and trees overlap as the dancers move through the lush vegetation of a sacred grove.

In the Tomb of the Ship (circa 450 BC or slightly later, Fig. 56.7),[23] the banquet taking place on the back wall and in the tympanum continues on to the side walls, thereby binding the distinct zones of side and back walls into a continuous spatial arrangement. Figures with their backs to the banquet announce a change in theme and perhaps also of space.[24] On the right wall a cortege moves toward the symposium, whereas on the left a small red tree separates the scene of banquet preparation, *kylikeon* and servants and musicians facing right, from an imposing male figure facing left gazing out to a marine landscape composed of two colorful rocks[25] and six boats. The boats are of varying sizes with a large merchant ship dominating the foreground. The disposition of ships and landscape elements suggests an attempt to create spatial depth.[26] Such spatial innovations,

Figure 56.5 Tarquinia, Tomb of the Mouse: detail with the mouse. Image courtesy of the Soprintendenza per i Beni Archeologici dell'Etruria Meridionale.

Figure 56.6 Tarquinia, Tomb of the Triclinium, right wall. Image courtesy of the Soprintendenza per i Beni Archeologici dell'Etruria Meridionale.

combined with the increased use of foreshortening in the depictions of figures coincide with a decline in the use of landscape elements, such as trees.

By the end of the fifth century BC the Etruscan artist, perhaps inspired by Greek innovations in perspective, especially the technique of *skiagraphia* (depicting shadows), begins to lose interest in "landscape" in favor of creating three-dimensional forms. A good example is the Tomb of Orcus II (Figs 56.8 and 56.9), where foreshortening and shading and highlighting are skillfully employed to populate the world of Hades. The few "landscape" elements, the rocks of the entrance to the Underworld inhabited by Theseus and Sisyphus, serve as locators. These paintings are not blown-up vase decorations, but reflect contemporary large-scale Greek paintings.[27] The purely Etruscan elements here are the demons, Tuchulcha, Charun and probably a Vanth who have invaded the Greek underworld in the tomb of the famous Spurinna family.[28]

These late paintings do not carry on the earlier Etruscan tradition of painting landscape elements teeming with life on the walls of their dark tombs. The torch or lamp light of a visitor to the Tomb of Orcus II (Figs 56.8–9) would have illuminated intimidating, large, seemingly three dimensional forms, as opposed to the earlier tombs where glimpses of trees, birds, dolphins over waves provided the setting for the human activities taking place on the walls.

Figure 56.7   Tarquinia, Tomb of the Ship. Right wall. Image courtesy of the Soprintendenza per i Beni Archeologici dell'Etruria Meridionale.

Figure 56.8   Tarquinia, Tomb of Orcus II, right wall (right). Image courtesy of Stephan Steingräber. (Photograph: Steingräber-Schwanke).

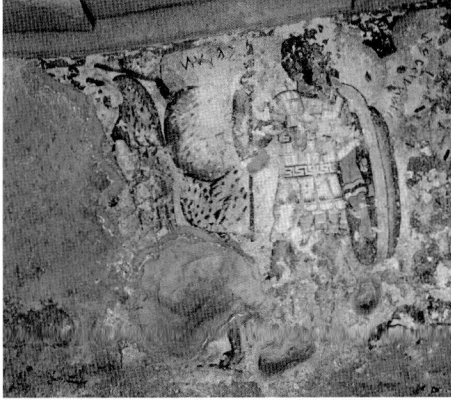

Figure 56.9 Tarquinia, Tomb of Orcus II, rear wall (left). Image courtesy of Stephan Steingräber. (Photograph: Steingräber, Schwanke).

NOTES

1   For example, Spivey 1997: 104; Steingräber 2006: *passim.* Haynes 2000: 225, 231, etc.; Pieraccini 2011: 65, suggests that in addition to Greek influence, one city may have inspired another artistically. See Chapter 48 on foreign artisans.
2   Brendel 1995: 120–121, while he recognized the strong influence of Greek art and culture on Etruscan.
3   Steingräber 2006: 63, 123–125. (Campana and Boccanera Plaques from Cerveteri. On formerly unpublished plaques: Pieraccini 2011: 55–70.
4   Moretti 1970: xxiii–xxv; Spivey 1997: 104–108; Steingräber 2006: 10, 20; Vlad Borelli 2003: 140–153.
5   Steingräber 2006: 16.
6   For example, Steingräber 2006: 62: Campana Plaque, circa 570 BC.
7   Archaeological evidence: Haynes 2000: 172–174, Gravisca as one example. See also 64–65 for sources on Greek immigrants, specifically Demaratos of Corinth. (Pliny *HN.* 35. 152).
8   Discovered in 2006. Boitani 2010: 23–47.
9   Boitani 2010: 23–24.
10 Steingräber 1986: No. 176, 374–376, with bibliography.
11 Corinthian and Etrusco-Corinthian painting: Amyx 1988; Szilágyi 1992.
12 Steingräber 2006: 58–60.
13 Brendel and Serra Ridgway 1995: 120–122, excellent discussion of what is and is not Greek about these paintings.
14 This is not to say that all Tarquinian tomb paintings from this period adhere to an identical scheme, but that most follow this general scheme.
15 Vlad Borelli, L. V. 1986: 83–84.
16 On the larger question of the reception of Greek myth and specifically on the imagery in this tomb see: Oleson 1975: 189–200. See also Osborne 2001: 277–295.
17 General description and bibliography: Steingräber (ed.) 1986: No. 50, 293–294; an informative study: Holloway 1965: 341–347.
18 A similar rocky formation separates the large ship from the depiction of the deceased about to partake in a banquet in the Tomb of the Ship. Steingräber 2006: 153.
19 Holloway (1965: 69) traces elements of the painting to Greek vase painting, but notes that in Greek vase painting "...the crucial effect of the open sky is always lacking." Examples

of landscape in contemporary black-figure Greek vase painting: "Olive harvest" on a neck amphora by the Antimenes Painter (London. British Musem B226; *ABV* 270.52) from Vulci, and "bathing women" by the Priam Painter (Villa Giulia Museum, Inv. No. 106463). Colonna 2003: 77, calls the walls of the back chamber a global landscape of the Elysian fields with birds as the unifying elements.

20 Steingräber (ed.) 1986: No. 119, plates 153–156.
21 Outside and tondo of kylix in Munich, Antikensammlung 2645, *ARV*371, 15.
22 Steingräber 2006: 138–139.
23 Most recently: Colonna 2003: 63–77.
24 Similar approach in the Tomb of the Funeral Couch (460–450 BC). Influence of 5th century BC. Attic vase painting noted here by Steingräber 1986: 320, especially in the rendering of the youth leading the blue horse on the right.
25 The one on the left mostly destroyed, the one on the right similar to its counterpart in the Tomb of Hunting and Fishing, with little plants growing on its edges.
26 Colonna 2003, 74–75, notes that this spatial arrangement calls to mind the innovations of Polygnotos (Pausanias 10.25.1; the Knidian *Lesche* at Delphi), and the work of Agatharchos of Samos. The latter was especially known for a form of linear perspective; see Vitruvius 7, praef. 11.
27 Apollodorus of Athens: Pliny *NH* 35.60 or Zeuxis of Herakleia, Pliny *NH* 61–66, according to Pliny, both known for "representing appearances."
28 For a description: Steingräber (ed.). 1986: 329–332; for context: Steingräber 2006: 185–206. On the style: Brendel 1995: 337–339. For more on mythical and underworld characters, see Chapter 25.

BIBLIOGRAPHY

Amyx, D. A. (1988) *Corinthian Vase-painting of the Archaic Period*, Berkeley: University of California Press.

Boitani, F. (2010) "Veio. La tomba dei leoni ruggenti. Dati preliminari" in P. A. Gianfrotta and A. M. Moretti (eds), *Archeologia nella Tuscia. Atti dell'incontro di studi (Viterbo 2 Marzo 2007), Daidalos* 10: 23–47.

Brendel, O. and Serra Ridgway, F. (1995) *Etruscan Art*, 2nd edition, New Haven: Yale University Press.

Colonna, G. (2003) "Osservazione sulla Tomba tarquiniese della Nave" in A. Minetti (ed.), 63–77.

Haynes, S. (2000) *Etruscan Civilization. A Cultural History*, Los Angeles: The J. Paul Getty Museum.

Holloway, R. R. (1965) "Conventions of Etruscan painting in the Tomb of Hunting and Fishing at Tarquinii," *American Journal of Archaeology,* 69: 341–347.

——(1986) "The Bulls in 'The Tomb of the Bulls' at Tarquinia," *American Journal of Archaeology*, 90: 447–452.

Minetti, A. (ed.) (2003) *Pittura etrusca: problemi e prospettive. Atti del convegno, Sarteano, Teatro comunale degli Arrischianti, 26 ottobre 2001, Chiusi, Teatro comunale Mascagni, 27 October 2001.* Siena: Amministrazione provinciale di Siena – Sistema dei Musei senesi, Siena: Protagon editori toscani.

Moretti, M. (1970) *New Monuments of Etruscan Painting*, trans. D. Kiang, University Park: Penn State University Press.

Oleson, J. P. (1975) "Greek myth and Etruscan imagery in the tomb of the Bulls at Tarquinia," *American Journal of Archaeology* 79: 189–200.

Osborne, R. (2001) "Why did Athenian pots appeal to the Etruscans?" *World Archaeology* 33: 277–295.

Pieraccini, L. (2011) "The colors of Caere in California," *Etruscan Studies,* 14: 55–70.

Rizzo, M. A. (ed.) (1989) *Pittura etrusca al Museo di Villa Giulia / nelle foto di Thashi Otamura*. Studi di Archeologia 6: Rome: Soprintendenza archeologica per l'Etruria meridionale. De Luca.

Roncalli, F. (2003) " La defininizione dello spazio tombale in Etruria tra architettura e pittura" in A. Minetti (ed.), 52–62.

Spivey, N. (1997) *Etruscan Art*, New York and London: Thames & Hudson.

Steingräber, S. (2006) *Abundance of Life: Etruscan Wall Painting*. trans. R. Stockman, Los Angeles: Johnson Reprint Corporation.

Steingräber, S. (ed.) (1986) *Etruscan Painting. Catalogue Raisonné of Etruscan Wall Paintings*, English-language editors: D. and F. R. Ridgway, New York: Johnson Reprint Corporation.

Szilágyi, J. Gy. (1992) *Ceramica etrusco-corinzia figurate. Parte I. 630580 a.C.* Florence: L. S. Olschki.

Torelli, M. (1997) *Il rango, il rito e l'immagine. Alle origini della rappresentazione storica romana*, Milan: Flecta

Vlad Borelli, L. V. (2003) "Profilo storico della tecnologia sella pittura tombale Etrusca" in A. Minetti (ed.), 140–153.

Vlad Borelli, L. V. (1986) "Techniques and Conservation of Etruscan Painting" in S. Steingräber (ed.), 83–91.

CHAPTER FIFTY SEVEN

THE TRADITION OF VOTIVE BRONZES IN ETRURIA

———•◆•———

Margherita Gilda Scarpellini

The Etruscans were famous among the peoples of ancient Italy for their production of valuable bronzes. The Roman poet Horace mentions the Etruscan statuettes, *tyrrhena sigilla*, which represented true treasures in the precious collections of the wealthy Romans at the time of Augustus (*Ep.* 2.2.180–181) and Pliny the Elder refers to large bronze statues, *signa tuscanica* that were known everywhere (*HN* 34.16.34). Pliny also talks about an incident, described by Metrodorus of Scepsis who reported the Roman theft of 2,000 statues in the temple at Volsinii in 264 BC, votive offerings of the faithful to the gods. The episode makes us realize how much interest there was for bronze in Antiquity, a material that could be melted down for other use. Furthermore, we see how much the Etruscans were dedicated to practices of devotion: the Etruscan votive bronze statuettes, the so-called "idols," constituted valuable offerings to the deities. Such *ex voto* bronzes were usually deposited at the sanctuaries, attached to a stone base through the bronze strips intentionally left underneath the feet after the statuette had been made. Nevertheless, when the cult place was moved, or the votive offerings had filled up all the available space, they were buried in large pits (*stipes*), always located within the sacred areas. We should also remember the presence of those votive bronzes thrown into sacred places such as rivers, springs, or wells, of which the territory around Arezzo preserves numerous examples (such as Brolio and Monte Falterona).

In ancient Italy, the production of anthropomorphic bronze statuettes begins in the later phase of the early Iron Age in the eighth century BC[1] and is particularly well documented in Etruria where the availability of metals (iron, copper, lead, and, in less quantity, silver and tin) present in the Colline Metallifere, in the Campiglese area, on the island of Elba, and in the Monti Rognosi in the Arretine territory,[2] provide the source for the formation of a specialized craftsmanship (see Chapter 37). In particular, it was the search for tin that determined the movement of groups from Etruria all over Europe, as is documented by the finds of Etruscan bronzes in the Loire district, in Cornwall, and in Pomerania.[3]

From the end of the eighth and in particular throughout the seventh century BC, following the Greek example, the bronzes representing living creatures, men, women, and animals, are an expression of their sacred destination in Etruria in general but beginning in the last thirty years of the seventh century BC, they become characteristic of northern Etruria and, in particular, the areas of Volterra and Arezzo; in these areas the human figures are rendered in a frontal position and stand with the arms folded in front in a "Hittite pose," or some female figures have their hands on their breasts or grasp the ends of their braids, all of them displaying Near Eastern influences. As far as the subjects are concerned, the earliest examples represent in ideal form male and female worshippers identified according to their specific social positions. The men in particular are represented with a display of their male features, but essentially as warriors (for example, the so-called "gladiators" from Volterra and Arezzo) (Figure 57.1a), and belong to societies organized around the military chieftains, while the women have clothing representing their high rank (Figure 57.1b).[4]

The presence of this kind of *ex voto* statuettes is sporadic and occasional in southern Etruria and Latium. Beginning in the fifth century BC analogous production in terracotta develops in these areas, probably through influences from Magna Graecia.[5]

Throughout the span of noteworthy diffusion of bronzes in the central and northern regions of Etruria and in the Po valley we see a change in the image of the worshippers. In fact, in the middle of the sixth century BC, they appear as a nude *kouros* or a *kore* dressed in a *tunica*, *tutulus*, and *calcei repandi* (tunic, conical headdress and shoes with upturned toes); towards the end of the sixth century BC there is added an offering in the right hand or prayer position with the arms along the body and the hands outstretched. In addition to the nude *kouroi*, figures of athletes appear with a display of physical qualities: these images of the worshippers in heroic nudity tend to disappear in the Classical and Hellenistic periods.[6]

During the Hellenistic period we find a series of worshippers (Figure 57.2), in both Etruria proper and in areas under Etruscan influence, that were produced from the third century BC to the Early Empire:[7] the male figures, characterized by a wreath crown of a

Figure 57.1a–b   Armed worshipper (late seventh century BC). Arezzo, Museo Archeologico Nazionale Mecenate. Inv. no. 11495 (Photo Tavanti, Arezzo). Female worshipper (600–575 BC). Arezzo, Museo Archeologico Nazionale Mecenate. Inv. no. 11501 (after Maetzke 1987, 187).

Figure 57.2 Worshippers of the Hellenistic period. Arezzo, Museo Archeologico Nazionale Mecenate. Inv. nos. 12033 and 11698 (Photo Tavanti, Arezzo).

type inspired from Magna Graecia, are dressed in a *himation* or *pallium* around the hips or a short toga, and the female figures, with a three-pointed diadem and torque necklace, hold a *patera* for the libation and box (*acerra*) for incense. This typology, the best-known examples of which are those from Nemi in the British Museum,[8] has a noteworthy distribution across sketchy and schematic products and relates to the Dionysiac cult. Still in the Hellenistic period we find a production of statuettes of young boys, *pueri*,[9] some belonging to the aristocratic social class, recognized by the *bulla* attached around the neck, as for example the putto Graziani[10] or the boy with the duck (in some publications referred to as a goose) from Montecchio (see Figure 57.8).

In the votive deposits we also find statuettes of animals such as horses, deer, and hares pertaining to the aristocratic hunt (Brolio) or domestic animals such as pigs, chickens, and ducks (Arezzo, Fonte Veneziana), and above all bovines (Arezzo, Volterra) (Figs. 57.3a, 3b and 3c). In connection with healing cults or waters with healing or therapeutic qualities we find human body parts such as heads, eyes, legs, arms, and breasts (for example, at Arezzo, Fonte Veneziana, and Monte Falterona). Furthermore, there are representations of divinities with their attributes, such as *Tinia* with the lightning bolt, *Aplu* with the lyre, *Fufluns*, *Laran*, *Hercle* and *Menerva*, and other deities of the Etruscan pantheon, identified by the dedicatory inscription (*Culsans*, *Thanr*, *Selvans*).

I will conclude this brief survey of the typological and chronological evolution of the bronze statuettes and statues from the sacred and devotional sphere by mentioning some unusual examples of large statues, such as the Mars from Todi,[11] the Chimaera from Arezzo, and *l'Arringatore*, votive offerings by communities or wealthy citizens who continued to exist in Etruria. Seeing that the tradition of production of votive bronzes has been particularly well documented in Arezzo and its territory, it is relevant to discuss the Chimaera, and, in view of recent studies and restorations, also the Minerva of Arezzo.

The Chimaera was discovered on November 15, 1553 in Arezzo near the Porta S. Lorenzo as a result of Cosimo I de' Medici's construction of the defensive walls of the city. It is considered an offering to *Tinia* because of the votive inscription *tinścvil* found on the right front paw of the animal. The statue should be considered a precious gift dedicated in a suburban sanctuary along the road to Fiesole by an individual aristocrat or by a group.[12] On the basis of stylistic comparisons with the art of Greece and Magna Graecia from the late fifth-century BC, the Chimaera enters into the Atticizing sphere and has therefore been dated to the early fourth century BC. The hypothesis has been proposed that the statue was made in Arezzo by a group of artisans representing the craftsmanship of Greece and Italy, and of southern Etruria, as documented by the letterforms used in the inscription executed before the statue was cast.[13]

We know from the archival documents that the Chimaera was discovered together with a large number of small bronzes representing young men and bearded men, birds and other animals, in fact, constituting a true votive deposit. Recently, Maggiani has discovered the bronze statuettes in the old Medici collections of the Uffizi galleries in Florence, which formed part of the deposit with the Chimaera: a statuette of *Tinia* (third century BC) (Figure 57.4a), a young worshipper with *pallium* (Figure 57.4b), and a griffin (fourth century BC).[14]

Figure 57.3a–c   Archaic statuette of bovine. Arezzo, Museo Archeologico Nazionale Mecenate. Inv. no. 11524 (after Maetzke 1987). Rooster from Arezzo: Fonte Veneziana (fifth century BC). Florence, Museo Archeologico Nazionale. Inv. 544 (after Scarpellini 2007, 47, fig.7). Statuette of wild boar from Arezzo: Fonte Veneziana (fifth century BC) Florence, Museo Archeologico Nazionale. Inv. no. 470 (after Scarpellini 2009B, 28).

Figure 57.4a–b   Statuette of *Tinia* from Arezzo: votive deposit of Chimaera (third century BC). Florence, Museo Archeologico Nazionale. Inv. no. 15 (after *Etruschi nel tempo*, 4). Young male worshipper from Arezzo: votive deposit of Chimaera (late fourth century BC). Florence, Museo Archeologico Nazionale. Inv. no. 4 (after *Etruschi nel tempo*, 5).

According to Colonna,[15] the statue known as the *Arringatore* originated in Arezzo in the early second century BC, as an *ex voto* dedicated to the god *Tece Sans*. Also in Arezzo, in 1541 the statue of Minerva was found in a well near the church of S. Lorenzo. Considered a cult statue, it was previously regarded as a Roman copy of a Greek original, dated to the mid-fourth century BC but, after a detailed scientific analysis and careful restoration, it is now dated to the early part of the third century BC and was the product of an "Italic" workshop, hence perhaps Arretine (Figure 57.5).[16]

The series of remarkable examples discussed above confirm the considerable ability in metallurgy that can be attributed to Arezzo, an Etruscan lucumony, known not only for its production of weapons (Livy 28.45.16–17)[17] but also, since the sixth century BC, for its production of large and small statues thanks to the presence of specialized artisans as well as mineral resources (copper and iron) at nearby Monti Rognosi and Staggiano (perhaps tin), of abundant water (Arno, Chiana, Tiber) and wood (forests in Casentino); all elements necessary for the production of metals. Such testimonies, even though they may be indirect, are clearly clues that allow us to speculate on the presence of local workshops, in addition to the many discoveries in the city of Arezzo and surroundings of votive deposits, isolated and sporadic bronze statuettes linked with the sacred areas of Valdichiana, of Casentino, and of Valtiberina. Furthermore, we should consider the fact that in the museums of Volterra and Arezzo as well as in the collections of the seventeenth–eighteenth centuries of these two centers, there are a large number of bronzes for which the two cities are the undisputed places of production.[18]

Undoubtedly, the Valdichiana together with the city of Arezzo exhibit the largest number of bronzes from the Archaic period to the late Hellenistic within the territory. Recent discoveries of votive bronzes of the Hellenistic period include finds from the temple at Castiglion Fiorentino (Figs. 57.6a, 57.6b),[19] at the small rural sanctuary at

Figure 57.5   Minerva from Arezzo after the recent restoration. Florence, Museo Archeologico Nazionale. Inv. no. 2 (after Cygielman 2008, Fig. 1).

Figure 57.6a–b Female worshipper (third–second century BC). Castiglion Fiorentino, Museo Civico Archeologico Inv. 205665A (Archivio fotografico Istituzione Culturale ed Educativa Castiglionese, Castiglion Fiorentino, Arezzo). Female worshipper (third–second century BC). Castiglion Fiorentino, Museo Civico Archeologico Inv. 205665 (Archivio fotografico Istituzione Culturale ed Educativa Castiglionese, Castiglion Fiorentino, Arezzo).

Ossaia-Terontola,[20] as well as the Late Archaic and Late Classical examples from the sanctuary at via Capitini at Camucia-Cortona.[21]

In 1863, along the east bank of the river Clanis near Castiglion Fiorentino, which is an Etruscan *oppidum* with an important acropolis of a sacred nature, the exceptional discovery was made of Etruscan bronzes (statuettes and luxury vessels) at Brolio, the so-called Brolio Deposit.[22] For a long time there has been discussion of the interpretation of the deposit, but the most prevalent theory is that it is a votive deposit. Maggiani has recently considered the site the result of a ritual of immersion, perhaps dedicated to *Hercle*,[23] thus a place of worship where the worshippers threw their votive offerings directly into the water, similar to what took place at the Lake of the Idols on Monte Falterona.

The best known finds from Brolio are three bronze warriors (Figure 57.7a), and a female, probably armed (Figure 57.7b), to be interpreted as supports of *perirrhanteria*, which are large basins used for ritual cleansing.[24] This use is suggested in particular by the female figure, which is reminiscent of the caryatids of the bucchero chalices from Cerveteri and Tarquinia, but in particular the Castellani bronze chalice used for a *lustratio*, or cleansing ritual in a funerary context.[25]

The Brolio complex is in fact one of the most important examples of Etruscan sculpture in the Archaic period of the sixth century BC. The bronze *anathemata* (votive offerings) from Brolio originate in workshops at Chiusi and Arezzo and represent both armed male figures, in the style of the god *Laran* and chief warriors, and female worshippers in aristocratic dress, in addition to bronzes of horses, deer (Figure 57.7c), and hares.[26]

Figure 57.7a–c   Warrior from Brolio (550 BC). Florence, Museo Archeologico Nazionale.
Inv. no. 562 (Archivio fotografico Istituzione Culturale ed Educativa Castiglionese, Castiglion
Fiorentino, Arezzo). Female armed figure from Brolio (550 BC). Florence, Museo Archeologico
Nazionale. Inv. no. 561 (Archivio fotografico Istituzione Culturale ed Educativa Castiglionese,
Castiglion Fiorentino, Arezzo). Statuettes of deer from Brolio (560–550 BC). Florence, Museo
Archeologico Nazionale. Inv. nos. 558 and 559 (Archivio fotografico Istituzione Culturale ed
Educativa Castiglionese, Castiglion Fiorentino, Arezzo).

In 1746, we have another extraordinary discovery, also near Castiglion Fiorentino, at
Montecchio. It consists of splendid bronzes of the Hellenistic period (third–second
century BC), produced in an Etruscan workshop in the north, perhaps in Arezzo, and
probably part of a votive deposit belonging to a nearby sanctuary. The group consists of
a *thymiaterion* (incense burner), a shovel, a female worshipper with a triangular diadem, a
young boy with a duck, and a female worshipper with a *patera*.[27]

The finds became part of the collection of a nobleman at Cortona, Galeotto Ridolfini
Corazzi, and in the early nineteenth century they were sold by Jean Emile Humbert
to the Rijksmuseum van Oudheden in Leiden, where they remain today. Two of these
bronzes, the *thymiaterion* and the statuette of the child with the duck (Figure 57.8) are
interesting because of the Etruscan dedicatory inscription to the goddess *Tufltha*,[28] a deity
perhaps linked to the sphere of fertility and the protection of childhood.[29]

In fact, the statuette of the child is a votive offering by *Velia Fanacnei* to the goddess on behalf of her son. The child is portrayed nude with a duck in his arms, and is characterized by his curly hair, a *bulla*, which is a sign that he had the status of *liber* (free), and by a bracelet with pendants. The statuette can be dated to the middle of the second century BC because of its baroque Hellenistic features and the style of the letters in the inscription.

As for Arezzo, one should mention first of all the votive deposit at Fonte Veneziana,[30] discovered in 1869 near a gate, still referred to during the Middle Ages as *"Augurata"* (inaugurated), an area which today is within the modern city, but which in ancient times corresponded with the north-east edge of the hill of S. Donato, where the Etruscan settlement of Arezzo was located.

The bronzes found in Arezzo, some 180 objects, consist in particular of figures of *kurai* and *kouroi* (Figs. 57.9a, 57.9b), dated to between 530 and 480 BC, and are the products of Arretine workshops in which the influence of the Ionic sculptural style is dominant. Among the figures are domestic animals and anatomical body parts such as heads, eyes, arms, and legs, which are connected with a healing cult as indicated by the presence of a fountain fed by the spring of the Alpi di Poti. It is interesting to notice the presence of bones of pigs, cows, and sheep, which may suggest the ritual practice of *suovetaurilia* at the closing of the votive deposit. Together with the bronze statuettes were found fibulae, rings, and Etruscan and Attic pottery, as also found in the deposit at Brolio, and at S. Bartolomeo, where the finds unfortunately were already dispersed at their discovery.[31]

From S. Giusto-Le Gagliarde, where there perhaps existed a small extra-urban sanctuary, and near the area of the deposit at Fonte Veneziana, derives the group of the *Aratore* (ploughman) found in the seventeenth century together with other bronzes, (Figure 57.10).[32] The ploughman with the animal skin tied in a knot at the neck, and a large *petasos* (hat) is shown intent on ploughing with the help of two oxen. In the *Museum Etruscum* by Francesco Gori, he is shown accompanied by a statuette of *Menerva* as *Athena Ergane*, and the group thus assumes a symbolic value, which may be connected with the rites of the foundation of the city.[33] The statuette was made in a north Etruscan workshop and can be dated to 430–400 BC.

Other votive statuettes illustrate the bronze production of Arretine workshops, such as two male figures, a nude *kouros* from Lignano (Figure 57.11), and an athlete from Quarata (Figure 57.12). The findspots of these votive statuettes are important for our understanding of Arezzo and its territory. The *kouros* with a pronounced chest and well-articulated legs suggests characteristic stylistic developments in relation to the *kouroi* of Fonte Veneziana. It is dated to 500–480 BC and comes from the peak of Monte Lignano, a stopping point with a spring and serving as passage between Valdichiana and the basin of Arezzo.[34]

The bronze statuette at the Bibliothèque Nationale in Paris, which depicts an athlete ready to jump with his *halteres* (counter weights), was found at Quarata near Arezzo at the confluence of the rivers Clanis and Arno.[35] On his right leg is an Etruscan inscription, *mi klaninśl*[36] which identifies him as the property of a man whose name was derived from the river name Clanis, or better, from a deity, in this case a river god (*Klanins*) to whom in all likelihood the statuette was given as a votive offering. Produced in 460–440 BC it belongs to a group of late Archaic athletic figures produced in Chiusi and Arezzo.[37]

To the north of Arezzo, in the Casentino area, on Monte Falterona at the source of the river Arno, we find the small lake known as Lake Ciliegeta or the Lake of the Idols.[38] The location ought to indicate a kind of station along a traveling route between northern

Figure 57.8 Putto from Montecchio (second century BC). Leiden, Rijksmuseum van Oudheden. Inv. no. CO4 (Archivio fotografico Istituzione Culturale ed Educativa Castiglionese, Castiglion Fiorentino, Arezzo).

Figure 57.9a–b *Kouros* from Arezzo: Fonte Veneziana (530–510 BC). Florence, Museo Archeologico Nazionale. Inv. no. 68 (after Cristofani 1985, Figure 3.2). *Kore* from Arezzo: Fonte Veneziana (520–500 BC). Florence, Museo Archeologico Nazionale. Inv. no. 264 (after Cristofani 1985, Figure 3.13).

Etruria and the Po valley. In fact, into the small lake, which is fed by an underground spring, and tied to *sanatio* (healing)[39] were thrown directly hundreds of votive bronzes, dated from the late sixth century BC to the Republican period. The sacred place was visited by soldiers and shepherds as part of transhumance, as is shown by the discovery in 1838[40] of more than 600 bronzes of males, females, and anatomical parts, about 1,000 pieces of *aes rude* and 2,000 arrow heads and javelin points that were scattered between local collections and large museums abroad.

Figure 57.10   Left leg of male statuette (400 BC). Arezzo, Museo Archeologico Nazionale Mecenate. Inv. no. 11023 (after Scarpellini Testi 2000, Figure 6).

Figure 57.11   *Kouros* from Arezzo: Monte Lignano (500–480 BC). Arezzo, Museo Archeologico Nazionale Mecenate. Inv. no. 11563 (after Scarpellini Testi 1996, 14).

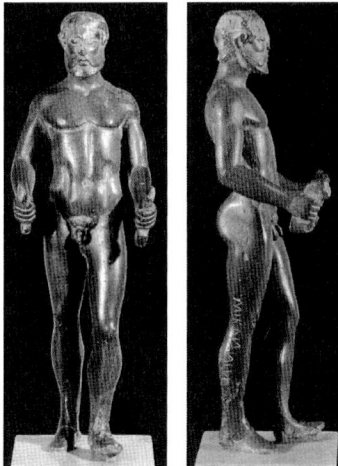

Figure 57.12   Athlete from Arezzo: Quarata (460–440 BC). Paris, Bibliothèque Nationale. Inv. no. 921 (after Scarpellini 2007, 48, Figure 9).

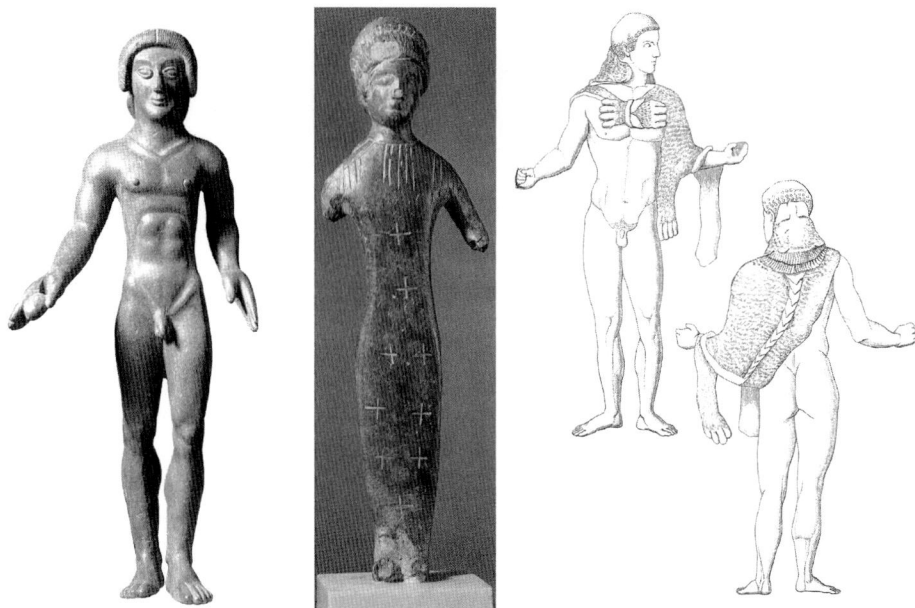

Figure 57.13a–c *Kouros* from Lago degli Idoli (480–460 BC). Paris, Musée du Louvre. Inv. no. 220 (after *Etruschi nel tempo*, 10). Female worshipper from Lago degli Idoli (500–450 BC). Paris, Musée du Louvre. Inv. no. 230 (After Cristofani 1985, fig. 4.4). *Hercle* from Lago degli Idoli. London, British Museum. Inv. no. 463 (Drawing after Micali 1844, tav.15).

At the Lake of the Idols one can follow the stylistic and chronological evolution of the votive bronze statuettes, the standing nude *kouros* (Figure 57.13a), the *kore* (Figure 57.13b) as a worshipper praying and presenting offerings, the armed youth, the almost portrait-like heads, the representation of deities such as *Hercle* at the British Museum (Figure 57.13c), dated to 450 BC, which could have served as the protective deity of the place itself.

While the Etruscans were united in terms of language, culture, and religion, this brief survey of production of bronze statuettes and statues provides a good example of how each city developed its own characteristic artistic and commercial interests. In the case of Arezzo and its immediate territory, including Brolio and Montecchio, the availability of metals and water enabled the inhabitants to develop a bronze industry, and the goods could be easily transported to communities both near and far. Like Volterra and other centers in northern Etruria, the city of Arezzo maintained a position of wealth and power that was ultimately derived from a successful balance between artistic production and trade contacts with its neighbors.

NOTES

1 Peroni 1994, 100.
2 Camporeale 1985, 25.
3 Cristofani 1978, 127, with bibliography; Cristofani 1985, 17; Richardson 1983, 81; *Gli Etruschi e l'Europa* 1992, 180–195.
4 Cristofani 1978, 129; Cristofani 1985, *passim*, Richardson 1983.

5   Turfa 2006, 96 and fig. VI.6, with bibliography.
6   Cristofani 1985, 18.
7   A great number of bronzes come from Bolsena, Carsoli, and Vetulonia and were particularly popular in central Etruria in the Volsinian or Volsinian/Umbrian workshops (Benz 1992, *passim*).
8   Haynes 1960, 34–45; Cristofani 1985, 274–276; Turfa 2006, 93 and Fig. VI.5.
9   See in addition to the well-known statuettes of children, a boy with a dedicatory inscription to *Mantrn* (CIE 447) from Castiglion Fiorentino (Cortona, MAEC) (Bruschetti 2002, 95–99) and the series of bronzes from the stipe of Colle Arsiccio at Magione (National Museum at Perugia) (Feruglio 1999, 116).
10 Benz 1992, 179–180; Fiorini 2005, 313; Turfa 2006, 92, Fig. VI.2.
11 Città del Vaticano, Museo Gregoriano Etrusco, Inv. 13886 (Roncalli 1973).
12 Colonna 1985, 174.
13 Maggiani 1990, 53–63 with bibliography, Maggiani 2001, 57–59; Warden 2011, 1–5.
14 Maggiani 2001, 60–64.
15 Colonna 1990, 110.
16 Cygielman 2008, 3–11, with bibliography.
17 The passage in Livy lists the large number of weapons and tools that Arezzo provided for Scipio's expedition to Africa.
18 Balty 1966; Maetzke 1987, 185–196.
19 Scarpellini 2009, 261–264; Scarpellini 2010, 88 and catalogue entries by P. Zamarchi Grassi, 104–105.
20 Fracchia 2005, 390–392, n. IX, 12.
21 Salvi and Zamarchi Grassi 2005, 286–290; Fedeli and Salvi 2006, 177–180.
22 Romualdi 1981 with bibliography and archival records, Scarpellini Testi 1995, 111–121.
23 Maggiani 1999, 188.
24 Scarpellini 2002, 66; Scarpellini 2009A, 72–72.
25 Colonna 1982, 33–44.
26 Scarpellini 2002, 65–83; Scarpellini 2008, 21–41; Scarpellini 2010A, 113–116.
27 Halbertsma 1991, 68–70; Scarpellini 2002A, 87–94, and in particular 88–89, where I attribute to the group a bronze of a female worshipper with a patera on the basis of the treatise of Coltellini 1750, 118–119, 163–164, tav. III, Fiorini 2005, 310–312.
28 *Thymiaterion* CIE 445; child with duck CIE 446.
29 Fiorini 2005, 294 with bibliography.
30 Bocci Pacini 1990, 73–91; Zamarchi Grassi 2001, 111–129 with bibliography.
31 For the votive deposit at S. Bartolomeo, see the document of Gamurrini in Zamarchi Grassi 1989 348 and Fig. 13, from which it is shown that the cult place connected with it was frequented at least from the last quarter of the sixth century BC as documented at Fonte Veneziana.
32 Rome, Museo di Villa Giulia, Inv. 24562. Cristofani 1985, n. 54, Cherici 2001, 77–78. For a bronze leg found at Le Gagliarde in 1903, see Scarpellini Testi 1997, 70 and Scarpellini 2000, 40.
33 Edlund-Berry 2006, 117, fig. VII.2.
34 Arezzo, Museo Archeologico Nazionale Mecenate, Inv. 11563. Bocci Pacini 1975, 67; Scarpellini Testi 1996, 14, figs. 3–4.
35 Cristofani 1985, 268, n. 48 with bibliography; Scarpellini 2007, 48, fig. 9.
36 CIE 380=TLE 668.
37 Arezzo is well represented through examples of this typology. In addition to the athlete from Quarata there are a javelin thrower from Fonte Veneziana (Firenze, Museo Archeologico Nazionale, Inv. 472), an athlete from Porta Colcitrone (Arezzo, Museo Archeologico Nazionale

Mecenate, Inv. 19528), and a jumper from the Duomo Vecchio (Arezzo, Museo Archeologico Nazionale Mecenate, Inv. 11595).

38 Fedeli 2001, 89–108 with bibliography.

39 The healing cult is connected with the presence of creosote, a balsamic substance for the lungs, but above all, used as an antiseptic, antihemorrhagic and healing agent, ancient medicinal purposes which the ancient Etruscans and Romans would have recognized.

40 For the discoveries in 1972, see Fortuna and Giovannoni 1975. The Soprintendenza per i Beni Archeologici della Toscana conducted excavations from 2003 to 2006, for which see Fedeli 2004, 29–31; Fedeli 2006, 143–145. The recent finds, about 100 in all, are typologically similar to the bronzes of the nineteenth century, and include 30 votive heads, 37 anatomical parts and four animals, which, however, do not provide evidence to identify the deity for whom the cult practices were intended.

BIBLIOGRAPHY

Balty, J. C. (1966) "Un centre de production de bronzes figurés de l'Etrurie septentrionale (deuxième moitié du VII – première moitié du VI siècle av.J.- C.): Volterra ou Arezzo?" in *Bulletin de l'Institut Historique Belge de Rome*, 33: 1–64.

Benz, M. (1992) *Etruskische Votivbronzen des Hellenismus*, Florence: Olschki.

Bocci Pacini, P. (1975) "Appunti su Arezzo arcaica" in *Studi Etruschi*, 43: 47–70.

— (1980) "La stipe della Fonte Veneziana ad Arezzo" in *Studi Etruschi*, 48: 73–91.

Bruschetti, P. (2002) "Statuetta bronzea di fanciullo" in P. Zamarchi Grassi and M. G. Scarpellini (eds), *Tesori Ritrovati*, Exhibition catalogue, Castiglion Fiorentino, Montepulciano (Siena): Le Balze, 95–99.

Camporeale, G. (1985) "Introduzione" in G. Camporeale (ed.), *L'Etruria mineraria*, Exhibition catalogue, Portoferrario, Massa Marittima, Populonia, Milan: Electa, 21–36.

Cherici, A. (2001) "Gruppo dell'Aratore" in *Etruschi nel tempo. I ritrovamenti di Arezzo dal 1500 ad oggi*. Exhibition catalogue, Arezzo, July – December 2001 Basilica Inferiore di S. Francesco, Museo Archeologico Nazionale Mecenate di Arezzo, Florence: Nuova Grafica Fiorentina, 77–78.

Colonna, G. (1982) "Di Augusto Castellani e del c.d. calice a cariatidi prenestino" in *Miscellanea Archeologica Tobias Dohrn dedicata*, Roma: G. Bretschneider, 33–44.

——(1985) "I santuari di Arezzo" in G. Colonna (ed.), *Santuari d'Etruria*, Exhibition catalogue, Arezzo, Milan: Electa, 172–174.

——(1990) "Il posto dell'Arringatore nell'arte etrusca di età ellenistica" in *Studi Etruschi*, 56: 99–122. Florence: Olschki.

Coltellini, L. (1750) *Due ragionamenti agli Accademici Etruschi di Cortona sopra quattro superbi bronzi antichi*, Venezia.

Cristofani, M. (1978) *L'arte degli Etruschi Produzione e consumo*, Torino: Giulio Einaudi editore.

——(1985) *I bronzi degli Etruschi*, Novara: Istituto Geografico De Agostini.

Cygielman, M. (2008) "La Minerva di Arezzo" in M. Cygielman (ed.), *La Minerva di Arezzo*, Exhibition catalogue, Arezzo, July 2008 – January 2009, Florence: Nuova Grafica Fiorentina, 3–11.

Edlund-Berry, I. E. M. (2006) "Ritual Space and Boundaries in Etruscan Religion" in N. T. de Grummond and E. Simon (eds), *The Religion of the Etruscans*, Austin: University of Texas Press, 116–131.

Fedeli, L. (2001) "La stipe votiva del Lago degli Idoli" in *Etruschi nel tempo. I ritrovamenti di Arezzo dal 1500 ad oggi*. Exhibition catalogue, Arezzo, July – December, 2001 Basilica Inferiore di S. Francesco, Museo Archeologico Nazionale Mecenate di Arezzo, Florence: Nuova Grafica Fiorentina, 89–108.

——(2004) "La stipe votiva del Lago degli Idoli" in M. Ducci (ed.), *Santuari etruschi in Casentino*, Exhibition catalogue, Stia e Partina, July – October 2004, Ponte a Poppi: Comunità Montana del casentino, 24–31.

——(2006) "Stia (AR). Lago degli Idoli: campagna di scavo 2006" in *Notiziario Soprintendenza per i Beni Archeologici della Toscana*, 2: 143–145.

Fedeli, L. and Salvi, A. (2006) "Camucia di Cortona (Ar). Saggi archeologici in via Capitini" in *Notiziario della Soprintendenza per i Beni Archeologici della Toscana. Scavi e Ricerche sul territorio*, 2: 177–180.

Feruglio, A. E. (1999), "Materiali da Colle Arsiccio" in G. Baronti (ed.), *Percorsi di protezione della gravidanza del parto e della prima infanzia*, Exhibition, Corciano – Chiesa S. Francesco, 7–22 agosto 1999, Perugia: Graphic Masters, 112–117.

Fiorini, L. (2005) "I santuari del territorio" in S. Fortunelli (ed.), *MAEC Il museo della città etrusca e romana di Cortona*. Catalogo delle collezioni, Florence: Edizioni Polistampa, 291–317.

Fortuna, A. M. and Giovannoni, F. (1975) *Il Lago degli Idoli. Testimonianze etrusche in Falterona*, Florence: Salimbeni.

Fracchia, H. (2005) "La fase precedente alla costruzione della villa" in H. Fracchia and M. Gualtieri, *La villa romana di Ossaia*, in S. Fortunelli (ed.), *MAEC Il museo della città etrusca e romana di Cortona*. Collection catalogue, Florence: Edizioni Polistampa, 390–392.

Gli Etruschi e l'Europa (1992), Exhibition catalogue, Paris and Berlin, Milan: Fabbri Editori.

Gori, A. F. (1737) *Museum Etruscum exhibens insignia veterum Etruscorum*, Florentiae: Caletanus Albizinius typographus.

Halbertsma, R. B. (1991) *Etruskische Cultuur. Rijksmuseum van Oudheden, Leiden*, Amsterdam: Bataafsche Leeuw.

Haynes, S. (1960) "The Bronze Priests and Priestesses from Nemi" in *Römische Mitteilungen*, 67: 34–45.

Maetzke, G. (1987) "Statuette etrusche in bronzo" in *Il Museo Archeologico Nazionale G.C. Mecenate in Arezzo*, Florence: Arti Grafiche Giorni e Gambi per Cassa di Risparmio di Firenze, 185–196.

Maggiani, A. (1990) "La Chimera di Arezzo" in P. Zamarchi Grassi (ed.), *La chimera e il suo mito*, Florence: Arti grafiche "Il Torchio," 53–63.

——(1999) "Culti delle acque e culti in grotta in Etruria" in *Ocnus* 7: 187–203

——(2001) "La Chimera di Arezzo e i "compagni" della Chimera" in S. Vilucchi and P. Zamarchi Grassi (eds), *Etruschi nel tempo. I ritrovamenti di Arezzo dal 1500 ad oggi*. Exhibition catalogue, Arezzo, July – December 2001, Basilica Inferiore di S. Francesco-Museo Archeologico Nazionale Mecenate di Arezzo, Florence: Nuova Grafica Fiorentina, 57–64.

Micali, G. (1844) *Monumenti inediti a illustrazione della Storia degli antichi popoli italiani*, Florence: Coi tipi della Galileiana.

Peroni, R. (1994) *Introduzione alla protostoria italiana*, Bari: Laterza.

Richardson, E. (1983) *Etruscan votive bronzes geometric, orientalizing, archaic*, Mainz an Rhein: P. von Zabern.

Romualdi, A. (1981) *Catalogo del Deposito di Brolio in Val di Chiana*, Rome: Libreria dello Stato.

Roncalli, F. (1973) *Il Marte di Todi: bronzistica etrusca ed ispirazione classica*, Atti della Pontificia Accademia Romana di archeologia. Memorie, vol. 11, 2. Rome: Tip. Poliglotta Vaticana.

Salvi, A., Zamarchi Grassi, P. (2005) "Il santuario di Camucia – Via Capitini (area dell'ex Consorzio Agrario)" in S. Fortunelli (ed.), *MAEC Il museo della città etrusca e romana di Cortona*. Collection catalogue, Florence: Edizioni Polistampa, 286–290.

Scarpellini Testi, M. G. (1995) "Nota su alcuni altri reperti da Brolio 'Deposito'" in P. Zamarchi Grassi (ed.), *Castiglion Fiorentino un nuovo centro etrusco*, Exhibition catalogue, Castiglion Fiorentino, Cortona: Calosci, 111–121.

——(1996) "La valle del Bagnoro nell'antichità presenze etrusche e romane" in *I Quaderni della Chimera*, 1: 11–76.

——(1997) "Guglielmo Maetzke, il Museo Archeologico Nazionale di Arezzo e le Carte Gamurrini" in *Annuario Accademia Etrusca Cortona*, 27: 59–75.

——(2000) "Il sacello tardo etrusco di Villa Fatucchi ed appunti sui santuari di Arezzo etrusca" in *Atti e Memorie Accademia Petrarca di Lettere Arti e Scienze Arezzo*, 59–60: 29–55.

Scarpellini, M. G. (2002) "Il deposito di Brolio" in P. Zamarchi Grassi and M. G. Scarpellini, (eds), *Tesori Ritrovati*, Exhibition catalogue, Castiglion Fiorentino, Montepulciano (Siena): Le Balze, 65–83.

——(2002A) "I bronzi votivi di Montecchio" in P. Zamarchi Grassi and M. G. Scarpellini (eds), *Tesori Ritrovati*, Exhibition catalogue, Castiglion Fiorentino, Montepulciano (Siena): Le Balze, 87–94.

——(2007) "Da Arezzo a Castiglion Fiorentino" in I. Biagianti (ed.) *La Valdichiana dai primordi al terzo millennio. Storia ragionata di un territorio*, Cortona: Tiphys editoria e multimedia, 46–53.

——(2008) "L'acqua degli Etruschi. Appunti per alcuni culti idrici della Valdichiana aretina" in *I sentieri dell'acqua. Culto ruolo e regime delle acque nel Castiglionese*, Master Conoscere l'Etruria Università degli Studi di Siena, Quaderno di Biblioteca 31, Arezzo: Centro Stampa, 21–41.

——(2009) "Castiglion Fiorentino" in G. Camporeale and G. Firpo (eds), *Arezzo nell'antichità*, Roma: Giorgio Bretschneider, 261–264.

——(2009A) "Le manifestazioni del sacro nella Valdichiana aretina" in *Hintial Il Sacro in terra d'Etruria*, Atti del convegno promosso dalla Quinta Commissione consiliare Attività culturali e turismo, Soci 17 October 2009, Florence: Consiglio Regionale della Toscana, 67–79.

——(2009B) (ed.) *Il cinghiale nell'antichità. Archeologia e mito*, Exhibition catalogue, Castiglion Fiorentino, Cortona: Tiphys editoria e multimedia.

——(2010) "Sacra mirabilia dagli scavi archeologici del piazzale del Cassero" in P. Torriti and M. G Scarpellini (eds), *Sacra Mirabilia Tesori da Castiglion Fiorentino*, Exhibition catalogue, February – April 2010 Rome - Castel Sant'Angelo, Florence: Edifir, 111–116.

——(2010A) "Il deposito di Brolio a Valdichiana" in P. Torriti and M. G. Scarpellini (eds), *Sacra Mirabilia Tesori da Castiglion Fiorentino*, Exhibition catalogue, Febuary–April 2010 Rome – Castel Sant'Angelo, Florence: Edifir, 113–116.

Turfa, J. M. (2006) "Votive Offerings in Etruscan Religion" in N. T. de Grummond and E. Simon (eds), *The Religion of the Etruscans*, Austin: University of Texas Press, 79–90.

Vilucchi, S., Zamarchi Grassi, P. (eds) (2011) *Etruschi nel tempo. I ritrovamenti di Arezzo dal 1500 ad oggi*, Exhibition catalogue, Arezzo, July – December 2001, Basilica Inferiore di S. Francesco, Museo Archeologico Nazionale Mecenate di Arezzo, Florence: Nuova Grafica Fiorentina.

Warden, P. G. (2011) "The Chimaera in Arezzo: Made in Etruria," *American Journal of Archaeology*, 115.1: 1–5.

Zamarchi Grassi, P. (1989) "Recenti scoperte archeologiche ad Arezzo e nel suo agro," *Atti e Memorie Accademia Petrarca di Lettere, Arti e Scienze*, 51: 333–356.

——(2001) "La stipe della Fonte Veneziana" in *Etruschi nel tempo. I ritrovamenti di Arezzo dal 1500 ad oggi*. Exhibition catalogue, Arezzo, July – December 2001, Basilica Inferiore di S. Francesco, Museo Archeologico Nazionale Mecenate di Arezzo, Florence: Nuova Grafica Fiorentina, 111–129.

ABBREVIATIONS

CIE: *Corpus Inscriptionum Etruscarum.*
TLE: Pallottino M. (1968), *Testimonia linguae etruscae*, Florence.

CHAPTER FIFTY EIGHT

MIRRORS IN ART AND SOCIETY

———·◆·———

Richard Daniel De Puma

Yet there is no branch of Etruscan antiquities more genuinely native – none more valuable to the inquirer, for the information it yields as to the mysterious language and creed of that ancient race; for the inscriptions being always in the native character, and designatory of the individual gods or heroes represented, these mirrors become a sure index to the Etruscan creed – "a figurative dictionary," as Bunsen[1] terms it, of Etruscan mythology; while at the same time they afford us the chief source and one of the most solid bases of our acquaintance with the native language.

George Dennis, *Cities and Cemeteries of Etruria*
(revised edition, London, 1878, p. lxxx).

INTRODUCTION: A BRIEF HISTORY OF RECENT MIRROR STUDIES

When J. D. Beazley, the renowned expert on Greek vases, published his only article on Etruscan mirrors he gave it this title: "The World of the Etruscan Mirror."[2] This may sound grandiose or exaggerated at first. Surely these small, utilitarian objects that many art historians would assign to the "minor arts" could not constitute a "world." But, as Beazley and others who had examined them closely realized, mirrors did indeed provide a significant window into the world of the Etruscans, despite their small scale and often unpretentious appearance. They surely appealed to Beazley because in many ways Etruscan mirrors document Etruscan culture in the same way that Greek vase paintings document Greek culture. Furthermore, because we possess relatively little information on the Etruscans from their own lost literature, the value of mirrors as documents becomes even more precious.

In the nineteenth century Eduard Gerhard (1795–1867) took on the herculean task of collecting, categorizing and publishing hundreds of Etruscan mirrors, many in his own collection.[3] Several twentieth-century scholars, among them Massimo Pallottino (1909–1995), Guido Mansuelli (1916–2001) and especially Roger Lambrechts (1927–2005), championed the study and publication of mirrors. They were instrumental in organizing and promoting an international effort to update and correct various inaccuracies in Gerhard's corpus. This new venture, called the *Corpus Speculorum Etruscorum* (*CSE*), published its first fascicules in 1981.[4] At the time of this writing a total of 31 fascicules representing 13 countries have appeared.

A number of significant improvements make the *CSE* an invaluable resource. As is well known, the engravings on Etruscan mirrors are usually very difficult to see thanks to the accumulation of corrosion products on the bronze surface. Thus, drawings of these engravings have always been a necessity in their study. The first four volumes of *ES* are illustrated with drawings of the engraved sides (reverses) of the mirrors. Relatively few drawings of the original reflecting sides (obverses) are included. Only the last volume, published in 1897, supplemented the drawings with a small number of photographs. By contrast, the *CSE* fascicules have drawings *and* photographs that are usually reproduced to scale of *both* sides of each mirror. Unengraved or minimally engraved mirrors, fragments, and isolated mirror handles (bronze, bone or ivory) are also included. In several cases there are also large, detailed photographs to illustrate especially interesting techniques or features of the engraved designs, while X-ray photos and microphotographs show details of metallurgical interest.

In addition to the visual documentation, the *CSE* also routinely includes "sections" (similar to vase profiles). These first appeared in the 1970s as another tool to understand the evolution of mirror types.[5] Over time, mirror sections evolve (Fig. 58.1) from thick and flat to thinner and more convex (on the reflecting side). The convex reflecting surface produced a wider than normal field of view.[6] Still another tool unavailable to earlier scholars is the chemical composition of the bronze alloy used to make the mirrors. Several, but unfortunately not all, of the *CSE* fascicules include these data, which often help to detect forgeries. Of course, the various committee members who oversee the editing of these *CSE* fascicules have attempted to bring a consistent approach to the textual documentation of each mirror as well. This often includes conservation reports and thorough discussion of the physical condition of each mirror, a complete list of previous publications, numerous measurements including weight, careful explication of any

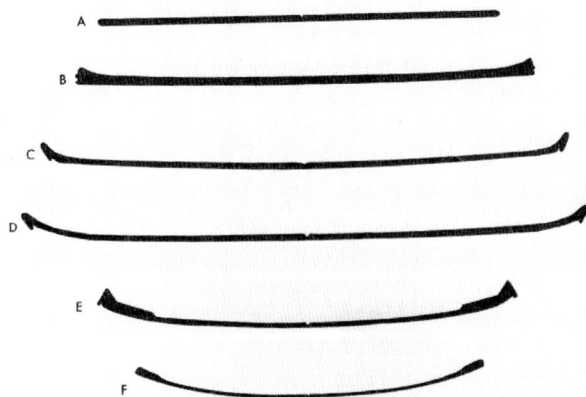

Figure 58.1 Typical mirror sections. A: Minneapolis Institute of Arts, inv. 57.198; B, C and D: Cleveland Museum of Art, inv. 52.259, inv. 20.170 and inv. 16.2012; E: Field Museum of Natural History, Chicago, inv. 24376; F: formerly Rockford College Art Collection, Rockford, IL, inv. 125. Drawings by the author.

inscriptions, complete discussion of the subjects or ornaments engraved on both sides of the mirror, citation of parallels and possible attribution to a regional workshop or artist, and finally a discussion of chronology. In the case of public and university museums there is usually a history of the collection and discussion of provenance for each object.

Even before the *CSE* began to appear in 1981, a number of major articles and books on various mirror topics had been published. In many ways these helped to determine the format the *CSE* would follow. Among the several important pre-*CSE* contributions are those of G. Matthies,[7] G. Mansuelli,[8] I. Mayer-Prokop,[9] D. Rebuffat-Emmanuel,[10] G. Pfister-Roesgen,[11] R. Lambrechts,[12] and U. Fischer-Graf.[13] These works attempted to define specific workshops or artists, to treat mirrors from specific periods, or to catalogue large public collections.[14] In an ideal world the collections with mirrors that have precise archaeological contexts would have been published in the *CSE* first. That way the authors treating collections of largely unprovenanced mirrors, which form the majority, could use these more archaeologically-secure examples to develop opinions about possible provenances. To a certain extent this happened with Sassatelli's two *CSE*s of the Bologna mirrors, several of which have good contexts. However, the majority of these mirrors are undecorated and, therefore, of limited potential for dating other engraved mirrors. Only recently have the excellent mirrors in the Museo Nazionale di Villa Giulia's extensive collection begun to appear in the *CSE*, and we have yet to see a *CSE* from the major holdings in Florence.[15] In the meantime, the majority of *CSE* fascicules published mostly treat unprovenanced mirrors; ultimately, many of the conclusions posited in them will need to be updated or refined as more mirrors with secure archaeological contexts are published.

THE BASIC CHARACTERISTICS OF ETRUSCAN MIRRORS

The Etruscans produced polished bronze mirrors throughout their history. Estimates of the surviving number of examples range between 3,000 and 4,000 if we include the many undecorated and fragmentary mirrors and independent mirror handles. Certainly, bronze was always the major medium for these mirrors, but a few silver examples have survived and it is possible that other more precious alloys like electrum were occasionally used. The earliest extant example, an undecorated tang mirror (Fig. 58.2), comes from the Villanovan period at Tarquinia and probably dates to the first half of the ninth century BC.[16] This simple mirror shares many features with standard Etruscan tang mirrors of later periods. It has a flat, thick, circular disc and the triangular tang is attached with three rivets similar to handle attachments on contemporaneous bronze razors.[17]

Tang mirrors (Fig. 58.3) that have an attached handle made of bone, ivory or wood continued to increase in popularity during the Late Archaic period, circa 525–450 BC. At this point some discs are still circular, flat and relatively heavy but many now have a concave section with a slightly raised rim on the non-reflecting surface.[18] This side is often decorated with chased or engraved figural or vegetal designs.[19] Perhaps the concavity and raised rim helped to protect the decorated surface from being marred when the mirror was placed facedown on a dressing table. Most bone or ivory handles have simple lathe-turned grooves or ridges. Some are ergonomically carved with concave grooves to accommodate the grip of fingers (Fig. 58.3c). Others have elaborate figural representations (Fig. 58.4), and at least one preserves vestiges of gilding and paint.[20]

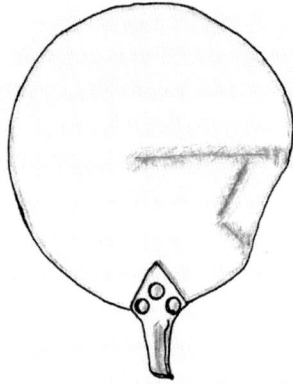

Figure 58.2   Undecorated tang mirror from Tarquinia. Drawing by the author based on H. Hencken, *Tarquinia and Etruscan Origins* (New York 1968), pl. 59.

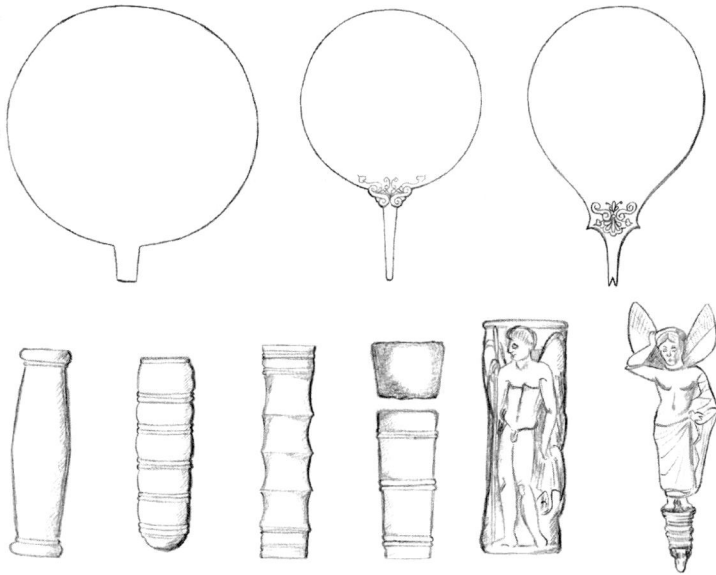

Figure 58.3a–c   Typical bronze tang mirrors and independent carved bone, ivory or cast bronze handles. Drawings by the author.

Another disc shape that appears during this early period of development is the "solar" or elliptical disc.[21] This type was probably influenced by Egyptian mirrors, which are normally of this "flattened" shape (Fig. 58.5a).

Still another mirror type is a simple circular disc with no tang or handle (Fig. 58.5b). These tend to be small, undecorated and have flat or slightly concave sections with rounded edges.

Almost certainly, many of these unpretentious mirrors were originally kept in boxes that functioned like modern compacts (Fig. 58.5c). Sometimes box mirrors of this sort appear in sculpted representations where the box might be square or rectangular but the

Figure 58.4   *"Atunis* (Adonis) and *Lasa Achununa,"* tang mirror with a well-preserved carved bone handle from the Sperandio Tomb, Perugia, circa 350–325 BC. (Museo Archeologico, Florence inv. 80933). Photo from the Museum.

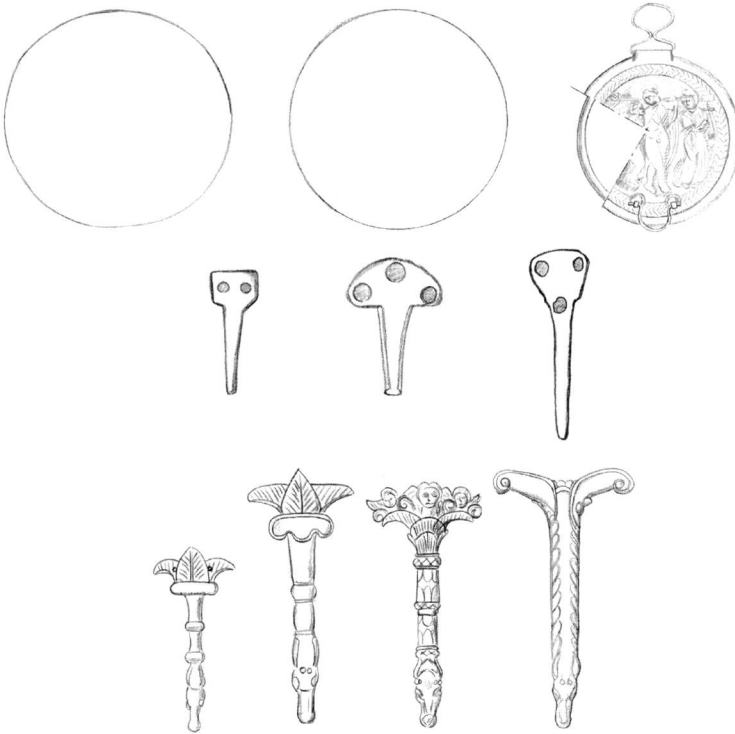

Figure 58.5a–c   Typical elliptical ("solar") and circular mirrors; independent tangs and handles. Drawings by the author.

mirror inside is circular. There is, indeed, a large corpus of well-preserved round box mirrors dating from the Late Classical and Hellenistic periods. These are usually made of bronze (although a few silver examples are known[22]) and their hinged covers are decorated with figural scenes in high relief. These sculpted reliefs were made from moulds and, therefore, there are numerous duplicates of individual types.[23] Simple round discs can also be turned into hand mirrors, even if they don't have tangs, by the addition of separately-cast bronze handles attached with solder or, less commonly, with small rivets (Fig. 58.5, 2 [a–c] and 3 [a–d]). There are numerous examples of this type but they have attracted relatively little scholarly attention because the discs are usually undecorated.[24]

Sometime in the later fourth century BC the Etruscans began to produce mirrors with discs and handles formed in one piece (Fig. 58.6). Exactly how these mirrors were made is the subject of considerable debate. For many years scholars assumed that the mirrors were cast in moulds and then polished. Many mirrors published in the *CSE* are said to have a "handle cast in one piece with the disc" but a close examination of the metallurgical features of several mirrors convinced four British researchers (Judith Swaddling, Paul Craddock, Susan La Niece and Marilyn Hockey) that this was not correct.[25] Instead, they proposed: "Etruscan metalworkers both made and decorated the mirrors by cold working" (p. 117). The authors examined mirrors carefully and noted various metallurgical clues that demonstrate the validity of many of their arguments. However, is it not possible that the Etruscans employed a combination of direct casting *and* cold working? Essentially, this was the hypothesis put forth in the 1950s by C. Panseri and M. Leoni.[26] In favor of this suggestion is the similarity of so many complicated handles, as well as the same or similar dimensions for disc diameters. The "mass production" of late Etruscan mirrors, especially during the late fourth and third centuries BC, would seem to require direct casting rather

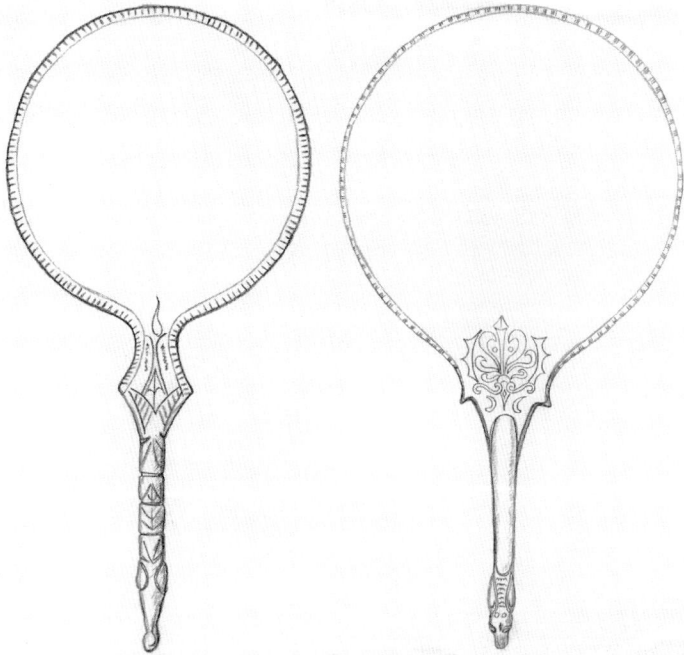

Figure 58.6 Typical handle mirrors: Etruscan (left) and Praenestine (right). Drawings by the author.

than the far more laborious and time-consuming efforts of pure cold working. In any case, all the mirrors, regardless of how they were made, required polishing and this because, like chasing or engraving, it is part of the cold working process.

It is likely that more than one artisan was involved in making a fine mirror. There might have been a metal smith who cast or hammered the disc to its proper shape; perhaps another artisan who executed the chased or engraved ornaments like frames and extension designs; a third, responsible for the primary figural design on the reverse; and a fourth, who carved (and perhaps sometimes painted or gilded) the bone or ivory handle for a tang mirror. One can imagine a workshop where individual artisans worked together to create a single, refined mirror. There is little evidence for this idea, although we know definitely that Greek pottery was often the product of two artisans: a potter who threw the vase on the wheel, and a painter who decorated it. Some have suggested that different painters may have been assigned to do decorative ornaments like frieze patterns while others were experts at painting figures (for example, Caeretan hydriai). In the case of Etruscan mirrors we have some examples that seem unfinished because they have only an ornamental frame waiting to be filled with a figural scene. In one case from Tarquinia, the frame is quite elegant and carefully executed but the figural scene is rather incompetent and seems to be the work of a different, far less skilled artist (Fig. 58.7 and compare with Fig. 33.3).[27]

The question of bronze alloy composition for mirrors is also highly debatable. A major problem is that only a small fraction of the mirrors so far published in the *CSE* has been analyzed. And, to complicate matters, different technical methods (not to mention different laboratories) have been used. Furthermore, it has been noted that samples taken from different areas of the same mirror often produce different results. Thus, the data are not always consistent and may be unreliable. Ideally, all mirrors and independent

Figure 58.7   "*Uni* (Hera) nursing *Hercle* (Herakles)," mirror from tomb 65, Tarquinia, Fondo Scataglini, circa 350–300 BC. (Soprintendenza Archeologica per l'Etruria Meridionale, inv. 68705). From Serra Ridgway 1996, pl. CXL.

bronze mirror handles should be sampled in the same manner and analyzed by the same technique in the same laboratory. This is unlikely to happen. However, despite these concerns, Judith Swaddling and her colleagues at the British Museum have determined some basic points: (1) Etruscan mirrors are made primarily of tin bronze, that is they have a relatively high concentration of tin when compared to bronze alloys used for statuettes, vessels or helmets, and contemporaneous Greek mirrors; (2) the percentage of tin is essentially consistent at about 10–11 percent over the entire time Etruscan mirrors are being produced; (3) very few Etruscan mirrors contain more than one percent lead, although over time lead content rises for all bronzes in Etruria and Greece. This last phenomenon is probably the result of the growing incidence of reused scrap bronze.[28]

A rare variation on these mirror types is the relief mirror where the figural scene is not chased or engraved but cast in shallow relief. Only about a dozen mirrors of this type are extant.[29] Some have additional metals inlaid in their designs to enhance the appearance and, no doubt, increase the cost. In the realm of mirrors, these are probably among the most expensive status symbols available to the Etruscan elite.

An important variant of the Etruscan tang and handle mirrors was developed at Praeneste, modern Palestrina. These mirrors have discs that are piriform rather than circular (Fig. 58.6, right). It is thought that this change in disc shape was an attempt to strengthen the most fragile part of the mirror, the area where disc joins handle (called the "extension" by mirror specialists). Many mirrors broke at this weak point and required repairs, usually with rivets or patches of various sorts. The Praenestine mirrors, because their shape gives them a wider extension, are perhaps more durable in this regard. However, the area is still relatively weak and broken examples exist.[30] In any case, the piriform shape is one of the distinctive hallmarks of mirrors produced in ancient Praeneste. This city was not Etruscan. The inhabitants spoke an archaic dialect of Latin and their mirrors are often inscribed in this Latin. But, despite these differences, Praeneste was heavily influenced by Etruscan culture and, at least for most archaeologists concerned with its material culture, it is virtually an Etruscan city.

ICONOGRAPHICAL CONSIDERATIONS

From the earliest beginnings of modern interest in Etruscan mirrors the aspect that has captivated attention is their iconography. What do the scenes on these mirrors depict and what do they tell us about Etruscan culture? This interest often determined the value of a mirror in the eighteenth and nineteenth centuries and – at least in most circles – it remains important today. A mirror with an elaborate depiction of an Etruscan myth or legend, perhaps accompanied by inscriptions, is certainly more interesting than a blank mirror or one minimally decorated with vegetal ornament. This is why so many authentic blank mirrors have been supplied with engraved designs by modern forgers.[31]

Many of the subjects depicted on Etruscan mirrors are recognizable because the characters portrayed carry specific attributes and/or are inscribed with their names. For example, figures of Herakles (Etruscan *Hercle*) often wear the lion-skin cloak and carry a club. Hercle is one of the most frequently depicted figures on Etruscan and Praenestine mirrors and, therefore, we can assume – even without other evidence – that he was a significant character in their mythology and religion.[32]

Perhaps more critical today are the many depictions on Etruscan mirrors that help us to understand Etruscan divinities, spirits, heroes or legendary characters. Most of these are known by their Etruscan names inscribed on the mirrors and can then be compared with other representations showing similar or identical attributes. These have been carefully collected by various authors in the *Lexicon Iconographicum Mythologiae Classicae* (*LIMC*), which has revolutionized the study of ancient Greek, Etruscan and Roman iconography in recent years.[33] (See also Chapter 25.)

Other important iconographical questions concern the patrons of mirrors and their functions. For example, we know that Etruscan mirrors were almost exclusively used by, or at least buried with women.[34] How then can we explain the popularity of violent battle scenes on articles supposedly made to appeal to women? There are, of course, numerous depictions that seem, to us at least, more appropriately feminine: bathing scenes, women or goddesses at their toilette, scenes with mythical or legendary lovers like Venus and Adonis, Eos and Tithonos, or Paris and Helen, or depictions that might be appropriate for a grieving mother.[35] In this context, dueling warriors seem out of place. However, the same "inappropriateness" also occurs on Etrusco-Hellenistic cinerary urns that show many battle scenes and even depictions of matricide on urns belonging to women. In the case of mirrors, Alexandra Carpino (2009) has recently tackled this problem. She lists only four male burials with mirrors,[36] but we can only guess at how many others may have gone unrecorded by the careless excavations of the nineteenth century when most mirrors were discovered. It seems unlikely that Etruscan men were unconcerned with their appearance and did not use mirrors. I suspect that they did but (1) we have lost the contexts of many male burials that may have contained mirrors, or (2) mirrors, for whatever reason, were not considered appropriate tomb gifts for Etruscan men although they may have used them while alive. Carpino, for her part, suggests that the subjects on mirrors that seem inappropriate for women may well have had other meanings that were significant for them at the time. For example, during much of the fourth century BC the Etruscans were under attack from various outside forces. Battle scenes with Homeric warriors like Achilles and Memnon may have symbolized the bravery and strength needed to defeat contemporary enemies. Mirrors depicting legendary Greek heroes "…not only associated the mirrors' patrons [whether men or women] with the grandeur of the Homeric heroes, but also functioned as inspirational calls to heroism."[37]

PROPOSED GROUPS OF MIRRORS: *KRANZSPIEGEL*, DIOSKOUROI AND LASA MIRRORS

Because so many mirrors have been deprived of their archaeological contexts, scholars have attempted to group related examples with the hope that these proposed groups might be assigned to specific sites and provide clues to dating.[38] In the case of the Praenestine mirrors, for example, we see that the disc shape is almost always a distinctive piriform rather than the standard Etruscan circular shape (Fig. 58.6). These piriform mirrors, even when undecorated, can be tentatively assigned to workshops in ancient Praeneste. But it is not only their distinctive shape that helps to identify them. There are other characteristics: their relatively large size compared to Etruscan mirrors; their archaic Latin inscriptions; their complicated and crowded mythological scenes, often with figures overlapping the ornamental borders.[39]

Three other types of mirrors have long attracted the attention of scholars because they seem to share iconographical, technical or stylistic features that suggest they were made in the same workshops or perhaps by the same artisans. The most characteristic feature of the first group is the elaborate decorative border or frame that surrounds the figural scene on the non-reflecting side of the mirror. This border is a spiky-leafed garland (hence the German designation for this type, *Kranzspiegelgruppe*) often bound at the cardinal points with "slide binders" (Fig. 58.8). Mirrors in this proposed group often depict four-figure compositions and sometimes the figures are identified by inscribed labels. Mirrors in the spiky-garland group have other features in common: a massive, modeled handle terminating in a stylized ram's head; a concave extension, often with an engraved "flame motif" on the obverse; a raised medallion border (engraved with the spiky-garland or other frame device); and a heavy rim profile with deep groove on the obverse. But can these similar mirrors be assigned to a specific workshop? A systematic investigation by Denise Emmanuel-Rebuffat[40] demonstrated that there is no direct correlation between the spiky-garland border and the various four-figure compositions they frame. In fact, a number of mirrors of this general type have laurel-leaf or guilloche borders and it is estimated that about 40 percent of them have no engraved border ornament at all. These differences suggest a flexible relationship between border design and figural composition and, I think, strengthen the idea that borders may have been executed by different artisans and bear no meaningful relationship to the figural scenes that they frame.[41]

The two most common subjects decorating fourth and third centuries BC Etruscan mirrors are the twin gods, Castor and Pollux, often called the Dioskouroi (or *Tinias Cliniar* in Etruscan)[42] and Lasa (Figs 58.9 and 58.10). Many of these mirrors are of relatively poor quality, both technically and aesthetically. They are thin, fragile and generally smaller than most earlier mirrors and the engravings are often crude, incompetent or, at best, perfunctory. Many have no frame or border for the figural scene on the reverse and no extension ornament on the reflecting side. These qualities have led some to speculate that

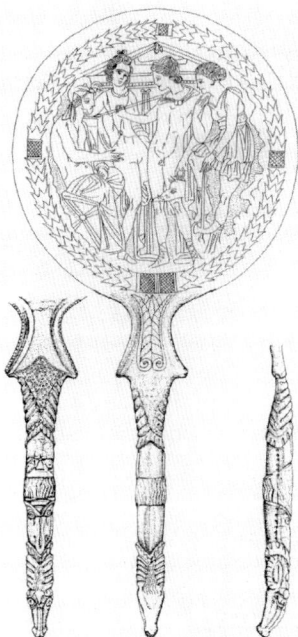

Figure 58.8 Spiky-garland mirror, provenance unknown, circa 300–250 BC. (Indiana University Art Museum, Bloomington, inv. 62.251). From De Puma 1987, no. 3. Drawing by the author.

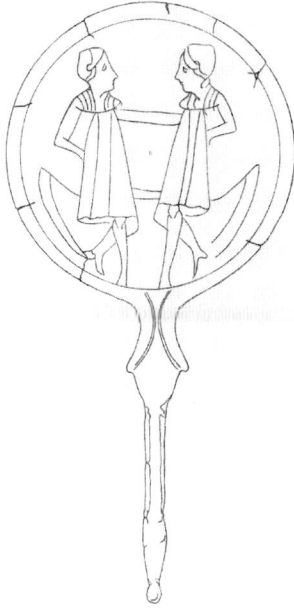

Figure 58.9 Dioskouroi mirror, provenance unknown, circa 300–250 BC. (Formerly Rockford College Art Collection, Rockford, IL, inv. 125, de-accessioned and on the Chicago antiquities market in 2009). From De Puma 1987, no. 33. Drawing by the author.

Figure 58.10 Lasa mirror, provenance unknown, circa 300–275 BC. (Museum of Art and Archaeology, University of Missouri, Columbia, MO, inv. 83.224). From De Puma 1987, no. 18. Drawing by the author.

these mirrors were made expressly for tomb use, and in some cases this is possible. At present, however, there is no definite proof of this practice for mirrors; in fact, many show evidence of repairs made in antiquity and thus demonstrate that they were used over long periods of time, perhaps by more than one owner.

Dioskouroi mirrors are especially difficult to understand because there are several variations on the common theme. Some representations are naturalistic, others are highly abstract. A variety of iconographical attributes accompany the figures and, in many cases, they are depicted in the presence of related mythical characters like Helen, Minerva, or others who cannot be easily identified. They are rarely shown in a specific mythical narrative, but rather appear simply grouped in "sacred conversation" scenes. Many of these groupings are formulaic and the figures seem interchangeable.[43]

Lasa mirrors are equally problematic. We know that this mythical Etruscan character is often depicted as a nude, winged female on late Etruscan mirrors. But sometimes Lasa can be a male figure (Fig. 58.11) and, on at least one mirror (Fig. 58.12) a group of both male and female Lasae appear together.[44] Some Lasae are named on mirrors (for example, Fig. 58.4) and we thus know that Lasa is really the designation for a large group of beings comprised of sometimes specific individuals. One can think of them like angels, a large group, with specific members (for example Michael, the Archangel). Lasae can appear nude or clothed, usually but not always winged, wearing elaborate jewelry and shoes, slippers or Phrygian hats, and carrying various attributes including alabastra and perfume-dipsticks. The late Etruscan mirrors with Lasae are a far cry from the elegant and complex depictions on the St. Petersburg mirror (Fig. 58.12). A typical range of examples will illustrate "the good, the bad and the ugly" for this common subject. A fine Lasa is engraved on a damaged tang mirror in Princeton (Fig. 58.13).[45] The running or flying pose is ubiquitous on Lasa mirrors, but in this case the figure carries no attributes. A handle

Figure 58.11   Handle mirror with male Lasa, from the Tomb of Fastia Velsi, Chiusi, circa 240–200 BC. (Museum of Fine Arts, Boston, inv. 13.2889). From De Puma 1993, no. 22. Drawing by the author.

Figure 58.12 Tang mirror with male and female Lasae forming border, provenance unknown, circa 330–320 BC. (Hermitage Museum, St. Petersburg, inv. V.505). From E. Mavleev in F. Roncalli (ed.), *Gens antiquissima Italiae. Antichità dall'Umbria a Leningrado* (Milan, 1990), no. 8.19, p. 416.

Figure 58.13 Lasa mirror, provenance unknown, circa 300–250 BC. (Princeton University Art Museum, inv. y1954–412). From De Puma 2005, no. 44. Drawing by the author.

mirror with Lasa in Boston (Fig. 58.14)[46] shows the same pose but this time the figure wears a Phrygian cap. The last mirror, said to be from Orvieto, is now in Philadelphia (Fig. 58.15).[47] Here the figure, again nude, winged and wearing the Phrygian cap, has become highly abstracted and, although competently executed, seems perfunctory and decidedly unattractive. All three examples are mirrors without decorative borders and depict the Lasa in an identical pose. These features are typical of the type in general.

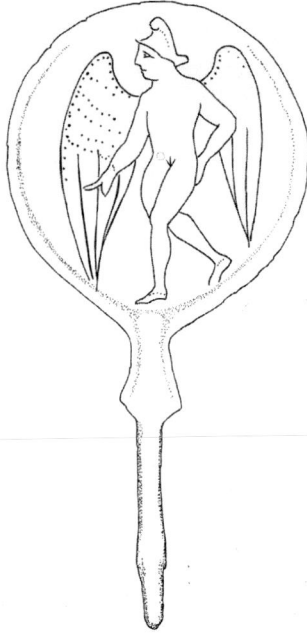

Figure 58.14   Lasa mirror, from the Tomb of Fastia Velsi, Chiusi, circa 200 BC. (Museum of Fine Arts, Boston, inv. 13.2890). From De Puma 1993, no. 23. Drawing by the author.

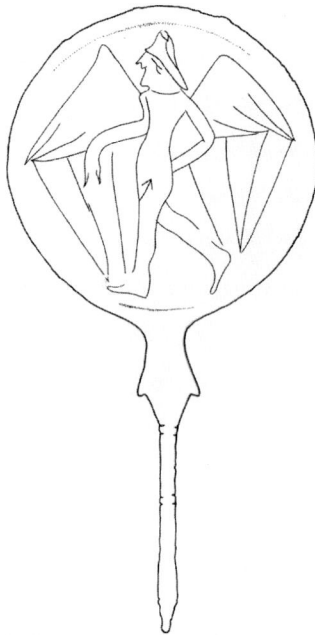

Figure 58.15   Lasa mirror, from Orvieto, circa 200 BC. (University Museum of Archaeology and Anthropology, University of Pennsylvania, inv. MS 3261). From De Puma 2005, no. 33. Drawing by the author.

What drove the demand for these mirrors in late Etruscan times? In the case of the Dioskouroi, their shared immortality (according to Greek and apparently Etruscan myth) may have been a factor in making them especially appealing for funerary purposes. Nancy de Grummond (1991), building on several previous investigations into the iconography and significance of the Dioskouroi in ancient Italy, has speculated that these twins had a special role on mirrors. She connects the divine twins with the concept of the double manifestation of the living woman using her mirror and her image in the mirror. A woman's reflection on an important mirror in the British Museum (Fig. 58.16)[48] is labeled *hinthial* (genitive of *hinthi*), a word that means "of the Underworld," "soul," "ghost," or "shade" in Etruscan. Furthermore, the association of the divine twins with the *dokana*, a gate-like attribute either visible or referenced symbolically on many Etruscan mirrors with the Dioskouroi, may represent the gate to the Underworld. These are fascinating and provocative interpretations. They help to explain the popularity of this type of mirror in the last phases of Etruscan culture. My only problem with this hypothesis is that it omits a significant population from consideration: Etruscan men. Are only Etruscan women able to use their mirrors to gain safe passage to the Underworld? If the mirror had such an important funerary function in Etruscan culture, how do we explain its absence in the tombs of almost all men and even many women? It would seem that everyone needs a mirror to assist in this ultimate journey, but we find them only in some tombs. Perhaps it means that not everyone shared this belief, but surely many, if not most, would have.

In the case of the Lasa mirrors, we can imagine that these characters acted somewhat like the popular contemporary belief in "guardian angels." For the Etruscans, the Lasa's functions include protecting innocent victims from harm, facilitating or encouraging lovers, and assisting brides in their grooming and adornment before marriage. The last two functions clearly demonstrate why Lasae often appear in the entourage of *Turan*, the Etruscan Aphrodite. These functions may help to explain the popularity of Lasa mirrors

Figure 58.16 "Toilette of *Malavisch*," provenance unknown, circa 350–325 BC. (British Museum, London, inv. 626). From *ES* II, pl. 213.

in late period Etruria. By this time, too, mirrors must have been less expensive and more accessible to a larger segment of Etruscan society. There is every indication that they were widespread and available from many bronze workshops.

THE POSSIBLE FUNCTIONS OF MIRRORS IN ETRUSCAN SOCIETY

It is obvious that mirrors in all ancient societies were used primarily to afford a view of a person using them. They are shown being used by women in several works of art, including on Etruscan bronze mirrors and Praenestine cistae. One can groom, inspect and refine one's image, check the appearance of the skin, the hair, or adjust jewelry or makeup. We have seen that, at present, the archaeological and artistic evidence suggests that in Etruscan society mirrors were used primarily by women. There is no evidence concerning the cost of a good Etruscan mirror, but many were not easy to produce and, I suspect, often involved the skills of more than one artisan working with costly materials like bronze, sometimes silver and ivory. We must assume that, at least until the late fourth century BC, they were expensive items and therefore status symbols.

Mirrors have often been considered marriage gifts, and certainly some subjects depicted on them (for example, elaborate toilette scenes that probably represent the bridal preparations) seem appropriate for such a purpose. Indeed, some inscriptions on mirrors indicate that they were marriage gifts, presumably from groom to bride or perhaps parents to their daughter. Recently, some interpretations of familiar and new inscriptions on mirrors have given more weight to this idea of mirrors as wedding gifts. A mirror in Florence showing the parents of Achilles, Peleus and Thetis (a frequent couple on Etruscan mirrors and one that may symbolize marriage), has an inscription with the word *malena*. It has often been assumed that this word means "mirror" because it appears in several inscriptions with proper names in the genitive preceded by the word *mi*. In the case of the Florence mirror the retrograde inscription reads: *mi malena larθia puruhenas*. If *malena* means "mirror" then the inscription would translate as "I am the mirror of Larthia Purubena," and thus belongs to a large class of objects, mostly vases, that address the reader: it is as if the vase is speaking.[49] But it now seems more probable that *malena* means "wedding gift" and the proper name is male so the inscription means "I am the wedding gift of Larth Purubena [to his bride]." The inscription on a recently-published mirror in a private Japanese collection supplements this interpretation: *mi malana larθiia cavis spuriiex* or "I am the wedding gift of Larth Cavi Spuriie [to his bride]."[50]

Many mirrors depict scenes of divination or prophesy and some scholars have interpreted mirrors themselves as possible instruments of prophesy.[51] A subdivision of this type shows the oracular head of Orpheus (*Urphe* in Etruscan). In his treatment of a mirror with this subject now in Siena (Fig. 58.17), Adriano Maggiani[52] suggested that Orpheus is prophesying a happy and fruitful marriage for a mythical couple with whom an Etruscan couple can identify. I have combined Maggiani's interpretation with the idea of the appropriate wedding gift. In my discussion of an elaborate mirror in Princeton (Fig. 58.18), I state:

> The symbolism of this subject, the consultation of the oracular head of Orpheus, would have reassured the [bridal] couple and their families…The Princeton mirror, then, was perhaps a wedding gift to a young Etruscan woman about to become a bride. Like all

the other mirrors with this subject, it was elaborately decorated, larger than usual, and surely expensive. It would have been an appropriate wedding gift, perhaps from the bride's parents, that would have reminded her of her duties and the expectations of her new role in society, a useful gift that she would have treasured throughout her life, taking it with her to the afterlife.[53]

Figure 58.17   "Oracular Head of *Urphe*," so-called Casuccini Mirror, from Chiusi, circa 300 BC. (Siena, Museo Archeologico, inv. 176). From R. Bianchi Bandinelli, "Clusium," *Monumenti antichi* 30, 1925, cols. 545-46, Fig. 10.

Figure 58.18   "Oracular Head of *Urphe*," provenance unknown, circa 300 BC. (Princeton University Art Museum, inv. 1998-46. Gift of Gillett G. Griffin in honor of J. Robert Guy). From De Puma 2005, no. 45. Drawing by the author.

INSCRIPTIONS ON ETRUSCAN AND PRAENESTINE MIRRORS

The previous discussions of mirrors demonstrate the importance of inscriptions.[54] Most inscriptions on mirrors are simple labels that identify characters portrayed in the scene. Almost all are engraved near the relevant figure but some examples place the inscriptions within cartouche-like frames (for example, Fig. 58.16). These identifying inscriptions are similar to those frequently painted on Greek vases to serve the same function. On the famous Attic black-figure amphora by Exekias showing Achilles and Ajax playing a board game, the artist has done something more elaborate. He records a brief conversation between the two contestants. This is very rare on mirrors. I know of only one example that portrays a conversation between a young couple, who are also playing a board game, on a Praenestine mirror (Fig. 58.19).[55] Here the figures speak in the archaic Latin of Praeneste. The young woman says: *devincam ted* ("I'm going to beat you.") to which the young man responds *opeinod* ("I believe you are.") Sometimes inscriptions describe the event depicted on the mirror. For example, Fig. 33.3 shows a bearded figure on the right who is holding a tablet with retrograde inscription in five lines with words separated by interpoints ("colons") that reads:

> *eca:sren:*
> *tva:iχna*
> *c:hercle:*
> *unial:cl*
> *an:θra:sce*

This may be translated as "This shows how Hercle, Uni's son, suckled [milk]." He thus became her legitimate son and was admitted to Olympos.

We have seen that mirrors intended as wedding gifts might carry an inscription identifying the donor. A few mirrors record the names of donors, owners and even artists. It is interesting that while the names of many potters and painters are recorded on vases in the Greek world, very few artists signed mirrors. One exception is on another Praenestine mirror (Fig. 58.20) that labels both figures depicted and identifies the artist: *painiscos* (Paniscos or "Little Pan") and *marsvas* (Marsyas, the satyr). The artist's signature appears vertically beside the satyr's left leg: *vibis pilipus cailavit* or "Vibius Philippus engraved [this mirror]." To explain the absence (at least so far) of Etruscan mirrors with "conversational" inscriptions and with artist signatures, Larissa Bonfante and Nancy de Grummond proposed an intriguing idea: that "There are important differences, not only of language, but of customs, between Etruscan and Praenestine mirrors." They imply a more serious tone in the use of the "adoption paper" recorded on the Hercle and Uni mirror (Fig. 33.3).[56]

MIRRORS IN FUNERARY CONTEXTS

There is another kind of mirror inscription that has been the focus of several studies in recent years. Approximately 21 extant mirrors were intentionally defaced by the normally rough engraving of the word *śuθina*, usually on their reflecting sides.[57] This word means "for the tomb" (*śuθi* = tomb), in other words, an object never again to be used by the living. Mirrors with this inscription have been known for a long time,[58] but now we are

Figure 58.19   Praenestine mirror with young couple playing a board game, probably from Praeneste, circa 300 BC. (British Museum, London, inv. 3213). From Count Michael Tyskiewicz, *Memories of an Old Collector* (London, 1898), opposite p. 186.

Figure 58.20   "Paniscos and Marsyas," Praenestine mirror, circa 300-250 BC. (Villa Giulia, Rome inv. 24898). From *ES* V, pl. 45.

in a better position to begin to understand the meaning of this word as part of Etruscan funerary ritual (see also Chapter 33). First, it must be noted that the term *šuθina* occurs on other kinds of objects besides mirrors, including bronze vessels, candelabra, incense burners, cistae, helmets and spear-points. There are also items of jewelry and, among the earliest appearances of *šuθina*, several Attic vases from Southern Etruria. Several of the metal objects, including some of the mirrors, also give the owner's name.[59] The other interesting phenomenon concerning this kind of inscription is that, except for the late fifth century BC Attic vases found mostly at Cerveteri, almost all the items come from Etrusco-Hellenistic tombs in the area between Orvieto and Lake Bolsena.[60] A single tomb-group might contain numerous objects that have been "*šuθinized.*" The Metropolitan Museum of Art's Bolsena tomb-group, acquired in 1903, presents ten objects (bronze and silver vessels, a bronze mirror, a silver strigil, a gold ring, etc.) with, for the most part, carefully engraved or punched *šuθina* inscriptions.[61] This was the tomb of a wealthy woman and apparently she, or her surviving family members, took precautions to discourage anyone from removing these objects from the tomb.

It is also important to realize that mirrors, and many other kinds of objects, were intentionally damaged (by bending, folding, perforating, etc.) even when not inscribed with *šuθina*. In the case of mirrors, Nancy de Grummond has provided a useful list of eleven examples that appear to have been intentionally mutilated as part of the funerary ritual.[62] No doubt more will be added to her list as more mirrors are carefully examined and published in the *CSE*. De Grummond proposes some provocative reasons why mirrors might have been purposely damaged and uses an excellent example in the Museo Faina at Orvieto to elucidate her points.[63]

If we are beginning to appreciate the ways mirrors functioned in Etruscan society, both in the everyday lives of women and in their preparations for death, we may come to a better understanding of their rituals and beliefs. Some recent examinations of specific tombs are shedding light on mirror functions that we had not suspected. For example, Alexandra Carpino recently examined the specific placement of mirrors in a series of carefully excavated tombs in the Monterozzi necropolis (Calvario area and Fondo Scataglini) at Tarquinia.[64] A close examination of 31 Etruscan tombs, several that contained mirrors,[65] is of utmost importance for understanding mirror funerary functions and, in many ways, it demonstrates how much precious information we have lost due to the haphazard or clandestine recovery of so many other mirrors. Admittedly, these Tarquinian tombs represent a very small sample of the thousands of known Etruscan tombs, and they belong to a single site at a single phase in Etruscan history. Still, given the fact that we have so few undisturbed tombs to study and that so few were methodically excavated and recorded in the nineteenth century, these Tarquinian tombs take on added significance. Fortunately, these tombs, which date from the late fourth to early second century BC, were all relatively intact. Therefore, the archaeologists who worked on them could recover not only ancient artifacts, systematically recording their precise locations, but also the skeletal material for numerous inhumation burials. These skeletons could then be studied so that the gender and approximate age at death for most could be determined. The results are interesting: (1) Some, but certainly not all of the adult women were buried with mirrors; this suggests that mirrors were not an essential element for female burials, at least at this time and place; (2) When mirrors were placed in these graves they were always oriented with their reflecting sides visible; (3) There was little consistency in the placement of mirrors relative to the skeletons associated with them, although a position between the lower legs or near the feet was most common in these graves; (4) The most common subject decorating the mirrors was the Lasa, or winged genius;[66] (5) Of the 31 Etruscan tombs studied, 14 had mirrors associated with them (circa 44 percent); they contained a total of 32 mirrors, some fragmentary.

A fascinating burial at the Cannicella necropolis, Orvieto, has a mirror propped up beside the skeleton's face as if she is looking at the non-reflecting side with a Lasa engraved on it (Fig. 58.21).[67] Nothing quite this dramatic was found at Tarquinia or, for that matter, anywhere else in Etruscan territory. From this small sample we see that mirror usage in burials varied according to time and place. In fact, some practices (for example, the use of *suθina*) seem to have been known as a concept for a long period of time but only used in a relatively localized area for a short period. The same seems to be true for the placement of mirrors relative to the body of the deceased. There is also the problem of quantity: how many mirrors should accompany the deceased? Usually, one mirror suffices, if we can trust our small sample size. But in one case, an alleged tomb group from Chiusi[68] excavated in the late nineteenth century, there are eleven associated mirrors! One possibility is that they did indeed all come from the same chamber tomb but that it contained several female cremation burials and all the mirrors were clustered together by the excavator or the antiquities dealer.

To conclude, mirrors are being studied with intense zeal today. Scholars are realizing that they have much to tell us on a variety of levels. The results are rewarding and are giving us a far more nuanced understanding of Etruscan culture.

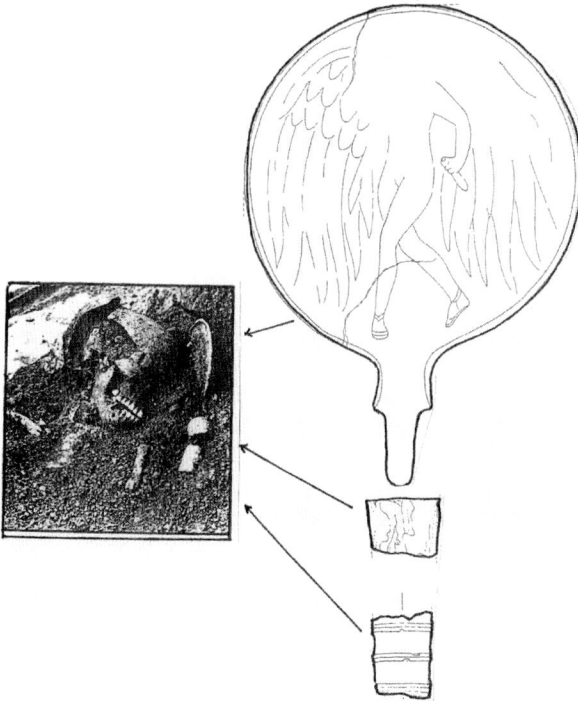

Figure 58.21   Female skeleton with Lasa mirror, from Tomb A, Cannicella necropolis, Orvieto. Adapted from Stopponi 1994, p. 217, Fig. 62 and p. 228, pl. XXXII.

NOTES

1 Christian Charles Josias, Baron von Bunsen (1791–1860), Prussian diplomat and scholar, ambassador to the Court of St. James and long-time resident of London.

2 J. D. Beazley, "The World of the Etruscan Mirror," *Journal of Hellenic Studies* 69, 1949: 1–17.

3 E. Gerhard, *Etruskische Spiegel*, vols. I–IV (Berlin, 1840–1867). Volume V was completed by A. Klügmann and G. Körte (Berlin, 1897). Approximately 911 mirrors are included in the five volumes, abbreviated here as *ES*. See also, Zimmer 1997.

4 Three *CSE* fascicules appeared in 1981: H. Salskov Roberts, *CSE* Denmark 1, Copenhagen, The Danish National Museum, the Ny Carlsberg Glyptotek; G. Sassitelli, *CSE* Italia 1, Bologna, Museo Civico I and II.

5 The first large collection of mirror sections was published by Denise Rebuffat-Emmanuel, *Le Miroir Étrusque d'après la collection du Cabinet des Médailles*. Rome: École Française de Rome, 1973. The sections appear on pls 94–110.

6 See Swaddling *et al.* 2000: 132, 137, Figs 14, 25.

7 G. Matthies, *Die Praenestinischen Spiegel*. Strassburg, 1912.

8 G. Mansuelli, "Materiali per un supplemento al 'corpus' degli specchi etruschi figurati, I–II, *Studi Etruschi* 16, 1942: 531–551 and *Studi Etruschi* 17, 1943: 487–521; "Gli specchi etruschi figurati," *Studi Etruschi* 19, 1946–1947: 3–137.

9 I. Mayer-Prokop, *Die gravierten etruskischen Griffspiegel archaischen Stils*. Heidelberg, 1967.

10 See above, note 4.

11 G. Pfister-Roesgen, *Die etruskischen Spiegel des 5.Jhs.v.Chr.* Frankfurt, 1975.

12 R. Lambrechts, *Les miroirs étrusques et prénestins des Musées Royaux d'Art et d'Histoire à Bruxelles*. Brussels, 1978.

13 U. Fischer-Graf, *Spiegelwerkstätten in Vulci*. Berlin, 1980.

14 Of course, there are many smaller studies that record various collections or treat specific groups of mirrors. Here I have not attempted to give a complete history of the study of Etruscan mirrors that, in fact, goes back to the Renaissance. See, for example, N. de Grummond (ed.), *A Guide to Etruscan Mirrors* (Tallahassee, 1982) pp. 1–7.

15 M. P. Baglione and F. Gilotta, *CSE* Italia 6, Villa Giulia I (Rome, 2007); E. Foddai, *CSE* Italia 6, Villa Giulia II (Rome, 2009), includes the collection of the Museo Archeologico, Palestrina; M. Pacetti, *CSE* Italia 6, Villa Giulia III (Rome, 2011).

16 H. Hencken, *Tarquinia, Villanovans and Early Etruscans* (Cambridge, 1968) pp. 47–49, Fig. 35, b; Hencken, *Tarquinia and Etruscan Origins* (London, 1968) pp. 45, 47, 117 and pl. 59. Hencken's dates for the Villanovan I period are circa 1000–750 BC.

17 V. Bianco Peroni, *I rasoi nell'Italia continentale* (Munich, 1979), pp. 28–30, pls 11–12, nos 125–138. For later mirrors with similar tangs attached by rivets, see R. De Puma, *CSE* USA 2: Boston and Cambridge (Ames, 1993) no. 37.

18 For mirror types in general, see De Puma, *CSE* USA 4: Northeastern Collections 2005, "Notes on Classification and Terminology," pp. 17–23, Figs A–G.

19 Technical definitions: "Engraving" is a process that removes metal with a V- or U-shaped tool. "Chasing" uses a small chisel-like tool that is hammered to push aside, but not remove, a line of metal. Although the "default" term used to describe decorated mirrors is "engraved," there are many that were actually chased. It is difficult to discern these differences with the naked eye and sometimes ancient polishing or subsequent corrosion obscures the characteristic markings of each technique.

20 For carved handles in general, see S. Weinberg, "Etruscan Bone Mirror Handles," *Muse* 9, 1975: 25–33; De Puma, *CSE* USA 1, no. 16.

21 See, for example, Mayer-Prokop 1967: 12, S1, pl. 1, 1; Rebuffat-Emmanuel 1973: 123–128, pl. 18 and pp. 370–374 for the type in general, see De Puma, *CSE* USA 1, nos 11, 29, 40 and *CSE* USA 2, no. 19, with additional parallels from dateable contexts.

22 De Puma, *CSE* USA 2, nos 15–16.

23 For the type in general, see E. Richardson "Covered Mirrors: Bronze" in N. de Grummond (ed.), *Guide* 1982: 14–21. See also, A. Stewart, "A Fourth-Century Bronze Mirror in Duneden," *Antike Kunst* 23, 1980: 25; E. Richardson, "A Mirror in the Duke University Classical Collection and the Etruscan Versions of Odysseus' Return," *RömMitt* 89, 1982: 27–34; D. Willers, "Vom Etruskischen zum Römischen: Noch einmal zu einem Spiegelrelief in Malibu," *J. Paul Getty Museum Journal* 14, 1986: 21–36.

24 For various examples of this type, their chronology and an interpretation, see De Puma, *CSE USA* 4, nos 6 and 41; Neri 2002, nos 199–235.

25 Swaddling *et al.* 2000.

26 Panseri and Leoni 1956; Panseri and Leoni 1957–1958.

27 Serra Ridgway 1996: Tomb 65 (= 4883), pp. 79–80, no. 2; pp. 287–288; pls XLIX, CXL. The subject is a famous one, Hercle being nursed by Uni, known from the mirror in figure 6. This subject appears on two other mirrors: Bologna, Museo Civico inv. It. 1075 (*CSE Bologna*, no. 15); Berlin, Antikenmuseum inv. Misc. 7769, from Vulci (*ES* V, pl. 59; Zimmer 1987: fig. 13, pl. 15)

28 Swaddling *et al.* 2000: 124–126.

29 For a comprehensive survey of the known examples, see Carpino 2003.

30 For example, a number of Praenestine mirrors show cracks at this weak area: Foddai, *CSE Villa Giulia* 2, nos 48, 85, 87, 90. Others have lost their handles: nos 20, 55. Of course, the mirrors with circular discs are perhaps even more vulnerable: nos 3, 24.

31 De Puma 1989; De Puma 2002.

32 Van der Meer 1995; Rallo 2000; for a brief survey, see De Puma 1982. Hercle was worshipped as a god by the Etruscans.

33 In addition to the *LIMC* entries for specific Etruscan gods, see also Jannot 2005, chaps. 8–9; Simon 2006; de Grummond 2006a. Publication of *LIMC* began in 1981, the same year that saw the first *CSE* fascicules.

34 Only a few mirrors can be definitely associated with male burials: see below, note 36. Of course, we do not know the archaeological context for the vast majority of mirrors excavated before the twentieth century. It is possible that men purchased and used mirrors in life but, due to funerary customs and rituals, were rarely buried with them.

35 De Puma 1994.

36 Carpino 2009: 190. The tombs are Tomb of the Ceicna, Castiglione sul Lago: see Sannibale 1994, pp. 126–129 (a simple Dioskouroi mirror); Tomb 5, Gioiella, near Chiusi; Tombs 5699 and 6093, Tarquinia (Calvario).

37 Carpino 2009: 191. For a contrary opinion, see Izzet 1998.

38 For a useful summary of the problems, see Szilágy 1995.

39 See Adam 1980; De Puma 1980.

40 Emmanuel-Rebuffat 1984. Indications of these problems were given by my earlier analysis of the four-figure Dioskouroi groups: see De Puma 1973. See also, Bonfante 1980.

41 A number of mirrors show elaborate borders but no figural composition in the medallion. Are these "unfinished" mirrors awaiting the attentions of master engravers who would have provided the figural scenes? Pericle Ducati (1912) suggested that these borders were executed by apprentices, but in my opinion they are often highly skilled demonstrations of the engraver's craft and seem on a par with (if not sometimes far better than) the work of the engraver of figural scenes (see, for example, fig. 7). For mirrors decorated with isolated borders, see A. Frascarelli, *CSE Italia* 2, no. 19; J. Swaddling, *CSE Great Britain* 1, no. 12; G. Heres, *CSE DDR* 1, nos 22 and 46.

42 For a summary of these gods in Etruscan art, see De Puma 1986b.

43 For an excellent summary of the iconographical types and chronological considerations, see A. Frascarelli, *CSE Italia* 2, *Perugia* I, pp. 37–40, no. 14 and pp. 47–48, no. 24. For a recent

discussion of attributions, see M. P. Baglione and F. Gilotta, *CSE Italia* 6, *Villa Giulia* I, pp. 96–97, no. 38.

44 Hermitage, St. Petersburg inv. V.505: *ES* IV, pl. 322; E. Mavleev in F. Roncalli (ed.), *Gens antiquissima Italiae. Antichità dall'Umbria a Leningrado* (Milan, 1990), no. 8.19, pp. 413–417.

45 De Puma 2005: no. 44, p. 60 (with parallels cited).

46 De Puma 1993: no. 23, p. 44. Compare the male Lasa on no. 22 and another in De Puma 1987, no. 10.

47 De Puma 2005: no. 33, p. 50.

48 British Museum inv. 626: *ES* II, pl. 213.

49 See, for example, L. Agostiniani, *Le 'iscrizioni parlanti' dell'Italia antica.* Florence, 1982.

50 For discussion of these mirrors and their inscriptions, see de Grummond 2000: 75–77 and Pandolfini 2000: 224. Note that *malana* is probably an alternative spelling of *malena*.

51 For a list of 38 examples, see de Grummond 2000a: 66–67. To this list may now be added the mirror in Princeton University Art Museum inv. 1998–46; see De Puma 2001.

52 Maggiani 1992. He treats the Casuccini Mirror from Chiusi, now Siena, Museo Archeologico inv. 176.

53 De Puma 2001: 27.

54 For a general survey of the topic, see Bonfante and de Grummond, "Inscriptions on Etruscan Mirrors" in de Grummond (ed.) 1982: 69–78.

55 British Museum inv. 3213: ES V, pl. 146. See also, Bonfante and de Grummond (n. 54), p. 75.

56 Ibid., p. 76.

57 De Grummond 2009, Appendix I (pp. 178–180) conveniently lists these with references.

58 For example, *ES* I, pl. XXII, 7–9 (published in 1843).

59 Fontaine 1995, Tables I–II (pp. 205, 207) list the types of objects and numbers as well as findspots, if known. His lists can now be supplemented by at least four more mirrors and one candelabrum. For a list of inscriptions that include owner's name, see Appendix II, p. 212.

60 For a map of the known findspots, thus far recorded, see Fontaine 1995, Fig. 1, p. 202.

61 See De Puma 2008b and 2013, nos 6.25–6.40. The tomb-group is on display in the newly-renovated Etruscan Gallery at the Museum and the objects can be accessed on the Museum's website: www.metmuseum.org.

62 De Grummond 2009, Appendix II (pp. 181–182). I wonder if the Villanovan tang mirror (fig. 2) was also intentionally damaged. Note the bent tang and heavy creases on the right side of disc. If this does represent intentional mutilation, it might push the beginnings of this funerary practice back to the ninth century BC.

63 For the mirror and her discussion, see Ibid., 175–177, Figs 44–45; the mirror is also discussed in *CSE Italia* 4, no. 6.

64 Carpino 2008.

65 Carpino 2008: 3, 13, Charts I–III. The tombs were excavated and first published by Lucia Cavagnaro Vanoni, Richard E. Linington and Francesca R. Serra Ridgway. For references, see Carpino 2008: 26, n. 4.

66 Rallo 1974; De Puma 1985.

67 Stopponi 1994: 207–209, fig. 62; pls XXXII, b–c and XXXV, c–d.

68 De Puma 1993: 37–45, nos 15–25; De Puma 2008a. This fine group, now in the Museum of Fine Arts, Boston, has several unusual mirrors. There are two silver box mirrors (nos 15–16), a silver handle mirror (no. 18, undecorated), a magnificent bronze tang mirror (no. 23), a bone mirror handle (no. 25), and a very small handle mirror (no. 24), which I have suggested may have been a toy mirror from Fastia Velsi's childhood.

BIBLIOGRAPHY

Adam, R. (1980) *Recherches sur les miroirs prénestins*, Paris: Presses de l'École Normale Supérieure.

Beazley, J. D. (1949) "The World of the Etruscan Mirror," *Journal of Hellenic Studies* 69: 1–17.

Bonfante, L. (1980) "An Etruscan Mirror with 'Spiky Garland' in the Getty Museum," *J. Paul Getty Museum Journal* 8: 147–154.

——(1997) *CSE USA* 3: *New York, The Metropolitan Museum of Art*, Rome: "L'ERMA" di Bretschneider.

Carpino, A. A. (2003) *Discs of Splendor: The Relief Mirrors of the Etruscans*, Madison: University of Wisconsin Press.

——(2008) "Reflections from the Tomb: Mirrors as Grave Goods in Late Classical and Hellenistic Tarquinia, *Etruscan Studies* 11. 1–33.

——(2009) "Dueling Warriors on Two Etruscan Bronze Mirrors from the Fifth Century B.C.E." in S. Bell and H. Nagy (eds), *New Perspectives on Etruria and Early Rome in Honor of Richard Daniel De Puma*, Madison: University of Wisconsin Press, pp. 182–197.

CSE Corpus Speculorum Etruscorum (1981–).

de Grummond, N. T. (ed.) (1982) *A Guide to Etruscan Mirrors*, Tallahassee: Archaeological News.

——(1991) "Etruscan Twins and Mirror Images: The Dioskouroi at the Door," *Yale University Art Gallery Bulletin* 10: 10–31.

——(2000a) "Mirrors and *Manteia*: Themes of Prophecy on Etruscan and Praenestine Mirrors" in M. D. Gentili (ed.), *Aspetti*, pp. 27–67.

——(2000b) "An Etruscan Mirror in Tokyo" in M. D. Gentili (ed.), *Aspetti*, pp. 69–77.

——(2000c) "Etruscan Mirrors Now," *AJA* 106: 307–311.

——(2002) "Mirrors, marriage and mysteries," *JRA Suppl.* 47: 62–85.

——(2006a) *Etruscan Myth, Sacred History, and Legend*, Philadelphia: The University Museum of Archaeology and Anthropology.

——(2006b) "Mariś, the Etruscan Genius" in E. Herring, I. Lemos, F. Lo Schiavo, L. Vagnetti, R. Whitehouse and J. Wilkins (eds), *Across Frontiers: Etruscans, Greeks, Phoenicians and Cypriots. Studies in honour of David Ridgway and Francesca Romana Serra Ridgway*, London: Accordia Research Institute, pp. 413–426.

——(2009a) "On Mutilated Mirrors" in M. Gleba and H. Becker (eds), *Votives, Places and Rituals in Etruscan Religion. Studies in Honor of Jean MacIntosh Turfa, Religions in the Graeco-Roman World* 166, Leiden and Boston: Brill, pp. 171–182.

——(2009b) "The Sacred Day on Etruscan Mirrors" in S. Bruni (ed.), *Etruria e Italia preromana. Studi in onore di Giovannangelo Camporeale, Studia erudita* 4, Pisa and Rome: Fabrizio Serra, pp. 285–294.

De Puma, R. D. (1973) "The Dioskouroi on Four Etruscan Mirrors in Midwestern Collections," *Studi Etruschi* 41: 159–170.

——(1980) "A Fourth Century Praenestine Mirror with Telephos and Orestes," *RömMitt* 87: 5–28.

——(1982) "Greek Gods and Heroes on Etruscan Mirrors" in N. T. de Grummond (ed.), *A Guide to Etruscan Mirrors*, pp. 89–100.

——(1985) "An Etruscan Lasa Mirror," *Muse: Annual of the Museum of Art and Archaeology*, University of Missouri: Columbia, 19: 44–55.

——(1986a) "A Fourth Century B.C. Etruscan Engraved Mirror," *Bulletin/Annual Report of the Elvehjem Museum of Art for 1985–86*, University of Wisconsin, Madison: 29–42.

——(1986b) "Dioskouroi/TINAS CLINIAR," *LIMC* 3: 597–608.

——(1987) *CSE USA* 1: *Midwestern Collections*. Ames: Iowa State University Press.

——(1989) "Engraved Etruscan Mirrors: Questions of Authenticity" in G. Maetzke (ed.), *Atti del Secondo Congresso Internazionale Etrusco: Florence 26 May – 2 June 1985*, vol. 2, Rome: Giorgio Bretschneider, pp. 695–711.

——(1993) *CSE USA* 2: *Boston and Cambridge*, Ames: Iowa State University Press.

——(1994) "Eos and Memnon on Etruscan Mirrors" in R. D. De Puma and J. P. Small (eds), *Murlo and the Etruscans: Art and Society in Ancient Etruria*, Madison: University of Wisconsin Press, pp. 180–189.

——(1998) "The Etruscan Rhadamanthys?," *Etruscan Studies* 5: 37–52.

——(2001) "An Etruscan Mirror with the Prophesying Head of Orpheus," *Record of The Art Museum, Princeton University* 60: 18–29.

——(2002) "Forgeries of Etruscan Engraved Mirrors" in C. Mattusch *et al.* (eds), *From the Parts to the Whole: Acta of the 13th International Bronze Congress, held at Cambridge, Massachusetts, May 28–June 1, 1996, JRA* Suppl. 39, vol. 2, Portsmouth, RI: Journal of Roman Archaeology, pp. 53–64.

——(2005) *CSE USA 4: Northeastern Collections*, Rome: "L'ERMA" di Bretschneider.

——(2008a) "The Tomb of Fastia Velsi from Chiusi," *Etruscan Studies* 11: 135–149.

——(2008b) "A Third-Century B.C.E. Etruscan Tomb Group from Bolsena in the Metropolitan Museum of Art," *AJA* 112: 429–440.

——(2013) *Etruscan Art in the Metropolitan Museum of Art*, New York and New Haven: The Metropolitan Museum of Art and Yale University Press.

Dobrowolski, W. (1991) "Il mito di Prometeo: Il limite tra il cielo e la terra nell'arte etrusca" in R. A. Staccioli (ed.), *Miscellanea etrusca e italica in onore di Massimo Pallottino* = *Archeologia Classica* 43, Rome: "L'ERMA" di Bretschneider, pp. 1213–1230.

——(1994) "I Dioscuri sugli specchi etruschi" in M. Martelli (ed.) *Tyrrhenoi Philotechnoi: Atti della Giornata di studio organizzata dalla Facoltà di Conservazione dei Beni Culturali dell'Università degli Studi della Tuscia in occasione della mostra "Il mondo degli Etruschi. Testimonianze dai Musei di Berlino e dell'Europa orientale" Viterbo, 13 October 1990*, Rome: Gruppo editoriale internazionale, pp. 173–181.

Ducati, P. (1912) "Contributo allo studio degli specchi etruschi figurati," *RömMitt* 27: 243–285.

Emmanuel-Rebuffat, D. (1984) "Typologie générale du miroir étrusque à manche massif," *Revue Archéologique*: 195–226.

ES E. Gerhard, *Etruskische Spiegel*, vols. I–IV (Berlin, 1840–1867); A. Klügmann and G. Körte, vol. V (Berlin, 1897).

Fischer-Graf, U. (1980) *Spiegelwerkstätten in Vulci* = Deutsches Archäologisches Institut, Archäologische Forschungen 8. Berlin: Gebr. Mann Verlag.

Foddai, E. (2009) with the collaboration of L. Galeotti, *CSE Italia 6, Roma-Museo di Villa Giulia, Palestrina-Museo Archeologico, fasc. II*, Rome: "L'ERMA" di Bretschneider.

Fontaine, P. (1995) "A propos des inscriptions šuθina sur la vaisselle métallique étrusque" in J.-R. Jannot (ed.), *Vaisselle métallique, Vaisselle céramique. Productions, usages et valeurs en Étrurie* = *REA* 97, pp. 201–216.

Gentili, M. D. (ed.) (2000) *Aspetti e problemi della produzione degli specchi Etruschi figurati. Atti dell'incontro internazionale di studio (Roma, 2–4 maggio 1997)*, Rome: Aracne.

——(2000) "Il 'maestro di *Phaun*' e la sua bottega. Considerazioni su un gruppo di specchi Etruschi figurati" in M. D. Gentili (ed.), *Aspetti*, pp. 115–141.

Gilotta, F. (2000) " Specchi prenestini tardo-classici: qualche appunto sugli avvii della produzione" in M. D. Gentili (ed.), *Aspetti*, pp. 143–163.

Izzet, I. (1998) "Holding a Mirror to Etruscan Gender" in R. D. Whitehouse (ed.), *Gender and Italian Archaeology. Challenging the Stereotypes*, London: Accordia Research Institute and Institute of Archaeology, pp. 95–126.

Jannot, J.-R. (2005) *Religion in Ancient Etruria*, Madison, University of Wisconsin Press.

Lambrechts, R. (1978) *Les miroirs étrusques et prénestins des Musées Royaux d'Art et d'Histoire à Bruxelles*, Brussels: Musées Royaux d'Art et d'Histoire.

Maggiani, A. (1992) "Iconografie greche e storie locali nell'arte etrusco-italica tra IV e III secolo a.C.," *Prospettiva* 68: 3–11.

Mayer-Prokop, I. (1967) *Die gravierten etruskischen Griffspiegel archaischen Stils* = *RömMitt* Erg. Heft 13. Heidelberg: F. H. Kerle Verlag.

Pandolfini Angeletti, M. (2000) "Iscrizioni e didascalie degli specchi etruschi: alcune riflessioni" in M. D. Gentili (ed.), *Aspetti*, pp. 209–224.

Panseri, C. and Leoni, M. (1956) "Sulla tecnica di fabbricazione degli specchi di bronzo etruschi," *Studi etruschi* 25: 305–319.

——(1957–1958) "The Manufacturing Technique of Etruscan Mirrors," *Studies in Conservation* 3: 49–63.

Pfister-Roesgen, G. (1975) *Die etruskischen Spiegel des 5.Jhs.v.Chr* = *Archäologische Studien* 2. Bern and Frankfurt: Herbert and Peter Lang.

Rallo, A. (1974) *Lasa. Iconografia e esegesi*. Florence: Sansoni.

——(2000) "Motivi ispiratori greci nella decorazione di alcuni specchi etruschi" in M. D. Gentili (ed.), *Aspetti*, pp. 225–248.

Rebuffat-Emmanuel, D. (1973) *Le Miroir Étrusque d'après la collection du Cabinet des Médailles*, Rome: École Française de Rome.

Sannibale, M. (1994) *Le urne cinerarie di età ellenistica* = *Museo Gregoriano Etrusco* catalogo 3, Rome: "L'ERMA" di Bretschneider.

——(2008) "Specchi" (nos 119–127, pp. 175–201) in *La raccolta Giacinto Guglielmi. Parte II: Bronzi e materiali vari. Musei Vaticani. Museo Gregoriano Etrusco. Cataloghi*, 4, Rome: "L'ERMA" di Bretschneider.

Serra Ridgway, F. R. (2000) "Etruscan Mirrors and Archaeological Context," *JRA* 13: 407–418.

Simon, E. (2006) "Gods in Harmony: The Etruscan Pantheon" in N. de Grummond and E. Simon (eds), *The Religion of the Etruscans*, Austin: University of Texas Press, pp. 45–65.

Stopponi, S. (1994) "Tomba A" in M. Bonamici, S. Stopponi and P. Tamburini (eds), *Orvieto, La necropoli di Cannicella. Scavi della fondazione per il museo "C. Faina" e dell'Università di Perugia (1977)*, Rome: "L'ERMA" di Bretschneider, pp. 207–231.

Swaddling, J., Craddock, P., La Niece, S. and Hockey, M. (2000) "Breaking the Mould: The Overwrought Mirrors of Etruria" in D. Ridgway, F. Serra Ridgway, M. Pearce, E. Herring, R. Whitehouse and J. Wilkins (eds), *Ancient Italy in its Mediterranean Setting: Studies in honour of Ellen Macnamara* = *Specialist Studies on the Mediterranean* 4, London: Accordia Research Institute, pp. 117–140.

Szilágyi, J. G. (1995) "Discourse on Method: A Contribution to the Problem of Classifying Late Etruscan Mirrors," *Etruscan Studies* 2: 35–52.

van der Meer, L. B. (1995) *Interpretatio etrusca: Greek Myths on Etruscan Mirrors*, Amsterdam: J. C. Gieben.

Wiman, I. (1990) *Malstria-Malena: Metals and Motifs in Etruscan Mirror Craft* = *Studies in Mediterranean Archaeology* 91, Gothenburg: Paul Åströms.

Zimmer, G. (1987) *Spiegel im Antikenmuseum*, Berlin: Staatliche Museen Preussischer Kulturbesitz, Antikenmuseum.

——(1997) "Eduard Gerhard und das Corpus der etruskischen Spiegel" in H. Wrede (ed.), *Dem Archäologen Eduard Gerhard 1795–1867 zu seinem 200. Geburtstag*, Winckelmann-Institut der Humboldt-Universität zu Berlin 2, Berlin: Arenhövel, pp. 107–117.

CHAPTER FIFTY NINE

SCIENCE AS ART: ETRUSCAN ANATOMICAL VOTIVES

———— .◆. ————

Matthias Recke

Figural representations of the human form have been known in Etruscan art in greater numbers since the Archaic period. Whether divine or mortal, in statues in the round or figurines, figural representations always concern the portrayal of the whole figure from head to toe. The pictorial dissection of the human body into isolated body parts is a phenomenon that occurs in the Etruscan-Latin sphere, especially in the Hellenistic period, in the form of votive models of body parts. Produced and dedicated in large numbers, the anatomical votives far exceed all other kinds of votive offerings in volume in the sanctuaries.[1] (As a phenomenon, this custom is related to the votives of isolated heads that begin around the end of the sixth century BC.)[2] Comparable phenomena of dedication of model body parts are known in ancient Greece and Cyprus,[3] although the practice is not nearly so widespread there. In the Gallo-Roman area also appropriate finds extend into the Imperial period.

THE DISSECTION OF THE BODY

Despite the large quantity of votives recovered, the repertoire of the various types is quite limited. The anatomical body-part dedications, in the narrower sense of the term, include, besides heads (and half-heads) (Figs. 59.1–2) – numerically certainly the most widely distributed category – the extremities of the human body (arms, legs) as well as parts thereof (lower arm with hand, lower leg with foot, knee, neck) and individual hands and feet. Even single fingers and toes were dedicated.

The division of the body into busts (from navel to head)[4] and corresponding counterparts such as the lower body from hip to feet are also known, as are torsos (and halved torsos)[5] without extremities. Isolated representations of the sense organs appear, namely eyes and ears (Fig. 59.3, see Fig. 59.11), (usually single organs, but sometimes in pairs), rarely also nose, tongue and mouth.[6] "Masks" show a cut out section of the face, which as a rule includes eyes and nose, sometimes also the mouth.[7] The representations of male genitalia always include the scrotum and the non-erect penis, often the pubic hair is also depicted (see Fig. 59.10). In the female representations, the vulva and also the female breast are depicted, usually not in pairs but as single objects (Fig. 59.4).

Figure 59.1   Male votive head, from Veii. Antikensammlung, Inv. Inv. T III-30 (formerly Sammlung Stieda), Giessen. Photo Matthias Recke.

Figure 59.2   Female votive head (half-head), from Veii. Antikensammlung, Inv. T III-36 (formerly Sammlung Stieda), Giessen. Photo Matthias Recke.

A special feature of the Etruscan-Italic anatomical votives (and in fact strictly limited to these cultures) is the dedication of reproductions of human internal organs.[8] The range of the representations is very large. Among the most elaborate are certainly the statues and busts of worshippers in which a window-like opening into the (clothed) body (see Fig. 59.7) furnishes a view of the interior and shows the internal organs.

Torsos without limbs or head in contrast are always nude (see Figs. 59.13, 59.15 and 59.16). Plaques with internal organs, blocks of viscera, or individual organs, especially heart, bladder, uterus (sometimes with additional body/appendix?) (Fig. 59.5, see Fig. 59.9); other organs such as lungs, liver, stomach and intestines as a rule only appear in association with the polyvisceral plaques, the ensembles of organs, or the models with open abdomens. There is a question of the interpretation of tubular-oval objects as single testicles (Fig. 59.5 center), which have often been interpreted as bladders as well. Representations of swaddled infants (Fig. 59.6) cannot be understood in the narrow sense of the term as anatomical votives, but they are usually treated under this heading.[9]

Figure 59.3   Right Eye. Göttingen, Archäologisches Institut, Inv. TC 136. Copyright: Archäologisches Institut der Universität Göttingen, Photo Stephan Eckardt.

Figure 59.4   Female breast, from Veii. Antikensammlung, Inv. T III-32 (formerly Sammlung Stieda), Giessen. Photo Matthias Recke.

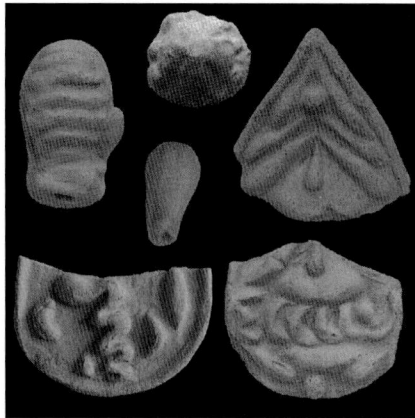

Figure 59.5   Uterus, heart, bladder and three fragments of polyvisceral plaques, from Veii. Antikensammlung, Inv. T III-7, T III-18, T III-16, T III-34, T III-10, T III-33 (formerly Sammlung Stieda), Giessen. Photo Matthias Recke.

Figure 59.6   Swaddled infant, from Veii. Antikensammlung, Inv. T III-38 (formerly Sammlung Stieda), Giessen. Photo Matthias Recke.

MATERIAL AND PRODUCTION

The bulk of the Etrusco-Italic anatomical votives consists of fired clay, thus terracotta. Rarely, there are representations in bronze, and then they are especially concentrated in the northern Etruscan region. The terracotta votives are usually moldmade, less often turned on a potter's wheel or hand-modeled. A combination of the various techniques is common. Thus moldmade objects can be reworked by hand or completed with appliqués, and hand- or wheel-made figures may be completed with parts drawn from a mold. Most of the extant anatomical votives however are obtained without extensive reworking or retouching. Since the production of such votives is a serial mass-production technique, there is usually little room for expression of artistic merit. In fact the molds were often used for a very long period of production, until they were heavily worn and details were only faintly visible. Differences in size between examples of identical types show that new molds were drawn from extant impressions, so that their products are then significantly smaller than the originals, due to the natural shrinkage of the clay in firing.[10] Individual molds and details thus become blurred over succeeding mold-generations. This means that an art-historical, stylistic dating technique can only be reliably applied to the original version of a mold. And this applies in principle only for the representations of heads (see Figs. 59.1–2), since the anatomical votives in the narrow sense do not conform to a stylistic dating.[11]

The fact that anatomical votives were moldmade in large numbers means that they were stock productions and have no real claim to individuality. That might be different in the case of large, expensive votives like the life-size statues and torsos with visible internal organs, because here at least the body was usually individually finished by hand (Fig. 59.7, see Fig. 59.13). The extant examples show, however, that even in these cases the heads were taken from the repertoire of stock head-types already to hand.[12]

Circular holes on the back or underside of the votive are sometimes identified as vent-holes for firing, to prevent bursting of the piece in the kiln. However, since they appear in the hollow heads and half-heads (Fig. 59.8) that are open on the underside, where this was not technically necessary, and appear to be made with great care in small objects that did not require a vent-hole, they are more likely to be understood as provisions for suspension. They allow the presentation, for example, of a breast- or heart-votive in an anatomically correct orientation.[13]

Figure 59.7 Fragment of a female votive statue with open abdominal cavity, from Veii. Antikensammlung, Inv. T III-37 (formerly Sammlung Stieda), Giessen. Photo Matthias Recke.

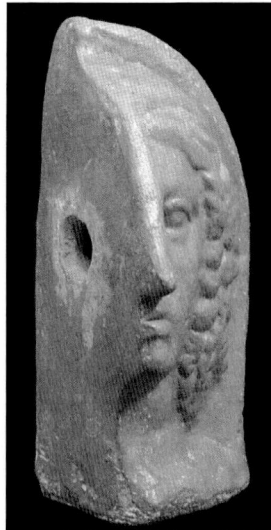

Figure 59.8 Female half-head, with hole for hanging, from Veii. Antikensammlung, Inv. T III-36 (formerly Sammlung Stieda), Giessen. Photo Matthias Recke.

Although the paint is usually poorly preserved, it is known that the anatomical votives (as also statues and heads) were painted. The repertoire of colors includes above all a strong reddish brown (for skin, but also for internal organs), and black (for hair or drawing of details), but also yellow and white. Very rarely, a red or white slip has survived as the base coat for paint.[14]

Since the paint was applied before firing in the kiln, we can hardly assume that the paint was applied according to the wishes of individual buyers. In any case we cannot exclude the fact that certain areas of a donor's votive were highlighted in color according to they buyer's directions. Since such labeling must be done after firing, because of the transience of certain colors, we should not expect that anything has survived of this.

Finds of molds show that anatomical votives were made in the immediate vicinity of the shrines and sold to visitors to the cult places.[15] Because formal characteristics allow the identification of local workshop groups, the anatomical votives of the great Etruscan cities may be divided into different regional styles.

DATING

Anatomical votive models in terracotta can hardly be exactly dated – except for complete votive statues or heads, whose underlying prototypes may be analyzed stylistically to some extent. This is partly because of low artistic aspirations and because the strong abstraction of the moldmade body parts makes a stylistic dating unlikely,[16] and also because only the design of the prototype can be chronologically classified. But since the mold was used over a long period of time or certain types have been produced over several generations by making new molds from extant models, an art-historical sort of dating cannot be achieved. Since votive inscriptions as a rule are lacking, the objects found in the same votive deposits are of utmost importance – insofar as they are chronologically informative. This consists mainly of (fine) pottery and coins. One of the main difficulties here is again the fact that any such *favissae, bothroi* (or *stipi*)[17] are usually secondary deposits, so that objects can only be linked to a broad time period. This usually covers the second half of the fourth century to the end of the second century BC.

SITES

Anatomical votives are found exclusively as votive offerings in sanctuaries.[18] Some 300 corresponding sites are known in the Etrusco-Italic region.[19] They range from the Arno in the north, to the east and south through the Etruscan core area bounded by the Tiber and to the Faliscan territory as well as to the south comprising Latium and Campania (down to Cales and Lucera). Geographically, a strong concentration may be recognized in southern Etruria and northern Latium: the most significant finds were made in the following places: Caere, Pyrgi, Tarquinia, Gravisca, Canino (Tessenano), Veii, Vulci (in Etruria), Falerii, Narce (Faliscan area), Fregellae, Gabii, Lavinium, Nemi, Ponte di Nona, Praeneste, Rome (in Latium), Cales and Lucera (in Campania).[20] The different kinds of sanctuaries are represented here – urban, rural, inland and coastal – thus encompass the entire known range of private and public cults.[21]

Unlike Greece, where stone carved anatomical votives are confined to the shrines of very few gods and those in terracotta were given exclusively in the Asklepieion of Corinth,[22] in the Etrusco-Italic region practically all the deities worshipped were offered such votives.[23]

This raises the problem that because of the lack of dedicatory inscriptions, the local deity can hardly ever be identified, and the votive gifts themselves are not so specific that the recipient can be read from them. The few epigraphically documented examples were compiled by Turfa: Vea, Uni, Turan, Menerva and probably Tiur and Selvans in Etruria, and Minerva, Diana, Juno, Mater Matuta, Ceres and Aesculapius in Latium and Campania.[24]

Although in some sanctuaries anatomical votives have been found as they were placed by the worshippers, namely on or at an altar in the sanctuary, or at least in the immediate vicinity,[25] the majority of the objects come from secondary depositions. These were in the form of pits in the area of the sanctuary, in order to make room for new offerings. These *bothroi* (or *stipes*) can contain several thousand objects[26] and they are occasionally sorted according to type,[27] but they often include other objects as well. Both find-situations illustrate clearly that among dedications the offering of anatomical votives was a very broad, widespread custom, which reflects an everyday, individual rite of the "private" religion, and that this communication between worshipper and deity stands in the foreground, and is by far much more crucial than any aspect of self-representation and self-portrayal of the dedicant in public inside the sanctuary.[28] It is questionable, though, to what extent we may read an indication of lower social status of dedicants from the low value of the material and its less costly manufacturing process.[29]

MEANING

Votive offerings are primarily gifts for the gods, tangible signs of reverence, and often they are the only surviving witness to ritual cult events. They are considered an expression of the interaction and communication between donor and deity. This also applies to the anatomical votives. Since dedicatory inscriptions are missing in general,[30] it is difficult to decide whether we are dealing with *ex-votos* in the strict meaning of the term, thus with thanks-offerings made because of a vow and after the petition has been fulfilled by a deity, or if they are gifts that emphasize the request and the prayers of the worshipper and are supposed to encourage the deity to an active participation.[31] In addition to the lack of dedicatory inscriptions, the solution to this question is complicated by the fact that the vast majority of votive offerings were found deposited in secondary contexts. It is striking, however, that the low value of the votive material suggests a minor role for the aspect of self-representation of the donor in front of other visitors to the sanctuary. Thus these votive offerings differ quite significantly from the practices in the Greek cultural area where this is a central element.

The most important basis, from which all interpretive approaches proceed, is the recognition that the anatomical votives, as well as the relevant statues and heads, do not depict the deity revered, but rather mortal men.[32] In favor of this is the adaptation of standardized head types with different physiognomic characteristics that typify human age and gender, without following the usual ideal for classical divine iconography, such as the dress and attitude of statues, especially the representation as gift-bearers or worshippers. From this it can still not be concluded that the votives always represent the donor himself (or a part of him). This is evident for example in the votives of swaddled infants (see Fig. 59.6) or small children, which they can hardly have consecrated themselves.[33] Therefore if a dedication for a third party is possible, then we must also expect that men sometimes could donate models of women's bodies, heads or body parts, on behalf of their wives, and vice versa. Equating the donor with the person depicted is indeed probable in most cases, but not provable exclusively.

Despite the popular view in the scholarship that the anatomical votives, just like all the complete figures and heads, are deputies representing the worshippers, as *pars pro toto,* the real question is: what are the meaning and purpose of such dedications? On account of the lack of dedicatory inscriptions, this is not at all clear.

The various interpretive approaches that have been found to date for the genre of Etruscan and Italic votive body-part models are also conditioned by the historic state of the research. Thus, the first scientists who studied the genre sought to recognize in it the representation of symptoms of illness.[34] Uterus-votives might be seen as representations of some incident involving the uterus (prolapse) (Fig. 59.9), hands holding votive offerings as depictions of a tumor,[35] half-heads a sign of unilateral headache (migraine) (see Fig. 59.2), heart-votives as boils, abscesses or even as "pathologically altered *glans* of the male member."[36] This specifically pathological interpretation is today, as a rule, no longer proposed. The only assumption that continues to be held is that penis-votives with closed, tightly pointed foreskin (Fig. 59.10) should be explained as images of the

Figure 59.9   Uterus from Veii. Antikensammlung, Inv. T III-7 (formerly Sammlung Stieda), Giessen. Photo Matthias Recke.

Figure 59.10   Penis. Göttingen, Archäologisches Institut, Inv. TC 135. Copyright Archäologisches Institut der Universität Göttingen, Photo Stephan Eckardt.

condition of phimosis. Generally, caution is advised because of the absolute rarity of representations addressable as disease – if there are any among anatomical votives – and because of the artistic conventions practiced in this period that conform to Greek norms as found in fine art. Instead of the representation of a diseased condition of phimosis, the intention to be sought here is surely in the realm of fertility and reproduction.[37]

Beside the interpretation in terms of a cure for diseases, or at least a concrete protection of specific members of the body and their capabilities (for example, vision, physical strength, virility), which are included under the term *sanatio* ("healing"), another, less literal interpretation is also conceivable. Thus, ear votives (Fig. 59.11) could be intended as a sign of being heard by the deity, and eyes show the god's attention. Raised hands[38] (Fig. 59.12) permanently express the prayer of the dedicant, just as individual heads, as representatives of the donor, perpetuate his presence in the sanctuary for all eternity.[39] The representation of human internal organs is sometimes explained by the great significance

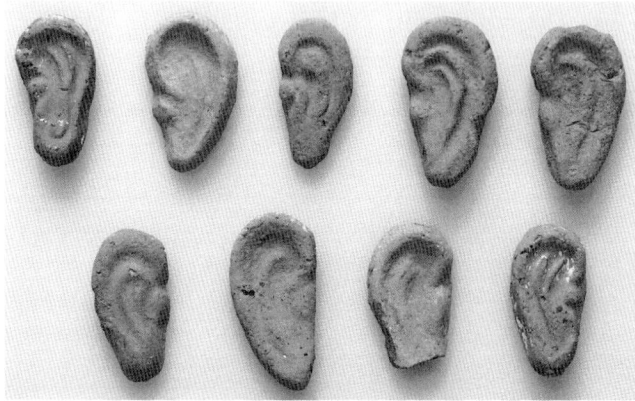

Figure 59.11   Votive ears, from Veii. Antikensammlung, Inv. T III-19 – T III-27 (formerly Sammlung Stieda), Giessen. Photo Matthias Recke.

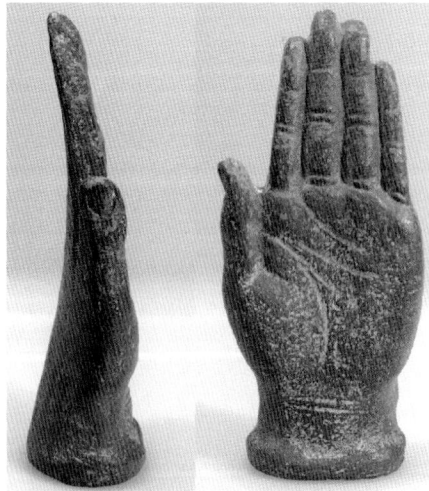

Figure 59.12   Outstretched votive hand, from Veii. Antikensammlung, Inv. T III-5 (formerly Sammlung Stieda) Giessen. Photo Matthias Recke.

placed by the Etruscans on divination by entrails. Other interpretive models see the dedicating worshippers in the role of haruspex and their placing of terracotta viscera on the altar as a symbolic self-sacrifice.[40]

MODELS

The anatomical votives are usually greatly simplified and are reproduced without specific details. This applies equally for the votives that show externally visible body parts as well as those portraying internal organs. Here there is a tendency to create symmetry, both in the form of the polyvisceral plaques which, like those images of bodies with openings, are usually teardrop-shaped (see Fig. 59.5), and also in the arrangement of the individual organs placed inside them (Fig. 59.13). This can also be seen in the design of isolated organs, such as the heart. Especially lifelike representations are known for feet (Fig. 59.14), on which veins are depicted,[41] although this should not be taken as evidence for the socially inferior status of the worshippers, but rather as a feature of the special care taken in the design, and as evidence for a positive connotation of veristic art which stands out from the mass of works that are not especially sophisticated artistic products.

Nevertheless, the obvious question is posed, regarding the artisans who designed the appropriate models, particularly the representations of internal organs: where did they acquire their knowledge? It has rightly been noted that a medically accurate description of anatomy could hardly have been the main interest of the buyer/dedicant.[42] However, since the order of the internal organs corresponds to reality (see Fig. 59.13), it has been proposed that such knowledge had been gained from the examination of the human body, for instance on the battlefield, or it could indicate a comprehensive medical knowledge obtained through surgery or dissection.[43] Other researchers suggest that the basically identical arrangement of animal viscera, for instance in pigs, served as a model for the artisans. The knowledge would have been acquired mainly through blood sacrifices in the context of religious cult.

Figure 59.13   Votive torso with internal organs. Rome, Therme Museum Inv. 14608. Photo DAI Rom, Sansaini, Neg. D-DAI-Rom 54. 105.

VOTIVES WITH OPEN BODY CAVITY

From the various interpretive models in the research,[44] the statues and torsos with open body cavity (see Figs. 59.7, 59.13) are conspicuous because of the discrepancy between the simultaneous representation of inside and outside and the window-like opening that completely ignores vitality in attitude and gesture. They are among the most characteristic examples of the genre of anatomical votives. Three different sub-types may be distinguished: small-scale statuettes in the style of Tanagra-figurines (originally a Hellenistic Greek style),[45] representations up to life-size (usually as busts, but also in the form of complete statues) of draped worshippers (see Fig. 59.7),[46] and torsos without heads where the arms and legs are only depicted as stumps (see Fig. 59.13).[47] In the statuettes and the large-scale statues there exists a serious contradiction between the attitude of a worshipper or offering-bearer and the gaping hole that is placed, without regard for the clothing, in the region of the abdomen, and that reveals the viscera, from heart, lungs placed above the liver, stomach, and kidneys to bowel and bladder. While with the draped figures it is evident through their attitude and gestures that living persons are being portrayed, in the usually nude torsos vitality is shown through a strong pose. In these contradictory representations they wished to recognize votives that thematized the inner diseases that could not be further defined. Against this is posed the absolute rarity – fewer than 40 examples are known today – but one must consider whether in this period a projection of the interior to the exterior of a body was even possible. That quite concrete incisions in the body, in the sense of an abdominal surgery, could be intended is shown by a torso in Ingolstadt: on the edge of the opening before firing small paired holes were carved that must be understood as stitches indicating a seam, by which the abdomen was closed again (Figs 59.15–16). Are the votive figures with open body cavity then evidence for major surgical operations? Any one subject to the opening of the chest that exposes the lungs would not survive due to the inevitably occurring condition of pneumothorax.[48] Based on written sources such as Celsus, we do know, in fact, that complicated abdominal surgeries were being performed by his time – but certainly without exposing the lungs. That the entire surgical site was shown from heart to intestine, would not be a literal representation but a symbolic image implying a major abdominal operation.[49] The polyvisceral plaques that show the complete surgical site from heart to intestine are to be understood as a less expensive version of this type.[50]

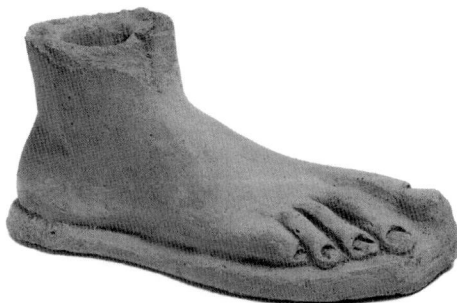

Figure 59.14   Right foot. Göttingen, Archäologisches Institut, Inv. TC 219 © Archäologisches Institut der Universität Göttingen, Photo Stephan Eckardt.

Figure 59.15   View of male torso. Male torso with open abdominal cavity. Ingolstadt, Deutsches Medizinhistorisches Museum, Inv. AB/720. Photo Matthias Recke.

Figure 59.16   Male torso with open abdominal cavity. Ingolstadt, Deutsches Medizinhistorisches Museum, Inv. AB/720. Photo Matthias Recke.

HISTORICAL CONTEXT

In connection with the emergence and spread of anatomical votives during the fourth century BC, it is worth noting the coincidence in time with the expansion of Roman military hegemony. This has led some researchers to consider the anatomical votives as cultic testimonies of the appearance of Roman and Latin colonists, who were mainly small farmers and artisans from the Roman *plebs*.[51] This fits the observation that the votive heads are mostly represented *capite velato* ("with veiled head") (see Figs. 59.1–2), in the Roman-Latin sphere, a specific custom for sacrificial rituals that was not practiced by Greeks or Etruscans. The representation of the *velum* (veil) is therefore interpreted as a sign of Romanization. Indeed, it is found in places like Veii, which in 396 BC was conquered by the Romans, and there is a change from bare-headed votive heads of late Archaic and Classical styles to corresponding representations with covered heads – a phenomenon that occurs at different times and different places in association with the founding of Roman or Latin colonies.[52] Around the end of the second century BC an evident, relatively abrupt end to the custom of dedicating anatomical votives on the one hand is associated with the historically tangible transformation of social structures, and on the other with a change in religious practices at this time.[53]

HISTORY OF RESEARCH

The genre of anatomical votives has attracted attention only relatively late in art-historically oriented archaeology. Although individual heads have been known in Italian antiquities collections since the seventeenth century,[54] a fundamental scientific examination of the genre and a classification according to formal criteria only took place at the end of the nineteenth century. Significantly, it was medical doctors interested in archaeology who first were interested in the material, namely Louis Sambon in England and Ludwig Stieda in Königsberg.[55] Both men, as was common practice in their day, also purchased objects: Sambon also furnished numerous appropriate pieces to Sir Henry Wellcome and to the Oppenheimer collection (which later was also acquired by Wellcome), and Stieda donated his extensive collection of anatomical votives from Veii to the Archaeological Institute of the University of Giessen, Germany, in 1913.

The reasons for the initial lack of interest by archaeologists, and also by museums and collections are manifold: first, the material is often quite coarse, has many inclusions and is not as fine or well fired as the terracottas from Tanagra and Myrina that were greatly prized by collectors and museums. Add to this the fact that products manufactured as mass-produced pieces are often in poor condition (see Figs. 59.3, 59.11). In their production worn molds may already have been used, so that – regardless of the artistic quality of the original design – the aesthetic appeal is low. And ultimately the question naturally arises, whether, apart from the complete statuettes and isolated heads, anatomical votives possess any aesthetic quality that meets the artistic taste of a public that has been schooled in the humanistic and Greek ideal.[56]

Therefore, even in the wake of scientific arguments, with the latter strongly influenced by medical issues,[57] it was not until the 1960s–1970s that the phenomenon (apart from the submission of excavation reports) was intensively investigated archaeologically.[58] Of great importance for the presentation of material is the series of the *Corpus delle stipi votive in Italia*, begun in 1986, that now comprises 21 volumes.[59] Currently the genre is considered especially in terms of its potential for religious, cultural and social-historical studies.[60]

NOTES

1   Only the pottery exceeds the anatomical votives in terms of quantity. However, it is not known, as a rule, whether this consisted of votive offerings or vessels intended for ritual meals.

2 The earliest examples of votive heads are found in Veii and Falerii. On the origin of Etruscan votive religion in the Protovillanovan and Villanovan periods and its development independent from Greece, cf. Turfa 2006, 90, 102–103.

3 Summaries: Forsén 1996; Forsén 2004, 311–313.

4 Also half-busts: Baggieri 1999, 36 fig. 1 (from Tessennano).

5 D'Ercole 1990, pl. 83 b.

6 Very rarely representations of the jaw with teeth: Pensabene 2001, pl. X.3 (from Palestrina); Baggieri 1999, 93 Fig. 10 (Lucus Feroniae).

7 Portions of faces ("masks") from Corvaro show a peculiarity of a profiled outline, a clear abstraction of the representation in the sense of an image, cf. Reggiani Massatini 1988, 27–34, Fig. 35–53.

8 This was already emphasized by Sticda 1901, 80. Old Babylonian and Hittite liver models depict (as does the Etruscan bronze Liver of Piacenza) the livers of animals.

9 Recke, Wamser-Krasznai 2008, 125 Nr. 27, fig. 50–52 (from Veii). Not addressed here are the anatomical votives that represent the body parts of animals, usually the limbs of cattle, but also of pigs and horses. The finds from Capua are published by Pesetti 1994, 96–100; cf. also a bovine hoof from Palestrina: Pensabene 2001, 373 Nr. 350. Still unpublished are the finds from the deposit of Fidenae, which are under study by L. Ceccarelli, Cambridge, among which is a large-scale bovine hoof. The body-part votives most likely have their counterpart in the Asklepieion of Corinth, where an isolated goat's foot was found (Roebuck 1951, 141, pl. 56.38).

10 This approach also explains the occurrence of identical types in different places: Although not excluding the possibility that molds were actually traded, there is the proliferation of types among impressions of the finished objects. Popular motifs of other workshops have been incorporated into the repertoire. The revision (retouching) and reworking of the new molds can over time lead to different variants (type conversion).

11 For the dating potential of votive heads, see the work of Papini 2004.

12 Votive heads in general do not represent physiognomic portraits, only types, cf. Hofter 1985, Papini 2004.

13 Recke 2008, 60–61; Recke – Wamser-Krasznai 2008, 88 Fig. 16.

14 Pensabene 1980, pl. A, 506, 515; Recke – Wamser-Krasznai 2008, 80 Nr. 3, Fig. 13.

15 Terracotta molds are known in Pyrgi, Tarquinia, Satricum and Cales, see Turfa 2004, 364–367.

16 Strictly speaking, only votive heads may be dated on stylistic grounds.

17 On terminology cf. Turfa 2006, 91.

18 An exception is the find of a terracotta votive foot in a tomb at Spina: Berti, Guzzo 1993, 358 Nr. 911, Ferrara inv. 9438 (from Tomb 300B VP).

19 Glinister 2006, 13, note 11; cf. also the presentation of the most important findspots in Turfa 2006, 95–102. Since then, new sites are known, for instance, Pellegrini, Rafanelli 2007, 189–212; or an as-yet unpublished deposit at Fidenae.

20 The most important literature on findspots is summarized by Turfa 2004, 364–367.

21 Cf. Edlund 1987. Not all sanctuaries in which anatomical votives have been found are necessarily healing shrines, as also emphasized by Glinister 2006, 13.

22 Summarized by Forsén 1996, esp. 133–159.

23 Turfa 2006, 92. Several shrines with anatomical models already existed in the Archaic period and then in the (late) fourth century BC they undergo a corresponding change in votive customs, identifiable in the finds.

24 Turfa 2004, 360. The founding of the Asklepios sanctuary on the Tiber Island in Rome as an offshoot of the sanctuary in Epidauros and thereby the introduction of the Aesculapius cult into Italy at the beginning of the third century BC is traditionally linked to the "plague" epidemic in Rome. The new cult melded with older, long-established cults of native

divinities, Turfa 2006, 104. The contemporaneous growth in the popularity of anatomical votives led Pensabene 2001, 111 to link it to the spread of the Asklepios cult in central Italy.

25 Gravisca: Comella 1981; Lavinium: Castagnoli 1975.

26 Tarquinia, Ara della Regina (1000+), Veii, Contrada Campetti (3000), Veii, Pendici di Piazza d'Armi (3000), Fregellae (3000+), Ponte di Nona (8000+, of which 3800 are anatomical votives), cf. the counts in Turfa 2004.

27 Some in Tarquinia, Ara della Regina (Turfa 2004, 365 Nr. 314).

28 In this sense even the uterus votives could have held a special meaning in the relationship between god and man, at least for the ones that are hollow inside. (Baggieri 1999, 68 fig. 68–69, 69 fig. 70, 99 figs. 21–22. The most significant inclusions of intrauterine "life" (pellets sealed into the hollow object) are not visible from outside (and can now only be detected by X-rays). They are a secret known only to the donor and the deity which would exclude all others from this close connection.

29 Glinister 2006, 27–30.

30 For dedicatory inscriptions preserved on anatomical votives, cf. De Cazanove 2009.

31 On the procedure cf. Turfa 2006, 91.

32 Turfa 2006, 104, as regards the portrayal of internal organs in statues and torsos sees a reference to the mortality of the person represented, and concludes that they cannot be images of gods. On analogy to this, identical figure types without incisions are also mortals.

33 Turfa 2006, 104, sees the dedication of images of swaddled infants not necessarily as representing the welfare of the child, but possibly as thanks-offerings on behalf of the mother, after conception or childbirth.

34 Sambon 1895; Stieda 1901; Alexander 1905; Holländer 1912.

35 Stieda 1901, 72; Recke – Wamser-Krasznai 2008, 101 Fig. 23–24.

36 Stieda 1901, 106.

37 Glinister 2006, 12 proposed an alternative explanation for the dedications of penis models, that they marked a transition, such as puberty.

38 It is striking that hands are not shown relaxed, but stiffly held up with flat palms. Furthermore, they always have the wrist truncated so that it forms a stand for the hand to be displayed, cf. Recke, Wamser-Krasznai 2008, 100 Fig. 21–22.

39 Foot votives as the expression of a trip completed safely were already indicated by Stieda 1901, 75.

40 Turfa 2006, 106. These interpretive approaches are heavily focused on the representations of internal organs and do not allow a comprehensive interpretation of the phenomenon of anatomical votive models and the visual analysis of the human body. Another problem is the verification of plausible-sounding aspects for some hypotheses.

41 Baggieri 1999, 96, Fig. 17 (Civita Castellana).

42 Glinister 2006, 11.

43 Krug 1984, 26–27, 61–62. Torsos with representation of internal organs are occasionally interpreted as teaching models for the appropriate medical operations for the purpose of developing surgical skills.

44 Summarized by Glinister 2006, 12.

45 Coarelli 1986, pl. 68, 3–4 (from Fregellae); Tabanelli 1962, 39 Nr. 6 (from Nemi).

46 Recke, Wamser-Krasznai 2008, 118 Nr. 24, 120 Nr. 25 (from Veii); Tabanelli 1962, Fig. 7 (from Canino / Tessennano, now in the Louvre).

47 Tabanelli 1962, Fig. 8–9 (Rome), Fig. 10 (Paris, from Palestrina?), Fig. 11 (from Veii).

48 This was only possible after 1904 with the invention of Ferdinand Sauerbruch.

49 Against the idea that in these representations is a dissection of the corpse are the attitude and gestures of the people depicted, and the function of objects as offerings. Other examples among the anatomical votives, which could be interpreted as an indication that surgery actually took place, are gathered by Turfa 2006, 104. Contra, however Glinister 2006, 12–13.

50   Normally, the polyvisceral plaques are not designated by gender. An important exception is a plaque from Tarquinia (Baggieri 1999, 97 Fig. 19), because here is shown below the intestinal loops and a uterus an organ which can only be the urinary bladder. This is an identification of major importance, since such objects when shown separately are often misunderstood as an isolated testicle (Baggieri 1999, 62 fig. 57). The opening shows that there is a hollow body, which is clearly seen in radiological investigations (Recke, 2008, 61 Fig. 7).

51   Comella 1981, 771–775. Generally Papini 2004, attributes this to the economic and cultural integration of central Italy during the Roman expansion into the Greek-Hellenistic world. The donors come, in the view of Torelli 1976 and Pensabene 1979, from the class of the plebeians. Critical to this Söderlind 2005, 363, notice of finds with anatomical votives in a purely Etruscan context, and Glinister 2006.

52   In Cales or Lucera, while in formally independent cities like Capua, Falerii or Tarquinia such specifically Roman customs are not adopted for the votive heads. Pensabene 1979, 217–222; Söderlind 2002, 381; Söderlind 2005, 359–365.

53   Söderlind 2005, 362; Glinister 2006, 30–31.

54   For example, anatomical votives from Veii in the De Medici Collection, today in Florence (Delpino 1985, 19–21). For early treatments, such as J. P. Tomasini, *De donariis ac tabellis votivis liber singularis* (Padua 1654), which was more concerned with the inscriptions accompanying votive offerings, but also illustrated uterus- hand- and head-votives, see the compilation in Tabanelli 1962, 4–6.

55   L. Stieda, *Anatomisches über alt-italische Weihgeschenke (Donaria). Anatomisch-Archäologische Studien* II (Wiesbaden 1901).

56   For example, of the approximately 6,000 votives discovered in 1885 in the Vignaccia deposit at Cerveteri, of which 800 objects went to the Phoebe A. Hearst (previously Lowie) Museum, Univ. of California, Berkeley, these consisted entirely of figural terracottas (heads and figurines), which expresses the taste of the times, cf. Nagy 1988.

57   We name Alexander 1905, Holländer 1912, but also Tabanelli 1962. Still in the tradition of this sort of research is the exhibition "Speranza e Sofferenza nei Votivi Anatomici dell'Antichità (Ancient Anatomy in the Art of Votive Offerings)" 1996 in Rome, see Baggieri 1999.

58   Bonghi Jovino 1965; Bartoloni 1970; Bonghi Jovino 1971; Vagnetti 1971; Torelli-Pohl 1973; Fenelli 1975; Bonghi Jovino 1976; Comella 1978. Earlier: Bartoccini 1940, 241–298.

59   Comella 1986; Bartoloni –Benedettini 2011.

60   Turfa 2006, 90–115; Glinister 2006, 10–33.

BIBLIOGRAPHY

Alexander, G. (1905) "Zur Kenntnis der Etruskischen Weihgeschenke nebst Bemerkungen über anatomische Abbildungen im Altertum," *Anatomische Hefte*, 30.1: 157–198.

Baggieri, G. (ed.) (1999) *L'antica anatomia nell'arte di donaria (Ancient Anatomy in the Art of Votive Offerings*, Rome: MelAMi.

Bartoccini, R. (1940) "Arte e religione nella Stipe votiva di Lucera", *Iapigia*, 11.4: 241–298.

Bartoloni, G. (1970) "Alcune terrecotte votive delle Collezioni Medicee ora al Museo Archeologico di Firenze", *Studi Etruschi*, 38: 257–270.

Bartoloni, G. and Benedettini, M. G. (2011) *Veio. Il deposito votivo di Comunità. Scavo 1889–2005. Corpus delle Stipi Votive in Italia XXI*, Rome: Giorgio Bretschneider.

Berti, F. and Guzzo, P. G. (eds) (1993) *Spina. Storia di una città tra Greci ed Etruschi*, Ferrara: Maurizio Tosi.

Bonghi Jovino, M. (1965) *Capua preromana. Terrecotte votive I. Teste isolate e mezzeteste*, Florence: Sansoni.

——(1971) *Capua preromana. Terrecotte votive II. Le Statue*, Florence: Sansoni.

——(1976) *Depositi Votivi in Etruria*, Milan: Cisalpino-Goliardica.

Castagnoli, F. *et al.* (1975) *Lavinium II. Le tredici Are*, Rome: De Luca.

Coarelli, F. (ed.) (1986) *Fregellae 2. Il santuario di Esculapio*, Rome: Quasar.

Comella, A. (1978) *Il materiale votivo tardo di Gravisca*, Rome: Giorgio Bretschneider.

——(1981) "Tipologia e diffusione dei complessi votive in Italia in epoca medio- e tardo-repubblicana", *Mélanges de l'Ecole Française de Rome. Antiquité*, 93: 717–803.

——(1986) *I materiali votive di Falerii. Corpus delle Stipi Votive in Italia I*, Rome: Giorgio Bretschneider.

D'Ercole, M. C. (1990) *La stipe votiva del Belvedere a Lucera. Corpus delle Stipi Votive in Italia III*, Rome: Giorgio Bretschneider.

De Cazanove, O. (2009) "Oggetti muti? Le iscrizioni degli ex voto anatomici nel mondo romano" in J. Bodel and M. Kajava (eds) *Dediche sacre nel mondo Greco-Romano. Diffusione. funzioni. tipologie. Acta Instituti Romani Finlandiae 35*, Rome: Institutum Romanum Finlandiae, pp. 355–371.

Delpino, F. (1985) *Cronache Veientane. Storia delle ricerche archeologiche a Veio. Dal XIV alle metà del XIX secolo*, Rome: Consiglio Nazionale delle Ricerche.

Edlund, I. E. M. (1987) *The Gods and the Place. Location and Function of Sanctuaries in the Countryside of Etruria and Magna Graecia (700–400 B.C.)*, Stockholm: Åström.

Fenelli, M. (1975) "Contributo per lo studio del votivo anatomico: i votivi anatomici di Lavinio," *Archeologia Classica*, 27: 206–252.

Forsén, B. (1996) *Griechische Gliederweihungen. Eine Untersuchung zu ihrer Typologie und ihrer religions- und sozialgeschichtlichen Bedeutung*, Helsinki: Suomen Ateenan-instituutin säätiö.

——(2004) "Models of body parts" in J. C. Balty *et al.* (eds), *Thesaurus Cultus et Rituum Antiquorum (ThesCRA) I*, Los Angeles, California: Getty Publications, pp. 311–313.

Glinister, F. (2006) "Reconsidering 'religious Romanization'" in C. E. Schultz and P. B. Harvey, Jr (eds), *Religion in republican Italy*, Cambridge: Cambridge University Press, pp. 10–33.

Hofter, M. R. (1985) *Untersuchungen zu Stil und Chronologie der mittel-italischen Terrakotta-Votivköpfe*, Bonn: Habelt.

Holländer, E. (1912) *Plastik und Medizin*, Stuttgart: Enke.

Krug, A. (1984) *Heilkunst und Heilkult. Medizin in der Antike*, München: C.H. Beck.

Nagy, H. (1988) *Votive Terracottas from the "Vignaccia", Cerveteri, in the Lowie Museum of Anthropology*, Rome: Giorgio Bretschneider.

Papini, M. (2004) *Antichi volti della Repubblica. La ritrattistica in Italia centrale tra IV e II secolo a.C.*, Rome: "L'ERMA" di Bretschneider.

Pellegrini, E. and Rafanelli, S. (2007) "La stipe votiva del Pantano," *Studi Etruschi*, 73: 189–212.

Pensabene, P. (1979) "Doni votivi fittili di Roma: Contributo per un inquadramento storico," *Archeologia Laziale*, 2: 217–222.

——(2001) *Le terrecotte del Museo Nazionale Romano, II. Materiali dai depositi votivi di Palestrina: collezioni ,Kircheriana' e ,Palestrina'*, Rome: "L'ERMA" di Bretschneider.

Pensabene, P. *et al.* (1980) *Terrecotte votive dal Tevere. (Studi Miscellanei, 25)*, Rome: "L'ERMA" di Bretschneider.

Pesetti, S. (1994) *Capua Preromana. Terrecotte votive VI. Animali, frutti, giacattoli, pesi da telaio*, Florence: Sansoni.

Recke, M. (2008) "Auf Herz und Niere. Etruskische Körperteilvotive der Gießener Antikensammlung," *Spiegel der Forschung*, 25.2: 56–63.

Recke, M. and Wamser-Krasznai, W. (2008) *Kultische Anatomie. Etruskische Körperteil-Votive aus der Antikensammlung der Justus-Liebig-universität Giessen (Stiftung Ludwig Stieda)*, Ingolstadt: Deutsches Medizinhistorisches Museum.

Reggiani Massatini, A. M. (1988) *Santuario degli Equicoli a Corvaro: oggetti votivi del Museo Nazionale Romano*, Rome: DeLuca.

Roebuck, C. (1951) *Corinth XIV. The Asklepieion and Lerna*, Princeton: American School of Classical Studies at Athens.

Sambon, L. (1895) "Donaria of medical interest", *British Medical Journal*, 2: 146–150, 216–219.

Söderlind, M. (2002) *Late Etruscan Votive Heads from Tessennano. Production, Distribution, Sociohistorical Context*, Rome: "L'ERMA" di Bretschneider.

——(2005) "Heads with velum and the etrusco-latial-campanian type of votive deposit" in A. Comella and S. Mele (eds), *Depositi votive e culti dell'Italia antica dall'età arcaica a quella tardo-repubblicana*, Bari: Edipuglia, pp. 359–365.

Stieda, L. (1901) *Anatomisch-Archäologische Studien II. Anatomisches über alt-italische Weihgeschenke (Donaria)*, Wiesbaden: Bergmann.

Tabanelli, M. (1962) *Gli "ex-voto" poliviscerali etruschi e romani. Storia – ritrovamenti – interpretazione*, Florence: Leo S. Olschki.

Torelli, M. (1976) "La situazione in Etruria" in P. Zanker (ed.), *Hellenismus in Mittelitalien*, Göttingen: Vandenhoeck and Ruprecht, pp. 97–110.

Torelli, M. and Pohl, I. (1973) "Veio. Scoperta di un piccolo santuario etrusco in località Campetti," *Notizie degli Scavi di Antichità*, 8.27: 40–258.

Turfa, J. M. (2004) "Anatomical Votives" in J.Ch. Balty *et al.* (eds), *Thesaurus Cultus et Rituum Antiquorum (ThesCRA) I*, Los Angeles, California: Getty Publications, pp. 359–368.

——(2006) "Votive Offerings in Etruscan Religion" in N. T. de Grummond and E. Simon (eds), *The Religion of the Etruscans*, Austin: University of Texas Press, pp. 90–115.

Vagnetti, L. (1971) *Il deposito votivo di Campetti a Veio (Materiale degli scavi 1937–1938)*, Florence: Sansoni.

CHAPTER SIXTY

ANIMALS IN THE ETRUSCAN HOUSEHOLD AND ENVIRONMENT

———·◆·———

Adrian P. Harrison

INTRODUCTION

It is now some 80 years since D. H. Lawrence, accompanied by his friend the artist Earl Brewster, set off in April of 1927 to visit the Etruscan sites. In his inevitable fashion, Lawrence details his travels and his descent into the lost world of the Etruscans, whilst all the while interjecting his observations with personal interpretations of the images and artifacts he finds, helped by a liberal dose of artistic license.

> …the tomb called the Grotta Bella is interesting because of the low-relief carvings and stucco reliefs…the dog who is man's guardian even on the death journey, the two lions that stand by the gateway of life or death, the triton, or merman, and the goose, the bird that swims on the waters and thrusts its head deep into the flood of the Beginning and the End…
>
> *Etruscan Places*, Chapter 1 (Lawrence, 1972)

Lawrence paints an idyllic and often romantic portrait of life for an Etruscan, with banqueting, music, sports and hunting as the norm. However, this can only have been the case for a chosen few, an elite, and would not have been something experienced by the everyday Etruscan man or woman. It is perhaps easy to understand the view adopted by Lawrence as what we know today of the Etruscan civilization is more often than not derived from the rich ruling class, expensive tombs, costly grave goods etc.

Lawrence also argues for a very "black and white" civilization understood from the perspective of life *versus* death, of a world of the living and a world of the dead, an underworld. He discusses the animal motifs he finds in tombs and on pottery in the context of this black and white world, with animals as protectors of grave goods, albeit mythical animals more often than not, and symbols of the world of the living.

...and death, to the Etruscan, was a pleasant continuance of life, with jewels and wine and flutes playing for the dance. It was neither an ecstasy of bliss, a heaven, nor a purgatory of torment. It was just a natural continuance of the fullness of life...

Etruscan Places, Chapter 1 (Lawrence, 1972)

But was life for an Etruscan so clear-cut? Moreover, do the fragments of artwork that remain support such a use of animal motifs or are they more mundane? In order to assess this point, one has first to amass a set of data pertaining to known Etruscan animal motifs, and thereafter examine the data for trends and changes.

CLASSIFICATION

Most of the objects tallied represent personal possessions, moveable objects that belonged to individuals in life, or that were given as grave gifts or votive offerings – such items were the result of personal selections, so we may assume that the decorative images (of animals) they feature were also a source of interest and prestige for the owners/givers. According to one scholar, pottery formed the most ubiquitous connection between life and art in Etruria, even if (at a guess) some 80 per cent of vessels in daily use carried little or no decoration as such (Spivey 1997: 35). However, such material as exists has not yet been classified. I therefore propose a form of classification that covers the domesticated, wild, exotic and also the mythical animals associated with tomb art, pottery finds, metal artifacts and jewelry – essentially an Aristotelian classification of animals (see Fig. 60.1). Besides this initial selection criterion, items of known source and age have been chosen in preference to others that were less clearly ascribed a region of manufacture or particular find site or indeed chronological date. Items shown in books have been given equal weighting to those displayed in museums around the world, although I have tried to describe or illustrate items that I have been able to see in person, and which readers may be able to visit for themselves.

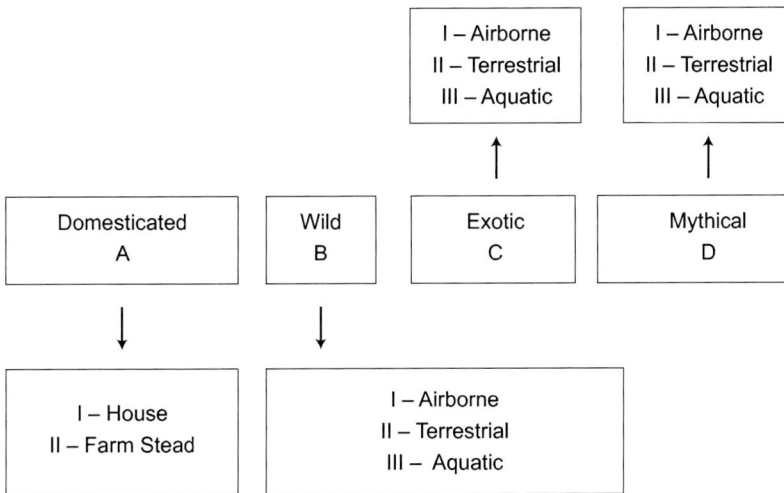

Figure 60.1   The classification system adopted for this chapter in terms of Etruscan animal motifs (see Table 60.1 for more details).

Table 60.1   Classification system adopted and animals listed.

Classification	Animals
A I	dog, cat, cockerel, partridge
A II	bull, mule, horse, ram, sheep, cattle (oxen), goat
B I	swan, geese, owl, partridge, eagle, heron and others
B II	deer, hare, boar, stag, snake, deer calf (fawn), mouse, tortoise
B III	dolphin, tuna, frog, turtle, fish, octopus
C I	not represented in Etruscan art
C II	ostrich, lion, leopard, panther, monkey, elephant
C III	tridacna shell
D I	griffin, winged horse, harpies, winged lion, typhon
D II	sphinx, centaur, satyr, chimera, 3-headed dog (cerberus), wolf-man, gorgon
D III	sea-monster (undefined), hippocamp, ketos, skylla

Sadly, the vicissitudes of preservation, display and publication preclude a thorough statistical analysis of the frequency or popularity of species in early Etruria, however, some animals are so commonly depicted that we may be sure they were everyday sights (horse, dog, waterfowl) or are acknowledged symbols of power or authority.

Of course this source material is biased in that it is mostly items from wealthy Etruscan families that have survived, and if this skew was not enough, museum curators have further selected the material on display in favor of complete, exotic, unique and elaborate pieces. Sadly, such biases are difficult to remove and the reader must therefore bear in mind that any results from this classification of Etruscan animal motifs and conclusions drawn therefrom may not be entirely representative of the whole of Etruscan society at any one period in time.

Museums

This classification is based on material located at, and published or on display in some 30 museums and art galleries around the world. These include: Museo Archeologico Arezzo, the British Museum, Florence Archaeological Museum, Villa Giulia in Rome, Vatican Museo Gregoriano Etrusco, Musée du Louvre in Paris, Poggio Civitate Museum Murlo, the Palatine Antiquarium in Rome, Bologna Museo Civico Archeologico, Munich Antikensammlung, Pigorini Museum in Rome, Ny Carlsberg Glyptotek in Copenhagen, Nationalmuseet Copenhagen, University of Pennsylvania Museum Philadelphia, Chiusi Museo Archeologico Nazionale, Tarquinia Museo Nazionale, Walters Art Gallery in Baltimore, The Metropolitan Museum of Art in New York, Hermitage Museum in St Petersburg, the Martin von Wagner Museum Würzburg, Palermo Museo Nazionale, Pierpont Morgan Library in New York, Bibliothèque Nationale in Paris, Villa Albani in

Rome, Fiesole Museo Archeologico, Volterra Museo Guarnacci, Viterbo Museo Civico, Museo Nazionale Cerite (Cerveteri) and The Boston Museum of Fine Arts.

Necropoleis/tombs

In addition to museums and art galleries, some of the catalogued material is still to be found at tombs or other archaeological sites, or has known provenance to certain tombs. These include: Cerveteri: the Regolini-Galassi Tomb, the Banditaccia Necropoleis, the Tomb of the Painted Animals (reliefs), the Sorbo Necropolis; Tarquinia: the Tomb of the Baron, the Tomb of the Augurs, the Bruschi Tomb, the Tomb of the Triclinium, the Temple of Ara della Regina, the Tomb of the Chariots, Monterozzi Necropolis; Castel san Mariano near Perugia; Palestrina: the Bernardini and Barberini Tombs, the Castellani Tomb; Vulci: the Isis Tomb, Tomb 177, the François Tomb; Chiusi: the Tomb of the Hill, Palazzaccio, the Purni family Tomb at Città della Pieve; Veii: the Tomb of the Ducks; Peschiera Necropolis; and the Certosa Necropolis in Bologna. Still other material has been catalogued simply according to city/region.

Animal motifs

Of the 433 animal motifs I have catalogued (260 artifacts), the most popular in terms of the Etruscan "Top 10," were, in descending order, the horse (see Fig. 60.2a, 2o, 2r); lion (see Fig. 60.2e, 2n, 2s); sphinx (see Fig. 60.2d); dog (see Fig. 60.2m: Jannot 1986: Fig. 5, British Museum GR1891.6–24.53, from Chiusi); bird (generic: see Fig. 60.2b, and Fig. 60.3); winged horse (Fig. 60.2j); deer/fawn (Fig. 60.2c, 2l); griffin (Fig. 60.2p); and goat (Fig. 60.2c). However, it should be noted that the most popular by far were the top three (horse, lion and sphinx), which together comprised some 35 per cent of all the animal motifs catalogued.

ANIMAL MOTIFS

Over the eons of human history, our species has had a close contact with living organisms and especially with those used to provide sustenance (Moore, 1988). Indeed, some cultures have even chosen to dress for ceremonies in such a way as to resemble and imitate the behavior of a protective animal "totem," for example, a bear or a wolf. Furthermore, in some cases, this tradition was extended to the belief that upon death, an individual would revert to becoming just such a protective animal. However, representational art is believed to have had its origins around 30,000 years ago, and the objects discovered so far tell us something about our early ancestors, and what they thought about, which was for the most part animals; those they chose to hunt for food and those they feared (Moore, 1988).

Early Paleolithic cave art reveals an insight into the artists' passion. Moore (1988) estimates that of all the known cave art more than 50 per cent represents wild horses, 16 per cent is of cattle, 11 per cent of deer, 2 per cent of cave lions and approximately 1 per cent is of mythical beasts, for example, unicorns. In another more detailed assessment of early cave art, Leroi-Gourhan (1967) analyzed the paintings of 72 late Paleolithic caves in France and Spain and found representations as follows: 28 per cent horse, 23 per cent bison, 11 per cent deer, 9 per cent mammoth, 8 per cent ibex, 6 per cent cattle, 5 per cent humans and less than 5 per cent in total of cave lions, bears, birds, fish and monsters.

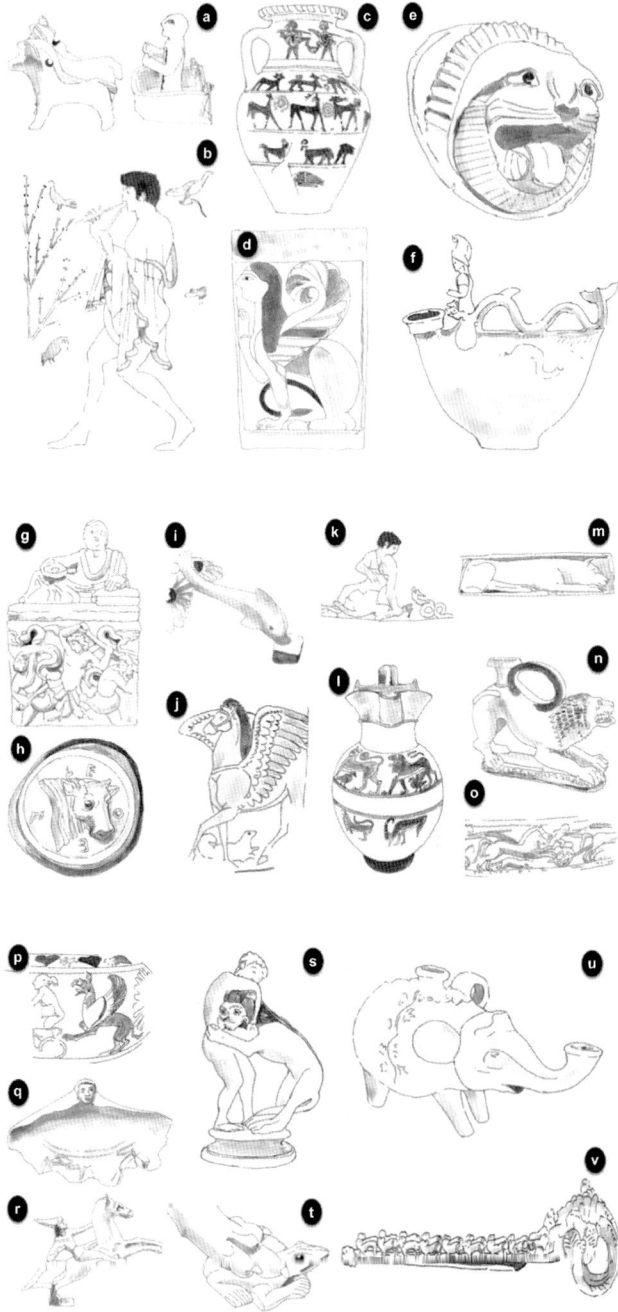

Figure 60.2a–v Examples of Etruscan animal motifs on an array of different artifacts and diverse materials (see text for more details). Source: Images a and e are of items on display at The National Museum of Copenhagen, Denmark. Image b is after Spivey 1997: 102 and color pl. 86, whilst the remaining objects are to be found on display in the British Museum as part of the Etruscan Gallery © www.bmmadsen.dk

Symbolism and mythology

The majority of the animals used as motifs by the Etruscans as decoration on their everyday as well as their more decorative and funereal items were no doubt animals they liked, were proud of, held in high esteem or deemed to be of high status. However, there may also have been a considerable degree of symbolism applied to their artwork. Symbolism is interesting in the context of portraying animal attributes that must have been noticed by the Etruscans as we ourselves tend to do today, however, symbolism relating to the zodiac as we know it originates from Babylon around 700 BC (Sachs, 1952), and is first thought to have been adopted by Greek astronomers around 400 BC in connection with Eudoxus of Cnidus, a Greek astronomer, mathematician and student of Plato, so these symbolic interpretations can only really be applied to animal motifs from the mid Classical and the Hellenistic periods of Etruscan civilization.

DOMESTICATED ANIMALS

Etruscan artisans in Archaic and Classical times sometimes used domestic animals as elaboration or complements to the main motifs. It is fair to assume that this trait was also borrowed from Greek black- or red-figured vases along with the main motifs, even if these small in-fill ornaments were treated with a distinct Etruscan touch of humor. In the later Etruscan period, however, such forms of elaboration seem to disappear (Wiman 2004).

The house

Etruscan animal representative art includes a number of domesticated species including cats and dogs. Indeed, the architectural frieze plaques with banqueting scenes from Aquarossa, Tuscania and Velletri all show dogs under the tables, hopefully awaiting crumbs from their master's meals (Wiman 2004) and there are similar examples in the British Museum (see Fig. 60.2m = GR 1891.6–24.53). However, there are also examples of another more exotic species, namely the monkey (Rm 25 Case 4; Villa Giulia, Rome), which is also depicted on a hydria found at Caere and dating circa 520 BC (Villa Giulia, Rome). This motif is also to be found in the Tomb of the Monkey (Tomba della Scimmia) at Chiusi dating from the early fifth century BC, which shows a little striated monkey tied on a leash to the acrobat troupe's dwarf and equilibrist (Steingräber 1985: 273–274 no. 25 rear wall left). Most likely these luxury pets came from North Africa and examples of this motif have been attributed to local memories of such an animal either in the possession of a mercenary of Chiusi who had fought in an African campaign, or given as a gift by a Punic businessman to a client in Chiusi (Heurgon 1961: 120).

The farmstead

The farmstead animals include pigs, horses, cattle, sheep, goats etc. and numerous examples are known, although by far the most popular of the farmstead species seems to have been the horse. There is evidence of an interchange between the Greeks and Etruscans in terms of horses and their breeding techniques. Moreover, discovery of early Celtic horses in northern Italy shows they were very small, although this did nothing to decrease the demand for them. At first, Greek horses were of the smaller variety, but this was soon improved by the importation of eastern horses by 700 BC coinciding with the early equestrian games (Bokonyi 1968). Subsequently, the Etruscans took rapidly to such events as chariotry (see Fig. 60.2 O = GR 1842.5–15.1; British Museum), which readily became associated with an extensive aristocratic prestige system requiring a considerable income in order to be able to breed and maintain such animals (Turfa and Steinmayer 1993). A frieze from the excavations at Murlo portrays a horse race and Livy writes (Livy 1.35.68) that when the first games at Rome were celebrated in the reign of the Etruscan king Tarquinius Priscus, most of the horses came from Etruria (cited in Bokonyi 1968).

In terms of symbolism, horses are often associated with the twins (the Dioscuri/ Gemini). Horses are also represented with one or two knights in a group, indicative of mobility, exchange and travel, and in association with *Turms*, the Hermes of the Etruscans. A good example of this is to be found in the Tomb of Bulls, Tarquinia, circa 530 BC (Bonfante and Swaddling 2006: 18; Steingräber 1985: 350 no. 120, color pl. 158), in which the ambush of the Trojan prince Troilos is depicted. This particular image is interesting for another reason, though, as the painter of this particular tomb appears unpracticed in working on the scale demanded by a wall space, being more used perhaps to painting pottery. One can see that the head of the horse being ridden by Troilos is very small in proportion to the body, and the horse's head appears to have been repainted a couple of times in an attempt to improve this error of size (Spivey 1997: 106).

Many of the Etruscan bronze sculptures depict the head of a horse reigned in and deep, what we refer to today as "deep and round," a typical position of control that calms any horse into submission. Horses were also controlled with the aid of a bit as on display at Villa Giulia in Rome (circa 800 BC; Rm 21 Case 1; references on early bits: Turfa 2005: 115–116 nos. 52–53; 148–150 nos. 110–111). Perhaps these sculptures and metal bits are indicative of the style of riding used by the Etruscans, but they may also serve as a visual attestation to the power the Etruscans wielded over their neighbors.

Another point of interest is the white horses pulling Amazons' chariots on the painted sarcophagus in Tarquinia of Ramtha Huscnai (Brendel 1978/1995: 342 Fig. 266). Such horses, especially if they are true "dominant whites," have characteristic pink skins, all-white hair and brown eyes, and are born white since one of the parents is a dominant white. This trait does not as a consequence "skip" a generation, as it is not recessive. Nonetheless, "dominant whites" are rare, and to have four matching horses for your chariot would be a clear sign to all that you had hundreds of horses in your breeding stable, and that you owned sufficient land to support that many horses. There are also suggestions that true homozygous "dominant whites," at least some forms of dominant white, may result in nonviable embryos, making breeding of these horses even more expensive. However, unlike other species, dominant white horses do not suffer the complications of anemia and sterility, although they are prone to sunburn.

The bull was a cult object in several Etruscan localities (Tarquinia, Volsinii) (see Fig. 60.2h = GM 1872.7–9.4; British Museum). It was a symbol of fecundity and force. Cattle also represented an agricultural asset as is beautifully illustrated by the plowing peasant on the bronze vessel found at Bisenzio in Olmo Bello necropolis tomb 22 (circa 730–700 BC; Rm 25 Case 2; Villa Giulia, Rome; drawing: Turfa 2012: Fig. 17). This simple motif tells the familiar story of man dependant on his oxen for his sustenance.

The rooster/cockerel is associated with all those who are dead and everything erotic. A famous example of this form of Etruscan representative art is that of the Tomba del Triclinio at Tarquinia (circa 470 BC; Steingräber 1985: 352–353 no. 121, color pls. 166–

171). The back wall of this tomb depicts banqueters and under the table is illustrated a cockerel. A beautiful facsimile of this tomb painting was made in 1895 and can now be seen at Ny Carlsberg Glyptotek in Copenhagen. Another fine example of cockerels is to be seen in the British Museum in the form of two exquisite gold earrings that were formerly part of the Castellani Collection. These two earrings which can be seen in Figure 60.3 (no. 10 = GR 1884.6–14.3) are said to have come from Vulci and have been dated to circa 300–200 BC.

The goose is often seen as the queen of the aquatic birds and it proved popular as an Etruscan animal motif. Indeed, the magical defense of Rome was entrusted to the geese of the Campidoglio. One of the earliest Etruscan items to bear this motif is the painted mixing bowl on high feet with geese adorning the neck and the handles. This item is from Bisenzio and is dated circa 800–700 BC (Villa Giulia, Rome, Brendel 1978: 27 and Fig. 6). Another fine example is that of the limestone base used to mark a tomb, a so called *cippus*, which depicts a hunting scene with dogs and geese and huntsmen carrying a dead hare slung from a pole, that was found at Chiusi circa 490–470 BC (British Museum: Camporeale 1984, pl. 58).

Livestock were also deemed the spoils of war and just such an illustrative piece is the famous sarcophagus from the Sperandio necropolis of Perugia (inv. no. 195) dated circa 490 BC which depicts cattle, goats, and pack-mules which all form part of the booty from a northern raid (Wiman 2004; Turfa 2012: Fig. 24).

Other items include the impasto vase in the shape of a bull that was found at Tarquinia circa 850 BC (Magagnini 2008: Fig. 33), and the impasto vase in the shape of a ram that came from Cerveteri circa 800 BC (Magagnini 2008: Fig. 38), both of which can be seen in the Villa Giulia. There is also the Plikaśna silver gilt vessel that was found at Chiusi (circa 650 BC), which depicts warriors and horsemen as well as sacrificial sheep and pigs (Museo Archeologico Nazionale, Florence; Turfa 2012: Fig. 19) (see Fig. 6.35 in this book). The Ny Carlsberg Glyptotek possesses a small terracotta figurine that originates from Veii circa 350 BC depicting a woman carrying by the legs a piglet which is thought to be a pre-harvest offering to the goddess *Ceres/Vei* (see Moltesen and Nielsen 1996, 150–151 no. 62; such images were common in Greek cults of Demeter and Kore). Finally, in this category I wish to mention the bucchero pyxis with a short foot stand and four handles in the form of goat's heads that was found at Caere at the Sorbo Necropolis circa 700–600 BC and is to be found in the Vatican Museo Gregoriano Etrusco.

WILD ANIMALS

The Etruscans often show wild animals on their objects and in their tombs, many of them in association with a hunting scene. Typically we are shown various hunting birds and wild boar, but also deer (see Fig. 21 GR 1978.5–2.1; British Museum – for more on wild species, see Camporeale 1984).

The red deer was associated with the beginning of spring and, in Roman art is often found at the flank of Diana-Artemis, the Goddess of the animals and the patroness of the awakening of wild nature in the month of March. A jug attributed to the Swallows Painter and found at Vulci circa 600 BC shows a number of male deer (stags) grazing, and this is very similar to the bucchero cup decorated with a frieze of grazing stags that was found at Tarquinia circa 600 BC on display at the British Museum (Magagnini 2008: 135 and Fig. 135). In another example, that of a small ivory plaque with shallow relief found in a tomb at Orvieto (circa 520–500 BC), two men are depicted wrestling a stag to the ground, perhaps some form of dangerous aristocratic sport (Museo Archeologico Nazionale, Florence). Finally, I should mention the vase from Orvieto that depicts a horseman startling a spotted fawn, illustrated in Fig. 52.11a, b in this book.

Hares are also depicted in connection with wild animal hunts. A Caeretan brazier found at Cerveteri (circa 550–530 BC) depicts, by means of a roller-stamped frieze, a hare hunt (British Museum and elsewhere: see Camporeale 1984: 116–118, pls. 48–49). Hares were also used as the motif for perfume bottles, as for example the terracotta perfume bottle from Nola, Campania (circa 600–550 BC) that was part of the Sir William Temple collection (British Museum; see also Turfa 2005: 169 no. 150).

Airborne

Etruscan representative art is very fond of all sorts of bird motifs, some rather more easily discernible than others. In an attempt to bring some structure to this particular aspect of Etruscan animals, I have chosen to identify not only a number of examples of Etruscan bird art, but also to combine this data into a table of Italian native bird species.

As Heurgon put it, the Tomb of the Triclinium at Tarquinia "is a veritable aviary of birds" (Heurgon 1961: 121; Steingräber 1985: 352 no. 121). In addition to a cock and hen watched by a cat beneath the banqueting couches, there are blackbirds and thrushes perched in the trees and a partridge on the ground. Then there is the Tomb of the Augurs, also at Tarquinia (Steingräber 1985: 283 no. 42, color pls. 13–22), which is marked by the flight of palmipeds (web-footed birds), which have been identified as cormorants. Then again in the Tomb of Hunting and Fishing at Tarquinia (Steingräber 1985: 293–294 no. 50, color pls. 41–51), hunters stand on a cliff and try to reach with their slings a multi-colored flight of wild duck. Strabo (cited in Heurgon 1961: 121) noted that Etruscan lakes and marshes were famous for waterfowl.

The eagle is seen as the king of everything that flies, just as the lion is the king of the terrestrial animals. The Etruscans saw the eagle as a source of omen and an example of this bird as an Etruscan animal motif can be found in the Caeretan hydria that depicts two eagles in flight, found near Chiusi (circa 600 BC) and currently residing at the Louvre (Camporeale 1984, pls. 40a and 54).

Swans appear on a number of Etruscan items, for example the limestone panel from a *cippus* depicting a banqueting scene that was found at Chiusi (circa 490–470 BC, British Museum GR 1873.8–20.752, Jannot 1984: 52–53 no. 14, Fig. 179).

A wonderful Etruscan example of ducks as an animal motif is the gold fibula found at Marsiliana d'Albegna (circa 650 BC), which depicts a number of ducks in a row on the catch (Museo Archeologico Nazionale, Florence). Another example is that of the red figured askos in the form of a duck that was discovered at Chiusi (circa 400 BC) and is now on display at the Louvre (Brendel 1978: 351 and Fig. 273). However, perhaps the most fascinating example is that of the duck pyxis (cosmetic box) to be found at the British Museum (see Figure 60.3 (8, GR 1884.6–14.37). This is a wooden carved duck that can be split apart, which has some residue of the original paint remaining. Based on the paint coloration and its specific application it is quite likely that this particular item represents a Common Shelduck, which tends to frequent salt marshes and estuaries.

The dove was the sacred bird of *Turan* (equated with Aphrodite/Venus), the goddess of passion and the world of form, beauty and harmony (see Fig. 60.3–9, GR 1873.8–20.211;

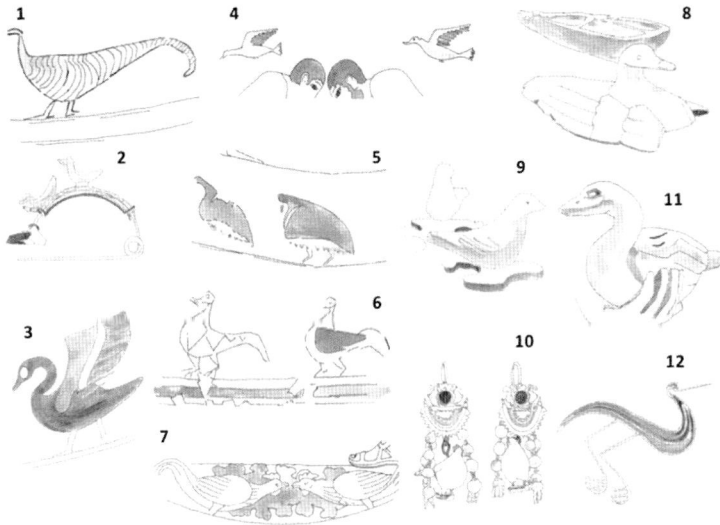

Figure 60.3 Examples of Etruscan bird motifs on an array of different artifacts and diverse materials (see text and Table 60.2 for more details). Source: Images 1, 2 and 12 are of items on display at the National Museum of Copenhagen, Denmark. Image 4 is of a wall painting on display at Ny Carlsberg Glyptotek, Copenhagen. The remaining objects are to be found on display in the British Museum as part of the Etruscan Gallery © www.bmmadsen.dk

British Museum). An example of this Etruscan animal motif is to be found on the bronze censer with shaft depicting a satyr that was found at Todi (circa 400 BC), four doves adorn the corners of the incense cup at the top (Villa Giulia, Rome: doves on the cup are favorites: see Haynes 1985, nos. 170, 181, 182, 184, fourth–third centuries BC) (see Figure 60.3 no. 9). Another example is the detail of the wall painting from the Golini II tomb at Orvieto (circa 300 BC, Steingräber 1985: 279 no. 33), which has now been detached and is on display in Florence. This painting shows a dove seated on a footstool. Then there is the *balsamarium* in the form of a dove that was found in the Necropoli di Monte Abatone (tomb 264) (circa 400–300 BC), which is currently on display in the Museo Nazionale Cerite. Finally, I should mention the dove on an Etruscan red-figured vase (circa 300 BC) to be found in Figure 52.13, which originally had a purple beak, although this has now vanished with time.

The owl was consecrated to Minerva (Minerva-Athena), and is a nocturnal predator that sees in the darkness. It was therefore a symbol of secret acquaintance and of generic wisdom. I have only come across a few examples of this Etruscan animal motif, and one may well be Faliscan in origin. It is of a red-figured calyx krater that is Faliscan-Caeretan in origin (circa 400 BC) and it depicts the Gods struggling for the possession of Athens with an owl flying above. Another object with this motif is a jug in superimposed color in the University of Pennsylvania Museum: a red painted and plump owl motif appears on the neck, in loose imitation of Attic red-figured owl-vases (see Beazley 1947: 201, E). Finally, I recently found a very cheeky looking owl sitting on the tail of a winged lion as part of the decoration of a red *olpe* (circa 600 BC) in the collection of the National Archaeological Museum of Florence (No. 71015–71016) said to have been manufactured in Etruria or Corinth.

Table 60.2 Examples of possible Etruscan bird motifs identified against the characteristics of Italian native bird species (see text for more details).

Fig 60.3 No.	Possible bird	Italian native species	Most likely
1	Pheasant	Common Pheasant – *Phasianus colchicus*	
2	Dabbling Duck	Northern Shoveler – *Anas clypeata*	
		Mallard – *Anas platyrhynchos*	*
3	Swan	Mute Swan – *Cygnus olor*	
4	Pigeon	Rock Pigeon – *Columba livia*	
		Stock Pigeon – *Columba oenas*	
		Wood Pigeon – *Columba palumbus*	*
5	Quail	Common Quail – *Coturnix coturnix*	
		Corncrake – *Crex crex*	*
		Rock Partridge – *Alectoris greca*	*
		Red-Legged Partridge – *Alectoris rufa*	
		Grey Partridge – *Perdix perdix*	
		Great Bittern – *Botaurus stellaris*	
		Little Bittern – *Ixobrychus minutus*	
		Capercaillie – *Tetrao urogallus*	
6	Ibis	Glossy Ibis – *Plegadis falcinellus*	*
		Hazel Grouse – *Bonasa bonasia*	
		Black Grouse – *Tetrao tetrix*	
		Common Snipe – *Gallinago gallinago*	
7 and 9	Dove	Eurasian Collared Dove – *Streptopelia decaocto*	*
		Turtle Dove – *Streptopelia turtur*	
8	Shelduck	Common Shelduck – *Tadorna tadorna*	
10	Cockerel	Bianca di Saluzzo	*
		White Leghorn (Livornese)	
11	Goose	Lesser Whitefront – *Anser erythropus*	
12	Heron / Stork / Egret	Great Egret – *Ardea alba*	*
		Cattle Egret – *Bubulcus ibis*	
		Little Egret – *Egretta garzetta*	*
		Great Heron – *Ardea cinerea*	
		Purple Heron – *Ardea purpurea*	
		Squacco Heron – *Ardeola ralloides*	
		White Stork – *Ciconia ciconia*	*
		Black Stork – *Ciconia nigra*	*

Aquatic

It is known that the Etruscans sailed boats that were guided from the rear by a tiller-oar, and that they sailed out seeking fish. Moreover, Etruscan fishermen threw harpoons and retrieved nets. Indeed, texts recount of tuna fishing, and there were on the promontories of Populonia and Monte Argentario, above Orbetello, two lookout points from which the arrival of fresh shoals of fish could have been observed. Furthermore, Pyrgi, the port of Caere (Cerveteri) was famous for its fisheries. It is also documented that the Etruscans stocked the lakes of Bracciano, Bolsena and Vico with carp, sea-dace and other salt-water fish that were capable of adjusting to the fresh water environment (Strabo 5.2.6; cited in Heurgon 1961: 122). In this way they could catch fresh fish at sea when the weather permitted, but also draw on farmed stocks when the seas prevented them from using their fishing craft. Etruscan representative art includes aquatic species, many of which are so clearly drawn as to be identifiable. An oinochoe found at Tarquinia (Pittore delle Palme, circa 700 BC) depicts a number of tuna swimming to the right (Museo Archeologico Nazionale, Tarquinia: Martelli *et al.* 1987: 78 no. 23). Likewise, part of a terracotta sarcophagus found at Tuscania circa 200 BC depicts in clear relief a dolphin (Museo Archeologico Nazionale, Florence: Gentili 1994: pl. 22 no. A45). The large vase by Aristonothos, from Cerveteri (circa 650 BC), depicts a naval battle, but in the sea around the two ships are clear motifs of fish, an octopus and a turtle (Louvre, Paris: see Fig. 40.8). Then finally, there is the Etruscan fish plate found in Monte Abatone tomb 264 (circa 400–300 BC) that clearly depicts all sorts of fish, an octopus (possibly a squid) and most interestingly, a flat fish (Museo Nazionale Cerite: Martelli *et al.* 1987: no. 154).

In the amphibian world, frogs are very often depicted in Etruscan art, more often than not as part of the support for an item (see Fig. 60.2t = GR 1849.5–18.21; British Museum), for example, take the cista in bronze to be found at Villa Giulia, Rome, that was discovered at Palestrina (circa 350 BC), depicting a horse-drawn chariot engraved on the body of the cista, whilst the feet are those of a lion, resting on a frog. Likewise, there is the bronze tripod depicting two satyrs that was found at Vulci (circa 490–470 BC) that has feet in the form of lion's paws resting on a frog. In each case the frog looks for all the world like a South American poison dart frog, but in fact a native frog with exactly the same features can still be found in Italy. The Italian stream frog (*Rana italica*), which inhabits rivers, swamps and freshwater marshes, although it is today seen as being threatened, very closely resembles the Etruscan images for this species. It is particularly interesting that animal motifs depicted on Etruscan tripods very often follow a pattern, namely an airborne species at the top, a terrestrial species in the middle and an aquatic/amphibian species for the feet, for example, dove, lion, frog/dolphin (see Fig. 60.2i = GR 1873.8–20.211; British Museum). Although it is tempting to read too much into this, perhaps they symbolize the Etruscan understanding of the world, the lion or terrestrial species representing their mortal time on Earth, the dove or bird representing the heavens/World of the Gods, and the amphibian or aquatic species symbolizing the connection with the underworld and the tomb (see Fig. 60.9).

EXOTIC ANIMALS

Gradually, Etruscan representative art began to include more exotic animal motifs, species that were not native to Italy, but that had been imported, or had been described or depicted on traded items.

The lion is the king of the animals and sometimes a replacement for the wolf and the chimera. It was the main symbol of royalty, but also of supreme force and power. One of the most famous examples of this form of representative art must be the gilded silver bowl from Cerveteri circa 650 BC, which was found in the Regolini-Galassi tomb (Vatican

Museum, Rome). It is an example of the means by which exotic images reached Etruria, for it is of Phoenician manufacture, a royal gift, no doubt, to the family of Larthia, wife of Velthur, the princess buried in the Regolini-Galassi Tomb (*Principi*: 222, 230–231 no. 257). It depicts three lions, resplendent with manes, in the centre, surrounded by a hunting scene in which one hunter appears to have become the prey of a large lion. Following on in the same theme is the bucchero kantharos found at Vulci (circa 620 BC; Villa Giulia, Rome and Rathje 1982: 12 and Fig. 8). This depicts a lion with a human leg hanging from its mouth and a spotted deer grazing from a nearby bush. Often, though, the lion motif is simplified as in the case of the huge red-ware storage jar from Cerveteri (circa 500–400 BC) in which lion-head motifs have been used to form four small handles to enable the jar to be hung or supported (National Museum, Copenhagen). Finally, lion motifs were often used in a more practical fashion, for example, the bronze boss, probably from the bolster of a funerary couch, in the form of a lion's head that was found in a rock-cut tomb near Tarquinia (circa 500 BC; National Museum, Copenhagen; corpus of these bosses: Scala 1993; Brendel 1978: 213–214).

The panther is the great, consecrated feline of Dionysos (Etruscan Fufluns). A wonderful example of Etruscan art in the form of a panther is that of the large stone sculpture of a crouching panther that was found at Vulci (circa 700–500 BC; Ny Carlsberg Glyptotek, Copenhagen). Then there are the two black-figured vases at the British Museum, the one an oinochoe from Vulci (circa 550–530 BC) depicting panthers as well as lions, griffins etc., the other, part of the Campanari Collection, an amphora with two panthers around the neck, also from Vulci (circa 530–520 BC). Finally, there is the rear wall painting of the Campana tomb at Veii (circa 600 BC), which depicts a horse and horseman leading with panthers following (Steingräber 1985: pl. 197).

Other exotic animal motifs used by the Etruscans include elephants and leopards. There is, of course, the beautiful little elephant askos (see Fig. 60.2u) that was found at Vulci (circa 300–200 BC) and may have been inspired by the first elephants to be seen in Italy in connection with either the invasion by Pyrrhus, King of Epirus, or the invasion by Hannibal of Carthage in the third century BC (GR 1849.6–20.4; British Museum). Another example is that of the plate in the Villa Giulia, which was found at Capena (circa 280 BC) and depicts a mother elephant upon which are seated three warriors, and holding on to its mother's tail is a baby elephant following along (Martelli *et al.* 1987: no. 158). This motif also features on a vase from Veii (Roman colony period) but here the baby elephant is being menaced by Cerberus. It is thought to have been a victory donation after the defeat of Hannibal (see Ambrosini 2006: pl. IV). With regard to leopards, there is of course the Tomb of the Leopards at Tarquinia (circa 480–470 BC), which depicts two facing male leopards in the pediment (Steingräber 1985: color pl. 105). An earlier testimony is the large bronze belt relief that was found at Capena (circa 575–550 BC), depicting leopard and lion motifs in relief (National Museum, Copenhagen – Rm 313).

The only exotic and aquatic Etruscan motif I have been able to find is not strictly an animal motif, but rather an item of trade. It is a Tridacna shell that has been carefully carved to portray a human head at the umbo of the shell, and it was found at Vulci (circa 650 BC; see Fig. 60.2q = GR 1852.0112.3; British Museum). This is interesting and important as Tridacna shells are to be found in the Red Sea and the Indian Ocean, which would suggest some trade with these regions and due to the novelty of the item, its conversion into an item of beauty (found in Etruscan "princely" tombs of women, and in Greek sanctuaries as votives, see Rathje 1986a).

MYTHICAL ANIMALS

The richest source of information about Etruscan mythological subjects is their art. The Etruscans decorated their pottery, their bronze furnishings and their chamber tombs with the figures and stories of Greek myth (see Chapters 24–25; Bonfante and Swaddling, 2006). They used the apotropaic power of images to protect their temples and tombs and to drive away evil demons. Some of the mythical images used by the Etruscans include the Sphinx, Hippocamp, Centaur, Griffin, Satyr, Harpy, Chimera, Typhon, Ketos and Skylla.

In *Etruscan Places* published two years after the author's death, D. H. Lawrence wrote of the sarcophagi he had seen in the Etruscan tombs:

> …urns representing "Etruscan" subjects; those of sea-monsters, the sea-man with fish-tail, and with wings, the sea-woman the same: or the man with serpent-legs, and wings, or the woman the same. It was Etruscan to give these creatures wings, not Greek.

> …other common symbolic animals in Volterra are the beaked griffins, the creatures of the powers that tear asunder and, at the same time, are guardians of the treasure. They are lion and eagle combined, of the sky and of the earth with caverns.
>
> *Etruscan Places*, Chapter 6 (Lawrence, 1972)

Griffins were seen as being protective, and perhaps for this reason they are often depicted in Etruscan tombs. They were also associated with gold, both in terms of its discovery, but also in terms of hoarding gold underground. Indeed, Flavius Philostratus writes of griffins in *The Life of Apollonius of Tyana*:

> …as to the gold which the griffins dig up, there are rocks which are spotted with drops of gold as with sparks, which this creature can quarry because of the strength of its beak. For these animals do exist in India, and are held in veneration as being sacred to the Sun; … in size and strength they resemble lions, but having this advantage over them that they have wings, they will attack them, and they get the better of elephants and of dragons.
>
> Flavius Philostratus 3.40.48. (Philostratus, 1921, vol. I, p. 333)

There are numerous examples of the griffin in Etruscan art (see Fig. 60.2p = GR 1887.7–25.30, British Museum), but to mention a few, one should perhaps list the bronze cauldron from the Regolini-Galassi Tomb (circa 650 BC), which is decorated with six repoussé griffin heads (Vatican Museo Gregoriano Etrusco). This particular piece is a Phoenician import and serves to highlight the entry of overseas influence on aristocratic Etruria. Then there is the sarcophagus from Vulci (circa 350–300 BC) depicting on the right side panel a griffin (Ny Carlsberg Glyptotek, Copenhagen; Moltesen and Nielsen 1996: 44 no. 7; cf. Tarquinia sarcophagus with griffin: 50 no. 8). Yet another example is that of the Faliscan krater from Civita Castellana (circa 400 BC) that depicts two griffins attacking a bull and a stag (Villa Giulia, Rome: Martelli *et al.* 1987: 199 no. 147).

The skylla was another mythical beast (see Fig. 60.2f = GR 1873.8–20.422, British Museum). The skylla, or Scylla, was a horrible sea monster with four eyes, six long necks equipped with grisly heads, each of which contained three rows of sharp teeth, and a body comprising 12 tentacle-like legs and a cat's tail and with four to six dog-heads ringing her waist. In Homer's *Odyssey* Book 12, Odysseus successfully sails his ship past Scylla and Charybdis, but Scylla manages to catch six of his men, devouring them alive: "...Scylla seized from out the hollow ship six of my comrades who were the best in strength and in might... then at her doors she devoured them..." (Murray 1998, Homer, *Odyssey* 12.245–258).

An example of the skylla in Etruscan art is given by the cinerary urn from the Purni family tomb at Citta Della Pieve near Chiusi (circa 160–130 BC) which depicts on the side panels a winged skylla sea-monster with an oar in her hand (Ny Carlsberg Glyptotek, Copenhagen; Moltesen and Nielsen 1996: 86 no. 28).

The Typhon, or marine dragon, was a form of guardian. An example is the Tomb of the Typhon at Tarquinia (circa 200 BC; Steingräber 1985: color pls. 150–151), which beautifully portrays this Etruscan demon of the Underworld as a half sea snake (legs) and half human (winged upper body, head) monster. Another example is that of the painted terracotta antefix molded in the form of a bearded typhon that was found at Capua (circa 500–450 BC; British Museum, GR 1877.8–2.14).

The face of the gorgon Medusa was another apotropaic symbol designed to ward off evil. An example is the Gorgon-head antefix found at Veii in the Portonaccio sanctuary dating from the late sixth century BC (Sgubini 2008: p. 32). Another example of a gorgon is to be found on the relief panel in nenfro found at Tarquinia circa 600 BC, in which the center panel depicts a winged gorgon (Tarquinia Museo Nazionale, Brendel 1978: 119 and Fig. 76).

The sphinx was represented also with other images of animal composites (see Fig. 60.2d = GR 1889.4–10, British Museum). An example of an Etruscan sphinx is to be found on the cauldron and stand found at Marsciano (circa 540 BC), which depicts warriors and a sphinx (Antikensammlungen, Munich). Another example is that of the bronze mirror from Vulci (circa 300 BC), which depicts Herakles on Olympus with a sphinx motif (Bibliotheque Nationale, Paris). Finally, I should mention the ivory comb in North Syrian style found at Marsiliana d'Albegna (circa 700–650 BC), which depicts two sphinxes facing each other (Museo Archeologico Nazionale, Florence, Steingräber 1981: 163 and Fig. 76).

A wonderful example of a centaur found at Vulci (circa 600 BC) is that of a terracotta figure some 77 cm in height and 80 cm in length to be found at Villa Giulia (Bloch 1957: pl. 31). It is there, too, that a plate with attached foot is on display, also originating from Vulci (tomb 177, circa 520 BC) and said to be by the Tityos painter, depicting a centaur, with long hair and fully human body with equine hind-portion, around its edge (see Fig. 25.12a – note also central wolf demon, Fig. 25.12b).

The siren is a funereal icon, which seems to fill the role of companion of the spirits in the world of the Afterlife. The more ancient sirens were rapacious birds whilst in successive eras they were associated with the aquatic world. The double tail is a symbol of great power, analogous with the iconography of the Hindu divinity with many limbs. A wonderful example of an Etruscan siren is to be found on an amphora found in Monte Abatone tomb 424 (circa 530 BC, Museo Nazionale Cerite). See also the sirens painted at the corners of a carved ceiling coffer in the Chiusine Tomb of the Monkey (Steingräber 1985: 274 no. 25).

The winged horse Pegasus was an immortal and divine horse of the celestial world (see Fig. 60.2j = GR 1884.6–14.33, British Museum). It serves as a symbol of the transformation of the wild and animal nature into a spiritual and divine nature. An example is represented by the bronze relief decoration on a bronze and ivory chariot found at Monteleone di Spoleto in Umbria, dating from the sixth century BC in which scenes from the life of Achilles are recounted (see Chapter 24, Fig. 24.8; Bonfante and Swaddling 2006: 17). Another example of winged horses is to be found on the terracotta relief for the pediment of the temple of the Ara Della Regina at Tarquinia, where they pulled the chariot of a goddess, perhaps Uni (circa 400 BC, Tarquinia, Museo Archeologico Nazionale).

The chimera was yet another popular Etruscan mythological motif, and a wonderful example of a chimera is to be found on the back of the Etruscan bronze mirror from Bolsena (dated circa 350–300 BC; Bonfante and Swaddling 2006: 47) in which Bellerophon, riding on the winged horse Pegasus, thrusts a spear into the lion mouth of the Chimaera. Another example is the bronze Chimaera of Arezzo to be found in Florence museum (fourth century BC), which was part of a life size group, although now it is sadly the sole survivor (Brendel 1978/1995: 326 Fig. 248).

Wings

Clearly, the Etruscans relied heavily on mythology for subjects for their early art, in much the same way as the Greeks. Take for example, the fabulous myth of the proto-craftsman, Daedalus, the man who made wings and flew westwards. In fact the very first attestation of Daedalus so far known comes from Etruria rather than from Greece. On a relief-decorated jug made of bucchero, found in a mid-seventh century BC tomb at Cerveteri, we see a winged figure inscribed as "*Taitale,*" the Etruscan transliteration of the Greek for Daidalos (see Fig. 24.2).

But the fascination for all things winged goes further than this. The Etruscans put wings on non-winged animals, almost as if to improve on their inherent properties. They added wings to lions and to horses and a number of other animals. Take for example the bucchero situla found at Cerveteri in the Tomb of the Painted Animals (circa 620 BC), which depicts two winged lions (Villa Giulia, Rome; Rathje 1982: 30). Of course the guardians of the Palace of Ashurnasirpal II (ninth century BC) at Nimrud include a winged lion and a winged bull (Layard, 1849); the original inspiration is no doubt Near Eastern. Aristotle, who examined things in terms of their structure and function, concluded that the purpose of wings is flight (Moore 1988) and so we should also consider that perhaps the Etruscans wished to give these special animals properties of flight for specific metaphysical (psychopompic?) purposes.

PERIOD-BASED INTEREST IN ETRUSCAN ANIMAL MOTIFS

The Villanovan Period

Whilst it is perhaps premature to speak of "art" in this period, as it is hard to imagine full-time "artists" operating before the eighth century BC, yet animal motifs (often rather crude in their execution) are occasionally found. An example is the helmeted and combative rider we see serving as the handle of a "duck-shaped" flask (*askos*) with bull's head found in a Villanovan tomb at Bologna, constituting as it does a simplified and abstracted form of ornament (Brendel 1978/1995: 90 Fig. 59).

The overall evaluation of the popularity of Etruscan animal motifs spanning from approximately 900 BC to 700 BC and including 20 items and 32 animal motifs are shown in Fig. 60.4. It is interesting to note that there are no strictly "mythical" animal motifs among those items catalogued for this period (although there are composite creatures, as on the Bologna askos). Likewise, very few "exotic" animals are represented, and those that are fall into the sub-category C II (exotic terrestrial).

The vast majority of animal motifs for this period are those assigned to A II (domesticated farmstead, e.g. horses, cattle, sheep), with B I (wild airborne, e.g. swan, geese, owl, partridge, eagle, heron (see Fig. 60.3 no. 11 = GR 1873.8–20.44, British Museum) and B II (wild terrestrial, e.g. deer, hare, boar, stag, snake, deer calf [fawn] and mouse) proving the second most popular. If we were to draw conclusions from these findings, bearing in mind the biases mentioned previously, it would appear that the early Iron Age Etruscan peoples were particularly taken with their domesticated farmstead animals and chose to represent them on their pottery and metal objects. They were also very fond of the wild species that surrounded them, depicting both wild birds and wild terrestrial animals on their possessions. This is perhaps not that surprising for a group of Iron Age Etruscans who were very dependent on hunting and farming for their existence.

Outstanding examples of such homestead and hunting motifs are to be found on the bronze trolley (Tomb 2) and bronze situla (Tomb 22) found in the Olmo Bello necropolis in Bisenzio – late eighth century BC (Sgubini 2008: 27). The bronze trolley of Tomb 2 is thought to be a censer or offering trolley, and its rich sculptural decoration is indicative of the emerging Etruscan aristocracy in its activities of war, hunting and farming. The situla of Tomb 22 is equally impressive, decorated with scenes of dancing and farming, around a top that shows a hunting or ritual scene with a chained bear in the centre of a ring of eight men bearing spears (Rm 25 Case 1; Villa Giulia, Rome; Haynes 1985: no. 5).

The Orientalizing period

In the first decades of the seventh century BC the phenomenon of Etruscan-geometric pottery rapidly develops from simple linear and circular patterns into systems of figurative motifs, for example, the heron and fish.

Importantly, lions begin to appear in Etruscan art as a result of the influences prevailing during the Orientalizing period (see Fig. 60.2n GR 1873.8–20.269 and Fig. 60.2s GR 1824.4–46.22; British Museum), although the Etruscan artists committed a great many errors in terms of representation, for example, multiple teats, which do not occur naturally (see William Llewelyn Brown, *The Etruscan Lion*, 1960), but since lions have never been indigenous to Italy, an Etruscan artist would not have had the opportunity for direct observation, and most likely used the wolf as the primary model. See the recently discovered Tomb of the Roaring Lions of Veii, Fig. 56.1.

The overall evaluation of the popularity of Etruscan animal motifs spanning approximately 780 BC to 600 BC: 86 items and 149 animal motifs are shown in Fig. 60.5. In contrast to the previous period, this phase of Etruscan civilization is dominated by the "exotic" type of animal motifs – C II (exotic terrestrial, e.g. lion, ostrich, leopard, panther, monkey and elephant).

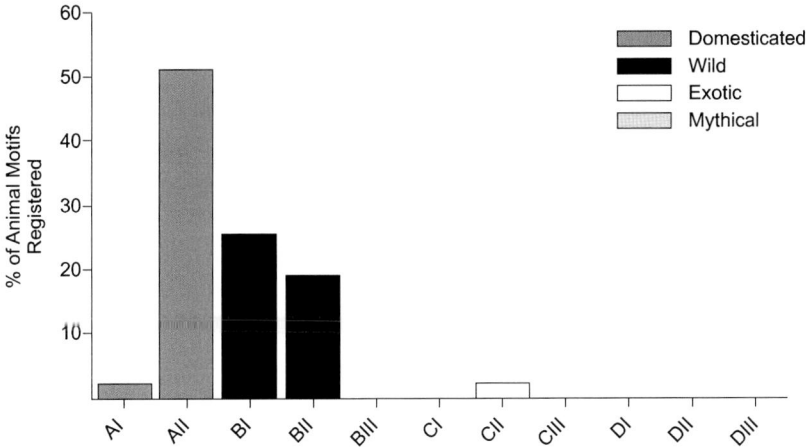

Figure 60.4   Villanovan period. A graphic presentation of some 20 items spanning the years 900–780 BC depicting or representing animal motifs classified as per Fig. 60.1.

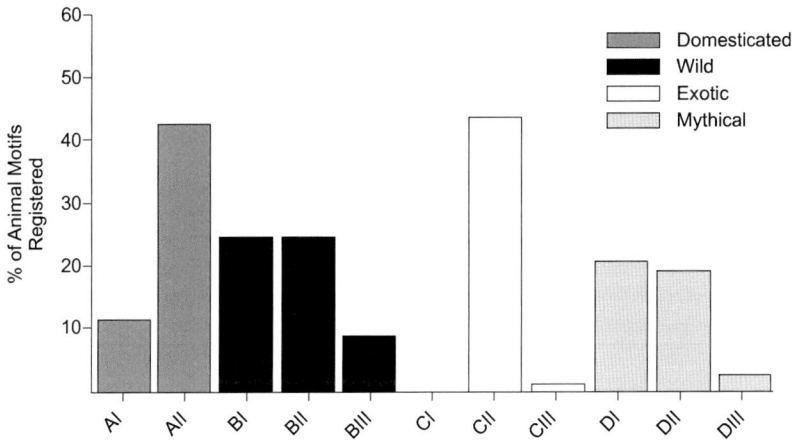

Figure 60.5   Orientalizing period. A graphic presentation of some 86 items spanning the years 780–600 BC depicting or representing animal motifs classified as per Fig. 60.1.

The Orientalizing period denotes a change from the hitherto animal motifs towards one that sets a high value on things exotic and mythical. Perhaps this represents the influence of external pressures or sources of inspiration. The Orientalizing phase of Etruscan art is not merely an aesthetic vogue for the exotic, it also represents an interaction with civilizations of the Near East and Egypt that were technically innovative. Samples of their work, when brought to the shores of Etruria, must have seemed exotically enchanting (for example the tridacna shell or the ostrich egg covered with miniature incised decoration (see GR 1850.7–27.5; British Museum, Rathje 1986b). But more importantly such items of oriental provenance most likely correspond to a need from the elite to set themselves apart with distinct personal ornaments. Indeed, the Greeks of Homer's time had a word for these prestige objects *"keimelia,"* implying "those things which are to be treasured when plundered or presented." Moreover, as a result of the Persian invasion of East Greece during the late sixth century BC, a number of immigrant artists made their way to Etruria. A good small-scale example of the immigrant artist phenomenon is the Swallows Painter, an Ionian vase painter who seems to have settled at Vulci (620–610 BC, see Chapter 52), and provided the locals with drinking vessels executed in the distinctive "Wild Goat" style of his homeland (see Chapters 48 and 52).

The Archaic period

As a result of the conflict between the Etruscans and Phocaeans (circa 540 BC: Herodotus 1.165–6) some Phocaean prisoners were stoned to death near to Cerveteri. This action ultimately led to a delegation of Etruscans travelling from Cerveteri to Delphi to consult the oracle about atonement. Clearly this delegation of Etruscans would have been exposed to the enormous display of sculpture and painting at Delphi, for example, the Naxian sphinx.

The overall evaluation of the popularity of Etruscan animal motifs spanning approximately 600 BC to 480 BC: 85 items and 141 animal motifs are shown in Fig. 60.6. During this period there is a slight revival in A II animal motifs which is at the expense of B I, B III and C II animal motifs.

During the Archaic period the sudden interest in things exotic, which was observed during the Orientalizing period, wanes and there is a loss of interest in wild animals as popular motifs. Instead, the Etruscan peoples continue to be fascinated with, and set considerable prestige on, mythical animals as decorative motifs for their possessions.

The Classical period

It is generally believed that due to some strong iconographic evidence that Etruscans, from the late fourth century BC onwards, invented mythical prehistories for themselves (Spivey 1997: 12). However, is this actually what the collated evidence indicates, or do other animal motifs prevail?

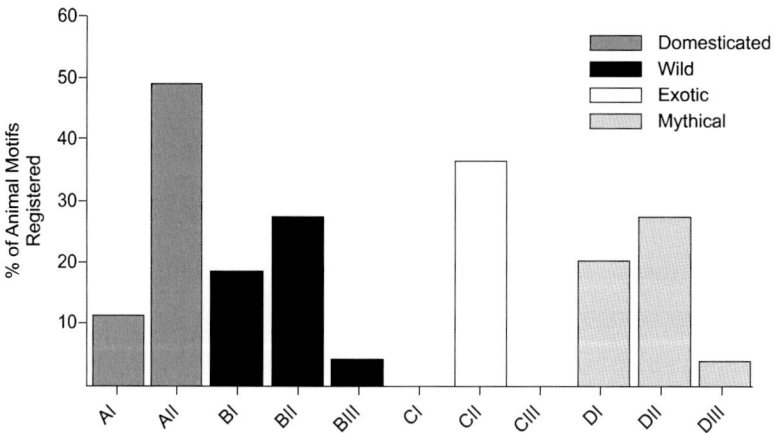

Figure 60.6 Archaic period. A graphic presentation of some 85 items spanning the years 600–480 BC depicting or representing animal motifs classified as per Fig. 60.1.

The overall evaluation of the popularity of Etruscan animal motifs spanning approx. 480 BC to 323 BC; 32 items and 59 animal motifs are shown in the Figure 60.7. During this period there is a continued decline in interest in "exotic" animal motifs, and perhaps more surprisingly we see a reduction in the popularity of "mythical" animal motifs. Instead we see what appears to be a return to "domesticated" and "wild" animal motifs, perhaps indicating a revival in interests from earlier periods of Etruscan civilization. Thus the top three most represented animals include in descending order, birds, horses and joint third snakes and lions.

The Classical period is quite interesting as suddenly we see a reversal of interest in mythical animal motifs, and a continued decline in the use of exotic animals as motifs on pottery, wall paintings and other objects. Rather, we see a return to "old fashioned" values and a revival of both wild and domesticated animals as decorative motifs. Perhaps these changes are indicative of real or feared threats to the continuance of things Etruscan, with value being attributed to a period that signified older and better times?

The Hellenistic period

The overall evaluation of the popularity of Etruscan animal motifs spanning approximately 323 BC to 100 BC: 35 items and 52 animal motifs are shown in Fig. 60.8. In this the final period of Etruscan civilization, we see a stable interest in "mythical" animal motifs and a slight resurgence of interest in "exotic" animals. However, there is a loss of interest in "wild" animal motifs, in fact the lowest level seen for any of the previous periods. In contrast, there is a continued increase in "domesticated" animal motifs, with A II attaining a level that matches that of the Archaic period, and A I attaining the highest level of interest seen to date. Thus the top three most represented animals include in descending order, horses, birds and joint third dolphins and lions. The Hellenistic period denotes a strengthening of interest in "old-fashioned" values albeit with a slight revival in exotic animal species. Yet, wild animals seem no longer to be highly valued, falling to an all-time low in terms of their occurrence on Etruscan objects. This particular period of Etruscan civilization is associated with a loss of political

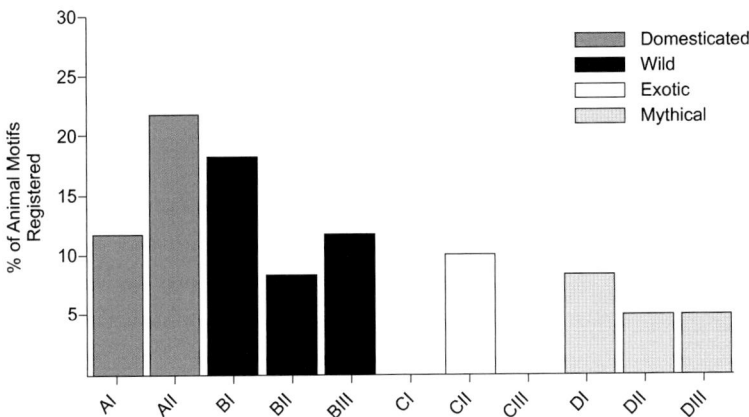

Figure 60.7   Classical period. A graphic presentation of some 32 items spanning the years 480–323 BC depicting or representing animal motifs classified as per Fig. 60.1.

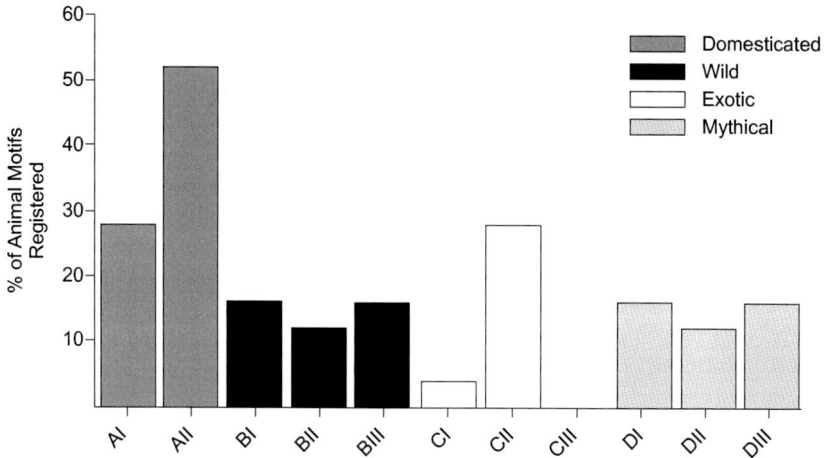

Figure 60.8 Hellenistic period. A graphic presentation of some 35 items spanning the years 323–100 BC depicting or representing animal motifs classified as per Fig. 60.1.

autonomy to Rome, which might also be expected to give rise to changes in identity markers. Moreover, most urbanites were no longer tied to the land, and as such, one would expect that there would be fewer aristocrats able to afford to hunt.

LOCATION-BASED INTEREST IN ETRUSCAN ANIMAL MOTIFS

Of the artifacts identified as coming from a specific Etruscan location that I have classified in this catalogue, 70.5 per cent of them can be attributed to the cities of Vulci, Chiusi, Cerveteri and Tarquinia. Moreover, these four cities differ in the frequency with which animal motifs occur.

In Vulci animal motifs A, B, C and D had a frequency of 22.7 per cent, 18.2 per cent, 13.6 per cent and 45.4 per cent, respectively. Clearly in this city mythical animal motifs were the most popular.

In Chiusi animal motifs A, B, C and D had a frequency of 57.1 per cent, 14.3 per cent, 0 per cent and 28.5 per cent, respectively. Interestingly, in Chiusi exotic animal motifs were not that popular, whilst domesticated animal motifs were the most frequently portrayed of all the categories investigated.

In Cerveteri the animal motifs A, B, C and D had a more even frequency of 33.3 per cent, 16.6 per cent, 25.0 per cent and 25.0 per cent, respectively, whilst in Tarquinia the animal motifs A, B, C and D had a frequency of 40.0 per cent, 28.0 per cent, 16.0 per cent and 16.0 per cent, respectively, showing a slight preference towards domesticated and wild animal motifs.

It is most likely that these differences between cities in terms of the portrayed animal motifs, represented on tomb paintings, pottery, metal work etc., are indicative of regional associations and ties with trade links and the prevailing association/influence that different cultures were able to impose.

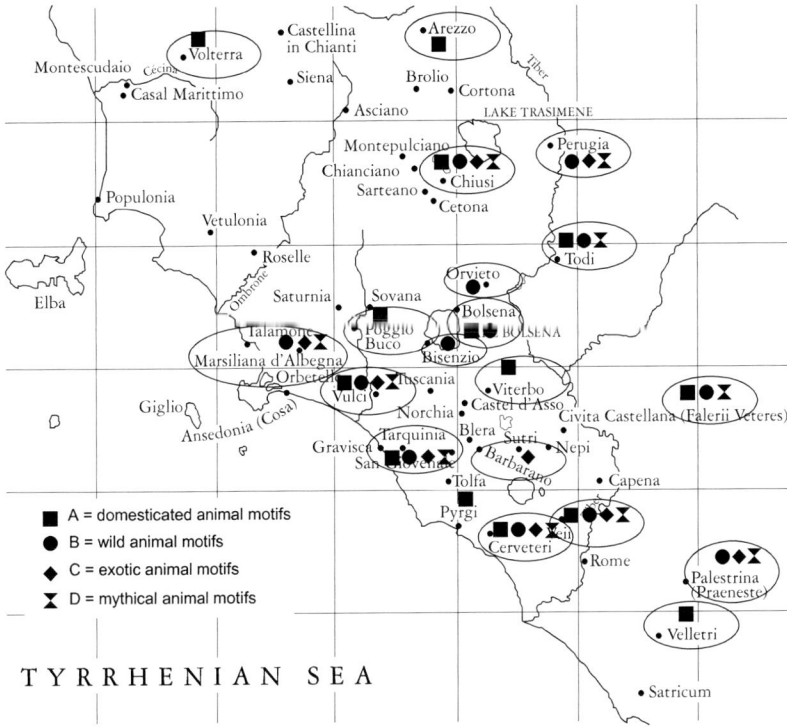

Figure 60.9   Etruscan animal categories collated according to find site.
Note that the cities of Vulci, Chiusi, Cerveteri and Tarquinia account for some 70% of the artefacts
catalogued. This may be biased because of the locations of major museums today – many small, regional
museums displaying recent discoveries can furnish different types or ratios of decorative motifs
(map modified after Spivey, 1997: p. 6).

ETRUSCAN ANIMAL MOTIFS AND WAR, SPORT, AGRICULTURE AND CULTURE

"…the horse is always the symbol of the strong animal life of man…"

Etruscan Places, Chapter 6 (D. H. Lawrence)

Certain animals have always been used as weapons on the battlefield and been seen as the spoils of war to be taken freely by the victor (see Fig. 60.2r = GR 1856.12–26.796; British Museum). Thus, put simply, the number and quality of, for example, horses owned by an individual would surely have served as a sign of that individual's status in Etruscan society. Moreover, horses are often represented as being connected to the life-style of the aristocrats and involved in hunting, competition and warfare (Wiman 2004).

If horses were seen as weapons by the Etruscans, then the number of horses that a given region was capable of mustering must also have been seen in terms of that region's strength. Likewise, with horses being seized as the spoils of war, this would tend to make wars with neighboring tribes a profitable enterprise. It is therefore perhaps not surprising that a number of Etruscan individuals are seen on horse-back and, on occasion, dressed for battle, take for example the Cerveteri Warrior on horse-back in the form of a *balsamarium* that was found in Banditaccia necropolis tomb 304 (circa 570–550 BC) and is now on display at the Museo Nazionale Cerite (Rossi 2011: 12).

Horses would also have offered the fastest mode of land transport, and would have been synonymous with speed. Numerous Etruscan items depict horses in motion with their legs fully stretched and their spines flexed. Others depict horses harnessed to a chariot for recreational racing and athletic competition, take for example the amphora by the Micali painter (circa 525–490 BC) which is believed to have been produced in Vulci, depicting a four-horse chariot with riders on display in the Ny Carlsberg Glyptotek in Copenhagen (circa 500 BC; HIN 676: Rm 21A, Case A-2: Moltesen 1982: Fig. 1), a clear example of a need for speed if ever there was one (for more on chariots, see Chapter 41). There is also the example of the painted vase from Narce (circa 700 BC) that shows a horse tamer and acrobats, the latter standing on the back of two horses (Philadelphia, University Museum, see Fig. 52.7). It seems that the Etruscans saw the horse as being a symbol of speed, of status and independence, as well as a sign of power and entertainment. We should not forget, however, that animals and agriculture are very much intertwined. Clearly, Etruscan society and individuals placed pride in their livestock, and rightly so as there was a very strong link with an individual's financial stability.

Animals and their motifs also form a very strong link with other cultures that were associated commercially with the Etruscans. Often, the introduction of animal motifs comes directly from other cultures through the telling of myths and the exchange of exotic and highly esteemed pottery, sculpture and art. Indeed, such exchange of animal motifs even occurs without the artist ever having seen the animals he attempts to portray on occasions.

ETRUSCAN ANIMAL MOTIFS AND RELIGION

Animals have always been closely linked with religion and the Afterlife. Used for sacrifices to the gods, or as omens of an impending tragedy they have become a pillar of religious belief that has been adopted up to the present day, where Christian saints are depicted by animal motifs (e.g. Eagle: John the Evangelist). For additional animal sacrifice scenes, see Chapter 28, Figs. 28.2 (goat), 28.5 (bovine), and 28.7a (fawn).

Animals: bringers of death

Just as today, in the past working with and handling animals was not without some element of risk. Racing horses either bare-back or in association with a chariot was a dangerous sport, likewise the handling of bulls and boars was not without risk of injury or death and the introduction of more exotic species such as lions, panthers and elephants must without doubt have cost some individuals their life. Indeed, some of the Etruscan art that has survived provides examples of just such dangers; 1) the Tomb of the Augurs, Tarquinia circa 510 BC depicting a man with a sack over his head battling with a dog – perhaps a form of sport, but more likely a funerary ritual evoking a blood sacrifice (Haynes 2000: 233 Fig. 190); 2) the cinerary urn from Volterra circa 200 BC that depicts the death of Actaeon being torn apart by his hounds (Haynes 2000: 365 Fig. 287); 3) the bucchero kantharos from Vulci circa 620 BC depicting a lion with a human leg in its mouth; 4) the bucchero model boat from Capena circa 675–650 BC illustrating a drowning man, which serves to remind us that not only the animals but the means by which they are caught can be life threatening; 5) the terracotta panel from Arezzo circa 500 BC depicting a horseman galloping after a fleeing enemy; 6) the bronze statuette from Vulci circa 425–400 BC of Herakles wrestling with the Nemean lion (Haynes 1985: 204 no. 136), and 7) the large bronze vessel with lid from Bisenzio (Necropoli Di Olmo Bello – tomb 22) adorned by seven men with spears attacking a chained animal, perhaps a bear or a wolf (circa 730–700 BC) – something that may depict a form of sport, but could equally be read as a ritual (Haynes 1985: no. 5).

Snakes

The serpent was an important part of general Mediterranean iconography and Etruscan religion, and whilst overlooked, they have a prominent place in funerary art. In the Tomba dell'Orco II at Tarquinia (fourth century BC), there is a clear depiction of the demon Tuchulcha, who is shown holding a bearded snake in his left hand and with two smaller snakes in his hair (Hostetler, 2007). The markings on the snake depicted in this tomb are similar to those of the adder, which is indigenous to Italy and most of Europe.

A number of examples of Etruscan representative art depicting snakes have survived. In Bologna, a gravestone with a relief of a snake fighting a hippocamp was found (circa 400 BC, Bologna Museum; Haynes 2000: 307 Fig. 247). Another motif from a sarcophagus from Vulci (circa 350–300 BC) depicts a griffin protecting a serpent (Ny Carlsberg Glyptotek, Copenhagen, Moltesen and Nielsen 1996: 44 no. 7). On a red-figured krater for mixing wine, found at Civita Castellana (circa 400 BC), the infant Herakles is shown strangling snakes with his bare hands (see Fig. 60.2k, = GR 1888.10–15.13, British Museum). Finally, note the bronze votive statuette of a winged female Vanth found near Mount Vesuvius (circa 425–400 BC) which shows her holding snakes in either hand – perhaps a symbolic protective role towards the souls of the departed (GR 1772.3–2.15; British Museum; Bonfante and Swaddling, 2006: Fig. 53; Haynes 1985: no. 142). Snakes have a close association with the earth, inhabiting subterranean lairs, and as such they have a cross-cultural association with death and the Underworld. The Etruscans shared the hilltops with such snakes as the adder, and their stone dwellings, which would have been relatively dark, cool and moist, would have been enticing for snakes (Hostetler, 2007).

Hostetler (2007) also points out that in the Tomba dei Caronti at Tarquinia (third century BC, Steingräber 1985: color pls. 61–63) the wall paintings depict several male demons, some labeled as Charu(n), which have a very distinctive blue colored skin. This apparently odd form of skin coloration may either symbolize the change in skin coloration that occurs with an adder bite, which is typically a blue to purple or black discoloration associated with the hemorrhage that follows the injection of venom. Alternatively, it may serve to symbolize the typical blue skin coloration that one finds with decaying flesh.

Animals: protectors of souls and wealth

Many of the Etruscan tombs and indeed funerary urns either depict or incorporate animal motifs. Moreover, a great many of these animal motifs appear to have performed a protective role, serving to stand guard over the entrance to a family tomb or to play a similar role with regard to an urn. Take for example the British Museum cinerary urn originating from Chiusi, and carved in the form of a house or temple with two panthers standing guard on the roof (GR 1873.8–20.757).

Other Etruscan items involve animals more in the events leading up to burial. They typically show the dead on foot, horseback, in a chariot sometimes preceded by a small hooded figure, or a covered wagon. Sometimes they use highly unusual forms of locomotion such as serpents, a hippocamp or a centaur to pull the vehicle. Then, at the start of the third century BC, the most frequent image is that of a cortege in which the deceased and his guides Charu(n) and Vanth appear, Charun holding his mallet with which he unlocks the great bar on the door of the World of the Dead, and the winged Vanth bearing a torch with which she lights the route (Jannot, 2000). An example of this can be found on the sarcophagus of a man from Volterra circa 150–130 BC, where the lower panel shows the journey to the land of the dead in relief. A woman leads a horse, upon which rides the deceased, while a slave holds the horse's tail (Ny Carlsberg Glyptotek, Copenhagen). In a similar setting, the end wall of the sarcophagus of Ramtha Viśnai found at Vulci (circa 350 BC) illustrates two women under an umbrella being drawn by two horses to the Underworld, led by a Vanth (Boston Museum of Fine Arts; Haynes 2000: 289 Fig. 232c).

The images left by the Etruscans are far from complete in terms of providing us with a clear picture of their near-death and after-life experiences and expectations. However, it is clear that Etruscans believed in ghosts, as there is mention of shades (ghosts), which are referred to by the Etruscans as *hinthial*, depicted in the Tomb of Orcus II, Tarquinia (circa 400 BC; Bonfante and Swaddling, 2006: 68).

It is also clear that griffins were seen as being protective, and could have been intended to protect the occupants of the tombs and their buried wealth. Winged lions may have served a similar guardian role in the tomb, as did the lions at the Palace of Ashurnasirpal II at Nimrud. However, it is possible that they performed a role as escorts for the soul as it was transported or carried to the World of the Gods (see Fig. 60.10). Indeed, there are many winged lion statues in the necropoleis of archaic Vulci, one would almost say it was their trademark, as they line the dromoi to big tombs (Van Kampen, 2007).

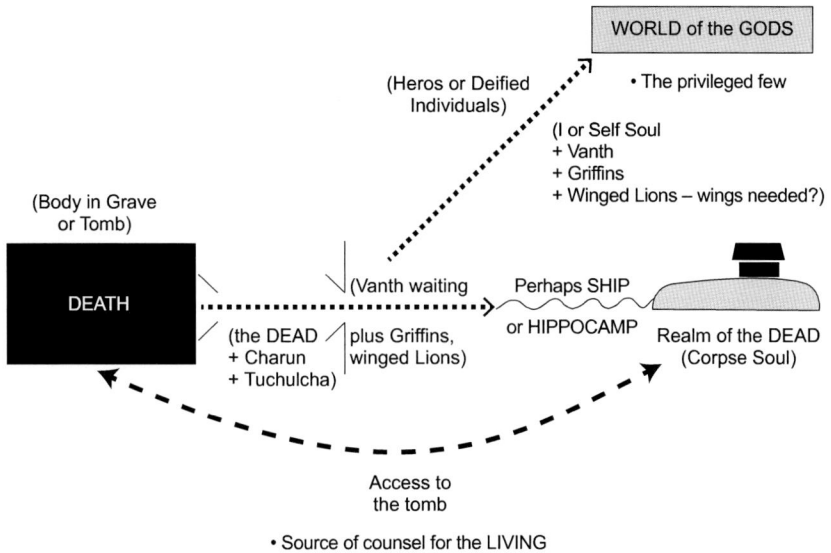

Figure 60.10 A possible role of animal motifs in the after-life beliefs of the Etruscans.

Animals: sacrifice and omens

A good many of the Etruscan funerary urns depict scenes of animal sacrifice (see Chapter 28). There was a tradition of sacrificing an animal, typically a sheep or ram, as part of the funeral celebrations. An example of this can be seen below on the front of an Etruscan alabaster casket at the British Museum (Fig. 60.11). It depicts in the bottom right-hand corner just such a ram being led to the entrance of a tomb.

However, the Etruscans considered omens as highly significant, in particular, it is said that omens coming from bees were considered to be sinister by the Etruscans after a swarm settled in the Forum at Cassino (Heurgon, 1961: 225). It is likewise reported that Tarquinius the Elder, on his arrival in Rome, saw an eagle steal his cap, carry it off and then put it gently back on his head, whereupon Tanaquil did not hesitate to entertain the highest hopes for the future (Heurgon 1961: 225).

Another form of prediction used the *Brontoscopic Calendar*, which was intended to function as a reference for priests who interpreted the phenomenon of "thunder" with regard to herds, flocks, deer, wild birds and fish of both river and sea (Turfa 2007, 2012). For example, such warnings relating to thunder on a specific day include:

June 9. If in any way it should thunder, there will be a loss of flocks through being overrun by wolves.

May 28. If it thunders, there will be a plenty of marine fish.

Highly specialized Etruscan religious practices were arranged into a systematic code in several sets of books written in Etruscan and known today under the generic Latin title *Etrusca Disciplina*. The *Libri Haruspicini*, for example, dealt with divination from the

Figure 60.11   The front panel relief of a Hellenistic Volterran alabaster urn showing a funeral celebration procession and the preparation of a ram for sacrifice at the tomb monument. (British Museum Collection D 69, *ThesCRA* vol. I: pl. 42, Etr. 138 = Rafanelli 2004; see Haynes 2000: 369 and Fig. 291) © www.bmmadsen.dk

entrails of sacrificed animals (Harrison *et al.* 2010). Haruspicy and the recognition of adverse conditions through haruspicy, the practice of scrutinizing the livers of sacrificed sheep (and later, during the first century BC, the entire viscera of various victims) would have furnished data on the relative health of the food supply and thus of humans in a given area. If the haruspex priest could see dire information in the livers of sacrificed victims, they could call for expiation, lustration or presumably other forms of group religious response to adverse phenomena.

Birds were also used as a means of predicting the future, and since the skies of Etruria were filled with birds, carefully studied by the haruspices. Pliny recounts that species, such as eagles (known from the glosses as Etruscan *antar*), hawks (Etr. *arac*) and falcons (Etr. *capu*) were present. Moreover, in the François Tomb we see a woodpecker on the verge of flying away in a scene denoting augury, in the observation of the flight of birds (*auspicium*, see Chapter 26).

Finally, there is mention of the ancient Etruscan ritual of *dii animales* in which the sacrifical offering of an animal could enable the soul of a departed relative to commune with the Gods, although sadly the ritual has been lost and all that remains are much later texts that attribute it to the Etruscans. Arnobius, writing around 305 AD, states that the Etruscan *libri Acherontici* say that through the offering of blood from particular animals, certain divinities can be summoned who have the power to overturn the rules of mortality and confer godlike status on the spirits of the dead. Sadly, there remains little indication as to which animals or indeed which gods were involved in this ritual (Becker *et al.* 2009: 104–108). Cremation burials ought to preserve some evidence of the procedure, but the only samples recovered by Becker and colleagues were found to be of immature mammals although whether these represented lambs, piglets, puppies or kit rabbits was not discernible owing to the fragmented nature of the material.

This study was initiated with the intention of suggesting some associations between animals and the beliefs and lifestyles of ancient Etruria. Since the topic and corpus of evidence are too vast to yield complete conclusions, this chapter should rather be considered as a work in progress. It has not yet been possible to catalogue all extant representations of all the creatures represented in the Etruscan artistic world, just as physical evidence of animal species (from food remains, votive deposits and other archaeological finds) has not been collated into a single source (cf. Turfa 2012, Chapter 5). However, it is hoped that readers with access to archaeological or art historical data will update this record with the findings of their own research.[1]

NOTE

1   The author is indebted to the enthusiastic help freely given by Birgitte Holle in connection with the cataloguing of Etruscan artifacts containing animal motifs. I would also like to thank especially Dr Judith Swaddling of the British Museum and Dr Jean MacIntosh Turfa at the University of Pennsylvania Museum for their support and help with this endeavor. I am also indebted to Dr Jan Kindberg Jacobsen from Ny Carlsberg Glyptotek for his kind and generous help, and to Bolette Madsen for her hard work in converting my many images into illustrations (www.bmmadsen.dk). Finally, but by no means least, I acknowledge the assistance and patience of those Museum attendants around the world who have put up with my cataloguing work over the past two years, and who continue to accommodate my eccentricities.

BIBLIOGRAPHY

Ambrosini, L. (2006) "Cerbero e l'elefante. Ipotesi sulla ricostruzione di un donario fittile dal santuario di Portonaccio a Veio" in A. Comella and S. Mele (eds.), *Depositi votive e culti dell'Italia antica dall'età arcaica a quella tardo-repubblicana* (Atti del Convegno di Studi, Perugia, 1–4 June 2000), Bari: Edipuglia, 189–208.

Banti, L. (1968) *The Etruscan Cities and their Culture*. Prescot, UK: C. Tinling & Co.

Beazley, J. D. (1947) *Etruscan Vase Painting*. Oxford: Clarendon Press.

Becker, M. J., Turfa, J. M., Algee-Hewitt B. (2009) *Human Remains – From Etruscan and Italic tomb groups in the University of Pennsylvania Museum*. Biblioteca Di "Studi Etruschi" 48, Rome: Ed. Fabrizio Serra.

Bloch, R. (1957) "Etruskerne," trans. Peter Grove, in Dr Glyn Daniel (ed.), *The Etruscans: Ancient Peoples and Places*, London: Thames & Hudson.

——(1970). *Archaeologia Mundi – Die Etrusker*. Nagel Verlag, Stuttgart.

Bonfante, L. and Swaddling, J. (2006) *Etruscan Myths, the Legendary Past*, London: The British Museum Press.

Bokonyi, S. (1968) *Data on iron age horses of central and eastern Europe*. American School of Prehistoric Research. The Peabody Museum, Harvard University.

Brendel, O. J. (1978) *Etruscan Art*, New Haven, CT: Yale University Press.

Camporeale, G. (1984) *La caccia in Etruria*, Rome: Giorgio Bretschneider.

Cristofani, M. (1979) *The Etruscans: A New Investigation. Echoes of the Ancient World*, trans. Brian Phillips, London: Orbis Publishing.

Gentili, M. D. (1994) *I sarcophagi etruschi in terracotta di età recente*, Rome: Giorgio Bretschneider.

Hall, J. (1974) *Dictionary of Subjects and Symbols in Art*, London: John Murray.

Harrison A. P., Cattani, I. and Turfa, J. M. (2010) "Metallurgy, environmental pollution and the decline of Etruscan civilization," *Environ.Sci.Pollut.Res.*, 7: 165–180.

Haynes, S. (1985) *Etruscan Bronzes*, London: Sotheby's Publications.

——(2000) *Etruscan Civilization. A Cultural History*. Los Angeles: J. Paul Getty Museum.

Heurgon, J. (1961) *Daily life of the Etruscans*, trans James Kirkup, 2002, London: Phoenix Press.

Hostetler, K. L. (2007) "Serpent Iconography," *Etruscan Studies: Journal of the Etruscan Foundation*, 10: 203–209.

Jannot, J-R. (1984) *Les reliefs archaïques de Chiusi* (Collection de l'École française de Rome – 71.) Rome: École française de Rome.

——(1986) "45. Sur les coffrets archaïques étrusques à decoration d'ivoire et d'os: hypotheses sur la production et la diffusion" in J. Swaddling (ed.) *Italian Iron Age Artefacts, Papers of the sixth British Museum Classical Colloqium*, London: The British Museum Press, 1982), 405–415.

——(2000) "Etruscans and the Afterworld," *Etruscan Studies – Journal of the Etruscan Foundation*, 7: 81–99.

Lawrence, D. H. (1972) *Etruscan Places*, London: The Folio Society, Norwich: Jarrold & Sons Ltd.

Layard, A. H. (1849) *Nineveh and its remains*, New York: Putnam.

Leroi-Gourhan, A. (1967) *Treasures of prehistoric art*, New York: Abrams.

Llewelyn Brown, W. (1960) *The Etruscan Lion*. Oxford: Clarendon Press.

Magagnini, A. (2008) *The Etruscans – History and treasures of an ancient civilization*. Novara: White Star Publishers.

Martelli, M. *et al.* (1987) *La ceramica degli Etruschi. La pittura vascolare*, Novara: Istituto Geografico De Agostini.

Moltesen, M. (1982) "Til væddeløb i Etrurien," *Meddelelser fra Ny Carlsberg Glyptotek*, 38: 53–72.

Moltesen, M. and Nielsen, M. (1996) *Catalogue: Etruria and Central Italy, 450–30 BC*, contributions by P. Guldager Bilde, T. Fischer-Hansen and A. M. Nielsen. Ny Carlsberg Glyptotek.

Moltesen, M. and Weber-Lehmann, C. (1991) *Catalogue: The Copies of Etruscan Tomb Paintings in the Ny Carlsberg Glyptotek*. Ny Carlsberg Glyptotek.

Moore, J. A. (1988) "Understanding Nature – Form and Function," *Amer.Zool.*, 28: 449–584.

Murray, A. T. (1998) *Homer – Odyssey*. Books 1–12, revised by G. E. Dimock. Loeb Classical Library, Bury St. Edmunds, Suffolk, UK: Edmundsbury Press Ltd.

Pallottino, M. (1956) *The Etruscans*. Harmondsworth, UK: Penguin Books Ltd.

Philostratus, F. (1921) *The Life of Apollonius of Tyana*, trans. F. C. Conybeare, volume I, book III. XLVIII., 333.

Principi = G. Bartoloni, F. Delpino, C. Morigi Govi and G. Sassatelli (eds) (2000) *Principi etruschi tra Mediterraneo ed Europa* (exhibition, Bologna Museo Civico Archeologico, 1 October 2000– 1 April 2001), Venice: Marsilio.

Rafanelli, S. (2004) "Il sacrificio nel mondo etrusco" in *ThesCRA* I, Processions. Sacrifices. Libations. Fumigations. Dédications, 2.a. Sacrifices / Sacrifices / Opfer / sacrifici, Etr., 136–182.

Rathje, A. (1982). *Etruskerne en antik kultur gennem 700 aar*. Gylendal. ISBN 87-00-70522-5.

——(1986a) "43. A tridacna squamosa shell" in J. Swaddling (ed.), *Italian Iron Age Artefacts, Papers of the sixth British Museum Classical Colloqium* (London, The British Museum Press, 1982), 393–96.

——(1986b) "44. Five ostrich eggs from Vulci" in J. Swaddling (ed.), *Italian Iron Age Artefacts, Papers of the sixth British Museum Classical Colloqium*, London: The British Museum Press, 1982, 397–404.

Roberts, H. S. (1982) *Etruskerne mennesker i hverdagen*, Copenhagen: Gylendal.

Rossi, D. (2010) *Cerveteri – A guided visit to the Banditaccia necropolis*, Cerveteri: Grafica e Stampa, Tip.

——(2011) *Cerveteri – Una visita guidata al Museo Nazionale Cerite*, Rome: Via Fontana Morella.

Sach, A. (1952) "A Late Babylonian Star Catalogue?" *Journal of Cuneiform Studies* 6: 146–150.

Scala, N. (1993) "I 'lacunari' bronzei di Tarquinia" in *Miscellanea Etrusco-Italica* I (Quaderni di Archeologia Etrusco-Italica 22) 149–184.

Sgubini, A. and Moretti, M. (2008) *The Villa Giulia National Etruscan Museum – Short Guide,* Rome: Soprintendenza Archeologica Per L'Etruria Meridionale.

Spivey, N. (1997) *Etruscan Art*, London: Thames & Hudson.

Steingräber, S. (1981) *Etrurien, Stadte, Heiligtumer, Nekropolen*, Munich: Hirmer Press.

——(1985) *Etruscan Painting: Catalogue Raisonné of Etruscan Wall Paintings*, D. and F. R. Ridgway (eds), New York: Harcourt Brace Jovanovich.

Turfa, J. M. (2005) *Catalogue of the Etruscan Gallery of the University of Pennsylvania Museum of Archaeology and Anthropology*, Philadelphia: Philadelphia University Museum.

——(2007) "The Etruscan Brontoscopic Calendar and Modern Archaeological Discoveries," *Etruscan Studies – Journal of the Etruscan Foundation.* 10: 163–173.

——(2012) *Divining the Etruscan World: The Brontoscopic Calendar and Religious Practice*. Cambridge: Cambridge University Press.

Turfa, J. M. and Steinmayer, A. G. (1993) "In Defence of Patroklos: A Plea to Common Sense," *Antichthon*, 27: 1–12.

van Kampen, I. (2007) "A Workshop of Stone Sculpture Production in South Etruria: la Bottega del Gruppo di San Donato," *Etruscan Studies*, 10: 35–46.

Wiman, I. M. B. (2004) "Who let the animals out? Changing modes in Etruscan mirror decoration," *PECUS. Man and animal in antiquity*. Proceedings of the conference at the Swedish Institute in Rome, September 9–12, 2002. Rome: Ed. Barbro Santillo Frizell (The Swedish Institute in Rome. Projects and Seminars, 1).

PART VIII
POST-ANTIQUE RECEPTION OF ETRUSCAN CULTURE

———·◆·———

CHAPTER SIXTY ONE

ANNIUS OF VITERBO

———•◆•———

Ingrid D. Rowland

The history of Etruscan studies has always featured an unusually large number of forgers, and for good reason. In the first place, there was the matter of patriotism: long after the rise and fall of the Roman Empire, the descendants of the Etruscans, well aware of their heritage, were tempted to embellish any ancestral story that glorified a culture conquered, but never entirely eradicated, by Rome. Furthermore, because the written Etruscan language largely disappeared from Italy at the time of the early Roman Empire, scholars from later periods were faced with a frustrating lack of first-hand information about one of the peninsula's most important ancient populations. Their hunger for knowledge, however far-fetched, often overruled their skepticism. Needless to say, people who traced their ancestry back to Etruscan forebears were especially eager to grasp at any trace of their heritage, in any form: object or text, real, embroidered, or invented. And because the line between a vivid historical imagination and a vivid imagination is not always an easy one to draw, fictions about the Etruscans have ultimately been as plentiful as facts, from the tall tales told by medieval chroniclers to the lyrical prose of a dying D. H. Lawrence in *Etruscan Places*.

The first serious student of Etruscan language, history, and culture was particularly good at mixing fact and fiction. The Dominican friar Annius of Viterbo (1432–1502; Fig. 61.1) was certainly a scholar of vivid imagination and definite talent, but from the outset he also acquired a reputation as a serious rogue. His contemporaries accused him of being a charlatan, a religious apostate, a forger, and a madman, and he may well have been all of these things, but he also rose to the third highest position in his large, important order, and distinguished himself, before his death in a Renaissance straitjacket, as a highly intelligent scholar, a real pioneer of Etruscan studies, and an acute observer of the world around him. Dismissing him as no more than a forger and a spinner of implausible tales means missing the real insights he has to offer, for the Viterbo of Annius of Viterbo was a city on which the Etruscan imprint was much fresher than it is today – fresher by 500 years. If his surroundings inspired him to leap to wild conclusions about past and present, they were still real surroundings, and some of his thoughts about his city's history were genuinely insightful. The more we know about Viterbo as it was in earlier times, the more we can admire the way in which this ingenious fifteenth-century scholar used history, archaeology, and eloquence (along with a few well-placed fabrications) to promote his own city, and – not quite incidentally – to save what seemed to be his own ruined career.

The strange career of Annius of Viterbo had a great deal to do with the peculiar qualities of his native city. Even today, Viterbo is a mysterious place, with plentiful, tantalizing evidence of its earlier history. Perched on the side of an extinct volcano, shaded by pines and hazel trees, watered by artesian springs, the city's steep, isolated buttes have hosted human communities ever since prehistoric times (Fig. 61.2). Despite centuries, if not millennia, of leveling and filling, Etruscan streets still wind their way around the hills that make up the city, and many of these roadways are still lined with rock-cut chamber tombs (Fig. 61.3). Modern builders have continued, like their Etruscan, Roman, medieval and Renaissance forebears, to use local volcanic stone for construction: the dark brown *tufa* was easy to cut in the quarry but hardened on exposure to air to become a tough, durable material. Statues, pottery, and metal artifacts emerged from tombs and sometimes from collapsed buildings – and still do. Already in the Middle Ages, these trophies of antiquity were taken home or displayed in Viterbo's churches as precious relics. Some of the local Christian ceremonies also bear a strong resemblance to ancient Etruscan rites, like the miracle of St. Mary the Liberator who calmed a violent, demon-filled thunderstorm on the day of Pentecost in 1320, a Christian version of the Etruscan thunder-diviners who used to foretell the future by interpreting the region's frequent electrical storms (in fact, Italy is the most thunder-prone country in the world).

All these curiosities must have tempted the curiosity of the young boy known as Giovanni Nanni (the story of how Giovanni Nanni became "Annius" will be told below). Born in Viterbo in 1437, he entered the Dominican convent of Santa Maria in Gradi, just outside the city walls, in 1448, thus becoming a member of the fifteenth century's most actively intellectual religious order.[1] The young man's religious education would have

Figure 61.1 Anonymous seventeenth-century painter, *Annius of Viterbo*. Museo Civico, Viterbo. Photograph: author.

Figure 61.2   View of Viterbo. Photograph: author.

Figure 61.3   Etruscan tombs along a street in Viterbo. Photograph: author.

been carefully prescribed, and closely attuned to medieval scholastic learning; typical topics for master's theses at Dominican colleges of the time were "Everything Thomas Aquinas says in the *Summa Theologiae* is correct" or "Everything Peter Lombard says in the *Sentences* (the standard theological textbook, written in the twelfth century) is correct" – needless to say, both Aquinas and Peter Lombard had been Dominicans themselves.[2] The Dominican order did more than provide a first-rate education in theology and careful argumentation. As the order's official designation, Ordo Praedicatorum (Order of Preachers), made clear, its priests were trained to sway crowds by public preaching, and they bore the letters O. P. after their names to indicate their dedication to that mission. In addition, from the outset the order's founder, Domingo de Guzmán, had offered its services to combat heresy, setting up the boards of inquiry called Inquisitions, and the Dominicans continued to play the dominant part in such investigations.

Giovanni Nanni did well in the Order of Preachers; by 1464 he had moved to the convent of Santa Maria Novella in Florence and was engaged in the course work that would lead to a degree as doctor of theology. By 1469 he was back in Viterbo as a *magister*, a professor; two years later he had been transferred to the Genoese convent of Santa Maria in Castello, where he would stay for 18 years.

True to his vocation, Magister Giovanni believed fervently in the righteousness of the Church and its cause, and became a fiery preacher on behalf of crusading against the infidel. Like many Dominicans of his epoch, he also thundered against the high interest rates charged by Jewish moneylenders, in a printed pamphlet.[3] He decried the feuds between noble families that had turned so many Italian cities, including Genoa and Viterbo, into bloody battlegrounds. In Genoa, in 1478, he also made a dramatic political speech; brandishing an intercepted letter from the Milanese warlord Francesco Sforza, Magister Giovanni induced the citizens of Genoa to resist the Milanese – which they did successfully – by the sheer force of his courage and eloquence.[4] In Genoa, too, he was sought after as an astrologer, and published a visionary prediction "About the Future Triumphs of the Christians" (*De futuris christianorum triumphis*), printed in 1484.[5]

All told, the friar from Viterbo seemed destined for a great career, until, in November of 1488, he fell sick with what he would describe as an ear infection that spread across the side of his head and turned into an abscess of the brain – an extremely dangerous condition even in our age of antibiotics and still more potentially lethal in the fifteenth century. Desperate, he called upon the Immaculate Virgin Mary for help, invoking her by a title no Dominican would ever normally use. Fifteenth-century Christians had been arguing strenuously with one another about whether Mary had been born, like her son Jesus, without sin, or as a normal human baby. The Dominicans were convinced that Mary had been born fully human and fallible, but the Franciscans and Augustinians insisted that she had been as pure as Christ from the very beginning, spotless – that is, "immaculate" – from the moment of her own conception by her parents Joachim and Anna. Magister Giovanni's prayer to the Virgin Immaculate tested the question by asking for a miracle, and the miracle took place. His terrible infection burst through his eardrum, Magister Giovanni began to recover, and on Christmas Eve of 1488 he made an official act of devotion, dedicating himself, body and soul, to the Immaculate Virgin Mary.[6]

Not everyone saw this sudden cure as a blessing, least of all Magister Giovanni's fellow Dominicans, for whom his combination of proven oratorical skills and new theological insight promised to make him a most inconvenient presence, a Dominican who favored the opposing side in a theological debate the order knew it was beginning to lose. His superiors interrogated him about the Immaculate Conception and he proved adamant in his newfound convictions, so they sent him into early retirement, returning him in spring of 1489 to Viterbo and his home convent of Santa Maria in Gradi. The transfer was an exile, but the city council of Viterbo made it a constructive exile, engaging Magister Giovanni to deliver a series of lectures on local history. Stubborn to the core, he continued to sign documents as "Iohannes Nannius, professor of theology."[7]

Although he claimed to know almost nothing about his city when he began, Magister Giovanni set to work on his new assignment as city historian with characteristic energy, and a remarkably wide-ranging idea of what might count as useful research.[8] Although his own training had been strictly traditional, running to the memorization of a demanding technical vocabulary, elaborate syllogisms, and long strings of questions and answers about Christian theology, metaphysics, and natural philosophy, the middle-aged friar knew that there were new educational philosophies afoot. In cities like Florence and Rome, the movement we know as humanism had begun to encourage new fields of endeavor, such as critical reading and comparison of ancient texts, a systematic study of ancient art and architecture, and an emphasis on a style of writing and speaking that drew its inspiration from the style of great classical orators like Cicero rather than the exhaustive precision of Scholastic learning. The University of Rome had introduced a humanist curriculum in the late 1460s (exactly when Nanni himself had begun teaching Scholastic theology in Viterbo), including courses on rhetoric and the beginnings of what would eventually be called archaeology.[9]

Giovanni Nanni may not have had a humanistic education himself, but he understood how the humanists worked, and began to use some of their methods himself. Like the students at the University of Rome who had begun to explore the ruins of the Imperial palace on the Palatine Hill, the Colosseum, and the Golden House of Nero, he examined Viterbo's buildings, streets, hills and bridges for clues to the past. At the same time he searched through the Dominican archive for early documents, and scoured the city's libraries to find books, both old and new, about Viterbo and its place in world history to add to the library of sources he had already amassed during his stay in Genoa.

Viterbo, as its citizens were well aware, had an important history of its own. For several decades in the thirteenth century, from 1257 to 1282, the city had housed the Pope and Curia, and had always served as an important base for military orders like the Knights Templar (before their suppression) and the Knights Hospitallers of St. John of Jerusalem and Rhodes – in fact, two decades after Giovanni Nanni's death, Viterbo would become the world headquarters for the Hospitallers of St. John, between their expulsion from Rhodes in 1522 and their definitive resettlement on Malta in 1530.

Strictly speaking, the Viterbo that Magister Giovanni and his fellow citizens knew, the bustling town with its scenic piazzas, impressive waterworks, and imposing city walls, had only existed since the early thirteenth century. In 1210 the first complete circuit of walls was erected in volcanic stone to enclose a series of separate settlements, each perched on its own distinct rocky outcrop, joining these scattered parishes (*pievi*) into a single community. The name "Viterbo" was a few centuries older than the town defined by that initial circuit wall: it first appeared on documents from the eighth century, but the eighth century was still well into the Middle Ages, an unimpressive millennium and a half after the foundation of Rome.[10] Magister Giovanni was convinced, however, that the center of Viterbo must have been settled as early as Rome itself; too many ancient artifacts had emerged from the soil for him to believe that the city had sprung up wholesale centuries after the fall of the Roman Empire. But that ancient city must have had another name.

Magister Giovanni's surviving writings show that his revisionist view of history developed gradually. He began by gathering together the information reported by ancient Greek and Latin writers and local chroniclers, comparing these textual sources with local names, recent archaeological discoveries, and the actual lay of the land, within the city limits of Viterbo and in its surrounding territories. His first concern, clearly, was to give his native city a respectable ancient pedigree, the older the better. For a fifteenth-century scholar there was no civilization more ancient than Egypt, thousands of years earlier than Greece, Etruria and Rome (more worryingly, the Egyptian king lists preserved in Greek writers like Manetho extended back beyond the traditional date for Creation). Happily for Viterbo, however, Magister Giovanni could report in 1491 that he had discovered the city's Egyptian roots. It had been founded as an Egyptian colony by Osiris and his nephew Italus Hercules with the name "Biturgion," an ancient title still echoed in the name of the little river, the Urcionio, that divided Viterbo in two until the 1930s.

Magister Giovanni's foundation myth may have been inspired in part by a tomb on the high altar of his own convent of Santa Maria in Gradi, adorned with a beautiful marble sphinx, signed and dated by the artist, Master Pasquale of Rome, in 1286 (Fig. 61.4). Several ancient Egyptian artifacts were on public display in thirteenth-century Rome, and Master Pasquale's figure is only one of several thirteenth-century sphinxes sculpted in a consciously antique style to decorate churches in the Eternal City and its environs. For many fifteenth-century scholars, artists, and architects, moreover, twelfth- and thirteenth-century works in the classical style were as important for inspiring their own designs as objects and monuments created a millennium earlier – in effect, these medieval, Romanesque works "counted" as classical antiquities.[11]

This Renaissance borrowing of Romanesque motifs stemmed from a certain broad-mindedness rather than ignorance about the past. The basic principles of classical design had not changed significantly before or after the advent of the Christian era; harmony, proportion, solid construction and human scale could be interpreted in various ways, but certain basic ideas about comfort and beauty provided working principles as durable as the law of gravity. Furthermore, in many ways Italian cities like Rome and Florence experienced a genuine classical revival in the late Middle Ages, with new urban layouts featuring long colonnaded streets, elaborately carved classical cornices, capitals, and friezes, statues and relief sculptures.[12] Thus Master Pasquale's crouching Sphinx may have dated from 1286, but the civilization it symbolized was older than Moses, and that fact must have been as clear in the late-thirteenth century to Master Pasquale and his patron Pietro di Vico as it was to Magister Giovanni two centuries later.

Very little information about Giovanni Nanni's public lectures in Viterbo survives, and some of what has survived is highly unflattering. But the friar also produced a short written history of Viterbo in 1491, a manuscript pamphlet dedicated to a local baron, Ranuccio Farnese, whose family kept a palazzo on the same hill as Viterbo's cathedral of San Lorenzo, incorporating an ancient Etruscan wall (still visible) and overlooking

Figure 61.4   Master Pasquale of Rome, *Sphinx*, signed and dated 1286, from the tomb monument to Giovanni Di Vico, Prefect of Rome, formerly in the church of Santa Maria in Gradi, Viterbo (destroyed during the Second World War by Allied bombs, 1944). Museo Civico, Viterbo. Photograph: Museo Civico, Viterbo.

an Etruscan bridge (also visible today).[13] This *Summary of the History of Viterbo (Viterbiae historiae epitoma)* focuses attention on the ancient city, but also on the surrounding territories that were of interest to the Farnese family, important feudal landlords.[14] Most importantly, in its few dozen pages Magister Giovanni presents his evidence that Viterbo was originally an Egyptian colony, founded by the great god Osiris, his son Libyus, nicknamed Hercules, and his son-in-law Italus:[15]

> When Osiris the Egyptian and his third son Libyus, nicknamed Hercules, his first son by his wife Isis, and Italus, nicknamed Atlas, his nephew by his cousin and close relative Corythus, established colonies, they entered this plain of ours, and chose it as the capital of Italy, as a place of delight, full of pleasantness and pleasure, supremely rich and suitable for every kind of human use; in this plain they founded this city of ours, which they called Biturgion, that is, "next to the flowing Urgion," and the Egyptians always called it by that name, as our illustrious Egyptian geographer Ptolemy agrees in his *Geography of Italy*.

The *Epitoma* proceeds with its roster of ancient heroes, tracing Viterbo's history through the rise and fall of the Roman Empire, the Middle Ages, and into the fifteenth century. It ends with words of high praise for Pope Innocent VIII, who died in 1492, the year after the *Epitoma* was written. But it was Innocent's successor, Alexander VI, the former Cardinal Rodrigo Borgia, who turned the renegade friar Magister Giovanni Nanni into the powerful, notorious Annius of Viterbo. It all happened because of a papal hunting expedition in October of 1493. Alexander's entourage was searching for rabbits in an area called Monte Cipollara, "Onion Hill," in the outskirts of Viterbo. When a rabbit disappeared into a hole in the ground, the Pope's retainers followed, and what they saw made them forget all about rabbits and hunting for the rest of the day. They had stumbled into an Etruscan tomb, filled with stone sarcophagi, and, still more excitingly, legible inscriptions. Word of the discovery spread quickly to Viterbo, and soon Pope and sarcophagi were entering the city in triumph. The sculpted coffins were put on display in the courtyard of Palazzo dei Priori, City Hall, where they probably sit today, though time and the elements have long since worn away their inscriptions (Fig. 61.5).

As Viterbo's local historian Magister Giovanni was quick to supply an explanation of this extraordinary find. In November 1493, one month after their discovery, he produced a pamphlet called *The Borgian Study (Borgiana Lucubratio)*, explaining that Monte Cipollara was not, in fact, "Onion Hill," but Mons Cybellarius, the mountain of the great mother goddess, Cybele. As for the sarcophagi, they were commemorative statues erected when Isis had come to visit Viterbo and happened on the wedding of the city's fifth king, Iasius Ianigena. The inscriptions celebrated the fact that she had used the occasion to bake Europe's very first loaf of bread.

With information like this to fire his imagination, the Pope seems to have decided that Magister Giovanni's talents were wasted in Viterbo. They seem to have kept in contact from 1493 onward, and in 1499 the Dominican was called to Rome to serve as Master of the Sacred Palace, chief theologian to the Pope. It was the third-highest position in the Dominican order, after Master General and Prior General. It is hard to imagine a more complete rehabilitation.

Contact with Rome expanded both Magister Giovanni's ambitions as a historian and his available resources. He sharpened his analytical tools to match the sophisticated

Figure 61.5   Etruscan sarcophagi in the courtyard of Palazzo Civico, Viterbo (formerly Palazzo dei Priori). Photograph: author.

scholarship of the curial staff. At the same time, his account of ancient history shifted its focus to satisfy new patrons, not only the Spanish pope, but also the Spanish sovereigns Ferdinand and Isabella. Magister Giovanni's scope became more international, and more keyed to a public of readers rather than listeners. In 1498, with the financial help of Ferdinand and Isabella, the papal printer Eucharius Silber published his latest book, an imposing quarto volume in Gothic typeface, with the title *Commentary on the works of Various Authors Speaking about Antiquities*.[16]

The compiler of this monumental tome no longer went by the title of Magister Iohannes Nannius. The Pope's theologian had changed his name to a much more impressive and ancient Iohannes Annius Viterbiensis, Annius of Viterbo. "Nanni" meant nothing more than "Johnson," but the ancient family of the Annii, as the new book revealed, had been an Etruscan dynasty of particular importance:[17] "The city of Etruria was both the native region of the early kingship and of the Annii Veri, an extremely ancient Etruscan family, adorned by the august Emperors Antoninus [Pius] and Commodus." Thus "Annius of Viterbo" was more than a pen name for the Master of the Sacred Palace: this Dominican of exceptional talents, exceptional bravery, and controversial opinions had taken on a whole new identity.

Nor was Annius the only protagonist of his tale to change names. The great city of Etruria, "native region of the early kingship" was his new title for Viterbo, and his latest work on the city showed that he had shifted his attention from its Egyptian founders to its long and important position at the center of an Etruscan Golden Age.

At the same time, however, Annius began to concentrate on the primeval history of Rome, and especially on the city's left bank, which lay on the Etruscan side of the traditional border that divided the Latins from the Etruscans. He also kept an attentive eye on the Vatican and the Spanish church of San Pietro in Montorio, set on the slopes of the Janiculum Hill, the outcrop that loomed over the Seven Hills across the river, and bore the name of Janus, the oldest of the Etruscan gods.[18]

Janus had always been a figure of particular interest in the Etruscan areas of Italy, the god who governed doors, openings, crossings, and beginnings, including the beginnings of civilization.[19] A twelfth-century guidebook to Rome, Peter the Deacon's *Graphia aureae urbis Romae* (*Map of the Golden City of Rome*), claimed that Janus was really the Biblical patriarch Noah, who had come to Italy after the Flood in order to replace its drowned population with the help of his wife, sons, and daughters-in-law.[20] In 1450, the Florentine humanist and architect Leon Battista Alberti credited "Father Janus" and the Etruscans with the invention of city walls, Doric architecture, and sculpture, all of these innovations developed in Italy long before the ancient Greeks ever set their hands to carving stone.[21] And during Viterbo's heyday in the thirteenth century as the home of the papacy, a local chronicler and curial official, Godfrey of Viterbo, identified Noah as the first king of Italy, succeeded by his son Janus.[22] Now Annius of Viterbo presented his own version of this complicated story. He agreed with Peter the Deacon that Janus had been Noah himself rather than Noah's son, basing his claim on a series of ancient texts he had collected during his time in Genoa, and a new series of archaeological finds to add to the repertory he mentions in his earlier writings.

This trenchant textual analysis represented a new horizon for Annius, and presumably reflects the influence of his Roman environment. Most of these newly discovered texts, like the fragments of Cato, the *Itinerary* of Antoninus Pius, the *Questions* of Xenophon, and the chronology of Berosus the Chaldaean were works mentioned by ancient authors, though no manuscripts had been known to survive of any of them (nor had Annius himself mentioned any such manuscripts in his earlier works). A few texts, like the chronicles of Metasthenes the Persian, were entirely unknown.

By 1498, Annius had also amassed an extensive collection of ancient inscriptions, in Greek, Latin, and Etruscan, some in marble, some in volcanic rock, some in alabaster, including one that glowed with a mysterious interior light. Three of these artifacts can still be seen on display in Viterbo's Civic Museum: two inscriptions on alabaster roundels and a carved marble stele that the good friar identified as a work of evident Egyptian manufacture.

Taken together, and analyzed in light of what the physical layout of Viterbo and Rome revealed about their urban history, this treasury of sources allowed Friar Annius to announce marvelous new revelations about the history of the whole world. This book, his masterwork, clearly contains material composed during his time in Viterbo as well as new material composed in Rome, with the result that its magnificent discoveries are sometimes inconsistent with one another. Just as often, however, these different kinds of evidence are interwoven with stunning ingenuity.[23]

If the chief concern of Magister Giovanni's Viterbo lectures had been to give that city a suitably ancient pedigree, the *Commentary* of Annius aims to provide the same favor for the papacy, an office he traces back, far beyond Saint Peter, to Janus, who is, of course, Noah by another name. If the Etruscans were famous throughout the ancient world for their devotion to religion, Annius showed, it was because they had been instructed in piety by their first king, Noah-Janus, and because of the Hebrew patriarch's nearness to God many Etruscan beliefs and rituals prefigured those of Christianity.

Here, as in his discussions of Viterbo, Annius was building on real traditions. Many trappings of the papacy do originate with Etruscan rituals, passed down to the Romans and absorbed by the Christians of the Roman Empire: the Pope's title *pontifex maximus*, supreme pontiff, is an ancient Roman priesthood that goes back to the period of Rome's

Etruscan domination. The bishop's crozier was an Etruscan priestly staff, the *lituus*, before it became a shepherd's crook. The Pope wears red shoes because Etruscan patricians wore red shoes, passing their privilege down to Roman Senators, who passed it in turn to Christian cardinals. Annius added plausible details: the keys of St. Peter, which symbolize the ability to do and undo all things in earth and heaven, were clearly the same keys as those of Janus, the god of doorways; hence Janus-Noah, not Peter, was the very first Pope. Noah drank too much because he was the inventor of wine – and Hebrew *yayin*, the word for wine, was obviously the same word as Janus.

He made flattering observations about his Spanish sponsors. The Borgia coat of arms featured a heraldic bull (originally it had been an ox, but the ambitious Rodrigo restored the beast's lost masculinity when he became a cardinal). Annius identified this creature as the sacred Apis bull of ancient Egypt, the reincarnation of Osiris, thus pushing the Borgia genealogy as far back in time as the founding of Viterbo. Spain itself was nearly as old, a colony founded by the same Egyptian Hercules, nephew of Osiris, who had helped his uncle establish Viterbo. Osiris, Isis, Egyptian Hercules, Noah-Janus and their relatives had been a race of giants; as the Bible said, "There were giants in those days."[24]

In Viterbo and Rome, Annius and his ideas captured people's imaginations so thoroughly that we can still see their effects today. The city seal of Viterbo still uses the four sacred letters, FAVL, by which he had identified its early, separate settlements: Fanum, Arbanum, Vetulonia, and Longula. In Rome, the Borgia Apartments, Pope Alexander's living quarters, still glitter with the paintings Bernardino Pinturicchio executed between 1492 and 1494. Alexander's successor, Julius II, loathed his predecessor, but he put equal faith in the tales of Janus and Noah – his favorite theologian, the Augustinian friar Egidio Antonini, was another native of Viterbo, and an enthusiastic follower of Annius. Michelangelo's Sistine Chapel ceiling begins its great chronicle of human salvation with the creation of the universe, and ends with three stories about Noah: the landing of the Ark, the drunkenness of Noah, and his sacrifice of thanksgiving, the precursors, according to Annius, of the Church, the sacramental wine, and the Mass.

Annius himself died on September 15, 1502, one year before his sponsor, Pope Alexander. One eighteenth-century author claimed that he had been poisoned by Cesare Borgia, though there is no contemporary evidence that this is so.[25] He may not have been well: a marginal note in one copy of his great book reports, "this man went insane twice and died in chains," that is, in the Renaissance equivalent of a straitjacket.[26]

The friar's ideas had never met universal approval. None of his surviving inscriptions, for instance, would convince a modern archaeologist that they are what Annius took them to be. The broken alabaster circle with the decree of Holy Roman Emperor Desiderius from the year 776 is carved in a curving script known as "Beneventan" that is otherwise known only in manuscripts (Fig. 61.6). The Egyptian stele combines two heads in bas relief and a sculpted vine; its original backing incorporated a grave marker inscribed in Hebrew and dated 1409, evidently removed from Viterbo's Jewish cemetery; this is now displayed separately (Fig. 61.7).[27] No one but Annius has ever reported seeing the inscription that glowed from within.

The literary texts preserved in his 1498 *Commentary* are equally dubious. Despite their varied age and varied authorship, they are remarkably uniform in their prose style, which in turn is extremely close to the style of the comments themselves. Skeptical readers like Erasmus began to suggest that Annius had written the whole compendium, from Berosus the Chaldaean to Fabius Pictor to Metasthenes the Persian.

Figure 61.6   "Desiderius decree," supposedly 776, probably circa 1493. Museo Civico, Viterbo.
Photograph: author.

Figure 61.7   "Egyptian" stele, pastiche made circa 1493. Photograph: author.

On the other hand, the inscriptions from Monte Cipollara were real Etruscan inscriptions, and Annius interprets their letters differently in his last book than he did in his initial study of 1493. Apparently, then, after producing the pamphlet that transformed his life, he made a genuine study of these genuine Etruscan texts, and began to make headway in reading them. By 1498, he had recognized that what looked like a letter "O" was a letter theta, and that the Etruscans must have pronounced the "o" sound as "u," so that Rome was pronounced "Ruma."[28] The word he had transcribed as "Laroal" in 1493 had become "Larthal" by 1498, and he knew that this, at least, was a genuinely Etruscan word. He decided that "Larth" must refer to the supreme leader of all the Etruscans (an office archaeologists now believe to have been called *zilath mechl rasnal*).[29] His analysis of Viterbo's historical topography is also based on genuine study of genuine evidence.

By the early sixteenth century, despite all the friar's careful claims to plausibility, many Italians believed that Annius of Viterbo was a forger, at the very least of the texts that appeared in his 1498 *Commentary*, and possibly of many of his artifacts as well. In 1636, the precocious young forger Curzio Inghirami subjected Annius to a thoroughgoing send-up in his own forged Etruscan texts, the "Volterran Antiquities."[30] And yet the last true believer in Annius of Viterbo lived well into the twentieth century. Mario Signorelli was the son of one of the city's most scrupulous historians, the lawyer Giuseppe Signorelli, who published his monumental *Viterbo nella Storia della Chiesa* in 1907. Mario, on the other hand, believed firmly in the full authenticity of Annius and his antiquities, and was confirmed in his convictions by mystical meetings with Etruscan ghosts.[31]

NOTES

1 1437 is the date that Annius supplies himself; see Fumagalli 195; 1432 is the date on his epitaph in Santa Maria Sopra Minerva in Rome; Roberto Weiss, "Traccia per una biografia di Annio da Viterbo," *Italia medioevale e umanistica* 5 (1962), 426.

2 Weiss, "Traccia," 427.

3 The undated *Pro Monte Pietatis*; Weiss, "Traccia," 430, 434.

4 Edoardo Fumagalli, "Aneddoti della vita di Annio da Viterbo, O.P., 1. Annio e la vittoria dei genovesi sui sforzeschi, 2. Annio e la disputa sull'Immacolata Concezione," *Archivum Fratrum Praedicatorum*, 50s (1980), 167–99.

5 *De futuris christianorum triumphis*; Weiss, "Traccia," 428–30.

6 Fumagalli, "Aneddoti," 189–191.

7 Giovanni Baffioni, *"Viterbiae Historiae Epitoma*: opera inedita di Giovanni Nanni da Viterbo," in Gigliola Bonucci Caporali, (ed.), *Annio da Viterbo, Documenti e ricerche*, Rome: Consiglio Nazionale delle Ricerche, 1981, 165.

8 Weiss, "Traccia," 430.

9 Charles Stinger, *The Renaissance in Rome*, Bloomington: Indiana University Press, 1985; revised edition 1998; Ingrid D. Rowland, *The Culture of the High Renaissance: Ancients and Moderns in Sixteenth-century Rome*, New York and Cambridge: Cambridge University Press, 1998.

10 Susanna Valtieri, *La genesi urbana di Viterbo e la crescita della città nel medioevo e nel '500*, Rome: Officina edizioni, 1977, 31–37.

11 Thus Filippo Brunelleschi modeled his arcades on the eleventh-century Baptistery of Florence; see Erwin Panofsky, *Renaissance and Renascences in Western Art*, New York: Harper and Row, 1969, 20–23.

12 Torgil Magnuson, *The Urban Transformation of Medieval Rome, 312–1420*, Stockholm: Paul Åströms Förlag, 2004.

13 Baffioni, *"Viterbiae Historiae Epitoma*," 11–254.

14 Baffioni, op. cit.

15 Cited in Baffioni, 78: "In tertio ineluctabilibus argumentis probavimus quotiens huius nostrae urbis variata sunt nomina et cognomina, et eius vetustissimam senectutem ab hac aetate ad Osirim Aegyptium et Italum, ipsius nepotem ex consobrino Ionico."

16 Iohannes Annius [Giovanni, Nanni, O.P.], *Commentaria...super opera diversorum auctorum de antiquitatibus loquentium*, Rome: Eucharius Silber, 1498.

17 Iohannes Annius, [Giovanni Nanni, O.P.], *Antiquitatum variarum volumina XVII a venerando et sacrae theologiae et praedicatorii ordinis professore Ioanni Annio*. Paris: Josse Bade and Jean Petit, 1512, reprinted 1515. This is the first paginated edition of the text, and is normally the one cited in footnotes. Because of the change in title between the first edition and the Parisian editions, the work is usually abbreviated as *Antiquitates*. Here the page is clxxiv recto.

18 Annius, *Antiquitates*, 3 verso: "Janus primam Etruriam regiam et Surrenam augustalem condidit."

19 Louise Adams Holland, *Janus and the Bridge, Memoirs of the American Academy in Rome*. Rome: American Academy in Rome, 1960.

20 Godfrey of Viterbo, *Pantheon sive Memoriae saeculorum*, published in J.-P. Migne, *Patrologiae Cursus Completus*, Vol. 198, Paris: J-P Migne Editeur, 1853, col. 1019:
Catalogus regum Italicorum
Italus, primus rex Italiae, regnavit annis quadraginta et uno
Janus, rex Italiae, regnavit annis viginti septem
Saturnus, rex Italiae, regnavit annis triginta quattuor
Picus, rex Italiae, regnavit annis triginta et uno
Faunus, rex in Laurento, id est in Sabinia provincia, regnavit annis viginti novem.

21 Ingrid D. Rowland, "Bramante's Hetruscan Tempietto," *Memoirs of the American Academy in Rome*, 51 (2006), 225–238

22 In Peter the Deacon's *Graphia aureae urbis Romae*, Janus is the son of Noah rather than the patriarch himself; Valentini and Zucchetti 1946, vol. III, 77–78: "Postquam filii Noë aedificaverunt confusionis turrem, Noë cum filiis suis ratem ingressus, ut Hescodius scribit, venit Ytaliam, et non longe ab eo loco ubi nunc Roma est, civitatem nominis sui construxit, in qua et laboris et vitae terminum dedit. Ianus vero filius, una cum Iano, filio Iapheth, nepote suo, et Camese indigena, civitatem Ianiculum construens, regnum accepit."

23 For Annius and his literary method, see Edoardo Fumagalli, "Un falso tardo-Quattrocentesco: lo pseudo-Catone di Annio da Viterbo," *Vestigia: Studi in onore di Giuseppe Billanovich*, (Rome: Edizioni di Storia e Letteratura, 1984), Vol. 1, 337–363; Christopher Ligota, "Annius of Viterbo and Historical Method," *Journal of the Warburg and Courtauld Institutes* 50 (1987), 44–56; Walter E. Stephens, Berosus Chaldaeus: *Counterfeit and Fictive Editors of the Fifteenth Century*, diss. Cornell University 1979; Anthony Grafton, *Forgers and Critics: Creativity and Duplicity in the Western World* (Princeton: Princeton University Press, 1980).

24 Walter E. Stephens, *Giants in Those Days: Folklore, Ancient History, and Nationalism*, Lincoln: University of Nebraska Press, 1989.

25 Weiss, "Traccia," 436, citing Apostolo Zeno, *Dissertazioni Vossiane*, Venice 1753, II. 92.

26 This copy of the 1515 edition of Annius is in Rome, Biblioteca Hertziana, Zn 500–1120 raro.

27 Brian Curran, "'De Sacrarum Litterarum Interpretatione.' Reticence and Hubris in Hieroglyphic Studies in the Renaissance: Pierio Valeriano and Annius of Viterbo," *Memoirs of the American Academy in Rome*, 43/44, 1999, 167–181.

28 See for example, *Antiquitates*, ix recto.

29 See, for example, *Antiquitates* clxix recto.

30 Ingrid D. Rowland, *The Scarith of Scornello: A Tale of Renaissance Forgery* (Chicago: University of Chicago Press, 2004).

31 Mario Signorelli, "Fra' Annio da Viterbo, umanista e storico," *Memorie domenicane*, n.s., vol. XLI, 1965, 102–112. Signorelli's Etruscan visions are recounted in *Il mondo allucinante degli etruschi*, Milan: SugarCo, 1977; *Colloqui con i perispiriti etruschi*, Rome: Edizioni Mediteranee, 1973.

CHAPTER SIXTY TWO

THE RECEPTION OF ETRUSCAN CULTURE: DEMPSTER AND BUONARROTI

——— •◆• ———

Francesco de Angelis

The publication of Thomas Dempster's treatise *De Etruria regali* in 1726, promoted by Thomas Coke and Filippo Buonarroti one century after the work had been composed, is an event that not only marks the rebirth of the interest for Etruscan antiquities in the eighteenth century, but also coincides with a more general renewal of antiquarianism in Tuscany and in Italy. This renewal does not simply occur on the scholarly level but has a strong political dimension. As the very title of the treatise suggests, its main aim is to affirm and celebrate the monarchic character of Etruria. The temporal distance separating the editors of the work from its author adds a further layer of complexity, since neither the intellectual nor the political conditions were the same in the seventeenth and in the eighteenth century. This chapter intends to jointly examine these aspects, all of which are important for our understanding of the genesis of Etruscan studies in the modern age.[1]

Thomas Dempster (1579–1625), a Scottish jurist and scholar, had composed the *De Etruria regali* upon commission of the Grand Duke of Tuscany Cosimo II de' Medici during his sojourn as professor of law in Pisa between 1616 and 1619, but he had left Tuscany before publishing it. The manuscript stayed in Florence where it was purchased in 1716 by the young Thomas Coke, future Earl of Leicester. Coke sent it back soon afterwards, entrusting Filippo Buonarroti (1661–1733), senator of the Grand Duchy and antiquarian, with the editorial work. The original text was articulated in seven 'Books': the first one treated the origins, the inhabitants, and the religion of Etruria; the second listed and discussed the Etruscan kings; in the third the inventions that could be attributed to the Etruscans were examined; Books 4–6 described the cities of Etruria, namely those that had not survived into the modern age (4), those still existing (5), and those founded after the fall of the Roman empire (6); and Book 7, finally, was a history of the Medici family through a series of short biographies. Buonarroti added to Dempster's text an apparatus of plates depicting Etruscan artifacts, both real and alleged. These plates required in turn a bulky appendix of *Explicationes et conjecturae* written by the senator himself.

The differences in method and scholarly approach between the two components of the final work are quite evident. While Dempster bases his analyses mainly on literary sources and textual criticism, Buonarroti focuses on artifacts and monuments, i.e. on material and visible evidence. Measured by current standards, Buonarroti appears more "advanced" than Dempster, almost like a forerunner of the modern discipline. The different uses that the two scholars made of their travel experiences are symptomatic in this respect. Buonarroti repeatedly made trips to the Etruscan countryside to explore ancient monuments, and even carried out excavations when possible, such as in Civita Castellana – ancient Falerii – in 1691. As for Dempster, the tour he made when writing his treatise in 1617 was significantly not to an ancient site but to England, in order to purchase books that were unavailable in Tuscany.[2] Equally eloquent are the divergences in their respective attitudes towards the monuments. Dempster almost never cites ancient remains in his descriptions of the cities of Etruria, the only exception being the Roman ruins of Florence, which he knows second-hand;[3] moreover, he is uninterested in the figural arts. By contrast, as to be expected from a descendant of Michelangelo, Buonarroti is not only interested in iconography and the materiality of objects, but also displays a keen sensitivity for stylistic features: on more than one occasion he dates objects based on their degree of formal development.[4]

Despite these differences, Buonarroti himself does not conceive his relationship to Dempster in terms of contrast but rather of complementarity. When talking of his predecessor, he does not present him as the representative of a superseded method but rather as an earlier colleague.[5] Nor is Buonarroti's approach invariably "progressive." As regards traveling, for example, it is significant that Buonarroti's archaeological tours all took place in an earlier period, when he was residing in Rome at the service of cardinal Carpegna, and that the publication of the *De Etruria regali* with its appendix did not entail any new investigation of the Tuscan territory. The illustrated plates are emblematic of the ambivalences in the relationship between the two components of the work: on the one hand, they are distributed among the pages of Dempster's text, which of course makes no reference to them; on the other hand, they are explicitly referenced in Buonarroti's appendix, which is, however, structured according to a different order than Demspter's text. As a result, the images are quite cumbersome to consult, as contemporary reviewers had already remarked.[6] In other words, the eighteenth-century publication of the *De Etruria regali* has clear transitional connotations.

It would be a mistake to understand this transition in teleological terms, as a gradual approximation to our own standards. In order to avoid this risk, the focus needs to shift from methodology to the broader visions of the Etruscan past developed by Dempster and Buonarroti, and specifically to their diverging ways of characterizing Etruscan identity and relating it to the political sphere.

The pivotal aspect of Dempster's whole endeavor clearly is the regal character of Etruria. This is not coincidental: the *De Etruria regali* is the culmination of a long elaboration process of the so-called "Etruscan myth" that played a crucial role in defining the ideology of grand ducal power in Tuscany since the Renaissance.[7] Dempster's work is the most systematic treatment aimed at legitimizing the Medici's hegemony and the autonomy of their state based on the ancient history of the region. Despite its courtly nature, however, Dempster's work is not the outcome of a banal operation. Dempster addresses the issue of Etruria's regality in such a way that it cannot be reduced to the mere celebration of the ruling dynasty; and some of his ideas have genuine historiographic value. For example, he refuses to acknowledge the antiquity of noble families when it is not supported by documentary evidence, and he does not make an exception for the Medici, about whom he writes: "Their antiquity is quite modest, of about 600 years, if we believe public records."[8] He mentions a possible etymological connection between the Medici's family name and the Etruscan (in fact, Italic) magistracy of the *meddix* only to underscore its conjectural nature.[9] Likewise, despite the treatise's ideological agenda, Dempster does not at all minimize Etruria's subjugation by the Romans. On the contrary, he uses it to reflect on the causes of the interruption of royal power in Etruria and attributes it to civic discord, that is, the lack of solidarity among Etruscan cities.[10]

Dempster's historical sensitivity does not imply that his approach to the past is an innovative one. On the contrary, even the traits just mentioned only acquire their sense within a typical seventeenth-century framework – and this is all the more true for Dempster's treatment of Etruscan regality. The initial part of Book 2 is in fact devoted to demonstrating the existence and the importance of a unified monarchic regime in Etruria, against those scholars who maintained that the region had only been ruled by aristocrats; and the rest of the book mainly consists of lists of alleged Etruscan kings and dynasties.[11] Even though Dempster criticizes predecessors such as the notorious fifteenth-century forger Annio da Viterbo, most of the names he gives are spurious, too. Moreover, he does not understand ancient and modern regality to be substantially different: in more than one passage he draws direct parallels between Etruscan dynasties and later ones.[12] He is aware of the paucity of mentions of Etruscan kings in the Latin sources, but he attributes this feature to the hostility of the Romans towards the Etruscans.[13]

The guiding principle of Dempster's historiographic vision is continuity.[14] This is particularly evident in Books 4–6, where the cities of Etruria are treated one by one. Significantly, the initial part of Book 4 is still global in character and describes the final Etruscan defeat in the battle of lake Vadimo (283 BCE) and the organization of the Roman province. With the ensuing treatment of the individual cities the emphasis shifts from history to geography. The historical nature of the account is not dismissed but gets split into the histories of the different cities, as if once the region had lost its independence and Etruscan kingship had ceased to exist it did not make any sense to follow its vicissitudes from a unitary point of view. Dempster's choice is driven by a quite perceptive concept of Tuscan history, according to which its protagonists are the single cities – they are the actual carriers of the continuity of Etruscan identity from the past to the present. This fragmented identity gets reunified in Book 7 that focuses on the ruling dynasty, the Medici. Etruria's identity for Dempster is therefore something that allows a multiplicity of dimensions and is articulated differently according to circumstances. On the one hand this characteristic allows him to adapt the treatise to the complexity of the topic, on the other hand, it provides the latter with a protean quality, so that the definition of Etruria can be expanded or restricted according to need. This is especially visibile as regards the relationship with Rome: the role that Dempster accords to the Romans to define a sense of "Etruscanness" by way of opposition is not carried out consistently throughout the treatise; the Roman origins of Florence, for example, do not prevent him from celebrating this city in Book 6, alongside the other still existing Etruscan centers. Nor is it by chance that the process of Romanization is only acknowledged for its institutional aspects – the passage of the region from a monarchic regime to provincial status – but does not appear to have consequences on the Etruscan character of Etruria even after antiquity in Dempster's eyes.

This weak definition of what is Etruscan clearly originates in the official ideology propagated by the Grand Dukes. The *De Etruria regali* is not only the culmination but also the endpoint of the Etruscan myth – it is not coincidental that the treatise remained unpublished for over a century. When Coke and Buonarroti started working on the publication, the political conditions had changed dramatically. The problem of the autonomy of the Tuscan state in the wake of the impending end of the Medici dynasty after Cosimo III and his successor Gian Gastone had become a burning issue. The publication of Dempster's treatise can be seen as part of a broader trend of interest in their own past by the Tuscan élites: as in the case of the coeval editions of sixteenth-century Florentine historians, this interest was due to a sense of uncertainty that led them to look back to the past in order to draw orientation principles for the present and the future.[15] The issue of Etruria's identity acquired a different flavor in this context. This is especially visible in Buonarroti's appendix. Other than Dempster, Buonarroti explicitly thematizes and discusses the question of what is Etruscan. At the same time, however, he applies it not to the history of the region in its entirety or to its cities, but exclusively to the artifacts. Apparently, the issue has lost its political connotations. As Buonarroti states at the very beginning of the appendix, he wants to identify objects that are undoubtedly Etruscan.[16] His aim, then, is both narrower and more specific – more specialized – than Dempster's one. To this effect he employs a whole array of criteria that range from the findspots of the artifacts to their inscriptions, and from style and decorative patterns to iconographic peculiarities.[17] The fact that not all of his conclusions are correct – for example, he believes he can prove that the vases found in the tombs of Italy are not Greek but Etruscan – does not diminish the relevance of his endeavor. For the first time the issue of the Etruscan origins of the artifacts found on Etruscan ground is pursued in a way that is not occasional or desultory. This attitude leads Buonarroti to quite remarkable insights, such as the following:

> It is likely that many Etruscan donaries and votive objects still exist but are hidden, as it were, among those innumerable statuettes that are found everywhere in Etruria and pertain to both the sacred and the domestic sphere, represent human beings as well as animals, and are made of either bronze or terracotta. I am thinking especially of the terracotta ones that were dug up few years ago near Viterbo and are kept in the collection of the most excellent cardinal Gualtieri. Since they bear no inscriptions, it is uncertain whether they pertain to the old Etruscans or to the more recent ones (*incertum an Etruscorum antiquorum sint, an potius recentiorum*), that is, those who converted to the Roman customs after the deduction of colonies and the attainment of Roman citizenship.[18]

As this passage shows, the focus on the objects has led Buonarroti to almost inadvertently raise and address a crucial theme such as that of the cultural Romanization of Etruria. In other words, Buonarroti identifies and expresses in clear terms the issue of identity that Dempster never defined once and for all. The most relevant consequence of this sharper focus is that the leading historiographic criterium for Buonarroti becomes distance rather than continuity. This is nowhere more evident than with regard to the issue of regality. Other than Dempster, Buonarroti thinks that the Etruscan cities were ruled by magistrates and that there was no unified monarchic state.[19] However, he does not criticize his predecessor; rather, he ignores him. Despite appearances, this lack of interest in the issue that had been at the core of Dempster's project does not imply that the character of the eighteenth-century enterprise was basically apolitical. On the contrary, the very editorial format of the *De Etruria regali* displays a clear awareness of some of the most urgent issues of contemporary politics, in particular that of succession. The two volumes into which the work is divided came out in 1726 but are dated to 1723 and 1724, so that each of them is dedicated to the then ruling Grand Duke, respectively Cosimo III (who died on 31 October 1723) and Gian Gastone. The two frontispieces with the ruler's name, the two portraits following each of them, Thomas Coke's distinct prefatory epistles addressing Cosimo III and Gian Gastone – everything contributes to emphasize and visualize at the very outset of the treatise the wish for an orderly transition from one Medici to the next. All the same, Buonarroti must have been aware that asserting Etruscan regality in a scholarly work was not sufficient to preserve the autonomy of the Grand Duchy; and indeed, shortly before Buonarroti's death in 1733, when Gian Gastone was still ruling, the Spanish troops accompanying the designated successor Don Carlos entered into Leghorn. Buonarroti's use of the past for present purposes was more subtle, and focused on practice rather than on content. In fact, it is the very engagement with Etruria's history, regardless of the specific nature of its ancient political regime, that allowed a redefinition of the Tuscan élites as *cultural* élites, who through their erudite interests would grant the continuity of Etruscan identity even after the Medici's demise and thereby open a new chapter in the study of the Etruscans.

NOTES

1 Main bibliography on Dempster and Buonarroti: Cristofani 1983; Gallo 1986; Leighton and Castelino 1990; Marchesano 2002; de Angelis 2009; Gialluca and Reynolds 2009.
2 See Cristofani 1978: 583–585; Leighton and Castelino 1990: 347.
3 Dempster 1726: vol. 2, p. 363.
4 See, for example, Buonarroti 1726: 74, 75–76, 108–109.
5 Buonarroti 1726: 3.
6 S. Maffei, *Osservazioni letterarie*, vol. 3, Verona: J. Vallarsi, 1738, pp. 241–242.
7 Cipriani 1980.
8 Dempster 1726. vol. 2, p. 453; see also *ibid.*, p. 451–453; vol. I, p. 210.
9 Dempster 1726: vol. 2, p. 462.
10 Dempster 1726: vol. 1, p. 226; see also *ibid.*, p. 106, 218–219; vol. 2, p. 4
11 Dempster 1726: vol. 1, pp. 106–111
12 Dempster 1726: vol. 1, p. 105, 117, 136, 190.
13 Dempster 1726: vol. 1, p. 103, 142, 160, 194, 227, 319, 335.
14 Dempster 1726: vol. 1, p. 104, 298.
15 Verga 1990: 13–45; Verga 1999: 130–131.
16 Buonarroti 1726: 4–5.
17 Buonarroti 1726: 16–17, 18, 26, 34–35, 43.
18 Buonarroti 1726: 35, 75; see also Demspter 1726: vol. 1, p. 281 note 1. For examples of such objects, see Chapters 54 and 57.
19 Buonarroti 1726: 21, 53, 78–79.

BIBLIOGRAPHY

Buonarroti, F. (1726) "Explicationes et conjecturae" in Dempster (1726), vol. 2.
Cipriani, G. (1980) *Il mito etrusco nel rinascimento fiorentino*, Florence: L. S. Olschki.
Cristofani, M. (1978) "Sugli inizi dell' 'etruscheria.' La pubblicazione del 'De Etruria regali' di Thomas Dempster," *Mélanges de l'École Française de Rome. Antiquité*, 90: 577–62; reprinted in *La scoperta degli Etruschi. Archeologia e antiquaria nel '700* (1983), Rome: CNR, pp. 13–43.

de Angelis, F. (2009) "L'Etruria regale, da Dempster a Buonarroti. Ricerca antiquaria e attualità politica in Toscana fra Sei e Settecento," *Rivista Storica Italiana* 121: 497–542.

Dempster, T. (1726) *Thomae Dempsteri De Etruria regali libri VII nunc primum editi curante Thoma Coke*, vols. 1–2, Florentiae: Typis Regiae Celsitudinis apud Joannem Cajetanum Tartinium et Sanctem Franchium.

Gallo, D. (ed.) (1986) *Filippo Buonarroti e la cultura antiquaria sotto gli ultimi Medici*, Florence: Cantini; Leighton and Castelino, 1990.

Gialluca, B. and Reynolds, S. (2009) "Il manoscritto Holkham Hall Ms 809 e la genesi del *De Etruria regali*. Novità e conferme," *Symbolae Antiquariae* 2: 19–60.

Leighton, R. and Castelino, C. (1990) "Thomas Dempster and Ancient Etruria: A Review of the Autobiography and 'De Etruria Regali'," *Papers of the British School at Rome*, 58: 337–352.

Marchesano, L. (2002) "Antiquarian Modes and Methods. Bellori and Filippo Buonarroti the Younger", in J. Bell and T. Willette (eds), *Art History in the Age of Bellori*, Cambridge: Cambridge University Press, pp. 75–93.

Verga, M. (1990) *Da "cittadini" a "nobili." Lotta politica e riforma delle istituzioni nella Toscana di Francesco Stefano*, Milano: Giuffrè.

——(1999) "La cultura. Dai Medici ai Lorena" in *Storia della civiltà toscana*, vol. 4, Florence: Le Monnier, pp. 125–151.

CHAPTER SIXTY THREE

MODERN APPROACHES TO
ETRUSCAN CULTURE

——— ·◆· ———

Marie-Laurence Haack

ETRUSCAN MYTH IN THE RENAISSANCE

The rediscovery of Etruscan culture in modern times dates back to the mid-nineteenth century when a movement for the promotion of the ancient past occurred. It was motivated both by scholarly curiosity for all things Etruscan and by a political will to appropriate the prestige of a brilliant civilization. Reminding citizens of the Etruscan past was first used by the Florentine Republic, at a time when it had designs on the neighboring cities; Tuscany was depicted as the most ancient cradle of Republican liberty: in that sense, it can be described as an "Etruscan myth".[1] The Florentine chronicler, G. Villani, in his *Nuova Cronica*, and the Florentine chancellor, L. Bruni, in his *Historiarum Florentini populi libri XII*, extolled an autochthonous Etruria that was independent from Rome. With the stranglehold of the Medici on local power in the fifteenth century, Etruria was then considered in its monarchic aspect. L. B. Alberti, in his *De re aedificatoria* (1485), prefaced with a dedication by Angelus Politianus to Lorenzo the Magnificent, mentioned the "admirable things that were said about the Etruscan kings." Among the Etruscan kings, the first to be taken into account is Porsenna. L. B. Alberti, B. Peruzzi and the Sangallo brothers, basing themselves on an account given by Varro and passed on by Pliny the Elder,[2] reconstructed his extraordinary monumental tomb with a maze.

The Dominican monk, G. Nanni, who called himself Annio da Viterbo, in his *Antiquitatum variarum* (1498), went so far as to assert the religious primacy of Tuscans on Romans (*see* Chapter 61). Thus he claimed to have found passages by ancient historians enabling him to reconstruct Etruscan history. In them the Etruscans were described as the first inhabitants of the world after the Flood, the heirs to a Janus-Hercules taken to Tuscany by Noah and initiated to the rites and the doctrine of ancient Jews. From the late fifteenth century onwards, the discovery of Etruscan vestiges launched a fashion for the Etruscans. Tarquinia's funeral chambers were discovered during the pontificate of Innocent VIII (1484–1492), large sarcophagi were brought to light near Viterbo in 1493, and then the "tomb of the she-mule" near Sesto Fiorentino in 1494, the hypogaeum of Castellina in Chianti in 1507, and numerous Arretine vases were found. Florentine patricians developed a taste for Etruscan vases, urns and statuettes. Artists started to adopt Etruscan motifs. The Pollaiuolo brothers reproduced in painting *putti* wearing garlands around their necks, fights between lions, fights between dragons and hunting scenes.

Lorenzo the Magnificent is described as being offered four "Etruscan" vases that were found in the course of excavations carried out in Arezzo. In the sixteenth century, the Medici having been driven out of Florence once again and the Republic restored and Pope Leo X, son of *Il Magnifico*, having a passion for Etruscan archaeology turned the Etruscans into his objective allies when his family returned to Florence. During the Roman ceremonies organized in 1513 to bestow the title of Roman citizen on Giuliano de Medici and Lorenzo de Medici, the idea of a cooperation between the Roman and Etruscan peoples in the service of the monarchic ideal embodied by the Tarquins was glorified. At that time, Etruria played an even more significant role under the reign of Cosimo I (1537–1574), because three exceptional bronze statues were discovered in Arezzo: the Minerva (1552), the Chimaera (1553) and the *Arringatore* (1566). Cosimo I immediately claimed the Chimaera and after its restoration by B. Cellini showed it to the public in the Leo X room of the *Palazzo Vecchio*. He thus revived the mythical Etruria in the guise of the Principate at the very time when he was gaining control of the Sienese State. G. Vasari, a propagandist of Cosimo's power, gave the statue of the Chimaera the value of a political symbol: in his *Ragionamenti* (1567), he compared Cosimo to Bellerophon and to Leo X, who through his liberality, subjugated all men as we are reminded by the frescoes of the very Vasari, in the eponymous room where the Chimaera was exhibited. Cosimo, heir of the two heroes, also tamed a chimera himself, namely the Florentines who felt nostalgic for the republican regime, which was blamed for arousing civil discord. The statue of the Chimaera also gave rise to speculation on the "Tuscan style" in art. In *Le Vite de' più eccellenti pittori, scultori e architettori* (1568), Vasari defined the "Tuscan style" by its realistic and dramatic treatment of the subject and by the adoption of a sophisticated posture. Men of letters worked to relate the story of Etruscan origins within a Florentine Academy founded by Cosimo in 1541. In 1546, Giambullari published *Il Gello*, a work officially approved by the Academy and dedicated to Cosimo. He used the same framework as Annio da Viterbo: he made the Florentine language derive from the Etruscan, which like Hebrew supposedly had Aramaic as its matrix.

In 1551, G. Postel published *Des origines, institutions et mœurs de la région d'Etrurie* in Florence, the first synthesis on knowledge about Etruria. Then, despite the lack of new discoveries and criticism of Annio's and Postel's Etruscan theories, Etruscan descent became a subject of major importance in political propaganda. In 1569, Cosimo had the Pope recognize the title of grand duke and had Etruscan descent mentioned in the title. M.-A. Muret, a French humanist at the court of Pius V, thus celebrated Cosimo as *Dux Magnus Etruscus*, the third one to hold the title after Janus and Porsenna. Ferdinando de Medici who built the villa Medici in 1576, rivaled his father's model resting on the exaltation of the figure of Augustus by having the gardens laid out as an Etruscan tumulus. The presence of underground galleries may allude to King Porsenna's labyrinthine tomb. In 1589, on the occasion of Ferdinando's wedding feast, a painting by J. Ligozzi, placed above the entrance to *Palazzo Vecchio*, showed Cosimo I crowning a woman who represents Tuscany while on her side King Porsenna holding a broken crown in his hands, ancient Etruria's crown, once worn by the king of Chiusi, a crown that was lost and that Ferdinando, in his turn, is about to receive in the name of his ancestors.

Interest for Etruscan culture faded away but it came back with a vengeance in the seventeenth century thanks to the influence of the Medici. Between 1616 and 1619, upon the request of Cosimo I, the Scottish humanist T. Dempster, professor of law at the University of Pisa, wrote a monograph in seven books on the Etruscans, *De Etruria regali* (*see* Chapter 62). Eventually, the book was published in two volumes in Florence, between 1720 and 1726, and then dedicated to Cosimo III and his successor, Gian Gastone de Medici, at the time when the dynasty, in steep decline, was attempting to strengthen its hand by insisting on its so-called Etruscan origins. The manuscript caught the attention of Sir T. Coke, an English nobleman, who brought it back from his grand tour in Italy; it was then sent back to Florence and, thanks to Coke's money, published by F. Buonarroti, a Florentine and a descendant of Michelangelo who took charge of the 93 plates illustrating Etruscan monuments known at the time. The published book turned out to be scholarly after all, thanks to Dempster, who divided it into sections on the customs, the history, the inventions and the cities that have vanished. Dempster did the real work of a philologist, while not questioning the validity of ancient literary sources, since he took up again the idea of Etruscan indigenous identity aired by Dionysius of Halicarnassus and underlined the difference between Etruscan and the other languages of the ancient world. He did not believe in the idea of an Aramaic origin for Etruscan, an idea supported by Annio da Viterbo and by Giambullari.

COLLECTIONISM IN THE EIGHTEENTH CENTURY

We then go from a simple description to a systematic and reasoned inventory of antiquities that reminds us of the work of B. de Montfaucon, *L'Antiquité expliquée et représentée en figures* (1719–1724), which made up a real encyclopedic book and in which, the language problem was treated as distinct from the script problem for the first time. The publication of Dempster's work gave impetus to a whole movement of collecting and Etruscomania fueled by new excavations, new collections and as a result, theoretical treatises on every aspect of Etruscan history, art and civilization. New collections were assembled, a thriving antiquities market developed, notables wanted their curio cabinet and real private museums were created.

In Volterra, Mario Guarnacci (1701–1785) gathered a collection chiefly made up of urns discovered in the city and the surroundings. The abbot published three volumes of *Origini italiche*, from 1767 to 1772, a highly scholarly work on the mythical and historical origins of the first peoples who lived in the Italian Peninsula. In this work, Guarnacci asserted the primacy of Etruscans who were supposed to have represented the first hotbed of civilization in Italy. He wanted to show that arts and sciences were not imported from Greece to Italy but exported from Italy to Greece. He reproached the Romans for being ungrateful to the Etruscans even though they owed them their laws, their arts, their monuments and their rites. In the same manner in the second half of the eighteenth century, in France, the Count of Caylus gathered a huge collection, which was published in seven volumes: *Recueil d'antiquités égyptiennes, étrusques, grecques, romaines et gauloises*; it was published in Paris between 1752 and 1767, and Sir W. Hamilton, British ambassador at the court of Naples, took advantage of his stay in Italy to assemble two big collections of Greek vases found in Campania that were described as Etruscan in their publication by P. F. d'Hancarville, *Antiquités étrusques, grecques, et romaines tirées du cabinet de M. Hamilton à Naples*, 1766–1767. So, under Hamilton's influence, an "Etruscan taste" was born in

England. It spread to wall and crockery decoration. In 1769, Josiah Wedgwood created a new factory of decorative vases in Burslem in Staffordshire, it was called the Etruria works, and shortly before 1768, he developed a fine-grained black stoneware he described as "Etruscan." Under the name of *Artes Etruriae renascuntur*, series of "Etruscan" vases were made, their decoration inspired by the Hamilton collection, but most of them were imitations of Greek art, not Etruscan art. The Adam brothers created an "Etruscan room" (1775–1777) for Osterley Park, an Elizabethan mansion on the outskirts of London.

In France, Jean-Jacques Lagrenée made tumblers with Etruscan handles and saucers of Marie-Antoinette's service, for the dairy of Versailles. Academies and learned societies multiplied, such as the Etruscan Academy of Cortona, founded in 1726 by a Cortona patrician, O. Baldelli, who owned a collection open to all scholars and who thus favored the development of Etruscan studies. Every year, it elected its president who was conferred the Etruscan title of *lucumon*; twice a month, the academicians, called "the very scholarly and famous associates," met during the "Cortona nights" and read "academic essays," published between 1738 and 1795, covering all the Etruscology subjects studied at the time: origins, language, alphabet, relations with Hebrews, Lydians and Egyptians. In 1750, it opened one of the first public collections. The Tuscan Academy of Science and Letters "La Colombaria" was created in 1735 in Florence by A. F. Gori, a scholar in the tradition of Florentine antiquarians, who published *Museum Etruscum* in Florence in three volumes, from 1737 to 1743, when he published inscriptions found in Etruria. Indeed, Gori collected Greek, Latin, Etruscan inscriptions, tracings and drawings. They were used in particular to support his theories on the place of Etruscans. They were published in the three volumes of *Inscriptiones antiquae in Etruriae urbibus existantes*, and in *Difesa dell'alfabeto degli antichi toscani*.

After this, collections and research developed outside the territory of ancient Etruria. In Verona, the Marquis S. Maffei gathered the important collections of *Museum Maffeianum*, and published them in his *Museum Veronense* in 1749. For many of those collectors, for whom Greek easily became Etruscan and Roman became Greek, the enthusiasm of discovery was a universal excuse, which lasted until the publication in 1789 by the Jesuit abbot, Luigi Lanzi, deputy keeper of the gallery of antiquities of Florence, of a book that revolutionized Etruscology. In *Saggio di lingua etrusca e di altre antiche d'Italia* Lanzi correctly interpreted almost the whole alphabet, and put the precise role and relation of Etruscans with Roman civilization and especially Greek civilization back in its context. He understood that a good many vases described as Etruscan were in fact Greek, a revolutionary idea at the time, and that they were made to order by Greeks. He made an inventory of 500 Etruscan inscriptions.

IDEAL OF AN ETRUSCAN SCIENCE IN THE NINETEENTH CENTURY

Through the rigor of his reasoning and through the widening of historical perspectives, Lanzi's work launched "scientific" Etruscology. It developed slowly in the nineteenth century. The attempt at a critical examination of sources was thus carried on by G. Micali in 1810 in *L'Italia avanti il dominio dei Romani*, in which he tried to bring out the specific contribution of the peoples Roman civilization had originally taken over, but the book was considered as an anti-Bonapartist pamphlet and, in the course of the century, because of its anti-Roman bias it became one of the bibles of the *Risorgimento* and was met with the opposition of the Germans who, following Niebuhr, made the Etruscans a Northern people and placed the cradle of their race in Tyrol.

At first, direct surveys of Etruria's territory multiplied. Wealthy amateurs directed excavation sites in southern Italy and in Etruria and marketed their finds. First, the Chevalier Edmond-Antoine Durand (1768–1835), thanks to several stays in the Italian peninsula, gathered bronzes, pieces of pottery, mirrors, arms etc., which the Louvre acquired in 1825. But systematic and large-scale excavations carried out from 1828 by Lucien Bonaparte, Prince of Canino (1775–1840), second brother of Napoleon I, were unquestionably the most productive. After the fall of the Empire in 1815, Lucien Bonaparte indeed devoted himself to archaeology and the excavations he carried out in the Etruscan necropoleis of Vulci, Corneto and Canino revealed between 15 and 20,000 vases which enabled him to overcome some financial difficulties, especially by organizing several major sales in 1834, 1837, 1838 and 1840. Conducted in an empirical way, the excavations supplied the art market and nourished the inspiration of artists and creators of the time. The vases of the Durand and Canino collections were irreparably scattered around the world: they were bought by major European museums Paris, London, Munich, Berlin but also by a new generation of wealthy collectors eager to put together an amateur cabinet for themselves.

In those years, the Campanari family, living in Tuscania, became famous for its archaeological discoveries in Veii, Vulci and Tuscania, and in their collection the Campanari possessed dozens of Etruscan sarcophagi found in those cities. In 1837, they organized an exhibition of Etruscan sarcophagi (placed in the decor of recreated tombs) in London in the West End district, at 121 Pall Mall. They came above all from Tuscania, and on this occasion were called "the city of Etruscan sarcophagi." After seeing the exhibition, G. Dennis decided to go to Italy, to Tuscania, to *see* the Campanari garden that had been turned into a small necropolis with the sarcophagi of the Vipinanas. In 1839, in their house at Toscanella, the Campanari faithfully reconstructed a *semidado* tomb where they had already placed the sarcophagi of the Vipinanas tomb (24 sarcophagi) discovered in the Calcarello necropolis. We owe them, among other discoveries, that of the Campanari tomb (1833) in Vulci, that of the *Statlanes* and the *Vipinanas* in Tuscania.

Foreigners were not outdone, for Italy occupied the place of choice in their grand tour. E. C. Hamilton-Gray gave an account of her visits in *Tour to the Sepulchres of Etruria* (1839). But above all, we should mention G. Dennis who, with his friend, artist Samuel James Ainsley, wrote *Cities and Cemeteries of Etruria*, published in 1848 by the British Museum, the fruit of field trips made in Etruria between 1842 and 1844; it is a sort of guide with lyrical evocations of Etruscan landscapes. It opened up the exclusive scholarship of the "cabinets" to adventure, to new horizons.

Scientists, travelers, local owners, amateurs, treasure hunters went all over the still-wild regions of Etruria, infringing legal limits. This was the case of Marquis Giampietro Campana di Cavelli, a passionate collector, who started excavation in Cerveteri and Veii and bought sculptures, terracotta ware, jewels, bronzes, paintings almost 15,000 works in total! In 1846, when the new Pope, Pius IX, visited his collection in the city of Campana the reputation of the collection was confirmed. He piled up his collections in Roman palaces but he lived in grand style and his fortune was swallowed up. Living on his fame, he ran up debts, and he was arrested in 1857. The Marquis' collections were seized and put up for sale by the papal government. On April 28th, 1859, he ceded his collection to the papal government. In 1861, Russia bought 467 pieces including ancient vases, statues and jewels. Finally, Napoleon III decided to buy all of the remaining collections, some 11,835 objects and 646 paintings. By imperial decree, the Campana collection was bought by France in 1861. The Campana collection left Italy to occupy the Palace of Industry in Paris, inaugurated in 1853, but, victim of jealousies and diverse schemes, the establishment rapidly closed its doors. In 1862, Napoleon III decided to share out the collection according to its content between the Louvre and the provinces of France.

It was the end of *etruscheria* and the beginning of the takeover of data on the Etruscans by scholars and institutions. In 1877, K. O. Müller's book on the Etruscans (*Die Etrusker*, Göttingen, 1828) was published at almost the same time as the second or the third edition of the first volume of Niebuhr's Roman history, and it was later revised and updated by W. Deecke (*Die Etrusker*, Stuttgart, 1877). It met the demands of savants and students, by presenting Etruscan influence on Roman political and religious institutions and showing the Etruscans as stemming from a mixture said to be between a Nordic population, the *Rasenna*, and an Eastern population, the *Tyrrheni*.

ETRUSCOLOGY AND EUROPEAN NATIONS IN THE TWENTIETH CENTURY

But the real birth of Etruscology was mainly the result of the chance discovery, between 1914 and 1920, of fragments of monumental statues in Veii. These statues, which did not fit the patterns of classical art, suddenly promoted Etruscan art to the rank of art that is original and timeless, art that is quite different from the provincial and minor art it had seemed to embody thus far in relation to the canons of classical Greek art. This viewpoint, inherited from J. J. Winckelmann, could be explained by the importance granted at the time to artistic personalities. Veian statues changed the point of view: they were thought to be the work of the Etruscan sculptor, Vulca, and their originality is interpreted through the prism of modern and African art. Thanks to the art historians R. Bianchi Bandinelli and G. Kaschnitz-Weinberg who discussed the cubist and expressionist character of the so-called bust of Brutus, the anti-classical character of Etruscan works began to be appreciated. This reappraisal had repercussions on overall research on the Etruscans. After art, the Etruscan language was considered for itself.

Recognizing Etruscan originality encouraged Etruscologists to make their discipline independent by giving it scientific legitimacy. The organization of conferences and the publication of a scientific journal contributed to the creation of university chairs of Etruscology. A. Minto, superintendent of Antiquities of Etruria, thanks to funding granted by the Director of the bank *Monte dei Paschi di Siena*, turned the *Ente per le attività toscane*, operating in Florence, into a *Comitato Permanente per l'Etruria*. In 1925, he became chairman of this committee to promote and coordinate all the initiatives on Etruscan civilization. This was instrumental in the founding of a journal exclusively devoted to Etruscology, *Studi Etruschi,* whose publication began in 1927. In 1926, the year when the first *Convegno nazionale etrusco* was held in Florence, a chair of Etruscology was created at the University of Rome. In 1928, the first *congresso internazionale etrusco* was organized in Bologna. In 1932, the standing committee for Etruria was transformed into the *Istituto di Studi Etruschi*, which was dedicated to organizing round tables on specific subjects and to launching index projects. In 1935, a chair of Etruscology was established in Florence, on the proposal made by the chief education officer to the minister of education.

However, while gaining in autonomy and legitimacy, studies were fragmented, as shown by the first issues of *Studi Etruschi*, which were divided into distinct sections on history and archaeology, on language and epigraphy and natural history and by dictionaries such as the *Reallexikon der Vorgeschichte* (Berlin, 1926, s. v. Etrusker, III, 132 ff.) in which Duhn dealt with the archaeological side, Herbig with the linguistic side and Reche with the anthropological side. From 1935 to 1947, the new academic discipline, "Etruscology," tried to solve the controversial issue of Etruscan origins but in the absence of any certainties on the subject Etruscology was subjected to the competition of Roman history. To gain recognition by the authorities that were very much aware of the themes of race, nation and empire, German and Italian Etruscologists gave priority to the theme of the origin of Etruscans. Traditionally, the Etruscans were recognized to be foreign in origin, either they came from overseas or they had a Lydian origin by relying on the claims of Herodotus, considered as the father of history. In the 1930s, the theory of Dionysius of Halicarnassus who thought the Etruscans were a native people, "since it has existed from time immemorial and bears no resemblance to any other race as regards language or customs," aroused new interest among German-speaking and Italian Etruscologists, even among its traditional opponents. In the wake of A. Trombetti, linguistic arguments in favor of the "Italianness" of the Etruscan nation and civilization were put forward.

In Germany, when the Etruscans were not seen as a foil for their luxurious manners, they generated the same desire for annexation. Some scholars sought traces of the Etruscans in northern Italy near the Austrian border. E. Fischer, a Nazi geneticist, attempted to challenge Italian anthropologists, by claiming to be able to isolate the Etruscan character of a race. In short, the origin of the Etruscans became a matter of rivalry between the Germans and the Italians. The interest taken by all these scientists in a historically isolated and once-spurned theory was a consequence of the Führer's and Il Duce's words on the purity of the race. In Italy, in 1938, the year when the "battle of the race" was launched, the "Manifesto of racist scientists" came out, according to which the Italian race existed and had been fixed for thousands of years in the peninsula. Accordingly, its physical and psychological characters must not be altered especially through crossbreeding with extra-European races. Etruscologists, however, sounded doubtful as to whether or not the language was native, non-specialists took it upon themselves to demonstrate, through the example of the Etruscan language, the unity and continuity of the Italian race. While Etruscology was being dogged by a discourse on origins, learned societies were becoming fascistic. The most fervent fascists among Etruscologists, like P. Ducati, were unable to strike out the theory of a heterochthonous origin, and we notice, if not a loss of interest in Etruscology, at least a new interest in Greek or Roman history on the part of many Etruscologists seeking to secure their careers. Indeed, in Italy, Roman history offered devotees of the fascist regime two key themes: the Empire and Augustus. On Augustus, imperator and conqueror, the shadow of Il Duce is cast, as M. Pallottino underlined in *Capitolium*, which unreservedly supported Il Duce's action. A victorious and grandiose Roman Empire was preferred to a still debated and actually questionable history of the Etruscans. M. Pallottino described the great Augustan exhibition of the Roman Empire as an undertaking sought by the Duce and worthy of fascist Italy.[3]

After the Second World War, pluridisciplinarity gave way to interdisciplinarity. The barriers between Etruscologically special fields broke down thanks to the emergence of new personalities with, at the same time, linguistic, historical and artistic competences. The most distinguished was unquestionably M. Pallottino who, in the midst of war, devoted himself to his book, *Etruscologia*, the second edition of which was published after the war ended, offered a "panorama of the knowledge and problems of Etruscan civilization" to the general public and was a tremendous success. M. Pallottino also wrote for the second 1948 appendix of the *Enciclopedia Treccani*, the article "Etruschi." This conception of a global Etruscology, a conception that was shared abroad, was evident in the exhibition displaying multiple aspects of Etruscan civilization: *Mostra dell'arte e della civiltà etrusca*, in 1955 and 1956. Taking into account different points of view went hand in hand with putting into perspective again the particularity of the Etruscans within the framework of pre-Roman Italy. The growth of economic, sociological and archaeological sets of issues makes it possible to map out other unities, different from linguistic or artistic unities. In 1951, the *Istituto di Studi Etruschi* became the *Istituto di Studi Etruschi ed Italici*, whose aim was to favor studies "on the origin and development of the Etruscans and ancient peoples." Henceforth, an attempt was made to understand the relations between different peoples and the role each of them played in the history of their time. The idea of a hierarchy between peoples was dismissed and the old problem of origins was simultaneously rethought.

Etruscology even underwent its Copernican revolution. The concept of derivation from a single origin was progressively discarded for the idea of a formation process for the Etruscan people and its civilization. M. Pallottino in *L'origine degli Etruschi* (1947), then F. Altheim in *Der Ursprung der Etrusker* (1950), voiced the idea of a very progressive ethnic formation, a far cry from the usual theory of an unknown invader. For them, henceforward, a people resulted from the melding of different elements, it did not prolong a previous single origin. The change of points of view can be perceived by comparing the first edition of *Etruscologia* in 1942 with the second edition in 1947 and the third edition in 1955, in which M. Pallottino noted that nobody wondered where the Italians or the French came from but the formation of the Italian or the French nation was discussed at length (*see* Chapter 2).

In the 1960s, the publication of discoveries of Etruscan objects in Ampurias, Spain; in Pech-Maho, in Saint Blaise; and in Burgundy, France, broadened further the scope of study (*see* Chapters 17 and 19). The Etruscans, once considered as an Italian people, became a European people. In 1957, *Studi Etruschi* asserted their international character: G. Devoto justified an application for funding by the international character of the *Istituto di Studi Etruschi ed Italici*. Although in the years that followed, M. Pallottino took on responsibilities within the *Associazione Internazionale di Archeologia Classica* and of the *Unione Internazionale degli Istituti di Archeologia*, major exhibitions kept nevertheless a continental, European character. Before the treaty of Rome was even signed, the 1954–56 Etruscan Art and Civilization exhibition moved from the Zurich *Kunsthaus* to the Milan *Palazzo reale* and to other European sites (The Hague, Paris, Oslo, Cologne) and people came in droves to *see* it: 140,000 in Zurich, 100,000 in Milan) thanks to the participation of German, French, Swiss, Austrian, English and American museums. Then, before the fall of the Berlin wall, the exhibition *Die Welt der Etrusker-Archäologische Denkmäler aus Museen sozialistischer Länder*, was presented at the Berlin Altes Museum. More recently, in 1992, when the Maastricht treaty on the enlargement of Europe was signed, the exhibition: "The Etruscans and Europe," conceived by M. Pallottino, G. Camporeale and F. Gaultier, placed the Etruscans within their European framework: Rome is presented both as heir to Etruscan civilization and as mediator between it and Europe.[4] Finally, in the twenty-first century we witnessed the return of the origin issue stemming from new DNA analyses[5] that showed that the Etruscans are related to Asia Minor populations and the repetition of these analyses in a European press where the place of Turkey in Europe is a contentious issue.

NOTES

1 I quote Cipriani's words (1980).
2 *HN*, 36, 91–93.
3 These elements are overlooked in Michetti, L. M. (ed.) (2007).
4 *Gli Etruschi e l'Europa* (1992).
5 *See* the international scientific project *Human Genome Diversity*.

BIBLIOGRAPHY

Barbanera, M. (2009) "Lo studio dell'arte etrusca era fermo al volume di Jules Martha, Le ricerche sugli Etruschi nel primo trentennio del Novecento" in *L'occhio dell'archeologo. Ranuccio Bianchi Bandinelli nella Siena del primo '900. {Siena, Complesso museale Santa Maria della Scala, 4 aprile 5 luglio 2009}*, Cinisello Balsamo, pp. 17–31.

Bartoloni, G. and Bocci Pacini, P. (2003) "The Importance of Etruscan Antiquity in the Tuscan Renaissance" in J. Fejfer, T. Fischer-Hansen and A. Rathje (eds), *The Rediscovery of Antiquity. The Rome of the Artist. Acta hyperborea*, 10, 449–479.

Borsi, F. (ed.) (1985) *Fortuna degli Etruschi*, Milan.

Briquel, D. (2005) "Lucien Bonaparte épigraphiste: les 'inscriptions d'ipogées' dans le Muséum étrusque" in F. Poli and G. Vottéro (eds), *De Cyrène à Catherine: trois mille ans de Libyennes, études grecques et latines offertes à Catherine Dobias-Lalou.*, pp. 301–314.

Bruni, S. (2008) "Anton Francesco Gori, Carlo Goldoni e La Famiglia dell'antiquario. Una precisazione," *Symbolae Antiquariae*, 1, 11–69.

Cagianelli, C. (2006) "La collezione di antichitá di Anton Francesco Gori. I materiali, la dispersione e alcuni recuperi," *Atti e memorie dell'Accademia Toscana di Scienze e Lettere La Colombaria*, 71, 99–167.

——(2008) "La scomparsa di Anton Francesco Gori fra cordoglio, tributi di stima e veleni," *Symbolae Antiquariae*, 1, 71–119.

Camporeale, G. (2001) *Gli Etruschi fuori d'Etruria*, Arsenale.

——(2007) "Dal'etruscheria all'etruscologia. Appunti per un problema" in D. Barbagli and M. Iozzo (eds), *Chiusi Siena Palermo. Etruschi. La collezione Bonci Casuccini*, Siena, pp. 25–38.

Cipriani, G. (1980) *Il mito etrusco nel Rinascimento fiorentino*, Florence.

Cristofani, M. (1978) "Sugli inizi dell' 'Etruscheria.' La pubblicazione del 'De Etruria regali' di Thomas Dempster," *MEFRA*, 90, 577–616.

——(1983) *La scoperta degli Etruschi. Archeologia e antiquaria nel '700*, Rome.

De Benedictis, C. (2004) "Contributo alla conoscenza del 'Museo Gorio'" in C. de Benedictis and M. G. Marzi (eds), *L'epistolario di Anton Francesco Gori. Saggi critici, antologia delle lettere e indice dei mittenti*, Florence, pp. 1–10.

Delpino, F. (2005) "Per una storia del Museo di Villa Giulia. Una visita del ministro Bottai e i progetti di ampliamento del museo" in *Aeimnestos. Miscellanea di studi per Mauro Cristofani*, Florence, pp. 958–969.

Döhl, H. (1990) "K. O. Müller und die Etrusker," in H. Heres (ed.), *Die Welt der Etrusker*, Berlin, pp. 351–356.

La Fortuna degli Etruschi nella costruzione dell'Italia unita. Atti del XVIII Convegno Internazionale di Studi sulla Storia e l'Archeologia dell'Etruria (2010). Annali della Fondazione Faina, 2011.

Gáldy, A. (2006) The Chimera from Arezzo and Renaissance Etruscology, in *Common Ground. Archaeology, art, science and humanities. Proceedings of the XVIth International Congress of Classical Archaeology, Boston (August, 23–26 2003)*, Oxford, pp. 111–113.

Gambaro, C. (2008) *Anton Francesco Gori collezionista. Formazione e dispersione della raccolta di antichità*. Accademia toscana di scienze e lettere "La Colombaria," vol. 244, Florence: Leo S. Olschki Editore.

Gialluca, B. (2008) "Anton Francesco Gori e la sua corrispondenza con Louis Bourguet," *Symbolae Antiquariae*, 1, 121–181.

Gli Etruschi e l'Europa (1992) Milan.

Haack, M. L. (2011) "L'étruscologie : une histoire contemporaine?," *Anabases*, 13, 266–270.

Heurgon, J. (1973) *La découverte des Etrusques au début du XIXème siècle, académie des Inscriptions et Belles-Lettres, Lecture du 30 novembre 1973*, Paris.

Isler-Kerenyi, C. (1998) "K.O. Müllers Etrusker" in W. M. Calder III and R. Schlesier, (eds), *Zwischen Rationalismus und Romantik. Karl Otfried Müller und die antike Kultur*, Hildesheim, pp. 239–281.

Maras, D. F. (2010) "Duecento anni di etruscologia pontificia a Roma" in *I duecento anni di attività della Pontificia Accademia romana di archeologia (1810–2010)*, Rome, pp. 179–200.

Massa-Pairault, F. H. (1982) "Le petit cheval de Volterra au Cabinet des Médailles du Paris ou de M. de Caylus et les 'Origini italiche'," *Rassegna Volterrana*, pp. 58, 1–14.

Michetti, L. M. (ed.) (2007) *Massimo Pallottino a dieci anni dalla scomparsa : atti dell'incontro di studio, Roma, 10–11 novembre 2005*, Rome.

Momigliano, A. (1984) "Gli studi classici di Scipione Maffei" in *Secondo contributo alla storia degli studi classici*, Rome.

——(1987) "Un 'ritorno' alla etruscheria setecentesca: K. O. Müller" in *Ottavo contributo alla storia degli studi classici e del mondo antico*, Rome, pp. 45–58.

Nadalini, G. (1993) "De Rome au Louvre, les avatars du Musée Campana entre 1857 et 1862," *Histoire de l'art*, no. 21/22, 47–58.

——(1998) "La collection Campana au musée Napoléon III et sa première dispersion dans les musées français (1862–1863)," *Journal des savants*, 2, 2, 183–225.

Pallottino, M. (1984) "L'Étrurie de S. J. Ainsley, paysagiste romantique," *Comptes-rendus des séances de l'Académie des Inscriptions et Belles-Lettres*, 3, 497–505.

Potter, T. W. (1998) "Dennis of Etruria: a celebration," *Antiquity* 72, 916–21.

Poucet, J. (2004) "Lucien Bonaparte à Vulci ou Les délires de Canino," *Bulletin de l'Académie royale de Belgique. Classe des Lettres et des Sciences morales et politiques*, 1–6, 7–22.

Rathje, A. (2006) "Etruscology through the looking glass or the eyes of the beholder" in *Across frontiers. Etruscans, Greeks, Phoenicians and Cypriots. Studies in honour of David Ridgway and Francesca Romana Serra Ridgway*, London, pp. 483–490.

van Heems, G. (2010) "Naissance de l'étruscologie et fantasmes linguistiques orientalistes: éléments de réflexion à partir du cas d'Adolphe Noël des Vergers" in B. Grévin (ed.), *Maghreb-Italie. Des passeurs médiévaux à l'orientalisme moderne, actes des journées d'étude*, Rome: Collection de l'École française de Rome 439, pp. 307–322.

Waquet, F. (1982) "Le premier public de l'étruscologie: les souscripteurs au Museum etruscum d'A. F. Gori," *Studies on Voltaire and the Eighteenth Century*, 208, 305–313.

Weiss, R. (1969) *The Renaissance Discovery of classical Antiquity*, New York.

INDEX

——•◆•——

Aborigines 40
Abraham 45
Abul (Portugal) 342
Accesa *see* Lago dell'Accesa
Acheloos 621, 937
Achilles (*Achle*) 434, 498, 500, 506, 518, 567,
    754, 931–934, 937, 938, 939, 954, 958,
    1019–1020
Achviser /Achvizr and *Ethausva* 517, 523
Acqua Acetosa Laurentina 771, 916
Acquarossa 121, 138, 659, 807, 814, 903–906
acromegaly 61
Actium, battle 548
Adad 548
Adam brothers 1139
Admetus & Alkestis 431–432, 468, 676–677
Adoni Villanova Tulo (Sardinia) 239
Adonis (*Atunis*) 117, 506, 608–609
Adrastus 508
Adria (Etruscan colony) 759, 760
Adriatic Sea/region 281–299
Aegina 606, 607
Aegina, Aphaia sanctuary 340
Aeginetans 764, 891
Aelian 516, 850
Aeneas 40, 48, 504, 761, 934
Aeolian Islands 198
Aeolians 44
Aeschylus 503–504, 687, 760
Aesculapius 865, 1074
Aethiopians 500, 506
Aetos 666 cup 312
Afuna (family) 161, 363, 709
Agde 378, 382, 392, 765
Ager faliscus (Faliscan region) 81, 259–276, 298

Ager picentinus (Picentine region) 304
aging 860–861
agriculture 65, 163–165, 178
Agrimensores 362
Agylla (Caere) 497
Aiakos 502
Ainsley, Samuel James 1140
Aita-Hades 520, 524–525
Aius Locutius 517
Ajax/Aifas 934, 937, 938
Alalakh 113
Alalia (colony site) *see* Aleria
Alalia battle (Battle of Sardinian Sea) 250, 516,
    615, 832
Alaric 169
Alberti, Leon Battista 1125, 1136
Aleria (Alalia, Corsica) 156, 237, 240–241, 244,
    249–254, 330, 341, 374–376, 393, 579
Alethna family 355
Alexander the Great 765, 923, 962
Alexander VI (Pope) 1123, 1126
Alpan/Alpnu 517
Alpenquai 374
alphabet 100, 430
    Greek 459
Alsium 156, 761
altars, Etruscan 566–570
Amasis Painter 787, 954
Amathus, Cyprus 393
"*Amazons' Sarcophagus*" (of Ramtha
    Huzcnai) 1092
amber 289–290, 433, 887–888
Amphiaraos 437, 503, 508
    Painter 954
Ampurias *see* Empuries-Ampurias

Amyntor 47
anatomical votives 692, 862, 1068–1080
Anaxilaos of Rhegion 760
ancestor cult, Etruscan 665–666
Anchises 504, 934
ancile/ancilia 94, 747
Ancus Martius 762
anemia 60–61
animal sacrifice, Etruscan 571–576, 578, 1111
animals in Etruria, Etruscan art 1086–1112
animals, wild 1093–1094
Annius of Viterbo (Annio da Viterbo) 1117–1128, 1132, 1136–1138
Antaios 935
antenna/*antenne* swords 374, 397, 886
anthrax 863
Antiati 765
Antibes, shipwreck 326, 395–6, 398, 986 (*see also* La Love)
Antigone 508
Antipater Cicuś 451
anti-Semitism 104–105
Antistius Labeo 690
Antium 865
Antonini, Egidio 1126
Apelles (naval personage) 765
Aphrodite (*Turan*) 500–502, 504, 506, 513, 516, 517, 605–606, 607–609, 618
Aphrodite Koltas, cult of 760
Apollo (*Aplu*) 287, 309, 505–507, 516, 607–609, 620, 621, 906, 1028
Apollo and Artemis (*Aplu* and *Artumes*) 1001
Apollo, *Śuri* 519 (*see also Śuri*, Soranus)
Apollodorus 763
Apollonia 63
Apennines 11, 62
Appenwihr 387, 393
Apuan Alps 724–725, 892
Apulia 665
aquatic animals 1096–1097
Aquileia 940
Ara del Tufo 907
Aranθ Heracanasa 451, 892
Arath Velavesna 919
Aratore d'Arezzo (statuette) 1033
Arcadians 40
Archaic period 1104
architectural terracottas 903–910
architecture, Etruscan 695–704
architecture, Etruscan, influence abroad 387–388
archon (Greek) 354
Ard el-Kheraib 329
Ard el-Mourali 329
Ardea 702, 908
Arene Candide site 863
Arenosola 83

Ares *see* Mars
Arezzo 155–156, 169, 188, 449, 457, 561, 729, 752, 813, 831, 1026–1036
Arezzo, Fonte Veneziana deposit 1033
Argive Painter 947
Argonauts 495–497
Argonauts Painter 957
Argos 383
Ariadne 945
Aricia (battle) 239
Arimnestos 351–352
Arion (on Exekias vase) 21
aristocracy, Etruscan 88, 429–430
Aristodemus of Cumae 239, 306, 314, 315
Aristonothos 126, 497, 768, 770, 889, 948
Aristotle 331, 427, 448–449, 761, 1101
Arles 325
arms and armor, Etruscan and Italic 747–756, 886
Arno 11
Arno Painter (Perugia Painter) 895
Arnobius 513, 546, 572
Arnth Churcles 356
Arnth/Arnthe Praxias 893–894, 896, 956
Arnth Tetnies 359–360
Arringatore see Oratore/ Avele Metelis
Arruns, son of Tarquinius Superbus 740–742
arsenic 13
arthritis 62
Artimino 657–658, 666, 689 (Montagnola tomb)
artists, East Greek 891, 907, 909, 919, 930, 953
Artumes (Artemis) 517, 906, 933, 1001 (*see also* Apollo/*Aplu*)
arx 287, 362, 709, 739
Aryan theories 105
Arzachena-Albucciu hoard 203
asbestos 799
Ashurbanipal 778
Ashurnasirpal II 108, 1101, 1110
Asia Minor (and Ionia), artisans 891, 907, 909, 919, 930, 953
askoid jug(s) (Nuragic type) 209–210, 224
Assyrian kings 108
Assyrian records 825
Astarte 352, 516, 572, 618
Asti 886
astral motifs (Near Eastern art) 108
Astypalaia 62
Atalanta 506
Atelier des petites estampilles 962
Athena (*Menrva*) 500, 502, 508, 513, 620, 933, 937, 999–1000 (*see also Menrva*/Minerva)
Athenaeus 426, 721, 827
Athenian theater 504
Athens 39, 294–295, 298–299, 354, 390, 626, 764, 827
athletic events in Etruria 835–837

athletics: combat sports 834–835
Athrpa (Atropos) 506
Ati (Attius family) 184
Atilius Regulus 651
Atrium-house 665, 698–699, 713
Attic pottery 328, 338, 623, 636, 891, 893, 934
    red-figure pottery 603, 624–627, 957
    vases, imports to Etruria 498, 672–678, 743
Attica 943
Attus Navius 545
Atunis see Adonis 506
Atys 38–39, 42, 43, 45
Aufidena 751, 754
auguraculum 287, 291, 484
augury 539
Augustus 184, 188
Aule Havranas 709
Aule Metellus (*Avle Metelis*) 168, 1013
aulos 844, 848, 849, 850
aurochs (*Bos primigenius*) 13
Aurora painter 895
autochthonist theory 36–50, 1136
avile vipiiennas 985–986 (*see also* Vibenna brothers)
Ayia Triada 203

Babylonian divination 547–548
Bacchus, cult of 163 (*see also* Dionysos/*Fufluns*)
baityloi 607
Bajo de la Campana (shipwreck) 396
banquet(ing) 100, 812–819, 823–829, 850
Barbarano Group 959
barbiton 845–846
Battle of Centaurs and Lapiths 188
Battle of Cumae 41, 314, 340, 390, 608, 618, 760,
    763, 765 (*see also* Cumae)
Battle of the Sardinian Sea *see* Alalia battle
Bearded Sphinx Painter 127, 890–891
Beazley, Sir John D. 1041
beech 16
Bellerophon 751
Berlin Painter 623
Bettona 363
Bianchi-Bandinelli, Ranuccio 1141
Bibbona 728
Bible 45
Bibliothèque Nationale 178 Painter 954
Bickermann, E. 49
biga(e) 793, 837–838
birds 1094–1096
birds, augury 550
Bisenzio 79, 134, 674, 768, 887, 915, 945
Bisenzio Group 955
Bithia 218, 233
Black Sea 383
Blera 570, 657, 660, 662
boar 19, 506, 525, 752, 813, 850, 905, 1029, 1093

boat models (Villanovan) 106
boat models, Nuragic 210–212, 226
Boccheggiano 724
Bocchoris Painter 945
Boii 755
Bologna (*Felsina/Bononia*) 79–81, 83, 281–282,
    283–288, 487, 724, 733, 801, 805, 915–916
    San Francesco hoard 725–726
Bolsena (Lake and city) 156, 159, 163, 361, 449,
    709, 727
Bolsena Group 950
Bomarzo 748, 755
Bon Porté 1 (shipwreck) 766
Bona Dea 663
Bonaparte, Lucien (Prince de Canino) 1140
Bonci Casuccini Painter 957
Book of Kings 113
Book of Maccabees 45
"*Book of the Heavenly Cow*" 109
Boreads 833
Borgia family 1126
Borgia, Rodrigo (Cardinal) 1123
Bos taurus 14, 19, 20
Bosa 218
Bourges, *oppidum* 328, 376, 382, 396
Bowls (cups), Cypro-Phoenician 102–103, 123
Bozzolo (Mantua) 859, 866
Bragny-sur-Saone 327
Brauron 49, 623, 760
Brendel, Otto 1007–1009, 1013, 1017
Broglio-Trebisacce 201
Brolio 1028, 1031, 1036
Brontoscopic Calendar 352, 360, 478, 548, 863–866,
    1111
brontoscopy 115
Bronze Age 79–81, 105
bronzes, Etruscan (sculpture) 1026–1036
Brucellosis 864
Brutus, Lucius Junius 740–742
"*Brutus*" (bronze head) 1013, 1141
Brygos Painter 625, 626, 1021
bucchero *olpe* with *Metaia* and *Taitale see* San Paolo
    (Cerveteri) bucchero *olpe*
bucchero pesante 980–984
bucchero pottery 974–986
bucchero sottile 974–980
bucchero transizionale 976
bucchero, decoration 984–985
    inscribed 985–986
    trade in 986
buccheroid impasto 974
bucina 842
Budrio 860
Buonarotti, Filippo 1130–1134, 1138
Busca (Piedmont) 458
Busiris Painter 953

Buso della Casara (Padua), aqueduct 710–711

Cacu 22, 167, 540
Cadiz 328, 760
Caecina (port) 761
Caecina Selcia, Aulus 861
Caecina (*Ceicna/ Keikna* family) 169, 183, 189–191, 544, 546
Caere (*Cisra*/Cerveteri) 46–47, 100, 121, 134–138, 141, 152–153, 156–9, 169, 241, 323–324, 328, 330, 331, 339, 352, 354, 356, 358–359, 451, 495–496, 506, 599, 613–627, 642, 658, 660, 663, 666, 672, 675, 721, 731, 761, 763, 786, 813, 814, 816, 826, 832, 887, 889, 891, 906, 907, 908–909, 915, 917, 943, 945, 950–951, 955, 956, 961, 962, 974–975, 977, 980, 993–1004, 1009, 1073, 1106, 1140, for tombs, *see also* Cerveteri.
    Montetosto site 125–126, 615
    Regolini-Galassi Tomb 104, 109–110, 113–115, 123, 125, 311, 658, 673, 782, 889, 917–918, 976, 978, 979, 985, 1097–1099
Caeretan Figured Group 959
Caeretan Hydriai 497, 953
Caeretan Red Ware 981
Caesar (Julius) 156, 184, 481, 488, 544, 690
Calendar, Gregorian 690
    Julian 690
Cales 1073
Calus 520
Calusna 573
Calydonian Boar Hunt 185, 186–188, 506
Campana Collection (Louvre) 920, 1140–1141
Campana di Cavelli, Marquis Giampietro 1140
Campana Group 953
Campanari family 1140
Campania 301–316, 665, 943
"*Campanian system*" (architectural decoration) 305, 307, 313
Campanizzante Group 958
Campetti sanctuary *see* Veii, Campetti sanctuary
Campiglia (Marittima) 13, 724, 725, 731
Campo della Fiera (Orvieto site) 365, 559, 561–562, 567–569, 571, 632–653
Camporeale, Giovannangelo 1143
Campus Martius 838
Camucia-Cortona 1031 (*see also* Cortona)
cancer (disease) 860
Cancer (zodiac) 498
Cancho Roano 333, 394
Canina, Luigi 614
Canino (Tessenano) 1073, 1140 (*see also* Tessennano and Vulci)
Cannae, Battle of 729
Cape Gelidonya (shipwreck) 202–203

Capena 267, 768,
Capenates 260–269, 365
capite velato (votive heads) 274, 1079–1080
Capo Piccolo 198
Capodifiume 83
Caprifico (Cisterna) 907
Capua 83, 301–310, 310–315, 315–315, 438
capyas/capys 858
Carambolo, El (Iberia) 209
cardiovascular disease 61
Caria 665
Carians 44
carpentum (cart) 188, 778
Carsac 325
Carthage (*Karthazie*), Carthaginians 157, 206–207, 209, 233, 235, 238–241, 328–341, 374, 389, 391, 393, 458, 607, 618, 929
carts, Etruscan and related 786–793
Casale Marittimo 805
Casale Rivalta 733
Casalecchio 726
Case Nuove di Siccomonte 733
Casentino 1030
Castel d'Asso 570, 662, 666
castella 298, 651
Castellaccio di Sorgenti della Nova 80–81
Castellani family (goldsmiths) 920
Castellina del Marangone 140–141, 729, 731, 907, 909
Castellina in Chianti, (including Montecalvario tomb) 655, 657–658, 1136
castellum aquae 294
Castelsecco, *auguraculum* 484
Castenaso 726, 860
Castiglion Fiorentino 703, 1030, 1031
Castiglioncello 762
Castrum Novum 156, 761
Cato (the Elder) 17, 315, 545
catoptromanteia 551
cattle 13, 19, 22, 24, 501, 571–573, 857, 1089–1093
Catullus 860
cauldrons (bronze) 125
Caunes-Minervois (grotto) 326
cavalry 740–742, 748
Cavatha (Kore/Persephone?) 516, 605, 607, 621, 642
Cavios Frenaios 896
Cayla de Mailhac 326, 392
Celle Sanctuary, *Falerii* 272
Cellini, Benvenuto 1137
Censorinus 80, 480, 546, 683
centaur 1100
centuriation 156
Ceramica argentata 159, 961
ceramics, Etruscan Hellenistic types 165
Cerberus/Kerberos 675, 1098

cereals 856
Ceres 1074 (*see also* Demeter/*Vei*)
Ceri, Tomb of the Statues 116, 889
Cerro del Villar 332, 334, 335, 339, 342
Cerveteri *see also* Caere
    Banditaccia necropolis 655, 657
    Manganello sanctuary 865, 1012, 1013
    Monte Abetone necropolis 672–678
    Tomb of the Alcove 662
    Tomb of the Colonel 689
    Tomb of the Demons 662, 667
    Tomb of the Five Chairs 116, 429, 667, 916
    Tomb of the Painted Animals 123, 949, 1101
    Tomb of the Painted Lions 123, 949
    Tomb of the Reliefs 660, 675, 815, 817, 849
    Tomb of the Shields and Chairs 659, 665
    Tomba Calabresi 124, 979
    Tomba del *Tablinum* 665
    Tomba Maroi 816–817
    Torlonia Tomb 662
Cesnola Painter 945
Cetamura del Chianti 566–567, 569, 571, 816–819
Chalchas 549
Chanenko Group 954
charcoal 17
Chariot, Castel San Mariano 722, 783–784, 787
    Monteleone di Spoleto 498, 722, 783–785
Charioteer of Delphi 837–838
chariots and carts, Etruscan and Italic 375, 430,
    650, 778–793, 779–786, 1108
Charu/Charun 434, 522, 579, 676, 678, 861, 1022,
    1110
Chassey-le-Camp (Saone-et-Loire) 327
cheese 817–818
cheese-grater (*gratattoio*) 19, 102, 383, 817–818
Cheiron 500, 502
chelys lyra 845–846, 850
chestnut (*Castanea sativa*) 17–18
Chianciano (Terme) 506, 805, 844
chickpeas 816
Chigi vase (olpe) 500–501, 950, 980
childbirth 434–436, 861
childhood illness 61
children 434–436
Chimaera of Arezzo (statue) 166, 509–510, 721,
    1028–1029, 1137
chimaera 938, 1101
Chiusi (*Clusium/Clevsin*) 126, 156, 162, 164, 166,
    182–183, 188, 274, 355, 357, 429, 451,
    498, 662, 665, 688, 750, 805, 813, 814,
    823, 826, 833, 835, 859–860, 870, 873,
    922, 957, 977, 981, 984, 1008–1009, 1031,
    1033, 1106
Chiusi, Tomba della Scimmia (Tomb of the
    Monkey) 836, 1091
chora 287

Churriana (Malaga) 328, 339
Ciba Foundation Symposium (1958) 33
Cicero 364, 543–544, 546–547
Cigarralejo (El), 332, 392, 806
Cilens 515
Cilnii (family) 156, 169
cilth 709
Ciminian Forest *(Silva Ciminia)* 15
Cincius 635
cippus, funerary (Caeretan) 330, 393, 398
Circus Maximus, Rome 831–832
Cisium 778
Civil War (Roman) 761
Civita Castellana *(Falerii Veteres)* see *Falerii*
Clanis River 688, 1033
Classes (social), Etruscan 162–177, 183
Classical period 1104–1105
Claudius (emperor) 169
Clavus annalis 635, 690
claw-foot 858
Clevsina family 356
clientela, system 115, 143
Cloaca Maxima 598, 687, 856, 958
clouds, Etruscan personifications 524
Cluj-Napoce 374
Clusium Group 958
Clusium Volaterrae Group 958
Clytemnestra 437
Coarelli, Filippo 710
Cogion-Coste di Manone 805
coinage, coins, Etruscan 397, 486–487
Coke, Thomas 1130–1134, 1138
Collatia 361
Colline Metallifere 724, 728, 731
Colonna, Giovanni 615
congenital conditions, deformities 857
constellations 691–692
cooking utensils 814–815
cooking, Etruscan 814–815
copper (ore) 12
copper trade 202–212
coppice woods– 17
Corchiano 260, 269, 275, 934
Corinth 340, 389, 397, 508–509, 764, 890–891,
    980
Corinth, *Asklepieion* 1073
Corinthian vases 500–501
Cornelius Nepos 840, 890
Corneto 594, 1140
cornu 842–843, 850
Corpus delle stipi votive in Italia 1080
Corpus Speculorum Etruscorum 1042–1043
Corsica 203, 237, 244–254
Corsini throne 169
Cortona 39, 48, 156, 362, 657–658, 662, 665,
    1032 (*see also* Camucia-Cortona)

Cortona, Melone/Tumulo del Sodo site 116, 666, 667, 689, 906, 907, 920–921

Cortona Lamp (Lampadario di Cortona) 485

Cortona Tablet (see also Tabula Cortonensis) 161, 355, 363, 460–462, 470, 471, 473

Cortona, Etruscan Academy 1139

Cortsen, S.P. 448

Coruncanius 651

Corvaro di Borgorese 61

Cosa 156, 702,761

cosmogony, Egyptian 112

cosmogony, Etruscan 683–684

Coste del Marano hoard (Tolfa) 721

Comte de Caylus 1138

Cozza Torta (Corsica) 246, 253

Cozza, Adolfo 712

Cranes Painter 948

Creusa-Dolon Group 957

cribra orbitalia 60–62, 856

Cristofani, Mauro 449

Croesus 45

Crostoletto di Lamone 81

crotalum 847, 848

Crotone (sanctuary of *Hera Lacinia*) 221

crux 291

Cuciurpula (Corsica) 246

cuirass, muscle 748–749, 754
triple-disc 749

Culsans/Janus 517, 1028, 1124–1125

Culsu (Etruscan demon) 621

Cumae 108, 302, 304, 306, 313, 916, 945

cuniculi 20, 358–359, 687, 712–717, 856

cup-spirals motif 111

currus (cart) 778

Cusu (family) 161, 363

Cutus (family, tomb) 181, 667

Cyclades 943

Cypro-Phoenician *oinochoe* 978–979

Cyprus (*Alashiya*) 201, 206–207, 665

Cyrene, Cyrenaica 44, 328, 383

d'Hancarville, P.F. 1138

Da Vinci, Leonardo 655

Daidalos (*Taitale*) 495, 834, 980, 985, 1101

daimon (Greek) 521

Damon 771

Damophilos 893

Danae 437

Dancing Satyrs Painter 956

Danube region (imports) 93

de Guzmán, Domingo 1119

De Montfaucon, B. 1138

Decima (Castel di) 438, 916

Decius Mus 651

Deecke, Wilhelm 447, 1141

deer 19, 1093–1094

Del Chiaro Painter 957

Della Seta, Alessandro 29

Delos 506, 760,

Delphi 47, 295, 375, 389, 506, 516, 764, 832, 839

Demaratus 107, 143, 495, 890, 896, 897, 993

Demeter-Ceres (*Vei*) 273, 516, 576, 579–580, 608, 620, 622–623, 642, 862, 867

Demetrios Poliorketes 765

demons, Etruscan 521–526

Dempster, Thomas 1130–1134, 1138

Dennis, George 13, 29, 697–698, 1041, 1140

dental appliances 59, 870–873

dentistry, dental health, Etruscan 870–873

Deorum sedes 521

Devoto, Giacomo 1143

Diana 1074

dice 478–479

Diespater Group 957 *see also Dis Pater* Painter

Dii animales ("Spirit gods") 572, 1112

Dii consentes or *complices* 513, 521

Dii superiores et involuti 513, 521

Dindia Macolnia 168

Dio Cassius 744

Diodorus Siculus 240, 688, 728–729, 759, 813, 855, 914

Dionysiac cult 163, 579–581, 622, 764, 922, 1028

Dionysios of Phocaea 763, 764

Dionysius (I) of Syracuse 41, 616, 765

Dionysius of Halikarnassos 36–50, 355, 365, 448, 457, 545, 739, 740–742, 759, 762, 813, 831, 838, 1142

Dionysos and Ariadne 433–434

Dionysos (*Fufluns*, Bacchus) 49, 435, 505–506, 521, 578, 579, 580, 642, 622, 764, 931, 1028, 1098

Diopos 890

Dioscorides 457, 687

Dioscuri 520, 580, 1050–1052, 1055, 1092

Diotimos 764

"Diptych Group" 189

Dis Pater (Diespater) Painter 266, 895

Dis Pater, cult (Marzabotto) 294, 516, 573, 576

disease 862–863

DISH (diffuse idiopathic skeletal hypertrophy 861

dissection (anatomical knowledge) 1068–1070

distaff(s) 801

divinità-atto 517, 521–522

DNA studies (of Etruscan/Italian populations) 57–58, 859, 1143

Dodecapolis 48, 281, 301, 839

Dodona 375

Dog Star (*Sirius*) 498

Doganella 134

dogs 574–575

Dokana 1055

Dominican Order 1119

donario (offering table) 636
Dorians 44
Douris 647
Ducati, Pericle 1142
Durand, Chevalier Edmond-Antoine 1140
Dutuit chariot, Capua 785
dwarfism 861
dyes, dyeing process 804–805
dynatotatos 739

E. Mizane (Corsica) 246
eagle 1094, 1111, 1112
Eagle Painter 953
Echemos (hero) 742
"economy of plunder" 91
Ecueil du Miet 3 (shipwreck) 326, 766
education, Etruscan 439, 683–692
eggs 816–817
Egypt 374, 383
Egyptian belief system, iconography 109–110, 112
Egyptian gods (Ra, Hathor) 109, 115, 117
Egyptians 428, 435
Eileithyia(-i) 513, 575
Eileithyia-Leukothea, sanctuary at Pyrgi 613–627
Ekman, Sten 16–17
Ekphantos 890
El Campello (Alicante) 342
El Turuñuelo 333
Elba (*Aithalia*) 12, 164, 222, 245, 249, 724, 725, 728–729, 731, 762
elephant(s) 1098
Eleusis 623
Elissa (Dido) 206
Elogia Tarquiniensia 354–355, 365, 449
Elongated Horses Painter 945
emporion/emporium 295
Empuries-Ampurias 325, 326, 332, 336, 337, 341, 375, 382, 383, 389, 391–393, 397, 986, 1143
Enotrian imports 88, 90
Ensérune 332, 390
environment, environmental pollution 856–857
Eos *see Thesan*
Ephorus 763
epidemic 832, 863
epilepsy 595
Eretum 787
Eros 506
Esarhaddon 99, 778
Eteokles & Polyneikes 508
Ethauśva 513
Ethiopians *see* Aethiopians
Etruria padana see Po Valley
Etruria, Twelve Peoples ["Etruscan League"] 365
etrusca disciplina 360, 364, 483, 546, 549–551, 557, 575, 597

Etruscan black-figure pottery 954–956
bronze vessels 378–382
bronzes, exports 395
exports, perishables 386–387
figurines 378
Geometric pottery 943–945
infundibula (strainers/funnels) 383
language 457–475, 478–488
language, phonology 470–472
language, vocabulary 474–475
mirrors 377, 1041–1061
pottery, exports 330
pottery, exports (fine wares) 383, 385, 395, 400–401 (*see also* Etrusco-Corinthian vases)
pottery, exports (utility wares) 385
pottery, exports, amphorae 385–386, 395
pottery, overpainted 961–962
pottery, painted 943–962
pyxides 377
red-figure pottery 957–960
shipbuilding 765–773
ships, representations 770–773
silvered pottery *see ceramica argentata*
Subgeometric pottery 945–947
terracottas, production techniques 993–995
tripods 382
utensils 383
women 426–440
women, abroad 390
Etrusco-Corinthian pottery 950–952
Euboea 377, 943
Eucheir 890
Eugrammos 890
Euphronios 675
Euripides 763, 764
Eusebius 759
Evan 517
Evander 40
evocatio (ritual) 153, 514
exchange system(s) 88
exotic animals 1097–1098
expositio 435

Fabii (family) 158
falcon 1112
Falerii (*Falerii Veteres*/Civita Castellana) 152–153, 156, 241, 260–276, 357, 561, 619, 748–749, 753, 887, 910, 957–959, 962, 1073, 1151
Falerii, liver model 542, 547
Falerii, Vignale-Tempio Maggiore 862
Faliscan culture, Faliscans 259–276, 365
Faliscan Figured Group 959
famine(s) 813, 855–856
Fanum Voltumnae 152–153, 156, 169, 269, 364–365, 515, 561, 567, 632–653, 839

"faretrine" (Nuragic miniature quivers) 223–224
farro (spelt) 813
fasces 356, 365, 850
Felsina stelai 288, 834
Fermo 83
Ferrara T 408 Group 962
   585 Group 962
Feruglio, Anna Eugenia 713–716
Fescennium 261
Festus 483, 489, 632, 687, 690, 692
fibers (in textile production) 799
fibula, Villanovan 108
Ficoroni cista 168
Fiesole 1013
figurines, anthropomorphic 105
Finlay, Moses I. 447
fir 16
Fischer, E. 1142
fish 1096–1097
flamen (flamines) 905
flanged axe(s) 374
floods 16
Florence 156, 657
   Baptistry 690
Florentine republic 1136
Fluid Group 959
focolare (brazier, Caeretan type) 322, 385, 815, 816
foculum (bucchero form) 984
Foied Group/Painter 895, 958
Follonica 729
fonduk (fondaco, fondouk, fonde) 336–342, 395
Fonteius Capito, C. 544, 546
food, Etruscan 812–819, 855–856
Forcello di Bagnolo San Vito 297
Formello *cuniculus* 687
Fortnum Group (rings) 923
Fortuna 314
Forum Group 958
foundation rites, Etruscan 709–710
François Tomb, Vulci 23, 352, 435, 541, 665, 677, 806, 808, 861, 1112 (*see also* Vulci)
Fratte di Salerno (Etr. *Marcina*) 306
freedman/freed slaves 450–451
Fregellae 865, 1073
Fregenae 156
Freret, Nicolas 36
frescoes, Etruscan 1017–1022
Fretum Gallicum (Strait of Bonifacio) 244
Fufluns see Dionysos/Bacchus
Full Sakkos Group 959
Fulvius Flaccus 156, 632, 636
funeral ritual, funerary cult (Etruscan) 80–81, 84–94, 116–118, 180–191, 655–668, 672–678
Funnel Group 958
Funtana Coberta-Ballao hoard 203

Furius Camillus 267
furnaces, smelting 730

Gabii (including Osteria dell'Osa) 21, 859, 1073
Galeotto Ridolfini Corazzi 1032
games 42–43, 831–839
Gaul 340, 391
Gaul, finds of Etruscan goods 396
gauloi (Phoenician) 772
Gauls 154, 157
   invasion of Italy 297–298
Gaultier, Françoise 1143
geese 1093
Gela Painter 787
Gemma Stosch 934
gems, Etruscan 502, 928–940
Genoa 729
gentilizio 305, 310
Genucilia plate(s) 241, 764, 959–961
Geras 502, 931
Gerhard, Edouard 1041
Germans 428, 435
Geryon 22, 40, 603, 938
Giacometti, Alberto 167
Giambullari 1137, 1138
Giens (Madrague de, shipwreck) 766
glosses, Etruscan 457, 869–870
Gnathia pottery 963
Gobbi krater 22
Godfrey of Viterbo 1125
Golasecca culture 282, 390
gold jewelry 108–126, 376–367
goldworking 888
Gordion 115–116
Gorgasos 893
Gorgon 1100
Gori, (Antonio) Francesco 1033, 1139
Gouraya (Gunugu) 329, 340, 388
Gozzadini, Giovanni 79
Grächwill 392
grain 813
Gran Carro (Bolsena) 727, 800
Grand Ribaud F (shipwreck) 326, 340, 382, 395, 766–767
granulation technique (goldsmithing) 108, 686, 722, 915–923
Grasceta dei Cavallari 568
grasses 15
Gravisca 21, 141, 164, 516, 559, 562, 567, 574, 605–609, 622, 732, 761, 762, 891, 909, 1073
Greece 340
Greek alphabet 21
   iconography (fantastic animals) 110
Greeks 435, 516
Gregory the Great (Pope) 218

griffin 1099
groma 483, 687, 710–711
Gromatici Veteres 478, 483, 544
Grotta Porcina (Blera) 570, 666, 831
Group of Alcestis/Painter of Alcestis 958
    of Florence 80675 955
    of *Kape Mukathesa* 955
    of La Tolfa 921
Guadocinto 907
Guarnacci, Mario 1138
Gubbio Tablets see Tabulae Iguvinae

Hades 621
Hades and Persephone 434
Hague Painter 958
Halesos (hero) 81
Hallstatt (culture, site) 374, 806, 886, 890
Hamae 314
Hamilton, Sir William 1138
Hamilton-Gray, Mrs. Elizabeth Caroline
    Johnstone 1140
hare(s) 1094
harpies 833
haruspex, haruspices/haruspicy 23, 160, 481,
    483–484, 539–551, 1077, 1112
Haspnas 739, 744
Hatrencu 431
Hawk 1112
Haynes, Sybille 1009–1010
health in Etruria 855–874
heavy metal(s) 13, 724, 726, 856, 870
Heba 156
Hebe 502, 677
Hecataeus of Miletus 46, 297, 759, 763
Helbig, Wolfgang 104
Helen 502
Helios 517
Hellanicus of Lesbos 37–39, 41, 45, 49
Hellen, son of Deucalion 44
Hellenistic period 1105–1106
helmet(s), bell-helmet 886
    Belmonte-type 751
    Corinthian type 739–740, 752
    crested 374, 390, 886
    Etruscan 390, 396
    Montefortino-type 752
    Montegiorgio Piceno-type 750–751
    Montelparo-type 750–751
helots 448
hematite (iron ore) 396
hepatoscopy 115
Hephaestus (*Sethlans*) 113, 513, 517, 606, 933
Heptachord Painter 778, 845, 889, 948
Hera (*Uni,* Juno) 327, 391, 430, 432, 439,
    500–501, 513, 516, 572, 575, 599, 606,
    607, 609, 617, 619, 677, 1074

Herakles and Athena (sculptural group) 907, 909
Herakles/Hercules/*Hercle* 19, 22, 23, 38, 40, 272,
    287, 431, 439, 468, 497, 502, 507, 513,
    515, 523, 524, 603–604, 617, 618, 621,
    622, 625, 672, 675, 676, 677, 931, 934,
    935, 937, 939, 954, 961, 1028, 1031, 1036
herbs, herbal remedies 15, 687, 869–870
Herculaneum 861, 863, 864
Hermes (*see also Turms*) 500–501, 503, 578, 937,
    938, 939
Hero of Alexandria 711
Herodian (grammarian) 479
Herodotus 37, 42, 50, 458, 516, 742, 760, 764,
    770, 832, 891, 986, 1142
Hescanas (family, tomb) 275
Hesychius 457
Heuneburg 376, 394
Hieron I of Syracuse 41, 61, 608, 765
hieros gamos ("sacred marriage") 308
Himera 607, 618
hinthial 1055, 1110
Hippokrates, Hippokratic corpus 764, 855, 863,
    864, 870
Hiram of Tyre 113
Hirpini 304
Hispellum (Spello, Rescript of) 169, 365, 632, 839
histriones 832
Hochdorf 375, 387, 392, 806
Hohmichele 806
Holaie Phokiaš 458
holm oak 16
Homer, Homeric epic/poems 99, 495, 817, 825
Homeric Hymn to Dionysos 505, 764
Hoof Painter 953
hoplite (tradition, armor) 742–744
Horace (Roman poet) 165, 1026
horse-racing 837–838
horses 1091–1092, 1107–1108
Hospitallers of St. John 1121
houses (Etruscan) 65–66, 292–293
Huelva 198, 209, 233, 319, 328, 332, 333, 336,
    338, 342, 379, 383, 392, 760
Humbert, Jean Emile 1032
Hutchinson, G. Evelyn 15
Hyakinthos 938
Hydra 498, 603, 937
hydraulic engineering, Etruscan 692, 710

Iberia 221, 235, 331–335, 374, 374, 375
Iberian connections with Etruria 207–209
Ibiza 393
"Iceman" (Similaun Man/"Oetzi") 19, 856, 859
Ides (Etr. *itus*) 471, 690
Iliad 498, 504, 550, 742, 919
Illa d'en Reixac, *oppidum* 338
immigrants, Sardinian 887

imports to Italy, Near Eastern 89, 915
imports to Italy, Phoenician 89
Impruneta 724
infant mortality 857–858
Inghirami, Curzio 1128
ingots, Etruscan bronze 487
Innocent I (Pope) 169
Innocent VIII (Pope) 1123, 1136
inscription(s), Etruscan 237, 324–325, 327,
    330, 340–341, 351–354, 360, 388–390,
    450–452, 457–475, 478–488, 606, 647,
    666, 861, 893–894, 919, 929, 934, 949,
    952, 985–986, 1028, 1033, 1056–1058,
    1127–1128
inscriptions, Greek 891
    Latin 1058
Intermediate Group 957
Iolaos 498
Ionia 606
iron (iron ore) 12
Iron Age 308–309
    (Sardinia) 217
    Etruscan 134–139
iron bloom 17
Ischia *see* Pithekoussai
Isernia 702
Isidore 759
Isola del Giglio (shipwreck) 395–396, 844
ivory, ivory trade 396, 888
Ivy Leaf Group 954

Jahn Painter 956
Janus *see Culsans*
Jason 495, 834
Jerusalem 113, 683
jewelry, Etruscan 914–924
Jews 45, 428, 435, 1136
journey to the Underworld 188
Judgement of Paris 500–501
Julius Obsequens 544, 863
Juno (statue at Veii) 514
Juno *see* Hera/*Uni*
Juno Curitis, sanctuary at *Falerii* (Vignale) 264–
    265, 272
Juno Regina (Rome) 515

Kadmos 937
Kainua (*see also* Marzabotto) 291
Kameiros (Rhodes) 393
kantharos 977, 982–983
Kanuta 450, 637, 642
Kapaneus (Capaneus) 508, 619, 934, 937, 938,
    939
Kape Muka0esa 451, 892, 955
Karalis (Cagliari) 218, 233, 241
Karmir-Blur 125

Karnak 328
Kaschnitz-Weinberg, G. 1141
Kassandra 934
Kastor/*Castur* 937
Kephalos 506
Kerberos (Cerberus) 937–938
ketos 525
king ("*rex*") 92–93
kišpu ritual (Near Eastern religion) 116
kitchens 814–815
kithara 845–846, 849
Kithara Painter 768
Kleitias krater (François Vase) 498
kopis (sword) 755–756
Kościelec (Poland) 986
kotyle 979
kourotrophos 436–439, 996–997
Kranzspiegel 1049–1056
Kreon 508
Kritias 721
Ksour es Saaf (Tunisia) 375
kykeon 817,
Kyknos Painter 955
Kyknos/*Kukne* 934
Kypria 500

La Algaida, sanctuary (deposit) 332, 335, 382, 391
La Love (Antibes) (shipwreck) 766
La Tolfa Group 954–955
Lago dell'Accesa 13, 16–18, 725, 729, 856
Lago di Bolsena, 558
    Bracciano 558
    Chiusi 558
    Monterosi 15
    Vico 558
Lagrenée, Jean-Jaques 1139
Lake Albano 688, 710–711
    Nemi 710–711
    Prile 762
    Trasimene 221, 558
    Vadimon (battle of) 154, 1132
Lambrechts, Roger 1041
Landscape painting, Etruscan 1017–1022
Lanuvium 747–750
Lanzi, Luigi 1139
Laran 513, 517, 816, 1028, 1031
Lares (Viales) 572
Laris Lethaies 952
Laris Pulena/Lars Pulenas 164, 439, 462–463, 540,
    677
Larnas (family) 363
Lars Felsnas 861
Larth Curunas 356
    Hulchnies 354
    Lapicanes 359
Larthia Telikles 430

Lasa 434, 1050–1055
Lasa Vecuvia ("Nymph Vegoia") 540–541, 686, 709
Latium Vetus 270
Lattes 325, 327, 332, 336, 338, 341, 390, 393
lautni/lautniθa ("freedman/woman") 162, 450–452
Lavinium 48, 1073
Lavinium, Sanctuary of Thirteen Altars 568
Lawrence, D.H. (*Etruscan Places*) 13, 29–30,
    1086–1087, 1099, 1107, 1117
Le Bouffens (Roc de Bouffens, Aude) 325, 386, 391
lead ingots 622
leannver 864–865
lictor 357
Leda and Tyndareus 434
Lefkandi 817
lekanomanteia 551
Lemnos (and Kaminia stele) 29, 33, 49, 458
Leo X (Pope) 1137
leopards 1098
leprosy 61
Letha 548
Leto and Apollo 438
Leukothea (or *Eileithyia*) 514, 516, 619–621
lex Julia 156, 161, 451
lex Plautia Papiria 156
libra (unit of weight) 486
Libri (religious books) 542–543
    Acheruntici 580, 1112
    fatales 481
    fulgurales 543, 685
    haruspicini 1111–1112
    lintei (textiles) 799
    rituales 80, 480, 483, 543, 575, 687
Lignano 1033
Ligozzi, J. 1137
limestone 12
Lindos (Rhodes) 383
linear enamel hypoplasia 61–62, 856
lion 1097–1098
Lipari 760, 763, 764
literacy, Etruscan 439
lituus 120, 360, 549, 1126
lituus (musical instrument) 842–843, 848, 850
Liver of Piacenza 485–486, 515-16, 542, 548, 557,
    642
livestock (assorted species) 1091–1093
Livia 188–189
Livius Andronicus 832
Livorno 762
Livy 37, 151, 267, 298, 301, 365, 449, 517,
    544–545, 605, 635, 651, 688, 690, 697,
    710, 729, 740–742, 756, 752, 759, 762,
    813, 831, 832, 833, 834, 839, 850, 863
longevity 861
loom weights, inscribed 439
loom(s) 801–803

Los Villares 332, 392
lotus flower(s) 112–113
Lotus Flowers Workshop 956
Lucanian Pottery 957
Lucca 156
Lucera 1073
Lucumo 352
Lucus Feroniae 60, 240–241, 364
ludi circenses 832
ludi scaenici 832
ludus, loidorein (Latin and Greek) 43
Luni (sul Mignone) 80, 156, 164, 166, 761–762
Lupercalia 064
Lustignano 728
Lycia 665
Lycophron 48
Lydia 665
Lydians (Lydian Theory) 37–50
Lydos/Lydus (mythical hero) 38, 43, 45
Lydus, Johannes (John the Lydian, Byzantine) 478,
    544, 546, 690
Lyre-Player seal 309
Lysikrates monument, Athens 764

Macedonia 665
Macmillan Painter 950
Macrobius 352, 690
Maecenas 169
Maenad(s) 434, 579, 617, 622, 833, 933
Maeonia, Maionians 38, 43
Maffei, Marquis S. 1139
magister 352
Magliano Lead Plaque 460, 463
Mainake (Toscanos?) 334, 339
Malacena Ware 976
Malaga (*Mainake*) 332, 335, 336, 339, 391
malaria 60, 13, 164, 864
Malavisch 22
malena 1056
Malta 328, 759
Mamurius Veturius 747
Mamurke Tursikina 919
Manetho 1121
"Manifesto of the Race" 105, 1142
Maniie ("Manios") 766
Mansuelli, Guido 1041
Mantua 281–282, 297, 298
marble (Greek and related) 892
Marce Caliathe 354
March, George Perkins 14
Marcina (Fratte di Salerno) 306
Marcus Junianus Justinus 206
Maremma 13, 724
Maris 523
marriage 182, 430–434
Mars *see Laran*

Mars of Todi (statue) 721, 752, 1028
Marseille (Massalia/*Matalia*) 320–341, 373–383, 389–391, 394, 400
Marseille, Place Jules-Verne (shipwreck[s]) 766
Marsiliana d'Albegna 100, 118, 656, 916–918, 979, 1010
Martanum 762
Martelli, Marina 943
Martianus Capella 483–484, 488, 513, 515, 546, 557, 683, 687, 869
Martini, Wolfram 937
marunch (maru) 356, 359, 362
Marzabotto 141, 282–283, 291–294, 298, 450, 569–570, 573, 655, 689, 699, 710, 712, 733, 870
maschialismos scenes 939
masonry (stone) 140–141
Massa Maritima 16, 725, 856
Massetano 16
Mastarna/Servius Tullius 351–352, 957, 985–986
Master of Animals 23
Master of the Boston Dionysos 502, 931, 933
    London Satyr 930
Master Pasquale of Rome 1122
Mater Matuta 314, 514, 516, 619, 1074
"*Mater Matuta*" statue 438
Matuna (family) 660
Mausoleum of Halicarnassus 961
Mazarrón (shipwreck) 396
meat 817
Medea (*Metaia*) 495, 834, 948, 980, 985 (*see also* San Paolo *olpe*)
Medici collection(s) 1028–1029
Medici family 1130–1134
Medici, Cosimo (I) de' Medici 169, 1028, 1137, 1138
    Cosimo (II) de' Medici 1130–1134
    Cosimo (III) de' Medici 1138
    Ferdinando de' Medici 1137
    Gian Gastone de' Medici 1133–1134, 1138
    Lorenzo (*Il Magnifico*) 1136–1137
medicine in Etruria 855–874
Megales (Phrygian seer) 547
Megara Hyblaea 438
Melanippus 619
Meleager 506
Meleager Painter 957
Memnon 500, 506, 518
Menrva (Minerva) 435, 482, 513, 519, 862, 1028, 1074 (*see also* Athena)
metallurgy, Corsican 246–248
    Etruscan 163–168, 178
    techniques (Villanovan-Etruscan) 721–723
Metaponto/Metapontum 63, 863
methlum 709
Metopengattung 947

Metrodorus of Scepsis 1026
Metru (menece) 894, 896
Mezentius 351
Mezzomiglio 870
Micali Group 891
Micali Painter 768, 771, 833, 834, 835, 848, 955
Micali, Giuseppe 1139
middle class (Etruscan) 65
milk, human 437
mineral resources, Etruria 724–725
Minerva *see* Menrva
Minerva of Arezzo (statue) 1028–1029, 1137
mining processes 856–857
    Etruscan 721–733
    Villanovan-era 725–728
Minio 761
Minto, Antonio 1141
mirror(s), Etruscan 21–23, 393, 397, 502, 1041–1061
mirrors, iconography 1048–1049
Mitza Purdia-Decimoputzu 200
MLK (Phoenician: "king") 352
model huts, hut urns 86
moldings, Etruscan 700–703
Molise 62
Mommsen, Theodor 36
Monfestino 726
monkey(s) 1091
monomachia 740, 742
Monte Amiata 558
    Bibele di Monterenzio 298, 733
    Falterona, 558, 1028, 1031, 1033, 1036
    Giovi 558
    Grande 198
    Li Santi-Le Rote sanctuary (Narce) 272–273
    Pezzola 726
    Polizzo 21
    Rombolo 724
    Ruvello 80
Montebello 873
Montecatini 725
Montecchio 1028, 1032, 1036
Montediano Painter 958
Montefiascone 722, 750
Monteleone di Spoleto, chariot 498, 722, 783–785
Montescudaio (funerary urn) 123, 823
Montieri 725
Mont-Lassois (Vix), *oppidum* 328, 394
Montoro-Cordoba 200
Morrius (king of Veii) 94
Morro de Mezquitilla (Malaga) 397
Mount Eryx 618,
Mount Soracte 260, 558, 560
Mozia/Motya (Sicily) 209
Muller, Karl Ottfried 447, 1141
mundus 294, 573

Muret, M.-A. 1137
Murila Hercnas 451
Murlo/Poggio Civitate 17, 121–122, 138, 434,
    561, 731, 787, 805, 807, 825–826, 834,
    837, 903–906, 930
Musarna 154, 158, 354–355, 479
music, Etruscan 841–850
musical instruments, Etruscan 842–847
musicians (figurines) 1000–1001
Mycenaeans (in west/Italian archipelago) 198–201,
    232
Myrsilus 39, 47
Mysians 44
mythical animals, monsters 1099

Nae Cicu 539
naming conventions, women 428
Nanas/Nanos 47–48
Nanni, Giovanni *see* Annius of Viterbo
Nanos-Ulysses 48
naper 486
Napoleon III 1141
Napoleon Bonaparte 864
Narce 261–276, 747, 817, 873, 1073
Narce Painter 264, 947
Narni 156
Naukratis 328, 986
Naxos 945
Nazi/Fascist scholarship 1142
Nazzano Painter 266, 895
Neapolis (Naples, Italy) 315
Neapolis (Sardinia) 233, 239
Near Eastern iconography 109–111
Nearchos 340, 389
Negau-type helmets 739, 750–752
Nemean Lion 937
Nemi (votive deposit) 1028, 1073
Neo-Assyrian kings, courts 547
Nepi 153, 157, 261–262
Nepi Painter 957
Neptune/*Nethuns* (Poseidon) 548, 938
Nereus 502, 650, 931
Nestor's cup 817
nettle 15
Newton, Sir Isaac 685
Niebuhr, B.G. 36, 1140–1141
Nigidius Figulus, Publius 352, 360, 478, 514,
    544, 546, 548, 550
Nikosthenes (Nikosthenic amphorae) 674, 893,
    954, 977
Nilén, John 17, 18
Ninhursag 111
Niobids 437
Nocera 306
nodus (Roman hairstyle) 188–189
Nola 306

Nola-Croce del Papa 857
nomen etruscum 80
Nora 233, 239–240
Norchia 275–276, 354, 356, 570, 662, 665, 666,
    859
Northampton Group 953–954
Nortia, sanctuary of 482, 635
Novios Plautios 168
Numa (Pompilius) 94, 567, 709, 747, 863
Numana 895
numbers, Etruscan 475, 478–480
numen 517
Nun Painter 958
Nuoro region (Sardinia) 218
Nuraghe Antigori-Sarroch 201
Nuraghe Arrubiu-Orroli 198–200
Nuraghe Serucci-Gonnesa 203
Nuragic bronzes 308–309, 885–886
    metallurgy 205
    pottery 201, 207, 330, 334
Nurdole (Sardinia) 239

oak 16
Oberwilflingen (hoard) 202
Obesus etruscus 860–861
obstetrical knowledge 866–868
Ocnus 281
Octavia 188
Octavian 156, 181, 481
Odysseus 495–496, 503, 948,
Odysseus and the suitors 624–627
Odysseus at Circe's Banquet 186–188
Odysseus/*Uthuze* 937, 939
Odyssey 303, 495, 497, 503, 550, 624–627
Oedipus Painter 957
Oetzi *see* "Iceman"
Oidipus with the Sphinx 939
Okeanos 517
Olbia 233, 237, 241
Old Testament 825
Olta 688
Oltos 672, 674, 678
Olympia 351, 374, 375, 383, 390, 765, 832,
    839
Olzscha, Karl 448
"*Ombra della serra*" ("Shadow of the Night"
    statuette) 167
Omphale 38
Onasias 626
Onesimos 625, 626
Oppidum 298
oral health (Etruscan/ancient) 59–60
Oratore ("*Arringatore*" statue of Avle Metelis) 166,
    168, 1028, 1029, 1137
Orbetello Group 955
Ordo LX haruspicum 169, 549

Orestes 437
Orgolnius 354
Orientalizing period 99–128, 138, 309–311,
    1102–1104
Orientalizing pottery, Etruscan 948
Oristano 237
Orpheus (*Urphe*) 496, 939, 1056,
Ortaglia 571–572, 575
Orthopedic problems, Etruscan 858
Orvieto (*see also Volsinii*) 141, 355, 450, 559, 660,
    632–653, 666, 673, 688, 768, 826, 856,
    910, 955–956, 957, 958, 981
Orvieto Group 955–956
    Belvedere temple 562, 573, 635, 689, 712
    Cannicella necropolis/sanctuary/"Venus"
        statue 561, 569, 576, 711, 870, 892,
        1061
    Crocofisso del Tufo necropolis 655, 711
    Settecamini necropolis 748, 754–755
    Tomba Golini (I and II) 452, 813, 827–828,
        848
    town-planning 708–717
Ossaia-Terontola 1031
osteoporosis 62
Osteria dell'Osa (*Gabii*) 439
Osterley Park 1139
Ostia 762
Otho (emperor) 169
Othoca, 218, 233, 239
Otricoli 907,
Oued Miliane (Bir Mcherga, Tunisia, Etruscan
    inscriptions) 164–165, 329, 388
Ovid 545, 747, 832, 864
owl(s) 1095
oxen 19
oxhide ingots 202–204

Paestum (*Poseidonia*) 157, 306
Painter of Achilles 957,
    of Amsterdam/ Amsterdam Painter 889, 948,
    of Bufolareccia 86 949
    of Civitavecchia 834, 889
    of Hesione 958
    of Kadmos 603
    of London F 484 958
    of London F 64 957
    of Louvre E 736 (Eight Painter) 953
    of Louvre E 737–E 739 (Ribbon Painter) 953
    of Lykurgus 603
    of Narce 264, 947
    of Silenus 954
    of Stamnos Casuccini 957
    of Stockholm 889
    of the Birth of Menerva 948–949
    of the Calabresi Urn 948–949
    of the Cranes, 889
    of the Fishes 889
    of the Heptachord 778, 845, 889, 948
    of the Pigmy Trumpeter (or Monteriggioni
        Painter) 958
    of the Tuscan Column 958
    of the Vatican *Biga* 958
    of Vatican 238 764, 955
    of Vienna 4008 957
Palaeolithic (art) 1089–1090
Palafitte (platform villages) 85
Palamedes 43
Palestrina (*Praeneste*), (including Barberini,
        Bernardini Tombs) 104, 166, 168, 439,
        889, 916, 918–919, 978, 979, 1048, 1073
Pallottino, Massimo 29–34, 36–50, 613, 615,
        1041, 1142–1143
Palmavera-Alghero 218
Panathenaic amphora(e) 674, 743
Pania *pyxis* 126, 768,
Pantheon, Rome 690
panther 1098
parasites 856
Pareti, Luigi 104
Paris and Helen 432, 435
Paris (son of Priam) 500–502
Paris Painter ("Pontic vases") 500–501, 891,
        954–955
Pater Soranus, cult of Apollo Soranus 260
paterfamilias (Roman) 429, 450, 665
pattern-welding 723
Pauli, Karl 447
Pausanias 742
Pava Tarchies 540, 549
Pech-Maho, *oppidum* (lead tablet) 324, 340, 364,
        389, 1143
Pegasus 751, 938, 1100–1101
Peirithöos 579
"Pelasgian Walls" of Pyrgi 613–614
Pelasgians 37–50, 497, 616, 760
Pelasgos (hero) 45
Peleus and Atalanta 434
Peleus and Thetis 432, 1056
Peleus/*Pele* 498, 937
Pelops and Hippodameia 185
Penates 521, 572
penestai 448, 739, 744
pentekonters 760
Penthesilea (*Pentasila*) 676
Perachora 340, 389–390
Perali, Pericle 713, 716
periplus 761
perirrhanteria 1031
Perizoma Group 674, 676, 678
Peroni, Renato 302
Perseus/*Pherse* 437, 937
personal effects (Etruscan) 399–400

Pertuis 326, 379, 392
Perugia (*Perusium*) 156–7, 159–160, 181, 281, 451, 544, 662, 753, 813, 833, 922
Perugia *cippus* 161, 363, 460, 462–463, 486, 709
Perugia Painter 957
Perugia, Tomb of the Volumnii *see Velimna*
Perusine War 181
Pesaro (bilingual inscription) 158, 539
Pézenas 326
Phaeton 938
Phalanthos/ Taras 938
Phantom Group 962
Pharmacopeia, Etruscan 687, 869–870
Phayllos 765
Pherekrates 721
Phersu 674, 835
Pheziu Paves 896
phyllobolia ("offering of leaves") 622
Philoktetes 939
Philostratus, Flavius 1099
Phineus 833
Phocaeans 250, 605, 833, 891
Phoenician cups (inscribed) 111
    jewelry (and iconography) 112–113
    Sardinia 308
Phoenicians 105, 235–239, 303–310, 919
Phorcys 763
Phoroneus (*Phoronis*) 39, 45, 47
Phrastor 47
Phrygia 665
Piana del Lago (Montefiascone) 567
Pianella di Monte Savino 733
Piano di Stigliano 732
Picentia, oppidum 307
Pietrabbondante 702
Pigorini, Luigi 203
pigs 20, 574–575, 578–579
pila (spears) 756
"pilgrim flasks" (Sardinian bronzes) 223–224
Pillars of Herakles 760
Pinza, Giovanni 104
pirates, piracy 20–21, 298, 505, 763–769
Pisa 11, 156, 252, 729, 761, 763
Pisaeus (son of hero Tyrrhenus) 768
Pithekoussai (Ischia) 237, 302–309, 396, 817, 857, 864, 943, 1018
Pittore delle Palme (Painter of the Palms) 768, 770, 945, 947
Pius IX (Pope) 1140
Pizzo Piede sanctuary, Narce 270–272
plantain 15
Plataea 626
Plato 428, 521, 684, 763
plebs/plebeian class (Roman) 163
Pleistocene 12
Plikaśna situla 126, 580, 850, 898, 1093

Pliny (the Elder) 17, 83, 169, 246, 301, 365, 486–487, 514, 545–6, 550, 632, 683, 688, 697, 709, 721, 759, 755, 768, 870, 887, 890, 993, 1026, 1112, 1136
Plutarch 365, 710, 813
Po Valley/*Etruria Padana* 281–299, 733, 760
Pocola deorum (vases) 962
Poggio Baccherina 802
    Buco 905, 907, 945
    Civitate *see* Murlo
    Colla 436, 566, 571, 575, 861
    Malinverno 724
Point du Dattier (shipwreck) 766
Pointe Lequin 1B (shipwreck) 766
poliomyelitis 864
Pollaiuolo brothers 1137
pollen 15
Polybius 239, 241, 762
Polychrome Group 127
Polygnotos (painter) 626
Polyphemus 497, 948
Polyxena 567, 954
pomerium 361–362, 545
Pompeii 306, 844, 861, 863
Pompeius Trogus 206
Pomponius Mela 761
Ponte di Nona 1073
Pontecagnano 63, 65, 111, 222, 302, 306, 307–315, 571, 791, 860, 864, 916, 978, 979
Pontic Group 891, 921, 954
Pontifex maximus 690
Poplia Genucilia 959
Populonia 11, 18, 83, 87, 120–121, 136, 164, 221–223, 226, 245, 248–249, 251–252, 397, 487, 657, 658, 660, 721, 725, 728, 729, 731, 762, 765, 766, 860, 887, 894–895, 917, 922, 933, 935
    Poggio del Molino 728
    ruler's house, (foundation) rituals 120–121
    Tumulo dei Carri 781–782, 786–787
    Val Fucinaia 728
porotic hyperostosis 60–61
Porsenna 351, 365, 653, 688, 1136–1137
Porto Perone 198
portolan 761
portraiture 185
portraiture, Etruscan 1007–1013
Portus 60
Posada 240
Poseidon *see* Neptune/*Nethuns*
Poseidonia see Paestum
Poseidonios/Posidonius of Apamea 448, 759, 688
Postel, G. 1137
Postumius 651, 765
pottery, black gloss 241, 296

Etrusco-Corinthian 127, 323–324, 336, 339, 672, 1018
Euboean 91–92, 309, 888–889
Nuragic 886–887
production 888
Pozo Moro 332, 392
Pozzuolo 863
Praeneste see Palestrina
praenomen 451–452
praetor 288, 353–355
Praxias Group 893–894, 956–957
Primacy Group 957
Principes 106, 235, 282, 310, 351, 364
prodigies (*prodigia*) 543
Prometheus 550, 939
"Prophecy of Vegoia" 160–161, 362, 448, 478
protein, in Etruscan diet 64
Protocorinthian pottery 980
Protogenes of Ialysos 963
Proto-urban (period, culture, sites) 81–82
Protovillanovan culture/period 80, 134
PseudoAristotle 728
Pseudo-Skylax 295
Ptolemy (geographer) 240–241
puls 813
Punic War(s) 157, 813
Punicum 761
purth 356
putto Graziani 1028
Pyla-Kokkinokremos (Cyprus) 201, 206
Pyrgi 11, 21, 41, 141, 156–157, 250, 508, 516, 519, 524, 559, 562, 566–567, 569, 570–573, 599, 607, 689, 702, 732, 761, 765, 891, 906, 909, 1073
Pyrgi Plaques 339, 352, 356, 460, 464, 479, 480, 482, 618
pyrrhiche (armed dance) 496, 574, 833

Q. Marcius Philippus 154
Qatna (Syria) 116–117
Quadriga(e) 781, 786, 837–838
Quarata 1033
Quercus cerris (Turkey oak) 17
Quinto Fiorentino, 657

Ramtha Viśnai 359–360
Ras el Bassit (Syria) 341, 393
Rasenna/rasna 36, 355, 362–363, 709, 1141
Rath 519
rattling-cup 847
Ratumenna 832
Ravenna 760
Recognition of Paris 185
Red-on-White pottery 949–950
Regisvilla (*Regae*) 141, 762
religion, Roman 517, 557

Rhaetians (Raeti) 36
Rhegion 44
ribbed bowls 100
Ricci Hydria 574, 953
Rimini 299
Rinaldone culture 33
Risorgimento 169
ritual meals 815–817
rituals, Etruscan 576–581
rivers, Etruria 11, 558–559
Rix, Helmut 448
road-inscription (Faliscan territory) 275
roads, Etruria 559, 644–645
Roc de Buffens *see* Le Bouffens
rocchetti (spools) 803
Rochelongue (Agde, underwater deposit) 396
Rognosi Mountains 724
Roman populations 60–61
Rome, *Auditorium* 699
    Capitoline Temple 482, 689, 696–698, 701–702, 907
    colonization (Sardinia) 240
    colonization of Etruria 156–177, 613–615, 619, 1079–1080
    Regia 907
    Romans 63, 151–152, 156, 164, 269, 607, 732, 865, 905, 907, 1073
    Sacred Area of Sant'Omobono/ *Mater Matuta* sanctuary 568, 636, 701–702, 907
    Temple of Castor 701–702
    Temple of Ceres, Liber and Libera 893
    Temple of Saturn 701–702
Romulus 574, 864
Romulus and Remus 550
roofs, Etruscan and related 903–910
Roselle (*Rusellae*) 134, 140, 156, 762, 813, 906, 907, 908
    House of the *Impluvium* 699
rostrum 768
Rubiera *cippi* 284, 286, 351
runes 21
Ruspi, Carlo 1021,
Rutile Hipucrates 107, 894

Sa Osa-Oristano 201
sacrifices 815–817
saeculum 80, 480–482
sailor (Tarquinia Pian di Civita burial) 21
Saint-Blaise 320, 336, 337, 389–390, 391, 1143
    oppidum 324–327
Saint-Marcel, *oppidum* 323, 327
Saint-Remy-de-Provence 327
Sala Consilina 83, 302, 886, 916
salaria 20
saleable goods (Etruscan) 398–399
Salii 94

salt 20
Salvii (family) 169
Sambon, Louis 1080
Samian Heraion 375, 760
Samians 606
Samos 49
San Giovenale 20, 138, 657, 731, 816, 864
San Giuliano 570, 657, 660, 662, 665, 666, 769
San Paolo (Cerveteri) bucchero *olpe* 126, 495, 834, 980, 985
San Paolo Belsito 856
San Valentin Group 962
sanatto 1034, 1076
Sanctuary of *Uni* (Fondo Patturelli, Capua) 314
Sangallo brothers 1136
Sant'Abbondio 856
Sant'Antioco *see Sulki*
Sant'Imbenia 212, 219–220, 222, 233
Santa Cristina in Paulilatino (Nuragic shrine) 690
Santa Marinella (Punta della Vipera) 568–569, 689, 761, 909
Santa Marinella Plaque 460, 463
Sarcapos (Sardinia) 241
Sarcophagus of the Married Couple ("degli Sposi") 430
Sarcophagus of Ramtha Višnai/Boston Sarcophagus 430
Sardinia 87, 216–243
Sardinia, Nuragic culture 216–230, 232
Sardis 42, 115
Sargon II 116
Sarteano 728
Sarteano Painter 958
Sarteano, Tomba della Quadriga Infernale 526, 667
Sasso di Furbara 768, 804, 805, 806, 807, 909
Satricum 138, 702, 871, 909
Saturnia 156, 164
Saturnus (*Satre?*) 513
Satyr and Dolphin Group 958
scarabs, Etruscan 928–938
Scarlino 856
Scasato, sanctuary at *Falerii* 265–267
Scevas (family) 161, 363
Schnabelkannen 320, 328, 329–330, 378–382, 392, 393
Schwarzenbach 335
science, Etruscan 683–692
Scipio 813
Scoglio del Tonno 198
sculptural style, Syrian 889
sculpture, Levantine 116
Scylax of Caryanda 761
Scylla 675, 763, 938, 1099–1100
seafaring, Etruscan 759–773
Second Punic War 729
Seianti Hanunia Tlesnasa 675, 860, 1012

Selinus, *Malophoros* sanctuary 576, 623
sella curulis 288
Selvans 520, 709, 1028, 1074
Semele (*Semla*) 434, 435, 506
Seneca 546, 581, 684–685
Senones 755
Sentinum (battle of) 154
Serra Ilixi 203
servi (Latin: slaves) 162
Servirola 733,
Servius (author) 80, 94, 365, 483, 546, 557, 572, 690, 759, 858
Servius Tullius (king of Rome) 352, 486–487, 545
Sesto Fiorentino 1136
Sethlans see Hephaistos
Setia 449
Settecamini Painter 958
Settefinestre 156, 162
Seven Against Thebes 166, 502, 508, 619, 626, 934
Sextii (family) 162
Sforza, Francesco 1120
Shamash 548
sheep/goats 19–20, 573–574, 856–857
Sheshonq I 113
shields, Etruscan 375, 390
shipwrecks 395–397, 765–767
Sicily 203
Siege of Syracuse 760, 762, 763
sigla 439, 457, 464, 597–599
signa tuscanica 1026
Signorelli, Giuseppe and Mario 1128
Silenus Painter 954
Silius Italicus 729
Silva Arsia, battle (Roman) 740–742
silver 487
siren 1100
Sirolo 790–791
sistra 847
Sisyphos 509, 678
situla 110
Situla Art 807
Six's technique 956, 977
skeletal studies (of Etruscan and Italic populations) 56–66, 859, 870–873
skeletons 751, 766
skiagraphia 1022
Skylla *see* Scylla
slave revolt(s) 156, 448–450
slavery, slaves 58, 362, 447–452, 744, 813, 827–828, 839–840
slaves, epigraphic evidence 451–452
Smyrna 42, 711
snakebite 861
snakes 1109
social inequality 64–65
Social War 156

Sokra Group 962
Sommavilla Painter 957
Sophocles 504, 759, 760
Sora 702
Soranus 516
Sorgenti della Nova *see* Castellaccio di Sorgenti della
     Nova
sorrels 15
Sorrento 306
Sostratos 607–608, 897
Sovana 570, 662, 665
     Tomba Ildebranda 662, 665
Spain 919
Spano, Giovanni 203
Spargi (La Maddalena shipwreck) 765–766
Spartans 45
"speaking inscriptions" (*iscrizioni parlanti*) 465, 985
"special gods" (*Sondergötter, indigitamenta*) 522
spectacles in Etruria 831–840
spelt 813
Sperandio sarcophagus 1093
sphinx 1100
Spina 46–47, 294–296, 298, 733, 760, 895, 922
spinning (spindles, spindle whorls) 800–801
sports in Etruria 834–837
spur/spura 360, 709
"Spurinas" plate 460
Spurinna (family) 1022
Spurinna, Aulus 156, 449
Spurinna, Velthur 762
Spurius Carvilius Maximus 267
"*Srdn*," "*Shardana*" 218
Stabiae 306
Statlanes family/tomb 1140
stature (ancient populations) 58–59, 63
Steingräber, Stephan 708–709
stenochoria ("lack of land") 43–44
Stična 374, 383
Stieda, Ludwig 1080
Strabo 254, 295, 301, 457, 711, 728, 759,
     761, 763, 850, 890
Strozzacaponi (Perugia) 166, 805
Studi Etruschi (Istituto, etc.) 1141
Su Monte (Nuragic sanctuary) 209
Suda (Byzantine text) 683, 686
Suessula and *Calatia* 306
Sulcus primigenius 574
Sulki (*Sulky*/Sulcis/Sant'Antioco) 201, 218, 222,
     233
Sulla 156, 388
sulphur 13
Summanus 513
surgery 692, 868–869, 1078
Śuri/Soranus/Apollo Soranus 516, 578, 605, 607,
     621
"*sutiles naves*" ("sewn ships") 211, 772

Sutri 153–154, 261
śuθina 1059–1061
Swallows Painter 127, 890–891, 1093, 1104
swan 525
swords, Sardinian types 226
Sybaris 914,
symposion/symposia 826
syngeneia, "matching" 44–47, 50
syphilis 863
Syracuse 607–608, 620, 763, 765, 895
Syria 665
syrinx 845

Tabanelli, Mario 855
tabby (tabbies) 802, 805
tablet-weaving 803, 806
Tabula Capuana 305, 314, 315, 460–461, 469,
     470, 480, 482
     Cortonensis see Cortona Tablet
     Peutingeriana 688
Tabulae Iguvinae 568, 578, 709
Tacitus 42
Tages 142, 541, 544–546, 548, 601, 686, 859
Talamone 157, 508
Talos Painter 957
"Tanagras" (figurines) 993
Tanaquil 1111
Tanchvil Catharnai 619
Taranto 963
Tarchon 23, 83, 142, 291, 294, 544, 601–604
"tare" (commercial concept) 692
Tarquinia (Tarquinii) 63, 79, 83, 134–142,
     152–158, 166, 222, 276, 308, 328,
     354–359, 374, 427, 495, 559–571, 657,
     660, 666, 674, 677, 721, 728, 740–742,
     762, 763, 769, 771, 805, 817, 826, 831,
     833, 850, 859–860, 885, 887, 891, 906,
     907, 908, 909, 915, 917, 944–945, 958,
     962, 975, 981, 1008, 1018–1022, 1043,
     1060–1061, 1073, 1106, 1136
"Ara della Regina" 562, 566, 600–605;
     Winged Horses group 603, 702, 1013
"Tumulus of the Queen" 118–120
Doganaccia necropolis 107, 667
Mercareccia Tomb 662
Pian di Civita (Area Sacra) 83, 120, 560, 566,
     567, 569, 571–572, 575, 594–599, 727,
     930
Tomb of Hunting and Fishing 813, 1020
Tomb of the Augurs 804, 1094, 1108
Tomb of the *Bigae* 831
Tomb of the Blue Demons 580, 667
Tomb of the Bulls 23, 1019–1020, 1092
Tomb of the Funeral Bed 839
Tomb of the Leopards 827, 1098
Tomb of the Lionesses 1020

Tomb of the Mouse (Topolino) 1020
Tomb of the Olympic Games 674
Tomb of the Painted Vases 817
Tomb of the Shields 828–829
Tomb of the Triclinium 1021, 1092–1093
Tomb of the Warrior 918
Tomba Bruschi 161
Tomba Cardarelli 834
Tomba degli Auguri 674, 835–836
Tomba degli Olimpiadi 835–837, 839
Tomba dei Caronti 861, 1109
Tomba dei Giocolieri 845
Tomba dell'Orco 1022, 1110
Tomba della Nave (Tomb of the Ship) 772,
    1021–1022
Tomba della Pulcella 849
Tomba Giglioli 756, 849
Tarquinius Priscus 352, 361, 365, 545, 598, 831,
    832, 834, 1092, 1111
    Superbus 151
Tarquitius Priscus 544
Tarragona 331
Tarsus 986,
Tartessos 394, 760
Tasma Śatnas 451
Tebenna 430
Tece Sans 1029
Teiresias 503
Telamon 761, 762
Telephos 38
Telikles 894
temples, Etruscan 700–703
templum (various kinds) 287, 291, 483–484,
    548–549, 683, 687, 688, 691
terminatio 687
Terminus (Terminalia) 687
terracotta (anatomical models), production
    techniques 1071–1073
terracottas (figurines), Etruscan 993–1004
Terramare culture 856
Tessennano 165, 868, 1013, 1073 (see also Canino)
tessera hospitalis 330, 340, 388–389, 398, 458
"Testa Malavolta" (Veii) 1013
Teutamides 47
Tevnalthia 261, 272
textiles (Etruscan) 107, 289–290, 798–808
    finishing process 803–804
thalassemia 60–61, 864
thalassocracy 759–760
Thalna 434, 513, 517
Thanatos 509
Thanr 513, 520, 1028
Tharros 218, 233, 239
theater in Etruria 833–834
theaters, theatral areas 831–832
Thefarie Velianas 352–356, 618

Theophrastus 240, 687, 869–870
Theopompus 48, 426–427, 827
therapontoi (Greek) 162
Thesan (Eos/Aurora) 20, 24, 506, 518, 619
Theseus and Ariadne 435
Theseus/These, 937, 938, 945, 981
Thetis 498, 518–519, 933
"Throne of Claudius" (Cerveteri) 763
thrones, Etruscan 375, 390
Thucydides 756, 759
Thufltha (Tufltha) 521, 1032
thunder 20
thunderbolt(s) 513, 607
thusia (Greek ritual) 574
Tiberius 42
Tiberius Coruncanius, Publius 155
Tiglath-pileser III 99, 778
Timaeus 427, 827
Timoleon 765
Tinia (Tin/Jupiter/Zeus) 435, 483, 518–520, 549,
    573, 575, 621, 632, 677, 933, 1028, 1029
Tinia, cult (Marzabotto) 293–294
tintinnabula (Sardinian rattle-pendants) 224
tintinnabulum (Bologna) 104, 107, 799, 801, 803
Tipasa 329
Tithonos 506
Tityos Painter 954–955
Tiur 1074
Tluschva deities 637, 642
Tocra 328, 986,
Tolfa (region/hills/metal deposits) 164, 724–725,
    732
Tolle 823, 919
Tolumnius 354
tomba a fossa (trench tomb) 84
tomba a pozzo (well-shaped tomb) 81
tombs, Etruscan 655–668
Torcop Groupp 959
Torre Mordillo 198
Torre San Severo (sarcophagus from) 567, 754
Toscanella 1140
Toscanos 332, 335, 339, 342
Toulouse 325
town-planning, Etruscan 708–717
trade, Etruscan 107
Tragliatella oinochoe/urn 435
transhumance 19, 80, 558, 1034
tratturi 80
trauma 859–860
treaty (foedus) 153, 239, 651
tree heather (Erica arborea) 18
trees 16
trepanation 61, 866
Trevignano Romano, Tomba dei Flabelli 791
Tridacna squamosa 1098
triga(e) 781, 786, 793, 837–838

Trigarium 838
tripod-bowls, ceramic 102
Triptolemos Painter 674
triumph (Roman ceremony) 154–156
Troilos 500 954, 1019–1020, 1092
Trojans 40
Trombetti, A. 1142
truphe/tryphè/luxuria 427, 447–448, 834
tuba 842, 844, 850
tuberculosis 859, 863
Tuchulcha 861, 1022
tuff (tufo, tufa) 12
tular 22, 295, 361–364, 709
tumor 860
tumulus/tumulus tombs 100, 115, 139–140
Turan and Atunis 433
Turan (Aphrodite/Venus) 432–433, 520, 523,
    1074
Turms (Hermes/Mercury) 356, 520, 933
"Turms of Tin" 507
Turmuca Group 958
turseis ("towers") 38, 41
Tuscan Academy of Science and Letters "La
    Colombaria" 1139
Tuscan temple 562–563, 618, 659, 689, 691, 909
Tuscania 166, 354, 478, 479, 570, 662, 722, 906,
    1140
Tuscania, Pian della Mola tomb 121, 665
Tuscanicus 695–698
"Tusci" 355
tuthina 709
Twelve Tables (laws, Roman) 450
twill(s) 805
Tydeus 508, 619, 934, 937, 939
tympanum 847, 849
typhoid 864
Typhon 1100
tyrrhena sigilla 165, 1026
Tyrrhenian Sea 20
Tyrrhenians/"Tyrrhenoi", "Tyrsenians" 38, 42–50,
    355, 759–760
Tyrrhenos (hero) 38, 44, 46, 755, 759, 763, 768,
tyrsenike salpinx 842, 848, 850

Ullastret 323, 325, 332, 336, 338, 382, 383, 393
Uluburun (shipwreck) 202, 205
Umaele/Eumalos 23, 540
Umbro 762
Underworld 24
Uni see Hera
Urartu 125
urbanization, Etruscan 134–144
urbs 298, 361
Urgulania 169
Urnfields culture (Urnenfeldern) 80, 887
Uşak (Turkey) 933

Usekhet (Egyptian pectoral) 109
Usil/Sol 24, 507
uterus models 866–868
Utica 329

Vada Volaterrana 762
Vadena-Pfatten 374
Vagnonville Group 956–957
Val di Cecina 724, 728
Valdichiana 1030
Valerius Maximus 632
Valtiberina 1030
Vanth 24, 434, 509, 522, 579, 676, 678, 1022,
    1110
Vanth Painter 958
Varro 22, 37, 80, 457, 471, 544–6, 632, 690, 813,
    833, 855, 893, 993, 1136
Vasari, Giorgio 1137
Vegoia *see* Lasa Vecuvia and "Prophecy of Vegoia"
Vei/Vea (Demeter/Ceres) 642, 816, 1074
Veii 79–81, 84, 88–89, 92–95, 116, 134–141,
    151–153, 262, 269–274, 308, 314, 331,
    353-4, 357–359, 365, 374, 504, 507, 659,
    710, 728, 739, 740–742, 762, 764, 768,
    805, 832, 839, 856, 887, 905, 906, 907,
    915, 944–945, 947, 975, 993–1004, 1012,
    1013, 1073, 1140, 1141
  Apollo (statue) 803
  Campetti sanctuary 996–998
  Campana Tomb 127, 1018, 1098
  Comunità deposit 865
  Piazza d'Armi 127, 138, 141
  Portonaccio sanctuary 271, 487, 560, 562–563,
    568–9, 657, 870, 907, 909–910, 952,
    985–986, 993, 998
  Tomb of Roaring Lions 123, 667, 947,
    1017–1018, 1102
  Tomb of the Ducks 123, 947
Veii-Rome-Velletri decorative system 907–908
Vel Hulchnie 354
Vel Kaikna (funerary stele of) 760, 768, 771–772
Vel Leinies 355
Vel Saties 21, 541–542, 806, 808, 861
vela (awnings) 831
Velcha family 828–829
Velia 250, 306
Velia Fanacnei 1033
Velimna/Volumnii (family and tomb) 159–160, 181,
    471, 665, 845
Velleius Paterculus 311
Velletri, Chiesa delle Stimmate (Etruscan temple
    site) 689, 907
Velthina (family) 161, 363, 709
Veltune(?) 645
Venetic culture, Veneti (people) 282, 283
Ver sacrum 262

Verrius Flaccus 83, 457
Versailles 1139
Versilia 762
Vertumnus 545, 640
Verucchio 83, 281–282, 289–290, 295, 374, 430,
    571–572, 726, 799, 803, 804, 805, 806,
    807, 857–858, 887
Verucchio (throne) 107, 290
Vesuna 816
Vetter, Emil 448
Vetulonia 136, 210, 221, 223–224, 226, 249,
    328, 374, 486–7, 656–658, 721, 728, 739,
    750–752, 755, 762, 763, 887, 890, 897,
    908, 915, 916, 917, 918, 979, 1009
Vetulonia, Avele (Auvele) Feluske stele 126, 755
Via Armerina 268
Via Aurelia 613
Via Cassia 15
Via Flaminia 268
Vibenna (brothers) (*Vipinas, Aule* and *Caile*) 22,
    167, 352, 541, 678, 957, 985–986 (*see also*
    avile vipiiennas)
vici 298
Vico Equense 306
Vienne 327
Vignanello 260, 269, 907
Villa Giulia Caeretan Painter 959
Villa Giulia Painter 8361 957
Villae rusticae (Roman) 268
Villani, Giovanni 690
Villanova (di Castenaso) 79
Villanovan bronze belt(s) 377
Villanovan culture/ period 79–95, 134–138, 302,
    1043, 1101–1102
Vipinanas (family/tomb) 1140
Virgil 448, 504, 508, 545–546, 761
Viterbo 1117–1128, 1136
viticulture 91
Vitruvius 562–3, 659, 684–685, 689, 691,
    695–704, 713, 857
Vivara 198
Vix 379, 382, 392
Voghiera 733
volcanoes, volcanic activity 12, 856–857
Volcanus (*Sethlans*) 513
Volnius 833–834
Volsinii (*Velzna*, Orvieto) 155–157, 274–275,
    357, 365, 449, 482, 632, 688, 690, 721,
    743–744, 975, 1026
Volterra (*Volaterrae/Velathri*) 156, 162, 166, 169,
    183–188, 331, 451, 487, 544, 571–2, 573,
    575, 576, 657, 728, 813, 833–834, 887,
    922, 1027, 1028, 1030, 1036, 1138
Volterra, Inghirami Tomb 184–188
Voltumna 515, 632, 839
Volturnum 315

Vulca of Veii 993, 1141
Vulcanius (*haruspex*) 481
Vulci 79–81, 111, 127, 134–141, 155, 156, 162,
    224, 240, 478, 487, 561, 578, 656–7, 660,
    666, 676, 721, 747, 749, 751, 756, 763,
    771, 805, 833, 873, 885–886, 887, 891,
    893, 896, 906, 907, 915, 918, 921, 922,
    944–945, 950–951, 953, 954, 957, 958,
    963, 981, 1073, 1106, 1140
    Biconic workshop 947
    Cuccumella Tumulus 568, 666–667, 831
    Fontanile di Legnisina 867–868
    Isis Tomb 124, 916, 1010
    Tomb of the [Bronze] Chariot 124, 782
    "Tomb of the Sardinian Bronzes" 224
    Tomb of the Warrior 743, 755, 817
vulture-demon 526

walls, Etruscan 703
warfare, Etruscan 738–744
water, healing 870
weaving 801–803
Wedgewood, Josiah 1139
weights, Etruscan 486–487
Wellcome, Sir Henry 1080
Western Mediterranean 197–212
wheat 15
White-on-Red pottery 949–950
Winckelmann, J.J. 502, 1141
wine 100, 210 (residues), 578
winged animals, wings 1101
wolves, wolf-demons 524, 576
women, Etruscan, position of 160
woodpecker 1112
Workshop of *Rasinius* (*terra sigillata*) 160
Workshop of the Civitavecchia Fishes 948
Workshop of the Stockholm Fishes 948
wormwood 15

Xanthos (Xanthus) of Lydia 37–39, 43–45
Xenophon 749
X-ray fluorescence (XRF) analysis 726–727

Zagreb, *liber linteus*/mummy wrappings 160, 340,
    360–362, 388, 397, 460–461, 464, 469,
    470, 480, 482, 515, 578, 799, 805
Zavadintsy 886
Zazoff, Peter 937
Zeus and Hera 433, 434
Zeus (*see also Tin*/Jupiter) 430, 439, 508, 513, 515,
    619
zilath 284, 288, 351–363, 467, 473, 838,
Zolyom 374
Zonaras 449, 744
Zosimus (author) 169

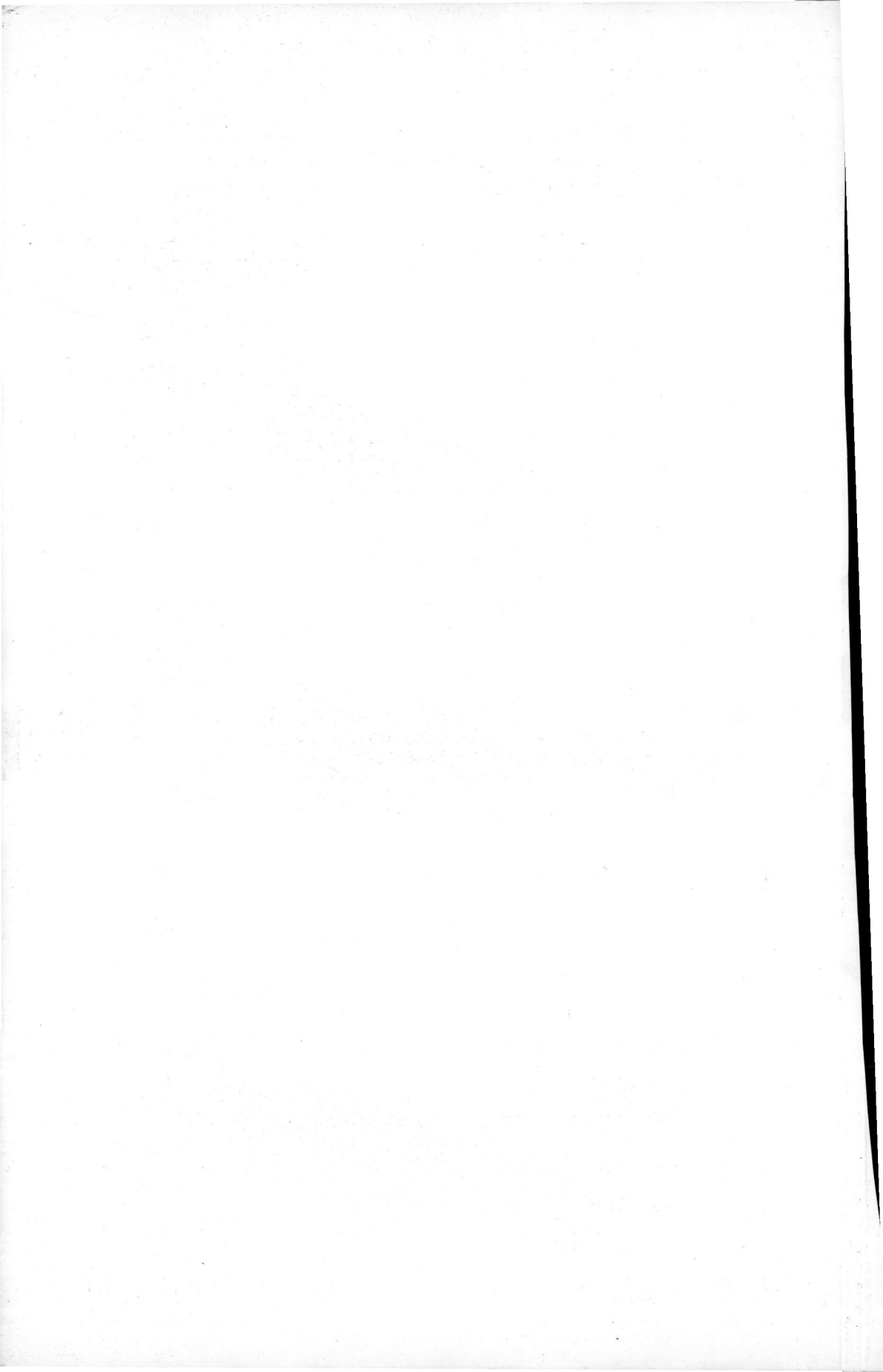